CONCISE BIOGRAPHICAL COMPANION TO INDEX ISLAMICUS

An International Who's Who in Islamic Studies from its Beginnings down to the Twentieth Century

Bio-bibliographical Supplement to Index Islamicus, 1665-1980, Volume Two

H-M

BY

WOLFGANG BEHN

909.09767
B 395
Vol. 2

BRILL
LEIDEN • BOSTON
2006

85609832

MACK LIBRARY
BOB JONES UNIVERSITY
GREENVILLE, SC

This book is printed on acid-free paper.

Library of Congress Cataloging-in-Publication Data

The Library of Congress Cataloging-in-Publication Data is available on
http://catalog.loc.gov

ISSN 0169-9423
ISBN 90 04 15037 4

© Copyright 2006 by Koninklijke Brill NV, Leiden, The Netherlands
Koninklijke Brill NV incorporates the imprints Brill Academic Publishers,
Martinus Nijhoff Publishers and VSP.

All rights reserved. No part of this publication may be reproduced, translated, stored
in a retrieval system, or transmitted in any form or by any means, electronic,
mechanical, photocopying, recording or otherwise, without prior written
permission from the publisher.

Authorization to photocopy items for internal or personal use is granted
by Brill provided that the appropriate fees are paid directly to
The Copyright Clearance Center, 222 Rosewood Drive,
Suite 910, Danvers MA 01923, USA.
Fees are subject to change.

PRINTED IN THE NETHERLANDS

Key to title codes for use in locating sources

The number in parentheses after an abbreviation refers to the number of references.
The sign | at the end of a source indicates the biographee's last entry in a serial publication.

Aa	van der Aa, Abraham Jacob. *Biografisch woordenboek der Nederlanden*. Haarlem, 1852-1878.
AALA	*Asien, Afrika, Lateinamerika*, Berlin.
Aalto	Aalto, Pentti. *Oriental studies in Finland, 1828-1918*. Helsinki, 1971.
ACAB	*Appleton's cyclopaedia of American biography*. New York, 1888-1901.
Adamec	Adamec, Ludwig W. *A biographical dictionary of contemporary Afghanistan*. Graz, 1987.
ADtB	*Allgemeine deutsche Biographie*. Leipzig, 1875-1912.
AfrA	Herdeck, Donald E. *African authors; a companion to Black African writing*, vol. 1. Washington, D.C., 1973.
AfrAmBi	*Who's who among African Americans*. Detroit, Mich., Gale, 1997- .
AfrBioInd	*African biographical index*, compiled by Victor Herrero Mediavilla. München, 1999.
AfricanExp	*Directory of African experts*, 1982.
AfricaWW	*Africa who's who*. 1- . London, Africa Books, 1981- .
Afrikanistik	*Lexikon der Afrikanistik*, ed. H. Jungraithmayr and W. J. G. Möhlig. Berlin, 1983.
AkKisL	*Akadémiai kislexikon*. Budapest, 1989-90.
AllgLBKünst	*Allgemeines Lexikon der bildenden Künstler von der Antike bis zur Gegenwart*, eds. Ulrich Thieme and Felx Becker. Leipzig, 1907-50.
Altpreuß	*Altpreußische Biographie*, ed. Christian Krollmann. Königsberg, 1941-1967.
AmAu&B	Burke, William Jeremiah & Will D. Howe. *American authors and books, 1640 to the present*, revised by I. and A. Weiss. New York, 1962.
AmIndex	*American biographical index*. 2nd ed., comp. by Laureen Baillie. München, 1998.
AmM&WSc P	*American men and women of science*: physical and biological sciences. New York, 1976- .
AmM&WSc S	*American men and women of science*: social and behavioral sciences. New York, 1973- .
AmPeW	Roberts, Nancy L. *American peace writers, editors and periodicals*. New York, 1991.
AMS	*American men of science*, New York.
AmWomM	Leavitt, Judith A. *American women managers and administrators*. Westport, Conn., 1985.
AnaBrit	*Ana Britannica*. İstanbul, 1987-1993.
ANB	*American national biography*. New York, London, 1999.
Andrieu	Andrieu, Jules. *Bibliographie générale de l'Agenais et des parties du Condomois et du Bazadais*. Paris, Agen, 1886-91.
AnEIFr	*Annuaire des études iraniennes en France*. 1ère éd., Paris, 1989- .
AnnDipl&C	*Annuaire diplomatique et consulaire de la République française*.
AnObit	*The Annual obituary*. 1- . New York, 1980- .
Arabismo	*Boletín informativo* (Agencia Española de Cooperación Internacional): Arabismo; estudios árabes en España. Madrid, Ed. Mundo Árabe e Islam, 1992- .

Artefici   *Artefici del lavoro italiano*. Roma, 1956-59. 2 vol.

ASTENE   Association for the Study of Travel in Egypt and the Near East.

AUB   American University of Beirut.

AUC   American University in Cairo.

AusBioInd   *Australasian biographical index*, ed. Victor Herrero Mediavilla. München, 1996.

AusDcBio   *Australian dictionary of biography*. Melbourne, 1966- .

Au&Wr   *Author's and writer's who's who.*

Awwad   'Awwad, Kurkis. معجم المألفين العراقيين . Baghdad, 1969.

Azan   Azan, Paul. *Les Grands soldats de l'Algérie*. Alger, 1930.

AzarbSE   *Азәрбајчан совет енсиклопедијасы*. Baku, 1976-1987.

Bacqué   *Représentants permanents de la France en Turquie, 1536-1991, et de la Turquie en France*, par Jean Louis Bacqué-Grammont, Sinan Kuneralp et Frédéric Hitzel. Istanbul et Paris, 1991.

BAEO   *Boletin de la Asociación Española de Orientalistas.*

Baker 78   Baker, Theodore. *Biographical dictionary of musicians*; completely revised by Nicolas Slonimsky. New York, 1978.

Baker 84   Baker, Theodore. *Biographical dictionary of musicians*. 7th ed., revised by Nicolas Slonimsky. New York, 1984.

Baldinetti   Baldinetti, Anna. *Orientalismo e colonialismo; la ricerca di consenso in Egitto per l'impreso di Libia*. Roma, 1997.

Ballesteros   Ballesteros Robles, Luis. *Diccionario biográfico matritense*. Madrid, 1912.

Baltisch   *Baltischer biographischer Index*, edited by Axel Frey. München, 1999.

BashkKE   *Башкортостан краткая энциклопедия*, general editor R. Z. Shakurov. Ufa, 1996.

BbD   *The Bibliophile dictionary*. Detroit, c1904, 1966.

BBHS   *Bio-bibliographisches Handbuch zur Sprachwissenschaft des 18. Jahrhunderts.* Tübingen, 1992- .

Behrmann   Behrmann, Georg. *Hamburgs Orientalisten*. Hamburg, 1902.

Bellier   Bellier de la Chavignerie, Émile, and Louis Auvray. *Dictionnaire général des artistes de l'école française*. Paris, 1882-85.

Bezemer   *Beknopte encyclopedie van Nederlandsch-Indië*, naar den 2. druk der *Encyclopedie van Nederlandsch-Indië*, bewerkt door Tammo Jacob Bezemer. s'Gravenhage, 1921.

BiBelgeOM   *Biographie belge d'outre-mer = Belgische overzeese biographie*. Vol. 8- . Gand, Bruxelles, 1968- .

BiBenelux   *Biografische index van de Benelux*. München, 1997.

BiBenelux²   *Biografische index van de Benelux*. München, 2003.

BiDAmL   *Biographical dictionary of American labor*, ed. by Gary M. Fink. Westport, Conn., 1984.

BiDAmS   Elliott, Clark A. *Biographical dictionary of American science, the seventeenth through nineteenth centuries*. Westport, Conn., 1979.

BiDInt   Kuehl, Warren F. *Biographical dictionary of internationalists*. Westport, Conn., 1983.

BiDLA   *A Biographical dictionary of the living authors of Great Britain and Ireland*. London, 1816; Detroit, 1966.

BiDMoPL   *Biographical dictionary of modern peace leaders*, ed. by Harold Josephson. Westport, Conn., 1985.

BiDMoER   *Biographical dictionary of modern European radicals and socialists*, ed. by D. Nicholls and Peter March. Vol. 1: 1780-1815. Brighton and New York, 1988.

BiDNeoM — *Biographical dictionary of neo-Marxism*, edited by Robert E. Gorman. Westport, 1985.

BiDrAC — *Biographical directory of the American Congress, 1774-1949*. Washington, D.C., United States Government Printing Office, 1950.

BiDrLUS — *Biographical dictionary of librarians in the United States and Canada*.

BiD&SB — *Biographical dictionary and synopsis of books*. Detroit, c1902, 1965.

BiDSovU — Vronskaya, Jeanne, with Vl. Chuguev. *A Biographical dictionary of the Soviet Union, 1917-1988*. London, 1989.

Bidwell — Bidwell, Robin L. *Travellers in Arabia*. Reading, 1994.

Bidwell² — Bidwell, Robin L. *Dictionary of modern Arab history*. London, 1998.

BiEncPak — *Biographical encyclopedia of Pakistan*, 1969-70. Lahore.

BiE&WWA — *The Biographical encyclopaedia & who's who of the American theatre*; edited by Walter Rigdon. Vol. 1- . New York, 1966- .

BiGAW — Ward, Robert E. *A Bio-bibliography of German-American writers*. White Plains, 1985.

BiLexDR — *Biographisches Lexikon zum Dritten Reich*, ed. Hermann Weiß. Frankfurt a. M., 1998.

BioB134 — *Bio-bibliographies de 134 savants*. Leiden, 1979. (Acta iranica; 4e sér.; Répertoires 1)

BiobibSOT — Биобиблиографический словарь отечественных тюркологов. Moskva, 1974.

Biograf — *Biográf ki kicsoda*. Budapest, 2001- .

BiogrLexOö — Khil, Martha. *Biographisches Lexikon von Oberösterreich*. Linz, 1955- .

BioHbDtE — *Biographisches Handbuch der deutschsprachigen Emigration, 1933-1945*. München, 1980-1983.

BioIn — *Biography index*, 1- . New York, 1949- .

BioJahr — *Biographisches Jahrbuch und deutscher Nekrolog*. 1-18. Berlin, 1897-1917.

BioNBelg — *Biographie nationale*; publiée par l'Académie royale des sciences, des lettres et des beaux-arts de Belgique. Bruxelles, 1866- .

Bitard — Bitard, Adolphe. *Dictionnaire général de biographie contemporaine française et étrangère*. Paris, 1878.

Bitard² — Bitard, Adolphe. *Dictionnaire de biographie contemporaine française et étrangère*. 3e éd. Paris, 1887.

BJMES — *British journal of Middle Eastern studies*.

BLC — *British Library catalogue*.

BlkwERR — *The Blackwell encyclopedia of the Russian revolution*, edited by Harold Shukman. New York, 1988.

BlueB — *The Blue book; leaders of the English-speaking world*. London, New York.

BN — *Catalogue général des livres imprimés de la Bibliothèque nationale de Paris*.

Boase — Boase, Frederic. *Modern English biography*. Truro, c1892-1921; London, 1965.

Boisdeffre² — Boisdeffre, Pierre de. *Histoire de la littérature de la langue française des années 1930 aux années 1980*. Paris, 1985.

Bonner — *Bonner Gelehrte; Beiträge zur Geschichte der Wissenschaften in Bonn*. 1- . Bonn, 1968- .

Brinkman's — *Brinkman's catalogus van boeken en tijdschriften*.

BRISMES — British Society for Middle Eastern Studies.

BritInd — *British biographical index*, 2nd cumulated and enlarged edition. München, 1998.

Brümmer — Brümmer, Franz. *Lexikon der deutschen Dichter*, 6. Aufl. Leipzig, 1913.

Brümmer²	Brümmer, Franz. *Deutsches-Dichter Lexikon.* Eichstädt, 1876-77.
BSMES	British Society for Middle Eastern Studies.
BSOAS	*Bulletin* of the School of Oriental and African studies.
Buckland	Buckland, Charles E. *Dictionary of Indian biography.* London, 1906.
Burkert	Burkert, Martin. *Die Ostwissenschaften im Dritten Reich.* 1. Teil. Wiesbaden, 2000.
Bursian	*Biographisches Jahrbuch für Alterthumskunde,* von Conr. Bursian. Berlin, 1879-1898.
BWN	*Biografisch woordenboek van Nederland.* 's-Gravenhage, 1979- .
Canadian	*Canadian who's who.*
Capeille	Capeille, Jean. *Dictionnaire de biographies roussillonaises.* Paris, 1914; reprint, Marseille, 1978.
Cappellini 1	Cappellini, Antonio. *Dizionario biografico di genovesi illustri e notabili.* Genova, 1941.
Carnoy 10²	Carnoy, Émile *dit* Henry. *Dictionnaire biographique international des écrivains.* Paris, 1903. 262 p.
Carnoy 11	Carnoy, Émile *dit* Henry. *Dictionnaire biographique international des artistes, peintres, sculptures etc.* Paris, n.d. 99 p.
Carnoy 11²	Carnoy, Émile *dit* Henry. *Dictionnaire biographique international des collectionneurs, ex-libris, livres, manuscrits etc.* Paris, 1895. 81 p.
Casanova	Casanova, Paul. *L'Enseignement de l'arabe au Collège de France.* Prais, 1910.
Casati	Casati, Giovanni. *Dizionario degli scrittori d'Italia.* A-K. Milano, 1925-1934-
Casati 2	Casati, Giovanni. *Scrittori cattolici italiani viventi.* Milano, 1928.
CasWL	*Cassell's encyclopaedia of world literature.* London, 1953, 1973.
CathWW	*The Catholic who's who and yearbook.*
ČBS	*Československný biografický slovník.* Praha, 1992.
CelCen	Sanders, Lloyd C. *Celebrities of the century.* 1881.
CentBbritOr	*A Century of British Orientalists, 1902-2001;* ed. C. Edmond Bosworth. Oxford, 2001.
Cesky	*Český biografický slovník XX. století.* Paseka, 1999. 3 v.
ChambrBrBi	*Chambers British biographies - the 20th century,* ed. Min Lee. Edinburgh, 1993.
Chi è	*Chi è?* Roma, 1928-1961.
ChineseBiInd	*Chinese biographical index,* compiled by Stephan von Minden. München, 2000.
Chi scrive	*Chi scrive? Repertorio bio-bibliografico degli scrittori italiani.* Milano, 1962.
Churan	Churaň, Milan. *Kdo byl kdo v našich dějinách ve 20. století.* Praha, 1994.
Clausen	Clausen, Ursel. *Tunisie; notes biographiques.* Hamburg, 1976.
CIDMEL	*Columbia dictionary of modern European literature,* ed. Horatio Smith. New York, 1967.
CnDiAmJBi	*The Concise dictionary of American Jewish biography,* edited by Jacob Rader Marcus. Brooklyn, N.Y., 1994. 2v.
CNRS	Centre National de la Recherche Scientifique, Paris.
ConAu	*Contemporary authors.*
Cordier	Cordier, Henri. *Bibliotheca Indosinica.* Paris, 1912-1932.
Coston²	Coston, Henry. *Dictionnaire de la politique française.* Paris, 1967-82.
Couceiro	Couceiro Freijomil, Antonio. *Diccionario bio-bibliográfico de escritores.* Santiago de Compostela, 1951-1953.

Cragg	Cragg, Kenneth. *Troubled by truth; life studies in interfaith concern.* Edinburgh, 1992.
C.S.I.C.	Consejo Superior de Investigaciones Científicas.
Cuenca	Cuenca, Francisco. *Biblioteca de autores andaluces.* La Habana, 1921-1925.
CUNY	City University of New York.
CurBio	*Current biography yearbook.*
Curinier	*Dictionnaire national des contemporains,* ed. C. E. Curinier. Paris, 1901-1906.
Czy wiesz	*Czy wiesz kto to jest?* Warszawa, 1938.
DAB	*Dictionary of American biography.*
DanskBL	*Dansk biografisk leksikon,* tredje udgave. København, 1979-1984.
DanskBL²	*Dansk biografisk leksikon.* København, 1933-1944.
Dantès 1	Dantès, Alfred Langue. *Dictionnaire biographique et bibliographique.* Paris, 1875.
Dawson	Dawson, Warren R. & Eric P. Uphill. *Who was who in Egyptology,* 2d ed. London, 1972.
DBEC	*Diccionario biografico español contemporáneo.* Madrid, 1970.
DBF	*Dictionnaire de biographie française.* Paris, 1933- .
DBFC	*Dictionnaire biographique français contemporain,* 2ème éd. Paris, 1954-55.
DcAfHiB	*Dictionary of African historical biography,* 2nd ed. by Mark R. Lipschutz and R. Kent Rasmussen. Berkeley and Los Angeles, 1986.
DcAfL	Núñez, Benjamin. *Dictionary of Afro-Latin American civilization.* Westport, Conn., 1980.
DcAmBC	Dickinson, Donald C. *Dictionary of American book collectors.* New York, 1986.
DcAmDH	Findling, John. *Dictionary of American diplomatic history.* Westport, 1980.
DcAmImH	*Dictionary of American immigration history;* edited by Francesco Cordasco. Metuchen, N.Y., 1990.
DcBiPP	Vincent, Benjamin. *Dictionary of biography, past and present.* 1877.
DcBMOuvF	*Dictionnaire biographique du mouvement ouvrier français.* Paris, 1964- .
DcBrA	Waters, Grant M. *Dictionary of British artists working 1900-1950.* Eastbourne, 1975-1976.
DcCanB	*Dictionary of Canadian biography.* Vol. 1- . Toronto, 1966- .
DcCathB	Delaney, John J. & J. E. Tobin. *Dictionary of Catholic biography.* Garden City, N.Y., 1961.
DcEnc	*Dicţionar enciclopedic.* Bucureşti, 1993- .
DcEnL	Adams, William Davenport. *Dictionary of English literature.* London, ca. 1885.
DcERomân	*Dicţionar enciclopedic Român.* Bucureşti, 1962-1966.
DcEuL	Magnus, Laurie. *A Dictionary of European literature.* London, 1926.
DcIrB	Boylan, Henry. *A Dictionary of Irish biography.* New York, c1978, 1998.
DcLEL	Meyers, Robin. *A Dictionary of literature in the English language from 1940 to 1970; complete with title-author index and a geographical-chronological index to authors.* Oxford, 1978.
DcNAA	Wallace, William Stewart. *Dictionary of North American authors.* Detroit, c1951, 1968.
DcNZB	*A Dictionary of New Zealand biography,* edited by G. H. Scholefield. Wellington, 1940.
DcOrL	*Dictionary of Oriental literatures.* London, New York, 1974. 3v.
DcScandB	*Dictionary of Scandinavian biography,* 2nd ed. Cambridge, 1976.
DcScandL	*Dictionary of Scandinavian literature,* edited by Virpi Zuck. New York, 1990.

DcScB	*Dictionary of scientific biography.* New York, 1970-76, 1978.
DcSpL	Newmark, Maxim. *Dictionary of Spanish literature.* New York, 1956.
DcTwHis	Teed, Peter. *A Dictionary of twentieth century history, 1914-1990.* Oxford, 1992.
DcWomA	Petteys, Chris. *Dictionary of women artists; an international dictionary of women artists born before 1900.* Boston, Mass., 1985.
De Rolandis	De Rolandis, Giuseppe M. *Notize sugli escrittori Astigiani.* Asti, 1859.
DeutschesZL	*Deutsches Zeitgenossen-Lexikon; biographisches Handbuch deutscher Männer und Frauen der Gegenwart,* ed. Franz Neubert. Leipzig, 1905.
Dezobry	Dezobry, Louis Charles & Jean Louis Théodore Bachelet. *Dictionnaire général de biographie et d'histoire* etc., 5e éd. rev. Paris, 1869.
Diaz	Díaz Díaz, Gonzales. *Hombres y documentos de la filosofia española.* Madrid, 1980.
Dicc bio	*Diccionari biográfic.* 1-3. Barcelona, 1966-1970.
DiccHist	*Diccionario historia de España.* Madrid, 1952.
Dickinson	Dickinson, Robert E. *Makers of modern geography.* London, 1969.
Dicţionar	*Dicţionar enciclopedic ilustrat.* Bucureşti, 1999.
DizBI	*Dizionario biografico degli italiani,* Roma, 1960- .
DizRN	*Dizionario del Risorgimento nazionale.* Milano, 1930-37.
DLB	*Dictionary of literary biographhy.* 1- . Detroit, Mich., 1978- .
DNB	*Dictionary of national biography.* London, Oxford University Press.
DNZB	*Dictionary of New Zealand biography.* Wellington, 1940. 2v.
DÖS	*Deutschlands, Österreich-Ungarns und der Schweiz Gelehrte, Künstler und Schriftsteller in Wort und Bild,* ed. Gustav Adolf Müller. Hannover, 1910.
DrAS	*Directory of American scholars.*
DrASCan	*Directory of Asia studies in Canada.* 1- . Ottawa, Ont., 1978- .
DrBSMES	*Directory of BRISMES members.*
DSAB	*Dictionary of South African biography.* v. 1- . Pretoria, etc., c1968, 1976- .
DtBE	*Deutsche biographische Enzyklopädie.* München, 1995-2000.
DtBiInd	*Deutscher biographischer Index.* 2. kumulierte und erw. Ausgabe. München, 1998.
DtBiJ	*Deutsches biographisches Jahrbuch.* Berlin, 1925-1929.
Dziekan	Dziekan, Marek M. *Polacy a świat arabski; słownik biograficzny.* Gdańsk, 1998.
Édouard-J.	Édouard-Joseph, René. *Dictionnaire biographique des artistes contemporains, 1910-1930.* Paris, 1910-1930.
EEE	*Εκπαιδευτική ελληνική ενκυκλοπαίδεια.* Athens, 1990-1991.
Egyptology	*Who was who in Egyptology,* 3d ed. by M. L. Bierbrier. London, 1995.
EI²	*Encyclopaedia of Islam,* 2d ed.
EIranica	*Encyclopédia Iranica.* London, 1985- .
EIS	Necatigil, Behçet. *Edebiyatımızda isimler sözlüğü,* 7th ed. Istanbul, 1972.
Elias	Elías de Molins, Antonio. *Diccionario biográfico y bibliográfico de escritores y artistas catalanes del siglo XIX.* Barcelona, 1889-95.
Elsie	Elsie, Robert, *History of Albanian literature.* Boulder, Colo., 1995.
Embacher	Embacher, Friedrich. *Lexikon der Reisen und Entdeckungen.* Leipzig, 1882.
Eminent	*Eminent Indians who was who, 1900-1980.* New Delhi, 1985.
EmOr	*Eminent Orientalists, Indian, European, American.* Madras, 1922.

EnBulg	*Енциклоредия България.* Sofia, 1978-1996.
EncAJ	Paneth, Donald. *The Encyclopedia of American journalism.* New York, 1983.
EncAm	*Encyclopedia Americana*; international edition. New York, 1966.
EncBrit	*Encyclopædia Britannica,* 11th ed. Cambridge, 1910.
EncCoWW	*An Encyclopedia of Continental women writers,* edited by Katharina M. Wilson. New York, etc., 1991.
EncFen	*Otavan iso tietosanakirja* (Encyclopedia Fennica). 1-10. Helsinki, 1967-68.
EncHung	*Enciclopedia Hungarica.* Budapest, 1992-1996.
EncicUni	*Enciclopedia universal ilustrada.* Barcelona, 1910-1930.
EncIran	*Encyclopaedia Iranica.* London, 1985- .
EncItaliana	*Enciclopedia italiana di scienze, lettere ed arti.* Roma, 1929-1949.
EncJud	*Encyclopaedia Judaica.* Jerusalem, 1971- .
EncJud²	*Encyclopaedia Judaica.* A-L. Berlin, 1928-1934.
EncJug	*Enciklopedija Jugoslavije.* A- . Zagreb, 1980- .
EncJug²	*Enciklopedija Jugoslavije.* Zagreb, 1955-1971.
EncLitu	*Encyclopeadia Lituanica.* 1-6. Boston, 1970-1978.
EncLZ	*Enciklopedija leksikografskog zavoda.* Zagreb, 1966-69.
EncNI	*Encyclopedie van Nederlandsch-Indië.* 2de druk. s'Gravenhage, 1917-1939.
EncO&P	*Encyclopedia of occultism and parapsychology.* Detroit, 1984.
EncPWN	*Encyklopedia PWN w trzech tomach.* Warszawa, 1999- .
EncSlov	*Encyklopédia slovenska.* Bratislava, 1977-1979 .
EncSlovenije	*Enciklopedija Slovenije.* 1-16. Ljubljana, 1987-2002.
EncTR	Snyder, Louis L. *Encyclopedia of the Third Reich.* New York, 1976.
EncTwCJ	Taft, William H. *Encyclopedia of twentieth-century journalists.* New York, 1986.
EncWL	*Encyclopedia of world literature in the 20th century,* edited by Wolfgang B. Fleischmann. New York, 1967-1975.
EncWM	*Encyclopedia of world Methodism.* Nashville, Tenn., 1974.
EnSlovar	*Энциклопедическій словарь.* S.-Peterburg, 1890-1904. 82 vols.
Erdélyi	*Erdélyi Magyar ki kicsoda.* Budapest, 2000.
Espasa	*Diccionario enciclopédico Espasa.* 1-12; apéndice 1 & 2. Madrid, 1978-1990.
EST	*Энциклопедияи совеетии точик.* 1-7. Dushanbe, 1978-1987.
EuAu	Kunitz, Stanley J. & V. Colby. *European authors, 1000-1900; a biographical dictionary of European literature.* New York, 1967.
EURAMES	*European expertise on the Middle East & North Africa, a directory of specialists and institutions*; eds. Emma Murphy, Gerd Nonneman, Neil Quilliam for EURAMES, 1993.
EVL	*Επίτομο βιογραφικό λεξικό,* Athens.
EvLB	Browning, David Clayton. *Everyman's dictionary of literary biography, English and American,* compiled after John W. Cousin. 3rd ed. London, 1962.
Facey Grant	Facey, William & Gillian Grant. *Kuwait by the first photographers.* London, 1998.
FarE&A	*The Far East and Australasia.* 1 (1969)- .
Faucon	Faucon, Narcisse A. *Le Livre d'or de l'Algérie de 1830 à 1889.* Paris, 1889.
Fekete	Fekete, Márton. *Prominent Hungarians, home and abroad.* 4th ed. London, 1985.

Ferahian	Ferahian, Salwa. *Handlist of M.A. and Ph.D. theses submitted to the Institute of Islamic Studies,* (McGill University,) *1954-1995.* Montreal, McGill University, 1996.
Féraud	Féraud, Laurent Charles. *Les interprètes de l'armée d'Afrique.* Alger, 1876.
Fernandez	Fernández y Sánchez, Ildefonso. *Año biográfico español.* Barcelona, 1899.
Figuras	*Figuras de hoy; enciclopedia biográfica nacional.* Madrid, 1951- .
Filipsky	*Čeští a slovenští orientalisté, afrikanisté a iberoamerikanisté,* by Jan Filipský a kol. Praha, 1999.
FilmgC	Halliwell, Leslie. *Filmgoer's companion,* 8th ed. New York, 1984.
Firenze	*Catalogo cumulativo 1886-1957 del bollettino delle pubblicazioni italiane ricevute per diritto di stampa dalla Biblioteca Nazionale Centrale di Firenze.* Nendeln, 1968-1969.
Frederiks	Frederiks, Johannes G. & F. Jos. van den Branden. *Biographisch woordenboek der Noord- en Zuidnederlandsche letterkunde.* 2e dr. Amsterdam, 1888-1892.
Freeth	Freeth, Zahra D. & H. V. F. Winstone. *Explorers of Arabia.* New York, 1978.
Fuad	Fuad, Kamal. *Kurdische Handschriften.* Wiesbaden, 1970.
Fück	Fück, Johannes. *Die arabischen Studien in Europa.* Leipzig, 1955.
Fusco	Fusco, Enrico Maria. *Scrittori e idee.* Torino, 1956.
Gabriel	Gabriel, Alfons. *Vergessene Persienreisende.* Wien, 1969.
GAL	Brockelmann, Carl. *Geschichte der arabischen Litteratur,* 1898-1942.
GAS	Sezgin, Fuat. *Geschichte des arabischen Schrifttums.* 1-12. Leiden and Frankfurt am Main, 1967-2000.
Gastaldi	Gastaldi, Mario. *Dizionario delle scrittrici italiane contemporanee.* Milano, 1957.
GdeEnc	*La Grande encyclopédie.* Paris, 1885-1901.
GdLaEnc	*Grand Larousse encyclopédique.* Paris, 1960-1964.
GDU	Larousse, Pierre. *Grand dictionnaire universel.* Paris, 1865-90.
GeistigeUng	Jásznigi, Alexander. *Das geistige Ungarn; biographisches Lexikon,* herausgegeben von Oskar von Krücken [pseud.] und Imre Parlagi. Wien & Leipzig, 1918.
GeistigeWien	Eisenberg, Ludwig Julius. *Das geistige Wien.* 1- . Wien, 1893- .
Geog	*Geographers; biobibliographical studies.* 1- . London, 1977- .
GER	*Gran enciclopedia RIALP.* 1-25. Madrid, 1984-1989.
Glaeser	Glaeser, Ernest. *Biographie nationale des contemporains.* Paris, 1878.
Goldschmidt	Goldschmidt, Arthur. *Historical dictionary of modern Egypt.* Boulder, Colo., 2000.
Građa	*Građa za hrvatsku retrospektivnu bibliografiju knjiga, 1835-1940.* Zagreb, 1982- .
GrBioInd	*Griechischer biographischer Index = Greek biographical index,* compiled by Hilmar Schmuck. Munchen, 2003. 3 v.
Gray	Gray, A. Stuart. *Edwardian architecture; a biographical dictionary.* London, 1985.
GrBr	Oxbury, Harold. *Great Britons; twentieth-century lives.* Oxford, 1985.
GSE	*Great Soviet encyclopedia.* New York and London, 1973-1983.
Gubernatis 1	Gubernatis, Angelo de. *Dizionario biografico degli scrittori contemporanei.* Firenze, 1879-1880.
Gubernatis 3	Gubernatis, Angelo de. *Piccolo dizionario dei contemporanei italiani.* Roma, 1895.
GV	*Gesamtverzeichnis des deutschsprachigen Schrifttums, 1700-1910.* München, 1979-1987. 160 v.; *Gesamtverzeichnis des deutschsprachigen Schrifttums, 1911-1965.* München, 1976-1981. 150 vols.
Haan	Haan, Wilhelm. *Sächsisches Schriftsteller-Lexicon.* Leipzig, 1875.

Hanisch	Hanisch, Ludmila. *Die Nachfolger der Exegeten; deutschsprachige Erforschung des Vorderen Orients in der ersten Hälfte des 20. Jahrhunderts.* Wiesbaden, 2003.
HanRL	*Handbook of Russian literature*, edited by Victor Terras. New Haven, 1985.
HbDtWiss	*Handbuch der deutschen Wissenschaft.* Berlin, 1949. 2 vols.
HBL	*Hrvatski biografski leksikon.* Zagreb, 1983- .
HE	*Hrvatska enciklopedija.* Zagreb, 1999- .
Hellenikon	*Ελληνικον who's who,* Athens.
Henze	Henze, Dietmar. *Enzyklopädie der Entdecker.* Graz, 1978- .
Hill	Hill, Richard. *A Biographical dictionary of the Sudan.* 2nd ed. London, 1967.
Hinrichsen	Hinrichsen, Adolf. *Das literarische Deutschland.* 2. Auflage. Berlin 1891.
Hirsching	*Historisch-litterarisches Handbuch berühmter und denkwürdiger Personen, welche in dem 18. Jahrhunderte gestorben sind*, herausgegeben von Friedrich Carl Gottlob Hirsching. Leipzig, c1794-1815, Graz, 1972-1976.
HisBioLexCH	*Historisch-biographisches Lexikon der Schweiz.* Neuenburg, 1921-1934.
HisDcDP	Cortada, James W. *Historical dictionary of data processing; biographies.* New York, 1987.
HL	*Hrvatski leksikon.* Zagreb, 1996-1997.
HnRL	*see* HanRL
Hoefer	*Nouvelle biographie générale*, edited by Johann C. F. Hoefer. Paris, 1852-1866.
Hofer	Hofer, Fritz and Sonja Hägeli, *Zürcher Personenlexikon.* Zürich, 1986.
HrvEnc	*Hrvatska enciklopedija*; general editor: Dalibor Brotović. Zagreb, 1999- .
Hvem	*Hvem er hvem,* Oslo.
IES	*Ilustrovaný encyklopedický slovník.* Praha, 1980-1982.
IJMES	*International journal of Middle East studies.*
Imperatori	Imperatori, Ugo E. *Dizionario di italiani all'estero.* Genova, 1956.
IndAu 1977	Thompson, Donald F. *Indiana authors and their books, 1917-1966.* Crawfordsville, Ind., 1974.
IndBI	*Indice biografico italiano,* 2a edizione, 1-7. München, 1997.
IndBiItal	*Indice biografico italiano*, 3a ed., edited by Tomasso Nappo. München, 2002.
IndexBFr	*Index biographique français.* London, 1993.
IndexBFr²	*Index biographique français*, 2ème édition cumulée et augmentée. München, 1998.
IndiaWW	*India who's who.*
IndianBiInd	*Indian biographical index*, compiled by Loureen Baillie. München, 2001.
IndiceE²	*Indice biográfico de España, Portugal e Iberoamérica.* 2a ed. München, 1995.
IndiceE³	*Indice biográfico de España, Portugal e Iberoamérica.* 3a edición corregida y amplicada, editado por Victor Herrero Mediavilla. München, 2000.
IntAu&W	*International authors and writers (who's who).*
IntDcAn	*International dictionary of anthropologists*, ed. Christopher Winters. New York, 1991.
IntMed	*International medical who's who.*
IntWW	*International who's who.*
IntWWM	*International who's who in music and musicians' directory.*
IntWWP	*International who's who in poetry.* London, 1958- .

IntYB — *The International year book and statesmen's who's who.*

IranWW — *Iran who's who.* Teheran, 1972- .

IWWAS — *International who's who in Asian studies,* Hong Kong.

JA — *Journal asiatique.*

JahrDtB — *Jahrbuch der deutschen Bibliotheken.* 1- . Leipzig, Wiesbaden, 1902- .

Jain — Jain, Naresh K. *Muslims in India.* New Delhi, 1979-83. 2v.

Jaksch — Jaksch, Friedrich. *Lexikon sudetendeutscher Schriftsteller für die Jahre 1900-1929.* Reichenberg, 1929.

Jalabert — Jalabert, Henri. *Jésuites au Proche-Orient; notices biographiques.* Beyrouth, 1987.

JAOS — *Journal* of the American Oriental Society.

JapAuFile — Kokuritsu Kokkai Toshokan (Japan). [Engl. alternative title:] *National Diet Library authority file for Japanese authors.* Tokyo, 1991.

JewEnc — *The Jewish encyclopedia.* New York & London, 1901-1906.

JNES — *Journal of Near Eastern studies.*

JRAS — *Journal of the Royal Asiatic Society.*

JRCAS — *Journal of the Royal Central Asian Society.*

JSS — *Journal of Semitic studies.*

JüdBiInd — *Jüdischer biographischer Index,* ed. Hilmar Schmuck. München, 1998.

JüdLex — *Jüdisches Lexikon.* A-R. Berlin, 1927-1930. v. 1-4.

JugoslSa — *Jugoslovenski savremenici; ko je ko u Jugoslaviji.* Beograd, 1970.

Juynboll — Juynboll, W.M.C. *Zeventiende-eeuwsche beoefenaars van het Arabisch in Nederland.* Utrecht, 1931.

Kazakhskaia — *Казахская ССР краткая энциклопедия,* vol. 1-4. Alma-Ata, 1985-1991.

KazakSE — *Казак Совет энцыклоредиясы.* Almaty, 1972-1982.

Kdo je kdo — *Kdo je kdo; osobnosti české současnosti = Who's who* Praha, 1991- .

KDtLK — *Kürschners deutscher Literatur-Kalender.* Leipzig & Berlin, 1887- . [1879-1886 entitled *Allgemeiner deutscher Literaturkalender* and *Deutscher Litteratur-Kalender.*]

Ki-kicsoda — *Ki-kicsooda? Kortársak lexikona.* Budapest, 1937.

Kim kimdir — *Günümü Türkiyesinde kim kimdir.* Istanbul.

Kirk — Kirk, John Foster. *A supplement to Allibone's critical dictionary of English literature.* Philadelphia, 1891.

KoBošnjaka — *Ko je ko u Bošnjaka* / redakcija Tufik Burnazović et al. Sarajevo, 2000.

Koi — *Кой кой е б България,* 1998. Sofia, 1998- .

Ko je ko — *Ko je ko u Jugoslaviji.* Beograd, 1957.

Ko je ko Srbiji — *Ko je ko u Srbiji; biografski leksikon.* Beograd, 1991- .

Kornrumpf — Hans-Jürgen & Jutta Kornrumpf. *Fremde im Osmanischen Reich, 1826-1912/13; bio-bibliographisches Register.* Stutensee, Privately published, 1998.

Kornrumpf[3] — Hans-Jürgen & Jutta Kornrumpf. *Fremde im Osmanischen Reich, 1826-1912/13; bio-bibliographisches Register.* 3. Auflage. Stutensee, Privately published, 2003. 2 vols.

Kornrumpf, N. — Hans-Jürgen & Jutta Kornrumpf. *Fremde im Osmanischen Reich, 1826-1912/13; bio-bibliographisches Register.* Nachträge. Stutensee, 2005.

Kosch — Kosch, Wilhelm. *Das katholische Deutschland.* Augsburg, 1933-38.

Kosel — *Deutsch-österreichisches Künstler- und Schriftsteller-Lexikon,* ed. Hermann Clements Kosel. Wien, 1902-1906.

Krachkovskii   Krachkovskii, Ignatii. *Die russische Arabistik*, von I. J. Kratschkowski, a translation of Очерк по истории русской арабистики. Leipzig, 1957.

Kraks   *Kraks blå bog*. København, 1910- .

KtoPolsce   *Kto jest kim w Polsce*.

Kuhn   Kuhn, Heinrich & Otto Boss. *Biographisches Handbuch der Tschechoslowakei*. München, 1961.

Kürschner   *Kürschners Deutscher Gelehrten-Kalender*.

KyrgyzSE   Кыргыз Совет энциклопедиясы. Ashgabat, 1974-1989.

Lamathière   Lamathière, Théophile de. *Panthéon de la Légion d'honneur*. Paris, 1875-1911.

LC   *Library of Congress catalog* and/or *Library of Congress name authority file*.

LEduc   *Leaders in education*. Lancaster, Pa., New York, 1932.

LexAfrika   *Lexikon der Afrikanistik*; ed. H. Jungraithmayr & W. J. G. Möhlig. Berlin, 1983.

LexFrau   *Lexikon der Frau*. Zürich, 1953-54.

LingH   *Linguisten-Handbuch*; herausgegeben von Wilfried Kürschner. Tübingen, 1994.

LitWho   *Literary who's who*. London, 1920.

LitYbk   *Literary yearbook (and who's who)*, vol. 1-22. London, 1897-1921.

Liudi   Люди и судьбы (Men and destiny), compiled by IAroslav V. Vasil'kov and Marina IU. Sorokina. Sankt-Peterburg, 2003.

LivesRem   *Lives remembered, The Times obituaries*. Pangbourne, 1991- .

Lodwick   Lodwick, Kathleen. *The Chinese Recorder index, 1867-1941*. Wilmington, Del., 1986.

LSE   London School of Economics.

LThK   Buchberger, Michael, *ed. Lexikon für Theologie und Kirche*. 2. Aufl. Freiburg, 1930-1938.

LuthC 75   *Lutheran cyclopedia*; edited by E. L. Lueker. St. Louis & London, 1975.

MacDCB 78   *The Macmillan dictionary of Canadian biography*, edited by William Stewart Wallace, 4th ed., by W. A. McKay. Toronto, 1978.

Magyar   *Magyar Nagylexikon*. Budapest, 1993- .

MagyarNKK   *Magyar és nemzetközi ki kicsoda*. Budapest, 1992-2000.

MagyarZL   *Magyar zsidó lexikon*. Budapest, 1929.

Makers   *Makers of modern Africa*. 1- . London, 1981- .

MaláČEnc   *Malá československá encyklopedie*. Praha, 1984-1987.

Manzanares   Manzanares de Cirre, Manuela. *Arabistas españoles del siglo XIX*. Madrid, 1972.

Martinek   Jiří & Miloslav Martínek. *Kdo byl kdo naši cestovatelé a geografové*. Praha, 1998.

Masarykův   *Masarykův slovník naučný*. Praze, 1925-1933.

Mason   Mason, Philip. *The Men who ruled India*. London, 1985. (An abridged version of the first edition in two volumes, 1953-1954).

Master   *Biography and genealogy master index*, 2d ed., vol. 1-8. Detroit, Mich., 1980- .

Matthieu   Matthieu, Ernest A. J. G. *Biographie du Hainaut*. Enghien, 1902-1905. 2 v.

Mayeur   Mayeur, Jean Marie & Yves Marie Hilaire. *Dictionnaire du monde religieux dans la France contemporaine*. Paris, 1985-1990.

MedWW   *The Medical who's who*. London, 1914.

Megali   Μεγαλη ελληνικη εγκυκλοπαιδεια. Athens, 1927-34. 24 vols.

MEJ   *The Middle East journal*.

MEL   *Magyar életrejzi lexikon.* Budapest, 1967-1969; 1978-1991.

MembriiAR   *Membrii Academiei Române, 1866-1999; dicţionar,* ed. Eugen Simion. Bucureşti,1999.

Men10   *Men of the time,* 10th edition. London, 1879.

Mendez   Méndez Bejarano, Mario. *Diccionario de escritores, maestros y oradores naturales de Sevilla y su actual provincia.* Tomo 1-3. Sevilla, 1922-1925.

Mennell   Mennell, Philip. *Dictionary of Australasian biography.* London, 1892- .

MES   *Middle Eastern studies.*

MESA   Middle East Studies Association of North America.

MEW   *Moderne encyclopedie van de wereldliteraturen.* Haarlem, 1980-1984.

Meydan   *Büyük lügat ve ansiklopedisi.* Istanbul, Meydan-Larousse, 1969-1976.

Meyers   *Meyers Großes Konversations=Lexikon,* 6. Aufl. Leipzig, 1907-1920.

MicDcEnc   *Mic dicţionar enciclopedic.* Bucureşti, 1986.

Michaud   *Biographie universelle (Michaud) ancienne et moderne.* c1854, 1967.

MidE   *The Middle East and North Africa.* 1- . London, 1948- .

MIDEO   *Mélanges* / Institut Dominicain d'Études Orientales du Caire.

Mifsud   Mifsud Bonnici, Robert. *Dizzjunarju bijo-bibljografiku nazzjonali.* Malta, 1960.

Miliband   Miliband, Sofiia D. *Биобиблиографический словарь советских востоковедо.* Moskva, 1975.

Miliband²   Miliband, Sofiia D. *Биобиблиографический словарь отечественных востоко-ведов с 1917 г.* Moskva, 1995.

MIT   Massachusetts Institute of Technology, Cambridge, Mass.

Morgan   Morgan, Henry J., ed. *The Canadian men and women of the time.* Toronto, 1898; 2nd ed., Toronto, 1912.

MW   *Moslem/Muslim world,* Hartford, Conn.

Nat   Nat, Jan, *De studie van de Oostersche talen in Nederland in de 18e en de 19e eeuw.* Purmerend, 1929.

NatCAB   *The National cyclopaedia of American biography,* vol. 1-63. New York, 1892-1984.

NatFacDr   *National faculty directory.* Detroit, 1970- .

NBN   *Nouvelle biographie nationale.* 1- . Bruxelles, 1988- .

NBW   *Nationaal biografisch woordenboek.* 1- . Brussel, 1964- .

NCCN   *New century cyclopedia of names.* New York, 1954.

NDB   *Neue deutsche Biographie.* Berlin, 1953- .

NDBA   *Nouvelle dictionnaire de biographie alsacienne.* Strasbourg, 1982- .

NDNC   *Nouveau dictionnaire national des contemporains,* 1-5. Paris, 1962-68.

NearMEWho   *The Near and Middle East who's who.* vol. 1. Jewrusalem, 1945.

NEP   *Nowa encyklopedia powszechna PWN.* Warszawa, 1995- .

NewC   *New century handbook of English literature.* New York, 1956.

NewCathEnc   *New Catholic encyclopedia.* Washington, D.C., c1967, 1981.

NewCEN   *see* NCCN

NewGrDM   *The New Grove dictionary of music and musicians.* London, c1980, 1995.

NieuwNBW   *Nieuw Nederlandsch biografisch woordenboek.* Leiden, 1911-1937.

NÖB   *Neue österreichische Biographie ab 1815; große Österreicher.* 1- . Wien, 1923- .

NorskBL	*Norsk biografisk leksikon.* 1-19. Oslo, 1923-1983.
NorskBL²	*Norsk biografsk leksikon.* Oslo, 1999- .
Note	Note about the author in a periodical or book.
NotWoAT	*Notable women in the American theatre; a biographical dictionary*, edited by Alice M. Robinson. New York, Greenwood Press, 1989.
NSB	*Neue schweizer Biographie.* Basel, 1938.
NSMES	Nordic Society for Middle Eastern Studies.
NUC	*National union catalog.*
NYC	New York City.
NYPL	New York Public Library, New York City.
NYT	*New York Times.*
ObitOF	*Obituaries on file*, compiled by Felice Levy. New York, 1979.
ObitT	*Obituaries from the Times.*
ÖBL	*Österreichisches biographisches Lexikon, 1815-1950.* Wien, 1957- .
Opać	*Opać enciklopedija.* Zagreb, 1980- .
OSK	Osteuropa Sammelkatalog, edited at the Staatsbibliothek zu Berlin. Not published.
Ossorio	Ossorio y Bernard, Manuel. *Ensayo de un catálogo de periodistas españoles del siglo XIX.* Madrid, 1903-4.
OttůvSN	*Ottův slovník naučný.* Praze, 1888-1909.
Oursel	Oursel, Noémie N. *Nouvelle biographie normande.* Paris, 1886-1888.
OxCan	Story, Norah. *Oxford companion to Canadian history and literature.* Toronto, 1967.
OxCLiW	*The Oxford companion to the literature of Wales.* Oxford, 1986.
OxEng	*Oxford companion to English literature*; 4th ed. by P. Harvey. Oxford 1969.
OxFr	*Oxford companion to French literature*; ed. P. Harvey, J. E. Hesseltine. Oxford, 1966.
OxGer	Garland, Henry and Mary. *The Oxford companion to German literature.* Oxford, 1976.
OxLaw	Walker, David M. *The Oxford companion to law.* Oxford, 1980.
OxMus	Scholes, Percy A. *The Oxford companion to music*, 10th ed. London, 1974.
OxSpan	*Oxford companion to Spanish literature*; ed. by Philip Ward. Oxford, 1978.
OxThe	*Oxford companion to the theatre*, 4th ed. by Phyllis Hartnoll. Oxford, 1983.
Özege	Özege, M. Seyfettin. *Eski harflerle basılmış Türkçe eserler kataloğu.* İstanbul, 1971-82
Pallas	*A Pallas nagy lexikona.* Budapest, 1893-1897.
PeoHis	*People in history*, edited by Susan K. Kinnell. Santa Barbara, Calif, 1988.
Peppin	Peppin, Brigid & Lucy Micklethwait. *Dictionary of British book illustrators; the twentieth century.* London, 1983.
Peyronnet	Peyronnet, Raymond. *Livre d'or des officiers des Affaires indigènes, 1830-1930.* Alger, Commissariat général du centenaire, 1930. Tome 2: Notices et biographies.
Pinto	Pinto, Juan. *Diccionario de la República Argentina.* Buenos Aires, 1950.
Poggendorff	Poggendorff, Johann C. *Biographisch-literarisches Handwörterbuch.* Leipzig & Berlin, 1863-1962.
PoIre	O'Donoghue, David James. *The Poets of Ireland.* c1912, 1968.
PolBiDi	*The Polish biographical dictionary; profiles of nearly 900 Poles*; by Stanley S. Sokol with Sharon F. Mrotek Kissane. Wauconda, Ill., 1992.

Polski	*Polski indeks biograficzny*, compiled by Gabriele Baumgartner. München, 1998.
Polski²	*Polski indeks biograficzny*, compiled by Gabriele Baumgartner, 2d ed. München, 2004.
PorLing	*Portraits of linguists; a biographical source book for the history of Western linguistics, 1746-1963*, edited by Thomas A. Sebeok. Bloomington, Ind., 1966. 2 v. [Reprint of obituaries, most of which in the original language.]
Private	Private information or questionnaire.
Prominent	*Prominent Hungarians*, ed. Márton Fekete. London, 1985.
PSB	*Polski słownik biograficzny*. 1- . Kraków, etc., 1935- .
PSN	*Příruční slovník naučný*. Praha, 1962-1967. 4 vol.
PTF	*Philologiae turcicae fundamenta*. 2v. Wiesbaden, 1959-1965.
Quem	*Quem é quem no Brasil.*
QuemPort	*Quem é alguém* (Who's who in Portugal). Lisboa, 1947.
Qui	*Qui est qui en Belgique francophone.*
Qui êtes-vous	*Qui êtes-vous*, 1908, 1924.
Quien	*Quién es quién en España.*
RCAJ	*Royal Central Asian journal.*
Rafols	Ráfols, José Francisco. *Diccionario biográfico de artistas de Cataluña*. 1-3. Barcelona, 1951-1954.
Ray	*Dictionary of national biography. Supplement*, edited by N. R. Ray. Calcutta, 1986- .
Reich	*Political leaders of the contemporary Middle East and North Africa*, edited by Bernard Reich. New York, 1990.
REJ	*Revue des études juives.*
RelLAm	Melton, J. Gordon. *Religious leaders of America; a biographical guide to founders and leaders of religious bodies, Churches, and spiritual groups*. Detroit, Mich., 1991 .
REnAL	*The Reader's encyclopeadia of American literature*. New York, 1963.
RHbDtG	*Reichshandbuch der deutschen Gesellschaft*. Berlin, 1931.
Richter	Richter, Julius. *A History of Protestant missions in the Near East*. New York, 1910.
Riddick	Riddick, John F. *Who was who in British India*. Westport, Conn., 1998.
RNL	*Révai nagy lexikona*. 1-21. Budapest, 1911-1935.
Robinson	Robinson, Jane. *Wayward women; a guide to women travellers*. Oxford, 1990.
Romaniai	*Romániai magyar ki kicsoda*. Kolozsvár, 1997.
ROMM	*Revue de l'Occident musulman et de la Méditerranée.*
Rosenthal	Rosenthal, Eric. *Southern African dictionary of national biography*. London, 1966.
Rovito	Rovito, Teodoro. *Letterati e giornalisti italiani contemporanei*. Napoli, 1922.
Ruiz C	Ruiz Cabriada, Agustín. *Bio-bibliografía del cuerpo facultativo de archiveros, bibliotecarios y arqueólogos, 1858-1958*. Madrid, 1958.
Sabater	*Diccionario biográfico español e hispanoamericano*, publicado bajo la dirección de Gaspar Sabater. Palma de Mallorca, 1959- .
Sainz	Sainz de Robles, Federico Carlos. *Ensayo de un diccionario de la literatura*, 2d ed., 1-3. Madrid, 1953-1956.
Salomone	Salomone, Sebastiano. *La Sicilia intellettuale contemporanea*. Catania, 1913.
Salses	Salses, Edmond de. *Livre d'or de valeurs humaines*. Paris, 1970.

Sampaio	Andrade, Arsénio Sampaio de. *Dicionário histórico e biográfico de artistas e técnicos portugueses.* Lisboa, 1959.
SBL	*Svenskt biografiskt lexikon.* Stockholm, 1918- .
ScBInd	*Scandinavian biographical index.* London, etc., 1994.
Schäfer	Schäfer, Richard. *Geschichte der Deutschen Orient=Mission.* Potsdam, 1932.
SchBiAr	Keller, Willy. *Schweizer biographisches Archiv.* 1-6. Zürich, 1952-1958.
Schoeberlein	Schoeberlein-Engel, John S. *Guide to scholars of the history and culture of Central Asia.* Cambridge, Mass., 1995.
Schwarz	Schwarz, Klaus. *Der Vordere Orient in den Hochschulschriften Deutschlands, Österreichs und der Schweiz.* Freiburg im Breisgau, 1980.
SchZLex	*Schweizerisches Zeitgenossen-Lexikon.* Bern, 1921.
Selim	Selim, George Dimitri. *American doctoral dissertations on the Arab world, 1883-1974.* Washington, D.C., 1976.
Selim²	Selim, George Dimitri. *American doctoral dissertations on the Arab world, 1981-1987.* Washington, D.C., 1989.
Selim³	Selim, George D. *American doctoral dissertations on the Arab world. Supplement, 1975-1981.* Washington, D.C., 1983.
Sen	*Dictionary of national biography,* edited by S. P. Sen. Calcutta, 1972-1974.
Sezgin	*Bibliographie der deutschsprachigen Arabistik und Islamkunde;* herausgegeben von Fuat Sezgin, I. Balçik, G. Degener, E. Neubauer. v. 1-21. Frankfurt a. M, 1990-1995.
Shavit	Shavit, David. *The United States in the Middle East.* New York, 1988.
Shavit, Africa	Shavit, David. *The United States in Africa.* New York, 1989.
Shavit, Asia	Shavit, David. *The United States in Asia.* New York, 1990.
SibirSE	*Сибирская советская энциклопедия.* 1-3. Moscow, 1929-1932.
Sigilla	*Sigilla veri; Lexikon der Juden, -Genossen und -Gegner.* Erfurt, 1929-1931.
SlovBioL	*Slovenski biografski leksikon.* Ljubljana, 1971-1991.
Sluglett	Sluglett, Peter. *Theses on Islam, the Middle East and North-West Africa.* London, 1983.
Smith	*The Admission register of the Manchester school;* ed. Jeremiah F. Smith. Manchester, 1866-1874.
SMK	*Svenska män och kvinnor.* Stockholm, 1942-1955.
SOAS	School of Oriental and African Studies, University of London.
Srodka	Śródka, Andrzej. *Uczeni polscy XIX-XX stulecia.* Warszawa, 1994-98.
Stache-Rosen	Stache-Rosen, Valentina. *German Indologists;* 2d ed. New Delhi, 1990.
Stenij	Stenij, S. Edv. "Die orientalischen Studien in Finnland, 1828-1875" in: *Studia orientalia* 1 (1925), pp. 271-311.
St&PR	*Standard & Poor's Register of corporations. directors and executives.* Charlottesville, Va., 1987- .
Suárez	Suárez, Constantino. *Escritores y artistas Asturianos; índice bio-bibliográfico. 7 vols.* Madrid, 1936-1959.
SUNY	State University of New York.
TatarES	*Татарский энциклопедический словарь,* ed. M. Kh. Khasanov. Kazan, 1999.
TB	*Türkiye bibliyografyası.*
Teichl	*Österreicher der Gegenwart,* hrsg. von Robert Teichl. Wien, 1951.

Temerson · *Biographie des principales personnalités françaises décédés au cours de l'année*, ed. Henri Temerson. Paris, 1956.

THESAM 1 · *Le monde arabe et musulman au miroir de l'université française*; répertoire des thèses soutenues dans les universités françaises, en sciences de l'homme et de la société, sur le monde arabe et musulman, 1973-1987. THESAM 1: Maghreb, Mauritanie, Maroc, par Marie Burgat, Danièle Bruchet. Aix-en-Provence, 1989.

THESAM 2 · *Le monde arabe et musulman au miroir de l'université française*; répertoire des thèses soutenues dans les universités françaises, en sciences de l'homme et de la société, sur le monde arabe et musulman, 1973-1987. THESAM 2: Algérie, Tunisie, Libye, par Jacqueline Quilès. Aix-en-Provence, 1990.

THESAM 3 · *Le monde arabe et musulman au miroir de l'université française*; répertoire des thèses soutenues dans les universités françaises, en sciences de l'homme et de la société, sur le monde arabe et musulman, 1973-1987. THESAM 3: Machrek, par Jacqueline Quilès. Aix-en-Provence, 1991.

THESAM 4 · *Le monde arabe et musulman au miroir de l'université française*; répertoire des thèses soutenues dans les universités françaises, en sciences de l'homme et de la société, sur le monde arabe et musulman, 1973-1987. THESAM 4: Monde arabe et musulman, Afghanistan, Empire ottoman, Iran, Pakistan, Turquie, par Marie-José Bianquis et Danièle Bruchet. Aix-en-Provence, 1992.

Thesis · Curriculum vitae in a doctoral dissertation.

ThTwC · *Thinkers of the twentieth century*, ed. E. Devine et al. London, c1983, 1987.

Traljić · Traljić, Hafiz Mahmud. *Istaknuti Bošnjaci*. Zagreb, 1994.

TurkmenSE · *Туркмен совет энциклопедиясы*, 1-10. Ashgabat, 1974-1989.

TwCAu · *Twentieth century authors*. New York, 1942, 1955.

TwCBDA · *The Twentieth century biographical dictionary of notable Americans*; edited by Rossiter Johnson. Detroit, c1904, 1968.

TwCPaSc · Spalding, Frances. *Twentieth century painters and sculptors*. Woodbridge, 1990.

UCLA · University of California, Los Angeles.

UjMagyar · *Új magyar lexikon*. Budapest, 1959-1972.

UjLex · *Uj idők lexikona*. Budapest, 1936-1942.

Uj lexikon · *Uj lexikon*. Budapest, 1936. 8 vol.

Unesco · UNESCO. *Social scientists specializing in African studies; directory = Africanistes spécialistes de sciences sociales; répertoire*. Prepared by the Secretariat of Unesco. Paris, 1963.

Uusi · *Uusi tietosanakirja*. Helsinki, 1966-68. 24 vol.

UzbekSE · *Узбек Совет энциклопедиясю*. 1-14. Toshkent, 1971-1980.

Vaccaro · Vaccaro, Gennaro, *ed. Panorama biografico degli italiani d´oggi*. Roma, 1956.

Van Ess · Van Ess, Dorothy. *Who's who in the Arabian mission*, by Mrs. John Van Ess. New York, ca. 1937.

Vapereau · Vapereau, Gustave. *Dictionnaire universel des contemporains*, 1861, 6e éd. Paris, 1893.

Vem är det · *Vem är det*, Stockholm.

Vem och vad · *Vem och vad*, Helsingfors.

VIA · *Voyageurs italien en Afrique*. Roma, Ministerio delle Colonie, Ufficio Studi e Propaganda, 1931.

Vogel · Vogel, Lester I. *To see a promised land*. University Park, Pa., 1993.

Vollmer · *Allgemeines Lexikon der bildenden Künste des XX.Jahrhunderts*, ed. Hans Vollmer. Leipzig, 1953-1961.

VostokMStP	*Востоковеды Москвы и Санкт-Петербурга* / Российская Академия Наук, Институт Востоковедения. Moskva, 2000.
Wer	*Wer ist wer; Lexikon österreichischer Zeitgenossen.* Wien, 1937.
WhAm	*Who was who in America.*
WhAmArt	*Who was who in American art.*
WhE&EA	*Who was who among English and European authors.*
WhNAA	*Who was who among North American authors.*
Who	*Who's who.*
WhoAm	*Who's who in America.*
WhoAmArt	*Who's who in American art.*
WhoAmJ	*Who's who in American Jewry.*
WhoAmL	*Who's who in American law.*
WhoAmM	*Who's who in American music.*
WhoAmP	*Who's who in American politics.*
WhoAmW	*Who's who of American women.*
WhoArab	*Who's who in the Arab world.*
WhoArt	*Who's who in art.*
WhoAtom	*Who's who in atoms.*
WhoAus	*Who's who in Australia.*
WhoAustria	*Who's who in Austria*
WhoBelgium	*Who's who in Belgium.*
WhoBIA	*Who's who among Black Americans.*
WhoChina	*Who's who in China; biographies of Chinese leaders.* 1st ed. - . Shanghai, China Weekly Review, 1918- .
WhoCon	*Who's who in consulting.*
WhoCroatia	*Who's who in Croatia.*
WhoE	*Who's who in the East.*
WhoEc	*Who's who in economics; a biographical dictionary of major economists, 1700-1986.*
WhoEcon	*Who's who in economics; a biographical dictionary of major economists, 1700-1981.*
WhoEduc	*Who's who in education.*
WhoEgypt	*Who's who in Egypt and the Near East.* [1959 edition entitled *Who's who in the U.A.R and the Near East.*] Cairo, 1952- .
WhoEIO	*Who's who in European institutions and organizations.*
WhoEmL	*Who's who of emerging leaders in America.*
WhoFI	*Who's who in finance and industry.*
WhoFr	*Who's who in France.*
WhoFrS	*Who's who in frontiers of science and technology.*
WhoGov	*Who's who in government.*
WhoGrA	*Who's who in graphic art,* edited by Walter Amstutz. Dübendorf, 1962- .
WhoIndia	*Who's who in India.*
WhoIsrael	*Who's who in Israel.*

WhoItaly	*Who's who in Italy.*
WhoLeb	*Who's who in Lebanon.*
WhoLib	*Who's who in librarianship.*
WhoLibI	*Who's who in library and information science.*
WhoLibS	*Who's who in library science.*
WhoLit	*Who's who in literature.* Liverpool, 1924-1934. (1897-1917 entitled *The Literary yearbook*, London).
WhoMilH	Keegan, John & A. Wheatcroft. *Who's who in military history.* 2nd ed. London, 1987.
WhoMus	*Who's who in music.*
WhoMW	*Who's who in the Midwest.*
WhoNL	*Who's who in the Netherlands.*
WhoNZ	*Who's who in New Zealand.*
WhoÖster	*Who is who in Österreich.*
WhoRel	*Who's who in religion.*
WhoRom	*Who was who in twentieth century Romania*, by Ş. N. Ionescu. Boulder, Colo., 1994.
WhoRomania	*Who's who în România.* Bucureşti, 2002.
WhoSAfrica	*Who's who in Southern Africa.*
WhoScand	*Who's who in Scandinavia.*
WhoScEu	*Who's who in science in Europe.*
WhoSocC	*Who's who in the Socialist countries*, edited by Borys Lewytzkyj and Juliusz Stroynowski. New York, 1978.
WhoSoCE	*Who's who in the Socialist countries of Europe*, edited by Juliusz Stroynowski. München, 1989.
WhoScot	*Who's who in Scotland.*
WhoSpain	*Who's who in Spain.*
WhoS&SW	*Who's who in the South and Southwest.*
WhoSwi	*Who's who in Switzerland.*
WhoUN	*Who's who in the United Nations and related agencies.*
WhoUSWr	*Who's who in U.S. writers, editors & poets.*
WhoWest	*Who's who in the West.*
WhoWor	*Who's who in the world.*
WhoWorJ	*Who's who in world Jewry.*
WhoWrEP	*Who's who in writers, editors & poets; United States & Canada.* Highland Park, Ill, December Press, 1989- .
WhWE	Carl Waltman and Alan Wexler, *Who was who in world exploration..* New York, 1992.
Widmann	Widmann, Horst. *Exil und Bildungshilfe.* Bern, 1973.
Wie is dat	*Wie is dat*, s'Gravenhage.
Wie is wie	*Wie is wie in Nederland*, s'Gravenhage.
Wieczynski	*Modern encyclopedia of Russian and Soviet history*, edited by J. L. Wieczynski. Vol. 1-60. Gulf Breeze, Fla., 1976-2000.
WielkoSB	*Wielkopolski słownik biograficzny*, Warszawa.
WieVlaand	*Wie is wie in Vlaanderen.* Brussel, 1980- .

Wininger	Wininger, Samuel. *Große jüdische National-Biographie.* Cernăuți, 1925-1932.
WomNov	Robinson, Doris. *Women novelists, 1891-1920.* New York, 1984.
WomWorHis	*Women in world history; a biographical dictionary.* Detroit, Mich., 1999-2002. 17 v.
WomWWA	*Woman's who's who of America*, 1914-1915.
WorAl	*The World Almanac Book of who*, edited by Hana U. Lane. New York, 1980.
WorAu	Wakeman, John. *World authors; a companion volume to Twentieth-century authors.* New York, 1975, 1980.
WrDr	*The Writers directory.* Chicago and London, 1976- .
Wrede	Wrede, Richard. *Das geistige Berlin.* Berlin, 1897-1898.
Wright	Wright, Denis. *The English amongst the Persians.* London, 1977.
WRMEA	*Washington report on Midle East affairs*, vol. 1- . Washington, D.C., 1982- .
Wurzbach	Wurzbach, Constant von. *Biographisches Lexikon des Kaiserthums Oesterreich.* Wien,
WW	*Who was who.* Vol. 1- . London, 1920- .
WWASS	*Who's who in Asian studies in Switzerland.* Geneva, 1989.
WWScand	*Who's who in Scandinavia.* A-K, L-Z. Zürich, 1981.
WWWA	*Who was who in America.* Chicago, 1963- .
WZKM	*Wiener Zeitschrift für die Kunde des Morgenlandes.*
Yonan	Gabriele Yonan and Bahman Nirumand. *Iraner in Berlin*. Berlin, Die Ausländer-beauftragte des Senats, 1994.
Zach	Zach, Michael. *Österreicher im Sudan, 1820 bis 1914.* Wien, 1985.
Zananiri	Zananiri, Gaston. *Figures missionnaires modernes.* Paris, 1963.
ZDMG	*Zeitschrift der Deutschen Morgenländischen Gesellschaft.*
ZKO	Zentralkatalog der Orientalia; Islamic publications down to 1993, edited by W. H. Behn at the Staatsbibliothek zu Berlin. Not published.
Zürcher	Zürcher, Erik J. *Turkey; a modern history.* London, 1993.

Haack, Hermann Oscar, born 29 October 1872 at Friedrichswerth, Germany, he studied geography and geology at the universities of Berlin and Halle/Saale, where he received a Dr.phil. in 1896 for *Die mittlere Höhe von Südamerika*. He subsequently entered the cartographic firm of Justus Perthes at Gotha where he became a scientific director. He died in Gotha on 22 February 1966. DtBE; GV; Sezgin; *Wer ist's*, 1922-1935

Haag, Wolfgang, born 12 May 1911 at Trier, Germany, he received a Dr.phil. in 1935 from the Universität Berlin for *Hālid b. Abd Allāh al-Qasrī, ein Statthalter der ausgehenden Umajjadenzeit*. He was a sometime academic assistant at the Seminar für Arabistik, Universität Berlin. After the second World War he entered the diplomatic service. Hanisch; Schwarz; Sezgin; Thesis

Haag-Higuchi, Roxane, born about 1950, she received a Dr.phil. for a study of a collection of Persian tales entitled *Untersuchungen zu einer Sammlung persischer Erzählungen*. She subsequently taught at the Universität Bamberg, where she was in 2004 a professor of Iranian studies. Her writings include *Geisteswissenschaftliche Lehr- und Forschungsinstitutionen in Iran* (1994), and she was a joint editor of *Erzählter Raum in Literaturen der islamischen Welt* (2001). Bamberg university calendar; Private

Haagensen, Cushman Davis, born 6 July 1900 at Hillsboro, N.Dak., he studied medicine. From 1933 to his retirement in 1966 he was a professor and researcher at the College of Physicians and Surgeons, Columbia University, New York. He was a joint author of *A Hundred years of medicine* (1943). He died in Palisades, N.Y., on 16 September 1990. AmM&WS, P, 12th ed. (1972); ConAu, 132; NYT, 18 Sep-tember 1990, p. B-10, cols. 1-2

Haarbrücker, Theodor, born 5 January 1818 at Elbing, Prussia, he studied at the Universität Halle, where he received a Dr.phil. in 1842 for *R. Tanchumi Hierosolymitani commentarii in prophetas Arabici specimen*. The second part of this work was submitted two years later as his *Habilitation*. He subsequently became a school teacher in Berlin. His writings include the translation from the Arabic, *Abu-'l-Fath Muhammad asch-Schahrastani's Religionspartheien und Philosophenschulen* (1850-51). He died in 1880. Flück; Sezgin; Thesis

Haardt, Georges Marie, born 12 July 1884 at Napoli, he was an engineer who became a director in the automobile industry. Befriended with André Citroën, he was since 1910 *directeur général* of the Usines Citroën. He was one of the great automobile explorers. In 1922 he succeeded in the first crossing of the Sahara by car with caterpillar wheels, from Touggourt to Timbuctu. He later crossed from Colomb-Béchar to Tananarive, and on his final exploit, from Beirut in ten months to China. He died in Hong Kong from influenza in 1932. His writings include *Le Raid Citroën; la première traversée du Sahara en automobile* (1923), its translations, *Across the Sahara by motor car* (1924), and *Die erste Durch-querung der Sahara* (1924). DBF; Peyronnet, 925

Haarmann, Ulrich Wilhelm, born 22 September 1942 at Stuttgart, Germany, he was a graduate of Princeton University, and received a Dr.phil. in 1969 from the Universität Freiburg im Breisgau for his study of source material for the early Mamlukes entitled, *Quellenstudien zur frühen Mamlukenzeit*. From 1978 to 1980, he was a director of the Orient-Institut der Deutschen Morgenländischen Gesellschaft, Beirut, and subsequently taught Islamic studies at Freiburg until 1992, and at Kiel until 1998, when he accepted the directorship of the newly established Zentrum Moderner Orient, Berlin, and concurrently a professorship at the Freie Universität, Berlin. He was editor of *Geschichte der islamischen Welt* (1987), and joint editor of *The Mamluks in Egyptian politics and society* (1998). He died in Berlin on 4 June 1999. Kürschner, 1976-1996; *MESA bulletin*, 33 ii (1999), pp. 294-5; Private; *Tagesspiegel* (Berlin), 11 June 1999, p. 30, col. 6; *Welt des Islams*, 40 (2000), pp. 335-343

Haas, Alois M., born 23 February 1934 at Zürich, he studied German language and literature, gaining a Dr.habil. in 1970 at the Universität Zürich for *Nim din selbes war; Studien zur Lehre von der Selbst-erkenntnis bei Meister Eckhart*. He was from 1969 to 1971 a professor in the German Department, McGill University, Montreal, P.Q., and subsequently until his retirement in 1999 at Zürich. His writings include *Parzivals tumpheit bei Wolfram von Eschenbach* (1964), and he was a joint author of *Deutsche Barocklyrik* (1973). Kürschner, 1976-2003

Haas, Cyril H., born about 1875, he graduated from the University of Michigan Medical School and then served under the American Board of Commissioners of Foreign Missions from 1910 to 1951 as a medical missionary in Turkey, first at the Anglican International Hospital, Adana; he later established his own clinic. After his service in the Near East, he became a volunteer staff physician at Pleasant Hill, Tenn., where he died 8 January 1961 at the age of eighty-six. N.Y.T., 12 January 1961, p. 29, col. 2

Haas, Ernst Anton Max, born 18 April 1835 at Coburg, Saxe-Coburg, he was educated at the Universität Berlin and received a Dr.phil. in 1859 from the Universität Tübingen for his thesis, *Die Heiratsgebräuche der alten Inder nach dem Grihyasûtra*, a work which was published, with additions from Albrecht Weber, in Berlin in 1862. From 1866 to his death in London on 3 July 1882, he was an assistant in the Department of Printed Books, the British Museum, and concurrently served since 1876 as a professor of Sanskrit at the University of London. His writings include the *Catalogue of Sanskrit and Pali books in the British Museum* (1876), and *Catalogue of the Sanskrit manuscripts in the Library of the India Office* (1887). Boase; Stache-Rosen, p. 80

Haas, Samuel Sheridan, born 22 March 1915 at N.Y.C., he graduated in 1936 from Columbia University, New York, and received a Ph.D. in 1942 from Princeton University for *The contribution of slaves to and their influence upon the culture of early Islam*. From 1947 to 1963 he was a professor of Hebrew and Old Testament studies at Bloomfield (N.J.) College and Seminary. DrAS, 1969 P; Selim

Haas, William (Wilhelm/Willy) S., born 13 July 1883 at Nürnberg, he studied law and philosophy at the universities of München, Berlin and Wien, and received a Dr.phil. in 1910 at München with a thesis entitled *Über Echtheit und Unechtheit von Gefühlen*. In America he was associated with the University of Denver. His writings include *Die Seele des Orients* (1916), *Die psychische Dingwelt* (1921), and *Iran* (New York, 1946). He died in 1956. Note about the author

Haase, Claus-Peter, born 15 January 1944 at Rawisch/Wartheland, Germany, he was educated at the Johanneum and the Universität, Hamburg, where he received his Dr.phil. in 1972 for a study of agriculture under the Umayyads entitled *Untersuchungen zur Landwirtschaftsgeschichte Nordsyriens in der Umayyadenzeit*. He spent 1968/69 as an exchange student in Istanbul. He was associated with the Seminar für Orientalistik in the Universität Kiel until 2002, when he was appointed director of the Museum für Islamische Kunst, Berlin. He was the com-mon-law husband of Petra Kappert. He edited the exhibition catalogue, *Morgenländische Pracht; islamische Kunst aus deutschem Privatbesitz* (1993), and he was a joint editor of *Memoiren eines Janitscharen, oder Türkische Chronik* (1975). Private; Thesis

Haberland, Eike, born 18 May 1924 at Detmold, she studied at Tübingen and received a Dr.phil. in 1950 from the Universität Frankfurt am Main, for *Das Gade-System der südwest-abessinischen Völker*, and a Dr.habil. in 1965 for *Untersuchungen zum äthiopischen Königstum*. She was for many years associated with Frobius-Institut, Universität Frankfurt/Main. Her writings include *Galla Süd-Äthiopiens* (1963), *Die Yimar am Oberen Korowori* (1974), *Ibaaddo ka-Ba'iso; culture and language of the Ba'iso* (1988), and *Hirarchie und Kaste; zur Geschichte und politischen Struktur der Dizi in Südwest-Äthiopien* (1993). On her sixty-fifth birthday she was honoured by *Afrika-Studien* (1989-90). GV; Unesco

Haberlandt, Arthur Ludwig Wolfgang, born 9 March 1889 at Wien, where he also studied archaeology, ethnography, and geography, gaining doctorates in 1912 and 1914. From 1924 to 1945 he was a director of Volkskundemuseum, Wien, and concurrently served as a professor at the Universität. His writings include *Trinkwasserversorgung primitiver Völker* (1912), *Kulturwissenschaftliche Beiträge zur Volkskunde von Montenegro, Albanien und Serbien* (1917), *Volkskunst der Balkanländer in ihren Grundlagen* (1919), and *Taschenwörterbuch der Volkskunde Österreichs* (1953-54). He died in Wien on 28 May 1964. DtBE; DtBilnd (1); Kürschner, 1926-1940/41, 1954, 1961; NDB; Teichl; Wer ist's, 1935

Haberlandt, Michael, born 29 September 1860 at Ungarisch-Altenburg (Mosonmagyaróvár), he studied Oriental languages, particularly Sanskrit, at Wien and received doctorates in 1882 and 1892. He subsequently became a professor of ethnography and a director of Völkerkundemuseum, Wien. He was for forty years an editor of *Zeitschrift für österreichische Volkskunde*. His writings include *Die Völker Europas und des Orients* (1920). He died in Wien on 14 June 1940. DtBE; DiBilnd (2); Kürschner, 1925-1935; ÖBL

Habermann, Stanley John, born 20th cent., he was a graduate of McGill University, Montreal, and Columbia University, New York. He was associated with the Foreign Production Division of a large American oil company. On a fellowship grant from the Ford Foundation he spent the year 1954 in the Middle East, studying the effects of economic development in Iraq Note about the author

Habib, Madelain Farah, born about 1940, she received a Ph.D. in 1976 from the University of Utah for *Islamic marital code; prolegomenon to and translation of al-Ghazālī's Book on the etiquette of marriage in Ihyā' 'ulūm al-dīn*. Selim[3]

Habib Edib, born 19th cent., his writings include *Türkisch; praktische türkische Sprachlehre* (1916), *Die Türkei; ein Beitrag zu den Friedenserörterungen* (1919); and he was the translator of *Türkische Geschichten* (Weimar, 1917). NUC, pre-1956; ZKO

Habicht, Christian Maximilian, born 8 March 1775 at Breslau, Prussia, he was a trained merchant and came to Oriental studies through his 1797 assignment to Paris as a secretary at the Prussian Legation. He there studied Arabic under Silvestre de Sacy. He pursued his Arabic studies after returning to

Breslau in 1806. He received doctorates in 1812 and 1813, and later became a professor of Arabic at the Universität Breslau, delivering his inaugural lecture on 10 July 1826 at the Philosophische Fakultät, entitled *Meidanii aliquot proverbia Arabica cum interpretatione Latina edit*. He was the first Arabist to edit the *Arabian nights* in Europe. He also edited *Episcolae quaedam arabicae a Mauris, Aegyptiis et Syris conscriptae* (1824), and he translated *Tausend und eine Nacht* (1825). He died in Breslau from a stroke on 25 October 1839. ADtB, vol. 10, pp. 283-284; DtBilnd (4); Fück; Krachkovskiĭ

Habraken, Nicolaas John, born 29 October 1928 at Bandung, Indonesia, he was educated at Technische Hogeschool Delft and was a practising architect, before he began teaching his subject at Technische Hogeschool Eindhoven, and Massachusetts Institute of Technology, Cambridge, Mass. Since 1989 he was a professor emeritus. His writings include *De dragers en de mensen* (1961), its translation, *Soportes; una alternativa al alojamiento de masas* (1975), *Denken in variaten*, its translation, *Variations; the systematic design supports* (1976), and *The Grunsfeld variations* (1981). IntWW, 1992/93-2002

von **Habsburg**-Lothringen, Otto, Archduke of Austria, born 20 November 1912 at Reichenau, Austria, he received a Dr.rer.pol. at Louvain. In 1987 he was honoured by *Einigen - nicht trenne; Festschrift für Otto von Habsburg zum 75. Geburtstag*. His writings include *Paneuropäische Idee* (1999). Au&Wr, 1963-1989; BioHbDtE; Bioln 17 (1); CurBio. 1946; IntWW, 1989-2006; WhoAustria, 1969/70-1982/83

Hacène, Ali, his writings include *Les Mahakmes; manuel à l'usage des mahakmas judiciaires, notariales et ibadites de l'Algérie* (Alger, 1923). His trace is lost after an articles in 1929. NUC, pre-1956

Hachtmann, Otto Wilhelm, born 10 December 1877 at Seehausen, Altmark, he was educated at the gymnasiums in Dessau and Bernburg, and subsequently studied modern languages and German literature at Bonn and Göttingen, where he received a Dr.phil. in 1902 for *Graf Julius Heinrich von Soden*. His writings include *Türkisch wie man es erlernt und lehrt* (n.d.), *Die türkische Literatur des zwanzigsten Jahrhunderts* (1916), *Europäische Kultureinflüsse in der Türkei* (1918), and *Die Direktoren des Dessauer Gymnasiums von 1785-1935* (Dessau, 1935). Thesis

Hacker, Jens, born 17 March 1933 at Kiel, Germany, he was a professor of political science and public law at the Universität Regensburg from 1981 to his death. His writings include *Der Ostblock; Entstehung, Entwicklung und Struktur* (1973). He died in Köln on 17 January 2000. Kürschner, 1987-2000

Hackin, Joseph, born 8 November 1886 at Boevange, Luxembourg, he was employed by the Musées nationaux, Paris, where he also served as a deputy secretary of the academic staff union. He later became a director of the Musée Guimet, Paris. He won abiding fame by his excavations in Bamyan and Begram in Afghanistan. At the time of his death by enemy action in 1941 he was *chef de Service des affaires étrangères* to General de Gaulle. His writings include *La Site archéologique de Bāmiyān* (1934), and *Recherches archéologiques au col de Khair khaneh près de Kābul* (1936). DcBMOuvF, vol. 31; JRCAS, 28 (July 1941), p. 309

Hackin, Ria née Parmentier, she was the wife of Joseph Hackin. During their expeditions she took charge of the photography and was, in many other ways, a most valuable assistant. Her own writings include *Recherches archéologiques à Begram* (1939), and she was a joint author, with Ahmad Ali Kuhzād, of *Légendes et coutumes afghans* (1953). She died with her husband by enemy action in 1941. JRCAS, 28 (July 1941), p. 309

Ritter von **Hackländer**, Friedrich Wilhelm, born 1 November 1816 at Burtscheid near Aachen, he was of humble parentage and lost his parents when he was still young. He was an apprentice to a textile merchant. In 1832 he joined the Prussian artillery, but he soon returned to his civilian occupation. In 1840 he settled in Stuttgart, where he tried unsuccessfully to get into the book trade or the theatre. However, he was able to publish a short story and subsequently find a place in the enourage of a nobleman travelling to the East. He became a courtier at the Württemberg Court and accompanied the crown prince on a two-year journey throughout Europe. He resigned in 1849 and became a war correspondent. Since 1859 he was a free-lance writer. His writings include *Daguerreotypen, aufgenommen während einer Reise in den Orient in den Jahren 1840 und 1841* (1842), and *Der Pilgerzug nach Mekka; morgenländische Sagen und Erzählungen* (1847). He died in Leoni, Starnberger See, on 6 July 1877. ADtB, vol. 10, pp. 296-97; DtBE; DtBilnd (2); Sezgin; Wurzbach

Hacquard, Augustin Prosper, born 18 September 1860 at Albestroff (Moselle), France, he studied at the Petit séminaire in Pont-à-Mousson (Meurthe-et-Moselle) and in 1878 entered the noviciate of the

Pères Blancs at Alger. After his ordination in 1884 he prepared a doctorate, specializing in Arabic and African languages. He subsequently participated in strictly colonial expeditions. In 1894 he led a French mission into Touareg country. He also headed the first caravan of missionaries to Timbuctu, which he reached from the south on 21 May 1895. In the following year, he accompanied the Mission Hourst down the Niger River. Since 1898 he was bishop of the French Sudan, comprising Mali and Upper Volta. He accidentally drowned in the Niger River on 4 April 1901. His writings include *Monographie de Tombouctou* (1900), and he was a joint author of *Manuel de la langue Soñgay* (1897). DBF; *Bulletin* de la Société de géographie d'Alger, 6 (1901), pp. 328-332

Hadamard, Jacques Salomon, born 8 December 1865 at Versailles, he was widely considered the pre-eminent French mathematician of the twentieth century. He was a sometime member of the French Palestine committee and of the administrative board of the Hebrew University, Jerusalem. He died in Paris on 17 October 1963. BioInd 17 (1); ConAu, 158; DBF; DBFC, 1954/55; IndexBFr² (4); WhoFr, 1953/54-1961/62

Hadank, Karl, born 21 February 1882 at Kesselsdorf, Silesia, he studied at Berlin, where he also received a Dr.phil. in 1905 for *Die Schlacht bei Cortenova am 27. November 1237*. He was associated with Oskar Mann's linguistic expedition to Kurdistan, 1906-1907. His writings include *Die Mundarten von Khunsâr, Mahallât, Natänz, Nâyin, Sämân, Sîvänd und Sô-Kohrûd* (1926), *Mundarten der Gûrân, besonders das Kändûlâî, Auramâî und Bâdschälânî* (1930), *Mundarten der Zâzâ, hauptsächlich aus Siwerek und Kor* (1932, and *Untersuchungen zum Westkurdischen, Bôti und Êzädî* (1938). Hanisch; Kürschner, 1928/29-1935|; Thesis; ZKO

Hadary, Gideon, fl. 20th cent., he was a research attaché with the American Embassy in Tehran from 1948 to 1950, and subsequently joined the division of research of the Department of State, Washington, D.C. His writings include *Handbook of agricultural statistics of Iran* (Tehran, 1949). Note

Haddad, George Meri, born 7 August 1910 at Homs, Syria, he was a graduate of A.U.B. and later studied at the Sorbonne, École nationale des langues orientales vivantes, Paris, and the Oriental Institute, University of Chicago, where he received his Ph.D. in 1949 for *Aspects of social life in Antioch in the Hellenistic Roman period*. He had taught at high schools in Syria and Palestine as well as at Damascus University, before emigrating to the U.S.A. in 1959. He subsequently taught Middle Eastern history for nearly twenty years at the University of California, Santa Barbara. His writings include *Fifty years of modern Syria and Lebanon* (1959), *Arab peace efforts and the solution of the Arab-Israeli problem* (1976) as well as Arabic textbooks for secondary schools. He died in San Francisco on 22 February 2000. ConAu, 17-20; DrAS, 1969 H; *MESA bulletin*, 34 (2000), pp. 154-55

Haddad, Malek, born 5 July 1927 at Constantine, Algeria, he was educated at a French school in his home town and briefly also taught there. He started to study at the Faculté de droit d'Aix-en-Provence, but the outbreak of the Algerian war of liberation turned him into a wandering writer. He was from 1968 to 1972 a *directeur de la culture* at the Ministry of Information and Culture in Alger, but above all he was a writer. He wrote in French, but never considered himself a French writer. His writings include *La Dernière impression* (1958), and its translation, *Die Brücken tanzen* (1961). He died after a long illness in Alger on 2 June 1978. *Annuaire de l'Afrique du nord*, 17 (1978), pp. 899-903; *Hommes et destins*, vol. 7, p. 230; Sezgin

al-Haddād, al-Tāhir, born in 1899 he belonged to the *'ulamā'* of the Zaytūna Mosque, Tunis, and was an advocate of enhanced rights of women, based on a liberal interpretation of the Koran. His writings include *al-'Ammāl al-Tūnisīyūn wa-zuhūr al-harakat al-niqābīyah* (1346/1927), *Imra'tunā fī al-sharī'ah wa-al-mujtama'* (1930), and *Les travailleurs tunisiens et l'emergence du mouvement syndical* (1985). He died in 1935. Note about the author; ZKO

Haddad, William Woodrow, born 20th cent., he received a Ph.D. in 1970 from Ohio State Universty for *Arab editorial opinion toward the Palestine question*. He was a professor at Illinois State University, Bloomington-Normal, before he was appointed a professor of history at California State University, Fullerton, a post which he still held in 2004. He was a joint editor of *Nationalism in a non-national state* (1977). MESA *Roster of members*, 1977-1990; NatFacDr, 1999; Note about the author

Haddad, Yvonne née Yazbeck, born 23 March 1935 at Alexandretta (İskenderun), Hatay, Turkey, she received a Ph.D. in 1979 from Hartford Seminary Foundation. She held teaching posts at a variety of American institutions before becoming a professor of history at the University of Amherst, Mass., a post which she still held in 1995; in 2004, she was associated with the School of Foreign Service, Georgetown University, Washington, D.C. Her writings include *Contemporary Islam and the challenge of history* (1982), *A Century of Islam in America* (1986), and *Islamic values in the United States* (1987). MESA *Roster of members*, 1982-1990; NatFacDr, 1995, 2004; ZKO

Hadley, Lawrence Hamilton, born 9 June 1945, he graduated in 1967 from Rutgers University, New Brunswick, N.J., and received his Ph.D. in 1975 from the University of Connecticut. He subsequently spent two years at the American University in Cairo doing field work, before being appointed a professor of economics at the University of Dayton, Ohio, a post which he still held in 2004. NatFacDr, 1994-2004; Private; WhoFI, 1992/93

Hadsel, Winifred N., he was in 1947 a research associate at the Foreign Policy Association, New York. His writings include *Allied military rule in Germany* (1945), and he was a joint author of *American policy toward Greece* (1947), and *The Turkish Straits and the great powers* (1947). Note about the author

Hadžibegić, Hamid, born 20th cent., he was for over twenty years a research fellow in the Institute for Oriental Studies, Sarajevo. He was a joint editor of *Oblast Brankovića; opširni katastarski popis iz 1455 godine* (1972), a detailed census of the Brankoviches region in Turkish (*Defter-i Vilayet-i Vulk*).

Hadžijahić, Muhamed, born 20th cent., he gained a doctorate. His writings include *Od tradicije do identiteta; geneza nacionalnog pitanja bosanskih Muslimana* (Sarajevo, 1974). OSK

Haeckel, Ernst Heinrich Philip August, born 16 February 1834 at Potsdam, he studied medicine at Berlin, Würzburg, and Wien. He practised his profession for a few years, before taking a second doctorate at the Universität Jena and later becoming a professor of zoology as well as a director of the zoological gardens. He went on several long travels. His writings include *Monismus als Band zwischen Religion und Wissenschaft* (1892), and *Von Teneriffa bis zum Sinai; Reiseskizzen* (1923). He died in Jena on 9 August 1919. ConAu, 157; DÖS; DtBE; DtBilnd (2); Master (6)

de **Haedo**, Diego, born about 1528 in the Valley of Carranza (Vizcaya), Spain, he was an *obispo* of Agrigento, Sicily, an archbishop of Palermo, and a Spanish member of the Benedictine Order. His writings include *Topografia e historia general de Argel* (1612), and its translation, *Histoire des reis d'Alger* (1881). He died an octogenarian in 1608. EnciUni

Haegg, Tomas, 1938- *see* Hägg, Eric Tomas

Haekel, Josef, born early 20th cent., he received a Dr.phil. in 1935 from the Universität Wien for *Totemismus, Mutterrecht und Zweiklassensystem im östlichen Nordamerika*. His writings include *Zum Individual- und Geschlechtstotemismus in den Kulturen Nordwestamerikas* (1955).

Haenisch, Erich, born 27 August 1880 at Berlin, he studied Chinese and Mongolian and received doctorates in 1904 and 1913. From 1912 to 1920 he was associated with the Museum für Völkerkunde, Berlin. He subsequently taught his subject successively at Berlin, Göttingen, Leipzig, Berlin, and München. His writings include *Kulturpolitik des mongolischen Weltreichs* (1943), and he edited *Mongolia der Berliner Turfan-Sammlung* (1954). He died in Stuttgart on 21 December 1966. DtBE; DiBilnd (2); Kürschner, 1925-1966; Wer ist's, 1935; Wer ist wer, 1955-1963

Haffner, August Otto Wilhelm, born 16 May 1869 at Witten, Westphalia, he studied theology and Oriental languages at Innsbruck and Wien and received a Dr.phil. in 1892 from the Universität Halle for *Das Kitab-al-chail von al-'Asma'i*; and gained a Dr.habil. in 1896 at Wien. From 1897 to 1899 he travelled in Egpyt, Palestine, and Syria, establishing close relations to the Arabists of the Université Saint-Joseph in Beirut. He edited *Texte zur arabischen Lexikographie* (1905), and he was a joint editor of *Dix anciens traités de philologie arabe* (1908). He died in Solbad Hall i. T. on 1 June 1941. DtBE; DtBilnd (1); Fück, p. 259; Hanisch; Kosch; Kürschner, 1935; ÖBL; Schwarz

Hafner, Donald L., born in 1944, he received a Ph.D. in 1972 from the University of Chicago for *Intervention in a "balance of power" system; case studies in nineteenth century Europe*. He was in 1995 a professor in the Department of Political Science, Boston College, a post which he still held in 2004. He edited *ATBMs and Western security; missile defenses for Europe* (1988). NatFacDr, 1995-2004

Hagedorn, Horst, born 17 May 1921 at Dresden, he received a Dr.habil. in 1971 from the Freie Universität Berlin for *Untersuchungen über die Relieftypen arider Räume*. He was a professor of geological sciences at the Universität Würzburg; his writings include *Natur- und wirtschafts-geographische Forschungen in Afrika* (1979), and *Geowissenschaftliche Untersuchungen in Afrika* (1988), and he was a joint author of *Les Sables éoliens - modelés et dynamique - le menace éolienne et son contrôle* (1984). On his sixtieth birthday he was honoured by *Geowissenschaftliche Beiträge zu Forschung, Lehre und Praxis* (1993). Kürschner, 2001-2003

Hagège, Claude Léon, born 1 January 1936 at Tunis, he was a graduate of the École normale supérieure and received a *doctorat de 3e cycle* in 1973 from the Université de Paris for *Les Juifs de Tunisie et la colonisation française jusqu'à la première guerre mondiale*; he also studied at Harvard. Since 1988 he was a professor at the Collège de France. His writings include *Profil d'un parler arabe du Tchad* (1973), *L'Homme de paroles* (1986), its translation, *Der dialogische Mensch* (1987), *Le Souffle de la langue; voies et destins des parlers d'Europe* (1992), its translations, *Storie e destini delle lingue* *d'Europa* (1995), and *Welche Sprache für Europa* (1996), *The Language builder* (1993), *L'Enfant aux deux langues* (1996), and *Halte à la mort des langues* (2000). THESAM 2; WhoFr, 1987/88-2003/2004

Hagel, Franz Josef, fl. 20th cent., his writings include *Zwanzig Jahre in Deutsch-Südwest* (Paderborn, 1933), and *An Gottes Fronten in Südafrika* (Rottemburg, 1962).

Hagelstein, Gabriel, born 1 June 1875 at Alger, he was a civil servant who worked at first in local administrations and, since 1895, with the *Gouvernement général de l'Algérie*. In 1914 he was a department head; he was still active in 1920. Peyronnet, p. 833

Hagemann, Ludwig, born 28 December 1947 at Niederlangen, Germany, he received a doctorate in Catholic theology in 1975 from the Universität Münster for *Der Kur'ān im Verständnis und Kritik bei Nikolaus von Kues*. He was successively a professor of religion at the universities of Koblenz, Würzburg, and Mannheim. His writings include *Das erwachende Asien; Arabien - Indien - China* (1962), *Christentum für das Gespräch mit Muslimen* (1982), *Moralische Normen und ihre Grundlegung im Islam* (1982), *Christentum und Islam zwischen Konfrontation und Begegnung* (1983), *Propheten, Zeugen des Glaubens; koranische und biblische Deutungen* (1985), and *Christentum contra Islam; eine Geschichte gescheiterter Beziehungen* (1999). Kürschner, 1987-2003

Hagemann, Walter, born 16 January 1900 at Euskirchen, Germany, he received a Dr.phil. in 1922 from the Universität Berlin. He was a journalist who travelled several times around the world. He spent six years with the daily *Germania* at the foreign affairs desk and subsequently became editor-in-chief. In 1946, he became a professor of journalism at the Universität Münster. An opponent of nuclear armament, he was ousted from his post and evaded justice by moving in 1961 to Communist Germany, where he became a professor of economic history of imperialism at Humboldt Universität, Berlin. His writings include *Das erwachende Asie; Arabien, Indien, China* (1926), *Gestaltwandel Afrikas* (1928), *Dankt die Presse ab?* (1957), and *Das Wagnis des Friedens* (1959). He died in Potsdam on 16 May 1964. DtBE

von **Hagemeister** (Гагемейстер), Julius (Юлий Андреевич), born in 1806, he received a Dr.phil. in 1843 from the Universität Berlin for *Des Rohrzuckers Erzeugung*. He was a director of the chancellery, Russian Ministry of Finance. His writings include *Rußland's Territorialvergrößerung von der Alleinherrschaft Peter's des Großen bis zum Tode Alexander's des Ersten* (Riga, 1834), *Report on the commerce of the ports of Russia, Moldavia, and Wallachia, made to the Russian Government in 1835, translated from the original, published at Odessa* (London, 1836), *Der europäische Handel in der Türkei und in Persien* (Riga, 1838), *Essai sur les ressources territoriales et commerciales de l'Asie occidentales, le caractère des habitants, leur industrie et leur organisation municipale* (St. Petersburg, 1839), and *Статистическое обозрение Сибири* (Sanktpeterburg, 1854). He died in 1878. EnSlovar; NUC, pre-1956; SibirSE

Hagenmeyer, Heinrich, born in 1834, his writings include *Peter der Eremite; ein kritischer Beitrag zur Geschichte des ersten Kreuzzuges* (1879), its translation, *Le vrai et le faux sur Pierre l'Hermite* (1883), *Chronologie de la première croisade* (Paris, 1902), and he edited *Die Kreuzzugsbriefe aus den Jahren 1068-1100; episcolae et chartae ad historiam primi belli sacri spectantes quae supersunt aevo aequales ac genuinae* (Innsbruck, 1901). He died in 1915. GV; NUC, pre-1956; Sezgin

Hager, Joseph (Giuseppe), born 30 April 1757 at Milano, he was a theologian and a Chinese scholar who had studied at the Orientalische Akademie, Wien, and subsequently at the Congregatio de Propaganda Fide, Roma. He spent some time with the Imperial Austrian Legation at Constantinople; and he was a sometime professor of German at Oxford. In 1809, he was appointed a professor of Oriental languages at Pavia. His writings include *Neue Beweise der Verwandtschaft der Hungarn mit den Lappländern* (1793), and *Memoria sulle cifre arabiche* (1813). He died in Pavia on 27 June 1819. DizBI; DtBE; DtBiInd (1); Kosch; Wurzbach

Hagerty Fox, Miguel José, born 20th cent., he received a doctorate in Semitic philology, with special reference to Andalusian literature. Throughout the 1990s he was a professor of Arabic language and literature at the Universidad de Granada. His writings include *Los cuervos de San Vicente; escatología mozárabe* (1978). Arabismo, 1992, 1994, 1997; EURAMES, 1993

Hägg, Eric *Tomas*, born 16 November 1938 at Uppsala, he was a lecturer in classics first at Uppsala and since 1977 at the Universitetet i Bergen. He spent 1992/93 in the Institute for Advanced Study, Princeton, N.J. His writings include *Narrative technique in ancient Greek romances* (1971), *Den antika romanen* (1980), its translation, *The Novel in antiquity* (1983), *Eros und Tyche* (1987), and *Greek biography and panegyric in late antiquity* (2000), and he was a joint author of *Studies on the history of late antique and Christian Nubia* (2002). ConAu, 111; Vem er hvem, 1984, 1994

Haggar, George Salem, born in 1935, he received a Ph.D. in 1966 from Columbia University, New York, for *The Political and social thought of G. D. H. Cole*. His other writings include *Imperialism and revolution in the Mideast* (Toronto, 1970). NUC

Haggard, Sir Henry Rider, born in 1856, he was a British adminstrator and novelist. For the Royal Colonial Institute he produced the report, *The after war settlement and employment of ex-servicemen in the overseas dominions* (1916). He died in 1925. DLB, 70 (1988), pp. 154-65, DLB, 156 (1996), pp. 124-136, DLB, 174 (1997), pp. 168-177, DLB, 178 (1997), pp. 109-120; BritInd (11); ConAu, 108, 148, new rev., 112; Dawson; DNB; Egyptology; MEW; *Who was who*, 2

Hagimihali (Chatzēmichalē/Χατζημιχάλη), Angelikē Platōnos (Kolyba), born 19 August 1895 at Athens, she was an ethnographer, painter, and novelist whose writings include Ἑλληνικη λαικη τέχνη; Σκύρος (1925), Ἑλληνικη λαικη τέχνη (1931), *L'Art populaire grec* (1937), *La Maison grecque* (1949), and *La Sculpture sur bois* (1950). She died in 1960 or 1965. EEE; GrBioInd (3); Hellenikon, 1965

Haglund, Åke, born in 1910, his writings include *Gudar och människor i Malaysia* (Stockholm, 1969), and *Contact and conflict; stories in contemporary religious attitudes among Chinese people* (Lund, 1972). NUC

Hagopian, Elaine Catherine, born 29 January 1933 at Cambridge, Mass., she received a Ph.D. in 1962 from Boston University for *Morocco; a case study in the structural basis of social integration*. She was in 1995 associated with the Department of Sociology, Simmons College, Boston. She was a joint author of *Arab Americans* (1969), and she was a joint editor of *South Lebanon* (1978). MESA Roster of members, 1977-1990; NatFacDr, 1995; Selim

von **Hahn** (Ганъ), Carl H., born 29 April 1848 at Friedrichsthal, Black Forest, Germany, he studied theology and philology at Tübingen. A curate since 1870, he went in 1872 to Tiflis, where he became a private teacher under the governor of the Caucasus. Since 1874, he taught at the German language gymnasium, Tiflis. In 1877/78, he was a Russian Red Cross representative during the war with Turkey. Since 1888, he made annual excursions in the Caucasus and Armenia, the results of which he published both in German and Russian. He translated Greek fairy tales into Russian. His writings include *Aus dem Kaukasus; Reisen und Studien* (1892), *Kaukasische Reisen und Studien* (1896), *Bilder aus dem Kaukasus* (1900), Опыт обяснения кавказских географичесеих названий (1909), *Erster Versuch einer Erklärung kaukasischer geographischer Namen* (1910), and *Kurzes Lehrbuch der Geographie Georgiens* (1924). He died in Tiflis on 16 August 1925. DtBE; Henze; NDB

Hahn, Eduard, born 5 August 1856 at Lübeck, he studied medicine and biology and wrote a zoological-geographical thesis at the Universität Leipzig for which he received a doctorate in 1887 from the Universität Jena. Financially independent, he took his time for the Dr.habil., which he gained in 1910. He taught until his death at Humboldt-Universität as well as the Landwirtschaftliche Hochschule, Berlin, but he was no popular teacher and few students ever attended his lectures. Opinions on him are diametrically opposed. His writings include *Das Alter der wirtschaftlichen Kultur der Menschheit* (1905), *Die Entstehung der Pflugkultur* (1909), and *Von der Hacke zum Pflug* (1914). He died in Berlin on 24 February 1928. Geographische Zeitschrift, 1928, pp. 257-58; Geographisches Taschenbuch, 1975/76, pp. 239-46, where there are five additional sources listed

Hahn, Ernest Norman, Dr., born 11 March 1926, he received an M.A. in 1965 from McGill University, Montreal, for *Mawlana Abu-l-Kalam Azad's concept of religions according to his "Tarjuman-i-Qur'an."* In 1974, he had "recently returned to India from Toronto, Ont." His writings include *How to respond to Muslims* (1995), and he was a joint author of *The Integrity of the Bible according to the Qur'an and the hadith* (1977). Ferahian; LC; Note about the author

Hahn, Ferdinand, born 19th cent., he was a missionary in the East Indies. His writings include *Kurukh (Orāõ)-English dictionary* (Calcutta, 1903), *Kurukh folk-lore, in the original* (Calcutta, 1905), *Blicke in die Geisteswelt der heidnischen Kols* (Gütersloh, Germany, 1906), and *Einführung in das Gebiet der Kols-Mission* (Gütersloh, 1907). Note about the author

Hahn, Georg, born 20th cent., he was a German aid worker in the Third World and became associated with Deutsche Stiftung für Entwicklungshilfe. His writings include *Economic planning and public utilities* (1962), and *The Nature, structure and functioning of local and regional administrations* (1963). Note

Hahn, Helmut, born 15 September 1921 at Boppard, Germany, he was a director of the Institut für Wirtschaftsgeographie, Universität Bonn. His writings include *Der Einfluß der Konfessionen auf die Bevölkerungs- und Sozialgeographie des Hunsrücks* (1950), and *Die Stadt Kabul und ihr Umland* (1964-65). On his sixty-fifth birthday he was honoured by *Beiträge zur empirischen Wirtschafts-geographie* (1986). Kürschner, 1976, 2001-2005

Hahn, Lorna Joan, born 16 June 1938 at Philadelphia, Pa., she received a Ph.D. from the University of Pennsylvania, and was in 1962 a research scientist at the Special Operations Research Office of the American University. In 1972, she was an executive director of the Association on Third World Affairs, and a lecturer in political science at Howard University. Her writings include *North Africa; nationalism to nationhood* (1960), *Morocco, old land, new nation* (1966), *Mauritius; a study and annotated bibliography* (1969), and *Historical dictionary of Libya* (1981). Note; Selim; WhoE, 1993/94

Hahn, Roland, born about 1940, he received a Dr.rer.nat. in 1970 from the Universität Stuttgart for *Jüngere Veränderungen der ländlichen Siedlungen im europäischen Teil der Sowjetunion.* He was a sometime professor of regional geography at the Pädagogische Hochschule Ludwigsburg. GV; Kürschner, 2001-2005

Hahn, Wiktor, born 9 September 1871 at Wien, he was a sometime lecturer in history of Polish literature at the Universities of Lwow and Warszawa. His writings include *Bibliografie bibliografij polskich* (1921), and *Shakespeare w Polsce* (1958). He died in Warszawa on 2 November 1959. Master (1); NEP; Polski (12); PSB

Haidari, Buland *see* al-Haydari, Buland

Haig, Felix Thackeray, born in 1827. His writings include the booklet, *Modern Christian missions in Arabia* (1895). He died in 1901. Kornrumpf, N; NUC, pre-1956

Haig, Malcolm Robert, major-general, born 19th cent., his writings include *The Indus Delta country; a memoir chiefly on its ancient geography and history* (London, 1894). BLC

Haig, Sir Thomas *Wolseley*, lieutenant-colonel, born in 1865, he had a career as a public servant, including a long term of service in Persia until his retirement in 1920. He was a great scholar, and it is remarkable that a soldier who had always been so busy in the service of the State should have found the time to become so intimately acquainted with the Persian sources of the history of the Muslim world. His two most important works were his translations from the Persian of 'Abd al-Qādir Badāyūnī, *Muntakhab ul-tawārīkh*, and of 'Alī Tabātabā'ī, *Burhān-i ma'āṣir*; his other writings include *Historic landmarks of the Deccan* (1907), *Comparative tables of Muhammadan and Christian dates* (1932), and he was a joint author of the *Cambridge history of India*. He died in 1938. IndianBiInd (1); Riddick; *Who was who*, 3; Obituary by E. Denison Ross in an unidentified periodical, pp. 498-99

Hailey, William Malcolm, Baron, born in 1872 and a Corpus Christi College scholar, Oxford, he entered the Indian Civil Service in 1895. His writings include *An African survey* (1938), and *The Future of colonial peoples* (1944). He died in 1969. Mason; Riddick; Unesco; Who, 1946; *Who was who*, 6

Haillot, *commandant* Charles William Robert Henri, born 4 October 1858 at Paris, he was educated at the Lycée Condorcet, Paris, and the military academies of Saint-Cyr, and Saumur. He served in Tunisia in 1881, and in Algeria from 1889 to 1892. From 1892 to 1901 he was a military attaché at the French Legation first in Bruxelles and later in den Haag. From 1908 to 1909 he was a *commandant de territoire* in Morocco. His writings include *Le Maroc, hier et aujourd'hui* (1912). Qui êtes-vous, 1924

Hailperin, Herman, born 6 April 1899 at Newark, N.J., he graduated in 1919 from New York University and was ordained a rabbi in 1922. From 1937 to 1941 he was a sometime professor and lecturer on Jewish history at Duquesne University, Pittsburgh. His writings include *Rashi and the Christian scholars* (1963). He died on 9 January 1973. Au&Wr, 1963; CnDiAmJBi; ConAu, 5-8, 103, new rev., 77; DrAS, 1969, vol. 1; Pamela S. Nadell, *Conservative Judaism in America* (1988), pp. 130-31; NYT, 10 January 1973, p. 44, col. 4; WhoWorJ, 1965

Haim, Sylvia G. *see* Kedourie, Sylvia G. Haim

Haim, Yehoyada, born about 1945, he received a Ph.D. in 1975 from Georgetown University, Washington, D.C., for *Zionist attitudes toward the Palestinian Arabs, 1936-1939.* He was in 1983 a political counsellor, Israeli Embassy, London. His writings include *Abandonment of illusions; Zionist political attitudes toward Palestinian Arab nationalism, 1936-1939* (1983). Note about the author; Selim[3]

Hainaut, Jean, fl. 20th cent., he was a joint author of *Les Arts décoratifs au Maroc* (Paris, 1925), *Sanctuaires et forteresses almohades* (Paris, 1932), *La Mosquée de Hassan à Rabat* (Paris, 1954), and *Islam d'Espagne* (Paris, 1958). NUC

Haines, Byron Lee, born 6 July 1928 at Casper, Wyo., his education included an A.B., M.Sc., and B.D. from a variety of institutions. After ordination he pastored a church in Wisconsin until 1956, when he moved to Lahore to work as chaplain and teacher at Forman Christian College. In 1960, he went to the Divinity School of Harvard University where he took a Th.D. in 1967 for *A paleographic study of Aramaic inscriptions antedating 500 B.C.* He spent the following ten years again in Pakistan, this time to help establish and staff the Christian Study Centre in Rawalpindi. In 1977, he returned to the U.S. where he began a pioneer effort as director, and later co-director, of the Office on Christian-Muslim Relations of the National Council of the Churches of Christ in the U.S.A. His writings include *The Islamic impact* (1984), and he edited *Christians and Muslims together* (1987). He died in Kearney, Nebr., on 21 June 1990. Muslim world, 80 (1990), pp. 290-91

Haines, Charles Grove, born in 10 December 1906 at Abbottstown, Pa., he was a university administrator and a diplomat. His writings include *The Origins and background of the second World War* (1943), *Trieste - a storm center of Europe* (1946), and *European integration* (1957), its translation, *Europäische Integration* (1958), *The Role of the Supreme Court in American government and politics* (1957), *Africa today* (1959). He died in 1976. DrAS, 1969 H; Washington Post, 28 May 1976, p. C-6, cols. 1-3

Haines, Stafford Bettesworth, captain, born about 1801, he served in the Bombay Marine. With the *Palinurus* of the East India Company he surveyed the Persian Gulf, the southern coast of Arabia, and Socotra. In January 1839, he occupied Aden with little bloodshed. He laboured to make the port an entrepôt which it was destined to become, but his interest in the hinterland was limited to the immediate aim of preventing attacks by hostile tribesmen. His writings include *Memoir of the south and east coasts of Arabia* (1845). He died in 1860. Bidwell; DNB, Missing Persons; Henze

Hair, Paul Edward Hedley, born 27 January 1926 at Amble, England, he graduated in 1950 from Cambridge University and received a doctorate in 1967 from Oxford University for *The Social history of British coalminers, 1800-1845*. He travelled a great deal, and taught in Africa, before joining the University of Liverpool as a reader in modern history, becoming chairman of department in 1979. His writings include *The Early study of Nigerian languages* (1967), and *English seamen and traders in Guinea, 1553-1565* (1992), a collection of his articles, *Africa encountered; European contacts and evidence, 1450-1700* (1997), and he was a joint author of *Black Africa in time perspective* (1990). He died in Upton, England, on 13 August 2001. ConAu, 202; Note about the author

Hajdarhodžić, Hamdija, born 25 March 1927 at Trebinje, Yugoslavia, he completed his secondary education in Dubrovnik and graduated in 1955 from the Univerzitet u Zagreb. He was from 1957 to 1969 a professor at Dubrovnik, taught from 1971 to 1974 philology at Bari, Italy, and was from 1975 to 1991 a librarian at Dubrovnik. He edited *Bosna Hrvatska, Hercegovina; zemljovidi, vedute, crteži i zabilješke grofa Luigija Ferdinanda Marsiglija krajem XVII. stoljeća* (1996). HBL; KoBošnjaka, 2000; OSK

Hajdarović, Rašid, born 2 April 1914 at Kalimanovićim near Rogatica, Bosnia, he was educated at Sarajevo, where he later became an archivist. He died 9 September 1980. Anali Gazi Husrev-Begove Biblioteke 7/8 (1982), pp. 277-278

Hajybăĭov, Uzair Abdul Gusein ogly (Узеир Әбдулһусейн оғлу һачыбәјов), *see* Gadzhibekob, Uzeir Abdul Gusein ogly

Hajyĭev, Magsud Ibragim ogly, 1935- *see* Gadzhiev, Maksud Ibragim ogly

Hajyĭev, Pasha A. *see* Gadzhiev, Pasha Azizbala ogly

Hajyĭev, Tofig I. *see* Gadzhiev, Tofig I

Haken, Johann Christian Ludwig, born 25 March 1767 at Jamund near Köslin, Pomerania, he studied from 1785 to 1788 Protestant theology at the Universität Halle. He first became a teacher for two years at the Cadettenhaus, Stolp, and later a pastor at a variety of churches in Pomerania. His writings include *Phantasus; Tausend und ein Märchen* (1802), *Tausend und eine Nacht; neue Märchen aus dem Arabischen übersetzt* (1808), and *Gemälde der Kreuzzüge nach Palästina zur Befreiung des Heiligen Grabes* (1808-20). He died in Treptow on 5 June 1835. ADtB, vol. 10, pp. 396-97; DtBilnd (4)

Hakov, Vahit H., 1926- *see* Khakov, Vakhit Khoziatovich

Halasi-Kun, Tibor, born 19 January 1914 at Zagreb of Hungarian parents, he obtained his doctorate at the University of Budapest, and from 1942 to 1952 served as a director of the Hungarian Institute at Ankara Üniversitesi. In 1953, he joined Columbia University, New York, and remained there until his retirement in 1982. He was a leading scholar of Turkic studies, a joint founder of the Near and Middle East Institute and the Department of Near and Middle East Studies at Columbia University, as well as the founding president of the American Research Institute in Turkey. He died of a heart attack on 19 (20 or 26) October 1991, according to obituaries. DrAS, 1982; Index Islamicus (2); MESA bulletin, 25 (1991), 311-312; WRMEA, 10 vi (December 1991/January 1992), p. 88

Halbout du Tanney, Dominique, born in 1942 at Paris, he received degrees from the École du Louvre, and École nationale des langues orientales vivantes, Paris. He was a professor in the Institut français d'études anatoliennes d'Istanbul. He was a joint author of *Le turc sans peine* (1992), *Parlons turc*

(2002), *Le persan* (2003), and he translated *Le Livre de l'amour sublime*, from the Turkish of Yunus Emre (1987). Note about the author; *Livres disponibles*; ZKO

Haldane, J. Duncan, born 20th cent., he received a Ph.D. in 1973 from the University of Edinburgh for *A Hariri manuscript and its relevance to Mamluk painting*. His writings include *Mamluk painting* (1978), and *Islamic book bindings in the Victoria and Albert Museum* (1983), and its Persian translation in 1987. Sluglett; ZKO

Haldane, James, born 19th cent., he was a missionary in Morocco. His writings include *Morocco in Mufti* (London, 1937), *Trekking among Moroccan tribes* (London, 1948), and his autobiographical reminiscences, *Missionary in Morocco* (1937). BLC

Haldon, John F., born about 1945, he received a Ph.D. in 1975 from the University of Birmingham for *Aspects of Byzantine military administration*. He became a professor of classics in the Centre for Byzantine Studies, Ottoman and Modern Greek Studies, University of Birmingham. His writings include *Byzantine praetorians* (1984), *Byzantium in the seventh century* (1990), and a collection of his articles, *State, army and society in Byzantium; approaches to military, social and administrative history, 6th-12th centuries* (1995). ConAu, 208; Sluglett

Hale, Charles, born in 1831 at Boston, Mass., he was a journalist, and from 1864 to 1871 he served as agent and consul general in Egypt. Francis Dainese wrote a memorial to the U.S. Congress in regard to Charles Hale, consul to Egypt, entitled *The History of Mr. Seward's pet in Egypt* (1867). He died in 1882. ACAB; AmIndex (1); DAB; Master (1); NUC, pre-1956; Shavit; WhAm, H

Hale, Gerry Alwyn, born in 1933, he received a Ph.D. in 1966 from the University of California at Los Angeles for *Cultivation terraces in western Darfur, Sudan*. He was from 1977 to 1993 a professor in the Department of Geography at the University of California, Los Angeles. LC; *MESA Roster of members*, 1977-1990; NatFacDr, 1993-1995

Hale, Sir John Rigby, born in 1923 at Ashford, Kent, he was since 1970 a professor of Italian at University College, London. His writings include *England and the Italian Renaissance* (1954), and *Napoleon; the story of his life* (1954). His book, *The Civilization of Europe in the Renaissance*, had just been finished in 1992 when he suffered a stroke which left him unable to speak or write. He died in 1999. Au&Wr, 1973; ConAu, 102, 183; IntWW, 1989/90-2000; *Who's who*, 1975-1999; WhoWor, 1991/92, 1993/94

Hale, Sonja, born about 1940, she received a Ph.D. in 1979 from University of California at Los Angeles, for *The changing ethnic identity of Nubians in an urban milieu; Khartoum, Sudan*. She was from 1989 to 2004 a professor of anthropology and women's studies at her alma mater. Her writings include *Nubians; a study in ethnic identity* (Khartoum, 1971), and *Gender politics in Sudan; Islamism, socialism, and the state* (1996). *MESA Roster of members*, 1990; NatFacDr, 1995-2004; Selim [3]

Hale, (Bill) William Mathew, born 17 November 1940 at Reading, England, he took his B.A. and M.A. at Oxford, and received his Ph.D. in 1966 from the Australian National University. His main research centred on modern Turkish political and economic development as well as foreign relations. He taught his subject at the University of Durham before he became a senior lecturer in politics at SOAS. Since 1993 he was chairman of its modern Turkish studies programme. In 1991, he was awarded the Turkish Ministry of Foreign Affairs' Exceptional Service Plaque. His writings include *The Republic of Turkey* (1978), *Turkish foreign policy, 1774-2000* (2000), and he edited *Aspects of modern Turkey* (1976). DrBSMES, 1993; Note about the author; Private

Haleber, Ron, born 20th cent., he was associated with the Middle East Research Associates in the Netherlands. His writings include *Discours islamiques et laïques au Magreb; à la recherche de la genèse de l'identité maghrébine; le cas du Maroc* (1990), *Morokko en de Sahara; deconstructie van een moderniseringsconflict* (1990), and *Islam en humanisme; de wereld van Mohammed Arkoun* (Amsterdam, 1992). Brinkman's, 1991-2000

Halecki, Oscar, Ritter von Chalecki, born in 1891 at Wien, he went to school at the local Schotten-Gymnasium and studied at Jagellonische Universität Krakau, where he received his doctorate and became a lecturer in Polish history. In 1918, he was invited to the Uniwersytet Warszawski, and in 1919, he became a professor of Polish history. From 1939 to 1940, he was president of the Polish University in exile, Paris. He subse-quently became a visiting profesor at a great variety of universities in the U.S. and Canada. He was granted numerous honorary doctorates. His writings include *Ostanie lata Świdrygielly i sprawa wolyńska za Kazimierza Jagiellończka* (1915), *Geschichte der Union Litauens mit Polen* (1919), *Dzieje unii jagiellońsiej* (1919-20), and *La Pologne de 963 à 1914* (1933), and its translation, *A History of Poland* (1961). He died in 1973. Au&Wr, 1963; DrAS, 1969 H; Master (2); NEP; Polski (7); *Slavic review*, 33 (1974), pp. 204; *Wer ist's*, 1935

Haleem, A. B. A., born about 1900, he was a historian and politician, and a sometime head of the History and Political Science Departments of the Muslim University, Aligarh, and later a Vice-Chancellor of the University of Sind and University of Karachi. He was a founding chairman of the Pakistan Institute of International Affairs. He died on 20 April 1975. *Pakistan horizon*, 28 ii (1975), pp. 3-4

Halén (Гален), Harry Thorvald, born to native Swedish-speaking parents on 24 May 1943 at Helsinki. Finnish became his first language when he went to the Finnish Normal Lyceum alias «Norsii» in Helsinki in 1955-1963. He studied Altaic philology, Sanskrit and comparative Indo-European linguistics at Helsinki University, becoming one of the most experienced and versatile Orientalists in Finland, and educating a generation of younger Orientalists. Since the early 1970s, he was associated in various capacities with the newly established Unit for East Asian and Altaic Studies of the University of Helsinki. "There is one aspect that perhaps explains something of his amazing productivity. He did not waste his time on foreign travel. In his youth he, like most Orientalists, dreamed of travels to exotic countries. Eventually his own relationship with the countries of the East has mostly remained platonic. He has commented his lack of fieldwork by saying, «I do not want to lose my illusions»." His writings, comprising also popular and belletristic works in the domestic languages of Finland, include *Handbook of Oriental collections in Finland* (Malmö, 1978), *A Biblio-graphical survey of the publishing activities of the Turkish minority in Finland* (1979), *Die uigurischen Mannerheim-Fragmente* (1979); he was a joint author of *The Middle Iranian fragments in Sogdian script from the Mannerheim Collection* (1980); and he edited *Nordmongolische Volksdichtung* (Helsinki, 1973-77). In 1998, he published his school reminiscences. On his sixtieth birthday he was honoured by *Remota relata; essays on the history of Oriental studies in honor of Harry Halén* (2003). Note about the author

Halepota, Abdul W. J., born in 1915, he received a D.Phil. in 1949 from Oxford University for *The practical theology and ethics of Shaikh Waliullah of Delhi*. His writings include *Philosophy of Shah Wakiullah* (Lahore, 197-), a work which was originally presented as his doctoral thesis at Oxford. He died in 2001. *Index Islamicus*; Note about the author; Sluglett

Halevi, Ilan, born 20th cent., his writings include *Sous Israel, la Palestine* (1978), *Question juive, la tribu, la loi, l'espace* (1981), its translations, *Auf der Suche nach dem gelobten Land* (1986),and *A History of the Jews* (1987), *De la terreur au massacre d'état* (1984).

Halévy, Joseph, born 15 December 1827 at Adrianople (Edirne), he first taught at Jewish schools in Adrianople and Bucureşti before he became a French Orientalist, archaeologist, and epigrapher who, in the service of the Académie des inscriptions et belles-lettres, Paris, visited the Yemen from 1869 to 1870 for the purpose of acquiring Sabaean inscriptions. He became the first European since Roman times to enter Najran and he returned through Marib bringing back a total of 685 inscriptions which greatly increased knowledge of pre-Islamic Arabia. Back in Paris, he became a professor of Ethiopian at the École pratique des hautes études. He died in Paris on 20 January 1917. Bidwell; Embacher; EncJud; GdeEnc; IndexBFr² (3); Vapereau

Halévy, Mayer Abraham, born 19th cent., he was associated with the Societăţii di Studii judaice, Bucureşti. His writings include *Moïse dans l'histoire et dans la légende* (Bucureşti, 1928), and he was an editor of *Sinai; anuar de studii judaice* (Iaşi, 1926). OSK

Halff, Bruno, born 20th cent., his writings include *Le Mahasin al-magalis d'Ibn al-'Arīf et l'œuvre du soufi hanbalite al-Ansari* (1972), and he was a joint author of *Dix ans de recherche universitaire française sur le monde arabe et islamique de 1968/69 à 1979* (1982), and *L'Orient au cœur; en l'honneur d'André Miquel* (2001). Livres disponibles, 2004; ZKO

Halford-Macleod, Aubrey Seymour, born in 1914, he was a graduate of Magdalen College, Oxford, who entered HM Diplomatic Service and served at Baghdad, in Libya, and in Kuwait as well as a great many other other assigments. He died 21 August 2000. Who, 1979-2000

Du Halgouet, Hervé A. Marie Louis de Poulpiquet, vicomte, born 25 July 1878, he served as an army officer in the first World War and later went into politics. He was a *conseiller général* of Morbihan and concurrently pursued an interest in the history of Bretagne. He became a president of the Société polymatique du Morbihan and a secretary general of the Société d'histoire et d'achéologie bretonnes. His writings include *Essai sur le Porhoët* (1906), *Archives des châteaux bretons; Tregranteur* (1909), *Tredion* (1911), *Grégo* (1913), *Le Duché de Rohan et ses seigneurs* (1925), and *Inventaire des archives de l'hôtel de Limur* (1927). He died about 1960. DBF

Halhed, Nathaniel Brassey, born in 1751 at London, he was educated at Harrow School and afterwards became a civil officer in the Honorable East India Company in Bengal, 1773-85. From 1790 to 1795 he was an M.P. for Lymington. His *Grammar of the Bengal language* (1778), is a remarkable work in so far as he was one of the first to draw attention to the similarity between Sanskrit and

European languages. He died in London in 1830. Rosane Rocher wrote Orientalism, poetry and the millenium; the checkered life of Nathaniel Brassey Halhed (1983). Buckland; IndianBiInd (3); Riddick

Halidé Edeb Hanım, 1885-1964 see Adıvar, Halide Edib

Halikova, E. A., 1930-1977 see Khalikova, Elena Aleksandrovna

Halil Hâlid (Khalil Khalid) Çerkeşşeyhizâde, born in 1869 at Ankara, after graduation from the local secondary school, he went to Constantinople and successively studied at the medrese of Beyazıt Mosque and the darülfünun (university), where he received a law degree in 1893. In the following year, he left for England, where he eked out a living by writing for newspapers and periodicals. In 1897, he was appointed a vice-consul at the Ottoman Embassy in London. From 1902 to 1911, he was a teacher of Turkish at Cambridge, where he was befriended with Elias J. W. Gibb and E. G. Browne. After his return to Turkey he was elected to the Ottoman Assembly, but resigned his mandate after ten months. Since 1922 he was teaching literary and theological subjects at the University in Constantinople. His writings include The Diary of a Turk (1903), and he is said to have written the introduction to Gibb's History of Ottoman poetry (1900-1909). He died at the end of March 1931. MES, 29 (1993), pp. 559-79; Türk ansiklopedisi

Halim Pasha, Said, 1863-1921 see Said Halim Pasha

Halit, Stella Reinhardt, fl. 1937, she was an American, did secretarial work in Chicago, Paris and Istanbul, and taught school in Bulgaria, and, in the meantime, wrote stories and articles. She married her Turkish husband in London in 1932. Note about the author

Halkin, Abraham Solomon, born in 1903 at Novo-Bykhov, Russia, he graduated in 1924 from Columbia University, New York, and became a professor of Semitic studies in N.Y.C. He edited Zion in Jewish literature (1961), and he jointly translated Moslem schisms and sects, from the Arabic of 'Abd al-Qāhir al-Baghdādī (1935). He died in Jerusalem in 1990. BioIn, 16, 17; CnDiAmJBi; ConAu, 131; DrAS, 1969, vol. 1; Selim; WhoWorJ, 1955, 1965

Halkin, François, S.J., born 1901 at Lille, he was a sometime president of the Société des Bollandistes, and an indefatigable editor of Greek hagiographic writings which include Inédits byzantins d'Ochrida (1963), Catalogue des manuscrits hagiographiques de la Bibliothèque nationale d'Athènes (1983), and a collection of his articles, Saints moines d'Orient (1973). He died in 1988. Nouveau dictionnaire des Belges (1992)

Hall, Ardelia Ripley, fl. 1934, her writings include Catalogue of color photographs of Korean monuments of architecture and sculpture (s.l., 1959). NUC, 1956-67

Hall, Edward Twitchell, born in 1914 at Webster Grove, Mo., he graduated in 1936 from the University of Denver, and received his M.A. in 1942 from the University of Arizona for Archaeological survey of Walhalla, and his Ph.D. in 1942 from Columbia University, New York, for Early stockaded settlements in the Governador, New Mexico. He subsequently held a great variety of posts as an anthropologist, archaeologist, and psychiatrist. His writings include The Silent language (1960), Handbook for proxemic research (1974), Beyond culture (1976), and he was a joint author of Intercultural communication (1960). ConAu, 65-68; NUC

Hall, Fitz-Edward, born 21 March 1821 at Troy, N.Y., he was a graduate of Harvard University and in 1846 went to India, where he stayed as instructor and professor of Sanskrit, with a three year interruption, until 1862. From 1862 until his retirement in 1869, he was at King's College, and the India Office, London. His writings include A Contribution towards an index to the bibliography of the Indian philosophical systems (1859), Benares, ancient and medieval (1869), Hindi reader (1870). He died in Marlesford, England, on 1 February 1901. ACAB; AmIndex (1); Buckland; DAB; DNB; IndianBiInd (1); Master (10); NatCAB, vol. 11, pp. 448-49; Shavit - Asia; WhAm, H

Hall, Harvey Porter, born 16 November 1909 at Beirut, he received his M.A. in modern European and Near Eastern history in 1934 from Harvard. Following a period of teaching at Robert College, Istanbul, he served as research analyst on Turkey with the Office of Strategic Services from 1942 to 1945. From 1946 to 1956 he was the first editor of The Middle East journal. He left the Journal to become involved in Ford Foundation activities. He edited Middle East resources (1954). He died in Oxford, N.H., on 18 June 1975. MEJ, 29 (1975), p. 433; Shavit

Hall, Isaac Hollister, born in 1837, he was an American lawyer who, from 1875 to 1877, taught at the Syrian Protestant College, Beirut. He died in 1896. AmIndex (3); DAB; NatCAB, v. 12, p. 143; Shavit; WhAm H

Hall, Leland Boylston, born in 1883, he was a faculty member of Smith College, who made two long and leisurely journeys into Morocco and other parts of Africa, settling down here and there for months at a time, and acquiring a working knowledge of Arabic as he went along. His writings include *Timbuctoo* (1827), and *Salah and his American* (1933). He died in 1957. Note about the author; LC

Hall, Lesley A., born 4 October 1949, she was a librarian and archivist at the India Office Library and Records, London, until the 1980s when she left to work at the Wellcome Institute Library, London, also as an archivist. Concurrently she was an honorary lecturer in the history of medicine at University College, London. Her writings include *A Brief guide to sources for the study of Afghanistan in the India Office Records* (1981), *Hidden anxieties; male sexuality, 1900-1950* (1991), and *Sex, gender and social change in Britain since 1880* (2000). Private

Hall, Marjorie J., born 20th cent., she was a joint author of *Sisters under the sun; the story of Sudanese women* (1981), and she translated from the Arabic, *Business laws of the United Arab Emirates* (1979).

Hall, Melvin Adams, born 14 April 1889 at Bellow Falls, Vt., he served with distinction with the British and American armies during the first World War, and subsequently, three years as aviation attaché to the American Embassy in London. He resigned from the services in 1922. From 1923 to 1927 he was a member of the first Arthur C. Millspaugh mission to Persia. From 1929 to 1935, he spent much of his time in Turkey in connection with the Turkish Government's aviation programme, and with matters of financing. His writings include *Journey to the end of an era; an autobiography* (1948). He died in N.Y.C. on 23 November 1962. Note about the author; NYT, 25 November 1962, p. 86, cols. 4-5; Shavit

Hall, Richard Seymour, born in 1925 at Margate, Kent., he wrote *Zambia* (1965), *The High price of principles; Kaunda* (1969), *Kaunda, founder of Zambia* (1965), *Stanley; an adventurer exposed* (1974), *The Great Uhuru Railway* (1976), and *Lovers on the Nile; the incredible African journeys of Sam and Florence Baker* (1980). IntAu&W, 1991|

Hall, William H., born about 1871, he was a missionary and teacher in Turkey and served for twenty-four years as a principal of the Preparatory School of the American University of Beirut. His writings include *Reconstruction in Turkey* (1918), and *The Near East, crossroads of the world* (1920). He died in Beirut on 8 January 1927, aged fifty-five. Note about the author; Shavit

Hallam, W. K. R., his writings include *The Nigerian safety manual* (Jos, Nigeria, 1970), and *The Life and times of Rabih Fadl Allah* (Ilfracombe, 1977). ZKO

Hallaq, Wael Bahjat, born 26 November 1955 at Nazareth, Israel, he received a Ph.D. in 1983 from the University of Washington, Seattle, Ore., for *The Gate of ijtihād; a study in Islamic legal history.* He was from 1992 to 2004 a professor in the Institute of Islamic Studies, and the Institute of Comparative Law, McGill University, Montreal, P.Q. His writings include *Law and legal theory in classical and medieval Islam* (1994), *A History of Islamic legal theories; an introduction to Sunni usūl al-fiqh* (1997), and he edited *Islamic studies presented to Charles J. Adams* (1991). Private; ZKO

Hallensleben, Horst, born 3 April 1928 at Evingsen, Altena, he received a Dr.phil. in 1963 for *Die Malerschule des Königs Milutin.* He was a professor of fine art at the Universität Bonn. Kürschner, 1976-2003

von Haller, Karl, born 19th cent., his writings include *Ein Ausflug nach Algier im Jahre 1857, nebst einem geographischen, statistischen und historischen Anhang* (Solothurn, 1859), and *Orientalische Ausflüge* (Ingenbohl, 1871). Sezgin

Hallet, Stanley Ira, born about 1940, he was a sometime Fulbright lecturer in architecture, and from 1995 to 2004 a Dean of Architecture, Catholic University of America, Washington, D.C. He was a joint author of *Traditional architecture of Afghanistan* (1980). NatFacDr, 1995-2004

Hallett, E., born about 1900, he received a Ph.D. in 1946 from the University of London for *Cotton finance and its relation to the currency and credit system of Egypt.* Sluglett

Halliday, Fred, born 22 February 1946 at Dublin, he studied at Queen's College, Oxford, SOAS, and LSE, where he obtained a Ph.D. in 1985. Since 1983 he taught at the LSE. He was on the editorial board of the *New left review*, and a fellow of the Transnational Institute, Washington, D.C. His writings include *Arabia without sultans* (1974), *Iran, dictatorship and development* (1978), *Revolution and foreign policy; the case of South Yemen* (1990), *Arabs in exile; Yemeni migrants in urban Britain* (1992), and *Islam and the myth of confrontation* (1995). Who's who, 1997-2004

Halliday, Jon, born in 1939 at Dublin, he graduated from Oxford University and served from 1974 to 1978 as a professor of comparative politics in Italy and Mexico. His writings include *Japanese imperialism today* (1973), *A Political history of Japanese capitalism* (1975), and *Korea; the unknown war* (1988). ConAu, 97-100

Halliday, Sir William Reginald, born in 1886 at Belize, British Honduras, he became a university administrator and served from1914 to 1928 as a professor of ancient history at the University of Liverpool. His writings include *Greek divination* (1913), *Folklore studies, ancient and modern* (1924), *The Greek questions of Plutarch* (1928), *Indo-European folk-tales and Greek legend* (1933), and *Greek and Roman folklore* (1959). He died in 1966. Au&Wr, 1963; *Who was who*, 6

Hallowes, Mary, born 19th cent., she was in 1926 the wife of a deputy secretary of the Indian Civil Service [possibly Basil John Knight Hallowes.] Note about the author

Halm, Heinz, born 21 February 1942 at Anderbach, Germany, he received a Dr.phil. in 1967 from the Universität Bonn for *Die Traditionen über den Aufstand 'Ali ibn Muhammads, des Herrn der Zang*, and a Dr.habil. in 1978 for *Kosmologie und Heilslehre der frühen Ismā'īlīyā*. A sometime *professeur associé* at the Sorbonne, he was since 1980 a professor of Islamic history at the Universität Tübingen. His writings include *Die Ausbreitung der šāfi'itischen Rechtsschule* (1974), *Kulturgeographische Grundlagen der islamischen Geschichte* (1975), *Ägypten nach den mamlukischen Lehensregistern* (1979-82), *Die islamische Gnosis* (1982), *Das Reich des Mahdi; der Aufstieg der Fatimiden* (1991), its translation, *The Empire of the Mahdi* (1996), *Der schiitsche Islam* (1994), and *Die Kalifen von Kairo, die Fatimiden in Ägypten, 973-1074* (2003). Kürschner, 1983-2003; Schwarz; ZKO

Halman, Talât Sait, born 7 July 1931 at Istanbul, he studied at Columbia University, New York, 1952-1955, and was granted an honorary doctorate from Boğaziçi Üniversitesi. He taught Turkish language and literature at Columbia, 1953-1960, and was appointed a professor at Princeton in 1966. In 1993, he was associated with the Department of Near Eastern Languages and Literatures, New Yok University. His writings include *Can kulağı; şiirler* (1968), *The Humanist poetry of Yunus Emre* (1972), *Turkey; from empire to nation* (1973), and he edited *Modern Turkish drama* (1976). ConAu, 53-56, new rev., 4; EIS; Master (1); NatFacDr, 1995; Private; Şükran Kurdakul, *Şairler ve yazarlar sözlüğü* (1973) ; WhoAm, 1990/91, 1992/93. [The reference in *Index Islamicus* to *Turkish review* is wrong.]

Halper, Benzion, born 15 April 1884 or 85 at Zhosly, Lithuania, he received a Ph.D. in 1915 from Dropsie College, Philadelphia, Pa., for *A Volume of the Book of precepts, by Hefes b. Yasliah*, edited from an Arabic manuscript in the Library of Dropsie College, translated into Hebrew, and provided with critical notes. His writings include *Post-Biblical Hebrew literature* (1921). He died in Philadelphia, Pa., on 21 March 1924. CnDiAmJBi; Selim

Halperin, Charles Jerome, born in 1946, he received a Ph.D. in 1973 from Columbia University, New York, for *The Russian land and the Russian tsar; the emergence of Muscovite ideology, 1380-1408*. His writings include *The Tatar yoke* (1985), and *Russia and the Golden Horde; the Mongol impact on medieval Russian history* (1986). ZKO

Halpérin, Vladimir, born 20th cent., he received a doctorate in 1950 at Paris for *Lord Milner et l'évolution de l'impérialisme britannique*. His writings include *L'Angleterre il y a 50 ans* (1948), and the translation of his thesis, *Lord Milner and the Empire* (1952).

Halperín Donghi, Tulio, born 20 October 1925 or 6 at Buenos Aires, he was a lawyer and a professor of history. His writings include *El pensamiento de Echeverría* (Buenos Aires, 1951), *Politics, economics and society in Argentina in the revolutionary period* (1975), and *Proyecto y construcción de una nación; Argentina, 1846-1880* (Caracas, 1980). *Quien es quien en la Argentina*, 1969

Halpern, Benjamin, born 10 April 1912 at Boston, he graduated from Harvard University, where he aslo received his Ph.D. He served with Jewish organizations and publishers until 1961, when he joined the Department of Near Eastern and Judaic Studies at Brandeis University, Waltham, Mass., the only formal academic position he ever held. His writings include *The Idea of the Jewish State* (1961), and *Jews and Blacks* (1971). He died in Boston on 5 May 1990. *American Jewish history*, 80 (1990), pp. 142-47; ConAu, 115, 131, 203; DrAS, 1969 H; NYT, 19 May 1990, p. 30, col. 3

Halpern, Daniel, born 11 September 1945 at Syracuse, N.Y., he graduated in 1969 from California State University at Northridge. He was an editor, poet, and translator. His writings include *On nature* (1987), *Selected poems* (1994), *Our private lives; journals, notebooks, and diaries* (1998), and he was a joint author of *Songs of Mririda, courtesan of the High Atlas* (1974). ConAu, 33-36, new rev., 93; IntWW, 1989-2002; Master (5); WhoAm, 1988/89-2003; WrDr, 1990-2004

Halpern, Manfred, born 1 February 1924 at Mittweida, Saxony, he graduated in 1947 from the University of California, Los Angeles, and received a Ph.D. in 1960 from Johns Hopkins University, Baltimore, Md. He was a political scientist who taught at a variety of American universities and also served as a consultant to RAND Corporation as well as the U.S. Department of State. His writings include *The Morality and politics of intervention* (1963), and *The Politics of social change in the Middle*

East and North Africa (1963). He died in 2001. ConAu, 9-12; *Index Islamicus*; *MESA Roster of members*, 1977-1990; Unesco; WhoAm, 1990-1998

Halphen, Louis Sigismond Isaac, born 4 February 1880 at Paris, he was educated at the Lycée de Versailles, and Louis-le-Grand de Paris; he received his first degree in 1899 from the Faculté des lettres de Paris, followed by study at the École pratique des hautes études, and the École des chartes, where he gained a diploma in 1904 for *Les transformations politiques du comté d'Anjou sous les premiers Capétiens.* After two years at the École française de Rome, he received his doctorate in 1906 from the Sorbonne for *Le comté d'Anjou au XI siècle.* He became a professor of history of the middle ages. His writings include *Les Barbares; des grandes invasions aux conquêtes turques du XIe siècle* (1926), *Initiation aux études d'histoire du moyen âge* (1940), and *Charlesmagne et l'empire caroligien* (1947). He died in 1950. DBF; IndexBFr² (2); *Qui est-ce*, 1934; *Qui êtes-vous*, 1924

Halsell, Grace Eleanor, born in 1923 at Lubbock, Tex., she was a writer who impersonated women from cultures other than her own and then wrote about her impressions. Her writings include *Soul sister* (1969), its translation, *Yo fui negra* (1973), *Black/white sex* (1972), *A Journey to Jerusalem* (1981), and her autobiography, *In their shoes* (1991). She died in Washington, D.C., on 16 August 2000. ConAu, 21-24, 189; NYT, 2 September 2000, p. A-17, cols. 5-6; WhoAm, 1988/89-1992/93; ZKO

Halstead, Charles Raymond, born 20th cent., he received a Ph.D. in 1962 from the University of Virginia at Charlottesville for *Spain, the powers, and the second World War.* NUC, 1956-67

Halstead, John Preston, born 10 May 1923 at Rome, N.Y., he graduated in 1948 from Dartmouth College and received a Ph.D. in 1960 from Harvard for *The origins of Moroccan nationalism, 1919-1934.* He subsequently became a professor of history at S.U.N.Y., Buffalo. His writings include *Rebirth of a nation; the origins and rise of Moroccan nationalism, 1912-1944* (1967), *Modern European imperialism* (1974), and *The Second British Empire* (1983). DrAS, 1969 H, 1974 H, 1978 H, 1982 H

Hamaker, Hendrik Arent, born 25 February 1789 at Amsterdam, he trained for business in accordance with his parents' wishes, but he also studied Arabic under Wilmet at the Athenaeum so successfully that he was nominated in 1815 a professor at Franeker Universiteit. Two years later he became a professor of Semitic languages and curator of Oriental manuscripts at Leiden. His research centred on the great Arabic collection of the Warner Collection. One of the great Dutch Orientalists, he was in constant contact with the giants of the day, Silvester de Sacy, Fleischer, Freytag, and Bernstein. His disapproval of Hammer-Purgstall's *Geschichte des osmanischen Reiches* cumulated in his *Réflexions critiques sur quelques points contestés de l'histoire orientales pour servir de réponse aux éclaircissements de M. de Hammer* (1829); he also wrote *Specimen catalogi codicum mss. orientalium Bibliothecae Academicae Lugduno-Batavae* (1820), *Miscellaneo phoeniciasive commentarii de rebus Phoenicum* (1828), and he edited *Incerti auctoris liber de expugnatione Memphidis et Alexandriae vulgo adscriptus Abou Abdallae Mohammedi Omari filio Wakidaeo, Medinensi* (1825). He died at his estate in Neerlangbroek on 7 October 1835. Aa; BiBenelux² (5); NieuwNBW, vol. 3, cols. 533-35

Hamalian, Leo, born 13 January 1920 at N.Y.C., he received a Ph.D. in 1955 from Columbia University, New York, for *The Voice of this calling; a study of the plays of T. S. Eliot.* He taught English at American universities and served from 1962 to 1964 as a Smith-Mundt Lecturer in Syria. He was a Fulbright scholar in Tehran and Hamburg. His writings include *International short novels* (1974), *Burn after reading* (1978), and he was a joint editor of *New writing from the Middle East.* ConAu, 5-8, new revision, 2; DrAS, 1969 E; ZKO

Hamani, Djibo, born in 1943, he received his doctorate from the Université d'Aix-en-Provence and became a professor of history and sociology. Since 1979 he was also a director of the Institut de Recherches en Sciences Humaines, Université de Niamey. His writings include *L'Adar précolonial; contribution à l'étude de l'histoire des états hausa* (1975), and *Au carrefour du Soudan et de la Berbérie; le sultanat touareg de l'Ayar* (1989). Note about the author; ZKO

Hamaoui, Ernest, born 20th cent., he was a sometime member of the Mission juridique française en Afghanistan, and in 1973, a lecturer in the Institut d'études juridiques, Université de Paris. His writings include *Les régimes politiques de la France, 1789-1958* (1970), *Cours de droit public* (1971), and he was an editor of *Le Juge administratif* (Paris, 1972-75). Note about the author

Hamarneh (Hamārnah), Sami Khalaf, born 27 February 1925 at Ma'dabā, Transjordan, he received a Ph.D. in 1959 from the University of Wisconsin for *Some pharmaceutical aspects of al-Zahrawi's al-Tasreef.* He was a sometime curator in charge of the Division of Medical Sciences, Smithonian Institute, Washington, D.C. His writings include *Ward min shawq* (1950), *A Pharmaceutical view of Abulcasis al-Zahrawi in Moorish Spain* (1963), *Bibliography on medicine and pharmacy in medieval*

Islam (1964), and *Catalogue of Arabic manuscripts on medicine and pharmacy in the British Library* (1976). AmM&WSc P, 1992-2003; IntWW, 1991-2002; Master (2); WhoAm, 1990-1996

Hambis, Louis, born in 1906 at Liugé (Vienne), France, he gained a diploma in 1943 at the École pratique des Hautes études. From 1942 to 1947 he was a lecturer at the École des Langues orientales, Paris. From 1947 to 1950 he served as an administrator at the Centre d'Études sinologiques of the Université de Paris at Peking. He subsequently taught at Paris, becoming a professor at the Collège de France in 1965. His writings include *Grammaire de la langue mongole écrite*, a work which won him the prix Volney for 1946, *Attila et les Huns* (1972), *Gengis-Khan* (1973), and he was a joint author of *L'Asie central; histoire et civilisation* (1978). He died in 1978. *Impressions*, 10 (1978), p. 43

Hambly, Gavin Richard Grenville, born 4 July 1934 at Sevenoaks, England, he received three degrees in history from Cambridge University. From 1961 to 1963 he was a British Council lecturer in Tehran and subsequently taught at Ankara, New Delhi, and New Haven, Conn. He was a professor in the Department of Fine Arts, University of Texas, Dallas, certainly from 1995 to 2000. His writings include *Cities of Mughul India* (1968), and he edited *Zentralasien* (1966), its translations, *Central Asia* (1969), and *Asie centrale* (1970). DrAS, 1969 H; NatFacDr, 1995-2000

Hambye, Edward René, S.J., M.A., Ph.D., born 20th cent., his writings include *1900 Jahre Thomas-Christen in Indien* (1972), *A Bibliography on Christianity in India* (1976), *Dimensions of Eastern Christianity* (1983), and he edited *Christianity in India* (1973).

Hamed, Ismaël, 1857-1932 or 33 *see* Hamet, Ismaël

Hamel, Louis, born 19th cent., his writings include *Les chemins de fer algériens; étude historique sur la constitution du réseau, le classement de 1857* (Alger, 1885). BN

Hamès, Constant, born 20th cent., he was a joint author of *Abd el-Kader au XIX siècle dans les collections du musée Condé à Chantilly* (Paris, 2003). *Livres disponibles*, 2004

Hamet, Ismaël, born 4 August 1857 at Alger, he changed his name from Hamed to Hamet. He was a military interpreter with the Ministère de la guerre before he became an *officier-interprète principal* at the French general staff. His writings include *Chronique de la Mauritanie sénégalaise* (1911), *Les Musulmans français du Nord de l'Afrique* (1916), and *Histoire du Maghreb* (1923). He died in 1932 or 1933. AfrBioInd (1); BN; Note about the author; NUC, pre-1956

Hamid, Abdul Hakk, 1852-1937 *see* Tarhan, Abdülhak Hâmit

Hamidullah, Muhammad, Dr., born in 1908 at Hyderabad, Deccan, he studied at Hyderabad as well as at Bonn and Paris. He has done library research in the Middle East, North Africa, and Europe. He was a sometime lecturer in Islamic law at İstanbul Üniversitesi Edebiyat Fakültesi. His writings include *Muslim conduct of state* (1941-42), *Introduction to Islam* (1957), *Le Prophète de l'islam* (1959), and he translated *Le Coran* (1959). He died in 2002. *Index Islamicus*; Note about the author; NUC

Hamidullah Khan, Sir, born in 1894 in India, he was a ruler of Bhopal. He died in 1960. Jain; *Who's who in India*, 1927; *Who was who*, 5

Hamilton, Adrian, born in 1944, he was in 1973 a correspondent for the London *Financial times*. He was a joint author of *Oil, the biggest business* (London, 1975). Note about the author

Hamilton, Archibald Milne, born about 1899, he was educated at Canterbury College, University of New Zealand, 1923-24. He subsequently spent two years with the Civil Engineering-in-Chief's Department, Admirality. In 1927, he was appointed to Public Works Department, Iraq, and was one of the five engineers who at one time or another were in charge of the Rowanduz Road work in Kurdistan, a project which he described in his *The Road through Kurdistan* (1957). After the completion of the project he returned to England. From 1936 to 1938 he served in Egypt as a captain with the Royal Engineers. BritInd = *Engineers who's who*, 1939

Hamilton, Bernard, born in 1932, he spent his entire academic career as a professor of history of the crusades at the University of Nottingham. His writings include *The Albigensian crusade* (1974), *The Latin Church in the Crusader States* (1980), *The Leper king and his heirs; Baldwin IV and the Crusader Kingdom of Jerusalem* (2000), and two collections of his articles, *Monastic reform, Cathorism and the crusades, 900-1300* (1979), and *Crusaders, Cathars and the holy places* (1999). WrDr, 1990-2004

Hamilton, Charles, captain, born about 1753 at Belfast, he went to India in the East India Company's military service in 1776 and became one of the first members of the Asiatic Society of Bengal. He served in the campaign against the Rohillas and wrote an account of them. He translated in 1791 the

Hedaya, or guide to Islamic law, from the Persian of ʿAlī ibn Abī Bakr Marghīnānī Farghānī. He died in England before he could take up the post of Resident in Oudh, to which he had been appointed. He died in Hamstead on 14 March 1792, aged thirty-nine. BLC; BritInd (1); Buckland; IndianBiInd (2); DNB; Riddick; ZKO

Hamilton, F. A., born 19th cent., he was a colonel and served with the former 3rd Cavalry, Indian Army, HQ Staff, South Persia, 1917-18. His trace is lost after an article in the *Cavalry journal* in 1940. Note about the author

Hamilton, James Russell, born in 1921, he received a doctorate in 1983 rom the Université de Paris for *Étude du corpus des manuscrits ouïgours de la grotte murée de Touen-Houang.* He was associated with the Institut des hautes études chinoises, Paris; his writings include *Les Ouïghours à l'époque des cinq dynasties* (1955), *Documents turco-sogdiens du IX-X siècle de Touen-houang* (1990), and he edited *Le Conte bouddhique du bon et du mauvais prince en version ouïgoure* (1971). In 2001 he was honoured by *De Dunhuang à Istanbul; hommage à James Russell Hamilton.* He died in 2003. Index Islamicus; Livres disponibles, 2004; THESAM, 4; Turcica, 35 (2005), pp. 5-6

Hamilton, John Almeric de Courcy, born in 1896, he graduated from King's College, Cambridge, and entered the Sudan Political Service. He subsequently was posted to Cairo and Beirut. His writings include *The Anglo-Egyptian Sudan from within* (London, 1935). He died in 1973. Who was who, 7

Hamilton, John Lushington Moore *Angus,* born 1874 at London, he was educated at Cheltenham College as well as in Germany and France. He was a newspaper correspondent and a lecturer. His writings include *The Siege of Mafeking* (1900), *Afghanistan* (1904), *Problems of the Middle East* (1909), *Somaliland* (1911), and *In Abor jungles* (1912). He died in 1913. Master (1); Who's who, 1904, 1908

Hamilton, Miss M. M., born 20th cent., she graduated from the London School of Economics. She made a study of social questions in the U.K., and in 1949 she went to Cairo and was attached to the British Embassy to assist in dealing with certain social problems there. During her three years in Egypt she visited also other countries in the Middle East. Note about the author

Hamilton, Robert Alexander B., 1903-1961 *see* Belhaven and Stenton, Robert Alexander Benjamin

Hamilton, Robert William, F.B.A., born 26 November 1905, he was a graduate of Magdalen College, Oxford, and was successively Chief Inspector of Antiquities in Palestine, lecturer in Near Eastern archæology at Oxford, and keeper of the Department of Antiquities, Ashmolean Museum, Oxford. His writings include *A Guide to Bethlehem* (1939), *The Church of the Nativity* (1947), and *Khirbat al Mafjar, an Arabian mansion in the Jordan Valley* (1959). He died on 25 September 1994. Who's who, 1979-1996

Hamilton, Thomas Jefferson, born 20 September 1909 at Augusta, Ga., he graduated in 1928 *magna cum laude* from the University of Georgia and went to Oxford as a Rhodes scholar. He was a newspaper correspondent and served as a member of the staff of the *New York Times* in Europe and Latin America. In 1946 he became chief of that newspaper's U.N. bureau, and followed closely the Palestine question. His writings include *Appeasement's child; the Franco regime in Spain* (1943). He died at his home in Southbury, Conn., on 8 January 1987. NYT, 9 January 1987, p. D-16, cols. 4-5; WhAm, 9

Hamilton, William John, born in 1805 at London, he was a geologist who had also studied history and philology at the Universität Göttingen. He subsequently had a brief career as an attaché at the British legations in Madrid and Paris. A fellow of the Geological Society, he visited, together with Hugh E. Strickland, Anatolia and Armenia, from 1835 to 1837. His writings include *Researches in Asia Minor, Pontus, and Armenia* (1842), and its translation, *Reisen in Kleinasien, Pontus und Armenien* (1843). He died in Lodnon in 1867. DNB; Embacher; Henze, vol. 2, pp. 444-50

Hamilton, William Richard, born in 1777 at London, he had a distinguished career as a diplomat and antiquarian, serving as under-secretary at the Foreign Office during the latter years of the Napoleonic Wars, and subsequently as one of the founding members of the Royal Geographical Society. As one of Lord Elgin's confidential clerks during the latter's posting as ambassador to the Sublime Porte, 1798-1803, Hamilton was sent to Egypt in 1801 as his representative with the British expeditionary force. In Egypt he also travelled up the Nile. His writings include *Remarks on several parts of Turkey* (1809), and its translation, *Aegyptiaca oder Beschreibung des Zustandes des alten und neuen Ägypten* (1814). He died in 1859. Boase; BritInd (4); *Bulletin* of the ASTENE, 19 (Spring 2004), pp. 23-24; Dawson; DNB; Egyptology; Hill

Hamilton-Grierson, Philip Francis, born in 1883, he graduated from Trinity College, Oxford, and was admitted to the Scottish Bar. He served as a judge in the Sudan. He died in 1963. Who, 1943-1963; Who was who, 6

Hamley, Sir Edward Bruce, born 27 April 1824 at Bodmin, Cornwall, he was educated at the Royal Military Academy, Woolwich, and served in the Crimean campaign, 1854-55. From 1859 to 1864 he was a professor of history at the Staff College, Sandhurst. He served with boundary commissions in Bulgaria, Anatolia, and Greece, and commanded an expeditionary force in Egypt. His writings include *The Story of the campaign of Sebastopol, written in the camp* (1855), and *The Operations of war explained and illustrated* (1866). He died in London on 12 August 1893. Alexander Innes Shand wrote *The Life of general Sir Edward Bruce Hamley, K.C.B., K.C.M.G.* (1895). Boase, vol. 5; BritInd (3); CelCen; DNB, vol. 22, pp. 807-10; Master (1)

Hamlin, Alfred Dwight Foster, born in 1855 at Constantinople, the son of Cyril H., he gratuted from Amherst College in the class of 1875 and then studied at the Massachusetts Institute of Technology, Cambridge, Mass., and École des beaux-arts, Paris. He taught architecural history at Columbia University, New York, where he later became head of the School of Architecture. He died in 1926. AmIndex (7); ANB

Hamlin, Cyrus, born in 1811 at Waterford, Me., he graduated in 1834 from Bowdoin College, Brunswick, Me., and from the Theological Seminary in Bangor, Me., a few years later. On 3 December 1838 he sailed for Turkey, where he became the most prominent American missionary educator in the Ottoman Empire during the nineteenth century. At Bebek, near Constantinople, he founded first the Bebek Seminary and later Robert College, the predecessor of to-day's Boğaziçi Üniversitesi. His writings include *Among the Turks* (1878), *My life and times* (1893), *Turkey and the Armenian atrocities* (1896), and he was a joint author of *Memoir on the language of the Gypsies, as now used in the Turkish Empire* (1861). He died in Lexington, Mass. in 1900. A. D. F. Hamlin wrote *In memoriam Rev. Cyrus Hamlin* (1903), and Marcia and Malcolm Stevens *Against the devil's current* (1988). AmIndex (4); ANB; NatCAB, vol. 10, pp. 491-92; Shavit

Hamm, Roberto, born in 1939, his writings include *Pour une typographie arabe; contribution technique à la démocratisation de la culture arabe* (Paris, 1975). NUC; ZKO

von **Hamm**, Wilhelm Philipp, born 5 July 1820 at Darmstadt, Hesse, he studied at Landwirtschaftliche Akademie, Hohenheim, 1838-39. After travels in Belgium, France, England, the Balkans, and Russia, he studied chemistry and natural sciences at the Universität Gießen. In 1843, he became a professor of agronomy at Hofwil, and in 1844, a director of the Ackerbauschule in Rütihobel near Bern. In 1847, he became an editor of the *Agronomische Zeitung*. In 1867, he went to Wien, where he entered the ministry of agriculture. He was knighted in 1871. His writings include *Südöstliche Steppen und Städte* (1862). He died in Wien on 8 November 1880. DtBE; DtBiInd (4); NDB; ÖBL

Hammarskjöld, Dag Hjalmar Agne Carl, born 29 July 1905 at Jönköping, Sweden, he was a statesman and became the second secretary general of the U.N.O. He died in a plane crash in northern Rhodesia in 1961. Posthumously he was awarded the Nobel Peace Prize for 1961. ConAu, 77-80; DcTwHis; Master (10); *Vem är det*, 1961; Who was who, 6

Hammer, Richard Milton, born about 1940, he received a Ph.D. in 1967 from the University of California, Los Angeles, for *Spatial distribution of rainfall in the Sudan*. Selim

von **Hammer-Purgstall**, Joseph, born in 1774 at Graz, he studied at the k.k. Orientalische Akademie, Wien, until 1799 when he was appointed to a postition at the Austrian legation in Constantinople. In 1807 he returned to Wien from the East, after which he was made a privy councillor. For fifty years he wrote incessantly on the most diverse subjects and published numerous texts and translations of Arab, Persian, and Turkish authors. It was natural that a scholar who covered so large a field should lay himself open to the criticism of specialists, and he was severely handled by Heinrich Fr. Diez who, in his *Unfug und Betrug* (1815), devoted to him 600 pages of abuse. His other contemporaries, H. L. Fleischer of Leipzig, Gustav Weil of Heidelberg, Adolf Fr. von Schack of München, and Hendrik A. Hamaker of Leiden in his *Réflextions critiques sur quelques points contestés de l'histoire orientale pour servir de réponse aux éclaircissements de M. de Hammer* (1829), as well as later Johann Fück of Halle in his *Arabische Studien*, all published scathing comments on his work. His *Literaturgeschichte der Araber* (1850-56) prompted W. Ahlwardt in his *Chalef elahmar's Qasside* (1859) to a very critical view of Hammer-Purgstall as an Arabist. His other works included *Morgenlaendisches Kleeblatt* (1819), to its 1981 reprint Andreas Tietze added a twentieth century biographical sketch; Konstantin Schlottmann wrote *Joseph von Hammer-Purgstall; ein kritischer Beitrag* (1857). In spite of many faults he did more for Oriental studies in the German-speaking world than most of his critics put together. He died in Wien in 1856. ADtB; AnaBrit; Dawson; Egyptology; EncBrit; DtBE; DtBiInd (12); Fück, pp. 158-166; GdeEnc; Krachkovskiĭ; Magyar; Megali, 24 (1934), p. 454; NDB; ÖBL; OttůvSN; OxGer, 1986; Pallas; RNL; Wurzbach

Hammerschmidt, Ernst E. M., born 29 April 1928 at Marienbad, Bohemia, he was professor of Coptic studies at the Universität Hamburg since 1970. His writings include *Grundriß der Konfessionskunde*

(1955), and *Ethiopian studies at German universities* (1970). He died in a highway traffic accident at night, 16 December 1993. Kürschner, 1992; *Who's who in Austria*, 1996

Hammershaimb, Erling, born 3 March 1904, he studied Oriental languages under Johannes Pedersen at Københavns Universitet, where he received a Dr.phil. in 1941 for *Das Verbum im Dialekt von Ras Schamra*. He was successively a professor of Biblical studies at København, and a professor of Semitic philology at Århus Universitet. His writings include *Amos* (1946), *Some aspects of Old Testament prophecy from Isaiah to Malachi* (1966). He died on 8 February 1994. DanskBL; IntWW, 1989/90, 1990/91; Kraks; ScBInd

Hammond, Paul Young, born 24 February 1929 at Salt Lake City, Utah, he was a political analyst for the Rand Corporation, Santa Monica, Cal., and a lecturer. He held a variety of teaching posts at American universities before he became a professor in the Department of Political Affairs, University of Pittsburgh, a post which he certainly held from 1995 to 2000. His writings include *Organizing for defense* (1961), *Foreign policymaking* (1965), *The Cold war years* (1969), and *Changing bargaining relations in the Atlantic Alliance* (1973). ConAu, 1-4, new rev., 2; NatFacDr, 1995-2000; WhoAm, 1990-2003; WhoE, 1991/92; WhoFI, 1992/93

Hammond (Hamui), Robert, O.F.M., born 19th cent., he was the author of the booklet, *The Philosophy of Al-Farabi and its influence on medieval thought* (New York, 1947). ZKO

Hamon, Léo, born 12 January 1908 at Paris, he was educated at the École alsacienne and the Facultés des lettres et de droit de Paris. From 1930 to 1969 he served as a barrister in the Cour d'appel de Paris. Since 1959 he was a professor at a variety of French universities. His writings include *Les parties politiques africains* (1961), *Histoire politique du Tchad de 1900 à 1962* (1963), *Le rôle extra-militaire de l'armée dans le tiers monde* (1966), *Les grands problèmes de la nouvelle constitution hellénique* (1979), *Le sanctuaire désenclavé* (1982), and *Avant les premières raffles; les Juifs à Paris sous l'occupation* (1992). He died on 27 October 1993. Unesco; Master (1); WhoFr, 1953/54-1993/94; WhoWorJ, 1965, 1972, 1978

Hamont, Pierre Nicolas, born in 1805, he contributed to the development of veterinary industry in France and was invited to Egypt by the Viceroy to look after his studs and establish a school of veterinary science at Abu Zabel near Cairo. The Académie royale de Médecine elected him a foreign associate member. His writings include *L'Égypte sous Méhémet-Ali* (1843). He died in 1848. Hoefer; IndexBFr² (1)

Hamori, Andras Peter, born 25 November 1940 at Budapest, he graduated in 1961 from Princeton University and received his Ph.D. in 1965 from Harvard University for *A Study of the Semitic infinitive*. He taught at Brandeis University, Waltham, Mass., until 1967 when he was appointed a professor in the Department of Near Eastern Studies at Princeton, a post which he still held in 2004. His writings include *On the art of medieval Arabic literature* (1974), and *The Composition of Mutanabbi's panegyrics to Sayf al-Dawla* (1992). AMS, 11th ed. (1968), Social and Behavioral Sciences; DrAS, 1969 F; NatFacDr, 1995-2004

Hamp (Хэмп), Eric Pratt, born 16 November 1920 at London, he graduated in 1942 from Amherst College, Mass., and received a Ph.D. in linguistics in 1954 from Harvard University. Since 1950 he was associated in various capacities with the University of Chicago. His writings include *A Glossary of American technical linguistic usage* (1957), and its translation, *Словарь американской лингвистической терминологии* (Moscow, 1964), and *Themes in linguistics* (1973). He was honoured by two jubilee volumes, *Celtic language, Celtic culture* (1990), and *Festschrift for Eric P. Hamp.* (1997). AmM&WS, 1976 P; BlueB, 1973/74, 1975, 1976; ConAu, 17-20; DrAS, 1969 F, 1974 F, 1978 F, 1982 F; WhoAm, 1974/75-1998|

Hampel, Adolf, born 7 September 1933 at Klein-Herlitz, he was a professor of moral theology and Church history at the Universität Gießen. His writings include *Glasnost und Perestroika; eine Herausforderung für die Kirchen* (1989), *Mit den Beneš-Dekreten in die EU? Anmerkungen zum Verhältnis von Sudetendeutschen und Tschechen* (2000). In 1993 he was honoured by *Politik - Religion - Menschenwürde; Herrn Prof. Dr. theol. Adolf Hampel zum 60. Geburtstag.* Kürschner, 1980-2003

Hampson, Geoffrey, born 14 April 1927 at Bolton, Lancs., he was since 1962 a librarian at the University of Southampton and also associated with the Southampton Museums and Art Gallery. His writings include *Southampton, old and new* (1975), *Records of the University of Southampton* (1980), and he edited *Southampton notarial protest books, 1756-1810* (1973). WhoLib, 1972

Hămraev (Hamrajev), Murat K. *see* Khamraev, Maratbek Karimovich

Hamrin, Josef *Agne*, born 15 September 1905 at Jönköping, Sweden, he graduated from Lunds Universitet and became an editor and writer. His writings include *Diktatorns fall* (1944), *Storm över*

Palestina (1948), *Nilen stiger* (1952), its translation, *Der Nil steigt; das heutige Ägypten und der Sudan* (1953), and *Resa bland rebeller* (1954). He died 22 September 1983. Sezgin; *Vem är det*, 1953-1983

Hamson, Charles John, born in 1905 at Constantinople, where his father was a vice-consul in the Levant Service. Educated at Trinity College, Cambridge, and Harvad Law School, he was called to the Bar in 1929 but chose an academic career over practising law. From 1953 to 1973 he was a professor of comparative law at Cambridge. He was a joint editor of the *Cambridge studies in international and comparative law*. He died in 1987. ConAu, 124; DNB; *Who was who*, 8

Hamui, Roberto *see* Hammond, Robert

Hamy, Théodore Jules *Ernest*, born 22 June 1842 at Bologne-sur-Mer, France, he completed his medical study with a doctorate at Paris. A member of the anthropological laboratory of the École des hautes études, he was appointed in 1867 to the Egyptian commission of the Exposition universelle, and two years later participated in the ceremony of the opening of the Suez Canal and remained three months in Egypt studying its civilization. Since 1880 he was associated with the Muséum d'histoire naturelle, Paris, as a professor of anthropology, and with the Musée d'ethnographie as a director. He died in Paris on 18 November 1908. BN; *Bulletin de géographie historique*, 24 (1909), pp. 165-66; *Bulletin de la Société de géographie de Marseille*, 33 (1908), p. 388; Dawson; DBF; Egyptology; IndexBFr² (3); IntDcAn; Master (2); NUC, pre-1956

Han, Verena née Manč, born 4 September 1912 at Vukovar, Croatia, she studied at Zagreb and received a doctorate in 1959. She served for twenty years as a museum curator. Her writings include *Umjetnička škrinja u Jugoslaviji* (1961), Интарзија на поøручу Пеħке патријарµије XVI-XVII вијек (1966), and she edited *La Culture urbaine des Balkans, XVe-XIXe siècles; recueil d'études* (1984-1991). She died in Beograd on 8 December 1993. HBL

Hanauer, Edmund R., born about 1945, he received a Ph.D. in 1972 from the American University for *An analysis of conflicting Jewish positions regarding the nature and political rule of American Jews*. NUC, 19773-77

Hanauer, James Edward, born in 1850, he was educated at Jerusalem and Malta, and ordained in 1889. He became a missionary under the London Society for Promoting Christianity among the Jews. His writings include *Folk-lore of the Holy Land* (1907), and *Walks in and around Jerusalem* (1926). He died in 1938. *Who was who*, 3

Hanaway, William Lippincott, born 22 September 1929 at N.Y.C., he graduated from Amherst College and received a Ph.D. in 1970 from New York University for *Persian popular romances before the Safavid period*. He was a professor of Persian, and sometime chairman, Department of Oriental Studies, University of Pennsylvania. He was a joint author of *Reading nasta'liq; Persian and Urdu hands from 1500 to the present* (1994), and he was a joint editor of *Studies in Pakistani popular culture* (1996). For the *Unesco collection of representative works* he translated *Love and war; adventures from the Firuz shāh nāma*, from the Persian of M. b. Hasan Bīghāmī. DrAS, 1974 F, 1978 F, 1982 F; *MESA Roster of members*, 1982-1990; NatFacDr, 1995; Schoeberlein; WhoLib, 1966

Hance, William Adams, born 29 December 1916 at N.Y.C., he graduated from Columbia University, New York, where he was professor of economic geography from 1942 until his retirement in 1982. During this period he frequently conducted field-work in Africa. He was a founding fellow of the African Studies Association as well as a honorary fellow of the American Geographical Society. His writings include *The Outer Hebrides in relation to Highland depopulation* (thesis, Columbia, 1949), *African economic development* (1958), *The geography of modern Africa* (1964), *Population, migration, and urbanization in Africa* (1970), *Black Africa develops* (1977). He died about 1990. AmM&WSc,1973 S; WhoAm, 1989-90

Hancock, Geoffrey H., O.B.E., born about 1900, he was educated at Tonbridge and Magdalen College, Cambridge, where he was a scholar taking a First Class in the Natural Science Tripos. Joining the Sudan Political Service in 1925, he served in the BLue Nile, White Nile and Upper Nile Provinces as a *bimbashi* in the Sudan Defence Force from 1940-1942. In 1946, he became the Governor of Kassalla Province, holding the post until his retirement in 1950. After his retirement from the Sudan, he was appointed adviser to the ruler of Qatar in 1953, a post which held until the early 1960s. He died about 1985. *Asian affairs*, n.s., 16 (1985), pp. 357-358

Handjéri (Χαντζερης), Alexandre, born in 1759, he was a prince of the Palaeologue family and a *hospodar* of Moldavia from 1807 to his resignation in 1821, when he went to Moscow. His writings include *Dictionnaire français-arabe-persan et turc* (Moscow, 1840-41), a work which, according to Krachkovskiĭ, was disappointing as far as Ottoman Turkish was concerned - not to mention Arabic. He died in 1854. BN; GdeEnc; Krachkovskiĭ, pp. 151-52; Megali

Handley, Hester Mervin, born in 1902, she was an American artist who developed her art chiefly - although she studied in Italy and had two years of sculpture under Albin Polasek - through sketching on her travels, most often in the Orient, which she visited on three trips, totalling almost three years and covering Japan, China, Malaya, Cambodia, India, and Afghanistan. Note about the author; NUC

Handley, Leonard Mourant H., born in 1890, he saw service in southwestern Arabia during the first World War as an officer in the Indian Cavalry. He retired with the rank of major. He later explored the Nile and other out-of-the-way places. His writings include *African wanderings* (1923), *Hunter's moon* (1933), *Remote journey* (1939), and *Luxury tour* (1941). BLC; Note about the author; NUC

Handley, William J., born in 1920, he "served as U.S. Labor Attaché in the Middle East from 1945 to 1948. Based on Cairo, he was also attached to the diplomatic missions at Jerusalem, Beirut, Damascus, Baghdad, Tehran, Jidda, and Addis Ababa. In 1949, he was a labor economist in the Office of International Labor Affairs, U.S. Department of Labor". LC; Note about the author

Handžić, Adem, fl. 1952-1995. His writings include *Population of Bosnia in the Ottoman period; a historical overview* (1994), and he was joint editor of *Dva prva popisa zvorničkog sandžka* (1986). LC

von **Haneberg**, Daniel Bonifatius, born in 1816 at Lenzfried, Allgäu, a farmer's son, he studied at the Universität München theology, philosophy, Hebrew, Syriac, Persian and Arabic, languages which he had started to learn during his school days. In 1837, he was ordained, received a doctorate, and became a university lecturer. In 1850, he entered the Benedictine Abbey St. Boniface, and in 1854, he became abbot, retaining his academic post. A delegate to the Vatican Council, he was a member of the Commission of the Oriental Churches. King Maximilian II effected his nomination as Bishop of Speyer against Roman opposition. His writings include *Die religiösen Irrtümer der Bibel* (1844), *Geschichte der biblischen Offenbarung* (1850), and its translation, *Histoire de la révélation biblique* (1856). He died in Speyer on 31 May 1876. DtBE

Haneda, Akira, born in 1910, he edited *Ajia shi kōza* (Tokyo, 1955-57). NUC, 1956-67

Hänel, Gustav Friedrich, born 1792 at Leipzig, he studied law at the Universität Leipzig and subsequently travelled for seven years in western Europe but also in Greece, where he studied the sources of Roman law at the monasteries of the Aegean Sea. Upon his return to Leipzig he became a professor of law. In 1847 he visited Palestine. He died in 1878. ADtB, vol. 49, pp. 751-55; DtBilnd (2); Sezgin

Hanf, Theodor, born in 1936, he studied sociology, political science and education at Bonn, Paris, Beirut, and Freiburg im Breisgau, where he also received a Dr.phil. in 1966 for a study of the Lebanese system of education entitled *Erziehungswesen in Gesellschaft und Politik des Libanon*. He was associated with Deutsches Institut für Internationale Pädagogische Forschung, Frankfurt am Main, Arnold-Bergstraesser-Institut, and Universität Freiburg im Breisgau. His writings include *Der Libanonkrieg* (1976), *Koexistenz im Krieg* (1990), its translation, *Coexistence in wartime Lebanon* (1993), and *Georgia lurching to democracy* (2000). Kürschner, 1983-2005; Note about the author in der Orient; Schwarz; Wer ist wer, 1999/2000-2005/2006

Hanika, Horst Michael, born 20th cent., he was in 1979 a retired German army major. He was a joint author of *Bundeswehr für Anfänger und Fortgeschrittene* (Frankfurt am Main, 1998).

Hanisch, Ludmila, born 3 December 1947 at Bad Godesberg, Germany, she studied sociology at Frankfurt am Main and Berlin, where she received a Dr.phil. in 1987 for a study of Algerian opposition from 1830 to 1919 entitled *Resistente Traditon und angepaßter Fortschritt; zu den Formveränderungen der religiösen Legitimation des algerischen Widerstands, 1830-1939*. She was the single-parent of two boys from a North African partnership. She worked as a student assistant in the Institut für Islamwissenschaft, Berlin. After completing her degree, she worked for humanitarian organizations until she successively obtained research fellow-ships in history of twentieth century Islamic studies in Germany in the Institut für Orientalistik, Uni-versität Halle. Her writings include *Verzeichnis der Orientalisten-nachlässe in deutschen Bibliotheken und Archiven* (1997), and she edited *Islamkunde und Islamwissenschaft im Deutschen Kaiserreich; der Briefwechsel zwischen C. H. Becker und Martin Hartmann* (1992), *"Machen Sie doch unseren Islam nicht gar zu schlecht;" der Briefwechsel der Islamwisschenschaftler Ignaz Goldziher und Martin Hartmann, 1894-1914* (2000), and *Die Nachfolger der Exegeten; deutschsprachige Erforschung des Vorderen Orients in der ersten Hälfte des 20. Jahrhunderts* (2003). Private; Thesis

Hankel, Hermann, born 14 February 1839 at Halle, Prussia, he studied at the universities of Leipzig, Göttingen and Berlin, and since 1863 taught mathematics, particularly its history, at Leipzig, and since 1869, at Tübingen. His writings include *Zur Geschichte der Mathematik im Altertum und Mittelalter* (1874). He died in Schramberg, Black Forest, on 29 August 1873. ADtB, vol. 10, pp. 516-19; DcScB; DtBE; DtBilnd (1); GdeEnc; NDB

Hankey, Vronwy, born 20th cent., he was a joint author, with Peter Warren, of *Aegean bronze age chronology* (Bristol, 1989).

Hankin, Ernst Hanbury, born in 1865 he was educated at Merchant Taylors', University College, and Bartholomew's Hospital, London, as well as St. John's College, Cambridge. He also studied medicine at Berlin under Robert Koch, and at Paris under Louis Pasteur. Since 1892, he was a chemical examiner and a bacteriologist in the North West Province and Oudh, India. His writings include *Animal flight* (1914), *The Drawing of geometric patterns in Saracenic art* (1923), and *Common sense and its cultivation* (1926). He died in 1939. Buckland; IndianBiInd (3); Master (2); WhE&EA; *Who was who*, 3

Hanks, Robert Jack, born 28 June 1923 at Marysvale, Utah, he was a U.S. Navy officer who retired with the rank of admiral. He had served at sea in the Pacific and the Indian Oceans as well as in the Persian Gulf. From 1972 to 1975 he was a commander of the Middle East Force. WhoAm, 1989/90-1999|

Hanlon, Henry, born in 1862, he was a missionary in Kashmir and Kafiristan, and was a sometime Vicar Apostolic of Uganda. He died in 1937. Master (1); *Who was who*, 3

Hanna, Nelly, born 20th cent., she became associated with the Institut français d'archéologie orientale, Cairo. Her writings include *An Urban history of Bulaq in the Mamluk and Ottoman periods* (1983), *Construction work in Ottoman Cairo* (1984), *Les Maisons moyennes du Caire et leurs habitants aux XVIIe et XVIIIe siècles* (1989), *Making big money in 1600; the life and times of Isma'il Abū Taqīyya, Egyptian merchant* (1998), and *Money, land and trade; an economic history of the Muslim Mediterranean* (2002). LC; ZKO

Hanna, Paul Lamont, born in 1913 at Paisley, Ontario, he graduated in 1935 from George Washington University and received a Ph.D. in 1939 from Stanford University for *British policy in Palestine*, a work which was published in 1942. He was a professor of social sciences at the University of Florida, Gainesville. AMS, 11th ed., Soc. & Behavioral Sciences, 1968; AmM&WSc, 1973 S, 1978 S

Hanna, Sami Ayad, born 3 October 1927 at al-Fayyum, Egypt, he graduated from Ain Shams University, Cairo, and Hunter College; he received a Ph.D. in 1964 from the University of Utah for *Problems of American college students in learning Arabic*. He was a professor, and sometime associate director, the Middle East Center of the University of Utah. His writings include *An Elementary manual of contemporary literary Arabic* (1962), *Writing Arabic* (1965), and he was a joint author of *Arab socialism* (1969). DrAS, 1969 F, 1974 F, 1978 F, 1982 F; DrBSMES, 1993

Hannay, David McDowall, born in 1853 at London, he was a journalist and a sometime vice-consul in Barcelona. His writings include *The Life of Tobias George Smollet* (1887), *The Navy and sea power* (1915), *The Great chartered companies* (1926); he was a joint author of *The later Renaissance* (1897), and *The Iberian Peninsula* (1910). *Who was who*, 3

Hannezo, Cyr-Gustave, born 19th cent., he was a French lieutenant-colonel and in 1905 a commandant in the service of the Ministère de l'Instruction publique. He wrote about the archaeology of Roman North Africa; his trace is lost after an article in 1912. Note about the author

Hannig, Gerhard, born about 1905, he received a Dr.phil. in 1930 from the Universität Tübingen for *Landesplanung mit besonderer Berücksichtigung des mitteldeutschen Industriebezirks*. He was a joint author of *Umlaufmittel in den volkseigenen Industriebetrieben* (1955). GV

Hanning, Hugh Peter James, born 5 February 1925 in Barrow-in-Furness, Cumbria, he graduated in 1949 from University College, Oxford. He was a defence and diplomatic correspondent to a variety of British newspapers. From 1968 to 1970 he served as an editor of the *Journal of the Royal United Service Institution*. His writings include *Britain and the United Nations* (1964), *The Peaceful uses of military forces* (1968), and *Defence and development* (1970). He died on 5 May 2000. ConAu, 25-28, 188; Who, 1998-2000; WhoWor, 1976/77; WrDr, 1976/78-1984/86

Hannoyer, Jean, born 20th cent., he received a doctorate in 1982 from the Université de Paris V for *Campagnes et pouvoir en Syrie; essai d'histoire socio-économique sur la région de Deir-ez-Zor*. In 1989, he was associated with the Institut du Monde Arabe, Paris. He was a joint author of *Essai et secteur public industriel en Syrie* (1979), and he edited *Guerres civiles; économies de la violence, dimensions de la civilité* (1999). Livres disponibles, 2004; THESAM, 3

Hanotaux, Gabriel Albert Auguste, born 19 November 1853 at Beaurevoir (Aisne), France, he grew up at Saint-Quentin. In 1871, he went to Paris to take his degree in law, but he later pursued an interest in history. About 1878 he became a lecturer at the École des hautes études, and in 1879, he entered the Archives of the Ministères des Affaires étrangères. After his diploma from the École des chartes, he entered colonial politics in 1885 as an adviser to the legation at Constantinople. A *député* since 1886, he remained in public service until 1920, concurrently pursuing his journalistic and historical writing, including *Le partage de l'Afrique; Fachoda* (1909), *La guerre des Balkans et l'Europe, 1912-1913* (1914), and *Regards sur l'Égypte et la Palestine* (1929). He was a member of the Académie française since 1897. He died in Paris on 11 April 1944. Alf A. Heggoy wrote the doctoral dissertation, *The colonial policies of Gabriel Hanotaux in Africa, 1894-1898.* BioIn, 17; DBF; IndexBFr² (9); *Who was who*, 4

Hanoteau, Louis Joseph *Adolphe* Charles Constance, général, born 12 June 1814 at Decize (Nièvre), France, he graduated in 1834 from the Polytechnique, and decided to serve with the Engineers. After some years spent at Paris, he became a captain at the Engineers' headquarters in Alger. From 1846 to 1848 he served with the *service central des affaires arabes*. From 1853 to his retirement in 1876, he served in a great variety of capacities with the Bureau Politique, and the Bureau des Affaires Arabes in Algeria. His writings include *Essai de grammaire kabyle* (1858), *Poésies populaires de la Kabylie, du Jurjura* (1867), and *La Kabylie et les coutumes kabyles* (1873). He died in Decize on 17 April 1897. DBF; IndexBFr² (2),, Vapereau

Hans, Josef, born 8 April 1888 at Klagenfurth, Austria, he received a Dr.jur. in 1913. After the war he became a banker and journalist. Since 1926 he worked for the official Austrian news service and was temporarily posted to London and Beograd. After 1945 he was with the Carinthian provincial government. His writings include *Geld und Gold in Asien* (1930), *Währungswandel im Orient* (1933), *Aus der Finanzwelt des Islams* (1938), its Japanese translation in 1940, *Homo oeconomicus Islamicus; Wirtschaftswandel und sozialer Aufbruch im Islam* (1952), and *Dynamik und Dogma im Islam* (1957). He died in Klagenfurth on 15 August 1968. DtBE

Hansal, Martin Ludwig, born in 1823 at Groß-Tajax, Moravia, he started life as a school master at the Pfarrhauptschule zu Maria Geburt, Wien, and later entered the Katholische Mission für Zentral-Afrika under Bishop I. Knoblecher. After completing his linguistic studies, he left in the summer of 1853 for Khartoum to become a secretary and teacher in the mission school for negroes. In 1855, he went with Alfred Peney from Khartoum to the country between the Blue Nile and Atbara. From 1857 to 1859 he spent at the mission station in Gondokoro, before returning to Wien. In 1861 he accompanied Martin Theodor von Heuglin's Sudan expedition as a secretary, interpreter, and treasurer. A successor to the Austrian consul Dr. Natterer, he ascended the Nile together with Ernst Marno in 1874, and explored the country up to Lado. He was in Khartoum during the siege and was killed by the Mahdists in the massacre which followed the taking of the city in 1885. His writings include *Neueste Briefe aus Chartum* (1855), and *Fortsetzung der neuesten Briefe aus Chartum* (1856). Embacher; Henze; Hill; Wurzbach

Hansberger, Robert Vail, born 1 June 1920 at Worthington, Minn., he received university degrees from the University of Minnesota and Harvard University, Cambridge, Mass., and became a lumber executive. He was a sometime member of the U.S. President's Committee on Urban Housing. He died about 1990. BioIn, 7, 9, 12; IntWW, 1974/75-1992/93|; Master (8); WhoAm, 1974-1989/90|

Hansen, Bent, born 1 August 1920 at Ildved, Denmark, and married with an Arab. He studied at the universities of København and Uppsala and since 1947 taught economics successively at Uppsala, Göteborg, and Stockholm. His writings include *A Study in the history of inflation* (1951), *Finanspolitikens ekonomiska teori* (Uppsala, 1955), *Inflation problems in small contries* (Cairo, 1960), *Cotton vs. grain on the optimum allocation of agricultural land* (Cairo, 1963), *Development and economic policy in the U.A.R* (1965), *Egypt and Turkey* (1991), and he was a joint author of *Egypt* (1975). IntWW, 1974/75-2002; *Vem är det*, 1979-2001; WhoEc, 1981, 1986, 1999; WhoFI, 1985/86

Hansen, Donald Percy, born about 1930, he received a Ph.D. in 1959 from Harvard University for *Phoenician art in the middle Bronze age; the origins of the international style.* He was in 1995 a professor in the Department of Fine Arts, New York University. His writings include *Temple of Enlil, scribal quarter, and surroundings* (1967), and he was a joint author of *Inscriptions from Tell Abū Salābikh* (1974). NatFacDr, 1995

Hansen, Erik, born 20th cent., his writings include *Motoring with Mohammed; journeys to Yemen and the Red Sea* (Boston, 1991). ZKO

Hansen, Gerda, born about 1945, she was a librarian who was associated with Deutsches Orient-Institut, Hamburg, for many years. Her writings include several biliographical introductions or documentations, *Wirtschaft, Gesellschaft und Politik der Staaten der Arabischen Halbinsel* (1976), *Wirtschaft, Gesellschaft und Politik Ägyptens* (1977), *Jerusalem, al-Quds; Literatur zur Situation in Jerusalem* (2000), and *Medien und Informationstechnologie in der arabischen Welt; Literatur seit 1995* (2002). Private; ZKO

Hansen, Harry, born in 1950, he took courses in Islamic, social, and political subjects at Göttingen, Cairo, and Berlin. A man of roving disposition, he still had not completed his thesis in 2004, when he was resident in Berlin. Note about the author; Private

Hansen, Henny Harald, born 18 April 1900 at København, she was an anthropologist who was since 1944 associated with the Department of Ethnography at the National Museum of Denmark, København. She did field-work in Bahrain, Iran, Turkey, and Egypt. Her writings include *Mongol costumes* (1950), *Klædedragtens kavalkade* (1954), its translation, *Histoire du costume* (1967), *The Kurdish woman's life* (1961), *I skyggen af Kerbela* (1961), *Islam, den yngste af de store verdensreligioner* (1964), *Investi-gations in a Shi'a village in Bahrain* (1967), *Alverdens klædedragter i farver* (1976), and *An Ethnog-raphical collection from the region of the Alawites* (1976). She died on 12 October 1993. IntDcAn; Kraks

Hansen, Kurt Heinrich, born 10 October 1913 at Kiel, Germany, he received a Dr.phil. in 1943 from the Universität Berlin for *Der Aretban des Shahname*. His writings include *Sprüche und Verse der Araber* (1954), *Das iranische Königsbuch* (1955), and *Go down, Moses; 100 spirituals* (1963). He died in Hamburg on 14 August 1987. Hanisch; KDtLK, Nekrolog, 1971-98

Hansen, Olaf, born 11 April 1902 at St. Petersburg, he was educated at Hamburg, where the family settled after their emigration by way of the Baltic provinces. After four years of study at the Universität Hamburg he received a Dr.phil. in 1927 for *Reste einer sogdischen Übersetzung eines Dhāna-Textes des Britischen Museums*. A travel fellowship enabled him to spent 1933-34 in India. In 1936, he received a Dr.habil. for *Mittelpersische Papyri*. In the following year, he was appointed a lecturer in Iranian philology at Berlin and concurrently became a member of the Oriental Section of the Prussian Akademie der Wissenschaften. After the war he served successively as a professor at Humboldt-Universität and Freie Universität, Berlin. He edited *Berliner soghdische Texte* (1941). He died on 10 January 1969. Hanisch; *Iranistische Mitteilungen*, 4 (1970), pp. 34-40; Kürschner, 1961-66; Schwarz; *Wer ist wer*, 1963-1967/68

Hansen, Svend Aage, born in 1919, he received a Dr.polit.; his writings include *Adelsvældens grundlag* (1964), *Økonomisk vækst i Danmark* (1974) *Early industrialization in Denmark* (København, 1970), *Tyrkisk teorieparlør* (Fredensborg, 1978), *Velfærdstaten, 1940-78* (1980), and *Sociale bryd-ninger, 1914-39* (1980).

Hansen, Thorkild, born 9 January 1927 at Ordrup, Denmark, he studied literature at Københavns Universitet, and from 1947 to 1952 worked in Paris as a journalist. He joined several archaeological missions that took him to Kuwait in 1960, to the Sudan in 1961, and Guinea in 1965. His writings include *Minder svøbt i Vejr; en studie i Jacob Paludans Digtning* (1947), *Syv seglsten* (1960), *Det lykkelige Arabien* (1962), its translations, *Reise nach Arabien* (1965), and *La Mort en Arabie; une expédition danoise, 1761-1767* (1988) , and *Slavernes kyst* (1967). He died in France on 4 February 1989. CasWL; ConAu, 184; DcScL; DLB, 214 (1999), pp. 134-47; Kraks, 1988; WhoWor, 1974/75

Hanser, Oskar, born 20th cent., his writings include *Turkmen manual; descriptive grammar of con-temporary literary Turkmen* (Wien, 1977). ZKO

Hansman, John F., born about 1940, he received a Ph.D. in 1969 from the School of Oriental and African Studies, London, for *Urban settlement and water utilization in south-western Khuzistan and south-eastern Iraq from Alexander the Great to the Mongol conquest*. His writings include *Julfār, an Arabian port; its settlement and Far Eastern ceramic trade from the fourteenth to the eighteenth centuries* (1985). Sluglett; ZKO

Hanson, Albert Henry, born 20 April 1913 at Swindon, Witshire, he graduated from Jesus College, Oxford, and pursued a career in secondary school education before he joined the University of Leeds as a reader in public administration. He spent 1953-54 with the Türkiye Orta Doğu Âmme İdare Enstitüsü. His writings include *Man; an introduction to history* (1949), *The Structure and control of state enterprises in Turkey* (1954), *Public enterprise* (1955), *The process of planning* (1966), *India's democracy* (1972), and he was a joint author of *Studies in Turkish local government* (1955). He died in London on 27 April 1971. Au&Wr, 1971; ConAu, 5-8, 89-92, new rev., 4; Unesco

Hansson, Michaël, born 19 November 1875 at Christiana, Norway, he was from 1906 to 1931 a judge in the Mixed Court of Appeal, Alexandria, Egypt, and since 1928 its president. A member of the Société Fouad Ier d'économie politique, de statistique et de législation, he served from 1936 to 1938 as a president of the League of Nations' International Nansen Relief for Refugees. His writings include *Kunsten at Dømme* (1916), and *25 år i Egypt* (1946). He died in Lillehammer, Norway, on 5 December 1944. NorskBL²

Hansson, Steinar, born in 1947, he was a cultural affairs editor with the Oslo *Dagbladet*. His writings include *Øperasjon Libanon; en reportasjebok on Israels okkupasjon av Sør-Libanon* (1978), *Makt og mannefall* (1992), and he was a joint author of *Socialisme på norsk* (1981). LC; Note about the author

Häntzsche, Julius Caesar, born in 1824 Saxony, he studied geography and medicine and received a Dr.med. in 1850 from the Universität Leipzig for *De natura rabiei caninae*. He was a sometime Russian diplomat in Persia, where he was also a physician in Rasht. He spent seven years in the Caspian region of Persia. His writings include *Talysch; eine geographische Skizze* (1867). He died on 18 September 1901, aged seventy-seven. BioJahr, 6 (1901), Totenliste, p. 39*; DtBilnd (1); Henze

Hanway, Jonas, born in 1712 at Portsmouth, he lost his father when still a child. The family moved to London and he was apprenticed to a merchant in Lisboa in 1729. He had been in business for himself in London for some time when in 1743 he became a partner with a merchant in St. Petersburg, and in this way was led to travel in Russia and Persia. Leaving St. Petersburg in the autumn of the same year, and passing south by Moscow and Astrakhan, he embarked on the Caspian Sea in November and arrived at Astrabad in December. There his goods were confiscated and it was only after great privations that he reached the camp of Nadir Shah, under whose protection he recovered most of his property. His return journey to the Russian capital was marred by sickness at Rasht, attacks from pirates, and by six weeks' quarantine. In 1750 he returned to London, where the narrative of his travels, *Historical account of British trade over the Caspian Sea, with a journal of travels* (1853), its translation, *Zuverläßliche Geschichte der englischen Handlung durch Rußland* (1769), soon made him a man of note, and where he devoted himself to philanthropy. He died in 1786. R. Everett Jayne wrote *Jonas Hanway, philanthropist, politician and author* (1929). BioIn, 3, 4, 10; DNB; EncBrit; Gabriel, pp. 61-64; Henze; Master (5)

Happel (Happelio), Eberhard Werner (Everhardo Guernero), born in 1647 at Kirchhain, Hesse, he was one of the most prolific authors in an age of highly productive writers. He was a polyhistor who tried to include the full spectrum of contemporary knowledge in his fiction and non-fiction writings. His writings include *Thesaurus exoticoorum oder eine mit Ausländischen Raritäten und Geschichten wohlversehene Schatz-Kammer ... darauffolgend eine Umständliche von Türckey Beschreibung ... wie auch ihres Propheten Mahometi Lebensbeschreibung, und sein Verfluchtes Gesetz-Buch oder Alkoran* (Hamburg, 1888), and *Africanischer Tarnolas, das ist eine anmuthige Liebes- und Helden-Geschichte von einem mauritanischen Printzen und einer portugallischen Printzessin worinnen ... die Africanischen Sachen ... angeführt werden* (Ulm, 1689). He died in Hamburg in 1690. ADtB; BiD&SB; CasWL; DLB, 168 (1996), pp. 180-84; DtBE; DtBilnd (4); Meyers; OxGer, 1976, 1986; Sezgin

Happold, David Christopher Dawber, born 19 April 1936 at Salisbury, Wiltshire, he graduated in zoology from Cambridge University and received a Ph.D. in 1963 from the University of Alberta. He taught successively at the University of Khartoum, and the University of Ibadan. His writings include *Wildlife conservation in West Africa* (1971), and *Geographical ecology in Nigerian mammals* (1905). AfrBioInd (1)

Haq, A. K. Fazlul, 1873-1962 see Fazlul Haq, Abul Kasem

Harant z Polžic a Bezdružic, Kryštof, Freyherr von Polschiz und Weseriz auf Pezka, born in 1564 in Moravia, he was an Imperial Austrian chamberlain who in 1591 fought in a campaign against the Turks. In the late 1590s he visited the Holy Land and Egypt, returning in 1599. Siding with the losing party in domestic politics, he was decapitated in Prag on 21 June 1621. His writings include *Cesta z království Českého do Benátek, odtud do Země Svatí, Země Judské a dalé do Egypta* (1608), the translation from the Bohemian, *Der christliche Ulysses, oder weit-versuchte Cavallier, fürgestellt in der denkwürdigen Bereisung sowohl des heiligen Landes, als vieler anderer Morgenländischer Provinzen, Landschaften und berühmter Städte* (Nürnberg, 1678), and its partial translation, *Voyage en Égypte*, by Cl. and A. Brejnik (1972). Jan Racek wrote *Kryštof Harant z Polžic a jeho doba* (1970). DtBilnd (4); Martinek; Master (2); OttůvSN; Sezgin; OSK

Harari, Maurice, born 26 June 1923 at Cairo, he graduated in 1949 from Columbia University New York, where he also received his Ph.D. in 1958 for *The Turco-Persian boundary question*. He taught international affairs and government successively at Columbia, Dartmouth College, Hanover, N.H., and Fort Lewis College, Durango, Col. His writings include *Government and policies in the Middle East* (1962). American men and women of science, 1973 S, 1978 S

Harari, Ralph Andrew, born in 1892 at Cairo, he was educated at Lausanne, Switzerland, and studied at Pembroke College, Cambridge. He participated in the Palestine campaign in the first World War. In 1916, he was an inspector of finances in Egypt and a member of the Société sultanieh d'économie politique, de statistique et de législation. Like his father, he became a merchant banker in Egypt. He was awarded O.B.E. for his economic efforts during the second World War. He died in London in 1969. *Dictionary of national biography; Who's who in Egypt and the Near East*, 1952

Harber, Charles Combs, born 20th cent., he received a Ph.D. in 1970 from Ohio State University for *Reform in Tunisia, 1855-1878*. In 1973, he was associated with Haigazian College, Beirut. He later served as a professor in the Department of History and Government, Point Loma Nazarene College, San Diego, Cal., a post which he certainly held from 1990 to 1995. *MESA Roster of members*, 1990, NatFacDr, 1995; Selim

Harbison, Frederick Harris, born in 1912 at Sewickley, Pa., he graduated in 1934 from Princeton, where he also received a Ph.D. for *Labor relations in the iron and steel industry*. He spent all his academic career at his alma mater, interrupted only by ten years with the Industrial Relations Center, Chicago, as executive director. His writings include *Patterns of union-management relations* (1947), *Educational planning and human resource development* (1967), and he was a joint author of *Human resources for Egyptian enterprise* (1958). He died in 1976. AmM&WS, 1973 S; ConAu, 65-68; NYT, 8 April 1976, p. 40, cols. 2-3; WhAm, 7; WhoAm, 1974-1976

Harbord, James Guthrie, born in 1866 at Bloomington, Illinois, he was a U.S. Army officer who headed a mission to Armenia in 1919. His writings include *America in the World War* (1933). He died in 1947. ANB; BioIn, 1, 4, 10; CurBio, 1945, 1947; DAB; Master (1); NatCAB, vol. 36, pp. 493-94; NYT, 21 August 1947, p. 23, cols. 1-2; Shavit

Harbottle, Michael Neale, born in 1917, he was a brigadier-general of the British Army who gained prominence when he founded the Centre for International Peacebuilding. His writings include *New roles for the military; humanitarian and environmental security* (1995). He died on 30 April 1997. ConAu, 29-32, 157, new rev., 45; IntAu&W, 1989-1993/94; Who, 1982-1997; WrDr, 1976/78-1996/98

Harbron, John Davison, born 15 September 1924 at Toronto, Ont., he graduated in 1946 from the University of Toronto where he also received his M.A. in 1948. He first served three years as chairman of the Department of History and Economics, Canadian Services College, Victoria, B.C., and later became an editor and social service executive. His writings include *Canada and the Organization of American States* (1963). Canadian, 1970-2004; ConAu, 9-12; Master (2)

Harbutt, Charles Henry, born 29 July 1935 at Camden, N.J., he graduated in 1935 from Marquette University, Milwaukee, and became a photographer and an editor. His writings include *America in crisis* (1969). Master (5); WhoAm, 1984-2003; WhoAmArt, 1984-2001/2002

Härd, Berit (Bertil), born in 1936, she was a writer on social problems and the moral aspects of arms transfer to underdeveloped countries. Her writings include *Tonåringer behöver föräldrar* (Stockholm, 1982), and she was a joint author of *Hot eller hopp; kapprustning eller utveckling* (Stockholm, 1982), and *Jesus var inte svensk* (Stockholm, 1986). Note about the author

Hardan, David, born in 1926, he edited Martin Buber's *From the treasure house of Hassidism* (1969), and he also translated Latin-American works into Hebrew. Note about the author

Hardee, Joseph Gilbert, born in 1924 in South Carolina, he received a Ph.D. in sociology in 1958. He taught rural sociology, demography and social change in the U.S.A. and abroad before he became associated with the Ford Foundation. In 1975, he was an adviser to the Population Section of the Pakistan Institute of Development Economics, Islamabad. His writings include *Evaluation of an educational program with part-time farm families, Transylvania County, N.C., 1955-60* (1963). *American men and women of science*, 1973 S; Note about the author

Harden, Evelyn Jasiulko, born about 1935, she received a Ph.D. in 1966 from Harvard University for *Truth and design; on the historical novels of Jurij N. Tynjanov*. In 1995, she was a professor in the Department of Foreign Languages, Simon Fraser University, Burnaby, B.C. NUC, 1956-67; NatFacDr, 1995

Harder, Ernst, born 29 November 1854 at Königsberg, East Prussia, he was educated at Neuwied and Elbing, and since 1874 studied history and modern languages first at Leipzig and later at Berlin. He then spent some time in Lisboa as a private teacher with an English diplomat. In 1882, he received a Dr.phil. from the Universität Königsberg for *Der Einfluß Portugals bei der Wahl Pius VI.* He subsequently lived in Berlin as a journalist of the *Tägliche Rundschau* as well as a teacher of Spanish and Portuguese. It was only later that he pursued an interest in Arabic. He wrote the heavily used *Arabische Konversationsgrammatik* (1898), a work which was also translated into English and French, and went through numerous printings. His other writings include *Deutsch-arabisches Handwörterbuch* (1902). He died in Berlin before 11 October 1927. DtBiInd (1); Hanisch; Kürschner, 1926

Hardgrave, Robert Lewis, born 6 February 1939 at Greensburg, Pa., he received a Ph.D. in 1966 from the University of Chicago for *The political culture of a community in change; the Nadars of Tamilnad*.

In 1967, he was appointed a professor of government at the University of Texas, Austin, a post which he still held in 2000. His writings include *The Dravidian movement* (1965), *The Nadars of Tamilnad* (1969), *India; government politics in a developing nation* (1970), *The Politics of bilingual education* (1975), and *India under pressure* (1984). AmM&WSc, 1973 S, 1978 S; ConAu, 25-28, new rev., 11; NatFacDr, 1995-2000; WhoAm, 1984-1990; WhoS&SW, 1986, 1993/94

Hardie, Peter, born in 1942 in England, he graduated from Oxford University and was since 1967 a curator of Oriental art at the City of Bristol Museum and Art Gallery. He organized, and wrote the text, of *The Japanese eye exhibition* in Washington, D.C., 1985. His writings include *A Descriptive a catalogue of the permanent collection of netsuke and related carvings* (1981). Note; WhoWor, 1987/88

Harding, Allan Francis (John), Baron Harding of Petherton, born in 1896, he was a soldier, who retired with the rank of field-marshal, a banker, and from 1955 to 1957 a governor and commander-in-chief, Cyprus. His writings include *Mediterranean strategy, 1939-1945* (1960). He died in 1989. DNB; *Who was who*, 8

Harding, Gerald William Lankester, born in 1901, he was since 1936 director of the Department of Antiquities, Jordan, and a fellow of University College, London. His writings include *Some Thamudic inscriptions from the Hashimite Kingdom of Jordan* (1952), *The Antiquities of Jordan* (1959), *Baalbek; a new guide* (1963), *Archaeology in the Aden Protectorate* (1964), and *An Index and concordance of pre-Islamic Arabian names and inscriptions* (1971). He died in 1979. Who, 1957-1979; *Who was who*, 7

Harding, Henry Gladstone, born in 1867 at Hammersmith, London, he was educated at Caterham Congregational College and the London College of Divinity. He was a lecturer in Old Testament and Arabic at London College of Divinity, 1906; a member of the Faculty of Theology and the Board of Oriental Studies, University of London; assistant secretary of the Church Missionary Society, London, 1910; vicar of Nettlebed, 1920; and Clerk in Holy Orders, the Vicarage, Nettlebed, Henley-on-Thames, 1936. His writings include *The Land of promise* (1919). NUC, pre-1956; *Who's who in Oxforshire*, 1936

Harding, Lesley E. née Forbes *see* Forbes, Lesley E.

Harding King, William Joseph, 1869-1933 *see* King, William Joseph Harding

Hardinge, H. R., born 19th cent., he retired from the Indian Army with the rank of lieutenant-colonel and was in 1935 a representative of the Marcony Company in India. Note about the author

Hardy, Auguste, born in 1819, he was in 1848 a director of the Pépinière centrale in Algeria. His writings include *Catalogue des végétaux cultivés à la pépinière centrale du gouvernement à Alger* (Alger, 1850), *Instruction sur la culture du coton en Algérie* (1855), and *L'Algérie agronomique devant l'Exposition universelle* (1878). BN; Note about the author; NUC, pre-1956

Hardy, Georges, born 5 May 1884 at Esquehéries (Aisne), France, he entered the École normale supérieure, Paris, in 1904, received his *agrégation* in history and geography as well as a diploma from the École pratique des hautes études, and subsequently taught first at Bourges and then at Orléans. In 1914, he was appointed to a post in education in French West Africa, but soon had to return to France for war-time service. After his doctorate in 1920, he was called to Morocco by Maréchal Lyautey as a director gen-eral of public education, fine art, and antiquities. Since 1926 he was successively an efficient and inspiring director of the École coloniale, *recteur* of the Académie d'Alger, and the Académie de Lille. After spending the years of the war at Alger, he became a mayor of Jaulgonne (Aisne), where he died in 1972. He was a member of the Académie des sciences d'outremer, whose writings include his two theses, *La mise en valeur du Sénégal de 1817 à 1854* and *L'enseignement au Sénégal, 1817-1854* as well as *Les Éléments de l'histoire coloniale* (1921), *Histoire de la colonisation française* (1928), *Le Sahara* (1930), *Géographie et colonisation* (1933), *Le Problème religieux dans l'Empire française* (1940), and *Histoire de la colonisation française* (1953). DBF; *Hommes et destins*, vol. 8, pp. 187-189

Hardy, Peter, born about 1920, he received a Ph.D. in 1952 from the School of Oriental and African Studies, London, for *The treatment of history by medieval Indian Muslim historians*. His writings include *Historians of medieval India; studies in Indo-Muslim historical writing* (1960), *Partners of freedom and true Muslims* (1971), and *The Muslims of British India* (1972). Sluglett; ZKO

Hare, Raymond Arthur, born 3 April 1901, he had a long career in the Near and Middle East first as a teacher at Robert College, Constantinople, and later as a diplomat to many of the countries. He died on 9 February 1994. IntWW, 1974-1993/94; Master (8); MidE, 1982/83; Shavit; WhoWor, 1974/75-1982

Hare, Tom, born in 1895, he was a pathologist, and a sometime president as well as member of council, Royal Central Veterinary Society. He died in 1959. *Who was who*, 5

Harenberg, Johann Christian, born 28 April 1696 at Langenholzen, Lower Saxony, he studied Protestant theology, classical and Oriental languages as well as history from 1715 to 1719. He was a private teacher before he became the principal of the Stiftsschule in Halberstadt. In 1745, he was invited to Pteach church history and classics at the Collegium Carolinum, Braunschweig, concurrently serving as dean of the Schöningen monastery. His writings include *Historia ecclesiae Gandershemensis cathedralis ac collegiatae diplomatica* (1734), and *Pragmatische Geschichte des Ordens der Jesuiten* (1760). He died in Braunschweig on 12 November 1774. ADtB; DtBE; DtBilnd (15); Master (1); Sezgin

Ritter von Harff, Arnold, a Rhinelander, born in 1471, he went to the East from 1496 to 1499, travelling from Cologne to Egypt by way of Venezia, visiting the Sinai and Palestine. His testimony to have also travelled to Mecca, Celyon and Madagascar - all achieved at jet-like speed - must be regretfully rejected. But his Arabic glossary and idioms contained in his travel account attest the first part of his journey. He wrote *Die Pilgerfahrt des Ritters Arnold von Harff von Cölln durch Italien, Syrien, Aegypten, Aethiopien, Nubien, Palästina, die Türkei, Frankreich und Spanien*, edited in 1860 by E. von Groote, English translation published in 1946, and an Italian one in 1876. He died in 1505. ADtB; Bidwell; Fück, p. 31; Henze; Hill; NDB

Harfield, Alan G., born in 1926 at Gosport, Hampshire, he was a free lance writer whose writings include *British and Indian armies in the East Indies, 1685-1935* (1984), *Christian cemeteries and memorials in Malacca* (1984), and *British and Indian armies on the China coast, 1785-1985* (1990). IntAu&W, 1986-2001/2002

Harford, Frederick Dundas, born in 1862 and a graduate of Christ Church College, Oxford, he entered the British diplomatic service in 1885. He was a member of the Royal Geographical Society. He died in 1931. Britlnd (5); *Who's who*, 1908-1931; *Who was who*, 3

Hargreaves, Harold, born 29 May 1876, he was a sometime superintendent, Archaeological Survey [of India], Frontier Circle; from 1928 to his retirement in May of 1931 he served as director general of archaeology. His writings include *Handbook to the sculptures in the Peshawar Museum* (1930); he was a joint author of *Excavations in Baluchistan, 1925* (1929), and *The Museums of India* (1936). IndianBilnd (1); Riddick; ZKO

Haringman, Henrik, born about 1767, he was the son of the sea captain Jan S. Haringman, 1747-1811. In the service of the Staten-Generaal he accompanied his father in the spring of 1788 on a mission to the Sultan of Morocco to establish friendly relations, a journey which he described in his *Beknopt dag-journaal van een verblyf van agt weeken in het kaizerryk van Marocco en landreize naar Mecquinez gedaan in den jaare 1788, by gelegenheid eener Hollandsche ambassade* (1803), and its translation, *Tagebuch einer Reise nach Marocco und eines achtwöchigen Aufenthaltes in diesem Lande* (1805). He died in Anholt on 5 March 1806. NieuwNBW, vol. 3, cols., 543-44 Sezgin

Harington, John Herbert, born in 1764, he joined the East India Company's service at Calcutta in 1780, and became a revenue Persian translator in 1780; he was a sometime professor of law and regulations at the College of Fort William, and president of the Council of the College. His writings include *The Persian and Arabic works of Sâdee in two volumes* (1791-95), and *An Analysis of the laws and regulations enacted by the Governor general in Council at Fort William in Bengal* (1805-1817). He died in 1828. Buckland; DNB; Riddick; ZKO

Hariz, Joseph, born 19th cent., he received a doctorate in 1922 from the Université de Paris for *La part de la médecine arabe dans l'évolution de la médecine française.*

Harkabi, Yehoshafat, born 21 September 1921 at Haifa, he studied at the Hebrew University, Jerusalem, and Harvard. A company commander in the 1948 Arab-Israeli war, he was a delegate to the 1949 Rhodes armistice talks; in 1955, became army intelligence chief; and in the 1960s, was strategic adviser to the Israeli defence minister. After the 1973 war, he became one of the first Israelis to support negotiations with the P.L.O. Until 1988 he was a faculty member of the Hebrew University. His writings include *Arab attitudes to Israel* (1972), *Palestine et Israël* (1974), *Palestinians and Israel* (1974), *Arab strategies and Israel's response* (1977), *The Palestinian covenant and its meaning* (1979), *The Bar Kokhbar syndrome* (1983), and *Israel's fateful decisions* (1988). He died in August 1994 of bone cancer in a Jerusalem hospital. Bioln, 16; ConAu, 73-76, 146, new rev., 27; Master (1); Note; WhoIsrael, 1980/81; WhoWorJ, 1965, 1972, 1978WRMEA, 13, no. 4 (Nov./Dec. 1994), p. 110

Harkavy (Гаркави), Abraham (Albert) Elijah IAkovlevich, born 20 November 1835 at Novogrudok, Lithuania, he was educated at Vilna, Berlin, and Paris and received a master's degree in 1868 in Semitic languages from the Oriental Faculty, St. Petersburg, for *Сказания мусульманских писателей о славянах и русских*, a work which was published in 1870. He was since 1877 a librarian at the Imperial Public Library, St. Petersburg, where he made important contributions to the study of

Judeo-Arabic literature. His writings include *Altjüdische Denkmäler aus der Krim* (1877). In 1908 he was honoured by *Festschrift zu Ehren des Dr. A. Harkavy aus Anlass seines vollendeten siebzigsten Lebensjahres*. He died in 1919. Egyptology; EncJud; JewEnc; JüdLex; Krachkovskiï, pp.133-34; Wininger

Harlan, Jack Rodney, born 7 June 1917 at Washington, D.C., he received a medical doctorate in 1942, and became a professor of agronomy and plant genetics as well as a member of the Crop Evolution Laboratory, University of Illinois at Urbana-Campaign, where his private papers are now in the Archives. He was particularly interested in the countries of the Muslim East. A member of the American Society of Agronomy, his writings include *Plant scientists, and what they do* (1964), and *Crops and man* (1975). He died on 26 August 1998. AmM&WSc, 1972 P - 20th ed. (1998/99); BioIn, 6, 9, 11; IntWW, 1989-1997/98; Master (1); Shavit; WhAm, 13; WhoAm, 1974-1996

Harlan, Josiah, born 12 June 1799 in Newlin Township, Chester County, Pa., he spent 1823 to 1841 in India as a soldier of fortune and adventurer. He was the first American to reside in Afghanistan first from 1827 to 1829 and again from 1836 to 1839, this time with the specific assignment to organize the Afghan infantry. His writings include *A Memoir of India and Avghanistan* (1842), and *Central Asia; personal narrative of General Josiah Harlan* (1939). He died in San Francisco in October 1871. ANB; Master (2); WhAm, H

Harlech, William George Arthur Ormsby-Gore, 4th Baron, 1885-1964 *see* Ormsby-Gore, William George Arthur, 4th Baron Harlech

Harley, Alexander Hamilton, born 11 June 1882, he studied Oriental languages at Glasgow, Edinburgh, and Berlin, graduating in 1902 from Glasgow University. He taught Semitic languages at Edinburgh before he went to India in 1910 to become a principal of Indian colleges, mainly in Calcutta, until 1937. He was a sometime reader at SOAS, London. His writings include *Colloquial Hindustani* (1944), and *Teach yourself Urdu* (1955). He died in 1951. IndianBilnd (2); Who was who, 5

Harlez de Deulin, Charles (Joseph), born 21 August 1832 at Liège, he completed his law at the local Université, and in 1858, entered the Benedictine Order, serving successively as director of the Collège St-Quirin at Huy, and the École Normale des Ecclésiastiques at Louvain. Frail health obliged him to resign his functions in 1865 and retreat to Deulin, where he devoted himself to the study of Oriental languages until 1871, when he started a twenty-five year academic career as a professor of Oriental languages at the Université de Louvain, teaching both Iranian and Chinese subjects. His writings, ranging from the religion of the Eastern Tatars to the monuments of the Easter Islands, and to the crusades, include the translation, *L'Avesta* (1875), and *Manuel de la langue de l'Avesta* (1878). He died in Louvain on 14 July 1899. BiBenelux² (2); BioNBelg, vol. 32

Harlow, Samuel Ralph, born in 1885 at Boston and a graduate of Harvard and Columbia universities, he spent ten years as a missionary and college professor of sociolgy at the International College, Smyrna. His writings include *Honest answers to honest questions* (1940), and *Life after death* (1961). He died in Oak Bluffs, Mass., in 1972. ConAu, 1-4; NYT, 23 August 1972, p. 44, cols. 3-4; Shavit; WhAm, 5, 7

Harman, Zena, born about 1915 at London, she was a graduate of L.S.E. and settled in Palestine in 1940. For two years she was in charge of the Children's Section of the Social Welfare Department of the Jerusalem Community Council, and was later attached to the Head Office of Youth Aliyah. In 1956, she was an adviser for social affairs in the Israeli delegation to the U.N.O.; in 1965, a chairman of U.N.I.C.E.F.; and in 1969, a member of the Knesset. Note about the author; WhoIsrael, 1956/57-2001; WhoWorJ, 1965, 1972, 1978

Harmatta, János (John), born 2 October 1917 at Hómezővásárhely, he studied classical and Oriental languages, history and archaeology at Budapest University, gaining a doctorate in 1941 for *Quellenstudien zu den Skythika des Herodot*. Since 1948 he taught at the Institute of Greek Classics at Budapest, being appointed to the chair of Indo-European linguistics in 1952. An editorial member of several scholarly journals since 1950, his writings include *Avarok nyelvének kérdéséhez*, its translation, *De la question concernant la langue des Avares* (1988), as well as a Turkish translation in the same year, and he edited *Studies in the sources on the history of pre-Islamic Central Asia* (1979). BioB134; Biograf, 2002; Magyar; MagyarNKK, 1992-2000; WhoSocC, 1978; WhoSoCE, 1989

Harmsen, L. K., born 19th cent., he was in 1875 associated with the Gouvernment van Nederlandsch-Indië. His writings include *Bahoewa mit kitab peladjarau* (Batawi, 1875), *Inilah kitab edja* (Batawi, 1887), and he edited *Catalogus der tentoonstelling van landbouw, veeteelt en nijverheid te Batavia, 1893* (Batavia, 1893). His trace is lost after an article in 1905. Brinkman's; NUC, pre-1956; ZKO

von **Harnack**, Adolf, born 7 May 1851 at Dorpat (Tartu), Estonia, he studied at the Universität Leipzig. From 1876 to 1921 he taught history of doctrinal theology at Gießen, Marburg, and Berlin. Concurrently he was chief librarian of the Preußische Staatsbibliothek zu Berlin from 1905 to 1921. His writings include *History of dogma* (1896-1899), *Lehrbuch der Dogmengeschichte* (1900), *Geschichte der Königlich Preußischen Akademie der Wissenschaftern zu Berlin* (1900). He died in Heidelberg on 10 June 1930. AnaBrit; *Byzantion* 6 (1931), pp. 963-965; DtBE; EncBrit; *Who's who*, 1905; *Who was who*, 3

Harnack, Anna, Miss, born 19th cent., she was a missionary in South Africa until 1902, when she went to Kho'i, Persia, to serve under J. Lepsius' Deutsche Orient-Mission. Her writings include the booklet, *Der Kurdenarschak; aus dem Leben eines armenischen Knaben* (Groß-Lichterfelde bei Berlin, 1905). Her trace is lost after an article in 1920. Note about the author; ZKO

Harney, Desmond, born 20th cent., he spent from 1958 to 1979 in Iran first on the staff of the British Embassy and then as a London merchant banker. He was a sometime vice-president of the Royal Society for Asian Affairs. His writings include *The Priest and the king; an eyewitness account of the Iranian revolution* (1998). Note about the author

von **Harnier**, Wilhelm, born in 1836 at Eckezell, Hesse, he entered the army but soon had to resign for reasons of health. In 1856, he went to Egypt; and in the summer of 1857 he was in Lebanon. In 1859, he travelled up the Nile to Khartoum and continued to Er Rosieres. In December of 1860 he set out for the Upper Nile, passing Gondokoro to the cataracts at Teremo Garbo. Without any particular destination in mind, he camped at 4° N. on the western bank of the Nile intending to spend the rainy season. He keenly, but leisurely, observed scenery and natives, documenting everything in words, but more so in pictures. He was killed on a buffalo hunt on 23 November 1861. His wrings include *Reise am oberen Nil nach dessen hinterlassenen Tagebüchern*, ed. Adolf von Harnier (1866). Embacher; Henze; Hill; Sezgin

Harning, Kerstin Eksel, also known as Eksel-Harning, born in 1948, she wrote *The Analytic genitive in modern Arabic dialects* (Göteborg, 1980). LC; ZKO

Haron, Miriam Joyce née Siegel, born 26 April 1936 at Schenectady, N.Y., she graduated from Columbia University and the Jewish Theological Seminary and received a Ph.D. in 1979 from Fordham University, N.Y.C., for *Anglo-American relations and the question of Palestine, 1945-1947*. Her writings include *Palestine and the Anglo-American connection, 1945-1950* (1986). She became a professor of history in the United States. DrAS, 1982 H; Selim[3]

Harper, Prudence Oliver, born 23 May 1932, her writings include *The Royal hunter* (1978), *Silver vessels of the Sasanian period* (1981), she was a joint author of *Egypt and the ancient Near East* (1985), she edited *Essays on Near Eastern art and archaeology in honor of Charles K. Wilkinson* (1983), *The Royal city of Susa; ancient Near Eastern tresures in the Louvre* (1992), and she was a joint editor of *Monsters and demons in the ancient and medieval worlds* (1987). ZKO

Harper, Richard I., born 20th cent., he received a Ph.D. in 1966 from Emory University for *The Kalendarium regime of Guillaume de St. Cloud*. NUC, 1973-77

Harper, Richard Perceval, born 3 August 1939 at London, he studied at the University of Durham. He was a sometime assistant director of the British School of Archaeology in Jerusalem. Interested in historical archaeology of the Middle East, he did field work, with Islamic interest, in northern Syria and Israel. He was a member of the Société asiatique. Private

Harper, Robert Francis, born 18 October 1864 at New Concord, Ohio, he studied at the University of Chicago and at Leipzig where he received a Dr.phil. in 1888 for *Cylinder A of the Esarhaddon inscriptions*. His writings include *The Code of Hammurabi* (1904). He died in London on 6 August 1914. DAB; Master (1); NatCAB, vol. 22, pp. 98-99; Schwarz; Shavit; WhAm, 1

Harper, Stephen Dennis, born 15 September 1924 at Newport, Wales, he was a journalist and foreign correspondent as well as a writer of fiction and non-fiction. His writings include *Last sunset* (1978). ConAu, 97-100; IntAu&W, 1982-2004

Harper, William Allen, born in 1880 at Berkley, Va., he graduated in 1895 from the local Military Academy and subsequently gained graduate degrees from a number of colleges and universities. He taught classics and religious studies at a variety of institutions. His writings include *The New layman for the new time* (1917), and *The Church in the present situation* (1921). He died in 1942. Master (5); WhAm, 2

Harré, Horace Romano, born 18 December 1927 in New Zealand, he graduated in 1948 from the University of Auckland, and received a B.Phil. in 1956 from Oxford University. He subsequently served as a professor of philosophy of science at a number of British universities. In 1995, he was a professor in the Department of Philosophy, State University of New York at Binghamton. His writings include *An Introduction to the logic of the sciences* (1960), its Spanish translation in 1967, *Theory and things* (1961), *Matter and method* (1965), *The Philosophy of science* (1972), *Personal being* (1983), and *The*

Encyclopedic dictionary of psychology (1983). ConAu, 5-8, new rev., 2, 21; NatFacDr, 1995; WhoWor, 1976/77, 1987; WrDr, 1976/78-2004

Harrell, Richard Slade, born 13 December 1928 at Fort Worth, Texas, he received a Ph.D. in 1956 from Harvard for *The phonology of colloquial Egyptian Arabic.* Since 1956 he was a professor of linguistics at Georgetown University, Washington, D.C., and a director of its Arabic Research Program. His writings include *A Linguistic analysis of Egyptian radio Arabic* (1960), *Contributions to Arabic linguistics* (1962), *Short reference grammar of Moroccan Arabic* (1962), and he was a joint author of *A Dictionary of Moroccan Arabic* (1963), and *A Basic course in Moroccan Arabic* (1965). He died in 1964. *Linguistic studies in memory of Richard Slade Harrell* was published in 1967 by Georgetown University Press. DrAS, 1963/64 F; Selim

Harrell, Roger Herman, born 20th cent., he studied Arabic at Tunis, 1965-1966, and he received a Ph.D. in 1970 from the University of Southern California for *Domestic violence and indicators of social change within nations; a regional perspective.* His trace is lost after an article in 1973. Note about the author; NUC, 1968-72

Harries, Jeanette, born 7 August 1923 at Minneapolis, Minn., she received a Ph.D. in 1966 in linguistics and subsequently taught her subject from 1966 to 1974 at her alma mater. DrAS, 1974 F, 1978 F

Harries, Lyndon Pritchard, born 11 January 1909 at Port Talbot, Wales, he graduated from St. Catherine's College, Oxford, was ordained in 1932, and received a Ph.D. in 1953 from the University of London for *The form and content of traditional Swahili literature.* He was a missionary in Tanganyika, and a member of the Translation Committee of the British and African Bible Society; he later taught successively at London, Madison, Wisc., and Dar-es-Salaam. His writings include *A Grammar of Mwera* (1950), *Islam in East Africa* (1954), *Swahili poetry* (1962), *Poems from Kenya* (1966), and *The Swahili chronicle of Ngazija* (1977). AfrBioInd (3); DrAS, 1969 F, 1974 F, 1978 F; Unesco; WhoAm, 1974-1980

Harries-Jones, Peter, born in 1937, he was a sometime professor of anthropology at York University, Toronto, Ont. His writings include *Freedom and labour; mobilization and political control on the Zambian copperbelt* (Oxford, 1975), and *A Recursive vision; ecological understanding and Gregory Bateson* (Toronto, 1995). LC; Note about the author

Harrigan, Anthony Hart, born 27 October 1925 at N.Y.C., he studied at a variety of American colleges and became a reporter, editor, and a lecturer at Harvard, the National War College, and Vanderbilt University. He published the pamphlets, *Our war with Red China and Viet Nam in the U.N.* (1966), *U.S.-Soviet relations; a strategy for the future* (1980), and he was a joint author of *American economic pre-eminence; goals for the 1990s* (1989), and he edited *Putting America first* (1987). ConAu, 21-24; Master (1); WhoAm, 1980-2003

Harrington, Charles W., born 20th cent., he received a doctorate in 1950 from the Université de Genève for *The problem of disarmament in the United Nations.* In 1958, he was a political scientist with the Arabian Research Division of the Arabian American Oil Company. Note; NUC, pre-1956

Harris, Christina née Phelps, born in 1902, she graduated in 1925 from Barnard College, N.Y.C., and received a Ph.D. in 1930 from Columbia University under the name of Chr. Phelps Grant for *The Anglo-American peace-movement in the mid-nineteenth century.* She taught history, with special reference to the Arab world, at a variety of American colleges, including Bryn Mawr College, Pa.. Her writings include *The Syrian Desert; caravans, travel and exploration* (1937), and *Nationalism and revolution in Egypt* (1964). She died in 1972. DrAS, 1969 H; Master (2); NatCAB, vol. 57, pp. 210-11; Note about the author; NUC, pre-1956; WhoAmW, 1968A, 1970

Harris, Elizabeth, born in 1883, her writings include *Friends of the caravan trails* (1926), and she was a joint author of *The Friendly farmers* (1931).

Harris, Franklin Stewart born in 1884 at Benjamin, Utah, he was a professor of agronomy. He was from 1939 to 1940 an agricultural adviser to the Iranian Government, and in 1950, the chairman of a mission on technical assistance to Iran. His writings include *Principles of agronomy* (1915), *Scientific research and human welfare* (1924), *The Book of Mormon; message and evidences* (1953), and he was a joint author of *The Fruits of Mormonism* (1925). He died in 1960. Master (2); NatCAB, vol. 53, pp. 67-68; NYT, 20 April 1960, p. 39, col. 1; Shavit; WhAm, 4

Harris, George Kaufelt, born in 1887, he was associated with the China Inland Mission and spent at least ten years successively in Sining and Kansu. His writings include *How to lead Moslems to Christ* (1947). He died in 1962. Malcolm R. Bradshaw wrote *Torch for Islam; a biography of George K. Harris* (1965). Lodwick; NUC

Harris, George Sellers, born in 1931, he studied Turkish history at Harvard and Ankara Üniversitesi, and also served with the U.S. Department of State in Ankara from 1957 to 1962. In 1970, he was a lecturer in Middle Eastern studies at the School of Advanced International Studies, Johns Hopkpins University, Baltimore, Md.; and in 1990, he was a director of the Office for Near East and South Asia, Bureau of Intelligence Research, U.S. Department of State. His writings include *The Origins of communism in Turkey* (1967), *Troubled alliance; Turkish American problems* (1972), and *Turkey; coping with crisis* (1985). Note about the author; ZKO

Harris, Sir John Hobbis, born in 1874 at Wantage, Oxfordshire, he spent some years in tropical Africa first as a missionary and later as a traveller. In 1922, he became a Member of Parliament. His writings include the pamphlet, *South Africa; from the Cape to the Zambesi* (1928). He died in 1940. Who, 1921-1938; *Who was who*, 3

Harris, Lawrence, born 19th cent., he was a traveller and in 1910 a member of the Royal Geographical Society. His writings include *With Mulai Hafid at Fez; behind the scenes in Morocco* (1909). Note

Harris, Lillian Craig, born 30 April 1943, she received a doctorate and worked as a political analyst for the U.S. Department of State, as a teacher, journalist, and U.N. information officer. In 1993, she was an independent writer and researcher. Her writings include *China's foreign policy toward the Third World* (1985), *Libya; Qadhafi's revolution and the modern State* (1986), *Sins of fathers* (1988), *Egypt; internal challenges and regional stability* (1988), and *China considers the Middle East* (1993). DrBSMES, 1993; LC

Harris, Norman Dwight, born 25 January 1870 at Cincinnati, Ohio, he graduated in 1892 from the Sheffield Scientific School of Yale University. After studying a year at the University of Chicago, he spent three years at the universities of Berlin and Leipzig. He received a Ph.D. in 1901 from the University of Chicago. For the next four years he served as an instructor in history in Lawrence College, Appleton, Wisc. In 1906, he was appointed a professor of European diplomatic history at Northwestern University, Evanston, Ill. Ten years later, he organized the Department of Political Science at Northwestern, and remained chairman of this department until his retirement in 1928. His writings include *History of Negro servitude in Illinois* (1904), *Colonization in Africa* (1914), *Europe and the East* (1925), and *Moving on* (1939). He died in Daytona Beach, Fl., on 4 September 1958. BioIn, 5; *Journal of Asian studies*, 18 (1958/59), pp. 309-310; Master (3); WhAm, 5

Harris, P. R., born 20th cent., he received an M.A. in 1952 from Birbeck College, University of London, for *The letter book of William Clarke, merchant in Aleppo, 1598-1602*. Sluglett

Harris, Sir Percy Alfred, born in 1876, he was a Cambridge graduate and called to the bar from the Middle Temple. He travelled around the world three times and became a politician and parliamentarian. His writings include *Forty years in and out of Parliament* (1947). He died in 1952. DNB; WhE&EA; *Who was who*, 5

Harris, Walter Burton, born in 1866, he was educated at Harrow and Cambridge. He was a traveller who first went to Morocco in 1888 where he became known as a master of disguise, penetrating where no other European would have been safe. He even visited the fanatical Riff Mountain region. Bluffing his way in 1892 across the Aden frontier in the character of a Greek merchant was a child's play for him. He went by way of Qataba, Yerim and Dhamar to San'a and from there on to Manakha and Hodeida on the Red Sea. He later also visited Persian Kurdistan. His writings include *Tafilet* (1895), *From Batum to Baghdad* (1896), *Morocco that was* (1921), its translation, *Maroc disparu* (1928), *East for pleasure* (1929), *East again; the narrative of a journey in the Near, Middle and Far East* (1933), and he was a joint author of *Modern Morocco; a report on trade prospects with some geographical and historical notes* (1919). He died on 4 April 1933. Bidwell, pp. 172-174; Embacher; Henze; *Who was who*, 3

Harris, William Wilson, born 20th cent., he received an M.A. and Ph.D. from the University of Otago, New Zealand, and he was associated with the Australian Middle East Studies Association. His writings include *Taking root; Israeli settlements in the West Bank, the Golan, and Gaza-Sinai, 1967-1980* (1980), *The Christian camp on the eve of the 1988 Lebanese presidential elections* (1988), *Faces of Lebanon; sects, wars, and global extensions* (1997), and *The Levant; a fractured mosaic* (2003). Note

Harris, Zellig Sabbettai, born 12 October 1909 at Balta, Russia, he graduated in 1930 from the University of Pennsylvania, where he received a Ph.D. in 1934 and there subsequently became Benjamin Franklin Professor of linguistics. His writings include *The Ras Shamra mythological texts* (1935), *Development of the Canaanite dialects* (1939), *Structural linguistics* (1951), and *Language and information* (1988). AnaBrit; BioIn, 9; BlueB, 1973/74, 1975, 1976; CnDiAmJBi; DrAS, 1969 F, 1974 F, 1978 F; Master (1); WhoAm, 1974-1988/1989|

Harrison, Austin F., born in 1873, he was educated at Harrow, and with a view to the diplomatic service he studied languages and history in Germany, France, Switzerland, and Spain. He was a correspondent and editor, and a literary editor of *The Observer*. His writings include *The Pan-Germanic doctrine* (1904), *England and Germany* (1907), *The Kaiser's war* (1914), *Before and now* (1919), and *Pandora's hope; a study of woman* (1925), and he edited the journal *The English Review*. He died in 1928. BLC; *Who's who*, 1909-1928; *Who was who*, 2

Harrison, David Lakin, born 10 January 1926 at Sevenoaks, Kent, he was a physician who had trained at St. Thomas' Hospital, London, and received a Ph.D. from Cambridge University. He was a fellow of the Linnean Society, and the Zoological Society, London. His writings include *The Mammals of Arabia* (1964-72). Au&Wr, 1971; ConAu, 117; IntAu&W, 1989; WhoWor, 1976/77; WrDr, 1976/78-2004

Harrison, Frederic, born in 1831 at London, he was educated at Oxford, and became a writer, political activist, and an editor of the *Fortnightly review* as well as the *Westminister review*. A member of the Positivist Society and the Metaphysical Society, his writings include *Byzantine history in the early middle ages* (1900), *The Creed of a layman* (1907), and *The German peril* (1915). He died in 1923. AnaBrit; Britd (13); ConAu, 175; DLB, 57 (1987), pp. 119-129; DLB, 190 (1998), pp. 132-138; EncBrit; Master (27); *Who was who*, 2

Harrison, John Vernon, born in 1892, he received a Dr.Sc. in 1931 from the University of Glasgow for *The geology of some salt plugs in Luristan, southern Persia*. He explored in Persia, Central and South America. In 1940, he was a geologist in charge of the Geological Section of the Oxford University Museum. He was a sometime reader in geology at Oxford. He was a joint author of the geographical handbook of the Naval Intelligence Division entitled *Persia* (1945). He died in 1972. Sluglett; *Who's who*, 1948-1972; *Who was who*, 7

Harrison, Marguerite Elton Baker, born in 1879, she was a college graduate and became a journalist, traveller, and intelligence agent. She visited Russia, and also travelled with the Bakhtiyaris on their annual spring migration across the Zagros Mountains. Her writings include *Marooned in Moscow* (1921), *Red bear of yellow dragon* (1924), and *Born for trouble; the story of a checkered life* (1936). She died in 1967. BioIn, 14, 15; Master (3); Note about the author; Shavit

Harrison, Paul Wilberforce, born 12 January 1883 in a Congregational home-missionary parsonage in Scribner, Nebraska. He was a graduate of the University of Nebraska and Johns Hopkins Medical School, after earlier education at Doane College. He renounced a promising medical career at home to serve under the Arabian Mission in Kuwait, Muscat, Oman, and Bahrain between 1909 and 1954. His profession as physician gave him access to many homes, high and low, and many out-of-the-way places in Arabia usually jealously guarded against Christians. He was a fellow of the American College of Surgeons. Honorary degrees in science and letters were conferred on him by Hope College, Michigan, and by Yale University. As the greatest honour of all, in 1944, he was awarded the British Government's gold Kaiser-i-Hind medal. The last years of his life were spent as physician in charge of the Memorial Community of Christian Retirees at Penney Farms in Florida. In the midst of a busy schedule he died on 30 November 1962 after only a fortnight of illness. His writings include *The Arab at home* (1924), and *Doctor in Arabia* (1940). The story of his life is told by his wife, Ann Monteith Harrison, in *A tool in His hand* (1958). MW 53 (1963), pp. 263-264; Shavit

Harrison, S. S., born 20th cent., he received an M.A. in 1977 from Manchester University for *Kinship and relations of the production; aspects of marriage in the Middle East*. Sluglett

Harrison, Selig Seidenman, born 19 March 1919 at Pittsburgh, Pa., and a graduate of Harvard, he became a reporter and foreign correspondent, a managing director, and was associated with the Associated Press, the *New Republic*, and the *Washington Post*, serving as a chief of the New Delhi and Tokyo bureaux as well as a lecturer throughout the United States. His writings include *India, the most dangerous decades* (1960), *The Widening gulf; Asian nationalism and American policy* (1978), *In Afghanistan's shadow* (1981), *Superpower rivalry in the Indian Ocean* (1889), and *India and Pakistan; the first fifty years* (1999). ConAu, 85-88; WhoAm, 1974-1994|; WhoWor, 1974/75-1876/77

Harrison, Thomas Skelton, born 19 September 1837 at Philadelphia, Pa., he was a local manufacturing chemist who travelled widely. He was a sometime diplomatic agent and consul-general of the United States to the Khedivial Court of Cairo. His writings include *The Homely diary of a diplomat in the East, 1897-1899* (1917). He died in 1919. NatCAB, vol. 27, p. 99; Note about the author; Shavit; WhAm, 1

Harrison-Church, Ronald James, born 26 June 1915 at Wimbleton, Sussex, he taught geography at the University of London, from 1944 to 1977. His writings include *Modern colonization* (1951), and *West Africa; a study of the environment and of man's use of it* (1957). He died on 30 November 1998. Au&Wr, 1963, 1971; ConAu, 172, new rev., 99; IntAu&W, 1976, 1977; Unesco; WhoWor, 1976/77; *Who's who*, 1969-1999; WrDr, 1976/78-1988/90

Harrisse, Henry, born 28 May 1829 at Paris, he grew up in France and came to the United States when still young, and received a Ph.D. for *Dictionary of philosophical sciences*. After briefly teaching French, and his bar admission, he practised law first at Chicago and later in New York. In 1870 he settled in Paris as an American lawyer. Endowed with a difficult personality and unsociable, he was at variance with all the scholars he met. He left a great literary opus, including *Les Colombo de France et d'Italie; fameux marins du XVe siècle* (1874), and *Christophe Colomb devant l'histoire* (1892). He died in Paris on 13 May 1910. CnDiAmJBi; DAB; DBF; DLB, 47 (1986), pp. 115-122; GdeEnc

Harrow, Leonard William, born 20th cent., he received a M.Phil. in 1974 from SOAS for *A study of the imagery of the eleventh century panegyricist Azraqi of Herat*. He was a writer on rugs, whose writings include *From the lands of sultan and shah* (London, 1987); and he was a joint author of *Iran* (London, 1977-78); and he edited *Oriental rugs in private collections* (London, 1982). Sluglett; SOAS; ZKO

Harsch, Joseph Close, born 25 May 1905 at Toledo, Ohio, he graduated from Williams College, 1927, and from Corpus Christi College, Cambridge, 1929. He was for sixty years associated with the *Christian science monitor*. His writings include *Pattern of conquest* (1941), and *At the hinge of history; a reporter's story* (1993). He died on 3 June 1998. Au&Wr, 1963, 1971; BlueB, 1973/74, 1975, 1976; ConAu, 102, 181; IntAu&W, 1976-1991; IntWW, 1974/75-1998/99; WhAm, 13; WhoAm, 1974-1992; *Who's who*, 1959-1998; WhoWor, 1974/75-1978/79

Harshe, Rāmakrshna Ganeśa, born in 1900, he received a doctorate in 1938 from the Université de Paris for *Observations sur la vie et l'œuvre de Bhavabhûti*. His writings include *A Descriptive catalogue of Sanskrit MSS. of the Vinayak Mahadev Gorhe collection* [of the Deccan College Post-graduate and Research Institute, Poona] (1942). IndianBilnd (1); LC

Hart, Albert Bushnell, born in 1854 at Clarksville, Pa., he was a professor of history and government at Harvard, where his private papers are kept. His writings include *The Romance of the Civil War* (1903), and *The Obvious Orient* (1911). He died in Waverley, Mass., on 16 June 1943. ANB; ConAu, 116; DAB; DLB, 17 (1983), pp. 198-207; Master (30); WhAm, 2

Hart, Sir Basil Henry Liddell, 1895-1970 *see* Liddell Hart, Sir Basil Henry

Hart, David Montgomery, born 18 May 1927 at Chestnut Hill, Pa., he graduated from Princeton, and received an M.A. from Harvard. He spent four years in Morocco on fellowships, and one year in Pakistan. He became an independent researcher whose writings include *The Aith Waryaghar of the Moroccan Rif; an ethnography and history* (1976), *Islam in tribal societies* (1984), *Banditry in Islam* (1987), and *Qabila; tribal profiles and tribe-state relations in Morocco and on the Afghanistan-Pakistan frontier* (2001). In 1991, he was honoured by *Tribe and state; essays in honour of David Montgomery Hart*. ConAu, 136; *MESA Roster of members*, 1982-1990; Note about the author; Shavit; Unesco; ZKO

Hart, Douglas M., born 20th cent., he was in 1986 a defence analyst at the Pacific Sierra Research Corporation. He was a joint editor of *Northern Europe; security issues for the 1990s* (Boulder, 1986).

Hart, Ernest Abraham, M.D., born in 1836, he was educated at London and Queen's College, Cambridge. He studied medicine and in 1856 became a member of the Royal College of Surgeons of England. His writings include *On diphteria, its history, progress, symptoms, treatment and prevention* (1859), and *Masters of medicine* (1897). He died in London on 7 January 1898. DNB; EncJud; JewEnc; *Who was who*, 1; Wininger

Hart, H. Gascoigne, fl. 1929, his writings include *Eva Chenholm* (London, Heath Crauton, 1924). BLC

Hart, Parker Thomas William, born 28 September 1910 at Medford, Mass., he graduated from Dartmouth College in 1933, obtained an M.A. in diplomatic history from Harvard, and also earned a diploma from l'Institut des hautes études internationales de Genève. He then entered the foreign service in 1938 and was the first Arabic-speaking foreign service officer to serve as assistant Secretary of State for Near Eastern and South Asian affairs. He was a sometime director of the Foreign Service Institute and a director of the Middle East Institute, Washington, D.C. His writings in-clude *Two NATO allies at the treshold of war: Cyprus* (1990), and *Saudi Arabia and the United States* (1998). He died at his Washington home, 15 October 1997. IntWW, 1974-1997/98; *MESA bulletin* 32 i (1998), p. 138; MidE, 1978-1982; Shavit; WhoAm, 1972/73-1978; WRMEA 16 v (Jan./Feb. 1998), p. 62

Hart, W. E., pseud., he was one of Britain's military analysts during the second World War, and the author of various books on strategy, *viz. Landmarks of modern strategy* (1942), *Hitler's generals* (1944), and *Defence of the Middle East* (1945). Note about the author

Hartert, Ernst Johann Otto, born 29 October 1859 at Hamburg, he was an ornithologist who did field-work in East Prussia and subsequently joined Eduard Flegel's expedition to western Africa, 1885-86. He was successively associated with the zoological garden, Frankfurt-on-Main, Baron Rothschild's natural history museum, Tring, Herfordshire, and the zoological museum, Berlin. His writings include *Aus den Wanderjahren eines Naturforschers* (1901), and *Another ornithological journey to Morocco in*

1925 (1926). In 1929, he was honoured by *Festschrift Ernst Hartert zum siebzigsten Geburtstag.* He died in Berlin on 11 November 1933. DtBE; Henze; *Who was who,* 3

Hartley, R. G., born about 1938, he received a Ph.D. in 1968 from the University of Durham for *Recent population changes in Libya; economic relationships and geographical patterns.* Sluglett

Hartman, Joan M., born 20th cent., her writings include *Chinese jade of five centuries* (1969), and the two exhibion catalogues, *Three dynasties of jade* (1971), and *Ancient Chinese jades from the Buffalo Museum of Science* (1975).

Hartman, Sven S., born 17 June 1922 at Högbo, Gävleborg, Sweden, he studied philology and theology at Uppsala, where he received a Ph.D. in 1953 for *Gayōmart; étude sur le syncrétisme dans l'ancien Iran.* He was from 1953 to his retirement in 1983 successively a professor of history of religion at Uppsala, Åbo, and Lund. He was also a sometime lecturer in comparative religion as well as a high school teacher at Haparanda. His writings include *Syncretism* (1969), *Mysticism, historical and contemporary* (1970), *Parsism, the religion of Zoroaster* (1980), and he was a joint author of *Vad funderar barn på?* (1973). He died on 2 April 1988. *Vem är det,* 1971-1991; ZKO

Hartmann, Anastasius, born Joseph Alois H. on 24 February 1803 at Altwis, Kanton Luzern, he entered the Capuchin friars in 1821 and was ordained in 1825. He served from 1826 to 1841 as a master of novices, lecturer in philosophy and theology as well as other capacities at Freiburg and Solothurn. He subsequently trained at the Capuchin missionary college in Roma, reaching Agra, India, in March 1844. He was appointed in 1845 Apostolic vicar of Patna and later titular bishop of Derbe. He built churches, schools, and orphanages. In 1849, he became Apostolic administrator in Bombay. He spent his last six years working at Patna, where he completed his translation of the Catholic New Testament into Urdu, noticing that the existing Protestant translations were useless in so far as they contained too many Arabic and Persian words, the meaning of which eluded the common people. His writings include *Monumenta Anastasiana* (1939-1948). He died in Patna on 24 April 1866. Adrian Imhof wrote *Anastasius Hart-mann von Hitzkirch, Kanton Luzern* (1903). DtBE; HisBioLexCH

Hartmann, Angelika, born 3 December 1944 at Kassel, Germany, she studied Islamic subjects at Göttingen, Hamburg, and Istanbul, gaining a Dr.phil. in 1971 for *An-Nāsir li-Dīn Allāh, 1180-1225; Politik, Religion, Kultur in der späten 'Abbāsidenzeit* (1975), and a Dr.habil. in 1982. She became successively a professor of Arabic and Islamic studies at the universities of Saarbrücken, Würzburg, and Gießen. Her writings include *Angewandte interdisziplinäre Orientforschung; Stand und Perspektiven im westlichen und östlichen Deutschland* (1991), and *Umar as-Suhrawardīs Streitschrift gegen die Philosophie* (2003). Kürschner, 1996-2003; Private; Schwarz

Hartmann, Anton Theodor, born 25 June 1774 at Düsseldorf, he studied Protestant theology and Oriental languages at Göttingen, 1793-96, and was employed as a private tutor in Düsseldorf, and served as an assistant principal at a number of schools until 1811. On the recommendation of his former professor, J. G. Eichhorn, he was in 1811 appointed a professor of theology at the Universität Rostock, concurrently serving since 1818 as director of the local numismatic cabinet. His writings include *Die asiatische Perlenschnur oder die schönsten Blumen des Morgenlandes* (1800-1801), *Morgenländische Blütenlese* (1802), *Aufklärung über Asien für Bibelforscher, Freunde der Kulturgeschichte und Verehrer der morgenländischen Literatur* (1806-1807), and he translated *Die hellstrahlenden Plejaden am arabischen poetischen Himmel, oder die sieben im Tempel zu Mekka aufgehangenen arabischen Gedichte* (1802). He died in Rostock on 20 April 1838. DtBE; *der Islam,* 54 (1977), pp. 133-35

Hartmann, Carl Eduard *Robert*, born in 1832 at Blankenburg, he was an anthropologist and ethnographer who in 1859 accompanied Baron A. von Barnim on an expedition to Khartoum and up the Blue Nile River to Fāzūghlī. His writings include *Reise des Freiherrn Adalbert von Barnim durch Nord-Ost-Afrika in den Jahren 1859 und 1860* (1863), and *Abessynien und die übrigen Gebiete der Ostküste Afrikas* (1883). He died in 1893. DtBiInd (2); Embacher; Henze; Hill

Hartmann, Hans Jürgen, born 26 March 1933 at Berlin, he trained as a library assistant and subsequently studied Romance languages, history, and education at Humboldt-Universität, Berlin, where he received a Dr.phil. for *L'Homme de guerre; Aspekte der Figurenwahl bei der Darstellung des Algerienkrieges und bei der Ausbildung imperialistischer Massenliteratur.* Since 1962 he was in charge of the library of the Institut für Romanistik at his alma mater. Kürschner, 1996; Thesis

Hartmann, Hans Walter, born in 1905, he received a Dr.phil. in 1930 from the Universität Zürich for *Korsika zur Zeit der französischen Revolution.* His other writings include *Die auswärtigen Politik der Türkei* (Zürich, 1941), and *Südafrika; Geschichte, Wirtschaft, Politik* (Stuttgart, 1968).

Hartmann, Johannes, born about 1905, he received a Dr.phil. in 1933 from Philosophische Fakultät, Universität Jena, for his prize-essay, *Die Persönlichkeit des Sultans Saladin im Urteil der abend-ländischen Quellen*. GV

Hartmann, Johann(es) Melchior, born 20 February 1764 at Nördlingen, Bavaria, he studied theology and Semitic languages at Jena and Göttingen. In 1793, he was appointed a professor of philosophy and Oriental languages at the Universität Marburg. Since 1819 he served also as a librarian. He was a joint editor of *Allgemeine Bibliothek der biblischen Wissenschaften*, and *Museum für biblische und orientalische Literatur*. His own writings include *Commentatio de geographia Africa Edrisiana* (1791), *Anfangsgründe der hebraeischen Sprache* (1798), *Erdbeschreibung und Geschichte von Afrika; Band 1, Das Paschalik Aegypten* (1799), and *Edrisii Hispaniae*, pt. 1-3 (1802-1818). He died in Marburg on 16 February 1827. ADtB, vol. 10, p. 687; DtBE; DtBiInd (6); GV; NUC

Hartmann, Joseph Alois, 1803-1866 *see* Hartmann, Anastasius

von **Hartmann**, Julius Hartwig Friedrich, born 2 March 1817 at Hannover, he joined the hussars in 1834, and studied at the war college from 1839 to 1842. Since 1844 he was attached to the topographic bureau; he transferred in 1847 to the high command of the army. An officer in the general staff since 1849, he participated in the Baden campaign, and became commander of a regiment in 1857. Since 1860 he was a member of the ministry of war in Berlin. A lieutenant-general since 1867, he participated in the Franco-Prussian war, 1870-71, and became governor of Straßburg. He resigned in 1875 with the rank of general of the cavalry. He died in Baden-Baden on 30 April 1878. ADtB, vol. 10, pp. 691-96; DtBE

Hartmann, Martin, born 9 December 1851 at Breslau, Prussia, he studied Oriental languages at Leipzig and served first with the German consulate general at Beirut from 1876 to 1887 as an interpreter, and then until his death at the Seminar für Orientalische Sprachen, Berlin, as a professor. He was a founding member of Deutche Gesellschaft für Islamkunde, 1912, as well as the periodical, *Welt des Islams*. His writings include *Chinesisch Turkestan* (1908), and *Der islamische Orient* (1899-1909). He died in Berlin on 5 December 1918. DtBE; Fück, p. 269; Hanisch; *Index Islamicus* (2)

Hartmann, Nils, born 20th cent., he was a joint author of *Sudan; stepperegionen* (København, 1978).

Hartmann, Regina, born about 1945, she received a Dr.phil. in 1974 from the Universität Erlangen for *Untersuchungen zur Syntax der arabischen Schriftsprache; eine generativ-transformationelle Dar-stellung*. ZKO

Hartmann, Richard, born 8 June 1881 at Neunkirchen bei Eberbach, Baden, he received a religious education and studied at Tübingen and Berlin and received a Dr.phil. in 1907 for *Die geographischen Nachrichten über Palästina und Syrien in Halīl az-Zāhirī's Zubdat kašf al-mamālik*, and a Dr.habil. in 1914 for *Das Sufitum nach al-Kuschairi*. He was a professor successively at Leipzig, Königsberg, Heidelberg, Göttingen, and Berlin. His writings include *Die Religion des Islam* (1944). He died in Berlin on 5 February 1965. DtBE; DtInd (1); Kürschner, 1926-1961; Schwarz; *Wer ist's*, 1928, 1935

Hartmann, Robert, 1832-1893 *see* Hartmann, Carl Eduard Robert

Hartmann, Walter, born 22 September 1889 at Pirna, Saxony, he studied at München and Jena, where he received a Dr.phil. in 1916 for *Der Mohn, seine Kultur, Geschichte und geographische Verbreitung*. Sezgin

Hartner, Willy, born 22 January 1905 at Ennigerloh/Westfalen, he studied natural sciences, particularly chemistry and astronomy, at Frankfurt am Main, where received a doctorate in 1928. From 1935 to 1938 he was a visiting professor at Harvard, where he came in contact with George Sarton. After his return to Frankfurt, he became a lecturer in 1940, and in 1943 he was instrumental in the establishment of the Institut für Geschichte der Naturwissenschaften. He was a sometime rector of the Universität Frankfurt. His writings include *Oriens - Occidens* (1968), he was a joint author of *Katalog der orientalischen und lateinischen Originalhandschriften, Abschriften und Photokopien des Instituts für Geschichte der Medizin und der Naturwissenschaften in Berlin* (1939), and he was a joint editor of *Klassizismus und Kulturverfall* (1960). He died in Bad Homburg on 16 May 1981. BioIn, 9, 13; DtBE; EncIran; Hanisch; IntWW, 1974/75-1981; *Journal for the history of Arabic science*, vol. 5, nos 1 & 2 (1981), pp. 109-110; Kürschner, 1961-1980; *Wer ist wer*, 1967/68-1979; WhoWor, 1974/75-1978/79

de **Hartog**, Leo, born 20th cent., he was a Dutch specialist in Mongol history, whose writings include *Djenghis Khan, conqueror of the world* (1979), and *Russia and the Mongol yoke; the history of the Russian principalities and the Golden Horde, 1221-1502* (1996). Note about the author; ZKO

Hartshorn, Jack Ernest, born 20th cent., he was a consultant in oil and energy matters at Walter I. Levy S.A. His writings include *Oil companies and governments* (1962), *Erdöl zwischen Mächten und Märkten* (1964), and *Oil trade; politics and prospects* (1993).

Hartvig, Torben, born 20th cent., he was a joint author of *Sudan; stepperegionen* (København, 1978).

Hartwig, Charles Walter, born 15 December 1941 at St. Charles, Mo., he graduated in 1964 from Southern Illinois University, and received a Ph.D. in 1975 from the University of Kentucky for *Health policies and national development in Kenya*. He spent two years in the U.S. Peace Corps in Liberia, and a year as a volunteer hospital administrator in Kenya. He was an assistant professor of political science at Arkansas State University, before he was appointed a professor in the Department of Political Science, Arizona State University, a post which he still held in 2000. AmM&WSc, 1978 S; Note about the author; WhoEmL, 1987/88; WhoS&SW, 1986, 1993/94

Hartwig, Otto, born 16 November 1830 at Wochmannshausen, Lower Hesse; in obedience to his father's wishes he studied theology. He became a librarian successively at Marburg and Halle/Saale; he established the *Zentralblatt für Bibliothekswesen*. His writings include *Ludwig Bamberger; eine biographische Skizze* (1900), *Aus dem Leben eines deutschen Bibliothekars; Erinnerungen und biographische Aufsätze* (1906), and he edited *Festschrift zum fünfhundertjährigen Geburtstage von Johann Gutenberg* (1900). He died in 1903. Note about the author

Hartzell, Joseph Crane, born 1 June 1842 at Moline, Ill., he was a graduate of Illinois Wesleyan University and Garrett Biblical Institute, Evanstone, Ill., and ordained in 1868. He was engaged in the race-adjustment in the American South until 1896 when he was consecrated missionary bishop for Africa. He served for twenty years, particularly in Liberia. His writings include *The African Mission of the Methodist Episcopal Church* (1909). On his eighty-sixth birthday he was assaulted by robbers in his home at Blue Ash, Ohio, and died 6 September 1928 from the effects of his injuries. DAB; Shavit - Africa; WhAm, 1

Harvey, Alexander, born in 1868 at Bruxelles, he came to America when still a child. He was a reporter, foreign editor, and Sunday editor. From 1898 to 1899 he was a diplomatic agent and counsel-general of the United States in Egypt. His writings include *Essays on Sophocles* (1923), *Essays on Euripides* (1923, and *Essays on Jesus* (1924). He died in 1949. Master (7); NYT, 21 November 1949, p. 25, col. 3; WhAm, 2

Harvey, David, born 20th cent., his writings include *Spoken Arabic* (London, 1979).

Harvey, Donald Joseph, born 4 October 1922 at N.Y.C., he graduated in 1943 from Princeton University, and received a Ph.D. in 1954 from Columbia University, N.Y.C., for *French concepts of military strategy, 1919-1939*. From 1951 until his retirement he was a professor of history at Hunter College, C.U.N.Y. His writings include *France since the Revolution* (1968). ConAu, 41-44; DrAS, 1969 H, 1974 H, 1978 H, 1982 H; WhoAm, 1974-1994

Harvey, Godfrey Eric, born 13 April 1889 at London, he was educated at the University of London, and Exeter College, Oxford. He entered the Indian Civil Service in 1912 and retired in 1935, when he became a lecturer in Burmese at Oxford. His writings include *History of Burma from the earliest times to 10 March 1824, the beginning of the British conquest* (1925). IndianBilnd (2); WhE&EA

Harvey, James, born 20th cent., he was associated with the University of East Anglia, Norwich; he was a joint author of *Subsistence farming in the dry savanna of western Sudan* (1977). Note about the author

Harvey, John Frederick, born 21 August 1921 at Maryville, Mo., he graduated in 1943 from Dartmouth College, and received a Ph.D. in 1949 from the University of Chicago. He was a librarian in a variety of capacities, cataloguer, reference librarian, chief librarian, professor of library science, and university administrator. From 1958 to 1971 he established a library system in Tehran, including the Iranian Documentation Centre, and the Book Processing Centre. His writings include *The Librarian's career; a study in mobility* (1957), *Report to Chancellor Torab Mehra covering recommendations for the development of Jundi Shapur University library services* (1968), and he edited *Comparative and international library science* (1977), and *Proceedings of the Southwest Asian Documentation Centre Conference* (1970). ConAu, 13-16, new rev., 8, 23; WhoLibS, 1955, 1966; WrDr, 1984/86-2004

Harvey, John Henry, aftwards John H. Barrington, he was an agent of the Secret Service of the French Foreign Legion in Tunis and Syria. His writings include *The Hell hounds of France* (1932), *With the Secret Service in Morocco* (1933), *The Arab patrol*, by ex-légionnaire 1384 (1935), and *The Devil's diplomats* (1935). BLC; NUC, pre-1956

Harvey, John Hooper, born 25 May 1911 at London, he was educated at Regent Street Polytechnic. He was a registered architect and worked in a variety of capacities at London and Jerusalem. He also served as a lecturer in conservation and restauration of medieval monuments. His writings include *The Plantagenets* (1948), *English medieval architects* (1954), *Early gardening catalogues* (1972), *Early horticultural catalogues* (1973), *Early Nurserymen* (1974), *The Black Prince and his age* (1976), and *Restoring period gardens, from the Middle Ages to Georgian times* (1988). ConAu, 5-8, new rev., 6, 21

Harvey, Leonard Patrick, born 29 February 1929, he graduated in modern languages in 1952 from Magdalen College, Oxford, and in 1954, in Oriental studies, and received a D.Phil. in 1958 for *The literary culture of the Moriscos, 1492-1608*. He taught Spanish at Queen Mary College, London, 1960-1973, and the subssequent twenty years until retirement at King's College, London. His writings include *Islamic Spain, 1250-1500* (1990), in the same year he was honoured by the publication, *Cultures in contact in medieval Spain.* Master (1); Sluglett; Who's who, 1974-2004

Harvey, Mary Frances, born 4 October 1911 at Orviston, Pa., she graduated in 1936 from Lock Haven State College and received her library degree in 1939 from Drexel University. She was a librarian in Pennsylvania. BiDrLUS, 1970

Harvey, Paul Dean Adshead, born 7 May 1930, he was educated at St. John's College, Oxford, where he also received a Ph.D. in 1960. An archivist until 1966, he successively taught medieval economy and social history at the universities of Southampton and Durham. His writings include *A Medieval Oxford village, Cuxham, 1240 to 1400* (1965), *The History of topographical maps* (1980), and *Mappa mundi; the Hereford world map* (1996). ConAu, 112; WrDr, 1982/84-20004

Harweg, Roland, born 20 August 1934 at Dortmund, Germany, he received a Dr.phil. in 1961 and a Dr.habil. in 1965, and subsequently became a professor of linguistics at the Universität Bochum. His writings include *Pronomica und Textkonstitution* (1979), *Studien zur Deixis* (1990), *Situation und Text im Drama* (2001), and *Sekundäre Unbestimmtheit* (2003). In 1994 he was honoured by *Text und Grammatik; Festschrift für Roland Harweg zum 60. Geburtstag.* Kürschner, 1970-2003

Hasak, Maximilian F. J., born 15 February 1856 at Wansen, Silesia, he studied from 1876 to 1880 at the Bauakademie, Berlin, and subsequently joined the Museum für Völkerkunde, Berlin. He later planned and built banks, churches, and museums. His writings include *Geschichte der deutschen Bildhauerkunst im XIII. Jahrhundert* (1899), and *Einzelheiten des Kirchenbaues* (1903). He died in Berlin on 14 September 1934. DtBE; Kosch; Sezgin

Hasan, Zakī Muhammad, 1908-1957 *see* Hasssan Zaky Mohamed

Hasandedić, Hivzija, born 1 July 1915 at Jablanici, his writings include *Katalog arapskih, turskih i perzijskih rukopisa* (Mostar, Arhiv Hercegovine, 1977), *Spomenici kulture turskog doba u Mostaru* (Sarajevo, 1980), and *Muslimanska bastina u istocnoj Hercegovini* (Sarajevo, 1990). KoBošnjaka, 2000; OSK

Hăsănov (həcəнов), I. M. *see* Gasanov, I. M.

Haschmi, Mohammed Jahia, 1903- *see* al-Hāshimī, Muhammad Yahyá

Hase, Christian Heinrich, born about 1730, he studied theology at the Universität Jena and became a pastor at Stadt-Sulze. In 1780, he was a superintendent at Altstädt, Thuringia. His writings include *De anima humana non medii generis inter simplicam et compositam substantiam* (Jena, 1756), *De lingva Carnorvm et Illyricorvm slavonica castiorbvs nostrativm sacris initiata* (Jena, 1759), as well as translations from Russian into German. He died in March 1791. DtBilnd (2); NUC

Häselbarth, Hans, born 20th cent., he was a missionary in Africa, whose writings include *Rassenkonflikt und Mission* (1970), *Die Auferstehung der Toten in Afrika* (1972), and *Lebenszeichen aus Afrika* (1978). NUC; Sezgin

Hasenclever, Adolf, born 2 October 1875 at Remscheid, Westphalia, he was a lecturer in modern history successively at the universities of Halle/Saale and Göttingen. His writings include *Die orientalische Frage in den Jahren 1838-1841* (1914), and *Geschichte Ägyptens im 19. Jahrhundert, 1798-1914* (1917). He died in 1938. Kürschner, 1925-1935; Wer ist's, 1928, 1935

Hashagen, Johann Friedrich, born in 1841, he was a Lutheran pastor whose writings include *Die kirchliche Armenpflege beleuchtet in einem Streifzug durch das Gebiet der Fürsorge für die Bedürftigen* (1901), and *Aus dem amtlichen Leben eines alten Pastors* (1911). He died in 1925. NUC; Sezgin

Hashagen, Justus, born 4 December 1877 at Bremerhaven, Germany, he was a professor of history successively at the universities of Bonn, Köln, and Hamburg. His writings include *Weltpolitische Entwicklungsstufen, 1895-1914* (1916), *Europa im Mittelalter* (1951), and *Das Zeitalter der Gegenrefor-*

mation und der Religionskriege, 1555-1660 (1957). He died in Wyk auf Föhr on 14 November 1961. DiBilnd (1); Kürschner, 1925-1954; *Wer ist wer,* 1950-1961

al-Hāshimī, Muhammad Yahyá (Mohammed Jahia Haschmi), born 10 December 1903 at Aleppo, he there went to school from 1910 to 1923, when he went to Germany to study chemistry at the Technische Hochschule, Stuttgart, and at Berlin. After gaining his diploma, he taught Arabic at the Seminar für Orientalische Sprachen, Berlin, from 1926 to 1935, when he received a Dr.phil. from the Universität Bonn for *Die Quellen des Steinbuches des Berūnī.* He subsequently lectured again at Berlin until 1937, when he returned to Syria to teach at Syrian schools until 1946, when he became for four years a professor of chemistry at the University of Damascus. Since 1950, he held prominent positions in Syrian industry, becoming president of the Society for Scientific Research. His writings include a consideration of atomic theory in Sufi thought, alchemical literature, and works dealing with the Sufi tradition, *al-Imām al-Sādiq fī mulham al-kīmiyā'* (1951), *al-Kīmiyā' fī al-tafkīr al-Islāmī* (1958), and *al-Mathal al-a'lá lil-hadārah al-'Arabīyah* (1964). Hanisch; Note about the author; Schwarz; WhoArab, 1978/79

Haskell, Edward Bell, born in 1865 in Turkey, he graduated from Oberlin College and became a missionary under the Congregational Mission Board and spent over twenty-seven years in European Turkey, Macedonia, Serbia, and Bulgaria. Note about the author

Haskell, Henry Charles, born 25 December 1835 at Anson, Me., he graduated in 1859 from Williams College, and in 1862 from Andover Seminary. He went directly to the foreign field and was stationed at Philippopolis (Plovdiv) from 1863 to 1870, at Eski Lagra, Ottoman Bulgaria, from 1870 to 1872. Returning to the United States he was released from connection with his Board in 1874, however, being reappointed in 1877, and from that time until 1912, when he finally resigned, he was stationed at Samokov, Ottoman Bulgaria. Since his return he and his wife lived at Oberlin, Ohio, where in spite of illness and gradually failing health his interest in Bulgaria never ceased. He died in Oberlin on 29 March 1914. *Missionary herald,* 110 (1914), p. 215

Haskell, William Nafew, born in 1878 at Albany, N.Y., he graduated from the U.S. Military Academy, and after the first World War supervised relief work among Greek refugees from Turkey. He died in 1952. BioIn, 3 (5); CurBio, 1947, pp. 25-27, 282-284; NatCAB, vol. 40, p. 516, cols 516-17; Shavit; WhAm, 3

Haskins, Charles Homer, born 21 December 1870 at Meadville, Pa., he received a classical education from his father, and graduated from Johns Hopkins University, Baltimore, Md., where he also received a Ph.D. in 1890. He was successively a professor of history at the University of Wisconsin, and Harvard. During the Treaty of Versailles negotiations, 1919, he served as an adviser to President Woodrow Wilson. His writings include *Norman Institutions* (1918), *Some problems of the Peace Conference* (1920). He died in 1937. ANB; BioIn, 5; ConAu, 201; DAB; DLB, 47 (1986), pp. 122-144; Master (7); WhAm, 1, Who was who, 3

Haskins, John Franklin, born 16 November 1919 at La Junta, Colo., he received a Ph.D. in 1961 from New York University for *The fifth Pazyrik kurgan and the "animal style."* He was a professor of art and archaeology successively at Columbia University, New York, and the University of Pittsburgh. His writings include the exhibition catalogues, *"Ch'ang-Sha," the art of the peoples of Ch'u* (1957), and *The Duke University Museum of Art presents imperial carpets from Peking* (1973). He died in 1991. DrAS, 1974 H, 1978 H, 1982 H; WhoAmArt, 1978-1991/92

Hasler, J. Ireland, born 19th cent., he was in 1916 resident in Bankipore. His writings include *The Messange of life; studies in the Epistles of St. John* (London, 1949). Note about the author

Hasluck, Frederick William, born 16 February 1878 at London, he was educated first privately, at Leys School, Cambridge, followed by King's College, Cambridge, and finally for one year at the British School at Athens. He remained at the School after his study, becoming first its librarian, and in 1906 assistant director, he post which he held until 1915. On 26 September 1912 he was married to Margaret Hardie. His writings include *Cyzicus, being some account of the history and antiquities of that city* (Cambridge, 1910), *Athos and its monasteries* (London & New York, 1924), *Christianity and Islam under the sultans* (Oxford, 1929), and he was a joint author of *The Church of Our Lady of the Hundred Gates in Paros* (London, 1920). He died of consumption in Switzerland on 22 February 1920. *Mitteilungen zur osmanischen Geschichte,* 2 (1923-26), pp. 321-23

Hasluck, Margaret Masson née Hardie, born in 1885 at Aberdeen, she studied at Aberdeen, Cambridge, and Berlin, and was since 1932 a correspondent for the Near East and India. Her writings include *Këndime englisht-shqip; or, Albanian-English reader* (1932), and she edited *The Unwritten law in Albania,* of her husband, F. W. Hasluck, 1878-1920, published in 1954. She died in 1948. WhE&EA

Haslund-Christensen, Henning, born 31 August 1896 at København, he was an infantry lieutenant and participated in the setting up of an experimental farm and fur trade station in northern Outer Mongolia, 1923-26. He later became a caravan leader for Sven Hedin. He died on his third expedition on 13 September 1948 in Kabul. His large collection of artifacts, folklore and music is now in the Danish Nationalmuseet, København. He had no academic training but reached a wide audience in Denmark and Sweden through his popular books and radio programs. His writings include *Jabonah* (1933), *Men and gods in Mongolia* (1935), *Zajagan* (1935), and *Mongolian journey* (1949). Henny Harald Hansen wrote *Mongol costumes; researches on the garments collected by the first and second Danish Central Asian expeditions under the leadership of Henning Haslund-Christensen, 1936-37 and 1938-39* (1950). DanksBL; IntDcAn; Kraks, 1948

Hassan, Mahmoud (Mahmud), born 7 May 1893 at Cairo, he received a law degree and entered the Egyptian civil service. He served as a minister of social affairs and from 1938 to 1948 he was Egyptian ambassador in Washington. He was a sometime president of the Egyptian Society of Internal Law. WhoArab, 1968

Hassan, Riaz ul, 1937- *see* Riaz Hassan

Hassan, Sana, born about 1930, the daughter of a former Egyptian ambassador to the U.S.A., she was studying at Harvard in 1974. Her writings include *Enemy in the Promosed Land; an Egyptian woman's journey into Israel* (1986), and she was a joint author of *Between enemies; an Arab-Israeli dialogue* (1974). Note about the author

Hassan (Hasan), Zaky Mohamed, born 17 July 1908 at Khartoum, he studied at the Faculty of Arts at Cairo and received degrees in 1929 and 1931. A fellowship enabled him to study history and Islamic art at the Sorbonne, gaining a doctorate in 1934 for *Les Tulunides; étude de l'Égypte musulmane à la fin du IXe siècle*, as well as a diploma in archaeology from the École du Louvre. He subsequently spent some months at Staatliche Museen, Berlin, under Ernst Kühnel. After returning to Cairo, he was a curator at the Museum of Islamic Art, concurrently teaching at the Cairo Faculty of Arts. Since 1939 he was a full-time staff member of the Archaeological Institute in Cairo University, successively holding the chair of archaeology, dean of faculty, and director of the Museum of Islamic Art. Two years after his 1952 retirement at Cairo, he was appointed to the chair of Islamic art at Baghdad. His writings include *Funūn al-Islām* (1948), and *Atlas al-funūn al-zakhrafīyah wa-al-tasāwīr al-Islāmīyah* (1956). He died on 31 March 1957. *Bulletin de la Société d'archéologie copte*, 14 (1950-57), pp. 251-52

Hassanein, Sir Ahmed Mohamed Pasha, born in 1889, he was a graduate of Oxford and became the first secretary of the Egyptian Legation in Washington. His writings include *The Lost oases* (1925). Barnaby Rogerson delivered a paper at the 4th biennial ASTENE Conference, Edinburgh, 2001, entitled "Ahmad Mohamed Hassanein, explorer in Egypt and Libya and royal chamberlain, 1920s and 1930s." He died in 1946. *Bulletin of the ASTENE*, no. 12 (October 2001), p. 7; *Who was who*, 4

Hasse, Johann Gottfried, born of humble parentage in 1759 at Weimar, he studied at the Universität Jena with a bursary. A professor at the Universität Königsberg since 1786, he taught Oriental languages, and since 1788 also theology. His writings include *Praktischer Unterricht über die gesammten orientalischen Sprachen* (1786-93), *Lectiones syro arabico samaritano aethiopicae* (1788), and *Praktisches Handbuch der arabischen und äthiopischen Sprache* (1793). He died in Königsberg on 12 April 1806. ADtB, vol. 10, pp. 758-59;DtBE; DiBiInd (3); Sezgin

Hasselquist, Frederik, born 3 January 1722 at Törnevalla, Östergötland, Sweden, he studied medicine and natural sciences at Uppsala. His writings include *Iter palæstinum, eller Resa til Heliga landet* (1757), and its translations, *Reise nach Palästina in den Jahren von 1749 bis 1752* (1762), and *Voyages and travels in the Levant* (1766). He died in Smyrna on 9 February 1752. Dawson; Egyptology; EncBrit; Henze; Master (2); SBL; Sezgin; SMK

van **Hasselt**, Frans G., born in 1927, his writings include *Griekenland; het failliet van een dictatuur* (1975), *Griekse tijd* (1985), *Verslaafd aan Griekse muziek* (1999), and he edited *Griekenland vrij!* (Amsterdam, 1967). Brinkman's

Hassenstein, Wilhelm, born 19th cent., he was an engineer in the German Civil Service. His writings include *Das Geheimnis um die Erfindung von Pulver und Geschütz* (Berlin, Verband Deutscher Ingenieure, 1939). NUC; Sezgin

Hassert, Ernst Emil Kurt, born 15 March 1868 at Naumburg/Saale, Germany, he studied at Leipzig and Berlin. He successively taught geography at the universities of Leipzig, Tübingen, Köln, and Dresden. From 1907 to 1908 he led an expedition to the Cameroons. His writings include *Reise durch Montenegro* (1893), *Das Türkische Reich* (1918), and *Die Erforschung Afrikas* (1941). He died in

Leipzig on 5 November 1947. DtBE; Geog, vol. 10 (1986), pp. 69-76; Kürschner, 1925-1940/41); NDB; RHbDtG; *Wer ist's*, 1922-1935

Hassid, Sami Youssef, born 19 April 1912 at Cairo, he graduated in architecture in 1935 from the University of London, and received a Ph.D. in 1956 from Harvard for *Rural housing reconstruction in Egypt*. He taught at Cairo, from 1934 to 1956, and subsequently at Berkely, Calif. His writings include *Architectural education U.S.A.* (1967), *Doctoral studies in architecture* (1971), and he was a joint author of *An annotated bibliography on urban aesthetics* (1960). Master (1); Selim; WhoAm, 1974-1998; WhoWor, 1974/75-1978/79; WhoWorJ, 1972, 1978

Hassing, Per Schioldborg, born 7 February 1916 in Sweden, he graduated in 1937 from Göteborgs Universitet, in 1948, from Hartford Seminary Foundation, and received a Ph.D. in 1960 from the American University, Washington, D.C., for *Christian missions and the British expansion in Southern Rhodesia, 1888-1923*. He served as a misionary in Rhodesia, 1939-1959, and subsequently until 1978 as a professor of Christianity at Boston University. ConAu, 37-40; DrAS, 1969 H; WhoRel, 1975, 1977

Hassinger, Hugo, born 8 November 1877 at Wien, he received a Dr.phil. in 1905 from the Universität Wien for *Morphogenese des südlichen Wiener Beckens*, and a Dr.habil. in 1914 for *Die Mährische Pforte und ihre benachbarten Landschaften*. He taught geography at Basel since 1918, at Freiburg im Breisgau since 1922, and at Wien since 1930. His writings include *Geographische Grundlagen der Geschichte* (1930), and its translation, *Fundamentos geográficos de la historia* (1958). He died on 13 March 1952 from a road accident. Dickinson, pp. 147-48; DtBE; *Mitteilungen der Geographischen Gesellschaft Wien*, 96 (1954), pp. 149-76; NÖB, 12 (1957), pp. 162-70; Sezgin; *Südost-Forschungen*, 12 (1953), pp. 293-94

Hassler (Haszler), Conrad Dietrich, born 18 May 1803 at Altheim, Bavaria, he studied theology and Oriental languages at the universities of Tübingen and Leipzig. In 1858, he became a conservator of historic monuments. He edited *Reisen und Gefangenschaft Hans Ulrich Kraffts aus der Originalhandschrift* (Stuttgart, 1861). He died in Ulm on 17 April 1873. ADtB, vol. 11, pp. 15-20, vol. 12, p. 795; DtBE; DtBilnd (1); NDB; Sezgin

Hassler, Joseph Louis François, born 10 April 1881 at Avesnes-le-Comte (Pas-de-Calais), he was from 1911 to 1914 associated with the École de Joinville-le-Pont. In 1920, he was posted to the Armée du Levant where he headed the office of the French High Commissioner in Syria and Lebanon, subsequently joining Intelligence of the Armée du Levant. A professor at the École supérieure de guerre in 1922, colonel in 1934, brigadier-general in 1937, he was from 1934 to 1939 commandant of the École militaire d'infanterie et des chars de combat at Saint-Maixent (Deux-Sèvres). After the 1940 armistice, he was commandant of the Département du Var until he went underground. His writings include *Ma campagne au jour le jour, août 1914 - décembre 1915* (1917). He died in Saint-Martin-Boulogne (Pas-de-Calais) on 4 November 1966. DBF

Hasson, Rachel, born in 1944 at Jerusalem, she was a sometime assistant to Leo A. Mayer and later became associated with the L. A. Mayer Memorial Institute for Islamic Art, Jerusalem. Her writings include *Early Islamic glass* (Jerusalem, 1979), *Pottery from Morocco* (1982), *Caucasian rugs* (1986), *Early Islamic jewellery* (1987), *Later Islamic jewellery* (1987), and she edited the exhibition catalogue, *Schmuck der islamischen Welt* (1988). WhoWor, 1987/88; ZKO

Hassouna (Hassūnah), Muhammad 'Abd al-Khāliq, born 28 October 1898 at Cairo, he was educated at Cairo and Cambridge and became a lawyer. He entered the Egyptian diplomatic service in 1926 as a diplomatic representative at Berlin. After the second World War, he served as an ambassador to the U.S.A. In 1952, he was elected secretary general of the Arab League. AfrBiolnd (4); WhoArab, 1967/68

Hatch, James Vernon, born 25 October 1928 at Oelwein, Iowa, he graduated in 1949 from State University of Northern Iowa, and received a Ph.D. in 1959 from the State University of Iowa for *Three original plays*. He subsequently taught English literature and drama at high schools and universities throughout the United States. From 1963 to 1965 he served as a Fulbright professor of cinematography in the High Institute of Cinematographic Arts, Giza, Egypt, and from 1995 to 2000 he was teaching in the Department of Theatre and Art, C.U.N.Y. His writings include *A history of African American theatre* (2003), and he was a joint editor of *Inside the mistrel mask* (1996). ConAu, 41-44; DrAS, 1974 E, 1978 E, 1982 E; NatFacDr, 1995-2000

Hatcher, William Spottswood, a Baha'i, born 20 September 1935 at Charlotte, N.C., he graduated in 1957 from Vanderbilt University, and received a Dr ès sciences in 1963 from the Université de Neuchâtel. He was a professor of mathematics in Switzerland, U.S.A., and Canada. His writings include *Foundations of mathematics* (1968), *The Logical foundations of mathematics* (1982), and *The Baha'i faith; the emerging global religion* (1984). AmM&WSc, 1973 P-2003; Canadian, 1983-1995|; ConAu, 123; WhoAm, 1984-1994|; WhoE, 1974, 1981, 1983

Hathaway, Robert Lawton, born 20 January 1932 at Fall River, Mass., he graduated in 1953 from Williams College, and received a Ph.D. in 1969 from Boston College, Providence, R.I., for *Love in the early Spanish secular theatre*, a work which was published in 1975. In 1964, he was appointed a professor in the Department of Romance Languages, Colgate University, Hamilton, N.Y., a post which he still held in 1995. DrAS, 1982 F; WhoAm, 1986-1998; WhoE, 1985-1989/90

Hatschek, Julius Carl, born 21 August 1872 at Czernowitz, Bukovina, he studied law at the universities of Czernowitz, Wien, and Heidelberg. Since 1905, he was a professor at the Prussian Civil Service Academy in Posen. In 1909, he was appointed a professor of law at the Universität Göttingen. His writings include *Englisches* Staatsrecht (1905-1906), and *Der Musta'min; ein Beitrag zum internationalen Privat- und Völkerrecht des islamischen Gesetzes* (1919). He died in Göttingen on 12 June 1926. DtBE; NDB; Sezgin

Hattis, Susan Lee, born in 1943, she received a doctorate in 1970 from the Université de Genève for *The bi-national idea in Palestine during mandatory regimes*. Schwarz

Hatto, Arthur Thomas, born in 1910, he was educated at the University of London. He was a lecturer in English at the Universität Bern, 1932-34, and a head of the Department of German, Queen Mary College, University of London, 1938-77. His writings include *Shamanism and epic poetry in Northern Asia* (1970), *The Memorial feast for Kökötöy-khan; a Kirghiz epic poem* (1977), *Traditions of heroic and epic poetry* (1980-89), and *The Manas of Wilhelm Radloff* (1990). IntAu&W, 1977; Who, 1969-2004

Hatton, Joseph, born in 1841 at Andover, Hampshire, he was a journalist, novelist, miscellaneous writer, and a sometime editor of the *Gentleman's magazine*, London. His writings include *Journalistic London* (1882), *Newfoundland* (1883), and *North Borneo; explorations and adventures on the equator* (1885). He died in London on 31 July 1907. BbD; DNB; OxCan; *Who was who*, 1

Hatton, Ragnhild Marie, born 10 February 1913 at Bergen, Norway, she received a Ph.D. in 1950 from the University of London for *Diplomatic relations between Great Britain and the Dutch Republic, 1714-1721*. She was associated with L.S.E. since 1949 and delivered her inaugural lecture on 1 May 1969 entitled *War and peace, 1680-1720*. Her writings include *Charles XII of Sweden* (1968), *Europe in the age of Louis XIV* (1969), and *Studies in diplomatic history* (1970). She died in London on 16 May 1995. ConAu, 25-28, 148, new rev., 12; IntAu&W, 1977-1991; WhoWor, 1976/77, 1982, 1984; WrDr, 1976/78-1990/92

Hau, Friedrun R., born 20th cent., he was a sometime professor of history of medicine at the Universität Bonn. He edited *Istorgia dalla Madaschegna; Festschrift für Nikolaus Mani* (1985). Kürschner, 2001, 2003

Hauber, Anton, born 14 November 1879 at Ellwangen, Württemberg, he studied history and Oriental languages at the Universität Tübingen and received his Dr.phil. in 1906 from the Universität München for *Die Stellungnahme der Orden und Stifter des Bistums Konstanz*. In 1908, he became an assistant at Tübingen University Library, and in 1914, he became an interpreter for Turkish with the German High Command. His writings include *Planetenkinderbilder und Sternbilder zur Geschichte des menschlichen Glaubens und Irrens* (1916), and he edited *Urkundenbuch des Klosters Heiligkreuztal* (1910). Poisoned by an insect, he died 9 June 1917. DtBiInd (1); Hanisch; *der Islam*, 8 (1918), pp. 134-135

Haubst, Rudolf, born 10 August 1893 at Zschopau, Saxony, he studied at München and Leipzig, where he received a Dr.phil. in 1921 for *Ein Münchner handschriftlicher Text angeblich des Alkindi; de signis astronomiae applicatis ad medicinam*. Thesis

Haubst, Rudolf, born 18 April 1913 at Masing, Prussia, he received a Dr.theol. in 1952 from the Universität Bonn for *Das Bild des Einen und Dreieinen Gottes in der Welt nach Nikolaus von Kues*, and a Dr.habil. in 1956 from the Universität Freiburg im Breisgau for *Die Christologie des Nikolaus von Kues*. He was a medievalist who taught dogmatics successively at the universities of Bonn and Mainz. His writings include *Der Friede unter den Religionen nach Nikolaus von Kues* (1984). He died about 1992. Kürschner, 1961-1992|

Haude, Waldemar, born about 1900, he was a meteorologist who was a member of Sven Hedin's expedition to Central Asia. In 1959, he was with the German meteorological service in Hannover. His writings include *Ergebnisse der allgemeinen meteorologischen Beobachtungen und der Drachenaufstiege an den beiden Stanglagern bei Ikengüng und am Edsen-Gol, 1931/32* (1940). Note

Hauer, Jakob *Wilhelm*, born 4 April 1881 at Ditzingen, Württemberg, the son of Pietists, he trained at Basel as a missionary and then studied Indian and religious subjects at Oxford. After obtaining a Dr.phil. in 1917 from the Universität Tübingen, he became a professor of Sanskrit successively at Marburg and Tübingen. His writings include *Glaube und Blut* (1938), *Ein arischer Christus?* (1939), *Urkunden und Gestalten der germanischdeutschen Glaubensgeschichte* (1940), *Was ist Religion* (1952),

Der Yoga (1958), *Toleranz und Intolerance in den nicht christlichen Religionen* (1961), and *Verfall oder Neugeburt der Religion* (1961). He died in Tübingen on 18 February 1962. DtBE; Kürschner, 1925-1961; Stache-Rosen

Haug, Martin H., born 30 January 1827 at Ostdorf, Württemberg, he studied classics and Oriental languages at the Universität Tübingen where he received a Dr.phil. in 1852 for *De fontibus Plutarchi*, and a Dr.habil. in 1854 from the Universität Göttingen for *Die Lehre Zoroasters nach den Liedern des Zendavesta*. In 1859, he was appointed superintendent and professor of Sanskrit at Poona College. For reasons of health he returned to Germany in 1866. From 1868 until his death on 5 June 1876 he was a professor of Sanskrit at the Universität München. Bonner, vol. 8, pp. 310-12; Buckland; EncIran; IndianBilnd (3); Master (1); Stache-Rosen, pp. 68-69

Haug, Walter, born 23 November 1927 at Glarus, Switzerland, he received a Dr.phil. in 1952 from the Universität München for *Zum Begriff des Theatralischen*. He was from 1973 until 1995 a professor of medieval literature at the Universität Tübingen. His writings include *Literaturtheorie im deutschen Mittelalter* (1985), its translation, *Literary theory in the German middle ages* (1997), and *Die Wahrheit der Fiktion; Studien zur weltlichen und geistlichen Literatur des Mittelalters und der frühen Neuzeit* (2003). DtBilnd (1); Kürschner, 1976-2003

Haughton, Sir Graves Champney, born in 1788, he was educated in England, and also studied under Silvestre de Sacy at Paris. In 1808 he entered the East India Company and proceeded to India. From 1812 to 1814 he studied Oriental languages in the College of Fort William, Calcutta. Ill-health obliged him to return on furlough to England at the end of 1815. From 1817 to 1827 he taught Oriental languages at the East India College, Haileybury. His writ-ings include *Rudiments of Bengálí grammar* (1821), and *A Dictionary, Bengálí and Sanskrit, explained in English*, (1833). He died of cholera at St. Cloud on 28 August 1849. Buckland; DNB; Fück, 156; IndianBid (2); Riddick

Haughton, Henry Lawrence, born 1 November 1883, he was educated at Winchester and the Royal Military College, Sandhurst. He was from 1922 to 1027 a commandant of the Prlnce of Wales Indian Military College and continued to serve in India until his retirement in 1940 with the rank of general. Concurrently he did archaeological work in the neighbourhood of Gandhara and the North-West Frontier. At the end of the second World War, he lived for four years in Cyprus. His writings include *Sport and folklore in the Himalayas* (1913). Note about the author; Who was who, 5

Haumant, Jean Camille, born about 1900, he received a doctorate in 1929 from the Université de Paris for *Les Lobi et leur coutume*. His other writings include *Initiation aux finances publiques des territoires d'outre-mer* (1952). NUC, pre-1956

Haumant, Juste Émile, born 17 April 1859 at Paris, he studied at the Faculté des lettres de Paris, École des chartes, and École des langues orientales. He obtained an *agrégation d'histoire* and subsequently taught first at lycées In Saint-Quentin and Amiens and later at the universities of Lille and Paris, where he held the chair of Russian literature. In 1893, he received a doctorate for his two theses, *La guerre du Nord et la paix d'Oliva, 1655-1660*, and *Quid detrimenti ex invasione Hungarorum Slavi ceperint*. His writings also include *La culture française en Russie, 1700-1900* (1910), *Le problème ukrainien* (1919), *Le problème de l'unité russe*, (1922), *La formation de la Yougoslavie, XVe-XXe siècle* (1930), *Histoire des Yougoslaves* (1932), and he was a joint author of *L'Europe et la résurrection de la Serbie, 1804-1834* (1907). DBF; Qui est-ce, 1934; Qui êtes-vous, 1924

Hauner, Milan L., born 4 March 1940 at Gotha, Germany, he received doctorates from the universities of Praha and Cambridge. He was in 1978/79 a visiting professor in the Department of History, University of Wisconsin; he subsequently settled in London. His writings include *India in axis strategy* (1981), *The Soviet war in Afghanistan* (1990), and *What is Asia to us? Russia's Asian heartland yesterday and today* (1992). Filipsky; Schoeberlein

Haunerová, Magdalena née Slavíková, born 30 April 1944 at Brno (Brünn), Czechoslavakia, she graduated in 1966 at Praha with the thesis, *Morphological statistics of Swahili newpapers and its application in the teaching process*; and she received a Ph.D. in 1975 from SOAS for *Relationships among six East African Bantu languages*. In 1979, she briefly taught African linguistics at the University of Wisconsin. Filipsky

Haupt, Ferdinand Carl Friedrich Lehmann, 1861-1938 *see* Lehmann-Haupt, Ferdinand Carl Friedrich

Haupt, Hermann Hugo *Paul*, born in 1858 at Görlitz, Silesia, he received a Dr.phil. in 1878 from the Universität Leipzig for *Sumerische Studien*. He became a professor of Assyriology successively at Göttingen and Johns Hopkins University, Baltimore, Md. He edited *Beiträge zur Assyriology und semitischen Sprachwissenschaft* (1899-1927). He died in Baltimore on 15 December 1926. DAB;

DtBE; EncJud; Kürschner, 1925, 1926; Master (6); NatCAB, vol. 22, pp. 157-58; NDB; WhAm, 1; *Who was who*, 2; Wininger

Hause, Helen Engel, born 28 October 1915 at Pottsville, Pa., she graduated in 1943 from the University of Pennsylvania and received a Ph.D. in 1948 from the University of Pennsylvania for *Terms for musical instruments in Sudanic languages; a lexicographic inquiry*. In 1957, she was appointed a professor of sociology and anthropology at Wayne State University, Detroit, Mich. AmM&WSc, 1973 S; AmM&WSc, 1976 P; Selim

Hauser, André, born 24 September 1924 at Paris, he was a somtime head of the Section sociologique of the Institut français de l'Afrique noire. Unesco

Hauser, Edmond *Fernand*, born 18 December 1869 at Toulon, France, he was a journalist who wrote for the *Figaro, Petit journal*, and *Écho de Paris*. He founded two journals around the turn of the century, but none of them survived the first year. His writings include poetry and biographies. He was a vice-president of the Société des poètes français. He died in 1941. Curinier, vol. 3 (1901), pp. 224-25; DBF

Hauser, Friedrich (Fritz) Ludwig Gustav, born 28 September 1889 at Erlangen, Bavaria, he studied sciences at the Universität München and after his Dr.rer.techn. in 1910 became an assistant to Eilhard Wiedemann at the Universität Erlangen. There he also gained a Dr.phil. and in 1913 a Dr.habil. in physics. After military service in the first World War, he was nominated a professor and elected to Deutsche Akademie der Naturforscher Leopoldina. He subsequently worked in industrial optics. His writings include *Über das Kitab al-Hiyal, das Werk über die sinnreichen Anordnungen, der Benū Mūsā* (1922), and he was a joint author of *Über die Uhren im Bereich der islamischen Kultur* (1915). DtBE

Hauser, Henri, born 19 July 1866 at Oran, he was a student at the lycée Condorcet, graduated from the École normale supérieure and received his *agrégation* in history and geography in 1888. He subsequently taught at the lycées of Bourges, Pau, and Poitiers. In 1892, he received a *doctorat ès lettres* for his theses, *François de La Noue*, and *De Cleone demagogo*. He successively served as a professor at the universities of Clermont-Ferrand, Dijon, and Paris. He occupied an important place among French historians during the first half of the twentieth century. His contributions to his field took the form of a very large number of articles, many of which were collected in three books, *Ouvriers du temps passé* (1899), *Travailleurs et marchands dans l'ancienne France* (1920), *Les débuts du capitalisme* (1927), and he was a joint author of *Notre empire coloniale* (1910), and *La France d'aujourd'hui et ses colonies* (1920). He was granted honorary doctorates by the universities of Riga, Toronto, and Tartu. He died in Montpellier on 27 May 1946. *American historical review*, 52 (1946/47), pp. 221-222; DBF; NYT, 15 July 1959, p. 29, col. 2; *Qui est-ce*, 1934; *Qui êtes-vous*, 1924

Hauser, Walter, born in 1893 at Middlefield, Mass., he was educated as an architect at M.I.T., where he taught both mathematics and drawing from 1914 to 1919, when he joined the staff of the Egyptian expedition of the Metropolitan Museum of Art. In 1931, he was in Iraq on a joint expedition of the Staatliche Museen, Berlin, and the Metropolitan Museum, which excavated the Sasanian site of Ctesiphon. In 1932, he was appointed to the Persian Expedition to Qasr-i-Abu-Nasr, a site near Shiraz; he later worked at Nishapur. In 1946, he was appointed curator of the Metropolitan Museum Library, later becoming research curator of Near Eastern archaeology. He retired in 1958 and died on 13 July 1959. *American journal of* archaeology, 64 (1960), p. 85; BioIn, 5; Egyptology; Shavit; WhAm, 4

Hausheer, Jacob, born 11 October 1865 in Switzerland, he studied Arabic under Heinrich Thorbecke and received a Dr.phil. in 1905 from the Universität Halle for *Kommentar des Abū Ga'far Ahmad Ibn Muhammad An-Nahhās zur Mu'allaka des Zuhair*. He became a secondary school teacher and subsequently a professor of Old Testament studies at the Universität Zürich. He died in 1943. Fück; HisBioLexCH; Schwarz

von **Hauslab**, Franz, born 1 February 1798 at Wien, he was a general, cartographer, and painter, who was educated at the Viennese Akademie der bildenden Künste and the Ingenieur-Akademie. He served as an officer with the Engineers as well as a professor at the Ingenieur-Akademie. Since 1828 he was repeatedly sent on lenghty diplomatic missions to the Levant and Russia. He died in Wien on 11 February 1883. DtBE; DtBiInd (3); ÖBL; Pallas

Hausmann, Rainer, born 20th cent., he received a Dr.jur. and was in 1978 an academic assistant at the Universität München, and subsequently became a professor of law at the Universität Konstanz. His writings include *Das Recht der nichtehelichen Lebensgemeinschaft; Handbuch* (1999). Kürschner, 2001, 2003

Haussig, Hans Wilhelm, born 3 October 1916 at Berlin, he received a Dr. phil. in 1939 from the Universität Berlin for *Das Chronicon Tuscanense des Floridus und einige damit zusammenhängende*

Quellen. He taught Byzantine history at the Freie Universität Berlin until 1969, when he became a professor of Byzantine and Central Asian history, and chairman of department, at Ruhr-Universität, Bochum. His writings include *Kulturgeschichte von Byzanz* (1959), its translation, *A History of Byzantine civilization* (1971), *Byzantinische Geschichte* (1969), *Geschichte Zentralasiens und der Seidenstraße in vorislamischer Zeit* (1983), *Die Geschichte Zentralasiens und der Seidenstraße in islamischer Zeit* (1988), and *Archäologie und Kunst der Seidenstraße* (1992). He died in Berlin on 27 April 1994. ConAu, 29-32; DtBE; GV; *Index Islamicus* (1); Kürschner, 1966-1992; Schoeberlein

Haussknecht, Heinrich *Carl*, born 30 November 1838 at Bennungen near Sangerhausen, Saxony, he was an pharmacist and since 1857 an assistant at Bremgarten (Canton Aargau) and Aigle (Canton Waadt), where he pursued an interest in the flora of the Swiss Alps. He subsequently took a degree in botany and pharmacy from the Universität Breslau in 1864. For the following five years he travelled as a private scholar in eastern Anatolia, Kurdistan, Luristan, to the Persian Gulf. He discovered antiquities and listed them on cartographic maps. He returned to Weimar with an important botanical collection which he then prepared for publication, 1867-84. He died in Weimar on 7 July 1903. DtBE; Henze; NDB

Haussleiter, Hermann, born 19th cent., his writings include the *Register zum Korankommentar des Tabari, 1321* (Straßburg, 1912). Sezgin

d'Hautpoul, Marie Constant Fidèle Henri *Amand*, born 26 September 1780 at Château de Lasbordes, comunauté Castelnaudary (Aude), he was educated at the Polytechnique, 1799-1802, and the École d'artillerie et du génie de Metz. He participated in the French military campaigns of the period up to the battle of Dresden in 1813, when he was seriously wounded and, with the rank of lieutenant-colonel, had to resign his active service. He became commander of the École d'artillerie de la garde royale in 1823, and of the École d'état-major in 1826. He retired in 1832 and died in Paris on 15 January 1853. His writings include *Souvenirs du général marquis Amand d'Hautpoul; quatre mois à la cour de Prague, l'éducation du duc de Bordeaux, 1833-1834*, ed. Maurice Fleury (1902). DDF; Hoefer; IndexBFr² (3); Master (1)

Hautreux, Joseph *Alfred*, born in 1826 at Bordeaux, he graduated from the École navale. He participated in expeditions to South America, the Crimea, Italy, and North Africa. He had to resign from active service for reasons of health and became director of the port of Toulon. He later pursued a scholarly interest in hydrography, meteorology, and oceanography. He died in Bordeaux on 7 January 1914. DBF

Hauziński, Jerzy, born 20th cent., he was associated with Uniwersytet Poznański. His writings include *Islam w feudalnych państwach arabskich i w krajach ościennych, VII-XV w* (1976), *Muzulmańska sekta asasynów w europejskim piśmiennictwie wieków średnich* (1978), and *Polityka orientalna Frydeyka II Hohenstaufa* (1978). Note about the author; OSK

Hava, Joseph Gabriel, born 20 February 1851 at Marseille to a Christian family from Ottoman Syria, he was educated at the collège de Vaugirard, Paris. Apart from French he had a good command of Turkish, Arabic, English, and Italian. He entered the Société de Jésus on 14 January 1882. He received his clerical training during two years each at Sidmouth, Devon, Beirut, and Mold, Wales, where he was ordained on 24 August 1888. In 1890 he returned to Beirut as a missionary. His writings include *Arabic-English dictionary for the use of students* (1899). When the war broke out he was in Saida, where he died in Bilad Bisharah of typhoid fever on 16 December 1916. *Arabica*, 10 (1963), pp. 61-62; Jalabert

Havass, Reszö (Rudolph), born 17 January 1852 at Pozsony (Pressburg/Bratislava), Slovakia, he obtained a doctorate and subsequently served for many years as head of the mathematics section in the First Hungarian General Insurance Company. He was a sometime vice-president of the Hungarian Geographical Society. His writings include *Magyar földrajzi könyvtár* (1893), and *Magyarország és a Balkan* (1913). His trace is lost after the seven-page publication, *Emeljünk muzulmán imaházat Budapesten* (1914). GeistigeUng; OSK; Pallas

Havell, Ernest Binfield, born 16 September 1861 at Reading, he was a prinicipal of the Madras School of Arts, from 1884 to 1892, when he returned to England. His writings include *The Basis for artistic and industrial revival of India* (1912), *A Handbook to Agra and the Taj, Sikandra, Fatehpur-Sîkrî and the neighbourhood* (1912), *Ancient and medieval art of India* (1915), *Hanbook of Indian art* (1920), and *The Himalayas in Indian art* (1924). He died in Oxford on 30 December 1934. DNB; IndianBiInd (3); Riddick; WhE&EA; *Who was who*, 3

Havelock, Sir Henry Marshman, born in 1830 in Bengal, he entered in 1846 the 39th Regiment in India, and served as assistant quatermaster-general in the Persian expedition of 1857, and later as assistant adjudant-general to his father in the campaign against rebels in Oudh. He retired in 1887 with the rank of lieutenant-general. He died in 1897. <small>Mason; Who was who, 1</small>

Havemann, Axel, born 20 February 1949 at Berlin, he studied since 1968 Islamic, Byzantine, and Iranian subjects at the Freie Universität, Berlin, where he received a Dr.phil. in 1983 for a study of rural movements in nineteenth century Lebanon entitled *Rurale Bewegungen im Libanongebirge des 19. Jahrhunderts.* He frequently visited the Near East during his student days. He served as an assistant at the Universität des Saarlandes at Saarbrücken before he started teaching at his alma mater, a post which he still held in 2004. His writings include *Ri'āsa und qaḍā'; Institutionen als Ausdruck wechselnder Kräfteverhältnisse in syrischen Städten vom 10. bis 12. Jahrhundert* (1975), and *Geschichte und Geschichtsschreibung im Libanon des 19. und 20. Jahrhunderts* (2002). <small>Kürschner, 2003; Sezgin; Thesis</small>

von Haven, Frederik Christian, born 3 July 1727 at Odense, Denmark, he was a philologist who accompanied in 1761 Carsten Niebuhr on his scientific expedition to the Arabian Pensinsula. His writings include *Om det hebraiske sprogs simpelhed og naturlighed* (København, 1827). His travel journal and papers are in the Royal Library in Copenhagen. He died of malaria at Mokha on 25 May 1763. <small>Bidwell; DanslBL; DanskBL²</small>

Haweis, Hugh Reginald, born in 1838 at Egham, Surrey, he was educated at Trinity College, Cambridge, receiving the M.A. in 1864. After filling two curacies, he was appointed rector of St. James', Westminister. In 1868, he became editor of *Cassell's Magazine*. He travelled throughout western Europe and Morocco. His writings include *Music and morals* (1874). He died in 1901. <small>BbD; BritInd (5); DNB; Master (6); Who was who, 1</small>

Hawi, Sami S., born about 1942, he received a Ph.D. in 1972 from State University of New York at Buffalo for *Naturalism and mysticism in Ibn Tufayl*. He subsequently became a professor in the Department of Philosophy at his alma mater, a post which he still held in 2004. His writings include *Islamic naturalism and mysti-cism; a philosophical study of Ibn Tufayl's Hayy bin Yaqzan* (1974). <small>NatFacDr, 1995-2004; Selim</small>

Hawkes, Charles Pascoe, born in 1877, he was educated at Dulwich College, Southwark. After graduating from Trinity College, Cambridge, he was called to the bar from the Inner Temple in 1901. He served in the European War and resigned in 1920 with the rank of lieutenant-colonel. He practised in a variety of courts until his retirement in 1950. His writings include *Mauresques, with some Basque and Spanish cameos* (1926). He died in 1956. <small>Who was who, 5</small>

Hawkes, James Woods, born in 1853 at Montezuma, Ind., he served as a missionary in Persia for fifty-two years under the Presbyterian Board of Foreign Missions. He was the founder of the American School for Boys at Hamadan, and was instrumental in establishing a hospital there. He was the compiler of a thousand-page Persian Biblical dictionary. He died in Hamadan on 21 April 1932. <small>Muslim world, 1923; Shavit</small>

Hawkes, Onera Amelia Merritt, 1887- see Merritt-Hawkes, Onera Amelia

Hawkins, Linda L, born 20th cent., she was still a doctoral candidate at the University of Wisconsin, Milwaukee, in 1979; she was a joint author of several scholarly papers dealing with the Middle East and North Africa, and published a number of articles on U.S. politics and urban politics. <small>Note about the author</small>

Hawley, Donald Frederick, born 22 May 1921 at Thorpe Bay, England, he graduated from New College, Oxford, and was called to the bar from the Inner Temple. He entered the Sudan Political Service in 1944 and subsequently served in the Foreign Service in a variety of capacities throughout the Muslim world. His writings include *The Trucial states* (1970), *Courtesies in the Gulf area; a diction-ary of colloquial phase and usage* (1978), *Oman and its renaissance* (1978), its translations *Oman et sa renaissance* (1978), *Oman y su renacimiento* (1978), and *Khartoum perspectives; a collection of lectures given at the Sudan Cultural Centre, Khartoum, in the 1940s and 1950s* (2001). <small>AfrBiInd (1); ConAu, 108; Master (2); Who, 1972-2004</small>

Hawley, Ruth, born 20th cent., her writings include *Omani silver* (London & New York, 1978), and the Arabic translation from her unidentified work, *al-Sinā'āt al-fiddīyah fī 'Umān* (Oman, 1980). <small>ZKO</small>

Haworth, Sir Lionel Berkeley Holt, born in 1873, he was educated at Dulwich College, Southwark, and Elizabeth College, Guernsey. He joined the Army in 1893 and served in India since 1898, holding polit-ical appointments in India and Persia. During the last ten years before his retirement in 1929, he was consul and political resident in the greater Persian Gulf region. He died in 1951. <small>Riddick; Who was who, 5</small>

Hawting, Gerald R., born 28 August 1944, he received a Ph.D. in 1978 from the School of Oriental and African Studies, London, for *Aspects of Muslim political and religious history in the 1st/7th century,* with special reference to the development of the Muslim sanctuary. He became a senior lecturer in the history of the Near and Middle East, and head of the Department of Religious Studies at SOAS. His writings include The First dynasty of Islam (1986), and he translated from the Arabic of al-Tabari, Approaches to the Qur'an (1993). DrBSMES, 1993; LC; Sluglett

Haxen, Ulf, born 28 July 1933 atb Frdbg, Denmark, he was a school teacher at the Copenhagen municipal school board, 1959-63, spent 1964-65 on a fellowship at Jerusalem, and from 1965 to 1969 served as headmaster at Carolineskolen, Copenhagen. He subsequently went for five years to Zambia as a consultant to the Ministry of Education. In 1974, he received an M.A. in Semitic philology from Københavns Universitet. Since 1979 he was in various capacities associated with the Royal Library, Copenhagen, as Hebrew and Jewish librarian. He was a joint author of A Guide to libraries of Judaica (1985). Kraks, 199-2004

Hay, Grace Marguerite Hay-Drummond née Lethbridge, born in 1895 or 96 at Liverpool. She was an English aviator, foreign correspondent, and the wife of Sir Robert Hay-Drummond Hay. She was the only woman on board the Graf Zeppelin on that airship's first flight across the Atlantic. She died in New York on 12 February 1946. Master (2); NYT, 13 February 1946, p. 23, col. 1

Hay, John Baldwin, born 19th cent., he "was a consular agent for Syria, working out of Beirut; in 1867, he received an appointment for the Jaffa post." Vogel, pp. 96, 110

Hay, John Milton, born in 1838 at Salem, Ind., he graduated from Brown College, Providence, R.I., and was admitted to the Illinois bar. He became acquainted with Abraham Lincoln when he was a lawyer practising in the building nex door. He campaigned for Lincoln; when elected he was appointed a White House secretary. Beginning in 1865 he held consular posts overseas until 1870 when he became editorial writer for the New York Tribune. From 1898 to his death in 1905 he was U.S. Secretary of State. AmIndex (3); ANB; ConAu, 108, 179; DLB, 189 (1993), pp. 138-43; Master (48); WhAm, 1

Hay, Michael Joseph, born in 1942, he received a Ph.D. in 1974 from the University of Minnesota at Minneapolis for An economic analysis of rural-urban migration in Tunisia. Selim³

Hay, Sir Robert Hay-Drummond, born 25 July 1846 at Tanger. After Eton and Trinity College, Cambridge, he entered the Foreign Service and remained in consular positions until his retirement in 1908, serving generally in the Middle East. He wrote a number of diplomatic and consular reports for the Foreign Office, including the Report on the methods adopted in Tunis for destroying locusts (1891). He died on 15 October 1926. Who was who, 2

Haycock, Bryan George, born in 1937, he graduated in ancient Egyptian and Nubian studies from Durham University and went on to take both D.Phil. and M.Litt. degrees in that order. He later became a member of the Sudanese Antiquities Service and the University of Khartoum, teaching alternately in the History and Archaeology departments. An accident in Kharoum involving his bicycle and a car resulted in his premature death in 1973. Journal of Egyptian archaeology, 60 (1973), p. 3

Haycraft, Sir Thomas Wagstaff, born in 1859, he was educated at St. John's College, Oxford, and called to the bar from the Inner Temple. He practised in a variety of courts in England as well as overseas, including as chief justice of Palestine. His writings include Palestine disturbances in May, 1921; report of the Commission of Inquiry (1921). He died in 1936. Who was who, 3

al-Haydari, Buland, born in 1926 in Irbil, Iraq, of a Kurdish family, he was a writer and a leftist opponent of one-party rule and left Iraq in 1982 to live in London, where he was literary critic for an Arabic-language weekly newspaper and a member of the dissident Iraqi Democratic Alliance. His writings include Khafqat al-ṭin (1974), and the English translation of his poems under the title Songs of the tired guard (1977). He died of complications following open-heart surgery in London on 6 August 1996. WRMEA 15 (December 1996), p. 126

Hayden, Sir Henry Hubert, born in 1869 at Londonderry, he was educated at Trinity College, Dublin, and in 1895 joined the Geological Survey of India, subsequently becoming its director. His writings include Sport and travel in the highlands of Tibet (1927), and he was a joint author of A Sketch of the geography and geology of the Himalaya Mountains and Tibet (1907), and The Geology of northern Afghanistan (1911). He died in 1923. Robert L. Praeger wrote Some Irish naturalists; a biographical note-book (1949). BLC; Riddick; Who was who, 2

Hayden, Lyle Johnson, born in 1903, he received a Ph.D. in 1945 from Cornell University, Ithaca, N.Y., for Characteristics of college curriculum for the education of teachers of vocational agriculture. From 1945 to 1948, he organized and directed the Near East Foundation's rural improvement demonstration in some 30 to 35 villages located in a restricted area to the southeast of Tehran. He and other members of the supervising staff concurrently served as counsellors and advisers to the Iranian

Government on various technical matters of interest to the Ministries of Agriculture, Education, and Health. He subsequently was in charge of the farm machinery program of the Economic Cooperation Administration, Paris. Note about the author; *Reader's digest*, 55 (December 1949), pp. 117-21 [not sighted]; Shavit

Hayden, Sherman Strong, born in 1908 at Cleveland, Ohio, he graduated from Harvard University and received his Ph.D. in 1942 from Columbia University, N.Y.C., for *The international protection of wild life*. He was since 1956 a professor of international relations at Clark University, Worcester, Mass. He was a joint author of *Non-selfgoverning territories; status of Puerto Rico* (1954). AmM&WSc, 1973 S

Haye, Kh. A., fl. 20th cent., he obtained a doctorate and was a sometime resident in Rawalpindi. His writings include *Education, old and new* (Chittagong, 1955), *Great lives* (Karachi, 1966), *General knowledge* (Karachi, 1967), and *Heroes and heroines of Islam* (Lahore, 1967). Note about the author

Hayes, Stephen D. born 20th cent., he was in 1977 a foreign affairs officer with the U.S. Treasury Department. Note about the author

Hayford, Elizabeth R., born in 1949, she received a Ph.D. in 1971 from Tufts University, Medford, Mass., for *The politics of the Kingdom of Libya in historical perspective*. LC: Selim

Hayit, Baymirza, born 17 December 1917 at Namangan, Turkestan, he graduated from Tashkent University and received a Dr.phil. in 1949 from the Universität Münster for *Die nationalen Regierungen von Kokand (Choqand) und der Alasch Orda*. He was associated with an East European research institute at Düsseldorf, 1953-64, and the Forschungs-Institut Turkestans, Köln, 1993. His writings include *Turkestan zwischen Russland und China* (1971), *Turkestan im Herzen Euroasiens* (1980), *Islam and Turkestan under Russian rule* (1987), *"Basmatschi;" nationaler Kampf Turkestans in den Jahren 1917 bis 1934* (1992), *Berichte und Forschungen über Turkestan* (1997). He was honoured by *Turkestan als historischer Faktor und politische Idee; Festschrift für Baymirza Hayit* (Köln, 1987), and *Dr. Baymirza Hayit armağanı* (İstanbul, 1999). EURAMES, 1993; Schwarz; WhoWor, 1980/81

Haynie, James *Henry*, born in 1841 at Winchester,Ill., he served in the U.S. Army from 1861 to 1864 and subsequently became a war reporter, foreign editor and correspondent. In 1876 he declined the offer of the Khedive to become a lieutenant-colonel in the Egyptian Army. He died in 1912. AmAu&B; DcNAA; WhAm, 1

Hayward, George S. W., born 19th cent., he made an impressive journey into eastern Turkestan in 1868-1869, penetrating into the dangerous and little-known country beyond the main Karakoram range as far as Kashgar and staying two months on the return journey at Yarkand. At the end of 1869, he was hoping to penetrate to the Pamir steppe and the source of the Oxus. The Kashmir authorities urged him repeatedly to abandon the expedition, but he resolved to persevere. He reached Gilgit on 7 July and, on the 13th of the month, Yasin. He was murdered at his camp at Darkhut, on his way from Yasin into Chitral, on 17 July 1869. Buckland; Embacher; *Geographical journal*, 122 (1956), p. 394; Henze; IndianBilnd (4)

Haywood, Ian, born in 1938 at London, he was an architect, town planner, and consultant, with Lebanese experience. His writings include *Working class fiction from Chartism to trainspotting* (1997), and he was a joint editor of *Implementation of urban plans* (1979). WhoWor, 1987/88

Haywood, John Alfred Algernon de, born 20 April 1913 ar Sheffield, he was from 1946 to 1955 an inspector of education in the Anglo-Egyptian Sudan. He subsequently taught Arabic at the University of Durham, where he became in 1967 a director of the Centre for Middle Eastern and Islamic Studies. His writings include *Arabic lexicography* (1960), *A New Arabic grammar of the written language* (1962), and *Modern Arabic literature, 1800-1970; an introduction with extracts in translation* (1971). ConAu, 17-20; Unesco

Hazai, György, born 30 April 1932 at Budapest, he studied Turkology at Eötvös Loránd Tudomány-yegyetem, Budapest, from 1950 to 1954. He was a sometime visiting lecturer at Sofia, and a visiting professor at Humboldt-Universität, Berlin, from 1963 to 1988. From 1993 to his retirement in 1997 he was chairman of the Department of Turkish in the University of Cyprus, Nicosia. He received honorary doctorates from the universities of Budapest and Ankara; he was general secretary of the International Union of Oriental and Asian Studies, vice-president of the Comité international des études ottomanes et pré-ottomanes, editor of *Bibliotheca orientalis hungarica*, as well as a joint editor of other scholarly journals. He was a member of the Academia Europea (London), the Hungarian Academy of Sciences, Körösi-Csoma Társaság, Société finno-ougrienne, Türk Dil Kurumu, and Türk Tarih Kurumu. His writings include *Das Osmanisch-Türkische im XVII. Jahrhundert* (1973), *Kurze Einführung in das Studium der türkischen Sprache* (1978), and he was a joint author of *Biographisches Handbuch der Turkologie* (1979-86). In 1997, he was honoured by *Studia Ottomanica; Festgabe für György Hazai*. Biograf, 2002, 2004; Fekete, 1985; MagyarNKK, 1992-1998; Private

Hazairin, Gelar Datuk Pangeran, born 28 November 1906, he was a professor of law at the Islamic University, Jakarta. He died in Jakarta on 11 December 1975. *Ensiklopdi Indonesia*

Hazam, John George, born in 1900, he received a Ph.D. in 1932 from the University of California at Berkeley for *Arab nationalism and Anglo-French imperialism on the eve of the World War*. He successively taught history at Yale, Stanford, University of California at Berkeley, University of Oregon, and the College of the City of New York. He died on 19 June 1951. *American historical review*, 57 (1952), p. 588; NYT, 20 June 1951, p. 27, col. 4; *School and society*, 73 (1951), p. 414; Selim

Hazard, Harry Williams, born in 1916 or 1918 at Plainfield N.J., he received a Ph.D. from Princeton University. His writings include *Atlas of Islamic history* (1951), *The Numismatic history of late medieval North Africa* (1952), a work which was originally accepted by Princeton University for a doctoral degree in Oriental languages and literatures, *Eastern Arabia* (1956), *Saudi Arabia* (1956), *A History of the crusades* (1977), and he edited *The Art and architecture of the Crusader states* (1977), and he was a joint editor of *The Idea of colonialism* (1958). He died in Rochester, N.Y., on 5 February 1989. LC

Hazard, John Newbold, born 5 January 1909 at Syracuse, N.Y., he received a J.S.D. from the University of Chicago's School of Law, and finished his academic career as an emeritus professor of law at Columbia University, N.Y.C. He was a specialist in the legal system of the Soviet Union. His writings include *The Soviet legal system* (1962), *Russia and the republics; legal materials* (1992), and he was a joint author of *Soviet policy toward Black Africa* (1972). He died in N.Y.C. on 7 April 1995. AmM&WSc, 1973 S, 1978 S; ConAu, 1-4, 148, new rev., 31; DrAS, 1974 P, 1978 P, 1982 P; IntAu&W, 1976, 1977; IntYB, 1998; WhoAm, 1974-1994; WhoAmL, 1978-1992; WhoE, 1991/92; WhoWor, 1974/75, 1993/94; WrDr, 1976/78-1994/96

Hazard, Louis Paul, fl. 1868-1911, he was a lawyer whose writings include *Des droits du conjoint survivant dans l'hérédité de l'époux précédé* (Niort, 1874), and *Note sur le Maroc* (Orléans, 1912). BN

Hazen, William Edward, born in 1933, he received a Ph.D. in 1976 from Johns Hopkins University, Baltimore, Md., for *Mustafá al-Nahhās, leader of the Wafd*. He worked for the American Institutes for Research and the Library of Congress, Washington, D.C., before he became affiliated with Abbott Associates, Inc. He was a joint author of *The Palestinian movement in history* (1976), and he was a joint editor of *Middle Eastern subcultures; a regional approach* (1975). Note about the author; LC

Hazleton, Jared Earl, born 12 September 1937 at Oklamoha City, Okla, he graduated in 1959 from the University of Oklahoma and received his Ph.D. in 1965 from Rice University, Houston, Tex. He was since 1976 a professor of public affairs in the University of Texas at Austin. In 1995, he was a professor in the Department of Finance, Texas A&M University, College Station, Tex., and in 2000, a dean of Business Administration, North Texas State University at Denton, Tex. His writings include *The Impact of the Texas constitution on natural resources* (1973). AmM&WSc, 1973 S

Head, Antony Henry, viscount, born in 1906, he was a British politician who was educated at Eton and the Royal Military College, Sandhurst. His writings include *Pattern of peace* (London, 1951). He died on 29 March 1983. BlueB, 1973/74, 1975, 1976; IntWW, 1974/75-1981; *Who's who*, 1959-1983; *Who was who*, 8

Headley, Rowland George Allanson Allanson-Winn, baron, born in 1855 at London, he studied mathematics and graduated from Trinity College, Cambridge. He spent many years in Kashmir as an engineer. In 1914, he converted to Islam. His writings include *A Western awakening to Islam* (1914), its translation, *Garpta Müslimanlik cereyani* (1928), and *The Affinity between the original Church of Jesus Christ and Islam*, by al-Hajj Lord Headley (1927). He died in 1935. Master (1); *Who's who*, 1929; *Who was who*, 3

Heaphey, James Joseph, born 28 June 1930 at Cleveland, Ohio, he graduated in 1957 from the local Western Reserve University and received his Ph.D. in 1962 from the University of California, Berkeley, for *Theoretical aspects of CPAC and ICP case studies*. He was successively a professor of public administration at the University of California, Berkeley, University of Pittsburgh, and S.U.N.Y. at Albany. He was a joint author of *Legislative institution building in Brazil, Costa Rica, and Lebanon* (1976), and he edited *Spatial dimensions of development administration* (1971). AmM&WSc, 1973 S, 1978 S; Master (1)

Heard-Bey, Frauke, born 21 October 1941 at Berlin, she studied history and political science at Heidelberg and Berlin. Under her maiden name, Frauke Bey, she received a Dr.phil. in 1967 from the Freie Universität Berlin for her thesis, *Räte und Gemeindewesen; ... in Berlin*. Since 1967 she was living in Abu Dhabi, where she was attached to the Centre for Documentation and Research. Her writings include *From Trucial States to United Arab Emirates* (1982), and *Die arabischen Staaten im Zeichen der islamischen Revolution* (1983). Thesis; ZKO

Heath, Lionel, born in 1872, his writings include the booklet, *Examples of Indian art at British Empire Exhibition, 1924* (London, 1925), and *Review of the conditions of hand weaving in the Punjab* (Lahore, 1930). NUC, pre-1956

Heath, Sir Maurice Lionel, born in 1909, he was a commander of the British Force, Saudi Arabia, 1957-1959, and retired with the rank of air marshall. Since 1966 he was gentleman usher to the Queen. He died on 9 July 1998. *Who's who*, 1959-1998

Heath, Michael John, born 20th cent., his writings include *Crusading commonplaces; La Noue, Lucinge and rhetoric against the Turks* (Genève, 1986), *Some Renaissance studies; selected articles, 1951-1991, with a bibliography* (1992), *Rabelais* (1996), and he edited *La soltane,* of Gabriel Bounin (1977), and *La manière de lire l'histoire,* of René de Lucinge (1993). ZKO

Heathcote, Dudley, his writings include *My wanderings in the Balkans* (London, 1925), and *Sweden* (London, 1927).

Heazell, Francis Nicholson, born in 1866 at Nottingham, he graduated in 1891 from University College, Nottingham. He became a missionary to the Assyrians in Kurdistan. His writings include *The History of S. Michel's Church, Croydon* (1934), *The Woes of a distressed people* (1934), and he was a joint author of *Kurds and Christians* (1913). BritBiInd (1); Note about the author

Hebby (Habbī), Antoine, born 20th cent., his writings include *Petite méthode de musique ecclesiastique byzantine à l'usage des paroisses grecques melkites catholiques de la diaspora* (Jounieh, 1987). ZKO

Hebenstreit, Johann *Ernst*, born in 1702 at Neustadt/Orla, Thuringia, he studied natural history and medicine at the universities of Jena and Leipzig, gaining a doctorate in 1730 for his thesis, *De viribus minerarum et mineralium medicamentosis*. In the service of August II, King of Saxony, he explored North Africa, collecting natural curiosities and wild animals. After his return he was appointed a professor of medicine at Leipzig. He died there on 5 December 1757. Martin Grosse wrote *Die beiden Afrika-Forscher Johann Ernst Hebenstreit und Christian Gottlieb Ludwig, ihr Leben und ihre Reise* (Leipzig, 1902). ADtB, vol. 11, p. 196; Bio, 17; DtBE; Henze; NDB

Heberer, Johann *Michael*, born about 1560 at Bretten, Baden, he studied at Wittenberg, Leipzig and presumedly at Heidelberg. He was in the service of a young Swedish nobleman. Since 1582 he accompanied a French earl on travels in France and Italy. In 1585 on board a Christian vessel in the Mediterranean, he was captured by Turks. After three years of slave labour in Egypt, and on a galley, he was freed at the end of 1587. He entered the service of the Elector of Palatinate and on account of his linguistic ability he accompanied several missions. In 1592 he was appointed registrar of the Palatinate chancellery. His experiences in Egypt are embodied in his *Aegyptiaca servitus* (1610), *Chur-Pfälzischer Robinson* (1747), *Der Pfälzer Robinson* (1906), and its translation *Ongelukkige voyagie door verscheyde gedeeltens van Asia en Africa in het jaar 1582* (1706). A partial French translation was published by Oleg V. Volkoff in his *Collection des voyageurs en Égypte*; vol. 6 (1976). He died after 1612. ADtB, vol. 11, 197-8; DtBE; DtBiInd (1); NDB

Hebert, Raymond J., born 20th cent., he was in 1973 associated with Smithonian Institute, Washington, D.C. He was the author of the exhibition catalogue, *Aditi; the monies of India* (1985), and he was a joint author of *Kirghiz manual* (1960). MESA Roster of members, 1990; Note about the author; ZKO

Hébrard, Ernest Michael, born in 1866 or 1875, he was an architect whose writings include *Le Palais de Dioclétien à Spalato* (Paris, 1911), *Spalato* (Paris, 1912), and he was a joint editor of *Creation of a world centre of communication* (Paris, 1913). Master (1)

Heck, Lewis, born 20 February 1889 at Heckton, Pa., he "was in the Near East in the consular service and later at the American Embassy at Constantinople almost continuously from 1909 through the busy years when the United States had charge of the interests of ten nations. He was appointed Turkish Secretary of the Embassy in 1916, and after the Armistice was put in charge of American affairs as Commissioner. He returned to the Near East several weeks ago to remain for an indefinite period." Kornrumpf; Note, *Asia*, July, 1920

Heckel, Jan-Uwe, born 20th cent., he was an aid worker in the Third World and associated with the Deutsche Gesellschaft für Technische Zusammenarbeit (German Agency for Technical Co-operation), Eschborn. Note about the author

Hecker, Hellmuth, born 12 October 1923, he received a Dr.jur. in 1948 from the Universität Hamburg and also a Dr.habil. in 1974. Since 1971 he was associated with the Institut für Internationale Angelegenheiten, Hamburg. His writings include *Die Kriegsdienstverweigerung im deutschen und ausländi-*

schen Recht (1954), and *Staatsangehörigkeitsrecht von Indien, Pakistan, Nepal* (1965). Kürschner, 1992-2003

Hecquard, Louis *Hyacinthe*, born in 1814 at Lisieux (Calvados), he was a spahi officer in Algeria and was later posted to Senegambia, where he explored Central Africa. He subsequently became a secretary to the French consulates in Scutari and Damascus. His writings include *Voyage sur la côte et dans l'intérieur de l'Afrique occidentale* (1853), its translation, *Reise an die Küste und in das Innere von West-Afrika* (1854), *Géographie générale du pachalik de Scutari* (1858), and *Histoire et description de la Haute Albanie ou Guégarie* (1858). He died in Beirut, 9 October 1866. Embacher; Henze; Kornrumpf

Hedayetullah, Muhammad, born 20th cent., he received his M.A. in 1954, and completed his formal education with a Ph.D. in 1973 from McMaster University, Hamilton, Ont., for *Kabir, the apostle of Hindu-Muslim unity*. In 1978, he was attached to the Institute of Islamic Studies, McGill University, Montreal. His writings include *Sayyid Ahmad; a study of the religious reform movement of Sayyid Ahmad of Ra'e Bareli* (1970). DrASCan, 1978; LC

Hedenström, Matthias, ca. 1780-1845 *see* Gedenshtrom, Matvei Matveevich

Hedin, Sven *Anders*, born in 1865 at Stockholm, he received a Dr.phil. in 1892 from the Universität Halle for *Der Demawend nach eigener Beobachtung*. He was the most successful and famous explorer of Central Asia and made great contributions to its geography and archaeology. His writings include *Central Asia and Tibet* (1903), *Ein Volk in Waffen; den deutschen Soldaten gewidmet* (1915), *Across the Gobi Desert* (1931), and *Tykskland och världsfreden* (1937). George Kish wrote *To the Heart of Asia; the life of Sven Hedin* (1984). He died in 1952. AnaBrit; EncIran; IntDcAn; Henze; Master (20); SBL; ScBInd (2); SMK; *Wer ist's*, 1909-1912; *Who was who*, 5; WhWE

Heepe, Martin, born 21 May 1887 at Leinde, Germany, he studied Oriental and African languages, and received a Dr.phil. in 1914 from the Universität Leipzig for a study of the dialects of the Comoro Islands entitled *Die Komorendialekte Ngazidja und Nzwani auf Grund älteren und neueren Materials*, a work which was published in 1920. He was doing field-work in eastern Africa when the first World War erupted and unable to return home until 1920. He was successively a lecturer at the Kolonialinstitut, Hamburg, a librarian at Preußische Staatsbibliothek, and a professor at Auslandshochschule, Berlin. He was a joint editor of *Lautzeichen und ihre Anwendung in verschiedenen Sprachgebieten* (Berlin, 1928). He died in Berlin on 11 December 1961. JahrDtB, 1922-25; Kürschner, 1928/29-1961; LexAfrika

Heer, Nicholas *Lawson*, born 8 February 1928 at Chapel Hill, N.C., he graduated in 1949 from Yale University and received his Ph.D. in 1956 from Princeton University for an edition and translation from the Arabic of al-Hakīm al-Tirmidhī, *The Bayān bayn al-sadr w-al-qalb w-al-fu'ād w-al-lubb*. He was a translator and analyst for the Arabian American Oil Company, Dhahran, 1955-57, and then taught Arabic at Stanford and Yale, before he was appointed in 1976 a professor of Arabic at the University of Washington, Seattle. His writings include *The Precious pearl; al-Jami''s al-Durrah al-fāqirah, together with his glosses and the commentary of 'Abd al-Ghafūr al-Lārī* (1979). DrAS, 1969 F, 1974 F, 1978 F, 1982 F; Selim; WhoAm, 1984-1994, 2003; ZKO

Heeren (Χέερεν/Геерен), Arnold *Hermann Ludwig*, born in 1760 at Arbergen near Bremen, he studied theology, history, and philology, and was since 1784 a professor at the Universität Göttingen. His great merit as an historian was that he regarded the states of antiquity from an altogether fresh point of view. His writings include *Über die Colonisation von Ägypten und ihre Folgen für das Europäische Staaten-system überhaupt und besonders für Russland* (Göttingen, 1805), *Versuch einer Entwicklung der Folgen der Kreuzzüge für Europa* (Göttingen, 1808), its translations, *Essai sur l'influence des croisades* (1808), *De volgen der Kruiztogten voor Europa* (1823), and *Ideen über die Politik ... der vornehmsten Völker der alten Welt* (1804-12), and its translations into Dutch, English, and French. He died in 1842. ADtB, vol. 11, pp. 244-46; BiB&SB; DtBE; DtBInd (14); EncBrit; EnSlovar; GdeEnc; Master (2); Megali, 24 (1934), p. 540; NDB; NUC, pre-1956; Sezgin

Heeres, Jan *Ernst*, born 30 May 1858 at Zuidhorn, the Netherlands, he started to study theology and letters at Groningen, but soon changed to law. In 1885, he received a doctorate from a Faculty of Law for *De wijzigingen in den reggeringsvorm van Stad en Lande in de jaren 1748 en 1749*, and in the following year he also completed his letters with a degree. In 1888, he entered the Algemeen Rijksarchief in Den Haag as a clerk. He rapidly advanced to become deputy archivist in charge of the East India section, where he catalogued the documents of the Verenigde Oost-Indische Compagnie, which he published between 1907 and 1934 entitled *Corpus diplomaticum Neerlando-Indicum*. Sharing wide-spread anti-British feelings, he published in 1898 *Abel Janszoon Tasman's journal of his dicovery of Van Diemensland and New Zealand in 1642*. In recognition of his historical research he was offered to teach colonial history at the Indian Foundation (Indische Instelling) at Delft. In 1902, he became a professor of history of the Dutch East Indies at the Rijskuniversiteit te Leiden. His Leiden period saw

MACK LIBRARY
BOB JONES UNIVERSITY
GREENVILLE, SC

his interest shift to social and political matters and he eventually went into politics. His other writings include *Daghregister gehouden int Casteel Batavia vant passerende daer ter plaetse als over geheel Nederlandts India* (1896), and *De afstand der Kaap de Goede Hoop aan Engeland in 1814* (1897). He died in s'Gravenhage on 16 February 1932. Benelux² (4); BWN, vol 5, pp. 184-87

Heers, Jacques, born 20th century, he received a doctorate in 1958 from the Université de Paris for *Gênes au XVe siècle; activité économique et problèmes sociaux*. He was a medievalist whose writings include *Les Merveilles en Andalusie* (1955), *L'Expansion maritime portugaise à la fin du moyen-âge* (1956), *Partis et la vie politique dans l'Occident médiéval*, its translation, *Parties and political life in the medieval West* (1977), a collection of his articles, *L'Ibérie chrétienne et le Maghreb, XIIe-XVe siècles* (1990), *Libérer Jérusalem; la première croisade* (1999), and *Les Barbaresques; la course et la guerre en Méditerranée, XIV-XVI siècle* (2001). In 1994 he was honoured by *Villes et sociétés urbaines au moyen-âge; hommage à M. le professeur Jacques Heers*. BN

Heffening, Wilhelm (*Willi*), born 2 June 1894 at Düsseldorf, Germany, he received a Dr.phil. in 1925 from the Universität Frankfurt for *Das islamische Fremdenrecht bis zu den islamisch-fränkischen Staatsverträgen; eine rechtshistorische Studie zum fiqh*. He was successively a librarian and professor of Islamic and Semitic studies at the Universität Bonn. His writings include "Die islamischen Handschriften der Universitätsbibliothek", Leuven (1937), *Die türkischen Transkriptionstexte des Bartholomaeus Georgievits aus den Jahren 1544-1548; ein Beitrag zur historischen Grammatik des Osmanisch-Türkischen* (1942). He died in Bonn on 3 March 1944. Hanisch; JahrDtB, 1937-1943|; Kürschner, 1926-1940/41|

Heffner, Ludwig, born about 1800, his writings include *Beitrag zur Geschichte der abendländischen Lepra in Ostfranken* (Würzburg, 1852), *Notice sur Auger-Ghislain de Busbeck* (Bruxelles, 1854), and *Die Juden in Franken; ein unparteiischer Beitrag zur Sitten- und Rechtsgeschichte Frankens* (Nürnberg, 1855). GV; NUC, pre-1956

Hegaard, Steven E., born 20th cent., he was a student of Turkic philology; his writings include *Karl Heinrich Menges Bibliographie* (Wiesbaden, 1979). LC

Hegelan, Faisal see Hejailan, Sheikh Faisal Abdul Aziz al-

Heggoy, Alf Andrew, born 15 December 1938 at Alger, the son of Norwegian Methodist missionaries. After schooling in Algeria, France, and the United States, he received his undergraduate education at Randolph-Macon College. He took a Ph.D. in history in 1963 from Duke University, Durham, N.C., for *The colonial policies of Gabriel Hanotaux in Africa, 1894-1898*. He subsequently joined the Department of History at the University of Georgia. His other writings include *Historical dictionary of Algeria* (1980), *Through foreign eyes; European attitudes toward North Africa* (1982), *The Military in imperial history; the French connection* (1984), and *The French conquest of Algiers, 1830; an Algerian oral tradition* (1986). He died in Athens, Ga., on 18 December 1987. ConAu, 37-40; DrAS, 1969 H, 1974 H, 1978 H, 1982 H; *Muslim world*, 78 (1988), p. 165

Heggoy, Willy Normann, born 20th cent., he received a Ph.D. in 1961 from Hartford Seminary Foundation for *Fifty years of Evangelical Missionary Movement in North Africa, 1881-1931*. He edited *I was an Algerian preacher*, of Said Abouadaou (1971). LC; Selim

Hegyi, Klára, born 27 December 1940 at Budapest, she was a historian whose writings include *Az oszmán birodalom Európában* (1986), its translation, *The Ottoman Empire in Europe* (1986), *Jászberény török levelei* (1988), *Muslime und Christen; das Osmanische Reich und Europa* (1988), and *Török berendezkedés Magyarországon* (1995). Biograf, 2002; MagyarNKK, 1994-2000

Hehir, Sir Patrick, born in 1859 at Templemore, Ireland, he was a medical doctor who was educated at Calcutta and Edinburgh and subsequently served as an army officer in India, Afghanistan, the Near and Middle East. In 1928 he served as a medical adviser to the British Red Cross Society's Mission to Greek refugees. He retired with the rank of major-general. His writings include *The Medical profession in India* (1923), and *Malaria in India* (1927). He died in 1937. Riddick; WhE&EA; *Who was who, 3*

Hehn, Johannes, born in 1873 at Burghausen, Germany, he studied at München, and in 1903 became a professor of Biblical studies and Semitic philology at the Universität Würzburg. His writings include *Der israelische Sabbath* (1909), *Wege zum Monotheismus* (1913), and *Der Untergang des alten Orients* (1928). He died in Würzburg on 9 May 1932. DtBilnd (2); Hanisch; Kosch; Kürschner, 1925-1931; *Wer ist's, 1928*

Heiberg, Johan Ludvig, born 27 November 1854 at Ålborg, Denmark, he was a scientist whose writings include *Om scholierne til Euklids Elementer* (1888), and he was joint author, with Eilhard Wiedemann, of *Naturwissenschaften und Mathematik im klassischen Altertum* (1912), and its translation, *Mathematics and physical science in classical antiquity* (1922). He died in København on 4 January 1928. DanskBL; DanskBL²; Kraks, 1927; NUC, pre-1956

Heichelheim, Fritz Moritz, born 6 May 1901 at Gießen, he studied at the local university as well as at München, receiving a Dr.phil. in 1925 for *Die auswärtige Bevölkerung im Ptolemäerreich*. He was a lecturer at Gießen from 1929 to 1933, when he emigrated to the United Kingdom, where he became in 1936 a lecturer in ancient history and archaeology at the University of Nottingham. From 1948 to his death on 22 April 1968, he served as a professor in the Department of Classics, University College, University of Toronto. His writings include *Wirtschaftsgeschichte des Altertums vom Paläolithikum bis zur Völkerwanderung der Germanen, Slaven und Araber* (1938), *An Ancient economic history* (1958), and he was a joint author of *Political refugees in ancient Greece* (1943). ConAu, 116; DrAS, 1963 H; DtBE; Egyptology; Private; WhoWorJ, 1965

Heidborn, Adolf, born 19th cent., his writings include *Manuel de droit public et administrative de l'Empire ottoman* (Wien & Leipzig, 1909). NUC, pre-1956

Heidemann, Stefan, born 24 May 1961 at Strang, he studied Islamic subjects and political economy at Regensburg, Berlin, Damascus, and Cairo, receiving his Dr.phil. in 1993 from Freie Universität, Berlin. In 2002, he was a lecturer in the Institut für Sprachen und Kulturen des Vorderen Orients, Universität Jena. His writings include *Das Aleppiner Kalifat vom Ende des Kalifats in Bagdad über Aleppo zu den Restaurationen in Kairo* (1994), *Islamische Numismatik in Deutschland; eine Bestandsaufnahme* (2000), *Die Renaissance der Städte in Nordsyrien und Nordmesopotamien* (2002). Kürschner, 2003; Note about the author

Heidenheimer, Heinrich, born 25 October 1856 at Mainz, he studied history and political economy at the universities of Tübingen, Leipzig, and Straßburg. Since 1887 he was a librarian at the public library, Mainz; and in 1933, he was nominated a professor. His writings include *Machiavelli's erste römische Legation* (1878), and *Petrus Martyr Anglerius und sein Opus epistolarum* (1881). He died in Mainz on 14 November 1941. DtBE; Kürschner, 1925-1935; Wer ist's, 1912-1928; Wininger

von **Heidenstam** (Heidenstamm), Carl (Charles) Peter, born 11 November 1792 at Smyrna, he graduated from the French military college, Saint-Cyr. A French officer since 1811, he participated in the Italian campaign and the battle of Tolentino. He subsequently went to Persia, where he became a colonel in the Persian army in 1816. Since 1818 he was in the Swedish army and advanced to lieutenant-colonel in 1836. He served from 1818 to 1824 as a Swedish attaché at Constantinople, later being posted to the Balkans. He died in Athens on 5 June 1878. SMK

Helderich, Franz, born 25 October 1863 at Wien, he there studied geography, gaining a Dr.phil. in 1889 and subsequently became academic director of the cartographic firm, Ed. Hölzel. He successively taught geography, agrarian statistics, economic geography, and history at Höhere Lehranstalt für Wein- und Obstbau, Konsularakademie, k.k. Exportakademie, and Hochschule für Welthandel, Wien. His writings include *Die Donau als Verkehrssraße* (1916), and *Wesen und wissenschaftliche Stellung der Wirtschaftsgeographie* (1923). He died in Badgastein on 27 July 1926. ÖBL

Heidermann, Ingrid, born 20th cent., she was associated with the Federal German Ministry of Labour and Social Affairs. Her writings include *Die Förderung der Eigentumsbildung im Ausland* (1965), *Neo-Kolonialismus oder Wirtschaftshilfe in Afrika* (1969) and she was a joint author of *Wirtschaftsorganisatorische Wege zum gemeinsamen Eigentum und zur gemeinsamer Verantwortung der Arbeitnehmer* (1959), *Erwachsenenbildung in Afrika* (1967), and *Erwachsenenbildung in Frankreich* (1973). GV

Heiduczek, Werner, born 24 November 1926 at Hindenburg, Germany. At the age of twenty, he had experienced the war and spent over a year in a Soviet POW camp. He became a manual labourer, student at the Universität Halle-Wittenberg, school master, teacher of German in Bulgaria, and freelance writer, novelist and playwright. His writings include *Die schönsten Sagen aus Firdausis Königsbuch* (1982), *Der Schatten des Sijawusch* (1986), and he translated from the Bulgarian of Ivan M. Vazov, *Im Schoße der Rhodopen* (1982). In 1996, he was honoured by *Werner Heiduczek zum siebzigsten Geburtstag* (1996). KDtLK, 1988-2003/2004; Kürschner, 2001, 2003; WhoSocC, 1878; WhoSoCE, 1989

Heilbrunn, Otto, born 7 March 1906 at Frankfurt am Main, he studied at the universities of Berlin, Frankfurt and München and received a Dr.jur. in 1929 at Frankfurt for a study of banking terms and conditions entitled *Auslegung nichtiger und billiger Klauseln der "Allgemeinen Geschäftsbedingungen" der Banken*. He subsequently emigrated to the U.K. He was a member of the Royal United Service Institution. His writings include *Der sowjetische Geheimdienst* (1956), its translation, *The Soviet secret services* (1962), *Partisan warfare* (1962), *Conventional warfare in the nuclear age* (1965), and its translation, *Konventionelle Kriegsführung im nuklearen Zeitalter* (1967). He died in 1969. Au&Wr, 1963; BioIn, 9; ConAu, 15-16; GV

54

Heilmann, Luigi, born 21 August 1911 at Portalberta (Pavia), Italy, he was since 1959 a professor of *glottologia* at the Facoltà di Lettere e Filosofia dell'Università di Bologna. His writings include *Grammatica storica della lingua greca* (1963), *Il lessico della Germania nazista* (1971), *Corso di linguistica teorica* (1971), *La linguistica* (1975), *Dizionario del dialetto cremonese* (1976), *Linguistica e umanismo* (1983), *Diacronica, sincronica e cultura* (1984). Chi è, 1957, 1961; Chi scrive; Lui, chi è; Wholtaly, 1980, 1983

Hein, Horst Adolf, born 4 May 1939 at Wihelmshaven, Germany, he changed school frequently as his parents were Silesian refugees in western Germany. He started his higher education at Leibniz-Kolleg, Tübingen, and concurrently studied history at the Universität. In 1961 he changed to the Universität Freiburg im Breisgau where he added Arabic to his subjects. Since 1963 he was a full-time student in Islamic and Judaic studies, taking Arabic, Persian, and Turkish. He received his Dr.phil. in 1968 for *Beiträge zur ayyubischen Diplomatik.* Thesis

Hein, Joachim Emil Peter, born 6 June 1891 at Hamburg, he studied Oriental languages and received a Dr.phil. in 1925 from the Universität Hamburg for a study of Ottoman archery entitled *Bogenhandwerk und Bogensport bei den Osmanen.* He was in 1949 a head of archives at Hamburgisches Welt-Wirtschafts-Archiv. His writings include *Das Buch des Dede Korkut* (1958), and *Das Buch der vierzig Fragen*, of Furati (1960). HbDtWiss; Schwarz; ZKO

Hein, Wilhelm, born 7 January 1861 at Wien, he studied Oriental languages, ethnography, history, and geography at Wien, where he received a Dr.phil. in 1885 for *Omar II. in seinem Verhältnis zum Staate.* He spent the following academic year at the Universität Straßburg pursuing Oriental studies. In 1887, he joined the Naturalien-Kabinett in Wien. He was one of the founders of the society of Austrian ethnology (Verein für Österreichische Volkskunde), and in 1895 established the Museum für Volkskunde, Wien, and became a joint author of its *Katalog der Sammlung des Museums für österreichen Vokskunde in Wien* (1897). His *Mehri- und Hadrami-Texte, gesammelt im Jahre 1902* (Wien, 1909), contains an obituary by the editor, pp. XXII-XXIV. In the service of the Austrian Academy of sciences he travelled to Southern Arabia for the purpose of linguistic and ethnographic research. He died in Wien on 19 November 1903. DtBilnd (1); Fück, p. 256; NDB; ÖBL; Schwarz

Hein, Wilhelm, born 20th cent., his writings include *Frühe islamische Keramik im Österreichen Museum für angewandte Kunst in Wien* (1963), and *Abhandlung über die Künste; der 5. Abschnitt aus dem Buch "Muqaddima"* (1988). ZKO

Heine, Peter, born 23 June 1944 at Warendorf, Westphalia, he received a Dr.phil. in 1971 for *Die westafrikanischen Königreiche Ghana, Mali und Songhai aus der Sicht der arabischen Autoren des Mittelalters.* He taught at the Universität Münster until 1994, when he became a professor in the Institut für Asien und Afrikawissenschaften, Humboldt-Universität, Berlin. His writings include *Geschichte der Arabistik und Islamkunde in Münster* (1974), *Weinstudien* (1982), *Ethnologie des Nahen und Mittleren Ostens; eine Einführung* (1989), *Konflikt der Kulturen oder Feindbild Islam; alte Vorurteile, neue Klischees, reale Gefahren* (1996), and he was a joint author of *Ethnizität und Islam* (1984). Kürschner, 1983-2003; Schwarz

Heine, Peter Bernhard *Wilhelm*, born 30 January 1827 at Dresden, Germany, he was a landscape artist and a traveller who, on his voyage to the Far East, visited Tripoli in Cyrenaica in 1859 and Egypt in 1860. From 1849 to 1859, he lived in New York City. His writings include *Reise um die Erde nach Japan* (1856). He died in Lößnitz near Dresden on 5 October 1885. Embacher; Henze; Kornrumpf; Shavit - Asia

Heinemann, Isaak, born 5 June 1876 at Frankfurt-on-Main, he studied classical antiquities at Straßburg, Göttingen, and Berlin, to which the Rabbinerseminar, Berlin, was added later. He taught at private schools until 1919 when he became a lecturer at Jüdisch-Theologisches Seminar, Breslau. From 1920 to 1938, he was editor of *Monatsschrift für Geschichte und Wissenschaft des Judentums.* He emigrated in 1939 to Palestine, where he died in Jerusalem on 29 July 1957. His writings include *Zeitfragen im Lichte jüdischer Lebensanschauung* (1921), *Vom jüdischen Geist* (1924), *Die Lehre von der Zweckbestimmung des Menschen im griechisch-römischen Altertum und im jüdischen Mittelalter* (1926), and *Philons griechische und jüdische Bildung* (1932). He died in Jerusalem on 29 July 1957. BioHbDtE; DtBE; JüdLex; Kürschner, 1925-1935; Master (1); Wer ist's, 1928; Wininger

Heinemeyer, Willem Frederik, born in 1922, he received a doctorate in 1968 from the Universiteit van Amsterdam for *Nationale integratie en regionale diversiteit; een sociografische studie van Marokko als ontwikkelingsland.* He retired as a professor of human geography. His writings include *De wereld is vol wonderen* (1956), *De sociale geografie in de rij van de sociale wetenschappen* (1968), and he was a joint author of *Het centrum van Amsterdam* (1968). Brinkman's

Heinen, Anton M., born 2 June 1939 at Hersdorf, an Eifel village in Germany, he joined the Society of Jesus in 1959 and studied philosophy and theology at Pullach. Because of his interest in Islam, he was sent to Lahore in 1964 to study Arabic, Persian, and Urdu. Later, he received a degree at the Weston School of Theology at Harvard and continued with history of science. In 1978, he received his Ph.D. from Harvard. He taught in Roma from 1981 to 1987 when he was elected director of the Orient-Institut of the Deutsche Morgenländische Gesellschaft, Beirut. On account of the events in Beirut, the Institute transferred to Istanbul where he remained until his return home to take up teaching at München and Innsbruck. His writings include *Islamic cosmology* (1982), a revision of his Harvard thesis. He died on 1 or 2 April 1998. Al-Furqan, the bi-annual newsletter, September 1998, p. 18; Kürschner, 1987-92

Heinisch, Reinhard Rudolf, born 3 August 1942 at München, he received a Dr.phil. in 1966 from the Universität Wien for *Salzburg im Dreißigjährigen Krieg*, and a Dr.habil. in 1977. Since 1980 he was a professor of history at the Universität Salzburg. His writings include *Die bischöflichen Wahlkapitulationen im Erzstift Salzburg, 1514-1688* (1977), and he was a joint author of *Kleine Landesgeschichte von Salzburg* (1979). GV; Kürschner, 1987-2003; WhoAustria, 1983

Heinitz, Wilhelm, born 9 December 1883 at Altona, Hamburg, he studied music at the Hamburg conservatory and became a teacher of music. An academic assistant at the Universität Hamburg since 1915, he there received a Dr.phil. in 1920. He was successively a lecturer, professor and head of comparative musicology at the Universität. His writings include *Phonographische Sprachaufnahmen aus dem egyptischen Sudan* (1917), *Arabischer Diwan* (1926), *Indianische Fantasie* (1928), *Instrumentenkunde* (1932), and he was joint author of *The Musical accent or intonation in the Kongo language* (1922). He died in Hamburg on 31 March 1963. DtBE; Kürschner, 1925-1961; Master (2)

Heinrich, Guillaume Alfred, born 4 December 1829 at Lyon, he graduated from the École normale supérieure in 1851. After the completion of his two theses in 1855, he was appointed to the chair of foreign literature at the Université de Lyon, and later served as a dean of the Faculté des lettres. In 1869, he was elected a member of the Académie des sciences, belles-lettres et arts de Lyon. His writings include *Les invasions germaniques en France* (1871), *La France, l'étranger et ses partis* (1873), *Le purgatoire de Dante* (1873), and *Histoire de la littérature allemande* (1888-1891). He died in Lyon on 19 May 1887. Bitard; DBF; Glaeser; IndexBFr² (2)

Heinrich, Lothar Alexander, born in 1946, he received a Dr.phil. in 1977 from the Universität Bonn for *Zur Herrschaftsideologie des präkolonialen Rwanda*. He was a free-lance journalist whose writings include *Die kurdische Nationalbewegung in der Türkei* (Hamburg, 1989). GV; Note about the author

Heinrichs, Jacob, born 2 March 1860 at Allenstein, Germany, he went in 1881 to the United States. After graduation from Rochester Theological Seminary, he was a missionary in India from 1889 to 1917. From 1918 to 1933, he was dean and professor of theology at the Northern Baptist Theological Seminary in Chicago. His writings include *Introduction to the books of the Old Testament with analyses* (1898). He died in Middlebury, Vt., on 30 August 1947. Shavit - Asia; WhAm, 2

Heinrichs, Wolfhart Peter, born 3 October 1941 at Köln, he studied at Köln, Tübingen, the School of Oriental and African Studies, London, and Gießen where he received a Dr.phil. in 1967 for a study of Arabic poetry and Greek poetics entitled *Arabische Dichtung und griechische Poetik; Hāzim al-Qartāgannīs Grundlegung der Poetik mit Hilfe aristotelischer Begriffe*. He was a lecturer at the Universität Gießen, 1972-1978, and subsequently a professor of Near Eastern languages and civilization at Harvard, a post which he still held in 2004. He was a joint editor of the *Encyclopaedia of Islam*, and a member of several learned societies. His other writings include *The Hand of the northwind; opinions on metaphor and the early meaning of isti'āra in Arabic poetics* (1977). MESA Roster of members, 1990; NatFacDr, 1995-2004; Private; Schwarz

Heinritz, Günter, born 12 August 1940 at Nürnberg, he received a Dr.phil. in 1970 from the Universität Erlangen-Nürnberg for *Die „Baiersdorfer" Krenhausierer; eine sozialgeographische Untersuchung*. He was successively a professor of economic geography at the Technische Universität München as well as the Universität München since 1975. His writings include *Dorfbewohner als Dorfentwickler* (1997), and *Sozialgeographie und Soziologie; Dialog der Disziplinen* (1998). Kürschner, 1983-2003

Heintze, Wilhelm, born 19th cent., he was in 1875 a director of the Ottoman Bank in Ruse, northern Bulgaria. His writings include *Türkischer Sprachführer* (Leipzig, 1882), a work which went through two editions until 1909. Kornrumpf; NUC, pre-1956

Heintzen, Harry Leonard, born in 1922 at New Orleans, La., he graduated in 1947 from Tulane University, and did postgraduate work on the Middle East and Africa at Columbia University, New York. He was a reporter and a free-lance correspondent since 1947, spending 1957-58 in French West Africa. In 1964 he joined the United States Information Agency. WhoGov, 1972, 1975, 1977

Heinz, Dora, born 20th cent., she received a Dr.phil. and became a curator of Textiles at Öster-reichisches Museum für Angewandte Kunst, Wien. Her writings include *Alte Orientteppiche* (1956), and *Europäische Wandteppiche* (1963). Note about the author

Heinz, Wilhelm, born 13 June 1932 at Wien, he received a Dr.phil. in 1960 for a study of Turkish cultural and intellectual life in the early eighteenth century entitled *Das kulturelle und geistige Leben der Türkei unter Ahmed III.*, and a Dr.habil. in 1971 for *Der indische Stil in der persi-schen Literatur*. He was a professor at the Universität Würzburg. His writings include the catalogue of Persian manuscripts in Germany entitled *Persische Handschriften* (1968). Kürschner, 1987-2003; Schwarz

Heinze, Christian, born 20th cent., his writings include *Cyprus conflict, 1964-1985* (London, 1986), and he was a joint author of *The Cyprus conflict; the Western peace system is put to test* (Nicosia, Public Information Office of the Turkish Federated State of Cyprus, 1977), and *Zum Zypernkonflikt* (London, 1988). ZKO

Heinzlmeir, Helmut, born about 1945, he received a Dr.phil. in 1976 from the Universität München for *Indonesiens Außenpolitik nach Sukarno, 1965-1970; Möglichkeit und Grenzen eines bündnisfreien Ent-wicklungslandes*. GV

Heinzmann, Roland, born 20th cent., his writings include *Baikalsee; eine Literaturdokumentation zur Umweltsituation am Baikalsee* (Köln, 1993), and *Arktische Gebiete; eine Literaturdokumentation zur Umweltsituation des russischen Arktik-Anteils* (1995).

Heissig, Walther, born in 1913, he received a Dr.phil. in 1941 from the Universität Wien for *Der mongolische Kulturwandel in den Hsingan-Provinzen Mandschukos*. He was a professor and chair-man, Seminar für Sprache und Kulturwissenschaft Zentralasiens at der Universität Bonn. His writings include *Ein Volk sucht seine Geschichte; die Mongolen und die verlorenen Dokumente ihrer großen Zeit* (1964), *Dschingis Khan; ein Weltreich zu Pferde* (1985), *Heldenmärchen versus Heldenepos? Strukturelle Fragen zur Entwicklung altaischer Heldenmärchen* (1991), and *Motive und Analysen mon-golischer Märchen* (2003). In 1983, he was honoured by *Documenta Barbarorum; Festschrift für Wal-ther Heissig*. Kürschner, 1954-2003

Heitmann, George Joseph, born 27 November 1933 at N.Y.C., he graduated in 1956 from Syracuse University and received a Ph.D. in 1963 from Princeton University. Since 1958 he taught management science at the University of Pennsylvania, University Park, Pa. From 1964 to 1966 he was an economic adviser to the Ministry of Planning and Development, Government of Libya; and from 1978 to 1987 he served as chairman of department at the University of Pennsylvania. AmM&WSc, 1973 S, 1978 S; WhoAm, 1990-1994, 2003; WhoE, 1974, 1989/90; WhoFI, 1992/93

al-Hejailan (Alhegelan/Hegelan), Sheikh *Faisal* Abdul Aziz, born 7 October 1929 at Riyadh, he studied at the Faculty of Law, Fuad University, Cairo, and subsequently entered the Saudi Arabian foreign service. Since 1984 he was a member of the Saudi Council of Ministers. His writings include *Perspectives on Saudi Arabia* (Washington, D.C., 1980). MidE, 1982/83; WhoArab, 1990/91

Hekekyan, Joseph, born in 1807 at Constantinople, he was educated in England, where he also trained as an engineer. Since 1830 he worked in Egypt as a civil engineer until dismissed in 1850. During his retirement in Egypt he made important archaeological discoveries. His writings include *A Treatise on the chronology of Siriadic monuments* (London, 1863). He died in Cairo in 1875. Dawson; Egyptology; ZKO

Hekler, Antal (Anton), born 1 February 1882 at Budapest, he completed his law at Budapest and subsequently went to München to study philosophy. Upon his return to Budapest he found employment at the Ministry of Cultural Affairs. Two years later, in 1907, he transferred to the National Museum as curator of archaeology. In 1911, he qualified at Budapest as university lecturer in classical archaeology. His writings include *Römische weibliche Gewandstatuen* (1908), *A budapesti Pázmány Egyetem sorskérdései* (1931), *Ungarische Kunstgeschichte* (1937). He died in Budapest on 3 March 1940. GeistigeUng; Ki=kicsoda, 1937; Magyar

Helbaek, Hans, born early 1900s in Denmark, he gained a status in the international scientific com-munity as the founder of the science of paleoethnobotany. But throughout his life he was without academic standing in his native country. He developed a system of identifying and dating plant impressions found in pottery shards and carbonized grain. His writings include *Cereals in Great Britain and Ireland in prehistoric and early historic* times (1944), *Queen Icheti's wheat* (1953), *Prehistoric investigations in Iraqi Kurdistan* (1960), and he was a joint author of *Luni sul Mignone e problemi della preistoria d'Italia* (1967). He died in Helsingen on 10 February 1981. AnObit, 1981, pp. 99-100

Helbock, Richard William, born 24 March 1938 at Portland, Ore., he graduated in 1960 from the United States Military Academy and received a Ph.D. in 1973 from the University of Pittsburgh for *Nodal settlement evolution in the Willamette Valley in New Mexico*. Since 1968 he was a professor of geography and sociology at New Mexico State University, Las Cruces. His writings include *Post offices in New Mexico* (1981). WhoWest, 1976/77, 1978/79

Helburn, Nicholas, born 20 December 1918 at Salem, Mass., he graduated in 1940 from the University of Chicago and received a Ph.D. in 1950 from the University of Wisconsin. He was a Ford Foundation scholar. From 1947 to 1964 he taught geology and geography at Montana State College, and since 1971 at the University of Colorado, Boulder. His writings include *Türk ziraatında bazı tahav-vül seyirleri. Some trends in the Turkish agriculture* (Ankara, 1953), and he was a joint author of *Montana in maps* (1962), and *Agriculture typology* (London, 1964). AmM&WSc, 1976 P; WhoAm, 1982-1999|

Helck, Hans *Wolfgang*, born 16 September 1914 at Dresden, he studied at the Universität Göttingen and was from 1907 to his retirement a professor of ancient Near Eastern studies and chairman of Egyptology at the Seminar für Geschichte und Kultur des Vorderen Orients, Universität Hamburg. He died in Hamburg on 27 August 1993. DtBE; Egyptology; Kürschner, 1992; *Wer ist wer*, 1963

Held, Hermann Josef, born 28 December 1890 at Freiburg im Breisgau, he received a Dr.jur. in 1920 from the local Universität and also studied at Heidelberg and Cambridge. From 1921 to 1937 he was associated with the Institut für Weltwirtschaft, Kiel, and since 1942 he was a professor of law at the Universität Kiel. His writings include *Volk, Recht und Staat im Lichte deutscher Rechtserneuerung* (1935), *Gebiet und Boden in den Rechtsgestalten der Gebietshoheit und Dringlichkeit* (1937), and *Wirtschaftliche Gleichberechtigung* (1937). He died in Malente, Holstein, on 8 September 1963. DtBE; Kosch; Kürschner, 1926-1961; *Wer ist wer*, 1955-1963

Held, Jean-Francis, born 9 July 1930 at Paris, he was educated at the Lycée Janson-de-Sailly, and the Faculté des Lettres de Paris. He was a journalist successively with *Libération* and *Nouvel observateur*. His writings include *Je roule pour vous* (1967), *La déchirure* (1983), he was a joint author of *Les Français et le racisme* (1965), *Israël et les Arabes* (1967), and he edited *Les dernières tribus* (1988). He died on 22 May 2003. Who's who in France, 1979/80-2003/2004

Held, Moshe, born 1 November 1924 at Warszawa, he was educated at the Hebrew University, Jerusalem, and received a Ph.D. in 1957 from Johns Hopkins University, Baltimore, Md., for *Studies in Ugaritic lexicography and poetic style*. Since 1970 he was a professor of Semitic languages at Columbia University, N.Y.C. He died in Beersheba, Israel, on 9 June 1984. CnDiAmJBi; DrAS, 1969 F, 1974 F, 1978 F, 1982 F

Held, Robert, born in 1929, his writings include *The Age of firearms* (New York, 1957). NUC, 1968-72

Helfen, Otto J. Maenchen, 1894-1969 *see* Maenchen-Helfen, Otto John

Helfer, James S., born 19 October 1933 at Syracuse, N.Y., he graduated in 1957 from Dartmouth College, and received his Ph.D. in 1962 from Princeton University. He taught at Oberlin College before he was appointed a professor of history and religion at Wesleyan University, Middletown, Conn. He edited *On method in the history of religions* (1968). DrAS, 1969 P, 1974 P, 1978 P, 1982 P

Helfer, Johann Wilhelm, d. 1840 *see* Helfer, Pauline

Helfer, Pauline (des Granges) Gräfin Nostitz-Rokitnitz., born early 19th cent., she was the wife of the Prague medical doctor, Johann (Jan) Wilhelm (Vilém) Helfer, who was overcome early in the ninteenth century by the desire to throw up his practice and journey East. So he went off to Smyrna, taking his young wife with him. After he was killed on 30 January 1840 by a poisoned arrow when they reached the Andaman Islands, she returned home and wrote *Travels of Doctor and Madame Helfer in Syria, Mesopotamia, Burmah, and other lands* (1878), and its translation, *Johann Wilhelm Helfer's Reisen in Vorderasien und Indien* (1873-77). Kornrumpf; Martinek; Note about the author; OttůvSN

von Helfert, Joseph Alexander, Freiherr, born 3 November 1820 at Prag, he studied law at the local Karls Universität where he received a Dr.jur. in 1842. He was a member of Königliche Böhmische Gesellschaft der Wissenschaften, Prag, and served in a variety of Austrian ministries as an expert on education and the preservation of historical monuments. His writings include *Königin Karolina von Neapel und Sicilien im Kampfe gegen die französische Weltherrschaft, 1790-1814* (1878), *Denkmalpflege* (1897), *Österreichische Geschichtslügen* (1897), *Aufzeichnungen und Erinnerungen aus jungen Jahren* (1904), and *An Ehren und Siegen reich; Bilder aus Österreichs Geschichte* (1908). He died in Wien on 16 March 1910. DtBE; NDB; ÖBL; *Wer ist's*, 1909

Helfgott, Leonard Michael, born in 1937, he received a Ph.D. in 1974 from the University of Maryland, College Park, for *The rise of the Qājār dynasty*. In 1982, he was a professor in the Department of History, Western Washington University, Bellingham, a post which he still held in 2000. His writings include *Ties that bind; a social history of the Iranian carpet* (1994). MESA Roster of members, 1982; NUC

Helfrich, Oscar Louis, born 6 October 1860 at Serang, Java, he was educated at Leiden and subsequently returned to Java until his retirement in 1912. From 1919 to 1921 he was a governor of Curaçao. His writings include *Bidragen tot de kennis van het Midden Maleisch* (Batavia, 1904), and *Nadere bijdragen tot de kennis van het Midden Maleisch* ('s-Gravenhage, 1927). Wie is dat, 1948

Helfritz, Hans, born 25 July 1902 at Hilbersdorf near Chemnitz, Saxony, he studied at the Hochschule für Musik, and the Universität, Berlin, as well as the Universität Wien. He was a writer, composer, ethnomusicologist, explorer and a lecturer on his travels. He was the first European to visit Shabwa, one of the cities claimed as the capital of ancient Sheba. His writings include *Entdeckungsreisen in Süd-Arabien; auf unbekannten Wegen durch Hadramaut und Jemen* (1935), *Glückliches Arabien* (1956), *Schwarze Ritter zwischen Niger und Tschad* (1958), *Berberburgen und Königsstädte des Islam* (1970), and the autobiography, *Neugier trieb mich in die Welt* (1990). He died in Duisburg on 24 October 1995. His large collection went to a number of public institutions in Berlin and Köln. Bidwell; ConAu, 41-42; DtBE; DtBIlnd (3); KDtLK, Nekrolog, 1971-1998; *Tagesspiegel* (Berlin), 24 Oktober 1995; Wer ist wer, 1955

Hélin, Jean-Claude, born 20th cent., he was associated with the Faculté de droit et des sciences politiques de l'Université de Nantes. A joint author of *Droit des enquêtes publiques* (1993), he edited *Les nouvelles procédures d'enquête publique* (1986), and he was a joint editor of *La norme, la ville, la mer; écrits de Nantes pour le doyen Yves Prats* (2000). Livres disponibles, 2004

Hélin de Fiennes, Jean Baptiste, 1669-1767 *see* Fiennes, Jean Baptiste Hélin de

de **Hell**, Ignace Xavier Morand Hommaire, 1812-1848 *see* Hommaire de Hell, Ignace *Xavier* Morand

de **Hell**, Jeanne Louise Adèle H., 1819-1883 *see* Hommaire de Hell, Jeanne Louise *Adèle* née Hériot

Hell, Joseph, born 14 June 1875 at Vilsbiburg, Bavaria, he studied Oriental languages under Fritz Hommel and received a Dr.phil. in 1902 from the Universität Leipzig for *Farazdak's Lobgedicht auf al-Walīd ibn Jazīd*. He was a professor of Oriental philology successively at the universities of München and Erlangen. His other writings include *Die Kultur der Araber* (1909), *Der Islam und die abendländische Kultur* (1915), *Von Mohammed bis Ghazālī* (1915), *Die Religion des Islam* (1915-23), *Neue Hudailiten-Diwane* (1926-33), and *Die arabische Dichtung im Rahmen der Weltliteratur* (1927). He died in Erlangen on 4 January 1950. Fück, p. 317; Hanisch; Kosch; Kürschner, 1928/29-1950; NDB; RHbDtG; Wer ist's, 1928, 1935

Ritter zur **Helle von Samo**, A., born 19th cent., he was a K.k. Ulanenoffizier who embraced Islam. His writings include *Die Völker des Osmanischen Reiches* (1877), and *Das Vilajet der Inseln des Weissen Meeres, das privilegirte Beylik Samos und das selbstständige Mutessariflik Cypern, 1876, nach geographischen, militärischen und national-ökonomi-schen Notizen* (Wien, 1878). Kornrumpf; ZKO

Heller, Bernát (Bernard), born 16 March 1871 at Nagybicse, Hungary, he obtained a doctorate in 1894 from Budapest University for *Az Evangeliumi parabola viszonya az Aggádához*. In 1894 he was ordained at the Landes-Rabbinerschule, Budapest, where he taught from 1922 to 1931. He contributed many articles to the first edition of the *Encyclopaedia of Islam*. His writings include *Az arab Antar-regény* (1918), *Die Bedeutung des arabischen Antar-Romans für die vergleichende Literaturkunde* (1931). In 1941, he was presented with the *Jubilee volume in honour of Prof. Bernhard Heller on the occasion of his seventieth birthday*. He died in Budapest on 26 February 1943. EncJud; Filipsky; Magyar; MagyarZL; *The Rabbinical Seminary of Budapest, 1877-1977* (1986), pp. 194-204

Heller, Erdmute, born 4 July 1930 at Schwäbisch-Hall, Germany, she was from 1949 to 1953 a journalist at Heilbronn and Stuttgart, and subsequently pursued Near Eastern studies, particularly Turkology, at the Universität München, where she received a Dr.phil. in 1961 for *Venedische Quellen zur Lebensgeschichte des Ahmed Paša Hersek-oghlu*. Her other writings include *Arabesken und Talismane; Geschichte und Geschichten des Morgenlandes in der Kultur des Abendlandes* (1992), *Islam, Demokratie, Moderne; aktuelle Antworten arabischer Denker* (1998), and she was a joint author of *Beduinen* (1985), and *Hinter den Schleiern des Islam; Erotik und Sexualität in der arabischen Kultur* (1993). GV; Thesis; ZKO

Heller, Joseph, born in 1937 at Tel Aviv, he graduated from the Hebrew University, where he also gained his M.A.; he received his Ph.D. in 1970 from the London School of Economics for *British policy towards the Ottoman Empire, 1908-1914*, a work which was published in 1983, the year in which he was appointed a lecturer in international relations at the Hebrew University, Jerusalem. His writings include *The Birth of Israel, 1945-1949; Ben-Gurion and his critics* (2000), and works in Hebrew. Note about the author; Sluglett

Heller, Lane Murch, born in 1929, he received his Ph.D. in 1958 from the University of Wisconsin for *Diderot's friend Melchior Grimm*. He was in 1995 a professor of French in the University of Western Ontario, London. His writings include *Bibliographie Blaise Pascal, 1960-1969* (1989), and *La poétique des Fables de La Fontaine* (1994). NatFacDr, 1995; NUC

Heller, Mark A., born 31 August 1946, he received a Ph.D. in 1976 from Harvard University for *Foreign occupation and political elites; a study of the Palestinians*. He was in 1991 a research fellow at Tel Aviv University. His writings include *A Palestinian state; the implications for Israel* (1983), *The New middle class and regime stability in Saudi Arabia* (1985), *No trumpets, no drums; a two-state settlement of the Israeli Palestinian conflict* (1991) as well as works in Hebrew. Note about the author; Selim[3]

Heller, Peter Bruno, born 20 August 1926 at Paris, he graduated in 1958 from New York University where he also received his Ph.D. in 1963 for *Demographic aspects of development in contemporary Egypt*. In 1972, he was appointed a professor of government at Manhattan College, Bronx, N.Y., a post which he still held in 1995. AmM&WSc, 1973 S, 1978 S; NatFacD, 1995; Selim

Heller, Peter Steven, born 16 June 1946 at N.Y.C., he received a Ph.D. in 1971 from Harvard, and was in 1992 associated with the International Monetary Fund. His writings include *A model of public investment expenditure dynamics in less developed countries; the Kenyan case* (1972), *An analysis of the structure, equity and effectiveness of public sector health services in developing countries* (1975), and he was a joint author of *International comparisons of government expenditure revisited; the developing countries, 1975-86* (1990). ZKO; WhoUN, 1992

Hellström, Bo Manne Olofson, born 3 November 1890 at Norrköping, Sweden, he received a doctorate in 1940 from Stockholms Universitet for *Wind effect on lakes and rivers*, and subsequently taught at his alma mater until his retirement. His writings include *The Israelites crossing of the Red Sea* (1950), and *Local effects of acclimatisation to cold in man* (1965). He died in Lidingö on 6 December 1967. SBL; Vem är det, 1949-1967

von **Hellwald**, Friedrich Anton, born 29 March 1842 at Padua (Padova), he was an Austrian army officer until 1872, when he resigned to pursue an interest in scholarly work. He first worked as an editor of *das Ausland* at Augsburg and later at Stuttgart. After ten years with the journal, he became a free-lance writer, addressing himself to the general public rather than the academic world. His writings include *Die heutige Türkei* (1878-79), *Centralasien* (1880), *Die Erde und ihre Völker* (1884), *Die menschliche Familie* (1889), *Die Welt der Slawen* (1990), and *Ethnographische Rösselsprünge* (1891). He died in 1892. ADtB, vol. 50, 173-81; Hinrichsen

Hellwig, Monika Konrad (Mary Cuthbert), born 10 December 1929 at Breslau, Germany, she was educated at Liverpool and received her Ph.D. in 1968 from the American University, Washington, D.C., for *Proposal towards a theology of Israel as a religious community contemporary with the Christian*. She subsequently held a great variety of posts at academic and religious institutions in the U.S.A. and abroad; she was the recipient of numerous honorary degrees. In 1995, she was associated with Georgetown University, Washington, D.C. Her writings include *What are the theologians saying?* (1970), *Tradition, the Catholic story today* (1974), and *Paul Tillich; a new assessment* (1994). ConAu, 37-40; Master (1); WhoRel, 1992

Helm, Sir Alexander *Knox*, born in 1893, he was educated at Dumfries Academy and King's College, Cambridge, after which he entered the Civil Service and was employed in the Foriegn Office, particularly in the Levant Consular Service. His writings include *The Middle East of to-day and its problems* (1956). He died in 1964. BritInd (1); Who was who, 6

Helmholdt, Wolfgang, born about 1937, he studied Arabic at the Universität Halle and collaborated with J. Fück in the publication of *Die arabischen Studien in Europa* (1955). He also studied library science and became an Arabic librarian at the Oriental Department of the Staatsbibliothek, Berlin. He was a difficult person and resigned after a few years on account of differences with his authorities. He subsequently worked in industry as a worker in a supply department. Private

Helms, Christine Moss, born about 1950, she graduated in 1973 from Oberlin (Ohio) College, and received her D.Ph. in 1979 from Oxford University for *Evolution of political identity in Saudi Arabia; delineation of a nation-state, 1901-1932*. She was in 1980 associated with Brookings Institution, Washington, D.C. Her writings include *The Cohesion of Saudi Arabia; evolution of political identity* (1981), *Iraq; the eastern flank of the Arab world* (1984), and *Arabism and Islam; stateless nations and nationless states* (1990). ConAu, 129; Sluglett; ZKO

Helsey, Lucien Edmond Marie Coulond *called Édouard*, born 17 April 1883 at Paris, he trained for the priesthood, but turned to journalism in 1906. He covered the Balkan conflict and, after the first World War, the campaigns in the Rif and the Jebel Druze. His writings include *L'an dernier à Jérusalem* (1930), *Pistes noires* (1945), and *Envoyé spécial* (1955). He died in Paris on 30 June 1966. DBF; WhoFr, 1955/56-1965/66

Hémardinquer, Jean Jacques, born 20th cent., he edited *Pour une histoire de l'alimentation* (Paris, 1970). NUC, 1968-72

Hemingway, Martha Ellis Gellhorn, 1908-1998 *see* Gellhorn, Martha Ellis

Hemmerdinger, Bertrand, fl. 20th cent., his writings include *Essai sur l'histoire du texte de Thucydide* (Paris, 1955), *Les manuscrits d'Hérodote et la critique verbale* (Genova, 1981), and he edited *Œuvres* d'Adolphe Dureau de la Malle (1986). Livres disponibles, 2004

Hempel, Helga, born 20th cent., she was in 2004 resident in Berlin. Her writings include *Dokumentation; Probleme der nationalen Befreiungsbewegung in den Dokumenten der internationalen Beratungen der kommunistischen und Arbeiterparteien, der Parteitage der KPdSU, der SED und ausgewählter theoretischer Konferenzen, 1949-1971* (Potsdam-Babelsberg, Deutsche-Akademie für Staats- und Rechtswissenschaft "Walter Ulbricht", Informationszentrum Staat und Recht, 1972), and she was a joint author of *Der Nahostkonflikt, Gefahr für den Weltfrieden; Dokumente von der Jahrhundertwende bis zur Gegenwart* (Berlin, Staatsverlag der DDR, 1987).

de **Hen**, Ferdinand J., born in 1933, he was an ethnomusicologist whose writings include *Beitrag zur Kenntnis der Musikinstrumente aus Belgisch Kongo und Ruanda-Urundi* (1960), and he was a joint author of *Musikinstrumente aus zwei Jahrtausenden* (1968). Master (1); NUC; ZKO

Henckel, Wilhelm Eduard, born 17 April 1825 at Burg near Magdeburg, Prussia, he was a publisher, translator and writer who attained great merits for popularizing Russian literature in Germany. His writings include *Russlands wirthschaftliche Lage im Jahre 1891* (1892), as well as translations from L. Tolstoi, and he was a joint author of *Wahnsinnige als Herrscher und Führer der Völker* (1910). He died in München on 30 November 1910. BioJahr, 15 (1913), Totemliste, col. 37*; KDtLK, 1895-1910

Henderson, Algo Donmyer, born 26 April 1897 at Solomon, Kan., he was a professor of business administration, particularly the administration of universities and colleges. His writings include *Policies and pratices in higher education* (1960), *Training university administrators* (1970), and its translation, *La formation des administrateurs d'université* (1972). He died in San Francisco on 20 October 1988. BioIn, 3; BlueB, 1973/74, 1975, 1976; ConAu, 1-4, 126; Master (1); NYT, 24 October 1988, p. B-12, cols. 4-5; WhAm, 9; WhoAm, 1978; WhoWor, 1978/79

Henderson, Eugénie Jane Andrina, born in 1914, she taught phonetics at the University of London since 1937, and delivered her inaugural lecture at SOAS on 5 May 1965, entitled *The domain of phonetics*. Her writings include *Tiddim Chin; a descriptive analysis of two texts* (1965), and she edited *Indo-Pacific linguistic studies*; papers of the Conference on Linguistic Problems of the Indo-Pacific Area (1965). She died in 1989. IntWW, 1989/90; Who, 1988-1989; Who was who, 8

Henderson, John Robertson, born 21 May 1863 at Melrose, Scotland, he entered the Indian Civil Service and was a superintendent, Government Museum and Principal Librarian, Connemara Public Library, Madras, 1911-1919. His writings include *The Coins of Haidar Ali and Tipu Sultan* (1921). He died in Edinburgh on 26 October 1925. Riddick; Who's who, 1921; Who was who, 2

Henderson, Keith Meader, born 24 May 1934 at Bakersfield, Calif., he graduated in 1956 from Occidental College, and received his Ph.D. in 1961 from the University of Southern California for *A content analysis and theoretic exploration of evasiveness of governmental administrators*. He was a professor of public administration in New York State, except for three years when he served as a professor at A.U.B. His writings include *The Study of public administration* (1983), *Public administration* (1984), and *Bureaucracy and the alternatives in world perspective* (1999). AmM&WSc, 1973 S, 1978 S; ConAu, 21-24; WhoE, 1974/75-1989

Henderson, Kenneth David Druitt, born 4 September 1903 at London, he was educated at University College, Oxford, and entered the Sudan Political Service in 1926. His writings include *Sudan Republic* (1966), *Set under authority* (1987), and he edited *The Making of modern Sudan; the life and letters of Sir Douglas Newbold, K.B.E., of the Sudan Political Service* (1954). He died on 23 March 1988. Au&Wr, 1963; IntAu&W, 1989; Who's who, 1959-1988; Who was who, 8; WrDr, 1976/78-1988/90

Henderson, Michael Magnus Thyne, born in 1942, he received a Ph.D. in 1972 from the University of Wisconsin for *Dari (Kabul Persian) phonology*. He was for many years a professor of foreign languages and literatures at Juniata College, Huntington, Pa. NatFacDr, 1995-2004; NUC, 1973-77

Henderson, William Otto, born 25 December 1904 at London, he was educated at Downing College, Cambridge, and received his Ph.D. from LSE. He taught at English universities and became a reader in international economic history. His writings include *Britain and industrial Europe, 1750-1870* (1954), *The Zollverein* (1959), *The Genesis of the Common Market* (1962), *The Industrialization of Europe, 1780-1914* (1969), *The Rise of German industrial power* (1975), and *Friedrich List* (1983). Au&Wr, 1963, 1971; ConAu, 1-4; IntAu&Wr, 1976-1989; WrDr, 1976/78-2000

Hendley, Thomas Holbein, born 21 April 1847, he was educated privately and at St. Bartholomew's Hospital. He joined the Indian Medical Service in 1869. From 1898 to his retirement in 1903 he was inspector-general of civil hospitals, Calcutta, with the rank of colonel. He died in London on 2 February 1917. Buckland; IndianBiInd (3); Riddick; *Who was who*, 2

Hendrickx, Benjamin, born 20th cent., he was a writer on Byzantine history. His writings include Οἱ πολιτικοί καὶ στρατιωτικοὶ θεσμοὶ τῆς λατινικῆς αὐτοκρατορίας τῆς Κωνσταντινουπόλεως κατκα τοὺς πρώτους χρόνους τῆς ὑπαρξεώς τῆς Θεσσαλονίκης (Thessalonica, 1970). NUC, 1973-77; OSK

Hendrikson, Kurt Heinrich, born 18 November 1913 at Podblon in one of the Baltic states, he received a Dr.rer.pol. in 1943 from the Universität Berlin. He was a barrister, and a consultant on corporation and credit law. His writings include *Die Technik der Kreditwürdigkeitsprüfung* (1956), *Rationelle* Unternehmensführung (1966), *Praktische Entwicklungspolitik* (1971), and he was a joint author of *Report on the progress of development projects in the Somali Republic* (Mogadishu, 1968). Wer ist wer, 1979-1991/2

Hendry, W., born 19th cent., he was in 1924 a chairman of the local committee of the British Empire Exhibition, Zanzibar, 1924. He edited *Zanzibar; an account of its people, industries, and history* (1924). His trace is lost after an article in 1927. NUC, pre-1956

Henggeler, Josef, born 28 February 1886 at Kreuzlingen, Canton Thurgau, he received a Dr.jur. in 1909 from the Universität Zürich for *Beiträge zur Lehre von Börsenstrafrecht*. He became a barrister and authority on Swiss fiscal and corporation law. His writings include *Die Praxis der Bundessteuern* (1943), and he was a joint author of *Das internationale Steuerrecht des Erdballs* (1936). WhoSwi, 1950/51

Henin, Roushdi A., born 13 November 1920 at Cairo, he was from 1953 to 1959 a senior statistician at the Department of Statistics, Republic of Sudan. In 1965, he received a Ph.D. from the University of London for *Fertility differentials in the Sudan, with reference to the nomadic and settled populations.* His writings include *Aspects of African demography* (1971), *Fertility, infertility, and sub-fertility in eastern Africa* (1982), *Population and development in Kenya* (1984), he was a joint author of *1967 population census of Tanzania* (1972), and he was a joint editor of *The Population of Tanzania* (1973). LC; Sluglett; Unesco

Henkel, Ludwig, born 19 May 1859 at Wasungen, Thuringia, he studied at the universities of Jena and Marburg, where he received a Dr.phil. in 1882. He was since 1886 a teacher at Königliche Landesschule Pforta near Naumburg, concurrently pursuing an interest in geography and geology. His writings include *Geologische Spaziergänge in Pfortas Umgebung* (1898), *Die Abhängigkeit der menschlichen Siedlungen von der geographischen Lage* (1898), *Geologische Heimatskunde der Naumburger Gegend* (1920), and *Von der Konvergenz zweier Geraden* (1931). Poggendorff

Henker, Fritz, born about 1910, he was a union official and served until 1970 as a committee member for foreign relations and migration as well as a member of the administrative council in the Institut für Auslandsbeziehungen. Note about the author

Hennebelle, Guy, born 20th cent., his writings include *Les Cinémas africains en 1972* (1972), *Quinze ans de cinéma mondial, 1960-1975* (1975), *Guide des films anti-impérialistes* (1975), *Grands cinéastes* (1981); he was a joint author of *Le Cinéma colonial; de "L'atlantide" à "Lawrence d'Arabie"* (1975); he edited *Algériens-Français; bientôt finis les enfantillages; Panoramiques, 62* (2003); and he was a joint editor of *La Palestine et le cinéma* (1977). Livres disponibles, 2004

Hennequin, Gilles, born 20th cent., he was associated with the Département des monnaies et médailles et antiques at the Bibliothèque nationale, Paris. His writings include *Catalogue des monnaies orientales* [du] *Cabinet des médailles, Archives de la Ville de Marseille* (1983), and he was a joint author of *Les Monnaies de Bâlis* (1978). MESA Roster of members, 1982-1990; ZKO

Hennig, Richard, born 12 January 1874 at Berlin, he there studied natural sciences, meteorology, and history, gaining a doctorate in 1897. A private scholar since 1909, he two years later established the journal, *Weltverkehr*, and, in 1919, was invited to teach geography of transport at Verkehrshochschule Düsseldorf, a post which he held until his retirement in 1939. His research focused on historical geography. He studied the reliability of legends and literature as well as Homer's knowledge of the Mediterranean Sea. His writings include *Deutsch-Südwest im Weltkriege* (1920), *Rheinschiffahrt und Versailler Friede* (1921), *Sturm und Sonnenschein in Deutsch-Südwest* (1926), *Terrae incognitae* (1936-39), and *Wege des Verkehrs* (1939). He died in Düsseldorf on 22 December 1951. DtBE; Kürschner, 1928, 1935; NDB; Wer ist's, 1928, 1935

Henniker, Sir Mark Chandos Auberon, born in 1906, he was educated at Marlborough College, the Royal Military Academy, Woolwich, and King's College, Cambridge. He joined the Royal Engineers and served in India both before and after the second World War. His writings include *Memoirs of a junior officer* (1951), *Red shadow over Malaysia* (1955), and *Life in the Army to-day* (1957). He died on 18 October 1991. Au&Wr, 1963, 1971; Who, 1969-1992

Henning, Max, born 18 December 1861 at Ruda, Pos., Germany, he was an Orientalist and novellist as well as the publisher and editor of the journal *Das freie Wort*. His writings include *Der Teufel, sein Mythos und seine Geschichte im Christentum* (1921), and he translated from the Arabic, *Tausend und eine Nacht* (1895-1900), and *Der Koran* (1901). He died in 1927. Hanisch; KDtLK, 1915-1926

Henning, Walter Bruno Hermann, born 26 August 1908 at Ragnitz an der Memel, East Prussia, he was educated at Köslin, Pomeria. He started his academic career in mathematics, but through an interest in the history of this subject, and the geography of the Middle East, he soon made Iranian and Arabic his major field of study, working under Friedrich Carl Andreas at the Universität Göttingen. After some time as an assistant to the *Concordance of Islamic tradition* at Leiden, he obtained a Dr.phil. *summa cum laude* at Göttingen in 1931 for *Das Verbum des Mittelpersischen der Turfanfragmente*, his dis-sertation being an award from the Philosophische Fakultät. He was appointed an editor of Manichean manuscripts for the Preußische Akademie der Wissenschaften, Berlin, a position he held until 1936 when he emigrated to Britain to become a lecturer in Iranian subjects at SOAS. In 1954 he became chairman of the executive council of the *Corpus Inscriptionum Iranicarum*, and also fellow of the British Academy. From 1958 he headed the Near and Middle East Department of SOAS until his departure for Berkeley in 1961 to accept the professorship in Iranian studies at the University of California, in which post he remained until his death on 8 January 1967 from complications resulting from an ac-cident which had occurred two weeks earlier. His writings include *Sogdica* (1940), *Zoroaster, politician or witch-doctor* (1951), and *A Fragment of a Khwarezmian dictionary* (1971). EncIran; Hanisch; *Iranistische Mitteilungen*, vol. 1 ii (1967), pp. 4-18, vol. 2 i (1968), pp. 86-92; *Indo-Iranian journal*, 10 (1967/68), pp. 308-13; Thesis

Henninger, Joseph Anton Martin, born 12 May 1906 at Wiesbaden, Germany, he studied philosophy and theology at St. Augustin near Bonn and the Pontificia Università Gregoriana, Roma, and ethnology and Oriental stududies at Wien and the Pontificium Institutum Biblicum, Roma. He taught at the Université de Fribourg, 1956-76, and Universität Bonn, 1964-74. In 1976 he was honoured by the jubilee volume, *al-Bahit, Festschrift Joseph Henninger zum 70. Geburtstag*. His writings include *Les fêtes de printemps chez les Sémites et la Pâque israélite* (1975). He died about 1993 in Switzerland. Hanisch; WhoSwi, 1986/87

Hennique, Privat Agathon Benjamin Arthur, born 19th cent., his writings include *Caboteurs et pêcheurs de la côte de Tunisie en 1882* (1884), and *Une Page d'archéologie navale; les caboteurs et pêcheurs de la côte de Tunisie* (1888). BN; NUC, pre-1956

Henrey, Katherine Helen, born about 1900, she was associated with the United Society for Christian Literature, London. Her writings include *An Historical background to the Old Testament* (London, 1951). BLC

Henriet, Marie Odile, born about 1940, she received a doctorate in 1972 from the Université René Descartes, Paris, for *Communauté villageoise et habit à Gozo* [Malta.] NUC

Henry, Jean Robert, born 20th cent., he was associated with the Institut de recherches et d'études sur le monde arabe et musulman. His writings include *Le Mouvement national algérien; textes, 1912-1954* (1978), *La Doctrine coloniale du droit musulman algérien; bibliographie* (1979), *Littératures et temps colonial* (1999); he was a joint author of *Nouveaux enjeux culturels au Maghreb* (1986), *Politiques méditerranéennes* (2000), *Où va l'Algérie?* (2001); and he was a joint editor of *Formation des normes en droit international du développement* (1984), *L'Enseignement du droit musulman* (1989), and *Le Maghreb dans l'imaginaire français* (2001). LC; *Livres disponibles*, 2004; Note about the author

Henry, Louis, born 20th cent., he was a writer on demography whose writings include *Anciennes familles genevoises; étude démographique* (Paris, 1956), *Leçons d'analyse démographique* (Paris, 1960), *Manuel de démographie historique* (Genève, 1967), *Démographie; analyse et modèles* (Paris, 1972), and its translation, *Population; analysis and models* (1976). BN; NUC

Henry, Paul, born in 1906 at Louvain, he went to school in England during the first World War. He then returned to Belgium, and studied philosophy and theology at Louvain, and joined the Society of Jesus. He did further studies at the Sorbonne, where he received a doctorate in 1938 for his two theses, *Les états du texte de Plotin*, and *La vision d'Ostie, sa place dans la vie et l'œuvre de Saint Augustin*. He then studied Arabic in Syria, Lebanon, and Palestine. In Roma he did further studies and received an S.T.D., as well as a licentiate in Sacred Scripture, from the Pontificia Università Gregoriana. He was appointed a professor at the Institut catholique de Paris. He published several fundamental studies on Plotinus and the development of Neo-Platonism in Western thought. He was a visiting professor at a variety of United States universities. His writings include *Plotin et l'Occident* (1934), and *Saint Augustine on personality* (1960). He died in Gand on 8 August 1984. Jalabert; *Journal of the history of philosophy*, 23 (1985), p. 453

Henry, René, born in 1871 at Limoges, he was a professor at the École libre des sciences politiques, Paris. His writings include *La Femme électeur* (1901), *Questions d'Autriche-Hongrie et question d'Orient* (1903), *Des Monts de Boême au Golfe persique* (1908), *La Question de Finlande au point de vue juridique* (1910), and *La Politique mondiale de l'Allemagne* (1918). IndexBFr² (1); Master (1)

Henry de Generet, Robert, born about 1900, he was associated with the Faculté de philosophie et lettres de l'Université de Liège. He edited and translated *Le Martyre d'Ali Akbar, drame persan* (Liège, 1946). ZKO

Henrys, Paul Prosper, born 13 March 1862 at Neufchâteau (Vosges), he was educated at the colleges at Verdun, St.-Mihiel, the lycée de Nancy, and the military academies of Saint-Cyr., and Saumur. He served in Algeria from 1887 to 1893, when he entered the École supérieure de guerre. He was posted to the French Soudan, where he participated in the campaigns against rebellious Touareg. Serving under General Lyautey since 1903, he served in Aïn Sefra, Algeria, Chott el-Gharbi, and various locations in Morocco until he was recalled to fight in Lorraine during the final years of the first World War. He spent the last two years before his retirement in 1924 with the Armée du Rhin. He died in Paris on 6 November 1943. DBF; *Qui êtes-vous*, 1924

Hensel, Howard Milton, born 21 August 1946 at Chicago, he graduated in 1968 from Texas A&M University and received a Ph.D. in 1976 from Virginia Polytechnic Institute and State University, Blacksburg, for *Soviet policy in the Persian Gulf, 1968-1975*. From 1983 to 1986 he was a visiting professor of national security affairs at the Air Command and Staff College, and since 1986 he was a professor of Soviet studies at the Air War College, Maxwell Air Force Base, Ala. His writings include *The Anatomy of failure* (1985). Selim³; WhoS&SW, 1993/94

Hensel, Wojciech, born in 1943, he was associated with Uniwersitet Warszawski and was, with Tadeusz Majda, a joint author of *Wybór tekstów z wspólczesnej literatury tureckiej; proza* (Warszawa, 1975), and *Wybór klasycznych i wspólczesnych tekstów tureckich; poezja* (Warszawa, 1982). He died in 1990. Index Islamicus; OSK

Henselmann, Manja, Miss, born about 1870, she arrived in Persia in 1899 and became the director of the orphanage at the Deutsche Orient-Mission in Khoi (Khvoy). An assassination attempt on 23 February 1901 failed, but the assassins were never caught. Note about the author

Henshaw, Thomas, born in 1618 at London, he was educated as a commoner at University College, Oxford, in 1634, and remained there five years without taking a degree. He entered the Middle Temple. He went to Holland and subsequently entered the French army, went to Italy, returned to England after the Restauration and became French secretary to the King. A fellow of the Royal Society, he edited *Etymologicon Linguae Anglicanae* (London, 1671). He died in 1700. BritInd (3); DNB

von Hentig, Werner Otto, born 22 May 1886 at Berlin, he there studied law and received a Dr.jur. in 1909 for *Die Exterritorialität in ihrer modernen Rechtserscheinung*, entering the diplomatic service two years later. Until the outbreak of the first World War he was posted successively to Peking, Constantinople, and Tehran. In 1915 he was sent on a horseback mission to the Emir of Afghanistan to incite him against the British in India, experiences which are embodied in his *Ins verschlossene Land; Kampf mit Mensch und Meile* (1918), and its translation, *Als diplomaat naar het gesloten land* (1918). In 1955, he was an adviser to King Sa'ūd. His writings include *Der Nahe Osten rückt näher* (1940), *Heimritt durch Kurdistan* (1943), and his biography, *Mein Leben eine Dienstreise* (1962). He died in Lindesnes, Norway, on 8 August 1984. DtBE; *Wer ist wer*, 1963

Hentsch, Thierry, born in 1944, he received a doctorate in 1973 from the Université de Genève for *Face au blocus; histoire de l'intervention du Comité international de la Croix-Rouge dans le conflit du Nigeria, 1967-1970*. He was a sometime professor of political science at the Université de Québec, Montréal. His writings include *L'Orient imaginaire; la vision politique occidentale de l'Est méditerranéen*

(1988), *Introduction aux fondements de la politique* (1993), *Raconter et mourir; l'Occident et ses grands recits* (2002), and *La Croyance* (2003). LC; *Livres disponibles*, 2004

Henze, Paul Bernard, born 29 August 1924 at Redwood Falls, Minn., he was a graduate of St. Olaf College and Harvard. He was a nomadic academic and a U.S. civil service officer who held positions in the Department of Defense, Radio Free Europe, the C.I.A. in Ethiopia and Turkey, and Johns Hopkins University, Baltimore, Md. In 1982, he became resident consultant to the RAND Corporation. His writings include *Ethiopian journeys* (1977), *The plot to kill the Pope* (1983), *The Horn of Africa from war to peace* (1991), *The Transcaucasus in transition* (1991), and *Turkish democracy and the American alliance* (1993). ConAu, 206; Master (2); Shavit - Africa; WhoAm, 1974-1999|; WhoWor, 1982-1989/90

Heper, Metin, born in 1940, he was successively a professor of political science at Middle East Technical University, Ankara, Boğaziçi Üniversitesi, Bebek, and Bilkent Üniversitesi, Ankara. He was a visiting scholar at Harvard, 1977-78, Southwest Texas State University, 1978, Hebrew University, Jerusalem, 1979-80, and University of Connecticut, 1981-82. His writings include *Modernleşme ve bürokrasi* (1973); and he was a joint author of *Development administration in Turkey* (1980). KimKimdir, 1997/98-2000; Note about the author

Hepper, Frank Nigel, born about 1930. For many years he was affiliated with the Herbarium, Royal Botanical Gardens, Kew (London). He was a member of ASTENE. His writings include *Pharaoh's flowers* (1990), *Luigi Balungani's drawings of African plants* (1991), and *The plants of Pehr Frosskĺhl's 'Flora Aegyptiaco-Arabica'* (1994).

Heradstveit, Daniel, born in 1940, he was a research fellow in the Norsk Utenrikspolitisk Institutt (Norwegian Institute of International Affairs), Oslo, and a college and university lecturer. His writings include *Palestinsk gerilja* (1969), *Brennpunkt i Midt-Austen* (1971), its translation, *Nahost-Guerillas; eine politische Studie* (1973), *Jews and Arabs* (1972), *Arab and Israeli elite perceptions* (1974), and *The Arab-Israeli conflict; psychological obstacles to peace* (1979). IWWAS, 1975/76; ZKO

Her, Michael, ca. 1490-1550 *see* Herr, Michel

Heras, Henry (Enrique), S.J., born in 1888 at Barcelona, he was a director and founder of the Indian Historical Research Institute, Bombay. His writings include *The Aravidu dynasty of Vijayanagara* (1927), *The Pallava genealogy* (1931), *The Conversion policy of the Jesuits in India* (1933), *Studies in Proto-Indo-Mediterranean culture* (1953), and a collection of his papers, together with a bibliography of 293 items, *Indological studies* (1990). He died in 1955. WhE&EA; ZKO

Heras'kova (Гераськова), Liubov' Sergeevna, born 20th cent., her writings include *Скульптура середньовічних кочовиків степів східної Європи* (Kyïv, 1991). LC; OSK

Héraud, Guy Maurice Émile, born 29 October 1920 at Avignon, he was educated at Reims and Pau, and studied law at the universities of Bordeaux and Toulouse, where received a doctorate in 1946 for *L'Ordre juridique et le pouvoir originaire*. He was successively a professor of law at Toulouse, Strasbourg, and Pau. In 1953 he served as a director of the Centres d'études juridiques du Maroc. His writings include *L'Europe des ethnies* (1963), *Les régions d'Europe* (1973), *Les Principes du fédéralisme et la fédération européenne* (1968), its translation, and *Die Prinzipien des Föderalismus und die Europäische Föderation* (1979), and he was a joint author of *Europe-Jura* (1965). He was honoured by *Fédéralisme, régionalism et droit des groupes ethniques en Europe; hommage à Guy Héraud* (1989), and *Regionalism, minorities and civil society in contemporary Europe; a volume in honour of Prof. Dr.h.c. Héraud* (1991). WhoFr, 1969/70-1987/88

d'Herbelot de Molainville, Barthélemy, born 14 December 1695 at Paris, he was educated at the Université de Paris and devoted himself to the study of Oriental languages, going to Italy to perfect himself in them by conversing with the Orientals who frequented its sea-ports. Upon his return to France after a year and a half, he was received into the house of Fouquet, *contrôleur général des finances*, who granted him a pension. Losing this on the disgrace of Fouquet in 1662, he was appointed secretary and interpreter of Oriental languages to Louis XIV. A few years later, he again visited Italy, when the Grand-Duke Ferdinand II of Tuscany presented him with a large number of Oriental maunuscripts, and tried to attach him to his court. However, he was recalled to France by Colbert, and received from the king a pension equal to the one he had lost. In 1692 he succeeded d'Auvergne in the chair of Syriac in the Collège de France. His great work, the *Dictionnaire orientale, ou dictionnaire universel contenant tout ce qui regarde la connoissance des peuples de l'Orient*, occupied him nearly all his life, and was completed in 1697 by Antoine Galland. A German translation, *Orientalische Bibliothek*, was published between 1785 and 1790. The work is based on Hājjī Khalīfah (Kâtib Çelebi's) *Kashf al-zunūn*. The manuscripts of Herbelot's other works are kept at the Collège de France. He died in Paris on 8 December 1695. Henry Laurens wrote *La Bibliothèque orientale de*

Barthélemi d'Herbelot; aux sources de l'orientalisme (1978). DBF; EncBrit; EncIran; EncItaliana; Füch, p. 98; GdeEnc; GDU

Herber, Joseph, his writings include *Tatouage et états mentaux* (Lyon, 1950). NUC, pre-1956

Herbert, Aubrey Nigel Henry Molyneux, born in 1880, he was educated at Eton and Balliol College, Oxford. A sometime attaché at Constantinople, and Conservative MP, he travelled extensively both in the Near and Far East and also knew the Balkans well. The first World War found him in Cairo before he was sent with Lawrence on the extraordinary attempt to bribe the Turkish general surrounding Kūt al-'Amārah to raise the siege. His writings include *Mons, Anzac, Kut* (1919), and *Ben Kendim, a record of Eastern travel* (1924). He died in 1923. Bidwell; DNB, missing persons; Kornrumpf; Who was who, 2

Herbert, Frederick William von, born 19th cent., he took part in the 1877 defence of Plevna, Bulgaria, with the rank of captain. His writings include *The Defence of Plevna* (1895), its Turkish translation, *Plevne müdafaasında bir İngiliz* (1938), *A Chronicle of a virgin fortress, being some unrecorded chapters of the Turkish and Bulgarian history* (1896), and *By-paths in the Balkans* (1906). BLC; ZKO

Herbert, Marie, pseud., 1859-1925 *see* Keiter, Therese

Herbert, Nicholas, born 20th cent., his writings include the pamphlet, *Jews and Arabs in conflict* (London, 1970). NUC, 1968-72

Herbert, Sir Thomas, born in 1597, he was a chamberlain to King Charles I and travelled in Persia, 1627-1629. His writings include *Some years travels into divers parts of Africa and Asia the Great, describing more particularly the empires of Persia and Indvustan* (1634), its translation, *Relation du voyage de Perse et des Indes Orientales* (1663), and *Travels in Persia, 1627-1629* (1928). He died about 1642. BritInd (2); Cambridge history of Iran; DNB; EncIran; Master (2); WhWE

Herbette, François, born 25 January 1885 at Paris, he graduated from the lycée Condorcet, the École normale supérieure, and received his *agrégation* in history and geography. He did not teach, preferring to devote himself to the study of economic problems. He was a *directeur général* of the Société d'études et d'information économiques, and a consultant to the Banque d'Indochine. His writings include *L'expérience marxiste en France; témoignage d'un cobaye conscient, 1936-1938* (1959). He died in Paris on 15 March 1960. DBF

Herbette, Jean, born 7 August 1878 at Paris, he studied at the Sorbonne, where he received degrees in arts as well as law, later gaining a doctorate in physical sciences for *Contribution à l'étude de l'isomorphisme*. He became a journalist with *le Temps* at the political desk, but also contributed to *Politique étrangère*. From 1924 to 1931 he served as ambassador at Moscow. His writings include *Un diplomate français parle du péril bolcheviste* (1943). He died in Clarens, Switzerland, on 21 November 1960. DBF; IndexBFr² (1)

Herbette, Maurice Lucien Georges, born 11 November 1871 at Paris, he was educated at the lycée Condorcet and Französisches Gymnasium, Berlin. After his study in 1896, he became a secretary at the Direction politique of the Quai d'Orsay. He played an important role in the 1912 Agadir affair. In 1917 he was nominated director of administrative and technical affairs at the Quai d'Orsay, and in 1922, he became French ambassador at Bruxelles, where he died on 4 November 1929. His writings include *Une ambassade turque sous le Directoire* (1902), *Une ambassade persane sous Louis XIV* (1907), and he translated from the German of Bernhard von Bülow, *La politique allemande* (1914). DBF; IndexBFr² (1); Qui êtes-vous, 1924

Herbordt, Oskar, born 19th cent. at Cassel, Hesse, he received a Dr.phil. in 1907 from the Universität Zürich for *Geologische Aufnahme der Umgegend von Rapperswil-Pfäffikon am Zürichsee*. He became a mining engineer. Thesis

Herczeg, Ferenc (Franz), born 22 September 1863 at Versec, Hungary, he studied law and did his articling at Temesvár and Budapest. He early in life began to write, his first literary works in 1886 being in German, but in the following year he began to publish in Hungarian. He became a successful and popular Hungarian literary figure of the early twentieth century. His writings, many of which were translated into German, include *Pogányok* (1902), its Turkish translation, *Paganlar* (1945), *Harcok és harcosok* (1935), and *Szelek számyán* (1957). He died in Budapest on 24 February 1954. CasWL; GeistigeUng; Magyar; Master (4)

Herdan, Gustav, born 21 January 1897 at Brünn, Moravia, he received a doctorate in 1923 at Praha and a Dr.phil. in 1937 from the Universität Wien for *Die Reduplicationen des Shih Ching*. He became a member of the Imperial College of Science and Technology, and was since 1948 a lecturer at the University of Bristol. His writings include *Small particle statistics* (1953), *Language as choice and chance* (1956), *Type-token mathematics; a textbook of mathematical linguistics* (1960), *The Calculus of lin-*

guistic observations (1962), and *The Advanced theory of language as choice and chance* (1966). ConAu, 1-4

von Herder, Johann Gottfried, born in 1744 at Mohrungen, East Prussia, he was one of the most prolific and influential writers that Germany has produced. He died in Weimar in 1803. DLB, 97 (1990), pp. 104-121; EncBrit; GdeEnc; *Geographers*, 10 (1986), pp. 77-84

Herfort, Paule, this was the pseudonym of a journalist born in the 19th century. She was educated at a girls religious institution at Tours and became a writer on political affairs with the journal *Minerva* . After the first World War she went to Paris, where she entered the Ministry of the Interior as an editor. She subsequently entered the Ministry of Foreign Affairs at the Service secret de la propaganda, a post which she held until the end of 1929. Her writings include *Chez les Romains fascistes* (Paris, 1934), *Échec au lion* (Paris, 1938), and *Sous le soleil levant* (Paris, 1943). Her trace is lost after an article in 1956. *Qui est-ce*, 1934

Hérin, Robert, born 20th cent., he was in the 1980s a *maître assistant* in the Institut de géographie de Caen. His writings include *Les travailleurs saisonniers d'origine étrangère en France* (1971), *Atlas de la France scolaire; de la maternelle au lycée* (1994), *Espaces et sociétés à la fin du XXe siècle; quelles géographies sociales?* (1998), and he edited *L'enseignement privé en Europe II; journées d'Angers, mai, 1998* (2001). LC; *Livres disponibles*, 2004

Hering, Gunnar, born 2 April 1934 at Dresden, Germany, he studied at the universities in Berlin, and Wien, where he received a doctorate in 1966. He travelled extensively in the Balkans and Turkey, and taught for five years at Göttingen, and four years at Salonika, before he was appointed chairman of the Institut für Byzantinistik und Neogräzistik at the Universität Wien. His writings include *Ökumenisches Patriarchat und europäische Politik, 1620-1638* (1968), and its translation, *Οικουμενικο πατραρχειο και ευρωπαικη πολιρτικη, 1620/1638* (1992). He died on 22 December 1994. WhoAustria, 1996; *Zeitschrift für Balkanologie* 33 (1997), pp. 127-31

Herkless, John L., born in 1940, his writings include the edition and translation, *Sir John Robert Seeley; a study of the historian* (Wolfeboro, N.H., 1987). LC

Herlihy, Patricia Ann McGahey, born in 1930, she received a Ph.D. in 1963 from the University of Pennsylvania for *Russian grain and Mediterranean markets, 1774-1861*. Her writings include *Odessa; a history, 1794-1914* (Cambridge, Mass., Harvard Ukrainian Research Institute, 1986). LC

Herlt, Gustav, born 25 April 1867 at Schönau, Bohemia, he studied at the Universität Wien and became a writer on economic and financial affairs. Stationed at Constantinople, he contributed to a variety of German-language journals and dailies; he was a sometime editor of the *Konstantinopler Handelsblatt*; and he was a joint author of *Geld, Industrialisierung und Petroleumschätze der Türkei* (Berlin, 1918). DtBiInd (1); Kornrumpf; *Wer ist's*, 1922-1928

Herman, Arthur Ludwig, born 16 November 1930 at Minneapolis, Minn., he graduated in 1952 from the University of Minnesota, where he also received his Ph.D. in 1970 for *The problem of evil and Indian thought*. After successively teaching philosophy at the University of Florida, Gainesville, and Hamilton College, Clinton, N.Y., he returned to his alma mater as a professor and there taught until his retirement. His other writings include *India folk tales* (1968), and *An Introduction to Indian thought* (1976). ConAu, 65-68; DrAS, 1974 P, 1978 P, 1982 P; NatFacDr, 1995; WhoRel, 1993/93; ZKO

Herman, Emil, S.J., born 5 April 1891 at Aachen, Germany, he was a professor of Oriental canon law at the Pontificio Istituto Biblico di Roma. His writings include *Leben aus Gott* (1936), and *Conspectus historiae iuris ecclesiastici Byzantini* (1953). He died in Münster on 20 January 1963. Kosch, Kürschner, 1954, 1961

Hermann, Alfred, born 11 May 1904 at Leipzig, he received a Dr.habil. in 1959 from the Universität Köln for *Altägyptische Liebeslieder*. He was an archaeologist and associated with museums in Berlin and Cairo, subsequently becoming a lecturer in Egyptology at Köln. His writings include *Die Welt der Fellachen* (1952). Hanisch; Kürschner, 1954-1996|; Schwarz; Sezgin

Hermann, Eduard, born 19 December 1869 at Coburg, Bavaria, he studied classical and comparative philology at the universities of Jena, Freiburg im Breisgau, and Leipzig, receiving a Dr.phil. in 1893 from the Universität Jena. After twenty years of school teaching, his publication of the *Griechische Forschungen* (1912), gained him a professorship of Indo-European philology successively at the universities of Kiel, Frankfurt am Main, and Göttingen. His other writings include *Die Sprach-wissenschaft in der Schule* (1923), *Litauische Studien* (1926), and *Lautgesetz und Analogie* (1931). He died in Göttingen on 14 February 1950. DtBE; Kürschner, 1926-1940/41; NDB; *Wer ist's*, 1922-1935

Hermann (Германъ), Karl August, born 11 September 1851 at Võhma, Livland, he started life as a teacher at the Parochial-Schule in Oberpahlen, and subsequently taught from 1873 to 1875 at St. Petersburg. He there studied theology from 1875 to 1878, when he went to the Universität Leipzig to study philology and take his Dr.phil. in 1880 for *Der einfache Wortstamm und die drei Lautstufen in der estnischen Sprache, mit vergleichenden Hinweisen auf das Suomi.* From 1880 to 1881 he was a free-lance writer in Reval and Dorpat; from 1882 to 1886, an editor of *Eesti Post*; and since 1889, owner and editor of the Dorpat newspaper, *Post*. In 1889, he became a lecturer in Estonian language and literature at Dorpat University. He was a member of the Estnische Gesellschaft zu Dorpat, a sometime conductor of Estonian choirs, and vice-president of the Estonian Literary Society. He also translated German literary works into Estonian. He died in Dorpat on 29 December1908/11 January 1909. Artur Vahter wrote *Karl August Hermanni päevik* (Tallinn, 1990), and Arnold Everaus wrote *K. A. Hermann, 1851-1909* (Tartu, 1996). Baltisch (8); OSK

Hermanns, Matthias, born in 1899, he received a Dr.phil. in 1948 from the Université de Fribourg for *Die A mdo pa-Grosstibeter; die sozial-wissenschaftlichen Grundlagen der Hirtenkultur Innerasiens*. His writings include *Die Nomaden von Tibet* (1949), *Indo-Tibetans* (1954), *The Evolution of man* (1955), *Mythen und Mysterien* (1956), *Die religiös-magische Weltanschauung der Primitivstämme Indiens* (1964), *Das National-Epos der Tibeter, Gling König Ge-sar* (1965), and *Schamanen - Pseudo-schamanen, Erlöser und Heilbringer* (1970). ZKO

Hermelin, Axel *Eric*, born 22 June 1860 at Svanshals, Sweden, into an aristocratic family, he studied at Uppsala Universitet without taking a degree. He soon in life took to alcohol and ended his life at a lunatic asylum in Lund, where he died on 8 November 1944. He was nevertheless a prolific translator of Persian works of literature, a great deal of which was published privately by his family. Per-Erik Lindahl wrote *"Jag kan hvissla Beethovens sonater!" En biografi om Erik Hermelin*, del I (Karls-krona,1982), and *"När man varit vagabond ... En biografi om Erik Hermelin*, del II (Karlskrona, 1985). EncIran; SBL

Hermelink, Heinrich, born 20th cent., he was a writer on Arabic exact sciences and a joint translator of *Über einander berührende Kreise*, from the Arabic of Archimedes (Stuttgart, 1975). Sezgin; ZKO

Hernández, Francesc Hernández, born 20th cent., he was a director of the Gabinet d'Investigació Sociologica i Economica. His writings include *La identidad nacional en Cataluña* (1983); he was a joint author of *La ideologia nacional catalana* (1981), and *Once tesis sobre la cuestión nacional en España* (1983); and he was a joint editor of *Estructuras sociales y cuestión nacional en España* (1986). LC

Hernández Giménez, Félix, born in 1889 at Barcelona, he there completed his architectural study in 1912. He served for fifty years as an *arquitecto conservador de monumendos* at Córdoba. He was granted honorary doctorates by the Universidad de Granada and Technische Universität Berlin. His writings include *El aminar de 'Abd al-Rahman III en la mezquita mayor de Córdoba; genesis y repercusiones* (1975). He died in Córdoba on 17 May 1975. al-Andalus, 40 (1975), pp. 225-31; Index Islamicus (5); IndiceE³ (1)

Hernández Juberías, Julia, born about 1960, she received a diploma in Semitic philology and in the mid-1990s a doctorate in Arabic philology. She was in 1993 associated with the Consejo Superior de Investigaciones Cientificas, Madrid. Her writings include *Peninsula imaginaria; mitos y leyendas sobre al-Andalus* (Madrid, C.S.I.C., 1996). EURAMES, 1992, 1994, 1997; LC

Hernández-Pachero de la Cuesta, Francisco, born 16 February 1899 at Valladolid, he was a profes-sor of applied physics and geological geography at the Universidad de Madrid. His writings include *Estudio de la región volcánica central de España* (1932), *Geomorfología de la cuenca media del Sil* (1949), and he was a joint author of *El Sahara español* (1962). Figuras, 1956; IndiceE³ (1)

Hernández Pacheco y Estevan, Eduardo, born 23 May 1872 at Madrid, he was a professor of natural sciences. In 1941 he led an expedition to the Sahara, a region which he knew from previous travels. His writings include *Los cinco ríos principales de España y sus terrazas* (1928), *El Sahara español* (1949), and *Prehistoria del solar hispano* (1959). He died in Alcuéscar, Cáceres, in 1965. Diccionario histórico de la ciencia moderna en España (Barcelona, 1983); Figuras, 1956; IndiceE³ (1)

Herr (Her/Herus), Michel (Michael), born about 1490 at Speyer (Spire) on the Rhine, he matricualted in the Universität Heidelberg on 28 December 1508. He was subsequently admitted to the Chartreuse de Strassburg without taking a vow. After the secularization of the Carthusian monasteries, he left the order. In June 1527 he matriculated in the Faculty of Medicine at Montpellier, but he was back in Strassburg in August 1528. Having been naturalized by his marriage on 13 August 1528, he served at the Corporation du Miroir. In addition to his post as town physician, he became in 1534 *médecin de l'hôpital*, where his brother-in-law, a lawyer, served as a manager. Concurrently to his medical duties he pursued an interest in liberal arts. He translated *Die ritterlich rayss des herren Ludowico Vartomans von Bolonia* (Strassburg, 1515), and *Schachtafelen der Gesuntheit* [Taqwīm al-sihhah] from the Arabic of Ibn Butlān (Strassburg, 1533, and re-issued, Leipzig, 1988). He died in Strassburg in 1550. NDB; NDBA; NUC; Sezgin

Herreman, Philippe, fl. 20th cent., he was a joint author of *L'année politique africaine, 1966* (Dakar, 1967). NUC, 1968-72

Herrera Escudero, María Luisa, fl. 20th cent., she was a director of the Museo del Pueblo Español de Madrid. Her writings include *El museo en la educación* (1971), and *Trajes y bailes de España* (1984). Note about the author

Herrero (y) **de Collantes**, Ignacio, marqués de Aledo, fl. 1952. His writings include *Salamanca* (1940), *Viajes oficiales por España de Isabel II* (1950). Figuras

Herrfahrdt, Heinrich Wilhelm, born 22 February 1890 at Genthin, Germany, he was a professor of law successively at the universities of Greifswald and Bonn, where he received a Dr.jur. in 1915 for *Lücken im Recht*. His writings include *Die Einigung der Berufsstände als Grundlage des neuen Staates* (1919), *Reich und Preußen* (1928), and *Werden und Gestalt des Dritten Reiches* (1933). In 1961 he was honoured by *Festgabe für Heinrich Herrfahrdt zum 70. Geburtstag*. He died in Marburg on 12 September 1969. DtBilnd (1); Kürschner, 1925-1970; Wer ist's, 1935

Herrick, George Frederick, born 19 April 1834 at Milton, Vt., he first went to Turkey as a missionary in 1861 under the American Board of Commissioners for Foreign Missions. He went on his last term there in 1905, retiring in 1912. His writings include *An Intense life* (1890), and *Christian and Mohammedan* (1912). He died in New York on 26 October 1926. AmIndex (2); Kornrumpf; Master (2); Shavit; WhAm, 1

Herrick, Helen Morris née Richards, born 13 June 1837 at Meriden, N.H., the daughter of Rev. Cyrus Richards, a long time principal of Kimball Union Academy, Meriden. In 1861, she married George Frederick Herrick and together they went to Turkey as missionaries. She made a happy home for her husband and for her children as they came. Hospitality was the rule, and the unexpected as well as the expected guest was made welcome. She learned Turkish and she was always seeking opportunity to become acquainted with Turkish women. She died in New York on 26 March 1920 from pneumonia. Her husband wrote her biography, *Helen Morris Richards Herrick* (1920). Missionary herald, 1920

Herring, Ronald J., born 21 January 1947, he received a Ph.D. in 1976 from the University of Wisconsin at Madison for *Redistributive agrarian policy; land and credit in South Asia*. While still a doctoral student he was associated with the Pakistan Institute of Development Studies. He successively became a professor of political science at Cornell University, Ithaca, N.Y., and the University of Wisconsin. His writings include *Land to the tiller; the political economy of agrarian reform in South Asia* (1983). Note about the author; NUC

Herringham, Christina Jane née Powell, born middle of the 19th cent., she was married to Sir Wilmot Parker Herringham, 1855-1936. She was a writer on fine art. Her writings include *Ajanta frescoes* (1915). She died in 1929. Chris. Petteys, *Dictionary of women artists* (1985).

Herriot, Marie *Édouard*, born 5 July 1872 at Troyes, (Aube), he was a graduate of the École normale supérieure and became a mayor of Lyon and a president of the Assemblée nationale. Jacques Louis-Antériou wrote *Édouard Herriot au service de la République* (1957), Michel Soulié, *La vie politique d'Édouard Herriot* (1962), Sabine Jessner, *Edouard Herriot, patriarch of the Republic* (1974). He died in Lyon on 26 March 1957. AnaBrit; CurBio, 1946, 1957; DBF; IndexBFr² (15); Master 20); ObitT, 1951-60, pp. 351-53; WhAm, 3; WhE&EA; WhoFr, 1953/54-1957/58; Who was who, 5

Herrlich, Albert, born in 1902, his writings include *Schwarze Reise, vom Roten Meer nach Südafrika* (Berlin, 1937), and *Land des Lichtes; deutsche Kundfahrt zu unbekannten Völkern am Hindukusch* (München, 1938). GV; NUC, pre-1956

Herrmann, Albert Adolf Ludwig, born 20 January 1886 at Hannover, he received a Dr.phil. in 1909 from the Universität Berlin for *Die alte Seidenstraße zwischen China und Syrien*. He was a historian of geography and cartography at the Universität Berlin. His writings include *Historical and commercial atlas of China* (1935), and *Das Land der Seide und Tibet im Lichte der Antike* (1938). He died in Pilsen on 19 April 1945. Isis, 40 (1949), p. 355; Kürschner, 1926-1940/41; Wer ist's, 1928, 1935

Herrmann, Ferdinand, born in 1904, he was an anthropologist whose writings include *Symbolik in den Religionen der Naturvölker* (1961), *Völkerkunde Australiens* (1967), and *Afrikanische Kunst* (1969).

Herrmann, Georgina, Dr., born 20th cent., she was an archaeologist whose writings include *Ivories from Nimrud* (Oxford, 1974),*The Iranian revival* (Oxford, 1977), *The Sasanian rock reliefs at Naqsh-i Rustam* (1989), *Monuments of Merv; traditional buildings of the Karakum* (London, Society of Antiquaries of London, 1999). ZKO

Herrmann, Hans, born 18 February 1922, his writings include *Omphalos* (1959), a work which was originally submitted as Dr.phil. thesis in 1951 to the Universität Münster, and *Die Kessel der orientalisierenden Zeit* (1966).

Herrmann, Klaus Jacob, born 21 July 1929 at Cammin, Germany, he graduated in 1954 from the University of Minnesota, where he also received a Ph.D. in 1960 for *Politics of administrative reorganization in Minnesota State Government, 1949-1959.* He taught at Lakehead College and the American University before he was appointed a professor of political science at Sir George Williams University, Montreal. AmM&WSc, 1973 S; ConAu, 37-40; Note about the author

Herrmann, Richard, born 19th cent., he was from Frankfurt am Main and spent many years in Anatolian agriculture and was in 1900 an inspector general with the Turkish Ministry of Agriculture and Forestry as well as the Ministry of the Imperial Civil List, Constantinople. His writings include *Anatolische Landwirtschaft auf Grund sechs-jähriger Erfahrung dargestellt* (Leipzig, 1900). Kornrumpf; Note about the author; NUC, pre-1956

Hershey, Amos Shartle, born 11 July 1867 at Hershey, Pa., he graduated in 1892 from Harvard, received a Dr.phil. in 1894 from the Universität Heidelberg for *Die Kontrolle über die Gesetzgebung in den Vereinigten Staaten von Nord-Amerika und deren Gliedern*, and subsequently studied law at Paris. He was from 1895 to 1933 a professor of political science and international law at Indiana University at Bloomington. His writings include *The international law and diplomacy of the Russo-Japenese war* (1906), *The essentials of international public law* (1912), and he was a joint author of *Handbook for the diplomatic history of Europe, Asia, and Africa, 1870-1914* (1918). He died on 12 June 1933. IndAu; WhAm, 1; Master (4)

Hershlag, Zvi Yehuda, born 23 June 1914 at Rzeszow, Poland, he studied at Uniwersytet Lwowski and the Hebrew University of Jerusalem, where he received his Ph.D. in 1952. He was successively a professor of economics at Jerusalem and Tel Aviv. His writings include *Turkey, an economy in transition* (1958), *Introduction to the modern economic history of the Middle East* (1964), *Turkey, the challenge of growth* (1968), *The Economic structure of the Middle East* (1975), *The Philosophy of development revisited* (1984), and *Contemporary Turkish economy* (1988). MESA Roster of members, 1982-1990; WhoWor, 1982/83; WhoWorJ, 1972, 1978

Hertel, Johannes, born 13 March 1872 at Zwickau, Saxony, he studied classical and Oriental languages at the Universität Leipzig, where he received a Dr.phil. in 1897 for *Text und Verfasser des Hitopadesha.* He taught modern languages at secondary schools until 1919, when he was appointed to the chair of Indian studies at the Universität Leipzig. His writings include *Das Pancatantra, seine Geschichte und seine Verbreitung*, a work which won him a prize from the Universität Straßburg. His other works include the translations *Bestrafte Neugier; Anekdoten und Schwänke aus dem Orient, ausgewählt aus indischen und persischen Sammlungen des 19. Jahrhunderts* (1979), and *Die zehn Prinzen; die merkwürdigen Erlebnisse und siegreichen Abenteuer des Prinzen von Magadha* (1985). He died in Leipzig on 27 October 1955. DtBE; EncIran; Kürschner, 1926-1940/41; Stache-Rosen; Wer ist's, 1935

Hertlein, Edgar, born 10 December 1935 at Würzburg, Bavaria, he received a Dr.phil. in 1963 for *Die Basilika San Francesco in Assisi*, and a Dr.habil. in 1970, subsequently becoming a professor of history of fine arts at the Universität Münster. His writings include *Masccios Trinität; Kunst, Geschichte und Politik der Frührenaissance in Florenz* (1979). Kürschner, 1973-1992|

Hertz, Allen Zangwil, born in 1946, he received a Ph.D. in 1973 from Columbia University, N.Y.C., for *The emergence of Ottoman Ada Kale, 1688-1753.* NUC, 1973-77

Hertz, Israel, fl. 20th cent., he was a political activist among the Arab minority in Israel. Note

Hertzberg, Gustav Friedrich, born 19 January 1826 at Halle/Saale, he studied history, classical and oriental languages as well as theology at the universities of Halle and Leipzig, and gained his Dr.phil. and Dr.habil. at Halle in 1848 and 1851 respectively. He there taught ancient history, and he concurrently served as an editor of a weekly and a daily newspaper. His writtings include *Geschichte Griechenlands unter der Herrschaft der Römer* (1866-75), and *Geschichte der Byzantiner und des Osmanischen Reiches bis gegen Ende des 16. Jahrhunderts* (1883). He died in Halle on 16 November 1907. DtBE; DtBIlnd (7); Hinrichsen; NDB

Hertzberg, Hans Wilhelm, born 16 January 1895 at Lauenburg, Prussia, he studied theology at Marburg and Berlin. A provost since 1923, he was a sometime superintendent of Deutsches Evangelisches Palästina-Institut, Jerusalem. From 1931 to 1947 he was a professor at the Universität Marburg and concurrently served from 1932 to 1936 as a pastor at Caldern near Marburg. In 1947 he was invited to teach Old Testament and Palestine studies at the Universität Kiel. His writings include *Blicke in das Land der Bibel* (1959), and *Gottes Wort und Gottes Land* (1965). He died in Kiel on 1 June 1965. DtBE

Herus, Michael, ca. 1490-1550 *see* Herr, Michel

Herval, René, born 11 April 1890 at Lille, France, he had barely completed his higher education at Lille, when he had to serve in the 1914-18 war. He was on a French mission to Russia when Czarist Russia collapsed. Upon his return to Rouen he published his first work, *Huit mois de révolution russe* (1918), and subsequently pursued a career in banking and law, but he devoted most of his time to writing, both prose and poetry, extolling and popularizing Normandy and the epic of the Normans in southern Italy. His writings include *Falaise, cité normande* (1929), and *L'Héroïque légende de Guillaume le Conqué-rant* (1987). He died in Rouen on 11 February 1972. DBF

Hervé du Halgouet, A. Marie Louis de Poulpique, 1878- ca. 1960 *see* Halgouet, Hervé A. Marie L. P.

Hervieux, Auguste *Léopold*, born 10 March 1831 at Elbeuf (Seine-Maritime), France, he was a lawyer who defended great cases in court, later becoming a judge, and municipal councillor in Paris, 1884-1887. His writings include *Notice sur les fables latines d'origine indienne* (1898). He died in Paris in 1900. DBF; IndexBFr² (4)

Herz, Max (Pasha), born in 1856, he was an architect who went to Egypt and became a director of the Museum of Arab Art, Cairo. His writings include *Catalogue sommaire des monuments exposés dans le Musée national de l'art arabe* (1895), *La Mosquée du Sultan Hassan au Caire* (1899), *La Mosquée el-Rifaï au Caire* (1906), *La Mosquée de l'Émir Ganem el-Bahlaouan au Caire* (1908), and *Die Baugruppe des Sultans Qalā'ūn in Kairo* (1919). He died in Switzerland in 1919. Dawson; Egyptology

Herzfeld, Ernst Emil, born 23 July 1879 at Celle, Lower Saxony, he studied architecture at Technische Hochschule, Berlin, and subsequently studied history, archaeology, and Oriental subejcts at München, and received a Dr.phil. in 1907 from the Universität Tübingen for *Pasargadae; Aufnahmen und Untersuchungen zur persischen Archaeologie*. Two years later he qualified as geographer of history at Berlin. Since 1918 a professor of Oriental archaeology, he was dismissed in 1935 while exavating at Persepolis. He did not return to Germany and instead emigrated to the United States by way of Britain. Until his retirement in 1944 he was a professor in the Institute for Advanced Study at Princeton, concurrently teaching in the Institute of Fine Arts at New York University. His writings include *Archaeological history of Iran* (1935). He died in Basel on 21 January 1948. BioHbDtE; BioInd, 1 (5), 2 (3), 11 (1); CnDiAmJBi; DtBE; EncIran; Fück, p. 291; Hanisch; Kornrumpf; Kürschner, 1926-1935; NDB; NYT, 23 January 1948, p. 23, col. 1; Schwarz; *Who was who*, 4; Wininger

Herzog, Chaim, born 17 September 1918 at Belfast, he was an ambassador to the U.N.O., and a president of Israel. His writings include *Kriege um Israel, 1948-1984* (1984), *The Arab Israeli wars* (1985), and *Living history; a memoir* (1997). He died on 17 April 1997. ConAu, 103, 157; CurBio, 1988; IntWW, 1977-1996/97; Master (5); MidE, 1982/83; WhAm, 12; Who, 1987-1997; WhoAm, 1976/77, 1978/79; WhoWor, 1978-1996; WhoWorJ, 1965, 1972, 1978

Herzog, David, born 7 September 1869 at Tyrnau (Nagyszombat), Slovakia, he studied at the Rabbinerseminar and the Universität in Berlin, and received a Dr.phil. in 1894 from the Universität Leipzig for *Maimonides' Kommentar zum Tractat Peah*. From 1896 to 1900, he pursued post-doctoral studies at Paris and Wien. He briefly served as a rabbi in Berlin and Prag. With a Dr.habil. in Semitic philology from Karls Universität, Prag, he started to teach his subject in 1908 at the Universität Graz, becoming a professor in 1926. After his dismissal in 1938, he went straight to Britain where he obtained a research position at the Bodleian Library, Oxford. His writings include *Zwei hebräische Handschriftenfragmente aus der Steiermark* (1911), *Der jüdische Grabstein in der Burg zu Graz* (1928), *Urkunden und Regesten zur Geschichte der Juden in der Steiermark, 1475-1585* (1934), and *Erinnerungen eines Rabbiners, 1932-1940* (1995). He died in Oxford on 6 March 1946. BioHbDtE; DtBE; DtBiInd (3); EncJud; ÖBL

Herzog, Rolf, born 14 May 1919 at Oppach, Oberlausitz (Upper Lusatia), he was a professor of anthropology at the Universität Freiburg im Breisgau. His writings include *Die Nubier* (1957), *Sudan* (1957), and *Seßhaftwerden von Nomaden* (1963). In 1984 he was honoured by *Wirtschaftsethnologische Studien Rolf Herzog zum 65. Geburtstag*. Kürschner, 1970-2003; Schwarz; Unesco

Heslot, Sylvie, born 20th cent., she was associated with the Centre de recherches et d'études documentaires sur l'Afghanistan, Paris. Her writings include *Lexique français-pashto* (1986), and she was a joint editor of Serge de Beaurecueil's letters from Afghanistan entitled *Chronique d'un témoin priviligé* (1992). BN; LC; Note

Hesronite, Jean (Joannes), born 16th cent., he was a Maronite priest and, with Gabriel Sionita, a joint author of *Grammatica Arabica Maronitarum* (Lutetiae, 1616), and *De nonnullis orientalium uibibus* (Amstelodami, 1633). BN; Casanova, pp. 49-50

Hess, Andrew Christie, born 25 September 1932 at Cleveland, Ohio, he graduated in 1954 from the University of Michigan, and received a Ph.D. in 1966 from Harvard for *The closure of the Ottoman frontier in North Africa and the origins of modern Algeria, 1574-1595*. He successively taught history, law and diplomacy at Tempel University, Philadelphia, and Tufts University, Medford, Mass. His writings include *The Forgotten frontier; a history of the sixteenth century Ibero-African frontier* (1978). DrAS, 1974 H, DrAS, 1978 H, 1982 H; *MESA Rosert of members*, 1982-1990; NatFacDr, 2000

Hess, Clyde Gardner, born in 1923 at Newton, Mass., he graduated in 1940 from Cornell University, Ithaca, N.Y. He was a Ford Foundation fellow at A.U.B., 1952-53, and subsequently conducted field research in Arab history and political institutions with a Ford Foundation Grant in 1954. In the following year he joined the United States Information Agency, serving as information officer with the United States Information Service throughout the world. He was a sometime editorial writer on the *Worcester Telegram*, and news analyst on radio station WTAF, Worcester, Mass. Note; WhoGov, 1972, 1975

Hess, Gary Ray, born 23 March 1937 at Pittsburgh, Pa., he graduated from the local university and received a Ph.D. in 1965 from Bowling Green (Ohio) State University for *Sam Higginbottom of Allahabad; the missionary as an advance agent of American economic and technical assistance in India*. He subsequently taught history at his alma mater. His writings include *America encounters India, 1941-1947* (1971), *The United States at war, 1941-1945* (1986), *The United States' emergence as a Southeast Asian power, 1940-1950* (1987), *Vietnam and the United States; origins and legacy of war* (1990), and *Presidential decisions for war: Korea, Vietnam, and the Persian Gulf* (2001). ConAu, 21-24; DrAS, 1974 H, 1978 H, 1982 H; WrDr, 1976/78-2004

Hess, Jean, born in 1862 at Courtavon (Haut-Rhin), he was a journalist, and an editor of *Le Commerce colonial*. His writings include *À l'Île du Diable* (1897), its translation, *Eine Reise nach der Teufelsinsel* (1898), *L'Âme nègre* (1898), *La Catastrophe de la Martinique* (1902), *La Question du Maroc* (1903), *La Vérité sur l'Algérie* (1905), and *Une Algérie nouvelle* (1909). BN; IndexBFr² (1)

Hess, Johann Jacob, 1866-1949 *see* Hess von Wyss, Jean Jacques

Hess, Peter, born 20th cent., his writings include *Bangladesh; Tragödie einer Staatenbildung* (Frauenfeld, Stuttgart, 1972). NUC, 1973-77

Hess, Robert Lee, born 18 December 1932 at Asbury Park, N.J., he graduated in 1954 from Yale University, New Haven, Conn., where he also received his Ph.D. in 1960. He taught history at Mount Holyoke College, Northwestern University, and the University of Chicago before he became a professor in 1979 at Brooklyn College, N.Y.C. His writings include *Italian colonialism in Somalia* (1966), *Ethiopia; the modernozation of autocracy* (1970), *Semper ex Africa...; a bibliography of primary source for 19th-century tropical Africa as recorded by explorers, missionaries, traders, travelers, administrators, military men, adventurers, and others* (1972), and *Library shelflist; Ethiopia and the Horn of Africa* (1973). He died in Manhattan, N.Y.C., on 12 January 1992. ConAu, 29-32, 136; DrAS, 1969 H; 1974 H, 1978 H, 1982 H; IntAu&W, 1977, 1982; WhAm, 10; WhoAm, 1986/87-1989//90; WhoE, 1991/92; WrDr, 1976/78-1994/96

Hess von Wyss, Jean Jacques, born 11 January 1866 at Freiburg, Switzerland, he went to school in Solothurn. He studied Semitic languages, Assyriology, Chinese, but particularly Egyptology for six semesters at the Universität Berlin; he spent his seventh semester at Straßburg and in the following spring term of 1889 obtained a Dr.phil. in Egyptology, Assyriology, and philosophy. At the end of this year, he was appointed a professor of his field at the newly established Universität Freiburg. Supported by a travel fellowship he first visited Egypt and Nubia in 1893/94. From 1896 to 1900 he spent his annual vacation in Egypt and concurrently studied the language of the Central Arabian Bedouins. As a personal friend of Khedive 'Abbās II Hilmī, he resigned his Freiburg professorship in 1908 and spent the following five years studying in Egypt. In 1918 he was appointed a professor of Oriental languages and ancient Near Eastern history at the Universität Zürich, a post which he held until 1936. His writings include *Die geographische Lage Mekkas und die Strasse von Gilda nach Mekka* (1900), *Beduinennamen aus Zentralarabien* (1912), and *Von den Beduinen des inneren Arabiens* (1938). He died on 29 April 1949. *Asiatische* Studien, 22 (1968), pp. 137-45; Dawson; Egyptology; Fück, p. 288; HisBioLexCH, vol. 4, p. 207, col. 2; Kornrumpf; Kürschner, 1926-1935; SchZLex

Hesse, Fritz, born in 1898, he received a Dr.phil. in 1923 from the Universität München for *Meso-potamien; Versuch eines geopolitisch erweiterten systematischen landeskundlichen Portraits.* He was a sometime editor of the *Mitteilungen* of Deutscher Orient-Verein. His other writings include *Die Mosulfrage* (1925), *Der Außenhandel Persiens, 1927/28* (Berlin, 1929), *Persien* (1932), and *Weltpolitik, 1945-1954* (1954). Schwarz; ZKO

Hesse, Reinhard, born 6 June 1945 at Warstein, Germany, he received a Dr.phil. and Dr.habil., and subsequently taught ethics, philosophy, and political science at teachers' colleges in Ludwigsburg, Gießen, and Freiburg. His writings include *Hausinschriften; Überlegungen zur Begründung und Methodik einer geschichtswissenschaftlichen Beschäftigung mit Bürger- und Bauernhausinschriften, erläutert an den Inschriften des Amtes Warstein* (1970), *Geschichtswissenschaft in praktischer Absicht* (1979), and *Die Einheit der Vernunft als Überlebensbedingung der pluralistischen Welt* (1994). Kürschner, 1996-2005; WhoWor, 1987/88

Hetherwick, Alexander, born 12 April 1860 at Savoch, Aberdeenshire, he graduated from Aberdeen University, where he was Simpson Mathematical Prizeman. He was ordained and became a missionary to Blantyre in Central Africa. He served as a chairman of the Nyanja Translation Board, and he was honorary life governor of the British and Foreign Bible Society. He died in 1939. WhE&EA; *Who was who,* 3

Hettner, Alfred, born 6 August 1859 at Dresden, he studied geography at the universities of Halle, Bonn, and Straßburg. He successively taught geography at Tübingen and Heidelberg. His writings include *Vergleichende Länderkunde* (1934), and *Allgemeine Geographie des Menschen* (1947-57). He died in Heidelberg on 31 August 1941. Dickinson, pp. 112-125; DtBE; DtBilnd (2); Geographers, 6 (1982), pp. 55-63; Henze; Kürschner, 1926-1940/41; NDB; RHbDtG; Wer ist's, 1909-1912

Hetzel, Gertrud, born 19th cent., she was associated with Deutsche Orient-Mission, Potsdam. Her writings include *Ein Heiliger, der kein Heiliger war; Schwänke aus dem Leben des Chodscha Nasr-ed-Din* (Potsdam, 1931). GV; Note about the author

Hetzel, Wilhelm Friedrich, 1754-1824 see Hezel, Wilhelm Friedrich

Hetzel, Wolfgang, born 26 January 1922 at Wörlitz, Anhalt, he received a Dr.phil. in 1952 for *Wiesenbewässerung und Agrarlandschaft des oldenburgischen Huntetals.* Since 1967 he was a professor of cultural and economic geography at the Universität Köln. His writings include *Studien zur Geographie des Handels in Togo und Dahomey* (1974), *N'Gaoundéré; Tradition und Wandel im Raum einer "Fulbe-Stadt" in Kamerun* (1983). He died on 2 May 1999. Kürschner, 1970-1992|

Hetzron, Robert, born 31 December 1937 at Budapest, he received a diploma in Hebrew in 1959 from the École des langues orientales vivantes, Paris, an M.A. from the Hebrew University, Jerusalem, and a Ph.D. in 1966 in Near Eastern languages from the University of California. In 1972 he was appointed a professor at the University of California, Santa Barbara. His writings include *The Verbal system of Southern Agaw* (1969), a work which he originally submitted as Ph.D. thesis to the University of California, *Ethiopian Semitic; studies in classification* (1972), and *The Semitic languages* (1997). He died in 1997. In 2001 was published *New data and new methods in Afroasiatic linguistics; Robert Hetzron in memoriam.* ConAu, 33-36; DrAS, 1974 F, 1978 F, 1982 F; IntAu&W, 1989; WhoAm, 1982-1996; WhoWest, 1976-1980 [not sighted]; WhoWor, 1982/83; WrDr, 1976/78-2002

Heubeck, Alfred, born 20 July 1914 at Nürnberg, he studied classical philology and received a Dr.phil. in 1936 for *Das Nationalbewustsein des Herodot.* He subsequently taught at secondary schools until 1961, when he was invited to teach classics at the Universität Erlangen. His writings include *Der Odyssee-Dichter und die Ilias* (1954), *Die homerische Frage; ein Bericht über die Forschung der letzten Jahrzehnte* (1974), and *Kleine Schriften zur griechischen Sprache und Literatur* (1984). He died in Erlangen on 24 May 1987. DtBE; Kürschner, 1961-1987

von Heuglin, Martin *Theodor*, born 20 March 1824 at Hirschlanden, Württemberg, he studied mining engineering and metallurgy. His extensive travels where financed with the publication his travel accounts, which include *Expedition nach Inner-Afrika zur Aufhellung der Schicksale Dr. Eduard Vogels und zur Vollendung seines Forschungswerkes* (1860), *Zur Fauna der Säugetiere Nordost-Afrikas* (1861), *Über die Antilopen und Büffel Nordost-Afrika's* (1863), *Reisen nach Abessinien, den Gala-Ländern, Ost-Sudán und Chartúm in den Jahren 1861 und 1862* (1868), and *Reise in Nordost-Afrika; Schilderungen aus dem Gebiete der Beni Amer und Habab nebst zoologischen Skizzen und einem Führer für Jagdreisende* (1877). He died of pneumonia in Stuttgart on 5 November 1876. ADtB; DtBE; DtBilnd (3); Embacher; Henze; Hill; Kornrumpf; NDB; Wurzbach

Heun, Irene, Mrs. Ortner, born about 1935, she received a Dr.phil. in 1952 from the Universität Freiburg im Breisgau for a study of contemporary journalist Arabic entitled *Die Sprache der arabischen*

Presse; Beobachtungen in der Entwicklung des neuklassischen Arabisch. She was for many years associated with the Federal German Bureau of Foreign Trade Information, Bonn. Her writings include *Das Entwicklungsland Somalia* (1963), *Das Entwicklungsland Libyen* (1965), *Tunesien als Wirtschaftspartner* (1970), *Die Rolle Libyens im Mittelmeerraum und die Bedeutung seiner politischen Neuorietierung* (Eggenberg, 1971), and *Algeriens Außenpolitik unter dem Einfluß des algerischen Nationalismus* (Eggenberg, 1972). Note; Schwarz; Sezgin

Heury, Joseph, born in 1824 at Avignon, he was a Jesuit missionary who published anonymously at the Imprimerie catholique de Beyrouth his *Vocabulaire français-arabe* (1857), and reprints in 1867 and 1885. This dictionary was republished in six successive editions until 1898, and possibly later. But during that period, Father J. B. Belot held such a place in Beirut Arabic lexicography that all the anonymous editions of the *Vocabulaire français-arabe* were attributed to him. It is sad that Father Heury's great endeavour was never appreciated on account of his modesty. He died in 1897. Arabica, 10 (1963), pp. 62-63; Fück, pp. 294-95; Jalabert

Heuser, Fritz, fl. 20th cent., he was a joint author, with Ilhami Şevket, of *Deutsch-Türkisches Wörterbuch* (1931), a work which went through five editions until 1962. ZKO

Heusinger, Carl Friedrich, born 28 February 1792 at Farnbroda near Eisenach, Germany, he studied medicine and natural sciences at the universities of Jena and Göttingen, gaining a doctorate in 1812. He became a military physician in the German War of Liberation, after which he remained in France until 1819. In 1821, he was invited to teach medicine at the Universität Jena, later moving on to Würzburg, and in 1829 to Marburg in the same capacity. His writings include *Grundriß der Encyclopädie und Methodologie der Natur- und Heilkunde nebst einer Übersicht der Geschichte der Medicin und des gegewärtigen Standes des Medicinal-Unterrichts in den europäischen Staaten* (Eisenach, 1839). He died in Marburg in 1883. DtBiInd (1)

Heuzé, Gérard, born 20th cent., he was a French sociologist and in 1989 associated with the C.N.R.S. His writings include *Inde; la grève du siècle, 1981-1983* (1989), *Iran au fil des jours* (1989), *Ouvriers d'un autre monde; l'exemple des travailleurs de la mine en Inde contemporaine* (1989), *Travailler en Inde* (1992), and *Politique et religion dans l'Asie du Sud contemporianes* (1998).

Heuzey, Léon Alexandre, born 1 December 1831 at Rouen, he was educated at lycées in Rouen and Paris, graduated from the École normale supérieure, and subsequently spent from 1855 to 1859 at the École française d'Athènes. In 1858 he was sent on a mission to Macedonia. In 1863 he became a professor of history and archaeology at the École nationale des beaux-arts, Paris, becoming deputy keeper in the Département des antiquités grecques et romaines du Louvre in 1870. Since 1881 he was a director of its Département des antiquités orientales. When he retired in 1908 he was awarded the *grand-croix* of the Légion d'honneur. A member of the Académie des inscriptions et belles-lettres since 1874, and the Académie des beaux-arts since 1885, he wrote *Mission archéologique de Macédoine* (1876), and *Catalogue des antiquités chaldénnes du Musée national du Louvre* (1902). He died in Paris on 8 February 1922. DBF; IndexBFr² (6); Kornrumpf; Kornrumpf, N

Hevener, Natalie T. Kaufman, she was in 1969 an assistant professor of political science at Columbia College, Columbia, S.C. Her writings include *The Dynamics of human rights in U.S. foreign policy* (1981), *International law and the status of women* (1983), and *Diplomacy in a dangerous world; protection for diplomats under international law* (1986). Note about the author

de **Hevesy**, André, born in 1882, his writings include *Nationalities in Hungary* (London, 1919), *L'Agonie d'un empire, l'Autriche-Hongrie; mœurs et politique* (Paris, 1923), as well as historical biographies. NUC, pre-1956

Hewitt, Brian George, born 11 November 1949, he received a Ph.D. in 1981 from Cambridge University for *Contrastive study of the subordinate clause syntax of Georgian and Abkhaz*. He was a reader in linguistics and Caucasian languages at SOAS, and since 1994, a director of its Centre for the Advancement of the Study of the Caucasus. His writings include the modified version of his thesis, *The typology of subordination in Georgian and Abkhaz* (1987), he was a joint author of *Abkhaz* (1979), *Nart sagas from the Caucasus; myths and legends from the Circassians, Abazas, Abkhaz, and Ubykhs* (Princeton, 2002), and he edited *Svan-English dictionary* (1985). Note about the author; ZKO

Hewitt, James Francis Katherinus, born in 1835, he was educated at Christ Church, Oxford, and entered the Bengal Civil Service; he retired in July 1885 as commissioner at Chota Nagpur, Bihar, India. His writings include *The Ruling races of prehistoric times in India, South-Western Asia and Southern Europe* (1894), *History and chronology of the myth-making age* (1901), and *Primitive traditional history* (1907). He died in 1908. IndianBiInd (1); Note about the author; NUC, pre-1956

Heyd, Uriel, born 26 July 1913 at Köln, he was a member of the Israeli Foreign Office, and a director of the School of Oriental Studies, Jerusalem. His writings include *Foundations of Turkish nationalism* (1950), *Language reform in modern Turkey* (1954), *Ottoman documents on Palestine, 1552-1615* (1960), and he edited *Studies in Islamic history and civilization* (1961). He died in Jerusalem in 1968. BioHbDtE; WhoIsrael, 1949, 1956-1966/67; WhoWorJ, 1965

von Heyd, Wilhelm, born 23 October 1823 at Markgröningen, Germany, he studied at the theological seminary at Blaubeuren and the Universität Tübingen. In 1857 he became a librarian at the public library in Stuttgart and there served from 1873 to 1897 as its director. His frequent research journeys to Italy resulted in his *Geschichte des Levanthandels im MIttelalter* (1879-80), and its translations, *Histoire du commerce du Levant au moyen-âge* (1885-86), and *Yakın doğu ticaret tarihi* (1975). He died in Stuttgart on 19 February 1906. DtBE; DtBilnd (2); NDB

Heyer, Anselm, born in 1919 at München, he studied performing arts and became a journalist with the *Neue Zeitung* and *Süddeutsche Zeitung*. In 1957, he was at the political desk of the German Tele-vision, and since 1962, he headed the Middle East desk on Channel 2 of the German Television network. His writings include *Untergang des Morgenlandes* (1966), and he was a joint author of *Berlin, Brandenburger Tor* (1956), and *Beiträge zu einer Soziologie der Polizei* (1971). Sezgin

Heyer, Friedrich, born 24 January 1908, he studied theology and received a doctorate in 1939. He was successively a pastor at Schloß Ernstbrunn/Niederösterreich, and Schleswig. He taught eccle-siastical history at the Universität Kiel until 1964, concurrently serving as a director of the Evangelische Akademie, Schleswig. Since 1964 he was a professor of religious knowledge at the Universität Heidel-berg. His writings include *Kirchengeschichte des Heiligen Landes* (1984), and *Die orientalische Frage im kirchlichen Lebenskreis; das Einwirken der Kirchen des Auslands auf die Emanzipation der orthodoxen Nationen Südosteuropas, 1804-1912* (1991). In 1994, he was honoured by *Horizonte der Christenheit; Festschrift für Friedrich Heyer zu seinem 85. Geburtstag.* DiBilnd (1); Kürschner, 1966-2003

Heyer, Richard, born 19th cent., he was a missionary at Lamu Island in the Indian Ocean just off the coast. Note about the author

Heyfelder (Гейфельдер), Oscar, born 7 April 1828 at Trier, Prussia, he studied medicine at Heidel-berg, Erlangen, Prag, Wien, and Paris. In Russian service since 1859, he participated in Russian mili-tary campaigns and expeditions. His writings include *Das Lager von Krasnoe Selo im Vergleich mit dem von Châlons; militärärztliche Studie* (Berlin, 1868), *Красносельский и шалонсіŭ лагерь въ военно-медицинскомъ отношеніи* (Sanktpeterburg, 1868), *Bericht über meine ärztliche Wirksamkeit am Rhein und in Frankreich während des Krieges 1870-1871* (St. Petersburg, 1871), *Manuel de chirurgie de guerre* (1875), *Bojeнa xupyprujcк* (Beograd, 1877), *Εγχειρίδιον χειρουργικής* (1881), and *Transkaspien und seine Eisenbahn nach den Acten des Erbauers General-lieutenant M. Annenkow* (Hannover, 1888). He died on 1 June 1890. BN; DtBilnd (2); *NYPL Library catalog*; OSK

Heymann, Egon, born 20th cent., his writings include *Balkan: Kriege, Bündnisse, Revolutionen; 150 Jahre Politik und Schicksal* (Berlin, 1938), *Da Varsavia a Londra* (Roma, 1940), *England und der abessinische Krieg* (Berlin, 1940), *Der Weg Italiens in den Krieg* (1940), and he was a joint author of *Amerikas zweiter Kreuzzug* (1952), and ... *und neues Leben* ... *Deutschlands Weg aus dem Elend* (1960), as well as numerous articles in *Die politische Meinung*. Sezgin; ZKO

Heymann, Hans, born 27 June 1885 at Königsberg, East Prussia, he studied philosophy, political economy, and law, gaining a Dr.phil. in 1920 for *Die Hauslebensversicherung als Teil der Sachwert-versicherung*. He became a banker and adviser on credit and currency to the German Foreign Office. In 1936 he went to the United States, where he was from 1939 to 1943 on the faculty of Rutgers University, New Brunswick, N.J. Since 1948 he served as a professor of economics at the University of Illinois. His writings include *Die Völkerbank* (1922). He died in Champaign, Ill., on 1 October 1949. BioIn, 2 (3); DcNAA; NYT, 2 October 1949, p. 82, cols. 5-6; WhAm, 2

Heymann, Michael, born about 1925, he received a Ph.D. in 1956 from Cambridge University for *British policy and public opinion on the Turkish question, 1908-1914*. His writings include the Hebrew work, *ha Tenu'ah ha-tsiyonit...* (1965), with the added t.p.: *The Zionist movement and the schemes for the settlement of Mesopotamia after Herzl*. NUC; Sluglett

Heyse, Théodore Jules Joseph Marie, born 7 February 1884 at Eine, East Flanders, he joined the Ministère des Colonies in 1910, and in 1925, he was appointed to the chairs of Droit public belge, and Charte coloniale at the Université coloniale de Belgique, Anvers. Concurrently he was an active mem-ber of the Commission belge de bibliographie. His writings include *Les Eaux dans l'expansion colo-niale belge* (1939), *Contribution au progrès des sciences morales, politiques et économiques relatives aux territoires d'outre-mer* (1957), *Documentation générale sur le Congo et le Ruanda-Urundi, 1958-*

1960 (1960), and *Bibliographie de H. M. Stanley, 1841-1904* (1961). He died at his place of birth on 7 February 1963. Benelux² (1)

Heywood, Colin J., born about 1940, he received a Ph.D. in 1969 from the School of Oriental and African Studies, London, for *English diplomacy between Austria and the Ottoman Empire in the war of the Sacra Liga, 1684-1699, with special reference to the period 1688-1699*. He was a joint author of *English and continental views of the Ottoman Empire, 1500-1800* (1972), and he edited *Studies in Ottoman history in honour of Professor V. L. Ménage* (1994). NUC; Sluglett; ZKO

Heyworth-Dunne, James, he was from 1928 to 1948 a senior reader in Arabic at the University of London. Thereafter he became a member of the staff of the Middle East Institute, Washingon, D.C. His writings include *Land tenure in Islam, 630 A.D. - 1915 A.D.* (1952), *Spoken Egyptian Arabic* (1961), and *An Introduction to the history of education in modern Egypt* (1968). He died on 9 June 1974). ConAu, 53-56; Note about the author

Hezel (Гецель/Hetzel), Wilhelm (Guilelmus) Friedrich (Fridericus), born 16 May 1754 at Königsberg, Franken, the son of a pastor; like his father, he also studied theology at the Universität Jena, gaining a doctorate in 1775. He lived on his inherited estate as a private scholar unitl 1786, when he became a professor of Oriental languages and Biblical literature at the Universität Gießen. In 1801, he became a professor of ethics and Oriental languages at the Universität Dorpat, with the titles of *wirklicher Hofrat* and *Kollegienrat*. His writings include *Erleichterte arabische Grammatik* (1776), *Ausführliche hebräische Sprachlehre* (1777), and *Anweisung zur arabischen Sprache bei Ermangelung alles mündlichen Unterrichts* (1784-85). He died in Domberg near Dorpat on 12 June 1824. Baltisch (5); DtBE; DtBilnd (10)

Hiç, Hüseyin Mükerrem, born 20 August 1929 at İstanbul, he there studied economics. After gaining a doctorate in 1958, he was appointed first a lecturer and later professor of economics at İstanbul Üniversitesi. From 1978 to 1983 he served as director of its Türkiye-Avrupa-Ortadoğu Ekonomik ve Sosyal Araştırmalar Institüsü (Europe and Middle East Economic and Social Relations Research Institute). He was a sometime visiting professor at Princeton and Columbia, a consultant to the World Bank, and a member of the Turkish Parliament. His writings include *Para teorisi* (1966), and *Kapitalizm, sosyalizm, karma ekonomi ve Türkiye* (1970). Kim Kimdir, 1985/86-2000

Hichens (Hitchens), Robert Smyth, born 14 November 1864 at Speldhurst, Kent, he was a journalist, music critic, and writer. Although he wrote more than seventy books, many of which were bestsellers, he is virtually forgotten today. His writings include *Egypt and its monuments* (1908), *The Holy Land* (1910), and *The Near East; Dalmatia, Greece and Constantinople* (1913). He died in Zürich on 20 July 1950. Bioln, 4, 14, 15; Britlnd (6); ConAu, 162; DLB, 153 (1995), pp. 106-119; DNB; Master (36); Who was who, 4

Hichens, William, born about 1900, he was a Swahili scholar whose writings include *The Azanian classics* (1932), and he edited and translated from the Swahili, *The Advice of Mwana Kupona upon the wifoly duty* (Medstaed, Hampshire, The Azania Press, 1934), and *Diwani ya Muyaka bin Haji al-Ghassaniy* (Johannesburg, University of the Witwatersrand Press, 1940). SOAS Library catalogue; ZKO

Hickmann, Hans Robert Hermann, born 19 May 1908 at Roßlau near Dessau, Anhalt, he took lessons in piano and composition before embarking on musicology at the universities of Halle/Saale and Berlin, gaining a doctorate in 1934. He subsequently went to Egypt where he spent twenty-five years as a musical director and producer for the Egyptian radio. In 1957 he was appointed a professor at the Universität Hamburg. His writings include *Le problème de la notation musicale dans l'Égypte ancienne* (1955), *Catalogue d'enregistrements de musique folklorique égyptienne* (1958), *Musikgeschichte in Bildern; Ägypten* (1961), and *Orientalische Musik* (1970). He died in Blandfort Forum, Dorset, on 4 September 1968. Baker, 1978; BioHbDtE; Dawson; DtBE; Egyptology; Kürschner, 1950-1966; Master (1)

Hicks, Harry Wade, born 19th cent., he was one of the secretaries of the American Board of Commissioners for Foreign Missions who, in 1909, visited missions in Turkey as a photographer for the *National geographic magazine* and made an outstation tour with Rev. James Luther Fowle of Kayseri. Missionary herald, 113 (1917), p. 319

Hidding, Klaas Albert Hendrik, born 23 April 1902, he received a doctorate in 1929 at Leiden for *Nji Pohatji Sangjang*. He spent from 1936 to 1948 at the Volkslectuur Batavia, and subsequently became a professor of ecclesiastical history and phenomenology at the Rijksuniversiteit te Leiden. His writings include *Mystiek en ethick in Schweitzer's geest* (1938), *Verscheidenheid der godsdiensten* (1955). *God en goden* (1960), and *De toekomst van het geloof* (1972). Wie is dat, 1948, 1956

Hiehle, Kurt, born 15 August 1882 at Riga, he graduated from a Moscow secondary school and took up engineering at Riga, a study which he completed at the Technische Hochschule (Berlin) Charlottenburg. Since 1907 he worked in industry as a mechanical engineer, including agricultural machinery. From 1926 to 1928 he travelled in North Africa, India, Indonesia, and Japan to study agricultural problems in arid regions, a subject which he pursued for the rest of his life. His writings include *Vom kommenden Zeitalter der künstlichen Klimagestaltung* (1947), and its English version, *On the coming age of controlled climate*(1947). He died on 28 July 1960. Kurt-Hiehle-Festschrift (1982), pp. 2-3

Hielscher, Friedrich, born 31 May 1902 at Plauen/Vogtland, Germany, he went to school at Guben and in 1919 served as a volunteer with the paramilitary border control. From 1920 to the winter term 1923/24 he studied law at the Universität Berlin, followed by one year of articling. After two more years at the Universität Jena he received a Dr.jur. *summa cum laude* for *Die Selbstherrlichkeit; Versuch einer Darstellung des deutschen Rechtsgrundbegriffes.* In 1928 he became editor of the conservative journal, *Der Vormarsch* (Berlin). His writings include the publication of his thesis in 1930 as well as *Das Reich* (Berlin, Das Reich, 1931), *Das Altvatergebirge* (Königsberg, 1936), and the autobiography, *Fünfzig Jahre unter Deutschen* (Hamburg, 1954). GV; Thesis

Higgins, Angus John Brockhurst, born in 1911 at Narberth, Wales, he received a Ph.D. in 1945 from Manchester University for *Tatian's "Diatessaron"; introductory studies, with a portion of the Arabic version.* From 1946 to 1970 he was successively a lecturer in New Testament at the universities of London and Leeds. His writings include *The Reliability of the Gospels* (1952), *The Historicity of the fourth Gospel* (1960), and *The Tradition about Jesus* (1969). Au&Wr, 1963, 1971; IntAu&W, 1976, 1977; Sluglett; WrDr, 1976/78-1986/88|

Higgins, Benjamin Howard, born 18 August 1912 at London, Ont., he graduated in 1933 from the local University of Western Ontario, later from LSE, and he received a Ph.D. in 1941 from the University of Minnesota. He taught economics at a variety of universities in the United States and Canada. He was a director of the Indonesian Project in the Center for International Studies of the Massachusetts Institute of Technology, and chief economist of the United Nations' mission of technical assistance in Libya in 1951-1952. After his retirement from the University of Ottawa, he became a professor emeritus. His writings include *Indonesia 1970* (1959), *Financing Lebanese development* (1960), *United Nations and U.S. foreign economic policy* (1962), and *Regional development theories and their application* (1995). In 1992, he was honoured by *Equity and efficiency in economic development; essays in honour of Benjamin Higgins.* He died in 2001. Index Islamicus; AmM&WSc, 1973 S; Canadian, 1970-1989|; Note; WhoEc, 1981, 1986, 1999

Higgins, Rosalyn Cohen, born 2 June 1937 at London, she graduated from Girton College, Cambridge as well as from Yale University, New Haven, Conn. In 1958, she was a U.K. intern at the United Nations. She successively held the chair of international law at the University of Kent at Canterbury, and L.S.E. Her writings include *The Development of international law through the political organs of the United Nations* (1963), *United Nations peacekeeping* (1972), *The EC and the new United Nations* (1994), and *Terrorism and international law* (1997). ConAu, 9-12, new rev., 3; IntAu&W, 1976, 1977, 1982; IntWW, 1990/91-2002; Who's who, 1981-2004; WhoWor, 1976/77; WrDr, 1976/78-2004

Higginson, Thomas Wentworth, born in 1823 at Cambridge, Mass., he graduated from Harvard University and Harvard School of Divinity. He was a writer, historian, Unitarian minister, and political activist who espoused anti-slavery, feminist, and labour causes. His writings include *Army life in a black regiment* (1870), its translation, *Vie militaire dans un régiment noir* (1884), *Common sense about women* (1882), its translation, *Die Frauenfrage und der gesunde Menschenverstand* (1895), and *Black rebellion* (1889). He died in 1911. James W. Tuttleton wrote *Thomas Wentworth Higginson* (1978). ConAu, 162; DLB, 64 (1988), pp. 108-113; DLB, 243 (2001), pp. 201-218; Master (42); WhAm, 1; Who was who, 1

Hilaire, Jean, born 16 November 1865 at Paillet (Gironde), France, he graduated in 1887 from the military academy, Saint-Cyr, and served in North Africa from 1892 to 1902, in Madagascar the following seven years, and subsequently in French Equatorial Africa and Chad, where he participated in the Ouadaï campaign. During the 1914-18 war he distinguished himself in the Champagne fighting, and was nominated brigadier-general in 1918. He served once again in French Equatorial Africa until 1919, when he was recalled to Marseille. He retired in 1925. His writings include *Du Congo au Nile ... cinq ans d'arrêt* (Marseille, 1930). He died in Bayonne (Pyrénée-Atlantiques), on 14 October 1931. DBF; NUC, pre-1956

Hilāl (Hlal), Yahyá, born 20th cent., he gained a *doctorat ès sciences* and became a lecturer in the École Mohamadia d'ingenieurs at Rabat. His writings include *Le Système documentaire arabe; contribution à l'indexation automatique de documents arabes* (Tunis, 1984). Note about the author; ZkO

Hildburgh, Walter Leo, born in 1876 at New York, he was an art collector and benefactor to the Victoria and Albert Museum, London, for more than forty years. He was trained as a scientist, and initially his interests veered in the direction of ethnology, but since the 1910s his researches became overlaid by an interest in the history of art, and he began slowly to amass the collections through which he was most widely known. His writings include *Medieval Spanish enamels and their relation to the origin and the development of copper champlevé enamels of the 12th and 13th centuries* (1936). He died on 25 November 1955. BioInd, 4 (2); *Burlington magazine*, 98 (February 1956), p. 56; NYT, 27 November 1955, p. 89, col. 1

Hildebrandt, Johann Maria, born 19 March 1847 at Düsseldorf, Prussia, he trained as an engineer, but had to forgo his profession when he lost an eye in an explosion. He became a "gardener." A secretary of the Berlin society of horticulture, he pursued entomological research and attended meetings of botanists and entomologists. In 1849 he began to travel, first both shores of the Red Sea until illness forced him to return home. Supported by the Berliner Gesellschaft für Erdkunde and the Afrikanische Gesellschaft, he set out again, visiting Somalia, and the Comoro Islands. Kenyan Massai, however, prevented him from entering East Africa so that he once more returned home. Supported by the same institutions, he reached Madagascar in 1879 and explored the island, collecting fossils as well as ethnographic material, all of which he sent to a Berlin museum. After seven years of wandering without comfort, the last two yeras of which without quinine in the Malagasy swamps, he died in Tananarive on 29 May 1881. ADtB; Embacher; *Hommes et destins*, 3, pp. 242-43; Kornrumpf; Kosch

Hildén, Kaarlo Thorsten Oskar, born 28 September 1893 at Helsinski, he was a geographer, anthropologist, and a professor at Helsinki. His writings include *Anthropologische Untersuchungen über die Eingeborenen des russischen Altai* (1920), *Die Runö-Schweden in anthropologischer Hinsicht* (1926), *Zur Frage der ostbaltischen Rasse* (1927), and *Studien über das Vorkommen der Darwinschen Ohrspitz in der Bevölkerung Finnlands* (1929), *Englannin kanaalisaaret ja niiden taloudelliset olot* (1955), and he edited *Across Asia from west to east in 1906-1908*, by Carl G. E. Mannerheim (1940). He died in Tammisaari (Ekenäs) on 15 July 1960. Aikalaiskirja, 1934; *Otavan iso tietosanakirja*; Van och vad, 1931-1957; *Unisi tietosanakirja*; ScBInd (1)

Hilder, Gisela, born about 1942, she received a Dr.phil. in 1972 from the Universität Göttingen for *Der scholastische Wortschatz bei Jean de Meun.* GV

Hilferding, A. F., 1831-1872 *see* Gil'ferding, Aleksandr Feodorovich

Hilgers [née] **Hesse**, Irene, born 17 January 1905 at Köln, she studied ethnology, Australasian civilization and classical archaeology, receiving a Dr.phil. in 1932 from the Universität Hamburg for *Darstellung der menschlichen Gestalt in Rundskulpturen Neumecklenburgs.* She worked as a private scholar until the outbreak of the second World War, when she was inducted into the armed forces. After her Dr.habil. in 1965 for *Beiträge zur Entwicklungsgeschichte der Bahasa Indonesia unter besonderer Berücksichtigung einiger syntaktischer Fragen*, she taught Southeast Asian studies at the Universität Köln. Her writings include *Indonesisch* (1955), *Indonesisch-deutsches Wörterbuch* (1962), and *Perlen im Reisfeld und andere indonesische Erzählungen* (1971). In 1992, she was honoured by *Kölner Beiträge aus Malaiologie und Ethnologie zu Ehren von Frau Professor Dr. Irene Hilgers-Hesse.* Kürschner, 1966-2005; Note about the author; ZKO

Hill, A. H., M.A., B.Sc., born about 1920, he received a D.Phil. in 1955 from Oxford for *An English translation of the "Hikayat Abdullah" and a critical examination of the subject-matter for the light it may throw on the history of the Far East, 1800-1850.* His wrings include *Malayan folk tales* (Kuala Lumpur, 1950), and *Hikayat Raja-Raja Pasai; a revised romanized version of Raffles MS67, together with an English translation* (1961). BLC; NUC, 1956-67; Sluglett; *SOAS Library catalogue*

Hill, Allan Graham, born 16 September 1944 at Bangor, Northern Ireland, he graduated from the University of Durham, where he also received his Ph.D. in 1967 for *Aspects of the urban development of Kuwait.* After teaching at the University of Aberdeen, he was in 1975 associated with the Office of Population Research, Princeton University. From 1979 to 1991 he was on the faculty of the School of Hygiene, University of London. He subsequently became a professor in the Department of Population Studies, Harvard School of Public Health, a post which he still held in 2004. His writings include *Population, health and nutrition in the Sahel; issues in the welfare of selected West African communities* (1985), *Health interventions and mortality change in developing countries* (1989), and he was a joint author of *Kuwait; urban and medical ecology; a geomedical study* (1971). DrAS, 10th ed. (2002), vol. 1 [not sighted]; NatFacDr, 1992-2004; Note about the author; WhoAm, 2001|

Hill, Arthur *Derek*, born 6 December 1916 at Bassett, Hampshire, he was educated at Marlborough College. He was a designer of sets and costumes for Covent Garden and Sadler's Wells, London, and he was a joint author of *Islamic architecture and its decoration* (1967), and *Islamic architecture in North Africa* (1976). He died on 30 July 2000. IntWW, 1990/91-2002; Note about the author

Hill, Donald Routledge, born 6 August 1922 at London, he served in the Middle East as a lieutenant with the Royal Engineers from 1941 to 1946, including two years in North Africa and Italy. In 1949 he graduated from Woolwich Polytechnic, University of London, and joined the Iraq Petroleum Company, for whom he worked in the Middle East for six years. From 1955 until his retirement in 1984 he held several senior positions in major petro-chemical companies, concurrently serving as a consultant to museums on Arabic technology. In 1985, he became an honorary research fellow, University College, London. He received an M.Litt. in Islamic history in 1964 from the University of Durham, and a Ph.D. in 1970 from the University of London for *The Termination of hostilities in the early Arab conquests*. His writings include *The Book of knowledge of ingenious mechanical devices* (1974), *Arabic water-clocks* (1981), *A history of engineering in classical and medieval times* (1984), *Islamic science and engineering* (1993), and he was joint author of *Islamic technology; an illustrated history* (1986). He died on 30 May 1994. Arabic sciences and philosophy 5 (1995), pp. 297-299; ConAu, 122; Sluglett

Hill, Enid, Mrs., born about 1937, she received a Ph.D. in 1967 from the University of Chicago for *Montesquieu's De l'esprit des lois; the necessity of relativistic political science to admit values*. She was in 1990 a professor of political science at the American University in Cairo. Her writings include *Mahkama; studies in the Egyptian legal system* (1979), *The Modernization of labor and labor law in the Arab Gulf states* (1979), and *Al-Sanhuri and Islamic law* (1987). DrBSMES, 1993; MESA Roster of members, 1977, 1990

Hill, Sir George Francis, born in 1867 at Berhampore, Bengal, he was the leading Greek numimatist of his time, and a director of the British Library, London. His writings include *The Development of Arabic numerals in Europe* (1915), and *Catalogue of the Greek coins of Arabia, Mesopotamia and Persia* (1965). He died in London in 1948. Biolnd, 1 (3), 2 (2); DNB; Enclran; WhE&EA; Who was who, 4

Hill, John Godfrey, born in 1870 in Sweden, he was a graduate of Cornell University, Ithca, N.Y., and he received a Ph.D. in 1905 and a D.D. in 1918. Since 1907 he was a professor of Biblical literature at the University of Southern California. His writings include *Christianity for today* (1924). He died in 1954. WhAm, 5; WhNAA

Hill, Peter Manners, born 16 October 1945 at Perth, Australia, he received a Dr.phil. in 1972 from the Universität Hamburg for *Die Farbwörter der russischen und bulgarischen Schriftsprache der Gegenwart; Versuch einer Klassifikation*. He was from 1983 to 1985 chairman of South Slavonic Studies, Macquarie University, Sydney, and subsequently became a professor in the Institut für Slavistik, Universität Hamburg. His writings include *The Macedonians in Australia* (1989), and he edited *Standard language in the Slavic world; papers on sociolinguistics by Hamburg Slavists* (1988). Kürschner, 1983-2005

Hill, Richard Leslie, born 18 February 1901 at Ramsbury, Wiltshire, he was brought up partly in New Zealand. He was recruited to the Sudan Civil Service in 1927 as a traffic trainee on the Great Western Railway and served from 1929 to 1944 as district traffic manager, Sudan Railways. He was seconded to University College of Khartoum, 1945-49, he then went to the University of Durham as a senior lecturer in Middle Eastern history, a post which he held until his retirement in 1966. During the early years of his appointment, he established single-handed the Durham Sudan Archive. His writings include *Sudan transport* (1965), *Slatin Pasha* (1965), *Biographical dictionary of the Sudan* (1967), *On the frontiers of Islam* (1970), *The Europeans in the Sudan, 1834-1878* (1980), and *The Sudan memoirs of Carl Christian Giegler Pasha* (1984). He died in Oxford on 21 March 1996. ConAu, 1-4, 151, new rev., 1; Note about the author; Unesco

Hill, Rosalind Mary Theodosia, born in 1908 at Neston, England, she graduated from St. Hilda's College, Oxford, and successively became a professor of medieval history at the universities of Leicester and London. Her writings include *Oliver Sutton, Dean of Lincoln, later Bishop of Lincoln, 1280-99* (Lincoln, Friends of Lincoln Cathedral, 1950). On the occasion of her seventieth birthday she was honoured by *Medieval women*, edited by Derek Baker (1978). She died on 11 January 1997. ConAu, 11-12, 156; WrDr, 1976/78-1998-2000

Hill, Samuel Charles, born in 1857 at Berhampton, India, he was educated at a school for sons of missionaries at Blackheath, England, and University College School, London, where he gained his B.A. and B.Sc. He went to India in 1881 and joined the Indian Educational Service at Dacca. Since 1885 he served as an inspector of schools and principal at a variety of colleges. In 1899 he was a director of the Imperial Records and Library, ex-officio assistant secretary to the Government of India, Home Department. He ended his career as a director of Public Instruction, Nagpur. His writings include *Three Frenchmen in Bengal* (1903), *Bengal in 1756-1757* (1905), and *Catalogue of the home miscellaneous series of the India Office Records* (London, India Office, 1927). He died in 1926. Cyclopedia of India (1907-09) [not sighted]; IndianBnd (2)

Hill, William Bancroft in 1857 at Colebrook, N.H., the son of a clergy, he graduated from Harvard as well as from Columbia Law School, Baltimore Law School, and Union Theological Seminary. He practised law until 1883, when he successively became a pastor at Athens, N.Y. and Poughkeepsie,

N.Y., later to become a professor of Biblical studies at Vassar College, Poughkeepsie. He died in 1945. Master (3); NatCAB, vol. 34, p. 212; WhAm, 2

Hillaireau, Julien Marie François Xavier, 1796-1855 see Hilléreau, Julien Marie François Xavier

Hille, Carl August, born about 1820, he received a medical doctorate in 1845 from the Universität Leipzig for *De medicia Arabibus oculariis prolegomena ad Alii Ben Isa monitorium ex cod. mst. in linguam latinam vertendum edendumque*. His trace is lost after an article in ZDMG in 1851. Sezgin

Hillelson, Sigmar, fl. 1939-41, he was a sometime member of the B.B.C.'s Near Eastern Service. His writings include *Sudan Arabic* (1925), and *Sudan Arabic texts* (1935). Note about the author

Hillenbrand, Carol (Carole), born about 1940, she received a Ph.D. in 1979 from the University of Edinburgh for *The History of the Jazira, 1100-1150; the contribution of Ibn al-Azraq al-Fariqi*. She was a reader in Arabic in the Department of Islamic and Middle Eastern Studies, University of Edinburgh. For a number of years in the 1990s, she was seconded part-time to the Enterprise Centre of her University as the Faculty of Arts Enterprise Adviser, responsible for a budget of £ 1 million. She was the British representative on the Union européenne des arabisants et islamisants, and the Islamic editor for Edinburgh University Press. Her writings include contributions to the *Encyclopedia of Islam* as well as *A Muslim principality in Crusader times, the early Artuqid state* (1990), *The Crusades; Islamic perspectives* (1999), she was a joint author of *Qajar Iran* (1983), she translated from the Arabic of al-Tabarī, *The Waning of the Umayyad Caliphate* (1989), and she was a joint editor of *Studies in honour of Clifford Edmund Bosworth* (2000). EURAMES, 1993; Sluglett

Hillenbrand, Robert, born about 1940, he received a D.Phil. in 1975 from Oxford University for *The Tomb towers of Iran to 1550*. He was a professor of fine art at the University of Edinburgh. His writings include *Imperial images in Persian painting* (1977), *Islamic architecture; form, function and meaning* (1994), *Shahnama* (2003)[not sighted], he was a joint author of *Islamic architecture in North Africa* (1976), *Ottoman Jerusalem, the living city, 1517-1917* (2000)[not sighted], *Studies in medieval Islamic architecture*, vol. 1 (2001), and he edited *Persian painting from the Mongols to the Qajars; studies in honour of Basil W. Robinson* (2000). Note about the author; Private; Sluglett

Hiller, Bruno Arthur, born 13 May 1875 at Berlin, he went to school at Leibniz-Gymnasium, Berlin, Collège Latin, Vervey, Switzerland, and Königliche Gymnasium, Wittstock. He studied theology and philosophy, particularly scholasticism, at Berlin and Erlangen, where received a Dr.phil. in 1900 for *Abälard als Ethiker*. His other writings include *Evangelische Bibelkunde für Lyzeen* (Leipzig & Berlin, Teubner, 1912). His trace is lost after an article in 1939. Thesis

Hilléreau (Hillaireau), Julien Marie François Xavier, born at a village in the diocese Luçon (Vendée) on 21 June 1796, he was educated at Chavagnes and Saint-Jean-d'Angély, before entering the seminary at La Rochelle, where he was ordained priest. Following a mission to Roma in 1830, he was in the following year appointed titular bishop of Caledonia as well as Apostolic visitor to the Diocese of Smyrna, and consecrated at the Congregation of Propaganda. He had hardly begun his mission when in 1833 he was nominated titular archbishop of Petra and assistant to the old and ailing vicar apostolic of the Patriarchate of Constantinople, whom he succeeded in 1835. During his episcopate, French and Italian communities flourished under a liberal Sultan. He died in office twenty years later in Constantinople from cholera on 1 March 1855. DBF; *Hommes et destins*, 7, pp. 239-41; Kornrumpf

Hillgarth, Jocelyn Nigel, born 22 September 1929 at London, he graduated in 1950 from Cambridge University and received a Ph.D. in history in 1957. He was successively a professor of history at Warburg Institute, University of Texas, Harvard University, Boston College, and the Pontifical Institute of Mediaeval Studies, University of Toronto. His writings include *The Problem of a Catalan Mediterranean empire, 1229-1327* (1975), *The Spanish kingdoms, 1250-1516* (1976-78), *The Register Notule communium 14 of the Diocese of Barcelona, 1345-1348* (1983), *The Liber communis curiae of the Diocese of Majorca, 1364-1374* (1989), and *Altercatio ecclesiae et synagogae* (1999). He was honoured by *Religion, text, and society in medieval Spain and northern Europe; essays in honor of J. N. Hillgarth* (Toronto, Pontifical Institute of Mediaeval Studies, 2002). ConAu, 37-40; DrAS, 1969 H, 1974 H, 1978 H, 1982 H; IntAu&W, 1982; WrDr, 1976/78-2004

Hillmann, Michael Craig, born 5 May 1940 at Baltimore, Md., he graduated from the local Loyola College. After serving two years with the American Peace Corps in Iran, he took his Ph.D. in 1974 at the University of Chicago for *Unity in the ghazals of Hafez*. He briefly worked as a Persian cataloguer at the University of Chicago Library, before being appointed a professor of Persian at the University of Texas, Austin. In 2004, he was associated with its Center for Asian Studies. His writings include *Twentieth century Persian literature in translation; a bibliography* (1976), *Literature and society in Iran* (1982), *Persian carpets* (1984), *A Lonely woman; Forugh Farrokhzad and her poetry* (1987), *Iranian* *culture; a Persianist view* (1990), and he edited *Hedayat's "The blind owl"* forty years after (1978). DrAS, 1978 F, 1982 F; NatFacDr, 1995-2004; Private

Hilprecht, Hermann Vollrat, born 28 July 1859 at Hohenerxleben, Anhalt, he studied theology, Oriental languages, and law at Leipzig where he received a doctorate in 1883. He became a professor of Assyriology and Semitic philology at the University of Pennsylvania in Philadelphia, and subsequently also served as a curator of the Semitic Section of the University Museum. He was the scientific director of the University's expedition to Babylonia, and he also made frequent scientific explorations in Asia Minor and Syria. His writings include *Explorations in Bible lands during the nineteenth century* (1903), *Assyriologische und archäologische Studien* (1909), and *Der neue Fund zur Sintflutgeschichte* (1910). He died in Philadelphia on 19 March 1925. ACAB; ANB; Bioln, 1; DAB; DtBE; Kornrumpf, N; NatCAB, vol. 10, p. 380; Shavit; WhAm, 1; WhoAm, 1899-1908/09

Hilsch, Peter, born 13 July 1938 at Warnsdorf, Germany, he received a Dr.phil. in 1969 from the Universität Tübingen for *Die Bischöfe von Prag in der frühen Stauferzeit; ihre Stellung zwischen Reichs- und Landesgewalt* (1969). After gaining a Dr.habil. in 2000, he became a professor of medieval history at Tübingen. His other writings include *Johannes Hus, Prediger Gottes und Ketzer* (1999). GV; Kürschner, 2003, 2005

Hilscher, Eberhard, born 28 April 1927 at Schwiebus, Mark Brandenburg, he became a novelist, essayist, and biographer whose writings include *Die Entdeckung der Liebe* (1962), *Arnold Zweig; Leben und Werk* (1968), *Gerhart Hauptmann* (1969), *Der Morgenstern, oder, Die vier Verwandlungen eines Mannes, Walther von der Vogelweide genannt* (1976), *Poetische Weltbilder* (1977), and *Dichtung und Gedanken; 30 Essays von Goethe bis Einstein* (2000). KDtLK, 1973-2002/2003

Hilton-Simpson, Melville William, born in 1881 at Albury, England, he was educated at Exeter College, Oxford, where received a B.Sc. in 1921 for *Medicine among the Berbers of the Aurès*. He was a traveller and ethnologist and had been engaged, together with his wife, for many years in ethnological study of Berber hill tribes of Southern Algeria, among whom they spent several winters. His writings include *Algiers and beyond* (1906), *Land and peoples of the Kasai* (1911), *Among the hill-folk of Algeria; journeys among the Shawia of the Aurès Mountains* (1921), and *Arab medicine and surgery; a study of healing art in Algeria* (1922). He died in 1938. BritInd (1); Sluglett; Who, 1929-1936; *Who was who*, 3

Hilty, Gerold, born 12 August 1927 at Samedan, Graubünden, Switzerland, he was a student of Romance languages and first taught at high schools, and since 1959 as a professor at the Universität Zürich. His writings include *Gallus und die Sprachgeschichte der Nordostschweiz* (2001), and he edited *El libro complido en los iudizios de las estrellas, por Aly aben Ragel* (1954). In 1987, he was honoured by *Romania ingeniosa," Festschrift für Professor Dr. Gerold Hilty zum 60. Geburtstag.* Kürschner; 1970-2005; WhoSwi, 1980/81

Himbury, Sir William Henry, born in 1871, he was in the cotton trade all his life, a pioneer of cotton growing within the Commonwealth, and the first Managing Director of the British Cotton Growing Association. He was on many government committees, and on boards of management connected with cotton growing, and also with agricultural development within the Commonwealth generally. He was a widely travelled man, for sixty-one years a fellow of the Geographical Association and for many years, right up to the time of his death in November 1955, was its higly esteemed treasurer. In 1930 he was awarded an honorary M.A. from Manchester University. *Geographical journal* 122 (1956), p. 140; Who, 1929-1955; *Who was who* 5

Himly, Carl/Karl Georg Friedrich Julius, born 4 December 1836 at Hannover, the son of chief surgeon Dr. G. Himly and his wife Louise von Bodungen, he went to school in Celle, Lüneburg, Goslar, and Clausthal. He studied Oriental languages first at the Universität Göttingen and later at Berlin. He taught at St. Petersburg, before becoming a student dragoman at Peking. He later was appointed an interpreter at the German consulate first at Che-foo and later at Shanghai. He was a sometime librarian to the North China Branch of the Royal Asiatic Society. He retired in 1876 first to Halberstadt and, after the death of his mother, to Wiesbaden. He collaborated with Ferdinand Frh. von Richthofen (1833-1905), and Sven Hedin. His writings include *Die Abteilung der Spiele im Spiegel der Mandschu-Sprache* (1895-1901), and he was a joint author of *Die chinesischen Handschriften und sonstige Kleinfunde Sven Hedins in Lou-Lan* (1920). He died of pneumonia in Wiesbaden on 1 June 1904. DtBIlnd (1); *T'oung pao*, 2e série, vol. 5 (1904), pp. 624-25

Himly, François Jacques, he was a deputy archivist of the Archives départementales, Bas-Rhin, Strasbourg. His writings include *Catalogue des cartes et plans manuscrits antérieurs à 1790* (Strasbourg, Archives départementales du Bas-Rhin, 1959), *Atlas des villes médiévales d'Alsace* (1970), *Fonds du Statthalter* (1980), and he was a joint author of *Dictionary of archival terminology* (1984).

Himly, Louis *Auguste*, born 28 March 1823 at Strasbourg, he received a Protestant secondary education, studied two years at German universities, and received his *agrégation* in history and geography in 1845. He graduated from the École des chartes in 1849. In 1863 he became a professor of geography at the Sorbonne, where he served from 1881 to his retirement in 1898 as a dean of the Faculté des lettres. He died in Sèvres (Hauts-de-Seine) in 1906. DBF; Geog, 1 (1977), pp. 43-47; NDBA

Himmel von Agisburg, Heinrich, born 3 May 1843 at Schönberg, Moravia, he was a lieutenant-colonel in the Imperial Austrian Army and a sometime education officer (*Erziehungsleiter*) to H.H. the Archduke Ladislas, residing in Budapest. He visited the Near East, particularly Palestine, experiences which are described in his *Eine Orientreise* (Wien, 1887). His other writings include *Freundesworte eines alten Soldaten an die heurigen Rekruten* (Brixen, 1908). GV; KDtLK, 1895-1900; Sezgin

von **Himpel**, Felix, born 28 February 1821 at Ravensburg, Bavaria, he studied at the Universität Tübingen and was ordained priest on 4 September 1845. A *Gymnasialprofessor* in Ehingen since 1849, he became in 1857 a profesor of Old Testament and Oriental studies at Tübingen. His writings include *Ursprung und Bedeutung der Sigfritssage* (1851), and *Die Unsterblichkeitslehre des Alten Testaments* (1857). Hie died in Tübingen on 18 February 1890. ADtB, vol. 50, pp. 342-43; GV; Kosch

Hincha, Georg, born about 1930, he received a Dr.phil. in 1961 from the Universität Hamburg for a study of current Persian grammar entitled *Beiträge zu einer Morphemlehre des Neupersischen*. He was for many years a professor at the Institut für Linguistik, Technische Universität, Berlin. Kürschner, 1976-2005; Schwarz

Hinchcliffe, Doreen, born 20th cent., she received a Ph.D. in 1971 from SOAS for *The Islamic law of marriage and divorce in India and Pakistan since partition*. "She taught Islamic law in general, and Islamic law of succession. In her practice she dealt not only with the law of personal status but also with the commercial law of the Middle East." She was a joint author of *Islamic marriage and divorce laws of the Arab world* (1996). Sluglett; *SOAS calendar*, 1997/98; ZKO

Hinckelmann (Hinkelmann), Abraham, born 2 May 1652 at Döbeln, Saxony. It is said that his grandfather, the pastor and *Magister* Balthasar Walther H., had travelled extensively in the East and knew Oriental languages. The grandson studied theology and Oriental languages since 1668 at the Universität Wittenberg where he obtained a *magister* degree at the age of seventeen. In 1672, he became a school principal in Gardelegen, Altmark, and three years later in Lübeck. In 1685, he was appointed a deacon at St. Nicholai Kirche in Hamburg. Since 1687, he served as a senior court preacher, elder, and superintendent-general in Hessen-Darmstadt as well as a professor of theology at the Universität Gießen. Recalled to Hamburg after a little more than a year, he became senior pastor of St. Catharinen Kirche, Hamburg, where he became involved in the Pietist controversies, which so weakened his health that he died in 1695. In the previous year, in the midst of the local religious unrest, during which he was accused of millenialism and pietism, he published the first printed Arabic Koran. His introduction is witness to his familiarity with Arabic literature. His other writings include *Auffrichtige Fürstellung des wahren Ursprungs der in Hamburg entstandenen und annoch währenden ärgerlichen und gefährlichen Unruhe* (1694). At the time of his death he was planning a lexicon of the Koran as well as an Arabic-Persian dictionary, the manuscript of which was in 1902 still at the Hamburg library. Behrmann, pp. 51-54; ADtB, vol. 12, pp. 460-62; Fück, p. 94; LuthC 75

Hinden, Rebecca Rita, born 16 January 1909 at Cape Town, South Africa, she was educated at the local seminary and university. About 1927 the family, intensely orthodox in its Jewish faith and strongly Zionist, moved to Palestine while she herself went to L.S.E. to take a B.Sc. In 1935, she and her husband moved off to Palestine, apparently for good, but in fact the move was unsuccessful and disturbing. Both of them rejected both Zionist nationalism and the Jewish faith so that in 1938 they returned to London disenchanted, and there she was to remain for the rest of her life. In 1939, she received a Ph.D. from the University of London for *Palestine, an experiment in colonisation*. From 1940 to 1950, she served as a secretary of the Fabian Colonial Research Bureau. In late 1951, she found a new role for herself in the Socialist Union. Soon afterwards she emerged as the editor of its journal, *Socialist commentary*, a post she retained until her death in 1971. Her writings include *Kenya, white man's country?* (1944), *Common sense and colonial development* (1949), *Empire and after* (1949), *No cheer for Central Africa* (1958), and she was a joint author of *Economic survey of Palestine, with special reference to the years 1936 and 1937* (1938), and *Must Labour lose?* (1960). Morgan, Kenneth O., *Labour people* (1987), pp. 239-45; Sluglett; WhE&EA; WhoWorJ, 1955, 1965

Hindle, Brian *Paul*, born 20th cent., he wrote *Maps for local history* (London, 1988), and *Maps for historians* (London, 1998).

Hindley, John Haddon, born in 1765 at Manchester, he graduated from Brasenose College, Oxford, and was elected chaplain of the Collegiate Church, Manchester, in 1790, and appointed librarian of

Chetham's Hospital in 1792. Although a "crotchetty" man, his poetical abilities were of a high order. He edited *Persian lyrics, or, Scattered poems from the Diwan-i Hafiz, with paraphrases* (1800), *Pendeh-i Attar; the counsels from Attar* (1809), and *Resemblances linear and verbal; nisāb-i tajnīs al-lughāt* (1811). He died unmarried in Clapham on 17 June 1827, having long laboured under mental infirmity. BiDLA; BritInd (2); DNB

Hinds, Douglas Lanford, born 25 May 1933, he graduated in 1955 from Furman University, and in 1963 from the Law School, University of South Carolina. He was admitted to the Bar of South Carolina. WhoAmL, 1979; WhoAmP, 1989-2003/2004

Hinds, Martin, born 10 April 1941 at Penarth, South Wales, he studied Arabic at SOAS and from 1963 to 1966 he there taught his subject. He subsequently became a lecturer in Arabic, and a fellow of Trinity Hall, Cambridge, until his death on 1 December 1988. From 1970 to 1972, he was a director of the Arabic Language Unit at the American University in Cairo. His publications, which reflect imaginative inside into Arab life, based on residence in Arab countries, include *Arabic documents from the Ottoman period from Qasr Ibrîm* (1986), *An Early Islamic family from Oman; al-'Awtabī's account of the Muhallabids* (1991), *Studies in early Islamic history* (1996), and he was a joint author of *God's caliph; religious authority in the first centuries of Islam* (1986). BSMES bulletin, 16 (1989), pp. 118-120; MESA bulletin, 23 i (July 1989), pp. 155-56

Hinkelmann, Abraham, 1652-1695 see Hinckelmann, Abraham

Hinkhouse, Paul McClure, 1892-1963. Encyclopedia of American biography (1934-70) [not sighted]

Hinnebusch, Raymond Aloysius, born in 1946, he graduated in 1968 from Duquesne University, Pittsburgh, Pa., and received a Ph.D. in 1976 from the University of Pittsburgh for *Political organization in Syria; a case of mobilization politics*, a work for which he had done field-work in Syria, 1973-74. Since 1976 he taught political science at Pittsburgh University, and in 1991, he was an associate professor of his subject at the College of St. Catherine. His writings include *Egyptian politics under Sadat* (1985), *Peasant and bureaucracy in Ba'thist Syria* (1989), *Authoritarian power and state formation in Ba'thist Syria* (1990), *Syria; revolution from above* (2001), and he was a joint author of *Syria and Iran; middle powers in a penetrated regional system* (1997). ConAu, 136; MESA Roster of members, 1982-1990; Selim³; WrDr, 1994/96-2000

de **Hinojosa** y **Naveros**, Eduardo, born 10 November 1852 at Alhama (Granada), he was a jurisconsul and historiographer who had studied law, philosophy, and letters at Garnada, gaining a doctorate in 1876 at the Universidad de Madrid. His writings include *Historia del derecho romano; segun las mas recientes invetigaciones* (1880-85), *Historia general del derecho español* (1887), and *Documentos para la historia de las instituciones de Léon y de Castilla* (1919). He died in Madrid on 19 May 1919. EncicUni; IndiceE³ (2); OxLaw

Hinsley, Sir Francis Harry, born 26 November 1918 at Walsall, Staffordshire, he served with the British Foreign Service in the 1939-45 war, and gained an M.A. in 1946 at Cambridge. A fellow of St. John's College, Cambridge, since 1944, he taught history of international relations at Cambridge from 1949 to his retirement. His writings include *Command of the sea; the naval side of British history* (1950), *Power and the pursuit of peace* (1963), *Power and the pursuit of peace; theory and practice in the history of relations between states* (1967), *Nationalism and the international system* (1973), and *British foreign policy under Sir Edward Grey* (1977). He died in Cambridge on 16 February 1998. ConAu, 17-20, 166; Who, 1973-1998; WrDr, 1986/88-1996/98

Hinterhoff, Eugène, born 3 March 1895 in Korea, he was educated at universities in Russia and Poland. In 1916 he entered the officers' artillery school at Petrograd, and was until 1917 at the front in the Russian army. At the beginning of the revolution, he passed into the 1st Polish Corps, and in 1918 entered the newly formed Polish army of independent Poland. In the interwar years he was sent for military studies to France, and subsequently served for three years on the high military council. In 1933 he left the army. After the second World War, he was the London foreign and diplomatic correspondent for the Polish Telegraph Agency, and since 1957 he served as defence correspondent for the London *Tablet*. He was a founding member of the Military Commentators' Circle, London. A good linguist, his writings include *Disengagement* (1959), *Pläne für ein militärisches Auseinanderrücken der Weltmächte in Deutschland* (1960), and he was a joint author of *Materielle Voraussetzungen für eine Wiedervereinigung Deutschlands in der Sicht nichtamtlicher Vorschläge* (1960). ConAu, 9-10; Note about the author

Hintze, Fritz, born 18 April 1915 at Berlin, he received a Dr.phil. from the Universität Berlin for *Untersuchungen zu Stil und Sprache neuägyptischer Erzählungen*. He was a professor of Egyptology at Humboldt-Universität, Berlin, and subsequently became a director of its Institut für Ägyptologie, and the Institut für Afrikanistik. His writings include *Sudan im Altertum* (1973). In 1977, he was honoured by *Ägypten und Kusch;* ... *Fritz Hintze zum 60. Geburtstag,* and in 1990, by *Studia in honorem Fritz Hintze.* He died in Berlin on 30 March 1993. Erika Endesfelder wrote *Von Berlin nach Meroe; Erinnerungen an den Ägyptologen Fritz Hinze* (2003). Egyptology; HbDtWiss; Kürschner, 1950-1976; Schwarz; *Wer ist wer*, 1955, 1958; *Wer war wer in der DDR* (Berlin, 2000)

Hintzen, Lothar, born about 1945, he received a Dr.jur. in 1974 from the Universität Köln for *Die Besteuerung der Kapitalgesellschaften in den Niederlanden im Vergleich zur Bundesrepublik Deutschland.* His other writings include *Steuerliche Behandlung deutscher Investitionen in Tunesien* (Köln, Deutsche Gesellschaft für Wirtschaftliche Zusammenarbeit; Bundesstelle für Außenhandelsbeziehungen, 1980). GV

Hinz, Walther, born 19 November 1906 at Stuttgart, he was an orphan since his youth and studied as a fellow of the Studienstiftung des Deutschen Volkes at Leipzig, München, and Paris. He received a Dr.phil. for a thesis on the cultural history of Russia under Peter the Great, and a Dr.habil. in 1936 for *Irans Aufstieg zum Nationalstaat im fünfzehnten Jahrhundert,* a work which was translated into Turkish (1948), and Persian (1968). A professor of Persian and dean of faculty at Göttingen since 1937, he served in the 1939-45 war as a staff officer, including a mission to Istanbul. Interned by the British from the summer of 1945 to autumn 1946, and disliked by many contemporaries for his political past, he returned to Göttingen to face the loss of his chair of Persian. Until 1957 he made a living as a translator, and an editor with the *Göttinger Tageblatt;* until his retirement in 1975 he was a director of the Seminar für Iranistik at Göttingen. His writings include *Altpersischer Wortschatz* (1942), *Islamische Maße und Gewichte* (1955), its translation, Мусульманские меры и веса с переводом в метрицескую систему (1970), *Das Reich Elam* (1964), *Altiranische Funde und Forschungen* (1969), and *Islamische Währungen des 11. bis 19. Jahrhunderts* (1991). He died in Göttingen on 12 April 1992. BioB134; DtBiInd (1); EncIran; Hanisch; Kürschner, 1983; *Wer ist wer*, 1967/68-1992/93; ZDMG, 143 (1993), pp. 241-47

Hippeau, Edmond Gabriel, born 14 October 1849 at Caen (Calvados), France, he was a private secretary before being attached to the Ministère des Affaires étrangères, from 1872 to 1879. In 1885 he entered the publishing house E. Dentu, Paris, as an administrator. He contributed to the journals *Événement, Télégraphe,* and *Bien public;* and he founded the ephemeral *l'Avenir diplomatique* (1880-81), and the *Renaissance musicale.* His writings include *Le Congrès* [de Berlin] *en miniature,* par un diplomate (1878), *Histoire diplomatique de la Troisième République* (1889), and *Les républiques du Caucase* (1920). He is mainly remembered for his writings on music. He died in 1921. DBF; Lamathière; Oursel; Vapereau

Hippisley Coxe, Antony Dacres, born 21 March 1912 at London, he attended the Royal Naval College, Dartmouth, and the Architectural Association School of Architecture. He was an international authority on the circus. His writings include *Haunted Britain* (1973). He died 28 January 1988. ConAu, 103, 124

Hiro, Dilip, born about 1930 at Larkana, Sind, India, he was educated in India, Britain and the United States. Since 1964 he was residing in London, where he became a full-time writer of novels, plays, poetry, and non-fiction on current affairs as well as a commentator on Muslim affairs on radio and television. His writings include *The Indian family in Britain* (1966), *A Triangular view; novel* (1969), *Black British, white British* (1971), *The Untouchables of India* (1975), *Inside the Middle East* (1982), *Iran under the ayatollahs* (1985), *Iran, the revolution within* (1988), *The Longest war; the Iran-Iraq military conflict* (1989), *Desert shield to desert storm; the second Gulf war* (1992), *Between Marx and Muhammad* (1995), *Sharing the promised land* (1996), *Dictionary of the Middle East* (1996), and *Neighbours, not friends; Iraq and Iran after the Gulf wars* (2001). ConAu, 77-80, new rev., 14, 32, 64; IntAu&Wr, 1977, 1991/92-1999/2000; *MESA Roster of members*, 1990 Note about the author; WrDr, 1976/78-2004

Hirsch, Abraham Menco, born in 1927 at Halberstadt, Germany, he graduated in 1949 from the City College of New York and received a Ph.D. in 1957 from Columbia University for *International rivers in the Middle East; a hydro-political study.* He subsequently became a senior research associate at the American University before becoming a program officer with the Agency for International Development, Washington, D.C. He was posted to Kabul from 1963 to 1966. Selim; WhoGov, 1972, 1975

Hirsch, David G., born in 1958 or 9 at Philadelphia, Pa., he gained an M.A. and M.L.Sc. He was a good linguist, fluent in Arabic, and served as a Middle Eastern studies librarian at Young Research Library, University of California, Los Angeles, certainly from 1990 to 2004. *MESA Roster of members*, 1990; Private

Hirsch, Ernst Eduard, born 20 January 1902 at Friedberg/Hesse, Germany, he studied law and received a Dr.jur. in 1924 at Gießen, and a Dr.habil. in 1930 at Frankfurt/Main. In the 1930s he emigrated first to the Netherlands and later to Turkey, where he became a professor of law at Ankara Üniversitesi, 1943-1952. After his return to Germany he was a professor of law at Freie Universität

Berlin, which post he held until his retirement in 1967. His writings include *Ticaret hukuku dersleri* (1939-40), *Fikri ve sinaî haklar* (1948), and *Die neuen Urherberrechtsgesetze der Türkei* (1951). In 1964 he was honoured by *Ord. Prof. Dr. Ernst E. Hirsch'e armağan*. He died in Göttingen on 12 April 1985. AnaBrit; BioHbDtE; DtBE; Hanisch; Kürschner, 1961-1983; Wer ist wer, 1958

Hirsch, Ferdinand Ludwig Richard, born 22 April 1843 at Danzig, Prussia, he studied history at the universitites of Königsberg, Göttingen, and Berlin, where he received a Dr.phil. in 1864 for *De Italiae inferioris annalibus saeculi et undecimi*. Since 1882 he was a professor at Königsstädtisches Real-gymnasium, Berlin. His writings include *Das Herzogthum Benevent bis zum Untergange des lango-bardischen Reiches; ein Beitrag zur Geschichte Unteritaliens im Mittelalter* (1871), and *Byzantinische Studien* (1876). He died in 1915. Hinrichsen

Hirsch, Hans Erich, born 25 September 1931 at Linz, Austria, he studied Semitic languages at the Universität Wien, where he received a Dr.phil. in 1958 for *Untersuchungen zur altassyrischen Religion*. From 1963 until his retirement he was a professor at his alma mater. Kürschner, 1966-2005; Schwarz; WhoAustria, 1967-1977/78

Hirsch, Leo, born middle 19th cent. in Germany, he was an Arabic and Himyarite scholar of repute, an expert on the law of Islam, and an archaeologist. In 1893 he received permission from the Governor of Aden to explore Southern Arabia. Although he travelled in the native dress, he admitted that he was a Westerner who had come to study Islam. He became the first European to reach the Wadi Hadhramaut. His writings include *Reisen in Süd-Arabien* (1897), an account of his journey which conforms exactly to what one might expect from a deeply learned Teuton. He edited and translated from the Arabic of 'Abd al-Qādir b. Muhammad al-Makkāwī, *Der überfließende Strom in der Wissenschaft des Erbrechts der Hanafiten und Schafeiten* (1891). Bidwell; Henze; Hogarth, David G., *The Penetration of Arabia* (1904), pp. 216-219

Hirsch, Max, born 30 December 1832 at Halberstadt, Germany, he studied political economy and received a Dr.phil. in 1855 from the Universität Greifswald for *De machinerum vi in quantitatem productionis*. He was a politician, member of the Reichstag, and active in the labour and trade union movement. In 1868 he visited England and Scotland. His writings include *Skizze der volkswirt-schaftlichen Zustände von Algerien mit Rücksicht auf die deutsche Auswanderung* (1857), *Reise in das Innere von Algerien durch die Kabylie und Sahara* (1862), and *Die Arbeiterfrage und die deutschen Gewerkvereine* (1893). He died in Bad Homburg in 1905. DtBE; NDB; Sezgin; Wininger

Hirschberg, Haim Zeev, born Joachim Wilhelm on 2 October 1903 at Tarnopol, Austrian Galicia, he was educated in Wien where he also received a Dr.phil. in 1935 from the Universität for *Jüdisches und christliches im vorislamischen Altertum; ein Beitrag zur Entstehungsgeschichte des Islams*. He emigrated to Palestine in 1943 and became a professor of Jewish history, and head of department, at Bar Ilan University. His writings include *A History of the Jews in North Africa* (1974-81), and the translation, *Der Diwan des as-Samaual ibn 'Adijā' und die unter seinem Namen überlieferten Gedichtfragmente* (1939). He died in 1976. BioHbDtE; WhoWorJ, 1965, 1972, 1978

Hirschberg, Harris Hans, born in 1908 at Berlin, he received a Dr.phil. in 1932 at Berlin for *Studien zur Geschichte Esarhaddons, König von Assyrien*, and was ordained rabbi in 1933. He subsequently served as a rabbi in Germany until 1936 when he emigrated to the U.S.A. His writings include *Hebrew humanism* (1964). BioHbDtE; Schwarz

Hirschberg, Joachim W., 1903-1976 *see* Hirschberg, Haim Zeev

Hirschberg, Julius, born 18 September 1843 at Potsdam, he studied medicine at the Universität Berlin. He was an ophthalmologist who became a professor of history of medicine at Berlin. His writings include *Eine Woche in Tunis; Tagebuchblätter* (1885), *Ägypten; geschichtliche Studien eines Augenarztes* (1890); and he was a joint translator of *Die Augenheilkunde des Ibn Sina* (1902), *Die arabischen Augenärzte* (1904-5), *Vorlesungen über Hippokratische Heilhunde* (1922); and he was a joint editor of *Die arabischen Lehrbücher der Augenheilkunde* (1905). He died in Berlin in 1925. DtBE; EncJud; Fück, p. 315; Hanisch; JewEnc; JüdLex; Master (1); NDB; Wininger

Hirschberg, Walter, born 17 December 1904 at Neugradiska, Croatia, he studied ethnology and anthropology at the Universität Wien where he received a Dr.phil. in 1928 for *Die Zeitrechnung in Afrika; ein Beitrag zur historisch vergleichenden Kalenderkunde*. He was since 1939 a lecturer in African ethnology at the Hochschule für Welthandel, Wien. His writings include *Völkerkundliche Ergebnisse der südafrikanischen Reisen Rudolf Pöch's in den Jahren 1907 bis 1909* (1936), and *Religionsethnologie und ethno-historische Religionsforschung* (1972). Note about the author; IntDcAn; Kürschner, 1950-1996]; Unesco; WhoAustria, 1967-1969/70

Hirschfeld (Χίρσφελντ), Gustav, born 4 November 1847 at Pyritz, Pomerania, he studied ancient history and archaeology at the universities of Berlin, Tübingen, and Leipzig, gaining a Dr.phil. in 1870 at Berlin for *De titulis statuariorum sculptorumque graecorum capita duo priora*. He was a professor of archaeology at the Universität Königsberg, and chairman of the Geographische Gesellschaft in Königsberg. He travelled in Italy, Greece, and Asia Minor and was an authority in classical topography. His writings include *Paphlagonische Felsengräber* (1885), *Aus dem Orient* (1897), and he was a joint author of *The Historical geography of Asia Minor* (1872), *Ausgrabungen zu Olympia* (1876-81). He died in Königsberg on 4 November 1895 (or 10 April in Wiesbaden). Deutsche Rundschau, 1895; DtBE; EncJud; Henze; Kornrumpf; Megali, vol. 24 (1934), p. 625; NDB

Hirschfeld, Hartwig, born 1854 at Thorn, Prussia, he received a Dr.phil. in 1878 from the Universität Straßburg for *Jüdische Elemente im Korân; ein Beitrag zur Korânforschung*. He was successively a professor of Semitic languages at Jews' College, Ramsgate, and University College, London. His writings include *Beiträge zur Erklärung des Korân* (1886), *Arabic chrestomathy in Hebrew characters* (1892), *New researches into the composition and exegesis of the Qoran* (1902), *Literary history of Hebrew grammarians and lexicographers, accompanied by unpublished texts* (1926), and he translated *Das Buch Al-Chazarî*, from the Arabic of Abu-l-Hasan Jehuda Hallewi (1885). He died in 1934. EncJud; JewEnc; Jews' College jubilee volume (1909), pp. 112-13 JüdLex; Schwarz; Wininger

Hirschfeld, Yair P., born in 1944, he emigrated to Israel in 1967. In 1978, he was a lecturer in Middle Eastern history at the University of Tel Aviv. His writings include *Deutschland und Iran im Spielfeld der Mächte; internationale Beziehungen unter Reza Schah, 1921-1941* (1980). Note about the author; ZKO

Hirst, David, born in 1936, he graduated from the American University of Beirut. He became a correspondent of the *Guardian* and worked for the Middle East Research and Publication Center, Beirut. His writings include *Oil and public opinion in the Middle East* (1966), *The Gun and the olive branch; the roots of violence in the Middle East* (1977), and he was a joint author, with Irene Beeson, of *Sadat* (1981). Note: ZKO

Hirst, Francis Wrigley, born in 1873, he was educated at Oxford and became a barrister-at-law, an editor of *the Economist*, from 1907 to 1916, and a governor of the London School of Economics. His writings include *Gladstone as financier and economist* (1931), *Liberty and tyranny and economic freedom* (1935), *Armaments* (1937), and *Gold, silver and paper* money (1943). He died on 22 February 1953. His friends wrote *F. W. Hirst* (O.U.P., 1958). BioIn, 1, 3 (2), 5; BritInd (2); DNB; Master (5); NYT, 23 February 1953, p. 25, col. 1; ObitT, 1951-60, p. 355; Who was who, 5

Hirszowicz, Łukacz, fl. 1955, his writings include *Iran, 1951-1953; nafta, imperializm, nacjonalizm* (Warszawa, 1958), *III Trzecia i Arabski Wschód* (1963), and its translations, *The Third Reich and the Arab East* (1966), as well as its translations into Hebrew (1965), and Arabic (1971). NUC; ZKO

Hirth, Friedrich, born 16 April 1845 at Gräfentonna near Gotha, he studied classical philology at the universities of Leipzig, Berlin and Greifswald, obtaining a doctorate in 1869. He subsequently entered the international maritime customs' service in China, being employed in various capacities at Canton, Amoy, Shanghai, and Hong Kong. He resigned in 1895 and settled in München. From 1902 to his retirement in 1917 he held the newly founded chair of Chinese studies at Columbia University, New York. He returned to München in 1920 and there died on 8 January 1927. His writings include *China and the Roman Orient* (1885), and *Die Länder des Islams nach chinesischen Quellen* (1894). Master (1); NDB; Wer ist's, 1909-1912; WhAm, 1

Hirtz, Georges, born 20th cent., his writings include *L'Algérie nomade et ksourienne, 1830-1954* (Marseille, 1989), and *Islam-Occident; les voies du respect, de l'entente, de la concorde; Abd El Qader, La Moricière, Aurélie Picard, Si Ahmed Tidjani* (La Roche-Rigault, 1998). Livres disponibles, 2004

Hiskett, Mervyn, born 20 May 1920 at St. Albans, Hertfordshire, he served in the British Army during the second World War. After the war, he served in mandated Palestine from 1946 to 1947. After demobilization in 1947, he studied at SOAS, graduating in Arabic. From 1952 to 1962 he served as a vice-principal at the School of Arabic Studies, Kano, Nigeria. He had published a steady stream of articles containing Arabic, and later Hausa, texts before he received a Ph.D. in 1968 from SOAS for *Hausa Islamic verse; its sources and development prior to 1920*. His writings include *A History of Hausa Islamic verse* (1975), *The Development of Islam in West Africa* (1984), *Some to Mecca turn to pray; Islamic values and the modern world* (1993), and *The Course of Islam in Africa* (1994). He died on 11 June 1994 after a long battle with cancer. ConAu, 61-64; Sluglett; Sudanic Africa, 5 (1994), pp. 1-6

Hitchcock, Richard, born 20th cent., he received a Ph.D. in 1970 from the University of St. Andrews for *An examination of the use of the "Mozarab" in eleventh and twelfth-century Spain*. He was a reader in Hispano-Arabic studies at the University of Exeter. His writings include *The "Kharjas;" a critical* *bibliography* (1977), and he was a joint editor of *Studies on the Muwaššah and the Kharja*; Exeter International Colloquium (1991), and *The Arab influence in medieval Europe* (1994). DrBSMES, 1993; EURAMES, 1993; Sluglett

Hitchens, Christopher, born 1949, he was educated at Leys School, Cambridge, and Balliol College, Oxford. He was a journalist, columnist, book reviewer, televison author, and contributor to the *New left review* as well as many other periodicals. His writings include *Inequalities in Zimbabwe* (1979), *Cyprus* (1984), *The Elgin marbles; should they be returned to Greece?* (1987), *Hostage to history; Cyprus from the Ottomans to Kissinger* (1989), *Blood, class, and nostalgia; Anglo-American ironies* (1990), *Unacknowledged legislation; writers in the public sphere* (2000), *The Trial of Henry Kissinger* (2001), and he was a joint author of *International territory; the United Nations, 1945-95* (1994). ConAu, 152, new rev., 89; Note about the author; WrDr, 1992/94-2000

Hitchens, Keith Arnold, born 2 April 1931 at Schenactady, N.Y., he received a Ph.D. in 1964 from Harvard for *The development of Rumanian nationalism in Transylvania, 1780-1849*. He also studied at Paris, Bucureşti, and Cluj. He was appointed a professor in the Department of History, University of Illinois at Urbana-Champaign in 1978, a post which he still held in 1990. His writings include the Rumanian and German translations of his thesis, *Studii privind istoria modernă a Transilvaniei*, and *Studien zur modernen Geschichte Transsylvaniens*, 1970 and 1971 respectively, *Cultură şi naţionalitate în Transilvania* (1972), and *Orthodoxy and nationality; Andreiu Şaguna and the Rumanians of Transylvania, 1846-1873* (1977). ConAu, 147, new rev., 98; DrAS, 1969 H, 1974 H, 1978 H, 1982 H; MembriiAR; NatFacDr, 1990; Note about the author; Schoeberlein; WrDr, 1998/2000-2004

Hitchens, Robert Smythe, 1864-1950 *see* Hichens, Robert Smythe

Hitti, Philip Khuri, born 24 June 1886 at Shimlan, Lebanon, he graduated in 1908 from AUB, and subsequently taught history until 1913 when he went to the United States, where he was awarded a Ph.D. 1915 by Columbia University. After five years at New York, he returned to AUB as a professor of Oriental history until he accepted an offer of professorship at Princeton in 1926. He there became one of the foremost Arabic scholars, a historian and authority of the Arab Near East. His writings include *History of the Arabs from the earliest times to the present* (1937), a work which went through eleven editions, and *Makers of Arab history* (1968). In 1959, he was honoured by *The World of Islam; studies in honour of P. K. Hitti*. He died on Christmas Eve, 1978. Au&Wr, 1963; BlueB, 1973/4, 1975; ConAu, 1-4, 91-84, new rev., 6; DrAS, 1969 H, 1974 H, 1978 H; IntWW, 1974-1978; MESA bulletin, 13 i (1979), pp. 1-2; Selim; WhAm, 7; WhE&EA; WhoAm, 1974-1978

Hitzig, Ferdinand, born 23 June 1807 at Hauingen near Lörrach, Germany, he studied theology at Heidelberg, Halle and Göttingen, where he received in 1829 a Dr.phil., and in the same year also obtained a Dr.habil. as well as a professorship in Old Testament theology at the Universität Heidelberg. In 1833, he was invited to the newly founded Universität Zürich, but returned to the Universität Heidelberg in 1841. In 1872, he became a Church administrator. His writings include *Geschichte des Volkes Israel* (1869). He died in Heidelberg on 22 January 1875. ADtB; DtBE; Hofer

Hjarnø, Jan, born in 1940, he was Danish ethnographer whose writings include *Fremmedarbejdere; en etnologisk undersøgelse af arbejdskrafteksportens virkninger* (1971), *Kurderne - et splittet folk* (1972), *Archaeological and anthropological investigations of late heathen graves in Upernavikdistrict* (1974), *Kurdiske indvandrere* (1991), and *Illegal immigrants and developments in employment in the labour markets of the EU* (2003), and he was a joint author of *Flygtninge og indvandrere* (1992). Note about the author

Hjärpe, Jan Östen, born 13 July 1942 at Göteborg, he received degrees in divinity from Uppsala Universitet, including a doctorate in 1972 for *Analyse critique des traditions arabes sur les Sabéens harraniens*. He was in 1982 a professor of history of religion at his alma mater and concurrently a research fellow at the Humanistik-Samhällsvetenskapliga Forskningrådet, and a special adviser for Islamic affairs at the Swedish Ministry of Foreign Affairs. He later was a professor at Lunds Universitet. His writings include *Politisk islam* (1980), and *Indvandrere fra Tyrkiet i Stockholm og København* (1988). IWWAS, 1975/76; Note about the author; Vem är det, 1997-2001

Hlal, Yahya *see* Hilāl, Yahyá

Hoag, John D., born 24 September 1919, his writings include *Western Islamic architecture* (1963), its translation, *Architektur des westlichen Islams* (1965), and *Islamic architechture* (1977), its translation, *Architecture islamique* (1991). LC; ZKO

Hobart, Augustus Charles, 1822-1886 *see* Hobart-Hampden, Augustus Charles

Hobart, Sir Percy Cleghorn Stanley, born 14 June 1885, he was educated in England and in 1904 he joined the Royal Engineers and subsequently went to India, where he served until the outbreak of the first World War, during which he served in Mesopotamia. He is best remembered for raising the 7th Armoured Division, Egypt, 1938-39. K. J. Macksey wrote *Armoured crusader; a biography of Major-General Sir Percy Hobart* (1967). He died in Farnham, Surrey, in 1957. DNB; ObitT, 1951-60, p. 356; Riddick; WhoIndia, 1927; *Who was who*, 5

Hobart-Hampden (Hobart Pasha), Augustus Charles, born 1 April 1822 in Leicestershire, he entered the Royal Navy in 1835 and served as a midshipman on the coast of Brazil in the suppression of the slave trade. In 1862 he retired from the navy with the rank of post-captain; but his love for adventure led him during the American Civil War to take the command of a blockade-runner. In 1867 he entered the Turkish service, and was immediately nominated to the command of that fleet, with the rank of *tuğamiral*, rear-admiral. In this capacity he performed splendid service in helping to suppress the insurrection in Crete, and was rewarded by Sultan Abdülaziz with the title of Pasha. At he outbreak of the Russo-Turkish war he was again in Turkish service. In command of the Turkish squadron he completely dominated the Black Sea, blockading the ports of South Russia and the mouth of the Danube, and paralysing the action of the Russian fleet. On the conclusion of peace he remained in the Turkish service, and in 1881 was appointed *müşir*, or field-marshal, being the first Christian to hold that high office. He wrote an autobiography, *Sketchs of my life* (1886), which must, however, be used with caution, since it contains many proved inaccuracies. He died in Milano on 19 June 1886. ACAB; AnaBrit; Boase; BritInd (5); DNB; EncAm; EncBrit; GdeEnc; Kornrumpf; *Nouvelle revue*, 46 (1887), pp. 429-61

Hobbs, John Alan, born 28 March 1935 at Aurora, Ill., he received a Ph.D. in 1961 from Princeton University for *The rise of scientific value realism in American political science*. He served as a professor of political science, particularly the politics of environmentalism, at Pennsylvania State University before his 1964 appointment as a professor at San Diego State University, a post which he still held in 1995. AmM&WSc, 1973 S, 1978 S; NatFacDr, 1990-1995

Hobbs, Nancy Outram, born 20th cent., her writings include *A Crewel embroidery primer* (New York, 1973), and *Imaginative canvas embroidery* (London, 1976).

Hobbs, William Herbert, born 2 July 1864 at Worcester, Mass., he was one of the leading geologists of the United States and was a recognized authority on earthquakes and glaciers and also on winds and weather and the origin of storms. From 1906 to his retirement in 1934 he was a professor of geology at the University of Michigan, Ann Arbor. His writings include *Meteorology, physiography, and botany* (1941), and *An explorer-scientist's pilgrimage* (1952). He died in Ann Arbor, Mich., on 1 January 1953. ANB; BioIn, 2, 3, 4; Master (2); NatCAB, vol. 42, pp. 34-35; ObitT, 1951-60, p. 356-57; WhAm, 3; WhNAA

Hobday, Peter, born 20th cent., his writings include *Man the industrialist* (London, 1973), and he was a joint author of *Industrial relations; the boardroom viewpoint* (London, 1972), and *Saudi Arabia today; introduction to the richest oil power* (London, 1978).

Hoberg, Otto, born 19th cent., he was in 1915 an editor-in-chief of the periodical, *Nord und Süd*. Note

Hobhouse, Sir Arthur, born 10 November 1819, he was educated at Eton and Balliol College, Oxford, and called to the bar from Lincoln's Inn in 1845. From 1872 to 1877 he served as a law member of the Council of Viceroy of India. He died in 1904. BritInd (3); Buckland; DNB; OxLaw; Riddick; *Who was who*, 1

Hobhouse, Charles Edward Henry, born in 1862, he was educated at Eton, Christ Church College, Oxford, and attended the Royal Military College, Sandhurst, but was diverted into politics both by his upbringing in a Liberal tradition and by his marriage. In 1907-1908 he served as Parliamentary Under-Secretary for India. His writings include *Inside Asquith's Cabinet; from his diaries*, edited by Edward David (1977). He died in 1941. BritInd (5); DBN; *Who was who*, 4

Hobman, Daisy Lucie née Adler, born in 1891, she was educated at St. Hilda's College, Oxford, and received a degree in economics. She was a contributor to several periodicals, a public speaker, translator, and a writer of biographies. Her writings include *The Welfare state* (1953), *Go spin, you jade* (1957), and *Cromwell's master spy* (1961). WhE&EA

Hobson, Robert Lockhart, born in 1872 at Lisburn, Ireland, he was educated at St. John's School Leatherhead and Cambridge University. He became a keeper at the Department of Oriental Antiquties and Ethnology in the British Museum, London. His writings include *A Guide to the Islamic pottery of the Near East* (1932), *The Romance of Chinese art* (1936), and, with Sir Aurel Stein, he was a joint author of *Archaeological reconnaissances in North-Western India and South-Eastern Iran* (1937). He died in 1941. WhE&EA; *Who was who*, 4

Hocart, Arthur Maurice, born 26 April 1883 in Guernsey (or at Etterbeck near Bruxelles), he was educated at Bruxelles and at Elizabeth College, Guernsey. From 1902 to 1906, he was a classical scholar of Exeter College, Oxford, to which a course of psychological research was added at Berlin.

He subsequently participated in a research expedition to the Solomon Islands, 1908-1909. He stayed on and was headmaster of a native school at Lau, Fiji, from 1909 to 1912, when he obtained a graduate research scholarship to investigate Fiji, Rotorua, Wallis Islands, Samoa, and Tonga. After the war he was appointed director of archaeology in Ceylon and carried out there important excavations and much ethnological research, besides making himself master of Sanskrit, Pali, Tamil, and Singhalese. In 1929, he retired on pension owing to ill-health and until his appointment to the chair of sociolgy in the Egyptian University, Cairo, in 1934, was engaged in writing and lecturing at University College, London. During the four years he spent in Cairo, he was eminently succesful as a teacher and lost no time in initiating field research into the social life of the Fellahin and in training Egyptian students to carry on this work. His last illness was due to infection while making ethnological enquiries in the Fayyoum. He died in March 1939. His writings include *Lau Islands, Fiji* (1929), *The Tempel of the Tooth in Kandy* (1931), *The Progress of man* (1933), its translation, *Les progrès de l'homme* (1935), *Les Castes*, traduit du manuscrit anglais (1938), *Caste; a comparative study* (1950), and *Imagination and proof; selected essays* (1987). E. E. Evans-Pritchard in *Man*, 39, nos. 114-115 (1939), p. 131; IntDcAn; Master (1); ZKO

Höcherl, Hermann, born 31 March 1912 at Brennberg, Bavaria, he studied law at Berlin, Aix-en-Provence, and München. In 1940 he became a public prosecutor; from 1953 to 1976 he served as a member of Parliament and at times as a minister. His writings include *Die Welt zwischen Hunger und Überfluß* (1969). He died in Regensburg on 18 May 1989. Reiner Vogel wrote *Hermann Höcherl; Annäherung an einen politischen Menschen* (1988). DtBE; IntWW, 1974-1989; *Wer ist wer*, 1971/72-1988/89; WhoWor, 1978-1980/81

Hochheim, Karl *Adolf*, born 16 January 1840 at Kirchheilingen/Kreis Langensalza, Prussia, he studied at the Universität Halle/Saale, where he received a Dr.phil. in 1864 for *De genere quodam curvarum orthogonalium*. He was successively a teacher at Erziehungsanstalt Schnepfenthal, Franckesche Stiftungen, Halle/Saale, and Guericke Realschule, Magdeburg. In 1885, he became a principal at Brandenburg/Havel, and in 1895, a school administrator at Berlin. He was one of the first to realize the importance of Arabic mathematics, and published a German translation of the Gotha Schloßbibliothek manuscript, *Kāfī fī al-hisāb*, from the Arabic of Abū Bakr Muhammad ibn al-Husayn al-Karkhī (1878-80). His other writings include *Leitfaden für den Unterricht in der Arithmetik und Algebra an höheren Lehranstalten* (1889). He died in Schnepfenthal near Gotha on 5 August 1898. DtBE; DtBilnd (4); NDB

Hochreutiner, Bénédict Pierre *Georges*, born 3 March 1873 at Genève, he was from an old St. Gallen family and was educated at the Collège de Genève and the Cantonal school, St. Gallen. He gained a Dr. ès sc. in 1896, and a theological degree in 1911. He was a sometime keeper of the Botanical Museum, Genève, and a professor of systematic botany at the Université de Genève. His writings include *Le Sud-oranais; études floristiques* (1904), and *La philosophie d'un naturaliste* (1911). He died in 1959. WhoSwi, 1950/51

Ritter von **Hochstetter**, Ferdinand, born 30 April 1829 at Eßlingen, Württemberg, he studied theology and natural sciences at the Universität Tübingen, where he received a Dr.phil. in 1852. He went on a research journey to Wien and there entered the Geologische Reichsanstalt. After his Dr.habil. in geology in 1856, he joined a scientific expedition on board the *Novara* around the world. Upon his return to Wien he became a professor of mineralogy and geology at Polytechnisches Institut. In 1869, he travelled to Constantinople for preliminary work on the construction of the Turkish railway, and in 1872, he went to the Ural Mountains for the planning of the Trans-Siberian railway. He was a founder of two Austrian learned societies. His writings include *Asien; seine Zukunftsbahnen und seine Kohlenschätze* (1876), *Leitfaden der Mineralogie und Geologie* (1876), *Gesammelte Reise-Berichte von der Erdumseglung der Fregatte Novara, 1857-1859* (1885), and *Allgemeine Erdkunde* (1886). He died in Oberdöbling near Wien on 18 July 1884. ADtB, vol. 50, pp. 500-502; DtBE; DtBilnd (7); Embacher; Henze; Kornrumpf; Master (2); NDB; NÖB, vol. 4, pp. 183-196; ÖBL; Wurzbach

Höck (Hoeck), Franz, born 11 October 1749 at Preßburg (Bratislava), he studied Oriental languages and subsequently entered the Society of Jesus. After the Jesuits had been banished in Austria he became an administrator at Orientalische Akademie, Wien, and concurrently a profesor of philosophy and Oriental languages. In 1785 Emperor Joseph II appointed him director of the Akademie and professor of "patriotic" and Oriental history as well as Oriental languages. In 1795, he became mitred abbot at Kács; and in 1818, abbot of Lekér. He retired in 1832 with the title *wirklicher Hofrat*. During his half a century at the Akademie he had brought together a collection of some twenty thousand items of Oriental business correspondence and similar documents which served as teaching aids for their students. His writings include *Historia priorum regum Persarum post firmatum in hoc regno islamismum* (Wien, 1782). He died in Wien on 12 December 1835. The firm Zehntmayer, Wien, published in 1837 the auction catalogue, *Manuscripten auf Pergament und Constantinopler Drucken aus dem Nachlasse Sr. Hochwürden Franz Hoeck*. Filipsky; Kosch; ÖBL; Wurzbach; ZKO

Hockey, Susan Margaret, born 13 November 1946 at Halifax, Yorks., she graduated in Oriental studies from Oxford University. Since 1969 she taught computing in the arts at the Oxford University Computing Service. Her writings include *Computing in the arts* (1978), and *A Guide to computer applications in the humanities* (1980). WhoWor, 1987/88; ZKO

Hocking, William Ernest, born 10 August 1873 at Cleveland, Ohio, he graduated in 1901 from Harvard, where he also received a Ph.D. in 1904. He pursued post-doctoral research at Göttingen, Berlin, and Heidelberg. He successively taught philosophy at Yale, Princeton, and Harvard. In 1938, he was a Hibbert lecturer. His writings include *Man and the state* (1926), *Types of philosophy* (1929), *Living religions and a world faith* (1940), and *The Coming world civilization* (1956). He died in 1966. ANB; DrAS, 1969 P; Master (27); WhAm, 4

Hodes, Aubrey, born 1 December 1927 at Cape Town, he was a kibbutz member, editor with an Israeli publishing house, translator and press analyst at embassies, teacher of English, and free-lance writer. From 1957 to 1965, he served as a non-party member of the Tel-Aviv *New outlook*'s editorial board. His writings include *Dialogue with Ishmael; Israel's future in the Middle East* (1968), and *Martin Buber, an intimate portrait* (1971). ConAu, 33-36; Note about the author

Hodge, Carleton Taylor, born 27 November 1917 at Springfield, Ill. he graduated in 1939 from DePauw University, Greencastle, Ind., and received a Ph.D. in 1943 from the University of Pennsylvania for *An Outline of Hausa grammar*. He was a language instructor with the U.S. Department of State before he served from 1947 to 1955 with its Foreign Service Institution. Since 1968, he was a professor of linguistics and anthropology at Indiana University, Bloomington. His writings include *Spoken Serbo-Croatian* (1945), *Hausa basic course* (1963), and *Afroasiatic; a survey* (1971). He died on 8 September 1998. DrAS, 1969 F, 1974 F, 1978 F, 1982 F; WhAm, 13; WhoAm, 1980-1998

Hodge, Humfrey Grose, 1891-1962 *see* Grose-Hodge, Humfrey

Hodgetts, Edward Arthur Brayley, born 12 June 1859 at Berlin. In 1867, his father accepted an appointment at Moscow University, and went to Russia, where his son was educated. For a time he was in the English Consulate at Moscow, and then served for two years in a bank. Subsequently, his father sent him to London, and he was appointed librarian to the Institution of Civil Engineers, a post which he held for five years, but resigned for the editorship of a monthly technical journal. In 1889, he was appointed St. Petersburg correspondent for the *Daily Graphic*. The year following, he became Reuter's special agent in Berlin. During the Russian famine of 1892, he travelled over the famine-stricken districts for Reuter's special service. He became for some time a foreign editor of *the World* in New York and later its Paris correspondent. In the service of the *Daily Graphic*, he investigated the Armenian atrocities. He proceeded to Constantinople and Trebizond, via Sofia. At Trebizond he was arrested by the Turkish police, but soon released. From thence he proceeded to Batum and Tiflis, but being prevented by the Russian authorities from entering Armenia, he went to Baku, and after crossing the Caspian Sea, rode on horseback to Tabriz, and from there reached Armenia. From 1902-1920 he was the London representative of Nobel's Explosives Co. Ltd. He died in 1932. BritInd (1); Master (2); Our contemporaries, 1897; Who was who, 3

Hodgkin, Edward Christian, a newphew of Sir Reader Bullard, he was born in 1913. Before his retirement, he was on the editorial staff of *the Times*, London. His writings include *The Arabs* (1966), and he edited *Letters from Palestine, 1932-36*, of Thomas Hodgkin (1986), and *Letters from Tehran*, of Sir Reader Bullard (1991). ZKO

Hodgkin, Robert Allason (Robin A.), born 12 February 1916 at Banbury, England, he was educated at Queen's College, Oxford. From 1937 to 1945, he was a teacher at a government school in Khartoum; in 1946, he was with the Translation and Publication Bureau, Bakht er Ruda, and in 1947 its managing editor; from 1949 to 1955, he was a principal of the Sudan Institute of Education; and from 1969 to his retirement in 1977, a lecturer in educational studies at Oxford. His writings include *Sudan geography* (1952), *Education and change* (1957), *Renaissance on an educational frontier* (1970), *Born curious; new perspectives in educational theory* (1976), *Playing and exploring* (1985), and he was a joint author of *How people live in the Sudan* (1963). Au&Wr, 1971; ConAu, 102; Note; WrDr, 1976/78-1996/98|

Hodgkin, Robin A., 1916- *see* Hodgkin, Robert Allason

Hodgkin (Χότζκιν), Thomas, born in 1798 at Tottenham, England, he graduated in 1823 from the Medical School of Edinburgh with a thesis entitled *De absorbendi functione*, enlarging his knowldege by post-graduate studies on the continent. Upon his return to England, he joined the group at Guy's Hospital, becoming curator of the pathological museum and demonstrator in pathology. He left Guy's Hospital after his unsuccessful candidature for the post of assistant physician and, since about 1840, devoted much of his time to philanthropic works, as did also his friend Sir Moses Montefiore, with whom he travelled to Morocco in his capacity as friend, philanthropist and personal physician. He was one of the brightest stars of British physicians of his day and is immortalized by the disease which bears his name. He was a Quaker, inwardly attached to the ideology of this group and, outwardly, wearing its characteristic garb. He was also styled a sound Greek and Latin scholar. His writings include *Narrative of a journey to Morocco, in 1863 and 1864* (1886). He died in Jaffa on 4 April 1886. *Clio medica*, 2 (1967), pp. 97-101; Boase; BritInd (3); DNB; EEE; IntDcAn; Kornrumpf

Hodgkin, Thomas Lionel, born 3 April 1910 at Oxford, he graduated from Balliol College, where he developed an interest in philosophy and archaeology, in the interest of which he went to Palestine in 1934 to work on John Garstang's dig at Jericho. After a brief period back in England, where he lectured in philosophy at Manchester University, he returned to Palestine in the British Civil Service. Ultimately the Administration's policy towards the growing wave of Arab unrest created a situation in which he could not longer square his position politically so that he handed in his resignation, which was followed immediately by his expulsion from Palestine. Returning to England he joined the Communist Party. In September 1939, he took a post as staff tutor of the Oxford Extra-Mural Studies Delegacy. In 1945, he bcame secretary of the Delegacy and a professional fellow of Balliol College, a post which he held until his resignation in 1952. All along he had developed an interest in Africa. In 1947, he went out to Nigeria, the Gold Coast, and Sudan to extend assistance to the fledgling university colleges. After leaving the Delegacy, he took a six-month journey across West Africa and the Sahara by lorry, river-steamer and camel, a trip which brought him into contact with many of the leaders of the developing African popular movements. In 1957, he spent several weeks living in disguise with the FLN guerillas in Algeria. The year 1957 also witnessed his re-entry into academic life successively at Montreal, P.Q., Evanston, Ill., Legon, Ghana, and, finally, Oxford. Since 1937, he was married with Dorothy Crowfoot, the later recipient of the 1964 Nobel Prize for Chemistry. His writings include *The Colonial empire; a students' guide* (1943), *Nationalism in colonial Africa* (1956), its translation, *Nazionalismo nell'Africa coloniale* (1959), and *Nigerian perspectives* (1960). He died on 25 March 1982. AfrBioIn (2); ConAu, 115; IntAu&W, 1977, 1982; IntWW, 1974-1982; Unesco; Who, 1963-1982; Who was who, 8

Hodgson, Brian Houghton, born 1 February 1800, he was educated at the India Company College at Haileybury. He joined the Bengal Civil Service and became widely known for his researches into the natural history of the eastern Himalayas, and the ethnology of the races and tribes of British India and the surrounding countries. His writings include *Illustrations of the literature and religion of the Buddhists* (1841), *Essays on the languages, literature, and religion of Nepal and Tibet* (1874), and *Miscellaneous essays relating to Indian subjects* (1880). He died in 1894. Sir Wm W. Hunter wrote *Life of Brian Houghton Hodgson, British Resident at the Court of Nepal* (1896). BritInd (2); Buckland; DNB; IndianBiInd (6); Riddick

Hodgson, James Flinn, born 26 May 1890 at Haddonfield, N.J., he graduated from the U.S. Military Academy and was promoted through the ranks to major. From 1921 to 1923, he was in charge of famine operations of the American Relief Administration in Odessa and Rostov. He subsequently was a commercial attaché in Warszawa, 1924, in Praha, 1925-26, and in Cairo, 1927-28. He later served as a lecturer in economics at the College of the City of New York and New York Universiry. He was a joint author of *Trade financing and exchange in Egypt, Greece and Turkey* (1927). He died before 1985. Note about the author; WhAm, 8

Hodgson, John Anthony, born 2 July 1777 at Sheraton, Durham County, he was baptized two days later at Bishop Auckland. He entered the Bengal Army in 1798 and arrived in March 1800 in India, where he served in Azimabad, Dariabad, Cawnpore, and Lucknow, later in Ceylon. He participated in the second Mahratta War, and at different times, he served with the Surveyor General of India. He died whilst on his way to Simla on sick leave at Ambalah on 28 March 1848. IndianBiInd (5)

Hodgson, Marshall Goodwin Simms, born 11 April 1922 at Richmond, Ind., he received a Ph.D. in 1952 from the University of Chicago for *A dissident community in medieval Islam; a general history of the Nizārī Ismāʿīlīʿs in the Alamūt period*. Since 1953 he was a professor of history at Chicago. His writings include *The Order of the Assassins* (1955), its Persian translation in 1967, *The Classical age of Islam* (1974), *The Venture of Islam* (1974), and he edited *Introduction to Islamic civilization; Course syllabus* (1958). He died in 1968. ConAu, 21-22; IndAu; Selim; WhAm, 5

Hodgson, William Brown, born 1 September 1801 at Georgetown, D.C., he served as a dragoman at the United States legations in Alger and Constantinople, later becoming a consul at Tunis. He was one of the founders of the American Oriental Society. His writings include *Grammatical sketch and specimens of the Berber language, preceded by four letters on Berber etymologies* (1829), *Notes on northern Africa, the Sahara and Soudan, in relation to the ethnography, languages, history, political and social conditions of the nations of those countries* (1844), and *The Foulahs of Central Africa and*

the African slave trade (1848). He died in New York on 26 June 1871.   DAB; Shavit; WhAm, Historical
volume

Hödl, Ludwig, born 19 November 1924 at Sonnen, Bavaria, he received a Dr.theol. in 1956 from the
Universität München for *Die Grundfragen der Sakramentenlehre nach Herveus Natalis O.P.*, and also
his Dr.habil. in 1960 for *Die Geschichte der scholastischen Literatur und der Theologie der Schlüssel-
gewalt.* Since 1965 he was a professor of systematic theology at Ruhr-Universität, Bochum. His writings include *Das Heil und die Utopien* (1977). On his sixtieth and sixtx-fifth birthday he was honoured
by *Renovatio et refomatio; wider das Bild vom "finsteren" Mittelalter; Festschrift*, and *Welt-Wissen und
Gottes-Glaube in Geschichte und Gegenwart*, 1985 and 1990 respectively.   Kürschner, 1970-2005

Hoekendijk, Johannes Christiaan, born 3 May 1912 at Garut, Indonesia, he studied theology at the
Rijksuniversiteit te Leiden and Utrecht where he received a doctorate in 1948 for *Kerk en volk in de
duitse zendingswetenschap*, a work which was published in 1967 in a German translation entitled
Kirche und Volk in der deutschen Missionswissenschaft. From 1939 to 1941, he was a secretary of the
Nederlandse Christelijke Studenten Vereiniging; in 1949, he became a secretary of the World Council
of Churches, Genève; from 1953 to 1965, he was a professor of theology at Utrecht; and from 1965 to
1975, he served as a professor of missions at the Union Theological Seminary, New York. His writings
include *De wereldzending in oorlogstijd, 1940-1944* (1945), *Zending in Indonesië* (1946), *De kerk
binnenste buiten* (1964), its translations, *Die Zukunft der Kirche und die Kirche der Zukunft* (1964), and
The Church inside out (1966). His private papers, *Inventaris van het archief van Johannes Christiaan
Hoekendijk* (1985), are in the Utrecht university library. He died on 25 June 1975.   WhAm, 6; WhoNL,
1962/63; *Wie is dat*, 1956

Hoell, Margaret Stevens, born 7 November 1921 at Vengurla, India, she graduated in 1942 from the
University of Arizona, received an M.A. in 1969 from the College of Wooster, and a Ph.D. in 1973 from
Ohio State University for *The Ticaret Odası; origins, function and activities of the Chamber of
Commerce of Istanbul.* She was successively a teaching assistant, 1971-73, and a lecturer in
continuing education, 1974-76, at Ohio State University.   IWWAS, 1976/77; *MESA Roster of members*, 1977-
1990

Hoenerbach, Wilhelm, born 21 March 1911 at Köln, he studied Islamic subjects, Romance and English philology at the universities of Köln and Bonn where he received a Dr.phil. in 1936 for *Deutschland
und seine Nachbarländer nach der großen Geographie des Idrīsī.* He subsequently went to the
Universität Breslau as an assistant to Otto Spies and received his Dr.habil. in 1939 for *Das
nordafrikanische Itinerar des 'Abdarī vom Jahre 688/1289.* After the war he returned to the Universät
Bonn where he taught in various capacities until 1959 when he became a visiting professor at U.C.L.A.
In 1962, he accepted an invitation to the re-established chair of Islamic studies at the Universität Kiel.
From 1970 to his retirement in 1976, he returned from the College of Orientalisches Seminar to Bonn to succeed Otto Spies to the directorship of
Orientalisches Seminar, and the Seminar für Orientalische Sprachen He was the contemporary
German authority in Spanish and North African Islam. He spent many years at his estate In the Sierra
Nevada near Granada Twenty-one of his works were published in Spanish. He participated in the
academic life of the universities of Granada and Barcelona. Since 1980, he was a joint editor of the
journal *Andalucía Islámica* (Granada). In 1964, he was elected a corresponding member of the Real
Académia de Buénas Létras de Barcelona, and in 1982, the Universidad de Barcelona conferred on
him an honorary doctorate. His writings include *Cervantes und der Orient; Algier zur Türkenzeit*
(1953), *Das nordafrikanische Schattentheater* (1959), *Spanisch-islamische Urkunden aus der Zeit der
Nasriden und Moriscos* (1965), *Dichterische Vergleiche der Andalus-Araber* (1973), *Agrarische
Vorstellungen in Nordafrika; Protokolle* (1984), he edited *Die vulgärarabische Poetik des Kitāb al-'Ātil
al-hālī wal-murahhas al-gālī des Safiyaddīn Hillī* (1956), and he translated from the Arabic *Watīma's
Kitāb ar-Ridda aus Ibn Hagars Isāba; ein Beitrag zur Geschichte des Abfalls der Araberstämme nach
Muhammeds Tod* (1951). He died in Troisdorf near Bonn on 10 May 1991.   Hanisch; Kürschner, 1961-1987;
Schwarz; *Welt des Islams*, 32 (1992), pp. 1-5; *Wer ist wer*, 1979-1990/91

Hoenigswald, Heinrich (Henry) Max Franz, born 17 April 1915 at Breslau, Prussia, he studied
classical and Indo-European languages at München, Zürich, and Padua before completing his D.Litt. in
1936 at Padua. For the following three years he was associated with the Istituto di Studi Etruschi,
Firenze. In 1939, he emigrated ot the United States where he held a variety of university posts until his
retirement in 1985. He was a prominent historical linguist whose writings include *Spoken Hindustani*
(1945), *Language change and linguistic reconstruction* (1960), and *Studies in formal historical
linguistics* (1973). He died in Haverford, Pa., on 16 June 2003.   ConAu, 13-16, 217, new rev., 39; DrASm 1969
F, 1974 F, 1978 F, 1982 F; Kürschner, 1983, 1987; (Master (1); WhoAm, 1974-1995, 2003; WhoE, 1993/94; WhoWor, 1978-
1993/94; WrDr, 1980/82-2004

Hoeppner, Rolf-Roger, born in 1941 or 42, he was associated with Deutsches-Orient Institut, Hamburg, and in 1980, he was a board member of Iran Commercial and Industrial Services, Ltd., Hamburg.

His writings include *Zur Entwicklung der Erdölwirtschaft Irans von 1954 bis 1973* (Hamburg, 1973), and *Praxis des iranischen Gesellschafts- und Steuerrechts* (Hamburg, 1975). Note about the author

Hoerburger, Felix, born 9 December 1916 at München, he was an ethnomusicologist who received a Dr.phil. in 1941 from the Universität München for *Musik aus Ungoni, Ostafrika*, and a Dr.habil. from the Universität Erlangen for *Tanz und Tanzmusik im Bereich der Albaner Jugoslawiens*. He was successively a professor at Regensburg, Erlangen, and again Regensburg. His writings include *Der Tanz mit der Trommel* (1954), *Die Zwiefachen* (1956), *Volkstanzkunde* (1961-1964), and *Volksmusik in Afghanistan, nebst einem Exkurs über Qor'ân-Rezitation und Thora-Kantillation in Kabul* (1969). On his sixtieth and seventieth birthdays, he was honoured by *Neue ethnomusikologische Forschungen; Festschrift*, and *Volksmusikforschung*, in 1976 and 1986 respectively. He died in Regensburg on 3 February 1997. Kürschner, 1966-1996; Master (1); NewGrDM

Hoernle, August Friedrich *Rudolf*, born 19 October 1841 at Sekundra near Agra to German missionary parents, he was educated at Stuttgart from the age of seven and subsequently studied at Basel and London. He returned to India in 1860 and remained there until 1899. He was successively a professor of philosophy at Jai Narain College, Benares, principal of the Cathedral Mission College, Calcutta, and principal of the Madrasa, Calcutta. His writings include *A Comparative grammar of the Gaudian languages, with special reference to the Eastern Hindi* (1880), *A Comparative dictionary of the Bihari language* (1885), *A Report on the British collection of antiquities from Central Asia* (1899-1902), and *A History of India* (1904). He died in Oxford on 12 November 1918. Buckland; DtBE; EncIran; NDB; Riddick; Stache-Rosen; Wer ist's, 1909-1912

Hoernle, Edward Frederick, born 15 August 1851 at Agra, India, he was educated at a secondary school and the university in Basel, Switzerland, graduated from the Edinburgh School of Medicine, and was ordained in 1879 in England. From 1879 to 1889, he served under the Church Missionary Society, London, as a medical missionary and assistant to Rev. Robert Bruce in Isfahan. After his return to Scotland, he was for three years an assistant superintendent, Edinburgh Medical Missionary Society. He subsequently held church, university and hospital posts in Edinburgh. His writings include *The Poetical works of Robert Browning* (1904). Edinburgh and the Lothians at the opening of the 20th century; contemporary biographies (Brighton, 1904); Wright, p. 118

Hoetzsch, Otto E. G., born 14 February 1876 at Leipzig, he studied history at the universities of Leipzig and München, gaining a Dr.phil. in 1900, and a Dr.habil. in 1906. He subsequently held a post at the Berlin Akademie der Wissenschaften before joining the Akademie in Posen as a professor of history. Since 1913, he was a professor of history, and director, Osteuropäisches Seminar, Berlin, but pensioned off early in 1935; he was reinstated after the war in 1945. His writings include *Russische Probleme* (1917), *Der Krieg und die große Politik* (1917-18), and *Südosteuropa und Naher Orient* (1933). He died in 1946. Gerd Voigt wrote *Otto Hoetzsch, 1876-1946* (1978), and Uwe Liszkowski, *Osteuropaforschung und Politik; ein Beitrag zum historisch-politischen Denken und Wirken von Otto Hoetzsch* (1988). DtBE; DtBIlnd (1); Kürschner, 1925-1935; Master (1); NDB; NYT, 31 August 1946, p. 15, col. 4; Wer ist's, 1922-1935

van **Hoëvell**, Wolter Robert, baron, born 15 July 1812 at Deventer, the Netherlands, he studied theology at Groningen and received a D.D. in 1836. He subsequently went to the Dutch East Indies where he became a minister at Batavia. He was a stout supporter of the Bataviaansch Genootschap van Kunsten en Wetenschappen, and served as their vice-president and president. His writings include *Reis over Java, Madura en Bali in het midden van 1847* (1849-54), *De emancipatie der slaven in Nederlands-Indië* (1848), and *Slaven en vrijen onder de Nederlandsche wet* (1854). He died in s'Gravenhage on 10 February 1879. Embacher; EncNI; NIeuwNBW, vol. 1 (1911), cols. 1128-29

Hoexter, Miriam, born 20th cent., her writings include *Endowments, rulers and community; waqf al-haramayn in Ottoman Algiers* (Leiden, Brill, 1998). ZKO

Hoff, Hellmut Eckart Walter, born 14 May 1924 at Rellingen near Hamburg, he studied history, Spanish, and ethnology and received a Dr.phil. in 1955 for *Der Niedergang des Konsulats der Kaufleute in der Stadt Mexiko, 1778-1827*. In 1958, he entered the German diplomatic and consular service; from 1962 to 1966, he was a first secretary at the Kabul Embassy. Wer ist wer, 1979-2004/2005 WhoWor, 1984-1989/90

Hoffer, Carl Ignaz, born 19th cent., he was a trained agronomist from Reichenau who spent two years carrying on field-work in the countries of the Nile, 1929-1930. His writings include *Ägypten im Weltkrieg* (Graz, 1916), and *Notwendigkeit der Wirtschaftsgeographie für den Landwirt und Agrarpolitiker* (Berlin, 1929). In 1931, he was resident in Berlin. Note about the author

Hoffherr, René, born 23 November 1893 at Lyon, he studied at the faculties of letters and law at the Université de Lyon where he received a doctorate in 1923 for *Le boycottage devant les courts anglaises, 1901-1923*. Twice wounded in the war and decorated Légion d'honneur, he thereafter became a director of the École de droit de Rabat as well as president of the Société d'études économiques, sociales et statistiques. After serving as an editor-in-chief of *la Revue*, he taught at the Institut d'études politiques de Paris and subsequently at the École nationale de la France d'outre-mer and the Centre de hautes études d'administration musulmane, Paris. His writings include *L'Économie marocaine* (1932), *Menaces allemandes sur l'Afrique* (1938), *Coopération économique franco-africaine* (1958), and he was a joint author, with Paul Mauchaussée, of *Formules modernes d'organisation minière africaine; Maroc français - Congo belge* (1933), and *Charbon et pétrole en Afrique du nord* (1935). He died in Paris on 30 March 1982. BN; DBF; BDFC, 1954/55; *Hommes et destins*, 9, p. 226; WhoFr, 1953/54-1965/66

Hoffman, Rolla Edwards, born in 1887, he went to Persia in 1915 as a medical missionary under the Foreign Missions Board of the Presbyterian Church in the U.S.A. He died in 1974. His papers, 1915-1949, are housed with the Presbyterian Historical Society, Philadelphia, Pa. LC; Note

Hoffman, Steven A., born 20th cent., he was in 1980 a professor of government at Skidmore College, Saratoga Springs, N.Y. Note about the author

Hoffmann, Andreas Gottlieb, born 13 April 1796 at Welpsleben near Mansfeld, Saxony, he studied theology and Oriental languages at the Universität Halle. In 1822 he accepted a professorship in theology from the Universität Jena, declining a concurrent offer from the Universität Königsberg. His writings include the widely used *Grammaticae Syriacae tres libri* (1827), and its abridged translation, *The Principles of Syriac grammar* (1858). He died in Jena on 13 March 1864. ADtB, vol. 12, pp. 571-72; DtBiInd (3)

Hoffmann, Birgitt, born 20 April 1953 at Offenburg, Germany, she studied Islamic subjects at the Universität Freiburg im Breisgau, where she received an M.A. In 1979 for *Eine Stiftungsurkunde des Turkmenen Yūsuf Mīrzā b. Gahānšāh Qara Qoyunlu aus dem Jahre 1464*, and a Dr.phil. in 1985 from the Universität Bamberg for *Persische Geschichte, 1694-1835, erlebt, erinnert und erfunden; das Rustam at-tawārīḫ in deutscher Bearbeitung*. After taking a Dr.habil., she became a professor in her field at the Universität Bonn. Her writings also include *Waqf im mongolischen Iran; Rašiduddins Sorge um Nachruhm und Seelenheil* (2000). Kürschner, 1996-2005; *MESA Roster of members*, 1990; Private; ZKO

Hoffmann, Christoph, born 2 December 1815 at Leonberg, Germany, he was an independent and eccentric theologian who had left the State Church in 1859 and founded a community called *Deutscher Tempel* (1861). He hoped to take a large number of followers to Palestine, but it was not until many years later that he established his first colony in Haifa, followed by others in Jaffa, Sarona and Jerusalem, none of which hardly survived its founder's death on 8 December 1885. His writings include *Christianity in the first century* (1860), *Blicke in die früheste Geschichte des Gelobten Landes* (1870), *Occident und Orient* (1875), and *Mein Weg nach Jerusalem* (1881-1884). ADtB; Kornrumpf; Richter, p. 234

Hoffmann, Eleanor, born 21 December 1895 at Belmont, Mass., she spent two years at a school in Germany before going to Radcliffe College, Cambridge, Mass., where she received her A.B. in 1917. She also studied at Massachusetts Agricultural College. Thereafter she had charge of a herd of cows and then did a year of landscape gardening for the Extention Department of the University of North Carolina. She then went to Hampton (Va.) Institute, where she taught for three years. She spent the years until 1932 driving cars across Europe and French North Africa and prowling about the West Indies in a freighter. Many of the summers were devoted to camping in the Sierras with her father, who was at work on his book on the birds of the Pacific Coast. Her writings include *Melika and her donkey* (1937), *Mischief in Fez* (1943), *Sierra Sally* (1944), *The Lion of Barbary* (1946), *White mare of the black tents* (1949), *The Mystery of the lion ring* (1953), and *The Charmstone* (1964). ConAu, 1, 15-16; Note about the author; WhoAmW, 1958/59, 1961/62

Hoffmann, Georg, 1845-1933 *see* Hoffmann, Johann Georg Ermst

Hoffmann, Gerhard Fedor Oskar, born 21 June 1917 at Weißenfels, Saxony, he studied law and, after bar admission, first became a lecturer at the Universität Erlangen, and from 1963 to his retirement in 1985, a professor of public and international law at the Universität Marburg. His writings include *Strafrechtliche Verantwortung im Völkerrecht* (1962), and he was a joint author of *Die Grenzen rechtlicher Streiterledigung im Völkerrecht und in internationalen Organisationen* (1969). In 1985 he was awarded an honorary doctorate by the University of Pécs. Kürschner, 1966-2005; WhoWor, 1991/92

Hoffmann, Herbert, born 3 April 1930 at Berlin, he was a keeper, Museum für Kunst und Gewerbe, Hamburg, and a lecturer in classical archaeology at the Universität Hamburg. His writings include *Attic*

red-figured rhyta (1962), *Greek gold* (1965), *Antiker Gold- und Silberschmuck* (1968), *Ten centuries that shaped the West; Greek and Roman art in Texas collections* (1970), and he was a joint author of *Sibui* (Bucharest, 1968). Wer ist wer, 1997/98-2004/2005

Hoffmann, Johann Georg Ernst, born 25 April 1845 at Berlin, he studied Semitic languages at the Universität Berlin where he received a Dr.phil. in 1868 for *De hermeneuticis apud Syros Aristoteleis*, a work which was published in 1873. He was a professor of Oriental languages and in 1906 he suceeded Th. Nöldeke, who went to Straßburg, in the chair of Oriental studies at the Universität Kiel, a post which he held until his retirement. He was awarded a D.theol.h.c. His writings include *Über einige phönikische Inschriften* (1890), *Mahdithum* (1899), and he edited the first half of Bar 'Alī's dictionary under the title *Syrisch-arabische Glossen* (1874), as well as *Auszüge aus syrischen Akten persischer Märtyrer, übersetzt und durch Untersuchungen zur historischen Topographie erläutert* (1880). He died in Berlin on 18 January 1933. Fück, p. 243; Hanisch; Kürschner, 1926-1931

Hoffmann, Johann Josef, born 16 November 1805 at Würzburg, Bavaria, he studied theology and classical philology at the Universität Würzburg, without taking a degree. Since 1825 he was a singer at the local theatre. While in Amsterdam in 1830, he met the Japanese scholar, Philip Franz von Siebold, who influenced him to study Japanese. He first became an interpreter of Japanese to the Dutch Government and, in 1855, a professor of Japanese and Chinese at the Rijksuniversiteit te Leiden. His writings include *Japansch-nederlandsch Woordenboek* (1881-1892), and *Japanese-English dictionary* (1881-1892). He died in Leiden on 19 January 1878. Franz Babinger wrote *Johann Josef Hoffmann, Professor der ostasiatischen Sprachen, 1805-1878* (1919). BiBenelux² (1); DtBE; Kosch; NDB

Hoffmann, Jonathan, born 19th cent., his writings include *De Pseudoapulejano libro de mundo* (Erlangae, 1880), and *De libro Pseudoapulejano de mundo* (Erlangae, 1881). ZKO

Hoffmann, Paul G., born 19th cent., he was a German vice-admiral who retired before 1913. His writings include *Die Abschaffung der Getreidezölle in England* (Berlin, 1904), and *Monarchisches Prinzip und Ministerverantwortlichkeit; eine politische Studie* (Jena, 1911). Note about the author

Hoffmann, Rudolf, born in 1925, he studied history and philosophy at Charles University, Praha. From 1962 to 1970, he served as a professor and vice-chancellor of the Academy of Military Policy. In 1970, he was ousted from the Czech Communist Party. WhoSoCE

von **Hoffmeister**, Eduard Carl Ludwig, born 7 July 1852 at Karlsruhe, Baden, he was a lieutenant-general as well as a Xenophon scholar who travelled extensively in the East, particularly in Armenia. His writings include *Meine Erlebnisse in China* (1903), *Die Rugardsage* (1905), *Die Witwe von Ephesus* (1906), *Aus Ost und Süd; Wanderungen und Stimmungen* (1907), *Kairo-Bagdad-Konstantinople; Wanderungen und Stimmungen* (1910), and *Durch Armenien* (1911). He died in Heidelberg on 19 May 1920. Kornrumpf, N; Wer ist's, 1909, 1912

Hoffmeister, Gerhart, born 17 December 1936 at Gießen, he received a Ph.D. in 1970 from the University of Maryland for *Die spanische Diana in Deutschland; zur Rezeption des Schäferromans im siebzehnten Jahrhundert.* He taught at a variety of American universities before he was appointed in 1975 a professor in the Department of German and Slavic Studies, University of California at Santa Barbara, a post which he held until his retirement. His writings include *European romanticims* (1990), and *Heine in der Romania* (2002). ConAu, 130; DrAS, 1974 H, 1978 H, 1982 H; Kürschner, 2001-2005; WhoWor, 1992/93, 1994/95

Höfig, Willi, born 22 November 1937 at Bremerhaven, Germany, he studied journalism and folklore and received a Dr.phil. in 1971 from the Freie Universität, Berlin, for *Der deutsche Heimatfilm, 1947-1960*. He was a newspaper librarian successively at the Staatsbibliothek, Berlin, and the library of the Universität Kiel. He was a joint author of *Zeitungen in Bibliotheken* (1986). It was his idea to publish the microfilm edition of anti-Shah periodicals which Wolfgang Behn then compiled and described in *The Dissident press of revolutionary Iran* (1983). JahrDtB, 1989-1997/98; Private

Höfler, Manfred, born 20th cent., his writings include *Untersuchungen zur Tuch- und Stoffbenennung* (1967), *Zur Integration der neulateinischen Kompositionsweise im Französischen* (1972), a revision of his 1968 Dr.habil. thesis submitted to the Universität Heidelberg, and *Dictionnaire des anglicismes* (1982). Mechthild Bierbach edited *Mélanges de lexicographie et de linguistique françaises et romanes dédiés à la mémoire de Manfred Höfler* (1997).

Hofman, Henry Franciscus, born 12 April 1917 at Amsterdam, he received a doctorate in 1969 from the Rijksuniversität te Utrecht for *A Specimen taken from the Chaghatayan section of the work "Turkish literature."* He was from 1969 to 1983 associated with the Turksch Afdeling at his alma mater. His writings include *Turkish literature* (1969), and *De Turcicis aliisque rebus* (1992). ZKO

Hofman, John Eric, born 29 November 1922 at Düsseldorf, he graduated in 1949 from the University of Michigan and received a Ph.D. in 1964 from New York University for *Attitude toward education and the meaning of educational concepts*. He was in 1976 associated with the Jewish-Arab Center of the University of Haifa. His writings include *Assessment of English proficiency in the African primary school* (1974), and he was a joint author of *Arab-Jewish relations in Israel* (1988). WhoWorJ, 1978, 1987

Hofman, Shlomo, born 24 April 1909 at Warszawa, he studied at the state conservatory, Warszawa, and the Sorbonne, Paris. He was a musicologist, composer, conductor and lecturer at Tel Aviv and Jerusalem. Baker, 1978, 1982, 1992; IntWWM; Wholsrael, 1966/67; WhoWor, 1974/75-1982/83; WhoWorJ, 1965

Hofmann, Inge, born 8 January 1939 at Essen, Germany, she received a Dr.phil. in 1967 from the Universität Hamburg for *Die Kulturen des Niltals von Assuan bis Sennar vom Mesolithicum bis zum Ende der christlichen Epoche*, and also a Dr.habil. in 1973 for *Wege und Möglichkeiten eines indischen Einflusses auf die meroitische Kultur*. She was a professor at the Seminar für Afrikanische Sprachen und Kulturen, Universität Hamburg, from 1971 to 1983, when she became a professor at the Institut für Afrikanistik, Universität Wien. Her writings include *Studien zum meroitischen Königtum* (1971), *Der Äthiopenlogos bei Herodot* (1979), *Der Sudan als ägyptische Kolonie im Altertum* (1979), *Das Islam-Bild bei Karl May und der islamo-christliche Dialog* (1979), *Unbekanntes Meroe* (1986), and *Steine für die Ewigkeit; meroitische Opfertafeln und Totenstelen* (1991). Kürschner, 1976-2005

Hofmann, Joseph/Josef Ehrenfried, born 7 March 1900 at München, he was associated with Deutsche Akademie der Wissenschaften, Berlin, before he became a professor of mathematics at the Universität Tübingen. His writings include *Geschichte der Mathematik* (1953-63), *Theory of mathematics* (1957), and he was a joint author of *Geschichte der Mathematik* (1951). In 1971 he was honoured by *Joseph Ehrenfried Hofmann zum 70. Geburtstag*. He died in Günzburg on 7 May 1973. DtBE; Kürschner, 1954-1970

Hofmann, Murad *Wilfried*, born 6 July 1931 at Aschaffenburg, Germany, he studied at Union College, Schenectady, N.Y., Universität München, and Harvard Law School. He received a Dr.phil. in 1957 at München for *Rechtsschutz vor Beeinflussung und Verunglimpfung der Gerichte durch die Presse nach dem Recht der Vereinigten Staaten von Nordamerika und dem deutschen Recht*. From 1961 until his retirement in 1994, he was in the German foreign service; from 1987 to 1990, at the German embassy in Alger, and thereafter he was posted as ambassador to Morocco. In 1980 he embraced Islam. His subsequent publications on Islam were critically acknowledged by his authorities: *Zur Rolle der islamischen Philosophie* (1984), *Tagebuch eines deutschen Muslims* (1985), *Islam als Alternative* (1992), *Islam, the alternative* (1993). He was also a joint author of *Three essays in dance aesthetics* (1973). He was married to a Turkish national; they maintained residences in Istanbul and Aschaffenburg. Wer ist wer, 1989/90-2004/2005; WRMEA 15 (October 1996), p. 65

Hofmann, Norbert M., born about 1940, he received a Dr.phil. in 1977 from the Universität Mainz for *Der islamische Festkalender in Java und Sumatra unter besonderer Berücksichtigung des Fasten-monats und Fastenbruchfestes in Jakarta und Medan*. GV

Hofmann, Tessa, born 15 December 1949 at Bassum/Grafschaft Hoya, Germany, she studied Slavic, Armenian, and sociological subjects at Freie Universität, Berlin. After her M.A. in 1974 she went for a year as a research scholar to Leningrad, Tiflis, and Erevan. She received a Dr.phil. in 1980 from the Freie Universität Berlin for *Das Bauernthema in der sowjetrussischen Prosa der 20er Jahre*. Since 1983 she was an academic staff member at Osteuropa-Institut, Berlin. Her writings include *Der Völkermord an den Armeniern vor Gericht; der Prozeß Talaat Pascha* (1980), *Die Nachtigall Tausendtriller; armenische Volksmärchen* (1983), *Das Verbrechen des Schweigens; die Verhand-lungen des türkischen Völkermords an den Armeniern vor dem Ständigen Tribunal der Völker* (1985), *Armenische Frage - türkisch behandelt; Dokumentation über eine antiarmenische Hetzkampagne in Berlin* (1988), *Armenien und Georgien; zwischen Ararat und Kaukasus* (1990), *Annäherung an Armenien; Geschichte und Gegenwart* (1997), and *Armenien; Stein um Stein* (2001). Note about the author; Thesis; ZKO

Hofmeier, Karl Wilhelm, born 19th cent., he received a Dr.phil. in 1909 from the Universität Wien for *Der Einfluss des genealogischen Moments auf die Thronfolge im Chalifate bis zum Untergang des Umaijadenreiches*. Schwarz

Hofmeyr, Adriaan Louw, born in 1873, his writings include *Het land langs het meer*, [Nyasaland] (Cape Town, 1910). He died in 1919. NUC, pre-1956

Höfner, Maria, born 11 October 1900 at Linz, Austria, she studied at the Universität Graz where she received a Dr.phil. in 1931 for *Die sabäischen Inschriften der südarabischen Expedition im Kunst-historischen Museum in Wien*. She successively taught Semitic philology at the universities of Wien and Tübingen as a lecturer and professor respectively. Her writings include *Altsüdarabische Grammatik* (1943), *Inschriften aus Sirwāh, Haulān* (1976-76), and *Sabäische Inschriften* (1981). In 1981 she was honoured by *Al-Hudhud; Festschrift Maria Höfner zum 80. Geburtstag* (1981). She died on 5 November 1992. DtBilnd (3); Hanisch; Kürschner, 1950-1992|; Note; Schwarz; Teichl; WhoAustria, 1977/78, 1982/83

Hofstetter, Johann (Jean) Baptist, born 18th cent., he wrote *Le Véritable conducteur viennois* (Vienne, 1818), *Galerie des voyages pittoresques dans l'Asie, l'Afrique, l'Amérique et les terres Australes = Gallerie malerischer Reisen in Asien, Afrika, Amerika und* Australien (Vienne, 1840), *Handbuch der französischen Sprache* (Wien, 1841), *Code de la morale et de la politique de la jeune noblesse de l'Autriche* (Vienne, 1844), and, with Georg Hudaj, he was a joint author of *Handbuch der arabischen Volkssprache = Manuale della lingua araba volgare* (Wien, 1846). BN; Sezgin; ZKO

Hogarth, David George, born 23 May 1862 at Barton-upon-Hunter (Lincolnshire) and educated at Winchester and Oxford, he was an archaeologist who made three journeys to Asia Minor. From 1897 to 1900 he was a director of the British School of Archaeology at Athens, and from 1908 until his death on 6 November 1927 he was a keeper at the Ashmolean Museum, Oxford. He excavated at Carchemish, a site of great historic and at that time strategic importance at the Syrian border. There can be little doubt that he was in close contact with the Secret Service, and at Oxford recruited potential future operators such as Lawrence, Woolley, and Pirie-Gordon. He appears to have got money for them to visit the East and given them assigments upon which they cut their teeth. His archaeological expeditions probably provided cover for the creation of a British intelligence network in the Levant. At the outbreak of war, he was commissioned in Naval Intelligence and posted to Cairo where he acted as first director of the Arab Bureau and edited the *Arab bulletin*. His writings include *A Wandering scholar in the Levant* (1896), *The Penetration of Arabia* (1904), *Accidents of an antiquary's life* (1910), and *The Ancient East* (1914). R. L. Bidwell, *Arab bulletin* 1 (1986 reprint), p. xxvi; DNB; Henze; Kornrumpf; Kornrumpf, N; *Who was who*, 2

Hogendorn, Jan Stafford, born 27 October 1937 at Lahaina, Hawaii, he graduated in 1960 from Wesleyan University, Middletown, Conn., and received his M.A. from Harvard University, and his Ph.D. from the London School of Economics. From 1963 until his retirement he was associated in various capacities with Colby College, Waterville, Me. He was a Ford Foundation professor at Robert College, Istanbul, 1971/72, and a Fulbright professor at Ahmadu Bello University, Zaria, Nigeria, 1975. His writings include *Managing the modern economy* (1972), *Markets in the modern economy* (1974), *Modern economics* (1975), *The Shell money of the slave trade* (1986), and he was a joint author of *Slow death for slavery; the course of abolition in Northern Nigeria, 1897-1936* (1993). AmM&WSc, 1973 S, 1978 S; ConAu, 37-40, new rev., 14, 43; IntAu&W, 1989; NatFacDr, 1990-2002; WrDr, 1976/78-2005

Hogg, Edward, M.D., he wrote *Visit to Alexandria, Damascus, and Jerusalem during the successful campaign of Ibrahim Pasha* (London, 1835), a work which was reviewed in the London *Athenæum*, 1835, p. 721. BritInd (1); Kornrumpf

Hogg, Edward Gascoigne, born 22 January 1882, he was a graduate of New College, Oxford, and was for twenty-five years in the Egyptian Civil Service until 1931, when he became an adviser to the Minstry of Finance, Iraq. He died in 1971. Who, 1936-1971; *Who was who*, 7

Hohenberger, Johannes, born 20th cent., his writings include *Semitisches und hamitisches Sprachgut im Masai* (1958), *The Nominal and verbal afformatives of Nilo-Hamitic and Hamito-Semitic* (1975), *Hamito-semitische Wortstämme im Bari und Lotuho sowie in verwandten Sprachen* (1979), and *Semitische und hamitische Wortstämme im Nilo-Hamitischen mit phonetischen Analysen* (1988). He died on 25 February 1983. LC; ZKO

Hohenwart-Gerlachstein, Anna, born 23 March 1909 at Wien, she received a Dr.phil. in ethnology in 1951 from the Universität Wien. She was a senior researcher in the Institut für Völkerkunde in the Universität Wien. Her writings include *Nubienforschungen; Dorf- und Sprachstudien in der Fadidja-Zone* (1979), and, with Josef Haekel, she was a joint author of *Die Wiener Schule der Völkerkunde* (1956). Unesco

Höhfeld, Volker, born in 1940, he studied geography, geology and cartography at the Universität Köln, from 1966 to 1972, and received a doctorate in 1976 from the Universität Erlangen-Nürnberg for a study of Anatolian small towns entitled *Anatolische Kleinstädte; Anlage, Verlegung und Wachstumsrichtung seit dem 19. Jahrhundert*. He was since 1975 successively an assistant in the Institut für Geographie, Erlangen, and at Geographisches Institut, Tübingen. His writings include *Die Türkei und die Türken in Deutschland* (1982), *Städte und Städtewachstum im Vorderen Orient* (1985), *Persistenz und Wandel der traditionellen Formen des Fremdenverkehrs in der Türkei* (1986), *Die Industrieachsen von Adana* (1987), *Türkei, Schwellenland der Gegensätze* (1995), and he was a joint author of *Kaffee aus*

Arabien; der Bedeutungswandel eines Weltwirtschaftsgutes (1979). EURAMES, 1993; Note about the author; Schwarz; ZKO

Höhl, Gudrun, born 21 January 1918 at Marktbreit/Main, she studied geography and German literature and history at Göttingen and Karls-Universität, Prag, where she received a Dr.phil. in 1940 for *Bayreuth, die Stadt und ihr Lebensraum*, and a Dr.rer.nat.habil. in 1960 from the Universität Erlangen-Nürnberg for *Fränkische Städte und Märkte in geographischem Vergleich*. She was successively a professor of geography at the universities of Erlangen-Nürnberg, Saarbrücken, and Mannheim. She was honoured by *Beiträge zur geographischen Methode und Landeskunde; Festgabe für Gudrun Höhl* (1977), and *Aspekte der Forschung; Gedanken zur Vielfalt des Denkens und Erkennens; Festschrift für Gudrun Höhl* (2002). HbDtWiss; Kürschner1966-1992

Hohlweg, Armin, born 10 April 1933 at Bayreuth, Bavaria, he received a Dr.phil. in 1962 from the Universität München for *Beiträge zur Verwaltungsgeschichte des Oströmischen Reiches unter den Komnenen*. After gaining a Dr.habil. he became successively a professor of Byzantine and Greek studies at the universities of Mainz and München. His writings include *Byzanz und seine Nachbarn* (1996), and he was, with Wolfgang Buchwald, a joint author of *Tusculum-Lexikon griechischer und lateinischer Autoren des Altertums und des Mittelalters* (1963), and *Dictionnaire des auteurs grecs et latins de l'antiquité et du moyen âge* (1991). Kürschner, 1976-2005; ZKO

Hoisington, William Arch, born 20 September 1941 at Chicago, he graduated in 1963 from Northwestern University, Evanston, Illinois, and received a Ph.D. in 1968 from Stanford University for *A businessman in politics in France, 1935-1955; the career of J. I. Dubreuil*. He taught in various capacities until his retirement in the Department of History in the University of Illinois, Chicago. His writings include *The Casablanca connection; French colonial policy, 1936-1943* (1984). DrAS, 1974 H, 1978 H, 1982 H; NatFacDr, 1990-2002

Holbach, Maude M., born 19th cent., her writings include *Dalmatia, the land where East meets West* (1908), *Dalmatien, das Land, wo Ost und West sich begegnen* (1909), *Bosnia and Herzegovina; some wayside wanderings* (1910), *Bible ways in Bible lands; impressions of Palestine* (1912), and *In the footsteps of Richard Coeur de Lion* (1912).

Holborn, Louise Wilhelmina, born 8 August 1898 at Berlin, she studied at Hochschule für Politik, Berlin, 1930-32, and received her Ph.D. in 1938 from Radcliffe College, Cambridge, Mass., for *The League of Nations and the problem of the refugees; a study of the development of international government and administration in post-war Europe*. Since 1939 she taught history and political science at a variety of American colleges and universities. Her writings include *L'Organisation internationale pour les réfugiés, agence spécialisée des Nations unies, 1946-1952* (Paris, 1955), *German constitutional documents since 1871* (1970), and *Refugees, a problem of our time; the work of the United Nations High Commissioner for Refugees* (1975). She died in 1975. BioHbDtE; ConAu, P-2, 25-28 (1971); WhoAmW, 1958/9

Holden, David Shipley, born 20 November 1924 at Sunderland, England, he received his higher education at Emmanuel College, Cambridge, and was then Middle East correspondent with the *Times* for four years, after which he became roving correspondent for the *Guardian*. He was one of Britain's most experienced foreign correspondents with an especial knowledge of the Arab world and had a wide rage of friends and contacts in the area. He was found murdered in Cairo in early December 1977. His writings include *Greece without columns; the making of modern Greeks* (1972), *Farewell to Arabia* (1966), and *Die Dynastie des Sauds; Wüstenkrieger und Weltfinanziers* (1983). BSMES bulletin; ConAu, 41-44

Holden, Edward Singleton, born in 1846 at St. Louis, Mo., he was a professor of mathematics at the Naval Observatory, Washington, D.C., until 1881, when he became a professor of astronomy at the University of Wisconsin. In 1888, he became director of the Lick Observatory, University of California. Although he was not much of an observer himself, he was a brilliant organizer, but his personality repelled most of his staff members, eventually precipitating a staff revolt in 1897. Most of his ideas were right, but he could not present them effectively to independent scientists who thought that he was treating them like privates in an infantry company. He became an outcast in American science. He moved to N.Y.C. and supported himself by grinding out magazine articles and books, many of them on astronomy, but others on subjects as diverse as poetry, heraldry, deportment, and travel. In 1901 his West Point background saved him. A fellow cadet succeeded in getting him appointed head of its library. His writings include *Flowers from Persian gardens; selection from the poems of Saadi, Hafiz, Omar Khayyam, and others* (1902). He died in 1914. ANB; DAB; DcScB; Master (14); NatCAB, vol. 7, pp. 229-230; WhAm, 1

Holden, Jeff, born 20th cent., he "first went to Ghana in 1960 to join the Institute of Extra-Mural Studies. In 1965, he moved to the Institute of African Studies, where, apart from a year at North-western [University, Evanston, Ill.], he carried out extensive field work on the political system of Samori Turay." His trace is lost after an article in 1970. Note about the author

Holdich, Sir Thomas Hungerford, born on 13 February 1843 at Dingley, Northamptonshire, and a graduate of Woolwich Academy, he served in India and Afghanistan, participating in several boundary expeditions and surveys. He retired from the Survey of India in time to have a share in the formation of the Central Asian Society. He was one of the early holders of its presidency. His writings include *The Indian borderland, 1880-1900* (1901), *India* (1904), *The Gates of India* (1910), and *Boundaries in Europe and the Near East* (1918). He died in 1929. Buckland; DNB; Enclran; Henze; IndianBilnd (2); Note about the author; Who, 1921-1929; Who was who, 3; Wright

Holdsworth, Mary Zvegintzov, born 24 October 1908 at Voronezh, Russia, she graduated from St. Hugh's College, Oxford, and successively became a teacher of adult education, senior research officer at Oxford University, and, since 1962, she served as principal of St. Mary's College, Durham. Her writings include *Soviet African studies and theories of nation-building as applied to emerging countries* (1959), *Turkestan in the nineteenth century* (1959), and *Soviet African studies, 1918-1959; an annotated bibliography* (1961). She died in 1978. ConAu, P-1, 15-16; Unesco; Who's who, 1969-1978; Who was who, 8

Holes, Clive Douglas, born 29 September 1948, he graduated in 1969 from Cambridge University where he also received his Ph.D. in 1981; he took an M.A. in 1972 at Birmingham. He did field-work in sociolinguistics and dialectology of the Gulf, and he had extensive experience as a consultant to universities and ministries of education in the Middle East on curriculum development. Fluent in Arabic, he had ten years of residence in the Middle East while a British Council officer. In 1997 he was appointed Khalid Bin Abdullah Al-Saud Professor for the Study of the Contemporary Arab World at Oxford University. His writings include *Colloquial Arabic of the Gulf and Saudi Arabia* (1984), *Language variation and change in a modernising Arab state; the case of Bahrain* (1987), *Gulf Arabic* (1990), and *Dialect, culture, and societyy in Eastern Arabia* (2001). Private; Who, 1997-2005

Holetschek, Johann, born 29 August 1846 at Thuma, Lower Austria, he studied mathematics and physics at the Universität Wien where he received a Dr.phil. in 1872. From 1878 until his retirement in 1919 he was an astronomer at the university observatory, Wien. He died in Wien on 10 November 1923. DtBE; DtBilnd (8); NDB; ÖBL

Holladay, Albert Lewis, born 16 April 1805 at Spotsylvania County, Va., he was educated at the University of Virginia. For some time he taught there and at Richmond, Va. He then took the presidency of Hampden-Sidney College, relinquishing it in 1833, when he took up the study of theology. For eleven years he was a missionary at Urmia, Persia, and achieved eminence as a scholar in Syriac literature. Returning home, he became a pastor at Charlotteville, Va. He died on 18 October 1856. *Encyclopedia of Virginia biography* (1915). NatCAB, vol. 2, p. 26

Holland, Frederick Whitmore, born in 1837 at Dumbleton near Evesham, he was educated at Eton and Trinity College, Cambridge. A vicar of Evesham since 1872, he visited the Sinai Peninsula in 1861, 1865, 1868, and 1878. His writings include *Sinai and Jerusalem; or, scences from Bible lands* (London, Society for Promoting Christian Knowldge, 1879). He died in 1880. Boase; Henze

Holland, Sir Henry Tristram, born in 1875, he graduated with distinction from the Edinburgh School of Medicine. He was a philanthpist and medical doctor who served for forty-eight years on the North West Frontier of India, mostly near Quetta. His writings include *Frontier doctor; an autobiography* (1958). He died in 1965. Bioln, 4; DNB; GrBr; Who was who, 6

Holland, Leicester Bodine, born in 1822, he studied architecture and achaeology at the University of Pennsylvania, Philadelphia, where he received all his degrees, including his Ph.D. in 1919. He first was a partner in an architectural firm in Philadelphia, later becoming a lecturer in architecture at his alma mater. In 1919 he was a fellow at the American School of Classical Studies, Athens, Greece. In 1925 he became a professor of fine arts at Vassar College, Poughkeepsie, N.Y., and in 1929 he was appointed chief of the division of prints at the Library of Congress, Washington, D.C., a post which he held until 1943. He died in Philadelphia, Pa., on 7 February 1952. Bioln, 2 (2), 3 (3); NatCAB, vol. 41, p. 270; NYT, 8 February 1952, p. 23, col. 1; WhAm, 3; WhE&EA

Holland, Sir Thomas Erskine, born in 1835 at Brighton, Sussex, he was educated at Balliol and Magdalen colleges, Oxford, and called to the bar from Lincoln's Inn in 1863. He taught for thirty-five years intenational law and diplomacy at Oxford. His writings include *The Elements of jurisprudence*

(1880), *The European concert in the Eastern Question* (1885), *Studies in international law* (1898), and *The Laws of war on land* (1908). He died in 1926. BiD&SB; DNB; Master (1); OxLaw; *Who was who*, 2

de **Hollander**, Joannes (Jan) Jacobus, born 28 August 1817 at Aartswoud, Noord-Holland, the Netherlands. He studied theology and letters at Leiden where he received his doctorate in 1840 with a thesis entitled *De Euripidis supplicibus*. From 1843 until his retirement in 1885 he taught Oriental languages in various capacities at the Koninklijke Militaire Akademie, Breda. Upon its reorganization in 1877, the subjects history, geography, and ethnology of the Dutch East Indies were added to his teaching load. He was an honorary member of the Bataviaasch Genootschap van Kunsten en Wetenschappen. His writings include *Handleiding bij de beoefening deer Javaansche taal en letterkunde* (1848), and he was a joint author of *Reizen in den Oost-Indischen Archipel* (1873). He died in Breda on 5 November 1886. EncNI, vol. 2, pp. 101-102; NieuwNBW

Hollatz, Günther, born 20th cent., his writings include *Auf den Spuren teppichknüpfender Nomaden* (Herford, 1984). Sezgin

Holle, Karel Frederik, born 9 October 1829 at Amsterdam, he went in 1843 with the family to the Dutch East Indies. He entered the civil service in 1846 at Tjiandjoer (Cianjur) and remained there until 1856 when he resigned to become an administrator in the tea business, founding his own enterprise, Waspada, in 1862. He became befriended with one Hadji Mohammed Moesa and devoted himself to the Sundanese's customs, habits, language, and religion. In 1866 he founded the native teachers' college at Bandung. In 1871 the Government nominated him an honorary adviser in native affairs. Since 1889 he was resident in Buitenzorg (Bogor), West Java, where he died on 3 May 1896. His writings include *Honderd en een Soendasche spreekwoorden* (1861-70). EncNI, vol. 2, pp. 102-103; NieuwNBW

Hollenbach, John Wiliam, born 10 February 1913 at Allentown, Pa., he was a graduate of Muhlenberg College and received a Ph.D. in 1941 from the University of Wisconsin. He was a professor of English first at Northeast Missouri State University and later at Hope College, Holland, Mich. In 1965/66, he served as a visiting professor at the American University of Beirut DrAS, 1969 E, 1974 E, 1978 E, 1982 E; WhoAm, 1964/65-1974/75

Höller, Ernst, born 15 January 1899, he was a secondary school teacher and a writer of juvenile literature. His writings include *Zeitgemäßer Rechtschreibunterricht* (Wien, Verlag für Jugend und Volk, 1953) *Zwei Jahrtausende in Sage und Anekdote* (Stuttgart, 1961), and *Theorie und Praxis des Schülergespräches* (Wien, Verlag für Jugend und Volk, 1970). KDtLK, 1963

Holley, Horace Hotchkiss, born in 1887 at Torrington, Conn., he graduated from high school in 1906, studied three years at college, before travelling and studying in Europe, 1909-14. He was a founder and director of a Paris art gallery, 1912-14. Since 1924 he was an administrative officer of the National Spiritual Assembly of Bahais of North America. His writings include *Bahaism, the modern social religion* (1913), *The Social principle* (1915), *Bahai, the spirit of the age* (1921), *Bahái scriptures* (1928), and *The World economy of Bahá'u'lláh* (1931). He died in 1960. Master (2); WhAm, 4

Holliday, Margaret Y., born 6 December 1843 in Indiana, she was educated at the McLean Female Seminary, Indianapolis, Ind., and at Dr. Lewis' School, Lexington, Mass. In September 1883, she sailed for Persia as a missionary of the American Presbyterian Mission in Persia. Her thirty-seven years of missionary life were spent in the Tabriz field. She started her work as an evangelist to the Armenians but soon began the direct evangelization of Muslims. She acquired an excellent command of Persian and, in 1901, she published anonymously the bilingual book entitled *Islam and Christianity*, composed of letters originally written to her Persian teacher, presenting in a convincing way the arguments of Christianity which would appeal to Persian Muslims. She was indefatigable in itinerating work in the towns and villages of western Persia, on horseback, or in a springless cart, accompanied only by a native woman and an evangelist. When the Turks drove out the Tabriz missionaries in 1918, she went to Qazvin for a brief period, before returning to the United States, where she died in Indianapolis, Ind., on 17 March 1920. MW, 10 (1920), pp. 304-305

Hollingbery, William, born 18th cent., he wrote *A History of his late Highness Nizam Alee Khaun, soobah of the Dekhan* (Calcutta, 1805), and *A Journal of observation made during the British embassy to the court of Persia in the years 1799, 1800 and 1801* (Calcutta, 1814), and its Persian translation in 1363/1984. BLC; ZKO

Hollingworth, Clare, born 20th cent., she was a special correspondent of *The Guardian* for some time, before she became their defence correspondent. Her writings include *Hitler's route to Bagdad* (1939), *The Arabs and the West* (1952), and *Mao and the men against him* (1985).

Hollis, George Edward (Ted), he was in 1979 associated with the Department of Geography in the University of London. He edited *Man's impact on the hydrological cycle in the United Kingdom* (Norwich, 1979). Note about the author

Hollis, Howard C., fl. 20th cent., throughout the 1930s and 1940s he contributed numerous articles on Islamic art to the *Bulletin* of the Cleveland Museum of Art.

Hollister, John Norman, born 20th cent., he received a Ph.D. in 1946 from Hartford Seminary Foundation for *The Shi'a of India*, a work which was published in 1953. He became a missionary in India. His other writings include *The Centenary of the Methodist Church in southern Asia* (1956), and *The Lucknow Publishing House, 1861-1961* (1961). Selim

Höllriegel, Arnold, pseudonym, born Richard Arnold Bermann on 27 April 1883 at Wien, he was a journalist, novelist, and writer of travel literature. His writings include *Die Derwischtrommel; das Leben des erwarteten Mahdi* (1931), and *Zarzura, die Oase der kleinen Vögel; die Geschichte einer Expedition in die Libysche Wüste* (1938). He died in Saratoga Springs, N.Y., on 3 September 1939. BioHbDtE; DtBiInd (1); EncJud; KDtLK, Nekrolog, 1936-1970; Sezgin; *Wer ist's*, 1935; Wininger, Nachtrag

Hollstein, Walter, born in 1939, he was educated at Basel, Frankfurt/Main, Osnabrück, and Lausanne, studied sociology at the universities of Basel and Münster, and obtained a Dr.phil. After practice work in journalism in Basel, he became a correspondent to newspapers in Switzerland for the Third World. He also taught soziology at Genève, Basel, and Berlin. His writings include *Der Untergrund* (1969), *Sozialarbeit unter kapitalistischen Produktionsbedingungen* (1973), and the fourth edition of his *Kein Frieden um Israel; zur Sozialgeschichte des Palästina-Konflikts* (1984). Note about the author; Sezgin; ZKO

Holm-Nielsen, Svend, born 15 January 1919 at Hellerup, Denmark, he studied theology and Oriental languages at Københavns Universitet where he also received a doctorate in 1960 for a thesis on the Psalms from Qumran. From 1961 to his retirement in in 1986 he was a professor of Old Testament at his alma mater. In 1987 Uppsala Universitet conferred on him an honorary doctorate. His writings include *Hodayot; psalms from Qumran* (1960), *Israel i den arabiske verden; krig eller fred?* (1967), *Historien bag Palæstina-problemet* (1975), *Palestina-konflikten, sett pa arabisk bakgrunn* (Oslo, 1978), and he edited *Retten til Palæstina; inledning og kilder* (1975). Kraks, 1990-2003/2004

Holma, Harri Gustaf, born 14 April 1886 at T:hus [!] , Finland, he received a doctorate in 1911 at Helsinki for *Die Namen der Körperteile im Assyrisch-Babylonischen.* He held several important positions as a libraian before entering the diplomatic field. From 1921 to 1943, he served as a minister to the German and French speaking countries in Europe as well as the Vatican. His writings include *Die assyrisch-babylonischen Personennamen der Form quttulu* (1914), *Muhammad* (1914), *Mainitseeko arabialainenmaantieteen kirjottaja Idrisi Turun kaupungin nimen?* (1917), *Arabian suuri profeta* (1943), its translation, *Mahomet, prophète des Arabes* (1946), and *Georg August Wallin, 1811-1852* (1952). He died in Capri, Italy, in 1954, one day after celebrating his sixty-seventh birthday. EncFen; NYT, 15 April 1954, p. 29, col. 5; ScBInd (2); Uusi; *Vem och vad*, 1931-1948

Holman, Sir Herbert Campbell, born in 1869, he was educated at Dulwich and Sandhurst and entered the army in 1889. From 1919 to 1920 he served as chief of the British Military Mission to South Russia. He retired with the rank of lieutenant-general. He was a sometime honorary treasurer to the Bible monthly, *The Bible speaks to Britain.* He died in 1949. *Who was who*, 4

Holmboe, Christopher Andreas, born 19 March 1796 at Vang, Oppland, Norway, he studied Oriental languages in Norway and, with a fellowship, also under Silvestre de Sacy and Caussin de Perceval at the Sorbonne, 1821-22. Since 1822 he taught his subject at the Universitetet i Christiania; in 1825 he was appointed a professor. He was also associated with its Universitetet Myntkabinett. He died in 1882. NorskBL [variant dates]; NorskBL²

Holme, John Gunnlaugur, born in 1878, he was a biographer whose writings include *The Life of Leonard Wood* (1920). He died in 1922. DcNAA; NUC, pre-1956

Holme, Winifred, born in 1903, his writings include *Tekhi's hunting* (1941), *An Introduction to Indian art* (1948), *Orient; a survey of films produced in countries of Arab and Asian culture* (1959), and *She was Queen of Egypt* (1959). WhE&EA

Holmes, Miss Mary Caroline, born in 1859 at Deposit, N.Y., she was for thirty years a missionary of the Presbyterian Board in the Near East. She was, for some time, a teacher in the girls' school of Tripoli, Syria. Her writings include *Who follows in their train* (1917), *A Knock at the door* (1918), and *Between the lines in Asia Minor* (1923). She died in N.Y.C. on 3 March 1927. Note about the author; Shavit; WhAm, 1

Holmes, Samuel, born 18th cent., he was a sergeant-major of the 11th Light Dragoons. He wrote *The Journal of Mr. Samuel Holmes ... during his attendance, as one of the guard on Lord Macartney's embassy to China and Tartary, 1792-3* (1798), and its translations, *Voyage en Chine et en Tartarie à la suite de l'ambassade de Lord Macartney* (1805), *Tagebuch einer Reise nach Sina und in die Tatarei* (1805), and *Viaggio di Samuele Holmes* (1817). BritInd (1)

Holmyard, Eric John, born 11 July 1891, he was a scholar of Sidney Sussex College, Cambridge, and received an M.Sc. in 1925 from the University of Bristol for *Rise and development of chemistry in medieval Islam*, and a D.Litt. in 1928 for (1) *Work on the history of chemistry in medieval Islam*. (2) *Work on the teaching of chemistry in this country*. From 1920 to 1940, he was head of the Science Department at Clifton College, and from 1941 to 1954, he served as editor of *Endeavour*. He is best remembered for his profound studies of Muslim chemistry. A good Arabist, he made a special study of Jābir ibn Hayyān and the writings attributed to him. His writings include *Science; an introductory textbook* (1926), *Makers of chemistry* (1931), and he edited and translated the Arabic alchemical text of Abū al-Qāsim Muhammad al-Simāwī al-'Irāqī, *K. al-'Ilm al-muktasab fī zirā'at adh-dhahab* (1923). BioIn, 5; DNB; *Nature*, 184 (31 October 1959), p. 1360; ObitT, 1951-60; Sluglett; WhE&EA; *Who was who*, 5

Holobuts'kyĭ (Голобуцкий), Volodymyr Oleksiĭovych (Vladimir Alekseevich), his writings include *Черноморское казачество* (Kiev, 1956), and *Дипломатическая история освободительной войны украинского народа, 1648-1654 гг.* (Kiev, 1962). OSK

Holod-Tretiak, Olga *Renata*, born 6 September 1942 at Rohatyn, Ukraine, she graduated in 1960 from Harbord Collegiate Institute, Toronto, Ontario, and subsequently pursued Islamic studies at the University of Toronto, graduating in 1964; she received a Ph.D. in 1972 from Harvard University for *The monuments of Yazd, 1300-1450*. She then served until her retirement as a professor of fine art in the University of Pennsylvania, Philadelphia, specializing in the architecture of Iran in the 14th to 16th centuries as well as urban planning. She was the editor of a number of collected works in both fields. ConAu, 119; *MESA Roster of members*, 1977-1990; NatFacDr, 2005; Private; Selim

Hołowiński, Ignazy, born 24 September 1807 at Owrucz, he studied theology at Vilna (Wilno), Russia, and in 1837 became a university professor at Kiev. As Ukrainian bishop he made a pilgrimage to the Holy Land, visiting on the way Turkey, Syria, and Lebanon. His writings, partly under the pseudonyms Ignacy Kefalinski and Zegota Kostrowiec, include *Pisma* (1848), and *Pielgrzymyka do Ziemi Swiętéj* (1853). He died in St. Petersburg on 13 October 1855. Dziekan; Polski (21); PSB

Holroyd, Arthur Todd, born 1806 at London, he took an M.D. in 1830 at Edinburgh and was subsequently admitted to the bar from Lincoln's Inn. He resolved first to travel. He spent a winter at Roma learning Italian and travelled in 1836-37 in the Sudan. He spent his later life in New South Wales, Australia. His writings include *Egypt and Mahomed Ali Pacha in 1837* (1838), *The Quarantine laws* (1839), and *Suakin and the country of Soudan* (1885). He died on 15 June 1887. AusDcBio, 1851-1890; Henze, HIII; Kornrumpf

Hölscher, Gustav Diedrich Hillard, born 17 June 1877 at Norden, East Friesland, he received his secondary education at Leipzig and studied theology and Semitic languages first at the Universität Erlangen and later at Leipzig where he received a Dr.phil. in 1902 for *Palästina in der persischen und hellenistischen Zeit*. He successively became a professor of theology at the universities in Gießen, Marburg, and Bonn. In 1917 the Universität Halle conferred on him a Dr.theol.h.c. His writings include *Landes- und Volkskunde Palästinas* (1907), and *Die Geschichte der Juden in Palästina seit dem Jahre 70 nach Chr.* (1909). He died in Heidelberg on 16 September 1955. DtBE; DtBiInd (2); Hanisch; HbDtWiss; Kürschner, 1926-1961; LuthC 75; NDB; *Wer ist's*, 1928-1935; Schwarz

Holsinger, Donald Charles, born about 1949, he received a Ph.D. in 1979 from Northwestern University at Evanston, Ill., for *Migration, commerce and community; the Mizabis in nineteenth-century Algeria*. He was successively a professor at George Mason University, Fairfax, Va., and Seattle Pacific University, Seattle, Wash. *MESA Roser of members*, 1982-1990; NatFacDr, 1990-2005

Holst, Hans Jørgen born 17 June 1891 at Drammen, Buskerud county, Norway, he studied classics at Kristiania and received a Dr.phil. in 1925 from the Universität Innsbruck for *Die Wortspiele in Ciceros Reden*. He was for thirty years a director of the Universitetets Myntkabinett, Oslo. He was a joint author of *Norges mynter efter 1814* (Oslo, 1927), and *Några undersökninger rörande skivor och höga balkar av armerad betong* (Stockholm, 1946). He died in Oslo on 23 September 1956. NorksBL²

Holst, Johann Jørgen, born 29 November 1937 at Oslo, he received a B.A. in political science in 1958 from Columbia University, New York, and subsequently studied at the Center for International Affairs, Harvard University. He became a politician and government official, and he served as a minister of defence. His writings include *Antorobotvapen - hot eller löfte* (1967), *Norsk sikkerhetspolitikk i*

MACK LIBRARY
BOB JONES UNIVERSITY
GREENVILLE, SC

strategisk perspektiv (1967), *Comparative U.S. and Soviet developments, doctrines, and arms limitation* (1971), *Security, order, and the bomb* (1972), *Rustingskontroll i norsk sikkerhetspolitikken* (1975), *Beyond nuclear deterrence* (1977), and *Exploring Europe's future* (1990). He died in Nesodden, Akershus, on 13 January 1994. ConAu, 25-28, new rev., 11, 143; *Hvem er hvem*, 1979; IntWW, 1990/91-1993/94; NorskBL²; WhAm, 11; WhoWor, 1978/79, 1989/90-1993/94

Holst, Marie Kristine Sofie, born 5 December 1866 at Virkelyst in Seest, Denmark, she took a medical doctorate in 1896 at the London School of Medicine for Women. She was a medical missionary under the Church of England Zenana Missionary Society in Bangalore. But she resigned from the Society, and with the help of a portable tent, the *Telkmission* (Tent Mission), and another missionary, Marie Rasmussen, took up itinerating work among the Pathans on the North-West Frontier of India, where she later operated a women's hospital at Hoti, near Peshawar. She intended to be ready with the Gospel whenever Afghanistan might be opened to preachers. She died in Mardan, India, on 18 February 1917. DanskBL; MW, 22 (1932, pp. 413-14

Holsten, Walter, born 29 March 1908 at Osnabrück, Germany, he received a Dr.theol. in 1932 from the Universität Göttingen for *Christentum und unchristliche Religion nach der Auffassung Luthers*. He was since 1947 a professor of missions and history of religions. His writings include *Das Evangelium und die Völker; Beiträge zur Geschichte und Theorie der Mission* (1939), *Das Kerygma und der Mensch; Einführung in die Religions- und Missionswissenschaft* (1953), and *Mission als Zeugendienst* (1972). He died in Alzey, Hesse, on 13 March 1982. HdDtWiss; Kürschner, 1950-1980; *Wer ist wer*, 1958-80

Holt, Eugene I., fl. 1958, he was a joint author of *Painted and printed textiles from A.D. 800 to 1961; catalog of a loan exhibition* (Pasadena, Calif., 1961). NUC, 1956-67

Holt, George Edmund, born in 1881 at Moline, Illinois, he was a novelist and writer of short stories who served as vice-consul at Tanger in 1907, and as consul-general, from 1909 to 1911. His writings include *Morocco, the bizarre; or, life in the sunset land* (1914). WhNNA; *Who's who in literature*, 1931

Holt, Peter Malcolm, born 28 November 1918 at Leigh, Lancs., he received a B.Litt. in 1951 from Oxford University for *Arabic studies in seventeenth-century England, with special reference to the life and work of Edward Pococke*, and also a D.Phil. in 1954 for *The personal rule of the Khalifat 'Abdallahi al-Ta'aishi*. He was for many years an archivist of the Sudanese Government, and since 1956 taught at SOAS. His writings include *Makers of modern Europe* (1955), *The Mahdist State in the Sudan* (1958), *A Modern history of the Sudan* (1961), *Egypt and the Fertile Crescent* (1966), *Political and social change in modern Egypt* (1968), *The Eastern Mediterranean lands in the period of the Crusades* 1977), *The Age of the crusades* (1986), and *The Sudan of the three niles; the Funj chronicle, 910-1288/1504-1871* (1999). EURAMES, 1993; IntWW, 1989-2002; Sluglett; Unesco; Who, 1974-2004; WhoWor, 1982 [not sighted]

Holter, Åge Standal, born 19 January 1919 at Ålesund, Norway, he graduated in 1942 from the Teachers' College, Volda; he gained a diploma in French language and literature in 1947 at the Université de Strasbourg, and a D.D. in 1957 at Oslo. He was a sometime professor of religion, missions, and Church history at the Universitetet i Trondheim. A member of the Norsk Vidensskaps-Akademi, he wrote *Moralundervisning og politikk* (1956), *Det Norske bibelselskap gjennom 150 år* (1966), *Arabisk statsreligion; det politiske og sosiale Islam; Nord-Afrika og Midt-Østen* (1976), and *Det levende ordet* (1989). *Hvem er hvem*, 1973-1994; WhoWor, 1974/75, 1976/77

Holter, Kurt, born 3 October 1911 at Wels, Upper Austria, he studied Oriental subjects and history of art at the Universität Wien where he received a Dr.phil. in 1934 for *Die Makamen des Hariri und die Golen-Handschrift der Wiener Nationalbibliothek*. He became a librarian at the Stiftsbibliothek, Kremsmünster. Since 1962 he was an editor of *Jahrbuch des Oberösterreichischen Musealvereins*. BiogrLexOö; Teichl

Holtkamp, Rudolf, born 20th cent., his writings include *Small four-wheel tractors for the tropics and subtropics; their role in agricultural and industrial development* (Weikersheim, 1990). ZKO

Höltker, Georg, born 22 May 1895 at Ahaus, Westphalia, he started life as a factory worker without formal secondary education but with missionary ambitions. He studied anthropology at the Theological Seminary St. Gabriel in Mödling and was ordained priest in 1925. From 1925 to 1929 he was an extension student at the universities of Wien and Berlin, obtaining a Dr.phil. in 1930 from the Universität Berlin. He subsequently did ethnological field-work in New Guinea, and since 1935 he served as a professor of ethnology at various universities in Switzerland and Germany. Since 1962 he was associated with the Anthropos-Institut in St. Augustin near Bonn, where he died on 22 January 1976. His writings include *Die Gende in Zentralneuguinea* (1940). In 1975 he was honoured by *Menschen und Kulturen in Nordost-Neuguinea: gesammelte Aufsätze; Festschrift Georg Höltker zu* *seinem 80. Geburtstag vom Anthropos-Institut gewidmet.* BioHbDtE; BioIn 11; *Neue Zeitschrift für Missions-wissenschaft,* 21 (1964), pp. 61-63; 31 (1975), p. 145; 32 (1976), pp. 148-150

Holtz, Bruno, born 20th cent., his writings include *Burundi; Völkermord oder Selbstmord* (1973); he was a joint editor of *Missionarische Kooperation morgen* (1975). ZKO

Holtzmann, Walther, born 31 December 1891 at Eberbach, Baden, he studied philology and history first at the Universität Straßburg and later the Universität Heidelberg, gaining a Dr.phil. in 1920 for a study of Papal history entitled *Die Beziehungen Papst Urbans II zu Frankreich,* and a Dr.habil. at Berlin for *Papsturkunden in England.* He subsequently taught medieval history first at Halle and since 1935 at the Universität Bonn. His writings include *Papsturkunden in England* (1930-1952), *Kanonistische Ergänzungen zur Italia Pontificia* (1959), and *Aus der Geschichte von Nardò in der normannischen und staufischen Zeit* (1961). He died in Bonn on 25 November 1963. *In memoriam Walther Holzmann* was published in 1965. Bonner, 7 (1968), pp. 398-409; DtBE; DtBild (1); HbDtWiss; Kürschner, 1931-1961; NDB; *Wer ist wer,* 1950-1962

Holý, Ladislav, born 4 April 1933 at Praha, he was a research fellow at the Czech Academy of Sciences, 1956-68, a director of the Livingstone Museum, Zambia, 1968-1972, and since 1973 a professor of social anthropology at the University of St. Andrews. His writings include *Afrika* (Praha, 1964), *Etnografie mimoevropských oblasti* (1964), *Neighbours and kinsmen; a study of the Berti people of Darfur* (1974), *Comparative anthropology* (1987), *Kinship, honour and solidarity; cousin marriage in the Middle East* (1989), *Anthropological perspectives on kinship* (1996), and *Malý český člověk a skvělý český národ* (2001). He died in St. Andrews on 13 April 1997. Český; ConAu, 141; Filipsky; Unesco

Holz, Robert I. Kenneth, born 3 November 1930 at Kankakee, Ill., he received a Ph.D. in 1963 from Michigan State University for *The area organization of national forests.* From 1962 to his retirement in 1995 he served as a professor in the Department of Geography, University of Texas at Austin; concurrently he was from 1991 to 1995 a director of its Center for Middle Eastern Studies. His writings include *Texas and its history* (1972), *The surveillant science; remote sensing of the environment* (1973), and he was a joint author of *Economics and populations growth* (1971). ConAu, 53-56; NatFacDr, 1990-1995; Private

Holzer, Herwig F., born 20th cent., he studied geology, palaeontology, and petrography at the Universität Wien where he received a Dr.phil. in 1949. He subsequently was associated with a variety of geological institutes in Wien, Ankara, and Delft. In 1956 he entered the Austrian federal goelogical administration (Geologische Bundesanstalt), Wien, as chief geologist. He successively worked in Egypt, Turkey, Greece, Ireland, Kuwait, East and West Pakistan as an expert exploration geologist in the service of the United Nations. Note about the author

Holzhausen, Rudolf Hermann Johannes, born 13 April 1889 at Nordhausen, Prussia, he studied law and political science and served during the first World War. In 1919 he entered the German diplomatic service, being successively posted to Wien, den Haag, and Praha. In 1937, he was sent into early retirement. After the second World War he became a government official in the Bavarian ministry of trade and commerce. In 1951, he returned to the foreign service and successively became ambassador at Pretoria and Cairo. He died in München on 9 June 1963. DtBE; *Wer ist wer,* 1955-1962

Holzhausen, Walter Heinrich Caecilius, born 23 August 1896 at Bonn, he received a Dr.phil. in 1922 from the Universität Bonn for *Die Entwicklung des deutschen Ornamentstichs im Zeitalter des Barocks.* In 1925 he started his career as an assistant at the collection of medieval artifacts (Grüne Gewölbe), Dresden, to become successively a director of Schloßmuseum, Altenberg/Thüringen, and Städtische Kunstsammlung, Bonn. His writings include *Das Grüne Gewölbe zu Dresden; Führer* (1927), and *Lackkunst in Europa* (1959). He died in Bonn on 31 October 1968. GV; Kürschner, 1950-1970; *Wer ist's,* 1928, 1935; *Wer ist wer,* 1958-1967/68

Holzwarth, Wolfgang, born 9 July 1952 at Asperg, Baden-Württemberg, Germany, he studied from 1972 to 1978 at the Freie Universität, Berlin, majoring in ethnology, and taking as minor subjects Iranian studies and political economy, gaining a master's degree in 1978. He subsequently spent three years carrying on field-work in Afghanistan, India, and Pakistan as a fellow of Stiftung Volks-wagenwerk. Concurrently to an assistantship, he started his doctoral program in 1981 at the Freie Universität, gaining a Dr.phil. in 1987 for *Vom Fürstentum zur afghanischen Provinz Badakhshan, 1880-1935; soziale Prozesse in einem zentralasiatischen Grenzgebiet.* From 1986 to 1990 he collaborated with a research project of the Freie Universität on the Ismailis in northern Pakistan. In 2004, he started a new three-year project financed by the German council. His writings include *Die Ismaeliten in Nordpakistan* (1994). Private; Thesis

Hóman, Bálint (Valentin), born 29 December 1885 at Budapest, he received a doctorate in philosophy from Budapest University and subsequently joined its library. His writings include a work on the

Oriental sources of Hungarian history, *Őstörténetünk keleti forrásai* (1909), *Magyar pénztörténet, 1000-1325* (1916), *A magyar történetírás új útjai* (1931), *King Stephen the Saint* (1938), *Gli Angioini di Napoli in Ungheria, 1290-1403* (1938), *Geschichte des ungarischen Mittelalters* (1940), and *Német-magyar sorsközösség* (1941). He died in Vác, Hungary, on 2 June 1951. GeistigeUng; Magyar

Homes, Henry Augustus, born 10 March 1812 at Boston, Mass., he was a sometime librarian of the New York State Library, Albany. His writings include works on bibliothecal subjects as well as *The Correct arms of the State of New York* (1880), and the translation from the Turkish of al-Ghazzālī, *The Alchemy of happiness* (1873). He died in Albany, N.Y., on 3 November 1887. BioIn, 3; Shavit; Master (6); NatCAB, vol. 13, p. 42; WhAm, Hist.

Hommaire de Hell, Ignace *Xavier* Morand, born 24 November 1812 at Altkirch (Haut-Rhin), he studied at the colleges of Altkirch and Dijon, and took civil engineering at the École des mineurs, Saint-Étienne, graduating in 1833. In 1834 he was employed by the inspector general of the Lyon-Marseille railway on a feasibility study. In October 1835 he left for Constantinople, with an appointment as engineer of public works. He constructed bridges and lighthouses along the Black Sea. From May 1838, he spent five years in southern Russia, visiting the country up to Astrakhan and discovering iron-ore fields on the Dnieper. In 1841 he explored and surveyed mines and means of communication in Moldavia. In 1843 he returned to France for three years before setting out in the service of several French ministries on a geographic mission to the regions of the Black Sea and the Caspian Sea. After over two years of exploration he succumbed to the hardships of the mission in Isfahan on 24 November 1848. His writings include *Les Steppes de la mer Caspienne, le Caucase, la Crimée et la Russie méridionale* (1844), a work to which his wife contributed the ethnographic parts as well as the illustrations, *Géographie historique du bassin de la Mer Caspienne* (1845), and *Voyage en Turquie et en Perse par ordre du Gouvernement français les années 1846-48* (1859). DBF; Enclran; Hoefer; IndexBFr² (3); Kornrumpf; NDBA; *Revue de l'Orient*, 5 (1849), pp. 63-64

Hommaire de Hell, Jeanne Louise *Adèle* née Hériot, born in 1819 in the Département Pas-de-Calais, she lost her mother when still quite young and had to travel with her restless father all around France before he put her in a boarding-school at Saint-Mandé (Val-de-Marne). After his death in 1833, her elder sister looked after her at Saint-Étienne, where she became acquainted with a recently graduated engineer, Xavier Hommaire de Hell. They got married the same year and she accompanied her husband on his Eastern travels. After his death in 1848, she returned to France first residing in Hyère and later in Paris, where she became a contributor to *la Presse* and other periodicals as well as seeing her husband's work through the press. In 1868 she went to live with her eldest son, a professor of mathematics in Martinique. Her writings include *Voyage dans les steppes de la Mer Caspienne et dans la Russie méridionale* (1860), and *Mémoires d'une adventurière, 1833-1852* (1934). Pavel P. Viazemskiĭ wrote Письма и записки Оммер де Геллъ (1990). She died in 1883. DBF; OSK; Vapereau

Hommel, Fritz, born 31 July 1854 at Ansbach, Bavaria, he studied at Leipzig where he received a Dr.phil. in 1878 for a study of mammal names in Arabic entitled *Die Säugetiernamen bei den Arabern*. Since 1885 he taught Semitic languages at the Universität München and continued to do so for years after his official retirement in 1925. His writings include *Die semitischen Völker und Sprachen* (1881-83), *Südarabische Chrestomathie* (1893), *Sumerische Lesestücke* (1894), *Geschichte des Morgenlandes* (1895), *The Oath in Babylonian and Assyrian literature* (1912), and *Zweihundert sumero-türkische Wortvergleichungen als Grundlage zu einem neuen Kapitel der Sprachwissenschaft* (1915). On his sixtieth birthday he was honoured by *Orientalische Studien Fritz Hommel zum sechzigsten Geburtstag am 31. Juli 1914 gewidmet* (1917-1918). He died in München on 17 April 1936. AfrBioInd (1); Dawson; DtBiInd (2); Egyptology; Hanisch; Kornrumpf; Kürschner, 1925-1935; LuthC 75; NDB; Wer ist's, 1908-1935

Homsy de Julliany, Gaston, born 4 April 1869 at Marseille, he studied classics and became a writer and contributor to a variety of periodicals. An *officier de l'Académie*, he was the recipient of numerous awards and decorations, including *Lion et de Soleil de Perse* as well as the Turkish *Medjidié*. His writings include *Le Général Jacob et l'expéditions de Bonaparte en Égypte, 1798-1801* (1921). Curinier, vol. 3 (19019, p. 200

de **Hond**, Meijer, born 30 August 1882 in a poor Jewish neighbourhood of Amsterdam, he began his education at the Nederlandsch-Israëlietisch Seminarium, and since 1901 at the Universiteit te Amsterdam, which was a prerequisite for the higher rabbinical examination. He studied classical philology, philosophy, and archaeology, graduating in 1904. In the same year, he gained the degree of *magid* , cand. rabbi, from the Seminarium. A recognized orator, he regularly preached to a large audience of the Touroh Our congregation at the newly established Nieuwe Synagoge. From 1905 to 1914 he was the chief contributor and editor of the monthly, *Libanon*. The congregation enabled him to go to Berlin in 1909 to complete his rabbinical studies in 1914 at the Rabbinerseminar, and also obtain a Dr.phil.

from the Universität Würzburg for *Beiträge zur Erklärung der Elhidrlegende und von Koran, Sure 18:59ff.* But he was a controversial rabbi, given to ghetto romantics and an idealized poverty, battling against the current and thus offending those who he meant to help. In the second World War, he and his family shared the fate of the majority of the poor Amsterdam ghetto Jewry. To the very end, even when he and his family were being led away to the camp in Westerbork (21 June 1943), he inspired faith and hope by his mystic words. Consonant with his belief and personality he replied on 20 July 1943 to the call to report for deportation to the east: "Hinneni" (Here I am' - Abraham's reply to God just before he received the order to sacrifice Isaac.) His writings include *Dr. Meijer de Hond; bloemlezing uit zijn werk* (1951). He perished in Sobibor, Poland, on 23 July 1943. BWN, vol. 3, pp. 263-265; EncJud; JüdLex

Honda, Minoba, born 20th cent., he received a Ph.D. in 1956 from Cambridge University for *Relations between Persia and China under the Mongol domination.* BLC; Sluglett

Hondrich, Karl Otto, born 1 September 1937 at Andernach, Germany, he received a Dr.phil. in 1962 from the Universität Köln for *Die Ideologien von Interessenverbänden.* He was a lecturer in economics at Kabul University, 1963-1965, and since 1972, a professor of economics at the Universität Frankfurt am Main. His writings include *Theorie der Herrschaft* (1973), *Menschliche Bedürfnisse und soziale Steuerung* (1975), *Die Bürger; Bedürfnisse, Einstellungen, Verhalten* (1979), *Krise der Leistungs-gesellschaft* (1988), *Wieder Krieg* (2002), *Enthüllung und Entrüstung* (2002), and *Die Kanäle der Macht* (2002). Kürschner, 1976-2003; WhoWor, 1991/92

Honey, William Bowyer, born in 1889 at Battersea, London, he won a scholarship from the local "board school'" to the Sir Walter St. John's School, Battersea. He left school at the age of fifteen to enter a department of the General Post Office. In 1926 came the turning point in his life when he found himself transferred from the clerical side of the Civil Service to an appoinment as assistant in the Department of Ceramics, Victoria & Albert Museum, London. From 1938 until 1950, he was a keeper of the Department. In 1951, following his retirement, he was honoured with the award of C.B.E. His wirtings include *Guide to later Chinese porcelain* (1927), *Dresden china* (1934), *The ceramic art of China and other countries of the Far East* (1945), *English glass* (1946), and *Wedgewood ware* (1948). He died in London on 13 September 1956, after a long illness. Artibus Asiae, 19 ii (1956), pp. 143-44; BioIn, 4 (1); BritInd (1); WhE&EA; *Who was who*, 5

Honeyman, Alexander Mackie, born in 1907, he was educated at the universities of Sr. Andrews, Edinburgh, SOAS, Zürich, and Chicago, where he received a Ph.D. in 1934 for *The Mission of Burzoe in the Arabic Kalilah and Dimnah.* From 1937 until 1967 he served as a professor of Semitic languages at the University of St. Andrews. He travelled and excavated repeatedly in Southern Arabia. He died on 28 August 1988. Who, 1969-1988

Honig, Nathan, born 19th cent., he received a Dr.phil. in 1917 from the Universität Berlin for *Die Stellung Konstantinopels in der asiatischen Türkei.* Schwarz

Honigberger, Johann *Martin*, born 10 March 1795 at Kronstadt, Transylvania, he pursued an interest personal physician to various potentates. His collection of numerous plants and herbs was edited by in medicine and pharmacy. In 1815 he left for the East, eventually reaching India where he became Stephan L. Endlicher (1804-1849) entitled *Serum Cabulicum enumeratio plantarum quas in itinere inter Dera - Ghazee - Khan et Cabul* (Vindobonae, 1836). He died in Kronstadt on 18 December 1869. ADtB, vol. 13, pp. 70-71; DtBE; DtBiInd (2); Embacher; Henze; Kornrumpf; NDB; ÖBL; Wininger; Wurzbach

Honigmann, Ernst, born 8 August 1892 at Breslau, Prussia, he received a Dr.phil. in 1920 from the Universität Breslau for *Historische Topographie von Nordsyrien im Altertum.* He was a librarian at the Preußische Staatsbibliothek, 1931-1933, and subsequently emigrated first to Belgium and then to France, before returning to Belgium after the war. His writings include *Die sieben Klimata und die πολεις επισημοι; eine Untersuchung zur Geschichte der Geographie und Astrologie im Altertum und Mittelalter* (1929), *Die Ostgrenze des Byzantinischen Reiches von 363 bis 1071 nach griechischen, arabischen, syrischen und armenischen Quellen* (1935), *Pierre l'Ibérian et les écrits du pseudo-Denys l'Aréopagite* (1952), and *Patristic studies* (1953). He died in Bruxelles on 30 July 1954. BioHbDtE; JahrDtB, 1931, 1933

Honigmann, John Joseph, born 7 June 1914 in Bronx, N.Y., he was since 1951 a professor of anthropology at the University of North Carolina and a research associate in the Institute for Research in Social Sciences. In 1952 he visited Pakistan to study the rural culture of West Pakistan, involving residence in three villages located in Sind, Punjab, and North West Frontier Provinces. His writings include *Ethnography and acculturation of the Fort Nelson Slave* (1946), *Information for Pakistan; report of research on intercultural communication through films* (1953), and *Three Pakistan villages* (1958).

He died in Chapel Hill, N.C., on 4 August 1977. AmM&WSc, 1973 S; AmM&WSc, 1976 P; ConAu, 1-4, new revision, 2; IntDcAn; WhAm, 7; WhoAm, 1976-1978

Honorat, Adrienne, born 20th cent., she received a doctorate in 1959 from the Université d'Alger for *Les innovations du décret du 20 mai 1955 relatif aux faillites et règlements judiciaires*. She was in 1960 an assistant at the Faculté de droit et des sciences économiques d'Alger. Throughout half a century she devoted herself entirely to the glory of collective procedures. She edited *L'application de la loi du 25 janvier 1985; bilan, actes du colloque, Sophia-Antipolis, 22 et 23 mars 1991* (1992). In 2000 she was honoured by *Procédures collectives et droit des affaires: morceaux choisis; mélanges en l'honneur d'Adrienne Honorat*. Note about the author; ZKO

Hony, Henry Charles, born in 1884 to a Wiltshire country clergyman, he was educated at Marlborough and Oxford where he was a scholar of Exeter College. He passed top into the Levant Service, studied simultaniously Turkish, Persian and Arabic under E. G. Browne at Cambridge University. He left London for Turkey via Marseille and arrived in Constantinople on Friday 5 Fenruary 1909. He served as vice-consul, dragoman and archivist at Constantinople and as vice-consul at Mosul (since 8 November 1911), and Beirut. During the first World War, he was an army interpreter in the Dardanelles and Mesopotamia; then retired, married and farmed in Wiltshire. He renewed his Turkish connections during the second World War, which led to his work as a lexicographer, producing the standard Turkish-English dictionary. It was recognized by the award of an Oxford D.C.L. He died in 1971. From his nephew's article "Fez and frock-coat; a very English consul in Ottoman Turkey," in *Asian affairs*, 15 (February 1984), pp. 65-76; Kornrumpf

van der **Hoog**, Pieter Henricus, born 17 August 1888 at s'Gravenhage, the Netherlands, he received a medical doctorate in 1922 from the Rijksuniversiteit te Leiden for *De bestrijding der geslachtsziekten*. He was in 1928 head of the Bacteriological Service of the Hijaz. His writings include *Pelgrims naar Mekka* (1935), *Ik, Ibn Sina* (1937), and *Rabbi Mozes Ben Maimon* (1938). Wie is dat, 1948, 1956

Hoogeweg, Hermann, born in 1857, he wrote on medieval archives and history, including *Die Schriften des Kölner Domscholasters, späteren Bischofs von Paderborn, Oliverus* (Tübingen, 1894), *Die Stifter und Klöster der Provins Pommern* (Stettin, 1924-25), and he edited *Inventare der nichtstaatlichen Archive im Kreise Alfeld* (Hannover, 1909). He died in 1930. NUC, pre-1956

Hooglund, Eric James, born 18 March 1944, he received a Ph.D. in 1975 from Johns Hopkins University, Baltimore, Md., for *The effects of the land reform program on rural Iran, 1962-1972*. He was a sometime profesor of political science at the University of California, Berkeley. His writings include *Land and revolution in Iran, 1960-1980* (1982), *Crossing the waters; Arabic speaking immigrants to the United States before 1940* (1987), *Twenty years of Islamic revolution; political and social transition in Iran since 1979* (2002), and he edited *Iran; the making of U.S. policy, 1977-1980* (Washington, D.C., National Security Archive, 1990). MESA Roster of members, 1982-1990

Hoogstraal, Harry, born 24 February 1917 at Chicago, he graduated in 1938 from the University of Illinois, and received doctorates in parasitology and medical zoology from the University of London in 1959 and 1971 respectively. He was a sometime head of the Department of Medical Zoology, U.S. Naval Medical Research Unit, Cairo, and a field associate in zoology, Chicago Natural History Museum. His writings include *Insects and their stories* (1941). AmM&WSc, 1973 P - 1992 P; Shavit

Hooker, Sir Joseph Dalton, born in 1817 at Halesworth, Suffolk, he was educated at Glasgow, and subsequently entered the Royal Navy's Medical Department. Apart form Antartica and North America, he visited the Himalayas, Syria, Palestine, and Morocco. His writings include *Journal of a tour in Morocco and the Great Atlas* (1878). He died in 1911. Buckland; DNB; Embacher; Henze; IndianBiInd (3); Master (19); Who was who, 1; WhWE

Hooker, Michael Barry, LL.M., he was a lecturer, Faculty of Law, University of Singapore. His writings include *A Sourcebook of adat, Chinese law and the history of common law in the Malayan Peninsula* (1967), *Readings in Malay adat laws* (1970), *Adat laws in modern Malaya* (1972), *The Personal laws of Malaysia* (1976), *Adat law in modern Indonesia* (1978), *Islamic law in South-East Asia* (1984), and he edited *Islam in South-East Asia* (1983). Note about the author; ZKO

Hooper, David, born in 1858 at Redhill, Surrey, he was educated at Chelmsford. In 1878, he was awarded the Herbarium Bronze Medal by the Pharmaceutical Society of Great Britain. In 1880, as a student at the Society's School, he qualified as a pharmaceutical chemist and distinguished himself by winning the Pereira Medal. In 1884, he was appointed quinologist to the Government of Madras, a post which he held until 1896. He subsequently served as curator of the Economic and Art Section of the Indian Museum until his retirement in 1914, when he returned to England. His last important task was the botanical investigation of native drugs and plants from south-western Asia. In 1907 he was awarded the Hanbury Gold Medal; in 1914, McMaster University, Hamilton, Ontario, conferred on him a LL.D. His writings include *Useful plants of Iran and Iraq* (1937). He died in Bromley, Kent, on 31 January 1947. Journal of the Chemical Society, February 1948, pp. 253-54; Riddick; WhE&EA; Who was who, 4

van **Hoorn**, Jan Willem, born 20th cent., he received a doctorate in 1960 from the Wageningen Agricultural Universiy (Landbouwuniversiteit) for *Grondwaterstroming in komgrond en de bepaling van enige hydrologische grootheden in verband met het ontwateringssysteem*. His writings include *Results of ground water level experimental field with arable crops on clay soil* (1958). Brinkman's, 1956-1960

Hooson, David John Mahler, born 25 April 1926 at Ruthin, Wales, he graduated from Oxford University and received his Ph.D. in 1955 from the University of London. He taught geography at universities in Scotland, Canada, and the United States. His writings include *The Soviet Union; people and regions* (1966), and *Geography and national identity* (1994). AmM&WSc, 1973 S; AmM&WSc, 1976 P; ConAu, 17-20

Hooton, Earnest Albert, born 20 November 1887 at Clemensville, Wisc., he grew up in a succession of small towns. After attending Appleton College in eastern Wisconsin and the University of Wisconsin as a student in classics, he left in 1910 for Oxford as a Rhodes scholar. There he ended up totally committed to anthropology. In 1913, after some negotiations, he settled for an instructorship in the Department of Anthropology at Harvard with the responsibility of covering the field of physical anthropology. And there he remained for the rest of his life. His writings include *The Ancient inhabitants of the Canary Islands* (1925), *The Indians of Pecas Pueblo* (1930), *Up from the ape* (1931), *Flesh of the wild ox* (1932), *Twilight of man* (1939), and *Why men behave like apes and vice versa*, or, *Body and behavior* (1940). He died in Cambridge, Mass., on 3 May 1954. American journal of physical anthropology, 56 (1981), pp. 431 34; ANB, Bloln, 3 (11), 4, 12, 13; CurBio, 1940, 1954; DAB; IntDcAn; Master (11); NatCAB, vol. 40, pp. 75-76; WhAm, 3

Hoover, Edgar Malone, born 22 February 1907 at Boise, Idaho, he studied at Harvard, where he also took all his degrees, include the Ph.D. in 1932. He taught economics in a great variety of capacities at American universities. His writings include *Location theory and the shoe and leather industries* (1937), *Economía geográfica* (México, 1943), *The Location of economic activity* (1948), *An Introduction to regional economics* (1971), *Spatial, regional and population economics* (1972), and he was a joint author of *Population growth and economic development in low-income countries* (1958). He died in 1992. AmM&WSc, 1973 S, 1978 S; ConAu, 13-16; LC; WhoAm, 1974, 1976

Hoover, Karl D., born 20th cent., he was in 1976 associated with Headquarters, Air Training Command, History and Research Office, Randolph Air Force Base, Tex. His writings include *Base closure; politics or national defense issue* (1989). LC; Note about the author

Hoover, Lyman, born about 1900, he studied at Yale University, New Haven, Conn., where he pursued special studies in Arabic and Islamic subjects. He maintained fairly direct contact with the Chinese community since he first went to China in 1930 as a Y.M.C.A. representative, a post which he still held in 1938. Note about the author

Hopen, Clarence Edward, born 11 September 1923 at Margo, Sask., he held research fellowships in social anthropology in Nigeria and Tanganyika from 1951 to 1959. In 1960 he obtained an M.A. from Columbia University, New York, and subsequently taught at the Department of Anthropology, University of Washington, Seattle. His writings include *The Pastoral Fulbe family in Gwandu* (1958). Unesco

Hopf, Carl, born 19th cent., his writings include *Die altorientalischen Teppiche; eine Studie über ihre Schönheitswerte* (Stuttgart, 1912), and *Die altpersischen Teppiche* (2nd ed., München, 1913). GV

Höpfner, Willi, born 20th cent., he was associated with Deutscher Evangelischer Missions-Rat, Frankfurt am Main. He edited *Der Islam als nachchristliche Religion* (1971), and he was a joint editor of *Muslime, unsere Nachbarn; Beiträge zum Gespräch über den Glauben* (1977). LC; Sezgin

Höpker, Wolfgang, born 8 February 1909 at Bromberg, Prussia, he studied political economy, sociology, and political geography, gaining a doctorate in 1934 at the Universität Jena for *Die Nationalwerdung des rumänischen Volkes, dargestellt an dem Spannungsverhältnis zwischen Altreich und Neureich*. He subsequently became a political editor with *Münchener Neueste Nachrichten*. Since 1958 he was a political commentator and correspondent at Bonn. Assignmets brought him to all parts of the globe. He wrote on the strategic importance of the oceans as well as the development of Africa. His writings include *Rumänien diesseits und jenseits der Karpathen* (1936), *Zwischen Ostsee und Ägäis* (1954), *Die Ostsee ein rotes Binnenmeer?* (1958), *Das Mittelmeer, ein Meer der Entscheidungen* (1961), *Wetterzone der Weltpolitik, der Indische Ozean* (1975), *Südafrika auf der Waage; ein Subkontinent zwischen Evolution und Revolution* (1978), *Aktionsfeld Pazifik* (1979), *Südatlantik,*

Machtvakuum der Weltpolitik (1983), and *Hundert Jahre Afrika und die Deutschen* (1984). He died in Bonn on 6 March 1989. DtBE; GV; *Wer ist wer*, 1979-1988/89

Hopkins, Clark, born 16 September in New York, he graduated in 1917 from Yale University, New Haven, Conn., and in 1921 went to Balliol College, Oxford, as a Rhodes scholar; he received his Ph.D. in 1924 from the University of Wisconsin. He was a Sterling Fellow at the American School of Classical Studies, Athens, and a senior Fulbright Fellow in Greece. He excavated in Syria, Mesopotamia and Libya, and subsequently taught English and classics at Yale and the University of Michigan, Ann Arbor. His writings include *Introduction to classical archeology: Crete and Greece* (1950). He died in Ann Arbor on 21 May 1976. Bioln, 8, 14; ConAu, 109, 129; DrAS, 1969 F, 1974 F; Master (3); NatCAB, 59, p. 175; Shavit

Hopkins, Garland Evans, born 28 December 1913 at Saluda, Va., he graduated in 1933 from Randolph-Macon College and subsequently studied law and theology before gaining an M.A. in international relations at the American University, Washington, D.C., in 1950. He served as a minister, deacon, and elder as well as in administrative and consulting capacities in a great variety of national and international organizations and societies. Since the second World War he established himself as a Church diplomat and persuasive lobbyist who fought for everything from labour peace to independence for Indonesia. In 1953, he served as executive vice-president of the American Friends of the Middle East. His writings include *Colonel Carrington of Cumberland* (1942), and he edited *The Mighty beginnings; sermons based on the Book of Genesis* (1956). WhoS&SW, 1959; *Christian century*, vol. 67 (26 April 1950), p. 517

Hopkins, Harry, born 26 March 1913 at Preston, Lancs., he was a graduate of Merton College, Oxford, and became a free-lance journalist and writer. He spent several yaers in Egypt. His writings include *New world arising; a journey of discovery through the new nations of South-East Asia* (1952), and *Egypt, the crucible* (1969). Au&Wr, 1971; ConAu, 29-32; IntAu&W, 1976-1982, 1991/92-1997/98; WhE&EA; WhoWor, 1976/77; WrDr, 1976/78-1994/96

Hopkins, Ian W. J., born 23 June 1941, he received a Ph.D. in 1969 from Oxford University for *The old city of Jerusalem; aspects of development of a religious centre*. His writings include *Jerusalem; a study in urban geography* (1970), *An Introduction to human geography* (1982), and he was a joint author of *Economics; a core text* (1995). LC; Sluglett

Hopkins, John Francis Price, born 14 December 1919, he received a Ph.D. in 1954 from the School of Oriental and African Studies, London, for *Early Islam in Barbary in relation to governmental activities*. His writings include *Medieval Muslim government in Barbary until the sixth century of the Hijra* (1958), its Arabic translation in 1980, *Arabic periodical literature* (1966), and *Corpus of early Arabic sources for West African history* (1981). LC; *SOAS Library catalogue*, ZKO

Hopkins, Lewis Egerton, born 21 January 1873 in England, he graduated from the Royal MIlitary College, Woolwich, and subsequently joined the Royal Engineers. Since 1894 he was employed on railways under the Government of India; and in 1899 he served with the Khyber Field Force. After his leave in England in 1903, he travelled overland to India through Turkey, Persia, Baluchistan and the Nushki route. Subsequently he was associated with the construction of the Nishpa Tunnel, and on the survey of the Makran Coast and Persian Baluchistan for the Trans-Persian Railway. He served in Persia from 1917 to 1919, and, with Eastern Bengal Railway, from 1920 to 1921 as chief engineer. His writings include *Nushki extension reconnaisance, 1918-19; a report* (1919), *Elementary politics of reform* (1935), and he was an editor of *Universal railway manual* (1911). He died on 7 January 1945. BritInd (1); IndianBiInd (1); WhoIndia, 1927; *Who was who*, 4

Hopkins, Nicolas Snowdon, born 20 February 1939 at Boston, Mass., he graduated in 1960 from Harvard and received a Ph.D. in 1967 from the University of Chicago for *Government in Kita; institutions and processes in a Malian town*. He taught anthropology at New York University from 1967 to 1975 and subsequently at the American University in Cairo until 1983. His writings include *Popular government in an African town; Kita, Mali* (1972), *Testour; ou, La transformation des champagnes maghrebines* (1983), *Agrarian transformation in Egypt* (1983), and he was a joint author of *Arab society in transition; a reader* (1977). ConAu, 77-80; *MESA Roster of memebers*, 1977-1990

Höpp, Gerhard, born 4 February 1942 at Berlin, he received a Dr.phil. in 1972 from the Universität Leipzig for a study of petty *bourgeoisie* in the Arab countries *Zur Rolle und Funktion kleinbürgerlicher Kräfte in den geistigen Auseinandersetzungen in den arabischen Ländern*. Since 1973 associated with the Akademie der Wissenschaften der DDR, he received a Dr.habil. in 1986, and specialized in the history of socialism in the Arab world. Since 1992 he was a member of the Centre for Modern Oriental Studies, Berlin-Nikolassee, concurrently lecturing in history of Islam in the early twentieth century

Germany. His writings include *Geistige Auseinander-setzung in Asien und Afrika* (1983). He died in Berlin on 7 December 2003. Kürschner, 1992-2003; Schwarz; *Tagesspiegel* (Berlin), 16 December 2003, p. 24

Hopp, Lajos, born 13 January 1927 at Zombor, Yugoslavia, he was a writer on Hungarian history and a member of the Hungarian Academy of Sciences. His writings include *A lengyel-magyar hagyományok újjászületése* (1972), *A Rákóczi-emigráció Lengyelországban* (1973), *A lengyel literatúra befogadása Magyarországon, 1780-1840* (1983), and *A fordító Mikes Kelemen* (2002). MagyarNKK, 1990-1996|; OSK

Hoppe, Ernst Max, born about 1900, he went in 1922 to Bulgaria as a missionary. During his stay there he began to translate the Koran into Bulgarian and succeeded in 1930. His trace is lost in 1935 at Sofia. Note about the author

Hoppe, Ralf, born in 1959, he studied social sciences at the Universität Göttingen. In 1985, he was an editor with the *Braunschweiger Zeitung*. His writings include *Volk ohne Raum; ein deutscher Sittenspiegel* (1999). Note about the author

Hopper, Bruce Campbell, born in 1892 at Lichfield, Illinois, he graduated in 1918 from Harvard, studied at the Sorbonne and Oxford and received a Ph.D. in 1930 from Harvard. He taught history and government at his alma mater until his retirement in 1961. He was a trustee, World Peace Foundation, and the recipient of American, French, and Moroccan decorations. His writings include *Pan-Sovietism* (1931). He died in 1973. NYT, 7 July 1973, p. 24, col. 4; WhAm, 6

Hopwood, Derek, born in 1933, he received a D.Phil. in 1964 from Oxford University for *A history of Russian activities in Syria in the nineteenth century*. A fellow of St Antony's College, he was a some-time director of the Middle East Centre, Oxford. He retired in 1998. He served as a president of BSMES, the Middle East Libraries Committee (UK), and represented U.K. on various Euro-Arab organizations. He was honoured with the award of O.B.E. in 1998. His writings include *The Russian presence in Syria and Palestine, 1843-1914* (1969), *The Arabian Peninsula* (1972), *British images of the Arab* (1980), *Egypt; politics and society, 1945-1981* (1982), *Syria, 1945-1986; politics and society* (1988), *Tales of Empire; the British in the Middle East, 1880-1952* (1989), and *Habib Bourguiba* (1992). EURAMES, 1993; Private; Sluglett

Horáček, Cyril, born 20 January 1896 at Prag, he was a professor, and sometime dean of the Faculty of Law, at Charles University. He died in Praha on 12 October 1990. Česky; Filipsky

Horálek, Karel, born 4 November 1908 at Rajhrad, Moravia, he studied at the University Brno and in 1947 became a professor of Slavic studies and folklore at Charles University, Praha. In 1950 he was appointed to the chair of Slavic languages and literatures. His writings include *Sborník slavistických prací* (1958), *Folklór a svetová literatura* (1979), *Studie o populární literature českého obrození* (1990), and he was a joint editor of *Les Relations entre l'Europe et l'Orient* (1969). He died in Praha on 26 August 1992. Česky; IES; MaláčEnc; Note about the author; OSK; PSN; WhoSocC 1978; WhoSocCE, 1989

Horeau, Hector, born 4 October 1801 at Versailles, he was an architect of chequered fortunes and left some forty projects, among them, *Panorama d'Égypte et de Nubie* (1841-1847) and *L'avenir du Caire au point de vue de l'édilité et de la civilisation* (1870). He died in Paris on 21 August 1872. DBF; Vapereau

Horelik, Arnold Lawrence, born 24 March 1928 at N.Y.C., he graduated *magna cum laude* in 1948 from Rutgers University, New Brunswick, N.J., and received an M.A. in 1950 from Harvard University. He became a political affairs analyst, specializing in the USSR and Eastern Europe, first with U.S. Government agencies and later with the RAND Corporation. His writings include *"Deterrent" and surprise attack in Soviet strategic thought* (1960), *The Cuban missile crisis* (1963), *Soviet policy dilemmas in Asia* (1976), *Soviet foreign policy under Gorbachev* (1986), *U.S.-Soviet relations; the next phase* (1986), *The West's response to Perestroika and post-Soviet Russia* (1995), and *Stopping the decline in U.S.-Russian relations* (1996). AmM&WSc, 1973 S; ConAu, 17-20, new rev., 8

Hörhager, Herbert, born about 1915, he received a Dr.phil. in 1944 from the Universität München for *Die Volktumsgrundlagen der indischen Nordwest-Grenzprovinz*. His writings include *Die deutsche Bundesrepublik* (1949). ZKO

von **Hörmann**, Albert, born 19th cent., he originated from Bregenz, Austria, and served from 1865 to 1867 as a *Rektor* of the Austrian hostel in Jerusalem. He was a writer on the Holy Land, who contributed to the journal *das Heilige Land* (Köln). His writings include *Gaza; Stadt, Umgebung und Geschichte* (Brixen, 1876). His trace is lost after an article in 1877. GV; Kornrumpf; Sezgin

Horn, Paul, according to the curriculum vitae in his thesis, he was born on 19 February 1863 at Halle where he was educated, first at the Latina of Franckesche Stiftungen, and later at the local Universität, receiving his Dr.phil. in 1885 for *Die Nominalflexion im Avesta und den altpersischen Keilinschriften* and gaining a Dr.habil. in 1889 at the Universität Straßburg. He became a lecturer in Indo-European literature at the Universität Straßburg. His writings include *Geschichte der persischen Literatur* (1901), *Grundriss der neupersischen Etymologie* (1893), *Das Heer- und Kriegswesen der Grossmoghuls* (1894), *Geschichte der türkischen Moderne* (1902), *Vom märk'schen Sand und türk'schen Land* (1903), *Die türkische Literatur* (1906), *Der Übermensch und anderes* (1909), and he edited *Asadī's neupersisches Wörterbuch Lughat-i Furs* (1897). He died in Straßburg on 11 November 1908. Enclran; KDtLK, 1897-1909; Kornrumpf; Schwarz; Thesis; *Wer ist's*, 1909

Horn, Siegfried Herbert, born 17 March 1908 at Wurzen, Saxony, he served from 1932 to 1940 as a missionary teacher in the Dutch East Indies, graduated in 1947 from the Seventh-Day Adventist Walla Walla College, College Place, Wash., and received a Ph.D. in 1951 from the University of Chicago. He subsequently served until his retirement in 1976 as a professor of archaeology and history of antiquity at Andrews University, Berrien Springs, Mich. His writings include *Entdeckungen zwischen Nil und Euphrat; erfolgreiche Ausgrabungen bestätigen die Bibel* (Zürich, 195-), *The Spate confirms the Book* (1957), *Mit dem Spaten an biblischen Stätten* (1971), and *Auf den Spuren alter Völker* (1979). In 1986 he was honoured by *The Archaeology of Jordan and other studies*. He died in 1993. ConAu, 37-40; DrAS, 1969 H, 1974 H, 1978 H, 1982 H; Master (1); WhoRel, 1975, 1977 [not sighted]; WrDr, 1976/78-1994/96

Hornaday, Mary, born 5 April 1906 at Washington, D.C., she was a journalist with the *Christian science monitor* from 1927 to 1945, when she became head of their West Coast Bureau. She travelled widely, and last visited Jordan in 1966. She died in 1982. BioIn, 13; Note about the author; WhoAmW, 1958/59, 1961/62, 1968/69, 1970/71

Hornblower, George Davis, born 19 September 1864 at London, he was a British civil servant with an interest in ancient Egypt. He died in Penzance, Cornwall, in 1951. Dawson; Egyptology

von **Hornborstel**, Erich Moritz, born 25 February 1877 at Wien, he grew up in a musical home frequented by musicians and composers. Despite interest in music, he studied science at the Universität Heidelberg, where he received a doctorate in chemistry. In 1900 he joined the Institute of Psychology at the Universität Berlin. In 1901 he changed to the newly established Berlin Phonogram Archive as an assistant. He then launched appeals to missionaries and travellers to provide him with barrel recordings of non-European music, which he then transcribed to sheet music and subsequently analysed; this was the beginning of ethnomusicology. In 1933 he emigrated first to Switzerland and then to the United States, where he was invited to teach at the New School of Social Research, New York. For reasons of health he moved to Britain, but for the same reason he had to decline an offer from Cambridge University in 1935. He died in Cambridge on 13 June 1935. He was a joint author of *Classification of musical instruments* (1961). Baker, 1978, 1982, 1992; BioHbDtE; DtBE; DtBilnd (6); Kürschner, 1925-1935; NDB; NewGrDM, 1980; ÖBL; *Wer ist's*, 1922-1935

Hornburg, Johann, born 19th cent., he received a doctorate and became a senior teacher at Kaiserliches Lyceum, Metz. He was associated with the Verein für Erdkunde zu Metz. His writings include *Die Composition des Beowulf* (Metz, 1877). Note about the author; NUC, pre-1956; Sezgin

Hornby, Arthur John Ward, born in 1893, he was educated at Edward's High School and Birmingham University, where he received a B.Sc. in 1914, and at Armstrong College, the University of Durham. From 1914 to 1918 he served with the R.A.F. Since 1921 he was an agricultural chemist in Nyasaland, becoming a director in 1934. In 1929 he was honoured with the award of M.B.E. His writings include *Tobacco culture; a comparison of methods adopted in the United States and in Nyasaland* (Zomba, 1926). BritInd (1); NUC, pre-1956

Horndasch, Georg, born in 1960, he studied geography, political economy and political science at the Universität Würzburg, made research visits to Syria and Qatar, and received a Dr.phil. in 1989 from the Universität Erlangen-Nürnberg for *Die wirtschaftliche Zukunft der petrochemischen Industrie in den Staaten des Golf-Kooperationsrats*, a work which was published in 1990. Note about the author; ZKO

Horne, Alistair Allan, born 9 November 1925 at London, he graduated from Jesus College, Cambridge, and became a journalist with the *Cambridge Daily News*. From 1952 to 1955 he was a correspondent to the *Daily Telegraph*, subsequently turning to free-lance writing. His writings include *Back into power; a report on the new Germany* (1955), *Canada and the Canadians* (1961), *The Price of glory; Verdun, 1916* (1962), *To lose a battle* (1969), its translation, *Über die Maas, über Schelde und Rhein* (1969), *A Savage war of peace; Algeria, 1954-62* (1977), its translation, *Histoire de la guerre d'Algérie* (1980), and *Seven ages of Paris* (2002). Au&Wr, 1963, 1971; ConAu, 5-8, new rev., 9; IntAu&W, 1976-1991; Who, 1970-2005; WhoWor, 1974/75, 1976/77; WrDr, 1971/73-2005

Horne, John, born 19th cent., he was an Englishman who lived for many years in the Near East and North Africa. His writings include *Many days in Morocco* (1925). His trace is lost after an article in 1929. Note about the author

Hornell, James born in 1865, he was educated in Scotland and at the University of Liverpool. He became one of the first marine biologists and fishery naturalists to be employed as such. His early experience was gained on a fisheries survey of the Channel Islands. In 1904 he was appointed marine biologist to the Government of Ceylon, and in 1908, director of fisheries, Government of Madras. His experience of the fisheries of warmer seas placed him in a unique position for many years. Later he urged the culture of fish in ponds and lagoons. In urging work of this sort, he produced a report on the conditions under which fish are farmed or cultured at Arcachon and Commachio, recommending similar action in India. His writings include *Report to the Government of Baroda on the marine zoology of Okhamandal in Kattiawar* (1909-16), *The Origins and ethnological significance of Indian boat designs* (1920), *The Boats of the Ganges; the fishing methods of the Ganges* (1924), and *Canoes of Oceania* (1936-38). He died in Hastings on 24 February 1949. IndianBilnd (1); *Nature* (London), 163 (7 May 1949), p. 714

Hornemann, Friedrich Conrad, born 15 September 1772, the son of a clergy, and, like his father, he also studied theology and natural sciences at the Universität Göttingen. With the recommendation of a local anthropologist, he travelled in 1797 to London to see Sir Joseph Banks and contact the Africa Association. In 1797 he set out for Cairo, where he joined in disguise a pilgrim caravan to Murzuq. His travel journal, *Friedrich Hornemanns Tagebuch seiner Reise von Cairo nach Murzuck*, he sent to Europe where it was published by Carl König in 1802, as well as the translations, *The Journal of Frederick Horneman's travels from Cairo to Mourzouk* (1802), and *Voyage de F. Hornemann dans l'Afrique septentrional depuis le Caire jusqu'à Mourzouk* (1803). On the route to Timbuctu he fixed the location of the Siwa and Aujila oases. He was the first European to cross and describe the Fezzan pilgrim route across the volcanic desert, *al-Haraj al-Aswad*. He returned by way of the Sudan. In 1800, he joined a caravan to Bornu. He reached Lake Chad and continued via Sokoto to the Niger River, where he died in Bokane in February of 1801. ADtB, vol. 13, pp. 149-50; DtBE; DtBilnd (4); Embacher; Henze; Master (2); NDB; WhWE

Horner, Leonard, born in 1785 at Edinburgh, he there received his education at a high school and the University. He became the most impressive and influential of the first English factory inspectors. From 1833 to 1859 he administered the Factory Act mainly in the textile district of Lancashire. A sometime president of the Geographical Society, he undertook the investigation of the alluvium deposited by the Nile. He died in London in 1864. Bioln, 8; Boase; Britlnd (4); Dawson; DNB; Egyptology; *International review of social history*, 14 iii (1969), pp. 412-13; Master (2)

Hornik, Marcel Paul, born about 1915, he received a Dr.phil. in 1938 from the Universität Wien for *Der Kampf der Großmächte um den Oberlauf des Nils*. His other writings include *Baron Holstein; studies in German diplomacy* (Vienna, 1948). NUC, 1956-67; Schwarz

Hornus, Jean Michel, born 20th cent., he received a doctorate in 1978 from the Université de Montpellier for *Le Mémoire sur les missions lazaristes et protestantes en Perse en 1854 du comte de Challaye*. THESAM, 4

Horon, Adolphe Gourevitch, fl. 20th cent., his writings include *L'Afrique et le Proche-Orient devant l'agression* (1959), and *Erets-ha-kedem* (Tel-Aviv, 1970). NUC

Horovitz, Jakob, born 30 April 1873 at Lauenburg, Pomerania, he studied philosophy, philology, and history at the universities of Marburg and Berlin, gaining a doctorate in 1899 for *Das platonische νοητον ζωον*; he later graduated from the Rabbinerseminar, Berlin. He became a prominent leader of the Frankfurt Jewish community. In 1929 he joined the Jewish Agency as a non-Zionist. Incarcerated at the Buchenwald concentration camp in 1938, he fled after his release to the Netherlands where he died from the effects of his arrest on 16 February 1939 in Arnheim. His writings include *Untersuchungen zur rabbinischen Lehre von den falschen Zeugen* (1914), and *Die Josephserzählung* (1921). BioHbDtE; DtBE; EncJud; JüdLex; Kürschner, 1925-1935

Horovitz (Χόροβιτς), Joseph, born 26 July 1874 at Lauenburg, Pomerania, he studied Oriental languages at the universities of Marburg and Berlin, where he received a Dr.phil. in 1898 for *De Wâqidii libro qui Kitâb al Magâzî inscribitur*, and a Dr.habil. in 1902. He subsequently visited Turkey, Syria, Palestine, and Egypt for the purpose of manuscript research. In 1907 he became a professor of Arabic at the Anglo-Oriental College, Aligarh, India. In 1915 he accepted an invitation to the chair of Semitic philology and Biblical literature at the Universität Frankfurt am Main, where he died on 5 February 1931. His writings include *Spuren griechischer Mimen im Orient* (1905), *Koranische Untersuchungen* (1926), *Indien unter britischer Flagge* (1928), and he edited *Epigraphica indo-*

moslemica (1907-1912).   DtBE;   DtBilnd (2);   EncJud;   Hanisch;   JüdLex;   Kürschner, 1925-1931;   Megali, vol. 24, p. 673;   NDB;   Schwarz;   *Wer ist's*, 1909-1928

Horovitz, Saul, born in 1859 at Szántó, Hungary, he was educated at Talmud schools in Poland and Hungary. Since 1880 he studied in Breslau at Jüdisch-Theologisches Seminar and the Universität, where he received a Dr.phil. in 1884. In the following year he became rabbi at Bielitz, Silesia, a post which he held for ten years until he became a lecturer in philosophy of religion and homiletics. Since 1917 he was a rabbinical tutor. His writings include *Die Psychologie bei den jüdischen Religionsphilosophen des Mittelalters* (1898-1912), *Der Mikrokosmos des Joef ibn Saddik* (1903), and *Über den Einfluß der griechischen Philosophie auf die Entwicklung des Kalam* (1909)   He died in 1921.   DtBE;   EncJud;   JewEnc;   JüdLex

Horowitz, David, born 15 February 1899 at Drohobycz, Galicia, he settled in Palestine in 1920. He became an economist, lecturer, politician, and a sometime Governor of the Bank of Israel. His writings include *Economic survey of Palestine, with special reference to the years 1936 and 1937* (1938), *Postwar reconstruction* (1943), *Hemispheres north and south; economic disparity among nations* (1966), *The Economics of Israel* (1967), and *The Enigma of economic growth* (1972). He died about 1979. IntAu&W, 1977;   IntWW, 1974/75-1978/79|;   WhoIsrael, 1949-1978;   WhoWor, 1974/75, 1976/77, 1978/79;   WhoWorJ, 1955, 1965, 1972, 1978

Horowitz, Michael M., born 2 November 1933 at N.Y.C., he graduated in 1955 from Oberlin, Ohio, College, and received a Ph.D. in 1959 from Columbia University, N.Y.C., for *Morne Payson; peasant community in Martinique*. In 1961 he was appointed a professor of anthropology at S.U.N.Y., Binghampton, a post which he held until his retirement. His writings include *Peoples and cultures of the Carribean; an anthropological reader* (1971).   AmM&WSc, 1973 S, 1978 S;   ConAu, 41-44, new rev., 15, 49;   NatFacDr, 1990-2002

Horrent, Jules Urbain, born 11 April 1920 at Seraing-sur-Meuse, he was a professor of Romance philology and literature at the Université de Liège and since 1965 held the chair of Romance languages and literatures. His writings include *La Chanson de Roland dans les littératures française et espagnole au moyen âge* (1951), *Roncesvalles* (1951), *Le pèlerinage de Charlemagne; essai d'explication littéraire* (1961), and *Cantar de mío Cid* (1982). He died in Malmedy on 11 September 1981.   BiBenelux² (1);   NBN, vol. 4, pp. 213-15;   *Who's who in Belgium and Luxemburg*, 1962

Horrocks, Sir Brian Gwynne, born in 1895, he graduated from the Royal MIlitary Collge, Sandhurst, and served during the second World War in the North African and Normandy campaigns as a general. After the war he embarked on a successful television career. He wrote his autobiography, *A Full life* (1960). He died in 1985. Philip Warner wrote *Horrocks, the general who led from the front* (1984). AnObit, 1985, pp. 27-29;   BioIn, 5, 11, 14 (2),   BlueB, 1973-1976;   ConAu, 114;   CurBio, 1945. 1985;   DNB;   IntAu&W, 1982;   IntWW, 1974-1985;   Who, 1959-1985;   WhoWor, 1974/75, 1976/77, 1978/79;   Who was who, 8

Horsfield, Agnes Ethel, née Conway, born in 1885 at London, she graduated from Newnham College, Cambridge, received her M.A. from the University of London, and her Litt.D. from the University of Dublin. She was an archaeologist who worked with her husband, G. Horsfield, a director of Antiquities, on archaeological excavations in the Near East, particularly in Transjordan. Her writings include *A Ride through the Balkans* (1917).   Lady's who's who, 1938/39;   WhE&EA

Horsman, Edward Imeson, born 10 March 1873 at Brooklyn, New York, he was an organist and choirmaster at New York churches and a sometime music and drama critic with the *New York herald*. He died in 1918. NatCAB, vol. 3, p. 274;   *Who's who in N.Y.C. and State*, 3 (1907)

Horst, Georg Conrad, born 26 June 1767 or 69 at Lindheim, Hesse, he studied theology and Oriental languages at the Universität Gießen and subsequently succeeded to his fathers pastorate, a post which he resigned in 1819. From then on he devoted himself to scholarly work, obtaining a doctorate in 1824 from the Faculty of Theology at Gießen. His writings include *Geschichte des letztern Schwedisch-Russischen Krieges* (1793), *Die Visonen Habakuks neu übersetzt mit historischen und exege-tisch-kritischen Anmerkungen* (1798), *Religion und Christenthum* (1809), and *Zauber-Bibliothek; oder von Zauberei, Theurgie und Mantik, Zauberern, Hexen und Hexenprocessen, Dämonen, Gespenstern und Geistererscheinungen* (1821-1826). He died in Lindheim on 20 January 1832. DtBilnd (5)

Horst, Heribert, born 7 September 1925, he received a Dr.phil. in 1951 from the Universität Bonn for a study of authorities in al-Tabari's Koranic commentary entitled *Die Gewährsmänner im Koran-Kommentar des Tabari; ein Beitrag zur exegetischen Überlieferung im Islam*, and a Dr.habil. in 1962 from the Universität Mainz for *Die Staatsverwaltung der Groß-Selgūken und H̲ōrazmšāhs, 1083-1231; eine Untersuchung nach Urkundenformularen der Zeit*. He was a professor of Persian at the Universität Mainz from 1963 to his retirement. Kürschner, 1987-2005

Horstmann, Julius Hermann Edward, Rev., born in 1869, he was associated with the Evangelical and Reformed Church. His writings include *Faithful unto death* (St. Louis, Mo., 1903), and *Through four centuries; story of the beginnings of the Evangelical and Reformed Church* (St. Louis, Mo., 1938). NUC, pre-1956

Horten, Max Joseph Heinrich, born 7 May 1874 at Elberfeld, Prussia, he studied theology, philosophy and Oriental languages at Fribourg, Switzerland, from 1893 to 1898, and subsequently spent two years in Jerusalem, Beirut and Egypt. He received doctorates in theology from the Dominican College, Jerusalem, and in scholastic philosophy from the Jesuit University, Beirut, where he was a student of Louis Cheikho. From 1900 to 1904 he studied Oriental lnaguages and philosophy at the Universität Bonn, where he received a Dr.phil. in 1904 for *Buch der Ringsteine Alfārābis neu bearbeitet und mit Auszügen aus dem Kommentar des Amīr Isma'il el Fārānī erläutert*, later also there gaining a Dr.habil. in Semitic languages and Islamic studies as well as an appointment as professor. From 1929 to 1935, he served as a librarian at the Staats- und Universitätsbiliothek Breslau, returning to Bonn after his retirement. Well-versed in scholastics, he endeavoured to popularize Islamic philosophy by translations from inadequate editions. His writings include *Die philosophischen Probleme der spekulativen Theologie im Islam* (1910), *Die spekulative und positive Theologie des Islams nach Razi* (1912), *Die Philosophie der Erleuchtung nach Suhrawardi* (1912), *Die Metaphysik des Averroes* (1912), *Die kulturelle Entwicklungsfähigkeit des Islam auf geistigem Gebiete* (1915), *Kleine türkische Sprachlehre* (1916), *Die religiöse Gedankenwelt der gebildeten Muslime im heutigen Islam* (1916), *Die religiöse Gedankenwelt des Volkes im heutigen Islam* (1917-18), *Die Philosophie des Islam in ihren Beziehungen zu den philosophischen Weltanschauungen des westlichen Orients* (1924), a survey which did not find general appreciation, *Indische Strömungen in der islamischen Mystik* (1927-28), and *Der Islam in seinem mystisch-religiösen Erleben* (1928). He spent the last years of the war at Dietingen on Neckar, where he died on 2 July 1945. Bonner, vol. 8, pp. 327-29; Fück, p. 322; Hanisch; JahrDtB, 1931-35; Kosch; Kürschner, 1925-1940/41; *Wer ist's*, 1912-1935

Horváth, Anna, born 20th cent., her writings include *Az európai szocialista orszagok törvényhozás* (Budapest, 1966), and *A társadalmi tulajdont sértő cselekmények bíróságon kivüli elbbírálása azóegyes európai szocialista országokban* (Budapest, 1969). OSK

Horváth, Jenő, born 16 November 1881 at Gyula, Hungary, he was a professor of history whose writings include *Magyar diplomácia, 1815-1918* (1928), *The Banat* (1931), *Transylvania and the history of the Rumanians* (1935), *Magyar diplomácia, magyar diplomaták* (1941), *Die Geschichte Siebenbürgens* (1943), and *Die kleine Entente* (1943). He died in Budapest on 20 January 1950. MEL

Horváth, Róbert Aurél, born 1 July 1916 at Győr, Hungary, he was a statistician and political economist who had studied at Szeged, Berlin, and Paris. His writings include *Laky Dezső, az egyetemi tanár* (Szeged, 1992), and *L'histoire de la pensée démographique hongroise de ses dóbuts jusqu'à l'avènement de la période de la statistique officielle* (Budapest, 1984). In 1986 he was honoured by *Studia in honorem Roberti Horváth septuagenarii*. MagyarNKK, 1990-1994; OSK

Horwood, Thomas Berridge, born 3 January 1888 at Somerton, Oxfordshire, he grew up in South Africa and graduated from Maritzburg College, Pietermaritzburg, Natal, and also from Oxford University. He entered the Indian Civil Service in 1910, arriving in India on 25 November 1911. He served in the United Provinces as an assistant magistrate and controller. He went to Natal for health reasons in 1920. In 1923 he was admitted as an advocate in the Natal Supreme Court. He was a joint author of *Voet's commentaries* (Cape Town, 1928), and *The Sale of goods in South Africa* (Cape Town, 1935). He died in Durban on 19 November 1938. DSAB, vol. 5; IndianBilnd (1)

Hoshangjī Jamaspjī Asa, born 26 April 1833 to a family of renowned Zoroastrian priests, he received a liberal education, on account of which he entered public service in British India. Through his service to the Government of India during the Mutiny, he made the acquaintance of Dr. Martin Haug, with whose assistance he studied Western languages. His scholarship received first recognition when he was appointed a professor of Persian at Deccan College. His writings include *An Old Zand-Pahlavi glossary* (1867), *An Old Pahlavi-Pazand glossary* (1870), and *Vendidad; Avesta text with Pahlavi translation and commentary* (1907). He was the recipient of numerous honours, a Fellow of Bombay University, First Class Sardar of the Deccan, Companion of the Order of the British Empire, and he was granted an honorary doctorate by the Universität Wien. He died on 23 April 1908. IndianBilnd (1); Note about the author

Hoskins, Halford Lancaster, born in 1891 near Carmel, Ind., he graduated in 1913 from Earlham College, Richmond, Ind., and received a Ph.D. in 1924 from the University of Pennsylvania for *British routes to India*. He was a professor of history and diplomacy at Middle West, and East Coast universities until 1949, when he started a fifteen-year service with the Library of Congress as a senior specialist in international relations in its Legislative Reference Service. As a director of the Middle East Institute, he was instrumental in 1946 in launching the *Middle East journal*. His writings include *European imperialism in Africa* (1930), *The Atlantic Pact* (1949), *Middle East oil in United States foreign policy* (1950), and *The Middle East, problem area in world politics* (1954). He died in 1967. IndAu, 1967; Master (2); NYT, 15 September 1967, p. 47, col. 3; WhAm, 4; WhE&EA

Hoskins, Harold Boies, born 19 May 1895 at Beirut; he was a Middle East expert, educator, and business executive. He died in 1977. NYT, 25 April 1977, p. 34 (not sighted)

Hosotte-Reynaud, Manon, fl. 1953-1960, her writings include *Publications de l'Institut des hautes études marocaines, 1936-1954; tables et répertoires* (Limoges, 1956). BN; NUC, pre-1956

Hospers, Johannes Hendrik, born 5 February 1921 at Eindhoven, Netherlands, he received a doctorate in 1947 from the Rijksuniversiteit te Utrecht for *De numeruswisseling in het boek Deuteronomium*. He was successively a professor of Semitic languages at the universities of Utrecht and Groningen. His writings include *Studia Semitica Neerlandica* (1973-74), and he was a joint author of *Gilgames, de elfde zang; de zondvloed en het levenskruid* (1985). Brinkman's; Wie is wie, 1984-1988

Hoßfeld, Paul, born 20th cent, he was associated with Albert-Magnus-Institut, Bonn. His writings include *Absolutheit des Christentums: ja oder nein?* (1964), *Die Jahrhunderte der Menschheit und ihr Philosophieren* (1969), *Pragmatismus mit dogmatischem Rückhalt* (1971), *Moses, Zarathustra, Buddha, Jesus, Mani, Mohammed; die großen Religionsstifter heute gesehen* (1974), and *Albertus Magnus als Naturphilosoph und Naturwissenschaftler* (1983). Note; NUC; ZKO

Høst, Georg (baptized Jørgen) Hjersing, born 8 April 1734 at Vitten, he studied theology at Århus, where he obtained a degree in theology in 1755. In 1760 he became associated with the Dansk-Afrikanske Kompagni as an assistant in Morocco. He there learned Arabic and was nominated vice-consul at Mogador. He later served as a secretary at St. Thomas in the Danish West Indies. His writings include *Efterretninger om Marókos og Fes, samlede der i Landenefra 1760 til 1768* (1779), its translation, *Nachrichten von Maroko und Fez* (1781), and *Den Marokanske Kajser Ben Abdallahs Historie* (1791). He died in København on 22 April 1794. DanskBL; DanskBL²; Sezgin

Hostachy, Victor, born 3 May 1885 at Saint-Firmin-en-Valgodemard (Hautes-Alpes), he was educated at the nearby École apostolique of La Salette and on 21 June 1901 entered the order of the Salésiens. In 1903 he left France and went to Roma where he studied at the Pontificia Università Gregoriana, taking a degree in theology and a doctorate in philosophy. Ordained in 1910, he was sent to the École apostolique of Tournai, Belgium, where he spent twenty years successively as professor, director of the *scolasticat*, and finally as superior, before becoming in 1931 superior of pilgrimage, Nôtre Dame de l'Hermitage in Loire, followed by superior of the École salettine of Suisse romande at Fribourg, 1938. In 1945 he became a permanent secretary of the Académie delphinale, which was a full-time position. For over forty years he was in charge of the *Bulletin des missionaires de La* Salette. His writings include *Les Missionaires de la Salette* (1930), *Les Indes et ses dieux-animaux* (1942). He died in La Tronche (Isère) on 26 January 1967. DBF

Hostelet, Georges, born 1 April 1875 at Chimay (Hainaut), Belgium, he graduated from Athénée, Chimay, and successively studied at the École militaire and the École d'application artillerie-génie. He subsequently went for study to Britain, returning to take a doctorate in physical chemistry at the Université de Liège in 1905. During the first World War he was implicated in the Edith Cavell affair and sentenced to hard labour in Germany until 1917. Having also been interested for a long time in the social sciences, he joined in 1919 the Institut de sociologie Solvay, Bruxelles. In 1924 he accompanied the Belgian Hellenist scholar Grégoire to establish social science teaching at the Faculty of Letters of the Eyptian University, Cairo. Soon after his return to Belgium in 1931 he began to teach public finance and Congo finances at the Université coloniale, Anvers, a post which he held until his retirement in 1947. His writings include *L'Œuvre civilisatrice de la Belgique au Congo de 1885 à 1953* (1954), *Comment atténuer le conflit scolaire* (1955), *Le Problème politique capital au Congo et en Afrique noire* (1959), and *L'Investigation scientifique des faits d'activité humaine avec application aux sciences et aux techniques sociales* (1960). He died on 4 November 1960. BiBelgeOM, 8 (1968), cols. 509-511

Hosten, Henry, Rev., born in 1873, his writings include *Jesuit missionaries in northern India and inscriptions on their tombs, Agra, 1580-1803* (Calcutta, Catholic Orphan Press, 1907), *Antiquities from San Thomé and Mylapore* (1936), and he edited *Mongoliæ legationis commentarius; or, the first Jesuit mission to Akbar* (Calcutta, 1914). BLC; NUC; ZKO

Hostler, Charles Warren, born 12 December 1919 at Chicago, he graduated from the University of California at Los Angeles, received his M.A. in 1955 from the American University of Beirut, and his

Ph.D. in 1956 from Georgetown University, Washington, D.C. He was a business executive, university professor, banker, colonel in the U.S. Air Force, and from 1989 to 1993 served as ambassodar to Bahrain. His writings include *Turkism and the Soviets; the Turks of the world and their political objectives* (1957), its translation, *Türken und Sowjets* (1960), and *The Turks of Central Asia* (1993). AmM&WSc, 1973 S; Au&Wr, 1963; BlueB, 1976; ConAu, 21-24; WhoAm, 1976-2003; WhoAmP, 1990/91-2003/2004; WhoGov, 1975, 1977 [not sighted]; WhoWor, 1993/94

Hottes, Karl Heinz, born 2 May 1925 at Köln, he received a Dr.phil. in 1952 from the Universität Köln for *Die zentralen Orte im Oberbergischen Land*. He was a lecturer at the Universität Gießen before he was appointed in 1966 a professor of economic geography at the Ruhr-Universität Bochum. He was a visiting professor at Kabul in 1975, and at Hyderabad, India, in 1979. His writings include *Ausländische Arbeitnehmer im Ruhrgebiet* (1977), *Entwicklungseffekte durch Verkehrserschließung in der Arabischen Republik Jemen* (1984), and he was a joint author of *Die Flurbereiningung als Instrument aktiver Landschaftspflege* (1974). He died on 1 February 2001. Kürschner, 1976-2001

Hottinger, Arnold J. C., born 6 December 1926 at Basel, he studied Romance, and later Oriental, subjects at Basel, Zürich, Paris and Chicago, and received a Dr.phil. in 1951 from the Universität Zürich for *Das volkstümliche Element in der modernen spanischen Lyrik*, a thesis which won him the *Hauptpreis* from Philosophische Fakultät, Zürich. He received a second Dr.phil. in 1958 from the same university for *Kalila und Dimna; ein Versuch zur Darstellung der arabisch-altspanischen Übersetzungskunst*. He became a commentator at the Swiss Radio and a correspondent to *Neue Zürcher Zeitung*, working at Beirut since 1955, Madrid since 1968, and Nicosia since 1982. His writings include *Die Araber* (1960), *Fellachen und Funktionäre* (1967), *10 mal Nahost* (1970), and *Islam in world politics* (1980). IntAu&W, 1977; Note; Schwarz

Hottinger, Johann Heinrich, born in 1620 at Zürich, he studied theology at Zürich, Genève, Groningen, and Leiden, where he was a student of the Arabist Jacobus Golius. He also took lessons from an Oriental Jew and a Turk. Obliged to decline an offer as preacher at the embassy of the Staten Generaal at Constantinople on the remonstrance of his Zürich authorities, he returned by way of England and France to Zürich, where he became in 1642 a professor of Church history, Oriental languages, rhetoric, and Old Testament theology. In 1655 the Elector of the Palatinate invited him to reestablish the theological faculty at the Universität Heidelberg and serve as a professor of Old Testament and Oriental languages. After the termination of the leave granted by his authorities, he returned to Zürich in 1661 to his former post. He was the first scholar to be interested in Arabic bibliography and literary history. His *Promtuarium sive Bibliotheca orientalis exhibens catalogum* (Heidelberg, 1658), contains a long chapter, *de bibliotheca arabica*, which enumerates Arabic works of Christian, Jewish, Samaritan, and Muslim authors. He lists many quotations in the original Arabic with Latin translation, and supplies an index of abbreviations of reciters of the Koran from a Basel manuscript of the Koran. The appendix includes a short list of manuscripts, including a repertory of 261 Arabic MSS from El Escorial. His other writings include *Historia orientalis* (1651), and *Historia ecclesiasticae* (1651-67). After declining invitations from the universities of Deventer, Marburg, Amsterdam, and Bremen, he accepted, with the approval of his authorities, a call from the Universiteit te Leiden. Before departure, while visiting his estate by boat, he and his three children drowned in the Limmat on 5 June 1667. Heinrich Steiner wrote *Der Zürcher Professor Heinrich Hottinger in Heidelberg, 1655-1661* (Zürich, 1886). DtBE; Fück, pp. 91-92; HisBioLexCH; Hofer; LuthC 75; Master (2)

Hotz, Robert, S.J., born in 1935 and officiating at Zürich. His writings include *Russland, Land der Dulder* (1962), *Allein der Wahrheit verpflichtet* (1972), *Sie kämpften für die Heimat* (1972), *Sie kämpften für ihre Freiheit* (1972), *Johannes XXIII., ein unbequemer Optimist* (1978), *Sakramente - im Wechselspiel zwischen Ost und West* (1979), and *Gebete aus der Orthodoxen Kirche* (1982). LC; ZKO

Houben, Joannes Josephus Antoon Maria, born 26 December 1904 at Valkenburg, Netherlands, he entered the Society of Jesus in 1924, and studied at the Jesuit Faculty of Philosophy, Nijmegen, and the Faculty of Theology, Maastrich. He was ordained in 1937. He spent the years from 1942 to 1946 in Great Britain, where he received a Ph.D. in 1951 from the University of London for *Supranaturalistic tendencies of Islamic theological thought*. He was successively a professor of Islamic subjects at the universities of Maastrich and Nijmegen. His writings include *De Koran als het woord van God* (1953), *De Oosterse mens* (1961), and he edited *Kitāb al-majmū' fi'l-muhīt bi'Itaklīf*, of Abu'l-Hassan 'Abd al-Jabbar (1965). Sluglett; *Wie is dat*, 1956

Houdas, Octave Victor, born 1 October 1840 at Outarville (Loiret), he grew up in North Africa and studied at Alger and Marseille. From 1860 to 1979 he was successively an interpreter and teacher of Arabic in Algeria. After five years as a colonial administrator, he was in 1884 appointed to the chair of colloquial Arabic at the École des langues orientales, Paris. Since 1892 he taught in concurrently Islamic law at the École libre des sciences politiques, becoming in 1895 inspector general of the

Algerian *medersas.* In 1905 he was commissioned to reform the Koranic schools in French West Africa. His writings include *Mission scientifique en Tunisie* (1882-84), *Ethnographie de l'Algérie* (1886), *Chrestomathie maghrébine* (1891), *L'Islamisme* (1904), and he jointly translated with William Marçais *Les Traditions islamiques* (1903-14) as well as classical Arabic textes. He died in Paris on 16 December 1916. DBF; *Hommes et dstins,* vol. 1, pp. 289-93

Houel, Guy Herbert Henry, born in 1914, he received a medical doctorate in 1938 from the Université de Bordeaux for *Les Cortico-surrénalomes; étude anatomo-clinique.* He was in 1951 chief medical officer with the Services de prophylaxie du Maroc, Institut d'hygiène, Rabat. His writings include *La Lutte antipaludique dans les zones rizicoles du Maroc* (Rabat, 1955). BN; Note; NUC, pre-1956

Hough, WIliam, born 1884, he graduated from Hulme Grammar School, Manchester, and entered the Levant Consular Service as a student interpreter in 1904. He served as a consul in the Ottoman Empire and Egypt until 1940, when he became British Commercial Agent at Jerusalem. In 1935 he received the Silver Jubilee Medal. He retired from the Foreign Service in 1944 and died in 1962. Kornrumpf; *Who's who,* 1932-1962; *Who was who,* 6

Houghton, John, born in 1640, he was a London dealer in tea, coffee, chocolate, and other luxuries, who, for a time, studied at Corpus Christi College, Cambridge, and became a fellow of the Royal Society of London. He died in London in 1705. BLC; DNB

Houille, René, born 20th cent., he received a doctorate in 1937 from the Université de Paris for *La politique monétaire de la Turquie depuis 1929.* NUC

Houis, Maurice Pierre, born 1 March 1923 at Saint-Nazaire (Loire-Atlantique), France, he was associated with the Institut français d'Afrique noire, Dakar. He was an anthropologist who received a doctorate in 1963 from the Université de Paris for *Les noms individuels chez les Mosi.* His writings include *La Guinée française* (1953), *Étude descriptive de la langue susu* (1963), *Anthropologie linguistique de l'Afrique noire* (1971), and *Intégration des langues africaines dans une politique d'enseignement* (1978). Unesco

Houminer, Ehud, born 20th cent. at Jerusalem, he was educated at the Hebrew University, Jerusalem, and the University of Pennsylvania. He was a sometime professor at the Graduate School of Business Administration, Columbia University, New York. Master (1); St&PR, 1991-2004

Hourani, Albert Habib, born 31 March 1915 at Manchester, he grew up in a Christian Lebanese home, where Arabic was spoken. He was educated at Oxford University, where he obtained a degree in 1936. He then had his first concentrated experience of life and work in the Middle East beginning as an instructor at the American University of Beirut, followed by war-time employment as a researcher and analyst by Chatham House and the British Middle East Office, Cairo, and finally post-war assistance to the Arab offices set up to present the Palestinian case to the international community. He returned to Oxford in 1948 as a Research Fellow of Magdalen College, and first university lecturer in the modern history of the Middle East. In 1958 he moved to St. Antony's College, Oxford, as director of its newly established Middle East Centre, staying there until his retirement in 1980. His writings include *Minorities in the Arab world* (1947), *Arabic thought in the liberal age* (1962), *Europe and the Middle East* (1980), *The Emergence of the modern Middle East* (1981, and *A History of the Arab peoples* (1991), and its translation, *Die Geschichte der arabischen Völker* (1992). He died in Oxford on 17 January 1993. Abdulaziz A. al-Sudairi wrote *A Vision of the Middle East; an intellectual biography of Albert Hourani* (1999). ConAu, 140; IJMES, 25 (1993), pp. i-iv; *Index Islamicus* (13); MES, 29 (1993), pp. 370-72; *Monde arabe dans la recherche scientifique,* 1 (1993), pp. 11-13

Hourani, Cecil Amin, born 6 April 1917 at Manchester, a younger brother of Albert Habib Hourani, he graduated from Magdelen College, Oxford. From 1946 to 1947 he served as a secretary of the Arab Office in Washington, D.C. He subsequently was a sometime professor of political science at the American University of Beirut, and an adviser to the Tunisian president Bourguiba. His writings include *Jerusalem and the world; a case of conscience* (1971), *The Arab cultural scene* (1982), and *An Unfinished odyssey; Lebanon and beyond* (1984). ConAu, 129; Note; ZKO

Hourani, George Fadlo, born 3 June 1913 at Manchester, he graduated in 1936 from Oxford University and received his Ph.D. in 1939 from Princeton University for his thesis *Arab navigation in the Indian Ocean in the ninth and tenth centuries.* After serving at a variety of posts, including several in the Middle East, he was at the Department of Near Eastern Studies, University of Michigan, from 1950 until 1967, when he accepted a position at SUNY, Buffalo, N.Y., where he remained until his retirement in 1983. At the close of his teaching career the latter institution made him a distinguished professor emeritus of Islamic culture and thought. His writings include *Averroes on the harmony of religion and philosophy* (1961), *Islamic rationalism* (1971), and *Essays on Islamic philosophy and science* (1975).

In 1984 he was honoured by *Islamic theology and philosophy; studies in honor of George F. Hourani.* He died on 19 September 1984. Bioln, 14 (2); ConAu, 45-48, 129, new rev., 23; DrAS, 1969 P, 1974 P, 1978 P, 1982 P; *Index Islamicus* (3); *Who's who in Asian studies,* 1975-1977; *Who's who in the Arab world,* 1967-1981

Hourcade, Bernard, born 17 March 1946 at Pau (Pyrénées-Atlantiques), he studied at Bordeaux and Paris, where he received a doctorate in 1975 for *La Haute vallée du Djadj-e Roud (Elbourz central, Iran); étude de géographie humaine.* In 1979, he became a director of the Institut français de recherche en Iran. In 1985, he succeeded to Ch. H. de Fouchécour as a director of *Abstracta iranica,* a journal to which he himself contributed regularly. As a geographer his early work centered on the Pyréneés, later turning towards the rural central Alborz Mountains and the social geography of Tehran, where he had resided for many years. His writings include *La Vie rurale en Haut-Ossau* (1970), and he was a joint author of *L'Iran au XXe siècle* (1996), and *Atlas d'Iran* (2002). AnEIFr, 1997; EURAMES, 1993; Private; THESAM, 4

Hours, Francis, born 20th cent., his writings include *Atlas des sites du Proche-Orient* (1994), he edited *Ta'rīkh Bayrūt,* from the Arabic of Sālih ibn Yahyá (1969), and he was a joint editor of *Chronologies du Proche-Orient* (1987), and *The Hammer on the rock* (1989). ZKO

Houry, Charles Borromée, born about 1800, his writings include *Du Droit des gouvernements sur l'instruction publique et du monopole de l'enseignement dans les Pays-Bas* (Bruxelles, 1829), *De l'Intervention européenne en Orient et de son influence sur la civilisation des Musulmans et sur la condition des Chrétiens d'Asie* (Paris, 1840), *De la Syrie considérée sous le rapport commercial* (Paris, 1842), *Plan de colonisation des contrées incultes de la Belgique* (Bruxelles, 1848), and *Coup d'œil sur l'état du commerce dans les États de l'Afrique septentrionale* (Arlon, 1850). BN

House, John Henry, born 29 May 1845 at Painesville, Ohio, he graduated in 1868 from Adelbert College, Western Reserve University, and later from Union Theological Seminary, New York. In 1872, he went as a Congregational missionary to Bulgaria and endeavoured to help the poverty-stricken people by giving them a scientific knowledge of agriculture. It was not until 1878 that he was able to secure a tract of desert land near Saloniki and opened the Thessalonica Agricultural and Industrial Institute, later known as the American Farm School. He and his wife spent sixty-four years in the Balkans, first at Samokov, Bulgaria, later at Constantinople and finally Saloniki. His his wife, Adeline Susan Beers, wrote *A Life for the Balkans; the story of John Henry House of the American Farm School, Thessaloniki,* as told by his wife (1939). He died at the Farm School on 19 April 1936. NatCAB, vol. 26, p. 329; WhAm, 1; WhoAm, 1908/9-1920/21

Housego, Jenny, born 20th cent., she was a founding member of the Tehran Rug Club, and an honorary secretary to the Oriental Rug and Textile Society, Great Britain. Her writings include *Tribal rugs; an introduction to the weaving of the tribes of Iran* (1978), and its translation, *Nomadenteppiche; eine Einführung in die Web- und Knüpfkunst der Stämme des Iran* (1984). Note; ZKO

Householder, Fred Walter, born in 1913 at Wichita Falls, Tex., he graduated in 1932 from the University of Vermont, and received a Ph.D. in 1941 from Columbia University, New York, for *Literary quotation and allusion in Lucian.* Since 1948, he taught classics and linguistics at Indiana University, Bloomington. His writings include *English for Greeks* (1954), *Problems of lexicography* (1962), *Basic course in Azerbaijani* (1965), *Linguistic speculations* (1971), *Greek; a survey of recent works* (1972), *The Syntax of Apollonius Dyscolus* (1981), and he was a joint author of *The Knossos tablets* (1959). DrAS, 1974 H, 1978 H, 1982 H; IndAu, 1967-1980

Houssay, Frédéric, born in 1859 at Lyon, he was accepted in 1879 simultaneously to the École normale supérieure and École polytechnique, opting for the former. After graduation he remained at E.N.S. as a *agrégé-préparateur.* In 1884 he received a doctorate in natural sciences for *Recherches sur l'opercule et les glandes du pied des gastéropodes.* After spending two years in Persia with the Mission Marcel Dieulafoy, he was appointed in 1886 *maître de conférences* in zoology at the Faculté des sciences de Lyon. Two years later, he was nominated to the identical post at the École normale supérieure, and in 1904 he was appointed a professor at the Sorbonne. His writings include *Les Races humaines de la Perse* (1887). He died in Lyon in 1920. DBF; IndexFr² (2)

Houssel, Jean Pierre, born 1934, he edited *Roanne et son arrondissement* (1984), and he was a joint editor of *Histoire des paysans français du XVIIIe à nos jours* (1958). LC

Houston, James Mackintosh, born 21 November 1922 at Edinburgh, he studied at the local University as well as at Hertford College, Oxford, where he became a fellow and bursar of his College in 1949. He was a townplanner whose writings include *A Social geography of Europe* (1953), and *The Western Mediterranean world; an introduction to its regional landscapes* (1964). Au&Wr, 1963, 1971; ConAu, 13-16

Houth, Émile, born in 1893, he was an editor at the Archives départementales, Seine-et-Oise, and associated with the Société historique de Pontoise et du Vexin. He edited *Recueil des chartes de Saint-Nicaise de Meulan, prieuré de l'Ordre du Bec* (Paris, 1924), and *Répertoire numérique de la série V (cultes) aux Archives départementales* (Corbeil, 1942). NUC, pre-1956

Houtum Schindler, Albert, 1846-1916 *see* Schindler, Sir Albert Houtum

Houtsma, Martijn Theodor, born 15 January 1851 at Irnsum, Friesland, the Netherlands, he studied Oriental languages at the Rijksuniversiteit te Leiden, where he received a doctorate in 1875 for *De strijd over het dogma in den Islâm tot op el-Askari*. He subsequently joined the Warneriaansch Legaat at the Leiden university library as an assistant in Oriental languages. From 1890 until his retirement in 1917 he was a professor of Oriental languages, particularly Persian and Turkish, at the Rijksuniversiteit te Utrecht. He was an editor of the *Encyclopaedia of Islam*. His writings include *Ein türkisch-arabisches Glossar* (1894), *Histoire des Seldjoucides d'Asie mineure, d'après l'abrégé du Seldjouknâmeh d'Ibn Bibi* (1902), *Textkritische Studien zum Alten Testament* (1925), and he was a joint author of *Catalogus codicum arabicorum* (Leiden, 1888-1907). He died in 1943. BiBenelux² (2); Fück, 325; Wie is dat, 1902

Hovannisian, Richard G., born 9 November 1921 at Tulare, Calif., he graduated in 1955 from the University of California, Berkeley, and received his Ph.D. in Russian and Near Eastern history in 1966 from the University of California, Los Angeles. He taught at public schools until 1962, when he was apppointed a professor of Armenian studies at U.C.L.A., a post which he held until his retirement. His writings include *Armenia on the road to independence, 1918* (1967), *The Republic of Armenia* (1971), *The Armenian holocaust; a bibliography* (1980), *Islam's understanding of itself* (1983), and he edited *The Armenian image in history and literature* (1981). ConAu, 21-24, new rev., 101; DrAS, 1969 H, 1974 H, 1978 H, 1982 H; IntAu&W, 1977-1999/2000; *MESA Roster of members*, 1977-1990; NatFacDr, 1990-2002; WhoAm, 1990-2003; WrDr, 1976/78-2004

Höver, Otto, born 14 December 1889 at Bremerhaven, Germany, he received a Dr.phil. in 1920 from the Universität München for *Spätstile deutscher Baukunst*. He was a historian of art, a private scholar, and from 1932 to his retirement, a director of the Stadtbibliothek Bremerhaven. His writings include *Kultbauten des Islam* (1922), *Indische Kunst* (1923), *Älteste Seeschiffahrt und ihre kulturelle Umwelt* (1948), and *Alt-Asiaten unter Segel im Indischen und Pazifischen Ozean* (1961). He died in Bremerhaven on 15 February 1970. GV; JahrDtB, 1936-1943; Kürschner, 1925-1961

Hövermann, Jürgen, born 15 March 1922 at Muschaken, East Prussia. After graduating from high school, he went straight into the army and served in the war until invalided home in 1943. He subsequently studied geography, history, and geology at the Universität Wien, and received a Dr.phil. in 1951 from the Universität Göttingen for *Morphologische Untersuchungen im Mittelharz*, and also a Dr.habil. for *Die Entwicklung der Siedlungsformen in den Marschen des Elb-Weser-Winkels*. He was successively a professor of geology at the universities of Berlin and Göttingen. In 1982, volume 56 of *Würburger geographische Arbeiten* was dedicated to him as "Festschrift für Jürgen Hövermann." GV; Kürschner, 1966-2003; Note about the author

Hovey, Esther Lancraft, born 21 August 1863 at New Haven, Conn., she graduated in 1886 from Mt. Holyoke College, and from 1909 to 1912 she served as a president of the New York Mt. Holyoke Alumnæ Association. WomWWA, 1914

Hovhannisyan, Abgar R., 1908- *see* Ioannisian, Abgar Rubenovich

Howard, Harry Nicholas, born 19 February 1902 at Excelsior Springs, Mo., he graduated in 1924 from William Jewell College, Liberty, Mo., and received his Ph.D. in 1930 from the University of California at Berkeley. He was a government official, a member of the U.S. delegation at the founding of the U.N.O. in 1945, and chief of the Near East Branch of the U.S. Division of Research for the Near East and Africa. He left the U.S. State Department in 1963 to become a professor of Middle Eastern studies at the American University, Washington, D.C. His writings include *The Partition of Turkey; a diplomatic history, 1913-1923* (1931), *U.S. policy in the Near East, South Asia and Africa* (1954), and *The King-Crane Commission; an American inquiry in the Middle East* (1963). BlueB, 1973/74, 1975, 1976; ConAu, 49-52, 123, new rev., 34; IntAu&W, 1977; IntWW, 1974-1993/94|; IntYB, 1978-1982; MidE, 1978-1982/83; Note; WhoAm, 1974-1988/89|; WhE&EA; WhNAA; WhoWor, 1974/75-1980; WrDr, 1976/78-1988/90|

Howard, I. K. A., born 20th cent., he received a Ph.D. in 1975 from Cambridge University for *Imami-Shi'i ritual in the context of early Islamic jurisprudence*. He was a lecturer in Arabic and Islamic studies at the University of Edinburgh. He translated *The Book of guidance into the lives of the twelve imams*, from the Arabic of Muhammad b. M. al-Mufīd (1981). Sluglett; ZKO

Howard, Sir Michael Eliot, born in 1922 at London, he was a graduate of Oxford and taught in various capacities war studies at the University of London since 1947. His writings include *Disengagement in*

Europe (1958), *Israel and the Arab world* (1967), *War in European history* (1976), *The Causes of war and other essays* (1983), and he was a joint author of *The Theory and practice of war* (1965). Au&Wr, 1963, 1971; IntAu&W, 1976-1989; IntWW, 1980-2005; Who, 1972-2005; WhoWor, 1978-1989/90

Howard, Nathaniel, born 18th cent., he was an English writer of poetry. His writings include *Bickleigh Vale, with other poems* (1804), he translated Dante's *The Inferno* (1807), and he published Greek and Latin educational works between 1804 and 1830. BLC; BritInd (1)

Howe, Marvine Henrietta, born 3 December 1928 at Shanghai, China, she was a newspaper reporter, and broadcaster for Radio Maroc's American program and a regular contributor to the Arabic Programme of the B.B.C. She was resident in Morocco from 1950 to 1955, when she went to Algeria as correspondent for Worldwide Press Service, *Time magazine*, and the Columbia Broadcasting System. Her writings include *The Prince and I; or, One woman's Morocco* (1956), and *Turkey today; a nation divided over Islam's revival* (2000). Note about the author; WhoAmW, 1958/59, 1961/62; ZKO

Howe, Mrs. Sonia Elizabeth, born in 1871 at St. Petersburg, she was a resident of Lausanne in 1928. Her writings include *A Thousand years of Russian history* (1915), *Real Russians* (1917), *Les Héros du Sahara* (1931), *Lyautey of Morocco* (1931), and *The Drama of Madagascar* (1938). Note; WhE&EA; ZKO

Howel, Thomas, born 18th cent., he was a medical doctor in the service of the Honourable East India Company. He wrote *A Journal of the passage from India by a route partly unfrequented through Armenia and Natolia or Asia Minor* (1789), its translation, *Voyage en retour de l'Inde* (1797). Its German translation was published in *Neue Beiträge zur Völker- und Länderkunde*, 3 (1790). BLC; Note

Howell, David, born in 1945, he was a sometime professor of politics at the University of York. His writings include *British social democracy* (1976), *Freedom and capital* (1981), *A Lost left; three studies in socialism and nationalism* (1986), *Respectable radicals; studies in the politics of railway trade unionism* (1999), and *MacDonald's party; labour identities and crisis, 1922-1931* (2002). LC

Howell, Sir Evelyn Berkeley, born 12 February 1877 at Calcutta, he was educated at Charterhouse School, Godalming, Surrey, and Emmanuel College, Oxford. He entered the India Civil Service and arrived in 1900 in India, where he served in the Punjab and the North-West Frontier Province as a revenue commissioner, political agent, and foreign secretary until his retirement in 1933, interrupted by four and a half years spent in Mesopotamia and Muscat. He died in 1971. BritInd (2); IndianBiInd (2); *Who was who*, 7

Howell, George, born in 1833, he was a British labour leader. His writings include *The Conflicts of capital and labour historically and economically considered* (1878), its translation, *Die englische Gewerksvereins-Bewegung* (1896), *Trade unionism, new and old* (1891), and *Labour legislation, labour movements and labour leaders* (1902). He died in 1910. F. M. Leventhal wrote *Respectable radical, George Howell, and Victorian working class politics* (1971). DNB

Howell, John, born in 1941, he was in 1989 a director of the Overseas Development Unit of the World Bank in London. His writings include *Borrowers and lenders; rural financial markets and institutions in developing countries* (1980), *Administring agricultural development for small farmers* (1981), *Small farmer services in India* (1984), he was a joint author of *Structural adjustment and the African farmer* (1992), and he edited *Local government and politics in the Sudan* (Khartoum, 1974). LC; NUC

Howell, John Bruce, born in 1941, he received a Ph.D. in 1984 from the University of Illinois at Urbana-Champaign for *The concept of "development literature" and the establishment of criteria for the creation of a development data base*. He became associated with the Reader Service Department of the Library of Congress, Washington, D.C. His writings include *East African community; subject guide to official publications* (1976), *Kenya; subject guide to official publications* (1978), *Tanganyika African National Union; a guide to publications by and about Tanu* (1976), *Zanzibar's Afro-Shirazi Party, 1957-1977* (1978), and, with Barbara M. Howell, he was a joint author of *Index to the African studies review/bulletin* and the *ASA review of books, 1958-1990* (1991). LC; Note; ZKO

Howell, Mortimer Sloper, born 3 February 1841 at Bath, he was educated at Corpus Christi College, Oxford. He entered the Indian Civil Service in 1862 and retired in 1896. His writings include *A Grammar of the classical Arabic grammar, translated and compiled from the works of the most approved native or naturalized authorities* (Allahabad, 1880-1911). He died in 1925. Buckland; Fück, p. 296; IndianBiInd (2); Riddick; *Who was who*, 2

Howell, Paul Philip, born 13 February 1917 at London, he received a Ph.D. in 1951 from Oxford University for *A Comparative study of customary law among cattle-owing tribes of the southern Sudan*. His writings include *A Manuel of Nuer law* (1954). He was with the Sudan Political Service, 1938-55, the British Foreign Service, 1961-69, and a director of Development Studies and Fellow of Wolfson College, Cambridge, 1969-1983. He died in 1994. ConAu, 135; Sluglett; Unesco; Who, 1965-1994

Howorth, Sir Henry Hoyle, born in 1842 at Lisboa, he was educated in England and called to the bar from the Inner Temple in 1867. He was a Conservative member of Parliament. His writings include *History of the Mongols* (1876-1927). He died in 1923. BiD&SB; BritInd (4); *Who was who*, 2

van **Hoyer**, Johann Gottfried, born 9 May 1767 to a family of Saxon soldiers, he entered the Prussian engineers in 1813 and participated in the German War of Liberation in 1815. He retired in 1825 with the rank of colonel and subsequently lectured in military sciences at Halle/Saale. Throughout his life he had pursued an interest in classics and modern languages. His writings include *Geschichte der Kriegskunst* (1797-1800), and *Geschichte Siciliens in der frühen Zeit und im Mittelalter* (1838). He died in Halle on 7 March 1848. ADtB, vol. 13, p. 218; DtBiInd (4)

Hoyle, Stephen Geoffrey, born 20th cent., he received a Ph.D. in 1977 from the School of Oriental and African Studies, London, for *The Settlement of nomads in the Sudan; the case of Khashm el-Girba agricultural scheme*. He was in 1979 associated with Bayero Unibersity, Kano, Nigeria. Note about the author; Sluglett; *SOAS Library catalogue*

Hoyt, Mont Powell, born 3 April 1940 at Oklahoma City, he graduated in 1962 from Northwestern University, Evanston, Illinois, and received his first law degree in 1965 from Oklahoma Law School; he was admitted to the Bar of Oklahoma in 1965. A licentiate in law to a Parisian advocate, 1967-68, he was admitted to the Bar of Texas in 1968. From 1970 to 1976 he served as an adjunct professor at the University of Houston. WhoAm, 1986-2003; WhoAmL, 1979-2003/2004; WhoEmL, 1987/88; WhoS&SW, 1991/92, 1993/94

Hoyt, Sally Foreman, Mrs. Spofford, born 11 April 1914 at Williamsport, Pa., she graduated in 1935 from Wilson College, and received a Ph.D. in 1948 from Cornell University, Ithaca, N.Y. for *A reference book and bibliography of ornithological techniques*. In 1951 he became a technical assistant in ornithology at Cornell University. She was a joint author of *Enjoying birds around New York City* (1966). AmM&WSc, 12th ed. (1972); WhoAmW, 1970/71

van **Hoytema**, Antoinette Agatha, born 6 December 1875 at Delft, the Netherlands, she was a painter, writer on art, and a member of De Onafhankelijken. Vollmer = Benelux²

Hrabak, Bogumil/Bohumír, born 20th cent., his writings include *Zapisnici sa sednica Delegacije Kraljevine SHS na Mirovnoj konferenciji u Parizu 1919-1920* (Beograd, 1960), *Jugosloveni zarobljenici u Italiji i njihovo dobrovoljačko pitanje 1915-1918* (Novi Sad, 1980), and he was a joint author of *Diferenčný slovník nárečia slovenského, vajnorského: jak nás učili matere viprávjat; ako sa rozprávalo vo Vajnoroch* (Bratislava, 2002). OSK

Hrabský, Jan, born in 1615 at Banská Bystrica-Radvaň, he studied Oriental languages, particularly Hebrew, at the Universität Wittenberg. His writings include *Dissertatio de utilitate et necessitate Arabismi at notitiam solidam Ebreae* (Wittenberg, 1654). He died in Bratislava in 1655. Filipsky

von **Hranilović-Czvetassin**, Oskar, born 19th cent., he was in 1903 a captain in the Austrian Imperial High Command. Note about the author

Hrastnik, Franz, born 19 September 1909 at Wien, he studied literature and music at the Universität Wien and became a novelist, playwright, and journalist. His writings include *Die Opernkonserve* (1957), and *Das Filmverdrehbuch* (1958). He died in Wien on 19 June 1978. IntAu&W, 1976; KDtLK, Nekrolog, 1971-1998; Master (1); Vollmer; WhoAustria, 1964-1977/78

Hrbek, Ivan, born 20 June 1923 at Praha, Czechoslovakia, he was an Arabist who researched medieval Arab relations with the Slavs. He later produced a long series of books and articles on the Prophet Muhammad and Islam. His twenty-year study culminated in his 1972 Czech translation of the *Korán*, with substantial introduction and explanatory notes. His writings include *Dějiny Afriky* (1966), *Muhammad* (1967), *Sjednocená Arabská Republika* (1969), *Libyská Arabská Lidová Socialistická Džamáhírija* (1982); and he was a joint author of *Charisteria orientalia* (1956), and Jan Rypka's *Dějiny perské a tádžické literatury* (1956), a work which became widely known through its translations into German and English in 1959 and 1968. He died in Praha on 20 March 1993. *Archiv orientální*, 62 (1994), Česky; pp. 79-80; Filipsky

Hřebíček, Luděk, born 9 June 1934 at Praha, he there studied Turkish and Persian. He was a research fellow at Ankara in 1990, and at the Ruhr-Universität Bochum in 1992. His writings include *Turečtina* (1969), *Turkish grammar as a graph* (1971), and *Quantities of social communication, with general applications to Islam and social morphogenesis* (1986). Česky; Filipsky

Hron, Carl, born 27 December 1852 at Wien, he was a professional soldier who participated in the 1878 campaign in Bosnia-Hercegovina. He resigned in 1883 to become successively an editor with a variety of conservative periodicals. His writings include *Wiens antisemitische Bewegung* (1890), *Ägypten und die ägyptische Frage* (1895), *Die Weltpolitik* (1898), and *In zwölfter Stunde; die Wahrheit über die Wiener Orientpolitik* (1909). He died in Wien on 22 Febrzary 1912. DtBilnd (2); ÖBL; Sezgin

Huang, Thomas Tin Fah, born 1919. His writings include *Loss of United States citizenship by expatriation* (1957).

Huard, Pierre Alphonse, born 16 October 1901 at Bastia, Corsica, he studied medicine at naval colleges in Brest and Bordeaux. After graduation he entered the Service de santé des troupes coloniales, posted to Cilicia and Alexandretta from 1925 to 1927. During his long carrer, he spent twenty-one years in French Indochina, he also served in French West Africa. He retired with the rank of *médecin général*. His writings include *Connaissance du Viêt-nam* (1954), *La Médecine des Chinois* (1967), and its translations, *Chinese medicine* (1968), and *Chinesische Medizin* (1968). He died in Paris in an accident on 28 April 1983. DBF; *Hommes et destins*, vol. 6, pp. 185-87; IndexBFr² (1); WhoFr, 1957/58-1981/82

Huart, Albin, born 19th cent., his writings include *La Révision douanière* (Paris, 1909), *Les Ports de commerce français* (Paris, 1911), *Finances de guerre comparées* (Paris, 1916), and *Étude comparée des principaux systèmes de banque* (Paris, 1913). BN; NUC

Huart, Marie Clément Imbault, he was born on 16 February 1854 at Paris. From the age of fourteen he studied Arabic concurrently with classical languages. He later studied at the École des languages orientales, Paris, where he received diplomas in Arabic, Turkish, Persian, and modern Greek. In 1875 he graduated from the École pratique des hautes études, Paris, with a translation from Sharaf al-Dīn Rāmī entitled *Anis-el-Ochchaq, traité des termes figurés relatifs à la description de la beauté*. He subsequently entered the Ministère des Affaires étrangères and was sent in August 1875 to Damascus as a student interpreter. In June 1878 he left for Constantinople, where he served for twenty-two years as vice-consul and consul. Recalled to France in 1898, he later was appointed to the chair of Persian at the École des languages orientales, and in 1908, a director of Islamic studies at the École pratique des hautes études. Concurrently he served as a secretary-interpreter at the Ministère des Affaires étrangères until 1912, when he resigned with the rank of consul-general. In 1919 he was elected to the Académie des inscriptions et belles-lettres to take the place of Gaston Maspéro, and would have become president of the Académie in 1927 if he had not died before taking office on 30 December 1926. His writings include *Bibliographie ottomane; notice des livres turcs, arabes et persans imprimés à Constantinople durant la période 1887-1891* (1881-95?), *Les Calligraphes et les miniaturistes de l'Orient musulman* (1908), *Histoire des Arabes* (1912-13), and *La Perse antique et la civilisation iranienne* (1925). DBF; Enclran; Fück; Kornrumpf; *Qui êtes-vous*, 1924 [Imbault-Huart]; Vapereau

Hubac, Pierre, comte Sarrus, born in 1894, his writings include *Les Masques d'argile, histoire carthaginoise* (1928), *Carthage* (1946), *Les Nomads* (1948), *Tunisie* (1948), and *Les Barbaresques* (1949). His trace is lost after an article in 1957. NUC

Hubay, Ilona, born 1 July 1902 at Pécz, Hungary, she studied history of art, classical and Christian archaeology, gaining a doctorate in 1938 at Budapest for *Magyar Hungarica; régi magyar misekönyvek*. She was an academic librarian at the National Library, Budapest, from 1929 to 1950, and subsequently at Coburg, Würzburg, and München. Her writings include *Egykorú újságlap Drakula vajdáról* (1948), *Die Handschriften der Landesbibliothek Coburg* (1962), *Incvnabvla der Universitätsbibliothek Würzburg* (1966), and *Incvnablvla der Staats- und Stadtbibliothek Augsburg* (1974). She died in München on 20 June 1982. JahrDtB, 1973-1981; MEL, 1978-1991

Hubbard, George David, born 12 May 1871 at Tolono, Illinois, he graduated in 1896 from the University of Illinois, and received a Ph.D. in 1905 from Cornell University, Ithaca, N.Y. He became a professor of geology and geography at various American universities until his retirement in 1936. His writings include *Quantitative vs. qualitative studies in geology* (1928), and *The Geography of Europe* (1937). He died in 1958. Bioln, 5; NYT, 13 June 1958, p. 23, col. 5; WhAm, 3; WhNAA

Hubbard, James Mascarene, born in 1836, he published two catalogues of the Barton Collection in the Boston Public Library, 1880 and 1888, and contributed articles on Central Asia and the Far East to a variety of periodicals. He died in 1932. Note; NUC

Hubbell, Lucy née Embury, born in 1883, she was an author of essays and poetry, and for eight years on the editorial staff of *Garden and home builder*, part of the time as its managing editor. She travelled in Central America, Europe, and North Africa to collect material for her articles. Her writings include

Persis, a pilgrim of to-morrow (1936), *The Listening man* (1940), a work for which she received the Julia Ellsworth Ford Foundation Award, and *The Golden football* (1948). LC; Note about the author

Huber, Barbara, born 1936, she received a Dr.jur. and became associated with Max-Planck-Institut für Ausländisches und Internationales Strafrecht, Freiburg im Breisgau. Her writings include *Das Recht der Tötungsdelikte in Nigeria unter vergleichender Einbeziehung verwandter Rechte Afrikas* (1983); she was a joint author of *Rechtliche Initiativen gegen organisierte Kriminalität* (2001); and she edited *Die christlich-islamische Ehe* (1984). *Papers in honour of Barbara Huber on her 65th birthday* was published in 2001.

Huber, Charles, born 19 December 1847 to a family of modest substance at Strasbourg. Some Arabic studies at Paris and two visits to Algeria constituted his preparation for his first journey to the Orient from 1878 to 1882. He visited Damascus, Palmyra, Baghdad, Hā'il, Buraydah, Khaybar, and Taymā'. In 1883 he returned in the company of Julius Euting. They succeeded in buying the Taymā' Stone, which had an important inscription, but the two travellers, who seem to have disliked each other intensely, separated as soon as they could. Huber left his papers and the Stone at Hā'il and went off to Mecca. On his way back he was murdered by two of his guides on 29 July 1884 near Rābigh. The French consul at Jiddah retrieved the Stone and Huber's diary. His writings include *Journal d'un voyage en Arabie* (1891). Bidwell; DBF; Henze; Kornrumpf; Kornrumpf, N; NDBA

Huber, Engelbert, born in 1873, he received a Dr.phil. in 1905 from the Universität Leipzig for *Die theophoren Personennamen in den Keilschrifturkunden aus der Zeit der Könige von Ur*. His writings include *Das Trankopfer im Kulte der Völker; die Rauschsehnsucht der Menschheit in der Völkerpsychologie* (1900), *Biblischer Bilderatlas* (1913), and *Der Kampf um den Alkohol im Wandel der Kulturen* (1930). NUC, pre-1956; Schwarz

Huber, Michael Joseph, born 26 January 1874 at Weil-Altomünster, Bavaria, he studied philosophy, theology, and philology at Roma, Würzburg, and München. He was ordained a Benectine priest in 1898. After extensive travels in Italy, Belgium, England, Egypt, Palestine, and Turkey, he became a teacher of modern languages at Stiftsgymnasium, Metten, Bavaria. His writings include *Beitrag zur Visionsliteratur und Siebenschläferlegende des Mittelalters* (1902-1908), *Wanderlegende von den Siebenschläfern* (1910), and *Vilsbiburg und sein Liebfrauenfestspiel* (1924). Kosch; Wer ist's, 1935, p. 725 [incorrect filing]

Hüber, Reinhard, born in 1905 he received a Dr.jur. in 1931 from the Universität Kiel for *Der Kartellcharakter von Gewerkschaft und Arbeitgeberverband*. He was for many years a director of the Nah- und Mittelost-Vereins, and in 1959 a journalist in Turkey. An editor of *Der Nahe Osten* (Berlin), he wrote *Deutschland und der Wirtschaftsaufbau des Vorderen Orients* (1938), *Der Nahe Osten* (1940), *Es wetterleuchtet zwischen Nil und Tigris* (1940), *Die Türkei* (1942), *Die Bagdadbahn* (1943), *Nah- und Mittelost zwischen Imperialismus, Freiheit und Kooperation* (1954), and *Nahost ruft* (1954). GV; NUC; ZKO

Hubert, Henry, born in 1871, he graduated from the École coloniale, but had a bad start in his career on account of administrative absudities. He received a doctorate in 1908 from the Université de Paris for *Contribution à l'étude de la géographie physique du Dahomy*. He subsequently spent twenty years in French West Africa reorganizing the Service météorologique colonial. His writings include *Mission scientifique au Dahomy* (1908), and *Mission scientifique au Soudan* (1916), and *Nouvelles études sur la météorologie de l'Afrique Occidentale Française* (1926). He died in 1941. AfrBioInd = *Hommes et destins*, vol. 8, pp. 193-196

Hubert, Klemens, born 16 October 1942 at Neumarkt, Germany, he studied mathematics and business administration at the Universität Freiburg im Breisgau, Freie Universität Berlin, and Technische Universität Berlin, where he received a Dr.agron. in 1972 for *Wirkung von Nahrungshilfe auf die wirtschaftliche Entwicklung*. In 1978 he was associated with the German Society for Technical Cooperation, Eschborn. He was a joint author of *Rehabilitation of rural roads in Handeni, Tanzania; project description and assessment* (1978). Note about the author; Thesis

Hubert, Lucien, born 27 August 1868 at Chesne-Populeux (Ardennes), France, he graduated from the École coloniale and successively became a journalist, editor of the *Petit Ardennais*, and, from 1897 to 1912, a *député* for Vouziers. He served in the Algerian administration under Charles Jonnard, advocating social reform in Algeria in respect to Muslims. His writings include *Politique africaine* (1904), *En Afrique centrale* (1906), *Notre colonie de Dahomy* (1906), *L'Afrique Occidentale Française* (1907), its translation, *Französisch Westafrika* (1907), *Avec ou contre l'islam* (1913), *La Question persane et la guerre* (1916), *L'Islam et la guerre* (1918), *Les Droits politiques des indigènes des colonies* (1927), and *L'Afrique Équatoriale Française* (1930). He died in Charleville (Ardennes) on 17 June 1938. *Correspondance d'Orient*, 31 (juin 1938), p. 266; IndexBFr² (5); *Qui est-ce*, 1934; *Qui êtes-vous*, 1924

Hubertus, Stephanus, born 16th cent., he had learned Arabic in the East and became a professor of Arabic at Paris. He was a court physician to Henri IV (1590-91). Flück, pp. 59-60

Hübinger, Paul Egon, born 4 February 1911 at Düsseldorf, he received a Dr.phil. in 1935 from the Universität Bonn for *Die weltlichen Beziehungen der Kirche von Verdun zu den Rheinlanden*. He subsequently served as a professor of history and auxiliary sciences at his alma mater until retirement. His writings include *Spätantike und frühes Mittelalter* (1959), *Bedeutung und Rolle des Islam beim Übergang des Islam vom Altertum zum Mittelalter* (1968), and *Zur Frage der Periodengrenze zwischen Altertum und Mittelalter* (1969). He died on 26 June 1987. DtBilnd (1); HbDtWiss; Kürschner, 1950-1987; Wer ist wer, 1955-1971/73

Hübner, Günter, born 24 November 1938 at Vietz/Landsberg an der Warthe, Germany, he was a forestry worker before graduating from the workers and peasants faculty of the Universität Greifswald. He subsequently studied economics and economic history, with special reference to the Near and Middle East, at the Universität Leipzig where he received a Dr.phil. in 1969 for *Der Einfluß der wirtschaftlichen Zusammenarbeit mit den sozialistischen Ländern auf den ökonomischen und sozialen Fortschritt der Staaten des Nahen und Mittleren Ostens*. Since 1965 he was an academic assistant in Orientalisches Institut, Universität Leipzig. His writings include *Das private Sparen in Ostafrika unter besonderer Berücksichtigung der Verhältnisse in Uganda* (1970). Schwarz; Thesis

Hübner, Max F., born 13 July 1854 at Oschatz, Saxony, he was a lieutenant colonel who taught mathematics at the *Kadetten-Korps*, and served as a lecturer in the technique of armaments at the *Kriegsschule* (war college). Concurrently he pursued an interest in colonial geography. He travelled in Asia Minor and North Africa. His writings include *Eine Pforte zum schwarzen Erdteil* (1904), *Militärische und militärpolitische Betrachtungen über Marokko* (1905), *Unbekannte Gebiete Marokkos* (1905), and *Die französische Sahara* (1907). Wer ist's, 1909-1912

Hübotter, Karl Arnold Franz, born 5 December 1881 at Weimar, he studied medicine, and concurrently Chinese and Manchuri at the universities of Jena, Berlin, and Heidelberg, gaining a Dr.med. in 1906 at Jena, and a Dr.phil. in 1912 at Leipzig with a thesis on Chinese history. He went to London for further medical studies. After his return to Berlin, he practised his profession, concurrently studying Arabic, Turkish, Persian, Assyrian, and Tibetan. In 1914 he took a Dr.habil. in history of medicine. After the first World War he spent four years in Japan, where he took the Japanese medical examinations; since 1925 he practised in China, returning in 1953 to Germany, where he applied Chinese cures. His writings include *3000 Jahre Medizin* (1920), he was a joint author of *Krankennot und Christenhilfe in China* (1929), and he edited *Biographisches Lexikon der hervorragenden Ärzte aller Zeiten und Völker* (1929). He died in Berlin on 23 March 1967. DtBE; DtBilnd (2); Kürschner, 1931-1966; NDB; NUC, pre-1956

Hübschmann, Heinrich, born 1 July 1848 at Erfurt, Prussia, he studied Indo-European languages at the universities of Tübingen, Leipzig, and München, where he received a Dr.phil. in 1870 for an annotated translation of *Das 30. Kapitel des Jasna mit Rücksicht auf die Tradition*. In 1877 he was invited to teach comparative philology at the Universität Straßburg, where he remained until his retirement. His writings include *Beiträge zur Erklärung des Avesta* (1872-74), *Die Umschreibung der iranischen Sprachen und des Armenischen* (1882), *Etymologie und Lautlehre der ossetischen Sprache* (1887), *Persische Studien* (1895), *Armenische Grammatik* (1897), *Die altarmenischen Ortsnamen* (1904), and he translated from the Armenian, *Zur Geschichte Armeniens und der ersten Kriege der Araber* (1875). He died in Freiburg im Breisgau on 20 January 1908. DtBE; DtBilnd (2); Enclran; NDB

Huby, Pamela Margaret Clark, born 21 April 1922 at London, she graduated in 1947 from Oxford University and successively became a lecturer in philosophy at St. Anne's College, Oxford, and the University of Liverpool. Her writings include *Plato and modern morality* (1972); she edited *The Criterion of truth; essays written in honour of George Kerferd* (1989); and she was a joint editor of *Theophrastus of Eresus' Commentary, vol. 4: Psychology* (1999). ConAu, 21-22; IntAu&WW, 1977, 1991; WhoWor, 1976/77; WrDr, 1976/78-2004

Huc (Гюк), Évariste Régis, born 1 June or August 1813 at Caylus (Tarn-et-Garonne), France, he was a missionary who, with a fellow priest, was ordered in the autumn of 1844 to explore the deserts of Tartary and go on to Tibet where, according to instructions from the Vicar Apostolic of Mongolia, they were expected to propagate Christianity and try to make converts. Dressed as lamas to escape attention, with only a young Christian native, they reached Kounboun, where they studied Tibetan. At the end of September 1845 they joined a caravane for Lhasa, arriving at the end of December. Prevented from going any further, they reached Macao in October of 1846. Abbé Huc's writings include *Souvenirs d'un voyage dans la Tartarie, le Thibet et la Chine, pendant les années 1844, 1845 et 1846* (1850), its translations, *Travels in Tartary, Thibet and China, 1844-1846* (1851), *Wanderungen durch die Mongolei nach Thibet zur Hauptstadt des Tale Lama 1844-1846* (1855), *Resa i Mongoliet* *och Tibet* (1862). *Воспоминанiя о путешествiи по Татарiи* (1866), and *Mais qui songe à la Tartarie; lettres de voyage, 1839-1848* (1993). He died in Paris on 25 March 1860. CasWL; DBF; Hoefer; IndexBFr² (4); Master (4); NewCathEnc; WhWE

Hucke, Ehrhart, born 20th cent., he was a trained political economist and associated with Internationale Raiffeisen-Union e.V., Bonn. In 1970 he was an aid worker in Iran. Note about the author

Hucul, Walter C., born 25 January 1922 at Stanislav, Russia, he received his M.A. in 1947 from the University of California at Berkeley, where he also gained his Ph.D. in 1953 for *The evolution of Russian and Soviet sea power, 1853-1953*. He was a lecturer in Russian history at West Coast colleges and universities until 1951, when he was appointed a research historian at the University of California, Berkeley. DrAS, 1969 H; Note about the author; NUC, pre-1956

Hudaj, Georg (Giorgio), he was, with Johann B. Hofstetter, a joint author of *Handbuch der arabischen Volkssprache = Manuale della lingua araba volgare* (Wien, 1846).

Huddleston, Willoughby Baynes, captain, born in 1866, he served with the Royal Indian Navy since 1887. During the first World War he was Principal Marine Transport Officer in Mesopotamia from 1915 to the surrender of Kut al-Amara in 1916. He died in 1953. Who was who, 5

Hudgell, Rev. E. W. G., M.A., of Port Said, he was in 1938 a secretary of the British and Foreign Bible Society. Note about the author

Hudson, Alfred Emmons, born in 1904 at New York, N.Y., he graduated from Yale University, New Haven, Conn., where he also received his Ph.D. He and his wife, Elizabeth Bacon, have done anthropological field work in Central Asia, the results of which are embodied in *Kazak social structure* (1938). Supported by Yale University, the Social Science Research Council, and the American Council of Learned Societies, they spent a year in study among the Hazara people. From 1939 to 1942 he was a professor of anthropology at the University of Washington. He died 25 May 1956. Note about the author; NYT, 27 May 1956, p. 89, col. 1

Hudson, Ellis Herndon, born in 1880 at Osaka, Japan, he received an M.D. in 1919 from the University of Pennsylvania and a diploma in tropical medicine from the London School of Hygiene and Tropical Medicine. In 1922 he joined the Syrian Mission of the Prebyterian Church in the U.S.A. and was posted to Deir-ez-Zor in Ottoman Syria, where he became the founding director of the Presbyterian Medical Center in 1924, returning to America in 1937. His writings include *Non-venereal syphillis* (1958). Au&Wr, 1963; WhAm, 9

Hudson, Geoffrey Francis, born in 1903 at Maple, Cheshire, he was educated at Shrewsbury and Queen's College, Oxford. A Fellow of All Souls College, Oxford, and the Royal Historical Society, he wrote *Europe and China* (1931), *Atlas of Far Eastern politics* (1938), its Japanese translation in 1941, *Turkey, Greece and the eastern Mediterranean* (1939), *The Sino-Russian dispute* (1961), *The Hard and bitter peace; world politics since 1945* (1966), and he was a joint author of *Second report upon the excavations carried out in and near the Hippodrome of Constantinople* (1929). He died in 1975. Who's who in Oxforshire, 1936

Hudson, James, born 20th cent., he was a sometime professor in the Department of Geography, American University of Beirut. In 1971), he served as a professor of geography at Morgan State College, Baltimore, Md. MESA Roster of members, 1982-1990; Note about the author

Hudson, Manley Ottmer, born in 1886 at St. Peters, Mo., he graduated in 1906 from William Jewell College, and received law degrees from Harvard University. He was a professor of international law at Harvard since 1923 and also served as a visiting professor abroad. He was a sometime judge of the Permanent Court of International Justice. He edited *World Court reports* (1936-42). He died in 1960. ANB; Bioln, 1, 2, 4, 5 (4); CurBio, 1944, 1960; DAB; Master (3); NYT, 14 April 1960, p. 31, col. 3; OxLaw

Hudson, Michael Craig, born 2 June 1938 at New Haven, Conn., he received all his degrees from the local Yale University, including his Ph.D. in 1964 for *Political changes in Lebanon, 1943-1963*. He was an associate professor of political science at Brooklyn College of the City of New York, before teaching his subject from 1970 to 1975 at the School of Advanced International Studies, Johns Hopkins University, Washington, D.C. He successively became director of Georgetown University's Center for Contemporary Arab Studies, and professor of international relations and government and Seif Ghobash Professor of Arab studies in the School of Foreign Service at Georgetown University, a post which he still held in 1995. His writings include *The Precarious republic; political modernization in Lebanon* (1968), and *Arab politics; the search for legitimacy* (1977). AmM&WSc, 1973 S; ConAu, 37-40; MESA Roster of members, 1977-1990; Note about the author; Selim; WhoAm, 1990-2003

Hudson, Norman Barrie, born 21 June 1937, he was educated at the University of Sheffield and University College, London. He was an economist and statistician in the civil service, and a sometime technical adviser in Lebanon and Jordan. Who, 1983-2004

von **Huebbenet**, Georg, born in 1925, his writings include *Arabisches Wirtschaftsleben* (1943), and *Die rote Wirtschaft wächst* (Düsseldorf, 1960).

Hueso Rolland, Francisco, fl. 1953, he was associated with the Sociedad Española de Amigos del Arte, Madrid. His writings include *Exposición de encuadernaciones españolas, siglos XII al XIX* (Madrid, 1934). NUC

Huet, Gédéon Busken, born 31 May 1860 at Haarlem, the Netherlands, he spent part of his youth at Batavia. In 1885 he graduated from the École des chartes, Paris, with a thesis on a medieval French poet. In 1888 he started his long association with the Bibliothèque nationale de Paris, where he edited the *Catalogue des manuscrits néerlandais* (1886), *Catalogue des manuscrits allemands* (1895), and the *Catalogue général des livres imprimés* (1915-20). He died in Paris on 10 November 1921. DBF

Huetz de Lemps, Alain, born 29 June 1926 at Bourges (Cher), France, he was a geographer who, since the 1960s, was associated with the Université de Bordeaux. His writings include *Australie et Nouvelle-Zélande* (1954), *Aumale, l'Algérien* (1962), *Géographie et Océanie* (1966), *Boissons et civilisation en Afrique* (2003), and he edited *Eaux-de-vin et spiritueux; colloque de Bordeaux - Cognac, 1982* (1985). Livres disponibles, 2003; Unesco

Hufbauer, Gary Clyde, born 3 April 1939 at San Diego, Calif., he graduated in 1960 from Harvard and received a Ph.D. in economics in 1963 from Cambridge University. Since 1963 he was a professor of economics at the University of New Mexico, Albuquerque. He served as an economic adviser in Lahore, 1967-68. His writings include *Synthetic materials and the theory of international trade* (1966), *Economic sanctions in support of foreign policy goals* (1983), *Trading for growth; the next round of trade negotiations* (1985), *North American economic integration; twenty-five years backward and foreward* (1998). and he was a joint author of *Overseas manufacturing investment and the balance of payments* (1968). AmM&WSc, 1973 S; Au&Wr, 1971; WhoAm, 1980-2003; WhoEc, 1981, 1986, 1999; WhoWor, 1980/81-1993/94

Huff, Dietrich, born 14 November 1934 at Zedlitzfelde near Stettin, Germany, he grew up at Helmstedt. After practice work in the construction industry, he began in 1955 to study architecture at Technische Universität Berlin. In the course of his study he participated in excavations, particularly in Takht-i Sulaiman, Iran. Supported by a travel grant from Deutsches Archäologisches Institut, he visited most of the eastern Mediterranean countries as well as North Africa. In 1971 he received a doctorate from Technische Universität Berlin for *Qal'a-ye Dukhtar bei Firuzabad; ein Beitrag zur sasanidischen Palastarchitecture.* Thesis

Huffman, Arthur Vincent, born 7 February 1912 at New Holland, Ill., he graduated in 1935 from McKendree College, Lebanon, Ill. A clinical pschologist, he was from 1943 to 1949 a professor in the University of Kabul and an adviser to the Ministry of Education. During part of this time he was also connected with the Office of International and Cultural Relations, U.S. Department of State. Since 1949 he was associated with the Department of of Public Safety and the Department of Corrections, State of Illinois. AmM&WSc, 1973 S; Note about the author; WhoAm, 1974/75; WhoWest, 1980/81, 1982/83

Huffman, Henry Russell, born in 1942, he received a Ph.D. in 1973 from the University of Wisconsin for *Syntactical influences of Arabic on medieval and later Spanish prose.* Selim; NUC

Hufnagel, Wilhelm Friedrich, born 15 June 1754 at Schwäbisch-Hall, Swabia, Germany, he studied theology successively at the universities of Altdorf, Bavaria, and Erlangen, where he received his degrees and served as a professor of theology and later also as a vice-chancellor. In 1788 he became pastor at the Erlangen university church and inspector of the ducal theological seminary. In 1781 he was invited to the city of Frankfurt's ministry of education (Predigerministerium) as preacher, educator, and superintendent, posts at the top of the Frankfurt educational system which he held until his retirement in 1822. He was a scholar well versed in classical and Oriental languages. His writings include *Handbuch der biblischen Theologie* (1785-89), and *Der Cherubhim Anfang und Ende im Paradiese* (1821). Wilhelm Stricker wrote *Erinnerungsblätter an Wilhelm Friedrich Hufnagel* (1851). ADtB; DtBE; DtBIInd (1); NDB

Hug, Georges, born about 1900, his writings include *Pour apprendre l'arabe* (Paris, 1928), *Méthode phonétique d'arabe dialectal algérien* (1958), and jointly with Jean Lozach *L'habitat rural en Égypte* (Le Caire, Institut français d'archéologie orientale, 1930). NUC, pre-1956

Freiherr von **Hügel**, Carl Alexander Anselm, born 25 April 1796 at Regensburg, Bavaria, he studied law at the Universität Heidelberg. In 1811 he joined the Austrian army to participate in the campaigns against Napoléon, later serving as a diplomat. In 1824 he resigned from the military with the rank of major in order to prepare for his journey to the East in 1830. During his seven-year travels he visited India, the Himalayas, and Southeast Asia, returning by way of the Cape of Good Hope in 1837. A friend of Prince Metternich, they went to England in 1848. Since 1849 he successively served as an Austrian ambassador in the Toscana and in Bruxelles, retiring in 1867. His writings include *Kaschmir und das Reich der Sieck* (1840-48), and its translation, *Travels in Kashmir and the Panjab, containing a particular account of the government and character of the Sikhs* (1845). He died in Bruxelles on 2 June 1870. ADtB; BLC; DtBE; Embacher; Henze; Kornrumpf; Kosch; Wurzbach

Hugessen, Sir Hughe Montgomery Knatchbull, 1886-1971 *see* Knatchbull-Hugessen, Sir Hughe M.

Huggins, Kenneth Herbert, born in 1908, he graduated from University College, London, and received a Ph.D. in 1940 from Glasgow University. He was a sometime lecturer in geography, a commercial counseller, and a consul-general. He died on 16 January 1993. Who, 1974-1993

Hugh-Jones, Llewelyn Arthur, born in 1888 at Wrexham, North Wales, he was an economist who was educated at Rugby and Oxford, subsequently holding government posts in the Near East and Greece. He died in 1970. Who was who, 6

Hughes, David Rees, born 23 April 1926 at Bodorgan, North Wales, he graduated from Cambridge University, where he also received a Ph.D. in ethnology in 1965. From 1950 to 1960 he served with H.M. Colonial Service in Singapore. In 1967 he was appointed chairman of the Deptment of Anthropology in the University of Toronto. His writings include *South-East Asia; a geographical notebook* (1957), *The Peoples of Malaya* (1965), and, with Evelyn Kallen, *Anatomy of racism; Canadian dimensions* (1974). AmM&WSc, 1973 P, 1976 P, 1979 P, 1982 P, 1986 P

Hughes, Thomas Patrick, born in 1838, he graduated in 1862 from the Church Missionary College, Islington, England, and was ordained in 1864. He subsequently served until 1881 as a missionary in Peshawar. In his intercourse with Muslims he dressed in Oriental fashion in order to facilitate his researches. For many years he was a government examiner in Pashto. One of the original fellows of the Oriental University of the Punjab at Lahore, he visited Egypt in 1876 to investigate the strength of Islam in that country. His witings include *Notes on Muhammadanism* (1877), *A Dictionary of Islam, being a cyclopædia of the doctrines, rites, ceremonies, and customs* (1885). He died in 1911. Kornrumpf; WhAm, 1; WhoAm, 1899/1900-1908/9; Who's who in New York City and State, 1907

Hughes-Buller, Ralph Buller, born in 1871, he was educated at Marlborough and Balliol College, Oxford. He entered the Indian Civil Service in 1892 and retired in 1917. He was a magistrate, controller, and inspector-general of police. His writings include *Makrán and Khárán* 1907). He died in 1949. IndianBilnd (1); Who was who, 4

Hugo, Just Abel, born 15 November 1798 at Paris, he grew up in various garrison towns in France, Italy, and Spain, where his father served as a general. In 1811 he became a page to the King of Spain. In 1813 he was attached to the general staff as a sub-lieutenant. He left the military in 1816 to pursue an interest in literature. He was a vice-president of the Société orientale. His writings include *Romances historiques, traduits de l'espagnol* (1822), its translation, *Abel Hugo und seine französischen Übersetzungen spanischer Romanzen* (1911), and *France militaire; histoire des armées françaises de terre et de mer de 1792 à 1833* (1834-38). He died in Paris in February 1855. DBF; IndexBFr² (1); OxFr

Hugon, Henri Louis Léon, born 27 August 1863 at Guéret (Creuse), he was a civil servant in France until 1885, when he left for Tunis to assume the directorship of agriculture and trade of the Régence de Tunis. After his return to metropolitan France he entered the financial administration, becoming first paymaster general at Tulle in 1914 and at Besançon in 1919. In 1924 he retired to Limoges. He was a member of several learned societies and a sometime president of the Société archéologique et historique du Limousin. His writings include *Les Emblèmes des beys de Tunis; étude sur les signes de l'autonomie husseinite, monnaies, sceaux, étendards, armoiries, etc.* (1913). He died in Limoges on 13 November 1953. DBF; BN

Hugonnard-Roche, Henri, born 20th cent., he successively associated with the Bibliothèque nationale de Paris, and the C.N.R.S. His writings include *L'Œuvre astronomique de Thémon Juif, maître parisien du XIV siècle* (1973), and he was a joint author of *Catalogue des cartes géographiques sur parchemin conservées au Département des cartes et plans* (Paris, Bibliothèque nationale, 1974), and *Introduction à l'astronomie de Copernic* (1975). EURAMES, 1993; Livres disponibles, 2004; Note

Hugonnet, Ferdinand Victor, he was born 22 May 1822 at Paris. After passing through the military college of Saint-Cyr, which he had entered in 1841, he received a commission as *sous-lieutenant* on 1 October 1843. He pursued a military career with the Bureaux arabes de l'Algérie. In 1853 he was awarded *chevalier de la Légion d'honneur*, and in the following year, captain. He left the military early in 1856. In 1858 he published his *Souvenirs d'un chef de Bureau arabe* which on account of the description of Arab customs, their progress and politics, was used for the first part of R. Peyronnet's *Livre d'or des officiers des Affaires indigènes*. His other writings include *Bugeaud, Duc d'Isly, maréchal de France, le conquérant de l'Algérie* (1859), and *Français et Arabes en Algérie* (1860). Peyronnet, 561; ZKO

Hugot, P., he was associated with the Centre des Hautes études d'administration musulmane, Paris. His writings include *Cours élémentaire de Hausa*, 2nd ed. (1957). NUC, 1956-67

Hugot, Pierre, born 20th ent., his writings include *Le Tchad* 1965), *Histoire de Djibouti* (1985), and *La Transhumance des Arabes Massirié et les batailles intertribales d'Oum Hadjer de 1947* (1997). Livres disponibles, 2004

Hugues, Luigi, born 28 October 1836 at Casale Monferrato, Piedmont, he graduated in engineering in 1859 at Torino and subsequently taught geography at his home town until 1896. A *dottore aggregato di geografia* since 1875, he was from 1897 to 1912 a professor at the Università di Torino. His writings include *Storia della geografia e delle scoperte geografiche* (1884-91). He died in Casale Monferrato on 5 March 1913. DizBI

d'**Hugues**, Ph.-Gustave, born 19th cent., he was a deputy administrator at Oum and Bouaghi, Province de Constantine, Algeria. His writings include *Sous la tente; types, scènes et paysages d'Algérie* (1895), and *Dans les douars; souvenirs d'Algérie, 1887-1888* (1897). BN; Note about the author

Huguet, J., born 19th cent., he was a French *médecin-major* who explored the Algerian Sahara since 1896. His trace is lost after an article in 1905. Note about the author

Huhn, Ingeborg nee König, born in 1940 at Hannover, Germany, she was married with children, and concurrently pursued a career as a free lance researcher. She received a Dr.phil. in 1989 from the Freie Universität Berlin for *Der Orientalist Johann Gottfried Wetzstein als preußischer Konsul in Damaskus, 1849-1861, dargestellt an seinen hinterlassenen Papieren*, a work which was used with much profit by Hans Jürgen Kornrumpf in his *Fremde im Osmanischen Reich, 1826-1912/13* (1998). Her other writings include *Der Nachlaß des Orientalisten Johann Gottfried Wetzstein in der Handschriften-Abteilung der Staatsbibliothek zu Berlin* (EDP: 2006). Note; Private

Huici Miranda, Ambrosio, born in 1880, he studied Arabic at the Université Saint-Joseph, Beirut, 1905 and 1906, subsequently taking philosophy and letters at the universities of Zaragoza and Salamanca, and earning his doctorate at the Universidad de Madrid. Unable to find a suitable Arabic post, he began in 1911 teaching Latin at the Instituto de Valencia, a city where he remained until the end of his days as a historian of the Muslims in Spain. His writings include *Historia política del Imperio almohade* (1956-57), *Historia musulmana de Valencia y su región* (1969-70), and *Colección diplomática de Jaime I., el Conquistador, años 1217 a 1253* (1916-18), as well as numerous translations of classical Arabic works and contributions to the *Cambridge history of Islam* and the *Encyclopaedia of Islam*. He died in Valencia on 9 November 1973. Boletín de la Asociación española de orientalistas, 10 (1974), pp. 7-8; Hespéris Tamuda, 14 (1973), pp. 5-6

Huillard-Bréholles, Jean Louis *Alphonse*, born 8 February 1817 at Paris, he was educated at the Lycée Charlemagne, Paris, where he later taught history, from 1838 to 1842. Since 1839 he was a member of the Commission des Monuments Historiques. A joint director of the *Bulletin des Comités Historiques* since 1843, he entered the Archives nationales in 1856 as an archivist, advancing to become head of its Section Législative et Judiciaire in 1868. On 29 January of the following year, he was elected member of the Académie des Inscriptions et Belles-lettres. His writings include *Recherches sur les monuments et l'histoire des Normands et de la maison de Souabe dans l'Italie méridionale* (1844), the five-volume *Historia diplomatica Frederici secundi* (1852-59), a work which won him the Grand Prix Gobert of the Académie des Inscriptions, and *Étude sur l'état politique de l'Italie depuis la paix de Constance jusqu'au milieu du XIV siècle* (1873). He died in Paris on 23 March 1871. Dantès 1; DBF; Hoefer; IndexBFr² (1); Vapereau

Huisman, August Jan Willem, born 22 October 1917, he prepared for a career in the Dutch East Indies by studying colonial law, first at Amsterdam and then changing to Utrecht, where he formally completed his studies in 1938. Before the outbreak of the war, he started on a degree in Semitic languages, which, however, he did not complete until 1954. From 1943 to 1947 he contributed to the *Concordance et indices de la tradition musulmane*. He subsequently served in two important capacities on Celebes until the independence of Indonesia. From 1954 until his retirement he was permanently associated with the Leiden University Library as a Near Eastern librarian. His writings include *Les Manuscrits arabes dans le monde; une bibliographie des catalogues* (1967). He died suddenly on 30 July 1983. *Manuscripts of the Middle East*, 1 (1986), pp. 100-102

Hulec, Otakar, born 23 March 1935 at České-Budějovice, Czechoslovakia, he studied history at Praha and received a doctorate in 1965 for *Zvláštní postavení Jižní Rhodesie mezi britskými koloniemi v Africe*. He became associated with the Czech Academy of Sciences. His writings include *Threefold wisdom; Islam, Arab world and Africa* (1993), and he edited *Cesta do země Mašukulumbů* (1973). Filipsky; OSK

Hull, Edward (Richard?), born in 1829 at Antrim, Ireland, he was for twenty years a member of the Geological Survey of Great Britain. In 1869 he became professor of geology at the Royal College of Science, Dublin; in 1883 he headed an expedition under the auspices of the Palestine Exploration Society to Arabia Petræa and Palestine. His writings include *Mount Seir, Sinai, and western Palestine, being a narrative of a scientific expedition* (1885), *Memoir on the geology and geography of Arabia Petræ, Palestine and the adjoining districts with special reference to the mode of formation of the Jordan Arabah Depression and the Dead Sea* (1886), and *Reminiscences of a strenuous life* (1910). He died in 1917. BbD; BiD&SB; Bioln, 2; Britlnd (1); Kornrumpf; *Who was who*, 2; ZKO

Hull, Richard William, born 29 August 1940 at Hackensack, N.J., he graduated in 1962 from Rutgers University, New Brunswick, N.J., and received his Ph.D. in 1968 from Columbia University, N.Y.C., for *The development of administration in Katsina Emirate, Northern Nigeria*. He was appointed a professor in the Department of History, New York University, a post which he still held in 2004. His writings include *African cities and towns before the European conquest* (1976), and *Modern Africa* (1980). ConAu, 45-48, new rev., 25; DrAS, 1969 H, 1974 H, 1978 H, 1982 H; NatFacDr, 2002-2005; NUC, 1968-72

Hulton, Jessop George de Blackburn, born about 1810, he took his M.D. at Edinburgh and obtained an appointment in the East India Company's service at Bombay. He accompanied a brig to the Red Sea and proceeded from Mocha into the interior and San'â'. He caught dysentery and died from fever on board the vessel in 1836. His writings include *The Journal of the late Jessop G. de B. Hulton, Esq., M.D., from 13th of August, 1832, to the 13th of May, 1836, and a paper on the Kooree Mooree Islands* (Preston, 1844). Britlnd (1); Henze

Hultsch, Friedrich Otto, 1833-1906 *see* Hultzsch, Friedrich Otto

Hultvall, John, born in 1911, he was a Swedish clergyman and teacher whose writings include *Mission och revolution i Centralasien; Svenska missionsförbundets i Östturkestan, 1892-1938* (Stockholm, 1981), and *Mission och vision i Orienten; Svenska missionsförbundets mission i Transkaukasien-Persien, 1882-1921* (Stockholm, 1991). LC; ZKO

Hultzsch, Eugen Julius Theodor, born 29 March 1857 at Dresden, Saxony, he studied classical and Oriental languages at Leipzig and Bonn, gaining a Dr.phil. in 1879 at the Universität Leipzig for *Prolegomena zu des Vasantarâja Çâkuna nebst Textprobem*. He became a librarian at London, and a professor at the Universität Wien before travelling in India from 1884 to 1885. He went out again to India in the following year as an epigraphist to the Government of India, concurrently acting as examiner of Sanskrit as well as fellow of the University of Madras. In 1903 he accepted an invitation from the Universität Halle to teach Indian subjects. His writings include *South Indian inscriptions* (1890-1916). He died in Halle on 16 January 1927. Buckland; DtBE; DtBilnd (2); IndianBilnd (2); Kürschner, 1925, 1926; NDB; Stache-Rosen; *Wer ist's*, 1909-1922

Hultzsch (Hultsch), Friedrich Otto, born 22 July 1833 at Dresden, Saxony, he studied classics at the Universität Leipzig where he received a Dr.phil. in 1855. He served in public education from 1857 to his retirement in 1884. His writings include *Griechische und römische Metrologie* (1862), *Der letzte Feldzug des Barkiden Hasdrubal und die Schlacht am Metaurus; eine historisch-topographische Studie* (1897), *Die Gewichte des Alterthums nach ihrem Zusammmenhang dargestellt* (1898), *Ptolemäische Münz- und Rechnungswerte* (1903), and *Münz- und Rechnungswerte* (1907). He died in Dresden on 6 April 1906. Dawson; DtBE; DtBilnd (9); Egyptology; NDB

Humbach, Helmut, born 4 December 1921 at München, he studied at München, where he received a Dr.phil. in 1951 for *Zum indogermanischen Femininum auf -os und -ä*. He was successively a professor of linguistics at the universities of Saarbrücken and Mainz. His writings include *Baktrische Sprachdenkmäler* (1966-67), *Die aramäische Inschrift von Taxila* (1969), and he was a joint author of *Die baktrische Inschrift IDN 1 von Dasht-e Nawur* (1976), and *Chwaresmischer Wortindex* (1983). In 1986 he was honoured by *Studia grammatica Iranica; Festschrift für Helmut Humbach*. GV; Kürschner, 1961-2005; WhoWor, 1991/92

Humbaracı, Aslan, born 21 August 1923 at Constantinople, he was educated at Robert College, Istanbul, and the Turkish Naval Academy. Since 1966 a naturalized British subject, he resided in London. He was a journalist and editor to a variety of English and French periodicals. His writings include *Middle East indictment* (1958), *Algeria; a revolution that failed* (1966), and *Portugal's African wars* (1974). ConAu, 49-52

Humberdrotz, Rudolf, born about 1900, he received a Dr.phil. in 1924 from the Universität Wien for *Onomatopoietika im Arabischen und Hebräischen*. He was a joint author of *Langenscheidts Taschenbuch der arabischen und deutschen Sprache* (1967), and he edited *Das Tagebuch des Johannes von Rost zu Kehlburg und Aufhofen* (Innsbruck, 1956). Schwarz; Sezgin

Humbert, Chantal, born 20th cent., he received a doctorate in 1976 from the Université de Nancy for *Les sources de l'orientalisme, son développement et son évolution sous Léopold I de Lorraine, 1698-1720*. His writings include *Les Arts décoratifs en Lorraine de la fin du XVIIe siècle à l'ère industrielle* (1993). Livres disponibles, 2004; THESAM, 4

Humbert, Claude, born 20th cent., he wrote *Ornamental design; Europe, Africa, Asia, the Americas, Oceania* (1970), *Label design* (1972), and *Islamic ornamental design* (1980). NUC

Humbert, Jean Pierre Louis, born 30 March 1792 at Genève, he studied Oriental languages under Silvestre de Sacy at Paris. In 1823 he was appointed a professor of Arabic at the Académie de Genève. He was one of the founders of the *Journal de Genève*. His writings include *Arabica chrestomathica facilior, quam, partim ex profans libris, partim e sacro codice collegit* (1834), *Guide de la conservation arabe; ou, vocabulaire français-arabe* (1838), and *Nouveau glossaire génevois* (1852). He died on 19 September 1851. Hoefer; ZKO

Humbert, Pierre Marie *Gustave*, born 15 May 1849 at Batterans (Haute-Saône), France, he graduated from the École polytechnique, Paris, and the École supérieure de guerre. He served in the 1881 Tunisian campaign, and in the 1882 Southern Oran campaign. With the rank of lieutenant-colonel he was sent in 1890-91 on a mission to the French Sudan, where he was later nominated a *commandant supérieure*. His writings include *Madagascar; l'île et ses habitants* (Paris, 1895), and *La Prochaine guerre, victoire ou défaite* (Paris, 1900). Curinier, 2 (1901), pp. 114-16

Humbertus de Romanis (Humbert of Romans), born about 1194 at Romans, a small town just north of Valence in the Dauphiné region of southeastern France, he became the fifth master general of the Dominicans. He left to posterity his *De praedicatione crucis contra Saracenos*, a manual written to assist those friars called to preach the crusade. He died in 1277. Edward Tracy Brett wrote *Humbert of Romans, his life and views of thirteenth-century society* (1984). BLC; Fück, 18-19; LC

Humblot, Paul, born 20 August 1886 at Paris, he graduated in 1907 from the École coloniale and subseqently journeyed for two years in Algeria and Tunisia to deepen his understanding of Islam and the Arabic language. In 1909 he began his military service at Mamou, Guinea, where he experienced the joys of a colonial administrator. He became one of the best French experts of the problems of the overseas territories. He died in 1878. Hommes et destins, 5, pp. 255-56

von **Humboldt** (Χούμπολτ, Гумбольдтъ), Friedrich Wilhelm Heinrich *Alexander*, born 14 September 1769 at Berlin, he was a natural scientist and geographer whose educational opportunities were worthy of his splendid intellectual gifts. He made a series of voyages which are memorable in the annals of science: to South America, the Ural and Altai mountains. His writings include *Kosmos* (1845-62). He died in Berlin on 6 May 1859. ADtB; AnaBrit; DLB, 90 (1989), pp. 193-99; DtBE; DtBilnd (23); EEE; Embacher; EncBrit; EncicUni; EncItaliana; EnSlovar; GdeEnc; Henze; Hoefer; Magyar; Master (90); NDB; WhWE

Hume, Elizabeth C., born about 1900, she was in 1932 associated with the Kennedy School of Missions, Hartford, Conn. Note about the author

Hume, William Fraser, born in 1867 at Cheltenham, England, he was educated at the Royal College of Science and the Royal School of Mines. He was associated with the Geological Survey of Egypt, 1897-1940, as a director and technical counseller. His writings include *The Topography and geology of the Peninsula of Sinai* (1906), *Geology of Egypt* (1925), and he was a joint author of *Topography and geology of the Eastern Desert of Egypt, central portion* (1902). He died in 1949. Bulletin de la Société de géographie d'Égypte, 23 (1949-50), pp. 63-74; WhE&EA; Who, 1921-1948; Who was who, 4

Hume, Wilson McClaughry, born about 1900, he received a Ph.D. in 1935 from the Hartford Seminary Foundation for a *Translation and notes of The Risalah of al-Qushairi concerning the science of Sufism*. NUC, pre-1956; Selim

Vicomte d'**Humières**, Marie Aymeric Eugène *Robert*, born 2 March 1868 at the Château de Conros, Aurillac (Cantal), France, he passed through the military college, Saint-Cyr, and was posted to the garrisons of Quimper and Compiègne. He resigned in 1892 to pursue an interest in letters. For fifteen years he was a great traveller: first in Algeria and Tunisia, then in Italy, in 1894 at Bayreuth, 1895 at Venice, the following year at Cairo, in 1897 at Athens and London. In 1898 he went for two years to India and the Himalayas; and since 1900 he visited Scandinavia and Spain. An established poet, writer, and translator, he was a sometime director of the Théâtre des arts. His writings include *Les essais sur l'île et l'empire de la Grande-Bretagne, Angleterre, Égypte, Inde* (1904), *Through isle and empire*, translated by Alexander Teixeira de Mattes (1905), and *Le livre de la beauté* (1921). Although under no obligation to serve in the war, he volunteered in 1914 and requested to fight at the front, where he was mortally wounded while leading his company in Lizerne, Belgium, on 26 April 1915. DBF

Humlum, Johannes, born 14 July 1911 at Holstebro, Denmark, he studied geography, geology and biology, and received a doctorate. He taught at trade and commercial colleges until 1939, when he became an assistant in cultural geography at Københavns Universitet, advancing to professor of geography, later also of cultural geography, at Århus Universitet, from 1943 to his retirement in 1981. In 1948 he participated in the third Danish expedition to Afghanistan. His writings include *Oversøiske transportproblemer* (1943), *Kulturgeografi* (1952), and *La géographie de l'Afghanistan* (1959). He died on 13 June 1990. Kraks, 1990

Hummel, Karl, born 25 April 1902 at Weiler/Allgäu, Bavaria, he received doctorates in 1927 and 1946 and taught pharmacy, pharmacognosy, and anthropology at the Universität Tübingen until his retirement in 1968. He was a joint author of *Die Grundlagen der europäischen Kultur und ihre Beziehungen zur orientalischen Kultur* (1968), and *Geistige Zusammenarbeit in der Ausbildung der Perser in Deutschland für Iran* (1970). He died on 28 December 1987. Kürschner, 1966-1987; ZKO

Hummel, Siegbert, born 18 July 1908 at Rodewisch/Vogtland, Germany, he received a Dr.phil. in 1948 for *Zum ontologischen Problem des Dauismus*. In 1949 he was appoined a director of Völkerkundliches Museum in Leipzig. His writings include *Das Gespenstige in der japanischen Kunst* (1949), *Die meroitische Sprache und das protoaltaische Sprachsubstrat als Medium zu ihrer Bedeutung* (1992), and *Sprache der Masai und ihre Beziehung zum Meroitischen* (1998). GV; Kürschner, 1950; WhoWor, 1982/83

Humphreys, Arthur Raleigh, born 28 March 1911 at Wallasey, England, he was a leading Shakespearean scholar who taught in many parts of the English-speaking world as well as in Turkey, Austria, and Denmark. His writings include *Steele, Addison and their periodical essays* (1959), and *Shakespeare's histories and 'the emotion of multitude'* (1968). He died on 9 August 1988. ConAu, 126; IntAu&W, 1976, 1977, 1982; Who, 1963-1988; *Who was who*, 8; WhoWor, 1978/79

Humphreys, Eileen, born 20th cent., she was a member of the British Institute of Persian Studies. Her wrings include *The Royal road; a popular history of Iran* (London, 1991). Note about the author; ZKO

Humphreys, Richard Stephen, born 11 August 1942 at Hutchinson, Kan., he graduated in 1964 from Amherst College, and received a Ph.D. in 1969 from the University of Michigan for *The Ayyubids of Damascus, 1193-1260*. He frequently did field-work in the countries of the Muslim Mediterranean from 1966 to 1990. He successively taught Islamic studies at S.U.N.Y., Buffalo, the University of Chicago, and the University of Wisconsin, Madison, from 1969 to 1990, when he was appointed to the chair of Islamic studies in the University of California, Santa Barbara, a post which he still held in 1995. His writings include *From Saladin to the Mongols; the Ayyubids of Damascus. 1193-1260* (1977), *Islamic history; a framework for inquiry* (1988), and he translated from the Arabic of al-Tabarī, *The Crisis of the early caliphate; the reign of Uthman* (1990). He also contributed articles to the *Encyclopaedia of Islam*. NatFacDr, 1995; Private; Selim; ZKO

Hunck, Josef Maria, fl. 20th cent., his writings include *Indiens landlose Revolution* (1957), its translation, *India's silent revolution* (1958), *India tomorrow; pattern on Indo-German future* (1963), and the booklet, *Presse in Japan* (1966). NUC

Hunfalvy, Pál (Paul), born 10 or 12 March 1810 to a family of modest substance at Nagy Szalok, Austria-Hungary, he was first educated at a village school, supplemented by the attention of a local pastor, then a secondary school in Késmark, and the Lutheran school in Miskolcz, where he studied Hungarian and classics. Some years after his graduation from the Lycæum, he was offered the turtorship to the sons of Baron Podmaniczky in Budapest. This gave him the opportunity to study law and become an advocate. But he never practised law and instead pursued an interest in linguistics, including Oriental languages. In 1841 he was elected a corresponding member of the Hungarian Academy of Sciences, and a year later, a similar distinction was offered to him by the Kisfaludy Társaság, the Literary Society. He was also invited to the professorship of law at his old Lycæum in 1842. After a brief parliamentary interlude, he was appointed librarian to the Hungarian Academy of Sciences, a post which he held until his death in Budapest on 30 November 1891. His writings include *A török, magyar és finn szók egybelhasonlítása* (1855), *Magyarország ethnographiája* (1876), and its translation, *Ethnographie und Ungarn* (1877). In 1891 appeared the commemorative volume *Hunfalvy album; Hunfalvy Pál félszázados akadémiai tagsága emlékére.* GdeEnc; JRAS, 1892, pp. 149-157; Magyar; ÖBL; Pallas; RNL; Wurzbach

Hunger, Herbert, born 9 December 1914 at Wien, he studied at the Universität Wien, where he received a Dr.phil. in 1936 for *Der Realismus in den Tragödien des Euripides.* He was a director of the Papyrussammlung, Österreichische Nationalbibliothek, and served from 1962 to1985 as a professor of Byzantine studies at the Universität Wien. A recipient of four honorary doctorates from international universities, his writings include *Lexikon der griechischen und römischen Mythologie mit Hinweisen auf das Fortwirken antiker Stoffe und Motive* (1953), *Aus der Vorgeschichte der Papyrussammlung der Österreichischen Nationalbibliothek; Brief* (1962), *Byzanz, eine Gesellschaft mit zwei Gesichtern* (1984), *Phänomen aus europäischer Sicht* (1984), *Byzanz und der Westen* (1987), and *Schreiben und Lesen in Byzanz; die byzantinische Buchkultur* (1989). He died on 9 July 2000. GV; IntWW, 1983-2002; Kürschner, 1976-1996; WhoAustria, 1959/60-1996

Hungerford, Edward, Rev., born in 1829, his writings include *Centennial sermons on the history of the Center Congregational Church, of Meriden, Conn.* (Hartford, 1877), and *American book of Church services* (1889). He died in 1911. NUC, pre-1956

Hunglinger von Yngue, Andreas Magnus, born 19 July 1763, he studied since 1771 at the Akademie der Künste, Wien, and became a landscape painter. He travelled in the Balkans and the East. In 1796 he taught drawing at Pest University. In 1798 he travelled in Greece and Turkey, where he spent some time in Smyrna and Constantinople. From 1808 to 1816 he was a drawing-master at the Theresianum and the Orientalische Akademie, Wien. In 1811 he opened the first Austrian modern gallery in Baden near Wien. His pictures of Oriental characters and street scenery appeal to the social historian rather than to artists. He published *Abbildungen und Beschreibungen herumziehender Krämer von Konstantinopel, nebst anderen Statdeinwohnern und Fremden aus Ägypten, der Barbarei und Archipelagus* (1803), and *Umm al-qurâ, Mekka, die Mutter der Städte der Mohammedanischen Religion* (1804). He died about 1830. ÖBL; Sezgin

Hunier, J., pseud. *see* Cloarec, Paul Jean Armand Marie, 1860-1951

Hunke, Sigrid, born 26 April 1913 at Kiel, Prussia, she received a Dr.phil. in 1941 from the Universität Berlin for *Herkunft und Wirkung fremder Vorbilder auf den deutschen Menschen.* She was a writer of fiction and non-fiction as well as scripts for radio and television, including *Am Anfang waren Mann und Frau* (1955), *Allahs Sonne über dem Abendland; unser arabisches Erbe* (1960), its translation, *Le soleil d'Allah brille sur l'Occident; notre héritage arabe* (1963), *Europas andere Religion* (1969), *Kamele auf dem Kaisermantel; deutsch-arabische Begegnungen seit Karl dem Großen* (1976), *Glauben und Wissen; die Einheit europäischer Religion und Naturwissenschaft* (1979), *Tod - was ist dein Sinn* (1986), and *Allah ist ganz anders* (1991). She died in Hamburg on 15 June 1999. KDtLK, Nekrolog, 1971-1999

Hunt, Chester Leigh, born 24 July 1912 at Duluth, Mich., he graduated in 1934 from Nebraska Wesleyan University and received his Ph.D. in 1948 from the University of Nebraska. He subsequently became a professor of sociology at Western Michigan University, Kalamazoo. His writings include *Cotabato, melting pot of the Philippines* (1954), *Sociology in the Philippine setting* (1954), *Social aspects of economic development* (1966), and he was a joint author of *Ethnic dynamics* (1974), and *Society and culture in the rural Philippines* (1978). AmM&WSc, 1973 S, 1978 S; ConAu, new revision, 5

Hunt, Kenneth, born 26 May 1914, he was associated in various capacities with the International Institute for Strategic Studies, London, from 1967 to 2000, concurrently serving as a visiting professor at home and abroad. His writings include *Defence with fewer men* (1973), and *Deterrend and defense in the North* (1985). He died on 27 March 1994. Who's who, 1980-2004

Hunter, Frederick Fraser, born 7 August 1876, he was with the military, from 1898 to 1905, when he was appointed assistant superintendent, Survey of India. He temporarily reverted to military duty from November 1914 to November 1919, when he was put in charge of the Mesopotamia survey party. From 1927 to his retirement in 1931, he was with the Map Publishing Office as a director. He published a *Map of Arabia and the Persian Gulf, 1908* (Calcutta, Survey of India Office, 1910). The India Office and Burma Office list, 1920, 1939; NUC, pre-1956

Hunter, Frederick Mercer, captain, born 19th cent., his writings include *The Aden hand-book; a summary of useful information regarding the settlement* (London, 1873), *An Account of the British settlement in Aden* (London, 1877), *A Grammar of the Somali language* (Bombay, 1880), and he was a joint author of *An Account of the Arabic tribes in the vicinity of Aden* (Bombay, 1886). BLC; NUC

Hunter, Frederick *Robert*, born about 1950, he was successively a professor in the history departments of Tulane University, New Orleans, La., and Indiana State University, Terre Haute, Ind. His writings include *Egypt under the khedives, 1805-1879* (1984), and *The Palestinian uprising* (1991). NatFacDr, 1995-2004

Hunter, George W., born in 1861 in Kincardineshire, he lost his mother when still a child. He made his first connection with institutional Christianity at the Y.M.C.A. Upon his second application to the China Inland Mission, in 1889, he was accepted by their Board to serve in China, where, for nearly a decade, he lived alone, surrounded by men to whom the most vital matters of his Christian faith were but an occasion for idle curiosity or even light jest. He returned to England for the first and only time in 1900, departing on 24 February 1902 for China, and arriving at his Urumchi, Sinkiang, station on 27 March 1906. Though he was first and foremost a missionary, he was also a great explorer, and knew Turkestan as no other Westerner did, and this at the time when the fast mail between Kobdo in Mongolia and Peking took a month. He died on 20 December 1946 as he had lived, a lonely man, unbroken by the post-war communist repressions, far from his fellow-missionaries, but cared for by faithful Chinese friends. Regrettably, he has not passed on more of the accumulated knowledge which he possessed. The honour which he coveted most was not the M.B.E. which King George VI was graciously pleased to grant him, but that of being a translator of the Scriptures into the language of some remote tribes who otherwise would not have known them. His writings include *Mohammadan "Narratives of the prophets"* covering the period from Zacharias to Paul; *Turki text with English translation* (Tihwafu [Urumchi], Sinkiang, 1916), and *Examples of various Turki dialects; Turki text with English translations* (Tihwafu [Urumchi], Sinkiang, 1918). *George Hunter, apostle of Turkestan*, by Alice Mildred Cable and F. L. French, London, 1948; MW 37 (1947), pp. 319-320

Hunter, Robert Edwards, born 1 May 1940 at Cambridge, Mass., he graduated in 1962 from Wesleyan University, Middletown, Conn., and received his Ph.D. in 1969 from L.S.E. He became a government consultant on foreign affairs, foreign policy adviser to several Democratic senators and presidential candidates, a professional lecturer in international affairs as well as university lecturer and fellow. His writings include *Israel and the Arab world* (1967), *Security in Europe* (1969), *Soviety dilemma in the Middle East* (1969), *NATO and Russia; bridge-building for the 21st century* (2002). ConAu, new rev., 33; Who's who in the East, 1981/82

Hunter, Thomas C., born about 1940, he received a Ph.D. in 1977 from the University of Chicago for *The development of an Islamic tradition of learning among the Jahanka of West Africa*. Selim[3]

Hunter, W. Patison, he wrote *Narrative of the late expedition to Syria, under the command of Admiral the Hon. Sir Robert Stopford* (London, 1841). Excerpts were published in the *United Service magazine*, and translations of portions of the work in the *Magazin für die Literatur des Auslandes*, in the same year. BLC; Sezgin

Hunter, William, born in 1755 at Montrose, Scotland, he studied at the University of Aberdeen, where he took an M.A. in 1777, later working on mechanical contrivances. After serving as apprentice to a surgeon, he became a ship's surgeon on an East Indiaman. For some time he was surgeon to the British Residency at Agra. On the foundation of the College of Fort William in 1801, he was appointed examiner in Persian and Hindustani. At the time of his death in 1812 he was superintendent-surgeon in the island of Java and its territories. Buckland; DNB; *Index Islamicus* (1); IndianBilnd (1); Riddick

Hunter, Sir William Wilson, born 15 July 1840, he was educated at the universities of Glasgow, Paris, and Bonn. He entered the Bengal Civil Service in 1861 and became Director-General of Statistics. His writings include *The Indian Musulmans* (1871), *The Indian Empire* (1882), *Life of Brian Houghton Hodgson* (1896), and *The India of the Queen* (1903). He died in Oxford, on 7 January 1900. BrtInd (1); CelCen [not sighted]; DNB; Note; Riddick; *Who was who*, 1

Hunth, Kenneth, born in 1914, he was a brigadier, and a director of the British Atlantic Committee, London. Note about the author

Huntingford, George Wynn Brereton, born 19 November 1901 at Newton Abbot, Devon, he graduated from Oxford University and received a Ph.D. in 1962 from the University of London. He was a lecturer at SOAS, who had lived in East Africa for twenty-five years. His writings include *The Northern Nilo-Hamites* (1953), *The Galla of Ethiopia* (1955), *The Kingdoms of Kafan and Janjero* (1955), *The Land charters of Northern Ethiopia* (1965), *Historical geography of Ethiopia* (1989), and he edited and translated *The Glorious victories of 'Āmda Şeyon, King of Ethiopia* (1965). He died in 1978. LC; Unesco

Huntington, Ellsworth, born in 1876, he graduated in 1897 from Beloit (Wisc.) College and subsequently spent four years teaching at Euphrates College, Harput, Turkey, concurrently mapping the area and exploring the Euphrates valley. He later spent altogether three years with expeditions to

Turkestan, Persia, Chinese Turkestan, India, China, and Siberia. From 1907 until his retirement in 1945 he was associated with Yale University. He was the recipient of numerous honours, awards, and medals. His writings include *The Pulse of Asia* (1907), *Palestine and its transformation* (1911), *Civilization and climate* (1915), *World power and evolution* (1919), and he was a joint author of *Principles of human geography* (1920). He died in 1947. Geoffrey J. Martin wrote *Ellsworth Huntington, his life and thought* (1973). ANB; BioIn, 1 (9); 10; DAB; EncIran; Kornrumpf; Kornrumpf, N; Master (9); NatCAB, vol. 37, p. 43; NYT, 18 October 1947, p. 15, col. 3; Shavit; WhAm, 2

Huntington, George Herbert, born in 1878 at Gorham, Me., he was a graduate of theological seminaries and Columbia University Teachers College. For thirty years he was a teacher at Robert College, Istanbul. He died in Portland, Me., in 1953. NatCAB, vol. 42, p. 316; Shavit; WhAm, 3

Huntington, Robert, born in 1637, he studied Oriental languages at Merton College, Oxford, and served from 1671 to 1681 as a chaplain to the merchants of the Levant Company in Aleppo. During this time he visited the Holy Land, Cyprus, and Egypt, including a visit to Saqqārah. Upon his request, Edward Pococke translated the Anglican catechism and liturgy into Arabic. He died in 1701. DNB; Egyptology; *Gentleman's magazine*, 95 i (1825), 11-15, 115-119. 218-221

Hunwick, John O., born in 1936 at Chard, Somerset, he obtained a B.A. in Arabic from SOAS, where he also received a Ph.D. in 1975 for *al-Maghili's replies to the questions of Askia al-Hajj Muhammad*. Some twenty years of his life were spent in Africa between Somalia, the Sudan, Nigeria, Ghana and Egypt. After military service in British Somaliland, 1955-56, and a year teaching at the Ahfad School, Omdurman, 1959-60, he was appointed to the University of Ibadan as a lecturer in Arabic in 1960. He remained of the faculty there until 1967, also initiating and directing a Centre of Arabic Documentation to preserve the Nigerian Islamic heritage. After teaching two years at his alma mater, he returned to Africa in 1969 - this time to Ghana - to teach Islamic and African history at the University of Ghana. In 1976 the Ghana Academy of Arts and Sciences honoured him by electing him a fellow. In 1977 he moved to Egypt where he spent four years directing programs of teaching Arabic to foreigners at the American University in Cairo. In 1981 he went to Northwestern University, Evanston, Ill., where he not only taught for two departments but was a chairman of the Department of Religion and, for two years, interim director of the University's Program of African Studies. He remained there until his retirement. He served as a consultant to Unesco on Arabic sources for African history, and from 1974 to 1988 was director of the Fontes Historicae Africanae project of the International Academic Union. He was a joint editor of *Sudanic Africa*. His writings include *Sharī'a in Songhay* (1985), *Timbuktu and the Songhay Empire; al-Sa'dī's Ta'rīkh al-Sūdān down to 1613* (1999), *The African diaspora in the Mediterranean lands of Islam* (2002), and he was a joint author of *The Writings of the Muslim peoples of Northeastern Africa* (2003). NatFacDr, 1990-2004; Private; Sluglett

Huober, Hans Günther, born about 1910, he received a Dr.phil. in 1934 from the Universität Hamburg for *Zinzendorfs Kirchenliederdichtung*. He was a sometime professor of education at Pädagogische Hochschule Reutlingen i. R. GV; Kürschner, 1970-1992|

Huot, *lt.-colonel*, born 1874 at Chalons-sur-Saône, France, he graduated from the military college of Saint-Cyr and entered the Bureau des Affaires indigènes de l'Algérie on 6 December 1899. He spent five years at various Saharan outposts and, in 1902, he founded Beni-Abbès, Algeria. In 1905 he was transferred to the Gouvernement général de l'Algérie and put in charge of native intelligence in Algeria as well as in Morocco, where he became head of the Service des renseignements in 1920. Peyronnet, p. 561

Huq, A. M. Abdul *see* Abdul Huq, A. M.

Hurault, Jean Marcel, born 30 August 1917 at Vincennes (Val-de-Marne), France, he graduated from the École polythechnique, Paris, and became an *ingénieur géographe* and associated with the Institut géographique national, Paris. His writings include *Problèmes de toponymie et de représentation du peuplement en Afrique noire* (1958), *Les Noires réfugiés Boni de la Guyane française* (1961), *La structure sociale des Bamiléké* (1962), *Applications de la photographie aérienne aux recherches de sciences humaines dans les régions tropicales* (1963), *La vie matérielle des Noirs réfugiés Boni et des Indiens Wayana du Haut-Maroni* (1965), and he was a joint author of *Mission d'étude des structures agraires dans le sud Dahomey, 1961* (1963). BN; Unesco

Hurault, Louis Aristide Alexandre, born 8 August 1886 at Attray-en-Gâtinais (Loiret), France, he graduated in 1906 from the École polytechnique, Paris, as a *lieutenant d'artillerie*. In 1912 he volunteered for the pacification of the Morroccan Rif. During the first World War, he used his scientifique background to improve artillery aiming with the aid of maps and arial photographs. After the war, he became director of the Service géographique de l'armée, rising to the rank of brigadier-general, and retiring in 1956 with the rank of *général de division*. He died in Vincennes (Val-de-Marne) on 2 November 1973. DBF; DBFC, 1954/55; *Hommes et destins*, 4, pp. 370-71; WhoFr, 1953/54-1971/72

Huré, Antoine Joseph Jules, born 11 February 1873 at Corbie (Somme), France, he graduated in 1895 from the École polytechnique, Paris, to which study at the École d'application de Fontainebleau and the École de supérieure de guerre was added later. He became a general staff officer with the French Engineers and served mainly in Morocco, resigning in 1938 with the rank of *commandant supérieur* of the French armed forces in Morocco. His writings include *La Pacification du Maroc; dernière étape, 1931-1934* (1952). He died in Pendé (Somme), on 17 March 1949. DBF; *Hommes et destins*, vol. 2, pp. 365-367

Huret, Jules (Жюль Гюрэ), born 8 April 1863 at Boulogne-sur-Mer, France, to a family of deep sea fishermen. Since the age of fifteen he had to support his parents by working at the municipality of Boulogne. Interested in journalism, he founded a literary circle, collaborating with local journals and becoming a correspondent for Parisian dailies. In 1886 he went to Paris, working for a variety of periodicals until 1890, when he entered full-time *l'Echo de Paris*. In the following year, he changed to *le Figaro*, producing the series *Enquête sur la question sociale en Europe*, published in one volume in 1897. Concurrently he was at the performing arts and social desks. In 1902 he began his ten-year period of extensive travels. In 1905 the Société de géographie commerciale de Paris awarded him its *Grande Medaille*. His writings include *De San Francisco au Canada* (1905), *Berlin* (1909), and *De Hambourg aux marches de Pologne* (1908). He died in Paris on 14 February 1915. DBF; OxFr

Hurewitz, Jacob Coleman, born 11 November 1914 at Hartford, Conn., he received his Ph.D. in 1951 from Columbia University, N.Y.C. for *The road to partition; the Palestine problem*. He started his career as a lecturer in Middle Eastern history at Dropsie College, Philadelphia, served as Palestine specialist during the war in the U.S. Office of Strategic Services and later in the Department of State, and as political affairs officer at the United Nations Secretariat in 1949. Since 1958 he was a professor of government at Columbia University, New York, and since 1971, a director of its Middle East Institute. He received grants from the Guggenheim Memorial Foundation, the American Philosophical Society, and the Rockefeller Foundation. His writings include *Diplomacy in the Near and Middle East; a documentary record* (1956), *Middle East politics* (1969), *Middle East dilemmas* (1973), and *Oil, the Arab-Israel dispute, and the industrial world* 1976). In 1990 appeared *The Middle East and North Africa; essays in honour of J. C. Hurewitz*. AmM&WSc, 1973 S, 1978 S; ConAu, 1-4, new rev., 2; Selim; WhoAm, 1982-1996; WhoE, 1989/90-1993/94; WhoWor, 1984-1989/90; WhoWorJ, 1965

Hurgronje, Christiaan Snouck, 1857-1936 *see* Snouck Hurgronje, Christiaan

Hurlaux, Édouard, born 19th cent., his writings include *Historique de la 19e section de commis et ouvriers militaires d'administration* (Paris, 1892), and the booklet, *L'Algérie, le tombeau de la chrétienne* (Paris, «les Actualités diplomatiques et coloniales» et «l'Africaines» 1905). BN

Hurst, Harold Edwin, born in 1880 at Wigston Magna, Leics., England, he was educated at Oxford and became a hydrological adviser to the Egyptian Ministry of Irrigation. During his term of duty he travelled extensively in the Nile Basin. His writings include *The Lake Plateau Basin of the Nile* (1925), *A Short account of the Nile Basin* (1944), *The Nile* (1952), and its translation, *Le Nil* (1954). He died in 1978. Au&Wr, 1963, 1971; *Who was who*, 7

Hurwicz (Hurwitz), Elias, born 1 May 1884 at Rogachov, Russia, he received a Dr.jur. in 1910 from the Universität Heidelberg for *Die Imperativtheorie und der §110 des Reichsstrafgesetzbuches; eine Studie zum Strafrecht*. He was resident in Berlin until 1934 when his trace is lost. His writings include *Die Orientpolitik der Dritten Internationale* (1922), and *Der neue Osten* (1927). EncJud²; KDtIK, 1925-1934; Wininger

Husayn, Rashid, 1936-1977 *see* Rashid Husayn Mahmud

Husayn (Hussein), Saddām, born 28 April 1937 at Tikrit, he was educated at Baghdad and Cairo. He became a leader of the Arab Socialist Ba'th Party and in 1979, a president and prime minister of Iraq. In 2003, during the American invasion of Iraq, he went underground, was subsequently betrayed by a body-guard, and captured by U.S. soldiers. His family then approached in 2004 the French lawyer J. M. Vergès to represent his interests in the subsequent trial at Baghdad. Efraim Karsh wrote *Saddam Hussein; a political biography* (1991). DcTwHis; IntWW, 1977-2005; IntYB, 1998; WhoArab, 2003/2004

Huseĭnov (hусеjнов), Beĭukaga Murtuza oglu, 1926-1983 *see* Guseĭnov, Beiukaga Murtazaevich

Huseĭnov (hусеjнов), Sadyg M. *see* Guseĭnov, Sadyg Mekhti-ogly

Huseĭnzadǎ (hүсеĭнзадǝ/Гусеĭнзфде), Ăli, fl. 20th cent., he was associated with Institute of History in the Azerbaijan Academy of Science. His writings include *XIX ǝсрин икинчи jарысында Азǝрбаjчан тарихшүнаслыFы* (Baku, 1967). OSK

Husik, Isaac, born in 1876 at Vascutinez, Russia, he received a Ph.D. in 1903 from the University of Pennsylvania for *Judah Messer Leon's commentary on the "Vetus logica."* He succesively served as a lecturer in philosophy in Philadelphia and New York City. His writings include *Three manuscripts with a glossary of Hebrew logical and philosophical terms* (1906), *Matter and form in Aristotle; a rejoinder* (1912), *A history of medieval Jewish philosophy* (1916), and he was a joint author of *Firdausī's Shahnāmáh and the Genealogica Regni Dei* (1935). He died in Philadelphia, Pa., on 22 March 1939. BioIn, 3; CnDiAmJBi; EncJud; Master (2); NatCAB, vol. 31, pp. 348-349; WhAm, 1

Hüsing, Richard *Georg*, born 4 June 1869 at Liegnitz, Prussia, he studied history and Indo-European languages, including Persian, and received a Dr.phil. in 1897 from the Universität Königsberg for *Die iranischen Eigennamen in den Achämenideninschriften*. He subsequently taught ancient Near Eastern history at the Universität Wien. His writings include *Der Zagros und seine Völker; eine archäologisch-ethnographische Skizze* (1908), *Die iranische Überlieferung und das arische System* (1909), and *Krsaaspa im Schlangenleibe und andere Nachräge zur iranischen Überlieferung* (1911). He died in Wien on 1 September 1930. DtBE; EncIran; Hanisch; Kürschner, 1925-1928/29; ÖBL; Schwarz; *Wer ist's*, 1922, 1928

Husmann, Heinrich, born 16 December 1908 at Köln, Germany, he studied philosophy, education, and mathematics, received a Dr.phil. in 1932 and a Dr.habil. in 1940. He successively taught music at the universities of Leipzig, Hamburg, and Köln. His writings include *Die dreistimmige Organa der Notre Dame-Schule mit besonderer Berücksichtigung der Handschriften Wolfenbüttel und Montpellier* (1935), and *Einführung in die Musikwissenschaft* (1958). He died in Göttingen on 8 November 1983. Baker, 1984, 1992; DtBE; Kürschner, 1950-1983; NewGrDM; *Wer ist wer*, 1955-1981

Hussain, Sajjad, born about 1920, he was educated at the Madrasah Aliya, Dacca College, and the University of Dacca. He was the first Muslim from Bengal to obtain a Ph.D. in English literature from the University of Nottingham in 1952 for his thesis *Kipling and India*. He was for many years chairman of the Department of English and dean of the Faculty of Arts, University of Dacca. He successively became vice-chacellor of the universities of Rajshahi and Dacca in East Pakistan. His writings include *Descriptive catalogue of Bengali manuscripts* (Dacca, Asiatic Society, 1960), *Mixed grill; a collection of essays on religion and culture* (1963), and he was a joint author of *Crisis in Muslim education* (1979). He died aged seventy-five in Dacca, on 12 January 1995. *Muslim world book review*, 15 iii (1995), pp. 67-68

von **Hussárd** (Huszár), Valentin, born 26 June 1787 or 88 at Wien, the son of a civil servant, he entered the Orientalische Akademie, Wien, in 1800, which he left in 1807 to become attached to the internuncio at the Porte in Constantinople, serving for twenty years as expert in Oriental languages and as interpreter In 1823 he was recalled to Wien to act as a legation secretary to Prince Metternich in Czernowitz at the meeting of the emperors of Austria and Russia. In 1824 he was nominated imperial court secretary. With the rank of imperial chancellery officer, he was entrusted in 1827 with an extraordinary mission to Constantinople. In 1830, when the situation at the Bosnian border became increasingly dangerous, he was sent on another extraordinary mission to Agram (Zagreb), in the course of which he travelled extensively in the area. On 29 May 1838 he was nominated *Hofrat* and confidential state officier. He was a corresponding member of the Société asiatique. Already in 1836 he had been decorated by Sultan Mahmud with the order *Nişani Iftihar*. He died in Wien in 1865. Fück, p. 160; Wurzbach

Hussein, Saddam, 1937- *see* Husayn, Saddām

Hussey, Eric Robert James, born in 1885 in Dorset, England, he was educated at Repton public school. He was an all-round athlete of considerable ability, specializing in the 120 yards hurdle. He was a member of the English team which participated in the 1908 Olympics. In the same year he took his degree at Hertford College, Oxford, and on going down entered the educational department of the Sudan Civil Service, his first post being as tutor in Gordon College, Khartoum. He was appointed chief inspector in 1918. In 1920 he was sent on an educational mission to Somaliland; in 1925 to Uganda, and in 1928 to Kenya. In 1928 he became Director of Education to Uganda and in 1929 was transferred to Nigeria as Director of Education, a post which he held until 1936. From 1942 to 1944 he served as educational adviser to the Emperor of Ethiopia. His writings include *Memorandum on educational policy in Nigeria* (1930), *Tropical Africa, 1908-1944; memoirs of a period* (1959), and he was a joint author of *Some aspects of education in tropical Africa* (London, 1936). He died on 19 May 1958. BritInd (2); *Who was who*, 5; ZKO

Husseynov, R. A., 1929- *see* Guseĭnov, Rauf Alishirovich

Huszar, G., born 19th cent., he was in 1928 an agent of Assicurazioni Generali di Trieste, resident in Cairo, and a member of the Société Fouad 1er d'économie politique, de statistique et de législation. Note about the author

Hutchins, Francis Gilman, born 29 October 1939 at Berea, Ky., he graduated in 1960 from Harvard University, where he also received his Ph.D. in 1966, and subsequently taught there in the Department of Government until 1973. During 1973/74 he was a member of the Institute for Advanced Study, Princeton University, N.J. His writings include *The Illusion of permanence; British imperialism in India* (1967), *Spontaneous revolution; the Quit India movement* (1971), a work which was published in 1973 entitled *India's revolution*. AmM&WSc, 1973 S, 1978 S; ConAu, 21-24; IntAu&W, 1977, 1982; WrDr, 1976/78-1994/96

Hutchinson, John P., born 20th cent., he taught at Clemson University, South West Missouri State College, and George Mason University. He did research while attached to the Social Research Group of George Washington University. In 1976, he was chairman of the Department of Sociology and Anthropology at Essex Community College, Baltimore, Md. From a graduate background of sociological theory and social psychology he proceeded into the area of political development in the Third World and into the areas of imperialism and nuclear weapon policies. Note about the author

Hutchinson, Martha Crenshaw, born about 1940, she received a Ph.D. in 1973 from the University of Virginia for *Revolutionary terrorism; the FLN in Algeria, 1954-1962*, a work which was published in 1978. In 1979 she was an assistant professor of government at Wesleyan University, Middletown, Conn. Selim

Hutchison, Alan Michael *Clark*, born in 1914, he was educated at Eton and Trinity College, Cambridge, and called to the bar from Gray's Inn in 1937. He served as a colonial administrator in the Muslim world, from 1946 to 1955, when he entered politics. He died in 1993. Who's who, 1969-1993

Hutchison, Elmo Harrison, born in 1910, he graduated from the University of Utah, and served in the US. Navy. A military observer with the U.N.O., he served with the Israel-Jordan Mixed Armistice Commission, and as a director of the American Friends of the Middle East. His writings include *Violent truth; a military observer looks at the Arab Israeli conflict, 1951-1955* (1956). He drowned in an inlet of the Red Sea in Saudi Arabia on 24 June 1964. Note; NYT, 26 June 1964, p. 29, col. 4; ObitOF, 1979 Shavit

Hutchison, John, born 19th cent., he studied medicine at Edinburgh and was a licentiate of the Royal College of Physicians and Surgeons. His writings include *Guide to Dalhousie, Chamba and the inner mountains between Simla and Kashmir* (Lahore, 1923), and he was a joint author of *History of the Panjab Hill states* (Lahore, 1933). BLC; Note about the author; NUC, pre-1956

Hutchison, Ralph Cooper, born in 1898 at Florissant, Colo., he graduated from Lafayette College, Harvard, and Princeton Theological Seminary, obtaining a Ph.D. in 1924 from the University of Pennsylvania for *Objectives and materials of the comprehensive program for young people of the Presbyterian Church, U.S.A.* He subsequently became associated with the national young people's work of the Presbyterian Church. He served in the war as a navy aviator, and after demobilization went out to Turkey to assist with the war and post-war emergency program of the Y.M.C.A. From 1925 to 1931 he was dean of the American College, Tehran. After his return to the United States, he was a university administrator and oil company executive. He died in Philadelphiy, Pa., in 1966. NatCAB, vol. 52, p. 593 [not sighted]; Note; NYT, 16 March 1966, p. 45, col. 1; Shavit; WhAm, 4

Huth, Hans, born 11 November 1892 at Halle/Saale, Germany, he received a Dr.phil. in 1922 from the Universität Berlin for *Das Zusammenwirken von Maler und Bildhauer an den plastischen Arbeiten der Spätgotik in Deutschland*. He successively served from 1924 to 1936 as a curator of the German national park service at München and Berlin. From 1944 to 1963 he was a curator of the Art Institute of Chicago; he subsequently was a lecturer in art at the University of California, Los Angeles. His writings include *Künstler und Werkstatt der Spätgotik* (1923), and *Der Park von Sanssouci* (1929). After his death in 1977 the Hans Huth Memorial Studies were established and financed by the Hans Huth Memorial Fund, dedicated to examining the inter-relationship between the decorative arts of Europe and the Islamic world. DrAS, 1969 H, 1974 H; Note about the author; WhoAm, 1974, 1976; WhoAmA, 1973-1978

Hutson, James, Rev., born 19th cent., his writings include *Chinese life in the Tibetan foothills* (Shanghai, 1921). NUC, pre-1956

Hutt, Anthony, born about 1952, he was educated at Mill Hill School, London, and studied on an open major scholarship since 1952 at Worcester College, Oxford. After reading history at Oxford, he went in 1966 to the School of Oriental and African Studies, London, as a post-graduate student, obtaining his M.Phil. in 1974 for *The development of the minaret in Iran under the Seljuks*. Since 1967 he was associated with the British Institute of Persian Studies, serving at one time as acting assistant director.

From 1971 to 1981 he served as associate editor of *Art and archaeology research papers*, and from January to May 1985, he was a visiting lecturer in Islamic art at the University of California, Berkeley. He was a joint author of *Iran* (1977-78), and *Persian landscape* (1978). He died on 13 October 1985, at the age of fifty-three. *Iran*, 24 (1986), p. iv; Sluglett

Huttenback, Robert A., born 8 March 1928 at Frankfurt/Main, Germany, he graduated in 1951 from the University of California, Los Angeles, where he also received a Ph.D. in 1959. He taught history at the California Institute of Technology from 1958 to 1969, when he became a professor of history, and later a chancellor, University of California at Santa Barbara. His writings include *British relations with Sind, 1799-1843* (1962), *The British imperial experience* (1966), *Racism and Empire; white settlers and colored immigrants in the British self-governing colonies, 1830-1910* (1976), and he was a joint author of *Mammon and the pursuit of empire* (1986). ConAu, 25-28; DrAS, 1969 H. 1974 H, 1978 H, 1982 H

Hütteroth, Wolf-Dieter, born 28 November 1930 at Königsberg, Germany, he received a Dr.phil. in 1959 from the Universität Marburg for a study of transhumance in the Kurdish Taurus Mountains entitled *Bergnomaden und Yaylabauern im mittleren kurdischen Taurus*, and a Dr.habil. in 1966 from the Universität Göttingen for *Ländliche Siedlungen im südlichen Inneranatolien in den letzten vierhundert Jahren*. He successively was a professor at the universities of Köln and Erlangen. His other writings incluce *Palästina und Transjordanien im 16. Jahrhundert; Wirtschaftsstruktur ländlicher Siedlungen nach osmanischen Steuerregistern* (1978), *Frühe Eisenbahnbauten als Pionierleistungen* (1993), and he was joint author of *Historical geography of Palestine, Transjordan and southern Syria in the late sixteenth century* (1977). Kürschner, 1970-2005; Schwarz

Hutton, James, born 1818, he was for a short time an officer in the Honorable East India Company. He was an editor of the *Delhi gazetteer*, *Bengal harkaru*, *The Englishman*, and *Madras Times*. He was later a newspaper editor in London until he became the proprietor of *The Day* until its bankrupcy in 1867. He subsequently turned to translating French monographs into English. His own writings include *A Popular account of the Thugs and Dacoits, the hereditary garotters and gang-robbers of India* (1857), and *Central Asia from the Aryan to the Cossack* (1875). He died in 1893. Boase; BritInd (1); Buckland; IndianBiInd (1); Riddick

Hutton, Thomas, born 4 March 1807 at Penang, he became a cadet in 1824, and arrived in India on 18 March 1826; he advanced to the rank of captain in the Bengal Army in 1838. Invalided on 24 December 1841, he died in Rajpur, near Mussoorie, on 19 December 1874. His writings include *The Chronology of creation; or, Geology and Scripture reconciled* (London, 1851), *Israel in the past, the present, and the future* (London, 1856), *Is Free Masonry of God?* (1856), and *Pre-Adamite death proved to be a geological delusion* (Agra, 1863). BLC; BritInd (1); IndianBiInd (2)

Huuri, Kalorvo, born 20th cent., he received a Dr.Phil. in 1941 at Helsinki for *Zur Geschichte des mittelalterlichen Geschützwesens aus orientalischen Quellen*. NUC, pre-1956; ZKO

Huxley, Aldous Leonard, born in 1894, he was educated at Eton and Balliol College, Oxford, and subsequently made his home in California. He was a major figure in the literary mainstream of his time. He died in 1986. ANB; Au&Wr, 1963; ConAu, new rev., 99; DLB, 36, 100, 162, vol. 195 (1998), pp. 155-67, vol. 255 (2002), pp. 97-105; DNB; Master (100); WhAm, 4; *Who was who*, 6

Hyde, Georgie D. M., born 20th cent., she wrote *Education in modern Egypt; ideals and realities* (London, 1978).

Hyde, Harford Montgomery, born in 1907 at Belfast, he was an attorney, private secretary, legislator, editor, and writer, particularly of historical biographies. His writings include *A History of pornography* (1965), *Cynthia, the spy who changed the course of the war* (1966), *Stalin* (1971), *Neville Chamberlain* (1976), and *Solidarity in the ranks; Lawrence of Arabia as airman and private soldier* (1977). He died in 1989. Au&Wr, 1963, 1971; BioIn, 10; ConAu, 5-8, 129; IntAu&W, 1976, 1977; Who, 1969-1989; WhoWor, 1976/77, 1987/88; WrDr, 1976/78-1986/88

Hyde, Thomas, born in 1636 at Billingsley near Bridgnorth, Shropshire, he received his first instruction in Oriental languages from his father, a vicar of the parish. About 1642 he went to King's College, Cambridge, where under Abraham Wheelock he made rapid progress in Oriental languages, so that after only one year of residence he was invited to London to assist Brian Walton with his edition of the *Polyglott Bible*. Besides correcting the Arabic, Persian and Syriac texts for that work, he transcribed into Persian characters the Persian translation of the Pentateuch, which had been printed in Hebrew letters at Constantinople in 1546. In 1658 he was chosen Hebrew reader at Queen's College, Oxford, and in 1659, he was admitted to the degree of M.A. In the same year, he was appointed under-keeper of the Bodleian Library, Oxford, and in 1665 librarian-in-chief. In 1691, the death of Edward Pococke opened up to him the Laudian professorship of Arabic; and in 1697, on the deprivation of Roger

Altham, he succeeded to the Regius chair of Hebrew and a canonry of Christ Church. Under three kings he discharged the duties of Oriental interpreter to the court. Worn out by his unremitting labours, he resigned his librarianship in 1701, and died in Oxford on 18 February 1703. His writings include *Historia religionis veterum Persarum eorumque Magorum* (1700) as well as a catalogue of the Bodleian Library in 1674. Britln (8); DNB; EncBrit; EncicUni; Enclran; Flück; GdeEnc; Master (5)

Hyer, Paul Van, born 2 June 1926 at Ogden, Utah, he received a Ph.D. in 1960 from the University of California at Berkeley for *Japan and the Lamaist world*. Since 1958 he taught history and Asian studies at Bringham Young University, Provo, Utah, a post which he still held in 1990. His writings include *A Mongolian living Buddha; biography of the Kanjurwa Khutughtu* (1983), and he was a joint author of *Mongolia's culture and society* (1979). ConAu, 104; DrAS, 1969 H, 1974 H, 1978 H, 1982 H; NatFacDr, 1990

Hyland, Michael Pearson, born 14 May 1936 at Denver, Colo., he graduated in 1960 from the U.S. Language School at Monterey, Calif., and had extensive residence, government work and academic research in Turkey before he became a research fellow Harvard University, from 1964 to 1970. He there received his Ph.D. in 1969 for *The party of Atatürk; tradition and change in Turkey*. Since 1989 he was associated with the United Nations Organization. Note about the author; WhoUN, 1992

Hyman, Anthony George, born 17 April 1946 in Sussex, England, he was in 1995 associated with Oxford University. His writings include *Afghanistan under Soviet domination, 1964-81* (1982), *Muslim fundamentalism* (1985), *Security constraints in the Gulf states* (1986), *Elusive Kurdistan; the struggle for recognition* (1988), *Pakistan; towards a modern Muslim state?* (1990), *Power and politics in Central Asia's new republics* (1994), *Russia's minorities in the near abroad* (1997), and he was a joint author of *Pakistan, Zia and after* (1988). Schoeberlein; ZKO

Hyman, Arthur, born 10 April 1921 at Schwäbisch-Hall, Germany, he received a Ph.D. in 1953 from Harvard for *Averroes' Sermo de substantia orbis*. He successively taught philosophy at the Jewish Theological Seminary of America, New York, Dropsie College, Philadelphia, Pa., and Yeshiva University, New York. His writings include *Philosophy in the middle ages* (1967), and *Eschatological themes in medieval Jewish philosophy* (2002). In 1988 appeared *A straight path: studies in medieval philosophy and culture; essays in honor of Arthur Hyman*, and in 1989 *Of scholars, savants, and their texts: studies in philosophy and religious thought; essays in honor of Arthur Hyman*. DrAS, 1969 P, 1974 P, 1978 P, 1982 P; Selim; WhoAm, 1974-1984; WhoWorJ, 1978 [not sighted]

Hymes, Dell Hathaway, born in 1927 at Portland, Ore., he graduated in 1950 from Reed College and received a Ph.D. in 1955 from Indiana University for *The language of the Kathlamet Chinook*. In 1965 he was appointed a professor of anthropology, folklore, linguistics, sociology, and education at the University of Pennsylvania; in 1990 he was associated with the University of Virginia. His writings include *Language in culture and society* (1964), *American structuralism* (1981), *Essays in the history of linguistic anthropology* (1983), and *Ethnography, linguistics, narrative inequality; toward an under-standing of voice* (1996). AmM&WSc, 1973 S, 1978 S; ConAu, 13-16; IntAU&W, 1977. 1982, 1986; DrAS, 1974 F, 1978 F, 1982 F; NatFacDr, 1990; WhoAm, 1974-2003; WhoS&SW, 1991/92, 1993/94; WhoWor, 1984-1989/90

Hyrtl (Гиртл), Josef, born 7 December 1810 at Eisenstadt, Austria, he studied medicine at Wien and after four years became a deputy dissector to the chair of anatomy. After gaining a Dr.med. in 1835, he became in 1837 a professor of anatomy at the Universität Prag, and in 1845 at Wien, where his lectures attracted crowds of students. In his inaugural address as chancellor of the Universität Wien in 1865 he denounced materialism and pleaded for the rule of the Church over science. In 1850 he founded the Museum für vergleichende Anatomie, Wien. He bequeathed his estate to the establishment of an orphanage and church in Mödling, and an institution for child welfare in Perchtoldsdorf. His writings include *Das Arabische und Hebräische in der Anatomie* (Wien, 1879), and *Руковоство орисательной анатомий* (1883). He died in Perchtoldsdorf, on 17 July 1894. DtBE; DtBilnd (10); ÖBL; Sezgin

Hyslop, John R., fl. 20th cent., he was a journalist whose writings include *Sudan story* (London, 1952), and *Sudan today* (London, 1954). BLC

Hytier, Jean Pierre, born 4 January 1899 at Paris, he studied at the Sorbonne, Paris, where he received all his degrees, including a doctorate in French literature. He taught some ten years each in Tehran and Alger before being invited in 1947 to teach his subject at Columbia University, N.Y.C. He retired in 1967. His writings include *Le Plaisir poétique; étude de psychologie* (1923), *Les Romans de l'individu* (1928), *Les Arts de littérature* (1945), *Les Dépêches diplomatique du Cte de Gobineau en Perse* (1959), *Questions de la littérature* (1967), and *La Poétique de Valéry* (1970). He died in Paris on 11 March 1983. ConAu, 109; DrAS, 1969 F; NYT, 13 March 1983, p. 44; WhoFr, 1971/72-1979/80

Hyvernat, Eugène Xavier *Henri*, born 30 June 1858 at Saint-Julien-en-Jarret (Loire), France, he studied at the Séminaire de Saint-Sulpice, 1877-1882, and was ordained priest in 1882 at Lyon. He subsequently studied at Roma, where he specialized in Oriental languages. In 1885 he was nominated a professor of Assyriology and Egyptology as well as a translator to the Congregatio de Propaganda Fide. In 1889 the French Government sent him on a mission to Armenia, as a result of which he published *Du Caucase au golfe Persique* (1892). In 1889 he was appointed to the chair of Biblical archaeology and Oriental languages at the Catholic University, Washington, D.C. In 1903 he established the publication of the *Corpus scriptorum christianorum orientalium*. His other writings include *Album de paléographie copte pour servir à l'introduction paléographique des Actes des Martyrs de l'Égypte* (1888). He died in Washington, D.C., on 29 May 1941. CurBio, 1941; DAB; DBF; Egyptology; Kornrumpf; NewCathEnc; WhAm, 1

IAblonskiĭ (Яблонский), Leonid Teodorovich, born 8 July 1950, he graduated in archaeology from Moscow University and became associated with the Archaeological Institute, Russian Academy of Sciences. He was joint author of *Древнейшее население низовий Амударьи* (1986), and *Антропология античного и средневекого населения Восточной Европы* (1987). LC; Schoeberlein

Iacopi (Jacopi), Giulio, born 7 September 1898 at Triest, he received a degree in humanities and a diploma from the Scuola Italiana di Archeologia. He became a superintendent of monuments and excavations at Rhodos and established the Istituto storico archeologico di Rodi, carrying on excavations and explorations also in Anatolia. He succesively served as superintendent of antiquities in Bologna and Reggio Calabria in 1942 and 1946 respectively. His writings include *Architettura turca in Rodi* (1932), *Lo spedale dei cavalieri e il Museo archeologico di Rodi* (1932), *Nuove epigrafi dalla Sporadi meridionali* (1932), *Rodi* (1933), *Museo archeologico dello spedale dei cavallieri di Rodi* (1935), and *Museo nazionale Tarquiniense* (1955-56). Chi è, 1940-1961; CurBio, 1959; Lui chi ; Master (1); Vaccaro; WhoItaly, 1963

IAdrintsev (Ядринцев), Nikolai Mikhailovich, born 18 October 1842 at Omsk, Russia, he was an archaeologist whose writings include *Сибирь какъ колония* (1892), and its translation, *Sibirien; geographische, ethnographische und historische Studien*, von N. Jadrinzew (1886). He died on 7 April 1894. BiobibSOT

IAgodin, Vadim Nikolaevich, born 5 February 1932 at Buzuluk, Orenburg Oblast, he was affiliated with the Institute of History, Archaeology, and Ethnography in the Karakalpak Branch of the Uzbekistan Academy of Sciences. He was a joint author of *Некрополь древнего Миздахкана* (1970); he edited *Вопросы антропологии и материальной культуры Кердера* (1973); and he was joint editor of *Археологические исследования в Каракалпакии* (1981). LC Schoeberlein

IAkovlev, Aleksandr Ivanovich, born 8 January 1950 at Moscow, he graduated in 1976 from the Regional Pedagogical Institute, Moscow, and received his first degree in 1980 for a study of capitalist influence on the social and economic development of Saudi Arabia entitled *Влияние государственного-монополистического капитализма на социально-экономом развитие Саудовской Аравии, 60-70 годы*. He was since 1967 affiliated with the Oriental Institute in the Soviet Academy of Sciences. His writings include *Саудовская Аравия и Запад* (1982), *Рабочий класс и социальная эволюция в нефтяных монархиях Востока* (1988), and he was joint author *Персидский залив в планах и политике Запад* (1985). Miliband²

IAkovlev, Nikolaĭ Feofanovich, born in 1892 in Russia, he graduated in 1916 from the Faculty of History and Philology at Moscow University. Since 1936 he was associated with the Institute of Linguistics, Soviet Academy of Sciences. His writings include *Словарь примеров к таблицам фонетики кабардинского языка* (1923), and *Таблицы фонетики каблардинского языка* (1923). He died 30 December 1974. Miliband; Miliband²

IAkovlev (Jakowlew/Yakovlev), Pavel Luk'ianovich, born in 1789, his writings include *Жизнь принцессы Анны* (Moscow, 1814), *Разказы лужницкаго старца и мои воспоминанія о немъ* (Moscow, 1828), and he was a joint author of *Russian missions into the Interior of Asia*; translated from the German (London, 1823). He died in 1835. NUC, pre-1956

IAkovleva, Nelli Sergeevna, born 2 April 1935 at Ilansk, Krasnoyarsk Territory, Siberia, she graduated in 1958 from the Oriental Faculty, Leningrad, and received her first degree in 1972 for *Сатирические новеллы Азиза Несина*, a work which was published in 1977. She subsequently joined the faculty of her alma mater. Her writings include *Турецкий рассказ; новей время* (1982). Miliband²

IAkubova, Él'vira Surenovna, born on 7 June 1928 at Andijan (Andizhan), East Fergana Valley, Uzbekistan, she graduated in 1951 from the Oriental Faculty, Tashkent, and received her first degree in 1985 for a study of Ahmad Shāh Durrānī's literary work entitled *"Диван" Ахмад шаха Дурани как источник по истории языка пашто и афганской литературы*. She subsequently joined the faculty of her alma mater. Her writings include *Афганские пословицы и поговорки на языке пашто* (1985). Miliband²

IAkubovskiĭ, Aleksandr IUr'evich, born in 1886 at St. Petersburg, he graduated from the Oriental Faculty in 1924 and in 1935 received a doctorate in history from Leningrad University. In 1949 he became a professor, specializing in the history of Central Asia and the development of the caliphate. His writings include *Самарканд при Тимуре и Тимуридах* (1933). He died on 21 March 1953. AzarbSE; EST; *Index Islamicus* (2); Krachkovskiĭ; Miliband; Miliband²; TatarES; UzbekSE; VostokMStP, p. 282

IAmpol'skiĭ, Zelik Iosifovich, his writings include *Древняя Албания; III-I вв. до н.э.* (1962). LC

IAnchevetskiĭ (Jan), Vasiliĭ Grigorevich, born in 1875 at Kiev, he graduated in 1897 from the Faculty of History and Philology at St. Petersburg. He subsequently travelled on foot for two years in northern and central Asian Russia, supporting himself by travel reports to newspapers. In 1901 he crossed the Karakum Desert by horse and visited Khiva and Bukhara. In the early years of the twentieth century he was a special correspondent for a St. Petersburg press agency, covering events in Port Arthur, Manchuria, Turkey, and the Balkans. He returned to Russia in 1918 and worked as a lecturer, school teacher, newspaper editor, and revolutionary stage producer. Since 1923 he resided in Moscow where he started his career as a writer of historical novels. In 1939 he was awarded a State Prize for the first part of his trilogy, *Чингиз-Хан*, its translation, *Jenghiz-Khan; a tale of the 13th century Asia* (1945), its sequel, *Батый*, its English translation, *Batu-Khan* (1945), and *К "Последнему морю"* (1955), all of which have also been translated into German. He died in 1954. Lev E. Razgon' wrote *В. Ян; дом детской книги* (1960). LC; Note about the author

IAnin, Valentin Lavrent'evich, born 20th cent., his writings include *Денежно-весовые системы русского средневековья* (1956), *Актовые печати Древней Руси XX-V вв.* (1970), and he edited *Археологические исследования в Верхневолжье* (1983). OSK

Iannettone, Giovanni, born 15 February 1928 at Carinola (Caserta), Italy, he graduated in colonial studies from the Università di Napoli, where he later lectured in Afro-Asian history and institutions. His writings include *La rivoluzione musulmana ed i paesi afro-asiatici* (1965), *Il Marocco negli atti consolari del regno delle due Sicilie* (1967), and *La Lega Araba* (Roma, 1979). IndBiltal (1)

IAralov (Yaralov), IUrii Stepanovich, fl. 1971, he wrote *Ереван* (1948), *Города Армении* (1950); he was joint author of *Архитектура Армении* (1950); and he edited *Архитектура республик Средней Азии* (1951). LC; OSK

Iatridis (Ιατρίδης), Demetrius S., born about 1940, he received a Ph.D. and became a professor of social planning at the School of Social Work, Boston College, Chestnut Hill, Mass., a post which he held until his retirement. His writings include *Social planning and policy alternatives in Greece* (Athens, 1980), and he was joint author of *Housing the poor in suburbia; public policy at the grass roots* (Cambridge, Mass., 1974). NatFacDr, 1995-2005

IAtsevich, Liudmila Stanislavovna, born 20th cent., her writings include *Неизвестный богатырь* (1961), *Заргуна* (1961), and she was joint author of *Русско-афганский словарь* (1973), and *Русско-дари разговорник* (1982). OSK; ZKO

IAstremskiĭ, Sergei Vasil'evich, 1857- *see* Jastrzębski, Sergiusz

IAukacheva, Mar'iam IAkubovna, born 9 May 1929 at Tashkent, she graduated in 1952 from the Oriental Faculty, Central Asian State University, Tashkent, and received her first degree in 1961 for a study of the theme of women's emancipation in contemporary Persian prose entilted *Тема освобождения женщины в современной персидской художественной прозе, 1920-1950 годы*. Since 1957 she was attached to the Oriental Institute in the Uzbek Academy of Sciences. Her writings include *Женщина в персидской прозе* (1964), and *Современнын прогрессивные поэтессы Ирана* (1978). Miliband; Miliband²

IAvich, Mirra M., fl. 1947, he edited *Народная поэзия Таджикистара* (Stalinabad, 1949). Note about the author; OSK

IAvorskiĭ (Jaworski), Ivan Lavrovich, born in 1853, he received a medical doctorate. From 1878 to 1879 he accompanied a Russian embassy to Afghanistan, and in 1894 he carried on orographic-geological exploration in Tien Shan, particular the mountain chains of Hasret-Sultan and Hissar. His writings include *Рутешествие русскаго посолъства по Афганистану и Бухарскому ханству в 1878-79 гг.* (1882-83), and its translation, *Reise der russichen Gesandtschaft in Afghanistan* (1885). Henze; Wieczynski; vol. 45, p. 24

IAzberdiev (IAzberdyev), Almaz, born 8 January 1939, he graduated in 1973 at Moscow and received his first degree in 1973 for *Проблемы библиорафирования национальной печати народов Средней Азии второй пол. XIX в. и первой четверти XX века.* He was since 1973 a director of library at the Turkmen Academy of Sciences. His writings include *Туркменская книга на арабской графике* (1981), *Мәмметназар Хыдыров* (1984), *Издательское дело в дореволюйионном Туркменистане* (1993), and *Гундогар метбечилиги ве көне туркмен басма китаплары* (2002). Miliband²

Ibáñez, Esteban, fl. 1955, he was affiliated with the Consejo Superior de Investigaciones Cientificas, Instituto de Estudios Africanos. His writings include *Diccionario español-rifeño* (Madrid, 1944), *Diccionario rifaño-español* (Madrid, 1949), *Diccionario español-baamarani; dialecto bereber de Ifni* (Madrid, 1954), *Diccionario español-senhayi* (Madrid, 1959), and *San Francisco el Grande en la historia y en el arte* (Madrid, 1962). Note; NUC, pre-1956-1967

Ibarra y Rodríguez, Eduardo, born in 1866 at Calatayud, Spain, he was a professor of history in the Universidad de Zaragoza and a sometime dean of the Facultad de Filosofía y Letras at Zaragoza as well as Madrid. He was also the founder and director of several periodicals. He died in Madrid in 1944. Espasa; IndiceE³ (2); Ossorio

Ibragimbeili, Khadzhi Murat, born 20th cent., his writings include *Россия и Азербайджан в первой трети XIX века* (1969), *Страничы истории боевого содружества русского и кавказских народов, 1853-1856 гг.* (1970), *Крах 'Эдельвейса' и Ближний Восток* (1977), and he edited *Турция и Адрианопольский мир 1829 г.* (1975), and *Османская империя в первой четверти XVII века* (1984). OSK

Ibragimov, Galimdzhan Girfanovich, born in 1887 at Sultanmuratovo, he was educated at *madrasahs* in Orenburg and Ufa. He was a Tatar scholar whose writings include *Дочьстепи* (1957), and *Наши дни* (1966). He died on 21 January 1938. F. G. Gabsaliamova wrote *Галимжан Ибрагимов; библиогра-фический указатель, 1907-1977* (1979). AzarbSE; BashkKE; BiobibSOT, pp. 167-68; GSE; KazakSE; *Казахская ССР краткая энциклопедия*, vol 4, p. 258; TatarES

Ibragimov, Mirza A., 1911- *see* Ibrahimov, Mirzä Äzhdär ogly

Ibragimov, Nematula, born 8 August 1945 at Margelan, Uzbekistan, he graduated in 1970 from the Oriental Faculty, Tashkent, received his first degree in 1975 with a dissertation on Ibn Battutah, and received his doctorate in 1984 fo a study of the Arabic popular novel entitled *Арабский народний роман* Since 1970 he was affiliated with his alma mater. He was appointed a lecturer in 1977, and a professor in 1985. His writings include *Ибн Баттута и его путешествия по Средней Азии* (1988), and he was a joint editor of *Повест о богатыре эмире Хамзе* (1990). Miliband²

Ibragimov, Sabirdzhan K., born in 1905 at Andijan (Andizhan), East Fergana Valley, he was a Turkologist whose writings include *Новые материалы по древнеи и средневековой истории Казахстана* (1960), and he was joint author of *Материалы по истории казахских ханств XV-XVIII веков* (1969). He died on 22 December 1974. *Советская тюркология*, 1975, no. 2, pp. 122-124; OSK

Ibragimov, Sagadat Mugallimovich, born 20th cent., his writings include *Аналитические конструкции и татарском языке* (Kazan, 1964). NUC, 1968-72

Ibragimov, Sapar Kamalovich, born 28 December 1929 in Kazakhstan, he graduated in 1950 from the Faculty of History, Kazakhstan State University, and received his first degree in 1953 from the Leningrad Branch of the Oriental Institute, Soviet Academy of Sciences for a study of democratic reform in Sinkiang, 1949-1951 entitled *Демократические преобразования в Синьцзяне после победы Китайской народной революции: 1949-1951 гг.* From 1953 to his death on 14 April 1960 he was a research fellow in Institute of History, Archaeology, and Ethnography, Kazakh Academy of Sciences. He was a joint author of *Краткий словарь к произведеиням узбекской клвссической литературы* (Tashkent, 1953). Miliband²

Ibragimov, T. A. *see* Ibrahimov, Tagi Äbulkasim ogly

Ibragimov, Z. I., 1910-1972 *see* Ibrahimov, Zulfäli Imamäli ogly

Ibrahimov (Ибрахимов/Ибрагимов), Mirzä Äzhdär ogly, born 28 October 1911 in Azerbaijan, he was writer and dramatist whose writings include *Избранные произведения* (1958), *Заметки о литера-*

туре, классики и современники (1971), and he edited *Azerbaijanian poetry, classical, modern, traditional* (ca. 1969), and *Azerbaijanian prose* (1977). AzarbSE, vol. 4, p. 361; KazakSE; OSK

Ibrahimov (ИбраҺимов), Tagi Äbulkasim ogly (Shahin), fl. 1963-1981, his writings include, *Иранда сијаси чәмијјәтләр вә тәшкилатларын јаранмасы вә онларын фәалијјәти, 1858-1906-чы илләр*, Russian colophon title, *Создание политических организаций в Иране и их деятельност, 1858-1906 гг.* (1967), and *Гашгајлар*, Russian colophon title, *Кашкайцы* (1988). NUC, 1968-72; OSK

Ibrahimov (Ибрахимов/Ибрагимов), Zulfäli Imamäli ogly, born 25 December 1910 in Azerbaijan, he wrote *Революция 1905-1907 гг. в Азербайджане* (1955). He died in Baku on 21 September 1972. AzarbSE

Ideler, Christian *Ludwig*, born in 1766 at Groß Breese, Prussia, he studied theology, philology, astronomy, and mathematics at the Universität Halle/Saale. In 1794 he was appointed at Berlin an astronomer for reckoning time, becoming a member of the "royal calendar deputation." A member of the Akademie der Wissenschaften since 1810, his writings include *Lehrbuch der mathematischen und technischen Chronologie* (1883). He contributed an edition and translation on the names of the stars from al-Qazwīnī's *'Ajā'ib al-makhlūqāt* to *Fundgruben des Orients*. He died in Berlin on 10 August 1846. ADtB; DcBiPP [not sighted]; DtBE; Fück, 160

Idelsohn, Abraham Zevi, born 1 July 1882 at Filzburg, near Libau, Courland, he studied at the conservatories of Berlin and Leipzig and in 1905 went to Jerusalem, where he founded the Institute of Jewish Music and the Jewish Music School. In 1922 he went to the U.S.A., where two years later he became a lecturer at the Hebrew Union College, Cincinnati, Ohio. His writings include *Liederbuch; Sammlung hebräischer und deutscher Lieder für Kindergärten, Volks- und höhere Schulen* (Berlin, Hilfsverein der deutschen Juden, 1912) and *Jewish liturgy and its development* (New York, 1932). Aron Friedmann wrote *Abraham Zwi Idelsohn zu seinem 50. Geburtstag; eine musikwissenschaftliche Studie* (Hamburg, 1932). He died in Johannesburg in August 1938. Baker, 1978, 1984, 1992; BioIn, 2; CnDiAmJB; ConAu, 109; DtBE; DtBInd (5); JüdLex; NewGrDM; Master (3); Wininger

Idowu, Hezei Olu, born 20th cent., he received a doctorate in 1966 from the University of Ibadan for *The Conseil general in Senegalm, 1879-1920.* He was a joint author of *History of West Africa; the revolutionary years, 1815 to independence* (1970). NUC, 1968-72; ZKO

Idris, Hady Roger, born 11 May 1912 at Paris, he received his secondary education at the Lycée Carnot, Tunis, and the Lycée Charlemagne, Paris. He then studied at the Faculté des Lettres de Paris under M. Gaudefroy-Demombynes, W. Marçais, and L. Massignon, obtaining a diploma in Arabic language and literature in 1935. In 1951 he became a professor in the Institut des Hautes Études de Tunis, concurrently preparing his principal thesis, *La Berbérie orientale sous les Zirides*, and his complementary thesis, *Les Manāqib d'Abū Ishāq al-Gabanyānī.* Since 1957 he taught history of the Arab West at the Faculté des Lettres d'Alger. In the course of the political events of 1962 his chair was transferred to the Université de Bordeaux, where he taught until his death on 29 April 1978. His writings include *L'Occident musulman à l'avènement des 'Abbāsides d'après le chroniqueur zīrīde al-Raqīq* (1974). NDNC, 5 (1968); *Revue des études islamiques*, 46 (1978), pp. 155-61

Ierusalimskaia, Anna Aleksandrovna, born 1 September 1928, she graduated in 1951 from the Faculty of History, Leningrad, and received her first degree in 1958 for *К истории племен эпохи бронзы степного Предкавказья.* She was since 1957 associated with the Oriental Section of the Hermitage Museum, Leningrad. Miliband; Miliband²

Iessen, Aleksandr Aleksandrovich, born 23 July 1896 at Peterburg, his writings include *Моздокский могильник* (1940), *Греческая колонизация северного Причерномоьря* (Leningrad, 1947), *Первобытная культура* (1955-56), and he was a joint author of *Из истории древней металлургии Кавказа* = *Гафгазда ән гәдим мис металлургијасы мәсәләсинә даир* (1935). He died in Leningrad on 31 May 1964. AzarbSE, vol. 4, p. 391; OSK

Igl, Gerhard, born 3 September 1947 at Berchtesgaden, Bavaria, Germany, he received a Dr.jur. in 1976 from the Universität Mannheim for *Die rechtliche Behandlung der Luftverunreinigung durch Industriebetriebe.* Since 1997 he was a professor of public and social law at the Universität Kiel. He was a joint author of *Einführung in das Recht der sozialen Sicherheit von Frankreich, Großbritannien und Italien* (1978). Kürschner, 2001-2005

Iglesias Laguna, Antonio, born in 1927 at Madrid, he received a degree in philosophy and letters. He resided for twelve years in Pakistan, India, and Germany. He was a literary critic, novelist, poet, editor, and a sometime lecturer in Spanish at Sindh Muslim Law College, University of Karachi. He travelled extensively in the Muslim world. His writings include *¿Por que no se traducela literatura española?* (Madrid, 1964), *Dios en el retiro* (Madrid, 1966), *La India, con vacas y sin ingleses* (Madrid, 1969),

Treinta años de novela española, 1938-1968 (Madrid, 1969), and *Literatura de España dia a dia, 1970-1971* (Madrid, 1972). He died in 1972. LC; IndiceE³ (1)

Ignatenko, Aleksandr Aleksandrovich, born 2 February 1947 in Russia, he graduated in 1970 from the Institute of Asian and African Studies and received his first degree in 1976 for a study of contemporary Islamic ideologies in the Arab world entitled *Основные направленния современная исламская идеологии в арабских странах*, and a doctorate in 1989 for *Общественно--политические взгляды арабо-исламских философов средневековья*. From 1981 to 1984 he served as director at the Soviet cultural centre in Alger. His writings include *Ибн-Халдун* (1980), *Халифы без халифата* (1988), *В поисках счастья; общественно-политические воззрения арабо-исламских философов средневековья* (1989), and he was a joint author of *Ислам на пороге XXI века* (1989). Miliband²

Ignat'ev, Nikolaï Pavlovich, born in 1832, he was a Russian statesman and diplomat who was conferred *graf* in 1877. An ardent patriot, imperialist and Panslav, he is best known for negotiating the Treaty of San Stefano with the Porte. His writings include *The Russian emerges; a native assessment of the Soviet experiment* (1932), and *Mission of N. P. Ignat'ev to Khiva and Bukhara in 1858*, edited and translated by John L. Evans (1984). He died in St. Petersburg in 1908. Bioln, 4; EnSlovar; Kornrumpf; Wieczinski, vol. 14, pp. 125-130

Igonetti, Giuseppina, born 20th cent., she was a joint author of *Rachid Boudjedra, un grande scrittore algerino* (1987). ZKO

Ijäs, Alexander (Александр Ияс), born in 1869, he graduated in 1891 with excellent marks from the Hamina Military Academy. From 1895 to 1898 he took courses in Oriental languages at the Asia Department of the Russian Foreign Office, and in 1900 was posted to the Turkestan military district. There he was used on diplomatic missions, e.g. in the Pamir expedition and on a commission sent to Persia to fight the plague. He was first stationed as consul in Khorasan, and in 1912 was sent to Soudj-Bulag, the capital of Persian Kurdistan as a Russian consul. He had a good command of Pashto and Persian, and soon acquired a command of Kurdish. In 1913 he made a journey of exploration in his consular district in connection with the diplomatic talks going on in Constantinople concerning the status of Kurdistan. When the World War broke out he remained at his post in order to pacify the Kurds. He was killed on 29 December 1914 in the Turkish invasion. Aalto, pp. 139-40

Ikram, Sheikh Mohammad, born in 1908 in a small town in the district of Faisalabad, India. In 1932, soon after receiving a master's degree in English from Government College, Lahore, he was selected for the Indian Civil Service and sent to Oxford. After his return followed a long administrative career in British India and Pakistan. Early in life he became attached to Sufism and he is best remembered as a historian and scholar. He was a sometime visiting professor of international affairs at Columbia University, N.Y.C. His writings include *Makers of Pakistan and modern India* (1950), and *History of Muslim civilization in India and Pakistan* (1963), as well as works in Urdu. He was joint editor of *The cultural heritage of Pakistan* (1955). He died in 1973. Afkar/Inquiry 2, no. 1 (January 1985), pp. 51-52

Sigmund Ritter von **Ilanor**, Carl Ludwig, born in 1810 at Schäßburg, Transylvania, he was a physician and a professor at the Wiener Hochschule. His writings include *Die Quarantäne; Reform und die Festfrage* (1850), *Südliche klimatische Kurorte mit besonderer Rücksicht auf Pisa, Nizza und die Riviera, Venedig, Meran und Gries* (1859), and *Über neuere Behandlungsweisen der Syphillis* (1876). He died in 1883. ADtB, vol. 34, pp. 300-301; DtBilnd (4); Wurzbach

Ilberg, Johannes, born in 1860 at Magdeburg, Prussia, he studied philology, archaeology, history, and philosophy at the universities of Leipzig, Bonn and Berlin, obtaining a Dr.phil. in 1883 from the Universität Leipzig for *Studia pseudippocratea*. He was a classicist and medieval historian who served successively as a principal at the leading secondary schools in Saxony. In 1897 he became a joint editor of *Neue Jahrbücher für das klassische Altertum, Geschichte und deutsche Literatur*, serving from 1914 to 1929 as its sole editor. His writings include *Die Sphinx in der griechischen Kunst und Sage* (1896), *Die Überlieferung der Gynäkologie des Soranus von Ephesos* (1910), *Rufus von Ephesos* (1930), and *Über die Schriftstellerei des Klaudios Galenos* (1974). He died in Leipzig on 20 August 1930. Bioln, 3; DtBE; Kürschner, 1926; NDB; Sezgin; Wer ist's, 1928

Ileri, Celal Nuri, born in 1877 at Gelibolu, Turkey, he was educated at the Galatasaray *lycée*, and graduated from the Constantinople Faculty of Law. He travelled in western Europe and was a member of the last Ottoman parliament as well as a deputy of the Türkiye Büyük Millet. He was a journalist whose writings include *Kutub musahabeleri* (1913), *'Ilel-i ahlâkiyemiz* (1916), *Ittihad-i Islâm ve Almanya* (1916), and *Taç giyen millet* (1923). He died in 1939 in Istanbul. Meydan; Özege

Iliescu, Octavian, born 22 August 1919 at Craiova, Rumania, he was a numismatist and historian whose writings include *Moneda în România, 491-1864* (Bucureşti, 1970); he was a joint author of *Constantin cel Mare* (1982); and he edited *Cultura bizantină în România; catalogul expoziţiei* (Bucureşti, 1971), and *La Numismatique, source de l'histoire de l'art et de l'histoire des idées* (1981). LC; OSK

Iliff, A. D., fl. 1955, he obtained a doctorate and subsequently spent twenty years in or near Waziristan as a medical missionary before joining the London Church Missionary Society's hospital on the North West Frontier of Pakistan. Note about the author

Il'inskii, Georgii Nikolaevich, born in 1903 at St. Petersburg, he graduated in 1930 from the Moscow Oriental Institute, and received his first degree in 1940 for a study of the Persian revolution, 1905-1911 entitled *Иранская революция, 1905-1911*. He was from 1941 to 1952 associated with the Ministry of Foreign Trade, nine years of which he spent in Iran. His writings include *Иран в период общего кризиса мировой капиталис-тической систем* (1953). He died 5 January 1960. Miliband; Miliband²

Ilisch, Ludger, born 2 July 1950 at Billerbeck, Westphalia, Germany, he studied Islamic and Byzantine subjects and history at the Universität Münster, where he received a Dr.phil. in 1985 for a study of the history of the Artuqids entitled *Geschichte der Artuqidenherrschaft von Mardin zwischen Mamluken und Mongolen, 1260-1410 A.D.* Thesis

Ilisch, Lutz, born 20th cent., he was in 1983 an editor of the *Münsterische numismatische Zeitung*. His writings include *Dirham und Rappenpfenning; Mittelalterliche Münzprägung in Bergbauregionen* (2003), and he edited *Sylloge numorum arabicorum Tübingen; Palästina, IV a, Bilād aš-Šām I* (1993). LC; Note about the author; ZKO

Illarionov, Sergeĭ Ivanovich, born 20th cent., his writings include *Государственный сектор в экономике Пакистана* (1979), *Роль государства в развитии экономики Пакистана 70-е годы XX в.* (1981), *Стратегия развития и внешнеэкономическая функция государства в странах Азии* (1982), and *Освободившиеся страны; роль внешне-экономических связей в развитии* (1987). LC; OSK

Il'minskiĭ, Nikolaĭ Ivanovich, born 23 April 1822 at Penza, Russia, he graduated in 1846 from the Ecclesiastical Academy (Духовная Акадннмия), Kazan, and subsequently began to teach there general arts subjects, including Arabic, but not Oriental subjects. During his time, the Academy was planning courses for missionaries and the establishment of an anti-Islamic department. He was selected to spent 1856 to 1854 in the Arab countries to perfect his Arabic. In the autumn of 1854 he began teaching at the department of missions, concentrating on language proficiency, including Tatar, over Islamic subjects. Soon to be suspected of being a partisan of Islam, he was obliged to resign his professorship in 1858 and go to Orenburg, where he was employed by the Commission for indigenous affairs. Having established himself with Turkological works, he was recalled to the chair of Turko-Tatar dialects at the University of Kazan in 1861. Two years later he was also reinstated to his professorship at the Academy. In 1872 he was appointed director of the Kazan Teachers College, a post which he held for the rest of his life, but which prevented him from academic work in Oriental studies. His writings include *О передаче звуков киргизкаго языка буквами русской азбука* (1862). He died on 27 December 1891. BashkKE; BiobibSOT, pp. 168-170; EnSlovar; Krachkovskiĭ, pp. 174-77; Miliband; Miliband²; VostokMStP, p. 250

Ilschner, Berhard Rudolf, born 13 December 1928 at Danzig, Germany, he studied applied science subjects at the universitites of Rostock, and Jena, obtaining a Dr.rer.nat. in 1954 from the Universität Bonn, and a Dr.habil. in 1963 from the Universität Göttingen. He was successively associated with the Akademie der Wissenschaften, Berlin, Massachusetts Institute of Technology, Cambridge, Mass., Zentralforschung Friedrich Krupp, Universität Erlangen-Nürnberg, Universität Göttingen, and from 1992 to his retirement in 1996 with the École polytechnique de Lausanne. His writings include *Neue Aufgaben der Werkstoffentwicklung* (1979), and *Forschung und Lehre im Spannungsfeld zwischen Universität und Industrie* (1986). Wer ist wer, 1989/90-2004/2005; WhoWor, 1974/75, 1976/77

Ilyas Ahmad, born 1891, he was a sometime district judge and, in 1958, a professor and head of the Department of Political Science in Karachi University. His writings include *Trends in socialistic thought and movement* (1937), *The social contract and the Islamic state* (1944), *Thoughts on the Indian constitutional problem, 1940-47* (1947), *The machinery of government* (1957). He died in 1960. LC

Imamnazarov, Mukhammad Sultanovich, born 6 February 1942 at Kokand, Uzbekistan, he graduated in 1966 from the Oriental Faculty, Tashkent State University, and received his first degree in 1975 for a study of Amīr Khusraw Dihlavī's poem Shirin and Khusraw entitled *Статистико-семантические*

исследование лексики поэмы "Ширин и Хосров" Амира Хосрова Дехлави. He was since 1979 associated with the Tashkent academy of Party Politics. Miliband²

Imamović, Mustafa, born 29 January 1941 at Gradačac, Bosnia, he studied at Beograd University, where he received all his degrees, including a doctorate. He subsequently became a professor at Sarajevo University. His writings include *Pravni položaj i unutrašnji politički razvitak Bosne i Hercegovine od 1878 do 1914* (Sarajevo, 1976), *Bošnjaci u emigraciji; monografija Bošanskih pogleda 1955-1967* (Sarajevo, 1996), and *Historija Bošnjaka* (Sarajevo,1998). KoBošnjaka, 2002

Imart, Guy G., born 20th cent., he received a *doctorat d'état* in 1979 from the Université d'Aix-Marseille for *Les Kirghiz; description d'une langue de littérisation récente,* a work which was published in 1981. He became associated with the Research Institute for Inner Asian Studies at Indiana University. His writings include *Islamic and Slavic fundamentalisms; foes or allies* (1987), *The limits of Inner Asia; some soul searching on new borders for an old frontier-land* (1987), *From roots to great expectations; Kirghizia and Kazakhstan between the devil and the deep ... green sea* (1990). Schoeberlein; THESAM, 4; ZKO

Imbart de la Tour, Joseph Jean Baptiste, born 22 July 1859 at Nevers, France, he studied law at the Institut catholique de Paris, where he received a doctorate in 1885 for *De la pêche en droit romain et dans le droit international actuel.* He became a barrister in the Cour d'appel de Paris, specializing in international and agricultural affairs. Concurrently he looked after his estate in the Département de Nièvre, where he was also active in municipal affairs. His writings include *L'Esclavage en Afrique et la croisade noire* (1894). His date of death has not been determined. DBF; *Qui êtes-vous,* 1924; ZKO

Imbault-Huart, Camille Clément, born 3 June 1857 at Paris, the brother of Clément Huart, he received a diploma from the École des langues orientales vivantes, Paris, and was nominated a student interpreter at Shanghai in 1878 and a deputy interpreter at Peking in 1880. In 1892 he was a consul at Canton. His writings include *Recueil de documents sur l'Asie centrale* (1881), *Manuel de la langue coréenne parlée à l'usage des Français* (1889), and *L'Île de Formose* (1893). He died in Hong Kong on 29 November 1897. BN; DBF

Imbault-Huart, Clément, 1854-1926 *see* Huart, Marie Clément Imbault

Imber, Colin H., born 20th cent., he received a Ph.D. in 1970 from Cambridge University for *The administration of the Ottoman navy during the reign of Sülaymān I, 1520-1566.* He was associated with the unidentified Seminar[?] of Early Islamic Science, [Manchester?]. His writings include *The Ottoman Empire, 1300-1481* (1990), and he was joint author of *The Da'ire-yi mu'addel of Seydi Ali Re'is* (1976), and the booklet, *The Aegean sea-chart of Mehmed Reis Ibn Menemenli* (1977). Sezgin; Sluglett

Imberg, Kurt Eduard, born 27 August 1887 at Berlin, he received a Dr.jur. in 1914 from the Universität Marburg for a study of the position of the U.S.A. regarding international court decisions entitled *Die Stellung der Vereinigten Staaten von Nordamerika zur internationalen Schiedsgerichtsbarkeit.* His writings Include *Der Nikaraguakanal* (1920). GV; NUC, pre-1956; Thesis

Imbert, Alfred, born 19th cent., his writings include *Le Droit abadhite chez les Musulmans de Zanzibar et de l'Afrique orientale* (Alger, 1903). ZKO

Imbert, François, he was born 1 October 1856 at Riom (Puy-de-Dôme), France. After passing through the military college of Saint-Cyr, he received a commission as *sous-lieutenant* and rose to the rank of general. He saw action in North Africa and French West Africa, particularly during the conquest of the French Soudan, 1894-1899. He retired from military service in 1917, and died in Marseille on 22 August 1930. DBF; Peyronnet, p. 745

Imbert, Léo Eugène, born 15 November 1879 at Roquemaure (Gard), France, he obtained a degree in law and subsequently graduated in 1903 from the École des chartes, Paris, with the unpublished thesis *Les péages du Rhône de Tournon à la mer; étude sur les droits de navigation au moyen âge.* Since 1904 he was an archivist successively at the *départements* of Tarn-et-Garonne, Charente, Vaucluse, and Alpes-Maritimes, where he served from 1928 to 1943 as keeper of antiquities and art objects. His writings include *Les Villes romaines de la Vallée du Rhône* (1926), and *Les Cites historiques de la Vallée du Rhône* (1928). He died in Nice on 12 February 1969. DBF; *Qui êtes-vous,* 1924

Imbert, Louis, born 19th cent., he was one of the earliest secretaries of the Société de géographie commercial de Bordeaux. He died on 16 October 1916. *Bulletin de la Société de géographie commerciale de Bordeaux,* 1917, p. 259

Imbrie, Robert Whitney, born in 1884 at Washington, D.C., he was a graduate of George Washington and Yale universities and practised law in Baltimore, Md. He volunteered for the American Ambulance

Service in 1915, experiences which are embodied in his *Behind the wheel of a war ambulance* (New York, 1918). He later entered the American consular service. He died at the hands of an unprovoked mob while taking pictures of a religious ceremony in Tehran in the summer of 1924. BioIn, 12, 15; DcNAA; NatCAB, vol. 54, pp. 123-124; Shavit

Imhoff (Paşa), Carl, born in 1854, he was a Royal Prussian and an Imperial Ottoman lieutenant-general, and a member of the Deutsch-Asiatische Gesellschaft. He was an expert in Near Eastern affairs, a champion of German-Turkish friendship and cooperation, and a friend of field-marshal Colmar Freiherr von der Goltz. His writings include *Hindenburg und Tannenberg* (1915), and *Die türkische Heeresmacht und ihre Entwicklung* (1916). He died in 1918. Asien, 15, Heft 6 (März 1918), pp. 91-92; Kornrumpf; NUC, pre-1956

Freiherr von Imhoff, Christoph Hans, born 11 April 1912, he received a Dr.jur. in 1937 from the Universität Erlangen for *Grundlagen und Grundzüge eines neuen Volksgruppenrechtes im Rahmen der politischen Lage Europas*. He started his writing career at the political desk of the *Dresdner neueste Nachrichten*. His writings include *Imperialismus oder völkische Politik* (1937), *Der Hölle entronnen; zwei deutsche Pioniere entkommen der englischen Gefangenschaft in Dünkirchen* (1941), *Die Einschmelzung Großbritanniens* (1943), *Duell im Mittelmeer* (1968), *Iran, Persien* (1977), and *Krisenquadrat Mittelost* (1978). His trace is lost after an article in 1985. KDtLK, 1943

Immanuel, Friedrich (*Fritz*), born 9 April 1857 at Frankfurt/Main, Germany, he was an army officer who retired with the rank of colonel. His rather nationalist writings include *Serbiens und Montenegos Untergang* (1916), *Fünfzig Jahre deutscher Geschichte* (1921), *Des Zaren Untergang* (1926), *Der große Zukunftskrieg keine Phantasie!* (1931), *Die deutsche Miliz der Zukunft* (1933), and *Der Untergang Abessiniens; der Krieg 1935/36* (1936). He died after 1935. KDtLK, 1916; Note about the author

Imperatori, Giulio C., born 28 December 1890 at Fiano Romano (Roma), Italy, he was a journalist and colonial administrator whose writings include *I Berberi* (Asmara, 1933), and *Fiano Romano* (1967). Firenze; *Lui, chi è*; Vaccaro

In der Smitten, Wilhelm Th., born 20th cent., he received doctorates for *Gottesherrschaft und Gemeinde* (1974), and *Einführung in die alttestamentliche Geschichte Israels* (1976). ZKO

İnalcık, Halil Ibrahim, born 26 May 1916 at Constantinople, he was a professor of Ottoman history at Ankara Üniversitesi until 1972, and subsequently became a professor at the University of Chicago. His writings include *Fatih devri üzerinde tetkikler ve vesikalar* (1954), *The Ottoman Empire in the classical age* (1973), *From Empire to Republic; essays on Ottoman and Turkish social history* (1995), and two collections of his articles, *The Ottoman Empire; conquest, organization and economy* (1978), and *Studies in Ottoman social and economic history* (1985). He was honoured by *Raiyyet rüsûmu; essays presented to Halil Inalcik on his seventieth birthday by his colleagues and students* (1986). AnaBrit; ConAu, 49-52; DrAS, 1974 F, 1978 F, 1982 F; Kimkimdir, 1997/98 *MESA Roster of members*, 1977-1990; WhoAm, 1984-1995; WhoMW, 1978, 1980 [not sighted]

Inbar, Efraim, born 22 January 1947 in Romania, he graduated in 1973 from the Hebrew University, Jerusalem, and received a Ph.D. in 1981 from the University of Chicago for *Problems of pariah states; the national security policy of the Rabin Government*. He was in the early 1990s a director of the Center for Strategic Studies, Bar-Ilan University. He was a sometime visiting professor at Georgetown University, Washington, D.C. His writings include *War and peace in Israeli politics* (1991), *Regional security regimes; Israel and its neighbors* (1995), and he edited *The Politics and economics of defence industries* (1998). ConAu, 195; *MESA Roster of members*, 1990; Private

Inchcape, Kenneth James Wiliam Mackay, 3rd Earl of, born 27 December 1917 at Uckfield, Sussex, he was a company executive. He died 17 March 1994. IntWW, 1982-1993/94; Master (1); Who, 1959-1994, WhAm, 11

Inchichean (Inchichian, Ingigian, Инджикян), Ghowkas (Ghukas, Loukas), born in 1758 or 1783 in Constantinople, he entered the Mechitharist congregation of Armenian monks in 1770 at San Lazarro near Venezia, and was ordained in 1779. He was a geographer and historian whose writings include *Amaranots' Biwzandean* (1794), and its translations, *Description du Bosphore* (1813), *Nachrichten über den Thrazischen Bosporus* (1814), *Villeggiature de' Bizantini sul Bosforo Tracie* (1831), and *Das russische Armenien* (1835). He died in San Lazarro on 2 July 1833. Kornrumpf; NUC; ÖBL

Inchikian, Hovhannes, 1913-1990 *see* Indzhikian, Oganes Grigor'evich

Indicus, *pseud. see* Bell, Thomas Evans, 1825-1887

Indyk, Martin, born 20th cent., his writings include *"To the ends of the earth;"* Sadat's Jerusalem initiative (Cambridge, Mass., 1984), and he was a joint author of *Israel and the U.S. Air Force* (Washington, American Israel Public Affairs Committee, 1983). LC; ZKO

Indzhikian (Inchikian), Oganes (Hivhannes) Grigor'evich, born in 1913 at Akhaltsikhe, Georgia, he graduated in 1939 from the Moscow Institute of Philology, Literature, and History, and received his first degree in 1954 with a thesis entitled *Революционная деятельность Богдана Кнунянца*. He was a research fellow successively at Moscow and Erevan. His writings include *Богдан Кнунянц* (1957), and *Буржуазия Османской Империи* (Erevan, 1977). He died on 5 April 1990. Miliband; Miliband²; ZKO

Ineichen, Gustav, born 6 June 1929 at Luzern, Switzerland, he received doctorates from the Université de Fribourg and the Universität Zürich in 1957 and 1963 respectively. He was a professor of linguistics at the Universität Göttingen and concurrently a director of a Swiss institute at Roma, Italy. His writings include *Repetitorium der altfranzösischen Lautlehre* (1968), *Arabisch-orientalische Sprachkontakte in der Romania; ein Beitrag zur Kulturgeschichte des Mittelalters* (1997), *Sprachen, Länder und Reisen; Erinnerungen eines Professors* (2000), and he edited and translated *Der Rosenroman* (1956). In 1989 he was honoured by *Variatio linguarum; Beiträge zu Sprachvergleich und Sprachentwicklung; Festschrift zum 60. Geburtstag von Gustav Ineichen.* Kürschner, 1970-2005; WhoWor, 1991/92

Ingham, Bruce, born 20th cent., he received a Ph.D. in 1975 from the School of Oriental and African Studies, London, for *The phonology and morphology of the verbal piece in an Arabic dialect of Khuzistan*. A sometime reader in Arabic at SOAS, his teaching covered dialectology, contrastive linguistics and American Indian studies. His writings include *North East Arabian dialects* (1982), *Bedouin of northern Arabia; traditions of the Āl-Dhafīr* (1986), and *Nadji Arabic, Central Arabian* (1994). Note; Sluglett; ZKO

Ingham, Kenneth, born 9 August 1921 at Harden, Yorks., England, he was educated at Keble College, Oxford, where he received a Ph.D. in 1950. He taught history at Makerere University, Kampala, Uganda, until 1962, when he started teaching the same subject successively at the Royal Military Academy, Sandhurst, and the University of Bristol. His writings include *Europe and Africa; a school certificate history* (1953), *Reformers in India; an account of Christian missionaries on behalf of social reform* (1956), *A History of East Africa* (1961), *The Kingdom of Toro in Uganda* (1961), *Politics in modern Africa; the uneven tribal dimension* (1990), and he edited *The Foreign relations of African states* (1974). Au&Wr, 1963, 1971; ConAu, 108, 110; IntAu&W, 1976, 1977, 1991/92; Unesco; Who, 1974-2005; WrDr, 1976/78-2005

Ingholt, Harald, born 11 March 1896 at København, Denmark, he was educated at the local university, where he received a Dr.phil. in 1928; he also received an M.A. from Yale University, New Haven, Conn., in 1960. He was a lecturer in archaeology at the American University of Beirut, from 1931 to 1938, and subsequently until 1940 a professor of Hebrew and Old Testament at Århus Universitet. From 1942 to his retirement in 1974 he taught in various capacities classics, Biblical exegesis, and archaeology at Calhoun College, Yale University. His writings include *Un nouveau thiase à Palmyre* (1926), *Rapport préliminaire sur sept campagnes de fouilles à Hama en Syrie, 1932-1938* (1940), *Parthian sculptures from Hatra* (1954), and he was a joint author of *Recueil des tessères de Palmyre* (1955). He died on 28 October 1985. DrAS, 1969 H, 1974 H, 1978 H, 1982 H; Kraks, 1985

Ingigian, Loukas, 1783-1833 *see* Inchichean, Ghowkas

Inglis, James William, born 12 September 1861, he was educated at Glasgow and from 1891 to 1938 served as a missionary in Manchuria. He died on 15 January 1943. Lodwick; *Who was who,* 4

Ingram, Edward, born 1940, he received a Ph.D. in international history in 1968 from the London School of Economics; in 1990 he was associated with Simon Fraser University, Burnaby, B.C. His writings include *The Beginning of the Great Game in Asia, 1828-1834* (1979), *Commitment to Europe* (1981), *In defence of British India* (1984), *Britain's Persian connection, 1798-1828* (1992), *The British Empire as a world power* (2001), and he edited *National and international politics in the Middle East; essays in honour of Elie Kedourie* (1986). MESA Roster of members, 1990; ZKO

Ingrams, Doreen Constance née Shortt , born in 1906, she was married to W. Harold Ingrams in 1930. Nine years later, she was awarded jointly with her husband the Royal Society for Asian Affairs' Lawrence of Arabia Memorial Medal in recognition of their outstanding role in bringing peace to the Hadhramaut. The couple also received awards from the Royal Geographical Society and the Royal Asiatic Society for their exploration and studies of the region. Her writings include *Survey of social and economic conditions in the Aden Protectorate* (1949), *A Time in Arabia* (1970), and she edited

Palestine papers, 1917-22; seeds of conflict (1973). She died on 25 July 1997. Asian affairs, 84 (1997), p. 438; Bidwell; BioIn, 12; ConAu, 33-36, 159, new rev., 12; IntAu&W, 1976, 1977, 1989

Ingrams, William *Harold*, born 3 February 1897, he was educated at Shrewsbury, England, and after service in the first World War, he joined the Colonial Service in 1919, being initially posted to Zanzibar. In 1930 he was married to Doreen Shortt. In 1933, after five years in Mauritania, he joined the political service of the Aden Protectorate, and there served until 1945. He spent the years until his retirement in 1948 in West Africa. His writings include *Zanzibar; its history and its people* (1931), *The Aden Protectorate* (1937), *Arabia and the isles* (1942), its translation, *Befriedete Wüste* (1950), *Uganda; a crisis of nationhood* (1963), and *Yemen* (1963). He died in December 1973. Au&Wr, 1963, 1971; *Geographical journal*, 140 (1974), pp. 353-54; Note; WhE&EA; Who, 1959-1974; *Who was who*, 7

Iñiguez Almech, Francisco, fl. 20th cent., he was an architect, a professor at the Escuela Superior de Arquitectura, and a *comisario general*, Patrimonio Artístico Nacional. His writings include *El Palacio de la Aljafería* (Zaragoza, 1947), *Trujillo; estudio histórico artístico* (Madrid, 1949), and *Geografía de la arquitectura española* (Madrid, 1957). IndiceE[3]; NUC, pre-1956

Inkizhekova-Grekul, A. I., fl. 20th cent., she was a joint author of Хакасско-русский словарь (1953).

Inlow, Edgar Burke, born in 1914 or 15 at Forest Grove, Oreg., he graduated in 1937 from Washington State University and received a Ph.D. in 1950 from Johns Hopkins University, Baltimore, for *The patent grant*. He was successively instructor at Princeton University, rector of a Protestant Episcopal Church, officer with the U.S. Department of Defense, and a professor of political science at the University of Calgary. His writings include *The Shahanshah; a study of the monarchy in Iran* (1979). AmM&WSc, 1973 S, 1978 S; Canadian, 1983-1989; WhoAm, 1974-1995; WhoWest, 1974/75-1978/79; WhoWor, 1980/81

Inman, Lawrence Lloyd, born 20th cent., he received a Ph.D. in 1957 from the University of Minnesota for *Studies on the methods of production and theoretical applications of large rings of chromosomes in maize*. NUC, 1956-67

Innes, Alfred Mitchell, 1864-1950 see Mitchell-Innes, Alfred

Innes, Neil McLeod, born in 1903, he was from 1953 to 1958 minister of foreign and external affairs, Sultanate of Oman. His writings include *Minister in Oman; a personal narrative* (1987). LC

Inostrantsev, Konstantin Aleksandrovich, born in 1876 at St. Petersburg, he graduated in 1899 from the Faculty of Oriental Languages, St. Petersburg, and received a doctorate in 1908 with a study of the Sāsānids entitled Сасанидские этюды, a work which was translated into Persian in 1973. He was a student of Baron Rosen and an authority in the material culture of the caliphate, and also the problem of Arab-Persian relations. His writings include Хунну и гунны (1926). He died at the end of December 1941. Krachkovskiĭ, pp. 242-43; Miliband; Miliband[2]

Insabato, Enrico, born 21 September 1878 at Bologna, Italy, he participated in several political missions as an expert in Oriental affairs. In 1902 he founded the first bilingual Italian-Arabic periodical in Egypt. His writings include *Gli Abaditi di Gebel Nefusa e la politica islamica in Tripolitania* (1918), *L'Islam et la politique des alliés* (1919), *La collaborazione italo-araba e il Sudan* (1950), and he was a joint author of *Der erlöschende Halbmond* (1909). He died on 6 March 1963. Chi è, 1928-1948; *Index Islamicus* (1); LC; Vaccaro

Ioannides, Christos P., born 7 April 1946, he received a Ph.D. in 1977 from the University of Pennsylvania; and he was in 1984 an adjunct professor of political science at Seton Hall University, South Orange, N.J. In 1990 he was a director of the S.B. Vryonis Center for the Study of Hellenism, Sacramento, Calif. His writings include *America's Iran* (1984), and *In Turkey's image; the transformation of occupied Cyprus* (1991). LC; *MESA Roster of members*, 1990

Ioannisian (Hovhannisyan), Abgar Rubenovich, born in 1908 at Tiflis, his writings include Россия и армянское освободительное движение в 80 годах XVIII столетия (1947), Присоединение Закавкаьзя к России и международные отношения в начале 19 столетия (1958), Коммунистические идеи в годы Великой Французкой Революции (1966), and Революция 1848 года во Франции и коммунизм (1989). WhoSocC, 1978

Iokhel'son (Jochelson), Vladimir (Waldemar) Il'ich, born in 1855 at Vilna, Russia, he was at one time associated with the Museum of Anthropology and Ethnography, Academy of Sciences, and St. Petersburg University as a professor. In 1885 he was banned to Yakutia and there studied the Yukaghirs. In 1922 he emigrated to the United States, where he died on 2 November 1937. His writings include *Religion and myths of the Koryak* (1905), *Material culture and social organization of the Koryak* (1908), Первые дни народной воли (1922), *The Yukaghir and the Yukaghirized Tungus* (1926), *Peoples of Asiatic Russia* (1928), and *The Yakut* (1933). BiDSovU; CnDiAmJB; GSE; SibirSE

Ion, Theodore P., born 19th cent., he was in 1908 associated with Boston University Law School. He contributed a critical introduction to *L'Hellénisme en Asie-mineure; le témoignage d'un Allemand*, translated from the German of Carl Dietrich (Paris, 1919). BN; Note about the author; NUC, pre-1956

Ionesco, Ion, fl. 1850-54 *see* Jonesco, Joan

Ionescu, Anca Irina, born 22 March 1946 at Bucureşti, she studied at the local university, gaining a doctorate in philology in 1975. She subsequently became a professor in the Faculty of Foreign Languages at her alma mater. Her writings include *Lingvistică şi mitologie; contribuţii la studierea terminologiei credinţelor populare ale slavilor* (Bucureşti, 1978). WhoRomania, 2002

Ionescu de la Brad, Ion, born in 1818, he wrote *Rapport du délégué officiel du gouvernement romain au 7e Congrès international de statistique sur les progrès statistiques en Roumanie* (s.l., 1869). He died in 1891. NUC, pre-1956

Ionescu-Nişcov, Traian, fl. 20th cent., his writings include *Acte de cancelarie domnească* (1974).

Ionides, Michael George, born in 1903, he was a trained civil engineer and employed as irrigation engineer in Iraq; he afterwards went to Transjordan as Director of Development in Amman. While employed in that capacity he prepared the Hydrographic Survey, which marched side by side with a similar survey that was being prepared in Palestine. His writings include *The Régime of the rivers Euphrates and Tigris* (1937), and *Report on the water resources of Transjordan and their development* (1939). He was a member of the Institute of Water Engineers and the Institution of Civil Engineers. His trace is lost after an article in 1953. Engineers' who's who, 1939; Note about the author

Ionov, Vsevolod Mikhailovich, born in 1851 at Astrakhan, Russia, he was educated at St. Petersburg. He was arrested for revolutionary activity in 1876 and sentenced to five years of hard labour in Siberia. Released in 1883, he pursued studies in Yakut ethnography and folklore. He died 2 February 1922. BiobibSOT, pp. 171-172; SibirSE; Wieczynski

Ionova, Alla Ivanovna, born 21 January 1936 at Minsk, Belorussia, she graduated in 1958 from the Faculty of History, Moscow State University, and received her first degree in 1965 with a study of Indonesian bourgeois politics entitled *Политика индонезийсеой буржуазии в рабочем вопросе, 1945-1960*. Since 1958 she was attached to the Oriental Institute of the Soviet Academy of Sciences. Her writings include *Индонезийская буржуазия и рабочий класс* (1966), «Мусульманский национализм» в современной Индонезии, 1945-1965 (1972), *Ислам в Юго-Восточной Азии* (1981), *Ислам; проблемы идеологии, права, политики и экономики; сборник статей* (1985), *Современный ислам, человек и общество* (1991), and she was a joint author of *Современный ислам, человек и общество* (1991). Miliband; Millband²; OSK

Ionova, Ol'ga Vsevolodovna, fl. 1952, her writings include *Из истории якутского народа* (Yakutsk, 1945). NUC, pre-1956

Iordanskiĭ, Anatoliĭ Mikhaĭlovich, fl. 20th cent., his writings include *История двойственного числа в русском языке* (1960), and he was a joint editor of *Избранные труды*, of Vasiliĭ Il'ich Chernyshev (1970). OSK

Iorga, Nicolae, born in 1871 in Botoşani, a small town in northern Moldavia, he studied history at the universities of Jassi, Paris and Leipzig. At Paris he submitted two theses, for the first of which, *Philippe de Mézieres et la croisade au XIVe siècle*, he obtained a diploma from l'École des Hautes Études, and for the second one, *Thomas III, marquis de Saluces,* he was awarded a Dr.phil. degree at the Universität Leipzig. In 1894 he was appointed to the chair of history at the University of Bucureşti, a position which he held until his assassination on 27 November 1940 in Romania. His writings include *Geschichte des Osmanischen Reiches* (1908), *Les Voyageurs français dans l'Orient européen* (1928), and *La France et la Terre sainte* (1934). In 1972, Maria Alexandrescu-Dersca published his biography, *Nicolae Iorga, a Roumanian historian.* CasWL; Dicţionar; EncItaliana; *Index Islamicus* (3); Magyar; Master (9); MembriiAR; MEW

Ioseliani (Osseliani), Platon Igniat'evich, born in 1810, he was a Georgian historian whose writings include *Краткая история Грузинской церкви* (1843), *Путевыя записки по Дагестану* (Tiflis, 1862), and *A Short history of the Georgian Church* (1866). He died in 1875. NYPL; OSK

Irandust, pseud., fl. 20th cent., his writings include *Движущие силы кемалистской революции* (1928), and *Персия* (Moscow, 1928). NUC, pre-1956

Iranshahr (Iranschähr), Husayn Kazim´zādah, 1884- *see* Kazim´zādah Īrānshahr, Husayn

MACK LIBRARY
BOB JONES UNIVERSITY
GREENVILLE, SC

Iranskiĭ, S., fl. 1925-30, he wrote, jointly with Mikhail L. Vel'tman, *Персия в борье за независимость* (1925), and its Persian translation, *Inqilāb-i mashrūtiyat-i Īrān va rīshah-hā-i ijtimāʿī va iqtisād-i ān* (Tehran, 1330/1951). OSK

Irechek, Konstantin, 1854-1918 *see* Jireček, Josef Konstantin

Iredell, Vernon Raymond, born 11 December 1929 at Pomona, Calif., he graduated in 1951 from Pomona College and received a Ph.D. in 1958 from the University of Chicago for *Procedures for maintaining peace according to the UN charter*. From 1958 until his retirement he was a professor of political science at the University of Tennessee, Knoxville. AmM&WSc, 1973 S, 1978 S; NatFacDr, 1990-1995

Ireland, John de Courcy, born 19 October 1911, he was a research officer of the Irish Commission on Maritime History; his writings include *Ireland and the Irish maritime history* (Dublin, 1986). Note about the author

Ireland, Philip Willard, born in 1902, he graduated from Ohio Wesleyan University, and received a Ph.D. in 1936 from the London School of Economics for *Government and administration of Iraq*. He taught at the American University of Beirut, the universitites of Harvard and Chicago, before joining the U.S. Foreign Service in 1941. In 1945, he served as liaison officer between the State Department and Arabic-speaking delegations at the formation of the UNO in San Francisco. He later served at Cairo, Baghdad, Thessaloniki, and Aleppo, before retiring in the mid-1960s. His writings include *Iraq; a study in political development* (1937), and he edited *The Near East; problems and prospects* (1942). He died of cancer on 30 December 1991. Sluglett; WRMEA 10 viii (February 1992), p. 90

Irisov, Abdusadyk, born 20 February 1928 at Tashkent, he graduated in 1951 from the Oriental Faculty, Tashkent Pedagogical Institute, and received his first degree in 1961 for a study of Avicenna's Salamān u Absāl entitled *Повесть Абу Али ибн Сины "Саламан и Ибсал."* From 1966 to 1969 he was employed by the Soviet legation in Damascus. His writings, all of which in Uzbek, include *Ибн Сина* (1962). Miliband²

Irmer, Dieter, born 9 February 1935, he received a Dr.phil. in 1961 from the Universität Hamburg for *Zum Primat des Codex S in der Demostheneskritik*. He subsequently became a research fellow and lecturer in classics at his alma mater. His writings include *Zur Genealogie der jüngeren Demosthenes-Handschriften* (1972), he edited and translated *Kommentar zu Hippokrates "De fracturis" und seine Parallelversion unter dem Namen des Stephanus von Alexandria* (1977), and he was a joint editor of *Kleine attische Redner* (1977). Kürschner, 1980-2005

Irmscher, Johannes, born 14 September 1920 at Dresden, Germany, he pursued Balkan and Byzantine studies at the Universität Leipzig. After the war he moved to Berlin where he received a Dr.phil. in 1947 with a thesis entitled *Götterzorn bei Homer*. He gained a Dr.habil. in 1951. Since 1953 he was a professor of classical antiquities at Humboldt Universität, Berlin, a post which he held until his retirement in 1985. His writings include surveys of Balkan studies in East European countries as well as numerous conference proceedings. He died in Roma, 23 May 2000. *Zeitschrift für Balkanologie* 36 (2000), pp. 246-47

Irnberger, Harald, born 24 August 1949 at Wolfsberg, Carinthia, Austria, he was a journalist and the publisher of *Extrablatt*. His writings include *Die Terrormultis* (1976), *SAVAK oder der Folterfreund des Westens* (1977), *Nelkenstrauß ruft Praterstern* (1983), and *Zentralamerika; Opfer, Akteure, Profiteure* (1989). WhoAustria, 1982/83

Irons, William, born 25 December 1933 at Garrett, Ind., he graduated in 1960 from the University of Michigan, where he also received a Ph.D. in 1969 for *The Yomut Turkman; a study of kinship in a pastoral society*. He was successively a professor of anthropology at Johns Hopkins University, Baltimore, Md., Pennsylvania State University, and Northwestern University, Evanston, Illinois. AmM&WSc, 1973 S, 1978 S; Schoeberlein; WhoAm, 1986-2003; WhoMW, 1984-1994/95

Irons, William Josiah, born in 1812, at Hoddesdon, Herts., England, he was educated privately and at Queen's College, Oxford. He was a sometime editor of the *Tracts of the Anglican Church*, and served successively as curate, vicar, rector and prebendary before he became a lecturer at Oxford in 1870. His writings include *The Bible and its interpreters* (1865). He died in London in 1883. Boase; BritInd (3); DcBiPP (not sighted); DNB

Ironside, Gilbert, born 12 December 1737 at London, he sailed for India in 1757 as ensign and returned to England shortly after his arrival in India, but he went back to India in the following year. Promoted Bt Major by Lord Clive in May 1766 in order to secure a sufficiency of field officers for the trial by C.M. of officers during the "Batta mutiny." He left India on 13 February 1786. His writings include *A Dissertation on horses* (1800). He died in London on 7 October 1802. IndianBiInd (1)

Ironside, Sir William Edmund, field-marshall, born in 1880, he commanded the British forces in Russia, 1918-19, and in Persia, 1921. His writings include *Tannenberg; the first thirty days in East Prussia* (1925), *Archangel, 1918-1919* (1953), and *The Ironside diaries, 1937-1940* (1962). He died in 1959. BioIn, 1, 6 (7); BritInd (2); DNB; Master (1); *Who was who*, 5

Irvine, A. K., born 20th cent., he obtained a D.Phil. and became a lecturer at the School of Oriental and African Studies, London, maintaining a general interest in Semitic languages, but particularly in the pre-Islamic Arabian epigraphic languages, Arabic, Ethiopic, and Amharic. He edited *A Miscellany of Middle Eastern articles in memoriam Thomas Muir Johnston, 1924-83, professor of Arabic in the University of London* (1988), and he was a joint translator of *Letters from Ethiopian rulers, early and mid-nineteenth century* (1985). SOAS, 1994 *Calendar*

Irvine, Francis, born in 8 February 1786 and baptized in Drumoak, Scotland, he was a cadet in 1804, and arrived in India in September 1805, being assigned to the 11th Native Infantry in 1806. From 1819 to 1822 he served as secretary to the Madrasa Committee in Calcutta and afterwards went home on furlow. He retired in England on 4 August 1824, his date of retirement being ante-dated to the 25th of November 1822. He died in Edinburgh on 16 December 1855. IndianBiInd (1)

Irvine, Keith, born 7 August 1924 at Ipswich, Suffolk, England, he was a Quaker who was educated at Friends' School, Saffron Walden, University of Manchester, Birkbeck College, London, University of Edinburgh, and the Sorbonne, Paris. He was an editor of dailies, journals, and encyclopaedias. From 1958 to 1969 he served with the Permanent Mission of Ghana to the U.N.O. His writings include *The Rise of the colored races* (1970), and he was the general editor of the *Encyclopedia of Indians of the Americas* (1974).

Irvine, William, born 5 July 1840, he was educated privately, at St. Anne's School, Brixton, and at King's College, London. He entered the Indian Civil Service and went out to the North West Province, India, in 1864. He rose to be magistrate-collector and retired in 1888. His writings include *The Army of the Indian Moghuls; its organization and administration* (1903), *Later Mughals* (1922), he compiled a supplementary index of the place names in *The Áín i Akbarí* (1873), and he translated from the Italian of Nicolao Manucci, *Storia do Mogor, or Mogul India, 1653-1708* (1907-1908). He died in 1911. BLC; DNB; IndianBiInd (2); Riddick

Irving, Clive, born 2 February 1933 at Luton, Beds., England, he was in various capacities an editor of weeklies and magazines as well as an editorial adviser. Since 1972 he was a free-lance writer. His writings include *Crossroads of civilization; 3000 years of Persian history* (1979), *Scandal '63; a study of the Profumo affair* (1963), its translation, *Escándalo en Inglaterra* (Barcelona, 1964), *Pox Britannica; the making of the British* (1974), and *True Brit* (1974). ConAu, 85-88, new revision, 22

Irving, F. F., born 19th cent., he was a missionary to the Assyrian Christians in Kurdistan. His writings include the two page pamphlet, *Litany in time of war* (Clevedon, Irving, 1915). ZKO

Irving, Sir Miles, born in 1876 at Singapore, he was educated at Balliol College, Oxford. From 1899 to his retirement in 1935 he was with the Indian Civil Service. He was a joint compiler of *Soldiers of the Raj* (Lahore, 1910-12). He died 24 June 1962. Riddick; *Who was who*, 6

Irving, Thomas Ballantine, born 20 July 1914 at Preston, Ont., Canada, he graduated in 1937 from the University of Toronto, and received a Ph.D. in 1940 from Princeton University for *A textual companion of a section of the Arabic Kalilah wa-Dimnah and the corresponding section of the old Spanish Calila e Digma*. An authority in Spanish language and history, he taught at a variety of international universities. From 1969 to his retirement in 1980 he was a professor of Romance history and Islamic studies at the University of Tennessee, Knoxville. A convert to Islam, his writings include *Falcon of Spain; a study of eighth-century Spain* (1954), *Profile of man and culture in Mexico* (1962), *Islam resurgent* (1979), *The World of Islam* (1984), and *The Qur'ān, basic readings* (1992). ConAu, 37-40; DrAS, 1969 F, 1974 F, 1978 F, 1982 F; IWWAS, 1976/77; *MESA Roster of members*, 1977-1990; Note; WhoMW, 1994/95

Irwin, Eyles, born in 1751 at Calcutta, he was educated in England, and became an officer of the East India Company in the Madras Presidency. He retired from the service in 1794. His writings include *A Series of adventures in the course of a voyage up the Red Sea, on the coasts of Arabia and Egypt* (1780), its translations, *Begebenheit einer Reise auf dem rothen Meer, auf der arabischen und ägyptischen Küste* (1781), and *Voyage à la mer rouge, sur les côtes de l'Arabie et l'Égypte et dans les déserts de la Thébaide* (1792). He died in Clifton near Bristol in 1817. BritInd (8); DNB; Master (4); Sezgin

Irwin, J. Mark, fl. 1945-46 at Abilene, Kansas, he was a sometime missionary in Meshed, Iran. Note about the author

Irwin, John Conran, born 5 August 1917 at Madras, he was a keeper of the Indian Section in the Victoria and Albert Museum, London. In 1956/57 he served as a Unesco expert in museum development. His writings include *Shawls; a study in Indo-European influences* (1955), *Indian painted and printed fabrics* (1971), *The Kashmir shawl* (1973), and *Treasures of Indian art at the Victoria and Albert Museum* (1977). He died on 23 January 1997. Au&Wr, 1963; IntAu&W, 1976; Who's who, 1979-1997

Irwin, Robert Graham, born 23 August 1946 at Guildford, Surrey, England, he graduated from Merton College, Oxford. He was a lecturer in history at the University of St. Andrews before he became successively a part-time teacher of Arabic and history at Cambridge, Oxford, and London. His writings include *The Middle East in the Middle Ages; the early Mamluk Sultanate* (1986). ConAu, 121, new rev., 48, 81; WrDr, 1992/94-2005

Isaac, Alfred, born 12 July 1888 at Köln, Germany, he was a professor at the Hochschule für Wirtschafts- und Sozialwissenschaften, Nürnberg, until sent into early retirement in 1934. He emigrated to Turkey, where he taught business administration at İstanbul Üniversitesi until 1951, when he was invited to the Universität Göttingen. From 1952 to 1955 he was at the Universität Nürnberg, where he died 9 June 1956. His writings include *Betriebswirtschaftliche Statistik* (1925), and *Der Industriebetrieb* (1930). BioHbDtE; Kürschner, 1950, 1954; RHbDtG; Wer ist wer, 1955; Widmann, pp. 126-127, 270-271; Wininger

Isaac, Auguste Paul *Louis*, born 6 September 1849 at Roubais (Nord), France, he was educated at Lyon, where his father ran a tulle and lace factory. He quickly rose to become one of the leading persons in the textile industry of the region. A president of the Chambre syndicale de la Fabrique lyonnaise in 1887, and president of the Chambre de Commerce in 1899, he entered politics in 1919 as a *député du Rhône*. He was a sometime member of the *Conseil d'administration de Suez*, and a member of the Académie de Lyon. He died in Lyon on 23 March 1938. DBF

Isaacs, Haskell Dawood, he was born 10 November 1912 at Baghdad; his mother tongue was Arabic, but at an early time he became proficient both in French and Hebrew, and much later, English. He studied medicine at the Royal College of Medicine, Baghdad, graduating B.Sc., M.D. in 1936, followed by internship. Since 1936 he served successively as civilian medical officer at Tiktrit, nort central Iraq, and as medical officer in the Army Reserve Corps until the end of the war, when he went to Britain. He obtained a post at St. Mary's Hospital, London. In 1947 he opted for general practice in the Manchester area. During thirty-five years at Manchester he devoted such spare time as he had to the pursuit of scholarship, culminating in a Ph.D. in 1969 from Manchester University for *A critical edition of the Arabic text of Isaac Israeli's Book of Fevers*. At the age of sixty-nine he received and accepted an invitation to join the Cambridge University Library's Taylor-Schechter Genizah Research Unit. His writings include *Medical and para-medical manuscripts in the Cambridge Genizah Collections* (1994), and he translated the *Book of counsel for kings*, of al-Ghazzālī (1964). He died on 1 November 1994. *British journal of Middle Eastern studies*, 21 (1994), pp. 331-32; *Index Islamicus* (1); Note about the author; Private; Sluglett

Isaev, Magomet Izmailovich, born 5 March 1928 in the Vladikavkaz, he graduated in 1951 from the Oriental Faculty, Leningrad, and received his first degree in 1954 with a study of Ossetic philology entitled *О фразеологии осетинского языка*. Since 1954 he was attached to the Institute of Linguistics at the Soviet Academy of Sciences. His writings include *Очерк фонетики осетинского литературного языка* (1959), *Очерки по фразеологии осетинского языка* (1964), *Дигорский диалект осетинского языка* (1966), *Очерки по истории изучения осетинского языка* (1974), *Языковое строительство в СССР* (1979), and *Василию Ивановичу Абаеву 100 лет; сборник статей по иранистике, общему языкознанию, евразийским культурам* (2000). Miliband; Miliband²; OSK

Isaev, Vladimir Aleksandrovich, born 24 April 1948 at Moscow, he graduated in 1971 from the Institute of Oriental Languages, Moscow State University, received his first degree in 1975 for a study of economic relations among the Arab countries entitled *Внешне-экономичие связи между арабскими странами, 1951-1971*, and his doctorate in 1993 for *Арабские страны в междунаром разделении труда; итоги пробенмы, перспективы, 1961-1990 гг.* He was since 1974 associated with the Oriental Institute in the Soviet Academy of Sciences. His writings include *Внешне экономические связи между арабскими странами, 1951-1975* (1978), *Эконо-мические отношения между арабскими и освободившимся странамы, 1961-1980 гг.* (1983), *Иордания; контуры перемен* (1987), *Арабские страны; проблемы социально-экономического и общественно-политиче-ского развития; сборник статей* (1995), *Российская востоковедная наука; прошлое и настоящее: библиография, 1726-1997* (1999), and he was joint author of *Катар; объединенные Арабские Эмираты* (1984), *Финансовые структуры Ближнего Востока* (1996), *Государство Кувейт; справочник* (1990), and *Soviet studies on the Middle East* (Tel Aviv, 1991). Miliband²; OLS

Isaeva, Fiia Abdulbarievna, born 1 March 1938 at Ufa, Russia, she graduated in 1962 from the Oriental Faculty, Leningrad State University and received her first degree in 1979 for a study of dialect in the Arabian nights entitled *Диалектизмы в "1001" ночи*. Since 1962 she was associated with Tajikistan State University. Her writings include *Арабская хрестоматия* (1970). Miliband²

Isambert, Émile, born in 1827 at Auteuil (Paris), he was a medical doctor who, during his early years, made a long journey throughout the Middle East in the company of Adolphe Chauvet. They published jointly *Itinéraire descriptif, historique et archéologique de l'Orient* (1861), and *Syrie, Palestine, comprenant le Sinai, l'Arabie pétrée et la Cilicie* (1882). He died in Paris on 27 October 1876. *Biographisches Lexikon der hervorragenden Ärzte aller Zeiten und Völker* (1962), vol. 3, pp. 378-79; DBF; Hoefer; Vapereau

Isazade, Akhmed I., born 20th cent., he was associated with the Institute of Architecture and Arts of the Azerbaijan Ministry of Cultural Affairs. His writings include *Инструментальное творчество композиторов Советского Азербайджана* (1961), *Летопись музыкальной жизни Советского Азербайджана, 1920-1915* (1965), and he edited *Слово об Узеире Гаджибекове* (1985). LC; Note

Ischchanian, Bachschi, born 15 July 1879 at Shusha, Azerbaijan, he studied at the universities of Leipzig and Berlin and received a Dr.phil. in 1912 from the Universität Heidelberg for a study of nature and history of foreigners in Russia entitled *Wesen und Geschichte des Ausländertums in Rußland*. His writings include *Die ausländischen Elemente in der russischen Volkswirtschaft* (Berlin, 1913), and *Nationaler Bestand, berufsmäige Gruppierung und soziale Gliederung kaukasischer Völker* (Berlin & Leipzig, 1914). He died 26 August 1921. LC; ZKO

Iselin, Ludwig *Emil*, born in 1861 at Basel, Switzerland, he became a pastor at Riehen. In 1917 he was awarded an honorable doctorate in divinity. His writings include *Der morgenländische Ursprung der Grallegende aus orientalischen Quellen erschlossen* (Halle an der Saale, 1909), *Der Untergang der christlichen Kirche in Nordafrika* (Basel, 1918), and *Geschichte des Dorfes Riehen* (Basel, 1923). He died in 1922. HisBioLexCH; Sezgin

Iseminger, Gordon Llewellyn, born 22 February 1933 at DeSmet, South Dakota, he graduated in 1959 from Augustana College, S.Dak., and received a Ph.D. in 1965 from the University of Oklahoma for *Britain's Eastern policy and the Ottoman Christians, 1856-1877*. Since 1968 he was a professor of history at the University of North Dakota, Grand Forks, a post which he still held in 2002. His writings include *The Americanization of Christiana Hillius* (1986). DrAS, 1969 H, 1974 H, 1978 H, 1982 H; NatFacDr, 1990-2002

Isenberg, Carl Wilhelm (Charles William), born 5 September 1806 at Barmen, Prussia, of humble and pious parentage, he early in life toyed with the idea of becoming a missionary, but in the circumstances had to train as a plumber. With the help of his pastor he was able to enter the Basler Missionshaus in 1824, completing his missionary training at Berlin in 1830, when he returned to Basel as a teacher of Greek. Upon a request from the Church Missionary Society (C.M.S.), London, he was sent to England to prepare for work in Ethiopia, studying first of all Arabic and Amharic. He left for Cairo in 1833, taking up his post at Tigre in 1835, but was expelled in 1838. After the attempt failed to re-establish himself in 1843, he left the country for good, and the C.M.S. sent him to Bombay, where he worked until exhaustion obliging him to travel to Düsseldorf, Germany, to recuperate. In 1854 he was back at Bombay, where he spent nearly ten more years until a cancer of the spleen obliged him to return to Germany, where he died in the same year. His writings include *A Small vocabulary of the Dankali language* (1840), *Grammar of the Amharic language* (1842), *Journals of...Isenberg and Krapf ... detailing their proceedings in the Kingdom of Shoa and journeys in other parts of Abyssinia* (1843), and *Abessinien und die evangelische Mission; Erlebnisse in Ägypten; Tagebuch* (1844). ADtB, vol. 14, pp. 614-618; Embacher; Henze; Kornrumpf

Isengalieva (Исенгалиева), Valentina Aĭtesevna (Aĭtesh kyzy), born 16 April 1924, she was a linguist and Turkologist who received a doctorate in 1967 and was appointed a professor in 1968. Her writings include *Служебные имена и послелоги в казахском языке* (1957), *Русские предлоги и их эквиваленты в казахском языке* (1959), *Употребление падежей в русском и казахском языках* (1961), and *Тюркские глаголы с основами, заимствованными из русского языка* (1966). KazakSE; Kazakhskaia, vol. 3, p. 231; OSK

al-Isfahānī, Nabīyah, fl. 1978. Her writings include *al-Tadāmun al-'Arabi al-Afriqi* (Cairo, 1977), and *Sīmūn Būlīfār, muharrir al-qārrah al-Amrīkīyah* (1983). LC

Isfandiyārī, Hasan, born in 1245 H. Sh., he was a Persian parliamentarian who wrote *Akhlāq-i muhtashamī* (Tehran, 1935). He died in 1323/1944.

İshaki, Mehmed *Ayaz*, born in 1878 at Kazan, Russia, he was educated at a local *medrese*, but he was also familiar with Russian. He was literary active from 1900 to 1903, when he returned to his home village as an *imam*. At the outbreak of the 1905 revolution, he immediately went to Kazan to enter the political scene, join the socialist revolutionary party, and edit the journal *Tan Yulduzi* for a group of militants. He was persecuted and incarcerated by the government. When all political agitation became impossible, he returned to a purely literary activity. After the 1917 revolution, he became a nationalist journalist, preoccupied with social and political problems. He died in Ankara in 1954. AnaBrit; Meydan; PTF, II, pp. 768, 772-73; TatarES; ZKO

Ishankhanov, Sattykhan Khabibovich, fl. 20th cent., his writings include *Каталог монет Коканда XVIII-XIX вв.* (Tashkent, 1976). OSK

Ishbulatov, Nagim Khazhgalievich, born 10 August 1928, he graduated in 1952 from the Bashkir State Pedagogical Institute, obtained a D.Phil. in 1975, and was appointed a professor in 1981. His writings include *Башкирская диалектология* (1963), and he edited *Некоторые вопросы урало-алтайского языкознания* (1970), and *Вопросы башкирского языкознания* (1972). BashkKE; OSK

Ishcherikov, Petr Fedorovich, born 15 June 1892, he was a historian and archaeologist. He died in Leningrad on 5 September 1961. BashkKE

Ishow, Habib, born 20th cent., he was in 1989 a research fellow in the Centre d'études et de recherches sur l'Orient arabe contemporain, and the Institut de recherches et d'études sur le monde arabe et musulman of the Centre National de la Recherche Scientifique. His writings include *Le Koweit; évolution politique, économique et sociale* (1989), *L'Irak; paysanneries, politiques agraires et industrielles au XXe siècle: contribution à la réflexion sur le développement* (1996) and *Les Structures sociales et politiques de l'Irak contemporain; pourquoi un État en crise?* (2003). Livres disponibles, 2003; ZKO

Iskanderov, Bokhodur Iskandarovich, born 12 April 1912 in a village in Tajikistan, he graduated in 1936 from the Leningrad Institute of History, Philology, and Linguistics, received his first degree in 1950 for *Бухара в 1918-1920 гг.*, and a doctorate in 1958 for *Восточная Бухара в последн. трети XIX в.* Since 1962, he was a director of the Institute of History, Soviet Tajik Academy of Sciences; in 1966, he was appointed a professor. His writings include *Из истории Бухарского эмирата* (1958), *Восточная Бухара и Рамир в период присоединенния Среднеи Азии к России* (1960), *Гиндукуш во второй половине XIX в.* (1968), *Бухара, 1918-1920 гг.* (1970), *Из истории дореволюцион. Таджикистана* (1974), and he was a joint author of *Россия и Таджикистан* (1984). Miliband[2]

Iskhakov, Damir M., born 20th cent., he was associated with the Institute of Language, Literature and History in the G. Ibragimov Kazan Branch of the Soviet Academy of Sciences. His writings include *Пермские татары* (1983), *Приуральские татары* (1990), *Историческая демография татарского народа* (1993), *Этнографические группы татар Волго-Уралского региона* (1993), *Татары* (1993), and *Нагайбаки* (1995). LC; Note about the author; OSK

Iskhakov, F. G., fl. 20th cent., he was associated with the Institute of Philology of the Soviet Academy of Sciences. His writings include *Хакасский язык; краткий очерк по фонетике* (1956), *Материалы и исследования* (Abakan, 1956), *Тувинский язык; материалы для научной грамматики: очерк по фонетике* (1957), and jointly with Nikolaĭ Konstantinovich Dmitriev, *Вопросы изученния языка и его диалектов; материалы для научной грамматики* (Abakan, 1954), and with A. A. Pal'mbakh, *Грамматика тувинского языка; фонетика и морфология* (1961). Note about the author; NUC; OSK

Iskhakov, Gegel' Mazhitovich, born 20th cent., his writings include *Этнографическое изучение уйгуров Восточного Туркестана русским путешественниками второй половины XIX века* (1975); he edited *Из истории международных отношений в Центральной Азии* (1990); and he was a joint author of *Краткая история уйгуров* (1991). LC; OSK

Iskhakova, Sofiia Munzirovna, born 20th cent., she was joint author of *Сибирские Татары; этнокультурные и политические проблемы возрождения* (1996). OSK

Islamov, Musa Isa oghlu, born 20th cent., his writings include *Түрк дилләриндә әвәзликләр; Азәрбајчан дилинин диалект материалы әсасында* (1986), and *Азәрбајчан дилинин диалектоложи атласы* (1990). OSK

Ismael, Jacqueline S., born 20th cent., she was a sometime professor of social work at the University of Calgary. Her writings include *Kuwait; social change in historical perspective* (1982), *Canadian social welfare policy* (1985), and jointly with Tareq Y. Ismael, *Kuwait; dependency and class in a rentier state* (1993), and *The Communist movement in Syria and Lebanon* (1998). MESA Roster of members, 1990; NatFacDr, 2002-2005

Ismael, Tareq Youssief, born about 1938, he graduated in 1958 at Baghdad and received a Ph.D. in 1967 from George Washington University for *U.A.R. policy in Africa*. He taught political science successively at Eastern Washington State College, and the University of Calgary, a post which he still held in 2005. His writings include *The Arab left* (1976), *Iraq and Iran; roots of conflict* (1982), *Middle East studies; international perspectives on the state of the art* (1990), and he was a joint editor of *Turkey's foreign policy in the twenty-first century; a changing role in world politics* (2003). ConAu, 125; MESA Roster of members, 1990; NatFacDr, 1995-2005

Ismagulov, Orazak, born 1 October 1930, he graduated in 1955 from the Kazan State University and became associated with the Institute of History, Archaeology, and Ethnography of the Kazan Academy of Sciences. He obtained a doctorate in 1984. His writings include *Население Казахстана от эпохи бронсы до современности* (1970), *Этническая антропологоя Казахстана* (1982), and he was a joint author of *Этническая одонтология Казахстана* (1989). Kazakhskaia, vol. 3, p. 232; OSK; Schoeberlein

Ismā'īl Hāmid, 1857-1932 or 33 *see* Hamet, Ismaël

Ismailov, Esmagambet (Есмағамбет) Samuratovich, born 15 October 1911, he graduated in 1934 from the Kazakhstan Pedagogical Institute and became a literary historian and critic, educator, lecturer, and professor who was associated with the Institute of Language and Literature in the Kazakhstan Academy of Sciences. He obtained a doctorate in 1958. His writings include *Ақындар* (1956). He died on 29 September 1966. KazakSE; OSK

Ismailov, IAkub *see* Ismaĭylov, Ĭagub

Ismailov, Il'ias A., born 20th cent., his writings include *Ответственность за причинение тяжких телесных повреждений по советскому уголовному праву* (1969), *Условия формирования значительных осадко над центральностепной зоной Азербайджанской ССР* (1969), and *Преступность и уголовная политика* (1990). LC; OSK

Ismailov, Mahmud A., born 20th cent., his writings include *Капитализм в сельском хозяйстве Азербайджана на исходе XIX- начале XX в.* (1964), *Промышленность Баку в начале XX века* (1976), and *События вокруг НКАО в кривом зеакале фальсификаторов* (1989). NUC, 1973-77; OSK

Ismailova (Ismailowa), Revmira IU., born 20th cent., she received a doctorate in 1959 from the Marxist-Leninist Institute of Social Sciences of the East German Communist Party for a study of the Turkestan labour movement entitled *Aus der Geschichte der Arbeiterbewegung in Turkestan am Ende des 19. und Anfang des 20. Jahrhunderts*, this thesis, unlike customary in Germany, does not include a curriculum vitae - probably for political reasons. Schwarz

Ismaĭylov (Исмајылов), Ĭagub (Јагуб), born 20th cent., his writings include *Обулһәсәнин јарадычылыгы* (Baku, 1986), and *Илјас Әфәндијевин јарадычылыг јолу* (Baku, 1991). OSK

Ismalun, Max, born 19th cent., he was a mining engineer and, in 1916, a member of the Société sultanieh d'économie politique, de statistique et de législation. In 1941, he was resident in Cairo. Note about the author

Isnard, Hildebert, born 4 April 1904 at Nice, France, he grew up and studied at Alger, becoming first a secondary school teacher and later an assistant at the local Institut de Géographie. He received a *diplôme d'études supérieure* and a doctorate in 1947 for *La Vigne en Algérie*, a work which was published in 1951. Since 1947, he taught geography in various capacities first at the Université d'Aix-en-Provence, and later at the Université de Nice. His writings include *La Réorganisation de la propriété rurale dans la Mitidja; ses conséquences sur la vie indigène* (1939), *L'Algérie* (1954), its translation, *Algeria* (1955), *Madagascar* (1955), *Le Maghreb* (1971), and *Pays et paysages méditerranéens* (1973). He died in July 1983. "Les Amis de la Revue *Méditerranée*" published in 1985 *Hommage en mémoire d'H. Isnard*, which contains a biographical note on pages 7-8. Unesco; ZKO

Isoart, Paul, born 20 January 1931 at Nice, France, he lost his father in 1940 and was able to complete his secondary education only with a Government scholarship. He studied law at the Institut d'études juridiques de Nice, obtaining diplomas in civil as well as public law. In 1953 he gained the *diplôme d'études supérieure* (D.E.S.) in public law. He served as a *Commissaire du Gouvernement chérifien au Maroc* until called for military service from 1956 to 1958 in Algeria. He submitted his *thèse d'état* in 1959, concurrently obtaining a second D.E.S. in political science; he completed his second thesis in 1964. Since 1968 he was associated with the Centre d'études politiques et constitutionnelles de l'Université de Nice as a professor. His writings include *Essai sur les solutions soviétiques au problème colonial russe* (1964), *Les états de l'Asie du Sud-est* (1978), *La situation au Kampuchea* (1983), and he was a joint editor of *Des républiques françaises* (1988). In 1996 appeared *Mélanges en* *l'honneur du doyen Paul Isoart*, where a full record of his memberships and activities will be found. Livres disponibles, 2004; ZKO

Israeli, Raphael, born on 15 or 19 September 1935 at Fès, Morocco, he graduated in 1963 from the Hebrew University, Jerusalem, and received a Ph.D. in 1974 from the University of California at Berkeley for *Chinese versus Muslims; a study of cultural confrontation*. He was a sometime lecturer at the Hebrew University, and a coordinator, Asia Research Unit, Truman Institute, Mount Scopus, Jerusalem, concurrently teaching Chinese and Islamic history. His writings include *The Public diary of President Sadat* (1978-79), *Muslims in China* (1980), *Peace is in the eye of the beholder* (1985), and *Palestinians between Israel and Jordan; squaring the triangle* (1991). IWWAS, 1976/77; Note; Selim³; ZKO

Issa Bey, Ahmed, d. 1946 *see* Ahmad 'Isá

Issawi, Charles Philip, born in 1916 at Cairo to Syrian parents, he spent his childhood in Cairo, Khartoum, and Lebanon and attended school in Alexandria. He matriculated at Magdalen College, Oxford. Upon graduation, he returned to Cairo in 1941 and began working for the National Bank of Egypt. By 1942, in the midst of working on his book, *Egypt; an economic and social analysis*, he accepted an offer to teach politics and economics at the American University of Beirut. In 1946, he was invited to work in the Arab Office in Washington, D.C., which soon led to a position at the United Nations where he worked on surveys of economic conditions in the Middle East. In 1951, he began teaching economics at Columbia University, N.Y.C., where he stayed until he accepted an endowed chair at the Department of Near Eastern Studies of Princeton University in 1975. He formally retired in 1986. He was a prolific scholar who established the economic history of the Middle East as a field of study. He was a president of Miidle East Studies Association of North America, and the Middle East Economic Association. His writings include *An Economic history of the Middle East and North Africa* (1982), a selection of his articles, *The Middle East economy; decline and recovery* (1995), and *Growing up different; memoirs of a Middle East scholar* (1999). In 1990 appeared *The Economic dimensions of Middle Eastern history; essays in honor of Charles Issawi*. He died on 8 December 2000. AmM&WSc, 1973 S, 1978 S; Au&Wr, 1963, 1971; ConAu, 5-8, 20, 42, 190, new rev., 4; IntAu&W, 1976; *MESA bulletin*, 35 (2001), pp. 148-149; MidE, 1982/83; WhoAm, 1974-2000; WhoArab, 1981-2002; WhAm, 14

Isserlin, Benedikt Sigmund Johannes, born 25 February 1916 at München, he studied history at the universities of Bern and Zürich, 1934-35, and then transferred to the University of Edinburgh to read for the M.A. degree in history and archaeology. At Edinburgh he also began to study Hebrew. He received his M.A. in 1939 and then went on to Magdalen College, Oxford, to read Oriental languages under A. F. L. Beeston, H. A. R. Gibb, H. Danby, Chaim Rabin, and G. I. Lewis. He was admitted to the degree of B.A. in 1943, with first class honours in Arabic and Hebrew. He proceeded to the Oxford M.A. in 1948, the B.Litt. in 1951 and the D.Phil. in 1954. In 1951 he was appointed an assistant lecturer in Semitic studies at the University of Leeds, becoming a full lecturer the following year. In 1960 he was appointed senior lecturer and head of the Department of Semitic Studies. His writings include *A Hebrew work-book for beginners* (1971), *The Israelites* (1998), and *Das Volk der Bibel* (2001). He was honoured by *Oriental studies presented to Benedikt S. J. Isserlin by friends and colleagues* (1980), a work which contains a biographical note. DrBSMES, 1993; WhoWorJ, 1965

d'Istria, Dora, pseud., 1828-1888 *see* Kol'tsova-Masal'skaia, Elena Mikhailovna

Istvánffy, Gyula (Julius), born 20 November 1863 at Miskolc, Hungary, he was in 1918 a profesor at a Hungarian school in Liptószentmiklós. His writings include *Palócz néprajzi tanulmányok* (1894). He died on 12 February 1921. GeistigeUng; Magyar

Istvanovits, Márton, born 20th cent., he was a joint author of *Magyar népköltészet* (Budapest, 1988).

Isusov, Mito TSekov, born 27 March 1928, he obtained a doctorate and became associated with the Bulgarian Academy of Sciences as a professor of history. His writings include *Револютсионното профсъюзно движение в България, 1903-1913 н.* (1962), *Д-р Йосуф Йосифов; биографичен очерк* (1968), *Работническата класа в България 1944-1947* (1971) and *Политическият живот в България 1944-1948* (2000). Koi, 1998; OSK; WhoSoCE, 1989

Italiaander, Rolf Bruno Maximilian, born 20 Feruary 1913 at Leipzig, Germany, he was for over forty years an explorer of Africa, and a visiting lecturer at home and abroad. His prolific writings include *Land der Kontraste, Orient und Okzident in Marokko* (1953), *1001 Weisheit; Sprichwörter der Araber und Berber* (1961), and *Schwarze Haut in rotem Griff* (1962). He died in Hamburg on 3 September 1991. ConAu, 5-8, new rev., 6, 23; CurBio, 1964; DtBE; IntAu&W, 1976-1989; IntWW, 1974-1991/92; IWWAS, 1976/77; KDtLK, Nekrolog, 1971-1998; Master (1); Sezgin; Unesco; WhoWor, 1974/75-1991

Italinskiĭ, Andreĭ IAkovlevich, born into a noble family in 1743 at Kiev, he was educated at the Ecclesiastical Academy (Духовная Акаднмия), Kiev, and became a Russian envoy to the Porte and the Italian states in the Napoleonic era. At Constantinople he made the acquaintance of Hammer-Purgstall. He died in Roma in 1827. Flück, p. 162; Wieczynski

I'timadzadah, Mahmud *see* Bih'azin (pseud.), Mahmud I'timadzadah

Itina, Marianna Aleksandrovna, born 5 November 1922 at Berlin, she became associated with the Institute of Ethnology and Anthropology of the Russian Academy of Sciences. Her writings include *Планирование розничного товарообота и товарных фондов* (1954), and *История степных племен Юзного Приаралья* (1977). OSK; Schoeberlein

Itscherenska, Ilse, born about 1944, she studied Indian subjects and Persian at Humboldt Universität, Berlin. She became associated with the Akademie der Wissenschaften, Berlin. She was a joint editor of *Der islamische Staat* (1983). Private

Itzkowitz, Norman, born 6 May 1931 at N.Y.C., he graduated in 1953 from the City College of New York and received a Ph.D. in 1960 from Princeton University for *Mehmed Raghib Pasha; the making of an Ottoman grand vezir*. In 1973 he was appointed a professor of Near Eastern studies at Princeton University. His writings include *The Ottoman Empire and Islamic tradition* (1972), and he was a joint editor of *Psychological dimensions of Near Eastern studies* (1977). DrAS, 1969 H, 1974 H, 1978 H, 1982 H; WhoAm, 1982-2003; WhoE, 1986, 1989 (not sighted); ZKO

IUdakhin (Юдахин), Konstantin Kuz'mich, born in 1890 at Orsk, Russia, he graduated in 1925 from the Turkestan Oriental Institute, Tashkent, and received a doctorate in 1949. His writings include *Киргизско-русский словарь* (1940), and *Хестоматия по уйгурскомы языку* (1948). He died on 22 March 1975. Index Islamicus (2); KazakSE; *Казахская ССР краткая энциклопедия*, vol. 3, p. 561; KyrgyzSE; Miliband; Miliband²; *Советская тюркология*, 1975, no. 3, pp. 123-125; TurkmenSE; UzbekSE

IUdin (Юдин), Beniamin Petrovich, born 1 February 1928 at Volgograd, Russia, he graduated in 1950 from the Oriental Institute, Moscow. He was an Uighur scholar who was successively affiliated with the Kazan State Pedagogical Institute, Kazan State University and the Kazan Academy of Sciences. He died on 12 May 1983. Miliband²

IUferev (Юферев), Viacheslav Ivanovich, born in 1876, his writings include *Из истории Туркестана* (Tashkent, 1911), and *Хлопководство в Туркестане* (1926). OSK

IUldashbaeva (Юлдашбаева), Fatima Khodzhamberdyevna, born in 1911 at Skobelev, Uzbekistan, she graduated in 1936 from the Institute of History at the Fergana Pedagogical State Institute, and received her first degree in 1953 at Tashkent with a study of British aggression in Central Asia and the Russo-Afghan border entitled *Английская агрессия в Средней Азии и русско-афганское разграничение 70-80-х гг. XIX в.* Her writings include *Из истории английской колониальной политики в Афганистане и Средней Азии* (1963) and *Моя судба* (1972). She died on 24 August 1983. Miliband; Miliband²

IUldashev (Юлдашев), Akhnef Akhmetovich, born 30 July 1920 near Ufa, Bashkir A.S.S.R, he received a doctorate in 1966 and was appointed a professor in 1967. His writings include *Аналитические формы глагола в тюрских языках* (1965), *Принципы составления тюруско-русских словарей* (1972), *Соотношение деепричастных и личкых форм глагола в тюркских языках* (1977), and he edited *Грамматика современного башкирского литературного языка* (1981). BashkKE; OSK

IUldashev (Юлдашев), Mukhamedzhan IUldashevich, born in 1904 in Russian Turkistan, he graduated in 1928 from the Central Asiatic Communist University and received his first degree in 1947 for a study of trade relations of Bukhara and Russia entitled «*Торговие отношения Бухары с Россей в XVI-XVIII вв.*» and his doctorate in 1953 for *Землевладение и государственное устройство феодальной Хивы XIX века в свете мате-риалов архива хивинских ханов*. He was appointed a lecturer in 1948 and a professor in 1960. His writings include *К истории торговых и посольских связей Средней Азии с Россией в XVI-XVIII вв.* (1964), and *К истории крестьян Хивы XIX века* (1966) as well as writings in Uzbek. He died on 3 September 1985. Miliband; Miliband²

IUnuskhodzhaeva (Юнусходжаева), Mubarak IUldashevna, born 20 December 1933 at Frunze, Kirgiz S.S.R., she graduated in 1957 from the Central Asian State University and received her first degree in 1964 for a study of the history of property ownership in Turkestan entitled *Из истории землевладения Туркестана*. She was since 1960 affiliated with the Oriental Institute in the Uzbek Academy of Sciences. Her writings include *Из истории землевладентя в дореволюционном Туркестане* (1970) as well as writings in Uzbek. Miliband; Miliband²

IUnusov (Юнусов), Kemal' Osmanovich, born 19 March 1931 at Gatchina, Russia, he graduated in 1955 the from Oriental Faculty, Leningrad, and received his first degree in 1973 for a study of the playwright Tawfiq al-Hakim entitled *Драматургия Тауфика аль-Хакима*, a work which was published in 1976. He was affiliated with his alma mater since 1960. In 1982 he was appointed a lecturer. His other writings include *Шесть гиней; новеллы египетских писателей* (1964), and *Тауфик аль-Хаким; библиографический указатель* (1968). Miliband²; OSK

IUrevich (Юревич), Liudmila Ieronimovna, born 23 October 1921 at Moscow, she graduated in 1944 from the Faculty of History, Moscow State University, and received her first degree in 1947 for *Саид Ахмад Хан и зарождение мусульманского общинного движения в Индии во второй половине XIX в.* She joined the Nauka publisher in 1960. When she retired in 1985 she was head of the South and Southeast Asia Division. Miliband; Miliband²

IUshkevich (Juschkewisch/Yushkevich), Adol'f Pavlovich, born in 1906 at Odessa, he graduated in 1929 from the Faculty of Physics and Mathematics, Moscow, received his first degree in 1935, and his doctorate in 1940. In the same year he was appointed a professor. His writings include *История математика в средние века* (1961), and its translation, *Geschichte der Mathematik im Mittelalter* (1964), a work in which he also referred to the algebra of Omar Khayyam. He died on 17 April 1993. Krachkovskiĭ, p. 266; Miliband; Miliband²

IUshmanov (Yushmanov), Nikolai Vladimirovich, born in 1896 at St. Petersburg, he graduated in 1923 from the Faculty of Oriental Languages, Petrograd, and received his first degree in 1929 for a study of irragularity of a Semitc root entitled, *Семитские корневые разновидности*, and a doctorate in 1938. He was affiliated with the Soviet Academy of Sciences. He was a linguist with a broad range of interests, encompassing Semitic as well as Hamitic philology. His writings include *Грамматика литературного арабского языка* (1928), *Амхарский язык* (1959), and *Краткая грамматика арабского языка* (1964). He died on 2 April 1946. Krachkovskiĭ, pp. 217-218; Miliband; Miliband²; VostokMStP, p. 282

IUsifov (Юсифов), IUsif Bakhlul-ogly, born 23 September 1929 in Soviet Armenia, he graduated in 1952 from the Oriental Faculty, Leningrad, received his first degree in 1958 for a study of Elam and Midian entitled *Царское ремесленное хозяйство в Мидии и Эламе*, and his doctorate in 1964 for *Элам; социально-экономическая история*, a work which was published in 1968. He was a scholar of the ancient Near East, and since 1952 associated with the Azerbaijan Academy of Sciences. Miliband; Miliband²

Iusifov (Јусифов), Khălil Gamid ogly, his writings include *Низаминин лирикасы* (Baky,1968), and *Шәргдә интибаһ вә Низами Кәнчәви* (Baky, 1982). LC; OSK

IUsipova (Юсипова), Roza Rizovna, born 9 November 1924 at Nizhni Novgorod (Gorki), she graduated in 1950 from the Oriental Institute, Moscow, and received her first degree in 1961 for a study of Turkish a dialect entitled *Устойчивые глагольные сочетания в турецком языке*. She was a Turkish scholar and from 1956 to 1980 associated with the Oriental Institute in the Soviet Academy of Sciences. Miliband; Miliband²

IUsupov (Юсупов), Daniil Ivanovich, born 10 October 1922 at Poltava, Ukraine, he graduated in 1945 from the Military Institute of Foreign Languages and received his first degree in 1954 for a study of the work of 'Umar Farid and his journal al-Tariq entitled *Творчество Омара Фахури и основное направление журнала «Ат-тарик»*. He was since 1954 associated with the Oriental Institute in the Soviet Academy of Sciences. The years from 1963 to 1967 he spent with Novosti Press Agency in Syria. His writings include *Современная ливанская литература* (1972), and he was a joint author of *Арабская литература; краткий очерк* (Moscow, 1964). He died on 23 March 1981. Miliband; Miliband²

IUsupov (Юсупов), Garun Valeevich, born in 1914, he was a Turkologist and ethnographer associated from 1946 to 1949 with Kazan University, and subsequently with the Institute of History of the Soviet Academy of Sciences, Bashkir Division. His writings include *Введение в булгаро-татарскую эпиграфику* (1960). He died in 1968.. OSK; TatarES

IUsupov (Юсупов), Iskander Azimovich, born 20 January 1928 at Tashkent, he graduated in 1951 from the Oriental Faculty, Central Asian State University, and received his first degree in 1955 for a study of establishment and development of Soviet-Iranian relations, 1917-1927, entitled *Установление и развитие советско-иранских отношений, 1917-1927 гг.* He was affiliated with the Uzbek Academy of Sciences since 1956. His writings include *Установление и развитие советско-иранских отношений* (1969). Miliband²

IUsupov (Юсупов), Khemra G., his writings include *Приузбойские туркменские племена XIV-XV вв.* (1975). OSK

IUsupov (Юсупов), Ruzal' Abdullazianovich, born in 1938, he was associated with Kazan Pedagogical University since 1970, and since 1986 its director. He received a doctorate in philology in 1984. He was a joint author of *Формирование и функционирование татарского языка* (1986), and *Вопросы структуры татарского языка* (1986). TatarES

IUsupov (Юсупов), Shakhzade, his writings include *Дружба, рожденная в труде* (Alma-Ata, 1970). LC

IUsopova (Юсупова), Zarė Alievna, born 16 December 1934 at Tiflis, she graduated in 1958 from the Oriental Faculty, Leningrad, and received her first degree in 1965 for a study of the Kurdish Sorani dialect entitled *Предлоги и послелоги в южном диалекте курдского языка соран.* She was since 1959 affiliated with the Leningrad Branch of the Oriental Institute in the Soviet Academy of Sciences. Her writings include *Сулейманийский диалект курдского языка* (1985), and she was a joint author of *Курдско-русский словарь* (1983). Miliband²

IUvachev (Ювачев/Youvatschef), Ivan Pavlovich, born in 1860, his writings include *Паломничество в Палестину к Гробу Господню* (1904), *Шлиссельбургская крепость* (1907), and its translation, *The Russian bastille; or, The Schlüsselburg fortress* (1909). NUC, pre-1956

Ivanics, Mária, born 20th cent., her writings include *A Krími kánság a tizenöt éves háborúban* (Budapest, 1994). OSK

Ivánka (de Draskócz et Jordanföld), Endre, born 24 September 1902 at Budapest, he was successively a professor of classics and Byzantine studies at the universities of Budapest, Wien, and Graz. His writings include *Die aristotelische Politik and die Städtegründungen Alexanders des Grossen* (1938), *Die letzten Tage von Konstantinopel* (1954), and *Rhomäervolk und Gottesvolk* (1968). He died in Wien on 6 December 1974. DtBilnd (3); Ki-kicsoda, 1937; Kürschner, 1950-1970; MEL, 1981; WhoAustria, 1969/70

Ivanov, Anatolii Alekseevich, born 3 July 1929 at Leningrad, he graduated in 1953 from the Oriental Faculty, Leningrad, and received his first degree in 1972 with a thesis entitled *Медине и бронзовые (латунные) изделия Ирана половины XIV- половины XVII вв.* He was a lecturer in Iranian history at Leningrad University from 1948 to 1956, when he joined the Oriental Section of the Hermitage Museum, Leningrad. He later was a keeper of Iranian metalwork and Syrian-Egyptian materials. Miliband; Miliband²; Schoeberlein

Ivanov, Mikhail Sergeevich, born in 1909 in Novgorod Oblast, he graduated in 1931 from the Oriental Section of the Leningrad State University, received his first degree in 1937 for *Бабидские восстания,1848-1852 гг. в Иране,* and his doctorate in 1953 for *Иранская революция, 1905-1911 гг.* He became a lecturer in 1939, and a professor in 1956. His writings include *Бабидские восстания в Иране* (1939), *Очерк истории Ирана* (1952), *Иранская революция, 1905-1911 годов* (1957), *Иран сегодня* (1969), *Новейшая история Ирана* (1965), *Рабочий класс современного Ирана* (1969), and *Иран в 60-70-х годах XX века* (1977). He died on 19 October 1986. Miliband; Miliband²

Ivanov, Nikolai Alekseevich, born 24 October 1928 at Viatka, Tatar Autonomous Soviet Republic, he graduated in 1951 from the Faculty of History, Moscow State University, and received his first degree in 1956, and a doctorate in 1972 with a thesis entitled *Кризис французского протектора в Тунисе, 1918-1939 гг.* Since 1951 he was attached to the Oriental Institute of the Soviet Academy of Sciences. His writings include *В борьбе за независимость* (1957), *Современные Тунис* (1959), *Государственныйстрой Туниса* (1962), *Османское завоевание арабских стран* (1984), and he was a joint editor of *Тунис; справочник* (1978), and *Ислат; краткий справочник* (1983). He died on 20 March 1994. Miliband; Miliband²

Ivanov, Pavel Petrovich, born in 1893 in Tiumen (Tyumen) Oblast, Russia, he graduated in 1924 from the Turkestan Oriental Institute, and received a doctorate in 1941. From 1934 to 1941 he was attached to the Oriental Institute of the Soviet Academy of Sciences. His writings include *К истории развития горного промысла в Средней Азии* (1932), *Восстание китай-кипчаев в Бухарском ханстве, 1821-1825 гг.* (1932), *Архив хивинских ханов XIX в.* (1940), and *Очерки по истории Средней Азии, XVI-XVII вв.* (1958) as well as catalogues of Oriental manuscripts. He died on 2 February 1942. Miliband; Miliband²

Ivanov, Sergeĭ Nikolaevich, born 11 June 1922 at Petrograd, he graduated in 1951 from the Oriental Faculty, Leningrad, and received his first degree in 1958 with a study of contemporary literary Uzbek entitled *Синтаксические функции формы на -ган в современном узбекском литературном*

языке. He was attached to the Bukhara Pedagogical Institute, before he joined in 1956 the Leningrad Oriental Faculty. He became a lecturer in 1961, and a professor in 1971. In 1970 he gained a doctorate. His writings include *Очерки по синтаксису узбексого языка* (1959), *Николай Федорович Катанов; очерк жизни и деятель-ности* (1962), and *Родословное древо тюрок Абу-л-Гази хана; грамматический очерк* (1969), *Арабизмы в турецком языке* (1973), *Курс турецкой грамматики* (1975), and he was a joint author of *Андрей Николаевич Кононов* (1980). Miliband; Miliband[2]

Ivanov, Viacheslav Vsevolodovich, born 21 August 1929 at Moscow, he graduated in 1951 from the Faculty of Philology, Moscow, and received his first degree in 1955 for a study of Indo-European philology entitled *Индо-европейские корни в клинописном хеттском языке и особенности их структуры*, and his doctorate in 1978 for *Отражение двух серий индоевропейских глагольных форм в балтийско-славянском*. His writings include *Санскрит* (1960), and *Хеттский язык* (1963). Miliband[2]

Ivanov, Vladimir, 1886-1970 *see* Ivanow, Vladimir Alekseevich

Ivanova, Inessa Il'inichna, born 4 May 1948 at Moscow, she graduated in 1971 from the Moscow State Institute of International Relations and received her first degree in 1975 for a study of the position of Turkey in the Arab-Israeli conflict entitled *Позиция Турции в отношении арабо-израильского конфликта*. She was since 1971 a research fellow in the Oriental Institute, Soviet Academy of Sciences. Her writings include *Турецко-арабские отношения и их место в системе меджу-народных связей на Ближнем Востоке* (1985). Miliband[2]

Ivanova, Inna Petrovna, born 29 July 1940 in Kirov Oblast, Russia, she graduated in 1962 from the Faculty of Economics, Moscow State University, and received her first degree in 1967 for a study of agrarian problems in the United Arab Republic entitled *Аграрные преобразования и развитие сельскохозяйственного производства в Объединеной Арабской Республике, 1952-1965 гг.* She was from 1950 to 1975 affiliated with the Oriental Institute, Soviet Academy of Sciences. Her writings include *Октябрьская революция и Иране в 1918-1922 гг.* (1958), *Национально-освободитное движение в Иране в 1918-1922 гг.* (1961), *Сельское хозяйство Объединенной Арабской Республики 1952-1965* (1970), and *Особенности воспроиз-водства общественного продукта в арабских странах* (1987). Miliband[2]

Ivanova, Mariia Nikolaevna, born in 1907, she graduated in 1929 from the Central Asian State University and received her first degree in 1949 for *Компартия Ирана в Гулянской революции*. Her writings include *Октябрьская революция и Иран* (1958). Miliband; Miliband[2]

Ivanow, Vladimir Alekseevich, born in 1886 in Byelorussia, he studied Oriental languages, mainly Persian and Arabic, under Victor von Rosen at St. Petersburg. He later became an assistant keeper of Oriental manuscripts at the Oriental Museum of the Russian Academy of Sciences, St. Petersburg. On the out-break of the revolution, he went to Central Asia looking for Islamic manuscripts. In 1918 he entered the service of the British Government, became a British subject, never to return to Russia. In the early 1920s he served as a Persian interpreter to H.M.'s Government in Persia. About this time, the Royal Asiatic Society of Bengal was looking for someone to catalogue its collection of manuscripts; he applied, was accepted, and successively catalogued five volumes of Persian, and one volume of Arabic manuscripts. His life work, however, was his contribution to the study of Ismailism, both Indian and Persian. His writings include *A Guide to Ismaili literature* (1933), *Ismaili tradition concerning the rise of the Fatimids* (1942), *The Alleged founder of Ismailism* (1946), *Studies in early Persian Ismailism* (1948), *The Truth-worshippers of Kurdistan* (1952), *Alamut and Lamasar* (1960), *Ismaili literature* (1963), and *Correspondance Corbin-Ivanow, lettres échangées de 1947 à 1966*, ed. Sabine Schmidtke (1999). "He came, lived his life 'like a lonely sea-bird on the wing', and went his way." He died an agnostic in Tehran on 19 June 1970. *Indo-Iranica* 23, no. 3 (1970), pp. 22-7; *Journal of the Asiatic Society of Bombay* 45/46 (1970/71), 92-97 (both by A. A.. Fyzee)

Iványi, Tamás, born 12 December 1944 at Budapest, he was an Arabist whose writings include *Gyöngyszemek klasszikus arab szövegekből* (1990), and he was a joint author of *Arab-magyar szótár* (1976-78), *Az arab írás* (1986), its translation, *Let's write Arabic* (1987), and *Indul a karaván; alapfolon arabul* (1995). Biograf, 2004

Iveković, Ivan, born in 1938, his writings include *Afrika u borbi za drugu nezavisnost* (Zagreb, 1990), and he edited *Afrika i socijalizm* (Beograd, 1976). LC

Ivonin, IUriĭ Evgen'evich, born 20th cent., his writings include *У истоков европейской дипломатии нового времени* (1984), and *Становление европейской системы государств; Англия и Габсбурги на рубеже лвух эпох* (1989). LC

d'**Ivray**, Jehan, pseud, 1861-1940 *see* Fahmy-Bey, Jeanne

Ivry, Alfred Lyon, born 14 January 1935 at Brooklyn, N.Y., he graduated in 1957 from Brooklyn College and received a D.Phil. in 1970 from Oxford University for *al-Kindi's 'First philosophy' and cognate texts; translation and commentary*. He was successively a professor of Jewish and Islamic philosophy at Brandeis University, Waltham, Mass., and New York University. His writings include *Middle commentary on Aristotle's De Anima* (2002), and he edited *al-Kindi's Metaphysics* (1974). DrAS, 1969 F; 1974 P, 1978 P, 1982 P; NatFacDr, 1990, 2002; WhoAm, 1984-2003

Iwamura, Shinobu, born in 1905, his writings include *Manuscripts and printed editions of Marco Polo's travels* (1949), and *The Zirni manuscript; a Persian-Mongolian glossary* (1961). NUC

Iwan, James L., born 14 December 1939 at Boonville, Mo., he graduated in 1964 from California State College, Long Beach, and received a Ph.D. in 1968. After a brief period with the International Agricultural Development Service, U.S. Department of Agriculture, Washington, D.C., he became a manager in industry. AmM&WSc, 1973 S

Iwarson, Jonas, born 28 August 1867 at Näskotts skn., Jämtland, Sweden, he was educated at Johanneslunds Missionsinstitut, in Linköping, and in Italy. He subsequently became a missionary in Eritrea. His writings include *Nya färdevägar i Ostafrika; resor i Eritrea* (Stockholm, 1936). SMK

Iwaszkiewicz, Leon *Jarosław*, born 29 February at Kalnik, Ukraine, he was a Polish poet and novelist, a prolific writer. He was a sometime president of the Union of Polish Writers. His writings include *Liryki* (1959), and *Gathering time; five modern Polish elegies* (1983). He died in Warszawa on 2 March 1980. CasWL; ConAu, 97-100; DLB, 215 (1999), pp. 152-60; Dziekan; IntWW, 1974-79; Master (16); NEP; Polski (5); WhoWor, 1974/75

Izmailova, Tat'iana Alekseevna, born in 1907 at Petersburg, she graduated in 1930 from the Leningrad Institute of History, Philology and Linguistics, received her first degree in 1944 for a study of Armenian art entitled "Декоративное убранство архитектурних памятников Армении XII-XIII вв.," and a doctorate in 1970 for *Армянская миниатюрная живопись XI века*. She was since 1930 a research fellow of the Ėrmitazh Museum, Leningrad. Her writings include *Культура и искусство Переднего Востока* (1960). Miliband; Miliband²

Izquierdo Benito, Ricardo, born 20th cent., he received a doctorate in history. A specialist in medieval history, he was a professor at the Universidad de Castilla-La Mancha, Ciudad Real, and a chairman of the Departamento de Historia. His writings include *Castilla-La Mancha en la edad media* (1985), *La sociedad medieval a través de la literatura hispanojudia* (1989), and he edited *Alarcos 1195; actas del Congreso Internacional Commemorativo del VIII Centenario de la Batalla de Alarcos* (1995). Arabismo, 1992, 1994, 1997

Izutsu, Toshihiko, born 4 May 1914 at Tokyo, he was a professor of linguistics and Oriental studies at Keio University, also serving from 1962 to 1968 as a visiting professor at the Institute of Islamic Studies in McGill University, Montreal. His writings include *Arabiago nyumon* (1950), *Language and magic* (1956), *The Structure of the ethical terms in the Koran* (1959), *God and man in the Koran* (1964), *The Concept of belief in Islamic theology* (1965), *A Comparative study of the key philosophical concepts in Sufism and Taoism* (1966-67), and a Japanese translation of the Koran in 1992. DrAS, 1969 F, 1974 F

Jaba, Auguste (Aleksandre Kościesza Żaba), born in 1801, he was a diplomat and orientalist who had studied at Wilna and St. Petersburg. His writings include *Recueil de notices et récits kourdes* (1860), and *Dictionnaire kurde-français* (1879). He died in 1894. Dziekan; Polski (4)

Jabcke, Peter, born 26 June 1935 at Braunschweig, Germany, he studied economics at the Universität Köln. From 1962 to 1964 he participated as an assistant in an exchange program of the Universität Köln at Kabul University. He received a doctorate in 1969 from the Ruhr-Universität, Bochum, for a study of financing development projects entitled *Probleme der Aufbringung von Eigenwährungsmittel bei der Finanzierung von Entwicklungsprojekten*. Thesis

Jabłonowski, Aleksander Walerian, born 19 April 1829 at Goźlin, Poland, he studied classics and German at the universities of Kiev and Dorpat. His writings include *Sprawy wołoskie za Jagiellonów* (Warszawa, 1878), and *Pisma* (Warszawa, 1910-13). BN; Dziekan; PSB

Jabłonowski, Wacław, Hrabia, he was born about 1800 in Poland. He had to leave his country after the 1831 revolution and went to France. His writings include *Esquisse d'un système de civilisation et*

colonisation de l'Algérie, par un étranger qui a habité ce pays et qui n'y possède rien (Paris, 1840), and *La France et la Pologne, le slavianisme et la dynastie polonaise*, par le comte Vinceslas Jablonowski (Paris, 1843). His trace is lost after a publication in 1853. BN; Dziekan

Jabłonowski, Władyslaw, born in 1841, he studied medicine at Kiev, Paris, and Kraków and received a medical diploma in 1865. In 1866 he entered the Ottoman service and a year later he was sent to Kirkuk as head of a hospital. He died in 1894. Dziekan; Kornrumpf; PSB

Jablonsky, Walter, born 20th cent., he was a German navy commander whose writings include *Taktische Nuklearwaffen der Marinen in der Konfrontation NATO Warschauer Pakt* (1979), and *Im Gleichschritt? Zur Geschichte der NVA* (2001).

Jaccard, Pierre, born 14 September 1901 at Sainte-Croix (Canton de Vaud), Switzreland, he was educated at Lausanne, Strasbourg, Paris and New York, and he received a doctorate in letters at Lausanne and a doctorate in theology at New York. He successively taught at Genève, Wooster, Ohio, Neuchâtel, and again Genève. Since 1952 he was a professor of sociology at l'École des sciences sociales et politiques de l'Université de Lausanne. His writings include *Histoire sociale du travail de l'antiquité à nos jours* (1960), *Sociologie de l'éducation* (1962), and *L'inconscient, les rêves, les complexes* (1973). SchBiAr, 4 (1954), pp. 70-71; WhoSwi, 1962/63, 1968/69, 1972/73

Jack-Hinton, Colin, born about 1930, he received a Ph.D. in 1962 from the Australian National University, Canberra, for *The European discovery, rediscovery and exploration of the Islands of Solomon, 1568-1838*. His writings include *A Sketch map history of Malaya, Sarawak, Sabah and Singapore* (1966), and *The Search for the Islands of Solomon* (1969). NUC, 1956-67

Jäckh, Ernst Friedrich Wilhelm, born 22 February 1875 at Urbach, Württemberg, Germny, he studied foreign languages, political economy, and history of philosophy at the universities of Heidelberg, Genève, Breslau, and München, obtaining a Dr.phil. in 1900 from the Universität Heidelberg for *Studien zu Kotzebue's Lustspieltechnik*. He subsequently became editor-in-chief of the Stuttgart *Schwabenspiegel*. Since 1913 he was associated with the Berlin weeklies *Die Politik*, and *Der Staat seid ihr*. In 1914 he was appointed a professor of Turkish history at the Universität Berlin. He was the founder and president of the Deutsch-Türkische Vereinigung, and the editor of the series *Deutsche Orientbücherei*. He served as president of the Hochschule für Politik, Berlin, from 1926 to 1933, when he emigrated to the UK. He had been a lecturer in America and Turkey before he started teaching Near Eastern subjects at Columbia University, N.Y.C. His many writings include *Der aufsteigende Halbmond* (1911), *Im türkischen Kriegslager durch Albanien* (1911), *Deutsch-türkische Waffenbrüderschaft* (1915), *Amerika und wir* (1929), *Politik als Wissenschaft* (1930), and the autobiography, *Der goldene Pflug* (1954); and he edited *Background of the Middle East* (1952). He died in New York on 17 August 1959. BioHbDtE; BioIn, 5; DtBE; KDtLK, Nekrolog, 1935-1970; Kornrumpf; Kürschner, 1925-1935; NDB; NYT, 18 August 1959, p. 29, col. 1; RHbDtG; Wer ist's, 1922-1935; WhE&EA

Jackson, Abraham Valentine Williams, born in 1862 at N.Y.C., he was educated at Columbia University and the Universität Halle/Saale. He taught Indo-Iranian languages at Columbia University, Ithaca, N.Y., until his retirement in 1935. He visited India and Ceylon in 1901 and travelled in Persia and Central Asia in 1903 for purposes of archaeological research, especially of Zoroastrianism. His writings include *An Avesta grammar in comparison with Sanskrit* (1892), *Persia, past and present; a book of travel and research* (1906), *From Constantinople to the home of Omar Khayyam; travels in Transcaucasia and northern Persia* (1911), *A Catalogue of Persian manuscripts, including also some Turkish and Arabic, presented to the Metropolitan Museum of Art, New York* (1914), *Early Persian poetry* (1920), and *Researches in Manichaeism* (1932). He died in 1937. Buckland; DAB; IndianBiInd (1); Master (80); NYT, 9 August 1937, p. 20, col. 1; Shavit; WhAm, 1

Jackson, Clarence J.-L., pseud. *see* Bulliet, Richard W., 1940-

Jackson, David Edward Pritchett, born 9 December 1941 at Calcutta, he graduated in 1964 from Pembroke College, Cambridge, and received a Ph.D. in 1970 from Cambridge University for *The Arabic version of the mathematical collection of Pappus Alexandrinus Book VIII*. He successively taught at the University of St. Andrew and at Cambridge. He was a joint author of *Saladin; the politics of the holy war* (1982). DrBSMES, 1993; *MESA Roster of members*, 1990; Sluglett; WhoWor, 1984-1989/90

Jackson, George *Colin*, born 6 December 1921, he graduated from St. John's College, Oxford, and was called to the bar from Gray's Inn. He was a Labour M.P., a broadcaster and journalist. He visited several Middle Eastern countries to collect material for his writings which include *The new India* (London, Fabian International Bureau, 1957), and *Labour in Asia* (London, Fabian Society, 1973). He died in 1981. Who's who, 1969-1981; Who was who, 8

Jackson, Henry Cecil, born 19th cent., he was a member of the Sudan Political Service. His writings include *Black ivory and white, or The story of El Zubeir Pasha, slaver and sultan, as told by himself,* translated and put on record (Khartoum, 1913), *Osman Digna* (1926), *The Fighting Sudanese* (1954), *Sudan days and ways* (1954), *Behind the modern Sudan* (1955), and *Pastor on the Nile* (1960). Note about the author; ZKO

Jackson, Sir Herbert William, born in 1861, he was educated at Rugby and the Royal Military College, Sandhurst. He joined the British Army in 1881 and served in the Egyptian war, 1882, and the Nile campaign, 1884-85. After the battle of Omdurman, he became a provincial governor in the Sudan. He retired from the service in 1923 with the rank of major-general. He died in 1931. Hill; *Who was who*, 3

Jackson, Jack, born 28 July 1938, he was a photographer, and an author of books on off-road four-wheel drives and diving sites. He was a joint author of *The Asian highway; the complete overland guide from Europe to Australia* (1979). LC

Jackson, James, born 19th cent., his writings include *Liste provisoire de bibliographies géographiques speciales* (Paris, Société de géographie, 1881). His trace is lost after an article in 1892. BN

Jackson, James Grey, born 18th cent., he was for sixteen years resident in western Africa. His writings include *An Account of the Empire of Morocco and the districts of Suse and Tafilelt* (1809), and *An Account of Timbuctoo and Housa* (1820). Brit Ind (4); Henze; Master (3)

Jackson, John, born 18th cent., he became a fellow of the Society of Antiquarians in 1787. His writings include *Journey from India towards England in the year 1797* (1799), its translation, *Tagebuch einer im Jahre 1797 unternommenen Landreise aus Ostindien nach Europa* (1803), and *Reflections on the commerce of the Mediterranean* (1804). DNB; Master (4); Sezgin

Jackson, John William, born about 1809, his writings include *The Peoples of Europe and the war in the East* (Edinburgh, 1854), and *Man contemplated physically, morally, intellectually and spiritually* (London, 1871-72). He died on 2 April 1871 in his sixty-second year. BLC; LC

Jackson, Paul, born 20th cent., his writings include *The Way of the Sufi; Sharafuddin Maneri* (1987), a work which was originally submitted as a Ph.D. thesis to Patna University in 1980 entitled *The life and teaching of a fourteenth century Sufi saint of Bihar,* and he translated from the Persian of Sharafuddin Maneri, *The hundred letters* (1980). ZKO

Jackson, Peter, born 20th cent., he received a Ph.D. in 1977 from Cambridge University for *The Mongols and India, 1221-1351.* His writings include *The Delhi Sultanate; a political and military political history* (1999). Sluglett; ZKO

Jacob, Abel, born 15 June 1939 at Tel Aviv, he graduated in 1962 from the University of California, Los Angeles, where he also received a Ph.D. in 1969 for *The political outcomes of foreign aid; Israel's foreign aid program to Africa.* In 1969 he was appointed an assistant professor of political science at York College, Jamaica, N.Y. AmM&WSc, 1973 S; NUC, 1968-72

Jacob, Alain, born 20th cent., his writings include *D'une Algérie à l'autre* (Paris, 1963), and *La Suède confiante en l'Europe* (Paris, 1963). BN; 1960-69

Jacob, Alain Paul Louis, born 5 July 1942 at Paris, he graduated in history of art and archaeology from the Sorbonne in 1971, and received a diploma from the École du Louvre in 1972. He was an editor-in-chief of A.B.C. Décor. His writings include *Bronzes de l'Afrique noire* (1974), *Armes blanches de l'Afrique noire* (1974), *Islam, les armes blanches* (1975), *Statuaire de l'Afrique noire* (1976), *Les Armes blanches du monde islamiques; arms de poing* (1985), *Costume de l'Afrique noire* (1980), and he was a joint author of *Céramique chinoise* (1976). IndexBFr^2 (1) = *Ceux qui font la presse,* 1979; ZKO

Jacob, Arthur Le Grand, born in 1867, he graduated from the Royal Military College, Sandhurst. Transferred to the Indian Staff Corps, he served in India until the outbreak of the first World War. After a brief employ during the 1920 Iraq rebellion, he returned to India, where he served until he retired in 1926 with the rank of major-general. He died in 1942. WhoIndia, 1927; Riddick; *Who was who*, 4

Jacob, Georg, 26 March 1862 at Königsberg, Prussia, he started to study theology, but soon changed to Oriental, Germanic, and ethnological subjects which he pursued successively at the universities of Leipzig, Straßburg, Breslau and Berlin, gaining a Dr.phil. in 1887 from the Universität Leipzig for a study of the Scadinavian trade of the Arabs in the middle ages entitled *Der nordisch-baltische Handel der Araber im Mittelalter.* From among his teachers, Eduard Reuss and Theodor Nöldeke influenced him most; he also studied under H. L. Fleischer, whose example induced him to combine the knowledge of Arabic, Persian, and Turkish. He served as a lecturer at the universities of Greifswald and Halle until 1901, when he was appointed a professor at the Universität Erlangen. In 1911 he was invited to a professorship at the Universität Kiel, where he remained until his retirement. Since 1896 he had devoted himself increasingly to Turkish studies. In 1904 he founded the *Türkische Bibliothek*. His writings include *Beiträge zur Kenntnis des Derwisch-Ordens der Bektaschis* (1908), *Schanfarā-Studien*: (1) *Der Wortschatz der Lāmīja*; (2) *Parallelen und Kommentare zur Lāmīja* (1914), *Der Einfluß des Morgenlandes auf das Abendland* (1924), and *Geschichte des Schattentheaters im Morgen- und Abendland* (1925). A bibliography of his writings is to be found in *Festschrift Georg Jacob zum siebzigsten Geburtstag 26. Mai 1932 gewidmet von Freunden und Schülern* (1932). He died on 4 July 1936. Islamic culture, 12 (1938), pp. 368-370; Fück, 319-322; Hanisch; Kürschner, 1935; Wer ist's, 1935; ZDMG, 91 (1937), pp. 486-500

Jacob, Harold Fenton, born in 1866, he graduated from the Royal Military College, Sandhurst, and joined the Indian Army, serving with the Indian Staff Corps since 1883. For over fifteen years he was intimately associated with Aden and its hinterland. He was a Political Officer on the disputed boundary between the Aden Protectorate and Yemen from 1904 to 1907 and later First Assistant Resident in Aden and Chief Political Officer with the Aden Field Force. In 1917 he was posted to Cairo as adviser to the High Commissioner who was responsible for Aden affairs and a member of the Arab Bureau. His writings include *Perfums of Araby* (1915), *Kings of Arabia* (1923), and its Arabic translation in 1983. He died in 1936. IndianBilnd (1); Note; Who was who, 3

Jacob, James Randal, born 28 August 1940, he received a Ph.D. in English literature from Cornell University, Ithaca, N.Y. He subsequently taught English history in various capacities at John Jay College of Criminal Justice, City University of New York, a post which he still held in 2004. His writings include *Henry Stubbe, radical Protestantism and the early Enlightenment* (1983). ConAu, 132; DrAS, 1974 H; NatFacDr, 1990-2004; WrDr, 1994/96-2005

Jacob, Xavier, Frère, born 20th cent., he received a *doctorat de 3ème cycle* in 1976 from the Université de Strasbourg for *L'enseignement religieux dans la Turquie moderne*. He was associated with the Centre for the Study of Islam and Christian-Muslim Relations, Birmingham, and Christlich-Islamische Begegnung, Frankfurt/Main. His writings include *Islamischer Religionsunterricht in der Türkei* (1983), *Das Christentum in der religiösen Literatur der Türkei* (1983), and *Christianity as seen by the Turks* (Birmingham, 1984). THESAM, 4; ZKO

Jacobé de Naurois, René Paulin, 1906- see Naurois, René Paulin de

Jacobi, Jürgen, born 20th cent., he translated from the Arabic of 'Abd al-'Azīz al-Dūrī, *Arabische Wirtschaftsgeschichte* (1969). His trace is lost after an article in 1992. Sezgin

Jacobi, Renate née Tietz, born 1 February 1936 at Volzrade, Mecklenburg, Germany, she grew up in Lüneburg and subsequently trained at Gemersheim as a translator of English and Swedish. In 1958 she began to study Islamic subjects at the Universität Tübingen, where she received her Dr. phil. in 1963 for a study of Koranic conditional sentences and expressions entitled *Bedingungssatz und Bedingungsausdruck im Koran*. In 1970, she gained her Dr.habil. at Saarbrücken for *Studien zur Poetik der altarabischen Qaside*. She subsequently became a professor of Islamic and Arabic studies at Saarbrücken until her retirement. Kürschner, 1980-2005; Schwarz; Thesis

Jacobowsky, Carl Ulf Vilhelm, born 23 April 1896 at Uddevalla, Sweden, he studied at the universitites of Göteborg and Uppsala, where he received a Dr.phil. in 1932 for *J. G. Sparwenfeld; bidrag till en biografi*. He was from 1930 to 1938 a librarian at Östersund and served from 1938 to his retirement in 1961 as chief librarian of Stifts- och Landsbibliotetek, Skara. His writings include *Svenskar i främmande land under gångna tider* (1930), and *Gustafsberg, Sveriges äldsta badort* (1958). He died on 17 December 1986. SMK; Vem är det, 1959-1987

Jacobs, Emil, born 25 April 1868 at Gotha, Germany, he studied classical philology and archaeology at the universities of Greifswald and Göttingen. Two years after having obtained a doctorate, he entered the Royal Library in Berlin. In 1912 he became head of the university library, Freiburg im Breisgau, and in 1914, a professor of library science. In 1929 he returned to Berlin where he remained until his retirement in 1935 as director of the Preußische Staatsbibliothek. His writings include *Untersuchungen zur Geschichte der Bibliothek im Serai zu Konstantinople* (1919). He died in Berlin on 18 March 1940. DtBE; JahrDtB, 1902-1939; NDB

Jacobs, Norman Gabriel, born 28 February 1924 at N.Y.C., he graduated in 1943 from the College of the City of New York and received a Ph.D. in 1951 from Harvard University. He was a sociologist who studied the problems of change and modernization in Asia. He had a first-hand acquaintance of Japan, China, and Iran, as a lecturer, adviser, and professor. He was a professor of sociology and Asian studies at the University of Illinois, Urbana Campus. His writings include *Japanese coinage* (1953), *The origin of modern capitalism and eastern Asia* (1958), *Culture for the millions?* (1961), *The Sociology of* *development; Iran as an Asian case study* (1966), *Modernization without development* (1971), and *Patrimonial interpretation of Indian society; contemporary structure and historical foundations* (1989). ConAu, 77-80; NatFacDr, 1990

Jacobs, Paul, born 24 August 1918 at N.Y.C., he was an author and activist who wrote on the Middle East, labour and minority problems. His writings include *Prelude to riot* (1966), *Between the rock and the hard place* (1970), and he was a joint author of *The New radicals* (1967), and its translation, *Die neue Linke in den USA* (1969), and *To search the devil* (1971). He died in San Francisco on 3 January 1978. CnDiAmJBi; ConAu, 13-16, 73-76; NYT, 5 January 1978, p. B-2, cols., 3-4; WhAm, 7; WhoAm, 1977-1978; WhoWor, 1974/75

Jacobs, S., fl. 19th cent., his writings include *Notice sur la carte centrale du théâtre des croisades* (Paris, 1844). BN

Jacobson, Alfred Léon, born 22 July 1883 at Rotterdam, he received his secondary school education at Bruxelles, and in 1902 entered the École centrale de Paris, where he graduated in 1905, first of a class of 223 students. He completed his French military service before joining the Société de constructions Coignet as an engineer, rising to the post of vice-president. His profession was engineering in public works, particularly in French Africa, where he had first served in 1912 as a commander of a platoon of Senegalese Spahis. In 1960, he was nominated president of the Société de géographie commerciale de Paris, and in 1961, elected to the Académie des Sciences d'Outre-Mer. He died on 6 July 1976. DBFC, 1954/55; *Hommes et destins*, vol. 4, pp. 383-84; WhoFr, 1953/54-1975/76

Jacoby, David, born 20th cent., his writings include *La féodalité en Grèce médiévale* (1971), *Société et démographie à Byzance et en Romanie* (1975), *Byzantium, Latin Romania and the Mediterranean* (2001), and a collection of his articles, *Recherches sur la Méditerranée orientale du XIIe au XVe siècle* (1979). OSK

Jacopi, Giulio, 1898- *see* Iacopi, Giulio

Jacotin, Pierre, born 11 April 1765 at Champigny-lès-Langres (Haute-Marne), France, to a family with a wealthy landed estate, he studied with a view to a career in the sciences. In 1780 he went to Corsica to work under his oncle at the Survey of Corsica, rising to be a geographical engineer. He returned to France in 1796. Two years later he was drafted into the Egyptian Expeditionary Corps with a view to producing a map of the country. In 1799 he became head of the geographical engineers of the Armée de l'Orient. In 1800 he became a member of the Institut d'Égypte and the Conseil privé de l'Égypte. He returned to Paris in 1801 and worked on maps of Egypt and Syria, which were completed in 1807, but kept secret by Napoleon. He published a *Mémoire sur la construction de la carte d'Égypte* (1823). He died in Paris on 4 April 1827. DBF; Hoefer; IndexBFr² (1)

Jacottet, Henri, born in 1856, he was a secretary to the journal *Tour du monde*, and a joint editor of *Nouvelles géographiques*. His writings include *Les Grands fleuves* (1887). BN; Note about the author

Jacquard, Albert, born 23 December 1925 at Lyon, he was a graduate of the École polytechnique, Paris, and obtained a doctorate in human biology. From 1968 to 1991 he was a *directeur de recherches* at the Institut national des études démographiques, concurrently serving as a visiting professor in Belgium, Switzerland, and U.S.A. His writings include *Structures génétiques des populations* (1970), its translation, *The genetic structure of populations* (1974), *Les Probabilités* (1974), *L'Explosion démographique* (1993), *Demain dépend de nous* (1999), *Science et croyances* (1999), and *J'accuse l'économie triomphante* (2000). WhoFr, 1990/91-2005/2006

Jacquart, Danielle, born 20th cent., her writings include *Le Milieu médical en France du XII au XV siècle* (1981), *La Formation du vocabulaire scientifique et intellectuel dans le monde arabe* (1994), *Les Voies de la science grecques; études sur la transmission des textes de l'antiquité au dix-neuvième siècle* (1997), jointly with Françoise Micheau, *La médecine arabe et l'Occident médiéval* (1990), and she was a joint editor of *Le Livre des anxiomes médicaux*, of Yūhannā ibn Māsawayh; texte arabe et versions latines avec traduction (1980). ZKO

Jacqueline, Bernard Henri René, born 13 March 1918 at Saint-Lô (Manche), France, he was educated at the Faculté des lettres de Caen, Séminaire Saint Sulpice, École nationale des chartes, Institut catholique de Paris, and the Pontificia Università Gregoriana, Roma. He became an archbishop and served in Morocco from 1986 to 1993. His writings include *Episcopat et papauté chez Saint Bernard de Clairvaux* (1975), a work which was originally submitted as his thesis to the Université de Paris in 1971 entitled *Episcopat et papauté selon Saint Bernard de Clairvaux*, and *Saint-Lô* (1996); he edited *L'Œuvres spirituelles de Charles de Foucauld* (1977-79). NUC; WhoFr, 1977/78-2005/2006; ZKO

Jacquemart, Albert, born in 1808 at Paris, he graduated from École des beaux-arts, where he specialized in drawing, particularly botanical subjects. He earned his living at the Ministère des finances, where he advanced to become a section head. His writings include *Les Merveilles de la céramique ou l'art de façonner et decorer les vases en terre cuite, faïence, grès et porcelaine depuis les temps antiques jusqu'à nos jours* (1866), and *Histoire de la céramique; étude descriptive et raisonnée des poteries de tous les temps et de tous les peuples* (1873). He died in Paris on 14 October 1875. DBF; IndexBFr² (3); Vapereau

Jacquemont, Venceslas *Victor*, born 8 August 1801 at Paris, he was educated at the Lycée Louis-le-Grand, and, until 1815, at the Collège de France, Paris. In 1817, he entered a chemical laboratory as an unpaid assistant, where he became gravely poisened during an experiment. To restore his health he went to castles of his family, where he became interested in botany. After spending the year of 1820 on botanical excursions in northern France, he returned to Paris, took formal courses at the Muséum d'histoire naturelle and became one of the founders of the Société d'histoire naturelle. In 1823, he briefly studied at the École de médecine; in 1827, he became associated with the Jardin du Roi in Paris; soon thereafter to be commissioned by the Muséum to travel to India by way of the Persian Gulf and return via Persia and Syria in order to collect objects of natural history. He fell ill at Tanna in Salsette and died in Bombay on 7 December 1832 after a month's agony. His writings include *Lettres from India* (1834). David Stacton wrote, *Ride on a tiger; the curious travels of Victor Jacquemont* (1954). Buckland; DBF; Embacher; Henze; *Hommes et destins*, vol. 2, pp. 370-71; IndexBFr² (4); IndianBiInd (6); Mason; Master (2); OxFr

Jacques-Meunié, Djinn, 1902- see Meunié, Germaine Amélie Popelin

Jacquet, Eugène Vincent Stanislas, born 10 May 1811 at Bruxelles, he came to Paris as a two-year old and never left. He was educated at the Lycée Louis-le-Grand and the École des language orientales, where he studied Arabic, Chinese, and Persian. His frail health prevented him from realizing his research projects. He was destined for a chair of Oriental languages to be established in Belgium in 1835, but the project failed. He died in Paris on 7 July 1838. BioNBelg, vol. 10 (1888/89), cols., 84-85; DBF; Hoefer; IndexBFr² (2)

Jacqueton, Jean Hugues *Gilbert*, born 31 October 1864 at Thiers (Puy-de-Dôme), France, he was educated at the Collège d'Ouillins, the École pratique des hautes études, Paris, as well as the École des chartes, where he graduated in 1888 with a thesis entitled *Essai sur l'histoire des relations diplomatiques de la France et de l'Angleterre pendant la deuxième régence de Louise de Savoie*, published in 1892 entitled *La Politique extérieure de Louise de Savoie*. He served from 1890 to 1894 as a deputy keeper at the Bibliothèque d'Alger, retaining an interest in North Africa for the rest of his life. His writings include *Les Archives espagnoles du gouvernement général de l'Algérie* (Alger, 1894), and the Guide Joanne, *Algérie et Tunisie* (1903). He died in Barrias (Puy-de-Dôme). BDF

Jacquey, Jules Joseph, born 19th cent., he received a doctorate in 1877 from the Faculté de droit de Nancy for *Droit de l'usage des indigènes dans les forêts de l'État en Algérie*. He obtained his *agrégation* in 1882. His trace is lost after a publication in 1927. BN; ZKO

Jacquier, Bernard, born 20th cent., he taught in 1974 at the Faculté de droit in the Université des sciences sociales de Grenoble. His writings include *Le Légitimisme dauphinois, 1830-1870* (1976), *Les États-Unis et le Nicaragua* (1983), *Les Rapports internationaux contemporains* (1993), and *Jalons pour une chronique grenobloise; du coup d'État au chemin de fer, décembre 1851-juillet 1857* (1998). LC; *Livres disponibles*, 2003; Note about the author

Jacquignon, Louis, born 20th cent., he received a doctorate in 1956 from the Université d'Alger for *Le Régime des biens des établissements nationaux*. His writings include *Le Droit de l'urbanisme* (1956). NUC, 1956-67

von **Jacquin**, Joseph Franz, Freiherr, born 7 February 1766 at Schemnitz (Selmecbánya), Austria-Hungary, he studied medicine at the Universität Wien, where he later taught chemistry and later botany until 1797, when he was appointed to the chair of botany; in 1820 he was admitted to the Deutsche Akademie der Naturforscher Leopoldina. His writings include *Lehrbuch der allgemeinen und medicinischen Chymie* (1793), *Eclogae plantarum rariorum* (1811), and *Die artesischen Brunnen in und um Wien* (1831). He died in Wien on 9 December 1839. DtBE; NDB

Jacquot, François *Félix*, born 6 January 1819 at St.-Dié (Vosges), France, he was educated at the local lycée and at Nancy. He studied medicine at Paris and became a military physician in Algeria. A *médecin major* with the Armée d'Orient in 1852, he received his *agrégation* in 1852, and in 1856, obtained the chair of military epidemiology at Val de Grâce. His writings include *Lettres d'Afrique* (1847), *Expédition du Général Cavaignac dans le Sahara algérien en avril et mai 1847* (1849), and *Du typhus de l'armée d'Orient* (1858). He died in Paris on 29 September 1857. Dantes 1; DBF

Jacquot, Lucien Marcel, born 3 October 1862 at Metz, France, he studied law and became a magistrate and judge in Algeria until he contracted typhoid fever in 1898 and had to return to metropolitan France, serving at Thonon and Grenoble until 1914, when he was again sent to Algeria. He again contracted the disease and died at Constantine on 2 November 1918. He is, however, best remembered as a remarkable archaeologist, who pursued this interest since 1890 in Algeria. His writings include *Monographie archéologique de la région de Mila* (1894), *Recherches étymologiques sur les noms de lieux en Chablais* (1901), and more than four hundred articles. BN; DBF; IndexBFr² (1)

Jadrinzew, N., 1842-1894 *see* IAdrintsev, Nikolai Mikhailovich

Jaeckel, Peter, fl. 20th cent., his writings include *Die Münzprägungen des Hauses Habsburg 1780-1918 und der Republik Österreich seit 1918* (1956), and he edited Eduard de Zambaur's *Die Münzprägungen des Islam, zeitlich und örtlich geordnet; der Westen und Osten bis zum Indus* (1968).

Jaeger, Christof T., born 29 June 1935 at Konstanz, Germany, he studied Islamic law, Arabic and Persian at the universitites of Tübingen, Tehran, and Cairo, obtaining a Dr.jur. in 1969 for *Die Stellung der Frau im islamischen Ehe- und Scheidungsrecht der Vereinigten Arabischen Republik unter besonderer Berücksichtigung der modernen Entwicklungstendenzen.* He was a sometime assistant to the legal counsellor at the German legation in Tehran, before he joined the U.N.O. as an area specialist for the Middle East and Asia. Schwarz; WhoUN, 1992

Jaeger, Friedrich (*Fritz*) Robert, born 8 January 1881 at Offenbach, Hesse, Germany, he studied mathematics, physics, geography and geology at the universities of Heidelberg, Zürich, and Berlin, obtaining a Dr.phil. in 1904 from the Universität Heidelberg for *Über Oberflächengestaltung im Odenwald*. He subsequently joined two expeditions to eastern Africa. In 1909 he received a Dr.habil. at Heidelberg for *Hochregionen des Kilimandscharo*. He was a professor of colonial geography at the Universität Berlin from 1911 until 1928, when he became a professor of geography at the Universität Basel, retiring in 1947. His writings include *Das Hochland der Riesenkrater in Deutsch-Südwestafrika* (1911-1913). He died in Zürich on 26 November 1966. DtBE; Kürschner, 1925-1966; Wer ist's, 1935

Jaenecke, Wilhelm, born 22 August 1896 at Berlin, he studied law at the universities of Berlin, Marburg, and Greifswald, where he received a Dr.jur. in 1918 for a study of Turkish criminal law entitled *Die Grundprobleme des türkischen Strafrechts; eine rechtsvergleichende Darstellung.* GV

Jäfär, Akrem, 1905- *see* Dzhafarov, Akrem Saftarovich

Ja'far Pasha al-'Askari, born in 1885 at Baghdad, he was educated at Constantinople and in Germany; he entered the Turkish Army in 1902. In the early stages of the Great War he directed the Sanūsī attack on the western frontier of Egypt, which won him the German Iron Cross. Friendship for the Amīr Faysal later enlisted him in the Arab revolt against the Turks. He joined the Army of the Hijaz and served with Faysal and Lawrence in command of the regular troops in Allenby's campaign up to the fall of Damascus. As prime minister of Iraq, he piloted through the constituent assembly of 1924, the law of the constitution, and the Anglo-Iraq Treaty, which secured the establishment of Faysal's monarchy and the ultimate independence of the country. During his term as Minister for Iraq in England, 1928-30, his own personal ability and perseverance secured his call to the English bar by Gray's Inn. He was assassinated and died 29 October 1936. Awwad; JRCAS, 24 i (1937), pp. 193-96; *The Times*, 2 November 1936 (not sighted); *Who was who*, 3

Jäfärov (Чәфәров, Dzhafarov), Sälim Äbdullätif oghlu, born 1 June 1907 at Indiki, Daghestan, he obtained a doctorate in linguistics in 1959, and was appointed a professor in 1961. His writings include *Муасир Азәрбајчан дилинин лексикасы* (1958), *Азәрбајчан дилиндә сөз јарадычлығы* (1960), *Муасир Азәрбајчан дылы; лексика* (1970); and he edited *Азәрбајчан әдәби дилинлә ишлэнән әрәб вә фәрс сөзларинин ғыса лугәти* (1960). He died on 30 April 1978. AserbSE, v. 10, p. 432; NUC, 1973-77

Jäfärzadä (Чәфәрзадә, Dzhafarzade), Äzizä Mämmäd gyzy, born 29 December 1921 at Baku, she received a doctorate in Azeri philology in 1970, and was appointed a professor in 1974. Her writings include *Әллэрини мэнэ вер ...* (Baku, 1970), *Алэмдэ сэсим вар мэним* (1972), *Бакы - - 1501; роман* (1981), *Звучу повсюду голос мой* (1981), *Сабир* (1989), and a Turkish translation of one of her works, *Anamın masalları* (İstanbul, 1990). AzarbSE, vol. 10, p. 430; NUC, 1973-1977

Jäfärzadä (Чәфәрзадә, Dzhafarzade), Ishag Mämmädriza ogly, born 14 August 1895 at Gandzha, Azerbaijan. He was an archaeologist and an ethnographer. He died in Baku on 5 January 1982. AzarbSE, v. 10, p. 430

Jaffa, George, pseudonym, 1916- *see* Wallace-Clarke, George

Jaffer, Ahmed Ebrahim Haroon, born 9 August 1909, he was educated in Poona at the Anglo-Urdu High School and the Deccan College. A member of the Muslim League Party, he entered the Central Legislative Assembly in 1934, later serving in the Legislative Assembly of Pakistan. A man with wide industrial interests, he was a president of the Pakistan Merchants' Association and head of a Karachi firm. In 1949, he was a member of the Pakistan trade delegation to West Germany and Czechoslovakia, and was also a delegate from his Parliament to the Council meeting of the Inter-Parliamentary Union, Nice, 1952. *Biographical encyclopedia of Pakistan*; Note about the author

Jager, Georges, born about 1900, he received a doctorate in 1935 from the Université de Montpellier for *L'Expropriation en droit public chérifien - zones française, espagnole et tangéroise du Maroc*. His trace is lost after an article in 1952. NUC, pre-1956

Jäger, Heinrich, born 15 September 1928, he received a Dr.phil. in 1953 from the Universität Frankfurt am Main for *Der kulturgeographische Strukturwandel des Kleinen Walsertals*. From 1963 to his retirement in 1993 he taught geography at the Institut für Didaktik der Geography, Frankfurt/Main. He conducted field work in Tunisia and Morocco. In 1993, he was honoured by *Geographische Lehrwanderungen und Exkursionen in Hessen und Nachbarräumen; Festschrift für Heinrich Jäger*. Kürschner, 1980-2003|; Sezgin

Jago, I. E., fl. 1946, he was a director of the British Council's work in the Black Sea area. Note about the author

Jagodic, Vladislav, born 20th cent., his writings include *Priročnik libijske arabščine* (Ljubljana, 1967). His trace is lost after an article in 1975. NUC

Jah, Omar (Umer), born in 1934 at Medina, Gambia, he studied at al-Azhar, Cairo, received a B.A. degree at Cairo, and a Ph.D. at McGill University, Montreal, for his thesis, *Sufism and nineteenth century jihad movements in West Africa*. In 1979, he was a senior lecturer in the Department of Islamic Studies, Bayero University, Kano, Nigeria. AfricaWW, 1991; Ferahian

Jahier, Henri, fl. 1951-58, he was an Arabist who was associated with the Institut d'études orientales, Faculté des lettres d'Alger. His several editions of classical Arabic texts, with translations, include *Le Jardin de consolation*, of Ibrahim al-Figuigui (Alger, 1958), and Avicenna's *Poème de la médecine* (1956). BN; Note about the author; NUC, 1956-67; ZKO

Jahn, Alfred, born in 1875, he received a Dr.phil. in 1898 from the Universität Wien for *Die Texte der Wenispyramide übersetzt, grammatisch erklärt und mit einer Grammatik ihrer Sprache versehen*. He was probably a member of the Austrian South Arabia expedition. His writings include *Die Mehri-Sprache in Südarabien; Texte und Wörterbuch*, a work which constitutes the third volume of *Schriften der Südarabien Expedition* (Wien, 1902), and *Somalitexte* (1906). His trace is lost after an article in *Mitteilungen des Bundes der Asienkämpfer* (Berlin, 1929). GV; Hanisch; Sezgin

Jahn, August Michael, born 9 August 1789 at Mainz, Hessen-Nassau, the son of a physician, he lost his parents early in life and had to forego a formal education. He first entered an interior decorating establishment, later joining large commercial enterprises, in whose service he travelled extensively throughout Europe. In the service of a Hannover trading firm, he went in 1826 on a two-year commercial journey to Cairo, returning by way of Jerusalem, Constantinople, and the Balkans, experiences which are embodied in his *Reise von Mainz nach Egypten, Jerusalem und Konstantinopel in den Jahren 1826-27* (Mainz, 1828-30). DtBilnd (1); Kornrumpf; Sezgin

Jahn, Gustav, born 11 June 1837 at Drossen (Neumark) Prussia, he studied Arabic, particularly al-Zamakhsharī's *Mufassal*, at the Universität Berlin under Emil Roediger. He received a Dr.habil. in 1879 at Berlin, where he served for ten years as a secondary school teacher until 1889, when he became a professor of Oriental languages at the Universität Königsberg. Encouraged by Heinrich L. Fleischer, he edited Ibn Ya'īsh's *Kommentar zu Zamachšarīs Mufassal* (1876-86), but without *apparatus criticus*. This was followed by *Sībawaihi's Buch über die Grammatik* (1894-1900), translated with a commentary based on Hartig Derenbourg's edition as well as Sīrāfī's commentary, a work which resulted in endless polemics with Franz Praetorius. He also became involved in literary controversies over his preference of the Septuagint over the Masoretic text because he challenged the authenticity of the Elephantine Papyri and the Mesa Stone, convictions to which he stubbornly adhered for the rest of his life. His writings include *Beiträge zur Beurtheilung der Septuaginta; eine Würdigung Wellhausenscher Textkritik* (1902); his final work was a study of the concept of God of the ancient Hebrews and their historiography, *Über den Gottesbegriff der alten Hebraeer* (1915). He died in 1917. DtBilnd (2); GV; Fück, p. 241

Jahn, Johann, born 18 June 1750 at Taswitz, Moravia, he was educated at Olmütz and the Praemonstratenser convent in Bruck, Styria, entered the order in 1774, and was ordained in 1775. After pastoral work in rural districts, he was recalled to Bruck to teach Oriental languages. He received a doctorate in divinity in 1782 at Olmütz. After the dissolution of the convent, he became a professor at the Universität Olmütz. In 1789, he was invited to teach Oriental languages, Biblical archaeology and dogmatics at the Universität Wien, a post which he held until 1806, when he was appointed canon of St. Stephan at Wien. His writings include *Arabische Sprachlehre* (1796), *Arabische Chrestomathie* (1802), *Archaeologia biblica* (1814), and its translation, *Archæologia Biblica; a manual of Biblical antiquities* (1836). He died in Wien on 16 August 1816. ADtB, vol. 13, pp. 665-67; DtBilnd (5); Master (1); Wurzbach

Jahn, Karl, born in 1906 at Brünn, Moravia, he studied at Brno, Praha, and Leipzig, gaining a Dr.phil. in 1931 from Karls Universität, Praha, for *Studien zur arabischen Epistologie*. His interest in Central Asia was related to his friendship with Zeki Velidi Togan, dating back to 1933. It is from then on that he pursued an interest in the work of Rashīd al-Dīn Tabīb (1247-1318), for whose *Geschichte Ġāzān Hān's des Rašīd ad-Dīn* he received a Dr.habil. at Praha, where he remained until the second World War as a lecturer (*Privatdozent*). The events of the war brought him first to the Universität Halle/Saale and later to the Rijksuniversiteit te Utrecht, the Netherlands, where he taught Turkish and Slavic philology since 1948, Iranian subjects being added to his teaching load later on. After his early retirement he lived until 1983 in Wien, where he was elected to the Österreichische Akademie der Wissenschaften. He was the main translator of Rašīd ad-Dīn Tabīb's works into German, *Die Geschichte der Oġuzen* (1969), *Die Chinageschichte* (1971), *Die Geschichte der Kinder Israels* (1973), *Die Frankengeschichte* (1977), and *Die Indiengeschichte* (1980). He died in Utrecht on 7 November 1985. Central Asiatic journal, 30 (1986), pp. 1-6 [not sighted]; Filipsky; Hanisch; der Islam, 64 (1987), pp. 4-5

Jahn, Samia Al-Azharia, born 20th cent., she was associated with the Water Purification Project, Khartoum, and the German Society for Technical Cooperation, Eschborn. Her writings include *Arabische Volksmärchen* (1970), *Traditional water purification in tropical developing countries; existing methods and potential application* (1981), and *Proper use of African natural coagulants for rural water supplies; research in the Sudan and a guide for new projects* (1986). Note about the author; LC

Jahncke, Ernst, born about 1880, he was from Neuhaus an der Oste, Lower Saxony, Germany, and received a Dr.phil. in 1903 from the Universität Göttingen for *Studien zum Wilhelm von Wenden Ulrichs von Eschenbach*. He was associated with the Deutsch-Türkische Vereinigung. His trace is lost after a publication in 1919. Note about the author; Thesis

Jaime, Jean *Gilbert* Nicomède, born 19th cent., he was a French navy lieutenant who went down the Niger River in a military vessel in the service of the French Government for the sole purpose of fostering good relations with the indigenous population. His experiences are embodied in his *De Koulikoro à Timbouctou, à bord du "Mage", 1889-1890* (1892). BN; Henze

Jaja, Goffredo, born in 1874, his writings include *L'isola di Rodi* (Roma, 1912), *L'Italia; geografico economica* (Milano, 1912), and *Istituzioni di geografica* (Livorno, 1917). NUC, pre-1956-1967

Jajko, Edward A., born 7 August 1940 at Philadelphia, Pa., he graduated in 1962 from the University of Pennsylvania and subsequently pursued graduate work there and at the American University in Cairo. After taking an M.Lib.Sc., he became a Near Eastern bibliographer at Yale University, New Haven, Conn., until 1983, when he became Middle East curator at Hoover Institution on War, Revolution, and Peace, Stanford, Calif. A member of the Turkish Studies Association, the Polish Institute of Arts and Sciences in America, and Middle East Librarians Association, he served at the latter as president, 1978/79, and 1980-89. His writings include *Iranian opposition literature in the Middle East Collection of the Hoover Institution* (1987). Private; ZKO

Jakobson, Roman, born 11 October 1896 at Moscow, he there graduated from the Lazarev Institute of Oriental languages and received his doctorate in 1930 at Praha. Since 1949 he was a professor of general linguistics and Slavic languages and literature at Harvard University. A visiting professor throughout the world, he was the recipient of numerous honours, awards, and honory doctorates. His writings include *Phonological studies* (1962), *Slavic epic studies* (1966), and he was a joint author of *Fundamentals of language* (1956), its translations, *Grundlagen der Sprache* (1960), *Podstay języka* (1964), and *Meine futuristischen Jahre* (Berlin, 1999). He died on 18 July 1982. CnDiAmJBi; ConAu, 77-80, 107, new rev., 31; DLB, 242 (2001), pp. 226-37; DrAS, 1974 F, 1978 F, 1982 F; Master (19); WhAm, 8; Who, 1969-1982; WhoAm, 1974-1982; Who was who, 8

Jakova-Mertury, Gaspare, born 19th cent., he was in 1904 a professor. His writings include *Grammatica della lingua albanese* (Frascati, 1904). NUC, pre-1956

Jakowlew, P. L., 1789-1835 see IAkovlev, Pavel Luk'ianovich

Jakšić (Јакшић, Yakschitsch), Grgur (Grégoire), born 21 February 1871 at Čačač, Serbia, he was a historian whose writings include *L'Europe et la résurrection de la Serbie, 1804-1934* (1907), *Evropa i vaskrs Srbije, 1804-1834* (1933), *Борба за слободу Србије 1788-1816* (1937), *La Bulgarie et les alliés* (1916), *Француска и Југославија у прошлости* (1938), *Босна и Херцеговина на Берлинском конгресу* (1955), and he was a joint author of *Србија од 1813 до 1858 године* (1937). He died in Beograd on 18 October 1955. EncJug; EncLZ

Jalabert, Henri, born in 1913, his writings include *Un Montagnard contre le pouvoir; Liban 1866* (1975), and *Jésuites au Proche-Orient; notices biographiques* (1987). NUC, 1956-67; ZKO

Jalabert, Louis, born 30 March 1877 at Lyon, France, he entered the Jesuit noviciate in 1895, and subsequently was sent to Beyrouth, where he taught at the Collège Saint-Joseph from 1901 to 1907, and at its Faculté orientale, from 1911 to 1914, when he was recalled to France to become an administrator of the periodical *Études*. His writings include *Syrie et Liban; réussite française?* (1934), and a *Recueil des inscriptions grecques et latines de Syrie* (1929-1939). He died in Nice on 12 August 1943. DBF; IndexBFr² (2)

Jalagania, Irine *see* Dzhalaganiia, Irina Levanovna

Jalil, Jalile, 1936- *see* Dzhalil, Dzhalile

Jałowiecki, Bohdan Maria, born 26 February 1934 at Warszawa, he studied philosophy and ethnography at Uniwersytet Jagielloński, Kraków, received doctorates in 1965 and 1975, and was appointed a professor of sociology in 1979. Since 1985 he taught at Uniwersytet Warszawski. His writings include *Człowiek w przestrzeni miasta* (1980), *Problematyka spoleczna w planowaniu przestrzennym* (1987), *Spoleczeńwo i gospodarka w Polsce lokalnej* (1992), *Polityka restrukturyzacji regionów* (1993), and *Oblicza polskich regionów* (1996), and he was a joint author of *The Brain drain in Poland* (1992). Kto jest kim w Polsce, 2001

al-Jamali, Mohammed Fadhel, born in 1902 at Kadhimain, Mesopotamia, he was a graduate of the American University in Beirut, and studied at Columbia University, NYC, where he obtained a Ph.D. in 1934 for his thesis, *The new Iraq; its problems of Bedouin education*. Subsequently he served Iraq's Ministry of Education until joining the Foreign Ministry in 1942. As foreign minister in 1945, he was Iraq's representative for the founding of the Arab League and the signing of the United Nations Charter. Under King Faysal II, he served two terms as prime minister. Following the 1958 military coup, he was sentenced to death, but his life was spared when Morocco intervened on his behalf. He later moved to Tunisia where he died of heart ailments on 24 May 1997. He wrote many works in Arabic as well as *Letters on Islam, written by a father in prison to his son* (1965). Harry J. Almond wrote his biography entitled *Iraqi statesman; portrait of Fadhel Jamali* (London, 1993). WRMEA 16, no. 2 (August/September 1997), p. 119

Jamasp, Hoshang, 1833-1908 *see* Hoshangjī Jamaspjī Asa

Jambu-Merlin, Roger, born 20th cent., he received a doctorate in law in 1947 from the Université de Paris for *La jurisprudence des prises maritimes et le droit international privé*. After his agrégation in law, he served in the 1950s in the Institut des Hautes Études de Tunis as a professor. His writings include *Cours élémentaire de droit international privé tunisien* (1956-59), *Le droit privé en Tunisie* (1960), and *Cours de droit civil* (1971). Note about the author; ZKO

Jameelah, Maryam *see* Maryam Jameela

James, Arthur Lloyd, born in 1884, he was educated at University College, Cardiff, and Trinity College, Cambridge, graduating in medieval and modern languages. He taught phonetics of English and French as well as West African languages at University College, London. In 1927 he became the first head of the Department of Phonetics at the School of Oriental and African Studies, London. His writings include *The pronounciation of foreign words* (1929), *The broadcast word* (1935), *A basic phonetic reader* (1938), and *Our spoken language* (1938). He was a man with a passion for punctuality and a scupulous regard for truth. During the stress and anxiety of the war he fell victim to depressive insanity and committed suicide on 24 March 1943. BritInd (1); DNB; Who was who, 4

James, David Lewis, he was born about 1940. For some years in the 1980s he was the Islamic curator of the Chester Beatty Library, Dublin, until dismissed for criminal conduct in 1990 as revealed by Estelle Whelan's researches. He was a specialist in Islamic calligraphy and a sometime lecturer in Arabic at University College, Dublin. His writings include *Arab painting* (1978), *Qur'ans and bindings from the Chester Beatty Library* (1980), and *The master scribes; Qur'ans of the 10th to 14th centuries A.D.* (1992). LC; Private

James, Edgar C., born 6 January 1933 at Bryn Mawr, Pa., he graduated in 1955 from Wheaton (Illiinois) College, and received a doctorate in divinity in 1962 from Dallas Theological Seminary. A non-denominational minister, he was since 1977 a professor in the Department of Theology, Moody Bible Institute, Chicago, a post which he still held in 1995. His writings include *II Corinthians, keys to triumphant living* (1964), *Arabs, oil and energy* (1977), and *Armageddon* (1981). ConAu, 13-16, new rev., 5; NatFacDr, 1990-95; WhoMW, 1992/93; WhoRel, 1975, 1977, 1992/93

James, Émile Pierre Marie, born 18 July 1899 at Riom (Puy-de-Dôme), France, he graduated from the Faculté de droit de Paris and served from 1934 to 1938 at the École française de droit, Cairo. He subsequently held the chair of political economy at the Sorbonne, Paris, until his retirement in 1970. A member of the Société Fouad Ier d'économie politique, de statistique et de législation, his writings include *Histoire de la pensée économique au XXe siècle* (1955), its translation into Czech, Polish and Russian, *Cours de théorie économique* (1963), and *Problèmes monétaire d'aujourd'hui* (1963). He died on 12 January 1991. DBFC, 1954/55; IndexBFr² (1); WhoFr, 1959/60-1991/92

James, John Morrice Cairns, Baron Saint Brides, born in 1916, he was educated at Balliol College, Oxford, and then entered the Dominions Office. After war-time service in the Middle East, he rejoined the Civil Service. In 1952 he began a unique series of postings to the Indian subcontinent where, with a few breaks, he served successively as deputy and high commissioner in both Karachi and New Delhi. It is worth looking at the entries in successive editions of *Who's who*. He died in 1989. DNB; IntWW, 1978-1981/82; IntYB, 1978-1981; Who, 1958-1988; *Who was who*, 8

James, Wendy R., born 4 February 1940, she received a D.Phil. in 1972 from Oxford University for *Principles of social organization among the Uduk-speaking people of the southern Fung region, Republic of the Sudan*. Her writings include *Kwanim pa, the making of the Uduk people; an ethnographic study of the survival in the Sudan-Ethiopian borderlands* (1979); she was a joint author, with Susan Jane Kedgley, of *The Mistress* (1973); she edited *Essays in Sudan ethnography presented to Sir Edward Evans-Pritchard* (1972), *Vernacular Christianity* (1988), *The Pursuit of certainty* (1995), and *Juan Maria Schuver's travels in North East Africa, 1880-1883* (1996), and she was a joint editor of *Remapping Ethiopia; socialism and after* (2002). LC; Sluglett; ZKO

Jamme, Albert Joseph, born 27 June 1916 at Senzeilles, Namur province, Belgium, he received a doctorate in divinity in 1946 from the Université catholique de Louvain, and also a doctorate in Oriental studies in 1952. He did post-doctoral research at Jerusalem, Tunis, and the Vatican. A priest of the Pères blancs, he was since 1955 associated with the Catholic University of America, Washington, D.C. His writings include *La Paléographie sud-arabe de J. Pirenne* (1957), *Sabaean inscriptions from Mahram Bilqîs, Mârib* (1962), and *Sabaean and Hasaean inscriptions from Saudi Arabia* (1966). ConAu, 5-8; WhoAm, 1986-2000; WhoE, 1983-1985/86 (not sighted); WhoRel, 1985; WrDr, 1976/78-1986/88|

Jamnig, Gustav, fl. 20th cent., he obtained a Dr.jur. and was since 1953 a member of the Austrian Federal Chamber of Commerce, Division of Trade Policy and Foreign Trade, where he was responsible for Africa and the Arab world. From 1955 to 1959, he was a member of the Austrian trade delegations to Paris, Casablanca and Cairo. He subsequently served as a consul in the Congo. Note about the author

Jan (IAn), W., 1875-1954 *see* IAnchevetskiĭ (Jan), Vasiliĭ Grigorevich

Janata, Alfred, he was born on 3 March 1933 at Wien. In the early fifties he belonged to the Viennese coterie of the Art Club which remained his intellectual home for the rest of his life. He started to study fine art, but after a summer's journey to India in 1953, he changed to ethnology. In 1958, he began his research on Afghanistan, culminating in his Dr.phil. in 1961 from the Universität Wien for *Die Bevölkerung von Ghor*. The previous year, he had joined the Museum für Völkerkunde, Wien, as an assistant, later to become head of the Islamic collection in the Museum. Since 1962 an editor of *Archiv für Völkerkunde*, and since 1975 a lecturer in the Institut für Völkerkunde, Universität Wien, he was also engaged in the friends of ethnology, *Freunde der Völkerkunde*. He regularly went on research travels to collect material for the Museum. His writings include *Außereuropäische Musikinstrumente* (1961), *Korean painting* (1964), *Das Profil Japans* (1965), and *Schmuck in Afghanistan* (1981). He died in Wien on 16 May 1993. *Archiv für Völkerkunde*, 47 (1993), pp. 1-12; DtBE; Private; WhoAustria, 1967

Janc (Jанц), Zagorka, fl. 20th cent., she was associated with the Museum for Applied Art, Beograd. Her writings include Исламски рукописи из југословенких колекција (1956), Кожни повези српске ћирилске од XII до XIX века (1974), Наслова страна српске штампане књиге (1965), and she was a joint author of Оријентални рукориси (Београд, Музеј Примењене Уметности, 1973). LC; ZKO

Jancigny, Adolphe Philibert Dubois de, 1795-1860 *see* Dubois de Jancigny, Adolphe Philibert

Jandin, R. B. de *see* Bernard de Jandin, R.

Jandora, John Walter, born about 1948, he graduated from Georgetown University in 1969. He was commissioned in 1969 and went to serve in Vietnam. Subsequently he worked for several years with Arab troops in the course of employment on a U.S. Military assistance program. He also managed English-Arabic translation projects in Europe and Saudi Arabia. In 1974 he earned an M.A. from the University of Chicago. In the period 1976-1986 he travelled extensively throughout the Near and Middle East. He subsequently became employed within the U.S. Defense establishment. In 1981 he received a Ph.D. from the University of Chicago for *Butrus al-Bustani; ideas, endeavors, and influence*. His writings include *March from Medina; a revisionist study of the Arab conquest* (1990). Note; Selim[2]

Janer i Graells, Florencio, born 11 May 1831 at Barcelona, he studied law and became an archivist, librarian, antiquary, and lecturer in history. His writings include *Exámen de los sucesos y circunstancias que motivaron el Compromiso de Caspe* (1855), *Condición social de los moriscos de España* (1857), and he edited *Poetas castellanos anteriores al siglo XV* (1864), He died in Escorial in August 1877. Dicc Bio; Elias; IndiceE³ (3)

Jangiże, V., 1928- *see* Dzhangidze, Verena Tarasovna

Janhunen, Juha Antero, born 12 February 1952 at Bborg [!], Finland, he was a professor at Helsinki University and associated with the Finnish Oriental Society. His writings include *Samojedischer Wortschatz; gemeinsamojedische Etymologien* (1977), *Glottal stop in Nenets* (1986), *Manchuria; an ethnic history* (1996); he edited *Writing in the Altaic world* (1999); and he was a joint editor of *Remota relata* (2003). LC; *Vem och vad*, 1996-2004; ZKO

Janicki, Stanisław, born in 1836 at Warszawa, he was a hydraulic engineer who was associated with Ferdinand de Lesseps on the construction of the Suez Canal. He died on 9 June 1888. Dziekan; PolBiDi; Polski (3); PSB

Janier, Émile, born 25 December 1909 in Normandie, France, he graduated in liberal arts. It was only later that he pursued an interest in Berber and Arabic philology, and more generally in the indigenous population of Algeria. In 1940 he became a teacher at the *médersa* in Tlemcen, whose director he became in 1950. His 1948 report «Les Ouléma d'Oranie et leurs médersa réformistes» established his association with the Centre de Hautes Études d'Administration Musulmane, Paris. Apart from his teaching duties, he served as a *madrasah* inspector, keeper of the Musée de Tlemcen and the archaeological sites of Ouest oranais, and also as a president of the Amis du Vieux Tlemcen. He wore himself out and paid with his life for the devotion to his ideal in the same way as did his friend Robert Montagne. He died on 12 January 1958. *l'Afrique et l'Asie*, n° 42 (1958), p. 77

Janin, Louis, born 17 October 1897, he gained a diploma in *Hautes études commerciales* as well as a doctorate in law. He subsequently pursued a career in international trade and commerce, becoming the director of a large Parisian bank. After his retirement in 1965, he pursued an increasing interest in sundials, particularly after discovering that there are no publications of the one in the Great Mosque of Damascus. He died on 29 December 1978. *Journal for the history of Arabic science*, 3, no. 1 (Spring 1979), pp. 85-87

Janin, Raymond, le Père, born 31 August 1882, he was ordained in 1911. In the same year, he joined the staff of *Echos d'Orient*, Constantionple, and became a member of the Institut français d'études byzantines. He remained associated with both institutions for sixty years. His writings include *Constantinople byzantine; développement urbain et répertoire topographique* (1950), and *La géographie ecclésiastique de l'Empire byzantine* (1969). He died on 12 July 1972. *Revue des études byzantines*, 30 (1972), p. 3

Janka, Lee, born 20th cent., he was a deputy Assistant Secretary of Defense for Middle Eastern and African affairs, and U.S. National Security Council senior staff member, before he became a consultant with DGA International, Inc., in Washington in 1980. He was a joint author of *Defense or aggression? U.S. arms export control laws and the Israeli invasion of Lebanon* (1982). Note about the author

Janke, Arthur W., he was born on 31 August 1843 at Bublitz, Prussia. His writings include *Reise-Erinnerungen aus Italien, Griechenland und dem Orient, mit besonderer Berücksichtigung der militärischen Verhältnisse* (Berlin, 1874). KDtLK, 1904-1917; *Wer ist's*, 1909

Jankó, János (Johann), born 13 March 1868 at Budapest, he gained a doctorate at the local University. With the support of the Budapest Chamber of Commerce, he travelled in Egypt and North Africa. His writings include *A Nilus deltája* (1890), its translation, *Das Delta des Nil* (1890), *A magyar halászat eredete* (1900) and *Dritte asiatische Forschungsreise* (1900). He died in Borszék on 28 July 1902. *Földrajzi közlemények*, 31 (1903), p. 165-172; GeistigeUng; *Index Islamicus* (1); Magyar; Pallas; RNL; OSK

von **Jankó**, Paul, born in 1856 at Tata, Hungary, he was a musician and engineer. His writings include *Eine neue Claviatur* (1886), and the article, "Türkische Nationalschrift Vorschlag zur Reform der türkischen Schrift" (1918). He died in Constantinople on 17 March 1919. Magyar; Master (2); NewGrDM

Jankowski, James Paul, born 17 July 1937 at Buffalo, N.Y., he graduated in 1959 from State University of New York at Buffalo and received a Ph.D. in 1967 from the University of Michigan for *The Young Egypt Party and Egyptian nationalism*. He spent his entire career teaching history at the University of Colorado, Boulder. His writings include *Egypt's young rebels;'Young Egypt,' 1933-1952* (1975), and he was joint author of *Egypt, Islam, and the Arabs; the search for Egyptian nationhood, 1900-1930* (1986), and *Redefining the Egyptian nation, 1930-1945* (1995). ConAu, 150; DrAS, 1974 H, 1978 H, 1982 H; MESA Roster of members, 1977-1990; Selim; WhoAm, 1988/89-1992

Jannasch, Robert, Dr.jur., Dr.phil., born 30 April 1845 at Cöthen (Köthen), Anhalt, Germany, he was a political economist and colonial politician, a joint founder and director of the Deutsche Exportbank, chairman of the Centralverein für Handelsgeographie und Förderung deutscher Interessen im Auslande zu Berlin as well as an editor of the journal *Export*. His writings include *Abhandlung über Nationalöconomie und Statistik* (1869), *Der Markenschutz und die Gewerbepolitik des Deutschen Reiches* (1873), *Die deutsche Handelsexpedition* (1887), and *Die Erschließung von China* (1895). He died in Berlin on 25 April 1919. DtBiJ, 2, 1917-1920 (1928), Totenliste, 1919, p. 722; Wer ist's, 1912

Jannequin, Claude, Sieur de Rochefort, he was born at Châlons-sur-Marne, France. In the early seventeenth century he accompanied the French diplomat de Bellièvre on a mission to England. After returning to Dieppe, he volunteered for service on a ship departing in 1638 on an exploration of the coast of western Africa. On board he was charged with keeping the log-book. His experiences are embodied in his *Voyage de Lybie au royaume de Sénégal, le long du Niger, avec la description des peuples qui sont le long de ce fleuve, leurs coutumes et façon de vivre, les particularités les plus remarquables de ce pays* (1643), a work which was reprinted in 1980. Hoefer; IndexBFr² (1); ZKO

Janner, Sir Barnett, born 20 June 1892 at Lucknick, Lithuania, he graduated from Cardiff College, University of Wales, and later practised law at Cardiff. He was a Labour M.P. and a Zionist politician. He died in 1982. Elsie Janner wrote *Barnett Janner; a personal portrait* (1984). BlueB, 1973/74, 1975, 1976; BritInd (1); DNB; NYT, 6 May 1982, D-27, col. 4; Who's who, 1948-1982; Who was who, 8; WhoWorJ, 1955, 1965, 1972, 1978

Janon, Michel, born 20th cent., his writings include *Le Décor architectonique de Narbonne; les rinceaux* (1986), and he collaborated with the publication of the *Inscriptions latines de Nabonnaise* (1985-1997), a project which was supported by the C.N.R.S. ZKO

Janowitz, Morris, born 22 October 1919 at Paterson, N.J., he received a Ph.D. in 1948 from the University of Chicago for *Mobility, subjective deprivation and ethnic hostility*. He taught sociology successively at the University of Michigan and the University of Chicago. Concurrently he served from 1962 to 1981 as a chairman of the Inter-University Seminar on Armed Forces and Society. His writings include *Sociology and the military establishment* (1959), *The New military* (1964), *On Military ideology* (1971), *The U.S. Forces and the zero draft* (1973), *Social control of the welfare state* (1976), and *On Social organization and social control* (1991). He died in 1988. AmM&WSc, 1973 S, 1978 S; CnDiAmJBi; ConAu, 13-16, 129; Master (1); WhAm, 9; WhoAm, 1974-1988/89; WhoWor, 1974/75; ZKO

Jansen, Godfrey Henry, born 2 December 1919 at Akyap, Burma, he was educated at the Christian College, Madras, and became a journalist and concurrently served with the Indian Diplomatic Service as a press officer in the Near East, Indonesia, and the U.N. His writings include *Afro-Asia and non-alignment* (1966), *Whose Suez?* (1968), *Zionism, Israel and Asian nationalism* (1971), *Militant Islam* (1977), its translation, *Islamischer Widerstand* (1984), and he was a joint author of *Der Islam in der Weltpolitik* (1982). ConAu, 114; IntAu&W, 1986, 1989; ZKO

Jansen, Herman Ludin, born 8 June 1905 at Halden, Norway, he studied theology at the Universitetet i Oslo and obtained his degree in 1933. After teaching for a few years at a secondary school, he turned to his true interest, the study of the religions of the Middle East and the classical world as well as Oriental languages, which he pursued at the universities of Uppsala, Strasbourg, Tübingen, and Heidelberg. From 1939 to 1943 he was a research fellow at Oslo, where he gained his doctorate in divinity in 1940. From 1953 to his retirement in 1975 he taught history of religion at Oslo. His writings include *Die spätjüdische Psalmendichtung* (1937), *Die Henochgestalt* (1939), *The Coptic story of Cambyses' invasion of Egypt* (1951), and *Islam, hengivelsens vei* (1973). In 1985 he was honoured by *The Many and the One; essays on religion in the Graeco-Roman world presented to H. Ludin Jansen*. He died in 1986. Hvem, 1984; IWWAS, 1976/77; NorskBL²; Temenos, 22 (1986), pp. 142-144

Jansen, Hermann, born 28 May 1869 at Aachen, Prussia, he trained as an architect at the local Technische Hochschule. After a brief employment with the city of Berlin until 1898, he became a successful free-lance architect, winning several competitions in town planning. He was an editor of the journal *der Baumeister*, 1903-1906. He won the first prize in the 1929 competition for the development of the projected Turkish capital, Ankara, and the plan's execution. He was a joint author of *Ankara şehrinin Profesör M. (Leon) Jausseley, Jansen ve Brix taraflarından yapılan plan ve projelerine ait izahnameler* (Ankara, 1929). He died in Berlin on 20 February 1945. AllgLKünst; AnaBrit; DtBE; DtBilnd (1); Kürschner, 1931-1940/41; NDB; *Wer ist's*, 1935; ZKO

Jansen, Hubert, born 2 November 1854 at Griethausen near Kleve, Prussia, he studied theology and philosophy from 1873 to 1874 at the Königliche Akademie, Münster, and subsequently taught for two years at a secondary school in Hüls near Krefeld. From 1877 to 1880, he studied Near Eastern and Indian philology at Münster. "A variety of unfortunate circumstances and events, primarily the death of all his family, obliged him again to interrupt his study for the better part of the 1880s" and work as an assistant in the Königlich Paulinische Bibliothek, Münster. From 1884 to 1887, he was the editor of the trade and commerce weekly, *Export*, and concurrently since 1885, secretary to the Centralverein für Handelsgeographie. From the autumn of 1887 to autumn 1889, he took courses in Hindustani and Persian at the Seminar für Orientalische Sprachen, Berlin. In the service of the Centralverein für Handelsgeographie he went to Morocco from July until December 1890 to study the customs and habits of Moors and Jews, but primarily to study Moroccan Arabic. It was not until the summer of 1893 that he again took up his Sanskrit study at Berlin. In the same year he received a Dr.phil. from the Universität Leipzig for *Bemerkungen zur Verskunst im Urdu*. His writings include *Verbreitung des Islams mit Angaben der verschiedenen Riten, Sekten und religiösen Bruderschaften* (1897). He died in 1917. NUC, pre-1956; Thesis

Jansen, Johannes J. G., born 17 November 1942, he studied Semitic languages at the universities of Amsterdam, Leiden, and Cairo, and obtained a doctorate in 1974 from the Rijksuniversiteit te Leiden for *The interpretation of the Koran in modern Egypt*. He taught Arabic at Leiden (1968-1975), and Groningen (1975-1978). He served as a director of the Dutch Institute for Egyptian Archaeology and Arabic Studies from 1979 to 1982, when he became a lecturer in Arabic at the Seminar for Arabic, Persian and Turkish at Leiden. His writings include *The Neglected duty; the creed of Sadat's assassins and Islamic resurgence in the Middle East* (1986), *Inleiding tot de Islam* (1987), and *The Dual nature of Islamic fundamentalism* (1996). Brinkman's, 1996-2000; LC; Note about the author; ZKO

Jansky, Herbert Emanuel Josef, born 25 June 1898, he studied Islamic subjects and political science at the Universität Wien, and economic subjects at the Viennese Hochschule für Welthandel, obtaining a Dr.phil. in 1922 from the Universität Wien for *Die Eroberung Syriens durch Selim I.* He was associated with the Österreich-Orientalische Handelskammer, and the Öffentliche Lehranstalt für orientalische Sprachen, Wien. His writings include *Lehrbuch der türkischen Sprache* (1960), *Deutsch-türkisches Wörterbuch* (1961), and he was a joint author of *Volksgesänge von Völkern Rußlands* (1952). In 1969 he was honoured by *Festschrift Herbert Jansky*. He died in Wien on 12 March 1981. Hanisch; *Index Islamicus* (3); Schwarz; Teichl; Wer; *Wer ist's*, 1935

Janssens, Émile, fl. 1972, his writings include *Trébizonde en Colchide* (Bruxelles, 1969), and he edited Aeschylus' *Agamemnon* (Namur, 1955). ZKO

Janssens, Gerard Hendrik Alfons, born 5 May 1923 at Antwerpen (Anvers), Belgium, he studied classical and Semitic philology at the universities of Gent and Leiden. Since 1959 he was a professor of Arabic and Hebrew at the Rijksuniversiteit te Gent. His writings include *Contribution to the verbal system in Old Egyptian* (Leuven, 1972), *Stress in Arabic and word structure in the modern Arabic dialects* (Leuven, 1972), and *Studies in Hebrew historical linguistics based on Origen's Secunda* (Leuven, 1982). WhoWor, 1980/81; WieVlaand, 1980

Janssens, Herman F., fl. 20th cent., his writings include *L'Entretien de la sagesse; introduction aux œuvres philosophiques de Bar Hebraeus* (1937), and *Ibn Batouta, le voyageur de l'islam* (1948). In 1966 he was honoured by the *Volume dédié à la mémoire de Henri Grégoire et Herman Janssens*, published by the Institut de philologie et d'histoire orientales et slaves, Université libre de Bruxelles. NUC; 1968-72

Janssens, Jules L., born 20th cent., his writings include *An annotated bibliography on Ibn Sīna, 1970-1989* (1991), and its *Supplement, 1990-94* (1999). ZKO

Jantzen, Günther, born about 1910, he received a Dr.phil. in 1934 from the Universität Hamburg for a study of East Africa and German-British politics entitled *Ostafrika in der deutsch-englischen Politik, 1884-1890*. He was an editor of the journals, *Neues Afrika*, and *Übersee-Rundschau*, and in 1968 served as chairman of the board of Deutsches Institut für Iberoamerika-Kunde, Hamburg. His writings include *Hamburgs Außenhandel im XX. Jahrhundert* (1953), *Ghana; Betrachtungen zum Unabhängigkeitstag* (1957), and he was a joint author of *Albert Ballin* (1969). GV; Note about the author

Japp, Alexander Hay, born in 1837 at Dun, Scotland, he started life as a tailor's book-keeper in Edinburgh, later taking classes in philosophy at Edinburgh University, but without taking a degree. In 1864 he settled in London as a journalist, general literary adviser, and writer. Busy to the last, he died in Surrey in 1905. DNB; Master (2)

Jaquet, Frits (Frédéric) George Peter, born in 1937, he was associated with the Netherlands' State Archives Service. His writings include *Gids van in Nederland aanwezige bronnen betreffende de geschiedenis van Nederlands-Indië/Indonesie, 1816-1942* (1970-80), and he was a joint author of *Java's onuitputtelijke natuur* (1980). Brinkman's, 1991-95

Jaray, Gabriel Louis, born 19th cent. at Lyon, France, he was a *maître de requêtes* in the French *Conseil d'État*, and a director-general of the Comité France-Amérique. His writings include *L'Albanie inconnue* (1913), *Au jeune royaume d'Albanie* (1914), *Un rempart contre l'Allemagne* (1918), *Les Albanais* (1920), *De Québec à Vancouver* (1924), *L'héritage du passé et les Français d'Amérique* (1937), and *Tableau du Japon et de la guerre du Pacifique* (1946). BN; Qui êtes-vous, 1924

Jardine, Alexander, born about 1740, he passed through the Royal Military Academy, Woolwich, and advanced to the rank of lieutenant-colonel in 1793. When stationed at Gibraltar in 1771, he was sent on a mission to the ruler of Morocco, experiences which are embodied in his *Letters from Barbary, France, Spain, Portugal* (1788), and its translation, *Bemerkungen über Marokko* (1790). He died in Portugal in 1799. DBN; Sezgin

Jardine, Sir John, born in 1844 in England, he entered the Bombay Civil Service in 1864. He was Political Officer to the Native States of Kattywar in 1871. In 1885, he served as Chief Secretary to the Bombay Government, holding the political, secret, educational, Persian, and judicial portfolios. His writings include works on Buddhist law. He died in 1919. Buckland; IndianBilnd (1); Riddick; Who was who, 2

Jardine, Robert Frier, born in 1894, he was educated at Cambridge, and served in the first World War in Egypt and Mesopotamia, with the rank of captain. After the war, he was in political charge of Kurdistan, where he was responsible for population repatriation and border settlement. His writings include *Bahdinan Kurmanji; a grammar of the Kurmanji of the Kurds of Mosul division and surrounding districts of Kurdistan* (Baghdad, 1922). He died in 1982. BritInd (1); Who, 1959-1983; Who was who, 8

Jargy, Simon Dominique, born 20 August 1920 at Mardin, Turkey, he was educated in Paris at the Sorbonne, l'École pratique des hautes études, and l'Institut catholique. In 1951, he received a doctorate from the Sorbonne for his thesis, *Le monarchisme syrien*. He was a professor in Paris, before he accepted a teaching position at the Université de Genève in 1964. His writings include *Syrie* (1962), its translation, *Syrien* (1963), *Guerre et paix en Palestine* (1968), *La poésie populaire traditionnelle chantée au Proche-Orient arabe* (1970), *La musique arabe* (1971), *Yémen avec les montagnards de la mer Rouge* (1978), *Islam et chrétienté* (1981), *L'Orient déchiré entre l'Est et l'Ouest* (1984), and he edited *Badr Shākir al-Sayyāb fī hayātih wa-adabih* (1966). WhoArab, 1981/82; WWASS, 1989

Jaritz, Günter, born 17 September 1934 at Heygendorf, Saxe-Anhalt, Germany, he went to school in Roßleben and Schulpforte, and studied geography, biology, and chemistry at Martin-Luther-Universität Halle, and Freie Universität Berlin, 1953-1960, where he received a teacher's certificate. He subsequently became an academic assistant in the Institut für Acker- und Pflanzenbau in the Universität Bonn, where he received a Dr.agr. in 1966 for *Untersuchungen an fossilen Tertiärböden und vulkanogenen Edaphoiden des Westerwaldes*. He became associated with governmental agencies in aid work in North Africa. His writings include *Weidewirtschaft im australischen Winterregenklima und ihre Bedeutung für die Entwicklung der Landwirtschaft in den nordafrikanischen Maghrebländern* (1973), *Amélioration des herbages et cultures fourragères dans le nord-ouest de la Tunisie* (1982), and he was a joint author of the booklet, *Situation und Perspektiven der Futterproduktion im Trockenanbau in Nordtunesien* (1973). GV; Thesis; ZKO

Jaritz, Kurt, born in 1926, he received a Dr.phil. in 1949 from the Universität Graz for *Die Inschriften der Kassitenkönige*. He taught ancient Near Eastern subjects and ethnography at his alma mater. His writings include *Babylon und seine Welt* (1964), *Utopischer Mond* (1965), and *Schriftarchäologie der altmesopotamischen Kultur* (1967). DtBilnd (1); Schwarz

Jarlot, Georges Marie Joseph, born 14 May 1894 at Saint-Aubin (Jura), France, he studied at the Jesuit College at Dôle (Jura) and entered the Compagnie de Jésus in 1912; he was ordained in 1925. A *maître agrégé* of the Pontificio Università Gregoriana, Roma, he taught *morale sociale* at Jersey,

Vals, Mongré (1930-1950), and subsequently taught at the Gregoriana until 1974, when he returned to France. His writings include *Le régime corporatif et les catholiques sociaux* (1938), *Compendium ethicae socialis* (1951), *Historia documentorum ecclesiae in re sociali a Leone XIII ad Pium XII* (1956), and *Doctrine pontificale et historie* (1964). He died in 1980. IndexBFr² (1); NUC

Jarosławiecka-Gąsiorowska, Maria, fl. 20th cent., her writings include *Architektura neoklasyczna w Krakowie* (1933), *Les principaux manuscrits à peintures du Musée des princes Czartoryski à Cracovia* (1935), *Oprawy artystyozne XIII-XVIII w. w zbiorach Czarttoryskich w Krakowie* (1952), *Malarstwo polskie XIX i XX wieku; katalog wystawy* (Toruń, 1952), and she was a joint author, with St. J. Gąsiorowski, of *Cracow, its antiquities and museums* (1924). NUC, pre-1956

Jarrett, Henry Sullivan, born in 1839, he was educated at Bath. He entered the army and served in India in the Mutiny, and later in Afghanistan. A secretary and member of the Board of Examiners at Fort-William, his writings include an Arabic edition of the *Arabian nights* (1880), and the translation, *History of the caliphs*, from the Arabic of al-Suyūṭī (1880-81). He retired with the rank of colonel and died in 1919. Buckland; IndianBiInd (1); Riddick; Who was who, 2

Jarring, Gunnar Valfrid, born 12 October 1907 at Brunnby, Sweden, he studied at Lunds Universitet, where he received a doctorate in 1933, and where he subsequently taught Turkic languages until 1940, when he entered the Swedish diplomatic service. He was a sometime under secretary general and special representative of the UN Secretary General on the Middle Eastern question. His writings include *Matter of ethnological interest in Swedish missionary reports from southern Sinkiang* (1979), *Some notes on Eastern Turki (new Uighur) munazara literature* (1981), *Return to Kashgar; Central Asian memoirs in the present* (1986), and *Culture clash in Central Asia* (1991). In 1988 appeared *Turcica and Orientalia; studies in honour of Gunnar Jarring*. He died on 29 May 2002. CurBio, 1957; Index Islamicus (4); IntWW, 1974-2002; IntWWAS, 1976/77; Master (9); Materialia Turcica, 3 (1977), pp. 164-166; MidE, 1982/83; Schoeberlein; Vem är det, 1969-2001; Who, 1974-2002; WhoUN, 1975; WhoWor, 1974/75-1984

Jarry, Jacques, born 20th cent., his writings include *Hérésies et factions dans l'Empire byzantine du IVe au VIIe siècle* (Le Caire, Institut Français d'Archéologie Orientale, 1968), and *L'Iconoclasme* (Hiroshima, 1991). ZKO

Jarvis, Claude Scudamore, born in 1879, he served as a trooper in the Imperial Yeomanry in the South African war, then in Special Reserve Dorsetshire Regiment, 1902; he served in France, Egypt and Palestine, 1914-18, when he entered the Egyptian Government Frontier Administration, serving two years in the Western Desert; then two years as Governor of the Oases of the Libyan Desert with headquarters at al-Kharga; and in 1922 he was appointed Governor of Sinai, a post which he held until his retirement in 1936 with the rank of major. He was for some time a member of Council, Royal Central Asian Society. His writings, partly under the pseudonym Rameses, include *Three deserts* (1936), *Desert and delta* (1938), *Yesterday and to-day in Sinai* (1938), and *Oriental spotlight* (1952). He died in 1953. Bioln, 3; DBN; *Journal of the Royal Asian Society*, 41 (1954), p. 93; NYT, 10 December 1953, p. 48, col. 3; WhE&EA; Who's who, 1943; Who was who, 5

Jarylgasinova, R. Sh., 1931- *see* Dzharylgasinova, Roza Shotaevna

Jarzębowski, Tadeusz, fl. 20th cent., his writings include *Wstechświat i jego zagadki* (Warszawa, 1956). NUC, 1956-67

Jašar-Nastena, Olivera, born 20th cent., her writings include *Турски елементи во јазикот и стилот на Македонската народна поезија* (Skopje, 1987), and she was a joint author of *Македонски текстови 10 - 20 век* (Skopje, 1966). OSK

Jäschke, Gotthard Friedrich Comenius, born 8 April 1894 at Reichenbach, he received a Dr.jur. in 1917 from the Universität Greifswald. He was a professor at the Universität Berlin from 1931 to 1945, and the Universität Münster from 1947 to 1959. His writings include *Die Entwicklung des osmanischen Verfassungsstaates von den Anfängen bis zur Gegenwart* (1917), *Türkei* (1941), *Turecko* (Praha, 1942), and, jointly with F. Taeschner, *Aus der Geschichte des islamischen Orients* (1949). He died in 1983. DtBE; DtBiInd (2); Hanisch; HbDtWiss; *Index Islamicus* (3); Kürschner, 1935-1983; *Welt des Islams*, 38 (1998), pp. 406-423; Wer ist wer, 1955-67/68; Widmann

Jashar-Nasteva, Olivera *see* Jašar-Nasteva, Olivera

Jasińska, Jolanta, fl. 20th cent., she was a joint author of *Nowa i wspóczesna literatura arabska 19 i 20 w* (Warszawa, 1978). NUC, 1979

Jasiński, Bogusław, born 18 October 1931 at Żydaczów (Zhydachir), Ukraine, he was an economist who received his degrees at Kraków, where he taught since 1964, first as a lecturer and later as professor. His writings include *Struktura rolna a wzrost gospodarczy* (Warszawa, 1965), and *Węlowe problemy gospodarcze świata arabskiego* (Warszawa, 1974). Kto, 1993, 2001

Jastrow, Morris, born 13/30 August 1861 at Warszawa, the son of Rabbi Mordechai/Marcus Jastrow, he was educated at Philadelphia, Pa., where he also graduated from the University in 1885. He subsequently studied at Breslau, where he was ordained rabbi; at Leipzig, where he gained a Dr.phil. in 1884 for *Abu Zakarijjä Jahjä ben Dawūd Hajjūǧ und seine zwei grammatischen Schriften über die Verben mit schwachen Buchstaben und die Verben mit Doppelbuchstaben*; he did post-doctoral research at the Collège de France, École des hautes études, École des languages orientales vivantes, Paris; and the Universität Straßburg. After his return to Philadelphia, he there became successively a lecturer and professor at the University of Pennsylvania; in 1898 he became a director of its University Library. His writings include *The Religion of Babylonia and Assyria* (1898), its translation, *Die Religion Babyloniens und Assyriens* (1902), *The War and the Bagdad Railway; the story of Asia Minor and its relation to the present conflict* (1918), and *Zionism and the future of Palestine* (1919). He died in Philadelphia in 1921. CnDiAmJBi; *Journal of the American Oriental* Society, 41 (1921), pp. 321-344; Master (9); NatCAB, vol. 11, pp. 372-373; WhAm, 1; *Who was who*, 2; Wininger; ZKO

Jastrow, Otto, born 19 February 1942 at Saarlouis, Germany, he received a Dr.phil. in 1967 from the Universität Saarbrücken for *Laut- und Formenlehre des neuaramäischen Dialektes von Miḏin im Tur 'Abdin*, and a Dr.habil. in 1974 from the Universität Erlangen, where he subsequently became a professor of Semitic and Arabic studies. His writings include *Daragözü, eine arabische Mundart der Kozluk-Sason-Gruppe* (1973), *Die mesopotamisch-arabischen qeltu-Dialekte* (1978-1981), and he was a joint author of *Lehrgang für die arabische Schriftsprache der Gegenwart* (1977-86). EURAMES, 1993; Kürschner, 1980-2005; *MESA Roster of members*, 1990; Schwarz

Jastrzębski, Sergiusz (Сергей Васильевич Ястремскнй), born 20 September 1857 at Khar'kov, Ukraine. His writings include *Fragments choisis du folklore iakoute* (Leningrad, 1929). He died after 1931. BiobibSOT, pp. 296-297; PSB, vol. 11, pp. 83-84

Jaubert (de Passa), Pierre *Amédée* Émilien Probe, born 3 June 1779 at Aix-en-Provence, France, he was educated at École des langues orientales, Paris, where he was a student of Silvestre de Sacy and upon whose recommendation he became *interprète en chef de l'armée d'Égypte* to Napoleon Bonaparte in 1799. After his return to Paris in 1801, he was appointed professor of Turkish at École des langues orientales. In the years 1805 and 1806 he went on a diplomatic mission to the Shah of Persia. He travelled from Constantinople by boat to Trebizond and overland to Tehran by way of Erzurum, Van, Bayazit, Tabriz and Ardabil. He published his *Voyage en Arménie et en Perse* in 1821; the German translation, *Reise durch Armenien und Persien*, appeared in 1822. He died in Auvers-S.-Georges (Esonne) on 21, 27 or 28 January 1847. DBF, Féraud, pp. 37-42; Henze; Hoefer; *Hommes et destins*, vol. 6, pp. 197-199; Index BFr² (3); Kornrumpf

Jauhri, Ramesh Chandra, born in 1933, he received a Ph.D. in 1968 from Agra University. His writings include *Firoz Tughluq, 1351-1388* (Agra, 1968), and *American diplomacy and independence for India* (Bombay, 1970). Note about the author; ZKO

Jaulin, Robert, born 7 March 1928 at Cannet (Alpes-Maritimes), France, he received a doctorate in philosophy from the Sorbonne in 1955 and became associated with the C.N.R.S. His writings include *La Géomancie* (1966), *La Mort sara; l'order de la vie ou la pensée de la mort au Tchad* (1967), *La Paix blanche; introduction à l'ethnocide* (1970), *Gens du soi, gens de l'autre* (1973), *Géomancie et islam* (1991), *L'Univers des totalitarismes; essai d'ethnologie du non-être* (1995), and *Exercises d'ethnologie* (1999). BN; Unesco

Jaulus, Heinrich, born early 19th cent., he was in 1862 a rabbi at Aachen, Prussia. His writings include *Goldene Schwerter* (Berlin, 1916), and *Worte der Mahnung zur Erfüllung der vaterländischen Pflicht, den Goldschmuck dem Vaterlande darzureichen* (Berlin, 1916). ZKO

Jaussaud, Robert Édouard, born 10 May 1913 at Draria, Algeria, he studied at the Université d'Alger, where he received a doctorate in 1940 for *Le rôle social de l'apprentissage*. He became a French *inspecteur général des Affaires sociales*. NUC, pre-1956; WhoFr, 1969/70-1979/80|

Jaussen, Joseph *Antonin*, born in 1871, his writings include *Coutumes des Arabes au pays de Moab* (1906), *La vie économique d'une famille demi-nomade à Madaba* (1914), *Coutumes des fuqarâ* (1920), *Les châteaux arabes de Qeṣer 'Amra, Harâneh et Tûba* (1922), *Naplouse et son district* (1927), *Coutumes palestinennes* (1927), and he was a joint author of *Mission archéologique en Arabie, mars-mai 1909*, par les RR. PP. Jaussen et Savignac (1909-22). He died in 1962. There was a colloquium held in June of 1998 entitled *Antonin Jaussen; sciences sociales occidentales et patrimoine arabe*, the

acts of which were published in 1999 at Beirut and contain a biographical itinerary [not sighted.]
Kornrumpf; Kornrumpf, N

Javadov, G. D. *see* Dzhavadov, G. D.

Javits, Jacob Koppell, born 18 May 1904 at N.Y.C., he was educated at Columbia University, New York, and New York University and admitted to the Bar of New York in 1927. He was from 1956 to 1981 a U.S. senator. His writings include *Who makes war; the President versus Congress* (1973). He died on 7 March 1986. CnDiAmJBi; ConAu, 118, new rev., 17; Master (75); WhAm, 9; WhoWorJ, 1965

al-Jawāhirī, Muhammad Mahdī, born 1900 in Iraq, he was a poet who lived in Damascus since 1979, having fled Iraq after the Government's crackdown on dissidents. Prior to 1958 he was a courtier of King Faisal, later becoming a journalist, writing against the monarchy and its British protectors. His writings include *al-Majmū'ah al-shi'rīyah al-kāmilah* (1968), and *Dhikrayātī* (1988). He died in Damascus on 27 July 1997. WRMEA, 16, no. 3 (October/November 1997), p. 120

Jawish (Schauisch/Shawish/Showesh), 'Abd al-'Aziz, he was born in 1872 or 1876 at Alexandria, Egypt. In 1915 he went to Berlin by way of Constantinople to solicit support for a German-Turkish alliance. With the help of theTurkish Government and the German Foreign Office he became joint founder the *Islamische Welt*, Berlin, a periodical which survived until the end of the Great War. He was a sometime president of the Egyptian National Party. He died in 1929. *Araber in Berlin* (1992), pp. 13-14; Goldschmidt; NUC, pre-1956

Jaworski, Ivan L., 1853- *see* IAvorskii, Ivan Lavrovich

Jayakar, Atmaram Sadashia Grandin, born in 1844, his writings include the translation from the Arabic of Muhammad ibn Mūsá al-Damīrī, *Hayāt al-hayawān; a zoological lexicon* (London, 1906-8). NUC

al-Jayyusi, Salma al-Kadra', born about 1922 at Safad, Palestine, she was educated at Schmidt's College, Jerusalem, and the American University of Beirut. In 1969 she received a Ph.D. from the Scoool of Oriental and African Studies, London, for her thesis, *Trends and movements in the contemporary Arabic poetry*. As the wife of a Jordanian diplomat, she travelled widely. She was active in literary journalism and broadcasting, and taught at colleges and universities throughout the Middle East and North Africa as well as North America. Her writings include works in Arabic, translations from and into English, and *Trends and movements in modern Arabic poetry* (1977); she edited *Modern Arabic poetry; an anthology* (1987), *The Literature of modern Arabia; an anthology* (1988); and she was joint editor of *The Legacy of Muslim Spain* (1992). LC; Sluglett

Jazayery, Mohammad Ali, born in 1924 at Shushtar, Persia, he graduated in 1950 from Tehran University with a *licence* in English. In 1951 he went with a Fulbright grant to the U.S.A., where he took a Ph.D. in linguistics and English in 1958 at the University of Texas. He taught at the University of Michigan from 1959 to 1962, when he returned to Texas, becoming first a professor of Oriental and African languages and later a chairman of department. He was a joint author of *English for Iranians* (1955), and *Modern Persian reader* (1963). In 1994 apperead *Persian studies in North America; studies in honour of Mohammad Ali Jazayery*. He died on 5 October 2001. BioB134; ConAu, 21-24, new rev., 9; DrAS, 1974 F, 1978 F, 1982 F; WhAm, 14; WhoAm, 1984-1995; WhoS&SW, 1982 (not sighted)

Jean, Charles *François*, born 20 March 1874, at Sauteyrargues (Hérault), France, he entered the Lazarists in 1891 at Paris, studied at the Sorbonne, École des hautes études, and École du Louvre, where he obtained a diploma. In 1898 he was appointed a professor of philosophy at the Grand séminaire d'Alger. After teaching from 1902 to 1905 at the Paris seat of the Lazarists, he was sent to China as a missionary, but stayed only for two years. After a brief teaching appoinment to Italy, he returend to Paris in 1914 to teach Hebrew and Semitic epigraphy at the École du Louvre until his retirement in 1949. His writings include *Les Lettres de Hammurapi à Sin-Idinnam* (1913), *Le Péché chez les Babyloniens et les Assyriens* (1925), and *Grammaire hébraïque élémentaire* 1943). He died in Paris on 15 May 1955. BN; DBF; DBFC, 1954/55

Jean-Darrouy, Lucienne, fl. 1945, her writings include *Au jardin de mon père; contes de la terre de l'Algérie* (Alger, 1942), and *Au pays de la mort jaune; ou, La Colonisation heroïque, roman* (Alger, 1945). BN; LC

Jeandet, Noël, fl. 20th cent., he was a diplomat whose writings include *Un golfe pour trois rêves; le triangle de crise Iran, Irak, Arabie: réflections géostratégiques sur un quart de siècle de rapports de forces* (1993). *Livres disponibles*, 2003

Jeanmougin, Gaston, born 20th cent., he received a *doctorat de 3ème cycle* in 1972 from the Université de Nice for *Les relations franco-turques de 1925 à 1935*. THESAM, 4

Jeanneret, André, born 5 June 1935 at Savagnier, Switzerland, he received a doctorate in 1967 from the Université de Neuchâtel for *La pêche et les pêcheurs du Lac de Neuchâtel*, and went on to Carleton College, Ottawa, for post-doctoral study. From 1959 to 1961 he served as a counsellor to the national Museum at Kabul. Since 1963 he was successively a keeper and director of the Musée d'ethnographie, Neuchâtel, concurrently serving at the local Institut d'ethnographie. His writings include *Aspects de la médecine primitive* (1966), *Genève, le Rhône et les Alpes à travers la collection G. Amoudruz* (1976), and he edited *Wow-ipitssj; sculptures Asmat* (1964). WhoSwiss, 1972/73; WhoWor, 1974/75, 1976/77

Jeannette, André, fl. 20th cent., he was a geologist associated with the Service géologique du Maroc. He was a joint author of *Carte géologique de la méséta entre Settat et Mazagan* (Rabat, 1954), and *Étude géotechnique de la région de Casablance* (Rabat, 1956). ZKO

Jeannot, Guissou née Jahangiri Tehrani, born 27 May 1962 at Tehran, she studied sociology at the École des Hautes études en Sciences sociales, Paris. She was a member of the editorial board of the weekly, *Courrier international*, and a collaborator with *Abstracta iranica*. AnEIFr, 1997; Note about the author

Jeanroy, Marie Henri Gustave *Alfred*, born 5 July 1859 at Mangiennes (Meuse), France, he was educated at the Collège de Verdun and the Lycée Louis-le-Grand, Paris, and since 1878 studied at the École normale supérieure. After his degree in letters in 1879 and his *agrégation* in 1881, he successively taught at secondary schools in Troyes, Besançon, and Paris. Since 1889 he taught Greek literature at Poitiers, later changing to Toulouse and Paris, where he became in 1911 director of the École pratique des hautes études. In 1923, he was elected a member of the Académie des inscriptions et belles-lettres, and in 1932, he was awarded officer of the Légion d'honneur. From 1898 to 1916 he was a director of the *Annales du Midi*. His writings include *Origines de la poésie lyrique en France* (1889), *Mystères provençaux du quinzième siècle* (1893), *La Poésie lyrique des troubadours* (1934), and he edited *La conquête de Constantinople*, of Geoffroy de Villehardouin (1932). In 1928 appeared *Mélanges de linguistique et de littérature offerts à M. Alfred Jeanroy par ses élèves et ses amis*. He died in S.-Jean near Castelmaurou (Haute-Garonne) on 4 March 1953. DBF; *Qui est-ce*, 1934; *Qui êtes-vous*, 1924; *Speculum*, 31 (1956), p. 569

Jeanselme, Édouard Antoine, born 14 June 1858 at Paris and a graduate of the Lycée Condorcet, he studied at the Faculté de médecine de Paris. In 1897 he was nominated *médecin des hôpitaux* of Paris. In 1898 the ministries of Instruction publique and Colonies en Extrême-Orient sent him to the East to study leprosy. Since 1901 he was a professor in the Institut de médecine coloniale de Paris. He was a prolific writer in the field and one of the great French historians of medicine. His writings include *Précis de pathologie exotique* (1909), and *Précis de syphiligraphie et des maladies vénériennes* (1925). He died in Paris on 9 April 1935. DBF; IndexBFr² (3); *Qui est-ce*, 1934

Jeanson, Francis, born in 1922 at Bordeaux, he received a *licence ès lettres* and a *diplôme supérieur* in philosophy. He became an essayist, novelist, literary critic, and a collaborator with, and student of Jean-Paul Sartre. He was the driving force behind the journal *le Temps modernes*. During the Algerian war he played an active role in the liberation movement. His writings include *Notre guerre* (1960), *La révolution algérienne* (1962), *L'action culturelle dans la cité* (1973), *Algéries; de retour en retour* (1991), and he was a joint author of *Algérie hors la loi* (1955), and its translation, *Algeria fuorilegge* (1956). IndexBFr² (2); ZKO

Jedin, Hubert, born 17 June 1900 at Großbriesen, Silesia, he studied Catholic theology and history at the universities of Breslau, München, and Freiburg im Breisgau, obtaining a Dr.theol. in 1925 at Breslau. He continued his study at the Vatican Archives. He gained a Dr.habil. at Breslau in 1930 and subsequently taught there until 1933. In 1939 he emigrated to Roma, continuing his study of ecclesiastical history. From 1949 to 1965 he was a professor of his field at the Universität Bonn, concurrently serving for three years as a consultant to the second Vatican Council. His writings include *Geschichte des Konzils von Trient* (1950), and its translation, *A History of the Council of Trient* (1949), and *Lebensbericht* (1984). He died in Bonn on 16 July 1980. BioHbDtE; DtBE; Kürschner, 1950-1980; *Wer ist wer*, 1955-1974/75

Jędrej, Marian Charles, born 20th cent., his writings include *Ingessana; the religious institutions of a people of the Sudan-Ethiopia borderland* (Leiden, Brill, 1995), and he was a joint editor of *Dreaming, religion and society in Africa* (Leiden, Brill, 1992). Brinkman's

Jefferson, John Howard Kettell, fl. 20th cent., his writings include *Soil conservation in the Sudan* (Khartoum, Ministry of Agriculture, 1952). BLC

Jefferson, M. M., born 20th cent., an author who received a M.A. in 1957/59 from Bedford College, University of London, for *The place of Constantinople and the Straits in British foreign policy, 1890-1902.* Sluglett

Jeffery, Arthur, born in 1892, he was educated at the University of Melbourne (B.A., 1918, M.A., 1920, B.Th.) He served under the Australian Methodist Church on the staff of the Madras Christian College from the first World War until 1921, when he joined the School of Oriental Studies, AUC. His scholarly ability placed him in the first rank of Western Orientalists. In 1929, he received a Ph.D. from Edinburgh University, and followed this with a D.Litt (*summa cum laude*) in 1938 from the same institution. His major interest was the textual criticism of the Koran, and on this he continued to work throughout his career. In 1938 he went to the Union Theological Seminary and Columbia University, N.Y.C. He offered courses in general history of religions, Biblical literature, and early Eastern Christianity. He not only headed the Department of Semitic Languages at Columbia, but was also chairman of the section on history of religions in the joint Committee on the Ph.D. degree in the field of religion, offered and administered by the Union Theological Seminary and Columbia University. His writings include *Materials for the history of the text of the Qurān* (1937), *The Foreign vocabulary of the Qur'an* (1938), *The Qur'ān as scripture* (1952), *The Koran: selected suras* (1958), and *A Reader on Islam* (1960). He died in 1959. Bioln, 3; *Journal of Biblical literature*, 79 (1960), pp. viii-ix; MW, 50 (1960), pp. 49-54; NYT, 5 August 1959, p. 27, col. 3

Jeffery, George H. Everett, born 19th cent., he was an architect and curator of ancient monuments. In 1892 he served as architect to Rt. Rev. Bishop in Jerusalem and the East. His writings include *A Description of the historic monuments of Cyprus* (1918), and he was a joint author of *An attempt at a bibliography of Cyprus* (1929). He died in 1935. Who's who, 1929; Who was who, 3

Jeffrey, Anne E. F., born 18 November 1941, she graduated in history from the University of Toronto in 1966. In second marriage she was married to the Montreal cardiologist Allan Sniderman, with whom she had two children, Sarah, born in 1969, and a son, born about 1972. After a successful business career with Anne Jeffrey & Associates in Prince George, B.C., she taught art, particularly modern, at the University of Tampa, Florida, a post which she still held in 2006, concurrently serving as a lecturer at the Museum of Fine Arts in St. Petersburg, Fla. She was a joint author of *Art lover's guide to Florida* (1998). LC; NatFacDr, 2003; Note; Private

Jeffrey, Thomas E., born in 1911, he received a Ph.D. in 1957 from the University of Chicago for *A factorial study of three space factors.* NUC, pre-1956

Jeffreys, Mervyn David Waldgrave, born 15 May 1890 at Johannesburg, South Africa, he was a Rhodes scholar at Oxford and received a Ph.D. from the University of London. He served as a magistrate and judge in British West Africa, before teaching social anthropology at the University of the Witwatersrand, Johannesburg, from 1945 to 1956. His writings include *Old Calabar and notes on the Ibibio language* (1935), *Some Semitic influence in Hottentot culture* (1968), and *Man and mythology* (1970). He died in Johannesburg on 21 March 1975. AfrBioInd (2); DSAB, vol. 5, pp. 383-384; Unesco; *Who's who in British science*, 1953

Jeffries, Joseph Mary Nagle, born in 1880 or 85, he was a journalist and a war correspondent of the *Daily Mail*. His writings include *The Palestine deception* (1923), *Front everywhere* (1935), and *Palestine, the reality* (1939). CathWW, 1920; NUC, pre-1956

Jehel, Georges, born 20th cent., his writings include *Aigues mortes, un port pour un rois; les Capétiens et la Méditerranée* (1985), *Débauche d'une stratégie pour un empire* (1993), *La ville médiévale de l'Occident chrétien à l'Orient musulman* (1996), *L'Italie et le Maghreb au Moyen âge; conflits et échanges du 7e siècle au 15e siècle* (2001); and he was a joint author of *Le christianisme; début du VIIe siècle - milieu du XIe siècle* (1997), and *Les relations des pays d'islam avec le monde latin* (2000). Livres disponibles, 2004

Jehenne, Aimable Constant, born 11 September 1799 at San-Malo-de-la-Lande (Manche), France, he was educated at the École spéciale de la marine, Brest (Finistère). A navy commander in 1830, he participated in this year's landing of troops for the conquest of Algeria; in the Crimean war he distinguished himself during the assault of Sebastopol (Sevastopol); and in 1861 in Syria, he assured the safety of the Lebanese Christians from Turkish persecution. In the same year he was made *grand officier* of the Légion d'honneur. He retired in 1863 and died in the same year at Brest. DBF

Jelavich, Barbara Brightfield, born 12 April 1923 at Belleville, Ill., she began her academic career in 1948 with a doctoral dissertation on the German Alliance system from 1939-41. In 1962 she started her teaching career at Indiana University, where the fruits of her labour helped make the University one of the premier centres of East European studies. Her writings include *Russia and the Rumanian*

Ottoman Empire, the great powers, and the Straits question, 1870-1887 (1973), *History of the Balkans* (1983), *Russia's Balkan entanglements, 1806-1914* (1991), and she was a joint author of *The Establishment of the Balkan nation states, 1804-1920* (1977). In 1992 appeared *Labyrinth of nationalism, complexities of diplomacy; essays in honor of Charles and Barbara Jelavich.* She died from cancer on 14 January 1995. ConAu, 53-56; DrAS, 1974 H, 1978 H, 1982 H; MembriiAR; *Südost-Forschungen,* 54 (1995), pp. 274-275; WhAm, 12; WhoAm, 1986-1994; WhoAmW, 1970/71; ZKO

Jelden, Helmut, born 20th cent., his writings include *Walddüngung* (1956), *Standortserkundungen mit Waldbaugrundlagen* (1965), and *Verzeichnis der Waldgemeinschaften Österreichs* (1965), all of which were published by the Austrian Bundesversuchsanstalt, Wien. Note about the author

Jellicoe, Susan, born 30 June 1907 at Liverpool, she was the second wife of Geoffrey Alan Jellicoe. From 1940 to 1944 she was in charge of counter-propaganda at the Ministry of Information, and from 1944 to 1945 she was press officer in the Information Department of U.N.R.R.A. She was a joint author of *Gardens* (1953), *Water; the use of water in landscape architecture* (1971), and *The Landscape of man* (1975). Au&Wr, 1971; IntAu&W, 1976, 1977, 1982

Jellinek, Adolf (Aaron), born 26 January 1821 at Drslawitz near Ungarisch Brod, Moravia, he studied philosophy and Semitic subjects at the Universität Leipzig, where he also served as a rabbi from 1845 to 1856, when he settled down in Wien. He was considered the most spirited and interesting preacher of his day. He died in Wien on 29 December 1893. BioIn, 17; DtBE; EncJud; JüdLex; LuthC 75; Wininger

Jemma-Gouzon, Danièle, born in 1943 at Constantine, Algeria, she graduated In ethnology from the Université de Montpellier and subsequently taught at the Université de Constantine. Her writings include *L'Algérie à la croisée des temps* (1989), and *Villages de l'Aurès; archives de pierres* (1989). LC; *Livres disponibles,* 2003

Jenkins, Hester Donaldson, born 6 July 1869 at Oshkosh, Wisc., she graduated in 1898 from the University of Chicago, and received a Ph.D. in 1911 from Columbia University, N.Y.C. for *Ibrahim Pasha, grand vizir of Suleiman the Magnificent.* She started her academic career at the American College for Girls, Constantinople, from 1900 to 1909, and subsequently taught at a variety of colleges in the American Midwest and East Coast. Her writings include *An Educational ambassador to the Near East* (1925), as well as translations from the Turkish, and short stories in periodicals. She died in 1941. NYT, 24 April 1941, p. 21, col. 4; WomNov; WomWWA, 1914

Jenkins, Jean L., born 20th cent., he was an ethnomusicologist. He was a joint author of *Eighteenth century musical instruments, France and Britain* (London, Victoria and Albert Museum, 1973), and he was a joint author of *Music and musical instruments in the world of Islam* (1976). LC

Jenkins, Marilyn, born 2 January 1940, she received a Ph.D. in 1978 from New York University for *Medieval Maghribi ceramics; a reappraisal of the pottery production of the western regions of the Muslim world.* She became an assistant curator of Islamic art at the Metropolitan Museum of Art, N.Y.C. Her writings include *Islamic jewelry in the Metropolitan Museum of Art* (1983), and she edited *Islamic art in the Kuwait National Museum; the al-Sabah Collection* (1983). LC; Selim[3]

Jenkins, R. G., born 20th cent., he received a Ph.D. in 1986 from the University of Melbourne for *The Old Testament quotations of Philoxenus of Mabbug,* a work which was published in 1989 by Peeters, Louvain. Note; ZKO

Jenkins, Romilly James Heald, born 10 February 1907 at Hitchin, Herts., England, he graduated from Emmanuel College, Cambridge, and subsequently studied at the British School of Archaeology, Athens. He became a professor of Greek and Byzantine subjects successively at Cambridge, London, Harvard, and Dumbarton Oaks Center for Byzantine Studies, Washington, D.C. His writings include *The Byzantine Empire on the eve of the crusades* (1953), *The Dilessi murders* (1961), and *Byzantium; the imperial centuries* (1967). He died on 30 September 1969. ConAu, 5-8, new rev., 5; WhAm, 5

Jenkinson, Sir Charles *Hilary*, born in 1882, he was educated at Dalwich College, and Pembroke College, Cambridge. He entered the Public Record Office in 1906 and retired in 1954. He was a president of the Society of Archivists in the UK from its formation in 1955 and long an honorary member of the Society of American Archivists. He was, almost certainly, the most eminent archivist of his generation in the English-speaking world. He was made C.B.E. in 1943 and was knighted in 1949. His writings include *Palaeography and the practical study of court hand* (1915), *Guide to the seals in the Public Record Office* (1954), and *A Manual of archive administration* (1965). In 1957 appeared *Studies presented to Sir Hilary Jenkinson.* He died on 5 March 1961. *American archivist,* 24 (1961), pp. 345-347; BioIn, 5, 15; DNB; ObitT, 1961-70, p. 400

Jenkinson, Emily J., born in 1879, she was a novelist, whose writings include *Silverwood* (1910), *Soul of unrest* (1912), and *Barbara Lynn, a tale of the dales and fells* (1914). Master (1); NUC, pre-1956

Jenks, David, born in 1866, he was a scholar of Pembroke College, Cambridge. From 1892 to 1899 he was with the Archbishop of Canterbury's Mission to the Assyrian Christians, serving from 1893 to 1896 as chaplain to the Sisters of Bethany at Urmia, Persia. His writings include *A Study of the mind of Christ* (1925), and *Six great missionaries of the sixteenth and seventeenth centuries* (1930). He died in 1935. Wo's who, 1921-1935; Who was who, 3

Jennings, Robert Carlton, Jr., born 6 May 1941, he spent two years in Turkey as a Peace Corps volunteer, teaching English at a college in Samsun, and learning Turkish at the same time. After finishing his studies at the University of California, Los Angeles, he became a member of the faculty in the History Department of the University of Illinois. He spent the entire year 1977/78 on leave from his university in the Turkish section of Cyprus. His writings include *The Judicial registers (şer'i mahkeme sicilleri) of Kayseri, 1590-1630, as a source for Ottoman history* (1972), *Christians and Muslims in Ottoman Cyprus and the Mediterranean world, 1571-1640* (1993), *Studies on Ottoman social history in the sixteenth and seventeenth centuries; women, zimmis and Sharia courts in Kayseri, Cyprus and Trabzon* (1999), and a great many substantial and careful studies, which were published in the very best journals of the field. "The tragedy of a hereditary deficiency, becoming apparent during his last decade, set an end to his research and to his still young life in January 1996." LC; *MESA Roster of members*, 1982-1990; *Turcica*, 29 (1997), pp. 13-14

Jennings-Bramley, Wilfred E., 1871-1960. Yvonne Neville-Rolfe and Joseph Bonomi delivered a paper at the 4th biennial ASTENE Conference, Edinburgh, 2001, entitled "W. E. Jennings-Bramley, explorer and surveyor in the Libyan Desert, Sudan and the Sinai Peninsula, authority on and friend of the Bedouin." *Bulletin of the ASTENE; notes and queries*, no. 12 (October 2001), p. 7, col. 2

Jenny, Ernest, born 16 April 1872 at Menton (Alpes-Maritimes), France, he was educated first at Zürich and later at Odessa until 1891. After the early death of his father, a Swiss vice-consul at Odessa, he looked after his landed estate for some time, before beginning to study first at the Landwirtschaftliche Akademie, Hohenheim, Württemberg, and then at the Universität Berlin, where he received a Dr.phil. in 1913 for *Der Teilbau, nebst der Monographie eines Teilbaugroßbetriebes in Rußland aus der Zeit von 1891-1910*. His writings include *Die Deutschen im Wirtschaftsleben Rußlands* (1920), and *Wie Rußland bolschewistisch wurde* (1921). Thesis

Jentsch, Christoph, born 21 December 1931 at Niederwartha/Meißen, Germany, he received a Dr.phil. in 1960 from the Universität Innsbruck for *Das Brunecker Becken*, and a Dr.habil. in 1973 from the University Saarbrücken for *Das Nomadentum in Afghanistan*. He was successively a professor of human geography at the universities of Saarbrücken, Stuttgart, and Mannheim. His writings include *Typen der Agrarlandschaft im zentralen und östlichen* Afghanistan (1966); he was a joint author of *Zur Geographie der ländlichen Siedlungen in Afghanistan* (1980); and he was a joint editor of *Afghanistan; Ländermonographie* (1986). Kürschner, 1983-2005; Schwarz

Jenyns, Roger *Soames*, born in 1904, he joined the British Museum, London, in 1931 to become a deputy keeper of its Department of Antiquities. His writings include *Japanese porcelain* (1965) and, jointly with William Watson, *Chinese art* (1963). He died 14 October 1976. Ronald Rompkey wrote *Soame Jenyns* (1984). *Burlington magazine*, 119 (February 1977), p. 119; ConAu, 69-72, 73-76

Jeol, Michel, fl. 20th cent., his writings include *La Réforme de la justice en Afrique noire* (Paris, 1963), *Cours de droit administratif mauritanien* (Bordeaux, 1964), *Cours de droit international public mauritanien* (Bordeaux, 1965), *Cours de droit judiciaire mauritanien* (Bordeaux, 1965), and *Droit public africain* (Paris, 1967). BN; NUC

Jeppe, Karen, born 1 July 1876 on a farm in Jylland (Jutland), Denmark, she was educated at the high school in Ordrup, where she lived until 1903 when she decided to serve as a teacher and missionary under the Deutsche Orient Mission in the Near East. For well over twenty years she cared for the Armenians, first at the Mission Orphanage in Urfa, Turkey, and later in Syria. Her writings include *Erlöst vom Mohammedanismus* (1926). Ingeborg Maria Sick wrote the biography *Karen Jeppe im Kampf um ein Volk in Not*, a translation from the Danish (Stuttgart, 1929).

Jernstedt, P. V., 1890-1966 see Ernshtedt, Petr Viktorovich

Jernudd, Björn H., born in 1942, he received a doctorate in 1979 from Umeå Universitet for *The language survey of Sudan; the first phase: a questionnaire survey in schools*. He was a joint author of *Language management in a multilingual state; the case of planning in Singapore* (1988); he edited *Aspects of Arabic sociolinguistics* (1986), *Chinese language planning; perspectives from China and* *abroad* (1986), *Language management and language problems* (2000); and he was a joint editor of *The Politics of language purism* (1989). LC

de **Jerphanion**, Guillaume, born 3 March 1877 at Château de Pontèves (Var), France, he was a missionary at Tokat, Turkey, from 1903 to 1907, and again from 1911 to 1914. In the post-war years, he was attached concurrently to l'Institut Biblique and l'Institut Oriental, Roma, teaching archaeology, history, institutions, and Byzantine epigraphy. His writings include *Le calice d'Antioche* (1926), *Mélanges d'archéologie anatolienne* (1928), and *Les miniatures du manuscrit syriaque n° 559 de la Bibliothèque vaticane* (1940). He died in Roma on 22 October 1948. Byzantion, 20 (1950), pp. 389-396

Jerusalemy, F., born 19th cent., his writings include *Le donne turche, loro vita e piaceri* (Milano, Treves, 1873). ZKO

Jeśman, Czsław, fl. 1958-68, his writings include *The Russians in Ethiopia; an essay in futility* (London, 1958), *The Ethiopian paradox* (London, 1963), and *Listy z Ameryki* (Londyn, Polska Fundacja Kulturalna, 1968). ZKO

Jessup, Henry Harris, born 19 April 1832 at Montrose, Pa., he was a missionary in Syria. His writings include *Women of the Arabs* (1873), *Syrian home life* (1874), *The Mohammadan missionary problem* (1879), *The Setting of the crescent and the rising of the cross* (1898), *Fifty-three years in Syria* (1910), and the translation, *Kamil Abdul Messiah el Aietany; ein Lebensbild* (1909). He died in Beirut on 28 April 1910. AmIndex (4); ANB; DAB; Kornrumpf; Kornrumpf, N; Master (10); NatCAB, vol. 10, p. 144; Shavit; WhAm, 1; ZKO

Jessup, Henry Wynans, born 20 January 1864 at Beirut, the son of Henry Harris Jessup, he graduated from Princeton University, was admitted to the Bar of New York, and until 1893 served as a professor of law at New York University. His writings include *The Law and practice in the Surrogates' Courts of the State of New York* (1899), *Justice through simplified legal procedure* (1917), and *The Professional ideals of the lawyer; a study of legal ethics* (1925). He died in 1934. Master (3); WhAm, 1

Jest, Corneille, born in 1930, he was an anthropologist who was associated with the Centre Nationale de la Recherche Scientifique, Paris. His writings include *Polpo; communautés de langue tibétaine du Népal* (1975), *L'Homme et son environnement à haute altitude* (1981), and he was a joint organizer of the seminar, *La Turquoise de vie; un pèlegrinage tibétain* (1985). LC; Master (1)

Jetter, Dieter, born 14 July 1929 at Stuttgart, Germany, he studied medicine and received a Dr.habil. in 1966 from the Universität Heidelberg for a study of lunatic asylums entitled *Zur Typologie des Irrenhauses von 1780-1840*. He was since 1971 a professor of history of medicine, and later director of the Institut für Geschichte der Medizin, Universität Köln. His writings include *Geschichte des Hospitals* (1966-81), *Das europäische Hospital von der Spätantike bis 1800* (1986), *Geschichte der Medizin; Einführung in die Entwicklung der Heilkunde aller Länder und Zeiten* (1992). Kürschner, 1983-2005

Jettmar, Karl Josef, born 8 August 1918 at Wien, he studied ethnology and early history at the Universität Wien, where he received a Dr.phil. in 1941 for a study on German blacksmiths entitled *Der Schmied im germanischen Raum*. He started his career at the Museum für Völkerkunde in Wien. He subsequently became a professor of ethnology and palaeoethnology successively at the universities of Wien, Mainz, and Heidelberg. He was a participant in the German Hindukush expedition to Afghanistan and Pakistan (1955/56), and the Austrian Haramash expedition (1958). His writings include *Die Religionen des Hindukusch* (1975), its translation, Религии Гиндукуша (1986), and *Bolar und Dardistan* (1980); he edited the conference papers, *Cultures of the Hindukush* (1974). In 1983 appeared *Ethnologie und Geschichte; Festschrift für Karl Jettmar*. He died on 27 March 2002. Kürschner, 1961-2001; Note; Schoeberlein

Jewett, Albert C., born about 1870, he was a hydraulic engineer and the first Westerner to spent eight years in Afghanistan. He was in the employment of Habib Allah Khan, Amir of Afghanistan, as chief engineer in charge of the installation of a hydro-electrical plant. He died in 1926. His writings include *An American engineer in Afghanistan; from the notes of A. C. Jewett*, edited by Marjorie Jewett Bell (1948). Note about the author; Shavit

Jewett, Iran Banu Hassani, born 20th cent., he received a Ph.D. in 1964 from the University of Maryland for *Kinglake and the English travelogue of the nineteenth century*. His writings include *Edward Fitzgerald* (1977), and *Alexander W. Kinglake* (1981). LC; NUC, 1968-72

Jewett, James Richard, born 14 March 1862 at Westport, Me., he graduated in 1884 from Harvard. After spending 1884-87 in Syria and Egypt on a Harvard fellowship, he received a Dr.phil. in 1891 from the Universität Straßburg for *Arabic proverbs and adverbial phrases collected largely during a stay in*

Syria in 1886. He taught Semitic languages and Oriental history at a variety of American universities from 1887 to his retirement in 1933. He died in 1943. CurBio, 1943; NatCAB, 35, pp. 126-27; WhAm, 2

Jiddou, Ahmed Ould, fl. 1969, he was an ambassador of the République islamique de Mauritanie.

Jik'ia, Sergi S., 1898- *see* Dzhikiia, Sergei Simonovich

Jikiev, Ata *see* Dzhikiev, Ata

Jiménez Castillo, Pedro, born 20th cent., he received a *licencio* in ancient history and archaeology, with special reference to Islamic archaeology. He became associated with the Centro de Estudios Árabes y Arqueologicos "Ibn Arabi" de Murcia. Arabismo, 1992; EURAMES, 1993

Jiménez de la Espada, Márcos, born 5 March 1831 at Cartagena, Spain, he studied natural sciences at the universities of Barcelona, Madrid, and Sevilla. Associated with both the Museo de Ciencias, and the Universidad de Madrid, he accompanied a Pacific expedition as natural scientist in 1862. He was a member of the Royal academies of history, and sciences. His writings include *España en Berberia* (1880), and *La guerra del moro a fines del siglo XV* (1940). He died in Madrid on 3 October 1898. EncicUni; IndiceE³ (6)

Jiménez Lozano, José, born 13 May 1930 at Landa/Ávila, Spain, he studied at the Universidad de Valladolid, received a *licencio* in law from the Universidad de Salamanca, and subsequently graduated in journalism from the Escuela Oficial de Madrid. He became an editor-in-chief of the *El Norte de Castilla*, Valladolid. His writings include *Un cristiano en rebeldía* (1963), *Historia de un otoño* (1971), *El sambenito* (1972), and *Judíos, moriscos y conversos* (1982). DBEC; IndiceE³ (3); WhoSpain, 2003

Jiménez Mata, Maria del Carmen, born 20th cent., she received a docatorate in Semitic philology and was throughout the 1990s a professor at the Universidad de Granada. She was a joint author of *Introducción al Jaén islámico* (1979). Arabismo, 1992, 1994, 1997; EURAMES, 1993; ZKO

Jiménez Sánchez, Sebastián, born 15 September 1904 at Palmas de Gran Canaria, he was a professor at a teachers' college and a patron of the Museo del Pueblo Español in Las Palmas de Gran Canaria. WhoSpain, 1963

Jindi, Hajji, 1908- *see* Dzhindi, Dzhauari Adzhie

Jireček (Иречек), Josef *Konstantin*, born 24 July 1854 at Wien, where he also grew up until 1872, when his parents moved to Prag. He there studied classical philology and history. At the end of 1875 he received his Dr.phil. for a study of the history of the Bulgarians entitled *Geschichte der Bulgaren*, a work which supported the claim to Bulgarian nationhood and which was concurrently published in a Bohemian edition. In 1877 he obtained a second doctorate for *Die Heerstraße von Belgrad nach Constantinople und die Balkanpässe*. He subsequently taught history until 1879, when he was invited to Sofia. Declining tenure at Sofia in 1883, he returned for ten years to the re-organized Czech university at Prag. In 1892 he accepted a professorship at the Universität Wien. His writings include *Dějiny národa bulharského* (1876), *Das Fürstenthum Bulgarien* (1891), *Geschichte der Serben* (1911), *Staat und Gesellschaft im mittelalterlichen Serbien* (1912-19), *Историја Срба* (1922-23), *Из архива на Константин Иречек* (1953-63), *История на българите* (1978), and he was a joint editor of *Plan eines Corpus der griechischen Urkunden des Mittlealters in der neueren Zeit* (1903). He died in Wien on 10 January 1918. DtBE; EnBulg; EnclZ; EnSlovar; *Études balkaniques*, 5 iii (1969), pp. 57-67; HL; *Jahrbücher für Geschichte Osteuropas*, 2 (1954/55), pp. 206-211; Kornrumpf; ÖBL; OSK

Jiriczek, Otto Luitpold, born 18 December 1867 at Ungarisch-Hradisch, Moravia, he studied philology at the Universität Wien, where he received a Dr.phil. in 1890, and a Dr.habil. in 1893 from the Universität Breslau for *Zur Geschichte der Bósa-Saga*. He taught English language and literature successively at the universities of Breslau, Münster, and Würzburg, where he died on 3 July 1941. His writings include *Die deutsche Heldensage* (1894), and *Specimens of Tudor translations from the classics* (1923). DtBE; KDtLK, Nekrolog, 1936-70; Kosel; Kürschner, 1925-1940/41; NÖB

al-Jirītlī, 'Alī Ahmad Ibrāhīm, 1913- *see* Gritly, Aly Ahmad Ibrahim

Jirku, Anton, born 27 April 1885 at Birnbaum, Moravia, he received a Dr.phil. in 1908 from the Universität Wien for *Die alte Landschaft Syrien*, and a Dr.habil. in 1914 from the Universität Kiel for *Die magische Bedeutung der Kleidung in Israel*. He was successively a professor of Old Testament at the universities of Kiel, Breslau, and Bonn. His writings include *Der Kampf um Syrien-Palästina, die Brücke zwischen Afrika und Asien* (1942), *Die Ausgrabungen in Palästina und Syrien* (1956), *Die Welt der Bibel* (1957), *Die ägyptischen Listen palästinensischer und syrischer Ortsnamen in Umschrift und mit historisch-archäologischem Kommentar* (1962), and *Von Jerusalem nach Ugarit* (1966). He died in Bonn on 3 December 1972. EncJud²; JüdLex; Kürschner, 1925-1976; Wer ist's, 1928, 1935

Jiskra, Carl, 1820-1879 *see* Giskra, Carl

Jisl, Lumír, born 18 April 1921 at Újezd u Svijan (Svijanský Újezd), Czechoslovakia, he received a doctorate in 1970 at Praha for *Balbals, Steinbabas und andere Steinfiguren als Äusserungen der religiösen Vorstellungen der Ost-Türken.* He was a Mongolian scholar and archaeologist, associated with the Náprstkovo Muzeum, Praha. His writings include *Mongolian journey* (1960), *Umění starého Mongolska* (1961), and *The Orkhon Türks and problems of the archaeology of the second Eastern Türk Kaghanate* (1997). He died in Praha on 22 November 1969. Filipsky; OSK

J.Nagy, László, born 14 June 1945 at Jászárkoszallás, Hungary, he received a doctorate in 1992 and wrote on Middle Eastern affairs. His writings include *La Naissance et développement du mouvement de libération nationale en Algérie, 1919-1947* (Budapest, 1989). MagyarNKK, 1998-2000; Biográf, 2002, 2004

Jndi, Hajie, 1908- *see* Dzhindi, Dzhauari Adzhie

Joalland, Paul, born 8 November 1870 in Guadaloupe, he was an officer in the French naval artillery. From 1894 to 1897 he served in the French Soudan and subsequently at the École de pyrotechnique de Toulon, where he was commissioned for a mission in Central Africa. He is mainly remembered for his role in the Mission Joalland-Meynier, 1899-1900, in the Zinder region of Niger. He died in an air-raid on Lorient (Morbihan) in September 1940. DBF; *Hommes et destins*, vol. 2, pp. 247-249

Joannou, Perikles Petros, born 27 November 1904 at Erzincan, Turkey, he studied at the Universität München, where he received a Dr.phil. in 1936 for *Die Erfahrung in Platons Ideenlehre.* He was a professor of Greek and Byzantine studies as well as canon law at his alma mater. His writings include *Christliche Metaphysik in Byzanz* (1956), and *Die Ostkirche und die Cathedra Petri im vierten Jahrhundert* (1972). He died near Mantua on 12 January 1972. Kürschner, 1961-1970

Job, Herbert Shipley, C.B.E., fl. 20th cent., he was a banker and, in 1941, a *sous-gouverneur* of the National Bank of Egypt, Alexandria, and a member of the Société Fouad Ier d'économie politique, de statistique et de législation. Note about the author; WhoEgypt, 1952, 1955

Jochelson, Waldemar, 1855-1937 *see* Iokhel'son, Vladimir Il'ich

Jochmus, August Freiherr von Cotignola, born 27 February 1808 at Hamburg, he pursued military studies at Paris in spite of the family's wishes to become a merchant like his father. In 1827 he joined the Greek war of independence, participating in the campaigns until the end of 1829. Since 1828 *aide-de-camp* to the British general, Sir Richard Church, he entered the Greek Ministry of War in 1832 with the rank of captain. With the recommendation of the British minister plenipotentiary at Athens, Edmund Lyons, he came in 1835 to London, where he joined the British Legion under Sir George Evans in the Spanish campaigns. At the end of 1838, he returned to London and was immediately commissioned to Constantinople to prepare the anticipated war in Syria. After the completion of the campaign he remained at the Porte until 1848. Early in 1849 he returned to Germany, but in December of the same year he resigned from the military. Thereafter he travelled extensively in Europe and the East. In 1859 he was raised to a hereditary Austrian peerage. In 1866 he was made lieutenant fieldmarshall without ever seeing action again. From 1870 to 1871 he made his last tour around the world. His writings include *Der syrische Krieg und der Verfall des Osmanen-Reiches seit 1840* (1856), and *The Syrian war and the decline of the Ottoman Empire, 1840-1848, in official and confidential reports, documents, and correspondences with Lord Palmerston, Lord Ponsonby, and the Turkish authorities* (1883). He died in Bamberg, Bavaria, on 14 September 1881. ADtB, vol. 50, pp. 745-46; DtBE; Kornrumpf; ÖBL

Joël, Manuel, born 19 October 1826 at Birnbaum, Prussia, he was first educated privately by his father, rabbi Hayyim Joël, and later studied at the universities of Berlin and Halle. Since 1854 he taught at Jüdisch-theologisches Seminar, Breslau, including German, history, philosophy of religion, and homiletics, concurrently taking a Dr.phil. in 1859 at the Universität Breslau for *Die Religionsphilosophie des Mose ben Maimon.* In 1869 he succeeded to Geiger in the Breslau rabbinate. His writings, in which he pointed out the mental stimulus to Christian scholasticsm, include *Spinoza's Theologisch-politischer Tractat auf seine Quellen geprüft* (1870), *Zur Genesis der Lehre Spinoza's* (1871), and *Beiträge zur Geschichte der Philosophie* (1876). He died in 1890. DtBE; DtBIlnd (2); EncJud; EncJud²; JewEnc; JüdLex; NDB; Wininger

Joesten, Joachim Franz, born 29 June 1907 at Köln, Germany, he studied at German universities and the Université de Nancy without taking a degree. He became a journalist with the Berlin *Weltbühne.* He left Germany in 1933, working first in Denmark and later in Sweden, subsequently emigrating to the United States. Since 1942 he was a news editor with *Newsweek.* His writings include *Rats in the larder* (1939), *Stalwart Sweden* (1943), *Gold today* (1954), and *Öl regiert die Welt* (1958). CurBio, 1942; BioHbDtE

Joffe, Ellis George Howard, born 20th cent., he was a research associate at the Centre for Near and Middle East Studies in the School of Oriental and African Studies, London, and a research fellow at the University of Exeter. His writings include *Social and economic development of Libya* (1982); he was a joint author of *Iran and Iraq; the next five years* (1991), *Social and economic development of Libya* (1982), *Chad* (1995); and he edited *Tribe and state; essays in honour of David Montgomery Hart* (1991). DrBSMES, 1993; EURAMES, 1993; Note about the author

Joffre, Joseph Jacques Césaire, born 12 January 1852 at Rivesaltes (Pyrénées-orientales), France, he graduated from the École polytechnique and the École d'application de l'artillerie et du génie de Fontainebleau. Having first served in the Far East, he was sent in 1892 to French West Africa as director of the railway of the French Sudan, where he took part in the occupation of Timbuctu in 1894. He died in Paris, 3 January 1931. DBF; DcTwHis; EncAm; IndexBFr² (7); Master (15); WhoMilH; *Who was who*, 3

Johannsen, Carl Theodor, born 8 November 1804 at Nortorf, Holstein, Germany, he received a Dr.phil. in 1828 from the Universität Kiel for *Historia Jemenæ e codice manuscripto Arabico cui titulus est Buǵjat al-mustafīd fī aẖbār madīna Zabīd*. He was successively a lecturer in Oriental languages at the univer-sities of Bonn, Kiel, and Copenhagen, where he fell ill soon after his arrival and died on 1 July 1840. His writings include *Die Lehre der lateinischen Wortbildung nach Anleitung der vollkommneren Bildungsgesetze des Sanskrit genetisch behandelt* (1832), and *Die kosmogonischen Ansichten der Inder und Hebräer* (1833). DtBilnd (4); Sezgin

Johansen, Baber, born 15 September 1936, he received a Dr.phil. in 1965 from the Freie Universität Berlin for *Muhammad Husain Haikal; Europa und der Orient im Weltbild eines ägyptischen Liberalen*. He served as a professor of Islamic studies at his alma mater until his retirement, when he settled in Paris. His writings include *Islam und Staat* (1982), *Islamic law on land tax and rent* (1988), and he was a joint author of *Law and society in Islam* (1996). Kürschner, 1980-1996; Private; Schwarz

Johansen, Ulla Christine, born 17 June 1927 at Tallinn, Estonia, she studied ethnology at the Universität Hamburg, where she received a Dr.phil. in 1953 for a study of Yakut ornamentation entitled *Die Ornamentik der Jakuten*. She subsequently spent fifteen months doing field-work among Turkish nomads in the Taurus Mountains, and she later spent ten months in the Soviet Union doing research. From 1962 to 1965 she was associated with the Museum für Völkerkunde, Hamburg. She received a Dr.habil. in 1968 from the Universität Heidelberg and there taught ethnology. She was a joint author of *Gastarbeiterfamilien* (1981), *Beruf und Ethik; Kriterien sozialer Schichtung bei Kleinstädtern in Estland* (1992), and *Symbolik der tibetischen Religionen und des Schamanismus* (2000). Kürschner, 2003, 2005; Note about the author; Schwarz; WhoWor, 1991/92

Johanson, Lars Erik Axel, born 8 March 1936 at Köping, Sweden, he studied at the universities of Stockholm and Uppsala, where he received a doctorate in 1966. He was a sometime professor of Turkology at the Universität Mainz. His writings include *Alttürkisch als "dissimilierende Sprache"* (1977), *Linguistische Beiträge zur Gesamtturkologie* (1991), and he edited *Türkisch und Deutsch im Vergleich* (1999), *Evidentials; Turkic, Iranian and neighbouring languages* (2000), and jointly with Bo Utas, *Arabic prosody and its applications in Muslim poetry* (1994). In 1996 appeared *Symbolae Turcologicae; studies in honour of Lars Johanson on his sixtieth birthday* , and in 2002, *Scholarly depth and accuracy; a festschrift to Lars Johanson*. IWWAS, 1976/77; Kürschner, 1980-2005; Schoeberlein; WhoWor, 1978/79

Johns, Anthony Hearle, born 28 August 1928 at Wimbledon, England, he received a Ph.D. in 1954 from the School of Oriental and African Studies, London, for *Malay Sufism as illustrated in an anonymous collection of seventeenth century tracts*. In 1963, he was appointed a professor of Indonesian languages and literatures at the Australian National University, Canberra. In 1997, appeared *Islam; essays on scripture, thought and society, a festschrift in honour of Anthony H. Johns*. He was a joint author of *Islam in Asia* (1984). IntWW, 1989-2002; *MESA Roster of members*, 1990; Sluglett; WhoAus, 1968-1992; WhoWor, 1980/81

Johns, Cedrid Norman, born in the early 20th cent., he joined the British School of Archaeology in Jerusalem in 1928 and in the following year he was working in the clearance and conservation of Ajlun castle in Transjordan. It was about 1930 that he was appointed as field archaeologist in the Palestine's Government Department of Antiquities; and from that time, for nearly twenty years, his contributions to the *Quarterly of the Department of Antiquities in Palestine*, ending in 1950, are an impressive memorial to his versatility as an archaeologist and, in particular, to his special interest and depth of research in the period of the Crusades. He left Palestine with the end of the Mandate in the spring of 1948. Some years later, after a spell of work in North Africa, he joined the Royal Commission on Ancient and Historical Monuments in Wales and Monmouthshire as a principal investigator, and moved to Aberystwyth. He died in September 1992. *Levante*, 25 (1993), p. iv

Johns, Richard, born 20th cent., he was in 1972 a Middle East correspondent of the *Financial Times*, and a joint author of *The House of* Saud (1981), and its translation, *Die Dynastie der Sauds, Wüsten-krieger und Weltfinanziers* (1983). Note about the author; ZKO

Johnson, Amy Jo, born in 1969 in Iowa, she graduated B.A. and M.A. in political science from Emory University, Atlanta, Ga., and received a Ph.D. in 1998 in history and Middle Eastern studies from Harvard University for a thesis on rural development in Egypt until 1952. She subsequently taught at Berry College, Mount Berry, Ga. Her writings include *Reconstructing rural Egypt; Dr. Ahmed Hussein and the history of Egyptian development* (2004). She died on 2 December 2004 of injuries sustained in a November automobile accident. *MESA bulletin*, 39 i (2005), pp. 157-58; NatFacDr, 2005

Johnson, Basil Leonard Clyde, born 21 November 1919 at Cockpen, Scotland, he graduated from King's College, London, where he also received a Ph.D. in 1947. Since 1971 he was a professor of geography at the Australian National University, Canberra. His writings include *South Asia; selective studies of the essential geography of India, Pakistan and Ceylon* (1969), *Bangladesh* (1975), *Pakistan* (1979), *Development in South Asia* (1983), *Geographical dictionary of India* (2001), and he was a joint author of *Place, people and work in Japan* (1972), and *Sri Lanka; land, people, and economy* (1981). ConAu, 120; WhoAus, 1971-1991|; WhoWor, 1978/79

Johnson, Douglas Leslie, born about 1940, he received a Ph.D. in 1972 from the University of Chicago for *Jabal al-Akhdar, Cyrenaica; an historical geography of settlement and livelihood*. He was in 1995 associated with the Department of Geography at Clark University, Worcester, Mass. His writings include *The Nature of nomadism; a comparative study of pastoral migration in southwestern Asia and northern Africa* (1969), and *Land degradation; creation and destruction* (1995). MESA *Roster of members*, 1977-1982; NatFacDr, 1995; Selim

Johnson, Frank Edward, born 3 July 1873 at Norwich, Conn., he was an artist and in 1926 a member of the Washington Water Color Club. AmIndex (2)

Johnson, Gail Cook, born in 1947, her writings include *High-level man-power in Iran; from hidden conflict to crisis* (1980), and *Recruiting, retaining, and motivating the federal workforce* (1991). LC

Johnson, George William, born 4 November 1802 at Blackheath, Kent, England, he was from 1839 to 1842 a professor of moral and political economy at Hindoo College, Calcutta, and concurrently edited in Calcutta the *Englishman newspaper*, and *Government gazette*. He was the owner of the Fairfax manuscripts published as *The Fairfax correspondence* (1848-67). His writings include *The Stranger in India* (1843), and its translation, *Ostindiens Gegenwart und Zukunft* (1844). He died in 1866. BioIn, 2; Boase; BritInd (7); DNB

Johnson, H. H., born 19th cent., his writings include *Reminiscences of the Near East, 1891-1913* (London, 1920). BLC; NUC, pre-1956

Johnson, Henry *Harrold*, born in 1869, he was a public lecturer and a secretary of the Moral Instruction League, London. His writings include *The House of life* (1911), *A Short life of Jesus* (1933), and *The Voice of one; empire lyrics* (1937). BLC; NUC, pre-1956; WhoLit, 1916

Johnson, J. Ray, he was in 1928 the editor of *The Interpreter*, organ of the Foreign Language Information Service in New York. Note about the author

Johnson, Jeremiah Augustus, born 3 June 1836 at Boston, Mass., he was a lawyer who served as consul and consul-general in Beirut from 1858-1867 and 1867-1870 respectively. He died on 28 February 1914. Kornrumpf; Shavit; TwCBDA, vol. 6; WhAm, 1

Johnson, Joseph Esrey, born 30 April 1906 at Longdale, Va., he graduated from Harvard, where he also received a Ph.D. in 1943. He was a professor and president of American universities, and from 1942 to 1947, he was associated with the U.S. Department of State. In August 1961, the Palestine Conciliation Commission appointed him president of the Carnegie Endowment for International Peace as its special envoy to the Middle East. He was charged with presenting proposals for the solution of the Arab refugee problem. His proposals were not accepted by Israel or the Arabs, and he resigned in February 1962. His writings include *Negotiating with the Russians* (1951), its translation, *Mit den Russen am Verhandlungstisch* (1953), and *China and the United Nations* (1959). He died in Lynchburg, Va., on 24 October 1990. AmM&WSc, 1973 S, 1978 S; CurBio, 1950, 1991; IntWW, 1974/75-1983; Note about the author; NYT, 27 October 1990, p. 28, cols. 5-6; WhAm, 10; WhoAm, 1974-1976/77; WhoWor, 1978/79

Johnson, Lee, fl. 20th cent., he was a historian of art, whose writings include *Delacroix* (1963), and *The Paintings of Eugène Delacroix; a critical catalogue, 1816-1831* (Oxford, 1981-86).

Johnson, Michael, born 20th cent., his writings include *Class and client in Beirut; the Sunni Muslim community and the Lebanese state, 1840-1985* (London, 1986), and *All honorable men; the social origins of war in Lebanon* (2001).

Johnson, Nels, born about 1948, he received a Ph.D. in 1978 from McGill University, Montreal, for *'Uthmān's shirt; aspects of Palestinian refugee ideology*. His writings include *Islam and the politics of meaning in Palestinian nationalism* (1982). Selim³; ZKO

Johnson, Pamela Ryden, born about 1950, she received a Ph.D. in 1979 from the University of California at Berkeley for *A Sufi shrine in modern Tunisia*. Her writings include *Egypt, the Egyptian American rural improvement service; a point four project, 1952-1963* (Washington, D.C., U.S. AID, 1983). LC

Johnson, Roswell Park, fl. 20th cent., he was a clergyman who in 1959 served as a Middle East representative of the Commission on Oecumenical Mission and Relations of the United Presbyterian Church in the U.S.A. His writings include *A Critical and explanatory translation of portions of the anonymous Ta'rīkh-i Sīstān* (1941), and *Middle East pilgrimage* (1958). Note about the author; NUC, pre-1956

Johnson, Vernon Webster, born 5 December 1899 at DeKalb, Illinois, he graduated from Northern Illinois State Teachers College, and received a Ph.D. in 1935 from the University of Wisconsin. He was an agricultural economist with the U.S. Department of Agriculture and served as a consultant in Lebanon from 1952 to 1956, and subsequently until 1961 in Iran. His writings include *Farm credit activities in selected countries* (1954), *Land problems and policies* (1954), and the pamphlet, *The Economics of land distribution with reference to Iran* (1960). AmM&WSc, 1973 S, 1978 S; NUC, 1967-1967

Johnson, W. H., born in 1831, the son of an ordnance officer in the Honorable East India Company, he was educated at Mussoorie, India, and became employed in the North-West Himalyan Survey, 1848 to 1852. He was the first European traveller who visited the plains of Khotan in 1865. From 1866 until his death in 1882 he was in the service of the Maharajah of Kashmir. Boase; Embacher

Johnson-Davies, Denys, born 20th cent., his writings include the translations from the Arabic, *Modern Arabic short stories* (1967), *Season of migration to the north* (1970), *The Wedding of Zein and other stories* (1970), *The Smell of it and other stories* (1971), *Egyptian short stories* (1978), *Egyptian one-act plays* (1981), *The Slave's dream and other stories* (1991), *Aladdin and the lamp* (1995), and *Bandarshah* (1996). ZKO

Johnston, Sir Alexander, born in 1775 in a British colony, from where he returned with his parents to England in 1792. He trained for the law, and studied for some time at the Universität Göttingen. He was called to the bar from Lincoln's Inn and became a colonial administrator. He died in London in 1849. BritInd (3); DNB

Johnston, Charles, born in 1867 at Ballykilbeg, Ireland, he was educated in England, and Dublin University. In 1886, he entered the Bengal Civil Service and reached India in November 1888. Two years later he was invalided. He travelled in Europe before going to the United States in 1896. In 1908, he was a special lecturer in political science at the University of Wisconsin. His writings include translations from the Sanskrit, Russian, and German. He died in 1931. DcNAA; Master (1); WhAm, 1; WhNAA

Johnston, Sir Harry Hamilton, born 12 June 1858 in South London, he was an explorer, naturalist, and painter who travelled extensively in Africa to gather geographic information and botanical samples as well as to record the languages and customs of native peoples. He is best remembered for his Imperialist British interests and for his ethnocentric attempts to make sense of the complex African continent. His writings include *A History of the colonization of Africa by alien races* (1930), and *The Story of my life* (1923). He died in obscurity in Nottinghamshire on 31 August 1927 while on a journey to visit his sister. Roland A. Oliver wrote *Sir Harry Hamilton Johnston and the scamble for Africa* (1957), and James A. Casada wrote *Sir Harry Hamilton Johnston; a bio-bibliographical study* (1977). BioIn, 11; BritInd (9); ConAu, 190; DLB, 74 (1997), pp. 191-200; DNB; Henze; LexAfrika; Master (12); Who was who, 2; WhWE

Johnston, Robert Lyon Nelson, born 19th cent., he was a British consular officer who was appointed a vice-consul at Mogador on 21 June 1878. He intermittently served as an acting consul until October 1892. He was Lloyd's agent at Mogador. His writings include *Morocco, the land of the setting sun* (London, 1902), *Tales from a Moorish nursery* (Mogador, 1914), and he was a joint author of *Moorish lotos leaves; glimpses of southern Morocco* (London, 1883), and he translated *The Songs of Sidi Hammo* (London, 1907). BLC; BritInd = *Foreign Office list*, 1900; NUC, pre-1956

Johnston, Scott Doran, born 8 October 1922 at Evanston, Illinois, he graduated in 1944 from the University of Minnesota, where he also obtained a Ph.D. in 1952. Since 1947 he taught political science at Hamline University, St. Paul, Minn., a post which he still held in 1990. AmM&WSc, 1973 S & 1978 S; *MESA Roster of members*, 1977-1990; NatFacDr, 1990

Johnstone, Barbara, born 24 March 1952, she taught English from the late 1980s to 2003 at Texas A&M University; in 2004 she was a professor of English at Carnegie Mellon University, Pittsburgh, Pa., a post which she also held in 2005. Her writings include *Stories, community, and place; narratives from middle America* (1990), *Repetition in Arabic discourse; paradigms, syntagms, and the ecology of language* (1991), *The Linguistic individual; self-expression in language and linguistics* (1996), and *Qualitative methods in socio-linguistics* (2000). LC; NatFacDr, 1990-2005

Johnstone, Charles, born in 1719 at Carrigogunnel, Limerick, Eire, he was educated at Dublin University. Although subsequently called to the bar, he pursued an interest in literature and wrote between 1760 and 1765 a novel, *Chrysal, or the Adventure of a guinee*, which made a sensation and was translated into German, *Chrysal oder Begebenheiten einer Guinee* (1775), and into French, *Les Aventures comiques et palisantes d'Antoine Varnish* (1788). He went to India in 1782, being shipwrecked on the way out. At Calcutta he acquired a fortune and became a joint proprietor of a newspaper in Bengal. He contributed regularly to the periodical press under the *nom de plume* Oneiropolos. He also wrote other novels. He died in Calcutta in 1800, though the place of his death has been disputed. BiD&SB; BritInd (14); Buckland; CasWL; DLB, 39 (1985), pp. 293-300; DNB; Master (15)

Johnstone, Penelope C., born 20th cent., she received a Dr.phil. in 1972 from Oxford University for *Arabic botany and pharmacology, with particular reference to the work of al-Zahrawi and Ibn Juljul in Muslim Spain*. She was a sometime secretary to the Centre for the Study of Islam and Christian-Muslim Relations, Selly Oak Colleges, Brimingham, and was later associated with the Oriental Institute, Oxford, as a tutor in Arabic. She edited *Studies in medieval Arabic medicine; theory and practice* (1984), a collection of Max Meyerhof's artices. DrBSMES, 1993; Sluglett

Johnstone, Thomas Muir, born 18 January 1924, he received a Ph.D. in 1962 from the School of Oriental and African Studies, London, for *Studies on the Arabic dialects of the Persian Gulf*. He was a professor of Arabic at the University of London from 1970 to 1982. His writings include *Eastern Arabian dialect studies* (1967), its translation into Arabic in 1975, *Jibbālī lexicon* (1981), and *Mehri lexicon and English-Mehri word-list, with index of the English definitions in the Jibbālī lexicon* (1987). In 1988 appeared *A Miscellany of MIddle Eastern articles in memoriam T. M. Johnstone*. He died on 11 January 1983. ConAu, 114; *Index Islamicus* (5); Sluglett; Who, 1972-1983; Who was who, 8; ZKO

Joiner, Charles Adrian, born 26 August 1932 at West Frankfort, Illinois, he graduated in 1954 from South Illinois University and received his Ph.D. in 1958 from the University of Illinois for *Administrative organization as a social system*. Since 1962 he was a professor of political science at Temple University, Philadelphia, Pa., a post which he still held in 1995. His writings include *Organizational analysis* (1964), and *The Politics of massacre* (1974). ConAu, 77-80; IWWAS, 1976/77; NatFacDr, 1990-1995

Joja, Constantin, born 20th cent., his writings include *Sensuri şi valori regăsite* (Bucureşti, 1981), and *Actualitatea tradiţiei arhitecturale româneşti* (Bucureşti, 1984). OSK

Joki, Aulis Johannes, born 2 June 1913 at Viipuri (Viborg), Finland, he studied at Helsinki University, where he received a doctorate in 1952 for *Die Lehnwörter des Sajansamojedischen*. He was a professor at his alma mater until his retirement. His writings include *Wörterverzeichnis der Kyzyl-Sprache* (Helsinki, 1953), *Der wandernde Apfel* (1964), *Masilman kielet* (1966), *Tutkimusmatkoilla Pohjolassa* (1967), *Uralier un Indogermanen* (1973), *Kaukomailta ja työkammioista* (1988), and he edited *Kai Donners kleinere Wörterverzeichnisse aus dem Jurak-, Jenissei- und Tawgy-samoje-dischen, Katschatatarischen und Tungusischen* (1956). He died on 8 February 1989. IWWAS, 1976/77; Vem och vad, 1970-1985

Joleaud, Jean *Léonce* François, born 8 November 1880 at Vincennes, France, he studied at the Faculté des sciences de Paris, where he graduated in 1903 and received a doctorate in 1912 for *Études géologique de la chaîne numidique et des monts de Constantine*. From 1907 to 1913 he was employed with the Service de la carte géologique de l'Algérie. During the war he was gravely injured in 1914 and left behind on the battle-field as dead, he was invalided seventy percent. He resumed his studies and petrochemical missions in North Africa in 1917 and became a professor of palaeotology at the Sorbonne. His writings include *Le Pétrole dans l'Afrique du nord* (1926). He died in Paris on 15 April 1938. BN; DBF; *Revue de géographie marocaine*, 22 (1938), pp. 272-73

Joliffe, Thomas Robert, 1780-1872 *see* Jolliffe, Thomas Robert

Jolivet, Jean Gaston Marie Louis, born 9 January 1925 at Saint-Cloud (Seine-et-Oise), France, he was educated at the Lycée Louis-le-Grand, École Normale Supérieure, and École Pratique des Hautes Études, Paris, gaining a diploma and a doctorate. He taught medieval Latin and Arabic philosophy at the École Pratique des Hautes Études, from 1965 to 1993. A member of the Société Internationale pour l'Étude de la Philosophie médiévale, and the Société Internationale d'Histoire des Sciences et de la Philosophie Arabes et Islamiques, his writings include L'Intellect selon Kindī (1971), Philosophie médiévale arabe et latine (1997), and La théologie et les Arabes (2002). In 1997 appeared Langages et philosophie; hommage à Jean Jolivet. AnEIFr, 1997; Private; WhoFr, 1977/78-2004/2005

Jolliffe (Joliffe), Thomas Robert, born in 1780, he was educated at Trinity College, Cambridge, and became a rector of Babington near Frome from 15 February 1810 to death on 15 June 1872 in Ammerdown Park near Bath. His writings include Letters from Palestine (1819), its translations, Palästina, Syrien und Ägypten im Jahre 1817 (1821), and Reis in Palestina, Syrië en Egypte, gedaan in het jaar 1817 (1822). Boase; Egyptology; Sezgin; ZKO

Jolowicz, Heimann (Heinrich, Heymann), born 23 August 1816 at Santomischl, Prussia, he studied at the Universität Berlin, without taking a degree, and then filled the position of preacher at Marienwerder, Kulm, and finally Köslin, Prussia. He belonged to the Jewish ultra-Reform Party and always expressed his views fearlessly. After he retired from office, he settled in Königsberg, where he delivered a series of lectures on the history and development of Judaism, and on the history of the Synagogue service. He established a radical Reform congregation, with Sunday service and German liturgy. His writings include Blüten rabbinischer Weisheit (1845), Der poetische Orient enthaltend die urzüglichsten Dichtungen der Afghanen, Araber, Amener (1853), Polyglotte der orientalischen Poesie (1853), Bibliotheca ægyptica (1858-61), Blütenkranz morgenländischer Dichtung (1860), and Geschichte der Juden in Königsberg (1867). He died in Königsberg on 31 January 1875. DtBiInd (1); EncJud²; JewEnc; JüdLex; Sezgin; Wininger

Joly, Alexandre, born 30 April 1870 at Montreuil-sous-Bois (Seine-S.-Denis), France, he graduated from the Lycée Henry-IV, Paris, and subsequently settled in Algeria for reasons of health. He became successively a public works' engineer at Alger, a teacher at the Medersa d'Alger in 1896, and, in 1901, at the Medersa de Constantine. In 1907, he was appointed to the public chair of Arabic at Alger. He accompanied the Mission Flamand to the Touat Oases, 1899-1900, as a geologist; went on a mission to southern Algeria to study the Muslim brotherhoods; and was a member of the scientific mission to Morocco, 1905-1906. He died in Constantine on 27 February 1913. DBF; Revue africaine, 57 (1913), pp. 5-6

Joly, E. Gertrude, born about 1900, she was in her younger years on the staff of the British Syrian Training College, Beirut. She married a business man (whose shipping firm claims to be the oldest British firm in Lebanon, and who was a Palestine Government official during the 1939-45 war) [possibly Kenneth Henry Joly, born 11 July 1892 at Beirut and partner of Henry Head & Co.] During the war, she was in charge of the training department of the Jerusalem Girls' College. During her long residence in the Near East she acquired a first-hand knowledge of the women of the region, particularly those of Lebanon. Her writings include The English-Arabic cookery book (Beirut, 1950). LC; Note about the author; WhoEgypt, 1955

Joly, Fernand, born 10 March 1917 at Rosny-sous-Bois (Seine), France, he was educated at the lycées Colbert and Chaptal, and studied at the Faculté des lettres et sciences, Paris. After his agrégation in history and geography, he taught at Oujda and Casablanca from 1942 to 1949; from 1946 to his retirement in 1986 he was a professor at the Université de Paris. His writings include Géographie du Maroc (1948), Études sur le relief du Sud-Est marocain (1962), La Cartographie (1976), and he was a joint author of Les hamada sud-marocaines; résultat de la mission d'étude, 1951 (Tanger, 1954), and Recherches sur la morphologie de la côte atlantique du Maroc (Tanger, 1954). WhoFr, 1977/78-1994/95|

Joly, Geneviève, born about 1945 in France, she was a librarian at the Société asiatique, Paris, until the 1980s, when she accepted a post in French archaeolgy at Luxor, Egypt. She was a founding member of the Middle East Libaries Committee International and served as its permanent secretary. Private

Joly, Robert, fl. 20th cent., he was a town planner and architect at the École d'architecture de Paris. His writings include Assistance architecturale du Lot (1975), La Ville et la civilisation urbaine (1985), and he was a joint author of Industrialisation du bâtiment (1978), and Le Paysage des lotissements (1978). LC; Livres disponibles, 2004

Jolyet, Antoine, born 19th cent., he wrote Le Transport des bois dans les forêts coloniales (1903), and he was a joint author of Traité pratique de sylviculture (1901). His trace is lost after an article in 1912.

Jomard, Edmé François, born 17 November 1777 at Versailles, France, he was educated at the lycées of Versailles, and Paris as well as the Collège Mazarin (Institut de France); he graduated from the École des ponts et chaussée, the Polytechnique, and the École d'application du génie. In 1798 he accompanied the French expedition to Egypt as captain and cartographer. In 1803 he became a member of the Commission d'Égypte which produced the official account of the Expedition, *Description de l'Égypte ou recueil des observations et des recherches qui ont été faites en Égypte pendant l'expédition de l'armée française* (1809-1822). A member of the Académie des inscriptions et belles-lettres since 1818, he became in 1828 a curator of the *dépôt de géographie* at the Bibliothèque nationale, Paris, and with Ferdinand de Lesseps, he was in 1855 one of the founders of the Compagnie du canal de Suez. He died in Paris on 23 September 1862. *Bulletin de la Société de géographie*, 5e série, 5 (1863), pp. 81-101; Dawson; DBF; Egyptology; EncAm; Goldschmidt; Hill; Hoefer; IndexBFr² (8); Pallas

Jomier, Jacques Louis Gaston, born 7 March 1914 at Paris, he was educated at the Lycée Janson-de-Sailly, Faculté des lettres de Paris, and the Facultés dominicains du Saulchoir; he obtained a *doctorat ès-lettres*. He entered the Dominicans in 1932 and was ordained in 1939. He studied Arabic at Paris from 1941 to 1944, and subsequently at Cairo. He later taught successively at the Institut dominicain d'études orientales in Cairo, as well as in Mosul, Ibadan, Kinshasa, and Toulouse. He served as a consultant to the Vatican's Secretariat for non-Christians. His writings include *Le mahmal et la caravane égyptienne des pèlerins de la Mecque, XIIIe-XXe siècles* (1953), *Le Commentaire coranique du Manār* (1954), *Bible et Coran* (1958), its translation, *Bibel und Koran* (1962), *Manuel d'arabe égyptien* (1964), *Grands thèmes du Coran* (1978), *Pour connaître l'islam* (1988), its translation, *How to understand Islam* (1989), and *L'Islam vécu en Égypte, 1945-1975* (1994). WhoFr, 1977/78-2001/2002|

Jónás, János, born 4 November 1848 at Kiskunhalas, Hungary, he studied classical and Oriental languages as well as ethnography. In 1885 he was appointed a principal of the Pozsony commercial college. His writings include *Mohammed elötli Moallakat* (1868) as well as tranlations from the German. He died in Eperjes (Prešov) on 3 January 1911. GeistigeUng; Pallas

Jonchay, Ivan du, 1899- *see* Du Jonchay, Ivan

Joncheray, Jean Pierre, born 20th cent., he was a marine archaeologist whose writings include *Essai de classification des amphores découvertes lors de fouilles sous-marines* (1970), its translation, *Amphoren; Bestimmung und Einteilung nach ihren Merkmalen* (1982), *Rencontre d'archéologie sous-marine de Fréjus-Saint-Raphaël, 1974* (1975), *Naufrages en Provence ou Livre des éspaves* (1984), and *50 épaves corses* (2002).

Jones, Alan, born 16 August 1933, he was a lecturer in Islamic studies at Oxford. His writings include *Romance kharjas in Andalusian Arabic muwaššah poetry* (1987), *Early Arabic poetry* (1992); he translated from the Arabic of al-Tabarī, *The Commentary on the Qur'an* (1987); he edited *The 'Uddat al-jalīs of 'Alī ibn Bishr; an anthology of Andalusian Arabic muwashshahāt* (1992), *Kitāb Jaysh al-tawsīh*, of Muhammad ibn al-Khatīb al-Salmānī's (1997); and he was a joint editor of *Studies on the Muwaššah and the Kharja*; Exeter International Colloquium (1991). LC; Note about the author; ZKO

Jones, Arleigh Willard, born in 1894 at Richmond, Iowa, he was the husband of Christina Hendry Jones. He served two long terms as principal of a Quaker boys school in Ramallah, Palestine. In 1963, he was an executive secretary of the Central Co-ordinating Committee of Volunteer Agencies. He died in 1973. Note about the author; Shavit

Jones, Christina Hendry, born 8 November 1896 at Greennock, Scotland, she was married to Arleigh Willard Jones. She graduated in 1921 from William Penn College, taught English and history at Ramallah, and served in various capacities with the Near East Christian Council Committee for Refugee Work, 1948-1962. Her writings include *Friends in Palestine* (1944), *American Friends in world missions* (Richmond, Ind., 1946), *The Untempered wind; forty years in Palestine* (1976), and the undated pamphlet, *Peasant life in Palestine among the villagers in the Holy Land* (Richmond, Ind., American Friends' Board of Missions). She died in 1984. ConAu, 73-76; NUC, pre-1956

Jones, Dalu, born 20th cent., he was an editor of *AARP; art and archaeology research papers*, and a joint editor of *International architect*. His writings include *Qallaline tile panels; tile pictures in North Africa, 16th to 20th century* (1979), and he was a joint author of *The Arts of Islam* (1976), *A Mirror of princes; the Mughals and the Medici* (1987), and *Lo specchio del principe; mecenatismi paralleli, Medici e Moghul* (1991). Note about the author; ZKO

Jones, Dorsey Dee, born 18 December 1898 in Greene County, Mo., he graduated in 1920 from Drury College, Springfield, Mo., and received a Ph.D. in 1929 from State University of Iowa for *Edwin Chadwick and the early public health movement in England*. From 1926 to his retirement in 1971 he taught history and political science at the University of Arkansas, Fayetteville. His writings include *Under the Russian canopy* (1936), and *Russia; a concise history* (1955). DrAS, 1974 H, 1978 H|

Jones, Eli *Stanley*, he was born on 3 January 1883 at Fairfield, N.Y., and graduated from Asbury College, and was ordained in 1908. He was a missionary in India from 1907 until his retirement in 1954. His writings include *The Christ of the Indian road* (1925), *Christ's alternative to communism* (1935), *The contribution of E. Stanley Jones*; edited by R. W. Taylor (1973). He died in Bareilly, India, on 25 January 1973. Shavit - Asia; WhAm, 7

Jones, Sir Harford, Baronet Brydges, born 12 January 1764 at Boultibrooke outside Presteigne in Radnorshire, England, he entered the East India Company early in life and spent nearly twenty years in Basra and Baghdad, during which time he paid two visits to Persia and learnt the language. In 1807 he was created Baronet Brydges for the sole purpose of representing British interests in Persia as a Crown's Envoy. In 1809 he successfully concluded a preliminary treaty of friendship and alliance with Fath 'Alī Shāh. He remained in Persia for four years, during which he travelled extensively in the Baluchistan region on the Arabian Sea coast, parts of Afghanistan, as well as the south shore of the Caspian Sea. He travelled home by way of Constantinople, where Sultan Mahmud II presented him with a royal gift for the help he had given the Turks in Persia. Though his Persian success was applauded in London, he was rewarded with neither honours nor with further employment. He retired to the life of a country gentleman and writer. His writings include *An Account of the transactions of His Majesty's Mission to the Court of Persia, 1807-1811* (1834), and he translated from a Persian manuscript *The Dynasty of the Kajars* (1833). He died in 1847 where he had been born. BritInd (2); DNB; IndianBiInd (3); WhWE; Wright, 5-8

Jones, Howard Palfrey, he was born on 2 January 1899 at Chicago, and graduated from Columbia University, New York. Until 1939, he was in the newspaper and publication business. After the second World War, he was engaged in United States foreign affairs, becoming ambassador to Indonesia from 1958 to 1965. His writings include *Indonesia; the possible dream* (1971). He died in Stanford, Calif., on 18 September 1973. Master (4); Shavit - Asia

Jones, James (Jack) Henry, born in 1894, he was educated at Port Talbot Elementary School and took a Workers' Educational Association course at Bangor University. During the 1914-18 war he served in the Imperial Camel Corps with Lawrence of Arabia. He was connected with the steel industry all his life, and was a trade unionist of knowledge and experience. During the 1939-45 war he was selected by H.M. Government to represent the war workers of Great Brtian on a mission to the United States of America. He was a member of a delegation sent out by H.M. Government, as a result of a certain amount of political agitation and consequent labour unrest in Persia, to enquire into the situation generally and to proffer the Anglo-Iranian Oil Company such advice and assistance as the delegation was able to give in connection with the Company's plans for the betterment of the welfare of its employees. In 1950 he was elected Labour M.P. for Rotherham. He died in 1962. Note; *Who was who*, 6

Jones, John Felix, born early 19th cent., he joined the Bombay Marine at the age of fourteen. He was employed in the survey of the Red Sea, from 1829 to 1834. By the late summer of 1839 he had begun work in the Persian Gulf, where he was to spend the next twenty-five years. He was a Political Agent in Bushire, Persia, from 1855 to 1862 and had an important role to play in the British invasion of southern Persia in 1856. His writings include *Topography of Niniveh* (1853), and *Vestiges of Assyria… constructed from trigonometrical survey … in 1852 at the command of the Government of India* (1855). He died on 3 September 1878. Buckland; DNB; NUC, pre-1956

Jones, John *Marsden* Beaumont, born about 1925, he received a Ph.D. in 1953 from the School of Oriental and African Studies, London, for *A critical text of al-Waqīdī, with an introduction and philological, historical and literary notes.* He was a professor of Islamic history and modern Arabic at the Center for Arabic Studies, American University in Cairo. He was a joint author of *A'lām al-adab al-mu'āsir fī Misr* (1975), and he edited *The Kitāb al-Maghāzī of al-Wāqidī* in three volumes (1966). Note about the author; Sluglett; SOAS Library catalogue; ZKO

Jones, Lewis Bevan, fl. 20th cent., he was a missionary of the Church Missionary Society, London, and, in 1930, became the first principal of the Henry Martyn School of Islamics, Lahore. His writings include *The People of the mosque* (1932), *Christianity explained to Muslims; a manual for Christian workers* (1938), and jointly with his wife, Violet Rhoda Stanford Jones, *Woman in Islam* (1941). He died on 31 March 1960. MW, 50 (1960), p. 303; 51 (1961), pp. 128-131

Jones, Lura *JaFran*, born 14 January 1941 at Holdrege, Nebr., she graduated in 1962 from Ottawa (Kans.) University and received her Ph.D. in 1977 from the University of Washington at Seattle for *The 'Isāwīya of Tunisia and their music.* From 1978 to 1993 she was a professor of ethnomusicology at Bowling Green (Ohio) State University, where she also served as chairman of the Department of

Composition and History during many of those years. She died on 1 March 1997 at her home after a two-year battle with cancer. *MESA bulletin*, 33 (1999), p. 149; *MESA Roster of members*, 1982-1990; ZKO

Jones, Marsden, born about 1925 *see* Jones, John *Marsden* Beaumont

Jones, Norman Leslie, born 27 April 1951 at Twin Falls, Iowa, he graduated in 1972 from Idaho State University, and received a Ph.D. in 1978 from Clare College, Cambridge. In 1977 he was appointed a professor of history at Utah State University, a post which he still held in 2005; he served as chairman of department during many of those years. His writings include *Faith by statute; Parliament and the settlement of religion, 1559* (1982), *God and moneylenders; usury and law in early modern England* (1990), *The English Reformation; religion and cultural adaptation* (2002), and he was a joint editor of *The Parliament of Elizabethan England* (1990). ConAu, 146; NatFacDr, 2005

Jones, Robert, born about 1945, he received a M.Phil. in 1981 from Warburg Institute, University of London, and subsequently pusued doctoral research on the subject of learning Arabic in Renaissance Europe. He was for many years employed by the antiquarian bookseller Bernard Quaritch, London, as a Middle East specialist. DrBSMES, 1993; *MESA Roster of members*, 1990; Private

Jones, Russell Albert, born 20th cent., he received a Ph.D. in 1968 from the University of London for *A study from Malay manuscripts of the legend of the Islamic Sufi saint Ibrahim ibn Adham.* Sluglett; SOAS library catalogue

Jones, Sarah A., born 20th cent., she received B.Litt. in 1976 from Oxford University for *The implications of ethnic division in Afghanistan, with particular reference to the Hazara Mongols.* Sluglett

Jones, Schuyler, born 7 February 1930 at Wichita, Kans., he received a M.A. in 1965 from Edinburgh University, and a D.Phil. in 1970 from Oxford University. In the same year he there began a teaching career in cultural anthropology. He was a museum director, and lecturer, Pitt Rivers Museum, School of Anthropolgy and Museum Ethnography, Oxford. He served as a trustee, The Horniman Museum, Forest Hill, London. Since the 1950s he was interested in Afghanistan, where he spent six years living in the country and conducting anthropological research in Nuristan. His writings include *An Annotated bibliography of Nuristan (Kafiristan) and the Kalash Kafirs of Chitral* (1966-69), *The Political organization of the Kam Kafirs* (1967), *Men of influence in Nuristan* (1974), *Afghanistan* (1992), *Tibetan nomads* (1996), and he was a joint author of *Nuristan* (Graz, 1979). DrAS, 1974 H, 1978 H; Private; Schoeberlein; Who, 1986-2005; WhoWor, 1984/85

Jones, Walter *Idris*, born 18 January 1900 at Llanelli, Carmarthenshire, Wales, he graduated from University College of Wales, Aberystwyth. He was a Rhondda and Frank Smart research student of Gonville and Caius College, Cambridge, where he took his Ph.D. in 1925. After leaving Cambridge, he became an industrial chemist, and from 1933 to 1946 served as director of research of the Powell Duffryn Company. He subsequently accepted the post of director-general of research for the National Coal Board. In 1940, he received a M.A. from the University of Wales for *The Aden dialect of Arabic; a study of its grammatical peculiarities as compared with the classical language.* He died in 1971. *Nature*, 158 (1946), p. 781; Sluglett; *Who was who*, 7

Jones, Sir William, born 28 September 1747, he was an extraordinary man; he learnt twenty-eight languages, including Arabic, Persian and Turkish during his studies at Oxford, became a judge of the Calcutta High Court, and was the leading Oriental scholar of his day. He is remembered above all for his translations from Sanskrit, but he did major work also from Arabic and Persian. He wrote sometimes in Latin and composed in Greek. His marriage was blissfully happy, although his wife had to wait many years before he felt he had a large enough income to propose. In the India of the period, he was one of the few whose integrity was total. He died in Calcutta on 27 April 1794. Muh. Abu Taher wrote *Sir William Jones; the romantics and the Victorians* (1976), and Garland H. Cannon, *The Life and mind of Oriental Jones* (1990). AnaBrit; *Asiatic review*, 40 (1944), pp. 186-96; BritInd (33); Buckland; DLB, 109 (1991), pp. 183-92; EncBrit; Fück, pp. 129-30; *Index Islamicus* (17); *Journal of the Asiatic Society*, Calcutta, 2 i (1960), pp. 47-61; Mason; PorLing, vol. 1, pp. 1-57 (3); Riddick

Jonesco (Ionesco), Joan (Ion), fl. 1850-54, his writings include *Excursion agricole dans la plaine de la Dobrodja* (Constantinople, Imprimerie du *Journal de Constantinople*, 1850). ZKO

de Jong, Frederick, born 20th cent., he received a doctorate in 1977 for *Turuq and turuq-linked institutions in nineteenth century Egypt; a historical study in organizational dimensions of Islamic mysticism*, and subsequently became a professor of Middle Eastern studies at the Rijksuniversiteit te Leiden. His writings include *Names, religious denominations, and ethnicity of settlements in western Thrace* (1980), *Islamic mysticism contested; thirteen centuries of controversies and polemics* (1999), *Sufi orders in Ottoman and post-Ottoman Egypt and the Middle East; collected studies* (2000), and he edited the conference proceedings, *Islam, sects and Sufism* (1992). LC; *MESA Roster of members*, 1990; Note about the author

de **Jong**, Karel Hendrik Eduard, born 9 February 1872 at Biebrich on Rhine, he went to school in Germany and Genève and since 1892 studied classics at Leiden, completing his study in 1900 with a doctorate for *De Apuleio Isiacorum Mysteriorum teste*. In 1910 he was appointed a lecturer in Roman philosophy at his alma mater, and in this capacity he taught for the rest of his life, specializing in psychical research. His particular interest in magic and mystery found expression in his *De magie bij de Grieken en Romeinen* (1921), and *De parapsychologie* (1936). In the 1920s he ventured into the political area when he was associated with first the Verbond van Actualisten and later the Vaterlandsch Verbond. He was a lifelong bachelor who, apart from his casual apparel, was a familiar ascetic apparition at the Royal Library in den Haag. His writings include *Das antike Mysterienwesen* (1909), *Rüdiger und ein Anfang! Kant und ein Ende!* (1931), *De zwarte magie* (1938), *Spinoza en de Stoa* (1939), *De Grieksche mysterien* (1943), and *Antieke welsprekenheid* (1949). He died in Zeist on 27 December 1960. NieuwNBW, vol. 2, pp. 264-65

de **Jong**, Pieter, born 3 March 1832 at Nieuwveen, the Netherlands, he studied theology and Oriental, particularly Semitic, languages, at the Rijksuniversiteit te Leiden, where he received a doctorate in 1857 for *Disquisitio de Psalmis Maccabaicis*. Already two years before the completion of his dissertation he had become an assistant to Th. W. J. Juynboll at the Legaat Warner; in 1859 he was appointed a lecturer in Persian and Turkish at the Universiteit; and after the death of Juynboll, he became acting *interpres*, and in 1866, *interpres*. In 1868 he succeeded to H. Chr. Millies in the chair of Oriental languages and literatures at the Rijksuniversiteit te Utrecht, delivering his inaugural lecture on 12 February 1869 entiled *Het belang dat de beoefenaar van het Hebreeuwsch heeft vij de kennis der overige semitische taten*. He died in office on 25 January 1890. His writings include *Over met ab, ach enz. zamengestelde Hebreeuwsche Eigennamen* (1881), and, jointly with H. E. Weijers, *Catalogus codicum orientalium Bibliothecae Academicae Regiae Scientiarum* (1862); and he was a joint editor with M. J. de Goeje of his first volume of the *Fragmenta historiorum arabicorum* (1867). Fück, p. 212; NieuwNBW

de **Jong**, Rudolf Erik, born in 1958, he received a doctorate in 1999 from the Universiteit van Amsterdam for *The Beduin dialects of the northern Sinai littoral, bridging the linguistic gap between the eastern and western Arab world*. He subsequently was a free-lance researcher. His writings include *A Grammar of the Beduin dialects of the northern Sinai littoral, bridging the linguistic gap between the eastern and western Arab world*. Brinkman's; Note

de **Jonge**, Henk Jan, born 28 September 1943 at Leiden, the Netherlands, he studied classics at the Rijkuniversiteit te Leiden (R.U.L.), where he received a doctorate in 1971 for *Daniel Heinsius and the textus receptus of the New Testament*. From 1970 to 1984 he was associated with the Universiteit van Amsterdam, and subsequently with R.U.L., where he delivered his inaugural lecture entitled *John Locke's interpretatie van Paulus' brieven* (Leiden, 1988). His writings include *De bestudering van het Nieuwe Testament aan de Noordnederlandse universiteiten en het Remonstrants seminarie van 1575 tot 1700* (1980), and he was a joint author of *Joseph Scaliger; a bibliography, 1852-1982* (1982). Brinkman's, 1971-80; *Wie is wie*, 1994/96

de **Jonge**, Morris/Moritz, born 3 November 1864 at Köln, Prussia, the son of the local head of the Jewish community, he studied law and took a Dr.jur. In 1890 he was baptized Christoph. He became an editor with the Berlin *Kreuzzeitung*, where he polemized against the Jews. Growing anti-Semitism, however, made him consider returning to Judaism under the condition that he retained his recognition of Jesus as a prophet. This the local rabbinate refused to consider. In his later years he espoused Zionist ideas. His writings include *Messias, der kommende jüdische Mann* (1904). He died in Berlin in 1920. EncJud²; JüdLex; Wininger

Jongmans, Deuwe Geert, born 9 January 1922 at Rotterdam, the Netherlands, he received a doctorate in 1955 from the Universiteit te Amsterdam for *Politiek in Polynesië*. He started his career as a professor of anthropology at his alma mater and ended it at the Rijsuniversiteit te Utrecht, where he had delivered his inaugural lecture in 1983 entitled *Naar vruchtbaar onderzoek*. His writings include *Van bron tot bron; onder der Berbers van de Marokkaanse Sahara* (1955); he was a joint author of *Marokkaanse moeders* (1984); and a joint editor of *Anthropologists in the field* (1967). In 1986 appeared *Vruchtbaar oderzoek; essays ter ere van Douwe Jongmans*. Brinkman's; NUC, pre-1956; Unesco

Jonnart, Charles Célestin Auguste, born 27 December 1857 at Flechin (Pas-de-Calais), France, he studied at the Faculté de droit de Paris, and the École des sciences politiques, gaining a doctorate in law. Upon the recommendation of the Ministère Gambetta, he was appointed in 1881 head of cabinet under the new governor-general of Algeria. He was an important and successful politician in North Africa, serving twice as governor of Algeria, 1900-1911 and 1918-1919, during which time he did much to develop its agriculture and educational facilities, including the establishment of the Université d'Alger. He was a foreign minister in 1913, and in 1917, an Allied high commissioner in Greece, and an ambassador to the Vatican, 1921 to 1923, when diplomatic relations with the Vatican were re-established. His writings include *Exposé de la situation générale des territoires du sud de l'Algérie* (1907), and he was a joint author of *L'Œuvre française en Algérie* (1912), and *Le Drame ignoré de l'armée d'Orient* (1927). He died in Paris on 30 September 1927. DBF; *Hommes et destins*, 8, 215-17

Jönsson, Lars, fl. 20th cent., he wrote *La révolution agraire en Algérie; historique, contenu et problèmes* (Uppsala, Scandinavian Institute of African Studies, 1978). LC

Jonveaux, Émile, born in 1819, his writings include *Deux ans dans l'Afrique orientale* (1871), and he translated from the English of William G. Palgrave, *Une Année dans l'Arabie centrale* (1872). He died in 1871. BN; NUC, pre-1956

Jooris, Joseph, born in 1831, his writings include *Aperçu politique et économique sur les colonies néerlandaises aux Indies orientales* (Bruxelles, 1884), and *L'Acte général de la conférence de Berlin* (Bruxelles, 1885). BN; NUC, pre-1956

Joost, Elisabeth, she was born on 14 February 1898 at Düsseldorf, Germany. Her writings, partly under the pseudonym Jonny Behm, include *Balkan, Bakschisch und Basare; zwei Reporterinnen auf Karl Mays Spuren* (Stuttgart, 1954), and *Fahrt zu tausend Inseln* (Stuttgart, 1955). She died in Friedberg/Hesse on 4 Decmber 1974. KDtLK, Nekrolog, 1971-98

Joppin, Émile, fl. 20th cent., his writings include *Une belle figure de missionnaire au Levant, le Réverent Père* [Ernest] *Sarloutte*, [1878-1944] (Paris, 1956). NUC, 1956-67

Joray, Malik see Allmen-Joray, Malik von

Jordan, Julius, born 27 October 1877 at Kassel, Prussia, he studied architecture at the Technische Hochschule Dresden, where he received a Dr.phil. in 1910 for a study of ancient Near Eastern architecture entitled *Konstruktions-Elemente assyrischer Monumentalbauten*. Since 1904 he was involved in a variety of excavations in Mesopotamia. From 1931 to 1934, he was in charge of the Iraqi Department of Antiquities. He had to leave the country in 1939. Later he became a visiting professor of history of architecture at the Technische Hochschule, Berlin. His writings include *Der Nahe Osten* (Stuttgart, 1942). He died in Berlin on 2 February 1945. DtBE; Hanisch; Kornrumpf; NDB; Sezgin

Jordan, Robert Paul, born 6 July 1921 at Omaha, Nebr., he served with the U.S. Signal Corps during the second World War and graduated in 1947 from George Washington University, Washington, D.C. In the same year, he started his career as a journalist with the *Washington Post*. In 1961 he became an assistant editor with the *National geographic magazine*. His writings include *Oklahoma, the adventurous one* (1971), and *The Civil War* (1969). ConAu, 29-32; WhoE, 1981/82; WhoS&SW, 1975/76

Jordan, Samuel Martin, Rev., born in 1871, he graduated from Lafayette College, and Princeton Theological Seminary, 1898, where he also took an M.A. in 1899. He subsequently went to Persia as principal of the American High School in Tehran; he later became president of the American College, later named Alborz College. In 1920 he received the Order of the Lion and the Sun from the Ministry of Education of the Persian Government for his service. He retired in 1941. He gained a D.D. in 1916 and a LL.D. in 1936. He died in Los Angeles on 21 June 1952. Arthur C. Boyce wrote a biography, *Alborz College of Teheran and Dr. Samuel Martin Jordan, founder and president* (1954). NatCAB, vol. 41, p. 146; NYT, 25 June 1952, p. 29, col. 3; *School and society*, 76 (1952), p. 14; Shavit; WhAm, 3

Jordan, Wilhelm, born 1 March 1842 at Ellwangen, Württemberg, Germany, he studied construction engineering and geodesy at the Polytechnikum, Stuttgart, and subsequently taught his field at the polytechnics of Stuttgart, Karlsruhe, and finally Hannover. He interrupted his teaching career from 1873 to 1874 to participate in Gerhard Rohlfs' expedition to the Lybian Desert as geodesist and astronomer. His writings include *Die geographischen Resultate der von G. Rohlfs geführten Expedition in die Libysche Wüste* (1875), and *Physische Geographie und Meteorologie der libyschen Wüste nach Beobachtungen ausgeführt im Winter 1873-74 auf der Rohlfs'schen Expedition* (1876). He died in Hannover on 17 or 24 April 1899. DtBE; DtBilnd (9); *Geographische Zeitschrift*, 5 (1899), unidentified pages; Henze; Kornrumpf, N; NDB

Jordana y Morera, José, born in 1836 at Cervera (Lérida), Spain, he was a head of the Escuela Práctica de Espinar, an inspector general of the Cuerpo de Montes as well as a member of the Consejo Superior de Agricultura, Industria y Comercio and the Cámara Agricola, Madrid. His writings include *La producción agricola y forestal de la Argelia en el concurso de Argel de 1881* (1882), and *Notas sobre los alcornocales y la industria corchera de la Argelia* (1884). He died in 1906. Elias; EncicUni; Ossorio

Jore, Léonce Alphonse Noël Henri, born 21 May 1882 at Helleville (Manche), France, he was educated at the Lycée de Cherbourg and the École coloniale, Paris. In 1904, he became a coloniale administrator successively at Bamako and Kita, French West Africa. In 1912, he received a doctorate for *La République du Liberia*. After the first World War, he was posted to Ivory Coast, Syria, Lebanon, Niger, and Senegal. He retired in 1939 as a governor of New Caledonia, and high commissioner of the Pacific. His writings include *L'Océan Pacifique au temps de la Restauration et de la monarchie de Juillet* (1959), and *Les Établissements français sur la côte occidentale d'Afrique de 1758 à 1809* (1965). He died in Vervey, Switzerland, on 29 September 1975. DBF; *Hommes et destins*, vol. 4, pp. 391-95

Jorga, Nicholas, 1871-1940 *see* Iorga, Nicolae

Jos Badiny, Francisco, fl. 1967, he wrote *The Sumerian wonder* (Buenos Aires, School for Oriental Studies of the University of Salvador, 1974). LC

Joseph, Brian Daniel, born 22 November 1951 at N.Y.C., he graduated in 1973 from Yale University , New Haven, Conn., and received a Ph.D. in 1976 from Harvard University for *Morphology and universals in syntactic change; evidence from medieval and modern Greek*. Since 1979 he served successively as a professor of linguistics and Slavic languages and literatures at Ohio State University, a post which he still held in 2005. His writings include *The Synchrony and diachrany of the Balkan infinite* (1983), *Studies on language change* (1986), *Language history, language change and language relationship* (1996), and *The Handbook of historical linguistics* (2003). DrAS, 1982 F; NatFacDr, 1990-2005

Joseph, Gaston Adrien, born 20 September 1884 at Sarralbe (Moselle), France, he was educated at the *lycées* Condorcet and Chaptal as well as the Faculté des sciences, and École coloniale, Paris. In 1907 he was posted to the Ivory Coast, where he served in a variety of posts, mainly at Dimbokro and Abengourou. He had a long and distinguished career as a colonial administrator in French West Africa, beginning with head of the Bureau des Affaires politiques indigènes before the first World War, becoming governor of the colonies in 1924, and serving from 1929 to 1940 as director of the Affaires politiques at the Ministry of France d'outre-mer. In 1951 he was elected secretary general of the Comité de l'Afrique française et du Comité du Maroc, where he remained until the disintegration of the Comité in 1959. His writings include *Manuel des palabres* (1916), *La Côte d'Ivoire* (1917), *Koffi roman vrai d'un noir* (1922), a work which won him the 1923 *grand Prix de littérature coloniale*. He died on 3 April 1977. *Hommes et destins*, vol. 8, pp. 217-18; IndexBFr² (1)

Joseph, Isya, born 19th cent., his writings include *Devil worship; the sacred books and traditions of the Yezidis* (Boston, 1919). NUC, pre-1956

Joseph, John Benjamin, born 1 September 1923 at Baghdad, he graduated in 1950 from Franklin and Marshall College, Lancaster, Pa., and received a Ph.D. in 1957 from Princeton University for *The Last phase of Nestorian history*. He successively taught at Princeton University and Thiel College. From 1961 until his retirement in 1988, he was Lewis Audenreid Professor of History and Archaeology at Franklin and Marshall, Lancaster, Pa. His writings include *The Nestorians and their Muslim neighbors* (1961), and *Muslim-Christian relations and inter-Christian rivalries in the Middle East; the case of the Jacobites in an age of transition* (1983). ConAu, 1-4; DrAS, 1974 H, 1978 H, 1982 H; WhoAm, 1984-2003

Joseph, Roger, born 23 July 1938 at Pasadena, Cailf., he graduated in 1960 from the University of Nevada, Reno, and received a Ph.D. in 1967 from the University of California, Los Angeles, for *Rituals and relatives; a study of the social uses of wealth in Morocco*, a work which was published in 1969. Since 1971, he was a professor of anthropology at California State University, Fullerton. AmM&WSc, 1973 S; AmM&WSc, 1976 P; NatFacDr, 1995; *MESA Roster of members*, 1977-1982; Selim

Joseph, T. K., born in 1884, his writings include *Malabar Christians and their ancient documents* (Trivandrum, 1929), and *Six St. Thomases of South India; a Muslim non-martyr (Thawwama) made martyrs after 1517 A.D.* (Chengannur, 1955). BLC; LC; NUC, pre-1956

Joseph-Jeanneney, Brigitte Claude Emma, born 4 January 1949 at Grenoble, France, she went to school in Paris and studied at the Sorbonne and the École normale supérieure de jeunes filles. She received a diploma from the Institut d'études politiques de Paris. After her *agrégation* in history, she briefly taught at Yale University, New Haven, Conn., and the Lycée Colbert at Paris. Since 1974 she was associated with social affairs on a national and municipal level. WhoFr, 1994/95-2004/2005

Josselin de Jong, Patrick Edward, born 8 July 1922 at Peking, he received the classical education of the day at Leiden, where he subsequently studied Malay language and literature, Arabic, Islamic subjects, and cultural anthropology. He received a doctorate in 1951 for *Minangkabau and Negri Sembilan; socio-political structure in Indonesia*. In 1957, he delivered his inaugural lecture as professor of cultural anthropology at the Rijksuniversiteit te Leiden (RUL) entitled *Eenige richtingen in de heden-*

daagse culturele antropologie. He was associated with RUL in various capacities since 1949. From 1953 to 1955 he served as a lecturer in Malay studies at the University of Malaya, Singapore. His writings include *Ruler and realm; political myths in western Indonesia* (1980), and *Unity and diversity; Indonesia as a field of anthropological study* (1984). He died in Leiden on 1 January 1999. American anthropologist, 102 (2000), pp. 577-588; WhoNL, 1962/63; Wie is wie, 1994-96

Josyer (Yosyar), Gomatham Rāmānuja, born in 1891, he was educated at Madras University and became a journalist who delivered an inaugural address in 1945 entitled *Philosophy and philosophers* (Mysore, 1945); his other writings include *History of Mysore and the Yadava Dynasty* (Mysore, 1950), and *Sanskrit wisdom* (Mysore, 1960). BLC; WhE&EA

Jouannet, Jacques, fl. 20th cent., he received a doctorate in law. His writings include *L'Évolution de la fiscalité marocaine depuis l'instauration du Protectorat* (Tanger, 1953). BN; Note about the author

Jouannin, André Pierre, born 20 March 1863 at Paris, he was educated at the Jesuit college in Vaugirard and the École des beaux-arts. In 1887 he went to New Caledonia, where he spent twelve years in a business entreprise. When he returned to Paris in 1899, he founded the Comité de l'Asie française and became its secretary general. From 1903 to 1906, he accomplished several missions for the governments of Arabia, Persia, and Mesopotamia. He contributed to several periodicals in the field. He died in Paris on 2 December 1922. Asie française, 1923.; DBF

Jouannin, Joseph Marie, born 6 September 1783 at Saint-Brieuc (Côtes-du-Nord), France, he was educated at the Prytanée français (Louis-le-Grand), from 1797 to 1802. Upon graduation, he was nominated by the minister of foreign relations a *jeune de langues de 2e classe* and sent in January 1803 to General Brune at the French embassy in Constantinople. From September 1803 to February 1804, he went to Trebizond to collect geographical information on the Black Sea, Anatolia, and the Crimea. From 1805 to 1810, he served as French agent to the Shah of Persia, returning to Paris in June 1810 to serve in Europe until 1817. He subsequently spent another five years at Constantinople until appointed in 1822 director of the École royale des jeunes de langues at Paris. Since 1826, he was a royal interpreter, and since 1837, a professor of Persian at the Collège de France in Paris. His writings include *Statu quo d'Orient; revue des événements qui se sont passés en Turquie pendant l'année 1838* (1838), and, jointly with Jules van Gaver, *Turquie* (1840). He died in Paris on 31 January 1844. DBF; Hoefer; IndexBFr² (2)

Joubin, André, born 11 April 1868 at Laval (Mayenne), France, he graduated from the École normale supérieure in 1886 and in 1889 became a member of the École d'Athène. An avid epigrapher, he returned to France to teach classical archaeology at the Université de Montpellier, but gradually his interest shifted towards modern art. In 1918, he became the first director of the Bibliothèque d'art et d'archéologie, Fondation de Jacques Doucet, in the Université de Paris. He is now best remembered as an expert on Eugène Delacroix. His writings include *Catalogue des sculptures grecques, romaines, byzantines et franques* (Constantinople, 1893), *Catalogue sommaire; Musée impériale ottoman: Monuments funéraires* (1893), *Le Musée de Montpellier, Musée Fabre* (Paris, 1929). He died in 1944. DBF; Revue archéologique, 36 (1949/50), pp. 97-101; ZKO

Jouffroy d'Eschavannes, Joseph Louis Édouard, born 10 February 1810 of French parents at Plaisance, Italy. He was a sometime keeper of the Musée du Louvre, and for ten years the editor-in-chief of *Revue de l'Orient*. He was awarded the Légion d'honneur. His writings include *Armorial universel* (1844-48), and *Traité complet de la science du blason* (1855). BN; Lamathière

Jouguet, Pierre Félix Amédée, born 14 May 1869 at Bessèges (Gard), France, he started his university education in 1889 at the Sorbonne, Paris, and one year later was admitted to the École normale supérieure. After his *agrégation* in grammar in 1893, he proceeded to the École d'Athènes, where he familiarized himself with the excavations at Delphi and Delos. He was soon sent to the Mission française du Caire, where he studied Egyptian antiquities, compiled a catalogue for the Museum of Gizeh, and deciphered certain Greek papyri. In the early years of the twentieth century he established the Institut de papyrologie at Lille, where he taught his subject and concurrently gave a similar course at the École des hautes études de Paris since 1912. A professor at the Faculté des lettres de Paris since 1920, he founded the Société française d'égyptologie in 1925. With the approval of King Fuad he founded in 1930 the Société royale égyptienne de papyrologie. After reaching retirement age in 1940, he remained in Cairo and headed the Comité national de la France libre. He returned to Paris in April 1949 and died there on the following ninth of July. His writings include *Impérialisme macédonien et l'hellénisation de l'Orient* (1926), and *Trois études sur l'hellénisme* (1944). In 1950 appeared *Hommage à Pierre Jouguet*. Dawson; DBF; Egyptology; Qui êtes-vous, 1924; Revue historique, 206 (1951), pp. 171-73

Jouhaud, Yves, born 31 January 1926 at Bourges (Cher), France, he was educated at the Lycée de Nevers and studied at the faculties of law and letters, Paris. He received degrees in law, medieval history and classical literature from a variety of institutions, including the École nationale de la France d'outre-mer. He served in various capacities in courts in metropolitain France as well as overseas; and he was the recipient of high honours and decorations. WhoFr, 1973/74-2004/2005

Jouin, Jeanne, born 31 October 1894, the daughter of a mayor of Bain-de Bretagne, she received the customary education of her class. After the first World War, she began to pursue an interest in the Arab world. She studied North African subjects at the École des langues orientales vivantes at the Sorbonne and subsequently made research visits to Syria, Egypt, Tunisia, and Morocco, publishing the results, predominantly of a sociological nature, in periodicals in the field. She died on 5 March 1986. *Littérature orale arabo-berbère*, 16-17 (1985-86), pp. 253-55

Jouin, Yves, fl. 20th cent., he was a joint author of *Historique des Goums marocains; la période de camouflage des Méhallas chérifiennes* (Paris, 1966). BN, 1960-69

Jouinot-Gambetta, François Léon, born 6 July 1870 at Paris, he joined for an initial five years the 6th Régiment de chasseurs d'Afrique, and in 1889 participated in the campaign in southern Morocco. He subsequently served in the desert regions of Morocco and Algeria, increasingly in the geographical section of the military, and as ordnance officer with the ministry of Affaires étrangères, advancing to the rank of colonel on the eve of the world war. With the rank of brigadier-general he served since 1917 with the Armée de l'Orient in Macedonia. He died in Antibes (Alpes-Martimes) on 9 November 1923. DBF; IndexBFr² (1); *Qui êtes-vous*, 1924

Joüon, Paul, born 26 February 1871 at Nantes (Loire-Atlantique), France, he entered the Compagnie de Jésus in 1890. He studied Semitic philology, mainly at Paris, before going to Cairo from 1896 to 1898 for private study and rest, and subsequently to Beirut for theological study from 1898 to 1901, when he returned to Paris. He later returned to Beirut to teach Hebrew at the Faculté orientale and the Jesuit Séminaire, from 1907 to 1914, when the Turks closed the university. He then taught at the Pontificio Istituto Biblico di Roma from 1915 to 1919. Failing health since 1920, restrained him to research, first at Roma and later at Paris. His writings include *Notes grammaticales, lexicographiques et philologiques sur les papyrus araméen d'Égypte* (1934), *A Grammar of Biblical Hebrew* (1923), and *Études de sémantique arabe* (1926). He died in Nantes on 18 February 1940. DBF; Jalabert, p. 414; *New Catholic encyclopedia* (Washington, D.C., c1967, 1981)

Jourdain, Amable Louis Marie Michel Bréchillet-Jourdain, born 25 January 1788 at Paris, he started life as a notary's clerk, but influenced by the example of a friend of the family, the Orientalist Abraham Anquetil-Duperron, he decided to pursue a literary interest. Since 1805 he studied Arabic and Persian under Louis M. Langlès and Silvestre de Sacy at the École des langues orientales, Paris. The latter found him a post as secretary at the ministry of foreign affairs and, shortly thereafter, as a deputy secretary at the École des langues orientales. His writings include *Notice de l'histoire universelle de Mirkhond intitulée «Le jardin de la pureté»*(1812), *La Perse ou tableau de l'histoire, du gouvernement, de la religion, de la littérature...de cet empire* (1814), *Recherches critiques sur l'âge et l'origine des traductions latines d'Aristote et sur des commentaires grecs ou arabes employés par les docteurs scholastiques* (1819), and its translation, *Forschungen über Alter und Ursprung der lateinischen Uebersetzungen des Aristoteles und über griechische und lateinische von den Scholastikern benutzte Commentare* (1831). He died in Paris on 12 February 1812. DBF; Hoefer; IndexBFr² (3)

Jourdan, Louis Charles, born in 1810 at Toulon (Var), France, he was educated at the Collège de Toulon and after graduation entered journalism. He later also studied at the Faculté de droit d'Aix-en-Provence. He participated in the 1830 campaign against Alger and subsequently pursued journalistic as well as commercial interests in the eastern and western Mediterranean. A Saint-Simonian since 1833, he was a recognized political editor with a variety of periodicals of his day. His writings include *Des intérêts de la France en Égypte* (1851). He died in Alger on 2 June 1881. Dantès 1; DBF; IndexBFr² (2); Vapereau

Jousse, Marcel, born 28 July 1886 at Beaumont-sur-Sarthe, France, he was early in life exposed to oral and epic culture and at the age of thirteen started to learn Hebrew, Latin and Greek. Ordained priest in 1910, he entered the Society of Jesus in 1913. In 1925 appeared his first study in linguistic psychology, *Le Style oral rythmique et mnémotechnique chez les verbo-moteurs*, and its translation, *The Oral style* (1990). He subsequently taught his subject at the Pontificio Istituto Biblico di Roma (1927), the Sorbonne (1931-1957), and the École d'anthropologie, where a chair of linguistics was founded especially for him (1932-1950). His writings include *Études de psychologie linguistique* (1925), *Les Rabbis d'Israël* (1930), *La manducation de la leçon dans le milieu ethnique palestinien* (1950), *Le Geste et la parole* (1965), and *L'Anthropologie du geste* (1969). He died in Fresnay-sur-Sarthe on 15 August 1961. DBF; IndexBFr² (2)

Joutard, Philippe Ernest Adolphe Jean, born 26 February 1935 at Paris, he was educated at the Institution Saint-Louis de Gonzague and the Lycée Louis-le-Grand, Paris, and subsequently studied at the Sorbonne, Paris, where he received a doctorate in letters and an *agrégation* in history. He started his career as a teacher and educator in 1958 at the Lycée Gouraud in Rabat, subsequently serving as a consultant, counsellor, director, and president in a great variety of educational institutions. His writings include *Les Cévennes de la montagne à l'homme* (1979), and he edited *Les Camisards* (1976). WhoFr, 1990/91-2004/2005

Jovanović, Jovan Zmaj, born 24 November 1833 at Novi Sad (Neusatz), Serbia, he studied law at Wien, Prag, and Pest and became an administrator in Austria-Hungary. In 1863 he was head of the Tököly Institution in Pest and concurrently completed his medical study with a doctorate. He subsequently practised his profession at a variety of places, including Wien. He also pursued an interest in writing and served as an editor of literary and satirical periodicals. He died in Kamenica on 3 June 1904. Grada; HrvEnc; ÖBL

Jovanović, Slobodan, Dr., he was in 1971 an editor with the Yugoslav news agency Tanjug. Note about the author

Jowett, William, born in 1787, he was educated at John's College, Cambridge. He became an Anglican clergyman who served as a missionary in the Near East under the Church Missionary Society of London. His writings include *Christian researches in the Mediterranean from 1815 to 1820* (1822), and *Christian researches in Syria and the Holy Land in 1823 and 1824, in furtherance of the objects of the Church Missionary Society* (1825). He died in Clapham on 24 February 1855. Boase; BritInd (2); Dawson; DNB; Egyptology

Joy, Sir George Andrew, born in 1896 at London, he entered the British Army in 1914 and served from 1917 to 1918 in Greater Syria. In 1924 he entered the Colonial Service. In 1940 he was Resident Adviser to sultans in the Hadhramawt states of southern Arabia, and from 1942 to 1946 he was Civil Secretary to the Government of Aden. He died in 1974. BritInd (2); EncO&P; Master (2); Who's who, 1948-1974; Who was who, 7

Joyaux, François, born 20th cent., his writings include *La Chine et le règlement du premier conflit d'Indochine* (1979), *La Nouvelle question d'Extrême Orient* (1985), *La Tentation impériale; politique extérieure de la Chine depuis 1949* (1994), and *La Rose, une passion française* (2002). ZKO

Joyce, James Avery, born in 1902, he was a public and university lecturer, broadcaster, pacifist, lawyer, and an authority on constitutional and international law. Admitted to the bars of Britain and Switzerland, he worked with a number of peace organizations. His writings include *Revolution on East River* (1957), *Red Cross International and the strategy of peace* (1959), *Capital punishment* (1961), *The Right to life* (1962), *The Story of international cooperation* (1964), *Decade of development; the challenge of the under-developed nations* (1967), *End of an illusion* (1969), *Human rights* (1978), and *World labour rights and their protection* (1980). He died in 1987. Au&Wr, 1971; BioIn, 11, 16; ConAu, 121, new rev., 10; IntAu&W, 1976, 1977, 1982; WhAm, 9; WhoAm, 1974-1986/87; WhoWor, 1974/75-1984

Joyce, Pierce Charles, lieut.-colonel, born in 1878 and educated at Beaumont College, he was attached to the Egyptian Army since 1907. In 1910 he fought in the Sudan. From November 1916 he was Political and Military Representative at Rābigh and then at Yanbu', Saudi Arabia. From March 1918 until after the end of the war, he commanded the northern Hejaz troops. H. W. Young, who served with him there and was later a leading adviser to Winston Churchill, minuted in 1921 that Joyce "deserves almost as much credit as Colonel Lawrence for the success of Faisal's campaign." He covered military and political matters for the *Arab bulletin*. After the war, Faisal took him to Iraq as military adviser. He died on 1 February 1965. R. L. Bidwell, *Arab bulletin* 1 (1986 reprint), p. xxvi; Who was who, 6

Joyce, Raymond H., born about 1910, he was a British born Canadian missionary in China and Arabia. In 1943 he was associated with the China Inland Mission. Lodwick

Józefowicz, Zdzislaw, fl. 20th cent., his writings include *Blokowo-kopleksowa koncepcja programo-wania dydaktycznego* (Gdansk, 1980). OSK

Juarros y Ortega, César, born 13 November 1879 at Madrid, he was a military physician and a director of the Escuela Central de Anormales. He served as a president of the Sociedad Española de Abolicionismo, and as a vice-president of the Liga Española para la Reforma Sexual. His writings include *La ciudads de los ojos* (1922), and *Atalayas sobre el facismo* (1934). He died on 24 October 1942. IndiceE³ (2)

Juchereau de Saint-Denys, Pierre *Antoine*, born 14 September 1776 at Bastia, Corsica, he was educated at the military schools of Pontlevoy and Brienne-le-Château, and the École du génie, Mézières (Ardennes), where he graduated in 1792. In the same year, he emigrated to Britain, where

MACK LIBRARY
BOB JONES UNIVERSITY
GREENVILLE, SC

he found a post with the English general staff. He subsequently served in British North America with the rank of captain. After the Peace of Amiens (1802), he went to Turkey, where he served as an engineer to the Sublime Porte since 1805. In cooperation with the French ambassador he planned the defence of the Straits as well as Constantinople, and also participated in the Turkish campaigns in the Balkans. For his accomplishments he was promoted in 1807 *baş mühendis*, chief military engineer of the Ottoman Empire. After the death of Sultan Mustafa IV and the following anarchy, he returned to France, and with the rank of colonel of engineers participated in Napoleon's Spanish campaign. In 1830 he served with the general staff in the campaign against Alger. His writings include *Révolutions de Constantinople en 1807 et 1808* (1819), *Considérations statistiques, historiques, militaires et politiques sur la régence d'Alger* (1831), and *Histoire de l'Empire ottoman depuis 1792 jusqu'en 1844* (1844). He died in Vierzon (Cher), France, on 19 September 1850. DBF; BN; Hoefer; *Hommes et destins*, vol. 7, pp. 270-273

Jucquois, Guy Paul André, born 19 December 1936 at Malines (Mechelen), Belgium, he studied classical philology and received a doctorate in Oriental philology and history from the Université catholique de Louvain (UCL); he was also a graduate of the École pratique des Hautes études, Paris. Since 1963 he was associated with UCL in a variety of capacities. From 1971 to 1975 he served as the founding director of the Institut de linguistique de Louvain. His writings include *Phonétique comparée des dialectes moyen-babyloniens du nord et de l'ouest* (1966), *La typologie linguistique* (1975), *Introduction à la linguistique différentielle* (1976), *La reconstruction linguistique* (1976), and *Pourquoi les hommes parlent-ils?* (2000). Qui est qui en Belgique francophone, 1981-85; WhoWor, 1980/81

Judas, Auguste Célestin, born in 1805, he received a doctorate. His writings include *Essai sur la langue phénicienne avex deux inscriptions puniques inédites* (1842), *Étude démonstrative de la langue phénicienne et de la langue libyque* (1847), and *Nouvelle analyse de l'inscription libyco-punique de Thugga en Afrique, suivie de nouvelles observations sur plusieurs épitaphes libyques dans le but exprès de faciliter en Algérie l'étude des langues phéniciennes et libyco-berbère* (1869). He died in 1872. BN; NUC; ZKO

Judeich, Walther, born 5 October 1859 at Dresden, Saxony, he took classics at university and received a Dr.phil. in 1884 from the Universität Straßburg for *Caesar im Orient*, and a Dr.habil. in 1889 from the Universität Marburg for *Persien und Aegypten im IV. Jahrhundert v.Chr.* He taught successively at the universities of Marburg, Czernowitz, Erlangen, and Jena. His writings include *Bericht über eine Reise im nordwestlichen Kleinasien* (1898), and *Topographie von Athen* (1905). In 1929 appeared *Festschrift Walther Judeich zum 70. Geburtstag überreicht von Jenaer Freunden*. He died in 1942. DtBilnd (1), Kürschner, 1925-1940/41; Wer ist's, 1928

Judet, Pierre, born 20th cent., he was associated with the Université des Sciences Sociales de Grenoble. His writings include *L'industrialisation dans les pays les moins avancés; orientations* (Paris, 1981), and *Les nouveaux pays industriels* (Paris, 1981). LC; Note

Jugant, Paul, he was in 1939 a *contrôleur des impôts et contribution* in Morocco. Note about the author

Jugašvili, Galina, 1938- *see* Dzhugashvili, Galina IAkovlevna

Jugie, Étienne, his clerical first name was *Martin*. He was born 3 May 1878 at Aubazine (Corrèze), France, entered the Assumptionists in 1895 at Livry, and took his monastic vow the following year at Jerusalem, where he continued his philosophical and theological study. After his ordination in 1901, he taught at the Greco-Slave Seminary at Kadıköy (Chalcedon), and started his association with the Russian archaeological institute at Constantinople. After the first Wold War, he was appointed a professor of orthodox theology at the newly established Oriental institute at Roma. In 1932, he taught at the Athénée du Latran and the Catholic faculties at Lyon, and in 1935, he became a consultant to the Sacred Congregation for the Eastern Church. In 1944, his duties brought him back to Roma once more, but ill health obliged him in 1952 to retire to Lorgues (Var), where he died on 29 November 1952. His writings include *Nestorius et la controverse nestorienne* (1912). In 1953 appeared *Mélanges Martin Jugie*. DBF

Juglar, Joseph *Clément*, born 15 October 1819 at Paris, he turned in the first instance to the study of medicine, taking his doctor's degree in 1846. After the 1848 revolution, he increasingly directed his attention to social maladies and economic problems. In 1851 he became editor of the *Journal des économistes*, and he founded the *Économiste français*. In 1860 he published his main work, *Des crises commerciales et de leur retour périodique en France, en Angleterre et aux États-Unis*, and its translation, *A Brief history of panics and their periodical occurence in the United States* (1893). He was a president of two learned societies, a professor of statistics at the École libre des sciences politiques, and elected a member of the Académie des sciences morales et politiques in 1892. He

died suddenly in Paris on 28 February 1905. BioIn, 16; Dantès, 1; DBF; *Economic journal*, 15 (1905), pp. 293-98; Master (1); WhoEc, 1981, 1986, 1991

Juhász, Kálmán (Koloman), born 28 August 1892 at Alibunár, Banat, Hungary, his writings include *Die Stifte der Tschanader Diözese im Mittelalter; ein Beitrag zur Frühgeschichte und Kulturgeschichte des Banats* (1927), *Das Tschanad-Temesvarer Bistum im frühen Mittelalter, 1030-1307* (1930), *Das Tschanad-Temesvarer Bistum während der Türkenherrschaft, 1552-1699; Untergang der abendländisch-christlichen Kultur im Banat* (1938), *Hajdani monóstorok a csanádi egyházmegye története* (Makó, 1941), *Laien im Dienst der Seelsorge während der Türkenherrschaft in Ungarn* (1960), and *Das Tschanad-Temesvarer Bistum im Spätmittelalter* (1964). He died in Szeged, Hungary, on 29 September 1966. MEL, 1981; OSK

Juillet Saint-Lager, Marcel, born 19th cent., he was a sometime section head in the French Ministry of the Interieur. His writings include *La Régence de Tunis; géographie physique et politique* (Alger, 1874), and *Elections municipales* (Paris, 1896). BN; LC

Juin, Alphonse Pierre, born 16 December 1888 at Bône, Algeria, he graduated from the military academy, Saint-Cyr, and was posted in 1910 to an Algerian regiment as an officer; he served from 1912 to 1914 in Morocco. After the war he went to the École de guerre in Paris, became chief of staff in France to Marshal L. H. Lyautey, and then returned to commands in Morocco. In the second World War he commanded the French forces first in Morocco and later in all of North Africa. After the war he served as Resident General in Morocco. His writings include *Mémoires* (1959), and he was a joint author of *Histoire parallele, La France en Algérie, 1830-1962* (1963). He died in Paris on 27 June 1967. Yves M. J. G. de Boissoisel wrote *Dans l'ombre de Lyautey* (1954). CurBio, 1943, 1967; DBF; DBFC, 1954/55; EncAm; *Hommes et destins*, vol. 1, pp. 310-12 HrvEnc; IndexBFr² (6); Master (8); NDNC, 1966; WhAm, 4; WhoFr, 1953-1967/68; *Who was who*, 6

Jukes, Worthington, Rev., born 19th cent. Around the turn of the century, he served for fifteen years as a missionary of the Church Missionary Society of London at Peshawar, where he was in charge of the Edwardes High School. He was a joint translator of the Bible into Pashto. His trace is lost after an article in 1927. Note; WhE&EA

Jülg, Bernhard, born 20 August 1825 at Ringelbach near Oberkirch, Baden, Germany, he went to school in Offenburg and Mannheim. Since 1844 a student in philology at the Universität Heidelberg, he was awarded a research travel grant for a prize essay and continued his study at Berlin, which included Far Eastern, Central Asian, and Middle Eastern languages. His first publication, *Initia linguae Calcuccicae* (1847), established his recognition. For several years he taught at schools in Baden until he was invited in 1851 by the Austrian ministry of education to teach classical philology and literature at the Universität Lemberg. Two years later he was invited to the Universität Krakau. In 1863 he became a professor in his field at the Universität Innsbruck, where he also served as chancellor since 1868. His writings include *Mongolische Märchen-Sammlung; die neun Märchen des Siddhi-kûr nach der ausführlichen Redaction und die Geschichte des Ardschi-Bordschi Chan, mongolisch mit deutscher Übersetzung* (1868). He died in Innsbruck on 14 August 1886. DtBE; DtBiInd (3); Kosch; NDB; ÖBL; Wurzbach

Julia de Fontenelle, Jean Sébastian Eugène, born 29 October 1790 at Narbonne (Aude), France, he started to study medicine at the Université de Montpellier but soon changed to pharmacy. He was the founding president of the Société des sciences physiques et chimiques, Paris. His writings include *Recherches historiques, chimiques et médicales sur l'air marécageux* (1823), *Manuel complet du blanchiment et du blanchissage* (1834), and its translation, *Vollständiges Handbuch der Bleichkunst* (1853). He died in 1842 in Paris. DBF; Hoefer IndexBFr² (5)

Julien, Charles André, born 2 September 1891 at Caen (Calvados), France, he studied at the Sorbonne, where he later taught in various capacities, from 1939 to his retirement in 1961. From 1957 to 1961 he also served as honorary dean of the Faculté des lettres de Rabat. His writings include *Histoire de l'Afrique du nord* (1931), its translation, История Северно Африки (1961), *Colonies et empires* (1946), *Géographie de l'Union française* (1953), *L'Histoire de l'Algérie contemporaine* (1964), *Le Maroc face aux impérialismes* (1978), and *L'Affaire tunisienne, 1878-1881* (1981). In 1964 appeared *Études maghrébines; mélanges Charles A. Julien*. He died in 1991. ConAu, 103; DBFC, 1954/55; DcBMouvF, vol. 32, pp. 314-16; IndexBFr² (1); Unesco; WhoFr, 1959/60-1984/85

Julien, Gustave Henri Jacques, born 15 March 1870 at Toulouse, he left France at the age of seventeen to study at the École des interprètes de Tananarive, Madagascar. After graduation in 1890, he became attached to the Résidence de France, becoming deputy administrator of colonies in 1899. Since 1903 he taught Malagasy at the École coloniale, Paris. From then on, he was intermittently a colonial adminstrator overseas and a professor at Paris. He was elected a member of the Académie des sciences coloniales. He was editor of the periodical *Bulletin de l'Union économique de Syrie*. His writings include *Cours public de langue malgache* (1901), and *Institutions politiques et sociales de Madagascar d'après des documents authentiques et inédits* (1909). He died in Paris on 2 August 1936. DBF; *Hommes et destins*, vol. 3, pp. 267-69

Julien, Noël Aignan *Stanislas*, born 21 September 1799 at Orléans, France, he was educated at the Petit séminaire d'Orléans and subsequently went to the Collège de France, Paris, to study first Greek and later Far Eastern languages, particularly under Abel de Rémusat, becoming one of the outstanding Chinese scholars of Europe. He eventually succeeded his teacher in the chair of Chinese at the Collège de France, concurrently teaching at the École des langues orientales. He died in Paris on 14 February 1873. Dantès, 1; DBF; Hoefer; Master (2); Vapereau

Julien, Raymond Charles, born in 1899, he received a doctorate in law in 1933 from the Université de Paris for *Le trafic du canal de Suez*. He was an agricultural engineer who, in 1951, was a lecturer in the Institut des Hautes études internationales. BN; Note; NUC, pre-1956

Julienne, Désirée, born 19th cent., he was an interpreter in the Corps des interprètes de l'armée d'Afrique. He was *interprète temporaire* in 1852, *interprète auxiliaire* in 1854, and *interprète titulaire de 3e classe* in 1858. Féraud

Jullian, Philippe, born 11 July 1919 at Bordeaux, he studied law and subsequently pursued an interest in painting, but it was as a writer that he became best remembered after 1950. He wrote fiction and non-fiction, including *Les Orientalistes; la vision de l'Orient par les peintres européens au 19e siècle* (1977), and its translation, *The Orientalists, European painters of Eastern scenes* (1977). He died in Paris on 1 October 1977. *Connaissance des arts*, no. 309 (9 novembre 1977) [not sighted]; DBF; IndexBFr² (3); ConAu, 73-77 [the biographical profile has been verified by his executor, G. de Diesbach]

Julliard, Émile Jean François, born in 1837 at Genève, he taught from 1869 to 1875 at the Galatasaray Lisesi, Constantinople, and subsequently became a teacher at the École des jeunes filles at Genève. His writings include *Nouvelles orientales* (1892), *Femmes d'Orient* (1896), and *Voyages incohérents* (1903). He died in 1907. HisBioLexCH; IndexBFr² (1)

Jullien, Léopold Joseph Eugène Charles, born in 1873, he was an agronomist, a sometime teacher at the Lycée français d'Alexandrie, a member of the Société sultanieh d'économie politique, de statistique et de législation, and in 1955 served as an honorary vice-consul of France at Alexandria. His writings include *Documents statistiques concernant l'étude des grossesses gémellaires* (Paris, 1897), and *Notions d'économie rurale égyptienne* (1943). NUC, pre-1956; WhoEgypt, 1955

Jully, Anthony (Antony/Antoine), born in 1862 in the Département de l'Aube, France, he studied at the École des beaux-arts of Paris, where he received a diploma in architecture. In 1888 he accepted the offer to build the Hôtel de la Residence de France at Tananarive, a project which he completed in 1892. During the subsequent fifteen years he was instrumental in the construction of numerous public buildings. His writings include *Madagascar au point de vue économique* (Marseille, 1900), and *Manuel des dialects malgaches* (1906). He died on 6 January 1907. *Hommes et destins*, vol. 3, pp. 270-71; *Bulletin de la Société de géographie de Marseille*, 31 (1907), p. 122; ZKO

Junck, Carl Franz Julius Heinrich, born in 1814 or 1816 in Hesse, he first entered the Hesse Army and in 1848 joined the Schleswig-Holstein Army. Three years later, he changed to the Austrian Army, where he was employed in the Ministry of War, with the rank of major. His writings include *Grundriß der Geschichte des Osmanischen Reiches mit besonderer Berücksichtigung der neuesten politischen Ereignissen im Orient* (Marburg, 1853), *Der russisch-türkische Krieg in der europäischen Türkei und in Asien in den Jahren 1828 und 1829* (Cassel, 1854), and *Der deutsch-französische Krieg, 1870 und 1871* (Leipzig, 1876). He died in Baden near Wien on 27 September 1878. DtBilnd (1); ÖBL

Jung, Carl *Emil*, born 1 February 1833 at Groß-Machnow near Berlin, he studied law and received a Dr.jur. He subsequently went to Eton to teach Latin and German. In the late 1850s he emigrated to Australia. He returned to Germany after twenty years and worked as a journalist and free-lance writer. His writings include *Lexikon der Handelsgeographie* (1886), and *Deutsche Kolonien* (1884). He died in Leipzig on 2 October 1902. DtBE; DtBilnd (4); NDB

Jung, Edeltrud, born 11 May 1948 at Linz, Austria, she grew up in Baden-Württemberg, Germany. After three years of practice work in a hospital she began in the summer semester of 1967 to study psychology at the Universität Tübingen, but after one semester she changed to Islamic studies, Oriental languages, and political science at the Universität Freiburg im Breisgau where she received a Dr.phil. in 1976 for *Ahmad Kasrawi; ein Beitrag zur Ideengeschichte Persiens im zwanzigsten Jahrhundert*. Schwarz; Thesis

Jung, Eugène Marie, born 13 November 1863 at Bordeaux, he was educated at the Prytanée militaire, La Flèche (Sarthe), and lycées in Lille, Clermont-Ferrand, and Paris. After graduating in law in 1886, he entered the colonial administration. His writings include *Les Puissances devant la révolte arabe* (1906), *La Révolte arabe* (1924), *L'Islam sous le joug et les réformes en Tunisie* (1926), *Questions d'Orient* (1926), *L'Islam et l'Asie devant l'impérialisme* (1927), *L'Islam et les Musulmans dans l'Afrique du nord* (1930), and *Le Reveil de l'islam et les Arabes* (1933). He died in Paris in 1936. Curinier, vol. 5 (1906), pp. 70-71; DBF; *Hommes et destins*, vol. 6, pp. 203-204

Jung, Leo, born 20 June 1892 at Ungarisch-Brod, Moravia, crownland of Austria, he studied at Wien and Berlin, and was ordained rabbi in 1920. In the following year he emigrated. In 1926 he received a Ph.D. from the University of London for *Fallen angels in Jewish, Christian and Mohammedan literature*. He became an Orthodox Jewish leader of the Jewish Center of New York. His writings include *Judaism in a changing world* (1939), *Guardians of our heritage* (1958), *Orthodox Judaism* (1959), and *Jewish leaders, 1750-1940* (1964). He died in N.Y.C. on 19 December 1987. Joshua Modlinger wrote *Leo Jung, Talmudist* (1950). CnDiAmJBi; ConAu, 124; EncJud; Master (3); WhAm, 9; WhoWorJ, 1965, 1972, 1978

Jungbauer, Gustav, born 17 July 1886 at Oberplan, Bohemia, he studied at Prag, where he obtained a Dr.phil., and subsequently taught until the outbreak of the first World War. In 1915 he became a prisoner of war, spending three years in a camp in Turkestan. In 1922, he received a Dr.habil. in German ethnology at Praha; in the following year he established the Böhmerwaldmuseum, Oberplan, and became an editor of the *Sudetendeutsche Zeitschrift für Völkerkunde*. His writings include *Märchen aus Turkestan* (1923), and *Deutsche Volkskunde, mit besonderer Berücksichtigung der Sudetendeutschen* (1936). He died in Praha on 23 October 1942. Franz Eduard Hrabe wrote *Universitätsprofessor Dr. Gustav Jungbauer, sein Wirken und Schaffen* (1936). DtBE; DtBilnd (1); Kosch; Kürschner, 1925-1940/41; ÖBL; *Wer ist's*, 1935

Junge, Friedrich, born 18 April 1941 at Bad Reinerz, Silesia, Germany, he received a Dr.phil. in 1970 from the Universität Göttingen for *Studien zum mittelägyptischen Verbum*, and a Dr.habil. in 1977 from the Universität Würzburg for *Syntax der mittelägyptischen Literatursprache; Grundlagen einer Strukturtheorie*. He was a professor of Egyptology at the Universität Göttingen. His writings include *Ein Jahrzehnt Erforschung orientalischer Religionen* (1982), and *Die Lehre Ptahhoteps und die Tugenden der ägyptischen Welt* (2003). Kürschner, 1980-2005; Schwarz

Junge, Reinhard, born 20 October 1888 at Goldberg, Silesia, Germany, he received a Dr.phil. in 1918 from the Universität Berlin for a study of Turkestan trade entitled *Der Waren- und Personenverkehr Turkestans in den Jahren 1901-1914*. He was an editor of *Archiv für Wirtschaftsforschung im Orient*, 1910-1919, and subsequeently became a professor of economic history at Humboldt-Universität, Berlin. His writings include *Das Problem der Europäisierung orientalischer Wirtschaft dargestellt an ... Russisch-Turkestan* (1915), *Weltgeschichte der Standortentwicklung der Wirtschaft in der Klassengesellschaft* (1961), and he was a joint author of *Das Türkische Reich* (1918). He died about 1975. Hanisch; *Wer ist wer*, 1955-1970

Jungfleisch, Marcel, fl. 1943-1952, he was associated with the Institut français d'archéologie orientale, Cairo. His writings include *La Trouvaille de Kom Denchal* (le Caire, 1948), and he was a joint author of *Les Moules de monnaies impériales romaines* (le Caire, 1952). NUC, pre-1956; ZKO

Junghuhn, Franz Wilhelm, he was born on 26 October 1809 at Mansfeld in ducal Saxony. In obedience to his father's wishes, he began to study medicine and also botany and geology at the Universität Halle. He became a Prussian military surgeon. After a duel in 1831, he was sentenced to twenty years in prison but escaped after twenty months from Feste Ehrenbreitstein near Coblenz to Algeria, where he was employed in 1834 at Bône as a medical officer in the Légion étrangère. Wounded, he resigned, went to Paris and from there, after being pardoned, went to Utrecht, where he passed the necessary examination to qualify for overseas service in Batavia as a health officer, arriving there in October 1835. In 1840, he was sent by the Dutch Government to the unknown lands of the Batta in Padang, Sumatra, on scientific, ethnographic, and statistical exploration. Having completed the mission, he returned in June 1842 to Batavia where he pursued his exploration as well as the topographical survey of Java. A member of the Naturkundigen Commission since 1845, he was nominated in February 1846 "governor general" of the entire geological survey of Java. For reasons of health he was obliged to return to Holland in 1849 by way of East India and Egypt. However, he returned in 1855 for renewed researches. His writings include *Java, deszelfs gedaante, bekleeding en inwendige structuur* (1850-53), its translation, *Java, seine Gestalt, Pflanzendecke und innere Struktur* (1857), and *Rückreise von Java nach Europa mit der sogenannten englischen Überlandpost im September und Oktober 1848* (1852). Much has been written about this "Humboldt of Java." He died on 24 April 1864. Embacher; EncNI; Henze; Master (2)

Jungnickel, Johann David, he wrote *Mahomet Maximus infernorum conquestor; das ist Mahomet der größte Seelen Verführer und Conquirant des Teuffels* (Erfurt, 1742). Sezgin

Jungraithmayr, Hermann, born 7 May 1931 at Eferding, Austria, he received a Dr.phil. in 1956 from the Universität Hamburg for *Untersuchungen zur Sprache der Tangale in Nordost-Nigerien*. After teaching at Goethe-Institut, Cairo, from 1956 to 1959, he became successively a professor of anthropology at the universities of Marburg and Franfurt/Main. His writings include *Die Ron-Sprachen; tschadohamitische Studien in Nordnigerien* (1970), *Gedächtniskultur und Schriftlichkeit in Afrika* (1981), *Märchen aus dem Tschad* (1981); he was a joint author of *Préables à la reconstruction du proto-tchadique* (1978), and *Einführung in die Ful-Sprache* (1988); and he edited *Wort und Religion* (1969). In 2001 appeared *Von Ägypten zum Tschadsee, eine linguistische Reise durch Afrika; Festschrift für Hermann Jungraithmayr zum 65. Geburtstag*. Kürschner, 1980-2005; WhoWor, 1991/92

Jungraithmayr, Wilhelmine, born 20th cent., she studied ethnography, ethnology, and history of art at the Universität Wien and received a Dr.phil. She spent 1957 to 1959 in Cairo, and in 1960 joined the Universität Hamburg. Since 1964 she was an assistant, and since 1969 also lecturer, at the seminary for German archaeology and folklore. She edited *Das historische Museum als Aufgabe; Forschungen und Berichte aus dem Museum für Hamburgische Geschichte, 1946-1972* (1972). Note

Jungwirth, Johann, born 25 August 1909 at Wien, he studied anthropology and early history at the Universität Wien, where he received a Dr.phil. in 1939. He subsequently was an assistant at his alma mater until 1947. From 1965 until his retirement in 1974, he was head of the anthropological section in Naturhistorisches Museum, Wien. He participated in several excavations in Egypt and Nubia. He was a joint author of *Die anthropologische Untersuchung der C-Gruppen und Pan-Gräber-Skelette aus Sayala, Ägyptisch Nubien* (1984). He died in 1980. LC; WhoAustria, 1977/78; WhoWor, 1974/75, 1976/77, 1978/79

Jungwirth, Wolfgang, born 9 August 1909 at Linz, Austria, he received a Dr.jur. in 1953 from the Universität Wien, and subsequently became associated with the Austrian federal ministry of foreign affairs. He was a sometime UN expert of public administration in Egypt, Turkey, and Iraq. Unesco

Junker, Heinrich F. J. born 26 March 1889 at Offenbach, Germany, he received a Dr.phil. in 1911 from the Universität Heidelberg for *The Frahang i Pahlavīk*, and a Dr.habil. in 1912 from the Universität Gießen. He taught comparative philology at the Universität Hamburg, from 1919 to 1926, when he was invited to become a professor at the Universität Leipzig. A member of the Saxon academy of sciences from 1926 to 1946, he was appointed in 1951 to the chair of Iranian studies at Humboldt-Universität, Berlin. He there headed the institute of Iranian and Caucasian languages which later also included Turkish and Arabic studies. He was with Bozorg Alavi, the joint author of *Persisch-deutsches Wörterbuch* (1965), and he edited and translated *Der wißbegierige Sohn* (1959). He died on 3 April 1970. *Iranistische Mitteilungen*, 4 (1970), pp. 60-61; Kürschner, 1950-1970; Schwarz; *Wer ist wer*, 1955-1967/68

Junker (Юнкеръ), *Wilhelm Johann*, born in 1840 at Moscow, he started his African exploration in 1873 in Tunisia, where he remained for nearly a year, before travelling on to Egypt, the Red Sea, and the Sudan. Since 1876 he explored eastern Equatorial Africa. He led a relief expedition to Emin Pasha who was besieged by the Mahdists at his headquarters. He returned to Europe by way of Zanzibar in 1886. His valuable ethnographical collection went to the Völkerkunde Museum in Berlin. The account of his years of exploration is embodied in his *Reisen in Afrika* (1889-91), and its translation, *Travels in Africa during the years 1879-1883* (1891). He died in St. Petersburg on 13 February 1892. ADtB, vol. 50, pp. 723-29; DtBE; Embacher; EnSlovar; Henze; Hill; Kornrumpf; Note; WhWE

Junker von Langegg, Ferdinand Adalbert, born in 1828, his writings include *El Dorado; Geschichte der Entdeckungsreisen nach dem Goldlande im 16. und 17. Jahrhundert* (Leipzig, 1888), and *Krypto-Monotheismus in den Religionen der alten Chinesen und anderer Völker* (1892).

Jürgens, Hans Wilhelm, born 29 June 1932 at Wolfenbüttel, Germany, he received a Dr.rer.nat. in 1959 from the Universität Kiel for a study of rural depopulation entitled *Beitrag zur Frage der geographischen und sozialen Mobilität bei der Abwanderung vom Lande*. He became successively a lecturer and professor of population studies until 1974, when he became a director of a variety of German federal institutes for the study of population and demography. In 1977 he prepared an expertise on Bangladesh for the German society for technical cooperation, Eschborn. His writings include *Beiträge zur Binnenwanderung und Bevölkerungsentwicklung in Liberia* (1965), and *Untersuchungen zur Binnenwanderung in Zanzania* (1968). Kürschner, 1992-2005; Note about the author; WhoScEu, 1991

Jurien de la Gravière, Jean Pierre *Edmond*, born 19 November 1812 at Brest (Finistère), France, he joined the French navy in 1828, plying the waters of the Levant, Senegal, and Brazil. At the time of the

Crimean War, he had advanced to become Admiral Bruat's chief of the general staff. From 1864 to 1870 he was A.D.C. to the *Empereur*; in 1871, he became director general of the Dépôt des Cartes et Plans; and since 1888 he was a president of the Académie française. His writings include *Le Drame macédonien* (1883), *Doria et Barberousse* (1886), *Les Chevaliers de Malte et la marine de Philippe II* (1887), *Les Corsairs barbaresques et la marine de Soliman le Grand* (1887), *La Guerre de la Chypre et la bataille de Lépante* (1888), and *La Flotille de l'Euphrate* (1892). He died in Paris on 5 March 1892. DBF; IndexBFr² (9); Master (1); Vapereau

Jurischitz (Jurišič), Nicolaus (Niklas, Miklós), born about 1490 at Zengg (Senj), Croatia, he entered the service of Ferdinand I of Austria, accomplishing important military and diplomatic missions. He is best remembered for his heroic defence of Güns against the large Turkish army of Süleyman II in August of 1532, a success for which he was knighted by Emperor Charles V. He subsequently achieved military and administrative honours in Lower Austria. In 1551, he again fought against the Turks in Hungary in the army of the Imperial Field Marshal Reinprecht von Ebersdorf. His writings include *Sendbrief vñ warhafte vrkundt Türckischer belaegerung, Stuermung vnd handlung, des Schloss vnd der Stat Güns* (Augsburg, 1532), and *Des Türcken erschröckenliche Belegerung der Stadt und Schloss Günss, uñ desselbigen nach zwelf verlorn Stürmen abzug* (Augsburg, 1532). He died in Wien in 1543 and was buried in Güns. ADtB, vol. 14, p. 743, vol. 21, p. 795; BLC; Magyar

Juritzky-Warberg, Alfred Antonin, born 30 August 1887 at Weißenbach on Traun, Austria, he was educated at Theresianische Akademie and subsequently studied law and history of art at the Universität Wien. The last descendant of an old noble family, he brought together a significant art collection at his castle, Schloß *Mon Repos*, in Gablitz. He was a sometime editor of the English-German art periodical, *Belvedere*. DiBilnd (1)

Jurquet, Jacques, born 20th cent., his writings include *Le Printemps révolutionnaire de 1968; essai d'analyse marxiste-leniniste* (Paris, 1968), *La Révolution nationale algérienne et le Parti communiste français* (1974-79), and *Mouvements communiste et nationaliste en Algérie* (1982). LC; ZKO

Jus, Henri, born 20 January 1832 at Ardendes (Indre), France, he was an agricultural engineer who, in the service of the Ministère de l'Instruction publique, worked on artesian wells in the south of Constantine Province, Algeria. His writings include *Les Forages artésiens de la province de Constantine, Algérie; résumé des travaux exécutés de 1856 à 1878* (1878), *Les Plantes textiles algériennes à l'Exposition universelle de 1878; histoire d'une botte d'alfa* (1878), *Les Sondages artésien de la province de Constantine, Algérie, et les oasis de l'Oued Rir'; résumé des travaux exécutés de 1856 à 1878* (1878), *Les Oasis de l'Oued Rir' en 1856 et 1879, suivies du Résumé des travaux de sondages exécutés de 1878 à 1879* (1897), *Résumé graphique des sondages exécutés dans la province de Constantine du 1er juin 1856 au 1er janvier 1890, suivi d'une notice sur la région de l'Oued Rir'* (1890), and *À travers les merveilles de Lourdes* (1911). AfrBiolnd; BN; ZKO

Juste y Garcés, Joaquin, he was a head of administration as well as an editor of*La República Federal* and other Madrid periodicals. He also contributed to the *Diario Mercantil* of Córdoba. Ossorio

Justel Calabozo, Braulio, born 20th cent., he received a doctorate in Semitic philology and a diploma in Romance philology. He was a professor of Arabic language and literature at the Universidad de Cádiz, a director of the Escuela Universitaria de Formación del Professorado de E. G. B. de la Linea de la Concepción, and librarian at the Real Biblioteca de El Escorial. His writings include *La Real Biblioteca de El Escorial y sus manuscritos árabes* (1978), *El Toledano Patricia de la Torre* (1991), and he edited and translated from the Arabic *La Hidāya de Al-Raŷrāŷī; un espejo de príncipes medieval* (1983). Arabismo, 1992; ZKO

Justi, Carl Wilhelm, born 14 January 1767 at Marburg, Hesse, he studied theology from 1782 to 1788 at the universities of Marburg and Jena. He was a private tutor to a princely family at Wetzlar, before he became in 1790 a deputy deacon at the Lutheran Pfarrkirche in Marburg. An archdeacon since 1801, he became in 1802 superintendent of the Lutheran congregations of Upper Hesse. Concurrently he taught since 1791 philosophy and later also theology at the Universität Marburg. He edited the *Hessische Denkwürdigkeiten* (1799-1805). His writings include the translations, *Nationalgesänge der Hebräer neu übersetzt* (1803-1815), and *Blumen althebräischer Dichtkunst* (1809). He died in Marburg on 7 August 1846. ADtB, v. 14, pp. 753-57; DtBE; DtBilnd (6)

Justi, Ferdinand, born 2 June 1837 at Marburg, Hesse, he studied German and comparative philology at the Universität Marburg, and Indo-European and Semitic languages at the Universität Göttingen, where he received both a Dr.phil. and Dr.habil. in 1861. Since 1865 he taught German philology at the Universität Marburg, but his research centred on Orientalism, mainly Iranian studies. Although he never visited Persia, he was considered the best Iranian scholar of his day. His writings include

Handbuch der Zendsprache (1864), Der Bundehesh (1868), Beiträge zur alten Geographie Persiens (1869-1870), Kurdische Grammatik (1880), Geschichte der orientalischen Völker im Altertum (1884), and Iranisches Namenbuch (1895). He died on 17 February 1907 where he had been born. AllgLKünst; DtBE; DtBiInd (3); EncicUni; NDB

Justinard, Léopold Victor, born 14 May 1878 at Nogent-sur-Seine, France, he graduated in 1899 from the military college, Saint-Cyr. Attracted by Africa, he volunteered for service with the *tirailleurs* in Morocco, where he spent his entire career, resigning, most highly decorated, with the rank of colonel. Early in life he had learned colloquial Arabic, and he continued reading and writing in order to perfect his competence. His writings include *Notes sur l'histoire de Sous au XVIe siècle* (1933), *Le Caid Goundafi* (1951), *Un Petit royaume berbère, le Tazeroualt* (1954), and he translated *La Rihla du marabout de Tasaft* (1940). He died at the Hôpital militaire du Val de Grâce on 16 February 1959. Hommes et destins, vol. 2, pp. 400-405

Juynboll, Abraham Willem Theodorus, born 28 October 1834 (according to family tradition) at Franeker, the Netherlands, he studied at Leiden, where he also received a doctorate in 1863 for his thesis, *Juda en de Assyrische macht*. He taught Javanese at the Indische Instelling tot Opleiding van Oost Indische Ambtenaren, Delft, until 1872, when he was appointed professor of Dutch East Indies studies. His writings include *Specimen e literis orientalibus, exhibens Kitabo'l-boldan* (1861); and he was joint editor of Yaqut's *Lexicon geographicum* (1852-1864). He died on 4 February 1887. Letter from G.H.A. Juynboll to the writer; EncNI; LC; NieuwNBW, v. 1, cols. 1237-1238

Juynboll, Gualtherus (*Gautier*) Hendrik Albert, born 20 October 1935 in the Netherlands, he received a Ph.D. in 1969 from the Rijksuniversiteit te Leiden with a thesis entitled *The Authenticity of the tradition literature; discussions in modern Egypt*. He was a sometime professor of Islamic studies at the University of Exeter until he resigned in the early 1990s to become a private scholar at Leiden. His writings include *Muslim tradition* (1983), and in the History of al-Tabari series, *The Conquest of Iraq, Southwestern Persia, and Egypt* (1989). In the mid-1990s he began research on a comprehensive study of the canonical *hadith* literature accompanied by an annotated English translation, a work which he planned to complete in the first decade of the twenty-first century. LC; Private

Juynboll, Hendrik Herman, born 24 July 1867 at Delft, the Netherlands, he studied classical and oriental philology at Leiden, where he took his doctorate in 1893 with a thesis which dealt with the Old-Javanese version of the Mahabharata. In 1899, he joined the staff of the Rijks Ethnografisch Museum Leiden. In 1909, he was appointed the Museum's director, a position which he held until his retirement in 1932. His writings include *Oudjavaansch-Nederlandsch woordenlijst* (1923), *Catalogus van de Maleische en Sundaneesche handschriften der Leidsche Universiteitsbibliothek* (1899) and *Javanische Altertümer* (1909). He spent the last years of his life in the home of his daughter at Bethesda, Md., where he died 25 October 1945. Far Eastern quarterly 5 (Feb. 1946), p. 216; LC; Private

Juynboll, Theodoor Willem, born 11 March 1866, he was a student of M. J. de Goeje and had studied also law, specialzing in *fiqh* and tradition. He received a doctorate in 1894 from the Rijkuniversiteit te Leyden with a thesis entitled *Over het historische verband tusschen de Mohammedaansche bruids-gave en het rechtskarakter van het oud-Arabische huwelijk*. He edited *Kitab al-kharaj* of Yahyá ibn Adam (1896), and also the fourth volume of al-Bukhari's *Musnad* (1907-1908). He is best remembered for his *Handleiding tot de kennis van de mohammedaansche wet volgens de leer der Sjafi'itische school*, a work which went through four editions between 1903 and 1925, and its translations, *Handbuch des islamischen Gesetzes* (1910), and *Manuale di diritto musulmano* (1916). He died in 1948. Fück, pp. 325-326

Juynboll, Theodorus Wilhelmus (Guilhelmus/Willem) Johannes (Jan), born 6 April 1802 at Rotterdam. He studied theology and Semitic philology at Leiden, where he received a doctorate in 1828 with a thesis entitled *De Amoso*. He was appointed professor of Semitic literature at Franeker in 1831, at Groningen in 1841, and finally at Leiden in 1845. He was a Samaritan scholar who also edited *Abu'l Mahasin ibn Tagri Bardii Annales*. His writings include *Letterkundige bijdragen* (1838). He died in Leiden on 16 September 1861. CelCen; DcBiPP; NieuwNBW, v. 1, col. 1238

Juynboll, Wilhelmina Maria Cornelia, born on 15 July 1898, she was the only daughter of Theodoor Willem Juynboll. She received a doctorate in 1931 from the Rijksuniversiteit te Utrecht for her thesis, *Zeventiende eeuwsche beoefenaars van het arabisch in Nederland*. She died on 5 August 1982. NUC, pre-1956; Private

Jwaideh, Albertine *see* Cox, Albertine née Jwaideh

Jwaideh, Zuhair E., born 3 June 1920 in Iraq, he received his law degree in 1944 from Baghdad University and practised his profession until 1948, when he emigrated to the United States. There he received his M.A, in comparative law in 1952 and his doctorate in juridical science in 1956 from George Washington University Law School. He subsequently joined the Library of Congress first as assistent chief of the Near East section of the Orientalia Division and then, since 1959, as chief of the Law Library's Near East and North African Division, a post which he held until May 1991. He died on 8 November 1991. He was instrumental in establishing a LC field office in Cairo in 1961. IWWAS, 1976/77; MESA bulletin 26 i (1992), pp. 153-54

Jyrkänkallio, Paul Georg, born 25 March 1922 at Björkö, Viipuri, Finland, he studied at Helsinki and also from 1950 to 1951 at Ankara Üniversitesi. He entered the Finnish diplomatic service and successively served as an ambassador in Paris, Moscow, Cairo, Sofia, and Budapest. His writings include the booklet, *Übersicht über die türkischen Völker unserer Zeit* (Helsinki, 1950). Vem och vad, 1975-1986

Kaba, Lansiné, born on 19 January 1941 at Kankan, Guinea, he was educated at the Sorbonne, Paris, where he received a degree in 1966, gaining a Ph.D. in 1972 from Northwestern University, Evanston, Illinois, for *Evolution of Islam in West Africa; the Wahhabi movement and its contribution to political development, 1945-1958*. He started to teach French in 1970 at the University of Minnesota, Minneapolis, and later became a professor of African studies at the University of Illinois, Chicago, a post which he still held in 2005. His writings include *The Wahhabiyya; Islamic reform and politics in French West Africa* (1974), *Le Guinée dit "non" à de Gaulle* (1989), and *Kwame N'Krumah et le rêve de l'unité africaine* (1991). ConAu, 61-64; NatFacDr, 1900-2005; Selim; ZKO

Kabátník, Martin, born 15th cent., he was a Bohemian who travelled to Jerusalem and Cairo from 1491-1492. He left the travel account, *Martina Kabátnika cesta z Čech do Jerusaléma a Kaira r. 1491 92*, edited by Justin V. Prášek (Praha, 1894). IES; Martinek; OSK; OttůvSN

Kabis, Marc, born 19th cent., his writings include *Introduction à l'étude de la langue copte* (Paris, 1862). His trace is lost after his article on the use of colloquial Arabic in teaching, which appeared in the *Bulletin de l'Institut égyptien* in 1880. Note about the author

Kabrda, Josef, born 3 February 1906 at Frýdlant nad Ostravicí, Moravia, he studied Turkology and Islamics, but considered it practical for his career to take a doctorate in history with a thesis on Moravian demography, followed by the prerequisites for teaching history and geography at secondary schools. In 1934 he set out for Bulgaria where he pursued his linguistic studies by teaching at a Muslim Turkish-speaking school at Kolarovgrad. Three years later, he moved on to Paris where, in 1939, he took diplomas in Bulgarian, Turkish, and modern Greek at l'École nationale des langues orientales vivantes. Returning to his occupied homeland in the summer of 1939, he found a post as substitute teacher at a secondary school at Německý-Brod (Havlíčkův-Brod). Declared unloyal, his activity was curbed until after the war. It was not until 1947 that he obtained a lectureship in history of South East Europe and the Middle East at Brno, where he later was instrumental in the creation of the Centre for Balkan and Hungarian studies at the Faculty of Arts. In the spring of 1968 he was granted the rare privilege of visiting Ankara Üniversitesi for a few days, a visit which turned into a few weeks spent in hospital after a heart infarct, but after the second attack he died on 27 May 1968. Archiv orientální 37 (1969), pp. 149-155; Filipsky

Kachel, Gustav, born 1 August 1843 at Karsruhe, Baden, Germany, he studied architecture at the Polytechnikum, Karsruhe, and subsequently made research visits to Italy, Egypt, Palestine, and Greece. In 1869, he was commissioned with the reconstruction and artist rennovation of Schloß Neuwied. Since 1872, he lectured at the Bauakademie, Berlin, with a cross-appointment to Lehranstalt des Kunstgewerbemuseums. In 1876, he became a curator of public monuments in Baden; two years later he became director of the Landesgewerbeschule. His writings include *Kunstgewerbliche Vorbilder aus dem Altertum* (Karlsruhe, 1879). He died in Karsruhe on 31 March 1882. DtBE

Kaddafi, Muammar *see* Qaddafi, Mu'ammar

Kaddoumi, Farouk, 1930- *see* al-Qaddūmī, Fārūq

Kadi, Leila, born 20th *see* Qadi, Laylá Salim al-

Kadi, Wadad A., 1943- *see* Qadi, Wadad A. al-

Kadymov, Ramiz Gulam oghly, his writings include Борьба рабочих за развитие нефтедобывающей промышленности Азербайджана (Baku, 1967). LC

Kaegi, Walter Emil, born 8 November 1937 at New Albany, Ind., he graduated in 1959 from Haverford (Pa.) College, and received a Ph.D. in 1965 from Harvard for *Byzantium and the decline of Rome*, a work which was published in 1968. After working at Dumbarton Oaks from 1963 to 1965, he started teaching Byzantine and Roman history at the University of Chicago, a post which he still held in 2005. His writings include *Byzantium and the early Islamic conquests* (1992). ConAu, 25-28, new rev., 10; DrAS, 1974 H, 1978 H, 1982 H; IndAu, 1967; NatFacDr, 1990-2005; ZKO

Kaempfer, Engelbert, born in 1651 at Lemgo, Westphalia, he studied medicine at Thorn, Krakau, and Königsberg and subsequently lived in Sweden until invited to join the embassy sent by King Charles XI of Sweden to the Shah of Persia. He lived in Isfahan, 1683-84, and left behind an excellent account of the Safavid capital and the country's court and administration, a work which was edited in 1977 by Walther Hinz entitled *Am Hofe des persischen Großkönigs, 1684-1685*; a Persian translation was published in 1350/1971. He later also visited Japan. He died in 1716, where he had been born. In 1982 appeared *Engelbert Kaempfer zum 330. Geburtstag; gesammelte Beiträge zur Engelbert-Kaempfer-Forschung und zur Frühzeit der Asienforschung in Europa*, edited by Hans Hüls. AnaBrtit; BbD; BiD&SB; Bioln, 8, 13; *Cambridge history of Iran*, vol. 6, p. 305, etc.; DcScB; DtBE; DtBiInd (9); Master (3); WhWE

Kafarov, Piotr Ivanovich, 1817-1878 *see* Palladius, archimandrite

Kaganė, Liudmila L'vovna, born 20th cent., her writings include *Испанская живопись в Эрмитаже* (1970), *Мурильо и художники Андалусии XVI века в собрании Эрмитажа* (1984), and she was a joint author of *Искусство семнадцатого века* (1964). LC; OSK

Kagramanov (Гəhрəманов), Dzhakhangir Vagid oghly, born 10 February 1927 in Soviet Azerbajan, he graduated in 1950 from the Oriental Faculty of the Azerbaijan State University and received his first degree in 1955 for *История философской терминологии азербайджанского литературного языка*. A lecturer since 1958, he received his doctorate in 1969 for *Научно-критический текст и лексика произведений Имадеддина Назими*, and subsequently became a professor in 1974 and a Merited Scholar of Azerbaijan in 1982. Since 1972, he was a director of the state manuscripts in the Azerbaijan Academy of Sciences. His writings include *Описание археографических документов* (1969), *Лексика "Дивана" Насими* (1970); he was a joint author of *Рукописи произведений Низами Гянджеви в мировых хранилищах* (1987); and he was a joint editor of *Мустафа Зərир: Jусиф вə Зулеjха; поəманын мəтни вə тарихи-грамматик очерк* (1991). Miliband²; OSK

Kahane, Henry (Heinrich) Romanos, born 2 November 1902 at Berlin, he studied at the universities of Berlin, Roma, and Greifswald, and received a Dr.phil. in 1932 from the Universität Berlin for *Bezeichnung der Kinnbacke im Galloromanischen*. He emigrated to Firenze, where he was a lecturer from 1934 to 1938. From 1941 to his retirement he was a professor of Romance languages at the University of Illinois at Urbana. He was a joint author of *Spoken Greek* (1945), *The Lingua franca in the Levant; Turkish nautical terms of Italian and Greek origin* (1958), *Structural studies on Spanish themes* (1959), and *The Krater and the grail; hermetic sources of the Parzival* (1965). He died on 11 September 1992. The University of Illinois Archives of Urbana-Champaign, hold the papers for Henry R. and Renée Kahane, 1939-1986. BioHbDtE; DrAS, 1974 F, 1978 F, 1982 F; WhAm, 12; WhoAm, 1974/75-1992

Kahane, Renée née Toole, born in 1907, she was a wife of Henry R. Kahane (1902-1992). She received a Dr.phil. in 1934 from the Universität Berlin for *Wort geschichtliche Studien toupin und bronze*. She was a joint author of *Romano-Aegytiaca* (1961), *The Krater and the grail; hermetic sources of the Parzival* (1965), and *Glossario degli antichi portolani italiani* (1967). The University of Illinois Archives of Urbana-Champaign hold the papers for Henry R. and Renée Kahane, 1939-1986. Bioln, 6; GV; LC; ZKO

Kahane, Reuben, born in 1931, he received a Ph.D. in 1970 form the University of California at Berkeley for *Higher education and political integration; the case of India*. His writings include *The Problem of political legitimacy in an antagonistic society; the Indonesian case* (1973), *The Origins of postmodern youth; informal youth movements in a comparative perspective* (1997), as well as writings in Hebrew; and he was a joint editor of *Orthodoxy, heterodoxy, and dissent in India* (1984). LC

Kahin, George McTurnan, bon 25 January 1918 at Baltimore, Md., he was from 1961 to 1970 a director of the Southeast Asia Program at Cornell University, Ithaca, N.Y. During the Vietnam war he loudly protested the United States' involvement in the war. His writings include *The Asian-African Conference, Bandung, 1955* (1956), *Nationalism and revolution in Indonesia* (1959), and he was a joint editor of *Major governments of Asia* (1959), and *Governments and politics of Southeast Asia* (1959). He died in Rochester, N.Y., on 29 January 2000. AmM&WSc, 1973 S, 1978 S; ConAu, 144, 187; WhAm, 14; WhoAm, 1984-2000

Kahl, Jewgenii Fe., 1861-1891 *see* Kal', Evgenii Fe.

Kahle, Erhart, born about 1942, he received a Dr.phil. in 1972 from the Universität Erlangen for *Studien zur Syntax des Adjektivs im vorklassischen Arabisch*, and a Dr.habil. in 1982 from the Universität Würzburg for *Die Kinderkrankheiten in mittelalterlichen arabischen Kinderregimina.* He taught history of medicine at the Universität Würzburg. His writings include *Al-Maǧusi über Kinderkrankheiten* (1980), and *Bibliographie der Hochschulschriften zur Geschichte der Medizin, Pharmazie und Naturwissenschaften der Universität Breslau, 1811-1945* (1986). Kürschner, 1987-2005; Schwarz

Kahle, Paul Ernst, born in 1875 at Hohenstein, East Prussia, he studied theology and Oriental languages, particularly Hebrew, at the universities of Marburg, Halle/Saale, and Berlin. He was a pastor and school principal at the German school in Cairo, from 1903 to 1908, and subsequently worked in Deutsches Institut für Altertumskunde in Jerusalem until 1914, when he was invited to teach Oriental languagues at the Universität Gießen. In 1923, he went to the Universität Bonn to teach in the same capacity. He emigrated in 1939 to Oxford, returning in 1963 to Germany, where he died in Düsseldorf on 24 September 1964. BioHbDtE; Bonner, vol. 8, pp. 350-53; DtBE; DtBilnd (3); Hanisch; *Index Islamicus* (3); JüdLex; Kürschner, 1961; NDB; *Who was who*, 6

Kahlenberg, Mary Hunt, born 19 October 1940 at Wallingford, Conn., she graduated in 1962 from Boston University and subsequently studied at art schools and academies at Wien, Berlin, and Chicago. She was associated with the Los Angeles County Museum of Art. She was a joint author of *The Navajo blanket* (1973); she also compiled several exhibition catalogues of museums in the Los Angeles area. ConAu, 45-48, new rev., 2; Master (1); WhoAmA, 1976-1986|; WhoEmL, 1989 (not sighted); WhoWest, 1984/85-1987

Kähler, Hans, born 16 February 1912 at Uetersen, Holstein, Germany, he received a Dr.phil. in 1937 from the Universität Hamburg for *Untersuchungen über die Laut-, Wort- und Satzlehre des Nias.* From 1919 until his retirement in 1978 he was a professor of Indonesian and South Sea languages at his alma mater. His writings include *Die Sichule-Sprache auf der Insel Simalur an der Westküste von Sumatra* (1955), *Studien über die Kultur, die Sprache und die arabisch-afrikaanse Literatur der Kap-Malaien* (1971), and he edited *Texte von der Insel Enggano* (1975). In 1982 appeared *Gava'; studies in Austronesian languages and cultures dedicated to Hans Kähler.* He died on 8 May 1983. Kürschner, 1950-1983

Kähler-Meyer, Emmi, born 30 November 1903 at Hamburg, she received a Dr.phil. in 1937 from the Universität Hamburg for *Etymologische Lautlehre des Nyanja*, and also a Dr.habil. in 1939/40 under her maiden name, Meyer. Since 1940, she taught African languages at her alma mater in various capacities. Her writings include *Die Ewe-Sprache in Togo* (1961), and she was a joint author of *Wörterbuch der Duala-Sprache* (1976). She spent the last years of her life at an old age home in Aumühle near Hamburg, where she died in 1998. *Afrika und Übersee*, 81 (1998), pp. 161-166, Kürschner, 1954-1996

Kahn, Margaret, born 9 April 1949 at N.Y.C., she graduated in 1971 from Barnard College, New York, and received a Ph.D. in 1976 from the University of Michigan, Ann Arbor, for *Borrowing and variation in a phonological description of Kurdish.* She was an English teacher at Rezaiyeh College, Urmia, Iran, in 1974/1975. Her "fascination with foreign languages and exotic cultures sidetracked her temporarily into an academic career" at a variety of American colleges and universities, but since the late 1970s she thought of becoming a writer. Her writings include *Children of the jinn; in search of the Kurds and their country* (1980). ConAu, 101; Selim³; ZKO

Kahrl, Faith née Jessup, born 18 September 1902 at Beirut, she graduated in 1925 from Vassar College, Poughkeepsie, N.Y., and was married in 1929 to George Morrow Kahrl. Her writings include *The Memoirs of Faith Jessup Kahrl*; edited by Rosemary O. Joyce (1989). LC; Note

Kahrstedt, H. G. Ulrich, born 27 April 1888 at Neiße, Prussia, he studied at Edinburgh, Straßburg, and Berlin, where he received a Dr.phil. in 1910 for *Die Politik des Demosthenes.* He was a professor of classics successively at the universities of Münster and München. His writings include *Pax Americana; eine historische Betrachtung am Wendepunkt der europäischen Geschichte* (1920), *Staatsgebiete und Staatsangehörigkeit in Athen* (1934), *Kulturgeschichte der römischen Kaiserzeit* (1944), *Beiträge zur Geschichte der thrakischen Chersones* (1954), and *Die wirtschaftliche Lage Großgriechenlands in der Kaiserzeit* (1960). He died in Göttingen on 27 January 1962. DtBilnd (1); Kürschner, 1928/29-1961; *Wer ist's*, 1928, 1935; *Wer ist wer*, 1950-1962

Kaĭdarov, Abduali Tuganbaevich, born 13 December 1924 in Kazakhstan, he graduated in 1951 from the Kazakhstan State University, received his first degree in 1955 for *Парные слова в современном уйгурском языке*, and a doctorate in Turkish philology in 1970 for *Уйгурские диалекты и диалектная основа литературного языка.* A director of the Institute of Linguistic Sciences, Kazakhstan Academy of Sciences, he was appointed a professor in 1982. His writings include *Уйгурский язык и литера-тура; аннотированный библиографический указатель* (1962),

Развитие казахского совет-ского языкознания (1980), *Проблемы этимологии тюркских языков* (1990), and he was a joint author of *Ьазирҗи заман уйгур тили* (1963). Kazakhskaia, vol. 3, p. 251; Miliband; Miliband[2]

Kail, Owen Cooke, born 28 April 1922 at Bombay, he was a business executive. A member of several learned societies, his writings include *Buddhist cave temples of India* (1975), *The Dutch in India* (1981), *Elephanta, the island of mystery* (1984), as well as contributions to journals in the field. IntAu&W, 1976, 1977, 1982; *Who's who of Indian writers*, 1983 (not sighted)

Kaim, Julius Rolf, Dr., born 19th cent., he visited Constantinople in 1927. His writings include *Der Sinn der Literaturwissenschaft* (1921), *Geist des Morgenlandes* (1927), *Der Balkan und seine Probleme* (1928), *Westöstliche Welt; unter Slawen, Griechen, Türken* (1930), *1001 Nacht heute; Menschen und Mächte im Orient* (1937), *Damals in Schanghai; Kaiser, Kaufleute und Kommunisten* (1963), and *Pariserinnen* (1965). Note; ZKO

Kaiser, Alfred, born about 1862, he studied natural sciences at Zürich and München and became a lifelong student of the Sinai, where he travelled extensively. His writings include *Die Sinaiwüste* (1922), and *Der heutigen Stand der Mannafrage* (1924). He died in Arbon, Switzerland, in April 1930. Note

Kaiser, Ernst, born 23 December 1885 at Hildburghausen, Saxe-Meiningen, Germany, he received a Dr.phil.nat. and became a *Akademie-Professor* at Erfurt. He died on 7 July 1961, where he had been born. Kürschner, 1950-1961

Kaiser, Henry John, born 9 May 1882 at Sprout Brook, N.Y., he was a contractor and industrial executive. The recipient of medals, honours, and honorary university degrees, his writings include *Management looks at the post-war world* (1948), and *Imagine your future* (1948). He died on 24 August 1967. Master (25); WhAm, 4, Addendum; *Who was who*, 6

Kaiser, Karl, born 8 December 1934 at Siegen, Germany, he received a Dr.rer.pol., a Dr.habil. (1968/69) and a French diploma. He was since 1971 a director of the research centre of the German association for foreign policy (Deutsche Gesellschaft für Auswärtige Politik,) Köln, concurrently serving as a professor at the Universität Köln. A visiting professor in Germany and abroad, his writings include *EWG und Freihandelszone* (1963), *Die neue Weltpolitik* (1995), and *Weltpolitik im neuen Jahrhundert* (2000). IntWW, 1993/93-2006; Kürschner, 1980-2005

Kajmaković, Zdravko, fl. 20th cent., his writings include *Šta je spomenik kulture* (Sarajevo, 1961), and *Зидно сликарство у Босни Херцеговини* (Sarajevo, 1971). OSK

Kakharova, Naima Abdulakhadovna, born 2 January 1942 at Pendzhikent, Tajikistan, she graduated in 1963 from the Arabic Section of the Tajikistan State University, and received her first degree in 1968 for *Рифа'а Рафи ат-Тахтави и его произведение "Извлечние чист. золота из посещения Парижа"*. She was associated with the Oriental Institute of the Tajikistan Academy of Sciences since 1963. Miliband[2]

Kakharova, Nazira Abdulakhadovna, born 24 November 1939 at Pendzhikent, Tajikistan, she graduated in 1962 from the Institute of History and Philology, Tajikistan State University, and received her first degree in 1970 for *Саади и его роль в развитии газели*. From 1962 to her death on 14 February 1984 she taught at her alma mater; in 1976 she was appointed a lecturer. Miliband[2]

Kakhiani (Кахиани), TSisia Prokof'efna, born 8 May 1925 at Tiflis, she graduated in 1947 from Tiflis State University, and received her first degree in 1966 for her monograph, *Арабские надписи из Дманиси*. She became associated first with the Institute of Linguistics, and since 1960 with Oriental Institute of the Georgian Academy of Sciences. Miliband; Miliband[2]

Kaklamanos (Caclamanos), Demetrios, born in 1872 at Nauplia, Greece, he studied at Athens University, where he also received a doctorate. He had a brief career as a publisher and editor before he started his foreign service career as chief of the Ministry of Foreign Affairs at Athens in 1907. He was posted to Paris in 1910 as first secretary of the legation, and to Roma as chargé d'affairs from 1912 to 1914. He represented Greece at the League of Nations on several occasions as well as at the Lausanne Peace Conference, 1922-1923. From 1918 until his retirement in 1935 he was Honorary Greek Minister in London. His writings include *Greece in peace and war* (1942), and *Greece, a panorama* (1943). He died in London on 7 June 1949. NYT, 8 June 1949, p. 30, col. 4; *Who was who*, 4

Kakuk, Zsuzsa (Suzanne), born 13 August 1925 at Nagytálya, Hungary, she was educated at a Catholic nun's school, and afterwards studied Hungarian and Latin linguistics at the University of Debrecen, where she also received her doctorate. Since 1951 she pursued Turkological studies at the Loránd Eötvös University, Budapest, where she received a doctorate in Turkology for her thesis,

Fejezetek oszmán-török jövevényszavaink történettéből, in 1955. When she retired in 1990, she was a professor and chairman in the Department of Turkology at her alma mater. Her writings include *Recherches sur l'histoire de la langue osmanlie des XVI. et XVII. siècles* (1973), *Cultural words from the Turkish occupation of Hungary* (1977), and *Hungarian Turcology, 1945-1974* (1981). Acta orientalia Academiae scientiarum hungaricae 48 (1995), pp. 247-259; Biograf, 2004; MagyarNKK, 1992, 1994, 1996

Kal' (Калъ/Kahl), Evgenii Fedorovich, born in 1861, he was one of the first to study Oriental languages under Viktor R. Rosen at St. Petersburg and completed his study with a gold medal in 1885. He entered the public administration in Tashkent, where he was able to pursue an interest in local archaeological and linguistic subjects. His writings include a catalogue of Oriental manuscripts in the Tashkent Public Library, *Персидская, арабская и тюркския рукописи Туркестанской Публичьной Библиотеки* (1889). He died in 1891. Krachkovskiĭ

Kalau vom Hofe, Kurt Karl Friedrich, also Eugen, born in 1850, he was a rear-admiral in the German navy, and a writer on naval operations. He wrote *Unsere Flotte im Weltkriege, 1914/15* (Berlin, 1915), *Die kämpfenden Flotten im Weltkriege* (1916), *Das Unterseeboot und der Krieg* (Berlin, 1918), and *Der Handelskrieg der Unterseeboote* (1919). GV; NUC, pre-1956

Kalb, Philine, about 1940, she received a Dr.phil. in 1969 from the Universität Freiburg im Breisgau for *Die Siedlungsarchitektur von Cerro de la Virgen bei Oce (Provinz Granada)*. She was associated with Deutsches Archäologisches Institut, Madrid, and a joint editor of *Die Megalithgräber der Iberischen Halbinsel* (1998). GV

Kaldy-Nagy, Gyula, born 14 July 1927 at Nagydém, Hungary, he was a Turkish scholar whose writings include *Harácsszedok és ráják* (1910), *Magyarországi török adóösszeírások* (1970), *Kanuni devri Budin tahrir defteri, 1546-1562* (1971), and he edited *The Muslim East; studies in honour of Julius Germans* (1974), and *Hungaro-Turcica; studies in honour of Julius Nemeth* (1976). Biograf, 2004; ZKO

Kaleši, Hasan, born 7 March 1922 at the village of Sërbicë near Kërçovë (Kičevo), Macedonia, he went to school first at the village school, and was later educated at the *medrese* in Skopje and the gymnasium in Priština. He studied Oriental and Romance subjects at Beograd, where he graduated in 1951. An assistant at its Faculty of Philosophy since 1952, he concurrently worked on his thesis, *Najstariji vakufski dokumenti u Jugoslaviji na arapskom jeziku* [The oldest vaqf documents in Arabic in Yugoslavia], a work which was accepted in 1960 and published in 1972. He subsequently spent two semesters at the Universität Hamburg, before becoming an academic member in the Institute of Albanian Studies, Prishtina, where he was appointed head of Oriental studies in 1970. In his writings he tried to demonstrate the advantages of Albania's long Turkish occupation which, far from being a period of barbarism and suppression, safeguarded the ethnic survival of the Albanians and prevented their being Slavonized or Græcized. He was a joint author of *Три вакуфнами на Качаникли Мехмед-Паша* (1958), *Srpskohrvatsko-arapski rječnik* (1988), and he translated *Haxhi Çelebiu dhe tregime tjera* (1968). He died from heart failure on 19 July 1976, three days after a guest lecture at the Universität München. Anali Husrev-Begove Biblioteke, 7/8, (1982), pp. 273-74; Index Islamicus (3); Prilozi za orijentalnu filologiju, 25 (1975), pp. 8-9; Südostforschungen, 35 (1976), pp. 252-53

Kalić-Mijušković, Jovanka (Јованка Калић), born 15 September 1933 at Beograd, she studied history at Beograd University, where she received a doctorate in 1967 for *Beograd u srednejem veku*. She became a lecturer in history at her alma mater. Her writings include *Срби у позном средњем веку* (1994). EncJug; JugoslSa, 1970; OSK

Kaliev (Қалиұлы), Gabdulla (Ғабдолла), born 20th cent., he was a joint author of *Қазақ диалектологиясы* (1991), and *Қазирги қазақ тилиниң лексикологиясы мен фразеологиясы* (1997). OSK

Kalimov, Abdurakhman, born 5 May 1923 at Irdyk, Kirgizia, he graduated in 1942 from the Kirgiz Pedagogical State University, and received his first degree in 1951 for *Грамматические особенности счетных слов, счетных суффиксов и единиц измерения в современном дунганском языке*. From 1951 to 1984 he was a researcher in the Oriental Institute of the Soviet Academy of Sciences. He was a joint author of *Русско-дунганский словарь лингвистических и литературоведческих терминов* (1971). Miliband; Miliband²

Kalinin, Nikolaĭ Filippovich, born in 1888, he was an archaeologist and historian, whose writings include *Горький в Казани* (1928), and *Казань; исторический очерк* (Kazan, 1955). He died in 1959. TatarES

Kalinin, Nikolaĭ Georgievich, born 22 June 1922 at Mikhaĭlovskiĭ, Uzbekistan, he graduated in 1949 from the Faculty of History, Moscow State University, and received his first degree in 1954/55 for *Национал-реформистскаяпартия ВАФД и национально-освободительное движение в Египте накануне второй мировой войны, 1934-1937 гг.* After spending the years from 1957 to 1960 in

Cairo, he became associated with the Insitute of Asian and African Studies, Moscow State University. He died on 8 August 1993. Miliband; Miliband[2]

Kalinina, Zoia Mart'ianovna, born 12 February 1923 at Moscow, she graduated in 1948 from the Oriental Institute, Moscow, and received her first degree in 1954 for *Наклонения в современном литературном пушту*. From 1975 to her death on 9 November 1987 she was associated with the Insitute of Asian and African Studies, Moscow State University. Her writings include *Учебник афганского пушту* (1966), and she was a joint author of *Учебник языка пушту* (1953), and *Учебник афганского языка, пушту* (1963). Miliband; Miliband[2]

Kalisky, René, born in 1936, his writings include *Le Monde arabe* (1968), *L'Islam; origine et essor du monde arabe* (1974), and *Sionisme ou dispersion* (1974). He died on 2 May 1981. LC

Kalkas, Barbara E., born about 1950, she received a Ph.D. in 1979 from Northwestern University, Evanston, Illinois, for *Aborted economic and social development in Egypt; new leaders in an old system.* Selim[3]

Kallenberg, Friedrich, born in 1856, he wrote *Auf dem Kriegspfad gegen die Massai; eine Frühlingsfahrt nach Deutsch-Ostafrika* (München, 1892). He died in Bayreuth on 27 May 1939. KDtLK, Nekrolog, 1935-1970

Kallner, David H., born in 1910 at Berlin, he later adopted the name David H. Amiran. He studied at Universität Bern, where he also obtained a doctorate. In 1935, he emigrated to Palestine, and in 1949 began teaching geography at the Hebrew University. He was a joint author of *Geographical conversion tables* (Zürich, 1961). BioHbDtE; EncJud

Kaloev, Boris Aleksandrovich, born 20th cent., his writings include *В. Ф. Миллер - кавказоев* (1963), *Осетины; глазами русских и иностранных путешественников* (1967), *Материальная культура и прикладное искусство осетин* (1973), *Земледелие народов Северного Кавказа* (1981), *Скотоводство народов Северного Кавказа* (1993), *Венгерские аланы (ясы); историко-этнографический очерк* (1996), *Осетинские историко-этнографические этюды* (1999), and he was a joint author of *Народы Кавказа; антропология, лингвистика, хозяйство* (1994). LC; OSK

Kalontarov, IAkub Iskhakovich, fl. 20th cent., his writings include *Таджикско-русский словарь* (1955), *Таджиксие пословицы и поговорки в аналогии с кусскими* (1965), *Таджиксие прсловицы и поговорки в сравнении с узбекскими* (1969), *Прицнпхои асосии терминологияи забони точики* (1971), *Карманный русско-таджикский словарь* (1972), and *Краткий русско-таджикский словарь политических терминов* (1975). OSK

Kaltbrunner, David, born in 1829, he wrote *Manuel du voyageur* (Zürich, 1879), *Aide-mémoire du voyageurs; notions générales de géographie ...* (Zürich, 1881), *Der Beobachter; allgemeine Anleitung zu Beobachtungen über Land und Leute für Touristen* (1888), and *L'Afrique en 1890* (Paris, 1890). He died in 1894. BN; NUC, pre-1956

Kaltenbrunner, Gerd Klaus, born 23 February 1939 at Wien, he wrote *Hegel und die Folgen* (1970), *Rekonstruktion des Konservatismus* (1972), *Geheimgesellschaften und der Mythos der Weltverschwörung* (1987), and he edited *Zur Kritik der deutschen Intelligenz*, of Hugo Ball (1970). KDtLK, 2004/5; Sezgin

Kalter, Johannes, born in 1943, he received a Dr.phil. in 1973 from the Universität Heidelberg for *Die materielle Kultur der Massai und ihr Wandel.* He was in charge of the Oriental Section, Linden-Museum, Stuttgart. His writings include *Schmuck aus Nordafrika* (1976), *Aus marokkanischen Bürgerhäusern* (1977), *Aus Steppe und Oase* (1983), and he was a joint author of the exhibiton catalogue, *Symmetrien in der islamischen Kunst* (1986), *Der lange Weg der Türken; 1500 Jahre türkische Kultur* (2003), and he edited *Erben der Seidenstraße; Usbekistan* (1995), and its translation, *Наследники шелкового пути - Узбекистан* (1997). Kürschner, 2005; LC

Kalus, Ludvik, born 20th cent., he received a *doctorat de 3ème cycle* in 1974 from the Université de Paris for *Contribution à l'étude des boucliers circulaires de l'Orient musulman*, and also a *doctorat d'état* in 1986 for *Les armes et leurs inscriptions dans l'art islamique de l'époque umayyade.* He was in 1993 associated with the Département d'études orientales at the Sorbonne. His writings include *Catalogue des cachets, bulles et talismans islamiques dans la Bibliothèque nationale* (1981), *Catalogue of Islamic seals and talismans in the Ashmolean Museum*, Oxford (1986), *Inscriptions arabes des îles de Bahrain; contribution à l'histoire de Bahrain* (1990), and he was a joint author of *Deux trésors monétaires des premiers temps de l'islam* (1984), and *Corpus d'inscriptions arabes et persanes en Chine* (1991). EURAMES, 1993; *Livres disponibles*, 2003, 2004; THESAM, 3, 4; ZKO

Kałużyński, Stanisław Paweł, born 6 August 1925 at Świerczów, Poland, he studied Oriental languages at the Uniwersytet Wrosławski, where he received doctorates in 1955 and 1963. He subsequently became a professor of Mongol philology at his alma mater, and concurrently served as editor-in-chief of the journal *Przegląd orientalistyczny*. His writings include *Mongolische Elemente in der jakutischen Sprache* (1962), *Die Sprache des mandschurischen Stammes Sibe aus der Gegend von Kuldscha* (1977), *Lacutice; prace jakutoznawcze* (1995), and he was a joint author of *Études maghrébines et soudanaises* (1983). KtoPolsce, 1993; WhoSocCE, 1989

Kalymon, Basil A., born 4 April 1944 at Horlyci, Ukraine, he graduated B.Sc. in 1966 from the University of Toronto, and received a Ph.D. in 1970 from Yale University, New Haven, Conn. He was a professor of business administration at a variety of universities in Canada and America, before he was appointed a professor of finance at the University of Western Ontario, London. His writings include *Rent control, myth and realities* (1981), *Global innovation and the impact on Canada's financial markets* (1989), and he was a joint author of *Studies in resource management* (1973). Canadian who's who, 1998-2005

Kamal, Ahmad, 1851-1923 *see* Ahmad Kamal

Kamali, Sabih Ahmad, born in 1927, he received an M.A. in 1955 from McGill University, Montreal, for his translation, *Ghazali's "Tahafut al-falasifah;"* and a Ph.D. in 1959 for his thesis, *The Concept of human nature in "Hujjat Allah al-Balighah" and its relation to Shah Waliullah's doctrine of fiqh*. He was a sometime professor in the Department for the Study of Religions, University of Ghana, Legan, as well as a member of the editorial board of the *Ghana bulletin of theology*. His writings include *Types of Islamic thought in criticism and reconstruction* (1963). He died in 1991. Ferahian; LC

Kamalov, Sabir (Sabyr) Kamilovich, born 10 September 1924 in the Karakalpak Autonomous Soviet Socialist Republic. His writings include *Каракалпакско-русские отношения в XVIII веке* (1966), *Каракалпаки в XVIII-XIX веках* (1968), and *Навеки вместе* (1973); he was a joint author of *Из истории взаимоотношений каракалпаков с другими народами Средней Азии и Казахстана* (1988); and he edited *Археология Приаралья* (1982-86), and *История каракалпакской литературы* (Tashkent, 1994). LC; OSK; Schoeberlein

Kamarić, Mustafa Emin, born 7 April 1906 at Gračanica, he completed his law with a doctorate and successively served as a superior official in Bosnia-Herzegovina, and as a professor and dean at Sarajevo University since 1945. His writings include *Problemi uredbe s naročitim obzirom na široka ovlašćenja* (1957), *Upravni postupak* (1962), and he was a joint editor of *Регистар прописа, објавлених "Службеном листу Народне Репуьлике Босне и Херцеговине,"* 1945-1950 (1951), and *Zbirka stanbenih i drugih komunalnih propisa* (1951). He died in Feldkirch, Austria, on 5 November 1973. Anali Gazi Husrev-begove biblioteke, 3 (1974), p. 260; EncJug; NUC, pre-1956; OSK

Kamarovskiĭ (Kamarowsky, Komarovskiĭ), Leonid Alekseevich, *graf*, born in 1846 at Kazan, Russia, he received a doctorate in 1884 at Moscow for *О междуеародеом судъ*, and subsequently became a professor of law at Moscow University. He was a member of the Institut du droit international, Bruxelles. His writings include the translation of his thesis, *Le Tribunal international*, (1887), *Обзоръ современной литературы по международому праву* (1887), *Über die Friedens-bestrebungen der Völker* (1890), and *О ролитических причинах войны в современной Европе* (1891). He died in 1912. EnSlovar; GSE, vol. 11, p. 375

Kamen-Kaye, Maurice, born 17 August 1905 at London, he graduated from the Royal College of Science, and the Royal School of Mines, London. He was a petroleum geologist and a consultant. His writings include *Bibliography of Great Basin paleozoic sediments, 1856-1971* (1972), and he was a joint author of *Subsurface exploaration geology* (1970). AmM&WSc, 1989, 1992 (not sighted); WhoE, 1993/94

Kamenev, Sergeĭ Naumovich, born 26 April 1951 at Moscow, he graduated in 1972 from the Moscow Regional Pedagogical Institute and received his first degree in 1976 for *Общественный продукт Пакистана*. Since 1971, he was a research fellow in the Oriental Institute of the Soviet Academy of Sciences. His writings include *Экономический рост Пакистрана* (1977), *Пакистан государств-енные финансы и экономическое развитие* (1982), and *The Economic growth of Pakistan* (1985). Miliband²

Kameneva, Marina Samuilovna, born 22 May 1947 at Moscow, she graduated in 1971 from the Insitute of Asian and African Studies, Moscow State University, and received her first degree in 1976 for *Социально-стилистическая дифференциация современного персидского языка*. She was since 1976 a research fellow in the Oriental Institute of the Soviet Academy of Sciences. Miliband²

Kamian, Bakary, born 26 December 1928 at San, French Sudan, present Mali, he graduated from the Sorbonne, Paris, and in 1972 he was appointed assistant director, Regional Office, Unesco, Dakar. His writings include *La République du Mali* (Bamako, 1961), and *Connaissance de le République du Mali* (1966). AfricaWW, 1996; Unesco; WhoUn, 1975

Kāmil, Murād, born 7 July 1907 at Cairo, he had lost his parents by the time he was thirteen years old, but nevertheless pursued a brilliant career, obtaining a Dr.phil. in 1937 from the Universität Tübingen for *Des Josef ben Gorion (Josippon) Geschichte der Juden nach den Handschriften in Berlin, London, Oxford, Paris und Straßburg*. He was a professor of Semitic languages in Egypt and abroad and an Egyptian government official, but above all he was closely associated with the Coptic Church and Coptic affairs in general. His writings include *Beiträge zur Entstehung der vierradikaligen Verben in den gesprochenen semitischen Sprachen* (1963), and *Aspects de l'Égypte copte* (1965). He died in Cairo on 16 January 1975. *Bulletin de la Société d'Archéologie copte*, 23 (1976/78), pp. 299-301; Sezgin

Kamioka, Kôji, born in 1938, he was affiliated with the Institute for the Study of Languages and Cultures of Asia and Africa, Tokyo, and later taught at Kyoto. He was a joint author of *The interregional trade in the western part of the Indian Ocean; the second report on the dhow trade* (Tokyo, 1979), and *Larestani studies; (1) Lari vocabulary* (Tokyo, 1979). LC; Note

Kamjaschott, J. B., born 18th cent., he wrote *Wanderungen durch Syrien, Egypten und einen Theil von Arabien* (Erfurt, 1806), and the second edition in 1810 entitled *Meine Schicksale in Syrien, Aegypten und Arabien*. BLC; Sezgin

El-Kammash, Magdi Mohamed, born 9 September 1931 at Cairo, his writings include *Economic development and planning in Egypt* (1968), a work which was originally submitted as a doctoral thesis at Duke University, Durham, N.C., in 1965. He was appointed a professor of economics at North Carolina State University, Raleigh, in 1967. AmM&WSc, 1973 S, 1978 S; Selim

Kammerer, Albert, he was born on 9 January 1875. After obtaining a doctorate of law and a *diplôme* from the École des sciences politiques, he entered the French diplomatic service. He was ambassador to Turkey from 1933 to 1936, at which time he took retirement. He wrote *La mer Rouge, l'Abyssinie et l'Arabie depuis l'antiquité* (1929), and *Petra et la Nabatène* (1929). Bacqué, pp. 84-85

Kámory (Kamori), Samuel, born 7 February 1830 at Pukanec, Slovania, he studied theology at Preßburg and briefly served as a substitute teacher at the local Lutheran gymnasium. He subsequently went to study theology and Oriental languages at the universities of Halle/Saale and Göttingen. After his return to Preßburg he was appointed *Gymnasialprofessor* at the Lutheran Hauptgymnasium, concurrently teaching at Lutherisches Theologisches Institut. His writings include translations of the Bible into Hungarian, and he left behind an unfinished Hungarian translation of the Koran. He retired in 1855, and died in Preßburg on 3 February 1903. Filipsky; Hinrichsen (not sighted); Jacksch (not sighted); ÖBL

Kämpfe, Hans Rainer, born about 1945, he received a Dr.phil. in 1974 from the Universität Bonn for *Die soziale Rolle des zweiten Pekinger Lčari skya-Qutuqtu Rol pa'i rdo rje, 1717-1786; Beiträge zu einer Analyse anhand tibetischer und mongolischer Biographien*. He became a professor of Central Asian studies, particularly Mongolian philology, at the Universität Bonn. His writings include *Abriß der tschuktschischen Grammatik auf der Basis der Schriftsprache* (1995). GV; Kürschner, 1996-2005

Kampffmeyer, Georg, born 8 July 1864 at Berlin, he studied philosophy, theology, Oriental and Romance languages at the universities of Bern, Lausanne, Firenze, and Berlin, gaining a Dr.phil. in 1892 at Leipzig. From 1890 to 1895 he was employed in the reorganization of the ecclesiastical library (Kirchenministerial-Bibliothek) at Celle. Since 1895 he pursued studies in Arabic dialects, obtaining a Dr.habil. in 1900 from the Universität Marburg for *Die arabische Verbalpartikel b (m)*. He subsequently travelled in Morocco. In 1906 he was invited to teach Arabic at the Seminar für Orientalische Sprachen, Berlin. His writings include *Marokko* (1903), *Marokkanisch-arabische Gespräche im Dialekt von Casablanca* (1912), *Im neuen Marokko* (1914), *Nordwestafrika und Deutschland* (1914), *Die deutschen Auslandsinteressen und das Seminar für Orientalische Sprachen zu Berlin* (1924), *Glossar zu den 5000 arabischen Sprichwörtern aus Palästina* (1936), and he was a joint author of *Leaders in contemporary Arabic literature* (1930). He died in Berlin on 5 September 1936. Fück, p. 315; Hanisch; NDB; Schwarz; Wer ist's, 1928

Kamphövener, Elsa Sophia, born 14 June 1878 at Hameln, Germany, the daughter of Louis von Kamphövener (1843-1927), a reformer of the Ottoman army, she lived in Turkey since the age of six and was educated privately, acquiring many foreign languages. Disguised as a man, she travelled for years throughout the Ottoman Empire and was even admitted to the Turkish guild of story-tellers. At an advanced age she broke her promise not to record the old tales in order to preserve this cultural heritage for posterity; she published them entitled *An Nachtfeuern der Karawan-Serail; Märchen und Geschichten alttürkischer Nomaden* (1956). She returned to Germany in 1921 and worked for ten years in the motion picture industry. Her other writings, partly under the pseudonym Else Marquardsen-Kamphoevener, include *Der weiße Scheich; eine Geschichte aus der Syrischen Wüste* (1957), *Damals im Reiche der Osmanen* (1959), and *Mohammed; die Legende des Islams* (1968). She died in Traunheim, Bavaria, on 4 August 1963. DtBE; EncCoWW; KDtLK, Nekrolog, 1935-70; Kornrumpf; Kornrumpf, N; LexFrau; NDB; Sezgin; *Wer ist wer*, 1962

Kampman, Arie Abraham, born 6 July 1911 at Dordecht, the Netherlands, he studied history and Oriental, particularly Hittite, archaeology at the universities of Leiden, Heidelberg, and Praha, and made six study tours to the Near East. He received a doctorate in 1945 from the Rijksuniversiteit te Leiden for *De historische beteekenis der Hethitiesche vestingsbouwkunde*. He participated in excavations in 1937 and 1952. He was a sometime director of the Nederlandsch Instituut van het Nabije Oosten, Leiden; he edited *Het Midden Oosten, centrum de wereld* (1959). Brinkman's, 1956-1960; *Wie is dat*, 1948, 1956; WhoNL, 1962/63

Kanaan, Haviv, born Lieber Krumholz in 1913 at Kuty, Poland, he trained for journalism in Warszawa. After his emigration to Palestine he joined the editorial staff of *Haaretz*. From 1948 to 1949 he was a press officer with the Israeli police. His Hebrew writings include *Be-'ene shoter Palestina'i* (1980). WhoIsrael, 1966/67-1980/81|; WhoWorJ, 1972, 1978

Kanchaveli, Nana Georgievna, borm 21 October 1930 at Tiflis, she graduated in 1954 from Tiflis State University and received her first degree in 1971 for *Арабоязычные документы дагестанского происхождения сороковых годов XIX столетия*. Since 1955 she was associated with the Institute of Manuscripts in the Georgian Academy of Sciences Her writings include *Каталог арабских рукописей Института рукописей нм. К.С. Кекелидже* (1978). Miliband²

Kandel', Volodymyr L'vovych, fl. 20th cent., his writings include *Розкажы правду людям* (1976). NUC

Kandiyoti, Deniz, born 15 March 1944 at Istanbul, she received a Ph.D. in 1970 from the London School of Economics for *A Social psychological study of a Turkish village*. She was in the 1990s a senior lecturer in the Centre for Development Studies, School of Oriental and African Studies, London, specializing in gender, family, development and the state, with special reference to Turkey, the Middle East and Central Asia. Her writings include *Women in rural production systems; problems and politics* (1985), she was a joint author of *Multinationales et inégalités de classe et de sexe* (1983), and she edited *Women, Islam and the state* (1991), and *Gendering in the Middle East* (1996). DrBSMES, 1993; EURAMES, 1993; LC; Schoeberlein; Sluglett

Kaneda, Hiromitsu, born 5 June 1934 at Osaka, Japan, he graduated in 1957 from Doshishak University and received a Ph.D. in 1957 from Stanford University, Palo Alto, Calif. Since 1963 he was associated with the Department of Economics, University of California at Davis, a post which he still held in 1995. He was a joint editor of *Agriculture and economic growth; Japan's experience* (1969). AmM&WSc, 1973 S, 1978 S; JapAuFile; Master (2); NatFacDr, 1995

Kaniki, Martin Hoza Yohana, born 2 December 1938 at Mlalo-Lushoto, Tanganyika, he was educated at University College, Dar-es-Salam, and the University of Birmingham. Since 1975 he taught history at the University of Dar-es-Salam. His writings include *Politics in the Usambara-Digo Lutheran Church, 1961-63*, his third year paper in political science; and he edited for the Historical Association of Tanzania, *Tanzania under colonial rule* (1979). AfricaWW, 1996; NUC

Kanitz, Felix Philipp, born 2 August 1829 at Pest, Hungary, he early in life displayed musical and free hand drawing abilities which he perfected at the Kunstakademie, Kassel, Hesse, from 1843 to 1847. He subsequently went to Wien, where he made a living as illustrator for the *Leipziger Illustrierte Zeitung*, concurrently pursuing an academic interest in ethnography and geography. Since 1858 he systematically explored the Balkans, Montenegro, Serbia, and Bulgaria, where he was remarkably successful thanks to his command of the Serbian and Bulgarian languages. His writings include *Serbiens byzantinische Monumente* (1862), *Serbien* (1868), *Katechismus der Ornamentik* (1870), *Donau-Bulgarien und der Balkan* (1875-79), its translation, *La Bulgarie danubienne et le Balkan* (1882), and *Das Königreich Serbien und das Serbenvolk* (1904). He died in Wien on 5 January 1904. AllgLKünst; EnBulg; GeistigeUng; Kornrumpf; ÖBL; Wininger; Wurzbach

Kaniukova, Aleksandra Semenovna, fl. 20th cent., her writings include *Чувашская диалектология; краткие очерк* (Cheboksary, 1965), and *Чӑвашла тӗрӗс те илемлӗ калаҫар* (Shupashkar, 1975). NUC, 1968-72; OSK

Kann, Peter, born about 1945, he received a Dr.phil. in 1972 from the Universität Wien for *Studien über Seelenvorstellung der Indianer Amazoniens*. His writings include *Brasiliens Indianer* (Wien, Museum für Völkerkunde, 1971). GV; NUC

Kann, Réginald, born in 1876 at Paris, he graduated from the Lycée Janson-de-Sally, Paris, and the military college, Saint-Cyr. Soon tired of garrison life, he resigned the French military in 1899 to participate actively in the Boer War. Since 1903 he was both a war correspondent to French newspapers and an active soldier in many of the war theatres in Europe and Asia. In 1924 he went to the Spanish Zone of Morocco; in the following year he once more put on his uniform of a lieutenant-colonel to participate at the front-line in the fight against Abd el Krim. Mortally wounded, he died on 30 September 1925. His writings include *Journal d'un correspondant de guerre en Extrême-Orient* (1905), *Impressions de campagne et de manœuvres* (1909), and *Le Protectorat marocain* (1921). Hommes et destins, vol. 7 , pp. 276-77

Kann, Robert Adolf, born 11 February 1906 at Wien, he there went to school and took a Dr.jur. in 1930, despite displaying a strong interest in history since his early years. After the *Anschluß* he emigrated to the U.S.A., where a took a B.Lib.Sc. in 1940 at Columbia University, subsequently working in a library. From 1942 to 1945 a member of the Institute for Advanced Study at Princeton, he received a Ph.D. in 1946 from Columbia University, New York, and in the same year started teaching modern European history, particularly the last phase of the Habsburg Empire, at Rutgers University, New Brunswick, N.J., a post which he held until his retirement in 1975. During his last years he was a visiting professor at the Universität Wien and at the Diplomatische Akademie, Wien. He died suddenly after boarding an excursion bus to Seggau on Sunday, 30 August 1981. BioHbDtE; DtBE; *Südost-Forschungen*, 40 (1981), pp. 283-84

Kannapin, Hans Eckhart, fl. 20th cent., his writings include *Der Strukturwandel des Zonengrenzraumes* (1953), and *Wirtschaft unter Zwang* (1966). NUC, 1956-67

Kannappan, Sam, born in 1943, he was an engineer who was associated with the Tennessee Vallley Authority, Knoxville, Tenn., in the 1970s. Note; *Who's who in technology today*, 1989 (not sighted)

Kanne, Jürgen, born 8 May 1943 at Dresden, Germany, he went to school in Detmold and Düsseldorf, and studied economics at the universities of Innsbruck, Bonn, and Köln, where he received a diploma in 1967. He subsequently spent three months in Afghanistan doing research, and then worked in an export firm in Déville-lès-Rouen, and in an international finance and consulting firm in Düsseldorf. From 1969 to 1972, he participated in a technical assistance programme at Kabul University. Supported by a two-year graduate scholarship, he completed his thesis at the Institut für Entwicklungsforschung und Entwicklungspolitik, Ruhr-Universität, Bochum, where he received a doctorate in 1974 for *Interne Investionsfinanzierung in Afghanistan*. He was a joint author of *Das System der Staatseinnahmen und seine Bedeutung für die Wirtschaftsentwicklung Afghanistans* (1975). Schwarz; Thesis

Kannenberg, Carl, born 15 March 1865 at Radem near Daber, Pomerenia, he was a Prussian lieutenant, and a joint author of *Kleinasiens Naturschätze* (Berlin, 1897). KDtLK, 1898; Kornrumpf

Kannenberg, Joachim, born about 1930, he received a doctorate in 1958 from the faculty of agriculture, Universität Göttingen, for *Physikalisch-chemische Veränderungen des Bodenzustandes durch Kleinpolderung von Sietländereien und deren ackerbauliche Nutzungsmöglichkeiten*. GV

Kannisto, Juha Artturi, born 12 May 1874 at Kylmäkoski, Finland, he became a professor at Helsingfors University. His writings include *Zur Geschichte des Vokalismus der ersten Silbe im Wogulischen vom qualitativen Standpunkt* (1919), *Wogulische und ostjakische Melodien* (1937), *Aufführungen beim Bärenfest* (1959); he was a joint author of *Materialien zur Mythologie der Wogulen* (1958); and he was a joint editor of *Yrjö Wichmanns Wörterbuch des ungarischen Moldauer Nordcsángó und des Hétfalurer Csángodialektes nebst grammatikalischen Aufzeichnungen und Texten aus dem Nordcsángodialekt* (1936). He died in Helsinki on 10 March 1943. Aikalaiskirja, 1934; EncFen; Magyar; *Vem och vad*, 1931-1941

Kanovsky, Eliyahu, born 25 March 1922 at Winnipeg, Manitoba, be graduated in 1942 from Yeshiva University, New York, and received a Ph.D. in 1961 from Columbia University, New York. Since 1962 he taught economics in various capacities at State University of New York, Stony Brook. His writings include *The Economy of the Israeli Kibbutz* (1966), *The Economic impact of the Six-Day-war* (1970), *The Economy of Jordan* (1976), *The Economic development of Syria* (1977), *Saudi Arabia's moderation in oil pricing* (1977), and *Iran's economic morass; mismanagement and decline under the Islamic Revolution* (Washington, D.C., 1996). AmM&WSc, 1973 S, 1978 S; ConAu, 33-36; *MESA Roster of members*, 1982-1990

Kansu, Şevket Aziz, born in 1903 at Edirne, Turkey, he was a professor of anthropology first at the Faculty of Medicine in Constantinople and since 1934 at the Faculty of Languages, History, and Geography, (D.T.C.F.) at Ankara, a post which he held until his retirement in 1973. His writings include *Les fouilles d'Etiyokusu* (1937), *Türk Antropoloji Enstitüsü tarihçesi* (1940), *Gençlikte irade eğitimi ve* *büyük adamlar* (1947) and he was a joint author of *Ökse otunun yem değen* (1938). He died in Ankara on 10 April 1983. AnaBrit; IntDcAn

Kantardžić, Muhammed, born 19 March 1900 at Sarajevo, he studied mathematics, physics, and chemistry at Zagreb University, obtaining a diploma in 1926. He retired in 1970. Traljić, pp. 61-65

Kanter, Helmuth August Heinrich, born 20 September 1891 at Königsberg, East Prussia, he studied at the Universität Hamburg, where he received a Dr.med. in 1921 for *Die Verbreitung der im Menschen parasitierenden Trematoden*, and a Dr.rer.nat. in 1922 for *Der Löß in China*. His two university subjects were a splendid prerequisite for research in the Far East and South America where he travelled as a ship's surgeon from 1922 to 1924. From 1925 to 1928 he made four extensive study tours in Italy. His research after 1933 centered on Libya. There, as well as on previous expeditions, he was probably one of the last explorers to travel the age-old way with local transport animals. He successively was a professor of geography at the universities of Hamburg and Marburg until 1945. His writings include *Kalabrien* (1930), *Der Gran Chaco und seine Randgebiete* (1936), and *Libyen-Libya; eine geographisch-medizinische Landeskunde* (1967). He died in Marburg on 8 January 1976. *Beiträge zur Kulturgeographie der Mittelmeerländer*, III (1977), pp. 1-10; Kürschner, 1931-1976; *Wer ist wer*, 1955-1973/74

Kantorowicz, Ernst Hartwig, born in 3 May 1895 at Posen, Prussia, he received a Dr.phil. in 1921 from the Universität Heidelberg for *Das Wesen der muslimischen Handwerksverbände*. He was a medieval historian successively at the universities of Frankfurt/Main, Oxford, Berkeley, Calif., and Princeton, N.J. His writings include *Kaiser Friedrich der Zweite* (1927). His scholarship is recognized in *On four modern humanists, Hofmannsthal, Gundolf, Curtius, Kantorowicz* (1970). He died on 9 September 1963. BioHbDtE; CnDiAmJBi; DtBE; EncJud; KDtLK, Nekrolog, 1935-70; Kürschner, 1931, 1935; NDB; *Wer ist wer*, 1962; WhAm, 4; WhoWorJ, 1965

Kanus-Credé, Hans *Helmhart*, born 26 March 1925 at Sagan, Silesia, he studied Iranian subjects and history of religion at the universities of Göttingen, Tehran (where he was in 1952 the first German exchange student), Marburg, and Tübingen, where he received a Dr.phil. in 1956 for *Lotfali Suratgar, ein Dichter und Denker des modernen Persien*. He was a private scholar and since 1967 an editor and publisher of *Iranistische Mitteilungen*. His writings include *Im Lande des Großkönigs; Erlebnisse in Persien, 1952-53* (1953), and *Türkisches Tagebuch* (1953). Private; Schwarz

Kanya-Forstner, Alexander *Sidney*, born 24 October 1940 at Budapest, he graduated in 1961 from Trinity College in the University of Toronto, and received a Ph.D. in 1965 from Cambridge University for *The Role of the military in the formulation of French policy towards the western Sudan, 1879-99*. From 1972 to his his retirement he was a professor of history at York University, Toronto, Ont. His writings include *The Conquest of the western Sudan* (1969), *The Sokoto Caliphate and the European powers, 1890-1907* (1994), and he was a joint author of *France overseas* (1981). ConAu, 25-28, new rev., 17; DrAS, 1982 H; Sluglett

Kapadia, Dinshah Dorabji, born 22 July 1874 or 1875 at Bombay, he was educated at Bombay University. In 1919 he joined the Indian Educational Service and served as a professor of mathematics at Deccan College until his retirement in 1930. His writings include *Glossary of Pahlavi Vendidad* (1953), and *The History of the "Sir Lawrence Jenkins" Lodge, no. 3275, 1933-1957* (Bombay 1958). IndianBiInd (2)

Kapadia (Kāpadiyā), Eruch Rustam, he received an M.A. in 1938 from the School of Oriental and African Studies, London, for *The Diplomatic career of Sir Charles Wade; a study of British relations with the Sikhs and Afghans*. His trace is lost after an article in 1944. Sluglett; SOAS Library catalogue

Kapanadze, David Georgievich, fl. 20th cent., his writings include *Грусинская нумизматика* (Moscow, 1955), and *Нумизматический сборник* (Tbilisi, 1977). NUC, pre-1956; OSK

Kapeliouk (Kapeliuk), Amnon, born about 1930 in Palestine, he majored in Oriental studies at the Hebrew University, Jerusalem, and was in 1957 a staff reporter for *al-Hamishmar*. His writings include *Israël; la fin des mythes* (1975), *Hébron; un massacre annoncé* (1994), and *Rabin; ein politischer Mord und rechte Gewalt in Israel* (1997), as well as works in Hebrew. NUC; ZKO

Kapeliuk, Amnon see Kapeliouk, Amnon

Kapeliuk, Menahem, born in 1900, he was a writer on Middle East affairs for the daily, *Davar*, specializing in the culture and history of the Arabian Peninsula. His writings, occasionally sighted Kapil or Kapil-Kapeliuk, include the translation from the Hebrew, *Los judíos del Yemen* (1971). Note; NUC

Kapeliuk, Olga, born 20th cent., she received a Ph.D. in 1968 from the Hebrew University, Jerusalem, with a thesis on Amharic syntax. Her writings include *Nominalization in Amharic* (1988), and *Syntax of the noun in Amharic* (1994). NUC; ZKO

Kapełuś, Helena, born 20th cent., her writings include *Stanisław z Bochnie, kleryka królewski* (1964), *Die Kuhhaut; 100 polnische Märchen* (1987), *Księga bajek polskich; wybór, wstęp i opracowanie* (1988), and she was a joint author of *Sto baśni ludowych* (1957). NUC; OSK

Kapferer, Reinhard Rochus, born 3 October 1932 at Ettlingen, Germany, he studied law at the Universität Heidelberg, and political science at the Fondation nationale des sciences politiques, Paris. He received a Dr.phil. in 1961 at Heidelberg for *Die Verfassung der 4. Französischen Republik*. After an assistantship in the Institut für Politische Wissenschaft, Universität Heidelberg, he became in the 1960s a lecturer in political science at the Universität Mainz. Note; Thesis

Kapidžić, Hamdija, born 1 February 1904 at Bileće, Herzegovina, he studied history at Beograd, where he also received his doctorate in 1957. He taught history at various schools in Sarajevo, from 1928 to 1948, and subsequently became a professor of local history at the newly established State University, where he remained for the rest of his life. His writings include *Призоли за историју Босне и Херцеговине у 19 вијуку* (1956), *Hercegovački ustanak 1882 godine* (1958), *Bosna i Hercegovina pod austrougarskom upravom* (1968), *Der Aufstand in der Hercegovina im Jahre 1882* (1972), and he was a joint author of *Bosna i Hercegovina u doba austrougarske okupacije 1878 godine* (1973). He died in Sarajevo on 16 January 1974. EncJug; EncJug²; HL; HrvEnc; JugoslSa, 1970; *Südost-Forschungen*, 33 (1974), pp. 321-323

Kapil-Kapeliuk, Menahem, 1900- *see* Kapeliuk, Menahem

Kapitánffy, István, born 20th cent., he was a joint author of *A bizánci és az újgörög irodalom története* (Budapest, 1989), *Ógörög-magyar szótár* (Budapest, 1990), and he was a joint editor of *A bizánci irodalom kistükre* (Budapest, 1974). LC

Kaplan, Frederick Israel, born 1 December 1920 at N.Y.C., he graduated in 1942 from the University of California, Berkeley, where, after war-time military service, he also received an M.A. in 1947, and a Ph.D. in 1957 for *Russian labor and the Bolshvik Party, 1917-1920*. Since 1958 he was associated with the Department of Humanities, Michigan State University, East Lansing; in 1960/61 he was a research scholar at Moscow University. His writings include *Bolshevik ideology and the ethics of Soviet labor, 1917-1920* (1968). ConAu, 21-24; DrAS, 1974 H, 1978 H, 1982 H

Kaplan, Marion, born 20th cent., she was a contributor to the *National geographic magazine*. Her writings include *Focus Africa* (London, Elm Tree Books, 1982). LC

Kaplan, Michel Lucien Gaston, born 15 April 1946 at Neuilly-sur-Seine, France, he studied at Paris, where he was since 1969 a professor of Byzantine studies at the Sorbonne; he was also associated with the Centre de recherches d'histoire et de civilisation byzantines. His writings include *Les Hommes et la terre à Byzance du VIe au XIe siècle; propriéte et exploitation du sol* (1992), *Tout d'or de Byzance* (1993), its translation, *Byzanz; früher Glanz von Istanbul* (1993); he was a joint author of *Le Proche-Orient médiéval des Barbares aux Ottomans* (1980); he edited *Les Propriétés de la Couronne et de l'Église dans l'Empire byzantin; documents* (1976), *Le Sacré et son inscription dans l'espace à Byzance et en Occident* (2001); and he was a joint editor of *La Chrétienté orientale du VIIe siècle au milieu du XIe; textes et documents* (1996). Note; WhoFr, 2002-2005

Kaplan, Nina Il'inishna, fl. 20th cent., her writings include *Русская народная резьба по мягкому камню* (1955), *Художественные изделия из кости, камня и дерева артелей промысловой кооперации РСФСР* (1956), *Очерк по народному искусство Алтая* (1961); she was a joint author of *Русская народная резьба и розпись по дерево* (1956); and she edited *Народное декоративное искусство РСФСР* (1957). OSK

Kaplowitz, Noel, born 20th cent., he received a Ph.D. in 1973 from Columbia University, New York, for *Attitudes of Arab and Israeli students in the United States regarding the Arab-Israeli dispute; a psychological study of international conflict*. Selim³

Kapoor, O. B. L. (Avadha-bihārī Lāla), born 20th cent., he was a sometime research fellow in the Indian Institute of Philosophy, and a head of department, Rajkia College. He was a writer on philosophy and religion, particularly Vaishnavism. His writings include *Vrajake rasikācārya* (1984), *Srī Caitanya mahāprahu* (1992), as well as other works in Hindi. Note about the author

Kapp, Albert Georg, born in 1904, he received a Dr.phil. in 1935 from the Universität Heidelberg for *Arabische Übersetzer und Kommentatoren Euklids*. NUC

Kappeler, Andreas, born 20 September 1943 at Winterthur, Switzerland, he received a Dr. phil. in 1972 from the Universität Zürich for *Ivan Groznyj im Spiegel der ausländischen Druckschriften seiner Zeit*, and also a Dr.habil. in 1979 for *Rußlands erste Nationalitäten; das Zarenreich und die Völker der*

Mittleren Wolga vom 16.-19. Jahrhundert. He was successively a professor of East European history at the universities of Zürich, Köln, and Wien. His writings include *Die Muslime in der Sowjetunion und in Jugoslawien* (1989), *Rußland als Vielvölkerreich* (1992), *La Russie empire multiethnique* (1994), *Kleine Geschichte der Ukraine* (1994), its translation, *Petite histoire de l'Ukraine* (1997), *Culture, nation, and identity; the Ukrainian-Russian encounter, 1600-1945* (2003), and *Geschichte Rußlands im 16. und 17. Jahrhundert aus der Perspektive seiner Regionen* (2004). Kürschner, 1983-2005; TatarES

Kappeler, Dietrich, fl. 20th cent., he received a doctorate in 1958 from the Universität Bern for *Les réserves dans les traités internationaux.* He was a joint author of *Traité de droit international public, avec mention de la pratique internationale et suisse* (1967).

Kappers, Cornelius Ubbo Ariëns, 1877-1946 see Ariëns Kappers, Cornelius Ubbo

Kappert, Petra K., born 3 April 1945 at Berlin, she studied Islamic subjects at the Universität Hamburg, where she also received her Dr.phil. in 1977 for *Die osmanischen Prinzen und ihre Residenz Amasya.* In 1979, she became a professor of Turkish at Hamburg, a post which she held until her death in Berlin on 23 May 2004. She was the common-law wife of Claus-Peter Haase. She translated from the Turkish, *Alte Märchen neu erzählt* (1981), *Die Friedenstorte*, of Fakir Baykurt (1982), and she edited a manuscript, *Tabakat ül-memalik ve derecat ül-mesalik*, of Celalzade Mustafa Koca Nişanci (1981), and *Türkische Erzählungen des 20. Jahrhunderts* (1992). Kürschner, 1992-2005; Private; Schwarz; ZKO

Kappler, Claude-Claire née Ancel, born 7 October 1946 in the Département Moselle, France, she was a medievalist and a student of the relations between Orient and Occident. After studying at Strasbourg, Aix-en-Provence, and Paris, she obtained a doctorate from the Sorbonne nouvelle in 1977. She was a member of the Société asiatique and the Societas Iranica Europea. Her writings include *Le monstre; pouvoir de l'imposture* (1980); she was a joint author of *Apocalypses et voyages dans l'au-delà* (1987); and, with René Kappler, she jointly edited *Voyage dans l'empire mongol,* de Guillaume de Rubrouck (1993). LC; Private

Kapranov, Vladimir Aleksandrovich, born 2 December 1927 in the northern Caucasus, he graduated in 1953 from the Oriental Faculty, Leningrad State University, received his first degree in 1959 for *"Лугати фурс" Асади Туси и его место в истории таджикскии (фарси) лексикологии,* and his doctorate in 1973 for *Фарсиязычная (тадж.-перс.) лексикология в Индии, XVI-XIX вв.* Since 1961 he was associated with the Institute of Language and Literature in the Tajikistan Academy of Sciences. His writings include *Лексическая контаминация в таджиксклм языке* (1979), *Русско-таджикская словарь* (1985), and *Таджикско-персидская лексикография в Индии XVI-XIX вв.* Miliband[2]

Kapteijns, Lidwien, born 20th cent., he received a doctorate in 1982 from Amsterdam University. About 1990 he was appointed a professor at Wellesley College, Wellesley, Mass., a post which he still held in 2005. His writings include *African historiography written by Africans, 1955-1973* (1977), *Mahdist faith and Sudanic tradition; the history of the Masalit Sultanate, 1870-1930* (1985), and he was a joint author of *Een kennlsmaking met de Afrikaanse geschiedenis* (1985). MESA Roster of members, 1990; NatFacDr, 1995 2003

Kapur, Ashok, born 28 January 1941, he was educated at Punjab University, and George Washington University, and received a Ph.D. from Carleton University, Ottawa, in 1974. Thereafter he was a professor in the Department of Political Science, the University of Waterloo, Ontario, where he was still active in 1997. His writings include *India's nuclear option* (1976), *Pakistan's nuclear development* (1987), and *Pakistan in crisis* (1991). DrASCan, 1978, 1983; LC

Kara, György, born 23 June 1935 at Budapest, he was a professor and chairman, Department of Altaic Studies, Budapest University. His writings include *A mongol irodalom kistükre; antológia* (1965), *Kőrösi Csoma Sándor* (1970), *Книги монгольсцих кочевников* (1972), and he was a joint author of *Fragmente tantrischer Werke in uigurischer Übersetzung* (1976), and *Die uigurischen Übersetzungen des Guruyogas "Tiefer Weg" von Sa-skya Pandita* (1977). Biograf, 2004; Schoeberlein; WhoSoCE, 1989; ZKO

Kara Krikorian, Hohannes, born in 1855, he was a professor whose writings include *Islam and Chrstianity face to face* (New York, 1937). He died in 1942. NUC, pre-1956; Note about the author

von **Karabaček**, Josef, born 20 September 1845 at Graz, Austria, he started to study law at the Universität Wien but in 1866 changed to Oriental subjects, gaining a Dr.phil. in 1868, and becoming in 1869 a lecturer in Islamic palaeography and numismatics, and in 1874 a professor of Oriental history and auxiliary sciences at his alma mater. Since 1882 a member of the Akademie der Wissenschaften, Wien, he was instrumental in acquiring in 1883 some ten thousand papyri from al-Fayyum for the Hofbibliothek, Wien, funded by the munificence of the Archduke Rainer. He was the most influencial of the Viennese Orientalists at the close of the nineteenth century, spending nearly fourteen years on deciphering approximately four thousand Arabic papyri. From 1899 to 1917 he concurrently served as a director of the Hofbibliothek. His writings include *Beiträge zur Geschichte der Mazjaditen* (1874), *Ergebnisse aus dem Papyrus Erzherzog Rainer* (1889), *Muhammedanische Kunststudien* (1913), and *Ein Koranfragment des 9. Jahrhunderts aus dem Besitz des Seldschukensultans Kaikubad* (1918). He died in Wien on 9 October 1918. DtBE; DtBilnd (2); Filipsky; Flück, pp. 254-55; *der Islam*, 10 (1920), pp. 233-38; Kosch; NDB; ÖBL; *Wer ist's*, 1909-1912

Karabaev, Berdimurad, born 15 August 1931 at Uzun-Su, Turkmenistan, he graduated in 1955 from the Turkmenistan State University and received his first degree in 1964 for *Политика Демократической партии Турции в крестьянском вопросе, 1950-1960 гг.*, a work which was published in 1966. Since 1963 he was a research fellow in the Institute of History, Turkmenistan Academy of Sciences. Miliband; Miliband[2]

Karabenick, Edward, born 24 August 1931 at Detroit, Mich., he graduated in 1954 from the local Wayne State University, and received a Ph.D. in 1962 from the University of Michigan for *A geographical analysis of population growth of Rome from 1871 to 1959*. From 1959 to his retirement he was associated in various capacities with California State University at Long Beach. AmM&WSc, 1973 S; AmM&WSc, 1976 P; NatFacDr, 1990-2005

von **Karacsay**, Feodor, Graf, born 3 October 1787, he attended the Wiener-Neustädter Akademie for some time and in 1805 entered the Hussars as a cadet. In 1813 he fought at Pirna, Saxony, with the rank of first lieutenant; and later at Lyons. For some time he was a courtier of Archduke Maximilian, became a major in the first Uhlanen-Regiment, and subsequently a colonel and commandant of Mantua, Lombardy. He then entered the service of the Qājār ruler Nāsir al-Dīn Shāh as an instructor in the training of the future high command. In 1854 he was chief of the Persian general staff with the rank of general. His writings include *Freymüthige Gedanken über die Theuerung in Wien* (Wien, 1816), *Der wechselseitige Unterricht nach der Ball-Lancaster'schen Methode* (Wien, 1819), and *Manuel du voyageur en Sicilie* (Paris, 1846). He died on 2 July 1859. DtBilnd (1); Wurzbach, vol. 10, p. 462

Karácson, Imre (Emerich), born 19 February 1863 at Veszprém, Austria-Hungary, he studied theology and in 1890 was appointed a director of the Györ (Raab) Catholic teachers' college. He repeatedly travelled to Turkey. His writings include *A mohammedanismus és a kereszténység* (1892), *III Károly háborúja a törökökkel* (1892), *Kelettröl* (1899), *Szent Imre herczeg* (Budapest, 1911); he edited *A Rákóczi-emigráczio török okmányai, 1717-1803* (Budapest, 1911); he was a joint author of *Illyrisch-albanische Forschungen* (1016); and he edited and translated *Evlia Cselebi török világutazó magyarországi utazásai* (1904-8). He met a tragic death on 2 May 1911 in Constantinople. His private papers are said to have been published by Gyula Szekfű. GeistigeUng; Pallas; RNL

Karadzhe-Iskrov, Nikolaï Pavlovich, born in 1896, his writings include *Les choses publiques en droit romain* (Paris, 1928), and *К вопросу о праве государства на землю* (Irkutsk, 1928). NUC, pre-1956

Karaev, Omurkul Karaevich, born 15 October 1930 in Kirgizia, he became associated with the Institute of History, Kirgiz Academy of Sciences. His writings include *Арабские и персидские источники IX-XII вв о киргизах и Киргизи* (1968), *Вопросы этнической истории киргизского народа* (1989), *Восточные авторы о кыргызах* (1994), *Чагатайский улус, государство Хайду, Могулистан; образование кыргызского народа* (1995), *Кыргызы; источники история, этнография* (1996), and he was a joint author of *Арабо-персидские источники о тюркских народах* (1973). Schoeberlein; OSK

Karahka, Eino, fl. 20th cent., his writings include *Zur Frage nach ursprünglichen Vokallängen im Tschuwassischen* (Helsinki, 1950); he edited *Gebräuche und Volksdichtung der Tschuwassen* (1949); and he edited and translated *Mischärtatarische Volksdichtung* (1953). NUC, 1956-67; OSK

Karakashly, K. T., fl. 20th cent., his writings include *Материальная культура Азербайджанцев северо-восточной и Центральной зон Малого Кавказа* (Baku, 1964). OSK

Karal, Enver Ziya, born in 1906 in Kosovo, he lost his parents when still a boy and had a late start with his higher education. In 1928 he won a scholarship to study history and geography at the Université de Lyon. After obtaining a doctorate on the Turkish revolution from the Sorbonne, he returned to Istanbul in 1933 to begin a teaching career at the Faculty of Letters. In 1940 he went to Ankara Üniversitesi, where he served successively as a lecturer, professor, dean of faculty, and university president. His writings include *Fransa, Mısır ve Osmanlı Imperatorluğu, 1797-1802* (1938), *Selim III. ün hatt-ı hümayunları* (1942), and *Türkiye Cumhuriyeti tarihi, 1918-1953* (1955). He died on 18 or 19 January 1982. AnaBrit; *Études balkaniques*, 18, no. 2 (1982), pp. 133-135; *Turcica*, 15 (11983), pp. 7-12

Karamshoev, Dodkhudo, born 5 May 1932 in Tajikistan, he graduated in 1956 from Dushanbe State Pedagogical Institute and received his first degree in 1963 for *Баджувский диалект шугнанского языка*, and his doctorate in 1979 for *Категория рода в памирских языках*. Since 1959 he was associated with the Institute of Languages and Literatures of the Tajik Academy of Sciences. In 1968 he was appointed a lecturer. His writings include *Шугнанско-русский словарь* (1988-1999). Miliband[2]

Karaś, Mieczysław, born 10 February 1924 at Przedzel, Poland, he studied at Uniwersytet Jagielloński, Kraków, where he also received a doctorate. He successively served at his alma mater as a professor of Slavic languages, chairman of department, and university president. His writings include *Nazwy miejscowe typu Podgóra, Zalas we językyu polskim i w innych językach słowiańskich* (1955), *Język polski i jego historia* (1986), and he was a joint author of *The Jagiellonian University; traditions, the present, the future* (1975). He died in 1977. NEP; OSK; WhoSocC, 1978 A;; WhoWor, 1974/75, 1976/77

Karasan-Dirks, Sabine, born 20th cent., she received a doctorate in 1975 under her maiden name, Dirks, from the Université de Paris V for her thesis, *Islam et jeunesse en Turquie d'aujourd'hui*. She became associated with the Übersee-Museum, Bremen. Her writings include *La famille musulmane turque* (1969), its translation, *Die türkische Familie zwischen gestern und morgen* (1980), and *Die Geschichte der Fatma Hanim in Köln* (1983). LC; THESAM, 4

Karelin, Grigorii Silych, born in 1801 in St. Petersburg Province, he graduated in 1817 from the cadet school, St.Petersburg, but five years later he was exiled to Ornenburg. From 1827 to 1829 he travelled in the western part of Kazakhstan, and in 1841 in Dzungaria (Sungaria). He was an explorer of the Caspian region. His writings include *Extrait d'un journal d'un voyage fait Djoungarie ou Sungarie en 1841* (Moscow, 1847), and *Путешествия по Каспийскому морю* (1866). He died in 1872. EnSlovar; GSE; Henze; Kazakhskaia, vol. 3, p. 260; SibisSE; Wieczynski

Karger, Mikhail Konstantinovich, Dr., born in 1903 at Kazan, Russia, he was an archaeologist and art historian at Leningrad, and a head of the Institute of Archaeology, Soviet Academy of Sciences. His writings include *Новгород Великий* (1946), *Археологические исследования древнего Киева* (1951), *Древний Киев* (1958), *Древнерусская монументальная живопись* (1963), *Зодчество древнего Смоленска, XII-XIII вв.* (1964), *Культура средневековой Руси* (1975), and he was a joint author of *Домонгольский период* (1948). OSK; WhoSocC, 1978

Karib, Ruel B., born about 1865 in Persia, a descendant of a well-known bishop of the Nestorians, he was educated in Persia, and spent two years in Russia and two in Germany studying medicine. In 1887 he went to the United States, where he received an M.D. in 1891 from the University of Pennsylvania. The Cosmopolitan, 13 (1892), p. 668

Karieva, Nasiba Sadirovna, born 13 October 1938 at Tashkent, she graduated in 1959 from ИИЯ, Tashkent, and received her first degree in 1979 for *Северная Индия во второй четверти XVI века*. Since 1970 she was associated with the Oriental Institute, Uzbekistan Academy of Sciences. Miliband[2]

Karimov, Akbar Umarovich, born 12 March 1939 in Uzbekistan, he graduated in 1963 from the Oriental Faculty, Tashkent State University and received his first degree in 1973 for *Йеменский диалект арабскых языка*. He repeatedly visited the Yemen, spending altogether five years in the country. He remained at his alma mater troughout his career, since 1982 as a lecturer. Miliband[2]

Kärimov (Кәримов), Kärim Jabbar oghlu, born 20 September 1921, he studied fine arts and received a doctorate in 1971 for *Тебризкая школа миниатурной живописи XVI века*. In 1975 he was appointed a professor. His writings include *Султан Мухаммед и его школа* (Moscow, 1970), *Азербаĵчан миниатюрлəри* (Baku, 1980), and he edited *Актуальные проблемы развития архитектуры и искусства Азербайджанв; сборник материалов конференции молодых ученых* (Baku, 1979). AzarbSE, vol. 5, p. 354; OSK

Karimov, Ubaïdulla Israilovich, born 1 April 1920 at Tashkent, he graduated in 1941 from the Institute of Asian and African Studies, Moscow State University, and in 1949 from the Central Asian State University, Tashkent; he received his first degree in 1953 for «*Неизвестное сочинение Абу Бакра ар-Рази "Книга тайны тайн" в свете других его трудов по химии*», and a doctorate in 1971 for *Китаб ас-сайдана ("фармакогнозия") Беруни*. He was associated with both the Central Asian State University and the Uzbekistan Academy of Sciences. Miliband; Miliband[2]

Karimullin, Abrar Gibadullovich, born 29 March 1925, he became associated with the Institute of History of the Uzbek Academy of Sciences. His writings include *Библиография литературы по татарскому языкознанию* (1958), *Татарская литература в переводах на русский язык; библиографический указатель, 1917-1960* (1962), *У истоков татарской книги* (1971), *Татарская* *книги начала XX века* (1974), and *Татарское Государственное Издательство и татарская книга Коссии, 1917-1932* (1999). Книга, 50 (1985), pp. 167-170 (not sighted); OSK; Schoeberlein; TatarES

Kariniyazov, T. M. *see* Kary-Niiazov, Tashmukhamed Niiazovich

Karkaria, Rustomji Pestonji, born in 1869 at Bombay, he graduated in 1888 from St. Xavier's School and College, and soon afterwards there became a senior fellow and professor. He was a sometime examiner in history and philosophy at Bombay University. His writings include *India; forty years of progress and reform* (1896), and *The Charm of Bombay* (1915). He died in 1919. Buckland; Eminent; *Who was who*, 2

Karklins, Rasma née Silde, born 7 June 1946 at Marburg, Germany, she studied at the Freie Universität Berlin, from 1965 to 1969, and subsequently went to the U.S.A., where she received a Ph.D. in 1975 from the University of Chicago for *The interrelationship of Soviet foreign policy and nationality politics; the case of the foreign minorities of the USSR*. After teaching three years at Boston University, she was appointed a professor in the Department of Political Science, University of Illinois at Chicago, a post which she still held in 2005. Her writings include *Interviews mit deutschen Spätaussiedlern aus der Sowjetunion* (1978), *Ethnic relations in the USSR; the perspective from below* (1986), *Nationality policy and ethnic relations in the USSR* (1986), *Determinants of ethnic identification in the USSR; the Soviet Jewish case* (1986), and *The Dissent coercion nexus in the USSR* (1987). NatFacDr, 1990-2005; OSK; WhoMW, 1994/95

Karlin-Hayter, Patricia, fl. 20th cent., her writings include *Vita S. Euthymii* (Bruxelles, 1957), and she edited *Vita Euthymii Patriarchae* (Bruxelles, 1970). OSK

Karlinger, Felix Josef, born 17 March 1920 at München, Germany, he received a Dr.phil. in 1949 from the Universität München for *Beiträge zu einer Volkskunde der Pyrenäen und ihrer Umwelt im Spiegel des Volksliedes*. He was a professor of Romance languages and literatures at the Universität Salzburg, and a member of two Italian academies. His writings include *Italienische Volksmärchen* (1973), and numerous similar publications. He died on 27 June 2000. GV; Kürschner, 1970-2001

Karliński, Justyn Józef Stanisław, born 23 July 1862 at Krakau, Austria, he was a physician and bacteriologist and became a district physician in Bosnia-Herzegovina. He visited Arabia and Asia Minor, a journey which he described in his *Über der gelben Flagge; Erinnerungen und Eindrücke von der Reise nach Arabien und Kleinasien* (Wien, 1894). His other writings include *Zur Hydrologie des Bezirkes Konjica in der Herzegovina* (Sarajevo, 1893), and *Über die geschichtliche Entwicklung der internationalen Gesundheitspflege und deren weitere Aufgaben* (Wien, 1895). He died in 1909. Dziekan; OSK Polski (1); PSB

Karmon, Yehuda, born 17 April 1912 at Oświęcim, Poland, he studied at the Universität Breslau from 1929 to 1933 and subsequently went to Palestine where he completed his study with an M.A. in 1953, and a Ph.D. in 1959. He became a professor of geography at the Hebrew University, Jerusalem. His writings include *A Geography of settlement in eastern Nigeria* (1966), and he was a joint author of *Atlas of the Middle East* (1971). WhoWorJ, 1972, 1978

Karmysheva, Balkis (Bėl'kis) Khalilovna, born 13 July 1916 at Kuldja, Sinkiang, she graduated in 1946 from Tashkent State University, received both her first degree in 1951 for a monograph, and also her doctorate in 1978. She was successively associated with the Institute of History, Tajikistan Academy of Sciences, and the Institute of Ethnography, Soviet Academy of Sciences. Her writings include *Очерки этнической истории южных районов Таджикистана и Узбекистана* (1976). Miliband²; Schoeberlein; TatarES

Karnapp, Walter, born 11 September 1902 at Baarenhof near Danzig, Prussia, he was from 1934 to 1939 a fellow of Deutsches Archäologisches Institut first at Istanbul and later at Athens. From 1939 to 1945 he was a professor of architecture and archaeology at the Technische Hochschule Danzig, subsequently serving in the same capacity at the Technische Hochschule München until his retirement in 1970. His writings include *Die Stadtmauer von Resafa in Syrien* (1976), and jointly with Alfons Maria Schneider, *Byzanz; Vorarbeiten zur Topographie und Archäologie der Stadt* (1936), and *Die Stadtmauer von Iznik, Nicaea* (1938). Kürschner, 1950-1992|

Karo, Georg Heinrich, born 11 January 1872 at the Palazzo Barbaro on Canale Grande, Venezia, the son of a wealthy business man in Berlin. German and Italian were native languages to him, but he spoke English and French and modern Greek equally well. Renowned German scholars were his teachers, and he received a Dr.phil. in 1896 from the Universität Bonn for *De arte vasevlaria antiqvissima qvaestiones*. In 1900 he went to Greece, soon to become secretary of Kaiserliches Deutsches Archäologisches Institut at Athens, where for fifteen years he was intensely active both in archaeology and higher social life. After the first World War he became the successor to Carl Robert in Halle, where he remained active as a professor until 1930. His writings include *Grundzüge der Kriegsschuldfrage* (1926), *Schachtgräber von Mykenai* (1930-33), *Athen und Umgebung* (1937), and his memoirs, *Greifen am Thron* (1959). He died in Freiburg im Breisgau on 12 November 1963. American journal of archaeology, 70 (1966), p. 73; BioHbDtE; DtBE; Kürschner, 1962; Wer ist wer, 1961

Károlyi, Árpád, born 7 October 1853 at Pest, Hungary, he was a Calvinist who studied history at the universities of Pest and Wien, where he received a Dr.jur. In 1875 he visited Wien where he worked at the Haus-, Hof- und Staatsarchiv, from 1877 to 1880, when he returned for three years to Budapest as a lecturer at the university. In 1883 he was appointed a professor of Hungarian at the Orientalische Akademie, Wien, and since 1897, a director of the Haus-, Hof und Staatsarchiv. As a historian he devoted some of his works to Hungary's wars with the Ottomans, particularly in the seventeenth century, *Buda és Pest visszavivása 1686-ban* (1886). In 1921 he became the first director of the Institut für Ungarische Geschichtsforschung, Wien. He died in Budapest on 26 October 1940. Dávid Angyal wrote *Károlyi Árpád emlékezete, 1853-1940* (Budapest, 1943). GeistigeUng; Magyar; Mitteilungen des Österreichischen Staatsarchivs, 15 (1962), pp. 577-94; ÖBL; Südost-Forschungen, 5 (1940), pp. 745-47

Karomatov, Feïzulla Muzafarovich, born 14 December 1925 at Bukhara, he graduated in 1944 from the Faculty of Philology, Tashkent Pedagogical Institute, and in 1950 from the Tashkent Conservatory. He received a doctorate in musicology in 1971 for *Узбекская инструментальная музыка*. His writings include *Узбек домбровская музыка* (1962), *Узбек чолгу мусикаси* (1972), *Музыкальные инструменты Средней Азии* (1980), and he was a joint author of *Музыкальное искусство Памира* (1978), and *Искусство туркменских бахши* (1985). Miliband[2]

Karouzis (Καρούζης), Geõrgios, he was born on 8 October 1934 in Cyprus. His writings include *Proposals for a solution of the Cyprus problem* (Nicosia, 1976), *Η Τουρκική Εισβολή και η Αντιμετώπισή της* (1976) *Land ownership in Cyprus - past and present* (Nicosia, 1977), *Γεωγραφική Εγκυκλοπαίδεια* (1978), and he was a joint author of *Ταξίδια στην Κύπρο* (1981-85), *Το Σύστημα ιδιοκτησίας στα Ομηρικά Έπη* (1983), *Περιδιαβάσοντας τη Βουλγαρία* (1986), and *Οικονομική γεωγραφία της Κύπρου* (1999). EVL, 1993/94-2001

Karpat, Kemal Hasim, born 15 February 1925 at Turda-Tulca, Dobruja, Romania, he completed his law in Turkey and subsequently earned his M.A. and Ph.D. in the U.S.A. After a year's teaching at the Middle East Technical University, Ankara, he became a professor in the Department of Government, Area Studies Program, New York University, 1962-67. Since 1968 he was a professor of history at the University of Wisconsin, Madison. His writings include *Turkey's politics* (1959), *Social change and politics in Turkey* (1973), *The Geçekondu* (1976), *Ottoman population, 1830-1914* (1985), *The Turks of Bulgaria* (1990), *Ottoman past and today's Turkey* (2000), and *Osmanlı modernleşmesi* (2002). AmM&WSc, 1973 S; ConAu, 21-24, 69-72, new revision, 11; MESA Roster of members, 1977-1990; Note; Schoeberlein; WhoE, 1974-1977 (not sighted); WrDr, 1976/78-1996/98

Kárpáti, János, born 11 July 1932 at Budapest, he graduated from Liszt Frenc Zenemüvészeti Fóiskola, Budapest, and received a doctorate in musicology from Budapest University with a thesis on Bela Bartók. Since 1961 he was a chief librarian of the F.Liszt Academy of Music. His writings include *Domenico Scarlatti* (1959), *Ferenc Liszt Musikakademie, Budapest* (1972), *Album d'un voyageur; F.-Liszt-Gedächtnisausstellung, 1981* (1981), and *Bartók's chamber music* (1994). Baker, 1984, 1992 (not sighted); Biograf, 2004; IntWWM, 1980, 1985, 1990 (not sighted); NewGrDM; WhoSoSoCE, 1989; WhoWor, 1991/92

Karpiński, Franciszek, born 4 October 1741 at Hołosków, Galicia, he was educated at Jesuit schools in Galicia and later at Wien, and became probably the foremost lyric poet of his age. He died in Chorowszczyzna on 16 September 1825. BiD&SB; CasWL; Dziekan; Master (2); Polski (23); PSB; Wurzbach

Karpinski, Louis Charles, born 5 August 1878 at Rochester, N.Y., he initially trained as a teacher at Oswego State Normal School. After obtaining a Dr.phil. in 1903 from the Universität Straßburg for *Über die Verteilung der quadratischen Reste*, he became associated in various capacities with the University of Michigan as a teacher of mathematics until his retirement in 1948. He was a joint author of *The Hindu-Arabic numerals* (1911), and he edited *Robert of Chester's Latin translation of the Algebra of Al-Khowarizmi* (1915). He died in Winter Haven, Fla., on 25 January 1956. DcScB, S 1; Master (3); WhAm, 3; WhNAA

Karpov, G. I., fl. 20th cent., he was a joint author of *Хивинские Туркмены конец Кунградской династии* (1930), *Туркменская ССР* (1945), and he was a joint editor and translator of *Творчество народов Туркменистана* (1936). His trace is lost after an article in 1947. NUC, pre-1956; OSK

Karpova, Nina Konstantinovna, born 21 August 1933 at Moscow, she graduated in 1958 from the Faculty of History, Moscow State University. She was since 1960 associated with the State Museum of Art of the People of the Orient, where she became a deputy section head in 1966. Miliband[2]

Karryev, Baĭmukhamed Atalievich, born in 1914 in Turkmenistan, he graduated in 1939 from the Turkmen Pedagogical Institute, reveived his first degree in 1942, and his doctorate in 1948 for *Махтум-Кули и его художественный язык*. From 1938 to 1945 he was associated with the Institute of Language and Literature, Turkmen Academy of Sciences, and subsequently served in various capacities in the Institute of Linguistic, Soviet Academy of Sciences. His writings include *Эпические сказантя о Кер-оглы у тюркоязычних народов* (1968), as well as numerous works in Turkmen. He died on 1 April 1981. Miliband; Miliband²

Karsenty, Jean Claude, born 26 May 1937 at Mostaganem, Algeria, he was educated in Mostaganem and Paris, where he received degrees in law and economics. He started his career in 1962 at the Office national de modernisation rurale du Maroc. After having served a number of years in Algeria, he became a financial director of a private society from 1979 to 1981, when he entered the socialist faction in the Assemblée nationale. He was an editor and joint author of *Les Restaurants scolaires municipaux; analyse et évolution depuis 1878* (1990). WhoFr, 1994/95-2004/2005

Karsh, Efraim, born 6 September 1953, he gained a doctorate and was a senior fellow at the Jaffee Centre for Strategic Studies, and a lecturer on international relations at Tel Aviv University, before he became a lecturer in regional security in the Department of War Studies, King's College, London. His writings include *The Iran-Iraq war; a military analysis* (1987), *Neutrality and small states* (1988), *The Soviet Union and Syria; the Asad years* (1988), *Empires of the sand; the struggle for mastery in the Middle East* (1999), and he edited *Israel, the Hashemites and the Palestinians; the fateful triangle* (2003). DrBSMES, 1993; EURAMES, 1993; Note

Kartsaklis, Renata, Dr., she was a student of underdeveloped countries, and a joint author of the booklets, *Interdependenzen zwischen Ost-Westhandel und Ost-Südhandel* (1970), and *Probleme der Familienplanung in Entwicklungsländern* (1970). Note about the author

Kartsev, Vladimir Nikolaevich, born 3 January 1925 at Moscow, he graduated in architecture in 1951 at СИМ, and he was from 1951 to 1960 a researcher associated with the МЖНИИ project, subsequently serving as head of the research division at the МАрхИ. From 1970 to 1974 he was employed by a Soviet institution in Afghanistan. His writings include *Зодчество Афганистана* (1986). Miliband²

Karunakaran, Kotta P., Dr., bon in 1925, he was a political scientist who was a sometime lecturer in the Institute for Advanced Study, Simla, and head of the Department of South Asian Studies at the Indian School of International Studies, New Delhi. His writings include *India in world affairs* (1952-58), *Outside the contest* (1963), *Modern Indian political tradition* (1968), *Modernization of capitalism, communism, and world politics* (1974), and *Gandhi interpretations* (1985). Note about the author; ZKO

Karutz, Heinrich Ludwig Matthias *Richard*, born 2 November 1867 at Stralsund, Prussia, he studied medicine and subsequently became a ship's surgeon, a post which afforded him travels and ethnographic studies. His writings include *Unter Kirgisen und Turkmen* (1911), its translation, *Среди Киргизов и Туркменов на Мангышлаке* (1910), *Die Völker Nord- und Mittel-Asiens* (1925), *Atlas der Völkerkunde* (1925-27), *Vorlesungen über moralische Völkerkunde* (1930-34), *Kirgisische Wanderhirten* (1933), and *Die afrikanische Seele* (1938). He died in Stuttgart on 10 February 1945. KDtLK, Nekrolog, 1935-71; *Wer ist's*, 1928

von **Karwath**, Cary, born 19th cent., he wrote *Das Buch der tausend Nächte und einer Nacht; vollständige und in keiner Weise gekürzte Ausgabe nach den vorhandenen orietalischen Texten* (Wien, 1906), *Die Erotik in der Kunst* (Wien, 1908), and he was a joint author of *Fünfzig erotische Grotesken* (Wien, 1909). Sezgin

Kary-Niiazov (Кары-Ниязов/Қориниёзов), Tashmukhamed Niiazovich, fl. 20th cent., his writings include *Очерк истории культуры Советского Узбекистана* (1955), *Совет Ўзбекистони маданияти тарихдан очерклар* (1956), *Socialist culture of Uzbek people* (1958), *О культурном наследии узбекского народа* (1960), *Астрономическая школа Улугбека* (1967), and *Размышления о пройденном пути* (1970). OSK

Kasack, Wolfgang, born 20 January 1927 at Potsdam, Germany, he received a Dr.phil. in 1953 and a Dr.habil. in 1968. He was since 1969 a professor of Slavic studies at the Universität Köln. His writings include *Heidelberger russische Periodica* (1952), *Die Technik der Personendarstellung bei Nikolaj Vasilević Gogol* (1957), *Die Akademie der Wissenschaften der UdSSR* (1967), and *Lexikon der russischen Literatur ab 1917* (1976). He died in München on 10 January 2003. Kürschner, 1976-2001; WhoWor, 1991/92

Käselau, Adolf, born about 1900, he received a Dr.phil. in 1927 from the Universität Heidelberg for *Die freien Beduinen Nord- und Zentral-Arabiens.* Schwarz

Kasem Beg, Mirza, 1802-1870 *see* Kazem-Bek, Aleksandr Kasimovich

Käser, Werner, born 20th cent., he wrote *Islam; Einführung in die jüngste Weltreligion* (München, Evangelischer Presseverband für Bayern, 1978).

Kasfir, Nelson M., born 20 June 1939, he was in 1990 a professor of government at Dartmouth College, Hanover, N.H., a post which he held until his retirement. He was associated with the American Universities Field Staff. His writings include *Still keeping the peace* (1976), *The Shrinking political arena; participation and ethnicity in African politics, with a case study of Uganda* (1976), *Soldiers as policymakers in Nigeria* (1977), and he edited *State and class in Africa* (1984). LC; NatFacDr, 1990-2005

Kashkaev, Badrutdin Omarievich, born 20th cent., his writings include *Борьба за Советы в Дагестане, 1917-1920 годы* (1963), *Красная Армия в Дагестане* (1964), *Деятельность партийной органзации Дагестана в послевоенный период* (1968), *Гражданская война в Дагестане, 1918-1920 гг.* (1976), and *Партийные организаций Северного Кавказа в условиях строистельства развитого социализма* (1985). LC; OSK

Kashtaleva, K. S., born in 1897, she was a student of Arabic, particularly the language and style of the Koran. She died 15 July 1939. Krachkovskii, pp. 220, 241

Kasi, Mirza Djevad Khan, 1884- *see* Qazi, Mirza Muhammad Javad Khan

Kasimov (Gasymov), Kubad (Gubad) Abdulla oghlu, born in 1885, he was a musicologist who was a joint author of *Азербайджанский государственный ордена Ленина театр, оперы и балета* (Moscow, 1959), *Гусейн Кули Сарабский; жизнь и творчество* (Baku, 1980), and he edited *Булбул; сечилмиш мэгалэ вэ мэ'рузэлэри* (Baku, 1968). NUC; OSK

Kasimova (Gazymova), Solmaz Dzhalal kyzy, born 20th cent., she was a musicologist whose writings include *Джанзир Джангиров* (Baku, 1964), *Оперное творчество композиторов Советского Азербайджана* (Baku, 1973), and *Азэрбаjчан совет мусиги эдэбиjjаты* (Baku, 1984). LC; OSK

Kaskabasov (Қасқабақов), Seit (Сейјт) Askarovich (Асқарулы), born 20th cent., his writings include *Казахская волшебная сказка* (Alma-Ata, 1972), *Родники искусства* (Alma-Ata, 1986), and he edited *Альын сандык*, of Wilhelm Radloff (Alma-Ata, 1993). LC; OSK

Kasozi, Abdu Basajabaka Kawalya, born in 1942, he received a Ph.D. in 1974 from the University of California at Santa Cruz for *The spread of Islam in Uganda, 1894-1945.* His writings include *The Social origins of violence in Uganda, 1964-1985* (1994), and jointly with Noel Q. King, *Islam and the confluence of religions in Uganda, 1840-1966* (1973). Selim[3]

Kasparian, Robert, born 20th cent., his writings include *Enquête sur la famille chrétienne au Liban* (Beyrouth, Centre d'Études et de Recherches sur l'Orient chrétien, 1989). ZKO

Kasper, Hans Erich, born 20th cent., he served for about ten years as a teacher at the Mittelschule St. Georg in Istanbul until he was appointed in 1963 head of Österreichisches Kulturinstitut, the Austrian Council, Istanbul. Note about the author

Kass, Ilana Dimant, born 20th cent., she was in 1979 a member of the Soviet and East European Research Center of the Hebrew University of Jerusalem. Her writings, partly under I. Dimant or Dimant-Kass, include *Pravda and Trud; divergent attitudes towards the Middle East* (1974), *The Lebanese civil war, 1975-1976; a case of crisis management* (1979), *The Deadly embrace; the impact of Israeli and Palestinian rejectionism on the peace process* (1997), and she was a joint author of *The Soviet military involvement in Egypt, January 1970- July 1972* (1974). NUC, 1968-77; ZKO

Kassarji, Lee G. (Kevork), born in 1912, he was before 1945 a sometime acting Canadian Trade Commissioner for the Middle East. His writings include *Behind the iron altar* (Philadelphia, Pa., 1950), and *Your love is your fortune* (New York, 1955). Note about the author; NUC, pre-1956

Kassavetes, N. *see* Cassavetes, Nicholas J.

Kaster, Heinrich Ludwig, born 20th cent., his writings include *Kleine Geschichte des Orients* (1955), *Abu Nawas oder Die Lust zu lügen* (1961), *Islam ohne Schleier* (1963), *Naher Osten; ein Zwischenkontinent in Aufruhr* (1969), *Iran heute* (1974), and *Die Weihrauchstraße* (1986). Sezgin

van **Kasteren**, Joannes Petrus, born in 1855 at Schijndel, Brabant, the Netherlands, he entered the Society of Jesus in 1874 and spent the years from 1886 to 1890 at the Université Saint-Joseph de

Beyrouth studying Semitic languages and Biblical subjects. In 1891, he became a professor of Hebrew at Collegium Canasianum, Maastricht. His writings include the German translation of one of his works, *Was Jesus predigte*, and *Eine Erklärung des Vaterunsers* (1920). He died in Maastricht on 15 September 1918. Jalabert; *Wie is dat*, 1902

Kästner, Hermann, born 20th cent., his writings include *Bibliographie zur Geologie Afghanistans und unmittelbar angrenzender Gebiete* (Hannover, 1971). ZKO

Kasturi, N., born about 1900, his writings include the *History of the British occupation of India*; being a summary of "Rise of the Christian power in India," by Major Baman D. Basu (Calcutta, 192--?). His trace is lost after an article in 1935. BLC; IndianBilnd (1)

Kasumović, Ismet, born 19 July 1948 at Pode near Travnik, Yugoslavia, he studied Arab history and education at Kuwait, where he received a graduate degree for his thesis, *Problem nihiliteta u arapsko-islamskoj filozofiji*, and registered his thesis, *Ali-Dede Bošnjak i njegova filozofsko-sufijska učenja*, at the Orientalnom Institutu u Sarajevu in 1991. He died in Sarajevo on 11 February 1995. *Prilozi za orijentalnu filologiju*, Sarajevo, 42/43 (1992-93), pp. 12-14

Katakura, Motoko, born in 1937, she was a social geographer and ethnologist. Her writings include *Bedouin village; a study of Saudi-Arabian people in transition* (Tokyo, 1977).

Katanov, Nikolai Fedorovich, born 6 May 1862, he studied Oriental languages, particularly Turkish, at at the Oriental Faculty, St. Petersburg. After graduation in 1888, he spent four years in Siberia, Mongolia, and Turkestan, studying the local Turkic dialects. Upon the recommendations of Radloff (Радлов, 1837-1918) and V. Rosen (Розен, 1849-1908), he was invited by the University of Kazan to teach Turkish dialects, starting in 1894, modern Persian and Arabic being added to his responsibilities in the following year. His interest included Arabic epigraphy, chronology, artifacts, and books current among Russian Muslims, particularly Tatars, which he reviewed. His monographs include *Опыт изследования урянхайскаго языка* (1903), and *Volkskundliche Texte aus Ost-Türkistan* (1933); his writings on current affairs of the regional Islamic communities largely appeared in the Kazan press. He died in Kazan on 10 March 1922. Sergei N. Ivanov wrote *Николай Федорович Катанов; очерк жизни и деятельности* (1962). BashkKE; BiobibSOT, pp. 183-184; GSE; Kazakhskaia, vol. 3, p. 263; Krachkovskii, p. 173; SibirSE; TatarES

Katarskiĭ, Igor' Maksimilianovich, born 29 October 1919, he was a Soviet literary historian whose writings include *Ликкенс; критико-биогпафический очерк* (1960), *Чарльз Диккенс* (1962), and *Диккенс в России* (1966). He died 19 October 1971. LC; OSK

Katibah, Habib Ibrahim, born about 1891 at Yabroud Syria, he graduated from the American University of Beirut in 1912, and Harvard School of Theology in 1918. He returned to the Near East in 1926 as correspondent for the *Brooklyn daily eagle*, *Detroit news*, *New York Times*, and the *Syrian world*, of which he also was a sometime editor. From 1936 to 1939 he served as director of the Arab National League, N.Y., and subsequently as secretary of the Institute of Arab American Affairs. In the second World War, he was with the Arab Office of the U.S. Office of War Information; after the War he was press attaché of the Syrian delegation to the United Nations. His writings include *The Case against Zionism* (1922), *Other Arabian nights* (1928), *Arabian romances and folk-tales* (1929), *The New spirit in the Arab lands* (1940), and *Arabic-speaking Americans* (1946). He died in Jacksonville, Fla., on 16 February 1951. Note; NYT, 17 February 1951, p. 15, col. 6; *Wilson library bulletin*, 25 (April 1951), p. 572 [not sighted]

Katibah, Nejib A., born in the 1870s in Ottoman Syria, he graduated from the American University of Beirut. Looking for adventure and a career, he served with the British forces in the conquest of the Sudan, 1898-99. He emigrated to the U.S.A. early in the twentieth century, and graduated from Williams College, Williamstown, Mass. In 1928 he was a dentist in Brooklyn, N.Y. Note about the author

Katırcıoğlu (Katirdschioglu), Mahmud Mukhtar Pasha, 1867-1935 *see* Mahmud Muhtar Pasha

Katona, Lajos (Ludwig), born 2 June 1862 at Vácz, Hungary, he studied at Berlin and subsequently taught at a Budapest secondary school from 1887 until 1900, when he received a doctorate. He became first a lecturer and later a professor of Hungarian literature at Budapest University. His writings include *Temesvári Pelbárt példái* (1902), *Petrarca* (1907), *Folklór-kalendárium* (1980), and he was a joint author of *Geschichte der ungarischen Literatur* (1911). He died in Budapest on 3 August 1910. GeistigeUng; Magyar; OSK

Katrak, Jamshid Cawasji, born 19th cent., he graduated in 1919 in Avesta and Pahlavi studies from Bombay University. and became a scholar of ancient Iran and Zoroastrianism. At the invitation of Shujā al-Dīn Shafā of the Pahlavi Library, Tehran, he worked there from March to May 1976 and completed a catalogue of manuscripts and books in Iranian and Indian languages. His writings include

Karachi, that was the capital of Sind (1963), *Marriage in ancient Iran* (1965), *The Age of Zarathustra* (1968), and a collection of his articles, *Iranian and Oriental papers* (1960). BioB134

Katsh, Abraham Isaac, born 10 August 1908 at Indura, Poland, he went in 1925 to the U.S.A., where he received a Ph.D. in 1944 from Dropsie College for Hebrew and Cognate Learning, Philadelphia, for *Aggadic background of the Qur'ān, Suras II and III.* He became an eminent authority on Jewish studies and was noted both for instituting the study of modern Hebrew in U.S. universities and for convincing the Soviet Government in the midst of the Cold War to allow him access to innumerable documents pertaining to Jewish history that had been hidden from Western eyes since the 1917 revolution. He was a professor of Hebrew culture and education at New York University. His writings include *Judaism in Islam* (1954), and *Catalogue of Hebrew manuscripts preserved in the USSR* (1957-58). He died in 1998. Au&Wr, 1963; BlueB, 1973/74, 1975, 1976; CnDiAmJBi; ConAu, 5-8, 169, new rev., 8; CurBio, 1962; DrAS, 1974 F, 1978 F, 1982 F; IntAu&W, 1977; Selim; WhoAm, 1974-1998; WhoE, 1974/75-1989/90; WhoWor, 1976/77-1989/90; WhoWorJ, 1955, 1965, 1972, 1978

Katsitadze, David Varlamovich, born 8 November 1928 at Tiflis, he graduated in 1955 from the Oriental Faculty, Tiflis State University, received his first degree in 1961 with a thesis entitled *Персидские источники продолжений «Картлис цховреба»*, and a doctorate in 1968 for *Грусия на рубеже XIV-XV вв.* He was appointed a lecturer in 1964, and a professor in 1974. He was a historian of Oriental history and was successively associated with the Institute of History, Georgian Academy of Sciences, and Tiflis State University. He was a joint author of *Грузино-иранские культурно-исторические связи* (1978). Miliband; Miliband²

von **Katte**, A., he was a German traveller in Abyssinia; his travel account is entitled *Reise in Abyssinien im Jahre 1836* (Stuttgart, 1838). NUC, pre-1956

Katz, Ze'ev, born 20th cent., he received a Ph.D. in 1957 from the University of London for *Party-political education in Soviet Russia.* He was in 1964 a member of the editorial board of the daily, *Ha'aretz.* His writings include *Soviet dissenters and social structure in the USSR* (1971), and he edited the *Handbook of major Soviet nationalities* (1975). NUC, 1956-77

Kaufhold, Hubert, born 19 March 1943 at Braunschweig, Germany, he received a Dr.phil. in 1970 from the Universität München for *Syrische Texte zum islamischen Recht*, and also a Dr.jur. in 1972 for *Die Rechtssammlung des Gabriel von Basra und ihr Verhältnis zu den anderen juristischen Werken der Nestorianer.* Since 1977 he was a professor of ecclesiastical and legal history of antiquity, particularly of the Christian Orient at his alma mater. His writings include *Syrische Handschriften juristischen Inhalts in südindischen Bibliotheken* (1989), and he edited *Syrische Texte zum islamischen Recht* (1971). Kürschner, 1983-2005

Kaufman, Richard Harris, born 30 January 1936 at Boston, Mass., he received a Ph.D. in 1963 from Harvard for *Exchange rate and economic development; the experience of Israel.* He was an economist and banker whose writings include *The Technology gap; United States and Europe* (1970). WhoE, 1974/75, 1976/77; WhoFI, 1974-75 (not sighted)

Kaufmann, David, born 7 June 1852 at Kojetin, Moravia, he was educated locally, where he studied the Bible and Talmud until 1867 when he went to the Rabbinerseminar, Breslau, concurrently also studying at the Universität Breslau. In the summer of 1874 he received his Dr.phil. from the Universität Gotha for *Die Attributslehre des Saadja Alfajjumi*; and on 29 January 1877 he was ordained rabbi. In the same year he declined a professorship at the Jewish Theological Seminary, Cincinnati, Ohio, preferring the chairs of history, philosophy of religion, and homiletics at the newly founded Landes-Rabbinerschule, Budapest, which he held until his death. Concurrently he taught Greek and German in the preparatory school of the same institution, carrying on this work in Hungarian, which he had rapidly mastered. He displayed a prolific literary activity; the bibliography in the *Gedenkbuch zur Erinnerung an David Kaufmann* (Breslau, 1900), includes 546 items, covering nearly every branch of Jewish science, and including *Die Spuren Al-Bataljūsī's in der jüdischen Religionsphilosophie* (1879), and *Die Sinne; Beiträge zur Geschichte der Psysiologie und Psychologie im Mittelalter aus hebräischen und arabischen Quellen* (1884). He died in Karlsbad, Austria, on 6 July 1899. ADtB, vol. 51, pp. 81-84; DtBE; GeistigeUng; JewEnc; JüdLex; *Revue des études juives*, 41 (1900), pp. 1-30; Wininger

Kaufmann, Max Rudolf, born 29 April 1886 at Basel, Switzerland, he studied at Bern and Heidelberg and received a Dr.phil. in 1908 from the Universität Bern for *Der Kaufmannsstand in der deutschen Literatur.* He was an editor of *Oriens*, Constantinople, 1912, *Osmanischer Lloyd*, Constantinople, 1910-1915, concurrently contributing to newspapers in Zürich, Frankfurt, and Wien; and an editor-in-chief of *Deutsche Allgemeine Zeitung*, Berlin, from 1916 to 1922. Since 1935 he was a writer and editor at Zürich. His writings include *Pera und Stambul* (1915), and *Türkische Erzählungen* (1916). NSB

Kaufmann, Wilhelm, born in 1858, he obtained a Dr.jur. and became a barrister-at-law and a lecturer at the Universität Berlin. His writings include *Das internationale Recht der egyptischen Staatsschuld* (Berlin, 1891), its translation, *The International state debt and its relation to international law* (1892), *Die mitteleuropäischen Eisenbahnen und das internationale öffentliche* Recht (1893), *Die Kommissare der Kasse der egyptischen Staatsschuld und das internationale Recht* (Berlin, 1896), *Zur Transvaalbahnfrage* (1901), and *Eine Sonderfahrt nach dem Orient* (1904). He died in 1926. GV; Note about the author; NUC, pre-1956

Kaul'bars, Aleksandr Vasil'evich, born in 1844 at St. Petersburg, he was a Russian officer and traveller who explored the western and central Tien Shan Mountains and the lower region of the Amu-Darya, the ancient Oxus. His last official position was a governor-general of Odessa, from 1905 to 1909. He died in 1929. Embacher; EnSlovar; Henze; Wieczynski

Kaunhoven, Friedrich, born 24 August 1860 at Straschin, Kreis Danzig, Prussia, he was educated at Danzig and studied natural sciences at the universities of Breslau and Berlin, where he received a Dr.phil. in 1887 for *Die Gastropenden der Maastricher Kreide*. He was subsequently a professor of geology at the Universität Berlin. He died in Berlin on 28 March 1940. DtBilnd (1)

von **Kaurimsky**, Emrich Fryda, born 19th cent., he received a Dr.phil. in 1914 from the Universität Wien for *Über das Ehe- und Familienrecht der Mohammedaner*. His writings include *Jugoslavien* (Berlin, Auswärtiges Amt, 1919). GV; NUC, pre-1956

Kauschansky, David Moiseevich, born about 1900, he received a Dr.jur. in 1923 from the Universität Heidelberg for *Rechtsvergleichende Darstellung des Rechtes des natürlichen Kindes nach modernen Rechten*. In 1934 he was resident in Paris. His writings include *Evolution des sowjetrussischen Eherechts; die Ehe im Gesetz und in der Gerichtspraxis* (1931), and *Evolution des sowjetrussischen Eherechts; die Familie im Gesetz und in der Gerichtspraxis* (1931). GV; Note; OSK

Kautzsch, Emil Friedrich, born 4 September 1841 at Plauen, Saxony, he studied theology and Oriental languages at the Universität Leipzig, where he received a Dr.phil. in 1863. He subsequently taught at schools. After his Dr.habil. in 1871 on the exegesis of the Old Testament, he successively taught at the universities of Basel, Tübingen, and Halle/Saale. His writings include *Die Grammatik des Biblisch-Aramaeischen* (1884), and a new edition of *Wilhelm Gesenius' Hebräische Grammatik, Gesenius' Hebrew grammar* (1880), a work which was reprinted repeatedly. He died in Halle/Saale on 7 May 1910. BLC; DtBE; DtBilnd (8); EncJud; EncJud²; JüdLex; LuthC 75; NDB; Wer ist's, 1909

Kawerau, Peter, born 13 March 1915 at Rawitsch, Prussia, he received a Dr.phil. in 1947 from the Universität Göttingen for *Die Jakobitische Kirche im Zeitalter der syrischen Renaissance*, and a Dr.habil. in 1956 from the Universität Münster for *Amerika und die orientalischen Kirchen; Ursprung und Anfang der amerikanischen Mission unter den Nationalkirchen Westasiens*. He taught ecclesiastical history first at the Universität Münster and since 1961 at the Universität Marburg. His writings include *Amerika und die orientalischen Kirchen* (1958), *Arabische Quellen zur Christianisierung Rußlands* (1967), *Geschichte der Alten Kirche* (1967), *Christlich-arabische Chrestomathie aus historischen Schriftstellern des Mittelalters* (1977), *Die Chronik von Arbela* (1985), and *Ostkirchengeschichte* (1984). He died on 8 September 1988. Kürschner, 1961-1987

Kay, Henry Cassels, born in 1827, his writings include *Yaman, its early mediæval history*; the original text, with translation and notes, from the Arabic of 'Umārah ibn 'Alī al-Hakamī (1892). He died in 1903. BLC; NUC, 1968-72

Kay, Shirley Mary née Clarke, born 13 May 1933 at Northampton, UK, she was a graduate of Cambridge and later studied at the Middle East Centre for Arab Studies, Lebanon, 1965-67, and the Institute of Archaeology, London, 1970-73, specializing in the history of the Persian Gulf region and the archaeology of the Arabian Peninsula. She was a member of the Society of Arabian Studies, and a lecturer on Middle Eastern topics. She lived in Arab countries for some twenty years between 1965 and 1990, working there as a journalist for radio and televison and as a free lance writer. Her writings include *Digging into the past* (1974), *The Egyptians* (1975), *The Bedouin* (1978), *Saudi Arabia* (1979), *Emirates archaeological heritage* (1988), *Enchanting Oman* (1988), *Portrait of Ras al Khaimah* (1990), *Seafarers of the Gulf* (1992), and *Wings over the Gulf* (1995). LC; Private

Kay, William, born 8 April 1820 at Pickering, Yorkshire, England, he was educated at Glygleswick and Lincoln College, Oxford, where he was a scholar, fellow, and tutor. A Pusey and Ellerton Hebrew Scholar, he was ordained in 1843, B.D. in 1849, and D.D. in 1855. From 1849 to 1865 he served as principal of Bishop's College, Calcutta. A Honorary Canon of St. Albans, he was one of the revisers of the Old Testament in 1870, and devoted his life to his parish and to critical and learned works on the Scriptures. He died in St. Albans on 16 January 1886. Buckland; DNB; Riddick

Kayaloff, Jacques, born in 1898 at Nakhichevan, Russia, where he was also educated, he went to the United States in 1924 and became an investment counsellor in New York. His writings include *The Battle of Sardarabad* (1973). WhoE, 1975/76, 1977/78, 1979/80; ZKO

Kaye, Alan Stewart, born 2 March 1944 (according to his own information) at Los Angeles, he received a Ph.D. in 1971 from the University of California at Berkeley for *Chadian and Sudanese Arabic in the light of comparative Arabic dialectology*, a work which was published in 1976. He spent his entire career with California State University at Fullerton as a professor of linguistics and director of phonetic research. His writings include *A Dictionary of Nigerian Arabic* (1982), and jointly with Garland H. Cannon, *The Persian contributions to the English language; an historical dictionary* (2001). MESA Roster of members, 1990; NatFacDr, 1990-2005; Private; Selim; WhoEmL, 1989 (not sighted); WhoWest, 1984-1987/88

al-**Kaylānī**, Rashīd ʿAlī, 1892-1965 *see* al-Kīlānī (Gailani, Gaylani, Gilani), Rashīd ʿAlī

Kayser, Friedrich, born 29 October 1843 at Mülheim an der Ruhr, Prussia, he gained a Dr.phil. and was ordained in Köln on 24 August 1868. He taught theology and served as a clergyman at Weinheim. From 1870 to 1877 he resided in Algeria and Egypt to recover from his pulmonary disease. He used these years for historical and ethnographical studies. His writings include *Eine Nilfahrt* (1878), *Ägypten einst und jetzt* (1884), and its translation, *Histoire d'Égypte* (1912). He died on 27 February 1900. DtBilnd (1)

Kayser, Walter, born 20th cent., he received a doctorate in 1949 from the Universität Münster for *Das physiologische Denken in der mittelalterlichen Medizin*. Schwarz

Kayser, Werner, born 20th cent., his writings include *Hamburger Bücher, 1491-11850* (Hamburg, 1973), *500 Jahre wissenschaftliche Bibliothek in Hamburg, 1479-1879; von der Ratsbücherei zur Staats- und Universitätsbibliothek* (1979); and he was a joint author of *Bibliographie der Hamburger Drucke des 16. Jahrhunderts* (1968).

Kayserling, Meyer (Moritz), born 17 June 1829 at Hannover, Germany, he studied Talmudic and rabbinical subjects at Halberstadt, Prag, and Würzburg, where he was ordained rabbi. He subsequently studied history at the universities of Berlin, and Halle, where he received a Dr.phil. for *Moses Mendelsohns philosophische und religiöse Grundsätze mit Hinblick auf Lessing*. He became a historian, and rabbi in Switzerland and Hungary. His writings include *Sephardim; romanische Poesien der Juden in Spanien* (1859), and *Geschichte der Juden in Spanien und Portugal* (1861-1867). He died in Budapest on 21 April 1905. DtBE; DtBilnd (3); EncJud; EncJud²; GeistigeUng; JewEnc; NDB; Wininger

Kazakov, Evgeniĭ Petrovich, born in 1934, he was an archaeologist who received a doctorate in 1994. Since 1995 he was associated with the Institute of History, Tatar Academy of Sciences. His writings include Памятники болгарского времени в восточных районах Татарии (1978), Археологические памятники Татарское АССР (1987), Булгарское село X-XIII веков низовий Камы (1991), and Культура ранней Волжской Болгарии (1992). OSK; TatarES

Kazakov, Miklaĭ, born 1918 in the Mari Autonomous Soviet Republic, he graduated from Gorkii Institute of Literature, Moscow. His writings include Поэзия - любимая подруга (Moscow, 1951), Корно ӱзеш; почеламут, муро, мускара (Ioshkar-Ola, 1972), Лесные напевы; Стихи (Moscow, 1976), and he was a compiler of Соловьиный подник; антология марийской поэзии (Ioshkar-Ola, 1970). He died in 1960. NUC, 1973-77; WhoSocC 78

Kazakov, Nikolaĭ Ivanovich, 1918-1960 *see* Kazakov, Miklaĭ

Kazanin, Mark Isaakovich, born in 1899 at Krivoĭ Rog, Ukraine, he graduated in 1927 from the Oriental Institute in the University of London. He was a first diplomatic secretary to the 1920/21 Far East Mission to Peking. His writings include Рубин эмира бухарского (1964), and *China in the twenties* (1973). He died on 11 January 1972. Miliband; Miliband²

Kazazis, Kostas, born 15 July 1934 at Athens, he was educated at Lausanne and received a Ph.D. in 1965 from Indiana University. After briefly teaching at the University of Illinois at Urbana, he taught linguistics in various capacities at the University of Chicago until his retirement. He was a joint author of *Reference grammar of literary Dhimotiki* (1964), and he was a joint editor of *Studies in modern Greek for American students* (1974). DrAS, 1974 F, 1978 F, 1982 F; NatFacDr, 1995-2002

Kazem-Bek, Aleksandr Kaslmovich, born Mirza Muhammad ʿAli on 22 July 1802 at Rasht, Persia, he was educated by his father as well as by Muslim teachers. Having completed his Islamic education at the age of twenty, he set out critically to review Islam with a view to disproving Christian polemics. Contrary to his intention, he became convinced of the superiority of Christianity and was baptized by Scottish missionaries in 1821 at Astrakhan. An account of his conversion is said to be found in the

Christian keepsake of 1836. He spent some five years with the missionaries acquiring a European education. In 1825 he was nominated a teacher of Tatar at the school in Omsk, concurently serving as an interpreter to the governor-general of Siberia. Soon thereafter he was invited to teach Oriental languages at the University of Kazan, gradually rising to become full professor of Arabic, Persian, and Turco-Tatar as well as director of the important numismatic collection of the University. When the Imperial Russian Government decided to establish a Faculty of Oriental Languages at St. Petersburg, he was appointed by the Ministry of Public Education to the chair of Persian, and on several occasions served also as dean of the Faculty of History and Philology. His writings include *Concordance complète du Coran* (St. Petersbourg, 1859), and *Избранные произведения* (1985). He died in 1870. Agababa Kasum ogly Rzaev wrote *Мухаммед Али М(ирза) Казем-Бек* (1989). BiobibSOT, pp. 175-178; EI²; GSE; *L'Orient, l'Algérie et les colonies françaises*, 2 (1867), pp. 62-64, 78-80; PTF, II, p. 780; TatarES; VostokMStP, p. 250

Kazemzadeh, Firuz, born 27 October 1924 at Moscow, he graduated in 1946 from Stanford University, Palo Alto, Calif., and received a Ph.D. in 1951 from Harvard. He was successively associated with the U.S. Department of State, Radio Free Europe, the Russian, and the Middle East centers at Harvard, before he began teaching at Yale University, New Haven, Conn., in 1956. His writings include *The Struggle for Transcaucasia* (1951), and *Russia and Britain in Persia, 1864-1914* (1968). ConAu, 21-24; DrAS, 1974 H, 1978 H, 1982 H; IntAu&W, 1977; NatFacDr, 1990; Schoeberlein; WhoAm, 1974-1996; WhoE, 1986-89 (not sighted); WhoRel, 1975, 1978, 1992/93; WrDr, 1976/78-1996/98

Kazi, Mirza Djevad Khan, 1884- *see* Qazi, Mirza Muhammed Javad Khan

Kaziev (Газыјев), Adil IUsif ogly, fl. 20th cent., his writings include *Очерки изобразительного искусства Советского Азербайджана* (1960), *Миниатюры рукописи "Хамсэ" Низами* (1964), *Художественно-технические материалы и терминология средневековой книжной живописи, каллиграфии и переплётного искусства* (1966), and *Художественное оформление азербайджанской рукописной книги XIII-XVII* (1977). NUC; OSK

Kaziev (Газыјев), Mamed Adil ogly, fl. 20th cent., his writings include *Из истории революционной борьбы бакинского пролетариата* (1956), *Жизнь и революционная деятельность Мешади Азизбекова* (1956), *Буниат Сардаров* (1964), *Мешади Азизбеков* (1966), *Нариман Нариманов, 1870-1925; жизнь и деятельность* (1970), *Мешади Азизбекав; жизнь и деятельность* (1976), and he edited *Памятники истории Азербайджана* (1956), and a brief guide to the Museum of the history of Azerbaijan, *Краткии путеводитель* (1959). NUC; OSK

Kazimirski-Biberstein (Kazimierski Bibersztein), Adalbert (Albert, Wojciech) de, born in 1808 at Lublin, Austria, he studied at the universities of Warszawa and Berlin. In the wake of the Polish revolution, he went into exile in Paris in 1831. From 1839 to 1840 he was a dragoman in French service in Tehran. His four-volume *Dictionnaire arabe-français* became the chief dictionary for French-speaking students for a hundred years. His other writings include *Le Koran; traduction nouvelle* (1840), *Enis el-Djélis; ou, histoire de la belle Persane* (1847), *Gulistan, to jest Ogród rózany Sa'dego z Szyrazu* (1876), and *Menoutchehri, poète persan du IXème siècle de notre ère; texte, traduction, notes et introduction his-torique* (1886). He died in Paris in 1887. Dziekan; NEP; PSB, 12, pp. 295-297; *Wielka encyklopedya powszechna illustrowana* (1904)

Kāzim'zādah Īrānshahr, Husayn, born in 1884 at Tabriz, he lost his parents early in life. Before the Persian revolution, he went by way of Batum to Constantinople where he remained until 1911 as an employee at the Persian Legation, concurrently studying law at the Darülfünun. In 1910-1911, he served as guide of the Persian Mecca pilgrims, an experience which he described in *Relation d'un pélerinage à la Mecque* (1912). In 1913, he was a lecturer in Persian at Cambridge; in 1915, he went to Berlin, where he was in 1918 a founding member of the Deutsch-Persische Gesellschaft. His writings include *Rahe nau, neue Methode; Entwurf einer Reform in Betreff der Alphabete der islamischen Sprachen und der Typographie der in diesen Sprachen verfaßten Werke* (Berlin, Büttner, 1919), *Râs-o-Niâs; der Seele Sehnen und Verlangen* (Berlin, Iranschähr, 1924), *Die Gathas von Zarathushtra* (Berlin, Iranschähr, 1930), and *Das Schicksal und seine Überwindung* (Olten, 1949). Sezgin; Yonan

Keall, Edward John, born 18 June 1939 in England, he received a Ph.D. in 1970 from the University of Michigan, for *The significance of late Parthian Nippur*. He was a curator at the West Asian Department, Royal Ontario Museum, Toronto, and from the early 1990s to his retirement he was a professor in the Department of Near and Middle Eastern Civilizations in the University of Toronto. He did field-work in Yemen and served as a member on the board of directors of the American Institute for Yemeni Studies. He was a joint author of *Silk roads, China ships* (1983). *MESA Roster of members*, 1990; NatFacDr, 2002-2004; Private; Schoeberlein

Keane, August Henry, born in 1833 at Cork, Eire, he was an emeritus professor of Hindustani, University College, London, and a sometime vice-president of the Anthropological Institute. His writings include *Ethnology* (1896), and *The World's peoples* (1908). He died in 1912. BritInd (2); *Who was who*, 1

Keane, John Freyer Thomas (Hajj Mohammed Amin), born 4 October 1854 at Whitby, England, he was the son of a clergyman and ran away to sea at the age of twelve. He spent most of the next nine years among Muslims, mainly as an officer on ships with Indian crews. About 1877 he arrived at Jiddah, attached himself to a suite of an Indian prince and visited Mecca and Medina. After his return he wrote his autobiography, *My journey to Medinah* (1881), *Six months in Mecca* (1881), *Six months in the Hedjaz; an account of the Mohammedan pilgrimages to Meccah and Medinah* (1887), and *Three years of a wanderer's life* (1887). He died on 1 September 1937. Bidwell, pp. 127-29; Kornrumpf; *Who was who*, 3

Kearney, Thomas Henry, born in 1874 at Cincinnati, Ohio, he studied at the University of Tennessee, Columbia University, New York, and the University of Arizona. He became a botanist successively at Columbia University, and the U.S. Department of Agriculture. His writings include *Date varieties and date culture in Tunis* (1906), and *Dry-land olive culture in northern Africa* (1908). He died in San Francisco in 1956. BioIn 4; NatCAB, vol. 45, pp. 565-66; NYT, 22 October 1956, p. 29, col. 2; Shavit; WhAm, 3

Keating, Michael F., born 28 August 1932 at Montreal, P.Q., he graduated in 1955 from Francis Xavier University. He was a free lance writer, photographer, and radio and television commentator as well as a sometime assistant professor of journalism at Rutgers University, Newark, N.J. He was a joint author of *White man, black man* (1974). ConAu, 49-52

Keating, Reginald *Rex* James Thomas, he was born in 1910 at London. In 1956, he became associated with the Unesco Secretariat, Paris. His writings include *Nubian twilight* (1962), and *Nubian rescue* (1975). Au&Wr, 1963

Keatinge, Margaret Clark, fl. 1972, her writings include *Beirut guidebook* (1953), *Costumes of the Levant* (1955), and she was a joint author of *Lebanon, land of the cedars* (1956), and *Food from the Arab world* (1959). NUC, pre-1956

Keay, John Seymour, born in 1839 and educated at St. Andrews, Scotland, he was for many years a banker in India and an M.P. His writings include *Spoiling the Egyptians; a tale of shame* (1882), and *The Landlord, the tenant, and the tax payer* (1890). He died in 1909. DNB; Riddick; *Who was who*, 1

Kebedgy, Michel S., born in 1865, he received a doctorate in 1890 from the Faculté de droit de Paris with his two theses entitled *De la tutelle des femmes pubères*, and *De l'intervention, théorie générale et étude spéciale de la question d'Orient*. His writings include *La question arménienne en 1895* (1896), *Die diplomatischen Privilegien* (1901), as well as contributions to the *Revue générale de droit international public*. BN

Kecskeméti, Istvan, born 6 March 1937 at Budapest, he was a scholar of Turkic philology who went to Austria in 1956, and to Finland two years later. His writings include *Rückläufiges Verzeichnis tatarischer Suffixe und Suffixkombinationen* (Helsinki, 1972), and *Die Frauensprache als Tabu im Oriotischen* (Helsinki, 1973). He died in Helsinki on 31 May 1975. MEL, 1987-1991

Kedar, Benjamin Ze'ev, born 2 September 1938 at Nitra, Czechoslovakia, he became a professor of history at the Hebrew University, Jerusalem. His writings include *Merchants in crisis; Genoese and Venetian men of affairs and the fourteenth-century depression* (1976), a work which was originally presented as his doctoral thesis at Yale University, New Haven, N.H. His other writings include *Crusade and mission; European approaches toward the Muslims* (1984), and he was a joint editor of *I comuni italiani nel regno crociato di Gerusalemme; atti del Colloquio "The Italian communes in the Crusading Kingdom of Jerusalem"* (1986). LC; WhoIsrael, 1980/81-2001

Keddie, Nikki Ragozin (Reinhard), born 30 August 1930 at N.Y.C., she graduated from Radcliffe College and received a Ph.D. in 1955 from the University of California at Berkeley for *The impact of the West on Iranian social history*. She had a number of minor university posts before 1961, when she was appointed a professor of history at the University of California at Los Angeles, a post which she held until her retirement. Her writings include *Religion and rebellion in Iran* (1966), *The Islamic response to imperialism* (1968), *Sayid Jamal al-Din "al-Afghani"* (1972), and a collection of her essays, *Iran; religion, politics and society* (1980). In 2000 appeared *Iran and beyond; essays in Middle Eastern history in honor of Nikki R. Keddie*. ConAu, 25-28, new rev. 13, 56; DrAS, 1974 H, 1978 H, 1982 H; NatFacDr, 1990-1995; ZKO

Keddie, Wells Hamilton, born in 1925, he received a Ph.D. in 1968 from Claremont Graduate School and University Center for *Democratic behavior and union bargaining power.* NUC, 1973-77

Kedourie, Elie, born in 1926 at Baghdad, he was educated at the local *lycée*, and subsequently went to the London School of Economics to study under Michael Oakeshott, whose conservative sympathies he shared. English was only his third language after French and Arabic, "but he commanded a mellifluous literary style, and could express opinions, which were often rebarbative, in remarkable seductive style." In 1964 he was appointed to the chair of political science at his alma mater, a post which he held until his retirement in 1990. His writings include *England and the Middle East* (1956), a work which was originally intended as a D.Phil. thesis at Oxford but which he decided to withdraw from the examination rather than change his conclusions to suit the opinion of his examiner H. A. R. (later Sir Hamilton) Gibb. His other writings include *Nationalism* (1960), *Nationalism in Asia and Africa* (1970), *The Chatham House version and other Middle-Eastern studies* (1970), and *Elie Kedourie, CBE, FBA, 1926-1992; history, philosophy, politics*, edited by Sylvia Kedourie (1998). He died in Washington, D.C., on 29 June 1992. In 1986 appeared *National and international politics in the Middle East; essays in honour of Elie Kedourie.* Au&Wr, 1971; BRMES *Newsletter*, no. 1 (November 1992), p. 1; ConAu, 21-24, 139, new rev., 10, 31; *Index Islamicus* (4); IntWW, 1989-1992/93; MES, 29 (1993), pp. 372-76; MidE, 1978-1982/83; *Political studies*, 40 (1992), pp. 581-82; *Proceedings* of the British Academy, 87 (1995), pp. 357-81; T.L.S., 4661 (31 July 1992), p. 7; *Who's who*, 1979-1992; WrDr, 1984/86-1992/94

Kedourie, Sylvia G. Haim, born 20th cent., she received a Ph.D. in 1953 from the University of Edinburgh for *The Ideas of a precursor, 'Abd al-Rahman al-Kawakibi, 1849-1902, in relation to the trend of Musilm-Arab thought.* She was an associate editor of *Middle Eastern studies* since the beginning. After the death of her husband, Elie, in 1992, she continued as editor of the journal. Her writings include *Turkey before and after Atatürk; internal and external affairs* (1998), *Seventy-five years of the Turkish Republic* (1999), and she edited *Arab nationalism* (1976), *Elie Kedourie, CBE, FBA, 1926-1992; history, philosophy, politics* (1998), and she was a joint editor of *Modern Egypt* (1980). Note about the author; Sluglett

Kedrov, Bonifatiĭ Mikhaĭlovich, born 10 December 1903, he was a specialist in the theory of materialist dialectics, the methodology of science, and the history of chemistry. His writings include Марксистская концепция истории естествознания (1985), Дисциплинарность и взаимодействие наук (1986), Науки в их взаимосвязи (1988), and Проблемы логики и методологии науки; избранные труды (1990). G. N. Finashina wrote Бонифатий Михайлов Кедров (1985). GSE; OSK

Keeley, James Hugh, Jr., born in 1895, he was from 1947 to 1950 a U.S. envoy extraordinary and minister plenipotentiary to Syria. He died in 1985. LC; Note about the author

Keeling, Cecil, born in 1912 at Teddington, Middlesex, England, he studied at schools of art while working for a printing firm. He later became associated with the BBC. After war-time service in Italy and the Middle East he became a designer, typographer, and illustrator in a variety of media. His writings include *A Modicum of leave* (1943), and *Pictures from Persia*, with 30 colour plates by the author (1947). Peppin; WhoGrA, 1962

Keeling, Edward Herbert, born 19th cent. at Bradford, Yorkshire, England, he took an M.A. in law at University College, Oxford. He was a barrister-at-law, soldier, writer, business man, and a Conservative M.P. He served in practically every country of the East, including India, Mesopotamia, Russia, Syria, Anatolia, the Black Sea, Armenia, and Kurdistan. He was the manager of the Turkish Petroleum Company. His writings include *Adventures in Turkey and Russia* (1924). He died in 1954. Note about the author; WhE&EA; *Who was who*, 5

Keenan, Edward Louis, born 13 May 1935 at Buffalo, N.Y., he graduated in 1957 from Harvard, where he also received his Ph.D. in 1966 for *Muscovy and Kazan, 1445-1552; a study in steppe politics.* He spent his entire career teaching history at his alma mater. During the last years of the Pahlavi dynasty he served on the board of governors of Reza Shah Kabir University. His writings include *The Kurbskiĭ-Groznyi opocrypha* (1971), and *Josef Dobrowský and the origins of the Igor' tale* (2003). NatFacDr, 1990-2004; OSK; Schoeberlein; WhoAm, 1976-1996

Keenan, Jeremy H., born in 1945 in Devon, England, he received a Ph.D. in 1970 from the University of London for *The social consequences of Algerian development policies for the Tuareg of Ahaggar.* He was a sometime senior lecturer at the University of Witwatersrand, Johannesburg. His writings include *The Tuareg, people of the Ahaggar* (1977). Note about the author; Sluglett;

Keene, Alfred, born 17 April 1855, he entered the British Army in 1874, and served in the Afghan War, 1878-80, and in Burma, 1885-86. For operations in Burma he was awarded D.S.O. He retired in 1905 with the rank of colonel. He died on 21 April 1918. BitInd (1); *Who was who*, 2

Keene, Henry George, born 30 September 1781, he was educated privately. He went out to the Indian Army in 1798 and participated in the siege of Seringapatam against Tipu Sultan in 1799. He subsequently passed to the Madras Civil Service, passed through the College of Fort William, Cacutta, and served in Madras but resigned his appointment in 1811. He graduated from Sidney Sussex College, Cambridge, in 1815, resigned the Indian Civil Service, and was ordained in 1817. In 1824, he became a professor of Arabic and Persian, and registrar, at the East India Company's college at Haileybury, a post which he held for ten years. His writings include *Persian fables for young and old* (1836), its translation, *Persische Fabeln für Jung und Alt* (1834), and *Akhlāq-i Muhsini*, a translation from the Persian of Husayn Vā'iz Kāshifī (1850). He died on 29 January 1864. BLC; Buckland; DNB; IndianBilnd (2)

Keene, Henry George, born in 1825 at Haileybury, England, he was educated at Rugby and Oxford. After passing through the East India Company's college at Haileybury, he entered the Indian Civil Service in 1847 and served in the North West Provinces as a magistrate and judge until he resigned in 1882. He officiated as commander of Agra in 1872 and 1875, and of Allahabad in 1874. His writings include *Delhi* (1873), *The Fall of the Moghul Empire* (1876), *The Turks in India; critical chapters on the administration of that country* (1879), *Fitfty-seven; some account of the administration of Indian districts during the revolt of the Bengal Army* (1883), *Madhava Ráo Sindhia* (1892), *History of India* (1898), *Hindustan under Free Lances, 1770-1820* (1907), and he edited *The Oriental biographical dictionary*, founded on the materials collected by Thomas Wm. Beale (1881). He died 29 March 1915. Buckland; IndianBilnd (3); Riddick; *Who was who*, 1

Keens, L. T., born about 1900, he was a group-captain in the R.A.F. and stationed to Aden from 1933 to 1937; he had another spell in Aden from 1948 to 1950. His trace is lost after an article in 1952. Note about the author

Kegel, Gerhard, born 26 June 1912 at Magdeburg, Prussia, he was a professor of law at the Universität Köln until his retirement. His writings include *Die Grenze von Qualification und Renvoi im internationalen Verjährungsrecht* (1962), *Ein Vierteljahrhundert danach; das Potsdamer Abkommen* (1970), and its translation, *25 years after Potsdam* (1979), and he was a joint author of *Die Einwirkung des Krieges auf Verträge in der Rechtssprechung* (1941). In 1987 appeared *Festschrift für Gerhard Kegel*. DiBilnd (2); IntWW, 1989-2002; Kürschner, 1954-2005; *Wer ist wer*, 1955-1979; WhoWr, 1974/75-1991/92

Kégl, Sándor, born 1 December 1862 at Pest, Hungary, he was a linguist who knew the major European languages as well as Arabic and Persian. He spent two years at Tehran and was since 1893 a teacher of Persian at Budapest. In 1906 he was appointed a professor. He contributed to the *Révai nagy lexikona*. His writings include *A persza néptal* (1899), *Szenáji és a persza vallásos költészet* (1904), *Dselâl ed-Dîn Rūmî négysoros versei* (1907), and *Emir Khoszrev* (1911). He died on 29 December 1920. GeistigeUng; Magyar; Pallas; RNL

Kehl, Camille, he was in 1941 a barrister at Oran, Algeria, and a president of the Société de géographie et d'archéologie d'Oran. Note about the author

Kehr (Керь), Georg Jacob, born 8 August 1692 at Schleusingen, Thuringia, he studied Oriental languages, particularly Arabic under S. Nehri, at the Universität Halle and gained a master's degree in 1722 at Leipzig where he became a lecturer in his field. Based on research on Kufic coins, he was in 1724 the first European to demonstrate that Kufic script was merely one particular style of writing, not a separate script as had been believed until then. It was he, too, who determined the Indian origin of the Arabic numerals. In 1732, he went to the Collegium of Foreign Affairs (Коллегия иностранных дель) at St. Petersburg as a translator, concurrently teaching Oriental languages. In 1735, the Imperial Academy entrusted him with the cataloguing of its coin collection. He also identified important sources relating to Russian history, and translated from the Chaghatai of Ebülgâzî Bahadır Han, "*Родословное древо турков.*" He is best remembered for his 1733 project of an "Academia vel Societas scientiarum atque linguarum orientalium in Imperii Ruthenici emolumentum et gloriam instauranda," which aimed at the training of young scholars for Oriental research as well as government service in Oriental countries, pleaded for the procurement of appropriate teaching aids, and provided a plan of research topics, emphasizing the importance of the material contained in the Arabic, Persian, Turkish, and Tatar "chronicles" for the Russian state and its history. But he was ahead of his time and died prematurely on 5 May 1740. His writings include *Saraceni, Hagareni et Mavri qvinam sint* (1723), and *Monarchae mogolo-indici* (1725). BiobibSOT, pp. 185-186; DtBlnd (1); EnSlovar; *Hamburgische Berichte von neuen gelehrten Sachen*, 1734, pp. 471-472, 479-81; Krachkovskiĭ, pp. 43-46; Sezgin

Kehren, Lucien, born 20th cent., his writings include *Tamerlan; l'empire du seigneur de fer* (1975), and he edited *La route de Samarkand au temps de Tamerlan; relation du voyage de l'ambassade de Castille à la cour de Timour Beg*, of Ruy Gonzales de Clavijo; traduit de l'espagnol et commenté (1990). *Livres disponibles*, 2004

Kehrer, Kenneth C., born in 1939, he was an economist whose writings include *Human resources development planning* (Washington, D.C., Department of State, 1967). LC

Keichel, Alfred, Dr., born 12 April 1893 at Posen, Prussia, he was a banker at Berlin and concurrently served as a lecturer in commercial and industrial law at the Handelshochschule, Berlin. His writings include *Die Aufbringung der Industriebelastung nebst den Texten des Aufbringungsgesetzes* (1926), *Zahlen aus Deutschlands Wirtschaft* (Berlin, 1931), and he was a joint author of *Die Goldbilanzverordnung vom 28. Dezember 1923* (1924). Kürschner, 1931, 1935

Keijzer, Salomo, 1823-1868 *see* Keyzer, Salomo(n)

Keil, Carl (Karl) Friedrich, born 23 February 1807 at Lauterbach near Oelnitz/Vogtland, Saxony, the son of a farmer, he was sent to St. Petersburg to train as a carpenter but instead went to the German Petrischule and turned out to be so gifted that a benefactor also enabled him to study theology from 1827 to 1833 at the universities of Dorpat and Berlin. He returned to Dorpat in 1838 as an orthodox Lutheran and became in 1839 a professor of exegesis and Oriental languages, a post which he held until 1858, when he returned to Saxony. His writings include *Apologetischer Versuch über die Bücher der Chronik und über die Integrität des Buches Esra* (Berlin, 1833), *Commentar über die Bücher der Könige* (Moskau, 1846), and he was a joint author of *Biblischer Commentar über das Alte Testament* (1861-85). He died in Rödlitz near Lichtenstein/Sachsen on 5 May 1888. DtBE; EncJud²; Krachkovskiï; NDB

Keimer, Ludwig, born 23 August 1893 at Hellenthal near Aachen, Prussia, he gained doctorates in philosophy, law, and political science. He became a specialist in natural sciences applied to Egyptology. His writings include his theses at the universities of Würzburg, and Münster, *Die privatrechtliche Sonderstellung des hohen Adeks einst und jetzt* (1922), *Ägypten in seinen staats- und völkerrechtlichen Beziehungen zur Türkei, zu den Mächten und zu England* (1924), as well as *Die Gartenpflanzen im alten Ägypten* (1924), *Histoire de serpents dans l'Égypte ancienne et moderne* (1947), and *Remarques sur le tatouage dans l'Égypte ancienne* (1948). He died after a long illness on 16 August 1957. Bulletin de la Société d'archéologie copte, 14 (1950/57), p. 252; Dawson; Egyptology; Schwarz

Keiser, Helen, born 27 June 1926 at Zug, Switzerland, her writings include the travel accounts *Sie kamen aus der Wüste; mit den Beduinen auf den Spuren der alten Nabatäer* (1964), *Salaam; Bordbuch einer Orientfahrt* (1958), *Vagabund im Morgenland* (1961), *Geh nicht über den Jordan* (1971), *Die kleine Beduinenfrau; Wege zwischen Wüste und Paradies* (1975), *Abenteur schwarzes Gold; Erlebnisse und Begegnungen in Saudi-Arabien* (1977), *Ruf des Muezzin; eine schwierige Liebe zwische Orient und Okzident* (1981), *Suche nach Sindbad; das Weihrauchland Oman und die altsüdarabischen Kulturen* (1979), and *Arabia* (1980). KDtKL, 1978-1998|; Sezgin

Keiser, R. Lincoln, born in 1937, he received a Ph.D. in 1971 from the University of Rochester, N.Y., for *Social structure and social control in two Afghan societies*. He became a professor in the Department of Anthropology, Wesleyan University, Middletown, Conn., a post which he held until his retirement. His writings include *The vice lords; warriors of the streets* (1969), and *Genealogical beliefs and social structure among the Sum of Afghanistan* (1973). NatFacDr, 1990-2004; NUC, 1973-77

von **Keiser**, Rolf, born 30 July 1908 at Oldenburg, Germany, he entered the foreign service and became head of Oriental trade relations in the German Foreign Office, posted successively to the Netherlands, India, Bulgaria, and Burma. Note about the author; Wer ist wer, 1955-1974/75

Keiter, Therese, born 20 June 1859 at Melsungen, Hesse, she was a prolific novelist and poet, writing under the pseudonym, Marie Herbert, on religious and historic subjects. She died in Regensburg on 5 April 1925. DtBE; KDtLK, 1916; Kosch

Keith, Arthur Berriedale, born in 1879, he was educated at the University of Edinburgh and Balliol College, Oxford. A barrister-at-law of the Inner Temple, he was Regius Professor of Sanskrit and comparative philology as well as a lecturer on constitution of the British Empire at the University of Edinburgh. His writings include *Dominion home rule in practice* (1921), *A History of Sanskrit literature* (1928), *Catalogue of the Sanskrit and Prakit manuscripts in the India Office Library* (1935), *The Governments of the British Empire* (1935), *A Constitutional history of India, 1600-1935* (1936), and *The Dominions as sovereign states* (1938). He died in 1944. Ridgway F. Shinn wrote *Arthur Berriedale Keith, the chief ornament of Scottish learning* (1990). BritInd (3); DNB; IndianBiInd (2); Riddick; WhE&EA; Who was who, 4

Keith-Falconer, Ion Grant Neville, born in 1856 at Edinburgh, he was educated privately, and afterwards at Cheam, Harrow, and Hitchin. After pursuing mathematics for one year at Trinity College, Cambridge, he changed to theological honours, graduating B.A. in 1878. After taking his degree, he devoted himself first to work among the poor, and later to Oriental languages, particularly Arabic at

Cambridge and Leipzig in 1880/81. The following winter he spent at Asyut, Egypt, where he turned his attention to colloquial Arabic. Since 1881 he was a lecturer in Hebrew at Clare Collge, Cambridge. About the mid-1880s he became engrossed with the idea of mission-work where Arabic might be useful. In 1886, he became Lord Almoner's Professor of England and soon thereafter went on his own cost to Shaykh 'Uthmān, Southern Arabia, taking along his wife and a medical doctor to establish a medical mission. He soon succumbed to attacks of Aden fever, of which he died on 11 May 1887. His writings include *Kalilah and Dimnah; or, The Fables of Bidpai, being an account of their literary history, with English translation of the later Syria version of the same* (1885). Boase; Buckland; DNB; LuthC 75; Richter

Keith-Roach, Edward, born in 1885 at Clifton, England, he was educated privately. He was in banking until the outbreak of the first World War during which he served in the Egyptian Army as a major, and in 1916 was seconded to the Sudan Government as intelligence officer. After the armistice, he served as a colonial adminstrator in Mandatory Palestine until the 1940s. He was a joint editor of the *Handbook of Palestine and Trans-Jordan* (1922), a work which went through several editions until 1934. He died in 1954. BritInd (1); Who was who, 5

Keizer, Mervyn Michael, born about 1938, he received a Ph.D. in 1969 from Harvard for *The technique of Latin didactic poetry*. His trace is lost after an article in 1977. NUC, 1968-72

Kekulé von Stradonitz, Stephan Carl, born 1 May 1863 at Gent, Belgium, he studied natural sciences at the universities of Bonn, and Straßburg, followed by six years as a professionel Prussian officer. He subsequently studied law and Oriental languages at the universities of Berlin and Halle, where he received a Dr.phil. in 1892 for *Über Titel, Ämter, Rangstufen und Anrede in der offiziellen osmanischen Sprache*; in 1895 he also gained a Dr.jur. He became a legal counsel, specializing in genealogical and heraldic cases. His writings include *Ausgewählte Aufsätze aus dem Gebiete des Staatsrechts und der Genealogie* (1903). He died in Berlin on 5 May 1932 or 1933. DtBE; DtBilnd (2); Kürschner, 1935; NDB

Keldani, 'Abdul-l-Ahad Dawūd, born in 1867 in Urmia or Digala, Persia, and baptized David Benjamin, he was educated in Urmia, and from 1886 to 1889 he was attached to the Archbishop of Canterbury's Mission to the Assyrian (Nestorian) Christians in Urmia. Sent by Cardinal Vaughan in 1892 to study philosophy and theology at the Collegio di Propaganda Fide, Roma, he was ordained in 1895. He returned to Persia by way of Constantinople, where he published a series of articles in French and English on the Greek-Orthodox Church in the *Levant herald*. In the same year, he joined the French Mission lazariste at Urmia and for the first time in the history of this mission he published a Syriac journal, *Qala la shārā*, the voice of truth. In 1897, the archbishops of the United Chaldaeans of Urmia, and Salamās sent him as their representative of the Greek-Orthodox Catholics to the Eucharistic Congress at Paray-le-Monial in France, where he denounced the prevalent Catholic education among the Nestorians. In 1898, he was nominated superintendent of the Diocese of Salamās, where he became a witness to the deadly rivalry among the five main Western missions. In the summer of 1900 he spent a month in prayer and meditation, at the end of which he resigned his post. For some months he was employed in the Persian postal and customs service at Tabriz, before he became a teacher and interpreter in the service of crown prince Muhammad 'Alī Mirzā. He visited England in 1903, and in 1904 he was asked by the British and Unitarian Foreign Association to continue his work among his countrymen. On the return journey to Persia he stopped at Constantinople where, after discussions with the şeyhülislâm Cemalüddin Effendi, he embraced Islam. His writings include *Muhammad in der Bibel* (München, 1992). From an unidentified German obituary, pp. 18-19

Keleita, Joh., fl. 1905-1915, a Nestorian (Assyrian) Christian, from Marbisho in Tergawar (Kurdistan), who was an in-law of the German pastor Otto Wendt of Lerbeck near Porta Westphalica, the chairman of the Komitee für die Liebesarbeit an den Nestorianern in Kurdistan. Note about the author

Keleita, Thoma J., fl. 1905-1915 in the vicinity of Urmia, Kurdistan, a brother of Joh. Keleita.

Kélékian, Dikran Garabed, born in 1868 Kayseri, Anatolia, the son of a banker, he was educated at the American Robert College, Constantinople, and at Paris. He immersed himself in archaeological lore of the Near East and at the same time maintained a keen interest in contemporary painting and painters in Paris. His success as a dealer soon resulted in the establishment of branches of his firm in New York, London, and Cairo. He first visited the United States at the time of the Chicago World's Fair in 1893. Though credited with having much to do with gaining recognition of French moderns, his chief interest was in the Near Eastern monuments he had assembled into a fabulous collection. His writings include *The Kelekian Collection of Persian art and analogous potteries, 1885-1910* (1910), and *Dictionnaire turc-français* (1911). He plunged twenty-one stories to his death from his suite in the Hotel St. Moritz, New York, on 31 January 1951. During his last years he suffered from lameness due to a hip injury, and from eyesight impaired by cataracts.   *Art digest*, 25 (15 February 1951), p. 10;   Dawson; Egyptology; NYT, 31 January 1951, p. 23 (not sighted)

Kelidar, Abbas, born about 1935, he received a Ph.D. in 1966 from the School of Oriental and African Studies, London, for *Shaykh Ali Yusuf, political journalist and Islamic nationalist; a study in Egyptian politics, 1889-1913.* He became a lecturer in the Department of Economic and Political Studies at his alma mater. He was a joint author of *Lebanon; the collapse of a state* (1976), *Egypt; the dilemmas of a nation, 1970-1977* (1977), and he edited *The Integration of modern Iraq* (1979).   Note;   Sluglett

Kellenbenz, Hermann, born 28 August 1913 at Süssen, Württemberg, he studied at the universities of Tübingen, München, Stockholm, Paris, and Kiel, where he received a Dr.phil. in 1940 for *Holstein-Gottorff, eine Domäne Schwedens.* He was a professor of economic and social history at a variety of German universities, and concurrently served since 1970 as a director of Fuggerarchiv in Dillingen. His writings include *Sephardim an der unteren Elbe* (1958), *Probleme der deutschen Sozialgeschichte* (1960), *Die Methoden der Wirtschaftshistoriker* (1972), *The Rise of the European economy* (1976), and he edited *Die Fugger in Spanien und Portugal bis 1560; Dokumente* (1990). He died on 26 November 1990.   HbDtWiss (not sighted); IntWW, 1989/90-1991/92; Kürschner, 1961-1992

Keller, Adolf (Adolph), born 7 February 1872 at Rüdlingen (Kt. Schaffhausen), Switzerland, he studied theology at the universities of Basel, Berlin, and Genève. Ordained in 1896, he then went to Cairo as a pastor. From 1899 to 1924, he served congregations at Burg (Kt. Schaffhausen), Genève, and Zürich. During this time he gained the international reputation as advocate of the oecumenical movement. Since 1924 he was at Zürich head of aid missions of the Churches.; and since 1928 he headed an international institute of social sciences at Genève. He was instrumental in organizing the first World Conference of Churches, 1948 at Amsterdam.   His writings include *Der Geisteskampf des Christentums gegen den Islam bis zur Zeit der Kreuzzüge* (1896), *Eine Sinaifahrt* (1901), *Protestant Europe, its crisis and outlook* (1927), *Kirchen und der Friede mit besonderer Berücksichtigung ihrer Stellung zum Völkerbund* (1927), and *Christian Europe today* (1942). He died in Los Angeles on 10 February 1963.   DtBE; DtBiInd (3); Kürschner, 1961; NDB; NSB; WhAm, 5; WhE&EA;   Who was who, 6

Keller, Helga, born in 1937 at Alt-Karbe, Germany, she was from 1961 to her retirement in December 2000 an East Asian librarian at the Deutsche Staatsbibliothek, Berlin.

Keller, Karel, born 8 April 1944 at Praha, he studied Arabic, Islamic, and Spanish subjects at the local Universita Karlova, from 1961 to 1969, and received a doctorate for *Sémantická analysa arabského slovesného systému.* He did post-doctoral work at the Institut Bourguiba, Tunis, 1982, the Université de Tunis, 1985-86, and Cairo University, 1989-90. Since 1988 he was a professor of Arabic at his alma mater.   Filipsky

von **Keller**, Otto, born 28 May 1838 at Tübingen, Germany, he studied classical, Romance, and Oriental philologies at the local university and at Bonn. After completion of his study with a Dr.phil. in 1860 for *Geschichte der griechischen Fabel,* he entered the secondary teaching profession successively as a teacher of classical philology and principal. In 1872, he was invited to the chair of classics and archaeology at the Universität Freiburg im Breisgau; in 1876, he went to the Universität Graz, and from 1882 to his retirement in 1909 he was a professor at Karls Universität, Prag. His writings include *Die antike Tierwelt* (1909-1913). He died in Stuttgart on 16 February 1927.   DtBE; DtBiInd (4); Hinrichsen; ÖBL; Wer ist's, 7 (1914)

Kellerhals, Emanuel, born 19 April 1898 at Basel, he studied theology in Switzerland and Germany. He was successively a pastor at Suhr (Kanton Aargau), inspector for the Basler Mission, and again a pastor at Basel. A member of the Synode der Evangelischen Reformierten Kirche, Basel, he wrote *Im Land der ewigen Sonne; Reisebilder aus Ägypten* (1938), *Evangelium und Islam* (1945), *Der Islam, die Versuchung der Kirche* (1945), *Der Islam; seine Geschichte, seine Lehre, sein Werk* (1945), *...Und Mohammed ist sein Prophet* (1961).

Kellermann, Mechthild, born 7 August 1935 at Berlin, she received a Dr.phil. in 1966 from the Universität Erlangen with a thesis entitled *Ein pseudoaristotelischer Traktat über die Tugend; Edition und Übersetzung der arabischen Fassungen.* From 1975 to her retirement she was an Arabic librarian at the university library, Tübingen.   JahrDtB, 1975-1999/2000; Schwarz

Kellersohn, Heinrich, born 2 July 1921, he received a Dr.phil. in 1951 from the Universität Köln for *Untersuchungen zur Morphologie der Talanfänge im mitteleuropäischen Raum.* From 1980 to his retirement he was a professor of geography at the Universität Siegen. In 1987 appeared *Festschrift für Heinrich Kellersohn zum 65. Geburtstag.* GV; Kürschner, 1980-2005

Kelley, Charles Fabens, born in 1885, he was a sometime curator of Oriental art at the Art Institute of Chicago. His writings include *Handbook of the Department of Oriental Art, The Art Institute of Chicago* (1933). LC

Kellgren (Челыгрен), Abraham *Herman* August, born 21 January 1822 at Kuopiossa, Finland, he studied Oriental languages at Helsingfors University and became a lecturer in Sanskrit at his alma mater. In 1854 he succeeded to the chair of Arabic left vacant by the death of G. A. Wallin. His writings include *Die Grundzüge der finnischen Sprache mit Rücksicht auf den ural-altaischen Sprachstamm* (1847), *Om affixpronomen i Arabiskan, Persiskan och Turkiskan* (1854), and *Ibn-Mâliks al-lâmijja med textkritik och anmärkningar* (1854). He died in Helsinki on 25 September 1856. EncFen; Krachkovskiĭ. 112; Stenij, pp. 282-84

Kellner, Wilhelm, born about 1835 at Witzenhausen near Cassel, Germany, he received a Dr.phil. in 1858 from the Universität Marburg for *De fragmentis Manethonianis quae apud Josephum contra Apionem sunt.* His writings include *Handbuch für Staatskunde* (1866), *Das türkische Reich* (1876), and its translation, *L'Empire ottoman* (1877). GV; NUC, pre-1956; Thesis

Kellner-Heinkele, Barbara Mechthild, born 15 February 1942 in Germany, she received a Dr.phil. in 1975 from the Universität Hamburg for her thesis, *Aus den Aufzeichnungen des Sa'id Giray Sultan.* Since the early 1990s, she was a professor of Turkish and the founding chairman of Turkologisches Institut, Freie Universität Berlin. Her writings include the exhibition catalogue, *Das Osmanische Reich im Spiegel europäischer Druckwerke* (1985), and jointly with György Hazai, *Bibliographisches Handbuch der Turkologie* (1986); she edited *Studia ottomanica; Festgabe* (1997), *Türkei; Streifzüge im Osmanischen Reich nach Reiseberichten des 18. und 19. Jahrhunderts* (1990), *Altaica Berolinensia; the concept of sovereignty in the Altaic world* (1993), *Laut- und Wortgeschichte der Türksprachen* (1995); and jointly with Jacob M. Landau, *Politics of language in the ex-Soviet Muslim states* (2001). Kürschner, 1992-2005

Kelly, George Armstrong, born in 1932 at Pittsburgh, Pa., he received an honor thesis award in 1953 from Harvard University for *History and tragedy in John Ford's Perkin Warbeck.* He was a professor of political science at Harvard, and Brandeis University, Waltham, Mass. His writings include *Lost soldiers; the French Army and empire in crisis* (1965), and *Idealism, politics, and history; sources of Hegelian thought* (1969). He died in N.Y.C., 23 December 1987. BioIn, 15, 16 (2); ConAu, 125; NUC, pre-56

Kelly, Henry Ansgar, born 6 June 1934 at Fort Dodge, Iowa, he graduated in 1959 from St. Louis University and received a Ph.D. in English from Harvard in 1965. He taught in various capacities English and medieval-renaissance studies at the University of California at Los Angeles from 1967 to his retirement. He was a Jesuit whose writings include *Towards the death of Satan* (1968), and *The Devil, demonology, and witchcraft* (1974). ConAu, 25-28, new rev., 30, 57; DrAS, 1974 E, 1978 E, 1982 E; IntAu&W, 1982 (not sighted); NatFacDr, 1990-2004; WhoAm, 1982-1998

Kelly, John Barrett, born in 1925, he received a Ph.D. in 1955 from Queen Mary College, University of London, for *British policy in the Persian Gulf, 1813-1843.* He was in the early 1960s a member of a Chatham House Study Group on the Persian Gulf. His writings include *Sultanate and imamate in Oman* (1959), *Eastern Arabian frontiers* (1964), *Britain in the Persian Gulf, 1795-1880* (1968), its Arabic translation, *Barītāniyā wa-al-Khalīj* (1979), *Arabia, the Gulf, and the West* (1980), and its translation, *Brennpunkt Golf* (1981). Note about the author; Sluglett

Kelly, Kathleen, born in 1942, she was a joint author of *Landscaping the Saudi Arabian desert* (Philadelphia, Pa., 1976). LC

Kelly, Lady Marie Noële, born in 1907, she was the daughter of Comte de Jourda de Vaux, Bruxelles, and since 1929 in second marriage the wife of the British diplomat Sir David Victor Kelly. Her writings include *Turkish delights* (1951), *Mirror to Russia* (1952), its translation, *Miroir de la Russie* (1953), *This delicious land, Portugal* (1956), and *Dawn to dusk* (1960). Note; NUC, 1956-67; WrDr, 1976/78-1996/98|

Kelly, Robert George Talbot, born 18 January 1861 at Birkenhead, England, he was a painter of almost exclusively Oriental subjects. He spent much of his life in Egypt, and was regarded as the most accurate delineator of desert life. He furnished the pictures for Slatin Pasha's well-known work, *Fire and sword in the Soudan.* His own writings include *Egypt, painted and described* (1902), and *Burma, painted and described* (1905). He died on 30 Decmber 1934. BritInd (1); Master (2); Note about the author; *Who's who in art*, 3 (1934); *Who was who*, 3

Kelly, Sir William Archibald *Howard*, born in 1873, he entered the British Navy in 1886. Apart from his naval career he had interests of a cosmopolitan character. As a young officer he qualified as a French interpreter and in 1908 he joined the French section of the Naval Intelligence Division. After the Great

War he headed a naval mission to Greece, and for two years held the rank of vice-admiral in the Royal Hellenic Navy, subsequently serving for two years as British naval representative with the League of Nations. In 1930 he was appointed commander-in-chief in China. In 1936 he began his long association with the Royal Central Asian Society, serving as a member of Council and chairman. During the second World War he spent four years in Ankara as a personal representative of the British naval commander-in-chief in the Mediterranean. He died on 14 September 1952. BioIn, 3; JRCAS, 40 (1953), pp. 4-6; ObitT, 1951-60; *The Times*, 15 September 1952 (not sighted); *Who was who*, 5

Kemal, Ali, 1869-1922 *see* Ali Kemal Bey

Kemal, Namık, 1840-1888 *see* Namık Kemal, Mehmed

Kemal Vlora, Alessandro *see* Vlora, Alessandro Kemal

Kemball, Sir Arnold Burrowes, born 18 November 1820, he was educated at the East India Company's college in Addiscombe, and in 1837 entered the Bombay Artillery, where he served in the first Afghan War at Ghazni and Kabul. In 1852, he was political resident, Persian Gulf; from 1855 to 1873, he served as consul-general at Baghdad, and political agent for Turkish Arabia; in 1873, he was a member of the Turko-Persian Boundary Commission; and in the Russo-Turkish war of 1876-77, he served as military attaché with the Turkish Army. He retired with the rank of general. He died on 21 September 1908. BritInd (2); Buckland; DNB; Kornrumpf; Riddick

Kemball, Charles Arnold, born in 1860, he was educated at Charterhouse School, Godalming, Surrey, and the Royal Military College, Sandhurst. He served with the Indian Army and was from 1900 to 1904 consul-general at Bushire, Persia. He retired in 1914 with the rank of lieutenant-colonel. He was a temporary assistant secretary in the Political Department, India Office, from April 1918 to March 1919. He died in 1943. IndianBiInd (1); *Who was who*, 4

Kemke, Johannes, born 20 January 1863 at Königsberg, East Prussia, he studied classical philology at the Universität Bonn, where he received a Dr.phil. in 1884 for *Philodemi de musica quae exstant*. He was a librarian successively at Göttingen, 1888, Königliche Bibliothek, Berlin, 1891-1901, Göttingen, 1901, Kiel, 1908, and finally Königsberg, from 1915 to his death on 20 October 1918. He edited *Patricius Junius* (Patrick Young), *Bibliothekar der Könige Jacob I. und Carl I. von England; Mittheilungen aus seinem Briefwechsel* (1898). JahrDtB, 1 (1902) - 14 (1920)

Kemp, Geoffrey, born 20th cent., he was in 1967 a research associate in the Institute for Strategic Studies, London. His writings include *Arms traffic and Third World conflict* (1970), *Nuclear forces for medium powers* (1974), and he was a joint author of *Arms to developing countries, 1945-1965* (1966), *Protection of power* (1982), and *India and America after the Cold War* (1993). Note about the author

Kemp, Percy E., born in 1952, he studied at the Sorbonne, Paris, and at Oxford. He received a *doctorat de 3ème cycle* in 1979 from the Université de Paris for *Pouvoir, discours et vision du monde chez Yasin Bin Khairallah al-'Umari al-Mausili*. He subsequently taught history at the Université Saint-Joseph de Beyrouth. His writings include *Des astres à Baabda* (Beyrouth, 1982), *Territoire d'islam; le monde vu de Mossoul au XVIIIe siècle* (Paris, 1982), and he was a joint author of *Majnûn et Laylâ* (Paris, 1984). LC; Note about the author; THESAM, 4

van der **Kemp**, Pieter Hendrik, born in 1845, his writings include *De leer der administratie van staatsfinanciën* (1878), *De administratie der geldmiddelen van Nederlandsch-Indië* (1881-82), *Handboek tot de kennis van 's lands zoutmiddel in Nederlandsch-Indië* (1895), *Java's landelijk stelsel, 1817-1819* (1916), *Oost-Indië's inwendig bestuur van 1817 op 1818* (1918), *Oost Indiës geldmiddelen* (1919), and *Sumatra in 1818* (1920). He died in 1921. Brinkman's; NUC, pre-1956; ZKO

Kemper, Engelbert, born the son of a clergyman on 16 September 1651 at Lemgo, Westphalia, he learned classical languages from his father and then became a vagrant scholar, attending schools at Hameln, Lüneburg, Lübeck, Danzig, and Thorn. From the spring of 1674 to 1677, he was matriculated in the Swedish university of Krakau, where he studied at the faculty of arts (*Artistenfakultät*) but also attended lectures in theology and law, to which medicine and botany were added later. He subsequently studied at Königsberg until 1681, when he went to Uppsala looking for a scholarly or scientific employment. Shortly thereafter, he made contacts in Stockholm which led to his appointment as secretary to a Swedish mission of forty men travelling to the Safavid ruler at Isfahan. By way of Moscow and Baku the party arrived in Isfahan on 30 March 1684 and remained there for two complete years, during which time he made the acquaintance of Raphaël du Mans, and immersed himself in Persian studies. Since 1685 he was toying with the idea of terminating his association with the Swedish embassy. Through the good offices of the Swedes, he found employment as a physician with the Verenigde Oostindische Compagnie at Bandar Abbas. On the way there he visited Persepolis and Shiraz. But the insalubrious climate of the location so taxed his health that he left the "hell of Ormuz" on 30 June 1688, sailing as a ship's surgeon on the Dutch *Coppelle* to Java. After a year and a half in Southeast Asia, he visited Japan, landing at Deshima on 25 September 1690. In the autumn of 1692 he started his return voyage to Europe, laden with a comprehensive area study of Japan, which was utilized as standard reference work until 1854, when Japan permanently opened its doors to foreigners. By way of Leiden, where he took a medical doctorate in 1694 for *Decas observationum exoticarum*, he returned to his family estate, the Steinhof at Lieme, near Lippe, where he died on 2 November 1716. His writings include *Amoenitatum exoticarum politico-physico-medicarum* (1712) (not sighted). All of his manuscripts and drawings were acquired between 1723 and 1725 by Hans Sloane, president of the Royal Society, London, and placed in Montague House (afterwards the British Museum). *Archiv für Kulturgeschichte*, 48 (1966), pp. 84-113

Kempf, Zdzisław, born 20th cent., his writings include *Próba teorii przypadków* (1978), *Orientalizm Wacława Sieroszewskiego* (1982), and *Nazwa Polski w językowej ocenie* (1989). OSK

Kempfner, Gaston, born 20th cent., his writings include *La Philosophie mystique de Simone Weil* (Paris, 1960). *Livres disponibles*, 2004; ZKO

Kempthorne, G. B., born 19th cent., he was a British Naval lieutenant who surveyed the coast of Makran and the eastern coast of the Persian Gulf. Henze

Kenderova, Stoianka, born in 1947, she received a doctorate in 2000 from the Université de Strasbourg for *Bibliothèques et livres musulmans dans les territoires balkaniques de l'Empire ottoman; le cas de Samokov, XVIII- première moitié du XIXe siècle*. She was a specialist curator at the SS Cyril and Methodius National Library in Sofia. Her writings include *Catalogue of Arabic manuscripts in SS Cyril and Methodius National Libray, Sofia* (1995), and she was a joint author of *Балканският полуостров изобразен в картите на Ал-Идриси; палеограско и историко-географско изследване* (Sofia, 1990). LC; Note about the author

Kendrik, Albert Frank, born in 1872, he entered the Victoria and Albert Museum, London, in 1897 and remained there until his voluntary retirement in 1924 as keeper, having become a leading authority on all forms of textile art. Between 1920 and 1925 he published a series of catalogues of cardinal importance: three volumes devoted to textiles from Egyptian burial grounds, a fourth volume concerned with Muslim textiles of the medieval period, and a fifth dealing with early medieval fabrics. In 1922 he was a joint author of *Handwoven carpets, Oriental and European*, and in 1933 he published the text-book *English needlework*. He died in St Peter's-in-Thanet, Kent, on 17 July 1954. BioIn, 12; *Burlington magazine*, 46 (1954), p. 290-91; *Who was who*, 5

Kenesbaev, Smet Kenesbaevich, born 15 February 1907 in southern Kazakhstan, he graduated in 1931 from the Leningrad Oriental Institute, received his first degree in 1939 for a teaching guide, and his doctorate in 1944 for *Устойчивые словосочетаннтя в казахском языке*. He was a pioneer in establishing Kazakh as a literary language. His writings include *Исследовантя по казахскому языкознания* (1987). On his seventieth birthday he was honoured by *Исследованнтя по тюркологии*. *Central Asiatic journal*, 21 (1977), pp. 1-3; Kazakhskaia, vol. 3, p. 266; Miliband[2]

Kenesbaeva, Saule Smetovna, born 3 May 1942 at Alma-Ata, she graduated in 1966 from the Faculty of Philology, Moscow State University, and received her first degree in 1982 for *Спектральный анализ гуттуральных согласных арабского литературного языка*. Since 1966 she was a research fellow in the Institute of Linguistics, Kazak Academy of Sciences. Her writings include *Фонетические модели арабизмов в казахском языке* (1987). Miliband[2]

Kenessey, Maria, born 1 April 1946 at Budapest, she studied at the universities of Budapest and Baku, and subsequently taught Turkish subjects at her alma mater. Biograf, 2004

Kennan, Elizabeth Topham, born 26 February 1938 at Philadelphia, Pa., she graduated in 1960 from Mount Holyoke College, South Hadley, Mass., in 1962 from Oxford University, and received a Ph.D. in 1966 from Washington University for *The "De consideratione" of Saint Bernard of Clairvaux* (1966). From 1985 to her retirement in 1995 she was a professor of medieval history and president of Holyoke College. DrAS, 1974 H, 1978 H, 1982 H; NatFacDr, 1990-95; WhoAm, 1982-2003; WhoAmW, 1983-1993/94; WhoE, 1986-1993/94

Kennan, George, born 16 February 1845 at Norwalk, Ohio, he was a telegraph engineer who was awarded honorary doctorates by Williams College (1910), and the University of Rochester (1916). He was a member of the Siberian expedition of the Western Union Telegraph Company, and lived in Siberia from 1865 to 1867. In 1870 and 1871 he explored the Caucasus and Daghestan. But above all, he was the most important interpreter of the Russian world to the American people in the decade of the 1890s: the exil camps, imprisonment or exile without benefit of trial, forced marches across the wastes of Siberia that damaged the health and morale of numerous Russians sentenced by an autocratic government to a form of living death. His writings include *Tent life in Siberia* (1870), a work which was translated into German, Hungarian, and Russian, and *Russische Gefängnisse* (1892), and *Жизнь политических-арестантов в русских тюьмах* (1904). He died in Elberton, N.J., on 10 May, 1924. ANB; BbD; BiD&SB Bioln, 1, 6, 12; DAB; Henze; Master (17); *Russian review*, 29 (1970), pp. 275-85; Shavit - Asia; WhAm, 1; *Who was who*, 2

Kennedy, Charles Henry, born in 1951, he received a Ph.D. in 1979 from Duke University, Durham, N.C., for *The context, content and implementation of Bhutto's administrative reforms in Pakistan, 1973-1977*. He became a professor in the Department of Politics, Wake Forest University, a post which he still held in 2005. His writings include *Bureaucracy in Pakistan* (1987), and he was a joint editor of *Ethnic preference and public policy in developing states* (1986), and *Civil military action in Asia and Africa* (1991). NatFacDr, 1990-2005; NUC, 1981

Kennedy, Edward Stewart, born 3 January 1912 in Mexico, he studied mathematics and received a Ph.D. in 1939. He started his career in 1932 as an instructor at Alborz College, Persia; from 1951 to 1977, he was a professor of mathematics at the American University of Beirut. His writings include *A Survey of Islamic astronomical tables* (1956), *A Commentary upon Bīrūnī's Kitāb Tahdīd al-amākin* (1973); he was a joint author of *Astronomical history of Masha'allah* (1971); he edited *al-Bīrūnī on transits* (1959), *The Planetary equatorium of Jamshīd Ghiyāth al-Dīn al-Kāshī, an edition of the anonymous Persian manuscript in the Garrett Collection* (1960); and he was joint editor of *The Life and work of Ibn al-Shātir* (1976). LC

Kennedy, Hugh N., born 22 October 1947 at Hythe, Kent, England, he graduated in 1969 from Pembroke College, Cambridge, and received a Ph.D. in 1978 at Cambridge for *Politics and the political elite in the early 'Abbasid Caliphate*. He was in 1993 a lecturer in the Department of Medieval History in the University of St. Andrews. His writings include *The Early Abbasid Caliphate* (1981), *The Prophet and the age of the caliphates; the Islamic Near East from the sixth to the eleventh century* (1986), *Muslim Spain and Portugal; a political history of al-Andalus* (1996), *The Historiography of Islamic Egypt, ca. 950-1800* (2001), and *The Armies of the caliphs; military and society in the early Islamic states* (2002). DrBSMES, 1993; ConAu, 127; Sluglett; ZKO

Kennedy, James, born the son of a missionary and minister in 1842, he was educated at Edinburgh High School and University. He entered the Indian Civil Service and went out to India in 1863, retiring in 1890. He served as a Magistrate and Collector of several districts. He contributed to journals in the field and also wrote *The Manor and Parish Church of Hampstead and its vicars* (London, 1906), and *The Story of Hamstead from the 10th to the 20th century* (1909). Buckland; IndianBilnd (4)

Kennedy, John *Clark*, born about 1800, he wrote *The Theory of Musketry* (London, 1855), and he was a joint author of *Algeria and Tunis in 1845; an account of a journey made through the two regencies*, by Viscount Feilding and Captain Kennedy (London, 1846), and its translation, *Algiers en Tunis in 1845; reistogt van Burggraf Feilding en capteen Kennedy naar het noorden von Afrika* (Amsterdam, 1846). BLC; NUC, pre-1956

Kennedy, John Fitzgerald, born in 1917 at Brookline, Mass., he was a president of the United States and assassinated in 1963. ANB; ConAu, new rev., 1; DAB; DcTwHis; Master (69); WhAm, 4

Kennedy, John Gordon, born 7 January 1927, he received a Ph.D. and became a professor of anthropology at the University of California at Los Angeles, a post which he still held in 1990. His writings include *The Flower of paradise; the institutionalized use of the drug qat in North Yemen* (1987); he was a joint author of *Struggle for change in a Nubian community* (1977); and he edited *Nubian ceremonial life* (1978). NatFacDr, 1990

Kennedy, Vans, born in 1784, he was educated at Edinburgh, Berkhamsted, Herfordshire, and Monmouth, Wales. He went to Bombay in the East India Company's military service in 1830. He studied languages and became Persian interpreter to the Peshwa's subsidiary force at Sirur in 1807. From 1817 to 1835 he served as judge-advocate-general to the Bombay Army, and from 1835 to his death he was Oriental translator to the Bombay Government. He was a major-general. His writings include *Treatise on the principles and practice of military law* (1823), *Abstract of Mohammedan law* (1824), *A Dictionary of the Maratha language* (1824), *Researches into the origin and affinity of the principal languages of Asia and Europe* (1828), and *Researches into the nature and affinity of ancient and Hindu mythology* (1831). He died in 1846. Bioln, 17; Buckland; DNB, suppl. 3; IndianBilnd (6); Riddick

Kennedy-Cooke, Brian, born 22 October 1894, he was educated at Worcester College, Oxford, and was attached to the Sudan Political Service from 1920 to 1943. He died 13 June 1963. *Who was who*, 6

Baron **Kennet**, Edward Hilton Young, 1879-1960 *see* Young, Edward Hilton Young, Baron Kennet

Baron **Kennet**, Wayland Hilton Young, 1923- *see* Young, Wayland Hilton, Baron Kennet

Kennett, Lee Broone, born 11 August 1931 at Greenboro, N.C., he graduated in 1952 from the University of North Carolina, and received a Ph.D. in 1962 for *The French armies in the Seven Years' War*. He started his career as a Fulbright lecturer at Toulouse, 1966-67, and subsequently became a professor of history and military science at the University of Georgia, Athens. His writings include *The French forces in America, 1780-1783* (1977), *The First air war, 1914-1918* (1991), and *Gettysburg, 1863; le tournant de la guerre de sécession* (1997). ConAu, 21-24, new rev., 109; DrAS, 1974 H, 1978 H, 1982 H

Kenny, Joseph P., Rev., O.P., born 20th cent., he studied at the University of Edinburgh, where he received a Ph.D. in 1970 for *Muslim theology as presented by M. b. Yusuf al-Sanusi especially in his al-'Aqida al-wusta.*. He was a sometime missionary in an Islamic area in northern Nigeria; in 1983 he was assocaited with the Department of Religious Studies, University of Ibadan. His writings include *The Catholic Church in Tropical Africa, 1445-1850* (1983). LC; Note about the author; Sluglett

Kenny, Lorne Milford, born 31 October 1918 at Seeley's Bay, Ontario, he was educated at Greenville College, Ashbury Theological Seminary, American University, Cairo, and McGill University, Montreal, where he received an M.A. in 1960 for *The khilafah al-rashidah period as presented by some Egyptian authors*. From 1938 to 1957 he was a missionary, and teacher of English, at the Canadian Mission in Asyut, Egypt. From 1962 until his retirement in 1984 he was professor of Arabic and Arab history in the Department of Islamic Studies, University of Toronto. DrAS, 1982 H; Ferahian; Private

Kensdale, William Elliott Norwood, born in 1926, his writings include *A Catalogue of the Arabic manuscripts preserved in the University Library, Ibadan, Nigeria* (1955-58), and the transcript of a lecture, *The Religious beliefs and practices of the ancient South Arabians* (1955). NUC, pre-1956

Kent, Clement Boulton *Roylance*, born in 1860, his writings include *Essays in politics* (1891), *The English radicals* (1899), and *The Early history of the Tories* (1908). BLC; NUC, pre-1956

Kent, Francis Lawrence, born 4 January 1908 at Gosport, Hampshire, England, he was educated at St. Paul's School, London, and Corpus Christi College, Cambridge. He started a library career in 1931 at the British Museum as an assistant keeper. During the second World War he joined the Near East Service of the BBC, London. He successively became a librarian at Bristol University Library, Unesco, Paris, and the Library of the American University of Beirut. He was a joint editor of the *World list of scientific periodicals published in the years 1900-1950* (1952). BioIn, 4; WhoLib, 1954, 1972

Kent, Marian R., born 27 November 1939, he received a Ph.D. in 1968 from the London School of Economics for *British government interest in Middle East oil concessions, 1900-1925*. He was a reader in history in the School of Social Sciences, Deakin University, Victoria, Australia. His writings include *Oil and Empire; British policy and Mesopotamian oil, 1900-1920* (1976), and *Moguls and mandarins; oil, impderialism, and the Middle East in British foreign policy, 1900-1940* (1993), and he edited *The Great Powers and the end of the Ottoman Empire* (1984). DrBSMES, 1993; Note; Sluglett

Kepel, Gilles Olivier, born 30 June 1955 at Paris, he received a *doctorat de 3ème cycle* in 1982 from the École des hautes études en sciences sociales, Paris, for *Le mouvement islamiste dans l'Égypte de Sadate*. He was a fellow of the Centre d'études et de documentation économiques et juridiques du Caire, 1980-1983. Since 2000 he was a professor in the Institut d'études politiques, Paris. His writings include *Le prophet et pharaon* (1984), its translation, *The Prophet and pharaoh* (1985), *Les Banlieus de l'islam; naissance d'une religion en France* (1987), *La Revanche de Dieu; Chrétiens, Juifs et Musulmans à la reconquête du monde* (1991), its translation, *Die Rache Gottes* (1991), *À l'ouest d'Allah* (1996), *Jihad; expansion et déclin de l'islamisme* (2001), and he was joint editor of *Intellectuels et militants de l'islam contemporain* (1990). EURAMES, 1993; THESAM, 3; WhoFr, 1995/96-2005/2006

Keppel, George Thomas, sixth Earl of Albemarle, born in 1799, the second son of the fourth earl, he idled at school from the age of nine to nearly sixteen, when the headmaster of Westminster School declared him unfit for any earned profession. An ensigncy was found for him and he became a soldier, serving first at Waterloo then in the Ionian Islands until ordered to India. In 1823 he obtained leave to return home overland, an experience which he described in *Personal narrative of a journey from India to England* (1927). He later studied at the Royal Military College, Sandhurst, obtained a majority on half-pay unattached and gradually attained the honorary rank of full general in 1874. Since the early 1830s he was a parliamentarian. After the deaths of his father, and brother, the fifth earl, 1851, he succeeded to the title. A trustee of Westminster School since 1854, he was popular in London society, holding receptions on each anniversary of Waterloo. He died at his London residence in his ninety-second year. Boase; BritInd (4); DNB; Kornrumpf

Ker', Georgiĭ IAkoblevich, 1692-1740 *see* Kehr, Georg Jacob

Kerblay, Basile H., born 25 May 1920, his writings include *Les marchés paysans en U.R.S.S.*(1968), a work which was originally submitted as a doctoral thesis at the Université de Paris, *L'Isba d'hier et aujourd'hui* (1973), *La Société soviétique contemporaine* (1977), its translation, *Modern Soviet society* (1983), *Gorbachev's Russia* (1989), and he edited *The Theory of peasant economy*, of A. V. Chaianov (1966). LC

van Kerckhoff, Charles Emile Pierre, born 11 November 1861 at Zwolle, the Netherlands, he entered in 1881 the Dutch civil service and was posted first to Batavia and in 1892 to the east coast of Sumatra, where he remained for two years until poor health obliged him to return to Holland. He died there on 7 October 1894. BiBenelux² (1); EncNI; NieuwNBW, vol. 8, col. 963

Kereeva-Kanafieva, Kal'sim Shakirovna, born 22 December 1920, she was since 1970 associated with the Kazakhstan State University and received a doctorate in 1972, and was appointed a professor in 1974. Her writings include *Русско-казахские литературные отношения* (1980). Kazakhskaia, v. 3

Kerestedjian, Bedros, born in 1840, he wrote *Quelques matériaux pour un dictionnaire étymologique de la langue turque*, edited by Haig Kerestdjian (London, 1912). He died in 1909. NUC, pre-1956

Kergomard, Joseph Georges, born in 1866, his writings include *Les départements envahis d'Alsace et de Lorraine* (Paris, ca. 1917), and he was a joint author of *Précis de géographie économique* (Paris, 1897). NUC, pre-1956

Kerim-Zade, Ramiz Ismail, born 15 September 1929 at Gandzha (Kirovabad), Azerbaijan, he graduated in 1963 from the Military Academy, and received his first degree in 1969 for *Парламент и парла-ментаризм в Турции*. He was associated with the Oriental Institute of the Soviet Academy of Sciences since 1965, interrupted only by a ten-year-spell in the Institute of Scientific Information on Social Sciences, 1970-1980 (ИНИОН). Miliband²

Kerimov, Ėmil' Ali ogly, born 20th cent., his writings include *Очерки истории этнографии Азербайджана и русско-азербайджанских этнографических связей, XVIII-XIX вв.* (Baku, 1985). LC; OSK

Kerimov, Gasym Mamed ogly, born 10 May 1930 at Gandzha (Kirovabad), Azerbaijan, he graduated in 1954 from the Oriental Faculty, Azerbaijan State University, studied 1963/63 at al-Azhar, Cairo, received his first degree in 1965 for *Суфизм в ортодоксальном исламе и отношение к нему аль-Газали*, and a doctorate in 1979 for *Шариат и его социальная-сущность*. He was from 1960 to 1967 associated with the Near and Middle East Institute, Azerbaijan Academy of Sciences, and subsequently with the *AOP* at the Central Committee of the Soviet Communist Party. His writings include *Аль-Газали и суфизм* (1969), *Ислам и его влияние на общественно-политическую народов Ближнего и Среднего Востока* (1982), *Учение ислама о государстве и политике* (1986), and he edited *Ислам; происхождение, истории и современность* (1984), as well as works in Azeri. Miliband²

Kerimov, Kerim Dzhabar-ogli, 1921- *see* Kărimov (Кәримов), Kărim Jabbar oghlu

Kerimov, Mustafa Abas Ali-ogly, born 14 February 1923 at Baku, he graduated in 1950 from the Oriental Institute, Moscow, and received his first degree in 1953 for *Борьба советских республик за прочный мир и добрососедские отношентя с Турцией, 1920-1922 гг.* He was from 1954 to his death on 26 October 1960 a research fellow in the Oriental Institute of the Soviet Academy of Sciences. He was a joint author of *Внешняя политика Турции* (1961). Miliband; Miliband²

Kerimova, Aza Alimovna, born 10 January 1925 at Bukhara, she graduated in 1950 from the Faculty of Philology, Moscow State University, and received her first degree in 1954 from the Institute of Linguistics, Soviet Academy of Sciences, for *Роль С. Айни в развитии современного таджикского литературного языка*. She subsequently joined the Institute of Linguistics, Soviet Academy of Sciences. Her writings include *Говор таджиков Бухары* (1959), *Гилянско-русский словарь* (1980), and she was a joint author of *Система таджикского глагола* (1964). Miliband; Miliband²; ZKO

Kéris, Georges Le Brun, 1910- *see* Le Brun Kéris, Georges

Kermarrec, Joël, born in July 1939 at Ostende, Belgium, he was a joint author of *Naissance et croissance de la République algérienne démocratique et populaire* (Paris, 1978). LC

Kern, Friedrich, born 28 July 1875 at Gleiwitz, Silesia, he received his secondary education at Joachimsthalsches Gymnasium, Berlin, and studied at the universities of Lausanne, Jena, Leipzig, and Berlin. Before the completion of his academic work, he went to Cairo where he wrote a comprehensive and remarkable thesis, *Molière's "Femmes savantes" neuarabisch bearbeitet von Muhammed Bey*

'Osmân Galâl unter dem Titel Innisâ'u-l-'âlimât; transkribiert, übersetzt, eingeleitet und mit einem Glossar versehen, with which he gained a Dr.phil. at the Universität Jena. He later studied half a year under Goldziher in Budapest, and spent six winters in Cairo. During the first World War, he was employed at the POW camp in Wünsdorf near Berlin. He spent the rest of his life as a private and lowly scholar in Berlin, pursuing his studies, neither holding nor endeavouring office, but always ready freely to give scholarly advice for the goodness of his heart to whoever needed it. He spoke Arabic fluently, including the Cairene dialect, and was well versed in Islamic literary history and with a phenominal memory, but he suffered from a nervous disorder which limited his literary production. His writings include an edition of al-Tabarî' Ikhtilâf al-fuqarâ' (1902). He died on 21 August 1921. From Eugen Mittwoch in der Islam, 14 (1925), pp. 88-91; Hanisch

Kern, Johan Hendrik Caspar, born 6 April 1833 at Poerwored, he studied at the universities of Utrecht, Leiden, and Berlin, where he received a Dr.phil. in 1855 for Specimen exhibens scriptores Graecos de Rebus Persicis Achaemenidarum monumentis collatus. After teaching Greek at the Koninklijke Athæneum, Maastricht, from 1858 to 1862, he was appointed in 1863 a professor of Sanskrit at Queen's College, Benares. Two years later, he started teaching his field at Leiden, delivering his inaugural lecture, Het aandeel van Indië in de geschiedenis der beschaving. His writings include Geschiedenis van het buddhismus in Indië (1882-84). After his retirement in 1903 he settled in Utrecht, where he died on 4 July 1917. BWN, vol. 3, pp. 320-22; EncNI

Kern, Montague, born 10 August 1941, he taught journalism in the early years of the 21st century at Rutgers University, New Brunswick, N.J. His writings include Television and Middle East diplomacy (1983), 30-second politics; political advertising in the eighties (1989), and he was a joint author of The Kennedy crises; the press, the presidency, and foreign policy (1983). LC; NatFacDr, 2002-2005

Kernan, Henry S., fl. 20th cent., he was associated with the State University College of Forestry at Syracuse, N.Y. His writings include The World is my woodlot (1962), Reforestation in Spain (1966), and Primary report on forestry in Vietnam (1968). Note; NUC, 1956-67

Kerner, Robert Joseph, born 26 August 1887 at Chicago of a Czech family, he graduated in 1908 from the University of Chicago and received a Ph.D. in 1914 from Harvard. During the next fourteen years, he taught history at the University of Missouri and, as a member of the Colonel House Commission from 1917 to 1919, participated in the deliberations that ultimately led to the establishment of an independent Czechoslovakia. In 1928, he joined the history department of the University of California at Berkeley, where in 1941 he became Sather Professor of History and in 1948 the first director of the Institute of Slavic Studies, which he had organized. In 1943, in recognition of his outstanding scholarship, he was elected faculty research lecturer. His writings include Social sciences in the Balkans and in Turkey (1930), The Urge to the sea; the course of Russian history (1942); he was a joint author of The Balkan conferences and the Balkan entente, 1930-1935 (1936); and he edited Czechoslovakia; twenty years of independence (1940). He died on 29 November 1956. American historical review, 62 (1956/57), pp. 800-801; BioIn (3); WhE&EA; WhAm, 3; WhNAA

Kernkamp, Willem Jan Arend, born 19 June 1900 at Edam, the Netherlands, he studied law at the Vrije Universiteit te Amsterdam, as well as law of the Dutch East Indies, and Islamic subjects, at the Rijksuniversiteit te Utrecht. From 1932 to 1933, he visited Egypt, Saudi Arabia, Palestine, and Syria. He received a doctorate In 1935 at Utrecht for De Islam en de vrouwen; bidragen tot de kennis van het reformisme, and there delivered his inaugural lecture in 1936 entitled Pan-arabische beweging en Islam. He was a sometime minister of overseas affairs. Brinkman's; Wie is dat, 1956

Kerr, Graham Burrell, born 20 January 1942 at Mountain Ash, Wales, he graduated B.A. in 1963 from Oxford University, received a diploma from the University of Ibadan, and a Ph.D. in 1970 from Michigan State University. His writings include Demographic research in Afghanistan (1977). AmM&WSc, 1973 S; Master (1)

Kerr, James, born 18th cent., he was a captain in the service of the East India Company who translated from the Persian A Short historical narrative of the rise and advancement of the Mahrattah State (1782). His traces is lost after an article in 1797. BLC

Kerr, Malcolm Hooper, born 8 October 1931 at Beirut of American parents, he graduated in 1953 from Princeton University, received his M.A. in 1955 from the American University of Beirut, and his Ph.D. in 1958 from Johns Hopkins University, Baltimore, Md., for Muhammad 'Abduh and Rashid Rida; contribution to the reinterpretation of Islamic constitutional and legal theory, a work which was published in 1966 under a slightly different title. He was a professor of political science successively at A.U.B., and the University of California, Los Angeles, and concurrently served as a consultant to RAND Corporation. His writings include Egypt under Nasser (1963), The Arab cold war (1965), The Middle East conflict (1968), Rich and poor states in the Middle East (1982), and he edited and translated

Lebanon in the last years of feudalism, 1840-1868 (1959). He was gunned down on 18 January 1984 as he left an elevator on going to his Beirut University office by members of the Islamic Jihad organization. In 1991 appeared *Quest for understanding; Arabic and Islamic studies in memory of Malcolm H. Kerr.* ConAu, 97-100, 111; *Index Islamicus* (2); Shavit; WhAm, 8; WhoAm, 1974-1982; WhoWest, 1974/75-1978/79 (not sighted)

Kerr, Robert, M.D., born 19th cent., he served from about 1885 to 1894 as a medical missionary in Morocco. His writings include *Pioneering in Morocco* (1894), *Morocco after twenty-five years* (1912), and *The "Gospel daybreak" in Morocco* (Glagow & London, Corquodale, n.d.) His trace is lost after an article in the 1913 issue of the *Missionary review of the world.* NUC, pre-1956; ZKO

Kerschagl, Richard, born 25 May 1896 at Wien, he received a Dr.jur. and Dr.rer.pol. and became a professor of political economy and finance at the Hochschule für Welthandel, Wien. Concurrently he served as an academic administrator, professor at the Universität Wien, and president of the Austrian Unesco Commission. His writings include his inaugural lecture as rector of the Hochschule für Welthandel, *Die Währungssteuerung in den Nationalstaaten* (1920), *Die Lehre vom Geld in der Wirtschaft* (1921), *Die Geldprobleme von heute* (1922), and *Die Methodenfrage in der theoretischen National-ökonomie* (1948). Kürschner, 1961-1966|; Note about the author; WhoAustria, 1955-1967|

Kerslake, Celia Jocelyn, born about 1945, she received a D.Phil. in 1975 from Oxford University for *A critical edition and translation of the introductory sections and the first thirteen chapters of the "Selimnâme," of Celâl Zade Musfata Çelebi.* She was Atatürk Lecturer in Turkish Studies at the University of Edinburgh until about 1989, when she started a long association with the Middle East Centre, Oxford, which lasted until the twenty-first century. Her writings include *The Prizegiving* (1988), a translation from the Turkish of Aysel Özakın. DrBSMES, 1993; EURAMES, 1993; Private; Sluglett

Kêrson (Кэрсонъ), George, 1859-1925 *see* Curzon of Kedleston, George Nathaniel

Kersten, Otto, born 23 December 1839 at Altenburg, Duchy Saxe- Altenburg, Germany, he studied at the Universität Leipzig, where he also received a doctorate in science. In 1861 he went to Berlin to prepare for a scientific expedition. Encouraged by Heinrich Barth, he decided to participate in the East Africa expedition of Baron Carl C. von der Decken to the Kilimanjaro. After the latter's murder in 1865, he complied with the family's wishes and edited, and saw through the press, the results of the expedition entitled *Baron Carl Claus von der Deckens Reisen in Ost-Afrika in den Jahren 1859 bis 1865* (1869-1879). Kersten then spent from 1870 to 1874 in Palestine, first as a member of the German Jerusalem consulate and later became attached to the Jerusalemverein, and Deutscher Verein zur Erforschung Palästinas. In 1883 he once more felt the urge to travel abroad, considering both Morocco and East Africa to be suitable for German colonial exploitation. He died in Altenburg on 22 November 1900. BioJahr, 5 (1900), pp. 72-73; DtBilnd (2); Embacher; Henze; Kornrumpf

Kervran, Monique, born 20th cent., she received a doctorate in 1987 from the Université de Paris for *Les structures funéraires et commémoratives en Iran et en Asie centrale du IXème au XIIème siècles.* She was associated with the Institut français d'archéologie du Caire, and was a joint author of *Index géographique du Répertoire chronologique d'épigraphie arabe* (1975). THESAM, 4; ZKO

Kerwin, Robert W., born 20th cent., he served in Turkey and other parts of the Middle East with the Office of Strategic Services during the second World War. Since 1948 he had been resident in Turkey on a grant from the Middle East Institute, Washington, D.C., and the American Social Science Research Council to study the industrialization of modern Turkey. He received a Ph.D. in 1956 from Johns Hopkins University, Baltimore, Md., for *Etatism and the industrialization of Turkey; a study of Turkish national economic policy and attitudes, 1933-1950.* Note about the author; NUC, 1968-77

Kesby, John Douglas, born 14 April 1938 at London, he graduated from Oxford University, where he also received his D.Phil. in 1971. From 1963 to 1966, he was a research associate in the East African Institute of Social Research, Kampala, Uganda. He was a lecturer at King's College, and Newnham College, Cambridge, before he joined Darwin College in the University of Canterbury. His writings include *The Cultural regions of East Africa* (New York, 1977). Private; WhoWor, 1987/88

Keseling, Paul, born 30 November 1892 at Duderstadt (Eichsfeld), Germany, he received a Dr.phil. in 1921 from the Universität Bonn for *Die Chronik des Eusebius in der syrischen Überlieferung.* He became a *Studienrat* at the Gymnasium Georgianum in Lingen on Ems, where he taught local history and classical as well as Semitic languages. His writings include the translations from Aurelius Augustinus, *Des Aurelius Augustinus Buch "Von den Sitten der katholischen Kirche"* (1948), *Die Enthaltsamkeit* (1949), and *Die Lüge und gegen die Lüge* (1953). GV; Kosch

Keshelava, Tengiz Georgievich, born 29 September 1930 at Tiflis (Tbilisi), Soviet Georgia, he graduated in 1953 from Tiflis State University and received hist first degree in 1958 for *Художественная проза Садека Хедаята*. He was associated with his alma mater since 1956, and in 1964 he was appointed a lecturer. Miliband; Miliband²

Kessler, Christel M., born 28 November 1922 at Idar-Oberstein, Pfalz, Germany, she lost her father and mother in 1928 and 1929 respectively and grew up in Nordhausen. After compulsory war-time military service, 1941-42, she began to study fine art, Arabic and Islamic subjects at Friedrich Wilhelm Universität, Berlin. She resumed her study in 1947, first at the Evangelisch-Theologische Fakultät and later at Orientalisches Seminar, Berlin. In 1948, she transferred to Freie Universität Berlin, where she was a student of Richard Hartmann and Walther Braune, and obtained a Dr.phil. in 1956 for *Abdurrahman al-Kawakibis Reform des Islam*. Her writings include *The Caved masory domes of medieval Cairo* (1976). She retired to Cambridge before 1993. DrBSMES, 1993; *MESA Roster of members*, 1977-1982; Schwarz; Thesis

Kessler, Gerhard, born 24 August 1883 at Wilmsdorf, East Prussia, he received a doctorate in 1906 from the Universität Berlin for *Die Tradition des Germanicus*, and later also a Dr.habil. Since 1927 he was a professor of sociology and political economy at the Universität Leipzig until dismissed in 1933. He emigrated to Turkey, where he taught at İstanbul Üniversitesi until 1951 when he was invited to the Universität Göttingen. His writings include *Kampf und Aufbau; junge deutsche Politik* (1933), *Die Familiennamen der Juden in Deutschland* (1935), *Die Familiennamen der ostpreußischen Salzburger* (1937), and *İçtimaiyata başlangıç* (İstanbul, 1938). He died near Kassel on 16 August 1963. BioHbDtE; DtBE; Kürschner, 1931, 1954, 1961; NDB; *Wer ist wer*, 1958-1963; Widmann, pp. 122-123, 271-272

Ketenensis, Robertus, fl. 12th cent., he was an English monk who was pursuing an interest in the astronomical and mathematical works of the Arabs. In the service of Petrus Venerabilis, Abbot of Cluny, he translated the Koran into Latin, a work which was handed over to Abbot Bernard de Clairvaux in 1143. But it was more of a paraphrase than a translation, without literal accuracy, a mere abstract of the separate sections of the *surahs*. Its printed edition is due to the Zürich theologian Th. Bibliander who published it four hundred years later, in 1543, entitled *Machumetis Saracenorum principis, eiusque successorum vitae, ac doctrina, ipseque Alcoran*. Flück, pp. 5-9

Keun, Odette, born 19th cent., her writings include *Mesdemoiselles Daisne de Constantinople, 1916-1917* (Paris, s.d.), *Les Oasis dans la montagne* (1919), *My adventures in Bolshevik Russia* (London, 1923), *In the land of the Golden Fleece; through independent Menchevist Georgia* (London, 1924), *A Foreigner looks at the British Sudan* (1930), *Dans l'Aurès inconnu* (1930), *Darkness from the North* (London, 1935), *I discover the English* (Leipzig, 1935), and *Trumpets bray* (1943). BLC; BN; Sezgin

Keworkian, Krikor, born 19th cent., he served as a missionary at Plovdiv (Philippopolis), Bulgaria, under the Deutsche Orient-Mission, Potsdam. He died at the Bulgarian mission on 14 April 1919. Note

Key, Kerim Kami, born 21 May 1913 at Constantinople, he graduated in 1932 from the local American Robert College, and received a Ph.D. in 1950 from the American University, Washington, D.C. After the second World War, he was an economist with the U.S. Government, and an occasional university professor. His writings include *Turkey's position in world affairs, 1923-1963* (1964), and *The State of Qatar; an economic and commercial survey* (1976). DrAS, 1969 H, 1974 H, 1978 H; Schoeberlein

Keyder, Çağlar, born in 1947 at Istanbul, he was a sometime professor of economics at the Middle East Technical University, Ankara. His writings include *State and class in Turkey; a study of capitalist development* (1987), a work which "consists of yards of unreadable sociologese," and *The Definition of a peripheral economy; Turkey, 1923-1929* (1981), and its translation, *Dünya ekonomisi içinde Türkiye, 1923-1929* (1982). zKO

Keyes, Charles Rollin, born 24 December 1864 at Des Moines, Iowa, he graduated in 1887 from State University of Iowa, and received a Ph.D. in 1892 from Johns Hopkins University, Baltimore, Md. He was a consultant in mining engineering and a geologist in U.S. federal and state institutions. He was a sometime editor of the *Pan-American geologist.*. He died in 1942. Master (2); NatCAB, vol. 13, p. 144, vol. 31, pp. 94-95; WhAm, 2

Keynes, John Maynard, born 5 June 1883 at Cambridge, he was educated at Eton and Cambridge. He was from 1906 to 1908 a civil servant at the India Office and subsequently became a lecturer in economics at Cambridge. In 1919, he served as representative of the Treasury at the Versailles Peace Conference. He subsequently excerted wide influence through his lectures at King's College, his Political Economy Club, and as a bursar of his College. He died in Tilton on 21 April 1946. BritInd (2); ConAu, 114, 163; DcTwHis; DNB; *Economic journal*, 57 (1947), pp. 1-68; Master (5); WhAm, 2; *Who was who*, 4

Keyser, James Moore Bryant, born 27 April 1932 at Philadelphia, Pa., he graduated in 1954 from Haverford (Pa.) College, and received his Ph.D. in 1969 from Harvard for *The effects of compulsory military service in rural Turkey*. In 1969, he was appointed a professor of anthropology at the University of California, Santa Barbara. AmM&WSc, 1973 S; Private

Keyzer (Keijzer), Salomo(n), born 18 January 1823 at Kampen, the Netherlands, he was a student of Roorda van Eysinga, and in 1847 received a doctorate in law for *De tutela secundum jus thalmudicum*, and a doctorate in letters for *De jurejurando Justiniano et Theodorae praestando*. In 1850, he began teaching Islamic and Dutch law at the Academie te Delft, to which also Javanese law was added later. A professor since 1859, he became in 1864 a director of the newly established Delft Gemeente-Instelling for the training of overseas civil servants in Islamic law as well as public and administrative law, and the history of the Dutch East Indies. Concurrently from 1860 to 1866 he served as head of a government commission drafting a criminal code for the Indies. His writings include *Handboek voor het mohammedaansch recht* (1853), *Kitab Toehpah* (1853), *Mawerdi's Publiek en administratief regt van den Islam* (1862), and a Dutch translation of the Koran, based on the French, German, and English versions, with a long introduction. From 1847 to 1848 he edited the journal *Palaestina; tijdschrift voor Hebreeuwsche taal, letterkunde, geschiedenis*. He died in Delft on 25 February 1868. BiBenelux (1); EncNI; NieuwNBW, vol. 8, col. 971

Khabichev, Magomed Akhiiavich, born 20th cent., he wrote *Местоимение и карачаево балкарском языке* (1961), *Карачаево-балкарское именное словообразование* (1971), *Социалистический образ жизни и языковые отношения* (1985), and he edited *Актуальные проблемы карачаева-балкарского и ногайского языков* (1981). NUC; OSK

Khachatrian, Aleksandr Arutiunovich, born 19 November 1948 in Syria, he graduated in 1972 from the Oriental Faculty, Erevan State University, and received his first degree in 1984 for *Арабие надписи Армении XI-XV вв. как историко-культурный памятник*. Since 1974 he was associated with the Oriental Institute, Armenian Academy of Sciences. Miliband²

Khadduri, Majid, born 27 September 1909 at Mosul, he received a Ph.D. in 1938 from the University of Chicago for *The Law of war and peace in Islam*. He was since 1956 a director of the Middle East Center, Johns Hopkins University, Baltimore, Md. His writings include *Republican Iraq* (1969), *Political trends in the Arab world* (1970), *Socialist Iraq; a study in Iraqi politics since 1968* (1978), *Arab personalities in politics* (1981), *The Islamic conception of justice* (1984), and he translated from the Arabic *Islamic jurisprudence; Shāfiī's Risala* (1961). In 1987 appeared *The Life and works of Majid Khadduri; law, personalities, and politics of the Middle East: essays in honor of Majid Khadduri*. AmM&WSc, 1973 S, 1978 S; ConAu, 1-4, new rev., 2; IntAu&W, 1989, 1991/92; IntWW, 1974-2006; Selim; Unesco; WhoAm, 1974-1996; WhoArab, 1990; WhoWor, 1974/75; WrDr, 1976/78-2006

Khadi-zade, Rasul, born 6 March 1928 at Samarkand, he graduated in 1950 from the Oriental Faculty, Central Asian State University, received his first degree in 1954, and his doctorate in 1969 for *Ахмад Дониш и таджикская просветительская литература*. He was since 1954 associated with the Institute of Language and Literature, Tajikistan Academy of Sciences. In 1984, he was appointed a professor. His writings include *Источники к изучению таджикской литературы второй половины XIX в.* (1956). Miliband²

Khaïtmetov (Хайтметов), Abdukadyr Khadzhimetovich, born 27 May 1926 at Tashkent, he graduated in 1949 from the Oriental Faculty, Tashkent State University, received his first degree in 1955, and his doctorate in 1965 for *Творческий метод Навои*. Associated with the Institute of Language and Literature, Uzbekistan Academy of Sciences, since 1953, he was appointed a professor in 1970. He wrote almost exclusively in Uzbek, including *Темурийлар даври ўзбек адабиёти; тадқиқотлар, мақолалар, лавқалар* (Toshkent, 1996). Miliband; Miliband²; OSK

Khaïrallah, Khairallah T., born in 1882, he was educated in France and Belgium. He was a regular contributor to *le Temps*, specializing in Middle Eastern political and religious affairs. His writings include *La Syrie; territoire, origines ethniques et politiques, évolution* (1912), *Le problème du Levant* (1919), and *Caïs* (1921). He died in the summer of 1930 in Tunis, where he had gone in the hope of recovering from a long illness. Correspondance d'Orient, 22 (août 1930), p. 96

Khăiretdinov, R. G., 1935- *see* Khairutdinov, Rif Galiautdinovich

Khairullaev, Muzaffar Mukhitdinovich, born 17 November 1931 at Kokand, Soviet Uzbekistan, he graduated in 1947 from Andizhan Teachers' Institute and in 1951 from the Faculty of Philology, Central Asian State University. He received his first degree in 1955 and his doctorate in 1966 for *Мировоззрение Фараби и его значение в истории философии*. He spent his academic career in Uzbekistan. His writings include *Фараби; эпоха учение* (1975), *Абу Наср ал-Фараби, 873-950*

(1982), *Социально-утопические идеи в Средней Азии* (1983) as well as writings in Uzkek.   LC; Miliband²

Khaĭrutdinov (Хәйретдинов), Rif Galiautdinovich, born in 1935, he was a historian who received a doctorate in 1979 and who was appointed a professor in 1982.   Since 1997 he was affiliated with the Tatarstan Republic's Kazan University.   His writings include *На путях к советской автономий* (1972), and he is said to have published *Республика Татарстан* in 1993.   TatarES

Khakhanov, Aleksandr Solomonovich, born in 1866, his writings, in addition to editions of Grusian literary texts, include *Грузинские рукописи* (1895), *Aperçu géographique et abrégé de l'histoire et de la littérature géorgienne* (1900), and *Материалие по грузинской агиологии* (1910); he also edited *Матеріалы по археологіи Кавказа* (1888-1916). He died in 1912.   NYPL

Khakimbaev, Alimdzhan Azizovich, born 9 May 1914 at Tashkent, he graduated in 1957 at Tashkent, received his first degree in 1961, and his doctorate in 1971.   Since 1969 he was successively associated with the Oriental Institute of the Uzbekistan Academy of Sciences and the Oriental Institute of the Soviet Academy of Sciences.   He wrote about non-Chinese minorities in Sinkiang during the 1930s and 1940s.   Miliband²

Khakimdzhanov, Askhadali IUnusovich, born 15 May 1948 at Kuldja, Sinkiang, he graduated in 1973 from the Oriental Faculty, Tashkent State University and received his first degree in 1984 for *Молодежние движение в Иране, 1940-1970*.   Since 1973 he was associated with the Oriental Institute of the Uzbekistan Academy of Sciences. Most of his writings are in Uzbek.   Miliband²

Khakimov, Ibragim Musaevich, born 15 May 1930 at Khuzhand (Ходжент), Tajikistan, he graduated in 1957 from the Moscow Institute of Oriental Laguages and received his first degree in 1971 for *Джамал ад-Лин аль-Афгани, его антиколониальн. взгляды и деятельгость, 1839-1897 гг.* He was since 1959 affiliated with the Oriental Faculty, Tashkent State University.   In 1983 he was appointed a lecturer.   He visited Egypt (1968-1970), Syria (1972-1976), and Jordan (1984).   Miliband²

Khakimova, Kaukab Zakhidovna, born 30 July 1921 at Tashkent, she graduated in 1944 from the Faculty of History, Tashkent State University, and received her first degree in 1966 for *Крестьянские движение в Бухарской ханстве в последней трети XIX века*.   She was successively associated with the Central Uzbekistan State Archives and the Institute of History in the Uzbek Academy of Sciences.   She was a joint author of *Социально-экономические отношения и классовая борьба в дореволюционном Узбекистане конец XIX- начадо XX в.* (1980).   Miliband²

Khakimzhanov, IUnus, born in 1893 at Tashkent, he graduated in 1925 from Kesak Kurgan Medrese. He was an Iranian scholar who was associated with the Oriental Institute, Uzbek Academy of Sciences from 1956 to 1974. He died on 27 December 1974.   Miliband²

Khakov, Dzhengis, born 20th cent., his writings include *Политиката на Турция в Арабския Изток* (Sofia, 1972), *Политическата борба в Турция, 1960-1971* (Sofia, 1979), *История на Турция през XX век* (2000), and he edited *Турция в българската литература* (Sofia, 1979).

Khakov (Hakov), Vakhit Khoziatovich, born in 1926, he received a doctorate in 1972.   Since 1960 he was associated with Kazan University as a teacher of philology; and in 1974, he was appointed a professor.   His writings include *Развитие татарского национального литературного языка 19-начало 20 вв.* (1971), *Татар әдәби тарихы* (1993), and he was a joint editor of *Формирование татарского литературного* (1989).   TatarES

Khalafallah, Muhammad, 1904- *see* Ahmad, Muhammad Khalaf Allah

Khalat'iants', Bagrat, fl. 1899-1904, he wrote in Armenian and German on Armenian history, and literature.   His writings include *Irani herosnerĕ hay zhoghovrdi mĕj* (1901).   LC; NUC, pre-1956

Khalfin, Naftula Aronovich, born 18 October 1921 at Kiev, he graduated in 1942 from the Northern Ossete Pedagogical Institute and received his first degree in 1946 for *Борьба за Памир, 1883-1895*, and his doctorate in 1961 for *Политика России в Средней Азии и англо-русское соперничество, 1857-1976 гг*.   Since 1957 he was affiliated with the Soviet Academy of Sciences; in 1973, he was appointed a professor.   His writings include *Провал британской агрессии и Афгавистане* (1959), *Борьба за Курдистан* (1963), *Россия и ханства Средней Азии* (1974), *Россия и Бухарский эмират на Западеом Памире* (1975), and *Саря свободы над Кабулом* (1985). He died on 4 August 1987.   Miliband; Miliband²

Khalid, Detlev H., who also calls himself Khalid Duran, born in 1939 or 1940 at Berlin, he studied political science.   These are the only facts concerning this researcher and perhaps impostor.   Other claims, and particularly his doctorate, cannot be ascertained - anywhere.   He was a joint editor of

Entwicklungspolitische Untersuchungen zur islamischen Herausforderung; Fallbeispiele Ägypten, Iran, Türkei (Hamburg, Deutsches Orient-Institut, 1983). IWWAS, 1976/77; Note about the author

Khalidov, Anas Bakievich, born 25 February 1929 in the Tatar Autonomous Republic, he graduated in 1951 from the Oriental Faculty, Leningrad, received his first degree in 1954 for *Художесивенная проза Таха Хусейа*, and his doctorate in 1983 for *Арабские рукописи и арабская рукописная традиция*, a work which was published in 1985. He was since 1962 affiliated with the Leningrad Branch of the Oriental Insitute, Soviet Academy of Sciences. His writings include *Каталог арабских рукописей Института народнов Азии Академии наук СССР* (1960). Miliband; Miliband²; Tatar ES

Khalidov, Baki Zakirovich, born in 1905 in the Tatar Autonomous Republic, he graduated in 1941 from Kazan State University and received his first degree in 1951 for *Арабские заимстовавия в современном литературном языке пушту*. His writings include *Учебник арабского языка* (1965). He died on 23 January 1968. Miliband; Miliband²; TatarES

Khalikov, Al'fred Khasanovich, born in 1929, he was an archaeologist and historian who was associated with the Tatar Academy of Sciences. His writings include *Древняя история Средного Поволжья* (1965), *Пепкинский курган (абашевский человек) Иошкар-Ола* (1966), *Приказанская культура* (1980); he was a joint author of *Материалы к древней истории Поветлужья* (1960); and he edited *Новое и археологии и етнографии Татарии* (1982). He died in 1994. NUC; OSK; TatarES

Khalikova (Chalikova/Halikova), Elena Aleksandrovna, born in 1930, she was an archaeologist who was associated with the State Museum of the Tatar Academy of Sciences. Her writings include *Altungarn an der Kama und im Ural* (1981), and *Мусульманские некропои волжской Булгарии X-начала XIII в.* (1986). Gyula László wrote *A zuevói temető; E. A. Halikova emlékének* (Budapest, 1993). She died in 1977. TatarES

Khalil Khalid, 1869-1931 *see* Halil Hâlid

Khalilov, Dzhabbar Asadulla ogly, Prof. Dr., fl. 1979, he was an archaeologist whose writings include *Материальная культура Кавказской Албании* (Baku, 1985). He was joint author of *Археологические памятники северо-восточного Азербайджана* (1991). LC

Khalilzad, Zalmay M., born in 1951 at Mazar-i Sharif, Afghanistan, he graduated from the American University of Beirut and received a Ph.D. in 1979 from the University of Chicago for *The political, economic and military implications of nuclear electricity; the case of the northern tier*. He was a sometime senior fellow, National Defense University. From 1983 to 1989 he served as a professor in the Department of Political Science, Columbia University, New York. He was a United States special envoy to Afghanistan in 2002, when the Loya Jirga elected Hamid Karsay president. During the 2003 war against Iraq, and in the aftermath, he again represented United States interests. His writings include *The return of the Great Game* (1980), *The security of southwest Asia* (1984), *Prospects of the Afghan interim government* (1991), and *From containment to global leadership? America and the world after the Cold War* (1995); he was joint author of *The government of God, Iran's Islamic Republic* (1984), and *The implications of the possible end of the Arab-Israeli conflict for Gulf security* (1997). Adamec; NatFacDr, 1983-1989|

Khamoian, Maksim Useinovich, born 25 December 1934 at Cobanmaz, Armenia, he graduated in 1959 from Erevan State University and received his first degree in 1966 for *Бахдинанский диалект курдов Ирака*. He was affilliated successively with the Armenian Academy of Sciences and Erevan State University. His writings include *Основы фразеологии курдского языка* (1988). Miliband²

Khamraev (Һәмраев/Hämraev), Maratbek Karimovich, born 20th cent., his writings include *Основы тюркского стихосложения* (1963), *Расцвет культуры уйгурского народа* (1967), *Веков неумирающее слово* (1969), *Пламя жизни* (1988), he was a joint author of *Нәсирдин Әпәндиниң ләтипилири* (1965), *Уйгурские юморески* (1969), and he was joint author and editor of *Әсирләр садаси* (1963) LC; OSK

Khamraev, Usman, born 20 December 1930 at Tashkent, he graduated in 1954 from the Oriental Faculty, Tashkent State University and received his first degree in 1970 for *Мухаммад Амин и его сочинение "Мухит ат-таварих"*. He was associated with the Oriental Institute of the Uzbek Academy of Sciences. He wrote mainly in Uzbek. He died in 1988. Miliband²

Khan, Chaudhri Nazir Ahmad *see* Chaudri, Nazir Ahmad Khan

Khan, Mahmood Hasan, born 8 August 1937 at Rampur, India, he received graduate degrees from universities in Sind, and a Ph.D. in 1966 from the Wageningen Agricultural University (Landbouwhoogeschool), the Netherlands, for his thesis, *The role of agriculture in economic development; a case*

study of Pakistan. He was for many years a professor in the Department of Economics and Commerce, Simon Fraser University, Burnaby, British Columbia, Canada. His writings include *Lectures on agrarian transformation in Pakistan* (1985), and *Rural change in the Third World* (1992). He was joint author of *Structural change in Pakistan's agriculture.* AmM&WS, 1973 S,1978 S; DrASCan, 1978, 1983

Khan, Muhammad Zafrulla(h), 1893-1985 *see* Zafrulla(h) Khan, Muhammad

Khan-Magomedov, Selim Omarovich, born in 1928, his writings include Народная архитектура Южного Дагестана (1956), Дербент (1958), Дербент; горная стена (1979), *Pioniere der sowjetischen Architektur* (1983), and *Pioneers of Soviet architecture* (1983). NUC; OSK

Khandalavala, Karl Jamshed, born 20th cent., he was admitted to the bar from the Middle Temple, London. He was a Chief Presidency Magistrate of Bombay, public prosecutor in some celebrated cases of national importance, and a senior advocate of the Supreme Court of India. He combined his legal career with an interest in the study of Indian art. He was associated with the Lalit Kala Akademi, New Delhi, since its inception in 1954, becoming honorary chief editor of the Akademi's publications on ancient Indian art. He also served as a chairman of the Board of Trustees of the Prince of Wales Museum, Bombay. His writings include *Indian sculpture and painting* (1938), *Gulshan-e musawwari; seven illustrated manuscripts from the Salar Jung Museum, Hyderabad* (1986), *Essays on Indian painting* (1991), *The Golden age; Gupta art* (1991), and he was a joint editor of *An Age of splendour; Islamic art in India* (1983). In 1995 appeared *Indian painting; essays in honour of Karl J. Khandalavala,* and in 1996, *Mr. Karl Jamshed Khandalavala felicitaion volume.* Note about the author

Khangil'din, Vali Nigmatullovich. born in 1891, he was a philologist, and from 1943 to 1966 associated with the Kazan Pedagogical Institute. His writings include Татар теле грамматикасы; морфология һәм синтаксис (Kazan, 1959). He died in 1971. TatarES

Khanykov, IAkov Vladimirovich, born in 1818, he was a geographer and a sometime governor of Orenburg. He was a joint author of Список мест северо-западной части Средней Азіи (1850), and he translated from the German of Ludwig A. Feuerbach, Сущность христіанства (1861). He died in 1862. EnSlovar; NYPL; Wieczynski

Khanykov, Nikolai Vladimirovich, born in 1819 or 1822, he was educated at the lycée of TSarskoe Selo, Russia. Early in life he succumbed to the lure of the East and participated in General V. A. Perovskii's (1794-1857) expedition to Khiva. In later years he visited Bukhara and parts of Khurasan and Afghanistan. He taught himself Persian and Arabic which stood him in good stead for his appointment as a Russian consul-general in Tabriz, 1854-57. Since 1860, he was resident in Paris. His writings include Описаніе Бухарскаго Ханства (1843), its translation, *Bokhara, its amir and its people* (1845), *Mémoire sur la partie méridionale de l'Asie centrale* (1861), and *Mémoire sur l'ethnographie de la Perse* (Paris, 1866), He died in Rambouillet, France, on 15 October 1878 and was buried in Paris. N. A. Khalfin wrote Н. В. Ханыков, востоковед и дипломат (1977). Das Ausland, 51 (1878), p. 1020; Embacher; EnSlovar; GSE; Henze; Krachkovskii, 189-191; VostokMStP, p. 257; Wieczynski

Khare, Ganeśa Harī, born in 1901 at Panvel, District of Kolaba, India, he was a writer on Indian history and art, and a teacher at Poona. His writings include *Persian sources of Indian history* (Poona, 1937), and *Select articles* (Poona, 1966). IndianBilnd (2)

Kharisov, Akhnaf Ibragimovich, born 15 June 1914, he was a scholar of Bashkir language and literature, who received a doctorate in 1966. His writings include Литературное наследие башкирского народа (1973). He died in Ufa on 15 May 1977. BashkKE

Khasanov, Akhadzhan Akhmedzhanovich, born 29 March 1940 at Pskent, Tashkent Oblast, he graduated in 1964 from the Oriental Faculty, Tashkent State University, and received his first degree in 1975 for Социально-политические строй мамлюкского Египта при черкесских султанах, 1382-1517. He was since 1964 affiliated with the Oriental Faculty, Tashkent State University. Miliband[2]

Khasanov, Saidbek Rustamovich, born 28 September 1945 in Uzbekistan, he graduated in 1967 from the Oriental Faculty, Tashkent State University, and received his first degree in 1972 for Трактат Бабура об арузе. Since 1967 he was associated with the Institute of Manuscripts, Uzbek Academy of Sciences. Miliband[2]

Khasanova (Ҳасанова), Z. Sh., fl. 20th cent., she was associated with the Oriental Institute of the Tajikistan Academy of Sciences. She edited Чоми ва робитаҳои адаби (Dushanbe, 1989). OSK

Khasenov, Manap Khasenovich, born 1 May 1915 at Akshar, Karaganda region of Kazakstan, he received a doctorate in philology. Since 1961 he was associated with the Institute of Literature and Arts, Kazakstan Academy of Sciences. His writings include Казак әдебиет (1963), Ғабиден

MACK LIBRARY
BOB JONES UNIVERSITY
GREENVILLE, SC

мұстафиннің шеберлігі (1987), and *Критика современной буржуазной историографии всеобщей истории* (1984). Kazakhskaia, vol. 3, p. 519

Khashimbekov, Khadiia, born 23 January 1932 at Kokand, Eastern Uzbekistan, he graduated in 1953 from the Oriental Faculty, Central Asian State University, and received his first degree in 1967 for *Актуальные вопросы терминологии языка дари*. He was since 1968 affiliated with the Oriental Institute, Soviet Academy of Sciences. Miliband²

Khaskashev, Talbak Nabotovich, born 20th cent., his writings include *Фонетическая природа словесного ударения в современном таджикском литературом языке* (1983), and jointly with Savlatsho Merganov, *Краткий русско-персидский геологический словарь* (1988). LC

Khatchadourian, Haig, born 22 July 1925 at Jerusalem, he was educated at the American University of Beirut, and received his Ph.D. in 1956 from Duke University, Durham, N.C. He had already been teaching in Nicosia and Beirut when he became a professor in the Department of Philosophy, University of Wisconsin, Milwaukee, a post which he held until his retirement. His writings include *The Coherence theory of truth; a critical evaluation* (1961), a work which in a somewhat different form was originally presented as his doctoral thesis at Durham, *A Critical study of method* (1967), *The Concept of art* (1971), a collection of his papers, *Philosophy of language and logical theory* (1995), *Community and communitarianism* (1999), and *The Quest for peace between Israel and the Palestinians* (2000). ConAu, 53-56; DrAS, 1974 P, 1978 P, 1982 P; IntAu&W, 1977-1995/96; NatFacDr, 1990-1995

Khatchatrian, Armen, fl. 20th cent., his writings include *L'Architecture arménienne* (Paris, 1949), its translation, *Monuments of Armenian architecture* (1972), *Les Baptistères paléochrétiens* (1962), *Inscriptions et histoire des églises arméniennes* (1974), and *Origine et typologie des baptistères paléochrétiens* (1982). He died in 1967. LC; OSK

Khater, Antoine, born 20th cent., he was associated with the Institut français d'archéologie orientale du Caire. His writings include *Le Régime juridique des fouilles et des antiquités en Égypte* (1960), and he was a joint author of the *Catalogue of the Coptic and Christian Arab MSS preserved in the Cloister of Saint Menas, Cairo* (1967), and *Catalogue of the Coptic and Christian Arabic MSS preserved in the Library of the Church of Saints Sergius and Bacchus, Cairo* (1977). ZKO

Khatsrevin, Zakhar L'vovich, born in 1903, his writings include *Лето в Монголии* (1939), *Подвиг и повести и рассказы* (1966), *Только стихи* (1976), and jointly with Boris M. Lapin, *Сталинабадский архив* (1932); and the translation, *Одина или похождения Таджика*, from Sadr al-Din Aini (1930). He died in 1941. Master (1); NYPL; OSK

Khayat, Marie Karam, fl. 20th cent., she was a joint author of *Lebanon, land of the cedars* (Beirut, Khayats, 1967). NUC, 1956-67

Khazanov, Anatoliĭ Mikhaĭlovich, born 1 May 1932 in Amur Oblast, Russia, he graduated in 1955 from the Faculty of History, Moscow State University, reveived his first degree in 1958 for *Освободительные движения в Бразилин в колониальный период, 1654-1792*, and his doctorate in 1972 for *Формирование португальского колониализма*. Since 1958 he was associated with the Oriental Institute of the Soviet Academy of Sciences. His writings include *Сомалийская республика* (1961), *Освободительная борьба народов Восточной Африки после второй мировой войны* (1962), *Colonialism without empire* (1965), and *Крушение последней колониальной империи* (1986). Miliband; Miliband²; OSK

Khazanov, Anatoly (Anatoliĭ) Michailovish, born 13 December 1937 at Moscow, he was an ethnographer who received a doctorate in 1966 at Moscow and subsequently was associated with the Soviet Academy of Sciences until 1985. He was a visiting professor at the Hebrew University, Jerusalem, 1985/86 and stayed on until 1990, when he became a professor of anthropology at the University of Wisconsin, Madison, a post which he held until his retirement. His writings include *Nomads and the outside world* (1984), *The Krymchaks, a vanishing group in the Soviet Union* (1989), *After the USSR; ethnicity, nationalism, and politics in the Commonwealth of independent states* (1995), and he was a joint editor of *Pastoralism in the Levant* (1992), and *Changing nomads in a changing world* (1998). BioIn, 14; ConAu, 154; NatFacDr, 1995-2004; Schoeberlein

Khazanov, Mikhail Evgen'evich, born 20th cent., his writings include *ООН и ближневосточный кризис* (1983). LC

Kheifets, Aleksandr Naumovich, born in 1917 in the Ukraine, he graduated in 1939 from the Faculty of History, Moscow State University, and received his first degree in 1964 for *Советско-турецкие отношения в 1918-1922*, and his doctorate in 1964 for *Советская Россия и страны Востока в первые годы после Великой Октябрьской социалистической революции*. He was during the last years of his life affiliated with the Oriental Institute, Soviet Academy of Sciences. His writings include *Ленин - великий друг народов Востока* (1960). He died on 4 September 1985. Miliband[2]

Khēmp, Ērik P., 1920- *see* Hamp, Eric Pratt

Kherumian, Rouben (Ruben), born in 1900, his writings include *Les Arméniens; race, origines ethno-raciales* (Paris, 1941), *Génétique et anthropologie des groupes sanguins* (Paris, 1951), and he was a joint author of *Hérédité et fréquence des anomalités congénitales du sens chromatiques* (1959). NUC

Khetagurov, Lev Aleksandrovich, born in 1901 in the North Ossetian Autonomous Republic, he graduated in 1930 from the Faculty of Language and Material Culture, Leningrad State University, and received his first degree in 1936 for *Категория рода в иранских языках*. He was associated with his alma mater from 1936 to his death on 12 March 1941; since 1938 he was a lecturer. Miliband[2]

Khevrolina, Viktoriia Maksimovna, born 20th cent., she became associated with the Institute of History, Soviet Academy of Sciences. Her writings include *Революционно-демократическая мысль о внешней политики России и международных отношениях* (1986), *Власть и общество; борьба в России по вопросам внешней политики, 1878-1894 гг.* (1999); she was a joint author of *Документы и материалы по истории Великой Октябрьской социалистической революции* (1970); and she edited *Внешняя политика России; источники и историография* (1991). Note about the author; OSK

Khikmatuallaev, Khamidulla, born 1 September 1929 at Tashkent, he graduated in 1955 from the Central Asian State University, and received his first degree in 1964 for *Трактат Ибн Сины "Сердечные лекарства."* Since 1962 he was associated with Oriental Institute of the Uzbek Academy of Sciences. Miliband[2]

Khlopin, Igor' Nikolaevich, born 7 June 1930 at Leningrad, he graduated in 1954 from the Leningrad Faculty of History and received his first degree in 1962 for *Племена раннего энеолита Южной Туркмении* and his doctorate in 1985 for his 1983 monograph, *Юго-Западная Туркмения в эпоху поздний бронзы*. He was since 1961 affiliated with the Leningrad Branch of the Archaeological Institute, Soviet Academy of Sciences. Miliband[2]; Schoeberlein

Khodorov, Abram Evseevich, born in 1886 at Odessa, he graduated in 1912 from the Odessa School of Law and received his first degree in 1947 for a work on imperial expansion in China. His writings include *Китай и Марокко в борьбе с мировым империализмом* (1925). He died on 12 August 1949. Miliband; Miliband[2]

Khodzhaev, Ablat, born 27 January 1942 at Kuldja, Sinkiang, he graduated in 1969 from the Oriental Faculty, Tashkent State University, and received his first degree in 1973 for *Карательные походы цинского правительства против восстаний народов Джунгарии и Восточного Туркестана в 1864-1878 годах*. Since 1973 he was associated with the Oriental Institute of the Uzbek Academy of Sciences. His writings include *Китай сегодня* (1979), and *Цинская империя, Джунгария и Восточный Туркестан* (1979). Miliband[2]

Khodzhaeva, Rano Umarovna, born 7 July 1941 at Tashkent, she graduated in 1963 from the Oriental Faculty, Tashkent State University, and received her first degree in 1968 for *Художественная проза и драматургия Абд ар-Рахмана ал-Хамиси*, a work which was published in 1975. Since 1967 she was associated with the Oriental Institute of the Uzbek Academy of Sciences. Her writings include *Абдурахман аль Хамиси* (1973), and *Очерки развития египетской поэзии* (1985). Miliband[2]

Khodzhaeva, Rukiia Dianatovna, fl. 20th cent., she was a joint author of *Казахская национальная одежда, XIX-начало XX вв.* (Alma-Ata, 1964). OSK

Khodzhaniiazov, Tirkesh *see* Khojanyiazov, Tirkes

Khodzhash, Andriana *Svetlana* Gulef Samuil-Izmailovna, born 10 November 1923 at Evpatoria, Crimea, she graduated in 1945 from the Faculty of Philology, Moscow State University, and received her first degree in 1949 for *Египетское художественное ремесло периода XVIII династии* and her doctorate in 1990 for *Древнеегипетск. глиптика; скарабеи*. She was an archaeologist and since 1944 affiliated with the State Museum of Decorative Arts, Moscow. Her writings include *Египетская пластика малых форм* (1985). LC; Miliband; Miliband[2]

Khodzhimuradov, Olimdzhon Khamroevich, born 29 July 1948 at Pendzhikent, Tajikistan, he graduated in 1970 from the Oriental Faculty, Tajik State University, and received his first degree in 1977 for *Стиль художой прозы Садека Хедаят*. He was from 1977 to 1984 affiliated with the Oriental Institute of the Tajik Academy of Sciences as a Persian scholar. Miliband[2]

Khojanyiazov (Ходжаниязов), Tirkes, fl. 20th cent., he was associated with the Turkmen Academy of Sciences. His writings include *Сырлы хазынлар* (1975), *Денежное обращение в государстве Великих Сельджуков; по данным нумизматики* (1977), *Каталог монет госуларства Великих Сельджуков* (1979), and *Гадым Бактрия топрагында* (1982). LC; OSK

Kholmogorov, Ivan Nikolaevich, born in 1818, he studied from 1837 to 1841 at Kazan University, where he received his first degree in 1865 with a thesis on Sa'dī. He was a man of roving disposition so that long periods of his career remain shrouded in mystery. He taught in various capacities at secondary schools and universities in Astrakhan, Penza, Kazan, and Simbirsk. In 1861, he delivered his inaugural lecture at Kazan University entitled, "*Очерки арабской речи и арабской письменности.*" Nothing is known about the years from 1876 to 1885, when he became a professor of Persian language and literature at the Moscow Lazarev Institute of Oriental Languages. He translated Sa'dī's *Gūlistān* into Russian (1882), as well as the "history of the caliphate", the so-called *Kitāb al-Fakhrī* entitled *Книга ал-Фахри* (1862-63). He died in 1891. EnSlovar; Krachkovskii, pp. 159-162; TatarES

Khouri, Fred John, born 15 August 1916 at Cranford, N.J., he graduated in 1938 from Columbia University, New York, where he also received a Ph.D. in 1953 for *The Arab states in the United Nations*. He taught at various colleges and universites before 1951, when he was appointed a professor of political science at Villanova (Pa.) University. In 1963 he served as a visiting professor at the American University of Beirut. His writings include *The Arab-Israeli dilemma* (1976). AmM&WSc, 1973 S, 1978 S; ConAu, 25-28; IntAu&W, 1977-1989; Note; Selim; WhoE, 1977-1989 (not sighted); WhoAm, 1984-2002|; WhoWor, 1989/90-1993/94; WrDr, 1976/78-1996/98

Al-**Khoury**, Farès, 1873-1962 *see* Khūrī, Fāris al-

Khoury, Fawzi W., born 8 April 1938, he was for many years a Middle East librarian at the University of Washington, Seattle, and an active member of the Middle East Librarians' Association in the United States. His writings include *The Middle East in microform* (1992), and he was a joint author of *National union catalog of Middle Eastern microforms* (1989). Private

Khoury, Paul, S.J., born in 1904 in northern Lebanon, he suffered greatly in his youth during the famine of the 1910s, during which many of his family members starved to death. (His father had emigrated to Brazil in a vain attempt to support his family.) In 1923, he entered the Maronites and spent the following ten years in France. Apart from two brief assignments to al-Minyā, 1937-38 and 1967-68, and the odd vacation in Lebanon, he spent fifty years at Cairo. His writings include *Une lecture de la pensée arabe actuelle; trois études* (1981). He died in the Italian Hospital in Cairo on 2 April 1984. Jalabert

Khoury, Raif Georges, born 22 April 1936 at Khabab, Syria, he received a doctorate from the Université de Paris in the 1960s for *Bibliographie raisonnée des traductions publiées au Liban à partir des langues étrangères de 1840 jusqu'aux environs de 1905*, and a Dr.habil. in 1970 at the Universität Heidelberg, where he subsequently taught Oriental subjects. His writings include *Codices arabici antiqui* (1972), *Der Islam* (1993), *Passé et présent de la culture arabe; ou, tradition, modernité et conservation d'identité selon Djubrān Khalīl Djubrān à l'image de la renaissance europénne* (1997); he was a joint author of *Papyrologische Studien zum privaten und gesellschaftlichen Leben in den ersten islamischen Jahrhunderten* (1995); and he edited *Les Légendes prophétiques dans l'islam* (1978). Kürschner, 1976-2005

Khrakovskii, Viktor Samuilovich, born 20 November 1932 at Leningrad, he graduated in 1955 from the local Oriental Faculty and received his first degree in 1961 for *Видовременные отношения в системе личных форм глагола и арабском языке*. He was since 1967 associated with the Leningrad Branch of the Philological Institute, Soviet Academy of Sciences. He received a doctorate in 1972 for *Проблемы деривацион. синтаксическ. теории и вопросы синтаксиса арабс. языка*. His writings include *Очерки по общему и араб. синтаксису* (1973), and *Типология конструкций с предикатными актантами* (1985). LC; Miliband; Miliband²

Khristov, Khristo Angelov, born 9 January 1915 at Kharmanli, he studied history, and was since 1949 a lecturer at Sofia University. In 1954, he was appointed a professor. His writings include *La Grande révolution socialiste d'octobre et le développement de la lutte de classe et du mouvement révolutionnaire en Bulgarie au cours de la période 1917-1944* (Sofia, 1967), *Освобождението на България и политиката на западгите държави, 1876-1878* (1968), *Пайсий Хилендарски; неговото време, жизнен път и дело* (1972), *Българските общини през Възраждането* (1973), *Аграргният въпрос в българската натсионална револютсия* (1976) and *Из историята на Добруджа, Тракия и Македония* (1990). In 1976 appeared *Акалемик Христо А. Христов; изследвания по случай 60 години от рождението му*. EnBulg; OSK

Khromov, Al'bert Leonidovich, born 28 August 1930 at Novgorod, he graduated in 1954 from the Faculty of Philology, Moscow, and received his first degree in 1963 for *Говоры филол. таджиков Матчинского района* and his doctorate in 1969 for *Историко-лингвистич. исследование Ягноба и Верхн. Зеравшана.* He was appointed a lecturer in 1966 and a professor in 1972. His writings include *Говоры таджиков Матчинского района* (1962), *Сборник статей по памирским языкам и истории таджикского языка* (1963), *Ягнобский язык* (1972), and he was joint author of *Из истории востоковедения в Таджикистане, 1917-1985 гг.* (1990), and *Проблемы деривационной ономасиологии современного персидского языка* (1990). LC; Miliband²; Shoeberlein; *Восток*, 1993, no. 5, pp. 218-219

Khrustalev, Mark Arsen'evich, born 24 August 1930 at Tver' (Kalinin), he graduated in 1953 from the Moscow Oriental Institute and received his first degree in 1969. He was since 1966 affiliated with the Moscow Institute of International Relations. In 1976 he was appointed a lecturer. His writings include *Системное моделирование международных отношений* (1987). Miliband²

Khuda Bakhsh, Salahuddin, born in 1877, a son of Muhammad Khuda Bukhsh (d. 1908), who in 1893 founded the Oriental Public Library in Bankipore. He was a barrister, whose years at Oxford, and his acquaintance with European languages as well as the work of European scholars, had given him a bent for the critical reconstruction of Islam's history, as well as the conviction that it was the duty of a good Muslim to spread, by translation and exposition, the knowledge of what scholars in other countries were thinking. He translated into English Gustav Weil's dated *Geschichte der islamischen Völker*, and partly Alfred von Kremer's *Geschichte der herrschenden Ideen des Islams* entitled *The Orient under the caliphs* (1920). He also took an active interest in Margaret Graham Weir's translation of Julius Wellhausen's *Das arabische Reich und sein Sturz* entitled *The Arab kingdom and its fall* (1927). His own writings include *Essays, Indian and Islamic* (1912), *Politics in Islam* (1920), and *Contributions to the history of Islamic civilization* (1929-30). He died on 12 August 1931. Fück, 270; *Moslem world*, 27 (1932), pp. 77-78

Khudadov, Vladimir Nikolaevich, born 19th cent., his writings include *Закавказье; историко-экономический очерк* (1926), *Армянка* (1927), and *Грузинка* (1928). OSK

Khudaĭberdiev, Aziz Kheliamovich, born 15 November 1949 at Tashkent, he graduated in 1974 from the Oriental Faculty, Tashkent State University, and received his first degree in 1979 for *Особенности колониальной политики бртьанского империализма в Йемене в первой трети XX века.* Since 1979 he was associated with the Oriental Faculty of his alma mater. Miliband²

al-Khūrī (Khoury), Fāris (Farès), born In 1877 at Kfir, Lebanon, he was a practising lawyer in Syria and a politician, who, before the first World War, fought for Syrian independence, and after the first World War, against the Ottomans and the French mandatory power, and subsequently for the Arab cause in the United Nations Organization after the second Word War. His writings include موجز في علم المالية (1924), *Le Droit civil et les finances.* He died in Damascus on 2 January 1962. Muhammad al-Farhanī wrote فارس الخوري و ايام لا تنى (1965). *Hommes et destins*, vol. 7 (1986), pp. 280-81

Khurshit, Ėnver Usmanovich, born 18 November 1939 in Russia, he graduated in 1969 from Tashkent State University, and received his first degree in 1982 for *"Тарих-и Кипчак-хани" - важный источник по истории Средней Азии и Северного Афганистана XVI-XVII вв.* He was from 1970 to 1978 an editor of *Фан* and subsequently joined the Oriental Institute of the Uzbek Academy of Sciences. Miliband²

Khuseĭn-zade, Matin Sharifovich, born 28 February 1939 at Tashkent, he graduated in 1964 from Leningrad State University, and received his first degree in 1967 for *Изображение крестьянск. жизни в литературе Египта.* He spent 1960-62 in Baghdad, and 1969-1970 in Alexandria, Egypt. He was successively associated with the Oriental Institute of the Tajik Academy of Sciences and the Oriental Faculty of the Tajik State University. His writings include *Феллах в литературе Египта* (1967). Miliband²

Khuseĭn-zade, Sharifdzhan, born 12 April 1907 in eastern Uzbekistan, he graduated in 1932 from the Oriental Faculty, Central Asian State University, receceived his first degree in 1953, and became a professor in 1966. His writings on Persian subjects were written almost exclusively in Tajik. Miliband²

Khushenova, Svetlana Vasil'evna, fl. 20th cent., her writings include *Изафетные фразеологические единицы таджикского языка* (Dushanbe, 1971), *Библиографический указатель литературы по таджикской фразеологии* (1977), and she edited *Помиршиноси; мас'алахой филология* (1975), and she was a joint author of *Забонхои Помири ва фольклор* (1972). LC

Khvol'son (Хвольсонб, Chwolson), Daniel Avraamovich, born 10 December 1819 at Vilnius, he was educated privately, before studying Oriental languages at the Universität Leipzig, where he received a Dr.phil. in 1850 for his thesis, *Die Ssabier und der Ssabismus*. After his return to Russia he considered it prudent for his career to be baptized Josef. In due course, he became the leading Orientalist in Russia of the time. Despite his conversion, he remained well disposed towards Jews and Judaism. He was active in Jewish community life and through his writings and personal conduct he achieved considerable success towards Jewish civil equality. He died in St. Petersburg on 6 April 1911. EncJud; GdeEnc; GSE; Krachkovskii; Meyers; VostokMStP, p. 257; Wininger

Khvostov, Vladimir Mikhaĭlovich, born in 1905, he was a specialist on modern history and international relations and adviser to Soviet policymakers on the conduct of foreign affairs. He was associated with the foreign ministry in the early postwar period, serving as director of the School for Higher Diplomats, Foreign Office, from 1945 to 1953. He acted as consultant to the Communist Party's Central Committee in the late nineteen-fifties. In 1959, he returned to academic life and headed an institute of the Soviet Academy of Sciences for eight years. He participated in international public forums of peace and disarmament, including the Pugwash conferences. His writings include *40 лет борьбы за мир* (1958), and he was a joint author of *История внешней политики СССР* (1966), and *Проблемы истории внешней политики СССР и международных отношений; избранные труды* (1976). He died in 1972. In 1976 appeared the commemoration volume *Вопросы имтории внешней политики СССР и международных отношений; сборнак статей памяти акад. Владимира Михайловиса Хвостова*. He died on 9 March 1972. NUC, pre-1956; NYT, 11 March 1972, p. 32, col. 5

Khydyrov, Мәмметназар (Mamed Nazarovich), born in 1905 at Beshir, Turkmenia, he received a doctorate in philology in 1948, and was since 1950 a professor of Turkic linguistics. He was associated with the Faculty of Turkmen Philology of the Ashkhabad State Pedagogical Institute im. A. M. Gorkiĭ. His writings include *Туркмен дилиниң тарыхындан материаллар* (1962). He died in Ashkhabad on 21 September 1977. Almaz IAzberdyev wrote *Мәмметназар Хыдыров* (1984). LC; OSK; *Советская тюркология*, 1975, № 4, pp. 118-19; TurkmenSE

Kiamilev, Khaĭbula, born in 1910 in the Crimea, he graduated in 1937 from the Moscow Oriental Institute, received his first degree in 1949 for «Намык Кемаль как драматург», and his doctorate in 1971 for *Развитие общественных мотивов в турецкой поэзии*. He taught at his alma mater from 1941 to 1952 and subsequently four years at the Moscow State Institute of International Relations. Since 1956 he was a research fellow in the Oriental Institute of the Soviet Academy of Sciences. His writings include *Хестоматия современных газетных текстов на турецком языке* (1950), *Назым Хидмет* (1952), *Анатолия глазами Сабахаттина Али* (1965), *У истоков современной турецкой литературы* (1967), and *Общественные мотивы в турецкой поэзии, конец XIX-середина XX века* (1969). He died on 18 February 1979. Miliband; Miliband[2]

Kiamilev, Said Khaĭbulovich, born 22 May 1937 at Moscow, he graduated in 1960 from the Moscow State Institute of International Relations and received his first degree in 1966 for *Марокканский диалект арабского языка*. He subsequently became a research fellow in the Institute of the People of Asia, Soviet Academy of Sciences. His writings include his published thesis in 1968, and he was a joint editor of *Социально-политические представления в Исламе* (1987). Miliband; Miliband[2]; OSK

Kiamileva, Alime Asai, born 15 September 1917 at Yalta, she graduated in 1941 from the Moscow State Library Institute and received her first degree in 1959 for *Наблюдения над лексикой художественной прозы Сабаттина Али*. From 1942 to 1954 she taught in the Moscow Oriental Institute; since 1956 she was a research fellow in the Oriental Institute of the Soviet Academy of Sceinces. Her writings include *Разговорник на турецком языке* (1951). Miliband; Miliband[2]

Kiazimov, Mekhti Davud ogly, born 18 August 1954 at Baku, he graduated in 1977 from Azerbaijan State University and received his first degree in 1981 for *Сравнительный анализ поэм "Семь красавиц" Низами Гянджеви и "Восемь райск. садов" Амира Хасрова Дехлеви*. He spent 1976/77 in Iran and was since 1980 affiliated with the Oriental Institute in the Azerbaijan Academy of Sciences. His writings include *"Хафт пейкар" Низами и традиция назире в персоязычной литературе XIV-XVI вв.* (1987). Miliband[2]

Kibe, Madhav Vinayak, born 4 April 1877 at Indore, Central India, he was privately educated at home, at Daly College, Indore, graduated in 1899 from Muir Central College, Allahabad, and took his M.A. in history and economics in 1901. He was an honorary attaché to the Agent to the Governor-General in Central India, and honorary magistrate in the Residency area, Indore, and in 1911 became dewan of the Dewas State Junior. He was awarded Rao Bahadur for his services in Dewas. He was then appointed Huzur Secretary to the Maharaja Tukojirao Holkar III, and became excise minister and retired as a deputy prime minister. In 1931 he was called by the Maharaja Holkar to London to be present at the second Round Table Conference. In 1933, he appeared before the Joint Parliamentary Committee on behalf of the land-holders of the Bombay Presidency. A member of the Royal Asiatic Society, London, and a fellow of the Royal Society of Arts, London, his writings include *Location of Lankā* (Poona, 1947). WhE&EA; *Who'swho in India* (1939?), p. 500-501; *Indian yearbook and who's who*, 1939/49 (not sighted)

Kibirov, Sh., fl. 20th cent., he was associated with the Uigur Division in the Institute of Philology of the Kazak Academy of Sciences. He was a joint author of Уйғур мақал вә тәмсиллири = Уйгурские пословицы и поговорки (Alma-Ata, 1978). OSK

Kidder, Homer Huntington, born in 1874, he was a physical anthropologist and an archaeologist. He died on 4 Decmber 1950 at the age of seventy-six. NYT, 6 December 1950, p. 33, col. 3

Kieffer, Charles Martin, born 14 June 1923 at Cernay, Haute-Alsace, France, he received a *doctorat d'état* in 1975 from the Université de Paris for *Les Parlers de la vallée du Logar-Wardak, Afghanistan*. He was in 1993 a *directeur de recherche* at the C.N.R.S., Paris. His writings include *Les Ghorides* (1962), and *Grammaire de l'ormuri de Baraki-Barak, Logar, Afghanistan* (2003). AnEIFr, 1997; BioB134; EURAMES, 1993; Private; THESAM, 4

Kieffer, Jean *Daniel*, born 4 May 1767 at Strasbourg, he studied at the local Université, where he received a doctorate in 1787. He pursued an interest in evangelical ministry, but also in Oriental languages. On 23 November 1794 he became a translator at the secretariat of the Comité du Salut public. A second secretary-interpreter at the French embassy in Constantinople since 3 March 1795, he became befriended with Pierre Ruddin, one of the great French Levant specialists. When diplomatic relations between France and the Ottoman Empire were broken off after the French invasion of Egypt in 1798, the two diplomats were locked up by the Turks until relations were re-established in 1801. He returned to France with the Turkish ambassador, Halet Effendi, and served as secretary-interpreter with the Grande Armée, translating military bulletins, foreign correspondence, and state treaties. On 9 November 1811, he was nominated first interpreter. Two days later, he succeded Pierre Ruffin as a professor of Turkish at the Collège de France; by royal decree of 11 September 1822, he was appointed to the chair of Turkish for life. During the rest of his life, he was occupied with the translation of the Bible into Turkish. From 1820 to 1832, he was the French representative to the British and Foreign Bible Society, London. He died in Paris on 31 January 1833, leaving his *Dictionnaire turc-français* to be completed by his collaborator, T. X. Bianchi, 1833-1835. *Bulletin de géographie historique et descriptive*, 35 (1920), pp. 133-162; DBF; Kornrumpf; NDBA

Kieffer, Louis, born about 1897 in France, he received degrees in arts, commerce, and foreign languages, particularly Russian. From 1925 until 1931, he was a trade attaché at the French Embassy in Moscow. Since 1939 he was attached to the Centre de Hautes Études d'Administration Musulmane, Paris. He served ten years as *directeur des affaires politiques* in the Middle East. During the last years of his active life he worked for l'Agence Havas, Paris. He died in his eighty-second year on 27 March 1978. *L'Afrique et l'Asie*, n° 117 (1978), pp. 64-65

Kiel, Machiel, born 25 February 1938 at Wormerveer, the Netherlands, his writings include *Art and society of Bulgaria in the Turkish period* (Assen, 1985), *Ottoman architecture in Albania* (1990), a collection of his articles, *Studies in the Ottoman architecture of the Balkans* (1990), *Ost-Lokris in türkischer und neugriechischer Zeit, 1460-1981* (Passau, 1994), and he was a joint author of *De Koerden* (Amsterdam, 1992). Brinkman's; LC; ZKO

Kielstra, Nicolaas Onno, born 20th cent., he received a doctorate in 1974 at Amsterdam for *Ecology and community in Iran; a comparative study of the relations between ecological conditions, the economic system, village politics and the moral value system in two Iranian villages*. His writings include *Two essays on Iranian society* (1976), *Fundamentalism; sect or mass movement* (Amsterdam, Middle East Research Associates, 1990), and he was a joint author of *De Koerden* (1992). Brinkman's

Kienast, Burkhart, born 3 July 1929, he received a Dr.phil. in 1956 from the Universität Heidelberg for *Die altassyrischen Texte des Orientalischen Seminars, Heidelberg*, and a Dr.habil. in 1978 for *Die alt-babylonischen Briefe und Urkunden aus Kisurra*. He taught ancient Near Eastern subjects succes-sively at the universities of Heidelberg and Freiburg im Breisgau. His writings include *Die altakkadi-schen Königsinschriften* (1990). Kürschner, 1983-2005; Schwarz

Kieniewicz, Jan, born 7 August 1938 at Warszawa, he studied history at Uniwersytet Warszawski, where he received doctorates in 1966 and 1974. He was a historian and diplomat whose writings include *Historia Indii* (1980), *Od eksansji do dominacji* (1986), and he was a joint author of *Historia Polski* (Paris, 1986). KtoPolsce, 1993, 2001; Polski²

Kienitz, Friedrich Karl, born in 1925, he received a degree in economics, and a Dr.phil. 1949 from the Universität Wien for *Die politische Geschichte Ägyptens vom 7. bis zum 4. Jahrhundert vor Christi Geburt*, a work which was published in 1953. His writings focus on the cultural and economic history of the Balkans and the Near East, including *Türkei; Anschluß an die moderne Wirtschaft unter Kemal Atatürk* (1959), *Existenzfragen des griechischen Bauerntums* (1960), *5000 Jahre Orient* (1962), *Städte unterm Halbmond* (1972), *Das Mittelmeer, Schauplatz der Weltgeschichte von den frühen Hochkulturen bis ins 20. Jahrhundert* (1976), and *Völker im Schatten* (1981). Note; ZKO

Kienle, Eberhard, born about 1960, he received French degrees, including D.E.S. (*diplôme d'études supérieures*), and a non-identified Dr.phil. in 1989 from Freie Universität Berlin. Since 1990 he was a lecturer in politics of the Near and Middle East at the School of Oriental and African Studies, London. His writings include *The Conflict between the Baath regimes of Syria and Iraq prior to their consolidation* (1985), *Ethnizität und Machtkonkurrenz in inter-arabischen Beziehungen; der syrisch-irakische Konflikt unter den Ba'th-Regimen* (1988), *Ba'th v. Ba'th; the conflict between Syria and Iraq, 1968-1989* (1990), *Entre jama'a et classe; le pouvoir politique en Syrie* (1991), *Contemporary Syria* (1994), *Liberalization between cold war and peace* (1997), and *A Grand delusion, democracy and economic reform in Egypt* (2001). Note about the author; ZKO

Kiep, Walther Leisler, born 5 January 1926 at Hamburg, he was educated at Hamburg, Istanbul, and Frankfurt am Main, and became a politician and business executive. He was awarded an honorary doctorate. His writings include *Good-bye America - was dann?* (1972), *A New challenge for Western Europe* (1974), and *Was bleibt ist große Zuversicht: Erfahrungen eines Unabhängigen; ein politisches Tagebuch* (1999). IntWW, 1989/90-2005; Wer ist wer, 1876/77-2004/2005

Kiepert, Johann Samuel *Heinrich*, born 31 July 1818 at Berlin, he studied classical philology at the Universität Berlin, and became an authority in classical geography and topography. From August 1841 to August 1842, he was able to visit Asia Minor in order to prepare a map of the region. After his return to Berlin he began to study Arabic, Persian, and Armenian as a prerequisite for the production of six maps of the Ottoman Empire in Asia, a task which he completed in 1844. After some years at Weimar as a cartographer, he returned to Berlin, where in 1853 he was elected to the Prussian Academy of Sciences. Since the same year he also lectured in historical geography at the Universität Berlin. In later years he served as a consultant to international border commissions. On his eightieth birthday he was honoured by *Beiträge zur alten Geschichte und Geographie*. He died in Berlin on 21 April 1899. ADtB; DtBE; DtBInd (7); Embacher; *Geographische Zeitschrift*, 7 (1901), pp., 1-21, 77-94; Henze; Kornrumpf; Kornrumpf², vol. 2; NDB

Kiepert, Richard K., born 13 September 1846 at Weimar, Duchy of Saxe-Weimar, Germany, the son of Heinrich Kiepert, he studied history and geography at the universitites of Berlin and Heidelberg, and subsequently travelled one year in the East. Since 1871 he was resident in Berlin. He was an editor of the journal, *Globus*, from 1875 to 1887. He collaborated with his father in his publications. His own writings include *Deutscher Kolonial-Atlas* (1893), and *Karte von Klein-Asien* (1912-1914). He died in Berlin on 4 October 1915. DtBInd (3); DtBiJ, vol. 1, 1914-1915 (1925), *Totenliste*, p. 331; *Geographische Zeitschrift*, 22 (1916), p. 121; *Deutsches Kolonial-Lexikon* (Leipzig, 1920); Kornrumpf; Meyers; Wer ist's, 1909-1912

Kieran, John A., fl. 20th cent., he jointly published, with Bethwell A., Ogot *Zamani; a survey of East African history* (New York, Humanities Press, 1968). NUC, 1968-72

Kiernan, E. Victor Gordon, born 4 September 1913 at Manchester, he was a fellow of Trinity College, Cambridge. From 1948 to his retirement he taught history in various capacities at the University of Edinburgh. His writings include *British diplomacy in China, 1880-1939* (1939), *Metcalfe's mission to Lahore, 1808-09* (1943), *The Revolution of 1854 in Spanish history* (1966), *The Lords of human kind* (1969), *Imperialism and its contradictions* (1995), and he translated *Poems from Iqbal* (1947), and *Poems from Faiz, translated from the Urdu* (1971). BioIn, 16; BLC; ConAu, 25-28, new rev., 11

Kiernan, Reginald Hugh, born in 1900 at Leeds, he was educated at the Jesuit College, Leeds, and the universities of Leeds and Manchester. His writings include *Lawrence of Arabia* (1935), *Unveiling Arabia; the story of Arabian travel and discovery* (1937), its translation, *L'Exploration de l'Arabie* (1938), and *Lloyd George* (1940). WhE&EA

Kiernan, Thomas, born 20th cent., he was a prolific professional writer of biographies, sports, and foreign policy. His writings include *The Negro impact on Western civilization* (1970), *Jane; an intimate biography of Jane Fonda* (1973), *The Arabs, their history, aims and challenge to the industrialized world* (1975), *Yasir Arafat, the man and the myth* (1976), and *Citizen Murdoch* (1986). ConAu, 113

Kiesewetter, August *Wilhelm*, born in 1811, he trained as a landscape painter under Carl Röthig in Berlin. He spent fifteen years travelling through northern Sweden, Russia, Central Asia, and the

Crimea. He returned with a rich collection of oil paintings of great ethnological importance, which was recommended for an exhibition by Alexander von Humboldt as well as the geographer Carl Ritter. His writings include *Mittheilungen aus dem Tagebuch zu Kiesewetters ethnographischen Reisebildern* (Berlin, 1855). He died in Gotha on 30 August 1865. AllgLKünst

von **Kiesling**, Hans, born 19th cent., he was a major with the Imperial German High Command under Field-Marshall Colmar von der Goltz in Mesopotamia. His writings include *Gefechtsbefehle* (1907), *Damaskus; Altes und Neues aus Syrien* (1919), *Rund um den Libanon; friedliche Wanderungen während des Weltkrieges* (1920), *Vorderasien* (1920), *Orientfahrten zwischen Ägeis und Zagros; Erlebtes und Erschautes aus schwerer Zeit* (1921), *Mit Feldmasrschall von der Goltz Pascha in Mesopotamien und Persien* (1922), and *Soldat in drei Weltteilen* (1935). Note about the author

Kieszkowski, Bohdan, born 24 December 1904 at Dębinie, Ukraine, he studied at Warszawa, where he also received a Ph.D. in 1934. He subsequently taught at his alma mater. His writings include *Platonizm renesansowy* (Warszawa, 1935), *Roczniki prac naukowych* (Warszawa, 1936), and *Studi sui platonismo del Rinascimento in Italia* (Firenze, 1936). Polski² (1); KtoPolsce, 1938

Kiker, Douglas, born in 1930 at Griffin, Ga., he graduated in 1952 from a Presbyterian college. He was a journalist of the *New York Herald Tribune*, and the *Chicago Tribune*, a correspondent for the National Broadcasting Corporation (NBC), and he served as a sometime government official. In his spare time he wrote novels. He died in 1991. Au&Wr, 1963, 1971; ConAu, 65-68, 135; WhAm, 10

Kiknadze, Otari Melitonovich, born 15 June 1924 in Soviet Georgia, he graduated in 1951 from the Oriental Faculty, Tiflis State University, and in 1961 from the School for Higher Diplomats at the Foreign Ministry, obtaining his first degree in 1983 at Tiflis for *Идеологическая экспансия ведущих капиталистических стран Зарада в Иране в 60-70-е годы XX века*. He served as a diplomat in Indonesia, 1962-64, and Iran, 1971-75. His writings include *История и искусствознагие* (1983). He died on 22 July 1984. Miliband²

Kiknadze, Revaz Kandidovich, born 7 June 1923 at Tiflis, he graduated in 1951 from the local Oriental Faculty and received his first degree in 1956 for *Города и городская жизнь в государстве хулагуидов*. He was since 1961 affiliated with the Georgian Soviet Academy of Sciences. His writings include *Очерки по источниковедения истории Грузии* (1980), as well as works in Georgian. Miliband; Miliband²

Kiknaże, Revaz, 1923- see Kiknadze, Revaz Kandidovich

Kikuchi, Tadayoshi, born in 1950, he was a lecturer in the Department of Arabic Studies, Osaka University. DrB3MES, 1993, JapAuFile; *MESA Roster of members*, 1982-1990

Kiladze Nana Valer'ianovna, born 3 May 1943 at Kutaisi, Soviet Georgia, she graduated in 1965 from the Oriental Faculty, Tiflis State University, and received her first degree in 1970 with a thesis on «*Ал-Газали и его Тахафут ал-фаласифа*», and a doctorate in 1980 for *Философская лексика средневекового Востока*. She wrote exclusively in Georgian. Miliband²

al-**Kīlānī** (Gailani, Gaylani, Gilani, Kaylani), Rashīd 'Alī, born in 1892 or 97 at Baghdad, he was a pro-Axis Iraqi politician who staged a *coup d'état* in Iraq in 1941, and subsequently sought Axis support for his leadership in the Arab world. He went to Berlin from Tehran by way of Turkey, where he was given asylum. He arrived in Berlin with his family in November 1941, and escaped from Berlin shortly before the German capitulation in May 1945. He died in 1965 or 68. *Die Araber in Berlin* (Berlin, 1998), p. 43; Awwad; DcTwHis; Majid Khadduri, *Arab contemporaries* (1973), pp. 77-79

Kil'berg, Khisia Izraelevna, born in 1902, she graduated in 1932 from the Oriental Institute, Moscow, and received her first degree in 1936 for her monograph, *Восстание Араби-паши в Египете*, a work which was published in 1937. Since 1950 she was affiliated with the Oriental Institute in the Soviet Academy of Sciences. Her other writings include *Египет в борьбе за независимость* (1950), and the translation from the Arabic of Amīn Sa'īd, *История арабской революции* (1940). She died on 3 March 1978. Krachkovskiĭ; Miliband; Miliband²

Kili, Suna, born 26 February 1939 at Istanbul, she studied at İstanbul Üniversitesi, Bryn Mawr (Pa.) College, the University of California, Columbia and Princeton universities, and gained a doctorate. She was a sometime fellow of the Fulbright Foundation. She subsequently became a professor of political science at İstanbul Üniversitesi. Her writings include *Turkey; a case study of political development* (1968), *Kemalism* (1969), *Turkish constitutional developments* (1971), *1960-1975 döneminde Cumhuriyet Halk Partisinde gelişmeler* (1976), and *Çayırhan* (1978). Note about the author; ZKO

Kilian, François Théodore *Conrad*, born 23 August 1898 at Château des Sauvages, commune de Désaignes (Ardèche), France, he was educated at Grenoble and studied at Paris until obliged to interrupt his course due to ill health. Since April 1917 he served in the war. In 1920, he continued his natural sciences at the Faculté des sciences de Grenoble. In 1922, he was enticed by a Swiss industrialist to participate in the futile attempt to locate the mysterious emeralds claimed to have been collected by Flatters in the Saharan Hoggar Mountains. After his return, he worked on his science degrees from Lyon and Grenoble. In the service of the Institut de France, he went from 1926 to 1929 on an exploration of the Sahara. In the remaining inter-war years he prepared the results of his explorations for publication and collaborated with the preparations for the 1934 Exposition internationale du Sahara at Paris. From 1942 to 1949 he accomplished more Saharan missions in the service of the Ministère des Affaires Étrangères. His writings include *Au Hoggar; mission de 1922* (1925). He was found with slashed chest and wrists hanging from the window fastener on 30 April 1950. Hommes et destins, pp. 322-26; *Travaux de l'Institut de Recherches sahariennes, 7 (1951), pp. 15-21*

Kilias, Doris (divorced Erpenbeck), born about 1942 in Germany, she studied Arabic and French and received a Dr.phil. in 1974 from the Universität Leipzig for *Die moderne ägyptische Kurzgeschichte*. Thereafter she was affiliated with the Department of Romance languages, Humboldt-Universität, Berlin. Her writings include the edition and translation of *Erkundungen; 22 syrische Erzähler* (1978). In the 1990s she translated the works of Najib Mahfuz, including *Die Kinder unseres Viertels* (1990), *Palast der Sehnsucht* (1993), *Zuckergäßchen* (1994), *Das Lied der Bettler* (1995), and *Ehrenwerter Herr* (2004). Private; Schwarz; ZKO

Killean, Mary *Carolyn* Garver, born 24 January 1936 at Columbus, Ohio, she graduated in 1952 from the University of Michigan, where she also received her Ph.D. in 1966 for *The deep structure of the noun phrase in modern written Arabic*. From 1967 to her retirement she taught in the Department of Linguistics, University of Chicago. She was a joint author of *A Comprehensive study of Egyptian Arabic* (1978-79). DrAS, 1974 F, 1978 F, 1982 F; NatFacDr, 1990; Selim

Killgore, Andrew Ivy, born 7 November 1919 at Greensboro, Ala., he graduated in 1943 from Livingston (Ala.) University, received a LL.D. in 1949 from the University of Alabama, and was admitted to the bar. From 1955 to 1957, he took Arabic language training at the U.S. Foreign Service Institute. A naval officer during the second World War, he became a career foreign service officer, mainly in the Muslim world. When he retired in 1980, he was U.S. ambassador to Qatar. He was a publisher of the *Washington report on the Middle East*. Note about the author; WhoAm, 1978-1996|; WhoGov, 1972, 1975 (not sighted); WhoWor, 1978/79-1989/90

Killian, Charles, born 18 February 1887 at Saverne (Bas-Rhin), Germany, he was educated at his native town and after passing his *Abiturium* in 1904, he went on to study at the universities of Berlin, Freiburg im Breisgau, and Straßburg. He received a doctorate in philosophy in 1911, and his *Staatsexamen* in 1912. He was a lecturer at the Botanische Institut, the later the Institut botanique, Strasbourg, from 1913 until 1926, when he was appointed lecturer in agricultural botany, with special reference to microbiology of desert soils, Faculté des sciences d'Alger, where he remained until his retirement. He was a member of the Institut de Recherches Sahariennes since 1940. His writings include *Biologie végétale du Fezzân* (Alger, 1947), and he was a joint author of *Recherches sur la microbiologie des sols désertiques; résultats des missions sahariennes Killian-Fehér* (1939). He died on 27 January 1957. DBF; Index BFr²; NDBA; *Qui êtes-vous, 1924*; *Travaux de l'Institut de recherches sahariennes, 16 (1957), pp. 11-13*

Kilner, Peter Pomfret, born 20th cent., he was a journalist and publisher, the editor of the *Arab report and record*, and a joint author of *The Gulf handbook, 1976-77* (1976). DrBSMES, 1993

Kilpatrick-Waardenberg, Hilary M. D. (Mrs. Jacobus Diederik Jan Waardenburg), born about 1930, she received a D.Phil. in 1971 from Oxford University for *Social criticism in the modern Egyptian novel*. She was a sometime talks writer in the Arabic Service of the BBC, and in 1993, a senior member of St. Antony's College, Oxford. Her writings include *The Modern Egyptian novel; a study in social criticism* (1974), *Making the great book of songs and the author's craft in Abū al-Faraj al-Isbahānī's "Kitāb al-Aghānī"* (2003), and she was a joint author of *Les Études sur l'Afrique du nord et l'Asie de l'ouest en Suisse; état des lieux et plaidoyer pour une réorganisation de la formation et de la recherche selon un approche "area-study"* (1993) DrBSMES, 1993; *MESA Roster of members*, 1990; Note about the author; Sluglett

Kim, Maksim Pavlovich, born in 1908 at Primorsky Kray (Putsilovka), Russia, he was a historian whose writings include *История и коммунизм* (1968), *Советское Крестьянстио* (1970), *Советское народ* (1972), and *Socialism and culture* (1984). In 1987 he was honoured by *Советская культура; 70 лет развития: к 80-летию академика М. П. Кима*. WhoSocC, 78

Kimball, Lorenzo Kent, he was born in 1922 in Utah, where he also spent most of his life. Upon graduation from high school he enlisted in the U.S. Army. His military career spanned from 1941 to his retirement from the U.S. Air Force in 1962 with the rank of lieutenant colonel. He then started a second career as a student of politics, particularly Middle Eastern, at the University of Utah. In 1963, he was awarded the graduate certificate in Middle Eastern studies, and in 1968, he completed a doctoral thesis on *The changing pattern of political power in Iraq, 1858-1966*, a work which was later updated to cover the period 1958-1971, and published in 1972. From 1965 to his retirement in 1987, he taught political science in various capacities at his alma mater. He died on 10 June 1999.
AmM&WSc, 1973 S, 1978 S; *MESA bulletin*, 35 (2001), p. 149; Selim; WhoAm, 1980-1982; WhoWest, 1976/77-1980/81

Kimble, George Herbert Tinley, born 2 August 1908 at London, he was educated at Eastbourne Grammar School, and graduated B.A. in 1929 with first class honours in geography at King's College, London. A year later, a degree in divinity was added, and in 1931 the M.A. in geography, all from his alma mater. Entering directly into teaching geography, he served at University College, Hull, from 1931 to 1936, and at the University of Reading, from 1936 to 1939. During World War two, he was an officer in the British Naval Meteorological Service. In 1945, he continued his teaching career at McGill University, Montreal, where he also completed the work for the Ph.D. in 1948. He later went to Indiana University to serve as chairman of the Department of Geography. His writings include *Geography in the middle ages* (1938), *The World's open spaces* (1939), *Ghana* (1960), and *Tropical Africa* (1960). AmAu&B; Au&Wr, 1963, 1971; BlueB, 1973/74, 1975, 1976; ConAu, 108; CurBio, 1952; *Geographical review*, 40 (1950), pp. 1-3; IntYB, 1978-82; Unesco

Kimche, David, born in 1928 at London, he grew up in England and went to Palestine in 1946 and studied at the Hebrew University, Jerusalem, where he also gained a Ph.D. He was a journalist who held senior positions in the Israeli Government, an intelligence agent, and a guest lecturer at Israeli universities. In 1968 he was a research fellow at the Reuven Shiloah Research Center, Tel-Aviv University. His writings include *The Afro-Asian movement* (1973), and he was a joint author of *The Secret roads* (1954), its translation, *Des Zornes und des Herzens wegen* (1956), and *A Clash of destinies* (1960). Au&Wr, 1971; BioIn, 15; ConAu, 103 (no substance); Note about the author; WhoIsrael, 1980/81-1985/86

Kimche, Jon, born 17 June 1909 at St. Gallen, Switzerland, he was a descendant of a Jewish family that settled in Switzerland and produced several famous rabbis. He was a journalist and active in Zionist politics after World War two. With the funding of the Israeli Government he edited and published the *Jewish observer and Middle East review* (1952-1977). In 1991, he was an editor of a London newsletter dealing with Afro-Asian affairs. His writings include *Seven fallen pillars* (1950), *The Second Arab awakening* (1970), its translation, *Zeitbombe Nahost* (1970), and *Palestine or Israel* (1973). Au&Wr, 1963; WhoWorJ, 1965; *Washington report on Middle East affairs*, 10, no. 4 (1991); WhE&EA; WhoWor, 1974-1976/77

Kimmerling, Baruch, born 10 October 1939 in Romania, he graduated in 1965 from the Hebrew University, Jerusalem, where he also received a Ph.D. in 1975. He taught sociology and anthropology in various capacities at his alma mater since 1978. His writings include *Inner dualism* (1973), *Zionism and territory; the socio-territorial dimensions of Zionist politics* (1983), *The Invention and decline of Israeliness* (2001), *Politicide; Ariel Sharon's war against the Palestinians* (2003); he was a joint author of *Palestinians; the making of a people* (1993); he edited *The Israeli state and society; boundaries and frontiers* (1988), and *Political sociology at the crossroads* (1996). ConAu, 141; ZKO

Kin, John, fl. 1942-43, he was a graduate of Yenching University, Peking, and associated for more than ten years with the editorial staff of the leading English-language newspapers, *North China daily news, Shanghai evening post & mercury*, and the *China press*, Shanghai. Since the Sino-Japanese war began, he covered Hankow, Ch'ang-sha, Chungking, and Cheng-tu as a free lance writer. Note

Kinberg, Naphtali, born in 1948, he received a Ph.D. in 1977 from the University of Michigan for *Hypothetical conditionals in Arabic; a study of "law" clauses*. His writings include *A Lexicon of al-Farrā's terminology in his Qur'ān commentary* (1996), and *Studies in the linguistic structure of classical Arabic* (2001). He died in 1997. In 1999 appeared *Compilation and creation in adab and luġa; studies in memory of Naphtali Kinberg*, edited by Albert Arazi. Selim[3]; ZKO

Kind (KИНД), Carl/Karl, born 7 October 1799 at Leipzig, he graduated from the Landesschule Pforta, and subsequently studied and completed his law at the Universität Leipzig, and practised his profession. In 1827 he gained a Dr.jur. at his alma mater for *De jure ecclesiae evangelicae*. In 1835, he became a member of the Faculty of Law at Leipzig, a post which he held until 1856, when he retired in order to pursue his long-standing interest in modern Greek history and literature. His writings include *Beiträge zur besseren Kenntniß des neuen Griechenlands in historisch-geographischer und* *literarischer* Beziehung (1831), *Neugriechische Chrestomathie* (1835), and *Anthologie neugriechischer Volkslieder* (1861). He died in Leipzig on 7 December 1868. ADtB; DcBiPP (not sighted); DtBE; Megali, vol. 14 (1930), p. 440; NDB

Kindermann, Hans, born 26 July 1902 in Prussia, he received a Dr.phil. in 1934 from the Universität Bonn for *"Schiff" im Arabischen; Untersuchungen über Vorkommen und Bedeutung der Termini*. He was a lecturer in Semitic languages and Islamic subjects at the Universität Köln. His writings include the translation, *Über die guten Sitten beim Essen und Trinken; das ist das 11. Buch von al-Ġazālīs Hauptwerk* (1964). He died in Köln on 29 December 1979. Hanisch; HbDtWiss; Kürschner, 1966-1980; Sezgin

King, Christopher Rolland, born 25 September 1938 at Taunton, Mass., he received a Ph.D. in 1974 from the University of Wisconsin for his thesis, *The Nagari Prachanrini Sabha of Benares, 1893-1914*. Thereafter he was a professor in the Department of Asian Studies of the University of Windsor, Ontario. DrASCan, 1978; IWWAS, 1976/77; LC

King, David Anthony, born 12 August 1939 at Durban, South Africa, he was a graduate of St. John's College, Johannesburg, and received a first Ph.D. in 1963 from the University of the Witwatersrand, and a second one in 1972 from Yale University, New Haven, Conn., for *The Astronomical works of Ibn Yunus*. He successively taught Near Eastern languages and literatures and history of science at New York University, physical chemistry at Cambridge University, served as a field director of the Smithsonian Institution Project in Medieval Islamic Astronomy, as chief scientific adviser to the UK Government, and as director of the Institut für Geschichte der Naturwissenschaften, Frankfurt am Main. His writings include *Spherical astronomy in medieval Islam* (1978), and a collection of his articles, *Islamic astronomical instruments* (1987). IntWW, 1992/93-2005; Kürschner, 1992-2005; Note; Selim; Who, 1979-2005

King, David James Cathcart, born 10 April 1913, his writings include *Llanstephan Castle, Carmarten-shire* (1963), *Castellarium Anglicanum* (1983), and *The Castle in England and Wales* (1991). He died on 29 September 1989. LC

King, Geoffrey Robert Derek, born in 1949, he received a M.Phil. in 1972 from the School of Oriental and African Studies, London, for *The Mosque Bab Mardum; its form and purpose in the 10th cent.*, and also a Ph.D. in 1976 for *The Origins and sources of the Umayyad mosaics in the Great Mosque of Damascus*. He was a senior lecturer in Islamic art at SOAS, and a sometime research fellow, King Saud University, Riyadh. From 1989 to 1992 he was a director of the British Archaeological Project at Julfār, subsequently doing archaeological field-work in the Yemen, particularly in the neighbourhood of Aden and Wādī Abyan, 1993-94. He also served as academic director of the SOAS/Sotheby's Asian Arts Programme. His writings include *The Historical mosques of Saudi Arabia* (1986), *A Survey of Islamic sites near Aden and in the Abyan district of Yemen* (1996), *The Traditional architecture of Saudi Arabia* (1998), and he edited *Land use and settlement patterns*; papers of the second Workshop on Late Antiquity and Early Islam (1994). LC; *MESA Roster of* members, 1982-1990; Sluglett; SOAS *Calendar*, SOAS *Library catalogue*; ZKO

King, Georgiana Goddard, born 5 August 1871 at West Columbia, W.Va., she was a graduate of Bryn Mawr (Pa.) College and became a teacher whose writings include *The Bryn Mawr spelling book* (1909), *Mudéjar* (1927), and she edited *Some account of Gothic architecture in Spain*, by George E. Street (1914). She died in Hollywood on 4 May 1939. AmAu&B; DcNAA; Master (2); WhNAA

King, Gilian, fl. 20th cent., he published in the series, *Chatam House essays* the monography, *Imperial outpost; Aden, its place in British strategical policy* (London, 1964).

King, James Roy, born 16 June 1926, he received a Ph.D. in English in 1952 from the University of Pennsylvania for *A study of the relationship of thematic and stylistic variation in Jeremy Taylor's prose*. He was from 1978 to 1990, a professor of English at Wittenberg University, Springfield, Ohio. His writings include *Studies in six 17th century writers* (1966), and he was a joint author of *The Middle East, crossroads of civilization* (1973), and *Islam; a survey of the Muslim faith* (1980). MESA *Roster of members*, 1982-1990

King, James Stewart, born 15 May 1848, he was educated at Fairfield, Wexford, Dublin University, and the Royal Military College, Sandhurst, and subsequently served with the Bombay Staff Corps until his retirement in 1892 with the rank of major. His writings include *Descriptive and historical account of the British outpost of Perim, Straits of Báb el Mándeb* (1877), and *The History of the Bahmani Dynasty* (1900). Buckland; Henze

King, Sir Lucas White, born in 1856, he was educated at Ennis College, and Dublin University. He entered the Indian Civil Service in 1878 and served as a political officer in India. From 1905 to his retirement in 1922 he was a professor of Oriental languages at Dublin, concurrrently serving as a Justice of the Peace. His writings include the edition and translation of Sa'dī's *Odes, Badāyi'*, with an introduction by R. A. Nicholson (Berlin, 1926). He died in 1925. Buckland; IndianBilnd (3); Kornrumpf², vol. 2; Riddick; *Who was who*, 2

King, Noel Quiton, born 9 December 1922 in India, he graduated in 1947 at Oxford, and received a Ph.D. in 1954 from the University of Nottingham. He successively taught comparative religion at the University of Nottingham, Makerere University, Uganda, and University of California at Santa Barbara. His writings include *The Emperor Theodorius and the establishment of Christianity* (1960), *Religions in Africa; pilgrimage into traditional religions* (1970), *Christian and Muslim in Africa* (1971), and jointly with A. B. K. Kasozi, *Islam and the confluence of religions in Uganda, 1840-1966* (1973), and he was a joint translator of *Ibn Battuta in Black Africa* (1975). ConAu, 1-4, new rev., 4, 19; DrAS, 1974 H, 1978 H, 1982 H; WhoRel, 1975, 1977, 1985, 1992

King, Russel(l), born 20th cent., he was associated with the Centre for Middle Eastern and Islamic Studies, University of Durham, and the Department of Geography, Trinity College, Dublin. His writings include *Visions of the world and language of maps* (1990), and he was a joint author of the *Bibliography of Oman, 1900-1970* (1973), *Bibliography of Saudi Arabia* (1973), and *Sunset lives; British retirement migration to the Mediterranean* (2000). Note

King, William Joseph Harding, born in 1869 in England, he was a graduate of Jesus College, Cambridge, who travelled a great deal in North Africa, experiences which are described in his *A Search for the masked Tawareks* (1903), and *Mysteries of the Lybian Desert* (1925). He died in 1933. AfrBioInd (1); WhE&EA; *Who was who*, 3; ZKO

Kingsford, W. E., born 19th cent., he was in 1925 a president of the British Union in Egypt. Note

Kingsmill, Thomas William, born in 1837, he was educated privately. He became an architect, and was largely engaged in exploration and survey work in China, especially geological. He made a special study of ancient literature and history of China, and contributed to knowledge of Central Asian ethnography. He died in 1910. Cordier; *Who's who in the Far East*, 1906/7 = BritInd = ChineseBilnd

Kiniapina, Nina Stepanovna, born 10 December 1920 at Kadom, Russia, she became a professor of nineteenth and twentieth century Russian history at Moscow State University. Her writings include *Внешняя политика России первой половины XIX в.* (1963), *Внешняя политика России второй половины XIX в.* (1974), *Балканы и проливы во внешней политике России в конце XIX века, 1878-1898* (1994), and she was a joint author of *Кавказ и Средняя Азия во внешней политике России вторая половина XVIII-80-е годы XIX в.* (1984). OSK; Schoeberlein

Kinnear, James E., he was in 1936 a secretary of the Nile Mission Press. Note about the author

Kinneir, Sir John Macdonald, born 3 February 1782 John Macdonald, he used his mother's surname, Kinneir, in his publications. (His and Sir John Malcolm's wife were sisters). He entered the Honorable East India Company as an ensign in the Madras Native Infantry. In 1824 he was nominated an envoy to Tehran with the rank of colonel. But it was not until two years later that he finally arrived there. He played an important role as peace-maker between the Persians and the Russians and was rewarded for his services with a knighthood and decoration and presents from both parties. His writings include *A Geographical memoir of the Persian Empire* (1813), *Journey through Asia Minor, Armenia, and Koordistan in the years 1813 and 1814* (1818), and its translation, *Reise durch Klein-Asien* (1821). He died in Tabriz on 11 June 1830. Kamran Eqbal edited the *Briefwechsel Abbas Mirzas mit dem britischen Gesandten Macdonald Kinneir im Zeichen des zweiten russisch-persischen Krieges, 1825-1828* (1977). Buckland; DNB; IndianBilnd (1); Kornrumpf; Wright

Kinney, Miss Mary E., born 27 October 1874 at Boston, Mass., she was for thirty years a missionary under the American Board of Commissioners for Foreign Missions, and a teacher at Adapazarı, and a principal of the American Academy for Girls in Scutari (Üsküdar). She died in Istanbul on 8 February 1930. Kornrumpf ; Note about the author

Kinross, Albert, born in 1870, he was a newspaper correspondent, journal editor, and art and drama critic until 1907, when he became a free-lance writer of novels. He joined the Army at the outbreak of the European War, serving for five years in France, Greece, Egypt, and Palestine. He retired with the rank of captain. He died in 1929. Master (3); *Who was who*, 3

Kinross, 3rd Baron of Glasclune, John Patrick Douglas Balfour, born in 1904, he was educated at Winchester, and graduated B.A. in 1925 from Balliol College, Oxford. He was a newspaper editor who travelled extensively in the Muslim world. After the second World War, he was a director of publicity at the British Embassy, Cairo. His writings include *Lords of the Equator* (1937), *Within the Taurus* (1955),

Portrait of Greece (1956), *Atatürk; the rebirth of a nation* (1964), *The Portrait of Egypt* (1966), *Between two seas* (1968), *Hagia Sophia* (1976), and *The Ottoman centuries; the rise and fall of the Turkish Empire* (1977). He died in 1976. Au&Wr, 1963; BioIn, 11; ConAu, 65-68, new rev., 6; WhE&EA; *Who was who*, 7

Kinzelbach, Gottlob *Theodor*, born 24 June 1822 at Stuttgart, Germany, the son of a renown maker of astronomical instruments, a trade which also the son learned and practised. After having worked in Germany and Switzerland, he realized a long entertained desire and settled in Constantinople in 1854. He subsequently travelled in the Ottoman Empire, partly as an official of the Austrian consulate. Upon his return to Germany in 1860, he joined Martin T. von Heuglin's search expedition to Central Africa to ascertain the fate of the traveller Ernst Vogel and recover his papers. He prematurely parted company with von Heuglin and travelled with Werner Munzinger to Kordofan by way of Khartoum, whence he returned home in 1862. He there spent two years learning Oriental languages and in 1864 went to Cairo. Two years later, he participated in the search expedition for Baron Carl Cl. von der Decken, then went in 1867 by way of Zanzibar to Barawa and Mogadishu, where died at the end of January 1868, physically and mentally ruined by his strenuous and unsuccessful travels. He was a joint author of *Die deutsche Expedition in Ost-Afrika, 1861 und 1862* (1864). ADtB; AfrBioInd (1); DtBiInd (1); Embacher; Henze; Hill; Kornrumpf; Kornrumpf², vol. 2

Kipling, John *Lockwood*, born in 1837 at Pickering, Yorkshire, England, he was educated at Woodhouse Grove. He became a teacher of architectural sculpture at the Bombay School of Art from 1865 to 1875, when he became principal of Mayo School of Art, and subsequently served until 1893 as curator of the Central Museum, Lahore. His writings include *Beast and man in India* (1891). He died in 1911. BioIn, 12, 15; Buckland; Master (4); Peppin; Riddick; *Who was who*, 1

Kippenberg, Hans *Gerhard*, born 5 February 1939 at Bremen, Germany, he received a Dr.phil. in 1968 from the Universität Göttingen for *Garizim und Synagoge; traditionsgeschichtliche Untersuchung zur samaritanischen Religion der aramäischen Periode*, a work which was published in 1971. He successively taught history and comparative religion in various capacities in the Seminar für Iranistik, Freie Universität Berlin, Rijksuniversiteit te Groningen, and Universität Bremen. His writings include *Neue Ansätze in der Religionswissenschaft* (1983), *Struggles of gods* (1984), *Die Entdeckung der Religionsgeschichte; Religionswissenschaft und Moderne* (1997), and he was a joint author of *Einführung in die Religionswissenschaft* (2003). In 2004 appeared *Religion im kulturellen Diskurs; Festschrift für Hans G. Kippenberg zu seinem 65. Geburtstag*. Kürschner, 1980-2005; Private

Kirakos, Gandzaketsi, born 1201, he was an Armenian historian, who, in his history of Armenia, relates the Khwarizm and Mongol-Tatar invasions of Armenia. His writings include *Deux historiens arméniens, Kiracos de Gantzac, Histoire d'Arménie; Oukhtanes d'Ourha, Histoire en trois parties*, traduits par Marie Félicité Brosset (St. Petersbourg, 1870-71), and *Извлечнïи из истории Киракоса Гандзакеци*, edited by K. P. Patkanov (1874). He died about 1272. GSE; NUC, pre-1956

Kiralfy, Alexander, fl. 1939-42, he was educated in American, Canadian, English, and French schools, and received his military training in an officers' training body in the United States. His extensive travels and proficiency in many languages aided his frequent contributions on naval and military problems to *Asia and the Americas*. A member of the United States Naval Institute, his writings include *Victory in the Pacific; how we must defeat Japan* (1942). Note about the author

Király, Péter, born 22 November 1917 at Málca (now Slovakia), he was a Hungarian philologist who received a doctorate in 1973. His writings include *A keletszlovák nyelvjárás nyomtatott emlékei* (1953), *Ismeretlen magyar glosszák* (1959), *Particles and fields in space* (1974), *Hungaro-Slavic* (1988), *Унгарска българистика* (Sofia, 1988), *A nyelvkeveredés* (2001), *A kelet-közép-európai helyesírások és irodalmi nyelvek alakulása* (2003), and he edited *Topographia Universitatis Hungaricae Budae, 1777-1848* (1983). Biograf, 2002, 2004; MagyarNKK, 1990-2000

Kiray, Mübeccel Belik, he was born on 21 February 1923 at Izmir, Turkey. After obtaining a Ph.D. degree in 1950 from Northwestern University, Evanston, Illinois, he taught at the Middle East Technical University, Ankara. His writings include *Yedi yerleşemeyen noktasında turizmle ilgili sosyal yapı analizi* (1964), *Örgütleşemeyen kent* (1972); and he was joint author of *Social stratification as an obstacle to development; a study of four Turkish villages* (1970). Kim kimdir, 1985/86

Kircher, Heidi *Gisela*, born about 1936, she received a Dr.phil. in 1966 from the Universität Bonn for her thesis, *Die "einfachen Heilmittel" aus dem "Handbuch der Chirurgie" des Ibn al-Quff*. She was a joint author of *Islamische Funde in Balaguer und die Aljafería in Zaragoza* (1971), and its translation, *Hallazgos islámicos en Balaguer y la Aljafería de Zaragoza* (1979). Schwarz

Kirchhammer, Alexander, born 27 February 1847 at Milano, he graduated in engineering from the Genieakademie, Wien, and in 1866 joined the 2nd Genieregiment as a lieutenant. He later transferred to the Department of Military History at the K.K. Kriegsarchiv, Wien. After his retirement with the rank of general, he remained active as a journalist. He edited *Feldzüge des Prinzen Eugen von Savoyen nach den Feld-Acten und anderen authentischen Quellen* (1885). He died in Wien on 18 February 1909. ÖBL

Kirchhoff, Alfred, born 23 May 1838 at Erfurt, Germany, he studied mainly natural sciences, but also history, at the universities of Jena and Bonn. From 1861 to 1873 he taught successively at high schools in Mühlheim/Ruhr, Erfurt, and Berlin, concurrently lecturing during the last two years in geography at the war academy (Kriegsakademie), Berlin. From 1873 to his retirement in 1904 he was a professor of geography at the Universität Halle. He died in Mockau near Leipzig on 8 February 1907. DtBE; DtBiInd (10); Geog, vol. 4, pp. 69-76

Kirchmair, Heinrich, born 1 April 1906 at Lübeck, Germany, he studied medicine, and became a professor successively at the universities of Hamburg, Würzburg, Berlin, and Rostock. From 1952 to 1955, he served as a medical consultant to the Iraqi Ministry of Health, and as a professor of pediatrics at Baghdad University. Kürschner, 1950-1976|; *Wer ist wer*, 1955, 1958

Kirdetsov, G., born 19th cent., his writings include *У ворот Петрограда, 1919-1920 г.г.* (Moscow, 1921), and the translation *Синдикализмъ*, of Enrico Leone (Moscow, 1907). NUC, pre-1956, 1968-72

Kireev, Akhnaf Nurievich, 1912-1984 *see* Kirei Mèrgèn

Kireev, Nikolai Gavrilovich, born 20 September 1929, he graduated in 1954 from the Faculty of History, Moscow State University, received his first degree in 1966 for a thesis on «*Национальные и иностранный капитал во внешней торговле Турции*» (a work which was published in 1968), and a doctorate in 1983 for *Развитие капитализма в Турции*. From 1955 to 1958 he was a research fellow at the All-State Library of Foreign Literature; he subsequently became associated with the Oriental Institute of the Soviet Academy of Sciences. He was a trade commissioner in Turkey, 1962-1964 and 1967-1969. His writings include *Анкара* (1972), *Турция вчера и сегодня* (1977), and *История этатизма в Турции* (1991). Miliband²

Kirei, Nikolaĭ Ivanovich, born 20th cent., his writings include *Алжир и Франция, 1962-1971* (1973), and he edited *Историографические исследования по африканистике и востоковедению; сборник научных трудов* (1986), *Проблемы археологии и этнографии Северного Кавказа; сборник научных трудов* (1988), and *Археологические и этнографические исследования Северного Кавказа; сборник научных трудов* (1994). OSK

Kirei Mèrgèn (Кирей Мэргэн or Ахнаф Нуриевич Киреев or Кирэи Мэргэн), born 11 July 1912 in Ufa Oblast, he graduated in 1949 from the Bashkir State Pedagogical Institute and received a doctorate in 1963. From 1965 to 1982 he was a professor of Bashkir literature and folklore at Bashkir State University. His writings include *Мэннгэнлек шиише* (1978), and he edited *Башкорт халык ижады* (1980). He died 24 January 1984. BashkKE; LC

Kirfel, Willibald, born 24 January 1885 at Reifferscheid/Eifel, Germany, he studied Oriental languages and Catholic theology at the Universität Bonn, where he received a Dr.phil. in 1908 for *Beiträge zur Geschichte der Nominalkomposition in den Upanisads und im Epos*. He was a librarian at the Universitätsbibliothek Bonn until he received Dr.habil. for *Die Kosmographie der Inder nach den Quellen dargestellt* in 1920, when he was appointed to the chair of Indian studies at his alma mater. His writings include *Der Rosenkranz; Ursprung und Ausbreitung* (1949), and *Kleine Schriften* (1976). He died in Bad Godesberg on 16 October 1964. DtBE; DtBiInd (4); Kürschner; NDB

Kirillina, Svetlana Alekseevna, born 20th cent., she wrote *Ислам в общественной жизни Египта; вторя половина XIX- начало XX в.* (Moscow, 1989). OSK

Kiripolská, Marta, born 27 April 1952 at Liptovský-Mikuláš, she was a Mongolian scholar at Prague University. Her writings include *King Arthasiddhi; a Mongolian translation of "The younger brother Don Yod"*; introduction, transcription with notes and facsimile of the Copenhagen manuscript Mong. 101 (Wiesbaden, 2001). Filipsky

Kirk, George Eden, born 3 February 1911 at Mansfield, Nottinghamshire, England, he was a Queen's College, Cambridge, graduate who was a research fellow at the British School of Archaeology at Athens. He taught modern Middle Eastern politics in Lebanon and America until 1966, when he began teaching his first love, ancient history, as a professor at the University of Massachusetts, Amherst. He was a meticulous scholar who held strong opinions about imperialism and nationalism in the Middle East, challenging many of the ideas fashionable among his students at the time. His writings include *A Short history of the Middle East* (1948), its translation, *Kurze Geschichte des Nahen Ostens* (1958), *The Middle East in war* (1952), and *Contemporary Arab politics; a concise history* (1961). He died of cancer on 18 February 1993 in Amherst.   Au&Wr, 1963, 1971; ConAu, 1-4; DrAS, 1969 H, 1974 H, 1978 H, 1982 H; *MESA bulletin*, 27 (1993), p. 154 (A. Goldschmidt); MidE, 1978/79-1982/83; Note

Kirk, Grayson Louis, born 18 October 1903 at Jeffersonville, Ohio, he graduated in 1924 from Miami (Ohio) University and received a Ph.D. in 1930 from the University of Wisconsin. He became a professor of government and a university administrator. His writings include *Philippine independence; motives, problems, and prospects* (1936), and *Uniting today for tomorrow* (1942). He died on 22 May 1995.   AmM&WSc, 1973 S; CurBio, 1951; IntAu&W, 1977; IntWW, 1974/75-1996/97; IntYB, 1978-82; Master (14); WhAm, 12; Who, 1974-1995; WhoA,, 1974-1994; WhoWor, 1974/75-1982/83

Kirk, Robert, born 26 January 1905 in Scotland, he received an M.D. in 1940 from the University of Glasgow for *The epidemiology of relapsing fever in the Anglo-Egyptian Sudan.* He became a professor of pathology, and dean, Faculty of Medicine in University College of Khartoum.   Sluglett; WhoEgypt, 1955

Kirk, Rupert, born 4 October 1806, he was a sometime assistant surgeon with the Bombay Establishment. He participated in the mission to Abyssinia, 1841-43, and the Afghanistan campaign of 1839-40. He died in Rajkot, Kathiawar, on 31 May 1852. IndianBilnd (1)

Kirkbride, Sir Alec Seath, born in 1897, he was a Mandatory administrator in the Middle East and a representative of HM Government to the Permanent Mandates Commission, Genève. His writings include *A Crackle of thorns; experiences in the Middle East* (1956), *An Awakening; the Arab campaign, 1917-18* (1972), and *From the wings; Amman memoirs, 1947-51* (1976). He died in 1978. Au&Wr, 1963, 1971; DNB; Who, 1959-1978; *Who was who*, 7; WrDr, 1974/76-1976/78

Kirketerp-Møller, Helge, born 17 May 1899 at Grinderslevkloster, Denmark, he was a barrister and from 1940 to 1973 an assistant in the Copenhagen Byrets Skifteret. He was a sometime member of the governing body of the Society of the Book Trade (Forening for Boghåndværk) as well as the Dansk Bibliofil-Klub. His writings include *Slægten Kirketerp-Møller* (København, 1971). He died on 17 November 1983. Kraks, 1983

Kirketerp-Møller, Hertha, born 20th cent., her writings include *Det islamiske bogmaleri* (København, 1974). LC

Kirkman, James Spedding, born 22 October 1906 at London, he graduated in 1928 from Caius College, Cambridge. He is best remembered as a pioneer in East African coastal archaeology. His writings include *The Arab city of Gedi* (1954), *Gedi, the palace* (1963), *Men and monuments on the East African coast* (1964), *Fort Jesus, a Portuguese fortress on the East African coast* (1974), and he edited *City of San'à, nomad and city exhibition* (1976). In 1982 appeared *From Zinj to Zanzibar; studies in history, trade and society on the Eastern Coast of Africa in honour of James Kirkman on the occasion of his seventy-fifth birthday.* He died on 26 April 1989. ConAu, 93-96, 128; *Kenya past and present*, 2 i (1973), pp. 40-41 (not sighted); *Paideuma*, 28 (1982), pp. 3-6 (not sighted)

Kirkpatrick, James Achilles, born in 1764, he was educated in France and at Eton. He joined the East India Company's Madras Army in 1780 and participated in the Mysore war, 1791-92. In the following year, he was in charge of the garrison at Vizianagram. A Resident at Hyderabad since 1795, he brought the Nizam of Hyderabad's continent of 60,000 men into the field against Tippoo Sultan. He died while still Resident at Hyderabad, on a visit to Calcutta on 15 October 1805. *Asiatic annual register*, 7 (1805), pp. 51-56; Buckland

Kirkpatrick, William, born in 1754, he joined the Bengal Infantry in 1773, and became a major-general in 1811. He was Persian interpreter to General Stibbert. For periods between 1777 and 1785, he was commander-in-chief in Bengal. In the Mysore war, 1791-92, he was Persian interpreter with Lord Cornwallis. After the fall of Seringapatam in 1799, he was made a commissioner for the partition of Mysore. Well versed in Oriental languages and Indian folklore, he translated Tippoo Sultan's diary and letters from the Persian. He died 22 August 1812. Buckland; DNB; Henze; Mason

Kirpichenko, Valeriia Nikolaevna, born 11 January 1930, she graduated in 1962 from the Oriental Institute, Moscow State University, received her first degree in 1970 for a thesis on «Творчество путь египетская новеллиста Юсуфа Идриса», and a doctorate in 1986 for *Египетская проза 60-70-х годов XX века.* Since 1974 she was associated with the Oriental Institute of the Soviet Academy of Sciences. Her writings include *Живи, Египет!* (1973), *Военное дело на Руси в XIII-XV вв.* (1976), *Юсуф Идрис* (1980), *Современная египетская проза* (1986); she was a joint author of *Викинги и славяне* (1998); and she edited *Славяне и финно-угри* (1997). Miliband²; OSK

Kirpichnikov, Anatoliĭ Nikolaevich, born 20th cent., he was a writer on arms and armory. His writings include *Древнерусское оружие* (1966), *Великая государева крепость* (1972), *Снаряжение всадника и верхового коня на Руси IX-XIII вв* (1973), *Военное дело на Руси в XIII-XV вв.* (1976),

Куликовская битва (1980), and he edited *Метательная артиллерия и оборонительные сооружения древней Руси* (1958).   Note about the author

Kirsch, Ottfried Conrad, born about 1937, he received a doctorate in agronomy in 1967 from the Universität Hohenheim for *Siedlungsgenossenschaften in West-Pakistan als besondere Genossenschaftsform*.   His writings on Third World coorporatives include *Formen und Funktionen ländlicher Genossenschaften in Entwicklungsländern; Kenia* (1969), *Agrarian reform in China* (1994), *Equitisation of agribusiness in Vietnam* (1999), and jointly with Johannes G. F. Wörz, *Genossenschaftliche Produktionsförderung in Ägypten* (1978), and its translation, *Cooperative promotion of products in Egypt* (1985).   GV

Kirste, Johann Otto Ferdinand, born 1 October 1851 at Graz, Austria, he studied classical philology and Sanskrit at the universities of Graz, Jena, Leipzig, Berlin, and Wien, where he received a Dr.phil. in 1876.   From 1881 to 1884, he studied Indo-Iranian languages at the École pratique des hautes études, Paris, followed by some months' immersion in the Slavic world at Beograd.   Since 1886, he taught comparative Indo-European linguistics, and Sanskrit at Wien, and since 1892 at the Universität Graz. During his last years he collaborated with the research in the languages of Eastern Turkestan.   His writings include *Die constitutionellen Verschiedenheiten der Verschlußlaute im Indogermanischen* (1881), *Die Bedeutung der orientalischen Philologie* (1892), *Die altindischen Platten* (1908), and *Kleine Schriften* (1993). He died in Graz on 2 May 1920.   DtBE; DtBilnd (2); NDB; ÖBL

Kirsten (Kirstenius), Petrus (Petrus/Piotr), born 25 December 1577 at Breslau, Austrian Silesia, he was educated at Posen and studied physics, botany and medicine at the universities of Leipzig, Wittenberg and Jena, and Arabic in France and the Netherlands.   In 1601 he received a doctorate at the Universität Basel. Aware of Avicenna's writings on medicine, he pursued a lifelong interest in Arabic for professional reasons, and maintained a private Arabic printing office at Breslau. He knew Hebrew from his student days, and had learnt Arabic probably from Christian Arabs on his travels. With the few and poor learning tools available to him, in addition to his professional duties, he cannot be expected to have done more than he did. He was a director of the schools of Breslau, from 1610 to 1616, when he resigned this post and again practised his profession, declining several offers as private physician to Austrian high nobility. He left Breslau about 1634 and went to Prussia, where he made the acquaintance of the Swedish chancellor Oxenstierna, who brought him in 1635 or 1636 to Uppsala to become a royal court physician and a professor of medicine at the university.   He died there on 8 April 1640.   His writings include *Grammatices arabicae, liber I-III* (Breslau, 1608-09), the last part of which containing the *Ājurrūmīyah* of the Rome edition, with Latin translation and notes, and the *Liber secundus De canone canonis a filio Sina* (Breslau, 1610), and *Notae in evangelium S. Matthaei ex collatione textuum Arabicorum Ægyptiac[um] Hebræa[um] Syriacor[m] Græcor[um] Latinor[um]* (1611). ADtB, vol. 16, pp. 34-35; DcBiPP (not sighted); DtBilnd (2), Dziekan; Fück, pp. 57-58; SBL; SMK

Kirwan, Sir Archibald *Laurence* Patrick, born 13 May 1907 in Ireland, he received a B.Litt. in 1935 from Merton College, Oxford, for his thesis, *Lower Nubia in the early Byzantine period*.   He was notable as director and secretary of the Royal Geographical Society for thirty years, but also as a distinguished archaeologist in Sudan, Nubia and the Aden Protectorate.   In 1929 he was involved with the rescue of Nubian sites threatened by the first Aswan High Dam. From 1934 to 1937 he was director of excavations in the Sudan where his most valuable discoveries, concerned with the Meroitic civilization, were made at Ballana and Qustal.   As president of the British Institute of Eastern Africa, he also encouraged interest in that region's wider contacts up the Red Sea and across the Indian Ocean.   He was a joint author of *Studies on the history of late antique and Christian Nubia* (2002).   He died in Ireland in March 1999.   Au&Wr, 1963; BlueB, 1975, 1976; *Bulletin* of the ASTENE, 8 (October 1999), p. 14; ConAu, 1-4, 177, new rev., 70; Sluglett; Who, 1965-1999; WhoWord, 1974/75, 1976/77

Kisch, Izaak, born 23 November 1905 at Amsterdam, he studied law at Amsterdam, Paris, and the London School of Economics, gaining a doctorate in 1932 at Amsterdam for *Beschouwingen over de onderscheiding tusschen zakelijke en personlijke rechten*. Since 1935 he taught law at the Universiteit van Amsterdam.   His writings include *Huwelijken van Nederlanders in het buitenland en van vreemdelingen in Nederland* (1935), and *Uitgelezen opstellen* (1981).   He died on 29 July 1980. BiBenelux² (1); IntWW, 1974/75-1977; WhoNL, 1962/63; WhoWor, 1974/75; Wie, 1956

Kiselev, Sergeĭ Vladimirovich, fl. 20th cent., his writings include *Разложение рода и феодализм на Енисее* (1933), *Древняя история южной Сибири* (1949), *Древнемонгольские города* (1965), *Новое в советской археологии* (1965), and he edited *Очерки по истории алтайчев* (1953). OSK

Kiselev, Vladimir Ivanovich, born 18 November 1924 in Ryazan Oblast, Russia, he graduated in 1948 from the Oriental Institute, Moscow, and received his first degree in 1954 for *Национально-освободительное движение в Судан после второй мировой войны*. He was since 1954 affiliated with the Oriental Institute in the Soviet Academy of Sciences. His writings include *Путь Судана к независимости* (1958), *Арабский мир* (1964), *СССР и Арабский Восток* (1971), and *Палестинская проблема и ближневосточный кризис* (1983). Miliband; Miliband²

Kiseleva, Lidia Nikolaevna Dorofeeva, born 26 December 1922 at Barnaul on the Turkestan-Siberian railway, she graduated in 1945 from the Oriental Institute, Moscow, and received a doctorate in 1955 for her thesis, *Опит лексико-грамматической характеристики кабули*. Thereafter she was a researcher at the Oriental Institute of the Soviet Academy of Sciences. Her writings include *Дари-русский словарь* (1978), *Язык дари Афганистана* (1985), and under the name L. N. Dorofeeva, *Язык фарси-кабули* (1960). She died on 15 April 1990. LC; Miliband; Miliband²

Kishibekov (Кішібеков/Кшибеков), Dosmukhambet, 1925- *see* Kshibekov, Dosmukhamed

Kisliakov, Nikolai Andreevich, born in 1901 at St. Petersburg, he received his first degree in 1935 for «Следы первобытного коммунизма у горных таджиков Вахиоболо» and his doctorate in 1951 for *Семья и брак у таджиков*. He was from 1943 to 1945 in diplomatic mission in Iran. His writings include *Патриархально-феодальные отношения среди оседлого сельского населения Бухарского ханства в конце XIX - начале XX века* (1962), and *Очерк по истории семьи и брака у народов Средней Ахии и Казахстана* (1969). He died on 8 October 1973. Miliband; Miliband²; UzbekSE

Kisliakov, Vladimir Nikolaevich, born 20 September 1946 at Leningrad, he received his first degree in 1983 for *История этнографического изучнеия народов Ближнего и Среднего Востока в русской и советской науке*. Since 1973 he was associated with the Institute of Ethnography, Soviet Academy of Sciences. Miliband²

Kislov, A., born in 1929, he was on the staff of the Institute of USA and Canada, Moscow, and a specialist in US foreign policy. He was a joint author of *USA and the Islamic world* (New Delhi, 1984). LC

Kissling, Hans Joachim, born 8 September 1912, at München, he studied Turkology, Islamic subjects, and law at the universities of München, Wien, and Breslau, and received a Dr.phil. in 1936 from the Universität Breslau for *Die Sprache des 'Asıkpasazade*. He subsequently obtained an assistantship at the Universität Leipzig until called to the colours in 1940. He received a Dr.habil. in 1956 for *Beiträge zur Kenntnis Trakiens im 17. Jahrhundert*. From 1955 to his retirement he was a professor in the Institut für Geschichte und Kultur des Nahen Orients, Universität München. His writings include *Osmanisch-türkische Grammatik* (1960), and *Rechtsproblematik in den christlich-muslimischen Beziehungen vorab im Zeitalter der Türkenkriege* (1974). He died on 10 October 1985. Hanisch; *Index Islamicus* (4); Kürschner, 1950-1983; Schwarz; *Südost-Forschungen*, 45 (1986), pp. 237-39

Kister, Meir Jacob, born in 1914, he studied at the Hebrew University, Jerusalem. His writings include *Tamim in the period of the Jahiliyya; a study in tribal tradition* (1964), a work which is a chapter from his Ph.D. thesis submitted at the Hebrew University, Jerusalem; he also published selections from the Koran translated into Hebrew (1963), *Hikre mizrah* (1979), two collections of his selected articles, *Studies in Jahiliyya and early Islam* (1980), and *Society and religion from Jahiliyya to Islam* (1990); and he edited *Ādāb al-suhbah*, of Muhammad ibn al-Husayn al-Sulamī (1954). In 1987 appeared *Jahiliyya and Islamic studies in honour of M. J. Kister septuagenarian*. LC

Kitaigorodskii, Paltièl Vol'kovich, born in 1883 in Russia, his writings include *Алжир, Тунис, Марокко в борьбе за независимость* (1925), *Египет в борьбе за независимость* (1925), *Сирия в огне восстаний* (1925), and *Түркҳе* (Baku, 1930). He died on 23 November 1956. Miliband; Miliband²

Kitchen, Helen Angell, born 28 June 1920 at Fossil, Ore., she graduated in 1942 from the University of Oregon. She lived in Cairo from 1944 to 1947, during part of which time she was a member of the Research and Analysis Branch of the (U.S.) Office of Strategic Services and was later attached to the American Embassy. In 1947 she joined the staff of the *Middle East journal*, Washington, D.C., becoming its editor-in-chief from 1960 to 1967. She later became associated with Georgetown University, Washington, D.C. Her writings include *The Press in Africa* (1956), *Footnotes to the Congo story* (1967), and she edited *Americans and the Middle East, partners in the next decade* (1950), *The Educated African* (1962), and *The Defence of white power; South African foreign policy under pressure* (1988). ConAu, 9-12, new rev., 8, 23, 47; Master (1); WhoAmW, 1968/69

Kitchener, Horatio Herbert, born 24 June 1850, he was educated at the Royal Military Academy, Woolwich, and subsequently joined the Royal Engineers. In 1882, he was appointed to an army command in the Egyptian Army, which he completely reorganized. A British field-marshall, he was widely honoured for his conquests in Africa. He was lost at sea in 1916. Samuel Daiches wrote *Lord Kitchener and his work in Palestine* (1915), Mortimer Menpes, *Lord Kitchener* (1915), and Ernest

Protheroe, *Lord Kitchener* (1916). Buckland; DcAfHiB, 1986; DcTwHis; DNB; Egyptology; EncAm; Goldschmidt; Henze; Hill; Kornrumpf; Master (14); Riddick; *Who was who,* 2

Kittary, Modest IAkovlevich, born in 1824, he gained a doctorate in chemistry in 1848, and taught chemical technology from 1844 to 1857 at Kazan University, and subsequently at Moscow. In 1850 he was appointed a professor. He died in 1880. EnSlovar; TatarES

Kittlaus, Ed., born 19th cent., he was successively a pastor at Buchholz, Nidden, and Gleißen in East Prussia. From 1912 to 1918 he was in charge of the missionary section of the *Mitteilungen* of Geographische Gesellschaft für Thüringen zu Jena. Note

Kiwi, Edith, 1908- *see* Gerson-Kiwi, Esther Edith

Kiwrlek'ian, Hakob *see* Gurlekian, Hagop

Klaczko, Julian (Yehuda), born 6 September 1828 at Vilna (Wilno), Russia, he studied at the universities of Königsberg, and Heidelberg and received a Dr.phil. in 1846. He subsequently collaborated with Gervinus' *Deutsche Zeitung* until 1849, when he went to Paris to join the staff of the *Revue des deux mondes*, concurrently serving as a librarian to the *Corps législatif*. In 1869, he was appointed court and government official with the Austrian Foreign Office. In 1870, he became a member of the Austrian Council of State as well as the Galician Diet. As a Francophile, he pleaded against Austrian neutrality in the Franco-Prussian War. As a consequence, he had to resign his ministerial post in September of 1870. He subsequently spent much of his time in Italy, but also in Paris and Krakau. In 1887, he was elected a corresponding member of the Académie des sciences morales et politiques, Paris. His writings include *Die deutschen Hegemonien* (1849), *Études diplomatiques contemporaines; les cabinets de l'Europe en 1863/64* (1866), *Deux chanceliers* (1876), a work which was translated into English (1876), German (1878), and Polish (1905), *Causeries florentines* (1880), and *Studya dyplomatyczne* (1903-4). He died either on 26 November 1906 in Wien or 27 November 1906 in Krakau. Ferdynand Hoesick wrote *Julian Klaczko; rys życia i prac* (1904), and Jan Bialostock, *Julian Klaczko, (1825-1906), uno storico dell'arte italiana* (1966). BiD&SB; DcCathB (not sighted); JewEnc; JüdLex; ÖBL; Polski (16); Wininger

Klado, N. N., fl. 20th cent., his writings include Декада таджиксой советской литературы в Москве (1950), Туркменская советская драматургия (1956), Таджикская советская драматургия (1957), and he edited Таджикская советская литературы; сборник статей (1954). NUC; OSK

Klaer, Wendelin, born 27 August 1925 at Zwinge, Germany, he took a doctorate in 1955 at the Universität Göttingen for *Verwitterungsbedingte Formen im Granit auf Korsika*, and a Dr.habil. in 1962 for *Untersuchungen zur klimagenetischen Geomorphologie in den Hochgebirgen Vorderasiens.* He became a professor of geography successively at the universities of Heidelberg and Mainz. In 1990 appeared *Festschrift für Wendelin Klaer zum 65. Geburtstag.* GV; Kürschner, 1987-2005

Klaić, Vjekoslav, born 28 July 1849 at Garčin near Slvonskog Broda, Croatia, he first studied theology, becoming an auxiliary teacher at the gymnasium in Varaždin, 1867-69; he subsequently studied history and geography at the Universität Wien, 1869-72, followed by a year's teaching at Agram (Zagreb). In 1884, he started his career at the university, first teaching geography of the southern Slavic countries, and later, general history. His writings include *Bosna* (1878), *Slavonien vom X. bis XI. Jahrhundert* (1882), *Provjest Hrvata od najstarijih vremena do svršetka XIX. stoljeća* (1899-1911), and *Knjižarstvo u Hrvata* (1922). He died in Zagreb on 1 July 1928. DtBilnd (1); EnclZ; GSE; HL; HrvEnc; Мала енциклопедија просвета (Beograd, 1978); ÖBL

Klamroth, Martin, born in 1855 at Fiddichow, Prussia, he studied at the universities of Tübingen, Leipzig, Göttingen, and Straßburg, taking a Dr.phil. in 1878 at Göttingen for *Gregorii Abulfaragii Bar Ebhraya in actus apostolorum et epistulas catholicas*. Since 1880 he was a school teacher at Hamburg. His writings include *Die fünfzig ältesten Suren des Korans in gereimter deutscher Übersetzung* (1890), *Ein Christ; wie ein ostafrikanischer Negerknabe zum Sklaven wurde* (1910), and *Der Islam in Deutsch-Ostafrika* (1912). DtBilnd (1)

Klaproth (Клапрот), Heinrich *Julius* (Jules), born 11 October 1783 at Berlin, he privately studied Chinese while still going to school, publishing his first two articles in 1800. In 1801 he matriculated at the Universität Halle, but in 1802 he was working at a library in Dresden. At the end of this year, he published the first issues of his *Asiatisches Magazin* at Weimar. He returned to Berlin in 1804, but already at the end of the year he accepted an assistantship in Oriental languages at the St. Petersburg Academy of Sciences. In the following year, he participated in Count Golovkin's embassy to China. After the failure of the mission in Ulan Bator, he returned on an individual route, acquiring linguistic and ethnographic expertise as he went along. In 1807, he was knighted for his services and elected

268

member of the St. Petersburg Academy of Sciences. In the service of the Academy he explored Central Asia and the Caucasus, from 1807 to 1809. From 1811 to 1814, he was in Berlin, preparing the results of his exploration for publication. Through the good offices of Alexander von Humboldt, he obtained a professorship in Oriental languages at the Universität Berlin. Relieved of academic duties, he was able to pursue his scholarly interests in Paris. His writings, partly under the pseudonym Louis d'Or and Wilhelm Lauterbach, include *Reise in den Kaukasus und nach Georgien* (1812-14), *Kaukasische Sprachen* (1814), *Abhandlung über die Sprache und Schrift der Uiguren* (1820), *Voyage à Peking à travers la Mongolie en 1820 et 1821* (1827), and *Briefe und Dokumente; Briefwechsel mit Gelehrten* (Wiesbaden, Hassassowitz, 1999-2002). He died in Paris in 1835. ADtB; BiobibSOT; DtBE; DtBiInd (3); Egyptology; Embacher; EnSlovar; Henze; *Index Islamicus* (3); Michaud; VostokMStP, p. 251

Klare, Michael Thomas, born 14 October 1942 at N.Y.C., he graduated in 1963 from Columbia University, New York, and received a Ph.D. in 1976 from Union Graduate School, Cincinnati, Ohio, for *Arms, oil and intervention; U.S. military strategy in the Persian Gulf during the Nixon era.* He subsequently held a great variety of posts *inter alia* professor of peace and world security studies at Hampshire College, Amherst, Mass. His writings include *The University-military complex* (1969), *War without end; American planning for the next Vietnam wars* (1972), its Persian translation, *Jang bī pāyān* (1977-78), *Low intensity warfare* (1988), and *Resource wars; the new landscape of global conflict* (2001). ConAu, 130; Selim²; WhoAm, 1982-2003; WrDr, 1994/96-2005

Klass, Rosanne, born in 1925 at Cedar Rapids, Iowa, she graduated from the University of Wisconsin, and received an M.A. Hunter College. From 1951 to 1954 she lived and taught in Afghanistan, and travelled in the Near East and Europe. The next several years were spent teaching in N.Y.C. public schools. Afterwards she became a free-lance writer; she published poetry and reviews, and in 1959 collaborated in the original idea which eventually became the Balanchine ballet "The figure in the carpet." She wrote *Land of high flags: a travel memoir of Afghanistan* (1964).

Klat, Paul J., born 20th cent., he received a B.Phil. in 1938 from Oxford University for *Land tenure in Syria and Lebanon and its economic effects, with some suggestions for reform.* He was associated with the American University of Beirut. His writings include *The Balance of payments of Lebanon, 1951 and 1952* (1954). His trace is lost after an article in 1962. Note; Sluglett

Klatt, Werner, OBE, born 22 May 1904 at Berlin, he studied agriculture at the Landwirtschaftliche Hochschule, Berlin, taking a doctorate in 1930 for *Die Milchversorgung Groß-Hamburgs.* He followed this with three years' research in agricultural economics. During the 1930s he worked in Berlin in the field of agricultural marketing and as an adviser to firm I. G. Farben. When war broke out, he and his wife took refuge in England and throughout the war he was employed by the British Government as an expert on European food and agriculture. From 1946 to 1949, he was in charge of the Supply Department of the German Section in the Foreign Office in London, working on both Europe and China, with an increasing emphasis on the latter. He retired from the Foreign Office in 1966, and thereafter he was associated with St. Antony's College, Oxford, and with the Contemporary China Institute at the School of Oriental and African Studies, London. His writings include *World sugar industry* (1954), its translation, *La economía mundial del azúcar* (1954), *The Chinese model* (1965), and *Volkswirtschaftliche Gesamtrechnungen für die Volksrepublik China; Ergebnisse westlicher Untersuchungen* (1979). He died on 21 January 1987 at his home in London. BioHbDtE; *China quarterly*, 111 (1987), pp. 473-474; FarE&A, 1978/79-1981

Klebe, Fritz, born 15 September 1896 at Prenzlau, Prussia, he successively studied at the universities of Bonn, Kiel, Berlin, and again Kiel, where he received a Dr.phil. in 1920 for *Beiträge zur islamischen Rechtskunde gegenüber Nichtmuslimen nach türkischen Urkunden aus dem 16. Jahrhundert.* Thesis

Klein, Adalbert, born 2 April 1913 at Düsseldorf, Germany, he received a Dr.phil. in 1940 from the Universität Bonn for *Zum Problem der Farbe; ihr Wesen und ein Teil ihrer Geschichte in der deutschen Malerei.* He became associated with Kunstmuseum, Düsseldorf, and since 1969 he was a director of Hetjens-Museum, Düsseldorf. His writings include *Moderne deutsche Keramik* (1956), *Keramik* (1966), *Das Hetjens-Museum* (1969), and *Islamische Keramik* (1976). He died about 1993. Wer ist wer, 1971/73-1993/94|; WhoWor, 1978/79

Klein (also Klein-Franke), Aviva née Sabri, born in 1936, she was an anthropologist who received a Dr.phil. in 1967 from the Universität Köln for a thesis on Yemenite Jews. In 1999 she was associated with Völkerkundliches Museum, Universität Köln. GV; Note

Klein, Ernst Ferdinand, born 18 April 1863 at Wohlau, Prussian Silesia, he was a pastor under the Deutsche Orient-Mission in Lichtenrade near Berlin and for many years a member of the Board. Since 1909 he was vice-president and in charge of publishing. His writings include *Das Urchristentum und unsere jetzigen Gemeinden* (1907), *Russische Reisetage* (1909), *Zeitbilder aus der Kirchengeschichte* *für die christliche Gemeinde* (Berlin, 1911-12), and *Der Große König und sein Glaube* (1936). GV; KDtLK, 1909-1943|; NUC, pre-1956

Klein, Friedrich August (Frederick Augustus), born 19th cent., he was a missionary who, with Dr. Sandreczky, began the Church Missionary Society's mission in Palestine in 1851. He became renown in Europe by his discovery of the Moabite Stone of Mesha. When the Society had to restrict its work in 1878 for want of means, he was recalled to Europe, but later, in 1882, he had the honour of beginning missionary work under the Society in Egypt. His writings include *The Religion of Islám* (London, 1906). He died in England on 1 December 1903. Kornrumpf ; Kornrumpf², vol. 2; Richter, p. 245

Klein, Ira Norman, born 7 December 1931 at N.Y.C., he graduated in 1956 from the local Columbia University, where he also took his Ph.D. in 1968 for *British imperialism in conflict and alliance; Anglo-French and Anglo-Russia relations in Asia, 1885-1914*. In 1972 he was appointed a professor of modern European and Asian history at the American University, Washington, D.C., a post which he still held in 2002. DrAS, 1969 H, 1974 H, 1978 H, 1982 H; NatFacDr, 1990-2002

Klein, Jules, born in 1894 at Bernhardsweiler, Alsace, he was a graduate of the École apostolique de la Province de Champagne (Belgique). He entered the Jesuits in 1911, but on account of the Great War was ordained only in 1922. He was a superintendent at Cairo, 1923-24, a student of Arabic at Bikfaya, Lebanon, 1924-26. In 1927, he became a director of the schools in Hawrān and the Djebel Druze, visiting the communities on foot or horse, later becoming responsible for the scholarly progress of the students of Arabic and residing in Damascus until 1937, when he was nominated *maître des novices* at Bikfaya. He remained there until he died at the Hôpital de Bhannès on 16 January 1980. He twice served as a deputy rector at Bikfaya, became an official of the Centre religieux d'études arabes, and served as a director-general of the sisters of Saints-Cœurs, 1944-47 and 1950-57. Jalabert, pp. 337-38

Klein-Franke, Aviva, 1936- see Klein, Aviva

Klein-Franke, Felix, born 29 November 1935 at Köln, Germany, he studied classical and Oriental philology and received a Dr.phil. in 1963 from the Universität Bonn for *Die Hamāsa des Abū Tammām; ein Versuch*. He was a lecturer in modern Hebrew at the Universität Köln, teaching also Arabic, Latin, and Greek. Since 1968 he was a professor at the Hebrew University, Jerusalem. His writings include *Die klassische Antike in der Tradition des Islam* (1980), *Vorlesungen über die Medizin im Islam* (1982), *Iatromathematics in Islam* (1984); he translated from the Arabic *Über die Heilung der Krankheiten der Seele und des Körpers*, of Ibn Bakhtīshū' (1977), *Das Ärztebankett*, of Ibn Butlān (1984); and he edited *The Physicians' dinner party*, of Ibn Butlan (1985). Kürschner, 1980-1992|; Note

Kleinknecht, Angelika, 1943- see Neuwirth, Angelika née Kleinknecht

Kleinman, Galina Aleksandrovna, born 30 October 1917 at Irkutsk, Russia, she graduated in 1940 from the Institute of Philosophy, Literature and History, Moscow, and received her first degree in 1949 for *Кризис военной системы феодальной Турции*. She was associated with the Tashkent Juridical Institute, 1941-1944, and Moscow State University, 1953-1962, when she joined the Oriental Institute of the Soviet Academy of Sciences. Her writings include *Армия и реформы; османский опыт модернизации* (1989). Miliband; Miliband²

Kleinmichel, Sigrid, born 29 April 1938 at Saarbrücken, Germany, she received a Dr.phil. in 1971 from Humboldt Universität, Berlin, for *Untersuchungen zu phonologischen, morphophonologischen und morphologischen Problemen im Marzubān-nāme*. Her writings include *Aufbruch aus orientalischen Dichtungs-traditionen; Studien zur usbekischen Dramatik und Prosa zwischen 1910 und 1934* (1993), *Ḫalpa in Chorezm (Ḫwārazm) und ātin āyi im Ferghanatal; zur Geschichte des Lesens in Usbekistan im 20. Jahrhundert* (2000), and she was a joint author of *Übungsbuch Usbekisch* (1995). Schoeberlein; Schwarz

Kleinpaul, Rudolf Alexander Reinhold, born 9 March 1845 at Groß-Grabe near Kamenz, Saxony, he studied philosophy at Leipzig, natural sciences at Berlin, and received a Dr.phil. in 1867 from the Universität Gotha for *Der Begriff der Erkenntniss in Plato's Theaetet*. He visited Italy, Greece, Egypt, and the Holy Land and subsequently took temporary residence in France, Switzerland, and Italy, before settling down in 1878 at Leipzig as a writer. His writings include *Die Dahabīye; Reiseskizzen aus Aegypten* (1879), *Mediterranea; Lebens- und Landschaftsbilder von den Küsten des Mittlemeers* (1881), *Menschen und Völkernamen; etymologische Streifzüge auf dem Gebiete der Eigennamen* (1885), and *Das Stromgebiet der Sprache* (1892). He died in 1918. BiD&SB; Hinrichsen; KDtLK, 1895

Kleiss, Wolfram, born 17 November 1930 at Berlin, he gained a doctorate in engineering in 1959, and subsequently joined Deutsches Archäologisches Institute successively working in Frankfurt/Main, Istanbul, and Tehran, where he was since 1971 its first director. His writings include *Die öffentlichen*

Bauten von Cambodunum (1962), *Topographisch-archäologischer Plan von Istanbul* (1965), *Zendan-i Suleiman; die Bauwerke* (1971), and *Die Entwicklung von Palästen und palastartigen Wohnbauten in Iran* (1989). Kürschner, 1983-2005

von **Kleist**, Hugo, born the son of a Prussia civil servant on 17 November 1842 at Heilsberg, East Prussia, he studied medicine and natural sciences at the universities of Jena, Greifswald, and Halle. He received his *candidatus medicinae* in 1864, and two years later his Dr.med. at Halle. After serving in the war against Denmark as a military physician, he took up private practice first in small towns and since 1870 in Berlin. He travelled widely, including visits to North Africa and the Far East. He was awarded the foreign class of the Tunisian *Nishān al-Iftikhār*. His writings include *Bilder aus Japan; Schilderung des japanischen Volkslebens* (1890) and, jointly with Albert Freiherrn von Schrenk von Notzing, *Tunis und seine Umgebung; ethnographische Skizzen* (1888), as well as contributions to newspapers on politics and current affairs. He died in Berlin in 1907. DtBilnd (4); Hinrichsen; KDtLK, 1907

Klekovskiĭ, Robert Valentinovich, fl. 20th cent., he was a joint author of *Арабские страны; экономика и внешнеэкономические связи; справочник* (Moskva, 1977), and *Объединенные Арабсие Эмираты* (Moskva, 1979) . NUC; OSK

Klemann, Peter, born about 1940, he received a doctorate in 1969 from the Universität Münster with a thesis on the cooperative movement, *Das Management in Genossenschaften des Lebensmittel-einzelhandels.* LC

Klemm, Ulf Dieter, born about 1945, he received a Dr.jur. in 1976 from the Universität Heidelberg for a thesis on the limits of the continental shelf, *Die seewärtige Grenze des Festlandsockels; Geschichte, Entwicklung und lex lata eines seevölker-rechtlichen Grundproblems.* He was a joint author of *Griechenland; Begegnung mit Landschaft, Kultur und Menschen* (2003).

Klemm, Verena, born in 1956 at Freiburg im Breisgau, Germany, she studied Islamic subjects and comparative religion at the Universität Tübingen, where she received a Dr.phil. in 1988 for *Die Mission des fatimidischen Agenten al-Mu'ayyad fi d-dīn in Šīrāz*, and a Dr.habil. in 1997 for *Literarisches Engagement im arabischen Nahen Osten; Konzepte und Debatten.* From 1989 to 1990, she was a fellow of the Orient-Institut of the Deutsche Morgenländische Gesellschaft, Istanbul. She was successively associated with Islamic institutes at the universities of Hamburg, Würzburg, and Leipzig. Her writings include *Memoirs of a mission; the Ismaili scholar, statesman and poet, al-Mu'ayyad fi'l-Din al-Shirazi* (2003), and she was a joint editor of *Understanding Near Eastern literatures; a spectrum of interdisciplinary approaches* (2000). EURAMES, 1993; Kürschner, 2003, 2005; Note; Publisher's catalogue

Klenk, Ursula, born 21 November 1943 at Dresden, Germany, she received a Dr.phil. in 1972 from the Universität Göttingen for *La Leyendad de Yusuf; ein Aljamiadotext.* After taking also a Dr.habil. in 1986, she became a professor at the Seminar für Romanische Philologie at her alma mater. Her writings include *Generative Syntax* (2003), and she edited *Kontextfreie Syntaxen und verwandte Systeme; Vorträge eines Kolloquiums in Ventron* (1985). Kürschner, 1987-2005; Schwarz

Klevenskiĭ, Mitrofan Mikhaĭlovich, born in 1877, his writings include *История Библиотеки московского публичного Румянческого Музея* (1953), and its translation, *Geschichte der Bibliothek des Moskauer Öffentlichen und Rumjančev-Museums* (1955). OSK

Klevtsova, Sofiia Dmitrievna, born 12 June 1925 at Moscow, she graduated in 1948 from the Oriental Institute, Moscow, and received her first degree in 1954 for *Местоимения в современном персидском языке.* She was since 1954 affiliated with the Moscow State Institute of International Relations. In 1967 she was appointed a lecturer. Her writings include *Учебник персидского языка* (1968), and *Русско-персидский словаь* (1975). Miliband; Miliband[2]

Kley, Otto, born 17 July 1882 at Oberursel/Taunus, Germany, he was a school teacher and member of a municipal school board in Trier. His writings include *Die deutsche Schulreform der Zukunft; Tatsächliches und Grundsätzliches zur Einheitsschulfrage* (1917), *Das Schulprogramm des Zentrums* (1919); he was a joint author of *Die Schulfrage und die Schulgesetzgebung in Deutschland* (1913), *Wege zur Gemeinschaft* (1926); and he was a joint editor of *Leben und Schaffen* (1927). GV; Kosch

Kliashtorina, Vera Borisovna, born 20 July 1927 at Chernigov, Ukraine, she graduated in 1951 at Moscow and received her first degree in 1955 for *Из истории персидской политической сатиры периода революции, 1905-1911 гг.* She was since 1955 associated with the Soviet Academy of Sciences. Her writings include *Современная персидская поэзия; очерки* (1962), *Новая поэзия в Иране* (1975), and *Иран 60-80-х годов от культурного плюрализма к исламизации духовных ценностей* (1990). Miliband; Miliband[2]

Kliashtornyĭ, Sergeĭ Grigor'evich, born 4 February 1928 at Gomel, Belorussia, he graduated in 1950 from the Oriental Faculty, Leningrad State University, and received his first degree in 1963 for *Древнетюркские рунические памятники как источник для истории Средней Азии.* Since 1957 he was associated with the Leningrad Branch of the Soviet Academy of Sciences; in 1990, he was head of the Division of Turkology and Mongolian history of Central Asia in the Institute of Oriental Studies, Leningrad. His writings include *Древние тюркские языки и литературы* (1986), and he was a joint author of *Восточный Туркестан глазами русских путешественников Восточный* (1988), *Туркестан глазами европейских путешественников* (1991), *Казахстан; летопись трех тысячелетий* (1992), *Государства и народы Евразийских степей; древность и средневековье* (2000), and *Народы степной Евразии в древтости* (2002). Miliband; Miliband²; OSK Schoeberlein

Klieman, Aaron S., born 27 July 1939, he received a Ph.D. in 1969 from Johns Hopkins University, Baltimore, Md., for *Foundations of British policy in the Arab world; the Cairo Conference of 1921.* He was a sometime professor of international relations at Tel-Aviv University. His writings include *Soviet Russia and the Middle East* (1970), *Emergency politics* (1976), *American Zionism; a documentary history, a fifteen-volume set of American Jewish and Zionist history from the nineteenth century to 1968;* and he was a joint editor of *Deterrent in the Middle East* (1993). Selim

Klíma, Otakar, born 15 November 1908 at Prag, Austria-Hungary, he studied from 1927 to 1931 Slavic, Germanic, and Oriental philology at the local university, and subsequently taught at high schools until 1953, when he started serving for twenty years as head of the Near Eastern Section in the Oriental Institute of the Czech Academy of Sciences. His writings include *Mluvnice hebrejštiny a aramejštiny* (1956), *Mazdak; Geschichte einer sozialen Bewegung im sassanidischen Persien* (1957), *Manis Zeit und Leben* (1962), and he was a joint author of Jan Rypka's *Dějiny perské a tádžické literatury* (1956). He died in Praha on 29 December 1988. In 1994 appeared *Iranian and Indo-European studies; memorial volume of Otakar Klíma.* BioB134; Filipsky

Klimburg, Maximilian, born about 1940, he studied history of art at the Universität Wien, and made several lengthy study visits to Afghanistan between 1956 and 1961. In 1956/57, he participated in the excavations of the Délégation archéologique française in Mundigak and Sorkh Kotal. He received a Dr.phil. in 1970 from the Universität Wien for *Die Entwicklung des zweiten indo-iranischen Stils von Kutscha; Untersuchungen zur buddhistischen Wandmalerei in Mittelasien.* His writings include *Afghanistan, das Land im historischen Spannungsfeld Mittelasiens* (1966), *The Kafirs of the Hindi Kush; art and society of the Waigal and Ashkun Kafirs* (1999), and he was a joint author of *Legende Afghanistan* (1959), *Die Religionen des Hindukusch* (1975), *The Religions of the Hindukush* (1985), and *The Religion of the Kafirs* (1986). GV; Note; ZKO

Klimburg-Salter, Deborah Elisabeth, born 13 March 1943, she received a Dr.phil. in 1976 from the Universität Wien, and also a Dr.habil. in 1991. She became a professor of history of art at her alma mater. Her writings include *The Silk route and the diamant path* (1982), *The Kingdom of Bāmiyān; Buddhist art and culture of the Hindi Kush* (1989), *Tabo, a lamp for the kingdom* (1997); she edited *The Inner Asian international style, 12th-14th centuries; papers* (1995); and she was a joint editor of *Coins, art, and chronology; essays on the pre-Islamic history of the Indo-Iranian borderlands* (1999). Kürschner, 1996-2005; Schoeberlein

Klimenko, A. A., fl. 20th cent., his writings include *Елементы фонетики узбекского языка* (Tashkent, 1958). NUC, 1956-67

Klimov, Ivan Mitrofanovich, born in 1907, he was associated with Kazan University from 1948 to 1963. He gained a doctorate in 1962, and was appointed a professor in 1963. His writings include *Образование и развитие Татарской АССР* (1960), *Татарская партийная организация в восстанновительный период, 1921-1925 гг.* (1961), *Образование Татарской АССР* (1963), *Татария в период Великой Отечественной войны* (1963), and *Воронежское краеведение* (1994). LC; TatarES

Klimovich, Liutsian Ippolitovich, born in 1907 at Kazan, Russia, he graduated in 1933 from the Faculty of Linguistics at Leningrad. He was from 1931 to 1953 successively affiliated with the Pedagogical Institute, Kazan, the Communist University of Workers of the East, and the Regional Pedagogical Institute, Moscow. His writings include *Содержание корана* (1930), *Мусульманам дают халифа* (1931), *Курбан-байрам* (1933), *Ислам и царской России* (1936), *Праздники и посты ислама* (1941), and *Наследство и современность* (1971). He died on 19 July 1989. Miliband; Miliband²

Klinge, Gerhard, fl. 20th cent., he received a theological degree and became a pastor in Berlin. His writings include *Lessings Bedeutung für die Geschichte und den Neuaufbau der christlichen Ethik*

(1930), *Der Aufbau* (1932), *Ist Gott tot?* (1932), *Glaube oder Wissenschaft* (1932), and *Die deutsche Bibel im deutschen Volk* (1934). His trace is lost after an article in 1941. GV

Klingenheben, Hermann *August*, born 11 May 1886 at Barmen, Prussia, he studied Oriental languages and, in 1911, he became an academic assistant at the Kolonial-Institut, Hamburg. Early in 1914, he went together with Carl Meinhoff on a linguistic research visit to the Anglo-Egyptian Sudan. During the first World War, he served as a Turkish first lieutenant in the Ottoman Empire. In 1920, he received his Dr.phil. from the Universität Leipzig, and in 1924 a Dr.habil. at Hamburg in African and Semitic philology. He was a professor and director, Afrikanistisches Institut, Leipzig, from 1930 to 1936, when he was appointed director of the Seminar für Afrikanische Sprachen, Universität Hamburg, a post which he held until his retirement in 1954. His writings include *Die Suffixklassen des Ful* (1941), *Die Sprache der Ful* (1963), and *Deutsch-amharischer Sprachführer* (1966). He died in Hamburg on 26 January 1967. IndDcAn; Kürschner, 1925-1966; LexAfrika; Unesco; WZKM, 61 (1967), pp. 7-8

Klinghardt, Karl, born 4 October 1884, he gained a Dr.ing. at a German university. His writings include *Angora - Constantinopel, ringende Gewalten* (1924), *Türkün Jordu; der Türken Heimatland* (1925), *Türkische Bäder* (1927), and he translated *Denkwürdigkeiten des Marschalls Izzet Pascha; ein kritischer Beitrag zur Kriegsschuldfrage* (1927). DtBilnd (1); Kürschner, 1931, 1935; ZKO

Klingmüller, Ernst, born 29 September 1914 at Berlin, he received a Dr.phil. in 1937 from the Universität Berlin for *Geschichte der Wafd-Partei im Rahmen der gesamtpolitischen Lage Ägyptens* and a Dr.habil. in 1943 for *Die Korrespondenz zwischen Sir Henry McMahon und dem Scharifen von Mekka*. He was an insurance expert and a director of the Institut für Versicherungsrecht, Köln, and a professor of insurance law at the universities of Karlsruhe and Köln. In 1974, he was honoured by *Festschrift für Ernst Klingmüller*. Hanisch; Kürschner, 1950-2005; Schwarz

Klinke-Rosenberger, Rosa, born in 1891, she received a Dr.phil. in 1941 from the Universität Zürich for *Das Götzenbuch, Kitab al-Asnām, des Ibn al-Kalbi*. Her writings include *Arabische Erzählungen* (Zürich, 1945), *Arabische Kadi-Geschichten nach arabischen Originalquellen* (Affoltern, 1953), and *Der Sänger der Barmakiden* (Affoltern, 1955). Schwarz; ZKO

Klinkhardt, Hans Eberhard, he received a doctorate in 1965 from the Universität Bonn for *Die Personensorge nach islamischem Recht*. Schwarz

Klinkott, Manfred, born 20 August 1936 at Berlin, he went to school in Naumburg and Berlin, and then studied architecture at the Technische Universität Berlin, where he received a doctorate in 1971 for *Martin Gropius und die Berliner Schule*. He became a professor of history of architecture in the Institut für Baugeschichte, Universität Karlsruhe. His writings include *Islamische Baukunst in Afghanisch-Sistan mit einem geschichtlichen Überblick von Alexander dem Großen bis zur Zeit der Safawiden-Dynastie* (1981). Kürschner, 1983-2005; Thesis

Klippel, Ernst August Josef, born 19 April 1872 at Liebau, Silesia, he studied architecture at the technical universities of München and Berlin. In 1895 he pursued archaeological study in Greece, Asia Minor, and Italy. Since 1897, he was employed by the Egyptian Government in the preservation of Roman, early Arab and Coptic historical monuments. In 1906, he was appointed an inspector of Upper Egyptian cultural buildings. From 1908 to 1912, he studied English, French and Arabic literature, as well as Semitic philology, at Cairo University. He also went on ethnological study visits to the Bedouins of Syria and Egypt. His writings include *Haschisch; ägyptische Skizzen* (1910), *Études sur le folklore bédouin de l'Égypte* (1911), *Betitkállim bil-'árabî? (Sprechen Sie Arabisch?); Handbuch* (1924), *Meine Pilgerfahrt nach Mekka* (1924), *Unter Drusen, Kurden und Teufelsanbetern* (1926), *Wanderungen im Heiligen Lande* (1927), *Als Beduine zu den Teufelsanbetern* (1932), and *Unter Senûsy-Brüdern, Drusen und Teufelsanbetern* (1942). He died in Berlin on 25 August 1953. DÖS; DtBE; Sezgin

Klitgaard, Robert E., born in 1947, he was in 1979 a professor in the Kennedy School of Government, Harvard University, and in 1990, a professor of social science at Wells College, Aurora, N.Y., a post which he still held in 2004. His writings include *Elitism and meritocracy in developing countries* (1986), *Controlling corruption* (1988), *Institutional adjustment and adjusting to institutions* (1995), and he was a joint author of *Corrupt cities; a practical guide to cure and prevention* (2000), as well as numerous brief reports for RAND Corporation. NatFacDr, 1990-2004

Klitzsch, Hans *Eberhard*, born 18 August 1933 at Remda, Germany, he received a Dr.rer.nat. in 1958 and became a professor of geology at the Technische Universität, Berlin. He edited *South-central Libya and northern Chad; a guidebook to the geology and prehistory* (Tripoli, 1966), *Research in Egypt and the Sudan* (1984), and *Research in Sudan, Somalia and Kenya; results of the special research project "geo-scientific problems in arid and semi-arid areas", period 1987-1990* (Berlin, 1990), and he was a joint editor of *Nordost-Afrika; Strukturen und Ressourcen* (1999). Kürschner, 2001-2005: WhoWor, 1987/88-1991/92

Kliuchnikov, Boris Ivanovich, born 18 July 1927 at Moscow, he graduated in 1952 from the Moscow Oriental Institute, received his first degree in 1964 from the School of Diplomats at the Soviet Foreign Office, and a doctorate in 1982 for a monograph. Associated with the Foreign Ministry since 1952, he spent eight years in Pakistan and India. For many years an active member of the Communist Party, he was since 1988 a research fellow in the Oriental Institute of the Soviet Academy of Sciences. His writings include *Русско-урду словарь* (1959), *Практический учебник языка урду* (1962), and *Урду-русский словарь* (1964). Miliband²

Kliuchnikov, Kamir (Boris) Fedorovich, born 21 October 1935 in the northern Caucasus, he graduated in 1958 from the Moscow State Institute of International Relations, received his first degree in 1963, and a doctorate in 1983 for *Концепции и прогнозы нового международного экономического порядка: горизонты 2000 года*, a work which was published in 1982. He was associated with Unesco, Paris, from 1965 to 1972 as an expert on human resources and education. In 1986 he was appointed a professor. His writings include *Пятая колонна в профсоюзах ФРГ* (1962), and *The Somali Republic: priority project for educational development* (Pars, Unesco, 1969). Miliband²

Klobb, Jean François Arsène, born 29 June 1857 at Ribeauville, Alsace, he was a graduate of both École polytechnique and École d'application de Fontainebleau. He spent nearly his entire career with the marines in the French Sudan. He was a commander of the newly acquired Timbuctu region, where he organized the first dromedary unit, forcing back the Touareg towards Gao. Nominated lieutenant-colonel and at the point of returning to France, he was ordered to leave Kayes on Senegal River and assume the command of the column under captains Voulet and Chanoine, who were guilty of cruelty on their advance on Chad. He was killed by order of these megalomaniac officers at Damangara near Zinder, Niger, on 14 July 1899. His writings include *Le Basin du Congo* (1898), *Dernier carnet de route au Soudan français; rapport officiel de M. le gouverneur Bergès sur la fin de la mission Klobb* (1905), and *À la recherche de Voulet; mission Klobb-Meynier* (1931). BN; NDBA

Klopfer, Fritz, 1864-1936 *see* Stumme, Hans

Klopfer, Helmut Ludwig, born 7 September 1926 at Leipzig, Germany, he went to school until 1944 when he was called to arms. After two years in a Soviet POW camp, he returned home and completed his high school. He subsequently studied Oriental languages and theology first at the Universität Leipzig and later at Freie Universität Berlin where he received a Dr.phil. in 1955 for *Das Kitāb al-Irshād des Imām al-Haramain al-Djuwainī*. He taught German at the Goethe-Institut in Egypt and Libya, and also spent some time as a librarian in Ankara. His writings include *Das Dogma des Imam al-Haramain al-Djuwaini und sein Werk al-'Aqīda an-nizāmīya übersetzt und erläutert* (1958), *Modernes Arabisch; eine Einführung ins heutige Zeitungs-Schriftarabisch* (1963), *Aspekte der Bewegung des Muhammad Ben Ali As-Sanusi* (1967), jointly with Fritz Steppat, *Deutsch für Araber* (1958), and he translated from the Arabic *Das arabische Traumbuch des Ibn-Sirin* (1989). Private; Sezgin; Thesis

Kloss, Heinz, born 30 October 1904 at Halle/Saale, Prussia, he studied at the Universität Halle and received a Dr.rer.pol. in 1939. He successively worked at Deutsches Auslandsinstitut, Stuttgart, and Forschungsstelle für Nationalitäten- und Sprachenfragen, Kiel. From 1947 to 1952 he collaborated with the American re-education program in Germany. His writings include *Fremdsprachige Einwanderung in das französische Sprachgebiet* (1935), *Brüder vor den Toren des Reiches* (1940), *Deutsche Einwanderung nach Algerien, 1832-1939* (1944), and *Algerien* (1959). He died in 1987. DcAnImH; Wer ist wer, 1955-1969/70

Klötzer, Wolfgang, born 8 April 1925 at Wiesbaden, Germany, he received a Dr.phil. in 1951 and subsequently became a professor of history, particularly local history, at the Universität Frankfurt/Main. His writings include *Zu Gast im alten Frankfurt* (1990), and he edited *Leben und Leistung; zur 150-Jahrfeier der Deutschen Burschenschaft* (1965). Kürschner, 1980-2005

Klöwer, Gerd Günter, born about 1947, he received a Dr.phil. in 1977 from the Universität Marburg for a thesis on the cooperative movement in the Third World, *Chancen von Genossenschaften in Entwicklungsländern; Chancen ihrer Entstehung und Chancen als entwicklungspolitisches Instrument gezeigt am Beispiel Ägyptens*. He became associated with governmental Third World aid agencies. His writings include *Genossenschaften in Entwicklungsländern* (1981), *Internationales Symposium "Islamic Banks and Strategies for Economic Cooperation"* (1982), and the pamphlet, *Financial co-operatives and credit insurance in Mongolia* (2001). Schwarz

von Klüber, Harald, born 6 September 1901 at Potsdam, Germany, he was born into a family which for generations had held high office in the civil, military, and diplomatic services. He became an internationally prominent astronomer who worked at the Potsdam observatory for a quarter of a century and after World War two was at the Solar Physics Observatory, Cambridge, England. His writings include *Das Vorkommen der chemischen Elemente im Kosmos* (1931). He died in Baden-Baden on 14 February 1978. DtBE; DtBilnd (1); Kürschner, 1966-1976; *Nature*, 273 (1 June 1978), p. 414; NDB; *Sky and telescope*, 56 (August 1978), p. 105

Klug, Tony, born 20th cent., his writings include *The Middle East; a tale of two peoples* (London, Fabian Society, 1973), and *The Middle East impasse; the only way out* (London, Fabian Society, 1977). LC

Kluge, Theodor, born in 1880, he received a Dr.phil. in 1906 from the Universität Gießen for *Die Darstellung der Löwenjagd im Altertum*, and a second doctorate in 1918 from the Universität Braunschweig in 1918 for *Versuch einer systematischen Darstellung der altgeorgischen (grusinischen) Kirchenbauten*. His writings include *Die Lykier, ihre Geschichte und ihre Inschriften* (1910), *Beiträge zur mingrelischen Grammatik* (1916), *Versuch einer Beantwortung der Frage: welcher Sprachengruppe ist das Sumerische anzugliedern* (1921), *Die Binden von Agram* (1936), *Die Zahlenbegriffe der Sudansprachen* (1937), *Das ossische Siedlungsgebiet* (1940), *Die Zahlenbegriffe der Dravida, der Hamiten, der Semiten und der Kaukasier* (1940), and *Die Völker und Sprachen des Indo-chinesischen Raumes* (1953). GV

Klunzinger, Carl Benjamin, born 18 November 1834 at Güglingen, Württemberg, he was a physician and zoologist who spent altogether eight years at Qusaiyr on the Red Sea, experiences which he described in his *Bilder aus Oberägypten, der Wüste und dem Rothen Meere* (1877), *Die Korallthiere des Rothen Meeres* (1877-79), and *Erinnerungen aus meinem Leben als Naturforscher und Arzt zu Koseir am Roten Meer* (1915). He died in Stuttgart on 21 June 1914. DtBE; DtBilnd (7); Embacher; Henze; Kornrumpf; *Wer ist's*, 1909, 1912

Klüver, Hartmut, born in 1952, he studied geography, German subjects, and education at the Universität Marburg, where he received a Dr.phil. in 1987 for *Bundeswehrstandorte im ländlichen Raum; wirtschaftsgeographische Auswirkungen der Garnisonen Diepholz und Stadtallendorf*. In 1984, he began a career as a teacher. His writings include *Sicherheitspolitik und Verteidigung in Südostarabien* (1990). Note about the author

Klychmuradov, K. K., fl. 20th cent., his writings include *Ашхабадское землетрясение и помощь народов СССР* (1977). OSK

Kment, Eugen, born 20th cent., he received a Dr.phil. in 1951 from the Universität Wien for *Die wirtschaftsgeographischen Grundlagen der Cyrenaica*. He was a joint author, with Heinrich Braitenberg-Zennenberg, of *Beiträge zur Wirtschaftsgeographie des Senusssistaates Libyen* (Wien, 1952). Sezgin

Kmietowicz, Anna, born 20th cent., her writings include *Skarb srebrny z miejscowośi Ochle, powiat Koło* (Wrocław, 1962), and she was a joint author of *Skarb monet arabskich z okolic Drohiczyna nad Bugiem* (1969). OSK

Kmietowicz (Kmietowitz), Franciszek (Frank), born in 1912, his writings include *Czarownina* (Surrey, England, 1951), *Wieża Babel* (Bradford, 1953), *Slavic mythical beliefs* (Windsor, Ont., 1982), and he was a joint author of *Skarb monet arabskich z okolic Drohiczyna nad Bugiem* (1960). LC

Kmoskó (Kmoško), Mihály (Michal), born 29 August 1876 at Illava (Ilava), Slovakia,, he completed his theological study at the Pazmaneum, Wien, and was ordained in 1898. With a travel grant from the Universität Wien, he subsequently studied Oriental languages at Beirut, Jerusalem, Oxford, and London. Since 1909 he was a professor at Budapest University. His writings include *Az emberiség első írott szabadságlevele* (1913), and *Az iszlám keletkezése* (1929). He died in Pusztazámor, Hungary, on 8 April 1931. Fililisky; GeistigeUng; *Index Islamicus*, (1); Magyar

Knabe-(Wohlfahrt), Erika, born about 1947, she received a Dr.phil. in 1977 from the Universität Köln for *Frauenemanzipation in Afghanistan; ein empirischer Beitrag*. Schwarz

Knabenshue, Paul, born in 1883 at Toledo, Ohio, he was educated at high school and privately. He was in business until 1906, when he entered the U.S. consular service, where he remained until 1933, serving exclusively in the Middle East from 1911 to his retirement. He died in Baghdad in 1942. CurBio, 1942; Shavit; WhAm, 1, 2

Knapp, Bettina Liebowitz, born 9 May 1926 at N.Y.C., she graduated in 1947 from Barnard College, New York, and received a Ph.D. in 1955 from Columbia University, New York. Since 1952 she was teaching in the Department of Romance Languages at Columbia; from 1990 to 1995, she was associated with Hunter College, City University of New York. Her writings include *French novelists speak out* (1973), *Céline, man of hate* (1974), *French theater since 1968* (1995), and *French fairy tales; a Jungian approach* (2003). ConAu, 13-16, new rev., 6, 21, 44; IntAu&W, 1976, 1977, 1982; Master (2); NatFacDr, 1990-95

Knapp, George Perkins, born of American missionary parents on 13 June 1863 at Bitlis, Anatolia, he graduated in 1887 from Harvard College, and in 1890 from Hartford Theological Seminary. In the same year he was ordained and married. He served under the American Board of Commissioners for Foreign Missions at Bitlis, 1890-96, Constantinople, 1896-97, Harput, 1899-1909, Bitlis, 1910-13, Harput, 1913-14, and again Bitlis, 1914. He had been witness of many dramatic events and had lived through several periods of massacre. He was the only American actually implicated in Armenian revolutionary schemes. He died suddenly some days before 17 August 1914 in Diyabakır, where he had arrived in a very sick condition, and stayed at a "hotel" near the Mardin gate. Kornrumpf ; *Missionary herald*, 111 (1915), pp. 511-12; Shavit

Knapp, Wilfrid, fl. 20th cent., his writings include *A History of war and peace, 1939-1965* (1967), *Unity and nationalism in Europe since 1945* (1969), *Tunisia* (1970), *France; partial eclipse* (1972), *North West Africa; a political and economic survey* (1977), and he was a joint author of *The Politics of African and Middle Eastern states; an annotated bibliography* (1976). ZKO

Knappen, Marshall Mason, born 6 January 1901 at Sioux Falls, N.Dak., he was in 1921 a Rhodes Scholar at Oxford, and held several degrees from American and British universities. He had a varied career in the fields of religion and education. At the time of his death, he was a professor of political science at Western Michigan University. Despondent over an illness, he was found dead in his apartment with several plastic bags tied over his head. His writings include *Tudor Puritanism* (1939), and he was a joint editor of *Two Elizabethan Puritan diaries* (Chicago, American Society of Church History, 1933). He died in 1966. NYT, 19 January 1966, p. 38, col. 1; WhE&EA

Knappert, Jan, born 14 January 1927 at Heemstede, the Netherlands, he gained a doctorate in 1958 at the Rijksuniversiteit te Leiden with a thesis entitled *Het epos van Heraklios*. He was a sometime senior research fellow at University College, Dar-es-Salaam, before he began a teaching career in languages and cultures of Africa at the School of Oriental and African Studies, London. His writings include *Four Swahili epics* (1964), *Myths and legends of the Swahili* (1970), *Four centuries of Swahili verse* (1979), *Islamic legends* (1985); and he was a joint editor and translator of *Textual sources for the study of Islam* (1987). AfrBiolnd (2); ConAu, 172; Unesco

Knatchbull-Hugessen, Sir Hughe Montgomery, born in 1886, he was educated at Eton, and Balliol College, Oxford. He entered the British Foreign Office in 1908 and became a diplomat. His writings include *Diplomat in peace and war* (1949). He died in 1971. Bioln, 9; CurBio, 1943, 1971; DNB; ObitT, 1971-75, p. 289; *The Times*, 23 March 1971 [not sighted]; Who was who, 7

Knauer, Elfriede Regina, fl. 20th cent., her writings on fine art include *Die Berliner Audokides Vase* (1965), *Das Reiterstandbild des Kaisers Marc Aurel* (Stuttgart, 1968), and *Ein Skyphos des Triptolemosmalers* (Berlin, 1973).

Knauerhase, Ramon, born 24 December 1929 at N.Y.C., he graduated in 1957 from Temple University, Philadelphia, and received a Ph.D. in economic history from the University of Pennsylvania in 1967. He started his career in teaching economics at Lehigh University, Bethlehem, Pa., and subsequently spent over twenty years at the University of Connecticut, Storrs, as a professor of economics. His writings include *An Introduction to national socialism, 1920-1939* (1972), and *The Saudi Arabian economy* (1975). AmM&WSc, 1973 S, 1978 S; MESA Roster of members, 1977-82; Who's who in the East, 1983/84, 1985/86

Knauss, Peter Richard, born in 1937, he received his Ph.D. in 1968 from Northwestern University, Evanston, Illinois, for *Whites under stress; communications and social change in two closed societies*. He subsequently taught political science at the University of Illinois at Chicago. He had also taught one year at the Université d'Oran as a Fulbright scholar. His writings include *The Persistence of patriarchy, class, gender, and ideology in twentieth-century Algeria* (1987). He died of AIDS in 1990. ConAu, 131; NatFacDr, 1990; NYT, 16 May 1990, p. B-8, col. 1

Knauth, Arnold Whitman, born in 1890 at N.Y.C., he graduated from Milton (Mass.) Academy, Harvard and Columbia universities, and was admitted to the Bar of New York. He there practised his profession and also taught at New York University. His writings include *The American law of ocean* (1953). He died in 1960. NatCAB, vol. 45, pp. 527-28; NYT, 15 October 1960, p. 23, col. 3; WhAm, 4

Knaysi, George Abdallah, born in 1898, he was in 1928 an instructor in bacteriology at Cornell University, Ithaca, N.Y. His writings include *Elements of bacterial cytology* (1944). Note; NUC, pre-1956

Knecht, Loring Dahl, born in 1921 at Wimbledon, N.Dak., he graduated in 1947 from Olaf College, Northfield, N.Mex., and received a Ph.D. in 1957 from the University of Wisconsin for *Sainte-Beuve en face de Montaigne et de Pascal*. He taught in various capacities French language and literature in the Department of Romance Languages at Olaf College. He was a joint author of *Échos de notre monde* (1975). DrAS, 1969 F, 1974 F, 1978 F, 1982 F; WhoAm, 1974-1988/89

Knibiehler, Yvonne, born 20th cent., she was in 1980 a professor at the University de Provence [*sic*]. Her writings include *Naissance des sciences humaines* (1973), *L'Histoire des mères du moyen âge à nos jours* (1980), *Histoire des mères et de la maternité en Occident* (2000), and she was a joint author of *La Femme et les médecins* (1983), and *Comettes et blouses blanches, 1880-1890* (1984). *Livres disponibles*, 2004; Note

Knight, Herbert *Gary*, he was born on 8 December 1939 at St. Joseph, Mo. By decree of Baton Rouge District Court his name was legally changed to Gary Knight on 16 August 1984. He graduated in 1961 from Stanford University, Palo Alto, Calif. He practised law at Los Angeles, before teaching it at Louisiana State University, Baton Rouge. His writings include *The Law of the sea* (1969), and *Managing the sea's living resources* (1977). DrAS, 1969 F, 1974 F, 1978 F|

Knight, Melvin Moses, born 29 April 1887, he graduated in 1913 from Texas Christian University, Fort Worth, and received a Ph.D. in 1917 from Clark University, Worcester, Mass. He was a professor of history, government, and economics successively in New York, Utah, and until his retirement in California. In 1919, he served as a member of the Roumanian Red Cross Commission; he first visited North Africa in 1925, and again in 1950-1951. During the second World War, he served in the U.S. Department of State. His writings include *Economic history of Europe* (1926), and *Morocco as a French economic venture* (1937). AmIndex (2); Note; PeoHis; WhE&EA

Knipp, Charles Christopher, born 28 December 1938 in the United States, he graduated in 1961 from Amherst (Mass.) College, and received his Ph.D. in 1974 from the University of California for *Types of orientalism in eighteenth-century England*. From 1970 to 1975 he taught successively at the University of California, University of Hawaii, and San Francisco State University. IWWAS, 1976/77

Knobel, Edward Ball, born 21 October 1841 at London, he was an astronomer and an Oriental scholar, who was awarded an honorary doctorate in science by Oxford University. He died in 1930. BritInd (1); *Who was who*, 3

Knobloch, Edgar, born 20th cent., at Prague, he studied at the local Charles University. His writings include *Beyond the Oxus* (1972), its translation, *Turkestan: Taschkent, Buchara, Samarkand; Reisen zu den Kulturstätten Mittelasiens* (1973), and he was a joint author of *Die Kunst Mittelasiens* (1965). Au&Wr, 1971; IntAu&W, 1976

Knoertzer, André Auguste, born 8 November 1887 at Alger, where he received a diploma in Algerian legislation and Islamic law. He was a sometime barrister, magistrate in Algeria as well as a president in the Court of Appeal in Alger and Rabat. He was a joint author of *Le Code forestier algérien* (1931). WhoFr, 1959/60-1967/68|

Knolles, Richard, born about 1550, a native of Northamptonshire, he was educated at Lincoln College, Oxford. He became a fellow of his college, and at some date subsequent to 1571 left Oxford to become master of a school at Sandwich, Kent, where he died in 1610. In 1603 he published his *Generall historie of the Turkes, from the first beginning of that nation to the rise of the Othoman familie*, of which several editions subsequently appeared, among them a good one edited by Sir Paul Rycaut in 1700. Knolles availed himself largely of Jean Jacques Boissard's *Vitae et Icones Sultanorum Turcicorum* (Frankfurt, 1596). BioIn, 2, 3; BritInd (14); DNB; EncBrit

Knollys, Denis Erskine, born in 1884, he passed through the Royal Military College, Sandhurst, and since 1903 served with the Indian Army in Europe, Mesopotamia, Persia, and Turkestan. He retired in 1931 with the rank of lieutenant-colonel. *Who's who*, 1929-1936

Knörzer, Jutta Edith, born 11 September 1954 in Germany, she received a Ph.D. in Persian from the Department of Islamic Studies, University of Toronto, and subsequently held a temporary teaching post at McMaster University, Hamilton, Ont. Her writings include *Ali Dashti's prison days; life under Reza Shah* (1994), and *Suri & Co.; tales of a Persian teenager*, translated from the Persian of Mahshid Amirshahi (1995). LC; *MESA Roster of members*, 1990; Private

Knowles, James Hinton, Rev., born 19th cent., his writings include *A Dictionary of Kashmiri proverbs and sayings* (Bombay, 1885), and *Folk-tales of Kashmir* (London, 1888), and its translation, *A gonosz királynek; kásmiri népmesék* (Budapest, 1958). NUC, pre-1956-1967

Knowles, Ruth Sheldon, born 23 April 1915 at Joplin, Mo., she studied at Smith College and the University of Tulsa. She became a petroleum specialist and a consultant to a variety of governments. Her writings include *Hubbin' it* (1938), *The Great gamblers* (1959), *Indonesia today; the nation that helps itself* (1973), and *America's energy famine, its cause and cure* (1980). WhAmW, 1961/62

Knox, Alexander A., born 19th cent., his writings include *The New playground; or, wanderings in Algeria* (London, 1883). His trace is lost after an article in 1909. BLC; NUC, pre-1956

Knox, Stuart George, born in 1869, he was educated at Elizabeth College, Guernsey, and after passing through the Royal Military College, Sandhurst, he entered the Army. He served as a political and consular officer in the Persian Gulf, Muscat, and Khuzistan from 1894 to 1915. He was a joint author of *Some plants of the Zor Hills, Koweit* (Calcutta, 1917). He died in 1956. IndianBilnd (1); Kornrumpf; *Who was who*, 5

Knox-Mawer, Ronald, born 3 August 1925 at Overton, Wales, he graduated from Emmanuel College, Cambridge, and was called to the bar from the Middle Temple in 1950. He was a judge in the Overseas Service and served as a chief justice in Aden. His writings include *The Sultans come to tea* (1961). Under the pseudonym Robert Overton he wrote his reminiscences, *Palm court* (1980). ConAu, 123; Who, 1999-2005

Knysh, Alexander D., born 20th cent., he was in 2002 associated with the University of Michigan at Ann Arbor. His writings include *Ibn 'Arabi in the later Islamic tradition; the making of a polemical image in medieval Islam* (Albany, N.Y., S.U.N.Y. Press, 1999), and *Islamic mysticism; a short history* (Leiden, Brill, 2000). LC

Kobeko, Dmitriĭ Fomich, born in 1837, his writings include Цесаревич Павел Петрович, 1754-1796 (1882), and its translation, *La Jeunesse d'un tsar* (1896), О разработке генеалогических данных в смысле пособія для русской археологіи (1887), Родословныя заметки о некоторых деятеляях Смутнаго Времени (1908), and Императорская публичнвя библіотека за сто, 1814-1914 (1914). He died in 1918. EnSlovar

Kobelt, Volker, born about 1940, he received a Dr.phil. in 1969 from the Universität Hohenheim for a thesis on the Third World cooperative movement, *Planung und Planrealisierung in der Landwirtschaft Tunesiens*. He was a joint author of *Staatliche geplante Produktionsgenossenschaften; das tunesische Modell der "Unités coopératives de production du Nord"* (1971). ZKO

Kobelt, Wilhelm, born 20 February 1840 at Alsfeld, Hesse, he studied medicine at the Universität Gießen, and obtained a Dr.med. in 1862. He subsequently practised his profession near Frankfurt until 1869. He later pursued an interest in zoology and geography and travelled in North Africa. His writings include *Reiseerinnerungen aus Algerien und Tunesien* (1885), and *Heimat und Heimatarbeit* (1912). In 1910 appeared *Festschrift zum siebzigsten Geburtstage von Wilhelm Kobelt*. He died in Schwanheim near Frankfurt on 26 March 1916. DtBE; *Geographische Zeitschrift*, 22 (1916), p. 229; *Wer ist's*, 1909, 1912

Kober, Leopold, born 21 September 1883 at Pfaffstätten, Austria, he completed his study of geology in 1907 with a Dr.phil. from the Universität Wien. He became an assistant at the local institute of geology until 1913, when he gained a Dr.habil. After military service during the first World War, he became a professor of geology at his alma mater in 1921. He did field work in North Africa, Greater Syria, and the Balkans. Dismissed from his post in 1938, it was not until 1945 that he re-entered his *Institut* as its chairman. His writings include *Bau der Erde* (1921), *Bau und Entstehung der Alpen* (1923), and *Vom Bau der Erde zum Bau der Atome* (1949). He died in Hallstatt, Austria, on 6 September 1970. DtBE; DiBilnd (1); Kornrumpf; Kornrumpf³, vol. 2; Kürschner, 1940/41-1970; Teichl

Köbert, Raimund, born 6 March 1903 at Frankfurt am Main, he received a Dr.phil. in 1939 from the Universität Wien for *Texte und Übersetzungen aus Ibn Furaks "Muškil al-ahadit" auf Grund der Handschriften im Vatikan, Leipzig, Leiden und London*. He became a lecturer in Arabic and Syriac at a Bible institute in Roma (Pontificio Istituto Biblico di Roma?). His writings include *Vocabularium syriacum* (1956). Kürschner, 1950-1980|; Schwarz

Kobidze, David Ivanovich, born in 1906 in Georgia, he graduated in 1933 from the Tiflis Faculty of Languages and Literatures of the Georgian Pedagogical Institute, received his first degree with a thesis on «Вопросы зачатия и развития новой персидской литературы», and a doctorate in 1946 for Персидские источники грузинских версий «Шах-намэ». He was appointed a lecturer in 1940, and a professor in 1949. He taught Iranian philology at the Oriental Faculty, Tiflis State University since 1953. His writings include *Muntakhabāt-i Fārsī* (Tbilissi, 1961), and Иранская филология в Грусии (1971). He died on 5 August 1981. Miliband; Miliband²; Народы Азии и Африки, 1982, no. 3, pp. 214-15

Kobishchanov, IUriĭ Mikhaĭlovich, born 8 October 1934 at Khar'kov, Ukraine, he graduated in 1958 from the Institute of Oriental Languages, Moscow State University, received his first degree in 1963 for *Древний Аксум; Аксумское царство в период возникновения и расцвета III-VII вв. н.э.,* and a doctorate in 1991 for *Значение комплекса полюдья в истории Африки.* Since 1964 he was associated with the African Institute of the Soviet Academy of Sciences. His writings include *Мелконатуральное производство в общинно-кастовых системах Африки* (1982), and *История разпространения ислама в Африка* (1987). Miliband; Miliband²

Købke (Köbke), Hans *Peter* Carl, born 5 July 1841, his writings include *Om runerne i Norden* (København, 1879), *De danske kirkebygninger* (København, 1883), and *Roskilde Domkirke* (København, 1895). He died on 30 January 1923. Kraks, 1922 [not sighted]; NUC, pre-1956

Kobychev, Veniamin Pavlovich, born 20th cent., his writings include *В поисках прародины славян* (1973), *Поселения и жилищенародов Северного Кавказа в XIX-XX вв.* (1982), and he was a joint author of *В краю гор, садов и виноградников; книга для чтения с коммент. и словарем на франц. языке* (1988), *Календарь и календарная обрядность народов Карачаево-Черкесий* (1989), and *Материальная культура; пища и жилище* (1995). OSK

Koch (Кохь), Carl (Karl) Heinrich Emil, born 6 June 1809 at Ettersberg near Weimar, Germany, he studied at the universities of Jena and Würzburg, and obtained a doctorate in 1834 at Jena. From 1836 to 1838 he visited Russia and the Isthmus of Caucasia. In the service of the academy of sciences, Berlin, he explored Asia Minor, Armenia, Kurdistan, the eastern Trans-Caucasus, and the Crimea. Although a dendrologist by profession, and a professor of botany at Jena, he settled in Berlin in 1847 because of the good research conditions. Some years later, he was appointed a professor at the Universität Berlin, concurrently serving as secretary-general of the society for the promotion of gardening in the royal Prussian estates. During the last years of his life, he was a director of the botanical gardens in Berlin. His writings include *Reise durch Rußland nach dem kaukasischen Isthmus in den Jahren 1836, 1837 und 1838* (1842-43), *Kaukasische Militärstraße, der Kuban und die Halbinsel Taman; Erinnerungen aus einer Reise von Tiflis nach der Krim* (1851), *Die Krim und Odessa* (1854), its translations, *The Crimea and Odessa; journal of a tour* (1855), and *De Krim en Odessa* (1855); he was a joint author of *Die kaukasischen Länder und Armenien in Reiseschilderungen* (1860), and its translation, *De caucasische landen en Armenië in reistafereelen* (1856). He died in Berlin on 25 May 1879. ADtB, vol. 16, pp. 395-98; BLC; DtBIlnd (2); Embacher; EnSlovar; Henze; Kornrumpf

Koch, Erich Friedrich Ludwig, 1875-1944 *see* Koch-Weser, Erich Friedrich Ludwig

Koch, Fridolin, born 28 May 1927 at Wien, he studied law at Wien and Paris, completing his study with a Dr.jur. He was associated with the Austrian chamber of retail industry, 1952; head of the foreign trade bureau, Léopoldville, 1956; Austrian trade commissioner in Cairo, 1957, returning in 1962 to his first post at the Bundeskammer der Gewerblichen Wirtschaft. Note; WhoAustria, 1959/60

Koch, Hans Theodor, born about 1940, he received a Dr.med. in 1969 from the Universität Halle for *Leben und Werk des halleschen Chirurgen Ernst Blasius.* He was a joint author of *Beiträge zur Geschichte des Gesundheitswesens der Stadt Halle und der Medizinischen Fakultät* (Leipzig, 1965).

Koch, Howard Everard, born about 1940, he received a Ph.D. in 1973 from Stanford University, Palo Alto, Cal., for *Permanent war; a reappraisal of the Arab-Israeli war.* Selim

Koch, Josef (Joseph), born 2 May 1885 at Münstereifel, Prussia, he studied Catholic theology, philosophy, and classical philology at the universities of Freiburg/Breisgau, Straßburg, and Bonn, where he received a Dr.phil. in 1915 for *Die Erkenntnislehre Hermann Schells;* in 1925 he received both a Dr.habil., and a Dr.theol. from the Universität Breslau for *Durandus de S. Porciano, O.P.* He subsequently taught at Breslau as a professor until 1945. He then briefly served as a professor in Bonn and Göttingen until 1948, when he was appointed to the chair of medieval philosophy in the Universität Köln, a post which he held until his retirement in 1956. He was an authority in medieval literature and theology. His writings include *Nikolaus von Cues und seine Umwelt* (1948), *Die Ars coniecturalis des Nikolaus von Kues* (1956), *Kleine Schriften* (1973), and he edited *Artes liberales von der antiken Bildung zur Wissenschaft des Mittelalters* (1959). He died in Köln on 10 March 1967. DtBE; Kürschner, 1940/41-1966; NDB

Koch, Josef, born in 1943, he studied geography, history, and theology at the universities of Münster, München, and Tübingen, where he received his Dr.phil. in 1975 for *Rentnerstädte in Kalifornien.* He was a Fulbright fellow in the Department of Geography, University of California at Los Angeles, and a sometime fellow in human geography in the Universität Tübingen research project on the Middle East. Note about the author

Koch-Weser, Erich Friedrich Ludwig, born 26 February 1875 at Bremerhaven, Germany, he studied law and political science and in 1901 became mayor of Delmenhorst in Lower Saxony. From 1913 to 1919 he was mayor of Kassel and in this capacity also a member of the House of Lords (Herrenhaus). He subsequently was first a member of the Weimar National Assembly and later of the Reichstag. He served as a minister of the interior as well as minister of justice. Concurrently he practised law at Berlin. He was dismised from office in 1933 on account of his Jewish background and emigrated to Brazil, where he died in Fazenda Janeta on 20 October 1944. His writings include *Deutschlands Außenpolitik in der Nachkriegszeit, 1919-1929* (1929), and its translation, *Germany in the post-war world* (1930). BioHbDtE; DtBE; DtBilnd (5); EncTR, 1991 (not sighted); NDB; RHbDtG; Wer ist's, 1935

Kochan, Ran, born 20th cent., he received a Ph.D. in 1969 from the London School of Economics for *Israel's relations with Asian states east of Iran, 1948 to 1967.* Sluglett

Köcher, Erika, born 20th cent., she was associated with the Institut für Orientforschung, Akademie der Wissenschaften zu Berlin, where she received an unspecified degree in 1958 for *Untersuchungen zu Gamīl al-Mudauwar's Hadārat al-islām fī dār as-salām* (Berlin, 1958). Note

Kochev, Nikolai TSviatov, born 20th cent., his writings include *Философската мисъл във Византия IX-XII в.* (Sofia, 1981), and *Античната литературна традиция и византийските автори* (Sofia, 1982.) LC

Kochnev, Boris Dmitrievich, born 30 October 1940 at Kostino, Russia, he graduated in 1964 from the Institute of History, Tashkent State University, and received his first degree in 1971 for his thesis *Мусалла Средн. Азии и их место в историчесой топографии феодального города.* He was a deputy director of the Museum of History at Frunze, from 1969 to 1971, when he became a research fellow in the Archaeological Institute of the Uzbekistan Academy of Sciences in Samarkand. His writings include *Средневековые загородные культовые сооружения Средней Азии* (1976). Miliband²; Schoeberlein

Kochwasser, Friedrich Helmuth, born 20th cent., his writings include *Kuwait; Geschichte, Wesen und Funktion eines modernen arabischen Staates* (1969), *Araber und Deutsche; Begegnungen in einem Jahrtausend* (1974), and he edited *Beziehungen im Bereich von Bildung und Wissenschaften zwischen dem Land Baden-Württemberg und dem Kaiserreich Iran* (1976). NUC; ZKO

Koecher-Henslowa, Agnieszka, born 20th cent., she was associated with the Polish Academy of Sciences. She edited *Art et liberté; exposition du théâtre polonais d'aujourd'hui, Maison de spectacle, La Bellone, Bruxelles* (Bruxelles, 1990). LC; Note

Koechlin, Raymond, born 6 July 1860 at Mulhouse, Alsace, he studied law and became a journalist. He spent the years from 1887 to 1902 at the foreign affairs desk of the *Journal des débats*, and subsequently taught at the École des sciences politiques. In later years, he pursued an interest in fine art. His writings include *Le Maroc en paix* (1917), *Oriental art* (1928), *Souvenirs d'un vieil amateur d'art de l'Etrême-Orient* (1930), and jointly with Gaston Migeon, *Islamische Kunstwerke: Keramik, Gewebe, Teppiche* (Berlin, 1928). He died in Paris on 9 November 1931. DBF; Qui êtes-vous, 1924; Who was who, 3

Koehler, Henry, born 23 June 1884 at Dôle (Jura), France, he entered the Franciscan Order in 1903 and received his religious education in Switzerland, concurrently also taking courses at the Université de Fribourg. After his ordination in 1907, he was a professor of humanities at the Petit Séminaire de Fribourg until 1912, when he became a chaplain in Morocco, remaining there until 1961. He established numerous Christian communities, built churches, and found time for archaeological excavations as well as historical researches in archives. He was a man in the best tradition of French Franciscan monkhood soldiers. His writings include *La Grotte d'Achakar au cap Spartel* (1931), and *L'Église chrétienne du Maroc et la mission franciscaines, 1221-1790* (1934). He died in Saint-Palais (Charente-Maritime) on 17 October 1965. DBF; Hommes et destins, vol 7, pp. 281-82

Koehler, Kurt, born 16 December 1883 at Leipzig, Germany, he studied at the universities of Leipzig, Berlin, Heidelberg, and again Leipzig, where he received a Dr.phil. in 1907 for *Die orientalische Politik Ludwig XIV., ihr Verhältnis zu dem Türkenkrieg von 1683 mit einem einleitenden Kapitel über die französisch-türkischen Beziehungen von Franz I bis zum Tode Mazarins.* He edited *Die neue Türkei, 1919-1927; Rede gehalten von Gasi Mustafa Kemal Pascha in Angora vom 15. bis 20. Oktober 1927* (1928). GV; Thesis

von **Koehne**, Bernard Carl, born 14 July 1817 at Berlin, he studied history and auxiliary sciences at the universities of Berlin and Leipzig, and received a Dr.phil. in 1840 from the Universität Berlin for *De numis Frederici II electoris Brandenburgici*, and a Dr.habil. in 1843 with a thesis on numismatics and archaeology. In 1841, he founded the *Zeitschrift für Münz-, Siegel- und Wappenkunde*, and two years later, the Numismatische Gesellschaft zu Berlin. In 1845, he left Berlin to enter the Russian civil service in St. Petersburg, where he spent many years with the Hermitage Museum. His writings include *Die auf die Geschichte der Deutschen und Sarmaten bezüglichen Römischen Münzen* (1844), *Description du Musée de feu le prince Basile Kotschoubey d'après son catalogue manuscrit et recherches sur l'histoire et la numismatique des colonies grecques en Russie* (1857), and *Berlin, Moskau, St. Petersbug, 1649 bis 1763; ein Beitrag zur Geschichte der freundschaftlichen Beziehungen zwischen Brandenburg-Preußen und Rußland* (1882). He died on 5 February 1886 in Würzburg, where he had gone for medical treatment. ADtB, vol. 51, pp. 318-20

Koelbing, Huldrych Martin, born 17 June 1923 at Reiden, Kanton Luzern, Switzerland, he studied medicine at the Universität Basel and since 1955 practised ophthalmology in Basel. He also received a Dr.habil. in 1965 from the Universität Basel and in 1971 was appointed a professor of history of medicine at the Universität Zürich, a position which he held until his retirement in 1988. His writings include *Renaissance der Augenheilkunde, 1530-1630* (Bern, 1967), *Im Kampf gegen Pocken, Tollwut, Syphillis* (Basel, 1974), *Arzt und Patient in der antiken Welt* (1977), *Die ärztliche Therapie* (1985), and he was a joint author of *Kurze Geschichte der ankylosierenden Spondylitis und Spondylose* (Basel, 1964). Volume 40 (1983) of the journal *Gesnerus* was dedicated to him as Festschrift für Huldrych M. Koelbing. Kürschner, 1976-2005; Note about the author

Koelle, Sigismund Wilhelm, born 14 July 1820 or 1823 at Cleebronn, Württemberg, he entered the Basler Missionshaus in 1841, and since 1847 he was a missionary under the Church Missionary Society, London, posted to Sierra Leone, where he became an authority in African languages. In 1855, he was sent to Egypt, in 1856 to Haifa; from 1862 to 1880, he was at Constantinople, where he acquired competence in Turkish. His writings include *African native literature* (1854), *Grammar of the Bórnu and Kánuri language* (1854), *Polyglotta Africana* (1854), *Über türkische Verbal-Wurzeln* (1870), and *Mohammed und Mohammedanism* (1889). He died in London on 18 February 1902. DcAfHiB, 1986; DtBE; DtBiInd (2); LexAfrika; LuthC, 75

Kœnig (Bey), Mathieu Auguste, born in 1802 at Paris, he was educated at the Collège Henri IV in Paris, where since his classes in rhetoric he also studied Oriental languages. In 1820, he went to Egypt, where he spent some time in Alexandria before embarking on a five-year exploration of the country as well as Syria and the Sudan under the auspices of the Société de géographie de Paris. In 1827, he settled at Cairo as a teacher of French at the Egyptian Staff College (*École d'état--major*) at Jihādābād outside Cairo, concurrently translating a number of scientific and military works into Arabic. In 1834, he became a tutor to the children of the viceroy Muhammad 'Alī. At the conclusion of his services, he was awarded the title of *Bey* and appointed director of the translation bureau in the Ministry of Foreign Affairs, a post which he also retained under the successive viceroys, 'Abbās I Pasha, and Sa'īd Pasha, whose private secretary he became. He died in Alexandria on 15 April 1865. DBF; Hill; Kornrumpf², vol. 2; Vapereau

Kœnig, René, 1906-1990 see König, René

Koester, Ulrich, born 20 May 1938, he studied at the Universität Göttingen, where he received a Dr.rer.pol. in 1968 for an analysis of the demand for food and coffee, *Theoretische und empirische Analyse der Nachfrage nach Nahrungs- und Genußmitteln*. He successively became a professor of agrarian and development economics at his alma mater and the Universität Kiel. His writings include *Alternativen der Agrarpolitik* (1976), and *Grundzüge der landwirtschaftlichen Marktlehre* (1981). In 1998 he was honoured by *Landwirtschaft in der Weltwirtschaft; Festschrift anläßlich des 60. Geburtstages von Prof. Dr. Ulrich Koester*. Kürschner, 1976-2005

Koestler, Arthur, born 5 September 1905 at Budapest, he was educated at the Universität Wien and at the Polytechnische Hochschule, Wien. He was a foreign correspondent successively in the Middle East, France, Germany, and Spain. His writings include *The Scum of the earth* (1941), *Promise and fulfilment* (1949), *The Thirteenth tribe, the Khazar Empire and its heritage* (1976), and its translation, *La Treizième tribu* (1976). He died in London on 3 March 1983. Iain Hamilton wrote *Koestler* (1982). Au&Wr, 1963; ConAu, 109, new rev., 33; CurBio, 1943, 1962, 1983; DNB; Hofer; IntAu&W, 1976, 1977, 1982; Master (100); WhAm, 8; Who was who, 8; WhoWor, 1974/75-1982/83; WhoWorJ, 1965, 1972, 1978

Koettlitz, Reginald, born in 1861, he was a ship's surgeon on scientific expeditions to the Arctic and the Abyssinian highlands. He died in 1916. Hill

Koev, Ivan, born 20th cent., his writings include *Облекло и жилища на старото българско население в Разградско* (Sofia, 1942), *Българската везбена орнаментика* (1951), *Бит на Партизанския Отряд 'А. Иванов' и песенно творчество за антонивановци* (1962), *Bulgarian embroidery and weaving designs* (Sofia, 1982), and he was a joint author of *Zehn Jahre bulgarische Ethnographie* (München, 1959). NUC; OSK

Koffsky, Peter Langer, born 22 September 1946 at Washington, D.C., he graduated in 1968 from Oberlin College, and received his Ph.D. in 1977 from the University of Wisconsin for *History of Takaunga, East Africa, 1830-1896.* His writings include *The Consul General's Shanghai Postal Agency, 1867-1907* (City of Washington, Smithsonian Institution Press, 1972). NUC, 1982; WhoE, 1989/90; WhoEmL, 1991/92 (not sighted)

Kofler, Johannes (*Hans*), born 30 January 1896 at Trient (Trento), Austria, he studied classics and Romance philology at the Universität Innsbruck, where he received a doctorate in 1919. Thereafter he was for twenty years a high school teacher and concurrently completed his legal studies with a Dr.jur. in 1926. He used his 1929-30 sabbatical to pursue his interest in Oriental philology, in particular Arabic, at the Universität Leipzig. From 1939 until his death in Wien on 20 March 1947, he was a professor of Arabic and Islamic studies at the Universität Wien. His writings consist of linguistic contributions to periodicals and his translation of Ibn al-'Arabi, *Das Buch der Siegelsteine der Weisheitssprüche*, published post-humously in 1970. Hanisch; Kürschner, 1940/41; WZKM 51 (1948/52), pp. 151-155

Kogan, Moisei Markovich, born in 1905 at Odessa, Ukraine, he graduated in 1928 from the Faculty of Economics, Institute of political economy, and received his first degree in 1930 for *Мировой рынок каучука.* Miliband; Miliband²; Unesco

Kőhalmi, Katalin (Catherine/Käthe) Uray, born 11 March 1926 at Wien, she was educated at Budapest, where she also received a doctorate in 1948. She became affiliated with the Hungarian Academy of Sciences. Her writings include *A steppék nomádja lóháton, fegyverben* (1972), *Chrestomathia Sibrica; Auswahl aus der Volksdichtung der sibirischen Urvölker* (Szeged, 1977), and she was a joint author of *Mythologie der Mandschu-Tungisischen Völker* (1997), and *Götter und Mythen in Zentralasien und Nordeurasien* (1999), both published as part of the *Wörterbuch der Mythologie* (Stuttgart, 1997 and 1999). Biograf, 2004; Schöberlein

Köhbach, Markus, born 16 January 1949 at Hainburg, Austria, he received a Dr.phil. in 1976 from the Universität Wien for *Die Feldzüge nach Neusäusel und Kanizsa in den Jahren 1599 und 1600 nach der osmanischen Chronik 'Abdu'l-Qadir Efendi.* He became a professor of Turkish studies in the Institut für Orientalistik, Universität Wien. Kürschner, 1996-2005; Schwarz

Kohl, Johann Georg, born 28 April 1808 at Bremen, Germany, he grew up among relatives who had travelled extensively in the East and West Indies as well as in America. He studied at the universities of Göttingen, Heidelberg and München from 1828 to 1830 and spent the following eight years in Kurland as a private tutor, a post which allowed him a bit time for travel in the Baltic provinces as well as writing. The success of his three travel accounts published in 1841, *Petersburg in Bildern und Skizzen, Reisen in Südrußland,* and *Reisen im Inneren von Rußland und Polen,* were the beginning of a career as travel writer. He spent long periods in Berlin, Paris, and London, before residing in the United States from 1854 to 1858. In the service of the U.S.Court Service Office he published the *History of the East Coast of North America, particularly the Coast of Maine* (1869). When he returned to Germany in 1858, he settled at Bremen where he became the city librarian, a post which offered him the chance for historical research. He was the recipient of two honorary doctorates and an honorary member of several learned societies. His writings include *Die geographische Lage der Hauptstädte Europas* (1874), and he edited *Pilgerfahrt des Landgrafen Wilhelm des Tapferen von Thüringen zum heiligen Lande im Jahre 1461* (1868). He died a bachelor in Bremen on 28 October 1878. ADtB; BbD; BiD&SB; DtBE; Embacher; Master (3)

Kohl, Karl, born in 1896 he received a Dr.phil. in 1923 from the Universität Erlangen for *Über die Theorie körperlicher Himmelssphären mit besodenrer Berücksichtigung von Ibn al-Haitams Schrift über die Gestalt der Welt* and, jointly with Axel Anthon Björnbo, *Thabit's Werk über den Transversalensatz* (1924). GV; Schwarz; Sezgin

Kohlberg, Etan, born about 1940, he received a D.Phil. in 1971 from Oxford University for *The Attitude of the Imami Shi'ites to the Companions of the Prophet.* His writings include *Belief and law in Imāmī Islam* (Aldershot, Variorum, 1991), *A Medieval Muslim scholar at work; Ibn Tāwūs and his library* (1992), and *Medieval Muslim views on martyrdom* (Amsterdam, Koninklijke Nederlandse Akademie van Wetenschappen, 1997), and he edited *Jawāmi' ādāb al-sūfiyya, and 'Uyūb al-nafs wa-mudāwātuhā,* by Abū 'Abd al-Rahmān al-Sulamī (Jerusalem, Jerusalem Academic Press, 1976). Brinkman's, 1996-2000; LC; Sluglett; ZKO

Kohlbrugge, Dina Johanna, born 20th cent., she received a doctorate in 1938 from the Rijks-universiteit te Utrecht for *Atharvaveda-Parisista über Omina.* In 1957, she delivered her inaugural lecture as a teacher of Iranian studies at her alma mater entitled *Individualistik tendencies in de wereld van de Islam.* Her writings include *De ware Jacob* (1973), *Konfrontatie met de Islam* (1980), and *De* *tijding van Job in de bijbel en in de koran* (1981); she also contributed to the *Historische encyclopaedie*. Brinkman's

Kohler, Charles Alfred, born 11 January 1854 at Genève, he studied at Paris, where he received a diploma from the École pratique des hautes études, and in 1879 he graduated from the École des chartes with a thesis entitled *Négociations diplomatiques entre les Suisses et les États qui ont pris part aux guerres d'Italie de 1506 à juin 1512*. A naturalized French citizen since 1884, he entered the Bibliothèque Sainte-Geneviève, Paris, where he remained until his death. Concurrently to his professional duty, he pursued an interest in research. An auxiliary member of the Académie des inscriptions et belles-lettres since 1891, he collaborated with the publication of the *Recueil des historiens des croisades*, publishing one volume of the section, *Historiens occidentaux*. In 1896, he became secretary to the *Revue de l'Orient latin*. His writings also include *Catalogue de la Bibliothèque Saint-Geneviève* (1893-98), and *Mélanges pour servir à l'histoire de l'Orient latin et des croisades* (1900-1906). He died in Fontenay-sous-Bois (Val-de-Marne) on 28 March 1917. DBF

Köhler, Johann Bernhard, born 10 February 1742 at Lübeck, Germany, he studied Arabic under Johann Jacob Reiske, and in 1766 became a professor of Oriental languages at the Universität Kiel. A professor at Göttingen since 1770, he resigned his post in 1773 and went back to Lübeck, where he pursued private research until 1781, when he became a professor of classical and Oriental languages at the Universität Königsberg. He once more returned to Lübeck in 1786, where he eked out his living by legal work until he found a post as a proof-reader in Basel, where he died in 1802. His writings include *Observationes in sacrum codicem ex scriptoribus profanis* (1759), *Observationes philologicae in loca selecta sacri codicis* (1765), *Notae et emendationes in Theocritum; accedit specimen emendationum in scriptores arabicos* (1767). ADtB, vol. 51, pp. 317-318

Kohler, Josef, born 9 March 1849 at Offenburg, Baden, he studied law at Freiburg im Breisgau, where he received a Dr.jur. and subsequently practised his profession. He was a judge at Mannheim from 1873 to 1878, when he became a professor at the Faculty of Law in the Universität Würzburg. Since 1888 he held the same post at the Universität Berlin. He was an editor of the *Zeitschrift für vergleichende Rechtswissenschaft*, and *Archiv für bürgerliches Recht*. He was a member of several learned societies. His writings include *Rechtsvergleichende Studien über islamisches Recht* (1889). In 1919 he was honoured by *Festgabe zum 70. Geburtstag Josef Kohlers am 9. März 1919*. He died in Berlin on 3 August 1919. DtBE; DtBilnd; Hinrichsen; Kosch; NDB; OxLaw; Wer ist's, 1909-1912

Kohler, Kaufmann, born in 1843 at Fürth, Bavaria, he studied at the universities of München, Berlin, Leipzig, and Erlangen, obtaining a Dr.phil. in 1868 from the Universität Leipzig for *Der Segen Jakobs*. In the following year, he accepted an invitation from Temple Beth-El in Detroit. He became a sometime president of the Hebrew Union College, Cincinnati, Ohio. His career embodied a sincere spiritual and scholarly struggle to understand the place of tradition and ritual in a world of science and reason. His writings include *Grundriss einer systematischen Theologie des Judentums auf geschichtlicher Grundlage* (1910), and *Heaven and hell in comparative religion, with special reference to Dante's Divine comedy* (1923). In 1913 appeared *Studies in Jewish literature issued in honor of Prof. Kaufmann Kohler on the occasion of his seventieth birthday*. He died in N.Y.C. on 28 January 1926. ANB; BioIn, 7, 16; CnDiAmJBi; DAB; DcNAA; EncJud; JüdLex; Master (9); NatCAB, vol. 13, p. 396; Wer ist's, 1909-1922; WhAm, 1; Wininger

Köhler, Ludwig Hugo, born 14 April 1880 at Neuwied/Rhein, Germany, he studied theology, Semitic languages, and education at the Universität Zürich, where he later received a Dr.phil. After his ordination in 1904 he successively became a pastor at Aeugst am Albis, and Langnau im Sihltal. His writings, partly under the pseudonym, Hugo Ratmich, include *Hebräisches und aramäisches Lexikon zum Alten Testament*, and its translation, *The Hebrew and Aramaic lexicon of the Old Testament* (1994). He died in Zürich on 25 November 1956. DtBE; DtBilnd (4); Kürschner, 1926-1954; NDB; OxLaw; Wer ist's, 1928, 1935

Köhler, Michael A., born in 1958, he studied history, comparative religion, theology, and international law at the universities of Bonn, Tübingen, and Hamburg, where he received a Dr.phil. in 1987 for *Allianzen und Verträge zwischen fränkischen und islamischen Herrschern im Vorderen Orient*, a work which was publlished in 1991, and translated by P. M. Holt entitled *Alliances and treaties between Frankish and Muslim rulers in the Near East* (2004). In 1987, he became a permanent representative of the Konrad-Adenauer-Stiftung in Morocco, and in the following year his responsibility was extended to include also Tunisia. GV; Note about the author

Köhler, Oswin, born 14 October 1911 at Tiefthal (Thüringen), Germany, he received a Dr.phil. in 1948 from Humboldt-Universität, Berlin, for *Die nilotischen Sprachen*, and also a Dr.habil. in 1952 for *Die Verbreitung und Gliederung der Gur-Sprachen*. He became a professor of African languages and culture at his alma mater. His writings include *Die Verbreitung und Gliederung der Gur-Sprachen* (1952), and *Geschichte der Erforschung der nilotischen Sprachen* (1955). In 1986 appeared *Contemporary studies on Khoisan in honour of Oswin Köhler on the occasion of his seventy-fifth birthday* (1986). Kürschner, 1950-1996|

Köhler, Reinhold, born 24 June 1830 at Weimar, Germany, he studied classical archaeology and philology at the universities of Jena, Leipzig, and Bonn, gaining a Dr.phil. in 1853 at Jena for *Über die Dionysiaka des Nonnus von Panopolis*. After his father's death in 1851, he abandoned all plans for the future, provided for the family and eked out his living by giving private lessons and working in the local library in a subordinate position. Only after five years as head of the library was he promoted senior librarian. He was a well-versed literary historian and critic. His writings include *Nasr-eddin's Schwänke und Nachtrag* (1862), *Dante's Göttliche Komödie und ihre deutschen Übersetzungen* (1865), *Herders Cid und seine französische Quelle* (1867). On 11 October 1890 he suffered a fracture of the tight at the library and died in agony on 15 August 1892. ADtB, vol. 51, pp. 317-318; DtBE; DtBilnd (2); NDB

Köhler, Wilhelm, born in 1870, he received a Dr.phil. in 1926 from the Universität München for *Die Kurdenstadt Bitlis nach dem türkischen Reisewerk des Ewlija Tschelebi*, and its Turkish translation by Hayder Işık, *Seyahatnamesinde Bitlis ve halkı* (1989). NUC, pre-1956; Schwarz

Köhler, Wolfgang Willy August, born in 1942, he received a Dr.phil. in 1969 from the Universität Frankfurt am Main for *Hugo von Hoffmansthal und "Tausendundeine Nacht;" Untersuchungen zur Rezeption des Orients*. From 1971 to 1974, he was a visiting lecturer at the universities of Bradford, England, and Alexandria, Egypt. In 1975 he was temporarily associated with Deutsches Orient-Institut, Hamburg. In 1993, he was a free lance Middle East correspondent to the *Frankfurter Allgemeine Zeitung*. His writings include *Muhammad Iqbal und die drei Reiche des Geistes* (1977). DrBSMES, 1993; Note about the author; Schwarz

Kohlhase, Norbert, born 24 September 1927, he received a Dr.rer.pol. in 1965 from the Freie Universität Berlin for *Dichtung und politische Moral, dargestellt am Beispiel von Brecht und Camus*. He was a civil servant of the European Economic Community. His writings include *Einheit in der Vielfalt; Essays zur europäischen Geschichte, Kultur und Gesellschaft* (1988). WhoEIO, 1982

Kohlhoff, Hartmut, born 20th cent., his writings include *Geld für jedermann; die verschiedensten neueren Kreditmöglichkeiten* (Düren/Rhld., Schweiger, 1961). GV

Kohlmeier, Johann, born about 1940, he received a Dr.phil. in 1969 from the Universität Freiburg im Üchtland for *Vita est actus primus; eine Untersuchung der Lebensmetaphysik des Petrus Hispanus*. GV

Kohlrausch, Ludwig Ludolph, born 12 August 1781 at Hannover, he was a student at the Universität Göttingen since 1798. In 1801, he became a tutor at its Faculty of Theology, and three years later, an auxiliary teacher at the Lyceum, Hannover, concurrently serving as a hospital priest as well as establishing an institution for boys. On 4 August 1811 he received his doctorate, and in 1814, he became parson of Deinsen and Marienhagen. His health soon deteriorated and he died on 14 March 1818. DtBilnd (1)

Kohlschütter, Andreas, born in 1935, he was a sometime Middle East correspondent of the Hamburg weekly, *die Zeit*. He was a joint author of *Ein Genie in chaotischer Zeit; Edmund H. Stinnes über seinen Vater Hugo Stinnes* (1979), and *Afghanistan, eine Sowjetrepublik?* (1980). LC

Kohn, Albert, born 14 September 1814 at Preßburg, Hungary, he was a student of Schotten-gymnasium, Wien, 1826-1832, and subsequently studied philosophy at the Universität Wien, gaining a Dr.phil. in 1834. A student of Arabic and Persian under Hammer-Purgstall, he served for three semesters as a lecturer at the Protestant Faculty, Wien. Upon Hammer-Purgstall's recommendation to Sylvestre de Sacy and J. T. Reinaud, he went in 1836 for two years to Paris, where he studied Arabic, Persian, Sanskrit, and Turkish under the eminent scholars of the day. Declining the chair of Arabic and Persian at Odessa, he preferred to accompany Baron James von Rothschild to Italy, and remained in his service for twenty years. In 1841, he went to Alger, where he established the first Jewish-French school. He subsequently founded Jewish benevolent institutions in many parts of the Ottoman Empire, in Jerusalem, Jaffa, Constantinople, Alexandria, Cairo, Korfu, and Saloniki. His writings include *Die Notablenversammlung der Israeliten Böhmens in Prag* (Wien, 1852). He died in Paris on 15 March 1877. NUC, pre-1956; Wininger

Kohn, Albin, born 19th cent., he was a joint author, with Richard Andree, of *Sibirien und das Amurgebiet; Geschichte und Reisen, Landschaften und Völker zwischen Ural und Beringstraße* (1876), and jointly with Christian Mehlis, *Materialien zur Vorgeschichte des Menschen im östlichen Europa* (1879). GV; NUC

Kohn, Hans, born 15 September 1891 at Prag, Austria, he received a Dr.jur. in 1923 from the local Karls Universität. He was a Middle East correspondent for Frankfurt and Zürich newspapers from 1925 to 1933. He emigrated to the United States and was successively a professor of history at Smith College, Northampton, Mass., and City College of C.U.N.Y. His writings include *Sinn und Schicksal der Revolution* (1923), *Geschichte der nationalen Bewegung im Orient* (1928), *Die Europäisierung des Orients* (1934), *Nationalismus und Imperialismus im Vorderen Orient* (1931), *Orient und Okzident* (1931), *Living in a world revolution* (1970), and he was a joint author of *Zionistische Politik* (1927). He died in Philadelphia, Pa., on 16 March 1971. Au&Wr, 1963; BioIn, 4, 8, 9, 11 (not sighted); CnDiAmJBi; ConAu, new rev., 4; DrAS, 1969 H; EncTR, 1976; Master (8); Note; WhAm, 9; WhE&EA; WhoWorJ, 1965; Wininger

Kohn, Samuel, born 21 September 1841 at Baja, Hungary, he was educated at the local secondary school and studied at Jüdisch-theologisches Seminar, Breslau, as well as the Universität Breslau. After completing his study in 1866, he was appointed rabbi in Budapest, where he was the first to introduce the Hungarian liturgy. Since 1898 he was a lecturer in homiletic at the Landesrabbinerschule in Budapest. His writings include *Zur Sprache, Literatur und Dogmatik der Samaritaner* (1876), *Héber kútforrások és adatok Magyarország történnetéhez* (1881), and *Die Sabbatharier in Siebenbürgen* (1894). He died in Budapest on 10 March 1920. GeistigeUng; JewEnc; JüdLex; MagyarZL; ÖBL; Wininger

Koht, Halvdan, born 7 July 1873 at Tromsø, Norway, he studied at the universities of København, Leipzig, Paris, and Oslo, where he received a doctorate in philosophy. He was a professor of history at Universitetet i Oslo, served as dean of faculty, visiting professor, and foreign minister, 1935-1941. His writings include *The Life of Ibsen* (1931), *Norsk vilje* (1933), *Saga litteraturen* (1938), *Essai sur l'étude de l'histoire du sentiment national* (1951), *Education of an historian* (1957), and *Minnearv og historie* (1965). On his sixtieth and eightieth birthdays he was honoured by *Festskrift til Halvdan Koht på sekstiårsdagen 7de juli 1933*, and *Norsk Folkemål; grunnskrifter og innlegg gjennom hundre år til Halvdan Koht på åttiårsdagen 7. juli 1953*. He died in Oslo on 12 December 1965. BioIn, 4, 7 (not sighted); ConAu, 85-88; NorskBL; NorskBL²; WhE&EA

Kohut, Alexander (Sandor), born 11 June 1842 at Félegyháza (Stuhlweissenburg), Hungary, he was an outstanding Orientalist of his age, who had received a Dr.phil. in 1866 from the Universität Leipzig for *Über die jüdische Angelologie und Daemonologie in ihrer Abhängigkeit von Parsismus*. He was a member of the Hungarian parliament, who emigrated to the United States, where he became a founder of the Jewish Theological Seminary in New York, and subsequently a professor. His writings include *Kritische Beleuchtung der persischen Pentateuch-Übersetzung des Jacob Ben Joseph Tavus unter stetiger Rücksichtnahme auf die ältesten Bibelversionen* (1871), *Notes on a hitherto unknown exegetical, theological and philosophical commentary to the Pentateuch composed by Aboo Manzur al-Dhamâri, with appendices containing Hebrew and Arabic extracts* (1892). He died in New York City on 25 May 1894. In 1897 appeared *Semitic studies in memory of Rev. Dr. Alexander Kohut*. ADtB, vol. 51, pp. 320-21; ANB; BbD; BiD&SB; BioIn, 16; CnDiAmJBi; DAB; DtDE; GeistigeUng; JewEnc; JüdLex; MagyarZL; Master (4); NatCAB, vol. 14 (not sighted); ÖBL; WhAm, H; Wininger

Kohut, George Alexander, born 11 February 1874 at Stuhlweißenburg (Székesfehérvár), Hungary, he studied three years at Columbia University, New York, as well as the Rabbinical Seminary, New York, to which two years at the Universität Berlin and the Hochschule für die Wissenschaft des Judentums were added. After ordination, he went for three years to Dallas, Tex., as a rabbi. Since 1900, he pursued a career in research and literature. In 1904 he became librarian at the Jewish Theological Seminary of America, New York. He died in New York on 31 December 1933. CnDiAmJBi; DAB; EncJud; EncJud²; JewEnc; JüdLex; Master (2); NatCAB, vol. 26 (not sighted)

Kojanec, Giovanni, born 9 January 1932 at Roma, he received doctorates at Roma and Trieste, and was admitted to the bar. He was a lawyer at the ministry of foreign affairs, before becoming a professor at the Università di Roma. His writings include *Trattati e terzi sati* (1961), *Investimenti all'estero* (1970), *L'Italiano nel mondo e la sua condizione giuridica* (1981), *Legislazione dell'Africa* (1982), *Legislazione dell'Asia* (1986), and *Nuove norme sulla cittadinanza italiana; reflessi interni ed internazionali* (1995). WhoWor, 1991/92

Kokiev, Georgiĭ Aleksandrovich, fl. 20th cent., his writings include Очерки по Осетии (1926), Склеповые сооружения Горной Осетии (1928), Крестьяанская реформа в северной Осетии (1940), Аграрное движение в Кабарде (1946), Борьба кабардинской бедноты за советскую власть (1946), Некоторые сведения из древней истории адыгов (1946), and Крестьяанская реформа в Кабарде (1947). NUC; OSK

Koklianova, Anna Aleksandrovna, born 26 July 1926 in the Tatar Autonomous Republic, she graduated in 1949 from the Faculty of Philology, Moscow, and received her first degree in 1953 for Сбособы синтакстческой связи слов в современном узбекском литературном языке. She was since 1952 affiliated with the Institute of Philology, Soviet Academy of Sciences. Her writings include *Категория времени в современном узбекском языке* (1963). Miliband; Miliband²; OSK

Kokovtsov, Pavel Konstantinovich, born in 1861 at Pavlovska, he graduated in 1884 from the Faculty of Oriental Languages, St. Petersburg, specializing in Judeo-Arabic. He was a fellow of the Soviet Academy of Sciences. His writings include *Еврейско-хазарская переписка в X веке* (1932). He died during the siege of Leningrad on 1 January 1942. BiobibSOT, pp. 191-92; Krachkovskii; Miliband; Miliband²; VostokMStP, p. 251

van **Kol**, Henri Hubert, born 23 May 1852 at Eindvoven, the Netherlands, he was educated at Turnhout and Roermond. Since 1870 he studied at Polytechnische School in Delft, during which time he was active in socialist politics at home and in France. In 1876, he started an eighteen-year career as engineer with the Indische Waterstraat in the Dutch East Indies, being posted successively to eastern and north-central Java, first with Sampean-Werken and later with Pemali-Werken, retaining his socialist connections with Holland throughout this period, even becoming in 1884 a regular contributor to the weekly *Recht voor Allen*, and always propagating ethical politics. In the service of the French Government he made a study of some French colonial schemes. His writings, partly under the pseudonym Rienzi, include *Socialisme en vrijheid* (1893), *Land en volk van Java* (1896), *Uit onze koloniën* (1903), and *In de kustlanden van Noord-Afrika* (1911). He died in Aywaille, Belgium, on 22 August 1925. BiBenelux² (3); BWN, vol. 3, pp. 346-48

Kol (Kolodny), Moshe, born 28 May 1911 at Pinsk, Belorussia, he was educated at Pinsk and Jerusalem. He was a member of Knesset, and served as a minister from 1966 to 1974. His writings include *Youth Aliyah* (1957), *Aliyah des jeunes* (1965), and *Mentors and friends* (1983). IntWW, 1974-1989/90|; WhoIsrael, 1958-1985/86; WhoWor, 1974/75; WhoWorJ, 1972, 1978

Kolankowski, Ludwig, born 21 June 1882 at Nadwónej, Poland, he studied history at Lwow, and Berlin, and received a doctorate in 1913 from Uniwersytet Jagielloński, Kraków. He was a historian, librarian, and politician whose writings include *Hold pruski, 10. IV 1525* (1925), *Dzieje Wielkiego Księstwa Litewskiego za Jagiellonów* (1930), *Polska Jagiellonów; dzieje polityczne* (1936), and *Ludwik Kolankowski, 1882-1982; materialy sesji w stulecie urodzin* (1983). He died in Toruń on 9 March 1956. Czy wiesz, 1938; OSK; Polski (12); PSB

Kolars, John F., born 25 March 1929 at Walla Walla, Wash., he graduated in 1953 from the University of Washington and received a Ph.D. in 1963 from the University of Chicago for *Tradition, season, and change in a Turkish village*. He successively taught cultural geography and geography of the Near East at Rutgers University, New Brunswick, N.J., and from 1961 to his retirement in the Department of Near Eastern Studies, University of Michigan. His writings include *On farm water management in Aegaean Turkey, 1968-74* (1983), and he was a joint author of *Geography; the study of location, culture, and environment* (1974), and *The Euphrates River and the southeast Anatolian development project* (1991). AmM&WSc, 1973 S; AmM&WSc, 1976 P; *MESA Roster of members, 1982-1990*; NatFacDr, 1990; WhoAm, 1974-1988/89

Kolarz, Walter J., born 26 April 1912 at Teplitz-Schönau, Bohemia, he was a socialist journalist from his early years. He was the representative of the Prague Orbis-Verlag, first in Berlin and later in Paris. In 1939 he settled in the UK. Since 1949 he was associated with the East European Service of the BBC, London. His writings, partly under the pseudonym Bernhard Vernier, include *Das Regime Blum* (Prag, 1935), *Stalin und das ewige Rußland* (1948), *Die Nationalitätenpolitik der Sowjetunion* (1956), *Islam in the Soviet Union, 1917-1960* (1960), *Religion in the Soviet Union* (1961), and *Die Religionen in der Sowjetunion* (1963). He died in London on 21 July 1962. AmAu&B; BioHbDtE; KDtLK, Nekrolog, 1936-1970; OSK

Kolchin, Boris Aleksandrovich, fl. 20th cent., he was an archaeologist whose writings include *Техника обработки в древней Руси* (1953), *Новгородские древности; деревянные изделия* (1968), *Археологическое изучение Новгорода* (1978), *Wooden artefacts from medieval Novgorod* (1989), and he was a joint author of *Древняя Русь; город, замок, село* (1985), and *Древняя Русь; быт и культура* (1997). NUC; OSK

Kolesnikov, Alii Ivanovich, born 5 December 1935 at Voroshilovgrad (Lugansk), Ukraine, he graduated in 1964 from the Oriental Faculty, Leningrad State University, and received his first degree in 1969 for *Иран накануне арабского завоевания*. Since 1967 he was associated with the Leningrad Branch of the Oriental Institute, Soviet Academy of Sceinces. He spent four years in Kabul. His writings include *Иран в начале VII века* (1970), its Persian translation, *Īrān dar āstānah-i yūrīsh-i tāzīyān* (1976), and *Завоевание Ирана арабами* (1982). Miliband; Miliband²; Schoeberlein; ZKO

Kolesnyk, Alexander, born 12 October 1933 at Wien, he was educated at German schools in Prag, 1939-1945, and subsequently in Bad Langensalza, Germany. From 1952 to 1957, he studied philosophy at Karl-Marx-Universität, Leipzig. In 1957, he became an academic assistant at the Academy of Sciences, Berlin. He later joined the Institut für Philosophie as a specialist in Marxist-Leninist philosophy. He was a joint author of *Über materialistische Dialektik; eine Studie* (Berlin, 1959), and *Das hussitische Denken im Lichte seiner Quellen* (Berlin, 1969). Thesis

Koleva, Elena, born 20th cent., she was a keeper of the Ethnographical Museum in Plovdiv and the editor of *Етнографски Музей Пловдив; народно изкуство* (Sofia, 1971). LC

van der **Kolff**, Gerard Hendrik, born 20th cent., he was associated with the Netherland's Koninklijk Instituut vor de Tropen. He became a professor of Oriental economics at the Universiteit van Amsterdam, where he delivered his inaugural lecture on 3 May 1957 entitled *De moeilijkkeden rondom het integratievraagstuk voor landen in versnelde sociaal-economische overgang.* His writings include *The social aspects of the Gezira scheme in the Sudan* (1957), *Tussen Steenbok en Kreeft* (1960), and he was an editor of the *Sticusa jaarboek.* Brinkman's, 1951-1960

Kolias, Taxiarchis Georgio, born 27 November 1951 at Thessaloniki, he received a Dr.phil. in 1980 from the Universität Wien for *Die Schutzwaffen der byzantinischen Armee.* He subsequently taught Byzantine history at the University of Ioannina. His writings include the enlarged version of his thesis, *Byzantische Waffen; ein Beitrag zur byzantinischen Waffenkunde von den Anfängen bis zur lateinischen Eroberung* (1988). EVL, 1998-2004

Kolinsky, Martin, born 24 June 1936 at Winnipeg, Man., he graduated in 1960 from the University of Saskatchewan, and received a Ph.D. in 1966 from the London School of Economics. He taught political science in various capacities at the University of Birmingham. His writings include *Law, order and riots in Mandatory Palestine, 1928-35* (1993), *Britain's war in the Middle East; strategy and diplomacy, 1936-42* (1999), and he was a joint editor of *Britain and the Middle East in the 1930s; security problems, 1935-1939* (1992). ConAu, 61-64, new rev., 8; Note; WrDr, 1980/82-2005

Koliqi, Ernest(o), he was born 20 May 1903 at Shkodër (Scutari), Ottoman Turkey, where he also received his first education at the Jesuit Collegio S. Francesco Saverio. In 1911, his family sent him for further study, particularly Italian language, to the Collegio Arici in Brescia, where Italian became his second mother tongue, and where he also showed an interest in journalism. He returned home in 1921 and two years later he was one of the founders of the periodical, *Ora e maleve*, concurrently contributing to Albanian dailies and journals. Political reasons obliged him to leave Albania in 1924, spending the next four years in Montenegro and Bosnia. In 1930 he returned to Albania and taught Albanian literature, first at the commercial school in Vlorë (Valona) and later at the State Lyceum in Shkodër. In 1933 he returned to Italy and in 1936 he became a lecturer in Albanian philology at Padua, where he completed his academic study in the following year. After the war, he taught Albanian language and literature at the Università di Roma until his death on 15 January 1975. His writings include *Shkrimtarët shqiptarë* (1941), and *Saggi di letteratura albanese* (1972). Chi è, 1961; Elsie; MEW; *Südost-Forschungen*, 32 (1973), pp. 321-322

Kolkowicz, Roman, born 15 November 1929 in Poland, he emigrated in 1949 to the United States, graduated in 1954 from the University of Buffalo, and received a Ph.D. in 1965 from the University of Chicago. He was a political scientist successively with Rand Corp., Santa Monica, Calif., and the University of California at Los Angeles. His writings include *The Soviet Union and arms control; a superpower dilemma* (1970); he edited *Soldiers, peasants, and bureaucrats* (1982); and he was a joint editor of *Arms control and international security* (1984). He also produced numerous short research reports for Rand Corporation. AmM&WSc, 1973 S, 1978 S; ConAu, 116, 154

Kollár, Johann (Ján), born 29 July 1793 at Mošove, Slovakia, to a Protestant family, he studied theology at Preßburg, where he graduated from high school and subsequently studied at the Universität Jena. After his ordination in 1819, he served as a preacher at Budapest until 1849, when he was appointed to the newly established chair of Slavic archaeology at the Universität Wien. His writings include *Über die literarische Wechselseitigkeit zwischen den verschiedenen Stämmen und Mundarten der slawischen Nation* (1837). He died in Wien on 24 January 1852. BiD&SB; BioIn, 7; CasWL; Filipsky; HrvEnc; Magyar; Master (6); Megali; ÖBL

Kollár von Keresztén, Adam Franz, born 15 April 1723 at Terchová, Hungary, he entered the Society of Jesus in 1838 but left ten years later in order to pursue an interest in philology at the Kaiserliche Hofbibliothek in Wien. When he died in 1783, he had become director of the *Bibliothek*. He published the second edition of Franciszek Meninski, *Institutiones linguæ Turcicæ* (1756). Two *defter* from his collection have survived in Göttingen. AAS (Bratislava) 16 (1980), p. 9; Wurzbach

Kollbrunner, Fritz, born 19 November 1937 at Wängi, Kanton Turgau, Switzerland, he received a doctorate in missionary sciences and subsequently taught in the Faculty of theology in Luzern from

287

1976 to 1990. His writings include *Die Katholizität der Kirche und die Mission* (1973). Kürschner, 1992, 1996|

Kollek, Theodore (Teddy), born in 1911 at Wien, he went to Palestine in 1934 and entered politics. He was a sometime mayor of Jerusalem. His writings include *My Jerusalem; twelve talks in the world's holiest city* (1990). ConAu, 29-32; CurBio, 1974, 1993; IntWW, 1974/75-2005; Master (8); MidE, 1978-1982/83; Wholsrael, 1972-2001; WhoWor, 1974/75-1978/79; WhoWorJ, 1965, 1972, 1978, 1987

Koller, Ange, born in 1896, he was a Franciscan Father whose writings include *Essai sur l'esprit du berbère marocain* (1946), and its translations *Los bereberes marroquíes* (1952), and *I berberi marocchini* (1953). He died in Jerusalem on 1 September 1955. LC; *Studia orientalia*, 1 (1956), p. 307

Köller, Ernst, born 8 October 1918 at Wien, he received a Dr.phil. in 1943 from the Universität Wien. He was subsequently associated with antiquities at the Dorotheum, Wien. He was a sometime editor of *Alte und moderne Kunst*, Wien. WhoAustria, 1964

Kollewijn, Roeland Duco, born 7 December 1892 at Amsterdam, he studied law at the Universiteit van Amsterdam and received his doctorate in 1917. He successively was a professor at the universities of Batavia, Groningen, and Leiden. His writings include *Intergentiel recht in Algerije* (1953), *American-Dutch private international law* (1955), and *Vier jaaren Nederlandse rechtspraak international privatrecht, 1964-1968* (1972). He died in Leiden on 1 September 1972. BWN, vol. 1 , pp. 310-11; *Wie is dat*, 1956

Kollotai, Vladimir Mikhaĭlovich, born 2 September 1927 at Berlin, he graduated in 1949 from the State Institute of International Relations, Moscow, and received his first degree in 1953 for «Англо-американская борьба за олово и каучук», and his doctorate in 1966 for *Проблемы экономического развития освободившихся стран*. He was since 1956 affiliated with the Institute of World Economy and International Relations. His writings include *Иностранные инвестиции в экономически славо-развитых странах* (1960), *Пути преодоления экономической отсталомти* (1967), and *Планирование и программирование в развивающихся* (1970). Miliband; Mliband²

Kollwitz, Johannes Franz, born 3 April 1903 at Magdeburg, Prussia, he studied Catholic theology at the universities of Paderborn, Freiburg/Breisgau, and Breslau. Ordained in 1928, he served two years as a clergy in Halle, before completing his formal education in 1930 with a Dr.theol. from the Universität Freiburg im Breisgau for *Die Lipsanothek von Brescia*. From 1932 to 1933, he visited the Balkans and Turkey, and from 1934 to 1937, he was attached to Deutsches Archäologisches Institut, Roma. During the war, he was a priest successively at Halle and Meinberg (Lippe). He subsequently became a professor of patrology and Christian archaeology, first at Erzbischhöfliche Akedemie, Paderborn, and later the Universität Freiburg im Breisgau. His writings include *Oströmische Plastik der theodosianischen Zeit* (1941). He died in Freiburg on 1 April 1968. DtBE; Kürschner, 1954-1966; NDB; *Wer ist wer*, 1955-1967/68

Kolman, Arnošt (Ernest), born 6 December 1892 at Prag, he studied at the local Universita Karlova and received a doctorate in 1934. Since 1917, he was living in the Soviet Union. He was a mathe-matician and philosopher successively at the universities of Moscow and Praha. His writings include *Ленин и новейшая физика* (1959), *Математика до эпохи возрождения* (1961), *Výhledy do budoucna* (1962), and *Мы не должны были так жить* (1982). He died in 1979. Bioln, 11; IntWW, 1974/75-1979; WhoSocC, 78; WhoWor, 1974/75

Kolmodin, Johannes Axel, born 22 February 1884 at Bromma förs., Stockholm, he studied Semitic languages at Uppsala Universitet, and Turkish at Orientalisches Seminar, Berlin. He served as a Swedish delegate to the Lausanne Conference of 1923. He was later posted to the Swedish Legation at Addis Abeba until his retirement in 1931. His writings include *Traditions de Tsazzega et Hazzega* (1912-15). Elizabeth Özdalga edited *The last dragoman; the Swedish Orientalist Johannes Kolmodin as scholar, activist, and diplomat* (2005). He died in Addis Abeba on 9 October 1933. Publisher's catalogue; SBL; ScBlnd (1); SMK

Kolodny, Émile Yerahmiel, born 20th cent., he was associated with the Institut de recherches méditerranéennes, Aix-en-Provence. His writings include *La population des îles de la Grèce; essai de géographie insulaire en Méditerranéen orientale* (Aix-en-Provence, 1974), and *Samothrace sur Neckar; des migrants grecs dans l'agglomeration de Stuttgart* (Aix-en-Provence, 1982). LC; OSK

Kolokol'tsov, Dmitriĭ Grigor'evich, born in 1918, his writings include *Экспедиция в Хива в 1873 году* (St. Petersburg, 1873). NYPL

Kol'tsova-Masal'skaia (Kolzow-Massalski), Elena Mikhailovna, born Helen Ghika into a noble family on 22 January 1828 or 1829 at Bucureşti, Walachia, she was educated by an English nanny, and from the age of seven by a Greek scholar. In 1841, forseeing the revolution which took place the following year, Prince Michael Ghinka took his family to Dresden, Saxony, to complete the education of his children. Here, Elena completed her studies of modern languages. In 1849, she was married to the Russian, Prince Kol'tsov-Masal'skiĭ, but the marriage was not a congenial one and lasted only six years. Being without children to link her in feeling to Russia, she left in 1855 for Ostende, Belgium, moving on to the Canton Tessin, Switzerland, where she spent some years, producing volume after volume. In 1860, she was in Athens, where she was made honorary member of the Archaeological Society of Athens. In 1866, she became a member of the Société de géographie, later being awarded a gold medal from the Institut Confucius for her Oriental studies. The Greek Chamber of Deputies in April 1868 awarded her with the citizenship of Greece for her efforts to assist the people of Candia to throw off the Turkish oppressor's yoke. In 1871 appeared her great work, *The Albanians in Roumania*. Her writings, largely under the pseudonym Dora d'Istria (Δωρα ντ Ιστρια), include *Αι Ιονιοι Νεσοι υπο την δεσποτειαν της ενετιας και την Αγγλικην προστασιαν* (1859), *Les Femmes d'Orient* (1859-60), a work which was translated into English, Russian, and Greek, *Excursions en Roumélie et en Marée* (1863), *Des Femmes d'une femme* (1865), *Fylétia e Arberaré préj Kanekate laoshima* (1867), *La Poésie des Ottomans* (1877). She died in 1888. Armand Pommier wrote a biography, *La comtesse Dora d'Istria, sa vie et ses œuvres sur la Russie et sur l'Orient* (Bruxelles, 1863). BbD; BiD&SB; DtBiInd (1); EncCoWW; Master (1); Megali, vol. 9, p. 609; *Rivista contemporanea*, Torino, 1869, fasc. 180, pp. 107-109; *Rivista Europea*, 4 (1873), pp. 54-71; *Scribner's monthly*, 17 (December 1878), pp. 225-233; *Unsere Zeit*, neue Folge, 2 (1866), pp. 431-444

Kolvenbach, Peter Hans, born in 1926 at Druten, the Netherlands, he was a Jesuit who studied at the Katholieke Universiteit Nijmegen and Université Saint-Joseph, Beirut, where he later also served as a professor of philology from 1968 to 1981. His writings include *Fedeli a Dio e all'uomo; i Gesuiti un'avanguardia obbediente di fronte alle sfide della modernità* (Torino, 1990). BioIn, 14, 17; CurBio, 1984; WhoWor, 1984-1989/90

Kolzow-Massalski, Helene, 1828-1888 *see* Kol'tsova-Masal'skaia, Elena Mikhailovna

Komakhidze, Nodar Vladimirovich, born 15 June 1931 at Akhaltsikhe, Soviet Georgia, he graduated in 1953 from the Oriental Faculty, Tiflis State University and received his first degree in 1966 for *Крушение колониализма на Востоке*. Since 1961 he was associated with the Oriental Institute of the Soviet Georgian Academy of Sciences. His writings include *Проблема преодоления социал-эконом. отсталости востока Турции в программн. установках буржуазн. политич. партии страны* (1985). Miliband; Miliband²

Komarov, Érik Naumovich, born 19 June 1927 at Moscow, he graduated in 1950 from the Moscow Oriental Institute and received his first degree in 1960 for *Аграрные отношения и земельно-налоговая политика английских колонизаторов в Бенгалии в XVII- второй половине XVIII века*. He was successively associated with Moscow State University and the Oriental Institute of the Soviet Academy of Sciences. His writings include *Мировоззрение Мохандаса Карамчанда Ганди* (1969), *Indo-Soviet cooperation* (1976), and *В России и Индии из воспомиваний и наблюдений индолога* (1998). Miliband; Miliband²

Komarov, Vladimir Leont'evich, born in 1869 at St. Petersburg, he graduated from the local university. He was a botanist, professor at his alma mater, and a sometime president of the Soviet Academy of Sciences. His writings include *Введение к флорам Китая и Монголии* (1908), *Кратки очерк растительности Сибири* (1922), and *Жизнь и труды Карла Линнея* (1923). He died in Moscow in 1945. GSE; Krachkovskiĭ, p. 256; OSK

Komarovskiĭ, Leonid Alekseevich, 1846-1912 *see* Kamarovskiĭ, Leonid Alekseevich

Komissarov, Daniil Samuilovich, born in 1907 in Turkmenistan, he graduated in 1934 from the Leningrad Institute of History, Philology and Linguistcis and received his first degree in 1948 for «К истории развития мысли о реформе алфавита новоперсидского языка» and his doctorate in 1965 for *Творчество Садека Хедаята и его место в современной персидской литературе*. He was from 1936 to 1941 a deputy dean at the Faculty of Philology, Leningrad, and from 1941 to 1950 a diplomat in Iran. In 1968 he was appointed a professor. His writings include *Садек Хедаят; жизнь и творчество* (1967). Miliband; Miliband²

Komorowski, Zygmunt, born 20th cent., his writings include *Szkolnictwo w kulturach Afryki* (1973), *Tradycje i współczesność Afryki Zachodniej* (1973), *Wśród legend i prawd Afryki* (1974), *Wprowadzenie do socjologii Afryki* (1978), and he was a joint author of *Ludy Afryki* (1985).

Kompantsev, Igor' Mikhaĭlovich, borm 13 January 1923 in the Ukraine, he graduated in 1951 from the Oriental Institute, Moscow, and received his first degree from a school of diplomatists. He was a sometime head of the Pakistan Section in the Asia Institute, Soviet Academy of Sciences. His writings include *Пакистан и Советский Союз* (1970). Miliband; Miliband²

Kondakchian, Raffi Pogosovich, born 13 October 1927 at Sukhumi, Georgian Soviet Republic, he graduated in 1951 at Erevan and received his first degree in 1964 for *Внутренняя политика демократической партии Турции, 1950-1960 гг.* He was since 1958 affiliated with the Armenian Academy of Sciences. His writings include *Внешняя политика Турции в годы второй мировой войны* (1978), and *Турция; внутренняя политика и ислам* (1983). Miliband; Miliband²

Kondakov, Nikodim Pavlovich, born in 1844 at Khalan, Russia, he was a professor of archaeology, architecture, and fine art at Novorossisk University. He emigrated after the 1917 revolution and became successively a professor of fine art at Sofia and Praha. His writings include *Путешесивие на Синай в 1881 году* (1882), *Русские клады* (1896), *О научных задачах истории древнерусскаго искусства* (1899), *Македонія; археологическое путешествіе* (1909), *Иконографія Богоматери* (1914-15), *The Russian ikon* (1928-29), *Die russische Ikone* (1928-29), *Очерки и заметки по истории средневековаго искусства и культуры* (1929), and *Histoire et monuments des émaux byzantins* (1992). In 1916 appeared *Recueil d'études dédiées à la mémoire de N. P. Kondakov*. He died in Praha on 17 February 1925. BiDSovU; Český; EnBul; EnSlovar; Kornrumpf³, vol. 2

Kondaraki, Vasilii Khristoforovich, born 19th cent., he was a historian, ethnographer, and geographer, whose writings include *Универсальное орисание Крыма* (Sankpeterburg, 1875), *В память столетія Крыма; историческія картины Тавриды* (Sankpeterburg, 1883), and *Эписоды и разсказы из Крымской Войны* (Moscow, 1883). BiobibSOT; NUC

Kondaurov, A. N., fl. 1935-1940, his writings include *Патриархальная домашняя община и общинные дома у ягнобце* (Moscow, 1940). NUC; OSK

Kondis (Κόντης), Basil (Βασίλειος), born about 1950, he received a Ph.D. in 1976 from a New York university for *Greece and Albania, 1908-1914*, and its Albanian translation *Greqia dhe Shqipëria në shekullin XX* (Selanik, 1997). He was associated with the Institute for Balkan Studies, Thessaloniki. His writings include *The Greek minority in Albania; a documentary record, 1921-1993* (1994), and he was a joint author of *Resurgent irredentism; documents on Skopje "Macedonian" nationalist aspirations, 1934-1992* (1993), *Η επεκτατιη πολιτικη των Σκοπιων; συλλογη εγγραφων, 1934-1992* (1993), and *Ελληνισμος της βορειου ηπειρουκαι ελληνοαλβανικες σχεσεις* (1995-1997). LC; Note; OSK

Kondrat'ev, Gelii Sergeevich, born 11 June 1930 at Sevastopol, Crimea, he graduated in 1954 from the Moscow Oriental Institute and received his first degree in 1967 for *Национальное-освободительное движение во Франции Судане и образование Республики Мали, 1945-1960.* Since 1968 he was associated with the Institute of Military History in the Ministry of Defence. His writings include *Пути Мали к независимости; очерк антиколониального движения, 1945-1960* (1970). Miliband²

Kondrat'ev, Vladimir Georgievich, born 8 July 1934 at Leningrad, he graduated in 1958 from the Oriental Faculty, Leningrad State University and received his first degree in 1965 for *Очерк грамматического строя языка памятников тюрской руническое письменности VIII в. из Монголии.* He was associated with his alma mater since 1961; in 1971, he was appointed a lecturer. His writings include *Очерк грамматики древне-тюркского языка* (1970), *Вводный фонетический курс турецкого языка XI* (1976), and *Грамматический строй языка памятников древнетюрской письменности VIII-XI вв.* (1981). Miliband²

Konduraki, Emil, 1912-1987 *see* Condurachi, Emil

Koner, Wilhelm David, born 6 August 1817 at Berlin, he received a Dr.phil. in 1843 from the Universität Berlin for *Commentationis de rebus Tegeatarum capita priora.* He became a librarian and professor. His writings include *Gelehrtes Berlin im Jahre 1845* (1846), *Repertorium über die vom Jahre 1800 bis 1850 in academischen Abhandlungen, Gesellschaftsschriften und wissenschaftlichen Journalen auf dem Gebiete der Geschichte und ihrer Hülfswissenschaften erschienen Aufsätze* (1852-1856), *Über die neuesten Entdeckungen in Afrika; zwei Vorträge* (1869), and jointly with Ernst Guhl, *Das Leben der Griechen und Römer nach antiken Bildwerken dargestellt* (1864). He died in 1887. KDtLK, 1884, 1885

Konetzke, Richard, born 20 March 1897 at Hangelsberg, Prussia, he studied at Friedrich-Wilhelms-Universität zu Berlin, where he was a graduate student of the historian Friedrich Meinecke, and pursued an interest in Spain's role in the nineteenth century. He went to Spain on a fellowship in 1925, and five years later published *Die Politik des Grafen Aranda; ein Beitrag zur Geschichte des spanisch-englischen Weltgegensatzes im 18. Jahrhundert.* In 1939, he published a survey of the history of the peoples of Spain and Portugal, *Geschichte des spanischen und portugiesischen Volkes* and subsequently *Das spanische Weltreich* (1943). In 1944, he was able to go to Sevilla for research on Spanish American colonial history at the Archivo general de Indias. In 1952, he was invited to Duke

University, Durham, N.C., as a research associate and lecturer. But he did not stay for long in the United States. From 1961 to his retirement in 1965, he was given a full chair in his field at Köln and became the director of a special section of its Historisches Seminar. He died in Gemünd on 29 May 1980. *Hispanic American historical review*, 61 (1981), pp. 87-89; Kürschner, 1961-1980

Konieczny, Mustafa Georg, fl. 20th cent., he was associated with the Berlin mosque, 1948-49. His writings include *Textiles of Baluchistan* (London, British Library, 1979), and he edited Laura Veccia Vagliera's translation from the Italian, *Apologie des Islam* (Berlin, 1948), and *Ernst Kühnel's Die Moschee* (Berlin, 1948). GV; LC

König, Friedrich *Eduard*, born 15 November 1846 at Reichenbach im Vogtland, Prussia, he studied philosophy and theology, gaining a Dr.phil. in 1874, and a Dr.habil. in 1879 at the Universität Leipzig for *De criticae sacrae argumento e linguae legibus repetito.* In 1885, he was appointed a professor. He later taught in the same capacity comparative linguistics, particularly Hebrew and Ethiopian, at the universities of Rostock and Bonn. His writings include *Historisch-kritisches Lehrbuch des Hebräischen* (1881-97), *Fünf neue arabische Landschaftsnamen im Alten Testament* (1901), *Neueste Principien der alttestamentlichen Kritik* (1902), and *Geschichte der alttestamentlichen Religionen* (1915). He died in Bonn on 10 February 1936. DtBE; EncJud²; JewEnc; JüdLex; Kürschner, 1925-1935; Wer ist's, 1912-1928

König, Hans, fl. 20th cent., he was a joint author of *Zentralasiatische Teppiche; eine eingehende Darstellung der Teppichknüpfkunst des 18. und 19. Jahrhunderts in Zentralasien* (Frankfurt am Main, Osterrieth, 1969), and *Alte Orientteppiche; Meisterstücke aus deutschen Privatsammlungen = Old Eastern carpets* (München, Callwey, 1978).

König (Koenig), René, born 5 July 1906 at Magdeburg to a family of industrialists, he grew up in France, where his mother originated. He studied Islamic languages, philosophy, amd sociology at the universities of Wien and Berlin, gaining a Dr.phil. in 1930 for *Die naturalistische Künstlerästhetik in Frankreich und ihre Auflösung.* Returning to Germany after research in Paris, his work, *Vom Wesen der deutschen Universität* (1935), met with such opposition and rejection that he decided in 1937 to emigrate to Switzerland. In 1949, he became a professor of sociology at the Universität Köln. Since 1955 he was an editor of the *Kölner Zeitschrift für Soziologie und Sozialpsychologie.* His writings include *Soziologie heute* (1949), *Soziologische Orientierungen* (1965), *Studien zur Soziologie* (1971), and *René König, Soziologe und Humanist; Texte aus vier Jahrzehnten* (1998). On his sixty-fifth and seventy-fifth birthdays he was honoured by jubilee volumes. He died in Köln on 21 March 1992. BioHbDtE; BioIn, 10; ConAu, 81-84, new rev., 15; DtBE; DtBiInd (4); IntAu&W, 1977, 1982; IntWW, 1974/75-1991; Kürschner, 1950-1987; Wer ist wer, 1955-1990/91

König, Wolfgang Walter, born 23 June 1925, he went to school in Heidenau and Pirna, Germany. He was a soldier in the war and spent the years from 1944 to 1948 in a Soviet prisoner of war camp. About 1950, he was delegated to study education, particularly adult education, and Russian. After the first semester he was enrolled in ethnology. From 1954 to 1957, he studied at Moscow Lomonosov State University. On 1 November 1958 he was appointed an academic assistant at the Museum für Völkerkunde, Leipzig. He received a Dr.phil. in 1959 from Karl-Marx-Universität, Leipzig, for *Zu einigen Fragen der Wirtschaft und Gesellschaft der Teke-Turkmenen Achals im 19. Jahrhundert.* Thesis

Koning, Karen Lee, born 20th cent., she received an M.A. in 1971 from McGill University, Montreal, for her thesis, *The crisis of the intellectual in the United Arab Republic, especially as reflected in Muhammad Husanayn Haykal's "Azmat al-muthaqqafin."* Ferahian

de **Koning**, Pieter, born 19th cent., he received a doctorate in 1877 from the Rijksuniversiteit te Leiden for *Beschrijving van Chinesische schedels.* His writings include *Quaestiones Atticae; de hypothesibus aliquot Muelleri Struebing* (Leiden, 1891) and he edited al-Rāzī's *Traité sur le calcul dans les reins et dans la vessie* (1896), and *Trois traités d'anatomie arabes* (Leiden, 1903). Fück, p. 215; ZKO

van **Koningsveld**, Pieter Sjoerd, born in 1943, he received a doctorate in 1976 from the Rijksuniversiteit te Leiden for *The Latin-Arabic glossary of the Leiden University Library.* He became a lecturer at his alma mater. His writings include *De islam; een eerste kennismaking met geloofsleer* (1988), *Snouck Hurgronje en de Islam; acht artikelen over leven en werk von een oriëntalist uit het koloniale tijdperk* (1988), *Yemenite authorities and Jewish messianism* (1990), and jointly with W. A. R. Shadid, *Beeldvorming en interculturelle communicatie; sociaal-wetenschappelijke en sociolinguistische studies* (1999), and he edited *Localities and dates in Arabic manuscripts* (1978). Brinkman's; LC; ZKO

Koniski, Joseph, born in 1908 at Beirut, he was a descendant of refugees who had fled Poland after the 1830 insurrection. In his youth he experienced the forced residence at Urfa in southwestern Anatolia, the difficult life in starving Beirut, and the death of his mother when he was ten years old. He studied philosophy at the Université Saint-Joseph de Beirut, from 1921 to 1927. In the same year, he entered the Jesuits, passing his noviciate at Yzeure in Borbonnais, France; he was subsequently educated at Cairo (1934-37) and Lyon (1937-41), before returning to Beirut. He became a minister at the Université Saint-Joseph (1945-51), and a superior at Homs (1951-55), Tanaïl (1955-59), and Aleppo (1959-62). In 1962, he was recalled to Beirut, where he became an administrator of the Province. A heart infarct in 1972 meant the end of his active religious life. He spent the summer of 1983 at Bikfaya amidst combat and explosions, circumstances which aggravated his condition. He was found dead on the morning of 12 September 1983. Jalabert, pp. 348-49

Konobeev, Vasiliĭ D., fl. 20th cent., his writings include *Русско-болгарское боевое содружество в Русско-турецкой войне 1877-1878* (Moscow, 1953), *Българското натсионалноосвоболително движение* (Sofia, 1972), and he was a joint author of *О связях русских, сербских и болгарских революционеров* (1966). NUC; OSK

Kononov, Andreĭ Nikolaevich, born in 1906 at St. Petersburg, he graduated in 1930 at Leningrad and received his first degree in 1939 for «*Система турецкой грамматики в изложении турецких авторов*» and his doctorate in 1949 for *Родословная туркмен; сочинения Абу-л-Гази хана Хивинского*. He was appointed a lecturer in 1941 and a professor in 1950. Since 1937 he was associated with Leningrad University. His writings include *Грамматика узбекского языка* (1948), *Грамматика сов-ременного узбекского литературного языка* (1960), and *История изучения тюркских языков в России* (1972). He died on 30 October 1986. GSE; *Index Islamicus* (4); Miliband; Miliband²; TatarES; UzbekSE

Konopacki, Maciej, fl. 20th cent., his writings include *Kaum Muslimin Polandia* (Djakarta, 1964). NUC

Konrad, Nikolai Iosifovich, born in 1891 at Riga, he graduated in 1912 at St. Petersburg. He was an East Asian scholar who spent the years from 1914 to 1917 in Japan. He was appointed a professor in 1926 and received a doctorate in 1934. He was affiliated with the Oriental Institute, Soviet Academy of Sciences. He wrote *Запад и Восток* (1966). He died on 30 September 1970. Miliband; Miliband²

Konrad, Walter, born 20th cent., he received a Dr.phil. in 1950 from the Universität Göttingen for *Friedrich Ratzel; sein Leben und Wirken als Völkerkundler*. His writings include *Zad, Geheimnis zwischen Niger und Nil; ein ethnographischer Beitrag zur Kenntnis der Tschadsee-Insulaner* (1955), and *Völkerkunde; vom Werden und Wesen einer Wissenschaft* (1969). GV

Konstantelos, Demetriu Io., 1927- *see* Constantelos, Demetrios John

Konstantinova, Ol'ga Aleksandrovna, fl. 20th cent., her writings include *Эвенкиский язык* (1964), and jointly with Elena Pavlovna Lebedevna *Русско-эвенский словарь* (1958). LC; OSK

Kontēs, Basileios *see* Kondis, Basil

Kontzi, Reinhold, born 22 December 1924 at Rot am See/Crailsheim, Germany, he received a Dr.phil. in 1956 from the Universität Tübingen for *Der Ausdruck der Passividee im älteren Italienischen*. After obtaining a Dr.habil. in 1969, he became a professor of Romance studies at his alma mater. His writings include *Zur Entstehung der romanischen Sprachen* (1978), *Substrate und Superstrate in den romanischen Sprachen* (1982); he was a joint author of *Wort und Schrift; des Kanonikus Fortunato Panzavecchia Bibelübersetzung ins Maltesiche* (1999); and he edited *Aljamiado Texte* (1974). In 1996, he was honoured by *Romania Arabica; Festsschrift für Reinhold Kontzi zum 70. Geburtstag*. He died in 2001. GV; Kürschner, 1976-2001|

Konzelmann, Gerhard, born 26 October 1932 at Stuttgart, Germany, he was a journalist as well as a radio and televison reporter and a prolific writer on many aspects of the Islamic world, based on less than scrupulous research. One of his books, *Mohammed, Allahs Prophet und Feldherr* (1980), had to be taken off the market. After a libel suit, he had to pay in excess of DM 35,000 to Gernot Rotter for plagiarism, and refrain from publishing new editions of some of his books. Rotter responded with a publication entitled *Allahs Plagiator; die publizistischen Raubzüge des "Nahostexperten" Konzelmann* (1992). Konzelmann's writings include *Vom Frieden redet keiner* (1971), *Die Araber und ihre Traum vom Großarabischen Reich* (1974), *Die Reichen aus dem Morgenlande* (1975), *Suez* (1975), *Die großen Kalifen* (1977), *Der befohlene Frieden* (1978), *Die islamische Herausforderung* (1980), *Arafat* (1981), *Der Nil* (1982), *Jerusalem* (1984), *Der unheilige Krieg* (1985), *Allahs neues Weltreich* (1986), *Der Diwan des Harun Al Rashid* (1987), *Der Jordan* (1990), *Der Golf* (1991), and *Die Emirate, das Paradies im Nahen Osten* (2005). Wer ist wer, 1991/92-1999/2000

Kopčan, Vojtech, born 1 May 1940 at Horná Žďaňa, he took archival and Turkish studies from 1957 to his graduation in 1964 successively at Comenius University, Bratislava, and Charles University, Prague. His research and writings concentrated on Ottoman Turkish documents from Slovakian archives, including *Turecké nebezpečenstvo a Slovensko* (1986); jointly with Pavol Horváth, *Turci na*

Slovensko (1971); jointly with Klára Krajčovičová, *Slovensko v tieni polmesiaca* (1983); and he translated from the Turkish of Evliya Çelebi, *Kniha ciest; cesty po Slovensko* (1978). He died in Banská Štiavnica on 2 September 2000. *Asian and African studies* (Bratislava), 9 ii (2000), pp, 145-47; Filipsky

Köpeczi, Béla, born 16 September 1921 at Nagyenyed, Romania, he was educated at Budapest and Paris, and became a politician, historian, minister of culture and education, and a member of the Hungarian Academy of Sciences. In 1979, he was granted an honorary doctorate by the Université de Paris. His writings include *Erdély rövid története* (1989), and *Nemzetképkutatás és a XIX. századi román irodalom magyarságképe* (2001), and he edited *History of Transylvania* (2001). Biograf, 2004; IntWW, 1974/75-2006; WhoSocC, 1978; WhoSocCE, 1989; WhoWor, 1974/75-1978/79

Kopf, David, born 12 March 1930 at Paterson, N.J., he graduated in 1951 from New York University, and received a Ph.D. in 1964 from the University of Chicago. In 1973 he was appointed a professor of modern Asian history at the University of Minnesota, Minneapolis, a post which he still held in 1995. His writings include *British Orientalism and the Bengal renaissance; the dynamics of Indian modernization, 1773-1835* (1969), and he edited *Bengal regional identity* (1969). ConAu, 89-92; DrAS, 1974 H, 1978 H, 1982 H; NatFacDr, 1990-1995; WhoMW, 1992/93

Kopf, Lothar, born about 1923, he received a Ph.D. in 1953 from the Hebrew University of Jerusalem for *Arabic lexicography; its origin, development, sources and problems*. His writings include *Studies in Arabic and Hebrew lexicography* (Jerusalem, 1976), and he edited and translated from the Arabic of Ibn Qutaybah, *The Natural history section from a ninth century "Book of useful knowledge"* (Paris, 1949). NUC, pre-1956-1967; ZKO

Kopp, Clemens, born 28 February 1886 at Wanne, Germany, he studied at Paderborn and the Universität Münster, gaining a Dr.theol. in 1911 for *Die Philosophie des Hermes, besonders in ihren Beziehungen zu Kant und Fichte*. He was a secondary school teacher at Paderborn. His writings include *Die heiligen Stätten der Evangelien* (1959), and its translations, *The Holy places of the Gospels* (1963), and *Itinéraires évangéliques* (1964). Kürschner, 1950

Kopp, Horst, born 12 May 1943 at Dresden, Germany, he received a Dr.phil. in 1973 from the Universität Erlangen-Nürnberg for *Städte im östlichen iranischen Kaspitiefland*. Since 1979, he was a professor of geography successively at the universities of Tübingen and Erlangen-Nürnberg. His writings include *Al-Qāsim; wirtschafts- und sozialgeographische Srukturen und Entwicklungsprozesse in einem Dorf des jemenitischen Hochlands* (1977), *Agrargeographie der Arabischen Republik Jemen* (1981); he was a joint author of *Kaffee aus Arabien; der Bedeutungswandel* (1979), and *Beiträge zur Stadtgeographie von San'a* (1990).; he edited *Jemen (Nord) im Aufbruch* (1988); and he was a joint editor of *Resultate aktueller Jemen-Forschung* (1978). EURAMES, 1993; Kürschner, 1980-2005; Schwarz; ZKO

Köppel, Robert, born 23 July 1882 at Karlsruhe, Baden, he was ordained in 1906 and subsequently served as a clergyman with the Archdiocese of Freiburg im Breisgau. In 1911, he entered the Jesuits and during the first World War served as a chaplain. From 1925 to 1930, he was a clergyman (*Spiritual*) at the Wilhelmsstift, Tübingen. He received a Dr.rer.nat. in 1929 from the Universität Tübingen for *Untersuchungen über die Steinzeit Palästina-Syriens*. He became associated with the Pontificio Istituto Biblico di Roma, and was in charge of excavations at the Dea Sea. His writings include *Palästina; die Landschaft in Karten und Bildern* (1930), *Zur Urgeschichte Palästinas; eine Übersicht aus Geologie, Prähistorie und Archäologie* (1937), and he was a joint editor of *Teleilat Ghassūl; compte rendu des fouilles de l'Institut biblique pontifical, 1932-1936* (1940). He died in 1943. GV; Kosch

von **Köppen**, Peter, 1793-1864 see Keppen, Petr Ivanovich

Köppen, Wladimir Peter, born 25 September 1846 at St. Petersburg, Russia, he studied botany and zoology at the universities of St. Petersburg, Heidelberg, and Leipzig, where he received a doctorate in 1870. When the Deutsche Wetterwarte in Hamburg was founded in 1875, he was nominated head of storm warnings and weather telegraphy. From 1879 to his retirement in 1919 he was on leave for private research. His writings include *Grundlinien der maritimen Meteorologie* (1899). He died in Graz, Austria, on 22 June 1940. DtBE; DtBiInd (4); Kürschner, 1926-1935; Master (1); NDB; Wer; Wer ist's, 1912-1935

Koppers, Wilhelm, born 8 February 1886 at Menzelen, Germany, he entered the Societas Verbi Divini and went to their secondary school at Steyl, the Netherlands. He studied at the Mission seats in St. Gabriel, Mödlingen, Austria, and Roma. Ordained in 1911, he joined the editorial staff of the journal *Anthropos* in the following year, and in 1914 began to study ethnology and Indian subjects at the Universität Wien, where he received a Dr.phil. in 1917 for *Die ethnologische Wirtschaftsordnung*. As a representative of the *Kulturkreislehre* he explored the Americas. In 1924, he gained a Dr.habil. and began a teaching career at the Universität Wien. In 1929, he was one of the founders of the Institut für

Völkerkunde. Dismissed in 1938, he emigrated, first to India and later to Switzerland. In 1945, he returned to his former post at Wien. His writings include *Anfänge des menschlichen Gemeinschaftslebens im Spiegel der neueren Völkerkunde* (1921), *Die Bhil in Zentralindien* (1948), *Der Urmensch und sein Weltbild* (1949) and its translation, *Primitive man and his world picture* (1952). BioHbDtE; DtBE; IntDcAn; Kosch; Kürschner, 1961; Teichl; *Wer ist wer*, 1950-1958

Koppes, Clayton R., born 24 September 1945 at Lincoln, Nebr., he graduated in 1967 from Bethel College, Kans., and received a Ph.D. in 1974 from the University of Kansas at Lawrence for *Oscar L. Chapman, a liberal at the Interior Department, 1933-1953*. In 1978, he was apointed a professor of history at Oberlin College, Ohio, a post which he still held in 2004; in 2005, he was chief academic dean. His writings include *JPL and the American space program* (1982), *Hollywood goes to war* (1987). DrAS, 1978 H, 1982 H; NatFacDr, 1990-2005

Köprülü, Mehmet *Fuat*, born in 1899 at Constantinople, he descended from a family of grand viziers and studied law without taking a degree. He taught Turkish language and literature at secondary schools from 1910 to 1913, when he was appointed a lecturer in Turkish literature at Darülfünun, Constantinople. He was one of the founders of modern Turkological studies in Turkey. In 1934, he was elected to the national assembly and in 1946 he joined the Demokrat Parti. He left politics in 1960 and died in İstanbul on 28 June 1966. AnaBrit; CasWL; CurBio, 1953, 1966; EIS; Meydan; *Index Islamicus* (3); PTF II, pp. 596-598; Zürcher

Kor-Ogly, Khalyk Guseinnovich, 1919- *see* Korogly, Khalyk Guseinovich

Korabinský (Korabinski/Korabinszky), Ján (Johann) Matthias, born of Slovak background on 23 February 1740 at Eperjes (Prešov), Hungary, he studied theology, philosophy, and history of philology. A Slovenian geographer, lexicographer, teacher, and editor of poor fortune, his writings include *Almanach von Ungarn auf das Jahr 1778* (1778), *Geographisch-historisches und Produkten Lexikon von Ungarn* (Pressburg, 1786), and *Versuch eines kleinen türkischen Wörterbuchs mit beygesessten deutsch-ungarisch und böhmisch Bedeutungen und einer kurzgefassten türkischen Sprachlehre* (Pressburg, 1788). He died in Pressburg on 23 June 1811. *Asian and African studies* (Bratislava), 16 (1980), p. 9; Filipsky, Magyar; OttůvSN; RNL; Wurzbach

Korbut, Mikhail Ksaver'evich, born in 1899, he was a historian whose writings include *Василий Константинович Магнацкий и его труды 1839-1901 гг.* (1929), and *Казанский Государственный Университет имени В. Л. Улянова-Ленинза 125 лет* (1930). He died in 1937. TatarES

Korczyn, Amos D., born in 1940 at Jerusalem, he gained science and medical degrees from the Hebrew University, Jerusalem. He was a sometime senior lecturer in pharmacy. WhoWorJ, 1978

Kordabaev (Qordabaev), Toleubaï Rakhimzhanovich (Төлеубай Қордабаев), he was born in 1915 in Semipalatinsk Oblast, received a doctorate in 1969, and was appointed a professor in 1970. He was a teacher at Dzhambul, Alma Ata, Aktiubinsk, 1935-39, and after the war at the Kazakhstan Pedagogical Institute. His writings include *Қазақ тіліндкгі құрмалас сөйлемдер синтаксисі* (1995). Kazakhskaia, vol. 3, p. 283; OSK; *Советская тюркология*, 1975, №, 4, pp. 119-120

Kordt, Erich, born 10 December 1903 at Düsseldorf, Germany, he completed his law with a doctorate and subsequently entered the diplomatic service being posted successively to Genève and Bern. In 1936, he went together with J. von Rippentrop to London. When the latter became German Foreign Minister in 1938, he was appointed head of his staff. In 1941 he went to Tokio as ambassador; at the end of the war, he was at Nanking in the same capacity. In 1948, he was a witness at the Nürnberg war tribunal. He subsequently gained a Dr.habil. and established the new German diplomatic service. His writings include *Wahn und Wirklichkeit* (1948), *Nichts aus den Akten* (1950), and *Neutrals facing global movements* (1965). He died in Düsseldorf on 11 November 1969. DtBE; KDtLK, 1952, 1958; Kürschner, 1950-1966

Korf (Корфъ), Fedor Fedorovich, 1795-1876 *see* Korff, Theodor von

Korfes, Sigrid Kumpf, 1933- *see* Wegner Korfes, Sigrid

von **Korff** (Корфъ), Theodor (Феодор Феодорович), Baron, born 3 July 1795, he was Russian officer, who retired in 1857 with the rank of general of cavalry, and in the same year acquired the estate Endenhof in Kurland. He died in 1876. Baltisch (1); NYPL; OSK

von **Korff** (Korf/Корфъ), Feodor Fedorovich, Baron, born 1803, he was attached to the Russian mission to Persia from 1834 to 1835. A sometime editor of *Русский инвалид*, his own writings include *Воспоминаня о Персии 1834-1835* (Sankpeterburg, 1838). He died in 1853. EnSlovar; NYPL; OttůvSN

Korgun, Viktor Grigor'evich, born 14 May 1940 at Leningrad, he graduated in 1968 from the Institute for Oriental Languages at Moscow State University, and received his first degree in 1975 for

Социально-полтич. кризис конца 20-х годов в Афганистане. He was since 1975 associated with the Oriental Institute of the Soviet Academy of Sceinces. His writings include *Афганистан в 20-30-е годы XX в.* (1979), its translation into Dari in 1365/1986, and *Интеллигенция в политической жизни Афганистана* (1983). Miliband²

Kori-Niëziï (Кары-Ниязов/Қориниёзов), T. M. *see* Kary-Niiazov, Tashmukhamed Niiazovich

Kořínek, Jan, born 7 December 1904 at Prag, Austria-Hungary, he graduated in 1923 from a secondary school in Poitiers, France. He was in Morocco in 1926, 1930-38, 1947, and 1956. His writings include *Maghreb el Aksa* (Praha, 1941), *Maroko, křížem krážem* (1959), its translation, *Kreuz und quer durch Marokko* (1962), *Maroko cestou-necestov* (Bratislava, 1961), *Umění prodávat* (1969), and *L'Historique des relations tchécoslovaques avec le Maroc* (Rabat, 1975). He died in Praha on 25 February 1984. Filipsky; OSK

von **Kořistka**, Carl (Karel) Franz (František) Eduard, born 7 February 1825 at Brüsau, Austrian Moravia, he studied science and mathematics at the Universität Wien, 1841-43, and at Berg- und Forstakademie, Schemnitz, 1843-48, where he subsequently became an assistant until 1854. He successively became a professor of mathematics and geodesy at Polytechnisches Institut, Prag, and at Deutsches Polytechnisches Institut, Prag. His writings include *Hypsometrie von Mähren und Österreichisch-Schlesien; die Resultate der Höhenmessungen* (1863), and *Die Markgrafschaft Mähren und das Herzogthum Schlesien in ihren geographischen Verhältnissen* (1861). He died in Prag on 19 January 1906. DtBE; DtBiInd (7); Hinrichsen; Martinek; ÖBL; OttůvSN; Wurzbach

Korkhmazian, Ripsimė Sergeevna, born 25 March 1940 at Tbilisi, she graduated in 1963 from the Faculty of History, Moscow State University, and received her first degree in 1975 for *Турецко-германские отношения в годы второй мировой войны: 1939-1945*, a work which was published in 1975. Since 1968 she was associated with the Oriental Institute, Armenian Academy of Sciences. Miliband²

Korkina, Evdokiia Innokent'evna, born 20th cent., her writings include *Наклонения глагола в якутском языке* (1970), *Глагольные лично-отношенные модальные конструкции в якутском языке* (1979), *Северо-восточная диалектная зона якутского языка* (1992); she was a joint author of *Якутско-русский словарь* (1972); and she edited *Якутский филологический сборник* (1976), and *Исследования по грамматике якутского языка* (1983). LC; ZKO

Korkut, Besim, born 25 November 1904 at Travnik, Bosnia, he studied at Sarajevo and in 1931 received a diploma from al-Azhar University, Cairo. He became associated with the Oriental Institute at Sarajevo. His writings include *Arapski dokumenti u Drzavnom Arhivu u Dubrovnuku* (Sarajevo, 1960-1969). He died in Sarajevo on 30 November 1975. *Gazi Husrev-begove Biblioteke*, 1 (1972), pp. 131-132; Grada; *Prilozi za orijentalnu filologiju*, 25 (1975), pp. 6-7

Kormushin, Igor' Valentinovich, born 25 January 1939 at Leningrad, he graduated in 1962 from the Oriental Faculty, Leningrad State University, and received his first degree in 1969 for *Категория каузатива в алтайских языках*. Since 1962 he was associated with the Institute of Philology, Soviet Academy of Sciences. His writings include *Системы времен глагола в алтайских языках* (1984), and *Удыхейский (удэгейский) язык* (1998). Miliband²; Schoeberlein

Korn, David, born 27 April 1934 at Kolbuszowa, Poland, he went to schools in Tashkent, Samarkand, and Kyzl Orda, from 1941 to 1945. He subsequently went to the United States, where he received all his degrees from Georgetown University, Washington, D.C., later becoming a professor of Russian at Howard University, Washington, D.C. His writings include *The Russian verb* (1966). He died on 30 July 1999. DrAS, 1969 F, 1974 F, 1978 F, 1982 F; Note about the author; WhAm, 13; WhoAm, 1974-1994; WhoWor, 1974/75-1978/79

Korn, Viktor Emanuel, born 1 July 1892 at Leiden, the Netherlands, he studied at the Rijksuniversiteit te Leiden, where he also received a doctorate in 1923 for *Het adatrecht van Bali*. He was a member of the Koninklijk Bataviaasch Genootschap van Kunsten en Wetenschappen. Since 1945, he was a professor of Islamic law at his alma mater. His writings include *Balische overeenkonsten* (1922), *De dorpsrepubliek Tnganan Pagringsingen* (1933), and *Adatgrodenrecht en domeinfictie* (1946). Brinkman's; *Wie is dat*, 1948, 1956; ZKO

Kornfilt, Jaklin, born 27 August 1946, he/she received a Ph.D. in linguistics in 1985 from Harvard University for *Case marking, agreement and empty categories in Turkish*, and subsequently became an assistant professor of linguistics and foreign languages at Syracuse University, N.Y., a post which he still held in 2005. A member of the Turkish Studies Association, writings include *Turkish* (1997). LC; *MESA Roster of members*, 1990; NatFacDr, 2005; Note; ZKO

Kornienko, Radmir Platonovich, born 8 June 1925 at Khar'kov, Ukraine, he graduated in 1952 from the Moscow Oriental Institute, and received his first degree in 1964 for *Рабочее движение в Турции в период между двымя мировыми войнами 1918-1939 гг.* He was associated with the Oriental Institute of the Soviet Academy of Sciences since 1956. His writings include the enlarged translation of his thesis, *The Labor movement in Turkey, 1918-1963* (1967). Miliband; Miliband²

Kornilov, Aleksandr Aleksandrovich, born in 1862 at St. Petersburg, he entered the Russian civil service and in 1909 became a professor of history at St. Petersburg Polytechnic Institute. His writings include *Крестьянская реформа* (1905), and *Общественное Движение при Александре II., 1855-1881* (1909). He died in 1925. BiDSovU; Wieczynski

Kornilov, Gennadiĭ Emel'ianovich, born 20th cent., his writings include *Имитативы в чувашском языке* (1984), and he edited *Летопись уральских деревень; тезисы докладов региональной научно-практической конференции* (Ekaterinburg, 1995). LC; OSK

Kornrumpf, Hans-Jürgen, born 18 July 1926 at Berlin, he was called to arms in March 1944 while still at school. After release from a Soviet prisoner of war camp in the autumn of 1945, he had to make up his lost school year at an evening school before taking up study at the Freie Universität Berlin, where he received a Dr.phil. in 1955 for *Das shi'itische Bild 'Alīs und des Islam nach Nahdj al-Balāgha des Sharīf al-Radī*, and a Dr.habil. in 1975 from the Universität Mainz for *Territorialverwaltung im östlichen Teil der europäischen Türkei*. In April 1954 he acted as religious guide to the Berlin mosque. From 1975 to his retirement he was a professor of Islamic studies at the Universität Mainz. His writings include *Syrien; Grundlagen und Möglichkeiten von Beteiligungen und Investitionen privater deutscher Firmen* (1965), *Osmanische Bibliographie mit besonderer Berück-sichtigung der Türkei in Europa* (1973), *Langenscheidts Universal-Wörterbuch Türkisch* (1976), *Fremde im Osmanischen Reich, 1826-1912/13; bio-bibliographisches Register* (1998), *Beitraege zur osmanischen Geschichte und Territorialverwaltung* (Istanbul, 2001). Kürschner, 1980-2005; Schwarz; Thesis; ZKO

Kornrumpf, Jutta, born in 1929 at Meißen, Germany, she studied Russian at the Universität Leipzig and subsequently worked as an interpreter. Since 1955 she was married with Hans-Jürgen Kornrumpf. She was a joint author of *Osmanische Bibliographie mit besonderer Berücksichtigung der Türkei in Europa* (1973), *Fremde im Osmanischen Reich, 1826-1912/13; bio-bibliographisches Register* (1998), and *An Historical gazetteer of Cyprus, 1850-1987, with notes on population* (1990). Note; Private; ZKO

Korobkova, Galina Fedorovna, born 9 March 1933, she became associated with the Institute of History of Material Culture in the Russian Academy of Sciences. Her writings include *Орудия труда и хозяйство неолитических идемен Средней-Азии* (1969). Schoeberlein

Korogly (Kor-Ogly), Khalyk Guseinovich, born 24 January 1919 at Ashkhabad, he graduated at Moscow and received his first degree in 1955 for «Шасенем и Гарып» - народный дастан» and a doctorate in 1969 for *Огузский героческий эпос*. In 1944 he became affiliated with the Oriental Institute, Moscow. His writings include *Современная персидская литература* (1965), *Туркменская литература* (1972), *Персидские пословицы, поговорки и крылатые слова* (1973), and *Взаимосвязи эпоса народов Средней Азии, Ирана и Азербайджана* (1983). Miliband; Miliband²

Korolec, Jerzy B., born 20th cent., his writings include *Filozofia moralna Jana Burydana* (Wrocław, 1973), and *Filozofia moralna* (Wrocław, 1980). LC; OSK

Korošec, Viktor, born 7 October 1899 at Laibach (Ljubljana), Austria, he received a doctorate in 1926 and became associated with the Universität Laibach. His writings include *Die Erbenhaftung nach römischem Recht* (1927), and *Hethitische Staatsverträge* (1931). He died on 16 November 1985. EnSlovenije

Kőrösi Csoma, Sándor, born 4 April 1784 at Kőrös, Hungary, he was a linguist. In quest of the origin of the geographical origin of the Magyar race, he set out, in 1820, overland through Syria, Central Asia, Kashmir to Tibet, where he studied at Lamaistic temples. He died in Darjeeling, India, on 11 April 1842. György Kara wrote *Kőrösi Csoma Sándor* (1970). A commemoration volume was published in 1985 entitled, *Studi miscellanei uralici e altaici dedicati ad Alessandro Kőrösi-Csoma.* Buckland; EncAm; EncBrit; GdeEnc; GeistigeUng; Henze; RNL; Magyar; UjLex; Uusi

Korostovets (Korostovetz), Vladimir Konstantinovich, born in 1888 in the Ukraine. His writings include *Neue Väter - neue Söhne* (1926), *Lenin im Hause der Väter* (1928), *The Re-birth of Poland* (1928), *Graf Witte, der Steuermann in der Not* (1929), *Polnische Auferstehung* (1929), *Quo vadis Polonia? Choses vues en Europe orientale* (Paris, 1929), *Seed and harvest* (1931), and *Europe in the melting pot* (1938). He died in 1980. NUC, pre-1956

Korotkova, Tat'iana Sergeevna, born 31 January 1921 at Ufa, Russia, she graduated in 1944 from Faculty of History, Moscow, and received her first degree in 1947 for «*Нейтралитет» Ирана в первой мировой войне*. She was since 1947 affiliated with the Oriental Institute, Moscow. In 1949 she was appointed a lecturer. She died 10 January 1982. Miliband; Miliband²

Korsh, Fedor Evgen'evich, born in 1843 at Moscov, he studied Arabic and Persian under Pavel Petrov, and succeeded Ivan N. Kholmogorov in the chair of Persian language and literature at the Moscow Lazarev Institute of Oriental Languages. He was a competent scholar of both Arabic and Persian. His writings include *Способы относительного подчинения* (1877). He died in Moscow on 16 February 1915. EnSlovar; *Index Islamicus* (2); Krachkovskiĭ, pp. 162-63; VostokMStP, pp. 251-52

Korson, Jay Henry, born 9 January 1910 at Philadelphia, Pa., he graduated in 1931 from Villanova University, Pa., and received a Ph.D. in 1947 from Yale University. From 1944 to his retirement in 1976, he was a professor of sociology at the University of Massachusetts, Amherst. He edited *Contemporary problems of Pakistan* (1974). AmM&WSc, 1973 S, 1978 S; WhoAm, 1974-1980

Kortepeter, Carl *Max*, born 27 May 1928 at Indianapolis, Ind., he was a graduate of Harvard University, received his M.A. in 1954 from McGill University, Montreal, for *Turkish language reform*, and his Ph.D. in 1962 from the School of Oriental and African Studies, London, for *The relations between the Crimean Tatars and the Ottoman Empire, 1578-1608*. He taught at Robert College, Istanbul, and for five years in the Department of Islamic Studies, University of Toronto, and from 1967 until his retirement in the Department of Near Eastern Languages and Literatures, New York University. His writings include *Ottoman imperialism during the Reformation; Eastern Europe and the Caucasus* (1973), his collected articles, *The Ottoman Turks* (1991), and he was joint editor of *The transformation of Turkish culture; the Atatürk legacy* (1986). His studies in general have focused on the relations between the Ottoman Empire and the peoples on the borderlands of this empire. ConAu, 41-44; DrAS, 1969 H, 1974 H, 1978 H, 1982 H; Ferahian; IndAu; LC; *MESA Roster of members*, **1977-1990**; Private; Sluglett

Kortum, Gerhard, born 19 February 1941 at Kiel, Germany, he studied geography and English from 1960 to 1966 at the universities of Kiel and Freiburg/Breisgau; from 1967 to 1970, he participated in an exchange programme with Pahlavi University, Shiraz. He received a Dr.phil. in 1974 from the Universität Kiel for *Die Marvdasht-Ebene in Fars*. He subsequently became a curator at the Institut für Meereskunde, Universität Kiel. His writings on Third World rural development projects include *Die iranische Landwirtschaft zwischen Tradition und Neuerung* (1977), *Entwicklunsprobleme und -projekte im bäuerlich-nomadischen Lebensraum Südpersiens* (1979), and *Zuckerrübenbau und Entwicklung ländlicher Wirtschaftsräume in der Türkei* (1986). Kürschner, 1992-2005; Schwarz

Korzhenevskiĭ, Nikolaĭ Leopol'dovich, born in 1879, he received a doctorate in 1937 and concurrently was appointed a professor of physical geography at the Central Asian University. His writings include *Главный туркменский канал и свяsanные с ним территории* (1951), *Ледники северного склона Алайского Хребта* (1955), *Природа Средней Азии* (1960); and he edited *Общество для изучения Таджикистана и иранских народностей за его пределами* (1925), and *Таджикистан; спорник статей* (1925). He died in Tashkent in 1958. GSE; UzbekSE; OSK

Kosack, Hans-Georg Fritz *Wolfgang*, born 29 October 1943 at Borkheide near Berlin, he studied Egyptology, ethnology, ancient history and Semitic philology at the Universität Bonn, where he received a Dr.phil. in 1970 for *Die Legende im Koptischen; Untersuchungen zur Volksliteratur Ägyptens*. He subsequently trained as a librarian but, unable to obtain a suitable post, he had to settle for employ with the German social security system in Berlin, a post which he still held in 2002. His writings include *Lehrbuch des Koptischen* (1974). Private; Sezgin; Thesis

Koşay, Hâmit Zübeyr, born in 1897 in the Volga-Urals ditrict into a leading Bashkir family, he was sent in 1909 to be educated at Selânik (Thessaloniki), later continuing at the teachers' college (Dârül-muallimin), graduating in 1916. He subsequently briefly taught at Kadıköy, concurrently studying ethnology and Hungarian philology at Darülfünun, Constantinople, until the end of 1917, when he cotinued at Budapest, where he received a diploma in 1921. Through the good offices of Gyula Németh, he was admitted to the pedagogical college (Eötvös Kollegium) and concurrently became a student at the Institute of Linguistics, Budapest University, gaining a Dr.phil. in 1923 in Turkish and Hungarian studies. He subsequently spent 1924-25 at Berlin. From 1925 to his retirement in 1962 he held important posts at Ankara in the Ministry of Education, such as inspector general of libraries, and director of museums. His writings include *Ankara budun bilgisi* (1935), and *1936 daki çalışmalara ke şiflere ait ilk rapor* (1938). He died in Ankara on 1 October 1984. AnaBrit; *Bulletin d'études karaïtes*, 2 (1989), pp. 100-101 (not sighted); *Materialia Turcica*, 3 (1977), pp. 152-159; Note

Kosbergenov, R. K., fl. 1954, he was a joint author of *Навееи вместе; к 100-летию добровольного присоединения Каракалпакии к России* (Nukus, 1973).

Koschmieder, Erwin, born 31 August 1895 at Liegnitz, Germany, he studied Slavic philology at the Universität Breslau, where he received a Dr.phil. in 1922 for *Über ein handschriftliches Euchologium in der Stadtbibliothek zu Breslau*, and a Dr.habil. in 1926. He subsequently became a professor at Wilna (1930-1938), and München, from 1939 until his retirement. His writings include *Zeitbezug und Sprache* (1929), its translation, *Les rapports temporels, leurs expression linguistique* (1996), *Phonationslehre des Polnischen* (1977), and *Gesammelte Abhandlungen zu Phonetik, Phonologie und Morphologie der slavischen Sprachen* (1979). He died in Ebersberg, Bavaria, on 14 February 1977. DtBE; Kürschner, 1931-1976; NDB; Polski (3); *Südosteuropa-Mitteilungen*, 17 (1977), Heft 1, pp. 86-90; *Südost-Forschungen*, 36 (1977), pp. 231-33; *Wer ist wer*, 1962-1971/72

Kościałkowski, Stanisław, born in 1881, he studied at Warszawa, Kraków, and Wilna. In 1941, he was deported to Central Asia, and in 1945 evacuated to Tehran. His writings include *L'Iran et la Pologne à travers les siècles* (1943), *Polacy a Liban i Syria w toku dziejowym* (Beirut, 1949), *Historyka; wsęp do studiów historycznych* (1954), *Studia i szkice przygodne z historii i z jej popranicza z literaturą* (Londyn, 1956), *Prace zebrane* (1958) and *Antoni Tyzenhaus; podskarbi nadworny litewski* (Lodndyn, 1970). He died in 1960. Dziekan; OSK

Kosegarten, Johann Gottfried Ludwig, born 10 September 1792 at Altenkirchen on the Isle of Rügen, Swedish Pomerania, he studied theology at the Universität Greiswald, 1808-1918, and Oriental languages at the Université de Paris, 1812-1814. Upon his return to Greifswald, he became an assistant in theology at the university. In 1817, he was appointed a professor of Oriental languages, a post which he held for seven years until recalled to Greifswald and appointed to the chair of theology and Oriental literatures, which post he held until his death. Apart from Arabic, Persian, and Turkish, he was competent in Sanskrit and Hebrew. His writings include *Von der religiösen Liebe der Mohammedaner* (1816), and *De Mohammede Ebn Batvta Arabe tingitano eiusque itineribus* (1818). He died in 1860. ADtB; Buckland; CelCen (not sighted); DcBiPP (not sighted); Egyptology; *L'Orient, l'Algérie et les colonies françaises*, 2 (1867), p.p. 15-16

Koshelev, Vladimir Sergeevich, born 20th cent., his writings include *Египет, уроки истории; борьба против колониального господства и контрреволюции, 1879-1981* (Minsk, 1984). OSK

Freiherr von **Kosjek**, Gustav, born 17 August 1838 at Mittertrixen, Austria, he was a graduate of the Orientalische Akademie, Wien. He started a diplomatic career on 17 August 1859 at the consulate in Galatz (Galaţi), Romania. Only a month later, he was posted to the internuncio of Constantinople as a dragoman assistant, advancing through the grades to become second dragoman in 1869, and first dragoman and secretary in 1877. Ennobled since 1870, he served as acting consul-general at Ruschuk (Ruse), Bulgaria, and in 1878, he was a delegate to the Congress of Berlin. On 31 October 1881, he was assigned to Cairo as diplomatic agent and consul-general, becoming minister plenipotentionary on 5 February 1883. He subsequently went to Tehran in the same capacity before becoming ambassador to Greece in 1887. His writings include *Aus den Papieren eines Verteidigers* (Graz, 1884). He died on 2 February 1897. BioJahr, 2 (1898), pp. 308-309; Kornrumpf; ÖBL

Kossak, Fortunat *Juliusz*, born 15 December 1824 at Wiśnicz, Austrian Galicia, he studied law and concurrently painting at Lemberg (Lwów), Austria. He was for thirty years head of the art section of the periodical *Tygodnik Ilustrowany*. He died in Krakau on 3 February 1899. Dziekan; ÖBL; Polski (20); PSB; Wurzbach

Kossak, Wojciech (Adalbert) Horacy, born 31 December 1856 or 1 January 1857 at Paris, he was a landscape painter whose work also include portraits of public figures as well as battle scenes. His writings include *Erinnerungen* (1913), and *Legjony polskie 1914* (1914). He died on 29 July 1942. Kazimierz Olzánski wrote *Wojciech Kossak* (1976). AllgLKünst; Dziekan; ÖBL; Polski (18); PSB

Kossovich, Kaétan Andreevich, born in 1815 at Polotsk, Russia, he was an Avesta and Sanskrit scholar whose writings include *Санскрито-русский словарь* (Sankpeterburg, 1854), *Decem Send-avestae excerpta* (Paris, 1865), *Inscriptiones palaeo-persicae Achaemenidarum quot hucusque repertae sunt* (1872), *Еврейская хрестоматия с ссылками на грамматику Гезениуса глоссарием еврейсео-русским составленная* (1878) and *Canticum canticorum ex Hebraeo convertit et explicavit* (1879). He died in St. Petersburg in 1883. EnSlovar; GSE; *Index Islamicus* (1)

Kossovitch, Nicolas, born a French national on 19 February 1884 at Beograd, he studied at Paris, where he received a degree in science, and in 1928 a doctorate in medicine from the Faculté de médecine de Paris. He was a professor at the École d'anthropologie de Paris and subsequently became *chef de service* at the Institut Pasteur de Paris. His writings include *Anthropologie et groupes sanguins des populations du Maroc* (Paris, 1953). He died in 1948. IndexBFr² (1); NUC

Kossuth, Lajos (Louis/Ludwig), born 19 September 1802 at Monok, Borsod-Abaúj-Zemplén County, Hungary, he was a lawyer and journalist. He was sentenced in 1837 to four years in prison for his political opposition. As editor-in-chief of the *Pesti Hirlap*, he successfully fought since 1841 for freedom and social reforms, and became the archpriest of the new crusades. His brilliant powers as orator and journalist, first directed towards securing the substitution of Magyar for Latin in the Hungarian Diet and afterwards employed in a passionate campaign for Hungarian independence, awoke in every part of the Austrian Empire the latent flames of a furious and disruptive racialism. He was elected into the government, but military misfortune compelled him to seek refuge abroad. He died in exile on 20 March 1894, as Turkey had declined to hand over him and other Hungarian fugitives to Russian or Austrian vengeance. EncBrit; GeistigeUng; GSE; Kornrumpf; Magyar; Master (30); Meyers; ÖBL; WhAm, H

Kostanick, Huey Louis, born 7 April 1918 at Horning, Pa., he graduated in 1940 from the University of Pittsburgh, and received a Ph.D. in geography in 1948 from Clark University. After service with the U.S. Goverment, he was appointed in 1946 a professor of geography at the University of California, Los Angeles. His writings include *Turkish resettlement of Bulgarian Turks, 1950-1953* (1957), and he edited *Population and migration trends in Eastern Europe* (1977). AmM&WSc, 1973 S; AmM&WSc, 1976 P

Kostenko, Lev Leofilovich, born in 1841, he was a Russian officer in the General Staff. In 1873 he participated in the campaign against Khiva, and subsequently explored the Pamirs. His writings include *Средняя Азія и водвореніе в ней русской гражданственности* (1870), *Туркестанскій край* (1880), *The Turkestan region* (1882-84), *Чжунгария*, and its Japanese translation, *Hokubu Shinkyō chishi* (1938). He died in 1891. Henze; LC; NYPL

Kostenkov, Kapiton Ivanovich, born 19th cent., his writings include *Очерк восточнаго и западнаго Манчуча* (1861), and *Историческія и статистическія свѣденія о калмыках кочующих в Астраханской Губернии* (S.-Peterburg, 1870). His trace is lost after an article on Khiva in *Globus* of 1875. NUC; NYPL

Kostiner, Joseph, born 20th cent., he received a doctorate and was in 1984 a lecturer at Shiloah Center, University of Tel-Aviv, and in 1990, a lecturer in the Department of Middle Eastern and African History, and a research fellow of the Dayan Center, Tel Aviv University. His writings include *The Struggle for South Yemen* (1984), a work which represents a revision of his M.A. thesis from the University of Haifa, *Yemen; the tortuous quest for unity, 1990-1994* (1996); he was a joint author of *Medinot ha-Mifrats ha-Parsi* (1992); and he edited *Middle East monarchies; the challenge of modernity* (2000). Note about the author

Kostof, Spiro Konstantin, born 7 May 1936 at Istanbul, he first graduated at Istanbul and later studied art history at Yale University, New Haven, Conn., specializing in architecture from classical history to the Renaissance. After taking a doctorate, he remained at Yale University until 1965, when he moved to the University of California at Berkeley. His writings include *The orthodox baptistery of Ravenna* (1965), *Caves of God* (1972), *The third Rome, 1870-1950; traffic and glory* (1973), *A History of architecture* (1985), and *The City shaped; urban patterns and meanings throughout history* (1991). He died at Berkeley, Cal., on 7 December 1991. AnObit, 1991, pp. 748-50; NYT, 10 December, p. B-20 (not sighted); WhoAm, 1976-1984 (not sighted)

Kostov, Konstantin, born 20th cent., his writings include *Архитектура на промишлените и гражданските сгради* (Sofia, 1975), *Типология на промишлените сгради* (Sofia, 1982), and *Мустантик ефенди* (Sofia, 1993). LC; OSK

Kostygova, Galina Ivanochna, born 13 January 1926 at Leningrad, she graduated in 1949 from the Oriental Faculty, Leningrad State University and reveived her first degree in 1954 for *Жизнь и творчество таджик. каллиграфа-художника Султан-Али Мешхеди*. Her writings include *Персидские и таджикские рукописи Государственной Публичной Библиотеки Имени М. Е. Салтыкова-Щедрина; алфавитный каталог* (1973-1988); and she was a joint author of *Образцы каллиграфии Ирана и Средней Азии XV-XIX вв.* (1963), as well as writings in Tajik. Miliband[2]

Košut, Jaromír Břetislav, born 18 January 1854 at Borová, [Ukraine ?], he first studied theology and later studied Semitic languages at the Universität Leipzig where he was a student of Heinrich L. Fleischer, gaining a Dr.phil. in 1878 for the edition and translation of *Fünf Streitfragen der Barenser und Küfenser über die Abwandlung des Nomens*, from the Arabic of Ibn al-Anbārī. He died in Prag on 6 December 1880. Filipsky; IES; MalaČEnc; PSN

Kosven, Mark Osipovich, born in 1885, his writings include *Очерки истории первобытной культуры* (1953), *История, география и етнография Дагестана XVIII-XIX вв.; архивные материалы* (1958), *Этнография и история Кавказа* (1961), *Семейная община и патронимия* (1963), and he edited *Народы Дагестана; сборник статей* (1955). NUC; OSK

Koszinowski, Thomas, born in 1938, he studied Islamic subjects and general history at Damascus and the Universität Göttingen, where received a Dr.phil. in 1967 for *Kitāb at-Tabaqāt von Ḥalīfa b. Haiyāt*. In 1968 he joined Deutsches Orient-Institut, Hamburg, as a permanent academic staff member, concurrently serving from 1981 to 1984 as representative of the Konrad-Adenauer-Stiftung (Foundation), at Cairo. His writings include *Zur politischen und wirtschaftlichen Situation des Jemen; Einführung und Dokumentation* (1980), and he edited *Saudi-Arabien, Ölmacht und Entwicklungsland; Beiträge* (1983). Note; Schwarz

Kotetishvili, Vakhushti Vakhtangovich, born 4 August 1935 at Tbilisi, Soviet Georgia, he graduated in 1959 from the Oriental Faculty, Tbilisi State University, and received his first degree in 1965 for a thesis entitled *«К вопросы о толковании лирики Хафиза,»* and a doctorate in 1975 for *Структура персидской классической рифмы*. He was associated with his alma mater since 1962; in 1977, he was appointed a professor. He translated classical Persian literature into Georgian, e.g. 'Umar Khayyām (1963), Jāmī (1966), and Ḥāfiz (1970). Miliband²

Kotlov, Lev Nikolaevich, born 9 May 1927 at Kineshma, Russia, he graduated in 1951 from the Faculty of History, Moscow, and received his first degree in 1954 for *Подъём национально-освоболительного движнеия и восстание 1920 г. в Ираке*. In 1952, he became associated with the Oriental Institute in the Soviet Academy of Sciences. His writings include *Йеменская арабская рес-публика* (1971), *Становление национально-освободительного движения на Арабих странах Азии, 1908-1914 гг.* (1986), and he was a joint author of *Юузныи Йемен* (1973). He died on 7 April 1983. Miliband; Miliband²; OSK

Kotobi, Mortéza, born 23 November 1932 at Tehran, he studied at the Université de Paris, where he received a *doctorat d'état* in 1974 for a sociological thesis. He was a sometime professor of social psychology. He edited *Iran, une première république; le grand satan et la tulipe* (Paris, 1983). AnEIFr, 1997; Private

Kotovskiĭ, Grigoriĭ Grigor'evich, born 6 February 1923, he graduated in 1949 from Moscow State University, and received his first degree in 1952 for *Аграрный вопросы на юге Индии в период общего кризиса капитализма*. He was a research fellow of the Oriental Institute in the Soviet Academy of Sciences from 1953 to 1958, when he joined the Institute of Oriental Languages in Moscow State University, a post which he held until 1981. His writings include *Аграрный реформы в Индии* (1959), its translation, *Agrarian reforms in India* (1964), and *The Human condition today; some new perspectives* (1988). He died in 1999. Index Islamicus; Miliband; Miliband²

Kotschy, Theodor Carl Georg, born 15 April 1813 at Unstron near Teschen, Austrian Silesia, he was the son of a botanist. In obedience to his father's wishes he began to study theology at Wien, but he also pursued his real interest, botany. From 1836 until 1843 he interrupted his study in order to accompany Joseph Russegger on his expedition to the Sudan. In 1846, he gave up theology for good and and jolned the k.k. Botanisches Hofkabinett. He again visited the Middle East in 1859-60. He died in Wien on 11 June 1866. ADtB, vol. 16, pp. 763-64; *Ausland*, 39, No. 33 (14 August 1866), p. 790; DtBE; DtBIlnd (1); Embacher; Henze; Hill; Kornrumpf; Kornrumpf², vol. 2; ÖBL; Wurzbach; Zach, pp. 39-45

Kotsones, Hieronymos (Ἰερωνιμος Ἰερωνιμου Κοτσωνης), born 25 November 1905 on the Island of Tenos, Greece, he studied theology and philology at the universities of Athens, München, Berlin, and Bonn. His writings include *Τα χρονολογικα ζητήματα του Σταυπου και των μονογραμμάτων X και P* (1939), *Ἡ Κανονικη ἀποψις περι της ἐπικοινωνίας των ετεροδόξων* (1957), the pamphlet, *A summary of the canonical view about the intercommunion with persons of different faith* (1957), and *Ἡ επι τεν νικεν πεποιθεσις των προτον χριστιανον ος ιεραττοστολικε δυναμις* (1958). Hellenikon, 1965

Kotwicz, Władysław, born 20 March 1872 at Vilna (Vilnius, Wilno), Russia, he completed his study at the Oriental Faculty of St. Petersburg and subsequently remained on the academic staff in order to prepare for a teaching career. In 1894 and 1896, he made study visits to the Kalmyk of the Astrakhan region. In 1900, he began his career, first teaching Mongolian and later also Manchu and Kalmyk. In 1923, he settled in his native Poland, where he became a professor of Oriental languages at Uniwersytet Lwowski. In 1939, he lost both country and teaching facilities. He died sick and starving in his home town a few weeks after the Soviet liberation on 3 October 1944. His writings include *Калмыксктя загадки и посдовицы* (1905), *Обзор современной постановки изучения восточных языков за границею* (1911), *Краткий обзор историй и современнаго политическаго положенiя Монголiи* (1914), *Le mouvement turc d'Ikhe-khuchotu* (1928), *Le dialecte tongous de Bargouzine* (1932), *En marge des lettres des il-khans de Perse retrouvées par Abel-Remusat* (Lwów, 1933), *Les pronoms dans les langues altaïques* (1936), and *Исследование по алтайским языкам* (Moscow, 1962). Maria Kotwiczówna and Marian Lewicki wrote *Wladislaw Kotwicz* (Hamburg, 1984). OSK; Polski (8); PSB; *Ural-altaische Jahbücher*, 26 (1954), pp. 118-123

Kotwiczówna, Maria, fl. 20th cent., she was a joint author of *Orijentalista Antoni Muchliński; życie b dziela* (Wilno, 1935), *Józef Kowalewski, orientalista* (Wrosław, 1948), *Bibliografia utworów Joachima Lelewela* (Wrosław, 1952), and *Wladiyslaw Kotwicz; eine bioblibliographische Skizze* (Hamburg, 1984). OSK

Kotzamanidou, Maria, born about 1950, she received a Ph.D. in 1983 from Columbia University, N.Y.C., for *Fasting and feasting; a study of an antithesis by analogy and association as an inquiry into literature and culture*. She was in 1995 associated with the Department of comparative literature, University of California, Berkeley. LC; NatFacDr, 1990

Koulytchizky, Serge, born in 1935, his writings include *L'autogestion, l'homme et l'état; l'expérience algérienne* (Paris, 1974), and *Contribution à l'étude de la formation des cadres du commerce* (Université de Bordeaux, Institut d'administration des entreprises, 1970). NUC; ZKO

Kourvetaris, George (Yorgos) Andrew, born 21 November 1933 at Elaiokhórion, Arcadia, Greece, he received a diploma from the Teacher's College, Tripolis, Arcadia, Greece; he graduated in 1963 from Loyola University, Chicago, and received a Ph.D. in 1969 from Northwestern University, Evanston, Ill., for *The contemporary army officer corps in Greece*. He subsequently served until his retirement at Northern Illinois University as a professor of sociology. His writings include *First and second generation Greeks in Chicago* (1971), *Political sociology; structure and process* (1997), *Studies on modern Greek society and politics* (1999), *The New Balkans; disintegration and reconstruction* (2002), and he was a joint author of *A Profile of modern Greece* (1987). AmM&WSc, 1973 S, 1978 S; ConAu, 127; NatFacDr, 1900-2004; WhoMW, 1984/85

Kouymijan, Dickran Karnick, born 6 June 1934 at Tulcea, Romania, he studied at the University of Wisconsin, the American University of Beirut, and Columbia University, New York, where he received a Ph.D. in 1969 for *A numismatic history of Southeastern Caucasia and Adharbayjan based on the Islamic coinage*. Afterwards he taught at various universities, terminating his teaching career as director of the Armenian Studies Program at California State University, Fresno. *Who's who in America*, 1994-2003

Kouznietsov, P. E., 1923- *see* Kuznetsov, Petr Evdokimovich

Kovačević, Ešref, born 1 September 1924 at Kovačevci near Glamoč (Glamoch), Herzegovina, he began his higher education during the last year of the second World War at Gazi Husrev-begov Madrasa, and the Advanced Islamic Theological School (Visotoka islamska teološka škola) in Sarajevo. In 1951, he began to study Oriental languages at the Faculty of Philosophy at Sarajevo, obtaining a diploma in 1958. He completed his study in 1971 at the Faculty of Philosophy, Beograd. He became an Ottoman-Turkish and Islamic scholar at Sarajevo. His writings include *Granice bosanskog pašaluka prema Austriji i Mletačkoj Republici po obredbana Karlovačkog mira* (Sarajevo, 1973). He died in Sarajevo on 2 March 1996. *Prilozi za orijentalnu filologiju*, 44/45 (1994/95), pp. 9-11

Kovacs, Helen Ilona von Magyar-Kossa, born 27 April 1912 in Hungary, she was a U.S. East Coast medical librarian. Her writings include *Historical review of medical libraries in Brooklyn* (Brooklyn, 1967), and she was a joint author of *Rare books in the collection of the Academy of Medicine of Brooklyn Library* (Brooklyn, 1972). WhoLibS, 1955, 1966

Koval', Antonina Ivanovna, born 20 July 1938 in Uzbekistan, she graduated in 1961 from the Faculty of Philology, Moscow State University, and received her first degree in 1976 for *Семантико-грамматическ. принципы имен. классификации в фула*. From 1963 to 1971 she was associated with the Soviet Academy of Sciences. Her writings include *Язык фула* (1986), *Эпос и литература фульбе* (1990), *Глагол фула в типологическом освещении* (1997), and she was a joint author of *Социолингвистическая типология; западная Африка* (1984). Miliband²; OSK

Kovalev, Aleksandr Aleksandrovich, born 27 November 1923, he graduated in 1945 from the Military Institute of Foreign Languages, received his first degree in 1950 for *Выражение категории времени в современном арабском литературном языке*. He taught Arabic at his alma mater and was from 1957 to 1982 associated with the Institute of Oriental Languages at the Moscow State University. He was appointed a lecturer in 1954, and became a professor in 1967. He was a joint author of *Учебнрк арабского языка* (1960), and *Арабская филология* (1968). Miliband; Miliband²

Kovalevskii, Andrei Petrovich, born in 1895 in the Ukraine, he graduated in 1922 at Kharkov, and received his first degree in 1937 and his doctorate in 1951 for *Ибн Фадлан*. He was from 1948 to 1969 affiliated with Kharkov State University as a professor, concurrently cataloguing the library's Oriental manuscripts. His writings include *Амин Рейхан* (1932). He died on 29 November 1969. BashkKE; *Index Islamicus* (1); Krachkovskii; Miliband; Miliband²

Kovaleskiĭ, Egor Petrovich, born in 1811 at the Ukrainian village of Iaroshevka, he studied at Khar'kov University. He became a mining engineer and explored eastern Siberia, the Kirghiz steppes, and Montenegro, publishing his results in the *Gornyĭ zhurnal* (*Горный журнал*). In the winter of 1847-1848, he and Pierre Trémaux went in the service of Muhammad ʿAlī Pasha on a mission to the gold-bearing region on the Nubian-Abyssinian border. He later undertook various diplomatic missions for the Russian Government to Peking. In 1856, he was nominated director of the Department of Asian Affairs, where he promoted expeditions, particularly to Khurasan and Kashghar. His writings include *Путешествие во Внутреннюю Африку* (1849), *Путешествие в Китай* (1853), *Война с Турцией и разрыв с западными державами в 1853 и 1854 годах* (1868), its translation, *Der Krieg Rußlands mit der Türkei und der Bruch mit den Westmächten* (1869). He died in St.-Petersburg on 20 September (2 October) 1868. EnSlovar; GdeEnc; GSE; Hill; Wieczynski

Kovalevskiĭ, Maksim Maksimovich, born in 1851 at Kharkov, Ukraine, he graduated in law in 1872 from Kharkov University and completed his education at Berlin, Wien, Paris, and London. He taught international law at Moscow University, from 1877 to 1887, when he was expelled for political reasons and went abroad, first to Stockholm and from 1889 to 1890 to Oxford University, where he delivered the Ilchester Lectures. In 1883, 1885, and 1887, he went on research visits to Dagestan. His writings include *Экономический строй России* (1900), *Modern customs and ancient laws of Russia* (1891), *Coutume contemporaine et loi ancienne; droit coutumier ossétien* (1893), and *La Russie sociale* (1914). He died in Petrograd in 1916. EnSlovar; GdeEnc; GSE; *Russian review*, 1 (June 1916), pp. 259-68; Wieczynski

Kovalevskiĭ, Osip Mikhaĭlovich (IUzef), 1800 or 1-1878 *see* Kowalewski, Józef Szczepan

Kovtunovich, Oleg Vital'evich, born 17 October 1930 at Moscow, he graduated in 1953 from the Moscow Oriental Institute and received his first degree in 1981. He was associated with the Ministry of Foreign Affairs from 1953 to 1979, being repeatedly assigned to Egypt, Syria, and Iraq. From 1979 to 1986, he was associated with the Oriental Institute of the Soviet Academy of Sciences. His writings include *Революция "Свободных офицеров" в Египте* (1984). He died on 17 March 1988. Miliband[2]

Kowalewski, David Alfred, born 8 September 1943 at Fargo, N.Dak., he graduated in 1965 from Mount Angel College, studied at the Defense Language Institute, Monterey, Calif., received M.A.'s in Soviet studies (1971), philosophy (1977), and East Asian studies (1980), and a Ph.D. in 1978 from the University of Kansas for *The protest uses of symbolic politics; the functions of symbolic resources for protest groups in the Soviet Union*. He was a sometime professor of political science. ConAu, 112

Kowalewski (Ковалевский), Józef Szczepan (Joseph Étienne), born 1800 or 1 in Gardinas (Grodno) county, Lithuania, he studied classical philology at the University of Vilnius from 1817 to 1823. In the following year, he was arrested as a member of a patriotic student organization and banned to Kazan, where he began to study Arabic, Persian, and Tatar. He later studied Mongolian and Tibetan in Siberia, where he remained until 1833, visiting the region beyond Lake Baikal, Mongolia, and even Peking. He returned to Kazan with a rich collection of books, manuscripts, and artefacts. He held the chair of Mongolian literature at Kazan until it was relocated to St. Petersburg, where he later also served as president of the university. In 1867, he was a professor of Tatar at Warszawa. He was a member of most of the European academies of sciences. His writings include *Монгольско-русско-французский словарь* (Kazan, 1844-49). He died in 1878. Maria Kotwiczówna and Władys Kotwicz wrote *Józef Kowalewski, orientalista* (1948). EncLitu; EnSlovar; Krachkovskiĭ; *L'Orient, l'Algérie et les colonies françaises*, 1 (1866/67), pp. 31-32; Polski (13); PSB; TatarES; VostokMStP, p. 251

Kowalska, Maria, born 20th cent., her writings include *Średniowieczna arabska literatura podróżnicza* (Kraków, 1973), and *Ukraina w połowie XVII wieku w relacji arabskiego podróznika Pawła, syna Makrego z Aleppo* (Warszawa, 1986). ZKO

Kowalski, Tadeusz, born 21 May 1889 at Châteauroux (Indre), France, he graduated in 1907 from a gymnasium at Krakau (Kraków), and studied Oriental subjects at the universities of Wien and Halle, where he received a Dr.phil. in 1911 for *Die vierte Kaside aus dem Diwan des Kajs ibn al-Ḥatim mit der Biographie des Dichters*. He went for post-doctoral study first to the Universität Straßburg, where Theodor Nöldeke and Enno Littmann were teaching, and then to Georg Jacob at the Universität Kiel. After two years of work at Orientalisches Institut, Wien, he received a Dr.habil. in 1914 from the Universität Krakau for a thesis on Arabic philology entitled *Der Diwān des Kais ibn al-Ḥatīm*. He subsequently taught Arabic, Persian, and Turkish at Uniwersytet Jagielloński, Kraków, for the rest of his life, declining tempting invitations from Ankara Üniversitesi before the war, and the School of Oriental and African Studies, London, after the war. He held several academic and administrative posts and was a member of numerous Polish and international learned societies. His writings include *Zagadki ludowe tereckie* (1919), *Turcja powojenna* (1925), *Karaimische Texte im Dialekt von Troki*

MACK LIBRARY
BOB JONES UNIVERSITY
GREENVILLE, SC

(1929), *Zur semantischen Funktion des Pluralsuffixes -lar, -lär in den Türksprachen* (1936), *Les Turcs et la langue turque de la Bulgarie du nord-est* (Kraków, 1933), and *Na szlakach islamu* (1935). He died in Kraków on 5 May 1948. Dziekan; *Folia orientalia*, 19 (1978), pp. 5-12; Hanisch; Schwarz

Kowalsky, Nikolaus (Nicholas/Nicolo), born 20 February 1911 at Berlin, he received a doctorate for *Die Errichtung der apostolischen Vikariate in Indien, 1834-1838*. He became a professor in the Pontifical Institute of Missions, Roma, and an archivist at the Santa Congregation de Propaganda Fide. His writings include *Pontificio Collegio Urbano de propaganda fide* (1956), and *Stand der katholischen Missionen um das Jahr 1765* (1957), and he was a joint editor of *Inventory of the historical archives of the Sacred Congregation for the Evangelization of Peoples* (1988), and *Bibiliotheca missionum*. He died in Bonn on 6 June 1966. Kürschner, 1966

Kozin, Sergei Andreevich, born in 1879 at Tuapse on the Black Sea coast, he graduated in 1903 from the Faculty of Oriental Languages, St. Petersburg, and received a doctorate in 1941. Since 1920 he was associated with Leningrad University. In 1943 he was appointed a professor. His writings include *Эпос монгольских народов* (1948). He died 16 October 1956. Miliband; Miliband[2]

Kozlov, G. I., fl. 20th cent., his writings include *Различия между таджикским и персидским языками* (Moscow, 1949). OSK

Kozlov, T. S., fl. 1930, his writings include *Красная Гвардия и Красная Армия в Туркмении* (Ashkhabad, 1928), *Зачатки большевизма в революционном движении Туркмении, 1904-1916 гг.* (Ashkhabad, 1928). NUC, pre-1956; OSK

Kozlova, Galina P., born 20th cent., she was a joint author, with Zakhar I. Faĭnburg, of *Научно-технический прогресс и совершенствование социалистических производственных отношений* (Moscow, 1987). OSK

Kozlowski, Gregory C., born about 1950, he received a Ph.D. in 1980 from the University of Minnesota, Minneapolis, for *Muslim endowments and society in British India*, a work which was published in 1985. He became a professor in the Department of History, De Paul University, Chicago, a post which he still held in 2002. NatFacDr, 1990-2002; Selim[3]

Koz'menko, I V., born 20th cent., his writings include *Сборник договоров России другими государствами, 1856-1917* (Moscow, 1952), and the Romanian translation of one of his works, *Руската дипломация и формирането на българската държавност след освобождението* (Sofia, 1982). LC; OSK

Koz'min, Nikolaĭ Nikolaevich, born in 1878 at Krasnoyarsk, Russia, he was a historian, ethnographer, and journalist. His writings include *Хакасы; историко-этнографический и хозяйственный очерк Минусинского края* (Irkutsk, 1925), *К вопросу о турецко-монгольском феодализме* (Irkutsk, 1934); and he was a joint editor of Mikhail N. Bogdanov's *Очерки прошлаго и настоящаго Сибири* (St.-Petersburg, 1910). NYPL; SibirSE; ZKO

Kozmoian, Armanush Kozmoevna, born 7 September 1945 at Erevan, he graduated in 1967 from the Faculty of Philology, Erevan State University, and received his first degree in 1976 for *Формирование рубаи в классической поэзии на фарси*, a work which was published in the same year. From 1967 to 1970 he collaborated with the publication of the *Армянский энциклопедический словарь*. Since 1971 he was associated with the Oriental Institute of the Armenian Academy of Sciences. Miliband[2]

Kozocsa, Sándor (Alexander), born 25 September 1904 at Dicsőszentmárton, Transylvania, he studied at Budapest and became a bibliographer, practising librarian, and a professor of library science. His writings include *Bevezetés a bibliográfiába* (1939), *Az orosz irodalom magyar bibliográfiája* (1949), *A bolgár irodalom magyar bibliográfiája* (1955), and he was a joint author of *Szindbád* (1957). He died in Budapest on 6 June 1991. Magyar; OSK; WhoSoCE, 1989

Krachkovskaia, Vera Aleksandrovna, born in 1884 at St. Petersburg, she graduated in 1923 from the local Institute of History of Fine Art and received a doctorate in 1944. From 1935 to 1950 she was associated with the Leningrad Institute of History, Philology and Linguistics, since 1935 as a professor. Her writings include *Арабские надгробия Музея палеографии Академии наук СССР* (1929), *Эпиграфика востока* (1947), and *Два забытых памятника архитектуры Ирана* (1948). She died on 4 January 1974. Miliband; Miliband[2]; OSK

Krachkovskiĭ, Ignatiĭ IUlianovich, born 4/16 March 1883 at Vil'na, Russia, he grew up in Tashkent after his father was transferred there as an administrator, learning Uzbek as a child from his nanny. His Russian education began five years later when the family returned to Vilna, where he graduated from the gymnasium as a gold medallist. He studied Oriental languages at St. Petersburg, gaining his first degree in 1905 with a dissertation on "the rule of Caliph al-Mahdī based on Arabic sources." Influenced by his teacher, Viktor R. Rosen, he prepared for a university career, obtaining his M.A. in 1915 for *Абу-л-Фарадж ал-Вафа Дамасский*, and his doctorate in 1921. His staff membership at St. Petersburg University since 1907 enabled him to spend the following two years on travels and study in Syria and Egypt. After his return, he was appointed director of the library of the Oriental Seminary, concurrently teaching and serving as a secretary of the Oriental Division of the Archaeological Society. In 1914 he went on his last travels abroad, studying manuscripts at Halle, Leipzig, and Leiden. In 1918 he was appointed secretary of the Oriental Faculty and professor. He became the leading Russian Arabist of his time. His writings include *Над арабскими рукописями* (1945), and its translations, *Über arabische Handschriften gebeugt* (1949), and *Avec les manuscrits arabes* (1954), *Очерки по истории русской арабистики* (1950), and its translation, *Die russische Arabistik* (1957). Anna A. Dolinina wrote the biography, *Невольник долга* (1994). He died in Leningrad on 24 January 1951. Fück, pp. 302-304; GSE; Miliband, Miliband²; TatarES; ZDMG, 105 (1955), pp. 5-17

Krader, Lawrence, born 9 December 1919 at N.Y.C., he graduated in 1941 from City College of New York, and obtained a Ph.D. in 1954 from Harvard University for *Kingship systems of the Altaic-speaking peoples of the Asiatic steppes*. He became a professor of anthropology at American universities; he was from 1970 to 1972 a chairman of the Department of Sociology and Anthropology, University of Waterloo, Ontario, and subsequently he was a professor of ethnology at the Freie Universität Berlin until his retirement in 1996. His writings include *Bibliography of Kazakhstan* (1954), *The Kazakhs* (1955), *Peoples of Central Asia* (1963), *Social organization of the Mongol-Turkic pastoral nomads* (1963), *Formation of the state* (1968), and *The Asiatic mode of production* (1975). In 1995, he was honoured by *Ethnohistorische Wege und Lehrjahre eines Philosophen; Festschrift für Lawrence Krader zum 75. Geburtstag*. He died in 1998. AmM&WSc, 1973 S; AmM&WSc, 1976 P; AMS, 1968; ConAu, 21-24; Kürschner, 1976-1996; Note; Schoeberlein

Kraeling, Carl Hermann, born 10 March 1897 at Brooklyn, N.Y., he graduated *magna cum laude* in 1918 from Columbia University, New York, where he also received a Ph.D. in 1927 for *Anthropos and Son of God*; in 1935, he gained a Dr.theol. at the Universität Heidelberg for *A Greek fragment of Tatian's Diatessaron from Dura*. He was ordained to the Lutheran ministry and became successively fellow, instructor, and assistant professor at the Lutheran Theological Seminary, Philadelphia, Pa., where he remained for nine years. He subsequently spent over twenty years at Yale University, New Haven, Conn., as a professor of New Testament criticism and interpretation before teaching Hellenistic Oriental archaeology at the University of Chicago from 1950 to his retirement in 1963. In 1947, he had succeeded Millar Burrows as president of the American Schools of Oriental Research. Few men in the history of the Schools have distinguished themselves so greatly as he did. His remarkable talents as organizer of scholarship, as academic administrator, and as diplomat brought him to the top in the learned world and led directly to results of the greatest value. He died on 14 November 1966. *Bulletin of the American Schools of Oriental Research*, no. 198 (April 1970), pp. 4-7; DrAS, 4th ed. (1963/64); Shavit

Kraelitz-Greifenhorst, Friedrich Johann, born on 12 July 1876 at Wien, he completed his law while concurrently taking courses in Arabic, Persian, and Turkish at the k.k. Öffentliche Lehranstalt für Orientalische Sprachen, Wien. He subsequently studied at the faculty of philosophy of the Universität Wien, where he received a Dr.phil. in 1903 for *Türkische Elemente im Neupersischen*. He spent a good ten years as keeper of Oriental manuscripts at the Hofbibliothek, Wien, concurrently gaining a Dr.habil. in 1913. Since 1916 he taught in various capacities Oriental languages at his alma mater. An authority in Turko-Tatar and Armenian linguistics as well as Ottoman-Turkish diplomatics, he was associated with the ministries of foreign, interior, and educational affairs, and also collaborated with the publication of the major Austrian Orientalist periodicals. His writings include *Studien zum Armenisch-Türkischen* (1912), *Die Verfassungsgesetze des Osmanischen Reiches* (1919), *Osmanische Urkunden in türkischer Sprache aus der zweiten Hälfte des 15. Jahrhunderts* (1920), and he translated *Die Verfassungsgesetze des Osmanischen Reiches aus dem Osmanisch-türkischen übersetzt* (1909). He died in Wien on 25 February 1932. DtBE; Hanisch; Kürschner, 1925-1931; ÖBL; Schwarz; *Wer ist's*, 1928; WZKM, 39 (1932), pp. 1-5; ZKO

Kraemer, Hendrik, born on 17 May 1888 at Amsterdam, he studied at the Rijksuniversiteit te Leiden, where he obtained doctorates in Oriental languages and religions. The Netherlands Bible Society sent him to Java in 1921 to translate the Bible into the indigenous Indonesian languages. During this work he began to realize that the methods of liberal theologians in trying to build bridges between Christianity and other religions were not well founded. He startled the Christian world in 1938 with his book *The Christian message in a non-Christian world* in which his unique and, perhaps, dogmatic claims for Christianity revealed the depth of the gulf between Christianity and the great Eastern faiths of which he was so profound a student. He parted company with those who believed there could be any compromise or any easy bridging of the gulf between the Christian faith and the living religions of the East. During the German occupation he was kept for a year in detention camps in South Holland. In the post-war years he became a world leader of Christian thought at the Ecumenical Institute near Genève. His writings include *De strijd over Bali en de zending* (1933), *Een nieuw geluid op het gebied der koranexegese* (1962), *Religion and the Christian faith* (1956), its translation, *Religion und christlicher Glaube* (1959), and *World cultures and world religions* (1960). He died at his home in Driebergen, Holland, on 11 November 1965. Arend Th. van Leeuwen wrote *Hendrik Kraemer, dienaar der wereldkerk* (1959), and work which was published in 1962 in a German translation. BiBenelux² (1); MW 56 (1966), p. 144; *Who's who in the Netherlands*, 1962/63

Kraemer, Joel Louis, born in 1933, he received a Ph.D. in 1967 from Yale University, New Haven, Conn., for *Abû Sulaymân as-Sijistânî, a Muslim philosopher of the tenth century*. His writings include *Humanism in the renaissance of Islam; the cultural revival during the Buyid age* (1986); and he edited *Jerusalem; problems and prospects* (1980), *Perspectives on Maimonides; philosophical and historical studies* (1991); and he was a joint editor of *Religion and government in the world of Islam; proceedings* (1980). WhoWorJ, 1978 (not sighted)

Kraemer, Jörg, born 20 December 1917 at Stuttgart, Germany, he received a Dr.phil. in 1947 from the Universität Tübingen for *Der Sturz des Königreiches Jerusalem in der Darstellung des 'Imād ad-Dīn al-Kātib al-Isfahānī*, a work which was published in 1952. He was a lecturer in Arabic and Islamic studies at his alma mater before he became a professor in his field at the Seminar für Orientalische Philologie in the Universität Erlangen. His writings include his inaugural lecture on 17 May 1958 at the Universität Erlangen, *Das Problem der islamischen Kulturgeschichte* (1959), and he was a joint author of *Wörterbuch der klassischen arabischen Sprache* (1970-). He died in Erlangen on 26 November 1961. Kürschner, 1950-1961; Schwarz

Krafft, Albrecht, born 25 February 1816 at Wien, he was educated at the local Benedictine Schotten-gymnasium, concurrently taking courses at the Akademie der bildenden Künste, Wien, where his father was a director. He began to study philosophy at the Universität Wien, but in 1835 transferred to the Orientalische Akademie, where he studied Oriental languages and literatures. He subsequently prepared the *Verzeichnis der K.K. Gemälde-Gallerie im Belvédère zu Wien* (1836), and its French edition, *Catalogue de la Galerie de tableaux impériale et royale au Belvédère à Vienne* (1845). From 1840 to 1842 he compiled the catalogue *Die arabischen, persischen und türkischen Handschriften der K.K. Orientalischen Akademie* (1842). In 1845, he was appointed to a clerical position at the K.K. Hofbibliothek, Wien, where he became a joint author of the catalogue of its Hebrew manuscripts. He died in Wien on 23 May 1847. AllgLKünst; *Journal asiatique*, 4e série, 10 (1947), pp. 174-76; Kosch; ÖBL; Wurzbach

von **Krafft**, Alexander, Baron, born 19th cent., he travelled to North Africa to continue Heinrich Barth's explorations in the Sahara and the Sudan. He stayed a year in Tripolis making preparations. He was obliged to return to Germany when the death of his mother reached him 1860 in Ghadames. Henze

Krafft, Hans Ulrich, born 25 March 1550 to a patrician family at Ulm, Swabia, he was sent in 1562 to Augusburg to train as a merchant, completing his training in Lyon, 1569, and Firenze, 1569. In 1573, he entered the service of the mercantile house of Melchior Manlich, which organized the German Oriental trade with its own fleet. He became head of their establishments in Aleppo, Tripolis, and Famagusta. After the bankruptcy of the firm, he was kept a prisoner of the Turks for three years. In 1577, he reached Marseille and returned to Germany. His *Reisen und Gefangenschaft* were published in 1843, 1862, and 1970. He died in Ulm on 21 February 1621. ADtB, vol. 17, pp. 11-13; DtBE; DtBilnd (1); NDB

Krafft, Hugues, born in 1853 at Paris, his writings include *Souvenirs de notre tour du monde* (1885), and *À travers le Turkestan russe* (1902). IndexBFr² (1)

Kraft, Gisela, born 28 June 1936 at Berlin, she received a Dr.phil. in 1978 from the Freie Universität Berlin for *Fazıl Hüsnü Dağlarca; Weltschöpfung und Tiersymbolik*. She was a novelist and translator from the Turkish. In the early 1980s she voluntarily settled behind the Iron Curtain in Weimar. Her writings include *Katze und Derwisch; Gedichte* (1989), *Sintflut; Märchen und Träume* (1990), *West-östliche Couch; zweierlei Leidensweisen der Deutschen* (1991), *Zu machtschlafender Zeit; ein postpolitisches Fragment* (1994), and the translations, *Privatexil; Gedichte*, of Aras Ören (1977), *Brot und Taube; Nachdichtungen*, of F. Hüsnü Dağlarca (1984), and *Südostverlies; drei literarische Reportagen über Anatolien*, of Bekir Yıldız (1987). KDtLK, 1984-1004/2005; Private; Schwarz

Kraft, Joseph, born 4 September 1924 at South Orange, N.J., he graduated in 1947 from Columbia University, N.Y.C. He became a journalist, staff writer with the *New York Times*, and a speech writer for John F. Kennedy during the 1960 presidential campaign. His writings include *The Struggle for Algeria* (1961), *The Grand design; from Common Market to Atlantic partnership* (1962), *Profiles in* *power* (1966), and *The Chinese difference* (1973). He died on 10 January 1986. ConAu, 9-12, 118, new rev., 34; Master (2); WhAm, 9; WhoAm, 1974-1984; WhoWor, 1976/77; WrDr, 1976/78-1984/86

Krahl, Günther, born about 1940, he received a Dr.phil. in 1967 from the Universität Leipzig for *Die technischen und wissenschaftlichen Termini im modernen Arabisch*, and also a Dr.habil. in 1985 for *Das arabische Adjektiv und die Substantiv-Adjektiv-Gruppe*. His writings include *Deutsch-Arabisches Wörterbuch* (1964), and he was a joint author of *Lehrbuch des modernen Arabisch* (1977), and *Wörterbuch Arabisch-Deutsch* (1984). ZKO

Krahlenbuhl, Margaret Flowers, born 26 July 1943, she received an M.A. in 1967 from the University of California, Los Angeles, and went the following year to Turkey as a Fulbright Fellow. She subsequently became a research associate in the Social Science Department of the Rand Corporation, Santa Monika, Calif. She produced research reports for her employer: *Turkish-American relations; an affair to remember* (1974), *Economic recovery following disaster* (1977), and *Lower level conflict on the Arabian Peninsula* (1982). LC; *MESA Roster of members*, 1982-1990; Note about the author

Krahmer, Gustav, born 29 December 1839 at Elbingerode, Germany, he was a professional soldier who retired with the rank of major-general. He served on boundary commissions in the Balkans. His writings include *Sibirien und die große sibirische Eisenbahn* (1897), its translation, *Сибирь и значеніе великаго сибирскаго пут* (n.d.), *Rußland in Mittel-Asien* (1898), *Die Geschichte des Russisch-Türkischen Krieges auf der Balkan-Halbinsel, 1877/78* (1902), and *Die Beziehungen Rußlands zu Persien* (1903). He died in 1905. BioJahr, 10 (1905), Totenliste, cols. 200*-201*; KDtLK, 1899-1904; Kornrumpf; *Soldatisches Führertum*, ed. Kurt Priesdorff, vol. 10 (1942).

Krall, Jakob, born 27 July 1857 at Volska, Istria, he studied at Trieste, Athens, and the Universität Wien, where he received a Dr.phil in 1879 and a Dr.habil. in 1881, and did post-doctoral work at the Collège de France, Paris. He became a professor of Egyptology at Wien. His writings include *Grundriß der altorientalischen Geschichte* (1899). He died in Wien on 27 April 1905. Dawson; DtBE; Egyptology; ÖBL

Krämer, Gudrun, born 3 August 1953 at Marburg, Germany, she studied general arts and Islamic subjects at the universities of Heidelberg and Hamburg, where she received a Dr.phil. in 1981 for *Minderheit, Millet, Nation; die Juden in Ägypten, 1914-1952*, a work which was also published in an English translation entitled *The Jews in modern Egypt* (1989); she received a Dr.habil. in 1993 from the Universität Hamburg for *Gottes Staat als Republik; Reflexionen zeitgenössischer Muslime zu Islam, Menschenrechten und Demokratie*. She was associated with Stiftung Wissenschaft und Politik, Ebenhausen, and taught at Orientalisches Seminar, Universität München, before she was appointed a professor and chairman of the Institut für Islamkunde, Freie Universität Berlin, a post which she still held in 2005. Her writings include *Ägypten unter Mubarak; Identität und nationales Interesse* (1986), *Arabismus und Nationalstaatlichkeit; Syrien als nahöstliche Regionalmacht* (1987), *Geschichte Palästinas von der osmanischen Eroberung bis zur Gründung des Staates Israel* (2002), and *Geschichte des Islam* (2005). Kürschner, 2005; Note

Krämer, Martin, born 9 February 1931 at Endigen, Germany, he received a Dr.rer.pol. in 1957 from the Universität Freiburg im Breisgau for *Die soziale Sicherung des Haushaltes im Lichte der modernen mikroökonomischen Spartheorie*. He became an executive member of the Africa Business Development Association, Hamburg. He was a joint author of *Afrika-Handbuch für Wirtschaft und Reise* (1967), and he edited *Recht und Rechtspraxis in Afrika* (1969). Unesco; *Wer ist wer*, 2004/2005

Kramer, Martin Seth, born 9 September 1954 at Washington, D.C., he received a Ph.D. in 1982 from Princeton University for *The congress in modern Islam; on the origins of an innovation*. Since 1981 he was associated with Moshe Dayan Center, Tel Aviv University, becoming its director in 1995. He also served as a visiting professor at U.S. universities. His writings include *Political Islam* (1980), *Islam assembled; the advent of the Muslim congresses* (1986), and *Ivory towers on sand; the failure of Middle Eastern studies in America* (2001). ConAu, 160, new rev., 114; Selim[2]

Kramer, Robert S., born 25 February 1956, he graduated in 1979 from Bard College, Columbia University, New York, studied Arabic at the American University in Cairo, 1980-82, received an M.A. in Middle East studies in 1984 from the University of Chicago, and a Ph.D. in African history in 1991 from Northwestern University, Evanston, Illinois. He was subsequently appointed a professor of history at St. Norbert College, De Pere, Wisc., a post which he still held in 2005. He was a joint author of *Historical dictionary of the Sudan* (1992). LC; NatFacDr, 2002-2005; Note

Kramers, Johannes Hendrik, born 26 February 1891 at Rotterdam, he was educated at the local Gymnasium Erasmianum and studied law and Arabic, at the Rijksuniversiteit te Leiden, where he was a student of Snouck Hurgronje. He received a doctorate in law and Oriental languages in 1915 for

Strafrechtspraak over Nederlanders in Turkije. In 1915, he went as a dragoman to the Dutch Legation in Constantinople, a post which he held until 1922, when he abandoned his consular career and entered the academic life at his alma mater on 22 February 1922 with his inaugural lecture, *Over de geschiedschrijving bij de Osmaanse Turken.* In 1939, he was appointed a professor of Arabic and Islamic studies. His writings include *De taal van de Koran* (1940), *De Semitische talen* (1949), and *Over de kunst van de Islam* (1953). For many years he collaborated with the English and French editions of the *Encyclopaedia of Islam.* He died after a long illness in Oegstgeest near Leiden on 17 December 1951. BWN, vol. 1, pp. 322-23; Fück; *Isis,* 43 (1952), pp. 118-119; *Wie is dat,* 1948; ZDMG, n.Folge 27 (1952), 10-13

Krammer, Arnold Paul, born 15 August 1941 at Chicago, he graduated in 1963 from the University of Wisconsin, Madison, where he also received a Ph.D. in 1970 for *Soviet Bloc relations with Israel, 1947-1953,* a work which was published in 1974 entitled *The forgotten friendship; Israel and the Soviet Bloc, 1947-1953.* From 1974 to his retirement he was a professor of history at Texas A&M University. His writings include *Nazi prisoners of war in America* (1979), *Public administration of prisoner of war camps in America since the revolutionary war* (1980), and *Undue process; the untold story of America's German alien internees* (1997). ConAu, 61-64, new rev., 11, 27; DrAS, 1974 H, 1978 H, 1982 H; NatFacDr, 1990-2002; Selim³; WhoS&SW, 1980, 1982, 1984 (not sighted)

Krámský, Jiří, fl. 20th cent., his writings include *Východ a nová doba* (Kladno, 1946), *The Article and the concept of definiteness in language* (The Hague, 1972), *Zvuková stránka jazyka ve vyucovvání cizim jazykům* (Praha, 1972), *The Phoneme* (The Hague, 1976), *Papers in general linguistics* (The Hague, 1976), and he was a joint editor of *Anglicko-česky slovník* (1960). NUC, pre-1956; OSK

Krane, Ronald E., born about 1940, he was a sometime professor in the Department of Sociology, California State University at Northridge. He edited *Manpower mobility across cultural boundaries; social, economic and legal aspects: the case of Turkey and West Germany* (1975), and *International labor migration in Europe* (1978). NatFacDr, 1990-2002

Kranz, Walther Friedrich, born 23 November 1884 at Georgsmarienhütte, Germany, he was a professor of classical philology at the Universität Halle/Saale, from 1923 until his emigration to Turkey. He taught at İstanbul Üniversitesi from 1942 to 1950 when he returned to the Universität Bonn. His writings include *Studien zu antiken Literatur und ihrem Fortwirken; kleine Schriften* (1967). He died in Bonn on 18 September 1960. BioHbDtE; DtBE; Kürschner, 1950, 1954; NDB; *Wer ist wer,* 1955, 1958; Widmann, pp. 109-110, 273

Krapf, Johann *Ludwig*, born 11 February 1810 at Derendingen, Württemberg, he was educated at a classicist school in Tübingen, where he came under the influence of James Bruce of Kinnaird's travel account as well as missionary endeavours. In 1827, he entered the Basler Missionshaus as a student. From 1829 to 1834 he completed his theology at the Universität Tübingen. In 1836, he accepted an invitation from the Church Missionary Society, London, to serve as a missionary in Abyssinia. He spent over twenty years in Africa and became a recognized explorer, ethnologist, and authority in Hamito-Semitic languages. His writings include *Journals of...Isenberg and Krapf ... detailing their proceedings in the Kingdom of Shoa and journeys in other parts of Abyssinia* (1843), *Outline of the elements of the Kisuaheli language, with special reference to the Kiníka dialect* (1850), *Afrika von Süd nach West und von West nach Ost endlich einmal durchkreuzt* (1857), *Reisen in Ost-Afrika, 1837-55* (1858), *The Acts of the Apostles translated into the Galla language* (1874), and *A Dictionary of the Suahili language* (1882). He died in Kornthal, Württemberg, on 27 November 1881. ADtB, vol. 17, pp. 49-55; BioIn, 6, 9; DcAfHiB, 1986; DtBE; Embacher, Henze; Hill; Kornrumpf; LexAfrika; LuthC, 75; WhWE

Krappe, Alexander Haggerty, born in 1894, he received a Ph.D. in 1919 from the University of Chicago for *Alliteration in the Chanson de Roland and in the Carmen de prodicione Guenonis.* He became a lecturer in Romance literature at Columbia University, N.Y.C. His writings include *The Legend of Rodrick, last of the Visigoth kings, and the Ermanarich Cycle* (1923), *Balor with the evil eye* (1927), and *Mythologie universelle* (1930). He died in 1947. AmIndex; BioIn, 1; Master (1)

Krása, Miloslav, born 6 January 1920 at Libočany, he studied Indian history at Praha, and Allahabad. His writings include *The Temples of Angkor* (1963), *Looking towards India* (1969), *Indie* (1972), and he edited the proceedings, *Unending discoveries of Eastern cultures* (1966). Český; Filipsky

Krasicki, Ignacy, born a nobleman on 3 March 1735 at Dubick, Galicia, he was a poet, writer, playwright, and clergyman. His writings include *Nikołaja Doświadczyńskiego przypadki* (1776), and its tanslations, *Begebenheiten des Nicolaus Doświadczyński in drey Büchern von ihm selbst beschrieben aus dem Pohlnischen übersetzt mit Anmerkungen* (Warschau, 1776), and *The Adventures of Mr. Nicholas Wisdom* (1992). He died in Berlin on 14 March 1801. BiD&SB;BioIn, 8; CasWL; DtBilnd (5); Dziekan; Master (12); Polski (30); Wurzbach

Krasner, Stephen D., born 15 February 1942 at N.Y.C., he received a Ph.D. in 1972 from Harvard University for *The politics of primary commodities; a study of coffee, 1900-1970*. He was a professor of government successively at his alma mater, the University of California, Los Angeles, and Stanford University, Palo Alto, Calif. His writings include *Defending the national interest* (1978), *Structural conflict; the Third World against global liberalism* (1985), *Sovereignty, organized hypocrisy* (1999), and *Problematic sovereignty; contested rules and political possibilities* (2001). AmM&WSc, 1978 S; ConAu, 85-88, new revision, 15; NatFacDr, 1990-2005

Krasnov, IUriĭ Alekseevich, born 20th cent., his writings include *Раннее земледелие и животновод-ство в лесной полосе восточной Увропы* (1971), *Древнейшие упряжные пахотные орудия* (1975), *Донская экспедиция* (1983), *Древние и средневековые пахотные орудия Восточной Европы* (1987), and he was a joint author of *Средневековные Чебоксары* (1978). LC; OSK; ZKO

Krasnov, Sergeĭ Arkhipovich, born in 1903, his writings include *Илыш шолеш; повесть* (Ioshkar-Ola, 1958). NUC, 1968-72

Krasnowolska, Anna, born 20th cent., she edited *Iranica Cracoviensia; Cracow Iranian studies in memory of Wladyslaw Duleba* (Kraków, 1996). OSK

Krassoeski, Andrzej, born 20th cent., he was associated with the Overseas Development Institute, London. His writings include *Aid and the British balance of payments* (1966), *The Aid relationship; a discussion of aid strategy with examples from the American experience in Tunisia* (1968), *Development and the debt trap; economic planning and external borrowing in Ghana* (1974), and he edited *British development policies* (1968). Note about the author

Kraus, Alessandro, barone, born 12 October 1853 at Firenze, he was a musicologist and a member of numerous international learned societies. He died in Fiesole on 21 May 1931. DizBI; IndBiltal (1)

Kraus, Joe, born 8 September 1931 at Portland, Oreg., he was a student at Citrus College and subsequently worked in public relations. Concurrently he contributed to American periodicals, including the periodical *Desert*, and *National wildlife*. His writings include *Desert survival* (1978). ConAu, 89-92; IntAu&W, 1982 (not sighted)

Kraus, Paul, born 11 December 1904 at Prag, he studied at the universities of Prag and Berlin, where he received a Dr.phil. in 1929 for *Altbabylonische Briefe aus den Staatsmuseen zu Berlin*. He subsequently spent four years at the Institut für Geschichte der Medizin und Naturwissenschaften, Berlin, where he was an assistant to Julius Ruska. In 1932, he became a lecturer in Semitic languages and Islamic studies at the Universität Berlin. Warned of the political growling of the time by Carl H. Becker, at that time Prussian minister of education, he emigrated to Paris, where he was found much support by Louis Massignon. For four years he taught at the Institut d'histoire des sciences at the Sorbonne. In 1936 he accepted an invitation from the University Fuad I in Cairo as a lecturer, later to lecture concurrently also at the University Faruq I at Alexandria. On 9 March 1942, he became a member of the Institut d'Égypte. His writings include *Jabir ibn Hayyam; contribution à l'histoire des idées scientifiques dans l'islam* (Cairo, 1942-43). He died on 10 or 12 October 1944. Max Meyerdorf wrote *Julius Ruska und Paul Kraus; der Zusammenbruch der Dschâbir-Legende* (1930). Bulletin de l'Institut d'Égypte, 27 (1946), pp. 431-441; Fück; Hanisch; Schwarz

Kraus, René Raoul, born 3 November 1902 at Wien, he studied at the universities of Berlin, Wien, and Paris. He served as press secretary to the German foreign minister Gustav Stresemann, 1923-28, periodical editor, 1928-35, and counsellor at the press department of the Austrian Government, 1935-38, during the last two years of which he was assigned to the United States, where he died on 17 July 1947. His writings in German, English, and French include *Spione im Geldkrieg* (1933), *Private and public life Socrates* (1940), and *The Men around Churchill* (1941). BioIn, 1 (4); CurBio, 1941, 1947; WhAm, 2

Kraus, Rüdiger W. H., born about 1950, he received a Dr.phil. in 1973 from the Universität Gießen for *Siedlungspolitik und Erfolg dargestellt an Siedlungen in den Provinzen Hilmend und Baghlan, Afghanistan*. Schwarz

Kraus, Wilhelm, born 27 October 1900 at Haibach, Austria, he studied German literature, history, and fine art successively at the universities of Innsbruck and Wien. Adverse economic conditions soon obliged him to take a part-time job with the library service of Public Instruction. He received a Dr.phil. in 1927 from the Universität Wien for *Die Geschichte des Zehents in Österreich von den Anfängen bis ins 13. Jahrhundert*. In 1929 he entered the Haus-, Hof- und Staatsarchiv, Wien, as a civil servant, a safe haven for successful research at one of the most prestigious Austrian archives where he remained until the end of the second World War. In 1950, he was assigned to the Kriegsarchiv (war archives), becoming its director in 1956. He died in Wien on 21 July 1978. Mitteilungen des Österreichischen Staatsarchivs, 32 (1979), pp. 487-92

Kraus, Willy, born 25 August 1918 at Düsseldorf, Germany, he taught Third World development policy at the universities of Köln, Kabul, and Gießen, before he became a professor and director, Institut für Entwicklungsforschung und Entwicklungspolitik, Ruhr-Universität, Bochum. His writings include *Nachhaltige räumliche Entwicklung auf dem europäischen Kontinent* (2000), and he edited *Nomadismus als Entwicklungsproblem; Bochum Symposium, 1967* (1969), and *Afghanistan; Natur, Geschichte und Kultur* (1972). In 1983 and 1998 he was honoured by the jubilee volumes, *Nationale Entwicklung und internationale Zusammen-arbeit; Festschrift zum 65. Geburtstag von Willy Kraus*, and *Rahmenbedingungen von Entwicklung; Festschrift zum achtzigsten Geburtstag von Willy Kraus*. Kürschner, 1966-2005

Krause, Albrecht Emil *Kurt*, born 20 April 1883 at Potsdam, Germany, he studied at the Universität Berlin, where he received a Dr.phil. in 1905 for *Beiträge zur Kenntnis der Flora von Aden*. He was in 1917 a keeper of Königliches Museum, Berlin-Dahlem. His trace is lost after an article in 1939. GV; Note about the author

Krause, Friedrich Ernst, born 23 August 1879, he received a Dr.phil. in 1914 from the Universität Berlin for *Fluß- und Seegeschichte nach chinesischen Quellen aus der Zeit der Chou- und Han-Dynastie und der drei Reiche*. He taught Chinese subjects successively at the universities of Heidelberg and Göttingen. His writings include *Cingis Han; die Geschichte eines Lebens nach den chinesischen Reichsannalen* (1922). He died in the 1930s. Kürschner, 1926-1935|; NUC, pre-1956

Krause, Gottlob Adolph, born 15 January 1850 at Ockrilla near Meißen, Saxony, he determined early in life to participate in the exploration and civilization of Africa. In 1868, he travelled to Tripolis and on to Murzuq where he encountered the explorer Gustav Nachtigal. He returned to Germany, fought in the Franco-Prussian war, 1870-71, studied natural sciences at the Universität Leipzig, 1873-76, and subsequently made several long visits and expeditions to the Gold Coast and Niger. He spoke Arabic and Hausa, and he adapted an African life-style. He was considered a vehement critic of European colonial policy. His considerable collection has disapperead and only few of the Hausa manuscripts which he collected have survived. Since 1915 he was resident in Zürich, where he died on 19 February 1938. His writings include *Ein Beitrag zur Kenntnis der fulischen Sprache in Afrika* (1884), *Proben der Sprache von Ghat in der Sáhara* (1884), *Die Musuk-Sprache in Central Afrika* (1886), and *Beitrag zur Kenntnis des Klimas von Salaga, Togo und der Goldküste* (1910). Embacher; Henze; Kornrumpf; LexAfrika

Krause, Max, born 20 April 1906 at Darmstadt, Germany, he studied Islamic and Semitic subjects as well as mathematics at the universities of Hamburg, München, and again Hamburg, where received a Dr.phil. in 1936 for *Die Sphärik des Menelaos aus Alexandrien in der Verbesserung von Abū Nasr ibn 'Alī ibn 'Irāq, mit Untersuchungen zur Geschichte des Textes bei den islamischen Mathematikern*, and he was a joint editor and translator of *Die Aufgangszeiten der Gestirne* (1966). He died on the eastern front in 1944. GV; Hanisch; Thesis; NUC, pre-1956; Sezgin

Krauß, Friedrich Salomon, born 7 October 1859 at Požega (Pozsega), Croatia, Austria-Hungary, he studied classic and Oriental languages, archaeology, and ethnography at the Universität Wien, where he received a Dr.phil. in 1881. In the service of Crown prince Rudolf of Austria, and with the support of the Viennese Anthropologische Gesellschaft, he travelled from 1884 to 1885 in the Balkans, visiting Bosnia, Herzegovina, Dalmatia, Slavonia, and Croatia, returning to Wien with valuable ethnographic material. He subsequently became a legal interpreter for Slavic languages, and a secretary to the Israelitische Allianz in Wien. From 1889 to 1898, he edited the monthly, *Am Urquell*. His writings include *Sagen und Märchen der Südslaven* (1883-84), *Ethnographische Fragebögen* (1884), *Tri riječi Hercegovca* (1885), *Wider die Unzuchtschnüffler der deutschen Justiz* (1928), *Friedrich Salomo Kraus, 1859-1938; Selbstzeugnisse und Materialien zur Biobibliographie des Volkskundlers, Literaten und Sexualforschers* (2002), as well as stories, novels, and plays. He died in 1938. DÖS; DtBE; EncJud; EncJud²; GeistigeUng; HL; KDtLK, 1914-16 & Nekrolog, 1936-1970; NDB; Pallas; Wer ist's, 1912-1928; Wininger

Krauss, Sámuel, born 18 February 1866 at Ukk, Austria-Hungary, he was educated at the Landesrabbinerseminar, Budapest, and concurrently studied since 1889 at Budapest University. He received a Dr.phil. in 1893 from the Universität Gießen with a thesis entitled *Zur griechischen und lateinischen Lexikographie aus jüdischen Quellen*. In 1894, he was appointed a professor of Hebrew at Jüdisches Lehrerseminar, Budapest. In 1906, he accepted an invitation from Israelitisch-Theologische Lehranstalt, Wien, where he then taught until 1937, when he emigrated to Cambridge. He died in Cambridge on 4 June 1948. BioHbDtE; DtBE; DtBIlnd (3); EncJud; EncJud²; GeistigeUng; JüdLex; Kürschner, 1925-1935; MagyarZL; NDB; ÖBL; Wer ist's, 1922-1935; Wininger

Kravets, Liudmila Nikitovna, born 20th cent., she was a joint author of *Социально-экономические отношения и классовая борьба в дореволюционном Узбекистане конец XIX- начадо XX в.* (Tashkent, 1980). OSK

Kravets (Kravetz), Nataliia, born 20th cent., she edited *Правовый захист біженців в Україні; збірка документів* (Kiev, 1998). OSK

Krawulsky, Dorothea, born about 1940, she received a Dr.phil. in 1971 from the Universität Freiburg im Breisgau for *Briefe und Reden des Abū Hāmid Muhammad al-Gazzālī*. She was in 2005 a lecturer in Islamic subjects at the Universität Tübingen. Her writings include *Iran, das Reich der Īlḫāne; eine topographisch-historische Studie* (1978), *Ḫorāsān zur Timuridenzeit nach dem Tārīḫ-e Hāfez-e Abrū* (1982-84), *Mongolen und Ilkhâne* (1989); she translated *Die Reise zum Imam; Kurzgeschichten und Satiren*, from the Persian of Sādiq Hidāyat (1997); and she edited volume seventeen of *Das biographische Lexikon des Salāhaddīn Ḫalīl ibn Aibak as-Safadī* (1982). Kürschner, 2005; Schwarz; ZKO

Krcsmárik, János (Johann), born in 1857 at Szarvas, Hungary, he completed his law and was from 1883 to 1890 in charge of Turkish affairs in the Bosnian provincial government. In 1891, he was appointed a judge at Szarvas. After gaining a Dr.habil. in 1901 at Budapest University, he there became a lecturer. His writings include *A török népdalról* (Budapest, 1879), and *A török jogrendszer és igazságszolgáltatás* (1899). GeistigeUng; Pallas; RNL

Krehl, Christoph *Ludolf* Ehrenfried, born 29 June 1825 at Meißen, Germany, he was educated at the renowned Fürstenschule St. Afra. From 1843 to 1846 he was a student of Friedrich Tuch, Hermann Brockhaus and Heinrich L. Fleischer at the Universität Leipzig, where he obtained a Dr. phil. in 1846. He did post-doctoral studies at Tübingen, Leipzig and, after the political turmoil of 1848 had subsided, Paris and St. Petersburg. Afterwards he was custodian of the Royal Public Library, Dresden, until 1861, when he was invited to become librarian of the Universität Leipzig and professor of Oriental philology, a position which he held until 1899. His writings include *De numis Muhammedanis in numophylacio Regio Dresdensi asservatis commentatio* (1856), *Die vorislamischen Araber* (1863), *Die Erfreuung der Geister, von Omar ben-Suleimân* (1898). In 1884, he published *Das Leben des Muhammed*, but, discouraged by his critics, its sequence, *"Die Lehre des Muhammed"*, remained in manuscript form. He is best remembered for his collaboration with Dozy, Wright and Dugat on al-Maqqari's *Nafh el-tîb*. He died in Leipzig on 15 May 1901. *Berichte über die Verhandlungen der k. Sächsischen Gesellschaft der Wissenschaften, Leipzig, Philologisch-historische Klasse* 53 (1901), pp 63-74

Kreiser, Klaus H., born in 1945, he studied Balkan and Islamic history at the universities of Köln, and München, where he received a Dr.phil. in 1972 for *Edirne im 17. Jahrhundert nach Evliya Çelebi*. He subsequently taught history at his alma mater until 1976, when he went for four years to Deutsches Archäologisches Institut, Istanbul, as a research fellow. After his return to München, he became an academic assistant in the Institut für Geschichte und Kultur des Nahen Orients, Universität München, until 1984, when he was appointed a professor at the Universität Bamberg, a post which he still held in 2005. His writings include *Edirne im 17. Jahrhundert nach Evliya Çelebi* (1975), *Siedlungsnamen Westthrakiens* (1978), *Türkische Studien in Europa* (1998), *Der osmanische Staat, 1300-1922* (2001), and he was a joint translator of *Evliya Çelebi in Albania and adjacent regions (Kosovo, Montenegro, Ohrid); the relevant sections of the Seyahatnâme* (2000). Kürschner, 2005; Note; Schwarz; ZKO

Krejčí, Jaroslav, born 13 February 1916, he received a Dr.jur. in 1945 from Charles University, Praha, and was subsequently associated with the Czech National Planning Office, Praha, until 1968. From 1970 to his retirement in 1983, he taught in various capacities comparative social and cultural analysis at the University of Lancaster, England. His writings include *Great revolutions compared; the search for a theory* (1983), *The Civilizations of Asia and the Middle East before the European challenge* (1990), *Dejiny a revoluce* (1992), and *Society in a global perspective* (1993). ConAu, 41-44, new revision, 14, 31, 57; IntAu&W, 1982, 1986, 1989; *Kdo je kdo*, 2002; OSK; WrDr, 1980/82-2005

Krek, Miroslav, born 30 July 1924 at Ljubljana, Slovenia, he studied geography and Oriental languages at the Universität Salzburg, Universität Wien, and the University of Chicago, where he received graduate degrees in arts, and library science. He was a head of acquisitions at the libraries of the University of Wisconsin at Madison, Brandeis University, Waltham, Mass., and a faculty associate, Harvard University, Center for Middle Eastern Studies. His writings include *A Catalog of Arabic manuscripts in the Oriental Institute of Chicago* (1961), *A Bibliography of Arabic typography* (1976), and *A Gazetteer of Arabic printing* (1977). Private; WhoLibS, 1966

Krekić, Barisa, born 14 October 1928 at Dubrovnik (Ragusa), Croatia, he graduated in 1951 from Beograd University and received a doctorate in 1954. He was since 1974 a professor of medieval and Balkan history in the Department of History of the University of California, Los Angeles, a post which he still held in 1995. His writings include *Dubrovnik i Levant, 1280-1460* (Beograd, 1956), *Dubrovnik (Raguse) et le Levant au moyen-âge* (1961), *Dubrovnik in the fourteenth and fifteenth centuries* (1971), *Urban society of Eastern Europe in premodern times* (1987), and two collections of his articles published by Variorum Reprints, *Dubrovnik, Italy and the Balkans in the late Middle Ages* (1980), and

Dubrovnik, a Mediterranean urban society, 1300-1600 (1997). DrAS, 1974 H, 1978 H, 1982 H; NatFacDr, 1990-1995; ZKO

Freiherr von **Kremer**, Alfred, born 13 May 1828 at Prenzig (Wien), he studied law and Oriental languages at the Universität Wien. Supported by a travel scholarship from the Orientalische Akademie, Wien, he went in 1849 to Damascus by way of Constantinople to study Arabic and collect Arabic manuscripts. From Constantinople he travelled in native costume to Aleppo, where he remained for three months, before going on to Damascus. Upon his return to Wien in 1851, he became a professor of colloquial Arabic at the Polytechnikum. In the following year, he entered the Austrian consular service, successively being assigned to Cairo (1852-59) and Galatz (Galaţi), Romania; in 1870 he became consul-general in Beirut. Since 1872, he was posted to the Austrian Foreign Office in a ministerial capacity. He was an Austrian representative on the Egyptian credit commission, 1876-80, and subsequently served for a brief period as Austrian minister of trade and commerce. Considered one of the founders of modern Islamic studies, his writings include *Mittelsyrien und Damaskus* (1853), *Geschichte der herrschenden Indeen des Islams* (1868), its translation, *Politics in Islam* (1920), *Kulturgeschichte des Orients unter den Chalifen* (1875-77), and its translation, *The Orient under the caliphs* (1920). He died in Döbling (Wien) on 27 December 1889. ADtB, vol. 51, pp. 374-376; BiD&SB; CelCen (not sighted); DtBE; Embacher; Fück, pp. 187-89; Henze; Kornrumpf; NDB; ÖBL

Kren, Claudia, born in 1929, she received a Ph.D. in 1966 from the University of Wisconsin at Madison for *The Questiones de spera, of Nicole Oresme*. She became a professor in the Department of History, University of Missouri, Columbia, Mo. Her writings include *Medieval science and technology; a selected, annotated bibliography* (1985), and *Alchemy in Europe; a guide to research* (1990). NUC, 1968-1972

Krenkow, Fritz, born 12 August 1872 at Schönberg, Mecklenburg, he graduated from high school, but the early death of his father prevented him from further fomal education. He became a merchant in Lübeck, Bremen, and Berlin. In 1894, he emigrated to Britain, becoming naturalized in 1911. For many years he ran a factory in Beckenham, England. In 1921, he began to pursue an academic interest. Soon after his arrival in England he had started to learn Persian in his spare time. Under the influence of Sir Charles Lyall, he also studied Arabic, at first poetry only, but later including also lexicography and biographical works. In the 1920s, he had become a recognized Arabic scholar, honoured by membership in learned institutions in Hyderabad, Deccan, Erlangen, and Damascus. Upon the recommendation of August Fischer, the Universität Leipzig granted him an honorary doctorate in 1929. In the same year, he was invited to teach Islamic studies at the Muslim University of Aligarh. Allergic to the Indian climate, he returned to Europe in 1930, teaching Arabic and Persian at Bonn until 1935, when he settled with his British wife at Cambridge, where he died on 7 June 1952. He donated his private library to the Seminar für Geschichte und Kultur des Vorderen Orients, Hamburg. His writings include several editions of classical Arabic texts. Fück, p. 280; Hanisch; *der Islam*, 31 (1953), pp. 228-236; *Wer ist's*, 1912

Krenn, Hilmar, born about 1945, he received a Dr.phil. in 1964 from the Universität Wien for *Die Bedeutung der Wüstungen für das Siedlungs- und Flurbild des nordöstlichen Weinviertels*. He was associated with the Hochschule für Sozial- und Wirtschaftswissenschaften, Linz, Austria. His writings on environmental development include *Regionales Strukturprogramm für den politischen Bezirk Rohrbach, Oberösterreich* (1975). GV

Kreševljaković, Hamdija, born 16 September 1888 to a Muslim merchant family in Sarajevo, he became a teacher at Bosnian primary and secondary schools as well as teachers' colleges from 1925 to 1945. Deprived of a university education, he pursued throughout his life an interest in the economic and social history of Bosnia under Turkish rule, having received the first impetus for the subject in his Imperial Austrian education. (He published a study of Otto H. Blau in German.) His writings also include *Sarajevo u doba okupacije Bosne 1878* (Sarajevo, 1937). He died in Sarajevo on 9 August 1959. *Südost-Forschungen*, 20 (1961), pp. 290-92; Traljić, pp. 83-90; ZKO

Kress, Hans Joachim, born about 1940, he received a Dr.phil. in 1968 from the Universität Marburg for *Die islamische Kulturepoche auf der Iberischen Halbinsel; eine historisch-kulturgeographische Studie*. Schwarz

Freiherr **Kreß von Kressenstein**, Friedrich Siegmund Georg, born 24 April 1870 at Nürnberg, Germany, he graduated from the Bavarian war college. In early 1918, he entered the Turkish army, serving with the eighth Turkish Army. From June 1918 to February 1919, he headed an Imperial German Delegation to the Caucasus; and during the Weimar Republik he served with the ministry of defence. His writings include *Mit den Türken zum Suezkanal* (1938), and its translation, *Türklerle beraber Süveyş Kanalına* (1943). DtBilnd (1); *Wer ist's*, 1922-1935

Kressel (Qresel), Gideon M., born in 1936, he was associated with the Hebrew University, Jerusalem. His writings include *Descent through males; an anthropological investigation into the patterns underlying social hierarchy, kinship, and marriage among former Bedouin in the Ramla-Lod area* (1992), *Ascendancy through aggression; the anatomy of a blood feud among urbanized Bedouins* (1996), and he was a joint editor of *Israel as center stage; a setting for social and religious enactments* (2001). LC; ZKO

Kretzenbacher, Leopold, born 13 November 1912 at Leibnitz, Austria, he was a professor of ethnology successively at the universities of Kiel and München. He received a Dr.habil. in 1941 from the Universität Graz for *Germanische Mythen in der epischen Volksdichtung der Slowenen* (1941). He was a professor of ethnology successively at the universities of Kiel and München. His writings include *Frühbarockes Weihnachtsspiel in Kärnten und Steiermark* (1952), *Seelenwaage* (1958), *Santa Lucia und die Lutzelfrau; Volksglaube und Hochreligion im Spannungsfeld Mittel- und Südosteuropas* (1959), *Bilder und Legenden* (1971), *Rituelle Wahlverbrüderung in Südosteuropa; Erlebniswirklichkeit und Erzählmotiv* (1971), and *Kettenkirchen in Bayern und Östrreich* (1973). IntDcAn; IntWW, 1989-2005; Kürschner, 1987-2005; OSK

Kreutel, Richard Franz, born 2 May 1916 at Wien, he completed his classics at the Universität Wien and did not turn to Turkish studies until 1943 after he had been seriously wounded and flown out of besieged Stalingrad to a military hospital. He received a Dr.phil. in 1948 at Wien for *Evlija Čelebi's Bericht über die Botschaftsreise Qara Mehmed Paschas nach Wien, 1665*. Although he held an academic post only for the subsequent eight years, he made outstanding contributions to Ottoman-Turkish studies. He established the monograph series *Osmanische Geschichtsschreiber*, in which he published no less than eight of his own voluminous translations. He is best remembered for his *Osmanisch-türkische Chrestomathie* (1965), and the edition *Die Autobiographie des Dolmetschers 'Osmān Aġa aus Temeschwar* (1980). He died 28/29 October 1981 of a heart infarct at the moment when he was ready to strike tent at Kabul after twenty years as head of the Austrian Legation. *Index Islamicus* (3); Schwarz; *Südost-Forschungen*, 41 (1982), pp. 353-54

Kreutz, Barbara McLaughlin, born in 1925, she received a Ph.D. in 1970 from the University of Wisconsin for *Amalfi and Salerno in the early Middle Ages*. Her writings include *Before the Normans; southern Italy in the ninth and tenth centuries* (Philadelphia, 1991). NUC, 1968-72; ZKO

Kreuzkam, Theodor, born in 1868, he received a Dr.phil. in 1897 from the Universität Leipzig for *Das Baugewerbe mit besonderer Rücksicht auf Leipzig; eine volkswirtschaftlich-statistische Untersuchung*. GV; NUC, pre-1956

Krey, August Charles, born 29 June 1887 in Germany, he graduated in 1907 from the University of Wisconsin, where he also received a Ph.D. in 1915 for *The Latin patriarchate in the Kingdom of Jerusalem*. In 1913, he went to the University of Minnesota where he became a professor of history and chairman of his department. From 1925 to 1929, he was chairman of the Committee of the American Historical Association on History in the Schools, and from 1929 to 1934, chairman of the Committee on Social Studies in the Schools. He was active in many organizations. He served terms as a member of the Board of Editors of the *American historical review* and as a member of the Council of the Minnesota Historical Society of which he became vice-president in 1947. His writings include *Bulletin for teachers of history* (1915), *The First Crusade; the accounts of eye-witnesses* (1958), a collection of his essays, *History and the social web* (1955), and he was a joint author of *Medieval foundations of Western civilization* (1929). The recognition of his work in the field of the crusades is evidenced by his inclusion among the four scholars to whom the extensive *History of the Crusades* is dedicated. He died on 28 July 1961. *American historical review*, 67 (1962), pp. 896-97; BioIn, 6 (2); Selim

Kreyenbroek, Philip Gregory, born 11 December 1948, he earned B.A., M.A., and Ph.D. degrees and became a lecturer in modern Iranian languages, teaching courses in Pashto and Kurdish, but also Zoroastrianism at the School of Oriental and African Studies, London. His writings include *The Kurds; a contemporary overview* (1992), *Yezidism; its background, observances and textual tradition* (1995), and *Living Zoroastrianism; urban Parsis speak about their religion* (2001). LC; Note; ZKO

Kriazhin, Vladimir Aleksandrovich, 1887-1931 *see* Gurko-Kriazhin, Vladimir Aleksandrovich

Krichewsky, S., born 19th cent., he was in 1928 a registrar in the Mixed Tribunal, Cairo, and a member of the Société Fouad Ier d'économie politique, de statistique et de législation. His trace is lost after an article in 1930. Note about the author

Krieger, Annie, her writings include *Le Pakistan; ou, l'état des purs* (1974).

Krieger, Kurt, born 17 January 1920 at Berlin, he received a Dr.phil. in 1942 from the Universität Berlin for *Perlen in Afrika*. He was a sometime keeper of the African section, Museum für Völkerkunde,

Berlin. His writings include *Geschichte von Zamfara, Sokoto Province, Nigeria* (1959), *Westafrikanische Plastik* (1965), *Ostafrikanische Plastik* (1990), and he was a joint author of *Westafrikanische Masken* (1960). Kürschner, 1987-1992; Unesco; ZKO

Krieger, Kurt, born 17 January 1920 at Berlin, he received a Dr.phil. in 1942 from the Universität Berlin for *Perlen in Afrika*. Unesco

Krieger-Krynicki, Annie, born 20th cent., she received a diploma in 1965 from the Faculté de droit et des sciences économiques, Paris, for *Essais sur l'économie de l'Algérie*. She was in 1982 a lecturer at the Université de Paris IX. Her writings include *Le Pakistan; ou, l'État des purs* (1974), *Zebunissa, princesse captive à la cour du Grand Moghol* (1990), *Le Pakistan* (1982), and she was a joint author of *Le Pakistan; les turbulences de l'État des purs* (1990). Livres disponibles, 2004; Note; ZKO

van **Krieken**, Gerardus Samuel, born in 1944, he received a doctorate in 1976 from the Rijksuniversiteit te Leiden for *Khayr al-Din et la Tunisie, 1850-1881*. His writings include *Kapers en kooplieden; de betrekkingen tussen Algiers en Nederland, 1604-1830* (1999), and he was a joint author of *Historysch verhael van den steden Thunes, Algiers en de andere steden in Barbarien gelegen* (s'Gravenhagen, 1975). Brinkman's

Krier, Fernande, born 20th cent., her writings include *Le maltais au contact de l'italien* (Hamburg, 1976), and *La zone frontière du francoprovençal et de l'alémanique dans le Valais* (Hamburg, 1985). NUC, 1973-77

Křikavová, Adéla, born 9 August 1938 at Praha, she was a joint author of *Islám; ideál a skutečnost* (Praha, 1990). OSK

Krikorian, Hohannes Kara, 1855-1942 *see* Kara Krikorian, Hohannes

Krischtschian, Melkon, Dr., born about 1900, he was associated with Deutsche Orient-Mission, Potsdam. His writings include *Deutschland und die Ausrottung der Armenier in der Türkei* (Potsdam, Missionsbuchhandlung, 1930). GV; NUC, pre-1956

Kristeller, Paul Oskar, born 22 May 1905 at Berlin, he received a Dr.phil. in 1928 from the Universität Heidelberg for *Der Begriff der Seele in der Ethik des Plotins*. He moved to Italy in the 1930s and successively became a lecturer in German in the Istituto superiore di magistero, Firenze, and the Universitè di Pisa, 1935-1938. In 1953, he emigrated to the United States, where he taught philosophy in various capacities successively at Yale University, New Haven, Conn., and Columbia University, New York. His writings include *The Philosophy of Marsilio Ficino* (1943), *Il pensiero filosofico di Marcilio Ficino* (1953), *The Classics and Renaissance thought* (1955), *Renaissance concepts of man* (1972), *Filosofi greci dell'età ellenistica*, and its translation, *Greek philosophers of the Hellenistc age* (1993), and *Medieval aspects of Renaissance learning; three essays* (1992). He died in N.Y.C. on 7 June 1999. In 2002 appeared *Florenz in der Frührenaissance; Kunst - Literatur - Epistolographie in der Sphäre des Humanismus; Gedenkschrift für Paul Oskar Kristeller, 1905-1999*. BioHbDtE; CnDiAmJBi; ConAu, 9-12, 181; DrAS, 1969 P, 1974 P, 1978 P, 1982 P; GV; WhAm, 13; WhoAm, 1974-1994; WhoWor, 1974/75

Kristensen, Thomas Møller, born 20th cent., he was in 1993 an assistant professor of Middle East sociology, Center for Contemporary Middle East Studies, Odense, Denmark. His writings include *Hvad må man i Mellemøsten* (1986), *Reklame i Mellemøsten* (1987), and *Saudi Arabien; håndbog for danskere som skal arbejde og leve i landet* (1986), and *Golfstaterne; håndbog for danskere som skal arbejde og leve i Bahrain, Emiraterne, Kuwait, Oman eller Qatar* (1988). DrBSMES, 1993; LC

Kristiansen, Knut, born 20th cent., he was a lecturer in the Indo-Iranian Institute (later the Department of East European and Oriental Studies), Universitetet i Oslo. His writings include *"The orange of love" and other stories* (1994), and he jointly edited with Inge Ross, *The Kalasha language; texts and translations, vocabulary and grammar* (1973). LC; ZKO

Kritzeck, James, born 6 July 1930 at St. Cloud, Minn., he graduated in 1949 from the University of Minnesota and received a Ph.D. in 1954 from Princeton University for *Peter the Venerable and Islam*. He was successively a professor of Oriental languages at Princeton University, and a member of the Institute of Advanced Study at Princeton, before he was appointed in 1965 a director of the Institute for Advanced Religious Studies and professor of Oriental languages and history at the University of Notre Dame, Ind. He served as a visiting professor in Morocco, Egypt, and Japan. In 1965, Pope Paul VI named him to the Papal Secretariat for Non-Christians, and he attended the fourth Session of the second Vatican Council. His writings include *Anthology of Islamic literature* (1964), *Sons of Abraham* (1965), *Modern Islamic literature* (1968), and he was a joint author of *Islam in Africa* (1969), and jointly with Philip Kh. Hitti he edited *The World of Islam* (1959). ConAu, 5-8; DrAS, 1969 P; DrAS, 1974 H, 1978 H; Master (1); Note; Selim

Krivonogov, Viktor Pavlovich, born 20th cent., his writings include *Хакасы* (1997), *Этнические процессы у малочисленных народов Средней Сибири* (1998), and *Западные эвенки на рубеже тысячелетий* (2001). LC; OSK

Krivov, M. V., born 20th cent., his writings include *Византия и арабы в раннем средневековье* (2002). LC

Graf von **Krockow-Wickerode**, Carl Johann Reinhold, born 27 January 1825 in Saxony, he went on a hunting expedition to the Sudan and travelled on the Red Sea to Suakin and on to Kassala, the Tekeze (Satit) River, Gedaref and Gallabat, returning via Kassala to Suakin, and then homewards to Dresden. On the way out he had encountered the Swiss explorer Werner Munzinger at Kassala, and together they surveyed the nearby Mukran Hills. His writings include *Der patentirte Krockow'sche Saamenleger und Untergiesser der Gewächse* (1863), and *Reisen und Jagden in Nord-Ost-Afrika, 1864-65* (1867). He died in 1901. Embacher; Henze; Hill; Kornrumpf

Kroell, Anne, born in 1939, she received a *doctorat de 3ème cycle* in 1975 from the Université de Paris for *Les relations diplomatiques entre la France et la Perse au début du XVIIIème siècle*. Her writings include *Louis XIV, la Perse et Mascate* (1977); she edited *Nouvelles d'Isphahan, 1665-1695* (1979); and she was a joint author, with J. L. Bacqué-Grammont, of *Mamlouks, Ottomans et Portugais en Mer Rouge* (1988). AnEIFr, 1997; THESAM, 4; ZKO

v. **Krogh**, Ferdinand Christian Herman, born 19 July 1815 at Favrvå in Tyrstrup, he went to school at Husum and studied at the universities of Kiel and München, and completied his law in 1841 at Kiel. In 1856, he became a customs officer at Nordborg. His writings include *Den høiere danske Adel* (1866), *De danske Majorater* (1868), *Erinnerungen aus Griechenland* (1874), *Dansk Adelskalender* (1878), and *Der Plon'sche Successionsvertrag; ein Beitrag zur Geschichte des Holstein-Sonderburg'schen Hauses* (1874). He died in Minden, Hannover, on 19 June 1891. DanskBL, DanskBL²

Kromann, Anne, born 20th cent., she was associated with the Royal Collection of Coins and Medals, Nationalmuseet, København. She was a joint author of *Inflation* (København, Nationalmuseet, 1976), and a joint editor of *Sylloge nummerorum Graecorum* (København, Munksgaard, 1979). LC; Note

Kromka, Franz, born 7 August 1944 at Marienhof, Steiermark, Germany, he studied agronomy and sociology at the Universität Wien, where he received a Dr.rer.soc. in 1975 and a Dr.agr.habil. in 1985. He was associated with the Institut für Wirtschafts- und Sozialwissenschaften, Technische Universität München-Weihenstephan, before he was appointed a professor in the Institut für Agrarsoziolgie, Landwirtschaftliche Beratung und Angewandte Psychologie, Universität Hohenheim, Stuttgart. His writings on local and foreign aid projects include *Soziokulturelle Integration und Machtverhältnisse in ehemals kleinbäuerlichen Dörfern* (1975), and *Unternehmen Entwicklungshilfe; Samariterdienst oder die Verwaltung des Elends?* (1991), and *Vitalreserven der Marktwirtschaft* (1995). Kürschner, 1992-2005; Note about the author

Krone, Max Thomas, born 21 August 1901 at Clarence, Pa., he graduated in 1923 from the University of Illinois and received a Ph.D. in musicology in 1940. He subsequently taught his subject at a number of American universities. He was a joint author of *Fundamentals of musicianship* (1934-37). He died on 24 June 1970. BioIn, 3; WhoAm, 5

Kronenberg, Andreas, born 30 September 1931 at Tarnow, Germany, he received a Dr.phil. in 1955 from the Universität Wien for *Die Teda von Tibesti*, and a Dr.habil. in 1972 from the Universität Frankfurt am Main for *Logik und Leben; kulturelle Relevanz der Didinga und Logarim, Sudan*. Since 1970 he taught anthropology and ethnology in various capacities at the Universität Frankfurt am Main. His writings on East African anthropology include *Nubische Märchen* (1978), and jointly with Waltraud Kronenberg, *Die Bongo; Bauern und Jäger im Südsudan* (1981). Kürschner, 1976-2005; Schwarz; Unesco

Kroner, Günter, born 20th cent., he received a doctorate in 1956 from the Universität Bonn for *Der Industriestandort Benel, seine industrielle Entwicklung und Struktur und seine Stellung im Rahmen der Industrien der südlichen Kölner Bucht*. His writings on industrial location and re-location include *Standortwahl und Entwicklung von Industriebetrieben sowie Stillegung in der Bundesrepublik Deutschland mit Berlin (West) von 1955 bis 1967* (Bonn, Bundesministerium für Arbeit und Sozialordnung, 1973), and he was a joint author of *Zentrale Orte und hochrangige Infrastruktur sowie sonstige Gemeinden in der Bundesrepublik Deutschland* (1983). GV

Kroner, Hermann, born 1870, his writings include *Ein Beitrag zur Geschichte der Medizin des 12. Jahrhunderts an der Hand zweier medizinischer Abhandlungen des Maimonides* (Frankfurt am Main, 1906), *Die Haemorrhoiden in der Medizin des XII. und XIII. Jahrunderts* (Harlem, Selbstverlag Oberdorf-Bopfingen, 1911), *"Zur Eschatologie und Dämonologie des Judentums und des Islams"*

(Breslau, 1916), and *Der Mediziner Maimonides im Kampfe mit dem Theologen* (Harlem, Oberdorf-Bopfingen, 1924). He died in 1930. GV; Hanisch; NUC, pre-1956; Sezgin

Krones von Marchland, Franz Xaver, born 19 November 1835 at Ungarisch-Ostrau, Austria-Hungary, he studied liberal arts at the Universität Wien, where he received a Dr.phil. Since 1856, he taught Austrian history at the Rechtsakademie, Kauschau (Kassa), Hungary, a post which he held until the revolutionary events of 1861 in Cisleithania obliged him to take a temporary professorship at a gymnasium in Graz. After his Dr.habil. in 1862 in Austrian history, he was appointed in the following year a professor of Austrian history at the Universität Graz, serving 1869 to 1873 as dean of the faculty of philosophy, and since 1877 as president of the university. His writings include *Handbuch der Geschichte Österreichs* (1876-80). He died in 1902. DtBE; DtBilnd (5); Hinrichsen; KDtLK, 1901; Kosch; NDB; ÖBL; Wer ist's, 1906; Wurzbach

Kropáček, Luboš, born 23 February 1939 at Praha, he studied Arabic at the universities of Praha and Cairo, and subsequently travelled in Equatorial Africa. After gaining a doctorate he taught Arabic and Islamic subjects in the Department of Asian and African Studies at Universita Karlova, Praha. His writings include *Slovník arabsko-český* (1972), *Arabsko-český, česko-arabský slovník* (1975), and he was a joint editor of *Variace na Korán; islâm v diaspore* (1999). Filipsky; Kdo je kdo, 2002

Kropf, Lajos (Lewis), born 18 August 1852 at Pest, Hungary, he was a contributor to, and collaborator with, the publication of periodicals in Budapest. He was a joint author of *The folk-tales of the Magyars* (1889). His trace is lost after an article in 1903. NUC, pre-1956; Pallas; RNL

Kropfitsch, Lorenz, born about 1942, he received a Dr.phil. in 1972 from the Universität Graz for *Einige ausgewählte parallele Entwicklungen in den altsemitischen Sprachen und in den neuarabischen Dialekten*. He edited Hans Wehr's fifth edition of *Arabisches Wörterbuch* (1985), and *Langenscheidts Taschenwörterbuch Arabisch* (2002). Schwarz; ZKO

Kropotkin, Petr Aleksandreevich, born in 1842 at Moscow into an aristocratic family, he first pursued a military career, and from 1864 to 1867, was in charge of a geographical survey expedition in eastern Siberia; he later sympathized with the lot of Russian peasants and labourers, and turned revolutionary and even anarchist. Since 1886 he spent most of his time in England, frequently going on lecture tours. He died in Russia in 1921. ConAu, 119; DLB, 277 (2003), pp. 191-98; EncAm; EncicUni; Geographers, vol. 7, pp. 57-62. 63-69; GdeEnc; Henze; Master (28); MEW; Meyers; Pallas; WhWE

Kropp, Manfred, born 14 June 1947 at Ludwigshafen, Germany, he received a Dr.phil. in 1975 from the Universität Heidelberg for *Die Geschichte der "reinen Araber" vom Stamme Qahtan*, and a Dr.habil. in 1985. He was since 1985 a professor of Semitic languages at the Universität Mainz. In 1991, he served as a visiting professor in the Department of Middle Eastern Languages, Lunds Universitet. His writings on East African history include *Die Geschichte des Lebna-Dengel, Claudius und Minas* (1988), *Die äthiopischen Königschroniken in der Sammlung des Däggazmac Haylu* (1989), *Der siegreiche Feldzug des Königs 'Amda-Seyon gegen die Muslime in Adal im Jahre 1332 n. Chr.* (1994), and he was a joint author of *Saints, biographies and history in Africa* (2003). Kürschner, 1987-2005; NSMES Bulletin of members, 1991; ZKO

Kropp, Wilhelm, born 19th cent., he was an Austrian naval officer and from 1868 to 1870 the commander of the *Narenta* operating in the Red Sea as protection of the merchant trade. His writings include *Beiträge zu den Segelanweisungen und zur physikalischen Geographie des Rothen Meeres* (1872), *Materiali per la geografia fisica e per la navigazione del Mar Rosso* (Fiume, 1872), and *Physical geography of the Red Sea, with sailing directions* (Washington, 1872). Kornrumpf

Krótki, Karol Józef, born 15 May 1922 at Cieszyn, Poland, he graduated from Cambridge University and received a Ph.D. in 1960 from Princeton University for *Estimating vital rates from peculiar and inadequate age distributions; Sudanese experiences*. He served successively in the Sudan and Pakistan as a professor of statistics and population development, became associated with the Dominion Bureau of Statistics, Ottawa, Ont., and was appoined in 1968 a professor of sociology at the University of Alberta, Edmonton. His writings include *The 1953 pilot population census for the first population census in Sudan* (1955), and he was a joint author of *The People of Karachi* (1964), *Seven years of clinic experience under the 'traditional planned parenthood approach' in Karachi* (1965), and *Demographic implications of the first six years of family planning in Karachi, 1958-1964* (1966). AmM&WS, 1973 S, 1978 S; Canadian, 1989-2005; ConAu, 41-44; Selim; WhoAm, 1982-1996; WhoWest, 1987-1994/95; WhoWor, 1982, 1991/92

Krotkoff, Georg (Georgiï Borisovich), born 21 May 1925 at Wien, where he received all his education, including a Dr.phil. in 1950 for *Al-Qarāfī's Schrift "Das Buch der genauen Beobachtungen dessen, was die Blicke erreicht."* He was a lecturer in German at 'Ayn Shams University, Cairo, 1951-55, and at Baghdad, from 1955 to 1959. From 1960 to his retirement in 1960, he taught Arabic at Johns Hopkins

University, Baltimore, Md. He did linguistic field work in Iraqi Arabic and Neo-Aramaic. His writings include *A Neo-Aramaic dialect of Kurdistan; texts, grammar and vocabulary* (1982), and he was a joint author of *Langenscheidts Taschenbuch der arabischen und deutschen Sprache* (1967). DrAS, 1969 F, 1974 F, 1978 F, 1982 F; Kürschner, 1992; *MESA Roster of members*, 1982-1990; Note; Private; Schwarz

Krueger, Hilmar Carl, born 19 April 1904 at Milwaukee, Wisc., he graduated in 1925 from Northwestern University, Evanston, Ill., and received a Ph.D. in 1932 from the University of Wisconsin for *Genoese trade with northwest Africa in the twelfth century*. He taught successively at the universities of Wisconsin and Cincinnati, Ohio. His writings include *Navi e proprietà navale a Genova; seconda metà del sec. XII* (1985). DrAS, 1969 H, 1974 H; Master (1); WhoAm, 1974, 1976

Krueger, John Richard, born 14 March 1927 at Fremont, Nebr., he graduated in 1948 from George Washington University and received a Ph.D. in 1960 from the University of Washington at Seattle for *The structure of discourse and poetry in the Mongolian chronicle of Sagang Sechen*. He taught Oriental languages, particularly Uralic and Altaic languages, successively at the University of California at Berkeley, and Indiana University at Bloomington. His writings include *Poetical passages in the Erdeni-yin Tobči* (1961), *Mongolian epigraphical dictionary in reverse listing* (1967); he was a joint author of *An Introduction to classical (literary) Mongolian* (1955), and *Mongolia and the Mongols* (1971). ConAu, 21-24, new rev., 10, 33; DrAS, 1969 F, 1974 F, 1978 F, 1982 F; IntAu&W, 1976, 1977; Schoeberlein

Krüger, Eberhard, born 20th cent., he received a Dr.phil. in 1977 from the Universität München for *Zum Verhältnis von Autor und Werk bei dem modernpersischen Erzähler Sâdeq Hedâyat*. His writings include *Siedlungsnamen Griechisch-Makedoniens nach amtlichen Verzeichnissen und Kartenwerken* (1984), *Zwei Beiträge zum iranischen Parlamentswesen* (1988), *Moderne iranische Presse, "Hamshahri" und "Iran"* (1999), and he was a joint author of *Traditionelle iranische Landwirtschaft in Dokumenten* (1995). Schwarz; ZKO

Krüger, Frédéric *Hermann*, born 13 February 1851 at Strasbourg, he studied theology at Strasbourg, from 1868 to 1870, served as a male nurse in the Franco-German war, and then completed his study of theology at the Faculty of Montauban in 1879. In 1882, he was assigned to Lesoto, where he trained the first native pastors. For reasons of health he returned to Europe in 1884. During the last years of his life he was in charge of the École des missions in Paris. His writings include *Essai sur la théologie d'Esaie XI-XVI* (Paris, 1881), and *Les huits premiers chapitres de la lettre de Paul aux Romains* (Lausanne, 1899). He died in Basel, Switzerland, on 21 July 1900. *Hommes et destins*, vol. 9, pp. 264-65; NDBA

Krüger, Hilmar, born 19 July 1938 at Halberstadt, Germany, he received a Dr.jur. in 1978 from the Universität Köln for *Fetwa und siyar; zur international-rechtlichen Gutachtenpraxis der osmanischen Şoyh ül-Islâm vom 17. bis 19. Jahrhundert unter besonderer Berücksichtigung des "Behcet ül-fetâvâ"*. Since 1986 he taught Islamic law at the Universität Köln. Concurrently he was associated with a federal bureau of foreign trade information, the Bundesstelle für Außenhandelsinformation, Köln. His writings on the law of Arab states include *Arabische Staaten; das Recht der Forderungsabtretung* (1988), *Vereinigte Arabische Emirate Handelsvertreterrecht* (1989), *Jemen; Handelsvertreterrecht* (1996), *Jordanien; Handelsvertreterrecht* (1996), *Kuwait; Handelsvertreterrecht* (1997), and *Vereinigte Arabische Emirate; Rechtstips für Exporteure* (Köln, Bundesstelle für Außen-handelsinformation, 1998). Kürschner, 2001-2005; Schwarz; ZKO

Krüger, Karl Otto Wilhelm, born 28 August 1897 at Berlin, he studied at the local Universität, particularly its Seminar für Orientalische Sprachen. After service in the first World War, he gained a diploma in Turkish, and a Dr.rer.nat. in 1920 for *Vorkommen, Gewinnung und Absatz des Kochsalzes im türkisch-arabischen Vorderasien*. He became first an academic assistant at the Technische Universität Berlin, and later a professor of mineralogy and economic geography. From 1929 to 1943, he was a joint editor of *der Neue Orient*; after 1945, he taught at Deutsche Hochschule für Politik, Berlin. His writings include *Deutsche Großraumwirtschaft* (1932), *Kemalist Turkey and the Middle East* (1932), *Erdölkrise* (1934), *Die Straßen der Welt* (1937), *Afrika* (1952), and *Weltpolitische Länderkunde* (1956). He died in Berlin on 26 August 1974. DtBE; Kürschner, 1940/41-1970; Schwarz; Wer ist wer, 1955-1971/72

Kruk, Remke, born 8 November 1942 at Apeldoorn, the Netherlands, he studied Arabic at the Rijksuniversiteit te Leiden, and received a doctorate in 1979 from the Universiteit van Amsterdam for *The Arabic version of Aristotle's Parts of animals*. In 1990, he was appointed a professor of Arabic and Arab culture at the Rijksuniversiteit te Utrecht. He was a joint translator of *De Ring van de duif*, from the Arabic of Ibn Hazm (1977). Wie is wie, 1994-96

Krumbacher (Κρούμπάχερ), Carl (Karl), born 23 September 1856 at Kürnach, Bavaria, he studied classical and German philology at the universities of München and Leipzig and subsequently taught

316

until 1891 at Ludwigs-Gymnasium, München. He then embarked on a career as Byzantine scholar, becoming instrumental in establishing the chair of Greek philology at the Universität München. In 1892, he founded the *Byzantinische Zeitschrift*, the first journal in the field. His writings include *De codicibus quibus Interpretamenta Pseudodositheana nobis tradita sunt* (1883), *Griechische Reise; Blätter aus dem Tagebuche einer Reise in Griechenland und in der Türkei* (1886), and *Geschichte der byzantinischen Literatur von Justinian bis zum Ende des Oströmischen Reiches, 527-1453* (1891), *Κρούμβαχερ Ἱστορία τῆς βυζαντήνης λογοτεχνίας* (1901), *Das Problem der neugriechischen Schriftsprache* (1902), and *Τό πρόβλεμα της νεωτέρας γραφομένης Ἑλληνικῆς* (1905). He died in München on 12 December 1909. DÖS; DtBE; Kosch; Megali, vol. 15 (1931), pp. 276-278; NDB; *Wer ist's*, 1909

Krumholz, Lieber, 1903- *see* Kanaan, Haviv

Krunić, Jovan, born 1 April 1915 at Budanovci, he was an architect, archaeologist, and preservator of monuments. He was a staff member of the Faculty of Architecture, Beograd University, from 1948 to 1958, later serving as a Unesco consultant in Iraq, Ghana, and North Africa. His writings include *Kuća i varoši u oblasti Stare Raške* (Beograd, 1994). Ko je ko Srbiji, 1996; OSK

Krupnitzky (Крупницький), Borys Dmytrovych (Boris), born 24 July 1894 at Medvedivets, near Kiev, he received a Dr.phil. in 1931 from the Universität Berlin for *Johann Christian von Engel und die Geschichte der Ukraine.* His writings include *Теофан Прокопович і шведы* (1934), *Гетьман Пилип Орлик, 1672-1742* (1937), *Geschichte der Ukraine* (1939), and *Українська історична наука під Совѣтами, 1920-1950* (1957). He died in Himmelpfort, Brandenburg, on 5 June 1956. NUC6 1956.67

Krupnov, Evgenii Ignat'evich, fl. 20th cent., his writings include *Краткий очерк археологии Кабардинской АССР* (1946), *Жемталинский клад* (1952), *Древняя история и культура Карбады* (1957), *Древности Нижнего Поволжья* (1959), and *Древняя история Северного Кавказа* (1960). LC

Krupp-Shamma, Alya, born about 1940, she received a Dr.phil. in 1969 from the Universität München for *Studien zum Menāqibnāme des Abu 'l-Wafá Tağ al-'Ārifīn*, a work which was published in 1976. Schwarz; ZKO

Kruse, Hans, born 26 September 1921 at Paderborn, Germany, he was interested in sciences and was thinking of going into chemistry after high school, but the war, and the foreign language school of the German army at Meißen, where he took his training, directed him elsewhere. Here, he chose Persian and Georgian as subjects, retaining a written and oral command of both of them for the rest of his life, even adding other languages in the course of his career. He received a Dr.phil. in 1953 from the Universität Göttingen for *Islamische Völkerrechtslehre; der Staatsvertrag bei den Hanifiten des 5./6. Jahrhunderts d.H.* Since 1955 he was actively concerned with the legal and ecological consequences of atomic energy on both the national and international level. By means of lectures and publications between 1964 and 1977, he assisted Muslim countries everywhere in solving newly arising international legal problems. His writings include *Besatzungsmacht und Freiheitsrechte* (1953), *Das Staatsangehörigkeitsrecht der arabischen Staaten* (1955), *The foundation of Islamic international jurisprudence* (1956), *Die internationale Zusammenarbeit auf dem Gebiet der friedlichen Verwendung der Atomenergie* (1956), and *Legal aspects of the peaceful utilization of atomic energy* (1960). He died on 1 May 1990. Kürschner, 1987; Schwarz; ZDMG, 142 (1992), pp. 237-246

Kruse, Rainer, born 20th cent., he received a Dr.phil. in 1969 from the Universität Göttingen for *Untersuchungen zum Prozeß der Rubefizierung mediterraner Böden am Beispiel kalkhaltiger marokkanischer Küsten-Dünen.* Schwarz

Kruse, Rainer, born 20th cent., he was a writer on Third World refugee affairs, which include *Reis für Indien; Bericht über die Kinderspeisung, 1966* (Stuttgart, Diakonisches Werk der Evangelischen Kirche in Deutschalnd, 1967). His trace is lost after an article in 1972.

Kryczyński, Leon Najman (Arslan), born 25 September 1887, he studied at Wilna and St. Petersburg, and became a lawyer and historian. His writings include *Bibljografija do historii Tatarów polskich; Bibliographie pour servir à l'histoire des Tartares polonais.* (Zamość, 1935). He died in 1939 or 1940. Dziekan; Polski (4); *Przeglad orientistyczny*, 49 (1964), pp. 27-36; PSB; TatarES

Kryczyński (Крышынский), Olgierd Najman Mirza, born 1884 or 1894 at Wilna, he studied at St. Petersburg, from 1903 to 1908, and subsequently became a lawyer. He died in 1940 or 1942. Dziekan; Polski (3); PSB; TatarES

Kryczyński, Stanisław, born in 1911, he was a philologist, whose writings include *Tatarzy litewszy; próba monografii historiczno-etnograficznej* (Warszawa, 1938). He died in 1941. NUC, pre-1956; Polski (2); PSB; TatarES

Krymskii, Agafangel Efimovich, born in 1871 at Vladimir-Volynski, Ukraine, he graduated in 1892 from the Lazarev Institute of Oriental Languages, Moscow, and subsequently studied four years at the Moscow Institute of History and Philology. He completed his formal education by spending two years, 1896-1898, in Syria. He was a Slavic as well as Oriental scholar, a poet and academic teacher as well as a popularizer of his field. His writings include *Історія Перії та її письменства* (1923*), Хафиз та його пісні (бл. 1300-1389) в його рідній Персії XIV в. та в новій Європі* (1924), and *История новой арабской литературы* (1971). He died 25 January 1941. BiobibSOT; *Index Islamicus* (5); Krachkovskii, pp. 163-167; Miliband; Miliband²; TatarES

Křziž (Křzyž), August Karl, born 12 May 1814 at Tábor, Bohemia, he joined the Austrian field artillery and advanced through the grades to first lieutenant in 1851. In the same year, he took an eight-year leave of absence and went with three fellow officers to Persia as a military consultant. He there set up several artillery units and introduced telegraph facilities in the Persian army. He concurrently served with the rank of general (*sartīp*) as an instructor in mathematics and science subjetcs at the newly established Persian military academy. At the end of his term of duty, he returned to Austria and was on 1 December 1859 reintegrated in the Austrian army with the rank of captain and posted to Prag. In the following year, he resigned and retired to Chrudim, Bohemia, where he died on 19 January 1886. His writings include a map, *Plan der Hauptstadt Teheran* (c1857, 1977). He was unsuccessful in finding a publisher for his travel account, *Reisen nach, in und aus dem Orient, mit Bildern aus Persien.* ÖBL; Wurzbach

Krzyzaniak, Marian, born 4 November 1911 at Starczanowo, Poland, he was educated at Poznan University, the University of Alberta, and Massachusetts Institute of Technology, where he received a Ph.D. in economics. He subsequently taught public finance and economics successively at the University of Michigan, University of Montana, Johns Hopkins University, Baltimore, Md., Wayne State University, Detroit, Mich., and Rice University, Houston, Tex. His writings include *Government expenditures, the revenue constraint and Wagner's law; the case of Turkey* (1972), *The Short-run burden of taxes on the Turkish agriculture in the sixties* (1974), and he was a joint author of *The Shifting of the corporation income tax* (1963), and *The distribution of income and the short-run burden of taxes in Turkey, 1968* (1972). He died in 1993. AmM&WS, 1973 S, 1978 S; WhoAm, 1974-1978; WhoS&SW, 1973 (not sighted)

Kshibekov (Кішібеков/Кшибеков), Dosmukhamed (Достмұхамбет/Досмухамед) Kshibekovich, born 15 December 1925 at Kyzyl-Orda (Perovsk), Kazakhstan, he graduated in 1948 from the Kyzyl-Orda Pedagogical Institute. Since 1964 he was associated with the Kazakhstan Academy of Sciences as a philosopher. He received a doctorate in 1965, and was appointed a professor in 1967. His writings include *О феодально-байских пережитках и их преодолении* (1957), *On feudal-bey survivals and their overcoming* (1958), *О закономерностях замены докапиталистических производственных отношений социалистическими* (1963), and *Кочевое общество: генезис, развитие, упадок* (1984). KazakSE; Kazakhskaia, vol. 3, pp. 297-98; OSK

Kubbel', Lev Evgen'evich, born 16 May 1929 at Leningrad, he graduated in 1951 from the Oriental Faculty, Leningrad State University, and received his first degree in 1963 for published works. He was a sometime teacher at his alma mater. Since 1972 he was associated with the Institute of Ethnography of the Soviet Academy of Sciences. His writings include *Страна зодота* (1966), *Путь в Томбукту* (1971), *Африка глазами насих соотечественников* (1974), *Сонгаская держава* (1974), *История Африки и древних и средневековых источниках* (1990), and he was a joint author of *В поисках держава* (1972). In 1993 appeared *Ранние формы социальной стратификации; генезис, историческая динамика, потестарно-политические функции памяти - Л. У. Куббеля.* He died on 23 November 1988. Miliband; Miliband²; Note about the author

Kubeš, Zdeněk, fl. 20th cent., his writings include *O Strednom Východe* (Bratislava, 1957), *Irak, Libanon, Jordánsko* (Bratislava, 1958), *Kdo s koho na Strednim Východe* (Praha, 1958), and *Izrael* (Praha, 1960). NUC; OSK

Kubesov, Audanbek Kubesovich, born 20th cent., his writings include *Математическое наследие аль-Фараби* (1974), and *Астрономия в трудах аль-Фараби* (1981). LC; NUC

Kubiak, Stanisław, fl. 20th cent., his writings include *Monety pierwszych Jagiellonów, 1386-1444* (Wrocław, 1970). NUC; OSK

Kubiak, Władysław B., born 1925, he studied Arabic at Uniwersytet Jagielloński, Kraków, where he obtained an M.A. in 1952 for "Relacja Ibn Fadlan o Kalifacie wschodnim i kraju Oguzów." He received a doctorate in 1966 from Uniwersytet Warszawski for "Archeologia muzułmańskiej Aleksandrii do okresu wypraw krzyżowch," and a Dr.habil. in 1979 for *Al Fustat, its foundation and early urban development*, a work which was published in 1982. His writings include a translation from the Arabian night, *Księga tysiąca i jednej nocy* (1959). He died on 27 September 1997. Afryka Azja Ameryka Lacińska, 75 (1999), pp. 166-67; Dziekan

Kubica, Václav, born 20th cent., his writings include *Hudební nástroje serní Afriky a arabského Orientu* (Praha, 1970), and jointly with Vladimir Klima, *Safari za africkou kulturou* (Praha, 1983). NUC, 1968-72

Kubíčková, Věra, born 16 December 1918 at Rybná nad Zdobnicí, she studied Persian at Praha under Jan Rypka and Felix Tauer, and obtained a doctorate in 1951. Her writings include *U studny Zemzem; arabská lidová poesie* (1954), *Persian miniatures* (London, 1960), *Persische Miniaturen* (Praha, 1960); she translated from the Persian of Firdawsi, *Zál a Rúdábe* (1958); she was a joint editor of *Charisteria orientalia* (1956); and she was a joint author of Jan Rypka's *Dějiny perské a tádžické literatury* (1956), a work which won wide recognition by its translation into English and other languages. Filipsky

Kubiëna, Walter Ludwig, born 30 June 1897 at Neutitschein, Moravia, he was a soil scientist and head of the research centre for soil science and forest ecology at the German Bundesforschungsanstalt für Forst- und Holzwirtschaft, Hamburg-Reinbek. His writings include *Micropedology* (1938), *Suelo y formación del suelo desde el punto de vista biológico* (1944), *Entwicklungslehre des Bodens* (1948), *Bestimmungsbuch und Systematik der Böden Europas* (1953), its translation, *The Soils of Europe* (1953), and *Micromorphological features of soil geography* (1970). In 1954, he was honoured by *Gedenkschrift zur Verleihung des Justus von Liebig-Preises der Gemeinnützigen Stiftung F. V. S. zu Hamburg durch die Landwirtschaftliche Fakultät der Christian Albrechts-Universität, Kiel, an Walter Kubiëna*. He died in Klagenfurth, Austria, on 28 December 1970. GV; Kürschner, 1961-1970

Kubik, István, born 20th cent., his writings include *A negyedik piramis* (Budapest, 1966). NUC, 1968-72

Kubinski, Z. M., born 20th cent., he was in 1958 associated with both the New South Wales University of Technology, Kensington, Australia, and the University of Khartoum. In 1974, he was a member of the American Economic Association. His writings include *Public finance for stability and growth* (1961). Master (1); NUC, 1968-72

Kuchkin, Andreĭ Pavlovich, born 25 November/7 December 1888 at Beloretsk, Bashkiria, he was a historian who received both his doctorate and professorsip in 1951. His writings include *СССР в период восстановления народного хозяйства, 1921-1925 гг. и исторические очерк* (1955), and *В боях и походах от Волги до Енисея* (1969). E. S. Sadyrina wrote *Андрей Кучкин* (1982). He died in Moscow on 30 March 1973. KazakSE; Kazakhskaia, vol. 3, p. 197

Kück, Gert, born 26 February 1939 at Bremen, Germany, he went to school in Leipzig, where he subsequently studied Third World political economy and sociology at Karl-Marx-Universität, Leipzig, and received a diploma in political economy as well as a Dr.sc.oec. in 1965 for a thesis on problems of economic cooperation between the Arab countries and the European Community, *Probleme der interarabischen wirtschaftlichen Zusammenarbeit unter besonderer Berücksichtigung der Wirkungen der Europäischen Wirtschaftsgemeinschaft*. He was a professor in the Sektion Afrika und Nahost-Wissenschaften of his alma mater until 1992, when he probably lost his tenure in the wake of German re-unification. He was a joint author of *Industrialisierung in Entwicklungsländern* (1975), *Wirtschaftliche Zusammenarbeit und Integration von Entwicklungsländern* (1976), and *International monopolies and developing countries* (1979). Thesis; ZKO

Kuckertz, Josef, born 24 November 1930 at Würselen, Kreis Aachen, Germany, he received a Dr.phil. in 1963 from the Universität Köln for *Gestaltvariation in den von Bartók gesammelten rumänischen Colinden*. He was a professor of musicology and ethnomusicology successively at his alma mater and Freie Universität Berlin, from 1970 to his retirement. His writings include *Form und Melodiebildung der karnatischen Musik Südindiens im Umkreis der vorderorientalischen und nordindischen Kunstmusik* (1970); he was a joint author of *Außereuropäische Musik in Einzeldarstellungen* (1980); and he was a sometime editor of the *Jahrbuch für musikalische Volks- und Völkerkunde*. He died on 25 March 1996. Kürschner, 1976-1996; Baker, 1992 [not sighted]; IntWWM, 1980 (not sighted); NewGrDM, 1980

Kuczynski, Liliane, born 20th cent., her writings include *Chemins d'Europe; les marabouts africain à Paris* (1995), and *Les Marabouts africains à Paris* (2002). Livres disponibles, 2004; ZKO

Kudelin, Aleksandr Borisovich, born 4 March 1944 at Moscow, he studied Arabic, spent 1966/67 at Tunis, graduated in 1967 from the Institute of Oriental Languages, Moscow State University, and received his first degree in 1970 for *Основные жанры арабо-испанской классической эпохи расцвета конец X- середина XX в.* He became associated with the Institute of World Literature, Soviet Academy of Sciences. His writings include *Классическая арабо-испанская поэзия конец X- середина XII в.* (1973), *Ближневосточная новелла; арабские страны, Иран, Турция* (1975), and *Средневековая арабская поэтика; вторая половина VIII - XI век* (1983). Miliband; Miliband²; OSK

Kuderna, Josef, born 19th cent., his writings include the German text to *Teppiche Zentralasiens aus der Sammlung Andreĭ A. Bogolubow* (Leipzig, 1911). NUC, pre-1956

Kudriashov, Konstantin Vasil'evich, born in 1885, his writings include *Александр I и тайна Федоора Козьмича* (1923), *Последний фаворит Екатерины II* (1925), *Половецкая степь; очерки исторической географии* (1948), *Москва в 1812 годы* (1962), and he was a joint author of *Москва в далеком пошлом* (1962). LC; OSK

Kudriavtsev (Кудрявцев), Alekseĭ Abakarovich, born 20th cent., his writings include *Древний Дербент* (1982), and *Дербенту - 5000 лет* (Moscow, 1989). LC

Kudriavtsev (Кудрявцев), Mikhaĭl Konstantinovich, born 31 December 1910/11 January 1911 at Orenburg, Russia, he graduated in 1939 from the Institute of History, Leningrad State University, received his first degree in 1952 for a dissertation entitled *Происхождение мусульманского населения Индии*, and a doctorate in 1972 for a monograph. Since 1948 he was associated with the Leningrad Branch of the Institute of Ethnography, Soviet Academy of Sciences. His writings include *Община и каста в Хиндустане* (1971). He died on 4 March 1992. Miliband²

Kudriavtsev (Кудрявцев/Kudryavtsev), Vladimir Leont'evich, born in 1903, he was a political observer to the Russian periodical *Известия*. His writings include *Peace programme for Europe* (1972), and *Которыы час в Каире?* (1976). WhoSocC, 78

Kudsi-Zadeh, Abdullah *Albert*, born 20th cent., he received a Ph.D. in 1968 from Indiana University for *The legacy of Sayyid Jamal al-Din al-Afghani*. He taught successively at Wisconsin State University, Stevens Point, Wisc., Concordia University, Montreal, P.Q., and the Department of Political Science, Dawson College, Montreal, P.Q. His writings include *Sayyid Jamāl al-Dīn al-Afghānī; an annotated bibliography* (1970). NatFacDr, 1990-2002; Selim

Kuentz, Charles, born in 1895 at New York, he studied Egyptology at the Université de l yon and the École Normale Supérieure, Paris. He was a Dominican priest who served as a school teacher and became a research fellow in the Institut français d'archéologie orientale du Caire, 1919-1934, successively serving as secretary, librarian, and director. He was a joint author of *Bibliographie des ouvrages arabes imprimés en Égypte en 1942, 1943 et 1944* (Le Caire, 1949). He died in 1979. Egyptology; NUC, pre-1956

Kuglin, Jörg, born 4 June 1945 at Garstedt near Hamburg, Germany, he was educated at the Johanneum, Hamburg, and studied modern philology, particularly Slavic languages, at the Universität Hamburg, from 1964 to 1971, concurrently teaching Russian at two local secondary schools between 1967 and 1969. He received a Dr.phil. in 1971 for *Die uneigentliche Verwendung von Wörtern aus dem tierischen Bereich im Russischen und Bulgarischen; ein Beitrag zur slavischen Lexicographie*. In May 1971, he became an academic assistant In the Institut für Slavistik und Balkanologie, Universität des Saarlandes, Saarbrücken. Thesis

Kuhn (Кунъ), Aleksandr Liudvigovich, 1840-1888 *see* Kun, Aleksandr Liudvigovich

Kuhn, Carl, born 1 September 1816 at Kunreuth, Bavaria, he studied mathematics at the Universität München and later taught physics and geometry at military institutions. He was a joint author of *Lehrbuch der Geometrie* (Landshut, 1850). He died in München on 5 January 1869. ADtB, vol. 17, pp. 340-41; DtBilnd (2)

Kuhn, Delia Wolf, born 2 October 1903 at N.Y.C., she graduated in 1925 from Horace Mann School, and from Vassar College, Poughkeepsie, N.Y. From 1926 to 1931 she was an associate editor of, and contributor to, *Current history* magazine, then published by the *New York Times*. From 1941 to 1953 she served with the United States Government as a writer and information officer in the Office of War Information, and subsequently in the Department of State and the Technical Co-operation Administration (Point 4). Since 1953, she and her husband, Ferdinand, collaborated as free lance writers and lecturers, and travelled widely in Asia, North Africa, and Europe for their material. They contributed articles on world affairs to many newspapers as well as to magazines such as *Harper's*, *The National geographic*, *Colliers*, and *Holiday*. She was a joint author of *Borderlands* (1962). She died in Washington, D.C. on 16 December 1989. ConAu, 130; Note; WhoAmW, 1961/62

Kuhn, Ernst Wilhelm Adalbert (or August), born 7 February 1846 at Berlin, he studied Indology and linguistics at the universities of Berlin and Tübingen and received doctorates from the Universität Halle-Wittenberg for *Kaccâyanappakaranae, specimen, 1 and 2*, in 1869 and 1871 respectively. He taught at the universities of Leipzig and Heidelberg before his appointment as professor of Indo-Aryan philology and comparatve Indo-European linguistics at the Universität München, 1877-1917. He was a joint editor of *Grundriß der iranischen Philologie* (1895-1904). He died in München on 21 August 1920. DtBE; DtBilnd (3); NDB; Stache-Rosen, p. 103; *Wer ist's*, 1909-1912

Kuhn, Ferdinand, born 10 April 1905 at N.Y.C., he graduated from Mount Vernon High School, and from Columbia University, New York, in 1925. He was on the staff of *The New York Times* from 1925 to 1940. For most of this period he was stationed in London, and was chief of the London bureau from 1937 until late in 1939. In 1941, he went to Washington as assistant to the Secretary of the Treasury, and subsequently served as deputy director of the Office of War Information. In 1946, he joined the *Washington Post*, and for seven years reported foreign affairs from the capital and abroad. His writings include *Commodore Perry and the opening of Japan* (1955), *The Story of the Secret Service* (1957), and jointly with his wife, Delia, *Borderlands* (1962). He died in Washington, D.C., on 17 December 1978. CnDiAmJBi; ConAu, 81-84, new rev., 36; IntWW, 1974/75-1978/79; Note; NYT, 19 October 1978 (not sighted); WhAm, 7; WhE&EA; WhoAm, 1974-78

Kühn, Peter, born in 1948, he studied the didactics of Arabic and French, and the pedagogics of university teaching at the Universität Leipzig, where he received a Dr.phil. in 1981 for *Die auswärtige Kulturpolitik der Bundesrepublik Deutschland gegenüber Entwicklungsländern*. He was an academic assistant until 1990. Since 1991 he was a consultant to publishers and an analyst of educational developments in the Arab world. Note; Sezgin

Kühne, Jörg-Detlef, born 6 March 1943 at Wriezen, Germany, he studied law and obtained a Dr.jur. in 1970, and a Dr.habil. in 1983 from the Universität Bonn. He was successively a professor of law at the universities of Köln, and Hannover. His writings include *Die Reichsverfassung der Paulskirche* (1985). Kürschner, 1987-2005

Kühne Brabant, Rosa, born in 1926 at Erfurt, Germany, she received a doctorate in Semitic philology and taught in the Departamento de Estudios Árabes e Islámicos, Universidad Complutense de Madrid. She was generally interested in medicine and related sciences in the medieval Arab world. She retired about 1993, and died in Madrid in 2002. Arabismo, 1992, 1994, 1997; *Index Islamicus = Anaquel de estudios arabes*, no. 14 (2003), pp. 323-26

Kühnel, Wilhelm *Ernst* Paul, born 26 October 1882 at Neubrandenburg, Germany, he studied at the universities of Paris, Wien, München, and Heidelberg. He began his career as a writer of travel accounts of his own research visits to Italy, Spain, and North Africa, 1906 to 1909. In the same year, he became a staff member of the museum of applied arts and handicrafts (*Kunstgewerbemuseum*), Berlin, where he collaborated with Friedrich Sarre in the first great exhibition of Islamic art (*Meisterwerke islamischer Kunst*) in 1910 in München. In 1911, he joined the Islamic section of the Berliner Museen, becoming keeper in 1922, and director in 1931. He participated in excavations at Samarra, 1912, and in 1915 was sent on a special political mission to Morocco by the German Government. He returned to Berlin by way of Spain, where he studied Moorish art and concurrently lectured at universities. A professor at the Universität Berlin since 1930, he was a visiting professor at Egyptian universities. After 1945, he organized the establishment of the Islamic section of the Staatliche Museen, Stiftung Preußischer Kulturbesitz, Berlin-Dahlem. In 1952, he catalogued the Islamic Collection of the Textile Museum, Washington, D.C. An editor of the journal *Kunst des Orients* since 1950, his own writings include *Granada*, (1908), *Algerien* (1909), *Maurische Kunst* (1924), *Islamische Kleinkunst* (1961), *Die Kunst des Islam* (1962), and *Die islamischen Elfenbeinskulpturen* (1971). He died in Berlin on 5 August 1964. BioIn, 3; DtBE; Hanisch; *Index Islamicus* (3); Kürschner, 1935-1963; NDB; *Wer ist's*, 1935; *Wer ist wer*, 1955-1963

Kuhnen, Frithjof Manfred, born 22 December 1927 at Dessau, Germany, he was educated at Dessau and Bernburg and subsequently inducted into the army in February 1945, experiencing the end of the war in an army hospital. After working successively on a farm and an agricultural experimental station, he studied agriculture at Landwirtschaftliche Hochschule, Hohenheim, gaining a Dr.agr. in 1954 for a thesis on agricultural secondary industries entitled *Der Charakter der landwirtschaftlichen Neben-erwerbsbetriebe*; in 1961 he received a second doctorate from the Universität Tübingen for a thesis on living conditions of rural families entitled *Lebensverhältnisse ländlicher Familien*. He became a professor and director in the Institut für Rurale Entwicklung, Universität Göttingen, where he specialized in agricultural problems of underdeveloped countries. His writings include *Agriculture and beginning industrialization; West Pakistan* (1968), *Agrarreform, ein Weltproblem* (1980), and *Land tenure in Asia; access to land, access to income: changing issues* (1996). Kürschner, 1976-2005; Thesis; WhoScEu, 1987-1991/93

Kuhnke, Laverne J., born about 1930, she received a Ph.D. in 1971 from the University of Chicago for *Resistance and response to modernization, preventive medicine and social control in Egypt, 1825-1850*. She was in 1972 with the U.S. Department of Commerce, Marine Administration, U.S. Merchant Marine Academy, King's Point, N.Y., and subsequently became a professor of history at Northeastern

University, Boston. In 1990 she was a professor emerita. *MESA Roster of members*, 1977-1990; NatFacDr, 1990; Selim

Kukanova, Nina Grigor'evna, fl. 20th cent., her writings include *Очерки по истории русско-иранских торговых отношений в XVII - первой половине XIX века* (Saranska, 1977), and *Русско-иранская торговля 30-50-е годы XIX в.; сборник документов* (Moskva, 1984). OSK

Kukhtina, Tat'iana Ivanovna, born 24 June 1926 at Ruza, Russia, she served in the Soviet Army from 1943 to 1955. She graduated in 1950 from the Military Institute for Foreign Languages, and received her first degree for a monograph. Since 1956 she was associated with the Oriental Institute of the Soviet Academy of Sciences. Her writings include *Просвещение в независимом Афганистане* (1961), and *Библиография Афганистана* (1965). Miliband; Miliband[2]

Kuksewicz, Zdzisław, born 11 March 1930 at Grodno, he was a professor of history of philosophy at Uniwersytet Warszawski, and a visiting member of the Institute of Advanced Study, Princeton University, 1974/75. His writings include *Averroïsme bolonais au XIVe siècle* (1965), *Awerroizm laciński trzynastego wieku* (1971), and *Filozofia czlowieka, teoria duszy* (1975), and he edited *Quaestiones super "De substantia orbis;" ein averroistischer Text aus dem 14. Jahrhundert* (1985). KtoPolsce, 1993, 2001; OSK

Kulagina, Liudmila Mikhaĭlovna, born 28 September 1927 at Leningrad, she graduated in 1950 from the Faculty of History, Moscow State University, and received her first degree in 1954 for *Экспансия английского капитализма в Иране в последней четверти XIX века*. Since 1954 she was associated with the Oriental Institute, Soviet Academy of Sciences. Her writings include *Иранистика в России и иранисты* (2001), and she was a joint author of *Азиатский Музей Институт востоковедения АН СССР, 1818-1968* (1969), and *Из истории советского востоковедения* (1970). Miliband; Miliband[2]; OSK

Kul'besherov, Biashim, he edited *Деятельность Совета национальнистей и его Президныма* (Moskva, 1929). NUC, pre-1956

Kuli-zade, Zumrud Ali Kuli kyzli, born 27 March 1932 at Baku, she graduated in 1954 from the Faculty of History, Azerbaijan State University, received her first degree in 1959 for *Марксизм-ленинизм о роли господствующей надстройки в антагонистич. обществе*, and her doctorate in 1968 for *Хуруфизм и его представители в Азербайджане*, a work which was published in 1970. Since 1959 she was associated with the Institute of Philosophy and Truth, Azerbaijan Academy of Sciences. Her writings include *Насими - философ и поэт Востока* (1973), *Закономерности развития восточной философии XIII-XVI вв. и проблема Запад-Восток* (1983), and *Теоретические проблемы истории культуры Востока и низамиведение* (1987). Miliband[2]

Kullev, Agamir Agasi ogly, born 23 March 1926 at Lenkoran, Azerbaijan, he graduated in 1957 from the Oriental Faculty, Azerbaijan State University, and received his first degree in 1963 for *Выдающийся азербайджанский ученый-путешественник Г. З. Ширвани*, a work which was published in 1964 at Baku in Azeri. Since 1958 he was associated with the Oriental Institute, Azerbaijan Academy of Sciences. He spent 1966-1970 in Afghanistan, and 1980-1983 in Iran. His writings include the Persian edition, *Haqīqat al-haqā'iq-i shāhīyah fī al-talvīh ilá tarjīh al-masālik al-ni'mah al-ilāhīyah*, of Muhammad 'Alī Shirvānī (1981). Much of his work is published in Azeri. Miliband[2]

Kuliev, O. K., fl. 20th cent., he edited *Материалы по археологии Туркменистана* (Ashkhabad, Izdat. Akad. Nauk Turkmenskoĭ SSR, 1956). OSK

Kuliev, Ovlia, fl. 20th cent., he was a joint author of *История Туркменсой ССР, лдя IX-XI классов* (Ashkhabad, 1963). NUC, 1956-67

Kulieva, Gevkhar Asad kyzy, born 15 January 1926 at Evlakh, Azerbaijan, she graduated in 1949 from the Oriental Faculty, Azerbaijan State University and received her first degree in 1969 for *Крестянскии вопрос в турец. прозе после второй мировой войны; в творчестве Факира Бейкурта, Самина Коджгёза и Кемала Тахира*. Since 1961 she was associated with the Oriental Institute, Azerbaijan Academy of Sciences. Her writings on Turkish literature are published almost exclusively in Azeri. Miliband[2]

Kulisch, Liselotte, born 28 October 1910 at Halle/Saale, she studied modern and Oriental languages at the universities of Halle, Rostock, Berlin, and Greifswald, where received a Dr.phil. in 1939 for a thesis on the early Turkish feudal system based on archival material entitled, *Die türkischen Lehnsbriefe in der Landesbibliothek zu Kassel mit einem Überblick über die Lehns-verwaltung in frühtürkischer Zeit*. Hanisch; Schwarz; Thesis

Kulkarni, Govind Trimbakrao, Dr., born 20th cent., he was a sometime head of the Department of History, Deccan College, Poona. His writings include *The Mughal-Maratha relations; twenty-five fateful years, 1682-1707* (Pone, 1983), *Tarif-i Husain Shah, Badshah of Dakhan,* edited and translated from the Persian of Aftabi (1987), and he was a joint editor of *Studies in Indology and medieval history* (1974). LC; Note

Kulke, Eckehard, born about 1940, he received a Dr.phil. in 1973 at Freiburg im Breisgau for *The Parsees in India; a minority as agent of social change.* His writings include *Die Parsen* (1968), *The Parsees of India* (1974), *Social class and primordial loyalty in rural India; an approach to the study of Indian untouchables* (Singapore, Department of Sociology, University of Singore, 1975), and *Die Abwahl einer Diktatur; Hintergründe und Auswirkungen der indischen Parlamentswahlen 1977* (1977). GV; Schwarz

Kulke, Holger, born 19 September 1938 at Goldberg, Germany, he received doctorates in 1967 and 1976, and became successively a professor of petrography at Ruhr-Univerität, Bochum, and Technische Universität Clausthal. His writings include *Tektonik und Petrographie einer Salinärformation am Beispiel der Trias des Atlassystems* (1978), and its translation, *Tectonics and petrography of a saline formation exemplified by the Triassic of the Atlas system* (1982). Kürschner, 1992-2005

Kultermann, Udo Rainer, born 14 October 1927 at Stettin, Germany, he studied at the universities of Greifswald, and Münster, where he received a Dr.phil. in 1953 for *Gabriel de Grupello.* He was a director of the Museum Schloß Morsbreich, Germany, before he became successively a professor of architecture at the Department of Architecture, Washington University, Saint Louis, Mo., and the University of Arkansas, Fayetevile. His writings include *Neues Bauen in der Welt* (1965), *Geschichte der Kunstgeschichte* (1966), *New architecture in the world* (1976), *Architecture of the twentieth century* (1993), its translation, *Architektur im 20. Jahrhundert,* and *Contemporary architecture in the Arab states; renaissance of a region* (1999). His works have also been translated into Dutch, Finnish, French, Italian, Romanian, Serbo-Croatian, and Spanish. ConAu, 85-88; IntAu&W, 1982-2005; NatFacDr., 1990-2002; WhoAm, 1984-2003; WhoAmA, 1976-2001/2002; WrDr, 1982/84-2005

Külz, Helmuth Robert, born 27 July 1903 at Meerane, Saxony, he studied law at the universities of Marburg, and Berlin as well as Columbia University, New York. He was a lawyer and politician, a sometime minister of justice, and president of court. In 1967 he was invited by the Government of Pakistan to deliver a series of lectures at the University of Peshawar. He died about 1985. DtBE; Wer ist wer, 1950-1985

Kumekov, Bulat Eshmukhabetovich, born 5 August 1940 at Jambul, Kazakhstan, he studied at Baghdad, 1962, graduated in 1963 from the Oriental Faculty, Tashkent State University, and received his first degree in 1970 for Государство кимаков IX-XI вв. по арабским источникам, a work which was published in 1972. Since 1974 he was associated with the Institute of History, Archaeology, and Ethnography, Kazakh Academy of Siences. His writings include Арабские и персидские источники по истории кыпчиаков XIII-XIV вв. (1987). Miliband²; Schoeberlein

Kümel, Friedrich, born 13 May 1908, he received a Dr.phil. and started a career as a secondary school teacher, later becoming chief geologist in the Austrian Federal Centre for Earth Sciences at Wien. He served as a geological consultant in tectonics to the governments of Iraq and Iran. Kürschner, 1950

Kumm, Hermann Karl/*Carl* Wilhelm, born 19 October 1874 at Hannover, Germany, he received a Dr.phil. in 1903 from the Universität Freiburg im Breisgau for *Versuch einer wissenschaftlichen Darstellung der wirtschaftlichen Verhältnisse Nubiens.* At the beginning of the twentieth century he began exploring the depth of north central Africa and became the first white man to pass the great divide between the Congo and the Nile. Later he founded a board for medical education and research in Africa. He was also prominent in opening up the Sudan to missionary endeavours. His writings include *The Sudan; a short compedium of facts and figures about the land of darkness* (1907), *From Hausaland to Egypt, through the Sudan* (1910), *Khont-hon Nofer, the land of Ethiopia* (1910), and *African missionary heroes and heroines* (1917). He died in California on 22 August 1930. DcNAA; NatCAB, vol. 23, pp. 323-324; Note; Schwarz; Wer ist's, 1922-1935; WhAm, 1

Kumm, Lucy Evangeline née Guiness Mrs. K., born in 1865, her writings include *Which house; a missionary study* (1896), its translation, *Welches Haus* (1897), *Across India at the dawn of the twentieth century* (1898), *African missionary heros and heroines* (1917), and *The Sudan; a short compendium of facts and figures about the land of darkness*; with an introduction by Mrs. Karl Krumm (1907). She died in 1905. BLC; NUC, pre-1956; ZKO

Kümmerer, Emil, born 19 April 1914 at Füßbach, Germany, he served with the German Army in North Africa during the second World War. In 1953, he obtained a Dr.phil. from the Universität Tübingen for

Die Ahmadiya; Beiträge zur Kenntnis eines ägyptischen Derwischordens. From 1953 until his retirement in 1979 he was affiliated with the Universitätsbibliothek Tübingen, the last five years of which as head of its Oriental Section. He edited Julius Euting's *Reise nach Innerarabien, 1883/84; Aquarelle aus den Skizzenbüchern* (1986), and he translated *Geschichte der Araber*, from the Italian of F. Gabrieli (1963), as well as the articles in the third edition of *Die Religion in Geschichte und Gegenwart* (1957-65). DtBiInd (1); JahrDtB, 1955-2001/2002

Kumpf-Korfes, Sigrid, 1933- *see* Wegner Korfes, Sigrid

Kun (Кун/Кунъ/Kuhn), Aleksandr Liudvigovich, born in 1840, he studied Oriental languages at the Oriental Faculty, St. Petersburg, where he graduated in 1865. He subsequently found employment at Orenburg but was assigned to Turkestan in 1868. He published articles on the 'Uthmān edition of the Koran, *waqf* law, and Central Asian affairs in the journals, *Туркестанский ведомости, Globus*, and *Russische Revue*. In 1882, he was transferred to Vilna, where he died in 1888. BiobibSOT; EnSlovar; Krachkovskiĭ, pp. 186-87

Kunaev, A. M., fl. 20th cent., his writings include *Каныс Имантаевич Сатпаев* (Moscow, 1982), and he translated from the Arabic of al-Fārābī, *О разуме и науке* (Alma-Ata, 1975). OSK

Kuneralp, Sinan, born 18 November 1947 at Ankara, he was a publisher and bookseller. In 1983, he set up Isis Press, Istanbul, which, over the years, published the works of Turkish and foreign scholars in the field of Turkish and Islamic studies. His company was also active as library supplier. His own field of interest was nineteenth-century Ottoman diplomatic history, late Ottoman travel literature, and the study of epidemics in the Ottoman Empire. He was the joint author of *Représentants permanents de la France en Turquie et de la Turquie en France* (1991). Kim kimdir, 1997/98-2000; Private

Kuniholm, Bruce Robellet, born 4 October 1942 at Washington, D.C., he graduated in 1964 from Dartmouth College, Hanover, N.H., and subsequently taught English for four years at Robert College, Istanbul. From 1967 to 1971, he served with the U.S. Marine Corps. He received a Ph.D. in 1976 from Duke University, Durham, N.C., for *The United States, the Northern Tier, and the origins of the Cold War; great power conflict and diplomacy in Iran, Turkey, and Greece*. In 1975, he became associated with Duke University, Durham, N.C., a post which he still held in 2002. His writings include *The Origin of the Cold War in the Near East; great power conflict and diplomacy* (1980), *The Persian Gulf and United States policy* (1984), and *The Palestinian problem in the Near East* (1986). ConAu, 93-96, new rev., 27; DrAS, 1978 H, 1982 H; *MESA Roster of members*, 1990; NatFacDr, 1990-2002

Kunik (Куникъ), Arist Aristovich (Ernst Eduard), born 14 October 1814 at Liegnitz, Prussia, he was educated in Germany and went to Russia in 1839. He developed the Norman theory of the origin of the Russian state. His writings include *Die Berufung der schwedischen Rodsen durch die Finnen und Slawen* (1844-45), and he jointly edited with Viktor Rosen *Известия ал-Бекри и других авторов о Руси и Слаянах* (1878). BioJahr, 4 (1900), Totenliste für 1899, col. 156*; DtBiInd (1); EnSlovar; GSE; GV

Kunin, Vladimir Nikolaevich, born in 1906, he was a Russian hydrologist whose writings include *Каракумские записки* (1950), its translation, *Bezwinger der Wüste* (1957), *Местные воды пустыни* (1959), *Временный поверхностный сток и искусственное формирование грунтовых вод в пустыне* (1960), and he edited *Очерки приводы Кара-Кумов* (1955). He died in 1976. LC; OSK; WhoSocC, 78

Kunisch, Johannes, born 31 January 1937 at Berlin, he received a Dr.phil. in 1963 from the Universität München and a Dr.habil. in 1971 from the Universität Frankfurt am Main. He was a professor of German history successively at the universities of Frankfurt/Main and Köln. His writings include *Der kleine Krieg* (1973), *Staatsverfassung und Mächtepolitik* (1979), *Absolutismus* (1986), and *Friedrich der Große und seine Zeit* (2004). Kürschner, 2005

Kunitzsch, Paul Horst Robert, born 14 July 1930 at Neu-Küssow/Ostprignitz, Germany, he received a Dr.phil. in 1956 from the Freie Universität Berlin with a thesis entitled *Arabische Sternnamen in Europa*, and a Dr.habil. in 1974 at München for *Der Amalgest; die Syntaxis mathematica des Claudius Ptolemäus in arabisch-lateinischer Überlieferung*. He spent his entire career at the Universität München as a professor of history of science. His writings include a selection of his articles, *The Arabs and the stars* (1989), *Neuzeitliche europäische Himmelsgloben mit arabischen Inschriften* (1995); he was joint author of *Maslama's notes on Ptolemy's Planisphaerium and related texts* (1994); and he edited and translated from the Arabic (of A. b. M.) *Ibn al-Salāh: Zur Kritik der Koordinaten-überlieferung im Sternkatalog des Almagest* (1975). In 2000, he was honoured by *Sic itur ad astra; Studien zur Geschichte der Mathematik und Naturwissenschaften; Festschrift für den Arabisten Paul Kunitzsch zum 70. Geburtstag.* IntWW, 1991/92-2005; Kürschner, 1980-2005; Schwarz; WhoWor, 1991/92; ZKO

Kunnert, Heinrich, born 17 April 1904 at Mödling, Austria, he studied history and geography at the Universität Wien, where he received a Dr.phil. for an Austrian local history of mining. In 1928, he entered the civil service in Burgenland, where he re-organized the provincial library and archives. For many years he taught history of mining at the Montan-Universität, Leoben, Styria. He was a member of numerous learned societies. In 1972, he became an honorary professor of the Montanuniversität. His writings include *Das Emstal und seine Berge* (1949). In 1969, he was honoured by *Festschrift für Heinrich Kunnert*. He died on 27 April 1979. Südost-Forschungen, 38 (1979), pp. 265-66

Kúnos, Ignácz, born Ignacz Lusztig on 21 or 22 September 1860 or 61 at Hajdusámson, Hungary, he was educated at Debrecen, and studied philology, particularly Hungarian and Turkish, at the Faculty of Philosophy in Budapest from 1879 to 1882, when he received a doctorate. Influenced by his teachers, Ármin Vámbéry and József Budenz, he left for Turkey and the Near East in 1885, devoting himself for five years to linguistic study. In 1891, he was appointed a lecturer in Turkish at Budapest, later to become a professor, and director of the Oriental Academy of Commerce. His writings include *Oszmán-török népköltési* (1887-89), *Anatóliai képek* (1891), *Köroglu* (1893), *Turkish fairy tales and folk tales* (1896), *Naszreddin Hodsatréfái* (1899), *Materialien zur Kenntnis des Rumelischen Türkisch; türkische Volksmärchen aus Adakale* (1907), *Das türkische Volkschauspiel Orta ojnu* (1908), and *Türkçe ninniler* (1341/1925). He died in 1945. Analecta linguistica, 6 (1976), pp. 178-91; GeistigeUng; JewEnc; JüdLex; Kornrumpf; Magyar; TatarES; Wininger

Künstlinger, David, born in 1867, he received a Dr.phil. in 1897 from the Universität Bern for a thesis on the theory of numerals in the Semitic languages entitled *Zur Theorie der Zahlwörter in den semitischen Sprachen*. His writings include *Altjüdische Bibeldeutung* (Berlin, 1911), *Die Petihôt der Pesiqtâ de Rab Kâhanâ* (Krakau, 1912), *Die Petichot des Midrasch rabba zu Leviticus* (Krakau, 1913), and he edited *Das Achtzehngebet mit arabischen Übersetzungen nach einer jemenitischen Handschrift* (Krakau, 1910). His trace is lost after an article in 1932. ZKO

Kunstmann, Friedrich, born 4 January 1811 at Nürnberg, he studied theology and law at the Universität Bamberg, gaining a Dr.phil. in 1834, and a Dr.theol. in 1836. He taught religion at the München trade school before he became a professor of canon law at the Universität München. Apart from publications in his field, he wrote *Afrika vor der Entdeckung der Portugiesen* (1853). He died in München on 15 August 1867. BiD&SB; DtBE; Kosch

Künzel, Georg, born 24 November 1885 at Meerane, Saxony, he was educated at Dresden and studied at the Universität Leipzig, where he received a Dr.phil. in 1910 for *Das zusammengesetzte Substantiv und Adjektiv in der englischen Sprache*. Thesis

Künzel, Hannelore, born 20th cent., she received a Dr.phil. in 1970 from the Universität Köln for a thesis on the influence of the ancient Orient on European art entiled *Der Einfluß des alten Orients auf die europäische Kunst*. Schwarz

Künzler, Jakob, born 8 March 1871 at Hundwil, Kanton Appenzell, Switzerland, he was a trained carpenter. In 1893, he started to train as a hospital orderly at the Basler Diakonenhaus, and in 1899 joined Johannes Lepsius' hospital of Deutsche Orient-Mission, Armenisches Hilfswerk, Urfa, Anatolia. He there initiated a school for Syrian Christians. During the first World War he headed the mission hospital, trained Armenian nurses, and saved hundreds of Armenians from deportation. In 1920, he qualified as surgeon at the Universität Basel and subsequently returned to his hospital. After its closure by the Turkish authorities, he and his wife organized the flight of eight thousand Armenian orphans from certain holocaust to Ghazir in the Lebanon. Since 1932, he was supported in his efforts by "Schweizer Armenienfreunde." His writings include *Im Landes des Blutes und der Tränen; Erlebnisse in Mesopotamien während des Weltkrieges* (1921), and *Dreißig Jahre Dienst am Orient* (1933). He died in Ghazir, Lebanon, on 15 January 1949. DtBE; HisBioLexCH; NSB

Kupferschmidt, Uri M., born 20th cent., he was since the 1980s associated with the Department of Middle Eastern History, University of Haifa. His writings include *The Supreme Muslim Council; Islam under the British Mandate for Palestine* (1987), part of which was submitted in 1979 to the Hebrew University, Jerusalem, as a doctoral thesis. He was a joint editor of *Studies in Islam, nationalism and radicalism in Egypt in the twentieth century* (1982), and *Islam, nationalism, and radicalism in Egypt and the Sudan* (1983). MESA Roster of members, 1982-1990; ZKO

von Kupffer (Купферъ), Adolph Theodor, born 6 January 1799 at Mitau (Jelgava), Kurland, he was educated at Mitau and studied medicine at the Landesuniversität Dorpat, 1816-19, mineralogy at the Universität Berlin, and chemistry at the Universität Göttingen, where he received a Dr.phil. in 1821 for *De calcule crystallonomico*. He subsequently went to Paris, where he won a prize for a physical essay. In 1824, he was invited to the professorship of physics and chemistry at Kazan University, but before taking office, he went in the service of the Russian Ministry of Public Instruction to Berlin, Wien, and

Paris, to purchase physical instruments for his future university. In 1828, he was nominated a fellow of the St. Petersbug Academy of Sciences. In 1829, he travelled in the company of Lenz and Ménétries in the Caucasus, experiences which are embodied in his *Voyage dans les environs du Mont Elbrouz dans le Caucase en 1829* (1830). He died in St. Petersburg on 23 May 1865. ADtB; DtBilnd (1); EnSlovar; Henze; TatarES

Küpper, Heinrich, born 10 February 1904 at Prag-Smichow, Austria-Hungary, he studied at the Universität Wien, where he received a Dr.phil. in 1926 for *Das Carbon der Karnischen Alpen*. He spent the following twenty years abroad as a geologist. In 1948, he joined the Geologische Bundesanstalt, Wien, becoming its chief geologist and director in 1950. His writings include *Geologie der Österreichischen Bundesländer, Wien* (1968). GV; Teichl; WhoAustria, 1954

Küppers, Norbert Ferdinand, born 20th cent., he received a Dr.phil. in 1953 from the Universität Bonn for a thesis on the terms of sale in Islamic law entitled *Der Lieferungsvertrag des islamischen Rechts nach klassischer hanafitischer Lehre*. He became associated with a German government information office of foreign trade (*Bundesstelle für Außenhandelsinformation*), Köln. His writings include *Der iraqische Fünf-Jahresplan, 1963/69* (1966), and the translations from the Arabic, *Das Arbeitsgesetz der Vereinigten Arabischen Republik* (1959), *Das Einkommensteuergesetz der Irakischen Republik* (1959), *Irakisches Arbeitsrecht; das irakische Arbeitsgesetz nebst Feiertagsgesetz und anderen neuen Regelungen der Irakischen Republik* (1959). GV; ZKO

Akdes Nimet who, in 1935, took the family name **Kurat**, was born on 9 (22) April 1903 at the village of Berkete in modern Tataristan, he was educated and home, but completed his secondary education in 1920 at a Russian school. In 1924, he went to Constantinople, became a Turkish national and enrolled in the Faculty of Letters, taking philosophy and history. His started his academy career on 25 August 1925 as an assistant to Fuat Köprülü in the Institute of Turkology. Supported by a scholarship, he went in 1929 to Germany. He studied at the universities of Breslau and Hamburg, where he received a Dr.phil. in 1933 for *Die türkische Prosopographie bei Lavnikos Chalkondyles*. Since 1944 he taught Russian language and literature as well as medieval history at Istanbul. With a British Council scholarship, he spent 1946-47 at the Bodleian Library, Oxford, and the British Museum Library, London. He died at the Marine Hospital in Kasımpaşa on 8 September 1971 from injuries sustained in a bus accident ten days earlier. AnaBrit; Note; Schwarz; TatarES

Kurbangaliev, Mukhitdin Khafizetdinovich, born in 1873, he was a philologist and educator. He died in 1941. Советская тюркология 1974, № 1, pp. 117-118; TatarES

Kurbanov, A. B., borm 20th cent., he was a poet and stage director. His writings include Əбдулһəг һамид (Baku, 1987). Note; OSK

Kurbanov (Гурбанов), Shikhali (Шыхəли) Kurbanovich, born 16 August 1925 at Baku, he was a philologist and writer who was associated with the Institute of Literature and Language im. Nizami, Azerbaijan Academy of Sciences. His writings include А. С. Пушкин и Азербайджан (1959), Этапы развития азербайджанско-русских литературных связей в XIX веке (1968), Əсəрлəри (1968-1970), Азəрбајчанрус əдəби əлагəлəри мəгалəлəр мəчмуəси (1969), Сечилмиш əсəрлəри (1974), and he was a joint author of Великая дружба азербайджанского и русского народов (1964). He died in Baku on 24 May 1967. AzarbSE, vol. 3, p. 277; NUC; OSK

Kurbatov, Khelif Rakhimovich, born in 1927, he was associated with the Institute of History, Language and Literatures im. G. Ibragimov. His writings include Татар теленең алфавит һəм орфография тарихы (1960), Хəзерге татар əдəби теленең стилистик системасы (1971), and Татарская лингвистическая стилистика и поэтиеа (1978); and he edited Современный татарский литературный язык (1969-70), and Исследования по татарском языкознанию (1984). TatarES

Kürchhoff, Detmar, born in 1875, he was a second lieutenant and editor of *Afrikanische Nachrichten*. His own writings include *Die Viehzucht in Afrika* (Berlin, 1907) as well as contributions to the journal *Geographische Zeitschrift*. He died 28 December 1909. GV

Kurdian (K'iwrtean), Haroutium Harry, born 9 August 1902, he was resident in Kansas and wrote on Armenian art as well as Armenians in the Ottoman Empire. His writings include *Armenian manuscripts; an exhibition at the University of Kansas Library* (Lawrence, 1955). His monographs are almost exclusively in Armenian. NUC, pre-1956; WhoAmA, 1973, 1976, 1978|

Kurdoev, Kanat (Qanat) Kalashevich, he was born in 1909 at Susuz in Kars Province under Russian rule. In the aftermath of the war, the family sought refuge at Tiflis, where he received his first education from Armenian teachers. When he completed school in 1928, he won a scholarship from the Central Committee of the Armenian Communist Party to study at Leningrad, where he became a student of

Aleksandr A. Freĭman, Iosif A. Orbeli, I. I. Zarubin, and IUriĭ N. Marr. He graduated in 1936 from the Oriental Faculty, Leningrad Institute of History, Philology, and Linguistics, and started his career as a teacher of Kurdish at the Faculty of Philology, and the Institute of Workers, Leningrad. He received his first degree in 1940 for *Образование сложнык глаголов в курдском яхыке*. In 1961, he was appointed director of the Department of Kurdish, *Курдский Кабинет*, of the Institute of the Peoples of Asia in the Soviet Academy of Sciences. His writings include *Курдско-русский словарь* (1960), *Грамматика курдского языка на материале диалектов курманджи и сорани* (1978), and *Курдский язык* (1961). He died in Leningrad on 31 October 1985. Miliband; Miliband²; *Studia iranica*, 15 (1986), pp. 249-56

Kurdziałek, Marian, born 12 August 1920 at Bobrownicki n. Wieprzem, he studied at Katolicki Uniwersytet Lubelski, where he received his first doctorate in 1961; in 1971, he was appointed a professor of history of philosophy. His writings include *Średniowiecze w poszukiwaniu równowagi między arystotelizmem a platonizmem; studi i artykuly* (1996); he edited *Towarzystwo Naukowe Katolickiego Uniwersytetu Lubelskiego* (Lublin, 1973); and he was a joint editor of *Saint Thomas d'Aquin pour le septième centenaire de sa mort; essais d'actualisation de sa philosophie* (1976), and *Theory of being to understand reality* (1980). Kto, 1993

Kurgantsev, Mikhail Abramovich, born 5 May 1931 at Moscow, he graduated in 1954 from the Faculty of Philosophy, Moscow State University. Since 1958 he was a member of the Soviet journalist union, and as such an editor of and consultant to journals dealing with Asian and African affairs. His writings include *Три арабских лирика* (1976), *Из афро-азиатыкой поэзии* (1981), *Лирика Востока* (1986), and *Поэты Востока* (1988). He died on 31 December 1989. Miliband²; OSK

Kurihara, Kenneth Kenkichi, born 8 January 1910 at Kutchan, Japan, he graduated in 1935 from Ohio Wesleyan University and received his Ph.D. in 1942 from the University of Iowa. He taught economics successively at Princeton University, Rutgers University, New Brunswick, N.J., and State University of New York at Binghamton. He was an editor of the *Indian journal of economics*. His own writings include *Labor in the Philippine economy* (1945). He died on 12 or 13 June 1972. ConAu, 1-4, 37-40, new rev., 6; NYT, 14 June 1972, p. 50, cols. 4-5; WhoE, 1974 (not sighted)

Kurilowicz, Jerzy, 1895-1978 see Kuryłowicz, Jerzy

Kurio, Hars, born 8 February 1943 at Berlin, he received a Dr.phil. in 1970 from the Universität Kiel for *Geschichte und Geschichtsschreiber der 'Abd al-Wadiden*. In 1972, he joined the Staatsbibliothek, Berlin, as an Arabic librarian and was in 2006 a deputy director of the Department of Oriental Books and Manuscripts. He was a good and helpful Arabist, but totally under-demanded and under-appreciated by a string of mediocre authorities; he was thus in many ways handicapped. His writings include *Arabische Handschriften der 'Bibliotheca orientalis Sprengeriana' in der Staatsbibliothek Preußischer Kulturbesitz, Berlin* (1981), and *Berberkönige und Schriftgelehrte; nordafrikanischer Islam in Tradition und Moderne* (1992). JahrDtB, 1973-2001/2002; Private

Kuripešić, Benedikt, fl. 1530, he was a German royal interpreter to the embassy of King Ferdinand I of Hungary to Constantinople and left *Itinerarium oder Wegrayß Küniglich Mayestät potschafft gen Constantinopel zu dem Türckischen Keiser Soleyman, Anno 1530* (1531), *Ein Disputation oder Gesprech zwayr Stalbuben am Hof des türkischen Sultans 1530 über Gebräuche, Glauben, Heerwesen, Politik der Türkei und ihr Verhältnis zum Deutschen Reich* (1532), a work which was edited by S. M. Džaja and Jozo Džambo entitled *Itinerarium der Gesandtschaft König Ferdinand I. von Ungarn nach Konstantinopel* (1983), and its translations, *Putopis kroz Bosnu, Srbiju, Bulgarsku i Rumeliju 1530* (Sarajevo, 1950), and *1530 yılında Bosna, Sırbistan ve Bulgaristan üzerinden İstanbul'a giden Joseph von Lamberg ile Niclas Jurischitz'in Elçilik günlüğü* (Ankara, 1977). NUC; ZKO

Kuroda, Toshio, born 27 August 1933 at Tokyo, he was a professor of Arabic and Islamic philosophy, and a director, Institute of Middle Eastern Studies, International University of Japan. He taught Islamic philosophy at Freie Universität Berlin, 1969-71, and also served as a visting professor at Cairo and Tehran. DrBSMES, 1993; JapAuFile; WhoWor, 1984/85

Kuroda, Yasumasa, born 28 April 1928 at Tokyo, he received a Ph.D. in 1962 from the University of Oregon. He was in 1990 a professor of political science at the University of Hawaii, Honolulu. His writings include *Japan in a new world order; contributions to the Arab-Israeli peace process* (1994), and he was a joint editor of *Political socialization in the Arab states* (1987). MESA Roster of members, 1990; NatFacDr, 1990-2002; Private

Kuropatkin, Alekseĭ Nikolaevich, born in 1848 in Pskov Oblast, Russia, he graduated from a military college and academy, advancing to the rank of general. He repeatedly served in Turkestan, and participated in the Russo-Turkish War, 1877-78. For seven years he was head of the Transcaspian region. His writings include *Кашгарія* (1879), its translation, *Kashgaria (eastern or Chinese Turkestan; historical and geographical sketch of the country* (1882), and *Завоеваніи* 1899), and its translation, *Geschichte des Feldzuges Skobelews in Turkmenien* (1904). He died in 1925. BiDSovU; Embacher; EnSlovar; GSE; Henze; Master (3); WhoMilH, 1976; Wieczynski

Kurtz, Eduard, born in 1846, he was a philologist whose writings include *Die Sprichwörtersammlung des Maximas Planudes erläutert* (Leipzig, 1886), *Zwei griechische Texte über die Hl. Theophano* (St. Petersburg, 1898), and he was a joint author of *Griechische Schulgrammatik* (Leipzig, 1879). He died in 1925. GV; NUC, pre-1956

Kurtzig, Michael E., born 20th cent., his writings include *Jordan's agriculture economy in brief* (Washington, D.C., U.S. Department of Agriculture, Economic Research Service, 1972), and *Iran; agricultural production and trade* (Washington, D.C., U.S. Department of Agriculture, Economic Research Service, 1974). NUC; ZKO

Kurylev, Vadim Petrovich, born 17 December 1928 at Leningrad, he graduated in 1951 from the Oriental Faculty, Leningrad State University, and received his first degree in 1969 for *Очерки хозяйства и материальной культуры турецкого крестьянства*. Since 1962 he was associated with the Leningrad Branch of the Institute of Ethnography in the Soviet Academy of Sciences. His writings include *Хозяйство и материальная культура турецкого крестьянства; новейсее время* (1976), and he edited *Памятники традиционно-бытовой культуры народов Средней Азии, Казахстана и Кавказа* (1989), and *Лавровские (Среднеазиатско-Кавказские) Чтения; краткое содержание докладов, 1998-1999 гг.* (2001). Miliband²; OSK

Kuryłowicz (Kurilowicz), Jerzy, born 26 August 1895 at Stanisławów (Stanislau), Austria-Hungary, he was educated at Lemberg (Lwów), and subsequently studied at the Hochschule für Welthandel, and Lehranstalt für Orientalische Sprachen, Wien, gaining diplomas at both institutions. Supported by a French scholarship, he studied at Paris from 1923 to 1925. He received doctorates at Lwów in 1923 and 1926. From 1927 to his retirement he was a professor of Indo-European linguistics at Lwów. His writings include *Traces de la place du ton en gathique* (1925), *Esquisses linguistiques* (1960), *Очерки по лингвистике* (1962), *The Inflectional categories of Indo-European* (1964), *Studies in Semitic grammar and metrics* (1972), *Metrik und Sprachgeschichte* (1975). In 1978, he was honoured by *Jerzy Kurylowicz, 1895-1978; materials from the scientific session organized by the Jagiellonian University*. He died on 28 January 1978. BioB134; *Folia orientalia*, 24 (1987), 255-62; IntWW, 1974/75-1978/79; Polski (7); *Romance philology*, 31 (1978), pp. 711-17; WhoWor, 1974/75, 1976/77

Kuryshzhanov, Abzhan Kuryshzhanovich, born 5 August 1930 in Kyzl-Orda Oblast, Kazakhstan. He was associated with the Institute of Language and Literature of the Kazak Academy of Sciences. In 1976 he obtained a doctorate. His writings include *Исследование по лексике старокыпцакского письменного памятника XIII в.* (1970), and *Куманско-казахский цастотный словарь* (1978). Kazakhskaia, vol. 3, p. 295, OSK; Schoeberlein

Kurz, Otto, born 26 May 1908 at Wien, he studied fine art and archaeology at the Universität Wien, where he also received a Dr.phil. in 1931. He spent 1932 to 1934 at Kunstwissenschaftliche Bibliothek Warburg, Hamburg, and remained with that institution when it removed in 1934 to London, eventually becoming the Warburg Institute in the University of London. Since 1965 he was a professor of fine arts in the University of London. In 1970/71, he was Slade Professor of Fine Arts at Oxford. His writings include *European clocks and watches in the Near East* (1975), *The Decorative arts of Europe and the Islamic East; selected studies* (1977), and he was a joint author of *Die Legende vom Künstler* (1980), and its translation, *Legend, myth, and magic in the image of the artist* (1979). He died in London on 3 September 1975. BioHbDtE; BioIn, 11; *Burlington magazine*, 118 (January 1976), pp. 29-30; ConAu, 104, 107; DtBE; NDB; Who, 1966-75; WhoLib, 1954; WhoWorJ, 1972

Kurzmann, Johann Philipp, born 18th cent. at Mühlhausen, Thuringia, he studied at the Universität Göttingen. His writings include *Commentatio de Africa geographi Nubiensis* (1791), and *Commentatio de VI symbolorum obligandi in veteri ecclesia* (1792). He died in Göttingen in March 1794. DtBiInd (3)

Kusch, Eugen, born 13 November 1905 at Danzig-Langfuhr, Germany, he was a private scholar of fine arts. His writings include *Ägypten im Bild* (1955), its translation, *Egypt in pictures* (1955), *Indien im Bild* (1959), and its translation, *India in pictures* (1960). He died in Neumark/Oberpfalz on 20 February 1981. KDtLK, Nekrolog, 1971-1998; Kürschner, 1970-1980

Kuschke, Arnulf, born 10 August 1912 at Kiel, Germany, he received a Dr.theol. in 1939 from the Universität Gießen for *Arm und reich im Alten Testament mit besonderer Berücksichtigung der nachexilischen Terminologie*. He was a professor of Old Testament and Biblical archaeology successively at the universities of Göttingen, Erlangen, and Mainz. He was a joint author of *Archäo-*

logischer Survey in der südlichen Biqā', Herbst 1972 (1976), and he edited *Archäologie und Altes Testament* (1970). DtBilnd (1); Kürschner, 1961-1992|

Kushev, Vladimir Vasil'evich, born 30 November 1927 at Leningrad, he graduated in 1950 from the Oriental Faculty, Leningrad State University, and received his first degree in 1974 for *Афганская рукописная книга; очерки афганской письменной культуры*, a work which was published in 1980. Since 1957 he was associated with the Leningrad Branch of the Oriental Institute in the Soviet Academy of Sciences. From 1975 to 1980 he served as ambassador to Iran in Tehran. His writings include *Описание рукописей на языке пашто Института Востоковедения* (1976). Miliband²; Schoeberlein

Kusheva, Ekaterina Nikolaevna, born 20th cent., her writings include *Народы Северного Кавказа и их связи с Россией* (1963), and she was a joint author of *Кабардино-русские отношения в XVI-XVIII вв.* (1957), *Русская подпольная и зарубежная печот* (1972), and *Русско-цеценские отношения ; вторая половина XVI-XVII в.* (1997). NUC; OSK

Kußmaul, Friedrich, born in 1920, he received a Dr.phil. in 1954 from the Universität Tübingen for *Zur Frühgeschichte des innerasiatischen Reiternomadentums*. He was associated with Linden-Museum, Stuttgart, which honoured him by the jubilee volume, *Friedrich Kußmaul zum Sechzigsten* (1981). His writings include *Ferne Völker, frühe Zeiten* (1982), and he edited the exhibition catalogues, *Chinesische Kunst* (1966), *Das Tier in der Kunst Irans* (1972), and *Linden-Museum Stuttgart; Staatliches Museum für Völkerkunde* (1987). Schwarz

Kutsch, Wilhelm, born in 1895, he entered the Society of Jesus in 1913, and in 1933 he received a Dr.phil. from the Universität Bonn for *In Lactanti de ira Dei librum quaestiones philologae*. He spent eleven years at Beirut, from 1948 to 1949, and from 1951 to 1961. He was *aumônier des sœurs de Saint-Charles-Borromée*. He edited *Ṭābit Ibn Qurra's arabische Übersetzung der Arithmētikē Eisagōgē des Nikomachus von Gerasa* (1959), and he was a joint editor of *Al-Farabi's commentary on Aristotle's Peri hermeneias* (1960). He died in Frankfurt am Main on 16 June 1966. Jalabert, p. 452

Kutscher, Eduard Yechezkel, born 1 June 1909 at Topolćany, Slovakia, he emigrated to Palestine in 1931. He was a lecturer in Hebrew at Israeli universities and a visiting professor in the United States. His writings include *The Language and linguistic background of the Isaiah scroll* (1974-79). He died in Jerusalem in 1971. EncJud; Filipsky; WhoWorJ, 1965, 1972

Kutschera, Chris, born in 1938, he was a photographer and journalist who contributed political eyewitness reports to *Le Monde diplomatique, Les Cahiers de l'Orient, Middle East magazine*, and *Jeune Afrique*. His writings include *Le mouvements national kurde* (1979), *Le défi kurde; ou, le rêve fou de l'indépendance* (1997), and he edited *Le Kurdistan* (1998). Livres disponibles, 2004; Note

von **Kutschera**, Hugo, Freiherr, born 16 March 1847 at Wien, he graduated from the local Orientalische Akademie. In 1871, he was an Austrian consul at Ruse (Rustschuk), Ottoman Bulgaria, and from 1876 to 1882 he was a secretary to the Austrian legation at Constantinople. He subsequently served for twenty years in the provincial government of Bosnia and Hercegovina. His writings include *Die Chasaren* (1909). He died in Vöslau, Austria, on 1 September 1909. BioJahr, 14 (1912), Totenliste, 1909, col. 49*; Kornrumpf; ÖBL

Kutsiia (Куция), Karlo Konstantinovich, born 2 February 1933 in Soviet Georgia, he graduated in 1958 from the Oriental Faculty, Tiflis State University, and received his first degree in 1967 for *Города и городская жизнь сефевидского Ирана*. Since 1960 he was associated with the Oriental Institute of the Georgian Academy of Sciences. His writings include *Социально-экономическая структура и социальная борьба в городах сефевидского Ирана* (1990). Miliband; Miliband²; OSK

Kutta, Wilhelm *Martin*, born 3 November 1867 at Pitschen/Schlesien, Prussia, he studied mathematics at the universities of Breslau, München, and Cambridge, and received a Dr.phil. in 1901 from the Universität München for *Beitrag zur näherungsweisen Integration totaler Differential-Gleichungen*. He taught mathematics in various capacities at the universities of München, Jena, Aachen, and Stuttgart. He died in Fürstenfeldbruck near München on 25 December 1944. Bioln, 12; DtBE; DtBilnd (3); Kürschner, 1931-1940/41; NDB; *Wer ist's*, 1912

Kütükoğlu, Bekir, born in 1926 at Ürgüp, central Anatolia, he went to school in Kayseri, and studied in Istanbul at a teachers college (Yüksek Öğretmen Okulu). He became a high school teacher of history first at Haruniye near Adana and later at Zonguldak. During the Congress of Orientalists in Istanbul, he became acquainted with Zeki Velidi Togan, whose assistant in Turkish history he became in 1953. In 1954, he was invited to the Türkiyat Enstitüsü as assistant at the Chair of Yeniçağ Kürsüsü. In 1957, he received a doctorate for *Osmanlı-İran siyasi münasebetleri, 1578-1590*, a work which was published in 1962. He became an authority in Ottoman Turkish and taught at Istanbul Üniversitesi in varied capacities and faculties. After his second doctorate in 1974 with a thesis entitled *Katib Çelebi, Fezleke'sinin kaynakları*, he was appointed a professor. When he retired in January 1990, he was chairman of the Department of History at the Faculty of Philosophy, Istanbul. He died in 1990. In 1991 appeared *Prof. Dr. Bekir Kütükoğlu'na armağan.* Materialia Turcica, 16 (1992), pp. 163-66

Kuun, Géza Lajos Lázlo József, Gróf, born 28 December 1837 at Nagyszeben, Hungary, he studied archaeology, history, and Oriental languages at the universities of Budapest and Göttingen, and repeatedly went on study journeys abroad. He contributed to *Rivista Europea, Bolletino italiano degli studi orientali, Revue internationale*, and *Revue d'ethnographie*. His writings include *Codex Cumanicus* (1880), *Additamentorum ad Codicem Cumanicum* (1883), *Relationum Hungarorum cum oriente gentibusque orientalis origines historia antiquissima* (1897), *Keleti kutfők* (1898), and *Gurdézi a törökökről* (1901/02). He died in Budapest on 9 April 1905. Ignaz Goldziher wrote *Emlékbeszéd Gróf Kuun Géza tiszt. ésigazgatótag fölött* (Budapest, 1907). GeistigeUng; Keleti Szemle, 6 (1905), pp. 178-79; Pallas; RNL

Kuuz, Aleksandr Al'bertovich, born 20th cent., his writings include *Аграрные отношения в Марокко* (Moscow, 1984). LC; OSK

Kuzeev (Kuziev), Rustem Gumerovich, born 5 January 1923, in Central Bashkiria, he received a doctorate in history in 1972, and, in 1975, was appointed a professor. His writings include *Рабочний класс-созидатель коммунизма* (1969); and he was a joint editor of *Формирование и развитие советского рабочего класса Башкирской АССР* (1975). He died in 1998. BashkKE; TatarES

Kuzmanić-Svete, Nila, fl. 1978, his writings include *Kraljevina Maroko* (Beograd, 1975). NUC, 1973-1977

Kuz'min, Ivan P., born 1893, he translated jointly with I. IU. Krachkovskiĭ *Роман о Хайе* from the Arabic of Ibn Tufayl, and *Калила и Димна* (1934). He died on 28 May 1922. Krachkovskiĭ; NYPL; Восток, 2 (1923), p. 164

Kuz'min, Stanislav Alekseevich, born 2 November 1930, he graduated in 1953 from the Moscow Oriental Institute, and received his first degree in 1958 for *Аграрные отношения в Синде во второй половине XIX в.* Since 1964 he was associated with the Soviet Academy of Sciences. His writings include *Экономическое развитие Пакистана и внешний рынок* (1960), *Развивающиеся страны* (1965), and *Системный анализ экономики развивающихся стран* (1972), and he was a joint author of *Указатели содержания русских дореволюционных газет* (1986). Miliband; Miliband²; OSK

Kuznetsov, Nikolaĭ Aleksandrovich, fl. 20th cent., he was a joint author of *Экономное использование нефтепродуктов* (1984), and he edited *Проблемы экономики и истории стран Ближнего и Среднего Востока* (1966), and *Иран; экономика, история, историография, литература: сборник статей* (1976). LC; ZKO

Kuznetsov (Kouznietsov), Petr Evdokimovich, born 19th cent., he taught Uzbek at the Oriental Faculty, Tashkent University, in the early years of the twentieth century. In 1912, he received a doctorate from the Université de Paris for *La lutte des civilisations et des langues dans l'Asie centrale*. His trace is lost after an article in 1927. BiobibSOT; NUC, pre-1956

Kuznetsov, Petr Ivanovich, born 10 April 1923 at Moscow, he graduated in 1945 from И.И.Я. [!], and received his first degree in 1950 with a thesis on «Условный период турецкого языка», and a doctorate in 1982 for *Система функционалных форм глагола в современном турецком языка*. He was member of the Red Army, 1941-45, and since 1949 successively associated with the Military Institute of Foreign Languages, and the Moscow State Institute of International Relations. His writings include *Учебное пособие по турецкому языку для 3-го курса* (1972-74), and *Курс общего перевода* (1973). Miliband; Miliband²

Kuznetsov, Viacheslav Semenovich, borm 29 August 1932 in Kirov Oblast, Russia, he graduated in 1955 from the Oriental Faculty, Leningrad State University, received his first degree in 1962, and a doctorate in 1985 for a monograph. He was a research fellow ща the Siberian Branch of the Institute of History, Archaeology and Ethnography of the Peoples of the Far East, 1965-69, and subsequently he was associated with the Far Eastern Institute, Soviet Academy of Sciences. His writings include *Амурсана* (1980), and *Нурхацы* (1985). Miliband²

Kuznetsova, IUlila Pavlovna, fl. 20th cent., her writings include *Михаил Иванович Пикоы* (Moscow, 1971), and jointly with Fedor D. Konstantinov, *Федор Денисович Константинов* (Moscow, 1965), and *Графические миниатюры* (Leningrad, 1979). OSK

Kuznetsova, Nina Alekseevna, born 17 January 1924 in Russia, she graduated in 1949 from the Faculty of History, Moscow State University, and received her first degree in 1952 for *Из истории*

социально-экономических отношений в Иране в первой трети XIX века; иранский город и городское ремесло. Since 1953 she was associated with the Oriental Institute, Soviet Academy of Sciences. Her writings include *Иран в первой половине XIX века* (1983); she was a joint author of *Из истории советского востоковедения: 1917-1967* (1970); and she edited *Иран, история и современность; сборник статей* (1983). She died on 30 June 1993. Miliband; Miliband[2]

Kuznetsova, Sof'ia Iosifovna, born 1 January 1923 at Vitebsk, Belo Russia, she graduated in 1946 from the Faculty of History, Moscow State University, received her first degree in 1950 for «Московский договор 16 марта 1921 г. между Советской Россией и Турцией», and a doctorate in 1972 for *Социальная структура африканского города.* She was successively associated with the Azerbaijan State University, Baku, and the Institute of Information Science, Soviet Academy of Sciences. Her writings include *Установление советско-турецких отношений* (1961), *Социальная структура африканского города; проблема формирования промышленного пролетариата и Тропической Африка* (1972). Miliband; Miliband[2]

Kverenchkhiladze, Roman Il'ich, born 20th cent., he obtained a doctorate in geography and subsequently became a professor. His writings include *Географические проблемы транспорта Грузии* (1976), and *Региональная география = Regional geography* (Tbilisi, 1983). LC

Kverfel'd, Ernest Konradovich, 1877-1949 *see* Querfeldt, Ernest Konradovich

Kvirkvelia, Georgiĭ Galaktinovich, fl. 20th cent., he was associated with the Geokgian State Museum im. S. N. Dzhanaskia. His writings include *Из истории материальной культуры Ирана; медно-латунные иранские сосуды XIX в.* (Tbilisi, 1968). Note; NUC, 1968-72

Kwanten, Luc Herman M., born 8 January 1944 at Bruxelles, he graduated from the universities of Gent and Louvain, and received a Ph.D. in 1972 from Columbia University, New York, for *Tibetan-Mongolian relations during the Yuan dynasty.* He was a professor of Chinese history at Indiana University, Bloomington, before he taught in the same capacity at the University of Chicago. His writings include *A History of Central Asia, 500-1500* (London, 1979), *Imperial nomads; a history of Central Asia, 500-1500* (New York, 1979), and he was a joint author of *Tangut (Hsi Hsia) studies; a bibliography* (1980). ConAu, 93-96; ZKO

Kwitny, Jonathan, born 23 March 1941 at Indianapolis, Ind., he received a college education in journalism and graduated with an M.A. from New York University in 1964. From 1965 to 1966 he served as an American Peace Corps volunteer in Nigeria. He became a reporter and journalist whose writings include *The Fountain pen conspiracy* (1973), *Endless enemies; the making of an unfriendly world* (1984), and *Man of the century; the life and times of Pope John Paul II* (1997). He died of cancer in N.Y.C. on 26 November 1998. ConAu, 49-52, 172, new rev., 1, 23, 92; EncTwCJ; IndAu

Kyas, Amand, born 19th cent., he wrote *Übersetzung ausgewählter Kapitel aus dem arabischen Geographen Ibn Rusta* (Braunau, 1905). GV; NUC, pre-1956

Kychanov, Evgeniĭ Ivanovich, born 22 June 1932 at Sarapul, Azerbaijan, he graduated in 1955 from the Oriental Faculty, Leningrad State University, and received his first degree in 1960 with a thesis on «Государство Си Ся (982-1227 гг.)», and a doctorate in 1970 for a monograph. He was since 1957 associated with the Leningrad Branch of the Oriental Institute in the Academy of Sciences. His writings include *Звучат лишь письмена* (1965), *Очерк истории тангутского государства* (1968), and he edited the exhibition catalogue, *Buddhistische Manuskripte der Großen Seidenstraße = Manuscripts and bloc prints from the collection of the St. Petersburg Branch of the Institute of Oriental Studies, Russian Academy of Sciences* (Sanktpeterburg, 2000). Miliband; Miliband[2]; OSK

Kyle, John Francis, born in 1943, he received a Ph.D. in economics from the University of Wisconsin. His writings include *Balance of payments in a monetary economy* (1976). Note; NUC, 1973-77

Kyle, Keith, born 4 August 1925 at Sturminster Newton, Dorset, he graduated from Magdalen College, Oxford. He spent some years with the BBC, London, before he became a correspondent, reporter, and newscaster in Africa, 1961-64. He was for many years a Middle East specialist at the Royal Institute of International Affairs (Chatham House) and was until 1990 Special Assistant to the director of that Institute. He was a sometime visiting professor of history at the University of Ulster, a fellow of the Institute of Politics, John F. Kennedy School of Government, Harvard, and a senior associate member of St. Antony's College, Oxford. At the time of Suez, he was the Washington correspondent of the *Economist.* He was known to a wider public for his work on television. He commented on events from around the world, in cluding the Middle East for the BBC in the sixties, seventies and early eighties. His writings include *Cyprus* (1984), and *Suez* (1991). ConAu, 137, new rev., 99; IntAu&W, 1977; Note about the author

Kyriakidès, Stilpōn Paraskeua, born in 1887 at Komotini, Thrace, he was a professor of ethnology and folklore. His writings include *Ελληνικη λαογραφία* (1922), *Ο διγενής Ακρίτας* (1926), *Neugriechische Volkskunde* (1936), *Τα βόρεια εθνολογικα ορια του Ελληνισμου* (1946), *Τρεῖς διαλέξεις* (1953), and *The Northern ethnological boundaries of Hellenism* (1955). He died in Thessaloniki in 1964. EEE; NUC

Kyriakos, Mansour, born about 1880 at Tall Kayf in northern Mesopotamia, he completed his education with a doctorate at Baghdad and went on to study theology at the Séminaire oriental Saint François Xavier in the Université Saint-Joseph, Beirut, where he was ordained at the Église de l'Université, on 20 May 1909. He became a Chaldaean priest in Aleppo. Together with Victor Yonan he published *L'action assyro-chaldéenne, 1920-1921*; his writings include the French translation *Le drame assyrien*, by Yusuf Malek (1940). Note about the author

Kyrris (Κύρρης), Costas (Konstantinos) P., born in 1928 at Cyprus, he received an M.A. in 1961 from the Royal Holloway College, London, for *Urban and rural conditions in the Byzantine Empire, from the end of the thirteenth to the middle of the fourteenth century*. His other writings include *Peaceful coexistence in Cyprus under British rule, 1878-1959, and after independence* (1977), *Κύπρος, Τουρκία και Ελληνισμός* (1980), and *Τουρκία και Βαλκάνια* (1986). EVL, 1996/97-2004; OSK

Kyzlasov, Igor' Leonidovich, born 28 August 1951 at Moscow, he graduated in 1974 from the Faculty of History, Moscow State University, and received his first degree in 1977 for *Аскизская культура Южной Сибири; происхождение и развитие X-XIV вв*, a work which was published in 1983. He was since 1978 associated with the Archaeological Institute of the Soviet Academy of Sciences. Miliband[2]

Kyzlasov, Leonid Romanovich, born 24 March 1924 in the Khakass Autonomous Region, he graduated in 1949 from the Faculty of History, Moscow State University, received his first degree in 1953 with a thesis on «Таштыкск. эпоха в истории Хакасско-Минустнск. котловины», and a doctorate in 1966 for *Истории Тувы в средние века*, a work which was published in 1969. Since 1952 he was associated with the Faculty of History, Moscow State University. He was appointed a lecturer in 1956, and a professor in 1969. His writings include *Древняя Тува* (1979), *История Южной Сибири в средние века* (1984), *Древнейсая Хакасия* (1986), *Очерки по истории Сибири и Центральной Азии* (1992); and jointly with Nikolaї Vladimirovich Leon'tev, *Народные рисунки хакасов* (1980), and jointly with Galina G. Korol', *Декоративное искусство средневековых хакасов как исторический источник* (1990); and he edited *История Хакасии; с древнейсих времен до 1917 года* (1993), Miliband[2]; OSK

La Names with the prefix La are entered under the prefix, or the part of the name following the prefix, variously in different languages. If the name looked for is not found under the prefix, search should be made under the part of the name following the prefix.

Laade, Wolfgang, born 13 January 1925 at Zeitz, Germany, he received a Dr.phil. in 1960 from Freie Universität Berlin, and a Dr.habil. in 1972 from the Universität Zürich. He was from 1976 to his retirement in 1995 a professor at Ethnologisches Seminar of the Universität Zürich. His writings include *Die Situation von Musikleben und Musikforschung in den Ländern Afrikas und Asiens und die neuen Aufgaben der Musikethnologie* (1969), *Gegenwartsfragen der Musik in Afrika und Asien* (1971), *Musik der Götter, Geister und Menschen; die Musik in der mythischen, fabulierenden und historischen Überlieferung der Völker Afrikas, Nordasiens, Amerikas und Ozeaniens; eine Quellensammlung* (1975), and *Musik und Musiker in Märchen* (1988). Kürschner, 1976-2005

Labadie-Lagrave, Gaston, born 15 August 1842 at Nérac (Lot-et-Garonne), he received a doctorate in law for *Essai sur la subrogation à l'hyothèque légale de la femme*. He was a journalist with the *Journal des débats, le Constitutionnel*, and *le Globe*. His trace is lost after an article in 1914. IndexBFr[2] (2)

Laban, Ferdinand, born 1 February 1856 at Preßburg, Slovakia, he studied German philology at the Universität Wien, where he received a Dr.phil. in 1879 and did post-doctoral work at the universities of Klausenburg and Straßburg. From his early years he was associated with literary and cultural circles in Bayreuth and Berlin, where he became in 1894 librarian of Berliner Königliche Museen. He was the most important German-Hungarian writer of the end of the nintheeth century. His writings include *Die Schopenhauer-Literatur* (1880), and *Verstreut und gesammelt; Aufsätze über Leben, Kunst und Dichtung* (1911). He died in Berlin on 30 December 1910. DtBiInd (5); ÖBL; Wer ist's, 1909

Labande, Edmond René Paul, born 11 June 1908 at Paris, he graduated from the École nationale des Chartes and the École pratique des Hautes Études, Paris. He subsequently spent from 1931 to 1933 with the École française de Rome. From 1934 to 1938 he was chief archivist of the Département d'Alger and subsequently was a lecturer in history of art in the Institut français de Florence. He submitted a *thèse complémentaire* to the Université de Paris in 1940 entitled *Étude sur Baudouin de Sebourc, chanson de geste*. He later taught at a lycée in Toulon, the Université d'Aix-en-Provence, the Prytanée national militaire, La Flèche, and the Faculté des Lettres de Poitiers. He was a medievalist whose writings include *L'Italie de la Renaissance* (1954), a collection of his articles, *Spiritualité et vie littéraire de l'Occident X-XIV siècles* (1974), and jointly with Marie Thérèse d'Alverny, *Répertoire des médiévistes européens* (1960), and he was a joint editor of *Instruments de musique du XIV siècle* (1932). He died about 1980. DBFC, 1954/55; WhoFr, 1967/68-1979/80|

Labaree, Benjamin, born 21 March 1834 at Columbia, Tenn., he graduated from Middlebury College, Vt., with the class of 1854, and taught for two years before entering Andover Theological Seminary. One year (1859-60) was spent in medical studies and other in preparation for his missionary career, after which he and his wife sailed in 1860 to join the American Mission to the Nestorians at Urmia, Persia. He was actively connected with the work in Persia until he died on his way for cancer treatment in the United States aboard the *Kaiserin Auguste Victoria* on 14 May 1906. Only for a few years he gave up his connection with the mission, on account of illness in his family, and spent seven years in America. During part of this time he was engaged in literary work in Syriac, and for several years was home secretary of the Presbyterian Board of Foreign Missions. Missionary review of the world, 19 (1906), pp. 915-919; NYT 19 May 1906, p. 11, col. 6; Shavit; Who was who in America, 1

Labaree, Benjamin Woods, born in 1871 at Newcastle, Ind., of American missionary parentage, he trained for the ministry in the United States and was a missionary in Urmia, Persia, from 1893 until he was killed by a fanatical Dasht Kurdish *sayyid* in a lonely mountain pass near Urmia while on an errand of mercy, 9 March 1904. Kornrumpf; NYT 19 May 1906, p. 11, col. 6; Richter, p. 315; Shavit

Labaree, Mrs. Benjamin Wood, 1868-1954 *see* Platt, Mary née Schauffler

Labarta Gomez, Ana, born 20th cent., she received a doctorate in Islamic studies and became a professor in her field in the Universidad de Córdoba. Her writings include *Vocabulario básico árabe-español* (1984), *La onomastica de los Moriscos valencianos* (1987); she was a joint author of *Numeros y cifras en los documentos arábigohispanos* (1988); and she edited and translated *Al-Kitāb al-kāmil, horóscopos históricos*, from the Arabic of Mūsá ibn al-Hasan al-Nawbakhtī (1982). Arabismo, 1992, 1994, 1997; EURAMES, 1993

Labarthe, André, born 26 January 1902 at Paris, he studied at the Sorbonne, where he received a doctorate in science in 1936 for *Nouvelles méthodes de mesures mécaniques*. He later entered the research department of the Ministère de l'Air. In June of 1940 he left France and went to Britain, where he became director of armaments under General de Gaulle. In November 1940 he became the founding editor of the monthly, *La France libre*; in 1843 he was nominated minister of information in North Africa; in May 1948 he established *Constellation*, Paris, a monthly which he managed until his death on 12 November 1967. His writings include *La France devant la guerre* (1938), *Retour au feu* (New York, 1943), *La Vie commence demain* (1947), and *Document sur le pétrole du Sahara* (1957). Master (2); NDNC, 1961/62; WhE&EA; WhoFr, 1959/60-1967/68

de **Labarthe**, Jean François *Charles*, born 27 May 1820 at Paris into an old Languedoc family, he was self educated, and pursued an interest in the exact sciences, ethnography, and philosophy. His writings include *De l'écriture et des alphabets chez les différents peuples* (1854), and he was a contributor to the *Presse algérienne*, and *Revue de l'Orient* of the Société orientale de France. He died in 1871. GDU; Hoefer

Labasse, Jean René François, born 10 July 1918 at Lyon, France, he was educated and studied at his home town and gained a degree in law and a doctorate in letters for *Le commerce des soies à Lyon sous Napoléon et le crise de 1811*. He was a banker since 1957 and concurrently served as a professour at the Institut d'études politiques de Paris, and the Université de Lyon. His writings include *Terres et hommes de la Communauté; France et pays-d'outre mer* (1959), *La Géographie au B.E.P.C.* (1966), *L'Organisation de l'espace; éléments de géographie volontaire* (1966), *L'Espace financier; analyse géographique* (1974), *L'Hôpital et la ville* (1981), *L'Europe des régions* (1991), and *Quelle régions pour l'Europe?* (1994). WhoFr, 1979/80-2000|

de **La Bastide d'Hust**, comte Henri Martin, born 14 December 1916 at Paris, he was a sometime *contrôleur civil* in Morocco, and professor (1961) and president (1976) of the École nationale des langues orientales vivantes, Paris. His writings include *Maghreb; Tunisie, Algérie, Maroc* (1973), and *Les quatre voyages; au cœur des civilisations* (1985). He died on 23 March 1986. WhoFr, 1985/86

Labatut, Augustin, born 19th cent., he was an Algerian veterinary from the École de Saumur, who served with the third Regiment de Casseurs d'Afrique with the rank of *lieutenant-vétérinaire*. He spent from 1908 to 1910 with the Bataillon du Tchad. Note about the author

Labaune, Patrick Francis, born 13 June 1951 at Paris, he went to school at Valence and gained a diploma and doctorate at the Institut d'études politiques in Grenoble and Paris, respectively. He was successively a secondary school teacher, lecturer at the Université de Grenoble, and a local and national politician. His writings include *La Rébublique arabe du Yémen* (Paris, 1985). WhoFr, 2000-2005/6

Labbé, Édouard Henri, born 3 July 1869 at Lille (Nord), France, he received a doctorate in law and successively served as a professor at the Faculté de droit de Lille, and as a judge and president of tribunal in Gabès, Sousse, and Tunis. Qui êtes-vous, 1924

Labbé, Ernest *Marcel*, born 2 December 1870 at Le Havre, France, he studied medicine and became a *professeur-agrégé* at the Faculté de médecine de Paris. His writings include *Maladies de l'appareil digestif et de la nutrition* (1922), and *Traité de l'éducation physique* (1930). He died in Paris on 29 May 1939. Dictionnaire national des contemporains, ed. Imbert Nath, 1936 (not sighted); Qui êtes-vous, 1924

Labbé, Paul Auguste, born 23 January 1867 at Arpajon (Seine-et-Oise), France, he received a classical education at the Lycée Michelet and studied at the École des Sciences politiques, Paris. He subsequently visited Italy, Germany, Austria, and Russia to learn foreign languages. In the service of the Ministère de l'Instruction publique he went between 1897 and 1900 on three missions to the Kirghiz in Central Asia, to the Bashkirs and Cossacks in the Urals, and lastly to Russian East Asia. In the service of the Russian Government he organized the Russian pavillon at the 1900 World Fair in Paris. His writings include *Les Russes en Extrême-Orient* (1904), *Sur les grandes routes de Russie entre l'Oural et la Volga* (Paris, 1905), *Chez les Lamas de Sibérie* (1909), and *La vivante Roumanie* (Paris, 1913). Curinier, 3 (1901), pp. 42-43; NUC, pre-1956

de **La Beaume**, Pierre Joseph *Jules* Jeanneau, born in 1806 at Grenoble, France, he entered the Ministère de la Guerre and subsequently became attached to the Gouvernement général de l'Algérie. Concurrently he was a contributor of miscellaneous articles to periodicals like *Univers pittoresque*, and *Magasin pittoresque*. His writings include *Le Koran analysé d'après la traduction de M. Kasimirski et les observations de plusieurs autres savants orientalistes* (1878). He died about 1876. GDU

Łabęcka-Koecherowa, Małgorzata, born 20th cent., she was a joint author of *Historia literatury tureckiej; zarys* (Wrocław, 1971). OSK

Labīb, Subḥī Yannī, born 27 March 1924 at Ṭanṭā, Egypt, he was educated at Coptic schools and studied at Alexandria University, where he received all his degrees, including a doctorate. He briefly headed the archives of his University until a French scholarship enabled him to go to Paris. Recommended by Fritz Meier, Basel, he went to the Universität Hamburg in 1954 as a lecturer in Arabic. In 1961 he became a lecturer at the Universität Kiel. He received his Dr.habil. in 1965 from the Universität Hamburg for *Handelsgeschichte Ägyptens im Spätmittelalter*. In 1970 he succeeded his Egyptian teacher 'Azīz Sūryāl 'Aṭīyah at the University of Salt Lake City. In 1973 he returned to Kiel to become a professor at the Historisches Seminar, which post he held until his death on 22 March 1987. der Islam, 65 (1988, pp. 1-4; Kürschner, 1980-1986; WhoWor, 1980/81

Labica, Georges, born 20th cent., he was a sometime *maître-assistant* at the Faculté des lettres et sciences humaines d'Alger, who became professor of philosophy at the Université de Paris. His writings include *Politique et religion chez Ibn Khaldoun* (1968), *De Marx au marxisme* (1986), *Robespierre; une politique de la philosophie* (1990), its translation, *Robespierre; eine Politik der Philosophie* (1994), and he was the editor of numerous collective works on Marxism. LC; Libres disponibles, 2004

de **La Bigne de Villeneuve**, Marcel, born in 1850 at Rennes (Ille-et-Vilaine), France, he studied medicine at the Université de Rennes, where he also received a doctorate in 1920 for *Un principe nouveau de législation du travail*. He became a professor at the Faculté libre de droit d'Angers. His writings include *Traité général de l'État* (1929). IndexBFr²

de **Laborde**, Alexandre Louis Joseph, Comte, born 15 September 1777 at Paris, he initially studied at the Collège de Juilly with a view to a navy career. After the revolution, he was sent to the Viennese Court of Kaiser Joseph II, with whom the family had long been on friendly relations. After the Treaty of Campo-Formio (1797), he returned to France, where he pursued an interest in arts and travel, visiting Britain, Holland, Italy, and Spain. Under the auspices of the diplomatic mission of Lucien Bonaparte, he had the opportunity to realize his survey of Spain which resulted in the publication of *Voyage pittoresque et historique de l'Espagne* (1806-20), its translations, *A view of Spain, comprising a descriptive itinerary of each province and a general statistical account of the country* (1809), and *Mahlerische und historische Reise in Spanien* (1809-1811). He was nominated auditor at the Conseil d'État in 1808, *maître des requêtes*, in 1809, and soon thereafter, director of the Service des ponts et chaussées of the Département de la Seine; in 1813, he was admitted to the Institut des Inscriptions et

Belles-Lettres. From 1822 to his death in 1842 he remained in politics. BiD&SB; DcBiPP (not sighted); EncicUni; GdeEnc; Hoefer; IndexBFr² (5); *Penny magazine*, 432 (29 December 1838), pp. 497-98

de **Laborde**, Léon Emmanuel Simon Joseph, he was born on 15 June 1807 at Paris. After completing his studies at Göttingen in 1825, he travelled overland to Petra and Cairo. In 1827 he explored Arabia together with Linant de Bellefonds. In his later years he was a keeper of antiquities at the Louvre, and director of the Archives de l'Émpire. He was a member of the Académie des inscriptions et belles lettres. His writings include *Voyage de l'Arabie petrée* (1830), its translation, *Journey through Arabia Petræa to Mount Sinai, and the excavated city of Petra* (1836), *Voyage de l'Asie mineure* (1838), *Histoire de la gravure en manière noire* (1839), and *De l'organisation des bibliothèques dans Paris* (1845-1846). He died at the château de Beauregard on 25 March 1869. DBF; Embacher; Henze; Kornrumpf; Kornrumpf³, vol. 2

de **Laboulaye**, Édouard René Lefebvre, born 18 January 1811 at Paris, he began life as a typefounder, then studied Fand from 1839 to 1845. He published works which were awarded by the Académie des Inscriptions and the Académie des Sciences morales, *Histoire du droit de propriété foncière en Occident* (1839), *Essai sur les lois criminelles des Romains concernant la responsabilité des magistrats* (1840), *Recherches sur la condition civile et politique des femmes depuis les Romains jusqu'à nos jours* (1843), and *Essai sur les lois criminelles des Romains concernant la responsabilité des magistrats* (1845). In 1849 he was appointed to the chair of comparative legislation in the Collège de France. During the Second Empire he took an active part in the efforts of the liberal party, and was consequently regarded with disfavour by the Government. He was an admirer of U.S. institutions, and both before and during the war of session threw his influence on the side of the Union, to which he rendered good service by his work, *The United States and France* (1862). His other writings include *Abdallah, ou, Le trèfle à quatre feuilles; conte arabe, suivi de Aizi et Aziza, contes des Mille et une nuits* (Paris, 1859), its translation, *Abdallah, oder das vierblättrige Kleeblatt* (1870), *Paris in America* (1863), and *О военной медицине во Франции и в Соединенных Штатах* (1870). He died in Paris on 25 May 1883. ACAB (not sighted); BbD; BiD&SB; BioIn, 2, 11; EncAm; Hoefer; IndexBFr² (4); Master (7); NUC, 1968-72; Sezgin; Vapereau

Laboulbène, Jean Joseph *Alexandre*, born 25 August 1825 at Agen (Lot-et-Garonne), France, he received a classical education at the Collège d'Agen and studied at the Faculté de médecine de Paris, where he received a doctorate in 1860 for *Des névralgies viscérales*. He subsequently practised and lectured in medicine at Paris. He died in 1898. IndexBFr² (7)

Labouret, Henri, born 27 May 1878 at Laon (Picardie), France, he joined the French Infanterie coloniale at the age of nineteen. After ten years of hard service and passing through the military college of Saint-Maixent (Deux-Sèvres) he became an officer and continued serving in the Ivory Coast, participating from July to December 1910 in the campaign with the Colonne des Agba. Seriously wounded in the operations at the Upper Bandama, he was awarded *chevalier de la Légion d'honneur* in 1911. On account of his injuries, he was transferred to the colonial military administration. In 1924 he was appointed to the Direction des Affaires politiques at the Ministère de la France d'Outre-Mer. In 1926 he was appointed to a professorship at the École Coloniale, and in the following year at the École des Langues Orientales Vivantes, Paris. His writings include *Le Royaume d'Arda et son évangélisation au XVIIe siècle* (1929), *Les Tribus du Rameau Lobi* (1931), *Monteil, explorateur et soldat* (1937), *La langue des peuls ou Foulbé; lexique français-peul* (Dakar, 1955), *Nouvelles notes sur les tribus du Rameau Lobi, leurs migrations, leur évolution, leurs parlers et ceux de leurs voisins* (1958), *L'Afrique précoloniale* (1959), and its translation, *Africa before the white man* (1962). He retired in 1945 to Levallois-Perret, where he died in 1959. *Hommes et destins*, vol.1, pp. 329-31; LexAfrika; ZKO

Labourt, Jérôme, Abbé, born in 1874 at Paris, he received a doctorate in theology in 1904 from the Université de Paris for *De Timotheo I Nestorianorum patriarcha* and later also a doctorate in letters. His writings include *Le christianisme dans l'Empire perse sous la dynastie sassanide* (1904), and he edited and translated *Lettres* [de Saint Jérôme] *choisie et présentées* (Namur, 1949-63). He was a sometime director of the Collège Stanislav in Paris. *Qui êtes-vous*, 1924

Labouz, Marie-Françoise, born in 1946, she received a doctorate in law. Her writings include *L'Organisation des Nations Unies et la Corée* (1980), *L'Usage orivé de l'écu* (1988), and she edited *Les Accords de Maastrich et la constitution de l'Union europeénne; actes du colloque* (1992), and *Le partenariat de l'Union europénne avec les pays tiers; conflits et convergences* (2000). LC; *Livres disponibles*, 2004

de **Labra** y **Cadrana**, Rafael Maria, born in 1841 at Habana, Cuba, he was educated at Madrid and became known at an early age as a lawyer, orator and writer, devoting himself to Antillan interests in general and especially to the cause of the abolition of slavery in the Spanish Antilles. He was an indefatigable agitator and parliamentarian of European reputation, an eminent publicist who wrote on judicial, historical, political and literary subjects. His writings include *Un viaje por Levante* (1892), and *El derecho internacional en España* (1905). He died in 1915 or 1918. DcAfL; EncicUni; IndicesE³ (14); Master (1)

Labroue, François Marie *Émile*, born 21 February 1847 at Moissac (Tarn-et-Garonne), France, he was a *professeur* at the Lycée de Bordeaux and a member of the Société de l'Histoire de France. From 1879 to 1882 he served as an editor-in-chief of the *Revue de géographie commerciale de Bordeaux*. Curinier, 5 (1906), p. 220; IndexBFr²

Labrousse, Henri Louis, born 8 October 1913 at Marseille, he was educated at Marseille and Paris, and gained a *baccalauréat*. He joined the French Navy and advanced to the rank of rear-admiral in 1970. Concurrently he held political appointments as a member of the Comité d'études de défense nationale as well as the French delegation to the Conference on the rights of the sea. His writings include *Le Golfe et le canal; la réouverture du canal de Suez et la paix internationale* (1973), *Le Droit de la mer; problèmes économiques et stratégiques* (1977), *Récits de la Mer Rouge* (1992), *Chroniques des mers orientales* (2001), and numerous articles on the Red Sea, the Indian Ocean, and the Middle East. *Livres disponibles*, 2004; WhoFr, 1979/80-2005/2006

Labrunie, Gérard de Nerval, 1808-1855 *see* Nerval, Gérard Labrunie de

La Bruyère, René, born 2 February 1875 at Jonzac (Charente-inférieure), France, he was successively a *contrôleur* de la Marine, administrator with the Compagnie des Messageries maritimes, and an editor of the *Journal des débats*. After participating in several campaigns with the French Navy and accomplishing numerous colonial missions, he became involved in Egyptian affairs and the French national armament. A member of the Académie de la Marine, he wrote on maritime affairs for a variety of periodicals throughout his career. His writings include *Deux années de guerre navale* (1916), *Notre marine marchande pendant la guerre* (1920), and *La guerre du Pacifique* (1945) Qui est-ce, 1934

Labuda, Gerard, born 28 December 1916 at Nowa Huta near Kartuzy, Poland, he was a professor of history at the Uniwersytet Poznański, and its sometime rector. His writings include *Pierwsze państwo słowiańskie; państwo Samona* (1949), *Źródła, sagi i legendy do najdawniejszych dziejów Polski* (1960), *Teksty źródłowe do ćwiczeń z historii Polski epoki feudalizmu, do połowy XIV wieku* (1961), and *Polsko-niemieckie rozmowy o przeszłości; zbiór rozpraw i artykułów* (1996). In 1987, he was honoured by *Profesorowi Gerardowi Lubudzie wybitnemu historykowi Pomorza w pięćdziesięciolecie pracy naukowej*. IntWW, 1976-2006; KtoPolske, 1993; Polski² (5); OSK; WhoSoC; WhoSoCE

Lacam, Jean, born 6 December 1907 at Bois-Colombes (Seine), France, he was educated at the Lycée Chaptal and the École du Louvre, Paris. He subsequently became attached to the C.N.R.S. as a specialist in Islamic ceramics, and excavated at Saracen sites in Provence; he also excavated in Iraq and Iran. He was successively a keeper of the Musée d'art et de céramique, Narbonne, and the Musées de Toulon (Var). His writings include *Les Sarrazins dans le haut moyen-âge français; histoire et archéologie* (1965). NDNC, 1964

Lacarelle, F., he was in 1937 a director of *Expérimentation fruitière et maraichère* of Morocco. His writings include *L'Orientation de la production frontière du Maroc* (Rabat, 1937). BN; Note; NUC, pre-1956

Lacarra y de Miguel, José María, born 24 May 1907 at Estella (Navarra), Spain, he was associated with the Universidad de Salamanca before he was appointed a professor of medieval history at the Universidad de Zaragoza. Concurrently he served as a director of the Centro de Estudios Medievales de Aragón. His writings include *Documentos para el estudio de la reconquista y repoblación del valle del Ebro* (1949), *La reconquista española y la repoblación des país* (1951), *Historia de la edad media* (1960), *El reino de Aragón bajo la dinastía pamplonesa* (1961), *Estudios de alta edad media española* (1971), *El juramento de los reyes de Navarra, 1234-1329* (1972), and he was a joint author of *Las peregri-naciones a Santiago de Compostela* (1948-1949). *Diccionario enciclopédico Espasa* (Madrid, 1978); LC; ZKO

Lacassagne, Bernard, born in 1903, he received a doctorate in 1929 from the Université de Nancy for *Contribution à l'étude du syndrome de Hanot*. NUC, pre-1956

Lacassagne, Jean *Alexandre* Eugène, born 17 August 1843 at Cahors (Lot), France, he studied at the École de santé militaire de Strasbourg, received his medical doctorate in 1867 at Paris and his *agrégation* in 1872 at Montpellier. A *médecin-major* since 1873, he entered the hospital Val-de-Grâce where he was responsible for hygiene and legal medicine. From 1880 to his retirement he was a professor of medicine and pharmacy at the Université de Lyon. He is best remembered for his part in the *Affaire Gouffé*. His writings include *Précis d'hygiène privée et sociale* (1876), *Précis de médecine* *judiciaire* (1878), *Les tatouages; étude anthropologique et médico-légale* (1881), *La verte vieillesse* (1920), and its translation, *A Green old age* (1923). He died in Lyon in 1924. BN; DBF

La Cava, Bertrand D., born 19th cent., he received a doctorate in medicine. His writings include *Étude sur les eaux minéro-thermales de Rouzat, Puy-de-Dôme* (Paris, 1863), and contributions to the journal *Gazette médicale d'Orient*, and *Journal des connaissances médicales*. BN

Lacaze, Édouard, born 19th cent., he received a doctorate in 1889 from the Faculté de droit de Paris for *Droit romain: de la Nature de la stipulation de peine. Droit français: de l'Inviolabilité du domicile.* His trace is lost after an article in 1921. BN; Kornrumpf

Lach, Donald Frederick, born 24 September 1917 at Pittsburgh, Pa., he graduated in 1937 from the University of West Virginia and received his Ph.D. in 1941 from the University of Chicago for *Contribution of China to German civilization, 1648-1740.* After four years of teaching at Elmira College he was appointed in 1948 a professor of modern history at the University of Chicago; since 1969 he there held the B. E. Schmitt Chair of History. His writings include *India in the eyes of Europe* (1968), and *Asia in the making of Europe* (1977). He died in Chicago on 26 October 2000. ConAu, 102, 192; DrAS, 1969 H, 1974 H, 1978 H, 1982 H; WhoAm, 1974-1889/90; WhoWor, 1980/81

Lach, Friedrich Wilhelm Viktor, born 18th cent., his writings include *Anleitung zur Kenntnis der Sternennamen mit Erläuterungen aus der arabischen Sprache und Sternkunde* (1796). He died in May 1796. DtBilnd (2); NUC, pre-1956; Sezgin

Lach, Robert, born 29 January 1874 at Wien, he was a civil servant who concurrently studied musicology at the Konservatorium der Gesellschaft für Musikfreunde in Wien, where he received a diploma in composition in 1899. In 1902 he received a Dr.phil. from the Universität Prag, and in 1915 a Dr.habil. from the Universität Wien. In 1911 he joined the Hofbibliothek in Wien, where he was head of the music collection from 1912 to 1920, when he became a professor of comparative musicology at the Universität Wien. Since 1924 he also held a cross-appointment at Staatsakademie für Musik und darstellende Kunst. His writings include *Zur Geschichte des musikalischen Zunftswesens* (1923), and *Gesänge russischer Kriegsgefangener* (1930-40). He died in Salzburg on 11 September 1958. Baker, 1978, 1984, 1992 (not sighted); DtBE; DtBilnd (4); Kosch; Kürschner, 1926-1954; NDB; NewGrDM; Teichl; Wer; *Wer ist's*, 1922-1935; WhoAustria, 1954

Lachal, Maurice, fl. 20th cent., he wrote on North African *zāwiyahs* and published in the *Bulletin* de la Société de géographie de Marseille. Note about the author

de **La Chambre**, Marin Cureau, born in 1594, he entered history in 1625 when his name appeared in a document at Le Mans (Sarthe), where he is referred to as *docteur en médecine.* On 12 June 1629 he was married to a lady from a family of physicians and surgeons. In 1630, he removed to Paris, where he was for thirty-five years the guest and commensal of Pierre Séguier (1588-1672), *chancellier de France.* In 1632, he is known to have been *médecin de Sa Majesté.* As physician, member of the Académie française, and philosopher his reputation and influence at the court was considerable. His writings include *Nouvelles pensées sur les causes de la lumière et du débordement du Nil et de l'amour d'inclination* (1634), *Discours sur les causes du descordement du Nil* (1655), *L'Art de connoistre les hommes* (1660), its translations, *The Art how to know men* (1665), and *Anleitungen zur Menschenkenntniß* (1794). He died on 29 November 1669 aged seventy-five. DBF; GdeEnc; GDU; Hoefer; IndexBFr² (8)

de **La Chapelle**, Frédéric, his writings include *Le Sultan Moulay Isma'il et les Berbères Sanhaja du Maroc central* (Paris, 1931); and he was a joint author of *Les Espagnols sur la côte d'Afrique au XVe et au XVIe siècles* (Paris, 1935). NUC, pre-1956; ZKO

de **Lacharrière**, Jacques, 1881-1958 *see* Ladreit de Lacharrière, Jacques

de **Lacharrière**, René, born 28 January 1915 at Coux (Ardèche), France, he was educated at the École secondaire libre et Lycée de Tunis; and he studied at the faculties of law and letters, Université de Paris. He was a professor at the universities of Lille, and Caen, 1942-44, and technical counsellor at the Cabinet of Ministers of National Education, 1944-45. After the second World War, he was associated with the Union française and the United Nations. From 1969 to his retirement he was a professor of law successively at the universities of Nanterre and Paris. He died on 16 July 1992. DBFC, 1954/55; IndexBFr² (1); WhoFr, 1953/54-1991/92

Lacher, Jörg, born 5 April 1941 at Wien, he grew up in Bavaria and went to school in Krefeld, Germany. After military service he studied law at the Universität München from 1961 to 1965. A French scholarship enabled him to study French civil and commercial law at the Faculté de droit de Nancy, gaining a *certificat de sciences juridiques* in 1966. In 1967 he entered the judiciary at Köln. In 1968, he received a Dr.jur. from the Universität Köln for *Der Verkauf von Handelsgeschäft und fonds de commerce; vergleichende Darstellung des deutschen und französischen Rechts.* Thesis

La Chesnais, Maurice, fl. 19th cent., he edited the *Journal de campagne de Claude Blanchard* (Paris, 1869). NUC, pre-1956

La Chica Garrido, Margarita, born 20th cent., she was associated with the Facultad de Filosofía y Letras, Universidad de Alicante. Her writings include *Almanzor en las poemas de Ibn Darrāy* (Zaragoza, 1979), and she translated from the Arabic of 'Abd al-Malik Ibn al-Kardabūs, *Historia del Andalus; España musulmana* (Alicante, 1984). Note; ZKO

Lachman, Samuel A., fl. 1969-1975 at Haifa, he was a joint author of *Countermarks of the Ottoman Empire* (London, 1974).

Lachmann, Robert, born 28 November 1892 at Berlin, he studied English, French and Arabic at Berlin and London and received a Dr.phil. in 1923 from the Universität Berlin for *Die Musik in den tunesischen Städten.* During the first World War he served as an interpreter at the prisoner of war camp for Arab and Central Asian soldiers at Wünsdorf near Berlin. After taking his doctorate he was associated with the Staatsbibliothek, Berlin, until 1935, when he emigrated to Jerusalem. His writings include *Musik des Orients* (1929), *Jewish cantillation and song in the Isle of Djerba* (1940), *Die Gesänge der Juden auf der Insel Djerba*, ed. by E. Gerson-Kiwi (1978), and he was a joint editor of *Risāla fī hubr ta'līf al-alhān*, of Ya'qūb ibn Ishāq al-Kindī (1931). He died in Jerusalem on 8 May 1939. Baker, 1978, 1984, 1992 (not sighted); BioHbDtE; DtBilnd (2); JahrDtB, 1928-1934; NDB; New GrDM; Schwarz

Lackany, Radames Sany, born 29 March 1921 at Cairo, he studied engineering at the universities of Alexandria and Manchester, taking a B.Sc. at both institutions. His writings include *Mersa Matruh and its environment* (1960), *The Egyptian Riviera; Sollum and its environment* (1962), *Quelques célèbres Allemands en Égypte* (1971), *Besson Bey, major-général de la flotte* (1989), and *Cerisy Bey, fondateur de l'arsenal d'Alexandrie et constructeur de la première flotte égyptienne* (1989). IntAu&W, 1982

Lackany, Sanny, fl. 1952, he was in 1928 a deputy auditor with the Egyptian State Railway, and a member of the Société Fouad Ier d'économie politique, de statistique et de législation. He was a sometime vice-president in the Cour des Comptes, Cairo. Note; WhoEgypt, 1955-1959

Lackner, Helen, born 20th cent., she was a rural development consultant in London. Her writings include *A House built on sand; the political economy of Saudi Arabia* (1978), and *P.D.R. Yemen, outpost of socialist development in Arabia* (London, 1985). DrBSMES, 1993; EURAMES, 1993

Lacombe, Oliver Auguste, born 2 July 1904 at Liège, Belgium, he graduated from the École normale supérieure, Paris, and received a doctorate in letters and his *agrégation* in philosophy. From 1928 to 1939 he pursued an academic interest in philosophy and orientalism. After a first visit to India, 1935-1936, he went to the University of Ankara, where he became the founding director of its Felsefe Araştırmaları Enstitüsü. He subsequently served as a cultural counsellor with the French diplomatic service in India. Upon his return to France he served in various capacities at the Faculté des lettres de Lille, becoming its dean in 1955. He also held a cross-appointment as *directeur d'études* at the École pratique des hautes études. Since 1959 he was a professor of comparative philosophy at the Faculté des lettres et des sciences humaines in the Université de Paris. His writings include *Au Service de l'homme* (1936), *L'Absolu selon le Védânta* (1937), and *L'Élan spirituel de l'hindouisme* (1986). He died on 2 July 2001. NDNC, 1964; WhoFr, 1979/80-2000/2001

Lacoste, Camille Andrée, 1929- *see* Lacoste-Dujardin, Camille Andrée

Lacoste, Yves Jean Paul, born 7 September 1929 at Fès, Morocco, he studied at the Sorbonne, Paris, taking a doctorate and *agrégation* and subsequently taught there geography until his retirement in 1999. Since 1990 he was a director of the Centre de recherches et d'analyses géopolitiques. His writings include *L'Afrique du nord* (1957), *Les pays sous développés* (1959), its translation, *I paesi sottosviluppati* (1963), *La géographie du sous-développement* (1965), its translation, *Geografia do subdesenvolvimento* (1966), *Ibn Khaldoun; naissance de l'histoire, passé du tiers-monde* (1966), *La géographie, ça sert d'abord à faire la guerre* (s.d.), its Persian translation in 1988, *Questions de géopolitique; l'islam, la mer, l'Afrique* (1988), *De la géopolitique aux paysages; dictionnaire de la géographie* (2003); he was joint author of *L'Algérie, passé et présent; le cadre et les étapes de la constitution de l'Algérie actuelle* (Paris, 1960); and he was a joint editor, with Camille A. Lacoste-Dujardin, of *Maghreb; peuples et civilisations* (1995) as well as a contributor to the Marxist journal *La Presse.* Livres disponibles, 2004; WhoFr, 2004/2005, 2005/2006

Lacoste-Dujardin, Camille Andrée, born 1 March 1929 at Rouen (Seine-maritime), France, she studied at the Sorbonne and the École nationale des langues orientales vivantes, Paris, taking degrees in geography (1954) and Berber language and literature (1961). She was an anthropologist associated with the C.N.R.S. as *directeur de recherches*. He writings include *Bibliographie ethnologique de la Grande Kabylie* (1962), *Le conte kabyle; étude ethnologique* (1970), *Un village algérien; structures et évolution récente* (1976), *Dialogue de femmes et évolution récente* (1977), *Des mères contre les femmes; maternité et patriarcat au Maghreb* (1985), its translation, *Mütter gegen Frauen; Mutterherrschaft im Maghreb* (1990), *Yasmina et les autres de Nanterre et d'ailleurs; filles de parents maghrébines en France* (1992); she edited and translated *Contes merveilleux de Kabylie* (1999); and she was a joint editor of *Maghreb; peuples et civilisations* (1995), and *Femmes et hommes au Maghreb et en immigration; la frontière des genres en question* (1998). EURAMES, 1993; *Livres disponibles*, 2004; Unesco; ZKO

Lacour, Jean Antoine *Armand*, born 19th cent., his writings include *Monographie de la marine française en Algérie* (Alger, 1877), and *L'esclavage africain* (Dunkerque, 1889) as well as contributions to the *Revue maritime et coloniale*. BN; NUC, pre-1956

Lacouture, Jean Marie Gérard, born 9 June 1921 at Bordeaux, he went to school at the Collège de Tivoli, Bordeaux, and studied law at the universities of Bordeaux and Paris, obtaining degrees in law and political science. He started his career in 1945 as a press attaché at Staff Headquarters in Indochina. From 1947 to 1949 he was in the same capacity attached to the Résidence général de France au Maroc. He subsequently spent ten years with a variety of publishing houses. From 1969 to 1972, he was a professor in the Institut d'études politiques de Paris. His writings include *Cinq hommes et la France* (1961), *Algérie, la guerre est finie* (1962); and jointly with Simonne Lacouture, *L'Égypte en mouvement* (1956), and *Le Maroc à l'epreuve* (1958). He was joint author of *Arabes et Israéliens; un premier dialogue* (1974). Au&Wr, 1963; ConAu, 101, new rev., 43, 92; DBF; WhoFr, 1971/72-2005/2006

Lacretelle (Лакретель), Charles Jean Dominique, born 3 September 1766 at Metz (Lorraine), France, he was educated at Nancy, particularly the Académie de Stanislas, where he received an honourable mention for his *Discours sur l'influence de la gloire relativement à l'éducation des princes*. A lawyer since 1784, he established himself in 1787 at Paris, where he collaborated with the publication of the *Encyclopédie par ordre des matières*, a position which brought him in contact with the eminent men of the time, Target, Malesherbes and Maret. The latter procured for him a position at the editorial office of the *Journal des débats*. As a royalist, he was imprisoned for twenty-three months. In prison, and on demand of the publishers Treuttel et Würtz, he wrote his *Précis historique de la Révolution française*, which appeared in five volumes between 1801 and 1806. In the same year Napoléon nominated him member of the Bureau de la presse; in 1810 he became imperial censor. He was an adjunct professor of ancient history and geography and a member of the Académie française. His numerous writings also include *Voyage pittoresque de Constantinople et des rives du Bosphore* (1819), and *Considérations sur la cause des Grecs* (1825). He died in Mâcon (Saône-et-Loire) on 26 March 1855. DBF; EncBrit; EncicUni; EnSlovar; Hoefer; IndexBFr² (5); Vapereau

Sieur de **La Croix**, born between 1630 and 1640. In August 1670 he accompanied the Marquis de Nointel, French ambassador to the Sublime Porte, as his secretary, arriving at Constantinople at the end of October 1670. Until his final return to France in January of 1686, he served under two French ambassadors, accomplishing missions in the Ottoman Empire, as well as reporting to the French Court in person. His writings include *Mémoires contenans diverses relations très-curieuses de l'Empire othoman* (1684), *Guerres des Turcs avec la Pologne, la Moscovie et la Hongrie* (1689), *Etat présent des Nations et Églises grecque, arménienne et maronite en Turquie* (1695), *État général de l'Empire othoman depuis sa fondation jusques à présent* (1695), *La Turquie chrétienne, sous la puissante protection de Louis-le-Grand, protecteur unique du christianisme en Orient, contenant l'état présent des Nations et lises grecque, arménienne et maronite dans l'Empire othoman* (1695), and the translations, *An Account of the Turks wars with Poland, Muscovy and Hungary* (1711), and *Geschichte des osmanischen Reichs* (1772). He died in Paris in 1704. GDU; Michaud; ROMM, 25 (1978), pp. 101-117

de **Lacroix**, Auguste, 1805-1891 *see* Lacroix, Gustave *Auguste* de

Lacroix, Frédéric, born about 1800, he was a geographer whose writings include *Guide du voyageur à Constantinople et dans ses environs* (Paris, 1839), *Question d'Orient* (Paris, 1839), and *Les mystères de la Russie; tableau politique et moral de l'Empire russe* (Bruxelles, 1844), its translation, *Die Mysterien Rußlands* (1845), and he was a joint author of *Projets de chemins de fer et de port dans la province de Constantine, Algérie* (1856). He died in 1864. BN; NUC, pre-1956

de **Lacroix**, Gustave *Auguste*, born 10 June 1805 at Lons-le-Saunier, France, he was a sometime *conseiller de préfecture*, and in 1862 he became adjunct chief at the Ministry of the Interior. His

writings include *De l'État actuel de la littérature et de la librairie en France* (1842), *Histoire privée et politique d'Abd-el-Kader*, publiée sur des notes communiqués par N. Manucci (Paris, 1845), its translation, *Geschichte von Abd-el-Kaders politischem und Privatleben* (Grünberg, 1846), *Les Reines de la nuits* (1869), and *Les Soirées de Saint-Germain* (Paris, 1883) as well as contributions to the Parisian journals, *le Temps*, *l'Époque*, and *le Constitutionnel*. He died on 2 December 1891. BN; GdeEnc; Sezgin

de **Lacroix**, Henri, born 30 August 1844 at the Ilet des Abymes (Grande Terre), Guadaloupe, he graduated from the military École de Saint-Cyr and the École de guerre. He was an active soldier and a brilliant military theoretician, participating in all the campaigns of the period and rising to the rank of general. The battle of Sedan cost him seven months as a German prisoner of war. Thereafter he served in the French colonies, 1875 to 1879 in Algeria. He died in Fleurier, Switzerland, on 30 August 1924. DBF; *Hommes et dsestins*, vol. 2, pp. 429-32; IndexBFr² (1); *Qui êtes-vous*, 1924

Lacroix, Jean Maurice Marc, born 14 May 1919 at Saint-Étienne (Loire), France, he went to school in Rabat and Paris and studied at the École Polytechnique, Paris. From 1942 to 1958 he was associated in various capacities with the Société chérifienne des pétroles. WhoFr, 1969/70-1978/79|

Lacroix, Léon, born 19th cent., he was a pharmacist and associated with the Société de géographie de Lille. His trace is lost after an article in 1884. BN; Note about the author

Lacroix, Louis, 1817-1881 see Lacroix, Pierre *Louis*

Lacroix, Napoléon, born 10 March 1855 at Paris, he enlisted in the army in 1875. He was a graduate of the military college of St-Cyr which he had entered in 1876. As *sous-lieutenant* he participated in the operations in Tunisia (1881), was present at the capture of Kef, and saw action at Ben Bechir and Ben Metir. Since 1883 he had been with the Service des Affaires indigènes de l'Algérie. He was a devoted and competent administrator, and an indefatigable writer and collaborator with other scholarly officers. He held offices in civilian learned institutions, and was awarded a gold medal by the Société de géographie de Paris in 1899. He was the author of *Les Derkaoua d'hier et d'aujourd'hui* (1902), besides being the joint author of *Documents pour servir à l'étude du Nord-Ouest africain* (1894-1897), *Algérie, historique de la pénétration saharienne* (1900), *L'évolution du nomadisme en Algérie* (1906), and *La pénétration saharienne* (1906). He died unexpectedly on 21 March 1910. Peyronnet, 467

Lacroix, Pierre Francis, born 1 May 1924 at Paris, where he was educated at both, the Lycée Carnot and the Lycée Louis-le-Grand. After passing through the École nationale de la France d'outre-mer, 1941-44, he went to the Cameroons where he successively served for six years as a chief of several sub-divisions. In the same capacity he was in Niger from 1952 to 1954. From 1955 to 1957 he was in charge of Muslim affairs in Nord-Cameroun, including the Meccan pilgrimage. In 1957, he received a diploma from the Centre d'études pratiques d'arabe moderne at Bikfaya, Lebanon. In 1958, he was appointed a professor of Peul at the École nationale des langues orientales, Paris, and since 1960, he also taught at the École pratique des Hautes études. In 1964 he received a doctorate in ethnography from the Université de Paris, and served, 1964-65, as a Unesco expect for the transcription of the languages in Niger. His writings include *Poésie peule de l'Adamawa* (1965), and he was a joint author of *Dictionnaire élémentaire fulfulde-français-english* (1971). In 1981 appeared *Itinérances - en pays peul et ailleurs; mélanges réunis par les chercheurs de l'E.R.A. 246 du C.N.R.S. à la mémoire de Pierre Francis Lacroix*. He died in Paris on 6 June 1977. *Hommes et destins*, vol. 5, pp. 311-12; Unesco

Lacroix, Pierre *Louis*, born 8 August 1817 at Paris, he went to school at the Lycée Louis-le-Grand, Paris. In 1836, he entered the École normale supérieure, taking a degree in letters, and an *agrégation* in history. He taught successively at Rennes, Louis-le-Grand, and Henri-IV, Paris. He received a doctorate in 1846 from the Université de Paris for *Recherches sur la religion des Romains d'après les Fastes d'Ovide* and then spent two years at the École française d'Athènes. After six years of school teaching in Paris and Nantes, he was appointed in 1854 a professor of history at the Faculté des lettres de l'Université de Nancy. Since 1864 he served as president of the Académie de Stanislas, Nancy. His writings include *Dix ans d'enseignement historique à la Faculté des lettres de Nancy* (1865). He died in Paris on 13 January 1881. BN; DBF; Note

Ladame, Paul Louis, born 25 June 1842 at Neuenburg (Neuchâtel), Switzerland, he studied medicine at the universities of Zürich, Würzburg, Bern, Paris, Wien and Berlin, taking a Dr.med. in 1866 at Bern for *Symptomatologie und Diagnostik der Hirngeschwülste*. He practised his profession in Canton Neuchâtel and later at Genève. In 1884, he received a Dr.habil. at Genève, where he then taught medical physics and neurology until his retirement in 1908. He was a writer on legal medicine and social health. He died in Genève on 21 October 1919. DtBilnd (2); HisBioLexCH; Note

Ladas, Mrs. Diana Margaret, born 8 February 1913, she graduated from Girton College, Cambridge. Before the second World War, she was a secretary in Genève, Malta and London. During the war, she worked as a Political Warfare executive in Cairo. She subsequently transferred first to UNRRA and later to the British Information Services, New York. Since 1955 she was in the English school system as vice-principal and head mistress. After her retirement she was a volunteer social worker and active in politics. She died on 8 October 2001. Who's who, 1969-2001

Ladd, Daniel, born in 1804 in New Hampshire, U.S.A., he served as a missionary in Turkey from 1836 to 1867. He died in Middlebury, N.H., in 1872. Shavit

Ladd, George Trumbull, born 19 January 1842 at Plainesville, Ohio, a graduate of Western Reserve College, Cleveland, Ohio, and Andower Theological Seminary. He was a pastor for ten years, and for twenty-five years until his retirement in 1906 a professor of philosophy at Yale University. His writings include *Philosophy of religion* (1905). He died in New Haven, Conn., 8 August 1921. DAB; Master (16); Shavit - Asia; WhAm, 1

Ladenson, Mark Lawrence, born 12 December 1941 at Chicago, he graduated in 1963 from the University of Wisconsin, received an M.B.A. in 1965 from the University of Chicago, and his Ph.D. in 1970 from Northwestern University, Evanston, for *Balance of payment of direct foreign investment of American firms*. Since 1974 he was a professor in the Department of Economics, Michigan State University at East Lansing, a post which he still held in 1995. In 1978, he served as a visiting professor of economics at Quaid-i-Azam University, Islamabad, Pakistan. AmM&WSc, 1973 S, 1978 S; NatFacDr, 1990-1995; Note; WhoMW, 1984/85

Ladero Quesada, Miguel Ángel, born about 1940, he received a doctorate in 1967 from the Universidad de Valladolid for *Castilla y la conquista del Reino de Granada*, a work which was published in 1988. He was a professor in the Departamento de Historia Medieval, Facultad de Geografia e Historia, Universidad Complutense de Madrid. His other writings include *Milicia y economía en la guerra de Granada; el cerco de Baza* (1964), *Granada; historia de un país islámico, 1232-1571* (1969), *Los mudéjares de Castilla en tiempos de Isabel I.* (1969), *Las Cruzadas* (1972), *Andalucía en el siglo XV; estudios de historia política* (1973), *El siglo XV en Castilla* (1982), *La España de los cincos reinos, 1085-1369* (1984), and *Granada despuésde la conquista* (1988). Arabismo, 1992, 1994, 1997; ZKO

Ladewig Petersen, Erling, born 1 April 1929, he was a Danish professor of history whose writings include *Historiske tekster til brug for undervisningen i historieforskningens metodelære* (1972), *'Ali and Mu'awiya in early Arabic tradition* (1974), *Veritas et honor regis* (1974), and *De fede år; Odense 1559-1660* (1984). He died on 25 June 2000. Kraks, Register, 2003/4

Ladey de Saint-Germain, born 19th cent., he was associated with the Société bourguignonne de géographie. His writings include *Le château de Montaigu et ses seigneurs* (Dijon, 1901). His trace is lost after an article in 1903. Note about the author

Ladouceur, Paul, born 20th cent., he was in 1975 a programme manager, Multilateral Programmes Branch, Canadian International Development Agency. Note about the author

Ladreit de Lacharrière, Jacques, born 14 June 1881, he studied history and after his degree in letters worked successively at the Bibliothèque de l'Arsenal and the Musée Carnavalet, Paris. During this period he produced remarkable work in nineteenth-century history; but after a mission to Algeria and Tunisia in 1909 his interest shifted to French North Africa. His 1919 award from the Société de géographie for his researches on Morocco caught the attention of Lyautey who entrusted him with the organization of the Moroccan exhibit at the Ghent World Exhibition. A correspondent of *le Temps*, he soon became Moroccan expert at the journal *l'Afrique française*. Since 1926 he taught political science at the École nationale de France d'Outre-mer, and two years later he was appointed to a chair, concurrently lecturing in the Institut colonial of the Faculté des Lettres de Bordeaux. In 1930, he became a member of the Académie des Sciences sociales. In 1957, he was still with the commission of admissions at the Centre de Hautes Études d'Administration Musulmane, Paris. His writings include *Le Rêve d'Abd el Kerim; esquisse d'histoire marocaine* (1925), *Au Maroc en suivant Foucauld* (1932); he was a joint author of *Pour réussir au Maroc* (1912); and he edited *Les Cahiers de Madame de Chateaubriand*, publiés intégralement avec introduction et notes (1909). He died on 26 February 1958. L'Afrique et l'Asie, n° 42 (1958), pp. 76-77; Revue africaine, 103 (1959), p. 168 (not sighted)

Ladrière, Jean, born in 1921, he was a professor of philosophy at the Université de Louvain until his retirement in 1986. On his seventieth and seventy-fifth birthdays he was honoured by jubilee volumes. His writings include *La décision politique en Belgique* (1965), *L'articulation du sens* (1970), its translation, *Language and belief* (1972), *La science, le monde et la foi* (1972), *Les enjeux de la rationalité; le défi de la science et de la technologie aux cultures* (1977), its translation, *The Challenge* *presented to cultures by science and technology* (1977), *Fondements d'une théorie de la justice* (1984), *L'Éthique dans l'univers de la rationalité* (1997), and *Le temps du possible* (2004). In 2002 appeared *La responsabilité de la raison; hommage à Jean Ladrière à l'occasion de son 80e anniversaire* (2002). Note about the author

de **Laet**, Johannes (Jean), born in 1582 or 1593 at Antwerpen (Anvers) into a Calvinist family, he entered history in 1617 with his *Commentarius de Pelagianis et Semipelagianis* published in Harderwijk. He was in 1618 and 1619 a member of the Synod of Dordrecht and, since 1621 he was associated with the newly established Westindische Compagnie, a post which afforded him time to collaborate with the publication of the Elzevir *Republicae*, a geographical series of forty-eight volumes, covering many a country. He supplied the following parts: *Hispania sive de regis Hispaniae regnis et opibus commentarius* (1629), *Galliae sive de Francorum regisdominiis et opibus commentarius* (1629), *Belgii Confoederati respublica* (1630), *Turcici Imperii status seu discursus varii de rebus Turcicis* (1630), *De imperio Magni Mongolis sive India vera commentata* (1630) - a work which was published in an English translation in 1928 and 1975 entitled, *The Empire of the Great Mogol*, and *A Contemporary Dutch chronicle of Mughal India* (1957) - *Persia vera seu regni status* (1633), *Portugallia seu de illius regnis et opibus commentarius* (1642), and *Respublica Poloniae, Lithuaniae, Prussiae et Livoniae* (1642). He died in Leiden in 1649. BiBenelux² (12); BioNBelg; GdeEnc; Master (1); NieuwNBW, vol. 8, cols. 991-92

de **Lafargue**, Max, born 19th cent., he was in 1910 a lieutenant in the 3e Spahis, and in 1914 he was assigned to the commander of the 1er Groupe d'aviation at Dijon. Note about the author

Lafaye, Jacques, born 20th cent., his writings include *Les conquistadores* (Paris, 1964), *Quetzalcóatl et Guadaloupe; la formation de la conscience nationale au Mexique* (1974), its English translation in 1976, and he edited *Histoire de la mission des pères capucins en l'isle de Maragnan et terres circonvoisins*, by Father Claude d'Abbeville (1963). NUC

de **La Faye**, Jean Baptiste, born 17th cent., he was a Jesuit whose writings include *État des Royaumes de Barbarie, Tripoly, Tunis et Alger; contenant l'histoire naturelle & politique de ces pais, la manière dont les Turcs y traitent les esclaves, come on les rachète, & diverses aventures curieuses, avec la tradition de l'Église pour le rechat ou le soulagement des captifs* (Rouen, 1703), its translation, *Allerneuester Zustand der Afrikanischen Königreiche Tripoli, Tunis und Algier, von einem gelehrten Jesuiten* (Hamburg, 1709), *Voyage pour la redemption des captifs aux royaumes d'Alger et de Tunis fait en 1720* (Paris, 1721), and its translation, *A Voyage to Barbary for the redemption of captives, performed in 1720*, by the Mathurin-Trinitarian fathers, Fran. Comelin, Philemon de la Motte, and Jos. Bernard (London, 1735). BN; NUC, pre-1956; Sezgin

Laffin, John Alfred Charles, born 21 September 1922 at Sydney, he was educated at the University of London. He taught at Mayfield College, Sussex, from 1959 to 1969, when he became a full-time writer, journalist, novelist, and broadcaster. His writings include *Boys in battle* (1966), *The Hunger to come* (1966), *Women in battle* (1967), *Anatomy of captivity* (1968), *Devil's Goad* (1970), *The Fedayeen; the Arab-Israeli dilemma* (1973), *The Arab mind considered* (1975), *The Dagger of Islam* (1979), its translation, *Islam; Weltbedrohung durch Fanatismus* (1980), *Damn the Dardanelles! The Story of Gallipoli* (1980), *The War of desperation, Lebanon, 1982-85* (1985), and *War annual; a guide to contemporary wars and conflicts* (1986-87). He died in 2002. ConAu, 53-56, new rev., 7, 23; IntAu&W, 1976-2004; WhoWor, 1976/77-1984; WrDr, 1976/78-2004

de **Lafitte-Clavé**, Jean, born in 1750, he was sent in 1783 to Turkey, where he participated in the war against Russia as a commander of a Turkish army corps. Upon his return to France, he became a colonel and director of the fortifications of Valenciennes (Nord). In 1792, he was a commander of the Engineers of the Armies of the North, participated in the Belgian campaign, and was subsequently assigned to the Army of the Pyrénées-Orientales, where he accomplished important services. But he was also included in a writ of attachment issued to twenty generals. When his innocence was proven he was promoted in 1793 to the rank of lieutenant general as indemnity. But he had died in the same year before the news could reach him. His writings include *Mémoire militaire sur la frontière du Nord* (1779), *Mémoire militaire sur la frontière de Flandre et de Hainaut depuis le mer jusqu'à la Meuse, c'est-à-dire depuis Dunkerque jusqu'à Charlemont* (Basle, 1797), and the two-volume work in Turkish (but not listed in Özege's *Eski harflerle basılmış Türkçe eserler kataloğu*), *Traité élémentaire de castramétation et de fortification passagère*, published in 1787 at Pera, and destined for use in the school established by the author in Turkey. GDU; ZKO

Lafont, F. D., born 19th cent., he wrote *L'Agriculture* (Paris, 1906), *La Lutte contre les insectes et autres ennemis de l'agriculture* (Paris, 1907), he was a joint author of *L'Industrie séricicole en Perse* (Montpellier, 1910), and a contributor to periodicals. His trace is lost after an article in 1914. BN

Laforgue, Pierre, born about 1900, he was in 1928 an *agent principal de classe exceptionelle* in the *Services civils* in French West Africa. In 1943, he was adminstrator-in-chief of the Colonies. He was a sometime lecturer at the Centre d'études musulmanes de Mauritanie. Note about the author

Lafuente y Alcántara, Emilio, born in 1825 at Archidona (Málaga), Spain, he participated in the Spanish campaigns in Africa of 1859 and 1860. He was an Arabist and historian. He was a member of the Academia de la Historia and an archivist and director of the Biblioteca de San Isidro. His writings include *Inscriptiones árabes de Granada* (1859), and *Catálogo de los códices arábigos adquiridos en Tetuan* (1862). He died on 3 June 1868. EncicUni; IndiceE³ (3); Manzaranes, pp. 168-172

Lafuente y Alcántara, Miguel, born 10 July 1817 at Archidona (Málaga), Spain, he studied law at Granada and was elected a deputy for Archidona at the Cortes in 1846. In the following year he was elected to the Academia de la Historia. In 1849, he went to Cuba as a fiscal officer. His writings include *Historia de Granada* (1843-46), and *El libro del viajero en Granada* (1843). He died in La Habana on 27 August 1850. EncicUni; IndiceE³ (4); Manzaranes, pp. 173-174

Lafuente Vidal, José, fl. 1930-1959, he was associated with the Museo Arqueológico Provincial de Alicante, Spain. His writings include *El Castillo de Santa Bárbara de Alicante; breve historia, plano y guía* (Alicante, 1952), *Las ruinas de la antigua Lucentum, la Alicante de hace veinte siglos* (Alicante, 1954), and *Breve historia documentada de Alicante en la edad antigua* (1957). Note about the author

Lagadec, Jean, born 20th cent., he was in 1978 a barrister in the Cour de Paris, and associated with the Association internationale des juristes démocrates. His writings include *Le Nouveau guide pratique du droit* (1994), and *Guide du droit de famille* (1999). Livres disponibles, 2004; Note

Lagarde, Michel, born 20th cent., he was a member of the Pères blancs whose writings include *L'Influence d l'arabe sur la langue bambara* (Falajé, Mali, Centre d'étude de langue Bambara, 1988), *Index du grand commentaire de Fahr al-Dīn al-Rāzī = al-Misbāh al-munīr lil-tafsīr al-kabīr* (1996), and he edited and translated from the Arabic of 'Abd al-Qādir al-Jazā'irī, *Le Livre des haltes* (Leiden, Brill, 2000-2002). Note about the author

de **Lagarde**, Paul Anton, born Paul A. Bötticher on 2 November 1827 at Berlin, he studied theology and Oriental languages at the Universität Berlin where he received a Dr.phil. in 1849 for *Initia chromatologiae Arabicae*. Adopted by a great aunt in 1854, he took her family name de Lagarde. In 1869, he succeeded Heinrich Ewald in the chair of Oriental languages at the Universität Göttingen, even though he never wanted to be nor claimed to be an Orientalist. He was a Biblical scholar who in his researches into the textual criticism of the Bible did not neglect the Arabic versions. He was a man inspired by late romanticism, rebelling against the materialism of the time, and striving for a conservative nationalism. Throughout his life he suffered from sensitivity for lack of recognition. His writings include *Die vier Evangelien arabisch, aus der Wiener Handschrift herausgegeben* (1864), *Armenische Studien* (1877), *Aus dem deutschen Gelehrtenleben* (1880), and *Übersicht über die im Aramäischen, Arabischen und Hebräischen ursprüngliche Bildung der Nomina* (1889-91). He died in Göttingen on 22 December 1891. Eduard Platzhoff-Lejeune wrote *Paul de Lagarde* (1903). BiD&SB; BioIn, 6; DtBE; DtBIlnd (14); EncTR; Fück, p. 244; GV; LuthC 75 (not sighted); NDB; *Der Orient* (Potsdam), 1937, pp. 41-45; OxGerm, 1976, 1986

Lagardère, Vincent, born 20th cent., he was a specialist in the history of the Muslim West and of the Mediterranean, particularly in the 11th-12th centuries. His writings include *Les Almoravides jusqu'au règne de Yūsuf B. Tāšfīn, 1039-1106* (Paris, 1991), a work which was originally submitted as a doctoral thesis to the Université de Bordeaux III. His other writings include *Le vendredi de Zallāqa; 23 octobre 1086* (1989), and *Campagnes et paysans d'al-Andalus, VIII-XV siècle* (1993), *Histoire et société en occident musulman au moyen âge; analyse du Mi'yār d'al-Wansarīsī* (Madrid, 1995), and *Les Almoravides; le djihâd anadolou, 1106-1143* (Paris, 1999). Livres disponibles, 2004; Note; ZKO

Lageman, Bernhard, born in 1948, he studied economics, particulalry socio-economic changes in Africa and underdeveloped countries. After gaining a Dr.oec. in 1977 from the Hochschule für Ökonomie, Berlin, for *Von der "bedarfs-" zur "beschäftigungsorientierten" Bildungsplanung; eine kritische Auseinandersetzung mit den in afrikanischen Staaten praktizierten Bildungsprogrammen*, he became a staff member in the Institut für Entwicklungsforschung, Ruhr-Universität, Bochum. His writings include *Wirtschaftswandel im Sudan; Ursprünge wirtschaftlicher Dynamik und Stagnation in einem arabisch-afrikanischen Entwicklungsland, 1898-1985* (1989), and he was a joint author of *Arabische Integrationsexperimente; der Sudan* (1980), and its translation, *Arab economic intergration, which way?* His later writings focus on the political economy of Eastern Europe. GV; Note

Lagerqvist, Lars Olof, born 8 February 1929 at Stockholm, he received degrees in 1952 and 1961 at Stockholm. He was a historian and numismatist, and a sometime director of the Statens Historisk

Museum, Stockholm. He retired in 1993. His writings include *Sverige och dess regenter under 1000 år* (1976), and he was a joint author of *Mynt och medaljer, och annan numismatik* (1960), and *Kungengräver; en bok om arkeologer och arkeologi* (1972). Vem är det, 1974-2001; WhoWor, 1978/79 (not sighted)

de **Laget**, Paul, born in 1883, he was a lawyer and a member of the Sociéte de géographie de Marseille. His writings include *Au Maroc espagnol* (Marseille, 1935), and *Le Château d'If; son histoire, ses prisonniers* (Saint-Étienne, 1956). Note about the author; NUC, pre-1956

Laging Tobias, Philip Franz, born in 1834 at Zwolle, the Netherlands, he entered in 1855 the Koloniaal Werfdepôt and arrived on 31 January 1856 at Batavia. He served to 29 December 1865, when he received an honoray discharge with the rank of first lieutenant. He then served as an administrator in the Netherlands' East Indies where he was from 1882 to 1886 governor of Atjeh. He retired to Nijmegen. His writings include *Phrasen en feiten; toelichting op "Mijne ervaring van Atjeh," door A. Pruys van der Hoeven* (Amsterdam, 1886). Brinkman's, 1882-1891; Wie is dat, 1902

de **La Gorce**, Paul Marie, born 10 November 1928 at Paris, where he was educated and received a doctorate in political science. He was a newspaper correspondent and editor, and a technical counsellor to successive French governments, a broadcaster and televison commentator. His writings include *La République et son armée* (1963), *Clausewitz et la stratégie moderne* (1964), *De Gaulle entre deux mondes* (1964), *La France pauvre* (1965), *La France contre les empires* (1969), and *Requiem pour les révolutions* (1990). He died on 1 December 2004. WhoFr, 1990/91-2004/2005

de **La Gorce**, Pierre François Gustave, born 29 June 1846 at Vannes (Morbihan), France, into a royalist and Catholic family, strongly attached to the *Ancien Régime*, he received an austere education, first in the north of France, where he spent his childhood, and later at Paris, where he received his doctorate in law in 1870 for *De la condition juridique des aliénés et des prodigues en droit romain et en droit français*. He started a promising public legal career successively at Rocroi, Montreuil, Béthune, and Saint-Omer, but under the decrees of 29 March 1880 he was dismissed. For some time he was a lawyer at S.-Omer, but his vocation was elsewhere. He became a historian of French history whose writings include *Histoire de la Second République française* (1887), *Histoire du Second Empire* (1887), *Histoire religieuse de la Révolution française* (1909-1923), *La Restauration* (1926-28), and *La conquête de l'Algérie* (1934). Elected to the Académie des sciences morales et politiques in 1907, he entered the Académie française in 1914, succeeding Thureau-Dangin. He died in Paris on 2 January 1934. Curinier (not sighted); DBF; IndexBFr² (2); Qui est-ce, 1934; Qui êtes-vous, 1924

Lagourgue, Domitille Claire Marie-Pierre, born 27 September 1963 at Saint-Quentin (Aisne), she was educated locally and received degrees from the École supérieure de commerce et de gestion de Paris, and the Institut national des lettres et civilisations orientales. She was a journalist who spent from 1986 to 1988 in Pakistan and Afghanistan. In 1991, she became a joint founder and director of the humanitarian organization, *Mission enfance*, Monaco. Her writings include *Espoir, j'écris ton nom* (1997), and she was a joint author of *Paona, une orpheline dans la tourmente roumaine* (1991). Who's who in France, 1997/98-2004/2005

de **Lagoy**, Louis *Roger* Xavier de Meyran, marquis, born 14 July 1790 at Saint-Rémy-de-Provence (Bouches-du-Rhône), France, he belonged to a noble family distinguished in arts and letters. His writings include *Description de quelques monnaies Mérovingiennes découverte en Provence* (1839), *Mélanges de numismatique, médailles inédites grecques, gauloises, romaines et du moyen-âge* (1845), and *Recherches numismatiques sur l'armement et les instrument de guerre des Gaulois* (1849). He died on 16 April 1860. DBF

Lagrange, Léon Marius, born 6 May 1828 at Marseille, he was a graduate of the Collège Charlemagne. He decided to forgo a legal career for painting, travelling to Italy, Egypt and Asia Minor. His writings include *Pierre Puget, peintre, sculpteur, architecte, décorateur de vaisseaux* (Paris, 1868) as well as contributions to the *Gazette des beaux-arts*. He died in Nice on 14 January 1868. Dantès 1; NUC, pre-1956; Vapereau

de **La Guérivière**, Jean Baptiste Joseph Marie Dupin, born 7 August 1937 at Paris, he was educated at Sarlat, Versailles, and Paris, where he received a *bachelier* in law. He spent years with *le Monde* at the foreign service desk. He was a correspondent successively at Alger and Bruxelles, from 1982 to 1996, when he became a free-lance journalist. His writings include the novel, *Hélène retrouvée* (1961), *Voyage à l'intérieur de l'eurocratie* (1992), *Les fous d'Afrique* (2001), *Exploration de l'Afrique noire* (2002), and *Amère Méditerranée* (2004). Livres disponibles, 2004; WhoFr, 2005/2006

Lagumina, Bartolomeo, born 14 July 1850 at Palermo, Italy, he had studied Arabic under Salvatore Cusa at Palermo. He became a bishop of Agrigento, Sicily, and pursued an interest in epigraphy and numismatics. His writings include *Il falso codice arabo-siculo della Biblioteca nazionale di Palermo* (1882), *Codice diplomatico dei giudei di Sicilia* (1884-95), *Catalogo delle monete arabe esistenti nella Bibliotheca comunale di Palermo* (1892), he edited *Il Libro della palma di Abu Hātim as-Siğistānī* (1891), and he was a joint editor of *La Cronaca siculo saracena di Cambridge con doppio testo greco* (1890). He died in Agrigento on 2 November 1931. DizBI; EncItaliana; Fück, p. 187; IndBiltal (3); ZKO

Laguna, Antonio Iglesias, 1927-1972 *see* Iglesias Laguna, Antonio

Lagus, Vilhelm (Wilhelm) *Gabriel*, born in 1837, he received a doctorate and subsequently taught at schools in Borgå (Porvoo), Finland., and Viborg. He was a historian of literature who succeeded A. Herman A. Kellgren in the chair of Oriental literature at Helsingfors' Universitet on 7 February 1857. His writings include *Den finsk-svenska litteraturens utveckling* (Borgå, 1866-67), and *Lärokurs i Arabiska Språket* (1869-78). He died in 1896. EncFen; ScBInd (1); Stenij, pp. 272, 284, 290; *Svensk uppslagsbok* (Malmö, 1963-64); Uusi

Lahache, Jean Antoine Étienne, born 13 July 1859 at Bruyère (Vosges), France, he was a pharmacist since 1884 and served with the rank of major successively at the hospitals of the Division de Constantine, Algeria, at Versailles and at Bourbonnes. He received a doctorate in pharmacy in 1900 from the Université de Paris for *Étude hydrologique sur le Sahara français oriental*. A member of the Société de pharmacie since 1899, and the Société nationale d'agriculture since 1904, he was awarded *chevalier* of the Légion d'honneur. His writings include *Le sel, le natron et les eaux de la région du Tchad* (1911), and he was a joint author of *La graine de coco épurée* (1912), and *Manuel des dames infirmières chargées dans les hôpitaux d'administrer les médicaments* (1916). IndexBFr² (2)

Lahaye, Rémy, born 20th cent., he received a doctorate in law in 1961 from the Université de Rabat for *Les entreprises publiques au Maroc; essai d'analyse des formes d'action médiate de la puissance publique*. BN, 1960-69; NUC, 1956-72

Lahbabi, Mohamed Aziz, born 22 or 25 December 1923 at Fès, Morooco, he was a graduate of l'École national des langues orientales vivantes, and the Sorbonne, Paris. Thereafter he was successively attached to the CNRS, and a professor of philosophy at the universities of Rabat and Alger. He was a prolific writer whose works have been translated into many languages and include *Le gouvernement marocain à l'aube du XXe siècle* (1957). He was widely acclaimed and was the recipient of numerous awards and distinctions. He died about 1994. *IRCICA newsletter* no. 33 (March 1994), p. 12; Unesco; WhoWor, 1974/75, 1976/77

Lahner, Lothar, born about 1940, he received a Dr.rer.nat. in 1970 from the Universität Erlangen for *Geologische Untersuchungen an der Westflanke des mittleren Amanos, Süd-Türkei*. He was a geologist with the German Federal Bureau of Geology and Mineral Resources. His writings include *Malaysia und Brunei* (1982). Schwarz; ZKO

Lahrkamp, Helmut, born 20th cent., he received a Dr.phil. in 1949 from the Universität Münster for *Ferdinand von Fürstenberg in seiner Bedeutung für die Geschichtsforschung seiner Zeit*. He was a local historian whose writings include *Der Friedenskongreß zu Münster im Spiegel der Ratsprotokolle* (1962). *Münsters Bevölkerung um 1685* (1972), *Beiträge zur Stadtgeschichte* (1984), *Beiträge zur neueren Stadtgeschichte* (1987), and *Münsters Rolle im Dreißigjährigen Krieg* (1998). GV

Laidlaw, Karen Anne, born 27 August 1949 at Akron, Ohio, she graduated in 1971 from Ohio Wesleyan University and received her Ph.D. in 1976 from Bowling Green (Ohio) State University for *A Comparative study of civilian and military rule in Peru, 1963-1974; implications for economic development*. She was a professor of sociology at Indiana University Northwest at Gary, Ind. She jointly wrote with Edward Grant Stockwell, *Third World development; problems and prospects* (1981). She died in 1979. AmM&WSc, 1978 S; LC

de **Laiglesia**, Antonio Carlos, his writings include *Breve estudio sobre las tribus moras de Mauritania* (Madrid, Istituto Hispano-Arabe de Cultura, 1985). ZKO

Laignel-Lavastine, Paul Marie *Maxime*, born 12 September 1875 at Évreux (Eure), France, he was a brilland student at school and at university, where he trained as a physician under eminent specialists. He received his medical doctorate in 1903, and his *agrégation* in psychiatry in 1910. Mobilized in 1914, he participated in the Artois and Somme campaigns before becoming head of the Centre de Psychonévrosés of the military government of Paris in 1915. After the war, he became head of the Hôpital Laennec. At the Faculté de médecine de Paris he held the chair of history of medicine, 1931-1939, and of clinical mental illness, 1940-1943. He was one of the great physicians of his time; his writings include *Histoire générale de la médecine, de la pharmacie, de l'art dentaire et de l'art vétérinaire* (1936). He died in Paris on 5 September 1953. BioIn, 3 (2); DBFC, 1954/55, Nécrologie; *Dictionnaire national des contemporains*, 1936

Laing, Alexander Gordon, born in 1793 or 94 at Edinburgh, he was educated by his father, who was a private teacher of classics, and at Edinburgh University. In 1811, he went to Barbados as a clerk and later obtained an ensigncy in the York Light Infantry. He was employed in the West Indies, and in 1822 was promoted to a company in the Royal Africa Corps. In that year, while with his regiment in Sierra Leone, he was sent by the governor to Mandino country, with the double object of opening up commerce and endeavouring to abolish slavery in that region. Later in the same year he visited Falaba and ascertained the source of the Rokell. He endeavoured to reach the source of the Niger, but was stopped by the natives. After active service in the Ashanti War of 1823-24, he was sent home. The secretary for the colonies then instructed captain Laing to undertake a journey, via Tripoli and Timbuktu, to further elucidate the hydrography of the Niger basin. He left England in February 1825 and on 16 July he started to cross the Sahara, being accompanied by a sheikh who was subsequently accused of planning his murder. Ghadames was reached in October, and in December he was in the Tuat territory, where he was well received by the Tuareg. In January 1826 he left for Timbuktu. His caravan suffered from fever and the plundering by Tuareg, Laing being wounded in the fighting. He reached the city on 18 of August and stayed despite the insecurity of his position until 21 September, intending two leave Timbuktu in three days' time. No further news was received from him. From native information it was ascertained that he left the city as planned and was murdered on the night of the 26th of September 1826. His papers were never recovered. His writings include *Travels in the Timanee, Kooranko, and Soolima countries in western Africa* (1825), and *The Letters of Major Alexander G. Laing, 1824-26* (1964). Albert Bonnel de Mézières wrote *Le Major A. Gordon Laing (Tombouctou, 1826); textes et documents nouveaux découverts à Tombouctou et Araouan* (1912). BioIn, 9; DcAfHi; DNB; EncBrit; GdeEnc; GDU; Henze; EncItaliana; Kornrumpf², vol. 2; Kronrumpf, N; LexAfrika; Master (2); WhWE; ZKO

Laing, Ellen Mae Johnston, born in 1934, she graduated in 1954 from the University of Missouri at Columbia, received her M.A. in 1956 from the University of Wisconsin at Madison, and her Ph.D. in 1967 from the University of Michigan at Ann Arbor for *Scholars and sages; a study in Chinese figure painting*. She was a professor of art and art history successively at Wayne State University, Detroit, Mich., and the University of Oregon at Eugene. Her writings include *Chinese paintings in Chinese publications, 1956-1968; an annotated bibliography and index to the paintings* (1969), *The winking owl; art in the People's Republic of China* (1988), *An index to reproductions of paintings by twentieth century Chinese artists* (1998), and she edited *Art and aesthetics in Chinese popular prints; selections from the Muban Foundation Collection* (2002). DrAS, 1974 H, 1978 H, 1982 H; NatFacDr, 1990

Laing, Samuel, born 12 December 1810 at Edinburgh, he graduated in 1827 from St John's College, Cambridge, was elected a fellow, and remained at Cambridge temporarily as a coach. He was called to the bar in 1837 and became private secretary to the president of the Board of Trade. In 1842, he became secretary to the railway department, and retained this post until 1847. An authority on railway operation, he was in 1848 appointed chairman and managing director of the London, Brighton & South Coast Railway. In 1852, he entered Parliament, and in 1859, he was appointed financial secretary to the Treasury; in 1860, he was made finance minister in India, returning to England in 1865. He later served as chairman of the Railway Debenture Tust and the Railway Share Trust. In later life he became well known as an author whose writings include *Modern science and modern thought* (1885), *Problems of the future* (1889), and *Human origins* (1892). He died in Sydenham on 6 August 1897. BiD&SB; Boase; BritInd (10); Buckland; DNB, vol. 22, supplement; EncBrit

Laissus, Yves, born 20th cent., his writings include *Les naturalistes français en Amérique du Sud, XVIe-XIXe siècles* (1995), and he was a joint author of *La découverte de l'Égypte* (1997), *Bonaparte et les savants français en Égypte, 1798-1801* (1998), and *L'Egypte, une aventure savante avec Bonaparte, Kléber, Menou, 1798-1809* (1998). Livres disponibles, 2004; ZKO

Laitman, Leon, born 20th cent., his writings include *Tunisia today; crisis in North Africa* (New York, 1954). He was in 1974 a member of the American Economic Association. Master

de La Jonquière, A., Vicomte, born 19th cent., his writings include *Histoire de l'Empire ottoman, depuis les origines jusqu'au traité de Berlin* (Paris, 1881), a second edition of which was published in 1914 also in Paris. BN

Lake, Kirsopp, born in 1872 at Southampton, England, he graduated in 1895 from Lincoln College, Oxford. He was a sometime curate of St. Mary the Virgin, Oxford, a cataloguer of Greek manuscripts at the Bodleian Library, and a professor of New Testament studies at the universities of Leiden, Boston, and Cambridge, Mass. In 1926 he married Silva New, who had been his student. In 1937 appeared *Quantulacumque; studies presented to Kirsopp Lake by pupils, colleagues and friends*. He died in 1946. DAB; DNB; Master (5); Shavit; WhAm, 1

Lake, Silva (Tipple) née New, born 18 March 1898 at New Haven, Conn., she graduated in 1924 from the University of Vermont. In 1926, she married her professor, Kirsopp Lake, and in 1934, received her Ph.D. from Brown University. She frequently went on archaeological expeditions to Turkey. She was a professor of archaeology and palaeography at Occidental College, Los Angeles, and also assisted her husband in writing *An introduction to the New Testament* (1937), and edited with him *Six collations of New Testament manuscripts* (1932). DAB; DrAS, 4th ed. (1963), vol. 1; WhE&EA

Lalive d'Epinay, Jean Flavien, born 1 May 1915 at La Chaux-de-Fonds, he was educated at the Université de Genève, Fletcher School of Law and Diplomacy, Medford, Mass., and Harvard and Columbia universities. He received a doctorate in law in 1941 from the Université de Genève for *Le droit de la neutralité et le problème des crédits consentis par les neutres aux belligérants*. He started his career as an attorney at Genève, followed by administrative positions with the International Red Cross and international legal organizations at Genève and den Haag. His writings include *Tibet and the Chinese People's Republic; a report to the International Commission of Jurists* (1960). He died about 1993. IntWW, 1989-1992/93|; WhoSwi, 1978/79-1992/93; WhoWor, 1974/75, 1976/77

Lalive d'Epinay, Pierre A., born 8 October 1923 at La Chaux-de-Fonds, he was educated at the Université de Genève and Cambridge University. After bar admission, he became successively a professor of law, director and dean at the Université de Genève as well as a senior partner in a private law firm. He received honorary doctorates from the universities of Lyon, Paris, and Bruxelles. His writings include *Réflections sur l'état et ses contrats internationaux* (1976). In 1993 appeared *Études de droit international en en l'honneur de Pierre Lalive*. IntWW, 1989-2005; WhoSwi, 1988/89-1992/93; WhoWor, 1974/75, 1976/77

Lallemand, Charles, born 19th cent., he was a French mining engineer with a strong interest in Asian geography, and a member of the Comité de l'Asie française since the early years of the twentieth century. He died in 1938. L'Asie française, 38 (1938), p. 138

Laloë, Francis, born 19th cent., he was in 1911 a judge in the Mixed Tribunal at Cairo, and in 1916, a counsellor in the Mixed Court of Appeal at Alexandria and Cairo, and a member of the Société sultanieh d'économie politique, de statistique et de législation. His writings include *Observations sur la compétence des conseils du guerre de l'armée de terre* (Paris, 1894). BN; Note; NUC, pre-1956

Laloire, Marcel, born 2 December 1903 at Uccle (Ukkel), Belgium, he studied at the Université catholique de Louvain, where he also received a doctorate in law. He held ministerial positions, served as a barrister in the Court of Appeal, Bruxelles, and taught at the École sociale de Louvain as well as the École catholique de service social de Bruxelles. In 1957, he served as a an expert to the Inter-office of Labour in Jordan and Syria. His writings include *Le Corporatisme* (1931), *L'Artisanat et la petite industrie* (1947), *De ondernemingsraden* (1949), and *Savoir vivre et morale des affairs* (1956). Le Livre bleu (Bruxelles, 1950); WhoBelgium, 1957/58; Who's who in Belgium and Luxemburg, 1962

La Mairesse, Pierre Eugène, born 14 July 1817 at Châlons-sur-Marne, France, he graduated from the École Polytechnique, Paris, and in 1840 became an enginer of *ponts et chaussée*. In 1865, he became a chief engineer employed in hydrology, particularly draining. Since 1867 he served in the same capacity in Algeria, where he was involved in the construction of ports and dams. He published several studies on Algeria, the Trans-Saharan railway project as well as on the role of the French in Africa. He was a competent linguist in his own right, including Arabic which he spoke fluently. His writings include *Manuel de drainage* (1853), *L'Inde après le Buddha* (1892), *La Vie du Bouddha suivie du Bouddhisme dans l'Indo-Chine* (1892), *Le Japon, histoire, religion, civilisation* (1892), *Vie de Mahomet* (1897-1898) as well as a translation of *Rawzat al-safā'* of Mīr Khwānd. BN; IndexBFr² (1); NUC, pre-1956

Lamare, Pierre, fl. 20th cent., he received a doctorate in 1936 from the Université de Paris for *Recherches géologiques dans les Pyrénées basques d'Espagne*. His writings include *Le pays basque - français et espagnol* (1926), its translation *The French and Spanish Basque country* (1928), *Structure géologique de l'Arabie* (1936), and *La feuille de Bayonne au 50.000e; son cadre morphologique et ses caractères géologiques* (1962). NUC

de **Lamarinière**, Louise, born about 1780 in France, she was for many years a governess at the court of 'Abbas Mirza as well as Fath Ali Shah, educating some of the young Persian princes, among them Malik Qasim. She died at the age of sixty after travelling from Isfahan to Shiraz, on 21 August 1840. Ausland, 14 (1841), p. 111

Lamarque, Jean *Maximilien* or Maximien, born 22 July 1770 at Saint-Sever (Landes), France, he was an army officer and military historian who retired with the rank of lieutenant general. His writings include *Mémoire sur les advantages d'un canal de navigation parallèle à l'Adour considéré sous le* *rapport agricole, commercial et militaire* (1825), and *Mémoires et souvenirs de général Maximilian Lamarque publiés par sa famille* (1835). He died in Paris on 1 June 1832. DBF; Master (2)

de **La Martinière** Poisson, Maximilian Antoine Cyprien *Henri*, born 18 July 1859, he was sent on a mission to Morocco (1887-91), attached to the Government of Algeria (1891), served as consul general at Tanger (1898), Warszawa (1903), Budapest (1904), was made deputy head of the Cabinet of ministers at Affaires étrangères (1906), and in 1907 was French minister at Tehran. His writings include *Morocco; journeys in the Kingdom of Fez and to the Court of Mulai Hassan* (1889), *Notice sur le Maroc* (1897), *Souvenirs du Maroc* (1919), and he was a joint author of *Documents pour servir à l'étude du nord ouest africain* (Alger, 1894-97). He died in 1922. NUC, pre-1956; Qui êtes-vous, 1924

Lamb, Alastair, born in 1930, he wrote *Britain and Chinese Central Asia; the road to Lhasa, 1767-1905* (1960), *The McMahon Line; a study in the relations between India, China and Tibet, 1904 to 1914* (1966), *Asian frontiers; studies in a continuing problem* (1968), *Tibet, China & India, 1914-1950; a history of imperial diplomacy* (1989), and *Kashmir, a disputed legacy, 1846-1990* (1991). ZKO

Lamb, Harold Albert, born in 1892 at Alpine, N.J., he graduated in 1916 from Columbia University, New York, after paving his way through college by writing fiction. He subsequently worked for some time in the financial and foreign news departments of New York newspapers. During the first World War he served as a private in the U.S. Army. In later years he was lured away from American fiction by the Chinese, Mongolian and Arabic chronicles and tempted to write only historical stories of Central Asia. Since his youth he was haunted by the name of Genghis Khan. He was one of the founders of the American Friends of the Middle East. His writings include *Genghis Khan, the Emperor of all men* (1927), its translation, *Dschingis Khan, Beherrscher der Erde* (1928), *Tamerlane, the earth shaker* (1928), *The Crusades* (1930-31), *Omar Khayyam; a life* (1934), its translation, *Omar Chajjam; das abenteurliche Leben des persischen Dichters und Astronomen* (1939), *The March of the Barbarians* (1941), *Alexander of Macedon* (1946), *Constantinople; birth of an empire* (1957), and *Cyrus the Great* (1960). He died on 9 April 1962. ConAu, 89-92, 101; Master (28), Note, WfAm, 4; WhE&EA

Lamba, Henri Gustave, born 1 January 1862 at Paris, he was educated at the Collège Stanislas, Paris, and subsequently took a doctorate in law. He was a sometime professor of law at Cairo as well as a legal counsellor at the League of Nations Secretariat, Genève. His writings include *Dictionnaire des codes égyptiens mixtes* (1888), *De l'évolution de la condition juridique des Européens en Égypte* (1896), *Droit public et administratif de l'Égypte* (1909), and *Code administratif égyptien* (1911). Qui êtes-vous, 1924; NUC, pre-1956

Lambdin, Thomas Oden, born 31 October 1927 at Frederick, Md., he graduated in 1948 from Franklin and Marshall College, Lancaster, Pa., and received his Ph.D. in 1952 from Johns Hopkins University, Baltimore, Md. for *Egyptian loan words and transcriptions in the ancient Semitic languages*. He was successively a professor at Johns Hopkins University and Harvard University. His writings include *Introduction to Biblical Hebrew* (1971), and *Introduction to Sahidic Coptic* (1983). WhoAm, 1974-1982

Lambert, Alexis, born 19th cent., his writings include *La Bourse à la portée de tout le monde; étude générale des opérations de Bourse* (Lyon, 1885). BN

Lambert, André, born about 1900, he was an agronomist from the I[nstitut] N[ational d']A[griculture], Paris. He was a sometime inspector at the Crédit foncier de France and, in 1943, served as a *chef de l'inspection* at the Crédit foncier égyptien. Note; WhoEgypt, 1955

Lambert, Denis Clair, born in 1932, he received a doctorate in economics and became a professor. His writings include *Les inflations sud-américaines* (1959), *Le développement agricole en Algérie* (1962), *Les Économies du Tiers-monde* (1974), *Le mimétisme technologique du Tiers-monde* (1979), *19 Amériques latines* (1984), and *L'Etat providence en question* (1990). Note; ZKO

Lambert, Édouard, born 22 May 1866 at Mayenne, France, he received a doctorate in law from the Faculté de droit de Paris, and his *agrégation* in 1896 from the Université de Lyon. Since 1900 he taught history of law at the Faculté de droit de Lyon. He was a sometime professor at the Khedivial Law School in Egypt. His writings include *Du contrat en faveur de tiers* (1893), and *L'Ancêtre américain du droit comparé* (1947). In 1938 appeared *Introduction à l'étude du droit comparé; recueil d'études en l'honneur d'Édouard Lambert*. NUC, pre-1956; Qui êtes-vous, 1924

Lambert, Élie, born 10 April 1888 at Bayonne (Pyrénées-Atlantiques), France, he graduated from École Normale Supérieure and passed his *agrégation* in German but soon abandoned this part of his education to devote himself to the history of Spanish art in the middle ages and in particular study Islamic architecture in the West. From 1919 to 1924 he was a professor at the Lycée français in Madrid. He returned to France in 1926 to teach history of medieval art at the Faculté des lettres de

Caen. Since 1944 he taught at the Sorbonne. In 1954 he was elected to the Académie des inscriptions et belles lettres. His writings include *Delacroix et les femmes d'Alger* (1937), *Histoire d'un tableau, l'Abd er Rahman, sultan du Maroc* (1953), *L'Art musulman et l'art chrétien dans la Péninsule ibérique* (1958), and *L'Art musulman d'Occident des origines à la fin du XVe siècle* (1966). He died in Paris on 23 April 1961. *Al-Andalus*, 26 (1961), pp. 477-78; BioIn, 6; DBF; WhoFr, 1959/60

Lambert, Georges Édouard, born 29 November 1923 at Ancelle (Hautes-Alpes), France, he received a medical doctorate in 1959 from the Université de Strasbourg with a thesis entitled *Évaluation bioclimatologique d'un site d'industrialisation saharien.* He was associated with the Laboratoire de physiologie appliquée au travail at the Faculté de médecine de Strasbourg and the Centre d'études et d'information des problèmes humains dans les zones arides, later becoming an inspector of *médecine de travail* of the City of Strasbourg. His writings include *L'Adaption physiologique et psychologique de l'homme aux conditions de vie désertiques* (1968). Unesco

Lambert, Jacques Joseph Édouard Numa, born 26 August 1910 at Alger, he received a doctorate in law, and also his *agrégation* in 1941 from the Université de Paris. He was a barrister in the Cour d'Appel d'Alger, professor at the Université d'Alger, and a director of the Institut d'études juridiques at Constantine, Algeria. He was a joint author of *Symboles et rites de l'ancestralité et de l'immortalité; le vent, la pierre, l'eau et le feu dans les mythologies* (1999). Unesco; ZKO

Lambert, Mayer, born 23 December 1863 at Metz, France, he was educated at the Lycée de Metz, the Séminaire israélite de France, Paris, the Sorbonne, and the École des hautes études, Paris. He was from 1889 to 1916 a professor at the École normale orientale israélite and concurrently since 1902 a professor at the École pratique des hautes études. His writings include *Éléments de grammaire hébraïque* (Paris, 1890), and he edited and translated *Commentaire sur le Séfer Yesira, ou Livre de la création* (1891), *Version arabe du Pentateuque de R. Saadia Ben Iosef al-Fayyoûmî, revué, corrigé et accompané de notes hébraïques avec quelques fragments de traduction française d'après l'arabe par J. Derenbourg* (1893), and *Version arabe des Proverbes* (1894). He died in 1930. Kürschner; Qui êtes-vous, 1924

Lambert, Paul, born early 19th cent., he was a French trader who spent the years from 1863 to 1868 in Marrakesh, Morocco. Henze

Lambert, Paul, born in 1875, he was the author of *Dictionnaire illustré de la Tunisie* (Tunis, 1912), and *Nos corps élus* (Tunis, 1913). NUC, pre-1956

Lambie, Thomas Alexander, born in 1885 at Pittsburgh, Pa., he was a graduate of the University of Pennsylvania and Western Pennsylvania Medical College. He served as a medical missionary in the Sudan, Ethiopia, and Palestine. His writings include *A doctor without a country* (1939), *A doctor carries on* (1942), *Boot and saddle in Africa* (1943), *A bruised reed* (1952), *A doctor's great commission* (1954). He died in 'Ayn 'Arrub, Jordan, on 14 April 1954. NUC; Shavit

Lambiotte, O. Ellesworth, born at East Orange, N.J., he was in 1941 and in 1952 a director of the Banque belge et international en Égypte, and a member of the Société Fouad Ier d'économie politique, de statistique et de législation. WhoEgypt, 1955, 1959

Lambton, Ann Katherine Swynford, born 8 February 1912, she received a Ph.D. in 1939 from the School of Oriental and African Studies, London, for *Contributions to the study of Seljuq institutions.* She had an affection for Persia and its people which ensured that, during her time as press attaché at the British Representative at Tehran, 1939-1945, the Persian point of view would never be overlooked. She subsequently taught Iranian subjects at the University of London until her retirement. She was a member of the British Academy. Her writings include *Three Persian dialects* (1938), *Landlord and peasant in Iran* (1953), *Persian grammar* (1953), *Islamic society in Persia* (1954), *Persian land reform* (1969), a collection of her articles, *Theory and practice in medieval Persian government* (1980), *State and government in medieval Islam* (1981), *Continuity and change in medieval Persia* (1988), and *Qajar Persia; eleven studies* (1988). DrBSMES, 1993; Sluglett; Who, 1969-2005

Lamec-Saad, J., born around the middle of the nineteenth century at al-'Abbadiyah, Lebanon, he obtained a Dr. med. degree in 1880 from the Universität Würzburg for his thesis *Die Catarrhe der weiblichen Sexualorgane* (1880). He spent thirty years in the Ottoman medical service. His writings include *Sechzehn Jahre als Quarantänearzt in der Türkei* (1913), and *Palästina-Erinnerungen; vierzehn Jahre Quarantänearzt in Jafa* (1929). Note about the author

Lami, Lucio, born in 1936, he was a journalist, editor, and war correspondent in the Third World, from Cambodia to Latin America. His writings include *Morire per Kabul; una lunga marcia afgana* (Milano, 1982), and *Giorno di guerra; un inviato nelle zone calde del mondo* (Milano, 1987). Wholtaly, 1992-1995|

Lamington, Charles Wallace Alexander Napier Cochrane Baillie, 2nd Baron, born 29 July 1860, he graduated from Eton and Christ Church College, Oxford. He was a member of Parliament, 1886-1890, a governor of Queensland, 1903-1907, and a governor of Bombay, 1903-1907. In 1919 he served as commissioner of the British Relief Unit in Syria. He died in Lanarkshire, Scotland, on 16 September 1940. Buckland; *Dictionary of Australian biography*, 1891-1939; IndianBilnd (2); Who, 1936; *Who was who*, 3

Lamm, Carl Johan, born 20 September 1902 at Stockholm, he graduated from Stockholms Universitet, where he also received a doctorate in 1933. He was a lecturer at an Egyptian university in Cairo from 1935 to 1937, when he started teaching Oriental art at Uppsala Universitet, a post which he held until his retirement in 1969. His writings include *Das Glas von Samarra* (1928), *Mittelalterliche Gläser und Steinschnittarbeiten aus dem Nahen Osten* (1929-30), *Glass from Iran in the National Museum* (1935), *Cotton in medieval textiles of the Near East* (Paris, 1937), *Oriental glass of mediaeval date found in Sweden and the early history of lustre-painting* (1941); he was a joint author of *Ambrosian fragments of an illuminated manuscript containing the Zoology of al-Ǧāhiz* (1946), and *Orientalische Briefumschläge in schwedischem Besitz* (1944). He died on 10 November 1981. BioIn, 13 = *Journal of glass studies*, 24 (1982), pp. 121-22 (not sighted); Sezgin; *Vem är det*, 1975-81

Lammens, Henri, S.J., born in 1862 at Gent, Belgium, he went to school at Turnhout and in 1877 he arrived in Beirut, where he went to college for a year. In 1878, he entered the Society of Jesus and was ordained in 1893. With the exception of two years of teaching at the Pontifico Istituto Biblico di Roma, and the years of the first World War, which he spent in Egypt, he passed the rest of his life at the Université de St. Joseph in Beirut. His writings include *Le triumvirat d'Abou Bakr, Omar et Abou 'Obaida* (1909), *Fatima et les filles de Mahomet* (1912), *Syrie, précis historique* (1921), *La Mecque à la veille de l'hégire* (1924), *L'islam; croyances et institutions* (1926), *L'Arabie occidentale avant l'hégire* (1928), and *Études sur le siècle des Omayyades* (1930). He died in Beirut on 23 April 1937. Fück, 292-293; *Index Islamicus* (4); Jalabert, pp. 196-97; Kornrumpf², vol. 2

Lamodière, Jean, born 20th cent., he received a *doctorat d'état* in 1976 from the Université d'Aix-Marseille for *Les Investissements privés étrangers au Maroc*. His writings include *L'Évolution des investissements étrangers au Maroc* (1977). THESAm, 1; ZKO

Lamont, Thomas Acquinas, born in 1938, he began teaching at the American University in Cairo after he had received an M.A. in English literature from the University of Arizona in 1963. He met his wife in Cairo and the city became their spiritual home. In 1972, he completed his doctorate in comparative literature at the University of Iowa. After his wife was diagnosed with breast cancer in 1980 the family moved to New York, where he directed the office of American University in Cairo until 1993, when he alone returned to his old department at A.U.C. and slipped into his pre-dean role as professor of English and comparative literature. He died on 31 January 1997 in Switzerland from an aneurysm that he suffered a week earlier in Cairo. *MESA bulletin* 32 (1998), pp. 139-140

La Monte, John Life, born 10 October 1902 at Columbia, Ohio, he received his M.A. in 1923 from Ohio State University with a thesis entitled *British diplomacy in the Near East, 1830-1841*, and his Ph.D. in 1928 from Harvard for *Kingship in the Latin Kingdom of Jerusalem*. He held academic posts at the universities of Nebraska, Minnesota, and Cincinnati, Ohio, and was awarded fellowships by the Social Science Research Council and the Guggenheim Memorial Foundation. In 1940, he went to the University of Pennsylvania. His career was interrupted by war-time service as a lieutenant in the U.S. Navy. In the realm of scholarship he was an authority on the history of the crusades and was engaged in editing an elaborate and comprehensive history of these great expeditions which he and scholars from all over the Western and Muslim world were to write. On 2 October 1949, on the eve of departing for the Near East upon an important scholarly mission, La Mote, Henry Charles Lea professor of medieval history in the University of Pennsylvania, was suddenly sticken and died without regaining consciousness. His writings include *Feudal monarchy in the Latin Kingdom of Jerusalem, 1100 to 1241* (1932). *American historical review*, 55 (1950), pp. 476-77; BioIn, 2 (3); Master (2); WhAm, 3; WhE&EA

de Lamothe, Henri Félix, born 8 August 1843 at Metz, France, he was ready to enter the École polytechnique in 1862, when instead he decided to get involved in Italy in the Hungarian Legion. In the following year, he fought in the ranks of Polish insurgents. After some more time spent in Italy, he joined the French Marine Infantry, spending from 1867 to 1871 in Senegal. From there he went to Algeria, where he collaborated with several journals. As a journalist he successively travelled in Canada, Herzegovina, U.S.A., Cuba, Haiti, Bulgaria, again Algeria, Tunisia, and Egypt. On account of his American experiences, he was made governor of the French islands of Saint-Pierre et Miquelon, south of Newfoundland. This was followed by assigments in Senegal, Guyana, the Congo, Indochina, Cambodia, Java, and the Philippines. He lost his only son in the first World War, and when he died on 20 Agust 1926, he left his wife to the mercy of the Government general of Indochina. His writings include *Cinq mois chez les Français d'Amérique* (1880). *Hommes et destins*, 8, pp. 233-34

de **Lamothe**, Léon Jean Benjamin, born 22 August 1849 at Metz, France, he was a graduate of the Collège de Metz, and the École polytechnique, obtaining degrees in the physical and natural sciences in 1870 and 1879 respectively. He became an army officer who served in the French wars of the period, retiring with the rank of general. In 1898-99, he was sent on a special mission to Algeria and Tunisia regarding the defence of the colonies. His writings include *Las anciennes lignes de rivage du Sahel d'Alger* (1911). IndexBFr² (1); Qui ets-ce, 1934

de **La Mottraye**, Aubrey, born about 1674, he settled in England freely to practise his Protestant belief, whence he visited the countries of northern Europe, Tatary, and Turkey. Upon his return from this long journey, he received a pension from King George I. Soon thereafter he began to travel in Europe, ending his life in France, where he died in Paris in 1743. His writings include *Travels through Europe, Asia, and into part of Africa, with proper cutts and maps, containing a great variety of geographical, topographical, and political observations on those parts of the world, especially on Italy, Turky, Greece, Crim and Noghaian Tartaries, Circassia, Sweden, and Lapland* (London, 1723), *Voyage en Europe, Asie et Afrique* (La Haye, 1727), and its translation, *Reisen in die Morgenländer* (Berlin, 1781), and *Voyages en anglois et en françois en diverses provinces et places de la Prusse ducale et royale, de la Russie, de la Pologne &* (La Haye, 1732). GdeEnc; GDU; Master (1); Sezgin

Lamouche (Ламуш), Léon, born in 1860, he was a French army engineer who retired with the rank of lieutenant colonel. His writings include *L'Organisation militaire de l'Empire ottoman* (1895), *La Peninsule balkanique* (1899), *Les Armées de la peninsule balkanique* (1901), *La Bulgarie dans le passé et le présent* (1892), *La Bulgarie* (1923), *Quinze ans d'histoire balkanique* (1928), *Les Bulgares en Macédoine dans les confins occidentaux et en Thrace* (1931), *Histoire de la Turquie depuis les origines juspu'à nos jours* (1934), and its Persian translation, *Tārīkh-i Turkiyah* (1316/1937). He died in 1945. BN; EnBulg; IndexBFr² (1); OSK

Lampe, Carl Emil *Felix*, born 31 July 1868 at Berlin, he studied geography, history, and literature at the universities of Bonn and Berlin, where he received a Dr.phil. in 1892 for *Qui fuerint Gregorii Mahni papae temporibus in imperii Byzantini parte occidentali exarchi et qualia eorum iura taque officia,* and his teacher's certificate in the following year. He taught at several Berlin schools until 1916, when he was appointed a deputy head of the Zentral-Institut for education and teaching as well as a director of its section of cinematography. He was a member of council of the Gesellschaft für Erdkunde. His writings include *Die transsibirische Eisenbahn* (1897), *Der mittelamerikanische Kanal* (1902), and *Kriegsbetroffene Lande* (1914). He died in 1946. Kürschner, 1926-1935; RHbDtG; Wer ist's, 1928, 1935

Lampérez y **Romea**, Vicente, born 24 March 1861 at Madrid, he was educated at the Instituto de Zaragoza, Escuela de Bellas Artes in that city, and Escuela Superior de Bellas Artes de la Villa y Corte. A bachelor of arts since 1879, he completed his architecture in 1885, and in 1894 he was appointed an *auxiliar profesor* in the Escuela de Artes y Oficios de Madrid. He subsequently taught at the Escuela Superior de Arquitectura de Madrid. His writings include *Historia de la arquitectura cristiana* (1904), *La Catedral de Burgos* (1912), *La Restauración de los monumentos arquitectónicos* (1913), and *Arquitectura civil española* (1922). He died in 1923. EncicUni

Lampreia, José Domingues, born 9 July 1927 at Beja, Portugal, he studied medicine and ethnology at the Universidade de Lisboa, where he received a doctorate in ethnology and a diploma in overseas administration. He was in 1960 a research fellow of the Centro de Estudos de Etnologia de Ultramar, Lisboa. Unesco

Lampué, Pierre, born 13 July 1899 at Paris, he was educated at the Collège Louis-le-Grand and Faculté de droit, Paris, where he received a doctorate in 1927 for *Les rapports entre l'État français et les compagnies de transport publics aériens.* He taught law in various capacities successively at the universities of Rennes, Caen, and Paris. From 1959 to 1961 he served as a judge. His writings include *Les Lois applicables en Algérie* (1950), and *La Justice administrative dans les états d'Afrique francophone* (1965). WhoFr, 1969/70-1979/80|

Lamy, Étienne Marie Victor, born 2 June 1845 at Cize (Jura), France, he was educated at the Collège dominicain de Sorèze, the Collège Stanislas, Paris, and received a doctorate in law in 1869 from the Faculté de droit de Paris. In 1871, he was elected a *député* for the Department of Jura as a Republican. After being defeated in the elections of 1881, he became a journalist, writing for the *Journal des débats, Revue des deux mondes,* and *le Correspondant.* From 1892 to 1898 he was active in Catholic politics, but without much success. He subsequently travelled to the Holy Land, experiences which are embodied in his *La France du Levant* (1900). A director of the *Correspondant* from 1904 to 1909, he devoted himself to literature and history. In 1905, he was elected to the Académie française. He participated in the first World War as a reserve *chef de bataillon.* His writings include *Études sur le second Empire* (1895), *Les luttes entre l'Église et l'État au XIXe siècle* (1895), *La* *femme de demain* (1901), and *L'Institut et la guerre* (1916). He was awarded *officier* of the Légion d'honneur. He died in Paris on 9 January 1919. Curinier, 5 (1906), pp. 377-38; DBF; IndexBFr² (8); Master (1)

Lamy, François Joseph Amédée, born 7 February 1858 at Mougins (Alpes-Maritimes), France, he entered the French army on 17 October 1877. After passing through the military college, Saint-Cyr, he next appears as a second lieutenant with the 1st Regiment of the Tirailleurs algériens at Blida (El Boulaïda) in northern Algeria. He later participated in the campaign against the Khroumir on the Algero-Tunisian border. Between 1885 and 1895 he was successively assigned to Indochina and Madagascar. When he returned to Algeria, he had been promoted battalion commander and was put in charge of the first platoon of Saharan *méharistes* at El Goléa. In 1898, he was assigned to head the Mission Foureau-Lamy, which assembled in November 1898 at Tamassinin in the southern Great Erg, some 280 miles south of Ouargla, for the purpose of reaching Lake Tchad. The Mission attained its goal in April 1900, culminating in the death of Rabah, the Pasha of Bahr el Ghazal, in Barguirmi. But in a futile counter offensive of the enemy forces at Koussouri, the Cameroons, François Lamy lost his life. Émil Reibell wrote a biography, *Le Commandant Lamy d'après sa correspondance et ses souvenirs de campagne* (1903). DBF; *La Géographie*, 7 (1903), pp. 113-115; *Hommes et destins*, v. 4, pp. 424-426

Lamy, Jacques Édouard, born 8 January 1915 at Neuilly-sur-Seine, France, he was a graduate of the École polytechnique, Paris, and the École nationale supérieure de l'aèronautique. Since 1938 he was a military aeronautics engineer, and from 1945 to 1968 he served as a professor at the École nationale supérieure de pétrole et des moteurs. He subsequently became an administrator with the Société des automobiles E. Bugatti. His writings include *Turbines à gaz* (Paris, 1958). WhoFr, 1969/70-1988/89|

Lamy, Thomas Joseph, born 27 January 1827 at Ohey (Namur), Belgium, he was educated at the Petit séminaire at Floreffe and the Grand séminaire at Namur. He was ordained priest in 1852 or 53. He taught Hebrew, Syriac, and sacred scriptures and was associated in other capacities with the Université catholique de Louvain from 1858 until his retirement in 1900. He died in Louvain on 30 July 1907. BiBenelux² (3); DcCathB; NewCathEnc

Lancaster, Joan Cadogan, 1918-1992 *see* Lancaster Lewis, Joan Cadogan

Lancaster Lewis, Joan Cadogan, born 2 August 1918, she was educated at the University of London. She was a librarian and archivist successively at Leicester and Conventry, an history librarian at the Commonwealth Office, London, and from 1972 to 1978 served as director of the India Office. She was a sometime editor of the journal *Archives*. Her writings include *Bibliography of historical works issued in the United Kingdom, 1946-1956* (1957), and *A Guide to lists and catalogues of the India Office and Records* (1966). She died on 31 December 1992. Who's who, 1974-1993; WhoWor, 1976/77

Lance, Frederick FitzHugh, born in 1873, the son of Sir Frederick Lance, 1837-1913, he was educated at Clifton and the Royal Military College, Sandhurst. He served in South Africa, India, and the European War, including Egypt. He retired with the rank of brigadier-general. Who's who in Kent, 1935

Lanchester, Henry Vaughan, born 9 August 1863 at London, he was articled to his father, an architect of London and Brighton. He entered the Royal Academy Schools in 1886 and began independent practice in 1887. In 1912, he visited Delhi to report on a new site for the new capital of India and prepared plans for other Indian cities; he also did plans for Zanzibar. He was a sometime professor of architecture at University College, London. His writings include *Town planning in Madras* (1918), *Zanzibar; a study in tropical town planning* (1923), and *The Art of town planning* (1925). He died in Seaford, Sussex, on 16 January 1953. BioIn, 3, 14; Gray; Riddick; Who's who, 1921-1953; Who was who, 5

de **Lancker**, Fritz, born 19th cent., he was an engineer and, in 1941, served as an administrator of the Société des tramways du Caire at Bruxelles. He was a member of the Société Fouad 1er d'économie politique, de statistique et de législation, Cairo. Note about the author

Lancrenon, Marie *Paul* Mathieu, born in 1857, his writings include *Trois mille lieus à la pagaie de la Seine à la Volga* (Paris, 1898), *L'impression d'hiver dans les Alpes* (Paris, 1906), and *Les travaux de la Mission télégraphique du Tchad, 1910-1913* (Paris, Comité de l'Afrique française, 1914). NUC, pre-'56

op 't **Land**, Cornelius, born 20th cent., he wrote *Werk in uitvoering; een analyse van drie ontwikkelings-objecten* (1970), a work which was originally presented as a thesis at the Rijkuniversiteit te Utrecht. LC

Land, James Wesley, born 12 April 1935 at Crockett, Tex., he graduated in 1957 from Southern Methodist University and received his Ph.D. in 1964 from Princeton University for *Factor-price equalization; an extension of a theorem in the pure theory of international trade*. He spent 1964-65 in Turkey with the support of a research grant from Yale University, New Haven, Conn., where he subsequently taught for five years. In 1969, he was appointed a professor of economics at Rice

MACK LIBRARY
BOB JONES UNIVERSITY
GREENVILLE, SC

University, Houston, Texas. His writings include *Economic accounts of government in Turkey, 1938, 1948, 1950, 1953-63; a statistical study* (1969). AmM&WSc, 1978 S

Land, Jan Pieter Nicolas, born 23 April 1834 at Delft, the Netherlands, he studied Semitic languages, philosophy and history of music at the Rijks-Universiteit te Leiden, where he was a student of Reinhart P. A. Dozy and Theodorus W. J. Juynboll (1802-1861), and received a doctorate in theology in 1857 for *De carmine Jacobi*. In 1859, he became a secretary of the Nederlandsch Bijbelgenootschap; in 1864, he succeded Pieter J. Veth as a teacher of philosophy and Oriental languages at the Athenaeum Amstelaedamse. It was during this period that he published his most important contribution to Oriental studies, the four-part *Anecdota Syriaca* (1862-75), a work which so pleased Th. Nöldeke that he dedicated to him his own *Kurzgefasste syrische Grammatik* (1880). After his 1872 appointment as a professor of philosophy at Leiden, his writings focus on philosophy, Spinoza and A. Geulincx, as well as musicology, including Arabic, Javanese and old Dutch. His other writings include *Hebreeuwsche Grammatica* (1869), and *Recherches sur l'histoire de la grammaire arabe* (1884). He died in Arnhem on 30 April 1897. BiBenelux²; NieuwNBW, vol. 9

Landa, Robert Grigor'evich, born 23 Mach 1931 at Moscow, he received his first degree in 1958 for *Национально-освободительное движение в Алжире после второй мировой войны, 1945-1951 гг.* He became a lecturer in 1973, received a doctorate in history in 1974, and was appointed a professor in 1990. Since 1957 he was associated with the Oriental Institute in the Soviet Academy of Sciences. His writings include *Алжир сбрасывает оковы* (1961), *У арабов Африки* (1967), *У арабов Азии* (1969), *Средиземноморье глазам востоковеда* (1979), *Кризис колониального режима в Алжире, 1931-1954* (1980), *История Алжирской революции, 1954-1961* (1983), *Марокко; 30 лет независимости* (1985), *Старина и новь Магриба* (1985), *Страны Магриба; общuство и традиции* (1988), *Оь руин Карфагена до вершин Атласа* (1991), *В стране аль-Андалус через тысячу лет* (1993), *Ислам в истории России* (1995), and *Социальный облик Востока* (1999). Miliband; Miliband²; OSK

Landau, Jacob M., born 20 March 1924 at Chişinău (Kishinv), Moldavia, he grew up in Palestine and studied at the Hebrew University, Jerusalem, and the School of Oriental and African Studies, London, where he received his Ph.D. in 1949 for *Parliamentary insitutions and political parties in Egypt, 1866-1924*. He became a professor at the Hebrew University as well as at univrsities in the United States and Turkey. His writings include *Electoral politics in the Middle East; issues, voters and elites* (1980), *Pan-Turkism in Turkey; a study of irredentism* (1984), *Atatürk and the modernization of Turkey* (1984), *Tekinalp, Turkish patriot* (1984), *The Arab minority in Israel, 1967-1991; political aspects* (1993), *Language and politics; theory and cases* (1999), and he was a joint author of *Politics of language in the ex-Soviet Muslim states* (2001). ConAu, 17-20, new rev., 8, 24; IntAu&W, 1977, 1982; *MESA Roster of members*, 1977-1990; Schoeberlein, Sluglett; WhoIsrael, 1973/74-2001; WhoWor, 1974/75, 1976/77; WhoWorJ, 1965

Landau, Rom, born 17 October 1899 in England, he was a sculptor until the late 1930s. During the second World War he was first with the Middle East Divison of the Ministry of Information, and also a member of the Arab Committee, and later with the Political Intelligence Department of the Foreign Office, London. From 1951 to 1967 he was successively a professor of Islamic art at the American Academy of Asian Studies, San Francisco, and the University of the Pacific, Stockton, Calif. He was an acknowledged authority on religion, metaphysics, and the Arab world for over thirty years. His writings include *Pilsudski and Poland* (1929), *God is my adventure; a book on modern mystics, masters and teachers* (1935), *Moroccan journal* (1952), *The Arabesque* (1955), *Moroccan drama, 1900-1955* (1956), *Mohammed V, King of Morocco* (1957), *Islam and the Arabs* (1958), *The Philosophy of Ibn 'Arabi* (1959), *Morocco independent under Mohammed the Fifth* (1961), and *The Kasba of southern Morocco* (1969). He died in Marrakesh on 2 or 3 March 1974. Au&Wr, 1963, 1971; ConAu, 49-52, new rev., 24; IntAu&W, 1976; Note; WhE&EA; *Who's who*, 1969-1974; *Who was who*, 7

Landauer, Samuel, born 22 February 1846 at Hürben, Bavaria, he was educated at the yeshibah of Eisenstadt, Hungary, and studied at the universities of Leipzig, Straßburg, and München, where he received a Dr.phil. in 1872 for *Beitrag zur Psychologie des Ibn-Sinâ*. He was appointed a lecturer (*Privatdozent*) in Semitic languages at the Universität Straßburg in 1875, and a librarian there in 1884. In 1894, he was named a professor. After being expelled from France in 1918, he settled at Augsburg, Germany, where he prepared an edition of the Targum on the later Prophets for the Akademie für die Wissenschaften des Judentums. His writings include *Katalog der hebräischen, arabischen, persischen und türkischen Handschriften in der Kaiserlichen Universitäts- und Landesbibliothek zu Straßburg* (1881), *Die Mâsôrâh zum Onkelos auf Grund neuer Quellen lexikalisch geordnet und kritisch beleuchtet* (1896), and *Themistii in libros Aristotelis De caelo paraphrasis hebraice et latine* (1902). He died in Augsburg on 18 February 1937. DtBE; DtBiInd (2); EncJud (1934, 1971); JewEnc; WhE&EA; Wininger

von **Landberg**-Hallberger, Carlo, Graf, born 24 March 1848 at Göteborg, Sweden, he studied Arabic under Heinrich L. Fleischer and spent two years and a half in Syria, Egypt, Nubia, and the Sudan, where he studied particularly colloquial Arabic. He was a private scholar whose writings include *I Öknar och palmlunder; skildringar från Österlandet* (1881), *Catalogue de manuscrits arabes provenant d'une bibliothèque privée à El-Medîna et appartenant à la Maison E. J. Brill* (1883), *Die Expedition nach Südarabien* (1899), *Die Hunde von 'Azzân und ihre Bestrafung durch die Engländer* (1903), *La Langue arabe et ses dialectes* (1905), *Langue des Bédouins 'Anazeh* (1919), and *Chez les Bédouins; récits arabes d'après un manuscrit de la Bibliothèque de l'Université d'Uppsala* (1970). C. U. Nylander wrote *C. Graf von Landberg als Kritiker beleuchtet* (1892), and Wilhelm Ahlwardt compiled *Kurzes Verzeichnis der Landberg'schen Sammlung arabischer Handschriften* (1885); in 1909 appeared the private publication in a small print-run entitled *Jeder tut was ihm paßt, denn reden werden die Leute immer*, arabisches Sprichwort im Dialekt von Haurân und Daṭînah mit Übersetzung und Kommentar; *Festgabe zu seinem 40. Jubiläum als Orientalist*. He died in Bern, Switzerland, on 20 July 1924.died in Bern, Switzerland, on 20 July 1924. Fück, p. 307; Hanisch; SBL; ScBlnd (1); SMK; ZKO

Landen, Robert Geran, born 13 July 1930 at Sundsvall, Sweden, he graduated in 1952 from the College of William and Mary, Williamsburg, Va., and received his Ph.D. in 1961 from Princeton University for *Modernization and imperialism in Oman in the late nineteenth century*. He subsequently taught social sciences, and Near Eastern and general history at a variety of American universities. His writings include *Oman since 1856* (1967), and *The Emergence of the modern Middle East* (1970). ConAu, 21-24; DrAS, 1969 H, 1974 H, 1978 H, 1982 H; LEduc; *MESA Roster of members*, 1977-1990; WhoAm, 1976-2003; WhoWor, 1982-1996

Landfried, Klaus, born 26 January 1941 at Heidelberg, Germany, he studied political science, history, German literature and political economy at the universities of Heidelberg and Basel, taking his doctorate in 1970 at the Universität Heidelberg for *Stefan George; Politik des Unpolitischen*, a work which was published in 1975. He was a research fellow in Iran and Afghanistan, 1972/73, and later a J. F. Kennedy Memorial Fellow at Harvard University. He was a professor of political science, with special reference to universities, successively at the universities of Heidelberg and Trier-Kaiserslautern. His writings include *Folgen neuer Informationstechniken* (1985), *Ausbildung versus Bildung; internationale Erfahrungen der Hochschulentwicklung* (1998), and *Steps towards a European higher education are without borders; annual report 2002 by the President of the Hochschulrektorenkonferenz* (Bonn, HRK, 2003). Kürschner, 1980-2005; Note about the author; WhoWor, 1980/81, 1982/83

Landis, James McCauley, born 25 September 1899 to American parents in Japan, he graduated from Princeton University in 1921, and from Harvard Law School in 1924; he also received a doctorate in law from the University Fouad I, Cairo. He was a professor of law at Harvard from 1926 to 1934, and a dean of its Law School from 1937 to 1946. He was also a partner in a law firm as well as a politician. From 1942 to 1943, he was a director of American Economic Operations and a minister to the Middle East. His writings include *Cases on labor law* (1934), *The administrative process* (1938), and its translation, *El poder administrativo* (1951). He died on 30 July 1964. Master (15); Shavit; WhAm, 4

Landis, Lincoln, born 5 August 1922 at Logansport, Ind., he graduated in 1945 from the U.S. Military Academy, West Point, received his M.A. in 1959 from Columbia University, New York, and a Ph.D. in 1969 from Georgetown University, Washington, D.C., for *Petroleum in Soviet Middle East strategy*. He spent four years as a senior research fellow at the Center of Strategic and International Studies, Georgetown University, until 1969, when he was appointed a foreign affairs analyst in Batelle Memorial Institute, Washington, D.C. His writings include *Politics and oil; Moscow in the Middle East* (1973), and he was a joint author of *Science, technology and development* (1974). ConAu, 45-48; IndAu; IntAu&W, 1976, 1977; Selim

Landolt, Hermann, born in 1935, he received a Dr.phil. in 1967 from the Universität Basel for his thesis, *Der Gebetstepptich als kultureller Faktor im Derwischtum*. Thereafter he was a professor of philosophy in the Institut of Islamic Studies, McGill University, Montreal. His writings include the translation, *Le révélateur des mystères* (1986); and he edited *Correspondance spirituelle échangé entre Nuroddin Esfarayeni et son disciple 'Alaoddawleh Semnani* (1972). AnElFr, 1997; DrASCan, 1983; LC; Schwarz; ZKO

Landon, Perceval, born 29 March 1869, he graduated in 1893 from Hertford College, Oxfors, and was called to the bar from the Inner Temple in 1895. He was a special correspondent for *The Times*. In 1900, he was a private secretary to the Governor of New South Wales. His writings include *The Opening of Tibet* (1905). He died in 1927. NUC, pre-1956; Who, 1909-1921; *Who was who*, 2

Landowski, Edward, born 14 October 1839 at Vilnius (Vilna), Lithuania, he studied medicine first at the Universität Breslau and later at Warszawa until 1863, when he had to emigrate. He subsequently continued his study at Zürich, completing his medicine in 1867 at the Université de Montpellier, France, with a thesis entitled *Essai sur la blennorrhagie uréthrale chez l'homme*. He settled in Sumène and later moved to Paris. During the Franco-Prussian war he served as a military physician in an ambulance in besieged Paris, which gained him French citizenship. In 1879, he settled in Algeria, where he established a clinical health resort at Mustapha supérieur. He died there on 7 November 1882. His writings include *L'Algérie au point de vue climato-thérapique dans les affections consomptives* (1877), and *L'Algérie au point de vue climato-thérapique dans les affections consomptives, création d'une station hivernale en Algérie* (1878); he also contributed to the *Journal de thérapeutique*. BN; Dziekan; Polski (9); PSB

Landreau, Anthony Norman, born 2 April 1930 at Washington, D.C., he received a B.A. in 1954, M.A. in 1993, and Ph.D. in 1996. He held a great variety of museums posts, including executive director of the Textile Museum, Washington, D.C. With grants from the National Endowment for the Humanities he repeatedly visited Turkey. His writings include *Traditional crafts of Saudi Arabia* (1981), *Flowers of the yayla; yörük weaving of the Toros Mountains* (1983); he was a joint author of *From the Bosporus to Samarkand; flat-woven rugs* (1969); and he edited *Yörük, the nomadic weaving tradition of the Middle East* (1978). WhoAmA, 1976-2001/2002

Clerc de **Landresse**, Ernest Augustin Xavier, born in 1800 near Louviers (Eure), France, he was an East Asian scholar and a librarian at the Institut de France. His writings include *Catalogue des livres imprimés, des manuscrits et des ouvrages chinois, tartares, japonais, etc., de la bibliothèque de M. Klaproth* (1839). He died near Pontoise (Val-d'Oise) in 1862. BN; DBF; NUC, pre-1956

Landuré, Jean-Louis, born 20th cent., he was in 1971 an assistant at the Faculté de droit et des sciences économiques d'Orléans. Note about the author

Lane, Edward *Arthur,* born 15 December 1909, he was educated at St. John's Leatherhead and proceeded as a scholar to St. John's College, Cambridge, where he took first class honours in both parts of the classical tripos. In 1952, he won a scholarship to the British School in Athens. After his appointment, in 1954, to an assistent keepership in the Victoria and Albert Museum, he was posted to the Department of Ceramics, which he never left. But his interest turned to the Near East, and his enthusiasm was strengthened by a spell on the excavations in northern Syria. His writings include *Early Islamic pottery* (1947), *Greek pottery* (1948), and *Later Islamic pottery* (1957). He died in 1963. BioIn, 6 (3), 7 (1); *Kunst des Orients*, 5 i (1968), pp. 79-80; *Oriental art*, n.s., 9 (1963), p. 174; *Who was who*, 6

Lane, Edward William, born 17 September 1801 at Hereford, England, he was educated at the grammar schools of Bath and Hereford, and subsequently went to Cambridge with the intention of taking orders. Dissatisfied with the way of living then prevalent at the University, he left almost immediately, but convinced himself of the thoroughness of his training by solving all the questions set one year in the Mathematical Tripos. Partly from weak health and partly from an increasing fondness for Oriental learning, he decided on travelling in Egypt with a view to devoting himself to Eastern studies. He visited Egypt three times, 1825 to 1828, 1833 to 1835, and 1842 to 1849. He acquired so perfect a knowledge of spoken Arabic that he was able freely to mix with the people as one of themselves. The result of his visits were *An Account of the manners and customs of the modern Egyptians*, and its translation, *Sitten und Gebräuche der heutigen Ägypter* (1852). From 1838 to 1840 he was occupied in the publication of a translation of the *Thousand and one Nights*. During his third visit he collected material for the composition of his *Arabic-English lexicon*, a work to which he devoted thirty-five years of his life, uneventfully spent in hard work from morning to night, week to week, year to year - single-handed. Few men have the courage thus to sacrifice a life. His drawings, notebooks, notes and correspondence are in the Griffith Institute, Ashmolean Museum, Oxford. His writings also include *Description of Egypt, notes and views in Egypt and Nubia, 1825-28*, edited by Jason Thompson (2000). He died on 10 August 1876. Obituary note, *The Times*, 15 August 1876; Fück, pp. 168-70; Goldschmidt; *Index Islamicus* (4); Kornrumpf; Kornrumpf², vol. 2

Laně, Tomás, born 29 December 1944 at Praha, he studied Turkic subjects at Universita Karlova, Praha, as well as at the Azerbaijan State University, Baku. He received a Ph.Dr. in 1988 and became a professor at his alma mater, concurrently serving as a diplomat in Turkey. Filipsky; *Kdo je kdo, 2002*

Lane, Winthrop David, born 29 May 1887 at Fort Wayne, Ind., he graduated in 1910 from the University of Michigan and subsequently attended the New York School of Social Work. He was a journalist who also held editorial positions and worked free-lance. He was a sometime director of the New Jersey Divison of Parole. His writings include *The Denial of civil liberties in the coal fields* (1924), and *Military training in schools and colleges of the United States* (1926). He died in 1962. IndAu

Lane-Poole, Stanley, born 18 December 1854 at London, he was educated at Corpus Christi College, Oxford, and was for eighteen years in the Coin Department of the British Museum. During this time he compiled a catalogue of Oriental and Indian coins in the Museum, which ran to fourteen volumes. Towards the end of the nineteenth century he was sent by the Government on archaeological missions to Egypt and Russia, and he had also been employed by the Egyptian Government on archaeological research at Cairo. From 1898 to 1904 he was professor of Arabic at Trinity College, Dublin. His writings include *Life of the Right Honorable Stratford de Redcliffe* (1888), *The Mohammedan dynasties* (1894), and its Ottoman Turkish translation, *Tabakāt-i salāṭīn-ül-Islām* (1928). He died in London on 29 December 1931. BbD; BiD&SB; BioIn, 1; DNB; Kornrumpf; *Who was who*, 3

de **Lanessan**, Jean Marie Antoine Belloguet, born 13 July 1843 at Saint-André-de-Cubzac (Gironde), France, he started his career as an *aide-médecin* with the French Navy in the Far East. During the war of 1870 he served as *chirugien-major des Mobiles* of Charente-Inférieure. His thesis in 1873 won him a bronze medal. In 1876 he received his *agrégation* in medical natural history, and he subsequently became a professor of zoology at the Faculté de médecine de Paris. Soon thereafter, he entered politics as a radical socialist and collaborated with the journals, *Réveil du peuple* and *le Siècle*. He successively entered municipal and national politics, devoting himself to French colonial affairs, serving as vice-president of the Commission des colonies. He was particularly successful in modernizing the ports of Dakar, Bizerte, Alger, and Saigon. His writings include *Les plantes utiles des colonies françaises* (1886), *L'expansion coloniale de la France* (1887), and *La Tunisie* (1887). He died in Écouen (Val-d'Oise) on 7 November 1919. DBF; *Hommes et destins*, vol. 7, p. 237; IndexBFr² (3)

Lanfry, J., born 20th cent., he was a priest of the Pères blancs, resident in Ghadamès, Libya, in 1945. He translated from Berber, *Anejmee n-taddart; l'assenblée du village* (Fort-National, Algérie, Fichier de Documentation berbère, 1946), and he edited *Textes du premier volume de Ghadamès* (Fort-National, Algérie, Fichier de Documentation berbères, c1968, 1971). Note; NUC, pre-1956, 1973-77

Lang, Andrew, born 31 March 1844 at Selkirk, Scotland, he studied at Scottish universities and took a first in classics at Oxford. He subsequently started a career in journalism, later becoming a historian, folklorist and writer of poetry and prose. His many writings include *Prince Darling and other stories* (1908), and *The Arabian nights entertainment* (1916). He died in Banchory, Scotland, on 20 July 1912. CasWL; ConAu, 114, new rev., 85; DNB; IntDcAn; Master (81); *Who was who*, 1

Lang, Carl, born in 1841 at Steinbach, Baden, Germany, he was an Arabist and a teacher at German secondary schools. His trace is lost after an article in 1897. DtBiInd (1)

Lang, David Marshall, born 1924 at Chislehurst, Kent, England, he was educated at Monkton Combe School and St. John's College, Cambridge, where he later held a fellowship. Military and official duties took him to Persia during the second World War, where from 1944 to 1946 he held the appointment of acting vice-consul in Tabriz. In 1949, he joined the School of Oriental and African Studies, London, as lecturer in Georgian, later becoming reader, and subsequently from 1964 to 1984 professor of Caucasian studies. During 1952/53 he held a senior fellowship at the Russian Institute, Columbia University, New York, and in 1964/65 was visiting professor of Caucasian languages at the University of California, Los Angeles. From 1962 to 1964 he served as honorary secretary to the Royal Asiatic Society. His writings include *Transcaucasia, based on the collection of the American Numismatic Society* (1955), *Lives and legends of the Georgian saints* (1956), *The last years of the Georgian monarchy, 1658-1832* (1957), *Catalogue of Georgian and other Caucasian printed books in the British Museum* (1962), *A Modern history of Georgia* (1962), *Armenia* (1970), and *The Armenians* (1981). He died on 30 March 1991. Au&Wr, 1963, 1971; BlueB, 1973/74-1976; *BRISMES newsletter*, 6 i (November 1991), p. 2; ConAu, 134, new rev., 2, 17; IntAu&W, 1977-1991/92; *Who's who*, 1969-1991; WhoWor, 1974/75, 1976/77; WrDr, 1976/78-1994/96

Lang, Hubert, born in 1947, he studied Romance and English linguistics at the Universität Freiburg im Breisgau, and Arabic in Lebanon and the Universität Bonn. He received a Dr.phil. in 1991 from the Universität Hamburg for *Der Heiligenkult in Marokko; Formen, Funktionen der Wallfahrt*, a work which was published in 1992. He entered the German foreign service in the 1970s and was assigned successively to the Persian Gulf and North Africa. His other writings include *Leitfaden für Geschäfte mit den Vereinigten Arabischen Emiraten* (1978). Note; ZKO

Lange, Antoni, born in 1861 at Warszawa, he was a linguist and a writer of poetry and prose. His writings include *Atylla* (1910), and he edited *Dywan wschodni* (Warszawa, 1921). He died in Pochowany near Powązkowskie on 17 March 1929. Hans-Peter Hoelscher-Obermaier wrote *Das lyrische Werk Antoni Langes* (1983). CasWL; Dziekan; Polski (16); PSB

Lange, Dierk, born 20th cent., he received a doctorate in 1974 from the Université de Paris for *Le Dīwān des sultans du (Kānem-) Bornu; chronologie et histoire d'un royaume africain*, a work which was published in 1977. His writings include *A Sudanic chronicle; the Borno expeditions of Idrīs Alauma,*

1564-1576, according to the account of Ahmad Furtū (1987), and the microfiche edition, *Contribution à l'histoire médiévale du Borno et des pays Hausa* (1987). LC; ZKO

Lange, Klaus, born 9 February 1935, in Germany, he studied at the Universität München, where he received a Dr.phil. in 1970 for *Grundzüge der albanischen Politik*, a work which was published in 1973. He was a professor of political science at the Hochschule für Politik, München, and a visiting professor at Moscow and Peshawar. Kürschner, 1992-2005

Lange, Michael, born in 1953, he received a Dr.phil. in 1986 from the Universität Bochum for a thesis on alternative forms of industrial cooperation in assistance in the Third World entitled *Der Beitrag alternativer Formen industrieller Kooperation zur Mobilisierung von Entwicklungspotentialen in Entwicklungsländern; Gegenüberstellung und Evaluierung westlicher und östlicher Kooperations-ansätze in den Mashreqländern.* He subsequently joined the Institut für Entwicklungsforschung und Entwicklungspolitik, Ruhr-Universität, Bochum. He was a joint author of *Deutsch-ägyptische Produk-tionskooperation* (1981), *Internationale Produktionskooperation in Jordanien* (1982), and *Internationale Produktionskooperation im Vorderen Orient; joint ventures und andere Formen unternehmerischer Zusammenarbeit* (1983). Note about the author; ZKO

Langella, Vittorina, born in 1921, she was a geographer who taught at the Istituto universitario orientale, Napoli. Her writings include *Il Malese* (1964), *Geografia e lingue in Europa* (1969), *Il quadro geografico-linguistico dell'Europa* (1971), *Oriente - Occidente* (1993), and she was a joint author of *Lingua, cultura, territorio - rapporti ed effetti geografici* (1992). She died in July 1990. LC

van **Langen**, Karel Frederick Hendrik, born 28 March 1848 in Java, he entered the Dutch East India Company in 1868 and in the following year he was sent to Borneo as a civil servant. In 1870 he was made a controller third class on the Sumatra West Coast, becoming controller first class in 1879. He successively served as Resident of the West Coast of Atjeh and Greater Atjeh until 1886 when he returned home for two years. Upon his return to Atjeh, he was first Assistent Resident at Meester Cornelis, later at Benkoelen (Bengkulu), and finally in charge of Atjeh Affairs with the Governor of Atjeh. His writings include *Handleiding voor de beoefening der Atjehsche taal* (1889). He died in Ede, the Netherlands, on 18 April 1915. EncNI

Langenderfer, Harold Quentin, born 21 July 1925 at Swanton, Ohio, he was a graduate of Miami University who received a Ph.D. in business administration in 1954 from Indiana University. From 1953 to his retirement in 1993 he was a professor of business at the University of North Carolina, Chapel, Hill. From 1961 to 1963 he served as a consultant in mangament development to the Ford Foundation, Cairo. His writings include *C.P.A examination* (1969), and *The Federal income tax, 1861-1872* (1980). NatFacDr, 1990; WhoAm, 1978-2000|

Langenfelt, P. Gösta, born 25 September 1888 at Örebro, Sweden, he received a doctorate in 1920 from Uppsala Universitet for *Toponymics or derivations from local names in English.* He served briefly as a Swedish consul before teaching Scandinavian languages at the Universität Berlin from 1923 to 1927. He was successively a lecturer at Yastad and Bromma from 1932 to his retirement in 1954. His writings include *Selected studies in colloquial English of the late Middle Ages* (1933), and *Namnproblem i de svenska städerna* (1939). He died on 21 April 1965. OSK; Vem är det, 1941-1965

Langer, Felicia, born in 1929 or 30, she was an Israeli lawyer. Her writings include במו עיני (1975), its translations, *With my own eyes; Israel and the occupied territories, 1967-1973* (1975), *La repressione di Israele contro i Palestinesi* (1976), *Mit eigenen Augen; Israel und die besetzten Gebiete* (1977), Они - мой братья (1979), *Prisonieros del sionismo* (1987); *Brücke der Träume; eine Israelin geht nach Deutschland* (1994), *"Laßt uns wie Menschen leben!" Schein und Wirklichkeit in Palästina* (1996) as well as the translations from an unidentified original, *An Age of stone* (1988), زمان الحجارة (1989), and *Die Zeit der Steine* (1990). BioIn, 12; NUC, 1973-77; ZKO

Langer, Gerd, born 20th cent., he was a writer on civil liberties whose writings include *Die Beteiligten in dem Verfahren vor dem Europäischen Gerichtshof für Menschenrechte* (1966).

Langer, Heinz, born in 1933, he received a medical doctorate, and went as a ship's surgeon to Japan, experiences which are embodied in his *Nach Yokohama und zurück; Gedanken und Bilder eines Schiffsarztes* (Leipzig, 1972). His other writings include *Indien* (1975), and jointly with Sigrun Langer, *Arzt am Rande der Sahara* (Leipzig, 1975), and *Algerische Sahara, Land zwischen Atlas und Ahaggar* (Leipzig, 1977). NUC; Sezgin; ZKO

Langer, Siegfried, born 1 September 1857 at Schönwald near Mährisch-Aussee, Moravia, he studied Oriental languages, geography and medicine at the Universität Wien. In June 1881 he went to Syria and subsequently stayed some six months at al-Salt, Jordan. At the end of December 1881 he sailed from Jaffa to Southern Arabia. By way of al-Hudaydah he reached San'ā' on 26 March, but after two weeks he was compelled to return to al-Hudaydah, since he was prevented from proceeding any further. In the middle of April he was at Aden where the Austro-Hungarian vice-consul introduced him to the British Resident. Although warned of the great danger of penetrating inland, Langer still began his journey on 20 May. He was murdered by his Arab companions. His writings include *Reiseberichte aus Syrien und Arabien und die von ihm endeckten und gesammelten Inschriften*, edited by his Vienna Arabic professor, David H. Müller (1884). Fück, 256; Kornrumpf; ÖBL

Langer, William Leonard, born 16 March 1896 at Boston, Mass., he studied at Harvard and at Wien, taking his B.A. and Ph.D. at Harvard in 1915 and 1923 respectively. He was a professor of history at Harvard until his retirement in 1964. He there served as a director of the Russian Research Center from 1954 to 1959 and concurrently in the same capacity at the Center for Middle Eastern Studies, 1954-56. His writings include *The Diplomacy of imperialism, 1890-1902* (1935), its translation, *La diplomazia dell'imperialismo* (1942), and *Encyclopaedia of world history, ancient, medieval and modern* (1940). He died in Boston on 26 December 1977. His personal papers are in the Harvard University Library Archives. ANB; ConAu, 29-32, 73-76, new rev., 14; DrAS, 1969 H, 1974 H, 1978 H, 1982 H; IntWW, 1974-1977; Master (16); WhAm, 7; WhE&EA; WhoAm, 1974-1978

Langerbeck, Hermann Karl Ernst, born 10 October 1908 at Bremen, Germany, he received a Dr.phil. in 1934 from the Universität Berlin for Δοξις ἐπίπυσμίη: *Studien zu Demokrits Ethik und Erkenntnislehre.* He was successively a professor of classics at the Universität Königsberg and Universität Frankfurt am Main. His writings include *Aufsätze zur Gnosis*, edited by Hermann Dörries (1967), and he edited *Gregorii Nysseni opera* (1952). He died in Bad Homburg on 16 February 1964. DtBiInd (1); Kürschner, 1954-61; Wer ist wer, 1958-1961

Langerhans, Heinz, born 22 February 1904 at Berlin, he studied at the universities of Berlin and Frankfurt/Main, where he received a Dr.phil. in 1931 for *Partei und Gewerkschaft; eine Untersuchung zur Geschichte der Hegemonie der Gewerkschaft in der deutschen Arbeiterbewegung.* He left Germany in 1939 and reached the United States by way of Belgium, France, and Martinique. After the war he taught sociology at Gettysburg College, Pa., from 1947 to 1959. Until his retirement in 1972 he was successively a professor at the universities of Saarbrücken and Gießen. From 1959 to 1963 he was a professor of sociology at the University of Dacca, East Pakistan. His writings include *Stalin und der deutsche Kommunismus* (1950), and *Partei und Gewerkschaft* (1957). He died in Bad Homburg on 4 May 1976. BioHbDtE; GV; Kürschner

Langerhans, Paul, born 25 July 1847 at Berlin, he was educated at Gymnasium zum Grauen Kloster, Berlin, and studied medicine at the universities of Jena and Berlin, where he received a Dr.med. in 1869 for *Beiträge zur mikroskopischen Anatomie der Bauchspeicheldrüse*; it was translated into English entitled *Contributions to the microscopic anatomy of the pancreas* (1937). He was a sometime professor of medicine at the Universität Freiburg im Breisgau until tuberculosis compelled him to settle in 1875 at Funchal on Madeira Island where he later practised his profession. He died there on 20 July 1888. In 1870 he had accompanied the German geographer Heinrich Kiepert on an expedition to Egypt and Palestine. DcScB; Master (4)

Langhade, Jacques, born 22 January 1935 at Beirut, he studied at 'Ayn Shams University, Cairo, and the Sorbonne, received a *doctorat d'état ès lettres* in 1987 for *La langue arabe et la formation du vocabulaire philosophique de Farabi*, and became associated with the Université Michel de Montaigne Bordeaux III. He was a member of the editorial committees of the *Annales islamologiques*, *Bulletin des études orientales*, and *Arabica*; he also served as a director of the Institut français de Damas. His writings include *Du Coran à la philosophy; la langue arabe et la formation du vocabulaire philosophique de Farabi* (1994); and he edited *Deux ouvrages inédits sur la réthorique*, of al-Fārābī (1971), and Taha Hussein; colloque de Bordeaux, 1989 (1991). LC; Private

Langlands, Bryan Wooleston, born 14 October 1928 at Eastbourne, Sussex, he was educated at Croydon, and the King's/LSE Joint School of Geography where he took a first-class B.A. Honours degree in 1952. Shortly afterwards he was appointed lecturer in the Department of Geography at Makerere University, Kampala, Uganda, then in special relationship with the University of London. He remained a member of that deparment for over twenty years, from 1967 as professor and head of department. In 1978, he was awarded an OBE for services to higher education overseas. In 1977, he became director of studies in the School of Environmental Sciences, Ulster Polytechnic. His writings include *Maps of Africa, 1540-1850* (1961), a series of studies in historical geography similar to *The Population geography of West Nile District* (Kampala, 1971), and *The Story of a continent; a display of decorative maps of Africa, 1500-1900* (1971). He was a victim of the British Midland air disaster at Kegworth on 8 January 1989. AfrBioInd (6); Geography, 74 (1989), p. 187

Langlès, Louis Mathieu, he was born on 23 August 1763 at Welles-Pérennes (Oise), France. After leaving school he obtained a post at the Garde des maréchaux de France. Ever since taking office he was determined one day to enter the Armée de l'inde. When he realized that this would take a long time, he abandoned pursuit of the military for the career of an academic Orientalist. For this purpose he enrolled at the Collège de France, where he studied Arabic and Persian under A. I. Silverstre de Sacy. At the age of twenty-four he published the *Instituts politiques et militaires de Tamerlan, proprement appelé Timour, écrits en mogol et traduits en françois sur la version persane d'Abou-Taleb al-Hosseïni* (1787), a work for which he was awarded a handsome scholarship. In 1792, he was made keeper of the Oriental manuscripts of the Bibliothèque royale. Soon thereafter he re-submitted his earlier petition to the French National Assembly, *De l'importance des langues orientales pour l'extension du commerce et le progrès des lettres et des sciences*, suggesting the establishment of three chairs of Arabic, Persian, and Turkish at both Paris and Marseille. Due to his endeavours the École spéciale des langues orientales was established in 1795 at Paris, and he served as its first administrator as well as professor of Persian. Twenty-six years later, he became also one of the founders of the Société de géographie de Paris. He was a member of the Institut national des sciences et des arts. He died in Paris on 28 January 1824. *Asiatic journal*, 22 (1826), pp. 257-61; Buckland; DBF; Fück, pp. 141-42; GdeEnc; Hoefer; IndexBFr² (5); *Revue encyclopédique*, 28 (1825), pp. 354-68

Langley, Kathleen Mary (Mrs. Stanley James Langley), born 24 January 1928 at Audley, England, she was a graduate of Birmingham University. She was associated with the Institute of Statistics, Oxford, from 1949 to 1953, served for three years as a senior lecturer at the College of Arts and Sciences, Baghdad University, and subsequently taught economics in various capacities successively at the Center for Middle Eastern Studies, Harvard, Boston University, and Mount Holyoke College. Her writings include *The Industrialization of Iraq* (1961). AmM&WSc, 1973 S, 1978 S; WhoAmW, 1974/75, 1975/76

Langley, Lester Danny, born 7 August 1940 at Clarksville, Tex., he graduated in 1961 from West Texas State University and received a Ph.D. in 1965 from the University of Kansas, Athens, Kan., for *The United States and Panama, 1933-41*. He taught history at Texas A & AT University before being appointed in 1970 a professor at the University of Georgia, a post which he held until his retirement. His writings include *The Cuban policy of the United States* (1968), *The United States, Cuba, and the Cold War* (1970), *Struggle for the American Mediterranean, 1776-1904* (1976), *The Banana wars* (1983), and *Mexico and the United States; the fragile relationship* (1991). ConAu, 102, new rev., 19, 41; DrAS, 1969 H, 1972 H, 1978 H, 1982 H; WhoAm, 2003; WrDr, 1990/92-2006

Langlois, Nicolas Elisa, born 4 January 1824 at Laffond (Haute-Marne), France. After graduating from the École polytechnique, which he had entered in 1840, he followed a military career and rose to the rank of captain in 1853. At the end of the same year, he transferred to the Bureaux arabes at Batna, Algeria. From 1855 until 1860 he was in charge of the Bureau arabe at Biskra. Thereafter he was at Djidjelli (1860), Constantine (1861), Sétif (1862), and, as *commandant supérieur du cercle*, at Téniet-el-Haâd from September 1866 until his return to metropolitan France in 1868. He retired from military service in 1878. Peyronnet, 330-333

Langlois, Victor, born in 1829 at Dieppe, France, he was a graduate of the École des chartes and the École des langues orientales vivantes, Paris. He entered history in 1852 with a publication on numismatics. In the same year the minister of public instruction sent him on a scientific mission to Cilicia and Lesser Armenia. He returned in 1853 with a collection of terracotta figurines and eighty Greek inscriptions found during excavations at the necropolis of Tarsus. In 1857 and 1861 he went to Italy for the purpose of collecting material on the relations between France and Armenia during the crusades. A competent scholar of Armenian, he subsequently pursued studies in the history and antiquities of Armenia. His writings include *Numismatique de la Géorgie au moyen âge* (1852), *Numismatique de l'Arménie* (1859), *Numismatique des Arabes avant l'islamisme* (1859), and *Hérat, Dost Mohammed et les influences politiques de la Russie et de l'Angleterre en l'Asie centrale* (1864). He died in Paris in 1869. GdeEnc; GDU; Henze; IndexBFr² (4); Kornrumpf; Kornrumpf³, vol. 2; Master (1)

Lanier, Lucien, born in 1848 at Louhans (Saône-et-Loire), France, he was for many years a *professeur agrégé* in history at the Lycée Janson de Sailly at Paris where he taught history and geography before becoming *inspecteur* of the Académie at Paris. An *inspecteur général de l'Enseignement secondaire*, he published a number of geographical lectures which were used in university courses, including *L'Afrique, choix de lectures de géographie* (1884), and *L'Asie, choix de lecture de géographie* (1889). He was awarded *chevalier* of the Légion d'honneur. He died in Branges (Saône-et-Loire) on 27 April 1908. *Bulletin de la Société de géographie de Marseille*, 32 (1908), p. 258; IndexBFr² (1)

Lankenau, H. von, born in 1831 at St. Petersburg, he was a sometime inspector at the Imperial Russian *cadet corps* and a novelist. In 1885 he retired to Wiesbaden, Hesse. His writings include *Das heutige Rußland* (Leipzig, 1876-77), *Die Klikuschka; Erzählung* (Berlin, 1881), *Turkmenenrache*

(Breslau, 1882), and *Gährende Kräfte; ein Roman-Cyclus aus der vornehmen russischen Gesellschaft,* freely translated from the Russian of Boleslav M. Markevich, and completed after his death (1889). He died in Wiesbaden on 27 October 1896. DtBilnd (1); BioJahr, 3 (1900), Totenliste für 1896, col. 135*; KDtLK, 1885; OSK

Lanne, Bernard, born 20th cent., he was from 1963 to 1974 a director of the École nationale d'administration de la République du Tchad at N'Djamena. His writings include *Tchad - Libye; la querelle des frontières* (1982), *Répertoire de l'administration territoriale du Tchad, 1900-1994* (1995), and *Histoire politique du Tchad de 1945 à 1958; administration, partis, élections* (1998). Note about the author; Livres disponibles, 2004; ZKO

Lanning, Ernest Christian, born 20th cent., his writings include *Uganda's past* (Nairobi, 1957), and *Senegal and the Ivory Coast* (London, 1969). BLC; NUC

Tugnot de **Lanoye**, Augustin *Ferdinand* (Fernand), born in 1810 at St. Saturnin (Vaucluse), France, he shared his father's exile after Waterloo, a fate which barred him from public offices under the second Restauration. Associated with the writers and the party of *le National*, he contributed since 1830 to radical publications. From 1848 to 1850 he was a section head in the Ministry of War. For some ten years he was an editor of the journal *le Tour du monde*. His writings include *L'Inde contemporaine* (1856), *Mémoires de Luftullah, gentilhomme mahométan* (1858), *Le Niger et les explorations de l'Afrique centrale depuis Mungo-Park jusqu'au docteur Barth* (1858), and *La Sibérie d'après les voyageurs les plus récents* (1879). He died in Vienne (Isère) on 10 April 1870. IndexBFr² (2); Vapereau; ZKO

Lanrezac, born 19th cent., he was in 1914 a captain with the Tirailleurs algériens; in 1939 he served as a vice-president of the Association française de la Sarre. Note about the author

Lansdell, Henry, born in 1841 at Tenterden, Kent, he was an ordained priest since 1867. Animated by the desire of visiting prisons and hospitals and of placing there copies of the Bible, he visited many parts of the world. On his long journey through Central Asia he was received by the Amir of Bukhara. His writings include *Through Siberia* (1882), its translation, *Durch Sibirien; eine Reise vom Ural bis zum Stillen Ocean* (Jena, 1882), *Russian Central Asia* (1885), its translation, *Russisch-Central-Asien nebst Kuldscha, Buchara, Chiwa und Merw* (Leipzig, 1885), *Through Central Asia* (1887), and *Chinese Central Asia* (1893). He died in 1919. BiD&SB; BritInd (4); Master (2); Note about the author; Who was who, 2

Lansing, John Gulian, born in 1851 at Damascus, he passed his early life in Egypt. After obtaining a Ph.D. degree, he became a professor of Old Testament languages and exegesis at the Theological Seminary of the Reformed (Dutch) Church in America, New Brunswick, N.J. He was also a preacher with a keen interest in the Arabian Mission. His writings include *An Arabic manual* (1891). He died in Denver, Colo., in 1906. DAB; Kornrumpf; *Muslim world*, 30 (1940), p. 270; Richter, p. 276

Lantenay, Roger, 1890- *see* Vaucher, Roger, pseudonym

Lantenois, Honoré, born 19th cent., he was a sometime *inspecteur général* of mines. In 1939 he had retired. Note about the author

Lanternari, Vittorio, born 1 November 1918 at Ancona, Italy, he first studied agricultural sciences and later took liberal arts subjects at the Università di Roma, where he received a doctorate in 1946 with a thesis on the history of religions. He became the major representative of the Italian historical school of religious studies. His writings include *La grande festa* (1959), *Movimenti religiosi di libertà e di salvezza dei popoli oppessi* (1960), its translations, *Les mouvements religieux de liberté et de salut des peuples opprimés* (1962), *The Religions of the oppressed* (1963), and *Religiöse Freiheits- und Heilsbewegungen unterdrückter Völker* (1968), *Occidente e Terzo Mondo* (1967), *Appunti sulla cultura nzima, Ghana* (1972), *Antropologia e imperialismo e altri saggi* (1974), *Protezioni antifurto ed etica social-religiosa fra i coltivatorinzima, Ghana* (1974), *Folklore e dinamica culturale; crisi e ricerca d'identità* (1976), *Incontro con una cultura africana* (1976), and *La mia alleanza con Ernesto de Martino* (1997). IndBiltal (2); IntDcAn; NUC

Lantier, Raymond, born 11 July 1886 at Lisieux (Calvados), France, he entered in 1911 the Musée de Saint-Germain, and from 1913 to 1914 he was a fellow of the École des hautes études hispaniques. From 1921 to 1926, he served as joint inspector of Antiquités de Tunisie. He subsequently entered the Musée des Antiqités nationales, Paris, becoming its *conservateur en chef* in due course. His primary research subject became Celtic art with special reference to the Iberian Peninsula. For thirty-two years he served as a joint director of the *Revue archéologique*. His writings include *Les Origines de l'art français* (1947), *L'Art prehistorique* (1961), and he edited *The Rise of the Celts* (1934). He died on 2 April 1980. DBF; DBFC, 1954/55; IndexBFr² (1); IntAu&W, 1977; IntWW, 1974-1980; *Revue archéologique*, n.s., 1984, p. 105; WhoFr, 1953/54-1979/80

Lantschoot, André *Arnold*, he was born 24 April 1889 at Ursel, Belgium. After taking doctorates in divinity and philology at the Université de Louvain, he was ordained in 1913. He was successively canon of l'Abbaye de Parc de l'Ordre de Prémonté, *consulteur* of the Congrégation pour l'Église orientale, and *consulteur* of the Commission biblique pontificale. Throughout his life he was a student of the Christian Orient. His writings include *Inventaires sommaires de MSS arabes d'Égypte, Bibliothèque de l'Université de Louvain* (1935). He died in Roma on 23 February 1969. Byzantion, 38 (1968), 620-630

Laor, Eran, born Erik Landstein on 1 June 1900 at Cifer (Cziffer) Austria-Hungary, he studied at Wien, and in 1925 left Europe for Constantinople where he studied Oriental languages and archaeology, and translated Turkish poetry. In 1934, he went to Palestine to become one of the pioneers of Israeli shipping. He spent the war years in Istanbul, Beirut, and Tehran on various missions. A student of Persian and Arabic, he was one of the founders of the Israel Oriental Society. His writings include *Orientalische Renaissance* (1958), *Umkehr und Aufstieg; Gedichte* (Wien, 1971), *Vergangen und ausgelöscht* (1972), *Maps of the Holy Land; cartobibliography* (1986), and *Wolkensäule, Feuersäule; Rückkehr ins Gelobte Land* (1987). He died in Jerusalem on 17 June 1990. Note about the author; WhoIsrael, 1973-1992/93; WhoWorJ, 1972, 1978

Laourdas, Basileios, born 12 March 1912 at Piraeus, Greece, he was a writer on Balkan history and the Greek Orthodox Church. His writings include Ή Πηνελόπη Δέλτα και ή Μακεδονία (1958), and Το Ελληνικον Γενικκον Προξενεῖον Θεσσαλονίκης, 1903-1908 (1961), and Ο Μακεδονικος άγών (1962). Hellenikon, 1965; NUC

Laoust, Émile, born 20 July 1876 at Fresnes-sur-Escaut (Nord), France, he graduated from the École normale de Douai and then went to Algeria to learn the local languages at the École de La Bouzaréa, in Arabic and Berber-speaking surroundings. He subsequently taught at Mouzaiaville and Marengo. When the French Resident general in Morocco, Lyautey, established the École supérieure de langue arabe in 1912 at Rabat, he was entrusted there to teach Berber. His writings include *Étude sur le dialecte berbère du Chenoua comparé avec ceux des Beni-Mevacer et des Beni-Salah* (1912), *Étude sur le dialecte berbère des Ntifa* (1918), *Mots et choses berbères* (1920), *Cours de berbère marocain* (1921), *Contes berbères du Maroc* (1949), *Noces berbères; les cérémonies du mariage au Maroc* (1993), and he was a joint author of *Notes d'ethnographie et de linguistique nord-africains* (1924). He died in Rabat on 20 September 1952. DBF; Hommes et destins, 7, pp. 293-94; ZKO

Laoust, Henri, born 1 April 1905 at Fresnes-sur-Escaut (Nord), France, he received his secondary education at Rabat and Paris. In 1928, graduated in Arabic and philosophy from the École normale supérieure, Paris. He spent 1929 at the Institut français de Damas. After his *agrégation* in Arabic in 1930, he spent five years at the Institut français d'archéologie oriental du Caire. In 1940, he received his *doctorat ès lettres* at Paris for *Essai sur les doctrines sociales et politiques d'Ibn Taymiyya*. He subsequently was director of the Institut français de Damas, held the chair of *Langue et civilisation arabes*, at Lyon, and finally succeeded Louis Massignon in the chair of Islamic sociology at the Collège de France. He was a member of academies in Syria, Egypt and France. His writings include *Les schismes dans l'islam* (1946), *Pluralismes dans l'islam* (1983), *Comment definir le Sunnisme et le Chiisme*(1985) as well as numerous translations from classical Arabic literature. He died on 12 November 1983. In 1990 appaered *Hommage à Henri Laoust*. Hommes et destins, vol. 7, pp. 194-95; Index Islamicus (5); LC; Revue des études islamiques, 52 (1984), pp. 3-11; WhoFr, 1967/68-1983/84

Laoust-Chantréaux, Germaine, born in the first half of the 20th century in Algeria. Her writings include *Kabylie côté femmes* (1990). LC

Lapanne-Joinville, Jean, born 19th cent , he was a sometime commissioner and inspector of the Jurisdictions chérifiennes, Morocco, as well as a counsellor in the Tribunal administratif de Constantine, Algeria. He edited and translated *Recueil de jurisprudence chérifienne* (Paris, 1920). Note about the author, NUC, pre-1956

Lapasset, Ferdinand Auguste, born 29 July 1817 at Saint-Martin, Île-de-Ré, France, he graduated from the two military colleges, the École spéciale, Saint-Cyr, and the École d'État-Major, as a *sous-lieutenant* in 1837. As a lieutenant he went in 1840 to Algeria to take an active part in the conquest of the colony. Promoted captain in 1845, he then entered the Bureaux arabes, where he became one of the most remarkable of its officers due to his personal qualities and his acquaintance with native customs as well as Arabic. He rose to become director of Arab Affairs of the Province of Oran in 1853. From 1854 to 1867 he was successively *commandant* at Philippeville, Sidi-Bel-Abbès, and Mostaganem. In the *Second Empire* he exercised considerable influence on the Algerian politics of the Emperor. His writings include *Mémoire sur la colonisation indigène et la colonisation européenne* (1848), and *Aperçu sur l'organisation des indigènes dans les territoires civils* (1850). He died in Toulouse on 16 September 1875. DBF; Hommes et destins, vol. 2, pp. 442-44

Lape, Ljuben, born 11 October 1910, he was a professor of Macedonian history at Skopje University as well as a director of its Институт за национала историја. His writings include *Одабрани четива за историјата на македонскиот народ* (1953), *Одбрани текстови за историјата на македонскиот народ* (1959), *Разловечкото востание од 1876 година и личноста на неговиот организатор Димитар Пол Георгиев Беровски* (Skopje, 1976), and *Македонја во XVIII, XIX и XX век; обрани трудови* (1992). JugoslSa; Ko je ko; NUC; OSK

Lapène, Blaise Jean François Édouard, born in 1790, he was a graduate of the École d'application de l'Artillerie et du Genie de Metz and was promoted captain on 28 June 1813. He participated in the final campaigns of the *Empire*. Under the *Restauration* he became a deputy director of the Manufacture d'armes in Tulle (Corrèze). A major since the *Révolution de Juillet*, he served in Africa and for a few months in 1836 was acting *commandant* of Bougie, Algeria, after his superior had been assassinated. He became lieutenant-colonel in 1839, colonel in 1843, advancing to brigadier-general after the revolution of February 1848. He was associated with the Académie de Metz. His writings include *Campagnes de 1813 et de 1814 sur l'Èbre, les Pyrénées et la Garonne, précédées de considérations sur la dernières guerre d'Espagne* (1823), *Vingt-six mois à Bougie* (1837), and *Tableau historique de l'Algérie, depuis l'occupation romaine jusqu'à la conquête par les Français en 1830* (Metz, 1845). He died in May 1854. GDU; Hoefer; IndexBFr² (1); NUC, pre-1956; Peyronnet, p. 154; ZKO

Laperrine, Marie Joseph François *Henri*, born 29 September 1860 at Castelnaudary (Aude), France, he received his first education from Dominicans at Sorèze. After graduation from the military college, Saint-Cyr, and the École d'application de la cavalerie, Saumur, he was posted to Sud-oranais and Tunisia as a *sous-lieutenant*, where he served with Charles de Foucauld in the same regiment. After some years spent in North Africa, he requested to be transferred to French Equatorial Africa where he spent twelve years of his life establishing himself as the pacificator of the Sahara. Since 1919 in charge of the newly established Commandement supérieur des territoires sahariens, he perished on 5 March 1920 from injuries received in a crash landing in the Sahara on a flight to Timbuctu. He was a joint author of *La Pénétration saharienne; 1906, le rendez-vous de Taoudeni* (1999). Pierre Gorrée wrote *Laperrine, la plus belle amitié du Père de Foucauld* (1948). DBF; Henze; IndexBFr² (1); Peyronnet, pp. 496-501

Lapham, Robert J., born about 1940, he received a Ph.D. in 1970 from the University of Michigan for *Fertility determinants in the Sais Plain of Central Morocco*. In the early 1970s he was associated with the Population Council, New York. He was a joint editor of *Research on the population of China; proceedings of a workshop* (1981). LC; *MESA Roster of members*, 1977-1982; Note about the author

Lapidoth, Ruth née Eschelbacher, born in 1930, she received a law degree from the Hebrew University, Jerusalem, and a doctorate in 1956 from the Faculté de droit de Paris. She became a lecturer at the Hebrew University, Jerusalem, as well as a legal adviser to the Israeli Ministry of Foreign Affairs. Her writings include *Les rapports entre le droit international public et le droit interne en Israël* (1959), *La conclusion des traités internationaux en Israël* (1962), *Les détroits en droit international* (1972), *Freedom of navigation* (1975), *The Red Sea and the Gulf of Aden* (1982), *Autonomy; flexible solutions to ethnic conflicts* (1997), and she edited *The Arab Israel conflict and its solution; selected documents* (1992). NUC; WhoWorJ, 1972, 1978

Lapidus, Ira Marvin, born about 1935, he received a degree in 1958 from Harvard for an honors thesis entitled *Saljug government and the Islamic community from Tughrul to Sanjar*, and also his Ph.D. in 1964 for *The Muslim city in Mamluk times*. He was a professor of history, and a sometime chairman of department, Center for Middle Eastern Studies in the University of California at Berkeley. His writings include *Muslim cities in the later middle ages* (1967), *Contemporary Islamic movements in historical perspective* (1983), and *A History of Islamic societies* (1988). *MESA Roster of members*, 1977-1990; NatFacDr, 1990-1995; Note about the author; Selim

Lapie, Pierre, born 11 August 1777 (not 1779) at Mézières, (Ardennes), France, he was a draughtsman at the École du génie de Mézières at the age of eleven, and in 1794 entered the Bureau topographique du Comité de Salut public. In 1799, he left his office post for field-work, first with the Armée des Alpes and later with the Grande Armée.. He became *premier géographe du roi* and director of his Cabinet topographique under the *Restauration*. During the Greek war of liberation, he produced the *Carte générale de la Turquie*. He was one of the great cartographers of all times, particularly the critical geography of Africa and Asia, including Algeria. He died in Paris on 30 December 1850. DBF; Hoefer; IndexBFr² (6)

Lapie, Pierre Olivier, born 2 April 1901 at Rennes Ille-et-Vilaine), France, he studied at the École libre des sciences politiques, and the Faculté de droit de Paris, taking his doctorate in 1925 for *L'État actionnaire*. He was a barrister in the Court of Appeal, specializing in international legal affairs. In

1939, he was mobilized as a *lieutenant d'infanterie coloniale*. In 1940, he went to London, where General de Gaulle took him into his cabinet as director of foreign affairs. In November 1940, he was made governor of Chad, where he remained for two years. After the war, he was a socialist *député*, holding high positions in international organizations. His writings include *Le Tchad fait la guerre* (1943), *Mes tournées au Tchad* (1944), and *Les déserts de l'action* (1946). He died in Paris on 10 March 1994. DBF; DBFC, 1954/55; IndexBFr² (3); WhoFr, 1961/62-1993/94

Lapinski (Lapinsky), Teofil (Theophil), also known as Tefik Bey, he was a born Pole and participated in the Hungarian revolution. Thereafter he lived for some time in Germany as a writer. In the late 1850s he organized an insurrection of the Abkhas against the Russians in the Caucasus. Subsequently he lived as a writer in Poland, Denmark, and Paris. His writings include *Feldzug der ungarischen Hauptarmee im Jahre 1849; Selbsterlebtes* (1850), and *Die Bergvölker des Kaukasus und ihr Freiheitskampf gegen die Russen* (1863). BN; GeistigeUng, p. 613; RNL

La Pira, Gaetano M., born 20th cent., he was a joint author of *Il Sud-Est asiatica* (Milano, Istituto per gli studi di politica internazionale, 1978). LC

Lapis, Bohdan, born 20th cent., his writings include *Poglądy na pracę we wczesno średniowiecznym piśmiennictwie łacińskim* (Poznań, 1977), *Rex utilis; kryteria oceny władców germańskich we wczesnym średniowieczu* (Poznań, 1986), and *U źródet polskich refleksji nad pracą* (1984). LC; OSK

Lapointe, Roger Lucien, born 28 July 1929 at Kénogami, P.Q., Canada, he received degrees in philosophy and theology in 1951 at Roma, where he also received a doctorate in 1966 from the Pontificio Istituto Biblico di Roma. He was a professor of theology and sociology of religion, first at St. Paul University and later at the University of Ottawa. His writings include *Les trois dimensions de l'herméneutique* (1967), *Consultation internationale sur le non-être; dialogue philosophique* (1969), *Dialogues bibliques et dialectique interpersonnelle; étude stylistique et théologique sur le procédé diagonal tel qu'employé dans l'Ancient Testament* (1971), *La Religion populaire au péril de la modernité* (1988), and *Cercle enchanté de la croyance* (1989). NatFacDr, 1990-1995|; WhoRel, 1975, 1977, 1985, 1992

LaPorte, Robert, born 12 February 1940 at Detroit, Mich., he graduated in 1962 from Wayne State University, Detroit, and received his Ph.D. in 1967 from Syracuse (N.Y.) University for *Public corporations and resource development in South Asia*. He spent his entire academic career with the Pennsylvania State University, University Park, Pa., as a professor of public administration. His writings include *Power and privilege; influence and decision-making in Pakistan* (1975), *Public enterprises in Pakistan; the hidden crisis in economic development* (1989), and he was a joint author of *Cultivating revolution; the United States and agrarian reform in Latin America* (1971). AmM&WSc, 1973 S, 1978 S; ConAu, 41-44; IWWAS, 1975/76; Private

Lapp, John Allen, born 15 March 1933 at Landsdale, Pa., he graduated in 1954 from East Mennonite College and received his Ph.D. in 1972 from the University of Pennsylvania for *The Mennonite Church in India, 1897-1962*. He was in 1995 a professor at Bible College, Lancaster, Pa. His writings include *The View from East Jerusalem* (1980). ConAu, 41-44; DrAS, 1969 H, 1974 H. 1978 H, 1982 H; LEduc, 1974; NatFacDr, 1995; WhoRel, 1992

de **Lapparent**, Albert Auguste Cochon, born 30 December 1839 at Bourges (Cher), France, he was a graduate of the École polytechnique as well as the École des mines, Paris, and subsequently served for thirty-three years as a professor of geology and mineralogy at the Institut catholique de Paris. He was one of the most distinguished French geologists of the nineteenth century. His writings include *Traité de géologie* (1882). He died in Paris on 4 May 1908. Curinier, 5 (1906), pp. 68-69; DBF; DcScB; IndexBFr² (2); Master (3); NewCathEnc

de **Lapparent**, Marie Félix *Albert* Cochon, born 9 September 1905 at Le Mont-Dieu (Ardennes), France, he studied at the Séminaire de Saint-Sulpice, entered the Compagnie de Jésus and was ordained priest in 1929. He took a doctorate in science in 1938 at the Sorbonne for *Études géologiques dans les régions provençales at alpines entre le Var et la Durance*. He subsequently taught at the Institut catholique de Paris, concurrently serving as a *directeur de recherches* with the C.N.R.S. He became a president of the Société de géologie de France in 1945, and was elected a corresponding member of the Académie des sciences in 1970. His principal research centred on North Africa and Afghanistan. He was a joint author of *Contribution à la géologie et à la paléontologie de l'Afghanistan central* (1968). He died in Paris on 28 February 1975. In 1977 appeared *Livre à la mémoire de Albert F. de Lapparent, 1905-1975, consacré aux recherches géologiques dans les chaînes alpines de l'Asie du sud-ouest*. DBF; ZKO

Lappe, John Allen, born 15 March 1933 at Landsdale, Pa., he graduated in 1954 from East Mennonite College and received a Ph.D. in 1959 from Western Reserve University, Cleveland, Ohio. His writings include *The View from East Jerusalem* (1980). DrAS, 1969 H

Geouffre de La Pradelle, Pierre Marie *Albert*, born 30 March 1871 at Tulle (Corrèze), France, he was educated at the colleges of Chartres and Alençon, and studied law at Paris, where he received both his doctorate and *agrégation*. He taught for nearly ten years at the Université de Grenoble before teaching public law, history of international treaties, and finally constitutional law at the Sorbonne, a post which he held until his retirement in 1939. In 1921, he there established the Institut des hautes études internationales. Having been jurisconsult of the French Foreign Ministry and of the Marine, he was designated by the Council of the League of Nations as a member of the committee which drafted the Statute of the International Court of Justice. He was a member of several learned societies and national academies, and the founder and director of journals in the field. Besides his own country, nine nations have awarded high decorations to this indefatigable fighter for justice and morality in the relation between men and nations. His writings include *La Mer territoriale* (1898), *Le Conflit italo-éthiopien* (1936), *La Paix moderne* (1945) as well as translations into French of other eminent jurists. He died on 2 February 1955. *American journal of international law*, 45 (1951), pp. 577-78; 49 (1955), p. 395; DBF; IndexBFr² (2)

de Lapresa Molina, Eladio, born 19 February 1907 at Granada, Spain, he received a degree in letters in 1927 and another one in law in 1929. He was a member of the Cuerpo de Archivos, Bibliotecas y Museos, a director of the Archivio de la Chancillería de Granada, and a professor at the Facultad de Filisofía y Letras, Universidad de Granada. His writings include *Historia del Ilustre Colegio de Abogados de Granada, 1726-1850* (Granada, 1976). IndiceE³ (2); WhoSpain, 1963

La Primaudaie, F. Elie de, fl. 19th cent. *see* Elie de la Primaudaie, F.

Laptev, Vladimir Viktorovich, born 28 April 1928 at Moscow, he received a doctorate in law and later held a chair of law at Moscow University. He was a member of the Soviet as well as the Russian Academy of Sciences. His numerous writings include Хозяйственное право (1986), and its translation, *Economic law* (1987), and Экономико-правовые проблемы перестройки хозяйственного механизма (1989). IntWW, 1991-2005; Master (1)

Laqueur, Hans Peter, born in 1949 at Istanbul, he received a Dr.phil. in 1979 from the Universität München for *Zur kulturgeschichtlichen Stellung des türkischen Ringkampfes einst und jetzt*. He was associated with Deutsches Archäologisches Institut, Abteilung Istanbul. His writings include *Osmanische Friedhöfe und Grabsteine in Istanbul* (1993), and jointly with J.-L. Bacqué-Grammont and Nicolas Vatin, *Stelae Turcicae; vol. 2: Cimitières de la mosquée Sokollu Mehmed Paşa à Kadırga Limanı, de Bostancı Ali türbe de Sokollu Mehmed Paşa à Eyüb* (1990). GV; Note; ZKO

Laqueur, Kurt, born 22 October 1914 at Berlin, he studied at the Universität Berlin until dismissed for political reasons in 1935. He came to in Ankara as the son of an emigré physician and initially pursued commercial interests in İstanbul until interned. After the war he was a lecturer at the Foreign language school (İstanbul Üniversitesi Yabancı Diller Okulu) from 1946 to 1952, when he returned to Germany to enter the German diplomatic service and became press attaché at the German legation, Ankara. In 1968, he was posted to Zagreb as consul general. BioHbDtE; Widmann, p. 108

Laqueur, Walter Ze'ev, born 26 May 1921 at Breslau, Germany, he went to Palestine in the late 1930s and began to study at the Hebrew University, Jerusalem. During the war, he was an agricultural worker in Palestine until 1944. He subsequently settled in London, where he became a historian and political commentator. He was for thirty years associated with the Institute of Contemporary History and the Wiener Library, London, as well as the Center for Strategic and International Studies, Washington. His many writings include *Nasser's Egypt* (1956), *Communism and nationalism in the Middle East* (1958), *The Soviet Union and the Middle East* (1959), *Europe in our time* (1992), *Fin de siècle and other essays on America and Europe* (1997), *No end to war; terrorism in the twenty-first century* (2003), its translation, *Krieg dem Westen* (2003); and he was a joint editor of *Polycentrism; the new factor in international communism* (1962). Au&Wr, 1963; CnDiAmJBi; ConAu, 5-8, new rev., 23, 94; IntAu&W, 1977-2006; IntWW, 1975-2006; Master (9); WhoAm, 1976-1996; WhoIsrael, 1972-76, 1990/91-2001; Who's who, 1973-2005; WhoWor, 1974/75-1984; WhoWorJ, 1965, 1972, 1978, 1987; WrDr, 1976/78-2006

Laquière, Emmanuel M., Colonel, born about 1850 at Foix, France, he graduated in 1877 from the military academy, Saint-Cyr, and then served with the Zouaves. In 1882, he entered the Algerian Service des Affaires indigènes where he remained until 1906. Three times he was awarded the Médaille d'or of the Société de géographie [de Paris?] for his Saharan travel account, for his map of the Oases, and for his pre-historical researches. Peyronnet

Lara, Oruno Dennis, born 20th cent., he was from Guadalupe and served as a director of the Groupe de recherches caraïbes-amériques de l'Université de Paris X - Nanterre. His writings include *Le Commandant Mortenol, un officier guadeloupéen dans la "Royale"* (1985), *Les Caraïbes* (1986), *Caraïbes en construction; espace, colonisation, resistance* (1996), *La naissance du pan-africanisme; les racines caraïbes, américaines et africaines au XIX siècle* (2000), *Mortenol ou Les infortunes de la servitude* (2001), and *Caraïbes entre liberté et indépendance; réflections critiques autour d'un bicentenaire, 1802-2002* (2002). LC; *Livres disponibles*, 2004

Laran, Michel, fl. 20th cent., his writings include *Russie-URSS, 1870-1970* (Paris, 1973), and, with Jean-Louis van Regemorter, *La Russie et l'ex-URSS de 1914 à nos jours* (Paris, 1996), and he edited *L'Époque contemporaine, 1871-1945* (Liège, 1960). NUC

Laranjo Coelho, Possidónio Mateus, born 16 November 1877 at Castelo de Vide, Portugal, he studied at Coimbra. He was a palaeographer who, in 1908, became a keeper of the Arquivo Nacional da Torre do Tombo, Lisboa. In 1923, he was a professor at the Lisboa Faculty of Letters. A member of several learned societies, his writings include *Documentos inéditos de Marrocos* (1943). *Quem é alguém*, 1947

Larcher, Eugène *Émile*, born 1 January 1869 at Nancy, France, he received his *licence en droit* in 1891; after he obtained also a doctorate in the following year, he taught for a year at the Faculty of Law in Paris, before going on to the Université d'Alger in 1896, where initially he taught civil law. After his bar admission in 1902, he became professor of criminal law. In 1905, he assumed also the editorship of the *Revue algérienne*, a position which he held until his death in Alger on 3 January 1918. His writings include *Traité élémentaire de législation algérienne* (1903).

Larchey, Étienne *Lorédan*, born 26 January 1831 at Metz, France, the son of an artillery captain, he began his education at the Lycée de Metz completing it at the Lycée Saint-Louis in Paris. After taking a law degree he enrolled in November 1849 in the École des chartes, Paris, but failed his second year and could not proceed to the final year. In June 1852, he entered the Bibliothèque Mazarin as a supernumerary. After also working at the Bibliothèque Ste.-Geneviève, Paris, he entered the Bibliothèque de l'Arsenal where he became keeper in 1880. He was sent on several library missions throughout France. He was a prolific writer on French affairs, including a dozen works in the series, *Documents pour servir à l'histoire de nos mœurs* (1869-1874). He died in Menton (Alpes-Maritimes) on 12 April 1902. DBF; IndexBFr² (7); Kornrumpf

Laredo, Abraham Isaac, born in 1895, he was a president of the Société d'histoire et d'archéologie de Tanger. His writings include *Bereberes y Hebreos en Marruecos* (1954), *Les Noms des Juifs du Maroc* (1978). In 1969 appeared *Hommage à Abraham I. Laredo, président de la Société d'histoire et d'archéologie de Tanger*. LC; ZKO

de **La Renaudière**, Philippe François, born in 1781 at Vire, Normandie, he started to write poetry when he was still young, but ceased to do so when he became president of the Tribunal de Vire. He was friends with the geographer Victor A. Malte-Brun and under his influence gave up his magistracy to pursue an interest in geography. He was a secretary of the Paris Société de géographie and in charge of its *Bulletin*, he was also one of the principal *rédacteurs-directeurs* of the *Annales des voyages* since 1823. He translated numerous English geographical works into French and contributed critical book reviews to French periodicals. He died in February of 1845. Hoefer; IndexBFr² (2)

Larew, Karl Garret, born 9 December 1936 at Ithaca, N.Y., he graduated in 1959 from the University of Connecticut and received his Ph.D. in 1964. He spent his entire academic career from 1966 to his retirement as a professor of modern European military and intellectual history in the Department of History, Towson State University, Baltimore, Md. His writings include *Garret Larew, Civil War soldier* (1975). DrAS, 1969 H, 1972 H, 1978 H, 1982 H; NatFacDr, 1990-2002; WhoE, 1993

Largeau, Étienne, 1867-1897 *see* Largeau, Victor Emmanuel Étienne

Largeau, Jean *Victor*, born in 1840 (or 42) at Niort (Deux-Sèvres), France, he was an explorer of the Sahara and French Sudan under commercial and scientific aspects. In 1875, he opended up the route from Biskra to Ghadamès. His writings include *Expédition de Rhadamès* (1876), *Sahara; premier voyage d'exploration* (1877), *Le Pays de Rirha, Ouargla; voyage à Rhadamès* (1879), *Le Sahara algérien* (1881), and he translated *Flore saharienne, histoire et légendes*, from the Arabic of 'Isá ibn al-Samātī al-Fallāī (1978). He died in Niort on 29 March 1897. DBF; *Bulletin de la Société de géographie d'Alger*, 2 (1897), pp. 372-73; Embacher; Henze; *Hommes et destins*, vol. 1, pp. 342-44

Largeau, Victor Emmanuel *Étienne*, born 11 June 1867 at Irgun (Spain), where his parents were travelling. He joined the French *infanterie de marine* in 1885, and in 1889 he entered the École militaire d'infanterie at Rochefort. After graduating the following year he served in the French Sudan for four years. In 1896, he was attached to the Mission Congo-Nil under Jean Baptiste Marchand, which ended in the Fashoda incident of 1898. From 1902 to 1915 he was head of the *Commandement du Territoire militaire du Tchad*. With the rank of brigadier-general he went into the first Word War at the *État-major général des troupes coloniales*. Mortally wounded before Verdun, he died two months later on 22 January 1916. His writings include *Encyclopédie pahouine, Congo français; éléments de grammaire et dictionnaire français-pahouin* (1901), and *La situation du territoire militaire du Tchad au début de 1912* (1913). DBF; Hill; *Hommes et destins*, vol. 1, pp. 342-44

Larguier, Jean, born 4 July 1925 at Montpellier, France, he studied law at the Université de Montpellier, there taking all his degrees, including a doctorate in law in 1948 for *La notion de titre en droit privé*, a work which was published in 1951. He subsequently taught law at the Université de Grenoble from 1949 to 1951, when he received his *agrégation* in *droit privé et sciences criminelles*. He then spent three years at the Institut des hautes études juridiques de Dakar. Upon his return to France in 1957 he became a professor of law at his alma mater. His writings include *Droit pénal* (1962), and *Droit pénal spécial* (1975). In 1993 appeared Mélanges en honneur du Professor Jean Larguier; droit pénal, procédure pénale. Note about the author

Larnaude, Marcel, born 24 April 1886 at Sainte-Adresse (Seine-maritime), France, he was a brilliant student at two Parisian colleges and received his *agrégation* in history and geography at the École normale supérieure in 1912. In the first World War he was seriously wounded in Flanders while serving with the 9e Zouaves. After recovery he was assigned to the Service des Affaires indigènes in Algeria. As an ordnance officer under General Laperrine, he accompanied his superior on his Saharan peregrinations, particularly Hoggar, much to the profit of cultural geography. In the inter-war years he taught geography first at the Université d'Alger and later moved to the Sorbonne to give the course, «Géographie et colonisation de l'Afrique du Nord», only to be mobilized once more. It was only after the war that he returned to his post at the Institut de géography. He retired in 1949. He was elected member of the Académie des sciences coloniales. His writings include *Algérie* (1950), and *La population musulmane de l'Algérie* (1956). He died in Paris on 15 January 1980. *Hommes et destins*, vol. 8, pp. 239-40

de **La Roncière**, Charles Germain Marie Bourel, born 24 October 1870 at Nantes, France, he was educated at the Collège S.-Charles at Saint-Brieuc and graduated in 1892 from the École des chartes, Paris, with a thesis entitled *Sur la marine française sous Louis XI*, a work which was later published in his two-volume *Histoire de la marine française* and gained him admittance to the École française de Rome. Upon his return to France, he entered the Département des manuscrits of the Bibliothèque nationale, Paris. In 1909, he was made deputy keeper of the Section des cartes et plans, and in November 1910, he became keeper of the Département des imprimés. His writings include *La découverte de l'Afrique au moyen âge; cartographes et explorateurs* (Le Caire, 1924-1925). He died in Gourin (Morbihan) on 15 June 1941. DBF; *Isis*, 40 (1949), p. 355 (not sighted); *Qui êtes-vous*, 1924

de **La Roncière**, Monique Bourel, she was a map librarian at the Bibliothèque National, Paris. Her writings include *L'amitié franco-canadienne de Jacques Cartier à Chateaubriand* (Paris, 1967), *Les portulans* (1984), its translation, *Portulane; Seekarten vom 13. bis zum 17. Jahrhundert* (1984), and she was a joint author of *Catalogue des cartes nautiques sur vélin conservées au Département des cartes et plans, Bibliothèuq Nationale* (Paris, 1963). BN; ZKO

de **La Roque**, Jean, born 16 February 1661 at Marseille, he entered the service of a *gros seignieur* of the Bouillon establishment which afforded him the opportunity to spend time in Constantinople and Jerusalem, and travel in Syria and visit Mount Lebanon in 1689, Arabia in 1708 and 1710, and the Yemen in 1711 and 1713. Upon his return to France, he settled in Paris, where he edited his travel accounts and worked at the *Mercure de France*. His writings include *Voyage de l'Arabie heureuse, par l'Océan oriental, et le Détroit de la Mer Rouge, fait dans les années 1708, 1709 et 1710; avec la relation particulière d'un voyage fait du Port de Moka à la Cour du Roy d'Yemen, dans la 2nde expédition des années 1711, 1712 et 1713* (1716), its translations, *Viaggio nell'Arabia felice per l'Oceano orientale e lo stretto del Mar rosso* (1721), *A Voyage to Arabia the Happy, by the way of the Eastern ocean, and the straights of the Red-sea* (1726), *Reise nach dem glücklichen Arabien* (1740); and *Voyage de Syrie et du Mont Liban* (1722). DBF; Hoefer

de **La Roquette**, Jean Bernard Marie Alexandre Dezos, 1784-1868 *see* Dezos de La Roquette, Jean Bernard Marie Alexandre

Laroui, Abdallah Muhammad, he was born 7 November 1933 at Azemmour, Morocco. Since 1964 he was a professor of history at Rabat and in 1969-1970 he was a visiting professor at the University of California at Los Angeles. His writings include *Histoire du Maghreb* (1970), *La Crise des intellectuels* *arabes* (1974), *The Crisis of the Arab Intellectual* (1976), *L'Algérie et le Sahara marocain* (1976), *El islam árabe y sus problemas* (1984), and *Islam et modernité* (1987). WhoWor, 1974/75

Larras, Nestor Prosper, general, born in 1868 at Alger, he was a graduate of the military college, Saint-Cyr, l'École nationale supérieure, and l'École polytechnique. He served between 1897 and 1907 in North Africa, mainly on diplomatic and cartographic missions, in particular the hydrographic mission to Morocco, where he was accompanied by A. Brives, who published its results entitled *Voyages au Maroc, 1901-1907* (1909). In 1905, he published maps of Fez and Marrakesh. He contributed numerous articles to scholarly journals, and was a member of the Académie des sciences coloniales since 1935. He died in 1955. *Hommes et destins*, vol. 1, p. 345; NUC, pre-1956

de **Larrea Palacín**, Arcadio, born in 1907 at Echávarri (Navarra), Spain, he was a musicologist, literary critic, member of numerous learned societies, and head of the Ethnology and Folklore Section at the *Enciclopedia de la cultura española*. His writings include *El dance aragonés y las representaciones de moros y cristianos* (1952), *Cancieones juglarescas de Ifni* (1956), *Cancieones populares de Ifni* (1957), *La música hispano-árabe* (1957), *El folklore y la escuela* (1958), and *La cancion Andaluza; ensayo de etnologia musical* (1960-61). He died in Madrid in 1985. IndiceE³ (3)

Larrey, Dominique Jean, Baron, born 8 July 1766 at Beaudéan (Haute-Pyrénées), France, he was one of the most famous physicians in military history, who participated in Napoleon's Egyptian campaign as chief medical officer, and as chief surgeon with the Grand Armée in the eastern campaign. Appalled by the sufferings and loss of wounded who were left for a day or more on the field, he devised light mobile ambulances to rescue them during battle and provide prompt surgical attention. His writings include *Mémoires de chirurgie militaires et campagnes* (1812-1817), its translation, *Surgical memoirs of the campaigns of Russia, Germany, and France* (1832), *Clinique chirurgicale exercée particulièrement dans les camps et les hôpitaux militaires depuis 1792 jusqu'en 1829* (1829), its translation, *Chirurgische Klinik* (1831), *Relation médicale de campagnes et voyages de 1815-1840* (1841), and *Les Rapports originaux de Larrey à l'armée d'Orient* (1936). He died in Lyon on 25 July 1842. DBF; Egyptology; Hoefer; IndexBFr² (7); Master (12); NewCathEnc

Larroumet, Christian, born 20th cent., his writings include *Droit civil: introduction à l'étude du droit privé; les biens droits réels principaux; les obligations* (1984-86), and he edited *L'Avenir de la codification en France et en Amérique Latine; colloque international* (2004).

Larroumet, Louis Barthélemy *Gustave* Paul, born 24 September 1852 at Gourdon (Lot), France, he was educated at Cahors (Lot) and Agen (Lot-et-Garonne) and became a teacher at the Collège d'Aix-en-Provence. He later taught at Paris and Vannes. After gaining a doctorate in letters in 1882, he successively taught French language and literature at the Sorbonne. Concurrently he served in 1888 as acting head of the Ministry of Public Instruction as well as director of Beaux-Arts. In 1891, he was elected a member of the Académie des Beaux-Arts, becoming its permanent secretary in 1898. His writings include *Études d'histoire et de critique dramatiques* (1892), *Vers Athènes et Jérusalem; journal de voyage en Grèce et en Syrie* (1898). He died in Paris on 25 August 1903. DBF; Curinier, 1 (1901), pp. 76-77; Vapereau

Larsen, Max, born in 1880, his writings, partly under the peseudonym Sven Larsen, include *Die Saat der Mohren; der Roman eines Herrnhuter Missionskindes* (Leipzig, 1927). NUC, pre-1956

Larsen, Sven, pseud., 1880- see Larsen, Max

Larsson, Thomas B., born 20th cent., his writings include *Approaches to Swedish prehistory* (Oxford, 1989), *Vistad; kring en befäst gård i Östergötland och östersjökontakter under yngre bronsålder* (Umeå, 1993), and *Materiell kultur och religiösa symboler; Mesopotamien, Anatolien och Skandinavien under het andra förkristna årtusendet* (Umeå, 1997). OSK

de **Lartigue**, Raoul Julien François, born 23 November 1857 at Avignon, France, he graduated in 1877 from the military academy, Saint-Cyr. As a *sous-lieutenant* he subsequently participated in quelling the insurrections in Algeria and Tunisia. As a captain he was sent on a topographic mission to the French Sudan (Mali) to mark out the railway track from Kita to Bamako. From 1895 to 1896 he was in charge of military operations against insurgents in the Cercle de Johel, particularly the Ouled Nocer Moors, the Kel Antassar Touareg and the Ouled Allouche Moors. In 1898, he was put in charge of the territory to the south of the French Sudan. He served in the European war until 1916 when he was sent back to Algeria with his native troops to fight insurgents in the Aurès region. He retired in 1919 with rank of *général de division*. He was awarded *Grand officier* of the Légion d'honneur. His writings include *Monographie de l'Aurès* (Constantine, 1904). Qui est-ce, 1934

de **Lasala** y **Samper**, Fernando María, fl. 20th cent., he was in 1957 a professor of international law at the Universidad de Zaragoza. His writings include *La protección a los heridos, enfermos y náufrages de las fuerzas armadas en campaña* (1964), and *Esta tierra aragonesa* (1982?). LC; Note

Lasbrey, Frederick Oakley, Dr., he wrote *The Livingstone Medical Mission* (Edinburgh, Edinburgh Medical Missionary Society, 1936), and *These fifty years; the story of the Old Cairo Medical Mission from 1889 to 1939* (Old Cairo, Church Missionary Society, 1939). BLC; NUC; ZKO

de **Las Cagigas**, Isidro, b. 19th cent. *see* Cagigas, Isidro de Las

Lascaris, Michel, 1903-1965 *see* Laskaris, Michael Th.

de **La Serna**, Alfonso, he wrote *Imagenes de Túnes* (Madrid, Instituto Hispano-Arabe de Cultura, 1979). ZKO

de **La Serre**, Françoise , born 20th cent., she was in 1979 associated with the Fondation nationale des Sciences politiques, Centre d'études et de recherches internationales. Her writings include *La Grand Bretagne et la Communauté européenne* (1987), and she was a joint editor of *French and British foreign policies in transition; the challenge of adjustment* (1990). NUC

Lashkov, F. F., born 19th cent., he edited Памятники дипломатических спошений Крымскаго ханства с Московским государством в XVI и XVII в.в. (1891). NYPL

Lashova, Galina Anan'evna, born 11 July 1948 in Cheliabinsk Oblast, Russia, she graduated in 1971 from Leningrad State Pedagogical Institute and received her first degree in 1975 for Тунис; проблема экономической географии. From 1976 to 1981 she was associated with the Soviet Ministry of the Interior and subsequently with the Leningrad Institute of Soviet Trade. In 1982, she was awarded a diploma from the Geographical Society of the USSR. Miliband[2]

Lashuk, Lev Pavlovich, fl. 20th cent., he was a writer on Central Asia ethnography. His writings include Формирование народности коми (1972), Происхождение народа коми; научно-популярный очерк (1961), and Очерк этнической истории Печорского края; опыт историко-этнографического исследоватия (1958). NUC; OSK

Lasinio, Fausto, born 1 December 1831 at Firenze, Italy, he was a professor of Hebrew and Greek at the Università di Siena in 1858; four years later, he was invited to teach comparative Semitic languages at Pisa. In 1873, he went to Firenze to teach at the Istituto di studi superiori, where Arabic was added to his teaching responisibilities. His writings include *Il commento medio di Averroe alla Retorica di Aristotele* (Firenze, 1877-78). He died in Firenze on 27 October 1914. DizBl; Fück, p. 199; *Giornale della Società asiatica italiana*, 26 (1913/14), pp. 317-20; IndBiltal (2)

Lask, Israel Meir, born 19 January 1905 or 1906 at London, he was a translator from the Jiddish and Hebrew. His writings include *The Palestine stories* (1942), *The Pessah Haggada, Jehuda edition* (1954), *The Bridal canopy*, of S. Y. Agnon (1967), and *The Enchanted land*, of Moshe Grossman (1960). NUC, pre-1956; WhoWorJ, 1972; ZKO

Laskaris (Lascaris), Michael Th. (Μιχαήλ Λάσκαρις), born 29 September 1903 on the Isle of Corfu, Greece, he received a doctorate in 1926 from Beograd University for Византиске принцезе у средњьвековној Србији. He was a professor of Byzantine and Balkan studies at Saloniki University and a corresponding member of the Academia Română. His writings include Ватопедската грамота на Царь Иван Асеня II (Sofia, 1930). He died on 7 November 1965. EEE; EnBulg; MembriiAR; Note about the author; OSK

Lasker, Daniel Judah, born 4 April 1949 at Flint, Mich., he graduated from Brandeis University, Waltham, Mass. He taught history in New York State, Ohio and Texas before settling in 1978 in Israel where he became a professor at Ben Gurion University of the Negev. His writings include *Jewish theological polemics against Christianity in the middle ages* (1977). WhoWor, 1989/90

Laskier, Michael M., born 5 May 1949, he graduated in 1971 from the University of California at Los Angeles, where he also received a Ph.D. in 1979 for *The Jewish communities of Morocco and the Alliance israélite universelle, 1860-1956*. He held a great many positions in the United States and Israel as a professor of modern Jewish and Islamic history and Western civilization. His writings include *The Alliance israélite universelle and the Jewish communities of Morocco* (1983), *The Jews of Egypt, 1920-1970, in the midst of Zionism* (1992), and *North African Jewry in the twentieth century; the Jews of Morocco, Tunisia, and Algeria* (1994). ConAu, 142; NatFacDr, 1990-1995; Selim[3]

Lassen, Christian L., born 22 October 1800 at Bergen, Norway, he studied Oriental languages at the universities of Heidelberg and Bonn. After study in Paris and London, 1824-26, he received a Dr.phil.

368

in 1827 from the Universität Bonn for *Commentatio geographica atque historica de Pentapotamia Indica*. From 1830 to his retirement he taught Indian philology at the Universität Bonn. His writings include *Essai sur le pali* (1826), *Die altpersischen Keilinschriften von Persepolis* (1836), *Zur Geschichte der griechischen und indoskythischen Könige in Baktrien, Kabul und Indien durch Entzifferung der altkabulischen Legenden auf ihren Münzen* (1838), and *Indische Alterthumskunde* (1858-74). He died in Bonn on 8 May 1876.   ADtB; BiD&SB; Bonner, vol. 8, pp. 296-99; Buckland; DcBiPP (not sighted); DtBE; GV; NDB; ScBInd (1) Stache-Rosen, pp. 17-19

Lasserre, Georges, born 8 September 1902 at Genève, Switzerland, he took a doctorate and agrégation in law and was successively a professor at the faculties of law in Lille, Bordeaux, Lyon, and Paris.   His writings include *Les obstacles au développement du mouvement coopérative* (1927), *Histoire du syndicalisme ouvrier* (1948-1950), *L'expérience coopérative de démocratie économique* (1957), *Réformer l'entre-prise en 1975* (1975) and he was a joint editor of *Management of coastal lagoon fisheries* (1984).   He was a sometime staff member of the Institut des hautes études d'outre-mer.   WhoFr, 1969/70-1979/80|

Lasserre, Henri, born 7 November 1866 at Granson (Switzerland), he came to Algeria when quite young and there completed his secondary education at the Lycée d'Alger. After the completion of his physics at the Université de Lille, he returned to Algeria to become a *professeur* at the colleges of Miliana and Blida, and later at the Lycée as well as the Faculté des Sciences d'Alger. In 1912, he was appointed director of the Service météorologique algérien. He is best remembered for the establishment of the Observatoire de Tamanrasset in the Algerian Sahara. He died in Alger on 28 August 1953.   *Travaux de l'Institut de recherches sahariennes*, 12, 2me semestre (1954), pp. 7-9

Lassner, Jacob, born 15 March 1935 at Brooklyn, N.Y., he graduated in 1955 from the University of Michigan and received a Ph.D. in 1963 from Yale University, New Haven, Conn., for his thesis, *The topography of Baghdad according to al-Khatib al-Baghdadi*. He was a professor of Near Eastern languages at Wayne State University, Detroit, Mich., from 1963 to 1993, and subsequently a professor of history and religion at Northwestern University, Evanston, Ill. His writings include *Topography of Baghdad in the early middle ages* (1970), *The shaping of Abbasid rule; an inquiry into the art of 'Abbasid apologetics* (1980), *Islamic revolution and historical memory* (1986), *The Middle East remembered; forged identities, competing narratives, contested spaces* (2000), and he is said to have translated al-Tabari's history series, *The End of the Zanj revolt* (1986).   ConAu, 29-32, new rev., 20, 42; NatFacDr, 1990-1995; Selim; WhoAm, 1988/89; ZKO

Lassus, Jean, born about 1900, he received a doctorate in 1944 from the Université de Paris for *Sanctuaires chrétiens de Syrie*, a work which was published in 1947. His other writings include *Inventaire archéologique de la région au nord-est de Hama* (1935-36), *Les dieux de Rome au Musée Gsell* (Alger, 1960), and *The Early Christian and Byzantine world* (1967).   NUC

Lassy, Ivar Frederik, born in 1889 at Baku, Azerbaijan, where he also grew up. He was the son of Captain Esaias Lassy, in the service of the Nobel Oil Company, and his wife Evelina Clement. He went to school in Helsinki and since 1903 studied aesthetics, Oriental literature, philosophy, and economics at Helsinki University. After taking his M.A. in 1913 and doctorate in 1916, he worked as a foreign correspondent. His political activity until 1918 was represented by his membership of an entente-minded group. In 1918, his life underwent a radical change when his idealistic leftism was faced with a real choice, and he made his decision by offering his linguistic skills to the Red Government (the Finnish People's Deputation) in Helsinki. But he was a loser in the struggle, received a nine-year sentence, conditionally discharged after seven months, with no prospects for an intelllectual who had belonged to the wrong side to get a post in academia. The press was the last chance for a left-wing intellectual and he became the motor of the left-wing *Sosialistinen Aikakauslehti*. His activities again resulted in a twenty-one month sentence for planning treason-felony. After being released in 1923, he moved to Soviet Karelia, where he worked as a minister of education and as a leader of the party school. Later he moved to Moscow as head of Comintern's Scandinavian department. During the purges in the 1930s his literary output, including his 1931 textbook, *Marxismin perusteet* (Fundamentals of Marxism), were declared anti-revolutionary. The last news of him came from a prison hospital in 1937. His writings include *The Muharram mysteries among the Azerbeijan Turks of Caucasia* (1916), and *Persiska mysterrier; legend, dikt, drama och ceremoni* (1917). He died about 1937.   *Studia orientalia*, 55 (1984), pp. 515-533; ZKO

Last, D. Murray, born 20th cent., he was associated with Ahmadu Bello University, Zaria, Nigeria, before he became a professor of history at Bayero University, Kano, Nigeria, from 1978 to 1980. In 1986, he was a lecturer in anthropology at University College, London. His writings include *The Sokoto Caliphate* (1977), a work which was based on his Ph.D. thesis submitted to the University of Ibadan.   Note about the author; NUC; ZKO

Lasz, Samu, born 18 December 1859 at Szergeny, Hungary, he was a geologist, geographer and climatologist, and, from 1882 to 1885, a teacher. MagyarZL; Pallas

László, Gyula, born 14 March 1910 at Kőhalom, Romania, he was an archaeologist and a sometime professor at Koloszvár University. His writings include *A népvándorláskor müvészte Magyarországon* (1970), its translations, *Steppenvölker und Germanen* (1970), *Steppevolken en hun kunst* (1970), and *The art of the migration period* (1974). MagyarNKK, 1992, 1994, 1996, 1998

Latham, John *Derek*, J.P., Manchester City Courts, Professor Emeritus, born 5 April 1927 in England, he graduated in 1949 with double honours in Classical Moderations and Oriental Studies (Arabic and Persian, first class), University of Oxford, from which he received, first in 1956 a D.Phil for his thesis, *Prolegomena to a study of Andalusian influences in the social life of North-West Africa* and, secondly, in 1981 the senior higher degree of D.Litt. From 1973 to 1981 he was Reader in Arabic, University of Manchester, in which he was appointed Honorary Research Fellow in 1990 after retirement from the posts of Iraq Professor of Arabic and Islamic Studies and Head of the Muir Institute, University of Edinburgh, 1982-88. He was Curator of Middle East Collections and Associate Professor at the Hoover Institution, Stanford University, 1957-58 and Visiting Fellow, St. Cross College, Oxford, 1975. He served as chairman, Sources of African History Committee, British Academy, 1971-79; was member of the advisory editorial board, the co-editor of, and contributor to, *Cambridge History of Arabic Literature*, 1983-91; chairman, Middle East Libraries Committee, 1971-79; editor of the *Bulletin of the Society for Middle Eastern Studies* (later BJMES), 1974-89, of which body he was president from 1985 to 1987. He is Specialist Consultant to the Oxford English dictionaries (1984-); etymological consultant and contributor to the British Academy's *Dictionary of Medieval Latin from British Sources* (1970-); member, Advisory Board, *Journal of Semitic studies* (1976-82), 1989-), *al-Masaq* (1996-), *British journal of Middle Eastern studies* (1991-); was Trustee, E. J. W. Gibb Memorial (1985-90). In 1970 he published (with W. F. Paterson) *Saracen Archery*, an English version and exposition of an authoritative Mamluk technical treatise, and in 1980 (with H. D. Isaacs) the first edition and annotated English translation of the discourse on pulmonary tuberculosis from the classic "Book of Fervers" of Ishaq al-Isra'lli. He published a large number of seminal articles, nineteen of which constitute his *From Muslim Spain to Barbary* (1986), contributed 20 to 30 articles to EI², of which the most prominent is the "Nasrids;" and also contributed to the *Encyclopaedia Iranica*, notably the article "Ebn al-Moqaffa." Approved by the author; *Who's who in Greater Manchester*, 1996; WhoScot, 1988

Latimer, Sir Courtenay, C.I.E., born 22 September 1880, he was educated at St. Paul's School and Christ Church College, Oxford. He entered the Indian Civil Service in 1903, went to India in the same year and transferred to the Political Department in 1908. He rose from Assistant Secretary in 1909 to Deputy-Secretary to the Government of India, Foreign and Political Department in 1923-25. His writings include *Monograph on carpet making in the Punjab, 1905-06* (Lahore, Department of Land Records and Agriculture, 1909), and *Census of India, 1911; North-West Frontier Province Administration report* (1913). He died on 14 July 1944. BLC; IndianBiInd (4); WhoIndia, 1927; *Who was who*, 4

Lator, Esteban, born 20th cent., his writings include *Parlez-vous arabe; arabe libano-syrien* (Beyrouth, 1953-56. ZKO

La Torre, Giuseppe, born 20th cent., he was a Waldensian pastor in Palermo, and an oecumenist. His writings include *L'Islam; conoscere per dialogare* (Torino, 1991). ZKO

La Touche, Emmanuel, born in 1849, his writings include *Pend-Nameh; ou, Le livre des conseils de Moula Firouz Ben Kaus, grand prêtre des Guèbres, suivi de plusieurs histoires du Bostan de Sadi et son traité de politique* (Paris, 1847). ZKO

La Touche, Theo W., fl. 1932, his writings include *India's premier ruling prince, a rapid sketch of the man and his work* (Bombay, 1946). NUC, pre-1956

Latour, Noël-Eugène, born 19 December 1818 at Paris, he was a military pharmacist who was an *aide-major* at hospitals of the Division d'Alger, and a major at Paris, Nancy, and Lyon. He retired on 2 April 1871 from the Hôpital Saint-Martin, Lyon. He contributed to the *Gazette médicale de l'Algérie* and *Journal de pharmacie et de chimie*. He died in Alger on 17 January 1888. IndexBFr² (1)

Latron, André, fl. 1934-38, his writings include *La Vie rurale en Syrie et au Liban; étude d'économie sociale* (Beyrouth, 1936). NUC, pre-1956

Latruffe, Marie *Camille* François, born 25 February 1847 at Lyon, he joined the French army and participated in the Franco-Prussian war, 1870-71, and subsequently in five campaigns in Algeria. On 29 December 1882 he was awarded the Légion d'Honneur. IndexBFr² (1)

Latter, Thomas, born 1816 in India, he joined the Bengal Native Infantry. He was chief interpreter to Sir Henry Thomas Godwin in the first Burmese war, 1824-26. He was resident deputy-commissioner at Prome, where he was murdered in his bed by the Burmese on 8 December 1853. His writings include *A Grammar of the language of Burmah* (Calcutta, Baptist Mission Press, 1845). Boase; DNB

Lattimore, Owen, born 29 July 1900 at Washington, D.C., he grew up in China and gave up an early career in business and journalism to indulge in what was to become his lifelong passion - travelling. He travelled widely in Chinese Turkestan unflanked by interpreters and electronic equipment, accompanied solely by a native of the area and nothing but native equipment. These early travels to Mongolia and Turkestan in 1926 and 1927 were pioneering journeys that led him to a belated academic training and the publication of his first book *The desert road to Turkestan* (1928). The next twenty or so years saw him established as the leading American scholar of contemporary China and Mongolia, to which two countries he returned several times. From his academic base as director of the Page School of International Relations, he published in 1940 probably his most influential book *Inner Asian frontiers of China*, and with his unique knowledge of the region became his government's adviser during the War - first seconded to advise Chiang Kai-shek, and later as director of Pacific Operations for the U.S. Office of War Information. His warm sympathies for the Chinese and Mongol people made him a target of the McCarthy witchhunt in the 1950s, leading to the loss of his academic base in America. He went to England as professor of Chinese studies at the University of Leeds, where he remained until his retirement in 1970. Fully exonerated he returned to his homeland, where he died in Providence, R.I., on 31 May 1989. *Asian affairs* 20 (1989), 386-387; *Geographical journal* (155 (1989), p. 448; IntWW, 1974-1978; Master (10); Shavit - Asia

de **Lattre**, Jean Michel, he received a doctorate in 1936 from the Université de Paris for *Le statut des commissaires de surveillance dans les sociétés anonymes*. His writings include *La mise en valeur de l'ensemble eurafricain français et la participation des capitaux étrangers; sociétés à participation étrangère, compagnies à charte* (1954), and *Les grands ensembles africains; aspects économiques et financières de l'industrie saharienne* (1956). NUC, pre-1956-67; ZKO

Latynin, Boris Aleksandrovich, born in 1899, his writings include *Мировое дерево, древно жизни в орнаменте и фольклоре восточной Европы к вопросу о пережитках* (Leningrad, 1933), and *Молоточковидные булавки, их культурнея атрибуция и датировка* (Leningrad, 1967). LC; OSK

Latysheva, Inessa Semenovna, born 25 June 1926 at Moscow, she graduated in 1949 from the Moscow Oriental Institute, where she also received her first degree in 1953 for *Малайя под гнетом английского империализма*. Her writings include *Малайзия* (1972). She was a foreign literature editor, 1952-56, and from 1957 to 1973 she was associated with the Oriental Isntitute of the Soviet Academy of Sciences. She twice worked for several years as a *Pravda* correspondent in Japan. Miliband; Miliband[2]

Lau, Linda Diana, born 3 July 1945, at Ann Arbor, Mich., she graduated in 1967 from the University of Massachusetts, received her M.A. in 1973 from the American University in Cairo, and her Ph.D. in 1980 from Indiana University for *Mus'ab b. al-Zubayr and his governorate of Iraq, 655-692 A.D.* She subsequently became a Middle Eastern research analyst, first with the Library of Congress, and later with the U.S. Department of Defense. DrAS, 1982 H; *MESA Roster of members*, 1982-1990; Selim[2]

Laubach, Frank Charles, born 2 September 1884 at Brenton, Pa., he was educated at Princeton, and Columbia universities, and the Union Theological Seminary. From 1915 to 1941, he served as a missionary and literacy campaigner in the Philippines. Afterwards he carried on his literacy campaign in southern Asia and, in his old age, in his homeland. His writings include *The People of the Philippines* (1925), *India shall be literate* (1940), *Forty years with the silent billion; adventuring in literacy* (1970). He died in his hometown on 11 June 1970. Master index (5); Shavit - Asia; WhAm, 5

de **Laubadère**, André, born 24 September 1910 at Paris, he studied law and letters at the Université de Bordeaux, where he received a doctorate in law in 1935 for *L'automobile et le régime de l'usage des voies publiques*, and also his *agrégation* in the following year. He successively taught at the universities of Bordeaux, Grenoble, and Montpellier, before he was sent in 1942 to Rabat as director of the Centres d'études juridiques du Maroc. Since 1951, he taught at the Faculté de droit de Paris He died on 17 October 1981. DBFC, 1954/55; WhoFr, 1979/80

Laude-Cirtautas, Ilse D., born about 1935 she received a Dr.phil. in 1961 from the Universität Hamburg for her thesis on the usage of colour description in the Turkic dialects, *Der Gebrauch der Farbbezeichnungen in den Türkdialekten*. In 1990, she was chairman and professor of Near Eastern languages and civilization at Washington University, Seattle, Wash., specializing in the peoples of Central Asia. Her writings include *Chrestomathy of modern literary Uzbek* (1980), and *Märchen der Usbeken* (1984). LC; MESA *Roster of members*, 1990; Schoeberlein

Lauer, Hans Hugo, born 18 April 1934 at Wetzlar, Germany, to a pastor's family, he studied medicine at the Universität Bonn. Since 1958 he also took courses in philosophy, psychology and history. He received a Dr.med. in 1962 from his alma mater. In 1961, he joined the staff of the Institut für Geschichte der Medizin at the Universität Heidelberg, concurrently pursuing his philosophical studies leading to his Dr.habil. From 1973 to his retirement in 1999 he was a professor of history of medicine at the Universität Marburg. Kürschner, 1976-2005; Thesis

Lauer, Jean *Philippe*, born 2 December 1874 at Lagny-Thorigny (Seine-et-Marne), France, he received degrees in law and letters, and graduated in 1897 from the École des chartes, Paris, with his thesis *Le règne de Louis IV d'Outremer; annales de l'histoire de France à l'époqie carolingienne*. After a diploma from the École pratique des hautes études, he became in 1898 a fellow of the École française de Rome. In 1902 he entered the Cabinet des manuscrits of the Bibliothèque nationale de Paris, becoming *conservateur en chef* in 1934. He was an editor of *La Conquêt de Constantinople*, of Robert de Clari (1924); and the *Catalogue général des manuscrits latins de la Bibliothèque Nationale* (1939). He died in Paris 3 February 1953. DBF

Laufer, Berthold, born 11 October 1874 at Köln, Germany, studied in Berlin, and received a Dr. phil. from the Universität Leipzig in 1897 for his thesis *Eine verkürzte Version des Werkes von den Hunderttausend Nâga's*. He settled in America in 1898, and became an East Asian ethnographer, anthropologist and linguist at American museums, and at Columbia University, New York. He died after a leap or fall from the upper storey of the hotel in which he resided in Chicago on 13 September 1934. DAB; Shavit - Asia; WhAm, 1

Lauffray, Jean Louis Raymond Marie, born 23 June 1909 at Alençon (Orne), France, he was educated at the Institution Marguerite Sainte-Marie, and the Facultés de droit et des lettres de Caen, Institut d'art et d'archéologie de Paris, École du Louvre, and École nationale supérieure des beaux-arts. He received degrees in law and letters, a *doctorat d'université* in archaeology, and a diploma in architecture. Since 1936, he was in various capacities an architect to French archaeological missions in Syria, Turkey, Lebanon and Egypt. Since the early 1950s he was reintegrated in France on a national level as a conservator of national monuments. He was a member of the Société française d'archéologie and the Société d'Égyptologie. His writings include *Halabiyya-Zenobia, place forte du limes oriental et la Haute-Mésopotamie au VIe siècle* (1983-2000); and he was a joint author of *Sidon, aménagement antiques du port de Saida* (1951), and *Beyrouth, ville romaine; histoire et monuments* (1952). He received numerous national and international decorations. He died on 5 March 2000. WhoFr, 1979/80- 2000

Laugier de Beaurecueil, Serge, born in 1917, he was a French Dominican priest who was from 1962 to 1983 head of an Afghan orphanage. His writings include *Mes enfants de Kabul* (Paris, 1983), *Wédâ, vingt ans, cellule 5, Kabul* (Paris, 1991), *Chronique d'un témoin privilige; lettres d'Afghanistan de Serge de Beaurecueil*, edited by Étienne Gille and Sylvie Heslot (1992), *Un chrétien en Afghanistan* (2001), and he edited *Abdullah Ansari and other Sufis of Afghanistan* (Kabul, 1976). Louis Dupree wrote the nine-page booklet, *Serge de Beaurecueil* (Hanover, N.H., American Universities Field Staff, 1976). LC; Livres disponibles, 2004; Note

Laugier de Tassy, born in the second part of the 17th cent., he was a French traveller. He was for several years attached to the French consulat at Alger and subsequently sent to Holland as a *commissaire de la marine*. His trace is lost in 1720. His writings include *Beschryving van het Koningryk en de Stadt Algiers* (Amsterdam, 1724) *Histoire du royaume d'Alger, avec l'état présent de son gouvernement, de ses forces de terre et de mer, de ses revenus, police, justice, politique et commerce* (Amsterdam, 1725), and its translations, *Historia del reyno de Argel* (Barcelona, 1733), *A Compleat [!] history of the piratical states of Barbary, viz. Algiers, Tunis, Tripoli and Morocco, containing their origin, revolutions, and present state of these kingdoms* (London, 1750), and *Die Staaten der Seeräuber; ausführlich beschrieben von einem englischen Consul* (Rostock, 1753). DBF; Hoefer; NUC, pre-1956

Laulan, Robert, born about 1895, his writings include *École militaire; aperçu historique et guide du visiteur* (Paris, 1918), he was a joint author of *École militaire et l'École supérieure de guerre* (Paris, 1937), and he edited *Mémoires de Monsieur de Pontis, qui a servi dans les armées cinquante-six ans, sous les rois Henri IV, Louis XIII, Louis XIV* (Paris, 1986).

de **Launay**, Louis Auguste Alphonse, born 19 July 1860 at Paris, he graduated in 1881 from the École polytechnique and subsequently also from the École des mines, Paris. From 1889 to 1935 he was a professor of applied geology at the École des mines, concurrently also teaching at the École des Ponts et Chaussée since 1907. He visited the Aegean Islands and Asia Minor from 1898 to 1900 as a geologist. His writings include *Chez les Grecs de Turquie* (1897), and *La Turquie que l'on voit* (1913). He died in 1938. DBF; Kornrumpf², vol. 2; *Qui est-ce*, 1934; *Qui êtes-vous*, 1924

de **Launay**, Marie, born 19th cent., her writings include *L'Architecture ottomane* (1873), and she was a joint author of *Les Costumes populaires de la Turquie en 1873* (1873).

Launay, Michel, born in 1933 at Paris, he received a doctorate for *Jean-Jacques Rousseau, écrivain politique*. He was a professor at the Université de Nice. His writings include *Paysans algérien; la terre, la vigne et les hommes* (1963). LC

Launay, Robert Gerard, born 23 October 1949, he was for over twenty years a professor in the Department of Anthropolgy, Nothwestern University, Evanston, Illinois. His writings include *Traders without trade; responses to change in two Dyula communities* (1982), and *Beyond the stream; Islam and society in a West African town* (1992). LC; NatFacDr, 1990-2005

Launois, A., born 20th cent., he was associated with the Institut français d'archéologie orientale du Caire and the Département des médailles et antiques, Bibliothèque nationale de Paris. His writings include *Estampilles et poids musulmans en verre du Cabinet des médailles* (Le Caire, 1959), and *Catalogue des étalons monétaires et autres pièces musulmanes en verre* (1960). NUC

Dr. **Laupts**, one of the pseudonyms of Georges Saint-Paul, who was born in 1870 at Metz, and who became a military physician attached to the Ministère de la Guerre, and a member of the Société d'anthropologie de Paris. His writings, under his real name as well as under the pseudonym G. Espé de Metz, include *Souvenirs de Tunisie et d'Algérie* (1904), and *Par les colons* (1914). He died in 1937. BN; IndexBFr² (1)

Laurens, Ferd., born 19th cent., he wrote *Le Réformes commerciales* (Alger, 1895). His trace is lost after an article in 1901.

Laurens, Henry, born 20th cent., he received a doctorate in 1989 from the Université de Paris for *La Révolution française et l'islam; histoire et significations de l'Expédition d'Égypte, 1798-1801*. His writings include *La Bibliothèque orientale de Barthélemi d'Herbelot; aux sources de l'orientalisme* (1978), *Les Origines intellectuelles de l'expédition d'Égypte; l'orientalisme islamisant en France, 1698-1798* (1987), *Le Royaume impossible; la France et la genèse du monde arabe* (1990), *Lawrence en Arabie* (1992), *La Question de Palestine* (1999-2002), and *L'Orient arabe; arabisme et islamisme de 1798 à 1945* (2002). *Livres disponibles*, 2004; ZKO

Laurens, Joseph Augustin *Jules*, born 26 July 1825 at Carpentras (Vaucluse), France, he studied at the École des Beaux-Arts. He went to Paris in 1842 and three years later he was admitted to the Salon with a painting entitled *Environs de Vaucluse*. In May of 1846 he received the unexpected offer to accompany I. X. M. Hommaire de Hell on a three-year scientific mission overland to the Black Sea through Asia Minor the Caspian Sea and ending at Tehran. He produced sketches of monuments and customary dresses on the way. At Tehran the mission was witness to the events which brought Nāsir al-Dīn Shāh to power. The graphic descriptions of this undertaking were published after the death of Hommaire de Hell by his widow, *Voyage en Turquie et en Perse* (1854-60) in three volumes. Upon Laurens' return to France, he settled at Paris, where his studio became a centre for artists. He produced illustrations for journals such as *L'Illustration, Le Tour du Monde*, and *Le Magasin pittoresque*. He died on 5 May 1901. DBF; IndexBFr² (1); Kornrumpf; Master (3)

Laurensen, Karsten, born 3 August 1933 at Esbjerg, Denmark, he was a professor of economics, political economy, and philosophy of economics successively at the universities of Århus and København. His writings include *Udviklingslandenes økonomi* (1986); he was a joint author of *The German inflation, 1918-1923* (1964); and he edited *The Trilateral countries in the international economy of the 1980s* (1982). Kraks, 1990-2000

Laurent, Joseph François, born 2 November 1870 at Bar-le-Duc, France, he was educated at the Lycée de Bar-le-Duc and studied at the universities of Nancy and Paris, where he completed his doctorate in 1913 with a *thèse complementaire* entitled *Byzance et les Turcs seldjoucides dans l'Asie occidentale jusqu'en 1081*. He was a sometime fellow of the École française d'Athènes who became a professor of ancient history at the Faculté des lettres de l'Université de Nancy. He also served as a mayor of Nancy. His writings include *L'Arménie entre Byzance et l'islam* (1919), *La Grèce antique* (1933), and *Études d'histoire arménienne* (1971). *Qui êtes-vous*, 1924

Laurent, Louis Olivier Philippe, born in 1896, he became known under his religious name, le Père Vitalien. He was an honorary director of the C.N.R.S. and a *conservateur honoraire émérite du médailler du Vatican*. His writings include *La Collection C. Orghidan; documents de sigillographie*

(1952), and *Le Corpus des sceaux de l'Empire byzantine* (1965). He died on 20 November 1973. LC; MembriiAR

Laurent-Chat, born 19th cent., he was a sometime president of the Section tunisienne de la Société de géographie commerciale de Paris. His trace is lost after an article in 1935 in the *Revue économique française*. Note about the author

Lauriol, Marc, born 18 August 1916 at Alger, he studied at the Faculté de droit d'Alger, where he also gained a doctorate in 1952 for *La subrogation rélle*, a work which was published in 1954. He was an *avocat-conseil juridique*, professor, commissioner of societies, deputy, and senator. From 1938 to 1951 he was a barrister in the Cour d'appel d'Alger. During the second World War, he was from 1943 to 1944 a professor at the Centre d'études juridiques de Tunis, and from 1943 to 1945, he also held the office of legal councillor to the Tunisian Government. Since 1951, he was a legal counsel to societies and concurrently a professor of law at the École supérieure de commerce d'Alger. He was *conseiller général d'Alger*, from 1960 to 1962, and a national delegate of the Grandes associations de rapatriés, 1969-71. He was subsequently politically active in the Rassemblement pour la République. His writings include *L'Algérie angoissée* (1956), *Le fédéralisme et l'Algérie* (1957), and *L'Europe anachronique* (1965). NDNC, 1961/62; WhoFr, 1965/66-1997/98|

Lautensach, Hermann, born 29 September 1886 at Gotha, Germany, he studied geography, mathematics and natural sciences at the universities of Göttingen, Freiburg im Breisgau and Berlin, taking a doctorate in 1910. A serious illness postponed his academic career until the 1930s so that he first entered high school teaching. He received his Dr.habil. in 1928 and became a professor of geography successively at Braunschweig, Greifswald and Stuttgart. In 1939, he was admitted to Deutsche Akademie der Naturforscher Leopoldina, and in 1957, he was honoured by *Hermann Lautensach Festschrift*. He died in Wildbach/Schwarzwald on 20 May 1971. BioIn, 1; *Geographers*, 4 (1980), pp. 91-101; Kürschner, 1935-1970; NDB; *Wer ist wer*, 1958-1970

Lauterbach, Walter, pseud. *see* Klaproth, Heinrich *Julius*, 1783-1835

Lauterpacht, Sir Elihu, born 13 July 1928 at London, he studied at Cambridge and was called to the bar from Gray's Inn in 1950. He was fellow and teacher in various capacities at Trinity College, Cambridge, from 1953 to his retirement in 1988. His writings include *Jerusalem and the holy places* (1968), *Aspects of the administration of international justice* (1991); he was a joint author of *Belize; joint opinion* (1978); and he edited *The Suez Canal settlement* (1960), and *The Kuwait crisis; basic documents* (1991). Who's who, 1974-2005; WhoWor, 1976/77; WhoWorJ, 1965

Lautour, J. B., born about 1800, he obtained a medical doctorate and became a medical official in the Ottoman Empire, serving as a veterinary at Damascus. His writings include *Rapport sur le voyage de la caravane de Damas à la Mecque* (Constantinople, Imprimerie du Journal de Constantinople, 1849). Kornrumpf; ZKO

Lauvergne, Hubert, born at the end of the 18th cent., he was in 1838 a professor of medicine at the École de Toulon and became *médecin en chef* of the Marine and the Hôpital du bagne in that city. His writings include *Souvenirs de la Grèce pendant la campagne de 1825; ou, Mémoires historiques et biographiques sur Ibrahim* (1826), *Histoire de la Révolution française* (1839), *L'agonie de la mort dans toute les classes de la société* (1842), and its translation, *Der Todeskampf und der Tod* (1845). He died at the age of sixty in January 1860. IndexBFr² (1); NUC; ZKO

Lauwerys, Joseph Albert, born 7 November 1902 at Bruxelles, he was a member of the Faculty of Education, University of London, for over thirty-five years. An authority on education, he helped estblished Unesco. In 1970, he went to Nova Scotia to become director of the Atlantic Institute of Education. His writings include *Morals, democracy and education* (1958), *History textbooks and international understanding* (1953), *A Handbook of British educational terms* (1963), and jointly with Gary J. Anderson, *Institutional leadership for educational reform* (1978); and he edited *Scandinavian democracy* (1958). He died in Guildford on 29 June 1981. BiBenelux² (1); ConAu, 13-16, 104; DNB; *Who's who*, 1969-1982; WhoWor, 1974/75, 1976/77; WrDr, 1976/78-1982/84

Lauzanne, Stéphane Joseph Vincent, born 22 January 1874 at Paris, he received a degree in law in France and then went to the United States where he received a Ph.D. from the University of Michigan at Ann Arbor. In 1898, he was the London correspondent of *le Matin*, a paper with which he remained associated until August 1944. He was an outstanding journalist who became vice-president of the Association des journalistes républicains. From March 1941 to the liberation of Paris he was responsible for the paper's editorials as approved by the German authorities. For this collaboration he was arrested on 30 October 1944 and sentenced to twenty years in prison, of which he served several years in the penitentiary on the Île de Ré. After his release from prison he collaborated with *Rivarol* and *France réelle*. His writings include *Au chevet de la Turquie; quarante jours de guerre* (1913), its translations, *Умирающа Турция* (1913), and *Hastanın başı ucunda kırk gün muhabere* (1331/1915), and *Fighting France* (1918). He died in Paris on 22 November 1958. DBF; IndexBFr² (1); Özege; *Qui êtes-vous*, 1924

Lavado Paradinas, Pedro José, born 20th cent., he received a doctorate in geography and history. He was a professor of history of art, who was associated with the Museo Arqueológico Nacional of the Instituto de Conservación y Restauración de Bienes Cuklturas, and the Instituto del Patrimonio Histórico Español, Madrid. Arabismo, 1992, 1994, 1997

Lavagnini, Bruno, born 3 October 1898 at Palermo, Italy, he received degrees from the Scuola di Archeologia di Atene as well as an honorary degree from Athens University. Since 1929 he was successively a professor of Greek literature at the universities of Catania and Palermo and concurrently served as a director of the Istituto Italiana di Cultura at Athens. His writings include *Storia della letteratura neoellenica* (1959), *Grecia 1859 nel diario di Francesco Crispi* (1967), and *Scritti di storia sulla Grecia antica, bizantina e moderna* (1997). He was honoured by *Hommage à Bruno Lavagnini* (1963). In 2000 appeared *Miscellanea di scritti in memoria di Bruno Lavagnini*. Chi è, 1928-1961; IndBiltal (1); Wholtaly, 1958, 1980

Lavallée, Théophile Sébastien, born 13 October 1804 at Paris, he spent his entire career at the École spéciale militaire de Saint-Cyr, first as a tutor in mathematics, later as tutor in history, and finally as a professor of geography and statistics of military art and science. His writings include *Histoire de l'Empire ottoman depuis les temps anciens jusqu'à nos jours* (1855). He died in Versailles on 29 August 1866. DBF; Hoefer; IndexBFr² (2); Vapereau

Lavan, Spencer, born 31 December 1937 at New York City, he was a graduate of Tufts University, Medford, Mass. In 1966, he received a M.A. degree, and in 1970, a Ph.D., from McGill University, Montreal, for his thesis, *The Ahmadiyah movement*. He wrote *The Ahmadiyah movement, past and present* (1974). ConAu, 57; DrAS, 1974 & 1982; Ferahian; LC

Lavauden, Adrien Joseph *Louis*, born 19 June 1881 at Grenoble, France, he was initially admitted to the Institut agronomique but decided against it when he ranked better in the admission to the École forestière, Nancy, in 1903; he graduated four years later. He started his career as a general forester, an experience which was useful when he subsequently started to study zoology and botany at the Université de Nancy. He became instrumental in the planning and organization of the parc national d'Oisans as well as the Société dauphinoise d'études biologique. In the first World War he served as a captain with the 68e *Bataillon de chasseurs alpins*. After demobilization, he was assigned to the Tunisian Government. In 1920 he had the chance to explore the Sahara from Tunisia to the Atlantic Coast. From 1928 to 1932 he was in Madagascar as chief forester of the Service forestier, later becoming a professor of zoology at the Institut agronomique at Digne (Alpes-de Haute Provence). His writings include *Les vertébrés du Sahara* (Tunis, 1926), *The Equatorial forest of Africa* (Hull, 1937), and *Le problème forestier colonial* (Paris, 1931). He died at his estate in Anjou (Isère) on 1 September 1935. *Hommes et destins*, vol. 3, pp. 291-92; IndexBFr² (1)

de **Laveleye**, Emile Louis Victor, born 5 April 1822 at Bruges (Brugge), Belgium, he started his humanistic education at the Athénée royal de Bruges, completing it at the Collège Stanislas in Paris. He studied philosophy at the Université de Louvain, and law at the Université de Gand, where he took his doctorate in 1844. He became a barrister-at-law in Gand, but spent most of his time writing. In 1863 he was appointed a professor of political economy at the Université de Liège. His prolific writings include *An account of the system of public instruction in Belgium, Russia, Turkey, Servia and Egypt* (1875), *La Péninsule des Balkans* (1886), and its translation, *The Balkan Peninsula* (1887). He died in Doyon (Namur), Belgium, on 2 January 1892. BiBenelux² (3); BioNBelg; IndexBFr² (5)

Lavergne, Alfred Adolphe *Bernard*, born 15 December 1884 at Nîmes, France, he was educated at Nîmes and studied at the Faculté de droit de Paris, where he received a doctorate in 1908 for *Les fédérations d'achat et de production des sociétés coopératives distributives*. From 1916 to 1918 he was a lecturer in law at the Faculté de droit d'Alger. After gaining his *agrégation* in political economy in 1920, he successively taught law at the law schools of Nancy, Lille, Alger and Paris, where he held the first chair of *insitutions et doctrines coopératives*, a field in which he became one of the great theoreticians. His writings include *Le problème des nationalisations* (1946), *Une révolution dans la politique coloniale de la France* (1948), *Les grands problèmes de l'Union française; l'Afrique du nord et l'islam, l'Indo-Chine* (1953), *L'Afrique du nord et l'Afrique noire* (1956), and *Le problème religieux à l'heure actuelle* (1967). He died in Paris on 8 October 1975. In 1977 appeared *Hommage à Bernard Lavergne*. DBF; IndexBFr² (3); IntWW, 1974/75-1978

Lavergne, Marc-Étienne, born 20th cent., he received a doctorate in geography in 1980 from the Université de Paris and became associated with the C.N.R.S. In 1989 he was a director of the Centre d'études et de recherches sur le Moyen-Orient contemporain, Amman and Beirut. His writings include *Le Soudan contemporain* (1989), and jointly with Brigitte Dumortier, *L'Oman contemporain; état, territoire, identité* (2002). EURAMES, 1993; *MESA Roster of members*, 1990; ZKO

de **La Véronne**, Chantal, born 20th cent., his writings include *Vie de Moulay Ismail, roi de Fès et de Maroc, d'après Joseph de Léon, 1708-1728* (1974), *Documents inédits sur l'histoire du Maroc* (1975), *Sources françaises de l'histoire du Maroc au XVIIIe siècle* (1981-83), and *Relations entre Oran et Tlemcen dans la première partie du XVIe siècle* (1983). NUC; ZKO

Lavers, John Ellis. born 22 July 1936, he was educated at Greenwich and did his national service with the Royal Medical Corps, stationed to Port Said during the Suez Crisis. He then studied at the University of London, graduating in anthropolgy in 1962 and taking his M.A. in 1964 for *The Organisation and distribution of trade in the Central Sudan in the pre-colonial period*. Shortly thereafter he went to Nigeria to work on the history of Bornu for his doctoral thesis, which he never wrote, but kept it all stored in his encyclopedic mind. He settled down in Nigeria making his home in Kano for almost thirty years. He was appointed assistant lecturer in history, particularly Bornu and Hausa history, at Abdullahi Bayero College in 1966, senior lecturer in 1979, became reader at what had long since become Bayero University in 1982, and professor in 1987. He died in Kano, Nigeria, on 16 May 1993. Sluglett; *Sudanic Africa*, 4 (1993), pp. 1-6

Lavička, Jan, born 20th cent., he was the translator and editor of *Antologie hussite* (Paris, Publications orientalistes de France, 1985). LC

Lavigerie, Charles Martial Allemand, born 31 October 1825 at Huire near Bayonne (Pyrénées-Atlantiques), France, and entered upon his studies in preparation for the priesthood as a student from his native diocese. He was ordained in 1849 and after four years of post-graduate work was appointed to a professorship at the Sorbonne. Here he made those contacts which made him to go, in 1860, on a mission of mercy to Lebanon. This resulted in his being honoured by France with the *croix de la Légion d'honneur*, and by the Holy See with a domestic prelature and the nomination as Auditor of the Roman Rota for France. In 1863 he was consecrated in Rome as bishop of Nancy, and four years later he consented to the request of Marshall MacMahon, the governor-general of Algeria, to become the archbishop of Algiers. This appointment brought many problems because the priests did not understand the Arabic of the natives; no attempt was being made to Christianize the non-European population. In 1868, three men from the diocesan seminary volunteered for the mission, and these with four others, on 2 February 1869, became the first members of the Société des missionnaires d'Afrique. They were clothed in the Arab costume, in a white tunic and a burnus, and became commonly known as Pères blancs. During his time as superior of the White Fathers he conducted an anti-slavery drive throughout Europe. In 1884 he was nominated the first modern primate of Africa. His writings include *L'esclavage africain* (1888), *Documents sur la fondation de l'œuvre anti-esclavagiste* (1889). A commemoration volume was published in 1927 entitled *Le Cardinal Lavigerie; échos et leçons du centenaire de sa naissance*. He died on 26 November 1892. *Hommes et destins* vol. 1, pp. 348-351; Kornrumpf; *Magyar*; MW 36 (1946), 88-89; NewCathEnc; Zananiri, pp. 122-140

Lavisse, Ernest, born 17 December 1842 at Nouvion-en-Thiérache (Aisne), France, he was educated at Laon and Paris, where he graduated from the École normale supérieure. He taught a year each at secondary schools in Nancy and Versailles before embarking on a brief career as secretary to the minister of Instruction public. After studies in Germany from 1872 to 1875 he received his *doctorat ès lettres* for a thesis on the origin of the Prussian monarchy. From 1879 to his retirement in 1919 he taught history in various capacities at the École normale supérieure, Faculté des lettres de Paris, and École de Saint-Cyr. His writings are much influenced by the disaster of 1870 and the Commune. In 1892 he was elected to the Académie française. He died in Paris on 18 August 1922. Curinier, 1 (1901), pp. 105-107; DBF; IndexBFr² (3); Master (4)

Lavoisier, Gaston, fl. 20th cent., he was a military engineer, and in 1960 an *ingénieur-en-chef*. His writings include *Moteurs à réaction; principe, description utilisation, entretien des réacteurs modernes* (Paris, Technique et vulgarisation, 1952). Note about the author; ZKO

Lavoix, Henri Michel, born 19 January 1820 at Nant (Aveyron), France, he started his secondary education at Poitiers and completed it at the Collège Ste.-Barbe in Paris. In 1840 he entered the Cabinet des médailles of the Bibliothèque nationale, Paris, where he became a keeper. His writings include *Monnaies à légendes arabes frappées en Syrie par les Croisées* (1877), and *Catalogue des monnaies musulmanes de la Bibliothèque nationale* (1887-1891). He died in Paris on 23 October 1892. DBF; Fück, p. 251

Lavollée, Charles, born 11 October 1823 at Paris, he accompanied a mission to China in 1843 under the French Minister de Lagrené. Upon his return in 1846, he received a decoration and entered the

Ministry of Commerce. In 1855 he changed to the Ministry of the Interior, where he became a *chef de bureau*. He later resigned his official functions to become an administrator with the Compagnie de omnibus de Paris. Since 1846 he had been a contributor to *Revue nouvelle, Revue de l'Orient, l'Assemblée nationale, l'Illustration*, but particularly to the *Revue de deux mondes*, where he wrote on commercial and economic affairs relating to his China experiences. His writings include *France et Chine* (1900). Vapereau

Lavrencic, Karl, born 20th cent. *see* Sylvester, Anthony

Lavrent'ev, Aleksandr Konstantinovich, born 20th cent., his writings include *Империалистическая политика США и Англии в Иране* (1960), *Тайная война против Индонезии* (1960), and *USA and Asia* (1982). LC; OSK

Lavrent'ev, Viacheslav Nikolaevich, born 13 April 1960 in Eniseĭsk Krasnoiarsk Krai, Russia, he graduated in 1982 from the Faculty of Economics, Moscow State University and received his first degree in 1987 for *Стратегия развития; Перестройка промышлен. структуры стран и территорий Юго-Вост. Азии и Далн. Востока*. Since 1986 he was associated with the Oriental Institute of the Soviet Academy of Sciences. His writings include *Новые индустриальные страны Азии* (1989). Miliband[2]

Lavroff, Dmitri Georges, born 10 November 1934 at Bordeaux, he there studied law and received his doctorate in 1960 from the Faculté de droit for *Les libertés publiques en Union soviétique*, and a diploma from the Institut d'études politiques. In 1960 he became a *professeur agrégé* in constitutional law at the Faculté de droit de Dakar and from 1964 to 1965 also served as a counsellor in the Cour suprême du Sénégal. Upon his return to France, he became successively director of the Département de droit public et sciences politiques, Bordeaux, academic director of the Centre d'étude d'Afrique noire de Bordeaux, professor in the Institut international d'administration publique de Paris, and president of the Université de Bordeaux. His writings include *Les constitutions africaines* (1961), *Les partis politiques en Afrique noire* (1970), *Les systèmes constitutionnelles en Afrique noire* (1976), and *Les institutions politiques de l'Espagne* (1981). In 2005 appeared *La constitution et les valeurs; mélanges en l'honneur de Dmitri Georges Lavroff*. WhoFr, 1979/80-2005/2006

Lavrov, Leonid Ivanovich, born in 1909 in Kubansk Gouvernement, Caucasus, he graduated in 1935 from the Leningrad Institute of History, Philology and Linguistics, and received his first degree in 1946 for a thesis on the *История абазинского народа*, and a doctorate in 1967 for *Эпиграфический памятники Северного Кавказа X-XIX в.в. как историко-этнографич. источник*. His writings include *Эпиграфические памятники Северного Кавказа на арабском, персидском и турецком языках* (1966), *Историко-этнографические очерки Кавказа* (1978), and *Этнография Кавказа* (1982). From 1957 to his death on 7 April 1982 he was successiveliy associated with the Institute of Ethnography, Soviet Academy of Sciences, Moscow and Leningrad. Miliband[2]

Lavrov, Sergeĭ Viktorovich, born 21 March 1950 at Moscow, he studied at the Moscow State Institute of International Relations (М.Г.И.М.О.) and in 1972 entered the diplomatic service. In 2004 he became Minister of Foreign Affairs. IntWW, 1993-2006

Lavy, Ernest Eduard, M.B.E., M.A., M.D., B.Ch., L.M., Clerk in Holy Orders, he was born 19th cent., and was educated at Rugby School, Pembroke College and Ridley Hall, Cambridge, as well as Trinity College, Dublin. He was a missionary under Church Missionary Society, London, assigned to Baghdad in 1903, and later also to India, Mesopotamia, Northern Sudan, Palestine. From 1917 to 1919, he was engaged in refugee relief work in Mesopotamia. Since 1931 he was a vicar of St. Andrew's, Watford. *Who's who in Herforshire*, 1936

Law, Bimala Churn, born in 1892 at Calcutta of well-to-do parents, he became a scholar of Pali language and literature as well as Indian history and culture. He was an early member of the Iran Society and served as its president for three terms. He was also associated in various capacities with numerous learned societies. His writings include *Historical gleanings* (1922), *Ancient Indian tribes* (1926), and *Buddhist studies* (1931). He died in 1969. *Indo-Iranica*, 45 (1992), pp. 27-77; ZKO

Law, Sir Edward Fitzgerald, born 2 November 1846 at Rostrevor, he was educated privately and at the Royal Military Academy, Woolwich. He entered the Royal Artillery in 1868, served in Suakin, Sudan, in 1885, and became major in the following year. In 1888, he entered the the Diplomatic Service as Financial and Commercial attaché for Russia, Persia, and Turkey, serving also as a British delegate to a variety of international financial commissions concerning Bulgaria, Greece, and Turkey. He was an active champion of imperial preference. He died in Paris in 1908. Buckland; DNB; IndianBilnd (1); Riddick; *Who's who*, 1897; *Who was who*, 1

Law, Henry Duncan Graves, born 13 August 1883, he was educated at Edinburgh University and Cambridge. He entered the Indian Civil Service in 1906 in the Foreign and Political Department of the Government of India. He retired in 1930 after his last appointment as consul general in Persia. He was a sometime honorary secretary of the Iran Society. His writings include *Persian letters; a manual for students of Persian* (1950). He died in 1951. BritInd (2); IndianBiInd (2); *Who's who*, 1946-1952; *Who's who in Kent*, 1935

Law, Thomas, born in 1759, he entered the East India Company and went to India in 1773. In the 1780s he was a member of the Council of Revenue at Fort William in Bengal. He resigned his post in 1791 and went first to England and in 1793 to the United States. His writings include *Thoughts on the moral system* (1833). He died in Washington in 1834. BritInd (1); DNB

Law, Vivien, born in March 1952, she received her first degree in classics and German from McGill University, Montreal, and received a Ph.D. in medieval studies. She taught history of linguistic thought at Cambridge University, since 1984 as a lecturer, and since 1998 as a reader. She was a founding member the the Henry Sweet Society and latterly chairman of the Executive Committee. Her writings include *The Insular Latin grammarians* (1982), *History of linguistic thought in the middle ages* (1993), *Grammar and grammarians in the early middle ages* (1997), and *The History of linguistics in Europe from Plato to 1600* (2003). She died in February 2002. In 2005 appeared *Flores grammaticæ; essays in memory of Vivien Law*. Note about the author

Lawal, Olayiwola Adejare, born 17 June 1943 at Ikirun, Nigeria, he received his first education at an African denominational school, and later studied at the universities of Ibadan and Lund, Sweden. He taught at a grammar school and Ibadan Polytechnic before becoming commissioner for Works and Housing in Oyo State, Nigeria. His writings include *'O' level economics of West Africa* (Ibadan, 1969), and *The Product life cycle model applied to export manufacturers and investment in a developing country* (Lund, 1974), AfricaWW, 1996; NUC, 1973-'77

Lawford, James Philip, born 29 December 1915 at Peking, where his father was an official in the Chinese Maritime Customs, he graduated M.A. from Cambridge University. He joined the Indian Army and served in the Far and Middle East as well as in North Africa. He retired with the rank of lieutenant colonel. His writings include *Solah Punjab; the history of the 16th Punjab Regiment* (1967), *Clive, Proconsul of India; a biography* (1976), *Britain's army in India* (1978), and he was a joint author of *A History of the British Army* (1970). He died in 1977. ConAu, 33-36, new rev., 28; IntAu&W, 1976;WrDr, 1976/78

Lawless, Richard Ivor, born 22 June 1943, he studied at the universities of Durham, London, Paris and Alger, gaining his B.A. and Ph.D. in Britain. He was a senior lecturer at the University of Durham, and an assistant director of its Centre for Middle Eastern and Islamic Studies. Concurrently he served as a member of the Council for Libyan Studies; he was also a regular contributor to the World Service of the BBC on North African Affairs. His writings include *Algerian bibliography; English language publications, 1830-1973* (1976); he was a joint author of *Work and company towns; settlement patterns and the Gulf oil industry* (1987); and he edited *Tlemcen; continuity and change in an Algerian Islamic town* (1976), *The Middle Eastern village* (1987), and *War and refugees* (1987). Note about the author

Lawrence, Bruce Bennett, born 14 August 1941, he received a Ph.D. in 1972 from Yale University, New Haven, Conn., for *Shahrastani on the Indian religions*. He subsequently became a professor of history of religion at Duke University, Durham, N.C., specializing in Indo-Muslim culture and medieval Sufism, a post which he still held in 2005. His writings include *An Overview of Sufi literature in the Sultanate period* (1979), *The Rose and the rock* (1979), *Ibn Khaldun and Islamic ideology* (1984), and *The Defenders of God; the fundamentalist revolt against the modern age* (1989). ConAu, 173; MESA Roster of members, 1990; NatFacDr, 2005; Selim; ZKO

Lawrence, Caleb W., born 19th cent. in Canada, he graduated from Queen's University, Kingston, Ont., and took post-graduate studies at Harvard. With the support of the Congregational Church of Melrose, Mass., he went in 1896 under the American Board of Commissioners for Foreign Missions to the Boys High School in İzmir (Smyrna), Turkey, later serving as a professor at the International College in that city. In 1922 he was head of the local relief association. Kornrumpf; *Missionary herald*, 1922

Lawrence, Rosamond née Napier, born in 1878, she wrote for magazins since she was sixteen. She was married to Sir Henry Lawrence, 1870-1949, who, besides holding other important official posts, served as a member of the Government of India and as governor of Bombay. Her writings include *The Faithful failure* (1910), and *Indian embers* (1941). BLC; Note about the author

Lawrence, Thomas Edward, born 18 August 1888 at Tremadoc, Wales, he studied at Oxford where he became a protégé of David G. Hogarth under whose auspices he first visited Syria in 1909. He travelled widely, often on foot, throughout the country and may have been in contact with Arab nationalists. From Jaunuary until March 1914 he was engaged with Sir Charles Leonard Woolley on a survey of Sinai. He was commissioned into the Geographical Section of the War Office and was assigned to Military Intelligence in Cairo. In the Great War he organized the Arab forces and led them in revolt against the Turks. He was a delegate to the 1919 Versailles conference, where he came to realize the hollowness of the Allies' war-time promises. He enlisted in 1922 in the Royal Air Force as a private under the name T. E. Shaw. He was killed in an accident when he crashed his motorcycle into a tree in 1935. His writings include *Seven pillars of wisdom* (1926), and *Secret dispatches from Arabia and other writings* (1991). Sir Basil H. Liddell Hart wrote *T. E. Lawrence* (1965), and Jean F. Bory, *Lawrence d'Arabie* (1989); Stephen E. Tabachnik edited *The T. E. Lawrence puzzle* (1984). AnaBrit; Bidwell, pp. 135-37; ConAu, 115, 167; Dawson; DcTwHis; DLB 195 (1998), pp. 194-203; DNB; Egyptology; *Index Islamicus* (10); Kornrumpf; Kornrumpf², vol. 2; Kornrumpf, N; Master (70); WhWE; *Who was who, 3*

Lawrence, Thomas Joseph, born in 1849 at Chesterton near Cambridge, he graduated in 1872 from Downing College, Cambridge, and was elected fellow and lecturer in law and history. Ordained in 1874, he served as a vicar of Tadlow from 1877 to 1888. Since 1883 he was a deputy professor of law in the University of Cambridge. His writings include *Essays on some disputed questions in modern international law* (1884), and *The Principles of international law* (1898). He died in 1919. BitInd (2)

Lawson, Ruth Catherine, born 18 April 1911 at Batavia, N.Y., she graduated in 1933 from Mount Holyoke College, South Hadley, Mass., and received her Ph.D. in 1951 from Bryn Mawr (Pa.) College for *The Compromise in international arbitration and judicial settlement*. From 1942 to her retirement in 1976 she was a professor of political science, and chairman of department, at Mount Holyoke College. Her writings include *International regional organizations; constitutional foundations* (1962). She died in December 1990. AmW&WSc, 1973 S, 1978 S; ConAu, 9-12; WhoAm, 1974, 1976; WhoAmW, 1958-1972/73; NYT, 18 December 1990, p. D-21 (not sighted)

Lawson, Fred Haley, born in 1952, he studied Middle Eastern politics and international relations at the University of California at Los Angeles, where he also received his Ph.D. in 1982 for *Social origins of aggresive foreign policy; the case of Muhammad 'Ali's Egypt*. He was successively a professor of government at Smith College, Northampton, Mass., and Mills College, Oakland, Calif. His writings include *Bahrain; the modernization of autocracy* (1989), and *The Social origins of Egyptian expansionism during the Muhammad 'Ali period* (1992). NatFacDr, 1995; Note about the author; ZKO

Layard, Sir Austen Henry, born in 1817, he was an archaeologist who directed excavations in Assyria from 1842 to 1851, when he turned to politics. He was elected as a Liberal member for Aylesbury in 1852. From 1877 to 1880, he served as a minister to Constantinople. His writings include *Nineveh and its remains, with an account of a visit to the Chaldaean Christians of Kurdistan, and the Yezidis, or Devil-Worshippers* (1849), *Early adventures in Persia, Susiana and Babylonia, including a residence among the Bakhtiyari and other wild tribes before the discovery of Niniveh* (1887), and *Sir A. Henry Layard; autobiography and letters, from his childhood until his appointment as H.M. Ambassador at Madrid* (1903). He died in 1894. Robert Silverberg wrote *The Man who found Niniveh* (1964). BritInd (11); DLB, 1666 (1996), pp. 200-208; DNB; Embacher; EncAm; EncBrit; Gabriel, pp. 118-28; Henze; Kornrumpf; Kornrumpf², vol. 2; Magyar; Master (20)

Layer, Ernest, born 7 June 1838 at Rouen (Seine-Maritime), France, he was a member of the Académie des sciences, belles-lettres et arts de Rouen and in 1911 submitted a report on the activities of the Classe des Belles-lettres et arts for the year 1910-11. His other writings include *Les Pères Blancs et la civilisation dans l'Ouganda* (1909), *De Tizi-Ouzou à Beni-Mengallet* (1911), *Par monts et par vaux; poésies populaires kabyles* (1913), *Confréries religieuses musulmanes et marabouts* (1916), *Note sur le panislamisme et la géographie équatoriale* (1916), *Les missions catholiques et la guerre* (1918), and *Quelques remarques sur le procès de Louis XVI* (1920). BN; IndexBFr² (1) = Oursel

Layish, Aharon, born 30 May 1933 at Suwalki, Poland, he studied at the Hebrew University of Jerusalem and the University of London, where he received his Ph.D. in 1973. He was a professor and chairman of the Department of Islamic and Middle Eastern Studies, Hebrew University of Jerusalem. He was a visiting fellow at Clare Hall, Cambridge, as well as the recipient of a scholar-in-residence award as Visiting Fulbright Professor, New York University. His writings include *Women and Islamic law in a non-Muslim state* (1975), *Marriage, divorce and succession in the Druze family* (1982), *Sharī'a and custom in Libyan tribal society; an annotated translation of decisions from the Sharī'a courts of Adjābiya and Kufra* (2004); he was a joint author of *The reinstatement of Islamic law in Sudan under Numayrī; an evaluation of a legal experiment in the light of its historical context* (2002); and he edited *Legal documents on Libyan tribal society in process of sedentarization* (1998). Private

Layna Serrano, Francisco, born 27 June 1893 at Luzón, Spain, he was a local historian and a member of the Hispanic Society of America. His writings include *El monasterio de Ovila* (1932),

Castillos de Guadalajara (1933), *La arquitectura romanica en la provincia de Guadalajara* (1935), *Historia de Guadalajara* (1942), and *Historia de la villa condal de Cifuentes* (1955). Figuras; IndiceE³ (2)

Lázár, Gyula (Julius), born 11 July 1841, he was since 1872 a secondary school teacher and ended his career as a professor of the Koloszvár Teachers' College. His writings include *Az ozmán uralom története Európában* (1877), *Regi Egyptom története & Assyria es Babylonia* (1878-79), *India története* (1879), *Das Judentum in seiner Vergangenheit und Gegenwart mit besonderem Hinblick auf Ungarn* (1880), and *A Török birodalom története* (1890). He died in Budapest in 1912. GeistigeUng

Lazar, Josef-Hans, fl. 20th cent., his writings include *Die Monstranz von Villalarga; Roman* (Innsbruck, Abendländische Verlags-Anstalt, 1953). Sezgin; ZKO

Lazar, Louis, born 20th cent., he received a *doctorat de 3ème cycle* in 1986 from the Université de Paris for *Quelques réflexions sur le législateur chez Ibn Roshd.* THESAM, 4

Lazard, Gilbert Léon Jean, born 4 February 1920 at Paris, he studied humanities and linguistics at Paris and Tehran, graduated from the École normale supérieure and the Sorbonne, received his *agrégation* in grammar in 1946, a diploma in Persian from the École nationale des langues orientales vivantes, Paris, in 1948, and a *doctorat ès lettres* in 1960 from the Sorbonne for *La langue des plus anciens monuments de la prose persane.* He was from 1948 to 1951 a fellow of the Institut franco-iranien at Tehran and was subsequently associated for seven years with the C.N.R.S. From 1958 to his retirement in 1981 he taught in various capacities Persian at Paris. In 1961-62 he was a visiting professor at the University of California at Los Angeles, and in 1980 he was elected to the Académie des inscriptions et belles lettres. His writings include *Grammaire du persan contemporain* (1957), *Les premiers poètes persans* (1964), *Dictionnaire persan-français* (1990), and *La formation de la language persan* (1995). In 1989 appeared *Etudes irano-aryennes offertes à Gilbert Lazard.* AnEIFr, 1997; BioB134; WhoFr, 1979/80-2005/2006

Lazare, Lucien, born 11 November 1924 at Strasbourg, France, he received teaching degrees at Lyon and Paris and became a Jewish community executive who also taught at Jewish schools in France and Belgium. His writings include *La résistance juive en France* (1987), and he was a contributing author to *Quatre approches différentes de la Bible* (1966), and its translation, *Die Eine Bibel auf vier Altären* (1968). WhoWorJ, 1965

Lazarev, Grigori, born 22 April 1936 at Marrakesh, he received degrees in sociology, economics and geography at Bordeaux and Paris. He was successively associated with the Société d'études agricoles et économiques, Moroccan governmental agencies, and the Food and Agriculture Organization. His writings include *Vers un éco-développement participatif; leçons et synthèse d'une étude thématique* (1993), and he was a joint author of *Développement local et communautés rurales approches et instruments pour une dynamique de concertation* (2002). Livres disponibles, 2004; Unesco

Lazarev, Mikhail Semenovich, born 8 May 1930 at Moscow, he graduated in 1952 from the Faculty of History, Moscow State University, reveived his first degree in 1956 for a thesis entitled «Крушение турецкого господства в арабских странах в годы первой мировой войны», and a doctorate in 1968 for *Курдский вопрос в сыязи с международными отношениями на Ближнем Востоке.* Since 1956 he was associated with the Oriental Institute of the Soviet Academy of Sciences. His writings include *Крушение турецкого господства на Арабском Востоке* (1960), *Курдистан и курдская проблема* (1964), *Курдский вопрос, 1891-1917* (1972), and *Империализм и курдский вопрос, 1917-1923* (1990). Miliband; Miliband²

Lázaro Durán, María Isabel, born 20th cent., she received a doctorate in 1986 from the Universidad de Granada for *Approximación a la "nahda" sirio-libanesa, la familia al-Bustānī; el pensamiento reformista del maesro Butrus.* She became a professor of Arabic at the Facultad de Filosofía y Letras at her alma mater. Arabismo, 1992; ZKO

Lazarus-Yafeh, Hava, born 6 May 1930 at Wiesbaden, Germany, he grew up first in Germany and since 1939 in Palestine. He received a Ph.D. in 1966 from the Hebrew University of Jerusalem for a Hebrew thesis on al-Ghazzālī's writings. He was a professor and chairman, Department of Civilization of Islam at the Hebrew University. His writings include *Studies in al-Ghazzali* (1975), *Some religious aspects of Islam* (1981), and *Intertwined worlds; medieval Islam and Bible criticism* (1992). BioHbDtE; IWWAS, 1975/76

Lazcano, Juan, born 14 September 1866 at Barrón (Ávala), Spain, he was an Augustinian priest and an Arabist and since 1881 a professor at the Universidad de Valladolid. In 1891 he went to Damascus for Arabic studies. He died in El Escorial on 17 December 1899. IndiceE³ (3)

Łazowski, Józef Feliks, born 20 November 1759 at Lunéville, Lorraine, he graduated in 1779 from the École des ponts-et-chaussée. As a captain in the French Engineers the Comité de salut public sent him in an *III* (1795/96) to Constantinople to undertake general reconnaissance work on Turkey's border, particularly the west coast of the Black Sea. When he returned to France in an *IV* (1796/97), he was promoted battailon commander. He later participated in the *Expédition d'Égypte* as well as the campaigns of the *Grande Armée*. He retired in 1811 with the rank of brigadier-general. He died in Paris on 8 October 1812. Dziekan; IndexBFr² (1); Polski (5); PSB

Lazreg, Marnia, born 10 January 1941 at Mostaganem, Algeria, she graduated in 1960 from the Université d'Alger, received her M.A. in 1970 from New York University, where she also obtained her Ph.D. in 1975 for *The emergence of classes in Algeria*. She became a professor in the Department of Sociology, Hunter College, C.U.N.Y., a post which she still held in 2005. Her writings include *The Emergence of classes in Algeria; a study of colonialism and sociopolitical change* (1976), and *Eloquence of silence; Algerian women in question* (1994). NatFacDr, 1990-2005; Selim³

Lazzaro, Nicola, born 6 January 1842 at Napoli, Italy, he received his first education at the Colegio dei Gesuiti and subsequently started to study engineering, but in 1860 he decided to enter the Ministerio di Agricoltura e Commercio. In the late 1860s he began a literary career with Italian periodicals. IndBiltal

Lazzerini, Edward James, born 14 September 1943 at Hartford, Conn., he received his Ph.D. in 1973 from the University of Washington for *Ismail Bey Gasprinskii and Muslim modernism in Russia, 1878-1914*. He was a professor of history at the University of New Orleans, La., from 1980 to his retirement. He was a joint editor of *Russia's Orient; imperial borderlands and peoples, 1700-1917* (1997). DrAS, 1982 H; *MESA Roster of members*, 1990; NatFacDr, 1995-2002; Selim; Schoeberlein

Lê, Thanh Khoi, born in 1923, he was in 1965 a *maître de recherche* in the Institut d'étude du développement économique et social, Université de Paris. His writings include *Le Viêt-nam, histoire et civilisation* (1955), *Histoire de l'Asie du sud-est* (1959), and *L'enseignement en Afrique tropicale* (1971). Note about the author; NUC

Leach, Robert, 1813-1845 see Leech, Robert

Leachman, Gerard Evelyn, born in 1880, he was educated at Charterhouse and entered the Royal Sussex Regiment in 1900. He served in the Boer War and explored Tibet before he wandered with the Anayzah tribe in Arabia in 1909. He returned to the Middle East in April 1915, and was present in person at many a decise battle in Mesopotamia as a lieut.-colonel and Political Officer on the Tigris. During September 1918 he was attached to the 1st Corps and took a prominent part in the operations leading to the surrender of the Turks at Shergat for which he received a D.S.O. by an immediate award in the field. He was present at the surrender of the Turks at Mosul, and was appointed Political Officer in charge of the Mosul Division, which post he held until he was compelled by sickness to take leave home. On his return he took over the Dulaim Divison. After the war he was attached to the Civil Administration of Mesopotamia. During the last few months of his life he performed some remarkable reconnaissances in Central Arabia. He was murdered in cold blood by the son of the chief of the Zoba tribe, in whose tents he had slept the night as a guest on 12 August 1920. His murder was one of the first events of the Iraqi rising. There are two biographies: *A Paladin of Arabia*, by N. N. E. Bray (1936), and *Leachman: O.C. desert*, by Harry V. F. Winstone (1982). Bidwell, pp. 158-59; *Journal of the Central Asian Society*, 8 (1921), pp. 70-75; Kornrumpf⁸, vol. 2; *The Times*, 20 August 1920 (not sighted); Who was who, 2;

Leaf, Walter, born in 1852 at Upper Norwood, England, he was a classical scholar, banker, and a Fellow of Trinity College, Cambridge. His writings include *Homer and history* (1915). He died in 1927. BbD; BiD&SB; DNB; EvLB; Master (11); Kornrumpf⁸, vol. 2

Leake, William Martin, born 14 January 1777 at London, he passed through the Royal Military Academy, Woolwich, and joined the artillery. Since 1800, he was sent on several diplomatic missions to the East. His writings include his travel accounts undertaken all in connection with his military service: *Travels in the Morea* (1830), *Travels in northern Greece* (1835-41), and *Greece and the end of twenty-five years protection* (1851). He died in Brighton on 6 January 1860. BbD; BiD&SB; BioIn, 7; DNB; Egyptology; Embacher; Henze; Kornrumpf; Kornrumpf, N; Master (6)

Léal, Numa F., born 19th cent., he received a doctorate in law in 1910 from the Université de Paris for *L'organisation de la police en Tunisie*. He subsequently served as a barrister in the Cour d'appel de Paris. Note; NUC, pre-1956

Leaman, Oliver Norbert Harold, Dr., born 16 October 1950, he was a senior lecturer in philosophy, first at Liverpool Polytechnic, and later at the Faculty of Education, Liverpool John Moores University, before he became a professor of philosophy at the University of Kentucky, Lexington, a post which he still held in 2005. His writings include *An Introduction to medieval Islamic philosophy* (1985), *Averroes* *and his philosophy* (1988); he edited *The Future of philosophy* (1998), *Friendship East and West; philosophical perspectives* (1996); and he was a joint editor of *History of Islamic philosophy* (1985). DrBSMES, 1993; EURAMES, 1993; NatFacDr, 2002-2005

Leander, Pontus Adalbert, born 18 September 1872 at Holsljunga (Älvsborg), Sweden, he studied Semitic languages at the universities of Göteborg, Uppsala, Leipzig, and Marburg, and received his doctorate in 1903 at Uppsala for *Über die sumerischen Lehnwörter im Assyrischen*, a thesis which won him a prize from his Philosophical Faculty. In 1910, he was appointed a lecturer in Assyriology and Hebrew at Lunds Universitet, and from 1917 to his death he was a professor of Semitic languages at Göteborgs Högskola. His writings include *Bibelns Konungsböcker i belysning av samtida inskrifter* (1927), *Laut- und Formlehre des Ägyptisch-Aramäischen* (1928), and jointly with Hans Bauer, *Historische Grammatik der hebräischen Sprache des Alten Testaments* (1922), and *Kurzgefasste biblisch-aramäische Grammatik* (1929). He died on Capri, Italy, on 12 August 1935. SBL; SMK; *Vem är det*, 1925

Leared, Arthur, born in 1822 at Wexford, Eire, he graduated in 1845 from Trinity College, Dublin, where he also received his medical degrees in 1847 and 1860; he was admitted M.D. at Oxford on 7 February 1861. He was a physician in County Wexford before going to India in 1851. Since 1852 he practised in London. He served as a physician to the British civil hospital in Smyrna during the Crimean War, 1854-56, and visited Morocco in 1872, 1877 and 1879. Since 1871 he was a Fellow of the Royal College of Physicians. His writings include *Morocco and the Moors; being an account of travels* (1876), and *A Visit to the Court of Morocco* (1879). He died in London on 16 or 17 October 1879. Boase; BritInd (1); DNB; Embacher; Kornrumpf; Master (3)

Leary, Allan, born 20th cent., he was in 1983 associated with the Centre of West African Studies in the University of Birmingham. He was a joint author, with Marion Johnson, of the exhibition catalogue, *African vision* (1988). LC; Note about the author

Leatherdale, Clive, born in 1949, he wrote *So you want to teach English to foreigners* (1980), *Britain and Saudi Arabia, 1925-1939; the Imperial oasis* (London, 1983), as well as science fiction writings. LC; Master (2)

Léaud, Aimé, born 20th cent., his writings include *Amnesty International; un combat de l'homme pour l'homme* (Choisy-le-Roi, 1983). LC

Le Balle, Robert, born about 1900, he received a doctorate in law in 1924 from the Université de Paris for *De la nature du droit du concessionnaire de sépulture*. His writings include *Cours de droit civil approfondi* (1955). NUC, pre-1956

Le Barrois d'Orgeval, René Robert, born in 1843 at Paris, he received a doctorate in law in 1868 from the Faculté de droit de Paris for *Du dominium, ou droit de propriéte, en droit romain De la propriété littéraire, en droit français*, a work which was published in the same year entitled *La Propriété littéraire en France et à l'étranger; son histoire, sa législation*. He became successively a counsellor at a prefecture and later a préfet. He died in 1928. BN; NUC, pre-1956; *Qui êtes-vous*, 1924

Lebault, G., born about 1900, he was in 1939 president of the Chambre d'agriculture de Casablanca. Note about the author

Lebeau, M., he was in 1955 director of the Caisse algériennne de crédit agricole mutuel. Note about the author

Lebedev, Evgeniĭ Aleksandrovich, born 31 December 1921 at Iaroslavl, Russia, he graduated in 1951 from the Moscow Oriental Institute, and received his first degree in 1954 for *Трансиордания - вассал английского империализма на Ближнем Востоке*. Since 1959 he was associated with the Oriental Institute of the Soviet Academy of Sciences. His writings include *Иордания в борьбе за независиность* (1956), *Иордания* (1959), *Демографические проблемы Иордании* (1972), *Иордания; контуры перемен* (1984), he was a joint author of *Суэцкий канал* (1956), and he was a joint editor of *Великий Октябрь и актуальные проблемы арабского мира* (1979). Miliband; Miliband²

Lebedev, German Aleksandrovich, born 20th cent., he was associated with the Oriental Institute of the Soviet Academy of Sciences. He was a joint author of *Южная Аравия без султанов; путевые заметки* (Moscow, 1971). NUC; OSK

Lebedev, Konstantin Aleksandrovich, born 20 March 1920 at Kolomna, Russia, he graduated in 1942 from the Moscow Oriental Institute and received his first degree in 1950 for his thesis «Внутренняя флексия в современном языке пушту», and his doctorate in 1962 for *Очерк по синтаксу простого предожения в современном литературном языке пушту*. He was associated with his alma mater from 1943 to 1954, when he was appointed to teach Afghan languages and literatures at the Moscow

State Institute for International Relations, Ministry of Foreign Affairs. In 1967 he became a *проректор.* His writings include *Грамматика языка пушту* (1945), *Русско-афгаискиий лексический минимум* (1957), *Карманны русско-афганский словарь* (1961), *Карманный афганско-русский словарь* (1962), *Грамматика языка пушту* (1970), and he was a joint author of *Русско-афганский словарь* (1973). Miliband; Miliband²

Lebedev, Nikolaĭ Ivanovich, born 20th cent., his writings include *Новый этап международных отношений* (1976), and its translations, *Eine neue Etappe der internationalen Beziehungen* (1978)., and *A New stage in international relations* (1978). OSK

Lebedev (Lebedew), V. I., born about 1800, he was a Russian "who had long lived among the Chuvash and was fluent in their language, but his competence in Turkish left something to be desired." He was a contributor to the *Журнал* of the Russian Ministry of the Interior, and the *Archiv für wissenschaftliche Kunde von Russland*, where he published articles between 1850 and 1854. BiobibSOT, pp. 203-204; Note about the author

Lebedev, Vasiliĭ Ivanovich, born in 1825 in Russia, he studied at the Theological Academy (Духовная Академия), Moscow, subsequently teaching there logic and history of philosophy. His writings include *О Сквернословіи* (Moscow, 1860), he edited *Душерользное чтеніе* (s.d.); he also contributed to the journal, *Москвитяніе.* He died in 1863. EnSlovar; NYPL

Lebedev, Viktor Vladimirovich, born 2 June 1940 at Leningrad, he graduated in 1962 from the local Oriental Faculty, and received his first degree in 1969 for a thesis on «Памятники арабской народной литературы в собрании А. С. Фирковича», and his doctorate in 1980 for *Проблемы источнико-ведения средневекового арабского фольклора.* Since 1962 he was associated with the State Public Library im. M. E. Saltykova-SHCHedrina, Leningrad. His writings include *Позний средне-арабский язык, XIII-XVIII вв.* (1977), *Арабские документы IX-XX вв; каталог* (1978), and *Арабские сочинения в еврейской графике; каталог рукописей* (1987). Miliband²

Lebedev, Vladimir Ivanovich, born 13 October 1894 at Riga, Latvia, he was a professor of history at Moscow, where he also died on 3 April 1966. BashkKE

Lebedev, Vladimir Vasil'evich, born 9 June 1945 at Moscow, he graduated in 1969 from the Institute of Oriental Languages, Moscow State University, and received his first degree in 1980 from the Institute of Asian and African Studies, Moscow, with a thesis on «Отрицание в арабск. литерат. языке.» Since 1969 he was associated with the Institute of Asian and African Studies. Miliband²

Lebedeva, G. D., fl. 1969, she was joint author of *Заколдованный город; новеллы афганских писателй* (1972). LC

Lebedeva, Irina Nikolaevna, born about 1935, she was a classicist whose writings include *Позние греческие хроники и их русские и восточные переводы* (1968), *Повесть о Варлааме и Иоасафе; памятник древнерусской переводной литературы XI-XII в.в.* (1985), and *Словоука-затель к тексту "Повести о Варлааме и Иоасафе"* (1988). OSK

Lebedinskiĭ, I. L., born 20th cent., he translated *Живой мост рассказы арабского сопротивления; перевод с арабского* (1972), and he translated from the Arabic and French, *Страшная ночь; новеллы алжирских писателей* (1966), and *Дорогая наса земля; новеллы писателей Марокко, Туниса, Ливии* (1967). ZKO

Lebedinskiĭ, Lev Nikolaevich, born 23 October 1904, he was a musicologist whose writings include two biographies of Bashkir composers, *Мажит Бурангулов* (1963), and *В. А. Белый; очерк жизни и творчества, статьи, воспоминания, материалы* (1987). He died in Moscow on 21 November 1992. BashkKE; OSK

Lebel, Roland, born in 1893, his writings include *L'Afrique occidentale dans la littérature française* (1925), *L'Impôt agricole au Maroc, "le tertib"* (1925), *Études de littérature coloniale* (1928), *Histoire de la littérature coloniale en France* (1931), and *Le Maroc chez les auteurs anglais du XVIe au XIXe siècle* (1939). His trace is lost after an article in 1959. NUC, pre-1956; ZKO

Le Berre, Marc, born 20th cent., his writings include *Monuments pré-islamiques de l'Hindukush central* (1987), and he was a joint author of *Monuments bouddhistes de la région de Caboul* (1976), and *Monuments préislamiques d'Afghanistan* (1964). *Livres disponibles*, 2004

Lebeuf, Jean Paul, born 30 January 1907 at Paris, he was a pioneer of African ethnology and took the required university courses as common at the time, degrees in *lettres* and *sciences humaines*, followed by study at the Institut d'ethnologie and the École pratique des hautes études. He was a deputy head of the Mission Dakar-Djibouti, 1936-37, experiences which are the basis of his later thesis on the Fali.

In 1937, he entered the Centre National de la Recherche Scientifique and there spent his entire career except for two years. Since his marriage to Annie Masson-Detourbet in 1943, he shared all his work with his wife. From 1961 to 1972, he was a director of the Institut national pour les Sciences humaines at Fort-Lamy. He was an officer of the Société des africanistes as well as the Académie des sciences d'outre-mer, and a corresponding member of the Académie des inscriptions et belles-lettres since 1985. His writings include *Quand l'or était vivant; aventures au Tchad* (1945), *Vêtements et parures du Cameroun français* (1946), *Fort-Lamy, Tchad, A.E.F.* (1951), *Bangui (Oubangui) A.E.F.* (1954), *Du Cameroun au Tchad* (1954), *L'Habitation des Fali* (1961), and he was a joint author of *La Civilisation du Tchad* (1950), and *Ouara, ville perdue* (1989). He died in Vaison-la-Romaine (Vaucluse) on 28 February 1994. DBF; *Journal des africanistes*, 64, no. 2 (1994), pp. 91-112; Unesco; WhoFr, 1979/80-1993/94

Leblanc, Ely Maximilien, born in 1871, he received a medical doctorate in 1897 from the Université de Paris for *Contribution à l'étude de l'hypertrophie congénitale unilatérale ou complète*. He became associated with the Institut de recherches sahariennes de l'Université d'Alger. His writings include *Choses et gens du Hoggar* (Alger, 1930), and *Anthropologie et ethnologie* (Alger, ca. 1945). BN; NUC, pre-1956

Le Blanc Hackluya, Frédéric, he wrote *Histoire de l'islamisme et des sectes qui s'y rattachent* (Paris, 1852). NUC, pre-1956

Lebling, Clemens, born 24 December 1884, he received a Dr.phil. in 1911 from the Universität München for *Geologische Beschreibung des Lattengebirges im Berchdesgadener Land*. He was associated with Columbia University, New York, in 1912. From 1919 until his retirement in 1934 he was a geographer at the Technische Universität München. His writings include *Forschungen in der Baharije-Oase und anderen Gegenden Ägyptens* (1919), and the novel, *Nandi und Kakamega; Erlebnisse in Ost-Afrika* (1954). Kürschner, 1926-35

Leblond, Ary, he was born Aimé Merlo on 30 July 1880 at Saint-Pierre, île de La Réunion, into a family originally from Provence, France. He was educated at the Collège de Saint-Denis which he left to continue at the Faculté des lettres de Paris, where he became acquainted with Georges Athénas. After his first novel in 1900, *Anicette et Pierre Desrades*, first serialized in *Revue hebdomadaire* and published in 1911, he joined forces with Georges Athénas and together published under the mutual pseudonym Marius et Ary Leblond or Marius-Ary Leblond. Their writings include *Après l'exotisme de Loti* (1926), *Lavigerie et les Pères blancs* (1938), and innumerable others. He later became a keeper of the Musée d'Outre-Mer. He died in Paris in 1958. Benjamin Cazemage wrote *La vie et l'œuvre de Marius et Ary Leblond* (1969). DBF; *Hommes et destins*, vol. 4 (1981), pp. 434-41

Leblond, Charles *Gaston*, born 19th cent., he was a lieutenant-colonel who, in the early years of the twentieth century, taught geography, with reference to Africa, at the École supérieure de guerre. Note about the author

Le Boeuf, Jules, born 19th cent., he was a lieutenant-colonel with the Bureau des Affaires indigènes de la Tunisie. His writings include *Les Confins de la Tunisie et de la Tripolitaine; historique du tracé de la frontière* (Paris, 1909). He died in 1916. NUC, pre-1956; Peyronnet, p. 628

Le Bon, Charles Marie *Gustave*, born 7 May 1841 at Nogent-sur-Retrou (Eure-et-Loire), France, he began life at the provincial bottom of the Administration de l'Enregistrement et des Domains. When he came to Paris, he broke off his medical studies, but with the support of Professor Piorry from the Académie de médecine, he began to publish in this field between 1862 and 1880, notably *La Vie, physiologie humaine appliquée à l'hygiène et à la médecine* (1874). He became a member of several learned societies so that his literary output took a bent towards history and ethnography, founded on his research travels in the East. He began to study crowd psychology and developed theories of social psychology that emphasized national character and racial superiority. His writings include *La Civilisation des Arabes* (1881), its translations, *Hadārat al-'Arab* (1948), and *Die mittelalterliche Welt der Araber* (1974), *L'Homme et les sociétés* (1881), *Les Monuments de l'Inde* (1893), *La Psychologie des foules* (1895), a bestseller which was also translated into Turkish, *Ruh ul-cama'at* (1907) and Arabic, *Rūh al-ijtimā'* (1909). He died in Marnes-la-Coquette (Hauts-de-Seine) on 15 December 1931. Alice Widener edited and translated, *Gustave Le Bon, the man and his works; a presentation with introduction, first translations into English, and edited extracts* (1979). BioIn, 10, 12; DBF; EncAm; GdeEnc; Master (5); Özege

Lebon, Gabriel, born in 1864 at Besançon, France, he was undoubtedly a student of the Marianists at Saint-Jean at Besançon and entered the Jesuits in 1884. He had his first contact with the East when he was in Alexandria from 1889 to 1892. He was ordained priest in 1895. Five years later, he was sent to the Mission d'Arménie as a professor of sciences in charge of the Latin parish at Amasya in northern Anatolia, where he remained until 1914, excepting one year each spent at Tokat and

Constantinople. His was a succesful apostolate even though he failed to master the Armenian language. But the first World War ruined everything. He became *operarius* at Besançon in 1915, and subesequently a chaplain with the French marine, based on a vessel in Malta. In 1919, he rejoined the Constantinople residence. He later spent some years at Aleppo before retiring in 1932 to Beirut. He died in Ghazir, Lebanon, on 22 January 1942. Jalabert, pp. 212-13

Lebon, John Harold George, he was in 1956 associated with the Department of Geography in the University of Khartoum. His writings include *The Evolution of our countryside* (1952), *An Introduction to human geography* (1952), and *Land use in Sudan* (1965).

Leboulanger, Philippe, born 20th cent., he graduated from the Faculté de droit de Paris, received a diploma in comparative law, and a doctorate in law. In the 1970s he was a barrister in the Cour d'appel de Paris, and in the 1980s, in the Barreau de Paris. He was a sometime lecturer in international law at the Faculté de droit du Caire. His writings include *Les Contrats entre états et entreprises étrangères* (1985). Note about the author

Lebourgeois, Stanislas, born 19th cent., his writings include *La question du Gouvernement générale de l'Algérie* (1895), and *Étude sur le transsaharien* (1899). His trace is lost after an article in 1903. BN; NUC, pre-1956

Le Bras, Gabriel, born 20th cent., his writings include *Études de sociologie religieuse* (Paris, 1955-56), and *L'Église et le village* (Paris, 1976). He was also a director of numerous works on the medieval Church of the East. Livres disponibles, 2004; NUC, 1973-77

Le Braz, Anatole, born in 1859 at Duault (Côtes-du-Nord), France, he was a professor of French literature in the Université de Rennes. He died in 1926. Master (1); NUC, pre-1956

Lebret, le Père Louis Joseph, born 26 June 1897 at Le-Minihic-sur-Rance (Ille-et-Vilaine), France, he joined the French navy in the first World War, trained at the École navale, and became an *enseigne de vaisseau*. In 1922, he was an instructor at the École navale. He had already been promoted lieutenant when he left the navy in the following year to enter the order of the *Frères prêcheurs*, where he devoted himself to social affairs of the merchant marine. Mobilized in 1939, he was made an economic expert at the French ministry of the merchant marine. Since that time he devoted himself to the aid of underdeveloped countries, for which purpose he established the Centre international de formation et de recherche en vue du Développement harmonisé. After the war he collaborated with the U.N.O., and in 1961 he headed a mission of the Institut de Recherches et de Formation en vue du Développement to the Lebanese Government. His writings include *Le Liban face à son développement* (1963), and *Dimensions de la charté* (1965), *Dynamique concrète du développement* (1967), *L'Économie au service des hommes* (1968), and its translation, *L'economia al servizio degli uomini* (1969). He died in Paris on 20 July 1966. BioIn, 5; DBF; DBFC, 1954/55; NDNC, 1966; Unesco

Le Brun Kéris, Georges, born 22 February 1910 at Paris, he received a diploma from the École libre des sciences politiques and a doctorate in 1938 from the Université de Paris for *Les Projets de réforme de la Société des nations et le développement du pacte*. He became a journalist and politician whose writings include *U.S.A. - U.R.S.S.* (Paris, 1947), *Mort des colonies?* (Paris, 1953), and *Afrique, quel sera ton visage?* (Paris, 1963). IndexBFr² (1)

Leca, Jean, 20 March 1935 at Alger, Algeria, he was educated at the Lycée d'Alger and studied at the law schools of Alger, Paris, and Aix-en-Provence. He received a diploma from the Institut d'études politiques d'Alger and a doctorate in law from the Université d'Aix-Marseille in 1959 for *Les techniques de révision des conventions internationales*, a work which was published in 1961. He taught successively at the Faculté de droit de Grenoble, Faculté de droit d'Alger and since 1979 at the Institut d'études politiques de Paris. He was a joint author of *Les Nationalismes maghrébins* (1966), and *L'Algérie politique; institutions et régime* (1975); and he edited *Les démocraties sont-elles gouvernable?* (1985). WhoFr, 1995-2005/2006

Lecerclé, Jacques, born about 1900, he received a doctorate in 1946 from the Université de Paris for *Bilans et monnaie; problèmes fiscaux posés par la dégradation monétaire et revision des bilans*. NUC

Lecerf, Jean, born 9 July 1894 at Orléans, France, he served in the Great War and was invalided home. In 1919, he entered the École normale supérieure, Paris, and subsequently served at the Collège Sadiki at Tunis. After some years as a fellow of the Institut Dominicain de Jérusalem, he taught first three years at the Mission Laïque and subsequently another two years under the same conditions at the Institut français de Damas. He returned to France about the time of the Munich Pact. In the ensueing war he fought with the Free French in Lebanon, Palestine, and Egypt. Demobilized in January of 1946, he had the chance to teach at the École nationale des langues orientales vivantes at

Paris but instead took Jean Cantineau's place at the Université d'Alger, teaching Arabic and Semitic philology, when asked by him because of his eye ailment. Upon the latter's premature death in 1956, he succeeded him in the chair of Arabic at the École des Langues orientales, a post which he then held until his retirement in 1964. His writings include *Littérature dialectale et renaissance arabe moderne* (1933), and he was a joint translator of *Le livre des jours*, from the Arabic of Taha Husayn (1947). He died in Paris on 14 March 1980. *Revue des études islamiques*, 48 (1980), pp. 1-7

Lech, Klaus, born about 1930, he received a Dr.phil. in 1962 from the Universität Bonn for *Al-'Umari's Bericht über die Reiche der Mongolen in seinem Werk "Masālik al-absār fī mamālik al-amsār,"* a work which was published in 1968 entitled *Das Mongolische Weltreich.* His other writings include *Geschichte des islamischen Kultus; rechtshistorische und hadīṯ-kritische Untersuchungen* (1979). ZKO

Le Chatelier, Frédéric *Alfred*, born 23 November 1855 at Paris, he was educated at the Collège Rollin and the Lycée de Bordeaux. After passing through the military college at Saint-Cyr, he was assigned to the Tirailleurs algériens in Blida as a *sous-lieutenant.* He was subsequently transferred, first to the Service des Affaires indigènes, and in March 1879 to the Bureau arabe in Boghar. In January 1880, he participated in the Trans-Saharan Mission Flatters. From 1882 to 1885 he was employed in artesian drilling at Ouargla in the Algerian Territoires du Sud. In February 1886, he was sent by the Governor General Tirman to Egypt to study Muslim brotherhoods. Although he resigned from the army in 1893, he still organized during the following year the expedition Foureau-Lamy. From 1902 to 1925, he held the newly instituted chair of *sociographie musulmane* at the Collège de France. In 1906, he became the founding editor of the *Revue du monde musulman.* His writings include *Les Confréries musulmanes du Hedjaz* (1887), *L'Islam au XIXe siècle* (1888), *Les Mégadanat* (1888), *Tribus du Sud-Ouest marocain; bassin côtier entre Sous et Drâa* (1891), and *L'Islam dans l'Afrique occidentale* (1899). He died in Paris on 9 August 1929. Raymond Messal wrote *La Genèse de notre victoire marocaine; un précurseur, Alfred Le Chatelier* (Paris, 1931). DBF; IndexBFr² (2); Peyronnet, pp. 385-86

Lechleitner, Herwig, born about 1900, he received a Dr.phil. in 1930 from the Universität Wien for *Neue morphologische Untersuchungen im alpinen Einzugsgebiet der Ybbs.* He was a professor at Wien, whose writings include *Die Rolle des Staates in der wirtschaftlichen und sozialen Entwicklung Libanons* (Wien, 1972). GV; ZKO

Lechner, Kilian, born 7 March 1920 at Rehling, Bavaria, Germany, he graduated from high school, completed his compulsory paramilitary national labour service (*Reichsarbeitsdienst*) and began to study classics at the Universität Würzburg. A few months later, war broke out and he was called up for military service. After the war, he continued with classics and Byzantine subjects at the Universität München, where he received a Dr.phil. in 1955 for *Hellenen und Barbaren im Weltbild der Byzantiner.* His writings include *Fatima* (Bamberg, 1988), and *Santiago de Compostela* (Bamberg, 2003) Thesis

Leclant, Jean, born 8 August 1920 at Paris, he was a student at the lycées Voltaire and Henri IV, Paris, and entered the École normale supérieure. Deeply interested in ancient Egypt, he majored in archaeology He gained his *agrégation* and a doctorate after the war and entered the Musée du Louvre. In 1948, he began a four-year association with the Institut français d'archéologie orientale du Caire; and in 1953, he became a professor of Egyptology at the Université de Strasbourg, a post which he held until 1963, when he received the chair of Egyptology at the Sorbonne. His writings include *Dans les pas des pharaons* (1958), and its translation, *In the stepps of the pharaohs* (1958). ConAu, 132; IntWW, 1989-2005|; NDNC, 1966; WhoFr, 1979/80-2005/2006

Leclerc, Jacques, born 7 June 1935, he received a *doctorat* in 1970 for his thesis, *La pensée des communistes indonésiens.* He was an historian, specializing in Indonesia. From 1973 to 1995, he was a research fellow of the C.N.R.S. at the Centre d'Étude et de Recherches Internationales de la Fondation Nationale des Sciences Politiques. He died on 20 April 1995. *Mouvement social*, 173 (1995), pp. 193-198

Le Clerc, Jean, born 19 March 1657 at Genève, Switzerland, he early in life displayed an interest in learning, which he was able to pursue in the rich private libraries of the family, particularly his grand-uncle Stephan de Courcelles, a champion of Arminianism. Since 1678, he was formally educated at Grenoble and Genève, where he was ordained an Evangelical minister. In 1680, he continued his theological studies, first at Saumur, and in 1682, went to London, concurrently also preaching in the Walloon Church and in the Savoy Chapel. For reasons of health he left England for Holland, where he became closely associated with Philips van Limborch, a famous professor at the Amsterdamsche Remonstrantsche Seminarium. This acquaintance with van Limborch strengthened his preference for the Remonstrant theology, already known to him by the writings of his grand-uncle and by those of Simon Episcopius. In 1684, he finally setttled at Amsterdam, first as a moderately successful preacher, until the ecclesiastical jealousy shut him out from that career, and he was named a professor of letters, philosophy and Hebrew at the Remontrantsche Seminarium. After the death of van Limborch in 1712, he succeeded him in the chair of ecclesiastical history, which post he held until 1728, when struck by paralysis. From 1714 to 1727, he had been an editor of *Bibliothèque ancienne et moderne*. He died in mental derangement in Amsterdam on 8 January 1736. EncBrit; Hoefer; Master (7); NieuwNBW, vol. 4 (1918), cols. 430-34

Leclerc, Max, born in 1864 at Paris, he was educated at the lycées de Vanves and Louis-le-Grand, Paris, and received degrees from the Faculté de droit de Paris, and the École des sciences politiques; he subsequently studied in Germany (Bonn) and Britain. From his time at the Universität Bonn originates his *La Vie municipale en Prusse*. Upon his return to Paris he collaborated with the foreign policy desk at the *Journal des débats*. In the course of his position he travelled extensively in the Americas, but particularly in Britain. Since the 1890s he collaborated with the French geographer Armand Colin and became a sometime editor of the *Annales de géographie*. As an old friend of Maréchal Lyautey, one of his last publications was *Au Maroc avec Lyautey* (1927). He died in 1932. *Annales de géographie*, 41 (1932), pp. 337-338; *Qui êtes-vous*, 1924

Leclerc, Nicolas *Lucien*, born 13 September 1815 at Ville-sur-Illon (Vosges), France, he received his first education at the Petit Séminaire de Châtel-sur-Moselle, his *baccalauréat ès lettres* in 1836 from the Collège royal de Nancy, and also his *baccalauréat ès sciences physics* in the follwing year. He then matriculated at the Université de Strasbourg with a view to a career as military physician. Since 1840 he served for four ywars with Algerian ambulances, concurrently studying Arabic philology and medicine, particularly as practised in Algeria. From 1844 to 1848 he passed successively through the teaching hospitals of Metz, Strasbourg, Paris, once again Paris, and finally Thionvillle, gaining his medical doctorate in 1849 at Paris for *Étiologie du goitre*. In the autumn of 1849 he went to Algeria as a *chirugien aide-major de 2e classe* to serve for five years with the Regiment de Zouaves, which post gave him a chance to perfect his competence in indigenous medicine and language. After a year in France, he was again assigned to Algeria from 1854 to 1864. He retired shortly after the Franco-Prussian War. His writings include *Une Mission médicale en Kabylie* (1864), and *Histoire de la médicine arabe* (1876). He died at his place of birth on 10 April 1893. DBF; Fück, p. 252

Leclercq, Jules Joseph, born 4 December 1848 at Bruxelles, he received a doctorate in law at Bruxelles and subsequently studied science subjects at the École polytechnic. He was a judge in the Court of first instance at Bruxelles. In whatever spare time he could find he travelled throughout Europe and beyond. His writings include *De Mogador à Biskra* (1881), *Du Caucase aux monts Alaï* (1890), and *Chez les Jaunes* (1910). He died in 1928. IndexBFr² (2); NUC; Vapereau

Lecocq, André, born 19th cent., he was in 1910 a professor at the Collège de Tlemcen, Algeria. Note about the author

Le Cœur, Charles, born 14 May 1903 at Paris, he graduated in 1924 from the École normale supérieure, Paris, and received a diploma from the École pratique des hautes études for *Le culte de la génération et l'évolution religieuse et sociale en Guinée*, a work which was published in 1932. In 1928, he went to Morocco, where he taught, first at the Muslim college of Rabat, and then joined the Institut des hautes études marocaines as a lecturer, later serving as a director of Moroccan studies in ethnography. In 1942, he submitted his two doctoral theses at the Sorbonne, *Le rite de l'outil* and *Textes sur la sociologie et l'école au Maroc*. He spent 1933 to 1935 on field-work in Tibesti on a Rockefeller fellowship. He died 20 July 1944 at the Italian front. *Hespéris*, 31 (1944), p. 70; *Hommes et destins*, vol. 2, pp. 452-57; *Travaux de l'Institut deRecherches sahariennes*, 3 (1945), pp. 7-11

LeCompte, Garé, born 15 September 1937 at Chicago, he graduated in 1959 from the University of Washington and received his Ph.D. in 1971 from the American University, Washington, D.C., for *Soviet Muslims and the Afro-Asian world*. He was a Ford Foundation visiting professor of social sciences at the Syrian National University, 1962-63; an associate director of the New York-Pennsylvania Health Management Corporation at Binghamton, 1971-73; and a dean and professor at the Ohio College of Pediatric Medicine at Cleveland. His writings include *Factors in the introduction of a new communications technology into Syria and Turkey* (Middletown, Conn., 1970). AmM&WSc, 1973 S; WhoMW, 1978/79, 1980/82 (not sighted); WhoWest, 1982/83, 1984/85

Lecomte, Gérard, born 20th cent., his writings include *Grammaire de l'arabe* (1968), *Éléments d'arabe de presse et de radio* (1979); he was a joint author of *Textes littéraires arabes des XIX e XXe siècles* 1969); and he translated from the Arabic, *Ibn Qutayba; le traité des divergences du hadith* (1962). LC

Lecomte, Paul *Henri*, born 8 January 1856 at Saint-Nabord (Vosges), France, he received a *doctorat ès sciences naturelles* in 1889 from the Université de Paris for *Contribution à l'étude du liber des angiospermes*, and also his *agrégation de l'université*. He taught at the Lycée Saint-Louis, 1884-1903, and the Lycée Henri-IV, 1903-1906; he subsequently was a professor at the Muséum d'histoire naturelle de Paris. In 1917, he was elected a member of the Académie des Sciences. He established the *Revue des cultures coloniales*, and was also its founding editor. His writings include *Le coton en Égypte* (1905), and *Les bois coloniaux* (1923). He died in 1934. NUC, pre-1956; *Qui êtes-vous*, 1924

von Le Coq, Albert August, born 8 September 1860 at Berlin, he trained as a merchant in England (London) and the U.S.A., concurrently studying medicine. Upon his return to Germany he entered the family firm at Darmstadt. He sold the business in 1900 to enter the Ethnological Museum, Berlin. He headed the German Turfan expeditions of 1904/5, 1905/6, and 1913/14. Since 1914 he was a keeper, and from 1923 to 1925 a director of the Indian section of Völkerkundliches Museum, Berlin. His writings include *Kurdische Texte* (1903), *Bilderatlas zur Kunst und Kulturgeschichte Mittel-Asiens* (1925), and *Von Land und Leuten in Ostturkistan* (1928). He died in Berlin on 21 April 1930. DtBE; DtBiInd (1); Hanisch; NDB; Stache-Rosen, pp. 141-142; *Wer ist's*, 1912

Lecoq, Pierre, born 9 March 1939 at Couthuin, Belgium, he received a *doctorat d'état* in 1984 from the Université de Paris for *Recherches sur les dialectes iraniens centraux*. In 1973, he was appointed academic assistant at the Université de Liège. His writings include *Le dialecte de Sivand* (1979). AnEIFr, 1997; BioB134; THESAM, 4

Le Coz, Jean Tristan, he was born of humble parentage on 31 May 1920 at La Forêt-Fouesnant, Bretagne, France. With a bursary for underprivileged students he completed his secondary education at Caen and le Mans. Influenced by his father's colonial military career, he wanted to attend the military college at Saint-Cyr, but the catastrophe of 1940 made him decide on the École normale de Saint-Cloud. After his *diplôme d'études supérieure* he started a colonial teaching career at Rabat, 1944-46, concurrently preparing his *agrégation*. He received a doctorate in letters in 1964 from the Université de Paris for both his theses, *Le Rharb, fellahs et colours; étude de géographie régionale*, and his *thèse complémentaire, Les Tribus Guichs au Maroc*. He remained associated with Morocco until 1965, when he was appointed a professor of geography at the Faculté des lettres in the Université de Montpellier. His writings include *Les Réformes agraires* (1974), and *Socialisme et localité; le deuxième cycle agraire de la Chine et de l'Algérie* (1984-91). He died in February 1991. Nearly the entire fascicule 3-4 of vol. 25 (1991) of the *Bulletin de la Société languedocienne de géographie*, entitled *Hommage à Jean Le Coz*, is dedicated to his work. Note

Lecq, Hippolyte, born in 1856, he was a joint author of *Manuel pratique de l'agriculteur algérien* (1900), *Cultures du Midi, de l'Algérie et de Tunisie* (1906), and, jointly with Charles Rivière, *Traité pratique d'agriculture pour le nord de l'Afrique; Algérie, Tunisie, Maroc, Tripolitaine* (1914). He died in 1922. NUC, pre-1956

Lecureul, Xavier Marie Vital Alphonse, born 2 September 1883, he gained degrees in letters and law, and also studied at the École des langues orientales vivantes, Paris. He was a student interpreter in Morocco in 1908, and at Cairo in 1909, successively becoming a consular officer at Cairo, Barcelona, Wien, Genève, and, since 1925, at Milano. IndexBFr² (1)

Lecuyer, Émile, born 20th cent., he was in 1950 a *professeur* at the Lycée moderne et technique de Tananarive, Madagascar. His writings include *Aide-mémoire de législation du travail malgache* (Tananarive, 1963). Note about the author

Lécuyer-Samanter, Nicole, born 20th cent., she wrote *Mohamed Abdulle Hassan, poète et guerrier de la Corne de l'Afrique* (Paris, 1979). Index Islamicus

Ledda, Romano, born in 1930, his writings include *Una rivoluzione africana* (1970), and *La battaglia di Amman* (1971).

Lédé, Marie-Louise, born about 1900, her writings include *Seule avec les Touareg du Hoggar* (1954). Her trace is lost after an article in 1957.

Ledeen, Michael Arthur, born 1 August 1941 at Los Angeles, Calif., he graduated in 1962 from Pomona College, Claremont, Calif., and received his Ph.D. in 1969 from the University of Wisconsin for *Fascismo universale; the theory and practice of Fascist International, 1928-1936*. His writings include *From Helsinki to Belgrade; issues and perspective* (1977), *Universal fascism* (1972), *Perilous statecraft; an insider's account of the Iran-Contra affair* (1988), *Grave new world* (1992), *Machiavelli on modern leadership* (1999), *Tocqueville on American character* (2000), and jointly with William Lewis, *Debacle, the American failure in Iran* (1981). ConAu, new rev., 103

Leder, Arnold, born about 1940, he received a Ph.D. in 1974 from Indiana University at Bloomington for *Kemalist rule and party competition in rural Turkey; politics and change in an Anatolian community*. He was a sometime chief, Azerbajani Service, Voice of America, Washington, D.C., and subsequently became a professor of political science at Southwest Texas State University, San Marcos, which post he still held in 2002. His writings include *Catalysts of change; Marxist versus Muslim in a Turkish community* (1977). MESA Roster of members, 1990; NatFacDr, 1990-2002; Note

Leder, Stefan, born 11 May 1951 at Göttingen, Germany, he received a Dr.phil. in 1982 from the Universität Frankfurt am Main for *Ibn al-Ǧauzi und seine Kompilation wider die Leidenschaft*, a work which was published in 1984; and he gained a Dr.habil. in 1988 for *Das Korpus al-Haiṯam Ibn-'Adī; Herkunft, Überlieferung, Gestalt früher Texte der aḫbār-Literatur*, published in 1991. His writings also include the edition, *Die arabische Ecloga; das 4. Buch der Kanones der Könige aus der Sammlung des Makarios* (1985). He was a professor in the Institut für Orientalistik in the Universität Halle-Wittenberg. Kürschner, 2001-2005

Lederer, Ivo John, born 11 December 1929 at Zagreb, Yugoslavia, he graduated in 1951 from the University of Colorado, and received his M.A. and Ph.D. from Princeton University. He taught Russian and Eastern European history successively at Princeton University, Yale University, New Haven, Conn., at Stanford University, Palo Alto, Calif. His writings include *The Versailles settlement - was it foredoomed to failure* (1960); he was a joint editor of *The Soviet Union and the Middle East* (1960), and *The Soviet Union and the Middle East; the post World War II era* (1974). He died of cancer on 18 June 1998 in New York City. ConAu, 9-12, 181; DrAS, 1969 H, 1974 H, 1978 H; IntAu&W, 1977, 1982; WhoE, 1977/78, 1979/80

Ledit, Canon Charles J., born 20th cent., his writings include *Mahomet, Israël et le Christ* (1956), *Le Coran; essai d'une exégèse structurale* (1983), and he was a joint author of *La Mosquée sur le roc* (1966). BN; ZKO

Ledoulx, Alphonse, born in 1846, he was a French consul-general at Jerusalem, and a dragoman at the French Legation in Constantinople. He died in 1898. Kornrumpf

de **Ledoulx**, Louis Henri Théodore Charles Alexandre Jules, born 24 September 1877, he entered the French consular service on 2 November 1898 at Montevideo as an *élève chancelier*. He served mostly in Latin America, but also in Malta, 1906 and 1917, as well as at Fiume (Rijeka), Croatia, 1920. IndexBFr² (1)

Leduc, Gaston Gabriel, born 27 July 1904 at Hérisson (Allier), France, he studied law at the Université d'Aix-en-Provence, gaining his *agrégation* in *scienes économiques et financières* in 1930. He began his teaching career at the Université de Caen, and was subsequently sent on missions to Brazil, 1936, 1937, and 1938, as well as to Egypt in 1938 and 1939. In 1941, he was a professor at l'École française de droit, Cairo, and a member of the Société Fouad Ier d'économie politique, de statistique et de législation. From 1942 to 1945, he served with the Free French as a financial adviser to the Délégation générale de la France Libre in the Levant. He subsequently became inspector general of French activities in the Levant. He taught at the Faculté de droit de Paris from 1947 to 1952, when he was appointed to the newly established chair of international economic relations. His writings include *La Théorie des prix de monopole* (1927), *Les Problèmes économiques de l'après-guerre* (Beyrouth, 1943), and *Cours d'économie d'outre-mer et du développement* (1958). He died on 6 December 1979. DBFC, 1954/55; Unesco; WhoFr, 1961/62-1979/80

Ledyard, Gari Keith, born 28 April 1932 at Syracuse, N.Y., he graduated in 1958 from the University of California at Berkeley, where he also received his Ph.D. in 1966 for *The Korean language reform of 1446*. He was appointed a professor of Asian studies at Columbia University, New York, which post he held until retirement. His writings include *The Dutch come to Korea* (Seoul, 1971). DrAS, 1969 F, 1974 F, 1978 F; NatFacDr, 1990-1995

Lee, Che-Fu, born 5 December 1941 at Tapei, Taiwan, he received a Ph.D. in 1971 from the University of North Carolina at Chapel Hill. He was appointed a professor of sociology at the Catholic University, Washington, D.C., which post he still held in 2005. From 1975 to 1976 he served as a United Nations senior population adviser to Iran. NatFacDr, 2005; WhoE, 1977/78

Lee, Conception E., born about 1950, she received a Ph.D. in 1979 from the University of Wisconsin for *Nomads, farmers, and migrant labor in southern Tunisia*. ZKO

Lee, David Raymond, born 31 December 1937 at Salt Lake City, Ut., he graduated in 1960 from Chico State College, Calif., and received his Ph.D. in 1967 from the University of California at Los Angeles for *The geography of rural house types in the Nile Valley of northern Sudan*. He was a lecturer in geography at the University of Khartoum, 1964-66, and a professor of geography at the University of California at Davis from 1966 to 1971, when he joined the Department of Geography at Florida Atlantic University, a post which he held until his retirement. He was a joint author of *Ländliche Siedlungen im nördlichen Sudan* (1971). AmM&WSc, 1973 S; AmM&WSc, 1976 P; NatFacDr, 1990-2005; Selim; Sezgin; WhoSSW, 1991

Lee, Dwight Erwin, born 3 June 1898 at Arcadia, N.Y., he graduated in 1921 from the University of Rochester, N.Y., and received his Ph.D. in 1928 from Harvard. He joined the staff of Clark University, Worcester, Mass., in 1927 and remained there until his retirement, serving as a professor of history and chairman of department. His writings include *Great Britain and the Cyprus convention policy of 1878* (1934), and *The Outbreak of the first World War; who was responsible* (1958). He died in 1986. In 1967 appeared *Statesmen and statecraft of the modern West; essays in honor of Dwight E. Lee and H. Donaldson Jordan.* ConAu, 5-8; DrAS, 1969 H, 1974 H; Master (2); WhAm, 10; WhE&EA

Lee, Hilda I., born 20th cent., she received an M.A. in 1949 from Beford College, University of London, for *Malta as a British colony, 1824-1851.* Her writings include *Malta, 1813-1914, a study in constitutional and strategic development* (Valetta, 1972). BLC; Sluglett

Lee, Julian F K., born 20th cent., he was "a chartered accountant who specialized in international taxation for a number of years; he was a tax partner in a firm of chartered accountants." Note about the author

Lee, Marc J., born 20th cent., he was in 1967 a tutor in international relations in the Department of Extra-Mural Studies in the University of Southampton. His writings include *United Nations and world realities* (1966). Note about the author

Lee, Robert Deemer, born 4 June 1941 at Estherville, Ia., he graduated in 1963 from Carleton College, and received his Ph.D. in 1972 from Columbia University, New York, for *Regional politics in a unitary system; colonial Algeria, 1920-1954.* From 1972 to his retirement he was a professor of political science at Colorado College, Colorado Springs. AmM&WSc, 1973 S, 1978 S; *MESA Roster of members*, 1982-1990; Selim; WhoWest, 1987/88, 1989/90

Lee, Samuel, born of poor parentage in 1783 at a Shropshire village, England, he was educated at the village charity school and apprenticed at the age of twelve to a carpenter. He managed to teach himself the classical languages and even made some progress in Oriental studies. Under the auspices of the Church Missionary Society he entered Queen's College, Cambridge, in 1813, proceeding D.D. in 1833. He became a professor of Arabic and Regius Professor of Hebrew in the University. His linguistic genius was chiefly exhibited in his scholarly editions of the New Testament in Syriac, Persian, and Hindustani. His writings include *A Grammar of the Hebrew language* (1844), he translated *The Travels of Ibn Batuta* (1829), and he was a joint author, with Henry Martyn, of *Controversial tracts on Christianity and Mohammedanism* (1824). He died in 1852. Boase; BritInd (11); DNB

Lee, Sherman Emery, born 19 April 1918 at Seattle, Wash., he graduated in 1938 from the American University, Washington, D.C., and received his Ph.D. in 1941 from Western Reserve University, Cleveland, Ohio, for *A critical survey of American watercolor painting.* He was successively associated in various capacities with Detroit Institute of Art, Seattle Museum of Art, Cleveland Museum of Art, Western Reserve University, and the University of North Carolina at Chapel Hill. His writings include *A History of Far Eastern art* (1964), its translation, *L'Art oriental* (1966), and *Chinese art under the Mongols* (1968). ConAu, 1-4, new rev., 1; Master (7); WhoAm, 1974-2003; WhoAmArt, 1973-1999/2000|

Leech (Leach), Robert, born 7 December 1813, he entered the Bombay Army in 1832 as a cadet of Engineers. He arrived in India in 1834 as a second-lieutenant and was attached to the Bombay Snappers and Miners. He was subsequently employed as an assistant to the Superintendent of Roads and Tanks until November 1836, when, in consequence of his proficiency in Oriental languages, he was selected for political employment under the Government of India and appointed to the future Sir Alexander Burnes, at the time proceeding on a special mission to the ruler of Afghanistan, arriving at Kabul on 20 September 1837. Three months later he was sent on a mission to Kandahar. Granted the local rank of major in Afghanistan, he was sent in the following year to Kalat on political duty in connection with the then impending invasion of Afghanistan. He later collected supplies in Sind and Baluchistan for the Army of the Indus, which he joined in February 1839, and accompanied it in the march to Kandahar, where he was left as a Political Agent, to act, on the part of Shah Shuja, under H.M. Envoy and Minister at the Court of Kabul until 1841. After weathering the defence of Kalat-i Ghilzai he returned to Kandahar. As a Political Officer, he took part in all the subsequent operations, including the re-capture of Ghazni, the actions of Beni Badam and Maidan, the re-occupation of Kabul, and various actions in the passes during the withdrawal from Kabul to Peshawar. For his services he was awarded a Companion of the Order of the Bath in 1841. He later became First Assistant to the Governor-General's Agent on the North-Western Frontier, an appointment which he held until his death at Ambala on 2 September 1845. His writings include *Vocabularies of seven languages spoken in the countries west of India, with remarks on the origin of the Afghan* (1838), and *A Grammar of the Pushtoo or Afghanee language* (Calcutta, 1839). BLC; IndianBilnd (2)

Leemhuis, Frederik, born 20th cent., his writings include *The D and H stems in Koranic Arabic* (Leiden, 1977), *De Koran; een weergave van de betekenis van de Arabische text in het Nederlands* (Houten, 2001), and he was a joint author of *The Arabic text of the Apocalypse of Baruch* (1986). Brinkman's; ZKO

Lees, George Martin, born in 1898, he was educated at St. Andrew's College, Dublin, passed through the Royal Military Academy, Woolwich, and at the age of seventeen was commissioned in the First World War, serving both in France and Mesopotamia. After the war he joined the Civil Administration of Iraq as Assistant Political Officer in Kurdistan. In 1921 he joined the Anglo-Persian Oil Company, taking courses at the Royal School of Mines, followed by a series of geological surveys throughout the Middle East. He received a Dr.phil. in 1927 from the Universität Wien for *Die Geologie Omans und von Teilen Südost-Arabiens*. After further surveys in many lands he was appointed chief geologist of the Anglo-Persian Oil Company in 1930, and under his direction during the next twenty years more oil was discovered by fewer wells than the world had yet seen. From 1951 to 1953 he was president of the Geological Society. He died on 25 April 1955. BriInd (1); *Geographical journal*, 121 (June 1955), pp. 252-53; JRCAS, 42 (1955), pp. 189-90; Master (3); ObitT, 1951-60, pp. 437-38; Schwarz; *The Times*, 26 January 1955 (not sighted); *Who was who*, 5

Lees, George Robinson, born in 1860 at Clayton West, Yorkshire, England, he was educated at the University of Durham and later served for several years as a head master at a school in Jerusalem. He travelled in eastern Palestine and Syria. His writings include *Village life in Palestine* (1897), and *The Witness of the wilderness* (1909). He died in 1944. Kornrumpf; *Who was who*, 4

Lees, Robert B., born 9 July 1922 at Chicago, he graduated in 1950 from the University of Chicago, and received his Ph.D. in 1959 from the Massacusetts Institute of Technology. He taught linguistics successively at the University of Chicago, Georgetown University, Washington, D.C., Ankara Üniversitesi and the University of Illinois at Urbana before becoming a professor of linguistics, and chairman of department, in Tel-Aviv University in 1969. His writings include *English for Turks* (1954), *The Grammar of English nominalizations* (1960), a work which is a revised version of his Ph.D. thesis, and *The Phonology of modern standard Turkish* (1961). In 1970 appeared *Studies presented to Robert B. Lees by his* students. DrAS, 1969 F, 1974 F, 1978 F, 1982 F; WhoIsrael, 1972-1985/86

Lees, William Nassau, born in 1825, he studied at Trinity College, Dublin, without taking a degree and subsequently entered the Bengal Native Infantry as an ensign, retiring in 1885 with the rank of major-general. He was a profound scholar in Arabic and Urdu and for some years principal of the Mohammedan College, Calcutta, where he also taught law, logic, literature and mathematics. He was granted honorary doctorates by the universities of Dublin and Berlin. His writings include *The Drain of silver to the East and the currency of India* (1867), *The Central Asian question* (1869), *The Indian Masalmans* (1871), and he edited al-Zamakhsharī's *Kashshāf* (1852-62), and the *Iqd-i Gul, being a selection from the Gulistan, and Anwar-i Sohaili* (1871). He died in London in 1889. Boase; Buckland; DNB; Fück, p. 177; Riddick

van Leeuwen, Arend Theodoor, born 1 September 1918 at Utrecht, the Netherlands, he studied theology at the Rijksuniversiteit te Leiden where he also received a doctorate in 1947 for *Ghazali als apologeet van de Islam*. He was from 1960 to 1971 director of the periodical, *Kerk en wereld*; and subsequently became a professor of theology at the Katholieke Universiteit Nijmegen. His writings include *Hendrik Kraemer, dienaar der wereldkerk* (1959), its translation, *Hendrik Kraemer, Pionier der Oekumene* (1962), *Christianity in world history* (1964), *Prophecy in a technocratic era* (1968), *Critique of heaven* (1972), *Critique of earth* (1974), and *De nacht van het kapitaal* (1983). He died in 1993. WhoNL, 1984-88

van Leeuwen, Jos, born in 1951, she studied modern history at the Rijksuniversiteit te Leiden, where she graduated in 1974. She successively became a research fellow in the Netherlands' Institute of Peace Research, den Haag, and the Institute of International Relations, Clingendael. Her writings include *Proliferatie in Zuid-Asië; hoe en warom* (1982), and *Den Haag, rampenstad?* (1998). Brinkman's; Note

Le Fanu, Henry, born 19th cent., his writings include *A Manual of the Salam District in the Presidency of Madras* (Madras, 1883), and *List of European tombs in the North Arcot District* (Chittoor, 1905). BLC; NUC, pre-1956

Lefébure, Adolphe, born 19th cent., he was a joint editor of *Code de l'Algérie annoté; recueil chronologique* (Alger, 1896-1907). BN; NUC, pre-1956

Lefébure, Claude, born 20th cent., he studied Berber language at the Institut national des langues et civilisations orientales, Paris. He edited *Noces berbères; les cérémonies du mariage au Maroc*, of Émile Laoust (1993). LC; Note

Lefébure, Jean Baptiste Louis Joseph *Eugène*, born 11 November 1838 at Prunoy (Yonne), France, he was an Egyptologist and a member of the Mission archéologique française au Caire. Not physically fitted for field-work, he was recalled in 1884 and worked at Lyon and Paris until about 1886. He subsequently went to the École des lettres d'Alger, where he remained until his death on 9 April 1908. His writings include *Le myth osirien* (1874-75), and *Œuvres diverses*, edited by Gaston Maspero (1910). Dawson; Egyptology

Lefebvre, Alain, born 20th cent., he received a *doctorat de 3ème cycle* in 1985 from the École des hautes études en sciences sociales, Paris, for *Étude comparative de l'émigration internationale à partir de deux villages pakistanais différents par leur agriculture.* He was in 1993 associated with the Centret for Udvik-lingsforskning (Centre for Development Research), København, Denmark, and the Université de Toulouse-Le Mirail, France. His writings include *Le District de Guanghan au Sichuan; matériaux pour l'étude de l'économie rurale chinois* (1979), *La Politique rurale de la Chine* (1984), *Islam, human rights and child labour in Pakistan* (Copenhagen, 1995), *Production de recherche en sciences sociales; un économiste dans la tourmente, 1965-1985* (1986), *Kinship, honour and money in rural Pakistan; subsistence economy and the effects of international migration* (1999), and he edited *La Coopération Europe-Maghreb; enjeux et perspectives* (1993). EURAMES, 1993; Livres disponibles, 2004; THESAM, 4; ZKO

Lefèbvre, Armand Édouard, born in 1800 or 1807 in the Netherlands, where his father was French minister plenipotentiary. His son, too, entered the foreign service, but lost his post under the July Revolution. During the Deuxième République he served as minister plenipotentiary successively at München and Berlin, and a member of the new Conseil d'État; on 14 April 1855, he was nominated a constituent member of the Académie des Sciences morales et politiques; and on 9 May 1856, he became *directeur des affaires politiques et du contentieux* in the Ministère des affaires étrangère. His writings include *Histoire des cabinets de l'Europe pendant le Consulat et l'Empire* (1845-1847). He died in 1864. Hoefer; IndexBFr² (2); Vapereau

Lefèbvre, Charlemagne *Théophile*, born 5 March 1811 at Nantes, France, he was educated at the Collège d'Angoulême and subsequently entered the navy, plying the waters from the Greek Archipelago to the South Sea. As a *lieutenant de frégate* in 1832, he visited Algeria, Brazil, and the coast of Africa. In 1836, he was sent by the French Government on a scientific mission to Abyssinia. Setting out from Cairo, the party went first to Jeddah and thence entered Abyssinia at Massawa (Messoah), penetrating as far as Aduwa (Adoua), the capital of Tigre, where he concluded a commercial treaty with the ruler. In subsequent years, he made several additional visits to the country, experiences which are embodied in his *Voyage en Abyssinie exécuté pendant les années 1839, 1840, 1841, 1842, 1843* (1845-51). He died in 1860. DcBiPP (not sighted); Henze; Hoefer; IndexBFr² (1); Vapereau

Lefebvre, Gilette, born 20th cent., she was in 1970 a research fellow with the C.N.R.S. She was a joint author of *Corpus des gravures et des peintures rupestres de la région de Constantine* (1967).

Lefebvre, Gustave Désiré Louis, born 17 July 1879 at Bar-le-Duc, Lorraine, he was an Egyptologist who studied at the Sorbonne. He was an inspector for Asyut in the Egyptian Antiquities Service, 1905-14, and a keeper of the Cairo Museum, 1919-28. His writings include *Essai sur la médecine égyptienne de l'époque pharaonique* (1956). He died in Versailles on 1 November 1957. Dawson; Egyptology

Lefèbvre, Henri, born 19th cent., he was a writer on forestry, whose writings include *Les Forêts de l'Algérie* (Alger-Mustapha, 1900). NUC, pre-1956

Lefebvre, Louis, born 20th cent., his writings include *Les Sources de la Semois* (Arlon, 1972), *Les Sculptures gallo-romaines du Musée d'Arlon* (Arlon, 1975), *Les 125 ans de l'Athénée royale d'Arlon* (Arlon, Association royale des anciens élèves de l'Athénée royale d'Arlon, 1977), and he was a joint author of *Corpus des gravures et des peintures rupestres de la région de Constantine* (1967). NUC

Lefèbvre, Théophile, 1811-1860 *see* Lefèbvre, Charlemagne Théophile

Lefebvre, Yvonne Mignot *see* Mignot-Lefebvre, Yvonne

Lefebvre de Villebrune, Jean Baptiste, born in 1732 at Senlis (Oise), France, he was a sometime physician who gave up his practice to pursue an interest in languages, attaining competence to translate widely from Romance, Germanic, and classical languages. In 1792, he became a professor of Hebrew and Syriac at the Collège de France. He subsequently became chief librarian of the Bibliothèque nationale de Paris, which post he held until 18 fructidor (4 September) 1797, after which date he left the city for political reasons and settled in Angoulême. He there obtained the chair of natural history at the École centrale and abandoned the idea of returning to Paris, where his merits were not appreciated. His contemporary philologists considered his pretensions not warranted. He died in Angoulême on 7 October 1809. Hoefer; IndexBFr² (4)

Lefeuvre-Méaulle, Hyacinthe Aristide, born 2 September 1863 at Rennes (Ille-et-Vilaine), France, he was educated at the Lycée and the Université de Rennes as well as the École des sciences morales et politiques. He subsequently entered the consular and diplomatic service. He served as commercial attaché in the Orient, as consul-general in England (London) and as minister in Chile. His writings include *La Grèce économique et financière en 1915* (1916). Qui est-ce, 1934; Qui êtes-vous, 1924

Lefevre, George Shaw, 1831-1928 *see* Eversley, George John Shaw-Lefevre, 1st Baron

Lefevre, Jean, born 20th cent., he jointly published with Jon Thompson, *The Persian carpet* (London, Lefevre & Partners, 1977). Index Islamicus, 1976-80

Lefèvre, Laure Marie Suzanne Bousquet, born about 1900, she received a doctorate in 1939 from the Université d'Alger for *Recherches sur la condition de la femme kabyle; la coutume et l'œuvre française*, work which was published in the same year entitled *La Femme kabyle*. NUC, pre-1956

Lefevre, Renato, born 5 October 1909 at Roma, he studied political science and history at the Università di Roma, where he also received his doctorate. He was a civil servant at the Italian National Archives and a journalist. His writings include *Politica somala, sotto gli auspici dell'Istituto coloniale fascista* (1933), *Terra nostra d'Africa* (1942), *L'Etiopia nella stampa del primo Cinquecento* (1966), and *Crociata di Tunisi del 1270* (1977). Chi è, 1940-1961; Firenze; IndBiltal (3); NUC, pre-1956

Lefèvre-Paul, J., born 19th cent., he graduated from the École normale supérieure, and served in 1939 as a barrister in the Cour d'appel d'Alger as well as president of the Société de géographie d'Alger et de l'Afrique du nord. Note about the author

Lefevre-Witier, Philippe, born in 1934, he was an anthropologist whose writings include *Idelès du Hoggar* (1995). LC; Master (1)

Le Flem, Jean Paul, born 20th cent., he was a joint author of *Rétables baroques de Bretagne et spiritualité au XVII siècle* (Paris, 1972), and *La frustración de un imperio* (Barcelona, 1984). LC

Lefranc, Jean Philippe, he was in 1957 associated with the Centre de Recherches sahariennes du Centre National de la Recherche Scientifique, Paris. Note about the author

Lefroy, Sir John Henry, born 28 January 1817 at Ashe, Hants., he was educated at Alton, Richmond, and the Royal Military Academy, Woolwich. He served twice as secretary of the Royal Artillery Institution, as director of the Observatory at Toronto, 1842-53, where, in 1842, he founded the Canadian Institute. As senior officer in the British War Office he was sent on a special mission to the Mediterranean, and also served as governor in British colonies. He died in Cornwall on 11 April 1890. His *Autobiography* was published posthumously. Boase; BritInd (3); DcCanB, vol. 11; DNB; Master (4); OxCan

Le Gall, Michel F., born about 1950, he received a Ph.D. in 1986 from Princeton University for *Pashas, Bedouins and notables; Ottoman administration in Tripoli and Benghazi, 1881-1902*. ZKO

Le Gallienne, Richard, born 1866 at Liverpool, he was a man of letters, literary critic, and a journalist. His writings include a freely rendered verse translation from Omar Khayyam. He died in Menton, France, in 1947. BbD; BritInd (4); ConAu, 107; Master (37); Who was who, 4

Le Gassick, Trevor John, born 19 August 1935 in Kent, England, he received a Ph.D. in 1959 from the School of African and Oriental Studies, London, for *Studies in contemporary Arab nationalist literature*. Since 1963 he taught in various capacities in the Department of Near Eastern Languages, University of Michigan at Ann Arbor, which post he held until retirement. He edited *Major themes in modern Arabic thought* (1979). DrAS, 1969 F, 1974 F, 1978 F, 1982 F; NatFacDr, 1995-2005; Sluglett

Legendre, Marcel, born in 1890, he was associated with the Société nationale d'acclimatisation et de protection de la nature. His writings include *Survivance des mesures traditionnelles en Tunisie* (Paris, 1958). Note about the author

Le Génissel, André, he was born about 1900 and was associated in the 1950s with the Institut de lettres orientales in the Université Saint-Joseph de Beyrouth. His writings include *L'Ouvrier d'industrie en Turquie* (1948), a work which was originally presented as the author's thesis at the Université de Grenoble, *Proche-Orient moderne: perspectives sociales; leçons données à l'Institut de lettres orientales* (1952), *Proche-Orient moderne* (1962), and *Manuel d'initiation sociale* (Beyrouth, 1965). NUC, pre-1956

Le Gentil, Jean Maxime *Georges*, born 3 December 1875 at Fère-Champenoise (Marne), France, he graduated from the Sorbonne and the École normale supérieure, Paris. He received his *agrégation* in 1901 and his doctorate in 1909 and subsequently became a professor of Portuguese language and literature at the Université de Paris. In 1935, he was granted an honorary doctorate by the

Universidade de Coimbra. His writings include *La littérature portugaise* (1935), *Les Portugais en Extrême-Orient* (1947), *Camoëns; l'œuvre épique et lyrique* (1954), its translation by José Terra, *Camões* (Lisboa, 1969), and *Découverte du monde* (1954). IndexBFr² (1); *Qui êtes-vous*, 1924

Le Gentil, Pierre Félix, born 1 November 1906 at Vertus (Marne); France, he graduated from the École normale supérieure, Paris, and received his *agrégation* in 1930. He became a lecturer at the Université de Rennes before the war, spent the war in a prisoner of war camp, and after the war returned to Rennes, becoming a professor in 1948. From 1949 to his retirement he was a professor of pre-classical French literature at the Sorbonne. His writings include *La poésie lyrique espagnole et portugaise à la fin du moyen âge* (Rennes, 1953), and *La littérature française du moyen âge* (1963). He died on 15 October 1989. DBFC, 1954/55; WhoFr, 1965/66-1989/90

Leger, Louis Paul Marie, born 13 January 1843 at Toulouse, France, he studied classics and law at Paris and subsequently became successively a professor at the Collège de France, École supérieure de guerre, and École des langues orientales vivantes, Paris. His writings include *Le monde slave* (1873), *Histoire de l'Autriche-Hongrie depuis les origines jusqu'à l'année 1878* (1879), its translation, *A History of Austria-Hungary* (1889), and *La littérature russe* (1892). He died in 1923. IndexBFr² (1); Vapereau

Legeza, Ireneus László, born 25 June 1934 at Debrecen, Hungary, he graduated in 1956 from Eötvös Loránd Tudomanyegyetem, Budapest, and, in 1960, from the University of London. He became associated successively with the University of Durham, England, as Chinese cataloguer, and the Gulbenkian Museum of Oriental Art and Archaeology, Durham, as a keeper. His writings include *Guide to transliterated Chinese in the modern Peking dialect, 1968* (1969), *Tao magic; the secret language of diagrams and calligraphy* (1975), its translation, *Magie et Tao* (1976), and he edited the exhibition catalogue, *Art and Tao* (Durham, Gulbenkian Museum, 1972). ConAu, 65-68, new rev., 32

Leggett, Eugene, born 19th cent., his writings include *A Treatise on the law of bills of landing* (London, 1880), *Notes on the mint-towns and coins of the Mohamedans* (London, 1885), and *A Treatise on the law of charter parties* (London, 1894). BLC; NUC, pre-1956

Le Glay, Maurice, born 19th cent., his writings include *Badda, fille berbère, et autres récits marocains* (Paris, 1921), *Récits marocains de la plaine et des mots* (Nancy, 1922), and *Chronique marocaine* (Paris, 1933). His trace is lost after an article in 1935. NUC

Legnani, Calisto, born 19th cent., he was an Italian trader and consular agent at Khartoum and Trieste. His trace is lost after an article in 1887. Hill

Legnaro, Aldo, born 29 June 1947 at Köln, Germany, he studied sociology and political economy at the Universität Köln, where he received a diploma as well as a doctorate in 1975 for *Drogen und sozial-kultureller Wandel*. He became associated with the Institut für Angewandte Sozialwisenschaft, Bad Godesberg. His writings include *Alkoholkonsum und Alkoholabhängigkeit* (1980), *Suchtwirtschaft* (2002), and *Rauchzeichen; zum modernen Tabakkonsum* (2003). Note; Thesis

Le Goff, Marcel, born 19th cent., he received a doctorate in law in 1905 from the Université de Poitiers for *Du Moulin et le prêt à intérêt*. He was in 1939 a vice-president of the Association nationale des avocats de France, and a lecturer in the Institut des Hautes études internationales. His writings inclunde *Traité théorétique de droit aérien* (1934), and *Manuel de droit aérien, proit public* (1954). Note; NUC

Le Goyet, Pierre, born in 1911, he wrote *La participation française à la campagne d'Italy, 1943-1944* (Paris, 1969), and *La guerre d'Algérie* (Paris, 1989). NUC

Legrain, Georges Albert, born in 1865 at Paris, he studied art and architecture as well as Egyptian archaeology and philology and since 1892 did field-work under the Institut français d'archéologie orientale du Caire. He later was made chief inspector of Luxor. Apart from numerous works on Egyptology he also wrote *Louqsor sans pharaons; légendes et chansons populaires de la Haute Égypte* (1914), *Une famille copte de Haute-Égypte* (1945), and he was a joint author of *Aux pays de Napoléon, l'Égypte* (1913). He died in 1917. Egyptology; NUC, pre-1956

Legrand, Émile Louis Jean, born 30 September 1841 at Fontenay-le-Marmion (Calvados), France, he was a lecturer in Greek at the École spéciale des langues orientales vivantes, Paris, until he was appointed to the chair of Greek in 1887. He died in Paris in 1903. EnSlovar; Oursel; Vapereau

Legrand, Étienne Antoine Mathieu, born in 1724 at Versailles, he spent years in Constantinople, Canea, Alexandria, Tripoli in Syria, Cairo, and Aleppo as a dragoman. When he returned to France, he was appointed *secrétaire interprète du roi*. He produced the Arabic version of the 1768 peace treaty between France and Morroco, a translation which found the admiration of Muhammad III ibn 'Abd Allāh, the Sharīf of Morocco. During the last years of his life he was befriended with A. I. Silvestre de Sacy. Of the many works which he translated only one saw the light of day, *Controverse sur la religion chrétienne et sur celle des mahométans* (1767), the translation of an Arabic dialogue of a Maronite and three Muslims, composed in 612/1215 by Giorgi. He died in Paris in August 1784. BN; Fück, 142; Hoefer; IndexBFr² (1)

Legrand, Gaston, born 19th cent., he was a secretary to Sir William Willcocks on his missions to Egypt, 1905, and Mesopotamia, 1911. Note about the author

Legrand, Léon Frédéric, born in 1861 at Saint-Pierre-les-Nemours (Seine-et-Marne), France, he was a deputy section head at the Archives nationales. His writings include *Les Sources de l'histoire religieuse de la révolution aux Archives nationales* (Paris, 1914). BN; IndexBFr² (1)

Legrand, Pierre *Maxime* Alexandre Amédée, born 15 January 1854, he wrote *Les Russes en Asie mineure, 1723-1877* (Paris, 1878), and *La Vallée du Nil* (Paris, 1892). He died on 22 September 1924. LC; NUC, pre-1956

Legras, Jules Émile, born in 1866, he was in 1897 a *maître de conférences* at the Université de Bordeaux. His writings include *Au pays russe* (1895), *En Sibérie* (1899), *L'âme russe* (1934), and he was a joint author of *Dans le monde des réprouvés* (1901). He died in 1939. LC; Note about the author

Leguèbe, Jacques, born in 1909, his writings include *Alerte en Afrique* (1954), and *Afrique du Sud et destin de l'Occident* (1974). NUC

Leguest, Charles, born 31 August 1824 at Dieppe (Seine-Inférieure), France, he was an *abbé* of the Alger diocese and a member of the Société asiatique. His writings include *Essai sur la formation et la décom-position des racines arabes* (1856), *Études sur la formation des racines sémitiques suivies de considérations générales sur l'origine et de développement du langage* (1858), *Y a-t-il ou n'y a-t-il pas un arabe vulgaire en Algérie?* (1858), and *Moyen de rechercher la signification primitive des racines arabes* (1860). He died at his place of birth on 11 August 1863. Oursel

Legum, Colin, born in 1919 at Kestell, South Africa, he was an associate editor and Commonwealth correspondet of the London *Observer*, and a writer on African affairs. His writings include *Must we lose Africa?* (1955), *Pan-Africanism; a short political guide* (1962), *Africa; a handbook* (1965), *Ethiopia* (1975), *The Horn of Africa; prospects for political transformation* (1992), and *Mwalimu; the influence of Nyerere* (1995); he edited *Crisis and conflict in the Middle East* (1981); and he jointly edited *Arab relations in the Middle East; the road to realignment* (1979). He died in 2003. Au&Wr, 1963, 1971; BioIn, 11; ConAu, 1-4, 217, new rev., 4; WhoWor, 1978/79-1982/83; WrDr, 1976/78-2005

Lehault, Philippe, born 19th cent., he wrote *La France et l'Angleterre en Asie* (Paris, 1892). BN; NUC

Lehfeldt, Werner, born 22 May 1943 at Perleberg, Germany, he received a Dr.phil. in 1967 from the Universität Bochum for *Das serbokroatische Aljammiado-Schrifttum der bosnisch-hercegovinischen Muslime; Transkription, 1919*, and a Dr.habil. in 1973. He was a professor of Slavic philology successively at the universities of Konstanz and Göttingen. His writings include *Einführung in die Sprachwissenschaft für Slavisten* (1995), *Eine serbisch-russische Sprachbegegnung vom Anfang des XVI. Jahrhunderts; zur Sprache der Moskauer Kopien von serbischen Briefen Sultan Selims I. an den Großfürsten Vasilij III. Ivanovič* (2000). In 2003 he was honoured by *Rusistika - Slavistika - Lingvistika; Festschrift für Werner Lehfeldt zum 60. Geburtstag*. Kürschner, 1976-2005; Schwarz

Lehmann, Alexander, born 18 May 1814 at Dorpat (Tartu), Estonia, he studied natural sciences at Kaiserliche Universität zu Dorpat and subsequently accompanied K. E. von Baer to Siberia, before setting out on the exploration of Central Asia to the borders of China. He died on his return journey to Dorpat at Simbirsk on 12 September 1842. His writings include *Reise nach Buchara und Samarkand in den Jahren 1841 und 1842* (St. Petersburg, 1852), and *Reisen in den mittleren und nördlichen Festländern Asiens* (1855). Baltisch (3); DtBiInd (1); Embacher

Lehmann, Carl Friedrich, 1861-1938 *see* Lehmann-Haupt, Ferdinand Carl Friedrich

Lehmann, Fritz L., born 26 December 1936 at Oak Park, Ill., he received a Ph.D. in 1967 from the University of Wisconsin for his thesis, *The 18th century transition in India; responses of some Bihar intellectuals*. After teaching at Temple University, he was appointed in 1972 a professor of Indian history at the University of British Columbia, Vancouver, B.C. DrAS, 1974-1982; DrASCan, 1878, 1983; IWWAS, 1975/76

Lehmann, Johannes *Edvard*, born 19 August 1862 at København, Denmark, he studied theology and philosophy at Københavns Universitet, where he also received his doctorate in 1896 for *Om Forholdet*

mellem Religion og Kultur i Avesta. From 1886 to 1892, he was a school teacher at København and Kalundborg, concurrently continuing his religious research, which won him a university gold medal in 1892. In 1900, he became the first lecturer in history of religion in Denmark, a post which he held until his retirement in 1927. His writings include *Zarathustra* (1899-1902), *Mystik i hedenskap og kristendom* (1904), its translations, *Mysticism in heathendom and Christendom* (1910), and *Mystik im Heidentum und Christentum* (1918), *Buddha* (1907), its translation, *Der Buddhismus als indische Sekte* (1911), *Opdragelse til Arbejde* (1909), its translation, *Erziehung zur Arbeit* (1914), and *Grundtvig* (1929). He died on 6 July 1933. DanskBL; Kraks

Lehmann, Walter, born 8 June 1891 at Schivelbein/Pomerania, Germany, he studied law at the Universität Berlin, and received a Dr.jur. in 1916 from the Universität Greifswald for *Die Aufhebung der Kapitulationen in der Türkei und ihre rechtliche Bedeutung*. His writings include *Die Kapitulationen* (1917). Thesis

Lehmann, Wilhelm, born about 1910 at Iserlohn, Germany, he received a Dr.phil. in 1936 from the Universität Bonn for *Der Friedensvertrag zwischen Venedig und der Türkei vom 2. Oktober 1549 nach dem türkischen Original herausgegeben und übersetzt*. Thesis

Lehmann-Haupt, Ferdinand *Carl Friedrich*, born 11 March 1861 at Hamburg, Germany, he studied law and Oriental languages at the universities of Heidelberg, Leipzig, Göttingen, Baltimore and Berlin, where he gained a Dr.jur. in 1886 for *De inscriptionibus cuneatis quae pertinent ad Šamaš-šum-ukīn regis Babyloniae regni initia*, followed by a Dr.phil. in 1886, and Dr.jur. in 1893. A member of the Ägyptische Abteilung, Königliches Museum, Berlin, since 1887, he was since 1901 a professor of ancient history successively at Berlin, Liverpool, Constantinople, and Innsbruck. He was in 1901 a founder of the journal, *Klio*. His writings include *Armenien, einst und jetzt; Reisen und Forschungen* (1910-31). In 1921, he was honoured by *Festschrift zu C. F. Lehmann-Haupts sechzigtem Geburtstage*. DtBE; EncJud; Fück, p. 290; Hanisch; Kornrumpf; Kornrumpf, N; Kürschner, 1926; NDB; ÖBL; *Wer ist's*, 1928; Wininger

Lehn, Walter Isaak, born 22 March 1926 at Herschel, Sask., Canada, he graduated in 1951 from Tabor College, Hillsboro, Kans., and received his Ph.D. in 1957 from Cornell University, Ithaca, N.Y., for *Rosental Low German, synchronic and diachronic phonology*. He was a professor of linguistics and director of English language instruction at the American University in Cairo, 1957-60, and he subsequently taught successively at the University of Texas at Austin, University of Minnesota at Minneapolis, Birzeit University and Najah University, Nablus. He was a joint author, with Peter Abboud, of *Beginning Cairo Arabic* (1965). DrAS, 1969 F, 1974 F, 1978 F, 1982 F; WhoAm, 1974-1980

Le Houérou, Henri Noël, born 25 December 1928, he received a doctorate in 1959 from the Université de Montpellier for *Recherches écologiques et floristiques sur la végétation de la Tunisie méridionale*, a work which was published in 1962. He was associated with both, the Institut de recherches sahariennes of the Université d'Alger, and the Food and Agriculture Organization of the U.N.O. His writings include *La Végétation de la Tunisie steppique* (1969), *An Eco-climatic classification of intertropical Africa* (1981), *The Grazing land ecosystem of the African Sahel* (1989), and he was a joint author of *Can desert encroachment be stopped? A study with emphasis on Africa* (Stockholm, 1976), and *Peut-on arrêter l'extension des déserts? Une étude plus particulièrement axée sur l'Afrique* (Stockholm, 1976). LC; Note about the author; ZKO

Lehrman, Harold (Hal) Arthur, born 7 January 1911 at New York City, he was a journalist and foreign correspondent who worked in Europe and the Middle East. He was a founding member of the Overseas Press Club in 1939. His writings include *Russia's Europe* (1947), and *Israel, the beginning and tomorrow* (1951). He died in N.Y.C. on 31 October 1988 of heart failure. ConAu, 127; NYT, 1 November 1988, B-13, cols. 1-2; WhoE, 1975/76; WhoWorJ, 1965, 1972, 1978, 1987

Lehuraux, Léon Joseph, born in 1885 in the Département du Nord, France, he joined the 1er Régiment de Zouaves at the age of eighteen. He was subsequently assigned to the Compagnie saharienne in Tidikelt as a non-commissioned officer. Beginning with the revolts of the desert in 1916, his name fills the annals of the *Compagnies méharistes* as a pacifier and diplomat, culminating in 1943 as honorary director of the Territoires du Sud, Algeria. He was a member of most of the scientific and literary societies of Alger. His writings include *Sur les pistes du désert* (1928), *Les Fondateurs d'empire* (1931), *Le nomadisme et la colonisation dans les hauts plateaux de l'Algérie* (1931), *Bou-Saada, cité de bonheur* (1934), *Les Français au Sahara* (1936), *Au Sahara avec le Père Charles de Foucauld* (1944), *Où va le nomadisme en Algérie?* (1948), and *Islam et chrétienté en Algérie* (1949). During a meeting at the Bureau de l'Institut de Recherches sahariennes on 30 May 1956 he suffered a first heart attack, but insisted on returning home alone. Some days later he died. *EuroAfrique, n.s., n° 7* (juillet 1956), pp. 70-73; Peyronnet, p. 822; *Travaux de l'Institut de Recherches sahariennes, Alger, 14 (1956), pp. 7-9; ZKO

Leibowitz, Isaiah (Yeshayahu), born 19 January 1903 at Riga, Latvia, he went to Berlin in 1919 to study chemistry, and received a Dr.phil. in 1924. Since 1928, he studied medicine at the universities of Köln and Heidelberg, obtaining his Dr.med. in 1934 from the Universität Basel. Since 1935 he taught biochemistry and neurophysiology at the Hebrew University, Jerusalem. From 1956 to 1972 he was editor-in-chief of the *Encyclopaedia Hebraica*. He predicted in early 1968 that Israel's occupation of Arab lands seized in 1967's Six-Day War would be a curse on the country. His writings include *Judaisme, peuple juif et État d'Israël* (1985), *The Faith of Maimonides* (1986), *Judaism, human values, and the Jewish state* (1992), and *La Foi de Maïmonide* (1992). He died on 18 August 1994 in his sleep in Jerusalem. BioHbDtE; BioIn, 17; EncJud; WhoIsrael, 1968-1992/93; WRMEA 13 iv (November/December 1994), p. 110

Leibowitz, Joshua Otto, born 25 April 1895 at Vilnius (Vilna), Lithuania, he was president of the International Academy of the History of Medicine, 1979-86. His writings include *Some aspects of Biblical and Talmudic medicine* (1969), and *The Histoy of coronary heart disease* (1970). EncJud; IntWW, 1989/90-1990/91; WhoIsrael, 1968-1985/86|; WhoWorJ, 1965, 1972

Leiden, Carl, born 6 February 1922 at Boone, Iowa, he graduated in 1945 from Iowa State College, and received a Ph. D. in 1949 from the State University of Iowa. He taught political science successively at State University of Iowa, Marshall University, Huntington, W.Va., American University in Cairo, and Texas University at Austin. He also served as a visiting profesor at Peshawar and Berkeley, Calif. His writings include *The Politics of violence* (1980); he was a joint author of *The Middle East; politics and power* (1974), *The Politics of assassination* (1970), *Politics in the Middle East* (1979); and he edited *The Conflict of traditionalism and modernism in the Muslim Middle East* (1966). AmM&WSc, 1973 S; ConAu, 5-8; WhoAm, 1984-1996

Leidlmair, Adolf, he was born 5 June 1919 at Linz, Austria. After graduation from secondary school, he began his compulsory twelve-month military service, which for him and many of his generation turned into an eight-year experience. He studied geography and history at the Universität Innsbruck, where he received a Dr.phil. in 1956 for *Die Formenentwicklung im Mitter Pinzgau*. From 1959 to 1963 he was an academic assistant to Hermann von Wissmann at the Universität Tübingen. After his Dr.habil. in 1958 from the Universität Tübingen for *Bevölkerung und Wirtschaft in Südtirol*, he successively taught geography at the universities of Karlsruhe, Bonn, and Innsbruck. His writings include *Hadramaut; Bevölkerung und Wirtschaft im Wandel der Gegenwart* (1961). He died about 1992. Kürschner, 1966-2005; *Mitteilungen der Österreichischen Geographischen Gesellschaft*, 121 (1979), pp. 304-312; WhoAustria, 1982/83, 1996

Leifer, Walter, born about 1900, his writings include *Indien, Pakistan, Ceylon* (1956), *Asien, Erdteil der Entscheidung* (1957), *Fünf Wege nach Asien* (1959), *Weltprobleme am Himalaya* (1959), *Hellas im deutschen Geisteswesen* (1963), *Indien und die Deutschen; 500 Jahre Begegnung und Partnerschaft* (1969), its translation, *India and the Germans; 500 years of Indo-German contacts* (1977), and he edited *Kenia* (1977). NUC; ZKO

Leighton, Neil Owen, born in 1937, he received a Ph.D. in 1971 from Indiana University for *The Lebanese middleman in Sierra Leone; the case of a non-indigenous trading minority and their role in political development*. NUC, 1968-1977; Selim

Leiser, Gary La Viere, born 9 April 1946, he received a Ph.D. in 1976 from the University of Pennsylvania for *The restoration of Sunnism in Egypt; madrasas and mudarrisūn, 495-647/1101-1249*. LC; Selim[3]

Leist, Arthur, born 8 July 1852 in southern Hungary, he was educated at Elisabeth-Gymnasium, Breslau, and subsequently completed Slavic studies with a doctorate. He was married to Marie Baitinger who originated from the German settlement Elisabethtal near Tiflis. For many years he was a correspondent for German daily newspapers as well as a private tutor in Poland. Since 1886 he was resident in Tiflis, where he established the German daily, *Kaukasische Post*. He travelled extensively in Italy, Greece, and Turkey. His writings include *Georgien; Natur, Sitten und Bewohner* (1885), *Alt-arisches jus gentium* (1889), *Alt-arisches jus civile* (1892-96), *Tagebuch eines Wanderers* (1909), *Sie ging den falschen Weg* (1923), and translations from the Armenian. Wer ist's, 1912

Leitenberg, Milton, born 20th cent., his writings include *Soviet submarine operations in Swedish waters, 1980-1986* (1987); he was a joint author of *The Vietnam conflict* (1973); and he was a joint editor of *Great Power intervention in the Middle East* (1979), and *The Structure of the defense industry* (1983). NUC

Leitenberger, Hermann, born about 1800, his writings include *Gemeinfassliche und erläuternde Darstellung der k.k. österreichischen Zoll- und Staats-Monopols-Ordnung, 1835, für den Handels- und Gewerbestand* (Wien, 1837). GV

Leiter, Hermann Julius, born 25 February 1882 at Deutsch-Liebau, Austria-Hungary, he was educated at Mährisch-Schönberg, and studied geography and history at the Universität Wien. He briefly worked at the Hofbibliothek Wien until 1905, when he became for eight years an assistant to Eugen Oberhummer. In 1908, he there received his Dr.phil. for *Die Frage der Klimaänderung während geschichtlicher Zei in Nordafrika*. In 1913, he entered the k.k. Exportakademie, Wien, where he received a Dr.habil. in 1916 as well as a lectureship. When the Exportakademie became the Hochschule für Welthandel in 1921, he was appointed a professor. From 1911 to 1950 he was concurrently honorary editor of both, the *Abhandlungen* and *Mitteilungen* of Geographische Gesellschaft in Wien. He died on 12 October 1958. DtBild (5); Kürschner, 1931-1954; *Mitteilungen der Geographischen Gesellschaft*, Wien, 94 (1952), pp. 5-10; Teichl; WhoAustria, 1954-1957/58

Leith, Edward Tyrrell, born 12 March 1842 at Calcutta, he was educated in Germany and Trinity College, Cambridge, and called to the bar from the Middle Temple on 26 January 1866. He practised law in Calcutta, 1867-85, and nearly concurrently served as a professor of law at Government Law School in that city. In 1886, he settled in Stuttgart, Germany. He was a member of the Bombay Branch of the Royal Asiatic Society. His writings include *On the legend of Tristan, its origin in myth and its development in romance* (Bombay, 1868). He died in Heidelberg on 10 December 1888. Boase

Leith-Ross, Sir Frederick William, born in 1887, he was educated at Merchant Taylors' School, and Balliol College, Oxford. He was a private secretary to Prime Minister Asquith, 1911-13, and British representative on the Finance Board of the Reparation Commission, 1920-25, and other international commissions, missions, and conferences. From 1946 to 1951 he was Governor of the Bank of Egypt. His writings include *Money talks; fifty years of international finance, the autobiography of Sir F. Leith-Ross* (1968). He died in 1968. DNB; *Who was who*, 6

Leitner, Gottlieb Wilhelm, born 14 October 1840 at Pest, Hungary, the son of a physician, he came to Turkey in 1847, where his father had established his practice. His school education was completed at the Malta Protestant College. In 1855, he gained by competitive examination the post of "First Class Inter-preter" to the British forces at Shumla, during the last eight months of the Crimean War. After the War, he attended a Muslim theological school in Constantinople. Since 1858 he studied at King's College, London, soon afterwards to be appointed lecturer in Arabic, Turkish, and modern Greek. In 1864, he was appointed principal of the newly founded Government College, Lahore, later also establishing the Anjuman-i Panjab, and also University College, Lahore, in 1870. Between 1866 and 1872 he undertook several explorations of the region between Kabul, Badakhshan, and Kashmir. In 1866, he was a founding member of the journal *Indian public opinion* and kept it going for ten years. Upon his return from India, he established the Oriental Institute in Woking. For his last nine years he was the proprietor and editor of the *Asiatic quarterly review*. For his work he was decorated by the emperors of Austria and Germany and granted honorary degrees by the Universität Freiburg im Breisgau. His writings include *History of the indigenous education in the Panjab* (1882), and *Dardistan in 1866, 1886 and 1893* (1893). He died in Bonn on 22 March 1899. Buckland; Embacher; EncJud; GeistigeUng; Henze; IndianBild (2); JewEnc; *Journal of the Royal Asiatic Society*, 1899, pp. 725-29; MagyarZL, Riddick; Wininger

Leitner, Wilhelm, born 26 February 1926 at Peggau/Steiermark, Austria, he studied geography and history at the Universität Graz, and received a Dr.phil. in 1949 and Dr.habil. in 1972. Since 1950 he successively taught at a secondary school and Bundeshandelsakademie Graz until 1976 when he was appointed to a chair in the Institut für Geographie der Karl-Franzens-Universität Graz. On his sixtieth and seventies birthdays he was honoured by jubilee publications. His writings include *Luxor (Theben); Aggressions- und Koexistenzforschung in einer oberägyptischen "Tempelstadt"* (1993), and *Geisteshaltung und Alltags-bewusstsein am Beispiel der türkischen (Kleinstadt-)Gemeinde Karahayıt* (1995). He died on 14 April 1999. Kürschner, 1976-1992; WhoAustria, 1996

Leitsch, Walter, born 26 March 1926 at Wien, he was since 1965 a professor of East European history at the Universität Wien. His writings include *Moskau und die Politik des Kaiserhofes im XVII. Jahrhundert* (1960), a work which was originally presented as a thesis at the Universität Wien in 1954, *Das Seminar für Osteuropäische Geschichte der Universität Wien, 1907-1948* (1983), and he was a joint editor of *Polen, Österreich; aus der Geschichte einer Nachbarschaft* (1988), and *Austria-Polska; z dziejów sąsiedztwa* (1989). Kürschner, 1976-2005

Lejean, Guillaume Marie, he was born in 1824 or 28 at Plouégat-Guérand (Finistère), France, to a poor Brittany peasant family. Since his early years he pursued an interest in history. After a brief employment with the *Sous-préfecture* of Morlaix (Finistère) as secretary, and the publication of a history of the Bretagne, he went in 1847 to Paris determined on geographical exploration. In the service of the Ministère de l'Instruction publique he went on research travel to the Balkans in 1857 and 1858. In 1860, he went by way of Suakin and Kassala to Khartoum to explore the region up to the

Upper Nile, including Bahr el Ghazal. After being appointed French vice-consul of Massawa he travelled in 1862 to Abyssinia in pursuit of French commercial and political interests. Between 1865 and 1869 he explored Asia Minor, Mesopotamia, Persia and Kashmir, before returning during his last years once again to the Turkish Balkans. His writings include *La Bretagne, son histoire et ses historiens* (1850), *Ethnographie de la Turquie* (1861), *Voyage aux deux Nils* (Paris, s.d.), and *Voyage en Abyssinie exécuté de 1862 à 1864* (1873). He died on 1 February 1871. BN; *Bulletin de la Société de géographie*, Paris, 6e s., 3 (1872), pp. 665-82; Embacher; Henze; Kornrumpf

Lejeune, Max, born 19 February 1909 at Flessilly (Somme), France, he received a degree in letters from the Sorbonne and a diploma in *Études supérieures d'histoire et géographie*. He was elected to the Chambre des députés in 1936, served in the second World War, and returned to politics in 1945. He served as a minister of the Sahara, 1958-59. He died on 23 November 1995. DBFC, 1954/55; BN; WhoFr, 1957/58-1995

Lekiashvili (Лекиашвили), Aleksei Semenovich, born 31 January 1920 at Tiflis, he received his first degree in 1946 for *Семасиологические и морфологические параллели корней в классическом арабском языке*, and a doctorate in 1965 for a monograph. He taught Semitics since 1943 at the Oriental Faculty, Tbilisi State University. He was appointed a lecturer in 1950, and a professor in 1967. He died on 20 March 1977. His writings are almost exclusively in Georgian. Miliband; Miliband[2]

Le Lannou, Maurice, born 8 May 1906 at Plouha (Côtes-du-Nord), France, he graduated in 1928 from the École normale supérieure, Paris. After teaching geography for two years at the Lycée de Brest, he spent two years in Sardinia on a Rockefeller scholarship. He received a doctorate in 1941 from the Université de Paris for *Pâtres et paysans de la Sardaigne*. He taught at the Université de Rennes from 1937 to 1945, when he had a brief career as a diplomat and visiting professor. In 1947, he was appointed a professor at the Université de Lyon, teaching at the Faculté des letters and concurrently serving as a director of the Institut de géographie du Proche et du Moyen-Orient. From 1970 to his retirement he held the chair of European geography at the Collège de France. His writings include *Pêches et pêcheurs de la Bretagne atlantique* (1944), *La géographie humaine* (1949), and *Les problèmes géographiques de la Méditerranée européenne* (1959). He died on 3 July 1992. NDNC, 1966; WhoFr, 1977-1990/91

Lelart, Michel Jean, born 2 August 1933 at Montreuil (Seine-St.-Denis), France, he received a doctorate in 1964 from the Université de Paris for *Les fondements actuels de la valeur de la monnaie*. He was successively associated with the Centre National de la Recherche Scientifique and the Université de Paris as an economist. His writings include *L'Emission de monnaie dans l'économie française* (1966), *Le Multiplicateur de crédit; analyse appliquée à l'économie canadienne* 1969), *Le dollar, monnaie international* (1975), and *La tontine, pratique informelle d'épargne et de crédit dans les pays en voie de développement* (1992). WhoWor, 1993/94

Lelekov, Leonid Arkad'evich, his writings include *Искусство Древней Руси и Восток* (1978). LC; OSK

Lelewel, Joachim Józef Benedykt, born 22 March 1786 at Warszawa, Poland, to a family that had left Prussia in the early years of the century. He was educated at the University of Vilna, and became, in 1807, a teacher at a school at Krzemieniec (Kremenets), Volhynia, in 1814, a history teacher at Vilna, and in 1818, professor and librarian at Uniwersytet Warszawski. He returned to Vilna in 1821, but was removed from his professorship in 1824, and returned to Warszawa, where he was elected a deputy to the diet in the same year. He joined the rebellion of 1830, but after its suppression made his way in disguise to Germany, and subsequently reached Paris in 1831. Ordered to quit French territory in 1833, he went to Bruxelles, where for nearly thirty years he earned a scanty livelihood by his writings. He died on 29 May 1861 in Paris, whither he had removed a few days earlier. His literary activity was enormous, extending from *Edda Skandinawska* (1807) to *Géographie des Arabes* (1851). One of his most important works was *La Géographie du moyen âge* in five volumes (1852-57). Dziekan; EncBrit; EncJud; *Geographers*, 4 (), pp. 103-12; Master (2); Polski (40); PSB; Sigilla

Lell, Hans Joachim, born 27 December 1933 at Stuttgart, Gemany, he was a trained mechanic who gained his university admission at evening school. He studied political economy at Stuttgart and Freiburg im Breisgau, and engineering at Technische Universität Berlin, from 1957 to 1960. With a French scholarship he studied at the École des hautes études en sciences politique, Paris, 1961/62. In 1965, he received a doctorate in economics at Berlin for a thesis on standarized social benefits in the European Community entitled *Die soziale Harmonisierung der Europäischen Wirtschaftsgemeinschaft und ihre wirtschaftlichen Auswirkungen, dargestellt an der Vereinheitlichung der Altersrenten und Familienbeihilfen in Frankreich und Deutschland*. Thesis

Lelong, Michel, born in 1925 at Angers (Maine-et-Loire), France, he was a Catholic priest who received a *doctorat ès lettres* in 1971 from the [Université de Aix-en-]Provence for *Le patrimoine musulman dans l'enseignement tunisien après l'indépendance.* He became responsible for relations with Islam at the Secrétariat de l'Église de France; he also taught at an Institut des sciences et de théologie des religions. His writings include *Pour un dialogue avec les athées* (1965), its translation, *Dialog mit den Atheisten* (1967), *J'ai rencontré l'islam* (1976), *Le don qu'il vous a fait; textes du Coran et de la Bible* (1977), *Deux fidélités, une espérance; Chrétiens et Musulmans aujourd'hui* (1979), *Guerre et paix à Jérusalem* (1982), *Islam et l'Occident* (1982), and *Jean-Paul II et l'islam* (2003). LC; Note; ZKO

Lelubre, Maurice, born 23 June 1926 at Paris, he was educated at the Lycée Chaptal and the Sorbonne, where he received a degree in natural sciences. He was a geologist in the Sahara until 1943. After the war, he was a staff member of the Service de la Carte géologique de l'Algérie, leading to his doctoral thesis in 1951 entitled *Recherches sur la géologie de l'Ahaggar central et occidental, Sahara central.* In 1957, he was appointed a professor at the Faculté des sciences de Toulouse. His writings include *L'Antécambrien de l'Ahaggar* (Alger, 1952) as well as numerous articles on the geology of the central Sahara, Fezzan, and Tibesti. NDNC, 1968

Lelyveld, David S., born 22 June 1941, he received a Ph.D. in 1975 from the University of Chicago for *Aligarh's first generation; Muslim solidarity and English education in northern India.* LC; Selim³

Lemaire, Paulin, born in 1896, he was a joint author of *Atlas biblique; hiistoire et géographie de la Bible* (1960), *Petit guide de la Terre Sainte* (Jerusalem, Impr. des PP. Franciscains, 1962), and *Guide de la Terre Sainte* (1971). He died in 1963. LC

Lemaire, William Lodewijk Gerard, born 25 September 1907 at Indramaju, Java, Dutch East Indies, where he served as a judge until 1941. Imprisoned during the war, he became a professor of law at the University of Batavia from 1949 to 1956. In that year he delivered his inaugural lecture as a professor of law in the Rijksuniversiteit te Leiden entitled *Kwesties bij de studie van het intergentiel recht.* His other writings include *Het Wetboek van strafrecht voor Nederlandsch-Indië vergeleken met het nederlandsche Wetboek van strafrecht* (1935), *Het recht in Indonesië* (1952), and *Nederlands internationaal privatrecht* (1968). Wie is dat, 1956; WhoNL, 1962/63

Le Maître, Isidore Charles Marie, born 7 February 1880 at Plouzelambre (Nord), France, he joined the French army in 1898, became captain in 1914, and battalion commander in 1926. Since 1920 he was associated with the geographical service of the French army, becoming head of the cartographic service at the general staff of the 19th Army Corps. He was a staunt supporter of the Transsaharian railway project. Peyronnet, p. 863

Lemay, Gaston, born in 1842 or 43, he was a French consular officer in the Sudan and Egypt. His writings include *À bord de la Junon* (Paris, 1879). He died in 1911. Hill; NUC, pre-1956

Lemay, Helen Rodnite, born 5 March 1942 at New York, she graduated in 1962 from Bryn Mawr (Pa.) College, and received a Ph.D. in 1972 in medieval history from Columbia University, New York. After three years spent at her alma mater as an assistant, she served since 1970 in various capacities as a professor in the Department of History, State University of New York at Stony Brook. Her writings include *Women's secrets; a translation of Pseudo-Albertus Mangnus' De secretis mulierum with commentaries* (1992). DrAS, 1974 H, 1978 H, 1982 H

Lemay, Richard Joseph, born 20th cent., he received a Ph.D. in 1958 from Columbia University, New York, for *The "Introductorium in astronomiam" of Abumasar and the reception of Aristotle's natural philosophy in the twelfth century.* His writings include *Abu Ma'shar and Latin Aristotelianism in the twelfth century; the recovery of Aristotle's natural philosophy through Arabic astrology* (1962). LC; ZKO

Lemercier, Robert Georges Antoine, born 2 August 1918 at Briare (Loiret), France, he was educated at the Lycée Louis-le-Grand and the Faculté de droit, Paris, and also received degrees from the École nationale de la France d'outre-mer, and École nationale des langues orientales vivantes. He served as an administrator of French overseas territories in various French ministries, and later as commercial adviser assigned to New York, Chicago, Karachi, and den Haag. WhoFr, 1973/74-1987/88|

Lemercier-Quelquejay, Chantal, born 20th cent., he was elected a member of the Académie des sciences, belles-lettres et arts de Rouen in 1971, and he was in 1981 *maître-assistant* at the École des hautes études en sciences sociales. His writings include *La Paix mongole, Joug tatar ou paix mongole?* (1970); he was a joint author of *Les Mouvements nationaux chez les Musulmans de Russie* (1960), *Les Musulmans oubliés; l'islam en U.R.S.S.* (1981), and *Sultan Galiev, le père de la révolution* *tiers-mondiste* (1986); and he edited *Passé turco-tatar, présent soviétique; études offertes à Alexandre Bennigsen* (1986). LC; Schoeberlein

Lemercinier, Geneviève, born in 1922 at Bruxelles, she gained a doctorate in sociology. Her writings include *Religion and ideology in Kerala* (Louvain-la-Neuve, 1983); she was a joint author of *The great Asiatic religions and their social functions* (1984); and she edited *Les Juifs dans la catéchèse*, of François Houtart (Bruxelles, 1972). LC; ZKO

Lemerle, Paul Émile, born 22 April 1903 at Paris, he was educated at the lycées Charlemagne and Louis-le-Grand at Paris, the Sorbonne, École pratique des hautes études, and École française d'archéologie d'Athènes. He was an archaeologist and Byzantine scholar who taught successively at the Université de Dijon, Faculté des lettres de Paris, École des hautes études, and finally the Collège de France. His writings include *Histoire de Byzance* (1943), its translation, *A History of Byzantium* (1964), *Le style byzantin* (1943), a collection of his articles, *Essais sur le monde byzantin* (1980), and *Byzantine humanism* (1986). He died on 17 July 1989. ConAu, 129; The Times, 27 July 1989 (not sighted); WhoFr, 1965/66-1988/89

Le Messurier, Augustus, born 23 June 1837, he was a British army officer who participated in two campaigns in Afghanistan. He retired with the rank of colonel. His writings include *Kandahar in 1879* (1880), and *From London to Bokhara and a ride through Persia* (1889). He died on 19 February 1916. IndianBilnd (1); Who was who, 2

Lemin, Iosif Mikhaĭlovich, born 21 December 1897 (2 January 1898) in Podolsk Gouvernement, he received his first degree in 1935, and a doctorate in 1941 for a thesis on Great Britain's foreign policy from Versailles to Locarno entitled *Внешняя политика Великобританни от Версаля до Локарно*. He was associated with the Institute of World Economics and World Politics, 1933-1948, the Institute of Economics, 1948-1956, and the Institute of World Economy and International Relations, 1956-1968. His writings include *Пропаганла войны в Японии и Германии* (1934), *Обострение кризиса Британской империи после второй мировой войни* (1951), *Англо-американские противоречия после второй мировой войны* (1955), *Международные отнтшения на новом этапе общего кризиса капитализма* (1961), and *Политика и стратегия* (1963). He died on 10 June 1968. Miliband; Miliband²

Lemke, Wolf-Dieter, born 4 September 1941, he received a Dr.phil. in 1977 from the Universität Köln for *Mahmūd Šaltūt (1893-1963) und die Reform der Azhar; Untersuchungen zu Erneuerungsbestrebungen im ägyptisch-islamischen Erziehungssystem*, a work which was published in 1980. LC; Sezgin; ZKO

Lemm, captain, born about 1800, he was a Russian officer in the Topographical Corps who supplied the basis for a new map of northern Persia by means of innumerable astronomical bearings. In 1838, he was put in charge of a caravan with presents for the Qajar ruler of Persia and the governor of Khurasan, and on this occasion determined the geographical position of all the major settlements on the way. Henze

Lemmleïn, Georgiĭ Glebovich, fl. 20th cent., he was associated with the Institut kristallografii in the Soviet Academy of Sciences. His writings include *Секториальное строение кристалла* (1948), and *Морфо-логия и генезис кристаллов* (1973). NUC; OSK

Lemoine, Jean Gabriel, born 10 March 1891 at Paris, he received degrees from the Faculté de droit de Paris, and the École du Louvre. He was for twenty years an art critic for *l'Intransigeant* and *l'Echo de Paris* before he became successively attached in various capacities with the Musée d'île de France, Sceaux, Musée des beaux-arts, Bordeaux, and Musée Bonnat, Bayonne. His writings include *Au Musée de peinture de Bordeaux* (1943), *Bourg et l'église de Brou* (1948), and *Les peintres primitifs sous un aspects nouveau* (1952). He died on 6 February 1970. WhoFr, 1959/60-1969/70

Lemoine, Paul, born 28 March 1878 at Paris, he studied earth sciences at Paris. In 1904, he went in the service of the Comité du Maroc on a geological exploration of the regions of Marrakesh and the Atlas Mountains. From 1907 to 1910, he was an assistant in geology at the Faculté des sciences de Paris; and from 1908 to 1919 he was in charge of the geological work at the Laboratoire colonial at the Muséum d'histoire naturelle. From 1921 to his death on 14 March 1940, he held the chair of geology at the Muséum national d'histoire naturelle. His writings include *Études géologiques dans le nord de Madagascar* (1906), *D'une rive à l'autre du Sahara* (1908), and *Géologie du bassin de Paris* (1911). Hommes et destins, vol. 4, pp. 445-50; IndexBFr² (1)

Lemoinne (Лемуанъ/Λεμουαν), John Émile, born 17 October 1815 at London, he was educated in England and France. He was for many years the political editor of the *Journal des débats*, Paris. His writings include *Études critiques et biographiques* (1852), and *De l'intégrité de l'Empire ottoman*

(1853). He died in Paris on 14 December 1892. BbD; BiD&SB; Bitard²; Coston²; Dantès 1; EnSlovar; IndexBFr² (4); Megali, vol. 15, p. 917; Vapereau

Lémonon, Ernest Marie Amédée, born 13 December 1878 at Bordeaux, he was educated at the Lycée Henri-IV, and the Faculté de droit de Paris, where he received a doctorate in law. He was a barrister at the French ministry of foreign affairs, and a representative of the French Goverment at den Haag. His writings include *L'Europe et la politique britannique, 1882-1909* (1910), *L'Italie économique et sociale, 1861-1912* (1913), *Les Alliés et les neutres* (1917), *La politique coloniale de l'Italie* (1919), *La nouvelle Europe et son bilan économique* (1926), and *Une étape de la démocratie anglaise, 1906-1914* (1947), many of which won awards from the Académie française. He was awarded *Officier de la Légion d'honneure* as well as foreign decorations. Qui est-ce, 1934; WhoFr, 1953/54-1955/56|

Le Myre de Villers (Vilers), Charles Marie, born 17 February 1833 at Vendôme, France, he passed through the École navale, and subsequently served to the rank of *lieutenant de vaisseau*. He resigned from the French Navy to pursue an administrative career in the *Corps préfectoral*. He became *sous-préfet* of Joigny, 1863, *préfet* of Alger, 1869, and head of the *préfecture* of the Département de la Haute-Vienne, 1873. In 1877, he became First Secretary General and later Director of Affaires civiles de l'Algérie, a first step in his career as a colonial administrator. He subsequently served in Cochin China and Madagascar. His writings include *Répertoire alphabétique des tribus et douars de l'Algérie* (1879), *Conquête de Madagascar, 1895-1896* (1902), and *Les Institutions civiles de la Cochinchine, 1879-1881* (1908). He died in 1918. Hommes et destins, vol. 8, pp. 251-54

Lenci, Marco, born 20th cent., his writings include *Lucca, il mare e i corsari barbareschi nel XVI secolo* (Lucca, 1987). LC

Lenczowski, George, born 2 February 1915 in Russia, he received a doctorate in 1938 from the Université de Lille for *Contributions à l'étude des obligations contractuelles en droit privé*. Since 1952 he was a professor of political science at the University of California at Berkeley, where he eventually attained professor emeritus status. He was a consultant to several American institutions concerned with the Middle East as well as Radio Free Europe. His writings include *Russia and the West in Iran, 1918-1948; a study in big power rivalry* (1949), *The Middle East in world affairs* (1952), *Soviet advances in the Middle East* (1972), *Middle Eastern oil in a revolutionary age* (1976); and he edited *Political awakening in the Middle East* (1970), *Political elites in the Middle East* (1975), and *Iran under the Pahlavis* (1978). In 1988 appeared *Ideology and power in the Middle East; studies in honor of George Lenczowski*. He died in 2000. AmM&WSc, 1973 S; 1978 S; ConAu, 1-4, 187, new rev., 4; IntAu&W, 1977, 1982; WhoAm, 1976-1984

von **Lendenfeld**, Robert, 1858-1913 see Lendelmayer von Lendenfeld, Robert J.

Lendelmayer (Lendlmayr) von **Lendenfeld**, Robert J., born 10 February 1858 at Graz, Austria, he studied natural sciences, mainly zoology, at the Universität Graz, where he received a Dr.phil. in 1881. He served for nearly ten years as a geologist in Australia, New Zealand, and England, before he was appointed a professor successively at the universities of Innsbruck, Czernowitz, and Prag, where he was concurrently director of the zoological institute. He died in Prag on 3 July 1913. Henze; Kosch; Martinek; ÖBL

Lendl, Egon, born 1 November 1906 at Trient (Trento), Austria, he graduated from a Viennese high school and subsequently studied geography at the Universität Wien where taught until 1963 when he moved to the Universität Salzburg. He there delivered his inaugural lecture in 1966 entitled *Salzburgs Stellung im österreichischen Raum*. In 1976 he was honoured by *Diskussionsbeiträge zu einem neuen Atlas von Salzburg, Egon Lendl zum 70. Geburtstag*. He died about 1987. Kürschner, 1961-1987|; WhoAustria, 1967-1977/78

Lenfant, Eugène Armand, born in 1865 at Mélun (Seine-et-Marne), France, he was a colonel and a commandant in the *Artillerie coloniale*, and an explorer of French Equatorial Africa. His writings include *Le Niger voie ouverte à notre empire africain* (1903), *La Grande route du Tchad, mission de la Société de géographie* (1905), and *29e Régiment d'infanterie; campagne contre l'Allemagne, 1914-1918* (1920). AfrBioInd (2); BN; IndexBFr² (1)

Lengyel, Emil, born 26 August 1895 at Budapest, he was conscripted into the Austro-Hungarian army and fought at the eastern front until captured by the Russians and sent to Siberia. He later emigrated to the United States to become, first a journalist, and later a historian and professor of social sciences. His writings include *The Soviet Union; the land and its people* (1956), *The Changing Middle East* (1958), *Africa in ferment* (1961), *They called him Atatürk* (1962), *The Countries of the Middle East* (1973), *Iran* (1978), and *Modern Egypt* (1978). He died in New York on 12 February 1985. Au&Wr, 1963; CnDiAmJBi; ConAu, 9-12, 115, new rev., 3; DrAS, 1969 H, 1974 H, 1978 H, 1982 H; Master (15); MEL, 1978-91; WhAm, 8; WhoAm, 1974-1978; WhoWorJ, 1965

MACK LIBRARY
BOB JONES UNIVERSITY
GREENVILLE, SC

Lenormant (Λενορμαν), Charles *François*, he was born on 17 January 1837 at Paris, the son of the Egyptologist Charles Lenormant (1802-1859), who was anxious that his son should follow in his steps. He made him begin Greek at the age of six. When he was fourteen, an essay of his appeared in the *Revue archéologique*. In 1856, he won the numismatic prize of the Académie des Insciptions. In 1862, he became *sous-bibliothécaire* of l'Institut. In the 1860s he visited Greece three times as well as the Near East. Since 1867 he turned his attention to Assyrian studies. In 1874, he was appointed professor of archaeology at the Bibliothèque nationale de Paris. He was a member of several learned societies. He was among the first to recognize in the cuneiform inscriptions the existence of a non-Semitic language. His writings include *Turcs et Monténégrins* (1866), and *Essai sur la propagation de l'alphabet phénicien dans l'ancien monde* (1872). He died in Paris on 9 December 1883 of injuries sustained in an accident during excavations in Calabria. BbD; BiD&SB; Bitard; Dantes 1; EncBrit; GDU; Glaeser; IndexBFr² (1); Master (2); Megali, vol. 15, p. 931; NewCathEnc; Vapereau

de **Lens**, Madame A.-R., fl. 1915, her writings, all of which were published in Paris, include *Le Harem entr'ouvert* (1919), *Derrière les vieux murs en ruines; roman marocain* (1922), *L'étrange aventure d'Aguida* (1925), and *Pratiques des harems marocains; sorcellerie, médecine, beauté* (1925). BN; NUC, pre-1956

Lenthéric, Charles Pierre Marie, born 15 May 1837 at Montpellier (Hérault), France, he graduated in 1858 from the École polytechnique, Paris, as an engineer of *ponts et chaussées*. He worked for some time at Nîmes and later became attached to the construction of the Canal du Rhône à Sète. His writings include *La Grèce et l'Orient en Provence; Arles, le Bas-Rhône, Marseille* (1878), and *L'Homme devant les Alpes* (1896). IndexBFr² (1); Vapereau

Lentin, Albert Paul, born 28 August 1926 at Constantine, Algeria, he was attached to the French delegation to the Nürnberg Tribunal, 1945, and subsequently became a press attaché to General Béthouart in Algeria. He then spent thirteen years with the Paris journal, *Libération*, and was sent to Algeria in 1961, but expelled. He was an ardent member of the French Communist Party and a partisan of Algerian independence. In 1962, he was the target of an assassination attempt. In 1979, he was a managing director of the journal, *Politique aujourd'hui*. His writings include *L'Algérie des colonels; journal d'un témoin* (1958), *Le dernier quart d'heure; l'Algérie entre deux mondes* (1963), and *La lutte tricontinentale; impérialisme et révolution après la conférence de La Habane* (1966). Coston²; IndexBFr² (1)

Lentin, Jérôme, born about 1945, he received a *doctorat de 3ème cycle* in 1982 from the Université de Paris for *Remarques sociolinguistiques sur l'arabe parlé à Damas*. In 1984 he was appointed an academic librarian at the Institut français d'études arabes de Damas. Since 1987 he was associated with the Institut national des langues et civilisations orientales, Université de Paris. He edited *Mélanges offerts à David Cohen présentées à l'occasion de son quatre-vingtième anniversaire* (2003). EURAMES, 1993; Private; THESAM, 3

Lents (Ленць, Lenz) Robert Émil'evich, born 16 November 1833 at St. Petersburg, Russia, he received a Dr.phil. in 1855 and became a professor of physics. His writings include *Изследованія в Восточной Персіи в Хератском владеніи* (1868), and *Unsere Kenntnisse über den früheren Lauf des Amu-Dara* (St. Petersburg, 1870). He died in Küjärvi, Finland, on 3 April 1903. Baltisch (2); BN; EnSlovar; NYPL

Lentz, Otto Helmut *Wolfgang*, born 23 March 1900 at Hameln, Germany, he studied Indo-European linguistics and Oriental languages at the universities of München and Göttingen, where he received a Dr.phil. in 1926 for *Die nordiranischen Elemente in der neupersischen Literatursprache bei Firdosi*. From 1924 to 1950 he was associated with the Preußische Akademie der Wissenschaften in Berlin and participated in the Alai-Pamir expedition of 1928, and the Hindukush expedition of 1934. In 1950 he entered the Seminar für Geschichte und Kultur des Vorderen Orients in the Universität Hamburg, where he was the most kind and civil counterpart to the ruling B. Spuler. His writings include *Auf dem Dach der Welt; mit Phonograph und Kamera bei vergessenen Völkern des Pamir* (1931), *Pamir-Dialekte* (1933), *Ein Lateinalphabet für das Paschto* (1937), *Zeitrechnungen in Nuristan und am Pamir* (1939), *Iran* (1952), and *Goethes Noten und Abhandlungen zum West-östlichen Divan* (1959). In 1974, he was honoured by *Neue Methodologie in der Iranistik*. He died in Marburg on 8 December 1986. BioB134; Hanisch; *der Islam*, 65 (1988), pp. 5-7; Kürschner, 1966-1987; Private

Lentzner, Karin R., born about 1950, she received a Ph.D. in 1977 from Georgetown University, Washington, D.C., for *Semantic and syntactic aspects of Arabic prepositions*. Selim³

Lenz (Ленць), Oskar, born 13 April 1848 at Leipzig, the son of a shoemaker, he studied natural sciences at the Universität Leipzig where he received a Dr.phil. in 1870 for *Über das Auftreten jurassischer Gebilde in Böhmen*. Two years later he entered the k.k. Geologische Reichsanstalt in

Wien, working in Hungary, Slavonia, and Vorarlberg, Austria. Since 1885 a professor of geography at the Universität Czernowitz, he headed the Austrian Congo expedition, 1887-89. Upon his return, he became a professor at Karls-Universität Prag until his retirement in 1909. His writings include *Timbuktu, Reise durch Marokko, die Sahara und den Sudan* (1884), its translation, *Timbouctou; voyage au Maroc, au Sahara et au Soudan* (1886-87), and *Wanderungen in Afrika; Studien und Erlebnisse* (1895). He died in Soos near Baden, Austria, on 2 March 1925. AfrBioInd (4); BiD&SB; DtBE; DtBiInd (5); EnSlovar; Henze; Martinek; ÖBL; *Wer ist's*, 1909-1922 WhWE

Lenz, Robert Émil'evich, 1833-1903 *see* Lents, Robert Émil'evich

Leo Africanus, Joannes, he was born between 894/1489 and 901/1495 at Granada and grew up at Fès, where he received a good education. He travelled to Timbuctu and Cairo. On the return voyage he was captured by Sicilian corsairs and taken to Roma, where he was persuaded to become a Christian. Before 1550 he went to Tunis, where his trace is lost. He wrote *Descrittione dell'Africa* (Venezia, 1550), of which there are several translations. Amin Maalouf wrote *Léon l'Africain* (1986). AfrBioInd; BiD&SB; Embacher; EI²; Fück, p. 35; *Geographers*, 15 (1994), pp. 1-9; Hill; Master (5); *Revue africaine*, 2 (1857/58), pp. 353-64

Leo Anderlind, Ottomar Viktor *see* Anderlind, Ottomar Viktor Leo

Leon, Edwin de, 1828-1891 *see* De Leon, Edwin

Léon, Henri Marcel, born in 1855 (or 1856), he was a physiologist, ethnologist, an honorary life-president of the Edingburgh University Oriental Students' Society, and a sometime dean of the London College of Physiology. His writings include *Sheikh Haroun Abdullah, a Turkish poet, and his poetry* (1916). He died in 1932. *Wo's who*, 1921-1932; *Who was who*, 3

Léon, Pierre Roger, born 12 March 1926 at Ligré (Indre-et-Loire), France, he studied at the Université de Paris, and received doctorates at Besançon and Paris as well as degrees in the United States. He was a linguist who taught successively at Paris, Besançon, Ohio State University, University of Toronto, and Pau. His writings include *Laboratoire des langues et correction phonétique* (1962), and *Aide-mémoire d'orthoépie des formes orales aux formes écrites* (1963). ConAu, 45-48, new rev., 1, 17, 43

Leon Tello, Pilar, born 8 December 1917 at Bujalance (Córdoba), Spain, he obtained a degree in Semitic languages from the Universidad Central. In 1950, he entered the Archivo Histórico Nacional, where he served in the Servicio Nacional de Microfilm. He subsequently entered the Sección de Manuscritos de la Biblioteca Nacional. His writings include *Los judíos de Palencia* (196-), *Judíos de Avila* (1963), *Diez años del Servicio Nacional del Microfilm* (1970), and he was a joint editor of *Archivo de los Duques de Frías* (1955). IntAu&W, 1982; IndiceE³ (1)

Leonard, Arthur Glyn, born 19th cent., he was a major, and appointed H.M. Vice-Consul and Deputy Commissioner for the Niger Coast Protectorate and adjoining Territories on 20 April 1897. His writings include *The Lower Niger and its tribes* (1906), and *Islam; her moral and spiritual value* (1909). BritInd (1)

Léonard, Guy, born 20th cent., he received a *doctorat de 3e cycle* in 1980 from the Université de Toulouse for *Étude de quartiers intercalaires d'une ville du Tiers-Monde, Casablanca*. He was a joint author of *Casablanca* (1987). *Livres disponibles*, 2004; THESAM, 1

Leonard, Henry Siggin, born 19 December 1905 at Newton, Mass., he graduated in 1927 from Harvard where he also received a Ph.D. in philosophy in 1931. In various capacities he taught philosophy at Harvard, Rochester, Duke University, Chapel Hill, N.C., and finally Michigan State University. He died in 1967. He was a sometime president of the American Philosophical Association. DrAS, 1964 P

Leonardi, Claudio, born 17 April 1926 at Sacco di Rovereto (Trento), Italy, he was a Latin scholar who was a *scrittore latine* at the Biblioteca Vaticana, 1963-68, and subsequently taught successively at the universities of Lecce, Perugia, Siena, and Firenze. His writings include *I codici di Marziano Capella* (Milano, 1961), and *La storia di Chiara da Montefalco* (1984). WhoItaly, 1992-2000

Léoncavallo, G., born 19th cent., his publications include *L'Ordre de succession au trône en Turquie* (Alexandrie, 1873), and he was a joint editor of *Manuale di diritto e privato ottomano* (Alessandria, 1865). BN

Leonclajus, Johannes, 1541-1594 *see* Löwenklau, Johannes

Leone, Enrico de, 1906-1983 *see* De Leone, Enrico

de **Léonessa**, André, born 19th cent., he was a Capuchin missionary at Salima, Lebanon. Note about the author

Leonhard, Richard, born about 1870 at Breslau, Germany, he received a Dr.phil. in 1893 from the Universität Breslau for *Der Stromlauf der mittleren Oder*, and also a Dr.habil. in 1898 for *Die Insel Kythera*. He was a lecturer in geography at his alma mater. His writings include *Paphlagonia; Reisen und Forschungen im nördlichen Kleinasien* (1915). *Geographische Zeitschrift*, 22 (1916), p. 346

Leonov, Nikolaï Ivanovich, fl. 1927, his writings include *Впервые в Алтай* (1951), *Петр Петрович Семенов-Тян-Шанский* (1957), *Научный родвиг самаркандских астрономов* (1960), *Александр Федорович Миддендорф* (1967), and he was a joint author of *По Алаю* (1962). NUC

Leopardi, Edoardo Romeo, born 21 July 1903 at Valetta, Malta, he was a librarian whose writings include *Malta's heritage; selected writings* (Valetta, 1969). Mifsud

Leopol'dov, Andreï Filippovich, born about 1800, he was a writer on the economic and political conditions in Seratov, Russia. His writings include *Историчкскии очерк Саратовскаго края* (Moscow, 1848) as well as articles in the journal *Северная пчела*. He died in 1875. NYPL

Leotard, Jacques, born 19th cent., he wrote *Le Port de Marseille* (Paris, 1922), and *Aperçu des colonies françaises* (Marseille, 1925). BN; NUC, pre-1956

Le Pape, Marc, born 20th cent., he received a *doctorat de 3e cycle* in 1980 from the Université de Paris for *Les voies de la mémoire; figures de l'espace, figures du père en Algérie*. He was associated with the Centre National de la Recherche Scientifique, and a joint editor of *Des Provinciaux en révolution* (1990), *Une Guerre contre les civils* (2001), and *Côte d'Ivoire; l'année terrible, 1999-2000* (2002). Livres disponibles, 2004; THESAM, 2

Le Parquier, E., born 19th cent., his writings include *Contribution à l'histoire de Rouen* (Rouen, 1895), *Département de la Seine-Inférieure* (Lille, 1922), and *L'Organistaion municipale de Rouen depuis le XIIe siècle jusqu'en 1449* (Rouen, 1932). BN

Le Portz, Yves, born 30 August 1920 at Hennebont (Morbihan), France, he was educated at the Sorbonne, École des hautes études commerciales, and École libre des sciences politiques. He was a civil servant and politician. He was a contributing author to *Les Problèmes de l'investissment dans les pays d'outre-mer* (Paris, 1961). IntWW, 1974-2000; IntYB, 1978-1982 (not sighted); WhoEIO, 1985; WhoFr, 1979/80-2005/6; Who's who, 1985-2005; WhoWor, 1974/75-1982/83

Lepsius, Johannes, born 15 December 1858 at Berlin, the son of Carl Richard Lepsius, he studied theology at the Universität Berlin, and, after his second theological examanation, he was assigned in 1884 to Jerusalem as auxiliary preacher and teacher at the German school in the old *Muristan-Kapelle*, which, before the construction of the Church of the Redeemer, was used by the German Evangelical community as place of worship. On 29 June 1886 he was married at Jerusalem to Margarete Zeller by her father, the pastor Johannes Zeller. Upon his return to Germany, he received his first and only pastorate at Friesdorf in the Harz mountains, a poor community of peasants and day-labourers, which post he held for ten years. During this period he established a cottage rug industry, employing forty girls. It was destiny that he was obliged to resign his pastorate at the very moment when the *Armenisches Hilfswerk* was able to take over and transfer his enterprise lock, stock, and barrel, including four of his trade associates to Urfa. Disguised as a carpet trader, he travelled in 1896 to Turkey to establish two orphanages in Urfa; in 1899 he spread his missionary activities to Urmia in Persia. His writings include *Rapport secret sur les massacres d'Arménie, 1915-1916* (1918), and *Der Todesgang des armenischen Volkes* (1919). He died in Merano (Meran), Italy, on 3 February 1926. Hanisch; KDtLK, 1925; Kornrumpf; Note in an unidentified issue of *Der christliche Orient*, pp. 110-111

Lepsius, Carl *Richard*, born 23 December 1810 at Naumburg, Ducal Saxony, Germany, and a graduate of Schulpforta, he studied the archaeological side of philology at Leipzig, Göttingen, and Berlin, where he received a Dr.phil. in 1833 for *De tabulis Eugubinis*. In the same year, he proceeded to study in Paris, where, in 1834, he took the Volny prize with his *Paläographie als Mittel der Sprachforschung*. After four years spent in visiting the major Egyptian collections in Europe, he returned to Germany. With royal support he subsequently went on a scientific expedition to Egypt. Upon his return he was appointed to a professorship at Berlin which afforded him the leisure necessary for the publication of the results of his research. In 1873, he was appointed keeper of the Königliche Bibliothek, Berlin. He was a corresponding member of the Academia Română and other learned societies. He died in Berlin on 10 July 1884. ADtB, vol. 51; DtBE; DtBIlnd (8); Egyptology; Embacher; EncBrit; EncItaliana; Henze; Hill; Kornrumpf; Kornrumpf², vol. 2; LexAfrika; MembriiAR

Le Puillon de Boblaye, Émile, 1792-1843 *see* Boblaye, Émile Le Puillon de

Leralle, André, fl. 20th cent., his writings include *Les armées de la Révolution et leurs marques postales* (1954), and he was a joint author of *Histoire postales des départements français d'Allemagne du Nord* (Amiens, 1957). NUC, pre-1956

Lerat, Serge, born 20th cent., he received a doctorate in 1963 from the Université de Bordeaux for *Les pays de l'Adour; structures agraires et économie agricole*. His writings include *L'ère des superpétroliers* (1971), *Géographie des mines* (1971), *L'or noire* (1971), and *Les populations du monde* (1995). *Livres disponibles*, 2004; NUC, 1956-77

Le Ray, Madame, born 19th cent., her writings include *Sixième voyage en Orient de Mme Le Ray; Damas, Palmyre, le désert, Babylone, le Tour de Babel, l'Euphrate, le retour* (Lyon, 1889), part of which was first published in the *Bulletin de la Société de géographie de Lyon*. BN

Lerch, P. I., 1827-1884 *see* Lerkh, Petr Ivanovich

Lerch, Wolfgang Günter, born 21 March 1946 at Friedberg/Hessen, Germany, he studied German literature, and religious, particularly Islamic, subjects at the universities of Tübingen and Freiburg im Breisgau. From the late 1970s to the early 2000s he headed the Middle East desk at the *Frankfurter Allgemeine Zeitung*. In the course of his work he visited Turkey, Iran, Syria, and Iraq. His writings include *Der Golfkrieg* (1988), *Ein Vorgeschmack auf Paradies* (1988), *Allahs neue Krieger* (1991), *Kein Frieden für Allahs Völker* (1991), *Halbmond, Kreuz und Davidstern* (1992), *Muhammads Erben; die unbekannte Vielfalt des Islam* (1999), *Der Kaukasus; Nationalitäten, Religionen und Großmächte im Widerstreit* (2000), and *Die Laute Osmans; türkische Literatur im 20. Jahrhundert* (2003). LC; ZKO

Lerche (Лерхе), Johann Jacob, born 26 December 1703 at Potsdam, Prussia, he studied at the universities of Halle, Jena and Berlin, and received a Dr.med. in 1730 from the Universität Halle for *Cryptographiam Halensem sive fossilium et mineralium in agro Halensi descriptiones*. He visited Holland and Wien. Upon the recommendation of the Halle professor Friedrich Hoffmann he was invited to Russia as a physician, and was subsequently sent to the Russian Army in Persia as an army-surgeon. He participated in campaigns against the Crimean Tatars on the western and south-western parts of the Caspian Sea. From 1745 to 1747 he went with an embassy to Nadir Shah, travelling by way of Darband, Baku and Lenkoran (Lankurān) to Rasht. He was later assigned to the second Russian Army at Bandar-i Shah. He played an important role in the fight against the plague epidemic current in Russia. His medical services were highly appreciated and rewarded. He was successively town physician at Moscow and St. Petersburg. He died in St. Petersburg on 23 March 1780. DtBE; DtBilnd (1); EnSlovar; Henze; Hirsching; NDB

Lerchundi, José, born 24 February 1836 at Orio (Guipúzcoa), Spain, he was educated privately by a Franciscan padre and showed an early predilection for Latin and music. At the age of seventeen he was an organist at the Santuario de Aranzázu. In 1856, he entered the Order of St. Francis and was ordained in 1860 at Tanger, where he began his missionary life, first of all as a student of Arabic. In 1864, he was appointed superior of the Misión de Tetuán. For some deplorable incident he was obliged to leave Morocco at the end of 1877 and collaborate in Granada with the publication of the *Chrestomatia arábigo-española* (1881). In September 1878 he was appointed a professor of moral theology and Arabic philology at the Colegio de Misiones, Santiago de Compostela, and already in November, its dean. Soon afterwards he was appointed Proprefecto de la Misión de Marruecos and took charge on 30 December 1879; he remained there until he died in Tanger on 18 March 1896. His writings include *Rudimentos del árabe vulgar que se habla en el imperio de Marruecos* (1872), its translation, *Rudiments of the Arabic-vulgar of Morocco* (1900), and *Vocabulario español-arábigo del dialector de Marruecos* (1892). *Boletin de la Asociacion española de orientalistas*, 33 (1997), pp. 5-12; EncicUni; Espasa; Fernandez, pp. 100-101; IndiceE³ (4); Manzanares

Lería y Ortiz de Saracho, Manuel, born in 1922 at Ceuta, Spain, his writings include *Un siglo medieval en la historia de Ceuta, 931-1031* (Ceuta, 1961), and *Ceuta y Mellila en la polémica* (Madrid, 1991). LC

Leriche, Albert, bon 14 June 1901 at Montfaucon d'Argonne (Meuse), France, he received a classical education, and did his military service in Morocco, where an uncle of his had served before 1910. He subsequently spent several years in the Ivory Coast with a private company. In 1932 he entered the Corps des Services civils in Mauretania as a special agent at Kaédi. He was an authority in the western Sahara, where he spent twenty-five years, during the first fifteen of which he never left Mauritania. His writings include *Terminologie géographique maure* (Saint-Louis, Sénégal, 1955), and an enormous French-Moorish dictionary which still awaits publication despite several attempts. He died in Nancy on 20 April 1957. *Bulletin de l'Institut français de l'Afrique noire*, série B, 19 (1957), pp. 333-36

Léris, Pierre, born 16 August 1881 at Nîmes (Gard), France, he studied law and received a doctorate in 1911 from the Faculté de droit d'Aix-Marseille for *Les communes et le Crédit foncier.* He was a sometime *président de Chambre* in the Cour d'appel de Rabat, Morocco, and a joint author of *Les ressources du travail intellectuel en France* (Paris, 1924). He was awarded *Chevalier de la Légion d'honneur*, and *Croix de guerre.* BN; Qui est-ce, 1934

Lerkh' (Lerch), Petr Ivanovich, born in 1827, his writings include Изслѣдованія об Иранских курдах и их предках сѣверных халдеях (1856-58), *Forschungen über die Kurden* (1857-58), Археологическая поѣздка въ Туркестанскій край въ 1867 году (1870). He died in 1884. EnSlovar; Kornrumpf², vol. 2; NYPL; Журнал / Russia. Ministervo narodnogo proveshcheniia, 11/12 (1884), 56-66

Lerner, Abba Petachja, born 28 October 1903 in Bessarabia, he graduated in 1932 from the University of London and received his Ph.D. in 1943. He taught economics in various capacities at a great number of U.S. colleges and universities. His writings include *Economics of control* (1944), *Everybody's business* (1961), and *Selected economic writings of Abba P. Lerner* (1983). He died on 27 October 1982. AmM&WSc, 1973 S, 1978 S; AnObit, 1982, pp. 519-21; CnDiAmJBi; ConAu, 1-4, new rev., 2; Master (6); WhAm, 8; WhoEc, 1981, 1986; WhoWorJ, 1965, 1972, 1978

Lerner, Daniel, born 3 October 1917 (or 30 November 1917) at N.Y.C., he graduated in 1938 from New York University, where he also received his Ph.D. in 1948. Since 1948 he was a professor of sociology at the Massachusetts Inistitute ofTechnology. His writings include *Tha Passing of traditional society* (1958), and he was a joint author of *Modernizing the Middle East; studies in communication and social change* (1955). He died on 1 May 1980. AmM&WSc, 1973 S, 1978 S; CnDiAmJBi; ConAu, 97-100, new rev., 6; WhAm, 7 & 8; WhoAm, 1974-1980; WhoWor, 1974/75-1976/77; WhoWorJ, 1965

Lerner, Ralph, born 20th cent., he edited *Averroes on Plato's Republic* (1974), and he was a joint editor of *Readings in American democracy* (1957), and, jointly with Muhsin Mahdi, *Medieval political philosophy; a sourcebook* (1963). LC; NUC, 1956-77

Leroux, Alcide, born in 1848, his writings include *Trois mois en Orient; le Liban et la mer, Beyrouth, Balbek, Damas* (Nantes, 1881), and *Esquisse sur l'Orient: Tyr, Sidon* (Nantes, 1882). He died in 1929. BN; NUC, 1956

Leroux, Hugues, originally Robert Charles Henri, born 1869 at Le Havre, France, he was a novellist who also contributed to the *Revue politique et littéraire, le Temps, le Matin, le Journal*, and *le Figaro*. His writings include *Le Sahara* (Paris, 1891), *En yacht: Portugal, Espagne, Maroc, Algérie, Corse* (Paris, 1892), *Chasses et gens d'Abyssinie* (Paris, 1903), and *Chez la Reine de Saba; chronique éthiopienne* (Paris, 1914). He died in Paris in 1925. BN; Larousse du XXe siècle

Le Roux des Hautesrayes (Deshauterayes), Michel Ange André, born 10 September 1724 at Conflans Sainte-Honorine, France, he grew up at his uncle's, an Orientalist, who initiated him to Hebrew, Arabic, Syriac and Chinese. He studied at the École des enfants de langues and in 1745 entered the Bibliothèque du Roi. In 1751 he was appointed to the chair of Arabic at the Collège de France, which post he held until 1777 when he retired to Rueil, where he died on 9 February 1795. Casanova; DBF; Fück, p. 142; GdeEnc; IndexBFr² (4)

Le Roy, Alexandre Louis Victor Aimé, born 19 January 1854 at Saint-Senier-de-Beuvron (Manche), France, he was educated at the seminary of the Abbaye-Blance at Mortain near Avranches, and later entered the Congrégation du Saint-Esprit, where he trained for missionary work in Africa. After his profession in 1877, he spent some years at the Island of Réunion, Pondichéry, French India, and Zanguebar, East Africa, where he was confronted with true missionary life and problems, particularly at Mombasa, where he established a mission in 1881 and there spent the following ten years. Upon his return to France, he was made vicar apostolic of Gabon and consecrated titular bishop of Alinda. From 1896 to his resignation in 1926, he was superior general of the Pères du Saint-Esprit. His writings include *À travers le Zanguebar, voyage dans l'Oudoé, l'Ouzigona, l'Oukwéré, l'Oukami et l'Ousagara* (1884), and *D'Aden à Zanzibar, un coin de l'Arabie heureuse, le long des côtes* (1894). He died in Paris on 21 April 1938. AfrBiolnd (1); Hommes et destins, vol. 1, pp. 379-80; IndexBFr² (2); Oursel; Qui êtes-vous, 1924

Leroy, Jean, born 19th cent., he was a judge in the Tribunal de la Seine, who had spent two years in Algeria. His writings include *Un Peuple de barbares en territoire français; deux ans de séjour en Petite Kabilie* (1911). BN; NUC

Leroy, Jules, born about 1900, he was associated with the Institut français d'archéologie de Beyrouth. His writings include *Introduction à l'étude des anciens codes orientaux* (1944), *Moines et monastères du Proche-Orient* (1958), its translation, *Monks and monasteries in the Near East* (1963), *Les manuscrits coptes et coptes-arabes illustrés* (1974), and *Les manuscrits syriaques à peintures conservés dans les bibliothèques d'Europe et d'Orient* (1964). NUC; ZKO

Leroy, Maurice A. L., born 23 January 1909 at Ath, Belgium, he studied at the Université de Bruxelles, where he received a doctorate in 1931; this was followed by advanced study at the Paris École pratique des Hautes études, and École nationale des langues orientales vivantes. He taught philology at a Bruxelles secondary school before the war, and from 1945 to 1979 at the Université de Bruxelles, where he also served several terms as its president. He was a member of numerous European academies of sciences. His writings include *Les Grands courants de la linguistique moderne* (1963), and its translations, *Profilo storico della linguistica moderna* (1965), *Introduction à la grammaire comparée des langues indo-européennes* (1963), *Main trends in modern linguistics* (1967), and *Las grandes corrientes de la lingüística* (1969). He died in 1990. BiBenelux²; ConAu, 25-28; *Qui est qui en Belgique francophone*, 1981-85; WhAm, 12

Leroy-Beaulieu, Jean Baptiste *Anatole*, born 12 February 1842 at Lisieux (Calvados), France, he was elected in 1881 a professor of contemporary history and Eastern affairs at the École libre des sciences politiques, Paris, becoming its director in 1906. Since 1887 he was a member of the Académie de sciences morales et politiques. His writings include *De la colonisation chez les peuples modernes* (1874), *L'Empire des tsars et les Russes* (1881-89), its translations, *The Empire of the tsars and the Russians* (1884), and *Das Reich der Zaren und die Russen* (1884), *Les Juifs et l'antisémitisme* (1891), *La Papauté, le socialisme et la démocratie* (1892), its translation, *Papacy, socialism, democracy* (1892), and *Les Arméniens et la question arménienne* (1897). He died in Paris on 15 June 1912. BbD; BiD&SB; Curinier, 1 (1901), pp. 148-51; EncBrit; IndexBFr² (2)

Leroy-Beaulieu, Pierre *Paul*, born 9 December 1843 at Saumur (Maine-et-Loire), France, he was educated at the Lycée Bonaparte and studied at the Faculté de droit, Paris. He afterwards studied at the universities of Bonn and Berlin, and on his return to Paris began to write for *le Temps, Revue nationale* and *Revue contemporaine*. In 1867 he won the first of many prizes from the Académie de sciences morales et politiques. In 1872 he became professor of finance at the École libre de sciences politiques, and in 1880 he succeeded his father-in-law, Michel Chevalier, in the chair of political economy in the Collège de France. His career was devoted to the study of economics and to its exposition in a series of works of classical reputation, including *Recherches économiques sur les guerres contemporaines* (1863-1869), *Traité de la science des finances* (1877), *Essai sur la repartition des richesses* (1882), *L'Algérie et la Tunisie* (1888), and *Question de la population* (1913). A large part of his contribution to the thought of his time is to be found in the weekly articles in the *Économiste français*, founded by him in 1873, over a period of nearly fifty years. He was widely honoured abroad, receiving honorary degrees of the universities of Cambridge, Edinburgh, Dublin, and Bologna. He died 9 December 1916. *Asie française* 16 (1916), pp. 148-149; Bitard; Bitard²; Curinier, 1 (1901), pp. 148-51; *Economic journal*, 26 (1916), p. 545; EncBrit; GDU; Glaeser; Vapereau; WhoEc, 1986, 1899

Lerski, George Jan (Jerzy Jur), born 20 January 1917 at Lwow, Poland, he received his LL.M. in 1946 from Oxford University, and his Ph.D. in American history in 1953 from Georgetown University, Washington, D.C. Since 1966 he was a professor of political science at the University of San Francisco. His writings include *The Economy of Poland* (1954). AmM&WSc, 1973 S; ConAu, 73-76; DrAS, 11th ed. (1968); DrAS, 1978 H, 1982 H

Leruth, Maurice Guillaume René Georges, born 31 March 1933 at Liège, Belgium, he was educated at the Collège des Jésuites Saint-Servais, Liège, and received degrees from the Institut d'études politiques and the Centre d'études supérieures de banque, Paris. He spent his entire career with the Banque régionale d'escompte et de dépôts. He was a joint author, with Yves Famchon, of *L'Allemagne et le Moyen-Orient; analyse d'une pénétration économique contemporaine* (Paris, 1957). NUC; WhoFr, 1979/80-1984/85|

Lesch, Ann Mosely, born 1 February 1944, she graduated in 1966 from Swarthmore (Pa.) College, and received her Ph.D. in 1973 from Columbia University, New York, for *The frustration of a nationalist movement; Palestine Arab politics*. She was associated with numerous U.S. organizations, including Rand Corporation, involved in Middle East research until 1987, when she was appointed a professor in the Department of Political Science, Villanova (Pa.) University, a post which she still held in 2005. Her writings include *Arab politics in Palestine, 1917-1939* (1979), *Political perceptions of the Palestinians on the West Bank and the Gaza Strip* (1980), *Egypt and the Palestinians* (1989), and she was a joint author of *The politics of Palestinian nationalism* (1973). *MESA Roster of members*, 1982-1990; WhoE, 1981, 1986, 1989 (not sighted); WhoAmW, 1983-1989/90

Lesch, David W., born 14 September 1960 at Baltimore, Md., he graduated in 1983 from Harvard, where he also received his M.A. in 1986, and Ph.D. in 1990. He held a variety of posts in Maryland before he was appointed in 1992 a professor of Middle Eastern history at Trinity University, San Antonio, Texas, a post which he still held in 2005. His writings include *Syria and the United States; Eisenhower's Cold War in the Middle East* (1992), and he edited *The Middle East and the United States; a historical and political reassessment* (1996). ConAu, 167; NatFacDr, 2005; ZKO

Leschi, Louis, born 2 December 1893, he was a graduate of the École normale supérieure, Paris, and the École française de Rome. He went to Alger in 1924 to work under Stéphane Gsell. He taught at the Lycée d'Alger until 1932, when he succeeded Eugène F. Albertini in the chair of North African archaeology at the Faculté des lettres d'Alger, and the directorship of the Service des Antiquités of the Gouvernement général de l'Algérie. He was an outstanding pre-historian and archaeologist of Roman North Africa. His writings include *Algérie antique* (Paris, 1952), and *Études d'épigraphie, d'archéologie et d'histoire africaines* (1957). He died on 7 January 1954. NUC, pre-1956; *Travaux de l'Institut de Recherches sahariennes*, Alger, 11 (1954), pp. 7-10

Lescot, Roger, born 18 March 1914 or 1917 at Lyon, France, he received degrees from the École pratique des hautes études, École nationale des langues orientales vivantes, and École libre des sciences politiques, Paris. In 1937, he entered the Institut français de Damas, serving from 1942 to 1944 as its secretary general. In that year, he joined the staff of the French foreign ministry, holding a variety of posts at Tunis and Cairo. After teaching Kurdish and Persian at the École nationale des langues orientales vivantes, from 1945 to 1947, he entered the diplomatic service, predominantly posted to Muslim countries and always in close relation to his academic subject. His writings include *Textes kurdes* (1940-1942), *Mam und Zin; kurdisches Volksepos* (1980), and he was a joint author of *Grammaire kurde* (1970), and its translation, *Kurdische Grammatik* (1986). He died in 1975. *Studia iranica*, 4 (1975), p. 240; WhoFr, 1965/66-1973/74

Leselbaum, Charles, born 10 December 1939 at Oran, Algeria, he there graduated from the Collège Ardaillon, and subsequently obtained a degree from the Faculté des lettres et sciences humaines de l'Université de Paris. He was a lecturer in French at the Universidad Autónoma de Madrid, from 1964 to 1968, and subsequently taught Spanish in various capacities at the Sorbonne. From 1980 to 2000 he was a director of the Centre d'études ibériques et latino-américaines appliquées at the Sorbonne. He was a recipient of Spanish and Venezuelan decorations. He edited *Epistolario de Rufino José Cuervo y Taymondo Foulché-Delbosc* (Bogotá, 1977). WhoFr, 2000/2001-2004/2005|

Leser, Paul W., born 23 February 1899 at Frankfurt a.M., Germany, he received a Dr.phil. in 1925 from the Universität Bonn for *Geschichte der Pflugforschung*. After his Dr.habil. in anthropology in 1929, he taught at the New School for Social Research, New York, Olivet College, and Black Mountain College, before teaching in the Department of Anthropology at Hartford Seminary Foundation, from 1951 to 1967. His writings include *Entstehung und Verbreitung des Pfluges* (1931). AmM&WSc, 1973 S; Unesco

Leshem (Lemberger), Moshe, born 30 September 1918 or 1919 in Russia, he was educated at Brno (Brünn) university and in 1949 entered the Israeli Ministry of Foreign Affairs, where he was since 1965 director of the African Division. His writings include *Israel alone; how the Jewish State lost its way* (1989), a work which was published earlier in the same year entitled *Balaam's curse*. WhoIsrael, 1966/67-1972; WhoWor, 1974/75; WhoWorJ, 1965, 1972, 1978

Leshnik, Lawrence (Lorenz) Saadia, born in 1933, he received a Ph.D. in 1964 from the University of Chicago for *Sociological interpretation in archaeology; some examples from a village study in Central India*. He was a sometime professor in the Department of Human Sciences, Pace University, Pleasant-ville, N.Y., a post which he certainly held from 1990 to 2002. His writings include *South Indian magalithic burials* (1974), and he was a joint editor of *Pastoralists and nomads in South Asia* (1975). NatFacDr, 1990-2002; NUC

Leslau, Wolf, born 14 November 1906 at Krzepice, Poland, he studied at the Sorbonne, where he received degrees in 1934 and 1953. Since 1942 he taught in the United States in various capacities: École libre des Hautes études, New York, Asia Institute, New York, Brandeis University, Waltham, Mass., and University of California at Los Angelos. His writings include *Lexique soqotri* (1938), *Documents tigrigna* (1941), *Falasha anthology* (1951), *English-Amharic context dictionary* (1973), *Concise dictionary of Ge'ez* (1989). On his eighty-fifth birthday he was honoured by the jubilee volumes, *Ethiopian studies, dedicated to Wolf Leslau on the occasion of his seventy-fiftth birthday* (1983), and *Semitic studies in honor of W. Leslau on the occasion of his 85th birthday* (1991). He was a member of numerous learned societies. CnDiAmJBi; ConAu, 104; DrAS, 1964 F, 1969 F; EncJud; Unesco; WhoAm, 1974-1976; WhoWorJ, 1965, 1972, 1978

Leslie, Donald Daniel, born 1 July 1922 at London, he graduated B.Sc. in 1943 from London University, obtained a diploma in Chinese in 1951 from Cambridge University, and received a doctorate in 1962 from the Sorbonne, Paris. He was a sometime teacher of mathematics and English at Haifa, Israel. Since 1963 he was associated with the Department of Far Eastern History in the Australian National University, Canberra, as research fellow, lecturer and professor, teaching history and philosophy. His writings include *Islamic literature in Chinese, late Ming and early Ch'ing* (1981), *Islam in traditional China* (1986), and he was a joint author of *Author catalogues of Western Sinologists*

(1966), and *Introduction to Palladii's Chinese literature of the Muslims* (1977).   ConAu, 102;   WhoWor, 1989/90

Leslie, Francis H., born about 1880 at Northport, Mich., he studied at Northport High School (1897), and the Art Academies of Chicago and Cincinnati, Fargo College as well as pursuing private theological study. He sailed for Turkey on 28 October 1911 destined for Urfa as the sole resident missionary. He there supervised carpentry and cabinet shops, iron and machine shops, tailor and shoes shops, besides the woman's department, with its extensive lace and handkerchief industries, the Shattuck School for the Blind, and the general evangelistic church work radiating from that centre. In 1913 he returned to Michigan on leave of absence and on 10 September 1913 was married to Miss Elvesta L. Thomas of Northport. They went back to Turkey a month later. During the war the Turkish Government interned many subjects of European countries brought to Urfa from different parts of Turkey. In view of the business involved, the American ambassador, Henry Morgenthau, had requested that Rev. Leslie be appointed consular agent at Urfa, but to this the Turkish Government would not consent In the summer of 1915 he fell ill, and while very sick drank some deadly carbolic acid. Death occured at the end of October or the beginning of November. *Missionary herald*, 112 (1916), pp. 18-19

Leslie, John Henry, born in 1858, he was educated at the Royal Military Academy, Woolwich. He retired with the rank of lieut.-colonel in 1897 and became a military historian. His writings include *The Services of the Royal Regiment of Artillery in the Peninsular War, 1808-1814* (1908-1912). He died in 1943 WhE&EA; *Who was who*, 4

Leśmian, Bolesław, born B. Lesman in 1877 at Warszawa, Poland, he was a poet and in ordinary life a notary public. In 1933, he became a member of the Polska Akademia Literatury. His numerous writings include *Przygody Sindbada żeglarza* (Warszawa, 1950). He died in Warszawa in 1937. CasWL; DLB, 215 (1999), pp. 220-26; Dziekan; Master (8); Polski (18); PSB

Lesne, Marcel, born 23 April 1916 at Fenain (Nord), France, he received a doctorate in 1959 from the Université de Paris for *Évolution d'un groupement berbère, les Zemmour.* He served successively as regional inspector of Muslim education at Rabat, and was chief of the Service de l'Enseignement technique of Morocco. In 1968, he was a lecturer at the Faculté des lettres et siences humaines d'Alger. Unesco

Lesný, Vincenc, born 3 April 1882 at Komarno (Komorn), Slovakia, Austria-Hungary, he studied Indo-European and classical philology at Prag, Oxford, and Bonn. He was an editor of *Nový Orient*, and from 1945 to 1952 a professor at Praha. His writings include *Duch Indie* (1927), *Rabíndranáth Thákar* (1937) and its translation, *Rabinath Tagore; his personality and work* (1939). He died in Praha on 9 April 1953. Český; Filipsky

Lesourd, Michel, born 17 December 1907 at Tours (Indre-et-Loire), France, he took the course of "Affaires indigène" at Alger, and subsequently entered the Corps des affaires musulmanes. Assigned to In-Salah, Algeria, in 1932, he was nominated head of post at Aoulef. In 1934, he was transferred to Fort (de) Polignac on the border to Fezzan, and instructed to maintain contact with the Touareg Ajjer, in the course of which he accomplished an intelligence mission in Italian territory up to Ghadames. In 1938, he was posted to Djanet near Gat, Fezzan, where he participated in the discovery of rock carvings in Tassili. During the war he was an intelligence officer, first in Niger, and later in the Annexe de Biskra in northern Touggourt, Algeria. From 1945 to 1946 he was transferred to the French ministry of national defence and sent on missions to Djibouti, Jeddah, San'ā', and Sheikh Sa'id. He later served as a military administrator. After his retirement he was a consultant to industry and business. He died in 1981. *Hommes et destins*, vol. 7, pp. 307-308

Lesourd, Michel, born in 1947, his writings include *État et société aux îles de Cap-Vert; alternatives pour un petit État insulaire* (1996), and he edited *Crises et mutations des agriculteurs et des espaces ruraux* (1997). LC; *Livres disponibles*, 2004

Lespés, René, born in 1870, his writings include *Alger; esquisse de géographie urbaine* (1925), *Alger, étude de géographie et d'histoire urbaines* (1930), *Pour comprendre l'Algérie* (1937), and *Oran; étude de géographie et d'histoire urbaines* (1938). He died in 1944. *Revue africaine*, 87 (1943), pp. 244-50 (not sighted)

Lespinasse, Émile, born 29 January 1841 at Nîmes, France, he was an interpreter in the Corps des interprètes de l'armée d'Afrique where he rose from the rank of *interprète auxiliaire de 2e classe* (28 February 1860) to *interprète titulaire de 2e classe* (6 March 1874). He still published in 1877. Féraud, p. 349

Lessar (Лессаръ), Pavel Mikhaĭlovich, born in 1851, he was a Russian engineer who explored and surveyed the Russo-Persian-Afghan border region with a view to railway construction in 1881 and 1882. His writings include *De la construction des chemins de fer en temps de guerre* (1879), and *Юго-Западная Туркменія* (1885). He died in 1905. EnSlovar; Henze

de Lesseps, Ferdinand Marie, vicomte, born in 1805 at Versailles, he was a French diplomat and the maker of the Suez Canal. His writings include *Le percement de l'isthme de Suez* (1855), and *Souvenirs de quarante ans* (1887), and work which was translated into English (1887), and German (1888). He died in Chesnaie (Indre) in 1894. Dawson; Egyptology; EncBrit; Goldschmidt; Hill; Hoefer; *Hommes et destins*, 4, pp. 457-66; Kornrumpf², vol. 2; Master (27); Megali, vol. 14, p. 15; Vapereau

de Lesseps, Théodore Antoine de la Sainte Trinité, comte, born 25 September 1802 at Cadix, Spain, the brother of Ferdinand, he was also a diplomat, particularly at Aleppo. He subsequently entered the central administration of the French Foreign Affairs as *rédacteur*. After the 1848 revolution, he became director of consulates. A minister plenipotentiary since 1853, he was made senator in 1860. He was greatly decorated in France and other countries. He died in Saint-Germain-en-Laye (Seine-et-Oise) on 19 May 1874. Hill; IndexBFr² (1); Vapereau

Lessner-(Abdin), Dietlinde, born about 1950, she received a Dr.phil. in 1978 from the Universität München for her thesis on the social status of women in underdeveloped countries, particularly Algeria, entitled *Zur sozialen Lage der Frau in Entwicklungsländern; eine Fallstudie - Algerien*. She was a joint author, with Angelika Schwarzbauer, of *Frauen im Sudan; Situationsanalyse und entwicklungspolitische Ansatzpunkte unter besonderer Berücksichtigung nichtstaatlicher Organisationen* (1979). GV

Lessona, Michele, born 29 September 1823 at Venaria Reale (Torino), Italy, he studied natural sciences and subsequently visited Egypt, Turkey, and Persia. He became a professor in his field at a variety of Italian universities, served as a director of the Museo di Zoologia e Anatomia comparata, Torino, and became elected a senator. His writings include *Le cacce in Persia* (1884), and *Gli animale nelle Divina commedia* (1895). He died in Torino on 20 July 1894. IndBiltal (5)

Lesure, Michel, born 20th cent., his writings include *Les Sources de l'histoire de Russie aux Archives nationale* (Paris, 1970), and *Lépante, la crise de l'Empire ottoman* (Paris, 1972). NUC

Lesthaeghe, Ron (Ronny), born 2 June 1945 at Oostende, Belgium, he received an M.A. in 1968 from Brown University, Providence, R.I., and a doctorate in 1970 from the Rijksuniveriteit te Gent for *Der ergodiciteit van de Leeftijdsstruktuur en de demografische transitie*. Since 1977 he was a professor of demography at Vrije Universiteit Brussel, where he also served from 1990-92 as dean of the Faculteit economische, sociale en politieke wetenschapen. In 1997 he was appointed to the Leclercq Chair at the Université catholique de Louvain. He was a visitng professor at Paris and Antwerpen. His writings include *The Decline of Belgian fertility, 1800-1970* (Princeton, N.J., 1977), *Indicatoren van integratie van etnische minderheden: Turkse en Marokkaanse vrouwen in Vlaanderen en Brussel; sociografische opstellen over sociale veranderingen* (Brussel, 1996), and he edited *Meaning and choice; value orientations and life course decisions* (The Hague, 2002). Qui, 1980, 2000/2002

Le Strange, Guy, born 24 July 1854 at Hunstanton, Norfolk, he was educated in England and later spent long periods abroad. It was during his years at Paris that his interest in Persian and Arabic was awakended by his contact with Julius Mohl and Stanislas Guyard. Sir Henry Rawlinson prompted him to edit and translate Ibn Serapion's description of Baghdad and Mesopotamia after he had already published *Palestine under the Moslems* (1890). He became a member of Pembroke College, Cambridge, of which his friend E. G. Browne was a fellow. His writings also include *Baghdad during the Abbasid Caliphate* (1900), and *The Lands of the Eastern Caliphate* (1905) as well as editions and translations of the E. J. W. Gibb Memorial Fund, a remarkable achievement for a man with his high degree of impaired sight. Since 1915 he was almost totally blind. He died in Cambridge on 24 December 1933. DNB; Fück, p. 275; JRAS, 1934, pp. 430-32; Kornrumpf, N; *Who was who*, 3

Leszczyński, Georg Léon, born 19th cent., he translated from the Persian, *"Hikayat," persische Schnurren übersetzt und mit Anmerkungen versehen* (Berlin, 1918), *Siyawush, eine alte persische Sage aus dem Schah-nameh des Firdus* (München, 1920), *Die Rubái'yát des Bábá Táhir 'Uryán, oder die Gottestränen des Herzens* (München, 1922), and he edited *Armegan; der Seele Sangesgabe*, of Hossein Kazimzadeh (Berlin, Schahin-Verlag, 1922). GV; BLC

Letellier, Camille, born 15 February 1835 at le Croisic (Loire-Atlantique), France, he graduated in 1852 from the military college, Saint-Cyr, and entered the 1er Zouaves in 1854, serving since 1855 with the Bureaux arabes in Algeria. In 1876 he was appointed *commandant supérieur* of Laghouat. Peyronnet, p. 692

Lethaby, William Richard, born 18 January 1857 at Barnstaple, Devon, England, he passed from the local school of art into the office of a Barnstaple architect. With an award from the Royal Institute of British Architects, and a studentship, he studied abroad from 1879 to 1881. It is as a teacher and critic rather than as a practising architect that he is remembered. He became the first professor of design at the Royal College of Art, South Kensington. His writings include *Leadwork, old and ornamental* (1893), *The Church Sancta Sophia, Constantinople* (1894), *Mediæval art* (1904), and *Form in civilization* (1922). He died in London on 17 July 1931. DNB; Master (20); *Who was who*, 3

Lethbridge, Sir Roper, born 23 December 1840 in Devonshire, England, he was educated at Mannamead School, just outside Plymouth. At Exeter College, Oxford, he won a Stapledon Scholarship in 1859. After leaving Oxford he was appointed to the Public Record Office, where he worked for five years. In 1868, his own and his wife's health compelled him to leave England, and he was appointed to the Indian Educational Department in Bengal. A professorship of history and political economy in the Presidency College, Calcutta, was his first post, from which he passed on to the Hugli College, and was thence transferred as principal to Krishnagar College; he also became a fellow of Calcutta University. In 1877, he was selected to be secretary to the Education Commission at Simla and appointed Press Commissioner with the Government of India and included in the Political Department. He retired from the Service in 1880 and was called to the bar from the Inner Temple in the same year. In the elections of 1885 and 1886 he was elected a Conservative M.P. for North Kensington. He was created K.C.I.E. in 1890, retiring in 1892 from Parliament. His writings include *The Golden book of India; a genealogiccal and biographical dictionary* (1893). He died on 15 February 1919. Asiatic review, n.s., 15 (1919), pp. 287-92; BbD; BiD&SB; BritInd (5); Buckland; IndianBiInd (1); Riddick; *Who's who*, 1909; *Who was who*, 2

Lethielleux, Jean, le Père, fl. 20th cent., his writings include *Le Fezzan, ses jardins, ses palmiers; notes d'ethnographie et d'histoire* (Tunis, 1948), and *Ouargla, cité musulman, des origines au début du XXe siècle* (Paris, 1984). LC; ZKO

Letnev, Artem Borisovich, born 20 December 1929 at Moscow, he graduated in 1952 from the Moscow State Institute of Foreign Relations, and received his first degree in 1963 for *Социальные отношения в деревне Западного Мали*. He was from 1952 to 1956 associated with the journal *Новое время*, and from 1958 to 1961 with Unesco, Paris. He subsequently joined the African Institute of the Soviet Academy of Sciences. His writings include *Деревня Западного Мали* (1964), *Общественная мысль в Западной Африке, 1918-1939* (1983), and he was a joint editor of *Из истории социалистических идей в Африке* (1990). Miliband; Miliband²

Leto, Pomponio, pseud., 1829-1906 see Nobili Vitelleschi, Francesco

Le Tourneau, Roger, born 2 September 1907 at Paris, he was educated at the Lycées Charlemagne and Louis-le-Grand, and l'École normale supérieure in Paris. In 1930, he became professor at the Collèqe Moulay-Idris, Fès, and later its director. The completion of his thesis, *Fès avant le protectorat*, started in 1935, but became delayed until after the war. Between 1958 and 1970 he gave seminars on North African history bi-annually at Princeton. His writings include *L'Islam contemporain* (1950), *Damas de 1075 à 1154* (1952), *Fez in the age of the Marinides* (1961), and *The Almohad movement in North Africa* (1969). He died in Aix-en-Provence on 7 April 1971. Hommes edt destins, vol. 7, pp. 308-309; Index Islamicus (9)

Letourneux, Aristide Horace, born in 1820, he was an honorary *conseiller* in the Cour d'Alger, and in the 1880s a member of the Mission scientifique tunisienne. His writings include *Catalogue des mollusques terrestres et fluviatiles recueillis dans le Département de la Vendée* (1869), *Excursions malacologiques en Kabylie et dans le Tell oriental* (1871), *La Kabylie et les coutumes kabyles* (1872-73), *Liste des coléoptères recueillis en Tunisie en 1883* (1885), *Rapport sur une mission botanique exécutée en 1884 dans le nord, le sud et l'ouest de la Tunisie* (1887). He died in 1890. BN; Note about the author; NUC, pre-1956

Letronne (Λετρον), Jean Antoine, born in 1787 at Paris, he became a keeper of the French Archives nationales. He wrote widely on the archaeology of Egypt. He died in Paris in 1848. BiD&SB; Dawson; DcBiPP (not sighted); Egyptology; EncBrit; EncItaliana; GdeEnc; Hoefer; IndexBFr2 (3); Megali, vol. 14, p. 19

Letteris, Max (Meir) Ha-Levi, born 30 August 1807 (or 1800 or 1804) at Żółkiew (Nesterov), Galicia, Austrian crown land, the son of a printer and writer; he himself started writing Hebrew poetry when still a youngster. He studied philosophy and Oriental languages at the Universität Lemberg (Lvov), gaining a Dr.phil. in 1844. For his *Sagen aus dem Orient nach den Quellen bearbeitet* he was awarded a gold medal in 1847. In 1848, he settled in Wien, where he was associated with the k.k. Hofbibliothek for some time. His collaboration with the publication of the 1852 Viennese Bible edition of the London Bible Society subjected him to the suspicion of supporting the Society's mission to the Jews, and estranged him from several of his friends. He is best remembered for his translations of European classics. His writings include רים ירבד (Żółkiew, 1822), *Andachtsbuch für israelitische Frauenzimmer zur öffentlichen und häuslchen Erbauung* (Prag, 1848), and *Oestliche Rose; Sagen und Dichtungen* (Prag, 1852). He died in Wien on 2 June 1871. ADtB, vol. 18, p. 461; CasWL; EncJud; JüdLex; ÖBL; Polski (5); Wininger; Wurzbach

Leuchs, Kurt, born 14 September 1881 at Nürnberg, Bavaria, he studied natural sciences at the Universität München, where he gained a Dr.phil. in 1906 and Dr.habil. in 1912. A good mountaineer since his student days, he accompanied G. Merzbacher in 1907 on an expedition to the Tien Shan Mountains. From 1915 to 1918, he was a war geologist on the western front and in Macedonia. In 1925, he was invited to teach at the Universität Frankfurt/Main. Three years later he went on his second large Central Asian expedition, which established his reputation as geologist of that region. In 1936, he accepted the directorship of the geological institute of Ankara Üniversitesi. In 1940, he became professor and chairman, Geologisches Institut, Universität Wien, a post which he held until removed from office in 1945. He was reinstated in 1948 but died shortly thereafter in Wien on 7 September 1949. His writings include *Aus den wissenschaftlichen Ergebnissen der Merzbacherschen Tian-Schan-Expedition* (1912), and *Geologie von Asien* (1935). DtBE; DtBiInd (1); Kürschner, 1926-1940/41; ÖBL; Wer ist's, 1922-1935

Leunclavius, Johannes, 1541-1594 *see* Loewenklau, Johannes

Leune, Jean, born in 1889, he was a writer of fiction and non-fiction. His writings include *Une Revanche, une étape; avec les Grecs à Salonique par Athènes et la Macédonie, campagne de 1912* (Paris, 1914), *L'Éternel Ulysée, ou La vie aventureuse d'un Grec d'aujourd'hui* (Paris, 1923), and *Le Miracle algérien* (1930). BN; NUC, pre-1956

Leuthold, Enrico, born 20th cent., his writings include *1056 dirhams Umaiyadi ed Abbasadi* (Milano, 1988), and *124 dirham dell'epoca di Kayqubādh I, Salgiuqide di Anatolia* (Milano, 1992). LC

Lev, Daniel Saul, born 23 October 1933 at Youngstown, Ohio, he graduated in 1955 from Miami University (Ohio) and received a Ph.D. in 1964 from Cornell University, Ithaca, N.Y., for *The Transition to guided democracy in Indonesia*, a work which was published in 1966. He taught at Cornell University, and the University of California, Berkeley, before he was appointed a professor in 1974 in the Department of Political Science, University of Washington, Seattle, a post which he still held in 1995. His other writings include *Islamic courts in Indonesia* (1972), *Legal aid in Indonesia* (1987), and *Legal evolution and political authority in Indonesia; selected essays* (2000). AmM&WSc, 1973 S, 1978 S; ConAu, 41-44; IntWWAS, 1976/77; NatFacDr, 1990-95; Private; WhoAm, 1980-1990

Leva, Antonio Enrico, fl. 20th cent., his writings include *Miti greci e scenari africani* (Roma, 1963), and *Il contributo italiano alla conoscenza delle lingue parlate in Africa* (Roma, 1969). NUC

Levainville, Jacques René, born in 1869, he graduated from the military college, Saint-Cyr, and served for twenty years as an officer in an infantry unit before he decided to prepare for higher grades by taking geography courses, first at the Université de Caen, and later at Lille. Since advancement in peace-time was slow, he terminated his military career in 1910. With the outbreak of the 1914 war, he could realize his ambitions and served as a battalion commander. Shortly after his demobilization, his family relations changed his orientation towards commercial iron ore exploration, a field in which he soon demonstrated administrative, technical, and logistic competence in metropolitan France as well as in Algeria and Morocco. His writings include *Le Morvan; étude de géographie humaine* (1909), a work for which he received a doctorate, *Rouen; étude d'une agglomération urbaine* (1913), and *L'Industrie de fer en France* (1922). He died aged sixty. *Annales de géographie* 41 (1932), pp. 217-218

Levasseur, Charles Jules Louis, he was born on 1 February 1856 at Aumale, Algeria. After study in Alger, he entered the Corps des interprètes de l'armée d'Afrique, where he rose to the rank of *interprète auxiliaire* on 29 June 1875. In 1906 he was *officier-interprète*. Féraud, p. 367

Levasseur, Émile, born in 1828, he was a graduate of the École Normale Supérieure, Paris, and received doctorates, and his *agrégation* in 1854. He taught at Besançon and Paris. Since 1870 he was one of the leading international figures of science, but of his considerable publications only some historical works are still known. All his numerous contributions to geography are forgotten even though he was a pioneer figure in the modern revival of French geographical studies. His numerous writings include *La France et ses colonies* (1890-93), *Le Dahomey* (1895), and *Elements of political economy* (1905). He died in 1911. Geographers, 2 (1978), pp. 81-87; WhoEc, 1981, 1986, 1991

Levasseur, Georges, born in 1907, he received a doctorate in law in 1931 for *Le domicile et sa détermination en droit international privé*. His writings include *L'Amnestie, son influence sur le droit disciplinaire* (1933), *Recherches historiques sur le système de Law* (1970), and he was a joint author of *L'Évolution de la procédure pénale en Égypte et dans les pays arabes* (1973), and *Human rights and the legal system in Iran* (Geneva, International Committee of Jurists, 1976). LC; ZKO

Levat, Édouard *David*, born 26 April 1855 at Montpellier, France, he was educated at Sainte-Barbe and Paris, where he graduated from the École polytechnique as well as the École des mines. He subsequently carried on mineral exploration in Italy, Greece, and the eastern Mediterranean Islands. From 1885 to 1889 he was a director-general of the Société de Nickel, Paris. In the service of the ministries of public education, and public works, he went on two missions of exploration to Siberia in 1894 and 1896 respectively, travelling from Moscow to Vladivostok. He later conducted similar explorations in the French colonies. He was a member of numerous learned societies. His writings include *L'Or en Sibérie orientale* (1897), *Mines et metallurgie* (1907), and *Richesse minérales de Madagascar* (1912). Curinier, vol. 3 (1901), pp. 215-17; Henze

Levchenko, Mitrofan Vasil'evich, born in 1890, he was a Byzantine scholar who was appointed a professor in 1938, and who received a doctorate in 1941. From 1944 to 1950 he was chairman of the Department of Byzantine Studies, Leningrad State University. His writings include *История византии* (1940), its translations, *Byzance des origines à 1453* (1949), and *Ιστορια της Βυζαντινης αυτοκρατοριας* (195-), and *Очерк по истории русско-византийских отношнеий* (1956). He died on 22 January 1955. LC

Levchine, Alexis, 1799-1879 *see* Levshin, Alekseĭ Iraklievich

Levé, Ferdinand Marie Gabriel Paul, born 25 March 1859, he was a graduate of the military academy, Saint-Cyr, who also passed through the École de guerre, 1885-1887. With the rank of general, he participated in the Algerian campaigns of 1896 and 1908. In 1911, he entered the Service des affaires indigènes as a military commandant of the Aïn Sefra Territory. In the first World War he served as brigadier-general of an infantry unit. His writings include the undated twenty-page booklet, *Le Rif et la politique marocaine.* BN; IndexBFr² (1); Peyronnet, pp. 524-28

Leveau, Philippe, born 20th cent., his writings include *Caesarea de Mauritanie, une ville romaine et ses campagnes* (1984), *L'Aqueduc sud des Alpilles* (1990); he was a joint author of *Campagnes de la Méditerranée romaine* (1993), *L'Alimentation en au de Caesarea de Mauritanie et l'aqueduc de Cherchell* (1976); he edited *L'Origine des richesses dépensées dans la ville antique* (1985); and he was a joint editor of *Villes et campagnes dans l'Empire romain* (1982). Livres disponibles, 2004

Leveau, Rémy Paul Jean Nicolas, born 6 July 1932 at Pierrelaye (Seine-et-Oise), France, he studied at the Faculté de droit de Paris and received degrees in political science from the Institut des études politiques, Paris. From 1958 to 1965 he was associated with the Faculté de droit de Rabat and the Moroccan Ministry of the Interior. He served in various capacities with the Food and Agriculture Organization, the French Embassy in Libya, the Université de Saint-Joseph, Beirut, the French Embassy in Egypt, and the Institut français des relations internationales. In 2002, he became a professor emeritus of his alma mater. His writings include *Le Fellah marocain, défenseur du trône* (1976), *Les Musulmans dans la société française* (1988); he was a joint author of *Acteurs et espaces politiques au Maroc et en Turquie* (1996), *Monarchies arabes* (2002); and he edited *Islam(s) en Europe* (1998), *L'Islam en France et en Allemagne* (2001), and *New European identity and citizenship* (2002). He died on 2 March 2005. EURAMES, 1993; *MESA Roster of members*, 1982-1990; Unesco; WhoFr, 1999-2005/2006; ZKO

Leveen, Jacob, born in 1891 at Jerusalem, he was educated at Jews' College, University of London, and the Sool of Oriental and African Studies. He joined the British Museum and retired in 1956 as keeper of the Department of Oriental Printed Books and Manuscripts. In 1939 he delivered the Schweich Lecture of the British Academy, entilted *The Hebrew Bible in art,* a work which was published in 1944. He died in 1980. Au&Wr, 1963, 1971; *Who's who*, 1968-1980; *Who was who*, 7; WhoWorJ, 1965

Levenberg, Alisa, fl. 1976, he was a veteran Israeli educator who had worked extensively in poverty neighbourhoods. His writings include *Welding a nation; education in Israel* (Tel-Aviv, 1958), *Pirke Kiryat-Shemonah* (Jerusalem, 1964), and *ha-Miflagot; madrikh la-boher* (Tel-Aviv, 1977). LC; Note

Levenq, Gabriel, born in 1868 at Marseille, he studied law and was for a year a teaching assistant at the Collège de Beyrouth before entering the Compagnie de Jésus at Ghazîr, Lebanon, in 1891. On account of an eye ailment, his education and training was somewhat irregular; he had to interrupt his philosophical studies at Jersey in 1895 for two years, completing it from 1897 to 1899 at Ghazîr, and subsequently returned to Europe for his theological work. Ordained in 1902, he served as a professor at Beirut from 1902 to 1906, and at Cairo from 1907 to 1912, teaching history and geography. After the first World War, he continued teaching his field at Beirut. Since 1923, he edited the journal *Relations d'Orient.* His writings include *La Syrie; géographie élémentaire à l'usage des écoles* (1923),

La Première mission de la Compagnie de Jésus au Liban et en Syrie (1925), and *La Nouvelle mission de la Compagnie de Jésus en Syrie, 1625-1774* (1925). He died in Beirut on 22 April 1938. Jalabert

Levental, Zdenko, born 20th cent., his writings include *Britanski putnici u našim krajevima od sredine XIX do početka XIX veka* (Gornji Milanovac, 1989), and *P. A. Рајс; швајцарац на Кајмакчалану* (1993), the first edition was entitled *Швајцарац на Кајмакчалану; књига о др. P. A. Рајс* (1984). OSK

Levering, Miriam Lindsey, born 1 January 1945 at Mt. Airy, N.C., she received her Ph.D. in 1978 from Havard University for *Ch'an enlightenment for laymen; Ta-hui and the new religious culture of the Sung*. She subsequently became a professor of religion and East Asian studies at Oberlin College (Ohio). In the 1990s she was a professor in the Department of Religious Studies, University of Tennessee at Knoxville. DrAS, 1978 P, 1982 P; NatFacDr, 1990-1995

Levey, Martin, born 18 May 1913 at Paris, he was a 1934 graduate of Temple University, Philadelphia, Pa., and received his Ph.D. in 1952 from Dropsie College for Hebrew and Cognate Learning, Philadelphia, Pa. He was a professor at Yale University, New Haven, Conn., and State University of New York, Albany. At the time of his death he was a member of the Institute for Advanced Study, Princeton. His writings include *Chemistry and chemical technology in ancient Mesopotamia* (1959), *Medieval Arabic toxology* (1966), *Medical ethics of medieval Islam* (1967), *Chemical aspects of medieval Arabic minting in a treatise by Mansūr ibn Ba'ra* (1971), *Substitute drugs in early Arabic medicine* (1971), *Early Arabic pharmacology* (1973), and he translated from the Arabic *The medical formulary or Aqrābādhīn of al-Kindī* (1966). He died on 22 August 1970. Au&Wr, 1963, 1971; CnDiAmJBi; ConAu, 13-16, new rev., 10; NatCAB, 56, pp. 233-34; WhAm, 5

Lévi, Isaac G., born 4 January 1878 at Constantinople, he studied at the Università di Napoli, and earned doctorates in law and political science as well as Semitic languages. He was a sometime director general of the Department of Statistics and Census, Cairo, an *administrateur-délégué* of the Usines textiles "Al Kahira," Cairo, a vice-president of the Communauté israélite, and a member of the Société Fouad Ier d'économie politique, de statistique et de législation, certainly from 1916 to 1952. Note about the author; WhoEgypt, 1955, 1959

Lévi, Sylvain, born 29 March 1863 at Paris, he was a Sanskrit scholar at the Sorbonne who received a *doctorat ès lettres* in 1890, presenting as his thesis *Quid de Græcis veterum Indorum monumenta tradiderint*. The same year saw the publication of his *Théâtre indien*, a standard work on its subject. In 1894, he was appointed professor of Sankrit in the Collège de France , a position which he held until his retirement. In 1897, he was sent on a mission to India by the Ministère de l'Instruction publique. His other writings include *Étude des documents tokhariens de la Mission Pelliot* (1911), and *Pre-Aryan and pre-Dravidian in India* (1929). In 1911, he was honoured by *Mélanges d'indianisme offerts par ses élèves à M. Sylvain Lévi le 29 janvier 1911*. He died in 1935. Buckland; EncJud; EncJud²; IndianBilnd (2); JewEnc; JüdLex; Qui êtes-vous, 1924; Who's who, 1928-1935; Who was who, 3; Wininger

Levi della Vida, Samuele Giorgio, born in 1886, he was a professor of Semitic languages and Islamic studies at the universitites of Napoli, Torino, and Roma, before emigrating to the United States, where he became a professor of his field at the University of Pennsylvania. His writings include *Storia e religione nell'Oriente semitico* (1924), *Arabi ed Ebrei nella storia* (1934), *Elenco dei manoscritti arabi islamici della Biblioteca Vaticana* (1935), *Frammenti coranici in carattere cufico nella Biblioteca Vaticana* (1947), *Aneddoti e svaghi arabi e non arabi* (1959), and *Linguistica semitica, presente e futuro* (1961). He died on 25 November 1967. In 1988 appeared *Giorgio Levi DellaVida nel centenario della nascita, 1886-1967*. Chi è, 1928-1961; Index Islamicus (9); IntBiltal (3); NYT, 27 November 1967, p. 47, col. 4; Wholtaly, 1967

Lévi-Provençal, Évariste, born 4 January 1894 in Algeria, he received a doctorate in 1922. He was initially a historian but early in his career his research included also Arabic literature and Islamic studies in general. He was successively a professor at the Faculté des lettres d'Alger, director of the Institut des hautes études de Rabat, and professor of Arabic language and civilization at the Sorbonne before he was appointed in 1950 director of the Institut d'études islamiques, Paris. Since 1944 he was in charge of the *Cahiers de l'Orient contemporain*. His universel reputation was recognized when he was entrusted with the revision of the French edition of the *Encyclopédie de l'islam*. His writings include *Les Historiens des Chorfa; essai sur la littérature historique et biographique au Maroc du XVI au XX siècle* (1922), *Extraits des historiens arabes du Maroc* (1923), *Documents arabes inédits sur la vie sociale et économique en occident musulman au Moyen âge* (1955). He died in Paris on 23 March 1956. In 1962 appeared *Études d'orientalisme dédiées à la mémoire de Lévi-Provençal*. L'Afrique et l'Asie, no. 34 (1956), p. 77; Hommes et destins, vol. 2, pp. 473-75; Index Islamicus (5); WhoFr, 1955/56

Lévi-Strauss, Claude Gustae, born 28 November 1908 at Bruxelles, he was an anthropologist and one of the great intellectuals of the twentieth century. He was successively a professor at the

Sorbonne and the Collège de France. His writings include *Race and history* (1952), *Anthropologie structurale* (1958), *Tristes tropique* (1961), its translation, *A World on the wane* (1961), *La Pensée sauvages* (1962), *Origine des manières de table* (1968), and its translation, *Origins of table manners* (1990). Jan P. B. de Josselin de Jong wrote *Lévi-Strauss' theory on kinship and marriage* (1952), and Denis Bertholet, *Claude Lévi-Strauss* (2003). ConAu, 1-4, new rev., 6, 32, 57; DLB, 242 (2001), pp. 278-92; IndexBFr² (4); IntWW, 1974-2006; EEE; Magyar; Master (33); WhoFr, 1965/66-2005/2006; *Who's who*, 1972-2005; WhoWor, 1974-2005

Lévi-Valensi, Jacqueline, born about 1927, she taught successively at the *lycées* at Aix-en-Provence and Laon, 1956-1959; at the Lycée Fromentin and the Faculté de lettres d'Alger, 1959-1965; and at the Collège littéraire universitaire, Amiens, and lastly at the Faculté des lettres, Université de Picardie, 1965-1997. A professor since 1981, she served as dean of the Faculté des lettres from 1989 to 1997, and as a director of the University's Centre d'études du roman et du romanesque from 1991 to 1997. She received a *doctorat d'état* in 1981 for *Genèse de l'œuvre romanesque d'Albert Camus*. Her other writings include *Aragon romancier* (1989); she was a joint author of *Diwan algérien; la poésie algérienne d'expression française de 1945 à 1965* (1967); and she edited *Les Critiques de notre temps et Camus* (1970), *Journalisme et politique; l'entrée dans l'histoire, 1938-1940* (1972), and *Camus et le théâtre* (1992). In 1999 she was honoured by *Pour un humanisme romanesque*. Note about the author

Levias, Caspar, born 13 February 1860 at Szagarren (Zhagory, Žagare), Lithuania, he received his elementary education in Russia, and received an M.A. after studying at Columbia College, New York, and Johns Hopkins Universty, Baltimore, Md. He was a fellow in Oriental languages of Columbia University, 1893-94, and a fellow in Semitic languages of Johns Hopkins University, 1894-95. Since 1895 he was an instructor at the Hebrew Union College, Cincinnati, Ohio. His writings include *The Justification of Zionism* (1899), and *A Grammar of the Aramaic idiom contained in the Babylonian Talmud* (1900). He died in Newark, N.J., on 18 February 1934. CnDiAmJBi; JewEnc

Levillain, Léon Octave, born 12 September 1870 at Deauville (Calvados), France, he studied at the universities of Caen and Paris and became a medievalist, archivist, and palaeographer. He taught history at a number of cities throughout France before he became a professor at the École nationale des chartes, Paris. He also served as a president of the Société des antiquaires de l'Ouest. His writings include *Examen critique des chartes mérovingiennes et carolingiennes de l'Abbaye de Corbie* (1902), *Recueil des actes de Pepin Ier et de Pepin II, rois d'Aquataine* (1926), and *Loup de Ferrières correspondance* (1927-1935). Oursel; *Qui est-ce*, 1934

Levin, Aryeh, born 6 Nissan 1885 at Urla near Belostok (Białystok), Russia, he was a professor of Arabic language and literature at the Hebrew University, Jerusalem. His writings include *A Tzaddik for our time* (1989), *Diḵduḵ ha-lahag ha-'Arvi shel Yerushalayim* (1994), and *Tsadiḵ yrsod 'olam* (1996). He died on 28 March 1969. LC; Note

Levin, Iosif Davidovich, born in 1901 at Warszawa, Poland, he graduated in 1922 from the Faculty of History and Philology, Moscow State University, and received a doctorate in 1939 for *Государственные формы на Востоке*. He was since 1927 associated with the Institute of State and Law in the Soviet Academy of Sciences. In 1939 he became a professor. His writings include *Современная Абиссиния; социальные сдвиги и политические реформы* (1936), *Египет* (1937), *Ирак* (1937), *Подготовка войны на Арабском Востоке* (1937), *Государственный строй стран Арабского Востока* (1957), *Государственный строй Индии* (1957), and *Конституции государств Африки* (1963). He died on 26 December 1984. Miliband; Miliband²

Levin (Lévine), Isaak Osipovich, born in 1876, he wrote *Эмиграция французской революции* (1923), and *La Mongolie historique, géographique, politique* (Paris, 1937). His trace is lost after an article in 1939. Note; NUC, pre-1956

Levin, Maksim Grigor'evich, born in 1904 in Belorussia, he was an ethnographer and anthropologist who conducted field-work in the Baikal and Altai regions. His writings include *Этническая антропология и проблемы этногенеза народов Дальнего Востока* (1958), *Очерки по истории антропология в России* (1960), *Историко-этнографический атлас Сибири* (1961), *Ethnic origins of the peoples of northeastern Asia* (1963), *The Peoples of Siberia* (1964), and he was a joint author of *Основы антропологии* (1955). He died in 1963. Bioln, 7; GSE; OSK

Levin, Sergeĭ Fridrikovich, born 30 May 1930 at Moscow, he graduated in 1953 from the Faculty of History, Moscow State University, and received his first degree in 1964 for *Торговая каста ходжа; из истории мусульманской буржуазии Индии и Пакистана*. Since 1956 he was associated with the Oriental Institute, Soviet Academy of Sciences. His writings include *Формировнте крупной*

416

буржуазии Пакистана (1970), *Экономическое развитие Пакистана* (1974), and *Государство и монополисти-ческая буржуазия в Пакистане* (1983). Miliband; Miliband²; OSK

Levin, Theodore Craig, born 9 August 1951 at Washington, D.C., he received a Ph.D. in 1984 from Princeton University for *The Music and tradition of the Bukharan Shashmaqām in Soviet Uzbekistan.* He was in 1995 a professor of music at Dartmouth College, N.H., a position which he still held in 2005. NatFacDr, 1995-2005; Schoeberlein

Levin, Zalman Isaakovich, born 17 July 1923 in Gomel Oblast, Belorussia, he graduated in 1947 from the Moscow Oriental Institute and received his first degree in 1956 for *«Природа деспотизма - социально-политический трактат Абд-ар-Рахмана аль-Кавакиьи».*, and a doctorate in 1971 for *Основные течення общественно-политической мысли в арабских странах.* Since 1953 he was associated with the Oriental Institute, Soviet Academy of Sciences. His writings include *Философ из Фурейки* (1965), *Развитие основных течений общественно-политической мысли в Сирии и Египте* (1972), *Развитие арабской общественной мысли* (1979), *Ислам и национализм в странах зарубежного Востока* (1988), and *Развитие общественной мысли на Востоке; колониальный период XIX-XXвв.* (1993). Miliband; Miliband²; OSK

Levinck, Anne, born 19th cent., her writings include *Les Femmes qui ne tuent ni ne votent* (Paris, 1882), and *Après la ruine* (Paris, 1884). BN

Levine, Daniel, born about 1940 at Denver, Colo., he received a Ph.D. in 1969 from Yeshiva University, New York, for *David Raziel, the man and his times.* After ordination from Yeshiva University he emigrated in 1970 to Israel where he resided in Jerusalem. He was a lecturer in the Department of Interdisciplinary Studies, Bar Ilan University. His writings include *The Birth of the Irgun Zvai Leumi; a Jewish liberation movement* (Jerusalem, 1991). LC; Note about the author; Selim

Levine, David, born 5 October 1876 at N.Y.C., he studied at the City College, New York, Columbia University, and the Jewish Theological Seminary, New York, gaining a Ph.D. in 1902 at Columbia for *The 'Bustan al-ukul,' by Nathanael ibn al-Fayyumi,* an edition and translation of the unique manuscript in Columbia University Library. His first charge as a rabbi was in Syracuse, N.Y. In 1904, after acting as rabbi in Portland, Oreg., he was called to Temple Emanu-El in Spokane, Wash. Since 1917 he was successively rabbi at the Temples Emanu-El in Brooklyn and Yonker, N.Y. He died in N.Y.C. on 26 June 1926. CnDiAmJBi; NYT, 28 June 1926, p. 17, col. 4; Selim

Levine, Donald Nathan, born 16 June 1931 at New Castle, Pa., he graduated in 1950 from the University of Chicago where he also gained a Ph.D. in 1957 for *Simmel and Parsons; two approaches to society.* He spent his entire career in various capacities with his alma mater. His writings include *Wax and gold; tradition and innovation in Ethiopian culture* (1967), *Greater Ethiopia; the evolution of a multiethnic society* (1974), *The Flight from ambiguity; essays in social and cultural theory* (1985), and *Visions and the sociological tradition* (1995). AmM&WSc, 1973 S, 1978 S; ConAu, 53-56; NatFacDr, 1990-2002; Unesco; WhoAm, 1980-1996; WhoMW (not sighted); ZKO

Lévine, J. O. *see* Levin, Isaak Osipovich

Levine, Louis David, born 4 June 1940 at N.Y.C, he graduated in 1962 from the University of Pennsylvania, where he also received a Ph.D. in 1969. He subsequently taught Hebrew at his alma mater until 1969 when he began a twenty-year association with the Royal Ontario Museum, Toronto, Ont. Since 1990 he was a director of the New York State Museum, Albany. His writings include *Two Neo-Assyrian stelae from Iran* (1972), a work which was partially submitted as a doctoral thesis, *Geographical studies in Neo-Assyrian Zagros* (1974), and he was a joint author of *Excavations of the Godin Project* (1974). WhoAm, 1992-2003;

Le Vine, Victor Theodore, born 6 December 1930 at Berlin, he graduated in 1950 from the University of California at Los Angeles, where he also received a Ph.D. in 1961 for *The Cameroun from mandate to independence.* He was a professor of political science at the University of Ghana and subsequently at Washington University, St. Louis, Mo., a post which he held until his retirement. His writings include his inaugural lecture delivered on 4 February 1971 at the University of Ghana entitled *Political corruption and the informal polity* (Accra, 1971), *The Political corruption; the Ghana case* (1975), and he was a joint author of *Historical dictionary of Cameroon* (1974), and *The Arab-African connection; political and economic realities* (1979). AmM&WSc, 1973 S, 1978 S; ConAu, 13-16; NatFacDr, 1995-2002; WhoAm, 1984-2003; WhoMW, 1994/95

Levitskaia (Левитская), Liia Sergeevna, born 23 November 1931 at Moscow, she graduated in 1955 from the Faculty of Philology, Moscow State University, and received her first degree in 1966 for *Историческая фонетика чувашского языка.* She was briefly an editorial assistant to the *Туркменская искра,* and a librarian, before she became associated in 1958 with the Institute of

Linguistics, Soviet Academy of Sciences. Her writings include *Историческая морфология чувашского языка* (1976), and *Теория и практика этимологических исследований; материалы к ЭСТЯ* (1988), and she was a joint author of *Общетюрксие и межтюркские лексические основы на букву "К"* (2000). Miliband²

Levitskiĭ, T., 1906-1992 *see* Lewicki, Tadeusz

Levkievskiĭ (Levkievsky), E. B., born about 1900, he translated from the Persian of Burhān al-Dīn Kūshgarī, *Каттаган и Бадахшан* (Tashkent, 1926). His trace is lost after an article in 1939. NYPL

Levkovskaia (Rafailova), Roza Georgievna, born 19 May 1923 at Kazan, Russia, she graduated in 1948 from the Faculty of Philology, Moscow State University, and received her first degree in 1956 for *Поэтич. творчество Мирсаида Миршакара*. She taught for four years at a university before becoming associated with the Institute of Asian and African Studies, Moscow State University in 1956. In 1963, she was appointed a lecturer in Persian. Her writings include *Учебник персидского языка* (1973). Miliband³

Levkovskiĭ, Alekseĭ Ivanovich, born 21 July 1924 at Moscow, he graduated in 1948 from the Faculty of Economy, Moscow State University, and received his first degree in 1952 for «Индия под гнётом английского империализма», and a doctorate in 1964 for a monograph. He was from 1953 to 1985 associated with the Oriental Institute, Soviet Academy of Sciences. Concurrently he collaborated from 1964 to 1967 as a research fellow with the publication of the Russian edition of the journal, *Problems of peace and socialism*, Prague. In 1971, he was appointed a professor. His writings include *Национально-освободительная борьба народнов Малайи* (1952), *Некоторые особенности развития капи-тализма в Индии до 1947 г.* (1956), *Capitalism in India* (1966), *Indépendance économique et secteur public* (1973), *Role of the public sector in achieving economic independence* (1973), and *Мелкая буржуазия; облик и судьбы класса* (1978). He died on 6 April 1985. Miliband; Miliband²; OSK

Levonian, Lootfy Hovannes, born 18 May 1881 at Aintab (now Gaziantep), Turkey, he was education at the local church schools, and graduated from Central Turkey College, Aintab. He subsequently went to Talas, where he taught for two years. He went back to teach at his alma mater from 1901 to 1915, interrupted for two years (1910-1912), when he went for special studies to Woodsbrooke College, a Quaker centre in England, which years later, in 1927, made him a honorary fellow. After the outbreak of the first World War, he was briefly arrested, but released and allowed to return to Aintab, where he taught in the Turkish schools for the duration of the war. From 1922 until his retirement in 1950, he was at the School of Religion (later the Near East School of Theology) at its changing localities in Istanbul, Athens and Beirut, and served as professor, dean, and at times as the principal. After his retirement he went to the United States where he was on two occasions a visiting professor at the Union Theological Seminary in New York, and the Pacific School of Religion in Berkeley, California. Death put an end to his lingering suffering in Los Angeles on 19 September 1961. His writings include *Moslem mentality* (1928), *The Turkish press: selections, 1925-1932* (1932), *The Turkish press: selections, 1932-1936* (1937), *Studies in the relation between Islam and Christianity* (1940). MW, 52 (1962), pp. 141-145

Levshin (Левшинъ), Alekseĭ Iraklievich, born in 1799, he was a prominent government figure during the preparations made for the emancipation of the Russian serfs. His writings include *Историческое и статическое обозрение уральских казаков* (1823), *Описание киргиз-казачьнихъ, или киргиз-кайсацких орд и степей* (1832), its translation, *Description des hordes et des steppes des Kirghiz-Kazaks* (1840), and *Прогулка русскаго в Помпеи* (1843). He died in 1879. EnSlovar; GSE; Henze; KazakSE; NYPL; Wieczynski

Levtzion, Nehemia, born 24 November 1935, he graduated in 1960 from the Hebrew University, Jerusalem, and received a Ph.D. in 1965 from the School of Oriental and African Studies, London, for his thesis, *The Spread and development of Islam in the Middle Volta Basin in the pre-colonial period*. He was a professor of history and chairman of the Institute of Asian and African Studies in the Hebrew University. His writings include *Muslims and chiefs in West Africa* (1968), *Ancient Ghana and Mali* (1973), *The History of Islam in Africa* (2000); he edited *Conversion to Islam* (1979); and he was joint editor of *Rural and urban Islam in West Africa* (1987). CoAu, 53-55, new rev., 4; MESA Roster of members, 1982-1990; Suglett; WhoWor, 1980/81; WhoWorJ, 1972, 1978

Levy, Avigdor, born 15 November 1933, he received a Ph.D. in 1968 from Harvard for *The Military policy of Sultan Mahmud II*. In 1990 he was a professor in the Department of Near Eastern Studies, Brandeis University, Waltham, Mass., a position which he still held in 2002. His writings include *The Sephardim in the Ottoman Empire* (1987), and he edited *Jews, Turks, Ottomans; a shared history, fifteenth through the twentieth century* (2002). MESA Roster of members, 1977-1990; NatFacDr, 1990-2002; ZKO

Levy, George(s) David, born 12 June 1925, he received diplomas in private law and a doctorate in law in 1949 from the Université de Paris. He was a sometime barrister in Casablanca. Unesco

Lévy, Isaac, born 20 January 1835 at Marmoutier, Alsace, he completed his rabbinical studies at Metz and successively served as a rabbi at Verdun, 1858-65, and at Lunéville from 1865 to 1869, when he was requested to succeed to Salomon Wolf Klein at Colmar. In spite of pressure from the German authorities, he opted for France and became rabbi at Vesoul. In 1887, he accepted an invitation from Bordeaux, where he remained until his retirement in 1906. His writings include *La Synagogue et M. Renan* (Lunéville, 1863), *Récits bibliques* (Verdun, 1864), and *Alsatiana; echos patriotiques de la chaire israélite* (Paris, 1873). He was awarded *chevalier de la Légion d'honneur*, and *officier de l'Instruction publique*. He died in Paris on 12 September 1912. EncJud; EncJud²; JewEnc; JüdLex; NDBA; Wininger

Lévy, Isidore, born in 1871 at Rixheim, Alsace, he taught archaeology, first at the Collège de France, and since 1919 at the Université de Bruxelles. His writings include *Recherches sur les sources de la légende de Pythagore* (1926), and *La Légende de Pythagore de Grèce et de Palestine* (1927). In 1955 he was honoured by *Mélanges Isidore Lévy*. He died in May 1959. Revue archéologique, 1959, p. 98

Lévy, Kurt, born in 1907, he received a Dr.phil. in 1933 from the Universität Bonn for *Zur masoretischen Grammatik; Texte und Untersuchungen*. He was an academic assistant at the universities of Halle and Bonn. He committed suicide in Köln in 1935. Hanisch; NUC, pre-1956; Sezgin; Thesis

Lévy, Raphaël Georges, born 24 February 1853 at Paris, he became a professor at the Association des cours commerciales, École des sciences politiques, and a member of the Académie des Sciences morales et politiques, Paris. A *conseiller municipal* of Deauville since 1900, he was elected senator for the Département de la Seine in 1920. In 1927, he gave up politics for reasons of health. His writings include *Le Péril financier* (1888), *La juste paix, ou, La vérité sur la traité de Versailles* (1920), and he was a joint author of *Au lendemain des guerres balkaniques* (1915). He died in Paris on 8 December 1933. BN; NUC, pre-1956; Qui êtes-vous, 1924.

Levy, Reuben, born in 1891, he graduated from University College of North Wales and subsequently studied Semitic languages, Persian and Turkish at Oxford. The first World War gave him practical application of his scholarship while posted to Mesopotamia. Since 1926 he taught Persian in the University of Cambridge. In 1950, he was appointed to the chair of Persian. He was a fellow of Christ's College. His writings include *The Three dervishes and other Persian tales and legends* (1923), *A Baghdad chronicle* (1929), *Mesopotamia* (1929), *The Persian language* (1951), *The Social structure of Islam* (1957), *Introduction to Persian literature* (1969), its translation, *Introduction à la littérature persane* (1973); and he translated from the Persian, *A Mirror for princes, the Qābūs nāma* (1951), as well as other works of classical Persian writers. He died in 1966. ObitT, 1961-70, p. 477 (8 September 1966); Who was who, 6; ZKO

Levy, Victor, born 19th cent., his writings include *La Serbie en 1900* (Vienne, 1900), and *Im belgischen Congostaate; Streiflichter aus dem modernen Afrika* (Wien, 1901). NUC, pre-1956

Levy, Walter James, born 21 November 1911 at Hamburg, Germany, he studied at the universities of Hamburg, Berlin, and Kiel. He was from 1936 to 1941 an editor with the Petroleum Press Bureau, London, and subsequently was an independent oil consultant and adviser to industry and the U.S. Government. His writings include *Petroleum prices in Peru* (1954), and *The Search for oil in developing countries* (1960). He died on 10 December 1997. AmM&WSc, 1973 S; BioHbDtE; IntWW, 1974-1997/98; Master (8); WhAm, 12; WhoAm, 1974-1996; WhoWorJ, 1965, 1978; WhoWor, 1974/75-1982

Lewan, Kenneth Melvin, born 26 April 1925 at Chicago, he received a Dr.phil. in 1972 from the Universität München for a thesis on the Middle East war in the West German press entitled, *Der Nahostkrieg in der westdeutschen Presse*. He was a lawyer and legal council to German ministries as well as to the U.S. Congress. He taught at both the Hochschule für Politik and the Universität in München before he was appointed a professor at the Fachhochschule Hagen. His writings include *Sechs Tage und zwanzig Jahre; Aufsätze zum Spannungsfeld Naher Osten* (1988). Kürschner, 1983-2003|; Schwarz

Lewando-Hundet, G. A., born 20th cent., she received an M.Phil. in 1978 from the University of Edinburgh for *Women's power and settlement; the effect of settlement on the position of Negev Bedouin women*. Sluglett

Lewcock, Ronald Bently, born 27 September 1929 at Brisbane, Australia, and a student at the University of Queensland and Columbia University, New York, he graduated from the University of Cape Town, where he also received his Ph.D. in architecture in 1961. From 1958 to 1969, he was a lecturer in architecture at the University of Natal, Durban, South Africa. He subsequently went to Clare College, Cambridge, as Whitehead Research Fellow. He was a member of the Council at the Middle East Centre when he went to the United States to become successively visiting Aga Khan Professor of Islamic architecture at Massachusetts Institute of Technology, and a professor at the Georgia Institute of Architecture. He served as technical coordinator of national and international campaigns for the conservation of the old cities of San'ā' and Shibām. His writings include *Early nineteenth century architecture in South Africa* (1963), *Traditional architecture in Kuwait and the northern Gulf* (1978), *The Old walled city of San'ā'* (1986), and *Wadi Hadramawt and the walled city of Shibām* (1986). ConAu, 121, new rev., 46, 96; IntAu&W, 1989; Private; WhoAm, 1988-2003; WhoWor, 1991/92, 1993/94

Lewenklaw, Johannes, 1541-1594 *see* Löwenklau, Johannes

Lewicki, Marian, born 15 August 1908 at Lemberg (Lwow), Austrian Galicia, he studied Turkic languages as well as Arabic and Persian, particularly under Zygmunt Smogorzewski. He received his first degree in 1931 for a paper on the plural in the Altaic languages, and four years later his doctorate for a thesis on the adverbial suffixes in certain Altaic languages. An assistant at the Uniwersytet Lwowski since 1929, he obtained a scholarship in 1937 to study Turkish and related languages under Jean Deny and Paul Pelliot at Paris. He returned home, and in December 1938 became a member of the Oriental Commission in the Polish Academy of Sciences and Letters, but the outbreak of the war degraded him to manual work. In August 1946, he resumed his academic work at Kraków, becoming assistant to the Chair of Oriental philology. In 1949 he was appointed a professor at the Uniwersytet Warszawski, a position which he held until his untimely death on 13 November 1955. He edited *La Langue mongole des transcriptions chinoises du XIVe siècle* (1949-59). NEP; Polski (1); PSB; *T'oung pao*, 44 (1956), pp. 444-48

Lewicki, Tadeusz, born 29 January 1906 at Lemberg (Lwów), Austrian Galicia, he graduated from Uniwersytet Lwowski, where he also received his doctorate in 1931. He subsequently went to Paris until 1934. In 1949, he was appointed to the chair of Oriental languages at Uniwersytet Jagielloński, Kraków. His writings include *Polska i kraje sąsiednie wśietle "Księgi Rogera," geografa arabskiego z XII w, al-Idrīsī'ego* (1954), *Études ibādites nord-africaines* (1955), *Les Ibadites en Tunisie au moyen âge* (1959), *Dzieje Afryki od czasów najdawniejszych do XIV w.* (1963), *Arabic external sources for the history of Africa to the South of Sahara* (1969), *Źródła arabskie o dziejów słowiańszczyzny* (1969), *West African food in the Middle Ages according to Arabic sources* (1974), *Études maghrebines et soudanaises* (1976),and a translation of the *Arabian nights* into Polish, *Księga tysiąca i jednej nocy* (1973). He died in 1992. Dziekan; *Index Islamicus* (2); WhoSocCE, 1986

Lewin, Bernhard J., born 16 November 1903 at Säbrå, Vnl., Sweden, he was from 1957 to 1970 a professor of Semitic languages at Göteborgs Universitet. His writings include *Ši'r 'Abdallah Ibn-al-Mu'tazz* (1945-50), *Den orientalska boken; skrift och bokväsen i Islams värld* (1951), *Notes on Cabali* (1969), *Arabische Texte im Dialekt von Hama* (1966), *A Vocabulary of the Hudailian poems* (1978), and he edited *The Book of plants of Abu ad-Dinawari* (1978). He died on 23 February 1979. SBL; *Vem är det*, 1975-1979

Lewin, David, 1889-1962 *see* Dallin, David Julievich

Lewin, Erwin, he was born on 5 September 1936 into a family of peasants at Hucisko, Poland. His father was missed in action during the war, and the family expelled from their home in January 1945. After completing grade school in Soviet occupied Germany, he became a carpender's apprentice. In 1953, he was sent to a workers' and peasants' faculty at Halle, where he studied Russian and prepared for a government-supported academic career. From 1956 to 1959 he studied Albanian language, literature, and history at Tirana. He subsequently completed his study at the Institute of history of the European people's democracies, Karl-Marx-Universität, Leipzig, where he received a Dr.phil. in 1965 for a thesis on the national liberation movement of the Albanian people entitled *Die nationale Unabhängigkeitsbewegung des albanischen Volkes von 1917-1920*. He was a joint author of *Einheit und Kampf gegen Faschismus und Krieg* (Berlin, Diez, 1975). A member of the East German Communist Party since 1959, his tenure at Leipzig was probably not renewed after German re-unification in 1990. Schwarz; Thesis

Lewin, Thomas, born in 1805 at Ifield, England, he was a miscellaneous writer who was educated at Merchant Taylors' School, London, and Worcester and Trinity colleges, Oxford, graduating M.A. in 1831. He was called to the bar from Lincoln's Inn in 1833. In 1852, he was appointed a conveyancing counsel in the court of chancery, a post which he held until his death. His writings include *Jerusalem; a sketch of the city and temple from the earliest times to the siege by Titus* (1861), *The Siege of Jerusalem of Titus* (1863), and *Fasti sacri; or a Key to the chronology of the New Testament* (1865). He died in 1877. Boase; BritInd (4); DcBiPP (not sighted); DNB; ZKO

Lewis, Archibald Ross, born 25 August 1914 at Bronxville, N.Y., he was a graduate of Princeton where he also obtained a doctorate in 1940. He was a medievalist who held teaching positions at various American universities. Since 1985 he was editor of the *American Neptun*. His research centred on the interaction among the sibling cultures of Byzantium, Islam, and the Latin West. His writings include *Naval power and trade in the Mediterranean, A.D. 500-1100* (1951), *Nomads and Crusaders* (1988). He died 4 February 1990. MESA bulletin, 24 i (July 1990), pp. 153-155; WhAm, 10

Lewis, Arnold, born in 1947 at Bridgeport, Conn., he received a Ph.D. in 1977 from Columbia University, New York, for *Sharonia; education and social inequality in an Israeli town*. He was a lecturer at Tel-Aviv University. His writings include *Power, poverty, and education* (1979). LC

Lewis, Bazett Annesley, born 4 June 1907 at Backhurst Hill, Essex, he studied at Oxford and Cambridge. His writings include *The Murle; red chiefs and black commoners* (1972). Note; NUC, 1973-77

Lewis, Bernard, born 31 May 1916 at London, he received his B.A. in 1936, a diploma in Semitic studies from the Université de Paris, and a Ph.D. in 1939 from the University of London for *Studies on the history of the Qarmati and Ismaili movements from the eighth to the eleventh centuries*. He taught at his alma mater until called to duty in the British armed forces. Being highly trained in Middle Eastern languages, he became an attractive recruit for British Intelligence. He served for five years before returning to academic life. He taught successively at the University of London, and Princeton University. His writings include *The Origin of Ismailism* (1940), *Turkey today* (1940), *The Arabs in history* (1950), *Semites and anti-Semites* (1999), *What went wrong? The clash between Islam and modernity in the Middle East* (2002), its translation, *Der Untergang des Morgenlandes* (2002), and he translated *Music of a distant drum; classical Arabic, Persian, Turkish, and Hebrew poems* (2001). In 1999 appeared *The Jewish discovery of Islam; studies in honour of Bernard Lewis*. BlueB, 1973/74-1976; CnDiAmJBi; ConAu, 113, 118, new rev., 44, 78; IntWW, 1974-2006; Master (2); MidE, 1978-1982/83; Who's who, 1969-2005; WhoAm, 1980-2003; WhoWorJ, 1965

Lewis, Geoffrey Lewis, born 14 June 1920 at London, he graduated in classics and Oriental languages from St. John's College, Oxford, in 1941 and 1947 respectively. After five years in the R.A.F., mainly in the Middle East, he returned to Oxford to read Arabic and Persian. For his *Teach yourself Turkish* (1950), he was awarded a D.Phil. from Oxford and was apointed a lecturer in Turkish. From 1959 to 1960 he taught at Robert College, Istanbul. He was a fellow of St. Antony's Collge, Oxford, and a visiting professor at Princeton University, 1970-71. His writings include *Turkey* (1955), its translation, *La Turquie* (1968), *Turkish grammar* (1967), *The Book of Dede Korkut* (1974), *The Turkish language reform, a catastrophic success* (1999), and he was a joint editor and translator of *On surgery and instruments* (1973). In 2000 appeared *The Balance of truth; essays in honour of Professor Geoffrey Lewis*. Au&Wr, 1963, 1971; ConAu, 13-16; EURAMES, 1993; Schoeberlein; Who, 1980-2005; ZKO

Lewis, Ion Myrddin, born 30 January 1930 at Glasgow, he graduated B.Sc. in 1951 from Glasgow University and received a D.Phil. in 1957 from Oxford University for *The Somali; some aspects of the social structure of a nomadic Muslim people*. He was associated with the Royal Institute of International Affairs, London, and taught at University College of the University of Rhodesia and Nyasaland, Salisbury, before he was appointed in 1969 a professor of anthropology at the London School of Economics and an honorary director at the International Africa Institute, positions which he held until his retirement in 1993. His writings include *Peoples of the Horn of Africa* (1955), *A Modern history of Somalia* (1965), *Social anthropology in perspective* (1976), *Blood and bone: the call of kinship in Somali society* (1994); and he edited *Islam in Tropical Africa* (1966). ConAu, 9-12, new rev., 5, 21; Sluglett; Who's who, 1984-2005

Lewis, Norman Nicholson, born 7 January 1919, during the second World War he was stationed in Syria from 1942 to 1945. He received an M.A. from Cambridge University in 1950, and was principal instructor at the Middle East Centre for Arab Studies, Shemlan, Lebanon, from 1948 to 1955, when he became an executive, Gulf Eastern Company, a post he held until his retirement in 1981. In 1999 he was a research fellow of the Institute for Lebanese Studies, Oxford. He published numerous articles on aspects of Syrian geography, history, ethnology and exploration, as well as *Nomads and settlers in Syria and Jordan, 1899-1980* (1987). DrBSMES, 1993; Private

Lewis, Philip, born 20th cent., he was a specialist in comparative religion, who spent six years in Pakistan. He was an adviser to the Bishop of Bradford on inter-faith issues, and represented the Bishop of Canterbury on the advisory committee of the Centre for the Study of Islam and Chrisitan-Muslim Relations in Selly Oak Colleges, Birmingham. His writings include *Pirs, shrines and Pakistani Islam* (1985), and *Islamic Britain; religion, politics, and identity among British Muslims: Bradford in the 1990s* (1994). Note

Lewis, Ralph Kepler, born 7 March 1912, he graduated from Missouri State College, received an M.A. in anthropology in 1939 from the University of Southern California, and a Ph.D. in 1967 from Columbia University, New York, for *Hadchite; a study of emigration in a Lebanese village.* He was a sometime field director of the Columbia University Middle East Project as well as a director of the Arabic Language and Training Center, Beirut. Selim; Unesco

Lewis, Robert Allen, born 4 June 1929 at Minot, N.D., he graduated B.Sc. in 1951 from Oregon State College and received a Ph.D. in 1964 from the University of Washington, Seattle, for *Early irrigation in West Turkestan.* He started his career as a professor of geography at San Diego State College and since 1966 taught at Columbia University, New York, where he also served as chairman of department. His writings include *Nationality and population change in Russia and the USSR; an evaluation of census date, 1897-1970* (1972), and he was a joint author of *Population changes in Russia* (1966). WhoAm, 1982-1984

Lewis, Stephen Richmond, born 11 February 1939 at Englewood, N.J., he graduated in 1960 from Williams College, Williamstown, Mass., and received a Ph.D. in 1963 from Stanford University, Palo Alto, Calif., for *Taxation and growth in the dual economy; an evaluation of tax devices in under-developed countries.* He taught successively at Stanford University, the Pakistan Institute of Development Economics, Karachi, Harvard University, and Williams College. His writings include *Economic policy and industrial growth in Pakistan* (1969), *Pakistan; industrialization and trade policies* (1970), and *Agricultural taxation and intersectoral resource transfers* (1971). AmM&WSc, 1973 S, 1978 S; ConAu, 41-44; WhoAm, 1978/79-1996; WhoMW, 1992/93

Lewis, Thomas Hayter, born 9 July 1818 at London, he articled to an architect and in 1837 became a student at the Royal Institute of Architects, which he left in 1839 as silver medalist for architectural drawing. After spending 1844 to 1845 with an architectural firm in London, he practised alone there since 1857. A fellow of the Society of Architects since 1862, he served as an honorary secretary of the Royal Institute of Architects from 1860 to 1865, when he was appointed a professor of architecture in University College, London, a position which he held until 1881 when he became a professor emeritus. His writings include *The Holy places of Jerusalem* (1888), and *Byzantine sculptures found at Ahnas* (1894). He died in London on 10 December 1898. Boase; BritInd (2)

Lewis, William Hubert, born 4 June 1928 at N.Y.C., he graduated in 1952 from George Washington University, Washington, D.C., and received a Ph.D. in 1960 from the American University, Washington, D.C., for *Morocco; the impact of social and political evolution on foreign policy.* He was associated with the U.S. Department of State as chief of North and East Africa, before he was appointed a professor of international relations at Georgetown University, Washington, D.C., a post which he still held in 1995. His writings include *New forces in Africa* (1962), *The Prevention of nuclear war* (1986), and he was a joint author of *Islam in Africa* (1969). ConAu, 13-16; DrAS, 1969 H, 1974 H, 1978 H, 1982 H; NatFacDr, 1990-1995; Unesco

Lewisohn, Alice, born 17 April 1883 in New York City, the eigth child of a millionaire industrialist, she was educated privately and encouraged in philanthropic and artistic pursuits on New York's Lower East Side. She and her sister built a small theatre at their own expense, the Neighborhood Playhouse, which opened in 1915 in N.Y.C. Together they visited Europe and the Orient in pursuit of their profession. Her association with the Playhouse ended shortly after she married in 1924. She died in Zürich on 6 January 1972. BiE&WWA, 1966; NotWoAT, 1989

Lewisohn, Irene, born 5 September 1892 at N.Y.C., the tenth child of a millionaire industrialist, she was educated privately and encouraged in philanthropic and artistic pursuits on New York's Lower East Side. She and her sister built a small theatre at their own expense, the Neighborhood Playhouse, which opened in 1915 in N.Y.C. Together they visited Europe and the Orient in pursuit of their profession. She died in N.Y.C. from cancer on 4 April 1944. BiE&WWA, 1966; NotWoAT, 1989; NYT, 5 April 1944, p. 13, col. 3 (not sighted)

Lewisohn, Leonard, born 20th cent., his writings include *Divani Nurbakhsh* (1980), and he translated from the Persian, *The Truths of love; Sufi poetry* (1982), and he edited *Classical Persian Sufism from its origins to Rumi* (1993). ZKO

Lewkowicz, Nancy Margaret Kennedy, born in 1929, she received a Ph.D. in 1967 from the University of Michigan for *A Transformational approach to the syntax of Arabic participles.* LC; Selim

Lewy, Ernst, born 19 September 1881 at Breslau, Prussia, he studied philology at the universities of Breslau, München and Leipzig, and received a Dr.phil. in 1904 from the Universität Breslau for *Die altpreußischen Personennamen.* He subsequently pursued Finnish, Hungarian, Basque, and Russian linguistic studies and earned a Dr.habil. He was appointed in 1925 a professor of Hungarian at the

Universität Berlin, a position from which he was dismissed in 1935. In 1937, he emigrated to Ireland, where he became a professor of linguistics in 1947. His writings include *Zur finnisch-ugrischen Wort- und Satz-verbindung* (1911), *Ungarische Zusammensetzungen* (1920), *Tscheremissische Grammatik* (1922), *Sprachgeographische Probleme des Mediterranen Gebietes* (1934), *Der Bau der europäischen Sprachen* (1942), and *Versuch einer Charkteristik des Awarischen* (1953). He died in Dublin on 25 September 1966. DtBE; GV; Kürschner, 1926-1935; Master (1); NDB

Lewy, Guenter, born 22 August 1923 at Breslau, Germany, he graduated in 1951 from City College of New York and received a Ph.D. in 1957 from Columbia University for *Constitutionalism and statecraft during the golden age of Spain.* He was successively a professor of government at Smith College, Northampton, Mass., and the University of Massachusetts, Amherst. His writings include *The Catholic Church and Nazi Germany* (1964), its translation, *Die katholische Kirche und das Dritte Reich* (1965), *Religion and revolution* (1974), *America in Vietnam* (1978), *Peace & revolution* (1988), *The Cause that failed; communism in American political life* (1990), and *Why America needs religion* (1996). AmM&WSc, 1973 S, 1978 S; BioHdDtE; ConAu, 9-12, new rev., 3, 21; IntAu&W, 1991/92; WhoE, 1991/92; WhoUSWr, 1988; WhoWrEP, 1989, 1992/93

Lewy, Hildegard née Schlesinger, born 17 October 1903 at Kolozsvár (Cluij), Hungary, she received a Dr.phil. in 1926 from the Universität Gießen. From 1963 to her death in 1967 she was a visiting professor of Assyriology at the Hebrew Union College, Cincinnati, Ohio. She died in Cincinnati in 1967. DrAS, 4th ed. (1964), vol. 3; Hanisch; NYT, 10 October 1967, p. 42, col. 1; WhoAmW, 1968/69; WhoWorJ, 1965

Lewytzkyj, Boris, born 20th cent., his writings include *Die Sowjetukraine, 1944-1963* (1964), *Who's who in the Soviet Union* (1984), *Politics and society in Soviet Ukraine, 1953-1980* (1987); he was a joint author of *Ideologie und Praxis in der sowjetischen Innen- und Außenpolitik* (1966); and he was a joint author of *Who's who in the socialist countries* (1978). LC; OSK

Lexa, František, born 5 April 1876 at Pardubitz (Pardubice), Austria, he received a Dr.phil. in 1903 from Karls Universität, Prag, for a thesis on the history of writing. He later turned to Egyptology, studying under Adolf Erman at Berlin, and under Wilhelm Spiegelberg at Straßburg, with whom he published *Das demotische Totenbuch der Pariser Nationalbibliothek, Papyrus des Pamonthes* (1903). He died in Praha on 13 February 1960. Český; Egyptology; Filipsky; IES; PSN

Ley, Hermann Hubert, born 30 November 1911 at Leipzig, he obtained a Dr.med. in 1944, and a Dr.habil. in 1948. He was a professor of dialectic materialism at Dresden, and also served as a director of Philosophisches Institut, Humboldt-Universität, Berlin. His writings include *Avicenna* (1953), *Studie zur Geschichte des Materialismus im Mittelalter* (1957), *Dämon Technik?* (1961), and *Geschichte der Aufklärung und des Atheismus* (1966). He died in Dresden on 24 November 1990. DtBE; IntWW, 1974/75-1991/92; Kürschner, 1961; Sezgin; Wer ist wer, 1955, 1958; WhoSocC, 1978; WhoSoCE, 1989; WhoWor, 1974/75-1984

von **Leyden**, Casimir Carl Maximilian, born 7 January 1852 at München, he was educated at the Königlich-bayerische Pagerie, München, and subsequently participated in the Franco-Prussian war of 1870-71. He then completed his law at the Universität München and entered the diplomatic service. He was in 1875 an attaché at London and subsequently served briefly in the German Foreign Office, Berlin. He was a German consul-general in Egypt, 1880-83, and subsequently served as ambassador in Bucureşti, Tokio, Stockholm, Constantinople, and Athens. He died in Territet, Switzerland, in 1938. DeutschesZL; Kornrumpf², vol. 2; Wer ist's, 1909-1922

Leyden, John, born in 1775, he went to school at Denholm, Roxburghshire, and here made excellent progress in Latin and Greek. From 1790 to 1793 he was a student in the Faculty of Arts and from 1793 to 1797 he was in the Faculty of Divinity, specializing in Hebrew, Old Testament as well as Syriac and Arabic. In 1800, he also completed medical studies. Soon thereafter he went to India, where his proficiency in Oriental languages led to an appointment as professor of Hindustani at Fort William College, Cacutta. His writings include the work published anonymously, *A Historica and philosophical sketch of the discoveries and settlements of the Europeans in northern and western Africa* (1799), its translation, *Historische und philosophische Skizze der Entdeckungen und Niederlassungen der Europäer in Nord- und West-Afrika* (1802), *A Comparative vocabulary of the Barma, Maláyu and Thai languages* (1810), *Historical account of discoveries and travels in Africa* (1817), and the translation, *Memoirs of Zehir-Ed-Din Muhammed Babur, Emperor of Hindustan* (1821). He died in Batavia, Java, in 1811. BbD; BiD&SB; Buckland; CasWL; DNB; IndianBiInd (4); Master (17); NewGrDM; *Revue des études islamiques*, 44 (1986), pp. 349-54

von **Leyden**, Rudolf, born 20th cent., his writings include *Die Welt der indischen Spielkarten* (1981), *Ganjifa; the playing cards of India; a general survey, with a catalogue of the Victoria and Albert Museum collection* (1982), *Die Welt der indischen Spielkarten; Geschichte, Systematik und* Herstellung

(1981), and jointly with Dorothea Duda and Mehdi Roschanzamir, *Spielkartenbilder in persischen Lackmalereien der Österreichischen Nationalbibliothek* (1981). ZKO

Leyerer, Constantin, born 17 January 1876 at Prag, he obtained a Dr.rer.pol. and became a professor of business administration at the Technische Hochschule Prag. Kürschner, 1931-1940/41; Wer ist's, 1935

Leymarie, Philippe, born in 1943, he was a journalist whose writings include *Océan indien, le nouveau cœur du monde* (1981). LC; Note; ZKO

Lézine, Alexandre, fl. 1958, he was associated with the Institut de France. His writings include *Notes sur la consolidation des monuments historiques de la Tunisie* (1953), *Architecture punique* (1959), *Sousse; les monuments musulmans* (196-?), *Architecture de l'Ifriqiya* (1966), *Mahdiya* (1968), *Carthage, Utique* (1968), *Utique* (1970), *Deux villes d'Ifriqiya, Sousse, Tunis* (1971), and *Deux palais d'époque ottomane au Caire* (1972). NUC

Lhéritier, Michel Jean-Baptiste Léon Claude, born 11 October 1889 at Bordeaux, he obtained his *agrégation* in history and geography in 1914 and a *doctorat ès lettres* in 1920. He taught at schools in Bordeaux, Tours, Rouen, and Paris, before he became a professor in the École des hautes études sociales, Paris, 1926-1944. His writings include *La Grèce* (1921), *Histoire diplomatique de la Grèce de 1821 à nos jours* (1925-26), *L'Europe orientale à l'époque contemporaine* (1938), and *La Russie* (1946). IndexBFr² (1); NUC, pre-1956

L'Hopital, Jean-Yves, born 20th cent., he received a *doctorat de 3ème cycle* in 1977 from the Université de Paris IV for *La Racine «Abada» dans le Coran*. THESAM, 4

Lhote, Henri Jacques René, born 16 May 1903 at Paris, he grew up an orphan without resources, thus being deprived of the average middle class education. He was a self-taught man who in his late youth took courses at the École d'anthropologie, a private institution, went to public lectures at the Musée d'histoire naturelle, and, finally, at the Institut d'ethnologie in the Université de Paris, where three *certificats de licence* were offered to students without *baccalauréat*. However, his credentials were insufficient for a *doctorat d'état*, but in 1944 he submitted an excellent thesis at the Université de Paris, based on his Saharan travels undertaken in the late 1930s. Throughout his life he remained an enthusiastic Saharan traveller and ethnographer, interests which were supported by the Musée de l'homme, Paris. His writings include *Aux prises avec le Sahara* (1936), *Le Sahara, désert mystérieux* (1937), *Le Niger en kayak* (1943), *Les Touaregs du Hoggar* (1944), *Comment campent les Touaregs* (1947), *Dans les campements touaregs* (1947), *La chasse chez les Touaregs* (1951), and *Vers d'autres Tassilis* (1976). He died on 26 March 1991. Master (1); *Revue des africanistes*, 64 i (1994), pp. 79-80; Unesco; WhoFr, 1977/78-1990/91

L'Hôte, Hippolyte Antoine *Nestor*, born 24 August 1804 at Köln, Germany, the son of a French customs official, he grew up in Charleville (Ardennes). He later worked in Paris, where he became befriended with Champollion who invited him to accompany him to Egypt as a draftsman. His writings include *Lettres écrites d'Égypte en 1838 et 1839, contenant des observations sur divers monuments égyptiens nouvellement explorés et dessinés* (1840), and *Sur le Nil avex Champollion; lettres, journaux et dessins inédits de Nestor L'Hôte* (1993). He died in Paris on 24 March 1842. Egyptology; Hill; Hoefer; IndexBFr² (1); Kornrumpf³, vol. 2

Li, IUliia (Юлия) Aleksandrovna, born 27 February 1932 at Leningrad, she graduated in 1956 from the Oriental Faculty, Leningrad State University, and received her first degree in 1975 for *Подготовка кадров средний и высший квалификации для народного хозяйства Турции, 1960-1970 гг.* Her writings include *Библиографический словарь отечественых тюркологов; дооктябрьский* (1974). Miliband²

Liakhov, Vladimir Platonovich, born in 1869, he rose to the rank of colonel. During the Persian revolution, 1905-1907, he led a Cossack unit and helped suppress rebellions in northern Persia. He was assassinated in 1919. Wieczynski

Liang, Hsi-Huey, born in 1929 in Europe, he graduated from Cambridge University and emigrated to the United States in 1951, where he received his Ph.D. from Yale University, New Haven, Conn. He was a sometime chairman of the Department of History and a professor emeritus of modern European history, Vassar College, Poughkeepsie, N.Y. He was married to Françoise Aguirre. His academic and artistic work was heavily influenced by his childhood experiences growing up as the son of the last Chinese diplomat in Berlin, and in China in the 1930s and 1940s. His writings include *The Berlin police force in the Weimar Republic* (1970), its translation, *Die Berliner Polizei in der Weimarer Republik* (1977), *The Sino-German connection; Alexander von Falkenhausen between China and Germany, 1900-1941* (1978), and *Berlin before the wall; a foreign student's diary* (1990). He died in Phoughkeepsie on 25 July 2004. From October to November 2005, the James W. Palmer III '90

Gallery at College Center, Vassar College, organized the exhibition "Houmptiphong - the art and life of Hsi-Huey Liang." He was a nice man.   Private

Liang, Yuen-li (Yün-li), born in 1900 at Sing-Chang, he studied at Nanyang University and received his LL.B. from the Comparative Law School.   While in law school, he was for two years an editor of the *China law review*.   After his bar admission in 1927, he was appointed secretary to the Ministry of Foreign Affairs, and in the following year to the same position in the Ministry of Justice.   He subsequently taught at Chinese universities before becoming an adviser to various Chinese delegations to conferences and the League of Nations.   After the war, he was a Chinese official at the United Nations Organization.   He was a joint author, with Neville Whymant, of *China* (London, 1946).   BioIn, 1; WhoChina, 5 (1936)

Liauzu, Claude, born 24 April 1940 at Casablanca, Morocco, he received a *doctorat d'état* in 1977 from the Université de Nice for *Naissance du salariat et du mouvement ouvrier en Tunisie à travers un démi-siècle de colonisation*.   In 1979, he was teaching at the Université de Jussieu, Paris VII.   His writings include *Salariat et mouvement ouvrier en Tunisie* (1978), *Militants, grevistes et syndicats* (1979), *Aux origines des tiers-mondismes* (1982), *Les Intellectuels français au miroir algérien* (1984), *L'Enjeu tiersmondiste* (1987), *L'Europe et l'Afrique méditerranéenne de Suez (1869) à nos jours* (1994), and *Passeurs de rives; changements d'identité dans le Maghreb colonial* (2000).   EURAMES, 1993; Livres disponibles, 2004; THESAM, 2; ZKO

Liauzu, Jean Guy, born 24 April 1934 at Casablanca, Morocco, he was educated at the Lycée Lyautey, Casablanca, and the Faculté des lettres d'Aix-en-Provence, completing his study with a *doctorat ès lettres*.   He was for four years a professor at lycées in Meknès and Rabat, and for two years an assistant at the Faculté des lettres de Rabat, before he became a cultural attaché at French embassies in Spain, Costa Rica, Cuba, Iraq, and Chile.   WhoFr, 1977/78-1992/93|

Libbrecht, Ulrich J., born in 1928 at Avelgen, Belgium, he obtained a doctorate and became a professor in the Department of Sinology, Katholieke Universiteit te Leuven.   His writings include *Chinese mathematics in the thirteenth century* (1973), *Oosterse wijsheid voor de westerse mens* (1974), *Scientific thinking in ancient China* (1976), and *Geen muren rond cultuuren* (1995).   LC; Note

Librande, Leonard Theodore, born 14 September 1943 at Rice Lake, Wisc., he was a graduate of St. Louis University and received an M.A. in 1972 and a Ph.D. in 1976 from McGill University, Montreal, for his thesis, *Contrasts in the two earliest manuals of 'Ulum al-hadith*.   Since 1976 he was a professor at Carleton University, Ottawa.   He was joint editor of *Iqbal - life, art, and thought; proceedings of the Iqbal Centennial Symposium* (1979).   Ferahian; LC; WhoWor, 1987

Lichtblau, John H., born 26 June 1921 at Wien, he graduated in 1949 from City University New York, where he also obtained his M.A. in 1951.   In 1961 he became a director of the Petroleum Industry Research Foundation, Inc., New York.   His writings include *United States oil imports* (19589, *The Outlook for world oil* (1978), and he was a joint author of *The Oil depletion issue* (1959), and *Energy policy and competition* (1961).   AmM&WSc, 1973 S; WhoAm, 1988/89-2000; WhoE, 1974/75-1981

Freiherr von **Lichtenberg**, Reinhold, born 15 December 1865 at Fiume (Rijeka), Austria-Hungary, he studied law at München and Wien, graduating in 1887; he then changed to fine art, archaeology, and Sanskrit, obtaining a Dr.phil. in 1892 for *Die Landschaftsmalerei bei den Niederländern im XVI. Jahrhundert*.   He subsequently made research travels to Italy, Greece, and Asia Minor.   In 1895, he entered the royal Kupferstichkabinett, München.   In 1899, he became a lecturer in fine art at Technische Hochschule, Karlsruhe; after his Dr.habil. in 1903, he was appointed a professor.   He resigned in 1908 to become a private scholar.   His scholarly work was mainly in classical antiquity, but he also published widely in German nationalist affairs, including *Beiträge zur ältesten Geschichte von Kypros* (1906), *Einflüsse der ägäischen Kultur auf Ägypten und Palästina* (1911), *Cypern und die Engländer* (1915), *Deutsches Land den Deutschen* (1921).   He died at Schloß Neubeuren am Inn, Bavaria, on 28 May 1927.   Kürschner, 1925, 1926; ÖBL; Wer ist's, 1905-1922

Lichtenstädter, Ilse, born 10 September 1907 at Hamburg, she received a Dr.phil. in 1931 from the Universität Frankfurt/Main for *Das Nasib der altarabischen Qaside*, and a D.Phil. in 1937 from Oxford for *An introduction to the Kitab al-Muhabbar of Muhammad ibn Habib, together with an edition of its first twenty folios, with indices and explanatory notes*.   She emigrated in 1935 to Britain and after the war to the United States.   She was a librarian at Cambridge, Oxford, and New York, before she became successively a professor and lecturer in Arabic and Islamic studies at New York University, Rutgers University, New Brunswick, N.J., and Harvard University, Cambridge, Mass.   Her writings include *Women in the Aiyām al-'Arab; a study of female life during warfare in pre-Islamic Arabia* (1935), *Islam and the modern age* (1958), and *Introduction to classical Arabic literature* (1976).   She died in Boston on 23 May 1991.   BioHbDtE; ConAu, 33-36, 134, new rev., 13; DrAS, 1969 P, 1974 F, 1978 F, 1982 F; Hanisch;

IntAu&W, 1977, 1982; *MESA bulletin*, 25 (1991), pp. 308-10; Schwarz; Sluglett; WhoWorJ, 1965, 1972, 1978; WrDr, 1976/78-1990/92

Lichtenstaedter, Siegfried, born in 1865, he was a civil servant and a writer. His works, partly under the pseudonyms Mehemed Emin Efendi and Dr. Efendi Neemān, include *Kultur und Humanität; völkerpsychologische und politische Untersuchungen* (1897), *Die Zukunft der Türkei; ein Beitrag zur Lösung der orientalischen Frage* (1898), *Das neue Weltreich* (1901-1903), *Der Kampf um Tripolis; ein Mahnruf an das türkische Volk* (1912), *Nationalitätsprinzip und Bevölkerungsaustausch* (1917), *Die Zukunft Palästinas* (1918), its translation, *The Future of Palestine* (1934), *Praktisches Judentum* 1931), *Naturschutz und Judentum* (1932), *Jüdische Politik* (1933), *Die siebenbürgische Frage* (1934), *Zionismus und andere Zukunftsmöglichkeiten* (1935), *Jüdische Fragen* (1935), *Jüdische Sorgen, jüdische Irrungen, jüdische Zukunft* (1937), and he translated from the Turkish, *Türkische Gedichte* (1919). There is no entry in Wininger as claimed by the editor of *Jüdischer biographischer Index*. JüdBilnd; NUC; ZKO

Lichtwardt, Hartman A., he was in 1934 a medical doctor at the American Hospital in Hamadan, Persia. His trace is lost after an article in 1945. Note about the author

Lida de Malkiel, María Rosa, born in 1910, she was an Argentine philologist whose writings include *Introducción al teatro de Sófocles* (1944), *Two Spanish masterpieces, the Book of good love and the Celestine* (1961), and *L'Idée de la gloire dans la tradition occidentale; antiquité, moyen âge occidental, Castille* (1968). In 1969, she was honoured by *Homenaje a María Rosa lida de Malkiel*. She died in 1962. BioIn, 6, 13; IndiceE³ (4); OxSpan

Liddell Hart, Sir Basil Henry, born in 1895, he graduated from Corpus Christi College, Cambridge, and subsequently joined the King's Own Yorkshire Light Infantry. He served in the First World War and retired in 1927 with the rank of captain. He was a military tactician, writer, and biographer. His writings include *Greater than Napoleon, Scipio Africanus* (1927), *The ghost of Napoleon* (1933), and *T. E. Lawrence* (1934). He died in 1970. BritInd (3); ConAu, 89-92, 103; CurBio, 1940, 1970; DNB; GrBr; Master (19); *Who was who*, 6

Lidén, Bror Per *Evald*, born 3 October 1862 at Sandared, Sweden, he was a professor of philology at Göteborgs Universitet. His writings include *Studien zur altindischen und vergleichenden Sprachgeschichte* (Uppsala, 1897), *Blandade språkhistoriska bidrag* (Göteborg, 1903-1934), and *Studien zur tocharischen Sprachgeschichte* (Göteborg, 1916). He died in Göteborg on 11 October 1939. SBL; SMK; *Vem är dat*, 1925

Lidzbarski, Marcellus (Mark), born Abraham Mordechai on 7 January 1868 at Płock (Plozk), Russia, he grew up in the mental confinement of the ghetto. Educated in rigid Hasidic piety since he was three years old, and weary to be exposed solely to Biblical and Talmudic studies, he ran away from home at the age of fourteen and matriculated at the gymnasium in Posen. Since 1889 he studied Semitic philology at Königliche Friedrich-Wilhelms-Universität zu Berlin under Eduard Sachau, and obtained a Dr.phil. in 1893 for *De propheticis, quae dicuntur, legendis Arabicis prolegomena*. He received his Dr.habil. in 1897, and since 1907 he served successively as a professor at the universities of Greifswald and Göttingen. In 1892, he was baptised a Lutheran. His writings include *Die neuaramäischen Handschriften der Königlichen Bibliothek zu Berlin* (1896), *Das Johannesbuch der Mandäer* (1905-15), *Handbuch der nordsemitischen Epigraphik* (1898), and *Auf rauhen Pfaden; Jugenderinnerungen eines deutschen Professors* (1927). He died in Göttingen on 13 November 1928. DtBilnd (2); DtBiJ, 10 (1928), pp. 154-57; EncJud²; Fück; Hanisch; JüdLex; NDB; Schwarz; *Wer ist's*, 1909-1928

Liebermann, Samuel S., born 6 August 1947, he was in 1972 a Ph.D. candidate in economics at Harvard University. His writings include *An Economic approach to differential demographic behaviour in Turkey* (1979), *Prospects for development and population growth in Iran* (1979), and he was a joint author of *An Econometric model of differential fertility in Iran* (1974), and *India; poverty, employment, and social services* (Washington, D.C., World Bank, 1990). LC; Note about the author

Liebeschütz, Hans, born 3 December 1893 at Hamburg, he studied at Lehranstalt für die Wissenschaft des Judentums, Berlin, and the universities of Berlin, and Heidelberg, where he received a Dr.phil. in 1920 for *Die Beziehungen Kaiser Friedrichs II. zu England seit dem Jahre 1235*. He then taught at secondary schools until 1929 when he was appointed a lecturer in medieval philosophy at the Universität Hamburg. Dismissed for political reasons in 1934, he became active in Jewish adult education. In 1936, he became a lecturer at the Lehranstalt für die Wissenschaft des Judentums, Berlin. He subsequently was arrested and sent to the concentration camp in Sachsenhausen but was able to escape in 1939 to Britain, and for the remainder of the war taught Latin at a school; from 1946 to 1960 he taught at the University of Liverpool. His writings include *Synagoge und Ecclesia im Mittelalter* (1983). He died in Liverpool on 18 October 1978. BioHbDtE; ConAu, 85-88; DtBE; Kürschner, 1928/29-1935; WhoWorJ, 1965

Liebesny, Herbert Joseph, born 6 March 1911 at Wien, he completed his law in 1935 at the Universität Wien with a Dr.jur. In 1939, he emigrated to the United States where he first lectured in colonial and African law and later served as a research analyst at the Office of Strategic Services, and the Department of State, Washington, D.C. From 1955 to his retirement he served in various capacities in the National Law Center, George Washington University. His writings include *The Government of French North Africa* (1943), *Materials on comparative law* (1974), *Law of the Near and Middle East* (1975), and *Foreign legal systems* (1981). BioHbDtE; DrAS, 1969 P, 1974 P, 1978 P, 1982 P; MESA Roster of members, 1977-1982; WhoAmL, 1978, 1979 (not sighted); WhoGov, 1972 (not sighted)

Liebrecht, Felix, born 13 March 1812 at Namslau, Silesia, he studied philology at the universitites of Breslau, München, and Berlin without taking a degree. He married at an early age and eked out his living by private teaching, concurrently reading immensely, and job-translating. It was only through the good offices of Alexander von Humboldt that he finally obtained a first teaching position in 1849 at the Collège communale in Liège, followed by a second one some years later at the Athénée royale, Liège, a position which he held until his retirement in 1867. Although best remembered as a writer on mythology and folklore, he purposely is limited his work to the collection of source material without analytical pretension. His writings include *Zur Volkskunde; alte und neue Aufsätze* (1879). He died in St. Hubert on 3 August 1890. ADtB, vol. 51; BiD&SB; DtBiInd (2); EncJud²; Wininger

Liechti-Stucki, Anneliese A. E., born 13 April 1944 at Bern, Switzerland, she was an anthropologist. MESA Roster of members, 1990; Schoeberlein

Lieder, Johann Rudolph Theophilus, born in 1797 at Erfurt, Germany, he started in 1825 to work as a missionary under the Church Missionary Society in Cairo, mainly among the Copts. He was permitted to distribute Protestant literature, and to preach in Coptic churches and even in the monasteries. He founded a training school for boys in Cairo, which gradually developed under his care into a theological institution for training priests for the Coptic Church. He laboured in Egypt unwearingly for thirty-five years, in face of many disappointments. He conducted services also for British residents and tourists in Cairo. He died from cholera in Cairo on 6 July 1865. His paper squeezes of monuments made in Egypt, 1850-53, are in the Archive of the Griffith Institute, Ashmolean Museum, Oxford. Dawson; Egyptology; Kornrumpf

Liedtke, Wolfgang, born 20th cent., he was an ethnographer whose writings include *Bibliographie deutschsprachiger Literatur zur Ethnographie und Geschichte der Ovambo, Nordnamibia, 1840-1915* (1986), *Samoa, 1880-1914; Bibliographie deutschsprachiger kolonialer Literatur zu Quellen der Ethnologie und Geschichte* (Dresden, Staatliches Museum für Völkerkunde Dresden, 1999), and he was a joint author of *Bibliographie deutschsprachiger Literatur zur Ethnographie und Geschichte der Ewe in Togo und Südostghana, 1840-1914* (1990). zKO

Liemen, Erhard, born in 1950, he obtained a Dr.jur. His writings on the legal aspects of international oil concessions include *Erdöl-Produktionsverträge des Iran; Rechtsgrundlagen und Praxis der Zusammen-arbeit mit transnationalen Unternehmen*. zKO

Lienau, Cay, born 3 July 1937 at Münster, Germany, he studied geography and completed his formal study with two doctorates. He served as a professor of human geography of the Balkans at the Universität Münster until his retirement in 2002. His writings include *Bevölkerungsabwanderung, demographische Struktur und Landwirtschaftsform im West-Peloponnes* (1976), *Malawi; Geographie eines unter-entwickelten Landes* (1981), and *Griechenland; Geographie eines Staates der europäischen Süd-peripherie* (1989). Kürschner, 1980-2005

Lienhardt, Peter Arnold, he was born on 12 March 1928 at Bradford, Yorks., England. After gaining an Open Scholarship in English at Downing College, Cambridge, he read English and the Arabic and Persian. After his military service he completed his B.Litt. in 1953 at Oxford with a thesis on *The northern Arabs; an account of the social and political organisation of some nomad and settled communities of northern Arabia and Greater Syria*. With the award of a Treasury Senior Studentship, he carried out his first intensive anthropological field-work in the Trucial States and Kuwait from 1953 until 1956. After his return to England he completed his D.Phil. thesis in 1957 on *The Shaykhdoms of Eastern Arabia*. In the same year he was appointed a senior research fellow in anthropology at the East African Institute for Social Research, Makerere, Uganda. On his return in 1960 he joined St. Antony's College, Oxford, where he served in various capacities as a teacher of Middle Eastern sociology until his death on 17 May 1986. He spoke Arabic, Swahili and Persian with fluency. His writings include *The Medicine man; Swifa ya Nguvumali, Hasani Bin Ismail* (1968). BRISMES bulletin, 13 (1986), pp. 131-33; Index Islamicus (1); Sluglett

Lieo Kai Lien, born 19th cent., he was a contributor to the *Chinese recorder*, and associated with a Christian mission in China. His trace is lost after a publication in 1918. Lodwick

van **Liere**, W. J., born 20th cent., his writings include *Report to the Government of Syria on the classification and rational utilization of soils* (Rome, Food and Agriculture Organization, 1965). NUC

Lieser, Peter, born 30 March 1938 at Hamburg, Germany, he left high school after grade ten and became an apprentice ship mechanic with a view to a career in the merchant marine. He later graduated at Hamburg as a ship's engineer. Since 1965 he studied political science and received a doctorate in 1976 from the Universität Hamburg for a thesis on the interdependence of German oil imports and Middle East policy entitled *Die Bedeutung der Ölimportabhängigkeit für die Nahost-Politik der Bundesrepublik Deutsch-land*. Note; Thesis

Lietzmann (Λιτσμαν), Hans, born 3 March 1875 at Düsseldorf, Germany, he completed his study of theology and classical philology at the universities of Jena and Bonn. After extensive research in European libraries, he took a Dr.habil. in ecclesiastic history in 1900 at the Universität Bonn and subsequently served as a professor at Jena until 1924 when he succeeded to Adolf von Harnack at the Universität Berlin. Elected a member of the Prussian Akademie der Wissenschaften in 1929, he was the leading patristic scholar in Germany. A member of the *Bekennende Kirche* since 1934, he was an active supporter of a university reform after Hitler. His writings include *Der Menschensohn; ein Beitrag zur neu-testamentlichen Theologie* (1896), and *Geschichte der alten Kirche* (1932-44). He died in Locarno on 25 June 1942. DtBE; Megali, vol. 16 (1931)

Lièvre, Daniel, born 19th cent., he was a *sous-commissaire* in the French merchant marine. His writings include *Les Volcans du Japaon* (Paris, 1890), and its translation, *I vulcani del Giappone* (Milano, 1900). His trace is lost after an article in 1908 in the *Bulletin* of the Sociéte de géographie commerciale du Havre. BN; NUC, pre-1956

Lifanov, Nikolaï Vasil'evich, born 26 September 1925 at Moscow, he graduated in 1954 from the Moscow Oriental Institute, and received his first degree in 1970 for Основные вопросы экономики развития современного Либана. From 1960 to his death he was associated with the Oriental Institute, Soviet Academy of Sciences. His writings include Ливан (1966). He died on 7 February 1987. Miliband[2]

Lifchitz (Lifshitz), Boris, 1895-1984 *see* Souvarina, Boris

Liger-Belair, Jean Bernard, born 20th cent., he received a doctorate in philosophy in 1989 from the Université de Paris for *Le corps, ontophanie du sujet*. His writings include *L'Ombre nécessaire; phénoménologie du corps* (1990), *Le Garçon qui disait suis moi* (1999), and *La Baisse tendancielle du taux de plaisir* (2002). Livres disponibles, 2004

Ligeti, Lajos (Louis), born 28 October 1902 at Balassagyarmat, Hungary, he studied at the University of Budapest, the Sorbonne and the Collège de France, Paris. He travelled widely in Central Asia before the war. Since 1931 he was associated in various capacities with the Budapest Oriental Institute. His writings include *Rapport préliminaire d'un voyage d'exploration fait en Mongolie chinoise, 1928-1931* (1933), *Afgán földön* (1938), *Catalogue du Kanjur mongol imprimé* (1942-44), he was a joint author of *Az magyar nyelv török kapcsolatai és körülöttük van* (1977), and he edited *Mongolian studies* (1970), and *Histoire secrète des Mongoles* (1971). Because he was a giant in Altaic studies, "no one will probably dare to note that, all in all, he was not a man easy to get on with, that he had little sense of humor and a great sense of his own importance. Yet he has always recognized something that was, in his eyes, much more important than his own person, something he has tried to serve with unswerving devotion probably throughout all his adult life: pure, unadulterated, honest scholarship." He died in Budapest on 24 May 1987. IntWW, 1974/75-1983; Magyar; MEL, 1978-1991; *Ural-Altaische Jahrbücher*, 60 (1988), pp. 195-196, 198-199; WhoSocC, 1979; WhoSoCE, 1989; WhoWor, 1974/75, 1976/77

Light, Sir Henry, born in 1782, he was an English army officer who, while serving with his regiment in Malta, obtained leave to explore Egypt, Nubia, and Palestine in 1814. His writings include *Travels in Egypt, Nubia, Holy Land, Mount Lebanon, and Cyprus in the year 1814* (1818), parts of which were published in a German translation in German periodicals in 1819 and 1820. He died in 1870. Dawson; Egyptology; Henze; Sezgin

Lightbown, Ronald William, born 2 June 1932 at Darwen, Lancs., England, he was a Latin scholar and a Cambridge graduate. He was in various capacities associated with the Victoria and Albert Museum, London, and since 1976 also a keeper of its Library. His writings include *Catalogue of Scandinavian and Baltic silver; Victoria and Albert Museum* (1975), *Donatello and Michelozzo* (1980), *Mediaeval European jewellery* (1992), and he was a joint author of *India observed* (1982). ConAu, 104; Who's who, 1982-2005

Lightner, Theodore McGraw, born 5 September 1934 at N.Y.C., he received a Ph.D. in 1965 from the Massachusetts Iinstitue of Technology for *Segmental phonology of modern standard Russian*. He was a professor of linguistics, particularly Slavic languages, at the universities of Illinois, Texas, and Paris. His writings include *Problems in the theory of phonology* (1972), and *Introduction to English derivational morphology* (1983). DrAS, 1969 F, 1974 F, 1978 F, 1982 F

Lighton, G., fl. 1936 at Timperley, Cheshire, England, he reveived an M.A. in 1935 from Manchester University for *The advance of Islam in western and central Sudan*. He was a contributor to the *Moslem world*. Note; Sluglett

Likhachëv, Dmitriĭ Sergeevich, born in 1906 he was a literary historian and a champion of the preservation of ancient monuments. He had a chekered career until the fall of the Soviet system. His writings include Культура Руси эпохи образования русского национального государства (1946). He died in St. Petersburg on 30 September 1999. BiDSovU; ConAu, 186; HanRL; IntWW, 1974/75-2000; WhoSocC, 1978; WhoWor, 1987-1997

Likhachëv, Nikolai Petrovich, born in 1862, he graduated in 1894 from Kazan University, and in 1892 he was appointed a professor in the Institute of Archaeology, St. Petersburg. His writings include Палеографическое значеніе бумажных водяныхзнаков (1899), *Russische Literatur und europäische Kultur des 10.-17. Jahrhunderts* (1977), and *Reflections on Russia* (1991). He died in 1936. BiD&SB; Egyptology; TatarES

Liley, Arthur V., born 19th cent., he was a British missionary of the North Africa Mission. He first sailed for Africa in 1882 and began work among the Muslims of Tunis in 1897. He died from heart failure on 24 June 1928 at Westcliff-on-Sea, England, the day following his arrival from Tunis for medical treatment. Note

Lilienthal, Alfred Morton, born 15 December 1913 at N.Y.C., he graduated from Cornell University, Ithaca, N.Y., and Columbia Law School, New York. He served in the Middle East with the State Department before the war as well as after a tour of duty in the U.S.Army. He practised law in Washington, D.C., and worked as a lecturer on foreign affairs. He was an accredited journalist to the U.N.O., and an editor and publisher of *Middle East perspective*. He frequently visited the Middle East. His writings include *What price Israel* (1953), *There goes the Middle East* (1957), *The Other side of the coin* (1965), and *Zionist connection - what price peace* (1978). ConAu, 37-40; IntAu&W, 1989-1997/98; Note; WhoAm, 1974-2003; WhoWor, 1974/75

Lilienthal, David Eli, bon 3 July 1899 at Morton, Ill., he was a founding director, and later chairman, of the Tennessee Valley Authority. His writings include *The TVA; an experiment in the "grass roots" administration of federal functions* (1939), *Big business; a new era* (1953), both of which have been translated into German, and *The Journals of David E. Lilienthal* (1964-71). He died in N.Y.C. on 14 January 1981. CnDiAmJBi; CurBio, 1944, 1981; IntWW, 1974/75-1980; Master (25); WhAm, 7; *Who was who*, 8; WhoWorJ, 1965, 1972, 1978

Lille, Odette, fl. 20th cent., she was a joint author of *Bibliographie marocaine, 1938-1951* (1955), and a contributor to the journal *Hespéris*. NUC, 1956-67

Lillo Alemany, Mercedes, born 20th cent., she was a *licenciada en filología y letras*, sección de historia, with special reference to Islamic art. She was in 1992 chief of the Sección de Becas in the Instituto de Cooperación con el Mundo Arabe, Madrid. Arabismo, 1992

Lilly, William Samuel, born in 1840 at Fifehead, Dorsetshire, England, he was eduacted at Peterhouse, Cambridge, and in 1862 entered the Madras Civil Service. He served as under-secretary to the Madras Government until he retired in 1872. He was a controversial writer, championing the Catholic point of view. His writings include *A Manual of the law, especially affecting Catholics* (1893), and *Christianity and the modern civilization* (1903). He died in 1919. BiD&SB; BritInd (4); Buckland; IndianBiInd (2); Master (4); *Who was who*, 2

Limbert, John William, born 10 March 1943 at Washington, D.C., he graduated in 1964 from Harvard University, where he also received his Ph.D. in 1974 for *Shiraz in the age of Hafez*. He taught English, first with the U.S. Peace Corps at Sanandaj, and later at Shiraz University before entering the U.S. Consular Service. His writings include *Iran at war with history* (1986). Master (2); *MESA Roster of members*, 1990; WhoE, 1991/92

van **Limburg Brouwer**, J. J. fl. 1879, he was an Assistant Resident at Sumanap (Madura), Java. His important collection of books was auctioned at Utrecht from 19 to 26 May 1883 by J. L. Beijers Booksellers, who issued the sales catalogue, *Catalogus van eene belangrijke verzameling boeken nagelaten door J. J. van Limbrug Brouwer*. Note; ZKO

Limongelli, Dominique, born end of the 19th cent., he was an engineer resident in Cairo, and a member of the Société Fouad Ier d'économie politique, de statistique et de législation. He died before 1934. Note about the author

Linant de Bellefonds, Louis Maurice *Adolphe*, he was born on 23 November 1798 at Lorient (Morbihan), France. He spent a few years in the French Navy charting and surveying along the coast of North America before accompanying the Comte de Forbin on an expedition to various countries in the Near East and produce drawings and maps as illustrations for works of various writers. He arrived in Egypt in 1818 and spent the rest of his life in the service of the Egyptian Government, becoming Minister of Public Works in 1869, and Pasha in 1873. He was a brilliant draftsman and artist, and his collection of drawings are extremely valuable today, as many of the monuments recorded have since been destroyed or damaged. His papers are now in the Griffith Institute, Oxford. His writings include *Account of a journey into the oases of Upper Egypt* (1822), *Mémoires sur les principaux travaux d'utilité publique exécutés en Égypte* (1872-73), and *Journal d'un voyage à Méroé dans les années 1821 et 1822*, edited by Margaret Shinnie (1958). He died in Cairo on 19 July 1883. Egyptology; Henze; Hill, Goldschmidt; *Hommes et destins*, 4, pp. 470-475; Kornrumpf; Kornrumpf², vol. 2

Linant de Bellefonds, Yvon, born 27 August 1904 at Cairo, he received a doctorate in law in 1935 from the Faculté de droit de Paris for *Traité de droit musulman comparé*. He was successively associated with the Faculté de droit de l'Université Fouad Ier, and the Centre National de la Recherche Scientifique, Paris, as a *maître de recherche*. His writings include *Cours de procédure civile, 1952-53* (1953), and *Traité de droit musulman comparé* (Paris, 1965-73). Unesco; ZKO

Lincoln, Joseph Newhall, born in 1892, he received a Ph.D. in 1930 from Harvard University for *La Leyenda de Yuçuf; an Aljamiado text with transcription and study*. His other writings include *Charts of Brazilian literature* (1947). He died in 1945. NUC, pre-1956

Lindau, Hans Rudolf David, born 12 August 1875 at Berlin, he studied philology at the universities of Jena, and Leipzig where he received a Dr.phil. in 1899 for *Johann Gottlieb Fichtes Lehren von Staat und Gesellschaft in ihrem Verhältnis zum neuen Sozialismus*. His other writings include *Die Theodicee im 18. Jahrhundert* (1911). NUC, pre-1956; Thesis

Lindau, Paul, born 3 June 1839 at Magdeburg, Prussia, he studied liberal arts at the universities of Halle, Leipzig, and Paris. He was a periodical editor, parliamentary correspondent, literary critic, stage manager, publisher, and novelist. His writings include *Aus dem Orient; flüchtige Aufzeichnungen* (1890), *Zwei Reisen in die Türkei* (1899), and *An der Westküste Klein-Asiens; eine Sommerfahrt* (1900). He died in Berlin on 31 January 1919. BbD; BiD&SB; DtBE; DtBilnd (3); Master (3); NDB; OxGer, 1976, 1986, 1997; *Wer ist's*, 1909-1912

Lindau, Rudolf, born about 1800, he wrote *Die Walachei und Moldau in Hinsicht auf Geschichte, Landesbeschaffenheit, Verfassung, gesellschaftkichen Zustand und Sitten der Bewohner, nach den besten Quellen bearbeitet* (Leipzig, 1829). GV; NUC, pre-1956

Lindau, Rudolf, born 10 October 1829 at Gardelegen (Altmark), Germany, he studied philology at the universities of Berlin, Gießen, Paris, Montpellier, becoming a private teacher as well as private secretary in France. He collaborated with the publication of the *Nouvelle biographie générale* and the *Revue des deux mondes*. In 1859, he represented Swiss economic interests in Japan, became consul-general and established the *Japan Times* and *Japan Punch*. As a correspondent to the Paris *Journal des débats*, he visited East Asia and California. In 1871, he began a career with the German diplomatic service in Paris. From 1878 to his retirement in 1892, he was associated with the German foreign office in Berlin. He subsequently spent ten years in Constantinople. His writings include *Un voyage autour du Japon* (1864), *Aus Paris; Beiträge zur Charakteristik des gegenwärtigen Frankreichs* (1865), *Erzählungen eines Efendi* (1896), *Türkische Geschichte* (1897), and *Morgenland und Abendland* (1917). He died in Paris on 14 October 1910. BiD&SB; DtBE; DtBilnd (8); Kornrumpf; NDB; *Wer ist's*, 1909

Lindau, Wilhelm Adolf, born 24 May 1774 at Düsseldorf, Germany, he studied law at the universities of Jena and Göttingen and subsequently articled at Wetzlar and Regensburg. From 1806 to 1815 he served as a police official in Dresden. He spent some years collaborating with Brockhaus publishers, Leipzig, in the production of an encyclopaedia, before retiring to Dresden and embarking on a career as novelist and translator, publishing under the pseudonyms Junius Lätus, Rudolf Wald, and Josef Aldoni. His writings include *Darstellung der Ereignisse in Dresden im Jahre 1813* (1816). He died in Dresden on 1 June 1849. DtBE

Lindauer, Gerhard, born about 1940, he wrote on urbanization of rural environments including *Beiträge zur Erfassung der Verstädterung in ländlichen Räumen* (1970), a work which was originally submitted as a doctoral thesis at Stuttgart. Note about the author

Lindbeck, George Arthur, born 10 March 1923 at Loyang Honan, China, he graduated B.A. in 1943 from Gustavus Adolphus College, Minnesota, and B.D. in 1946 from Yale University, New Haven, Conn., where he also received his Ph.D. in 1955. Since 1967 he was a professor of theology at Yale University. His writings include *The Future of Roman Catholic theology; Vatican II* (1970), *Infallibility* (1972), *University divinity schools* (1976), *The Nature of doctrine* (1984), and he edited *Dialogue on the way* (1965), and its translations, *Dialog unterwegs* (1965), *El dialogo esta abierto* (1965), and *Le Dialogue est ouvert; le Concil vu par les observateurs luthériens* (1965-67). DrAS, 1969 P, 1974 P, 1978 P, 1982 P; WhoAm, 1974-1976/77

Lindberg, David Charles, born 15 November 1935 at Minneapolis, Minn., he wa a graduate of Wheaton College and Northwestern University and received his Ph.D. from Indiana University. Since 1965 he was a professor of history, particularly history of science, at the University of Wisconsin at Madison. His writings include *The Perspectiva communis of John Peckham* (1965), *A Catalogue of medieval and renaissance optical manuscripts* (1975), *Theories of vision from al-Kindi to Kepler* (1976), *Roger Bacon's philosophy of nature* (1983), and he edited *John Peckham and the science of optics* (1970). A selection of his articles was published in 1983. ConAu, 69-72, new rev., 11; WhoMW, 1984/85, 1986/87

Lindberg, John, born in 1901, he wrote *Food, famine, and relief, 1940-46* (Geneva, League of Nations, 1946), *A General ecomonic appraisal of Libya* (1952), *Foundations of social survival* (1953), and *Spelet om Arabien* (Stockholm, 1956). LC

Lindberg, Otto Emil, born 3 May 1850 at Kila, Sörmland, Sweden, he studied English and Hebrew at Uppsala Universitet and received his doctorate in 1894. Since 1898 he was a professor of Semitic languages at Göteborg. His writings include *Mohammed och Qoranen* (1897), and *Vergleichende Grammatik der semitischen Sprachen* (1897). He died in 1920. NUC, pre-1956; Vem är det, 1912; ZKO

Linde, Gerd, born in 1933, he received a Dr.phil. in 1962 from the Universität Münster for a thesis on German politics in Lithuania during the First World War entitled *Die deutsche Politik in Litauen im ersten Weltkrieg*, a work which was published in 1965. He became a staff member of a German federally financed institute located in Köln, for which he produced numerous brief studies in contemporary international affairs. These include *Exodus '72; zur Ausweisung der sowjetischen Militärberater aus Ägypten* (1972), *Saudi Arabien auf neuem Kurs?* (1979), *Das Viereck Moskau - Damaskus - Bagdad - Teheran und die Kräftekonstellation in Mittelost* (1980), *Gemäßigte Araber zwischen den Großmächten* (1982), *Andropov - Assad - Arafat* (1983), *Afghanistan, Iran und Camp David als Probleme sowjetischer Mittelostpolitik* (1984), *Der Faktor Afghanistan in den sowjetisch-pakistanischen Beziehungen* (1986), and *Krieg um Kuwait* (1991). GV; LC; ZKO

Lindemann, Hans, he was in 1937 a professor whose writings include *Islam im Aufbruch, in Abwehr und Angriff* (Leipzig, 1941). Note

Lindenbaum, Shirley, born in 1933, she obtained a Ph.D. and became a professor of anthropology at the Graduate Faculty, New School for Social Science, N.Y.C., a position which she still held in 1990. From 1963 to 1965 she conducted field-work in East Pakistan. Her writings include *The Social and economic status of women in Bangladesh* (1974), and *Women in Bangladesh* (1976). NatFacDr, 1990

Linder, Sven Vilhelm, born 31 December 1887 at Längjum, Skaraborg, Sweden, he received a doctorate in 1922 from Uppsala Universitet for *Sauls Gibea*. He became a professor at his alma mater. His writings include *Studier till Gamla Testamentets föreställingen om Anden* (1926), *Kring språkdräkten i Gustav Vasas bibel* (1941), and *Palästinische Volksgesänge; aus dem Nachlaß herausgegeben von Helmer Ringgren* (Uppsala, 1952-55). He died on 2 August 1947. Vem är det, 1914-1949

Linder-Welin, Ulla S., 1909-1983 see Welin, Ulla S. née Linder

Lindgren, Uta, born 2 March 1941 at Chemnitz, Germany, she was a professor of medieval social history, particularly history of science, successively at the universities of Köln, München, and Bayreuth. She received a Dr.habil. in 1978 from the Universität Köln for *Bedürftigkeit, Armut, Not; Studien zur mittelalterlichen Sozialgeschichte Barcelonas*. Her writings include *Gerbert von Aurillac und das Quadrivium* (1976), *Naturwissenschaft und Technik im Barock* (1997), and the translation, *Clavijos Reise nach Samarkand, 1403-1406* (1993). Kürschner, 1992-2005; ZKO

Lindholm, Charles Thomas, born 18 December 1946 at Mankato, Minn., he was a graduate of Barnard College, New York, and obtained a Ph.D. He was a professor of anthropology successively at Columbia, Harvard, and Boston universities. His writings include *Generosity and jealousy; the Swat Pukhtun* (1982), and he was a joint author of *Is America breaking apart?* (1982). ConAu, 134; Schoeberlein; WhoE, 1993/94; WrDr, 1994/96-1998/2000

Lindisfarne-Tapper, Nancy Tapper née Starr Self, born 10 October 1944 at St. Louis, Mo., she graduated from Washington University, St. Louis, Mo., and received a M.Phil. in 1969 from the School of Oriental and African Stuides, London, with a thesis entitled *The role of women in selected pastoral Islamic societies* and also a Ph.D. in 1979 for *Marriage and social organisation among Durrani Pashtuns in northern Afghanistan*. She did field-work with Richard Tapper in Afghan Turkistan, 1970-72. She was in 1994 a lecturer in the anthropology of the Arab world at SOAS. Her writings include *Bartered brides; politics, gender, and marriage in an Afghan tribal society* (1991), and she was joint editor of *Dislocating masculinity; comparative ethnographies* (1993). ConAu 143; *MESA Roster of members*, 1990; Sluglett; SOAS, *1994 calendar*, WrDr, 1996/98-2005

Lindley, William Ralston, born 14 April 1923 at Portland, Ore., he was a 1955 graduate of the University of Oregon and received his Ph.D. in 1970 from the University of Washington at Seattle for *Approaches of selected American universities to the education of journalists*. He was a Fulbright visiting professor of journalism at Baghdad University, 1964-65, and since 1967 a professor of journalism at Idaho State University, Pocatello. His writings include *20th century American news-papers in content and production* (1993). AmM&WSc, 1973 S, 1978 S; WhoWest, 1974/75, 1976/77

Lindner, Jerzy, born 20th cent., his writings in economics include *Problemy uprzemysłowienia Algerii* (Warszawa, 1969), *Stosunski gospodarecze Francjiz byłymi krajami zależnymi w Afryce* (Warszawa, 1972), and he was a joint author of *Krótkoterminowe kredyty i rozrachunki* (Warszawa, 1953). NUC, 1968-1972; OSK

Lindner, Rudi Paul, born 17 July 1943 at Stockton, Calif., he was a 1965 graduate of Harvard College and received a Ph.D. in 1976 from the University of California at Berkeley for *Ottoman government and nomad society, 1261-1501*. Since 1977 he was a professor in the Department of History, University of Michigan at Ann Arbor, a position which he still held in 2005. His writings include *Nomads and Ottomans in medieval Anatolia* (1983). DrAS, 1982 H; NatFacDr, 1990-2005; Schoeberlein

Lindsay, Alexander William, Earl of Crawford, born 16 October 1812, he was educated at Eton and Cambridge, and "spent his life in studious pursuits, in the collection of a magnificent library, and in travel." He travelled in Nubia as far south as the second cataract in 1836 to 1837, a journey which he described in *Letters on Egypt, Edom, and the Holy Land* (1838). He died in Firenze on 13 December 1880. DNB; Egyptology; Hill; Kornrumpf; Kornrumpf², vol. 2

Lindsay, Kenneth Martin, born in 1897, he was educated at Worcester College, Oxford, and became a politician and M.P. He was active in the field of education and served as a visiting professor at many American universities. His writings include *Social progress and educational waste, being a study of the "free-placee" and scholarship system* (1926), *Eldorado, an agricultural settlement* (1931), *English education* (1941), *Towards a European parliament* (1958), its translation, *Ein Parlament für Europa* (1959), and *European assemblies* (1960). He died on 4 March 1991. Who, 1969-1991

Lindt, August(e) Rudolphe, born 5 August 1905 at Bern, Switzerland, he studied law at the universities of Genève and Bern, where he received a Dr.jur. in 1927 for *Das sowjetische Aktienrecht*. He became a journalist and a contributor to leading Swiss and German newspapers, covering the crises from Manchuria to Liberia that led up to the second World War. After demobilization in 1945, he was sent by his Government on a special political mission to London. After a brief service with the International Red Cross, he became, first a press attaché, and later a counsellor at the Swiss Legation, London. A staff member of UNICEF since 1948, he later served for four years as U.N. High Commissioner for Refugees. His writings include *Special correspondent; with bandit and general in Manchuria* (1933), *Im Sattel durch Mandschukuo* (1934). He died on 14 April 2000. CurBio, 1959; Facey Grant; IntWW, 1974/75-1994/95; Master (2); NSB; SchBiAr, 6 (1958); WhoAm, 1954/55-1958/59; Who's who, 1959-2000; WhoSwi, 1964/65-1998/99

Linehan, Edward J., fl. 20th cent., he was in 1961 a staff member of the *National geographic magazine*. His writings include *Norway, land of the generous sea* (Washington, D.C., National Geograhic Magazine, 1971). NUC, 1973-77

Ling, Dwight Leroy, born 9 October 1920 at Johnstown, Pa., he was a 1948 graduate of Pennsylvania State University and received a Ph.D. in 1965 from the University of Illinois at Urbana for *The French occupation and administration of Tunisia, 1881-1892*. He was since 1955 successively, and in various capacities, a professor at DePauw University, Greencastle, Ind., and Marietta College, Ohio. His writings include *Tunisia, from protectorate to republic* (1967), and *Morocco and Tunisia, a comparative history* (1979). ConAu, 21-24, new rev., 11; DrAS, 1969 H, 1974 H, 1978 H, 1982 H; LEduc, 1974 (not sighted); Selim; WhoAm, 1986-1996; WhoS&SW, 1978/79

Lings, Martin, born 24 January 1909 at Burnage, Lancs., England, he was an Oxford graduate in English, who subsequently taught at Cairo University until 1952. Took a B.A. and Ph.D. in Arabic at the

University of London for a thesis entitled *The Spiritual heritage and legacy of Shaikh Ahmad al-Alawi, a twentieth century Moslem mystic.* Since 1955 he was in charge of Arabic manuscripts in the Department of Oriental Printed Books and Manuscripts, British Library, London. From 1974 to 1976 he was a consultant to the World of Islam Festival Trust. His writings include *A Moslem saint of the twentieth century* (1961), *Sufis of Andalusia* (1971), *What is Sufism?* (1975), its translations, *Che cos'é if sufismo* (1978), *Qu'est-ce que le soufisme* (1977), *Was ist Sufismus?* (1985), *Quranic art of calligraphy and illumination* (1976), *Ancient beliefs* (1980), and he was a joint author of the *Third supplement catalogue of Arabic books in the British Library, 1958-69* (1976). ConAu, 57-60; IntAu&W, 1977, 1982; Note; Sluglett; Who, 1974-2005

Liniger, Jean, born 20th cent., his writings include *En toute subjectivité; cent ans de conquêtes démocratiques locales et régionales, 1880-1980* (1980). Livres disponibles, 2004

Liniger-Goumaz, Max, born in 1930, he received degrees in geography, social sciences, and a doctorate in economics. He was an authority in Equatorial African matters and a Unesco expert. His writings include *Réflexions sur antiféminisme suisse* (1959), *La Suisse, sa neutralité et l'Europe* (1964), *Pygmées et autres races de petite taille* (1968), *Villes et problèmes urbains de la République démocratique du Congo* (1968), *L'Eurafrique* (1972), *Historical dictionary of Equatorial Guinea* (1979), *ONU et dictatures* (1984), and *À l'aune de la Guinée équatoriale* (2003). In 2001 he was honoured by *Mélanges euro-africains offerts au professeur Max Liniger-Goumaz.* AfrBioInd (1); Livres disponibles, 2004

Linke, Lilo, born in 1906 at Berlin, she emigrated in the 1930s, and after the war served as a consultant to Unesco on Latin American affairs. Her writings include *Restless flags; a German girl's autobiography* (1935), *Allah dethroned; a journey through modern Turkey* (1937), *Andean adventure* (1945), and *Ecuador, country of constrasts* (1954). NUC, pre-1956; WhE&EA

Linke, Max, born about 1935, he studied geography at the Universität Halle an der Saale, where he also received his two doctorates in geography. He was a professor of history of geography at his alma mater. He probably lost his tenure after the reunification of Germany. His writings include the booklet, *Ritters Leben und Werk; ein Leben für die Geographie* (Halle an der Saale, 2000). Kürschner, 1992

Linton, James Henry, born in 1879 at Hawick, Scotland, he was educated at the Church Missionary College, London, and St. John's College, Durham. He spent two years with the Church Missionary Society in Yoruba, West Africa, before joining the Persian Mission in 1908, being successively stationed at Isfahan and Shiraz. From 1919 to 1935 he served as Bishop of Persia. His writings include *Persian sketches* (1923). He died in 1958. Birmingham Post year book and who's who, 1949; WhE&EA; Who was who, 5

Linz, Storch de Gracia, Juan José, born 24 December 1926 at Bonn, Germany, he was educated at Madrid and gained a Ph.D. in 1959 from Columbia University, New York, for *The social bases of West German politics.* He taught successively at his alma mater and Yale University, New Haven, Conn., where he was, in 1991, Sterling Professor of Political and Social Sciences. His writings include *El sistema de partidos en España* (1976), *Atlas electoral del País Vasco y Navarra* (1981), *Totalitäre und autoritäre Regime* (2000), and he was a joint author of *Problems of democratic transition and consolidation* (1996), *Sultanistic regimes* (1998), and *Political parties; old concepts and new challenges* (2002). AmM&WSc, 1973 S, 1978 S; ZKO

Lipets, Rakhil Solomovna, born in 1910, her writings include Рыбный Мурман (1933), Эпос и Древняя Русь (1969), Этническая история и фольклор (1977), Из истории русской сов. фольклористики (1981), Фольклор и историческая этнография (1983), and Образы батыра и его коня в тюрко-монгольском эпосе(1984). LC; OSK

Lipinskaia, Viktoriia Anatol'evna, born 20th cent., her writings on the material culture of Central Asia include Русское население Алтайского края; народные традиции в материальной культуре, XVIII-XX вв. (1987), Старообрядцы в Румынии; русские писатели о липованах (1994), and Старожилы и переселенцы; русские на Алтае, XVIII - начало XX века (1996). OSK

Lipiński, Edward, born 18 June 1930 at Łódź, Poland, he grew up in Belgium and graduated in 1950 from the Collège de Saint-Trond (Sint-Truiden). He studied Oriental languages and received a doctorate in 1960 from the Université catholique de Louvain. His writings include *Studies in Aramaic inscriptions and onomastics* (1975-94), and *Itineraria Phoenicia* (2004); he was general editor of the *Dictionnaire de la civilisation phénicienne et punique* (1992). WhoWorJ, 1972, 1978

Lipp, Vilmos (Wilhelm), born 11 December 1835 at Pest, Hungary, he studied theology and was ordained in 1868. After gaining a teacher's certificate for Latin, Greek, and German in 1878 from Pest University, he also obtained a Dr.phil. in 1878. He was since 1880 a principal of the Prämonstratenser-Gymnasium in Keszthely. He pursued an interest in archaeology and conducted excavations of local burial sites from the time of the Barbarian invasion as well as the Avar period. His writings include *Die Gräberfelder von Keszthely* (1885). He died in Keszthely on 3 January 1888. GeistigeUng; Magyar; ÖBL

Lippert, Julius, born 9 September 1866 at Stannaitschen, East Prussia, he went to school in Gumbinnen and studied classical and Oriental languages at the Universität Berlin, where he was a student of Eduard Sachau. He received his Dr.phil. in 1891 from the Universität Halle for *De epistula pseudoaristotelica περι βασιλείας*, and subsequently entered the royal library at Berlin. In 1897 he spent nine months in Tunisia and Cyrenaica studying Hausa. Upon his return to Berlin in the same year, he became a lecturer in West African geography and Hausa, Ful and Ewe at the Seminar für Orientalische Sprachen, Berlin. He was a joint translator of *Die Augenkunde des Ibn Sina* (1902), and, based on the preliminaries of August Müller, he edited *Ibn al-Qiftī's Ta'rīḫ al-hukamā'* (1903). He died on 29 June 1911. DÖS; Fück, 315; Hanisch; LexAfrika; Sezgin; Thesis

Lippich von Lindburg, Friedrich, born in 1834 at Laibach (Ljubljana), Austria-Hungary, he graduated from the Orientalische Akademie, Wien, and subsequently served for twenty-four years in Albania, first at Prizren and since 1878 at Scutary (Shkodër) as a consul-general, becoming an expert in local affairs. His reports on developments, particularly popular resistance to the implementations of the resolutions of the Berlin Congress, are contained in government documents of the Austrian foreign office. He died in Wien on 3 July 1888. Kornrumpf; Kornrumpf, N; ÖBL

von **Lippmann**, Edmund Oskar, born 9 January 1857 at Wien, he studied at Technische Hochschule Zürich and the Universität Heidelberg, where he received a Dr.phil. in 1878. He subsequently was a business executive in the sugar industry until ill-health obliged him to resign in 1925. Until 1933 he continued as a lecturer in history of chemistry at the Universität Halle. His writings include *Zur Geschichte des Schießpulvers und der älteren Feuerwaffen* (1899), *Entstehung und Ausbreitung der Alchemie* (1919), and *Beiträge zur Geschichte der Naturwissenschaften und der Technik* (1923-53). He died in Halle an der Saale on 24 September 1940. Bioln, 1; DtBE; Kürschner, 1925-1935; Master (1); ÖBL; Wer ist's, 1905-1935; Wininger

Lipset, Seymour Martin, born 18 March 1922 at N.Y.C., he graduated in 1943 from the City College of New York, and received his Ph.D. in 1949 from Columbia University, New York. He began his university teaching career in 1946 at the University of Toronto and after many appointments ended it at retirement in 1992 at Stanford University, Palo Alto, Cal., as Caroline S. G. Munro Professor of political science and sociology. His writings include *Agrarian socialism* (1950), *Political man* (1960), *The Confidence gap* (1983), and *Consensus and conflict; essays in political sociology* (1985). On his seventieth birthday he was honoured by two separate jubilee volumes, *Comparative perspectives on democracy* (1992), and *Reexamining democracy* (1992). AmM&WSc, 1973 S, 1978 S; Au&Wr, 1963; ConAu, 1-4, new rev., 1, 69, 106; IntWW, 1989-2005; Master (20); WhoAm, 1974-2002|; WhoWest, 1992/93, 1994/95; WhoWor, 1974/75; WhoWor, 1974/75; WhoWorJ, 1965; WrDr, 1976/78-2005

Lipshits, Flena Ėmmanuilovna, born 20th cent., she was a Byzantine scholar whose writings include, *Byzanz und die Slaven* (1951), *Очерки истории византийского общества и культуры VIII - первая половины IX века* (1961), *Право и суд в Византии в IV-VIII вв.* (1976), *Законодательство и юриспруденция в Византии и IX-XI вв.; историко-юридические этюды* (1981), and *Византийский земледельческий закон* (1984). LC; OSK

Lipsker, Erika, called Zarden, 1909- *see* Spivakovsky, Erika Lipsker called Zarden

Lipskiǐ (Lipsky), Vladimir Ippolitovich, born in 1863, he was a director of the Botanical Gardens in Odessa. His writings include *Горная Бухара; результаты трехлетних путешествий в Среднюю Азию в 1896 и 1899 году* (1902), *Florae Asiae mediae seu Turkestaniae rossicae inclusis chanatis Buchara et Chiwa* (1902-1905), and *Labiatae altaicae novae* (1905). He died in 1937. GSE; NUC; OSK

Lipstein, Kurt, born 19 March 1909 at Frankfurt am Main, Germany, he studied law at Grenoble and Berlin and subsequently entered the German judicial service, later also called to the bar from the Middle Temple. From 1946 to 1976 he taught at Cambridge University. He was a fellow of Clare College, Cambridge. His writings include *Le Système romaniste comparé avec le système de la common law* (1958), *The Law of the European Economic Community* (1974), and he edited *Private international law* (1972). BioHbDtE; ConAu, 117; Who's who, 1974-2005; WrDr, 1976/78-1996/98

Lipták, Pál, born 14 April 1914 at Békéscaba, Hungary, he was a professor of anthropology at Szeged University. His writings include *A magyar gyógyszerésztudományi Társaság értesítője* (1930), *Embertan és emberszármazástan* (1969), *Das bronzezeitliche Gräberfeld bei Pápé* (1975), and *Avars and ancient Hungarians* (1983). Biograf, 2004; OSK; WhoSoCE, 1989

Lirola Delgado, Jorge, born 20th cent., he received a doctorate in Semitic languages, particularly Arabic, and subsequently taught in the Departamento de Estudios Árabes e Islámicos, Universidad de

Almería. His writings include *El poder naval de al-Andalus* (1993), and he edited the *Enciclopedia de al-Andalus* (2002). Arabismo, 1992, 1994, 1997; ZKO

Lirola Delgado, Pilar, born 20th cent., she received a doctorate in Semitic philology and became a professor at the Facultad de Filosofía y Letras in the Universidad de Cádiz. Her writings include *Aproximación al teatro egicio moderno* (1990). Arabismo, 1994, 1997

Lisbonne, Jean, born 9 June 1912 at Paris, he went to school at the École alsasienne, Paris, and studied at the Facultés de droit et des lettres de Paris. He obtained a doctorate in law and a diploma at the École libres des sciences politiques. He practised law from 1933 to 1999. He subsequently served as an honorary barrister in the Cour d'appel de Paris, as well as a legal counsel to the Ministère des affaires étrangères. From 1984 to 1988 he was a president of the International Law Association. He died on 14 February 2004. WhoFr, 1977/78-2004

Lisev, Strasmir, fl. 20th cent., his writings on the history of feudalism in Bulgaria include *За стоковото производство във феодална България* (1957), *За проникването и ролята на парите във феодална България* (1958), *За генезиса на феодализма в България* (1963), and *История на България* (1982). OSK

Lisitsyna (Масюкоав), Irina Viktorovna, born 18 June 1951 at Moscow, she graduated in 1973 from the Moscow Regional Pedagogical Institute and received her first degree in 1983 for *Компартия Израиля в борьбе за политическое урегулирование арабо-израильских конфликта 1967 - начало 80-х гг.* Since 1973 she was associated with the Oriental Institute, Soviet Academy of Sciences. Her writings include *Коммунистическая партия Израиля в борьбе против политики сионистск. партий* (1987). Miliband²

Lisovskaia, Nonna Aleksandrovna, born 16 August 1919 at Petrovsk-Port, she received her first degree in 1962 for *Условный период в современном азербайджанском литературном языке в сопоставлении с другими языками юго-западной группы.* Since 1963 she was associated with the Oriental Institute, Soviet Academy of Sciences. Miliband; Miliband²

Lisowski, Jerzy, born 10 April 1928 at Epinay-sur-Seine, France, he was educated at the Lycée in Villard de Lans (Isère) and studied Romance and Polish philology at the Université de Lille, obtaining degrees in 1948 and 1949. A member of the French Communist Party, he emigrated in 1950 to Poland, where he became a translator, literary critic, and editor of literary periodicals. He edited *Antologia poezji francuskiej* (1967-68), and he was a joint author of *Poezje wybrane* (1967). KtoPolsce, 1993, 2001; OSK; WhoSoCE, 1989

Lissauer, Abraham, born 29 August 1832 at Berent (Kościerzyna), Prussia, he studied medicine at the universities of Berlin and Wien. He received his Dr.med. in 1856 from the Universität Berlin for *De digitalis in pulsum efficacitate in pneunomia.* He subsequently practised his profession in Danzig until 1892 when he accepted an appointment at the Anthropologische Gesellschaft, Berlin, as an anthropologist, ethnog-rapher, keeper, and librarian. His writings on pre-historic remnants in eastern Prussia and adjacent regions include *Neue Beiträge zur pommerellischen Urgeschichte* (1873), *Führer durch die anthropologische Sammlung der naturforschenden Gesellschaft in Danzig* (1874), and *Die prähistorischen Denkmäler der Provinz Westpreußen und der angrenzenden Gebiete* (1887). He died in 1908. DtBE; DtBilnd (3); Sigilla; *Wer ist's*, 1909; Wininger

Lissé, Pierre, fl. 20th cent., he was a joint author of *Les Poitiers de Nabeul; étude de sociologie tunisienne* (Tunis, 1967). NUC, pre-1956

Lissitzyn, Oliver James, born 21 March 1912 at Moscow, he was a 1933 graduate of Columbia University, New York, where he also gained a LL.B. in 1935, and a Ph.D. in 1942 from Columbia University, New York, for *International air transport and international policy.* After his bar admission in 1936 he practised his profession in N.Y.C. From 1946 to his retirement in 1980 he was a professor of international law and diplomacy at his alma mater. His writings include *The International Court of Justice; its role* (1951), *International law in a divided world* (1963), *International law today and tomorrow* (1965), and he was a joint author of *Creation of rights of sovereignty trough symboblic acts, 1400-1800* (1938). He died in 1994. DrAS, 1969 P, 1974 P, 1978 P, 1982 P; ConAu, 45-48; WhoAm, 1974-1980

Lissner, Will, born 11 November 1908 at New York, he was educated successively at Rand School of Social Science, and New School of Social Research, New York. He was associated with *Yorkville spirit* and *Harlem press* before joining the *New York Times*, where he spent fifty-three years. From 1953 to 1970 he taught business economics at the New School of Social Research. He was the editor of numerous monographs in the field. He died in Dunedin, Fla., on 25 March 2000. ConAu, 101, 189; WhoE, 1974/75-1981

Listfeld, Hans Guenther, born 23 November 1919 at Brandenburg, Germany, he graduated in 1956 from Loyola College, received his M.Lib.Sc. in 1960, and a Ph.D. in 1967 from the Catholic University of America for *Aristotle's astronomy and the principle of motion as expressed in the primer mover*. He was a librarian in Maryland. BiDrLUS, 1970; WhoLibS, 1966

Liszt, Franz Eduard, born 2 March 1851 at Wien, he studied law at the universities of Wien, Göttingen and Heidelberg, and received his Dr.habil. in 1879 at the Universität Graz. He subsequently was a professor of criminal law and justice at Gießen, Marburg, Halle and Berlin. He was a joint editor of *Zeitschrift für die gesamte Strafrechtswissenschaft*. He was in 1914 a founding editor of *Deutsche Strafrechts-Zeitung*. His writings include *Das deutsche Reichs-Presserecht* (1880), and *Das Völkerrecht* (1898). He died in Seeheim an der Bergstraße, Hesse, on 21 June 1919. BiDMoPL; DtBE; DiBilnd (4); Kosch; NDB; ÖBL; OxLaw; *Wer ist's*, 1909-1912

van der **Lith**, Pieter Antonie, born 31 May 1844 at Utrecht, the Netherlands, he received a doctorate in law from the local university in 1867 and in the following year passed the bar admission for the Dutch East Indies. On 1 October 1868 he was appointed a university teacher at the government institution (*Rijks-instelling*) for the education in East Indian languages, geography, and ethnology. Expected to teach also history, he handed over the latter subject to Pieter J. Veth in exchange for Islamic law. For this purpose he took up the study of Arabic under de Goeje. When the position was abolished in 1876, he became a professor of his subjects at Leiden University. In 1886, he became the director of a newly established institute for the training of Dutch East India officials. His writings include *Nederlandsch Oost-Indië* (1875), *Het doel en de methode der wetenschap van het koloniale recht* (1877); he was a joint author of *De staatsinstellingen van Nederlandsch-Indië* (1871); he edited the *Encyclopædie van Nederlandsch-Indië* (1897-1902); and he edited and translated into French the *K. 'Ajā'ib al-Hind*, from the Arabic of Buzurg ibn Shahriyār (1883-86). He died in Leiden on 17 March 1901. Fück, 214; NieuwNBW, vol. 8, cols., 1063-64

Lithgow, William, born about 1582, "he was in many ways the archetype of a Reformation Scotsman and, indeed, of subsequent generations of Scots who intrepidly explored so many unknown and little-known areas of the world. Combining a sturdy Protestantism with an intense intellectual curiosity, he had a fervent belief in the correctness of his own views linked with great physical stamina, both of which latter characteristics enabled him to survive first, the invariably contemptuous and at times violent treatment meted out to Christian unbelievers travelling through the Islamic lands, and second, the malevolence of the Spanish Inquisition when he fell into its hands in 1620." He visited the Balkans and the Near East. His writings include *The Totall discourse of the rare adventures & painfull peregrinations of long nineteene yeares travayles from Scotland of the most famous kingdomes in Europe, Asia and Affrica* (1906), a work which was first published in 1614, and in a Dutch translation in 1653. He died about 1645. C. E. Bosworth in *Bulletin of the John Rylands University Library*, 65, no. 2 (1983), pp. 8-36; BritInd (17); CasWL; DNB; Egyptology; EncBrit; EncicUni; GdeEnc; Master (7)

Litten, Wilhelm, born 5 August 1880 at St. Petersburg, Russia, he went to school in Italy and Germany, where he also studied law and Oriental languages at the Universität Berlin. He entered the German foreign service in 1902 and served as a consul in Constantinople, Tabriz, Bern, Libau, Latvia, Baghdad, and had several spells of duty in Tehran. His writings include *Persisch* (1919), *Persien von der "pénétration pacifique" zum "Protektorat"* (1920), *Wer hat die persische Neutralität verletzt?* (1920), *Lettisch* (1923), *Persische Flitterwochen* (1925), and *Das Drama in Persien* (1929). He died in Baghdad on 28 January 1932. Hanisch; Kürschner, 1928/29, 1931; *Wer ist's*, 1928

Little, Donald Presgrave, born 21 October 1932 in U.S.A., he graduated from Vanderbilt University, Nashville, Tenn., in 1953, from Stanford University, Palo Alto, Cal., in 1955, and received his Ph.D. in 1966 from the University of California at Los Angeles for *An analysis of the annalistic and biographical sources in Arabic for the reign of al-Malik al-Nasir Muhammad ibn Qala'un*. He spent some twenty-five years as a professor of Mamluk history, historiography and diplomatics in the Institute of Islamic Studies, McGill University, Montreal, P.Q., where he also served from 1982 to 1990 as its director. His writings include *An Introduction to Mamlūk historiography* (1970), *A Catalogue of the Islamic documents from al-Haram aš-Šarīf in Jerusalem* (1984), and a collection of his articles, *History and historiography of the Mamlūks* (1986). MESA *Roster of members*, 1977-1990; Private

Little Edward Campbell, born in 1858 at Newark, Ohio, he graduated in 1883 from the University of Kansas and passed his bar admission in 1886. He was a congressman who was awarded the Grand Cordon of the Medjidieh from the Sultan of Turkey for his diplomatic service. His writings include *The Armenian question in the American House of Representatives* (1918). He died in 1924. BiDrAC; Master (1); WhAm, 1; ZKO

Little, Ian *Malcolm* David, born 12 December 1918 at Rugby, England, he graduated from Oxford University where he also obtained his D.Phil. in 1949. He was a professor of economics, particularly economics of underdeveloped countries. Concurrently he served with international institutions and projects as well as the World Bank and the Organisation for Economic Co-operation and Development. His writings include *A Critique of welfare economics* (1950), *The Price of fuel* (1953), *Aid to Africa* (1964), *Estudio social del costo-beneficio en la industria de países en desarrollo* (1973), *Economic development* (1982), and *Macroeconomic analysis and the developing countries* (1993). Au&Wr, 1971; BlueB, 1976; ConAu, 21-24, new rev., 15, 34; IntAu&W, 1977, 1989; IntWW, 1991-2006; WhoEc, 1981, 1986, 1999; *Who's who*, 1974-2005; WrDr, 1980/82-1996/98

Little, Kenneth Lindsay, born 19 September 1908 at Liverpool, England, he graduated in 1941 from Cambridge University and received a Ph.D. in 1945 from the University of London. He taught anthropology successively at the London School of Economics and the University of Edinburgh, where he was a sometime professor of African urban studies. His writings include *Negroes in Britain* (1948), *The Mende of Sierra Leone* (1951), *Race and society* (1952), its French edition, *Race et société* (1952), *African women in town* (1973), *Urbanization as a social process* (1974), and *The Sociology of urban women's image in Africa* (1980). He died on 28 February 1991. ConAu, 17-20; IntAu&WW, 1976, 1977; Unesco; *Who's who*, 1973-1991

Little, Otway Henry, born 19th cent., he was in the 1940s for several years a director of the Geographical Survey of Egypt, Cairo. His writings include *The Geography and geology of Makalla, South Arabia* (Cairo, 1925), *Preliminary report on the water supply of Kharga and Dakhlah oases* (Giza, 1932), *The Deep bores in Kharga and Dakhla oases* (1942), *A Report on some studies of underground water flow and about subsoil pollution* (Cairo, 1942), and *The Development of the Aswân district* (Giza, 1943). NUC, pre-1956

Little, Stephen Lee, born 1 May 1954 at Ann Arbor, Mich., he graduated in 1975 from Cornell University, Ithaca, N.Y., and received his M.A. in 1977 from the University of California at Berkeley. In 1978, he joined the Asian Museum of San Francisco. His writings include the exhibition catalogue *Realm of the immortals* (1987), *Chinese ceramics of the transitional period, 1620-1683* (1983) [not sighted], and *Visions of the Dharma; Japanese Buddhist paintings in the Honolulu Academy of Arts* (1991). WhoAmArt, 1980, 1982

Little, Thomas (Tom) Russell, born 8 May 1911 at Tynemouth, England, he joined the British-owned Arab News Agency in 1943 after war-time military service. He served as diplomatic correspondent in New York, Washington and Paris, as general manager in Cairo and London, and since 1962 was managing director and general manager. He contributed regularly from the Middle East to the *Times*, *Observer* and *Economist*, and in the 1960s, when he was based in London, he was a frequent broadcaster on Middle East affairs as well as contributor of articles to *The World today* and similar periodicals. In 1971 he became the first editor of the *Middle East international*, and during the last years of his life he was the London representative of the Saudi News Agency and acted as correspondent for *al-Ahrām*. His writings include *Egypt* (1958), *High Dam at Aswan* (1965), *South Arabia* (1965), and *The Arab world in the twentieth century* (1972). He died on 22 February 1975. Au&Wr, 1963, 1971; *BRISMES Bulletin*, 2 (1975), pp. 119-120; ConAu, 13-16

Little, Tom, 1911-1975 *see* Little, Thomas Russell

Littledale, St George R., born 19th cent., he was a British traveller who, together with his wife, crossed the Pamirs from north to south between 1893 and 1895, and later travelled overland from Batum to Peking, achievements about which he reported in the *Geographical journal* and the *Proceedings of the Royal Geographical Society*, London. His trace is lost after an article in 1903. Henze; Note

Littmann, Ludwig Richard *Enno*, born 16 September 1875 at Oldenburg, Germany, he studied theology, classics and Oriental languages at the universities of Berlin, Greifswald, Halle and Straßburg. In 1899/1900 and 1904 he participated in Princeton University expeditions to Palestine and Syria. In 1906, he was appointed to the chair of Oriental languages at the Universität Straßburg, a position which he held until 1914 when he moved on successively to Göttingen, Bonn and finally Tübingen. His main field of research was epigraphy and Ethiopian philology. After the Second World War he was married to a grand daughter of Theodor Nöldeke. His writings include *Arabische Beduinenerzählungen* (1908), *Ägyptische National-lieder und Königslieder der Gegenwart* (1938), *Arabische und abessinische Dichtungen aus vierzehn Jahrhunderten* (1958), and the work for which he is probably best remembered, *Die Erzählungen aus den Tausend und ein Nächten* (1921-28). He died in Tübingen on 4 May 1958. Bonner, vol. 8, pp. 328-44; DtBE; DtBiInd (2); Hanisch; LexAfrika; Kornrumpf; Kürschner, 1925-1958; *Wer ist's*, 1928, 1935; *Wer ist wer*, 1958

Litvinskiĭ, Boris Anatol'evich, born 17 April 1923 at Tashkent, he graduated in 1946 from the Faculty of History, Central Asian State University, received his first degree in 1951 for «*Средневековые поселения области Нисы севернее Копет-Дага в IX-XV годах*», and a doctorate in 1969 for *Истории и культура восточной части Средней Азии от поздней бронзы до раннего* *средневековья.* He was since 1951 associated with the Institute of History, Tajik Academy of Sciences, as archaeologist and numismatist. In 1971 he was appointed a professor. His writings include *Археологическое изучение Таджикистана советской наукой* (1954), *Древнейшие страницы истории дела Таджикистана и других республик Средней Азии* (1954), *Кангюйско-сарматский фарн* (1968), *История таджикского народа* (1998), *La civilisation de l'Asie centrale antique* (1998), *Die Geschichte des Buddhismus in Ostturkestan* (1999), *Восточный Туркестан в древности и раннем средневековье; архитектура, искусство, костюм* (2000), and he edited *История и культура еародов Средней Азии* (1976). Miliband; Miliband²; OSK; Schoeberlein

Liubarskaia, Alla Mikhaĭlovna, fl. 20th cent., her writings include *Вилфрид Скоуэн Блант* (1969), *Горас Тробел; слава и забвение* (1980), and *Том с ленинской полки* (1981). NUC, 1968-71; OSK

Liubimov, Konstantin Mikhaĭlovich, born in 1907 at Moscow, he graduated in 1939 from the Moscow Oriental Institute and received his first degree in 1950 for *Образование значения и употребление времен в турецком языке*. Since 1956 he was associated with the Oriental Institute, Soviet Academy of Sciences. His writings include *Учебник старой турецкой письменности* (1951), as well as contribu-tions to the Turkish liguistic periodical *Türk dili dergisi*. Miliband; Miliband²

Liubimova, Gemma Nikolaevna, fl. 20th cent., her writings include *Народная архитектура Юзного Дагестана* (1956), and *Новое в архитектуре ГДР* (1965). OSK

Liushkevich, Fania Davydovna, born 5 December 1927 at Leningrad, she graduated in 1950 from the Oriental Faculty, Leningrad State University and received her first degree in 1977 for *Особенности этнической истории и этнографических черт культуры таджикского населения Бухарского оазиса конец XIX- начало XX в.* Since 1951 she was associated with the Leningrad Division of the Soviet Academy of Sciences. Miliband²; OSK

Liveran, Arthur Chaim, born 3 February 1919 at Beerfelden, Germany, he was educated at Teachers' College, Jerusalem, and subsequently took law degrees at the University of London. He was associated with the American Jewish Congress, New York, before he served successively with the Israeli Ministry of Foreign Affairs, and the United Nations Organization. WhoUN, 1975

Liverani, Giuseppe, born 17 September 1903 at Faenza, Italy, he was a keeper and director of the Museo Internazionale delle Ceramiche, Faenza, from 1924 until his death in 1961. His writings include *Il Museo delle Ceramiche in Faenza* (1936), *La maiolica italiana sino alla comparsa della porcellana europea* (1957), *Five centuries of Italian majolica* (1960), and *La ceramica popolare ligure* (1964). ConAu, 5-8, new rev., 6; IndBiltal (3); IntAu&W, 1976 (not sighted)

Livermore, Harold Victor, born in 1914, he was a graduate of Cambridge University. His writings include *A History of Portugal* (1947), *A History of Spain* (1958), *The Origins of Spain and Portugal* (1971), *Portugal; a short history* (1973), and *Origens das relações luso-britânicas* (1976). In 1985 appeared *Iberia; literary and historical issues: studies in honour of Harold V. Livermore*. LC; ZKO

Livingston, John William, born in 1932, he received a Ph.D. in 1968 from Princeton University for *'Ali Bey al-Kabir and the Mamluk resurgence in Ottoman Egypt, 1760-1772*. NUC, 1968-72; Selim

Livne, Moshe (Mosheh Livneh Vais), he was in 1977 a teaching assistant in the Depatment of Sociology and Anthropology, Tel Aviv University. He died on 28 April 1992. LC

Livneh, Eliezer, born Eliezer Liebenstein on 2 December 1902 at Lodz, Galicia, he went to Palestine in 1920 to become a journalist and periodical editor. His writings include *State and diaspora* (1953). WhoIsrael, 1966/67-1973/74; WhoWorJ, 1955, 1965, 1972, 1978

Livotova, Ol'ga Ėmanuilovna, fl. 20th cent., her writings include *Основная литература об Азиатском мусее-Институте востоковения Академии наук СССР, 1776-1954* (1956), and *Востоковедение в изданиях Академии наук, 1726-1917* (1966). LC; OSK

Livshits, Vladimir Aronovich, born 6 October 1923 at Petrograd, Russia, he served with the Red Army until 1945, when he began his Iranian study at the Oriental Faculty, Leningrad, gaining his first degree in 1952 for *Местоимения в афзанском языке*. At that time it was impossible to find any suitable work in his field within Russia, so that he had to go to Tajikistan as a school teacher, concurrently doing research in Tajik academic institutions. It was not until the years around the 1960 International Congress of Orientalists in Moscow that he was invited to return to Leningrad to the Oriental Institute, Soviet Academy of Sciences. He there received his doctorate in 1965 with a thesis on Sogdian juridical documents and letters. In 1972 he was nominated a professor. His writings include *Юридические документы и письма* (1962). *Bulletin of the Asia Institute,* 10 (1996), pp. 1-9; Miliband; Miliband²; Schoeberlein de **Lizáur** y **Roldán**, Juan, fl. 20th cent., his writings include *Expedición del Museo Nacional de Ciencias Naturales de Madrid a la Guinea continental española en 1940* (Madrid, 1941). His trace is lost after an article in 1951. NUC, pre-1956

Llavero Ruiz, Eloísa, born 20th cent., she reveived a liberal arts degree as well as a doctorate in Semitic languages. She became a professor at the Facultad de Filología, Universidad de Las Palmas de Gran Canaria. Arabismo, 1992, 1994, 1997; EURAMES, 1993

Llewellyn, Bernard, born in 1919, his writings include *I left my roots in China* (1953), *From the back streets of Bengal* (1955), *China's courts and concubines* (1956), *With my back to the East* (1958), and *The poor world* (1967). LC; ZKO

Llobregat, Enrique A., 1941- *see* Llobregat Conesa, Enrique

Llobregat Conesa, Enrique A., born in 1941, he obtained a doctorate in history. He was a sometime director of the Museo Arqueológico Provincial de Alicante. His writings include *En el ocre infinito* (1971), *Contestanía Ibérica* (1972), *Teodomiro de Oriola* (1973), *La festa d'Elx* (1975), *Iniciación a la arqueologia alicantina* (1976), and *El corpur de Valencia* (1978); he was joint author of *Historia de l'art al País Valencia* (1986-1988), and he was joint editor of *Homenage a Lluis Guarner, 1902-1986* (1988). Arabismo, 1992 LC

Llord O'Lawlor, Manuel, fl. 20th cent., his writings include *Regimen de la propiedad en Marruecos* (1935), and *Apuntes de derecho administrativo del Protectorado de España en Marruecos* (1952). NUC, pre-1956

Lloyd, George Ambrose, born in 1879, a member of the banking house, he was educated at Cambridge and started travelling in the Middle East in 1900. In 1905, he was an honorary attaché in Constantinople, specializing in the Baghdad Railway. In 1907, he led a trade mission to Iraq. In December 1914, by then an MP, he was posted to Military Intelligence in Cairo as an expect on Iraq, and early in 1916, he was sent there to advise the new British administration on financial policies. In June 1917, he was put in charge of Sinai Intelligence, staying there until 1918, when he was appointed Secretary to the British Delegation at Versailles. After the first World War, he was High Commissioner in Egypt. He died in 1941 while a member of Churchill's wartime Cabinet. R.L. Bidwell, *Arab bulletin* 1 (1986 reprint), p. xxvii; CurBio, 1941; DNB

Lloyd, Seton Howard Frederick, born 30 May 1902 at Birmingham, England, he was a trained architect who became an outstanding archaeologist of Mesopotamia and Turkey. After his initial experience gained at Tel el-Amarna in Egypt, he transferred to Iraq to join his friend, Henri Frankfort, in his pioneering excavations in the Diyala valley. In 1939, he was appointed archaeological adviser to the Directorate of Antiquities in Iraq, where he had planned the then Iraq Museum in Baghdad. He encouraged the British School of Archaeology in Iraq and succeeded Sir Max Mallowan as its president. His skills made him an obvious choice to become the first director of the British Institute of Archaeology at Ankara in 1948. Before his retirement fourteen years later, he made a name by his work at Polatı, Haran, Sultantepe and Beyce Sultan. Apart from full scholarly report of his activities, he found time to publish works of appeal to the general reader. In 1962, he was appointed a professor at the University of London, a position which he held until 1969. His writings include *The Ruined cities of Iraq* (1942), *Twin rivers; a brief history of Iraq from the earliest times to the present day* (1943), *Foundations in the dust* (1947), *World architecture* (1963), *The Archaeology of Mesopotamia*, its translations, *Die Archäologie Mesopotamiens* (1981), and *Археология Месопотамии* (1984), *Ancient Turkey; a traveller's history of Anatolia* (1989), and an account of his own life in Near Eastern archaeology, *The Interval* (1986). He died 7 January 1996. *Asian affairs*, 1996; ConAu, 132, 151; IntWW, 1974-1995/96 MidE, 1978-1982/83; Note; *Who's who*, 1962-1996; WhoWor, 1974/7-1978/79, WrDr, 1994/96-1998/2000

Lloyd, Sir William, born 29 December 1782 at Wrexham Regis, County Denbigh, Wales, he was a British army officer who was posted in 1801 to the Native Infantry in India. He served in the Bombay Marines and also participated in the third Mahratta War. He was in active service until 1820. From 1820 to 1821, he travelled in Upper India. In 1923, he went on furlough until he retired with the rank of major in 1825. In 1854, he became an honorary lieutenant-colonel. His writings include *Narrative of a journey from Caunpoor to the Boorendo Pass in the Himalaya Mountains, viá Gwalior, Agra, Delhi, and Sirhund* (1840). He died in Llandudno on 16 May 1857. IndianBilnd (1)

Lloyd James, Arthur, 1884.1943 *see* James, Arthur Lloyd

Llubiá i **Munné**, Luis Maria, fl. 1951, his writings include *Terminología tipológia de la cerámica española y etimología de la palabra mayólica* (Barcelona, 1955), *Cerámica medieval española* (1967), and he was a joint author of *Cerámica catalana decorada* (1949), *La cerámica murciana decorada* (1951), and *La cerámica de Teruel* (Teruel, 1962). NUC

Lluis y **Navas Brusi**, Jaime.fl. 20th cent., he obtained a doctorate. His writings include *Consideraciones en torno al perpetuo problema de la divinidad* (1950), *Las cuestiones legales sobre la amanedación peninsular en la edad antigua* (Madrid, 1953), *Las restricciones al trabajo de extranjeros en España* (Madrid, 1958), *Crisis de trabajo y modificación de condiciones laborales* (Barcelona, 1960), *Las cuestiones legales sobre la amenedación española bajo los Reyes Católicos* (Madrid, 1960), *Las actas de la inspeccion de trabajo* (Barcelona, 1961), *Medidas provisionales en relación con la mujer casada* (Barcelona, 1962), *Las bases de la sociedad y el problema social* (Barcelona, C.E.A.H.E., 1964), and *El régimen jurídico de facultades y deberes laborales del director de empresa* (Barcelona, C.E.A.H.E., 1979). NUC

Lo Giudice, Barbaro, born 5 January 1917 at Paternò, Sicily, he was a lawyer and a Christian Democrat parliamentarian. His writings include *Reddito e tributi in Sicilia* (Palermo, 1956). Firenze; IndBiltal (2)

Lo Jacono, Claudio, fl. 1974. His writings include *Partiti politici e governi in Iraq, 1920-1975* (1975); he was a joint author of *Maometto in Europa; arabi e turchi in Occidente, 622-1922* (1982). LC

Lo Verde, Giuseppe, born 2 August 1906 at Hamburg, Germany, he was a lawyer, university professor, and journalist who received doctorates in law and political science from the Università de Palermo in 1929 and 1931 respectively. His writings include *Die Lehre vom Staat im neuen Italien* (1934), *La nazionalsocialismo* (1939), and *Das faschistische Imperium* (1942). IntAu&W, 1976

Loarer, Édouard, fl. 19th cent., he wrote *Le Phylloxera, puceron de la vigne* (Paris, 1842), *L'Himalaya, ses produits naturelles, culture du thé dans l'Inde* (Paris, 1868), and *L'Invasion anglaise et le comité de défense des ports de la Manche* (Paris, 1869). BN

Lobacheva, Nina Petrovna, born 31 January 1924 at Khimki, Russia, she was associated with the Institute of Ethnography and Anthropology, Russian Academy of Sciences. Her writings include *Формирование новой обрядности узбеков* (1975), and *Традиционная одезда народов Средней Азии и Казахстана* (1989). Schoeberlein

Lobanov-Rostovsky, André Anatol'evich, he was born in 1892 at Yokohama, Japan, to a family with connections to Turkestan, where they owned extensive properties; and he was educated in Russia and France. In the late 1910s he was attached to the staff of General Denikin in the section of foreign relations, in which capacity he was in a position to obtain valuable information to current developments in Central Asia. He was a foreign correspondent in London from 1924 to 1930 when he went to the United States to teach history, first at the University of California, and from 1945 to his retirement in 1962 at the University of Michigan. His writings include *Russia and Asia* (1933), *The Grinding mill* (1935), *Illusions and realities of international coöperation* (1935), and *Russia and Europe, 1789-1825* (1947). DrAS, 1969 H; Note

Lobashev, Aleksandr Ivanovich, fl. 20th cent., his writings include *Сельское население и сельское хозяйство Афганистана в цифрах* (1967). OSK

Lobban, Carolyn Fluehr, 1945- see Fluehr-Lobban, Carolyn

Lobban, Richard Andrew, born 3 November 1943 at Baltimore, Md., he graduated in 1966 from Bucknell University, Lewisburg, Pa., and received a Ph.D. in 1973 from Northwestern University, Evanston, Ill., for *Social networks in the urban Sudan*. He taught at a variety of American universities, including the American University in Cairo, before he was appointed a professor in the Department of Anthropology, Rhode Island College, Providence, R.I., a position he still held in 2002. Since 1985 he there was a director of African and Afro-American Studies. He was a founder, and a sometime president, of the Sudan Studies Association. His writings include *Eritrean Liberation Front* (1972), *Historical dictionary of the republics of Guinea-Bissau and Cape Verde* (1979), *Urban research strategies for Egypt* (1983), and with Carolyn Fluehr-Lobban, *Historical dictionary of the Sudan* (1992). ConAu, 144; NatFacDr, 1990-2002; Note; Selim; WhoE, 1993/94

Lobel, Eli, born 20th cent., he was a joint author of *Les Arabes en Israël* (Paris, 1969), *Les Juifs et la Palestine* (Paris, 1969), *The Arab world and Israel* (New York, 1970), and *Die Araber in Israel* (München, 1970). ZKO

Lobingier, Charles Sumner, born 30 April 1866 at Lanark, Ill., he was a graduate of the University of Nebraska. From 1892 to 1903, he practised law in his home state. From 1905 to 1923, he was judge in the Philippines and in China, returning to his homeland in 1924 to become a government lawyer. His writings include *A treatise on Philippine practice including the law of evidence* (1907). He died in Washington, D.C., on 28 April 1956. Master (3); Shavit - Asia

Lobmeyer, Hans Günter, born in 1957, he went to Berlin to study political science at Otto-Suhr-Institut, Freie Universität Berlin, gaining a diploma in 1984 for his unpublished thesis, *Die Herausbildung von Regionalismus und ethnisch-religiösen Grenzziehungen in der Arabischen Sozialistischen Ba'th-Partei*. He subsequently went to Damascus to learn Arabic. Upon his return to Berlin he wrote a four hundred-page thesis on the contemporary Islamic opposition in Syria, a work which apparently was never completed. His qualifications came at the wrong time and at the wrong place. He went to Paris, where he eked out his living in a *chambre de bonne* as an honorary joint editor of a Middle Eastern periodical. After a few years he left expensive Paris and settled in Tarbes (Hautes Pyrénées), where he survived on casual Arabic translations, keeping in touch with his customers by way of e-mail. In 2001, he ought to have had heart surgery; for the subsequent operation he lacked the travel funds to go back to Berlin. He died in Tarbes in 2003. Note; *Tagesspiegel*, Berlin, 31 October 2003, p. 10

Łobodowski, Józef, born 19 March 1909 at Purwiszkach (Сувалки, Sudauen), Poland, he was a dissident poet and writer who spent the last part of his life in Spain. He frequently used Near Eastern and Hispano-Islamic themes in his writings, which include *Pieśń o Ukraine* (1959), *Terminatorzy rewolucji* (London, 1966), *Ukraina, 1956-1968* (Paris, 1969), and *Dwie książki* (Paris, 1984). He died in Madrid on 18 April 1988. Czy wiesz; Dziekan; NEP; OSK; Polski (8)

Lochbrunner-Paulenbach, Margarete, born in 1892. Her writings include *Dantes Weg durch die drei Seelenbereiche* (Marburg/Lahn, 1948), and *Die Göttliche Komödie, Dantes Botschaft aus neuer Sicht* (Köln, 1978).

Lock, Cecil *Max*, born 9 June 1909, he was an architect, trained at the Architectural Association. He established his own architectural and development consulting firm Max Lock & Associates, which became particularly concerned with underdeveloped countries. His writings include *A Plan for Middlesborough; the proposal in outline* (1945), *Outline plan for the Portsmouth district* (1949), *Municipality of Basrah; survey and plan* (1956), *Port of Basrah; the survey and plan for Margil* (1956), and *Kaduna, 1917, 1967, 2017; a survey and plan of the capital territory for the Government od Northern Nigeria* (1968). He died in 1988. Who's who, 1969-1988; Who was who, 8

Lock, Walter, born in 1846 at Dorchester, Dorset, England, he was a college warden and a professor of divinity. His writings include *John Keble, a biography* (1893), *A Critical and exegetical commentary on the Pastoral epistles* (1924), and *Oxford memories* (1932). He died in 1933. BritInd (4); DNB; WhE&EA; Who was who, 3

Lockett, Abraham, born 21 June 1781 at Clondeafe, County Tyrone, Ireland, he became a cadet in 1800 and arrived in India on 23 August 1811. He advanced through the grades to become lieutenant-colonel in the Bengal Native Infantry in 1829. He was on leave in Iraq and Arabia, 1810-12, and from 1821 to 1824 served as secretary to the Council of the College of Fort William, Calcutta. His writings include *The Miut Amil [Mi'at al-'amil] and Shurhoo (commentary) Miut Amil; two elementary treatises on Arabic syntax, translated from the original Arabic with annotations* (Calcutta, 1814). He died in Cape Town on 10 May 1834. IndianBiInd (1)

Lockhart, Donald Merritt, born 14 March 1923 at Cambridge, Mass., he graduated in 1948 from Bowdoin College, Brunswick, Me., and received his Ph.D. in 1959 from Harvard for *Father Jeronymo Lobo's writings concerning Ethiopia*. He was a professor of modern languages, particularly Romance languages, at Norwich University, Vt., a post which he still held in 1990. His writings include *The Itinerário of Jerónimo Lobo* (1984). DrAS, 1969 F, 1974 F, 1978 F, 1982 F; NatFacDr, 1990

Lockhart, Laurence, born in 1891, he studied Arabic and Persian, from 1910 to 1914, at Pembroke College, Cambridge, where he was a student of E. G. Browne, taking an honours degree in historical and Oriental studies. During the first World War, he served in the Foreign Office, then later combined cultural work for the Anglo-Persian Oil Company with the pursuit of research into eighteenth-century Persian history. During the 1939-45 war he served in the R.A.F., chiefly in the Middle East, and also on liaison with the Russian forces. His journeys to Iran were initially in connection with his work for the A.P.O. but he also visited the country after he left the Company in 1948. He served on the Council of the Iran Society, the Governing Council of the British Institute of Persian Studies and the Editorial Board for the *Cambridge history of Iran*. In the mid-1960s he was a visiting professor at the University of Toronto. In his retirement he lived close to Cambridge and wrote articles and books on Iran, which include *The Fall of the Safavi dynasty and the Afghan occupation of Persia* (1958), and *Persian cities* (1960). After his death in 1975, all his books, papers and photographic material - covering Egypt, Palestine, Iraq, Turkey, and Iran as well as Western countries - were given to the Faculty of Oriental Studies at Cambridge. Pembroke College organized an exhibition of fifty photographs from Iran, 1927-1928, during the third bi-annual Conference on Travellers on Egypt and the Near East, Newnham College, 15-18 July 1999. Note; Private; Sluglett

Lockroy (Λοκκρουα), Édouard Étienne Antoine Simon, son of Joseph Philippe Simon, he was born on 18 July 1838 at Paris and later took the name of Lockroy. He began to study art, but in 1860 enlisted as a volunteer under Garibaldi. The next three years were spent in Syria as secretary to Ernest Renan, and on his return to Paris he embarked in militant journalism against the second *Empire* in the *Figaro,* the *Diable à quatre,* and eventually in the *Rappel.* In 1871, he was elected to the Assemblée nationale where he sat on the extreme left and protested against the preliminaries of peace. In March 1871, he signed the proclamation for the election of the Commune, and resigned his seat as deputy. Arrested at Vanves (Hauts-de-Seine), he remained a prisoner in Versailles and Chartres until June when he was released without being tried. He was more than once imprisoned for violent articles in the press. He was returned to the Chambre des députées in 1873. In 1886, he was a minister of commerce and industry, and in 1888, minister of public instruction. His writings include *Les aigles du Capitole* (1869), and *Ahmed le boucher; la Syrie et l'Égypte au XVIIIe siècle* (1888), *Au hasard de la vie; notes et souvenirs* (1913). He died in 1913. BbD; BiD&SB; Curinier; EncBrit; EncicUni; GdeEnc; GDU; IndexBFr² (15); Megali, vol. 16, p. 215, cols. 2-3; Meyers; *Who was who,* 1

Lockwood, Wilfrid, born about 1936 in England, he was a sometime Orientalist librarian at Cambridge University Library and concurrently a joint compiler of the *Quarterly index Islamicus* from 1982 to 1983, when he moved to Dublin to serve for some six years as librarian of the Chester Beatty Library. His writings include *The Word of God; Biblical manuscripts at the Chester Beatty Library, Dublin* (1987), and jointly translated with Bruno Chiesa *On Jewish sects and Christianity,* from the Arabic of Ya'qūb al-Qirqisānī (1984). Private; ZKO

Lockwood, William Grover, born 25 May 1933 at Long Beach, Calif., he graduated in 1955 from Fresno (Calif.) State College, and received his Ph.D. in 1970 from the University of California at Berkeley for *Selo and Čaršija; the peasant market place as a mechanism of social integration in western Bosnia.* From 1969 to his retirement he was a professor of anthropology at the University of Michigan, Ann Arbor. His writings include *European Moslems; economy and ethnicity in western Bosnia* (1975), *Gypsies and travelers in North America; an annotated bibliography* (1994), and he edited *Essays in Balkan ethnology* (1967). AmM&WSc, 1973 S; AmM&WSc, 1976 P; NatFacDr, 1990-1995

Lodge, Henry Cabot, Jr., born 5 July 1902 at Nahant, Mass., he graduated from Harvard University. After a brief career as journalist, he became a state and federal politician as well as a diplomat. He died in Bervely, Mass., 27 February 1985. Master (16); Shavit - Asia; WhAm, 8

Loeb, Lauwrence (Lawrence) Delemos, born in 1942, he received a Ph.D. in 1970 for *The Jews in southwest Iran; a study of cultural persistence.* He was a professor in the Department of Anthropology, University of Utah, Salt Lake City, certainly from 1977 to 2005. His writings include *Outcaste; Jewish life in southern Iran* (1977). MESA Roster of members, 1977-1990; NatFacDr, 1990-2005; NUC, 1968-72

Loebenstein, Helene, born 20th cent., her writings on the Islamic collection in the Austrian National Library include *Katalog der arabischen Handschriften der Österreichischen Nationalbibliothek* (1970), *Koranfragmente auf Pergament der Österreichischen Nationalbibliothek* (1982), and she was a joint author of *Die Papyrussammlung der Österreichischen Nationalbibliothek; Katalog der Sonderausstellung 100 Jahre Erzherzog Rainer* (1983). ZKO

Loeffler, Reinhold L., 1932- *see* Löffler, Reinhold L.

Loehlin, Clinton Herbert, born in 1897, he was for many years associated with the Hartfort Seminary Foundation, where he also received a degree in 1958 for his thesis, *The Granth of the tenth Guru Gobind Singh, and the Khalsa Brotherhood,* a work which was published in 1971. His other writings include *The Sikhs and their book* (1946), *The Sikhs and their scriptures* (1958), and *The Christian approach to the Sikh* (1966). Note; NUC, 1968-72

Loehr, Max Johannes Joseph, 1903-1988 *see* Löhr, Max Johannes Joseph

Loelinger, Phyllis, born 20th cent., she was resident in Turkey from 1960 to 1962, when she was closely associated with many of the Turkish artists working in Ankara. When she and Lt.-Col. Edmond Louis Loeliger, USAF, returned to Washington, they brought back a number of paintings. Note about the author

Loewe, Fritz, 1870- *see* Löwe, Fritz

Loewe, Louis, born 24 June 1809 at Zülz, Prussian Silesia, he was educated at various cities before he took a Dr.phil. at the Universität Berlin. His knowledge of languages and numismatics was even at this period considerable. During a visit to Hamburg, he was entrusted with arranging a private collection of Oriental coins. He then went to London, where he became known to many leading scholars and patrons of learning. Under the auspices of benefactors he spent three years in the East.

From 1839 to 1874 he accompanied Sir Moses Montefiore on thirteen journeys. He was appointed first principal of Jews' College, London, and for twenty years served as principal and director of the Judith Theological College at Ramsgate (Kent). His writings include *A Dictionary of the Circassian language* (1854). He died in London on 5 November 1888. DNB; EncJud²; JewEnc; JüdLex; Wininger

Loewenklau, Hans (Johannes), 1541-1594 see Löwenklau, Johannes

Loewenstein, Fritz E., born about 1895, he received a Dr.phil. in 1922 from the Universität Würzburg for *Die Handzeichungen der japanischen Holzschnittmeister.* GV

Loewenthal, Isidor, born about 1827 in Prussian Poland, he received a liberal education as well as an introduction to the tenets of the Jewish faith and Hebrew. He became implicated in political affairs and emigrated to the United States in 1846. He became a Presbyterian, graduated from Princeton Theological Seminary, and went as a missionary to India. Although his missionary life was only seven years, he translated the whole of the New Testament into Pashtu, and had nearly completed a dictionary in that language when he was shot down by his Afghan watchman on 27 April 1864. DtAB; Enc. Jud.; MW 8 (1918), 131-136; Shavit - Asia; WhAm, H

Loewy, Karl, born about 1895, he received a Dr.phil. in 1922 from the Universität Wien for *Affektbezeichnungen im Semitischen.* GV

Lofchie, Michael F., born 23 April 1936 at Boston, Mass., he received a Ph.D. in 1964 from the University of California at Berkeley for *Constitutional change and political conflict in Zanzibar.* In 1966, he was appointed a professor in the Department of Political Science, University of California at Los Angeles, a position which he still held in 2005. His writings include *Zanzibar; background to revolution* (1965). AmM&WSc, 1973 S, 1978 S; NatFacDr, 1990-2005

Löffler, Paul, born 29 October 1931 at Łódź, Poland, he received a Dr.theol. in 1958 from the Universität Bonn for *Die Trinitätslehre des Bischofs Hilarius von Poitiers zwischen Ost und West.* Since 1960, he was associated with the Commission on World Mission and Evangelism of the World Council of Churches, London. His writings include *A Layman abroad in the mission of the Church* (1962), *Conversion to God and service to man* (1966), *Secular man and Christian mission* (1968), and *Arabische Christen im Nahostkonflikt* (1976). DtBiInd (1); GV

Löffler (Loeffler), Reinhold L., born 13 May 1932 at Innsbruck, Austria, he received a Dr.phil. in 1963 from the Universität Mainz for *Soziale Stratifikation im südlichen Hindukusch und Karakorum.* In 1967, he was appointed a professor of anthropology at Western Michigan State University, Kalamazoo, a position which he still held in 1990. His writings include *Islam in practice; religious beliefs in a Persian village* (1988). AmM&WSc, 1973 S; MESA Roster of members, 1990

Löfgren, Oscar Anders Valfrid, born 13 May 1898 at Larv, Skaraborg, Sweden, he received a doctorate in Semitic languages in 1927 from Uppsala Universitet. He was a professor in his field at Göteborg, 1951-1956, and Uppsala, from 1956 to his retirement in 1964. His writings include *Ein Hamdānī-Fund; über das Berliner Unikum der beiden ersten Bücher des Iklīl* (1935), *Studien zu den arabischen Daniel-übersetzungen mit besonderer Berücksichtigung der christlichen Texte* (1936), and he edited *Arabische Texte zur Kenntnis der Stadt Aden im Mittelalter* (1936-50), *Südarabisches Muštabih* (1953), *Al-Hamdānī, al-Iklīl, erstes Buch in der Rezension von Muhammad ibn Našwān ibn Sa'īd al-Himyarī* (1954-65), and *Katalog über die äthiopischen Handschriften in der Universitätsbibliothek Uppsala* (1974). He died in Uppsala on 23 April 1992. Rivista degli studi orientali, 67, i-ii, 1993 (1994); Vem är det, 1969-1991; ZKO

Loftus, August *William* Frederick Spencer Kenneth, Lord, born in 1817. His writings include *Travels and researches in Chaldaea and Susiana* (1857). He died on the voyage home from India in 1904. Kornrumpf; Kornrumpf³, vol. 2

Loftus, John Alphonsus, born in 1911, he received a Ph.D. in 1941 from Johns Hopkins University, Baltimore, Md., for *Investment management; an analysis of the experiences of American management investment trusts.* He was in the late 1940s chief of the Petroleum Division, U.S. Department of State, serving during the period when the Anglo-American intergovernmental discussions on petroleum were particularly concerned with questions affecting current and future status of Middle East oil. He subsequently became a professor of international economic relations at the School of Advanced International Studies, Washington, D.C. Note about the author

Loftus, Patrick Joseph, born 3 March 1912 at Dublin, he received a Ph.D. in 1948 from the University of London for *The National income of Palestine.* He was from 1944 to 1948 director-general, Department of Statistics, Government of Paestinel, and served in a similar capacity with the U.N.O.

from 1948 to 1961. His writings include *National income of Palestine, 1944* (1946), and *National income of Palestine, 1945* (1948). AmM&WSc, 1973 S; BLC; NearMEWho, 1945/46; Sluglett; WhoWor, 1978/79

Loftus, William Kennett, born about 1821 at Rye, Sussex, England, he was educated at Newcastle, Twickenham, and Cambridge without taking a degree. He acted for some time as secretary to the Newcastle Natural History Society and from 1849 to 1852 served as geologist on the Turko-Persian frontier delimitation commission. On his return to England he published what was for many years to be the most complete geological report in existence of any part of Persia. He also provided Kew Gardens with a number of botanical specimens. His writings include *Travels and researches in Chaldaea and Susiana* (1857). He died in November 1858 on the return voyage on board the *Tyburnia* within a week of starting. DNB; Embacher; Henze; Kornrumpf; Wright, p. 141

Logashova, Bibi-Rabiza, born 16 July 1931 at Baïram-Ali, Turkmen Soviet Republic, she graduated in 1954 from the Moscow Faculty of History, and received her first degree in 1958 for *Туркмены Ирана; историко-этнографическое исследование*, a work which was published in 1976. She was since 1966 associated with the Russian Academy of Sciences. She was a joint editor of *Московский регион; этноконфессиональная ситуация* (2000). Miliband²; OSK

Logemann, Johann Heinrich Adolf, born 19 January 1892 at Rotterdam, the Netherlands, he studied at the Rijksuniversiteit te Leiden, where he prepared for a civil service career in the Dutch East Indies, concentrating on linguistic studies and law. In 1923, he received a doctorate in Oriental languages, and also in law for *De grondslagen der vennootschapsbelasting in Nederland en Indië*. In 1924, he was appointed inspector of the Generale Thesaurie in the Departement van Financiën, Batavia, a position which held for fifteen years. During the 1940 to 1945 war he was a hostage. On 31 October 1947 he delivered his inaugural lecture as professor of East Indian law at the Rijksuniversiteit te Leiden entitled *Staatsrecht van Indonesië*, a work which was published in 1954. Subsequent political developments reduced much of his early publications to academic interest. He died in Noordwijkerhout (Z.H.) on 12 November 1969. BWN, vol. 4, pp. 316-18; Wieis dat, 1948

Loggin, George Nicholas, born in 1882, he was educated at University College, London, and subsequently held appointments in Public Works Departments in Ceylon, Kenia, Nigeria, the Sudan, and Iraq. He died in 1955. Who was who, 5

Login, Sir John Spencer, born in 1809 at Stromness, Scotland, he received a medical doctorate in 1831 from the University of Edinburgh and became an assistant surgeon in the East India Company's service. He was appointed to the Bengal Horse Artillery and served with the Nizam's army. He served in the first Afghan War and in 1839 accompanied the British Mission to Herat under Major D'Arcy Todd in a medical and political capacity. He later was named surgeon to the British Residency at Lucknow, and superintendent of hospitals to the King of Oudh. Knighted in 1854, he died in Felixstone, Suffolk, on 18 October 1863. Boase; Buckland; IndianBilnd (2)

Logio, George Clinton, born 19th cent., his writings include *Bulgaria; problems and politics* (London, 1919) and *Rumania; its history, politics and economics* (Manchester, 1932), and *Bulgaria, past and present* (Manchester, 1936). One of his works was translated into Romanian. BLC; NUC, pre-1956; OSK

Lohéac, André, born 13 November 1908 at Gourin (Morbihan), France, he was a graduate of the École spéciale militaire de Saint-Cyr. Since 1935 he served with the Services spéciaux du Levant of the French High Commission in Syria and Lebanon, where he was responsible for the administrative control and counsel to the local authorities in al-Hasakah (Hassetché), eastern Syria, soon gaining the confidence of the Kurdish population. In 1938, he was transferred to the Sanjak of Alexandretta, and after its incorporation into Turkey, he was sent on to a difficult district populated by Alawis, Turkomans, and Armenians. Since 1942 he cooperated with the Free French forces who controlled the French Mandatory Levant as an inspector in the Services spéciaux du Levant, first at Beirut, and later in the same year at Hassetché. For reasons of ill-health, he was posted from December 1943 to April 1946 to Beirut as a deputy chief of the *Services*. Based on his studies "Les Yézidis du Djebel Sindjar" (1935), and "Le peuplement chrétien de la Haute Djézireh" (1936), he was admitted to the Centre de Hautes Études d'Administration Musulmane, Paris, with the remarkable memorandum on "La confédération kurde des Millis." At the same time, he obtained diplomas in Turkish and Kurdish from the École nationale des Langues orientales vivantes, Paris. In the post-war period he was a U.N. observer in Palestine, and a French representative at Supreme Headquarters Allied Powers in Europe. He retired with the rank of lieutenant-colonel. He was an officer of the Légion d'honneur and awarded the Médaille de la Résistance. He was married to the painter and writer Blanche Ammoun. He died on 7 May 1966. L'Afrique et l'Asie, 74 (1966), pp. 72-74

Lohéac, Lyne, born 20th cent., she obtained a doctorate in history. Her writings include *Ammoun et la création de l'état libanais* (1977), a work which was reprinted in 1995. LC; *Livres disponibles*, 2004

Lohéac-Ammoun, Blanche, born 20th cent., she was a descendant of an old Maronite family from Mount Libanon and the wife of André Lohéac. Her writings include *Zénobie, reine de Palmyre* (Beirut, 1964), and *History of Lebanon* (1972). BN; Note; NUC

von **Löher**, Franz, born 15 October 1818 at Paderborn, Prussia, he studied philosophy, history and law at the universities of Halle and Freiburg im Breisgau. From there in the Black Forest, he went on foot by way of southern France and northern Italy to the Universität München where he completed his letters.   In 1841, he finished his law at Berlin and subsequently articled at Paderborn.   Before embarking on a civil service career, he travelled from June 1845 to October 1847, first to England, and then on to North America, experiences which are embodied in his *Geschichte und Zustände der Deutschen in Amerika* (Cincinnati, 1848). Foregoing plans for a journey to the Orient at the time of the 1848 revolution, he established and edited the *Westphälische Zeitung*. In 1852, he published *System des preußischen Landrechts in deutschrechtlicher und philosophischer Beziehung*, a work which gained him a Dr.jur. h.c. from the Universität Freiburg. After a Dr.habil. from the Universität Göttingen he taught there. In 1855, he was offered, more or less simultaneously, a professorship at Graz and a position at the court of the Bavarian King Maximilian II concurrent with a professorship at the Universität München. He accepted the latter royal offer.   In 1863, the directorship of the Bavarian Allgemeines Reichsarchiv was added to his responsibilities.   He also enjoyed the confidence of the next king, Ludwig II. In the service of this monarch, he travelled to the Canary Islands and the eastern Mediterranean in search of a royal refuge for the king, travels which he described in *Griechische Küstenfahrt* (1876), and *Cypern in der Geschichte* (1878). He was highly decorated for his political and literary achievements, including the Mecidiye Order, and Officier de la Légion d'honneur. He died in München on 1 March 1892. ADtB, vol. 52, pp. 56-62; BiD&SB; Embacher; Kornrumpf; Kornrumpf², vol. 2; Master (1); NDB

Lohmann, Johannes, born 9 July 1895 at Diensthop near Verden/Aller, Germany, he was a professor of comparative linguistics at the Universität Freiburg im Breisgau from 1949 to his retirement in 1963. His writings include *Philosophie und Sprachwissenschaft* (1965), and *Musiké und Logos* (1970). He died in Freiburg im Breisgau on 3 May 1983. Kürschner, 1940/41-1983; *Wer ist wer*, 1955-1974/75

Lohmann, Paul, born in 1886, he received a Dr.phil. in 1910 from the Universität Rostock for *Die anonymen Prophetien gegen Babel aus der Zeit des Exils*. He was an editor of the *Palästinajahrbuch* of Deutsches Evangelisches Institut für Altertumswissenschaft des Heiligen Landes zu Jerusalem. He died in 1915. Kornrumpf; NUC, pre-1956

Lohmann, Theodor, born 22 June 1928 at Dresden, Germany, he studied Lutheran theology at Kirchliche Hochschule, Berlin-Zehlendorf, and at the Universität Jena, where he received a Dr.theol. in 1952. After his Dr.habil. in 1957, he taught religious studies and New Testament and also served as chairman of the Institut für Allgemeine Religionsgeschichte, Jena, from 1958 to his retirement in 1993. His writings include a selection of his articles entitled *Religion, Religionen, Religionswissenschaft; Festschrift zum 70. Geburtstag* (1998). Kürschner, 1992-2005; Note

Lohr, Charles Henry, born 24 June 1925 at New York, he graduated in 1947 from Fordham University, New York, and received a Dr.phil. in 1967 from the Universität Freiburg im Breisgau for *Raimundus Lullus' Compendium logicae Algazelis; Quellen, Lehre und Stellung in der Logik*. Since 1963 he was associated with the Raimundus-Lullus-Institut der Universität Freiburg; from 1974 to 1990 he served as its chairman.   He was granted an honorary doctorate in divinity by the Université de Fribourg, Switzerland.   His writings include *St. Thomas Aquinas Scriptum super sententiis; an index of authorities cited* (1980). DrAS, 1969 P, 1974 P, 1978 P, 19982 P; Kürschner, 1980-2005; WhoWor, 1993/94

Löhr (Loehr), Max Johannes Joseph, born in humble circumstances on 4 December 1903 at Chemnitz, Saxony, he was obliged to leave school and take a job when he was sixteen. He worked for eleven years and had to study privately for his extramural high school graduation. He was then admitted to history of art at the Universität München in 1931. For five years he studied classical archaeology, Sanskrit and Chinese. He received his Dr.phil. in 1936 with a thesis on Chinese bronzes and subsequently entered the Museum für Völkerkunde, München. In December 1940 he was sent overland to Peking to study for three years at the Sino-German Institute in Peking. The war and its aftermath turned this into a nine-year stay, during which he became a director of the Institute. Upon his return he was offered, more or less simultaneously, the directorship of the Museum in München and a professorship at the University of Michigan. He chose the latter and went first to Ann Arbor, Mich., later moving to Harvard where he retired from his chair in June 1974. His writings include

Chinese art (1967). He died on 15 September 1988. Ars orientalis, 10 (1975), pp. 1-10; DrAS, 1969 H, 1974 H, 1978 H; WhAm, 9; WhoAm, 1974-1976/77; WhoAmArt, 1973-1986; WhoWor, 1974/75

Löhr, Max Richard Hermann, born 30 April 1864 at Stettin, Prussia, he studied theology, philology and philosophy at the universities of Königsberg and Göttingen, where he received his Dr.phil. in 1889 for *Gregorii Abulfaragii Bar Ebhraya in Epistulas Paulinas adnotationes* as well as a doctorate in divinity in the following year. He was a lecturer in theology and Old Testament at Königsberg until 1892 when he was invited to teach his field at the Universität Breslau. He went on research travel to the Jerusalem Deutsches Evangelisches Institut für Altertumswissenschaft des Heiligen Landes in 1903/4 and again in 1908/9. From 1909 to 1929 he was a professor in his field at the Universität Königsberg. His writings include *Der vulgärarabische Dialekt von Jerusalem* (1905), *Altestamentliche Religions-Geschichte* (1906), its translation, *A History of religion in the Old Testament* (1936), and *Volksleben im Lande der Bibel* (1907). He died in Königsberg on 21 October 1931. DtBE; EncJud²; JüdLex; Kürschner; NDB; Sezgin; Thesis; Wer ist's, 1909-1928: ZKO

Lohr, Otto, born 23 April 1872, he was continually since 1934 a staff member of the Institut für Auslandsbeziehungen (International Relations), Stuttgart, where he specialized in German-American matters and cultural exchanges. His writings include *The first Germans in North America and the German element of New Netherland* (1912), *Große deutsche im Ausland* (1939), and *Deutschland und Übersee* (1962). He died in Stuttgart on 18 June 1962. Mitteilungen des Instituts für Auslandsbeziehungen, 12 (1962), p. 261

Lohre, Nels J., born 25 May 1873 at Vermilion, S.D., he studied at the University of Minnesota and was ordained to the Lutheran ministry in 1897. He subsequently graduated in 1900 from the University of South Dakota, where he also obtained his M.A. in 1912. In the same year he became president of the Inter-Synodical Evangelical Lutheran Orient-Mission Society. He did pioneer work among the Kurds. In 1931, he received a D.D. from Carthage (Illinois) College. He died on 9 December 1933. WhAm, 1

Loi, Salvatore, born 20th cent., his writings include *Cagliari medaglia d'oro* (Cagliari, 1952), *Jugoslavia, 1941* (Torino, 1953), *Proverbi sardi* (Milano, 1972), *Le operazioni delle unità italiane in Jugoslavia* (Roma, 1978), *I rapporti fra alleati e italiani nella cobelligeranza* (Roma, 1986), and he was a joint author of *La popolazione dei comuni sardi dal 1688 al 1991; circoscrizioni dell'epoca e al 1991* (Cagliari, 1997). Firenze; NUC; OSK

Loir, Adrien Charles Marie, born in 1862 at Lyon, France, he had travelled in Africa before serving in 1911 as a keeper of the Musée d'histoire naturelle in Le Havre. His writings include *Canada et les Canadiens* (1908), *Thérapeutique et voyages au long cours* (1924), and *À l'ombre de Pasteur; souvenirs personnels* (Paris, Mouvement sanitaire, 1938). He died in 1941. IndexBFr² (1); Note

Loir, Raymond, fl. 1955, his writings include *Vieux Damas* (Avignon, 1947). NUC, pre-1956; Sezgin

Loiseau, Georges, born 19th cent., he received a doctorate in 1913 from the Faculté de droit de Paris for *Les doctrines économiques de Cournot.* BN; NUC, pre-1956

Loizos, Peter, born in 1937, he received a Ph.D. in 1971 from the London School of Economics for *Social organisations and political change in a Cypriot village.* He was a sometime lecturer in social anthropology at LSE. His writings include *The Greek gift; politics in a Cypriot village* (1975), *The heart grown bitter* (1981), *Innovation in ethnographic film; from innocence to self-consciousness, 1955-1985* (1994), *Conceiving persons; ethnographies of procreation, fertility, and growth* (1999); he was a joint author of *Cyprus* (London, Minority Rights Group, 1976); and he was a joint editor of *Contested identities; gender and kinship in modern Greece* (1991). Note; Sluglett

Lokke, Carl Ludwig, born in 1897, he graduated B.A. and M.A. from the University of California at Berkeley and received a Ph.D. in 1932 from Columbia University, New York, for *France and the colonial question; a study of contemporary French opinion, 1763-1801.* In 1935, he began his career at the National Archives in the Division of Classification and served in various capacities since that time. As head of the Foreign Affairs Branch of the Archives he shared with historians his amazing knowledge of the United States records from overseas. He died on 3 April 1960. American historical review, 66 (1960), p. 297; BioIn, 5 (3)

Løkkegaard, Frede, born 27 January 1915, he studied theology and Semitic languages. He held the chair of Semitic philology at Københavns Universitet from 1950 to his retirement in 1985. His writings include *Islamic taxation in the classical period with special reference to circumstances in Iraq* (1950), *Otte arabiske digtere* (1970), and he was a joint author of *1001 nat* (1961). In 1990 appeared *Living waters; Scandinavian orientalistic studies presented to Frede Løkkegaard on his senty-fifth birthday* (1990). Kraks; Note about the author

Lokotsch, Karl, born 3 February 1889 at Köln, Germany, he received a Dr.phil. in 1912 from the Universität Bonn for *Ein Beitrag zur Geschichte der Mathematik; Avicenna als Mathematiker*. He was a school teacher at Köln and since 1916 served as a lecturer at both the Handelshochschule and the Universität in Köln. His writings include *Türkische volkstümliche und Volkspoesie für Übungen in türkischer Originalschrift* (1917), and *Etymologisches Wörterbuch der europäischen (germanischen, romanischen und slavischen) Wörter orientalischen Ursprungs* (1927). Kürschner, 1931, 1935|; Schwarz

Loliée, Frédéric Auguste, born 14 October 1856 at Paris, he was a novelist, literary critic and contributor to the major European periodicals. He was in particular one of the main collaborators with the publication of the ten-volume *Dictionnaire de l'ancienne langue française et de tous ses dialectes du IXe au XVe siècle* (1881-1902). His writings include *Nos gens de lettres* (1887), *L'évolution historique des littératures* (1904), *Les Femmes du second Empire* (1906); he was a joint author of the *Dictionnaire-manuel illustré des écrivains et des littératures* (1898); and he edited the *Encyclopédie universelle du XXe siècle* (1912). He died in 1915. Curinier, vol. 1(1901), pp. 323-26; GdeEnc

Lomba Fuentes, Joaquín, born about 1940, he received a doctorate in philosophy and letters as well as a diploma in Semitic philology, specializing in philosophy and Spanish-Muslim culture. He was in 1993 a director of the Departamento de Filosofía e Historia de la Ciencia at the Facultad de Filosofía y Letras in the Universidad de Zaragoza. His writings include *La filosofía islámica en Zaragoza* (1987), and *La filosofía judia en Zaragoza* (1988). Arabismo, 1992-1997; EURAMES, 1993; ZKO

Lombard, Alexandre, born 19th cent., his writings include *Le Repos du dimanche devant la presse quotidienne* (Genève, 1869), *Isabeau Menet, prisonnière à la Tour de Constance, 1735-1750* (Genève, 1873), *L'État en face de la loi divine et du dimanche* (Genève, 1875), *Pauliciens, Bulgares et bons-hommes en Orient et en Occident; étude sur quelques sectes du moyen-âge* (Genève, 1879), *Jean Louis Paschale et les martyrs de Calabre* (Genève, 1881). BN; NUC, pre-1956

Lombard, Alf, born 8 July 1902 at Paris, he studied philology at Uppsala Universitet, where he also received his doctorate in 1930 for *Les constructions nominales dans le français moderne*. He was a lecturer in Romance philology at his alma mater from 1930 to 1938 and subsequently taught at Lund until his retirement in 1969 as a professor. He was a member of the Roumanian Academy of Sciences. His writings include *L'Infinitif de narration dans les langues romanes* (1936), *Le Verbe roumain; étude morphologique* (1954-55), *La langue roumaine; une présentation* (1976), *Le î prosthétique du roumain* (1976), and *Dictionnaire morphologique de la langue roumaine* (1981). In 1969 appeared *Mélanges de philologie offerts à Alf Lombard*. He died on 1 March 1996. IntAu&W, 1976, 1977, 1982; MembriiAR; Vem är det, 1941-1995; Who Wor, 1978/79

Lombard, Auguste, born 19th cent., he received a *doctorat ès sciences économiques* in 1911 from the Faculté de droit de Montpellier for *La Banque d'état du Maroc*. BN

Lombard, Denys Marius Claude Louis Jean Étienne, born 4 February 1938 at Marseille, France, he received a doctorate from the Sorbonne and a diploma from the École des langues orientales, Paris. In 1969, he joined the École des hautes études en sciences sociales where he headed the Division des aires culturelles until, in 1993, he became director of l'École française d'Extrême-Orient, a post which he held until his death on 8 January 1998. His writings include *Le Sultanat d'Atjéh au temps d'Isander Muda, 1607-1636* (1967), and *Histoires courtes d'Indonésie* (1968). IIAS newsletter 16 (1998), p. 5; WhoFr, 1993/94-1997/98

Lombard, Maurice, born in 1904, his writings include *Islam dans sa première grandeur* (1971), its translations, *The Golden age of Islam* (1975), and *Blütezeit des Islam* (1992), *Monnaie et histoire d'Alexandre à Mahomet* (1971), and *Études d'économie médiévale* (1978). He died in 1965. LC; ZKO

Lombard-Dumas, Armand, born 19th cent., he was a local historian whose writings include *Catalogue descriptif des monuments mégalithiques du Gard* (Nîmes, 1894), *La Botanique dans le Gard; biographies sommaires des botanistes nés dans le Gard* (Sommières, 1900), and *Une page d'histoire locale; l'hôpital de Sommières* (Sommières, 1901). His trace is lost after an article in 1905. BN; NUC, pre-1956

Lombardini, Elia, born 11 October 1794 at Labroque (Vosges), France, into a family originating from Milano. He was a mathematician, hydrographer, and engineer who also served as a senator. He was a member of the R. Istituto Lombardo di Scienze e Lettere. His writings include *Intorno al sistema idraulico del Po* (1840), *Della condizione idraulica della pianura subapennina fra l'Enza ed il Panaro* (1865), *Essay sur l'hydrologie du Nil* (1865), and *Studi idrologici e storici sopra il grande estuario adriatico* (1868). He died in Milano on 19 December 1878. IndBiItal (3)

Lomholt, Asger, born 2 August 1901, he received a Danish degree in theology and became an archivist of the Kongelige Danske Videnskabernes Selskab, from 1925 to 1975. His writings include

Kongelige Danske Videnskabernes Selskabs publikationer (1957-1968), and *Manuskripter og tegninger i Selskabets arkiv* (1973). He died on 26 December 1990. Kraks, 1990

Lommatzsch, Alfred, born in 1832 at Johanngeorgenstadt, Erzgebirge, Saxony, he was educated at the Fürstenschule, Grimma, Saxony, and subsequently studied law at the Universität Leipzig without taking a degree. He then joined the army and advanced through the grades to first lieutenant. In 1865 he took temporary retirement; in the same year he changed to Roman Catholicism. He went with his wife on lenghty journeys, visiting places as far away as Alger. He returned at the end of 1866 and died in Baden near Wien in the same year. DtBiInd (1)

London, Dr. B., born 19th cent., his writings include *Die Cholera und deren Vorbeugung für Laien dargestellt* (Wien, 1865), and he was a joint author of *A Medical treatise on the use of the (Carlsbad) waters* (London, 1886). BLC; GV

Londonderry, Frances Anne Emily Vane Tempest, 3rd marchioness of, born in 1800, she was married on 3 April 1819 to general Charles William Stewart whom she accompanied on his travels, the account of which she published under the title, *Narrative of a visit to the courts of Vienna, Constantinople, Athens, Naples ...* (1844), and *Russian journal, 1836-37*, edited by W. A. L. Seaman and J. R. Sewell (1973). She died in 1865. Edith H. V. T. Stewart wrote a biography *Frances Anne, the life and times of Frances Anne, Marchioness of Londonderry* (1958). Robinson, p. 117

Long, Charles, born 19th cent., he was in 1939 a president of the Comité central des industriels du Maroc. Note about the author

Long, Charles William *Richard*, born 20th cent., he obtained a Ph.D. and was in 1979 an exhibitioner, St. Catherine's College, Cambridge, and in 1993, a director of the International Office, University of Newcastle. His writings include *Tawfiq al-Hakim, playwright of Egypt* (1979). EURAMES, 1993; Note

Long, Charlotte R., born about 1950, she received a Ph.D. in 1980 from Case Western University, Cleveland, Ohio, for *The twelve gods in Greek and Roman art.* Her writings include *The Ayia Triadha sarcophagus* (1974), and *The twelve gods of Greece and Rome* (1987). Note about the author

Long, Colin D., born 20th cent., he was a solicitor who worked in private pratice and industry. He set up offices of his firm in Dubai and Sharjah. He spent two years working in the Persian Gulf before returning to London in 1978 where he specialized in the whole of the Middle East. His writings include *Telecom-munications law and practice* (1988), and *Competition aspects of interconnection agreements in the telecommunication sector; report to the European Commission* (Luxembourg, 1995). Note; ZKO

Long, David Edwin, born 21 November 1937 at Washington, Ga., he received his Ph.D. in 1973 from George Washington University, Washington, D.C. for *The Hajj today.* He was a senior analyst in the Office of Research for Near East and South Asia in the Department of State, Washington, D.C., and served in posts in the Sudan, Morocco, Saudi Arabia, and Jordan. He was a sometime executive director of the Center of Contemporary Arab Studies at Georgetown University, while on leave of absence from the U.S. Foreign Service, and a senior fellow at the Georgetown University Center for Strategic and International Studies. His writings include *The Persian Gulf* (1976), *Saudi Arabia* (1976), and *The United States and Saudi Arabia; ambivalent allies* (1985), *The government and politics of the Middle East and North Africa* (1986), and *The anatomy of terrorism* (1990). ConAu, 89-92; Note; Selim

Long, Edward Ernest, born in 1880 at Sutton Valence, Kent., England, he was a journalist who at one time contributed travel articles to the *Illustrated London News.* He travelled widely and was an editor of the *Rangoon Times* in 1905 and later of the *Indian Daily Telegraph.* During the first World War he was in charge of the eastern section of the News Department at the Foreign Office. He was the author of a book and a one-act play. He died on 10 November 1956. BioIn, 4 (1); *Illustrated London News*, 229 (17 November 1956), p. 853; *Who was who*, 5

Long, George, born 4 November 1800 at Poulton, Lancs., England, he was educated at Trinity College, Cambridge, and became a fellow of his College in 1823. In 1824, he was elected professor of ancient languages in the newly established University of Virginia at Charlottesville. After four years he returned to England as the first Greek professor at the University of London. In 1842, he became a professor of Latin at University College; from 1846 to 1849, he was reader in jurisprudence and civil law in the Middle Temple, and finally classical lecturer at Brighton College. Subsequently he lived in retirement at Portfield, Chichester. He was a founder, and for twenty years an officer, of the Royal Geographical Society and an active member of the Society for the Diffusion of Useful Knowledge. He died on 10 August 1879. BiD&SB; Boase; BritInd (7); DNB; Egyptology; EncBrit; Master (6); PeoHis

Long, George W., born in 1913 at Haddonfield, N.J., he graduated B.A. and M.A. in American history from Amherst College, Hanover, Mass. He taught this subject for ten years, before joining the staff of the *National geographic magazine* in 1945, becoming an assistant editor in 1953 of the *National* *geographic magazine.* On 9 November 1958 he was lost in line of duty when a Portuguese seaplane flying from Lisboa to Madeira was forced down at sea and vanished without trace. *National geographic magazine*, 115 (February 1959), p. 215 (not sighted)

Long, John Edward, born 16 March 1941 at Philadelphia, Pa., he graduated in 1963 from the local Temple University, received his B.D., Th.M. and M.A. elsewhere, before taking a Ph.D. in 1978 in classical and Oriental studies at Brandeis University, Waltham, Mass., presumingly for *Futūh Ifrīqiyā*. He had studied Arabic also at Tunis. In 2004 he was a professor in the Department of Philosophy and Religion, Western Kentucky University at Bowling Green. *MESA Roster of members*, 1982-1990; WhoBIA, 1980-2005

Long, P. Walter, born in 1895, he was in 1936 a flight-sergeant in the Royal Air Force. His writings include an account of his experiences as a prisoner of war in Mesopotamia after the fall of Kut in 1916, *Other ranks of Kut* (1938). BLC; LC

Longás y Bartibás, Pedro, born 1 July 1881 at Tauste, Spain, he was educated at Zaragoza, and Huesca, particularly at the Seminario Conciliar de Santa Cruz. After his ordination in 1904, he took courses in philosophy and history at the Universidad de Zaragoza. He was a sometime director of the Colegio de San Juan Bautista de Santoña (Santander), and a research fellow in the Sección de árabe in the Centro de Históricos de Madrid. His writings include *La representación aragonesa en la Junta Central Suprema* (1912), *Vida religiosa de los Moriscos* (1915), and *Catálogo de códices latinos* (1935). He died in Madrid in 1968. Ruiz C

Longhurst, Margaret Helen, born in 1882, she was educated privately and pursued a career with the Victoria and Albert Museum, London, where she retired as a keeper of the Department of Architecture and Sculpture. Her writings include *English ivories* (1926), and *Catalogue of carvings in ivory* (1927-29). She died in 1958. *Illustrated London News*, 232 (8 February 1958), p. 233 (not sighted); *Who's who*, 1948-58; Who was who, 5

Longley, Clifford Edmund, born 6 June 1940, he was a correspondent in religious affairs, leader writer and columnist to various British dailies, free-lance broadcaster, and author. His writings include *The Times book of Clifford Longley*, edited by Suzy Powling (1991), and *Chosen people; the big idea that shaped England and America* (2002). Note about the author; *Who's who*, 2001-2005

Longnon, Jean Baptiste Augustin, born 5 July 1887 at Paris, he was educated at the Collège Stanislav, École nationale des chartes, and École pratique des hautes études, Paris. He became an archivist and palaeographer. Since 1954 he was an honorary *conservateur* at the Bibliotheque de l'Institut de France. His writings include *Les Français d'outre-mer au moyen âge; essai sur l'expansion française dans le bassin de la Méditerranée* (1929), *Recherches sur la vie de Geoffroy de Villehardouin* (1939), *L'Empire latin de Constantinople et la principauté de Morée* (1949), and *Les Compagnons de Villehardouin; recherches sur les Croisés de la quatrième croisade* (1978). He died on 31 October 1980. WhoFr, 1955/56-1979/80

Longo, Francesco, born 19th cent., his writings include *Il canale di Messina e le sue correnti* (Messina, 1882). NUC, pre-1956

de **Longpérier**, Henri *Adrien* Prévost, born in 1816, he was educated at Meaux (Seine-et-Marne), France, and subsequently entered the Cabinet des médailles de la Bibliothèque du Roi in Paris. He served for some years as a joint editor of the *Revue numismatique*, Paris. His writings include *Description des médailles du Cabinet de M. de Magnoncour* (1840). He died in 1882. Dawson; CelCen (not sighted); Egyptology; Hoefer; IndexBFr² (5); Vapereau

Longrigg. Stephen Hemsley, born 7 August 1893 at Sevenoaks, Kent, England, he served in the first World War, and in 1918 entered the British Administration of Iraq. Two years later he took service with the Iraqi Government, in which he worked from 1920 to 1931. During the second World War he was governor of Eritrea from 1942 to 1944. He was made a doctor of letters by the University of Oxford on the strength of his historical work, and in 1969 he was awarded the Burton Memorial Medal for his eminent services in Oriental exploration and research. His writings include *Four centuries of modern Iraq* (1925), *A Short history of Eritrea* (1945), *Iraq, 1900-1950; a political, social, and economic history* (1953), *Syria and Lebanon under French mandate* (1958), and *Oil in the Middle East* (1961). He died in Guildford in 1979. Au&Wr, 1963, 1971; ConAu, 89-92; Note; JRCAS, 1970, p. 98; Who, 1956; Who was who, 7

Longuenesse, Elisabeth, born 20th cent., she received a *doctorat de 3ème cycle* in 1977 from the Université de Paris for *La Classe ouvrière en Syrie, une classe en formation*. In 1993, she was a research fellow of the Maison de l'Orient méditerranéen, Centre National de la Recherche Scientifique, Lyon. Her writings include *Le Golfe au sortir de la guerre* (1988); she edited *Bâtisseurs et bureaucrates; ingénieurs et sociétés au Maghreb et au Moyen-Orient; table ronde* (1991), *Santé,* *médecine et société dans le monde arabe* (1995); and she was a joint editor of *Professions scientifiques en crise; ingénieurs et médecins en Syrie, Égypte et Algérie* (1995). DrBSMES, 1993; EURAMES, 1993; *Livres disponibles*, 2004; THESAM, 3

Longuet, Henry, fl. 1935, his writings include *Introducton à la numismatique byzantine* (London, Spink & Son, 1961). BLC

Longuet, Robert Jean Gustave, born 9 December 1901 at Paris, he was a lawyer who started a career as journalist when still a university student. In 1926, he became one of the founders of the *Journal des retraités* and concurrently contributed to *le Populaire, le Quotidien, le Soir, la Nouvelle revue socialiste, la Presse*, and *Études nord-africaines*. In 1934, he became the founder and director of *Maghreb*. During the Spanish civil war he was a correspondent of the Agence Télégraphique-Radio. Prevented in 1939 from returning to Europe from the United States, he represented French mercantile interests and served as an expert in the court of New York. He later joined the Office (Bureau) of War Information, served as a lecturer in French civilization at Rutgers University, New Brunswick, N.J., as a delegate to U.N.R.R.A., and adviser to the Jewish Labor Committee. In 1950, he returned to France to become active in Third World affairs, particularly in Morocco and Madagascar. His writings include *Karl Marx, mon arrière-grand-père* (1977). He died on 19 March 1987. IndexBFr² (1); NDNC, 1961/62; NYT, 21 March 1987, p. 34, col. 5;

Longworth, Philip, born 17 February 1933 at London, he graduated in 1956 from Balliol College, Oxford. He was successively associated with the Central Asian Research Centre, London, the Commonwealth War Graves Commission, University of Birmingham, and University of London before he was appointed a professor of history at McGill University, Montreal, P.Q. in 1984, a position which he held until his retirement. His writings include *The Art of victory* (1965), *The Unending vigil* (1967), *The Cossacks* (1969), its translation, *Die Kosaken* (1971), *The Three empresses* (1972), *The Rise and fall of Venice* (1974), its translation, *Aufstieg und Fall der Republik Venedig* (1976), and *The Making of Eastern Europe, from prehistory to postcommunism* (1992). ConAu, 21-24, new rev., 10, 28; IntWW, 1977-2005; NatFacDr, 1990; WrDr, 1976/78-2005

Longworth Dames, Mansel, 1850-1922 *see* Dames, Mansel Longworth

Loomis, Louise Ropes, born in 1874 at Yokohama, Japan, she grew up in the United States and graduated in 1897 from Wellesley College. She subsequently held the position of instructor in classics and history at Whitman College, Walla Walla, Wash., until 1901 when she went for graduate study to Columbia University, New York, gaining her A.M. in 1902 and Ph.D. in 1906 for *Medieval Hellenism*. She briefly was an assistant in history at Barnard Collge, New York, before becoming, in 1905, a warden of Sage College and lecturer at Cornell University, Ithaca, N.Y. She subsequently taught Greek and history at a variety of colleges and universities in the United States. Her writings include *The Law of war and peace* (1949), and she edited *On man in the universe* (1943), and *The Council of Constance; the unification of the Church* (1961) as well as editions from the classics. She died in 1958. AmAu&B; Bioln, 4 (2); WhAm, 3; WhE&EA; WomWWA, 1914

Looney, Robert Edward, born 16 June 1941 at San Jose, Calif., he graduated B.Sc. in 1963 from the University of California at Davis where he also received a Ph.D. in 1969. He was successively a professor at the University of Santa Clara, Calif., and the Institute of International Studies, Monterey, Calif., before he became a professor of national security affairs at the Naval School of Postgraduate School in Monterey, Calif. His writings include *The Economic development of Iran* (1973), *Income distribution policies and economic growth in semiindustrialized countries* (1975), *The Economic development of Panama* (1976), *A Development strategy for Iran through the 1980s* (1977), and *Iran at the end of the century; a Hegelian forecast* (1977); he was joint author of *Economic causes and consequences of defense expenditures in the Middle East and South Asia* (1995). AmM&WSc, 1973 S, 1978 S; ConAu, 104; MESA Roster of members, 1990; NatFacDr, 1995-2005; Note; WhoCon, 1973; WhoWest, 1984/85

Loose, Rainer, born 4 June 1946 at Berlin, he received a Dr.phil. in 1974 from the Universität Frankfurt/Main, and a Dr.habil. in 1981 from the Universität Mannheim. Since 1992 he was a professor of geography at Mannheim. His writings include *Agrargeographie des südwestlichen Trentino* (1983); and he was a joint author of *Zur Geographie ländlicher Siedlungen in Afghanistan* (1977). Kürschner, 1992-2005

Loosen, Paul, born in 1886, he received a Dr.phil. in 1912 from the Universität Bonn for *Die weisen Narren des Naisaburi*. His trace is lost after two articles in 1935. Sezgin; Thesis

Łopaciński, Hieronim Rafał, born 30 September 1860 at Ośno, Poland, he studied at Uniwersytet Warszawski. He was a philologist, historian and ethnographer. He edited *Glosy polskie zawarte w rękopisie z kazaniami łacińskiemi z połowy wieku XV* (Krakowie, 1893). He died in Lublin on 25 August 1906. Feliks Araszkiewicz wrote *Hieronym Łopaciński, 1860-1906* (Lublin, 1928). Polski (12); OSK; PSB

MACK LIBRARY
BOB JONES UNIVERSITY
GREENVILLE, SC

Lopašić, Alexandar (Alexander), born 13 September 1928 at Beograd, he was for many years a lecturer in the Department of Sociology, University of Reading and served as a visiting professor in Germany. He edited *Mediterranean societies; tradition and change* (Zagreb, 1994). DrBSMES, 1993; Private; Unesco

Lopes, David de Melo, born in 1867 at the little town of Serta in Portugal, he made his first studies in Lisboa and later at the École des hautes études and the École des langues orientales, Paris. He taught for six years at a lyceum at Lisboa until 1902 when he was appointed to teach the advanced course in literature at the Universidade de Lisboa. In 1911, he there became director of the Faculty of letters, a position which he held until his retirement in 1937. His writings include *Textos em aljamia portuguesa* (1897), *Os Arabes nas obras de Alexandre Herculano* (1911), *Historia de Arzila durante o dominio portugués* (1924); and he edited and translated from the Arabic of Qutb al-Dīn al-Nahrawānī, *Extractos da conquista do Yaman pelos Othomanos* (1892), and from Zayn al-Dīn al-Ma'barī, *Historia dos Portugueses no Malabar*. In 1945 appeared *Mélanges d'études luso-marocaines dédiés à la mémoire de D. Lopes et P. de Cenival*, and in 1969, *Cultura islâmica e cultura árabe; estudios em honra de David Lopes*. He died in Lisboa on 13 February 1942. Buckland; IndiceE³ (1); *Islamic culture*, 21 (1947), pp. 1-2; ZKO

Lopez, Atanasio, O.F.M., born 12 October 1876 in the Province of Léon, Spain, he was educated in Galicia, at Madrid, and the international college at Quaracchi, Italy. He was in 1914 a founding member and editor of the *Archivo Ibero-Americano*, a periodical which he headed from 1919 to 1930. His writings include *Los obispos de Marruecos desde el siglo XIII* (1920), and its revised edition, *Obispos en el Africa septentrionale* (1941). He died from angina pectoris in Satiago de Compostela on 1 March 1944. Hespéris, vol. 31 (1944), p. 69; IndiceE³ (1)

Lopez, Robert(o) Sabatino, born 8 October 1910 at Genova, Italy, he taught medieval history in Italy until 1939 when he went to the United States. He successively taught at the University of Wisconsin and briefly at Columbia University, New York. From 1946 to his retirement in 1971 he was a professor at Yale University, New Haven, Conn. His writings include *Studi sull'economia genovese nel medio evo* (Torino, 1936), *Storia delle colonie genovese nel Mediterraneo* (Bologna, 1938), and *Medieval trade in the Mediterranean world* (1955). He died on 6 July 1986. BioIn, 15, 16; CnDiAmJBi; ConAu, 112, 119; DrAS, 1969 H, 1974 H, 1978 H, 1982 H; IntWW, 1981/82-1986/87; WhAm, 9; WhoAm, 1974-1986/87; WhoWorJ, 1965, 1972, 1978

López Anglada, Luis, born in 1919, he was a poet and novelist whose writings include *La arena y los sueños; poemas del Sahara* (1972), and *Canto de Tarik; poemas de la conquista de España* (Madrid, Instituto Hispano-Árabe de Cultura, 1984). IndiceE³ (7); LC; ZKO

López de Ayala, Jerónimo Conde de Cedillo, visconde de Palazuelos, he was born on 4 December 1862 at Toledo, Spain. His writings include *Toledo; guía artístico-práctica* (1890). He died on 15 March 1934. Ossorio; Ruiz C; Sainz

López Baralt, Luce, born 21 August 1944 at Rio Piedras, Puerto Rico, he graduated in 1966 from the local University of Puerto Rico and received his Ph.D. in 1974 from Harvard University, Cambridge, Mass. He then did postgraduate studies at the American University of Beirut, and the universities of Madrid and Santander. Since 1969 he taught Spanish at the University of Puerto Rico, Rio Piedras. His writings include *Huellas del Islam en la literatura español; de Juan Ruiz a Juan Goytisolo* (1985), its translation, *Islam in Spanish literature from the Middle Ages to the present* (1992), *San Juan de la Cruz y el Islam; estudio sobre las filiaciones semiticas de su literatura mistica* (1985); and he edited *El sol a medianoche; la experience mistica, tradicion y actualidad* (1996). WhoS&SW, 1982/83; ZKO

López-Cuervo, Serafín, born 20th cent., his writings include *Medina Az-Zahra; ingeniería y formas* (Madrid, Ministerio de Obras Públicas y Urbanismo, 1985), and he was a joint author of *Parque nacional de Timanfaya* (Madrid, Instituto Nacional para la Conservación de la Naturaleza, 1985). ZKO

López Dominguez, José, born 29 November 1829 at Marbella (Málaga), Spain, he was a military officer, who retired with the rank of general, and a politician. His writings include *San Pedro de Abanto y Bilboa; operaciones del Ejército del Norte, mandado por el Capitan General Duque de la Torre, en 1874* (Madrid, 1876), and *Cartagena; memoria y commentario sobre el sitio de Cartagena* (1877). He died in Madrid on 17 October 1911. EncicUni; IndiceE³ (14)

López Elum, Pedro, born 20th cent., his writings include *La alquería islámica en Valencia* (1994), and he edited *Historiarum Ferdinandi regis Aragoniae*, of Lorenzo Valla (Valencia, 1970), and *Crónica* (Valencia, 1973), and *La conquista y repoblación valenciana durante el reinado de Jaime I* (Valencia, 1995). LC

López Estrada, Francisco, born 21 May 1918 at Barcelona, he was a professor of Spanish successively at the universities of La Laguna, Santiago de Compostela, Sevilla, and Madrid. His writings include *Introducción a la literatura medieval española* (1952), *Tradiciones andaluzas* (1958), *La toma de Antequera* (1964), *Métrica española del siglo XX* (1969), *Notas sobre la espiritualidad española de los siglos de oro* (1972), *Poética para un poeta* (1972), *La Galatea* (1995); and he edited *Embajada a Tamerlán*, of Gonzáles de Clavijo (1943). DBEC; IndiceE³ (2); WhoSpain, 1963

López García, Bernabé, born 4 December 1947 at Granada, he studied at the Universidad Autónoma de Madrid, where he received a doctorate in 1973 in philosophy and letters, specializing in Semitic philology. He was a professor in the Departamento de Estudios Árabes e Islámicos of his alma mater, and he did field-work in Moroccan elections and at the Université Sidi Mohamed Ben Abdallah, Fès. An authority in migration and sociology of the Maghreb, his writings include *Contribución a la historia del arabismo español, 1840-1917* (1974), *Procesos electorales en Marruecos, 1960-1977* (1979), *Política y movimientos sociales en el Magreb* (1989), and he edited *Europa y mundo árabe en la política mediterránea* (1989), *Elecciones, participación y transiciones políticas en el Norte de Africa* (1991), and *Inmigración magrebi en España; el retorno de los Moriscos* (1993). Arabismo, 1992, 1994, 1997; EURAMES, 1993; Private; ZKO

López Guijarro, Salvador, born in 1834 at Granada, he received a degree in philosophy and letters and became a politician, diplomat and writer, and a sometime Spanish minister plenipotentiary to Greece. His writings include *Colección de articulos politicos* (Madrid, 1872), and *Tierra y cielo* (1886). He died in 1904. EncicUni; IndiceE³ (6); NUC, pre-1956

López y López, Ángel Custodio, born about 1945, he received a doctorate in Semitic philology. He became a professor in the Universidad de las Palmas de Gran Canaria, where he specialized in Arabo-Spanish culture and civilization. He edited and translated *Kitāb fī tartīb auqāt al-ǧirāsa wa'l-maǧrūsāt; un tradado agricola andalusi anónimo* (Granada, Consejo Superior de Investigaciones Cientificas, 1990). Arabismo, 1992, 1994, 1997; EURAMES, 1993; ZKO

López Morales, Gloria, born 29 May 1940 at Mexico City, she studied in Mexico and France. After a diploma in political science and a doctorate she worked since 1985 for Unesco, Paris. She was a joint author of *The missing half, woman, 1975* (Rome, Food and Agriculture Organization, 1975). WhoUN, 1992

López Morillas, Consuelo, born 7 July 1944 at Iowa City, Iowa, she graduated in 1965 from Bryn Mawr (Pa.) College and received her Ph.D. in 1974 from the University of California at Berkeley for *Lexical and etymological studies in the Aljamiado Koran based on manuscripts 4938 of the Biblioteca Nacional, Madrid*. After briefly teaching at Ohio State University, she was appointed in 1982 a professor in the Department of Spanish, Indiana University at Bloomington, a position which she still held in 2005. Her writings include *The Qur'ān in sixteenth-century Spain; six Morisco versions of sura 79* (1982). Arabismo, 1992; DrAS, 1982 F; *MESA Roster of members*, 1990; ZKO

López Ortiz, José, O.S.A., born 10 July 1898 at San Lorenzo de El Escorial, Spain, he studied arts and philosophy at the Seminario Conciliar de Madrid and in 1917 entered the Orden Agustiniana at the Real Monasterio del El Escorial. After further theological study he was ordained in 1922. He obtained a *licenciatura* and a doctorate in law in 1932 from the Universidad Central for *Derecho musulmán*. Since 1934 he taught history of jurisprudence at the Universidad de Santiago. He was a sometime bishop of Tuy-Vigo and later became an archbishop. Ciudad de Dios, 156 (1944), pp. 417-27; IndiceE³ (6); Quien, 1985; WhoSpain, 1963

López Otero, Modesto, born 24 February 1885 at Valladolid, Spain, he was a Spanish architect whose writings include *Una influencia española en la arquitectura norteamericana* (1926). Figuras; IndiceE (3)

López Pereira, José Eduardo, born 20th cent., his writings include *Estudio crítico sobre la Crónica Mozárabe de 754* (Zaragoza, 1980). LC; ZKO

Lopez Serrano, Matilde, born 6 October 1899 at Badajoz, Spain, she received a diploma in arts, and a doctorate, and became an archivist specializing in the art of the book. In 1942, she became the founding editor of *Bibliografía de arte español y americano*. Her own writings include *Incunables desconocidos* (1947), *Incunables españoles* (1947), *Lámparas, relojes y porcelanos del Palacio Nacional* (1950), *El Escorial* (1963), and *El Códice aureo* (1974). IndiceE³ (3); WhoSpain, 1963

Loprieno, Antonio, born 20th cent., he received a Ph.D. in 1979 from the University of California with a thesis on ancient Near Eastern studies. He was a professor of Egyptology at the Universität Basel, Switzreland, and concurrently associated with the Department of Near Eastern Languages and Cultures, University of California, Los Angeles, and the Dipartimento orientale, Università di Torino. His writings include *Sequential forms in late Egyptian and Biblical Hebrew* (1980), *Das Verbalsystem im Ägyptischen und im Semitischen* (1986), *Topos und Mimesis* (1988), and *Ancient Egyptian literature* (1996). Kürschner, 2003-2005

Loraine, Sir Percy Lyham, born 5 November 1880, he was educated at Eton and then went up to New College, Oxfod, in 1899, but on the outbreak of the South African War he joined the Imperial Yeomanry and served in South Africa until the end of the campaign. He entered the Diplomatic Service in 1904 and served in Turkey, Persia, Roma, Peking and Paris. In 1916, he was posted to Madrid as First Secretary and head of the Chancery. In 1921, he became Minister at Tehran, where he served five years, being then transferred to Athens and in 1929 to Cairo, where he had the difficult task of succeeding Lord Lloyd. In 1933, he was posted as ambassador to Ankara, where he achieved outstanding success and won the esteem and intimate friendship of Kemal Atatürk. After six years in Turkey, he was transferred as ambassador to Roma on the eve of the second World War, but too late to influence the minds of Mussolini and Ciano. He retired from the Foreign Service in 1940. In 1924, he was elected fellow of the Royal Geographical Society. He died on 23 May 1961. Gordon Waterfield wrote *Professional diplomat, Sir Percy Loraine of Kirkhale* (1973). Bioln, 5 (2); DNB; *Geographical journal*, 127 (1961), p. 387; Goldschmidt; ObitT, 1961-70, pp. 492-93; *Who was who*, 6; Wright, pp. xv, 37

Lorandi, Marco, born 17 April 1942 at Bergamo, Italy, he was a lecturer in history of modern and contemporary art at the Facoltà di lingue e lettere straniere, Università di Bergamo. His writings include *I Fantoni* (1978), *Alberto Martini, 1876-1954* (1985), *Tà erotikà* (1987), and *Il mito di Ulisse nella pittura a fresco del cinquecento italiano* (1996). Note

Lorch, Netanel, born 24 May 1925 at Künzelsau, Germany, he came to Palestine in 1935, graduated in 1943 from the Teachers' College, Jerusalem, and graduated M.A. in 1951 from the Hebrew University, Jerusalem. He was a government official and diplomat. His writings include *The Edge of the sword* (1961), *Israel's war of independence* (1968), and *One long war; Arab versus Jew since 1920* (1976), its translation, *Las guerras de Israel* (1983), and he edited *Major Knesset debates, 1948-1981* (1993). WhoWorJ, 1965, 1972, 1978; WhoIsrael, 1973/74-1992/93; WhoWor, 1978/79

Lorch, Richard P., born 13 June 1942 in England, he received a Ph.D. in 1971 from the University of Manchester with a thesis entitled *Jabir Ibn Aflah and his influence in the West*. In 1977-78 he taught mathematics at the University of Bir Zeit; 1978-80, was a Humboldt Fellow at München; and 1980-82, he was at the Institute of the History of Arabic Science, Aleppo. Thereafter he was for about twenty years at München, mostly involved with research projects. He was joint author of *The Da'ire-yi Mu'addel of Seydi 'Ali Re'is* (1976), *The Aegean sea-chart of Mehmed Reis Ibn Menemenli* (1977), *Maslama's notes on Ptolemy's Planisphaerium and related texts* (1994), and *The melon-shaped astrolabe in Arabic astronomy* (1999). A collection of his articles was published in 1995 entitled *Arabic mathematical sciences; instruments, texts, transmissions*. Private; Sluglett; ZKO

Lord, Albert Bates, born 15 September 1912 at Boston, Mass., he graduated in 1934 from Harvard where he subsequently served for thirty-three years as a professor of Slavic studies. He repeatedly conducted research in Yugoslavia, Albania, and Bulgaria. His writings include *Serbo-Croatian folk songs* (1951), *Slavic folklore* (1956), *Beginning Serbocroation* (1964), *The Singer of tales* (1965), *Russian folk tales* (1970); and he was a joint author of *A Bulgarian literary reader* (1968). He died in Boston on 29 July 1991. In 1981 appeared *Oral traditional literature; a festschrift for Albert Bates Lord.* Bioln, 17; ConAu, 103, 135, new rev., 85; WhAm, 10; WhoAm, 1974/75-1980

Lord, Percival Barton, born 1808, he studied at Dublin University and received a medical doctorate in 1832 from the University of Edinburgh. In 1834, he became an assistant surgeon in the service of the East India Company at Bombay. He was a medical officer with Sir Alexander Burnes on his mission to Kabul in 1836. He was later made political assistant to Sir William H. Macnaghten. He was present in the fighting in the Khyber in 1839; he was sent to obtain information, in 1839/40, of the Amir Dost Muhammad after his flight. He spent the winter at Bamian. He was killed when Dost Muhammad defeated the British force at Parwandarra on 2 November 1840. His writings include *Popular psychology* (1834), and *Algiers, with notices of the neighbouring states of Barbary* (1835). Buckland; DNB

Lorent, Jacob August, fl. 19th cent., he travelled in Egypt in 1842-43. His writings include *De animalculis infusoriis* (Mannheim, 1837), *Wanderungen im Morgenlande während den Jahren 1842-1843* (Mannheim, 1846), and *Egypten, Alhambra, Tlemsen, Algier; Reisebilder aus den Anfängen der Photographie* (1861). BLC; GV; Sezgin

Lorentz, John Henry, born 7 June 1940, he graduated from Miami University, gained his M.A. at Harvard, and received his Ph.D. in 1974 from Princeton University for *Modernization and political change in nineteenth-century Iran; the role of Amir Kabir*. He resided over five years in the Middle East, mostly in Iran, as a U.S. Peace Corps volunteer. He subsequently worked as a consultant on Middle East affairs and as director of American Aid for Afghans. In the 1980s he began an academic career as a teacher and administrator, lastly at the Department of Social Science, Shawness State

University, Portsmouth, Ohio, a position which he held until his retirement. His writings include *Historical dictionary of Iran* (1995). *MESA Roster of members*, 1982-1990; NatFacDr, 1995-2005; Note about the author

Lorenz, Charlotte, born 26 July 1895 at Oschersleben, Germany, she studied modern languages, including Turkish, and political economy at the Universität Berlin, where she received a Dr.phil. in 1919 for *Die Frauenfrage im Osmanischen Reiche mit besonderer Berücksichtigung der arbeitenden Klasse*. She then entered the German Bureau of Statistics in Berlin. After her Dr.habil. in 1927, she taught political economy and statistics at her alma mater. After the second World War, she was a professor at the Universität Göttingen. Her writings include *Die Statistik in der Kriegswirtschaft* (1935), and *Zehnjahres Statistik des Hochschulbesuchs und der Abschlußprüfungen* (1943). She died in Berlin on 1 April 1979. DtBE; DtBilnd (3); Hanisch; Kürschner, 1935-1976; LexFrau; Schwarz; *Wer ist wer*, 1950-1971/73

Lorenz, Manfred, born 6 October 1929 at Triebes/Thüringen, Germany, he originally trained as a Russian teacher at Pädagogische Fachschule, Weimar, and then taught at a school in Neustadt/Orla until 1952, when he started to study Slavic and Oriental languages at Humboldt-Universität, Berlin. He spent 1957-58 at the Tajikistan State University, Dushanbe, and in 1961 received his Dr.phil. at Berlin for *Untersuchung über Verschiedenheiten im tağikischen und persischen Satzbau*. He subsequently taught Iranian philology at his alma mater until his retirement. His writings include a *Lehrbuch der persischen Sprache* (1967), *Lehrbuch des Pashto* (1979), *Der Zauberbrunnen; Märchen und Geschichten aus Afghanistan* (1985) as well as translations from the modern writers, ʿAbd al-Husayn Nūshīn and Sadr a-l-Dīn ʿAinī. BioB134; Kürschner, 1992-2005; Private; Schoeberlein; Schwarz

Lorenz, Reinhold, born 24 January 1898 at Zittau, Saxony, he studied modern history, geography and philosophy and received a Dr.phil. in 1921 from the Universität Wien for *Volksbewaffnung und Staatsidee in Österreich, 1792-1797*. He later became a historian at his alma mater. His writings include *Das großdeutsche Problem* (1930), *Türkenjahr 1683; das Reich im Kampf um den Ostraum* (1933), and *Drei Jahrhunderte Volk, Staat und Reich* (1942), *Japan und Mitteleuropa* (1944), *Der österreichische Heil-quellenkataster* (1953). Kürschner, 1935-1940/41, 1955-1980|; Teichl; WhoAustria, 1959/60-1969/70

Loret, Victor Clément Georges Philippe, born 1 September 1859 at Paris, he initially studied at the Conservatoire de Paris but his acquaintance with Gaston Maspéro at the Musée du Louvre changed his direction of study so that he continued at the École des Hautes Études and the Collège de France. He afterwards went to Cairo as an Egyptologist. As an musicologist he there also pursued an interest in popular Egyptian music. From 1886 to his retirement in 1929 he taught Egyptology at the Université de Lyon. He died in Lyon on 3 February 1946. Egyptology; *Revue archéologique*, 6e série, 38 (1951), pp. 54-55; Vapereau

Loria, Gino, born 19 May 1862 at Mantua, Italy, he graduated from the Università di Torino. From 1884 to his retirement in 1935 he held the chair of geometry at the Università di Genova. His writings include *Guida allo studia della storia delle matematiche* (1916), and *Metodi matematici* (1935). He died in Genova on 30 January 1954. BioIn, 3; *Chi è*, 1928-1936; DcScB; IndBiItal (2)

Lorimer, David Lockhart Robertson, born 24 December 1876, he entered the British Army in 1896, and in 1903 joined the Indian Political Department. Before the first World War, he held the post of Political Agent at Bahrain, and spent the years 1912-12 as H.M. Consul in Kirman and Persian Baluchistan. There followed a short period when he was Political Agent in Chitral, but he was soon on war service with the Indian Expeditionary Force in Mesopotamia. He became Civil Governor of Amara in 1917. After the war, he returned to India, and became Political Agent at Gilgit. During his four years there, he and his wife made a detailed study of the Hunza country, where they were pioneers in recording the local language. After his retirement he did useful work in postal censorship during the second World War. His writings include *The Dumaki language* (1939), and *The Wakhi language* (1958). He died 26 February 1962. *Geographical journal* 128 (1962), pp. 369-70; Master (2); Riddick; *Who was who*, 6; Wright, p. 84

Lorimer, Emily née Overend, born in 1881 at Dublin, she studied at Alexandra College, Dublin, Somerville College, Oxford, and graduated from the Royal University of Ireland. While in Hunza with her husband, Lt.-Col. D. L. R. Lorimer, she was a Kashmir correspondent for the London *Times*. She was a keen student of languages and in addition to her own work of authorized translations from the German, she was her husband's amanuensis, indexer and collaborator in his studies of Persian dialects, Pashtu and languages of the Hinku Kush and Karakoram. Her writings include *What the German needs* (1942). She died in 1949. Master (1); Note; WhE&EA; *Who was who*, 4

Lorimer, Frank, born 1 July 1894 at Bradley, Me, he graduated in 1916 from Yale University, New Haven, Conn., and received his Ph.D. in 1929 from Columbia University, New York, for *The growth of*

reason. He was a Baptist minister in New York before he embarked on a career as a scientist of human population, covering such diverse areas as Soviet and African societies. He was from 1938 to 1964 a professor of sociology at the American University Graduate School, Washington, D.C. His writings include *Dynamics of population* (1934), and *The Population of the Soviet Union* (1946); he was a joint author of *Culture and human fertility* (1954); and he edited *Population in Africa* (1960). He died in Waketane, New Zealand, on 23 June 1985. AnObit, 1985, pp. 315-16; BioIn, 14; ConAu, 116; Unesco; WhAm, 10; WhoAm, 1974/75-1980

Lorimer, John Gordon, born in 1870, he was educated at Edinburgh University and Christ Church College, Oxford. He then entered the Indian Civil Service and arrived in India in 1891. He became a deputy commissioner in 1902; political officer in North Waziristan, 1898-99, and in the Khyber, 1899; and assistant secretary in the Foreign Department of the Government of India, 1899-1901. His writings include *Customary law of the main tribes in the Peshawar District* (Lahore, 1899), *Grammar and vocabulary of Waziri Pashto* (Calcutta, 1901), and *Gazetteer of the Persian Gulf, 'Omān, and Central Arabia* (Calcutta, 1908-15). He died in 1914. IndianBilnd (1); Kornrumpf; NUC, pre-1956; Who was who, 1

Lorimer, William Laughton, F.B.A., LL.D., born in 1885 at Strathmartine, Scotland, he was successively a professor of classics at University College, Dundee, and the University of St. Andrews. His writings include *The Text tradition of pseudo-Aristotle "De mundo"* (1924), and *Aristotelis qui fertur libellus; de Mundo* (1933). He died in 1967. Au&Wr, 1963; Who was who, 6

Lorin, Henri, born 2 July 1866 at Bayonne (Basses Pyrénées), France, he received a doctorate in 1895 from the Université de Paris and became a professor of colonial geography at the Université de Bordeaux and was a sometime professor at Tunis. He was a *député* for Gironde and a chief editor of the *Revue de géographie commerciale de Bordeaux*. His writings include *Promenade en Tunisie* (1896), *La France, puissance coloniale; étude d'histoire et de géographie politique* (1906), *L'Afrique du nord; Tunisie, Algérie, Maroc* (1908), *L'héroique Serbie* (1915), *Bordeaux, la Gironde* (1921), *L'Égypte d'aujourd'hui* (1926), and *Bibliographie géographique de l'Égypte* (1928-29). He died in 1932. Qui êtes-vous, 1924

Lőrincz, László, born 15 June 1939 at Szilvásszentmárton, Hungary, he was a Mongolian scholar whose writings include *Az éjszakai kutya* (1966), *A mongol népköltészet* (1969), *Mongólia története* (1969), its translation, *Histoire de la Mongolie* (1984), *Mongolische Märchentypen* (1979), *A Nagy fa árnyékában* (1979), and *Kéz a sziklán* (1997). Biograf, 2004

Lőrinczi, Marinella, born 20th cent., her writings include *Nel dedalo del drago; introduzione a Dracula* (1992), *Paesaggio marino con dame vittoriane* (1995), and *Giorno del giudizio* (2002). Catalogo dei libri in commercio, 2003

Loring, Ulick, fl. 20th cent., he wrote *The Yemeni monarchy; with a genealogy compiled by Jeffrey Finestone* (London, MPA Publications for the Hamid Ed-Din Order of the Crown of Yemen, 1977). LC

Lorini, Eteocle, born in 1865, he was an Italian economist whose writings include *La questione della valuta in Austria-Ungharia* (1893), *La riforma monetaria della Russia* (1897), *La Persia economica contem-poranea e la sua questione monetaria* (1900), *Il profitto* (1901), and *La Repubblica Argentina e la sua odierna crisi* (1902). He died in 1919. NUC, pre-1956

Lortat-Jacob, Bernard, born in 1941, he was an ethnomusicologist whose writings include *Musique et fêtes au Haut-Atlas* (1980), *Ballades et fêtes en Roumanie* (1985), *L'improvisation dans les musiques de tradition orale* (1987), *Chroniques sardes* (1990), *Indiens chanteurs de la Sierra Madre; l'oreille de l'ethnologue* (1994), and he was a joint author of *La Saison des fêtes dans une vallée du Haut-Atlas* (1978), and *A tue-tête; chant et violon au pays de l'Oach, Roumanie* (2002). LC; Livres disponibles, 2004

Lortet, Louis Charles, born 22 August 1836 at Oullins (Rhône), France, he was a professor of zoology at the École de médecine de Lyon, and in 1877 became a director of the Muséum d'histoire naturelle, and dean of the Faculté de médecine in Lyon. He went on special missions to Greece and Syria. In 1872, he was decorated with the Légion d'honneur. His writings include *Syrie d'aujourd'hui; voyages; voyages dans la Phénicie, le Liban et la Judée, 1875-1880* (1884). He died in Lyon on 25 December 1909. Dawson; Egyptology; IndexBFr² (3); Kornrumpf; Kornrumpf, N; Vapereau

Lory, Pierre, born 22 April 1952 at Paris, he studied at the Université de Paris, where he also received a *doctorat de 3ème cycle* in 1983 for *Édition, traduction et commentaire de dix traités de Gabir Ibn Hayyan*. He was in 1993 a *directeur d'études* at l'École pratique des Hautes études, Paris, specializing in Sufism, philosophy and occult sciences. In 1997, he was affiliated with the Université de Bordeaux. His writings include *Les commentaires ésotériques du Coran d'après 'Abd ar-Razzâq al-Qâshâni* (1980), *Alchimie et mystique en terre d'islam* (1989), and he edited *L'Elaboration de l'elixir suprême*

(1988), and *Les Orients des lumières* (1996). AnEIFr, 1997; EURAMES, 1993; *Livres disponibles*, 2003; Private; THESAM, 3

Losa Palestra, António, fl. 20th cent., his writings include *Raizes judaico-cristãs do islamicmo* (Braga, 1963). NUC, 1968-72

Losado Campos, Teresa, born about 1945, she received a doctorate about 1977 from the Universidad de Barcelona for *Estudios sobre Coranes aljamiados.* LC

Löschner, Harald, born 15 December 1940, he studied law and Oriental languages at the universities of Erlangen-Nürnberg, Lausanne, and Tehran and received a Dr.phil. in 1971 from the Universität Erlangen for a thesis on nationality and Islam entitled *Staatsangehörigkeit und Islam*, and also a Dr.jur. in the same year for a thesis on the dogmatic foundation of Shi'ite law entitled *Die dogmatischen Grundlagen des ši'itischen Rechts.* On 1 April 1971 he joined the German Foreign Office; from 2003 to his retirement in 2005 he was an ambassador to Tajikistan. Schwarz; Thesis; *Wer ist wer*, 2005/2006

Losman, Donald Lee, born 15 July 1942 at Pittsburgh, Pa., he graduated in 1966 from the University of Florida, where he also received his Ph.D. in 1969 for *International economic sanctions; the boycotts of Cuba, Israel, and Rhodesia*, a work which was published in 1979. He was successively a professor of economics at the University of Tennessee, Chattanooga, and Loyola University, New Orleans. His writings also include *The Promise of American industry; an alternative assessment of problems and prospects* (1990), and he was a joint author of *Overall economic development program* (1970). WhoCon, 1973

Lot-Falck, Éveline, born in 1915, she was a joint author of *Les Religions de l'Europe du nord* (Paris, 1974). NUC, 1973-77

Loth, Gaston, born in 1866, he received a doctorate in 1905 from the Université de Paris for *Arnoldo Soler, chargé d'affaires d'Espagne à Tunis, et sa correspondance, 1808-1810.* His writings include *Histoire de la Tunisie depuis les origines jusqu'à nos jours* (1898), *Le Peuplement italien en Tunisie et en Algérie* (1905), *Petite histoire de France et de l'Afrique du nord* (1907), and *L'Enfida et Sidi-Tabet* (1910). BN; NUC, pre-1956

Loth, Otto, he was born6 March 1844 at Meißen, Germany. After education at the renowned Fürsten-schule St. Alfa, he studied at Leipzig under H. L. Fleischer and L. Krehl from 1863 to 1866, submitting his thesis, *Über Leben und Werke des Abdallah Ibn el Mu'tazz*, in 1866 (published posthumously in 1882). From 1874 until his death he was a professor at the Universität Leipzig and, almost concurrently, editor of the *Zeitschrift der Deutschen Morgenländischen Gesellschaft.* It was only a year before his death that he acquired a first-hand knowledge of the Islamic world through travels to Constantinople, Cairo and Damascus in the winter term, 1879-1880. His writings include *Das Classenbuch des Ibn Sa'd* (1869), and the *Catalogue of the Arabic manuscripts in the Library of the India Office* (1877). He died after a sickness of only two days on 17 March 1881. *Otto Loth; ein Gedenkblatt für seine Freunde*; edited by August Müller, Halle, 1881

Lottin de Laval, Victorien Pierre (or René), born 19 September 1810 at Orbec-en-Auge (Calvados), France, he was an archaeologist who, in the service of the Ministère de l'Instruction publique, went on several scientific missions to Italy, Greece, Asia Minor and Persia, which are embodied in his *Un an sur les chemins* (1837). His other writings include *Voyage dans la Peninsule arabique de Sinaï et de l'Égypte moyenne* (1855-59). He died in Menneval (Eure) in February 1903. Dawson; Egyptology; Glaeser; IndexBFr² (4); Kornrumpf; Vapereau

Lotz, John (Lájos), born 23 March 1913 at Milwaukee, Wisc., he finished his first grade in a German Lutheran school at Detroit, but was taken to Hungary by his parents when he was about seven years old. He continued his education in small Hungarian towns and studied philology at Budapest University, where he received his doctorate in 1935. In the same year, he went to Stockholm, with a fellowship from the Swedish Government for Germanic studies and philosophy, while also serving as lecturer in Hungarian and director of the Hungarian Institute at Stockholms Universitet. In 1947, he joined the Faculty of Columbia University, New York, first as a visitor, and later as a permanent member of both the linguistics department and the Department of Uralic and Altaic Languages, which he founded and chaired. From 1959 to 1965 he was a director of research of the American Council of Learned Societies. He was a visiting professor in Stockholm, 1962-63, and in Budapest in 1966 and again in 1972. The Hungarian Academy of Sciences elected him a member in 1973. His writings include *A történelmi világkép* (Pécsett, 1936), *Das ungarische Sprachsystem* (Stockholm, 1936), *Hungarian reader* (1962), and *The Uralic and Altaic program of the American Council of Learned Societies* (1966). He died in Chevy Chase, Md., on 25 August 1973. DrAS, 1969 F; *Slavic review*, 33 (1874), pp. 417-418; WhAm, 6

Loubignac, Victorien, born 26 September 1892 at Geyrac (Dordogne), France, he was educated at the École normale d'instituteurs at Bouzaréa, Algeria. From the outset he pursued an interest in the country and quickly obtained diplomas in Arabic at the Faculté des lettres d'Alger. At that time the French army needed interpreters for the Bureau des Affaires indigènes. In 1916, he became the personal Arabic interpreter to Maréchal Lyautey, later adding competence in Berber dialects. Having also been trained in French law, he advanced to the position of inspector in 1928. In subsequent years he also taught at the Institut des hautes études marocaines at Rabat. His writings include *Étude sur le dialecte berbère des Zaïan et Aït Sgougou* (1924), and *Textes arabes des Zaër* (1952). He died of a pitiless disease in 1946. Hespéris, 33 (1946), pp. 1-2; NUC, pre-1956

Loucatos, Sp. D. *see* Loukatos, Spyridon D.

Loucel, Henri, born 20th cent., he was in 1969 a *maître assistant* at the École nationale des langues orientales vivantes, Paris. Note about the author

Louis, André Marie, Rev.P., born 30 September 1912 at Ay-Champagne (Marne), France, he was educated at the Séminaire de Reims and entered the novitiate at the Pères Blancs in Carthage, where he was ordained in 1938. In 1941, he began to study Arabic at the Institut des Belles Lettres Arabes (I.B.L.A.), Tunis, in due course becoming librarian, archivist, and editor of the Institute's journal *I.B.L.A.* A this time he began his anthropological field-work among peasants, fishermen, and nomads, concurrently giving evening courses to Tunisian students. From 1956 to 1964, he was in charge of a private secondary school at El-Menzah but also teaching colloquial Arabic. At the same time, he received his doctorate from the Université de Paris for *Les Îles Kerkena (Tunisie); étude d'ethnographie humaine*. Since 1964 he taught North African sociology, social anthropology, and ethnology at the Université de Tunis. In 1972, he was appointed a *maître de recherche* at the Centre National de la Recherche Scietifique. He died in the midst of an active life while on a short visit to Paris on 8 November 1978. His writings include *Documents ethnographiques et linguistiques sur les îles Kerkena* (1961-62), *Tunisie du sud; ksars et villages de crêtes* (1975), *Bibliographie ethnosociologique de la Tunisie* (1977), and *Nomades d'hier et d'aujourd'hui dans le Sud tunisien* (1979). Hommes et destins, vol. 7, pp. 314-321

Louis, Georges, born 20th cent., his writings include *Report to the Government of Ethiopia on the development of school gardens in Ethiopia* (Rome, Food and Agriculture Organization, U.N.O., 1964). NUC

Louis, Herbert, born 12 March 1900 at Berlin, he recceived a Dr.phil. in 1927 from the Universität Berlin for a thesis on the geography of Albanian Epirus entitled *Beiträge zur Landeskunde des albanischen Epirus*. He was a professor of geography at Berlin before he accepted in 1935 the chair of geography at Ankara, which he held until 1943, when he returned to Germany to become director of Geographisches Institut in the Universität Köln. He later moved to München where he held a similar post. His writings include *Albanien; eine Landeskunde vornehmlich auf Grund eigener Reisen* (1927), its translation, *Албания* (Moscow, 1948), *Das natürliche Pflanzenkleid Anatoliens* (1939), and *Morphologische Studien in Südwest-Bulgarien* (1930). He died in München on 11 July 1985. Kürschner, 1935-1983

Louis, William *Roger*, born 8 May 1936 at Detroit, Mich., he graduated in 1959 from the University of Oklahoma, and received his D.Phil. in 1962 from Oxford. He subsequently spent eight years as a professor of history at Yale University, New Haven, Conn. From 1970 to 1985 he held the Kerr Chair of English History and Culture at the University of Texas, Austin. He later became associated with St. Antony's College, Oxford. His writings include *Ruanda-Urundi, 1884-1919* (1963), *Britain and Germany in Africa* (1967), *Great Britain and Germany's lost colonies, 1914-1919* (1967), *More adventures with Britannia; personalities, politics and culture in Britain* (1998), *Still more adventures with Britannia* (2003), he was a join editor of *A Revolutionary year; the Middle East in 1958* (2002), and he was editor-in-chief of the *Oxford history of the British Empire*. In 1999 appeared *The Statecraft of British imperialism; essays in honour of Wm. Roger Louis*. Who's who, 1996-2005; WhoWor, 1993/94

Louis d'Or, pseud. *see* Klaproth, Heinrich *Julius*, 1783-1835

Louis-Lucas, Paul, born 6 August 1924 at Dijon (Côte d'Or), France, he studied at the faculties of law in Dijon, Paris, and Besançon. He taught law at Caen and Paris, and concurrently served as a professor at Tunis and Beirut. WhoFr, 1973/74-1983/84|

Louis Salvator, Archduke of Austria, 1847-1915 *see* Ludwig Salvator, Archduke of Austria

Loukatos (Loucatos), Spyridon D., fl. 20th cent., his writings include Έλληνες και Φιλέλληνες των Ίνδιων κατα την Έλληνικην Έπανάστασιν (Athens, 1965). NUC

Loukomski, Georges, 1884-1954 see Lukomskiĭ, Georgiĭ Kreskent'evich

Loupias, Bernard, born 20th cent., he received a *doctorat d'état* in 1987 from the Université de Paris X for *L'image du Maroc dans la littérature espangnole des origines au terme des Lumières*. THESAM, 1

Lourdjane, Ahmed, born 20th cent., he obtained a diploma at the Institut d'études politiques de Grenoble and also gained a *doctorat en science pénitentiaire*. He became attached to the Cour d'appel de Grenoble. His writings include *Le droit civil algérien* (1985). LC; Note about the author

Lourido Díaz, Ramón, born 20th cent., he received a doctorate in Semitic philology. He was a student of eighteenth and nineteenth-century Moroccan history. In 1947, he was a professor at the Université de Rabat, and in 1997 he was residing in Tanger. His writings include *Ensayo historiográfico sobre el sultano de Sīdī Muhammad B. 'Abd Allāh* (1967), *El sultano de Sīdī Muhammad b. 'Abd Allāh, 1757-1790* (1970), *Un fragmento de la obra de Ibn al-Šabbāt sobre al-Andalus* (1973), and *Marruecos en la segunda mitad del siglo XVIII* (1978), Arabismo, 1992, 1994, 1997; Note about the author

Lourie, Elena, born 20th cent., she was a historian of medieval Spain. Her writings include a collection of her articles, *Crusade and colonisation; Muslims, Christians and Jews in medieval Aragon* (1990). In 2004 appeared *Jews, Muslims and Christians in and around the Crown of Aragon; essays in honour of Professor Elena Lourie*. LC

Loutskaia, N. S., 1916-1984 see Lutskaia, Natal'ia Sergeevna

Love, Kennett, born 17 August 1924 at St. Louis, Mo., he graduated in 1948 from Columbia University, New York. He was a correspondent to the *New York Times*, served with the U.S. Peace Corps, 1963-64, and was a research associate at Princeton University before serving as a professor at the American University in Cairo. His writings include *Suez; the twice-fought war* (1969). ConAu, 77-80

Loveday, Anthony J., born 20 November 1925 at Manchester, he was a librarian in the UK and in Third World countries. Since 1972 he served as executive secretary of the Standing Conference of National and and University Libraries. Note; Private; WhoWor, 1989/90

Lovejoy, Paul Ellsworth, born 6 May 1943 at Girard, Pa., he received his Ph.D. in 1973 from the University of Wisconsin for *The Hausa kola trade, 1700-1900; a commercial system in the continental exchange of West Africa*. He was a sometime professor in the Department of History, York University, Toronto, Ont. His writings include *The Ideology of slavery in Africa* (1981), *Salt of the desert sun; a history of salt production and trade in the central Sudan* (1986); he was a joint author of *Slow death for slavery; the course of abolition in northern Nigeria, 1897-1936* (1993); and he edited *Africans in bondage* (1986). Canadian, 1987-2005; ConAu, 115; DrAS, 1982 H

Lovell, Emily Kalled, born 25 February 1920 at Grand Rapids, Mich., she graduated B.A. in 1944 from Michigan State University, and M.A. in 1971 from the University of Arizona. She was a journalist and an occasional university lecturer in English writing. Her writings include *A Personalized history of Otero County, New Mexico* (1963), *Weekend away; short trips from Alamogordo* (1964), *Lebanese cooking, streamlined* (1972), and *A Reference handbook for Arabic grammar* (1974). WhoAmW, 1970/71-1991/92; WhoWest, 1976-1992/93; WhoWor, 1984-1993/94

Lovett, C. Beresford, born in 1839, he graduated from the Addiscombe Military College and joined the Royal Engineers in 1858. He served in the Sistan Boundary Commission under major-general Frederic Goldsmid, 1870-71. He participated in the Afghan war, 1878-79, and then briefly served as consul at Astarabad. He retired with the rank of major-general in 1894. He died in 1926. Henze; Who was who, 2; Wright

Lovett-Cameron, Verney, 1844-1894 see Cameron, Verney Lovett

Lovsky, Fadiey (Fadiedy), born in 1914 at Paris, he was a sometime history professor. His writings include *Antisémitisme et mystère d'Israel* (1955), *L'Église et les malades depuis le IIe siècle jusqu'au début du XX siècle* (1958), *L'antisémitisme chrétien* (1970), *La déchirure de l'absence* (1971), and *Un passé de division; une promesse d'unité* (1990). LC

Löw, Conrad, born 16th cent., he wrote *Mahometische History; was der gottlose und falsche Prophet Mahomet für eine falsche verführerische Ketzerey und Lehr erdacht...; mit angehengter Ungarischer Chronik* (Cölln, 1596), and *Könige Buch, oder Register darin fein ordnetlich erzehlet werden die Könige aller fürnehmsten Königreichen des Christenthumbs...; hiezu ist auch gethan das Register der Türckischen Fürsten vnd Keiser* (Cölln, 1598). Sezgin

Löw, Immanuel, born 20 January 1854 at Szegedin, Hungary, he was educated at his native town as well as in Berlin, where he was ordained rabbi and obtained a Dr.phil. at the Lehranstalt für die

Wissenschaft des Judentums and the Universität respectively. He was an international Talmud authority. His writings include *Aramæische Pflanzennamen* (1881), *A Szegedi Zsidók 1785-től 1885-ig* (1885). In 1934, he was honoured by *Festschrift Immanuel Löw zum 80. Geburtstage*. He died in Budapest on 19 July 1944. In 1947 appeared *Semitic studies in memory of Immanuel Löw*. DtBE; EncJud²; GeistigeUng; *Isis*, 39 (1948), p. 241; JewEnc; JüdLex; Magyar; MagyarZL; Wininger

Low, Sir Sidney James Mark, born 1857, he graduated from Balliol College, Oxford and was admitted to the bar from the Inner Temple. He was a university teacher and journalist. His writings include *A Vision of India* (1906), *The History of England during the reign of Victoria* (1907), *Egypt in transition* (1914), *Italy in the War* (1916), and *The Indian states and ruling princes* (1929). He died in 1932. DNB; IndianBilnd (1); NewC; *Who was who*, 3

Löwe (Loewe), Fritz, born in 1870, he was a traveller whose writings include *Das Land der hellen Sommernächte; Schwedenfahrt* (1929), *Fahrten durch Norwegens Märchenwelt* (1929), and *Unter der Sonnen des Südens; eine Mittelmeer- und Orientfahrt* (1930). Sezgin

Löwenklau (Leunclavius, Leonclavius, Lewenklaw), Johannes, born, according to Fr. Babinger's recent study, at the end of July 1541 at Coesfeld, Westphalia, he came from a family of modest substance so that his education was greatly determined by his oncle, a vicar at Münster. He studied at the universities of Wittenberg, Heidelberg, and Basel. At Heidelberg he served as a dean of the Faculty of Arts, but his anticipated appointment as a professor of classics came to nothing for religious considerations. His domestic circumstances obliged him to dedicate many of his works to his patrons. In the service of Calvinist masters, but also imperial officials, he was frequently sent on missions throughout the realm, even to Hungary, Italy, and Constantinople. He made full use of his jouneys for his personal scholarly works, establishing lasting contacts with a large circle of scholars at home and abroad. His writings include *Annales sultanorum Othmanidarum* (1588), *Pandectes historiae turcicae* (1590), *Annales sultanorum Othmanidarum* (1650), as well as translations from the Greek Fathers of the Church and historians, works which were probably the reason that he was put in the front row of heretics on the Papal index. He died in Wien in June 1594 from the effects of an illness which he suffered in the camp at Turkish Gran (Esztergom) on Danube, where he had been obliged to accompany his patron Zierotin. ADtB; DtBilnd (5); GdeEnc; NDB; *Südost-Forschungen*, 9/10 (1944/45), pp. 165-74 (Franz Babinger)

Lowick, Nicholas Manning, born in 1941 or 42, he was educated at Clifton College, and Christ's College, Cambridge, and joined in 1962 the Department of Coins and Medals in the British Museum. He soon became proficient in Arabic and was soon known at home and abroad as a rising authority on Islamic coinage and epigraphy. He was a joint author of *The Mardin found; Islamic countermarks on Byzantine folles* (1977). He died on 11 November 1986 at the age of forty-five. *Iran*, 25 (1987), pp. v-vi (not sighted); JRAS, 1987, pp. 306-307

Lowry, Heath Ward, born 23 December 1942, he graduated in 1966 from Portland State University and received his Ph.D. in 1977 from the University of California, Los Angeles, for *The Ottoman tahrir defters as a source for urban demographic history; the case of Trabzon, ca. 1486-15*. He was successively a lecturer in history at Bosporus Üniversitesi, and associated with Dumbarton Oaks Research Library, Harvard, and the Department of Near Eastern Languages, Princeton University. His writings include *The Story behind Ambassador Morgenthau's* [1856-1946] *story* (1990), *Studies in defterology* (1992), and he was a joint editor of *Continuity and change in late Byzantine and early Ottoman society; papers* (1986). DrAS, 1982 H; NatFacDr, 1995

Löwy, Heinrich, born 7 April 1884 at Wien, he studied physical sciences at the universities of Wien and Göttingen, where he received a Dr.phil in 1908 for *Beiträge zur Ionentheorie des Phosphors*. He was a scholar of applied geophysics and mineralogy. His writings include *Elektrodynamische Erforschung des Erdinnern und Luftschiffahrt* (1920). His trace is lost after an article in 1942. DtBilnd (2); Thesis

Lowy, Paul, born about 1940, he received a *doctorat de 3ème cycle* in 1973 from the Université de Caen for *La Médina de Tunis, ses quartiers*, where he also received his *doctorat d'état* in 1986 for *Le Modèle d'organisation spatiale des médinas en Tunisie*. THESAM, 2

Loy, Friedrich, he was in 1932 a pastor at Hamborn, Germany. A member of *Bekennende Kirche*, he was active in the German alcoholic anonymous movement. His writings include *Die Alkoholfrage und der Islam* (1934), *Die bekennende Gemeinde* (1934), *Menschenfragen und Gottes Antwort; Rundfunk-Reden* (1934), *Verjudung des Evangeliums* (1935), *Die Christuswahrheit* (1937), and *Glaube und Leben* (1940). GV; Sezgin

Loya, Arieh R., born 25 February 1926 at Baghdad, he graduated in 1956 from the Hebrew University, Jerusalem, and received his Ph.D. in 1968 from the University of Pennsylvania for *The achievement of*

Badr Shakir al-Sayyab; a study in contemporary Arabic poetry. He was for some years an Israeli ambassador to Chad and subsequently held positions as teacher of Arabic and Hebrew at a great variety of American universities. His writings include *Israeli Hebrew method* (1977). DrAS, 1982 F; *MESA Roster of members*, 1982; Selim

Loyrette, Jean, born 1 May 1927 at Neuilly-sur-Seine, France, he received a diploma from the Institut d'études politiques and a doctorate from Oxford University. He was a barrister in the Cour d'appel de Paris, from 1952 to 1957, when he became a partner in a legal firm. He was a sometime deputy secretary general of the Association de Droit Minier et Pétrolier. His writings include *Le code pétrolier saharien* (Paris, 1961), *Les offres publiques d'achat; étude juridique des O.P.A.* (1971), *Dénationaliser; comment réussir la privatisation* (1986), and he was a joint author of *Sahara; organisation politique et administrative, droit pétrolier, régime des investissements* (1959-1960). WhoFr, 1969/70-2005/2006

Loytved, Ernst, born in 1871, he received a Dr.med. in 1898 from the Universität Kiel. He was in 1912 a physician at Aleppo. Kornrumpf

Löytved, J. H., Dr., born 19th cent., his writings include *Konia; Inschriften der seldschukischen Bauten* (Berlin, 1907). GV; NUC, pre-1956

Lozach, Jean, born about 1900, he received a doctorate in 1935 from the Université de Paris for *Le delta du Nil*. He jointly published with Georges Hug, *L'Habitat rural en Égypte* (Le Caire, Institut français d'archéologie orientale, 1930) Note about the author; NUC, pre-1956

Lozamo y **Muñoz**, Francisco, born 19th cent., he was a sometime Spanish consul at Larache and Essouira (Mogador), Morocco, and also for many years at Tanger and Oran. His writings include *Cronica de la provincia de Jaen* (Madrid, 1867). His trace is lost after an article in 1903. IndiceE³ (2)

Lozinskiĭ (Lozinsky), Mikhail Leonodivich, born in 1886, he began to study law at St. Petersburg but soon changed to philology. He was one of the great translators in all of Russian literature, but also a poet in his own right. He is particularly noted for his translation of Dante's *La Divina commedia*. He died in 1955. HanRL; Master (2)

de **Lozoya**, Juan Contreras y López de Ayala, Marquis, he was born in 1893. His writings include *El arte gótico en España* (1935), *Escorial e San Ildefonso* (1965), its translations, *The Escorial and La Ganja de San Ildefonso* (1967), *L'Escurial et la Granja* (1965), and *Los origines del Imperio* (1966). IndiceE³ (2); NUC

Lübbert, Hans, born 20 August 1870 at Hamburg, Germany, he became a director of fishery of the City of Hamburg and was awarded a Dr.med. h.c. From 1905 to 1915 he was an editor of the journal *Der Fischerbote* and later became a lecturer in fishery at the Universität Hamburg. His own writings include *Kriegskost* (1914 1915; *Die großen Seefischereien der Erde* (1950). Kürschner, 1931, 1935|; RHbDtG

Lubbock, Sir John, 1834-1913 see Avebury, Sir John Lubbock, Lord

Lubell, Harold, born 29 March 1925 at N.Y.C., he graduated in 1944 from Bard College and received a Ph.D. in economics in 1953. He was successively associated with the International Labour Office, Genève, and the U.S. Department of State. His writings include *Middle East crisis and world petroleum movements* (1958), *Middle East oil crises and Western Europe's energy supplies* (1963), *The Informal sector in the 1980s and 1990s* (1991), and he edited *Employment and unemployment problems of the Near East and South Asia* (1971). AmM&WSc, 1973 S; ConAu, 9-12; WhoAm, 1974/75-1998; WhoGov, 1972 (not sighted); WhoUN, 1975

Lubenau, Reinhold, born 5 August 1556 at Königsberg, East Prussia, he attended the local parochial school and subsequently trained as an apothecary. From 1580 to 1586 he travelled through Germany, Austria, and Hungary. After spending some time at Riga and Vilna he went to Wien, where he joined an Austrian imperial embassy to Constantinople, returning in 1589 to Königsberg. Since 1603 he was a councillor at Königsberg, where he died on 17 May 1631. His experiences in Egypt are embodied in his *Beschreibung der Reisen des Reinhold Lubenau*, edited by W. Sahm (1912-30); a partial French translation of his travels in Egypt is contained in Serge Sauneron's *Voyages en Égypte pendant les années 1587-1588* (Le Caire, 1972). DtBE; Egyptology; LC

Lubo-Lesnichenko, Evgeniĭ Iosifovich, born 23 September 1929, he graduated in 1953 from the Oriental Faculty, Leningrad State University, received his first degree in 1959 for Китайски шелковые ткани периода Хань в собрании Эрмитажа, and a doctorate in 1989 for Китай на Шелковом пути. He was associated with the Hermitage Museum, Leningrad. Miliband; Miliband²

Lubomirski, Prince Józef, born 25 August 1829 at Dubno, Ukraine, he lived for some time at the Russian Court before he settled in France. His writings include *Un nomade, Safar-Hadji; les Russes à Samarqand* (1874), its translation, *Safar-Hadgi; or, Russ and Turcoman* (1878), *Les pays oubliés, la Côte barbaresque et le Sahara; excursions dans le vieux monde* (1880), *Jérusalem, un incrédule en Terre sainte* (1882), *Autour de Jérusalem; le christianisme et la société* (1884), *Histoire contemporaine de la transformation politique et sociale de l'Europe* (1889-1896), and *Mémoires, 1839-1869* (1911). He died in 1911. BN; Dziekan; IndexBFr² (1); Polski (2)

Lucas, Alfred, born in 1867 at Manchester, he was educated at the School of Mines, London, and the Royal College of Science. Lung trouble brought him in 1897 to Egypt, where he became a chemist to the Antiquities Service. His writings include *Alcoholic liquors and the liquor trade in Egypt* (1916), *Antiques, their restoration and preservation* (1924), and *Ancient Egyptian materials* (1926). He died in 1945. Some of his papers are in the Archiv of the Griffith Institute, Ashmolean Museum, Oxford. Dawson; Egyptology

Lucas, Georges, fl. 20th cent., his writings include *Fès dans le Maroc moderne* (Paris, 1937). NUC

Lucas, Paul, born the son of a goldsmith on 31 August 1664 at Rouen, France, he went to the Levant to trade in precious stones. Between 1688 and 1736 he visited Greece, Asia Minor, particularly Constantinople and Smyrna, Egypt, Syria, and Spain. He returned to France in 1696 with numerous antiquities and medals for the Cabinet du roi. He wrote *Voyage au Levant; on y trouvera entr'autre une description de la haute Égypte, suivant le cours du Nil, depuis le Caire jusques aux cataractes* (La Haye, 1705), and its translation, *Reise nach der Levante* (1708). He died in 1737. Dawson; DcBiPP (not sighted); Egyptology; GDU

Lucas, Philippe Paul, born 4 October 1940 at Neufchâteau (Vosges), France, he studied at the facultés des lettres et de droit, Nancy, and the École pratique des Hautes études, Paris, and received a *doctorat d'état* in 1975 for *Socialisme et décolonisation; le "transformisme algérien," 1962-1972*. He taught in Algeria from 1965 to 1971 and subsequently was a university professor and president at Paris, and Lyon, and rector of academy successively at Brodeaux and Caen. His writings include *Sociologie de Frantz Fanon* (1971), *Socialisme et décolonisation* (1976), and he was a joint author of *L'Algérie des anthropologues* (1975). He died on 11 August 1997. THESAM, 2; WhoFr, 1987/88-1996/97

Lucchetta, Francesca née Picchetti, born 8 March 1930 at S. Dona' di Piave (Venezia), she graduated from the Università di Padova. She was a student of Arabic philosophy, and history of Venetian relations to the Near East. In 1994, she was a professor of Islamic philosophy at the Università di Venezia, a director of the journal *Quaderni di studi arabi*, and a member of the Union européenne des arabisants et islamisants as well as the International Society for the Study of Medieval Philosophy. Her writings include *Il medico e filosofo bellunese Andrea Alpago, traduttore di Avicenna; profilo biografico* (Padova, 1964), *Veneziani in Levante, musulmani a Venezia* (1997), and she edited and translated Avicenna's *Epistola sulla vita futura* (1969), and al-Fārābī's *Epistola sull'intellecto* (1974). Private; ZKO

Lucchini, Laurent, born 20th cent., he was certainly from 1969 to 1978 a professor at the Faculté de droit et des sciences économiques d'Orléans. In 1967, he served as a *maître de conférences* at the Université de Tunis. He was a joint author of *Les États et la mer; le nationalisme maritime* (1978), and *La Mer et son droit; les espaces maritimes* (1990). LC; Livres disponibles, 2004; Note about the author

Luccioni, Joseph, fl. 20th cent., he was in 1934 a section head in the Moroccan *waqf* administration, and received a doctorate in 1942 at Alger for *Le Habous ou wakf, rites malékite et hanéfite*. In 1955, he was a *maître de conférences* in the Institut des hautes études marocaines, Rabat. Note; NUC, pre-1956

Luce, Sir William Henry Tucker, born in 1907 at Alverstoke, Hampshire, England, he was educated at Clifton College and Christ's College, Cambridge. From 1930 to 1956 he served in various capacities in the Sudanese Government. He later became successively Governor of Aden, and Political Resident in the Persian Gulf. He died in 1977. IntWW, 1974-1977; Who was who, 7

de **Lucena Parades**, Luis Seco, 1901-1974 *see* Seco de Lucena Parades, Luis

Luchaire, François, born 1 January 1919 at La Rochelle, France, he studied la at the Université de Caen and since 1938 articled in the Cour d'appel de Caen, obtaining a doctorate in 1942 for *La court supérieure d'arbitrage, juridiction administrative*. He started his career as a professor of law at the Université de Nancy, later becoming a president of university and tribunal. His writings include *Manuel de droit d'outre-mer, Union française, Afrique du nord, teritoires d'outre-mer, Indochine* (1949-51), *L'Aide aux pays sous-développés* (1967), *Cours de droit constitutionnel étrangers* (1967), *La Protection constitutionnelle des droits et des libertés* (1987), and *Le Droit de décentralisation* (1989). He was highly decorated and honoured. WhoFr, 1971/72-2005/2006

Luciani, Giacomo, born in 1948, he received his M.A. in 1971 from Yale University, New Haven, Conn. His writings include *L'Opec nella economia internazionale* (1976), *Il potere multinazionale* (1977), *Compagnie petrolifere e paesi arabi* (1981), its translation, *The oil companies and the Arab world* (1984); and he edited *Nation, state, and integration in the Arab world* (1987-90), and *The Politics of Arab integration* (1988). LC; *MESA Roster of members*, 1990; ZKO

Luciani, Jean Dominique, born 2 July 1851 at Partinello (Corsica), he graduated from the Collège d'Ajaccio and subsequently went to Constantine, Algeria, where a relative was secretary general of the *préfecture*. On 1 July 1870 he, too, entered the public administration and began a career which was spent entirely in Algeria. During the following war he participated in the campaign against Kabylie. In 1875, he was nominated *rédacteur principal* in the administration, concurrently pursuing his studies in Islamic law, which he completed with a degree from the Faculté de droit d'Aix-en-Provence. During visits to Aurès and Kabylie, he became acquainted with Berber dialects, which he learnt to speak as fluently as Arabic. He was successively administrator at Aïn Mlila (1877), Batna (1880), and Attia (1885). In 1888, he was transferred to the Gouvernement général as *sous chef* responsible for native affairs, advancing to the position of full chief twelve years later. In 1900, he became head of the newly established Direction des Affaires Indigènes, a position which he held for over seventeen years until his retirement. His writings include *Biskra; le Marabout de Sidi Zerzour et le Beït el-mãl* (1924), the translations, *Traité des successions musulmanes; extrait du commentaire de la Rahbia par Chenchouri de la glosse d'el-Badjouri et d'autres auteurs arabes* (1890), *Petit traité de théologie musulmane*, par Muhammad ibn Yūsuf al-Sanūsī (1896); and the edition and translation, *El-Irchad*, par Imam el-Harameïn [al-Juwaynī] (1938). He died on 21 July 1932. BN; *Revue africaine* 73 (1932), pp. 161-177; ZKO

Lucidi, Mario, fl. 20th cent., his writings include *Saggi linguistici* (Napoli, Istituto universitario orientale di Napoli, 1966). NUC; ZKO

Lucini Baquerizo, Maria Mercedes, born 20th cent. After a degree in Semitic languages, she was a research fellow in the Instituto de Cooperación con el Mundo Arabe at the Consejo Superior de Investigaciones Científicas, Madrid. Arabismo, 1992, 1994, 1997

Luckaja, N. S., 1916-1984 *see* Lutskaia, Natal'ia Sergeevna

Luckerts, I., fl. 1899-1910, this is a frequent misprint for Jules Duckerts in the journal *Mouvement économique*.

Luckey, Paul, born 26 December 1884 at Wuppertal, Germany, he received a Dr.phil. in 1944 from the Universität Tübingen for *Die Schrift des Ibrahim b. Sinan b. Ṯabit über die Schatteninstrumente*. He was a secondary school teacher successively at Wuppertal and Marburg. His writings include *Lehrbrief über den Kreisumfang von Ğamšīd ibn Mas'ūd al-Kāšī*, edited by Alfred Siggel (1953). He died in Leipzig on 20 July 1949. Hanisch; Kürschner, 1050

Luckij, V. B., 1906-1962 *see* Lutskiĭ, Vladimir Borisovich

Luckwaldt, Friedrich, born 25 November 1875 at Stettin, Prussia, he received a Dr.phil. in 1897 from the Universität Göttingen for *Österreichs Friedensverwendung zu Beginn des Befreiungskrieges von 1813*, a work which was published a year later entitled *Österreich und die Anfänge des Befreiungskrieges von 1813*. He was for ten years a secondary school teacher at Stettin, before he became a professor of modern history successively at the Universität Bonn and the Technische Hochschule Danzig. His writings include *Die Vorgeschichte des Krieges* (1915), and *Deutschlands Anspruch auf einen Rechtsfrieden* (1919). Kürschner, 1925-1935|; Wer ist's, 1922-1935|

Ludén, Bo., born 20th cent., he edited and translated *Mawā'iz al-abrār*, from the Arabic of Baybars al-Mansūrī (Leiden, 1983). His writings also include *(Re)educating the reader* (1999) [not sighted.] LC; ZKO

Lüders, Ewald, born 15 September 1884 at Hamburg, he studied law at the universities of Heidelberg and Berlin and received a Dr.jur. in 1913 from the Universität Göttingen for *Das Jagdrecht der deutschen Schutzgebiete*. He subsequently became an academic assistant at the Seminar für öffentliches Recht as well as bibliographical expert in Islamic legal publications to the periodical *der Islam*, concurrently preparing for his Dr.habil. He was wounded on 8 September 1914 at Vltry-le-François, France, and died on 22 October 1914 at a military hospital in Merseburg. *Islam*, 6 (1915/16), p. 90; Thesis

Lüders, Michael, born 8 May 1959 at Bremen, Germany, he spent his grade twelve in the United States as an exchange student. From 1979 to 1981 he spent a year and a half as aid worker in Israel. He subsequently studied Islamic subjects, political science, and journalism at the Freie Universität Berlin, where he received a Dr.phil. in 1988 for *Gesellschaftliche Realität im ägyptischen Kinofilm von*

Nasser zu Sadat, 1952-1981. He became a free-lance journalist whose writings include *Im Herzen Arabiens; Stolz und Leidenschaft - Begegnung mit einer zerrissenen Kultur* (2004); he was a joint author of *Blick zurück ohne Haß* (1981); and he was a joint editor of *Palästina-Protokolle* (1981), and *PLO; Geschichte, Strategie, aktuelle Interviews* (1982). Thesis

Ludin-Jansen, Herman, 1905-1986 *see* Jansen, Herman Ludin

Ludlow, James Minor, born 27 May 1917 at Wareham, Mass., he graduated in 1939 from Williams College, and received his A.M. in 1940 from Columbia University, New York. He entered the U.S. Department of State in 1942, working on munitions control. He later became a specialist on United Nations affairs and an adviser on Near Eastern and South Asian matters to the American Government. In 1964, he joined the Foreign Service Institute faculty. He died in Arlington, Va., on 8 August 1974. NYT, 13 August 1974, p. 38, col. 3; *Washington Post*, 10 August 1974, p. D-6, col. 5; WhAm, 6: WhoAm, 1974/75, 1976/77; WhoGov, 1972 (not sighted)

Ludolf, Heinrich Wilhelm, born 20 December 1655 at Erfurt, Germany, he there learned Oriental languages, and since 1674 studied at the nearby Jena. In 1678, he first went to England, and subsequently entered the Danish diplomatic service, becoming a confidential secretary to Prince Georg of Denmark, from 1685 to 1691. He then travelled extensively in Holland, England, and Russia. After his return, he composed the first Russian grammar, *Grammatica Russica* (1696), - a Russian translation of which was published in 1937 at Leningrad entitled *Русская грамматика* - and began to pursue oecumenical ideas of the Russian and Slavonic Orthodox Church. He worked on a universal missionary scheme, and in 1702 he became instrumental in the establishment of August Hermann Francke's Collegium orientale in Halle/Saale, in which Oriental and Slavic languages were to be taught. He died in London on 25 January 1712. In 1954 Joachim Tetzner received a Dr.phil. for his thesis, *H. W. Ludolf und Rußland*. DtBE; DtBiInd (1); GDU; Master (1); NDB

Ludolf, Hiob (Job), born 15 June 1624 at Erfurt, Germany, he studied philology at Erfurt and Leiden and then travelled in order to perfect his linguistic competence. While in Italy, he became acquainted with an Abyssinian scholar, and acquired from him an intimate knowledge of the Ethiopian language. In 1652, he entered the service of Duke Ernst of Sachsen-Gotha, in which he continued until 1678, when he retired to Frankfurt am Main. In 1683, he visited England to promote a cherished scheme for establishing trade with Abyssinia, but his efforts were unsuccessful, chiefly through bigotry of the authorities of the Abyssinian Church. Returning to Frankfurt in 1684, he gave himself wholly to literary work, which he continued almost to his death on 8 April 1704. His writings include *De bello turcico feliciter conficiendo* (1686), and *Grammatica linguæ amharicæ quae vernacula est Habessinorum* (1698). DtBE; DtBiInd (6); EncBrit; EncicUni; GdeEnc; GDU; NDB; Pallas; RNL

Ludshuveït, Evgeniï Fedorovich, born in 1899 at Moscow, he received his first degree in 1950 for *О предпосылках и начальной стадии кемалистской революции*. He was from 1930 to his death on 26 December 1966 associated with the Faculty of History, Institute of Oriental Languages, Moscow State University. His writigs include *Турция* (1955), and *Турция в годы Первой Мировой войны, 1914-1918 гг.* (1966). Miliband; Miliband²

Lüdtke, Helmut Hermann Wilhelm, born 26 November 1926 at Osnabrück, Germany, he received a Dr.phil. in 1952 from the Universität Bonn for *Der lateinisch-romanische Vokalismus in struktureller Schau*, and a Dr.habil. in 1963 from the Universität Basel. He was a professor of Romance and general linguistics successively at the universities of Freiburg im Breisgau, Berlin and finally Kiel, where he retired in 1992. His writings include *Geschichte des romanischen Wortschatzes* (1968), and its translation, *Historia del léxico románico* (1974). GV; Kürschner, 1976-2005; WhoWor, 1987, 1993/94

Lüdtke, Willy August Fürchtegott, born 4 November 1875 at Körlin, Prussia, he studied theology and Christian archaeology, and received a Dr.phil. in 1897 from the Universität Greifswald in 1897 for *Untersuchungen zu den Miniaturen der Wiener Genesis*. He became a librarian at Kiel and Hamburg. His writings include *Evangelientexte, besonders aus Harmonien* (1965). JahrDtB, 1926-43; Kürschner, 1931

Ludwig (Louis/Luigi) **Salvator**, His Imperial and Royal Highness, the Archduke of Austria, Ludwig Salvator of Habsburg-Lothringen and Bourbon was born in Pitti Palace at Firenze on 4 August 1847. In 1859, he and his family had to leave Toscana and settled in Austria. He studied law and also pursued an interest in natural science and nautical matters. An unconventional younger member of the Austrian royal family, he started, in the 1870s, a life of extensive travels in the Mediterranean on his own yacht. He first visited Mallorca when it was still considered by many people to be exceedingly remote and more than a little civilized. Some time later, he returned to the island and bought the seventeenth century villa Miramar. Once he had settled permanently he built a tiny chapel in memory of the Raimon Lullus. By this time he began to study the legends and culture of his adopted island and for the rest of his life he devoted his scholarly gifts to the task of making the beauties of Mallorca widely known. His

writings include *Die Balearen* (1869-91), its translation, *Las Baleares* (1886-90), *Levkosia, die Hauptstadt von Cypern* (1873), its translation, *Levkosia, the capital of Cyprus* (1881), *Die Karawanenstraße von Aegypten nach Syrien* (Prag, 1879), *Bizerta und seine Zukunft* (Prag, 1881), *Um die Welt, ohne zu wollen* (Prag, 1881), *Bougie, die Perle Nord-Afrikas* (Prag, 1899), *Bizerte et son passé* (1900), *Die Felsenfeste Mallorcas* (Prag, 1901), and *Voci di origine araba nella lingue delle baleari* (1901). He died an avid pacifist at Schloß Brandeis/Elbe on 12 October 1915. Contemporary review, 233 (1978), pp. 157-60; DtBE; Kornrumpf; Kosch; NDB; ÖBL; Sezgin; Wer ist's, 1905-1912

Ludwig, Alfred, born 9 October 1832 at Wien, he studied classical and Oriental languages at the universities of Wien and Berlin. After teaching for some time at Wien, he became a professor of classics and comparative linguistics at Karl's Universität, Prag. He was a versatile but eccentric scholar, who knew Semitic and Iranian languages, and is best known for his translation of the *Rigveda*. He was a member of the Königlich Böhmische Gesellschaft der Wissenschaften. He died in Prag on 12 June 1912. Filipsky; ÖBL; Stache-Rosen, pp. 76-77

Ludwig, Emil, born Emil Ludwig Cohn on 15 January 1881 at Breslau, Germany, he studied law and history at the universities of Heidelberg, Lausanne, Breslau, and Berlin. Baptized in 1902, he resided since 1906 in Switzerland as a free-lance writer. In protest against the 1922 assassination of the German foreign minister, Walther Rathenau, he publicly renounced Christianity. In the 1930s he was naturalized in Switzerland and actively supported the literary opposition to German national socialism. In 1940, he emigrated to the U.S.A., where he became president Roosevelt's special envoy in the campagne for German re-eductation. He is best remembered as a writer of historical biographies. He died in 1948 in Switzerland. CnDiAmJBi; DtBE; DtBilnd (4); EncJud; Master (20); WhAm, 2; Wininger

Luethy, Herbert, born 15 January 1918 at Basel, Switzerland, he received a Dr.phil. in 1943 from the Universität Zürich for *Die Tätigkeit der schweizer Kaufleute und Gewerbetreibenden in Frankreich unter Ludwig XIV und der Regentschaft*. For some years he was a correspondent for the Swiss periodical *die Tat*. He delivered his inaugural lecture at the Eidgenössische Technische Hochschule, Zürich, entitled *François Quesnay und die Idee der Volkswirtschaft* (1959). He later became a professor in the Department of Mathematics, Universität Basel. His writings include *Frankreichs Uhren gehen anders* (1954), its translations, *À l'heure de son clocher* (1955), and *France against herself* (1955), *Nach dem Untergang des Abendlandes; zeitkritische Essays* (1964), *Die Schweiz als Antithese* (1969), *Wozu Geschichte* (1969), *Fahndung nach dem Dichter Bertold Brecht* (1972), and *Tugend und Menschenrechte* (1974). Kürschner, 1983-2005

Luft, Gerda, born 20 April 1898 at Königsberg, Germany, she studied at the universitites of Königsberg, and Berlin. In 1924, she went to Palestine; since 1960, she was a free-lance Istraeli correspondent to German as well as English-language periodicals. Her writings include *Heimkehr ins Unbekannte* (1977), and *Chronik eines Lebens für Israel* (1983). WhoWorJ, 1965, 1972

Luft, Johann Paul, born 24 September 1934 at Dresden, Germany, he received a Dr.phil. in 1969 from the Universität Göttingen for *Iran unter Schah 'Abbas II*. He was a lecturer in Persian studies, first at the University of Manchster, and later at the Centre for Middle Eastern and Islamic Studies, University of Durham, a position which he held until his retirement. He was a joint author of the catalogue, *Persische Handschriften und einige in den Handschriften enthaltene arabische und Türkische Werke* (Wiesbaden, 1980). DrBSMES, 1993; Private; Schoeberlein

Luft, Ulrich, born in 1941 at Dresden, Germany, he received a Dr.phil. in 1970 from the Universität Leipzig for *Die ägyptische Theokratie*. His writings include *Beiträge zur Historisierung der Götterwelt und der Mythenschreibung* (1978). Schwarz

Lugan, Jean, born 15 June 1921 at Alger, he received in that city all his education, including a diploma from the Faculté de droit. He subsequently practised his profession for ten years in Morocco, serving as member of the Conseil de l'ordre as well as the Association des barreaux du Maroc. When Morocco became independent in 1956, he settled in Paris, where he became an adviser to French and international firms as well as the Portuguese embassy and the consulate general in Paris. NDNC, 1961/62

Luganskiĭ, K., pseud., 1801-1872 see Dal', Vladimir Ivanovich

Lugard, Lady Flora Louisa (Shaw), born in 1852 at Dublin, she was a journalist specializing in colonial affairs, and headed the Colonial Department of the London *Times*. In 1902, she was married to Sir Frederick Lugard. In 1905, she published a history of northern Nigeria, *A Tropical Dependency; an outline of the ancient history of the western Sudan with an account of the modern settlement of Northern Nigeria*. Her other writings include *The Work of the War Refugees Committee* (1915). She died in 1929. Enid H. C. M. Bell wrote *Flora Shaw* (1947). Master (3); NewC; Robinson, pp. 193-194; *Who was who*, 3

Lugard, Sir Frederick John Dealty, born in 1858 at Fort St George, Madras, he was educated at the Royal Military College, Sandhurst, and served in India until 1885. He participated in the Sudan campaign for the relief of Khartoum. In 1888-89, he led a small force against Arab slave traders in the Lake Nyasa region of southeastern Africa. In 1894, he was engaged by the Royal Niger Company, becoming High Commissioner of Northern Nigeria in 1900, a post which he held until 1906 when he resigned. From 1922 to 1936 he was a member of the Permanent Mandates Commission of the League of Nations. He was married in 1902 to Flora Louisa Shaw. His writings include *The Rise of our East African empire; early efforts in Nyasaland and Uganda* (1893), *Uganda and its people* (1901), *Northern Nigeria* (1907), and *The Dual mandate in tropical Africa* (1922). He died in Abinger, Surrey, in 1945. DcTwHis; DNB; GrBr; Hill; Henze; Master (2); *Who was who*, 4

Luigi, Giuseppe De', 1881- *see* De' Luigi, Giuseppe

Luigi Salvadore d'Austria, 1847-1915 *see* Ludwig Salvator, Archduke of Austria

de **Luis Martínez**, Esmeralda, born 20th cent., she received a degree in Semitic philology and subsequently taught Arabic at the Instituto Cervantes, Madrid. Arabismo, 1992, 1994, 1997; EURAMES, 1993

Lukach, Harry Charles Joseph, 1884-1969 *see* Luke, Sir Harry Charles Joseph

Luke, Sir Harry Charles Joseph, born in 1884 at London, he was educated at Eton and Trinity College, Oxford, where he received a B.Litt. in 1919 for *Cyprus under the Turks, 1571-1878*. He was a colonial officer and served as Commissioner of Famagusta, Government Secretary at Mudros, 1915-16, British Chief Commissioner in Georgia, Armenia and Azerbaijan, 1920, as well as Colonial Secretary of Sierra Leone, 1924-28. His writings include *The City of the Dancing Dervishes, and other sketches and studies from the Near East* (1914), *Mosul and its minorities* (1925), and *The Making of modern Turkey* (1936). He died in 1969. Au&Wr, 1963; DNB; Master (3); Sluglett; *Who was who*, 6

Luke, John, born 17th cent., he was a nonentity who succeeded Edmund Castell in the Cambridge Adams professorship of Arabic from 1685 to 1702. His chief qualification appears to have been a seven years' sojourn in Smyrna.

Luke, Timothy Wayne, born 28 June 1951, he was in 1990 a professor in the Department of Political Science, Virginia Polytechnic Institute and State University, a position which he still held in 2005. His writings include *The Guerrilla counter-state; the case of Portuguese Angola* (1978), *Ideology and Soviet industrialization* (1985), *Screens of power; ideology, domination, and resistance in informational society* (1989), *Social theory and modernity; critique, dissent, and revolution* (1990), and *Shows of force; power, politics, and ideology in art exhibitions* (1992). LC; NatFacDr, 1990-2005

Lukens, Marie G., fl. 20th cent., she published the New York Metropolitan Museum of Art's *Guide to the collections; Islamic art* (1965). NUC, 1956-67

Lukomskiĭ (Loukomski), Georgiĭ (Georges) Kreskent'evich, born in 1884, he wrote Волынская старина (1913), *La Ville sainte de Russie, Kiev* (Paris, 1929), *L'Architecture religieuse russe du XIe siècle au XVIIIe siècle* (Paris, 1929), and *Les Théâtres anciens et modernes* (Paris, 1935). He died in 1954. NUC, pre-1956; OSK

Lukonin, IUriĭ Vladilavovich, born 28 May 1922 at Piatigorsk, Russia, he received his first degree in 1956 for Компартии Сирии и Ливана в борьбе за укрепление национальной независимости, 1945-1947. He was since 1960 associated with the Africa Institute, Soviet Academy of Sciences. From 1964 to 1967 he served as an ambassadorial researcher to Morocco, and in a similar capacity from 1974 to 1976 with the journal *Problems of peace and socialism* at Praha. Miliband; Miliband²; Unesco

Lukonin, Vladimir Grigor'evich, born 21 January 1932 at Leningrad, he received his first degree in 1961 for Иран в III-IV вв., and his doctorate in 1970 for Раннесасанидский Иран; некоторые проблемы истории и кулътуры. He was for more than twenty years head of the Oriental Section at the Hermitage Museum, Leningrad, and published widely on the cultural history of Iran from antiquity to the middle ages. He died 10 September 1984. Miliband; Miliband²

Lüling, Günter, born the son of a pastor on 25 October 1928 at Warna, Bulgaria, he went to school at Köslin until called to arms on the 1st of June 1944. After his release from a POW camp, he trained as a bricklayer in Wolfenbüttel and concurrently prepared for university admission as a mature student. He studied theology, classical and Oriental languages and social sciences at the universities of Erlangen and Göttingen, from 1950 to 1961. From 1962 to 1965 he was a director of the Goethe-Institut, Aleppo, and from 1965 to 1967 he was an assistant professor at the Seminar für Geschichte der Medizin, Erlangen. He subsequently was associated with Orientalisches Seminar of the Universität Erlangen-Nürnberg, where he received a Dr.phil. in 1970 for a study of the text of the Koran entitled *Kritisch-exegetische Untersuchung des Qurāntextes*, a work which was graded *eximium opus* which meant "acceptance of the work as admission to habilitation for professorship. Nevertheless, at the end of 1972, he was dismissed from the university by the establishment because of the revolutionary scholarly results he had offered. He published in 1974 a comprehensive version of his Koran criticism, *Über den Ur-Qur'ān*, which was hushed up by the official Western Koran scholarship for the next thirty years. An unemployed private scholar without private means, he lived of unemployment benefits until 1991, when he qualified for old age pension." His writings include *Die einzigartige Perle des Suwaid b. Abī Kāhil al-Yaškurī* (1973), *Der christliche Kult an der vorislamischen Kaaba als Problem der Islamwissenschaft und christlicher Theologie* (1977), *Die Wiederentdeckung des Propheten Muhammad* (1981), *Sprache und archaisches Denken* (1985), and the English translation of his *Über den Ur-Qur'ān*, entitled *A Challenge to Islam for reformation* (Delhi, 2003), as well as regular contributions to the German congresses of Orientalists. Letter from Dr. Günter Lüling to the writer; Thesis

Lullus (Llull/Lull/Lulle/Люллий/Λουλλος), Raimon (Raimundo Lulio/Raymond), born the son of a Catalan nobleman in 1235 or 1232 at Palma de Mallorca, six years after the island had been liberated from the Almohads. Inheriting the estate conferred upon his father for services rendered during the victorious 1229 expedition against the Balearic Islands, he was married at an early age, and, according to his own account, led a dissipated life until 1266 when, on five different occasions, he beheld the vision of Christ crucified. After his conversion, he resolved to devote himself to evangelical work among the heathen, to write an exposure of infidel errors, and to promote the teaching of foreign languages in seminaries. He devoted nine years to the study of Arabic, and in 1275 showed such signs of mental exaltation that at the request of his wife and family an official was appointed to administer the estate. He withdrew to Randa, there wrote his *Ars major* and *Ars generalis*, visited Montpellier, and persuaded the King of Mallorca to build a Franciscan monastery at Miramar. There for ten years he acted as professor of Arabic and philosophy, and composed many controversial treatises. After a fruitless visit to Roma in 1285-1286, he travelled to Paris, where he resided from 1287 to 1289 and expounded his bewildering theories to auditors who regarded him as half insane. In 1289, he went first to Montpellier and then to Genova, where he translated his treatise, *Ars veritatis inventiva*, into Arabic. In 1291, he sailed for Tunis where he publicly preached Christianity for a year. He was finally imprisoned and expelled. His efforts to interest the popes Clement V and Boniface VIII in his favorite project of establishing missionary colleges were unavailing. Neither was he successful in Paris and Cyprus or, some years later, in Bougie where he preached the gospel until imprisoned there for six months. Though close to eighty years of age in 1314, he once more went to Bougie on a crusade against Islam, but only raised the fanatical spirit of the inhabitants, was stoned and died of his wounds on 29 June 1315. Dicc bio; EncBrit; EncicUni; EnSlovar; Fück, pp. 16-22; GdeEnc; Krachkovskiï; Magyar; Megali, vol. 16 (1931), p. 296; MEW

Lumbroso, Giacomo, *barone*, born 9 October 1844 at Bardo, Tunisia, he was a professor of classical antiquity successively at the universities of Palermo, Pisa, and Roma. His writings include *Recherches sur l'économie politique de l'Égypte sous les Lagides* (1870), *Sulla storia dei Genovesi avanti il MC* (1872), *Descrittori italiani dell'Egitto e di Alessandria memoria* (1879), *L'Egitto al tempo dei Greci e dei Romani* (1882), and *Memorie italiane del buon tempo antico* (1889). In 1925 appeared *Raccolta di scritti in onore di Giacomo Lumbroso, 1824-1925*. He died in Rapallo on 27 March 1925. EncItaliana; Hill; IndBiltal (2)

Lumby, Christopher, fl. 1937, his writings include *Cook's Traveller's handbook to Palestine, Syria and Iraq*, 6th ed. (1934). NUC, pre-1956

Lumley, Lawrence Roger, 11th Earl of Scarbrough, born in 1896, he was educated at Eton and Oxford. After returning from his governorship of Bombay, he accepted in 1944 the chairmanship of a committee that was to look into the facilities already in existence at British institutions for the study of Oriental, Slavonic, and African languages and cultures, and come up with recommendations as to what could be done to improve upon the existing opportunities. The "Scarbrough Report" was submitted in 1946 and published the following year entitled *Report of the interdepartmental commission of enquiry on Oriental, Slavonic, East European and African studies*. Lord Scarbrough was president of the Royal Asiatic Society from 1946 to 1949 and continued his active interest in its work until he died in 1969. DNB; *Who was who*, 6

Lummau, Jean, born in 1908, he received a doctorate in 1933 from the Université de Bordeaux for *Le traitement de la syphillis par la méthode de Pollitzer; application à l'étude de la prophylaxie des maladies vénériennes chez les indigènes marocains*. NUC, pre-1956

Lumsden, Malvern, fl. 20th cent., his writings include *Napalm and incendiary weapons; legal and humanitarian aspects* (Stockholm, Stockholm International Peace Research Institute, 1972). NUC, 1973-77

Lumsden, Matthew, born in 1777, he was educated at King's College, Old Aberdeen, and in 1794 went to India in the service of the East India Company. He studied Persian and Arabic and since 1803 taught both languages at the College of Fort William, Calcutta, becoming a professor in 1808. Four years later, he was appointed secetary to the Calcutta Madrasa, and from 1814 to 1817 he was in charge of the Company's press at Calcutta. He made an overland journey to England by way of Persia, Georgia, and Russia in 1820. He was back in Calcutta in 1822 to serve as a professor until his retirement in 1826, when he returned to England. His writings include *A Grammar of the Persian language* (1810), *A Grammar of the Arabic language* (Calcutta, 1813), and an edition of Firdawsi's *Shāhnāmah*. He died in 1835. Buckland; DNB; Fück, pp. 137-38; Master (3)

Lumsden, Sir Peter Stark, born 9 November 1829, he was educated at the East India Company's college at Addiscombe, England. He joined the Indian Army in 1847 and served in the North West Frontier campaign from 1851 to 1854. In 1857, he was sent on special mission to Kandahar. He served in the China war and with the Bhutan Field Force in 1865. He was a Quartermaster-General until 1873, when he became Deputy Resident at Hyderabad. From 1884 to 1885 he was British Commissioner for the demarcation of the north west boundary of Afghanistan. He was a joint author of *Lumsden of the Guides; a sketch of the life of. Lt.-General Sir Harry Burnett Lumsden* (1899). He died in 1918. Buckland; IndianBilnd (1); Riddick; Who was who, 2

Lundbæk, Torben, born 20th cent., his writings include *Afrikas kultur* (København, 1965), *Afrikas kunst* (København, 1968), and he was a joint editor of *Etnografiske genstanden i det Kongelige Dansk Kunstkammer, 1650-1800 = Ethnographic objects in the Royal Danish Kunstkammer* (1980), and the exhibition catalogue, *Sultan, shah, and great Mughal; the history and culture of the Islamic world* (Copenhagen, National Museum, 1996). NUC; ZKO

Lundgreen, Friedrich, born 22 February 1869 at Erfurt, Germany, he studied theology and philosophy at the universities of Halle/Saale and Straßburg, and he received a Dr.phil. in 1911 from the Universität Jena for *Wilhelm von Tyrus und der Templerorden*. He was a writer on ancient Egypt as well as local Saxon history. His writings include *Die Benutzung der Pflanzenwelt in der alttestamentlichen Religion* (1908), *Aus Alt-Ägyptens Kulturwelt; nach eigenen Anschauungen* (1913), *Geschichte des Marktfleckens Schwarza/Saale* (1928), *Geschichte des Dorfes Zeigerheim* (1932), and *Im Stausee von Hohenwarte verschwunden* (1938). His trace is lost after an article in 1939/40. Note; Sezgin; Thesis

Lundin, Avraam Grigor'evich, born 25 December 1925 at Leningrad, he graduated in 1951 from the Oriental Faculty, Leningrad, and received his first degree in 1958 with a thesis entitled Южная Аравия в VI в. н. э. He gained a doctorate in 1968 also at Leningrad with a thesis entitled Государство мукаррибов Саба (Сабейский эпонимат). Although he worked all of his life on the subject of both of his theses, he had to wait until he was fifty-seven before he had a chance to visit the region of his studies. Not having been a Communist Party member prevented his participation in international meetings until the Gorbachev era. He nevertheless made important contributions to his field of study. At the end of his career in 1986 he became a senior research fellow at the Leningrad Oriental Institute. He was an editorial member of the journal *Arabian archaeology and epigraphy* from its inception in 1991. He died in 1994. Chroniques yéménites, 1995, pp. 9-15; Miliband; Miliband[2]

Lundman, Bertil Johs., born 20th cent., he received a doctorate in 1945 from Uppsala Universitet for *Dala-allmogens antropologi*. He was an anthropologist whose writings include *Nordens rastyper* (1940), *Umriß der Rassenkunde des Menschen in geschichtlicher Zeit* (København, 1952), a translation from an unidentified work, *Stammeskunde der Völker* (1961), *Jordens folk* (1962), *Geographische Anthropologie* (1967), and *The Races and people of Europe* (1977). NUC; Sezgin

Lundson, Thomas, he translated into German from an unidentified English work, *Reise von Indien durch Persien und Armenien nach England* (Jena, Germany, 1824). GV

Lundsten, Mary E. H., born about 1945, she received a Ph.D. in 1976 from the University of Minnesota, Minneapolis, for *Abraham and Ibrahim; a formal conflict model applied to Palestine, 1920-1931*. She was a sometime staff member in the Department of Political Science, Augsburg College, Minneapolis, Minn. NatFacDr, 1995-2002; Selim[3]

Lunet, Pierre Roger Louis, born 25 March 1921 at Paris, he was educated at the Lycée Lakanal, Sceaux, and the Faculté de droit de Paris. After degrees in political science and law he entered the French diplomatic service in 1945 as a *contrôleur civil* in Tunisia. WhoFr, 1967/68-1987/88|

Lunet de Lajonquière, Étienne Edmond, born 8 August 1861 at Rodez (Aveyron), France, he was educated at Rodez and Paris, where he obtained a *baccalauréat ès-lettres* in 1878. In 1879, he joined the French colonial infantry and served throughout his military career in the Far East, becoming a *commandnat* in 1911. He was a member of the Société asiatique and a corresponding member of the École française de l'Extrême-Orient. His writings include *Le Siam et les Siamois* (1904). Curinier, vol. 6 (1906)

Lungu, Traian P., born 20th cent., he was a joint author of *Viaţa politică in România, la sfîrsitul secolului al XIX-lea, 1888-1899* (Bucureşti, 1977). NUC; OSK

Lunin, Boris Vladimirovich, born 18 July 1906 at Genève, he graduated in 1922 from the Institute of Archaeology, Rostov-on-Don and received his first degree in 1956 at Tashkent for *Из истории русского востоковедения и археологии,* and his doctorate in 1967 for a monograph. Since 1953 he was associated with the Institute of History, Soviet Uzbek Academy of Sciences. In 1970, he became a professor. His writings include *Из истории русского востоковедения и археологии в Туркестане; туркестанский кружок в Туркестане* (1958), and *Средняя Азии в дореволюционном и советском востоковедении* (1965), *Историография общественных наук в Узбекистане; биобиблио-графические очерки* (1974), *Жизнь и деятельность академика В. В. Бартольда; Средняя Азия в отечественном востоковедении* (1981), and *История Узбекистана в источниках* (1984). Miliband; Miliband²; OSK; Schoeberlein; TurkmenSE

Lunina, Svetlana Borisovna, born 7 October 1932 at Rostov-on-Don, she graduated in 1955 from the Faculty of history, Tashkent State University, and received her first degree in 1961 for *Гончарное производство Мерва X - начала XIII в.* Since 1960 she was associated with her alma mater. Her writings include *Города Южного Согда в VIII-XII вв.* (1984), and *Древние города в долине Кашкадарьи* (1988); she was a joint editor of *Материалы по археологии Средней Азии* (1983), and *Култьура юга Узбекистана в древности и средневековье; сборник научых трудов* (1987). Miliband²; Schoeberlein

Luniya, Bhanwarlal Nathuram, born 12 November 1917 at Indore, India, he received his M.A. in history in 1946. His writings include *Evolution of Indian culture* (1951), *Some historians of medieval India* (1969), and he edited *Phases of freedom struggle in Madhya Bharat* (1957). BLC; IndianBilnd (2)

Lunt, James Doiran, born 13 November 1917 at Liverpool, he joined the British Army in 1937 and served many years in the East, most notably with the Arab Legion. He retired in 1972 with the rank of major-general. His writings include *Charge of glory* (1961), *The Barren rocks of Aden* (1966), *Bokhara burns* (1969), *John Burgoyne of Saratoga* (1976), *Glubb Pasha; a biography* (1984), *A Hell of a licking; the retreat from Burma, 1941-42* (1986), *Hussein of Jordan* (1989), and *The Arab Legion* (1999). He died on 1 October 2001. ConAu, 1-4, 202, new rev., 3; IntAu&W, 1971-1989; Who, 1969-2001; WrDr, 1976/78-2002

Lupton, Frank Miller, born 1854 at Ilford, Essex, England, he was originally a mercantile marine officer, and merchant. In 1879, he went by way of Suakin to Khartoum, where he entered the service of Ch. G. Gordon. In the rank of lieutenant-governor he went in early 1881 to Equatorial Province, Sudan, where he explored together with Emin Pasha the country east of the Nile between the fourth and fifth parallel. In late 1881 he was appointed governor of Bahr el-Ghazal Province. Having been obliged to surrender to the Mahdi in 1884, the khalifah 'Abd Allāh gave him an appointment in the Arsenal at forty dollars a month to maintain the captured British Nile steamers. He died in 1888 in Omdurman. *Bulletin* of the ASTENE, 15 (2003), p. 12, col. 1; Henze; Hill; Kornrumpf; Kornrumpf², vol. 2

Luquet, A., fl. 20th cent., he was a joint author of *La grande mosquée de Taza, avec une étude d'épigraphie historique, plans et relevés* (Paris, 1948). ZKO

Ritter von Luschan, Felix, born 11 August 1854 at Hollabrunn near Wien, he received several doctorates, including a Dr.phil. in 1891 from the Universität München for *Die Tachtadschy und andere Überreste der alten Bevölkerung Lykiens.* He was a physician, anthropologist, ethnographer, and archaeologist, but his radical social Darwinism did not contribute to his popularity, and his lasting fame relies chiefly on his activities as curator, and director, of the Völkerkunde Museum, Berlin. From 1909 to 1922, he was a professor of anthropology at the Universität Berlin. His writings include *Völker, Rassen, Sprachen* (1922), and he was a joint author of *Kriegsgefangene: ein Beitrag der Völkerkunde im Weltkriege; Einführung in die Grundzuge der Anthropologie* (1917). He died in Berlin on 7 February 1924. DtBE; DtBilnd (7); EncJud; EncJud²; Henze; JüdLex; Kornrumpf; Kornrumpf³, vol. 2; NDB; ÖBL; Schwarz; *Wer ist's,* 1909-1922

Luschey, Heinz, born 3 December 1910 at Berlin, he studied classics and received a Dr.phil. in 1939 from the Universität München for *Die Phiale,* and a Dr.habil. in 1956 from the Universität Tübingen for *Rechts und Links.* He began his academic teaching at Heidelberg and continued since 1971 at

Tübingen. Between 1956 and 1971 he served as a director of Deutsches Archäoligesches Institut, first at Istanbul and later at Tehran. His writings include *Funde zu dem großen Fries von Pergamon* (1962), and he was a joint author of the exhibiton catalogue, *Symmetrien in der islamischen Kunst* (1986). He died in Tübingen on 1 January 1992. Kürschner, 1970-1992; *Spektrum Iran*, 5 no. i (1992), pp. 91-92 (not sighted); ZDMG, 143 (1993), pp. 1-4

Luschey-Schmeisser, Ingeborg, born 20th cent., she received a Dr.phil. in 1951 from the Universität Tübingen for *Spätgotische und spätgotisch-barocke Tendenzen im Gewandstil der italienischen Kunst des Quattrocento*. Her other writings include *The Pictorial tile cycle of Hašt Behest in Isfahān and its iconographic tradition* (Roma, Istituto italiano per il Medio ed Estremo Oriente, 1978). LC; ZKO

Lushnikova, Larisa Ivanovna, born 22 June 1939 at Kiev, she graduated in 1962 from the Faculty of Economics, Moscow State University and received her first degree in 1967 for Государственные финансы ОАР, 1952-1966 гг., a work which was published in 1971. Since 1962 she was associated with the Oriental Institute, Soviet Academy of Sciences. Miliband; Miliband²

Lusi, Luigi, *capitane*, his writings on Italian military history include *Sintesi della guerra italo-austriaca 1915-1918* (1934), *Manuale di cultura militare per le scuole italiane dell'estro* (Roma, 1935), and *Genova cavalleria* (Roma, 1939). Firenze

Lusignan, Saveur, fl. 18th cent., his writings include *A History of the revolt of Ali Bey, against the Ottoman Porte, including an account of the form of government of Egypt; together with a description of Grand Cairo and of several celebrated places in Egypt, Palestine and Syria; to which are added, A short account of the present state of the Christians who are subjects to the Turkish government, and The journal of a gentleman who travelled from Aleppo to Bassore* (London, The author, 1783), and its translation, *Geschichte der Empörungen des Aly Bey wider die ottomanische Pforte* (Leipzig, 1784), its French translation in the Staatsbibliothek, Berlin, entitled *Histoire de la revolte d'Ali Bey contre la Porte Ottomane* (Hamburg, n.d.), *A Series of letters addressed to Sir William Fordyce ... containing a voyge and journey from England to Smyrna, from thence to Constantinople, and from that place over land to England ... together with the treaty of commerce between the court of Great Britain and the Sublime Porte*, translated from the original into English by the author (London, 1788), and a partial translation, *Reise nach der Türkei und einem Theil der Levante nebst einer Beschreibung von Palästina*, aus den Briefen des Herrn Saviour Lusignan an Sir Wm. Fordyce (Hamburg, 1789). BN; NUC; Sezgin

Lusk, Hugh Hart, born in 1837 in Britain, he came in 1849 with his family to New Zealand, where he was educated at Auckland and practised as a barrister and solicitor. In 1870, he entered politics, supporting the principle of free education. In 1890, he went to Australia and the U.S.A. He published widely, including *Social welfare in New Zealand; the result of twenty years of progressive social legislation and its significance for the United States and other countries* (London, 1913). He died in 1926. DcNZB

Lussu, Joyce Salvadori, born 8 May 1912 at Firenze, she studied at the universities of Heidelberg, Lisboa, and the Sorbonne, where she received a degree in 1941. She was a militant anti-fascist and from 1943 to 1945 served with the rank of captain in the Italian Liberation Corps. After the war, she was a chairman of friendship associations with China and Albania. She travelled in Africa and the Near and Middle East. Her writings include *Fronti e frontiere* (1945), its translation, *Freedom has no frontier* (1969), *Padre, Padrone, padreterno* (1976), *L'acqua dell 2000* (1977), *Lotte, ricordi e altro* (1992), *Il turco in Italia* (1998) and *Le inglesi in Italia* (1999). She died in 1998. ConAu, 29-32, new rev., 14; IntBiItal (6); Master (1)

Lustick, Ian Steven, born 4 October 1949 at Syracuse, N.Y., he graduated in 1971 from Brandeis University, Waltham, Mass., and received a Ph.D. in 1976 from the University of California at Berkely for *Arabs in the Jewish State; a study of the effective control of a minority population*, a work which was published in 1980. He was a professor of government at Dartmouth College, Hanover, N.H., before he was appointed a professor of politics at the University of Pennsylvaia, Philadelphia, a position which he still held in 2005. AmM&WSc, 1978 S; ConAu, 117, new rev., 40; *MESA Roster of members*, 1990; NatFacDr, 1994-2005; Selim³

Lusztig, Ignaz, 1860 or 1-1945 *see* Kunós, Ignácz

Luther, Kenneth Allin or Alun, born 22 January 1934 at Denver, Colo., he graduated in 1955 from the University of Florida and received a Ph.D. in 1964 from Princeton University for *The political transformation of the Seljuk sultanate of Iraq and western Iran, 1152-1187*. He was a professor of Persian studies in the Department of History, University of Michigan at Ann Arbor. His writings include *The History of the Seljuq Turks; from the Jāmiʿ al-tawārīkh, an Ilkhanid adaption of the Saljūq-nāma*, edited by C. Edmund Bosworth. He died about 1996. DrAS, 1969 H, 1974 H, 1978 H; *MESA Roster of members*, 1990; NatFacDr, 1995; Society for Iranian Studies, *SIS Newsletter*, 27, no. 2 (1997), pp. 6-7 (obituary - not sighted)

Lutskaia (Luckaja), Natal'ia Sergeevna, born in 1916 at Moscow, she graduated in 1947 from the Moscow Oriental Institute and received her first degree in 1950 for a study of the war of national liberation in Morocco, 1921-1926, entitled *Национально-освободительная война в Марокко в 1921-1926 гг.* Since 1958 she was associated with the Oriental Institute, Soviet Academy of Sciences. Her writings include *Республика Риф* (1959), and *Очерки новейшей истории Марокко* (1977). She died on 21 September 1984. Miliband; Miliband²

Lutskiĭ (Luckij), Vladimir Borisovich, born in 1906 at Bardiask (Osipenko), Ukraine, he graduated in 1930 from the Moscow Oriental Institute and received his first degree in 1935 for a study of the cntemporary history of the Arab countries entitled *Новая история арабских стран.* He was associated with the Institute for Oriental Languages, Moscow, from 1936 to 1958 when he joined the Africa Institute in the Soviet Academy of Sciences. His writings include *Узбекистан и Египет; итоги двух систем* (1934), *Национально-освободительная война в Сирии, 1925-1927 гг.* (1964), *Новая истории арабских стран* (1965), and *Арабские страны* (1966). He died on 17 December 1962. Index Islamicus (1); Miliband; Miliband²; Unesco

Luttor, Ferencz, born 19th cent., his writings include *Róma; a város a történelen türkrében* (Budapest, 1931). NUC, pre-1956

Luttrell, Anthony Thornton, born in 1932 at London, his writings include two collections of his articles, *The Hospitallers in Cyprus, Rhodes, Greece and the West, 1291-1440* (1978), *The Hospitallers state on Rhodes and its western provinces, 1306-1462* (1999), and he edited *Medieval Malta; studies on Malta before the Knights* (London, The British School at Rome, 1975).

Luttwak, Edward Nicolae, born 4 November 1942 at Arad, Transylvania, he was educated at Palermo, Milano, and London, where he graduated from the London School of Economics. In 1972, he went to the U.S.A., where he received a Ph.D. in 1975 from Johns Hopkins University, Baltimore, Md. He was an analyist of political, military and economic trends as they related to the United States and its relations with other countries. He served as a consultant to the U.S. Department of State as well as professor of international security affairs at Georgetown University, Washington, D.C. His writings include *The strategic balance, 1972* (1972), *Political uses of sea power* (1974), *Strategic power* (1976), *Coup d'etat; a practical handbook* (1979), *Sea power in the Mediterranean* (1979), and *Strategy and politics* (1980). Au&Wr, 1971; ConAu, 25-28, new rev., 11, 48, 88; IntAu&W, 1977-2005; IntWW, 1989-2005; WhoAm, 1982-2003; WhoWorJ, 1972, 1978; WrDr, 1982/84-2005

Lutz, Eberhard, born in 1953, he studied Islamic subjects, political science and sociology at Freie Universität, Berlin, and graduated M.A. He was from 1979 to 1981 an Arabic teacher with a German Third World aid organization. In 1982, he entered the employ of a German society for technical cooperation in afforestation in the Yemen. Note about the author

Lutz, Henry Ludwig Frederick, born 16 February 1886 at New York, he was an Egyptologist and Assyriologist who received his Ph.D. in 1916 and subsequently became a professor at the University of Chicago. He died in Berkeley in 1973. AmIndex (1); Egyptology

Lutz, Hermann, born 14 April 1881 at Stuttgart, Germany, he was a writer on contemporary history and politics, including *Wilhelm II. periodisch geisteskrank!* (1919), *Der Weg zum Kriege* (1922), *Lord Grey und der Weltkrieg* (1927), and its translation *Lord Grey and the World War* (1928), *An Appeal to British fair play* (1924), and *Die europäische Politik in der Julikrise, 1914* (1930). KDtLK, 1926-1943|

Luvsanbaldan, Ch., fl. 20th cent., he edited *Монгол хэлний товч тайлбар толь* of IA. TSevel (Ulaanbaatar, 1966). NUC; OSK

de **Luxán Meléndez**, Santiago, born 20th cent., his writings include *La industria tipográfica en Canarias, 1750-1900; balance de la produción impresa* (Las Palmas, 1994), and he was a joint author of *Publicidad Atlantis, 1945-1995; historia de una empresa familiar* (Las Palmas, 1997). LC

Duc de **Luynes d'Albert**, Honoré Théodore Paul Joseph, born 15 December 1802 at Paris, he early in life began to pursue an interest in archaeology and languages. When the Musée des Antiquités grecques et égyptiennes was established, he became its honorary deputy director. In 1830, he was elected an independent member of the Académie des Inscriptions et Belles-Lettres. The Duke made the most noble use of his great wealth by financing magnificent publications and lavishly spending money on the restauration of statues. In 1848, the Département de Seine-et-Oise elected him member of the Assemblée constituante. His writings include *Voyage d'exploration à la mer Morte, à Petra et sur la rive gauche du Jourdain* (1874). He died in 1867. DBF; Egyptology; Embacher; Henze; Hoefer; IndexBFr² (4); Kornrumpf; Kornrumpf³, vol. 2; Master (1); Vapereau

Luzhetskaia, Nina Leonidovna, born 5 February 1952 at Leningrad, she graduated in 1974 from the Oriental Faculty, Leningrad State University, and received her first degree in 1984 for a study of nineteenth century British colonial expansion in the Hindukush entitled *Государства и народы Восточного Гиндукуша во 2-й половина XIX в. и английская колониальная экспансия*. Since 1974 she was associated with the Leningrad Branch of the Oriental Institute, Soviet Academy of Sciences. Her writings include *Очерки истории Восточного Гиндукуша во второй половине .XIX в.* (1986). Miliband²

Luzzatto, Gino, born 9 January 1878 at Padova, Italy, he graduated in 1898 from the Università di Padova and subsequently taught for ten years at a secondary school. From 1910 to 1944 he was a professor of history of trade and commerce successively at the universities of Padova, Bari, Trieste, and Venezia. He was a sometime joint director of the Banca Commerciale Italiana per l'Egitto, and from 1928 to 1941 a member of the Société Fouad Ier d'économie politique, de statistique et de législation. His writings include *Storia economica di Venezia dell'XI al XVI secolo* (1961), *Storia economica d'Italia; il medioevo* (1963), and *Il rinnovamento dell'economica e della politica in Italia; scritti, 1904-1926* (1980). He died in 1964. *Chi è*, 1947, 1957, 1961; Note about the author; Wholtaly, 1958

L'vov, Andreĭ Stepanovich, born in 1905, his writings include *Очерки по лексике памятников старославянской письменности* (1966), and *Лексика "Повести временных лет"* (1975). LC

Lyall, Sir Alfred Comyn, born in 1835 at Coulsdon, Surrey, England, he was educated at Eton and the East India Company's college at Haileybury, and was assigned in 1856 to the North-West Provinces. He served in the cavalry during the Mutiny. He became a Foreign Secretary in the Indian Government and went on to be Lieutenant-Governor of the North-Western Provinces. To some he seemed "distrustful of his own powers and judgment, indecisive because he saw both sides of almost every question, too much a poet to be an administrator, too much a scholar to be a statesman, too diffident of himself, his interests too diffuse, to win complete success in any field." - "If all Englismen had been like Lyall, the English would perhaps never have been in India at all; empires are not made by men who see both sides of a question. But there would have been fewer who wanted the English to go." [Mason] His writings include *Asiatic studies, religious and social* (1882), its translation, *Études sur les mœurs religieuses et sociales de l'Extrême-Orient* (1885), and *The Rise and the expansion of the British dominion in India* (1893). He died in Farrington, Somerset, in 1911. H. M. Durand wrote *Life of the Right Honourable Sir Alfred Comyn Lyall* (1913). BiD&SB; Buckland; DNB; EncAm; IndianBiInd (4); Mason; Master (12); *Who was who*, 1

Lyall, Sir Charles James, born in 1845 at London, he was educated at King's College, London, and Balliol College, Oxford, and in 1867 entered the Bengal Civil Service in the North West Province, India, where he served in various capacities until 1898, when he became secretary at the India Office, London, in the Judicial and Public Department. As a private scholar of Arabic, he published *Translations of ancient Arabic poetry, chiefly pre-Islamic, poetry* (1885), he edited *A Commentary on ten ancient Arabic poems, namely, the seven mu'allaqāt*, of al-Tibrīzī (1891-94), and he edited and translated the *Dīwān al-Mufaddalīyāt; an anthology of ancient Arabian odes* (1918-1921). He received honorary degrees from the universities of Edinburg, Straßburg, and Oxford. He died in London in 1920. Buckland; DNB; EncAm; Fück, pp. 279-280; IndianBiInd (3); Riddick; *Who was who*, 2

Lyautey, Louis Hubert Gonzalve, born in 1854 at Nancy, France, he passed through the military college, Saint-Cyr, and became a cavalry officer and served seven years in Algeria until 1887. In 1897, he was assigned to the governor-general of Madagascar, Gallieni, as his chief of staff. After his promotion to colonel in 1903, and a short period spent in France, he was appointed commander of the Territoire d'Aïn Sefra, Algeria, and promoted to general. In 1912, he was nominated French Resident-General to Morocco, where he succeeded in the French attempts at pacification and colonization. During the first World War, he was Minister of War. He returned to Morocco in 1917 to deal with the Riff revolt under Abd el-Krim. Appointed *maréchal de France* in 1921, he retired in 1925. He was a prolific writer and the subject of a large literature; recent biographers are André Maurois (1938), Alan Scham (1970), André LeReverend (1976), and Maurice Durosoy (1984). He died in 1934. Curinier, vol. 6 (1906) (not sighted); DcTwHis; EncAm; *Hommes et destins*, vol. 1, pp. 399-413; IndexBFr² (8); Master (10); Peyronnet, p. 488; *Qui êtes-vous*, 1924; *Who was who*, 3

Lyautey, Pierre, born in 1893, he was educated at the Collège de Lunéville (Alsace-Lorraine). When he was fifteen he accompanied his oncle, the future *maréchal de France*, on a trip to Africa. He received degrees in law and political science. In 1921, he was appointed head of the *Cabinet civil* at the French High Commission in Lebanon and Syria. Dazzled by the East, he concurrently began to write. After the death of his oncle in 1934, Pierre Lyautey's life revolved around three centres, the cult around his oncle, his works, and his public addresses. His writings include *Le Drame oriental et le rôle de la France* (1923), *La Guerre du Rif et la Tache de Taza* (1929), *L'Empire colonial français* (1931),

Chevauchées impériales (1939), *Lyautey et le protectorat* (1947), *Le duel en Orient* (1957), *Iran secret* (1963), *Galieni* (1959), *Liban moderne* (1964), *Charles de Foucauld* (1966), *La Jordanie nouvelle* (1966), and *Turquie moderne* (1970). He died in 1976. Hommes et destins, vol. 7, pp. 321-32; IndexBFr² (2)

Lybarger, Lee Hartshorne, born in 1934 at Cleveland, Ohio, he graduated in 1956 from the College of Wooster, Ohio, and received graduate degrees from Case Western Reserve University, Cleveland, Ohio, and the University of Illinois. He was a social service worker of the United Presbyterian Church of the U.S.A. who spent ten years in Pakistan as an urban mission developer of his Church, serving as director of the Office of Urban-Industrial Affairs, Lahore Church Council, Lahore. Note; WhoE, 1991/92

Lybyer, Albert Howe, born in 1876 near Putnamville, Ind., he graduated from Princeton University, Princeton Theological Seminary, and received his Ph.D. in 1909 from Harvard University. An ordained Presbyterian minister since 1900, he served the following seven years as a professor of mathematics at Robert College, Constantinople. He then returned to America and until his retirement in 1944 taught history at various universities. In 1919, he served as a technical adviser to the American Commission on Mandates in Turkey. His writings include *The Government of the Ottoman Empire in the time of Suleiman the Magnificent* (1913). He died in 1949. IndAu; Kornrumpf; Master (3); WhAm, 2; WhE&EA

Lyde, Samuel, born 1825, he was an English independent Anglican missionary who settled in northern Syria in 1854, interesting himself much in the Nusayriyah, among whom he began evangelistic work, starting from Bahamrat (?). His writings include *The Ansyreeh and Ismaeeleh; a visit to the secret sects of northern Syria, with a view to the establishment of schools* (1853), and *The Asian mystery illustrated in history, religion, and present state of the Ansaireeh or Nusairis of Syria* (1860). He died in 1860. J. Richter, *History of Protestant Missions*, p. 209; Kornrumpf

de **Lyée de Belleau**, Manette, born 4 November 1873 at Courrières (Pas-de-Calais), France, she was a sculptor and potter whose writings include *Du Cameroun au Hoggar* (Paris, 1945). BN; DcWomA; Edouard-J.

Lydford, Air Marshall Sir Harold Thomas, he was educated privately. He was from 1940 to 1945 an air officer in charge of administration at Aden. He died in 1979. Who's who, 1959-1979; Who was who, 7

Lykke Nielsen, Helle, born 20th cent., she gained a doctorate and became a professor of Arabic at the Centre for Contemporary Middle East Studies in Odense Universitet. She wrote *Kvindens rolle i den algeriske revolution* (1996), she was joint author of *Den Arabiske halva; kultur og samfund* (1986), *Saudi Arabien; håndbog for danskere som skal arbejde og leve i landet* (1986), and she was joint editor of *Den Arabisk Golf, GCC* (1987). DrBSMES, 1993; EURAMES, 1993; NSMES, Directory of members, 1991

Lyko, Dieter, born about 1935, he received a doctorate in divinity in 1962 from the Universität Marburg for a thesis on the history of Christian Churches in Iran entitled *Gründung, Wachstum und Leben der evangelischen christlichen Kirchen in Iran*, a work which published in 1964. Schwarz

Lykoshin, Nil Sergeevich, born 19th cent., his writings include *Мурадбек и Фатима* (1896), and he translated from the Arabic of Muhammad ibn Ja'far al-Narshakhī, *Исторія Бухары* (1897). [To be added to GAS, vol. 1, p. 352.] LC

Lyman, Benjamin Smith, born 11 December 1835 at Northampton, Mass., he was a graduate of Harvard University, and the École des mines, Paris, and also studied at the Bergakademie, Freiberg, Germany. He was a mining engineer who spent years in private geological work before being engaged by governments the world over. From 1870 to 1871 he was in India. His writings include *General report on the Punjab oil lands* (1870). He died in Philadelphia, Pa., on 30 August 1920. Henze; Master (6); Shavit - Asia; WhAm, 1

Lyman, James K., born about 1880, he graduated from Whitman College and Oberlin (Ohio) Seminary. In 1913, he went out to Turkey as a missionary. He was assigned to Maraş in southeastern Turkey. He saw the deportations of 1915; he went to the rescue of a lady missionary at Haçın (Saimbeyli), southeast of Kayseri, where she held on alone for three years. He witnessed the atrocities under the nationalists in Cilicia in 1920; and he went through the siege of Maraş. Missionary herald, 1922 or 1926

Lynch, Henry Blosse, born in 1807, he joined the Indian navy in 1823 and was employed for several years in the survey of the Persian Gulf. On his promotion to lieutenant in 1829, he had learnt enough Persian and Arabic to act as an interpreter. In 1834, he was despatched to explore the Euphrates route to India, an enterprise lasting until 1842. From 1843 to 1851 he was employed as assistant to the superintendent of the Indian Navy, and a member of the Oriental Examination Committee at Bombay. In 1856, he retired from the service and settled in Paris. At the conclusion of the Persian war of 1856-57, he was delegated by Lord Palmerston to conduct the negotiations with the Persian plenipotentiary, which resulted in the treaty of Paris of 4 March 1857. He died in 1873. Buckland; DNB; Henze; IndianBilnd; Kornrumpf; Riddick

Lynch, Henry Finnis Blosse, born in 1862 at London, he was educated at Eton, Trinity College, Cambridge, and called to the bar from the Middle Temple in 1887. He was a senior partner of Lynch Brothers, Eastern merchants. He travelled widely in the countries between Turkey and India. For years he pressed, in and out of Parliament, the claims of Persia for sympathetic consideration and insisted on the enormous importance of maintaining its independence as a state. His writings include *Armenia; travels and studies* (1901). He died in 1913. Henze; Kornrumpf; Kornrumpf², vol. 2; Who was who, 1; Wright

Lynch, William Francis, born in 1801 in Virginia, he was a captain in the U.S. Navy who made, in 1848, a thorough exploration of Lake Tiberias, the Jordan River, and the Dead Sea. He resigned in 1861, when he became commodore in the Confederate navy. He died in Baltimore, Md., on 17 October 1865. ACAB; AmIndex (3); DAB; NatCAB; WhAm, H

Lyon, Caleb, born 8 Decmber 1822 at Lyonsdale, N.Y., he was a graduate of Norwich University, Northfield, Vt. In 1841, he went to Europe, where he travelled for several years. In 1847, he was appointed U.S. consul at Shanghai. He returned to the United States in 1849 and entered politics, first on the West Coast, and later at the East Coast and the Middle West. In the mid-1850s he went abroad again in the rescue of Martin Koszta from an Austrian brig in the Port of Smyrna. He died in 1875. ACAB; AmIndex (2); Master (8); WhAm, H

Lyon, George Francis, born in 1795 at Chichester, Sussex, he entered the British Navy in 1808 and took part in the battle of Alger on 27 August 1816. In 1819, he accompanied a British reconnaissance to Tripolitania from which he returned more dead than alive in March 1819. He is now best remembered for his arctic explorations. His writings include *A Narrative of travels in northern Africa in the years 1818, 1819, and 1820* (1821). He died in 1832. ACAB; BioIn, 1; BritInd (2); DNB; Embacher; Henze; Master (1); OxCan; WhWE

Lyon, Harold L. T., born 19th cent., he was a joint author of *Proposed scheme for a new Turkish grammar, together with a method of transcribing that language into the Latin character* (Cairo, 1888).

Lyon, Wallace A., born in 1892 in Ireland, he was provincial administrator and administrative inspector in northern Iraq between 1918 and 1945. His task was to administer what at the time was a fairly wild and remote province, while protecting the Kurds from a predatory and unstable Iraq and safeguarding British imperial interests in the area. His writings include *Kurds, Arabs and Britons; the memoir of Col. W. A. Lyon in Kurdistan, 1918-1945*, edited by D. K. Fieldhouse (2001). He died in California in 1977. Note

Lyons, Sir Henry George, born 11 October 1864 at London, he was educated at Wellington College and the Royal Military Academy, Woolwich, after which he joined the Royal Engineers. At the age of nineteen, he was elected a member of the Royal Geological Society. He was posted to Gibraltar and Cairo, where he carried out the cadastral survey. He later pursued an interest in Egyptology. His writings include *On the Nile flood and its variation* (1905), *The Physiography of the River Nile and its basin* (1906), *The Cadastral Survey of Egypt, 1892-1907* (1908), and *The Royal Society, 1660-1940* (1944). He died in 1944. BritInd (1); Dawson; Egyptology; Hill; WhE&EA; Who, 1909; Who was who, 4

Lyons, Malcolm Cameron, born 11 February 1929 at Indore, India, he was educated at Pembroke College, Cambridge, and received a Ph.D. in 1957 from Cambridge University for *An Arabic translation of the commentary of Themestius on Aristotle's De anima*. From 1989 to 1993 he was Sir Thomas Adam's Professor of Arabic at Cambridge. His writings include *An Elementary classical Arabic reader* (1962), *Identification and identity in classical Arabic poetry* (1999), he was a joint author of *Saladin; the politics of holy war* (1982); and he was a joint editor of Galenus' *On anatomical procedures, the later books*; a translation by W. L. H. Duckworth (1962). Sluglett; Who, 1988-2005

Lyssaridēs, Vasos, born 13 May 1920 at Lefkara, Cyprus, he was educated at Athens University and in 1960 he entered politics. He was a president of the Socialist Party of Cyprus. BioIn, 11; EVL, 1993/94-2004; IntWW, 1989-2006

Lytkin, Vasiliĭ Il'ich, born 15 (27) December 1895 at the village of Tentiukovo, Gouvernement Vologda, (present Syktyvkar, Komi Republic). He studied at the teachers' college, Tot'ma, 1912-16, and subsequently served until 1917 in the czarist army. After two years of teaching, 1921-22, he studied at the Moscow State University, 1925-28, and then joined the Institute of the Peoples of the East, Moscow. During this time he spent some time at Helsinki and Budapest studying Finno-Ugric philology and obtaining a doctorate in philosophy from Budapest University for *Az -s névszóképzők a permi nyelvekben*. From 1929 to 1933, he served as a lecturer at Moscow State University as well as research fellow of the Institute of the Peoples of the North at the Central Excecutive Committee of the USSR. In 1932, he was appointed to the chair of language and literature in the Komi Pedagogical Institute, Syktavkar. Convicted on spurious charges, he spent 1933-1935 in prison in Khabarovsk. During the second World War, he taught linguistics at the Pedagogical Institute, Orenburg. It was not until 1946 that his work was fully recognized and he was given a full chair in his field at Moscow. His writings include Древнепермский язык (1952), Историческая грамматика коми языка (1957), Комипермятский язык (1962); he was a joint author of Краткий этимологический словарь коми языка (1970); and he edited Комирусский словарь (1961), and Основы финно-угорского языкознания (1974-1976). Adolf Turkin and Wolfgang Veenker published in 1995 at Hamburg the bilingual Vasilij Il'ič zum 100. Geburtstag = К 100-летию со дня рождения Василия Ильича Лыткина. (Mitteilungen der Societas Uralo-Altaica; 17.) He died in Moscow on 27 August 1981. Note about the author

Ma, I-yü, born in 1900, he was an Islamic scholar and a teacher, whose writings include Chung-kuo hui chiao shih chien (1944). He died in 1961. ChineseBiInd (1); LC; ZKO

Maamouri, Mohamed, born in 1941 in Tunisia, he received a Ph.D. in 1967 from Cornell University, Ithaca, N.Y., for his thesis, The Phonology of Tunisian Arabic. NUC, 1973-1977

Maas, Otto, born in 1867, he received a Dr.phil. in 1890 from the Universität Berlin for a thesis on the evolution of fresh-water sponges entitled Über die Entwicklung des Süßwasserschwamms. He was a professor of zoology, particularly animal geography, at the Universität Mümchen and a contributor to Geographische Zeitschrift. He died in München on 21 March 1916. GeographischeZeitschrift, 22 (1916), p. 229

Maas, Otto, O.F.M., born 24 October 1884 at Neheim/Ruhr, Germany, he was baptized Ludwig Maas. He received a Dr.theol. in 1925 from the Universität Freiburg im Breisgau for a thesis on the re-opening of the Franciscan mission in China in modern times entitled Die Wiedereröffnung der Franziskanermission in China in der Neuzeit. He entered the Franciscan order and in 1921 became editor of Antoniusbote; Missionsblatt für die Franziskanermission. He later became a lecturer in Catholic missionary science at Paderborn. His other writings include Las órdenes religiosas de España y la colonización de América en la segunda parte del siglo XVIII (1929), Die Franziskanermission in China während des 19. Jahrhunderts (1933), and Heilige Stunden an heiligen Stätten (1936). He died in Wiedenbrück on 17 January 1945. DtBE; Kosch; Kürschner, 1931; Wer ist's, 1935

Maas, Wilhelm, born in 1937 at Witten-Annen, Germany, he studied classical philology, philosophy, and theology, and received a doctorate in 1974 at Paderborn for a thesis on the unchangeable nature of God as a dogmatic problem entitled Die Unveränderlichkeit Gottes als dogmatisches Problem. His writings include Arabismus, Islam, Christentum; Konflikte und Konvergenzen (1991). ZKO

Mabro, Robert Emil, born 26 Decmber 1934, he graduated B.Sc. from Alexandria University, Egypt, and the School of Oriental and African Studies, London. He was a director of the Middle East Centre, St. Antony's College, Oxford. His writings include The Egyptian economy, 1952-1972 (1974), its trans-lation, al-Iqtisād al-Misrī (1976); and he was a joint author of The Industrialization of Egypt (1976), and Nature gas; governments and oil companies in the Third World (1988). EURAMES, 1993; Who, 1999-2005

Macabich y LLobet, Isidoro, born 10 September 1883 at Ibiza, Spain, he was ordained a Presbyterian minister in 1907. He taught at the local Seminario and served as canónigo archivero of the Cathedral from 1913 to 1951, when he was nominated arcipreste, concurrently serving as a professor of religion in the Instituto de Enseñanza Media, 1937-1959. He was editor-in-chief of the Diario de Ibiza, 1907-36 and 1938-73. His writings include El feudalismo en Ibiza (1922), Historia de Ibiza (1966), and he edited Romancer tradicional eivissenc (1954). DBEC; IndiceEª (2)

McAfee, Helen Flora, born 1 June 1884 at New Milford, Conn., she graduated B.A. in 1903 from Smith College, and was a head of the English Department at the College for Women, Constantinople, from 1909 to 1912. She subsequently served as an editor of The Yale review until 1954. She died in 1956. NatCAB, vol. 43, p. 213; WhAm, 7

Macalister, Robert Alexander Stewart, born in 1870 at Dublin, he was educated in Germany and at Cambridge. He was an archaeologist who served from 1900 to 1909 as director of excavations with the Palestine Exploration Fund, and subsequently until 1943 as professor of Celtic archaeology at University College, Dublin. His writings include A Text-book of European archaeology (1925), A Century of excavation in Palestine (1926), and The Secret languages of Ireland (1937). He died on 26 April 1950. BritInd (2); DcIrB; Kornrumpf, N; Who was who, 4

Macaluso-Also, Giuseppe, fl. 20th cent., his writings include *Turchi, Senussi e Italiani in Libia* (Bengasi, 1930), *Dante e Maometto* (Roma, 1953), and *Scritti per l'Oriente e l'Occidente* (1967). Firenze; NUC, 1968-72

Macan, Turner, major, born 18th cent., he was an Arabic and Persian scholar, poet, and historian. He edited *The Shah Nameh; an heroic poem collated with a number of the oldest and best manuscripts, with an introduction and life of the author in English and Persian* (Calcutta, 1825-29). Flück, p. 138

Macartney, Carlile Aylmer, born in 1895, he was an acting British consul at Wien, 1919-1925, and later served with the League of Nations at the Intelligence Department. From 1936 to 1965 he was a research fellow of All Souls College, Oxford. His writings include *Refugees, the work of the League* (1931), *Hungary and her successors* (1937), *Studies on the earliest Hungarian historical sources* (1938-51) and *Problems of the Danube basin* (1942). He died on 18 June 1978. ConAu, 17-20, 125, new rev., 86; *Who was who*, 7

Macartney, Carlile Henry Hayes, born in 1842, he graduated in 1864 from Clare College, Cambridge, and was called to the bar from the Inner Temple in 1870. His writings include the edition of the *Dîwân of Ghailân ibn 'Uqbah known as Dhu'r-Rumma* (1919). He died in 1924. BritInd (1)

Macartney, Lady Catherine Theodora (Borland), born about 1877 in Scotland, she was the wife of Sir George Macartney and was with him at Kashgar until 1914, when she returned home overland by way of Scandinavia on account of the war. She wrote *An English Lady in Chinese Turkestan* (1931). She died in 1949. Robinson, pp. 242-43

Macartney, Sir George, born 19 January 1867 at Nanking, China, he was educated in Europe and entered the service of the Government of India in 1889. He served in Chinese Turkestan and with the Anglo-Russian Pamir Boundary Commission. He retired to Jersey. He died in 1945. BritInd (1); IndianBiInd (2); Riddick; *Who was who*, 4

Macartney, Maxwell Henry Hayes, fl. 1921-1945. His writings include *Five years of European chaos* (1923), *One man alone; the history of Mussolini and the Axis* (1944), and *The Rebuilding of Italy* (1945); and he was a joint author of *Italy's foreign and colonial policy, 1914-1937* (1938). He was a contributor to the *Fortnightly review*.

Macaulay, Denzil Ibbetson Michael, born in 1871 or 1872 at Bankura, West Bengal. Sotheby, London, published a *Catalogue of a small but very choice collection of Persian and Indian miniatures, manuscripts and calligraphs, the property of the late Major D. I. M. Macaulay which will sold by auction by Messrs Sotheby & Co. on 24 June 1941* (London, 1941). BritInd (1); NUC, pre-1956

McAuliffe, Jane Dammen, born 16 April 1944, she received a Ph.D. in 1984 from the University of Toronto for *Perceptions of the Christians in Qur'anic tafsir*. Her research centred on the Koran, Islamic history and thought, and Muslim-Christian relations. She was director of the Centre for the Study of Religion in the University of Toronto until 1999, when she accepted a position, first at Emory University, Atlanta, Ga., and later at Georgetown University, Washington, D.C., where she was dean of George-town College in 2001. Her writings include *Qur'anic Christians; an analysis of classical and modern exgesis* (1991); and she was general editor of the *Encyclopaedia of the Qur'ān* (Leiden, 2001-2004). MESA Roster of members, 1982-1990; NatFacDr, 1990-2005; Private; Selim[2]

McBarnet, Alexander Cockburn, born in 1868, he graduated from Balliol College, Oxford, and was called to the bar from the Inner Temple in 1892. He was a sometime lecturer in the Cairo law school, and in 1928, an adviser in the Mixed Court of Appeal, Cairo, and a member of the Société Fouad Ier d'économie politique, de statistique et de législation. He was a joint author of *Notes on the duties of volunteer mounted troops* (1903); and he was a joint editor of *A Handy book of the fishery laws* (1903). He died in 1934. BritInd (2); Note about the author; *Who was who*, 3

McCall, Daniel Francis, born 3 March 1918 at Westfield, Mass., he graduated in 1949 from Boston University and received a Ph.D. in 1956 from Columbia University, New York, for *The effect on family structure of changing economic conditions of women in a Gold Coast town*. In 1954, he was appointed a professor of anthropology at Boston University. His writings include *Africa in time-perspective* (1964; and he edited *Aspects of West African Islam* (1971), and *African images* (1975). AmM&WSc, 1973 S; AmM&WSc, 1976 P; ConAu, 17-20

McCall, William Alexander, born 3 September 1897 at Providence, R.I., he graduated in 1923 from Lafayette College, received graduate degrees at Princeton, and his Ph.D. in 1940 from Hartford Seminary Foundation for *The Book of knowledge, being a translation with introduction and notes of al-Ghazzali's book of the Ihya, Kitab al-'ilm*. He taught at a boy's school in Tripoli, Lebanon, from 1928 to 1939. He subsequently taught French and Greek at Hastings College, Nebr., from 1941 to 1967, and since 1967 he served as a professor of French at Pershing College, Beatrice, Nebr. DrAS, 1969 F; Selim

McCallum, Sir Duncan, born in 1888, he was educated at Filey, East Yorkshire, and Christ's Hospital, London. In 1914, he was with the French in the Cameroons as intelligence officer; after the war he was sent to Germany on the staff of the U.K. Military Mission in Berlin. Fluent in French, and with a good knowledge of Arabic, he went in 1919 to Syria as British liaison officer and there served until 1924. He retired in 1928 with the rank of major. He was later posted in a variety of capacities to British legations in China, Bulgaria, and Egypt. His writings include *From China to Chelsea* (1930). He died in 1958. *Illustrated London news*, 17 May 1958, p. 833 (not sighted); Note; *Who was who*, 5

MacCallum, Elizabeth Pauline, born about 1900, she was for many years affiliated with the research department of the Foreign Policy Association, New York. Her writings include *The Nationalist crusade in Syria* (1928), *Twenty years of Persian opium* (1928), and *Rivalries in Ethiopia* (1935). LC; Note

MacCallum, Frederick Lyman, born 19th cent., he was a Canadian missionary posted to Maraş, Turkey, in 1895. He was a sometime advisory editor to the *Moslem world*, and spent thirty years in Constantinople. His writings include the translation, *The Mevlidi sherif*, by Süleyman Chelebi (London, 1943). He died in January 1955. Kornrumpf; Note; NUC, pre-1956

McCarthy, John Joseph, born about 1950, he received a Ph.D. in 1979 from the Massachusetts Institute of Technology for *Formal problems in Semitc phonology and morphology*, a work which was published in 1985. He was a joint editor of *The Logical problem of language acquisition* (1981). ZKO

McCarthy, Justin Andrew, born 27 January 1945 at Evanston, Ill., he graduated in 1967 from John Carroll University, Cleveland, Ohio, and received his Ph.D. in 1978 from the University of California, Los Angeles, for *The Muslim population of Anatolia, 1878 to 1927*. He was a teacher of English at the Middle East Technical University, Ankara, from 1967 to 1969. In 1978, he was appointed a professor of history at the University of Louisville, Ky. His writings include *The Arab world, Turkey, and the Balkans* (1982), *Muslims and minorities; the population of Ottoman Anatolia and the end of the Empire* (1983), and *Death and exile; the ethnic cleansing of Ottoman Muslims* (1996). ConAu, 163; DrAS, 1982 H; *MESA Roster of members*, 1982-1990; NatFacDr, 2002; Selim³; WhoS&SW, 1980-84 (not sighted)

McCarthy, Justin Huntly, born in 1861, he was a dramatist, novelist, and historian. He was a joint translator of Hafiz and Omar Khayyam, and editor of *Lady Burton's edition of her husband's Arabian nights* (1886-87), and *The Thousand and one days; Persian tales* (1892). He died on 20 March 1936. Master (10); *Who was who*, 3

Mac Carthy, Louis Alfred Oscar, he was born 2 April 1815 at Paris, but little is known about his early life. He was a geographer and an equally talented scholar in history and archaeology. He travelled extensively and was a prolific writer of descriptive geography. He went to Algeria in 1848. He was fluent in Berber and Arabic before setting out on a life of solidary desert exploration in disguise of a ragged traveller between 1851 and 1863., concurrently supplying the French Government with information for its railway plans in North Africa. His writings include *Géographie, économique et politique de l'Algérie* (1858), and *Note et notices algériennes* (1859). He died on 28 December 1894. Geographers, 8 (1984), pp. 57-60; IndexBFr² (1); *Revue africaine*, 57 (1913), pp. 191-217; *Revue de l'Orient*, 13 (1853), pp. 53-54

McCarthy, Richard Joseph, S.J., born in 1913, he was in Iraq from 1953 until his expulsion as president of the Jesuit University al-Hikmah in 1970. For the next seven years, he continued his teaching at Oxford, where he had once been a post-graduate student. He spent the last four years of his life in his native United States, where he died from hemiplegia on 24 January 1981. His writings include *The Theology of al-Ash'ari* (1953), and he was a joint author of *Spoken Arabic of Baghdad* (1964). MIDEO 15 (1982), pp. 315-316; ZKO

McCarus, Ernest Nasseph, born 10 September 1922 at Charleston, W.Va., he graduated in 1945 from the University of Michigan and received his Ph.D. in 1956 for *Descriptive narrative of the Kurdish of Sulaymaniya, Iraq*. In 1967, he was appointed a professor of Near Eastern studies at the University of Michigan, Ann Arbor, becoming in 1974 a director of the Center of Arabic Studies Abroad. His writings include *A Kurdish grammar* (1958), *Kurdish-English dictionary* (1967), and he was a joint author of *First level Arabic* (1964). DrAS, 1969 F , 1974 F, 1978 F, 1982 F; *MESA Roster of members*, 1977-1990; Selim; WhoAm, 1974-1996; WhoWor, 1980 (not sighted)

Maccas, Leon, 1892-1972 see Makkas, Leon

McCauley, Robert Neil, born 20th cent., his writings include *The Euro and European financial markets* (1997); and he was a joint author of *The Anatomy of the bond market turbulence of 1994* (1995), and *The Economics of recent bond yield volatility* (1996).

McChesney, Robert Duncan, born about 1945, he received a Ph.D. in 1973 from Princeton University for *Waqf in Balkh*. He taught Middle Eastern studies at New York University. His writings include an

476

expanded version of his thesis, *Waqf in Central Asia; four hundred years in the history of a Muslim shrine, 1480-1880* (1991), *Kabul under siege; Fayz Muhammad's account of the 1929 uprising* (1999); and he was a joint author of *A List of Persian serials in the Princeton University Library as of September 1971* (1971). NatFacDr, 2002-2005; Selim

Macciocchi Jacoviello, Maria Antonetta, born 22 July 1922 at Isola Liri, Italy, she received doctorates from the Università di Roma and the Sorbonne, Paris. She was a political journalist. Her writings include *Persia in lotta* (1952), *Lettere dall'interno del P.C.I. a Louis Althusser* (1969), *Dalla Cina* (1971), its translations, *De la Chine* (1971), *Daily life in revolutionary China* (1973), *Per Gramsci* (1974), its translation, *Pour Gramsci* (1975), *La donna nera; consonso femminile e fascismo* (1976), and *L'amante della rivoluzione; la vera storia di Luisa Sanfelice e della Repubblica napoletana del 1799* (1998). ConAu, 73-76; IndBiltal (7)

McClain, Ernest G., born about 1930, he received a Ph.D. in 1959 from Columbia University, New York, for *A guide to the major clarinet compositions of Mozart, Weber and Brahms*. His writings include *The Myth of invariance; the origin of the gods, mathematics, and music from the Rg Veda to Plato* (1976). Master (2)

McClean, Sir William Hannah, born in 1877 in Scotland, he was educated privately and at the University of Glasgow. He became associated with the Colonial Office as a town planner and became engaged in Khartoum, Alexandria, Egypt, and Jerusalem. He served many years with the Advisory Committee on Education in the Colonies. He died in 1967. Au&Wr, 1963; Who was who, 6

McClellan, George Brinton, born 3 December 1826 at Philadelphia, Pa., he graduated in 1846 from the U.S. Military Academy, West Point. He was a Union general in the American Civil War and a politician. In 1855, he became a member of a board of officers assigned to the overseas study of European military organization. During this tour he had the opportunity to witness the siege of Sevastopol. In 1864, he was the Democratic presidenticial candidate. His writings include *McClellan's own story* (1887). He died in Orange, N.J., on 29 October 1885. Master (66); NCCN; WhAm H

McClellan, Grant Samuel, born 16 November 1914 at Stratton, Nebr., he was a 1936 graduate of Nebraska University and did post-graduate work at the London School of Economics, Columbia University, New York, and George Washington University, Washington, D.C. He was a foreign affairs analyst for the Intelligence Office, U.S. Department of State, from 1948 to 1953. He subsequently served as editor in charge of American world affairs for the Council on Foreign Relations. His writings include *India* (1960); and he edited *The Middle East in the Cold War* (1956), *U.S. Foreign aid* (1957), and *America's educational needs* (1958). He died in 1989. AmM&WSc, 1973 S, 1978 S; ConAu, 114

McClelland, David Clarence, born 20 May 1917 at Mount Vernon, N.Y., he graduated in 1938 from Wesleyan University, Middletown, Conn., and earned a Ph.D. in 1941 in psychology, particularly various aspects of human motivation. He successively taught at Wesleyan University and Harvard University, where he was a sometime chairman of the Center for Research in Personality. His writings include *Motivation and society* (1982), and *Motives, personality, and society; selected papers* (1984). He died in Lexington, Mass., on 27 March 1998. AmM&WSc, 1973 S, 1978 S; ConAu, 25-28, 165; WhoAm, 1974-1984

McClelland, Donald, fl. 20th cent., he was associated with the National Collection of Fine Arts in the National Museum of American Art, Washington, D.C. He edited *Paintings of Edwin Scott* (1970). LC

McClenaghan, P. J. W., born about 1898, the second son of the Venerable Henry St. George McClenaghan, Rector of Codwall, Letterkenny, County Donegal, northern Ireland, and Archdeacon of Raphoe, he was educated at the Royal School, Armagh, and passed into the Indian Army in 1915 at the early age of seventeen, proceeding to India in the same year. He served with distinction in Iraq, 1917-18, in Egypt in 1918, and in Waziristan in 1923-24. Before rejoining his regiment in India, he spent two years in Persia studying to pass the interpreter's examination. He resided in Isfahan, where he acted as British vice-consul, and became most popular with both Persians and Europeans. He took great interest in Persia, and lost no opportunity of touring about the country. In this way he visited the constructional work on the northern section of the Trans-Persian Railway. On 9 December 1930, while on parade in the Lahore cantonments, he was shot dead by an N.C.O. of his regiment, who had become temporarily insane owing to some trifling grievance which he attributed to the deceased officer. Journal of the Royal Central Asian Sociery, 18 (1931), pp. 296-97

McClenahan, Robert Stewart, born in 1871, he taught at a mission college in Norfolk, Va., and in Phillips Academy, Andover, Mass., before going to Egypt in 1897 under the United Presbytarian Church of North America to assume the post of professor of religion and ethics at Assiut College, Cairo, of which he became president from 1910 to 1918. He then joined the faculty of the American

College at Cairo and served as dean from 1928 to 1932. He died in Philadelphia, Pa., on 8 November 1949. NYT, 9 November 1949, p. 28, cols. 4-6; *School and society*, 70 (1949), p. 335; Shavit

McClintock, David William, born 11 April 1932 and a 1954 graduate of the University of California, Los Angeles, and received his Ph.D. in 1973 from the University of Michigan for *Foreign exposure and attitudional change; a case study of foreign policy makers in the Yemen Arab Republic*. He was for over twenty years associated with the U.S. Department of State, first attached to American embassies in the MIddle East, and later served as its Food and Agriculture Adviser to the Bureau of Oceans and International Environmental and Scientific Affairs. In 1990, he was a professor of political science at North Carolina State University, Raleigh. NatFacDr, 1990; Selim; WhoAm, 1974-1984; WhoGov, 1975, 1977 (not sighted)

McClintock, Marsha Hamilton, born 1 May 1952, she was a sometime secretary-treasurer of the Middle East Librarians Association. Her writings include *The Middle East and North Africa on film; an annotated filmography* (1982), and she edited *Training users of online public access catalogs; proceedings of a conference* (1983). LC; ZKO

McClinton, Katherine Morrison, born 23 January 1899 at San Francisco, she was a 1921 graduate of Stanford University, Palo Alto, Calif., and was awarded a doctorate in 1961 from Wheatin College, Illinois. She was a decorator, art critic, and lecturer in fine arts. Her writings include *Antique collecting for everyone* (1951), *Christian church art throughout the ages* (1962), *Antiques in miniature* (1970), and *Antiques, past and present* (1971). She died in N.Y.C. on 27 January 1993. ConAu, 1-4, 140, new rev., 5; CurBio, 1958, 1993; Master (4); WhoAm, 1974-1984; WhoAmW, 1958/59-1974/75

McClure, William Kidston, born 19th cent., his writings include *Italy in North Africa; an account of the Tripoli enterprise* (London, 1913), and *Italy's part in the War* (Firenze, 1918). NUC, pre-1956; ZKO

McCoan, James Carlile, born in 1829 in Ireland, and a student at Homerton College, London, he was called to the bar from Inner Temple in 1851, but did not practise. He became a war correspondent during the Crimean War and subsequently travelled in the region, and afterwards settled in Constantinople, where he founded and edited the *Levant herald*. He later became an M.P. His writings include *Egypt as it is* (1877), *Our new protectorate, Turkey in Asia* (1879), its translation, *Наc новый протекторат* (1884), *Egypt under Ismail* (1889), and *Egypt* (1900). He died in 1904. BritInd (2); DNB; OSK

MacColl, Dugald Sutherland, born in 1859 at Glasgow, he was educated at London and Oxford. An art critic since 1890, he was a sometime lecturer in history of art at University College, London, and a keeper of the Tate Gallery, London. He was an editor of the quarterly *Artwork*. His own writings include *Confessions of a keeper, and other papers* (1931). He died on 21 December 1948. DNB; TwCPaSc; *Who was who*, 4

MacColl, Malcolm, born in 1831 at a Scottish vIllage, he studied theology at Trinity College, Glen Almond, Scotland, and was ordained deacon in 1856, and priest in 1857. A well-known Scottish supporter of Gladstone's anti-Ottoman policy, his writings include *My reviewers reviewed* (1875), *The Eastern question* (1877), *England's responsibility towards Armenia* (1896), *The Sultan and the Powers* (1896), its translation, *Le sultan et les grandes puissances* (1899), and *Malcolm MacColl; memoirs and correspondence* (1914). He died suddenly in London in 1907. DNB; *Who was who*, 1

McCown, Chester Charlton, born 26 November 1877 at Orion, Ill., he was a 1898 graduate of De Pauw University, Greencastle, Ind., and received a B.D. from Garrett Biblical Institute in 1902, after which he spent four years in India as principal of the American Methodist Institution in Calcutta. Ill health forced him to retire from the missionary field in 1906. He began graduate studies in the field of New Testament at the universities of Heidelberg and Berlin. After his return to America, he taught Bible at Wesley College in North Dakota from 1909 to 1912 and the YMCA College in Chicago from 1912 to 1914. In Chicago he also completed his doctorate in New Testament in 1914. In the same year, he was invited to the Pacific School of Religion at Berkeley, Calif., as professor of New Testament literature and interpretation, a post which he held until 1947, concurrently serving as dean for two turns. He frequently visited Palestine and became a director of the American Schools of Oriental Research. His writings include *The Genesis of the social gospel* (1929), and *The Ladder of progress in Palestine* (1943). He died on 9 January 1958. *Bulletin of the American Schools of Oriental Research*, 149 (1958), pp. 3-4; *Journal of Biblical literature*, 78 (1959), pp. x-xi; Shavit; WhAm 5; WhNAA

McCrackan, William Denison, born 12 February 1864 of American parents in München, Germany, he was a graduate of Trinity College, Hartford, Conn. His writings include *The Rise of the Swiss Republic* (1892), *Teutonic Switzerland* (1894), and *Die Christliche Wissenschaft als Erklärung des Ideal-Menschen* (1914). He died in 1923. BiD&SB; DcNAA; Master (1); NatCAB, 19, p. 146; Shavit; WhAm 1; ZKO

McCrank, Lawrence Joseph, born 17 April 1945 at Fargo, N.Dak., he was a 1967 graduate of Moorhead State University, Minnesota, took an M.Lib.Sc. in 1976 at the University of Oregon, and a Ph.D. in medieval and Iberian history in 1974 at the University of Virginia for *Restoration and reconquest in medieval Catalonia*. He taught history at a number of colleges and universities before he became head of Rare Books and Special Collections at Cunningham Memorial Library, Indiana State University, Terre Haute. He subsequently served as a dean at Auburn University, Montgomery, Ala., and Ferris State University, Big Rapids, Mich. His writings include *Automatic the archives* (1981), and a selection of his articles, *Medieval frontier history in New Caledonia* (1996). ConAu, 110, new rev., 29; DrAS, 1978 H, 1982 H; IntAu&W, 1986 (not sighted); WhoLibl, 1982

McCreery, Ruth, fl. 1946 in Santa Barbara, Calif., she was a joint author of *The Other side of darkness* by Gidada Solon (New York, 1972). Note about the author; NUC, 1968-72

McCullagh, Francis, born in 1874 at Omagh, County Tyrone, Eire, he was a journalist who covered the Russo-Japanese War, the Balkan War, and the first World War. At one time or another he was expelled from Agadir, taken prisoner by the Bulgars, attached to the Turkish Army, acted as divisional intelligence officer in Serbia and Macedonia, captured by Bolsheviks, and represented the *New York Herald* in Russia until requested by the Soviet Government in 1924 to leave. His writings include *The Fall of Abd-Ul-Hamid* (1910), *Italy's war for the desert, being some experiences of a war-correspondent with the Italians in Tripoli* (1912), *A Prisoner of the Reds; the story of a British officer captured in Siberia* (1921), and *Bolshvik persecution of Christianity* (1924). He died in 1956. Bioln, 1 (1); Kornrumpf; Master (3); NYT, 26 November 1956, p. 27, cols. 2-3; *Who was who*, 4

MacCullagh Torrens, William, born in 1813, he was educated at Trinity College, Dublin, and graduated B.A. in 1833, and LL.B. in 1842. He was a barrister, politician, M.P., and historian, whose writings include *The Life and times of the Right Honourable Sir James R. G. Graham* (1863), *Empire in Asia, how we came by it; a book of confessions* (1872), *Reform of procedure in Parliament to clear the block of public business* (1881), and *History of Cabinets* (1894). He died in 1894. Boase; BritInd (4); DNB

McCutchen, Robert T., born 19th cent., his writings include *Practical English-Sulu vocabulary* (Zamboanga, P.I., 1918), and *Yakan-English, English Yakan vocabulary* (Zamboaga, P.I., 1918). NUC

McDaniel, Robert Aisnworth, born 25 November 1933 at Dixon, Ill., he received a Ph.D. in 1966 from the University of Illinois at Urbana for *The Shuster Mission of the Persian revolution of 1905-1911*, a work which was published in 1974. He was a professor of history at Purdue University, West Lafayette, Illinois, from 1974 to his retirement. DrAS, 1969 H, 1974 H, 1978 H, 1982 H; *MESA Roster of members*, 1982-1990; NatFacDr, 1995

McDermott, Anthony M., born 20th cent., he was a journalist, specializing in Arab affairs, and a contributor to *The Guardian*, and *The Financial Times*. His writings include *Egypt from Nasser to Mubarak* (1968); and he was a joint author of *The Kurds* (1975). LC; Note; ZKO

McDermott, Martin J., born 20th cent., he received a Ph.D. in 1971 from the University of Chicago for *The theology of al-Shaykh al-Mufid, its relation to the Imamite traditionalists and to the Baghdad Mutazilites*, a work which was published in 1978. He was a sometime director of the Bibliothèque orientale, Beirut. *MESA Roster of members*, 1990; ZKO

MacDiarmid, D. N., fl. 1921, he was associated with the Missions Committee of the Presbyterian Church of New Zealand. His writings include two undated booklets, *The Sudan and its evangelisation* and *Meet the New Hebrides*. Note; NUC, pre-1956

Macdonald, Alan David. His writings include *Euphrates exile* (London, 1936).

MacDonald, Callum A., born 11 November 1947 in Scotland, he graduated M.A. in 1969 from the University of Edinburgh and received a D.Phil. in 1973 from Oxford University. He was a professor of modern history, particularly American history, successively at the universities of Warwick and Liverpool. His writings include *The United States, Britain and appeasement, 1936-1939* (1980), *Korea; the war before Vietnam* (1986), and *Britain and the Korean war* (1990). ConAu, 144

MacDonald, Charles Gordon, born about 1945, he received a Ph.D. in 1976 from the University of Virginia for *Iran and Saudi Arabia in the Persian Gulf; a study in the law of the sea*. He was a visiting assistant professor, Woodrow Wilson Department of Government and Foreign Affairs, University of Virginia, before he was appointed a professor, and later chairman, International Relations, Florida International University, North Miami, a position which he still held in 2005. His writings include *Iran, Saudi Arabia, and the law of the sea* (1980). *MESA Roster of members*, 1982-1990; NatFacDr, 2005

Macdonald, Duncan Black, he was born on 9 April 1863 at Glasgow, where he took his college and seminary courses, and then went to Berlin for graduate study under Eduard Sachau. In 1892, he went to the United States as a teacher of Semitic literature in Hartford Theological Seminary, where he devoted half a century to the study of the Islamic, Hebrew, and Christian traditions. His writings include *Development of Muslim theology, jurisprudence and constitutional theory* (1903), *Aspects of Islam* (1911), *The Hebrew literary genius* (1933). On his seventieth birthday he was honoured by *The Macdonald presentation volume* (1933). For the last two years of his life he lived at a nursing home in South Glastonbury, Conn., where he died on 6 September 1943. Fück, 285-286; Master (5); MW 34 (1944), pp. 1-6; WhAm, 2

MacDonald, Eileen, born 20th cent., she was an *Observer* journalist. Her writings include *Brides for sale; human trade in North Yemen* (Edinburgh, 1988), and *Shoot the women first* (New York, 1991). LC

Macdonald, James Ramsay, born in 1866 at a Scottish village, he was reared in poverty. Interest in social reforms led him to the Social Democratic Federation and the Fabian Society. He became M.P. and prime minister in the first Labour Government of Britain. His writings include *Parliament and revolution* (1919). He died suddenly on a holiday voyage to South America in 1937. BioIn, 17 (2); BritInd (8); DcTwHis; DNB; EncAm; *Who was who*, 3

Macdonald, Sir John Kinneir, 1782-1830 *see* Kinneir, Sir John Macdonald

McDonald, Michael V., born about 1935, he received a Ph.D. in 1966 from Cambridge University for *The language and thought of Nizami of Ganja*. He was in 1993 a senior lecturer in Arabic in the Department of Arabic and Middle Eastern Studies, University of Edinburgh. DrBSMES, 1993; Sluglett

McDonald, W. Norman, fl. 1977-79, he was an engineer by profession who for many years lived and worked in the Persian Gulf. Note about the author

Macdonnell, Arthur Anthony, born in 1854 at Muzaffarpur, Bihar, India, he went to school in Germany at Dresden and Göttingen from 1866 to 1875. He studied for one year at the Universität Göttingen and then continued at Corpus Christi College, Oxford, where he won scholarships in German, Chinese, and Sanskrit. In 1884, he gained a postgraduate degree at the Universität Leipzig. From 1888 to his retirement in 1926 he was professor of Sankrit at Oxford and keeper of the Indian Institute. He died in Oxford in 1930. Buckland; DNB; IndianBilnd (2); *Who was who*, 3

McDonough, Sheila Doreen, born 13 December 1928 at Calgary, Alta., she received an M.A. in 1955 from McGill University, Montreal, for her thesis, *Eschatology in the Qur'an in the light of recent Biblical criticism*, and in 1963, a Ph.D., for her thesis, *An ideology for Pakistan*. From 1957 to 1960, she taught at the Kinnaird College for Women, Lahore. Since 1964, she was a professor of religion at Sir George Williams College, Concordia University, Montreal. Her writings include *Pakistan and the West* (1960), *The Authority of the past* (1970), and *Muslim ethics and modernity* (1984). ConAu, 77-80; DrAS, 1969 H, 1974 P, 1978 P, 1982 P; DrASCan, 1978; Ferahian; WhoRel, 1975-1976; WhoWor, 1987/88

M'Douall (McDouall), William, born in 1855 at Oswen Rectory, Suffolk, he became the first British vice-consul at Mohammerah, Persia. He had originally gone as a young telegraph clerk to Persia, but after twenty years had more or less 'gone native' and after the discovery of oil was not considered up to the new demands of the post. He was therefore transferred in 1909 to Kermanshah and two years later to Hamadan. He retired his consular service in 1918 and entered the Mesopotamia Civil Administration. He died in 1924. *Who was who*, 2; Wright, p. 84

MacDowall, David, born 20th cent., his writings include *Palestine and Israel; the uprising and beyond* (1989), and *A Modern history of the Kurds* (1996). ZKO

MacDowall, David William, born in 1930, he was educated at Liverpool, Corpus Christi College, Oxford, and the British School at Rome. He was an assistant keeper of the Department of Coins and Medals, British Museum, London, a university administrator, and lecturer in classics and Oriental studies, University of Durham. In 1998 appeared *Ex moneta; essays on numismatics, history and archaeology in honour of Dr. David W. MaDowall*. *Who's who*, 1990-2005; ZKO

McDowell, Charles M., fl. 20th cent., he was associated with the Institute of Administration, Ahmado Bello University, Zaria, Nigeria. His writings include *The Alien businessman in Nigeria* (Zaria, 1966), and *An Introduction to the problems of ownership of land in Northern Nigeria* (Zaria, 1966). Note about the author; NUC, 1956-1972

McDowell, David D., fl. 1963, he was a sometime director, American Friends of the Middle East. Note

McDowell, Edmund Wilson, born in 1857, he was a Prebyterian missionary who spent nearly forty years in Persia and Mesopotamia. He was instrumental in developing mission work in Urmia,

Kurdistan, organizing a chain of village schools and churches. He died in 1939. NYT, 10 April 1939, p. 17, col. 3; Shavit; WhAm, 4

McDowell, Joan Allgrove *see* Allgrove, Joan

McDowell, Margaret Dean, born in 1872, she was a teacher, relief worker, and the wife of Rev. Edmund Wilson McDowell. She died in 1927. Shavit

McElroy, Paul Simpson, born 29 August at Chicopee Falls, Mass., he was a 1926 graduate of Wesleyan University, Middletown, Conn., received an M.A. in 1931 from Columbia University, New Yorkk, and a B.D. in 1932 from Union Theological Seminary, New York. He taught English for three years at the American University in Cairo, during which time he made a trip up the Nile to its source. He subsequently served as a minister, chaplain, and church administrator in the United States. He was granted an honorary doctorate from Piedmont College. His writings include *Protestant beliefs* (1940), *Wings of recovery* (1947), *Moments of meditation* (1961), and *Quiet thoughts* (1964). He died in 1989. ConAu, 5-8; Master (1)

MacEoin, Denis Martin, born 26 January 1949, he received a Ph.D. in 1979 from Cambridge University for *From Shaykhism to Babism; a study in charismatic renewal in Shi'ite Islam*. He taught religion and philosophy successively at the universities of Newcastle-upon-Tyne, and Durham. His writings include *The Sources for early Bābī doctrine and history; a survey* (1992). LC; EURAMES, 1993; Sluglett

MacEwan, Arthur, born 7 April 1942, he received a Ph.D. in 1969 from Harvard University for *Development alternatives in Pakistan; a multisectorial and regional analysis of planning problems*, a work which was published two years later. In 1975, he was appoined a professor in the Department of Economics, University of Massachusetts, Boston, a post which he held until his retirement. His other writings include *Revolution and economic development in Cuba* (1981), *Instability and change in the world economy* (1989), and *Neo-liberalism or democracy? Economic strategy, markets and alternatives for the 21st century* (1999). ConAu, 222; NatFacDr, 1990-2002

McEwen, Alexander, born 19th cent., he was a political writer whose writings include *The Need of protection; free imports, not free trade* (London, 1880), and *Reasonable protection* (London, 1887). BLC; NUC, pre-1956

McEwen, Edward, born about 1937, he was a Fleet Street compositor who lived in Wanstead, London. He was an editor of the Society of Archer-Antiquarians, and a fellow of the Royal Asiatic Society. He made it a hobby of reconstructing Oriental composite bows and subsequently made a short film at the Tower of London for the Central Office of Information called *The Art of the bowman*. He was also engaged in researching Persian archery texts at the School of Oriental and African Studies, London. Note about the author

Macey, Roy Edgar Gene, fl. 20th cent., his writings include *Oriental prayer rugs* (Leigh-on-Sea, 1961). BLC; ZKO

McFadyean, Sir Andrew, born in 1887, he was educated at the universities of London and Oxford, and in 1910 enterd the Treasury. He was a sometime private secretary to P.M. Stanley Baldwin and served as secretary to the British Delegation Reparation Commission. From 1933 to 1967, he was a member of Council of the Royal Institute of International Affairs. His writings include *Reparation reviewed* (1930), *Government intervention in industry* (1935), and *The Liberal case* (1950). He died in 1974. Who was who, 3

MacFie, Alec (Alexander) Lyon, born in 1931, he received a Ph.D. in 1972 from Birbeck College, London, for *The Straits questions, 1908-1936*, a work which was published in 1993. His other writings include *Atatürk* (1994), *The End of the Ottoman Empire, 1908-1923* (1998), *Orientalism* (2002), and he edited *Orientalism; a reader* (2000). LC; Sluglett; ZKO

Macfie, John Mandeville, born in 1891, he was from 1926 to 1929 a deputy assistant director of pathology, India. His writings include *The Laws of Manu* (19219, and *Myths and legends of India* (1924). He died in 1985. Who was who, 8

MacGaffey, Wyatt, born in 1932 in England, he received a Ph.D. in 1967 from the University of California, Los Angeles, for *Structure and progress in a Kongo village*. He was a professor of sociology and anthropology at Haverford, Pa., College from 1967 to his retirement. His writings include *Custom and government in the Lower Congo* (1970), *Modern Kongo prophets; religion in a plural society* (1983), *Religion and society in Central Africa; the BaKongo of Lower Zaire* (1986), *Art and healing of the Bakongo commented by themselves* (1991), and *Kongo political culture; the conceptual challenge of the particular* (2000), and he was a joint author of *Cuba, its people, its society, its culture* (1962). ConAu, 72-76; NatFacDr, 1990-1994; WhoAm, 1990-1994|

MacGahan (Макгахан), Januarius Aloysius, born in 1844 on a farm in Ohio, he held odd jobs as clerk, and teacher, while contributing to a local periodical. In 1868, he travelled to Europe, learned French and taught English in France. He gained special correspondent credentials for the *New York Herald*. After the Franco-Prussian war he was given a roving commission for two years to visit the great cities of Europe and write for the newspaper. In 1873, he was sent to Central Asia to report on the Russian incursion into Turkestan; five years later, he covered Turkish reprisals in the Balkans for British newspapers. His writings include *Campaigning on the Oxus, and the fall of Khiva* (1874), its Turkish translation, *Hive seyahatnamesi ve tarihi-i musavver* (1292/1876), *Turkish atrocities in Bulgaria; letters of the special commissioner of the "Daily news"* (1876), and he was a joint author of *The War correspondence of the "Daily news," 1877, with a connecting narrative forming a continuous history of the war between Russia and Turkey to the fall of Kars* (1878). He died from typhus in Constantinople on 9 June 1878. ANB; DcAmDH; EnBulg; Kornrumpf; Kornrumpf, N; Özege; WhAm H

McGeachy, James Burns, born in 1899, he was a Canadian journalist who spent the war years in London as a broadcaster of BBC war and other commentaries. He returned to Canada in 1946 to join the editorial staff of the Toronto *Globe and mail*. From 1957 to 1964 he was an associate editor of the *Financial Post*, Toronto. His writings include *Provinces and Dominion* (1938), and *A Touch of McGeachy; a collection of the best from the pen of J. B. McGeachy* (1962). He died in 1966. Canadian; Master (1); NYT, 29 August 1966, p. 29, col. 4;

McGhee, George Crews, born 10 March 1912 at Waco, Texas, he graduated in 1933 from the University of Oklahoma and received a D.Phil. in 1937 from Oxford University. In the early 1940s he entered the U.S. Department of State, where he was responsible for economic and political affairs in the Balkans, Near East, South Asia, and South Africa. From 1951 to 1953 he served as an ambassador to Turkey. His writings include *Coordinating foreign aid* (1948), *Natürliche Hilfsquellen der Welt = The world's natural resources position* (Köln, 1964), *Envoy to the middle world; adventures in diplomacy* (1983), *National interest and global goals* (1989), and *The US-Turkish-NATO Middle East connections* (1990). ConAu, 152; IntWW, 1974-2006; Master (24); Shavit; Who, 1969-2005; WhoAm, 1974-1996

McGowan, Bruce William, born in 1933, he received a Ph.D. in 1967 from Columbia University, New York, for *Defter-i mufassal-i Liva-i Sirem, an Ottoman revenue survey dating from the reign of Selim II*. He was a sometime director of the American Center, Ljubljana. His writings include *Economic life in Ottoman Europe; taxation, trade and the struggle for land, 1600-1800* (1981), and *Sirem sancağı mufassal tahrir defteri* (1983). LC; NUC, 1968-72; ZKO

MacGowan, David Jerome, born in 1815, he was a medical missionary in China. His writings include *The Claims of the missionary enter on the medical profession* (1842). He died in 1893. LC; Lodwick

McGrath, Joan *Rosita* née Torr, 1895-1967 *see* Forbes, Joan *Rosita* née Torr

MacGregor, Sir Charles Metcalfe, born 12 August 1840, he was educated at Marlborough and entered the Indian Army in 1856. He served primarily in India and Afghanistan. His writings include *Narrative of a journey through the province of Khorassan and on the N. W. frontier of Afghanistan in 1875* (1879), *Diary of the 3rd Afghan war* (1880), *Wanderings in Balochistan* (1880), and *War in Afghanistan, 1879-80; the personal diary of Major General Sir Carles M. MacGregor*, edited by William Trousdale (Detroit, 1985). His *Defence of India*, privately published in 1884, was acknowledged to be the most perfect work of its kind, but was rigorously surpressed by the British Government. He superintended the compilation of the *History of the second Afghan War* in six volumes (1885-86), which, however, was surpressed by the Indian Government. He died in Cairo on 5 February 1887. Boase; Buckland; DNB; IndianBiInd (1); LC; Riddick

MacGregor, Sir George Hall, born 1 May 1801, he was educated at the East India Company's college in Addiscombe, England, and in 1826 he was commissioned in the Bengal Artillery. He was a political assistant and military secretary to Sir W. H. Macnaghten, accompanied him as envoy to Shah Shuja in 1838, and was present at the caputure of Ghazni, 1839, and Lucknow, 1858. He retired as major-general in 1859. He died in Glencarnock, Torquay, on 2 January 1883. BritInd (2); Buckland; IndianBiInd (2); Riddick

MacGuckin de Slane, William *see* Slane, William MacGuckin de

McGuire, Carl Wilburn, born 8 April 1911 at Shenandoah, Iowa, he was a 1935 graduate of the University of Colorado and received a Ph.D. in economics in 1939. Since 1941 he was a professor of economics at the University of Colorado. He was a Fulbright Lecturer at the University of Alexandria, 1952-53, and a visiting professor at the American University of Beirut, 1956-57. He was an editor of *Energy and development* (1974). AmM&WSc, 1973 S, 1978 S; Note about the author

Mach, Rudolf, born 28 October 1922, he received a Dr.phil. in 1957 from the Universität Basel for *Der Zaddik in Talmud und Midrasch*. His writings include *Catalogue of Arabic manuscripts (Yahuda Section) in the Garrett Collection, Princeton* (1977), and he was a joint author of *Handlist of Arabic manuscripts (new series) in the Princeton University Library* (1987). He died on 8 July 1981. MELA notes, 24 (1981), pp. 16-18 (not sighted)

Machado, José Pedro, born 8 November 1914, at Faro, Portugal, he was a Romance philologist whose writings include *Influência arábica no vocabulário português* (1958-61), *Vasco da Gama e a sua viagem de descobrimento* (1969), *Factos, pessoas e livros* (1971), and *Vocabulário portugués de origem árabe* (1991). In 1979 appeared *O Professor José Pedro Machado*. LC; *Quem é alguém*, 1947

Machalski, Franciszek, born in 1904 at Braddock, Pa., the son of Polish immigrants, he returned in 1910 with his parents to Poland. He studied Polish and Oriental philology at Uniwersitet Jana Kazimiersza at Lwów, Poland. In 1930, he received a doctorate in Islamic history. During the second World War he spent three years in Iran as secretary of a society of Iranian studies established by Polish refugees. When he returned to Poland he taught for four years at a secondary school. From 1951 to his retirement in 1974, he taught Iranian philology in various capacities at Uniwersitet Jagielloński, Kraków; since 1959, he was editor-in-chief of *Folia orientalia*. His writings include *Historyczna powieść perska* (1952), *Od Cyrusa do Mosaddeka* (1960), *La littérature de l'Iran contemporain* (1965), *Kultura arabska i jej wpływ w Europie* (1968), and *Firdausi i jego "Szāh-nāme"* (1970). He died in 1979. In 1985 appeared *Irania; studies in memory of Prof. Franciszek Machalski*. BioB134; NEP; Polski

McHardy, William Duff, born 26 May 1911 at Cullen Banffs, he was a professor of Syriac and Aramaic at Selly Oaks Colleges, Birmingham, and the University of London before becoming Regius Professor of Hebrew at Oxford from 1960 to1978. He edited *Hebrew and Semitic studies* (1963). He died on 9 April 2000. IntWW, 1991-1995/96; Who's who, 1961-2000

Machat, Jules, born 19th cent., he received a doctorate in 1905 from the Université de Paris for *Documents sur les établissements français de l'Afrique occidentale au XVIIIe siècle*. His writings include *Le Développement économique de la Russie* (1902), *Les Rivières du sud et le Fouta-Diallon* (1906), and *Cours de géographie* (1914). BN; NUC, pre-1956

Machatschek, Alois, born 12 November 1928 at Bratislava, Slovakia, he studied architecture, archaeology and fine art at both, Technische Hochschule, and the Universität, Wien. After his Dr.phil. in 1964, he went for research to Roma. Since 1967 he was a lecturer in fine art and preservation of monuments at Technische Hochschule Wien. His writings include *Die Nekropolen und Grabmäler im Gebiet von Elaiussa Sebaste und Korykos im Rauhen Kilikien* (1967), *Denkmalpflege in Europa* (2001), and he was a joint author of *Bauforschungen in Selge* (1981). In 1993, appeared *Von der Bauforschung zur Denkmalpflege; Festschrift für Aloys Machatschek zum 65. Geburtstag*. Note about the author; Kürschner, 1992-2005

Machatschek, Fritz, born 22 September 1876 into a German family at the German-speaking enclave, Wischau (Vyškov), Moravia, he studied geography and history at the Universität Wien in preparation for a teaching career. After his Dr.phil. in 1899, he did post-doctoral work at Berlin and Zürich. From 1900 to 1915 he taught at schools, concurrently gaining his Dr.habil. at the Universität Wien and serving as editor of three geographical periodicals. In 1911 and 1914 he was in Turkestan, experiences which are embodied in his *Landeskunde von Russisch Turkestan* (1921). In 1915, he was appointed to the chair of geography at the German Karls-Universität, Prag. The unbearable conditions in Czechoslovakia after 1918 persuaded him to accept successively the same chair at Zürich in 1924, at Wien in 1928, and at München in 1935. Until the end of his days, which came on 25 September 1957, he remained a native of Greater Germany. DtBE; Filipsky; Kürschner, 1925-1954; Martinek; *Mittelungen der Geographischen Gesellschaft in München*, 42 (1957), pp. 203-232; NDB; Teichl; *Wer ist's*, 1928, 1935

McHenry, Donald Franchot, born 13 October 1936 at East St. Louis, Ill., he graduated from Illinois State University and received an M.Sc. from Southern Illinois University. He served as U.S. Permanent Representative to the U.N.O. from 1979 to 1981. He subsequently became a university research professor of diplomacy and international affairs at Georgetown University, Washington, D.C. His writings include *Micronesia, trust betrayed* (1975), and *United States firms in South Africa* (1975). AfrAmBi, 2004; CurBio, 1980; IntWW, 1980-2006; Master (18); NatFacDr, 1995-2005; WhoAm, 1980-1996; *Who's who*, 1982-2005

McHenry, Stewart Gaylord, born about 1945, he received a Ph.D. in 1973 from Syracuse University for *The Syrians of upstate New York*. He was a sometime professor in the Department of History, Castleton State College, Rockville, Md. NatFacDr, 1990-2005; Selim

Machordom Comíns, Alvaro, born in 1923, he wrote *Muhammad, profeta de Dios* (Madrid, 1979), and *La expulsión de los moriscos* (2000) (not sighted). LC

Machover, Moshe, 1936- *see* Mahover, Mosheh

Machray, Robert, born in 1857, he was a journalist and novelist whose writings include *The Little Entente* (1929), *The Struggle for the Danube and the Little Entente* (1929-38), *The Eastern question revived* (1939), *East Prussia, menace to Poland and peace* (1943), and *The Problem of Upper Silesia* (1945). He died in 1946. Master (1); *Who was who*, 4

Machuel, Louis Pierre, born in 1848 at Alger, he had close contacts with Arabs from his early childhood, when he had attended, at the same time, both a French primary school and a Koranic school. He began his career in education as a teacher, serving successively at the Franco-Arab Collège at Constantine and the Lycée d'Alger. Later he was appointed to the chair of Arabic at Oran and was also made inspector by the French Government of the *madrasah* of Tlemcen. His competence and knowledge in matters relating to Muslim education became so widely known in pedagogical circles that in 1880 he was entrusted with heading a mission to Tunisia to study the organization of Zaytuna Mosque and Sādiqī College. In 1883, he was put in charge of all educational matters in Tunisia. By the early 1890s his reorganization of education in the Regency was pretty much completed to his satirfaction. His writings include *Manuel de l'arabisant; ou, Recueil de pièces arabes* (1885), *L'enseignement public dans la Régence de Tunis* (1889), *Grammaire élémentaire d'arabe régulier* (1892), *L'enseignement de la langue arabe* (1919), and he was a joint author of *Hygiène du colon; ou, Vade-mecum de l'Européen aux colonies* (1902). He died in 1922. LC; *Revue d'histoire maghrebine*, 3 (1975), pp. 45-55; ZKO

Machut-Mendecka, Ewa, born 20th cent., her writings include *Współczesny dramat egipski lat 1870-1975* (Warszawa, 1984), *Główne kierunki rozwojowe dramaturgii arabskiej* (Warszawa, 1992), and *Studies in Arabic theatre and literature* (Warsaw, 2000). OSK

McIlwraith, Sir Malcolm, born 1865, he was educated at Marlborough, Universität Berlin, Faculté de droit de Paris, and called to the bar from Lincoln's Inn in 1890. He was for eighteen years a judicial adviser to the Egyptian Government. He died in 1941. BritInd (2); *Who was who*, 4

MacInnes, Angus Campbell, born in 1901, a graduate of Trinity College, Cambridge, he was for two years a teacher at the Jerusalem Men's College and served from 1943 to 1951 as archdeacon of Jerusalem. He died in 1977. *Who was who*, 7

Macintosh, Edward Hyde, born in 1895, he served in the Palestine campaign during the First World War. From 1921 to 1945 he was in the Sudan Political Service, ending as governor of Khartoum Province. He died in 1970. *Who was who*, 6

McIntosh, Ian Graham, fl. 20th cent., he was a joint author of *The Face of Scotland* (Oxford, 1966).

Macintyre, James Lewis, born in 1868, his writings include *Giordano Bruno* (London, MacMillan, 1903), and jointly with W. A. Banfield, *A Grammar of the Nupe language, together with a vocabulary* (London, Society for Promoting Christian Knowledge, 1915). NUC, pre-1956; ZKO

Macintyre, Ronald R., born 20th cent., he was in 1975 a lecturer in political science at the University of Canterbury, Christchurch, New Zealand. Note about the author

McKane, William, born 18 February 1921 at Dundee, Scotland, he graduated from the universities of St. Andrews and Glasgow, where he also received a Ph.D. in 1956. He started his teaching career at the University of Glasgow and finished as a professor of Hebrew and Oriental languages and principal of St. Mary's College in the University of St. Andrews. His writings include *Prophets and wise men* (1965), *A Critical and exegetical commentary on Jeremiah* (1986-96), *Selected Christian Hebraists* (1989), and the translation from the Arabic, *Al-Ghazali's Book of fear and hope* (1963). In 1986 appeared *A Word in season; essays in honour of William McKane*. He died on 4 September 2004. ConAu, 117; IntWW, 1989/90-2005; *Who's who*, 1982-2004

Mackay, Alexander Murdoch, born 13 October 1849 at Rhynie near Aberdeen, he was an engineer who had studied at Edinburgh and Berlin and became a missionary in East Africa, where he arrived in May 1876, never to return home. He died from malaria in Usambiro, 8 February 1890. His sister, Alexina Harrison, wrote his biography, *The story of the life of Mackay of Uganda, pioneer missionary* (1891). A German translation was published in 1891.

Mackay, Angus Iain Kenneth, born in 1939, he graduated from the University of Edinburgh, where he also received his Ph.D. He there taught history in various capacities since 1977. His writings include *Spain in the middle ages* (1977), and *Atlas of medieval Europe* (1997). In 2002 appeared *Medieval*

Spain, culture, conflict, and coexistence; studies in honour of Angus Mackay. Who's who, 1994-2005; ZKO

Freiherr von Mackay, Ben Lawrence, born 2 September 1870 at Köln, Germany, he received an unidentified doctorate. He was resident in München and wrote on current history, including *China, die Republik der Mitte* (1914), *Italiens Verrat am Dreierbund* (1915), *Die moderne Diplomatie, ihre Entwicklungsgeschichte und ihre Reformmöglichkeiten* (1915), *Der Orient in Flammen* (1915), *Der Vierbund und das neue europäische Weltbild* (1916), and *Volksführer und -verführer* (1917). He died in 1918. GV; KDtLK, 1916; Note about the author

McKay, Donald Vernon, born 8 October 1912 at Independece, Kan., he was a 1933 graduate of Baker University, Oregon, and received a Ph.D. in 1939 from Cornell University, Ithaca, N.Y., for *The French acquisition of Tunis*. He was a research associate successively with the Foreign Policy Association and the U.S. Department of State before he became a professor of African studies at the School of Advanced International Studies, Johns Hopkins University, Baltimore, Md. His writings include *Africa in world politics* (1963), and he edited *African diplomacy* (1966). He died in 1985. AmM&WSc, 1973 S, 1978 S; ConAu, 5-8; Master (1); Selim; Unesco; WhoA, 1974-1980; WrDr, 1976/78-1988/90

Mackay, George Anthony, born in 1947, he studied at the universitites of Canterbury, and Reading, gaining a B.A. and M.A. He became a research assistant at the University of Aberdeen, concurrently serving as economic adviser to the United Nations Development Programme as well as the World Bank Mission to Oman. He was a joint author of *The political economy of North Sea oil* (1975), and *North Sea oil and the Aberdeen economy* (1980). Note about the author

Mackay, Mercedes Isabelle, born in 1906 at Poltesco, Cornwall, she studied English philology and drama and received a diploma from the University of London. She was a correspondent for African newspapers and travelled widely in the Third World. She was a contributor to a great variety of periodicals, and a writer of short stories and novels. ConAu, 11-12

Mackay, Pierre Antony, born 19 February 1933 at Toronto, Ont., he graduated in 1954 from Yale University, New Haven, Conn., and received his Ph.D. in 1964 from the University of California at Berkeley for *Studies in the history of Republican Macedonia, 168-146 B.C.* He taught classics successively at the University of Oregon and Bryn Mawr (Pa.) College before he was appointed in 1976 a professor in the Department of Classics, University of Washington at Seattle, a post which he still held in 1990. His writings include *Certificates of transmission on a manuscript of the Maqāmāt of Harīrī, MS Cairo, Adab, 105* (1971), and he edited *Computers and the Arabic language* (1990). DrAS, 1969 F, 1974 F, 1978 F, 1982 F; NatFacDr, 1990; WhoA, 1990-1994|

MacKay, Theodora née Stillwell, born in 1938, she was a graduate of Bryn Mawr (Pa.) College, where she also took a doctorate with a dissertation on the small Roman client state of Olba in Rough Cilicia. She excavated with George Scanlon at Fustat and later with George Miles at Heraclion. From 1980 to 1992, she served as associate editor of the *MESA Bulletin* and was compiler of its *Index, volumes 1 to 20*. During the last years of her life she turned to academic publishing successively for the university presses of Washington, California, and Princeton. She died of cancer on 17 January 1998 at the age of fifty-nine. *MESA bulletin* 32 (1998), pp. 140-141

McKay, Vernon, 1912-1985 *see* McKay, Donald Vernon

Mackeen, Abdul Majeed Mohamed, he received a Ph.D. in 1960 from the School of Oriental and African Studies, London, for *Studies in the origins and development of al-Shādhiliyyah*. In the 1960s he was associated with the University of Malaya, Kuala Lumpur. His other writings include *Contemporary Islamic legal organization in Malaya* (1969). Note; Sluglett; SOAS *Library catalogue*

Macken, Richard Alan, he received a Ph.D. in 1973 from Princeton University for *The Indigenous reaction to the French Protectorate in Tunisia, 1881-1900*. In 1982, he was associated with Gulf Oil Corporation, Pittsburgh. *MESA Roster of members*, 1977-1982; Selim

Mackenzie, Colin, born about 1753 in the British Isles, he left England in 1783 as a subaltern officer to serve in the East India Company, rising to the rank of colonel. From 1783 to 1796, he was "employed in all the campaigns of the time: Kimbatore, Dindigul, Madras, Nellore, Guntore, and Mysore." It was not until 1792 that he was "employed in the Nizam's dominions, for the purpose of acquiring some information of the geography" of the Dekkan, a task which resulted in his submitting a general map of the Nizam's dominons in 1796. By 1807, he had completed a first survey of the geography of Mysore which filled seven folio volumes. In 1810, he was made the first holder of the office of surveyor-general of Madras, and in 1811, surveyor-general of India, a post which he still held in 1817. By that time he had "resided in that climate, without the benefit of once going to Europe, or even to any other presidency, on account of health or private business." His writings include *Extracts from Capt. C. Mackenzie's work, regarding the dominions of the late Tippoo Sultaun* (1854), *Mackenzie collection; a descriptive* *catalogue of the Oriental MSS* (1828). A biography entitled *Colonel Colin Mackenzie*, by William Cook Mackenzie, was published in 1952. He died in 1821. Henze; *Journal of the Royal Asiatic Society of Great Britain and Ireland* 1 (1834), pp. 333-343

MacKenzie, David Neil, born 8 April 1926 at London, he became interested in Oriental subjects during his military service, especially in Iranian matters, and subsequently took up Oriental studies at the School of Oriental and African Studies, London. In 1955, he was appointed lecturer at SOAS and after extensive field-work in Kurdistan he obtained his Ph.D. in 1957 with the results of his research on Kurdish dialects for his thesis, *A dialectological survey of northern and central Kurdish*. He was promoted to reader in the University of London in 1963. His international reputation in the field of Iranian linguistics led to his appointment in 1975 as professor at the Seminar für Iranistik in the Universität Göttingen. He retired to Cyprus at the end of 1995. His writings include *Kurdish dialect studies* (1961-1962), *The Dialect of Awroman* (1966), *The 'Sūtra of the causes and effect of actions' in Sogdian* (1970), the collection of his articles, *Iranica diversa* (1999); he was a joint author of the *Catalogue of Pashto manuscripts in the libraries of the British Isles* (1965); and he translated from the Pashtu *Poems from the divan of Khushâl Khân Khattak* (1965). In 1991 appeared *Corolla iranica; papers in honour of Prof. Dr. David Neil MacKenzie*. He died in Bangor, Wales, on 13 October 2001. Kürschner, 1992-2003; Private; Sluglett

Mackenzie, Donald, born about 1840, he was a British trader and the founder of the British settlement at Cape Juby, Morocco. He went down in history of western Sahara as the founder of "Port Victoria," an initially successful but controversial trading station on the coast of Tarfaya in the late nineteenth century and as the author of the fantastic idea of creating a canal from the Saharan coast to Timbuctu to tap the wealth of Central Africa. He wrote *The Flooding of the Sahara; an account of the proposed plan for opening Central Africa to commerce and civilization from the north-west coast, with a description of Soudan and western Sahara* (London, 1877), and *The Khalifate of the West, being a general description of Morocco* (1911). BLC; Tony Hodges, *Historical dictionary of Western Sahara* (1984)

Mackenzie, Donald Alexander, born in 1873, he was a journalist, archaeologist, and lecturer. His writings include *Indian myth and legend* (1913), *Myths of Babylonia and Assyria* (1915), *From all the fronts* (1917), *Great deeds from the Great War* (1917), *Myths of China and Japan* (1923), *The Migration of symbols and their relations to beliefs and customs* (1926), *Fairy tales from many lands* (1930). He died in 1936. *Who's who*, 1929-1936; *Who was who*, 3

Mackenzie, Franklin, born in 1910, his writngs include *The Ocean and the steppe; the life and times of the Mongol emperor Genghis Khan* (1963), and its translation, *Dschingis Khan; der Fürst der aus der Steppe kam* (1977). ZKO

Mackenzie, Kenneth, fl. 20th cent., he was a writer on conflict affairs, including *Turkey after the storm* (1974), *Turkey under the generals* (1981), *Greece and Turkey; disarray on NATO's southern flank* (1983), *Turkey in transition* (1984), and he was a joint author of *Oppression and discrimination in Bulgaria; the case of the Muslim minority* (1986). LC; ZKO

MacKenzie, Kenneth Malcolm, fl. 1972 at Tenafly, N.J., he was a joint author of *Countermarks of the Ottoman Empire, 1880-1922* (London, 1974). Note about the author; ZKO

Mackenzie, Marcus, born 19th cent., he served in the British Army during the First World War, an experience which is embodied in his personal narrative, *From China to Baghdad* (1919). He subsequently went to Egypt for employment in the National Bank of Egypt. When the Second World War broke out he volunteered for military service and served with the Sanūsī for something over six months. After that, for four-and-a-half years he was Assistant Director of Land in Transjordan. His trace is lost after an article in 1946. Note about the author

Mackenzie, Molly, born 20th cent., her writings include *Turkish Athens; the forgotten centuries, 1456-1832* (Reading, 1992). ZKO

Mackenzie, Neil Donald, born 10 October 1941 at Everett, Mass., he received a Ph.D. in 1986 from the University of Michigan for *A topographical [sic] study of Cairo under the Ayyubids*. He was an independent researcher and archaeologist who participated in excavations of Sijilmasa, Morocco. He was a fellow of the American Research Center in Egypt, 1968-69, and was awarded a Fulbright grant to Syria, 1987-88. He was a member of the Middle East Institute, Washington, D.C. His writings include *Ayyubid Cairo; a typographical [sic] study* (1992). *MESA Roster of members*, 1990; Private; Selim[2]

Mackenzie, Peter Zambra, fl. 20th cent., he was a joint author of *The African veterinary handbook* (1956), a work which went through several editions. NUC

Mackenzie, Roderick Duncan, born 3 February 1885 at Carman, Ont., he graduated in 1912 from the University of Manitoba, and received his Ph.D. in 1920 from the University of Chicago. He was a sociologist who successively taught at Ohio State University, and the universities of West Virginia, Washington at Seattle, and Michigan. His writings include *The Neighborhood* (1923), *Oriental exclusion; the effect of American immigration laws, regulations, and judicial decisions upon the Chinese and Japanese on the American Pacific Coast* (1928), *The Metropolitan community* (1933), and *Readings in human ecology* (1934). He died 6 May 1940. AmIndex (2); CurBio, 1940; NUC, pre-1956; WhAm, 1; WhoAm, 1932/33-1940/41

Mackerras, Colin Patrick, born 26 August 1939 at Sydney, he graduated in 1961 from Melbourne University, reveived an M.Litt. in 1964 from Cambridge University for *Some aspects of the Uighur Empire, 744-840*, and his Ph.D. in 1970 from the Australian National University, Canberra. He taught English at Peking and worked as a research fellow at Canberra before he became a professor of modern Asian studies at Griffith Universty, Nathan, Australia. His writings include *The Uighur Empire (744-840) according to the T'ang dynastic histories* (1968), *China's minority cultures; identities and integration since 1912* (1996), *China in transformation, 1900-1949* (1998), and *China's ethnic minorities and globalisation* (2003). ConAu, 85-88, new rev., 15, 33, 86; IntAu&W, 1991/92-2006; Schoeberlein; Sluglett; WhoAus, 1977-2005; WhoWor, 1991/92; WrDr, 1990/92-2006

Mackeson, Frederick, born 28 September 1807 at Woodbridge, Kent, he was educated at Canterbury and in France. He entered the 14th Native Infantry in Bengal in 1825 and was subsequently stationed as assistant Political Agent at Ludhiana. He accompanied Sir Alexander Burnes to Kabul in 1837. He distinguished himself as a frontier and political officer in the first Afghan War, in the Khyber and at Peshawar. In 1842, he was awarded Companion of the Bath. In 1851, he became commissioner of Peshawar. He was assassinated by a religious fanatic from Koner on 10 September 1853 and died four days later. His writings include *Two letters to Major-General Pollock, commanding troops in Afghanistan* (1842). Bucklnad; DNB; IndianBilnd (3); Mason; Riddick

Mackey, Sandra, born 13 September 1937 at Oklahoma City, Okla., she graduated in 1958 from Central State College, Edmond, Okla., and received her M.A. in 1966 from the University of Virginia. She became a writer and public lecturer. Her writings include *The Saudis; inside the desert kingdom* (1987), *Lebanon; death of a nation* (1989), *Passion in politics; the turbulent world of the Arabs* (1992), *The Iranian; Persia, Islam and the soul of a nation* (1996), and *The Reckoning; Iraq and the legacy of Saddam Hussein* (2003). ConAu, 127, new rev., 54, 123; ZKO

Mackie, Louise W., born 20th cent., she received an M.A. in Islamic art in 1971 from New York University. She was in 1983 a curator of the Textile Department in the Royal Ontario Museum, Toronto, Ont. Her writings include *The Splendour of Turkish* weaving (1973), *Masterpieces in the Textile Museum, Washington, D.C.* (1976), and she was a joint editor of *Turkmen; tribal carpets and traditions* (1980). LC; *MESA Roster of members*, 1990; Note

MacKinnon, Colin R., born about 1940, he received a Ph.D. in Near Eastern languages and literatures in 1974 from the University of California, Los Angeles, and in 1976 he was a director of the American Institute of Iranian Studies, Tehran Center. His writings include *Finding Hoseyn; a novel* (1986). MESA *Roster of members*, 1990; Note about the author

McKitterick, Thomas Edward Maurice, fl. 1955, his writings include *Russian economic poliy in eastern Europe* (1948), *Wages policy?* (1949), and *Conditions of British foreign policy* (1951), all of which were Fabian Publications, London. NUC, pre-1956

MacLachlan, Alexander, born about 1865 at Erin, Ont., he graduated in 1884 from Queen's University, Kingston, Ont., and in 1887 from Union Theological Seminary, New York; in 1910 he received a D.D. from New York University. In November 1890 he went to St. Paul's College, [Tarsus,] Turkey, as a Presbyterian missionary. Soon thereafter he was assigned to the International College, Smyrna, where he served as its president from 1896 to 1926. His trace is lost in 1930. AmIndex (1); Kornrumpf; *Missionary herald*, 1926, p. 478

McLachlan, Keith Stanley, born 19 February 1937 at Warrington, England, he graduated in 1958 from the University of Durham, where he also received his Ph.D. in 1961 for *A geographical study of the coastal zone between Homs and Misurata, Tripolitania.* He taught geography in the Department of Geography, University of Durham before joining the School of Oriental and African Studies, London, as a professor of geography of the Near and Middle East in its Geopolitics and International Boundaries Research Centre. He was a joint author of *Social and economic development of Libya* (1982), *A Bibliography of the Iran Iraq borderland* (1987), *The Neglected garden; the politics and ecology of agriculture in Iran* (1987); he was a joint author of *A Bibliography of Afghanistan; a working bibliography of materials on Afghanistan, with special reference to economic and social change in the* *twentieth century* (1983), *Iran and Iraq; the next five years* (1987); and he edited *The Developing agriculture of the Middle East* (1977), and *The Boundaries of modern Iran* (1994). DrBSMES, 1993; Sluglett; Unesco

Maclagan, Sir Edward Douglas, born 25 August 1864 in the Punjab , he was educated at Winchester and New College, Oxford, and passed the examination for the Indian Civil Service in 1883. In 1906, he became chief secretary to the Government of the Punjab, and in 1910, secretary of the Revenue and Agriculture Department to the Government of India. From 1915 to 1918 he was secretary to the Education Department. In 1919, he suceeded O'Dwyer as lieutenant-governor of the Punjab and was its governor from 1921 until 1924, when he returned to England. His writings include *The Jesuits and the Great Mogul* (1932). He died in London on 22 October 1952. IndianBiInd (4); JRCAS, 1953, p. 90; *Who was who*, 5

Maclagan, Robert, born 14 December 1820 at Edinburgh, he was educated at Edinburgh and the East India Company's college at Addiscombe. He entered the Engineer Service in 1839. In 1842, he joined the Bengal Corps of Sappers and Miners and in the following year was apponted Surveyor of Canals and Forests in Sind. In 1847, he was selected for the post of first Principal of the Government of Civil Engineering, a post which he held until 1860. In 1852, he took his first furlough, and devoted part of it to a tour through Palestine to Baalbek, Damascus, and Constantinople. From 1860 to his retirement in 1879, he held the appointment of chief engineer and secretary to the Government of the Punjab in the Department of Public Works. He was a contributor to many learned journals as well as the *Encycloædia Britannica*. He died on 22 April 1893. JRAS, 1894, pp. 603-607

McLaren, Donald Stewart, born 4 February 1924 at London, he earned an M.D. in 1947 at Edinburgh and a Ph.D. in 1957 at London. He was a medical officer in India under the Baptist Missionary Society from 1949 to 1954, a medical research officer in the East African Institute of Medical Research, Tanzania from 1957 to 1962, a professor at the American University of Beirut from 1962 to 1976, and subsequently a professor at the University of Edinburgh. His writings include *Nutrition and its disorders* (1972), and *Nutrition in the community* (1983). WhoScEu, 1991 (not sighted); WhoWor, 1987/88

McLaren, Miss Grisell M., born 19th cent. in the United States, she was in 1901 a teacher and missionary at Van, and until the outbreak of the First World War did much touring and evangelistic work in Van and the sourrounding region. Like all missionaries, when sickness came and the wounded soldiers were brought in, she joined forces caring for them. When the Americans with the Armenians were shut up by the Turkish forces in that part of the city called the Gardens, she elected to stay in the Turkish military hospital with the Armenian nurses, who feared to remain without her presence. For a time messages were exchanged between her and the rest of the mission, but at last the Turkish officers forbade any further communication, and she was completely shut off from the other missionaries. Then the Russians came and the Turks evacuated the city. The Americans rushed over to the hospital to find some trace of her. The servants and those left said that she had gone with the wounded across Lake Van. No word of reassurance was she alllowed to send, but she was evidently shown personal kindness and allowed to stand by the nurses and carry on the work among the sick. She was last reported to be at Bitlis. She was a joint author of *The Tragedy of Bitlis* (New York, 1919). Kornrumpf; *Missionary herald*, 111 (1915), p. 460; NUC, pre-1956

McLaughlin, Gerald T., born about 1940, he was in 1990 associated with Brooklyn Law School, and in 1995 held the post of Dean of Law at Loyola Law School, Los Angeles, where he was still active in 2005. He was a joint author of *The Evolution of Federal drug control legislation* (1973). NatFacDr, 1990-2005; NUC, 1973-77

Maclaurin, Evan Colin Briarcliffe, born 14 September 1912 at Sydney, he graduated B.A. from the University of Sydney, and received his M.A. from Emmanuel College, Cambridge University. Since 1945 he was a professor, and later chairman, Department of Semitic Studies, University of Sydney. In 1966/67 he was a visiting professor at Leeds. His writings include *The Hebrew theocracy in the tenth to the sixth centuries B.C.* (1959), and *The Dead Sea scrolls* (1967). WhoAus, 1955-1977|

McLaurin, Ronald De, born 8 October 1944 at Oakland, Oreg., he was a 1965 graduate of the University of Southern Cailfornia, having spent 1964/65 at the Université de Tunis under the Year Abroad in the Maghreb Program. He also earned a Ph.D. degree. Since 1967 he briefly taught international relations at Merrimack College, North Andover, Mass., before embarking on a career with the U.S. Department of Defense. He later became an independent research scientist with Abbott Associates, Inc. He was a joint author of *The Soviet Middle East policy since the October War* (1976), *Foreign policy making in the Middle East* (1977), *Beyond Camp David* (1981), *Middle East foreign policy* (1982); and he edited *The Political role of minority groups in the Middle East* (1979), and *Military propaganda* (1982). AmM&WSc, 1973 S, 1978 S; ConAu, 65-68, new rev., 17; WhoAm, 1988/89-1996; WhoEmL, 1987/88; WhoS&SW, 1984-1986 (not sighted); WhoWor, 1989/90, 1991/92

Maclean, Arthur John, born in 1858, he was educated at Eton and King's College, Cambridge, and ordained an Anglican priest in 1882. He headed the Archbishop of Canterbury's Assyrian mission, 1886-91, designed to supply British assistance, partly in order to help resist the proselytising activities of the American Presbyterians and French Catholic missionaries, partly in order to secure British political protection against the Turks, Persians and Kurds. Under Canon A. J. Maclean, the Mission established schools for boys, two in Urmiyah, and two outside on the plain. He returned to Britain in 1891 to take up congregational duties. From 1903 to 1905 he was Canon of Edinburgh Cathedral. His writings include *The Catholicos of the East and his people, being the impressions of five years' work in the "Archbishop of Canterbury's Assyrian Mission;" an account of the religious and secular life and opinions of the Eastern Syrian Christians of Kurdistan and northern Persia* (1892), *Grammar of the dialects of vernacular Syriac as spoken by the Eastern Syrians of Kurdistan, North-West Persia and the Plain of Mosul* (1895), and *A Dictionary of the dialects of vernacular Syria as spoken by the Eastern Syrians of Kurdistan* (1901). He died in 1943. Who was who, 4; Wright, p. 121; ZKO

Mclean (MacLean), Derryl N., born about 1950, he received an M.A. in 1974 from McGill University, Montreal, for *Sind at the time of the Arab conquest*, and also a Ph.D. in 1985 for *Religion and society in Arab Sind*, a work which was published in 1989. He was a sometime professor of history at Simon Frazer University, Burnaby, B.C. MESA Roster of members, 1990; Selim²

Mclean of Dunconnel, Sir Fitzroy Hew, born 11 March 1911 in Cairo to Scottish parents, he was educated at Eton and Cambridge. He served in the Foreign Office until 1939 when he resigned and enlisted in the Cameron Highlanders. After war he was a lecturer and M.P. For his services in the British Military Mission to Yugoslav partisans, he received Yugoslav awards in 1969 and 1981. He was a Fellow of the British Academy. His writings include *Eastern approaches* (1949), *To the back of beyond; an illustrated companion to Central Asia and Mongolia* (1974), and *To Caucasus; the end of all earth* (1976). He died on 15 June 1996. Au&Wr, 1963; BritInd (1); DcLEL, 1940; EncZL; Who, 1951-1996

Maclean, Gerald M., born in 1952, he was in 1990 a professor of English at Wayne State University, Detroit, Mich., a post which he still held in 2005. He was also a visiting professor at Bosphorus University, Istanbul, and the Institute of Arab and Islamic Studies, University of Exeter, Devon. His writings include *The Rise of Oriental travel; English visitors to the Ottoman Empire, 1580-1720* (2004), and he was a joint editor of *The Country and the city revisited; England and the politics of culture, 1550-1850* (1999). LC; NatFacDr, 1990-2005; ZKO

McLean, John Godfrey, born 29 June 1917 at Portland, Oreg., he graduated B.Sc. in 1938 from the California Institute of Technology and received a Ph.D. in 1948 from Harvard, where he taught in a variety of capacities until 1956 when he became a business executive. His writings include *The Growth of integrated oil companies* (1954), and he was a joint author of *Manufacturing policy; a casebook of major production problems in six selected industries* (1957). He died in 1974. Master (6); NYT, 21 May 1974, p. 44, col. 4; WhAm, 6; WhoAm, 1964/65-1974/75; WhoE, 1974 (not sighted)

McLean, Neil Loudon Desmond, born 28 November 1918, he was educated at Eton and the Royal Military College, Sandhurst, and in 1938 posted to Palestine. He became an expert on guerrilla warfare, be it in Ethiopia, Albania, Vietnam or Algeria. He had travelled widely in the Middle East, the Horn of Africa, the subcontinent and China, and was one of the few British Orientalists who was accepted by Arabs and Israelis alike. In 1954, he was elected a Conservative MP for Inverness. He died 17 November 1986. Xan Fielding wrote *One man in his time; the life of lieutenant-colonel N.L.D. McLean* (1990). Asian affairs, n.s. 18 (1987), pp. 246-47; Who was who, 8

Mclean, Sir William Hannah, born in 1877, he was a town planner who planned Khartoum under the direction of Lord Kitchener, and also the protective planning scheme of Jerusalem, officially approved by Lord Allenby. He died in 1967. Master (1); Transactions of the Glasgow Oriental Society, 6 (1929-33), pp. 46-47 (not sighted); WhE&EA; Who was who, 6

Macleod, Aubrey Seymour Halford, 1914-2000 see Halford-Macleod, Aubrey Seymour

Macleod, Sir George Husband Baird, born in 1828, he studied medicine at Glasgow (M.D.), Paris, and Wien. He was a senior surgeon of the civil hospital at Smyrna, from February 1854 to 1856, when he returned to the Glasgow Royal Infirmary. Concurrently he lectured on surgery at Anderson's College. In 1869, he was appointed Regius Professor of Surgery at Glasgow University. His writings include *Notes on the surgery of the war in the Crimea* (1858), and *The Four apostles of surgery; an historical sketch* (1877). He died in Glasgow on 31 August 1892. Boase

MacLeod, Sir James McIver, born in 1866 at Glasgow, he served in various consular capacities, including interpreter and consul, mainly in Fez, where he also represented Portuguese and American interests, 1892-1917. From 1923 to his retirement in 1930 he was British consul-general at Tunis. His writings include the translation from the Spanish of José Lerchundi, *Rudiments of the Arabic-vulgar of Morocco* (Tangier, Catholic Mission Press, 1900). He died in 1944. BritInd (1); *Who was who*, 4

MacLeod, William Hewat, born 20th cent., his writings include *Guru Nanak and the Sikh religion* (1968), *The Evolution of the Sikh community* (1976), *Early Sikh tradition* (1980), and *Who is a Sikh? The problem of Sikh identity* (1989). NUC; ZKO

Macler, Frédéric, born in 1869, he obtained a doctorate in 1895 at the Université de Paris for his thesis, *Les apocalypses apocryphes de Daniel*. In 1920, he was appointed to the chair of Armenian at the École Nationale des Langues Orientales Vivantes, Paris. His writings include *L'apocalypse arabe de Daniel* (1904), and *Autour de l'Arménie* (1917). He died in 1938. *Byzantion* 13 (1938), pp. 764-765

Macleroy, Campbell Maqueen, Rev., B.D., born 19th cent., his writings include *The Garden in the waste, and other addresses to young people* (London, 1918), and he translated from the German of Gustav Warneck, *Outline of a history of Protestant missions from the Reformation to the present time* (New York, 1901). NUC, pre-1956

McLoughlin, Leslie J., born 24 February 1935, he studied Arabic at Manchester, Leeds, and London, becoming a teacher of Arabic in Aden, Lebanon, Britain, and the U.S.A. Since 1993 he was a consultant on the Arab world with McLoughlin Associates. His writings include *A Course in colloquial Arabic* (1974), *Colloquial Arabic* (1982), *Ibn Saud, founder of a kingdom* (1993), *In a sea of knowledge; British Arabists in the twentieth century* (2002), and he translated *Death in Beirut; a novel by Tawfiq Yusuf Awwad* (1976). DrBSMES, 1993; ConAu, 146; Private

McLoughlin, Peter Francis Martin, born 31 August 1928 at Comox, B.C., he received a Ph.D. in 1961 from the University of Texas for *The methodology of regionalizing and distributing African income; the Sudan*. He served as a lecturer in economics at the University of Khartoum, and as a district officer in Tanganyika. His writings include *Language-switching as an index of socialization in the Republic of the Sudan* (1964), *Research on agricultural development in East Africa* (1967), *African food production systems* (1970), *Agriculture in East and Central Africa* (1970), and *Research for agricultural development in northern Sudan to 1967* (1971). Selim; Unesco

McMahon, Arthur Henry, born in 1862, he was educated at the East India Company's college in Haileybury, and the Royal Military College, Sandhurst. He successively entered the Indian Staff Corps and the Indian Political Department. He made a name for himself by first settling the Afghan-Baluch border and later fixing the new Helmand boundary in 1903-1905. He was decorated for his later services in the Middle East and retired with the rank of colonel. He died in 1949. BioIn, 2 (2); Buckland; DNB; Goldschmidt; IndianBiInd (5); Riddick; *Who's who, 1936-1949*; *Who was who*, 4; Wright, pp. 145-46

MacManus, Emily Elvira Primrose, C.B.E., born in 1886, she was educated privately and became a registered nurse. She was active in professional organizations and became a president of the Royal College of Nursing. Her writings include *Hospital administration for women* (1934), and she was a joint author of *Nursing in the time of war* (1939). She died in 1978. BritInd (2); *Who*, 1951; *Who was who*, 7

MacMichael, Sir Harold Alfred, born in 1882, he was educated at King's Lynn and Bedford schools. After graduating from Magdalene College, Cambridge, he joined the Sudan Political Service in 1905, retiring in 1934. His writings include *The Tribes of northern and central Kordofán* (1912), *A History of the Arabs in the Sudan* (1922), *The Anglo-Egyptian Sudan* (1934), and *A History of the Sudan* (1955). He died on 19 September 1969. BritInd (2); DNB; *Who was who*, 6

Macmichael, William, born in 1784 in Shropshire, he studied at Christ Church College, Oxford, where he took all his degrees, including an M.D. Supported by a travelling fellowship, he visited Russia, the Balkans, and Turkey in 1811, and again in 1817 and 1818, experiences which are embodied in his *Journey from Moscow to Constantinople, in the years 1817, 1818* (1819). A member of the College of Physicians since 1818, he practised in London. His other writings include *Lives of British physicians* (1830). He died in 1839. BritInd (1); DNB

Macmillan, Sir Gordon Holmes Alexander, born in 1897, he was educated at Canterbury. After passing through the Royal Military College, Sandhurst, he was commissioned in Argyll and Sutherland Highlanders. During the second World War he served in North Africa, and after the war, in Palestine. He retired with the rank of general. He died in 1986. *Who was who*, 8

Macmillan, Maurice Harold, Earl of Stockton, born in 1894 at London, he was a graduate of Balliol College, Oxford. He was an officer in the first World War, was aide-de-camp to the Governor-General of Canada, 1919-1920. For twenty years a director of the family's Macmillan Publishing House, he sat in Parliament near continuously after 1924. He served as parliamentary undersecretary of state for the colonies, and prime minister of Britain. He died on 10 March 1986. AnaBrit; BritInd (1); ConAu, 113, 121, 128; DcTwHis; DNB; Master (8); WhAm, 10; *Who was who*, 7

McMillan, Wendell Marlin, born 14 June 1923 at Dallastown, Pa., he graduated in 1948 from Juniata College, Huntingdon, Pa., and he received a Ph.D. in 1955 from Pennsylvania State University for *Financial analysis of farmer purchasing cooperatives in Pennsylvania.* He was an agricultural economist who successively served with the U.S. Department of Agriculture, the Food and Agriculture Organization of the U.N.O., and the International Bank of Reconstruction and Development. His writings include *Fruit and vegetable bargaining cooperatives* (1958), and *A Bibliography of dissertations and theses on cooperatives* (1964). AmM&WSc, 1973 S, 1978 S; WhoFI, 1992/93

McMullan, Joseph Vincent, born in 1896, he was a collector of Oriental rugs. His writings include *Islamic carpets* (1965), *Rugs from the Joseph V. McMullan Collection* (1966), and *The George Walter Vincent and Belle Townsley Smith collection of Islamic rugs* (1971). He died in 1973. NatCAB, 57, pp. 45-46; NYT, 4 June 1973, p. 38, col. 4

McMullen, Christopher J., born about 1950, he received a Ph.D. in 1980 from Georgetown University, Washington, D.C., for *Calles and the diplomacy of revolution; Mexican-American relations, 1924-1928.* His writings include *Resolution of the Yemen crisis, 1963; a case study in mediation* (1980). LC

McMullen, Horace Martin, born 5 April 1913 at Montreal, P.Q., he was a 1935 graduate of the University of Vermont, and received an M.Div. in 1938 from Andover Newton Theological Seminary, Newton Centre, Mass. He was a principal of the Near East School of Theology, Beirut, 1947-1954, and a president of Aleppo College, 1954-1958. He subsequently served as a minister to several American congregations as well as a visiting lecturer and professor. WhoRel, 1992/93

MacMunn, Sir George Fletcher, born in 1869 at Chelsea, he was educated at the Royal Artillery Institution, the United Service Institution of India, and the Staff College. He served in India, the Dardanelles, and Mesopotamia. He retired in 1925. His writings include *The Armies of India* (1911), *Afghanistan from Darius to Amanuallah* (1929), *Behind the scenes in many wars, being the military reminiscences* (1930), *The Indian Mutiny in persepctive* (1931), *Religious and hidden cults of India* (1931), and he was a joint author of *The Official history of the World War; Egypt and Palestine* (1928)., and its translation, *Le operazioni militari in Egitto e Palestina* (1937). BritInd (4); IndianBilnd (1); Riddick; *Who was who*, 5; ZKO

MacMurdo (M'Murdo), James, born about 1789, he entered the military service of the Hon. East-India Company at a very early period of life. In India he was present at the taking of Baroda, Sunkra Pawaghur, Malia, and the Isle of France. His later years were passed in the civil and political departments, and he was successively appointed Agent in Kathiawar, and Resident in Kutch. He was eminently qualified for he possessed an accurate knowldge of Persian and Hindustani, and he spoke and wrote Gujarati with fluency. While proceeding on a tour to the frontiers of Wagen, for the purpose of establishing a military post, he was attacked by the fatal epidemic which had been ravaging India for four years. He died about 1822, aged thirty-three. *Asiatic journal*, vol. 14 (1822), pp. 5-9

MacNaghten, Sir William Hay, born in 1793, he was educated at Charterhouse School, London, and in 1809 he went to Madras in the Army and served in the Governor's bodyguard. He gained prizes in languages. In 1814, he was appointed to the Bengal Civil Service. From 1822 to 1830 he was registrar of the *Sadt Diwani Adalat* and published *Principles and precedents of Moohummudan law* (1825), and *Principles and precedents of Hindu law* (1829). From 1833 to 1837 he was secretary in the Secret and Political Departments. He made the treaty with Ranjit Singh and Shah Shuja in June 1838. He was appointed Envoy and Minister at the Afghan Court of Shah Shuja and accompanied the Army of the Indus to Kabul, but had great troubles with Shah Shuja and the Afghan tribes. He was nominated Governor of Bombay in September 1841. In the ensuing negotiations with Akbar Khan, son of Dost Muhammad, and at an interview on 23 December 1841 was treacherously killed by Akbar himself. AnaBrit; BritInd (6); Buckland; IndianBilnd (6)

McNair, William Watts, born 13 September 1849 in India, he joined H.M. Indian Survey Department on 1 September 1867, and was posted to the Rajputana Topographical Party where he was soon recognized as an accomplished surveyor, rising to 3rd grade. In the autumn of 1879 he accompanied the Khyber Column of the Afghan Field Force, and was present with that force during the severe fighting that occurred before Kabul in the winter of 1879-80, and the subsequent defence of Sharpur. Whilst in Afghanistan he mapped a large portion of hitherto unknown country, and having a perfect command of Urdu, he explored the Adrak-Badrak valleys with a native escort, and made himself acquainted with the route from Kabul to Jalalabad, via Lughman, which had not been explored by any European officer. At the close of the Afghan war he was attached to the Kohat Survey, particularly in the risky mapping of the frontier line from Kohat to Bannu. He later transferred to various Baluchistan parties. His ability as an observer, his readiness of resource under difficulties, and his power of attaching the frontier people to him personally have contributed greatly to his success as geographical topographer. He has won a lasting name as an explorer by his adventurous journey to Kafiristan in 1883, as he was the first European to set foot on that country. His lecture before the Royal Geographical Society in 1884 was the only time he had visited the land of his fathers. His services to geographical science were recognized by the R.G.S., who awarded him the Murchison Grant. *The memoir of W. W. McNair*, by J. E. Howard (1889), contains an account of his Kafiristan explorations. He died in Mysore on 13 August 1889. Proceedings of the Royal Geographical Society, October 1889, November 1889

McNeile, Robert Fergus, born 19th cent., he published his first article in 1916 and also wrote *Christianity in southern Fenland* (Cambridge, 1948). NUC, pre-1956

McNeill, N G., fl. 20th cent., his writings include *Business law in the Gulf* (London, 1977).

McNeill, William Hardy, born 31 October 1917 at Vancouver, B.C., he was a 1938 graduate of the University of Chicago, and received a Ph.D. in 1947 from Cornell University, Ithaca, N.Y. He taught history in varied capacities from 1947 to his retirement. His writings include *The Greek dilemma; war and aftermath* (1947), *Past and future* (1954), *The Rise of the West* (1963), *Europe's steppe frontier, 1500-1800* (1964), *The Pursuit of power* (1982), its translation, *Krieg und Macht* (1984); and he was a joint editor of *The Islamic world* (1973). Au&Wr, 1975; BioIn, 6, 14, 15, 17; ConAu, 5-8, new rev., 7; DrAS, 1974 H, 1978 H, 1982 H; IntAu&W, 1986; WhoAm, 1974-2003; WhoWor, 1991/92, 1993/94; WrDr, 1976/78-2005

McNicoll, Anthony, born about 1940, he received a Ph.D. in 1971 from Oxford University for *Hellenistic fortifications from the Aegean to the Euphrates*. He became associated with the British Institute of Archaeology. His writings include *Taşkun Kale; Keban rescue excavations, eastern Anatolia* (1983), and he was a joint author of *Pella in Jordan, 1; an interim report on the joint University of Sydney and the College of Wooster excavations, 1979-1981* (1982), and *Excavations at Kandahar, 1974 and 1975; the first two seasons at Shahr-i Kohna (Old Kandahar) conducted by the British Institute of Afghan Studies* (1996). LC; ZKO

Macomber, William Francis, S.J., born in 1921, he received a degree in 1964 from the Pontificium Institutum Orientalium Studiorum for *The Theological synthesis of Cyrus of Edessa*. His writings include *A Catalogue of Ethiopian manuscripts microfilmed for the Ethiopian Manuscript Microfilm Library, Addis Ababa, and for the Monastic Manuscript Microfilm Library, Collegeville, Minn.* (1975). ZKO

Macquart, Émile, born 19th cent., his writings include *Les Traités de commerce* (Paris, 1900), and *Les Réalités algériennes étude sur la situation économique de l'Algérie, 1881-1905* (1906). His trace is lost after an article in 1909. NUC, pre-1956

Macridy (Makridy) Bey, Theodor, born 19th cent., he was an archaeologist who excavated at Boğazköy and Alacahöyük. His writings include *Une Citadelle archaïque du Pont, fouilles du Musée Impérial Ottoman* (Berlin, 1907), and *La Porte des sphinx à Euyuk; fouilles du Musée Impériale Ottoman* (Berlin, 1908). His trace is lost after an article in 1931. BN; Kornrumpf; NUC, pre-1956; ZKO

Macro, Eric L., born 5 March 1920 at London, he was educated at Royal Air Force colleges and became a squadron-leader. He pursued an interest in the Middle East, and particularly Middle Eastern bibliography. He lectured widely. His writings include *Bibliography of the Arabian Peninsula* (1958), *Bibliography on Yemen and notes on Mocha* (1960), and *Yemen and the Western world since 1571* (1968). ConAu, 29-32, new rev., 32

McTague, John J., born 30 December 1944 at Albany, N.Y., he was a 1966 graduate of Siena College, Loudonville, N.Y., and received a Ph.D. in 1974 from the State University of NewYork at Buffalo for *British policy in Palestine, 1917-1922*. He was a lecturer in history at Buffalo before he was appointed a professor in 1976 at Sain Leo College, St. Leo, Fla. DrAS, 1978 H, 1982 H; MESA Roster of members, 1982-1990; Selim[3]

Macuch, Rudolf, born 16 October 1919 at Dolné Bzince, Czechoslovakia, he was one of the founders of the Institut für Semitistik und Arabistik at Freie Universität Berlin. His writings include *Neu-mandäische Texte im Dialekt von Ahwāz* (1993). He died in Berlin on 23 July 1993. In 1992 ppeared *Studia semitica necnon Iranica Rudolpho Macuch septuagenario ab amicis et discipulis dedicata*. Archív Orientální, 62 (1994), pp. 333-40 (not sighted) ; Filipsky, Kürschner, 1966-1992; WhoWor, 1991/92, 1993/94

Macůrek, Josef, born 31 March 1901 at Chomýž near Holešov, Moravia, he was educated at the archbishopric gymnasium in Kroměříž and studied history at Praha. He was a famous and productive Slavic historian who was competent in German, French, Hungarian, and Rumanian. From 1935 until his retirement in 1970 he was a professor of history at Brno (Brünn). His writings include *Dozvuky polského bezkrálovi z roku 1587* (1929), *Zápas Polska a Habsburků o přístup k Černému Moři na* *sklonku 16. stol* (1931), and *Dějiny mačrůa uherského státu* (1934). He died in Brno on 20 April 1992. Südost-Forschungen, 52 (1993), pp. 297-99

McVaugh, Michael Rogers, born 9 December 1938 at Washington, D.C., he graduated in 1960 from Harvard University with an honors thesis entitled *The De simplicibus of Arnald of Villanova*, and received a Ph.D. in 1965 in history from Princeton University. In 1976, he was appointed a professor of history of science and medieval history at the University of North Carolina, Chapel Hill, N.C. Since 1996 he was William Smith Wells Professor of History in the Institute for Advanced Study, Princeton. His writings include *The Tabula antidotarii of Armengaud Blaise and its Hebrew translation* (2000). ConAu, new rev., 99; DrAS, 1969 H, 1974 H, 1978 H, 1982 H; ZKO

McWilliam, Henry Ormiston Arthur, born 20th cent., his writings include *Muhammad and the world of Islam* (London, 1977), and he was a joint author of *The Development of education in Ghana* (1975). LC

Madale, Abdullah T., born 20th cent., he was in 1979 associated with Mindano State University, Marawi City, Philippines. His writings include *The Maranao* (Manila, 1975), and *The Remarkable Maranaws* (Quezon City, 1976). LC: ZKO

Madan, Triloki Nath, born 12 September 1931 at Srinagar, Kashmir, he received his M.A. in 1951 from Lucknow University and his Ph.D. in 1960 from the Australian National University for a thesis on family and kinship in rural Kashmir. For at least ten years he was a professor at the Institute of Economic Growth, Asian Research Center, University of Delhi. He edited *Muslim communities of South Asia; culture and society* (1976). IWWAS, 1975/76

Madani, Hamid, 1312/1934- *see* Bihzadi, Hamid

de **Madariaga**, Maria-Rosa, born 20th cent., she received a doctorate in 1987 from the Université de Paris for *L'Espagne et le Rif; pénétration coloniale et résistances locales, 1909-1926.* ZKO

Madden, Edward Harry, born 18 May 1925 at Gary, Ind., he graduated in 1946 from Oberlin College, Ohio, and received an undisclosed Ph.D. in 1950. He taught at a great variety of academic institutions, including the University of Toronto, and American University of Beirut, before he was appointed in 1982 a professor in the Department of Philosophy, University of Kentucky, Lexington, a post which he still held in 1990. His writings include *The Structure of scientific thought* (1960), *Philosophical problems of psychology* (1962), and he was a joint author of *Freedom and grace; the life of Asa Mahan* (1982). ConAu, 1-4, new rev., 1; DrAS, 1969 P; NatFacDr, 1990; WhoAm, 1990-2003

Maddick, Henry William, born 3 June 1915 at Totnes, Devon, he graduated M.A. in 1952 from Oxford University. He was a sometime lecturer in political science at Wadham College, Oxford. On 12 May 1970 he delivered an inaugural lecture at the University of Birmingham entitled *Mud walls and metropolises.* He was associated with the Birmingham Institute of Local Government Studies. His writings include *Democracy, decentralisation and development* (1963), and *Panchayati raj; a study of rural local government in India* (1970). Note; Unesco

Maddison, Francis Romeril, born 20th cent., he was in 1962 an assistant curator of the Museum of the History of Science, Oxford. His writings include *Sir William Dugdale, 1605-1686* (1953), *Medieval scientific instruments and the development of navigational instruments in the XVth and XVIth centuries* (1969); he was a joint author of *Mechanical universe, the astrarium of Giovanni De'Dondi* (1966); and he was a joint editor of *Science and technology in Islam; an exhibiton at the Science Museum, London, 1976* (1976). NUC; ZKO

Madelung, Wilferd Willy Ferdinand, born 26 December 1930 at Stuttgart, Germany, he graduated from Cairo University and received a Dr.phil. in 1957 from the Universität Hamburg for *Qarmaten und Fatimiden, ihre gegenseitigen Beziehungen und iihre Lehre vom Imamat*, and also a Dr.habil. in 1963 for *Der Imam al-Qāsim ibn Ibrāhīm und die Dogmatik der Zaiditen.* He was a German cultural attaché at Baghdad, and a lecturer at his alma mater before his was appointed a professor of Islamic history at the University of Chicago. From 1978 to 1998 he was Laudian Professor of Arabic in Oxford University. His writings include a collection of his articles, *Religious schools and sects in medieval Islam* (1985), *The Succession to Muhammad; a study of the early caliphate* (1997); he edited and translated *An Ismaili heresiography, the "Bāb al-shaytān" from Abū Tammām's Kitāb al-shajara* (1998), *Struggling with the philosopher; a refutation of Avicenna's metaphysics* (2001); he edited *Streitschrift des Zaiditenimams wider die ibaditische Prädestinationslehre* (1985), and *Arabic texts concerning the history of the Zaydi imāms of Tabaristān, Daylamān, and Gīlān* (1987). DrAS, 1969 H; Schwarz; Who's who, 1990-2005; ZKO

Mader, Andreas Evaristus, born in 1881, he was a scholar of Christian antiquity. His writings include *Altchristliche Basiliken und Lokaltraditionen in Südjudäa; archäologische und topographische Unter-suchungen* (Paderborn, 1918). NUC, pre-1956

Madeyska, Danuta, Mrs., born 20th cent., she received a doctorate in 1979 from Universytet Warszawski for her thesis, *The ideal of the Arab woman in the light of the epos Sirat al-Amira Ḏat al-Himma and historical reality*. Her writings include *Poetyka siratu; studium o arabskim roansie rycerskim* (1993), and *Historia świata arabskiego; okres klasyczny od starożytności do końca epoki Umajjadów* (1999). Note; OSK

Madigan, Cecil Thomas, born in 1889 at Renmark, South Australia, he was educated at the University of Adelaide and was a Rhodes Scholar at Oxford, where he took degrees in geology. He participated in the geographical survey of Sudan from 1920 to 1921. He subsequently was a lecturer in geology at the University of Adelaide until 1940. His writings include *Central Australia* (1935), and *Crossing the dead heart* (1946). He died in 1947. Hill; *Who was who*, 4

Madinier, Paul, born in 1836, he was an agriculturalist and African explorer who served from 1860 to 1862 as editor of the *Annales de l'agriculture des colonies*. His own writings include *Journal de l'agriculture des pays chauds* (1865-67). BN; NUC, pre-1956

Madkur (Madkour), Ibrahim, born in 1902 at Abu al-Numrus (Giza), he was educated in Egypt and Paris, where he received two doctorates in 1934 for his theses, *L'Organon d'Aristote dans le monde arabe* and *La place d'al-Fârâbî dans l'école philosophique musulmane*. After his return home, he was a professor at Cairo University until 1945, when he joined the ministry of social affairs. He later was affiliated with the Arabic language academy. He died on 4 December 1995. MIDEO, 23 (1997), pp. 477-479

Madraimov, Abdumadzhid Abduraimovich, born 5 April 1946 at Anduzhan, Uzbekistan, he received his first degree in 1979 at Tashkent for *Индийские миниатюры конца XVI- начала XVII веков к историческим хроникам; миниатюры к "Бабцр-наме."* Since 1978 he was associated with the Oriental Institute, Uzbek Academy of Sciences. He was a joint author of *Шарқ миниатюра мактаблари; мақолалар тўплами* (1979). Miliband²; OSK

Madurell i **Marimón**, José María, born in 1893 at Grácia near Barcelona, he was an historian and art critic and became associated with the Consell d'Estudis Medievals i d'Etnologia Peninsular. His writings include *Documentos para la historia de la imprenta y librería en Barcelona, 1474-1553* (1955), and *La Capilla de la Inmaculada Concepción de la Seo de Tarragona* (1958). Dicc bio; NUC

Maeder, Herbert, born in 1930, he was a (Swiss?) photographer and mountaineer whose writings include *Toggenburg* (1958), *Die Berge der Schweiz* (1967), *Afghanistan* (1980), *Gipfel und Grate; das Erlebnis der Schweizer Berge* (1980), and he edited *Berge, Pferde und Bazare; Afghanistan, das Land am Hindukusch* (1972). LC; Note; ZKO

Maenchen (Mänchen)-**Helfen**, Otto John, born 26 July 1894 at Wien, he studied Chinese, ethnology, history of art and archaeology at the universitites of Wien, Göteborg and Leipzig. After gaining a Dr.phil. in 1923 at Wien for *Über die späteren Bücher des Shan-hai-King*, he became a private scholar at Wien. From 1927 to 1929 he was head of the sociological-ethnological section at Marx-Engels Institute, Moscow. He then travelled in Central Asia, Mongolia, Nepal, Kashmir, and Afghanistan, before settling in 1930 in Berlin, where he received a Dr.habil. in 1933. In the same year, he went to Wien, where he received a second Dr.habil. in 1938, but soon had to emigrate for political reasons. In 1939, he was appointed a professor of Oriental studies at Mills College, Oakland, Calif. From 1947 to his retirement in 1962 he was a professor at the University of California, Berkeley. From 1957 to 1969 he was one of the editors of the *Central Asiatic journal*. A specialist in Hun studies, his writings include *Reise ins asiatische Tuwa* (1931), *Ein Drittel der Menschheit; ein Ostasienbuch* (1932), *The World of the Huns* (1973), its translation, *Die Welt der Hunnen* (1978); jointly with Boris I. Nikolaevskiĭ, he published *Karl und Jenny Marx* (1933). He died in Berkeley, Calif., on 29 January 1969. BioHbDtE; ConAu, 109; DrAS, 1969 H; DtBE; NDB

Maercker, Georg, born 21 September 1865 at Baldenburg, Germany, he was an army captain who travelled in Turkey and explored the Lower Kızılırmak River in the summer of 1893. He read a paper on his explorations at the Gesellschaft für Erdkunde, Berlin, on 6 January 1894. He died in Dresden, 31 December 1924. Henze

Maeso, David Gonzalo, 1902- *see* Gonzalo Maeso, David

Maev, Nikolaĭ Aleksandrovich, born in 1835, he was a Russian army colonel who headed the Russian Hissar Expedition to the northern tributaries of the Upper Oxus between Bukhara and Wakhan. In 1879, he participated in the Samara Expedition to prepare a railway through western Turkestan from Tashkent to Samarkand. He was a joint author of *Catalogue de la section du Turkestan de l'Exposition universelle de Vienne en 1873* (1873). He died in 1896. Embacher; EnSlovar; Henze

Maevskiĭ, Viktor Vasil'evich, fl. 20th cent., he was a *Pravda* commentator whose writings include *Когда шатаются небоскребы* (1962), *Европа без джентльменов* (1967), and *Сражения мирных дней* (1971). NUC; OSK

Magali-Boisnard, 1882-1945 *see* Boisnard, Magali

Magdalena, Federico V., born 20th cent., he was an instructor in sociology and community development at Mindanao State University, Philippines. In 1977, he went to study at Hawaii on a scholarship grant from the East-West Center. He was a joint author of *The Madrasah institution in the Philippines; historical and cultural perspectives, with a directory* (Iligan City, Philippines, 1987). Note; LC

Mage, Abdon *Eugène*, born 30 July 1837 at Paris, he entered the École Navale in 1850 and subsequently went to sea. In 1856, he was posted to West Africa, the French *Station navale des Côtes occidentales d'Afrique*. Three years later, he was hired by L. Faidherbe at Saint-Louis for the local naval station of the Circumscription of Gorée and Dependencies. He was charged with the exploration of Senegal and Mauritania, and he established good relations with the natives. He is best remembered for his mission to Ségou on the Niger river, 1863-66. On his return to Paris, he was promoted and awarded *Officier de la Légion d'Honneur*. His experiences are embodied in *Voyage dans le Soudan occidental*, published in 1868, a work which disproved the notion of a populated, rich and fertile Soudan and revealed a country devasted by intestine wars and slavery. He was preparing yet another expedition, starting at the estuary of the Niger when his vessel was lost at sea with all men abord on the cliffs of Ouessant off the tip of Brittany in the night from 18 to 19 December 1869. He also wrote *Du Sénégal au Niger* (1867). Embacher; Henze; *Hommes et destins*, 1, pp. 413-16; IndexBFr² (2)

Mage, Tristan, born 20th cent., he received a doctorate in sociology and became a political activist whose publications are so numerous - four pages in *Livres disponibles*, 2004 - that he seems to have had a way of getting his name on every title page he ever touched. They include *La Diplomatie iranienne, 1915-1978; index chronologique avec classement* (Paris, 1987).

Mager, Henri, born 17 May 1859 at Paris, he graduated from the Lycée Henri IV, Paris, and the École de droit de Paris. He was a geographer and colonial administrator. In 1892, he was elected *délégé des Colonies près des Pouvoirs publics*. His writings include *Lecture des cartes étrangères* (1883), and *Atlas colonial* (1885). IndexBFr² (2)

Magerramov, Takhir Akhmed ogly, born in 1916 at Nizhniaia Aksipar, he graduated in 1951 from the Oriental Faculty, Azerbaijan State University, and received his first degree in 1963 for *Поэма «Меджнун и Лейла» Амир Хусрова Дехлеви* and his doctorate in 1975 for *Научно-критический текст "Матла ал-анвар" Амир Хосрова Дехлеви*. He was since 1958 associated with the Institute of the People of the Near and Middle East, Azerbaijan Academy of Sciences. Miliband; Miliband²

Magitot, Louis Félix *Émile*, born 14 December 1833 at Paris, he gained a medical doctorate and became an ethnographer and folklorist. His writings include *Traité des anomalies du système dentaire chez l'homme et les mammifères* (1877), and its translation, *Treatise on dental caries* (1878). He died in Paris on 23 April 1897. Alfred Kühnöl received a Dr.med. in 1940 with a thesis entitled *Das Leben und das Wirken des französischen Zahnarztes Émile Magitot*. GV; IndexBFr² (2)

Magnanini, Pietro, born 20th cent., he was associated with the Istituto di studi del Vicino oriente, Roma. His writings include *Le iscrizioni fenicie dell'Oriente; testi, tradizioni, glossari* (Roma, 1973). LC

Magnarella, Paul Joseph, born about 1939, he graduated in 1959 from the University of Connecticut, spent 1963 to 1965 in Turkey as a U.S. Peace Corps volunteer, and received his Ph.D. in 1971 from Harvard University for *Tradition and changes in a modernizing Turkish town*, a work which was published in 1974. He also gained a J.D. at the College of Law, University of Florida in 1991. He taught in the Department of Anthropology, University of Vermont, from 1971 to 1975, when he was appointed a professor of anthropology and law at the University of Florida, Gainesville, a post which held until his retirement. He served as a president of the Association of Third World Studies, 1992-93. His writings include *The Peasant venture* (1979), and *Human materialism; a model of sociocultural systems and a strategy for analysis* (1993). ConAu, 93-95; *MESA Roster of members*, 1982-1990; NatFacDr, 1990-2005; Private; Schoeberlein

Magne, Jean-Henri, born 15 July 1804 at Sauveterre (Aveyron), France, he graduated from the Collège de Rodez and the École vétérinaire de Lyon. His writings include *Principes d'hygiène vétérinaire* (1842), its translation, *Grundlehren der Veterinär-Hygiene* (1844) *Choix du cheval* (1853), and *Rapport sur les progrès de la médecine vétérinaire* (1867). He died in Corbeil (Seine-et-Oise) on 27 August 1885. IndexBFr² (5)

Magnes, Judah Leon, born in 1877 at San Francisco, he was educated at Hebrew Union College, Cincinnati, Ohio, and graduated B.A. in 1898 from the local University. He did post-graduate work at the universities of Berlin and Heidelberg, where he received a Dr.phil. in 1904 for *A Treatise as to (1) neccessary existence, (2) the procedure of things from the neccessary existence, (3) the creation of the world, by Joseph ibn Aknin, edited and translated into English.* He was a reformed rabbi, a prominent member of the Civil Liberties Union, and became the first president of the Hebrew University, Jerusalem. His writings include *Arab-Jewish unity* (1947). He died in 1948. EncJud; GV; RelLAm; JüdLex; WhAm, 2; *Who was who,* 4

Magnin, Jean Gabriel, born in 1910 at Lyon, France, he was an Arabic scholar and a translator of classical and modern Tunisian works. From 1957 to 1973 he was a contributor to, and editor of, *IBLA*, the review of the Institut des Belles lettres arabes, Tunis. He died on 23 December 1977. IBLA, 41 (1978), pp. 3-20

Magnino, Leo, born 20th cent., his writings include *La scuola nel mondo arabo e in Israele* (1950), and *Organizzazione scolastica dei paesi africani* (Roma, Istituto italiano per l'Africa, 1961). Firenze

Magnus, Ralph Harry, born in 1936, he received a Ph.D. in 1971 from the University of California at Berkeley. He was in 1984 a professor and coordinator of Middle Eastern studies at the Naval Postgraduate School at Monterey, Calif. His writings include *Gulf security in the 1980s; perceptual and strategic dimensions* (1984), and *Afghan alternatives* (1985). He died on 25 October 2000. MESA bulletin, 34 (2000), p. 302; *MESA Roster of members,* 1982-1990; NatFacDr, 1990-1995

Magomedov, Murad Gadzhievich, born 20th cent., his writings include *Образование Хазарского каганата по материалам археологических исследований и письменным данным* (1983), and he edited *Археологические памятники раннесредневе кового* (1977). LC; OSK

Magomedov, Rasul Magomedovich, fl. 20th cent., *Общественно-экономический и политический строй Дагестана в XVIII- начале XIX веков* (1957), *Хонология истории Дагестана* (1959), *История Дагестана с древнейших времен до начала XIX века* (1961), *Легенд и факты; из записных книжек историка* (1963), and *Новое время и старые обычаи; из записных книжек историка* (1966). NUC; OSK

Magometov, Akhsarbek Khadziretovich, fl. 20th cent., he wrote *Культура и быт осетинского народа* (Ordzhonikidze, 1968). NUC, 1968-72

Magrini, Liliana, born in 1917 at Venezia, Italy, she was a writer and journalist resident in Roma. Her writings include *Carnet vénitien* (Paris, 1956), and she edited *La Coszienza dell'altro* (Firenze, 1974). Chi scrive; IndBiltal (6)

Maguelonne, Jeanne, Mlle., born in 1899, she received an doctorate In 1926 from the Faculté de droit d'Alger for *Le préapprentissage et l'enseignement technique et professionnel en Algérie.* BN; NUC, pre-1956

Maguelonne, Jules, born 19th cent., he was associated with the Ministère de l'Instruction public et des Beaux-arts. His writings include the two off-prints, "Les Essais de colonisation militaire en Algérie de 1830 à 1848" (1906), and "La Propriété en Algérie avant et depuis la conquête de 1830." BN

Mahan, Alfred Thayer, born 27 September 1840 at West Point, N.Y., he was a lecturer at the U.S. Naval War College and served two terms as its president. He is better known as a theorist of U.S. expansionism and author of numerous writings supporting expansion, including *The Influence of sea power upon history, 1660-1783* (1890), and its translation, *Der Einfluß der Seemacht auf die Geschichte* (1896-99). He died in Washington, D.C., on 1 December 1914. ANB; DcAmDH, 1989; DLB, 47 (1986), pp. 162-73; EncAm; EncBrit; Master (7); WhAm, 1; *Who was who,* 1

Mahdesian, Arshag D., born in 1873 at Palou, Armenia, he graduated in 1896 from Euphrates College, Harput, Turkey, and subsequently taught there until 1900, when he went to the United States. There he studied at Yale University, New Haven, Conn., for a while. His life was one long urge to get the English-speaking public acquainted with the soul of the Armenian people. For this purpose he published *The New Armenia,* and other periodicals in Armenian. His own writings include *Armenia, her culture, and aspirations* (1938). He died in Fresno Calif., on 4 April 1950. Armenian affairs, 1, no. 2 (Spring 1950), pp. 201-203

Mahé, Jean Baptiste, born in 1830, he received a medical doctorate and served as sometime *médecin sanitaire de France* at Constantinople. In 1883, he headed a medical mission to Egypt to research the origin of cholera. His writings include *Manuel pratique d'hygiène navale* (1874). He died in 1896. BN; NUC, pre-1956

Maher, Vanessa A., born 20th cent. in Kenya and educated in Tanganyika and England where she received a Ph.D. in 1972 from Cambridge University for *Social stratification and the role of women in the Middle Atlas of Morocco*. She conducted research in Morocco, in England in a working-class neighbourhood, and in Italy among migrant workers. In 1978, she taught anthropology in Italy. Her writings include *Women and property in Morocco; changing relation to the process of social stratification in the Middle Atlas* (1974). Note about the author; Sluglett

Mähl, Sibylle née Ermeler, born 20th cent., she received a Dr.phil. in medieval social history in 1955 from the Universität Hamburg for *Quadriga virtutum; die Kardinaltugenden in der Geistesgeschichte der Karolinerzeit*, a work which was published in a slightly revised edition in 1969. GV

Mahler, Eduard, born 28 September 1857 at Cziffer (Cifer), Hungary, he was a trained mathematician and astronomer and began his career at the observatory in Wien. His writings include *Chronologische Vergleichungs-Tabellen* (1889). On the occasion of his eightieth birthday the *Jubilee volume in honour of Edward Mahler* was dedicated to him (Budapest, 1937). His home of forty years was hit by a bomb, and his library completely ruined, at the end of 1944, when the siege of Budapest began. He died on 29 June 1945. EncJud; *Isis*, 38 (1948), p. 108; *Ki kicsoda*, 1937; Magyar; RNL; UjLex

Mahmoud Essad, fl. 1926, he received a doctorate in 1918 from the Université de Fribourg for his thesis, *Du régime des capitulations ottomanes*. In 1926, he was a Turkish minister of justice. LC; NUC

Mahmud, 'Abd al-Halim, born 20th cent., he was educated at al-Azhar, Cairo, and the Sorbonne, Paris, where he received a doctorate in 1940. He lectured in psychology and philosophy at al-Azhar. At the time of his death on 17 November 1978, he was Shaykh al-Azhar. *Hamdard Islamicus* 2 iii (1979), p. 89

Mahmud, Rashid Husayn *see* Rashid Husayn Mahmud

Mahmud Muhtar Paşa, born in 1867 at Constantinople, a son of Ahmed Muhtar Pasha, 1839-1919, he was educated at Galatasaray Lisesi and the military college Harbiye (1885). After passing through the Metz Militärakademie, Lothringen, he received a commission as lieutenant (1888). He served for some time in a Prussian regiment. During the Greco-Turkish war of 1897 he rose to the rank of colonel. In 1909, he became commander of the Constantinople garrison and in 1912, Minister of the Navy. In 1913, he was ambassador in Berlin. His writings include *Événements d'Orient* (1909), *Die Welt des Islam im Lichte des Koran und Hadith* (1915), *Ruzname-i harb* (1915), *La Turquie, l'Allemagne et l'Europe depuis le Traité de Berlin jusqu'à la guerre mondiale* (1924), *Maziye bir nazar* (1925), and *The Wisdom of the Qur'an* (1937). He died at sea on a voyage from Alexandria to Naples in 1935. AnaBrit; Meydan; Özege

Mahn-Lot, Marianne, born 20th cent., her writings include *Cristophe Colomb* (1960), its translation, *Columbus* (1961), *La découverte de l'Amérique* (1970), *Bartolomé de Las Casas; une théologien pour le Nouveau Monde* (19919, *Las Casas moraliste; culture et foi* (1997), and she edited and translated Columbus' *Les plus belles lettres* (1961). Livres disponibles, 2004; NUC

Mahon, Sir Bryan MacMahon, born in 1862 at Belleville, County Galway, Ireland, he joined the King's Royal Irish Hussars in 1883 and served in the Sudan, Egypt, India, and the Gallipoli campaign. He retired with the rank of general; he died in 1930. DclrB; *Who was who*, 3

Mahover (Machover), Moshe(h), born in 1936, his writings include *Lectures on non-standard analysis* (1969), *Set theory, logic and their limitations* (1996), and he was a joint author of *A Course in mathematical logic* (1977), *Laws of chaos* (1983), and *The Measurement of voting power; theory and practice, problems and paradoxes* (1998). LC

Maidhof, Adam, born 20 April 1885 at Wenighösbach, Bavaria, he studied classics at the universities of Würzburg and München, where he received a Dr.phil. in 1912 for *Zur Begriffsbestimmung der koine besonders auf Grund des Attizisten Moiris*. He subsequently became a secondary school teacher in Hameln and Dresden. From 1911 until 1914 he taught at the German-Greek school in Smyrna, a post which afforded him researches in Byzantine-Greek philology as well as travels in the Near East. After his return to Bavaria, he taught successively at schools in Dillingen, Eichstätt, München, and Passau. Since the summer of 1921 he concurrently taught history and auxiliar sciences at Philosophisch-Theologische Hochschule, Passau. He later pursued an interest in the local history. His other writings include *Unterrichtliche Verwertung der Sprachwissenschaft in der griechischen Laut- und Formenlehre* (1920-21), *Das Passauer Sadtrecht* (1927), and *Neugriechische Rückwanderer aus den romanischen Sprachen* (1931). He died in Passau on 2 May 1945. Anton Mayer, *Adam Maidhof zum Gedächtnis* (Passau, 1945).

Mailáth von Székhely, János(Johann) N. J., Earl, born 5 October 1786 at Pest, Hungary, he completed his philosophy at Erlau (Eger) and law at Raab (Győr) and subsequently entered the civil service, where he remained for ten years until an eye ailment obliged him to resign. He became a private scholar in literature and history, but without private means. Financial difficulties drove him first to become an informer of the Viennese police and later to drown himself in Lake Starnberg on 3 January 1855. He wrote *Magyarische Sagen und Mährchen* (1825), *Vallás-mozgalmak Magyarországban* (1844-46), *Die Religionswirren in Ungarn* (1845), and *Neuere Geschichte der Magyaren* (1853). GeistigeUng; ÖBL

Maillard, Monique, born 20th cent., she was affiliated with the École française d'Extrême-Orient. Her writings include *Essai sur la vie matérielle dans l'oasis de Tourfan pendant le haut moyen âge* (1973), *Grottes et monuments d'Asie centrale; essai sur l'architecture des monuments civils et religieux* (1983), and she was a joint author of *Buddhisme in Afghanistan and Central Asia* (1976). Livres disponibles, 2004

Maillard, P., born 19th cent., he translated *Nachr al-mathâni*, t. 1, from the Arabic of Muhammad b. al-Tayyib b. Abi Muhammad Sīdī 'Abd al-Salam al-Sharīf al-Qādirī (Paris, 1913). His trace is lost after an article in 1917. BN; GAL S II, p. 697, where Meillard

Maillart, Ella Katherine, born 20 March 1903 at Genève, Switzerland, she became one of the heroic figures in the West's involvement with Central Asia. She was much more than a traveller, having made herself a niche in relation to Central Asia like that of Freya Stark in the Middle East. She ranks with the best of men. Her qualities showed early. In 1924, she represented Switzerland in the single-handed Olympic sailing competition, she captained the Swiss hockey team in 1931 and skied for Switzerland in 1931-1934. Her earliest sorties, to Russian Turkestan in 1932 and Manchukuo in 1934 (as a journalist for *Le Petit Parisien*), settled the direction of her interest. She developed a great photographic skill in the course of her travels. Her writings include *Turkestan solo* (1934), its translation, *Des Monts célestes* (1934), *Oasis interdites* (1937), its translations, *Forbidden journey* (1937), *Verbotene Reise* (1988). She died in Chandolin, Switzerland on 27 March 1997. Asian affairs, 84 (1997), p. 437; ConAu, 158; DLB 195 (1998), pp. 204-215; EncCoWW; IntWW, 1989-1996/97; Master (3); Robinson, pp. 51-53; Who, 1943-1997; WhoSwi, 1950/51-1992/93|

Maíllo Salgado, Felipe, born 20th cent., he received a doctorate in Arabic and Islamic studies and became a professor in the Facultad de Filologia, Universidad de Salamanca. His writings include *Los arabismos del castellano en la Baja Edad Media* (Salamanca, 1983), and *Vocabulario básico de historia del islam* (Madrid, 1987). Arabismo, 1992, 1994, 1997; EURAMES, 1993

Maillot, Dominique, fl. 20th cent., his writings include *Le Régime administratif du cinéma au Maroc* (Rabat, 1961). ZKO

Main, Ernest B., M.A., born in 1889, he was a sometime editor of the *Times of Mesopotamia* and the *Baghdad Times*. His writings include *In and around Baghdad* (1935), *Iraq; from mandate to independence* (1935), and *Palestine at the crossroads* (1937). BLC

Mainguet-Michel, Monique, born 13 February 1937, she gained a doctorate and became a professor in the Laboratoire de géographie physique zonale, Université de Reims. Her writings include *Le Modelé des grès; problèmes généraux* (1972), *L'Homme et la sécheresse* (1995), *Desertification; natural background and human mismanagement* (1994), and *Les Pays secs; environnement et développement* (2003). Livres disponibles, 2004; Note about the author

Mainguy, Marc-Henri, fl. 1961, his writings include *La Musique au Liban* (Beyrouth, 1969).

Mainz, Ernst, born 22 September 1905 at Hamburg, he was educated at the Talmud-Tora-Schule, 1913-1922, and Thaer-Oberschule, 1922-1925, Hamburg, and subsequently studied Semitic languages, philosophy, Islamic subjects, history, and fine art successively at Hamburg, München, Berlin, and again Hamburg, where he received a Dr.phil. in 1931 for *Zur Grammatik des modernen Schriftarabisch*, a subject suggested by his teacher A. Schaade. Schwarz; Thesis

Maisey, Frederick Charles, born 27 August 1825 at Neuchâtel, Switzerland, he entered the Bengal Army in 1842, arrived in India in 1843, and was posted to the 32rd Native Infantry at Dinapore. From December 1845 to May 1846 he was sent to Kalinjar in Bundelkhand on special duty under the orders of the Government of the North-West Provinces to examine and report upon the ruins and antiquities of the place. He also served in the Burmese war, 1852-53, and throughout the siege of Delhi. A colonel since 1876, he was placed on unemployed supernumerary list on 16 July 1883. He attained the rank of general, 1 De-cember 1888. His writings include *Military law and the procedure of military courts* (1874), *Central Asia* (1878), and *Sánchi and its remains* (1892). He died in Eastborne, Sussex, on 2 September 1892, from the effects of a fall down a flight of stairs. Boase; IndianBiInd (3)

Maĭskiĭ, Ivan Mikhaĭlovich, born I. M. Liakhovskiĭ in 1884 at Kirillov, he was expelled from St. Petersburg University in 1902, and exiled to Siberia in 1903. He emigrated to Switzerland and graduated from the Universität München in 1912. In 1917, he returned to Russia, later to become a diplomat. From 1919 to 1921 he held a political post in the Mongolian central government. His writings include *Современная Монголия* (1921), *Монголия накануне революции* (1959), *Путешествие в прошлое* (1960), its translation, *Journey into the past* (1962), *Memoirs of a Soviet ambas-sador* (1967). He died on 3 September 1975. BiDSovU; Miliband²; *Who was who*, 7

Maitre, Luce Claude, fl. 20th cent., his writings include *Introduction to the tought of Iqbal* (Karachi 19-), and he edited *Mohammad Iqbal* (Paris, 1964). ZKO

Maître-Devallon, Charles Jules, born 28 September 1880 at Paris, he graduated from the École polytechnique, and the École nationale des Ponts et Chaussée, Paris. In 1912, he was sent on a mission to the Sahara to make a preliminary study of the Transsaharan railway project. Interreputed by the first World War, he completed the study between 1919 and 1929 as chief engineer and deputy director of the Travaux Publics du Maroc. At the end of this period he was appointed overlord of the Organisme d'études du Transsaharien. But eighteen years after the initial start of the project, the chance for great public works had been missed. In 1930, he was attached to the Ministère des Colonies, becoming in 1938 a director of public works in the Ministère des Colonies, and, in 1942, associated with the Centre d'études économiques et sociales de l'Afrique française. His writings include *Quelques considérations sur l'industrialisation en Algérie* (Alger, 1946). He died in Alger on 28 February 1958. Travaux de l'Institut de recherches sahariennes, 17 (1958), pp. 7-9

Maitrot, Albert-Charles, born 19th cent., he was a French army captain who wrote *Le Recrutement des indigènes algérien; impressions d'un officier d'Afrique* (Paris, 1913). BN

Maitrot de la Motte-Capron, A., fl. 1939, his writings include *Sidna Moulay Ismail, prince magnifique du Maghreb invincible* (Paris, 1929). BN

Maĭzel', Saliĭ (Solomon) Sergeevich, born in 1900 at Lepel Vitebskoĭ, Belarus, he received his first degree in 1944 for *Турецкий изафет*. He was from 1944 to 1952 a lecturer in Middle Eastern studies at Moscow State University. His writings include *Учебник турецкого языка* (1946), *Изафет в турецком языке* (1957), and *Пути развития корневого фонда семитских языков* (1983). He died on April 1952. Miliband; Miliband²

Majda, Tadeusz, born 20th cent., his writings include *Rozwój języka tureckiego w XVIII wieku* (1985); and he was joint author of *Skrypt do nauki języka tureckiego* (Warszawa, 1965), and *Rysunki kostimów tureckich z kolekcji króla Stanisława Augusta w Gabinecie Rycim Biblioteki Uniwersyteckie w Warszawie* (1973). OSK

Majer, Friedrich, born in 1772, his writings include *Geschichte der Ordalien* (Jena, 1795), *Zur Kulturgeschichte der Völker* (1798), *Allgemeines mythologisches Lexikon* (Weimar, 1803-1804), *Geschichte aller Religionen* (Weimar, 1811-1813), and *Brahma; oder, die Religion der Indier als Brahmaismus* (Leipzig, 1818). He died on 15 May 1818. GV; NUC, pre-1956

Majer, Hans Georg, born 12 July 1937 at Stuttgart, he received a Dr.phil. in 1978 for *Vorstudien zur Geschichte der Ilmiye im Osmanischen Reich* from the Universität München, where he also gained a Dr.habil. in 1979. From 1981 to his retirement he was a professor of Middle Eastern history and Turkish studies at München. His writings include *Das osmanische Registerbuch der Beschwerden* (1984), *Die Staaten Südosteuropas und die Osmanen* (1989), and he was a joint author of *Lexikon der islamischen Welt* (1974). Kürschner, 1983-2005; Schwarz

Majewska, Barbara Łucja, born 10 February 1933 at Inowroław, Poland, she completed her history in 1955 at Warszawa and became associated with the Oriental Committe in the Polish Academy of Sciences. Her writings include *Bibliografia polskich prac orientalistycznych, 1945-1955* (Warszawa, 1957). KtoPolsce, 2001

Majumdar, Ramesh Chandra, born in 1888 at Kandarpara, India, he was educated at Calcutta, where he also received a Ph.D. in 1918. He taught Indian history at Calcutta and Dacca, before he became successively a principal of the College of Indology, Banares Hindi University, and the University of Nagpur. His writings include *The Delhi Sultanate* (1967), *The Arab invasion of Bengal* (1974), and he edited *The History of Bengal* (1963). He died on 2 February 1980. ConAu, 33-36; Eminent; IndianBiInd (3)

Makaev, Ênver Akhmedovich, born in 1916, his writings include *Проблемы индоевропейскей ареальной лингвистики* (1964), *Язык древнейских рунических надписей* (1965), its translation, *The Language of the oldest Runic inscriptions* (1996), *Структура слова в индоевропейских и германских языках* (1970), *Общая теория сравнительного языкознания* (1977), and he edited *Проблемы лингвистического анализа* (1966). LC; OSK

Makarczyk, Janusz, born 25 March 1901 at Łódź, Russia, he studied at Poznań and Paris. He served as a diplomat until 1947, when he resigned. In the following year, he took a doctorate for a thesis on the history of Sudan, and subsequently became a lecturer at the Uniwersytet Jagielloński, Kraków. His writings include *Bezdroża pragnień* (1926), *Dzafar z Bagdadu* (1950), *Kobieta zawsze płaci* (1959), *Po orostu kobieta* (1960), and *Diabeł jest meskiego rodzaju* (1961). He died about 1960. Dziekan; Polski (4); *Polski słownik biograficzy*

Makarov, Alexander Nikolaevich, born in 1888 at TSarskoe Selo (Pushkin), the son of an architect, he completed his law in 1914 and in 1919 was appointed a professor of international law. From 1921 to 1925 he also lectured in international private law at the Institute of Political Science, concurrently teaching law of the sea at the Naval Academy. In 1923 he was dismissed by the Soviet authorities. In 1925 he emigrated to Berlin, where he was successively a subject specialist and head of department in Kaiser-Wilhelm-Institut of international law, 1928-1944. In 1945 he removed with the Berlin Max-Planck-Institut of international law to Tübingen. An academic staff member since 1952, he concurrently held a cross-appointment at the Heidelberg institute of international law. His writings include *Allgemeine Lehren des Staatsangehörigkeitsrechts* (1947), and *Deutsches Staatsangehörigkeitsrecht* (1971). He died in Heidelberg on 13 May 1973. DtBE; GV; NDB

Makarova, Svetlana Mikhaïlovna, born 12 March 1933 at Bryansk, Russia, she graduated in 1955 from the Faculty of Economics, Moscow State University and received her first degree in 1965 for *Об особенностях развития капитализма и промышленности Бирме*. She was since 1971 associated with the Institute of Information Science in the Soviet Academy of Sciences. Her writings include *Современная экономическая доктрина ислама* (1983), and she was a joint editor of *Проблема нефтедолларов* (1984). Miliband[2]

Makdisi, George, born 15 May 1920 at Detroit, Mich., he graduated in 1947 from the University of Michigan and received a *doctorat ès lettres* in 1964 from the Sorbonne, Paris. He was successively a professor of Middle Eastern and Arabic studies at the University of Michigan, Harvard University, and the University of Pennsylvania at Philadelphia. His writings include *Ibn Aqīl et la résurgence de l'islam traditioniste au XIe siècle* (1963), *The Rise of colleges* (1981), *L'Islam hanbalisant* (1983), *The rise of humanism in classical Islam and Christianity* (1990), and a collection of his articles, *Religion, law and learning in classical Islam* (1991). He received the Giorgio Levi Dela Vida award in Islamic studies, 1993. DrAS, 1969 H, 1974 H, 1978 H, 1982 H; *MESA Roster of members*, 1982-1990

Makeev, Dmitriĭ Alekseevich, born 17 August 1937 in Russia, he graduated in 1964 from the Faculty of History, Moscow, received his first degree in 1973 for *Помощь СССР странам Африки в борьбе за экономическою независимость*, and his doctorate in 1985 for *Становление и развитие внешнеторговых связей Ближнего Востока*. Since 1977 he was associated with the Vladimir State Pedagogical Institute, where he became deputy director in 1985, and professor in 1987. His writings include *Внешнеторговые связи СССР со странам Арабском Востока* (1983), *Международные отношентя на Ближнем Востоке и Северо-Востоке Африки в новейшее время* (1985), *СССР и страны Ближнего Востока и Среднего Востока; из истории внешне экономических связей 1921-1928 годы* (1990), and he was a joint editor of *Политика великих держав на Арабском Востоке в новейшее времтя* (1982). Miliband[2]; OSK

Makgakhan (Макгахан), Dzh. A., 1844-1878 *see* MacGahan, Januarius Aloysius

Makhkamov, Kakhar Makhkamovich, born 16 April 1931, he was a Tajik politician and a sometime president of the Tajik Soviet Republic. His writings include *Экономика Таджикской ССР* (1967). EST, vol. 4, p. 298, col. 881; IntWW, 1989/79-1992/93; Master (2)

Makhmadshoev, Rakhmatsho, born 20 January 1950 in Tajikistan, he graduated in 1972 from the Faculty of History, Tajikistan State University, and received his first degree in 1989 at Dushanbe for *Таджики Афганистана в новое врема*. After spending 1978 to 1982 in Kabul, he was since 1982 associated with the Oriental Institut of the Tajikistan Academy of Sciences. Miliband[2]

Makhmudbekov, Shukhrat Makhmudovich, born 10 August 1949 at Tashkent, he graduated in 1971 from the Oriental Faculty, Tashhkent State University, and received his first degree in 1977. He visited Egypt as a Soviet official in 1970-71, 1971-72, and 1975. Since 1977 he was affiliated with the Oriental Faculty, Tashkent. His writings include *Рабочий класс Египта, 50-70-е годы* (1993). Miliband[2]

Makhmudov, Akhmad, born 20th cent., his writings include *Словесное ударение в узбекском языке* (Tashkent, 1960), and *Сонорные узбекского языка* (Tashkent, 1980). OSK

Makhmudov, Akhmed Ramazanovich, born 20th cent., his writings include *Сравнительная типология русского и азербайджанского языков* (Baku, 1982). OSK

Makhmudov, Gasan Shakhmakhud-oglu, born in 1925 at Kuba, Azerbaijan, he graduated in 1951 from the Oriental Faculty, Azerbaijan State University, and received his first degree in 1954 for a study of dialects in contemporary Persian entitled *Управление глаголов дополнениями в современном персидском литературном языке*, and his doctorate in 1981 for *Проблема структурных типов и членов простого предложения современных персидского языка.* He was affiliated with the Azerbaijan State University since 1953. In 1964, he was appointed a lecturer. His writings include *Синтаксическая связь глагола с дополнениями в современном персидском языке* (1967). Miliband; Miliband²

Makhmudov, Khaïrolla Khabibullaevich, born 8 May 1909 in Russia, he received a doctorate in philosophy in 1970 and in the following year was appointed a professor. He was a Turkologist and from 1945 to 1983 a lecturer at Kazakhstan State University. He edited *Лингвостилитический анализ текста* (1982), and he was a joint editor of *Краткий русско-казахский словарь* (1959). He died in Alma Ata on 28 October 1983. Kazakhskaia, vol. 3; OSK

Makhmutov, Mirza Ismailovich, born 1 May 1926 at Altar, Mordovian Autonomous Soviet Republic, he graduated in 1955 from the Military Institute of Foreign Languages, Moscow, and received his first degree in 1966 for *О фонетическом грамматическом освоенин арабских заимствований в татарском литературно языке*, and his doctorate in 1973 for a monograph. His writings include *Школьный русско-татарский словарь* (1967), *Теория и практика проблемного обучентя* (1972), and he was a joint author of *Арабско-татарско-русский словарь заимствований* (1965). Miliband²; OSK; TatarES

Makhmutova (Мэхмутова), Liaïlia Tagirovna, born in 1925, she was from 1952 to 1986 associated with the Institute of Language, Literature, and History of the Kazan Branch of the Soviet Academy of Sciences. Her writings include *Опыт исследования тюркских диалектов* (1978); she edited *Исследования по исторической диалектологии татарского языка* (1979-82), *Исследования по татарскому языкознагию* (1984); and she was a joint editor of *Взаимовлияние и взаимо-обогащение языков народов ССР* (1982). TatarES

Makhova, E. I., she was a joint author of *Инструкция по сбору материалов по теме "Одежа народов Средней Азии и Казахстана" для Историко-этнографического атласа Средней Азии и Казахстана* (Москва, Изд-во восточной лит-ры, 1958). NUC, 1968-72

Maki, Dennis R., born in 1938, he received a Ph.D. in 1967 from Iowa State University for *A forecasting model of manpower requirements in the health occupations.* He was successively a professor in the Division of Counselor Education, University of Iowa, and in the Department of Economics, Simon Fraser University, Burnaby, B.C. His writings include *Search behaviour in the Canadian job market* (1972), *Major investments in British Columbia, 1983 to 1995* (1983), and *Applied rehabilitation counseling* (1986). NatFacDr, 1995-2000; Note about the author

Makinda, Samuel M., born in 1949, he was a sometime staff member of the Foreign Affairs Group, Legislative Research Service, and in 1990, associated with Murdoch University, Australia. His writings include *Kenya's role in the Somali-Ethiopian conflict* (1982), *Soviet policy in the Red Sea region* (1984), *The Coup in the Sudan* (1985), *Superpower diplomacy in the Horn of Africa* (1987), and *Security in the Horn of Africa* (1992). Note about the author

Makino, Shinya, born in 1930, he received in 1968 his doctorate which was published in an English edition in 1970 in Tokyo entitled *Creation and termination; a semantic study of the Qur'anic world view.* He became affiliated with Keio University. His other writings include *Zum semantischen Aufbau der neuarabischen Verben* (Tokyo, 1963), and he edited *Imi no kozo*, by Toshihiko Izutsu (1972). LC

Makkas (Μακκάς/Maccas), Leon, born 24 June 1892 at Athens, he was a lawyer, politician, and journalist. His writngs include *Les cruautés allemandes; requisitoire d'un neutre* (1915), *German barbarism; a neutral's indictment* (1916), *L'Héllenisme de l'Asie mineure, son histoire, sa puissance, son sort* (1919), *La question gréco-albanaise* (1921), *Quelques vérités sur la question d'Orient et la révolution grecque* (1922), *Έθνικαι άγωνίαι και προσδοκίαι, 1937/1945* (1945), and he edited *Les Études franco-grecques* (1918-21). He died in 1972. EEE; GrBiolnd; Hellenikon, 1965

Makofsky, David, born about 1945, he received a Ph.D. in 1972 from the University of California for *The capitalist factory, the socialist factory; class conflict in Turkey and Yugoslavia.* He was in 1990 a statistician, Occupational Health Center, San Francisco General Hospital. MESA Roster of members, 1990

Makovel'skiĭ, Aleksandr Osipovich, born in 1884 at Grodno, Lithuania, he graduated in 1907 from Kazan University, and received a doctorate in 1946. His writings include *Авеста* (1960), and *История логики* (1967). He died 16 December 1969. Miliband; Miliband²; TatarES

Makramalla, Maurice Wassef, born 3 October 1927 in Egypt, he obtained a law dedree in 1948 in Egypt, and a doctorate in political science in 1955 from the Sorbonne, Paris. He subsequently entered the Egyptian civil service.. Unesco

Makridy, Theodor *see* Macridy, Theodor

Maksimenko, Vladimir Il'ich, born 19 June 1948 at Odessa, he graduated in 1971 from the Faculty of International Journalism, Moscow, and received his first degree in 1977 for *Национальная непролетарская интеллигенция в общественно-политической жизни развивающихся стран; на примере Туниса и Алжира*. He was since 1977 affiliated with the Oriental Institute, Soviet Academy of Sciences, and since 1994 a deputy director. His writings include *Интеллигенция в странах Магриба* (1980), and *Политические партии в переходном общетве; Марокко, Алжир, Тунис, 20-80-е годы XX в.* (1985), *Ориентация - поиск; Восток в теориях и гипотезах* (1992), *Цивилизация и способ общения* (1993), and he was a joint editor of *Некоторые проблемы истории стран Ближнего и Среднего Востока и Африки* (1987). Miliband²; OSK

Maksimova, Anna Georgievna, born 20th cent., she was associated with the Institute of History, Archaeology and Ethnography, Kazak Academy of Sciences. Her writings include *Наскальные изображения урохища Тамгалы* (1985), and she was joint author of *Древности Чардары* (1968). Note about the author

Maksiutova (Мэксутова), Nadzhiba Khaerzamanovna, born 27 November 1932, she graduated in 1951 from the Bashkir State Pedagogical Institute; since 1957, she was associated with the Institute of History, Languages and Literatures, Uzbek Academy of Sciences. Her writings include *Восточный диалект башкирского языка сравнительноисторическом освещении* (1976), *Вопросы диалектологии тюрксих языков* (1985), *Проблемы диалектологии и лингвогеографии тюркских языков* (1986), *Ареальные исследования по башкирской диалектологии и ономастике Башкирии* (1988), *Башкирские говоры находящиеся в иноязычном окружении* (1996), and she edited *Словарь башкирских говоров* (1970), and she was joint editor of *Вопросы лексикологии и лексикографии башкирского языка* (1983). BashkKE; OSK

Maksoud, Clovis F., he was in 1966 chief representative of the Arab League in India. His writings include *The Arab image* (1963), and *On non-alignment* (1966). Note

Maktos, John, born in 1901 or 1902 in Greece, he graduated from Harvard and subsequently studied at the Sorbonne, Paris, and held a Carnegie fellowship in international law at Oxford. He was admitted to the bars of several American states, and served with U.S. Government claims commissions from 1929 to 1966. He was a joint author of *American-Turkish claims settlement, 1923; opinion prepared* (1937). He died in Washington, D.C. on 26 February 1977. ConAu, 69-72; WhAm, 7

Makulski, Jan Krzysztof, born 20th cent., his writings include *Guide to the exhibitions* (Warszawa, Państwowe Muzeum Etnograficzne w Warszawie, 1976), and *Stulecie działalności, 1888-1988* (1988). LC; OSK

Malabard, Jean, born in 1913, he received a doctorate in law in 1939 from the Sorbonne, Paris. He wrote for several official, semi-official and general periodicals in France. In 1950 he visited and studied in Iran and Turkey. His writings include *Jean Malabard, 1913-1955*, présentation de Wladimir d'Ormessen (S.l., n.d.) He died in 1955. BN

Malafosse, Paul, born in 1865, he received a medical doctorate in 1890 from the Université de Lyon for *Des fractures de la base du crâne par contre-coup*. He served as a *médecin major de 2e classe* from 17 November 1902 to 16 August 1905 at Géryville, Algeria,. NUC, pre-1956; Peyronnet, p. 824

Malakhovskiĭ, Kim Vladimirovich, born 27 January 1925 at Moscow, where he graduated in 1949 from the Moscow School of Law. He received his first degree in 1963 for *Система опеки* and his doctorate in 1967. Appointed a professor in 1970, he was since 1971 a deputy director of the Oriental Institute, Soviet Academy of Sciences. His writings include *Система опек; разновидность колониализма* (1963). Miliband; Miliband²

Malashenko, Alekseĭ Vsevolodovich, born 2 February 1951 at Moscow, he graduated in 1974 from the Institute of Asian and African Studies, Moscow State University, and received his first degree in 1978 for *Ислам и официальная идеология Алжира, 1965-1976 гг.* He worked for several years in North Africa and Praha, and from 1983 to 1985 published the political journal, *Проблемы мира и социализма*. In 1994 he was a section head in the Institute of Oriental Studies, Russian Academy of Sciences. His writings include *Официальная идеология современного Алжира* (1983), *Три города на севере Африки* (1986), *В поисках альтернативы* (1991), *Мусульманские страны; религия и*

MACK LIBRARY
BOB JONES UNIVERSITY
GREENVILLE, SC

политика (1991), and he was a joint author of *Islam in Central Asia* (1994), and *Ислам в СНГ* (1998). Miliband²; Note about the author

Malaurie, Jean Léonard, born 22 December 1922 at Mainz, Germany, he was since 1957 a professor of Arctic geomorphology and anthropogeography at l'École des Hautes Études en Sciences Sociales, Paris. His writings include *Hoggar, Touaregs, derniers seigneurs* (1954), and *Les derniers rois de Thulé* (1955), a work which has been translated into over twenty languages. IntWW, 1991/92-2006; WhoFr, 1984/85-2005/2006

Malavialle, Léon, born 29 July 1860 at Tuchan (Aude), France, he taught geography at the Faculté des lettres and the École supérieure, Montpellier. Elected in 1910 to the Chambre des Députés, he submitted in 1912 a feasibility report to the Commission des affaires extérieures of the Chambre des Députés with respect to a railway service between Tananarive and Antsirabe. Index BFr² (1); NUC, pre-'56

Malcolm, James Aratoon, born in 1867 at Bushire, Persia, he gradculated on 10 February 1886 from Cliftonville School, Margate, Isle of Thanet, Kent, England. BritInd (1)

Malcolm, Sir John, born in 1769 at Burnfoot on the Esk, Scotland, he had been commissioned by the East India Company at the early age of thirteen. He spoke Persian; and in 1792 he was appointed Persian interpreter to the Nizam of the Deccan. He had already made his mark in India when he became an envoy in Persia from 1799 to 1801. He returned on other missions in 1808-9, and 1810. He retired to England where he died in 1833. His writings include the *History of Persia* (1815). BritInd (19); *Cambridge history of Iran*, vol. 7; Buckland; Dawson; DNB; Egyptology; EnBrit; Henze; Mason; Wright, pp. 4-10

Malcolm, Napier, born 17 March 1870 at Ranley Grange near Worcester, he was a graduate of New College, Oxford; curate of St. Andrew, Eccles, Manchester, 1894-96, St. John Evangelist, Higher Broughton, Manchester, 1896-98; chaplain of the Church Missionary Society at Yazd, Persia, 1898-1903, Shiraz, 1904-7; curate of St. John, Altrincham, 1908; and subsequently rector of St. John Evangelist, Broughton, Manchester. His writings include *Five years in a Persian town* (1905). He died in 1921. BritInd (2)

Malcolmson, John Grant, born 17 December 1862, he was a Madras medical officer from 1823 to 1840, and since 1836 a surgeon, Madras Establishment. He was an editor of the *Journal* of the Bombay Branch of the Royal Asiatic Society, and its secretary. He died in Dhulia on 23 March 1844. IndianBiInd (2); Note about the author

Maldidier, Denise, born 20th cent., she was in 1990 a lecturer in linguistics at the Université de Paris X (Nanterre). Her writings include *Analyse de discours nouveaux parcours; hommage à Michel Pêcheux* (1986); she was joint author of *Langage et idéologie; le discours comme objet de l'histoire* (1974), *Discours et archive; expérimentations du discours* (1994); and she was joint editor of *L'Inquiétude du discours* (1990). Livres disponibles, 2004; Note about the author

Maldonado Macanaz, Joaquín, born 16 February 1833 at Iscar (Valladolid), Spain, he received in 1857 a doctorate in law from the Universidad de Madrid for *Paz universal*. He was a professor of colonial administration and history at Madrid and a member of the Academia de la Historia. His writings include *Principios generales del arte de la colonización* (1873). He died in Madrid on 17 September 1901. EncicUni; IndiceE³ (2)

Mâle, Émile, born 2 June 1862 at Commentry (Allier), France, he was an iconologist who started his career at St-Étienne, from which he passed to the Université de Toulouse and then to the Sorbonne, where he taught for many years. He later became a director of l'École française de Rome. He was a member of the Académie des Inscriptions and the Académie Française. He died in Chaalis near Senlis on 6 September 1954. DBFC, 1954/55; IndexBFr² (1); *Revue archéologique*, 1959, p. 98; *Speculum*, 34 (1959), p. 534; Who, 1936-1955; *Who was who*, 5

Malečková, Jitka, born 23 May 1960 at Praha, she studied history and Oriental languages at Universita Karlova, Praha, where she received a doctorate in 1983. Her writings include *Úrodná půda; žena ve službách národa* (Praha, 2002). Filipsky

Malekhova, Alla N., born 20th cent., she received a degree in 1978 at Tashkent for *Поэта Алишера Навои "Лисан-ат-тайр;" поэтика композиционных и образных средств*. Her writings include *Моя тетушка выходит замуж; новеллы турецеих писателей Болгарии* (1973), and a translation of *Kutadgu billiğ* entitled *Благодатное знание* (1990). OSK

Malet, Albert, born in 1864 at Cermont-Ferrand, France, he was a *professeur agrégé* in history and geography at the Lycée Louis-le-Grand, Paris. His writings include *L'Orient et la Grèce* (1923). He died in 1915. IndexBFr² (1); NUC, pre-1956

Maletin, Nikolaĭ Pavlovich, born 28 November 193- at Yaroslavl, Russia, he graduated in 1965 from the Moscow State Institute of International Relations and received his first degree in 1969 for *Некоторые аспекты внешние политики республики Индонезии, 1959-1965*. He was appointed a lecturer in 1973 and a professor in 1983. In 1981 he gained a doctorate. Since 1969 he was associated with the Institute. His writings include *Внешняя политика Индонезии* (1973), *Внешняя политика Филиппин* (1983), and *Внешняя политика Таиланда,1945-1983* (1986). Miliband[2]

Malfatti, Bartolomeo, born in 1828, he graduated at Trento and received a doctorate in law from the Università di Pisa. In 1860, he was appointed a professor of history at the Accademia Milanese di Belli Arti; and in 1878, he taught geography and ethnography at the Istituto Superiore di Studi, and the Scuola di Scienze Sociali, Firenze. His writings include *Scritti geografici ed etnografici* (1869), *Imperatori e papi ai tempi della signoria dei Franchi in Italia* (1876), and *Etnografia* (1878). He died in Firenze on 15 January 1892. IndBiltal (6); Kornrumpf; Kornrumpf[3], vol. 2

Malfray, Marie Agnès, born 20th cent., she was an *animatrice* with the Télévison Française. Her writings include *L'Islam* (1980), and she was a joint editor of *Les plus grands textes de la philosophie orientale* (1992), and *Les pages les plus célèbres de la philosophie occidentale* (2000). *Livres disponibles*, 2004; Note about the author

Malgo, Wim, Dr., he was affiliated with the Missionswerk Mitternachtsruf, Thun, Switzerland. His writings include *Jerusalem, Brennpunkt der Welt* (1971), *Israel aber wird den Sieg haben* (1971), its translation, *And Israel shall do valiantly* (1971), *Ägypten im Aufbruch* (1978), and *Der beschleunigte Aufmarsch Russlands nach Israel* (1980). LC; Note about the author

de **Malherbe**, Raoul, he was the author of *L'Orient, 1718-1845; histoire, politique, religion, mœurs* (Paris, 1846), and a member of the Société orientale, Paris. Note about the author

Malhomme, Jean, born 6 June 1895 at Mirepoix (Gers), France, he was successively a teacher in his home *Département*, in Madagascar, and from 1932 until his retirement in 1953 in Morocco, where he taught at the Lycée Mohamed V at Marrakesh. He took great interest in Moroccan customs and the country's fauna, pre-history, and particulalry in its inscriptions, which he described in his *Corpus des gravures rupestres du Grand Atlas* (1959-61). He died in 1963. Hommes et destins, vol. 7, pp. 327-28; Libyca, 11 (1963), pp. 261-65

Malhotra, Ravi Inder, born in 1935, he obtained an M.A. and Ph.D. and was in 1982 a reader in the Department of History, Panjab University, Chandigarh. His writings include *Afghan search for identity; frontier settlements, 1872-1893* (1982). Note about the author; ZKO

Maliavkin, Anatoliĭ Gavrilov, born 20th cent., he was a historian of Central Asia, whose writings include *Материалы по истории уйгуров в IX-XII вв.* (1974), *Историческая география Центральной Азии* (1981), *Уйгурские государства в IX-XII вв* (1983), *Танские хроники о государствах Центральной Азии; тексты и исследования* (1989), and *Борьба Тибета с Танским государством за Кашгарию* (1992), and he was a joint editor of *Проблемы реконструкций этнографии* (1984). OSK

Maliepaard, Cornelius Henricus Johan, born in 1901, he was educated at Wageningen Agricultural University, the Netherlands. He served as an adviser to the Dutch Ministry of Agriculture, and he was an expert for the Middle East with the Food and Agriculture Organization. His writings include *Zwervend tussen Arabieren en Koerden* (1953), its translation, *Wasserräder am Euphrat; ein Reisebuch* (1954), *Witte steden, zwarte zelten* (1955), its translation, *Weiße Städte, schwarze Zelte* (1956), *Dieren sterven uit* (1961), and *Spoken jagen mee* (1974). Brinkman's; Sezgin; WhoNL, 1962/62

Malik, Charles Habib, born 11 February 1906 at Bitirram, Lebanon, he was a Greek-Orthodox, and educated at A.U.B., Harvard, and Freiburg im Breisgau. He was a professor and university administrator in Lebanon and the U.S.A. He also served as a Lebanese diplomat throughout the world. His writings include *Christ and crisis* (1962), *Man in the struggle for peace* (1963), and *The wonder of being* (1974). He died after a long illness in Beirut in 1987. ConAu, 45-48, 124, new rev., 86; DrAS, 1969; MidE, 1982/83

Malinas, Alfred Frédéric Fructus, born 19th cent., he received a doctorate and was in 1905 a *médecin principal de première classe*, a director of the Service de Santé de la Division d'occupation de Tunisie, officer of the Légion d'honneur, and officer of Instruction publique. His trace is lost after an article in 1908. BN; Note about the author

Maling, Joan Mathilde, born about 1945, she received a Ph.D. in 1973 from Massachusetts Institute of Technology, Cambridge, Mass., for *The theory of classical Arabic metrics*. She was in 1995 associated with the Department of English, Brandeis University, Waltham, Mass. NatFacDr, 1995

Malinjoud, J., born 19th cent., he was a *commandant* whose writings include *Choses et autres sur la Syrie* (Damas, 1924), and *Guide de l'interprète en Syrie* (Damas, 1924). Note about the author

Maliukovskiĭ, Magarif Vagizovich, born 22 January 1925, he graduated in 1951 from the Oriental Institute, Moscow, and received his first degree in 1954 for *Начальный этап мусульманской реформации в Египте.* Since 1989 he taught in the Moscow State Institute of International Relations. Miliband; Miliband²

Malka, Élie, born 1 March 1911 at Fès, he graduated from the Institut des Hautes Études Marocaines and received diplomas in ethnography as well as government and law. In 1931, he became an interpreter in Morocco, and in 1963, he was appointed section head, Service nationale de la Protection civile, Paris. His writings include *Dictionnaire pratique français-arabe des termes administratifs* (1939), *Glossaire judéo-arabe de Fès* (1940), *Essai d'ethnographie traditionnelle des Mellahs* (1946), *Essai sur la condition juridique de la femme juive au Maroc* (1952), *Essai de folklore des Mellahs* (1954), and *Pour rédiger et traduite* (Rabat, 1961). IndexBFr² (1); NDNC, 1964

Malkiel, Yakov (Jacques), born in 1914 at Kiev, he received a Dr.phil. in 1938 from the Universität Berlin for *Das substantivierte Adjektiv im Französischen.* He emigrated in 1940 to the U.S.A., where he became a professor of linguistics, mainly Romance languages, at the University of California, Berkeley. His writings include *Essays in linguistic themes* (1968), *Diachronic problems in lexicology, affixation, phonology* (1992), and a collection of his articles, *Theory and practice of Romance etymology* (1989). He died in 1998. Henry Romanos Kahane wrote *Yakov Malkiel, a tentative autobiography* (1988). CnDiAmJBi; ConAu, 25-28; DrAS, 1969 F; WhoAm, 1990-1998; WhoWorJ, 1965; WrDr, 1990/92-2002

El **Mallakh**, Ragaei William, born in 1925 at Tanta, Egypt, he graduated from Cairo University and received his Ph.D. in 1955 from Rutgers University, New Brunswick, N.J., for *The effects of the second World War on the economic development of Egypt.* He was an economic consultant to the International Bank of Reconstruction and Development as well as a professor at the University of Colorado. His writings include *Industrial development of the Arab states* (1955), *Economic development and regional cooperation; Kuwait* (1968), *Kuwait; trade and development* (1979), and *The Economic development of the Yemen Arab Republic* (1986). ConAu, 112; Note about the author

Mallarmé, André, born 6 August 1877 at Bouzaréa, Algeria, he obtained a doctorate in law in 1901 from the Sorbonne, Paris, for *L'organisation gouvermentale de l'Algérie.* He was a professor of constitutional and administrative law at the Université d'Alger and also served as a barrister in the Cour d'appel. A *député* for Alger since 1924, he later became a senator. His writings include *Emer de Vattel* [1714-1767] *et son droit des gens* (1904), and he was a joint autor of *Code de l'Algérie, annoté* (1908). DBFC, 1954/55; IndexBFr² (2); NUC, pre-1956

Mallat, Hyam Georges, born 26 July 1945 at Baabda, Lebanon, he was educated at the American University in Cairo, and the Université St.-Joseph, Beirut. He was a lawyer and sociologist. His writings include *L'Amenagement de territoire et de l'environement au Liban* (1971), and *Politique, économie et société du Liban de 1516 jusqu'à nos jours* (1977). WhoLebanon, 1977/78-2005/2006

Malle, Elisabeth, born 20th cent., she was in 1960 a journalist in Tehran. She was a joint author of the travel guide *Iran (Persien)*, a work which went through four editions from 1960 to 1974. Note

Malleson, George Bruce, born 8 May 1825 at London, he joined the Bengal Native Infantry in 1844, served in the second Burmese war, and subsequently in the Commissariat Department until 1856. He later served as an administrative officer, with the rank of colonel, until his retirement in 1877. He was a regular contributor to the *Calcutta review.* His writings include *The Mutiny of the Bengal Army* (1857-1858), *History of the French in India* (1868), its translation, *Histoire des Français dans l'Inde* (1874), *An Historical sketch of the native states of India* (1875), *The Russo-Afghan question and the invasion of India* (1878), and *Herat, the granary and garden of Central Asia* (1880). He died in 1898. Boase; BritInd (1); Buckland; DNB; IndianBiInd (1); Riddick; Who, 1897; Who was who, 1

Malleson, Sir Wilfrid, born in 1866, he was educated at Wimbledon and the Royal Military Academy, Woolwich. He joined the Royal Artillery in 1886 but transferred to the Indian Army in 1904. He served in Persia, Afghanistan and Turkestan until his retirement, with the rank of major-general, in 1920. He died in 1946. Riddick; Who, 1921-1946; Who was who, 4

Malleterre, Pierre Marie *Gabriel*, born in 1858, he was a captain and professor at l'École spéciale militaire, Saint-Cyr. His writings include *Un Court récit de la grande guerre, 1914-1919* (1921), and *La Guerre sur le front oriental* (1926). BN; IndexBFr² (1)

Mallison, Sally Vynne, born about 1920, she was a research associate of the International and Comparative Law Program, Washington, D.C., and the wife and long-time collaborator of W. Thomas

Mallison, both at George Washington University, and in dozens of legal assignments on behalf of the Palestinians. In 1988, the couple jointly received the Human Rights Award of the American-Arab Anti-Discrimination Committee and also the Elmer Berger Award for the promotion of human rights and peace in the Middle East. Her writings include *Armed conflict in Lebanon; humanitarian law in a real world setting* (1982); she was a joint author of *The Palestine problem in international law and world order* (1986). LC; Note about the author

Mallison, William Thomas, born in 1917 at Pago Pago, American Samoa, he graduated from Vanderbilt University Law School and received a doctorate in international law from Yale University. He was a professor and director of the International and Comparative Law Program at George Washington University until his retirement in 1987. Concurrently he held the Stockton Chair of International Law at the Naval War College in Newport, R.I., in 1960-61, and again in 1974-75. His writings, partly with his wife Sally, include *Studies in the law of naval warfare* (1968), and *The Palestine problem in international law and world order* (1986). In 1988, the couple jointly received the Human Rights Award of the American-Arab Anti-Discrimination Committee and also the Elmer Berger Award for the promotion of human rights and peace in the Middle East. He died in Silver Spring, Md., 24 November 1997. Palestine yearbook of international law 10 (1998/99), pp. xvii-xxiv; WRMEA 16 v (Jan./Feb. 1998), p. 63

Mallitskiĭ, Nikolaĭ Gur'evich, born in 1873, he graduated from the Faculty of History and Philology, St. Petersburg, and became successively associated with the Tajik Pedagogical Institute, Dushanbe, and the Central Asian State University, Tashkent. He died on 31 October 1947. BiobibSOT; UzbekSE

Mallmann, Wolfgang, born 20th cent., he was for many years associated with the German Federal Institute of East European and International Studies, Bonn. His writings on armanent, security, and economics include *Rüstung und Wirtschaft am Golf* (1978), *Die Weltraumpolitik der Sowjetunion in den 80er Jahren* (1989), and he was a joint author of *Sicherheit und Zusammenarbeit in Europa* (1973). Note about the author

Mallon, Marie *Alexis*, S.J., born in 1875 at La Chapelle-Bertrin (Haute-Loire), France, he was a Copticist who taught at Beyrouth, 1902-1905, and Jerusalem, from 1913 to 1914, when he was expelled from Palestine. He returned in 1920. His writings include *Grammaire copte avec bibliographie, chresto-mathie et vocabulaire* (1904). He died in Bethlehem on 7 April 1934. Dawson; Egyptoloy; Jalabert

Mallon, Richard Dicks, born 27 August 1926 in California, he graduated in 1949 from Princeton University and received his Ph.D. in 1964 from Harvard University for *Economic development and foreign trade of Pakistan*. He was an economic adviser to national and international organizations, particularly in the underdeveloped countries. His writings include *Economic policymaking in a conflict society; the Argentine case* (1975). WhoE, 1991/92

Mallowan, Sir Max Edgar Lucien, born in 1904, he was an archaeologist, and the husband of Agatha Christie. He excavated in Syria, Iraq, and Egypt. His writings include *Mallowan's memoirs* (1977), and he was a joint editor of *Ivories from Nimrud* (1967-70). Henrietta McCall wrote *Max Mallowan; archaeology and Agatha Christie* (2001). He died in 1978. ConAu, 69-72, 81-84, new rev., 21; DNB; Who was who 7

Malmusi, Benedetto, born 28 August 1839 at Parma, Italy, he was a biliophile and archaeologist. His writings include *Monte dei Sassanidi e dei Mongoli di Persia, appartenenti al Museo civico di Modena* (1887), *Una lettera d'Abd el Kader nella collezione Campori* (Modena, 1889), and *Giuseppe Malmusi; nelle vicende politiche dei suoi tempi* (1894). His trace is lost after an article in 1900. Firenze; IndBiltal (1)

Malo, Henri, born in 1868 at Boulogne-sur-Mer, France, he was a keeper of a museum and a writer. His writings include *Au Temps des châtelaines* (1894), *Ces Messieurs du Cabinet* (1905), *Les Corsairs, mémoires et documents inédits* (1908), *Les Corsairs* (1913-14), and *Corsairs et flibustiers* (1932). BN

Malone, Joseph James, born 18 April 1924 at San Francisco, he began his college education at the University of Washington. After war-time service with the U.S. Navy, he returned to the University and gained his B.A. and M.A. In 1956, he was awarded a Ph.D. in modern history from the University of London. His post-doctoral study included a fellowship at St. Antony's College, Oxford, the certificate in Arabic from the British Foreign Office's Middle East Centre for Arab Studies in Lebanon, and a diploma from the National War College. From 1959 to 1971, he was a chairman of the Department of History at the American University of Beirut. He subsequently taught at the University of Pittsburgh, and Kansas State University. In 1978, he had completed a three year term as director of Middle Eastern studies at the National War College. In 1974, he had established the Middle East Research Associates, serving as its president until his death on 4 December 1983. His writings include *The Arab lands of western Asia* (1973). The *Catalog, the Joseph J. Malone Collection on Arabian affairs in the William R. Perkins Library, Duke University* was edited by Jane Sturgeon, with an introduction by Ralph

Braibanti, in 1985. ConAu, 111; DrAS, 1978 H; *Journal of South Asian and Middle Eastern studies*, 7 ii (1983), pp. 1-2; *MESA Roster of members*, 1982; NatFacDr, 1975

Freiherr von **Malortie**, Carl, born in 1838, he was a Hanoverian who accompanied Archduke Maximilian to Mexico. After the latter's death, he returned to Europe; during his last years he was a cor-respondent for British papers in Egypt. His writings include *Dem Recht die Ehre* (Halle, 1864), *Mexikanische Skizzen* (Leipzig, 1882), *Egypt; native rulers and foreign interference* (London, 1882), and *Twixt old times and new* (London, 1890). He died in Cairo on 13 May 1899. BioJahr, 4 (1900), Toten-liste, pp. 161*-162*

Maloumian, Khatchadour, born in 1863, his writings, partly under the pseudonym E. Aknouni and Aknowni, include *Les Plaies du Caucase* (1905), and *Political persecution; Armenian prisoners of the Caucasus* (1911). He died in 1915. LC

Malov, Sergeï Efimovich, born in 1880 at Kazan, he there graduated in 1904 from the Ecclesiastical Academy (Духовная Академия), and in 1909 from the Oriental Faculty, St. Petersburg; he gained a master's degree in Turkish literature in 1916, and his doctorate in 1935. He twice spent two years in China. His writings include *Уйгурский язык* (1954), *Лобнорски язык* (1956), *Язык желтых уйгуров; словарь и грамматика* (1957), *Памятники древнетюркской письменноста Монголии и Кир-гизии* (1959), and *Уйгурские наречия Синьсзяна; тексты, переводы, словарь* (1961). He died on 7 September 1957. BioibSOT; *Index Islamicus* (6); Kazakhkaia, vol. 3; Miliband; Miliband²; TatarES; UzbekSE; VostoMStP

Małowist, Marian, born in 1909, he was since 1952 a professor at Uniwersytet Warszawski. His writings include *Kaffa, kolonia genueńska na Krymie i problem wschodni w latach 1453-1475* (1947), *Historia powszechna 14-15 w.* (1954), *Wielkie państwa Sudanu Zachodniego w późnym średniowieczu* (1964), *Europa a Afryka Zachodnia w dobie wczesnej ekspansji kolonialnej* (1969), and *Tamerlan i jego czasy* (1985). He died in 1988. NEP; OSK

Malpica Cuello, Antonio, born 20th cent., he received a doctorate in history and became a professor in the Departamento de Historia Medieval, Universidad de Granada, a post which he still held in 1997. He specialized in the history of the Mudejars and Moriscos of Granada. His writings include *Andalucía en el siglo XVI* (1981), *Turillas, alqueria del alfoz sexitano* (1984), he was joint author of *El azúcar en el encuentro entre dos mundos* (1992), and he was joint editor of *Colección diplomatica del Archivo de la Casa de Cázulas* (1982). Arabismo, 1992, 1994, 1997

Malte Brun, Conrad, he was born 12 August 1775 at Thisted, Denmark. On account of the violence of his political pamphleteering he was banished from his home country in 1800, and found permanent exile in Paris, where he became recognized as one of the best geographers of France. He was a founding member of the Société de géographie de Paris, and the founder of *Annales des voyages*. His writings include *Précis de la géographie universelle* (1810-1829), an epitome of universal geography. He died in Paris on 14 December 1826. BiD&SB; Dansk BL; EncBrit; Meyer

Malte-Brun, Victor Adolphe, born 23 or 25 November 1816 at Paris, the son of Conrad M.-B., he was educated at the Collège de Versailles. In 1838, he started a career in history, teaching successively at Pamiers (Ariège), Sainte-Barbe, and the Collège Stanislas, Paris. Since 1847, his interest began to shift increasingly towards geography. A member of the Société de géographie, he became its secre-tary general in 1855. His writings include *La France et ses colonies* (1857), and *Les Nouvelles acquisi-tions des Russes dans l'Asie orientale* (1860). He died in Marconssis (Seine-et-Loire) on 15 or 16 April 1889. Dantès 1; GdeEnc; Hoefer; IndexBFr² (1); Vapereau

von **Malten**, Heinrich, he wrote *Beschreibung aller berühmten Bäder in der Schweiz* (Aarau, 1830), and from 1834 to 1842 he contributed articles on French North Africa and Egypt to the Aarau periodical, *Bibliothek der neuesten Weltkunde*. GV; Sezgin

Maltese, Paolo, born in 1936, he wrote *La terra promessa; la guerra italo-turco e la conquista della Libia, 1911-1912* (1968), *Perchè il IV° conflitto arabo-israeliano?* (1974), *Storia del Canale de Suez* (1978), and *Nazionalismo arabo e nazionalismo ebraico, 1798-1992; storia e problemi* (1992). Catalogo dei libri in commercio, 2004

Malti-Douglas, Fedwa, born 12 January 1946 at Beirut, she graduated in 1970 from Cornell University, Ithaca, N.Y., and received her Ph.D. in 1977 from the University of California, Los Angeles. She was successively appointed a professor of Near Eastern languages and literature, comparative literature, and women's studies at Indiana University at Bloomington, a post which she still held in 2005. Her writings include *Structures of avarice* (1985), *Woman's body, woman's world* (1991), and she was joint author of *The treatment by computer of medieval Arabic biographical data* (1976). DrAS, 1982; NatFacDr, 1995-2005; ZKO

Mal'tsev, IUriĭ Stepanovich, born 31 July 1936 at Vladivostok, he graduated in 1959 and received his first degree in 1972 at Dushanbe for *Анонимная персоязычная космография XII века "Аджаиб ал-махлукат на гара`иб ал-мавджудат" как историко-географический источник.* He was since 1965 associated with the Oriental Institute, Tajik Academy of Sciences. He edited *Институт истории имени Ахмада Дониша* (Dushanbe, 1981), *Общественно-политическая деятельность Мальком-хана* (1984), and he edited the translation, *Завоеванние Хорасана,* of al-Balādhurī (1987). Miliband²; OSK

Freiherr von Maltzan zu Wartenberg und Penzlin, Heinrich Carl Eckard Helmuth, born 6 September 1826 at Dresden, Saxony, the son of a Bavarian major. From 1846 to 1850 he studied law and Oriental languages at München, Heidelberg and Erlangen. He briefly served in the Saxon civil service which he resigned in 1851. When he succeeded to his hereditary rights, he went on a research visit. After travelling in Europe, he reached Algeria by way of the Near East and there settled in 1852. In 1857, he travelled first to Abyssinia and later back to North Africa. He spent the years 1867 to 1869 in Malta, Sardinia and Sicily and later visited southern Arabia. Among his friends was an Algerian with a gargantuan appetite for hashish, who, in return for a supply guaranteed to last six months, allowed von Maltzan to use his name on a passport to Mecca for the pilgrimage. He reached Mecca but had to escape in disguise. His writings include *Meine Wallfahrt nach Mekka* (1865), *Drei Jahre im Nordwesten von Afrika* (1868), and *Reisen in Arabien* (1873). He committed suicide in Pisa on 22 February 1874. Bidwell; DtBE; Fück; *Globus,* 25 (19874), p. 231-34; Henze; Kornrumpf; NDB; *Unsere Zeit,* 10 (1874), pp. 351-52

Malvezzi de' Medici, Aldobrandino, marchese, born 26 May 1881 at Bologna, he served from 1913 to 1920 with the Ministero delle Colonie, and subsequently lectured on colonial affairs. His writings include *L'Italia e l'islam in Libia* (1913), *Odierne questioni politiche dell'Oriente musulmano* (1920), *Elementi di diritto coloniale* (1928), *La politica indigena nelle colonie* (1933), *Il rinnovamento del mondo musulmano; Eggitto contemporaneo* (1951), and *L'islamismo e la cultura europea* (1956). He died in 1960. Chi è, 1928, 1931, 1936, 1940, 1948; LC

Malyon, Frank Hailstone, born 19th cent., he was a joint editor of *Pushto folk stories* (1980).

Malysheva, Dina Borisovna, born 11 June 1944 at Moscow, she graduated in 1967 from the Faculty of History, Moscow State Pedagogical Institute and received her first degree in 1972 at Moscow for *Религия и политика в странах Восточной Африка.* Since 1967 she was affiliated with the Institute of World Economy and International Relations, Soviet Academy of Sciences. Her writings include *Концепции революции в развивающихся странах* (1979), and *Религия и общественно-политическое развитие арабских и африканских стран 70-е-80-е годи* (1986). Miliband²

Mamatakhunov, Usman, born 12 April 1925 in Sinkiang, he graduated in 1949 from Central Asian State University, Tashkent, and received his first degree in 1963 for *Жизнь и творчество уйгурского поэта XX века Билляль Назима.* From 1945 to his death on 9 August 1985 he was affiliated with the Oriental Faculty, Tashkent State University. Miliband²

Mamatsashvili (Mamac'ašvili/Мамацашвили), Marina Georgievna, born 7 November 1930 at Tiflis, she graduated in 1955 from the Oriental Faculty, Tiflis State University, and received her first degree in 1964 for *К вопросу о персидском источнике поэмы Теймураза Первого "Луйлмаджнунини,"* and her doctorate in 1974 for *О художественной специфике грузинскою перевода "Вис о Рамин."* Since 1958 she was affiliated with the Institute of Manuscripts in the Soviet Georgian Academy of Sciences. Her writings include *Каталог персидских рукописей Института Рукорисей Им. К. С. Кекелидже* (1977), and she was a joint auhor of *Каталог тюркских и персидских рукописей Института Рукописей Им. К. С. Кекелидзе* (1969), as well as other writings in Georgian. Miliband²

Mamedaliev, Vasim Mamedali ogly, born 27 September 1942 at Baku, he graduated in 1964 from the Oriental Faculty, Azerbaijan State University, received his first degree in 1968 for *Сравнитый-типологичий анализ временних форм глагола в современном арабском и азербайджанском литературых языках и багдадском диалекте,* and his doctorate in 1977 for *Категории времени, лица и наклонения в современном арабском литературном языке.* Since 1958 he taught at Azerbaijan State University. His writings on Arabic linguistics are largely in Azeri. Miliband²

Mamede, Suleiman Valy, born about 1900, he was in the 1960s a president-director of the Islamic community in Lisboa. His writings include *Maomé e o islamismo* (1967), *Contacto com as communidades Muçulmanas de Moçambique* (1970), *O Islão no mundo* (1971), *Curiosidades linguísticas da problemática islâmica* (1972), *Socialismo islamico* (1974), and *Vinte capitulos de Alcorão* (1977). Note; ZKO

Mamedov (Мәммәдов), Ali Asker Dzhafar ogly, born 10 October 1919 at Kishly, Azerbaijan, he graduated in 1941 from Azerbaijan State Pedagogical Institute and received his first degree in 1953 for a study of grammar in contemporary literary Arabic entitled *О простом предложении в современном арабском литературном языке*. His writings include *Эрэб дили* (Baku, 1971), and other works in Azeri.   Miliband; Miliband²

Mamedov, Aziz Aga Gadzhi Ali ogly, born 15 May 1918 at Lenkoran, Azerbaijan, he graduated in 1941 from Azerbaijan State Pedagogical Institute and received his first degree in 1949 for *Творчество Шах Исмаила Хатаи*, and a doctorate in 1971 for *Текстологические исследованния и научно-критические текст произведений Шах Исмаила Хатаи*. He was since 1957 associated with the Azerbaijan Academy of Sciences. His writings include *Журнал "Молла Насреддин" об американо-английском империализме* (1952), and *Шах Исмаил Хатаи* (1961).   Miliband²

Mamedov, Nadir, fl. 20th cent. *see* Mămmădov, Nadir Jalil oghlu

Mamedova, Asmetkhanym Bekakhmed kyzy, born 5 March 1941 at Baku, she graduated in 1965 from the Oriental Faculty, Azerbaijan State University and received her first degree in 1972 for *Фонетическая природа и место словесного ударения в современном персидском языке*. Since 1969 she taught at the Oriental Faculty, Azerbaijan State University. Her writings on Farsi phonetics are mainly in Azeri.   Miliband²

Mamedova, Mazara Gasan kyzy, born 25 March 1932 at Erevan, she graduated in 1956 from the Faculty of Philology, Baku, where she also received her first degree in 1968 for *Основные принципы составления персидских толковых словарей IX-XVII вв.* Since 1970 she was affiliated with the Oriental Faculty, Azerbaijan State University, Baku. Her writings are largely in Azeri.   Miliband²

Mamedova, Nina Mikhaĭlovna, born 25 October 1938 at Moscow, she graduated in 1961 from the Moscow Institute of Political Economy and received her first degree in 1971 for *Кооперативное движение в Иране*. Since 1969 she was associated with the Oriental Institute of the Soviet Academy of Sciences. Her writings include *Кооперация в Иране* (1973), *Концентрация производства и капитала в Иране* (1982), and *Городское предпринимательство в Иране* (1988).   Miliband²

Mamedzade, Kiamil' Mamedovich *see* Mămmădzadă, Kamil Mămmădăli oghlu

Mamikonov, Levon G., fl. 1959, he was associated with the Institute of Architecture and Art, Azerbaijan Academy of Sciences. His writngs include *Дома Правительства республик Закавказья* (1978), and he edited *Вопросы реставрации памятнико зодчества Азербайджана* (1960).   OSK

Mămmădov, Ali Asker Dzhafar ogly, 1919- *see* Mamedov, Ali Asker Dzhafar ogly

Mămmădov, Azizăghă Gadzhi Ali ogly, 1918- *see* Mamedov, Aziz Aga Gadzhi Ali ogly

Mămmădov, Nadir Jalil oghlu (Надир Чалил оғлу Мәммәдов), fl. 20th cent., his writings include *М. Ф. Ахундов реализми* (Baku, 1978), and he edited *Мирза Фәтәли Ахундов* (1962) as well as Akhundov's comedies in 1982.   OSK

Mămmădzadă, Kamil Mămmădăli oghlu (Камил Мәммәдәли оғлу Мәммәдзадә), born 20th cent., he received a degree in 1983 for a thesis entitled *Строительное искусство Азербайджана*. His other writings include *Азәрбаjчанда иншаат сәнәти* (1978), *Народный архитектор СССР Михаёль Усейнов* (Baku, 1989), and he was joint author of *Аразбочу абидәлəр* (Baku, 1979).   OSK

Mammarella, Giuseppe, born in 1929 at Firenze, Italy, he was a professor of contemporary history, and until 2001, a vice-president of the Università Internazionale dell'Arte, Firenze. His writings include *L'Italia dopo il fascismo* (1963), *Italy after Fascism* (1964), *Il Partito communista italiano, 1945-1975* (1976), *Imparare l'Europa* (1994), and *Destini incrociati* (2000).   Catalogo dei libri in commercio, 2002; Wholtaly, 2003

Mamoli, Pietro, born 19th cent., he travelled in 1881 in Cyrenaica. His writings include *La Cirenaica* (Napoli, 1912).   Kornrumpf; Kornrumpf⁵, vol. 2

Mamopoulos, Pierre (Petros) Iōannou, born 17 November 1892 at Constantinople, he received a doctorate in 1916 from the Sorbonne, Paris, for *Du recours de l'assureur contre le tiers responsable du sinistre et du cumul des indemnités au profit de l'assuré*. He was a barrister in the Court of Appeal, Athens, and a sometime adviser to the Commission mixte pour l'échange des populations grecques et turques. His writings include *Μέρες αγωνίας αί Πάτραι κατα την απελευθέρωσι* (Athens, 1949), and he translated the *Code civil hellénique* (1956).   Hellenikon, 1965; Note about the author

Mamuliia (Мамулия), Éteri Vissarionovna, born 15 September 1934 at Potskho, Georgia, she graduated in 1958 from the Oriental Faculty, Tiflis, and received her first degree in 1971 for *Идеоматические выражения в турецком*. Since 1960 he was affiliated with the Oriental Institute, Georgian Academy of Sciences. She was a joint author of a catalogue of Arabic manuscripts in the

Kekelidze Institute of Manuscripts, Georgian Academy of Sciences (1978), written in Georgian. Miliband²

Mamuliia, Lia (Лиа) Il'inichna, born 1 January 1933 at Tiflis, she graduated in 1956 from the Oriental Faculty, Georgian Academy of Sciences, and received her first degree in 1970 for *ал-Идах Абу Али ал-Фариси*. Since 1960 she was associated with the Oriental Institute, Georgian Academy of Sciences. Her writings are mainly in Georgian. In 1978, she published a catalogue of Arabic manuscripts in Tiflis. Miliband²

Manandian, IAkov (Akop) Amazaspovich, born in 1873 at Akhaltsikhe, Georgia, he received a Dr.phil. in 1897 from the Universität Jena for *Beiträge zur albanischen Geschichte*. He was from 1920 to 1931, dean and rector, Erivan State University, and from 1939 to 1940 he was associated with the Institute of History, Armenian Academy of Sciences. His writings include *История Армении в период тюрко-татарских нашествий* (1922), *О торговле и городах Армении в связи и мировой торговлей древних времен* (1954), *О некоторых спорных проблемах истории и географии древней Армении* (1956), and the translations, *Tigrane II and Rome* (1963), and *The Trade and cities of Armenia in relation to ancient world trade* (1965). He died in 1952. Miliband; Miliband²; VostokMStP

Manasse, E., born 19th cent., he received diplomas from the Faculté de droit, and the École des sciences politiques, Paris. His writings include the Turkish *Loi, concernant l'impôt sur les bénéfices* (1926). Note about the author

Mance, Sir Harry Osborne, born in 1875, he was since 1895 an officer with the Royal Engineers and was employed in African railway construction. He retired from the Army in 1924 with the rank of colonel. His writings include *The Road and rail transport problem* (1940), *International telecommunications* (1943), *International river and canal transport* (1944), and *International sea transport* (1945). He died in 1966. BritInd (2); Who, 1909-1967; *Who was who*, 6

Mänchen-Helfen, Otto John, 1894-1969 *see* Maenchen-Helfen, Otto John

Manchez, Georges, born 12 January 1851 at Paris, he was a journalist who spent the years from 1881 to 1887 with *le Figaro* at the economic desk, and until 1891 he edited the journal *le Capital*. A member of the Société d'économique politique, and the Société de statistique de Paris, he was awarded *chevalier* of the Légion d'honneur. His writings include *La Séparation de l'épargne et de l'État* (1910), and *La Bourse de Paris après la guerre* (1918). Curinier, vol. 3 (1901), pp. 128-29

Mańczak, Witold, born 12 August 1924 at Sosnowiec, Poland, he studied linguistics at Uniwersytet Jagielloński, Kraków, where he received a doctorate in 1950. He was appointed a lecturer in 1957, and a professor in 1971. His writings include *Phonétique et morphologie historiques du français* (1962), *Polska fonetyka i morfologia historyczna* (1965), *Gramatyka hiszpańska* (1966), and *Z zagadnień językoznawstwa ogólnego* (1970). Poloc, 1993, 2001

Mandaville, James P., born 6 March 1935, his writings include *A List of desert plants of eastern Arabia* (1964), *Wild flowers of northern Oman* (1978), and *The Flowers of eastern Saudi Arabia* (1990). LC

Mandaville, Jon Elliott, born in 1937, he received his Ph.D. in 1969 from Princeton University for *The Muslim judiciary of Damascus in the late Mamluk period*. He subsequently was appointed a professor at the Middle East Studies Center, Portland State University, a post which he still held in 2004. Master (1) = DrAS, 1999 (not sighted); *MESA Roster of members*, 1977-1990; NatFacDr, 1995-2004; Selim

Mandel, Gabriele, born 12 February 1924 at Milano, he studied classics, music, and Oriental subjects and became a sometime director of the Istituto Europeo di Storia dell'Arte, Milano. His writings include *Gengis Kan* (1969), *Maometto* (1976), *Mohammed und seine Zeit* (1976), *Il sufismo, vertice della piramide esoterica* (1977), *Come riconoscere l'arte islamica* (1979), as well as its translations into English and German in the same years, *I detti di al Hallaj* (1980), *La chiave; storia e simbologia di chiavi lucchetti serrature* (1990), *Il Corano senza segreti* (1991), *Storia del Sufismo* (1995), and *Arabic script; styles, variants, and calligraphic adaptions* (2001). Many of his works have been translated into other languages. Chi scrive; IndBiltal (3); Note about the author; ZKO

Mandel, Neville J., born 20th cent., his writings include *The Arabs and Zionism before World War one* (1976), a work which was originally presented in 1965 as his thesis at Oxford, entitled *Turks, Arabs, and Jewish immigration into Palestine, 1882-1914*. Note about the author; Sluglett

Mandelbaum, David Goodman, born 22 August 1911 at Chicago, he was an anthropologist who carried out field-work in northern India in 1963-1964. His writings include *Society in India* (1970), *Human fertility in India* (1974), *Women's seclusion and man's honor; sex roles in North India, Bangladesh, and Pakistan* (1988). He died in Berkeley, Cal., on 19 April 1987. Master (3); Shavit - Asia; WhAm, 9

Mandel'shtam, Anatolii Maksimilianovich, born 11 August 1920 at Voronezh, Russia, he graduated in 1941 from the Faculty of History, Leningrad, received his first degree in 1951 for *Сложение таджикской народности в среднеазиатском Междуречье*, and his doctorate in 1973 for *История скотоводческих племен и ранних кочевников на юге Средней Азии*. He was from 1951 to his death on 8 September 1983 affiliated with the Leningrad Branch of the Archaeological Institute, Soviet Academy of Sciences. His writings include *Кочевники на пути в Индию* (1966), *Памятники эпохи бронзы в Южном Таджикистане* (1968), and *Памятники кочевников кушанского времени Северной Бакмрии* (1975). Miliband; Miliband²; ZKO

Mandelstam, Andreï (André) Nikolaevich, born in 1869, he received a doctorate in law from the University St. Petersburg, and he was in 1907 associated with the Institute of International Law. His writings include *La Société des nations et les puissances devant le problème arménien* (1926), *Das armenische Problem im Lichte des Völker- und Menschenrechts* (Berlin, 1931), and *Le Conflit italo-éthiopien devant la Société des nations* (Paris, 1937). He died in 1949. Kornrumpf ; LC; Note

de **Mandeville**, John (Jean), fl. 14th cent., he was the ostensible author of a book of travels in the East, written in French and published between 1357 and 1371. The work has been translated into numerous languages. Recent editions are *Jean de Mandeville; le livre des merveilles du monde* (2000), *The Book of John Mandeville; an edition of the Pynson text* (2001), and *The Defective version of Mandeville's travels* (2002). DLB, vol. 146 (1994), pp. 269-73; DNB; EncBrit; EncicUni; GdeEnc; Meyers; Pallas

Mandleur, Alain, born in 1944, he was a joint author of the guide-book, *Découverte de Marrakech* (Rabat, 1973). Note about the author

Mandonnet, Pierre-Félix, born in 1858 at Beaumont near Clermont-Ferrand, France, he was since 1884 a Dominican priest; he became a professor of ecclesiastical history in the Université de Fribourg, Switzerland, and later served until 1902 as its *recteur*. His writings include *Siger de Brabant et l'averroïsme latin* (1899), *Dante le théologien* (1935); he was a joint author of *Bibliographie thomiste* (1921); and he edited *Opuscula omnia*, of Thomas Aquinas, in five volumes (Paris, 1927). IndexBFr² (1)

de **Mandrot**, Bernard Édouard, born 7 November 1848 at le Havre, France, he was a graduate of l'École des chartes, Paris, and became a palaeographer and archivist. His writings include *Relations de Charles VII et de Louis XI* (1881), and *Ymbert de Batarnay, seigneur du Bouchage* (1886). He died in 1920. Oursel

Maneca, Constant, born 20th cent., he wrote *Lexicologie statistic romanica* (Bucureşti, 1978), and he was a joint author of *Dicţionar de neologisme* (1961). OSK

Manera Regueyra, Enrique, born 19 September 1908 at Madrid, he was in 1957 a *capitán de fregata*. He became a deputy director of the Madrid school of naval warfare. IndiceE³ (1) = WhoSpain, 1963; Note

Manesse, Jacques, born 20th cent., he gained a doctorate in law and was in 1977 an assistant in the Département des sciences politiques, Université de Paris I. His writings include *L'Aménagement du territoire; des instruments pour quelles politiques* (1998). Livres disponibles, 2004; Note about the author

Maneville, Roger, fl. 1951, he was a joint author, with Jean Mathieu, of *Les Accoucheuses musulmanes traditionnelles de Casablanca* (1952).

Manfroni, Camillo, born 13 June 1863 at Cuneo (Piedmont), he was a professor of history of Italian colonization at the Accademia Navale di Livorno, 1886-96, Università di Genova, 1896-1900, and Università di Padova, 1900-1925. He subsequently taught at the Facoltà di scienze politiche dell'Università di Roma. His writings include *Guerra italo-turca, 1911-12; cronistoria delle operazioni navali* (1918-26), *Storia della marina italiana, 1914-1918* (1923), and *I colonizazioni italiani durante il medio evo e il rinscimento* (1933). He died on 16 June 1935. Chi è, 1928, 1931; IndBiltal (5); Rivista delle colonie italiane, 9 (1935), pp. 655-58

Manga, János, born 24 June 1906 at Pereszlény, Hungary, he was an ethnologist and a university lecturer. His writings include *Pásztorművészet* (1963), *Magyar népdalok, népi hangszerek* (1969), its translations, *Hungarian folk song and folk instruments* (1969), *La Musique populaire hongroise et ses instruments* (1969), *Ungarische Volkslieder und Volksinstrumente* (1969), and *Magyar pásztorfaragások* (1972), and its translations, *Hirtenschnitzereien* (1972), and *Herdsmen's art in Hungary* (1976). He died in Budapest on 2 September 1977. Magyar; MEL, 1981

Mangasarian, Mangasar Mugurditch, born in 1859 in Turkey, he was educated at Robert College, Constantinople, and Princeton Theological Seminary. He served from 1878 to 1880 as a missionary at Marsovan (Merzifon), Amasya Province, Turkey. He later was a lecturer of the Independent Religious Society of Chicago at Orchestra Hall. His many writings include *The Bible unveiled* (1911). He died in 1943. WhAm, 4

Mangeot, Pol Victor, born in 1869, he was associated with the Comité d'études historiques et scienti-fiques de l'Afrique Occidental Française. His writings include *La Vie ardente de van Vollenhoven, gouverneur général de l'A.O.F., un grand colonial et un grand Français* (1943). Note about the author

Mangin, Charles Marie Emmanuel, born 6 July 1866 at Sarrebourg (Meurthe), France, he grew up at Alger and in 1886 entered the military college of Saint-Cyr. After graduation he opted for the marines, serving in the French Sudan until 1889. Influenced by Louis Archinard, lieutenant-governor of French West Africa, he developed a fondness for Negroes which increased in time. Involved in the preparations for the Fashoda campaign, he recruited the native escort which, under his command, pacified the Congo, reached Fashoda, and triumphantly participated in the Paris victory parade. In 1912, he conquered southern Morocco with his Negroe troops. During the first World War he was instrumental in the recruitment of over a hundred thousand Senegal *tirailleurs*, with whom he later led the operations of the Armée du Rhin. His writings include *La Force noire* (1910), *Regards sur la France d'Afrique* (1924), *Lettres du Soudan* (1930), *Lettres de la mission Marchand, 1895-1899* (1931), and *Souvenirs d'Afrique* (1936). He died in 1925. Hill; *Hommes et destins*, vol. 8, pp. 279-81; IndexBFr² (2); Master (1); *Qui êtes-vous*, 1924; WhoMilH

Mangion, Giovanni, born in 1938 in Żurrieq, Malta, he studied at Malta and received a B.A. in classics in 1958 and a doctorate in 1963. His writings include *Per una storia di Malta secolo XIX; breve studio sulla opinione pubblica maltese della metá del secolo scorso* (1965). Mifsud

Mangion, Paul, he was in 1942 a *professeur* at the Lycée Gautier, Alger. His writings include *Cent textes d'arabe dialectal algérien* (Alger, 1959), and he was a joint author of *Vocabulaire de base de l'arabe dialectal algérien et saharien* (1961), and he edited *Les Milles et une nuits* (1961). Note; ZKO

Mango, Andrew J. A., born in 1926 at Constantinople, he was educated in Turkey. He subsequently gained his Ph.D. in 1955 at the School of Oriental and African Studies, London, for *Studies on the legend of Iskandar in the classical literature of Islamic Persia, with special reference to the work of Firdawsi, Nizami and Jami*. He was a head of the South European Service of the BBC, an honorary research associate at SOAS, and a lecturer at the Royal College of Defence Studies. His writings include *Turkey* (1968), *Discovering Turkey* (1971), *Turkey, a delicately poised ally* (1975). *Turkey; the challenge of a new role* (1994), and *Atatürk* (2000). DrBSMES, 1993; Note; Sluglett

Mango, Cyril Alexander, born 14 April 1928 at Istanbul, he gained an M.A. in 1949 at St. Andrews and a doctorate in 1953 at the Sorbonne, Paris. He was a professor of Byzantine studies in the U.K. and U.S.A. His writings include *The Brazen house* (1959), *Materials for the study of the mosaics of St. Sophia at Istanbul* (1962), *Byzantium and its image* (1984), *Le Développement urbain de Constantinople* (1985), *Studies on Constantinople*, a selection of his periodical articles (1993), and *The Oxford history of Byzantium* (2002). *Bosphorus, essays in honour of Cyril Mango* was published in 1995. ConAu, 109; DrAS, 1969 H; Who, 1995-2005

Mangold, Peter, born about 1942, he received his Ph.D. in 1972 from the London School of Economics for *The Role of force in British policy towards the Middle East, 1957-66*. He was a sometime member of the Foreign and Commonwealth Office Research Department. His writings include *Superpower intervention in the Middle East* (1978), *National security and international relations* (1990), and *Success and failure in British foreign policy; evaluating the record, 1900-2000* (2001). Note; Sluglett

Manguin, Pierre Yves, born 20th cent., he was affiliated with the École française d'Extrême-Orient. His writings include *Les Portugais sur les côtes du Viêt-Nam et du Campa; études sur les routes maritimes* (1972), *Les Nguyên, Macau et le Portugal* (1984), and he was a joint author of *Un Siècle pour l'Asie; l'École française d'Extrême-Orient, 1898-2000* (2001). Note about the author

Manik, Liberty, born about 1935, he received a Dr.phil. in 1968 from the Freie Universität Berlin for *Das arabische Tonsystem im Mittelalter*. His writings include *Batak-Handschriften* (1973). ZKO

Man'kina, Sof'ia Solomonovna, born 30 Decmber 1908 (12 January 1909) in Bryansk Oblast, she graduated in 1941 from the Moscow Oriental Institute, and received her first degree in 1954 for *Аффиксы, образующие имена существительных и прилагательных в турецком языке*. Since 1954 she was associated with the Moscow State Institute of International Relations. She was a joint author of *Турецко-русский разговорник* (1950). Miliband²

Man'kovskaia, Liia IUl'evna, born 2 January 1932 at Moscow, she graduated in 1955 from the Central Asian Polytechnic Institute, and received her first degree in 1964, and her doctorate in 1982 for *Типологические основы зодчества Средней Азии*. Since 1966 she was associated with the Institute of Fine Art im. Khamzy. Her writings include *Бухоро; осиқ осмон остидаги музей* (1991), and she was a joint author of *По древним городам Усбекистана: Ташкент, Самарканд, Шах-рисябз, Бухара, Хива* (1988). She died in 1988. Miliband²

Mańkowski, Tadeusz, born 2 August 1878 at Lwów (Lemberg), Austria, he was an art historian and a member of the Lwów and Kraków Academies of Sciences. His writings include *Sztuka islamu w Polsce v XVII i XVIII wieku* (1935), *Genealogia sarmatyzmu* (1946), and *Dzieje wnętrz wawelskich* (1952). He died in Kraków on 8 August 1956. Czy wiesz, 1938; Polski (2); PSB;

Mann, Cameron, born in 1851 in N.Y.C., he was a clergyman who was consecrated bishop of North Dakota in 1901. His writings include *Five discourses on future punishment* (1888). He died in 1932. Master (2); NatCAB, vol. 13, p. 220; WhAm, 1; Who was who, 3

Mann, Carl Heinrich, born 4 January 1839 at Zürich, Switzerland, he lost his father when still quite young. After completing his secondary education at Schaffhausen he became a bookseller, concurrently pursuing an interest in writing. He spent some years in Dresden, where he wrote his first publication, a *Christian Gedenkbuch*. Since 1861 he was in Bern, where he became in 1866 an editor of the journal *Der Pilger*. Until 1885 he was successively an editor at Basel and Bern. Thereafter he became a free-lance writer on social and legal subjects. His writings include *Spiess und Nägel eines Friedfertigen; Erinnerungen aus den Jahren 1832-1885* (1885), *Bilder aus Nord=Afrika* (1888), and *Kreuz und quer durch den Kanton Bern* (1900). GV; Hinrichsen = DtBilnd

Mann, Gottlieb Bernhard Oskar, born 18 September 1867 at Berlin, he received a Dr.phil. in 1891 at Berlin for *Das Majmil et-tarikh-i ba'd nâdirîje des Ibn Muhammad Emin Abu'l-Hasan aus Gulistâne nach der Berliner Handschrift*. He became a librarian at the Berlin royal library and a university professor. In the service of the German emperor he went in 1901/3 and 1906/7 on linguistic expeditions to Kurdistan, returning with valuable collections. His writings include *Die Mundart der Mukri-Kurden* (1905-9), and *Die Mundart der Luristämme im südwestlichen Persien* (1910). He died in Berlin on 5 December 1917. The first *Year book of the Kurdish Academy*, 1990, was dedicated to him. DtBiJ, 2 (1917-1920), Totenliste, p. 664; Hanisch; JahrDtB, 1902-1916; Wer ist's, 1912

Mann, Jacob, born in 1888 at Przemyśl, Austria, he received his Ph.D. in 1920 from the University of London for *The Jews of Egypt and in Palestine under the Fatimid caliphs*. He became a professor of Jewish studies at Hebrew Union College, Cincinnati, Ohio. His writings include *Text and studies in Jewish history and literature* (1931-35), and *The Bible as read and preached in the old synagogue* (1946-66). He died in 1940. CnDiAmJBi; Master (1); WhNAA; Who was who, 4

Mann, Traugott, born 5 January 1881 at Bielefeld, Germany, he studied at the universities of Greifswald, Halle, and Berlin, where he received a Dr.phil. in 1904 for *Beiträge zur Kenntnis arabischer Eigennamen*. His other writings include *Der Islam einst und jetzt* (1914), and he edited *Über Namen und Nisben bei Bohārî, Muslim, Mālik*, by Ibn Khatīb al-Dahshah (1905). GV

Mannanov, Abdurakhim Mutalovich, born 22 December 1942 at Tashkent, he graduated in 1966 from the Oriental Faculty, Tashkent State University, and received his first degree in 1970 for *Суффийско-пантеистического направление в афганской литературе XVI-XVII вв.* Since 1979 he was a lecturer at his alma mater. He published in Pushto periodicals. Miliband²

Mannanov, Bakhritdin Salakhitdinovich, born 10 September 1930, he graduated in 1951 from the Oriental Faculty, Central Asian State University, and received his first degree in 1963 for *Русско-иранские отношения конца XIX и начала XX века*. He became associated with the Oriental Institute, Uzbekistan Academy of Sciences. His writings include *Из истории русско-иранских отношений в конце XIX- начале XX века* (1964), and he was a joint author of *Современная Иран* (1960), as well as writings in Uzbek. Miliband²

Manndorff, Hans, born 26 April 1928 at Hinterbrühl, Austria, he received a Dr.phil. in 1953 from the Universität Wien for *Kulturpflanzen Indiens in Wirtschaft und Brauchtum; eine kuturhistorische Untersuchung*. He joined the Museum für Völkerkunde, Wien, in 1956. In 1965, he gained his Dr.habil. He was a sometime university professor. His writings include *Indien - 400 Millionen suchen einen Weg* (1958), and *Völker der Tundra und Taiga* (196-?). Kürschner, 1980-1996|; WhoAustria, 1967-1996; WhoWor, 1978/79, 1989/90

Mannin, Ethel Edith, born in 1900, she was the author of over ninety books, and a keen political observer. Foreign governments in search of a glossy image recognized the sanitizing effect of a visit by her and would invite her to stay with them for a while and within a year a book would appear. Her books bearing on the Middle East include *South to Samarkand* (1937), *Moroccan mosaic* (1953), *Aspects of Egypt* (1964), *The Lovly land, Jordan* (1965), *Bitter Babylon* (1968), and *Mission to Beirut* (1973). She died in 1984. Au&Wr, 1963; ConAu, 53-56, 114; DLB, 191 (1998), pp. 217-221; DLB, 195 (1998), pp. 216-234; DNB; IntAu&W, 1977, 1982; IntWW, 1974/75-1983; Master (5); Robinson, pp. 183-85; Who, 1964-1984; *Who was who*, 8

Mano, G. A., he was in 1828 a lecturer at Genève, Switzerland. His writings include *Alexandre-le-Grand d'après les auteurs orientaux* (1828), *L'Orient rendu à lui-même* (1861), *La Grèce et le Danemark* (1863), and *Des Intérêts religieux de l'Orient au sujet des biens conventuels dans les Principautés-Unies* (1864). He died in 1868. BN; Note; NUC, pre-1956

Manolescu, Radu, born 20th cent., his writings include *Studiul comportării sub trafic şi sub diverse condiţii microclimatice a sistemelor rutiere uzuale* (Bucureşti, 1963), and *Comerţul Ţării Romîneşti şi Moldovei cu Braşsovul* (Bucureşti, 1965). OSK

Manomohana Lala Agarvala see Agarwala, Manmohan Lal

Manor, Yohanan, born 20th cent., his writings include *Naissance du sionisme politique* (Paris, 1981). NUC, 1982

Manousakas, Manousos Iōanni, he was born 2 December 1914 at Rethymnon, Crete. His writings include Χειρόγραφα και εγγραφα του Άγγιου Όρους (1958), Ἡ εν Κρήτη συνωμοσία του Σήψη Βλαστού, 1453-1454 (1960), and Ανέκδοτα πατριαρχικά γράμματα (1547-1806) προς τους εν Βενετία μητροπολίτας Φιλαδελφείας και την Ορθόδοξον Ελληνικήν Αδελ-φότητα (1968). EVL, 1993/94-2001; Hellenikon, 1965; NUC, 1968-72

Manousakis, Gregor M., born in 1935, he received a Dr.phil. in 1965 from the Universität Bonn for *Das Verhältnis von Militär und Politik in Griechenland von 1900-1952*, a work which was published in 1967 entitled *Hellas - wohin?* Since 1976 he was a German news correspondent in Athens. His other writings include *Die Rückkehr des Propheten* (1979), *Der Islam und die NATO; Bedrohung an der Südflanke* (1980), *Die Re-Islamisierung als politisches Phämomen* (1980), and *Weg zum Öl* (1984). GV; Sezgin

Mansel, Arif Müfid, born in 1905 at Constantinople, he was an archaeologist who received a Dr.phil. in 1929 for *Stockwerkbauten der Griechen und Römer*. He was since 1938 a member of Deutsches Archäologisches Institut, Istanbul. His writings include *Ege ve Yunan tarihi* (1947), and *Die Ruinen von Side* (1963). He died in Istanbul on 18 January 1975. AnaBrit; Widmann

Manselli, Raoul, born 8 June 1917 at Napoli, he received a doctorate in philosophy and became a medieval historian successively at the universities of Perugia, Torino, and Roma. His writings include *Studi sulle eresie del secolo XII* (1953), *I fenomeni di devianza nel medio evo* (1972), *La religione popolare nel medioevo* (1974), and its translation, *La religion populaire au moyen âge* (1975). He died in 1984. IndBiltal (1); Liu, chi è

Manser, Gallus Maria, born 25 July 1866 at Brüslisau (Appenzell), Switzerland, he came from a rural environment and studied at Monza, Milano, and Fribourg. Since 1892 he taught philosophy at Wenesh, England. A Dominican priest since 1897, he was in 1898 a lecturer in moral theology at Dominikanerstudium, Düsseldorf. He later returned to Fribourg as a vice-prefect of the theological seminary Canisianum, where he served from 1899 to 1942 as a professor of logic, ontology, and medieval history. His writings include *Das Naturrecht in Thomistischer Beleuchtung* (1944), and *La esencia del tomismo* (1947). In 1936 he was honoured by *Festgabe P. Gallus M. Manser zum siebzigsten Geburtstag.* He died in Fribourg on 20 February 1950. DtBE; DtBilnd (1); Kosch; Kürschner, 1926-1935; NDB

Mansfield, Peter J., born 1928 in India, he was educated at Winchester and was president of the union at Cambridge. In 1955, he joined the Foreign Office which sent him, in 1956, to Lebanon's Middle East Centre for Arabic Studies. This was the turning point in his life, but before he finished the course, the 1956 Suez crisis erupted. He disagreed with the British Government's position and resigned. He stayed on in Lebanon working as a free-lance journalist. From 1958 to 1961, he was editor of the *Middle East forum*, and from 1961 to 1967, he became the Cairo-based Middle East correspondent of *The Sunday Times*, and contributed also regularly to *The Financial Times*, *The Economist*, *The Guardian*, and *The New Statesman*. His writings include *Nasser's Egypt* (1965), *Nasser* (1969), *The British in Egypt* (1971), *The Ottoman Empire and its successors* (1973), *The Middle East: a political and economic survey*, 5th ed. published by O.U.P. under the auspices of St. Antony's College, Oxford (1980), *The new Arabians* (1981), *Kuwait, vanguard of the Gulf* (1990), *A History of the Middle East* (1991). He will be remembered best for his 1976 book, *The Arabs*, (3rd rev. ed., 1992). He was a leading light in the Council for the Advancement of Arab-British Understanding, a member of the Royal Institute of International Affairs, and a founding fellow of the British Society for Middle Eastern Studies, at whose annual conferences he was a regular participant. He was committed to the Arab cause, espousing positions which were often unfashionable, but he was always respected, even by those who did not share his views. He died in the first half of 1996. DrBSMES, 1993; *BRISMES newsletter*, 10 iii (July 1996); Private

Mansion, Auguste, fl. 1940-46, he wrote *Het Aristotelisme in het historisch perspectif* (1954), and its translation, *Introduction à la physique aristotélicienne* (1963); he also edited *Aristoteles latinus* (Bruges, 1957).

Mansoor, Menahem, born 4 August 1911 at Port Said, he received a B.A. from the University of London, and a B.A. (Hons.) from Trinity College, Dublin; in 1944, he gained a doctorate. From 1944 to 1954, he was in British government service as a teacher of Hebrew and Arabic, employed in Britain as well as in Israel. Since 1954 he taught Hebrew and Semitic studies, first at Johns Hopkins University, Baltimore, Md., and later at the University of Wisconsin, Madison, where he died on 21 October 2001. His writings include *Listen and learn modern Hebrew* (1962), *The story of Irish orientalism* (1944), and *Legal and documentary Arabic reader* (1965). BlueB, 1973/74, 1975, 1976; ConAu, 41-44, 202, new rev., 15; DrAS, 1969 F, 1974 F, 1978 F, 1982 F; Master (1); NUC, 1956-67; WhoWorJ, 1965, 1972, 1978; WrDr, 1976/78-2003

Mansour, Atallah B., born in 1934, born at Jish, Palestine, he was educated at Ruskin College, Oxford. He was an agricultural worker, writer, and a correspondent of *Ha'aretz* in Nazareth and Gaza. His writings include אור שדה‎ = *Be-'or hadash* (1966), its translation, *In a new light* (1969), and *Waiting for the dawn; an autobiography* (1975). Bioln, 6; WhoIsrael, 1976-2001

Mansour, Jacob, born in December 1924 at Baghdad, he received graduate degrees from the Hebrew University, Jerusalem, in 1949 and 1965. Since 1961 he was successively associated with Bar-Ilan University, and the University of Haifa as a lecturer and head of department. His writings include *The Jewish Baghdadi dialect; studies and texts in the Judeo-Arabic dialect of Baghdad* (1991). IWWAS, 1975/76; WhoWorJ, 1978 (not sighted)

Mansur, Abullah, born 1874 see Bury, George *Wyman*

Mansur, W. A., born 19th cent., he was a Palestinian Arab who had a foretaste of education in missionary schools in Syria, before entering McCormick Seminary in Chicago from which he graduated with honours, and was subsequently ordained a minister in the Presbyterian Church. In 1926, he was president, Santee (Nebr.) Normal Training School; and from 1930 to 1931, he was a minister at the First Methodist Church of Winside (Nebr.) Note about the author

Mantel-Niećko, Joanna (Mrs.), born 14 August 1933 at Warszawa, she graduated in 1956 in Ethiopic philology from Uniwersytet Warszawski. She subsequently became associated with the Department of Semitic Languages at her alma mater. Her writings include *Les Verbes de type A/B-C en amharique* (1969), *The Role of land tenure in the system of Ethiopian Imperial Government in modern times* (Warszawa, 1980), and she was a joint author of *Historia Etiopii* (Warszawa, 1971), and its translation, *История Эфиопии* (1976). OSK; Unesco

Mantran, Robert, born 19 December 1917 or 1918 at Paris, he studied at the Sorbonne, École des langues orientales vivantes, and École pratique des hautes études, Paris. After the war he conducted epigraphic research at Damascus and Beirut, subsequently moving on to Istanbul as a fellow of the Institut français d'archéologie, and teaching from 1947 to 1952 at Galatasaray Lisesi. He spent the remainder of the 1950s with the Centre National de la Recherche Scientifique in Paris and in Tunis. In the early 1960s he settled in Aix-en-Provence, where he became a founding or active member of a number of research centres and scholarly journals. A visiting professor at the University of Mexico and University of California, Los Angeles, he became professor emeritus following his retirement in 1985. In 1990, he was elected member of the Académie des Inscriptions et Belles Lettres. His writings include *Istanbul dans la second moitié du XVIIe siècle* (1962), *Histoire de la Turquie* (1975), and *L'Empire ottoman du XVI au XVIIIe siècle* (1984). He died in Aix-en-Province on 24 September 1999. MESA bulletin, 34 (2000), pp. 302-303; Revue des mondes musulmans et de la Méditerranée, 89-90 (2000), pp. 376-82; Unesco

Manu, Maurycy, born in 1814, he studied at the universities of Kraków, Genève, and Paris. He became a journalist and editor of the Kraków *Czas*. In the mid-1850s, he travelled to Egypt and Palestine. He died in 1876. Dziekan

Manucci, Nicola or Niccolò, born in 1638 or 39 at Venezia, he was a medical doctor and a traveller. His writings include *Storia generale dell'imperio del Mogol dopo la sua fondazione* (Venezia, 1731), and its translations, *Histoire générale de l'empire du Mogol depuis sa fondation* (La Haye, 1708), and *Storia do Mogor, or Mogul India, 1653-1708* (1907). He died about 1710, certainly after February 1709. Enciclopedia italiana di scienze, lettere ed arti (Roma, 1929-1949)

Manue, Georges R., born Georges Luc François Roulain on 2 November 1901 at Estavayer, Canton Fribourg, Switzerland, he joined the Légion étrangère on 24 April 1921 and participated in the Riff campaign as a sergeant. Since this time he is known only by the name Manue. He left the French Foreign Legion in 1926 and became a reporter for *le Journal*, a post which he held until 1930. In 1929, he made a Sahara crossing, and continued to Dakar by way of Gao, Timbuctu and Bamako, an experience which he described in his *L'Appel du Sud* (1931). Since 1930 the owner and director of the journal *Bravo*, he still contributed to *La Revue des deux mondes, La Revue de Paris* and other periodicals. In 1931, he published his experiences as a *légionnaire, La Retrait du désert,* a work which won him an award from the Académie française. On the eve of the second World War he was editor-in-chief on the *Annales coloniales.* On 9 September 1939, he joined for a five-year term, and subsequently volunteered for the remainder of the war. After the war he served until 1948 in Indochina, returning to Paris in 1949. His other writings include *Têtes brûlées; cinq ans de Légion* (1929), *Sur les marches du Maroc insoumis* (1930), and *Caméroun, création française* (1938). He died in Paris in 1980. Hommes et destins, vol. 4, pp. 481-82

Manuel, Frank Edward, born 12 September 1910 at Boston, Mass., he graduated in 1930 from Harvard, where he also received his Ph.D. in 1933. He was successively a professor of history at Harvard, Brandeis University, New York University, and again Brandeis. In 1979, he was granted a Litt.D. by the Jewish Theological Seminary of America. His writings include *The Politics of modern Spain* (1938), *The Realities of American-Palestine relations* (1949), *The Age of reason* (1951), *Shapes of philosophical history* (1965), *Freedom from history* (1971), and *The Changing of the gods* (1983). ConAu, 9-12, new rev. 6, 29, 53, 92; DrAS, 1969 H, 1972 H, 1978 H, 1982 H; IntAu&W, 1976, 1977; Master (4); WhoAm, 1974-1984

Manuk, P. C., born 19th cent., his writings include the *Catalogue of Persian, Mogul and Indo-Mogul pictures, comprising the collection of the P. C. Manuk* (s.l., 1912). His trace is lost after an article in 1943.

Manylov, IU. P., born 20th cent., he received a degree in 1972 at Tashkent for a thesis entitled *Археологические памятники Султануиздага эпохи античности и средневековья.* OSK

Manz, Beatrice Forbes, born 21 November 1947 at Boston, Mass., she received a Ph.D. in 1983 from Harvard University for *Politics and control under Tamerlane.* She subsequently was appointed a professor in the Department of History, Tufts University, Medford, Mass., a post which she still held in 2004. Her writings include *The Rise and rule of Tamerlane* (1989), and *Central Asia in historical perspective* (1994). MESA Roster of members, 1982-1990; NatFacDr, 1995-2005; Schoeberlein; ZKO

Manzanares (Manzares) **de Cirre**, Manuela, born in 1910, she received a Ph.D. in 1958 from the University of Michigan for *Los estudios árabes en España en el siglo XIX.* She was an emerita professor of Wayne State University, Detroit, Mich. Her other writings include *Arabistas españoles del siglo XIX* (1972). Arabismo, 1992; LC

Manzano Lizandro, Alberto, born in 1955, his writings include *Leonard Cohen* (1978), *Señales para una muerte* (1983), and a selection of *Poemas sufies,* of Jalāl al-Dīn Rūmī (1988). ZKO

Manzano Martos, Rafael, born in 1936 at Cádiz, Spain, he was in 1992 at keeper of the Reales Alcázares, Sevilla. His writings include *La Alhambra; el universo mágico de la Granada islámica* (1992), and he was a joint author of *Tres estudios sobre Sevilla* (1984). Arabismo, 1992; ZKO

Manzano Moreno, Eduardo, born about 1940, he received a doctorate in medieval Islamic history. Throughout the 1990s, he was associated with the Departamento de Historia Medieval, Centro de Estudios Históricos, Consejo Superior de Investigaciones Cientificas, Madrid. His writings include *La frontera de al-Andalus en época de los Omeyas* (1991), *Historia de las sociedades musulmanas en la edad media* (1992), and he edited *Métodos y tendencias actuales en la investigación geográfica y histórica; actas de las Journadas de Madrid* (1988), and *Diario de Jerusalen, 1914-1919,* of Antonio de la Cierva Lewita (1996). Arabismo, 1992, 1994, 1997

Manzano Rodriguez, Miguel Ángel, born about 1950, his writings include *La intervención de los Benimerines en la Península Ibérica* (1991), a work which was originally submitted in 1990 as a doctoral thesis at the Universidad Complutense de Madrid. He edited the *Actas* of the 16th Congress of the Union Européenne des Arabisants et Islamisants (1995). Arabismo, 1992, 1994, 1997

Manzenreiter, Johann, born about 1950, he received a Dr.phil. in 1981 from the Universität Bochum for *Die Bagdadbahn als Beispiel für die Entstehung des Finanzkapitalismus in Europa, 1873-1903.* His writings include *Die Bagdadbahn* (1982). Sezgin; ZKO

Manzoni, Renzo, born in 1852 at Milano, Italy, he was the grandson of the poet Alessandro Renzoni, and early in life became exposed to travel literature at home. In 1876, he made his first encounter with the Orient in Morocco. A year later, he landed at Aden, from where he made three visits to San'ā', each time taking a different route, staying in Arabia from September 1877 to March 1880, an experience which he described in his *El Yemen; tre anni nell'Arabia felice* (1884). He died in Roma in 1918. Henze; IndBiltal (4); Kornrumpf

Ma'oz, Moshe M., born about 1935, he received a D.Phil. in 1965 from Oxford for *The Tanzimat in Syria and Palestine, 1840-61; the impact of the Ottoman reforms.* He was a professor of Islamic and Middle East studies at the Hebrew University of Jerusalem. His writings include *Ottoman reform in Syria and Palestine* (1968), *Studies on Palestine during the Ottoman period* (1975), *Asad, the sphinx of Damascus* (1988), *Syria and Israel, from war to peacemaking* (1995), *Middle Eastern politics and ideas* (1997), *Modern Syria; from Ottoman rule to pivotal role in the Middle East* (1999), and *Middle Eastern minorities and diasporas* (2002). DrBSMES, 1993; MESA Roster of members, 1977-1990; Note; Sluglett; ZKO

Mar Shimun XX, d. 1918, *see* Benjamin Shimun, Mar Shimun

Maracchi Biagiarelli, Berta, born 6 July 1908 at Firenze, she was a chief librarian of the Biblioteca Medicea Laurenziana, Firenze. Her writings include *La Bibliotheca Medicea-Laurenziana nel secolo della sua apertura al pubblico* (1971). Chi è, 1961; IndBiltal (2)

Marais, Benjamin (Barend) Jacobus, born in 1909, he was a theologian, religious leader, and a professor of history of Christianity. His writings include *De kleur-krisis en de Weste* (Johannesburg, 1952), and its translation, *Colour, unsolved problem of the West* (Cape Town, 1952), *Die kerk deur die eeue* (Kaapstad, 1960), and *The two faces of Africa* (1964). AfricanBilnd (1); WhoSAfrica, 1986/87

Maraval-Berthoin, Angèle, Mrs., she was a novelist who collected some of her material in the Sahara. Her writings include *Chants du Hoggar* (1924), *La Légende de Lalla Maghnia d'après la tradition arabe* (1927), *Le Chapelet des vingt et une koubbas* (1930), *Hoggar, chants, fables, légendes* (1954), *La Voix du Hoggar* (1954), and *Le Drac* (1959). AfricanBilnd (1); BN

Maravent, Victor, fl. 20th cent., he received a doctorate in law in 1949 at Paris for *L'Enrichissement sans cause en droit égyptien et dans le projet de code civil égyptien revisé.* He was a lawyer resident in Cairo, and in 1952 a member of the Société Fouad Ier d'économie politique, de statistique et de législation. He was a joint author of *L'Impôt sur les bénéfices des professions non-commerciales en droit égyptien* (Le Caire, 1951). BN; Note about the author

Marazzi, Ugo, born 20th cent., his writings include *Tevārīḫ-i āl-i 'Oṣmān* (1980), *Maday Qara, an Altai epic poem* (1986), and *La Grande Madre in Siberia e Asia centrale; aspetti del principio femminile nella religiosità* (Napoli, 1989). Catalogo dei libri in commercio, 2002

Marc, E., born 19th cent., he was a sometime editor of the *Revue de géographie commerciale de Bordeaux.* Note about the author

Marc, Lucien François, born in 1877 at Rouen, France, he graduated from the military college, Saint-Cyr, and became a colonial officer in Mossi and Gourounsi towns, before he was posted to Timbuctu. He subsequently received a doctorate in 1909 from the Sorbonne for *Le Pays Mossi.* He died in the Great War in the early months of 1914. AfricanBilnd (1); NUC, pre-1956

Marçais, Georges, born 11 March 1876 at Rennes, France, he was a graduate of the École des Beaux-Arts de Paris. He received a doctorate in 1913 from the Sorbonne, Paris, for *Les Arabes en Berbérie du IXe au XIVe siècle.* He was from 1919 to 1944 a professor at the Faculté des Lettres de l'Université d'Alger, a director of its Institut d'Études Orientales, and a member of the Académie des Inscriptions et Belles-Lettres de l'Institut de France. His writings include *L'Art de l'islam* (1946), *L'Art musulman* (1981), and its translation, *El arte musulmán* (1983). He died 20 May 1962. Arabica, 11 (1964), pp. 1-4; Index Islamicus (2)

Marçais, Jean, fl. 20th cent., he was associated with the Service géologique du Maroc, and a joint author of *La géologie marocaines* (1948), *Lexique stratigraphique du Maroc* (1956), and he edited the *Notes* of the Service géologique du Maroc. Note about the author

Marçais, Philippe André, born 16 March 1910 at Alger, the son of William Marçais, he was educated at the École nationale des langues orientales vivantes, Paris, and subsequently taught in Algeria and metropolitan France. His writings include *Textes arabes de Djidjelli* (1954), *Le Parler arabe de Djedjelli* (1956), *Esquisse grammaticale de l'arabe maghrébin* (1977), and he was a joint author of *Au service de l'Algérie nouvelle* (1960). In 1985, a memorial volume was published entitled *Mélanges à la mémoire de Philippe Marçais.* IndexBFr² (1); WhoFr, 1961/62-1981/82|

Marçais, William, born 6 November 1872 at Rennes, France, he received a classical education and studied Semitic languages, particularly Arabic, on his own; he did not collect degrees. In 1898, the Govern-ment of Algeria nominated him *professeur-directeur* of the Médersa de Tlemcen, later to become a director of the Médersa supérieure d'Alger. Above all, he was a scholar of the living Arabic of North Africa and he continued to teach there several weeks every year even after he had been appointed to the École des Hautes Études and the Collège de France in Paris. His writings include *Les*

Monuments arabes de Tlemcen (1903), and he jointly translated with O. Houdas *Les Traditions islamiques* (1903-1914). In 1951, he was honoured by *Mélanges offerts à William Marçais par l'Institut d'Études Is-lamiques de Paris.* He died in Paris on 1 October 1956. BioIn 6 (1); IndexBFr² (4); *Index Islamicus* (6)

Marcas, Z., *pseud.,* he was born Georges Biard d'Aunet on 21 August 1844 at Paris. He was a naval officer who served from 1879 to 1883 successively as a consul at Algeciras, Aden, and Bizerte. His writings include *L'Organisation consulaire française au point de vue de nos intérêts commerciaux* (1883), *La Diplomatie, les consulats et le commerce français* (1890), *La Politique et les affaires* (1918), and *Après la guerre* (1918). BN; IndexBFr² (1)

Marcel, Gabriel Alexandre, born 7 April 1843 at Paris, he trained for some years to be an architect like his father, but his interest in the world of learning made him enter the Bibliothèque impériale on 16 December 1868. He remained there for the rest of his life, becoming successively librarian in 1885, and deputy keeper of the department of geography in 1894. Concurrently he was from 1877 to 1879 a lecturer in commercial geography at the Association philotechnique. Since 31 May 1892 a member of the Comité des Travaux historiques et scientifiques, he had just been nominated on 28 December 1908 vice-president of its Section de géographie, when he suffocated and died a day later on 26 January 1909. He published widely in periodicals. *Bulletin de géographie historique et descriptive,* 24 (1909), pp. 167-68; Curinier, vol. 4 (1903), pp. 146-47

Marcel, Jean Joseph, born 24 November 1776 at Paris, he was a student of Louis M. Langlès and Silvestre de Sacy, and, as director of the Imprimerie nationale, he accompanied the French expedition to Egypt, where he was the editor of the *Courier de l'Égypte, Décade égyptienne* and the *Rapports de l'Institut d'Égypte.* Upon his return to France, he became one of the editors of *Descriptions de l'Egypte.* He was a member of many international learned societies, and a founding member of the Société asiatique. In later life he lost his hearing and sight and was able to complete his *Histoire de Tunis* (1834) only thanks to his wife's devoted assistance. His other writings include *Histoire de l'Egypte* (1834). He died in Paris on 11 March 1854. Egyptology; EnclcUni; Feraud, pp. 37-42; *Journal asiatique,* 5e série, 3 (1954), pp. 553-562; GdeEnc; GDU; Hoefer; IndexBFr² (3); Master (1)

March, Frederic William, born 6 March 1847 at Cheshire, Conn., he was an active missionary in Syria, under the Board of Foreign Missions of the Presbyterian Church in the U.S.A., from 1873 to his honourable retirement with his wife in 1924. He was engaged in field itineration, in teaching, and literary work. He died in Suq al-Gharb, Syria, on 28 September 1935. Note about the author; Shavit

Marchand, Georges, born 19th cent., his writings include *Conte en dialecte marocain* (1906), and *Français, d'abord* (Casablanca, 193-?). BN; NUC, pre-1956

Marchand, Hans, born 1 October 1907 at Krefeld, Germany, he received a Dr. phil. in 1933 from the Universität Köln for *Ernst Hello.* He emigrated to Turkey and was a lecturer in philology at Istanbul until 1953 when he went to Yale University, New Haven, Conn. In 1957, he became a professor of English at the Universität Tübingen. His writings include *The Categories and types of present-day English word-formations* (1960). He died in Genova on 13 December 1978. Kürschner, 1960-1976; Widmann, p. 107

Marchand, Henri, fl. 20th cent., he wrote *Mélanges d'anthropologie et de sociologie nord-africaine* (Alger, 1951), *L'Islam avec nous!* (Alger, 1952), and *Les Mariages franco-musulmans* (Alger, 1954). BN; NUC, pre-1956

Marchand, Henri François, he wrote *Les Sablier d'argent; poèmes* (Alger, 1938). NUC, pre-1956

Marchand, Jean, he was a French general whose writings include *Vérités sur l'Afrique noire* (Paris, 1959). BN

Marchand, Jean Baptiste, born 22 November 1863 at Thoissey (Ain), France, he worked for some years as a clerk in a lawyer's office, before embarking on a splendid military career. A graduate of the military college, Saint-Maixent, he participated in the expansion of French Equatorial Africa to the Nile. He became a heroe when he reached Fashoda on 10 July 1898. His expulsion by Kitchener was the base of the Fashoda incident. He died in 1934. AfricanBiInd (2); Hill; *Hommes et destins,* vol. 9, pp. 307-310; IndexBFr² (3); Master (7); *Qui êtes-vous,* 1924; WhoMilH

Marchand, Pierre *Joseph* Abel, born in 1855, his writings include *Le Commerce de Marseille avec le Levant pendant les croisades* (1890). BN; NUC, pre-1956

Marchat, Henry, born 21 May 1893 at Saint-Jean-d'Angély (Charente-maritime), France, he studied at Paris, where he received degrees in law and political science. He entered the consular service, where he became a specialist in Moroccan affairs. His writings include *La Conférence d'Algésiras* (1959). IndexBFr² (1); NDNC, 1961/62; WhoFr, 1955/56-1981/82|

Marchat, Philippe Raphaël Pierre Henry, born 12 January 1930 at Saint-Jean-d'Angély (Charente-maritime), France, he graduated from the Lycée Gouraud, Rabat, and received degrees in law and political science. After post-graduate study at Cambridge and London, he entered the French government service as an *inspecteur des finances*, later serving some years overseas. His writings include *L'Orga-nisation du crédit au Sénégal* (1962), and *L'Économie mixte* (1971). IndexBFr² (1); WhoFr, 1971/72-2005/2006

von **Marchesetti**, Carlo, born 17 January 1850 at Triest, Austria, he studied medicine at the Universität Wien and briefly practised his profession. He subsequently pursued an interest in botany. From 1875 to 1876 he travelled in the East Indies. Upon his return, he became a director of the Museo di storia naturale di Trieste. Since 1903 he was a director of the botanical gardens in the city. Concurrently he served from 1901 to 1921 as president of the Società adriatica di scienze naturali. He died in Trieste on 1 April 1926. IndBiltal (2); ÖBL

Marchet, Gustav, born 29 March 1846 at Baden, Austria, he studied law and political science at the Universität Wien, where he subsequently became a professor of political economy and forest legis-lation at a college of earth sciences in Wien. He was a sometime minister of culture and education in the Austrian government. His writings include *Studien über die Entwicklung der Verwaltungslehre in Deutschland* (1885). He died in Schlackenwerth (Ostrov), Bohemia, on 27 April 1916. DtBE; ÖBL

Marchionini, Alfred, born 12 January 1899 at Königsberg, Germany, he was a professor of derma-tology at the university hospital in Freiburg im Breisgau, from 1934 to 1938, when he was successively appointed head of the dermatological section at the Ankara Nümune Hastanesi and a professor at the newly established Ankara Tıp Fakültesi. He returned in 1949 to Germany where he served as a professor for eighteen months at Hamburg before he moved in the autumn of 1950 to München, where he died on 6 April 1965. BioHbDtE; DtBE; Kürschner, 1950-1961; Wer ist's, 1935; Widmann, pp. 154, 275

Marcillac, Paul, born about 1855, he was associated with the Service technique des Télégraphes, Marseille, and privately pursued an interest in meteorology and assisted in the technical operations of the Société de géographie et d'études coloniales de Marseille. He was an officer of the Nicham Iftikar, and a knight of the Italian Crown. His writings include *La Lutte contre la grêle et la foudre* (Paris, 1919). He died in Montélimar on 27 November 1918. Bulletin of the Société de géographie et d'études coloniales de Marseille, 42 (1918/19), p. 135

Marco Rodríguez, María del Rosario, born 20th cent., her writings include *Catálogo de las armas del fuego* (Madrid, 1980), and *El verbo español* (Madrid, 1984).

Marcos Marín, Francisco, born 20 June 1946 at Madrid, he graduated at Granada and received his doctorate at Madrid. He successively became a professor of Romance languages at the universities of Madrid, Montréal, Zaragoza, Valladolid, and again the Universidad Autónoma de Madrid. His writings include *Poesía narrativa árabe y épica hispánica* (1971), *El comentario filológico con apoyo informático* (1996), and he was a joint author of *Textos para la historia del Proximo Oriente antiguo* (1980). WhoWor, 1989/90, 1991/92

Marcoux, Alain, born 20th cent., he was associated with the Food and Agriculture Organization of the United Nations. His writings include *Planification agricole, population et société* (1985), its translation, *Population, society, and agricultural planning* (1987), and he was a joint author of *Demographic change in coastal fishing communities and its implications for the coastal environment* (2000).

Marcum, John Arthur, born 31 August 1927 at San Jose, Calif., he was educated at Stanford Uni-versity, Palo Alto, Calif., and the Sorbonne, Paris. He received his Ph.D. in 1955 from Stanford for *French North Africa in the Atlanic community*. He successively became a professor of political science at Lincoln University, Pa., and Merrill College, University of California. His writings include *The Angolan revolution* (1969), and *Education, race, and social change in South Africa* (1982). AmM&WSc, 1973 S, 1978 S; ConAu, 25-28, new rev., 14; Selim; Unesco

Marcus, Abraham, born in 1948, he received a Ph.D. in 1979 from Columbia University, New York, for *People and property in eighteenth-century Aleppo*. In the 1980s he was appointed a professor in the Department of History, University of Texas at Austin, a post which he still held in 2005. In 2003, he accepted an invitation to serve as one of the editors of the third edition of the *Encyclopedia of Islam*. His writings include *The Middle East on the eve of modernity; Aleppo in the eighteenth century* (1989). Center for Middle Eastern Studies newsletter (Austin), 29 (2002/3), p. 5; MESA Roser of members, 1990; NatFacDr, 1989-2005; Selim³

Marcus, Alfred, born about 1874, he received a Dr.jur. in 1899 from the Universität Breslau for *Die Wahlschuld des Bürgerlichen Gesetzbuches für das Deutsche Reich*. His other writings include *Die wirtschaftliche Krise der deutschen Juden; soziologische Untersuchungen* (1931). GV

Marcus, Harold Golden, born 8 April 1936 at Worcester, Mass., he graduated in 1958 from Clark University, Worcester, Mass., and received his Ph.D. in 1964 from Boston University. After serving as a visiting professor of history for two years at Addis Ababa, he successively became a professor at Howard University, Washington, D.C., and Michigan State University, East Lansing. His writings include *A Modern history of Ethiopia and the Horn of Africa; a select and annotated bibliography* (1972), *Ethiopia, Great Britain, and the United States* (1983), *Haile Selassie* (1987), *A History of Ethiopia* (1994), and *The Life and times of Menelik II* (1995). ConAu, 37-40; DrAS, 1969 H, 1974 H, 1978 H, 1982 H; WrDr, 1976/78-2003

Marcus, Margaret, 1934- *see* Maryam Jameela

Marcus, Margaret Fairbanks, fl. 20th cent., she was associated with the Cleveland Museum of Art. Her writings include *Flower painting of the great masters* (1954), and its translation, *Tableaux de fleurs par les grands maîtres* (1957). ZKO

Marcus, Ralph, born 17 August 1900 at San Francisco, he received his Ph.D. in 1927 from Columbia University, N.Y.C., for *Law in the Apocrypha*. He was a professor of Semitic philology in the Jewish Institute of Religion, from 1927 to 1943, when he went to the University of Chicago to teach Hellenistic culture until his death on 25 December 1956. He was a member of the Academy of Jewish Research; at various times an editor of the *Journal of Biblical literature; Classical philology; Review of religion; Jewish social studies*. During 1954-55 he was a visiting professor in the Universität Frankfurt am Main, directing a joint seminar of the universities of Frankfurt and Chicago. BioIn, 4 (3); CnDiAmJBi; *Journal of Near Eastern studies*, 16 (1957), pp. 143-44; WhAm, 3

Marcy, Georges, born 21 March 1905 at Granville (Manche), France, he arrived in 1928 at Rabat as a research fellow of the Institut des hautes études marocaines. Two years later, he there became a lecturer, and in 1934, a *directeur d'études* of Moroccan sociology. Since 1936, he taught Berber languages and culture, and since 1937, North African sociology and ethnography. His writings include *Les Inscrip-tions libyques bilingues de l'Afrique du nord* (Paris, 1936), and *Le Droit coutumier zemmoûr* (Paris, 1949). He died on 21 March 1946. Hespéris, 34 (1947), pp. 1-3; *IBLA*, 10 (1947), pp. 79-87; *Index Islamicus* (1); *Isis*, 41 (1950), p. 56

Mardek, Helmut, born 4 April 1939 at Buchenhain/Großwartenberg, Germany, he studied law at Leipzig, where he received a Dr.phil. in 1966 for a thesis on the constitutional foundation of Ghana entiled *Die politischen und verfassungsrechtlichen Grund-lagen des ghanesischen Staates, 1960-1965*; he there also gained a Dr.habil. in 1970. He spent 1961-1962 in Moscow, and 1965-1966 in Ghana. In 1962, he became an academic assistant in the Afrika-Institut, Universität Leipzig. Until about 1992 he was a professor of international relations, with special reference to anti-imperialist liberation movements and class struggle, at Hochschule für Recht und Verwaltung, Potsdam-Babelsberg. His tenure was probably terminated after German re-unification. His writings include *Der Nahostkonflikt; Ursachen und Lösungswege* (1977), *Der Nahostkonflikt, Gefahr für den Weltfrieden; Dokumente* (1987), and *Regional Konflikte und Ihre politische Regelung* (1990). Kürschner, 1992|; Thesis

Marden, Henry, born 9 December 1837 at New Boston, N.H., and united with the Presbyterian Church, New Boston, in 1857. He graduated in 1862 from Dartmouth College, Hanover, N.H., from Andover Theological Seminary, in 1869, and was ordained on 2 September 1869 at Francetown, N.H. He was married to Mary L. Christy on 10 September 1869, and the following day they sailed for Turkey, where he was first assigned to Aintab (Gaziantep) and then to Maraş. On 17 April 1890, he set out on his long ovedue furlough after twelve years, during the last year of which he had been absent from the mission for 189 days, and travelled over 1,500 miles on horseback, visiting forty-three towns. The couple sailed from Mersin via Smyrna to Athens, where he succumbed to a malignant form of typhus on 13 May 1890. *Missionary herald*, 86 (1890), pp. 270-271; Shavit

Mardersteig, Hans (Giovanni) M., he was born on 8 January 1892 at Weimar, Germany, the son of a lawyer. In obedience to his father's wishes he studied law and received a Dr.jur. in 1915. He subsequently pursued an interest in fine art, first in exhibitions and later in publishing. In 1922, he established the private press, Officina Badoni in Montagnola near Lugano. His writings include *Ein Leben den Büchern gewidmet* (1968), *Liberale ritrovato nell'Esopo Veronese del 1479* (1973), and he edited *The Making of a book at the Officina Bodoni* (Verona, 1973). He was the greatest scholar-printer of modern times, whose researches into Renaissance printing and lettering were published in magnificent books, printed at his Officina Bodoni in hand-set types on a hand press. He died in Verona on 27 December 1977. Sebastian Carter, *Twentieth century type designers* (1987), pp. 96-100; DtBE; Master (4); NDB

Mardonov, Tadzhiddin Nuriddinovich, born 4 December 1947 in Tajikistan, he graduated in 1972 from the Faculty of Oriental Languages, Tashkent State University, and received his first degree in 1986 for *Возникновение и развитие традиции двуязычия в персидско-таджикской поэзии IX-X вв.*

Associated with the Oriental Institute, Tajik Academy of Sciences since 1973, he spent 1979-1983 in Iraq. His writings include *МирзоТурсунзода ва чахони араб* (1990). Miliband²; OSK

Mardrus, Joseph Charles Victor, born in 1868 at Cairo, he received his early education at Cairo and went for medical studies to Paris. Later he went on offfical missions to the Orient and Morocco. For many years he had been a picturesque figure of St.-Germain-de-Près. He married the French novelist Lucie Delarue. He is best remembered for his translation of the *Arabian nights, Mille nuits et une nuit*, 1898-1904 in 16 vols. (much more colourful than that of Antoine Galland), *La Reine de Saba* (Paris, 1918), and *Le Koran qui est la guidance et le différenciateur* (1926). He died in 1949. BioIn, 2 (1); BN; NYT, 28 March 1949, p. 21., col. 1; OxFr

Maréchal, Joseph Marie François, born 1 July 1878 at Charleroi, Belgium, he was educated at the local Collège du Sacré-Cœur, where he graduated first class, despite persistant megrim from which he suffered throughout his life. In 1895, he started his novitiate in the Compagnie de Jésus, and since 1898, he spent three years studying scholastic philosophy. Under the influence of his superiors, he turned to natural sciences, leading to a doctorate in 1905 in biology from the Institut Carnoy, Université de Louvain, to which several years of theology were added. An ordained priest since 1908, he spent from 1909 to 1910 at Linz, Austria. Since 1912, he taught biology and experimental psychology at Louvain. His writings include *Le Point de départ de la métaphysique* (1922), its translation, *El Punto de partida de la metafisica* (1957), *Études sur la psychologie des mystiques* (1924-37), and *Studies in the psychology of mystics* (1927). *Mélanges Joseph Maréchal* was published in 1950. BiBenelux² (2); NBN, vol. 3 (1994), pp. 255-56

Maréchaux, Pascal, born 20th cent., he was the author of the coffee-table books, *Villages d'Arabie heureuse* (1979), its translations, *Arabia felix; the Yemen and its people* (1980), and *Jemen; Bilder aus dem Weihrauchland* (1980), and *Lune d'Arabie* (1987). ZKO

Marek, Jan, born 31 August 1931 at Praha, Czechoslovakia, he studied Hindi and Urdu under Jan Rypka at Praha, and did post-graduate study at Delhi and Aligarh. He received a Dr.phil. in 1960 from Universita Karlova, Praha, with a thesis on Muhammad Iqbal; he there also gained a Dr.habil. in 1992. His writings include *Po stopách sultánů a rádžů* (Praha, 1973), its translation, *По следам султанов и раджей* (Moscow, 1987), and he was a joint author of *Dvarát Pákistán* (1964), and its translations, *Два Пакистана* (Moscow, 1966), *Zweimal Pakistan* (Leipzig, 1966). Filipsky; OSK

Marengo, M., born 19th cent., he was in 1881 a Spanish vice-consul in Trebizond. Kornrumpf ; Note about the author

Marès, Paul, Dr., born 19th cent., his writings include *L'Agriculture en Algérie* (Alger, 1889), and he was a joint author of *Catalogue raisonné des plantes vasculaires des Îles Baléares* (Paris, 1880). *Bulletin de la Société de géographie d'Alger*, 5 (1900), p. 219

Marès, Roger, born 19th cent., he grew up in Algeria and studied at the Institut agronomique, Paris. He subsequently returned to Algeria and served eighteen months as an inspector of agriculture in the Régence de Tunisie, a post which he resigned in order to become a *colon*. At the end of his life, he was a professor in the Département d'agriculture d'Alger. From 1891 to 1911, he was an editor of the *Bulletin agricole de l'Algérie et de la Tunisie*. He was a joint author of *L'Algérie agricole en 1906* (1906). His trace is lost after an article in 1912. Note about the author

Maretić, Tomislav, born 13 December 1854 at Virovitica, Croatia, he studied classical and Slavic philology at the universities of Zagreb and Leipzig, and subsequently taught his subject at Zagreb. His writings include *Slavini u davnini* (1889), and *Naša narodna epika* (Zagreb, 1909). He died in Zagreb on 15 January 1938. EncLZ; HL

Maretin, IUriĭ Vasil'evich, born 3 March 1931 at Kronshtadt, Russia, he graduated in 1955 from the Oriental Faculty, Leningrad, and received his first degree in 1962 for a monograph. He was from 1955 to 1980 associated with the Institute of Ethnography, Soviet Academy of Sciences, and subsequently served with the State Public Library, Leningrad. His writings include the bibliographies *Бирма* (1983), *Вьет-нам* (1983), and *Индонезия* (1987). He died 4 August 1990. Miliband; Miliband²; OSK

Marey-Monge, Guillaume Stanislas, born 19 February 1796 at Nuits (Côte-d'Or), France, he graduated in 1814 from the École polytechnique and went to Algeria at the time of its conquest. On account of his proficiency in Arabic as well as his interest in the indigenous population, he played an important role in native politics. He was an officier in the Sphahis and resigned with the rank of general. He published a report of his *Éxpédition de Laghouat* (1845). After his military career he became a senator. He died in 1863. Hoefer; IndexBFr² (2); Vapereau

Marfil García, Mariano, born in 1883, he was a lawyer, soldier, politician, and from 1918 to 1933 an editor-in-chief of the journal *La Época*, Madrid. He died in 1939. IndiceE³ (1)

Margadant, Christiaan Willem, born 19th cent., his writings on Dutch East Indian law include *Het regeeringsreglement van Nederlandsch-Indië* (Batavia, 1894-97), and *Verklaring van de Nederlandsch-Indische strafwetboeken* (Batavia, 1895). NUC, pre-1956

Margalioth, George, 1853-1924 *see* Margoliouth, George

Mărgăn, Kirăi, 1912-1984 *see* Kirei Mĕrgĕn

Margat, Jean François, born 11 November 1924 at Paris, he was from 1947 to 1960 associated with the Centre d'études hydrogéologiques, Rabat, and later entered the Minstère de l'Environnement. His writings include *Bibliographie hydrogéologique du Maroc* (Rabat, 1958), and *Les Eaux salées au Maroc* (Rabat, 1961), and he was a joint author of *Dictionnaire français d'hydrogéologie* (1977). WhoWor, 1989/90

de **Margerie**, Marie Pierre Martin *Emmanuel* Jacquin, born in 1862, he held no academic degree, even of the lowest rank, and occupied no chair of learning or other official position to speak of, but he was an outstanding figure in geological and geographical circles. For three-quarters of a century he unselfishly placed his immense reading, infallible memory, and untiring energy at the service of his fellow workers and of science in general. His writings include *L'Œuvre de Sven Hedin et l'orographie du Tibet* (Paris, 1929), and *Notice sur les traces scientifiques de M. Emm. de Margerie* (Macon, 1938). But his masterpiece was the French edition of Eduard Suess' *Das Antlitz der Erde* in its new garb, *La Face de la terre*, in three large volumes (1897-1918). He was a member of the Royal Society, London. He died on 21 December 1953. BioIn, 4, 15; Dickinson; *Geographical review*, 44 (1954), pp. 600-602

Margold, Stella K., born about 1910 in New York, she graduated in 1931 from the University of Michigan, gained an M.A., and continued with post-graduate study in the U.S.A. and U.K. She was a specialist on foreign export matters and later covered international affairs as a journalist for various U.S. periodicals. She was a member of the Overseas Press Club. ConAu, 81-84; IntAu&W, 1976, 1977

Margoliouth (Margalioth), David Samuel, born 17 October 1858 at London, he was elected in 1881 a fellow of New College, Oxford, and in 1889 succeeded to the Laudian Professorship of Arabic at Oxford. In this position, under obsolete statutes, he was able to block all advancement at Oxford for forty-eight years until forced to retire at the age of seventy-nine. His name is connected - though by no means exclusively - with Arabic and Islamic studies, in which he was professionally interested, and to every branch of which he made notable contributions. His writings include *Mohammed* (1905), *Early development of Mohammedanism* (1914), and *Letters of Abu'l-'Ala'* (1898). In 1935, he was awarded the Sir Richard Burton Medal of the Royal Asiatic Society. He died in London on 23 March 1940. DNB; *En terre d'islam*, 16 (1941), pp. 126-127; Fück, 273-278; *Index Islamicus* (2); *Who was who*, 3; Wininger

Margoliouth (Margalioth), George, born 1853 at Wilkowicki, Poland, he studied Semitic subjects in the U.K. and Germany and was ordained in 1881. A Semitic scholar, he entered the British Library, London, in 1891. His writings include *Catalogue of the Hebrew and Samaritan manuscripts in the British Museum* (1899-1905). He died in 1924. BritInd (1); Who, 1905-1923; *Who was who*, 2; Wininger

Margos, Ara, born 20th cent., her writings include *Чудната кеменна гора* (Varna, 1960), *Текето "Ак Язълъ баба"* (Tolbykhin, 1971), *Побитите камъни* (Varna, 1973), and *Провадия* (Sofia, 1981). OSK

Margulan (Марғұлан), Al'keĭ (Әлкей) Khakanovich (Хакан ұлы), born in 1904, he graduated in 1929 from the Faculty of Philology, Leningrad Oriental Institute, and received his first degree in 1943 for *Историческое значение ярлыков и пайцзе*, and a doctorate in 1946 for *Эпические сказаний казахского народа*. He became a director of the Institute of History, Archaeology and Ethnography, Kazakh Academy of Sciences. He edited *Культура и быт казахского колхозного аула* (1967). He died on 12 January 1985. IntDcAn; KazakSE, vol. 7, pp. 459-60; Kazakhkaia, vol. 3; Miliband[2]

Marguliés, Alfons, born 17 July 1897 at Prag, Bohemia, he received a Dr.phil. in 1922 from the Universität Königsberg for *Die Verba reflexiva in den slavischen Sprachen*. He became a lecturer in Slavic philology at the Universität München. His writings on Slavic social history include *Volklieder der Serben* (1925), *Der alt-kirchenslavische Codex Suprasliensis* (1927), and *Entwicklungsphasen der südslavischen Kulturen* (1930). Kürschner, 1926-1928/29|

Margvelashvili, Tinatina Semenovna, born 12 December 1924 at Tiflis, Georgia, she graduated in 1946 from the Faculty of Philology, Moscow State University, and received her first degree in 1952 for *Языковые особенности арабоязычных памятников Северного Кавказа*. She was since 1949 associated with Tiflis State University, and since 1957 as a lecturer. She published in Georgian on Persian and Arabic philology as well as on the history of Daghestan and Georgia. Miliband; Miliband[2]

Marial, Waille, born 19th cent. *see* Waille-Marial, Alexandre

Marian, Iulia, born 20th cent., her writings include *Antologie de texte în limba amhară* (Bucureşti, 1974).

Mariani, Vittorio Giulio, born 19th cent., his writings include *Il fato di Tripoli e il fato latino* (Roma, 1912), and *Condottieri italiani in Germania* (Milano, 1941). Firenze

Marie, René, fl. 1954-1964, he was a French *commandant*, and a sometime member of the Centre de Hautes Études d'Administration Musulmane, Paris. Note about the author

Marie de Saint Elie, Anastase, 1866-1947 *see* Anastas Mari, al-Karmili

de **Marignolli** (Marignola), Giovanni (Johannes), born in 1297 at Firenze, Italy, he was a notable traveller to the Far East, and in 1354 became a bishop of Bisignano. His writings include *Chronicon reverendissimi Joannis dicti de Marignolis* (Pragæ, 1764), and *Reise ins Morgenland vom Jahre 1339-1353*, aus dem Lateinischen von Johann G. Meinert (Prag, 1820). He died in Praha in 1359. EncBrit; EncItaliana; IndBiltal (8); Martinek; Sezgin

de **Marigny**, François Augier, born about 1690, he became a clergyman and soon received a canonry. He led a modest life, given to study, particularly Semitic languages. In his writings he seems to have borrowed freely from B. d'Herbelot. His writings include *Histoire des Arabes sous le gouvernement des califes* (1750), its translations, *Geschichte der Araber* (1750), *Storia degli Arabi* (1753-4), *The History of the Arabians under the government of the caliphs* (1758), and *Histoire des révolutions de l'empire arabe* (1750-52). He died in Paris on 9 October 1762. Hoefer; IndexBFr² (2); Master (1)

Marill, Alain, born 20th cent., he gained a doctorate in political science, and he was in 1965 an assistant at the Faculté de droit et des sciences économiques, Université de Paris. He was a joint author of *Essais sur l'économie de l'Algérie nouvelle* (1965). Note

Marín, F. M., an author who wrote *El comentario filológico con apoyo informático* (Madrid, 1996). LC

Marin, Louis, born in 1871 at Faulx-Saint-Pierre (Meurthe-et-Moselle), France, he graduated from the École des sciences politiques, Paris, and in 1905 entered politics as a *député*; thereafter he held various ministerial posts beginning in 1924. As minister of state in 1940, when the Germans invaded France, he was one of the small group of French leaders who argued unsuccessfully for continuation of the war against Germany, and in 1944 escaped to Britain in disguise. After the war, he was re-elected twice. He was regarded as a representative French scholar-statesman. He prepared a report on Afghanistan for the Commission des Finances de la Chambre des Députés. His other writings include *Le Partage équitable des charges de la guerre* (1925), its translation, *The Equitable division of the war charges* (1925), *Les Accords de Locarno* (1926), and *Frontières d'Asie* (1993). He died in 1960. Fernande Marin wrote *Louis Marin, 1871-1960, homme d'état, philosophe et savant* (1973). IndexBFr² (2); *Hommes et destins*, vol. 2, pp. 511-521; WhoFr, 1953/54-1959/60

Marín Guzmán, Roberto, born about 1945, he was a professor of Middle Eastern history at the University of Costa Rico, who in 2003 served as a visiting Fulbright scholar at the Center for Middle Eastern Studies in the University of Texas at Austin. His writings include *La guerra civil en el Líbano* (1985), *El Islam; ideología e historia* (1986), and *El Islam; religion y politica; interpretación mesiánica del movimiento mahdista sudanés* (1986). Note about the author; ZKO

Marín Morales, José Alberto, born 4 March 1924 at Madrid, he studied law at Valladolid and Madrid and subsequently entered the legal profession. In 1965, he was a municipal judge in Yecla, but he was also a novelist and essayist. His writings include *Carril de un cuerpo* (Barcelona, 1968), and *Gota a gota* (Barcelona, 1972). IndiceE³ (2)

Marín Niño, Manuela, born in 1945 at Madrid, she received a doctorate in Semitic philology, specializing in social and cultural history of al-Andalus. She was a sometime chairman of the Departamento de Estudios Árabes at an unidentified Institute in Madrid. She was an active member of the Middle East Libraries Committee (Iternational). Her writings include *Estudios onomástico-biográficos de Al-Andalus* (1988-90), and *Individuo y sociedad en al-Andalus* (1992). She was a joint editor of *The Legacy of Muslim Spain* (1992) as well as chief consultant to its second edition in 1994, *Kanz al-fawa'id fi tanwi' al-mawa'id* (1993), *La alimentación en las culturas islámicas* (1994), *The Formation of al-Andalus* (1998), and *Writing the feminine; women in Arab sources* (2002). LC; Private; Publisher's catalogue

Mariñas Otevo, Luis, born 9 January 1928 at Mugardas (La Coruña), Spain, he gained a degree in law as well as a doctorate in political science and economics. He entered government service and later joined the consular service. His writings include *Las constituciones de Guatemala* (1958), *La herencia del 98* (1967), and *La literatura filipina en castellano* (1974). He died in 1968. IndiceE³ (2); Note about the author; WhoSpain, 1963

Marinelli, Olinto, born 11 February 1874 at Udine, Italy, he was a geographer and a lecturer at Firenze, who visited Chinese Turkestan as well as the countries of the eastern Mediterranean. His writings include *Atlante scolastico de geografia moderna* (Milano, 1912), and he edited *La Cirenaica; geografica, economica, politica* (Milano, 1923). He died in Firenze in 1926. IndBiltal (4)

Marinescu, Beatrice, born 20th cent., she was a Romanian historian whose writings include *Bucureşti şi eporea inndependenţei, 1887-1978* (Bucureşti, 1978), *Romanian-British political relations, 1848-1877* (1983), and she was a joint author of *Bucureştii în anii primului război mondial, 1914-1918* (1993), and *Instaurarea totalitarismului comunist în România* (Bucureşti, 1995). OSK

Marinescu (Marinesco), Constantin, born in 1891 at Şerbăneşti-Poduri, he was a professor successively at Cluj and Bucureşti, later in life also at Paris. His writings include *La Politique orientale d'Alfonso V d'Aragon* (1994), and he edited *Mélanges d'histoire générale* (1927). WhoRom

Marinetto Sánchez, Purificación, born 20th cent., he obtained a doctorate in Islamic art. In 1992, he was head of the Departamento de Conservación at the Museo Nacional de Arte Hispanomusulman, Granada. His writings include *Los capiteles del Palacio de los Leones en la Alhambra* (1996). Arabismo, 1992

Marinho, João Augusto, born 20th cent., his writings include *Apontamentos sobre selos da India Portuguesa* (Luanda, 1964), *Apontamento sobre selos de Angola e Congo* (Luanda, 1965), and *Três para a história postal da India Portuguesa* (Luanda, 1973).

Marinov, Vasil Aleksandrov, born in 1907, he was a Bulgarian anthropologist whose writings include Делиорманъ, южна частъ; областно географско изучване (Sofia, 1941), Принос към изучаванего на бита и културата на турците и гагаузите в Североизточна България (1956), Принос към изучаването на произхода, бита и културата на Каракачаните в България (1964), and Гердово (Sofia, 1970). Master (1); OSK

Mariotti, André Kanüth Lindorff Louis, *capitain*, born 19th cent., his writings include *Notes sur le service dans les états-majors en campagne* (1879), *Du Droit des gens en temps de guerre* (1883), and *Canons français et canons allemands* (1886). BN; NUC, pre-1956

Mariotti, Louis and Luigi, 1810-1895, pseud. *see* Gallenga, Antonio Carlo Napoleone

Maris, Maurice, his writings include *La Réforme municipale* (Paris, 1921). BN

Marissal, Jacques, born 20th cent., he was a professor at the École normale supérieure, Université de Burundi. His writings include *Le Burundi à la fin du XIX siècle* (1977).

Mariti, Giovanni, born 4 November 1736 at Firenze, Italy, he was a merchant at Livorno, before he became a vice-chancellor at the British Consulate in Cyprus. In this capacity he travelled in Syria, Palestine and Egypt. His writings include *Viaggi per l'isola di Cipro, e per la Soría e Palestina, 1760 al 1768* (1769-1770), its translations, *Travels through Cyprus, Syria, and Palestine* (1792), *Travels in the Island of Cyprus* (1971), *Istoria della guerra accesa nella Soría l'anno dalle armi de Aly-Bey dell'Egitto* (1772), *Cronologia de' Re Latine di Gerusalemme* (1784), and *Istoria dello stato presente della città di Geru-salemme* (1790). He died in Firenze on 13 September 1806. EncicUni; GdeEnc; Master (1)

Mariwalla, C. L., fl. 20th cent., he was a sometime professor of history at the D. J. Sind College, Karachi. His writings include *Ancient Sind* (1940), *Essays on British policy towards Sind up to the first Afghan War, 1839* (c1947, 1982), *World history* (1950-51), and *When the storm came... 1857, Sind* (Bombay, 1957). Note about the author; ZKO

Mark, Peter Allen, born in 1948, he received a Ph.D. in 1976 from Yale University, New Haven, Conn., for *Economic and religious change among the Diola of Boulouf (Casamance), 1890-1940; trade, cash cropping and Islam in southwestern Senegal*. His writings include *Africans in European eyes in 14th and 15th century Europe* (1974), *A Cultural, economic and religious history of the Basse Casamance since 1500* (1985), and *The Wild bull and the sacred forest: form, meaning and change in Sene-gambian initiation masks* (1992). LC

Markevich, Arseneĭ Ivanovich, born in 1855, his writings include Опыть указателя сочиненій, касающихся Крыма и Таврической губерніи вообще (Simferopol, 1894), Таврическая губерния во времия крымской воины (Simferopol, 1905), and he edited Путеводитель по Крыму, 2d ed., rev. and enl. (Simferopol, 1925). His trace is lost after a publication in 1928. NYPL; OSK

Markgraf, Carl August *Hermann*, born 30 May 1838 at Cottbus, Germany, he was a local historian and a director of the public library and the city archives, Breslau, Silesia. His writings include *Annales Glogovienses bis zum Jahre 1493 nebst urkundlichen Beilagen* (1877), *Breslauer Studien* (1901),

Kleine Schriften zur Geschichte Schlesiens und Breslaus (Breslau, 1915). He died in Breslau on 12 January 1906. BioJahr, 11 (1908), Totenliste, cols. 42*-43*; DtBiInd (2)

Markham, Sir Clements Robert, born in 1830 at Stillingfield, Yorkshire, he served in the Royal Navy from 1844 to 1852 and subsequently spent twenty years with the India Office. He was a comparative and historical geographer whose writings include *Travels in Peru and India* (1862), *A General sketch of the history of Persia* (1874), and its Persian translation in 1985. He died in London on 30 January 1916. BbD; Buckland; DcScB; DNB; Embacher; Henze; IndianBiInd (2); Master (10); Riddick; *Who was who*, 2

Márki, Sándor (Alexander), born 27 March 1853 at Kétegyháza, Hungary, he studied philosophy, and in 1877 he was appointed a teacher at the secondary school in Arad, Hungary. Transferred in 1886 to Budapest, he there gained a Dr.habil. in 1888 and became a lecturer in history. In 1892, he was appointed a professor at Kolozsvár University. He later returned to Budapest in the same capacity. His writings include *II. Rákóczi Ferencz* (1907-10), *Rákóczi adriai tervei* (1915), *Magyar középkor* (1917), and *A M. Kir. Ferencz József-Tudományegyetem története* (1922). He died in Gödöllő on 1 July 1925. GeistigeUng; Magyar

Makides, Kyriacos Costa, born 19 November 1942 at Nicosia, he received a Ph.D. in 1970 from Wayne State University, Detroit, for *The Greek unification movement in Cyprus*. He was since 1972 a professor of sociology at the University of Maine, Orono, a post which he still held in 2004. His writings include *The Rise and fall of the Cyprus Republic* (1977), *Retirement in industrialized societies* (1987), *Aging & ethnicity* (1987), and *Aging, stress and health* (1989). AmM&WSc, 1973 S, 1978 S; ConAu, 81-84; NatFacDr, 1995-2004

Markish, David Peretsovich, born 24 September 1938 at Moscow, he graduated in 1962 at Moscow and subsequently went to Israel. He was a writer and translator, and a member of P.E.N. international. ConAu, 69-72; Master (1); WhoIsrael, 1992/93-2001; WhoWor, 1982/83

Markoff, Alexis de, 1858-1920 *see* Markov, Alekseï Konstantinovich

Markoff, Irene Judyth, born 17 April 1944, she received a Ph.D. in 1986 from the University of Washington, Seattle, for *Musical theory, performance, and the contemporary bağlama specialist in Turkey*. She was in 1990 a lecturer in ethnomusicology at her alma mater. MESA *Roster of members*, 1990

Markon, Isaak Dow Ber, born in 1875 at Rybinsk-on-Volga, he studied law and Oriental languages at St. Petersburg, and subsequently entered the Russian public service. He went to Germany in 1926, to the Netherlands in 1938, and to the U.K. in 1940. His writings include *Die Bennenung der Türkei in der jüdischen Literatur* (Berlin, 1926). He died in London in 1949. BiHbDtE; EncJud; JüdLex; Wininger

Markov (Markoff), Alekseï Konstantinovich, born in 1858, he graduated from the École nationale spéciale des langues orientales vivantes, Paris, and the Oriental Faculty, St. Petersburg. He was from 1886 to his death in 1920 a keeper of Oriental numismatics at the Hermitage Museum. His writings include *Les Monnaies des rois parthes* (1877), *Catalogue des monnaies arsacides, subarsacides, sassanides, dabweihides, ainsi que des pièces frappées par les Ispehbeds arabes du Tabaristan* (1889), *Registre général des Monnaies orientales de l'Institut des langues orientales du ministère des Affaires étrangères* (1891), *Неизданныя арсакидскія монеты* (1892), *Инвентарный каталогъ мусульманскихъ монетихъ императорскаго Эрмитажа* (1896-1904), and *Каталогъ джелаиридскихъ монетъ* (1897). BN; EnSlovar; Krachkovskiï; Wieczynski

Markov, Gennadiï Evgen'evich, born 21 June 1923 at Moscow, he graduated in 1951 from the Faculty of History, Moscow State University, received his first degree in 1954 for *История формирования северных туркмен*, and his doctorate in 1968 for *Кочевники Азии*. Since 1954 he was associated with the Faculty of History, Moscow. His writings include *Этнография* (1982), *Скотовот у туркмен в XIX- начале XX в.* (1995), and he was joint author of *Кочевники Азии* (1976). Miliband²; Schoeberlein

Markov, Walter Mulec, born 5 October 1909 at Graz, Austria, he studied at the universities of Leipzig, Köln, Berlin, Hamburg and Bonn, where he received a Dr.phil. in 1934 for *Serbien zwischen Österreich und Rußland, 1897-1908*. A member of the Communist Party, he was sentenced to a long prison term, which he served until liberated after the war in 1945. In 1946, he went to Leipzig, where he received a Dr.habil. in 1947 and there taught from 1949 to his retirement in 1974. He was an important scholar of revolutions as well as liberation movements in the Third World. His writings include *Grand Empire; Sitten und Unsitten der Napoleonzeit* (1984), its translation, *Grand Empire; virtue and vice in the Napoleonic era* (1990), *Grundzüge der Balkandiplomatie* (1999), he was a joint author of *Geschichte der Türken von den Anfängen bis zur Gegenwart* (1978), and he edited *Kolonialismus und Neokolonialismus in Nordafrika und Nahost* (Berlin, 1964), and *Nordafrika und Nahost im Kampf für nationale und soziale Befreiung* (Berlin, 1968). He died in Leipzig on 3 July 1993. DtBE; GV; Kürschner, 1992; WhoSocC, 1978

Marková, Dagmar, born 12 August 1935 at Gablenz an der Neiße, Germany, she studied Indian subjects, particularly Hindi and Urdu, at Universita Karlova, Praha, and Humboldt-Universität, Berlin. She became associated with the Institut für Orientforschung, Akademie der Wissenschaften, Berlin. Her writings include *Die Frau im modernen Hindi-Roman nach 1947* (1970); and, jointly with Mohamed Ahmed Ansari, *Chrestomathie der Urdu-Prosa des 19. und 20. Jahrhunderts* (1965), and *Gesprächsbuch Deutsch-Hindi* (1981); she was also a joint author of *Variace na Korán; Islám v diaspore* (Praha, 1999); and she edited *Chrestomathie der Hindi-Prosa des 20. Jahrhunderts* (1967). Filipsky; OSK

Marková, Ol'ga Petrovna, fl. 20th cent., she was associated with the Institute of History, Soviet Academy of Sciences. Her writings include *Восстанние в Кахетии 1812 г.* (1951), and *Россия, Заекавказье и международные отношения в XVIII веке* (1966). OSK

Marková Ansari, Dagmar, 1935- *see* Marková, Dagmar

Markovitz, Irving Leonard, born 9 August 1934 at McKeesport, Pa., he received a Ph.D. in 1967 from the University of California at Berkeley for *Léoplod Sédar Senghor; a case study of Senegalese ideology*. Since 1966 he was a professor of political science at SUNY, Queen's College, Flushing, N.Y., a post which he still held in 2004. His writings include *Léopold Sédar Senghor and the politics of negritude* (1969), *African politics and society* (1970), and *Power and class in Africa* (1977). AmM&WSc, 1973 S, 1978 S; ConAu, 33-36; NatFacDr, 1995-2004

Marks, John Henry, born 6 August 1923 at Denver, Colo., he graduated in 1946 from the University of Denver, received a B.D. in 1949 from Princeton University, and a Dr.theol. in 1953 from the Universität Basel. In the same year, he started his long association with Princeton University. In 1966-67, he was a director of the American Schools of Oriental Research, Jerusalem, Jordan. His writings include *A Beginner's handbook to Biblical Hebrew* (1958), *Visions of one world; legacy of Alexander* (1985), and he jointly edited *Love and death in the ancient Near East* (1987). ConAu, 17-20; DrAS, 1969 H, 1974 H, 1978 H, 1982 H; WhoAm, 1984-2003

Markwart, Josef, born Joseph Marquart on 9 December 1864 at Reichenbach, Baden-Württemberg, he studied history, classical and Oriental philology, and received a Dr.phil. in 1892, and a Dr.habil. in 1897. He was from 1912 to his death on 4 February 1930 a professor of Armenian and Iranian philology at the Universität Berlin. His writings include *Die Chronologie der alttürkischen Inschriften* (1898), *Ērānšahr nach der Geographie des Ps. Moses Xorenac'i* (1901), *Die Entstehung und Wiederherstellung der armenischen Nation* (1919), and its translation, *L'Origine et la reconstruction de la nation arménienne* (1919), and *Südarmenien und die Tigrisquellen nach griechischen und arabischen Quellen* (1930). DtBE; Hanisch; Kürschner, 1926-1928/29; NDB

Marlet, Mara Cop, 1859-1910 *see* Berks, Marie Edle von

Marlowe, John, born in 1909, his writings include *Rebellion in Palestine* (1946), *Anglo-Egyptian relations, 1800-1953* (1954), *Arab nationalism and British imperialism* (1961), *The Persian Gulf in the twentieth century* (1962), *Iran; a short political guide* (1963), *Four aspects of Egypt* (1966), *Cromer in Egypt* (1970), *Perfidious Albion* (1971), *Cecil Rhodes, the anatomy of Empire* (1972), *Spoiling the Egyptians* (1974), and *Milner, apostle of Empire* (1976). NUC, pre-1956

Marmier, Xavier, born 24 June 1809 at Pontarlier (Doubs), France, he was a journalist and later travelled widely in central Europe, Russia, Algeria, America, and the East. In 1835, he accompanied the scientific voyage of the *Research* to the Arctic regions and then acquired a wide knowledge of the Scandinavian and Finnish languages and customs. In 1839, he became a professor of foreign languages at Rennes, and in 1841 held a position at the Ministère de l'Instruction publique. In 1846, he was appointed curator of the Bibliothèque Sainte-Geneviève, Paris. His writings include *Du Danube au Caucase* (1854). A. Estignard wrote *Xavier Mamier, sa vie et ses œuvres* (1893). He died in Paris on 11 October 1892. Embacher; EnclZ; EncicUni; GdeEnc; Kornrumpf; Master (3); Megali; Pallas; RNL

de **Marmont**, August Frédéric Louis, Duc de Raguse, born 20 July 1774 at Châtillon-sur-Seine, France, he entered the army. At Toulon he became acquainted with Napoléon Bonaparte, who chose him for his aide-de-camp. For several years after 1805 he was military and civil governor of Dalmatia, where he initiated important public works. Created *maréchal de France* by Napoleon, he participated in the military campaigns until 1814. His writings include *Voyage en Hongrie, en Transylvanie, dans la Russie méridionale, en Crimée ... et quelques parties de l'Asie mineure, en Syrie, en Palestine et en Égypte* (1837-38), its translations into English and German, and *The Present state of the Turkish Empire* (1839). He died in Venezia on 2 March 1852. BioIn 9; EncBrit; EncicUni; EncItaliana; EnclZ; HL; Hoefer, pp. 867-99; IndexBFr² (10); Kornrumpf; Master (4); Megali

Mamorstein, Emile, he was born in 1909 of Austro-Hungarian parentage. After the second World War he worked for the BBC, London. His writings include *Heaven at bay, the Jewish Kulturkampf in the Holy Land* (1969). He died in 1983. Middle Eastern studies, 20 (1984), pp. 131-32

Marmottan, Paul Albert Jules, born 26 August 1856 at Paris, he was a lawyer since 1880, and a *conseilleur de préfecture* in the Département Eure from 1881 to 1882, when he resigned from public life to pursue his own interests. He was an art critic and a historian of private means. His writings include *L'École française de peinture* (1886). He died in 1932. Carnoy, 11, pp. 60-61; NUC, pre-1956

Marmura, Michael Elias, born 11 November 1929 at Jerusalem, where he lived until 1948. He graduated from the University of Wisconsin with the class of 1953, and received his Ph.D. in 1959 from the University of Michigan with a thesis entitled *The Conflict over the world's pre-eternity in the Tahafuts of al-Ghazali and Ibn Rushd*. From 1959 until his retirement in 1995 he was professor of Arabic and Islamic philosophy in the Department of Islamic Studies, the University of Toronto. He was a nice man and teacher. His writings include *First readings in classical Arabic* (1961), *The Incoherence of the philosophers; parallel English-Arabic text of al-Ghazzālī* (1997), and he edited *Islamic theology and philosophy; studies in honor of George F. Hourani* (1984), as well as a number of monographs, both in English and Arabic. Canadian, 1994-1996|; DrAS, 1978 P, 1982 P; Private; Selim

Marno, Ernst Joseph Katejan Franz, born 13 January 1844 at Wien, he studied zoology at the local Universität. In 1866/67, he was with a dealer in wild animals in Abyssinia, and in 1869, he tried to explore the country from the Blue Nile to the Indian Ocean but had to give up at Fadasi. Two years later, he travelled in the region of Bahr al-Zeraf and reached Gondokoro. On the invitation of Ch. G. Gordon, he went to the Sudan and accompanied Charles Chaillé-Long on an exploration of the water resources of the Nile. In 1878, Gordon appointed him *mudīr* of Galabat province. From 1878 to 1879, he was employed with a fleet of steamers clearing vegetable obstructions from the Bahr al-Jabal. Nominated a *bey*, and *mudīr* of Fazogli at Famaka, he fought against the followers of the Mahdi, and the slave trade. His writings include *Reisen im Gebiete des Blauen und Weissen Nil, im egyptischen Sudan und den angrenzenden Negerländern in den Jahren 1869 bis 1873* (1874), and *Reise in der egyptischen Aequatorial-Provinz und in Kordofan in den Jahren 1874-1876* (1878). He died in Khartoum on 31 January 1883. Embacher; Henze; Kornrumpf; Kornrumpf³, vol. 2; Kosch; Hill; LexAfrika; ÖBL

Marquardsen, Hugo, born 2 February 1869 at Porto Alegre, Brazil, he graduated in 1889 from a high school in Kiel, Germany, and then entered the Prussian army, concurrently studying geography and geology. He subsequently was sent on a mission to the Cameroons to settle the boundary of the German protectorate between Yola on the Benuë River and Lake Chad. He resigned in 1907 with the rank of captain to complete his study. He received a Dr.phil. in 1909 from the Universität Göttingen for *Ober-flächengestaltung und Hydrographie des saharisch-sudanischen abflußlosen Gebietes*. He later served at Berlin with the ministry of reconstruction as well as the bureau of the colonies. Since 1911 he was an editor of the *Mitteilungen aus den deutschen Schutzgebieten*. His own writings include *Der Niger-Benuë* (1909), *Die Grenzgebiete Kameruns im Süden und Osten* (1914), *Die Kolonial-Kartensammlung des Reichs-Kolonialamts* (1915), *Belgisch-Kongo* (1916), *Unsere Kolonien* (1917), and *Angola* (1920). He died in Berlin on 17 May 1920. DtBiJ, 2 (1917-20), p. 754; Thesis

Marquardsen-Kamphövener, Else, 1878-1963 see Kamphövener, Elsa Sophia von

Marquart, Joseph, 1864-1930 see Markwart, Josef

Marquet, Yves, born 20th cent., he received a *doctorat d'état* in 1971 from the Université de Paris IV for *La Philosophie des Ikhwan as-Safa; de Dieu à l'homme*. His other writings include *Poésie ésotérique ismaïlienne; la Tā'iyya de 'Āmir b. 'Āmir al-Basrī* (1985), and *La Philosophie des alchimistes et l'alchimie des philosophes; Ibn Jâbir ibn Hayyân et les "Frères de la pureté* (1988). THESAM, 4; ZKO

Marr, IUriĭ Nikolaevich, born in 1893 at St. Petersburg, he there completed his secondary school in 1913, and his university studies in 1917 in the Arabo-Perso-Turco-Tatar section, concurrently taking courses in Armenian and Georgian philology. From 1919 to 1921 he was a librarian in the Georgian University, acting at the same time as a translator to the local telegraph agency. In 1922 and 1923, he was an academic assistant at the Asiatic Museum of the Academy of Sciences, and a lecturer in the Institute of Oriental Languages, Petrograd. From 1922 to 1925 he was also associated with the Institute of Scientific Research for the Comparative History of Occidental and Oriental Literatures and Languages. After a stay in Persia, 1925-26, he returned with the first symptoms of tuberculosis and from that time on he was obliged to live at the health resort of Abast'uman, Georgia, paying only short visits to Leningrad and Moscow, and sometimes spending the winter in Tiflis. During his final seven years he carried on research in association with the Caucasian Institute of History and Archaeology as well as the Georgian Branch of the Academy of Sciences, and Tiflis State University. His writings include *Материалы для персидско-руссеого словаря* (1974), and *Письма о персидской литературе* (1976). He gained a doctorate on 25 October 1935 and died in Abast'uman on 1 December 1935. Georgica, 1, nos. 4-5 (1937), pp. 278-86; *Index Islamicus* (3); Krachkovskiĭ, p. 200; Miliband²

Marr, Nikolaĭ IAkovlevich, born in 1864 or 65, he was an archaeologist, ethnographer, folklorist and, above all, a specialist in Caucasian languages. His writings include *Археологическая експедиція 1916 года в Ванъ* (1922), *Der japhetische Kaukasus* (1923), *Абхазский аналитический алфавит* (1926), and *Тристан в Изольда* (1932). He died on 20 January 1934. GSE; *Index Islamicus* (5); KazakSE; Kornrumpf³, vol. 2; Miliband, pp. 336-340; Miliband²; *Советская этнография*, 1935, no. 1, pp. 8-17; VostokMStP, p. 253

Marr, Phebe Ann, born 21 September 1931 at Mt. Vernon, N.Y., she received a Ph.D. in 1967 from Harvard University for *Yasin al-Hashimi; the rise and fall of a nationalist*. From 1960 to 1966, she was successively a research assistant with the Arabian-American Oil Company, Saudi Arabia, and a director of the Middle East Program, Foreign Service Institute, U.S. Department of State. She subsequently was a professor of Middle Eastern history successively at California State University, Stanislaus, and University of Tennessee, Knoxville. In 1990, she was a senior fellow in the Institute for National Strategic Studies of the National Defense University, Washington, D.C. Her writings include *The Modern history of Iraq* (1985), *Riding the tiger; the Middle East challenge after the cold war* (1993), and *Egypt at the crossroads; domestic stability and regional role* (1999). DrAS, 1974 H, 1978 H, 1982 H; *MESA Roster of members*, 1977-1990; Note about the author; Selim; WhoAmW, 1979/80-1993/94; WhoS&SW, 1986/87

Marr, S. M., fl. 20th cent., he was joint author of *Письма о персидской литературе* (Tbilisi, 1976). OSK

Marracci, Lodovico (Luigi), born in 1612 at Torcigliano (Lucca), Italy, he was a theologian, an Arabist, Pope Innocent XI's confessor, and author of the first useful translation of the Koran and its refutation entitled *Refutatio Alcorani in qua ad Mahumetanicae superstionis radicem securis appenitur* (1698). He died in Roma on 5 February 1700. EncicUni; EncItaliana; Fück, p. 78; GdeEnc; *Rendiconti della R. Accademia dei Lincei*, s. 5, vol. 7 (1931), pp. 303-349

Marrassini, Paolo, born 20th cent., he was associated with the Istituto di Linguistica e di Lingue Orientali, Firenze. His writings include *Formazione del lessico dell'edilizia militare nel semitico di Siria* (Firenze, 1971), *Scettro e la croce; la campagna di 'Amda Seyon I contre l'Ifat, 1332* (1993), and *Gadla Yemrehanna Krestos* (1995). Catalogo dei libri in commercio, 2002, 2003; ZKO

Marrast, Augustin, born in 1829, his writings include *La Philosophie du droit de Hégel* (1869), *Esquisses byzantines* (1874), and *La Vie byzantine au VIe siècle* (1881). He died in 1877. BN; NUC, pre-1956

Marre, Eugéne Aristide, born 7 March 1823 at Mamers (Sarthe), France, he graduated from the military college at La Flèche. In 1840, he went to Paris, where he devoted himself to the study of Oriental languages and also mathematics, becoming for some time a teaching assistant at the Collège Henri IV, Paris. Since 1886 he taught Malay and Javanese at the École spéciale des langues orientales vivantes, Paris. He was a corresponding member of numerous European learned societies. Endowed with a remarkable aptitude for languages, and accompanied with broad learning, he published widely on Oriental literature and Arabic mathematics. He was a contributor to the *Grande encyclopédie*. His writings include *Petit vocabulaire des mots malays que l'usage à introduits dans les langues d'Europe* (1866), and he edited and translated *Malâka; histoire des rois malays de Malâka et cérémonial de leur cour, extrait du Livre des Annales malayses, intitulé en arabe Selâlet al Selâtyn* (1874), *Extrait du Kitâb al mobârek d'Abu'l Wafa al Djoueini* (1974), *Code malais des successions et du mariage* (1889), and *Le Sadjarah Malayou, ou, Histoire des radjas et des sultans malais depuis les origines jusqu'à la conquête de Malaka par Alphonse d'Abuquerque en 1511* (1896). He died in 1918. Cordier; GdeEnc

Marriott, Constance Sutcliffe, born 19th cent., her writings include *Love lyrics, and snatches to set to music* (Westminster, 1900). Master (2)

Marriott, Sir John Arthur Ransome, born in 1859, he was educated at New College, Oxford, where he subsequently became Dunkin Lecturer in sociology. He later was a member of Parliament. His writings include *The Eastern question* (1917), *The English in India* (1932), and *Memories of four score years* (1946). He died in 1945. Master (4); Who, 1909-1945; *Who was who*, 4

Marriott, Sir William Thackeray, born in 1834, he was educated at St. John's College, Cambridge, and called to the bar from Lincoln's Inn in 1879. His writings include *Clerical disabilities* (1865), *The Khedivial family* (1889), and *War and its cost* (1901). He died in 1903. DNB; *Who was who*, 1

Marrison, Geoffrey Edward, born 11 January 1923 at Ulverston, Cumbria, he became a director and keeper at the British Library, Department of Oriental Manuscripts and Printed Books. He served as a secretary and treasurer of the International Association of Orientalist Librarians. His writings include *Christian approach to the Muslim* (1959), and *A Handlist of Tai and Mou-Khmer manuscripts in the British Library* (1968). Beween 1989 and 1993 he also published three catalogues of special South-East Asian collections in the Brynmor Jones Library, University of Hull. Who, 1976-2005

Marro, Giovanni, born 28 January 1875 at Limone Piemonte (Cuneo), Italy, he was an anthropologist who in 1926 established the Istituto etrusco di antropologia presso l'Università di Torino. His writings include *Caratteri fisici e spirituali della razza italiana* (Roma, 1939), and *Primato della razza italiana* (Milano, 1940). Chi è, 1940, 1948; Note about the author

Mars, V. de, *pseud.* see Aumale, Henri Eugène Philippe Louis d'Orléans, Duc d'

Marschall von Bieberstein, Adolf Hermann, born 12 October 1842 at Karsruhe, Bade, he studied law at the universities of Heidelberg and Freiburg im Breisgau, and served as public prosecutor at Mosbach from 1871 to 1882. He was a sometime member of the German Diet. He was head of the German foreign office from 1890 to 1897, when he became ambassador at Constantinople. In April 1912 he was appointed to the same office at London. His writings include *Juristische Daten zur Repitition aus den verschiedenen Rechtsgebieten chronologisch zusammengestellt* (Berlin, 1881). He died in Badenweiler on 24 September 1912. DtBE; Kornrumpf; Kornrumpf, N; Wer ist's, 1909, 1912

Marsden, Arthur, born about 1930, he received a Ph.D. in 1962 from LSE for *British policy towards Tunis, 1875-1899*. His other writings include *Britain and the end of the Tunis treaties, 1894-1897* (1965), and *British diplomacy and Tunis, 1875-1902* (1971). Sluglett; ZKO

Marsden, D. J., fl. 20th cent., an author of the booklet, *The Qashqai 'tribe' and tribal identity* (Swansea, Centre for Development Studies, U.C., 1978). ZKO

Marsden, William, born 16 November 1754 at Verval, Ireland, he received the usual education at Dublin and subsequently entered the Indian Civil Service, arriving in 1771 in India. During the eight years he spent there, he had enough time to learn the Malay language. In 1779, he returned to England, where he resolved on literary retirement. He was a fellow of the Royal Society. His writings include *History of Sumatra* (1783), *A Catalogue of dictionaries, vocabularies, grammars and alphabets* (1796), and *A Dictionary of the Malayan language* (1812), a work which was translated into Dutch and German. He died in Kemal Green, 6 October 1836. Buckland; DNB; IndianBind (2); Master (6); Riddick

Marseille, Jacques Robert Henri Maurice, born 15 October 1945 at Abbeville (Somme), France, he was educated at Amiens and Lille, and gained an *agrégation* in history and a doctorate in humanities. Since 1985 he taught economic history at Paris universities. His award-winning books include *Empire colonial et capitalisme français; histoire d'un divorce, 1880-1960* (1984), *La France travaille trop; éloge du jeune rentier* (1989), and *La Révolution commerciale en France; du bon marché à l'hypermarché* (1997). WhoFr, 1997/98-2005/2006

Marsh, Charles R., born in 1958 at Mobile, Ala., the son of a minister, he studied philosophy and theology at Harvard University and gained a Ph.D. at the University of Virginia. He was a minister and civil rights leader. His writings include *Share your faith with a Muslim* (1975), its translation, *Le Musulman, mon prochain; un manuel destiné à ceux qui désirent présenter l'évangile aux Musulmans* (1977), and *The Challenge of Islam* (1980). ConAu, 200

Marsh, Hippisley Cunliffe, born 27 February 1837 at Kurnal, India, he was educated in England and became a captain in the 18th Bengal Cavalry. A fellow of the Royal Geographical Society, his writings include *A Ride through Islam, being a journey through Persia and Afghanistan to India viâ Meshed, Herat, and Kandahar* (London, 1877). BritInd (1) = Who's who in Kent, 1911-12 (not sighted)

Marshak, Boris Il'ich, born 9 July 1933 at Luga, Russia, he graduated in 1956 from the Faculty of History, Moscow State University, received his first degree in 1965 for Керамика Согда V-VII вв, and his doctorate in 1981 for История восточной торевтики в III-XI вв. Since 1961 he was associated with the Oriental section of the State Ėrmitazh, Leningrad. His writings include Согдийское серебро (1971), Восточные аналогии зданиям типа вписанного креста (1983), *Silberschätz des Orients; Metallkunst* (1986), *Peerless images; Persian painting and its sources* (2002), and he was joint author of Анализ археологических источников (1975). Miliband²; Schoeberlein

Marshall, Charles Burton, born 25 March 1908 at Catskill, N.Y., he received a Ph.D. in 1939 from Harvard for *The relation of the Neutrality Act to the control of foreign relations*. He was a staff consultant for the U.S. House of Representatives' Committee on Foreign Affairs, from 1947 to 1950, and subsequently became associated with the U.S. Department of State until 1957, when he started teaching international politics at a variety of institutions. His writings include *The Limits of foreign policy* (1956), *The Cold war* (1965), *The Exercise of sovereignty* (1965), and *Crisis over Rhodesia* (1967). He died in Portland, Ore., 22 December 1999. AmM&WSc, 1973 S, 1978 S; WhoAm, 1974-1999; WhoWor, 1991/92, 1993/94

Marshall, Dara Nusserwanji, born 25 April 1906 at Bombay, he became a librarian and head of the Department of Library Science, Bombay University. His writings include *Mughals in India* (1967), *The Afghans in India under the Delhi Sultanate and the Mughal Empire* (1976), and he was joint author of *Mughal bibliography* (1962). IndianBilnd (1)

Marshall, David R., born 20th cent., he received his Ph.D. in 1962 from the University of Durham for *The Accusative in Arabic grammatical literature*. He became associated with the Royal University of Malta. His writings include *History of the Arabic language in local education* (Malta, 1971), and he edited the *Proceedings* of the 1st Congress on Mediterranean Studies of Arabo-Berber Influence, 1972 (1973). Note about the author; Sluglett

Marshall, Edward Asaph, born in 1866 at Cambridge, N.Y., he was for over ten years a lecturer at Moody Bible Institute of Chicago. His writings include *Christianity and non-Christian religions compared* (Chicago, 1910). WhAm, 4

Marshall, Frederick Henry, born in 1878 at Hampstead, he was a lecturer in classics at Emmanuel College, Cambridge, and a professor of modern Greek and Byzantine history at King's College, London. His writings include *Catalogue of the jewellery, Greek, Etruscan, and Roman, in the departments of antiquities, British Museum* (1911), *Old Testament legends* (1925), and he edited and translated *The Siege of Vienna by the Turks in 1683, translated into Greek from an Italian work published anonymously in the year of the siege, by Jeremias Cacavelas* (Cambridge, 1925). He died on 9 November 1955. Master (2); WhE&EA; *Who was who*, 5

Marshall, John Edwin, born 3 March 1864 near West Hartlepool, he was educated at Durham School and called to the bar from the Middle Temple in 1886. He became a judge in the Egyptian Supreme Court of Appeal. He was a member of the Société sultanieh d'économie politique, de statistique et de législation. His writings include *The Egyptian enigma, 1890-1928* (London, 1928). He died in 1937. BritInd (2); Master (1); Note about the author; Who, 1929-1936; *Who was who*, 3

Marshall, Sir John Hubert, born 19 March 1876 at Chester, England, he graduated in classics from King's College, Cambridge, and from 1901 to 1931 served as a director general of Archaeology in India. A member of the major Oriental societies, he was awarded numerous gold medals. He died in 1958. BioIn, 5 (4); Buckland; DNB; IndianBilnd (4); Master (2); NYT, 19 August 1958, p. 28, cols. 1-2; *Revue archéologique* 1959, t. 1, pp. 206-208; Riddick; WhE&EA; WhoIndia, 1927; ZDMG, 109 (1959), pp. 16-25

Marshall, Peter James, born 28 October 1933, he was a Rhodes Professor of Imperial History, King's College, London. His writings include *The Impeachment of Warren Hastings* (1965), *Problems of Empire; Britain and India, 1757-1813* (1968), *The British discovery of Hinduism in the eighteenth century* (1970), *East Indian fortunes* (1976), *Bengal, the British bridgehead; eastern India, 1740-1828* (1987), and a collection of his articles, *Trade and conquest; studies on the rise of British dominance in India* (1993). Who, 1982-2005

Marshall, Susan Elaine, born in 1950, she received a Ph.D. in 1980 from the University of Massachusetts at Amherst for *The Power of the veil; the politics of female status in North Africa*. She became a professor in the Department of Sociology, University of Texas at Austin, a post which she still held in 2005. Her other writings include *Splintered sisterhood; gender and class in the campaign against women suffrage* (1997). LC; NatFacDr, 2005; Selim³

Marshall Cornwall, Sir James Handyside, Colonel, born 27 May 1887 at Karachi, he was a graduate of the Royal Military Academy, Woolwich, and served in the forces as well as military attaché in Europe. In 1919, he attended the Paris Peace Conference as a member of the British delegation. He went out in January 1920 to Turkey with a brigade of the Royal Field Artillery, and then in April of the same year, he was appointed to the command of the British troops at Chanak (Çanakkale), Dardanelles. In August 1921, he was appointed intelligence officer to General Sir Charles Harington in Constantinople until the evacuation of the British forces in October 1923. He remained in Constantinople after the evacuation in order to study Turkey and the Turks. His writings include *Geographic disarmament* (1935). He died on 25 December 1985. ConAu, 107, 118; Who, 1974-1985; *Who was who*, 8

Marsili (Marsigli/Μαρσίλι), Luigi Fernandino, comte, born 10 July 1658 at Bologna, he was interested in the Ottoman Empire from his early years, and had the good fortune of being taken in the train of senator Ciurani, the new Venetian ambassador to the Porte, and made a stay of eleven months in Constantinople, from 1679 to 1680, sparing neither labour nor money in the pursuit of his object, which was to study the Turkish military system. Although warned of the dangers involved, to his surprise the Turks, far from viewing this interest with suspicion, gave him assistance in his researches, even procuring for him - at a very high price - a copy of the *Kanunname*, especially the part containing the schedules of the imperial revenues, army establishments, and regulations. With the help of an interpreter, he set himself to master the contents of this work, which he found dealt with military administration rather than the training of troops. His writings include *Stato militare dell'Imperio Ottomano* (1732), *Scritti inediti di Liugi Ferdinando Marsigli* (1930), and *La schiavitù del generale Marsigli sotto i Tartari e i Turchi, da lui stesso narrata* (1931). He died in Bologna on 1 November 1730. There is now a collection Marsigli at Bologna. EncicUni; EncItaliana; EncLZ; GdeEnc; IndBiltal (2); Magyar; Master (3); Megali; Note about the author; Pallas; RNL

Marsot, Afaf Lutfi al-Sayyid, born about 1930 at Cairo, he was in 1979 a president of MESA, and certainly from 1977 to 1990, he served as a professor of history at the University of California, Los Angeles. His writings include *Women and men in late eighteenth-century Egypt* (1995). DrAS, 1974 H, 1978 H,1982 H; *MESA Roster of members*, 1977-1990; Who Arab, 2001/2002, 2002/2004

Marston, Thomas Ewart, born 7 November 1904 at Chicago, he graduated in 1927 from Yale University, New Haven, Conn., and received a Ph.D. in history in 1939 from Harvard University, Cambridge, Mass.; from 1940 to 1971 he was a curator of classics, medieval and renaissance literature at Yale University Libraries. His writings include *Incunabula in the Yale University Libraries* (1955), *Britain's imperial role in the Red Sea area* (1961), and he was a joint author of *The Vinland map and the Tartar relation* (1965). He died in Leesburg, Va., on 25 February 1984. BioIn, 13 (1); ConAu, 112; DrAS, 1974 H; NYT, 28 February 1984, p. D-27, col. 1

Martel, André Étienne, born 4 May 1930 at Cavaillon (Vaucluse), France, he was educated at Avignon and Aix-en-Provence. After teaching in southern France, he taught from 1952 to 1957 at the Lycée Sadiki, Tunis, and subsequently for two additional years at the Faculté des lettres. He spent three years with the Centre National de la Recherche Scientifique, before joining the Université de Paul-Valéry, Montpellier III, successively serving as a professor, vice-president, and president. His writings include *Les Confins saharo-tripolitains de la Tunisie* (1965), *Luis-Arnold et Joseph Allegro, consuls du Bey de Tunis à Bône* (1967), and *La Libye, 1835-1990; essai de géopolitique historique* (1991). Unesco; WhoFr, 1981/82-1985/86|

Martel, Gordon Andre, born 14 January 1946, he received a Ph.D. in 1977 from the University of Toronto, and became a professor at Trent University, Peterborough, Ont. He subsequently taught at a variety of universities and colleges in British Columbia, before he was appointed in 1995 a professor of history at the University of Northern British Columbia, a post which he still held in 2004. His writings include *The Origins of the second World War reconsidered* (1986), and *Modern Germany reconsidered* (1992). ConAu, 208; NatFacDr, 2000-2004; Private

Martel, Pierre Albin, born 20th cent., his writings include *Habib Bourguiba, une homme, un siècle* (Paris, 1999). LC; *Livres disponibles*, 2004

Martel, René, born about 1900, his writings include *La Pologne et nous* (Paris, 1928), *Les Frontières orientales de l'Allemagne* (Paris, 1930), *Le Mouvements antireligieux en U.R.S.S.* (Paris, 1933), *La Ruthénie subcarpathique* (Paris, 1935), *La France et le corridor polonais* (Paris, 1941), and *Principes du national-socialisme* (1941). BN

Martelli, George Ansley, born in 1903, he was a chief foreign correspondent of the *Morning Post*, London. During the second World War he served with the U.K. Political Warfare Executive. He subsequently became a public relations consultant. His writings include *Italy against the world* (1937), *Whose sea? A Mediterranean journey* (1938), *Leopold to Lumumba; a history of the Belgian Congo* (1962), *Experiment in world government* (1966), and *Livinstone's river* (1970). WrDr, 1976/78-1996/98

Martellotto (Martellotus), Francesco, born 16th cent., he was a Minorite who in the service of Pope Paul V wrote *Institutiones linguae arabicae*, published posthumously in 1620 at Rome. He died in 1618. Fück, p. 77

Martens, Fedor Fedorovich, born in 1845, he was a member of the Cour permanent d'arbitage de la Haye. His writings include *Das Consularwesen und die Consularjurisdiction* (1874), *Russia and England in Central Asia* (1879), Восточная война; Брюссельская конференция, 1874-1878 (1897), Россія и Англія в Средней Азіи (1880), and Россія и Китай (1881). He died in 1909 or 1910. EnSlovar, vol. 36, pp. 691-92; NYPL

Martens, Jean Claude, born 20th cent., his writings include *Le Modèle algérien de développement; bilan d'une décennie, 1962-1972* (Alger, 1973).

Marthe, Johann Gottlob *Friedrich* Heinrich, born 17 July 1832 at Niemegk, Mark Brandenburg, Germany, he studied philosophy, history and geography at the universities of Berlin and Halle, where received a Dr.phil. in 1856 for *De legibus Romanorum agraiis*. In the same year, he obtained a post as private tutor in Odessa and the Crimea. He was since 1861 a teacher at Dorotheenstädtisches Gymnasium, Berlin, and concurrently taught geography at the war college. In 1884, he became a professor. He died in Berlin on 11 June 1893. Poggendorf = DtBilnd

Marthelot, Pierre, born 28 February 1909 to a family of *instituteurs laïques* at Joigny (Yvonne), France, he went to Paris in 1926, and to Strasbourg in 1930, where he received a degree in medieval studies. After a thesis on the geography of the Vosges, he taught geography from 1945 to 1950 at the Université de Strasbourg. He subsequently spent ten years teaching in Tunis, becoming the founding director of the journal, *Cahiers de Tunisie*. After his return to France, he pusued a career as director of the École des hautes études en sciences sociales. He was a joint author of *Islam; civilisation et religion* (1965). He died in 1995. *Cahiers de Tunisie*, n° 164 (1993), pp. 5-6; Unesco; WhFr, 1969/70-1979/80

von **Martin**, Alfred, born 21 January 1862 at Köln, Germany, he was a graduate of McGill and Harvard universities, and was ordained a Unitarian minister in 1888. Since 1907 he was a leading member of the Ethical Culture Society. His writings include *Ideals of life; or, the soul's way to God as taught in the sacred scriptures of antiquity* (1893), *Great religious leaders of the East* (1911), and *Great moral leaders* (1933). He died in N.Y.C. on 15 October 1932. Bioln, 2; Master (3); NatCAB, vol. 23, p. 138; WhAm, 1

Martin, Alfred Georges Paul, *commandant*, born in 1863 at la Mayenne (Orne), France, he was an expert on North Africa, which he knew at first hand and which he had studied comprehensively, from Alger to the Sahara and theTripolitanian border to Sous on the Atlantic Coast. As an *officier interprète de première classe* for more than a quarter of a century, he was an eyewitness to all the great political movements, starting with the Bou-Amama rebellion to the pacification of the Moroccan Chaouïa; he was an alert investigator of Muslim mentality as well as a direct witness to the social development of both, the native population, and the European colonists. He was fully aware of the conflict of interests between the French and Moroccan authorities in their struggle for the domination of Touat and the Sahara. A sometime professor at the École supérieure de commerce de Bordeaux, his writings include *À la frontière du Maroc* (1908), *Géographie nouvelle de l'Afrique du nord* (1912), *Méthode déductive d'arabe nord-africaine* (1919), *Précis de sociologie nord-africaine* (1913-20), *Quatre siècles d'histoire marocaine au Sahara de 1504 à 1902; au Maroc de 1894 à 1912, d'après archives et documentations indigènes* (1923), and *Le Maroc et l'Europe* (1928). Curinier

Martin, Basil *Kingsley*, born 2 December 1897 at Pershore, England, he was a fellow of Magdalen College, Cambridge, and briefly served as an assistant lecturer at the London School of Economists, before becoming an editor. His writings include *The British public and the general strike* (1926), *War, history, and human nature* (1959), and *The Magic of the British Royalty* (1962). He died in Cairo on 16 February 1969. Bioln, 2, 5, 7, 8, 9, 10; ConAu, 5-8, 25-28, new rev., 11; DNB; GrBr; Master (2); Who was who, 6

Martin, Bernadette, born 20th cent., she received her university agrégation and was in 1980 a *maître-assistant d'histoire*. She was joint author of *Le Proche-Orient médiéval des Barbares aux Ottomans* (Paris, Hachette, 1980). Note about the author

Martin, Bradford Garey, born 14 August 1925 at Boston, Mass., he graduated from Harvard and received a Ph.D. in 1958 from Princeton University for *German-Persian diplomatic relations, 1873-1912*. From 1960 to 1966, he was a senior lecturer and research fellow in Ghana. He subsequently served as a professor of African Islamic history at Indiana University, Bloomington. His writings include *Muslim brotherhoods in ninenteenth century Africa* (1976). Note about the author; WhoAm, 1984-1988/89

Martin, Charles D., born 19th cent., he was in 1927 an assistant chief of the Agricultural Implements Division, U.S. Bureau of Domestic and Foreign Commerce. His writings include *Modern farm equipment in India* (1926), and *Foreign markets of agricultural implements* (1927). Note about the author; NUC, pre-1956

Martin, Colin Henri, born 11 March 1906 at Froideville (Canton de Vaud), Switzerland, he received a doctorate in law in 1939 from the Université de Lausanne with a thesis entitled *La législation monétaire bernoise au pays de Vaud, de 1536 à 1623*. Since 1937 he was a director of the Cabinet des médailles du Canton de Vaud, and since 1940 a director of the Musée romain de Vidy (Lausanne). He was a sometime president of the Société suisse de numismatique. His writings include *La règlement bernoise des monnaies au pays de Vaud* (1940), and *Essai sur la politique monétaire de Berne, 1400-1798* (1978-1983). SchBiAr, 6 (1958), p. 69; WhoSwi, 1962/63, 1968/69, 1972/73

Martin, Denis (Denis-Constant), born 20th cent., he was a research fellow of the Fondation nationale des sciences politiques. His writings include *Tanzanie, l'invention d'une culture politique* (1988), *Nouveaux langages du politique en Afrique orientale* (1998), and, jointly with Tatiana Yannopoulos, *L'Afrique noire* (1973), with Gene Dauch, *L'Héritage de Kenyatta* (1985), and with Fred Constant, *Les Démocraties antillaises en crise* (1996); and he edited *Sur la piste des OPNI* (2002). Livres disponibles, 2004; Note about the author

Martin, Fredrik Robert, born 8 May 1868 at Stockholm, he received a Dr.phil. in 1901 from the Universität Wien for *Figurale persische Stoffe aus dem Zeitraum 1550 bis 1650*. He was an Orientalist, historian of art, and art collector. He collaborated in 1910 with Friedrich Sarre in the exhibition of Islamic art at München and its catalogue, *Die Austellung von Meisterwerken mohammedanischer Kunst in München* (1912). His other writings include *Svenska kungliga gåfvor till ryska zaren, 1647-1699* (1899), *The Miniature painting and painters of Persia, India and Turkey* (1912), *The Nizāmī MS from the library of the Shah of Persia now in the Metropolitan Museum at New York* (1927), *Il lustro sul vetro e la ceramica in Egitto da Adriano a Saladino* (1929), his memoirs, *Sett, hört och känt* (1933), and he edited *Siberica* (1897). He died in Cairo on 19 April 1933. SBL, pp. 192-94; ScBlnd; SMK; *Vem är det*, 1925

Martin, Godefroy, he was born in 1875 at Sancerre (Cher), France. After passing through the military college of Saint Cyr, he received a commission as *sous-lieutenant* in 1896. He entered the Bureau des Affaires indigènes de l'Algérie in 1903 and served at Méchéria, Marnia, and Touat-Gouarar from 1904 to 1908. Afterwards he was *chef du bureau* and *commandant* at Bou-Sâada, Saoura and Laghouat respectively. From 1916 to 1918 he was at the French front, but returned to Algeria to become *commandant supérieur* at Colomb-Béchar from 1919 to 1922 when he was transferred to the Service des renseignements du Maroc. From 1924 to 1928 he was *commandant* at the Cercle d'Azilal in eastern Morocco. He was awarded *Officer de la Légion d'honneur*. Peyronnet, p. 552

Martin, Hugh Gray, lieutenant-general, born 28 February 1887 in Dunbartonshire, he graduated from the Royal Military Academy Staff College and became a military correspondent to the London *Daily Mail*. His writings include *The History of the fifteenth Scottish Division, 1939-1945* (1948), and *Sunset from the main* (1951). He died in 1969. Au&Wr, 1963; WhE&EA; *Who was who*, 6

Martin, J. D., born 20th cent., he received a Ph.D. in 1969 from Glasgow University for *The Zuhdiyat of Abu'l-Atahiya*. Sluglett

Martin, James Walter, born 11 September 1893 at Muskogee, Okla., he was a professor of economics at the University of Kentucky from 1948 to his retirement. His writings include *Southern state and local finance trends and the war* (1945). WhAm, 10

Martin, Janet Louise Block, she was born on 24 January 1945. Her writings include *Treasure of the land of darkness; the fur trade and its significance for medieval Russia* (1986), and *Medieval Russia, 980-1584* (1995). LC

Martin, Jean Pierre Paulin, Abbé, he was born in 1840. His writings include *La Chaldée; esquisse historique suivie de quelques réflexions sur l'Orient* (1867) *Chronique de Josué le Stylite* (1876), *De la métrique chez les Syriens* (1877), and *Description technique des manuscrits grecs relatifs au Noveau Testa-ment conservés dans les biliothèques de Paris* (1884) He died in 1890. BN; NUC, pre-1956

Martin, Lawrence, born 14 February 1880 at Stockbridge, Mass., he graduated in 1904 from Cornell University, Ithaca, N.Y., where he also received his Ph.D. in 1913. He taught geography at a variety of American universities, before he served from 1924 to 1946 as chief of the Library of Congress' Map Division. Concurrently he was since 1927 a member of the United States' Board on Geographic Names. He died in Washington, D.C., on 12 February 1955. BioIn, 3, 4 (3); Master (2); NatCAB, vol. 44, pp. 42-43; WhAm, 6; WhE&EA

Martin, Lenore Greenslag, born about 1950, she received a Ph.D. in 1979 from the University of Chicago for *A systematic study of boundary disputes in the Persian Gulf, 1900 to present*. She was in 1984 a professor of political science at Emmanuel College, Boston, a post which she still held in 2004. Her writings include *The unstable Gulf; threats from within* (1984). NatFacDr, 2004; Note about the author

Martin, Lucien, born 19th cent., he was a first *maître mécanicien* in the French navy. His writings include *Voyage autour du monde, 1903-1904* (Villedieu-Vaison, 1906). His trace is lost after an article in 1923. BN

Martin, M. E., bon 20th cent., he received an M.A. in 1972 from the University of Birmingham for *Venice and the Byzantine Empire before the fourth crusade*. Sluglett

Martin, Marie H., born 20th cent., he was a joint author of *Iran; Protoiraner, Meder, Achämeniden* (1964), and *La tradition manuscrite des quatorze hymnes attribués à Saint Ambroise jusqu'à la fin du XIe siècle; étude codicologique, critique et ecdotique* (1987).

Martin, Maurice, S.J., born 20th cent., he had been living in Egypt long before he started writing about the country in the late 1960s. He taught history and philosophy to boys at the schools of Sainte-Famille in Cairo, and to girls at Mère-de-Dieu. In their company he explored the country and became confronted with the terrible misery of the villages as they went about in the countryside. His writings include *La laure de Dêr al Dîk à Antinoé* (1971), and he was a joint author of *Arab culture and society in change* (1973). In 1992, he was honoured by *Itinéraires d'Égypte; mélanges offerts au Père Maurice Martin*. Note about the author

Martin, Thomas Henri, born 4 February 1813 at Bellesme (Orne), France, he was educated at Séez and Avranches, and taught literature at schools in Dijon and Caen. After gaining a doctorate in 1836 at the Faculté des lettres de Paris, he became a professor of classical literature at the Faculté des lettres, Université de Rennes, and in 1838, a dean of his faculty. His writings include *Mémoire sur la période égyptienne du Phénix* (Paris, 1864), and *Les sciences et la philosophie; essais de critique philosophique et religieuse* (1869). He died in 1884. Hoefer; IndBFr² (6); Vapereau

Martin, Thomas Josiah, born in 1945, he received a Ph.D. in 1975 from the University of St. Andrews for *The Arabic translation of Theodosius' "Sphaerica."* His writings include *North American collections of Islamic manuscripts* (1977). LC; Sluglett

Martin, Vanessa, born about 1950, she was a lecturer in modern Middle Eastern history at the Royal Holloway College, University of London. Her writings include *Islam and modernism; the Iranian revolution of 1906* (London, 1989), *Creating an Islamic state; Khomeini and the making of a new Iran* (London, 2000), and *The Qajar pact; bargaining, protest and the state in nineteenth-century Persia* (2005). Note about the author; Publisher's catalogue

Martin, William James, born 25 May 1904 at Broughshane, County Antrim, Ireland, he went to school in Cross and subsequently attended Ballymena Academy. He was a 1927 graduate of Trinity College, Dublin; two years later he graduated from Princeton Theological Seminary. From 1929 to 1936, he successively studied at the universities of Berlin and Leipzig, where he received a Dr.phil. in 1936 for *Tribut und Tribut-leistungen bei den Assyrern*. His writings include *Letters and documents of the Old-Babylonian period* (1953), and *Stylistic criteria and the analysis of the Pentateuch* (1955). Schwarz; Thesis

Martin, Wulf, born 11 April 1933 at Heinsberg (Rheinland), Germany, he studied law at the universities of Tübingen, Bonn, and Mainz, where he received a Dr.jur. in 1965 for a thesis on the development of modern rural self-government in India entitled *Panchayati Raj; die Entwicklung der modernen ländlichen Selbstverwaltung in Indien*. He was from 1965 to 1968 associated with Deutsch-Indische Handelskammer, in the latter period, as head of its main bureau in Bombay. He subsequently served for six years with the foreign trade section of Verein Deutscher Maschinenbau-Anstalten. He was a sometime a lecturer in Deutsches Maschinenbau Institut, and in 1975 became head of the German Iranian Chamber of Commerce. He was a joint author of *Der internationale Lizenzverkehr* (1973). Note about the author; Thesis

Martín de la **Escalera**, Carmen, he was an author who flourished between 1945 and 1962, whose writings include *Fatma; cuentos de mujeres marroquíes* (Madrid, 1945), and *Argelia u su destino* (Madrid, Instituto de Estudios Políticos, 1956). NUC, pre-1956

Martín Gonzalez, Juan José, born 8 February 1923 at Alcazarquivir, Morocco, he was a professor of history of art successively at the universities of La Laguna, Santiago de Compostela, and Valladolid. His writings include *La huella española en la escultura portuguesa, renacimiento y barroco* (1961), *Historia de la escultura* (1964), *Historia de la arquitectura* (1965), and *Historia del arte* (1974). DBEC; WhoSpain, 1963

Martineau, Alfred Albert, born 18 January 1859 at Artin (Loir-et-Cher), France, he received degrees in law as well as archival palaeography and became a barrister in the Cour de Paris; he ran for elections in 1889. During his term of office, he pursued a strong interest in colonial politics. His writings include *Madagascar* (1894), *Le commerce français dans le Levant* (1902), *Les derniers années de Dupleix* (1929), *Mémoires* (1931-34), and *Tableau de l'expansion européenne à travers le monde de la fin du XIIe au début du XIXe siècle* (1935). He died in 1941. IndexBFr² (1); Hommes et destins, vol. 5, pp. 369-74; Vapereau

Martinet, André, born 12 April 1908 at Saint-Albans-des-Villards (Savoie), France, he received a doctorate in 1937 for two theses entitled *La gémination consonantique d'origine expressive dans les langues germaniques*, and *La phonologie du mot en danois*. He was since 1938 associated with the École pratique des hautes études, Paris. His other writings include *Économie des changements phonétiques* (1955), *Éléments de linguistique générale* (1960), its translation, *Elements of general linguistics* (1964) as well as its translations into German in 1963, and Spanish in 1965, *Mémoires d'un linguiste* (1993), and he edited *Linguistics today* (1954). He died on 16 July 1999. ConAu, 11-12; WhoFr, 1979/80-1999; WhoWor, 1987/88; WrDr, 1976/78-1990/92

Martinez, Nadine, born 20th cent., her writings include *"Quand le serpent parle le bummō le répète …; étude des surfaces planes dans les œuvres d'art des Dogon, Bamana et Sénoufo du Mali, de la Côte d'Ivoire et du Burkina Faso* (1997).

Martínez Bara, José Antonio, born 20th cent., his writings include *Licencias de exencion de aposento del Madrid de Felipe II* (1962), and *Catálogo de informaciones genealógicas de la Inquisición de Córdoba conservadas en el Archivo Histórico Nacional* (1970). NUC, 1956-'72

Martínez Caviró, Balbina, born about 1930, she received a doctorate in history as well as a law degree. She specialized in Arab and Mudejar art, particularly ceramics. She was a professor of fine art at the Universidad Complutense de Madrid and an honorary director of the Museo Valencia de Don Juan. Her writings include *Catálogo de cerámica española* (1968), *Porcelana del Buem Retiro* (1973), and *Mudéjar toledano* (1980). Arabismo, 1992; EURAMES, 1993; LC

Martínez de Leiva (Leyva), Sancho, born 16th cent., he was *capitan general* of the Armada of Naples. He died in the seventeenth century. IndiceE³ (3)

Martínez Lillo, Rosa Isabel, born 20th cent., she received a doctorate in Arabic and Islamic studies and became a professor in the Departamento de Estudios Árabes e Islámicos, Universidad Autónoma de Madrid. Arabismo, 1992, 1994, 1997; EURAMES, 1993

Martínez Lillo, Sergio, born 20th cent., he received a degree in archaeology and prehistory, with special reference to Islam and became associated with the Departamento de Estudios Árabes e Islámicos, Universidad Autónoma de Madrid. He was a joint author of *II curso de arqueología subacuática* (1993). Arabismo, 1992, 1994, 1997; LC

Martínez Loscos, Carmen, born 20th cent., she received a degree in Semitic philology, with special reference to Islamic history and archives. She was associated with the Cuerpo de Archivos, Bibliotecas y Museos con destino en la Real Cancillería de Granada. Her writings include *Origines de la medicina en Aragon; los médicos árabes y judíos* (1958). Arabismo, 1992; NUC

Martínez Martín, Leonor, born 1930, she received a doctorate in Semitic philology, with special reference to Arabic literature. She was a professor at the Facultad de Filología, Universidad de Barcelona. Her writings include *Antología de poesía árabe contemporanea* (1972), and *Al Andalus* (1987). Arabismo, 1992, 1994, 1997; EURAMES, 1993; LC; WhoSpain, 1963

Martínez Montávez, Pedro, born 30 June 1933 at Jódar (Jaén), Spain, he received a doctorate in Arabic language and literature, and taught his subjects in the Departamento de Estudios Árabes e Islámicos in the Universidad Autónoma de Madrid, where he also served as chairman of the department. His writings include *Ensayos marginalos de arabismo* (1977), *Exploraciones en literatura neoarabe* (1977), *Literatura iraqui contemporanea* (1977), *Literatura árabe de hoy* (1990), he was joint author of *Europa islámica; la magia de una civilisación milenaria* (1991), and he translated *Poemas amoroso arabes*, from the Arabic of Nizār Qabbānī (1965). Arabismo, 1992, 1994, 1997; LC

Martínez Núñez, Maria Antonia, born about 1935, she received a doctorate in Semtic philology, with special reference to modern Arabic literature and Arabic epigraphy. She was a professor in the Departamento de Lengua y Literatura Árabes, Universidad de Málaga. She was a joint author of *Catálogo de las inscripciones árabes del Museo de Málaga* (1982). Arabismo, 1992, 1994, 1997; EURAMES, 1993

Martínez Ruiz, Juan, he was born on 10 November 1922 at Granada. His writings include *Inventarios de bienes moriscos del reino de Granada* (1972), and he was a joint author of *Los Ogijares; estructura socio-económica, toponimica, onomástica segun el libro de Habices de 1547-1548* (Granada, 1983). An un-identified *festschrift* was dedicated to him in 1991. LC; Note about the author

Martínez Yagüez, F., born 19th cent., he was a lawyer and editor of the journal *La Correspondencia Alicantina*. Ossorio = IndiceE³

Martini, Aldo, fl. 20th, he was an engineer whose writings include *Iran; analisi di mercato, asseto industriale e dinamica di sviluppo* (Torino, 1976). Note about the author

Martini, Erich Christian Wilhelm, born 19 March 1880 at Rostock, Germany, he received a Dr.phil. in 1903 from the Universität Rostock for *Über Furchung und Gastrulation bei Cucullanus elegans Zed.* He was from 1912 to his retirement an entomologist at the Tropeninstitut, Hamburg. His writings include *Berechnungen und Beobachtungen zur Epidemiologie und Bekämpfung der Malaria auf Grund von Balkanerfahrungen* (1921). He died in Hamburg on 5 December 1960. DtBilnd (1); Kürschner, 1926-1954; *Wer ist's*, 1935

Martino, Pierre, born 29 June 1880 at Clermont-Ferrand, France, he was a graduate of the École normale supérieure, Paris, and received a doctorate in 1906 from the Sorbonne for *L'Orient dans la littérature française*. He was a professor of French literature, and sometime dean, Faculté des lettres d'Alger. His other writings include *L'Époque romantique en France, 1815-1830* (1945). He died on 9 November 1953. Qui êtes-vous, 1924; *Revue de littérature comparée*, 28 (1954), pp. 114-15; WhE&EA

Martinovitch (Мартинович), Nicholas Nikolaevich, born 27 April 1883 in Russia, he went to the United States, where he became associated with the New York Public Library and the Metropolitan Museum of Art. His writings include *A Catalogue of Turkish and Persian manuscripts belonging to Robert Garrett and deposited in the Princeton University Library* (1926), and *The Turkish theatre* (1933). He died in N.Y.C. on 18 September 1954. BiobibSOT, pp. 213-14; NYT, 19 September 1954, p. 88, col. 6; *Wilson library bulletin*, 29 (1954), p. 200

Martins, Charles Frédéric, born 5 or 6 February 1806 at Paris, he studied medicine at the Sorbonne, Paris. A botanist and meteorologist, he was appointed to the chair of botany at the Université de Montpellier shortly after 1846. His writings include *Promenade botanique le long des côtes de l'Asie-Mineure, de la Syrie et de l'Égypte à bord de l'Hydaspe* (1858), and *Du Spitzberg au Sahara; étapes d'un naturalist* (1866). He died in 1889. Bitard; Bitard²; Dantes 1; Glaeser; Hoefer; Master (1); Vapereau

Martins, José V. de Pina, he was born 20th cent.; his writings include *L'Humanism portugais, 1500-1580, et l'Europe* (1978), and *Erasmo na Academia das Ciências de Lisboa, século XVI* (1987).

Martins de Carvalho, Henrique see Carvalho, Henrique Martins de

Martiny, Günter, born in 1903, he received a Dr.phil. in 1932 from the Technische Hochschule Berlin for a thesis on temple architecture in ancient Mesopotamia entitled *Die Kultrichtungen in Mesopotamien*. In 1933, he became an editior of the journal, *Architectura; Jahrbuch für Geschichte der Baukunst*. His writings include *Die Gegensätze im babylonischen und assyrischen Tempelbau* (1936). His trace is lost after an article in 1961. GV

de **Martoni**, Nicolas, born 14th cent., he was an Italian notary who made the pilgrimage to Jerusalem which is described in his *Relation du pèlerinage à Jérusalem de Nicolas de Martoni, notaire italien, 1394-1395*, publiée par Léon Le Grand (Paris, 1895). Note about the author

de **Martonne**, Édouard Guillaume, born in 1879, he was a *commandant* and a sometime director of the Service géographique in French West Africa as well as head of the Service topographique du Maroc. In 1939, he was a president of the Société de Topographie de France. His writings include *Le Savant colonial* (1930), *La Carte de l'empire colonial français* (1931), and *Cartographie coloniale* (1935). BN; Note about the author; NUC, pre-1956

de **Martonne**, Louis Eugène *Emmanuel*, born in 1873 at Chabris (Indre), France, he was admitted to the École normale supérieure, Paris, in 1892 and successively became a professor of geography at the univer-sities of Rennes, Lyon, and Paris, where he also served as a director of the Institut de géographie, from 1927 to 1944. He was a founding editor of the *Annales de géographie*. His writings include *La Valachie* (Paris, 1902). He died in Paris on 25 July 1955. *Bulletin* de la Société de l'Égypte, 29 (1956), pp. 5-6; DcScB; Dickinson, pp. 229-31; *Geographical journal*, 121 (1955), 547-49; *Geographical review*, 46 (1956), pp. 277-279

Martos O'Neale, José, born 19th cent., his writings include *Peligro nacional; estudios é impresiones sobre el catalanismo* (Madrid, 1901). His trace is lost after a periodical article in 1913. NUC, pre-1956

Marty, Paul Nicolas, born 6 July 1882 at Boufarik, Algeria, he went to school in Algeria first in Castiglione and then in Saint-Eugène; he received a degree in humanities at Aix-en-Provence, and in law at Alger. In 1901, he joined the 1st Regiment of the Zouaves, and one year later he became a military interpreter, being assigned mainly to Saharan regions of French North Africa as well as to French Equatorial Africa. His writings include *L'Études sur l'islam au Sénégal* (1917), *L'Émirat des Trarzas* (1919), *Études sur l'islam et les tribus du Soudan* (1920-21), and *Études sur l'islam au Dahomy* (1926). He died in Tunis on 11 March 1938. Hommes ed destins, vol. 7, pp. 329-32; Index Islamicus (1)

Martyn, Henry, born in 1781, he was a graduate of St. John's College, Cambridge, and in 1805 ac-quired a chaplaincy from the Honorable East India Company. He translated Christian literature into Urdu, Persian, and Judeo-Persian. His writings include *Christian India* (Calcutta, 1811), and he was a joint author, with Samuel Lee, of *Controversial tracts on Christianity and Mohammedanism* (1824). He died in 1812. A first biography, by J. Hall, appeared in 1832 entitled *The Life of Rev. Henry Martyn*; this was followed by at least three more by various writers. BioIn, 5, 6, 14, 17; Buckland; DNB; IndianBiInd (7); Master (5); Riddick

Martyntsev, Andreĭ Evgen'evich, born 27 April 1945, he graduated in 1968 in Turkish philology from the Oriental Faculty, Leningrad. He subsequently spent some years with the USSR Embassy in Turkey. From 1972 to his death on 31 March 1975 he was a research fellow of the Oriental Institute of the Soviet Academy of Sciences. Советская тюркология, 1975, no. 3, p. 125

Marufova, S. B., born 20th cent., she received a degree in 1969 for a work on Tajik literature and philology entitled Сложные слова в современном таджикском литературном языке и принципы их в большом таджикско-русском словаре. OSK

Marugan Güémez, Marina, born 20th cent., she received a doctorate in Semitic philology, with special reference to Arabic and Islam. In the early 1990s she was associated with the Departamento de Estudios Árabes e Islámicos, Universidad Complutense de Madrid. Her writings include El refranero andalusi de Ibn 'Āsim al-Garnāṭī (1994), and she edited Acta del Congreso International sobre Interferencias Lingüísticas Arabo-Romances y Paralelos Extra-Iberos, 1990 (1994). Arabismo, 1992; EURAMES, 1993; LC

Marunov, IUriĭ Vladimirovich, fl. 1961, his writings on current Arab-Turkish relations include Арабо-турецкие отношения на совре-менном этапе (Moscow, 1961). OSK

Marvin, Charles Thomas, born in 1854 at Plumstead, Kent, England, he spent the years from 1870 to 1876 with his father in Russia. In the following year, he entered the Foreign Office, London, but was fired after thirteen months on account of unprofessional conduct, although he had not committed any offence known to the law. He subsequently wrote numerous books on Central Asian affairs, including The Russian advance towards India (1882), The Russians at Merv and Herat (1883), The Region of eternal fire; an account of a journey to the petroleum region of the Caspian in 1883 (1884), and The Russians at the gate of Herat (1885). He died in 1890. DNB

Marvin, Francis Sydney, born in 1863 at London, he graduated from St. John's College, Oxford, and became successively an elementary school teacher, extension lecturer, inspector, and consultant to teachers' colleges. In 1929-30, he served as a professor of modern history in Egypt. His writings include The Living past (1913), The Century of hope (1919), and India and the West (1927). He died in 1943. Master (3); TwCAu; WhE&EA; Who was who, 4

Marvin, George, born 31 July 1873 at Brewster, N.Y., he graduated from Harvard University and Harvard Law School. He had a brief career in the U.S. Consular Service. During the Balkan war of 1912-1913, he was a correspondent for Colliers weekly. Afterwards he did editorial work in New York and Washington, D.C., where he died on 21 or 22 December 1955. Shavit - Asia; WhAm, 3

Marx, Emmanuel Erich, born 8 May 1927 at München, Germany, he received a Ph.D. in 1963 from the University of Manchester for A sociological analysis of kinship and corporate groups among the Bedouin of the Negev. Afterwards he taught social anthropology at the University of Manchester and in Israel. Under a grant from the Ford Foundation he and Yoram Ben-Porath published the report, Some sociological and economic aspects of the refugee camps on the West Bank (1971). His own writings include Bedouin of the Negev (1967), and The Social content of violent behaviour (1976). He was a joint editor of The changing Bedouin (1984), and The Bedouin of Cyrenaica, by Emrys L. Peters (1990). MESA Roster of members, 1982-1990; Sluglett; WhoWorJ, 1972, 1978

Marx, Gustaf A., 1855-1941 see Dalman, Gustaf Hermann

Maryam Jameela(h), born Margaret Marcus in 1934 at New York City; she became a Muslim and adapted the name Maryam Jameelah; she emigrated to Pakistan and married Mohammad Yusuf Khan. She reviewed books regularly for the Muslim world book review. Her writings include Islam versus the West (1962), The Resurgence of Islam and our liberation from the colonial yoke (1980), and two autobiographies, Memoirs of childhood and youth in America (1989), and At home in Pakistan (1990). LC

Marye, Georges, born 19th cent., his writings include Notes sur l'état de l'industrie des théâtres depuis le décret de 1864 (1877), Catalogue officiel de l'Exposition d'art musulman, Palais de l'Industrie (1893), and he was joint author of the Catalogue du Musée national des antiquités algériennes (1899). BN

Marzari, Frank O., born 1 August 1938 at Pola, Italy, he graduated in 1962 from the University of Toronto and received a Ph.D. in 1966 from the London School of Economics. He subsequently became a professor of history in the University of British Columbia, specializing in diplomatic history and international affairs. He was a joint author of Italian foreign policy, 1870-1940 (1975). He died in 1971. DrAS, 1969 H; NUC, 1973-77

Di **Marzo**, Costanza, born in 1899, he was a writer on political and colonial affairs, whose writings include Origine e sviluppi della colonizzazione belga (Napoli, 1938), and he edited Annali dell'Istituto superiore orientale di Napoli. IndBiltal (1)

Marzolph, Ulrich, born 2 May 1953 at Landau (Pfalz), Germany, he received a Dr.phil. in 1981 from the Universität Köln. He was from 1981 to 1982 a research fellow in the Oriental Institute of the German Oriental Society, Beirut. He then spent four years as an academic assistant with the Universität Köln, before joining the research project of the Akademie der Wissenschaften, Göttingen, *Enzyklopädie des Märchens*. His own monographs include *Die vierzig Papageien, čehel tuti, das persische Voksbuch* (1979), *Typologie des persischen Volkmärchens* (1981), *Der weise Narr Buhlūl* (1983), *Arabia ridens* (1992), *Wenn der Esel singt, tanzt das Kamel; persische Märchen und Schwänke* (1994), *Nasreddin Hodscha; 666 wahre Geschichten* (1996), and *Narrative illustration in Persian lithographed books* (2001). Kürschner, 1996-2005

de **Mas**, Paolo, born in 1948, he was in 1978 associated with the Sociaal-Geografisch Instituut, Universiteit van Amsterdam. He was a joint author of *A Balance of curses and blessings; government policy and development in Beni Boufrah, a small valley in the Moroccan Central Rif region* (1981), *De gezinshereniging van Marokkanen in Nederland, 1968-1984* (1985), and *Geschiedenis van Marokko* (1999). Brinkman's

de **Mas Latrie**, Jacques Marie Joseph *Louis*, Comte, born 9 April 1815 at Castelnaudary (Aude), France, he studied mathematics at military colleges but later changed to law at the Université of Paris. He subsequently joined the École des chartes, Paris. In the service of the Ministère de la Guerre he visited over a period of four years the national archives of Italy, Sicily, and Spain, investigating the relations of the Christians and North African Arabs in the middle ages prior to the Turkish rule in Alger, a project which he described in *Traités de paix et de commerce et documents divers concernant les relations des Chrétiens avec les Arabes de l'Afrique septentrionale au moyen âge* (1865). His other writings include *L'Île de Chypre* (1879), and *La Prise d'Alexandrie; ou, Chronique du Roi Pierre I de Lusignan* (1877), and *Relations et commerce de l'Afrique septentrionale; ou, Magreb avex les nations chrétiennes au moyen âge* (1886). He died in Paris on 3 January 1897. Bibliothèque de l'École des chartes, 60 (1899), 617-39 = Comptes-rendus des séances de l'Académie des Inscriptions, Paris, 4e série, 27 (1899), 711-737; GdeEnc; Glaeser; Hoefer; IndexBFr* (1); Vapereau

de **Mas Latrie**, René Marie Louis, Comte, born in 1844, he was associated with the École des chartes, Paris. His writings include *Du droit de marque, ou Droit de représailles au moyen âge* (1866). His trace is lost after an artile in 1894. BN; NUC, pre-1956

Masala, Anna, born 20th cent., her writings include *La banda militare ottomano, mehter, con l'aggiunta di testi musicali* (Roma, Università, Facoltà di Lettere e Filosofia, Lingua e Letteratura Turca, 1978). LC

Masani, Sir Rustom Pestonji, born in 1876, he was a journalist, banker, and, for six years, served as a president of the Anthropological Society of Bombay. His writings include *Folklore of wells* (1918), *Evolution of local self-government in Bombay* (1929), *Court poets of Iran and India* (1938), *The Religion of the good life, Zoroastrianism* (1938), *Education for world understanding* (1954), *The Role of wealth in society* (1956), and he translated *The Conference of the birds, a Sufi allegory*, from the Persian of Farīd al-Dīn 'Attār (1924). He died on 14 November 1966. B. K. Karanjia wrote *Rustom Masani; portrait of a citizen* (1970). Eminent; IndianBiInd (6); Master (1); Who was who, 6

Masannat, George Suleiman, born 15 October 1933 at Madaba, Transjordan, he received a Ph.D. in 1964 from the University of Oklahoma for *Aspects of American foreign policy in the Arab Middle East*. He was since 1967 a professor of government, and sometime chairman of department, at Western Kentucky University, a post which he still held in 2004. His writings include *The Political arena* (1969), and he was the compiler of *International politics* (1970), and *The Dynamics of modernization and social change* (1973). AmM&WSc, 1973 S, 1978 S; ConAu, 25-28; NatFacDr, 1995-2004; Selim

Masanov, Édige Aïdabek ogly, born 9 February 1922 at Semeĭ/Semey, Kazakstan, he was an ethnographer whose writings include *Очерк истории изучения казахского народа в СССР* (Alma-Ata, 1966). He died on 14 July 1965. KazakSE

Maschino, Maurice, fl. 1960, his writings include *Le Refus* (1960), *L'Engagement; le dossier des réfractaires* (1961), and *L'Algérie des illusions; la révolution confisquée* (1972). NUC; ZKO

Mashiah, Ya'akov, born 20th cent., he received a Ph.D. in 1972 from Columbia University, New York, for *The terminology of Hebrew prosody and rhetoric, with special reference to Arabic origins*. His writings include a collection of Persian short stories translated into Hebrew entitled *Mi-sipure Paras hahadashah* (Tel-Aviv, 1967). NUC, 1968-72; Selim

Mashtakova, Elena Innokent'evna, born in 1916 at Novonikolaevsk, she graduated in 1940 from the Faculty of Philology, Leningrad, received her first degree in 1948 for *Творческий путь Сабахаттин Али*, and her doctorate in 1982 for *Типологические модификации в турецкой литературе пере-*

ходного периода. Since 1958 she was affiliated with the Oriental Institute of the Soviet Academy of Sciences. Her writings on Turkish literature include *Из истории сатиры и юмора в турецкой литературе* (1972), and she edited the *Диван* of Mihrī Hātūn (1967). Miliband; Miliband[2]

Masià de Ros, Maria dels Àngels, born in 1907 at Figueras, Province of Gerona, Spain, she studied liberal arts, particularly history, at Barcelona, where she graduated in 1927. She received her doctorate in 1931 from the Universidad de Madrid for *Gerona en la guerra civil en tiempo de Juan II*, a work which was published in 1943 by the Consejo Superior de Investigaciones Cientificas. Since 1933 she was a lecturer. Her other writings include *La Corona de Aragón y los estados del norte de África* (1951), and *Jaume II - Aragó, Granada i Marroc; aportació documental* (1989). Dicc bio

Masiutova, Nadzhiba Khaerzamanovna, she was born on 27 November 1932. Her writings on Bashkir philology include *Восточный диалект башкирского языка* (1976), and *Башкирские говоры, находящиеся в иноязычном окружении* (1996). BashkKE

Mas-Latrie, Louis, 1815-1897 *see* Mas Latrie, Jacques Marie Joseph Louis

Maslenitsyna, Svetlana Petrovna, born 20th cent., her writings on Iranian art include *Искусство Ирана в собрании Государственного Музея Искусства Народов Востока* (Leningrad, 1975). OSK

Maslova, Gali Semenovna, born 20th cent., her writings on Oriental handicrafts include *Орнамент русской народной вышивки как историко-этнографический источник* (1978), and *Народная одежда в восточно-славянских традиционных обычаях и обрядах XIX- начала XX в.* (1984). OSK

Maslow, Boris, fl. 20th cent., he wrote on Islamic architecture and was a joint author of *Les Mosquées de Fès et du nord du Maroc* (Paris, 1937).

Maslow, Will, born in 1907 at Kiev, he came to the U.S.A. as a boy, graduated in 1929 from Cornell University, Ithaca, N.Y., and received a LL.B. 1931 from Columbia University, Ithaca, N.Y. In the following year he was admitted to the Bar of New York. He became a journalist, lawyer, administrator and executive of societies. Since 1931 he was a lecturer at the New York School for Social Research as well as the City University of New York. His writings include *How Israel will be governed* (1948), and *The Structure and functioning of the American Jewish communities* (1974). BlueB, 1973/74-1976; Master (2); WhoAm, 1974-2003; WhoE, 1991/92; WhoWor, 1974/75; WhoWorJ, 1965-1987

Masmoudi, Mohamed, he was born on 29 May 1922 or 1925 at Mahdia, Tunisia. After secondary education in Tunis, he studied at the Université de Paris, where he obtained a *licence de lettres*. Through his journalistic activities with *al-Sabah* and *al-Hurriyah*, he established important political connections so that he was appointed to the first Tunisian cabinet after independence. He held government or diplomatic posts ever since. He wrote *Les Arabes dans la tempête* (1977). Africa who's who, 1996; AfrBioInd (5); Clausen

Masnovo, Amato, born 2 November 1876 or 1880 at Parma, Italy, he was a clergyman and a professor of scholastic philosophy at the Università di Parma. His writings include *Introduzione alla Somma teologica de San Tommaso* (1918), *Il neo-Tomismo in Italia* (1923), *Problemi di metafisica e di criteriologia* (1930), *Da Guglielmo d'Auvergne a S. Tommaso d'Aquino* (1930-34), and *La filosofia verso la religione* (1948). He died in 1955. Chi è, 1928-1948; IndBiItal (1)

Mason, Alexander Herbert, born 19th cent., he served as a lieutenant with the Royal Engineers. His writings include *Operations of the Zhob Field Force under Major-General Sir G. S. White in 1890* (1892-1902), and, jointly with W. H. Paget, *A Record of the expeditions against the North-West Frontier tribes, since the annexation of the Punjab* (1884). BLC

Mason *Bey*, Alexander McComb, born 10 November 1841 at Washington, D.C., he was a graduate of Annapolis Naval College, and a veteran of the Confederate Navy during the Civil War. In 1870, he entered the service of the Egyptian Government and became a favourite with the Khedive. At first employed as officer in the Khedivial steamer service plying between Alexandria and Constantinople, he later travelled in the Sudan, making reconnaissances as far as the White Nile. His report was published in the *Bulletin de la Société khédiviale de géographie*. He was a sometime chief of the anti-slavery organization on the Red Sea coast, governor of Equatorial Africa, associated with the development of the Sudan railway, and served with General Gordon in Khartoum. In 1885, he retired from the Egyptian service. He died in Washington, D.C., on 17 March 1897. ACAB, Suppl. (not sighted); AmIndex (1); Embacher; Henze; Hill; Kornrumpf; Kornrumpf[2], vol. 2; Shavit

Mason, Herbert Warren, born 20 April 1932 at Wilmington, Del., he graduated from Harvard University, where he also received his Ph.D. in 1969 for *Two statesmen of medieval Islam, Vizir Ibn*

Hubayra and Caliph an-Nâsir li-Dîn Allâh. He was since 1972 a professor of Islamic history and religion at Boston University. His writings include *Reflections on the Middle East crisis* (1970), *Gilgamesh; a verse narrative* (1972), *The Death of al-Hallaj; a dramatic narrative* (1979), *Memoir of a friend, Louis Massignon* (1988), and *al-Hallāj* (1995). BioIn, 10; ConAu, 85-88, new rev., 16, 38; Selim; WhoAm, 1974-2003; WhoRel, 1992/93

Mason, Isaac, born about 1865 at Leeds, Yorkshire, he was a missionary who spent his first twenty-three years of service in the western provinces of China, but, in 1915, the Friends' Mission, to which he belonged, released him for literary work in Shanghai in connection with the Christian Literature Society of China. He knew that to prepare the type of Christian literature most effective for the Christian cause, he must understand Islamic literature. Thus he built up the finest collection of the time, a catalogue of which was published in the *North China Branch of the Royal Asiatic Society journal* for 1925. (This library collection was subsequently acquired by the New York Public Library.) He left China in March 1932 and retired in England. He was an authority on Chinese Islam, its literature and history. His writings include *A primer on Islam and the spiritual needs of Mohammedans in China* (1928). He was a joint author of *Life in west China* (1905), and the translator of *The Arabian prophet; a life of Mohammed from Chinese and Arabic sources, by Liu Chai-lien* (1921). At the time of his death in 1939, he was preparing a new book on "Islam in new China." *Chinese recorder*, 70 (1939), 247-248; MW, 30 (1940), p. 84

Mason, John Paul, born 1941, he received a Ph.D. in 1971 from Boston University for *The social history and anthropology of the Arabized Berbers of Augila Oasis in the Libyan Sahara Desert.* His writings include *Island of the blest; Islam in a Libyan oasis community* (1977). Selim

Mason, Kenneth, lieutenant-colonel, born in 1887 at Sutton, Surrey, England, he had a distinguished career in the Survey of India. During the First World War he was a soldier, and in the twenties, a leader of a successful expedition in the Karakorams. In 1932, he was appointed the first professor of geography at the University of Oxford, a post which he held until his retirement in 1953. His writings include *Exploration of the Shaksgam Valley and Aghil Ranges* (1928), *Abode of snow; a history of Himalayan exploration and mountaineering* (1955). For the British Naval Intelligencce Division he edited *Italy* (1944-45), and *Persia* (1945). He died on 2 June 1976. BritInd (1); *Geographical magazine*, 48 (1976), p. 267; WhE&EA; Who, 1957-1976; *Who was who*, 7

Mason, Mary Augusta, b. 1861 *see* Poynter, Mary Augusta née Mason (Dickinson)

Mason, Richard Anthony, born 22 October 1932 at Bradford, Yorkshire, England, he studied at the universities of St. Andrews and London, and became an Air Vice-Marshall. He was a joint author of *Air power in the nuclear age* (1983), and he edited *War in the third dimension* (1986). ConAu, 119; Who, 1987-2005

Mason Bey, 1841-1897 *see* Mason, Alexander McComb

Maspéro, Sir Gaston Camille Charles, born in 1846 at Paris, he was educated at the Lycée Louis-le-Grand and the École normale supérieure, Paris. He was appointed in 1869 a professor of Egyptology at the École des hautes études, Paris, and in 1874, he became a professor of Egyptian philology and archaeology at the Collège de France. He died in Paris in 1916. BiD&SB; BioIn, 1; Bitard²; Curinier, vol. 1 (1901), pp. 131-32; Dawson; Egyptology; EncBrit; EncLZ; GdeEnc; Goldschmidt; Kornrumpf; Master (4); Megali; Pallas; TwCAu; Vapereau; *Who was who*, 2

Maspéro, Jacques *Jean*, born in 1885 at Paris, he was an archaeologist, numismatist, and art collector. His writings include *Organisation militaire de l'Égypte byzantine* (1912), and *Matériaux pour servir à la géographie de l'Égypte* (1914). His collection is now in the Bibliothèque nationale, Paris, and was described by A. Launos in *Catalogue des étalons monétaires et autres pièces musulmanes en verre, de la collection Jean Maspéro* (1960). He was killed in action in 1915. Dawson; Egyptology

Masqueray, Charlemagne *Émile*, born 20 March 1843 at Rennes, France, he entered in 1866 the École normale supérieure, Paris, received his *agrégation* in history and geography, and, in 1869, obtained a post at Bastia. After serving in the 1870-71 war, he accepted a post at Alger. A trained archaeologist and particularly a sociologist, he began in 1873 with field-work in Kabylie. Since 1875 he camped for two years with Berbers of the Aurès Mountains, followed by a stay in the Mzab, where he obtained permission to copy a "sacred" text, the *Chronique d'Abou Zakaria*, which he translated and published in 1878. In 1880, he was commissioned to organize Algerian higher education; he established the École des lettres d'Alger together with its *Bulletin de correspondance africaine*, and concurrently encouraged social research. His writings include *Note concernant les Aoulad-Daoud du Mont Aurès* (1879), *For-mation des cités chez les populations sédentaires de l'Algérie* (1886), *Dictionnaire français-touareg* (1893), and *Souvenirs et visions d'Afrique* (1894). He died from heart failure in Normandie on 19 Au-gust 1894. *Hommes et destins*, vol. 7, pp. 333-34; IndexBFr² (1); ZKO

Masraff, P. M., born 19th cent., he was in 1916 an administrator with the Société Matossian, Cairo, and a member of the Société sultanieh d'économie politique, de statistique et de législation. Note

Massa, Charles André, born 6 March 1913 at Alger, he studied law at Paris and Bordeaux, and received a degree from the École nationale des langues orientales vivantes, Paris. He was in 1950 an *inspecteur des colonies*. He died on 8 March 1993. WhoFr, 1975/76-1992/93

Massa, Daniel, born 20th cent., he edited *Across cultures; Festschrift edition in honour of Professor Ġużè Acquilina* (1977). NUC

Massara, Massimo, born 20th cent., his writings include *I communist raccantato* (1972), *Storia d'Italia in date* (1973), *La Chiesa cattolica nella seconda guerra mondiale* (1977), and *La terra troppo promessa; sionismo, imperialismo e nazionalismo arabo in Palestina* (1979). LC

Massari, Claudia, fl. 20th cent., her writings include *Resultati scientifici della missione alla Oasi di Giarabùb, 1926-27* (Roma, 1928-31), and *Corso di etnologia* (Firenze, 1959). NUC

Massé, Henri Marie Nicolas Philippe, born 2 March 1886 at Lunéville, (Alsace-Lorraine), he was a professor at the Faculté des lettres d'Alger and the École nationale des langues orientales vivantes, Paris. His writings include *Contes en persan populaire* (1925), *L'Islam* (1930), *Les Épopées persanes* (1935), *Croyances et coutumes persanes* (1938), its translation, *Persian beliefs and customs* (1954), and *Antologie persane, XIe-XIXe siècles* (1950) as well as editions of classical texts. In 1963 he was honoured by *Mélanges d'orientalisme offerts à Henri Massé*. He died on 9 November 1969. Index Islamicus (5); Qui est-ce, 1934; WhoFr, 1953/54-1969/70

Massé, Pierre, born 13 January 1898 at Paris, he was a graduate of the École polytechnique, Paris. He directed several hydro-electric power projects, before he became in 1948 a deputy director general of Electricité de France. From 1965 to 1967 he was an associate professor at the Faculté de droit de Paris. His writings include *Les Reserves et la régulation de l'avenir dans la vie économique* (1946), *Les Choix des investissements* (1959), and its translation, *Optimal investment decisions* (1962). IntWW, 1974/75-1988/89|; WhoFr, 1959/60-1987/88|; WhoWor, 1974/75

Masselos, James (*Jim*) Cosmas, born 20th cent., he gained a doctorate and became a sometime reader in history at the University of Sydney. His writings include *Nationalism on the Indian Sub-continent* (Melbourne, 1972), *Towards nationalism* (Bombay, 1974), and he edted *India, creating a modern nation* (1990). LC

Freiin von **Massenbach**, Gertrud Dorothea, born 6 January 1883 at Pinne, Prussia, she was from 1909 to the outbreak of the First World War a missionary under the Sudan-Pionier-Mission in Aswan. In 1924, she returned to Nubia until the outbreak of the Second World War. In 1952, she made her last study visit to Egypt. She was also associated with the Seminar für Orientalische Sprachen, Universität Berlin. Her writings include *Als das Morgenland noch christlich war* (Wiesbaden, Evangelische Muhammadaner=Mission, 1928), and *Nubische Texte im Dialekt der Kunuzi und der Dongolawi* (1962). She died in Espelkamp, Germany, on 5 March 1975. GV; LC; LexAfrika

Massey, R. E., fl. 20th cent., his writings include *Sudan grasses* (Khartoum, Dept. of Agriculture and Forests, 1926), and, jointly with Alfred F. Broun, *Flora of the Sudan* (London, 1929).

Massey Stewart, John, born 20th cent., his writings include *Across the Russias* (London, 1969), and he edited *The Soviet environment; problems, policies, and politics* (Cambridge, 1992). LC

Massignon, Geneviève, born in 1920 or 1921, her writings include *Contes de l'Ouest* (1954), *Les Parlers français d'Acadie* (1955), *Contes corses* (1963), and *Folktales of France* (1968). She died aged forty-five in 1966. LC

Massignon, Louis, born 25 July 1883 at Nogent-sur-Marne, France, he taught at the Collège de France for nearly thirty years; in 1933 he became director of l'École pratique des hautes études, Paris, where he remained until his retirement in 1954. At the very outset of his career at the Collège de France, he founded the *Revue des études islamiques* and at the same time gave the impetus to the *Abstracta islamica*. For posterity he remains foremost the historian of Sufism. His writings include *La Passion d'al-Hallaj* (1922), and *Essai sur les origines du lexique technique de la mystique musulmane* (1922). He died in Paris on 31 October 1962. Giulio Basetti-Sani wrote the biography, *Louis Massignon* (1971), and Herbert W. Mason, *Memoir of a friend, Louis Massignon* (1988). Archives de sociologie des religions, 8 xv (1963), pp. 3-4; Hommes et destins, vol. 1, pp. 435-436; Index Islamicus (27); Kornrumpf; WhoFr, 1961/62

Massip, Jean Maurice Daniel, born 28 February 1910 at Cahors (Lot), France, he studied at the Faculté de droit de Paris and received a diploma in études supérieures de droit public et d'économie politique. He subsequently entered the Services extérieurs des régies financières. Since 1940, he was employed in a variety of government agencies. In 1966, he became the founding president of the Association pour l'étude et la prospection du marché international de l'équipement scolaire et des collectivités. WhoFr, 1969/70-1987/88|

de **Massol**, Louis Marie Antoine Ernest, Marquis, fl. 1852, his writings include *France, Algérie, Orient; souvenirs, études, voyages* (Versailles, 1860). BN

Masson, Charles, born the son of George Lewis in 1800 in England, he was a traveller in Asia, where he attempted without success to engage in trading. He therefore joined the Indian Army and was present at the 1825 siege of Bharatpur, but shortly thereafter he deserted. After his desertion he assumed the new identity of Charles Masson and became an adventurous traveller in the Valley of the Indus, in Afghanistan and in Baluchistan. He also sailed from Karachi to Muscat and back, visiting western Persia on the way. After some more travel in Baluchistan he headed again for Kabul, where he encountered Alexander Burnes. His writings include *Journeys in Balochistan and the Punjaub* (1842), its translation, *Reisen in Beludschistan, Afghanistan und dem Pendschab während eines 12jährigen Aufenthalts in diesen Ländern, 1826-1838* (1843), *Narrative of a journey to Kalât, including an account of the insurrection at that place in 1840* (1843), and *Legends of the Afghan countries* (1848). He died in 1853. One modern Indian source says he was an American, born about 1798. Embacher; Henze; IndianBiInd (4); Riddick

Masson, Denise, she was born early 20th cent., her writings include *Le Coran et la révélation judéo-chrétien* (1958), *Monothéisme coranique et monthéisme biblique* (1976), *Les Trois voies de l'Unique* (1983), *Porte ouverte sur un jardin fermé; valeurs fondamentales et traditionnelles d'une société en pleine évolution, Marrakech, 1930-1989* (1989), and in 1967, she published a French translation of the Koran. ZKO

Masson, Mikhail Evgen'evich, born in 1897 at St. Petersburg, he had hardly begun his course in engineering, when the revolutionary turmoil of 1917 put an end to his formal education. He was quite young when he sided with the new rulers, who entrusted him with important administrative and scientific responsibilities, thus complementing his academic training with field-work. In 1936, he received a doctorate in archeology, and in 1939, he was appointed to the chair of archaeology at Tashkent University, a post which held for thirty years. His writings include *Из истории горной промышленности Таджикистана* (1934), and *Падающий минарет* (1968). He was married to Galina A. Pugachenkova. He died in Tashkent on 2 November 1986. KazakSE; Kazakhskaia, vol. 3; Miliband; Miliband²; *Studia Iranica*, 17 (1988), pp. 243-246; TurkmenSE; UzbekSE

Masson, Oliver Jean Gabriel, born 3 April 1922 at Paris, he was educated at the Lycée Charlemagne and the Faculté des lettres, Paris. He subsequently taught classics at the Université de Paris. His writings include *Les Inscriptions chypriotes syllabiques* (1961), *Recherches sur les Phéniciens à Chypre* (1972), and he was a joint author of *Objets pharaoniques à inscription carienne* (1956). He died on 23 February 1997. WhoFr, 1974/75-1996/97

Masson, Paul, born in 1863 at Freyming (Moselle), France, he became a professor at the Université d'Aix-Marseille. His writings include *Histoire du commerce français dans le Levant au XVIIe siècle* (1896), *Histoire des établissements et du commerce français dans l'Afrique barbaresque* (1903), *Marseille et la colonisation française* (1906), and *Histoire du commerce français dans le Levant au XVIIIe siècle* (1911). He died in 1938. IndexBFr² (1)

Masson, Vadim Mikhaïlovich, born 3 May 1929 at Samarkand, he graduated in 1950 in history from Central Asian State University, received his first degree in 1959 for *Древняя культура Дахистана*, and his doctorate in 1963 for *Древнейшее прошлое Средней Азии*. Since 1981 he was associated with the Soviet Academy of Sciences, Institute of Archaeology, Leningrad Branch. His writings include *Экономика и социальный строй древних обществ* (1976), and he was joint author of *Central Asia; Turkmenia before the Achaemenids* (1972). Miliband; Miliband²; Schoeberlein

Massonié, Gilbert, born 19th cent., he received a doctorate in law in 1890 from the Université de Paris for *Droit romain: De la confusion dans les obligations; droit français: De la reconnaissance des enfants illégitimes*. His writings include *Les Tribunaux répressifs indigènes en Algérie* (1904), *Législation algérienne* (1909), and *Traité théorique & pratique de la compétence et de la procédure en matière musulmane; Tell, Kabylie, Sahara* (1909). BN; ZKO

Massy, Henry (Harry) Stanley, born in 1855, he was an officer in the 19th Bengal Lancers and served against Javākī-Afridis, 1877-78; in the Afghan war, 1878-80; the second Miranzai expedition, 1891; and the Tirah campaign, 1897-98. In 1900, he was a lieutenant-colonel. Dressed as a native officer of distinction and attended by his military orderly, he visited in 1893 the shrine of Imam Reza in Mashad. He died in 1920. Buckland; Note; Riddick

Massy, Percy Hugh Hamon, born in 1857, he graduated from the Royal Militray College, Sandhurst. He served in the Afghan war and also under the War Office and Foreign Office in Asia Minor and Bulgaria. He retired with the rank of colonel. His writings include *Turkey; suggestions for British traders with Turkey in Asia* (1901), and *Eastern Mediterranean lands; twenty years of life, sport and travel* (1928). He died in 1941. Kornrumpf², vol. 2; Who, 1932-1940; Who was who, 3

Master, Alfred, born 12 January 1891, he entered the Indian Civil Service in 1906 and served in India until 1934. A lecturer in Indian languages at the School of Oriental and African Studies, London, since 1937, he served from 1951 to 1957 as an assistant keeper of the India Office Library, London. His writings include *Introduction to Telugu grammar* (1947), *A Grammar of old Marathi* (1964), and, jointly with J. F. Blumhardt, *Catalogue of the Gujarati & Rajasthani manuscipts in the India Office Library* (1954). He died in 1977. Who was who, 7

Masterman, Ernest William Gurney, born in 1867, he was a fellow of the Royal College of Surgeons of England, and since 1920 an honorary secretary of the Palestine Exploration Fund, London. His writings include *Cook's Handbook for Palestine and Syria* (1907), *Studies in Galilee* (1909), *Delivrance of Jerusalem* (1918), and *Hygiene and disease in Palestine in modern and in Biblical times* (1920). He died in 1943. BioIn, 3; Kronrumpf, N; WhE&EA

Mate, Madhukar Shripad, born 20th cent., his writings include *Maratha architecture, 1650 A.D. to 1850 A.D.* (1959), *Deccan woodwork* (1967), *Nasik rāgamālā* (1982), *Daulatabad; a report on the archaeological investigations* (1992), and he was a joint author of *Paintings from the Bhagavata Purana in the Bharata Itihasa Samsodhaka Mandala* (1979). ZKO

Mateer, Mrs. Ada Haven, born 19th cent., she was the wife of an American missionary in China. Her writings include *China* (Chicago, 1886), *Siege days* (1903), *New terms for new ideas; a study of the Chinese newspaper* (Shanghai, 1913), and *Hand book of new terms and newspaper Chinese* (Shanghai, 1917). Her trace is lost after an article in 1919. Lodwick

Mateescu, Tudor, born 20th cent., he was associated with the Romanian State Archives. His writings include *Păstoritul mocanilor în teritoriul dintre Dunăre şi Marea Neagră* (Bucureşti, 1986), and he edited *Documente privind istoria Dobrogei, 1830-1877* (Bucureşti, 1975), and *Publicaţtiile Arhivvelor Statului, 1860-1977* (Bucureşti, 1978). Note; OSK

Mates, Leo, born in 1911 at Osijek, Croatia, he studied at Zagreb University. He was a diplomat, ambassador to the U.S.A., an U.N.O. official, and a sometime director of the Belgrade Institute for International Politics and Economy. His writings include *Non-alignment theory and current policy* (1972), *Koegzistencija* (1974), and *Es begann in Belgrad* (1982). He died on 9 September 1991. CurBio, 1956; HL; IntWW, 1974/75-1989; JugosISa, 1970; Ko je ko, 1957; WhoSocC, 1978; WhoWor, 1974/75

Mateu Ibars, Josefina, born 20th cent., she was associated with the Universidad de Barcelona. Her writings include *Los virreyes de Valencia* (Valencia, 1963), *Los virreyes de Cerdeña* (Padova, 1964), *Paleografía de Andalucía oriental* (1973), *Colectánea paleográfica de la Corona de Aragón, siglos IX-XVIII* (Barcelona, 1980), *Braquigrafía de sumas; estudio analitico en la traditio de algunos textos manuscritos, incunables e impresos arcaicos, siglo XIII-XVI* (1984); she was a joint author of *Bibliografía de fuentes históricas e instrumentales en bibliotecas de Granada* (Granada, 1972), *Bibliografía paleográfica* (1974); and she edited *La librería de la Orden de Montesa en el siglo XVIII* (1974). Note

Mateu Ibars, Maria de los Dolores, born 20th cent., her writings include *Iconografia de San Vicente Mártir* (Valencia, 1980); and she was a joint author of *Bibliografía de fuentes históricas e instrumentales en bibliotecas de Granada* (Granada, 1972), and *Bibliografía paleográfica* (1974). NUC

Mateu y Llopis, Felipe, born 15 November 1901 at Valencia, he studied at the local university and received a doctorate in 1926 from the Universidad Central. He was an archivist and librarian who successively served as a director of the Museo Arqueológico, the Biblioteca Provincial, Tarragona, and the Bibliotheca de Catalunya, Barcelona. His writings include *Bibliografía de Felipe Mateu y Llopis, reunida en su LXX aniversario* (1972), *El pais valencià* (1933), *Glossario hispánico de numismática* (1946), *Monedas de Mauritania* (1949), *Bibliografía de la historia monetaria de España* (1958), *Lérida y sus relaciones con Valencia* (1976). Dicc bio; IndiceE³ (2)

Matgaziev, Akbar, born 20th cent., he received a doctorate in early Uzbek philology in 1979 at Tashkent for *Исследованние по морфологии староузбекского языка; конеч XVIII - до семидесятых годов XIX в.* OSK

Matgioï, pseud. *see* Pouvourville, Eugène *Albert* Pouyou de, 1861-1939

Mather, Loris Emerson, born in 1886 at Manchester, he was educated at Harrow and Trinity College, Cambridge. In 1919, he retired from the Royal Engineers with the rank of captain and became associated with Manchester University. He was a business executive and a president of the Manchester Engineering Council. He edited his father's *The Right Honourable Sir William Mather* (1925). He died in 1976. BLC; Who, 1948-1976; *Who was who* 7

Matheson, Virginia, born about 1945, she received a Ph.D. in 1973 from Monash University, Melbourne, for *Tuhfat al-nafis = the precious gift; a nineteenth century Malay history.* Her writings include *Perceptions of the hajj* (1984), and she jointly translated from the Malay of Raja Ali Haji ibn Ahmad, *The Precious gift* (1982). LC; ZKO

Mathews, Basil Joseph, born in 1879 at Oxford, where he was also educated. He became a theologian who was successively associated with the World's Alliance of Young Men's Christian Associations, Genève, the Missionary Society, London, and, as a professor of missions, with universities and colleges in the U.S.A. and Canada. His writings include *The Riddle of Nearer Asia* (1918), *The Book of missionary heroes* (1924), *Torchbearers in China* (1924), and *Consider Africa* (1935). He died in 1935. BioIn, 2 (2), 7 (1); DNB; Lodwick; NYT, 30 March 1951, p. 23, col. 5; WhAm, 3; WhE&EA; *Who was who*, 5

Mathews, Felix A., he was born on 15 March 1835 at Tanger, the youngest son of Dr. J. A. Mathews, of Louisiana, and was educated, first at Tanger, and then at Gibraltar and the College of Stepone. Apart from English, he spoke Arabic and the Romance languages. Having lost his parents at the age of fifteen, he embarked for America to join his uncle, but was shipwrecked on the voyage at the island of Lanzarote. He entered the American navy in 1852 and served in the Mediterranean as well as on the west coast of Africa engaged in the suppression of the slave trade. He resigned in 1857 and went to California, where he later joined an expedition to British Columbia and the Frazer diggings, but soon returned to California and, in 1858, opened a school for foreign languages, painting in oil and water colours, and draughting. In 1860, he was an interpreter to the courts in California; in 1861, appointed a U.S. District Marshall for northern California; in 1869, he became a U.S. Consul to Tanger. In the summer of 1871 he went to Fes on a visit to the Sultan of Morocco. His trace is lost after an article in 1881. AmInd (1); Master (1)

Mathey, Alphonse Auguste Louis, born 5 June 1862 at Thurey (Saône-et-Loire), France, he was educated at the École forestière and became a *conservateur des eaux et forêts.* From 1900 to 1901, he was an inspector at Mostaganem, Algeria. He retired in 1922. His writings include *La Pasturage en forêt* (1900), and *Traité d'exploitation commerciales des bois* (1906-1908). He died in Flers (Orne), on 22 August 1927. IndexBFr² (1)

Mathieu, Antoine *Auguste*, born 14 March 1814 at Nancy, France, he graduated in 1835 from the École forestière, where he served from 1838 to 1851 as a professor. His writings include *Flore forestière; description et histoire des végétaux ligneux qui croissent spontanément en France et des essences importantes de l'Algérie* (1860), and *Les Hautes-plateaux oranais* (1891). He died in Nancy on 13 November 1890. IndexBFr² (1); *Mémoires* de l'Académie de Stanislas, 5e série, 9 (1891), pp. 1-48

Mathieu, Jean, fl. 20th cent., he was a joint author, with Roger Maneville, of *Les Accoucheuses musulmanes traditionnelles de Casablanca* (1952). NUC, pre-1956

Mathieu, Joseph, born in 1829, he was a head of the secretariat of the Marseille Chambre de commerce. His writings include *Les Grandes processions à Marseille depuis le moyen âge jusqu'à nos jours* (1864), and *Marseille, statistique et histoire; population, consommation* (1879). BN; NUC, pre-1956

Mathieu, Marcel, colonel, born 17 May 1909, he wrote *Une vie exaltante* (Annecy, 1981). LC

Mathieu, Marguerite, fl. 20th cent., her writings include *La Sicile normande dans la poésie byzantine* (Firenze, 1954), and she edited *La Geste de Robert Guiscard* (Palermo, Istituto Siciliano di Studi Bizantini e Neoellenici, 1961).

Mathiopoulos, Basil Vasos/*Wassos* Petros, born in 1928, he received a doctorate in 1954 from the Universität Bonn for *Geschichte und Entwicklung des Sozialismus in Griechenland.* His other writings include *Die Geschichte der sozialen Frage und des Sozialismus in Griechenland, 1821-1961* (1961), *Athen brennt; der 21. August 1967 in Griechenland* (1967), and its translations, *Athènes brûle* (1968), and *Il colpo dei colonnelli* (1968). GV; LC

Mathorez, Jules Michel Henri, he was born in 1873; his writings include *Guillaume aux Blanches-Mains, évêque de Chartres* (1911), and *Les Étrangers en France sous l'ancien régime* (1919-21). He died in 1923. BN; NUC, pre-1956

de **Mathuisieulx**, Henri Méhier, 1860- *see* Méhier de Mathuisieulx, Henri

Matiakubov, Otanazar, born 25 August 1946 at Khiva, he graduated in 1970 from Tashkent State Conservatory, and received his first degree in 1977 for *Хорезмские макомы*. He later taught at the Conservatory, since 1980 as a professor of Oriental music. His writings include *Фараби об основах музыки Востока* (1986). Miliband²

Matiukhin, Ivan Semenovich, born 17 February 1928 in Russia, he graduated in 1951 from the Institute of Foreign Trade of the Ministry of Foreign Trade, and received his first degree in 1964 for *Внешнеэкономические связи ОАР*. He was associated with the Ministry in a variety of posts since 1951. From 1955 to 1958, and again from 1962 to 1965, he was assigned to Egypt. His writings include *Объединенная Арабская Республика* (1966). Miliband²

Matković, Petar, born 18 June 1830 at Senj, Croatia, he was a geographer who had studied at the universities of Wien, Prag, Berlin, and Göttingen. He became a professor at Zagreb University. His writings include *Hrvatska i Slavonija* (1873), and *Reisen durch die Balkanhalbinsel während des Mittelalters* (1880). He died in Wien on 25 March 1898. EncLZ; HL

Matkovski, Aleksandar, born 30 May 1922, he gained a doctorate. His writings include *Диетот - крвнината во Македонија и на балканскиот полуостров за време на турското владеење* (Skopje, 1973), *A History of the Jews in Macedonia* (Skopje, 1982), *Македонскиот полк во Украина* (1985), *Кануни и фермани за Македонија* (1990), and he edited *Macédonie; articles d'histoire* (Skopje, 1981). Note about the author; OSK

Matl, Joseph, born 10 March 1897 at Schirmdorf, Styria, Austria, he was educated at Humanistisches Knabenseminar, Graz, and studied Slavic languages at the Universität Graz. After 1945 he taught first at Grazer Handelsakademie and later at the Universität Graz. His writings include *Europa und die Slawen* (1964), *Südslawische Studien* (1965), and *Die Kultur der Südslawen* (1970). He died on 14 June 1974. A memorial volume, *Gedenkschrift für Josef Matl*, was published in 1977. Kürschner, 1954-1966; SlovBioL; *Südost-Forschungen*, 33 (1974), pp. 320-21; WhoAustria, 1955-1969/70

Matley, Ian Murray, born 23 October 1921 at Edinburgh, he received an M.A. from the local University, and a Ph.D. in 1961 from the University of Michigan, Ann Arbor, for *The Soviet approach to geography*. He was since 1967 a professor of geograpgy at Michigan State University. His writings include *Romania; a profile* (1970), *The Geography of international tourism* (1976), and he was a joint author of *Economic atlas of the Soviet Union* (1960), and *An Atlas of the Russian and East European history* (1967). AmM&WSc, 1973 S; AmM&WSc, 1976 P

Matouš, Lubor, born 2 November 1908 at Náchod, he became a professor of Assyriology at Praha. His writings include *Bedřich Hrozný, the life of a Czech Oriental scholar* (1949), *Základy akkadské gramatiky* (1952), and he edited *Die lexikalischen Tafelserien der Babylonier und Assyrer in den Berliner Museen* (1933), and he translated *Epos o Gilgamešovi* (1971). In 1978 he was honoured by *Festschrift Lubor Matouš*. He died in Praha on 2 April 1984. Filipsky; Hanisch; OSK

Matringe, Denis, born 26 May 1953 at Belfort, France, he studied at Strasbourg and Paris, where he received a doctorate in 1982. He was an editor of the *Journal asiatique*, and associated with the C.N.R.S. as a *directeur de recherche*. He conducted field-work in Pakistan and India. His writings include *Hīr Vāris̲ Šāh* (1988), he edited and translated *Masnavîs, poèmes d'amour de l'Inde moghole*, of Mīr Taqī Mīr (1993), and he translated from the Panjabi of Amrita Pritam, *Pinjar le squelette* (2002). AnElFr, 1997; *Livres disponibles*, 2004; Private

Matsakov, Ivan Matsakovich, born 20th cent., his writings on Kalmuck literature include *Калмыцкая советская художест-венная литература* (1967), *Современная калмыцкая проза* (1970), *Ветераны калмыцкой лите-ратуры* (1976), and *Писатель и время* (1987). OSK

Matson, Frederick Rognald, born 29 July 1912 at Chicago, he graduated in 1933 from the University of Illinois and received a Ph.D. in 1939 from the University of Michigan for *A technological study of the unglazed pottery and figurines from Seleucia on the Tigris*. He participated in 1936-37 in the University of Michigan expedition to Iraq as a field archaeologist. He was since 1949 associated with the University of Pennsylvania as an anthropologist, archaeologist, teacher, and administrator. He was a joint author of *Early Arabic glass weights and stamps* (1948), and he edited *Ceramics and man* (1965). AmM&WSc, 1973 S; AMS, 1968; Bioln, 2, 13; WhoAm, 1974/75-1976/77

Matsson, G. Olof, he was born in 1891; his writings include *A Historical outline of Palestine* (Stockholm, 1958), and *The Gods, goddesses and heroes on the ancient coins of Bible lands* (Stockholm, 1969). NUC

Matteo, Ignazio di, 1872-1948 *see* Di Matteo, Ignazio

Mattern, Joseph, S.J., born in 1869 at Andlau, France, he was educated at the École apostolique de la Province de Champagne. He spent many years in the East studying philosophy and Arabic, which he knew well. A *supérior de la mission*, he served as a director-general of the Sœurs des Saints-Cœurs, and rector of the Séminaire maronite de Rome. His writings include *À travers les villes mortes de Haute Syrie; promenades archéologiques en Syrie, 1928, 1929, 1931* (1933), *Villes mortes de Haute Syrie* (1944), and he was a joint author of *Dair-Solaib* (1939). He died in 1943. BN; Jalabert

Mattes, Hanspeter, born 6 July 1951 at Schwäbisch-Hall, Germany, he studied political economy, spent 1976-79 as a scholarship student in Tunisia and Libya, and received a Dr.phil. in 1982 from the Universität Heidelberg for *Die Volksrevolution in der Sozialistischen Arabischen Volksgamahiriyya*. In 1983 he joined the Deutsches Orient-Institut, Hamburg, a post which he still held in 1993, concurrently teaching at the Universität Hamburg. In 1986 he became the founding publisher and editor of the journal *Wuqūf*. His writings include *Aspekte der libyschen Außeninvestitionspolitik, 1972-1985* (1985), *Al-Da'wa al-islamiya; die innere und äußere islamische Mission Libyens* (1986), *Die islamistische Bewegung des Senegal zwischen Autonomie und Außenorientierung* (1989), and *Qaddafi und die islamistische Opposition in Libyen; zum Verlauf eines Konflikts* (1995). EURAMES, 1993; Private

Matthee, Rudolph (*Rudi*) P., born 18 November 1953 at Oosterhout, the Netherlands, he studied Arabic as well as Islamic and Iranian subjects at the universities of Utrecht, Tehran, Cairo and Los Angeles, and received a doctorate in 1991. He taught at Utrecht, conducted field-work at the East India Company's archives, and in Egypt. In 1993, he was appointed a professor of Middle Eastern history in the University of Delaware, Newark, Del., a post which he still held in 2005. His writings include *The Politics of trade in Safavid Iran; silk for silver, 1600-1730* (1999), and he was a joint editor of *Iran and beyond; essays in Middle Eastern history in honor of Nikki R. Keddie* (2000). AnEIFr, 1996; *MESA Roster of members*, 1990; NatFacDr, 1995-2005; Private

Matthes, Benjamin Frederik, born 16 January 1818 at Amsterdam, he studied humanities and theology, from 1835 to 1838 at Leiden, and from 1838 to 1841 at the Luthersche Seminarium, Amsterdam. He subsequently joined the service of the *Evangelisch-Luthersche* church. After a brief period at Rotterdam, he continued his study at Heidelberg, and served from 1844 to 1848 as a deputy director at the missionary institute, Zendeling-Instituut, Rotterdam. In 1848, he went to southern Celebes as a delegate of the Nederlandsch Bijbelgenootschap, with a view to learn the local languages in order to translate the Bible. Except for two long interruptions, he remained in Celebes until he retired to 's Gravenhage at the end of October 1879. As a result of his efforts, he established a teachers' seminary for native teachers as well as interpreters. His writings include *Makassaarsche chrestomathie* (1860), *Boeginesche chrestomathie* (1864-72), *Bijdragen tot de ethnologie van Zuid-Celebes* (1875), and he was a joint editor of the Arabic *Annales* of Abū al-Mahāsin ibn Taghrībirdī (1855-61). He died in Nijmegen on 9 October 1908. BiBenelux² (1); EncNI; NieuwNBW

Matthew, John Godfrey, born 14 March 1881, he joined the Sudan Political Service and served in Sennar and the Red Sea provinces. He died on 3 June 1947. Who, 1932-1946; *Who was who*, 4

Matthews, Ahmed Thomas James, born 19 January 1921 at Seattle, Wash., he graduated in 1948 from Washington State College, and received a Ph.D. in 1953 in sociology and anthropology from Cornell University, Ithaca, N.Y. He taught in the Near and Middle East, before becoming in 1971 a professor in his subject at Mansfield (Pa.) State College. AmM&WSc, 1973 S, 1978 S; *MESA Roster of members*, 1977-1990

Matthews, Charles D., born 15 January 1901 at Piedmont, Ala, he graduated in 1922 from Birmingham-South College, Ala., and received a Ph.D. in 1932. He taught foreign languages at his alma mater until 1943 and subsequently held a variety of posts until 1961, when he was appointed a professor of linguistics at the Middle East Center, University of Texas at Austin. His writings include *Palestine, Mohammedan Holy Land* (1949), and he edited *Kitāb bā'iṭu-n-nufūs of Ibnu-l-Firkāh* (1935). DrAS, 1969 F, 1974 F; Note about the author

Matthews, Geoffrey Frank, born in 1937, he was in 1967 a tutor in international relations, Department of Extra-Mural Studies, University of Southampton. His writings include *The Re-conquest of Burma* (1966). LC; Note about the author

Matthiessen, Ludwig, born 22 September 1830 at Fissau near Eutin, Holstein, Germany, he studied mathematics, astronomy, and natural sciences at the Universität Kiel. After teaching for fifteen years at schools in Jever and Husum, he became in 1874 a professor of physics at the Universität Rostock. A *Rektor* of the Universität, 1885/86, he was appointed director of the observatory in 1888. His writings include *Grundzüge der antiken und modernen Algebra der litteralen Gleichungen* (1878). He died in Rostock on 15 November 1906. DtBE; DtBiInd (3)

Mattison, Beatrice McCown, born early twentieth century, she resided in the Middle East for some time prior to the second World War. From 1945 to 1947, she was assistant professor of political science at Bryn Mawr College, Pennsylvania. Afterwards she was special assistant at the Division of Near Eastern Affairs, U.S., Department of State, 1947-1948. In 1951, she was resident in Egypt. Middle East journal

Mattock, John Nicholas, born 6 January 1938 at Horsham, Sussex, he was a graduate of Pembroke College, Cambridge, where he also received a Ph.D. in 1969 for *A Critical edition of the Arabic version of Aristotle's "De animalibus historia."* He taught in the Department of Arabic and Islamic Studies, University of Glasgow. He was a joint author of *Kitāb al-ajinna li-Buqrāt; Hippocrates on embryos* (1978), and he edited *Kitāb Buqrāt fī tābi'at al-insān; On the nature of man, of Hippocrates* (1968), *Kitāb Buqrāt fi'l-amrad al-biladiyya; On endemic diseases, of Hippocrates* (1969), and *Kitāb Buqrāt fi'l-akhlāt; On humours, of Hippocrates* (1971). DrBSMES, 1993; Sluglett; WhoWor, 1989/90-1993/94

Matton, Sylvain, born 20th cent., his writings include *La Magie arabe traditionnelle; Ibn Khaldun, al-Kindi, Ibn Wahshîya, Picatrix*, traduit de l'arabe (Paris, 1977), and he edited *Les Aventures du philosophe inconnu en la recherche et l'invention de la pierre philosophale* (Paris, 1978), and *Le Dernier testament*, of Basile Valentin (Paris, 1977).

Mattušová, Miroslava, fl. 20th cent., her writings include *La letteratura italiana in Cecoslovacchia dal 1945 al 1964* (Praga, P.E.N. Club cecoslov., 1965). OSK

Matunák, Michael, born 17 July 1866 at Šurancy, he trained for the priesthood at the Catholic Seminary, Budapest, and in 1898 became a director of a school in Korpona (Krupina), Slovenia. In 1922, he was an archivist at Kremnica, where he died on 5 December 1932. His writings include *Z dejín slobodného a hlavného mesta Kremnice* (1928), and he was a joint author of *Život a boje na slovensko-tureckom pohraničí* (1983). Filipsky; GeistigeUng; LC

Matuz, Josef Eugen, born 27 October 1925 at Budapest, he received a Dr.phil. in 1961 from Freie Ukrainische Universität München for a thesis on the diplomatic relations of the Crimea and Denmark in the eighteenth century entitled *Diplomatische Beziehungen zwischen dem Chanat der Krim and Dänemark in der zweiten Hälfte des 17. Jahrhunderts*, and a Dr.habil. in 1974 at Freiburg for *Das Kanzleiwesen Sultans Süleymans des Prächtigen.* He was a professor of Islamic studies at the Universität Freiburg. His writings include *Herrscherurkunde des Osmanensultans Süleyman des Prächtigen* (1971), *Das Osmanische Reich; Grundlinien seiner Geschichte* (1985), *Die Steuerkonskription des Sandschaks Stuhlweißenburg aus den Jahren 1563 bis 1565* (1986), *Ottoman records on the history of the Christians in Palestine* (1992). In 1992, he was honoured by *Osmanistik, Turkologie, Diplomatik; Festgabe an Josef Matuz.* He died in Freiburg im Breisgau on 20 December 1992. Kürschner, 1970-1992; Private; Schwarz

Matveev, A. M., fl. 20th cent., his writings include *Социально-политическая борьба в Астрабаде* (1957), and *Зарубежные выходцы в Туркестане на путях к Великому Октябрю* (1977). OSK

Matveev, Konstantin Petrovich, born 10 December 1934 at Voronezh, Russia, he there graduated from the Pedagogical Institute, and received his first degree in 1966 at Moscow for *Ассирийцы в период 1914-1933 гг*, and his doctorate in 1983 for a thesis on the modern Assyrians entitled *Национально-освободительная борьба ассирийского народа за свободы и независимость как часть национально-освободительного движения.* He was appointed a lecturer in 1975, and a professor in 1987. He was since 1975 a member of the journalists' association. His writings include *Истребителькольюцек* (1974), *Ассирийцы и ассирийская проблема в новое и новейсее время* (1979), *Ассиро-вавилонская символика и образы в мировой художественной литературе, публицистике и поэзии* (1992), and he was a joint author of *Пять жизней древней Сури* (1989), *История и этнография ассирийцев* (1990). Miliband; Miliband[2]

Matveev, Viktor Vladimirovich, born 1 September 1928 at Moscow, he graduated in 1951 from the Oriental Faculty, Leningrad, and received his first degree in 1955 for a thesis entitled *Из истории русского востоковедения.* Since 1956, he was associated with the Leningrad Division of the Institute of Ethnography in the Soviet Academy of Sciences. His writings include *Средневековая Северная Африка* (1993), and he was a joint author of *Египет - сын тысячелтий* (1959). Miliband; Miliband[2]; Unesco

Matyukhin, I. S., 1928- see Matiukhin, Ivan Semenovich

Matzke, Monika, born about 1950 in Germany, she completed her Persian studies under Buzurg Alavi at Humboldt Universität, Berlin, and subsequently taught Persian at her alma mater well into the twenty-first century. She was a joint author of *Kurzgefaßte praktische Grammatik der persischen*

Sprache (Zwickau, Zentralstelle für Lehr- und Organisationsmittel des Ministeriums für Hoch- und Fachschul-wesen, 1985), and she translated from the Persian of Fahimeh Farsaie, *Hüte dich vor den Männern, mein Sohn* (Köln, 1998). Private; ZKO

Mauchaussée, Paul, fl. 20th cent., he received a doctorate in 1931 from the Université de Paris for *L'Évolution des principes dominants du régime minier au Maroc.* He was a joint author, with René Hoffherr, of *Formules modernes d'organisation minière africaine; Maroc français - Congo belge* (1933), and *Charbon et pétrole en Afrique du nord* (1935). BN

Maud, Constance Elizabeth, born 19th cent., she was a novelist whose writings include *An English girl in Paris* (1890), *Wagner's heroes* (1895), *Felicity in France* (1906), *A Daughter of France* (1908), and *Sparks among the stubble* (1924). She died in 1929. Obituary in the Times, London, 21 May 1929, p. 16, col. 3 (not sighted); Master (1); WomNov

Maude, James Ashley, born 18th cent., he was a British sea captain who, in July 1816, discovered eight islands in the southern Persian Gulf. Henze

Maudoodi, Syed Abu'l Ala, Maulana, born in 1903 in India, he became a Pakistani by virtue of the partition of 1947. His writings and influence have been a major factor in shaping twentieth century developments in the Sub-continent. He was a traditionalist in the sense that he adhered firmly to the orthodox teachings of Islam. Yet, at the same time, he was a modernist because he himself sought to influence political and social change. His interest in politics led him to form one of the leading political parties in Pakistan, the Jama'at-i Islami. In the English-speaking world he is probably best known for his book *Towards understanding Islam* (1940). He died on 22 September 1979, in Buffalo, N.Y., while visiting his son. ConAu, 89-92

Mauger, Roger Paul Jean, born in 1908, he received a doctorate in law in 1944 from the Université d'Alger for *Le contrôle des prix en Algérie aux points de vue administratifs et pénal.* BN; NUC, pre-1956

Maugini, Armando, born 1 May 1889 at Messina, he received a doctorate in agricultural sciences in 1912 from the Università di Bologna. He became a professor of Tropical agriculture at Firenze, and a director of the Istituto agronomico per l'Otremare. His writings include *Le Colonie italiane di diretto dominio* (1931), *El Trabajo italiano en Africa* (1948), and he was a joint author of *Le Pecore e le lane dell'Africa settentrionale* (1929), and *Food aid from the EEC to developing countries* (1965). Unesco

Mauguin, Georges Charles, born 4 June 1881 at Paris, he graduated from the military college of Saint-Cyr and the École de guerre. Gravely injured in the first World War, he was invalided (80%) home. He subsequently pursued a literary interest in the period of the first *Empire*. He was a chief editor of the *Revue des études napoléoniques.* His writings include *Le Maréchal Ney et le Maréchal Blücher à Nancy en 1814* (1930), *Napoléon et la superstition* (1946), and *Le Napoléon de Sainte-Hélène* (1951). He died 13 May 1961. NDNC, 1964

Mauldin, Wayman Parker, born 18 October 1914 at Six Mile, S.C., he graduated in 1935 from Clemson College, S.C. Since 1976, he was associated with the Population Council, New York, as a statistician and demographer. His writings include *The Population of Poland* (1954). AmM&WSc, 1973 S, 1978 S; WhoE, 1974-1977/78

Maula, Erkka, born 3 September 1935, he gained a doctorate in philosophy and was in 1980 a member of the Interdisciplinary Academy, Hauho, Finland. His writings include *Studies in Plato's theory of forms in the Timaeus* (Helsinki, 1970), *On the semantics of time in Plato's Timaeus* (Åbo, 1970), *Studies in Eudoxus' homocentric spheres* (Helsinki, 1974), and he was a joint author of *Enklima* (Athens, 1982), and *Les Débuts de l'astronomie de la géographie et de la trigonométrie chez les Grecs* (Paris, 1986). LC

Maull, Hanns Walter, born 5 October 1947 at Augsburg, Germany, he received a Dr.phil. in 1975 from the Universität München for *Konflikt und Konfliktverhalten; eine Fallstudie; die Rolle Ägyptens, Syriens und Jordaniens im Konflikt mit Israel.* He was a journalist for the Bavarian radio, before he obtained his Dr.habil. and successively became a professor of international politics at the Universität Trier, and the Katholische Universität Eichstätt. His writings include *Ölmacht; Ursachen, Perspektiven, Grenzen* (1981), *Bowing to the winds of change* (1994), *Regionalismus in Asien-Pazifik* (1998), and *Multilateralismus in Ostasien-Pazifik* (2001). Kürschner, 1992-2005; Schwarz; Wer ist wer, 1994/95-2005/2006

Maull, Otto, born 8 May 1887 at Frankfurt am Main, he studied at Frankfurt, Berlin, and München, and he received a doctorate in 1910 at Marburg for *Die bayerische Alpengrenze.* He served as a professor of geography, from 1919 to 1929 at Frankfurt, and from 1929 to 1945 at Graz. His writings include *Griechisches Mittelmeergebiet* (1922), its translation, *Geografía del Mediterráneo griego* (1928), *Politische Geographie* (1925), *Geographie der Kulturlandschaft* (1932), and *Frankreichs Überseereich*

(1935). The University of Athens granted him an honorary doctorate. He died on 16 December 1957. DtBE; Kürschner, 1925-1954; *Mitteilungen der Geographischen Gesellschaft in München*, 42 (1957), pp. 233-47; NDB; *Südost-Forschungen*, 17 (1958), pp. 412-16; *Wer ist's*, 1935

Maumené, Charles Gustave Vincent, he was born 19th cent.; his writings include *Histoire de 3e régiment du cuirassiers* (Paris, 1893), and he was a joint author of *Iconographie des rois de France* (Paris, 1929-1932). BN; NUC, pre-1956

Maunier, René, born 26 August 1887 at Niort (Deux-Sèvres), France, he received a doctorate in law in 1909 from the Université de Paris for *La localisation des industries urbaines*. He was a professor at l'École khédiviale de droit du Caire, 1911-18; a director at the Egyptian Ministry of Justice, 1918-20; and in 1924 he was appointed a professor at the Faculté de droit de Paris. He was a member of the Société sultanieh d'économie politique, de statistique et de législation. His writings include *La Vie municipale en Égypte* (1914), *Manuel bibliographique des sciences sociales et économiques* (1920), *La Construction collective de la maison en Kabylie* (1926), *Mélanges de sociologie nord-africaine* (1930), *Loi française et coutume indigène en Algérie* (1932), *Coutumes algériennes* (1935), *Introduction au folklore juridique* (1938), and *Sociologie coloniale* (1949). *Dictionnaire nationale des contemporains*, 1936

Maunoir, Charles Jean, born 23 June 1830 at Poggibonsi (Toscana), he joined the French army and served until discharged after an accident in 1853. For the rest of his life he devoted himself entirely to the Société de géographie, Paris, where he served from 1867 to 1897 as general secretary. He was also an editor of the *Année géographique*. He edited *Journal de route Henri Duveyrier* (1905). He died in Paris on 22 December 1901. IndexBFr² (2); Note

Maunsell, Eustace Ball, lieutenant-colonel, born 19th cent., his writings include *Prince of Wales's Own, the Scinde Horse, 1839-1922* (London, 1926). NUC, pre-1956

Maunsell, Francis Richard, born in 1861 at Limerick, Ireland, he was a graduate of the Royal MIlitary College, Woolwich, and served two years as a military vice-consul in Anatolia. He explored eastern Anatolia, particulary Kurdistan, journeys about which he reported in geographical journals. He died in 1936. Kornrumpf³, vol. 2; Who, 1921-1936; *Who was who*, 3

Mauny, Raymond Auguste René, born 12 January 1912 at Nogent-sur-Marne (Seine), France, he studied law at Poitiers, and law and humanities at both Poitiers and Paris, where he gained a doctorate in 1940 for *La Question coloniale dans les rapports franco-italien depuis 1918*. He became an administrator with La France d'outre-mer in 1942, an assistant in the Institut français d'Afrique noire, Dakar, in 1947, and a *directeur de recherches* at the Office de la recherche scientifique et technique outre-mer in 1959. After two theses for the Université de Paris, *Les Navigations médiévale sur les côtes sahariennes antérieures à la découverte portugaise, 1434* (1960), and *Tableau géographique de l'Ouest africain au moyen âge* (1961), he began lecturing at the Sorbonne. He served as a visiting professor at the University of California, Los Angeles, 1963, 1966, and 1969. His other writings include *Gravures, peintures et inscriptions rupestres de l'Ouest africain* (1954), and he was a joint author of *The Historian in Tropical Africa* (1964). Unesco; WhoFr, 1974/75-1981/82|; WhoWor, 1974/75, 1976/77

Maupin, Georges, born in 1867 at Landerneau (Finistère), France, he was a professor of mathematics at the Collège de Saintes (Charente-maritime), and a member of the Société mathématique de France. His writings include *Questions d'algèbre* (1895), and *Opinions et curiosités touchant la mathématique* (1898). IndexBFr² (1)

Maupoil, Bernard, born 17 November 1906 at Paris, he received a degree in 1932 from the École Coloniale, and subsequently served in Dahomey, Dakar, and Guinea. He became a stout defender of African culture and religions. Mobilized in 1939, he was assigned to Dakar. As an opponent to the Vichy government, he was sent to Guninea as an archivist. In 1942, he went on furlough to France, where he joined the Résistance at Lyon. He received a doctorate in 1943 for his two theses, *La Géomancie à l'ancienne Côte des esclaves*, and *Contribution à l'ètude de l'origine musulmane de la géomancie dans le Bas-Dahomey*. Arrested in the summer of 1943, he was sent a year later to Germany, where he died from exhaustion in December 1944 in a labour camp in Hersbruck. *Hommes et destins*, 1, pp. 439-40

Maura y Gamazo, Gabriel, Duque de Maura, born in 1879 at Madrid, he was a historian whose writings include *La cuestion de Marruecos desde el punto de vista español* (1905), its translation, *La question du Maroc au point de vue espagnol* (1911), *El convenio entre España y Francia relativo á Marruecos* (1913), *Rincones de la historia siglo VIII al XIII* (1941), and *La crisis de Europa* (1955). He died in 1963. CIDMEL; Espasa; IndiceE³ (10)

Maurach, Reinhart, born 25 March 1902 at Simferopol, Crimea, he studied law at the universities of Würzburg and Breslau, where he received his Dr.jur. in 1927 for a thesis on the legal status of foreigners in Russia entitled *Die Rechtsstellung der Ausländer in der U.d.S.S.R.* He became a judge at Breslau and concurrently was associated with the local Osteuropa-Institut as an expert in Soviet law. Although dismissed for political reasons in 1937, he was appointed in 1944 a professor in the Universität Königsberg. He returned from a Soviet POW camp in 1947 and subsequently served as a professor of criminal and East European law at the Universität München. His writings include *Grundlagen des räterussischen Strafrechts* (1933), *Kritik der Notstandslehre* (1935), and *Die Kriegs-verbrecherprozesse gegen deutsche Gefangene in der Sowjetunion* (1954). He died in Salo, Italy, on 11 June 1976. DtBE; Kürschner, 1950-1976; NDB; Wer ist wer, 1958-1974/75

Mauran, Dr., born 19th cent., his writings include *Le Maroc d'aujourd'hui et demain* (Rabat, 1909), *La Société marocaine; études sociales* (Paris, 1912), *L'Organisation et les buts du service de la Santé et de l'hygiène publiques du protectorat du Maroc* (Casablanca, 1918), and he was a joint author of *Le Ministère de la Santé et de l'hygiène publiques du Maroc* (Casablanca, 1925). BN; NUC, pre-1956

Maurer, Franz, born 19th cent., he was a Prussian journalist who visited the Balkans at his own expense. His writings include *Die Nikobaren; Colonial-Geschichte* (Berlin, 1867), and *Eine Reise durch Bosnien, die Saveländer und Ungarn* (Berlin, 1870). Kornrumpf

Maurer, Gérard, born in 1924, he was a geographer whose writings include *Le Rif central; carte géomorphologique* (1965), and *Les Montagnes du Rif central; étude géomorphologique* (1968). He was honoured by *Hommage à Gérard Maurer* (Poitiers, Centre interuniversitaire d'études méditer-ranéennes, 1987). LC; ZKO

Mauret, Élie, born 1 December 1925 at Saint-Palais (Charente-Maritime), France, he studied at the École de Versailles, where he specialized in landscape gardening, and subsequently graduated also from the Institut d'urbanisme de Paris. He received a doctorate from the Université de Paris for *L'Urbanisme et la poussée démographique au Maroc.* He started his career with the Ministère de la Construction pour la Seine-et-Oise, where he worked as an engineer from 1947 to 1950. He then worked until 1953 as an *architect urbaniste* at Rabat-Salé in the Services de l'Urbanisme du Maroc, followed by three more years studying development projects in the same region as well as in some other Moroccan rural com-munities. When he returned to France, he entered the Compagnie nationale d'aménagement of the Région Bas-Rhône and Languedoc as a *chef de service.* His writings include *Pour un équilibre des villes et des campagnes; aménagement, urbanisme, paysage* (Paris, 1974). NDNC, 1963

Maurette, Fernand, born in 1878, his writings include *La France et ses colonies* (1922), *Géographie de la France* (1923), and *Afrique équatoriale, orientale et australe* (Paris, 1938). He died in 1937. BN; NUC, pre-1956

Maurice, Sir Frederick Barton, he was born in 1871 at Dublin, and graduated from the Royal Military College, Sandhurst. He was one of the foremost British military critics and interpreters of the War. Following his frank speaking on the conduct of military operations early in the War, he devoted himself to interpreting the First World War ever since his resignation as director of military operations of the General Staff of the British Army. His writings include *The Last four months* (1919), *The Life of Lord Wolseley* (1924), *Government and war* (1926), and *The Maurice case; from the papers of Major-General Maurice*, edited by Nancy Maurice (1972). He died in 1951. BioIn, 2, 9; DNB; GrBr; NYT, 20 May 1951, p. 88, cols. 5-6; Who was who, 5

Maurice, Godfrey Kindersley, born in 1887, he entered the Royal Army Medical Corps, and served in Egypt and the Sudan; he retired with the rank of colonel. He died in 1949. Who was who, 4

Maurício Gomez dos Santos, Domingos, born 29 March 1896 at Perafita (Matozinhos), Portugal, he studied at the Pontificia Università Gregoriana, Roma. In 1910, he entered the Society of Jesus as a noviciate. In 1915, he went to Spain for literary studies, returning once more to the Gregoriana, where he received a doctorate in 1923. In 1929, he joined the editorial staff of the journal *Brotéria.* His writings include *A mensagem artística de Antero do Figueiro* (Lisboa, 1945), and he was a joint author of *À memória do Dr. António de Vasconcelos* (Lisboa, 1948). QuemPort, 1947

Maurin, Claude, born 17 March 1925 at Oran, Algeria, he studied biological sciences and received a doctorate. He started his career in 1954 as an oceanographer in the Institut des pêches du Maroc. Employed in France since 1957, he was in 1979 an administrator in the Centre national d'exploitation des océans. His writings include *Les Merles du Maroc et leur pêche* (Casablanca, 1954). IndexBFr² (1); WhoFr, 1971/72-1983/84|

MACK LIBRARY
BOB JONES UNIVERSITY
GREENVILLE, SC

Maurizi, Vincenzo, born 18th cent., he was an Italian adventurer who claimed to have been born in Roma but had left Italy to avoid becoming involved in the civil strife which followed the French revolution. In Constantinople he had doctored the admiral of the Turkish fleet and fought at sea against the Russians. He then practised in Cairo and Yemen before reaching Muscat. He moved on to Baghdad where he again worked as a doctor, and then to Kurdistan where he commanded the artillery of a Persian prince. He was captured by the Russians in Azerbaijan but was soon released to resume his travels. He subsequently worked in India and Brazil before returning destitute to Europe. He wrote *History of Seyed Said, Sultan of Muscat, together with an account of the countries and people on the shores of the Persian Gulf, particularly of the Wahabees*, by Shaik Mansur (London, c1819, 1984). Bidwell, 199-200; ZKO

Mauro, Frédéric Joseph Fernand, born 24 October 1921 at Valenciennes (Nord), France, he studied at Paris, and qualified for both law and humanities. He was a professor of modern history as well as economic history at a variety of universities in France and abroad, and a member of the Académie des sciences d'outre-mer. His writings include *Commerces et marchands* (1954), *Expansion européenne* (1963), its translation, *Die europäische Expansion* (1984), *Des produits et des hommes* (1972), and he was a joint author of *Histoire économique du monde; l'ère des ruptures, 1950-1996* (1997), and *Economic integration and FDI; an empirical analysis of foreign investment in the EU and in Central and Eastern Europe* (1998). He died on 11 June 2001. WhoFr, 1969/70-2000/2001

de **Mauroy**, Hubert, born 20th cent., he was in 1978 associated with the Département de géographie of the Université de Paris. His writings include *Les Assyro-Chaldéens dans l'Iran d'aujourd'hui* (Paris, 1978). LC; Note; ZKO

Maury, Roger, born in 1938, he went to Tunisia in 1961. In 1972, he received a history degree from the Faculté des lettres et sciences humaines at Tunis, and in 1980, he received his *doctorate de 3e cycle* from the Université de Paris I for a partial edition of Jamāl al-Dīn al-Watwāt's *Mabâhig al-fikar wa-manâhig al-'ibar*. He was subsequently associated with the Institut des Belles Lettres Arabes, Tunis, and a director of its library. He died in 1985. *IBLA*, 48 (1985), pp. 213-14

Mauss, Christophe Édouard, born 18 March 1829 at Rouen (Seine-Maritime), France, he was an architect who was sent by the French government on several archaeological missions to the Ottoman Empire. In 1862, he was in Jerusalem for the restauration of the Church of St. Anne. He also accompanied Louis Félicien de Saulcy on explorations of the Dead Sea region. In 1866, he and the Russian architect Eppinger were working on the restauration of the great cupola of the Church of the Holy Sepulchre in Jerusalem. His writings include *Loi de la numismatique musulmane; classement par séries et par ordre de poids des monnaies arabes du Cabinet de médailles de Paris* (Paris, 1898). Henze; IndexBFr² (2)

de **Maussion de Favières**, Jacques Ghislain, born in 1929, his writings include *Damas, Bagdad, capitales et terres des califes* (1971), and he edited *Mémoires du chevalier d'Arvieux; voyage à Tunis* (1994), and *Les Voyages et observations du sieur de La Boullaye-Le Gouz* (1994). LC; Livres disponibles, 2004; ZKO

Mavlianov, Abdumanon M., born 20th cent., he received a degree in 1972 at Dushanbe for Развитие таджикской советской сатиры и юмора послевоенных лет и журнал "Хорпуштак." His writings include Представительные органы госу-дарственной власти Таджикистрна в период строительства социализма (Dushanbe, 1973). LC; OSK

Max Müller, Friedrich, 1823-1900 see Müller, Friedrich Wilhelm Max

Maxey, Edwin, born 26 October 1869 at Royal, Pa., he was a professor of constitutional and international law at a variety of American colleges and universities. In 1915, he was associated with Blackstone Institution, Chicago. His writings include *Some questions on larger politics* (1901), and *International law* (1906). AmInd (3); Master (1); WhAm, 5

Maxim, Mihai, born 20th cent., his writings include *Țările Române și Înalta Poartă* (1993), *L'Empire ottoman au nord du Danube et l'autonomie des principautés roumaines au XVIe siècle; études et documents* (İstanbul, 1999), *Romano-Ottomanica; essays & documents from the Turkish archives* (2001), and he edited *Culegere de texte otomane* (București, 1973). LC; OSK

Maximoff, Matéo, born in 1917, his writings include *Le Prix de la liberté* (Paris, 1955), *Savina* (1986), and jointly with Otto Daettwyler, *Tsigane; wanderndes Volk auf endloser Straße* (Zürich, 1959). LC; Livres disponibles, 2004

Maximos V Hakim, born 18 May 1908 at Tanta, Egypt, he was a Lebanese ecclesiastic, and formerly the Archbishop George S. Hakim. WhoWor, 1974/75; IntWW, 1974/75-2002; MidE, 1978-82 (not sighted)

Maxwell, Ian Stanley, born 20th cent., he was associated with the Department of Geography, University of Sheffield. His writings include *Historical atlas of West Penwith* (1976), and he was a joint author of *Domesday geography of northern England* (1962). Note abut the author

Maxwell, Sir William George, born in 1871 in Malacca, he was educated at Clifton College and was called to the bar from the Inner Temple. He became a colonial civil servant in the Far East, and was awarded the Royal Humane Society's Medal. His writings include *In Malay forests* (1907), and *Treaties and engagements affecting the Malay states and Borneo* (1924). He died in 1959. BritInd (3); WhE&EA; Who was who, 5

Maxwell-Hyslop, Kathleen Rachel, born 27 March 1914 at London, she was an archaeologist and lectured from 1947 to 1966 in the Institute of Archaeology, Unversity College, London. Her writings include *Western Asiatic jewellery, circa 3000-612 B.C.* (1971), and she was a joint author of *Everyday life in Babylon and Assyria* (1955). Schoeberlein; Who, 1993-2005

May, C. J. Delabère, born 19th cent., his writings include *How to identify Persian rugs* (1920), and *How to identify Persian rugs and other Oriental rugs* (1952). NUC

May, Carl (Karl) Friedrich, born in 1842 in Saxony, he was the sixth of fourteen children of a poor weaver. Educated at a theological seminary, he became a newspaper editor, private tutor and teacher until discharged for misdemeanour. He subsequently became a successful and prolific writer of travel literature which to this day appeals largely to juveniles. A great many of the plots are set in the Muslim world. He died in 1912. CIDMEL; DLB, 129 (1993), pp. 241-51; DÖS; DtBE; Kornrumpf; Master (16); Sezgin

May, Lini Saïah, born 20 January 1930 at Amsterdam, she graduated in 1951 from Columbia University, New York, where she also received her Ph.D. in 1963 for *Muslim thought and politics in India after 1857*. In 1960, she was appointed a staff member at the New School of Social Research, New York, and concurrently served as a lecturer in Jewish history at Rutgers University, New Brunswick, N.J. Her writings include *The Evolution of Indo-Muslim thought after 1857* (1970), and *Iqbal; his life and times, 1877-1938* (1974). DrAS, 1969 P, 1974 H, 1978 H; Selim

Mayall, Robert Cecil, born in 1893, he was educated at Sidney Sussex College, Cambridge, and served from 1920 to 1940 as a colonial civil servant in the Sudan. From 1941 to 1951, he was Sudan Agent in London. He died in 1962. Who was who, 6

Maybaum, Ignaz, born 2 March 1897 at Wien, he was a rabbi from 1926 to 1939 in Germany, and from 1947 to 1963 in England. His writings include *Parteifreies Judentum* (1935), *Man and catastrophe* (1941), *Trialogue between Jew, Christian and Muslim* (1973), and *Happiness outside the state; Judaism, Christianity, Islam* (1980). He died on 12 March 1976. Au&Wr, 1963, 1971; BioHbDtE; ConAu, 9-10; EncJud; WhoWorJ, 1965, 1972

Maydon, Hubert Conway, Major, born in 1884, his writings include *Simen, its height and abysses; a record of travel in Abyssinia* (1925), *Big game of Africa* (1935), and *Big game of India* (1937). BLC; NUC, pre-1956

Mayer, Adrian Curtius, born 12 December 1922 at London, he graduated in 1943 from St. John's College, Annapolis, Md., and received his Ph.D. in 1953 from the University of London. He taught at the Australian National University, Canberra, and the University of British Columbia, Vancouver, before teaching Asian anthropology at the School of Oriental and African Studies, London. His writings include *Land and society in Malabar* (1952), *Caste and kinship in central India* (1961), and he edited *Culture and morality; essays in honour of Christoph von Fürer-Haimendorf* (1981). ConAu, 1-4; WrDr, 1976/78-1996/98|

Mayer, Ann Elizabeth, born 5 May 1945 at Seguin, Tex., she graduated in 1964 from the University of Michigan, and received her Ph.D. in 1978 from the University of Pennsylvania; in the same year she was admitted to the Bar of Pennsylvania. In 1982, she was appointed a professor of legal studies at the University of Pennsylvania, Philadelphia, a post which she still held in 2005. Her writings include *Islamic law in Libya* (1977), *Property, social structure, and law in the modern Middle East* (1985), and *Islam and human rights* (1991). Master (1); *MESA Roster of members*, 1982-1990; NatFacDr, 2005; WhoE, 1991/92

Mayer, Claudius Francis/Frank/Franz, born 6 July 1899 at Eger, Hungary, he graduated in 1918 from the Universität Innsbruck and gained medical doctorates at Budapest and Cornell University, Ithaca, N.Y. He was from 1931 to 1954 associated with the Surgeon General's Library, Washington, D.C., and subsequently until 1974 with the U.S. Department of Defense. His writings include *Bio-bibliography of XVIth century medical authors* (1941). AmM&WSc, 1972 P, 1976 P; IntAu&W, 1989; Master (1)

Mayer, Egon, born 23 December 1944 at Caux sur Montreux, Switzerland, he graduated in 1957 from Brooklyn College, received his M.A. in 1969 from the New School of Social Research, N.Y.C., and his

Ph.D. in 1975 from Rutgers University, New Brunswick, N.J. Since 1975, he was a professor of sociology at New York University. His writings include *Intermarriage and the Jewish future* (1979), and *Marriage between Jews and Christians* (1985). AmM&WSc, 1978 S; Note about the author

Mayer, Ferdinand, born 21 April 1927 at Ybbs on Donau, Austria, he studied at Hochschule für Welthandel, Wien, where he received a Dr.phil. in 1961 for *Erdöl im Mittleren Osten*. He was associated with Shell, Austria, as well as Geographisches Institut in the Hochschule für Welthandel as an academic assistant. His writings include *Erdöl Weltatlas* (1966), and he was honoured by *Beiträge zur Geographie und Kartographie; Festschrift für Ferdinand Mayer* (1989). Note; Sezgin

Mayer, Hans Eberhard, born 2 February 1932 at Nürnberg, Germany, he was a professor of medieval history successively at the universities of Innsbruck and Kiel as well as a visiting professor abroad. His writings include *Die Geschichte der Kreuzzüge* (1965), its translation, *The Crusades* (1988), *Bistümer, Klöster und Stifte im Königreich Jerusalem* (1977), *Die Kreuzfahrerherrschaft Montréal* (1990), and *Die Kreuzfahrerstaaten als multikulturelle Gesellschaft* (1997), as well as collections of his articles in 1983 and 1994. Kürschner, 1970-2005

Mayer, Jenny E. de, b. 19th cent. *see* De Mayer, Jenny E.

Mayer, Leo(n) Aryeh (Ari), born 12 January 1895 at Stanislawow, Galicia, he studied at the universities of Lausanne, Berlin and Wien, where he received a Dr.phil. in 1917 for a thesis on Islamic town planning entiled *Studien zum islamischen Städtebau*. A convinced and staunch Zionist, he emigrated to Palestine in 1921. His first appointment there was as inspector in the Department of Antiquities, Jerusalem, and he was soon promoted to be librarian of the Department. When the Hebrew University was founded in 1929, he was first appointed lecturer in Islamic art and archaeology and became the first Sir David Sassoon Professor of Near Eastern art and archaeology in 1932. He served terms as dean of the Faculty of Arts, and as rector. His writings include *Islamic astrolabists and their works* (1956), *Islamic architects and their works* (1956), *L'Art juif en terre de l'islam* (1959), *Islamic armourers and their works* (1962), and *Bibliography of the Samaritans* (1964). He died in Jerusalem on 6 April 1959. Ars orientalis, 4 (1961), pp. 454-55; EncJud; Index Islamicus (3); Master (1)

Mayer, Thomas, born in 1949, he gained a doctorate for his thesis *Egypt and the Palestine question, 1936-1945*. He was successively associated with the London School of Economics and the Shiloah Center for Middle Eastern and African Studies, Tel Aviv, from 1977 to 1981. Since 1982, he was a lecturer in history and politics in the Department of Middle Eastern and African Studies, Tel Aviv University. Note about the author

Mayer, U. P., born 20th cent., he received a D.Phil. in 1944 from Oxford University for *The Agrarian question in Iraq*. Sluglett

Mayer, Wolfgang, born 20 January 1950 at Langwetzendorf, Germany, he studied political science and sociology and received a Dr.phil. in 1977 from the Universität Erlangen-Nürnberg for *Penetration und Transformation in Französisch-Westafrika* (1977). He became a newspaper editor; his writings include *Schwarz-Weiß-Rot in Afrika; die deutschen Kolonien, 1883-1918* (1985). GV; Note about the author

Mayers, Carl, born 21 September 1841 at Stuhlweißenburg (Székesfehérvár), Hungary, he was a graduate of the military college in Wiener Neustadt as well as the Austrian war college and served in the general staff until 1874, when he became a war correspondent to *Neue Freie Presse*. He covered the 1876 Serbo-Turkish war, the 1877 Russo-Turkish war, the 1878 occupation of Bosnia and Herzegovina as well as the 1882 insurrection in southern Dalmatia. His writings include *Der serbisch-türkische Krieg im Jahre 1876* (1877). He died in Abbazia (Opatija), Istria, on 18 April 1903. Kornrumpf; ÖBL

Mayers, William Frederick, he was born on 7 January 1831 in Tasmania, where his father was chaplain and private secretary to the governor. In 1842, the family returned to England and he was educated at Woolwich and Liverpool. He spent a year in America in journalistic work and then went to China as student-interpreter. He served as an interpreter at Canton until 1870, and subsequently as Chinese secretary to the British Legation in Peking. His writings include *Treaties between the Empire of China and foreign powers* (1877). He died of typhus fever in Shanghai on 24 March 1878, when on his way to England on leave of absence. Boase; ChineseBiInd (1); Cordier; DNB

Mayerson, Philip, born 20 May 1918 at N.Y.C., he graduated in 1947 from New York University, where he also received a Ph.D. in 1956 for *Arid zone farming in antiquity*. He was since 1968 a professor of classics at his alma mater. His writings include *The Ancient agricultural regime of Nessant and the Central Negeb* (1961), and *Classical mythology in literature, art, and music* (1971). ConAu, 41-44; DrAS, 1969 F, 1974 F, 1978 F, 1982 H; Master (2); WhoAm, 1978-2003; WhoWorJ, 1965, 1972, 1978

Mayes, Stanley Herbert, born 19 November 1911 at Liverpool, he graduated in 1934 from Wadham College, Oxford. From 1940 to 1946, he served with the British Army, mainly in Egypt and Greece, and from 1946 to 1947, he was an information officer with the British Embassy in Greece. Since 1947, he was a writer and broadcaster in the B.B.C.'s External Service. His writings include *An Organ for the sultan* (1956), *The great Belzoni* (1959), and *Cyprus and Makarios* (1960). Au&Wr, 1963, 1971; ConAu, 1-4

Mayet, Valéry, born in 1839, he was a viticulturist and associated with the Ministère de l'Instruction publique. His writings include *Voyage dans le sud de la Tunisie* (Paris, 1887), and *Les Insects de la vigne* (Montpellier, 1890). BN; NUC, pre-1956

Mayne, Peter Howel, born in 1908 at Christian Malford, Wiltshire, England, in the early 1950s, he lived in Morocco and took up an antique life style in the alleys of Marrakesh, where time does not exist. He was in Kashmir when the British moved out; the Pakistanis, whom he had come to admire, invited him to serve them in their newly set up government. For two years he worked without stint in the Ministry of Refugees and Rehabilitation. Then, when tensions eased off, he decided to retire to another part of the Muslim world and invite his toughts. His writings include *The Alleys of Marrakesh* (1955), *Journey to the Pathans* (1955), *The Saints of Sind* (1956), *The Private sea* (1958), *A Year in Marrakesh* (1990), and its translation, *Ein Jahr in Marrakesch* (1992). He also contributed to periodicals. Au&Wr, 1963, 1971; Note about the author

Maynial, Édouard, born 9 December 1879 at Moulins (Allier), France, he graduated from the École normale supérieure, Paris, and was a fellow of the École française de Rome. He became a *professeur* at a variety of *lycées*. His writings include *Flaubert et son milieu* (1927), and he edited *Anthologie des poètes du XIXe siècle* (1929). DBFC, 1954/55

Mayr, Joachim, born about 1900, he was from Walchsee, Tirol, Austria. His writings include *Umrechnungstafeln für Wandeljahre* (1932); he contributed to Franz Babinger's *Geschichtsschreiber der Osmanen* (1927); and he was a joint author of *Arabische Chronologie* (1966).

Mayr, Josef Karl, born 21 August 1885 at Salzburg, Austria, he studied geography and history at the universities of Innsbruck and Wien, where he received a Dr.phil. in 1909, and subsequently trained as an archivist in the Institut für österreichische Geschichtsforschung, Wien. In 1912, he entered the Austrian national archives, where he was acting director in 1945. He was pensioned off four years early for political reasons on 7 February 1946. He had received a Dr.habil. in 1925, and in 1932, he had been nominated a university professor. His writings include *Metternichs geheimer Briefdienst* (1935), and *Wien im Zeitalter Napoleons* (1940). He died on 2 December 1960. Kürschner, 1926-1954; *Mitteilungen* des Österreichischen Staatsarchives, 13 (1960), pp. 604-607

Mayrhofer, Manfred, born 29 September 1926 at Linz, Austria, he received his doctorates from the Universität Graz, and successively served as a professor of Indo-European linguistics at the universities of Würzburg, Saarbrücken, and Wien. He was a member of several learned societies. His writings include *Indo-iranisches Sprachgut aus Alalah* (1960), *Indo-Arier im alten Vorderasien* (1966), *Sanskrit-Grammatik* (1965), its translation, *A Sanskrit grammar* (1972), and *Die Arier im Vorderen Orient - ein Mythos?* (1974). IntWW, 1989-2001|; Kürschner, 1983-2005; Note; Schoeberlein; WhoAustria, 1983; WhoWor, 1974/75, 1976/77

de **Mazade-Percin**, Louis *Charles* Jean Robert, born in 1821 at Castelsarrasin (Tarn-et-Garonne), France, he studied at the Collège de Bazas and the Faculté de droit de Toulouse. In 1841, he went to Paris, where he wrote for the periodicals, *la Presse*, *Revue de Paris*, and *Revue des deux mondes*. He was a literary critic, biographer, and historian who, on several occasions, visted Spain and Italy. His writings include *L'Espagne moderne* (1855), and *L'Italie et les Italiens* (1864). He died in Paris on 27 April 1893. Bitard; Bitard²; Dantès 1; IndexBFr² (2); Vapereau

Mazard, Jean, born about 1900, he was a public prosecutor and a vice-president of the Société française de numismatique. His writings include *Histoire monétaire et numismatique des colonies et de l'Union française, 1670-1952* (1953), *Corpus nummorum numidiae mauretaniaeque* (1956), and *Histoire monétaire et numismatique contemporaine, 1790-1963* (1965-68). Note about the author

Mazarredo y **Salazar**, José Maria, born in 1745 at Bilbao, Spain, he joined the Spanish navy in 1760 and distinguished himself in the campaign against Alger in 1775 when he rescued the remnants of the army. He rose to the rank of admiral and also served in 1804 as an ambassador in Paris, and in 1808 as minister of the navy. His writings include *Instrucciones y señales para el regimen y maniobras de escuadra* (1781), its translation, *Instructions et signaux pour la régie et les manœuvres de l'escadre* (1782), *Rudimentos de táctica naval* (1776), and its translation, *Rudiments de tactique navale* (1875). He died in 1812. Espasa; GdeEnc; IndiceE³ (6)

Mazas, Antoine, fl. 20th cent., his writings include *L'Abus des droits dans les codes libanais de 1932-1933* (Beyrouth, 1945), and *Divorce mixtes au Liban* (Beyrouth, 1947).

Mazas, Pierre, fl. 20th cent., he studied at the École française de droit, Beirut, and received a doctorate in 1936 from the Université de Paris for *Le Fondement de l'obligation aux allocations familiales*. Note about the author; NUC, pre-1956

Maze-Sencier, Georges, born in 1866, his writings include *Une Enquête sur la crise agricole dans l'arrondissement de Confolens* (Angoulême, 1898), *Le Rôle social et moral de la presse* (Paris, 1911), *Vies héroïque* (1916), *Les Orphelins de la guerre* (Paris, 1918), and *Le Général de Saint-Just, 1862-1933* (1937). BN; NUC, pre-1956

Mazeaud, Léon, born 7 March 1900 at Limoges, France, he received a doctorate from the Université de Lyon for his two theses, *La preuve intrinsèque* (1921), and *Le problème des unions de producteurs devant la loi française* (1924). He was a professor at the Faculté de droit de Grenoble (1928), at Cairo University (1931), a sometime director of the Maison franco-japonaise at Tokyo, and, from 1941 to his death, at the Faculté de droit, Paris. His writings include *Droit commercial* (1942), *Cours de droit civil* (1953), and *Cours de droit commercial* (1956). He died on 22 August 1970 on a mountain excursion in the vicinity of Argentière (Haute-Savoie). DBFC, 1954/55; IndexBFr² (1)

de **Mazières**, Marc, born 19th cent., he was an administrator of the Compagnie des chemins de fer P[aris]-L[yon-M[arseille], who also represented the company at Casablanca. His writings include *Promenades à Fès* (1934), and he was a joint author of *Promenades à Marrakech* (1937). BN; Note about the author; NUC, pre-1956

Mazoillier, J., fl. 19th cent., he was in 1853-54 a vice-consul in Syria. His writings include *Les Chevaux arabes de la Syrie* (Paris, 1854). BN; Kornrumpf; NUC, pre-1956

Mazour, Anatole Gregory, born A. G. Mazurenko on 24 May 1900 in a village near Kiev, he graduated in 1917 from the Kiev gymnasium. He fought with the White Guards against the Bolsheviks. Seeing no future in Russia for a White Guard soldier and son of a middle-class family, he slipped out of Russia via the Black Sea and ultimately reached Berlin. But inflation-ridden Germany offered bleak prospects for Russian émigrés, and he availed himself of a Nasen passport and went to the U.S.A. He settled in Lincoln, Nebr., where he graduated in 1930, and subsequently earned an M.A., and Ph.D. at Yale University, New Haven, Conn., and the University of California, Berkeley, in 1931 and 1934 respectively. He held various academic positions before he went to Stanford University, Palo Alto, Calif., in 1945 to teach Russian civilization and history; he remained there until his retirement in 1965. His writings include *The first Russian revolution, 1825* (1937), and *Russia, past and present* (1951), *Finland between East and West* (1956), and *Modern Russian historiography* (1975). He died on 26 January 1982 from cardiac arrest. Au&Wr, 1963, 1971; BlueB, 1973/74, 1975, 1976; ConAu, 13-16; DrAS, 1969 H, 1974 H, 1978 H; IntAu&Wr, 1976; WhoAm, 1974-1978/79; *Russian review*, 41 (1982), pp. 362-64; *Slavic review*, 42 (1983), pp. 165-66

Mazoyer, Henri Francis, born 16 May 1906 at Autun (Saône-et-Loire), France, he received degrees in public law and political economy, and in 1930 entered the Contrôle civil du Maroc successively with the Service central du contrôle civil in Rabat, the Cabinet du Résident général Noguès, and the Bureau du Cercle de Beni-Amir-Moussa. After the war, he held administrative, political, consular, and ambassadorial posts in the Middle East and North Africa. In 1974 he became a member of the Académie des sciences d'outre-mer. He died in Dreux (Eure-et-Loir) on 29 September 1979. *Hommes et destins*, vol. 7, pp. 342-43

Mazoyer, Pierre, born 7 February 1840 at Lyon, he studied at the theological seminaries of Lyon and Saint-Sulpice, and in 1861 entered the Society of Jesus; he was ordained priest in 1866. He was a sometime superior (*procureur général*) of the Jesuit missions in Armenia, Syria, and Egypt. He dedicated most of his life to the spirituel development of young Jesuits at Fourvière and Cantorbéry. His writings include *Rapport sur les missions de la Compagnie de Jésus en Syrie, en Égypte et en Arménie, présenté au Congrès de Lille, 1881* (Lille, 1881), and *Le Cœur de Jésus, source de toute pureté* (1915). He died in Cannes on 22 January 1918. BN; IndexBFr² (1); Jalabert

Mazuel, Jean, fl. 20th cent., he submitted two doctoral theses in 1937 to the Université de Paris, *L'Œuvre géographique de Linant de Bellefonds*, and *Le Sucre en Égypte; étude de géographie historique et économique*. NUC, pre-1956

Mažuranić, Vladimir, born 16 October 1845 at Karlstadt (Karlovac), Austrian crownland Croatia and Slavonia, he studied law at the universities of Wien and Agram (Zagreb), and served as a judge and public procecutor. His writings include *Grof Ivan* (1883), *Prinosi za hrvatski pravno-povjestni rječnik*

(1908-22), and *Südlaven im Dienste des Islams*, compiled and edited by Camilla Lucerna (Zagreb, 1928). He died in Zagreb on 17 January 1928. EncLZ; HL; ÖBL

Mazzarella, Pasquale, born 20th cent., he gained doctorates in philosophy and law. In 1948/49, he was an academic assistant at the Università di Catania, and subsequently became a professor of history of medieval philosophy at the Facoltà di Lettere, Università di Napoli. His writings include *Il pensiero de Giovanni Scoto Eringena* (1951), *Il pensiero speculativo di s. Anselmo d'Aosta* (1962), *Il neoplatonismo di Teodorico di Vriberg* (1972), and *Controversie medievali; unità e pluralità delle forme* (1978). IndBiltal (1)

Mead, Donald C., born in 1935, he received a Ph.D. in 1962 from Yale University, New Haven, Conn., for *Monetary analysis in an underdeveloped economy; a case study of three East African territories*. His writings include *Growth and structural change in the Egyptian economy* (1967), *Regionalism and United States aid in East Africa* (1969), and he was a joint author of *Small enterprises and economic development* (1999).

Meade, Malcolm John, born in 1854, he entered the British Army in 1873, and in the same year he was posted to India, where he served under the military and foreign departments of the Indian Staff Corps. Since 1879, he was for various periods Assistant to Governor-General's Agent in Central India, and from 1900 to 1901, he served as Political Resident in the Persian Gulf. He then served in India until 1911, when he retired with the rank of lieutenant-colonel. In 1900, he was awarded Compagnion of the Indian Empire. He died in 1933. Who, 1921; Who was who, 3

Meakin, Annette M. B., born 19th cent., she was educated in England and Germany. She travelled by train to Siberia and was probably the first European woman to study at first hand the domestic life of the secluded women of Bukhara. Her writings include *In Russian Turkistan* (1903), *Woman in transition* (1907), and *Enlistment or conscription* (1915). She died in 1959. WhE&EA; Who was who, 5

Meakin, James Edward Budgett, born in 1866, he was from 1884 to 1893 an editor of *the Times of Morocco*. His writings include *Introduction to the Arabic of Morocco* (1891), *The Moorish Empire* (1899), *The Land of the Moors* (1901), *The Moors* (1902), and *Life in Morocco and glimpses beyond* (1905). He died in 1906. DNB; Who was who, 1

Means, Gordon Paul, born 9 May 1927 at Spokane, Wash., he received a Ph.D. in 1961 from the University of Washington at Seattle for *Malayan government and politics in transition*. He taught political science at various U.S. universities before he was appointed a professor at McMaster University, Hamilton, Ont. His writings include *Malaysian politics* (1970), and *Malaysian politics; the second generation* (1991). AmM&WSc, 1973 S, 1978 S; ConAu, 33-36; IntAu&W, 1977, 1982, 1986; WhoWor, 1991/92; WrDr, 1976/78-2004

Meath, Mary Jane Brabazon née Maitland, she was born about 1840. In 1868, she married Reginald Brabazon, Earl of Meath. She and her husband devoted much time and money to philanthropic objects. Her husband edited *The Diaries of Mary, Countess of Meath* (1928). She died in 1918.

Earl of **Meath**, Reginald Brabazon, 1841-1929 *see* Brabazon, Reginald

Mécérian, Jean Hovhannès), born in 1888 at Erbaa (Tokat Province) to an Eastern Orthodox family, he went to school in Tokat, where he became a Roman Catholic at the age of seventeen. He entered the Society of Jesus in 1911, and was ordained in 1921. For the rest of his life he devoted himself to the service of the survivors of the 1915-18 Armenian genocide. His writings include *Inscriptions de l'Amanus et de Séleucie* (1942-43), *Le Livre de prières* (1961), *Expédition archéologique dans l'Antiochène occidentale* (1965), *Le Génocide du peuple arménien* (1965), and *Histoire et institutions de l'Église arménienne* (1965). He died in Jamhour on 16 August 1965. Jalabert, pp. 294-95

Meckelein, Richard, born 13 September 1880 at Arnstein, Bavaria, he received a Dr.phil. in 1913 from the Universität Berlin for *Die finnisch-ugrischen, turko-tatarischen und mongolischen Elemente im Russischen*. He became a professor at the Seminar für Orientalische Sprachen, Berlin, concurrently serving as a librarian. His writings include *Lehrbuch der deutschen Sprache für Georgier* (1931), *Polnisches Lesebuch mit Glossar* (1932), and *Deutsch-Georgisches Wörterbuch* (1937-43). Kürschner, 1926-1935; JahrDtB, 1934-42|

Meckelein, Wolfgang, born 27 February 1919 at Berlin, the son of Richard Meckelein, he returned seriously wounded from the war, studied since 1947 geography at Humboldt-Universität, Berlin, and received his Dr.phil. in 1951 from the Freie Universität Berlin for *Nordkaukasien*. He remained at Berlin as an academic assistant and lecturer until he obtained his Dr.habil. in 1957 for *Forschungen in der zentralen Sahara*. In 1959, he accepted an invitation from the Technische Hochschule Stuttgart as professor of geography and director of its geographical institute. His writings include *Ortsumbenen-*

nungen und -neugründungen im europäischen Teil der Sowjetunion. In 1979, he was honoured by *Festschrift für Wolfgang Meckelein.* He died in Stuttgart on 6 December 1988. DtBE; Schwarz; Unesco

Medico, Henri E. Del, 1896- *see* Del Medico, Henri E.

Medico, Salvatori, Dr., born 18th cent., he was at one time attached to the French Legation in Persia. Note about the author

Médina, Gabriel, born 19th cent., his writings include *Étude critique sur l'établissement d'une zone franche à Bizerte* (Tunis, 1904). ZKO

Medley, Rachel *Margaret*, born 6 March 1918 at London, she was a librarian at Courtauld Institute, University of London, before she became a librarian of Eastern art at the School of Oriental and African Sudies, London, where she also taught Chinese art for ten years. Her writings include *Illustrated catalogue of underglaze blue and copper red decorated porcelains* (1963), and *The Chinese potter; a practical history of Chinese ceramics* (1976). She died on 12 June 2000. ConAu, 13-16, 188

Medlicott, William Norton, born in 1900 at Wandsworth, London, he received his M.A. in 1926 from the University of London for *British foreign policy in the Near East from the Congress of Berlin to the accession of Ferdinand of Coburg.* He taught history at the University of Exter and the University of Texas before becoming a professor of international history at the University of London from 1953 to 1967. His writings include *The Congress of Berlin and after* (1938), *British foreign policy since Versailles* (1940), *The Economic blockade* (1952), and *Studies in international history* (1967). He died on 7 October 1988. AnObit, 1987, pp. 608-9; Au&Wr, 1963, 1971; BlueB, 1973/74, 1975, 1976; ConAu, 9-12, 123; IntAu&W, 1976, 1977, 1982, 1986; Master (1); WhE&EA; Who, 1959-2004; WrDr, 1976/78-2004; Sluglett

Mednick, Melvin, born in 1923, he received a Ph.D. in 1965 from the University of Chicago for *Encampment on the lake; the social organization of a Moslem-Philippine Moro people.* NUC, 1968-'72

Mednikov, Nikolaĭ Aleksandrovich, born in 1855 at St. Petersburg, he graduated from the Faculty of Oriental languages, St. Petersburg, where he later became a professor. He is best remembered for his four-volume collection of Arabic material on Palestine from the Arab conquest to the crusades, Палестина, от завоеванія ея арабами до крестовых походов по арабским источникам (1897-1903). He died in 1918. GSE; Index Islamicus (1); Krachkovskiĭ, p. 140; Wieczynski

Medovoĭ, M. I., born 20th cent., he was a Russian mathematician who wrote about the work of the Arab mathematician Abū al-Wafā' al-Būzajānī. He was a joint editor of Русские ночи, of V. F. Odoevskiĭ (Leningrad, 1975). GAS, v. 5, p. 322

Medvedev, Evgeniĭ Mikhaĭlovich, born 23 November 1932 at Moscow, he graduated in 1956 from the Faculty of History, Moscow State University, and received his first degree in 1967 for Возникновение феодализма в Северной Индии. From 1960 to his death, he was associated with the Institute of Asian and African Studies, Moscow. His writings include Индия в литературных памятниках III-IV веков (1984), and Очерки истории Индии до XIII века (1990). He died on 27 October 1985. Miliband; Miliband²

Medvedev, Roĭ (Roy) Aleksandrovich, born in 1925 at Tiflis, Soviet Georgia, he was a high school teacher and principal before he joined a Moscow publishing house. After serving for ten years at an institute of vocational education, he became a free-lance writer. From 1989 to 1991 he was a member of the Supreme Soviet of the USSR. His writings include К суду истории (1974), Связь времен (1992), Время Пу-тина (2001), Солзеницын и Сахаров (2002), and the translations, *Der Produktionsunterricht an sowjetischen Schulen* (1962), *Faut-il réhabiliter Staline?* (1969), *Riabilitare Stalin* (1970), and *Let histo-ry judge* (1971). ConAu, 81-84, new rev., 110; IntAu&W, 1991-2004; IntWW, 1975-2002; Master (8); WrDr, 1980-2004

Medvedko, Leonid Ivanovich, born 25 December 1928, he graduated in 1952 from the Oriental Institute, Moscow, and received his subsequent degrees for monographs in 1973 and 1983 respectively. From 1962 to 1982, he was a correspondent for *TASS* and *Pravda* in the Middle East. Since 1983, he was associated with the Africa Institute, Soviet Academy of Sciences. His writings include Ветры перемен в Персидском Заливе (1973), К востоку и западу от Суэца (1980), ...Этот Ближний буржящий Восток (1985), Проблема номер один (1987), Именем Аллаха (1988), and he was a joint author of Княжества Персидского Залива (1970), and Вся Сирия, 2nd. ed. (1995). LC; Miliband²

Medvedko, Sergeĭ Leonodovich, born 23 October 1952 at Saratov, Russia, he graduated in 1976 from the Institute of Asian and African Studies, Moscow, and received his first degree in 1988 for Арабское единство в теории и практике Партии арабского социалистического возрождения Сирии,

1947-1982 гг. His writings include *"Седьмая" ближневостная война* (1993), and he was joint author of *Ваш лучший спутник по Сирии Дамаск: Аль-Ахали* (1992). Miliband[2]

Medzini, Meron, born 2 September 1932 at Jerusalem, he received a Ph.D. in 1964 from Harvard University, Cambridge, Mass., for *French policy in Japan during the closing years of the Tokugawa regime*. He was from 1962 to 1970 a director of the Government Press Office, Jerusalem. WhoIsrael, 1980/81-2001; WhoWorJ, 1978, 1987

Medzini, Ronnie, born 20th cent., he was in 1971 associated with the Hebrew University, Jerusalem. His writings include *Israel and the Arab states* (1956). Note; NUC, 1956-'67

Meek, Christine, born 20th cent., she received post-graduate degrees at Dublin and Oxford, and also a D.Phil. from Oxford University. In 1978, she was a lecturer in medieval history and fellow of Trinity College, Dublin. Her writings include *Lucca, 1369-1400* (1978), *The Commune of Lucca under Pisan rule, 1342-1369* (1980), and *Women in renaissance and early modern Europe* (2000). Note

Meek, Theophile James, born 17 November 1881 at Port Stanely, Ont., he was a graduate of the University of Toronto, and received at Ph.D. from the University of Chicago in 1915. He was a professor of Biblical studies at a number of American universities before he was appointed professor of Oriental languages at University College in the University of Toronto, from 1923 to 1952. He visited the Shi'ite holy cities while he was in Iraq, 1930-1931, as annual professor of the American Schools of Oriental Research in Baghdad, and epigraphist for the Harvard-Baghdad School Expedition at Nuzi. His writings include *The Hebrew origins* (1936). He died in 1966. Canadian, 1955/57; LC; Master (6)

Meeker, Michael Elliott, born 2 November 1935 at Fort Worth, Tex., he studied at the Massachusetts Institute of Technology, Cambridge, Mass., and the University of Chicago, where he received a Ph.D. in 1970 for *The Black Sea Turks; a study of honor, descent, and marriage*. He did field-work in Trabzon, Antalya, and Istanbul. After teaching for four years at Cornell University, Ithaca, N.Y., he became a professor of anthropology at the University of California, San Diego, a post which he still held in 2000. His writings include *Literature and violence in North Arabia* (1979), *The Pastoral son and the spirit of patriarchy* (1989), and *A Nation of empire; the Ottoman legacy of Turkish modernity* (2002). AmM&WSc, 1973 S; AmM&WSc, 1976 P; *MESA Roster of mem-bers*, 1977-1990; NatFacDr, 1995-2000; Private

Meersman, Achilles, O.F.M., fl. 20th cent., his writings include *The Friars Minor or Franciscans in India, 1291-1942* (1943), *The Franciscans in Bombay* (1957), *The Franciscans in Tamilnad* (1967), *The Franciscans in the Indonesian Archipelago* (1967), and *The Ancient Franciscan provinces in India* (1971).

Megaw, Arthur Hubert Stanley, born in 1910 at Dublin, he was a director of Antiquities, Cyprus, 1936-1960, and a director of the British School of Archaeology, Athens, 1962-68. He was a joint author of *The Church of the Panagia Kanakariá at Lythrankomi in Cyprus* (1977). Master (1); WhE&EA; Who, 1962-2005

Mège, Charles, born 19th cent., he was in 1922 head of the Services des renseignements au Camp Bordeaux, and a member of the Société de géographie du Maroc. Note about the author

Megerlin, David Friedrich, born 18th cent. at Stuttgart, he studied for five years at the monasteries of Blaubeuren, and Maulbrunn, and then thirteen years at Tübingen, where he graduated in philosophy and Hebrew. About 1729 he was the oldest academic assistant at Tübingen. He subsequently was appointed a professor at Maulbrunn and then pastor and rector at Lambach (Wetterau). In 1769, he retired to Frankfurt, where he tried to convert Jews. His writings include *Sammlung merkwürdiger Rabbiner-zeugnisse* (1754), *Neue Erweckung der zerstreuten Judenschafft durch eine allgemeine Rabbiner-Versammlung* (1756). *Grundriß eines Offenbahrungsschlüssels von Mahomed* (1768), and *Die türki-sche Bibel oder des Korans allererste teutsche Übersetzung aus der arabischen Urschrift selbst verfertigt* (1772). He died in 1778. DtBiInd (3)

Megrelidze, Iosif Varfolomeevich, his writings include *Ласский мегрельский слои в гурийском* (1938), *Руставелии фольклор* (1960), he was a joint author of *Переписка по вопросам ира-нистики и грузиноведения* (1980), and joint editor of *Описание грузинских рукописей Синанского монастыря* (1940). NUC, pre-1956

Mehemed Emin Efendi, 1865- *see* Lichtenstädter, Siegfried

de **Méhier de Mathuisieulx**, Henri Jean Marie, born 29 July 1860 at Roma of French parents, he received a classical education from Jesuits at Lyon and at the Collège Stanislas, Paris. He entered the French navy and participated in the Tonkin campaign. After his return to France, he resigned in order to pursue an interest in literature, particularly to do some work for Louis Vivien de Saint-Martin on a geographical publication on Africa. In 1900, he was sent by the Ministère de l'Instruction publique on an important archaeological mission to Tripolitania. He was a member of the Comité de l'Afrique française. His writings include *À travers la Tripolitaine* (1903), its translation, *Attraverso la Libia* (1912), *La Tripolitaine d'hier et de demain* (1912), and *Histoire des zouaves pontificaux* (1913). Curinier, 4 (1903), pp. 162-63; Kornrumpf², vol. 2

Mehinagić, Hafiz Ibrahim, born 11 March 1894 at Gračanica, Bosnia, he was educated at Constantinople and Sarajevo. He later was an imam at his home town, where he died 30 July 1976. Anali Gazi Husrev-Begove Biblioteke 7/8 (1982), pp. 274-275; Traljić, pp. 95-102

Mehlan, Arno, born 8 March 1902 at Berlin, he was a trained economist who entered the civil service in the German Federal Ministry of Economics. He published widely on the economic history of the Balkans. Kürschner, 1935-1992|

Mehlis, Christian, born 28 April 1850 at Herschberg (Palatinate), Germany, he studied philology and history at Erlangen, Leipzig and München, and received a doctorate. He was a high school teacher in his home region and also pursued an interest in the archaeology of the German-speaking countries. He was a joint author, with Albin Kohn, of *Materialien zur Vorgeschichte des Menschen im östlichen Europa* (1879). He died on 8 April 1933. Hinrichsen = DtBilnd; Kürschner, 1931, 1935

Mehner, Harald, born about 1920, he received a doctorate in 1950 from the Faculty of Agriculture, Universität Gießen, for *Die Siedlung Lettgenbrunn-Vilbach als Planungs- und Siedlungsbeispiel*. He was in 1978 head of a research centre of Tropical and Sub-Tropical agriculture and forestry at the Universität Göttingen. He visited Iran on several occasions. His writings include *Stand und Formen der Mechanisierung der Landwirtschaft in den asiatischen Ländern* (1968), and he was a joint author of *Naher und Mittlerer* Osten (1968), and *Iran; Natur, Bevölkerung, Geschichte, Kultur, Staat, Wirtschaft* (1975). GV; ZKO

Mehnert, Klaus, he was born on 10 October 1906 of German parents at Moscow; the family returned to Germany in 1914, and his father became a casualty of the First World War. He received a doctorate at Berlin and fellowships at the University of California, Berkeley, and Stanford University, Palo Alto, Calif. In 1930s he became an editor of *Osteuropa*. During the Second World War he returned to Berkeley to teach, was a guest lecturer at Hawaii, and spent five years in China. After the war, he taught political science at Aachen, Germany. His writings include *Asien, Moskau und wir* (1956), *Der Sowjetmensch* (1958), its translation, *Soviet man and his world* (1958), *Peking und Moskau* (1962), its translation, *Peking and Moscow* (1962), and his autobiography, *Ein Deutscher in der Welt* (1981). He died in 1984. Bioln, 1; ConAu, 111, new rev., 2; DtBE; IntAu&W, 1976, 1977, 1982; IntWW, 1974/75-1983; Kürschner, 1966-1983; NDB; NYT, 4 January 1984, p. B-6, col. 3, Slavic review, 43 (1984), pp. 550-51; WhoWor, 1974/75-1982; WrDr, 1976/78-1986/88

Mehra, Eileen N., born 20th cent., she was in the 1950s and 1960s an American nurse and social worker at the Lions Clinic, Shiraz. Her trace is lost after an article in 1965. Note about the author

van **Mehren**, August Ferdinand Michael, born 6 April 1822 at Helsingør, Denmark, he studied classical philology in Denmark, Arabic under Heinrich L. Fleischer at Leipzig, and Old Testament subjects and Persian under J. Oslhausen at Kiel, where he received a Dr.phil. in 1845. From 1849 until his retirement he was a professor of Semitic philology at Københavns Universitet. His writings include *Die Rhetorik der Araber* (1853), *Câhirah og Kerâfat; historiske studier under et ophold i Aegypten, 1867-68* (1869-70), *Les Rapports de la philosophie d'Avicenne avant l'islam* (1883), *Om oprindelsen til det i den orientalske filosofi oftere forekommende Hay ben Yaqzân* (1886), *L'Oiseau, traité mystique d'Avicenne* (1887), and *Traités mystiques d'Avicenne* (1889-99). He died in Fredensborg on 14 November 1907. Fück, p. 200; DanskBL; DanskBL²

Mehring, Gottlieb Gerhard, born 18th cent., his writings include *Das Jahr 2500, oder der Traum Alradi's* (Berlin, 1794-95), an outline of an Utopian state, translated from an Arabic manuscript of the sixteenth century. Sezgin, vol. 11, p. 410

Mei, Yi Pao, born in 1900 at Tientsin, China, he graduated in 1924 from Oberlin College, Ohio, and received his Ph.D. in 1927 from the University of Chicago. He held a great variety of positions at numerous U.S. colleges and universities before he was appointed a professor of Oriental studies at the University of Iowa in 1955. His writings include *The Ethical and political works of Motse* (1929), *Motse, the neglected rival of Confucius* (1934), and *Yenching University in Chengtu* (1959). DrAS, 1969 P; ZKO

de **Meibohm**, Anatole, his writings include *Proverbes arabes* (Le Caire, 1948), and *Démons, derviches et saints* (Paris, 1956).

Meid, Wolfgang, born 12 November 1929 at Pfungstadt (Hesse), Germany, he received a Dr.habil. in 1963 for a thesis on Old Irish verbal inflexion entitled *Die indogermanischen Grundlagen der altirischen absoluten und konjunkten Verbalinflexion*. He was a professor of linguistics at the Universität Innsbruck. His writings include *Indogermanisch und Keltisch* (1968), *Das germanische Praeteritum* (1971), and *Kleinere keltiberische Sprachdenkmäler* (1996). On his seventieth birthday he was honoured by *Studia celtica et indogermnica; Festschrift für Wolfgang Meid* (Budapest, 1999). Kürschner, 1966-2005; WhoAustria, 1969/70-1996

von **Meïendorf** (Мейендорфъ/Meyendorff), Georg (Egor) Konrad Woler, Freiherr, also called Aleksandr Kazimirovich, born in 1795 at the family's country estate Klein-Roop, Livland (Livonia), he was for some time a pupil at Metz before studying two years at the Universität Göttingen. He subsequently joined the Russian army and advanced through the grades to become colonel at the Imperial High Command. He accompanied a mission under von Negri to Bukhara from October 1820 to May 1821. He resigned in 1826 and entered the Russian civil administration. His writings include *Voyage d'Orenbourg à Boukhara* (1826), and *Journey of the Russian Mission from Orenbourg to Bokhara* (1840). He died in Würzburg, Bavaria, in 1863. Baltisch (5); DtBiInd (2); EnSlovar; Henze; Wieczynski

Meier, Ernst Heinrich, born in 1813, he was a German philologist and a Hebrew scholar, whose writings include *Hebräisches Wurzelwörterbuch* (1845), *Die Bildung und Bedeutung des Plural in den semitischen und indogermanischen Sprachen* (1846), *Deutsche Volksmärchen aus Schwaben* (1852), and *Morgenländische Anthologie; eine Auswahl klassischer Dichtungen* (1869). He died in 1866. NUC

Meier, Fritz (Friedrich) Max, born 10 June 1912 at Gelterkirchen (Basel-Land), Switzerland, he studied at Basel and Istanbul, and received a Dr.phil. in 1937 from the Universität Basel for *Die Vita des Abu Ishaq al-Kazaruni*. Thereafter he taught Islamic studies at Orientalisches Seminar in the Universität Basel until his retirement. He was awarded honorary doctorates from the universities of Tehran and Freiburg im Breisgau. His writings, mostly in radical non-capitalization, include *Die schöne Mahsati* (1963), and *Baha'-i Walad; Grundzüge seines Lebens und seiner Mystik* (1989). In 1974 he was honoured by *Islamwissenschaftliche Abhandlungen Fritz Meier zum 60. Geburstag* (1974). He died in the late after-noon of his eighty-sixth birthday, returning from a small celebration, a bouquet of roses in his hand. BioB134; Hanisch; Kürschner, 1970-96; *Persica*, 16 (2000), 1-7; SchBiAr 1 (1952), p. 98; *Welt des Islams*, 39 (1999), pp 143-48; WWASS, 1989

Meier, Georg Friedrich, born about 1925, he received a Dr.phil. in 1953 from the Universität Leipzig for *Beitrag zur Erforschung der Zusammenhänge von Sprache und Denken*, and also a Dr.habil. in 1958 for *Das Zéro-Problem in der Linguistik*. He was a joint author of *Handbuch der Linguistik und Kommunikationswissenschaft* (1979).

Meier, Helga, born 30 September 1939 at Freiberg, Germany, she received her university admission from a workers' and peasants' faculty from the Universität Halle and successively studied Indian subjects at Leipzig and Humboldt-Universität, Berlin. Since 1962 she was an academic staff member of the Institut für Orientforschung, Deutsche Akademie der Wissenschaften, Berlin. In 1969, she received a Dr.phil. from Humboldt-Universität for *Zur nationalen Befreiungsbewegung im Punjab in den Jahren 1905-1908*. Thesis

Meïer, Mikhail Serafimovich, born 30 August 1936 at Moscow, he graduated in 1960 from the Institute of Asian and African Studies, Moscow, received his first degree in 1965 for *Народние выступления в городах Османской империи в конце XVII - начале XVIII в.*, and his doctorate in 1989 for a thesis on eighteenth century Ottoman history entitled *Социально-политический кризис Османской империи в XVIII веке*. He was associated with his Institute since 1963, and was appointed its director in 1994. His writings include *Османская империя в XVIII веке* (1991), *Востоковедные историко-экономические чтения; памяти В. И. Павлова* (1993), and he was a joint author of *История Турции в средние века и говое время* (1992). Miliband²; OSK

Meile, Pierre, fl. 20th cent., his writings include *Introduction au tamoul* (1945), *Histoire de l'Inde* (1951), and he was joint author of *L'Inde* (1955), and *Application de la cartographie à l'histoire de l'Indo-aryen* (1963). ZKO

Meilink-Roelofsz, Marie Antoinette Petronella, born 6 December 1905 at s'Gravenhage, the Netherlands, she was an archivist who started her career in 1930 as an unpaid volunteer at the Algemeen Rijksarchief, den Haag, becoming a junior archivist in 1937. From 1947 to 1951 she studied history at Amsterdam where she received her doctorate in 1962 for *Asian trade and European influence in the Indonesian Archipelago between 1500 and about 1630*. From 1964 to 1971 she was *Rijksarchivaris* at the National Archives of the Netherlands. In 1970, she became a professor of history of European overseas expansion at the Rijksuniversiteit te Leiden. Her writings include *De Vestiging der Nederlanders ter kuste van Malabar* (1943). She died in s'Gravenhage on 23 September 1988. BWN; *Itinerario*, 12 ii (1988), pp. 8-9

Meillassoux, Claude Albert, born 26 December 1925 at Roubaix (Nord), France, he studied until 1950 in France, and obtained his M.A. in 1950 from the University of Michigan. He worked from 1950 to

1957 in a factory, in advertising, and as an interpreter. From 1957 to 1964, he was an academic assistant at the École pratique des hautes études, Paris. After receiving his doctorate in 1964 from the Sorbonne, he became associated with the Centre National de la Recherche Scietifique. His writings include *Anthropologie économique des Gouro de Côte d'Ivoire* (1964), *Urbanization of an African community; voluntary associations in Bamako* (1968), *Femmes, greniers et capitaux* (1975), its translation, *Maidens, meal, and money* (1980), *Anthropologie de l'esclavage* (1986), its translation, *The Anthropology of slavery* (1991), and *Mythes et limites de l'anthropologie* (2001). ConAu, 25-28; IntAu&W, 1977, 1982; *Livres disponibles*, 2004; Unesco

Meillet, Antoine, born in 1866, he was a linguist whose writings include *Altarmenisches Elementarbuch* (Heidelberg, 1913), *Les dialectes indo-européens* (1950), *Esquisse d'une grammaire comparée de l'arménien classique* (Vienne, 1903), *Lettres de Tiflis et d'Arménie du 29 avril au 3 août 1891* (1987). He died in 1936. *Byzantion*, 12 (1937), pp. 710-712

Meinardus, Otto Friedrich August, born 29 September 1925 at Hamburg, Germany, his writings include *Monks and monasteries of the Egyptian desert* (1961), *Cradles of the faith* (1966), *Christian Egypt, ancient and modern* (1970), *Patriarchen unter Nasser und Sadat* (1998), and *Coptic saints and pilgrimages* (2002). IntAu&W, 1977, 1982|; ZKO

Meinecke, Max, born in 1912 at Düsseldorf, Germany, he studied at Staatliche Kunstacademie, Düsseldorf, and became a stage director at a variety of theatres in Wien. In 1952, he became a director of the Istanbul municipal theatre. Since 1952 he was successively a lecturer in performing arts at Istanbul and the Ankara Devlet Konservaturarı. *Kürschners biographisches Theater-Handbuch*, 1956; Widmann

Meinecke, Michael, born 6 November 1941 at Wien, he grew up in Istanbul where his father, Max Meinecke, was a stage director. He graduated in 1959 from the German school, Istanbul, and began his studies at Wien, but continued since 1964 at Hamburg where he received his Dr.phil. in 1976 for *Fayencendekoration seldschukischer Sakralbauten in Kleinasien*. He spent ten years in the service of Deutsches Archaeologisches Institut, first in Cairo, and later in Damascus, before becoming in September 1988 a director of the Museum für Islamische Kunst, Berlin, a post which he held until his death from a heart attack on the steps of his office on 10 January 1995. *Artibus Asiae*, 55 (1995), pp. 382-387; DcBiPP (not sighted); DtBE; Kürschner, 1987-1992; Schwarz

Meinecke-Berg, Viktoria, born 13 July 1941 at Eberswalde, Germany, she studied history and history of art at the universities of Wien, Hamburg, and München, where she obtained a Dr.phil. in 1971 for *Die Fresken des Melchior Steidl*. She pursued an interest in Islamic art since 1969, when her husband, Michael Meinecke, obtained a position at the German Archaeological Institute, Cairo. She was a contributor to *Ägypten* (Kohlhammer Kunst- und Reiseführer, 1982.) LC

Meiners, Christoph, born 31 July 1747 at Warstade (Land Hadeln), Holstein, Germany, he taught since 1772 philosophy at the Universität Göttingen. His writings on social history include *Grundriß der Geschichte aller Religionen* (1785), *Geschichte des weiblichen Geschlechts* (1788-1800), its translation, *History of the female sex* (1808), *Geschichte des Verfalls der Sitten* (1791), its translation, *Storia della decadenza dei costumi* (1817), and *Untersuchungen über die Verschiedenheiten der Menschennaturen in Asien und den Südländern* (1811). He died in Göttingen on 1 May 1810. ADtB; DtBE;; DtBiInd (6); Master (1)

Meinhof, Carl/Karl, born 23 July 1857 at Barzwitz, Prussia, he studied at the Universität Halle and became a high school teacher for seven years, and subsequently served for seventeen years a pastor in Pomerenia. In 1902, he went to Zanzibar for research, and then taught at the Seminar für orientalische Sprachen, Berlin, until 1909, when he joined the Kolonialinstitut, Hamburg, where he founded the *Zeitschrift für Kolonialsprachen*. He was one of the great figures in comparative Bantu philology. His writings include *Grundriß einer Lautlehre der Bantusprachen* (1899), *Die moderne Sprachforschung in Afrika* (1910), its translation, *An Introduction to the study of African languages* (1915), and *Die Sprache der Suaheli in Deutsch-Ostafrika* (1928). On his seventieth birthday he was honoured by *Festschrift Meinhof; sprachwissenschaftliche und andere Studien* (1927). He died in Hamburg (or Greifswald) in 1944. DtBE; Kürschner, 1925-1940/41; LexAfrika; PorLing., v. 2, pp.110-122

Meininger, Thomas A, born 30 June 1941, he received a Ph.D. in 1974 from the University of Wisconsin for *The Formation of a nationalist Bulgarian intelligentsia, 1835-1878*, a work which was published in 1987. Note about the author

Meir, Golda, born in 1898 at Kiev, she became an Israeli politician and served from 1969 to 1974 as prime minister of Israel. She died in 1978. CnDiAmJBi; ConAu, 81-84, 89-92; DcTwHis; IntWW, 1974/75-1978; Master (40); Who, 1959-1979; WhoIsrael, 1958-1978; *Who was who*, 7; WomWorHis

Meisami, Julie Scott, born 29 July 1937 at Berkeley, Calif., she received a Ph.D. in 1971 from the University of California at Berkeley for *New forms in modern Arabic poetry, 1900-1965*. For the next ten years she taught English and comparative literature at the University of Tehran, including the Department of Arabic. In 1985, she was appointed a lecturer in Persian and Oriental studies at the University of Oxford. Her writings include *Medieval Persian court poetry* (1987), *Persian historiography to the end of the twelfth century* (1999), *Structure and meaning in medieval Arabic and Persian poetry* (2003), and she translated from the Persian, *The Sea of precious virtues; a medieval Islamic mirror for princes* (1991). She also contributed to the *Encyclopedia of Arabic literature*. Private; Selim³

Meiseles, Gustav, born 20th cent., his writings include *Reference literature to Arabic studies* (Tel Aviv, 1978), a work which was originally published in 1970 in Hebrew entitled *Sifrut 'ezer la-limudim ha-'arviyim*. NUC, 1968-72

Meissner, Boris, born 10 August 1915 at Pleskau (Pskov), Russia, he received a Dr.jur. in 1955 from the Universität Hamburg for *Die sowjetische Intervention im Baltikum*. He was from 1964 to 1984 a chairman of the Institut für Ostrecht, Universität Köln. His numerous writings include *Das Ostpakt-System* (1951). Kürschner, 1966-2003

Meißner, Bruno Ernestus, born 25 April 1868 at Graudenz (Grudzią), Prussia, he was an Assyriologist who successively taught Oriental languages at Breslau and Berlin. His writings include Arabic riddles, poems, and stories, which he had collected while excavating in Babylon, *Neuarabische Geschichten aus dem Iraq* (1903). He died in Zeuthen near Berlin on 13 March 1947. DtBE; Hanisch; Kürschner, 1925-1941; NDB; Schwarz; Wer ist's, 1912-1935; Wininger

Meissner, Frank, born in 1923 at Trest, Czechoslovakia, he received a Ph.D. in 1957 from Cornell University, Ithaca, N.Y., for *Production - consumption balance in Rochester, New York, milkshed*. He was in 1953 a teaching assistant in economics at the Agricultural College, University of California at Davis. His writings include *Technology transfer in the developing world; the case of the Chile Foundation* (1988), and he was a joint editor of the *Proceedings* of the International Conference on Marketing Systems for Developing Countries (1976). AmM&WSc, 1973 S

Meissner, Marek, born 20th cent., his writings include *Śladami arabskich kupców i piratów* (1977), and its two translations, *Die Welt der sieben Meere; auf den Spuren arabischer Kaufleute und Piraten* (Hanau, 1980), and its second edition entitled, *Das goldene Zeitalter Arabiens; unter den Abbasiden* (Hanau, 1988). OSK; ZKO

Meissonier, Georges, born 20th cent., he was a sometime director of the legal division of the Groupe SCOA [Société commerciale de l'Ouest africain]. His writings include *Droit des sociétés en Afrique* (1978). Note about the author

Meister, Michael William, born 20 August 1942 at West Palm Beach, Fla., he graduated B.A. in 1964 from Harvard University, Cambridge, Mass., with the honours thesis, *The Use of aesthetics in America*; in 1974 he there also received his Ph.D. for *Form in the North Indian temple*. He was since 1976 a professor of art at the University of Pennsylvania, Philadelphia. His writings include *Discourses on Śiva* (1984), and he edited the *Ency-clopedia of Indian temple architecture* (1986). DrAS, 1982 H; WhoAmA, 1976-2001/2; WhoE, 1986-1993/94; WhoEmL, 1987/88

Meister, Peter Wilhelm, born 16 May 1909, he was associated with the Museum für Kunst und Gewerbe, Hamburg, and an editor of the *Jahrbuch der Hamburger Kunstsammlungen*. He jointly edited *Schöne Möbel im Laufe der Jahrhunderte* (1958), *Das Handbuch der Orientteppiche* (1970), and *Persische Teppiche* (1971). He was honoured by *Festschrift für Peter Wilhelm Meister zum 65. Geburtstag am 16. Mai 1974* (1975). Note about the author

Meister, Wilhelm, born 7 July 1854 at Lüneburg, Lower Saxony, he studied law at Leipzig and Göttingen and received a Dr.jur. He entered the Prussian judiciary. His writings include *Repertorium des europäischen Völkerrechts* (1886), *Zeitbetrachtungen* (1905), and *Allgemeines deutsches Staatsrecht sowie europäisches Völkerrecht* (1912). He died in 1914. DtBilnd (1); NUC, pre-1956

Mejcher, Helmut J. F., born 17 September 1937 at Viersen, Germany, he received a D.Phil. in 1969 from Oxford University for *The Birth of the mandate idea and its fulfilment in Iraq up to 1926*. He was since 1977 a professor of modern history, with special reference to the Middle East and the Mediterranean, at the Universität Hamburg. His writings include *Die arabische Welt; Aufbruch in die Moderne* (1976), *The Imperial quest for oil; Iraq, 1910-1928* (1976), *Die Politik und das Öl im Nahen Osten* (1980), and he was a joint author of *Die Palästina-Frage, 1917-1948* (1981). DrBSMES, 1993; EURAMES, 1993; Kürschner, 1987-2005; Sluglett

Mekarska-Kozłowska, Barbara, born 20th cent., her writings include *Polskie drogi do Anglii poprzez stulecia* (Londyn, 1971). *Lwów, twierdza kultury i niepodległości* (1991), and *Mozaika wspomnień* (Londyn, 1994).

Mekhitarian, Arpag, fl. 20th cent., his writings include *Ägyptische Malerei* (1954), *Egyptian painting* (1954), *Introduction à l'Égypte* (1956), *L'Égypte* (1964), and he was a joint author of *Histoire de la civilisation de l'Égypte ancienne* (1961-63), *Les Arts de l'islam* (1976), and *Armenian miniatures from Isfahan* (1986).

Melamid, Alexander, born 28 March 1914 at Freiburg im Breisgau, Germany, he graduated from the London School of Economics and completed his Ph.D. in 1953 at the New School for Social Research, N.Y.C. He taught from 1954 to 1957 at the Sorbonne, Paris, as well as at the New School, where he was a member of the Graduate Faculty, and a professor of economics and political economy. From 1957 until his retirement he was a professor at New York University. He was a visiting research professor at the University of Lagos (1964), and a Fulbright Visiting Professor at Wien (1980/81). His writings include *Turkey* (1967), and he was a joint author of *Oil and the economic geography of the Middle East and North Africa* (1991).   AmM&WSc, 1973 S; AmM&WSc, 1976 P; BioHbDtE; ConAu, 45-48; Unesco; WhoE, 1975/76-1986; WhoFI, 1987/88

Mel'chuk (Mel'čuk), Igor' Aleksandrovich, born 19 October 1932 at Odessa, he was educated at Moscow, where he also received a doctorate. Since 1978 he was a professor of linguistics at the Université de Montréal. The recipient of numerous awards and an honorary doctorate, his writings include *Опыт теории лингвистических моделей "смысл - текст": семантика, синтаксис* (1999), *Communicative organization in natural language; the semantic-communicative structure of sentences* (2001), and he was a joint author of *Тохарские языки* (1959), *Автоматический перевод, 1949-1963* (1967), and *Elements of mathematical linguistics* (1974).   Canadian, 1997-2004; OSK

Mel'gunov (Melgounof), Gregoriĭ Valerianovich, born 19th cent., he travelled in northern Persia in 1858 in the service of a trading company, and again in 1860, when he accompanied B. von Dorn to the Persian provinces of Gurgan, Mazandaran, and Gilan, experiences which he described in *О южномь береге Каспійскаго моря* (1863), and its translation by J. Th. Zenker, *Das südliche Ufer des Kaspischen Meeres; oder, die Nordprovinzen Persiens* (1868).   Henze

Mel'gunov (Melgounov), Sergeĭ Petrovich, born in 1879 in Russia, he began his political and scholarly career in Imperial Russia, where he belonged to a party who regarded terror, dictatorship of a minority, and violence used as a means to establish liberty, as fatal to liberty itself. He was among the small number of socialists who advocated taking up arms against Bolshevism. He was arrested and sentenced to life in prison. A lucky coincidence allowed him to leave prison and go to France, where he remained until his death in Champigny on 26 May 1956. His writings include *Красный террор в России* (1924), and its translations, *Der rote Terror in Rußland* (1924), *Red terror in Russia* (1925), *De roote terreur in Rusland* (1928), and *Легенда о сепаратном мире, 1918-1923* (1957).   BiDSovU; *Russian review*, 17 (1958), pp. 193-200

Mélia, Gabriel, born 19th cent., he was in 1910 a consultant in foreign trade, a tobacco manufacturer as well as a Chilean consul.   Note about the author

Mélia, Jean, born 19th cent. at Alger to an Italian family, he pursued a career in the government of Algeria and the French High Commission in Syria in addition to missions to Beirut and Jerusalem. At Alger he was one of the founders of the Ligue française en faveur des indigènes musulmans. His writings include *Algérie et la guerre* (1918), *Laghouat* (1923), *Pour la représentation parlementaire des indigènes musulmans* (1927), *Le Centenaire de la conquête de l'Algérie et les reformes indigènes* (1929), *La triste sort des indigènes musulmans d'Algérie* (1935), and *Dans la patrie française, la patrie algérienne* (1952).   DcBMOuvF, vol. 36 (1991), p. 206; ZKO

Mel'iantsev, Al'bert Nikolaevich, born 9 December 1929 at Novozybkov, Russia, he graduated in 1952 from the Moscow Oriental Institute and received his first degree in 1978 for a study of the *masdar* in literary Arabic entitled *Структурно-функциональная характеристика масдара в арабском литературном языке*. He was since 1961 associated with the Institute of Asian and African Studies, Moscow. His writings include *Масдар в теории и структуре арабского языка* (1990).   Miliband[2]

Mel'iantsev, Vitaliĭ Al'bertovich, born 20 January January 1956 at Moscow, he graduated in 1977 from the Institute of Asian and African Studies, and received his first degree in 1981 for a study of economic growth of the Maghreb entitled *Экономический рост стран Магриба*, a work which was published in 1984. Since 1981 he was associated with the Institute.   Miliband[2]

Melich, János (Johann), born 16 September 1872 at Szarvas, Hungary, he studied at Kolozsvár, Wien and Budapest, where he received a doctorate in philosophy. He worked for five years at the Hungarian national museum before he started in 1901 on an academic career as philologist. His writings include *Szláv jövevényszava* (1903-1905), *Nyelvünk szláv* jövevényszavai (1910), *A magyar nyelv etimológiai szótára* (1914), and he was joint author of *Deutsche Ortsnamen und Lehnwörter des ungarischen Sprachschatzes* (1910). He died in Budapest on 20 November 1963. GeistigeUng; MEL, 1967-69

Meliczek, Hans Alfred, born 30 July 1932 at Dresden, Germany, he received a Dr.agr. in 1966 at Berlin for a study of the economic and social situation of Iraq entitled *Die wirtschaftlichen und sozialpolitischen Verhältnisse im Irak*. He was affiliated with the Deutsche Stiftung für Entwicklungsländer, and since 1989 associated with the Food and Agriculture Organization of the United Nations, Roma, where he was responsible for agrarian reform and rural development. His writings include *Socio-economic conditions of a Libyan village and proposals for future development* (1964), and he was a joint author of *Training of European experts and specialists within the framework of agricultural development assistance* (1962). Kürschner, 2001-2005; Schwarz; WhoUN, 1992

Mélida y Alinari, José Ramón, born 26 October 1856 at Madrid, he graduated from the Instituto de Madrid and susequently studied at the Escuela Superior de Diplomática. In 1875, he qualified as an archivist and archaeologist. Since 1881 he was associated with the Museo Arqueológico Nacional, and in 1916 became its director. A member of many Spanish and international learned societies, he was since 1912 also a lecturer in archaeology at the Universidad Central. His writings include *Historia de el arte griego* (1897), and *Arqueologia española* (1929). He died in 1933. EncicUni; Espasa; IndiceE[3] (3); RuizC

Meliev, Kamil M., born 20th cent., he was associated with the Institute of Languages and Literatures, Uzbek Academy of Sciences; his writings include *Имена действия в современном уйгурском языке* (Moscow, 1964), and an Uzbek work on participles in the modern Turkic languages with the Russian parallel title *Причастие в современных тюрских языках* (Tashkent, 1974). OSK

Melikhov, Georgiĭ Vasil'evich, born 14 June 1930 at Harbin, China, he graduated in 1964 from the Institute of Asian and African Studies, Moscow, and received his first degree in 1968 for a study of the history of Sinkiang entitled *К истории освоения Цинской империей периферии Северо-Восточного Китая, 1583-1689*, and his doctorate in 1986 for *Россия и Цинская империя на Дальнем Востоке, 40-е - 80-е годы XVII в.*, a work which was published in 1989. Since 1980, he was associated with the Institute of History at the Soviet Academy of Sciences. His writings include *Маньчжуры на Северо-Востоке, XVII в.* (1974), *Маньчжурия далекая и ближкая* (1991), and *Российская эмиграция в Китае, 1917-1924 гг.* (1997). Miliband[2]; OSK

Melikian, Levon Hagop, born about 1926, he received a Ph.D. in 1956 from Columbia University, New York, for *Some correlates of authoritarianism in two cultural groups*. His other writings include *Jassim; a study of the psychosocial development of a young man in Qatar* (1981). ZKO

Melikian-Chirvani, Assadollah Souren, born 5 December 1936 at Paris, he received degrees in Arabic and Persian language and literature from the École nationale des langues orientales vivantes, Paris, including a *doctorat d'état* in 1972 for *L'Argenterie et le bronze iraniens, VIIème - XIème siècles; essai sur la naissance et l'évolution de l'Iran islamique*. He was associated with the Centre National de la Recherche Scientifique. His other writings include *Le Roman de Varque et Golšâh* (1970), *Islamic metalwork from Iranian lands* (1976), and *Les Frises du Shāh Nāme dans l'architecture iranienne sous les Ilkhān* (1996). AnEIFr, 1989, 1997; IntAu&W, 1986; THESAM, 4; ZKO

Mélikoff, Irène, born in 1917 at Petrograd, she came with her family in 1919 to Paris, where she later studied at the École nationale des langues orientales vivantes, taking a *doctorat d'état* under Claude Cahen. After the second World War she spent seven years in Turkey, before starting a seventeen-year career with the Centre National de la Recherche Scientifique in Paris. In 1968, she joined the Université de Strasbourg, and in the following year, she became a director of the Institut d'études turques et d'études persans, a post which she held until her retirement in 1986. She was married to Faruk Sayar. Her writings include *La Geste de Melik Dānişmend* (1960), *Abū Muslim, le «Porte-Hache» du Khorassan* (1962), a collection of her articles, *Sur les traces du soufisme turc* (1992), *De l'épopée au mythe; itinéraire turcologique* (1995), *Hadji Bektach, un mythe et ses avatars* (1998), and *Au banquet des quarante; exploration au cœur du Bektachisme-Alevisme* (2001). She died about 1990. Schoeberlein; Turcica, 21-23 (1991), pp. 9-19

Melikov, Oktaĭ Suleĭman-ogly, born 10 December 1925 at Baku, he graduated in 1949 from the Moscow Oriental Institute and received his first degree in 1954 for a study of the rise of Reza Shah's rule in Persia entitled *Установление реакционной диктатуры Реза-шаха в Иране*. He was from 1960 to 1982 associated with the Institute of the People of the Near and Middle East of the Azerbaijan Academy of Sciences. His writings include *Установление дикратуры Реза-шаха в Иране* (1961). Miliband; Miliband[2]

Melikov, Tofik David ogly, born 31 August 1942 at Shamkhor, Azerbaijan, he graduated in 1965 from the Oriental Faculty, Baku, and received his first degree in 1968 for a study of twentieth century study of Turkish poetry entitled *Турецкая поэзия 60-х годов XX века*. He was since 1969 associated with the Oriental Institute of the Soviet Academy of Sciences. His writings include *Турецкая поэзия 60-х - начала 70-х годов; основные тенденции и направ-ления* (1980), *Назым Хикмет и новая поэзия Турции* (1987), and he translated from the Turkish *Из современной турецкой поэзии* (1975). Miliband[2]; ZKO

Melikset-Bek, Leon Meliksetovich, born in 1890, he was associated with Tiflis University. His writings include *Полная библиография печатных работ по арменоведению, грузиноведению, кавказо-ведению* (Tbilisi, 1960). He died in 1963. NUC, pre-1956

Melioranskiĭ, Platon Mikhaĭlovich, born in 1868 at St. Petersburg, where he studied Oriental languages, particularly Turkish, and later there became a professor. He edited *Араб филолог о турецком языке* (1900). He died in St. Petersburg on 16 May 1906. BiobibSOT; GSE; ZKO

Melis, Federigo, born 31 August 1914 at Firenze, he was successively a professor of economic history at the universities of Pisa, Roma, and Firenze. A member of the Académie royale de Belgique, he was associated with the Istituto internazionale di storia economica, and was the recipient of several honorary doctorates. His writings include *Aspetti della vita economica medievale* (1962), *Documenti per la storia economica dei secol XIII-XVI* (1972), and *L'economica fiorentina del Rinascimento* (1984), and *I vini italiani nel medioevo* (1984). Lui, chi è; Note

Melka, Robert Lewis, born 31 July 1932 at Chicago, he graduated in 1955 from Georgetown University, Washington, D.C., and received his Ph.D. in 1966 from the University of Minnesota for *The Axis and the Arab Middle East, 1930-1945*, a work which was published in 1980. He was in 1965 appointed an assistant professor of history at Wisconsin State University. DrAS, 1969 H; Selim; ZKO

Melkonian, Vartan, fl. 20th cent., his writings include *My diary* (1927), *The Iraqi home of medicine* (1932), *Occult sciences and arts in Iraq* (1936), *Your Oriental polyglossary* (1943), and *An Historical glimpse of the Armenians in Iraq* (Basra, 1957). NUC, pre-1956-1967

Melkumian, Elena Surenovna, born 8 July 1944 at Kirovakan (Karaklis), Soviet Armenia, she graduated in 1968 from the Institute of Asian and African Studies, Moscow State University, and received her first degree in 1978 for a social and political study of twentieth century Kuwait entitled *Особеннсти социально-политического развития независимого Кувейта*. Since 1969 she was associated with the Oriental Institute of the Soviet Academy of Sciences. Her writings include *Кувейт в 60-80-е годы; социально-политические процессы и внешняя политика* (1989). Miliband[2]

Mellaart, James, born in 1925, he excavated at archaeological sites in Turkey from 1951 to the mid-1960s when he was accused of stealing ancient artifacts from tombs near the village of Dorak and was subsequently denied permission to direct further excavations at Çatal Hüyük. From 1964 to 1991 he was a lecturer in archaeology and ancient history at the University of London. A member of the British Institute of Archæology, his writings include *The Earliest civilizations of the Near East* (1965), *Çatal Hüyük, a neolithic town in Anatolia* (1967), its German (1967), and French (1971) translations, *Excavations at Hacılar* (1970), and *The Archaeology of ancient Turkey* (1978). Kenneth Pearson and Patricia Connor wrote *The Dorak Affair* (1967). BioIn (1); ConAu, 118, 161; Who, 1979-2005; Master (1)

Mellema, R. L., born about 1900, he was in 1961 head of the Islamic Studies Section in the Koninglijk Instituut voor de Tropen, Amsterdam. His writings include *Purâna çâstra* (Groningen, 1934), *De Islam in Indonesië* (Amsterdam, 1947), *Wayang puppets* (1954), and *De islamietische Staat en de Grondwet* (1956). Brinkman's; Note about the author

Mellor, Francis Horace, born in 1897 at Lytham, Lancs., England, he was educated at King William's College, Isle of Man. He served in the Army of the Black Sea, 1920-22, the British South African Police, 1923-1924, and the Northern Nigeria Police, 1924-1930. His writings include *Papal forces* (1933), *Sword and spear; autobiographical reminiscences* (1934), *Quest Romantic* (1935), *Morocco awakes* (1939), and *The True Morocco* (1952). BLC; WhE&EA

Melnik, Rivanne née Sandler *see* Sandler, Rivanne

Mel'nikov, Evgeniĭ Nikolaevich, born 20th cent., he was in 1972 a Soviet ambassador to the Central African Republic. His writings include *Политический и государственный строй Ливана* (1974), and *Государственный строй Центральноафриканской Республики* (1984). WhoSocC, 1978; OSK

Mel'nikova, Alla Sergeevna, born 20th cent., she was a numismatist who was associated with the State Historical Museum, Moscow. Her writings include *Москов-ские клады* (1973), *Новые нумизма-*

тические исследованния (1986), *Русские монеты от Ивана Грозного до Петра Первого* (1989), *Булат и злато* (1990), *Константиновский рубль* (1991), *Монеты, медали, жетоны; сборник статей* (1996), and she edited *Очерки по истории Отдела Нумисматики* (1993). LC; OSK

Meloni, Gerardo, born 10 January 1882 at Urbino, Italy, he graduated in classics from the Universita di Roma, and subsequently studied ancient Near Eastern subjects at the universities of Heidelberg and Paris. From 1910 until his death in Cairo on 28 February 1912, he lectured in Arabic in ancient Near Eastern history at the Egyptian University. Baldinetti, pp. 80-82; IndBilTal (1)

Melvill van Carnbee, Pieter Baron, born 20 May 1816 at s'Gravenhage, the Netherlands, he graduated from the Marine-Instituut, Medemblick; as a cadet he first went to the Dutch East Indies in 1835, remaining there until 1837. With the rank of lieutenant he made a voyage to Batavia in 1839, where he was posted to the Hydrographisch Bureau. In 1845 he returned home and became attached to the Ministerie van Marine. Five years later, he was again sent to the East Indies as head of the Hydrographic Office in Batavia. Since 1853 attached to the Sedentair Zeewesen, he was promoted lieutenant-commander and director of the Maritiem Etablissement, Onrust, in 1856. He died in the same year on 24 October. He is best remembered for his cartographic achievements, including *The Seaman's guide round Java* (1850), and *Algemeene atlas van Nederlandsch Indië* (1853-62) EncNI; NieuwNBW, vol. 1, cols. 1323-24; Master (1)

Melville, Charles Peter, born 5 October 1951 at London, he was a graduate of Pembroke College, Cambridge, where he also received his Ph.D. in 1978 for *Arabic and Persian source material on the historical seismicity of Iran from the 7th to the 17th centuries*. He taught twelve years in the Department of Civil Engineering, Imperial College, London, before he was appointed in 1984 a lecturer in Islamic studies at Cambridge, a post which he still held in 1993. His writings include *The Seismicity of Egypt, Arabia, and the Red Sea; a historical review* (1994), and he was a joint author of *Christians and Moors in Spain* (1988-1992). DrBSMES, 1993; ConAu, 138; Note about the author; Sluglett

Melvinger, K. *Arne*, born 18 March 1909 at Risinge, Östergötland, Sweden, he received a doctorate in 1955 from Uppsala Universitet for *Les Premières incursions des Vikings en Occident d'après les sources arabes*. He became chief librarian at Uppsala Universitetsbibliotek. He contributed to the second edition of the *Encyclopedia Islamica*. He died on 27 June 1997. Vem är det, 1969-1997

Melzer Edler von Tapferstein, Uto Ottomar, born 18 October 1881 at Graz, Austria, he was an Oriental linguist and translator of Persian literature, and a private scholar who made a living as school teacher at an Austrian provincial *Hauptschule* in Graz. He obtained a Dr.phil. for his thesis *Beitrag zur Erklärung der semitischen Wörter im Mittelpersischen* (Graz, 1923). N. Rastegar and W. Slaje published his biography entitled *Uto von Melzer; Werk und Nachlaß* (1987). He died in Graz on 22 February 1961. Note about the author

Melzig, Herbert, born 10 May 1909 at Stuttgart, he was in 1934 resident in Berlin and later became a lecturer in German at Istanbul. His writings include *Resa Schah; der Aufstieg Irans und der Groß-mächte* (1936), *Kamâl Atatürk; Untergang und Aufstieg der Türkei* (1937), *Timur; Verhängnis eines Erdteils* (1940), *Atatürk bibliyografyası* (1941), *Büyük Türk Hindistan kapılarında Kanuni Sultan Süleyman devrinde amiral Hadım Süleyman Paşa'nın Hint seferi* (1943), and the translations from the Turkish of Aziz Nesin, *Meister Mateh* (1961), *Die skandalösen Geschichten vom türkischen Erzgauner Zübük* (1968), and *Zwischen Bosporus und Anatolien* (1975). KDtLK, 1934, 1937/38; Widmann

Membré, Michele, born 1509, he visited the court of Shah Tahmāsp on behalf of the Venetian Republic, a journey which he described in his *Relazione di Persia* (1542). A. H. Morton published its edition and translation in 1993, entitled *Mission to the Lord Sophy of Persia, 1539-1542*. He died in 1595. Note about the author

Memetov, Aider, born 20th cent., his writings include *Источники формирования лексики кримско-татарского языка* (Tashkent, 1988). LC; ZKO

Memmi, Albert François, born 15 December 1920 at Tunis, he was educated at the Lycée Carnot, Tunis, the universities of Alger and Paris, as well as l'Ecole pratique des hautes études. He was a professor of social sciences successively at Tunis and Paris. His writings include *Juifs et Arabes* (1974), its translation, *Jews and Arabs* (1975), *Portrait du colonisé*, and its translation, *The Colonizer and the colonized* (1991). AfrBioInd (7); Au&Wr, 1963, 1971; ConAu, 81-84, new rev. 14, 32; DcOrL, vol. 3; IndexBFr² (3); IntAu&W, 1976-1989; IntWW, 1974-2006; Master (17); Unesco; WhoArab, 1981/82-2005/2006; WhoFr, 1971/72-2005/2006; WhoWorJ, 1978-1987

Memminger, Lucien, born 11 August 1879 at Tampa, Fla., he graduated in 1900 from the University of the South, Sewanee, Tenn., and served from 1907 to his retirement in 1944 with the U.S. Consular Service. WhAm, 6

Ménage, Victor Louis, born about 1920, he received a Ph.D. in 1962 from the School of Oriental and African Studies, London, for *A Survey of the early Ottoman histories, with studies on their textual problems and their sources.* He was a professor of history at SOAS until his retirement in 1985. His writings include *Neshri's history of the Ottomans* (1964), and he was a joint editor of *Qasr Ibrim in the Ottoman period; Turkish and further Arabic documents* (1991). In 1994, he was honoured by *Studies in Ottoman history in honour of Professor V. L. Ménage,* edited by Colin Heywood (1994). Private; Sluglett; ZKO

Menant, Mlle. Delphine, born 10 October 1850 at Cherbourg (Manche), France, her writings include *Les Parsis; histoire des communautés Zoroastriennes de l'Inde* (1898), and its translation, *The Parsis in India* (1917). BN; Oursel

Ménant, Joachim, born 16 April 1820 at Cherbourg (Manche), France, he studied law at the Faculté de Caen. He was an Orientalist and a sometime judge in the Tribunal civil du Havre. Concurrently with his legal profession he had the reputation of a distinguished Assyriologist. His writings include *Les Langues perdues de la Perse et de l'Assyrie* (1885). He died in 1899. Dantes 1; Glaeser; IndexBFr² (1); Oursel; Vapereau

Ménard, Alphonse, fl. 1934-35, he gained doctorates in letters and law and was a sometime barrister in the Tribunal mixte. His writings include *Etude critique du régime spécial de la zone de Tanger, Maroc* (1932), *Traité de droit international privé marocain* (1936), and *La Radio-diffusion à Tanger* (1939). BN; NUC, pre-1956

de **Menasce**, Jean Pierre, born 24 December 1902 at Alexandria, Egypt, to a wealthy Judeo-Egyptian family, he was educated at the Ecole française de droit, Cairo, and Balliol College, Oxford. Having been a secretary of the Bureau sioniste at Genève since 1925, it was a spiritual clap of thunder when on 19 May 1926 he was baptized in the Eglise St. Etienne du Mont, Paris. In 1930, he entered the noviciate of the Dominicans at Amiens. He spent from 1935 to 1945 at Fribourg, where he gained the reputation as Iranian scholar, earning his doctorate for *Le Skand Gumanik Vicar ou solution décisive des doutes.* In 1948, he returned to Paris to hold the chair of *Religions de l'Iran* at the Ecole pratique des hautes études. Since 1951 he suffered from failing health and died after a long illness on 24 November 1973. His writings include *Situations du Sionisme* (1928), *Quand Israël aime Dieu* (1930), and *Le Porte sur le jardin* (1975). Hommes et destins, vol. 4, pp. 510-11; Index Islamicus (3)

Menashri, David, born in 1944, he received a Ph.D. in 1982 from Tel Aviv University. He was successively a research fellow of the Shiloah Center for Middle Eastern and African Studies and a professor in Moshe Dayan Center for Middle Eastern and African Studies, Tel Aviv University. In 1977, he was in Iran. His writings include *Iran; a decade of war and revolution* (1989), *Education and the making of modern Iran* (1992), *Post-revolutionary politics in Iran* (2001); and he edited *The Iranian revolution and the Muslim world* (1990), and *Central Asia meets the Middle East* (1998). Note

Menchikoff, Nicolas N., born 22 November 1900 at Moscow, he studied at Paris, where he received his *doctorat ès science* in 1930 for *Recherches géologiques et morphologiques dans le nord du Sahara occidental.* In 1934 he joined the Centre National de la Recherche Scietifique. Since 1957 he was a member of the Comité national de la recherche scientifique. Interested in Saharan exploration since 1924, he became a director of the Centre de recherches sahariennes. NDNC, 1961/62; WhoFr, 1959/60-1971/72|

Menck, Karl Wolfgang, born in 1942, he received a doctorate in 1972 from the Universität Hamburg for a thesis on taxes and foreign investments entitled *Steuern und Auslandsinvestitionen.* He was a joint author of *Elemente einer internationalen Stratogie für die dritte Entwicklungsdekade* (1980).

von **Mende**, Gerhard Roman, born 25 December 1904 at Riga, he was educated at Mitau, Misdroy and from 1920 to 1923 at Schulpforta, Germany. From 1927 to 1932 he studied history, Russian, and Turkish at Berlin, and subsequently one year at the Econle national des langues orientales vivantes, Sorbonne, Paris. He received his Dr.phil in 1933 from the Universität Breslau for *Studien zur Koioni-sation in der Sovetunion,* and his Dr.habil. in Slavic studies from Wirtschaftshochschule (Berlin?). He travelled in the Balkans before he was appointed a professor successively at Berlin, Posen, and Hamburg. His writings include *Der nationale Kampf der Rußlandtürken* (1936), *Die Völker der Sowjetunion* (1939), and *Nationalität und Ideologie* (1962). He died in Düsseldorf on 16 December 1963. Baltisch (1); Kürsch-ner, 1940/41-1954; TatarES; *Türk kültürü,* no. 15 (January 1964), p. 43

Mende, Tibor, fl. 20th cent., his writings include *Hungary* (1944), *Wold power in the balance* (1953), *South-east Asia between two worlds* (1955), and its translation, *L'Asie du sud-est entre deux mondes* (1954). NUC

Mendel, Gustave, born in 1873, he was a sometime keeper of the Musées impériaux, Constantinople. His writings include *Catalogue des figurines grecques de terre cuite* (Constantinople, 1908), and *Catalogue des sculptures grecques, romaines et byzantines* (Constantinople, 1912-14).   Kornrumpf; Note about the author; NUC, pre-1956

Mendel, Miloš, born 22 April 1952 at Praha, Czechoslovakia, he studied at Universita Karlova, Praha, and Institut Bourguiba des langues modernes, Tunis. He received his doctorate in 1992 at Praha for *Islámský fundamentalismus na Blízkém východé; Egypt a Sýrie v 50.-70. letech*. His writings include *Svět Arabů* (1989), and he was a joint author of *Islám; ideál a skutečnost* (1990), and *Islám a české země* (1998).   Filipsky; *Who is ... ? (České republice)*, 3 (2004)

Mendelsohn, Isaac, born 31 October 1898 at Kremenicz, Ukraine, he was a Semitc scholar and historian who emigrated in 1920s to the United States, where he received an M.A. from Columbia University, New York, in 1930, and also a Ph.D. two years later for *Legal aspects of slavery in Babylonia, Assyria and Palestine*. He later joined the Columbia libraries as curator and compiled a catalogue of Hebrew manuscripts for the University. He joined the Faculty in 1942 and was named a full professor in 1959. He died in N.Y.C. on 20 May 1965.   CnDiAmJBi; NYT, (22 May 1965), p. 31, col. 3

Mendel'son, Elena Solomonovna, born 27 January 1930 at Artemovsk, Donets Basin, she graduated in 1952 at Tashkent and received her first degree in 1978 for a study of production and trade in Afghanistan entitled *Некоторые проблемы истории ремесленного производства и торговли в Афганистане, XIX в. - начало XX в.* She was since 1958 affiliated with the Tashkent Oriental Institute for Foreign Languages, Uzbekistan Academy of Sciences. Her writings include *Ремесленное производство иторговля в Афганистане* (1983).   Miliband[2]

Mendelssohn-Bartholdy, Albrecht, born 1874 at Karlsruhe, Germany, he studied law at Leipzig, where he received a Dr.jur. He was from 1920 to 1930 a professor of law at the Universität Hamburg. In the early 1930s his tenure was revoked and he went to Britain, where he died in Oxford on 26 November 1936. His writings include *Grenzen der Rechtskraft* (1900), and *The War and German society* (1937).   BioHbDtE; KDtLK, Nekrolog, 1936-1970; Kürschner, 1925-1931; NDB; *Wer ist's*, 1922, 1928; Wininger

Mendelssohn-Bartholdy, Carl/Karl, born 7 February 1838 at Leipzig, Saxony, he was a historian who received a Dr.phil. in 1860 from the Universität Heidelberg for *De monitione canonica*. His writings include *Geschichte Griechenlands* (1870-74), and its translation, *Ἱστορία τῆς Ἑλλάδος* (1873-1876). He died in Brugge (Bruges), 23 February 1897.   EEE; GV; Megali, vol. 16 (1931), p. 907; Wininger

Mendenhall, George Emery, born 13 August 1916 at Muscatine, Iowa, he graduated in 1936 from Midland College, Neb., was ordained a Lutheran minister in 1942, and received a Ph.D. in 1947 from Johns Hopkins University, Baltimore, Md. He was a professor of ancient Near Eastern studies at a variety of academic institutions in America. His writings include *The Tenth generation* (1973), and *The Syllabic Inscriptions from Byblos* (1985).   ConAu, 33-36; DrAS, 1969 H, 1974 H, 1978 H, 1982 H; Master (1); WhoAm, 1974-1986/87; WhoRel, 1975, 1977, 1992; WrDr, 1976/78-2006

Mendes Pedro, Albano *see* Pedro, Albano Mendes

Mendras, Henri, born 16 May 1927 at Boulogne-Billancourt, he studied at the Sorbonne and the University of Chicago and received a *doctorat ès lettres*. He was from 1956 to 1997 a professor of sociology at the Institut d'études politiques de Paris. His writings include *Études de sociologie coloniale* (1953), *Sociologie rurale* (1957), and *Sociétés paysannes* (1976). He died on 5 November 2003.   ConAu, 73-76, new rev. 13; IndexBFr[2] (1); Master (1); WhoFr, 2000-2003/2004

Menéndez y Pelayo, Marcelino, born in 1856 at Santander, Spain, he was the major Spanish literary historian and critic of the 19th century. He was honoured by *Homenaje a Menéndez y Pelayo en el año vigesimo de su profesorado* (1899). He died in Santander in 1912.   AnaBrit; EncBrit; IndiceE[3] (19); Megali, vol. 16 (1931), p. 902; OxSpan; RNL; *Who was who*, 1

Menéndez Pidal, Gonzalo, fl. 20th cent., he wrote *Lengua española* (1942), *Mozarabes y Asturianos en la cultura de la alta Edad Media* (Madrid, 1954), *Romancero español* (Barcelona, 1957), *Sobre miniatura española en la alta Edad Media* (Madrid, 1958), *La España del siglo XIII* (Madrid, 1986), and *La España del siglo XIX vista por sus contemporáneos* (Madrid, 1988).

Menéndez Pidal, Ramón, born in 1869 at La Coruña, Spain, he was the leading Hispanist of his age, specializing in medieval Spanish literature. He was a professor of Romance philology at the Universidad de Madrid. His writings include *Castilla, la tradición, el idioma* (1945), *La Chanson de Roland* (1959), and he edited *Poema de Yúçuf; materiales para su estudios* (1952). He died in Madrid in 1968.   AnaBrit; ConAu, 116, 153; IndiceE[3] (20); Master (9); OxSpan;

and his *agrégation* in 1892 from the Faculté de médecine de Paris. He was a chief medical officer, Hôpitaux de Tesson, 1899, and l'Hôtel de Dieu, 1919. A member of the Académie de médecine since 1914, he was since 1919 also a professor of history of medicine at the Faculté de médecine de Paris. He also served as a president of a variety of French societies. He died in Lisieux (Calvados) on 22 August 1935. IndexBFr² (2); *Qui est-ce*, 1934

Mengeot, Albert, born 19th cent., he was associated with the Société de géographie commerciale de Bordeaux. His writings include *De la Création à Bordeaux d'un musée commercial et colonial, musées étrangers et français* (1900). BN

Menges, Josef, born 19th cent., he repeadedly visited Berbera, Ethiopia, since 1862. In 1873, he belonged to General Gordon's *entourage* at Khartoum. He subsequently went to the eastern Sudan and Somaliland as a hunter and animal dealer in the service of the Hamburg zoologist Carl Hagenbeck. Later he established his own entreprise with depots at Aden, Massawa (Mesewa), and other places. His cartog-raphical explorations were not without value at the time. AfrBioInd (1); Henze; Kornrumpf; Kornrumpf², vol. 2

Menges, Karl Heinrich, born 22 April 1908, he left Germany in protest against the political conditions in the 1930s, and taught Slavic and Oriental studies at the Dil ve Tarih-Coğrafya Fakültesi, İstanbul, from 1935 to 1939, when he was invited to Columbia University, New York, where he became a professor of Altaic and Uralic languages for thirty-six years. On his seventy-fifth birthday he was honoured by the jubilee volume, *Eurasia Nostratica; Festschrift für Karl Heinrich Menges* (1977). He died in Wien on 20 September 1999. Steven E. Hegaard wrote *Karl Heinrich Menges Bibliographie* (1979). BioHbDtE; ConAu, 37-40, 185; DrAS, 1969 F, 1974 F; Hanisch; *Index Islamicus* (2); Schoeberlein; Widmann; WrDr, 1976-1984/86

Menghin, Oswald Franz Ambrosius, born 19 April 1888 at Meran, Austria, he studied history at Wien, where he received a Dr.habil. in 1913. A professor of prehistory since 1918, he served 1935/36 as a chancellor of the Universität Wien. His tenure was revoked in 1945 for political reason and he emigrated to Buenos Aires, where he became a professor. His writings include *Einführung in die Urgeschichte Böhmens und Mährens* (Reichenberg, 1922), *Geist und Blut* (Wien, 1934), and he was a joint author of *The Excavations of the Egyptian University in the neolithic site at Maadi* (Cairo, 1932). He died in Buenos Aires on 29 November 1973 or 74. DtBE; IntWW, 1969/70-1974/5; Kürschner, 1925-1970; NDB

Mengin, Félix, fl. 19th cent., he wrote *Histoire de l'Égypte sous le gouvernement de Mohammed-Aly, ou Récit des événements politiques et militaires qui ont eu lieu depuis le départ des Français jusqu'en 1823* (Paris, 1823), *Considérations sur l'opportunité de reconnaître l'indépendance de l'Egypte, sous le gouvernement de Mohammed-Aly* (Marseille, 1839), and *Histoire sommaire de l'Egypte sous le gouvernement de Mohammed-Aly* (Paris, 1839). BN; Sezgin

Meniaud, Jacques, born 1 September 1877 at Paray le Monial (Saône-et-Loire), France, he was a scholarship student at *lycées* and colleges in Macon, Lyon, and Paris, before entering the Ecole polytechnique in 1898. He became a director of the Services économiques et financiers des Mines, and from 1906 to 1909 he served as a secretary-general of the Haut Sénégal-Niger. After the war, he was an agriculturist. In 1932, he was elected a member of the Académie des sciences d'outre-mer. His writings include *Le Transsaharien et le Transafricain* (1930), and *Les Pionniers du Soudan avant, avec et après Archinard, 1879-1894* (Liège, 1931). He died suddenly in Bruxelles in 1938. *Hommes et destins*, vol. 5, pp. 379-80

Menicoff, Ulrico, born 19th cent., he received a doctorate. His writings include the booklet, *Gli Abbasidi sul trono dell'impero arabe* (Sondrio, 1898). His trace is lost after an article in 1901. Firenze

Menin, Lodovico, born 7 September 1783 at Ancona, Italy, he was a professor of history and historico-auxiliatory sciences at the Università di Padua, as well as a member of the Real Istituto veneto di scienze, lettere ed arti. His writings include *Il Costume di tutte le nazioni e di tutti i tempi* (1834-37). He died in 1868. IndBiltal (1); NUC, pre-1956

Meniński (Mesgnien), Franciszek (François), born in 1628 in Lorraine, he studied at Roma. In 1652, he accompanied the Polish ambassador to Constantinople and there learned Turkish. Two years later, he was an interpreter at the Polish diet. Soon thereafter he was appointed a Polish representative at the Porte. In appreciation of his services he was naturalized and knighted by King John III Sobieski. When he entered in 1661 the service of Emperor Leopold I, he continued his functions at the Porte. In 1669, he travelled to Jerusalem. After his return to Wien in 1669 he resided there until his death in 1698. His writings include *Thesaurus linguarum Orientalium Turcicae, Arabicae, Persicae* (Wien, 1680-1687), and *Francisci à Mesgnien Meninski Institutiones linguæ Turcicæ, cum rudimentis parallelis linguarum Arabicæ & Persicæ*; edited by Adam F. Koller (Wien, 1756). DtBiInd (1); Dziekan; EncicUni; Fück, p. 93; Hoefer; IndexBFr² (2); PSB

Mennel, Rainer, born 21 September 1938 at Berlin, he received a Dr.rer.nat. in 1971 from the Freie Universität Berlin for *Italien 1943-1945; ein Beitrag zur politischen Geographie*, and a Dr.habil. in 1979. He was successively a professor of geography at the universities of Berlin, Koblenz, and Mannheim. His writings include *Der nordafrikanisch-italienische Kampfraum, 1943-1945* (1983), and *Der Balkan; Einfluß- und Interessensphären* (1991). Kürschner, 1983-2005; Thesis

Mennessier, Guy Pierre, born 8 November 1928 at Sceaux (Seine), France, he was a graduate of the Lycée Saint-Louis and the Faculté des sciences, Paris, where he received a doctorate in 1959 for *Étude tectonique des confins alpino-provençaux entre le Verdon et l'Argens*. He was a professor of geography at various French universities. From 1975 to 1979 he was a director of the Mission scientifique permanente du Centre National de la Recherche Scientifique en Afghanistan. His writings include *Contributions à la géologie et paléontologie de l'Afghanistan central* (1968), and *Stratigraphie, évolutions paléogéographique et structural; géologie de la Picardie* (1980). He died on 30 November 1985. WhoFr, 1977/78-1985/86|; WhoWor, 1980/81

Meno von Minutoli, 1772-1846 *see* Minutoli, Johann Heinrich von

Menouillard, H., born 19th cent., he was in 1904 affiliated with the Service des Affaires indigènes in French North Africa. Note about the author

Mensching, Gustav, born 6 May 1901 at Hannover, Germany, he studied theology, philosophy and comparative religion at the universities of Göttingen, Marburg and Berlin. He received a Dr.habil. in 1927 at Braunschweig, and in the same year became a professor at Riga. Since 1936 he taught comparative religion at the Universität Bonn, where he held since 1942 the newly established chair of comparative religion. His writings include *Das heilige Schweigen* (1926), *Religion, Rasse und Christentum* (1947) *Soziologie der Religion* (1947), its translation, *Sociologie religieuse* (1951). He died in Düren in 1978. DtBE; Kürschner, 1961-1976; DtBilnd (2); NDB; Wer ist wer, 1955-1976/77; WhoWor, 1974/75

Mensching, Horst Georg, born 5 June 1921 at Möllbergen-Porta, Germany, he received a Dr.rer.nat. in 1949 from the Universität Göttingen for *Eiszeit-Schotterfluren und Talauen*, and a Dr.habil. in 1952 for *Morphologische Studien im Hohen Atlas von Marokko*. In 1951, he made a four-month research visit to Morocco. He was successively a professor of geography at Hannover and Hamburg. His writings include *Zwischen Rif und Draa; geographische Reise in Marokko* (1955), *Tunesien; eine geographische Landeskunde* (1979), and he was a joint author of *Sudan, Sahel, Sahara; geomorphologische Beobachtungen auf einer Forschungsexpedition* (1970), and *Nordafrika und Vorderasien* (1977). IntWW, 1989-2000; Kürschner, 1961-2005; Unesco; WhoScE, 1991; WhoWor, 1976/77

Mensching, Wilhelm, born 5 October 1887 at Lauenhagen, Schaumburg-Lippe, he was a pastor and founder of Freundschaftsheim, an international trainings centre for peace workers. He wrote *Im vierten Erdteil* (1925), *Jesus im politischen Zeitgeschehen* (1954), and *Conscience* (1961). Note: Sezgin

Menu von Minutoli, Johann Heinrich, 1772-1846 *see* Minutoli, Johann Heinrich von

Menzel, Theodor, born 2 December 1878 at München, Germany, he received a Dr.phil. in 1905 from the Universität Erlangen for *Mehmet Tevfiq; ein Jahr in Konstantinopel*. He was in 1921 a professor at the Archaeological Institute, Odessa, and since 1924 a professor at the Universität Kiel. His writings include *Meddâh, Schattentheater und Orta ojunu* (1941), and he was a joint editor of *Beiträge zur Märchenkunde des Morgenlandes* (1923). He died in Kiel on 10 March 1939. Hanisch; Kürschner, 1928/29-1935; Schwarz

Meo, Leila Marie-Therese, born 20th cent., she received a Ph.D. in 1961 from Indiana University, Bloomington, for *The Separation of Lebanon from Greater Syria; a case study in Lebanese politics*. Her writings include *Lebanon, improbable nation* (1965); she was a joint author of *The Arab boycott of Israel* (1976); and she edited *U.S. strategy in the Gulf* (1981). Selim; NUC

Merani, Peter Pritam Tarachand, born 3 May 1933 at Hyderabad, India, he graduated from Johns Hopkins University, Baltimore, Md., where he also received a Ph.D. in 1964 for *India's territorial disputes; a legal analysis*. He was from 1975 to his retirement a professor of political science at Townson State College, Baltimore, Md. In 1980 he was admitted to the Bar of Maryland. AmMWSc, 1973 S, 1978 S; IWWAS, 1975/76; NatFacDr, 1995; WhoE, 1985/86-1991/92

Merbach, Paul Alfred, born 14 September 1880 at Dresden, Germany, he studied German literature at the universities of Berlin and Leipzig, and was from 1904 to 1908 successively a stage manager at Nürnberg, Gaudenz, and Berlin. His writings include *Otto v. Bismarck; ein biographischer Abriß* (1915), and *Festschrift zum hunderjährigen Bestehen des Mainzer Stadttheaters* (1933). He died in Bad Gandersheim in 1951. KDtLK, 1925-1937/38|, Nekrolog, 1936-1970; Wer ist's, 1922-1935

Mercadier, G., he was a French lieutenant who was a joint author of *L'Oasis rouge; impressions sahariennes* (Alger, 1946). BN

Mercadier, Gédéon, born 19th cent., he received a *bachelier en théologie* in 1906 from the Faculté de théologie protestante de Montauban (Tarn-et-Garonne) for *Mohammed et son œuvre*. BN

Mercadier, Maurice, born 19th cent., he was a lieutenant in the 2e Tirailleurs algériens in 1910, a member of the Mission (Jean) Tilho in Central Africa, a *capitaine directeur* of the Centre d'instruction de mitrailleurs at Blois in 1916, and a commandant in 1922. He retired with the rank of colonel. His writings include *L'Armée noire anglaise en Afrique occidentale; notes sur la West African Frontier Force* (1913), and *Quelques considérations sur les Etats-Unis* (1922). He died in 1938. Note

Mercanton, Jacques, born 16 April 1910, he received the classical education of the time and completed his studies with a *licence* and a *doctorat ès lettres*. He subsequently was a professor of French literature at Lausanne from 1935 to 1941. He was a sometime secretary to James Joyce. His writings include *Les Heures de James Joyce* (1967), *L'Eté des sept-dormants* (1974), and *Ceux qu'on croit sur parole* (1985). CasWL; IndexBF² (1); Master (1); WhoSwi, 1950/51-1992/93

Mercati, Angelo, born in 1870 at Villa Gaida (Emilio Reggio), Italy, he was a keeper at the Biblioteca vaticana since 1919, and became prefect of the Archivio vaticano in 1925. He was an editor of Vatican documents. His writings include *Miscellanea archivistica Angelo Mercati* (1952). He died in 1955. LC; IndBI (3)

Mercati, Giovanni, cardinal, born 17 December 1866 at Gaida (Regio Emilia), Italy, he was an archivist, philosopher, linguist, and librarian and moved from a position as *dottore* at the Biblioteca Ambrosiana, Milano, to that of *scrittore* of the Biblioteca Vaticana, where he spent fifty-nine years keeping up his studies. His writings include *Notizie varie di antica letteratura medica e di bibliografia* (1917). He died in Vatican City on 22 August 1957. BioIn, 4 (4); *Chi è*, 1936-1967; DcCathB; IndBiItal (4); NewCathEnc; NYT, 23 August 1957, p. 19, col. 3; *Speculum*, 33 (1958), pp. 462-463

Mercer, Graeme, born 4 July 1764, he received his M.D. in 1784 from Edinburgh University and in 1804 became a surgeon. He participated in the third Maisur war, 1790-91, and the second Maratha war, 1803-04. He died in Mavisbank, Midlothian, on 6 October 1841. IndianBiInd (1)

Mercer, John, born in 1934, his writings include *Spanish Sahara* (1876), *The Sahrawis of Western Sahara* (1979), *Slavery in Mauretania today* (1982), its translation, *Haratim, Mauretaniens Sklaven* (1982), *Communes; a social history and guide* (1984), and he was a joint editor of *The City in cultural context* (1984). LC; ZKO

Mercer, Patricia Anne, born 20th cent., she received a Ph.D. in 1975 from the School of Oriental and African Studies, London, for *Political and military developments within Morocco during the early 'Alawi period.* Sluglett; SOAS Library catalogue

Merchant, Jules W., born 19th cent., his writings include the booklet, *La Commission de Constantinople et le nouveau tonnage officiel pour le canal de Suez* (Paris, 1874). BN

Merchier, Albert, born 19th cent., he was from 1890 to his death in 1911 a deputy secretary general of the Société de géographie de Lille as well as a sometime editor of its *Bulletin*. His writings include *Les Conseillers du grand Roi; Colbert, Louvois, Yauban* (1889). BN; Note about the author; NUC, pre-1956

Mercier, Ernest, born in 1840 at La Rochelle, France, he was there educated at the Collège municipal until the age of fourteen, when his family moved to the newly established colonial centre of Aumale in Algeria (1854). Despite the vicissitudes of life, he passed his Arabic examinations with excellent marks and, in 1865, was appointed military interpreter at Sebdou. In the following year, he became court interpreter, first at Ténès, then at El Harrouche, and, in 1873, at Constantine. During the last thirty-four years of his life he was an important municipal politician in Constantine, being elected its mayor in 1883, 1896, and 1900. Apart from his political duties, he found time for historical research. According to the Académie des inscriptions et belles-lettres, his *Histoire de l'Afrique du nord* alone would suffice to secure lasting memory for him. His *Histoire de l'établissement des Arabes dans l'Afrique septentrionale*, first published in 1875, was awarded posthumously a silver medal by the Académie des sciences coloniales in 1938. His writings also include *Le Cinquantenaire d'une colonie* (1880), *Le Code du hobous selon la législation musulman* (1899), *La Condition de la femme musulmane dans l'Afrique septentrionale* (1895), *La Question indigène en Algérie au commencement du XXe siècle* (1901), and *Histoire de Constantine* (1903). He died in 1907. *Bulletin de la Société de géographie et d'études coloniales de Marseille* 59 (1938), pp. 84-89

Mercier, Ernest Frédéric Honorat, he was born in 1878 at Constantine, Algeria, (a son of Ernest

Mercier, 1840-1907)   He was a graduate of the École polytechnique, and, as president of the Compagnie française des pétroles, became instrumental in the development of the French petroleum industry. He was also a member of the Conseil de l'ordre de la Légion d'honneur, and a founder of the Redressement français. His writings include *La Production et le travail* (1927), *Résurrection française* (1937), *La France devant son destin* (1939). He died on 11 July 1955.   *L'Afrique française*, september-octobre 1955, p. 114

Mercier, Gustave Louis Stanislas, born on 31 October 1874 at Constantine, Algeria, (a son of Ernest Mercier, 1840-1907), he was educated at the Lycée de Constantine, but learned Arabic from his father well enough to finish first in the competition for military interpreters. He became an officer in Tunisia, and was later assigned to Aurès, Algeria, where he also learned Berber. After finishing his legal study, he resigned from the military in 1896 and became active in public affairs, while concurrently practising law in Alger. His writings include *Le Chaouia de l'Aurès* (1896), *Corpus des inscriptions arabes et turques de l'Algérie* (1902), *Le Centenaire de l'Algérie* (1931), *Le Dynamisme ascensionnel* (1949). He died in Algiers on 17 April 1953. *Hommes et destins*, vol. 7, pp. 344-346; *Index Islamicus* (2); Peyronnet, 677

Mercier, Henry, born 8 December 1903 at Tunis, he began his military career in Morocco with the 1er Chasseurs d'Afrique and became a military interpreter. In 1923, he was an *interprète stagiaire* with the Service de renseignement at the Résidence générale. In 1925, he was assigned to the Bureau des Affaires indigènes at a variety of stations in Morocco. He later wrote the script for the movie *Le Maroc d'aujourd'hui*. After the war, he taught Arabic at the Institut des hautes études. His success brought him finally to Paris, where he taught Islamic institutions at the Ecole nationale d'administration. In 1960, with the rank of commandant, he left Morocco for good and retired to Magagnosc near Nice, where he died on 17 March 1982. His writings include *Méthode moderne d'arabe parlé marocain* (1942-51), *Dictionnaire français-arabe* (1945), *Grammaire arabe* (1945), *L'arabe par l'image* (1946), *La politesse arabe au Maroc* (1957), as well as French selections from the Koran in 1956.   *Hommes et destins*, vol. 7, p. 347

Mercier, Louis Charles Émile, born 13 November 1879 at Constantine, Algeria, and a graduate of the École des Lettres d'Alger, he entered the Corps des officiers interprètes de l'armée d'Afrique and served in Sud-oranais, Taghit and Colomb-Béchar, where he made the acquaintance of Colonel Lyautey and Father de Foucauld. With the exception of one year, which he spent in Algeria, he was a high official in Morocco from 1905 until the outbreak of the first World War. From 1917 to 1921 he represented French interests in Greater Syria, much to the annoyance of the British. Thereafter, he held diplomatic posts at home, in Morocco, Guatemala, and Albania. Apart from his administrative and diplomatic abilities, he was an accomplished Arabist. In 1929, he was elected to the Académie des sciences d'Outre-Mer. His writings include *La Parure des chevaliers et l'ensigne des preux* (1922), *La Chasse et les sports chez les Arabes* (1927), *L'Ornament des âmes et la devise des habitants d'el Andalus* (1939); he was a joint author, with Maurice Gaudefroy-Demombynes, of *Manuel d'arabe marocain* (1917). He died in 1945. *Hommes et destins*, vol. 7, pp. 347-348

Mercier, Marcel, born in 1899, he received a doctorate in 1922 from the Université d'Alger for *La civilisation urbaine au Mzab*. His other writings include *Étude sur le waqf abadhite et ses applications au Mzab* (1927). His trace is lost after an article in 1960. ZKO

Mercier, Maurice, born in the 1870s at Constantine, Algeria, (a son of Ernest Mercier, 1840-1907). He obtained a diploma in Arabic and collaborated with his brother Ernest (1878-1955) at the Compagnie française des pétroles as general secretary. He was elected to the Académie des sciences coloniales in 1948. Note about the author

Mercken, Henri Paul Florent, born 28 June 1934 at Louvain, Belgium, he graduated at Louvain, where he also received a doctorate in philosophy in 1959. About 1970 he was for several years a professor of philosophy at Florida State University, Tallahassee. His writings include *Aristoteles over de menselijke volkomenheid* (1963), and *The Greek commentaries on the Nicomachean ethics of Aristotle* (1973). DrAS, 1969 P, 1974 F

Meredith-Owens, Glyn Munro, born in 1921, in Amlwch, on the Isle of Anglesey. He was proud of being Welsh, with a Scottish admixture. During the second World War he served in the Royal Navy, and was a "shipmate" of the late Peter Swann, sometime Director of the Royal Ontario Museum, Toronto. He was an assistant lecturer in Oriental Studies (Persian and Turkish) at Cambridge 1950-1953, and then became curator at the British Museum. He went in 1968 to the Department of Islamic Studies, the University of Toronto, as a professor of Turkish and remained there until his retirement in 1986, when he quietly retreated to Switzerland, where he died in Basel in 1997, after a long illness. He was a highly erudite, eccentric scholar of the old-school, Oxbridge-style, a nice man. His writings include *Turkish miniatures* (1963), *Persian illustrated manuscripts* (1965), and *Handlist of Persian manuscripts acquired by the British Museum, 1895-1966* (1968). Letter from Prof. G. M. Wickens to the writer

Merensky, Alexander, born 8 June 1837 at Panten bei Liegnitz, Silesia, he was a missionary in South Africa until 1882, and in 1889 he founded missions in German East Africa. His writings include *Deutsche Arbeit am Njassa, Deutsch-Ostafrika* (1894), and his autobiography, *Erinnerungen aus dem Missionsleben in Transvaal, 1859-82* (1889). He died in Berlin on 22 May 1918. DtBE; DtBilnd (2); LuthC 75; Sezgin; Wer ist's, 1909-1912

Merewether, Sir William Lockyer, born in 1825 at London, he was educated at Westminster School and in 1841 joined the Bombay Army. In 1865, he was appointed political agent at Aden. From 1866 to 1867 he conducted the negotiations with King Theodore of Abyssinia. In 1877, he became a member of the Council of India. He died in London in 1880. Buckland; DNB; Mason; Riddick

de **Mergelina** y **Luna**, Cayetano, fl. 1925-45. His writings include *El santuario hispano de la sierra de Murcia; memoria de la excavaciones* (1926). NUC, pre-1956

Mèrgèn, Kirai, 1912-1984 see Kirai Mèrgèn

Mergenthaler, Erich, born 20th cent., he was a joint editor of the legal loose-leaf collection, *Standesamt und Ausländer* (1973). NUC, 1973-77

Merglen, Albert, born in 1915, he received a doctorate in 1969 from the Université de Bordeaux for *Les Forces allemandes sur le front de l'Ouest en septembre 1939*. His other writings include *Novembre 1942, la grande honte* (1993), and *Le Parfum de l'aventure* (2001). Livres disponibles, 2001, 2002

Merhav, Peretz, fl. 1952-1971, he was one of Mapam's theoreticians and headed the party's international bureau. He also was a member of *New outlook*'s editorial board. His writings include *La Gauche israélienne* (1973), *Storia del movimento operaio in Israel, 1905-1970* (1974), and *The Israel left; history* (1980). Note about the author

Meriage, Lawrence Paul, born 3 February 1943 at East Liverpool, Ohio, he received a Ph.D. in 1975 from Indiana University for *Russia and the first Serbian insurrection*, a work which was published in 1987. He was since 1986 a director of industry analysis for the Occidental Petroleum Corporation, Los Angeles. WhoFI, 1987/88

Meriggi, Piero, born 12 January 1899 at Como, Italy, he was a linguist who taught at the Universität Hamburg until 1940, when he lost his tenure for political reasons. After the war he was a professor in his field at the Università di Padua. His writings include *Die längsten Bauinschriften in "hethitischen" Hieroglyphen* (Leipzig, 1934), *Primi elementi di mimoico A* (Salamanca, 1956), *Manuale di eteo geroglifico* (Roma, 1966), and *La scrittura proto-elemica* (Roma, 1971). Chi è, 1957, 1961; Kürschner, 1931, 1935; Wholtaly, 1958. 1980, 1983, 1986

Merigoux, Jean Marie, born 20th cent., he received a doctorate in 1987 from the Université de Dijon for *Les grandes religions de l'Orient à la fin du XIIIè siècle vues par Riccoldo da Monte di Croce; le monde de l'islam*. His writings include *Va à Ninive; un dialogue avec l'Irak, Mossoul et les villages chrétiens* (2000). Livres disponibles, 2002; THESAM, 3

de **Mérionec**, Alain, born 19th cent., his writings include *Chharagatt-Ouddourr* (Le Caire, 1889), and *La Dejanira, Maria Zanella, Pauvre petit* (Paris, 1892). BN

Merkel, Hans *Ulrich*, born 4 September 1934 at Stuttgart, Germany, he studied German and Romance philology and received a Dr.phil. in 1964 from the Universität Tübingen for *Maske und Identität in Grimmelshausens „Simplicissimus."* He was for twenty years a director of the Goethe-Institut, Tunis. Wer ist wer, 1998/99-2005/2006

Merkel, Rudolf Franz, born in 1881, he received a Dr.phil. in 1912 from the Universität Straßburg, Alsace, for *Der Naturphilosoph Gotthilf Heinrich Schubert*, and a second doctorate in 1920 at Göttingen for *G. W. von Leipnitz und die China-Mission*. He was a pastor and affiliated with Allgemeiner Evangelisch-Protestantischer Missionsverein, Berlin. His other writings include his inaugural lecture, *Mission und Wissenschaft* (Herrnhut, 1921), *Mystik im Kulturleben der Völker* (1940), and he edited *Gebete der Völker* (1954). GV; NUC, pre-1956

Merklinger, Elizabeth Schotten, she took two graduate degrees before she received her Ph.D. in 1977. In 1978 she was a lecturer in history of art at the Smithsonian Institute, Washington, D.C. Her writings include *Indian Islamic architecture; the Deccan, 1347-1686* (1981). DrASCan, 1978; LC

Merlan, Philip, born 20 December 1897 at Kolomyja, Austria, he received a Dr.phil. in 1924 from the Universität Wien for *Prinzipien der Aristotelischen Psychologie*. He was from 1942 to his retirement affiliated with Scripps College, Claremont, Cal. His writings include *From Platonism to Neoplatonism* (1953), and *Studies in Epicurus and Aristotle* (1960). He died in 1968. DrAS, 1969 P

Merle, Jean Toussaint, born in 1785 at Montpellier, France, he was a dramatist, journalist, and critic whose writings include *Anecdotes historiques pour servir à l'histoire de la conquête d'Alger en 1830* (Paris, 1831), and *La Prise d'Alger; racontée par un témoin* (1930). He died in Paris in 1852. BiD&SB; IndexBFr. (4); NUC, pre-1956; ZKO

Merle, Philippe Jean Gabriel, born 1 October 1940 at Pont-à-Mousson (Meurthe-et-Moselle), France, he studied law and was from 1972-75 a professor at the Université Saint-Joseph de Beyrouth, from 1976-1992 at the Faculté de droit de Nancy, and since 1993 at the Université de Paris. His writings include *Les Présomptions légales en droit pénal* (Paris, 1970), and *L'Application jurisprudentielle de la loi du 24 juillet 1966 sur les sociétés commerciales* (Paris, 1976). NUC, 1968-77; WhoFr, 2000-2005/2006

Merlet, Henry, he was in 1957 an administrator of the Services civils d'Algérie. Note about the author

Merlin, Maurice Joseph *Alfred*, born 13 March 1876 at Orléans (Loiret), France, he was educated at the Lycée Henri-IV, École normale supérieure, and received a *doctorat ès lettres*. He was an archaelogist and from 1905 to 1920 a director of Antiquités et Arts de la Tunisie. He successively became deputy keeper of Greek and Roman antiquities at the Musée du Louvre, and finally honorary chief keeper of Musées nationaux, and a member of l'Institut. He was a joint author of *Cratères et candélabres de marbre trouvés en mer près de Mahdia* (Tunis, 1930), and *Guide du Musée Alaoui* (Tunis, 1950). He died in Paris in 1965. Qui êtes-vous, 1924; WhoFr, 1953/54-1963/64

Merlin, Samuel, born 17 January 1910 at Kishinev, Russia, he was educated at the local secondary school and the Université de Paris. He was a Zionist leader, member of the first Knesset, and director of the Institute for Mediterranean Affairs, New York. His writings include *The Search for peace in the Middle East* (1969), and its translation, *Guerre et paix au Moyen-Orient* (1970). ConAu, 115; MidE, 1978-1982/83; WhoIsrael, 1949

Mernissi, Fatima, born 1941 at Fez, she grew up in traditional Muslim family surroundings, largely without her father who died in 1946. After attending the local Koranic school, she started in 1960 political and social studies at the Université de Rabat - which she never completed - to be followed by a brief interlude in public service. From 1966 to 1970, she studied sociology at the Sorbonne, Paris, and, at the same time, she was a free-lance translator for the journal, *Jeune Afrique*, where she became involved in the Paris student movement. In 1969, her non-Muslim Ghanian fellow student talked her into going to the USA, where they got married. Divorced after only seven months, she spent the years from 1970 to 1973, thanks to a scholarship from the Pathfinder Foundation, at Brandeis University, Waltham, Mass., working on her Ph.D. thesis, *The effects of modernization of the male-female dynamics in a Muslim society; Morocco.* Her published thesis, *Beyond the veil* (1975), led to the appointment as a professor of literature at Rabat (1974 1980). She formally ended her academic career in 1982 to work on feminist Islamic historiography. She wrote an autobiography, *Dreams of trespass; tales of a harem girlhood* (1994). N. Nagie published her biography in 1992 entitled *Fez-New York und zurück: Fatima Mernissi.* ConAu, 152; Master (1); Selim³

Meron, Theodor, born 28 April 1930 at Kalisz, Poland, he was educated at the Hebrew University, Jerusalem, and Harvard University, Cambridge, Mass. He became an Israeli ambassador to Canada and a professor of law in New York. His writings include *The United Nations Secretariat* (1971), and *Investment insurance in international law* (1976). ConAu, 130; DrAS, 1982 P; Master (2); WhoE, 1991/92; WhoIsrael, 1968-1985/86

Meron, Ya'akov, born 20th cent., his writings include *L'Obligation alimentaire entre époux en droit musulman hanéfite* (Paris, 1971), and *Lexique juridique d'après Kâšânî* (Paris, 1981). LC; ZKO

Merpert, Nikolai IAkovlevich, he received a doctorate and became a professor of prehistory. His writings include Древнейшие скотоводы Волжско-Уральского межлуречья (1974), he was a joint author of Древномти нашей земли (1961), Раннеземледельческие поселения Северной Месопотамии (1981), *Early agricultural settlements in northern Mesopotamia* (1972), and he edited Энеолит Восточной Европы (1980). LC; OSK

Merriam, Gordon P., fl. 1926-28, he was a sometime American vice-consul in Aleppo. Note about the author

Merrick, James Lyman, born 17 December 1803 at Monson, Mass., he graduated in 1830 from Amherst College and in 1833 from Columbia Theological Seminary, S.C. After being ordained a Presbyterian evangelist in 1834, he served from 1835 to 1845 in Persia, successively assigned to Tabriz, Shiraz and Urmia. He subsequently served as a pastor in South Amherst, where he died in

1866. His writings include *An Appeal to the American Board of Commissioners for Foreign Missions* (1847), and *The Life and religion of Muhammad*, from the Arabic of Muhammad Bāqir al-Majlisī (1850). ACAB; Master (3); Shavit; TwCBDA

Merrilees, Brian Stuart, born in 1938 at Roxburgh, New Zealand, he received a doctorate in 1965 from the Sorbonne, Paris. He was successively a professor of French, chairman of department, and vice-provost of Victoria College in the University of Toronto. He edited *Le Petit plet*, from Chardri (1970). Canadian, 2003, 2005; NatFacDr, 1995-2004

Merrill, Frederick Thayer, born 5 February 1905, he was a graduate of Phillips Academy, Andower, Mass., and Princeton University; he received his M.A. from Columbia University, New York. He had been a research fellow of the Foreign Policy Association, before joining the U.S. Foreign Service in 1940. His writings include *Marihuana* (1938), and *Japan and the opium menace* (1942). He died on 30 November 1974. ConAu, 53-56; NYT, 2 December 1974, p. 36, col. 2; WhoAm, 1962/63-1974/75; *Washington Post*, 2 December 1974, p. C8, cols. 1-4

Merrill, John Ernest, born 9 May 1872 at Medina, N.Y., he was educated at the University of Minnesota (B.A., 1891, Ph.D., 1894), and Hartford Theological Seminary, which awarded him the Wells Fellowship for study in Europe upon graduation in 1896. Two years later, he joined the Central Turkey College at Aintab (Gaziantep), whose president he became in 1905. During the First World War, he shared the tragic experiences of the Armenian population of Turkey. He saved the College from extinction but, more than that, he ministered to the needs of the oppressed and suffering. When the College transferred operations to Aleppo and became Aleppo College in 1924, he was its president until his retirement in 1937. For ten more years he served the cause of Muslim evangelization by leading a seminary three times a year, usually at Hartford Theological Seminary. He died in Bellows Falls, Vt., on 22 September 1960. Kornrumpf; *Muslim world*, 51 (1961), pp. 53-54; Shavit

Merriott, A. C., fl. 1972, he was an International Labour Office expert on co-operative development in the Yemen Arab Republic. Note about the author

Merritt-Hawkes, Onera Amelia, born in 1887 in New York, she was educated at London and Birmingham. She researched in genetics in her own laboratory from 1905 to 1929 and subsequently travelled for journalism until 1938. Her writings, partly under the pseudonym Mary Weston, include *Persia, romance and reality* (1935). Lady's who's who, 1938/39; WhE&EA

Merruau, Paul François, he was born on 30 June 1812; his writings include *Les Convicts en Australie* (1853), and *L'Egypte contemporaine, 1840-1857, de Méhmét-Ali à Said Pacha* (1858). He died in Vésinet (Yvelines), 20 February 1882. Vapereau

Merry del Val, Alfonso, born in 1864, he was educated at Beaumont College, and Saint Michel, Bruxelles, and entered the Spanish diplomatic service in 1882. His writings include *Spanish Basques and separation* (London, 1939). He died 26 May 1943. NUC, pre-1956; Who was who 4

Merry y Colom, Francisco, born in 1829 at Sevilla, he was a Spanish diplomat whose writings include *Telavion del viaje a la ciudad de Marruecos* (1864), and *Mi embajada extraordinaria á Marruecos en 1863* (1894). He died 4 January 1900. EncicUni; IndiceE³ (1); NUC, pre-1956

Mersanne, Norbert, born 19th cent., his writings include *Les Ascensions mystiques; poèmes et méditations* (Paris, 1922). BN

Merton, Arthur S., he was from 1928 to 1941 resident in Cairo, and a member of the Société Fouad Ier d'économie politique, de statistique et de législation. Note about the author

Merton, Robert King, born 5 July 1910 at Philadelphia, Pa., he graduated in 1931 from Temple University and received his Ph.D. in 1935 from Harvard University for *Sociological aspects of scientific development in seventeenth century England*. He was a professor of sociology as well as a university administrator in the U.S.A. His writings include *Mass persuasion* (1946), *Social theory and social structure* (1949), and *Sociology of science* (1973). He died in 2003. AmM&WSc, 1992 P - 2003 P; AmM&WSc, 1973 S, 1978 S; CnDiAmJBi; ConAu, 41-44, new rev., 31; IntAu&W, 1982-1991/92; IntWW, 1974-2002; Master (15); WhoAm, 1974-2003; WhoE, 1974, 1991/92; WrDr, 1986/88-2004

Mertz, Robert Anton, born 20th cent., he received a Ph.D. in 1975 from Johns Hopkins University, Baltimore, Md., for *The United Arab Republic, 1958-1961; Arab unity on trial*. He was a joint author of *Arab aid to Sub-Saharan Africa* (1983). Selim³

Mertzios, Konstantinos D., born about 1900, his writings include Ὀ μικρος Ἑλληνομνήμων (1939), Μνημεῖα Μακεδονικης ἱστορίας (1947),and Πατριαρχικα, 1556-1702 (1951). NUC, pre-1956

Merwe, Willem Jacobus van der, 1906- see Van der Merwe, Willem Jacobus

Merx, Ernst Otto *Adalbert*, born 2 November 1838 at Bleicherode/Harz, Germany, he took classical languages at school and studied theology and philology, including Oriental languages, at the universities of Marburg, Halle, Breslau, and Berlin, receiving a Dr.phil. in 1861, a Lic.theol. in 1864, and his Dr.habil. in 1865 from the Universität Jena for *Cur in libro Danielis iuxta hebraeam aramaea adhibita sit dialectus explicatur*. He taught Old Testament studies at Jena, where he also lectured in Arabic, Persian, and Ethiopic. He subsequently was a professor successively at Tübingen and Gießen. His writings include *Türkische Sprichwörter* (1877), and *Documents de paléographie hébraïque et arabe* (1894). He died in Heidelberg on 4 August 1909. DtBE; DtBilnd (4); *Wer ist's*, 1909

Méry, Gaston, born 19th cent., he was a Saharan explorer who, early in 1893, travelled in the service of an Algerian exploration institution in Ouargla from el-Oued south to Hassi Mey, and continued to Wadi Igharghar, the Timassini Oasis, and Lake Menkhough. In October 1893 he set out for the territory of the Azdjer Tuareg, but had hardly started when he had to return for reason of ill-health. He died in October 1896. Henze; Sezgin

Meserve, Walter Joseph, born 10 March 1923 at Portland, Me., he was educated at Bates College, Boston University, and the University of Washington, where he received a Ph.D. in 1952. He became a professor of theatre and English at a variety of American universities. His writings include *An Outline history of American drama* (1965). ConAu, 1-4, new rev., 1, 100; DrAS, 1969 E, 1974 E, 1978 E, 1982 E; IntAu&W, 1982-2003; Master (3); WhoAm, 1986-1994, 2003; WhoWor, 1984/85-1987; WrDr, 1976/78-2003

Meshchaninov, Ivan Ivanovich, born in 1883 at Ufa, Russia, he was educated at St. Petersburg. He was a philologist and an authority in Caucasian languages and for many years affiliated with the Soviet Academy of Sciences. His writings include *Проблема классификации языков* (1935), and *Члены предложения и части речи* (1945). He died in 1967 in Leningrad. GSE; *Казахская ССР краткая энциклопедия*, vol. 3; VostokMStP

Meshkeris, Veronika Aleksandrovna, born 14 October 1927 at Vladivostok, Russia, she graduated in 1952 from Tashkent State University and received her first degree in 1964 for a study of Sogdian art entitled *Коропластика Согда*, a work which was published in 1977. She was from 1953 to 1979 affiliated with the Institute of History in the Tajik Academy of Sciences and gained a doctorate in 1992 in Sogdian studies. Her writings include and *Согдийская терракота* (1989). Miliband²; Schoeberlein

Mesić, Matija, born 19 February 1826 at Bosanski Brod, Bosnia, he was a professor of Biblical and Semitic studies at Zagreb University and its sometime president. His writings include *Ilirska čitanka za gornje gimnazĺje* (1856-1860), *Život Nikole Zrinjskoga, Sigetskoga junaka* (1866). He died in Zagreb on 6 December 1878. *Grada za hrvatsku retrospektivnu bibliografijn knjiga*, 1835-1940; HL; *Hrvatski opći leksikon* (1996)

Mesnard, André-Hubert, the son of Pierre Mesnard (1900-1969), he was born about 1935. He received a doctorate in law and became associated with the Faculté de droit et des sciences économiques de Paris. His writings include *L'Action culturelle des pouvoirs publics* (1969), *La Politique culturelle de l'état* (1974), and *Droit de l'urbanisme communal* (1993). Livres disponibles, 2003; Note about the author

Mesnard, Pierre Eduard Charles Marie, born 3 November 1900 at Surgères (Charente-Inférieure), France, he was educated at the Lycée de Poitiers, and studied at l'Ecole normale supérieure, Faculté des sciences, and École nationale des langues orientales vivantes, Paris. He was a philosopher, professor, and writer who taught at Iaşi, Rochefort, Poitiers, Bône, Alger, and Tours, where he founded the Centre d'études supérieures de la Renaissance in 1956. He was a *membre de l'Institut*. His writings, partly under the pseudonym Le Maga, include *La France catholique* (1943), and *La Vrai visage de Kierkegaard* (1948). He died on 12 March 1969. MembriiAR; WhoFr, 1959/60-1967/68

Mesnier, born 19th cent., he was in 1914 a French army captain and head of the Bureau de compabilité des Oasis sahariennes. Note about the author

Mesplé, Armand Antoine, born 1 May 1853 at Paris, he was educated at the École normale supérieure and École des hautes études, Paris. He started his career at the Lycée de Bourges teaching history later becoming a professor of *littérature étrangère* at the Faculté des Lettres d'Alger. He was a founding member, and a sometime president, of the Société de géographie d'Alger et de l'Afrique du nord. He died in Alger on 1 March 1927. Curinier; *Qui êtes-vous*, 1924

Messal, Raymond, born 19th cent., he was a French lieutenant-colonel who wrote *La Genèse de notre victoire marocaine; un précurseur, Alfred Le Chatelier* (Paris, 1931). His trace is lost after a publication in 1932. Note about the author; NUC, pre-1956

Messana, Gaspare, born 20th cent., his writings include *L'architettura musulmana delle Libia* (1973), and its translation *Originalité de l'architecture musulmane libyenne* (1977). ZKO

Messenger, Ruth Ellis, born in 1884, she graduated from Normal College of the City of New York, now Hunter College, with the class of 1905, and became a teacher of classics at high schools. After her Ph.D. in 1930 from Columbia University for *Ethical teachings in the Latin hymnes of medieval England*, she pursued a teaching career at her alma mater until her retirement in 1950. Her other writings include *The Medieval Latin hymn* (1953), and *A Short bibliography for the study of hymns* (1964). She died in 1964. DrAS, 1963, vol. 1; NatCAB, 51 (1969), p. 566; NYT, 4 March 1964, p. 37, col. 1

Messerschmidt, Ernst August, born 13 November 1913 at Straßburg, Alsace, he studied medicine and liberal arts at the universities of Freiburg im Breisgau and Hamburg, where he received a Dr.phil. in 1939. During his military service in the Second World War he spent much time in Switzerland and Italy, where he remained until 1949 as a correspondent for German and Italian newspapers. In 1950, he began his involvement with the Muslim world in the field of trade and commerce. Until 1957 he spent two years each in Pakistan and Iran, and three years in Lebanon. In 1958, he was recalled to Hamburg, where he held a cross appointment as director of Nah- und Mittelost Verein and the German-Iranian Chamber of Commerce. His writings include *Pakistan; Wirtschaftsgrundlagen und Außenhandelsmöglichkeiten* (1952), and *Iran (Persien); Wirtschaftsgrundlagen und Außenhandelsmöglichkeiten* (1953). He died after two years of illness on 18 October 1971. Note about the author

Messier, Ronald Albert, born 8 December 1944 at Providence, R.I., he graduated in 1966 from the University of Rhode Island and received a Ph.D. in 1972 from Michigan State University for *Muslim exploitation of West African gold during the period of the Fatimid Caliphate*. In 1972, he was appointed a professor of medieval Islamic and North African history at Middle Tennessee State University; in 2004 and 2005, he was a professor of history at Vanderbilt University, Nashville, Tenn. DrAS, 1974 H, 1978 H, 1982 H; *MESA Roster of members*, 1990; NatFacDr, 1995-2005

Messina, Giuseppe, S.J., born 6 January 1893 at San Cataldo, Sicily, he was for many years a professor of Iranian languages and a director of religious studies at the Pontificio Istituto Biblico di Roma. His writings include *Ursprung der Magier und die zarathuštrische Religion* (1930), *Libro apocalittico persiano* (1939), *Notizia su un diatessaron persiano, tradutto dal siriaco* (1943), *Cristianesimo, buddhismo, manicheismo nell'Asia antica* (1947), and *La religione Mazdea* (1951). He died in 1951. Chi è, 1948

Messina, Salvatore, born 2 April 1882 at Prizzi (Palermo), Sicily, he was a sometime consul in Alexandria, Egypt, and since 1905 a magistrate. His writings include *La Juridiction administrative des tribunaux mixte en Egypte* (1923), *Traité de droit civil égyptien mixte* (1927), *La carta del lavoro nei principi generali del diritto fascista* (1941), and *Teoria generale dei delitti contro l'onore* (1953). Chi è, 1931-1948|

Messing, Simon David, born 13 July 1922 at Frankfurt am Main, he was educated in America and in 1953/54 did ethnographic field-work among the Amhara of Ethiopia's central plateau, while on a research grant from the Ford Foundation. He received his Ph.D. in 1957 from the University of Pennsylvania for *The Highland plateau Amhara of Ethiopia*. He became a professor of social sciences at a variety of American universities. His writings include *A Holistic reader in applied anthropology* (1973), and he edited *Rural health in Africa* (1972). AmM&WSc, 1973 S; AmM&WSc 1976 P - 2003 P; ConAu, 57-60; Note about the author; Unesco; WhoE, 1993/94

Messiqua, Marcel, fl. 20th cent., he was a merchant residing in Cairo in 1928, and a member of the Société Fouad Ier d'économie politique, de statistique et de législation, certainly from 1928 to 1952, when he was residing in Paris. Note about the author

El-Messiri (Elmessiri), Abdelwahab Mohammad, born in 1938, he was in 1966 a graduate student at Rutgers University, New Brunswick, N.J., and associated with the Committee to Support Middle East Liberation, New York. He was a sometime professor of literature at Ain Shams University, Cairo. His writings include *The Land of promise; a critique of political Zionism* (1977); he was the compiler of *A Lover from Palestine, and other poems* (1970), *The Palestinian wedding; a bilingual anthology* (1982), and he was a joint editor of *Israel and South Africa* (1976), and *A Land of stone and thyme; an anthology of Palestinian short stories* (1996). LC; Note about the author

Mestre, Achille, born 20th cent., he received his *agrégation* from the Faculté de droit et des sciences politiques et économiques de Tunis, and there served as a lecturer in 1973/74. In 1982 he was a professor at the Université de Paris XII. His writings include *Le Conseil d'Etat* (1974), *Les Services publics de l'administration tunisienne* (1977), and he was a joint author of *Constitutionalisme jacobin et constitutionalisme soviétique* (1971). Note about the author; NUC

Mészáros, Gyula (Julius), born 28 March 1883 at Szakcs, Hungary, he studied Oriental languages at Budapest, where he also gained a doctorate. He was one of the most gifted students of A. Vámbéry. From 1904 to 1906 he studied at Constantinople and subsequently went in the service of the Hungarian Academy of Sciences to the region east of the Volga River to study the Tatar and Chuvash peoples. In 1910, he went on a scientific expedition to Asia Minor. He later was named a keeper of the ethnographical section in the Hungarian National Museum. His writings include *A csuvas ősvallás emlékei* (1909), *A Boszporusz partjain* (1910), *Magyarországi kun nyelvemlékek* (1914), and *Die Päkhy-Sprache* (Chicago, 1934). He died in New York in 1957. GeistigeUng; MEL, 1967-69

Metcalf, Barbara Daly, born 13 September 1941, she was successively a professor at the University of Pennsylvania, and the University of California at Davis, a post which she still held in 2005. Her writings include *Islamic revival in British India* (1982), *Perfecting women; Maulana Ashraf 'Ali Thanawi's Bihishti zewar* (1990), and she edited *Moral conduct and authority; the place of adab in South Asian Islam* (1984). LC; NatFacDr, 2005

Metcalf, David Michael, born 8 May 1933, he was educated at St. John's College, Cambridge. A numismatist, he was a keeper of the Ashmolean Museum, Oxford, president of the Royal Numismatic Society, and for ten years an editor of the *Numismatic chronicle*. His writings include *Coinage in the Balkans, 820-1355* (1966), *Classification of Byzantine stamena* (1967), *The Origins of the Anastasian currency reform* (1969), and *Coinage of the Crusades and the Latin East in the Ashmolean Museum* (1983). Who's who, 1985-2004

Metcalf, Thomas Richard, born 31 May 1934 at Schenactady, N.Y., he graduated in 1955 from Amherst College and received a Ph.D. in 1960 from Harvard University for *Victorian liberalism and the Indian Empire; the impact of the Mutiny of 1857 on British policy in India*. He served as a professor of history at a variety of American universities. His writings include *The Aftermath of the revolt; India, 1857-1870* (1964), *Land, landlords, and the British Ray* (1979), and *An Imperial vision; Indian architecture and Britain's Ray* (1989). ConAu, 13-16; DrAS, 1969 H, 1974 H, 1978 H, 1982 H

Metgé, A., fl. 19th cent., his writings include *Grammaire philosophique et raisonnée* (Toulouse, 1828), *Mes loisirs* (Castelnaudary, 1840), *Projet de colonisation en Algérie* (Paris, 1855), *Colonie de l'Aude dans l'Afrique française* (Villefranche, 1856), and *Mémoire sur l'immigration des enfants trouvés en Algérie* (Castelnaudary, 1860). BN; NUC, pre--1956

Métin, Albert, born in 1871 at Besançon, France, he received his doctorate in letters in 1907 from the Université de Paris for *La Mise en valeur de la Colombie Britannique; étude de colonisation*, and subsequently his *agrégation* in history and geography. He was a sometime directeur of the Cabinet et du Personnel at the Ministère du Travail, as well as a professor at l'Ecole coloniale. His writings include *Socialisme en Angleterre* (1897), its translation, *Социализм в Англии* (1898), *L'Inde d'au-jourd'hui, étude sociale* (1903), *La Transformation de l'Egypte* (1903), and *Histoire moderne, 1715-1815* (1904). He died in 1918. IndexBFR² (1); Note about the author

Métois, Florentine *Alexis*, born 2 April 1868 at Ayron (Vienne), France, he was a graduate of the military college, Saint-Maixent (Deux Sèvres), and subsequently spent his military career essentially in Africa - Algeria, Sahara, Tunisia, Morocco. In 1925, he entered French politics as a militant socialist. His writings include *De l'Algérie au Congo par le Tchad*, par capitain Métois, de la Mission Fourreau-Lamy (1901), *Impressions sahariennes* (1901), *Pour les femmes de France: au désert* (1901), and *Essai de transcription méthodique des noms de lieux touaregs* (1908). He died in Cissé (Vienne) on 5 November 1955. DcBMOuvF, vol. 36 (1990)

Métral, Jean, born 20th cent., he was in 1982 an assistant at the Université de Lyon II, I.R.M.A.C. [Institut de recherches et d'études sur le monde arabe contemporain?], and a joint editor of *L'Homme et l'eau en Méditerranée et au Proche Orient* (1981-82). Note about the author; ZKO

Métro, André, fl. 1946-1958, he was associated with the Food and Agriculture Organization of the United Nations. His writings include *L'Ecologie des eucalyptus, son application au Maroc* (1938), *Les Pépinières forestières au Maroc* (1951), *Les Eucalyptus dans les reboisements* (1954), *Eucalypts for planting* (1955), *Forêts* (1958), and he was a joint author of *Flores des végétaux ligneux de la Marmora* (1955).

Mettmann, Walter, born 25 September 1926 at Köln, Germany, he received a Dr.phil in 1951 from the Universität Köln for *Studien zum religiösen Theater Tirso de Molinas*. He was since 1962 a professor, and later director, the Seminar für Romanische Philologie at the Universität Münster. His other writings include *Der Tristanroman* (1962). Kürschner, 1966-2005

Metzemaekers, Louis Antoine Vincent, born 23 May 1912 at Vilvoirds, Belgium, he studied philosophy, economics, and Arabic at Leiden. After three years as a keeper at the Rijksmuseum voor Volken- kunde, Leiden, he became a journalist, editor, and foreign correspondent. His writings include *Groot- Britannië in de Europese Gemeenschap! Verslag van enkele discussies* (Den Haag, 1967). WhoWor, 1976/77

Metzger, Carl Albert *Emil*, born 19 October 1836 at Coblenz, Prussia, he was a first lieutenant in the Prussian Engineers. About 1862 he went as an officier to Java, returning to Württemberg in 1875. He resigned in 1877 from the military. He remained active as a secretary of Württembergischer Verein für Handelsgeographie, Stuttgart. His writings include *Geographisch-statistisches Welt-Lexikon* (1883). He died in Stuttgart on 9 July 1890. DtBiInd (1)

van der **Meulen**, Daniël, born 4 September 1894 at Laren, Gelderland, the Netherlands, he pursued Oriental studies at Leiden and became a career diplomat, until the second World War in Arabia, and subsequently in Dutch East India. His writings include *Aden to the Hadhramaut, a journey in South Arabia* (1947), *Onbekend Arabië* (1951), *Mijn weg naar Arabië en de Islam* (1954), *Ik stond er bij* (1955?), *The Wells of Ibn Sa'ud* (1957), and the autobiography, *Don't you hear the thunder* (1981). He died in 1989. Au&Wr, 1963; MidE, 1980-1982/83; WhoWor, 1974/75, 1976/77; WhoNL, 1962/63; *Who was who*, 8; *Wie is dat*, 1956

van der **Meulen**, J. F. W., born 19th cent., he was a joint author of *Agrarische regelingen; handleiding voor de toepassing van de wettelijke bepalingen an administratieve voorschriften betreffende het agrarisch recht in Nederlandsch-Indië* (Batavia, 1911). Brinkman's; NUC, pre-1956

Meunié, Germaine Amélie Popelin, called Djinn, Madame Jacques-Meunié, born 24 May 1902 at Paris, she studied Berber language at the École nationale des langues orientales, Paris, and was later associated with the Institut des hautes études, Rabat. Her writings include *Greniers-citadelles au Maroc* (1951), *Sites et forteresses de l'Atlas* (1951), *Cités anciennes de Mauritanie; province du Tagannt et du Hodh* (1961), *Architectures et habitats du Dandès, Maroc présaharien* (1962), *Le prix du sang chez les Berbères de l'Atlas* (1964), *Le Maroc saharien des origines au XVIe siècle* (1982), and she was joint a author of *Nouvelles recherches archéologiques à Marrakech; la coupole almoravide de Marrakech* (1957). BN; Unesco

Meunier, Albert, born 8 September 1861 at Bignicourt (Ardennes), France, he was educated at the École normale, Charleville. He received a teacher's certificate and a doctorate in law in 1911 from the Faculté de droit de Caen for *L'Association agricole dans les Ardennes.*. He was a senator for the Ardennes and a president of the Syndicat agricole des Ardennes. His writings include *Voyage en Algérie* (1909). BN; *Qui êtes-vous*, 1924

Meunier, Dominique, born 20th cent., he edited *Le Consulat anglais à Tetouan sous Anthony Hatfield; études et édition de textes* (Tunis, 1980). ZKO

Meunier, Georges Jean, born 20 May 1910 at Montceau-les-Mines (Saône-et-Loire), France, he graduated from the Lycée Saint-Louis, and the École polytechnique, Paris, and received a degree in law, and a diploma from the Centre des Hautes Études administratives. He was from 1946 to 1956 associated with public works in Tunisia. He subsequently became director of *Bases Aériennes*. His writings include *Conception, construction et gestion des aérodromes* (1969). He died about 1980. WhFr, 1971/72-1979/80|

Mew, James, born in 1837, his writings include *Types from Spanish Story; or, the old manners and customs of Castile* (1884), *Traditional aspects of hell* (1903), and he was a joint author of *Drinks of the world* (1892). BLC; NUC, pre--1956

Meyendorff, Baron Georges de, 1795-1863 *see* Meïendorf, Georg

Meyendorff, John, born 17 February 1926 at Neuilly-sur-Seine, France, he received a *doctorat ès lettres* in 1948 in Byzantine history from the Sorbonne, and also graduated from St. Vladimir's Orthodox Theological Seminary, Tuckahoe, N.Y., where he taught for over twenty-five years. He served as the editor of its quarterly, and became its dean in 1984. His writings include *Le Christ dans la théologie byzantine* (1969), its translation, *Christ in Eastern Christian thought* (1975), *Byzantine theology* (1974), and a collection of his articles, *Byzantine heschasm* (1974). He died from cancer in Montreal in 1992. ConAu, 21-24, 138, new rev., 9; DrAS, 1969 P - 1982 H; Master (1); WrDr, 1976/78-1994/96

Meyer, Albert Julius, born in 1919 at Hawarden, Iowa, he received a Ph.D. in 1950 from Johns Hopkins University, Baltimore, Md., for *History of the California Fruit Growers Exchange, 1893-1920*. He was from 1955 to 1983 a faculty member of Harvard University His writings include *Middle Eastern capitalism* (1959), and *The Economy of Cyprus* (1962). He died in Boston on 31 October 1983. ConAu,

111; *MESA Roster of members*, 1982; NYT, 4 November 1983, p. B14, col. 4; Shavit; WhAm,8; WhoAm, 1970/71-1982/83; WhoWor, 1974/75

Meyer, Alphonse, born 19th cent., he was a French military interpreter who, in 1881, was in retirement. His writings include the annotated translation *Don précieux aux amis traitant des qualités des végétaux et des simples* تحفة الاحباب في ماهية النبات والاعشاب (Alger, 1881). BN

Meyer, Bärbel, born 21 September 1938 at Stolp, Germany, she was educated, first in an internment camp in København, from 1945 to 1949, and, after the family's return to Germany, in Castrop-Rauxel. After completing a library science course, she studied at Heidelberg, Hamburg, and the London School of Economics, where she was awarded a post-graduate diploma in social anthropology. In 1975, she received a Dr. phil. from the Universität Hamburg with a thesis entitled *Wissen und Kontrolle: zur Geschichte und Organisation islamischen Elite-Wissens im Zentralsudan*. Since 1988 she was employed at the Deutsches Orient-Institut, Hamburg. Private

Meyer, Eduard, born 25 January 1855 at Hamburg, he studied Oriental languages at the universities of Bonn, and Berlin, and received a Dr.phil. in 1875 as well as a Dr.habil. in 1879. He was appointed in 1885 a professor of ancient history at the Universität Breslau. He subsequently moved in 1889 to Halle and finally, in 1902, to Berlin, where he remained until his retirement in 1935. His writings include Пабство в древности (1899), *Die Israeliten und ihre Nachbarstämme* (1906), *Kleine Schriften zur Geschichtstheorie* (1910), and *Preußen und Athen* (1919). He died in Berlin on 31 August 1930. DtBE; Egyptology; Kürschner, 1925-1928/29; Wininger

Meyer, Egbert, born about 1938 he, received a Dr.phil. in 1968 from the Universität Köln for a thesis on the historical content of ancient Arabic poetry entitled, *Der historische Gehalt der Aijām al-'Arab*, a work which was published in 1970.

Meyer, Emmi, 1903-1998 *see* Kähler-Meyer, Emmi

Meyer, Erich, born in 1884, his writings include *Deutschland und Ägypten* (1915), *Deutsch-Evangelisch im Orient* (1916), *Das Dommuseum Halberstadt* (1938), and he was a joint author of *Deutsche Arbeit und deutsche Kriegserlebnisse in Ägypten* (1916). NUC, pre-1956; Sezgin

Meyer, Georges Séverin, born 12 April 1897 at Paris, he was a sometime correspondent in Bruxelles and the Middle East for *le Temps*, *le Figaro*, *le Petit Parisien*, and *le Soir*. He was since 1930 a lecturer at the Faculté de droit du Caire, as well as a member of the Société Fouad Ier d'économie politique, de statistique et de législation. His writings include *L'Égypte contemporaine et les capitulations* (1930). He died on 23 February 1971. IndexBFr, (1); WhoFr, 1959/60-1971/72

Meyer, Günter, born about 1945, he received a Dr.rer.nat. in 1978 from the Universität Erlangen-Nürnberg for a thesis on local social history entitled, *Junge Wandlungen im Erlanger Geschäftsviertel; ein Beitrag zur sozialgeographischen Stadtforschung*. He was in 1993 a professor in the Department of Geography, Erlangen. His writings include *Ländliche Lebens- und Wirtschaftsformen Syriens im Wandel* (1984), *Arbeitsmigration, Binnenwanderung und Wirtschaftsentwirklung in der Arabischen Republik Jemen* (1986), and *Kairo; Entwicklungsprobleme einer Metropole der dritten Welt* (1989). DrBSMES, 1993; EURAMES, 1993; ZKO

Meyer, Gustav, born 25 November 1850 at Groß-Strehlitz, Silesia, he studied classical philology, including Sanskrit, at Breslau and Leipzig, gaining a Dr.phil. in 1871. He was a school teacher at Gotha until 1876, when he started his university career at Prag as a lecturer in his subject. Since 1881 he was a professor of Sanskrit and comparatve philology at the Universität Graz, a post which he held until 1897, when failing health obliged him to resign. Since 1875 he had frequently gone on research travels to Italy, the Balkans, and Turkey, where he collected lexicographical and ethnological material. His writings in-clude *Griechische Grammatik* (1880), *Etymologisches Wörterbuch der albanesischen Sprache* (1888), *Türkische Studien* (1893), and *Neugriechische Studien* (1894-95). He died in Graz on 28 August 1900. DtBE; DtBiInd (4); ÖBL

Meyer, Henry Cord, born 12 February 1913 at Chicago, he graduated in 1935 from the University of Colorado, studied 1935/36 at the Universität Wien, and received a Ph.D. in 1941 from Yale University, New Haven, Mass. He was a professor of history at Pomona College, Claremont, Calif., until his retirement in 1980. His writings include *Mitteleuropa in German thought and action, 1815-1945* (1955), *Five images of Germany* (1960), and *The Long generation* (1973). DrAS, 1969 H, 1974 H, 1978 H, 1982 H

Meyer, Johann Jacob, he was born on 25 April 1870 at Frankenmuth, Mich., to a family of poor farmers. The hard work on the family's farm left a mark on his health throughout life. He took Latin, Greek, and Hebrew at high school and studied Sanskrit privately. After graduating from Concordia Theological Seminary, St. Louis, Mich., he learnt modern languages, including Persian, to train his memory while working in the fields. From 1898 to 1900 he formally studied comparative linguistics and German, obtaining in the same year a Ph.D. in Indian studies from the University of Chicago. He subsequently became a lecturer in ancient Indian languages at Chicago, a post which he held until his early retirement on account of ill health. He retired to Chur, Switzerland, where he died of a stroke on 2 April 1939. His writings include *Das Weib im altindischen Epos* (1915), and its translation, *Sexual life in ancient India* (1952). DtBE; Kürschner, 1926-1935; Master (1); Sezgin; Stache-Rosen, pp. 171-172

Meyer, Paul, born in 1840 at Paris, he was successively an archivist at the Archives nationales, Paris, a director of the École des chartes, Paris, and a professor at the Collège de France, Paris. He was a medievalist, and a member of the French Institut; his writings include *Alexandre le Grand dans la littérature française du moyen âge* (1886), and he edited and translated *La Chanson de la croisade contre les Albigeois* (1875-79). He died in 1917. IndexBFr² (1); *Who was who*, 2

Meyer, Rudolf Adalbert, 1880-1936 *see* Riefstahl, Rudolf Meyer

Meyer, Sir William Stevenson, born 13 February 1860 at Galați, Moldavia, the son of a clergyman, he was educated at London University and in 1881 entered the Indian Civil Service. After serving in the Madras Presidency, where he rapidly rose to the post of Secretary of the Board of Revenue in 1890, he joined the Government of India in 1895 as deputy secretary in the Finance Department. He retired from service in India in 1918. He edited the *Imperial gazetteer of India* (1907). He died from heart failure on 19 October 1922. DNB; IndianBilnd (4); *Journal of the Central Asian Society*, 10 (1923), pp. 81-82; Master (1); Riddick; Wininger

Meyer-Ingwersen, Johannes Christian, born in 1940 at Hamburg, he pursued Iranian and Turkish studies at the Universität Hamburg, where he also received a Dr.phil. in 1966 for a study of Pashto gramar entitled *Untersuchungen zum Satzbau des Paschto*. After employment with a variety of German universities, he became a faculty member of the Universität Essen. A member of the Kurdish Academy, his writings include *Zur Sprachentwicklung türkischer Schüler in der Bundesrepublik* (1977). Note about the author; Private

Meyer-Oehme, Detlef, born 20th cent., he received a doctorate in 1956 from the Universität Freiburg im Breisgau for a study of vision among trained squirrels entitled *Dressurversuche an Eichhörnchen zur Frage ihres Helligkeits- und Farbsehens*. His trace is lost after an article in 1974. GV

Meyer-Ranke, Peter, born 20th cent., his writings include *Der rote Pharao, Ägypten* (1964), and *Die arabischen Staaten Vorderasiens* (1970). Sezgin

Meyerhof, Max, born 21 March 1874 at Hildesheim, Germany, he studied medicine at the universities of Heidelberg, Berlin, and Straßburg. He was practising ophthalmologist with a social commitment at Cairo from 1903 to 1914; the outbreak of the First World War prevented him from returning from his vacation to Egypt until 1922. In the same year, he declined an invitation from the Universität Leipzig to succeed K. F. J. Sudhoff in the chair of history of medicine. His writings include *Le Monde islamique* (1926); he edited and translated *The Book of the ten treaties on the eye, ascribed to Hunain ibn Ishâk* (1928), *Un Glossaire de matière médicale de Maïmonide* (1940); and he was joint editor and translator of *Galen über die medizinischen Namen* (1931). He died in Cairo on 19 April 1945. *Al-Andalus* 10 (1945), pp. 460-462; DtBE; DtBilnd (1); Hanisch; *Index Islamicus* (3); Kürschner, 1928/29-1935; NDB; *Wer ist's*, 1935; ZDMG, 99 (1945/49), pp. 11-14

Meyering, Harry Ralph, born in 1899, he received a Ph.D. in 1937 from the University of Michigan for *Behavior problems encountered in a camping situation*. NUC, pre-1956

Meyerovitch, Eva Lamacque de Vitray *see* Vitray-Meyerovitch, Eva Lamacque de

Meyerowitz, Mrs. Eva Leonie Lewin-Richter, born 3 November 1899 at Berlin, she studied fine art at colleges in Berlin. She spent much of her life with her husband in South and West Africa as an anthropologist. Her writings include *Akan traditions of origin* (1952), *The Akan of Ghana* (1958), *At the court of an African king* (1962), and *Mystique et poésie en islam* (1972). AfrBiolnd (1); ConAu, 9-12; IntAu&W, 1977, 1982; Unesco

Meyers, Allan Richard, born 25 November 1946 at Holyoke, Mass., he graduated in 1968 from Dartmouth College, Hanover, N.H., and received a Ph.D. in 1974 from Cornell University, Ithaca, N.Y., for *The 'Abīd 'l-Bukhārī; slave soldiers and statecraft in Morocco, 1672-1790*. He was since 1975 a professor of anthropology at a variety of American universities; in 2005 he was a professor of cultural studies at Eckerd College, Saint Petersburg, Fla. AmM&WSc, 1976 P; Master (1); *MESA Roster of members*, 1977-82; NatFacDr, 2005 Selim³

Meyners d'Estry des Frames, Guillaumes Henry Jean, comte, born in 1829, he was from 1878 to 1891 an editor of the *Annales de l'Extrême Orient et de l'Afrique*. His own writings include *La*

Papouasie, ou Nouvelle-Guinée occidentale (1881), and *Le Souveraineté du peuple* (1889). NUC, pre-1956; (a cross-reference in DBF refers to a forthcoming entry)

Meynet, Roland, born 7 July 1939 at Thonon-les-Bains (Haute-Savoie), France, his writings include *L'Écriture arabe en question; les projets de l'Académie de langue arabe du Caire* (1971), and he was a joint editor of *Ouvrier les écritures; mélanges offerts à Paul Beauchamp* (1995). LC; *Livres disponibles,* 2003; ZKO

Meynier, Gilbert, born in 1942 at Lyon, France, he received a *doctorat d'état* in 1979 from the Université de Nice for *L'Algérie révélée; la guerre de 1914-1918 et le premier quart du XXème siècle*, a work which was published in 1981. He was in 1981 affiliated with the Université de Nancy. His other writings include *L'Emir Khaled, premier za'im?* (1987), he was a joint author of *Histoire de la France coloniale, 1871-1931* (1996), and he edited *L'Europe et la Méditerranée* (1999), and *L'Algérie contemporaine* (2000). *Livres disponibles*, 2003; THESAM 2

Meynier, Octave Frédéric François, born 22 February 1874 at Saint-Yriex-la-Perche (Haute-Vienne), France, he passed through the military college, Saint-Cyr, and then opted for the *infanterie coloniale* in French Equatorial Africa. In 1896, he participated in the pacification of the loop of the Niger region. A joint commander with Paul Joalland, they defeated the forces of the Sultan of Zinder in 1899. La Mission Joalland-Meynier was awarded the *grande médaille d'or* of the Société de géographie de Paris. After passing through the École de Guerre, 1906 to 1907, he served until 1910 at Niamey, before being nominated a professor of military history at Saint-Cyr. In 1911, he became chief of battalion and deputy head of the Cabinet militaire of the governor-general Lutaud at Alger. He subsequently was a member of the mission d'études du transsaharien and succeeded Commandant Romain F. Payn at the head of the Territoire des Oasis. In 1916, he participated in the operations against the Sanusi brotherhood. He entered the Algerian military government in 1923 and was from 1925 to 1935 a director of the Territoires du Sud. He was a member of the Académie des sciences d'outre-mer, and a sometime director of the journal, *Eurafrique*. His writings include *L'Afrique noire* (1911), *Les Conquérants du Tchad* (1923), *La Pacification du Sahara et la pénétration saharienne* (1930), and *La Mission Joal-land-Meynier* (1947). He died in Alger on 31 May 1961. *Eurafrique*, n.s., 27 (juillet 1961), pp. 2-10; *Hommes et destins*, vol. 9, pp. 323-24; Peyronnet, p. 637; *Travaux de l'Institut de Recherches sahariennes*, 20 (1961), pp. 7-10

Mez, Adam, born in 1869 at Freiburg im Breisgau, Germany, he received a Dr.phil. in 1892 from the Universität Straßburg for a study of the history of Harran in Mesopotamia before the Arab conquest entitled *Geschichte der Stadt Harran in Mesopotamien bis zum Einfall der Araber*. He was a professor of Semitic philology at the Universität Basel. Joh. Fück and C. H. Becker contradict each other regarding his background. His writings include *Die Renaissance des Islams* (1922), its translations, *The Renaissance of Islam* (1937), الحضارة الاسلامية (1940); and *Мусулманский ренессанс* (1966), and he edited *Abulkâsim, ein bagdâder Sittenbild von Muhammad ibn Ahmad Abu'l-Mutahhar al Azdi*. He died in 1917. DtBilnd (2); Fück, p. 287; *der Islam*, 13 (1923), pp. 278-80; ZKO

Mez, Theodor, born 20th cent., he received a doctorate in 1954 from the Universität Freiburg, Switzerland, for a study of the market for Egyptian cotton entitled *Der Markt ägyptischer Baumwolle unter besonderer Berücksichtigung seiner Struktur*. His trace is lost after an article in 1960. Schwarz

Miachina, Ekaterina Nikolaevna, born 29 November 1931 at Leningrad, she graduated in 1955 from the Oriental Faculty, Leningrad, and received her first degree in 1967 from the Military Foreign Language Institute, Moscow, for a study of Swahili language and literature entitled *Система суффиксов в глаголе языка суахили*. Her writings include *Учебник языка суахили* (1973), *The Swahili language* (1981), and she was joint author of *Суахили-русски словарь* (1987). Miliband[2]

Miaille, Michel, born in 1941, he was a *maître de conférences agrégé* successively at the schools of law at Alger and Montpellier. His writings include *Une Introduction critique au droit* (1976), and *Constitutions et luttes de classes de 1789 à nos jours* (1978). LC

Micacchi, Rodolfo, fl. 20th cent., he was associated with the Istituto coloniale fascista. His writings include *Sculptures antiques en Libye* (1931), *La rapporti fra il regna di Francia e la Reggenza di Tripoli di Barberia nella prima meta' del secolo XVIII* (Rocca San Casciano, 1934), *La Tripolitania sotto il dominio dei Caramánli* (Intra, 1936), and *L'exploration italienne du Sahara* (Roma, 1938) Firenze; Note about the author; ZKO

Micaletti, Raffaello, born 24 April 1892 at Frattamaggiore (Napoli), he was a graduate of the Istituto orientale di Napoli and the Université de Grenoble. He became an official in the Italian colonial administration and a general. His writings include *Sangue italiano in Etiopia* (1933), *Colonie di agni paese* (1934), and *Al servicio della patria* (1954). IndBiltal (2); *Lui chi è*, 1969

Micara, Ludovico, born in 1942, his writings include *Architetture e spazi dell'islam* (1985), and he was a joint author of *Sabbioneta* (1979). LC

Micaud, Charles Antoine, born 26 November 1910 at Bourg-en-Bresse (Ain), he received a law degree in 1933 from the Université de Lyon and a Ph.D. in 1943 from Columbia University, New York, for *The French right and nazi Germany*, and its translation, *La Droite devant l'Allemagne* (1945). He was a professor at a variety of American universities, and from 1959 to 1961 associated with the International Cooperation Administration mission in Tunis. He was a joint author of *Tunisia; the politics of modernization* (1964), and he was a joint editor of *Arabs, Berbers, from tribe to nation in North Africa* (1972). ConAu, 5-8; NYT, 27 June 1974, p. 48, cols., 5-6; ZKO

Michael, Heimann Joseph, born 12 April 1792 at Hamburg, he was a student of the local Rabbi Lazarus Joseph. He became a private scholar and bibliophile, particularly of Hebrew literature. He left an important library of Hebraica which found its way to the British Museum, London, and the Bodleian Library, Oxford. He died in Hamburg on 10 June 1846. DtBE; Sezgin; Wininger

Michaelis, Adolf Theodor Friedrich, born 22 June 1835 at Kiel, he studied classical philology at the universities of Kiel and Berlin, gaining his Dr.phil. and Dr.habil. at the Universität Kiel. He spent some years in Italy and Greece, before serving successively as a professor at Greifswald, Tübingen, and Straßburg. His writings include *Die archäologischen Entdeckungen des neunzehnten Jahrhunderts* (1906), and its translation, *A Century of archaeological discoveries* (1908). He died in Straßburg on 12 August 1910. DtBE; Kornrumpf², vol. 2; Μεγαλη ελληνικη εγκυκλοπαιδεια, vol. 17 (1931), pp. 270-71; NDB; NDBA

Michaelis, Alfred, born in 1901, he received a Dr.rer.pol., he was a sometime editor of the *Middle East economist*, New York, as well as a professor at the Asia Institute, New York. He spent considerable time in the Middle East as a writer and correspondent. His writings include *Wirtschaftliche Entwicklungsperspektiven des Mittleren Ostens* (1956), *Wirtschaftliche Entwicklungsprobleme des Mittleren Ostens* (1960), and *Erdöl in der Weltwirtschaft* (1974). Note about the author; ZkO

Michaelis, Johann David, born 27 February 1717 at Halle/Saale, he studied at the Universität, where he received a magister artium in 1739. He subsequently travelled to Holland and England. After his return in 1742, he became a lecturer at Halle until 1746, when he went to Göttingen, where he became a professor of philosophy. Since 1751 a member of Göttinger Gesellschaft der Wissenschaften, he served as their director from 1761 to 1770. In 1771, he founded the *Orientalische und exegetische Bibliothek*. He took an active interest in the 1761-68 Danish Arabia expedition. Though for many years the most famous teacher of Semitic languages in Europe, he had little of the higher philological faculty, and neither his grammatical nor his critical work has left a permanent mark, with the exception of his text-critical studies on the *Pshitta*. His *Litterarischer Briefwechsel* (1794-1796) contains much that is of interest for the history of learning. He died in Göttingen on 22 August 1791. *Allgemeine Bibliothek der biblischen Litteratur*, 3 (1790/92), pp. 827-906; Bidwell, pp. 32-33; DtBE; EncBrit; Fück, p. 119; Master (5); Μεγαλη ελληνικη εγκυκλοπαιδεια, vol. 17 (1931), p. 271

Michaelson, Karen Lee, born 11 March 1944 at N.Y.C., she graduated in 1966 from the University of Miami and received her Ph.D. in 1973 from the University of Wisconsin for *Class, caste, and network in suburban Bombay*. In 1974, she was appointed a professor of anthropology at State University of New York at Binghamton. She was a joint author of *Childbirth in America; anthropological perspectives* (1988), and she edited *And the poor get children; radical perspectives on population dynamics* (1981). AmM&WSc, 1976 P

Michalon, Thierry, born 20th cent., he received a diploma from the Institut d'études politiques de Grenoble, a degree from Tulane Law School, New Orleans, La., and a *doctorat de 3ème siècle* from the Université d'Aix-Marseille for *Les Collectivités locales algériennes d'hier à aujourd'hui*. His writings include *Quel état pour l'Afrique* (1984). He was a sometime *enseignant-chercheur* at the Faculté de droit et des sciences économiques, Université du Tchad. Note about the author; THESAM 2

Michalopoulos, André/Andreas C., born 1 March 1897 at London, he was educated at St. Paul's School, London, and Oriel College, Oxford. He was for over twenty years in the service of the Greek Government and concurrently from 1957 to 1964 a professor of classics at Fairleigh Dickinson University, Teaneck, N.J. His writings include *Greek fire* (1943), and *Homer* (1966). He died about 1990. ConAu, 23-24; DrAS, 1974 F; Who, 1963-1991|

Michałowski, Kazimierz, born 14 December 1901 at Tarnopol, Poland, he studied classical archaeology at Lwów, Berlin, Heidelberg, Münster, Paris, Roma, Athens, and Cairo. He held the chair of classical archaeology at Warszawa, and concurrently served as a deputy director of the National Museum. He died in 1981. AnObit, 1981, pp. 3-5; BioIn 12; ConAu, 108; Dziekan; Egyptology; IntWW, 1966/67-1980/81; Master (2); WhoWor, 1974-1978/79

Michałowski, Piotr, born 25 June 1800 at Kraków (Cracow), Austria-Hungary, to an old Polish family, he was educated privately and later studied at the universities of Krakau and Göttingen, where he was a student of the Orientalist Johann G. Eichhorn. Recommended by Count Łubecki, he entered the public service in 1823. He went to Italy in 1825 to recuperate from over-work, and in 1832 he was sent on a mission to France to study the mining industry. In 1832 he resigned his public office to pusue an interst in fine art. He became a landscape and portrait painter of Oriental subjects in the fashion of Eugène Delacroix. He died in Kraukau on 9 June 1855. Dziekan; NEP; PolBiDi (not sighted); Polski (14); Wurzbach

Michaud, Claude, born 20th cent., his writings include *L'Europe de Louis XIV* (1973), and he was a joint editor of *L'Intendance d'Orléans à la fin du siècle* (1989).

Michaud, Joseph François, born in 1767 at Albens (Savoie), France, he was educated at Bourg-en-Bresse (Ain), and afterwards engaged in literary work at Lyon, where the events of 1789 first called out the strong dislike to revolutionary principles which manifested itself throughout the rest of his life. In 1791, he went to Paris as an editor of several journals. In the early 1900's he began to write or edit books. His writings include *Histoire des croisades* (1812-22), a work, though translated into English, German, and Spanish, is more interesting than exact. In 1830-31, he travelled in Syria and Egypt for the purpose of collecting additional material for the *Histoire*. He is, however, best remembered for starting in 1811 the *Biographie universelle, ancienne et moderne*. He died in Passy in 1839. BiD&SB; EncBrit; IndexBFr² (6); Hoefer; Kornrumpf; Kornrumpf³, vol. 2; Kornrumpf, N; Master (1); NewCathEnc; OxFr

Michaux, André, born in 1746 at Versailles, he spent some time botanizing in England, and in 1780 he explored Auvergne, the Pyrénées and the north of Spain. In 1782, he was sent by the French Government on a botanical mission to Persia. His journey began unfavourably, as he was robbed by Arabs of all his equipment except his books; but he gained influential support in Persia, having cured the ruler, Muhammad Karīm Khān Zand, of a dangerous illness. After two years he returned to France with a fine herbarium, and also introduced numerous Eastern plants into the botanical gardens of France. He was in 1785 sent to North America. He died in 1803 of fiver on Madagascar. EncBrit; Hoefer, *Hommes et destins*, 4, pp. 511-513; IndexBFr² (5)

Michaux-Bellaire, Edouard, born 3 November 1857 at Ouen, he was in 1911 a French consular officer at El-Ksar, and chief of the Mission scientifique française au Maroc. His writings include *Quelques tribus de montagnes de la région du Habt* (1911), *Le Gharb* (1913), *Registre des habous de Tanger* (1914), and *Apuntes para la historia de Rif* (1926). He died in Rabat on 13 May 1930. BN; Note about the author; ZKO

Micheau, Françoise, born 20th cent., she received a *doctorat de 3ème cycle* in 1973 from the Sorbonne for *Les traductions imprimées d'œuvres en langues occidentales*. She was a joint author of *La médecine arabe et l'Occident médiéval* (1990), *Communautés chrétiennes en pays d'islam du début du VII siècle au mileu du XI siècle* (1997), *Les Pays d'islam, VII-XV siècle* (2000), she was a joint translator of *Chronique des Ayyoubides*, from the Arabic (1994), *Histoire de Yahyá Ibn Sa'īd d'Antioche* (1997), and she was a joint editor of *Vivre au moyen âge, d'après un manuscrit du XIIIe siècle* (1980). THESAM, 4

Michel, Aloys Arthur, born 9 September 1928 at Brooklyn, N.Y., he graduated in 1950 from Harvard University, where he also received a Ph.D. in 1959 for *The Kabul, Kunduz and Helmand valleys and the national economy of Afghanistan*. He successively served as a professor at Columbia and Yale universities, and the University of Rhode Island, Kingston. His writings include *The Indus rivers* (1967). AmM&WSc, 1973 S; AmM&WSc, 1976 P; WhoAm, 1974/75-1978/79

Michel, André, born 20th cent., his writings include *Sociologie de la famille et du mariage* (1972), its translation, *Sociologia della famiglia* (1974), and *The Modernization of North African families in the Paris area* (1974). ZKO

Michel, Bernard, born 19th cent., he was in 1916 associated with the Caisse hypothécaire d'Égypte; in 1928, he was a director of the Compagnie immobilière d'Égypte resident in Cairo, and a member of the Société sultanieh d'économie politique, de statistique et de législation. His writings include *Les Musulmans d'Egypte et la vie économique moderne* (1926), and *L'Evolution du budget égyptien* (1932?). Note about the author; NUC, pre-1956

Michel, Carl (Karl), born 4 July 1885 at Habitzheim, Hesse, Germany, he studied at København and Gießen, where he received a Dr.phil. in 1912 for a study of Old-German verbs entitled *Die mit -j- abgeleiteten denominativen verba im Alt-germanischen*. GV

Michel, Hubert, born in 1935 at Toulon, France, he received a diploma in political science and became an assistant to Roger Le Tourneau at the Centre de Recherche sur l'Afrique méditerranéenne at Aix-en-Provence. He was a joint author of *Technologies et développement au Maghreb* (1978), and a joint editor of *Le Maghreb et l'Afrique subsaharienne* (1980). Note about the author

Michel, Karl August, born 26 May 1875 at Straßburg, Alsace, he studied at the Universität Straßburg and Universität Berlin and received a Dr.phil. in 1902 for a study of prayer and image in early Christianity entitled *Gebet und Bild in frühchristlicher Zeit*. He subsequently spent two years as a private teacher in Constantinople, during which time he visited central Anatolia. He made archaeological excursions to Roma, Athens, southern Russia, and Macedonia, experiences which are embodied in his articles. In 1910 he was resident in Allenweiler, Unter-Elsaß. DÖS

Michel (Mişel Paşa), Marius, born about 1819 at Sanary-sur-Mer (Var), France, he was a naval officer who entered the Ottoman public service. He introduced lighthouses, making a fortune, and was named admiral of the fleet. He was chief administrator of lighthouses in the Ottoman Empire, a president of the Administrative Council of the Society of Quays, Docks,and Bonded Warehouses, Constantinople, and the Steam-Packet Service. At home, he was a founding member of the Société de géographie de Marseille; he retired to Tamaris-sur-Mer, where he died on 6 January 1907 at the age of eighty-eight. *Bulletin of the Société de géographie de Marseille*, 31 (1907), p. 122; Kornrumpf

Michel, Pierre, le père, born in 1855, he was a missionary whose writings include *La Question religieuse en Orient et l'union des Églises* (1893), and *L'Orient et Rome; étude sur l'union* (1894). He died in 1926. BN; NUC, pre-1956

Michelini Tocci, Franco, born 4 February 1937 at Pesaro (Urbino), Italy, he was a Hebrew scholar and a professor of religion who served from 1963 to 1966 at the Università Roma and subsequently at the Università di Venezia. His writings include *La Siria nell'età di Mari* (1960), *Visita a Tamerlano* (1988); he edited *Il commentaro di Emanuelo Romano al capitolo I della Genesi* (1963); and he edited and translated *I manoscritti del Mar Morto* (1968). IndBiltal (1); *Lui, chi è*; Wholtaly, 1980

Michell, George, born 16 December 1944, he was a joint author of *The Arts of Islam* (1976), *Firuzabad, palace city of the Deccan* (1992), and he edited *Architecture of the Islamic world* (1978).

Michell, George Babington, born in 1864 at Bangalore, E.I., he was educated at King's College School, London, and served as a lay missionary in Tunis and Tripoli under the North African Mission, from 1887 to 1902. In the following year, he entered the British Consular Service as vice-consul at Casablanca. He was a lifelong student of Hamito-Semitic languages. His writings include *The Historical truth of the Bible* (1927), and he was a joint translator of the eleventh-century Archbishop of Canterbury Anselm's *Cur Deus Homo*, from the Latin into Arabic, published at Beirut in 1896. He died in 1936. Who, 1929-1936; *Who was who, 3*

Michell, Robert, born 19th cent., his writings include *Eastern Turkestan and Dzungaria* (1871), *Report on the overland trade between Russia and China* (1871), and he was a joint translator of *The Chronicle of Novgorod, 1016-1471* (1914). NUC, pre-1956

Michell, Roland Lyons Nosworthy, born in 1847, he was educated at Christ Church College, Oxford. His "friends know something of the immense width of his knowledge, but, unfortunately, he never collected or published his recollections. It will be a great misfortune if his notes on the dervish sects are not put together, for he himself said he probably knew more about them than any other living man. His friendship with many of the various sects when he was in Egypt, first in charge of Prince Ibrahim Pasha, son of the Khedive, from 1870 to 1878, and then as chief of the Statistical Department of the Egyptian Revenue Survey, and other posts, enabled him to collect much first-hand information which would be invaluable to scholars." He was from 1879 to 1911 Commissioner of Limassol. He wrote *An Egyptian calendar for the Coptic year 1617, corresponding with the Mohammedan years 1318-1319* (1900). He died in 1931. Note about the author; *Who's who*, 1921-1931; *Who was who 3*

Michon, Jean Hippolyte, abbé, born 21 November 1806, he received the classical education of his day at Angoulême, to which theological studies at Saint-Sulpice were added. After two years as a *professeur* of rhetoric at the Petit séminaire in Larochefoucauld (Charente), he was ordained in 1830. Being more inclined towards preaching than teaching, he established in the same year an ecclesiastic institution in les Thibaudières, which later was transferred to Lavalette. Although he left Lavalette in 1845, he remained a much sought-after Lenten preacher at Paris, Bordeaux, Périgueux, and other places. In 1850 and 1863 he accompanied Félicien de Saulcy on explorations in Palestine. His writings include *Solution nouvelle de la question des lieux saints* (1852). He died in Montauzier (Charente) on 8 May 1881. Glaeser; Vapereau

Michon, Jean Louis, born 20th cent., his writings include *Le Soufi marocain Ahmad Ibn 'Ajiba et son mi'rāj* (1973), *Lumières d'islam; institutions, art et spiritualité dans la cité musulmane* (1994), *Le*

Shaykh Muhammad al-Hāshimī et son Commentaire de l'échiquier des gnostiques (1998), and he translated from the Arabic *L'Autobiographie du Soufi marocain Ahmad ibn Agiba, 1747-1809* (1982). *Livres disponibles,* 2003; ZKO

Michon, Louis Marie, fl. 1927-1951, his writings include *Inventaire des incunables de la Bibliothèque Sainte-Geneviève* (1943), *Les Reliures mosaïques du XVIIIe siècle* (1956), and he was a joint author of *L'Art du livre en France des origines à nos jours* (1931).

Michot, Jean R., born 20th cent., his writings include *La Destinée de l'homme selon Avicenne* (Louvain, 1986), and he edited and translated from the Arabic, *Lettres à un rois croisé*; présentation et traduction de la Risâla Qubrusiyya d' Ahmad ibn Taymiyya (1995). *Livres disponibles,* 2003; ZKO

Mickiewicz (Μιτσκεβιτς), Adam Bernard, born 24 December 1798 in Lithuania, he studied philology, literature, and history at Vilnius University, graduating in 1819. He subsequently taught for four years at Kaunas. A member of the secret patriotic society of Philomaths, he was arrested by the Russians and exiled to Russia, where he nevertheless was well received by Russian *littérateurs.* In 1828, he was permitted to go abroad. He taught Latin at the Université de Lausanne, 1839-1840, and Slavic literature at the Collège de France, Paris, from 1840 to 1844. In 1855, at the outbreak of the Crimean War, he left for Turkey to organize a Polish regiment for service against the Russians. He died in Constantinople on 26 September 1855. Baltisch (2); ConAu, (3); Dziekan; EEE; EncBrit; GdeEnc; JüdLex; Kornrumpf², vol. 2; Krachkovskiĭ; Magyar; Master (39); Megali, vol. 17 (1931), p. 268; MEW; Meyers; Polski (20); PSB

Middendorf, John William, born 22 September 1924 at Baltimore, Md., he was educated at Harvard University, and the New York Graduate School of Business Administration. He became an investment banker, diplomatist, government official, and business executive. BlueB, 1976; IntWW, 1974/75-2002; WhoAm, 1976/77-2003; WhoWor, 1993/94

von Middendorff, Alexander Theodor, born in 1815, he graduated from the Universitas Dorpatensis (Tartu). He was an explorer, whose travels, which took him to Siberia, were of great scientific importance. His writings include Бараба (1871), Путнишествие на север и восток Сибири (1876-77), *Einblicke in das Fergana-Tal* (1881), and *Auf Schlitten, Boot und Renntierrücken* (1956). He died in 1894. Nikolaĭ Ivanovich Leonov wrote Александр Федорович Миддендорф (1967). Embacher; EnSlovar; Henze; SibirSE; Wieczynski

Middleton, Drew, born in 1913 or 1914 at New York City, he graduated in journalism in 1935 from Syracuse University and received an honorary LL.D. in 1963. He was a journalist and a correspondent attached to a variety of allied forces as well as chief correspondent for the *New York Times,* reporting on global events for over forty years. His writings include *Our share of night* (1946), *The Struggle for Germany* (1949), *These are the British* (1957), and *Submarine, the ultimate naval weapon* (1976). He died in N.Y.C. on 10 January 1990. Au&Wr, 1963, 1971; ConAu, 110, 130; IntAu&W, 1976-1991/92; IntWW, 1983-1989/90; WhAm, 10; Who, 1969-1990; *Who was who,* 8

Middleton, James, fl. 19th cent., he was a fellow of the Geographical Society, whose writings include *Astronomical excercises for acquiring a knowldge of the fixed stars* (1828), and *Astronomy and the use of the globes* (1848). BLC

Middleton, Wilfred Lawson, born in 1881, his writings include *The French political system* (London, 1932). BLC

Miège, Émile, born 14 July 1880 at Paris to a family of modest substance, he lost his parents when he was quite young so that he had to work throughout his education. He became an agricultural engineer with degrees from the École supérieure d'agronomie in Grignon as well as in Rennes, and a doctorate from the Sorbonne. After the first World War he was called to Morocco by General Lyautey to establish the Service de recherches agronomiques, which he then headed for the next twenty years. He was a member of several academies. His writings include *Recherches sur la composition et la valeur industrielle des blés marocains* (1930), *Les Cultures complémentaires au Maroc* (1938), and *L'Orientation de l'agriculture marocaine* (1946). He died in Aix-en-Provence on 18 July 1969. *Hommes et destins,* vol. 7, pp. 349-50; NDNC, 1964

Miège, Jean Louis, born 22 September 1922 (or 23 August 1923) at Rabat, he was educated at Rabat, Toulouse, and Paris. He taught at schools and the university at Rabat, before he was appointed a professor at the Université d'Aix-Marseille. He there successively headed the Institut d'études politiques, the Centre de recherches sur l'Afrique méditerranéenne, and the Institut d'histoire des pays d'outre-mer. His writings include *Le Maroc* (1952), and *Les Européens à Casablanca au XIX siècle* (1954), and *Le Maroc et l'Europe, 1830-1894* (1961). Unesco; WhoFr, 1977/78-2003/2004

Miegel, Alfred Günther, born 8 May 1940 at Altsee, Pomerania, he attended school in Hüttenrode, Harz, where he also trained as a mechanic. Since 1959 he studied at a workers' and peasants'

preparatory school in Potsdam for his matriculation. He subsequently trained as a geographer and Slavic studies teacher but became an assistant in problems of underdeveloped countries at Karl Marx Universität Leipzig. In 1971, he there received a Dr.phil. in Marxist-Leninist administrative sciences for a study of the role of mineral resources for the Iraqi industry entiled *Zur Rolle der Energie- und Rohstoffgrundlagen für die aktuelle Entwicklung und territoriale Verteilung der Industrie in der Republik Irak*. His writings include *Die Moldanische Sozialistische Sowjetrepublik* (1967). Schwarz; Thesis

Miégeville, J.-J., born about 1900, he received a doctorate in 1926 from the École nationale vétérinaire de Toulouse for *Contribution à l'étude de l'anémie infecteuse des équides au Maroc*.

Mielck, Reinhard Bertram, born 3 November 1883 at Hamburg, he was educated at the Johanneum, Hamburg, and studied at the universities of Heidelberg, Freiburg im Breisgau, Berlin and Breslau, where he received a Dr.phil. in 1913 for a study of the nomenclature of millers bakers in the Islamic middle ages entitled *Terminologie und Technologie der Müller und Bäcker im islamischen Mittelalter*. His trace is lost after an article in 1923. Schwarz; Sezgin

Mieli, Aldo, born 4 December 1879 at Livorno, Italy, he graduated in chemistry from the Università di Pisa. Since 1912 he pursued an interest in the history of science. Political considerations forced him to leave Italy in 1928. He went first to France and then to Argentina. His writings include *Studi su Dante* (1923), *La Science arabe et son rôle dans l'évolution scientifique mondiale* (1938), *La época medieval; mundo islámica y occidente cristiano* (1946), *El mundo islámico y el occidente medieval cristiano* (1946), and *La ciencia del Renacimiento* (1952). He died in Florida, Argentina, on 16 February 1950. BioIn 2 (1); Chi è, 1928, 1931, 1936; DcScB; IndBiltal (1)

Miette, Roland, fl. 1957-62, he was associated with the Centre de hautes études de l'Afrique et l'Asie moderne, Paris. His writings include *Les Prémisses de l'insurrection algérienne* (Paris, 1977).

Miéville, Sir Walter Frederick, born in 1855, he was educated at Christ's College, Finchley. He was in the British Consular Service from 1874 to 1884, and subsequently served until 1897 as a president of the Egyptian Maritime and Quarantine Board of Health. His writings include *Under Queen and Khedive; the autobiography of an Anglo-Egyptian official* (1899). He died in 1929. BritInd (1); Who was who, 3

Migaux, Léon, born 15 October 1897 at Gennevilliers (Hauts-de-Seine), France, he graduated from both, the École polytechnique, and École normale supérieure, Paris. After fighting in the First World War, he participated in the Ruhr Basin Allied Control Commission. In 1925, he was appointed manager of Montpellier's mining district, where he had his first contacts with the petroleum industry. In 1929, he was promoted to organize and manage the Bureau de recherches pétrolières et minières in Morocco and thereafter its subsidiary, the Société chérifienne des pétroles. He played a prominent role in the first French petroleum discoveries, such as the gas field of Lacq and the oil fields of Parentis in France, the fields of Hassi Messaoud and Hassi R'Mel in the Sahara, and all the early producing fields in Gabon and Equatorial Africa. After his retirement in 1967, he pursued until his death a continuing and extremely prolific activity in scientific research. He was a joint author of *Conrad Schlumberger et la prospection électrique* (Paris, 1942). He died on 9 November 1974, after a long and painful illness. American Association of Petroleum Geologists bulletin, 59, no. 8 (1975), pp. 1508-1509

Migeod, Frederick William Hugh, born in 1872 at Chislehurst, Kent, England, he was educated at Folkestone, and served from 1889 to 1898 in the Royal Navy (Pay Department). After a brief service with the Royal Niger Company in 1898, he served until 1899 with the West African Field Force in Lokoja, Nigeria, as an assistant transport officer. He subsequently served until his retirement in 1919 with the Colonial Civil Service (Gold Coast). During the next five years he travelled extensively in Africa south of the Sahara. After 1925 he headed various expeditions in the service of the British Museum. He was an example of the gifted amateur who despite limited formal education developed wide interests and wrote prolifically on many subjects. He was a sometime president of the Worthing Archaeological Society, as well as its honorary secretary. His writings include *The Languages of Africa* (1911-1913), *A Grammar of the Hausa language* (1914), *Across Equatorial Africa* (1923), *Through Nigeria to Lake Chad* (1924), and *Aspects of evolution* (1932). He died in Worthing, Sussex, in 1952. AfrBioInd (1); LexAfrika; Who's who in Sussex, 1935

Migeod, Heinz Georg, born early 20th cent., he studied Arabic under Helmut Braun at the Universität Göttingen, where he received a Dr.phil. in 1956 for a study of Persian society under Nāsir al-Dīn Shāh entitled *Über die persische Gesellschaft unter Nāsiru'd-Dīn Šāh*. Note about the author; Schwarz

Migeon, Gaston born in 1861 at Vincennes near Paris, he joined the Musée du Louvre in 1869, first in the library and later in the Département des Objets d'Art which, at that time, was limited to European objects. It was during his time as assistant curator that this changed to include Islamic as well as Far

Eastern art. His writings include *Le Caire, le Nil et Memphis* (1906), *Les Arts musulmans* (1926), *Cent planches en couleur d'art musulman* (1929), and he was a joint author of *Islamische Kunstwerke; Keramik, Ge-werbe, Teppiche* (Berlin, 1928). He died in Paris on 29 October 1930. *Eastern art*, 3 (1931), pp. 2-3; *Syria*, 11 (1930), pp. 309-310

Migliorini, Elio, born 9 March 1902 at Rovigo, Italy, he took a doctorate in law and successively became a professor of political geography, and director, in the Istituto universitario orientale di Napoli, and Istituto di geografia di Napoli. His writings include *Strade e commercio dell'Iran* (1939) *La Siria* (1941), *La Tunisia* (1941), and *Profilo geografico dell'Africa* (1955), *Profilo geografico del Vicino Oriente* (1956), *L'esplorazione del Sahara* (1961), *L'uomo e la terra* (1971), and he was a joint editor of *Terra, mari e uomini* (1967-68). *Chi è*, 1948, 1957, 1961; IndBiltal (3); *Lui, chi è*; Wholtaly, 1957/58

Mignan, Robert, born about 1800, he entered the Bombay Army in 1819 and served in the first European Regiment until death. He was brevet lieutenant-colonel. His writings include *Travels in Chaldaea, including a journey from Basrah to Bagdad, Hillah, and Babylon, performed on foot in 1827* (1829), *Notes extracted from a private journal, written during a tour through a part of Malabar* (1834), and *A Winter journey through Russia, the Caucasian Alps and Georgia… into Koordistaun* (1839). He died in Poonah on 3 June 1852. Boase; Henze

Mignon, Jean-Marie, born in 1947, he received a doctorate in public law in 1977 from the Université de Paris for *Organisation de l'espace urbain et étude des fonctions sociales; le cas de la ville de Saida, Algérie*. He was a sometime lecturer in the Institut de Technologie, de Planification et d'Economie appliquée d'Alger. His writings include *Afrique; jeunesses uniques, jeunesse en cadrées* (1985), and he was a joint editor of *Education en Afrique* (1980). *Livres disponibles*, 2003; THESAM 2

Mignot, Vincent, born about 1730 at Paris to a family originally from Sedan, he was a nephew of Voltaire. He became an ecclesiastic, although not ordained, and obtained benefice of clergy at the Abbaye de Scellières, among others. He was with Voltaire when he was dying and, together with the Marquis de Villevieille, signed his religious credo. He was also a historian whose writings include *Histoire de l'Empire ottoman* (1771), its translations, *Geschichte des Osmanischen Reichs* (1774), and *The History of the Turkish, or Ottoman Empire* (1787). He died in Paris in 1791. Hoefer; IndexBFr² (4)

Mignot-Lefebvre, Yvonne, born 20th cent., she was in 1974 a researcher in the Institut d'études du développement économique et social, Université de Paris. She was a joint author, with Michel Lefebvre, of *La société combinatoire; résaux et pouvoirs dans une économie en mutation* (1989), *Les patrimoines du futur; les sociétés aux prises avec la modialisation* (1995), and she was a joint editor of *Education en Afrique* (1980), *Les télévisions arabes à l'heure des satellites* (1996), and *Xoana 6-7; multimedia en recherche; nouvelles pratiques en sciences sociales* (1999). *Livres disponibles*, 2003, 2004; Note about the author

Migoń, Krzysztof, born in 1940 in Poland, he was since 1982 a professor at Uniwersytet Wrocławski. His writings include *Recepcja książki orientalistcznej na Śląsku do końca XVIII wieku* (Wrocław, 1969). NEP; *Who's who w Polsce*, 2005

de **Miguel Zaragoza**, Juan, fl. 20th cent., he wrote *Ensayo sobre el derecho de los pamues de Río Muni* (Madrid, 1963). NUC, 1956-67

Mihaéloff, Simantov, born about 1900, he received a doctorate in 1923 from the Université de Genève for *Contribution à l'étude des bacteries anaerobies et anaerobies facultatives.*

Miiatev (Миятев), Petur, fl. 20th cent., his writings include, *Török iratok Bulgáriában* (Budapest, 1937), *Les Monuments osmanlis en Bulgarie*, its English translation, *Ottoman monuments in Bulgaria* (Ankara, 1987); he edited *Маджарски пътеписи за Балканите: XVI-XIX в.* (Sofia, 1976); and he was a joint editor of *Документи за историята на Българското книжовно дружество в Браила, 1868-1876* (Sofia, 1958-1966). NUC; NYPL; OSK; ZKO

Mijatovich, Chedomil', born in 1842 at Beograd, he studied at the universities of München, Leipzig, and Zürich. He was a professor of political economy at Beograd, before he entered Serbian politics and subsequently the foreign service. When he resigned from politics in 1883, he was appointed chargé d'affaires in London. Recalled in 1887, he remained in London, where he died on 14 May 1932. His writings include *Constantine Palaeologus, the last emperor of the Greeks* (c1892, 1968), *Servia and the Servians* (1908), *The Memoirs of a Balkan diplomatist* (1917) as well as a number of novels. Kornrumpf; *Мала енциклопедија просвета* (1978); Meyers; Who, 1908-1932; *Who was who*, 3

Mikaelian, Nina Rubenovna, born 16 August 1957 at Moscow, she graduated in 1980 from the Institute of Asian and African Studies, Moscow, and received her first degree in 1984 for a study of traditional forms of social protest in India and Pakistan entitled *Традиционые формы социального*

протеста в Индии и Пакистане. She spent 1979-80 in Karachi. Since 1984 she was associated with the Oriental Institute, Soviet Academy of Sciences. Her writings include *Общественно-политические движенния и религиозная традиция в Индии и Пакимтане* (1989). Milband²; OSK

Mikesell, Marvin Wray, born in 1929 or 1930 at Kansas City, Mo., he graduated in 1952 from the Universtity of California, Los Angeles, and received a Ph.D. in 1959 from the University of California at Berkeley for *The northern zone of Morocco; a study of rural settlement and its effect on the land.* He was since 1958 associated with the University of Chicago, finishing his career in its Department of Commercial Geographic Studies. His writings include *Northern Morocco* (1961), and *Patterns and imprints of mankind* (1969). AmM&WSc, 1976 P; ConAu, 1-4, new rev., 4; NatFacDr, 1995-2003; Selim; Unesco; WhoAm, 1984-2003

Mikesell, Raymond Frech, born 13 February 1913 at Eaton, Ohio, he graduated in 1935 from Ohio State University, where he also received a Ph.D. in 1939 for *The marginal productivity theory and unemployment.* He was a government economist and a professor of economics at a variety of institutions. His writings include *United States economic policy and international relations* (1952), *Foreign exchange in the postwar world* (1954), and he was a joint author of *Arabian oil, America's stake in the Middle East* (1949). AmM&WSc, 1973 S, 1978 S; ConAu, 1-4, new rev., 4, 19, 41; Shavit; WhoAm, 1974/75-2003; WhoEc, 1986; WhoWor, 1974/75

Mikhail, Mona Naguib, born 18 October 1940 at Cairo, she studied at Cairo and received a Ph.D. in 1972 from the University of Michigan for *Major existentialist themes and methods in the short fiction of Idris, Mahfouz, Hemingway and Camus.* She was a professor of Arabic literature and Islamic studies at New York University for well over twenty-five years, a post which she still held in 2005. She was a member of the Board of Governors, American Research Center in Egypt. Her writings include *Images of Arabic[!] women; fact and fiction* (1979), and *Studies in the short fiction of Mahfouz and Idris* (1992). MESA Roster of members, 1977-90; NatFacDr, 1995-2005; Private; Selim

Mikhaĭlov, Georgiĭ Ivanovich, born 23 December 1908 (5 January 1909), at St. Petersburg, he graduated in 1930 from the Leningrad Oriental Institute, and received his first degree in 1952 for a study of Mongol literature entitled *Возникновение и развитие современной монголской литературы,* and his doctorate in 1970 for *Литературное наследие монголских народов.* He was from 1950 to 1986 associated with the Oriental Institute, Soviet Academy of Sciences. His writings include *Культурное строительство в МНР* (1957), *Литературное наследство монголов* (1969) and *Проблемы фолбклора мон-гольских народов* (1971). He died 26 July 1986. Miliband; Miliband²

Mikhaĭlov, IA, fl. 1923, he was a writer on communism who published under the pseudonym IA. M. Zakher. His writings include *Парижские секции 1790-1795 гг.* (1921), and *История Великов французской революции* (1923). NUC, pre-1956; NYPL

Mikhaĭlov, Mikhaĭl Semenovich, born 23 March 1896, he was a Soviet Turkologist whose writings include *Исследования по грамматика турецкого языка* (1965), and he was a joint author of *Русско-турецкий словарь* (1943). Народы Азии и Африки, 1966, no. 2, pp. 229-30

Mikhaĭlova, Aleksandra Ivanovna, born 19 November 1923 at Perechivno (Novgorod Oblast), she graduated in 1949 from the Oriental Faculty, Leningrad. She was from 1950 to 1979 associated with the Leningrad Branch of the Oriental Institute, Soviet Academy of Sciences. Her writings include *Каталог арабских рукописей Института народов Азии АН СССР* (1965). Miliband; Miliband²

Mikhaĭlova, Irina Borisovna, born 16 June 1940 at Leningrad, she graduated in 1962 from the Oriental Faculty, Leningrad, and received her first degree in 1983 for a study of popular movements in medieval Baghdad entitled *Народные движения в Багдаде в X-XII вв.* Her writings include *Библиография арабских рукописей / АН СССР* (1982), *Установления и обычаи двора* (1983), and *Средне-вековый Багдад* (1990). Miliband²

Mikhal'chenko, S. E., born 20th cent., he was associated with the Archaeological Institute in the Russian Academy of Sciences. He was a joint author of *Археологическая карта России; Рязанска область* (1993). Note about the author

Mikhalevich, Galina Pavlovna, born 16 August 1926 at Leningrad, she received her first degree in 1953 for a study of progressive poetry in contemporary Iran entitled *Прогрессивная поэзия современного Ирана; по материалам демократической прессы 1944-1949 гг.* Since 1954 she was associated with the Hermitage Museum, Leningrad. Miliband; Miliband²

Mikhneva, Rumiana, born 20th cent., her writings include *Россия и Османская империя в международных отношениях в середине XVIII века, 1739-1756* (1985), and she was a joint author of *От Галиполи до Гепанто; Балканите, Европаи османското нашествие, 1354-1571 гг.* (Sofia, 1988).

Mikkola, Jooseppi Julius, born 6 July 1866 at Ylöjärvi, Finland, he received a doctorate in 1893 from Helsingfors University for *Berührungen zwischen den westfinnischen und slavischen Sprachen*. He was a professor of Slavic philology at Helsingfors. His writings include *Urslavische Grammatik* (1913-1950), *Die älteren Berührungen zwischen Ostseefinnisch und Russisch* (1938), and *Hämäran ja sarastuksen ajoilta* (1939). He died in Helsinki on 28 September 1946. Aikalaiskirja, 1934; Otavan iso tietosanakirja = Encyclopaedia Fennica; Vem och dat, 1931, 1936

Miklashevskaia, N. N., fl. 20th cent., she was a joint author of *Growth and development in high altitude regions of southern Kirghizia*, translated by Barbara Honeyman Heath (Coconut Grove, Miami, Fla., 1973). NUC, 1973-77

Ritter von **Miklosich** (Miklošič), Franz (Ferenc) Xaver, born 20 November 1815 at Radmescak, he studied law at Wien and subsequently practised his profession until 1844, when he accepted a post at the Hofbibliothek, concurrently pursuing an interest in Slavic studies. He later was appointed a professor of this subject at the Universität Wien, a post which he held until 1885. His writings include *Beiträge zur Kenntnis der Zigeunermundarten* (1874-79), *Die slawischen Elemente im Magyarischen* (1884), and *Die türkischen Elemente in den südost- und osteuropäischen Sprachen* (1884). He died in Wien in 1891. BiD&SB; HL; Magyar; Megali, vol. 17 (1931), p. 174; Pallas; RNL; SlovBioL

Miklukho-Maklai, Nikolaï Dimitrievich, born in 1915 at Kiev, he graduated in 1938 from the Oriental Faculty, Leningrad, and received his first degree in 1941 for a study of Afghan conquests in Persia entitled *Афганское завоевание Ирана в 1722-1736 гг.* He was from 1942 to 1975 associated with the Oriental Institute, Soviet Academy of Sciences. His writings include *Описание персидских и таджикских рукописей Института народов Азии* (1961-1975), and he edited *Nāmah'-i 'ālam ārā-yi Nādirī*, of Muhammad Kāzim (1960-61). He died on 8 April 1975. Millband; Miliband²

Mikoian (микоян), Anastas Ivanovich, born in 1895 in Armenia, he was a Soviet politician, whose writings include *Дорогой борьбы* (1971), *Fünfzig Jahre Sowjetunion* (1972), and *Советскому Союзу пятьдестят лет* (1972). He died in 1978. BiDSovU; Bioln, 4, 5, 6, 7, 9, 11, 12, 16; WhoSocC, 1978; Who was who, 7

Mikul'skaia, Elena Georgievna, fl. 1960, her writings include *Абылхан Кастеев, народыи художеник Казахстина* (Alma-Ata, 1956). OSK

Mikul'skiĭ, Dmitriĭ Valentinovich, born 13 December 1954 at Moscow, he graduated in 1978 from the Institute of Asian and African Studies, Moscow, and received his first degree in 1981 for a study of al-Mas'ūdi's prose and the Arabic historiographic tradition entitled *Проза ал-Масуди и арабская историографическая традиция*. He was since 1993 associated with the Oriental Institute, Russian Academy of Sciences. His writings include *Социальное учение исламского возрождения* (1990), and *Ислам в России и Средней Азии* (1993). Miliband²

von **Mikusch-Buchberg**, Dagobert, born 11 November 1874 at Berlin, he was a writer of historical biographies, including *Muhammed; Tragödie des Erfolgs* (1932), *Wassmuss, der deutsche Lawrence, auf Grund seiner Tagebücher* (1937), and *König Ibn Saud* (1942). He died in Berlin on 11 October 1950. KDtLK, Nekrolog, 1936-1970

Milanova, Elena Valentinovna, born 28 July 1937 at Moscow, she graduated in 1959 from the Faculty of Geography, Moscow, and received her first degree in 1969 for a study of the contemporary landscape of the Levant entitled *Современные ландшафты стран Леванта*. She spent 1969/70 in Guinea, and subsequently became associated with the Faculty of Geography, Moscow. In 1982, she was appointed a lecturer. Her writings include *Географические аспекты охраны природы* (1979). Miliband²

Milcent, Ernest, born 20th cent., he was in 1969 a correspondent to *le Monde*, specializing in religion. His writings include *L'A.O.F. entre en scène* (1958), *À l'est du Vatican* (1980), *L'Année religieuse dans le monde, 1983* (1984), and he was a joint author of *L'Avenir de Dieu* (1974). LC; Livres disponibles, 2004

Mildenberger, Michael, born in 1934, he was associated with the Evangelische Zentralstelle für Weltanschauungsfragen (Protestant clearing-house for philosophy of life) His writings include *Heil aus Asien?* (1974), *Muslime in unserer Gesellschaft* (1983), and he was a joint author of *Moslems unter uns* (1974). ZKO

Edler von **Mildenstein**, Leopold Itz, born in 1902 at Prag (Praha), he was a qualified engineer, with a passion for journalism. He grew up in the twilight of the Habsburg multi-national empire - which predisposed him to viewing the solution of the Jewish problem along the lines of national self-determination. For such reasons, he appreciated the Zionists' promotion of Jewish emigration to Palestine, and he himself became an ardent Zionist, even attending their congresses. His peculiar fascination soon earned him the reputation among his superiors of both, the Nazi party, and Hitler's elite bodyguard, the S.S., of being an expert on Zionism. In the spring of 1933, it was arranged that he visit Palestine in order to acquaint the German public with the Zionist cause and the progress of Jewish efforts in Palestine, by means of a series of periodical articles in a prominent party organ. The articles won him promotion, and, in the summer of 1935, he was assigned to the Jewish desk in the security service. But after ten months he resigned, the victim of internal rivalries and jealousies and more specifically, for the failure of his policy. He wrote *Rings um das brennende Land am Jordan; eine Fahrt bis zu den Quellen des flüssigen Goldes* (1938), and *Naher Osten vom Straßenrand erlebt; Reisebericht* (1941). *History today*, 30 (January 1980), pp. 33-38; KDtLK, 1943

Milé, Ligor K., born 20th cent., he was associated with the Institute of History, Tirana University. His writings in Albanian political and social history include *Kryengritjet popullore në fillim të rilindjes sonë 1830-1877* (Tiranë, 1962), *Çështje të historisë agrare shqiptare* (Tiranë, 1984); and he edited *Shqipëria në vitet e Lidhjes Sqiptare të Prizrenit; dokumente arkivore franceze* (Tiranë, 1986). LC; OSK

Milenković, Milutin A., born 3 December 1925 at Mladenovac, he was a chief editor at Radio Belgrad. His wrings include *Jemen bez imama* (1962), *Petrolej u politici* (1966), *Arapi između juče i sutra* (1974), and he was a joint author of *Bliski ostok* (1967). Ko je ko, 1957; JugoslSa, 1970

Miles, George Carpenter, born 30 September 1904 at St. Davids, Pa., he graduated in 1926 from Princeton University. He taught at Robert College, İstanbul, in a variety of capacities from 1926 to 1933. He subsequently served until 1937 as an epigrapher and assistant field director with the University of Pennsylvania and Boston Museum of Fine Arts' expedition to Persia. He received a Ph.D. in 1937, and later became a curator of Islamic coins at the Museum of the American Numismatic Society. His writings include *Rare Islamic coins* (1950); *Early Arabic glass weights and stamps* (1951), and *Excavation coins from the Persepolis region* (1959). He died in Ardsley-on-Hudson, 15 October 1975. BioIn, 1, 11; ConAu 61-64; DrAS, 1969 H, 1974 H; *Index Islamicus* (5); Master (1); NYT, 16 October 1975, p. 42, col.s. 5-6

Miles, Samuel Barrett, born 1838, he became an ensign in the Bombay Infantry in August 1857. He was appointed assistant Resident at Aden in November 1867; assistant Political Agent Makran Coast in 1871; Political Agent and Consul at Muscat in October 1872; Political Agent, Turkish Arabia, and Consul-general at Baghdad, 1879-1880; Political Agent, Zanzibar, 1881. He returned to the Agency of Muscat in 1883, and became acting Political Resident, Persian Gulf, in April 1886; and Political Resident, Mewar, December 1886. In December 1893 he reverted to the Military Department with the rank of colonel. He was one of the first to explore the Aden hinterland. As an excellent Arabic linguist, he became the second European to reach Buraymi (Trucial Oman), and the first to approach it from the east. His writings include *The Countries and tribes of the Persian Gulf* (c1919, 1966). He died in 1914. Bidwell; BritInd (1); Henze; IndianBilnd (1); Kornrumpf; Kornrumpf², vol. 2

Miles, William, born 18th cent., he joined the Bombay Native Infantry in 1800. He concluded several treaties with indigenous rulers. In 1829 he was Political Officer at Palanpur. In the same year, he retired with the rank of major-general. His writings include three major translations from the Persian, *The Shajrat ul Atrak, or, Genealogical tree of the Turks and Tatars* (1838), *The History of Hydur Naik* (1842), and *The History of the reign of Tipú Sultán* (1864 [i.e. 1844.]) He died in 1860. Buckland; IndianBilnd (1)

Mileski, Witold (Witold Muttermilch, pseud. Andrzej Tenczyński), born in 1904, he was a Polish lawyer with an interest in the Near East. He died about 1940. PSB

Milewski (Milevskiĭ), Tadeus, born 17 May 1906 at Kolomiyya (Kołomija), Ukraine), he was a philologist who was associated with the Catholic University of Lublin. His writings include *L'Indo-hittite et l'indo-européen* (1936), *Język a społeczeństvo* (Lublin, 1947), *Zarys językoznawstwa ogólnego* (Lublin, 1947), and *Językoznawstwo* (Warszawa, 1965). He died in Kraków on 5 March 1966. PSB

Milhac, Louis, born 19th cent., he received a doctorate in 1911 from the Université de Paris for *Les subdélégues en Champagne sous l'Ancien régime*. BN; NUC, pre-1956

Miliband, Sofiia Davidovna, born 17 July 1922 at Moscow, she graduated in 1945 from the Oriental Division in the Faculty of History. She was a bibliographer from 1950 to 1965 and subsequently became a member of the Institute of Information Science in the Soviet Academy of Sciences. Her writings include Биобиблиографический словарь советских востоковедо (1975), and Биобиблиографический словарь отечественных востоковедов с 1917 г (1995), and she edited *Soviet Oriental* *studies today; bibliographies of papers by Soviet Orientalists published abroad, 1945-1979* (1980). Note about the author

Militarev, Aleksandr IUr'evich, born 14 January 1943 at Tomsk, he received his first degree in 1973 for a study of consonantal variations in Semitic roots entitled *Варьирование согласных в семитиском корне*. He was associated with the Oriental Institute, Soviet Academy of Sciences, from 1973 to 1994, when he became a deputy director, Institute of Oriental Cultures, R.G.G.U. Miliband[2]

Milkova, Fani Ganeva, born 20th cent., her writings, all of which were published in Sofia, include *История еа българската буржоазна и право през периода 1918-1944 г.* (1969), *Реакционният заком за заштита на държавата вато изключителен наказателен закон в България през периода 1924-1934* (1973), *История на българската буржоазна държава и право през периода 1918-1944 г.* (1976), and *История на българската държава и право* (1985). OSK

Millant, Richard Alexandre Théodore, born 28 February 1876 at Paris, he received a medical doctorate in 1902 from the Université de Paris for *Castration criminelle et maniaque; étude historique et médico-légale*. He was associated with the Société antiesclavagiste. His writings include *Les Eunuques à travers les âges* (1908), *"La droge;" fumeurs et mangeurs d'opium* (1910), *L'Esclavage en Turquie* (1912), and *La Culture du pavot et le commerce de l'opium en Turquie* (1913). In the First World War he served as a *médecin-major* with the 26e Bataillon de Chasseurs and died in Souain-Perthes-lès-Hurlus (Marne) on 13 January 1916. BN; IndexBFr[2] (1)

Millar, Thomas Bruce, born in 1925 at Kalamunda, Western Australia, he graduated in 1944 from the Royal Military College, Australia, and received a Ph.D. in 1960 from the London School of Economics. He was a professor of Australian history, and a chairman of the Sir Robert Menzies Centre for Australian Studies in the University of London. His writings include *Australia's defense* (1965), *Foreign policy; some Australian reflections* (1972), and *East-West strategic balance* (1981). ConAu, 29-32, new rev., 26; WhoAustralia, 1980-1994; WhoWor, 1974/75

Millard, Charles Warren, born 20 December 1932 at Elizabeth, N.J., he graduated in 1954 from Princeton University, and received a Ph.D. in 1971 from Harvard University. He served as a curator, or director, at a variety of American museums as well as a professor of art history. His writings include *The Degas bronzes* (1974). ConAu, 153; Master (1); WhoAm, 1980-2003; WhoAmA, 1976-2001/2002; WhoS&SW, 1988-1993/94

Millás Bendrell, Eduardo *see* Millás Vendrell, Edouardo

Millás y Vallicrosa, José Maria, born 29 November 1897 at Sta. Coloma de Farnés (Gerona), Spain, he studied at the Universidad de Barcelona, where he later became a professor of Hebrew language and literature. His writings include *La poesía sagrada hebraicoespañola* (1940), *Estudios sobre Azarquiel* (1943-50), and *Textos dels historiados árabs referentes a la Catalunya carolingia* (1987). He died in Barcelona on 26 September 1970. Index Islamicus (5); IndiceE[3] (5); WhoSpain, 1963

Millás Vendrell (Bendrell), Eduardo, he was born about 1935. In 1962, he received a doctorate in science, with special reference to the history of Arabic science, from the Universidad de Barcelona for *El commentario de Ibn al-Muthannā' a las tablas astronómicas de al-Jwārizmī*. He was in 1992 a professor in the Departamento de Árabe, Universidad de Barcelona, a post which he still held in 1997. Arabismo, 1992, 1994, 1997; EURAMES, 1999

Mille, Pierre, born in 1864 at Choisy-le-Roi near Paris, he was educated at the Collège Rollin, and studied at the Faculté de droit de Paris, obtaining degrees from the École des sciences politiques. After participating in several African missions, he became a correspondent to *le Temps*, *Journal des débats*, *Revue des deux mondes*, and *Revue de Paris*. He was not only also a war correspondent during the 1897 Greco-Turkish conflict, but one of the most eminent writers and journalists on colonial affairs of his day. His writings include *Madagascar* (1930), his autobiography, *Mémoires d'un vagabond en retraite* (1932), and *L'Empire coloniale et la guerre* (1939). He died in Paris on 12 January 1941. Curinier; *Hommes et destins*, vol 1, pp. 442-43, vol. 6 , p. 291; *Qui est-ce*, 1934; *Qui êtes-vous*, 1924

Miller, Aaron David, born in 1949, he received a Ph.D. in 1977 from the University of Michigan for *Arabian oil and American foreign policy, 1941-1948*. He served in the U.S. State Department's Office of the Historian and in the U.S. Bureau of Intelligence and Research, before he became a member of the Policy Planning Staff of the Department of State. His writings include *Search for security; Saudi Arabian oil and American foreign policy* (1980). MidE, 1982/83; Note about the author; Selim[3]

Miller, Anatoliĭ Filipovich, born in 1901 at Novorossisk, Rusia, he graduated in 1926 from the Oriental Institute, Moscow, with a study of the national liberation movement in Tureky entitled *Национально-освободительное движение в Турции*, and received a doctorate in 1943 for *Мустафа паша*

Байрактар, a work which was translated and published in 1973 at Bucureşti entitled *Mustapha Pacha Baïraktar*. He was from 1937 to 1960 associated with Moscow State University. He was a scholar of Turkish and Balkan history, and a corresponding member of the Bulgarian Academy of Sciences. His writings include *Краткая история Турции* (1948), *Очерки новейшей истории Турции* (1948), and *Турция; актуальные проблемы новой и новейшей* (1983). He died on 3 October 1973. Études balkaniques, 10 (1974), p. 147; GSE; Index Islamicus (2); Miliband; Miliband²

Miller, Barnette, born in 1875, she was a professor at American colleges, before she taught at the Constantinople College for Girls. Since 1917, she was engaged in historical research work in that city as well as in Paris and London. In 1920 she was back in the United States. Her writings include *Beyond the Sublime Porte* (1931), and *The Palace school of Muhammad the Conqueror* (1941). She died in 1956. Asia, 20 (1920), p. 302; Shavit

Miller, Boris Vsevolodovich, born in 1877 at Moscow, he graduated in law and Oriental languages at Moscow. He was from 1924 to 1956 associated with the Institute of Linguistics in the Soviet Academy of Sciences. A professor since 1935, he received a doctorate in philology in 1939. His writings include *Конспект лекции по истории Персии* (1926), *Талышские тексты* (1930), and *Талышский язык* (1953). He died on 6 August 1956. Index Islamicus (1); Krachkovskiĭ; Miliband; Miliband²; Wieczynski

Miller, Conrad, born 21 November 1844 at Oppelthofen, Swabia, he was a farmer's son and studied since 1862 philosophy, theology, and natural sciences at the Universität Tübingen. Ordained in 1868, he received a doctorate in 1871. He served as a secondary school teacher from 1882 until his retirement in 1910. He subsequently pursued an interest in the history of cartography. His writings include *Mappae Arabicae, arabische Welt- und Länderkarten des 9.-13. Jahrhunderts in arabischer Umschrift, lateinischer Transkription und Übertragung in neuzeitliche Kartenskizzen*, 6 v. in 3 (1926-1931). He died in Stuttgart on 25 July 1933. DtBE; GAS, vol. 10; Kornrumpf; Kosch; Kürschner, 1925-1931; NDB; Wer ist's, 1909

Miller, IUriĭ Aleksandrovich, born 26 August 1928 at Leningrad, he received his first degree in 1953 for a study of Turkish ornamental blades entitled *Художественное производство холодного оружия в Турции в XVI-XVIII веках*. He was in 1979 a curator of arms and armour at the State Hermitage Museum, Leningrad. His writings include *Искусство Турции* (1965), and *Художественная керамика Турции* (1972). Miliband; Miliband²

Miller, James Andrew, born 15 July 1947, he was a Fulbright scholar in Morocco and received a Ph.D. in 1981 from the University of Texas for *Imlil, a Moroccan mountain community in change*, a work which was published in 1984. He was a Fulbright fellow in Morocco and in 1990 a professor of geography at Clemson University, S.C., a post which he still held in 2005. ConAu, 137; MESA Roster of members, 1982-1990; NatFacDr, 1995-2005; Note about the author; Selim²

Miller, John Donald *Bruce*, born 30 August 1922 at Sydney, he was for twenty-five years a professor of international relations, Research School of Pacific Studies, Australian National University. His writings include *Australian government and politics* (1954), *The Commonwealth in the world* (1958), *The Politics of the Third World* (1966), and *Survey of Commonwealth affairs* (1974). Unesco; Who, 1979-2005; WhoAustralia, 1977-1996|; WhoWor, 1974/75; WrDr, 1976/78-1986/88

Miller, Joyce Laverty, born 16 September 1941 at Coral Gables, Fla., she graduated in 1963 from Boston University, and received a Ph.D. in 1970 from Bryn Mawr (Pa.) for *Henry de Jouvenel and the Syrian Mandate*. She became a promotional writer. Selim; WhoAmW, 1989/90

Miller, Roland Eric, born 22 June 1927 in Canada, he received a Ph.D. in 1973 from Hartford Seminary Foundation for *The Mappila Muslims of southwest India; a study in Islamic trends*, a work which was published in 1976 entitled *Mappila Muslims of Kerala*. He had lived in Malabar (Kerala) for nearly a quarter of a century, before he became successively a professor of Islam and world religions at Luther College, University of Regina, Sask., and Luther Northwestern Theological Seminary, Saint Paul, Minn. NatFacDr, 1995-2000; Note about the author; Selim

Miller, Ronald, born 21 August 1910 at Stromnes, Orkney, he was a superintendent of education in Nigeria, before he became a professor of geography at Glasgow University in 1953. His writings include *Africa* (1967), *Orkney* (1976), and he was joint editor of *Geographical essays in memory of Alan G. Ogilvie* (1959). He died 10 August 1990. Bioln 3; IntAu&Wr, 1977, 1982; Unesco; Who, 1969-1990; Who was who, 8

Miller, Roy Andrew, born 5 September 1924 at Winona, Minn., he graduated in 1946 from Gustavus Adolphus College, and received a Ph.D. in 1953 from Columbia University, N.Y.C., for *Problems in the study of Shuo-wen chieh-tzu*. He had a varied career at home and abroad as a researcher and teacher of Asian languages before joining the University of Washington, Seattle, from 1972 to 1981.

His writings include *The Tibetan system of writing* (1956), and *Japanese and the other Altaic languages* (1971). ConAu, 5-8, new rev. 2, 18, 40; DrAS, 1969 F - 1982 F; WhoAm, 1976/77-1982; WhoWor, 1974/75

Miller, Susan (L.) G., born in 1944, she received a Ph.D. in 1975 from Michigan University for *A Voyage to the Land of Rum; the Rihlah of the Moroccan Muhammad al-Saffār to France, 1845-46*. She was associated in a variety of capacities with Harvard University, posts which still held in 2005. ConAu, 197; *MESA Roster of members*, 1990; NatFacDr, 1995-2005; Selim³

Miller, Vsevolod Fedorovich, born in 1848, he graduated from Moscow University, where he became a professor. He was a folklorist, linguist, and ethnographer. His writings include Осетинские этюды (1881-82), Очерки русской народной словесности (1897-1924), *Die Sprache der Osseten* (1903), Осетинско-русско-немецкий словаь (1927-34), and he was a joint author of *Fünf ossetische Erzählungen in digorischem Dialekt* (1891). He died in 1913. Boris A. Kaloev wrote В. Ф. Миллер - кав-казоев (1963). HanRL; Krachkovskiĭ, p. 153; EnSlovar; VostokMStP, p. 253; Wieczynski

Miller, Walter Richard Samuel, born in 1872, he was a missionary who carried on remarkable work under difficult conditions among Muslims in northern Nigeria, where he joined the Church Missionary Society in 1898. His writings include *Hausa notes* (1901), *Reflections of a pioneer* (1936), *Yesterday and to-morrow in northern Nigeria* (1938), *Have we failed Nigeria?* (1947), *For Africans only* (1950), and *Walter Miller; an autobiography* (1949). He died in 1952. Note about the author; NUC, pre-1956

Miller, William, born 8 December 1864 at Wigton, Cumberland, he was educated at Rugby and Oxford, and admitted to the bar from the Inner Temple in 1889. He never practised his profession but turned instead to writing and became one of the first authorities in medieval Greek history and the Balkans. He frequently visited the area. His writings include *The Latins in the Levant* (1908), Ἰστορία της φραγκοκρατίας ἐν Ἑλλάδι, 1204-1566 (1909-10), *Essays on the Latin Orient* (1921), Ἰστορία της Βουλγαρίας (1921), *A History of the Greek people* (1922), *The Ottoman Empire and its successors* (1923), and *Trebizond, the last Greek empire* (1926). He died in Durban, South Africa, on 23 October 1945. *American historical review*, 52 (1946/47), p. 223; BioIn, 2; DNB; EEE; Megali, vol. 17 (1931), p. 222; WhE&EA; Who, 1932-1943; *Who was who*, 4

Miller, William Green, born 15 August 1931, he was educated at Williams College, Oxford, and Harvard University. He was a Foreign Service officer and a presidential emissary to Iran, and subsequently became a legislative assistant for foreign affairs to Senator John Sherman Cooper of Kentucky. He also served as an associate dean, Fletcher School of Law and Diplomacy, Medford, Mass. He was a joint editor of *Perspectives on the Middle East; proceedings of a conference* (1983). Master (1); Note about the author; WhoAmP, 1981-2004-2005

Miller, William McElwee, born 12 December 1892, he graduated in 1919 from Princeton Theological Seminary, and subsequently served in Iran as a missionary under the Presbyterian Church in the U.S.A. until his retirement in 1962. His writings include *Ten Muslims meet Christ* (1969), *The Baha'i faith* (1974), *A Christian response to Islam* (1980), *Tales of Persia* (1988), and *My Persian pilgrimage* (1989), and he translated from the Persian, *Al-Babu 'l-hâdî 'ashar* (1928). ConAu, 57-60, new rev. 6; Shavit

Milleron, Jacques, fl. 1956, his writings include *Le Contrôle des engagements de dépenses au Maroc* (Paris, 1932), *Regards sur l'économie marocaine* (Rabat, 1954), and *Étude sur l'économie espagnole* (Rabat, 1955).

Millet, Philippe, born in 1880, the son of René Philippe Millet (1849-1919), he was educated in France, Tunisia, and Great Britain, where he spent many years. He was a novelist and also a colonial editor to *le Temps*, a diplomatic editor to *le Petit Parisien* as well as a director of *l'Europe nouvelle*. He was devoted to the cause of North African Muslims, an attitude which is reflected in his *La Délivrance de Zacouren* (1922). His other writings include *La Crise anglais* (1910), and *En liaison avec les Anglais* (1916). He died in 1923. Qui êtes-vous, 1924; *Revue indigène*, septembre/octobre 1923, pp. 272-73

Millet, René Philippe, born in 1849 he was a civil servant and a diplomat who from 1893 to 1900 served as a *résident général* at Tunis. His writings include *Souvenirs des Balkans; de Salonique à Belgrade et du Danube à l'Adriatique* (1891), *La Colonisation française en Tunisie* (1899), *L'Avenir colonial de la France* (1902), and *France d'Outre-Mer; la conquête du Maroc; la question indigène* (1913), and *Les Almohades* (1923). He died in 1919. BN; Kenneth J. Perkins, *Historical dictionary of Tunisia* (1997); Note about the author in an unidentified issue of the *Revue indigène*

Millies, Henricus Christiaan, born 15 October 1810 at s'Gravenhage, the Netherlands, he trained as a pastor at the Luthersch Seminarie, Amsterdam, and successively served at Kuilenburg, Haarlem, and Utrecht. A university professor since 1847, he concurrently served with the Netherland's Bible Society. In 1856 he became a professor of Oriental languages and literatures at Utrecht. His writings include *De Chinezen in Nederlandsch Oost-Indië en het Christendom* (1850), and *Recherches sur les* *monnaies des indigènes de l'archipel Indien* (1871). He died in Utrecht on 26 November 1868. EncNI, vol. 2 (1918), cols. 729-30, NieuwNBW, vol. 8, col. 1157; vol. 9, cols. 679-80

Millingen, Charles, born 19th cent., he was a British physician who travelled in 1873 from al-Hudaydah to San'ā', where he stayed for four days and returned by way of Kawkabah, Tawīlah. Henze

Millingen, Frederick, fl. 19th *see* Osman Bey

Millingen, Julius Michael, born in 1800 at London, he studied medicine at Roma and Edinburgh, and was since 1821 a member of the Royal College of Surgeons. He settled in Constantinople in 1827, and became court physician to five successive sultans. He died in Constantinople on 30 November 1878. Dawson; DNB; Egyptology; Kornrumpf

Milliot, Louis, born 13 October 1885 at Bugeaud, Algeria, he grew up in a multi-lingual environment, becoming acquainted with French, Arabic, and Berber. He studied law at Alger and Paris, where he received a doctorate in 1910 for *Étude sur la condition de la femme musulmane au Maghreb*. Since 1945 he was a professor of Islamic law at the Sorbonne and concurrently associated with the Centre de Hautes Études d'Administration Musulmane à Paris. His writings include *L'Association agricole chez les Musulmans du Maghreb* (1912), *Le Gouvernement de l'Algérie* (1930), *Introduction à l'étude du droit musulman* (1953), he was joint author of *L'Œuvre legislative de la France en Algérie* (1930), and he edited and translated *Recueil de jurisprudence chérifienne* (Paris, 1920-24). He died in 1961. Hommes et destins, vol. 7, pp. 350-53; WhE&EA

Millot, Albert, born about 1900, he received a doctorate in political science and economics in 1924 from the Université de Paris for *Contribution à l'étude des mandats internationaux*. His writings include *Les Mandats internationaux; étude sur l'application de l'article 22 du pacte de la Société des nations* (Paris, 1924). BN

Millot, Jacques, born 9 July 1897 at Beauvais (Oise), France, he received doctorates in medicine and science from the Université de Paris. Since 1931 he taught at the Faculté des sciences de Paris, and concurrently at the Institut d'ethnologie. From 1943 to 1957 he was successively a professor at the Musée d'histoire naturelle, director of the Institut scientifique de Madagascar, president of the Conseil scientifique africain, and president of the Association scientifique des pays de l'Océan indien. A member of the Académie des sciences d'Outre-Mer since 1948, and its president since 1963, he became in the same year a member of the Institut de France. Since 1960 he was a director of the Musée de l'Homme, Paris. He was a joint author of *Archéologie malgache; comptoirs musulmans* (1971). He died on 23 January 1980. IntWW, 1974/75-1980; NDNC, 1966; WhoFr, 1959/60-1979/80

Millot, Stanislas Joseph Émile Albert, born in 1875, his writings include *Dictionnaire des formes cursives des caractères chinois* (1909), *Pour défendre l'idéalisme français; la France et l'Algérie* (1928), *La Language de Jeanne d'Arc* (1931), and *Nouvelles méthodes pour la transciption et l'identification des incunables* (1931). NUC, pre-1956

Mills, Arthur E., born 20th cent., he received an M.Sc. as an external in 1958 from the University of London for *Private enterprise in Lebanon*. His writings include *The Dynamics of management control systems* (London, 1967), and he was a joint author of *Management for technologists* (London, 1968). Sluglett

Mills, Charles, born in 1788 at Greenwich, England, the son of a court surgeon, he trained as a lawyer, but ill health and the attraction of literature prevented him from practising his profession. His writings include *History of Muhammadanism, comprising the life of the Arabian prophet* (1817), its translation, *Histoire de Mahométisme* (1826), *History of the crusades* (1820), and *History of chivalry* (1825). He died in 1826. BritInd (1);DNB; Master (3); Sezgin

Mills, John FitzMaurice, born in 1917 at Cheam, Surrey, England, he was educated at an architectural school. His writings include *The Painter and his materials* (1960), *The Care of antiques* (1965), *The Pergamon dictionary of art* (1965), and *How to detect fake antiques* (1972). Au&Wr, 1963, 1971; ConAu, 103

Mills, Lawrence Heyworth, born in 1837 at New York, he was educated at New York University and Theological Seminary, Virginia. He went to Oxford in 1887 on the invitation of Max Müller. In 1898 he there became the first and only professor of Zend philosophy for life. His writings include *Avesta, Pahlavi and ancient Persian studies* (1904), *Avesta eschatology* (1908), and *Our own religion in ancient Persia* (1913). He died in Oxford in 1918. Buckland; DAB; DcNAA; Master (1); Who, 1903-1916; Who was who, 2

Mills, Margaret Ann, born 9 November 1946 at Boston, Mass, she graduated in 1968 from Harvard University where she also received a Ph.D. in 1978 for *Oral narrative in Afghanistan*. She taught briefly at the universities of Tehran and Babolsar before the Iranian revolution. She was in 2003 a professor of Near Eastern languages and literature at Ohio State University, Columbus, a post which she still held in 2005. Her other writings include *Cupid and psyche in Afghanistan* (1978), and *Rhetorics and politics in Afghan traditional storytelling* (1991). ConAu, 141; NatFacDr, 2003-2005; ZKO

Mills, Mark Carter, born in 1893, he received a Ph.D. in 1924 from Columbia University, New York, for *The wood industries in New York and its environs.* He was a joint editor of *Readings in public finance and taxation* (1o32). He died in 1966. IndAu, 1967-80; NUC, pre-1956

Millspaugh, Arthur Chester, born in 1883, he received a Ph.D. in 1916 from Johns Hopkins University, Baltimore. He was an economic adviser with the U.S. State Department, who also served as an administrator-general of the finances of Persia from 1922 to 1927, and again from 1943 to 1945. His writings include *The American task in Persia* (1925), *The Financial and economic situation of Persia, 1926* (1926), *Crime control of the national government* (1937), *Peace plan and the American choice* (1942), and *Americans in Persia* (1946). He died of a heart attack in 1945. James A. Thorpe wrote a doctoral thesis, *The Mission of Arthur C. Millspaugh to Iran, 1943-1945.* Shavit; WhAm, 3; *Who was who*, 5; *Wilson library bulletin*, 30 (November 1955), p. 220

Millward, William Guy, born 20th cent., he received a Ph.D. in 1962 from Princeton University for *A Study of al-Ya'qubi, with special reference to his alleged Shi'a bias.* He was at some time associated with McGill University, Montréal, P.Q. He was a joint author of *Social and cultural selections from contemporary Persian* (1973), and he edited *Mashākalat al-nās li-zamānihim,* of Ahmad ibn Ishāq al-Ya'qūbī (1962). MESA Roster of members, 1977-1990; Selim; ZKO

Mil'man, Aron Shmul'evich, born 20th cent., his writings include Бакы Совети-Азэрбайчанда пролетар органыдыр; октябр 1917-чи илиюл 1918-чи ил (1957), Управление здравоохранегием и социальным в СССР (1960), Подитический строй Азербайджана в XIX- начале XX веков (1966), and Азербайджанская ССР - суверенное государство в составе СССР (1971). LC; OSK

Milne, Janet Catherine Murray, born 20th cent., she received a M.Phil. in 1976 from the School of Oriental and African Studies, London, for *The changing pattern of mobility and migration of the Amarar tribe of eastern Sudan.* Sluglett; *SOAS Library catalogue*, 1979

Milne, John Sidney, 1879-1967 *see* Wardlaw-Milne, Sir John Sidney

Milogradov, Petr Vladimirovich, born in 1904 in Russia, he graduated in 1931 from the Institute of Political Science, and in 1941 from the Moscow Oriental Institute. He received his first degree in 1944 for a study of south-western Iran in the Second World War entitled Юго-Западный Иран во время 2-ой мировой воины, and a doctorate in 1954 for Руководящая роль Народной партии в борьбе народов Ирана за национальную независимость и демократию, 1941-1949 гг. He was appointed a lecturer in 1946, and a professor in 1960. Since 1954 he was associated with the Moscow State Institute of International Relations in the Ministry of Foreign Affairs. His writings include Арабский Восток в международных отношениях (1946), and Объединенная Арабская Республика (1968). He died on 2 October 1980. Miliband; Miliband[2]

Milone, Ferdinando, born 1 February 1896 at Napoli, he received a doctorate in letters. He was a professor of economics and/or economic geography successively at the universities of Bari, Napoli, and Roma. He was a member of several learned societies. His writings include *La regione carpatico-danubiana; lezioni di geografia economica* (1927), *La grano; le condizione geografiche della produzione* (1929), *L'Albania economica* (1941), *L'Albania* (1943), *L'universo e la terra* (1943), *Il confine orientale* (1945), *Lezioni di geografia economica* (1954). *Chi è*, 1931-1961; *Lui, chi è*; IndBiltal (2); Vaccaro; Wholtaly, 1958

Milosavljević, Petar, born 14 December 1925 at Beograd, Yugoslavia, he received a doctorate in 1967 and became associated with the Institute for Balkan Studies, Serbian Academy of Sciences, Beograd. His writings include *Velika oktobarska socijalistička revolucija* (1967), Петар Радовановић (1968), and Положај радничке класе Србије 1918-1929 (1972), *Radničiki pokret u Rumuniji* (1977-1981), and *Reč i korelativ* (1983). *Ko je ko u Srbiji*, 1996; OSK

Miloslavskiĭ, Georgii Vasil'evich, born 29 August 1946 at Moscow, he graduated in 1978 from the Moscow Regional Pedagogical Institute. He was successively associated with the State Historical Museum, and the Oriental Institute in the Soviet Academy of Sciences. His writings include Ибн Баттута (1974), Интеграционные процессы в мусульманском мире; очерки исламской цивилизации (1991), and he was a joint author of Ислам; энциклопедический словарь (1991). Miliband[2]

Milot, Jean-René, born 20th cent., he took an M.A. in 1970 at McGill University, Montreal, and also a Ph.D. in 1978 for his thesis, *Une analyse structuraliste du thème faqr (pauvreté) en sufisme classique.* Ferahian

Milson, Menahem, born in 1933, he received a Ph.D. in 1964 from Harvard University for an edition and abbreviated translation of *Kitāb Adab al-muridīn of Abu al-Najīb al-Suhrawardī.* He became a professor of Arabic at the Hebrew University, Jerusalem. He edited *Society and political structure in the Arab world* (1973), and he translated from the Arabic of 'Abd al-Qāhir ibn 'Abd Allāh al-Suhrawardī, *A Sufi rule for novices* (1975). LC; Note about the author; Selim

Milstein, Rachel, born in 1946, she was affiliated with the Hebrew University, Jerusalem. Her writings include *Ottoman painting in Ottoman Baghdad* (1990), and *Miniature painting in Ottoman Baghdad* (1990). LC; ZKO

Miltner, Vladimír, born 6 July 1933 at Plzeň, Czechoslovakia, he received a doctorate in 1966 at Praha for *Early Hindi morphology and syntax*, and subsequently taught Indian subjects at the Université de Paris. Since 1974 he was an Oriental editor and a correspondent at Praha. His writings include *The Hindi sentence structure in the works of Tulsīdās* (1967), *Theory of Hindi syntax* (1970), *Příběhy bájné Indie* (1973), *Sagen und Märchen aus Indien* (1977), *Lékarství staré Indie* (1986), and *Našim v Indii, Pákistánu a Bangladéši* (1991). He died in Surír, India, on 13 January 1997. Český; Filipsky, pp. 329-32

Milton-Edwards, Beverley J. P., born 22 February 1964, she received her Ph.D. in 1991 from the University of Exeter for *The Rise of the Islamic movement in the West Bank and Gaza since 1967.* Since the early 1990s she was a lecturer in politics at Queen's University of Belfast, where she established a Middle East politics programme. In the early part of the "intifada" she spent one year working for a Palestinian newspaper in Jerusalem. Her writings include *Islamic politics in Palestine* (1996), and *Conflict in the Middle East since 1945* (2001). Note about the author

Milykh, Mariia Karpovna, fl. 20th cent., she was a linguistic, whose writings include *Прямая речь в художественной прозе* (Rostov-on-Don, 1958), and *Конструкции и косвенной речью в современном русском языке* (Rostov-on-Don, 1975). OSK

Mimaut (Mimaud/Mimault), Jean François, born in 1774 at Méru (Oise), France, he was educated at the Collège de Beauvais, and the Collège des Grassius, Paris, and subsequently entered the diplomatic service. He was a sometime consul at Cagliari, Cartagena, Venezia, and Alexandria, Egypt. His writings include *L'Auteur malgré lui* (1823), *Histoire de Sardaigne* (1825), and *Description des antiquités égyptiennes, grecques et romaines, monuments coptes et arabes, composant la collection de feu m. J. F. Mimaut* (Paris, 1837). He died in Paris on 31 January 1837. Dawson; Egyptology; Hoefer; Kornrumpf², vol. 2; Kornrumpf, N

Minault, Gail (Mrs. Thomas Graham, Jr.), born 25 March 1939 at Minneapolis, Minn, she was a graduate of Smith College and spent her junior year at École nationale des sciences politiques, Paris. She received a Ph.D. in 1972 from the University of Pennsylvania for her thesis, *The Khilafat movement; a study of Indian Muslim leadership*, a work which was published in 1982. From 1961 to 1964, she was Assistant Cultural Affairs Officer at the U.S. Information Agency in Beirut and Dacca. Her research focuses on Indo-Islamic history; she was a member of the Association for Asian Studies. She repeatedly conducted field-work in India and Pakistan. In 1993, she had been professor of history at the University of Texas, Austin, Tx., for a number of years. She was a joint author, with Ian H. Douglas, of *Abul Kalam Azad; an intellectual and religious biography* (1989), she edited *The extended family; women and political participation in India and Pakistan* (1981); and she translated *Voices of silence; Altaf Husain Hali's "Majalis un-nisa"* (1986). DrAS, 1982 H; NatFacDr, 1995-2000; Selim

Minces, Juliette, born in 1927 or 1937, she was a writer on social and socialist affairs whose writings include *Un Ouvrier parle* (1969), *L'Algérie de Boumediène* (1978), *La Femme dans le monde arabe* (1980), its translation, *The House of obedience* (1982), *La Génération suivante* (1986), *L'Algérie de la révolution* (1988), *La Femme voilée* (1990), its translations, *Frauen im Islam* (1992), *Veiled* (1993), and *Le Coran et les femmes* (1996). BN; Livres disponibles, 2004

Minenko, Nina Adamovna, born 20th cent., she gained a doctorate in history. Her writings on Central Asia and Siberia include *Северо-Западная Сибирь в восемнадцатом-первой половине XIX в.* (1975), *Культурно-бытовые процессы у русских Сибири* (1985), *Проблемы истории Сибири* (1990), *Казаки Урала и Сибири в XVIII-XX вв.* (1993), and *История казачества азиатской* (1995). Note about the author; OSK

Miner, Horace Mitchell, born 26 May 1912 at St. Paul, Minn., he was educated at the universities of Kentucky and Chicago, and received a Ph.D. in 1937, part of which was published as *Changes in rural French-Canadian culture.* From 1946 until his retirement in 1980 he was a professor of sociology and anthropology at the University of Michigan. He repeatedly conducted field-work in Algeria and Morocco; in 1961-1962 he was Fulbright lecturer at Makerere University, Uganda. His writings include *The primitive city of Timbuctoo* (1953); with George De Vos he published *Oasis and casbah; Algerian culture and personality in change* (1960). He died on 26 November 1993. AmM&WSc, 1973 S, 1978 S; Shavit - Africa; Unesco; WhAm, 12; *Who's who in America*, 1988/89-1994; WhoWor, 1974/75

Minerbi, Sergio Itzhak, born 3 August 1929 at Roma, he graduated in 1960 from the Hebrew University, Jerusalem, and received a doctorate in 1967 from the Sorbonne, Paris. He was an Israeli diplomat whose writings include *L'Italie et la Palestine, 1914-1920* (1970), *ha-Vatikan, Erets ha-Kodesh veha Tsiyonut* (1985), and its translation, *The Vatican and Zionism; conflict in the Holy Land* (1990). WhoIsrael, 1968-2001; WhoWor, 1974/75; ZKO

Mines, Mattison, born 18 January 1941 at Seattle, Wash., he received a Ph.D. in 1970 from Cornell University, Ithaca, N.Y., for *The Muslim merchants of Pallavaram, Madras*. He was since 1975 associated with the Department of Anthropology, University of California at Santa Barbara, a post which he still held in 2005. His writings include *Muslim merchants* (1972), and *Warriors merchants* (1984). AmM&WSc, 1973 S; AmM&WSc, 1976 P; NatFacDr, 1995-2005

Mingana, Alphonse, born 23 August 1881 near Mosul, he was successively a student and teacher at the Syro-Chaldean Seminary in Mosul. In 1913 he made his home in England, until 1915 in Birmingham, but thereafter moved to Manchester when invited to join the John Rylands Library, eventually becoming keeper of the Oriental manuscripts. In 1932 he returned to Selly Oak, Birmingham, to become curator of the manuscript collection. He made three journeys to the East, to the Mosul district, in 1924, to Kurdistan in 1925, and to Egypt and the Sinai in 1929; each time succeeding to assemble for the Selly Oak Library an amazing collection of Syriac and Arabic manuscripts. An appreciation of his life and work is *Alphonse Mingana, 1878-1937, and his contribution to early Christian-Muslim studies*, by Samir Khalil Samir (1990). The *Catalogue of the Mingana Collection* in Selly Oak Colleges Library was published in 1985. He died in Birmingham on 5 December 1937. Fück, p. 277; MW, 28 (1938), 186-188; WhE&EA; *Who was who*, 3

Minganti, Paolo, born in 1925 at Roma, he graduated in 1952 from the Istituto Orientale di Napoli. He taught successively Arabic and Islamic subjects at the universities of Roma, Torino, Cagliari, and again Roma. An editor of *Oriente moderno* since 1953, he became its director in 1965. After the death of Maria Nallino in 1974 he became chairman of the Istituto di studi orientali in the Università di Roma. His writings include *L'Egitto moderno* (1959), *I movimenti politici arabi* (1971), its translation, *Os movientos políticos árabes* (1976), *Vicino Oriente* (1979), its translation, *Proche-Orient* (1980), and he was a joint author of *Storia della letteratura araba* (1971), as well as translations from the Arabic of Badr Shākir al-Sayyāb and Nizār Qabbānī. He died on 12 December 1978. *Index Islamicus* (2); *Rivista degli studi orientali*, 52 (1978), pp. 149-51

Mingote y **Tarazona**, Policarpo, born in 1847 at Granada, Spain, he gained a doctorate in letters and philos-ophy and became a professor and director, Instituto de segunda enseñanza de Valladolid. He was a corresponding member of the Real Academia de la Historia, and a honoray professor of the Real Colegio de San Lorenzo del Escorial. His writings include *Guía del viajero en Leon y su provincia* (1879), *Varones ilustres de la provincia de Leon* (1880), and *Compedio de geografía de España*, 2nd ed. (1909). EncicUni

Minio-Paluello, Lorenzo, born 21 September 1907 at Belluno (Veneto), Italy, he received a doctorate in 1929 at Padua for *Terria della storia e gnoseologia in Kant*. For three years afterwards he was assistant librarian, in charge of the library of the Facoltá di Lettere e Filosofia, and working on Isocrates, Plato, and Spinoza. In 1932-33, he studied at the Sorbonne, Paris, also taking courses at the École des hautes études, and the Collège de France. When he returned to Padua in 1933 he was again offered the library post, on the condition that he join the Fascist party, but he refused. He then taught at a school until 1935, concurrently beginning an Italian translation of Aristotle's works on logic. When he was excluded even from public teaching, he accepted an invitation from Oriel College, Oxford. He there took a D.Phil. for *The methods of the translators of philosophical works from Greek into Latin in the middle ages*, and became senior lecturer in medieval philosophy at Oxford in 1948. He was elected a professorial fellow of Oriel in 1962. He was the moving spirit behind one of the most important academic enterprises of the twentieth century, the Aristoteles Latinus. But his interests were even broader and extended to Boethius and Abelard, to Dante, and to a native son of his own city, James of Venice. On the basis of James' translations made directly from the Greek, he disproved the hoary legend that most of the West's knowledge of Aristotle in this period came through the Arabic language and Arabic schools. His writings include *Education in fascist Italy* (1946), *Opuscula; the Latin Aristotle* (1972), and he edited *Twelfth century logic* (1956), and *Aristotles Latinus* (1961). He died in Oxford on 18 October 1986. ConAu, 119; Who, 1969-1985; *Speculum*, 62 (1987), pp. 789-91; *Who was who*, 8

Miniscalchi Erizzo, Francesco, born 25 September 1811 at Verona, Italy, he was a philologist and ethnographer who was nominated a senator in 1866. His writings include *Le scoperte artiche* (1855). He died in Padova on 27 December 1875. Atti del R. Istituto veneto di scienze, lettere ed arti, serie 5, vol. 2 (1875/76), pp. 645-660; IndBiltal (1); *Index Islamicus* (1)

Minissi, Nullo, born 8 August 1921 at Viterbo (Latium), Italy, he was a professor of Slavic philology, and a director of the Istituto di fonetica sperimentale e di linguistica in the Istituto universitario orientale di Napoli. His writings include *Prinicipi di trascizione e traslitterazione* (1964), *Manuale di fonetica* (1969), *Come utilizzare la documentazione finnougristica nella linguistica indoeuropea* (1970), *Scritture fonetiche e traslitterazioni convenzionali* (1970), and he was a joint author of *Фонетика на македонскиот јазик. The phonetics of Macedonian. La fonetica del macedone* (1982). IndBiltal (3); *Lui, chi è*

Minkarah, Eleanor C., born 20th cent., she received a Ph.D. in 1978 from the University of Cincinnati, Ohio, for *The Evolution of the zejel from the fourteenth to the sixteenth century.* Selim[3]

Minorsky, Vladimir Fed'orovich, born in 1877 at Korcheva, Russia, he graduated in law and Oriental languages at Moscow, and entered the foreign service, first in Turkey and later in Persia, from where he did not return to Russia after the Bolshvik revolution. He successively lived in Persia, France, and England, where he became a professor at the University of London. He was a fellow of the British Academy. In 1962, he was awarded the Sir Richard Burton Medal of the Royal Asiatic Society, and in 1969, he was honoured by *Yād-nāmah-i Īrānī-i Minorskī*. His writings include a collection of his articles, *The Turks, Iran and the Caucasus in the middle ages* (1978), and *Medieval Iran and its neighbours* (1982) as well as many editions and translations of classical Persian texts. He died in 1966. Au&Wr, 1963; BiDSovU; BiobibSOT, pp. 217-18; CentBritOr, pp. 202-218; *Index Islamicus* (3); Kornrumpf; Krachkovskiĭ, p. 166; WhE&EA; *Who was who*, 6; Wieczynski

Minost, Émile Charles, born 3 October 1893 at Provins (Seine-et-Marne), France, he received a doctorate in 1917 from the Université de Paris for *Une méthode internationale d'exploitation; l'intervention gouvernementale ou diplomatique dans les grandes entreprises contemporaines.* He became a banker who was a member of the Société Fouad Ier d'économie politique, de statistique et de législation, from 1928 to 1941. He was a sometime directeur general of the Crédit foncier égyptien in Cairo, and a vice-president of the Compagnie financière de Suez. His writings include *De l'intervention des puissances dans les entreprises contemporaines d'intérêt international* (1917), *Aux confins de la politique et de l'économie internationales; les coopérations inter-étatistes* (1929), and *Histoire d'un petit Français, 1919-1942* (Beyrouth, 1943). BN; WhoFr, 1965/66-1973/74|; WhoWor, 1974/75

Mintjes, H., born 20th cent., he was a staff member of the Christian Study Centre, Rawalpindi. His writings include *The Doctor and the ladies; a new debate on "women and Islam" in Pakistan* (1984). Note about the author

Mints (Минц), Semen Veniaminovich, fl. 1923, he writings on commercial law include *Советское промышленное право* (Moscow, 1925). OSK

Mintslov, Rudolf, 1811-1883 *see* Minzloff, Carl Rudolph

Menu von **Minutoli**, Johann Heinrich (C.), born 12 May 1772 at Genève, Switzerland, he was the son of a watchmaker and went to school in Karlsruhe, Baden. In 1786 he joined the Prussian army. Seriously wounded in the war of 1794, he became an instructor in the officers' training school (Adliges Kadettenkorps), Berlin, and was appointed tutor to two royal princes in 1810 and 1813 respectively. In the service of the Prussian State, he went to Egypt in quest of antiquities, which he sold to the state in 1823. His collection of manuscripts is now in the Staatsbibliothek, Berlin. In subsequent years he supported excavations, museums and archaeological societies. His writings include *Reise zum Tempel des Jupiter Amnon in der Libyschen Wüste und nach Ober-Aegypten, 1820 und 1821* (1824), and *Einige Bemerkungen über die Pferdezucht in Aegypten* (1932). He died in Berlin on 16 September 1846. ADtB; Dawson; DtBE; DtBilnd (5); Egyptology; Embacher; Henze; HisBioLexCH; Kornrumpf[2], vol. 2; NDB; *Zeitschrift für Kunst, Wissenschaft und Geschichte des Krieges*, 71 vii (1847), pp. 36-63

Minvielle, Émile, born 19th cent., he received a doctorate in 1907 from the Université de Toulouse for *La maison habitée et les lieux assimilés en droit pénal.* He was a joint editor of *Code foncier* [marocain;] *texte de législation* (1952). BN; NUC

Minzloff (Минцловъ), Carl (Charles) *Rudolph*, born in 1811 at Königsberg, Prussia, he went to St. Petersburg, where he became keeper of the Imperial Public Library. His writings include *Die altdeutschen Handschriften der Kaiserlichen Öffentlichen Bibliothek zu St. Petersburg* (1853), *Catalogue des publications de la Bibliothèque impériale publique de Saint-Petersbourg, depuis sa fondation jusqu'en 1861* (1861), *Pierre le Grand dans la littérature étrangère* (1872), and *Петръ Великій въ иностранной литературе* (1872). He died in 1883. EnSlovar

Mioni, Albertto M., born 23 February 1942 at Schio, Italy, he received a doctorate in letters in 1964 from the Università di Padua. He was successively a professor of linguistics at the Università di Urbino, Università della Calabria, Cosenza, and again the Università di Padua. From 1967 to 1968 he was a Unesco expert in Burundi. His writings include *Problèmes de linguistique, d'orthographie et de coordination culturelle au Burundi* (1970), and *Fonematica contrastiva* (1973). WhoWor, 1993/94

Mioni, Ugo, born in 1870 at Triest, Austria, he was a journalist and a professor at the Istituto tecnico di Trieste. His writings include *La mamma delle missioni africane; la contessa Maria Teresa Ledóchowska* (1930), *Manuale di sociologia* (1932), and *Girolamo Savonarola* (1941). IndBiltal (2)

Miquel, André Raymond, born 26 September 1929 at Mèze (Hérault), France, he was educated at Montpellier and Paris (École normale supérieure.) He was a fellow of the Institut français d'études arabes de Damas, and the recipient of awards tenable at a variety of institutions in the Middle East and Africa. In 1976 he was appointed to the chair of Arabic at the Collège de France. His writings include *La géographie humaine du monde musulman jusqu'au milieu de 11e siècle* (1967-75), *L'Islam et sa civilisation* (1968), its translation, *Der Islam von Mohammed bis Nasser* (1970), *Un Conte des Milles et une nuits* (1977), *Layla; ma raison* (1984), its translation, *Layla; eine orientalische Liebesgeschichte* (1986), *Au Mercure des nuits* (1986), and *L'Événement; le Coran, sourate LVI* (1992). Note about the author; WhoFr, 1977/78-2005/2006

Mir Montilla, Rafael, born 20th cent., he was a colonel in the Ingenieros D.E.M. and a corresponding member of the Real Academia de Córdoba, resident in Cádiz. He pursued an interest in Arabo-Spanish numimatics and architecture. Arabismo, 1992

Mirakhmedov, Äziz Mirfeizulla oghlu, (Əзиз Мирфејзулла оғлу Мирәһмәдов), born 11 February 1920 at Baku, he was an Azeri scholar who received a doctorate in 1975. His writings include *Әдәбијјат-шунаслығ терминләри лүғәти* (1957), *Поэт, призванный революцей; жизнь и творчество М. А. Сабира* (1964), *Плачущий смехач; жизнь и творчество М. А. Сабира* (1989), and he was a joint author of *Совет Азәрбајчанынын китаб мәдәнијјәти; күтләви очерк* (1975), and *Азәрбајчан китабы* (1982). AzarbSE, vol. 6, p. 589; OSK

Mirambel (Μιραμπέλ), André, born 1 October 1900 at Paris, he gained a diploma at the École des Langues Orientales, Paris, a doctorate as well as *agrégation*. He started his career as a *professeur* at the Lycée de Reims in 1924, followed by a fellowship at the Institut français d'Athènes. In 1938 he was appointed a lecturer at the Sorbonne, Paris. He served as a director of the Institut d'Études byzantines et néo-helléniques in the Université de Paris as well as a deputy administrator at the École des Langues orientales. In addition, he was from 1931 to 1954 an adminstrator of the Société de Linguistique de Paris. He was awarded an honorary doctorate by the University of Saloniki. His writings include *La France devant l'hellénisme* (1962), and *Grammaire du grec moderne* (1969). He died in 1970. DBFC, 1954/55; EEE; NDNC, 1964

Miranda Calvo, José, born 20th cent., he was a colonel in the infantry, and affiliated with the Instituto de Estudios Visigótico-Mozárabes de San Eugenio-Toledo, and a member of the Real Academia de Bellas Artes y Ciencas Historicas de Toledo. His writings include *La reconquista de Toledo por Alfonso VI* (1980), and *La campaña de 1809 sobre la Provincia de Toledo durante la Guerra de Independencia* (1982). Note about the author

Mirante, Jean, he was born on 13 December 1868 at Sévignacq-Meyrarc (Basse-Pyrénées), France. After some years of teaching, he entered the *Corps des interprètes* in 1893 and advanced steadily to become *interprète de 1ère classe* with the *Gouvernement général de l'Algérie*. Since 1906 he was attached to the cabinet of the governor and also editor-in-chief of *al-Mubashshir*. In 1922 he became head of the *Direction civile* of the *Bureau des Affaires indigènes*. In 1922 he retired from the military but continued to guide the native affairs of the Tell, certainly until 1931. Peyronnet, p. 866

Mircea, Ion-Radu, fl. 1967, he was a Roumanian author whose writings include *Catalogul documentelor Ţării (or Rării) româneşti, 1369-1600* (Bucureşti, 1947). NUC, pre-1956; OSK

Mirel, Pierre, born 20th cent., he received a *doctorat d'état* in 1980 from the Université de Poitiers for *Recherches sur le sytème politique égyptien, 1967-1977*. His writings include *L'Égypte des ruptures* (1982). THESAM, 3; ZKO

Miret y Sans, Joaquim, born 9 April 1858 at Barcelona, he was an eminent historian who visited the Balkans and the Middle East between 1901 and 1905, and Tunisia in 1909. He was a member of the Institut d'Estudis Catalans. His writings include *Les Cases de Templers y Hospitalers en Catalunya* (1910). He died 30 December 1919. Dicc bio; EncicUni

MACK LIBRARY
BOB JONES UNIVERSITY
GREENVILLE, SC

Mirete Navarro, José Luis, born 20th cent., his writings include *El doctrinarismo filosófico-político y la Restauración en España* (Murcia, 1981).

de **Mirimonde**, Albert Pomme, born in 1897, he was an art historian, collector, and benefactor of the Musée de Gray. He was a member of the Conseil artistique des Musées, a member of council of the Société de l'Histoire de l'art français, a corresponding member of the Institut de France, *commandeur* of the Légion d'honneur, and *commandeur* of des Arts et des Lettres. His writings include *Sainte Cécile; métamorphoses d'un thème musical* (1974), *L'Iconographie musicale sous les rois Bourbons* (1975), *Astrologie et musique* (1978), and shortly before his death, a kind of testament, *Le Language secret de certains tableaux du Musée du Louvre* (1984). He died in 1985. Gazette des beaux-arts, série 6, vol. 105: suppl. (Fevrier 1985), p. 30

Mirkhasilov, S. M., fl. 1963, he edited *Тезисы докладов и сообщений по этнографии* (1973), and *Ветровая ерозия и агролесомелиорация в Узбекистане* (1973). LC

Mirkine-Guetsevitch, Boris, born in 1892 at Kiev, he received a doctorate in law in 1914 and then taught law at Petrograd. About 1920 he went to France, where he was from 1926 to 1936 a professor in the Institut supérieure des études internationales at the Sorbonne. In 1941, he went to the United States, where he taught at the New School for Social Research, New York, and became a founder and administrator of the École libre des Hautes études. Since 1947, he spent part of each year in New York and part in Paris. He was granted honorary membership by several learned societies, several honorary degrees, and was made *chevalier* of the Légion d'honneur in 1932 and *officier* in 1948. His writings include *Les Juifs et la révolution russe* (1921), *Les Constitutions de l'Europe nouvelle* (1928), *Droit international et droit constitutionnel* (1932), and *Droit constitutionnel international* (1933). He died in Paris on 1 April 1955. American historical review, 61 (1955), pp. 260-61; NYT, 7 April 1955, p. 27, cols. 2-3; WhAm, 3

Miron, François, born in 1861 at Paris, he was a civil engineer whose writings include *Les Huiles minérales* (1897), *Les Eaux souterraines* (1902), and *Gisements miniers* (1903). BN; NUC, pre-1956

Mironov, Leonid Kupriianovich, born 20th cent., he supplied the text to the pictorial work *Афганистан сегодня,* and its translation, *Afghanistan today* (1981). LC

de **Miroschedji**, Pierre R., born 20th cent., he was associated with the Centre de recherche français de Jérusalem. His writings include *L'Époque pré-urbaine en Palestine* (1971), and he edited *L'Urbanisation de la Palestine à l'âge de Bronze ancien* (1989).

Miroshnikov, Lev Ivanovich, born 30 March 1924 at Astrakhan, he graduated in 1952 from the Moscow Oriental Institute and received his first degree in 1955 for a study of Iran as stage for anti-Soviet intervention, 1918-1920, entitled *Иран как плацдарм антисоветской интервенции 1918-1920 гг.* He was associated with the Soviet Unesco Commission; since 1984, he was a research fellow of the Oriental Institute of the Soviet Academy of Sciences. His writings include *Английская экспансия в Иране, 1914-1920* (1961), and he was a joint author of *Изучение цивилизаций Центральной Азии* (1976). Miliband; Miliband²; ZKO

Mirot, Marie Léon, born in 1870 at Clamency (Nière), France, he studied at l'École française de Rome and became an archivist at the Archives nationales, Paris. His writings include *Les Ambassades anglaises pendant la guerre de Cent ans* (1900), and *Une Expédition française en Tunisie au XIVe siècle; la siège de Mahdia* (1932). He died in 1946. BN; IndexBFr² (1)

Mirsaidov, Dzhamol, born 28 May 1938 in Uzbekistan, he graduated in 1963 from the Faculty of Philology, Samarkand State University, and received his first degree in 1970 for a study of the poetry of Amīr Khusraw Dihlavī entitled *Текстологические исследование поэмы "Зеркало Искандера" Амира Хосрова Дехлеви.* Since 1964, he taught Oriental languages and literature at Samarkand State University. He received a doctorate in 1985 for *Принципы составления критического текста произведений Амира Хосрова Дехлеви.* In the same year, he was appointed a professor. Miliband²

Mirskiĭ (Mirsky), Georgii Il'ich, born 27 May 1926 at Moscow, he graduated in 1952 from the Moscow Oriental Institute and received his first degree in 1955 for a study of British imperialist rule in Iraq and Iraqi reaction, 1930-1941, entitled *Господство английского империализма в Ираке и национально-освободительное движение иранского народа, 1930-1941,* and his doctorate in 1967 for *Политическая роль армии в развивающихся странах.* He was an editor of the journal *Новое время* from 1955 to 1957, when he joined the Moscow State Institute of International Relations. In 1969 he was appointed a professor. His writings include *Багдадский пакт - орудие колониализма* (1956), *Азия и Африка - континенты в движении* (1963), *Арабские народы продолжают борьбв*

(1965), *Soviet view of Arab nationalism* (1967), *Армия и политика в странах Азии и Африки* (1970), *Третий мир* (1976), and *On ruins of empire* (1997). Miliband; Miliband[2]

Mirza, Youel Benjamin, born of Persian Christian parentage in 1886 (or 1888) at Nazie near Urmia, Persia. He studied at Johns Hopkins University, Baltimore, Md., and gained a Ph.D. in 1920. He enlisted in the U.S. Navy, and served with the Office of Naval Intelligence. His writings include *Iran and the Iranians* (1913), and *Myself when young* (1929). He died in Dayton, Ohio, on 29 September 1947. Asia, 22 (April 1922), p. 325; BioIn, 1 (2); DcNAA; Master (1); NYT, 1 October 1947, p. 29, col. 6; WhAm, 2; WhE&EA; WhNAA

Mirzhanova, Sariia Fazullovna, born 24 December 1924, she gained a doctorate in philology in 1985 and was since 1956 affiliated with the Bashkir State Pedagogical Institute. Her writings include *Южный диалект башкирского языка* (1979), and *Северо-западный диалект башкирского языка* (1991). BashkKE

Mirzoev, Abdulgani Mukhammadovich, born in 1908 at Kitab, Uzbekistan, he graduated in 1939 from the Oriental Faculty, Leningrad, and received his first degree in 1947 for a study of Tajil literature entitled *Майдо и его место в истории таджикской литературы*. He received a doctorate in 1958 and was appointed a professor in 1960. Since 1953 he taught Oriental and Arabic literature at the Tajik State University. His writings include *Рудаки; жизнь и творчество* (1968), and he was a joint author of *Хрестоматия адабиёт* (1955). He died 14 August 1976. EST; Miliband[2]; UzbekSE

Mirzoev, Sobir Mirzoevich, born 3 October 1930 at Ura-Tiube, Tajikistan, he graduated in 1954 from the Tajik State University and received his first degree in 1964 for a literary study of M. Tarzī and his fortnightly, *Sirāj al-akhbār*, entitled *Литературно--просветительская деятельность М.Тарзи и его газета "Сирадж-ул-Ахбар,"* a work which was published in 1973. Since 1964 he was associated with the Dushanbe State Pedagogical Institute. In 1971 he was appointed a lecturer. His writings are largely in Tajik and Dari. Miliband[2]

Mischlich, Adam, he was born on 23 August 1864 at Nauheim, Hessen, the son of a railway labourer. From 1885 to 1890 he trained at the Basel Mission. After being ordained, he was first sent to Britain to study English and then served until 1897 as a missionary in the Gold Coast and Togo, concurrently exploring the countryside. In the same year, he entered the service of the German protectorate government, continuing his explorations. The outbreak of the First World War in 1914 caught him on furlough in Germany. He lived in Germany ever since. His writings include *Lehrbuch der hausanischen Sprache* (1902), *Wörterbuch der Hausasprache* (1906), *Haussa* (1914), *Neue Märchen aus Afrika* (1929), and *Über die Kulturen im Mittel-Sudan; Landwirtschaft, Gewerbe, Handel, unter Beifügung der Hausa-Texte* (1942). He died in Frankfurt am Main on 13 December 1948. DtBE; LexAfrika

Mişel Paşa, ca. 1819-1907 *see* Michel, Marius

Misermont, Lucien, born 16 July 1864, he was a clergyman who had trained at the Séminaire de Dax (Landes), where he was ordained in 1889. He gained a doctorate in law. He was a sometime father superior of the Séminaire académique de Lille at Beaumont-du-Périgord. His writings include *Les Vénérables Filles de la Charité d'Arras* (1914), and its translation, *The Blessed Sisters of Charity of Arras* (1926). He died on 16 May 1940. BN; IndexBFr[2] (1)

Mishkurov, Éduard Nikolaevich, born 2 February 1940 at Omsk, Russia, he graduated in 1963 from the Institute of Asian and African Studies, Moscow, and received his first degree in 1973 for a study of Algerian colloquial Arabic entitled *Система глагола в алжирском диалекте арабского языка*, and a doctorate in 1985 for *Типология диалектного и литературного грамматического строя современного арвбского языка*. Since 1964 he taught at the Military Institute for Foreign Languages, where he was appointed a lecturer in 1979 and a professor in 1990. His writings include *Учебник алжирского диалекта арабского языка* (1972), and *Алжирский диалект арабского языка* (1982). Miliband[2]

Misiorowski, Andrzej Jan, born 22 January 1930 at Warszawaб pe graduated in 1965 from the Warsaw Polytechnic Institute, and received a doctorate in 1978. He was an architect and active in restoration, particularly in Egypt. KtoPolsce, 1993

Misiugin, Viacheslav Mikhaĭlovich, born 19 October 1924 in Russia, he received his first degree in 1966 at Leningrad for a study of Swahili entitled *Основные черты этнической истории суахили*. He was since 1957 affiliated with the Oriental Faculty, Leningrad. In 1969 he was appointed a lecturer. Miliband[2]

Miské, Ahmed Bâba, born 20th cent., his writings include *al-Wasît; tableau de la Mauritanie au début du xxe siècle* (1970), *Front Polisario, l'âme d'un peuple* (1978), and *Lettre ouverte aux élites du Tiers monde* (Paris, 1981). ZKO

Miskolczy, Gyula (Julius), born 14 October 1892 at Szeged, Hungary, he wrote *A Kamarilla a reform-korszakban* (1938), and *Ungarn in der Habsburger Monarchie* (1959). He died in Bécsújhely on 6 July 1962. Magyar; MEL, 1967-69

Mislin, Jacques, Mgr., born in 1807, he made the pilgrimage to the Holy Land in 1848. His writings include *Les Saints lieux; pèlerinage à Jérusalem en passant par l'Austriche, la Hongrie, la Slavonie, les provinces Danubiennes, Constantinople, l'archipel, le Liban, la Syrie, Alexandrie, Malte, la Sicilie et Marseille* (1851), and its translation, *Die heiligen Stätten; Pilgerreise nach Jerusalem* (1852-53), and *La Très sainte Vierge est-elle née à Nazareth ou à Jérusalem?* (1863). He died in 1878. Kornrumpf; NUC, pre-1956; Sezgin

Misra, Satish Chandra, born 22 July 1925, he studied at Agra University and received a Ph.D. in 1950 from Banares Hindi University. He was a professor of history at M. S. University, Baroda, Gujarat. His writings include *Muslim communities in Gujarat* (1964), and *The Rise of Muslim power in Gujarat* (1981). IndianBiInd (1); ZKO

Miss X., pseud., 1857-1931 *see* Goodrich-Freer, Ada

Missiroli, Mario, born 25 November 1886 at Bologna, Italy, where he also gained a liberal arts degree. He was a correspondent to many Italian newspapers, and from 1955 to 1961 served as a director of *Il Corriere della Sera*. His writings include *Una battaglia perduta* (1924), *Cosa deve l'Italia a Mussolini* (1936), its translations, *Ce que l'Italie doit à Mussolini* (1936), *What Italy owes to Mussolini* (1938), *Da Tunisi a Versailles* (1939), and its translations, *From Tunis to Versailles* (1939), and *De Tunis à Versailles* (1942). G. Afeltra wrote *Missiroli e i suoi tempi* (1985). He died in Roma after a long illness on 29 November 1974. Chi è, 1928-1961; Chi scrive; IndBiItal (13); IntWW, 1974/75; NYT, 30 November 1974, p. 34, col. 2; Vaccaro; Washington Post, 1 December 1974, p. D 16, col. 2; Wholtaly, 1957/58

Mitchell, Roland, C.M.G., born 19th cent., he was a sometime Commissioner of Limasol. His trace is lost after an article in 1920. Note about the author

Mitchell, Terence Frederick, born 3 May 1919, he was a professor of linguistics and head of department, University of Leeds. His writings include *Writing Arabic* (1958), *Colloquial Arabic* (1970), *The Principles of Firthian linguistics* (1978), An *Introduction to Egyptian colloquial Arabic* (1978), and *Pronouncing Arabic* (1990), and he was a joint author of *Modality, mood, and aspect in spoken Arabic* (1991). Note about the author; ZKO

Mitchell, Timothy, born 14 August 1955, he received a Ph.D. in 1984 from Princeton University for *As if the world were divided in two; the birth of politics in turn-of-the-century Cairo*. He became a professor of political science at New York University, a post which he still held in 2005. His writings include *Colonising Egypt* (1988), and *Rule of experts; Egypt, techno-politics, modernity* (2002). MESA Roster of members, 1990; NatFacDr, 2004 & 2005; Selim[2]

Mitchell, William A., he was born on 21 April 1940, he received a Ph.D. in 1974. He was a captain in the U.S. Air Force and taught geography at the U.S. Air Force Academy, Colorado. Certainly from 1995 to 2001 he was a professor at Baylor University, Waco, Tex. He was joint author of *The Euphrates River and the southeast Anatolia development project* (1991). MESA Roster of members, 1990; Note about the author

Mitchell-Innes, Alfred, born in 1864, he was educated privately, and subsequently entered the British Diplomatic Service in 1890; in the following year, he was appointed to Cairo. In 1899, he was Under-Secretary of State for Finance in Egypt. He died in 1950. Who was who, 4

Mitev, Ĭono M., born 23 April 1916 at Chekhlare, Bulgaria, he was a historian whose writings include *Героизмът на Българската армия през Балканската война* (1953), *Героизмът на Българската българския народ през Балканската война* (1958), *Исторически студии* (1963), *Генерал Никола Генев* (1966), and the translation from the Bulgarian, *Der Aprilaufstand von 1876* (1976). EnBulg; NUC; OSK

Mitford, Bertram Reveley, born 6 February 1863, he was a British major-general who served in the Egyptian Army from 1882 to 1899. He died in 1936. Hill; Who, 1903-1936; Who was who, 3

Mitjana y **Gordón**, Rafael, born 6 December 1869 at Malaga, he was a Spanish diplomat who served in Russia, Turkey, Morocco and Sweden, and who pursued a strong interest in musicology. His writings include *Ensayos de critica musical* (1904), *En el Magreb-el-Aksa; viaje de la Embajada*

española a la Corte del Sultán de Marruecos en el año 1900 (1915), and *Estudios sobre algunos músicos españoles del siglo XVI* (1918). He died in Stockholm on 15 August 1921. Baker, 1978, 1984, 1992; IndiceE³ (5); NewGrDM, 1980, 1995

Mitler, Louis, born 5 April 1944 at Lexington, Ky., he graduated from Edebiyat Fakültesi, İstanbul Üniversitesi, gained an M.A. in history from the University of Kentucky, and a M.Div. from Lexington Theological Seminary. While working in real estate management and investment in Washington, D.C., he remained actively interested in Turkish history and literature. His writings include *Contemporary Turkish writers; a critical bio-bibliography* (1988), and *Ottoman Turkish writers; a bibliographical dictionary* (1988). Note about the author; ZKO

Mitrovic, Václav Vratislav, Hrabé, 1576-1635 *see* Vratislav z Mitrovic, Václav, Hrabé

Mittelberger, Theodor, born about 1900, he received a doctorate in 1923 from the Universität Erlangen for a study of medieval astronomy entitled *Über die Verwendung des Astrolabs zur mechanischen Lösung astronomischer Aufgaben unter vorwiegender Berücksichtigung der Universalscheibe nach Alfons von Kastilien.* He was a joint author of *Das kugelförmige Astrolab nach den Mitteilungen von Alfons X. von Kastilien und den vorhandenen arabischen Quellen* (1925). His trace is lost after an article published in 1926.

Mittelsten Scheid, Jörg, born in 1936, his writings include *Die Teilung Indiens; zur Zwei-Nationen-Theorie* (1979), a work which was originally submitted as a doctoral thesis to the Universität Würzburg in 1964. Note about the author

Mittwoch, Eugen, born 4 December 1876 at Schrimm, Prussia, he studied Semitic languages under the leading orientalists of his day, particularly Eduard Sachau, whose friend he became until he died. He received a Dr.phil. in 1899 at Berlin for *Proelia arabum paganorum, ajjām al-'Arab, quomodo litteris tradita sint.* He became a professor of Semitic languages at the Universität Berlin, and in 1927 a director of its Seminar für Orientalische Sprachen. He lost this post in 1933, but continued to teach his subject until 1936. It was not until 1938 that he finally left Germany for Britain. His main field of research was Abyssinian philology. His *Aus dem Jemen* (1926), shows that he was also interested in Sabaean studies. Together with Julius Lippert and Julius Hirschberg he had published a German translation of *Die arabischen Augenärzte* (1904-5). His other writings include *Deutschland, die Türkei und der heilige Krieg* (1914), *Die traditionelle Aussprache des Äthiopischen* (1926). He was a joint author of *Erzeugnisse islamischer Kunst* (1906-1909), and *Literaturdenkmäler aus Ungarns Türkenzeit* (1927). He was a lifelong rival of E. Littmann. According to Richard Walzer, "he was a good scholar and a charming man, but had no interest in teaching and shunned academic responsibility." He died on 8 November 1942. BioHbDtE; *Bulletin* de la Société d'archéologie copte, 8 (1942), pp. 201-203; Fück, pp. 314-15; Hanisch; *Index Islamicus* (1); Kürschner, 1925-35; RHbDtG; *Wer ist's*, 1922-1935

Mizanur Rahman Shelley, born in 1943, he taught political science at Dacca University until 1967, and was a member of the Pakistan higher civil service. He later was affiliated with the Institute of Commonwealth Studies. In 1994, he was a chairman, Centre for Development Research, Bangladesh. Under the name Rafiq Rahbar he published articles in the monthly "Concept of Pakistan," which appeared in 1970 entitled *Pakistan, the second republic.* He also was the author of Bengali novels. LC; Note about the author

Mizon, Louis Alexandre Antoine, born 16 July 1853 at Paris, he was a *lieutenant de vaisseau* who was attached to the Ministère des Colonies. In the 1890s he explored the Ogowe region and the Cameroons. He shot himself in Dzaoudzi on 11 March 1899. *Annales de géographie,* 8 (1899), p. 280; Henze; *Hommes et destins,* vol. 8, pp. 290-95

Mizzi, Giuseppe (Jos), born 21 July 1911 at Sliema, Malta, he received a religious education at Seminarju Arċiveskovili, Furjana, a Valetta suburb, and was ordained in 1937. He subsequently trained as a palaeographer and archivist and became associated with the Bibljoteka Rjali, Malta. His writings include *Catalogue of the records of the Order of St. John of Jerusalem in the Royal Malta Library* (1964). Mifsud, p. 362

Mladenov, Stefan, born 27 December 1880 at Widin, Bulgaria, he was a professor of philology at Sofia University. His writings include *Sur l'étymologie de quelques mots turcs et grecs en bulgare moderne* (1926), *Geschichte der bulgarischen Sprache* (1929), История на българскиятъ език (1935), Първобългарско, а не печенежко е т. н. Антилово златно съкровище отъ *Nagy-Szent-Miklós* = *Protobulgarisch, und nicht pečenĕgisch ist der Goldschatz von Nagy-Szent-Miklós* (1935), and Съвременниятъ български книжовенъ езикъ (1943). He died in Sofia on 1 May 1963. EnBulg; Kürschner, 1926-1935; Magyar

Mladenović, Miloš, born 20 August 1903 at Valjevo, Serbia, he completed his law at Beograd, and subsequently studied at the École des langues orientales vivantes, Paris. He received a doctorate in 1930 from the Sorbonne for *Le caractère de l'état serbe au moyen âge*, work which was published in the following year. In 1950, he was appointed a professor of history of Eastern Europe at McGill University, Montreal, P.Q. DrAS, 1969 H, 1974 H

Mlaker, Karl, born 29 July 1897 at Wien, he received a Dr.phil. in 1919 from the Universität Graz for a study of historical commentaries to Roman-Iranian treaties entitled *Historische Glossen zu den römisch-iranischen Staatsverträgen*. He was a lecturer in Semitic philology at his alma mater. His writings include *Die Hierodenlisten von Maccīn, nebst Unters-chungen zur altsüdarabischen Rechts-geschichte und Chronologie* (1943). He died in Graz on 1 Octo-ber 1951. Hanisch; Kürschner, 1950

M'Murdo, James, ca. 1789- ca. 1822 see MacMurdo, James

Moberg, Carl *Axel*, born 15 June 1872 at Norrköping, Sweden, he studied Oriental languages, particularly Arabic, under Zetterstéen, and received a doctorate in 1918 from Lunds Universitet for *Babels torn en översikt*. He became a professor at Lund; his writings include *The Book of the Himyarites; fragments of a hitherto unknown Syriac work* (1924), *Arabiska myter och sagor* (1927), *Über einige christliche Legenden in der islamischen Tradition* (1930), *An-Nasi' (Koran 9, 37) in der islamischen Tradition* (1931), and he edited *Gedichte von 'Obeidallāh b. Ahmed al-Mīkālī* (1908). Fück, p. 309; Vem är det, 1925-1953|

Moberly, John Campbell, born 27 May 1925 at Exmouth, Devon, England, he was educated at Winchester College and Magdalen College, Oxford. He entered the Foreign Service and served largely in the Middle East. He was from 1973 to 1975 a director of the Middle East Centre for Arab Studies at Shemlan (Shimlān), Lebanon. He died on 14 September 2004. IntWW, 1976-1992/93|; MidE, 1978-1982/83; Note about the author; Who, 1971-2004; WhoWor, 1974/75, 1976/77

Mochi, Aldobrandino, born 19th cent., he was a medical doctor and from 1928 to 1941 a professor at the Italien hospital in Cairo as well as a member of the Société Fouad Ier d'économie politique, de statistique et de législation. Note about the author

Mockler, Edward, born about 1835, he served in August 1859 with the Bombay Infantry as an officer. From 1866 to 1873, he was an assistant Resident at Aden, and subsequently was in civilian employment on the Makran Coast. In October 1879, he was appointed assistant to the governor-general's agent in Baluchistan; and in November 1881, he became assistant agent and consul at Basra. He served as Political Agent at Basra from 1883 to 1886, and at Muscat from 1886 to 1891. In May 1892, he was appointed Political Resident, Turkish Arabia, a post which he resigned in April 1899, with the rank of colonel. His writings include *A Grammar of the Baloochee language as it is spoken in the Makrān, in the Persi-Arabic and Roman characters* (London, 1877). IndianBilnd (*India list and India Office list*, 1900, 1920); Kornrumpf

Modinos, Polys (Polykarpos), born in September 1899 at Alexandria, Egypt, he was a lawyer and diplomat. He was a sometime judge in the mixed courts of Egypt. In 1968 he was honoured by *Mélanges offerts à Polys Modinos*. His writings include Τρεις επιστολες του Καβαφη (1980). He died 31 May 1988. GrBiolnd (2)

Moersch, Karl, born 11 March 1926 at Calw, Germany, he was a free-lance journalist, politician, and parliamentarian. IntAu&W, 1982-1989; IntWW, 1979-2006; Wer ist wer, 1979-2005/2006; WhoWor, 1974/75, 1976/77

Moeser, Hermann, born 19th cent., he received a Dr.phil. in 1897 from the Universität Bern for *Gottfried von Ville-Hardouin und der Lateinerzug gen Byzanz; ein quellenkritischer Beitrag zur Kreuzugsgeschichte*. NUC, pre-1956

Moesgaard, Kristian Peder, born 15 March 1939 in Denmark, he was a lecturer in the history of science at the universities of Århus and København. His writings include *Kosmos af chronos; træk af en udviklingshistorie for vort astronomiske verdensbillede* (1977). Kraks, 1999-2003/2004

Moezzi, Mohammad Ali Amir see Amir Moezzi, Mohammad Ali

Moffa, Claudio, born 20th cent., he was a writer on international social and political affairs. His writings include *Etiopia dietro la trincea* (1978), *La Rivoluzione etiopica* (1980), *Saggi di storia africana* (1996), *La Favola multietnica; per una critica della sociologia dell'immigrazione facile* (2002), and he edited *La Resistanza palestinese; dalla nascita del sionismo alla straga di Tall El Zaatar* (1976). Catalogo dei libri in commercio, 2002

Moffat, Abbot Low, born 12 May 1901 at N.Y.C., he graduated in 1923 from Harvard University, Cambridge, Mass., and received a law degree in 1926 from Columbia University, New York. In government service since 1929, he was from 1954 to 1956 with the International Bank for Reconstruction and Development, Washington, D.C., and as a staff member of department in charge of Arab states. ConAu, 1-4

Moffet, Cleveland Langston, born 27 April 1863 at Boonville, N.Y., he was a journalist and an author of books, plays, and short stories. He died in Paris on 14 October 1926. DAB; Master (4)

Mogannam, Elias Theodore, born in 1921, he was a member of the Palestine and Jordan bars, and a legal adviser to the Arab Bank, Ltd., and to the Income Tax Department of the Ministry of Justice of the Hashimite Kingdom of Jordan. Master (1); Note about the author

Mogenet, Joseph, born 26 February 1913 at Melreux, Belgium, he studied at the Université de Louvain and was ordained in 1935. During the Second World War he was arrested, escaped, and joined the résistance. Since 1951, he taught classics at Louvain. His writings include *L'introduction à l'Almageste* (1956). He died on 18 February 1980. Byzantion, 50 (1980), pp. 636-641; LC

Mogilevkin, Il'ia Moiseevich, born 20th cent., he gained a doctorate in economics. His writings include *Бизнес и море* (1982), *Тайная стратегия Уолл-стрит* (1985); he was joint author of *Наука и техника против целовека* (1985); and he was a joint editor of *Проблемы развития морского судоходства* (1983). LC; Note about the author; OSK

Mohan, Vasundhara *see* Vasundhara Mohan

Mohedano Barcelo, José, born 20th cent., he received his *bachillerato* at Barcelona and a degree in Semitic studies and medieval history, with special reference to classical Arabic poetry and history of Islam and Andalusia. He was in 1992 a *profesor agregado*. His writings include *Ibn 'Abdūn de Evora, c. 1050-1135* (1982). Arabismo, 1992; LC

von **Mohl**, Jules (Julius), born 25 October 1800 at Stuttgart, Württemberg, he studied theology for five years at the Universität Tübingen, but abandoned the idea of entering the Lutheran ministry and instead went to Paris in 1823 to pursue studies in Oriental languages. From 1826 to 1833 he was nominally professor at Tübingen, but had permission to continue his studies abroad; he passed some years at Oxford and Paris. In 1838, he was charged by the French Government with the preparation of an edition of Firdawsi's *Shah-nāmah*. Discerning this to be his life's work, he resigned his chair at Tübingen in 1834 and settled permanently in Paris. In 1844, he was nominated to the Académie des inscriptions, and in 1847, he became a professor of Persian at the Collège de France. He served for many years as secretary, and then as president of the Société asiatique. His annual reports on Oriental studies entitled *Vingt-sept ans d'histoire des études orientales* (1879), are an admirable history of the progress of Oriental learning during these years. He died in Paris in 1876. Ausland, 49 (1876), pp. 117-18; BiD&SB; Buckland; Contemporary review, 33 (1878), pp 1-21; EncBrit; Fück, p. 154; GDU; Glaeser; Hoefer; IndexBFr² (2); Master (3)

Möhler, Johann Adam, born in 1796 at Igersheim in Württemberg, he studied philosophy and theology at the Universität Tübingen and was ordained in 1819. He was appointed to a curacy at Riedlingen, but soon returned to Tübingen where he joined the academic staff, becoming a full professor in 1828. His lectures drew large audiences, including many Protestants. But the controversies excited by his *Symbolik* (1832) proved so unplesant that in 1835 he accepted an invitation from the Universität München. In 1838, he was appointed to the deanery of Würzburg, but he died shortly afterwards on 12 April 1838. His writings include *Einheit der Kirche* (1825), its translation, *Unity in the Church* (1995), *Neue Untersuchungen der Lehrgegensätze zwischen den Katholiken und Protestanten* (1834), and *On the relation of Islam to the Gospel*, translated by J. P. Menge (Calcutta, 1847). Hervé Savon wrote *Johann Adam Möhler* (Paris, 1965), and its translation, *Johann Adam Möhler, the father of modern theology* (1966). ADtB, vol. 22, pp. 59-61; BLC; DtBE; DtBilnd (6); EncBrit; GdeEnc; GDU; Master (3)

Mohn, Kurt Johannes *Paul*, born 12 December 1871 at Insterburg, Prussia, he received a Dr.jur. in 1896 from the Universität Greifswald for *Beitrag zur Lehre von der Beschränkung des freien Arbeitsvertrages*. He was a legal counsel to Deutsch-Technische Gesellschaft, and a sometime editor of *Magazin für Technik und Industriepolitik*, and *Deutsche Monatsschrift für Kolonialpolitik und Kolonisation*. His writings include *Marokko; eine politisch-wirtschaftliche Studie* (1902), *Algerien; eine Studie über die französische Land- und Siedlungspolitik* (1907), *Politische Probleme im westlichen Mittelmeer* (1914), and *Der Kampf um deutsche Kulturarbeit im nahen Osten* (1915). KDtLK, 1915-1917

Mohn, Paul Erik Alfred, born 24 May 1898 at Stockholm, he studied at den Haag, Zürich, Stockholm, and Uppsala, and subsequently entered the Swedish foreign service. He was a sometime president of the Aid Committee of the International Red Cross in Greece. His writings include *Resa till Afghanistan*

(1930), *Sverige i utrikspolitiskit perspektiv* (1937), and *Hjälp till underutvecklade länder* (1952). He died on 18 February 1957. SBL; *Vem är det*, 1941-1957

Mohr, Richard Joseph, born 27 May 1900 at Daleiden, Germany, he was a Roman Catholic priest who received a Dr.phil. in 1934 from the Universität Wien for *Untersuchungen über Sexualethik ost- und zentralafrikanischer Volksstämme*. Since 1956 he was a professor of cultural anthropology at the Universiteit te Nijmegen, the Netherlands, where he delivered his inaugural lecture in 1956 entitled *Missionsethnologie*. His writings include *Totenbrauch, Totenglaube und Totenkult um den oberen Nil und Viktoriasee* (1961). GV; Unesco; WhoNL, 1962/63; *Wie is dat*, 1956

Mohtar Katırcıoğlu, M. *see* Mahmud Muhtar Pasha

Moir, George *Guthrie*, born 30 October 1917, he was a sometime chief officer of St. John Ambulance Brigade Cadets, and a president of the World Assembly of Youth. His writings include *Teaching and televison; ETV explained* (1967), and he edited *Why I believe; fifteen lay Christians in "Last programmes" on Independent Television* (1964). He died on 29 November 1993. *Who's who*, 1979-1994

Moiseev, Petr Pavlovich, born 6 July 1922 at Staro-Seslavino, he graduated in 1949 from the Moscow Oriental Institute, received his first degree in 1952 for a study of Turkey's economic crisis entitled *Кризис экономики Турции во время второй мировой войны*. He received a doctorate in 1968 for *Социально-экономический строй современной турецкой деревни*. He regularly attended international conferences and congresses. Since 1953 he was a research fellow of the Oriental Institute of the Soviet Academy of Sciences, and since 1976 he was associated with the Institute of Asian and African Studies, Moscow State University. His writings include *Аграрные относения в современной Турции* (1960), *Турция ждет перемен* (1963), *Турция* (1965), *Аграрный строй современной Турции* (1970), and *Турецкая Республика; крестьянство и социально-политические процессы в деревне* (1994). Miliband; Miliband²

Mojuetan, Benson Akutse, born 20th cent., he received a Ph.D. in 1970 from the School of Oriental and African Studies, London, for *The Rise of the 'Alawi dynasty in Morocco, 1631-1672*. Sluglett; SOAS Library catalogue

Mokrynin, Vladimir Petrovich, born in 1937, his writings include *По следам прошлого; научно-популярный очерк* (1986), and he was a joint author of *Арабо-персидские источники о тюркских народах* (1973). LC; OSK

Mokwa, Marian, born 9 April 1889, he was a Polish landscape painter who frequently travelled in the Near East and Africa. He died 15 June 1987. Krzysztof Wójcicki wrote *Rozmowy z Mokwa* (1989). Dziekan; NEP; Note about the author

Molan, Peter D., born 20th cent., he received a Ph.D. in 1978 from the University of California at Berkeley for *Medieval western Arabic; reconstructing elements of the dialects of al-Andalus, Sicily and North Africa from the lahn al-'āmmah literature*. MESA Roster of members, 1982-1990; Selim³

Moldobaev, Imel' Bakievich, born 15 February 1942 at Karakol (Przhevalsk), Kirgizia, he received his first degree in 1979 for a study of Kirghiz literature entitled *Эпос "Заныс и Байш" как историко-этнографический источник*, a trade edition of which was published in 1983. He became affiliated with the Institute of History, Kirghiz Academy of Sciences. His other writings include *Отражение этнических связей киргизов в эпосе "Манас"* (1985), *Эпос "Манас" как источник изучения духовной культуры киргизского народа* (1989), and *"Манас;" историко-культурный памятник кыргызив* (1995). OSK; Schoeberlein; ZKO

Molé, Marian, born 20th cent., he received a doctorate in 1964 from the Sorbonne for *Le problème zoroastrien et la tradition mazdéenne*. He became affiliated with the Institut d'études iraniennes de l'Université de Paris. His writings include the trade edition of his thesis, *Culte, mythe et cosmologie dans l'Ian ancien* (1963), *L'Iran ancien* (1965), *Les Mystiques musulmans* (1965), and he edited *Le Livre de l'homme parfait*, of 'Abd al-'Azīz ibn Muhammad al-Nasafī (1962). BN; ZKO

Moleah, Alfred Tokollo, born in 1937, he received a Ph.D. in 1973 from New York University for *The Republic of South Africa and revolution*. He was in 1980 a professor of political science at Temple University, Philadelphia, Pa., a post which he still held in 1995. His writings include *Namibia, the struggle for liberation* (1983), and *South Africa* (1993). NatFacDr, 1995; Note about the author

van der **Molen**, Gerben, born 20th cent., his writings include *A Case study of a university project in technical sciences in Zambia* (The Hague, Centre for the Study of Education in Developing Countries, 1978). LC

Molero, Rodríguez, born in 1918, he was a Jesuit priest who received a doctorate in 1949 with his thesis entitled *Anatomía y fisiología de Averroes; texto, traducción, glosario y estudio de los libros I y II del Kulliyyat*. He died in 1998. *.Miscelánea de estuudios árabes y hebraicos; sección árabe.islam*, 48 (1999), pp. 475-7

Molesworth, George Noble, born 14 July 1890, he graduated from the Royal Military College, Sandhurst, and subsequently served in India. He retired with the rank of lieutenant-general. His writings include *Afghanistan, 1919* (1963), and *Curfew on Olympus* (1965). He died in 1968. Riddick; Who was who, 6

Molin, Georg, born 23 October 1908 at Meran, Austria, he received a Dr.phil. in 1931 from the Universität Wien for a study of popular seventeenth century German literature entitled *Jan Perus und Jan Rebhu; ein Beitrag zur Geschichte des volkstümlichen Romans im 17. Jahrhundert*, and eight years later also gained a Dr.theol. A lecturer at the Universität Graz since 1960, he was appointed in 1966 a professor of ancient Near Eastern studies and archaelogy. His writings include *Die Söhne des Lichtes; Zeit und Stellung der Handschriften vom Toten Meer* (1954), and *Lob Gottes aus der Wüste* (1957). GV; Kürschner, 1966-2005; Note about the author

Molina Fajardo, Eduardo, born 14 November 1914 at Granada, he was a periodical editor, editor-in-chief, and director at Almería, Huelva, and Granada. His writings include *Manuel de Falla y el "cante jondo"* (1962), *Cante jondo granadino* (1972), *El flamenco en Granada* (1974), and *Los últimos días de García Lorca* (1983). He died on 3 November 1979. IndiceE³ (1)

Molina López, Emilio, born 20th cent., he received a doctorate in Semitic philology. He was throughout the 1990s a professor at the Facultad de Filología y Letras, Universidad de Granada, and a director of the Grupo de Investigación "Ciudades andaluzas bajo el Islam." His writings include *Ceyt Aby Ceyt; novedades y rectificaciones* (1977); he was a joint author of *Los Almorávides* (c1956, 1990); and he edited *La cora de Tudmir según Al-'Udri (s. XI); aportaciones al estudio geográfico-descriptivo del S.E. Peninsular* (1972), and *al-Andalus fī iqtibās al-anwār wa-fī ikhtisār iqtibās al-anwār* (Madrid, 1990). Arabismo, 1992, 1994, 1997; EURAMES, 1993

Molina Martínez, Luis, born 20th cent., he received a doctorate in Semitic philology, and later specialized in the history and geography of Muslim Spain. He was throughout the 1990s a director of the Escuela de Estudios Árabes, Granada. Arabismo, 1992, 1994, 1997; EURAMES, 1993

Molina Pérez, María Elisa, born 20th cent., she received a doctorate in modern history, specializing in history of the Maghreb. She was throughout the 1990s a professor in the Departamento de Estudios Árabes y Islámicos in the Universidad Autónoma de Madrid. Arabismo, 1992, 1994, 1997; EURAMES, 1993

Molina Rueda, Beatriz, born 20th cent., she received a doctorate in Semitic philology, specializing in Arabic language. She was throughout the 1990s a professor in the Departamento de Estudios Semíticos, Universidad de Granada. She jointly translated from the Arabic of Muhammad Zafzāf, *l a mujer y la rosa* (1997). Arabismo, 1992, 1994, 1997; EURAMES, 1993

de **Molinari**, Gustave, he was born on 3 March 1819 at Liège, Belgium. About 1840 he went to Paris filled with the spirit of economic propagandism. He believed in scientific and industrial progress, and he was an opponent to protectionism and socialism. He published his ideas in two booklets, *L'organisation de la liberté industrielle et l'abolition de l'esclavage* (1846), and *Histoire du tarif* (1847). Carried away by his sense of logic, he went to extremes in his opposition to all state intervention. He returned to Belgium, where his countrymen were well inspired to found for him a chair of political economy at the Musée royale de l'industrie, Bruxelles, to which another chair at the Institut supérieure du commerce, Anvers, was added later. About 1860 he returned to Paris, and in 1867 entered the office of the *Journal des débats*, of which he became editor, concurrently travelling a great deal until 1881. He subsequently devoted his life until November 1909, to the *Journal des économists*. His writings include *Les clubs rouges pendant le siège de Paris* (1871), and *Le mouvement socialiste et les réunions publiques avant la révolution du 4 septembre 1870* (1872). He died in Adinkerque on 28 January 1912. BiBenelux² (1); *Economic journal*, 22 (1912), pp. 152-56; IndexBFr² (6); WhoEc, 1981, 1986, 1999

Molino, Giovanni, born 16th cent., he was a dragoman for Turkish, and for this reason spent a lenghty period in Constantinople, first in the service of the King of France and later in that of the Republic of Venice. His origin from Venezia seems to be ascertained by the distinctive Venetian characteristics of his Italian. He left us a Turkish dictionary, *Dittionario della lingua italiana turchesca* (1607), and a Turkish grammar. Since both works are written throughout in the Roman alphabet they are of prime importance for Turkish linguistics, representing the colloquial language of Constantinople under total disregard of the Arabic script. The *Dittionario* was publihed "*con licenza de' superiori*" and was dedicated to the *camerlengo* (chamberlain) of the Roman Church, Cardinal Antonio Barberini. Acta linguistica hungarica, 24 (1974), pp. 37-67; IndBiltal (1)

Moll, Friedrich Rudolf Heinrich Carl, born 31 January 1882 at Culm, West Prussia, he began life as a railway worker, stevedore, and carpenter. From 1902 to 1907 he studied ship-building at Technische Hochschule, Berlin, and received a doctorate in 1909 for a study of causes for the loss at sea of fishing vessels entitled *Untersuchung über die Ursachen des Unterganges der verschollenen Fischdampfer*. He was a lecturer on the preservation of wood, from 1922 to 1936 at his alma mater. His other writings include *Untersuchung über Gesetzmäßigkeiten in der Holzkonservierung* (1920), and *Das Schiff in der bildenden Kunst*. He died in Berlin on 8 May 1951. DcScB; DtBE; Kürschner, 1935; NDB

Molla, Claude F., born about 1900, he was a sometime director-general of the Centre de littérature évangélique pour l'Afrique d'expression française, Yaoundé, and in 1967, a minister at Lausanne. Note

Mollat du Jourdin, Michel Jacques Yves Marie, born 13 July 1911 at Ancenis (Loire-inférieure), France, he was educated at Nantes and Rennes and successively became a professor of history of the middle ages at the universities of Lille and Paris. He was a member of numerous academies, including the Institut de France. His writings include *Pauvres au moyen âge* (1978), its translations, *Poor in the middle ages* (1986), and *Die Armen im Mittelalter* (1988), *Le Pouvoir central et les villes en Europe de l'est et du sud-est du XVe siècle aux débuts de la révolution industrielle* (1985), *La Cartographie reflet de l'histoire; recueil d'articles* (1986), *Jacques Cœur ou l'esprit d'entreprise au XVe siècle* (1988), and its translation, *Der königliche Kaufmann, Jacques Cœur* (1991). IntWW, 1989/90-1996/97|; WhoFr, 1969/70-1997/98|

Møller, Bjørn, born 2 February 1953, he was associated with the Center for Peace and Conflict Research in Københavns Universitet. His writings include *Norden atomvåbenfri zone* (1985), *Common security and nonoffensive defense* (1992), *Non-offensive defence in the Middle East?* (1998), and he edited *Oil and water; cooperative security in the Persian Gulf* (2001). Note about the author

Möller, Detlef, born 20th cent., he received a Dr.phil. in 1963 from the Universität Münster for a study of medieval Arabic literature on falconry entitled *Studien zur mittelalterlichen arabischen Falknerei-literatur*, a work which was published in 1965. Schwarz

Möller, Georg Christian Julius, born 5 November 1876 at Caracas, he was an Egyptologist and a sometime deputy director of the Ägyptische Abteilung in the Staatliche Museen zu Berlin. His writings include *Hieratische Lesestücke für den akademischen Gebrauch* (1910-27). He died suddenly in Uppsala on 2 October 1921. Dawson; Egyptology

Møller (Möller), Martin Thomas *Hermann*, born 13 January 1850 at Hjerpsted, Denmark, he received a Dr.phil. in 1875 from the Universität Leipzig for *Die Palatalreihe der indogermanischen Grundsprache im Germanischen*. He was a sometime professor at the universities of København and Kiel. His writings include *Das Beowulfepos* (1883), and *Indoeuropaeisk-semitisk sammenlignende glossarium* (1909). He died in Frbg., Denmark, on 5 October 1923. DanskBL; DanslBL²; Kraks, 1923

Mollov (Mollof), Riza Mustafov, fl. 1970, his writings on Turkish literature, both old and contemporary, include Христоматия на нова и съвременна турска литература (Sofia, 1959), and he edited *Köroğlu* (Sofia, 1957). NUC, 1973-77; OSK

Mollova, Mefiure (Mefküre), fl. 1962 in Sofia, she received her first degree in 1974 at Moscow for a study of Turkic dialects entitled Восточнородопский турецкий диалект (фонология) и его отношение к другим тюркским языкам и диалектам огузской группы. OSK

Molostvova, Elizaveta Vladimirovna (Behr), born in 1873, her writings on religious affairs include Иеговисты; жизнь и сочиненія кап. Н.С. Ильина; возникновеніе секты и ея развитіе (S. Peterburg, 1914). NYPL; OSK

Molyneux, Maxine D., born 20th cent., at Karachi, she was in 1980 a lecturer in sociology at Essex University, and an editor of *Feminist review*; in 1997, she was a senior lecturer in the Institute of Latin American Studies, University of London. Her writings include *State policies and the position of women workers in the People's Democratic Republic of Yemen, 1967-77* (1982), *Gender justice, development, and rights* (2002), and with Fred Halliday she wrote *The Ethiopian revolution* (1981). Note about the author

Molyneux, Thomas Howard, born about 1800, he was a lieutenant in the Royal Navy and explored the Jordan River and the Dead Sea. He died from exhaustion in Jaffa in November 1847. Henze; Kornrumpf³, vol. 2; Note about the author

Momirović, Petar, born 20th cent., his writings include Манастир Бођани (Bodani, 1980), and he edited *Popis; slikarskih i vajarskih dela u muzejima i galerijama slika Vojvodine* (Novi Sad, 1965), and he was joint editor of *Popis; prinovljenih slikarskih i vajarskih dela u vojvođanskim muzejima i galeirjama slika od 1963. do 1975. godine* (Novi Sad, 1978). OSK

Mommsen, Katharina née Zimmer, born 18 September 1925 at Berlin, she received a Dr.phil. in 1956 from the Universität Tübingen for *Goethe und 1001 Nacht*, and a Dr.habil. in 1962 from the Freie Universität Berlin for *Goethe und* [Heinrich Fr.] *Diez* (1962). She was a Goethe scholar who taught at Berlin until 1970, when she became for four years a professor of German at Carleton University, Ottawa. From 1974 to her retirement she was a professor of German at Stanford University, Palo Alto, Calif. Her writings include *Goethe und die Moallakat* (1960), *Goethe und der Islam* (1964), *Who is Goethe* (1983), and *Goethe und die arabische Welt* (1989). ConAu, 69-72; DrAS, F 1974, 1978 F, 1982 F; IntAu&W, 1989-1999/2000; Kürschner, 1966-2003; Master (1); WhoAm, 1978-2003; WhoAmW, 1977-1981/82; WhoWest, 1978-1994/95

Monaco, Adriano, born about 1900, his writings include *L'Azerbeigian persiano* (Roma, 1928), *Periplo di Mitilene; viaggio in Oriente* (Milano, 1928), and *Morti in Libia; cronache dei battaglioni d'Africa* (Verona, 1930). Firenze; NUC, pre-1956

Monaco, Attilo, born 19th cent., his writings include *Gli Accadi; note d'assyriologia* (Roma, 1886), *Orientalia* (1891), *Early printed books* (Shanghai, 1908), *Raccolta tibetana* (1923?), and *Un attendibile* (1927). Firenze; IndBiltal (1); NUC, pre-1956

Monaco, Riccardo, born 2 January 1909 at Genova, Italy, he studied law and received a doctorate in international law in 1933. He was successively a professor of law at the universities of Torino, Cagliari, Modena, and again Torino. In 1947, he entered the ministry of foreign affairs, and in 1960, he was appointed a professor in the Facoltà di scienze politiche nell'Università di Roma. He served as an Italian delegate to the U.N.O. and Unesco. He was a recipient of numerous awards, and a member of several learned societies. His writings include *Enti spaziali internazionali* (1962), *Lineamenti di diritto pubblico europeo* (1975), and *Scritti di diritto delle organizzazioni internazionali* (1981). On his eightieth birthday he was honoured by *Studi di diritto europeo in onore di Riccardo Monaco*. Chi è, 1948, 1957, 1961; IndBiltal (2); Lui, chi è; Vaccaro; Wholtaly, 1980-1988

Moncelon, Léon, born 19th cent., his writings include *Les Colons, les transportés, les récidivistes à la Nouvelle-Calédonie* (1885), *Les Canaques de la Nouvelle-Calédonie et des Nouvelles-Hébrides; la colonisation européenne en face de la sauvagerie locale* (1886), *De la Main-d'œuvre agricole dans les colonies et spécialement du métayage* (1900), and *Quel est le régime économique qui favorise le plus la colonisation* (1900). His articles appeared in the *Bulletin* de la Société de géographie commerciale de Bordeaux. BN

Monchanin, Jules, he was born in 1895 and became a clergyman. His writings include *De l'esthétique à la mystique* (Tournai, 1955), *Écrits spirituelles* (Paris, 1965), and he was a joint author of *A Benedictine ashram* (Douglas, Engl., 1964), a work which was originally published in 1951 entitled *An Indian Benedictine ashram*. He died in 1957. Henri de Lubac wrote *Images de l'Abbé Monchanin* (Paris, 1967). BLD; Zananiri, pp. 287-296

Moncharville, Maurice, born 6 April 1864 at Bar-le-Duc (Meuse), France, he was a professor of law at lthe Université de Strasbourg, chevalier de la Légion d'honneur, and officier de l'Instruction publique. In 1902, he served as a professor at the École française du droit at Cairo. His writings include *Monaco; son histoire diplomatique* (1898), and his memoirs, *Au fil des ans et des latitudes* (1939). Note about the author; Qui êtes-vous, 1924; Revue générale de droit international public, 3e série, t. 16 = 49 (1941/45), pp. i-iv (These pages are not included in every copy, even though they are listed in the table of contents.)

Monchi-Zadeh, Davoud, born 28 August 1914 at Tehran, he went in 1933 as a scholarship student to France, where he graduated in 1937 from the Université de Dijon. Since 1945 he studied Oriental languages at München and Berlin, where he seems to have been one of the few students to receive a Dr.phil. in 1945 for a thesis entitled *Ta'ziya, das persische Passionsspiel*. He was successively a lecturer in Persian at München, 1947-50, a visiting professor at Alexandria, Egypt, 1950-51, a free-lance writer, translator, and teacher in Iran, 1951-58; he subsequently was on a study visit in the U.S.A., 1958-61. From 1964 to his sudden death on 13 July 1989, he was a lecturer in Persian at Uppsala Universitet. BioB134; IWWAS, 1975/76

Monchicourt, Charles, born in 1873, he was in 1903 a deputy chief at the Bureau du contrôle civil of the Résidence générale de France in Tunis. He completed his formal education with two theses in 1913, *La région du Haut-Tell en Tunisie*, and *L'expédition espagnole de 1560 contre l'Île de Djerba*. His other writings, partly under the pseudonyms Rodd Balek, and Cave, include *La Tunisie et l'Europe* (1905), *La steppe tunisienne chez les Frechich et les Majeur* (1906), *Relations inédites de Nyssen, Filippi et Calligaris, 1788, 1829, 1834* (1929), and *Les Italiens de Tunisie et l'accord Laval-Mussolini de 1935* (1938). He died in La Goulette, Tunisia, on 20 August 1937. Note about the author; Questions nord-africaines, 4, n° 10 (15 janvier 1938), pp. 3-4. In the footnote, P.-E. Viard mentions also the following obituaries which, however, have not been sighted: Dépêche tunisienne, 21 août 1937, and Bulletin du Comité de l'Afrique française, 47e année, nos. 8 and 9 (août-september 1937).

de **Monconys**, Balthasar, born in 1611 at Lyon, he was educated at Salamanca, Spain, where he was sent by his parents to evade the pestilence ravaging his home town. Later he succumbed to the lure of Oriental philosophy and travelled to the East in quest of the ancient religions. He visited Persia, India, and Arabia. His writings include *Journal des Voyages* (1666), and its translation, *Ungemeine Beschreibung seiner gethanen Reisen in Asien und das Gelobte Land* (1697). He died in Lyon in 1665. Egyptology; GDU; Hoefer; IndexBFr² (3); Master (2); Sezgin

Moncrieff, A. M. Scott *see* Scott-Moncrief, A. M.

Moncrieff, Sir Colin Campbell, 1836-1916 *see* Scott-Moncrieff, Sir Colin Campbell

Moncrieff, Sir George Kenneth, 1855-1924 *see* Scott-Moncrieff, Sir George Kenneth

Mondain, Gustave Stéphane, born 18 May 1872 at Paris, he was a brilliant student in English and physical sciences at the Lycée Condorcet and the École normale supérieure, Paris, as well as a Sunday school teacher in his Protestant congregation in les Batignoles. Since 1896 he was a science teacher at Toulon, where he learned of the demand for missionaries in Madagascar, and offered his service to the Société des Missions Évangéliques de Paris. He spent an initial six years in Madagascar, returning to Paris in 1903 to take his theological training. He spent nearly sixty years altogether on the island. His writings include *Les tribus de l'Imoro au XVIIIe siècle, d'après un manuscrit historique arabico-malgache* (1910), *Un siècle de mission protestante à Madagascar* (1920), and *Un siècle de mission à Madagascar* (1948). He died in Pau (Pyrénées Atlantiques) on 9 August 1954. Hommes et destins, vol. 3, pp. 337-39

de **Monfreid**, Henri, born in 1879 at Leucate (Aude), France, he was an engineer who in 1910 went to eastern Africa and settled in Obock from where he travelled. His writings include *Les secrets de la mer Rouge* (1931), its translation, *The Secrets of the Red Sea* (1934), *La croisière du hachich* (1933), its translation, *Hashish; the autobiography of a Red Sea smuggler* (1973), *Les derniers jours de l'Arabie heureuse* (1935). He died in 1974. Georges M. Poisson wrote, *Henry de Monfreid; le passionné de l'aventure* (1966). IndexBFr² (2)

Monfrin, J., fl. 1976, he was a medievalist who edited *Historia calamitatum*, of Pierre Abailard (1959).

Mongaït, Aleksandr L'vovich, born 24 April 1915 in the Ukraine, he was an archaeologist whose writings include *Археология в СССР* (1955), its translation, *Archaeology in the USSR* (1959), he jointly translated from the Arabic of Abu Hamid al-Andalusi al-Gharnātī *Путешествие в Восточную и Центральную Европу* (1971), and he was a joint author of *Клад из Старой Рязани* (1978). He died in Moscow on 20 August 1974. GSE; OSK

Mongeri, Luigi (Louis), born 19th cent., his writings include *Étude sur l'épidémie de choléra qui a regné Constantinople en 1865* (Constantinople, 1866), and *Notice statistique sur l'asile des aliénés Solimanié à Constantinople, 1857-1867* (Constantinople, 1867).

de **Monglave**, François *Eugène* Garay, born 5 March 1796 at Bayonne (Pyrénées-Atlantiques), France, he was a political activist who spent five years of his youth first in Brazil and then in Portugal. After his return to France, he began to write for small periodicals, frequently getting in trouble with the courts. In 1833 he became the founding permanent secretary of the Institut historique, Paris. His writings include *Siège de Cadiz par l'armée française en 1810, 1811 et 1812* (1823), *Histoire des conspirations des Jésuits contre la maison de Bourbon en France* (1825), and *Résumé de l'histoire du Mexique* (1826). He died in Paris on 21 April 1873. Hoefer; IndexBFr² (2); Vapereau

Monglond, André, born 2 March 1888 at Sornac (Corrèze), France, he was a lecturer at the Institut français, Firenze, and later taught French literature at the Université de Grenoble. After taking a doctorate in 1929, he became a professor. His writings include *Vies préromantiques* (1925), *Histoire intérieure du préromantisme français* (1929), and *La France révolutionnaire et impériale* (1930). DBFC, 1954/55; IndexBFr² (1)

Monier, Eugène Alphonse, born 6 December 1826 at Ollioules (Var), France, he entered the French army in 1845 and joined the Bureaux arabes on 13 April 1855, being successively assigned to Bougie, Souk-Ahras, Bel-Abbàs, Daya, Ad'n-Témouchent and Ammi-Moussa. In 1865, he transferred to the Bureau politique at Ad'n-Témouchent. He was captain in 1866, *chef de bataillon* in 1877, and retired as *commandant supérieur* at Bordj-Bou-Arréridj on 22 June 1881. Peyronnet, p. 161

Monier, Raymond, born about 1900, he completed his law at the Université de Paris with two theses, *Les institutions judiciaires des villes de Flandre des origines à la rédaction des coutumes* (1924), and *Le contentieux administatif au Maroc* (1935). His other writings include *Droit romain* (1941-42). His

Manuel élémentaire de droit romain went through six editions between 1935 and 1947. BN; NUC, pre-1956

Monier-Williams, Sir Monier, born in 1819 at Bombay, he came to England in 1822, where he was educated, and became a professor of Sanskrit, Persian, and Hindustani at the East India Company's College, Haileybury, from 1844 to 1858. In 1860 he was appointed Boden professor of Sanskrit at Oxford. He was a founding member of the Indian Institute, Oxford. His writings include *An easy introduction to Hindústânî* (1858), *Bág-O-Bahár; the Hindustani text of Mir Amman, edited in Roman type* (1859), and *Brahmanism and Hinduism* (1887). He died in Oxford on 11 April 1899. Concise DNB; DNB; Riddick; *Who was who*, 1

Moniot, Henri, born 20th cent., he was a sometime *maître-assistant* at the Université de Paris VII. He was a joint author of *L'histoire en partage; le recit du vrai, questions de didactique et d'historiographie* (1994), and he was a joint editor of *L'Afrique noire de 1800 à nos jours* (c1974, 1980), *Dialoguer avec le léopard?* (1988), and *L'histoire et ses fonctions; une pensée et des pratiques au présent* (2000). *Livres disponibles*, 2003, 2004; Note about the author

Monjauze, Alexis Fernand Marcel, born 18 April 1906 at Paris, he graduated from the Institut national agronomique as well as the École nationale des eaux et forêts, Paris. He began his career as a forest ranger and retired as a director general of environment in France. He spent over fifteen years in Algeria and was from 1957 to 1961 a director of the École supérieure d'agriculture africaine. His writings include *Le groupement à micocoulier en Algérie* (1958), *Les plantations forrestières sur bourrelets en Israël* (1959), and he edited *Parc national des Cévennes* (1973). WhoFr, 1971/72-1979/80|

Monlezun, Jules Frédéric, born 19th cent., he was a French army colonel whose writings include *Bataille de Rocroi* (Paris, 1877). His trace is lost after an article in 1889. BN

Monmarché, Marcel, born in 1872, he contributed to the journal *le Tour du monde*, and he was in 1921 a director of the *Guides bleus*. His writings include *De Paris à Constantinople* (1920). Note

Monneret de Villard, Ugo, born 16 January 1881 at Milano, Italy, he studied history of architecture. After graduating in Italy, he studied Oriental archaeology in Germany and Britain. Since 1908 he spent twenty years in archaeological travels, mainly in Egypt and Nubia. He died in Roma on 4 November 1954. Chi è, 1948; Dawson; Egyptology; IndBiltal (2); *Index Islamicus* (4)

Monnerot-Dumaine, Marcel, born 28 November 1903 at Paris, he studied medicine at Paris, and was from 1931 to 1956 a medical officer with the Compagnie de Suez. IndexBFr² (1)

Monnot, Guy, born 28 December 1928 at Paris, he received a theological degree in 1958, an M.A. in 1969 at Tehran, a *doctorat de 3ème cycle* from the Université de Paris in 1972 for *La réfutation des dualistes et des mages par Abd al-Jabbar*, and also a *doctorat d'état* in 1986 for *Histoire musulmane des religions*. In 1987 he was associated with the École pratique des Hautes études, Paris. His writings include *Penseurs musulmans et religions iraniennes* (1974), and *Islam et religions* (1986). AnEIFr, 1997; IWWAS, 1975/76; THESAM, 4

Monod, André *Théodore*, born 9 April 1902 at Rouen, France, he was educated at Paris, where he received a doctorate in 1926 from the Sobonne for *La région de la basse Seulle; étude bionomique*, as well as a diploma from the École nationale des langues orientales vivantes. He subsequently joined the Musée national d'histoire universelle. From 1938 to 1965 he also served as a director of the Institut français d'Afrique noire. His writings include *L'élevage au Maroc* (1931), *L'Adrar Ahnet; contribution à l'étude archéologique* (1932), *Méharées, explorations au vrai Sahara* (1937), *L'Adrar mauritanien, Sahara occidental* (1952), *Les déserts* (1973), *De Tripoli à Tombouctou; le dernier voyage de Laing, 1825-1826* (1978), and he was a joint author of *Études sur la flore et la végération du Tibesti* (1950). IntWW, 1969/70-2000|; WhoFr, 1983-2001|

Monogarova, Lidiia Fedorovna, born 9 October 1921 at Moscow, she graduated in 1946 from the Faculty of History, Moscow State University, received her first degree in 1951, and a doctorate in 1993 for a study of contemporary Tajik and Pamir families entitled *Современная семья таджиков и памирского народов*. Since 1959 she was affiliated with the Institute of Ethnology and Anthropology in the Soviet Academy of Sciences. Her writings include *Преобразования в быту и культуре припамирских народностей* (1972), and she was a joint author of *Современная сельская семья таджиков* (1992). Miliband²; Schoeberlein

Monro, James, born 25 November 1835 at Edinburgh, he was educated at Edinburgh and Berlin. He joined the Bengal Civil Service and arrived in India on 27 January 1858. He served with the judiciary and the police until 1883, when he returned to London. He went to India again about 1892 to organize and superintend the Ranaghat Medical Mission until 1905. His writings include *Christianity and*

Hinduism; five lectures to Hindu gentlemen (Calcutta, 1892-1893). He died in 1920. BritInd (2); Buckland; IndianBiInd (1); Riddick, *Who was who*, 2

Monroe, Elizabeth, Mrs. Humphrey Neame, born 16 January 1905 at Great Malvern, England, she worked successively as an information officer at the League of Nations, the Royal Institute of International Affairs, and the Ministry of Information, London. She subsequently spent eighteen years with the *Economist* at the Middle East desk. From 1958 until her retirement she was a research fellow of St. Antony's College, Oxford. Her writings include *Mediterranean politics* (1938), *The awakening Middle East* (1948), *Britain's moment in the Middle East* (1965), and *Philby of Arabia* (1973). She died in 1986. AnObit, 1986, pp. 194-96; ConAu, 13-16, 118; Who, 1969-1986; *Who was who*, 8

Monroe, James Thomas, born 21 December 1921 at Dallas, Tex., he graduated in 1959 from the University of Houston, and received a Ph.D. in 1964 from Harvard University, Cambridge, Mass., for *Main currents in Spanish Arabism*. In the same year he was appointed a professor of Arabic and Spanish literature at the University of California, San Diego. His writings include *Islam and the Arabs in Spanish scholarship* (1970), *The shu'ūbiyya in al-Andalus* (1970), and *The art of Badī' az-Zamān al-Hamdhānī as picaresque narrative*(1983). Directory of American scholars, 1969 F; Selim; ZKO

Monson, Terry Dean, born 9 October 1945 at Petoskey, Mich., he received a Ph.D. in 1972 from the University of Michigan. He was successively a professor of economics at Illinois State University, and Michigan Technical University, Houghton, a post which he still held in 2005. His writings include *The effects of domestic and international competition upon Michigan's iron ore and steel industries* (1980), and he was a joint author of *An evaluation of expatriate labor replacement in the Ivory Coast* (1976). NatFacDr, 1995-2005; Note about the author; WhoMW, 1988/89

Monsour, Sally A., born 24 May 1929 at Valentine, Nebr., she received her M.A. in 1952 from Columbia University, New York, and her Ph.D. in 1960 from the University of Michigan for *The establishment and early development of beginning piano classes in the public schools*. Since 1979 she was a professor in the Department of Music, Georgia State University, Atlanta, a post which she still held in 1995. Her writings include *Music in open education* (1974), and she was a joint author of *Music in recreation and leisure* (1972). ConAu, 21-24; NatFacDr, 1995

Montagne, H. Ambroise, O.P., born 19th cent., he was associated with the Institut catholique de Toulouse. His writings include *Études sur l'origine de la société* (Paris, 1900), *Panégyrique de saint Thomas d'Aquin* (1900), and *Saint Thomas d'Aquin à Toulouse, ses reliques, son culte* (1923). BN; Note about the author

Montagne, Robert Louis André, he was born on 19 January 1893 at le Mans (Sarthe), France. After war-time service, he was in command of a maritime aviation centre in Morocco, where he began to study Arabic. In 1924, he became a lecturer in Muslim sociology at the Institut des hautes études marocaines in Rabat. This was the beginning of a career which was to culminate in his appointment to the chair of history of colonization at the Collège de France in 1948. His writings include his thesis, *Les Berbères et le makhzen dans le sud du Maroc* (1930), *Un magasin colletif de l'Anti-Atlas, l'Agadir des Ikounda* (1930), *La civilisation du désert* (1947), *Naissance du prolétariat marocain* (1952), and *Révolution au Maroc* (1954). He died in Paris on 27 November 1954. *L'Afrique et l'Asie*, n° 29 (1955), pp. 57-60, n° 32 (1955), pp. 3-4, 5-8, 9-15, 16-35, 36-43, 44-49, 50-57, 58-60; *Hommes et destins*, vol. 1, pp. 446-447; IndexBFr² (1); WhoFr, 1953/54; *Index Islamicus* (4); NYT, 27 November 1954, p. 14, col. 3

Montagno, George Lucien, born 2 January 1923 at Waterbury, Conn., he graduated in 1927 from Middleburg College, and received a Ph.D. in 1954 from the University of California for *Matthew Lyon, radical Jeffersonian*. Sponsored by the Asia Foundation, he was from 1960 to 1962 a visiting professor of American history at Karachi University. He subsequently taught history at Mount Union College, Alliance, Ohio. DrAS, 1969 H; Note about the author

Montagu, Edward Wortley, born in 1713, he was a son of Lady Mary Pierremont Wortley. Undisciplined in his youth, he briefly held a commission in the army. He was a man of roving disposition who had been to Egypt. His writings include *Reflection of the rise and fall of the ancient republics* (1759), and its translations, *Betrachtungen über die Aufnahme und den Verfall der alten Republiken* (1761), and *De la naissance et de la chute des anciens républiques* (1793), and *Nachrichten über Sitten und Gebräuche des Morgenlandes* (1779). He died in 1776. Jonathan Curling wrote *Edward Wortley Montagu, the man in the iron wing* (1954). BritInd (13); DNB; Master (2)

Montagu, John Walter Edward Douglas-Scott-Montagu, born in 1866, he was educated at Eton and Oxford, and was interested in all transport matters. He died in 1929. BritInd (6); DNB; Who, 1909, *Who was who*, 3

Montagu, Lady Mary Pierremont Wortley, born in 1689, she was known in her lifetime as a wit and poetess; she has since been admired as a letter writer whose accounts of the East convey its atmosphere and show unusual sympathy for Islam. She introduced vaccination against small-pox into England. A tempestuous character, she traded insults with Swift and Pope and conducted a series of dramatic love affairs. She died in 1762. Isobel Grundy wrote *Lady Mary Wortley Montagu; comment of the Enlightenment* (2000). BritInd (21); DLB, vol. 95 (1990), pp. 145-58; DLB, vol. 101 (1991), pp. 240-51; DNB; Master (60); WomWorHis

Montagu-Stuart-Wortley, Edward James, 1857-1934 *see* Stuart-Wortley, Edward James Montagu

Montague, Joel G., born 20th cent., he was a graduate of Johns Hopkins University School of Advanced International Studies, Washington, D.C., who had spent years doing field-work in Iran. In 1966, he was an assistant mission chief for CARE, Cairo, and in December of the same year he was a director of CARE/MEDICO, Tunisia. In 1974, he was a regional director for the Near East and Africa in the Population Council, Tehran. He was a joint author of *Primary health care;bibliography and resource directory* (1982). LC; Note about the author

Montaldo y Pero, Federico, born 11 July 1859 at Sevilla, Spain, he was educated at Sevilla, Valencia and Madrid, and obtained a medical doctorate. He was a corresponding member of the Real Academia de Medicina, a sometime deputy first inspector of health in the Spanish Armada, and a director of the Hospital Militar de Marina at Cartagena. He later served as an editor of the journals, *El Resumen*, and *Diario de Marina*. His writings include *Nuestras colonias en Guinea* (Madrid, 1902), and *Higiene de la habitación* (1904). His trace is lost after an article in 1914. EncicUni; IndiceE³ (2)

de **Montaut**, Henry, born in 1830, he was from 1864 to 1868 an editor of the Paris *Journal illustré*. His writings, partly under the pseudonym H. de Hem, include the booklet, *Projet d'irrigation pour l'Egypt* (Paris, 1869). He died in 1890. BN; NUC, pre-1956

Montefiore, Judith née Cohen, 1784-1862, she was the wife of Sir Moses, who documented his visits abroad in official papers, while she wrote conventional journals, published anonymously: *Private journal of a visit to Egypt and Palestine by way of Italy and the Mediterranean* (1836), and *Notes from the private journal of a visit to Egypt and Palestine by way of the Mediterranean* (1844). EncJud; JewEnc; Robinson

Montefiore, Sir Moses Haim, born 24 October 1784 at Leghorn (Livorno), Italy, he was a philanthropist who invested his money in the regeneration of Jerusalem's Jews. In recognition of his general public services, he was made a baronet in 1846. His writings include *Diaries of Sir Moses and Lady* [Judith] *Montefiore* (1890). He died in Ramsgate, 28 July 1885. DNB; EncJud; Kornrumpf; Wininger

Montégut, Émile, born 24 June 1825 or 1826 at Limoges, France, he went in 1844 to Paris to study law, a purpose from which he was soon turned by the attractions of literature. He became a journalist and miscellanous writer who was for over forty years associated in various capacities with the *Revue des deux mondes*. His writings include *L'Angleterre et ses colonies australes* (Paris, 1880), and *Livres et âmes des pays d'Orient* (Paris, 1885). He died in 1895. BiD&SB; CIMEL; OxFr

Monteil, Charles Victor, born 22 February 1871 at Paris, he joined the Infanterie de Marine and served for three years until 1892 when, through the good offices of his brother, Louis Monteil (1855-1925), he went to Africa in 1893 as a *commis* in the Affaires indigènes, successively assigned to Sahou and Dabou, Ivory Coast. At the beginning of 1897 he became deputy *commandant* at Khayes, and subsequently spent until 1899 at Médine, the commercial centre on the Senegal River, followed by his final African assignment to Djenné. After his return to Paris in 1903, he remained two years with the Office colonial. He subsequently taught African languages at the École nationale des langues orientales vivantes, Paris, from 1904 to 1909. From 1911 to his retirement in 1936 to Tulle (Corrèze), he was successively a provincial *receveur des finances* at Bellac, Orthez, Lisieux, Bergerac and Epernay. His writings include *Monographie de Djenné* (1903), *Contes soudanais* (1905), *Les Khassonké* (1915), *Les Bambara du Ségou et du Kaarta* (1924), *Les empires du Mali* (1929),and *La langue azer* (1939). He died in 1949. Hommes et destins, vol. 5, pp. 403-406

Monteil, Parfait *Louis*, born 18 April 1855 at Tulle (Corrèze), France, he enlisted in the French army and from 1874 to 1876 passed through the École spéciale militaire de Saint-Cyr. He served as a colonial officer in French colonies, mainly in Africa, and retired in 1896 with the rank of lieutenant-colonel. Apart from many missions, he explored the Upper Senegal and made a feasibility study of a railway track between Bafoulabé and Bamako on the Niger River. His writings include *De Saint-Louis à Tripoli par le lac Tchad* (1894), *La Colonne de Kong, 1894-1895* (1902) and *Quelques feuillets de l'histoire coloniale Souvenirs vécu* (1924). He died in Herblay (Val d'Oise) on 29 September 1925.

Henri Labouret wrote *Monteil, explorateur et soldat* (1937).   Henze; *Hommes et destins*, vol. 5, pp. 406-10; IndexBFr³, Kornrumpf⁴, vol. 2

Monteil, Vincent Mansour, born 27 May 1913 at Bellac (Haute-Vienne), France, the son of Charles Victor Monteil (1871-1949), he passed through the military college, Saint-Cyr, 1934-36, and in the Second World War enlisted in the Forces Françaises Libres. He became a Muslim and was in 1963 a director of the Centre d'études pratiques de l'arabe moderne at Bikfaya, Lebanon. He was a sometime director of the Institut français de l'Afrique noire, and an honorary professor at the Université de Paris. His writings include *Note sur les Tekna* (1948), *Un écrivain persan du demi-siècle, Sadeq Hedâyat* (1951), *Persan contemporain* (1954), *Iran* (1957), *Islam* (1963), *Le monde musulman* (1963), its translation, *Muselmanische Welt* (1964), *L'islam noire* (1964), *Aux cinq couleurs de l'islam* (1981), and he translated from the Arabic, *Abû-Nuwâs; le vin, le vent, la vie* (1979). He also contributed the biographical notes of his father, and his oncle, Louis Monteil (1855-1925) in *Hommes et destins*, vol. 5, pp. 402-409.   BN; Note; Unesco

Monteith, William, he was born in 1790 at Paisley, Scotland. As a colonel of the Madras Engineers, he spent from 1810 until late 1829 much of his time with Persian forces on the Caucasian front, and assisted in delimiting the new frontier after the treaties of Gulestan and Turkmanchai. He retired with the rank of general. His writings include *Notes on Georgia and the new Russian conquest beyond the Caucasus* (183-), *Kars and Erzeroum; with the campaigns of Prince Paskiewitch, in 1828 and 1829* (London, 1856). He died in London on 18 April 1864.   Boase; Buckland; DNB; Henze; IndianBilnd (1); Kornrumpf; Riddick; Wright

de **Montémont**, Albert Étienne, born 20 August 1788 at Remiremont (Vosges), France, he graduated from the local college and subsequently became a teacher of general arts subjects, before entering the Ministère des finances. He was an author of poetry and travel books. His writings include *Voyages en Afrique* (1853), and *Voyages en Asie* (1855). He died in Paris on 31 December 1861.   Dantès 1; Hoefer; Vapereau

Montenant, Christian, born 20th cent., he obtained a doctorate in science, and became affiliated with the Société de géologie de France. He was a joint author of *Les empreintes de pas de reptiles de l'Infralias du Veillon, Vendée* (1967), and *Pour lire la création dans l'évolution* (c1984, 1994).   Note about the author; *Livres disponibles*, 2003

de **Montêquin**, François Auguste, born about 1935, he studied at Perugia, where he also obtained a certificat in fine art in 1969. He received a doctorate in 1970. In the 1970s he taught for a few years in the U.S.A. His writings include *Classicisme et anti-clasicisme anadolous* (1982), *Muslim architecture of the Iberian Peninsula* (1987), and he was a joint editor of *Art of the Eastern world; Orientalia from the Moreen O'Brien Maser Memorial Collection* (1982).   LC; WhoAmA, 1976, 1978; ZKO

Monterin, Umberto, born 19th cent., he was a meteorologist and geophysicist, and became a director of the RR. Osservatori Metereologici e Geofisici del Monte Rosa. His writings include *Il ghiacciaio del Lys al Monte Rosa del 1901 al 1917* (Firenze, 1918), and *Richerche sull'ablazione e sul deflusso glaciale nel versante meridionale del Monte Rosa* (1931).   Chi è, 1940, 1948; Firenze

Montet, Édouard Louis, born 12 June 1856 at Lyon, he received a doctorate from the Faculté de théologie de Genève in 1877 for *Étude littéraire et critique sur le livre du prophète Joël*, and a second doctorate in 1880 from the Faculté de théologie protestante de Paris for *La légende d'Irénée et l'introduction du christianisme à Lyon*. He taught Hebrew, Aramaic, Syriac, and Arabic at the Université de Genève. From 1910 to 1912 he served as a rector of the university. His writings include *Le culte des saints musulmans dans l'Afrique du nord et plus specialément au Maroc* (1909), *L'état présent et l'avenir de l'islam* (1911), *L'islam* (1923), its translation, *Der Islam* (1923), and he translated *Le Coran* (1925). He died in 1934.   SchZLex

de **Montety**, Henri, born about 1900, he received a doctorate in 1927 from the Université de Toulouse for *Une loi agraire en Tunisie*. His other writings include *Le mariage musulman à Tunisie* (1941), and *Femmes de Tunisie* (Paris, 1958). His trace is lost after an article in 1972.

de **Montferrat**, Barral, 1854- *see* Barral de Montferrat, Horace Dominique, marquis

Montgomerie, Thomas George, born 23 April 1830 in Ayrshire, Scotland, he was educated at the East India Company's college, Addiscombe, and in 1851 went to India with the Bengal Engineers. In the following year he joined the Trigonometrical Survey, and from 1855 to 1864 he was in charge of the topographical survey of Jammu and Kashmir, for which he received the Royal Geographical Society's medal. He died in Bath on 31 January 1878.   Bioln, 12; Buckland; DNB; Embacher; Henze; Riddick

Montgomery, A. E., born 20th cent., he received a Ph.D. in 1970 from Birkbeck College, London, for *Allied policies in Turkey from the Armistice of Mudros, 30 October 1918, to the Treaty of Lausanne, 24 July 1923*. Sluglett

Montgomery, David Christopher, born 16 January 1940 at Chicago, he received a Ph.D. in 1971 from Indiana University for *Some characteristics of a basic vocabulary for the Soviet Uzbek literary language*. He was appointed a professor in the Department of History, Brigham Young University, Provo, Utah, a post which he still held in 2004. He visited Tashkent in 1969, 1977-78, and 1982. He was a member of the Turkish Studies Association. His writings include *Mongolian newspaper reader* (1970). MESA *Roster of members*, 1990; NatFacDr, 1995-2004; Schoeberlein

Montgomery, George Redington, born 17 June 1870 at Maraş, Turkey, he graduated in 1892 from Yale University, New Haven, Conn., where he also received his Ph.D. in 1902. From 1897 to 1898 he studied at the Universität Berlin. An ordained minister, he was in 1916 a special assistant to the American anbassador at Constantinople. In 1918, he was attached to the Peace conference. He was a sometime lecturer at Yale and New York universities. His writings include *The Place of values* (1903), *The Unexplored self* (1910), and *English language sounds for learners of English* (1942). He died in Stamford, Conn., on 29 November 1945. DcNAA; WhAm, 2; WhNAA

Montgomery, Giles Foster, born 8 November 1835 at Walden, Vt., he graduated in 1860 from Middlebury College, and in 1863 from Lane Theological Seminary, Chicago. He arrived at Aintab (Gaziantep) on 23 December 1863. In 1883/84, he founded a girls' school and residence at Adana, Turkey. He was a Presbyterian missionary, one of the strongest men, a good business man, a strong preacher, and unusually successful in the management of men. He died in Adana on 4 December 1888. Kornrumpf; *Missionary herald*, 85 (1889), pp. 58-59; Shavit

Montgomery, James Alan, born in 1866 at Germantown, Pa., he was from 1899 until 1935 a professor of Old Testament studies at Philadelphia Divinity School, and from 1921 until 1934 he served as a president of the American Schools of Oriental Research. On his retirement he became a professor emeritus of Hebrew at the University of Pennsylvania. He died in Philadelphia on 6 February 1949. ANB; BioIn, 1 (1), 2 (3), 14 (1); DAB, S 4; NYT, 8 February 1949, p. 26, col. 3; Shavit; WhAm, 5

Montgomery, John Warwick, born 18 October 1931 at Warsaw, N.Y., he graduated in 1952 from Cornell University, Ithaca, N.Y., and received a M.Div. in 1958 from Wittenberg University, a Ph.D. in 1962 from the University of California, a doctorate in theology in 1964 from the Université de Strasbourg, and a LL.B. in 1977 from the University of Chicago. He was a professor of jurisprudence and administration, divinity, and philosophy at a variety of universities and colleges in the U.S. and Canada. In 1966 he was a director of the European program in the Université de Strasbourg. His writings include *The writing of research papers in theology* (1959), *Crisis in Lutheran theology* (1967), and *The law above the law* (1975). ConAu, 21-24, new revision, 10, 25, 89; DrAS, 1969 P, 1974 P, 1978 P, 1982 P; Master (2); WhoAm, 1974/75-2003; WhoAmL, 1979-2003/2004; WhoFr, 1977/78-2003/2004; WhoWor, 1974/75-2003

Monti, Gennaro Maria, born 16 November 1896 at Napoli, he completed his studies in 1919 at Roma and became successively a lawyer and professor of jurisprudence and maritime trade at the universities of Sassari, Bari, and Napoli. His writings include *Studi letterari* (1924), *Le confraternite medievali dell'alta e media Italia* (1927), and *Lo stato normanno svevo* (1934). Chi è, 1928-1957|; IndBiltal (1)

Monticone, Giuseppe, born 24 July 1886 at Torino, Italy, he graduated in theology. He served as a chaplain in the First World War and subsequently became an archivist at the S. Congregazione della Propaganda Fide. Vaccaro; Wholtaly, 1958

de **Montmarin**, A., fl. 20th cent., his writings include *Étude hydrologique de l'Oued el-Lil et de l'Oued Rhezala* (Tunis, 1952). His trace is lost after an article in 1958.

Montoro Murillo, Rosario, born 20th cent., she received a doctorate in Semitic philology. She was a professor who taught contemporary Arabic literature since 1992 in the Departamento de Filologio Moderna, Facultad de Letras, Universidad de Castilla-La Mancha, Ciudad Real, a post which she still held in 1997. Arabismo, 1992, 1994, 1997; EURAMES, 1993

Montoy, Louis Pierre, born 20th cent., he received a *doctorat d'état* in 1982 from the Université d'Aix-Marseille for *La Presse dans le département de Constantine, 1870.1918*. He was a joint author of *Géographie de l'Afrique noire* (Paris, 1970). NUC, 1968-72; THESAM 2

Moody, Ernest Addison, born 27 September 1903 at Cranford, N.J., he graduated in 1924 from Williams College and received a Ph.D. in 1936 from Columbia University, New York, for *The logic of William of Ockham*. He taught philosophy at Columbia from 1939 to 1953, and from 1961 to his retirement in 1961. From 1953 to 1958 he was owner and operator of a cattle ranch in Texas. His writings include *The medieval science of weights* (1952), *Truce and consequence in medieval logic* (1953), and *Studies in medieval philosophy, science, and logic; collected papers, 1933-1969* (1975). He died in 1975.   ConAu, 13-16, 61-64; DrAS, 1969 P, 1974 P; NYT, 23 December 1975, p. 28, col. 5; WhAm, 6

Moon, Frederick William, born 19th cent., he wrote *Preliminary geological report on Saint John's Island, Red Sea* (Cairo, 1923), and he was a joint author of several other geological reports on the western Sinai and other places, between 1920 and his death in 1925.   Note about the author

de **Moor**, Eduardus Cornelius Maria, born in 1936, he wrote *Basis woordenlijst arabisch* (1984), *Arabisch voor beginners* (1984), *Sluit aan bij; arabisch voor beginners* (1984) *Arabisch uitgesproken en geschreven* (1989); he was a joint author of *De Iraanse revolutie; achtergronden* (1980); he edited *Vrouwen in het Midden-Oosten* (1982), and *Arabisch en Turks op school; discussies over eigen taal- en cultuuronderwijs* (1985).   Brinkman's, 1981-85

Moor, Edward, born in 1771, he went early in life to India, where he served with the Mahratta army against Tīpū Sultān, 1790-91. From 1799 until his retirement in 1805 he was a commissary-general at Bombay. He was a member of several learned societies. His writings include *A Narrative of the operations of Captain Little's detachment, and ot the Mahratta Army, commanded by Purseram Bhow* (1794), *The Hindu pantheon* (1809), *Hindu infanticide* (1811), *Suffolk words and phrases* (1823), and *Oriental fragments* (1834). He died in 1848.   Buckland; DNB; IndianBilnd (2); Riddick

Moór, Elemér, born 1 December 1891 at Hárspatak, Hungary, he was at one time affiliated with the Collegium Hungaricum, Berlin. His writings include *A magyar néo eredete* (1933), *Westungarn im Mittelalter im Spiegel der Ortsnamen* (1936), and *A honfoglaó magyarság megtelepülése és a székelyek eredete* (1944). He died in Szeged on 22 April 1974.   MEL, 1981

Moorcroft, William, born about 1765 in Lancashire, he was baptized on 25 June 1767. He was educated at Liverpool as a surgeon and subsequently studied veterinary science in France. In 1808 he joined the East India Company as a superintendent of military studs. In 1811-12 he crossed the Himalaya and traced the sources of the Satlaj and Indus. In 1819 he travelled to Lahore, Ladakh, Kashmir, Peshawar, Kabul, and Bukhara, desposing of his merchandise. He started his return journey in August 1825, but died of fever in Andhkhui on 27 August. His writings include *Cursory account of the various methods of shoeing horses* (1800), and *Travels in the Himalayan provinces of Hindustan and the Panjab from 1819 to 1825* (1841). Gerry Adler wrote *Beyond Bokhara; the life of William Moorcroft* (1985).   Asian affairs, 18 (1987), pp. 3-10; Buckland; DNB; Embacher; Henze; Mason; WhWE

Moore, Arthur, Major, born 19th cent., he had a long and varied experience in the Near East as foreign and war correspondent of the London *Times*. In 1922 he became proprietor and editor of *The New age*, a weekly review published in London. His writings include *The Orient express* (1914).   Note

Moore, Clement Henry, born 2 February 1937 at N.Y.C., he studied political science at Harvard University, where he received a Ph.D. in 1963 for *Tunisia's single party system*. He successively served as a professor at the University of California, Berkeley, American University in Cairo, University of Michigan, American University of Beirut, University of California, Los Angeles, and the University of Texas, Austin, a post which he held until 1994. His writings include *Tunisia since independence* (1965), *Politics in North Africa* (1970), *Images of development; Egyptian engineers in search of Industry* (1980).   AmM&WSc, 1973 S, 1978 S; MESA Roster of members, 1977-1982; Note; Selim

Moore, Frederick, born 17 November 1877 at New Orleans, he was a correspondent for various newspapers, including the *New York sun*, in the Balkan states, Morocco, and Turkey until 1909. His writings include *The Balkan trail* (1906), *The passing of Morocco* (1908). He died in 1956.   Kornrumpf; LC; Shavit - Asia; WhAm

Moore, Laurence Shaw, born 19th cent., he had a long acquaintance with Turkey and the Near East. He first visited Constantinople in 1902. A year after the 1914-18 War, he went to Constantinople again with the King-Crane Commission, which investigated the Turkish mandate question. He stayed on as a teacher of history at Robert College, Constantinople, and as executive secretary of the American Chamber of Commerce for the Levant. His trace is lost after an article in 1923.   Note about the author

Moore, Raymond Arthur, born 5 July 1925 at Towanta, Pa., he received a Ph.D. in 1961 from Columbia University, New York, for *The foreign policy image of Aneurin Bevan*. Since 1958 he taught in a variety of capacities in the Department of International Studies, University of South Carolina, Columbia. In 1963/64 he was a Fulbright senior lecturer in Panjab University. His writings include *Nation building and the Pakistan Army, 1947-1969* (1979), and he edited *The United Nations reconsidered* (1963).   AmM&WSc, 1973 S, 1978 S; ConAu, 5-8

Moore, Thomas, 1779-1852, he was a poet who became the national lyrist of Ireland by his publication of *Irish melofies* (1807-1834). DNB

Moore, William Arthur, M.B.E., born in 1880, he was educated at Belfast and Oxford. He was a special correspondent of *the Times*, notably during the 1914-18 War, and later an editor of the Calcutta *Statesman*. He died 23 July 1962. ObitT, 1961-70, pp. 558-59; Riddick; *Who was who*, 6

Moore, William Robert, born in 1899 in Butler Township, Mich., he was educated at Hillsdale College, and the University of Michigan. He joined the staff of the *National geographic magazin* in 1931 and became chief of the foreign editorial staff in 1953. Au&Wr, 1963

Mooren, Thomas, born 1947 at Dortmund-Kurl, Germany, he received a theological degree in 1979 from the Institut catholique de Paris. His writings include *Auf der Grenze; die Andersheit Gottes und die Vielfalt der Religionen* (1991), its translation, *On the border; the otherness of God and the multiplicity of the religions* (1994), *Macht und Einsamkeit Gottes; Dialog mit dem islamischen Radikal-Monotheismus* (1991), *Purusha oder der messerscharfe Weg zum Selbst; Selbst und Selbsterfahrung in islamischer und hinduistischer Mystik* (1993), *Es gibt keinen Gott außer Gott; der Islam in der Welt der Religion* (1996), *Making the earth a human dwelling place* (2000), and *Gewürzstraße des Glaubens - eine interreligiöses Tagebuch; Bausteine zu einer narrativen Missiologie* (2001). ZKO

Moorhead, Helen Armstrong Howell, born in 1882 at New Brunswick, N.J., she graduated in 1904 from Bryn Mawr (Pa.) College and received a graduate degree in 1907 at the Université de Grenoble. In 1927, she joined the Foreign Policy Association, New York, where she became chairman of its Opium Research Committee. She was a joint author of *International limitation of dangerous drugs* (1931). She died on 6 March 1950. Master (1); NYT, 10 March 1950, p. 27, col. 3

Moosa, Matti, born in 1924 at Mosul, he received a law degree from Baghdad University, and also took degrees at the University of Wales, and Columbia University, New York. He received an American Ph.D. in 1965. He was an attorney in Iraq until 1953, when he entered the U.S. Mission in Iraq as a civilian employee. After his immigration to the States he was a professor of history at Gannon University, Erie, Pa. His writings include *The Origins of modern Arabic fiction* (1983), and *Extremist Shi'ites* (1988). ConAu, 127, new rev. 55; *MESA Roster of members*, 1977-1990; Note; ZKO

Mooyer, Ernst Friedrich, he was born on 6 August 1798 at Minden, Germany. In obedience to his father's wishes, he trained as a merchant, later entering the family business. Concurrently he pursued his long-standing interest in history and languages. As a private scholar he published *Nekrologium des Klosters Weissenburg* (s.l., n.d.), *Die Einfälle der Normannen in die Pyrenäische Halbinsel. Les invasions des Normannes dans la péninsule pyrénéenne; collection de renseignements sur ce sujet, traduite en grande partie du danois* (Münster, Paris, 1845), *Über die angebliche Abstammung des normannischen Königsgeschlechts Siziliens von den Herzögen der Normandie; eine genealogische Untersuchung* (1850), and *Onomasticon chronographicon hioarchiae germanicae* (1854), a work which took him twenty years to complete, and for which he was awarded Rother Adlerorden fourth class; the King of Belgium presented him the gold medal for arts and science. He died in Minden on 8 May 1861. ADtB, vol. 22, p. 210; BN; GV

Mor, Carlo Guido, born 30 December 1903 at Milano, Italy, he was a professor of law and taught successively at the universities of Ferrara, Cagliari, Modena and Trieste until 1957, when he became a professor at Padua. Concurrently he served from 1944 to 1947 as a rector of the Università di Modena. He was a member of several learned societies. His writings include *Lex romana canonice compta* (1927), and *L'età feudale* (1952-53). He died in Cividale del Friuli in 1990. Chi è, 1948, 1957, 1961; IndBiltal (1); Lui, chi è; Vaccaro; Wholtaly, 1958

Morabia, Alfred, born 20th cent., he received a *doctorat d'état* in 1974 from the Université de Paris for *La Notion de gihâd dans l'islâm médiéval*, a work which was published in a trade edition in 1975. His writings include *Le gihâd dans l'islam médiéval; le combat sacré des origines au XIIe siècle* (Paris, 1993). Livres disponibles, 2004; THESAM, 4

Moraes, Francis (Frank) Robert, born 12 November 1907, he received his B.A. at Bombay, M.A. at Oxford, and was called to the bar from Lincoln's Inn. He was a journalist and newspaper editor who from 1938 to 1946 was an assistant editor of the *Times of India*. His writings include *The Story of India* (1942), *Yonder one world; a study of Asia and the West* (1958), *India today* (1960), and *The Importance of being black* (1965). He died in 1974. CurBio, 1957; ConAu, 13-14, 49-52; IndianBilnd (9); NYT, 4 May 1974, p. 44, col. 4; WhE&EA; WhoWor, 1974/75; ZKO

Moraes, George Mark, he was affiliated with Konkan Institute of Arts and Sciences, Bombay, and St. Xavier's College, Bombay. His writings include *Mangalore, a historical sketch* (1927), *Bibliography of Indological studies* (1945), and *A History of Christianity in India* (1964). Note about the author de **Moraes Farias**, Paulo Fernando, born 20th cent., he was a sometime lecturer in African history in the Centre of West African Studies, University of Birmingham. His writings include *Self-assertion and brokerage; early cultural nationalism in West Africa* (1990). Note about the author

Moraht, Ernst, born 19th cent., he was a soldier and retired with the rank of major. He later became a journalist at the military desk of the *Berliner Tageblatt* and *Neue freie Presse*. His writings include *Die Ostfront; der Krieg an der Ostfront von Kurland bis Constantinopel* (1915), *Unser gemeinsamer Krieg* (1915), and *Tage des Krieges; militärische und politische Betrachtungen, 1914-1916* (1916). He died in Berlin on 22 March 1918. DtBiJ, 1917-1920, Totenliste, 1918, p. 699; KDtLK, Nekrolog, 1901-1935

del **Moral Molina**, Celia, born 20th cent., she received a doctorate in Semitic philology, with special reference to Arabic literature of Granada. She was in 1997 a professor in the Departamento de Estudios Semíticos, Facultad de Filosofía y Letras, Granada. Her writings include *Un poeta granadino del s. XII, Abū Ya'far Ibn Sa'īd* (1987). Arabismo, 1992, 1994, 1997

Moraleda y Esteban, Juan, born 8 February 1857 at Orgaz (Toledo), Spain, he graduated in 1873 from a provincial institution, and completed his medical study in 1880 at Madrid. Since 1888 he was a member of the Real Academia de la Historia. His writings include *Cantares populares de Toledo* (1889), *Médicos y farmacéuticos célebres de Toledo* (1890-1911), *Mártires mozárabes de Toledo* (1911), and *Notas médicas toledanas* (1912). His trace is lost after an article in 1928. EncicUni

Moralejo Laso, Abelardo, born 20th cent., his writings include *Toponomia gallega y leonasa* (1977), and he was a joint author of *Galicia e a seitura en Castela* (1997). LC

Morales Delgado, Antonio, born 20th cent., he received a doctorate in Semitic philology, and became a professor of Arabic literature, particularly contemporary Palestinian literature, at the Univerdad de Granada. Arabismo, 1992, 1994, 1997; EURAMES, 1993

Morales Lezcano, Victor M., born 30 January 1939 at Las Palmas, Spain, he received a doctorate in modern history. He was successively a professor at the Universidad Autónoma de Madrid, and the Universidad Nacional de Educación a Distancia, Madrid. His writings include *Sintesis de la historia economica de Canarias* (1966), *Relaciones mercantiles entre Inglaterra y los archipiélagos del Atlántico ibérico* (1970), and *El colonialismo hispano-francés en Marruecos, 1898-1927* (1979). Arabismo, 1992, 1994, 1997; WhoWor, 1989/90

Morales Oliver, Luis, born 1 April 1895 at Pasajes de San Pedro (Guipúzcoa), Spain, he graduated from the Instituto Nacional de Enseñanza, Huelva, and subsequently studied liberal arts at Madrid, where he received a doctorate in 1922. He was a professor of Hispanic-American literature at Madrid and Sevilla. His writings include *Arias Montana y la política de Felipe II en Flandes* (1927), *Africa en la literatura española* (1957-64), *La novela mosrisca de tema granadino* (1970), and *El pota Miquel Melendres* (1975). Figuras; IndiceE³ (1); Sainz; WhoSpain, 1963

Morán Bardón, César, Padre, O.S.A., born 7 October 1882, he was associated with the Museos del Pueblo Español and Arqueológico Nacional. His writings include *El paleolítico de Beni Gorfet, Marruecos* (1941), and *Vías y poblaciones romanas en el norte de Marruecos* (1948). He died in Madrid on 19 January 1952. *Archivo español de arqueología*, 25 (1952), p. 210; NUC, pre-1956

Morand, Marcel Ludovic Alexandre, born 17 March 1863 at Saint-Amand (Nord), France, he studied at Paris, where he received a doctorate for his thesis, *Droit romain: les accusations populaires à Rome; droit français: les conflits de lois en matière d'hypothèque maritime*, in 1888. He held two brief teaching positions at Montpellier and Poitiers before he went to the École de droit d'Alger in 1894, where he was a member of its teaching staff, and since 1906, its director until his death. He was a specialist in Islamic law and an adviser to the Algerian administration as well as the French government. Shortly before his death in Algiers, in 1931, he published *Études de droit musulman et de droit coutumier berbère* (1931). *Revue africaine*, 72 (1931), p. 370

Morandini, Giuseppe, born 19 May 1907 at Predazzo (Trento), he received a doctorate in natural sciences, and became successively a professor of geography at the universities of Messina, Roma, Pisa, and Padova. Chi è, 1957, 1961; Vaccaro; Wholtaly, 1958

Moranvillé, Louis Henri, born 9 August 1863 at Paris, he gained a law degree and became an archivist and palaeographer. He was a sometime vice-president of the Société de l'Histoire de France and an honorary libarian at the Bibliothèque nationale, Paris. His writings include *Étude sur la vie de Jean le Mercier* (1888), and *Chroniques de Perceval de Cagny* (1902). Qui êtes-vous, 1924

Morata, Nemesio, born about 1886, he was an Augustinian father and an Arabist who specialized in Islamic asceticism and mysticism. A director of the Biblioteca Escurialense, Madrid, he contributed to

Al-Andalus, Ciudad de Dios, and *Religión y cultura*. He died at the Real Monasterio de El Escorial on 23 March 1960 at the age of seventy-four. *Al-Andalus*, 25 (1960), pp. 469-470

Moravcsik, Gyula, born 29 January 1892 at Budapest, he was a professor of Greek philology and Byzantine studies at Budapest University. A member of numerous learned societies, he was granted an honorary doctorate by the University of Athens. His writings include *Byzantinoturcica* (1942-43), *Bevezetés a byzantinológiába* (1966), and its translation, *Einführung in die Byzantinologie* (176). He died on 10 December 1972. *Etudes balkaniques*, 9 (1973), pp. 147-48; Magyar; MEL, 1981

Morawetz, Sieghard Otto, born 25 November 1903 at Knittelfeld, he received a Dr.phil. in 1926 from the Universität Graz for *Kenntnis der Oberflächenformen der Kreutz-Eck-Gruppe*. After his Dr.habil. he taught geography from 1932 until his retirement at the Universität Graz. His writings include *Hundert Jahre Geographie an der Karl-Franzens-Universität in Graz, 1871-1971* (1971). He was honoured by *Festschrift für Sieghard O. Morawetz zum 80. Geburtstag* (1983). He died about 1992. DtBilnd (1); GV; Kürschner, 1935-1992|

Ritter von **Morawitz**, Carl (Charles/Karl), born 9 March 1846 at Triesch (Třešt), Austrian Moravia, he trained as a banker in Prag, and worked at banks in Austria and Germany before going in 1868 to Paris, where he worked for the Banque de Paris et des Pays-Bas. In 1870 he entered the Banque Impériale Ottoman. As a financial director and administrator of the Ottoman railway company, he played an important role in the financing of the track to Constantinople. Resident in Wien since 1885, he became an outstanding personality of the Viennese financial world. From 1906 to 1914 he served as president of the Anglo-Österreichische Bank. His writings include *Les finances de la Turquie* (1902), its translation, *Die Türkei im Spiegel ihrer Finanzen* (1903), *Aus Arbeitstagen und Mußestunden* (1911). He died in Wien on 13 January 1914. DtBE; Kornrumpf; NDB; ÖBL; Wininger

Morcos, Soliman, Dr., he was in 1935 a lecturer in civil law at the Faculté de droit, Cairo, and in 1941 at the Faculté de droit, Zaytun, as well as a member of the Société Fouad Ier d'économie politique, de statistique et de législation, Cairo, and in 1971, a chairman of the Department of Legal Studies and Islamic law at the Institute of Arab Research and Studies. Note about the author

Mordell, Phineas, born in 1861 or 62 in Lithuania, he studied at Elizavetgrad (Kirovograd), Ukraine. In 1881 he emigrated to the United States, where he settled in Philadelphia, Pa. His writings include *The origin of the letters and numerals according to the Sefer Yetzirah* (1914). He died in Philadelphia, Pa., on 22 June 1934. CnDiAmJBi; EncJud

Mordini, Antonio, born 14 February 1904 at Barga (Lucca), Italy, he was an ethnologist and anthropologist. He explored South America, Southern Arabia, the Sahara, Abyssinia, Socotra, and East Africa. *Chi è*, 1940, 1948, 1957, 1961; Vaccaro; Wholtaly, 1958

Mordochai Abi Serour, born in 1831 at Akka, Morocco, he visited Timbuctu about 1870. He died in Alger in 1886. Sanford H. Bederman wrote *God's will; the travels of Rabbi Mordochai Abi Serour* (1980). NUC, 1981

Mordtmann, Andreas David, born 11 February 1811 at Hamburg, Germany, he taught himself Oriental languages and received a Dr.phil. in 1845 from the Universität Kiel. From 1847 to 1859 he was a chargé d'affaires and consul-general at Constantinople. He subsequently entered the Turkish service and became a judge in the commercial tribunal, concurrently acting as a corresopndent to the *Augsburger allgemeine Zeitung*. His writings include *Belagerung und Eroberung Constantinoples durch die Türken im Jahre 1453* (1858); he translated from the Arabic of al-Istakhrī, *Das Buch der Länder* (1845); he also published the undated *Guide de Constantinople*. He died in Constantinople on 30 December 1879. ADtB, vol. 22, p. 219; BN; DtBE; DtBilnd (2); Fück, p. 212; Embacher; Henze; Kornrumpf; NDB

Mordtmann, Johannes Heinrich Hermann, born 11 September 1852 at Pera (Constantinople), he studied classical and Oriental philology at the universities of Bonn and Leipzig, and received his Dr.phil. in 1874 at Berlin for an epigraphical work entitled *Marmora Ancyrana*. He was successively a dragoman, consul, and consul-general at Thessaloniki, Constantinople, and Smyrna (Izmir). Since 1910 he lectured at the Darül-fünun, Constantinople. Obliged to leave Turkey after the 1914-18 War, he settled in Berlin, where he joined the Orientalisches Seminar. He was one of the pioneers of South Arabian studies as well as Ottoman diplomatics. He was a joint author of *Literaturdenkmäler aus Ungarns Türkenzeit* (1927). He died in Berlin on 3 or 4 July 1932. DtBE; Fück, p. 256; Hanisch; Kornrumpf; Kürschner, 1925-1931; NDB

Moreau, Laurent Adolphe, born in 1882, he received a doctorate in 1913 from the Université de Paris for a thesis on tropical botany. His writings include *À bord du cuirassé "Gaulois"; Dardanelles - Salonique, 1915-1916* (Paris, 1930). BN; NUC, pre-1956

Moreau, René Luc, born in 1929 at Angers (Maine-et-Loire), France, he was a Dominican father who, in 1982, taught at the Institut catholique de l'Afrique de l'ouest at Abidjan. His writings include *Africains musulmans; des communautés en mouvement* (Paris, 1982). ZKO

Moreau-Defargues, Philippe, born 20th cent., he graduated from the École nationale d'administration, Paris. He was a sometime *directeur d'études* at the Institut d'études politiques de Paris. His writings include *Le problème de l'eau dans le département de l'Ardèche* (1968), *L'Europe et son identité dans le monde* (1983), *La politique internationale* (1990), *La France dans le monde du XXe siècle* (1994), *Introduction à la géopolitique* (1994), *Les relations internationales depuis 1945* (1996), *Repentance et réconciliation* (1999), *La communauté internationale* (2000), and *La gouvernance* (2003). Livres disponibles, 2004; Note about the author

Moreh, Shmuel Sami Ibrahim, born 22 December 1932 at Baghdad, he received his M.A. in 1962 from the Hebrew University, Jerusalem, and his Ph.D. in 1966 from the School of Oriental and African Studies, London, for *Strophic, blanc and free verse in modern Arabic literature*. Since 1966 he was associated with the Hebrew University. His writings include *Arabic works by Jewish writers, 1863-1973* (1973), *Live theatre and dramatic literature in the medieval Arab world* (1992), *The Book of strangers; medieval Arabic graffiti on the theme of nostalgia, of Abū al-Faraj al-Isfahānī* (2000), and he was joint editor of *Jewish contributions to nineteenth-century Arabic theatre; previously unknown plays from Algeria and Syria* (1996). ConAu, 141; IWWAS, 1975/76; Private; Sluglett; Wholsrael, 1978-2001

Moreing, Charles Algernon, born 19th cent., he was head of the firm Benwick, Moreing & Co., London, mining engineers and mine managers. His writings include *Telegraphic mining code* (1888), and he was a joint author of *The New general and mining telegraph code* (1895), a work which went through five editions until 1905. BritInd (2)

Morel, André, born 19th cent., he received a doctorate in 1904 from the Université de Paris for *La Jurisdiction des administrateurs actifs*. He was in 1903 a founding editor of the *Revue de science et de législation*. BN

Morel, Bénédict Auguste, born 22 November 1809 to French parents at Wien, he lost his father when quite young and grew up under difficult conditions in Luxembourg and St.-Dié. He went to Paris, where he eked out his living by journalism. In most miserable conditions he completed his medicine in 1839 at the Université de Paris with the inaugural thesis, *Questions sur les diverses branches des sciences médicales*. He spent two years studying lunatic asylums in the Netherlands, Switzerland, Germany, and Italy. Upon his return to France in 1848, he became chief medical officer of the asylum at Maréville (Meurthe), where he initiated fundamental changes in the treatment of patients. Since 1856 he headed the important institution at Saint-Yon (Seine-inférieure). His writings include *Traité des dégénérescences physiques, intellectelles et morales de l'espèce humaine et des causes qui produisent ces variétés maladives* (Paris, 1857), and *Traité de médecine légale des aliénés* (1866). He died in Saint-Yon in 1873. GdeEnc; IndexBFr² (1); Master (1)

Morel, Edmund Dene, born Georges Edmond Pierre Achille Morel de Ville in 1873 at Paris, he was an international issues campaigner, journalist, and member of Parliament. His writings include *Affairs of West Africa* (1902), *Morocco and Armageddon* (1915), *Morocco in diplomacy* (1912), and *Africa and the peace of Europe* (1917). He died in 1925. Catherine A. Cline wrote *E. D. Morel, 1873-1924; the strategies of protest* (1980). DNB, *Missing Persons*; Master (2); *Who was who*, 2

Morel-Fatio, Alfred Paul Victor, born in 1850 at Strasbourg, France, he was a Romance scholar, and was successively a lecturer at the École supérieure des lettres d'Alger, École pratique des hautes études, and the Collège de France, Paris. He died in Versailles in 1924. GdeEnc; *Qui êtes-vous*, 1924

Moreland, William Harrison, born 13 July 1868 at Belfast, he was educated at Clifton College, and Trinity College, Cambridge. He took a First in law tripos and became an LL.B. in 1889. He joined the Indian Civil Service and went to India and served as a magistrate in the North West Province and Oudh. Since 1899 he was a director of Land Records and Agriculture. His writings include *India at the death of Akbar; an economic study* (1920), *From Akbar to Aurangzeb; a study in Indian economic history* (1923), and *The Agrarian system of Moslem India* (1929). He died on 28 September 1938. Index Islamicus (1); IndianBiInd (4); Riddick; *Who was who*, 3

Morelet, Arthur, born in 1809 at Lays (Saône-et-Loire), France, he was a natural scientist and a president of the Académie des sciences de Dijon. He made scientific journeys to Algeria, Portugal, and Central America. He translated *Journal du voyage de Vasco de Gama* (Lyon, 1864). He died in 1892. BN; IndexBFr² (1)

Morelon, Régis, born 20th cent., he received a *doctorat de 3ème cycle* in 1983 from the Université de Paris V for *Les Textes astronomiques arabes de Thabit B. Qurra*. He translated from the Arabic of al-Ghazzālī, *Le Livre du licite et de l'illicite* (1981), and he edited and translated from the Arabic of Thābit ibn Qurrah, *Œuvres d'astronomie* (1987). THESAM, 4; ZKO

Moreno, Antonio Elosegni, born 1 March 1918 at San Sebastian, Spain, he graduated in 1945 from the Universidad de Madrid and received a B.A. in 1955 from the University of California, Berkeley, and a Ph.D. in 1960 from St. Thomas Aquinas College, River Forest, Illinois. In 1959, he was appointed a professor of philosophy at the University of Notre Dame. ConAu, 33-36; DrAS, 1978 P, 1982 P; Master (2)

Moreno, Martino Mario, born 8 September 1892 at Torino, Italy, he entered the colonial service in 1914 and served in Tripolitania and Cyrenaica until 1926, when he became for a year a consul in Egypt. From 1931 to 1934 he was a director of political affairs in the Eritrean government. In 1936 he became vice-governor of Galla and Sidama, and in 1938 he was appointed director-general of press in the Ministero dell'Africa Italiana. He taught at the Università di Roma during the 1939-1945 War, and again from 1949 to 1952. In 1955-56 he taught at a university in Beirut. In the post-war period he was sent on missions to Somalia, Lebanon, and the Sudan. His writings include *Brevi nozioni d'islam* (1927), *Grammatica teorico-pratica della lingua galla con esercizi* (1939), *L'islamismo* (1947), and *L'islamismo e l'educazione* (1952). He died in Roma on 13 June 1964. *Annali* / Istituto universitario orientale di Napoli, n.s., 15 (1965), p. 355; Chi é, 1940, 1948, 1957, 1961; LexAfrika; Vaccaro; Wholtaly, 1958

Moreno Casado, J., fl. 20th cent., his writings include *Los concilios nacionales visigodos* (1946), *Las capitulaciones de Granada en su aspecto jurídico* (1949), *Los gitanos desde su penetración en España* (1949), and *Fuero de Baza; estudio y transcripción* (1968).

Moreno Nieto y **Villarejo**, José born in 1823 or 1825 in Badajoz province, Spain, he studied law at Toledo. His writings include *Gramática de la lengua arábiga* (1872). He died in Madrid on 24 February 1882. EnicUni; Manzanares, pp. 165-168

Moreno Olmedo, María Angustinas, born 20th cent., her writings include *Heráldica y genealogía granadinos* (Granada, 1976), a second edition was published in 1989. ZKO

Morère, Maurice M., fl. 20th cent., his writings include *Une symbiose juridique au Maroc; la condition civile des étrangers* (1955), *La cour suprème, organisation et procedure* (Casablance, 1961), *Manuel d'organisation judiciaire au Maroc* (1961), *L'influence de l'amour courtois hispano-arabe sur la lyrique des premiers troubadours* (1972), and he edited *Codes marocains annotés* (1935), and *Code de la route au Maroc* (1946).

Moreux, René Jean Marie, born 17 March 1976 at Sury-près-Léré (Cher), France, he graduated in humanities and German, and subsequently taught German at the Lycée de Douai until entering the economic desk at the journal, *le Temps*. He later became a parliamentary editor at *Le Siècle*. From 1947 to 1952 he served as a *conseiller* to the Union Française. His writings include *Les trafics et l'outillage des ports nord-africains* (Paris, 1927), and *Principes nouveaux d'économie coloniale* (1951). He was an editor of the Paris monthly, *Industries et travaux d'outre-mer* as well as *Marchés tropicaux du monde*. He died in July of 1957. BN; BDFC, 1954/55; WhoFr, 1953/54-1957/58

Morewedge, Parviz, born 30 January 1934 at Bābulsar on the Caspian Sea, he graduated in 1957 from the University of California, Los Angeles, where he also received his Ph.D. in 1969 for *A Study of Ibn Sina and Sufism*. He subsequently taught philosophy at a great variety of U.S. colleges and universities. His writings include *The Metaphysica of Avicenna* (1973), and he edited *Islamic philosophical theology* (1979). ConAu, 93-96; *MESA Roster of members*, 1977; Master (1); NatFacDr, 1995; Selim

Morey, Charles Rufus, born in 1877 at Hastings, Mich., he graduated in 1899 from Michigan University. From 1918 to his retirement he was a professor of fine art and archaeology at Princeton University. He was the compiler of the Princeton index of Christian art, a catalogue from the birth of Christ until 1500. His writings include *Christian* art (1935), and *Early Christian art* (1942). He died in 1955. BioIn, 2, 4 (8), 11; NYT, 30 August 1955, p. 27, col. 3; WhAm, 3; WhNAA

Morfill, William Richard, born in 1834 at Maidstone, Kent, England, he was educated at Oriol College, Oxford, and remained there for the rest of his life as a Slavonic scholar. His writings include *Russia* (1880), *Poland* (1893), *Short grammar of the Bulgarian language* (1897), and *A Grammar of the Bohemian or Čech language* (1899). He bequeathed his Slavonic library to Queen's College, Oxford. He died in 1909. BritInd (2); DNB, Suppl., 1901-11; *Who was who*, 1

Morgan, David Orrin, born 20th cent., he received a Ph.D. in 1977 from the School of Oriental and African Studies, London, for *Aspects of Mongol rule in Persia*. He was throughout the 1990s a reader in history of the Middle East, particularly Il-Khanid Persia, at S.O.A.S, and an editor of the *Journal of* *the Royal Asiatic Society.* His writings include *The Mongols* (1987), and he edited *Medieval historical writing in the Christian and Islamic worlds* (1982). Note about the author; Sluglett; SOAS *Library catalogue*; ZKO

Morgan, Edward Delmar, born in 1840 at Stratford, Essex, England, he travelled in Persia and Central Asia. A member of the Royal Geographic Society, he contributed much to its journal. He was also an honorary secretary of the Hakluyt Society. His writings include a translation from the Russian of Nikolai M. Przheval'skiĭ's travels, and he edited *Early voyages and travels to Russia and Persia* (London, 1886). He died in London in 1909. BritInd (1); DNB

Morgan, Helen Gertrude Louise, born in 1921 at Ilford, Essex, England, she was a writer of Children's books. She died in 1990. ConAu, 57-60

de **Morgan**, Jacques Jean Marie, born in 1857 at Huisseau-sur-Cosson (Cher), France, he studied at École des mines, Paris. From 1882 to 1883, he travelled to the East Indies and there in 1884 explored the Malacca Peninsula. From 1886 to 1889, he visited southern Russia, mainly the Caucasus and the Asian and European parts of Turkey. Before returning to France in 1891, he made his first explorations in Persia. Until 1895 he served under the Ministère de l'Instruction publique et des Beaux-Arts as a director-general of the Service des Antiquités. In 1897 he left for Persia, where he continued his archaeological work. His writings, partly under the pseudonym Karagueuz Effendi, include *Catalogue des monuments et inscriptions de l'Egypte antique* (1894-1905), *Les premières civilisations* (1909), *Alaric; roman historique* (1914), *Essai sur les nationalités* (1917), and *Contre les barbares de l'Orient; études sur la Turquie* (1918). He died in Marseille in 1924. Curinier, vol. 1 (1901), pp. 337-338; Dawson; Egyptology; EncIran

Morgenstern, Julian, born 18 March 1881 at Francisville, Illinois, he graduated from the University of Cincinnati in 1901, from Hebrew Union College, Cincinnati, in 1902, and received a Dr.phil. in 1905 from the Universität Heidelberg for *The Doctrine of sin in the Babylonian religion*. He was since 1907 a professor of Semitic languages at Hebrew Union College, and since 1912 also its director. He died in Macon, Ga. on 4 December 1976. CnDiAmJBi; ConAu, 19-20, 89-92; Schwarz; WhoWorJ, 1965; Wininger

Morgenstern, Laura, born in 1897, she received a Dr.phil. in 1921 from the Universität Bern for a study of grief in Christian art entitled *Die Ausdrucksbewegung des Schmerzes in der christlichen Kunst.* Her other writings include *Etsétiques d'Orient et d'Occident* (Paris, 1937). She died in 1936. NYPL

Morgenstern, Oskar, born in 1902 at Görlitz, Silesia, he received a Dr.rer.pol. in 1925 at Wien, and subsequently became a lecturer at his alma mater until 1935. Since 1941 he successively taught at Princeton and New York universities. His writings include *Wirtschaftsprognose* (1928), *International financial transactions and business cycles* (1959), and *The Question of national defense* (1959). He died in N.Y.C. in July 1977. AnaBrit; BioHbDtE; CnDiAmJBi; ConAu, 9-12, 73-76, new rev. 5; IntAu&W, 1976, 1977; Master (6); NatCAB, 54, pp. 241-42; WhoAm, 1974/75, 1976/77; WhoEc, 1981, 1986, 1999; WhoWor, 1974/75

Morgenstierne, Georg Valentin, born 3 January 1892 at Oslo, he received a Dr.phil. in 1918 from the Universität Berlin for *Über das Verhältnis zwischen Cārūdatta und Mrcchakatikā*, on an aspect of the history of Indian literature. He served as a professor at Göteborg, 1930-37, and Oslo, 1937-63. He received honorary doctorates at Göteborg, Bern, and Tehran. His research was mainly in the field of the Indian and Iranian frontier languages, undertaken for the Institute for comparative research in human culture, Oslo. His writings include *Reports on a linguistic mission to Afghanistan* (1926), *Notes on Phallūra* (1941), *Notes on Gawar-bati* (1950), *Irano-Dardica* (1973), and *Etymological vocabulary of the Shugni group* (1974). He died 3 March 1978. BioB134, pp. 369-70; IWWAS, 1975/76; Hvemer hvem, 1948-1973; Index Islamicus (6); Studia iranica, 7 (1978), pp. 281-82

Morgenthau, Hans Joachim, born 17 April 1904 at Coburg, Bavaria, he studied law at the universities of Berlin, München, and Frankfurt am Main. Since 1932 he successively taught political science at Genève, Madrid, and since 1935 in the U.S.A. His writings include *Die internationale Rechtspflege* (1929), *Politics among nations* (1948), and *In defense of the national interest* (1951). He died in N.Y.C. on 19 July 1980. AmM&WSc, 1973 S, 1978 S; AnaBrit; AnObit, 1980, pp. 418-22; BioHbDtE; CnDiAmJBi; ConAu, 9-12, 101, new rev., 82; CurBio, 1963, 1980; Master (14); NYT, 21 July 1980, p. A14, cols. 1-3; WhAm, 7; WhoAm, 1974/75-1980; WhoWor, 1974/75; WhoWorJ, 1965, 1972, 1978

Morghen, Raffaello, born in 1896 at Roma, he was a professor of medieval history successively at the universities of Roma, Palermo, Perugia, and again Roma. He retired in 1971. His writings include *Il tramonto della potenza sveva in Italia* (1936), *Gregorio VII* (1942), *Il medioevo nella storiografia* (1953), and *Civiltà mediovale al tramonto* (1973). He died in 1983. Chi è, 1931-1961; ConAu, 109; IndBiltal (1); IntAu&W, 1977; IntWW, 1974/75-1983; Master (1); Vaccaro; Wholtaly, 1958-1983

Mori, Attilio, born 12 September 1865 at Firenze, Italy, he was for many years a topographer and librarian in the Istituto Geografico Militare. A lecturer in geography at the R. Università di Messina, he successively became a professor of geography in the Istituto Superiore di Magistero, Firenze, taught economic and political geography in the Istituto Superiore di Scienze Economiche e Commerciale, Firenze, and the R. Istituto Superiore "Cesare Alfieri." He retired in 1934. He was a member of several national and international learned societies. His writings include *L'esplorazione geografica della Libia* (Firenze, 1927), *La Tunisia* (Roma, 1930), and *Africa in generale* (Milano, 1936). He died on 16 December 1937. *Isis*, 40 (1949), p. 355; *Rivista delle colonie*, 11 (1937), p. 1592-93

Mori, Fabrizio, he was born in 1925; his writings include *Tadrat Acacus, arte rupestre e culture del Sahara preistorico* (1988). NUC; ZKO

Mori, Masao, born 30 March 1921, he gained a doctorate and became a director of the Center for East Asian Cultural Studies in Toyō Bunko. His writings include *Toruko no shakai to keizai* (Tokyo, 1971)., he was a joint author of *Arabu to Isuraeru* (Tokyo, 1986), and he edited *Modern China studies in Japan* (Tokyo, 1982). JapAuFile

Morier, James Justinian, born about 1780 at Smyrna, Turkey, of a Swiss father and a Dutch mother, his father having migrated to Smyrna as a young man and become a naturalized British subject. As a member of Sir Gore Ouseley's Mission to Persia, he landed in 1811 at Bushire. He was the first European traveller to publish an illustrated account of the Sassanian ruins and bas-relief at Shapur. After 1815 he devoted himself to writing, achieving fame with his amusing satire of the Persians in *The Adventures of Hajji Baba of Isfahan* (1835), a work which was translated into Persian in 1996. His other writings include *Journey through Persia, Armenia, and Asia Minor to Constantinople in the years 1808 and 1809* (1812), and its translation, *Reisen durch Persien in den Jahren 1808 bis 1816* (1985). He died in Brighton in 1849. AnaBrit; DLB, 116 (1992), pp. 223-27; *Cambridge history of Iran*, vol. 7; DNB; Embacher; Henze; Master 24), Wright

Morier, John Philip, born in 1776 at Smyrna, Turkey, he was attached to the British embassy at Constantinople, 5 April 1799, despatched to special service to Egypt, 22 December 1799. He was appointed consul-general in Albania, 3 December 1803, secretary at legation at Washington, 5 April 1810, and envoy extraordinary to the Court of Saxony, Dresden, 5 February 1816. He retired on pension, 5 January 1825. His writings include *Memoir of a campaign with the Ottoman Army in Egypt* (1801), German extracts of which were published in *Minerva* (Hamburg), 1802, no. 1. He died in London, 20 August 1853. Boase; BritInd (1); DNB; Sezgin

Morimoto, Kosei, born 20th cent., he was in 1981 a lecturer at Kyoto University. His writings include *The fiscal administration of Egypt in the early Islamic period* (Kyoto, 1981). ZKO

Moris, Roger Louis Jean, born 24 July 1906 at Sète (Hérault), France, he received a doctorate in economics in 1930 from the Université de Paris for *Le cinéma*. He became a French administrator in Morocco and Algeria, 1933-1943, and subsequently in metropolitan France. He was a joint author of *Revenus et niveaux de vie indigènes au Maroc* (1934). He died on 28 May 1987. DBFC, 1954/55; NDNC, 1966; WhoFr, 1969/70-1987/88

Morison, Antoine, born 17th cent., his writings include *Relation historique d'un voyage nouvellement fait au Mont de Sinai et à Jérusalem* (Toul, 1704), its translation, *Reisebeschreibung nach Jerusalem und Cairo* (1704), and *Voyage en Egypte, 1697*, edited by Georges Goyon (1976). ZKO

Morison, David Lindsay, born 15 October 1920 at Roslin, Scotland, he graduated in 1947 from Merton College, Oxford, and served with the B.B.C. monitoring service from 1948 to 1959, when he joined the Central Asian Research Centre, London. His writings include *The U.S.S.R. and Africa* (1964). ConAu, 13-16

Morison, Sir Theodore, born in 1863 in Malta, he graduated from Trinity College, Cambridge, and in 1885 he became a tutor to princes in India. He subsequently joined the staff of the Muhammadan Anglo-Oriental College, Aligarh, and served as its principal from 1899 to 1905, when he returned to England. His writings include *Imperial rule in India* (1899), *History of the M.A.O. College, Aligarh* (1903), and *The Economic transition in India* (1911). He died in Paris on 14 February 1936. DNB; Riddick; WhE&EA; *Who was who*, 3

Moritz, Bernhard, born 14 September 1859 at Guben, Prussia, he received a Dr.phil. in 1882 from the Universität Berlin for *Gregorii Barhebraei in duodecim prophetas minores scholia*. He was for many years a librarian at the Seminar für Orientalische Sprachen, Berlin. In 1896 he became a chief librarian at Cairo. He had a first-hand acquaintance of the Muslim world, from Mesopotamia to Morocco. Influenced by Heinrich Kiepert, he pursued an interest in historical geography. His writings include *Sammlung arabischer Schriftstücke aus Zanzibar und Oman* (1892), *Arabic palaeography* (1905), *Wie Ägypten englisch wurde* (1915), *Bilder aus Palästina, Nord-Arabien und dem Sinai; 100 Bilder nach Photographien mit erläuterndem Text* (1916), *Arabien; Studien zur physikalischen und historischen*

Geographie des Landes (1923). He died in 1939. Fück, p. 316; GV; Hanisch; Kornrumpf², vol. 2; Kürschner, 1926-1935; *Wer ist's*, 1909-1912; ZKO

Morizot, Jean, born 20th cent., his writings include *L'Algérie kabylisée* (1962), *Les Kabyles; propos d'un témoin* (Paris, Centre de hautes études d'administration musulmane, 1985), and *Aurès, ou le Mythe de la montagne rebelle* (1991). *Livres* disponibles, 2004; ZKO

de **Morla**, Vidal, pseud., 1892-1981 *see* García Figueras, Tomás

Morley, Grace Louise (McCann), born in 1900, she studied at the University of California as well as at Paris and Grenoble. She was a historian of art, who in 1934 established the San Francisco Museum of Art. Involved since the early 1940s in museum projects of international scope, she was the first head of the Museum Division of Unesco. She was a sometime director of the National Museum, New Delhi, and a founder of the International Council of Museums, Regional Agency in Asia, New Delhi. Her writings include *Le Sentiment de la nature en France dans la première moitié du dix-septième siècle* (Nemours, 1926). She died in Berkeley, Calif. in 1985. BioIn, 15 (1); BlueB, 1976; IntWW, 1974/75-1983; Note; NYT, 26 January 1985, p. 26, col. 4; WhAm, 8; WhoAmA, 1966-1978; WhoAmW, 1958/59

Morley, Sylvanus Griswold, born 23 February 1878 at Templeton, Mass., he graduated in 1898 from Tufts College, and received a Ph.D. in 1902. He was a scholar of Romance languages and successively taught Spanish in Massachusetts, Colorado, New Mexico, and California. He died in 1970. BioIn, 9 (2); ConAu, 5-8; DrAS, 1969 F; LC; WhE&EA

Morley, William Hook, born in 1815, he was called to the bar from Middle Temple in 1840. As a notable Arabic and Persian scholar, he became connected with appeal cases from India. A member of the Royal Asiatic Society, he was since 1859 a librarian to the Society. In 1838, he discovered a manuscript of Rashīd al-Dīn Fadl Allāh's *Jāmi' al-tawārīkh*. His writings include *Desciptive catalogue of the historical manuscripts in the Arabic and Persian languages, preserved in the Library of the R.A.S. of Great Brtain and Ireland* (1854), *Administration of justice in British India* (1858), and he edited *The History of the Atábeks of Syria and Persia*, of Mirkhond (1848). He died in London, 21 May 1860. Boase; BritInd (2); Buckland; DNB, vol. 22; ZKO

Mornand, Félix, born in 1815 at Mâcon (Saône-et-Loire), France, he studied at Lyon. In 1833, he was attached as a secretary to the Commission d'enquête de l'Algérie, and in the following year he entered the service of the Ministère de la Guerre, a post which he resigned in 1844 in order to pursue an interest in literature. His writings include *La Vie arabe* (1855), *En peu partout* (1857), and he was a joint author of *Tableau historique, politique et pittorique de la Turquie et de la Russie* (1854). He died in Paris on 16 June 1867. Dantes 1; Hoefer; Vapereau; ZKO

Mornet, J., colonel, born in 1877, he graduated in 1897 from the École polytechnique, and from the École d'application de Fontainebleau in 1901. In 1903, he was sent to the Ivory Coast to prepare railway construction. Until the first World War he was involved in the planning of the track from Brazzaville to the coast. After the war, he returned to West Africa on a similar project of communication between the Mediterranean and Niger. He was a vice-president of the Société de géographie commerciale de Marseille. He died in an accident on 22 March 1948. *Hommes et destins*, vol. 9, pp. 332-33; Note about the author

Morony, Michael Gregory, born 30 September 1939, he received a Ph.D. in 1972 from the University of California, Los Angeles, for *Transition and continuity in seventeenth-century Iraq*. He was a professor in the Department of History, U.C.L.A., a post which he still held in 2000. His writings include *Iraq after the Muslim conquest* (1984), and he translated *Between civil wars*, from the Arabic history of al-Tabarī (1987). *MESA Roster of members*, 1977-1990; NatFacDr, 1995-2000; Selim

Morozova, Anna Stepanovna, born 18 February 1898 at Fergana, she went to school in Tashkent and studied at the Central Asian State University. She was an ethnographer. Her writings include Машинная декоративная вышивка Узбекистана (1960), and she edited Ковры народов Средней Азии (1970), and *Die Teppiche der Völker Mittelasiens im späten XIX. und XX. Jahrhundert* (1970). UzbekSE

Morpurgo, Giulio, born 9 February 1865 at Görz (Gorizia), Austria, he was a director of a private chemical laboratory in Triest, and editor-in-chief of the *Giornale di chimica farmaceutice e affini*, Triest, from 1895 to 1906. A teacher at the Università commerciale, Triest, since 1901 (and director since 1926), he also served as a director of the Musei commerciali (Handelsmuseum) and the Camera del commercio, Triest, 1906-1920. His writings, both in German and Italian, include *L'organizzazione et lo scope dei Musei commerciali* (Trieste, 1906), and *I prodotti del Levante* (Trieste, 1925). Chi è, 1931

Morpurgo, Giuseppe, born 16 July 1887 at Ancona, Italy, he was a teacher successively at Perugia and Torino. His writings include *Novelle del trecento* (1920), and *Italia, Francia, Tunisia; la condizione giuridica degli italiani in Tunisia* (Livorno, 1938). Chi è, 1931, 1936|

Morpurgo, Victor (Vittorio), born at Triest, Austria, he studied at Pisa, where he also received a doctorate in 1828. Since 1838 he was a practising physician in Paris, and was also attached to the Turkish legation, supervising Turkish students in France on Turkish scholarships. He was a sometime chief surgeon at the central hospital in Cairo. His writings include *Politique de la Russie en Orient; avenir de la Turquie* (1854), and *Considerations sur la question d'Orient à la Chambre des députés* (1859). He died in Paris in 1856. IndBiltal (1); Wininger

Morrell, Philip Edward, born 4 June 1870 at Oxford, he was educated at Eton and graduated from Balliol College, Oxford. He became a solicitor to the University. In 1906 he was elected a member of Parliament. His writings include *The Rural problem* (1913). He died in 1943. BritInd (2); Who was who, 4

Morrill, Warren Thomas, born 5 November 1929 at Portland, Me., he received a Ph.D. in 1961 from the University of Chicago for *Two urban cultures of Calabar, Nigeria*. He was since 1970 a professor of anthropology, and a sometime chairman of department, at Pennsylvania State University, University Park, Pa., a post which he still held in 1995. AmM&WSc, 1973 S; AmM&WSc, 1976 P; NatFacDr, 1995; Unesco

Morris, Colin, born 16 September 1928, he was associated with Pembroke College, Oxford, before became a professor of medieval history in the University of Southampton. His writings include *The Discovery of the individual, 1050-1200* (1972), and *The Papal monarchy; the Western Church from 1050 to 1250* (1989). LC; Note about the author

Morris, Harold Stephen, born 22 March 1913 at Weymouth, Dorset, England, he gained degrees at London and Edinburgh, and became successively a solicitor at the Supreme Court of Justice, England, a research fellow at the Colonial Social Science Research Council, Sarawak, and in the East African Social Science Research Institute Kampala, Uganda. He subsequently became a lecturer at the London School of Economics. Unesco

Morris, James A., born in 1918 he was in 1960 a professor of economics in the University of South Carolina at Columbia. Since 1948 he was a labour arbitrator on panels of the American Arbitration Association and the Federal Mediation Service. In 1953-54 he was a visiting professor at Oxford University, and in 1956-57 he was a special economic advisor to the Director, United States Operation Mission in Turkey. His writings include *South Carolina, a location for the woolen and worsted industry* (1950), and *Woolen and worsted manufacturing in the southern Piedmont* (1952). LC; Note

Morris, L. P., born about 1935, he received his Ph.D. in 1969 from the School of Slavonic and East European Studies, London, for *Anglo-Russian relations in Central Asia, 1873-1887*. He became a lecturer in history in the University of Exeter. His writings include *Eastern Europe since 1945* (1984). Sluglett

Morrison, Barrie McAcra, born in 1930, he took degrees at the University of Saskatchewan, and Oxford, and received his Ph.D. in 1966 from the University of Chicago for his thesis, *The property-transfer inscriptions of Bengal from the fifth to the thirteenth century*. Thereafter he was a professor in the Department of Asian Studies in the University of British Columbia, Vancouver, B.C. His writings include *Political centers and cultural regions in early Bengal* (1970). In 1991 he was a joint author of *Rice science and development policies*. DrASCan, 1983; LC

Morrison, George, fl. 1966, he was a joint author of *History of Persian literature* (Leiden, 1981).

Morrison, Godfrey, born 20th cent., he was associated with the Minority Rights' Group, London. He was an editor of *Africa confidential*. His writings include *Eritrea and the southern Sudan* (1971), and he was a joint author of *Eritrea and Tigray* (1983). Note about the author

Morrison, Michael Andrew, born 19th cent., his writings, partly under the pseudonym Oliver M. Norris, include *The Stundists; the story of a great religious revolt* (London, 1893). BLC

Morrison, Stanley Andrew, born 19th cent., he was a missionary of the Church Missionary Society in Cairo, and since 1920 engaged in evangelistic work among the Muslim students of Cairo. He also served as chairman of the Egypt Inter-Mission Council, and as a secretary of the Committee of Liaison between the Non-Moslem Communities in Egypt. His writings include *Religious liberty in the Near East* (1948), *Middle East survey* (1954), and *Middle East tensions* (1954). Note about the author

Morrison, William David, born 19 August 1940 at Philadelphia, Pa., he graduated in 1962 from Princeton University, and in 1965 from Yale University, New Haven, Conn. After bar admission in New York and California he practised law. WhoAm, 1994-2003; WhoAmL, 1983-87

Morrisson, Christian, born 20 October 1936, he was a sometime head of the research programme in the Organization for Economic Co-operation, Development Centre, Paris. His writings include *Questions financières aux XVIIIe et XIXe siècles* (1967), *La Répartition des reserves dans les pays du*

Tiers-monde (1968), *Ajustement et équité au Maroc* (1991), and its translation, *Adjustment and equity in Morocco* (1992); and he was a joint author of *Justice et redistribution* (1977), *Economic policies and agricultural performance* (1985), *Long-term growth in Tunisia* (1996); and he edited *Dépenses d'éducation, de santé et réduction de la pauvreté en Afrique de l'Est* (2002). LC; Livres disponibles, 2004

de **Mortillet**, Adrien, born in 1853 at Genève, the son of Gabriel de Mortillet, he was an honorary president of the Société historique de France. His writings include *Les Monuments mégalithiques de la Lozère* (1905); he was a joint author, with his father, of *Musée préhistorique* (1881); and he edited *Homme préhistorique* (1903-1927). He died in 1931. BN

de **Mortillet**, Louis Laurent Marie *Gabriel*, born 29 August 1821 at Meylan (Isrère), France, he was educated at a Jesuit institution in Chambéry and completed his study in Paris at the Musée d'histoire naturelle and the Conservatoire des arts et métiers. He was an archaeologist, geologist, and a political thinker. A participant in the revolution of 1848, he had to spend a few years in exile in Savoie and Switzerland. He organized and classified the museum collections at Genève and Annecy (Haute Savoie). Since 1868 he was attached to the Musée des antiquités nationales de Saint-Germain-en-Laye. Günther Junghans wrote *Gabriel de Mortillet, 1821-1898; eine Biographie* (1987). He died in 1898. DcScB; GdeEnc; IndexBFr² (4); Master (1); Vapereau

Mortimer, Edward, born in 1943, he was in 1981 a foreign special and editorial writer on the *Times* of London. His writings include *France and the Africans, 1944-1960* (1969), *The News bulletins of the Committee for the Defence of Political Prisoners in Iran* (1979), *The Rise of the French Communist Party, 1920-1947* (1984), and *Roosevelt's children; tomorrow's world leaders* (1987). LC; Note

Mortimer, Mildred Palmer, born about 1935 at New York, she received a Ph.D. in 1969 from Columbia University, New York, for *The Algerian novel in French, 1945-1965* and subsequently became a professor of French and Italian at the University of Colorado, Boulder, a post which she still held in 2000. Her writings include *Mouloud Mammeri, écrivain algérien* (1982), and *Journeys through the French African novel* (1990). MESA Roster of members, 1990 NatFacDr, 1995-2000; Selim

Mortimer, Robert Amsden, born 16 October 1938 at N.Y.C., he received a Ph.D. in 1968 from Columbia University, New York, for *Foreign policy and its role in nation-building in Algeria*. He was appointed in 1966 a professor of political science at Haverford (Pa.) College, a post which he still held in 2000. His writings include *The Third World coalition in international politics* (1980). AmM&WSc, 1973 S, 1978 S; MESA Roster of memvers, 1990; NatFacDr, 1995-2000; Selim

Morton, Alexander (*Sandy*) H., born about 1940, he was certainly from 1994 to his retirement a senior lecturer in Persian at the School of Oriental and African Studies, London, where his research centred on Islamic Persia. His writings include *A Catalogue of early Islamic glass stamps in the British Museum* (1985), and he edited and translated *Mission to the Lord Sophy of Persia, 1539-1542*, of Michel Membre (1993). Note about the author; Private

Moscati, Sabatino, born 24 November 1922 at Roma, he was an archaeologist and linguistic, specializing in Semitic languages. Since 1954 he held the chair of Semitic philology at the Università di Roma. He excavated in Israel and in North Africa. His writings include *Ancient Semitic civilizations* (1957), *The face of the ancient Orient* (1960), *Lezione di linguistiche semitica* (1960), and *L'ancora d'argente* (1989). He died in Roma on 8 September 1997. Au&Wr, 1963; Chi e, 1961; ConAu, 77; IntAu&W, 1976-1977; WhoItaly, 1958, 1988; WhoWor, 1978; WRMEA 16, no. 4 (December 1997), p. 136

Moscati Steindler, Gabriella, born 20th cent., her writings include *Hayyim Habšuš, immagine dello Yemen* (Napoli, Istituto Orientale, 1976). ZKO

Moschonas, Theodores Demetriou, born in 1892, he was a librarian of the Patriarchal Library of Alexandria, Egypt. His writings include Κουρτέα ντε Αρτζες και αλλες ταξιδιωτικες ιστορίες (Alexandria, 1960), Κασρ αλ Χάμσα και αλλα στιγμιότυμα αλο τεν Ἰσπανία (Alexandria, 1963), Ἀγγλία και Ἀγγλοι (Alexandria, 1964), and *Mélanges historiques* (Alexandrie, 1964). He died in 1983. GrBioInd (2); LC

Moschopoulos, Nikephoros, born in 1871, his writings include *La question de Thrace* (Athènes, 1922), *La Presse dans la renaissance balkanique* (Athènes, 1931), *La Question de l'Épire du nord* (1946), *La Question de Palestine et le patriarcat de Jérusalem* (Athenes, 1948), *La Terre Sainte; essai sur l'histoire politique et diplomatique des lieux saintes de la chrétienté* (Athènes, 1956), and Ἱστορία της Ἑλληνικης Ἐπαναστάσεως κατα τους Τούρκους ιστοριογράφους εν αντιπαραβολη και προς τους Ἑλληνας ιψτορικούς (Athens, 1960). NUC, 1956-67

Mosconas, Th. D., 1892-1983 *see* Moschonas, Theodores Demetriou

Mosely, Philip Edward, born 21 September 1905 at Westfield, Mass., he graduated in 1926 from Harvard University, Cambridge, Mass. After research in Moscow (1930-32) and the Balkans (1935-1936), he taught international relations at Princeton and Cornell universities. He also served as adviser to U.S. delegations at international conferences. His writings include *Russian diplomacy and the opening of the Eastern question in 1838 and 1839* (1934), *Face to face with Russia* (1948), *Russia after Stailin* (1955), and *The Soviet Union since Khrushchev* (1966). He died in 1972. NYT, 14 January 1972, p. 36, cols. 1-2; WhAm, 5

Moser, Charles Kroth, born 27 August 1877 at Marion, Va., he graduated in 1901 from the University of California, and spent a few years as a sports writer and reporter in San Francisco. He was later admitted to the bar and practised in San Francisco, and from 1904 to 1909 he was an editorial writer on the *Washington Post*. He then entered the U.S. Foreign Service and served as consul at Aden, Harbin, Tiflis, with special detail in Constantinople. When he retired in 1947, he joined the staff of the Bureau of Foreign and Domestic Commerce, first as assistant chief, and later as chief of the Far Eastern Division. He also lectured at many universities and colleges and for a number of years gave courses at the School of Foreign Service, Georgetown University, Washington, D.C. His writings include *The Cotton textile industry of Far Eastern countries* (1930), and *The United States in India's trade* (1939). He died in 1968. Foreign commerce weekly, 29 (11 October 1947), p. 15; Shavit; WhAm 5

Moser, Heinrich (Henri), born 1 (13) May 1844 at Villa Charlottenfels, in Neuhausen, Kanton Schaffhausen, Switzerland he was a Swiss traveller with a passion for the unknown rather than scientific exploration. He made two journeys to Tashkent, 1868 and 1883, and spent some years in Central Asia immediately after the Russian conquest. He was a guest at the courts of St. Petersburg, Wien, and Paris, where he advanced the interests of Bosnia and Herzegovina. He bequeathed his private collection to Historisches Museum, Bern. His writings include *À travers l'Asie centrale; la steppe Kirghize, le Turkestan russe, Boukhara, le pays des Turcomans et la Perse* (1885), its translation, *Durch Central-Asien* (1888), *L'Irrigation en Asie centrale* (1894)., *À travers la Bosnie et l'Herzégovine* (1895), *La Bosnie-Herzégovine au seuil du XXe siècle* (1995), and *Collection Henri Moser-Charlottenfels* (1912). In 1992, Roger N. Balsinger and Ernst J. Kläy edited *Bei Schah, Emir und Khan; Henri Moser-Charlottenfels, 1844-1923*. He died in Vevey, 15 August 1923. Carnoy 11², pp. 70-72; Henze; HiBioLexCH, vol. 5, p. 171ª; Sezgin

Moser-Charlottenfels, Heinrich (Henri), 1844-1923 *see* Moser, Heinrich (Henri)

Moshaver, Ziba, born 12 February 1952, she received a doctorate in 1987 from Oxford University for *Nuclear weapons proliferation in the Indian Subcontinent*, a work which was published in 1991. She was a Stanford Lecturer in international relations at Magdalen College, Oxford, a visiting scholar at the University of São-Paulo, Brazil, and a research fellow of the École des hautes études en sciences sociales, Paris. LC; Note; ZKO

Mosher, Lawrence Foryth, born 12 July 1929 at Los Angeles, he graduated in 1952 from Stanford University, Palo Alto, Calif., and became a journalist. In 1967, he was the Beirut bureau chief of the Copley News Service; in 1977-79, writer-in-residence at the Foreign Service School, Georgetown University, Wsshington, D.C.; and in 1989/90, editor of the *Middle East insight*. WhoAm, 1994-1998; WhoE, 1991/92

Moshin, Vladimir A., 1894-1987 *see* Mošin, Vladimir A.

Moshkova, Valentina Georgievna, born in 1902 at Fergana, Uzbekistan, she graduated in 1925 from the Central Asian Oriental Institute, Tashkent. She was an ethnographer and a doctoral candidate when she died in 1952. Her writings include Ковры народов Средней Азии конца деевятнадцатого до начала двадцатого веко (1970), and its translation, *Die Teppiche der Völker Mittelasiens im späten XIX. und frühen XX. Jahrhundert* (1977), and *Carpets of the people of Central Asia of the late XIX and XX centuries* (1996). ZKO

Mošin (Мошин), Vladimir A., born 26 September 1894 at Petrograd, he studied at his home town as well as in Kiev. In 1921, he became a secondary school teacher in Yugoslavia; in 1928, he received his doctorate at the the Philosophical Faculty, Zagreb; and in 1930, he successively became a lecturer in Byzantine studies at Skopje, Beograd, and again Skopje. From 1947 to 1959 he was a director of the Archives of the Yugoslav Academy of Sciences, Zagreb. His writings include *Ćirilski rukopisi Jugolavenske Akademije* (1952-55), *Δουλικον ζεγάριον* (1941), and he was joint author of *Filigranes des XIIIe et XIVe ss.*(1957). He died in Skopje on 3 February 1987. EnJug²; HL

Moskalenko, Vladimir Nikolaevich, born 21 or 22 January 1932 in Russia, he graduated in 1955 from the Faculty of History, Moscow State University, and received a doctorate in 1967 for a monograph. He was since 1967 associated with the Oriental Institute in the Soviet Academy of Sciences. His writings include *Проблемы современного Пакистана* (1970), he was joint author of *Пакистан; трудный путь развития* (1979), and he was joint editor of *Пакистанское общество; экономическое развитие и социальная структура* (1987). Miliband; Miliband²; OSK

Moskalev, Vladimir Sergeevich, born in 1906 at Lugansk (Luhans'k/Voroshilovgrad), Ukraine, he graduated in 1934 from the Moscow Oriental Institute; he received his first degree in 1953 and his doctorate in 1955. Since 1959 he was associated with Tashkent State University. His writings include the Urdu dictionary, *Русско-урду словарь* (Tashkent, 1943). He died 14 July 1982. Miliband; Miliband²

Moss-Blundell, A. S., fl. 1924-26 *see* Blundell, A. S. Moss

Mossa, Vico, born 15 October 1914 at Serramanna (Cagliari), Italy, he graduated in architecture. He practised his profession and served as a part-time lecturer at the Università di Cagliari. His writings include *Architettura religiosa minore in Sardegna* (1953), *Architettura domestica in Sardegna* (1953), *Architetture sassaresi* (1965), and *Dal gotico al barocco in Sardegna* (1982). Chi scrive

Mosse, Werner Eugen Emil, born 5 February 1918 at Berlin, he graduated from Corpus Christi College, Cambridge, and successively taught Russian history at London, Glasgow, and Norwich. His writings include *Alexander II and the modernization of Russia* (1958), *The European powers and the German questions, 1848-71* (1958), and *The Rise and fall of the Crimean system, 1855-71* (1963). Au&Wr, 1963; BioHbDtE; ConAu, 9-12; IntAu&W, 1976, 1977, 1982

Mosséri, Victor M, born in 1873, he was an agronomist and, in 1916, resident in Cairo and a member of the Société sultanieh d'économie politique, de statistique et de législation. His writings include *Contribution à l'étude des moyens de destruction des insectes ravageurs du cottonier* (1910), *L'Utilisation du réservoire souterrain de l'Égypte* (1914), and he was a joint author of *Les Constructions rurales en Égypte* (1921). He died in 1928. Note about the author; NUC, pre-1956

Mössner, Jörg Manfred, born 1 October 1941 at Köln, Germany, he received a Dr.jur. in 1968 from the Universität Köln for a study of international law in the Barbary states entitled *Die Völkerrechtspersönlichkeit und die Völkerrechtspraxis der Barbareskenstaaten*. He was successively a professor of international law at the universities of Köln, Hamburg, and Osnabrück; he also served for fifteen years as a judge. Kürschner, 1976-2003; Schwarz; Wer ist wer, 1994/94-2003/2004

Mostaert, Antoine, born 10 August 1881 at Bruges, Belgium, he early in life received a good training in classical philology. When after his novitiate he began to study Chinese as a seminarian of the Congregatio Immaculati Cordis Mariae, commonly known as the Scheut Society for Foreign Missions, his linguistic talents as applied to this language proved to be such that he was urged to study Mongolian as well. In 1905, he was commissioned to China as a missionary. There, his superiors, taking into account his knowledge of Mongolian, decided to sent him to Boro Balgasu in the south Ordos region, where a Roman Catholic mission was located. He remained there until 1925 when he left for Peking where he lived until 1948. His writings include *Dictionnaire ordos* (1941-44). He died in Arlington, Va., on 2 September 1971. Harvard journal of Asiatic studies, 19 (June 1956), pp. vii-xiv

da **Mota**, Avelino Teixeira, born about 1900, he was a naval officer whose writings include *Guiné Portuguesa* (Lisboa, 1954), *A cartografia antiga da Africa Central e a travessia entre Angola e Moçambique, 1500-1860* (Lourenço Marques, 1964), and he was a joint author of the six-volume *Portugaliae monumenta cartographica* (Lisboa, 1960). He died 1 April 1982. ConAu, 106; LC

Motalová, Ludmila, born 22 April 1935 at Kroměříž (Kremsier), Czechoslovakia, she was an Armenian scholar whose writings include *Arménská literatura, její tradice a současnost* (Praha, 1972). She died in Praha on 29 August 1975. Filipský, pp. 334-335; OSK

Mote, Victor Lee, born 2 November 1941 at Corpus Christi, Texas, he graduated in 1964 from the University of Denver, and received his Ph.D. in 1971 from the University of Washington for *The geography of air pollution in the U.S.S.R.* From 1971 to his retirement he taught in the Department of Political science, University of Houston, Texas. His writings include *An Industrial atlas of the Soviet successor states* (1994), and he was joint author of *Gateway to Siberian resources* (1977). AmM&WSc, 1973 S; AmM&WSc, 1976 P; NatFacDr, 1995-2004; Schoeberlein

Moti Chandra, 1909-1974 *see* Chandra, Moti

Mott, John R., born 25 May 1865 at Livingston Manor, N.Y., given no middle name - he added early the initial R[aleigh]. After graduating from Cornell University, Itahaca, N.Y., in 1888, he entered on a life-long lay ministry through his enthusiasm for, and involvement in, the student YMCA. In 1895, he founded the World's Student Christian Movement, the nursery of the ecumenical movement of the twentieth century. From 1900 until 1941 he made repeated tours throughout the world in the interest of world mission to Christianity. He was a gifted orator and hundreds of his addresses were published, apart from a score of books. In 1946 he shared the Nobel Peace Prize with Emily Greene Balch. He died in Orlando, Fla., 31 January 1955. DAB; Master (6)

Mott-Smith, May, born 17 March 1879 at Honolulu, Hawaii. She spent her early life in Hawaii, studied art in Paris, and became an accomplished jewelry and medal designer who exhibited for seven consecutive years in the Paris Salon. In the 1920s, she travelled widely into places that were still free from a stream of tourists. She travelled alone two years around Africa which she described in *Africa from port to port* (1930). She was the third lone American woman to reach Kabul by motor-car over the Khyber Pass in 1929. During the Second World War she served in the Office of Strategic Services. She died in New York City, 5 June 1952. Shavit - Africa; WhNAA, 1927-28

Motte, Thomas, born 18th cent., he was a British traveller who in 1766 visited Sambalpur, northern Orissa, on behalf of Lord Clive to find out whether the diamond trade could be channelled by way of Calcutta. Henze; Note about the author

Motyliński, Kalasanty Gustaw Adolf, 1854-1907 *see* Calassanti-Motylinski, Adolphe de

Motzki, Harald, born 25 August 1948 at Berlin, he studied at the universities of Bonn, Paris (Ecole pratique des Hautes études), Köln, and again Bonn, where he received a Dr.phil. in 1978 for a study of non-Muslim minorities in nineteenth century Egypt and the French expedition entitled *Dimma und égalité; die nicht muslimischen Minderheiten Ägyptens in der zweiten Hälfte des 18. Jahrhunderts und die Expedition Bonapartes, 1798-1801*, and a Dr.habil. in 1989 for *Die Anfänge der islamischen Jurisprudenz*, a work which was published in 1991. In the same year, he was appointed a university *hoofddocent* at the Katholieke Universiteit Nijmegen, the Netherlands. He was the 1980 recipient of the Heinz-Maier-Leibnitz-Preis. Private

Motzkin, Aryeh Leo, born in 1934, he received his Ph.D. in 1965 from the University of Pennsylvania for *The Arabic correspondence of Judge Elijah and his family; papers from the Cairo Geniza*. He was in 1970 a senior lecturer in Arabic at the University of Haifa, and in 1995 in the Department of Philosophy, Boston University. His writings include *Mavo le-limude ha-Islam* (Jerusalem, 1967). Harvard College Library; Selim

Mouat, Frederic John, born in 1816 at Maidstone, England, he was educated at London, Paris, and Edinburgh, receiving an M.D. in 1839. He served in India as Local Government Inspector and Deputy Inspector-General, Bengal Army for many years. He was a professor of medicine, and first physician of the Meidcal College, Calcutta. From 1890-92 he served as president of the Royal Statistical Society. His writings include *Rough notes on a trip to Reunion, Mauritius, and Ceylon* (1852), and *History of the Statistical Society of London* (1885). He died in London, 12 January 1897. Buckland; Henze; Riddick

Mougel (Mougel-Bey), Dieudonne Eugène, born 19th cent., he was a French mining engineer who, since 1842, worked for twenty years unsuccessfully at the construction of a barrage in the Nile Delta. He subsequently entered the service of Midhat Paşa in Baghdad. His trace is lost after an article in 1869. Kornrumpf; Kornrumpf², vol. 2

Mougenot, Fabien, born 19th cent., he was a French captain whose writings include *Mes gibernes* (Paris, 1911), and *Un sabre; histoire contemporaine* (Paris, 1913). BN

Moughtin, J. *Cliff*, born 20th cent., he received an M.A. in 1965 from the University of Liverpool for *Traditional architecture of the Hausa people*. He delivered his inaugural lecture before Queen's University of Belfast on 3 May 1972, entitled *Planning for people*. He pursued a career in under-developed countries, before he joined the Department of Architecture and Planning, University of Nottingham. His writings include *Hausa architecture* (1985), *Who needs development? Planning with the poor in Third World countries* (1992), and *Urban design; green dimensions* (1996). Note

Mougin, Louis, born in 1910 at Lalla Marnia, he graduated in 1931 from the École polytechnique and entered the French Army. After a brief assignment to an artillery unit, he was soon tranferred to Rafai, on the Riff frontier, as an officer with the Service des Affaires indigènes. There he was mobilized in 1939, but since he rejected the armistice, he first lost his office in Clermont-Ferrand and later his post altogether. His involuntary leisure gave him a chance to complete his history degree and to work on his literary Arabic. When the war was over, he took leave fom the army and turned to economic ques-tions. In the service of Unesco and financial institutions, he accomplished missions in the Third World, staying for considerable periods in Alger, Dakar, Yaoundé, Brazzaville, and Tananarive. In 1965, he finally settled down in Aix-en-Provence, where he became a collaborator of Roger Le Tourneau, whom he had know from his Moroccan days. After the latter's death, he completed his unfinished translation of al-Zayyānī's chronicle, *Histoire de la dynasty Sa'dite*. He died after months of suffering in July 1980. ROMM, 31 i (1981), pp. 5-6

Mougin, Louis Jean Laurent, he was born on 10 November 1873 at Mostaganem, Algeria. After passing through the military college of Saint-Cyr, which he had entered in 1894, he received a commission as *sous-lieutenant* on 1 October 1896. From 1902 to 1903 he was with the Service des Affaires indigènes de l'Algérie. The following five years where spent with the Mission militaire du Maroc before returning to Algeria for a last time. In 1911, he became a member of the Cabinet du ministère de la guerre. In the post-war era he accomplished important missions in Syra and Turkey (1920) and Morocco (1925). In 1928, he resigned from active service when he had reached the position of Chef du cabinet militaire du Résident général at Rabat. Peyronnet, p. 860

Mouliéras, Auguste (Augustin) St-Jean, he was born on 22 December 1855 at Tlemcen, Algeria. After study at Bône, he became *interprète auxiliaire de 2e classe* (5 November 1875), and served at Takitount (1876-1877), Batna (1878), Algiers (1879), Tunisia (1881-1883), and Géryville (1884). Although he had advanced to the rank of *interprète de 3e classe* in 1882, he left the *Service de l'interprétriat* three years later in order to go into teaching at Oran, where he came to hold the chair of Arabic. He published numerous translations, articles and monographs which include *Manuel algérien: grammaire* (1888), *Nouvelle chrestomathie arabe* (1889), *Le Maroc inconnu: vingt-deux ans d'explorations dans cette contrée mystérieuse de 1872 à 1893* (1895-1899), *Une tribu zénète antimusulmane au Maroc* (1904). Féraud, p. 368; Peyronnet, p. 376

Moulin, René, born in 1880, he was an editor of *La Revue hebdomadaire*. His own writings include *La Guerre des neutres* (1915), *L'Année des diplomates, 1919* (1920), *La Paix assassinée* (1941), and its translation, *Der Mord am Frieden* (1943). BN; NUC, pre-1956

Mountjoy, Alan B., born about 1920, he graduated in 1940 from the University of Reading, where he also received his M.A. in 1949 for *Geographical features in the future development of Egypt*. He was a reader in his field in the University of London, and retired after thirty-nine years of service in the summer of 1985. Between 1967 and 1970, he acted as the external examiner in the Department of Geography in the University of Khartoum and visited Sudan each year. His writings include *Industrialization and underdeveloped countries* (1963), and he was joint author of *Africa; a geographical study* (1965). In 1989 he was honoured by *The Geography of urban rural interaction in developing countries; essays for Alan B. Mountjoy*. Note about the author; Sluglett

Mouradgea d'Ohsson (Мураджа д'Оссонъ/Оссонъ), Ignatius, born 31 July 1740 at Constantinople to Armenian parents. In 1815, he became a Lutheran. In 1763, he was appointed a secretary of the Swedish embassy at the Ottoman Court. A first dragoman since 1768, he was married in 1774 to Eva Couleli, the daughter of a rich Armenian banker. In 1775, he was nominated secretary to the King, ennobled in 1780, and in 1782 received the title *chargé d'affaires*. For his succesful negociation of a treaty of peace and commerce between Sweden and the Porte, he was awarded a decoration. He resigned in 1784 and went to Paris, where he published the first two volumes of his *Tableau général de l'Empire othoman* (1787-1820), and its translations, *Oriental antiquities, and general view of the Othoman customs, laws, and ceremonies* (1783), *Vollständige Beschreibung des Othomanischen Reiches* (1788), and Полная картина Оттоманской имперіи (1795). In 1787, he was given permission to take the name d'Ohsson; in 1791, he departed for Constantinople by way of Wien; in 1795, he was first nominated *chargé d'affaires* and then minister plenipotentiary. His French leanings, however, resulted in an unlimited suspension and he returned to France in 1799. After the break-off of relations between Sweden and France in 1804, he received permission from both governments to retire to the châteaux de Bièvre near Paris, where he died on 27 August 1807. AnaBrit; Dantès 1; Master (1); NYPL; *Revue de l'Orient*, n.s., 4 (1856), pp. 158-167; Gunnar Jarring in SMK, vol 25, pp. 753-755

Mourant, Arthur Ernest, born in 1904 on Jersey, he was educated at Voctoria College, Jersey, Exeter College, Oxford, and St. Bartholomew's Hospital, London; he gained a Ph.D. as well as a medical doctorate. He was a director of the Serological Population Laboratory. His writings include *The Distribution of the human blood groups* (1954), he was a joint author of *The ABO blood groups; comprehensive tables* (1958), and he was a joint editor of *Man and cattle* (1963). He died 29 August 1994. IntWW, 1974/75-1994/95; Who, 1968-1994; WrDr, 1976/78-1996/98

Mourey, Charles, born in 1872 at Marseille, he was a sometime head of the commerce section in the French Office Colonial, and he edited the journal *L'Année coloniale*, Paris, from 1899 to 1905. He was a joint author of *L'expansion française et la formation territoriale* (Paris, 1910). IndexBFr² (1)

Mourgues, Gaston, born in 1895, he was a joint author of *Le Moyen Niger et sa bouche dans la région de Tombouctou* (Paris, 1933). NUC, pre-1956

Mourier, Jules, born in 1846, his writings include *L'Art religieusx au Caucase* (Paris, 1887), *Contes et légendes du Caucase* (Paris, 1888), *Guide au Caucase* (Paris, 1894), *L'Art au Caucase* (Paris, 1896), and *Ivan Serguévitch Tourguéneff à Spasskoé* (St. Petersbourg, 1889). BN; NUC, pre-1956

Mouriez, Paul, fl. 19th cent., his writings include *Des intérêts européens en Orient* (Marseille, 1852), *Histoire de Méhémet-Ali, vice-roi d'Égypte* (Marseille, 1855-58), *La Mer Rouge* (Paris, 1862), and *Les Guerres commerciales, 1486-1850* (Paris, 1863). BN

Mourin, Elie, *capitaine*, born 19th cent., his writings include *En Tunisie, 1885-1888; notes d'un chasseur à pied* (Nancy, 1891), and *Esai historique sur l'armée Russe* (Paris, 1889). BN

Mourin, Maxime, born in 1902, his writings include *Le Drame des états satellites de l'Axe, de 1939 à 1945* (1957), *Le Vatican et l'U.R.S.S.* (1965), its translation, *Der Vatikan und die Sowjetunion* (1967), *Les Relations franco-soviétique, 1917-1967* (1967), and *Reddition sans conditions* (1973). NUC

Mouskhéli, Michel, born in 1903, he was throughout the 1940s a professor at the Ecole française de droit, Cairo. His writings include *La Théorie juridique de l'état fédéral* (1931), *La Loi et le règlement* (1943), and he was a joint author of *L'Europe face au fédéralisme* (1949). He died in 1964. Note

Moussard, Paul, fl. 1924-1946, he was a joint author, with Henri Bruno, of *Répertoire alphabétique de la jurisprudence de la Cour d'appel de Rabat* (Casablanca, 1947). BN

Mousseron, Jean-Marc, born 20th cent., he received a doctorate in 1958 from the Université de Montpellier for *Contribution à l'analyse objective du droit breveté d'invention*, a trade edition of which was published in 1961 entitled *Le droit breveté d'invention*. He was a professor at the Faculté de droit, Montpellier, a professor at the Universität Heidelberg, and associated with the Centre de recherche sur le droit des affaires. His writings include *Producteurs, distributeurs, quelle concurrence?* (1986), and he was a joint author of *Les biens de l'entreprise* (1972), and *L'avant-contrat* (2001). Livres disponibles, 2004; Note about the author

de **Moustier**, Audéric, *comte*, born 12 June 1823 at Paris, he had finished his study, followed by travelling, when the revolution of 1848 broke out. He was nominated a battailon commander with the Garde nationale in the Département Seine-et-Marne. He subsequently was elected *conseiller général* of the same *département*, where he served successively until 1871. He was associated with the Société des agriculteurs de France. His writings include *Les Publications populaires en France* (Paris, 1863), *Chemins de fer départementaux de Seine-et-Marne* (Meaux, 1872), *Viaggio da Constantinopoli ad Efeso per l'interno dell'Asia Minore, Bitinia, Frigia, Lidia, Jonia* (Milano, 1873), and *Souvenirs et pensées* (Paris, 1890). Glaeser; Note about the author; ZKO

Mout, Marianne Elisabeth Henriette *Nicolette*, born 31 May 1945 at Wassenaar, the Netherlands, she studied at Amsterdam and received a doctorate in 1975 from the Rijksuniversiteit te Leiden for a study of Bohemia and the Netherlands in the sixteenth century entitled *Bohemen en de Nederlanden in de zestiende eeuw*. She was successively a professor of modern history at the universities of Utrecht and Leiden. Her writings include *"Het bataafse oor"; de lotgevallen van Erasmus' adagium "Ausris Batava" in de Nederlandse geschiedschrijving* (1993), *Die Kultur des Humanismus* (1998), and she was joint editor of *Bestuurders en geleerden* (1985). Brinkman's, 1971-1981; IntWW, 1991-2002

Mouterde, René, born 20 November 1880 at Tarare (Rhône), France, he entered the noviciate of the Society of Jesus at the age of eighteen in Aix-en-Provence. He spent two years studying literary subjects and three years philosophy at Laval and Jersey respectively. In 1905, he was assigned to Beirut, where he became a collaborator of Louis Jalabert. In 1908, he went to Britain, where he spent five years completing his religious training. Upon his return to Beirut, he became chancellor of the École de droit française. This appointment would have been permanent if it had not been for the Great War which kept him in France until 1919. The Turkish rule terminated, he found himself under French mandatory powers and returned to his post for another twenty-two years. In 1955 he resigned his last formal post as director of the Institut de Lettres Orientales. He was a joint author of *Dair-Solaib* (Beyrouth, 1939). He was found dead in his bed in the morning of 27 December 1961. Jalabert; *Mélanges* de l'Université Saint-Joseph, Beirouth, 38 (1962), pp. 1-9

Movers, Franz Carl, born 1806 at Coesfeld, Westphalia, he studied theology and Oriental languages at the Universität Münster. In 1829 he was ordained a Roman Catholic priest at Paderborn. Much later he became a professor of Old Testament exegesis at the Universität Breslau. His writings include *Kritische Untersuchungen über die biblische Chronik* (1834), *Loci quidam historiae canonis Veteris Testamenti illustrati* (1840), and *Das phönizische Alterthum* (1849-56). He died in Breslau in 1856. ADtB, vo. 22, pp. 417-18; BN; Fück, p. 195; Master (1)

Movsesian, Grair Oganesovich, born 9 October 1924 at Anzali, Caspian province of Persia, he graduated in 1951 from the Erivan Г.П.И.И.Я., and received his first degree in 1962 for a study of the Persian writer Bozorg Alawi, 1904-1997, entitled *Новеллистическое Бузурга Алави, 1930-1952*. He was since 1961 with the Oriental Institute in the Armenian Academy of Sciences. His writings include *Творчество Бозорга Аляви* (1980). Miliband; Miliband[2]

Mowat, Robert Case, born 11 May 1913 at Oxford, he received his D.Phil. in 1970 from Oxford University for *Lord Cromer and his successors in Egypt*. Since 1947, he was successively a senior lecturer in history at the Royal Naval College, Greenwich, University of Ibadan, and Oxford Polytechnic. His writings include *Climax of history* (1951), *Middle East perspective* (1958), *Ruin and resurgence, 1939-1965* (1968), and *Decline and renewal; Europe - ancient and modern* (1991). ConAu, 29-32; IntWW, 1977; Sluglett

Moyal, Munir Abdallah, fl. 1944 in Jaffa, he was a Palestinian who gained a doctorate at the Université de Marseille, and held a commission in the French cavalry. He subsequently was a correspondent for French newspapers in North Africa. Note about the author

Moyne, John Abel, born 6 July 1920 at Yazd, Persia, he received his Ph.D. in 1970 from Harvard University, Cambridge,Mass., for *Structure of verbal constructions in Persian*. Since 1971, he was a professor of computer science in N.Y.C. His writings include *Georgetown automatic translation* (1962), and *Understanding language* (1985). AmM&WSc, 1979 P, 1982 P, 1986, 1989, 1992; WhoAm, 1988-2003; WhoE, 1981-1995/96

Moynet, E., fl. 1860, his writings include *Il Volga, il mar Caspio e il mar Nero* (Milano, 1875). NUC

Moynihan, Daniel Patrick, born in 16 March 1927 at Tulsa, Okla., he was educated at City College of New York, Tufts University, and Fletcher School of Law and Diplomacy. He was a politician, university professor, and diplomat. His writings include *Beyond the melting pot* (1963), *On the law of nations* (1990), *Pandaemonium; ethnicity in international politics* (1993), *Secrecy; the American experience* (1998). He died in 2003. ConAu, 5-8, new rev. 43; IntAu&W, 1991-2004; IntWW, 1974/75-2002; Master (60); Who, 1983-2003; WhoAm, 1974-2003; WhoE, 1974-1993/94; WhoWor, 1974/75-2002; WrDr, 1980/82-2004

Mozley, Alan, born in 1904, his writings include *The Control of Bilharzia in Southern Rhodesia* (Salisbury, 1944), *Sites of infection; unstable areas of sources of parasitic diseases* (London, 1955), and *Reconnaissance; an approach to exploration* (1965). NUC

Mrkos, Josef, born 2 January 1869 at Malostovice, he studied Oriental languages and philosophy and received a doctorate in 1895 for a thesis on Sa'di's *Gulistan*. He died in Praha in 1927. Filipsky, p. 336

Mroz, Edward Anthony, born 24 March 1913 at Morawianki, Poland, he fought in the second World War and subsequently studied at Paris and den Haag. He was attached to international organizations and was a sometime professor at the universities of Moncton, N.B., and Notre Dame, Ind. His writngs include *Return to disengagement in Europe* (1964). AmM&WSc, 1973 S; WhoAm, 1976

Mrozek, Anna, born 20th cent., her writings include *Koran a kultura arabska* (Warszawa, 1967), *Średniowieczna filozofia arabsk* (Warszawa, 1967), and *Islam a naród w Afryca; Somalia, Sudan, Libia* (Warszawa, 1973). OSK

Mrozek, Antoni *Bogusłav*, he was born on 9 June 1930 at Poznań (Posen). After completing his studies with two doctorates, he was appointed a professor at Uniwersytet Warszawski in 1972.. His writings include *Pakistan, przeszłość* (1966), *Historia najnowsza Azji poludiowo-wschodniej, 1917-1970* (1973), and *Indie, Pakistan, Bangladesz; studia historyczno-polityczne* (1976). KtoPolsce, 1993

Mrozowska, Alina, born 20th cent., her writings include *Tureckie stroje i seny rodzajowe* (1991), and with Tadeus Majda she jointly wrote *Rysunki kostimów tureckich z kolekcji króla Stanisława Augusta w Gabinecie Rycim Biblioteki Uniwersyteckie w Warszawie* (1973). ZKO

Much, Mathäus (Matheus), born 18 October 1832 at Göpfritz an der Wild, Austria, he studied law at the universitles of Wien and Graz and received a Dr.jur. in 1858. He entered the public service but resigned two years later to manage his father-in-law's zither factory. Concurrently he pursued an interest in prehistoric research. A member of the Viennese Anthropologische Gesellschaft since 1870, he served from 1876 to 1883 as their secretary, and editor of the society's *Mitteilungen*. His writings in European prehistory include *Die Kupferzeit in Europa* (1886), *Die Heimat der Germanen im Lichte der urgeschichtlichen Forschung* (1902), and *Die Trugspiegelung orientalischer Kultur in den vorgeschichtlichen Zeitaltern* (1907). He died in Wien on 17 December 1909. DtInd (2); Kosch; ÖBL; Wer ist's, 1909

Muchliński (Мухлинский), Anton (Antoni/Antoine) Osipovich, born in 1808, he was a professor of Arabic at St. Petersburg, and from 1859 to 1866 a dean of its Faculty of Oriental Languages. His writings include *Османская хрестоматія* (1858). He died 13 October 1877. Władysław Kotwicz and Maria Kotwiczówa wrote *Orijentalista Antoni Muchliński; życie i dziela* (Wilno, 1935). BiobibSOT, pp. 221-222; Dziekan; EnSlovar; OSK; Polski (7); PSB

Mückenhausen, Eduard, born 7 February 1907 at Enzen, Germany, he received a Dr.phil. in 1934 from the Universität Bonn for a study of soils in Prussia entitled *Die Böden der weiteren Umgebung von Landsberg/Warthe*. He was a professor and director, Institute of Soil Science at his alma mater. His writings include *Entstehung, Eigenschaften und Systematik der Böden der Bundesrepublik Deutschland* (1962), and *Die Bodenkultur und ihre geologischen, geomorphologischen, mineralogischen und petrologischen Grundlagen* (1975). GV; Kürschner, 1976-2005

Mueller-Werthmann, Gerhard, 1951- *see* Müller-Werthmann, Gerhard

Muftić, Teufik, born 28 November 1918 at Sarajevo, he was a sometime professor in the Orientalni Institut, Sarajevo. His writings include *Infinitivi triletera u arapskom jeziku; odnos oblika i značenja* (1966), *Arapsko-Srpskohrvatski rieečnik* (1973), and *Arapsko pismo* (1982). JugoslSa, 1970; ZKO

Muggeridge, Thomas*Malcolm*, born in 1903 at Croydon, England, he studied natural sciences at Selwyn College, Cambridge. He was a magazine editor, novelist, and a familiar figure on British television. In the late 1920s he taught some English at Cairo University, before becoming a leaderwriter on the *Manchester Guardian*. He died in 1990. Au&Wr, 1963; ConAu, new rev., 33, DNB; Who, 1969-1991; Who was who, 8

Mughul, Muhammad Yakub, born in 1935 at Tando Bago, Sind, he was a graduate of the University of Sind, and received a doctorate from Ankara Üniversitesi Dil ve Tarih-Cografya Fakültesi in 1967 for a thesis on Ottoman policy in the Indian Ocean and Indo-Ottoman relations in the face of Portuguese aggression. He was a sometime lecturer in Islamic history as well as Turkish language in the University of Sind. He was an honorary joint secretary of the Mehran Arts Council, Hyderabad. His wiritings include *Kanunî devri* (1987).

Muginov, Abdulladzhan Muginovich, born in 1896 at IArmukhamet, he was educated at Leningrad, where he received his first degree in 1945 for a study of Persian lexical elements in Uzbek prose entitled *Иранские лексические элементы в узбекской художественной прозе*. His writings include *Орисание уйгурских рукописей Институа Народов Азии* (1962), and *Описание тюркских рукописеи И.Н.А.* (1965). He died on 12 January 1967. Miliband; Miliband²

Muhammad, Muhammad 'Awad, born 3 April 1896 at al-Mansurah, Egypt, he was educated at a local *kuttāb* school and at Cairo. As a student agitator still in his early twenties, he was banished by the British to Malta. After his release, the Egyptians supported his studies at Liverpool and at London, where he obtained his Ph.D. in 1926. He pursued a teaching career at Egyptian universities. For some time he held the position of director general of Cultural Relations at the Ministry of Education, of which he became Minister in 1954. He was active in the U.N. and, in the mid-1950s, he became chairman of the Executive Board of Unesco. For the U.N. Human Rights Commission he wrote *Report on slavery* (1966). His other writings include *Nahr al-Nil* (1948), and *Fann al-tarjamah* (1969). He died on 9 January 1972. Bulletin de la Société de géographie d'Égypte 41-42 (1968-69), pp. 1-4

Mühlau, Heinrich *Ferdinand*, born 20 June 1839 at Dresden, Saxony, he studied theology and, under his father-in-law, Heinrich L. Fleischer, Oriental languages at Leipzig, where he received a Dr.phil. in 1869 for *De proverbiorum quae dicuntur Aguri et Lemuelis origine atquae indole*. He was successively a professor of theology at the universities of Dorpat and Kiel. He died in 1914. Baltisch (4); DtBilnd (3); Wer ist's, 1909-1912

Mühlmann, Felix, born 4 September 1846 at Beverungen, Bavaria, he studied at the universities of Halle an der Saale, and Berlin. He was from 1879 to 1887 director of the two German schools in Constantinople. From 1895 to 1905 he was a member of the Merseburg School Board. He belonged to the *entourage* of the German Emperor during his 1898 visit of the Holy Land. Kornrumpf; Wer ist's, 1909

Mühlmann, Wilhelm Emil, born 1 October 1904 at Düsseldorf, he received a Dr.phil. in 1932 from the Universität Berlin for *Die geheime Gesellschaft der Arioi*. He was a professor of anthropology successively at the universities of Berlin, Mainz, and Heidelberg. His writings include *Krieg und Frieden* (1940), *Assimilation, Umvolkung, Volkswerdung* (1944), *Dreizehn Jahre; Tagebuch, 1932-1945* (1947), and *Geschichte der Anthropologie* (1948). He died in Wiesbaden, 11 May 1988. DtBE; DtBilnd (3); IntDcAn; Kürschner, 1940/41-1987; Wer ist wer, 1955-1974/75

Mühsam (Muhsam), Helmut Victor, born 12 August 1914 at Berlin, he was educated at the local Collège français and received a Dr.sc. in 1937 from the Université de Genève. In the same year he emigrated to Palestine as a statistician. In 1958 he was appointed a professor in the Hebrew University, Jerusalem. His writings include *Beduin of the Negev* (1960). BioHbDtE; WhoIsrael, 1949, 1969/70; WhoWor, 1980/81; WhoWorJ, 1965, 1972, 1978

Muhtar Pasha, Mahmud *see* Mahmud Muhtar Pasha

Muir, Sir William, born in 1819 at Glasgow, he was educated at Edinburgh, Glasgow, and the East India College, Haileybury. A devout Christian, he took an active interest in Christian missionary work at Agra since 1847. In 1857, he was in charge of Intelligence Department of the Government of the North-West Provinces of India, and from 1868 to 1874 he there served as lieutenant-governor. In 1903, he was awarded the Sir Richard Burton Medal of the Royal Asiatic Society. His writings include *The Life of Mahomet and history of Islam* (1858), *The Corân, its composition and teaching* (1878), *Annals of the early Caliphate* (1883), and *The Caliphate* (1891). He died in 1905. BiD&SB; BritInd (5); Buckland; DNB; Fück, 180-81; Riddick; Who, 1897-1905; *Who was who*, 1

Mujahid, Sharif, born 1 July 1926 at Madras, India, he received an M.A. in 1954 from McGill University, Montreal, for *Sayyid Jamal al-Din al-Afghani; his role in the nineteenth century Muslim awakening*. From 1962 to 1972, he was a professor in the Department of Journalism, University of Karachi; since 1976, he was attached to the Quaid-i-Azam Academy, Karachi. His writings include *Indian secularism* (1970), *Ideology of Pakistan* (1974), and *Quaid-i-Azam Jinnah* (1981). Ferahian; IntAu&W, 10 (1986); LC

Mujezinović, Mehmed, born 29 July 1913 at Sarajevo, he wrote *Islamska epigrafika Bosne i Hercegovine* (1974), he was a joint author of *Stari mostovi u Bosni i Hercegovini* (1969), and he translated *Ljetopis*, from the Turkish of Mula Mustafa Ševki Bašeskija (1987). He died 14 May 1981. Anali Gazi Husrev-Begove Bibliotke, 9/10 (1983), pp. 327-333; Traljić, pp. 117-122

Mujibur Rahman, Sheikh, born in 1920, he was a Pakistani judge and a Bangladesh political leader. Kazi Kamal wrote *Sheikh Mujibur Rahman; man and politician* (1970), and Yatindra Bhatnager *Mujib, the architect of Bangladesh* (1971). He died in 1975. BioIn, 9, 10; CurBio, 1973, 1975; DcTwHis; IntWW, 1974/75, 1975/76; Master (5)

Mujić, Muhamed A., born 29 May 1920 at Mostar, Yugoslavia, he was since 1950 attached to the Orijentalni Institut, Sarajevo; he died in Sarajevo, 14 March 1984. Anali Gazi Husrev-Begove Biblioteca, 11/12 (1985), pp. 333-34

Mukanov, Marat Sabitovich, born 14 November 1929, he was associated with the Institute of History and Ethnology in the Kazak Academy of Sciences. His writings include Этнический состав и расселение казахов Среднего жуза (1974), Казахские домашние художественные ремесла (1979), and Казахская юрта (1981). Schoeberlein

Mukarovsky, Hans Günther, born 2 October 1992 at Wien, he received a Dr.phil. in 1948 from the Universität Wien. He was a free-lance journalist before he was appointed a professor of African languages at the Universität Wien. From 1963 until his retirement, he was director of the Institut für Afrikanistik in Wien. His writings include *Die Sprache der Kisi in Liberia*, and *Die Grundlagen des Ful und des Mauritanischen*. He died in Wien, 29 November 1992. Africa (Roma), 49 (1994), pp. 126-127; WhoAustria, 1967-1982/83

Mukhamed'iarov, Shamil' Fatykhovich, born 17 June 1923 at Kazan, Russia, he graduated in 1946 from the Kazan Institute of Law and received his first degree in 1950 for a study of the social-economic and political organization of the Kazan Khanate entitled Социально-экономическии и государственный строй Казанского ханства. He was from 1970 to 1996 a lecturer and affiliated with the Institute of History in the Soviet Academy of Science. He was joint editor of Вопросы историографии и источниковедения Якутии (1971). Miliband²; TatarES

Mukhamedova, Nadida Akhsanovna, born 17 November 1924 at Semipalatinsk, Kazakhstan, she graduated in 1949 from the Oriental Faculty, Central Asian State University, and received her first degree in 1956 for a study of contemporary literary Persian entitled Словообразование имен существительных и прилагательных современного персидского литервтурного языка. Since 1949 she was associated with the Oriental Faculty, Tashkent State University. She edited Востоковедение; языкознаие (1973), Вопросы востоко-ведения; языкознание (1981); and she was a joint editor of Вопросы грамматики и лексикологии восточных языков (1984). Miliband; Miliband²

Mukhamedova, Zuleikha Bakievna, born 9 January 1922 at Mary (Merv), she gained a doctorate in philology. Her writings include Исследования по истории туркменского языка XI-XIV веков (1973). She died in Ashkhabad, 7 May 1984. TurkmenSE, vol. 6, pp. 92-93

Mukhamedzhanov, Abdullakhad Rakhimdzhanovich, born 26 December 1928, he was a professor associated with the Institute of Archaeology in the Uzbek Academy of Sciences. His writings include История орошения Бухарского оазиса (1978), and Городище Пайкенд; к проблеме изучения средневекового городо Средней Азии (1988). Schoeberlein

Mukhiddinov, Ikromiddin, born 6 February 1933 in Tajikistan, he graduated in 1957 from the Institute of History and Philology, Tashkent, received his first degree in 1972 for a study of historical agriculture in Central Asia entitled *Земледеле памирских таджиков Вахана и Ишкашима в XIX-начале XX в.*, and his doctorate in 1984 for *Этногра-фические аспекты высокогорного Земледелия Западного Памира и сопредельных областнй*. Since 1957 he was affiliated with the Institute of History in the Tajik Academy of Sciences. His other writings include *Особенности традиционного земледельче-ского хозяйства припамирских народностей в XIX- начале XX века* (1984), and *Реликты доисламских обычаев и обрядов у земледельцев Западного Памира* (1989). Miliband²; Schoeberlein

Mukhlinskii, Anton Osipovich, 1808-1877 *see* Muchliński, Anton Osipovich

Mukhtarov, Akhror Mukhtarovich, born 5 November 1924 at Ura-Tyube, Tajikistan, he received his doctorate in 1971 at Dushanbe for a study of epigrafic monuments, eleventh to nineteenth century entitled *Эпиграфические памятники XI-XIX вв.* He was since 1954 affiliated with the Institute of History in the Tajik Academy of Science and was appointed a lecturer in 1956 and a professor in 1982. His writings include *Материалы по истории Ура-Тюбе* (1963), *Очерк истории Ура-Тюбинского владения в XIX в.* (1964), *Дильшод и ее место в истории общественной мысли таджикского народа и XIX- начале XX вв.* (1969), *Эпиграфические памятники Кухистана* (1978), *Подне-средневековый Балх* (1980), and *Из истории народных движений в Средней Азии* (1988); and he was joint author of *Historiography of Tajikistan, 1917-1969* (1970), and *Путешествие в Согдиану* (1982); and he edited *Резьба по дереву в долине Зерафшана* (1966). Miliband²; Schoeberlein

Mukimov, Rustam Samatovich, born in 1946, he was a lecturer in architecture at the Tajik Poly-technical Institute. Schoeberlein

Mukminova, Roziia Galievna, born 30 December 1922 at Kazan, Russia, she graduated in 1944 from the Faculty of History at Tashkent and received her first degree in 1949 for a study of the history of Timuride Transoxania entitled *Борьба за Мавераннахр между тимуридами и шейбанидами*, and her doctorate in 1986 for *Ремесло в Самарканде и Бухара XVI в.* Her writings include *К истории аграрных отношений в Узбекистане XVI в.* (1966), *Очерки по истории ремесла в Самарканде и Бухара в XVI веке* (1976), and *Социальная дифференциация населения городов Узбекистана в XV-XVI вв.* (1985). Miliband; Miliband²; Schoeberlein; TatarES; UzbekSE

Mulack, Gunter, born 23 September 1943 at Landsberg/Warthe, Prussia, he received a Dr.jur. in 1972 from the Universität Göttingen for a study of legal aspects of Middle Eastern oil concessions entitled *Rechtsprobleme der Erdölkonzessionsabkommen im Nahen Osten*, and subsequently gained an LL.M. at the University of California, Berkeley. He was briefly an assistant at the Institut für Völkerrecht, Göttingen. He then entered the German foreign service and served since 1990 as a consul and ambassador in Middle Eastern countries. Note; *Wer ist wer*, 1994/95-2002/3

Mulder, Dirk Cornelis. born 5 October 1919 at Leiden, he studied law, theology and Islamic subjects at Amsterdam and Aligarh, and received a doctorate in philosophy in 1949 from Vrije Universiteit te Amsterdam. He was from 1950 to 1965 a lecturer at theological schools in Djakarta and concurrently at the State University Gadjah Mada Djokjakarta. From 1965 to his retirement in 1985 he served as a professor of religious studies at his alma mater; from 1983 to 1992 he was chairman of the Council of Churches in the Netherlands. His writings include *Pembimbing kedalam Perdjandjian Lama* (1963), *Bronnen van herinnering* (1993), and *Kinderen in Kamp esterbork* (1994). Wie is wie, 1984-88, 1994-96

Mulertt, Otto Emil Paul *Werner*, born 23 December 1892 at Halle an der Saale, Prussia, he studied Romance philology and received both a Dr.phil. in 1918 from the Universität Halle for *Laissenverbindungen und Laissenwiederholung in den chansons de geste*, and a Dr.habil. in 1919 for *Studien zu den letzten Büchern des Amadisromans*. He was successiveley a professor of Romance philology and literature at the universities of Danzig, Innsbruck, and again Halle. His writings include *Die Stellung der "Marokkanischen Briefe" innerhalb der Aufklärungsliteratur* (1937), and *Literarische Frauen-Idealbilder* (1941). Kürschner, 1940/41

Mulhall, Michael George, born 29 September 1836 at Dublin, he was educated at Irish College, Roma. He was a statistician who spent the years from 1858 to 1878 in South America. His writings include *The progress of the world in arts, agriculture, commerce, manufacture, instruction, railways, and public health since the beginning of the nineteenth century* (1880), and *Industries and wealth of nations* (1896). He died in 1900. BiD&SB; DclrB, 1978, 1988, 1998; DNB; Master (1); Who was who, 1

Graf von **Mülinen**, Eberhard Friedrich, Dr., born 6 September 1861 at Bern, Switzerland, he was a sometime dragoman at the German consulate in Constantinople. He wrote *Die Lateinische Kirche im Türkischen Reiche*, 2nd ed. (Berlin, 1903), and he was joint author of *Das Heiligtum al-Husains in Kerbalâ* (1909). He died in 1927. GV; Hanisch; Kornrumpf

Muliukov, Farid M. S. *see* Seiful'-Muliukov, Farid Mustaf'evich

636

Mul'kamanov, Abdyrakhman, born 9 December 1932 in Turkmenistan, he graduated in 1955 from Turkmen State University and received his first degree in 1963 at Ashkhabad for a thesis on Дестан "Шабехрам" Шабенде и его связь с сюжетом о Бахраме Гуре. Miliband²

Mulladzhozova, Zul'fiia Abdugafarovha, born 20 March 1952 at Stalinabad (Dushanbe), she graduated in 1974 from the Oriental Faculty, Dushanbe, and received her first degree in 1985 for a study of the sources and evolution of Firdawsi's *Shahname* entitled *Истоки и эволюция образа Искандара в "Шах-наму" Фирдоси.* Miliband²

Mullaly, Major-General Sir Herbert, K.C.M.C., C.B., C.S.I., born 4 June 1860, he graduated from the Royal Military College, Woolwich, and subsequently served with the Royal Engineers in India until his retirement in 1920. He died in 1932. Riddick; Who, 1909-1932; *Who was who*, 3

Müller, August, 1848-1892 *see* Müller, Friedrich August

von Müller, David Heinrich, born 6 July 1846 at Buczacz, Austrian Galicia, he studied at Jüdisch-Theologisches Seminar, Breslau, and the Universität Wien. A student of H. L. Fleischer at Leipzig and Th. Nöldeke at Straßburg, he held the chair of Semitic languages at Wien from 1881 to his retirement in 1912. He collaborated with the Leiden edition of al-Tabari's *Annals* and concurrently edited Hasan b. Ahmad al-Hamdani's geographical description of Arabia, a project which led him to pursue studies in pre-Islamic South Arabia. His other writings include *Südarabische Alterthümer im Kunsthistorischen Hofmuseum*, (Wien, 1899). He died in Wien on 27 December 1912. DtBE; DtBilnd (3); Fück, pp. 255-57; Hanisch; *Jahrbuch für jüdische Geschichte und Literatur*, 17 (1914), pp. 145-157; JewEnc; JüdLex; Kornrumpf; ÖBL; Pallas; RNL; *Wer ist's*, 1905;1911; Wininger

Müller, Dorothea, born 7 October 1939 at Heiningen, Germany, she studied German literature, history and education, and until 1963 trained as a teacher at the Universität Münster. She subsequently changed to Islamic studies and received a Dr.phil. in 1968 for a study of animals in the life and belief of early Islamic society entitled *Das Tier im Leben und Glauben der früh-islamischen Gesellschaft.* She edited *Ambivalenzen der Okzidentalisierung; Zugänge und Zugriffe* (1998). Thesis

Müller, Ernst Wilhelm, born 21 April 1925 at Gelsenkirchen, Germany, he was an anthropologist who taught at Heidelberg, before he was appointed a professor at Mainz. Kürschner, 1970-2005; Unesco

Müller, Friedrich *August*, born 3 December 1848 at Stettin, Prussia, he studied classical and Semitic philology at the universities of Halle an der Saale, and Leipzig, gaining a Dr.phil. in 1868 at Halle for *Imrvvlkaisi Mu'allaka commentario critico illvstrata.* After his Dr.habil. he was successively a professor at Königsberg and Halle. His writings include *Hebräische Schulgrammatik* (1878), its translation, *Outlines of Hebrew syntax* (1882), *Der Islam im Morgen- und Abendland* (1885-87), its translations, *Исторія истама с основанія доновейших времен* (1895-96), *L'islamismo in Oriente ed in Occidente* (1898), and *Türkische Grammatik* (1889). He died in 1892. DtBE; DtBilnd (1); Fück, pp. 236-239; ZDMG, 46 (1892), pp. 775-779

Müller, Friedrich Wilhelm Karl, born 21 January 1863 at Neudamm near Frankfurt/Oder, he was educated at Französisches Gymnasium, Berlin, and subsequently studied theology and Oriental languages at the Universität Berlin. After his doctorate he joined in 1887 the newly founded Museum für Völkerkunde, Berlin, serving from 1906 to 1928 as director of the East Asian Section. He published the Uighur manuscripts brought to Germany by four successive Turfan expeditions. His writings include *Uigurica* (1908-1931) and *Zwei Pfahlinschriften aus den Turfanfunden* (1915. He died in Berlin on 18 April 1930. DtBE; Hanisch; NDB; Stache-Rosen, p. 150

Müller, Friedrich Wilhelm *Max*, born 6 December 1823 at Dessau, of humble parentage, having lost his thirty-three old father, when he was still a child. He studied classical and Oriental philology at Leipzig. After post-doctoral study at Berlin and Paris he went in 1846 to London. He subsequently was appointed a professor of comparative linguistics at Oxford. In 1872 he declined a professorship at the Universität Straßburg. He was a fellow of All Souls' College, Oxford, and a member of the Académie des Inscriptions et Belles-Lettres, Paris. His writings include the Gifford Lecture delivered before the University of Glasgow, 1888, entitled *Natural religion* (c1889, 1975), and *My autobiography* (1901). BioJahr 5 (1900), pp. 273-88; DNB; DtBE; DtBilnd (7); PorLing, vol. 1, pp. 395-99; Riddick; Stache-Rosen; *Who was who* 1

Müller, Gottfried, born 31 October 1942 at Görlitz, Germany, he graduated in 1963 from Evangelisches Gymnasium zum Grauen Kloster, Berlin, and subsequently studied Islamic subjects at Freie Universität Berlin. From 1964 to 1966 he was a teacher of German at Goethe Institut, Tripoli, Lebanon. After his M.A. in 1970, he became first an assistant and later lecturer in Islamic studies in the Institut für Islamwissenschaften, Berlin, a post which he still held in autumn of 2005. He took a Dr.phil. in 1978 at Berlin for *Ich bin Labid und das ist mein Ziel; zum Problem der Selbstbehauptung in* *der arabischen Qaside*, a work which was published in 1981. His writings include *Araber in Berlin* (1992). Private; Thesis

Müller, Hans, born 22 October 1927 at Heuchelheim, Germany, he was a trained political economist and gained a Dr.habil. From 1981 to his retirement he taught Islamic studies at Freiburg im Breisgau. His writings include *Lehr-, Lern- und Arbeitsmittel für Arabisch, Persisch und Türkisch* (1977), and *Die Kunst des Sklavenkaufs* (1980). Kürschner, 1983-2003

Baron von **Müller**, Johann Wilhelm, born 4 March 1824 at Heilbronn, Baden, he studied natural sciences and from 1845 to 1849 travelled in Algeria, Morocco, and northeastern Africa to Kordofan. He died in 1866. Embacher; Henze; Hill; Kornrumpf

Müller, Josef Franz, born 29 April 1811 at Reichenau (Rychnov) on Kněžna, Bohemia, he completed his medical studies at Padua and Prag, becoming a sometime public health official in Zara (Zadar), Croatia. His writings, probsably articles, include *Albanien, Rumelien und die österreichisch-montenegrische Gränze* (1843), and *Über die Analogie des öffentlichen Volkslebens und der inneren Regierungspolitik der westlichen Türken mit denen des slawischen Mittelalters* (1845). He died in Prag on 23 March 1845. Kornrumpf; ÖBL; OttůvSN

Müller, Julius Otto, born 24 March 1931 at Trier, Germany, he gained a Dr.rer.hort. in 1962 and a Dr.habil. in 1970 and became a professor of rural and agrarian development in the Third World at Göttingen from 1973 to his retirement. He was joint author of *On the evaluation of rural cooperatives, with reference to governmental development policies; case study Iran* (1976), and he edited *Gesellschaftspolitische Konzeptionen der Förderung von Selbsthilfe durch Fremdhilfe in Afrika* (1981). Kürschner, 1976-2001|

Müller, Karl, born 2 January 1879 at Thannsüß, Germany, he gained a doctorate and was in 1935 a director of the Reichsbank, Berlin. Wer ist's, 1935

Müller, Kurt, born 20th cent., he received a Dr.phil. in 1949 from the Universität Bonn for *Al-Malik al-Ašraf Salah ad-Din Ḥalil, ein Mamlukensultan am Ausgang der Kreuzzüge*. Schwarz

Müller, Marcus Joseph, born in 1809 at Kempten, Bavaria, he studied, particularly Oriental languages, from 1826 to 1830 at München and became a school teacher. A Bavarian travel fellowship enabled him in 1833 to study Pahlavi and Arab geographers at Paris and Leiden. He failed to obtain a professorship at München as the university saw no need to offer such studies. A full member of the Bavarian Academy of Science since 1841, he was from 1852 to 1870 secretary of its Philosophisch-philologische Classe. The King of Bavaria sent him from 1856 to 1858 to study the Arabic manuscripts at the Escurial Library. He was invalided to retirement in 1862 and died after an illness of twelve years on 28 March 1874. His writings include *Über die oberste Herrschergewalt nach dem moslemischen Staatsrecht* (1847), *Philosophie von Averroës* (1859), and *Beiträge zur Geschichte der westlichen Araber* (1866-76). ADtB, vol. 22, p. 651-52; DtDE; Kosch

Müller, Max, 1823-1900 *see* Müller, Friedrich Wilhelm Max

Müller, Max born about 1850, he entered in 1862 the Potsdam cadet corps (Cadettenhaus) and subsequently served with the Prussian Hussars. He resigned in 1876 with the rank of lieutenant and went to Egypt. About 1881 he was hired by one Morice Bey as a deputy inspector of Coast Guards for the coastal region between Ramlah and Abukir, experiences which he described in his *In ägyptischen Diensten; Erlebnisse eines ehemaligen preußischen Husarenoffiziers* (Leipzig, 1888). In 1887 he was resident in Berlin. Note

Muller, Robert, born 29 September 1917 at Strasbourg, he graduated second of the 1938 class of 360 students from l'École spéciale militaire de Saint-Cyr. Since 1939 he served with the Troupes de marine in French Somalia. In 1942 he joined the Free French Forces in Ethiopia and in the following year served with the Division française libre in Tunisia. In 1946 he became director of Affaires politiques et du cabinet militaire in French Somalia. Since 1949 he served successively in French Equatorial Africa and Algeria. He retired in 1976 with the rank of general to the Côte d'Azur and died in Saint-Laurent-du-Var, 3 January 1990. NDBA

Müller, Sigrid Flamand, 1904- *see* Müller Christensen, Sigrid Flamand

Müller, W. Max, 1823-1900 *see* Müller, Friedrich Wilhelm Max

Müller, Walter Wilhelm, born 26 September 1933 at Weipert, Sudentenland. In the wake of the war, his education in his home town was interrupted for two years and a half. After the expulsion of the family, he went to high school in the Odenwald region and began to study Catholic theology at Mainz, soon to change to Oriental studies at Tübingen, concurrently working as a student assistant in the repository of the Prussian Oriental manuscripts. He spent 1960-61 as a research assistant in the Near Eastern Center, U.C.L.A., where he gained an M.A. in 1961. He received his Dr.phil. in 1963 from Tübingen for *Die Wurzeln mediae und tertiae y/w im Altsüdarabischen*, and also his Dr.habil. in 1968 for *Vergleichendes Wöterbuch der neusüdarabischen Mehri-Sprache*. He was successively a professor at Tübingen and Marburg, specializing in pre-Islamic South Arabia, Semitic epigraphy, and comparative Semitics. EURAMES, 1993; Kürschner, 1976-2003; Thesis

Müller, Wilhelm, born about 1895, he received a Dr.phil. in 1922 from the Universität Erlangen for *Über die Musik der muslimischen Völker*.

Müller, Wilhelm Max, born in 1862 in Bavaria, he received a doctorate and in 1888 emigrated to America, where he became a professor of ancient Near Eastern studies and Egyptology in Philadelphia. His writings include *Studien zur vorderasiatischen Geschichte* (1898-1900). He died in 1919. DAB; Dawson; Egyptology; NatCAB, 21, p. 413; Shavit; WhAm, 1; Who was who 2

Müller, Zdeněk, born 12 February 1947 at Praha, he studied philosophy and Arabic at Universita Karlova, Praha, and received a Ph.Dr. in 1971 for *Fuád Mursí a pojetí egyptské cesty k socialismu*. He became affiliated with the Oriental Institute, Praha. He was joint author of *Svět Arabů* (1989), and *Islám; ideál a skutečnost* (Praha, 1990). Filipsky

Müller née **Christensen**, Sigrid Flamand, born in 1904, she received a Dr.phil. in 1931 from the Universität München for *Die männliche Kleidung in der süddeutschen Renaissance*. Her writings include *Alte Möbel vom Mittelalter bis zum Biedermeier* (1948), and *Das Gunthertuch im Bamberger Domschatz* (1966). NUC, pre-1956

Müller-Hohenstein, Klaus, born 15 August 1936 at Neusalz, Silesia, he received a Dr.habil. in 1978 from the Universität Erlangen-Nürnberg for *Die ostmarokkanischen Hochplateaus*. He was a professor of biogeography at Bayreuth from 1979 until his retirement. His other writings include *Die Wälder der Toskana* (1969), a work which was originally presented as a doctoral thesis at Erlangen, *Marokko, ein islamisches Entwicklungsland mit kolonialer Vergangenheit* (1990), and he was joint author of *An Introduction to the vegetation of Yemen* (1984). Kürschner, 1983-2003; WhoScEu, 1987-1993

Müller-Werthmann, Gerhard, born in 1951, he wrote *Konzern der Menschlichkeit; die Geschäfte des Deutschen Roten Kreuzes* (1984). LC; Sezgin

Müller-Wiener, Wolfgang Karl Heinz Albert, born 17 May 1923 at Friedrichswerth, Thuringia, he trained as a carpenter and later studied architecture at Technische Hochschule Karsruhe, where he received a Dr.phil. in 1954 and a Dr.habil. in 1965. Except for seven years, when he was a professor at Darmstadt, he spent the rest of his career with Deutsches Archäologisches Institut in Cairo and Istanbul respectively. His writings include *Burgen der Kreuzfahrer im Heilgen Land, auf Zypern und in der Ägäis* (1966), its translation, *Castles of the Crusaders* (1966), *Bildlexikon zur Topographie Istanbuls* (1977), *Istanbul-Zeyrek* (1982), and *Die Häfen von Byzantium, Konstantinupolis, Istanbul* (1994). He died in Istanbul, 25 March 1991. DtBE; Kürschner, 1983-1992; NDB; WhoWor, 1974/75, 1976/77

Mullet, Clément, 1796- ca. 1865 *see* Clément Mullet, Jean Jacques

Mullick, Muhammad Anwar *Hussein*, born in 1928, he received a Dr.phil. in 1967 from the Universität Bonn for a study of the German system of agrarian credit entitled *Die Entwicklung des deutschen Agrarkreditsystems*. His writings include *Wastewater treatment in the Middle East* (1987). NUC, 1969-72

Mullina, R. M., born about 1900, she was affiliated with the Kazak State University, Alma Ata. She was joint author of *Руководство к изучения крымско-татарского языка* (1931), and *Казахски язык* (1960). OSK; NUC, 1968-72

Mulloakhmedov, Mirzo, born 20 February 1948 in Tajikistan, he graduated in 1969 from Tajik State University and received his first degree in 1975 at Dushanbe for *Творчество Фирдоси*, a work which was published in 1978. His writings include works in Tajik. Miliband[2]

Mumford, Ethel Watts, 1878-1940 *see* Grant, Ethel Watts Mumford

Mumford, Philip Stearn, born in 1894 at Colchester, Essex, he was eduated at Charterhouse School and Jesus College, Cambridge, and in 1914 commissioned in the Westminster Dragoons. In the 1920s he was with the Colonial Service in Zanzibar and Kenya, and subsequently with the British Army in Iraq. From 1928 to 1931 he was with Air Staff Intelligence, R.A.F., in Kurdistan. His writings include *Introduction to pacifism* (1937). BritInd (1)

Muminov, Khalim Kakhkharovich, born 15 October 1934 at Bukhara, he graduated in philology at Tashkent, where he also received his first degree in 1975 for a study of Mikha'il Nu'aymi and his place in Arabic literature entitled *Михаил Нуайме как теоретик критического реализма в арабской литературе*. Miliband[2]

Comte de **Mun**, Gabriel, born 12 August 1885 at the chateau de Lumigny (Seine-et-Marne), he was educated at the Collège Stanislas and later gained a diploma in letters. He was an archivist, palaeographer, and a sometime *secrétaire interalliés de la Commission des Reparations*. His writings include *Deux ambassadeurs a Constantinople* (1902), and *Richelieu et la maison de Savoie* (1907). *Qui etes-vous*, 1924

al-Munayyar, 'Afīf, 1910-1996 *see* Myers, Eugene Abraham

Mundy, Martha, born 20th cent., she completed her graduate work at Columbia University, New York, and from 1982 to 1992 she worked at Yarmouk University, Jordan, where she was a founding member of the Institute of Archaeology and Anthropology In 1995 she taught anthropology at the American University of Beirut. Her writings include *Part-time farming; agricultural development in the Zarqa River basin* (1990), *Domestic government, kinship, community and polity in North Yemen* (1995), and she was joint author of *al-Qaryah mā bayna al-numūw wa-al-takhṭīṭ* (1990). DrBSMES, 1993; EURAMES, 1993; LC; Note

Munholland, John *Kim*, born 5 November 1934 or 1935 at Long Beach Calif., he graduated from Stanford University and received his Ph.D. in 1964 from Princeton University for *The emergence of the colonial military in France, 1880-1905*. Since 1963 he was affiliated with the University of Minnesota at Minneapolis. His writings include *The Origins of contemporary Europe, 1880-1914* (1970). ConAu, 29-32, new rev., 25; DrAS, 1974 H, 1978 H, 1982 H

Munier, Adolphe *Henri*, born 14 July 1884 at Meursault (Côte d'Or), France, he came to Egypt as a youngster, when the family moved to Cairo. He returned to France for his education, which he completed at the Faculté des lettres de Dijon. He studied Hebrew and Coptic at Cairo and subsequently served from 1908 to 1924 as librarian with the Service des antiquités de l'Egypte. From 1925 to his death on 20 August 1945 he was secretary to the Société royale de géographie d'Egypte. His writings include *Tables de la description de l'Egypte, suivies d'une bibliographie sur l'expédition française de Bonaparte* (1943). Dawson; Egyptology; *Hommes et destins*, vol. 7, pp. 376-77

Munier, Bertrand René, born 2 May 1943 at Rabat, he received a *doctorat d'état* in 1969 from the Université d'Aix-Marseille for *Le Cambisme et les mouvements de capitaux à court terme*. He was a professor of economics successively at Lyon, Marseille and Cachan (Val-de-Marne). His writings include *La Banque nationale pour le développement économique et l'industrialisation du Maroc* (1967), and he was joint author of *Compromise, negation, and group decision* (1987). WhoWor, 1982/83, 1991/92

Munirov, Kuvamiddin/Quvamiddin, born 5 May 1928 at Tashkent, he graduated in 1949 from the Oriental Faculty, Central Asian State University and received his first degree in 1961 for *Историче-ские труды Муниса, Агакхи и Баяни*. Since 1949 he was affiliated with the Oriental Institute in the Uzbek Academy of Science. His other writings include *Сокровищница восточных рукописей* (1988). LC; Miliband; Miliband[2]

Munk, Salomon, born 14 May 1805 at Glogau, Prussia, he studied at Berlin and Bonn and then emigrated to Paris, where he became a keeper at the Bibliothèque Nationale. He was a member of the Académie des Inscriptions and a professor at the Collgège de France. In his later years he lost his eyesight. His writings include *Palestine; description géographique* (1845), *Mélanges de philosophie juive et arabe* (1859), and he edited and translated *Le Guide des égarés*, of Moses ben Maimon (1856-66). He died in Paris, 6 February 1867. ADtB, vol. 23, pp. 16-18; Dantès 1; Dezobry; DtBiInd (2); EncJud; Fück; JewEnc; JüdLex; Vapereau; Wininger

Munkácsi, Barnát (Bernard), born 12 March 1860 at Großwardein (Nagyvárad), Austria-Hungary, he studied ethnology and comparative Ural-Altaic languages and was appointed a professor in 1885. He made extensive travels in Siberia. His writings include *Votjak népköltészeti hagyományok* (1887), *Blüten der ossetischen Volkdichtung* (1932), and *Volksbräuche und Volksdichtung der Wotjaken* (1952). He died in 1937. GeistigeUng; *Index Islamicus* (1); JewEnc; JüdLex; MEL, 1967-69; ÖBL; Wininger

Munkuev, Nikolai TSyrendorzhievich, born 1 July 1922 in Buriat Autonomous Soviet Republic, he graduated in 1950, received his first degree in 1962 and his doctorate in 1970 for a study of thirteenth century Mongol history entitled *Некоторые проблемы истории монголов в XIII в. по новым материалам*. From 1957 to 1985 he was affiliated with the Oriental Institute in the Soviet Academy of Sciences. He died 29 April 1985. Miliband[2]

Münnich, Jerzy Wilhelm, he was a professor of classical philology and Oriental languages, particularly Hebrew, Arabic, Persian and Turkish, and successively taught at Kraków and Wilna. He died in 1829. Dziekan; Polski (1)

Muños y Bosque, Angel, born 19th cent., he wrote *Gui manual de la conversación marroqui* (1914).

Muños Jiménez, Rafael, born early 20th cent., he received a doctorate in Semitic philology and later was successively a professor of Arabic and Islamic studies, and a director, Departamento de Fililogía Clásica y Arabe in the Universidad de La Laguna, Santa Cruz de Tenerife. His writings include *Temas de literatura árabe* (1991). He died on 8 September 1999. Arabismo, 1992, 1994, 1997; EURAMES, 1993; LC

Muños Vázquez, Miguel, born 16 March 1909 at Villenueva de Córdoba, he received a diploma from a teachers' college. His writings include *Historia de El Carpio* (Córdoba, 1963). LC; WhoSpain, 1963

Munro, Dana Carlston, born in 1866 at Bristol, R.I., he graduated from Brown University and successively served as a professor of Roman and medieval history at the universities of Pennsylvania, Wisconsin, and Princeton. He writings include *A history of the middle ages* (1902), *Medieval civilisation* (1904), and *The Kingdom of the Crusaders* (1935). He died in 1933. BioIn 5, 11; DAB; Master (3); NatCAB, vol. 23, pp. 81-82; WhAm 1

Munro, John Murchison, born in 1932 at Wallasey, Cheshire, he graduated from the University of Durham and received a Ph.D. in English literature in 1960 from Washington University, St. Louis. He taught in America, Canada, Lebanon and Egypt, and he was a consultant to universities and governments throughout the Middle East. His writings include *A mutual concern; the story of the American University of Beirut* (1977), *The Nairn way; desert bus to Baghdad* (1980), and he was joint author of *Cyprus between Venus and Mars* (1984). ConAu 69-72, new rev. 11; IntAu&W 1986-2003; Note

Munson, Henry Lee, born 1 November 1946 at N.Y.C., he was a graduate of Columbia University and received his Ph.D. in 1980 from the University of Chicago for *Islam and inequality in northwestern Morocco*. Since 1982 he was a professor in the Department of Anthropology, University of Maine at Orono. His writings include *Islam and revolution in the Middle East* (1988), and *Religion and power in Morocco* (1993). ConAu 115, new rev. 40; NatFacDr, 1995-2003; Private; Selim²

Münter, Friedrich Christian Carl Hinrich, born 14 October 1761 at Gotha, Thuringia, he was a bishop of Sjaelland, Church historian and archaeologist. His writings include *Versuch über die keilförmigen Inschriften zu Persepolis* (1802), *Om Frankernes mynter i Orientem* (1806-21), *Aus den Tagebüchern Friedrich Münters; Wander- und Lehrjahre* (1937) as well as the translations *Nachrichten von Neapel und Sizilien, 1785 und 1786* (1790), and *Viaggio in Sicilia* (1990). He died in København, 9 April 1830. DanskBL; DanskBL²; LuthC 1975

Munthe, Ludvig, born 22 April 1920 at Hjelmeland, Norway, he studied missionary science at Stavanger and received a doctorate in 1964 at Paris. He went in 1946 to Madagascar as a missionary. From 1966 to 1977 he was a professor at Misjonsskolen, Stavanger. His writings include *Misjonæren Lars Dahle* (1968), *La Bible à Madagascar* (1969), *La Tradition arabico-malgache vue à travers le manuscrit A-6 d'Oslo* (1982), and *Venstrehandsmisjon* (1985). Hvem er hvem, 1979-1994

Muntner, Süßman, born 17 September 1897 at Kolomea, Galicia, he came to Berlin at the age of five. There he grew up, studied medicine and practised until the last year of the Weimar Republic, 1932, when he went to Palestine, where he died on Saturday, 21 January 1973. As a scholar he worked in the field of Jewish medical history, devoting himself to editing and translating medieval Jewish classics, particularly Moses Maimonides, of whom he published ten medical books. He was modest and kind and only through extraordinary industry and devotion did he succeed in creating, simultaneously with his practical activities, a medico-historical *œuvre*, which in quality and quantity surpasses that of many "fulltime" men. BioHbDtE; DtBE; WhoIsrael, 1969/70; WhoWorJ, 1965; Unidentified obituary by E. H. Ackerknecht in *News and Notes*, p. 241

Munzel, Kurt, born about 1920, he received a Dr.phil. in 1948 at Erlangen for a study of the genetive in Egyptian Arabic entitled *Der Gebrauch der Genitivexponenten im arabischen Dialekt von Ägypten*. His writings include *Ägyptisch-Arabischer Sprachführer* (1958).

Munzinger, Johann Albert *Werner*, he was born in 1832 at Olten, Switzerland. After studying natural sciences, Oriental languages and history at Bern, München and Paris he went to Egypt in 1852 and spent a year at Cairo perfecting himself in Arabic. Entering a French mercantile house, he went as a leader of a trading expedition to various parts of the Red Sea, fixing his quarters at Massawa. In 1861, he joined an expedition to Central Africa, and in 1862 he travelled to Kordofan. He was British consul at Massawa in 1865, French consul in 1868, and in 1871 named governor by the Khedive Ismail. He, his wife, and nearly all his companions were killed in 1875 in an expedition in Abyssinia. His writings include *Über die Sitten und das Recht der Bogos* (1859), *Ostafrikanische Studien* (1864), its translation, *Studi sull'Africa orientale* (1890), *Vocabulaire de la langue tigre* (1865), and *Die Barea-Sprache* (1874). A. Kitt wrote the biography, *Werner Munzinger Pascha* (Basel, 1912). ADtB, vol. 23, pp. 50-51; DtBE; DtBiInd (2); Embacher; EncBrit; EncicUni; GDU; Kornrumpf; Kornrumpf³, vol. 2; Kosch; Henze; Pallas; RNL

Muracciole, Luc Marcel Martial, born 16 March 1923 at Médéa, Algeria, he went to school in Blida and Alger and started to study law at the Université d'Alger, gaining a doctorate, as well as a *licence ès lettres*, at Paris. In addition, he received a diploma in North African legal studies and a certificate from the Académie internationale de La Haye. A barrister at Alger since 1946, he served from 1953 to 1968 as a professor of law at the Ecole nationale supérieure des P.T.T. and concurrently as a secretary general of the *Revue juridique et politique d'outre-mer*. His writings include *L'Emigration algérienne* (1950), and *République du Tchad; les constitutions des états africains d'expression française* (1962). NDNC, 1963; WhoFr, 1971/72-1992/93|

Murad Efendi, 1836-1881 *see* Werner, Franz von

Murad, Hasan Qasim, born 20th cent., he received an M.A. in 1968 from McGill University, and also a Ph.D. in 1981 for *Ethico-religious ideas of Umar II*. In 1978, he was a professor in the Department of Islamic History, Karachi University. Ferahian

Muradov, Gulam, born 20th cent., he wrote Демократическая Республика Афганистан (1982). OSK

Muradzha d'Osson (Мураджа д'Оссон), I., 1740-1807 *see* Mouradgea d'Ohsson, Ignatius

von **Muralt**, Jürgen, born about 1935, he studied political economy at Marburg, Frankfurt am Main and Berlin and received a Dr.rer.pol. in 1964 for a study of cooperative movement in Egypt entitled *Entwicklung und Struktur des Genossenschaftswesens in Ägypten*. Fellowships had enabled him to perfect himself in Arabic in various Arab countries. He was joint author of *Plantations and plantation workers* (1987). Note

Murányi, Miklos, born 26 September 1943 at Kiskörös, Hungary, he studied German and Islamic subjetcs at Eötvös Loránd University, Budapest, and Arabic at Cairo University, 1967-68, gaining his first degree at Budapest in 1969. He then emigrated to Germany and pursued Islamic studies at Bonn, where he received a Dr.phil. in 1973 for a study of the companions of the Prophet in early Islamic history entitled *Die Prophetengenossen in der frühislamischen Geschichte*. His writings include *Materialien zur malikitischen Rechtsliteratur* (1984), and *Ein altes Fragment medinensischer Jurisprudenz aus Qairawan* (1985). Thesis

Murarka, Dev, fl. 1965, he wrote *The Soviet Union* (1971), and *Gorbachov* (London, 1988). LC

Muratore, Dino, born 19th cent., he wrote *Corso pratico di geografia moderna* (Novara, Istituto geografico d'Agostini, 1914-1916). NUC, pre-1956

Muratov, Khikmatulla Il'iasovich, fl. 1940, he wrote Крестьянская война 1773-1775 гг. в России (1954), and Революционное движение в русской армии в 1905-1907 нн.(1955). OSK; NUC, pre-1956

Muratov, Saifi Nizamovich, born 30 November 1919 in Bashkiria, he graduated in 1952 from the Oriental Faculty, Leningrad, where he also received his first degree in 1955 for a study of Bashkir linguistics entitled Сложные имена в системе башкирского словосложению. He was from 1957 to 1966 affiliated with the Leningrad Branch of the Institute of the Peoples of Asia. His writings include Устойчивые словосочетания в тюркских языках (1961), and he was joint author of Описание тюркских рукописей Института народов Азии (1965). Miliband; Miliband[2]

Murav'ev (Karskiĭ), Nikolai Nikolaevich, born in 1794, he entered the army in 1811 and served in the Polish and Turkish campaigns. In 1819 he was named to lead an expedition to Central Asia, an experience which he described in Путешевские в Туркмнения и Хиву в 1819 и 1820 годах (1822), and its translations, *Voyage en Turcomanie et à Khiva* (1823), *Reise durch Turkomanien nach Chiwa* (1824), *Journey to Khiva through the Turkoman country* (1977), and Русскіе еа Восфоре в 1833 годы (1869). He died in 1869. BioIn 11; Embacher; EnSlovar; GSE; Henze; Kornrumpf; Wieczynski

Murdoch Smith, Sir R., 1835-1900 *see* Smith, Sir Robert Murdoch

Muret, Jules Henri *Maurice*, born 11 June 1870 at Morges, Switzerland, he studied liberal arts at Lausanne, Leipzig, München and Paris and was resident in Paris from his student days. He was a sometime editor of the *Journal des débats* and *Gazette de Lausanne*. He had travelled widely. His writings include *L'Esprit juif* (1901), *Le Crépuscule des nations blanches* (1925), and its translation, *The twilight of the white races* (1926). He died in 1954. DBFC, 1954/55; *Qui etes-vous, 1924*; WhoFr, 1953/54

Murkos (Murqus), Georgi Abramovich, born in 1846, he was an Arab from Damascus and had gone to a Greek school on the Island of Khalkë, Dodecanese. He studied at Moscow, where he graduated in 1868 from Lazarev Institute of Oriental Languages. He was strongly committed to the cause of

Christian Arabs. His writings include the translation, *Путешествие антиохийскаго патриарха Макария в Москву* (1898), of the Archdeacon Paul of Aleppo. He died in 1911. Krachkovskii, pp. 156-59

Murmann, Heinz, born 15 November 1909 at Hammelburg, Bavaria, he received a Dr.phil. in 1957 from the Universität Tübingen for *Der Redestiel früher englischer Labourpolitiker.* He was a foreign editor of the Düsseldorf Handelsblatt. GV; Wer ist wer, 1988/89-1999/2000|

Murodov, Otamurod, he received a degree in 1975 for *Пережитки ранних верований у таджиков долины Зеравшана.* His writings include *Древние образы мифологии у таджиков долины Зеравшина* (1979), and he was joint author of *Трансформация мифологических и легендарных образов в таджикско-персидских хрониках XI-XV вв.* (1986). LC; OSK

Murphey, Rhoads, born 13 August 1919 at Philadelphia, Pa., he graduated *magna cum laude* from Harvard, where he also received his Ph.D. in 1950 for *The economic geography of Shanghai.* He was a professor of geography successively at the University of Washington, Seattle, and the University of Michigan, Ann Arbor, where he also served from 1969 to 1976 as director of the Center for Chinese Studies. His writings include *Shanghai, key to modern China* (1953), and *The outsiders; the Western experience in India and China* (1977). BlueB, 1973/74, 1975, 1976; ConAu 33-36; IntAu&W, 1989-2003; WhoAm, 1974/75-1999; WhoMW, 1994/95; WrDr, 1980/82-1992/94, 2002, 2003

Murphy, Charles Cecil Rowe, born in 1872 at Woolwich, he was educated at a private school. He was from 1913 to 1922 a naval and military intelligence officer successively posted to the Persian Gulf, Mesopotamia, Turkey and Persia. He retired with the rank of lieutenant-colonel. His writings include *Soldiers of the Prophet* (1921), and *A Mixed bag* (1936). Who' who in Essex, 1935

Murphy, Lawrence Richard, born 4 October 1942 at Sacramento, Calif., he graduated in 1964 from the University of Arizona and received a Ph.D. in 1968 from Texas Christian University. He was a professor of history successively at Western Illinois University and Central Michigan University. From 1971 to 1973 he was a visiting professor at the American University in Cairo. His writings include *The American University in Cairo, 1919-1987* (1987), and *Perverts by official order* (1988). He died 26 September 1987. ConAu 105; DrAS, 1974 H, 1978 H, 1982 H; LC; WhoMW, 1984/85

Murqus, Sulayman *see* Morcos, Soliman

von **Murr**, Christoph Gottlieb, born in 1733 at Nürnberg, he studied law at the nearby Altdorf Universität, where he gained a doctorate. During travels from 1756 to 1761 in the Netherlands, Britain, Austria and Italy he established contacts with numerous scholars, acquiring at the same time an important collection in arts and literature. Upon his return home, he became an excise official. From 1775 to 1789 he published the *Journal zur Kunstgeschichte und zur allgemeinen Literatur.* His writings include *Drei Abhandlungen von der Geschichte der Araber, derselnben Münzen und Siegeln* (1770), and *Beiträge zur arabischen Literatur* (1803). He died in Nürnberg in 1811. ADtB, vol. 23, pp. 76-80; DtBE; Master (1); Sezgin

Murray, Charles Adolphus, Earl of Dunmore, born 24 March 1841 at London. He was educated at Eton. He was an army officer, and a Conservative politician. From 1892 to 1893 he made a journey through Kashmir, Western Tibet, Chinese Tartary and Russian Central Asia. He died in 1907. DNB; Henze; Who was who, 1

Murray, Geoffrey, born 20th cent., he was at the time of the 1956 Suez crisis a senior counsellor in the Permanent Mission of Canada to the U.N.O. and later served a two-year secondment in the Secretariat, before returning in 1960 to the Department of External Affairs. In 1973 he was a coordinator, corporate policy, in the Canadian Department of Indian Affairs and Northern Development. Note

Murray, George William Welsh, born in 1885, he was since 1907 associated with the Survey of Egypt. His writings include *An English-Nubian comparative dictionary* (1923), *Sons of Ishamel; a study of the Egyptian Bedouin* (1935), *The Egyptian desert and ist antiquities* (1959), *The Survey of Egypt, 1898-1948* (1950), *The Artesian water of Egypt* (1952). He died in 1966. Who, 1953-1966; Who was who 6

Murray, Hugh, born in 1779 at North Berwick, Scotland, he was a clerk in the excise office, Edinburgh, devoting his time to literature, especially geography. He was the editor of the *Scots magazine.* He wrote *Morality of fiction* (1805), and *History of British India* (1849). He died in London in 1846. BiD&SB; BitInd (7); DNB; Master (2)

Murray, Sir James Augustus Henry, born in 1837, he was a lexicographer and the first editor of the *Oxford English Dictionary.* He died in 1915. BritInd (4); DNB; GrBr; Master (19); Who was who 1

Murray, Keith Anderson Hope, born in 1903 at Edinburgh, he was educated at Edinburgh University, where he gained the B.Sc. in agriculture. On a Commonwealth Fellowship he then went to Ithaca, N.Y.

to take his Ph.D. in 1929 at Cornell University, Ithaca, N.Y., for *Some aspects of the supply and prices of meat in Great Britain*. He spent the subsequent ten years with the Oxford University Agricultural Economics Research Institute. He was made a fellow and bursar of Lincoln College in 1937 and was a member of the Oxford City Council from 1937 to 1939. He was with the Ministry of Food from 1939 to 1941, following which he was in the Royal Air Force, 1941-42, on special duties, and was seconded by the R.A.F. to the Middle East Supply Centre, 1942-45, as director of Food and Agriculture. His writings include *The Planning of Britain's food imports* (1934), and *Milk consumption* (1937). Note; WhE&EA

Murray, Margaret Alice, born in 1863 at Calcutta, she studied Egyptology at University College, London, where she later served as a professor. Her writings include *Excavations at Malta* (1923-25), *Egyptian sculpture* (1930), *The splendour that was Egypt* (1949), and *The genesis of religion* (1963). She died in 1963. ConAu 5-8; Dawson; DNB; Egyptology; EncO&P; GrBr; Master (14); WhE&EA

Murray, Rosalind, 1890- see Toynbee, Rosalind née Murray

Murtonen, A., born 20th cent., he received a doctorate in 1958 at Helsinki for the first volume of his *Materials for a non/Masoretic Hebrew grammar*. He was in 1969 affiliated with the University of Melbourne, Victoria. His writings include *A philological and literary treatise on the Old Testament divine names* (1952), *The living soul* (1958), *The broken plurals* (1964), *Early Semitic* (1964), and *Hebrew in ist Semitic setting* (1986-90). Brinkman's; LC; Note

Mury, Francis, born 1 November 1866 at Saint-Georges (Rhône), France, he took classical subjects at the Collège d'Autun and the Lycée de Moulins and subsequently studied at the Faculté des lettres de Dijon and the Faculté de droit de Paris, to which a course at l'Ecole coloniale was added later. He served in Indo-China, Martinique and French Africa. He was one of the founders of the Congrès coloniaux français and in 1908 a member of the Conseil supérieur des colonies. His writings include the booklet, *Les Troubles dans l'Inde et en Indo-Chine* (1909). His trace is lost after a publication in 1913. Cordier; Curinier, vol. 5 (1906), pp. 335-37

Murzaev, Éduard Makarovich, born in 1908 at Simferopol, Crimea, he graduated in 1930 from the Faculty of Geography, Leningrad, and received his first degree in 1940 for «Территории, прилегающие к верхней части Узбоя (Сев. Зап. Туркмения)» and his doctorate in 1948 for *Основные вопросы физической географии Монгольской Народной Республики*. He was since 1931 affiliated with the Soviet Academy of Science. His writings include *Средняя Азия* (1947), *Географические исследования Монгольской Народной Репуьлики* (1948), and *Первые исследователи Каркумор* (1983). Miliband; Miliband²

Murzakevich, Nikifor Adrianovich, born in 1769, he wrote *Исторія губерускаго города Смоленска* (1804), and the undated booklet, *Краткая исторія древняго Херсона*. He died in 1834. EnSlovar

Musabaev, Gainetdin Galievich, born 17 September 1907 at Osmk, he was a professor of Kazakh who received a doctorate in 1960 and was appointed a professor in 1968. He wrote *Современный казахский язык* (1959), *Эпиграфика Казахстана* (1971), and he edited *Краткий казахско-русский словарь* (1954). He died 28 November 1981. Казахская ССР краткая энциклопедия, vol. 3 (1989), p. 346

Musaélian, ZHakelina Surenovna, born 24 June 1933 at Leningrad, she graduated in 1957 from the Oriental Faculty, Leningrad, and received her first degree in 1978 from the Oriental Institute of the Soviet Academy of Sciences for a study of Kurdish literature entitled *Курдская поэма "Замбильфрош" и ее фольклори версии*. Since 1958 she was affiliated with the Leningrad Branch of the Oriental Institute in the Soviet Academy of Science. Her writings include *Библиография по курдоведения* (1963), and she edited *Курдские народные песни из рукописного собрания ГПБ им. М.Е. Салтыкова-Щедрина* (1985). Miliband²

Musaev, Kenesbai Musaevich, born 24 March 1931 in Kazakhstan, he graduated in 1952 from the Faculty of Philology in the Kazakhstan State University. He received his first degree in 1957 for a study of contemporary Kazakh dialects entitled «О глагольно-именных конструкциях в современном казахском языке» and his doctorate in 1968 for *Строй караимского языка*. Since 1956 he was affiliated with Institute of Philology in the Soviet Academy of Science. His writings include *Алфавиты языков народнов СССР* (1965), *Лексика тюркских языков* (1975), *Краткий грамматический очерк караимского языке* (1977), and *Лексикология тюрских языков* (1984). Казахская ССР краткая энциклопедия, vol. 3 (1989), p. 347; Miliband; Miliband²; Schoeberlein

Musaeva, T. A., born 20th cent., her writings include *Борьба за рахвитие народного образования в Азербайджана в годы первой пятилетки* (1964), and *Социалистическое соревнование трудящихся Азербайджана в период развитого социализма, 1971-1979 гг.* (1980). OSK; NUC, 1956-67

Museur, Michel, born 20th cent., he was in 1979 a research fellow at the Institut de sociologie de l'Université libre de Bruxelles. Note

Mushegian (Moushelean), Khach'atur Artashesovich, born 20th cent., he received a degree in 1975 at Erevan for Денежное обращение в античной и среднев ековой Армений по нумизматическим данным. His writings include Денежное обращние Двина по нумисматическим данным (Erevan, 1962), and other writings in Armenian. LC; OSK

Mushkat, Marion, born in 1919 at Suwalki, Poland, he served in the war, became a POW and served on the Committee for Investigation of War Crimes, Nürnberg, 1945-48. He gained a doctorate in 1947 at Nancy, and a LL.D. in 1949 at Warszawa. He was successively a professor of law at Warszawa and Tel-Aviv. His writings include Polish charges against German war criminals (1948), Interwencja - zbrodniczy oręż polityki Stanów Zjednoczonych (1953), its translation, Титервенция - преступное орудние политики США (1954), and The Third World and peace (1982). ConAu 120; Master (1); WhoIsrael, 1969/70-1990/91; WhoWor, 1974/75, 1975/76, 1980

Mushketov, Ivan Vasilievich, born in 1850 in the settlement of Alekseevskaya on the Don to a family of modest substance, he became a major geologist and physical geographer, a student of Central Asia, the Caspian steppes, the Caucasus and other regions of Russia. He organized many geological and geographical expeditions. He died in St. Petersburg in 1902. DcScB; EnSlovar; Geographers, 7 (1983), pp. 89-91; TurkmenSE

Mušić, Omer, born in 1903 at Sarajevo, he was a professor of Arabic and Persian at the Oriental Institute, Faculty of Philosophy, Sarajevo. He died in Sarajevo, 10 April 1972. Anali Gazi Husrev-Begove Biblioteke2-3 (1974), pp. 103-108, 261-263

Musil, Alois, born 30 June 1868 at Richterdorf (Rychtářov), Moravia, he studied Catholic theology at the Universität Olmütz, where he received a doctorate in 1895 and there also was active as a professor of Biblical studies from 1902 to 1909. Through the good offices of Josef von Karabacek, he was invited to the Catholic Faculty of the Universität Wien as a professor of Biblical auxiliary sciences and Arabic, a post which he held until 1920, when he accepted the chair of Oriental studies at Praha. He there founded the Oriental Institute. He is best remembered for four great journeys from 1908 to 1915 in the region between the Gulf of Aqaba, the Tigris, Aleppo and the borders of Najd. He was an indefatigable collector of data, both in the field and in the library. In recognition of his contribution to geography he was awarded the Charles P. Daly Gold Medal of the American Geographical Society in 1928. His writings include Arabia Petraea (1907-1908), Zur Zeitgeschichte von Arabien (1918), The northern Hegâz (1926), The middle Euphrates (1928), Northern Arabia (1928), Lev ze kmene Judova; nová Habeš (1934). He died in far-away Otryby in eastern Bohemia on 12 April or 30 June 1944. DtBE; DtBilnd (4); Filipsky; Flück, pp. 260-65; Geographical review 36 (1946), pp. 686-87; Hanisch; IES; Index Islamicus (4); Kornrumpf; Kornrumpf³, vol. 2; Martinek; Mitteilungen der Österreichischen Geographischen Gesellschaft, Wien, 110 (1968), pp. 277-79; ÖBL; PSN

Musrepov (Müsrepov), Gabit Makhmudovich. born in 1902 in Kazakhstan, he gave up his education at an agricultural institute to become a journalist and writer on Kazakh subjects. His writings include Солдат из Казахстана (1950), Пробужденный край (1958), and Пьесы (1958). He died in Alma-Ata, 31 December 1985. DrOrL, vol. 3; Казахская ССР краткая энциклопедия, vol. 4, pp. 398-400; WhoSocC, 1978

Mussel, Louis Jean Laurent, born 10 November 1873 at Mostagem, Algeria, he entered the French military college, Saint-Cry, in 1894. Since 1902 he was attached to the Bureaux des Affaires indigènes, posted to Géryville in the Saharan Atlas. After secondment to Morocco from 1903 to 1908, he returned to Algeria, spending three years at Marnia, near the Moroccan border first as deputy and later as chief of the Bureaux des Affaires indigènes. A captain since 1905, he departed from Algeria in 1911 to join the Cabinet du Ministre de la guerre. With the rank of colonel he accomplished important missions to Syria and Turkey in 1920, and to Morocco in 1925. Promoted brigadier general, he served as head of the military cabinet with the Résident général at Rabat until retired in 1928. Peyronnet, p. 860

Musset, René, born in 1881, he was a professor of history and geography at the Université de Rennes. His writings include Le Bas-Maine; étude géographique (1917), Le Blé dans le monde (1923), and La Bretagne (1937). LC

Musso, Gian Giacomo, born 20th cent., he wrote Navigazione e commercio genovese con il Levante nei documenti dell'Archivio di Stato di Genova (1975), and the booklet, Mgr Agostino Giustiniani (Bastia, 1986). LC

Musso, Jean Claude, fl. 1970, he wrote Dépots rituels des sanctuaires ruraux de la Grande Kabylie (1971), and he was joint author of Corpus des peintures et gravures rupestres de Grande Kabylie (1969). LC

Mustafa Kemal Paşa, 1881-1938 see Atatürk, Mustafa Kemal

Mustafaev, Dzhamal Mekhti ogly, born 20th cent., he wrote *Северные ханства Азербайджана в Россия конец XVIII- начало XIX в.* (1989). LC

Mustafaev, Dzhamal Vali ogly, born 15 April 1928 in Georgia, he graduated in 1952 from Moscow State University, received his first degree in 1961 for a study of Nizami's ethics entitled «Философские и этические воззрения Низами», and his doctorate in 1968 at Baku for *Мир идей Низами и современность.* Since 1957 he was affiliated with the Philosophy Division in the Azerbaijan Academy of Science. In 1969 he was appointed a professor. His writings include *Философские и этические воззрения Низами* (Baku, 1962). Miliband; Miliband²

Musul'mankulov (Musulmonqulov), Rakhim, born 20th cent., he was a Tajik philologist whose writings include *Атаулла Махмуд-и Хусайни* (1983), *Сохиб Шухратиевич Табаров* (1984), and *Персидско-таджикская классическая поэтика* (1989). LC

Mutafchieva, Vera Petrovna, born 28 March 1929 at Sofia, she received a doctorate in history in 1978. Her writings include *Рицарят; роман* (1970), *Нероика* (1972), *Процесът* (1972), *Кърджалийско време* (1977), and she was joint author of *Турски извори за Българската имтория* (1964), *Sur l'état du système des timars des XVII.-XVIII ss.* (1968), *Agrarian relations in the Ottoman Empire in the 15th and 16th centuries* (1988), and *Bulgarische Vergangenheit* (1969). DLB 181 (1997), pp. 187-96; EnBulg; Koi, 1998

Mutin, Georges, born in 1934, he was in 1995 a professor at the Institut d'études politiques de Lyon. His writings include *La Mitidja; décolonisation et espace géographique* (1977), a work which was originally presented as thesis for his *doctorat d'état* in 1974 at Lyon. He also wrote *L'Eau dans le monde arabe* (2000), and he was joint editor of *Afrique du Nord, Moyen-Orient, Monde indien* (1995). Livres disponibles, 2002; THESAM 2

Muttermilch, Witold, 1904-1940 *see* Mileski, Witold

Muzikář, Josef, born 15 March 1932 at Stříbrná Skalice (obr. Český Brod), Czechoslovakia, he studied at Praha, where he received a doctorate in law in 1966, and subsequently pursued studies at Nancy and Moscow. He was from 1972 to 1990 head of the Arab and Middle East section of the Oriental Institute in the Czech Academy of Science. His monographs, mostly as lead writer of a Czech authors' collective, include *Les Perspectives de l'intégration des pays maghrébins et leur attitude vis-à-vis du Marché commun* (1968), *Libanon* (1981), *Islám a současnost* (1985), *Islám v politice* (1987), and *Zápas o novodý stát islámkém světě* (1989). Filipsky; LC

Muztar, Allah Ditta, born 20th cent., he gained an M.A. in 1964 at Manchester with a thesis entitled *The Sultans of Delhi and their non-Muslim subjects* and his Ph.D. in 1966 for *An annotated history of the Jahan-Gusha-yi-Qu'an of Muhammad Ali Nura.* His other writings include *Khāksār tahrīk aur āzādī-yi Hind* (1985). LC; Sluglett

Muzzio, Douglas, born about 1945, he was successively associated with both, the Department of Political Science, and Department of Public Administration in City University of New York. His writings include *Watergate; strategies, choices, outcomes* (1982). NatFacDr, 1995-2003

Mveng, Engelbert, born 1930 in French West Africa, he studied at Dakar, Lyon and Paris, where he received a doctorate in 1972 for *Les Sources grecques de l'histoire négro-africaine depuis Homère jusqu'à Strabon.* He was a Cameroon Jesuit priest and a professor whose writings include *L'Art et artisanat africains* (1980), *Histoire du Cameroun* (1984-85), *L'Afrique dans l'Eglise* (1985); he was joint author of *Manuel d'histoire du Cameroun* (1969); and he edited *Histoire des églises chrétiennes au Cameroun* (1990). AfrBioInd (8); IntWW, 1989-1995/96|

Myers, Charles Samuel, born in 1873, he was a director of the Psychological Laboratory and reader in experimental psychology in Cambridge University. His writings include *Industrial psychology* (1925), and *In the realm of the mind* (1937). He died in 1946. BritInd (2); DNB; Master (5); Who was who 4

Myers, Eugene Abraham, born 'Afīf al-Munayyar on 10 March 1910 at Amyun, Lebanon, he was Greek Orthodox and graduated in 1934 from the University of Pittsburgh, where he also gained a Ph.D. in 1946. Since 1947 he was a professor of economics in the University of Pennsylvania at University Park, Pa. His writings include *Cases on state and local taxation* (1961), and *Arabic thought and Western world in the golden age of Islam* (1964). He died in 1996. AmM&WS, 1973 S, 1978 S; ConAu 45-48

Myers, George Hewitt, born 10 September 1865 or 1875 at Cleveland, Ohio, he was a financier, authority on textiles, and museum director. His writings include the pamphlet, *Catalogue of an exhibition of embroideries from the Greek Islands,* held at the Century Club, N.Y. (1928). He died in 1957. NatCAB, vol. 49, pp. 532-533; WhAm 3

MACK LIBRARY
BOB JONES UNIVERSITY
GREENVILLE, SC

Myers, Oliver Humphreys, born in 1903 at Shoeburyness, he was an archaeologist in the Middle East and during the war served with UK Intelligence in the region. He taught at Gordon College, Khartoum, and the University of Ibadan. His writings include *Some applications of statistics to archaeology* (1947), and he was joint author of *The Bucheum* (1934), and *The Cemeteries of Armant* (1937-40). AfrBioInd = Dawson; Egyptology; NUC, pre-1956

Mygind, Eduard, born 19th cent., he wrote *Vom Bosporus zum Sinai; Erinnerungen an die Einweihung der Hamidié-Pilgerbahn des Hedjas* (Constantinople, 1905), and *Syrien und die türkische Mekkapilgerbahn* (Halle, 1906). His trace is lost after a publication in 1908. GV

Mylès, Henri, born 19th cent., his writings include *La Fin de Stamboul* (1921), *Clair de lune sur le Bosphore; histoire orientale* (1926), *L'Autre carrière; scènes de la vie consulaire* (1927), and *Perdreaux manqués* (1932). NUC, pre-1956

Freiherr von **Mylius**, Hermann, he was in 1967 affiliated with the Faculty of Agriculture in the Universität Kiel. His writings include *Nachkommenbeurteilung bei Bullen, künstlicher Besamung und Milchleistungsprüfung in England und Schottland* (1957). NUC, 1973-77

Mylius, Norbert, born 3 April 1906 at Wien, he studied law and ethnology at Wien until called to arms from 1940 to 1945. After his release from an American prisoner of war camp in 1946, he entered the Museum für Völkerkunde, Wien, and received his Dr.phil. in the following year. His interests ranged from Inonesia to Africa. His writings include *Afrika-Bibliographie, 1943-1951* (1952), and *Antlitz und Geheimnis der überseeischen Maske* (1961). He died in Wien on 29 December 1981. *Archiv für Völkerkunde* 36 (1982), pp. 161-64; Kürschner, 1961-1980; WhoAustria, 1964-1977/78

Mylrea, Clarence *Stanley* Garland, born 19th cent., at London, he saw some service with the American Board of Foreign Missions in Turkey as a very young man, before his medical training at the Medico Chirurgical College and Medical School, Philadelphia. In 1906, he went out as a medical missionary to the Arabian Mission of the Reformed Church in America, at first stationed in Bahrain, and from 1913 onwards in Kuwait where he was still active in 1939. In his later years, he lived in Hartford, Conn., where his mimeographed memoirs, *Kuwait before oil; memoirs written between 1945 and 1951,* and edited by Samuel M. Zwemer, are deposited at the Hartford Seminary Foundation. Facey Grant; Van Ess

Mynors, T. H. B., born 1 August 1907 at Chippenham, England, he gained his B.A. at Oxford and became a sometime editor of *Sudan notes and records.* WhoEgypt, 1951

Myntti, Cynthia L., born in 1949, she was affiliated with the German Agency for Technical Cooperation, Eschborn, and wrote *Women and development in Yemen Arab Republic* (1979). LC

Myres, Sir John Linton, born in 1869 at Preston, Lancs., he was an archaeologist and historian. He prepared for the U.K. Naval Intelligence Division *Dodecanese* (1943), and *Albania* (1945). His other writings include *The Dawn of history* (1911). He died in 1954. BioIn 3, 4; DBN; WhE&EA; *Who was who* 5

Myrsiades, Linda Suny, born 26 August 1941, she received a Ph.D. in 1973 from Indiana University for *The Karaghiozis tradition and Greek shadow puppet theater.* Between 1995 and 2003 she was a professor of English at West Chester University, Pa. Her writings include *The Karagiozis heroic performance in the Greek shadow theater* (1988), *Karagiozis; culture and commedy in Greek puppet theater* (1992), and she was joint editor of *Margins in the classroom* (1994). LC; NatFacDr, 1995-2003

von **Mžik**, Hans, born 24 July 1876 at Rzeszow, Galicia, he studied at Wien and Leiden and received a Dr.phil. in 1903 at Wien for a study of the Arab wazirate entitled *Das Vezirat bei den Arabern.* Since 1903 he was associated with Öster-reichische Nationalbibliothek, Wien, concurrently lecturing at the Universität. His writings include *Erdmessung, Grad, Meile und Stadion nach den altarmenischen Quellen* (1933); he edited *Das Kitāb al-Wuzarā' wa-l-kuttāb des al-Gahšiyārī* (1926-28), and *Das Kitāb Sūrat al-ard wa-l-kuttāb des al-Huwārizmī* (1963). He died in Wien on 4 March 1961. DtBiInd (1); GAS, vol. 10; Hanisch; Kürschner, 1931-1961; Schwarz; Teichl; *Wer ist's*, 1928